P9-AZV-100

PSYCHOLOGY

FRONTIERS AND APPLICATIONS

THIRD CANADIAN EDITION

Michael W. Passer
University of Washington

Ronald E. Smith
University of Washington

Michael L. Atkinson
University of Western Ontario

John B. Mitchell
Brescia University College
University of Western Ontario

Darwin W. Muir
Queen's University

Toronto Montréal Boston Burr Ridge, IL Dubuque, IA Madison, WI New York
San Francisco St. Louis Bangkok Bogotá Caracas Kuala Lumpur Lisbon London
Madrid Mexico City Milan New Delhi Santiago Seoul Singapore Sydney Taipei

The McGraw·Hill Companies

McGraw-Hill Ryerson

Psychology: Frontiers and Applications
Third Canadian Edition

ISBN-13: 978-0-07-098592-6
ISBN-10: 0-07-098592-8

2 3 4 5 6 7 8 9 10 QPD 0 9 8

Printed and bound in the United States of America.

Editorial Director: Joanna Cotton
Publisher: Nicole Lukach
Director of Marketing: Jeff MacLean
Managing Editor, Development: Jennifer DiDomenico
Senior Developmental Editor: Denise Foote
Editorial Associate: Marina Seguin
Manager, Editorial Services and Design: Kelly Dickson
Supervising Editor: Joanne Limebeer
Copy Editor: Imogen Brian
Senior Production Coordinator: Paula Brown
Cover Design: Michelle Losier
Cover Image: © Digital Vision Ltd./SuperStock
Interior Design: Michelle Losier
Page Layout: Bookman Typesetting Co. Inc.
Printer: Quebecor Printing Dubuque

Library and Archives Canada Cataloguing in Publication Data

Psychology : frontiers and applications / Michael W. Passer . . . [et al.]. — 3rd Canadian ed.

Includes bibliographical references and indexes.
ISBN 978-0-07-098592-6

1. Psychology—Textbooks. I. Passer, Michael W.

BF121.P833 2008 150 C2008-900246-6

About the Authors

Michael W. Passer, Ph.D.

Michael Passer coordinates the introductory psychology program at the University of Washington, which enrolls about 2,500 students per year, and also is the faculty coordinator of training for new teaching assistants (TAs). He received his bachelor's degree from the University of Rochester and his Ph.D. in Psychology from the University of California, Los Angeles, with a specialization in social psychology. Dr. Passer has been a faculty member at the University of Washington since 1977. A former Danforth Foundation Fellow and University of Washington Distinguished Teaching Award finalist, Dr. Passer has had a career-long love of teaching. Each academic year he teaches introductory psychology twice and a required pre-major course in research methods. Dr. Passer developed and teaches a graduate course on the Teaching of Psychology, which prepares students for careers in the college classroom, and has also taught courses in social psychology and attribution theory. He has published more than 20 scientific articles and chapters, primarily in the areas of attribution, stress, and anxiety, and has taught the introductory psychology course for almost 20 years.

Ronald E. Smith, Ph.D.

Ronald E. Smith is Professor of Psychology at the University of Washington, where he has served as Director of Clinical Psychology Training and as Head of the Social Psychology and Personality area. He received his bachelor's degree from Marquette University and his Ph.D. from Southern Illinois University, where he had dual specializations in clinical and physiological psychology. His major research interests are in anxiety, stress and coping, and in performance enhancement research and intervention. Dr. Smith is a Fellow of the American Psychological Association. He received a Distinguished Alumnus Award from the UCLA Neuropsychiatric Institute for his contributions to the field of mental health. He has published more than 140 scientific articles and book chapters in his areas of interest and has authored or coauthored 21 books on introductory psychology, human performance enhancement, and personality, including *Introduction to Personality: Toward an Integration*, with Walter Mischel and Yuichi Shoda (Wiley, 2004). An award-winning teacher, he has more than 15 years of experience in teaching the introductory psychology course.

Michael L. Atkinson, Ph.D.

Mike Atkinson is an associate professor of psychology at the University of Western Ontario in London, Ontario. Atkinson received his B.Sc. from Dalhousie University in 1975 and his M.Sc. (1978) and Ph.D. (1982) from the University of Wisconsin, Madison. Atkinson's training is in social psychology, but his research and teaching interests place him more in the field of educational psychology. "Dr. Mike," as he is known to his students, has been featured in *Maclean's* magazine, *Media Television*, and the *Globe and Mail.* He has also received numerous teaching awards, including the University of Western Ontario Professor of the Year award five times, as well as the Student's Council/Alumni Western Teaching Award of Excellence, and the Pleva Award for Excellence in Teaching. He has also received the 3M Canada Teaching Fellowship for his pioneering work in large-scale multimedia instruction, the "Superclass."

John B. Mitchell, Ph.D.

John B. Mitchell, Department of Social Sciences, Brescia University College, University of Western Ontario, received his B.A. and M.A. from Queen's University and his Ph.D. from Concordia University. Following completion of his Ph.D., Dr. Mitchell did post-doctoral research at the Douglas Hospital Research Centre in Montreal and at the University of Colorado Health Sciences Center in Denver. Dr. Mitchell has taught Introduction to Psychology at Boston College, Brescia University College, and the University of Western Ontario in classes that have ranged in size from 50 to 500 students. He has also taught courses in behavioural neuroscience, psychopharmacology, memory, research methods, and, more recently, educational psychology. Dr. Mitchell has authored or co-authored research papers and book chapters on memory, the effects of early experience on the ability to recover from stress, and motivation.

Darwin W. Muir, Ph.D.

Darwin W. Muir is a professor of psychology at Queen's University. He received his B.S. and M.Sc. from Eastern Michigan University and his Ph.D. in Experimental Psychology from Dalhousie University. Dr. Muir has been in the Psychology Department at Queen's University since 1974 where he has held an NSERC operating grant that supported the publication of approximately 90 journal articles and book chapters on topics ranging from the study of concept formation in pigeons, the visual acuity of visually deprived cats, and social learning in snails to human fetal, neonatal, and infant sensitivity to tactile, auditory, and visual stimulation. Recently he has been studying the role played by adult auditory, visual, and tactile stimulation in the regulation of infant affect and attention during face-to-face interactions. He is married with three daughters and three grandsons. Dr. Muir is Fellow of the Canadian Psychological Association and a member of the International Society for Infant Studies, the Society for Research on Child Development, the American Psychological Society, and the Canadian Society for Brain, Behaviour & Cognitive Sciences.

Brief Contents

Contents

CHAPTER 3
BIOLOGICAL FOUNDATIONS OF BEHAVIOUR 82

CHAPTER 4
GENES, EVOLUTION, AND BEHAVIOUR 132

CHAPTER 5
SENSATION AND PERCEPTION 168

CHAPTER 6
STATES OF CONSCIOUSNESS 214

CHAPTER 7
LEARNING AND ADAPTATION: THE ROLE OF EXPERIENCE 264

CHAPTER 8

MEMORY 310

CHAPTER 9
THOUGHT, LANGUAGE, AND INTELLIGENCE 352

CHAPTER 10
MOTIVATION AND EMOTION 400

CHAPTER 11

DEVELOPMENT OVER THE LIFE SPAN 456

CHAPTER 12

PERSONALITY 508

CHAPTER 13
PSYCHOLOGICAL DISORDERS 548

CHAPTER 14
TREATMENT OF PSYCHOLOGICAL DISORDERS 598

Preface

There is nothing more fascinating than the study of the mind and behaviour. But we didn't recognize this when we entered university. In fact, the study of psychology wasn't even on our radar screens. Some of us had planned careers in the "hard" sciences (MP, MA) and others were focused on the "softer" side (RS). One of us (JM) was pretty sure he would pursue psychology, although philosophy was an attractive alternative. Then something unexpected occurred. Each of us took an introductory psychology course, and suddenly our life paths changed. Because of instructors who brought psychology to life, we were hooked, and that initial enthusiasm has never left us.

Now, through this textbook, we have the pleasure and privilege of sharing our enthusiasm with today's instructors and a new generation of students. We've endeavoured to create a thoughtfully integrated book and multimedia package that strikes just the right balance between student friendliness and scientific integrity—a teaching tool that introduces students to psychology as a science, while highlighting its relevance to their lives and society. We want students to experience, as we did, the intellectual excitement of studying the mind and behaviour. We also seek to help students sharpen their critical thinking skills, dispelling some commonly held myths. We have used clear prose, careful explanations, engaging examples, and supporting artwork to make the book and multimedia accessible to a wide range of students. All of this is done within a conceptual framework that emphasizes relations between biological, psychological, and environmental levels of analysis.

We are particularly excited about the unique way in which our third Canadian edition text is integrated with its supplements. This integration results in a learning package that "uses science to teach science." Specifically, we are impressed with research (e.g., Moreland et al., 1997; Pauk & Fiore, 2000) showing that recall of textual material is significantly enhanced by specific focus questions and learning objectives that serve as retrieval cues and help students identify important information and assess their mastery of the material. In addition, the opening vignettes are presented as Problem-Based Learning (PBL) case studies. PBL generates a deeper understanding of material and provides the student with critical problem-solving skills (see Aspy et al., 1993; Vernon & Blake, 1993). It is for precisely this reason that PBL is used in the curriculum of so many medical schools. Over the years, our students have profited from these pedagogical tools; consequently, we have retained these popular features from the second Canadian edition.

One of the fastest-evolving areas in psychology is neuroscience, particularly in the use of neuroimaging. By some estimates, published studies involving some aspect of neuroimaging have increased by 3000 percent over the past decade! We are now able to examine the neural substrates for most topics in psychology including attitude change, fabricated memory, and psychological disorders, in addition to the more traditional topics of brain function and sensory processing. In an effort to embrace this fast-moving area of research, we have included a neuroscience feature in each chapter. Here we will examine how neuroimaging has provided a much more detailed understanding of how the mind and brain work.

Let's take a look at the features of our third edition.

OVERVIEW OF FEATURES

- **Problem-Based Learning:** Chapter-opening vignettes, identified by the compass icon, are Problem-Based Learning tools that introduce real-world cases closely related to the topics presented in each chapter. The compass icons in the margins throughout the chapters identify points at which an element of the corresponding text relates directly back to the case introduced in the opening vignette. These vignettes are revisited in the Instructor's Manual.
- **Focus on Scientific Psychology:** Throughout the book, psychology is portrayed as a contemporary science without becoming excessively formal or terminological. *Psychology: Frontiers and Applications*, Third Canadian Edition, focuses both on principles derived from research and on how good research is done.
- **Focus on Relations between Basic Science and Applications:** Whether in the context of students' personal lives or larger societal issues, many questions studied from a basic science perspective are inspired by real-world questions and issues, and basic research findings often guide solutions to social and individual problems. In this way, students can be guided by their knowledge in other aspects of their lives.
- **Integrated Coverage of Cultural and Gender Issues:** Cultural and gender issues are at the forefront of contemporary psychology, and rather than isolating this material within dedicated chapters, we integrate it

throughout the text. Our Levels of Analysis approach conceptualizes culture as an environmental factor and also as a psychological factor that reflects the internalization of cultural influences.

- **Levels of Analysis:** A unifying framework students will remember: To help students become more sophisticated in their everyday understanding of behaviour, we present a simple framework that emphasizes how to study behaviour at biological, psychological, and environmental levels, and how these explanations are related to one another. While we carry this Levels of Analysis framework throughout the book in textual discussion, we apply it selectively without being overly repetitious for students or confining for instructors.

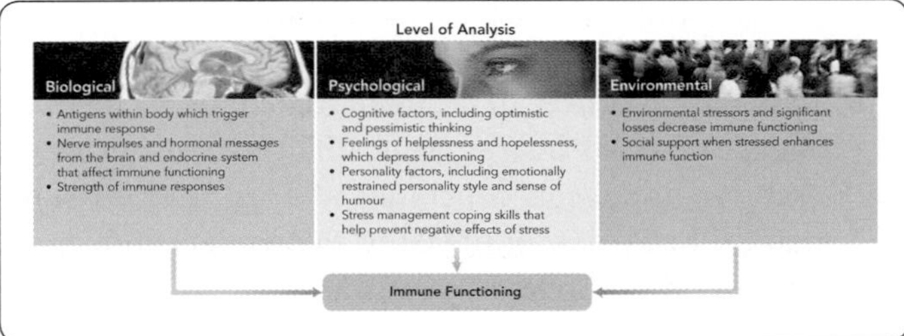

- **Reader's Guide:** To help familiarize students with the pedagogical features incorporated in *Psychology: Frontiers and Applications*, Chapter 1 contains a number of call-outs written by the authors to draw attention to specific features in the text and illustrate why they have been incorporated. These notes will help guide students in their understanding of the features to come throughout the text, and ultimately help their learning of the material.

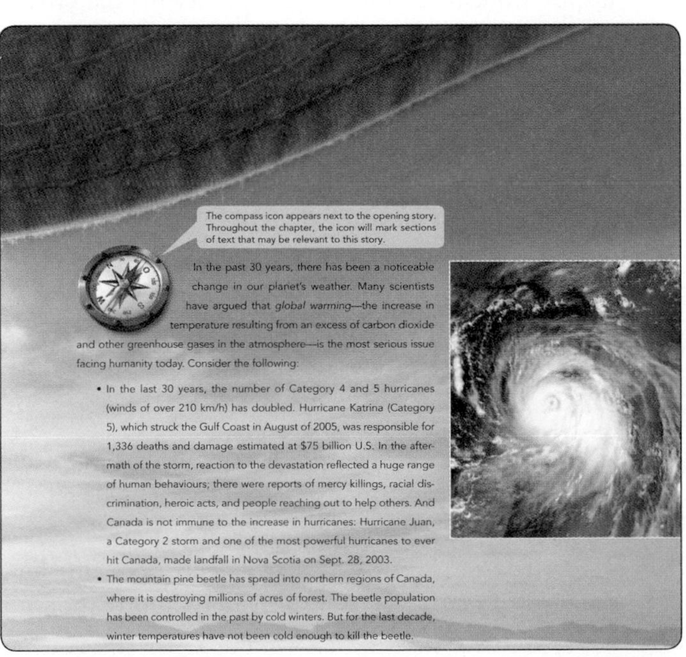

The compass icon appears next to the opening story. Throughout the chapter, the icon will mark sections of text that may be relevant to this story.
In the past 30 years, there has been a noticeable change in our planet's weather. Many scientists have argued that global warming—the increase in temperature resulting from an excess of carbon dioxide and other greenhouse gases in the atmosphere—is the most serious issue facing humanity today. Consider the following:
• In the last 30 years, the number of Category 4 and 5 hurricanes (winds of over 210 km/h) has doubled. Hurricane Katrina (Category 5), which struck the Gulf Coast in August of 2005, was responsible for 1,336 deaths and damage estimated at $75 billion U.S. In the aftermath of the storm, reaction to the devastation reflected a huge range of human behaviours; there were reports of mercy killings, racial discrimination, heroic acts, and people reaching out to help others. And Canada is not immune to the increase in hurricanes: Hurricane Juan, a Category 2 storm and one of the most powerful hurricanes to ever hit Canada, made landfall in Nova Scotia on Sept. 28, 2003.
• The mountain pine beetle has spread into northern regions of Canada, where it is destroying millions of acres of forest. The beetle population has been controlled in the past by cold winters. But for the last decade, winter temperatures have not been cold enough to kill the beetle.

- **NEW! Focus on Neuroscience Box:** The Focus on Neuroscience feature in each chapter highlights how rapidly developing cutting-edge technology is paving the way for groundbreaking imaging studies that give new insights into the workings of the human brain and its relationship to behaviour.

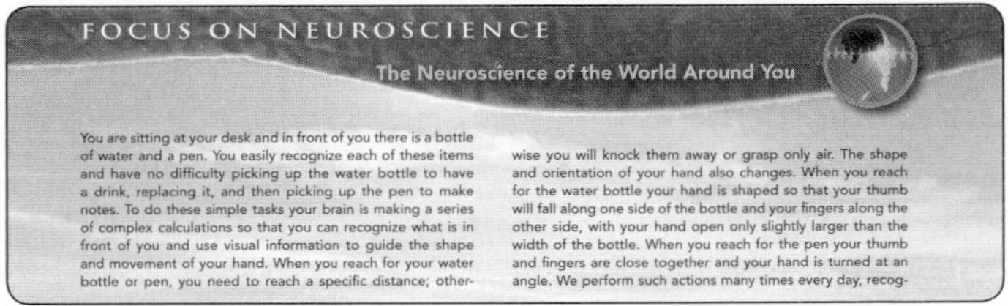

- **Research Frontiers Box:** This in-depth feature highlights both current and future directions in psychological theory and research, illustrating the dynamic nature of psychological science and ways in which it can promote human development.

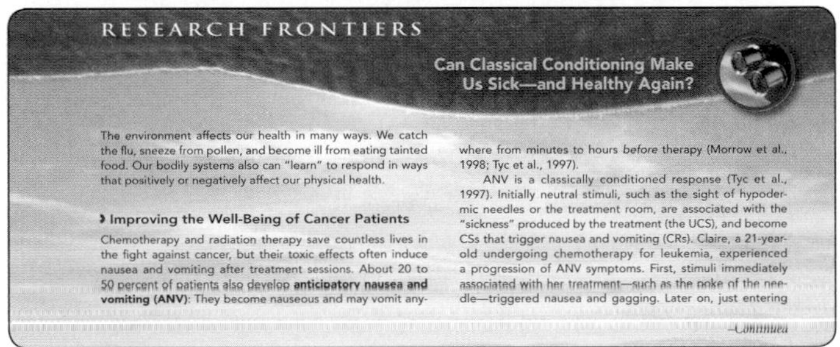

- **Research Foundations Box:** Each Research Foundations box describes and critically evaluates a high-interest study. Presented in a simplified journal format (background, method, results, critical analysis), these studies represent a diversity of research methods to engage students in the process of critical thinking.

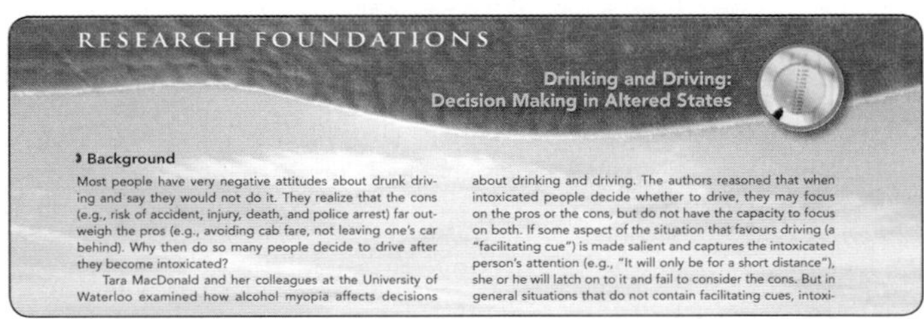

- **Psychological Applications Box:** In each chapter, this feature brings a key concept into the realm of real-life application. Many of these boxes throughout the book focus on important skills that can enhance students' learning and performance. For example, in Chapter 1, this feature comprises a discussion of good study habits and other ways that students can enhance their learning.

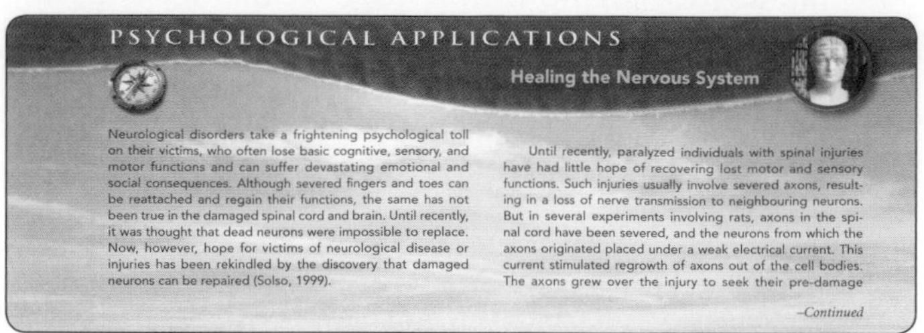
PSYCHOLOGICAL APPLICATIONS

Healing the Nervous System

Neurological disorders take a frightening psychological toll on their victims, who often lose basic cognitive, sensory, and motor functions and can suffer devastating emotional and social consequences. Although severed fingers and toes can be reattached and regain their functions, the same has not been true in the damaged spinal cord and brain. Until recently, it was thought that dead neurons were impossible to replace. Now, however, hope for victims of neurological disease or injuries has been rekindled by the discovery that damaged neurons can be repaired (Solso, 1999).

Until recently, paralyzed individuals with spinal injuries have had little hope of recovering lost motor and sensory functions. Such injuries usually involve severed axons, resulting in a loss of nerve transmission to neighbouring neurons. But in several experiments involving rats, axons in the spinal cord have been severed, and the neurons from which the axons originated placed under a weak electrical current. This current stimulated regrowth of axons out of the cell bodies. The axons grew over the injury to seek their pre-damage

–Continued

- **Directed Questions:** Each chapter includes directed questions in the margin of the text adjacent to important material. When author Ron Smith took introductory psychology in university, he wrote questions in the margin of the text to help him study for exams. It was of such benefit to him that we have continued this practice to help all students, both in first reading the chapter, and in later revisiting the material. These directed questions enhance student concept mastery, serve as retrieval clues during review, and act as a performance feedback measure for students. They are available on the test bank to give instructors the option of including them on exams.

18. How does negative reinforcement differ from positive reinforcement and from punishment?

- **Canadian Content:** Times have changed and work that once was considered classic is now being performed in labs all across North America. Thus, we have included a large number of studies by both Canadian and U.S. authors. The text has been written to be relevant in a Canadian context, using examples our students can relate to, statistics that reflect the Canadian and North American scene, and stories and vignettes that occur in Canadian locations. By so doing, psychology is brought to life for students.
- **Gaining Direction:** At the end of each chapter, the opening vignette is revisited with the new "Gaining Direction" box that suggests some answers to the questions posed at the beginning of the chapter. In the spirit of Problem-Based Learning, these answers are not definitive, but merely suggest a set of issues to be explored and some sources of information. With this feature, students will be able to apply the newly learned material to these real-world situations, thus enhancing their understanding of the topics in the text and the use of psychology in real life.

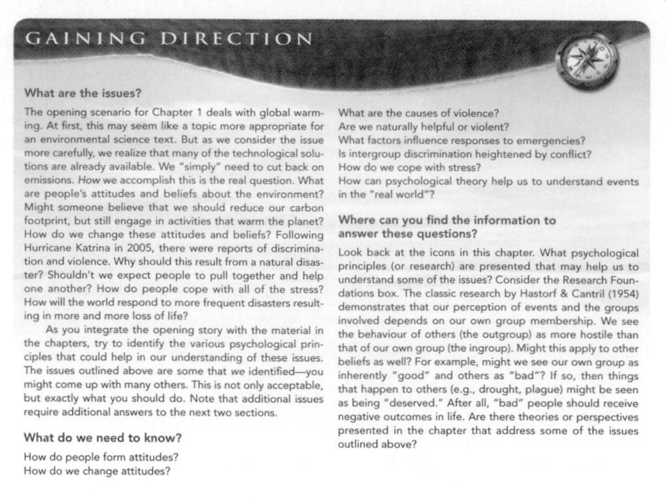
GAINING DIRECTION

What are the issues?

The opening scenario for Chapter 1 deals with global warming. At first, this may seem like a topic more appropriate for an environmental science text. But as we consider the issue more carefully, we realize that many of the technological solutions are already available. We "simply" need to cut back on emissions. *How* we accomplish this is the real question. What are people's attitudes and beliefs about the environment? Might someone believe that we should reduce our carbon footprint, but still engage in activities that warm the planet? How do we change these attitudes and beliefs? Following Hurricane Katrina in 2005, there were reports of discrimination and violence. Why should this result from a natural disaster? Shouldn't we expect people to pull together and help one another? How do people cope with all of the stress? How will the world respond to more frequent disasters resulting in more and more loss of life?

As you integrate the opening story with the material in the chapters, try to identify the various psychological principles that could help in our understanding of these issues. The issues outlined above are some that *we* identified—you might come up with many others. This is not only acceptable, but exactly what you should do. Note that additional issues require additional answers to the next two sections.

What do we need to know?

How do people form attitudes?
How do we change attitudes?
What are the causes of violence?
Are we naturally helpful or violent?
What factors influence responses to emergencies?
Is intergroup discrimination heightened by conflict?
How do we cope with stress?
How can psychological theory help us to understand events in the "real world"?

Where can you find the information to answer these questions?

Look back at the icons in this chapter. What psychological principles (or research) are presented that may help us to understand some of the issues? Consider the Research Foundations box. The classic research by Hastorf & Cantril (1954) demonstrates that our perception of events and the groups involved depends on our own group membership. We see the behaviour of others (the outgroup) as more hostile than that of our own group (the ingroup). Might this apply to other beliefs as well? For example, might we see our own group as inherently "good" and others as "bad"? If so, then things that happen to others (e.g., drought, plague) might be seen as being "deserved." After all, "bad" people should receive negative outcomes in life. Are there theories or perspectives presented in the chapter that address some of the issues outlined above?

- **In Review Feature:** To facilitate student understanding and provide for instructor flexibility on assignments, each major section concludes with an interim summary ("In Review"), breaking the content into more manageable modules or segments.

In Review

- *Genetic determinism assumes that if a characteristic is genetically based then it is invariant and unalterable. This view ignores the fact that genes and the environment constantly and necessarily interact.*
- *Social Darwinism arose from a poor understanding of the principles of natural selection and has been used to justify the exploitation of others. Social Darwinism confuses the Darwinian idea of fitness and the time course of changing adaptations with the erroneous idea that there is some genetic superiority of individual members.*
- *Although genetic and evolutionary arguments have been used to justify the status quo as "right" or "moral," such arguments ignore the fact that natural selection is neither "moral" nor "just." The real perspective in evolutionary psychology, as in much of psychology, is for increased understanding so that appropriate changes can be made to better quality of life. An evolutionary analysis suggests environmental interventions as it attempts to explain human behaviour.*

- **Additional Pedagogical Features:** A textbook should inspire students and help them master the material at hand. To accomplish these goals, our book incorporates *chapter outlines, boldfaced key terms* in the narrative, *summaries,* and an *end of chapter list of key terms.*
- **Updated coverage:** Our third Canadian edition is rich in discussions of research and new references, many from the years 2000 and beyond.

CONTENT CHANGES IN INDIVIDUAL CHAPTERS

Chapter 1

- The opening vignette now features a discussion of the psychological factors in people's attitudes and reactions to environmental disasters.
- A new feature, Focus on Neuroscience, explains how the field of neuroscience is providing information for

almost every area of psychology. In this chapter, we examine the proliferation of neuroimaging over the past two decades.

- A new Research Frontiers box examines the relationship between culture and behaviour, focusing on the work of Li-Jun Ji at Queen's University.
- The Gaining Directions feature focuses students' attention on the problem of global warming and how psychology may provide some of the approaches necessary to address the problem.

Chapter 2

- A new Focus on Neuroscience box, The Neuroscience of the Human Brain, looks at imaging technology as a powerful tool for neuroscientists to study localization of function.

Chapter 3

- Neurotransmitter content has been updated.
- New Focus on Neuroscience box, The Neuroscience of the World Around You, highlights the work of Melvyn Goodale, of the University of Western Ontario, and colleagues.
- New Research Frontiers box, Gliotransmission?, highlights Canadian research (Richard Robitaille of the Université de Montréal).

Chapter 4

- Revisions and updates to the material on mapping the Genetic Code.
- Canadian statistics such as homicide rates.
- Revised explanation of the heritability coefficient.
- More on genetic counselling.
- New Focus on Neuroscience box: The Neuroscience and Genetics of Dyslexia.

Chapter 5

- The opening vignette looks at the perceptual basis for the phenomenon of gravity hills, such as Moncton's famous Magnetic Hill.
- Focus on Neuroscience addresses subliminal perception by looking at the work of Jody Culham and Mel Goodale on patients' awareness of objects following brain damage.
- Research Foundations looks at the work on critical periods in the development of feature detector cells in the cat's visual cortex.
- Gaining Directions explains gravity hills as optical illusions.

Chapter 6

- The opening vignette looks at fear of flying and how one Montreal firm is addressing this issue.
- Many minor revisions plus several major changes including a new Research Frontiers box, To Sleep, To Dream, Perchance to Learn, which highlights work by C. Smith of Trent University.
- Updated material on crystal methamphetamine and NMDA (ecstasy).
- A new Focus on Neuroscience box: The Neuroscience of Meditation.
- Gaining Directions focuses on fear of flying as an anxiety disorder. The treatment described in the vignette is a form of behaviour therapy.

Chapter 7

- A new Psychological Applications box highlighting the use of VR: Learning, Virtual Reality, and Therapy.
- A new Focus on Neuroscience box: The Neuroscience of Fear Conditioning.

Chapter 8

- In the Research Foundations feature, we examine the work of Sperling on memory traces.
- Focus on Neuroscience addresses methods to distinguish accurate from fabricated memories.
- A new table summarizing information on some hunger and satiety signals such as CCk and leptin.
- A new Research Frontiers section, Excessive Exercise: Activity Anorexia, highlights the work of Virginia Grant and colleagues at Memorial University in Newfoundland.
- A new neuroscience feature, Affective Neuroscience.

Chapter 9

- In the Focus on Neuroscience box, we examine the issue of brain size and intelligence, looking at specific brain regions.

- Research Foundations looks at the classic study by Hampson & Kimura on the influence of hormones in cognitive functioning.

Chapter 10

- A new table has been added to summarize signals that help to control hunger and eating.
- A new Research Frontiers box on excessive exercise and activity anorexia highlights work by Dr. Virginia Grant and colleagues at Memorial University, Newfoundland.
- Revised and rewritten section on motivational conflict and delay discounting.
- Focus on Neuroscience box discusses the emerging area of affective neuroscience.

Chapter 11

- A new Focus on Neuroscience box, The Neuroscience of the Teenage Brain, investigates ground-breaking imaging research that has established a link between various aspects of brain maturation and behavioural changes during adolescence.

Chapter 12

- A new opening vignette examines astrology as a predictor of personality.
- Extensive revisions to the section on the Psychodynamic Perspective.
- A new Research Frontiers: Stressed by Success highlights research by Joanne Wood and Sara A. Heimpel of the University of Waterloo, and their colleagues.
- A new Focus on Neuroscience box: The Neuroscience of the Big Five.
- A new Research Foundations section highlights the contributions of Albert Bandura, a Canadian and one of the most influential of all modern psychologists.
- Gaining Directions invites the reader to consider both what personality is and how it should be measured.

Chapter 13

- Research Foundations examines the classic work of Robert Rosenthal on being sane in insane places.
- Eating disorders are now discussed in this chapter rather than in Chapter 15.
- Focus on Neuroscience examines two competing neural theories for obsessive-compulsive disorder.

Chapter 14

- In Focus on Neuroscience, we examine the neural underpinning for the successful treatment of unipolar depression.

Chapter 15

- Expanded and extensively revised section on Post Traumatic Stress Disorder (PTSD).
- A new Focus on Neuroscience box: The Neuroscience of Social Support.
- Revisions to the Optimism and Personality Factors sections.
- Updated statistics on causes of death in Canada, health costs in Canada, and drug use in Canada.
- A new research foundations section, Research Foundations: Life Events, Illness, and the Emergence of Health Psychology.

Chapter 16

- A new opening vignette challenges students to think about the shootings at Montreal's Dawson College.
- The Focus on Neuroscience feature looks at the involvement of brain structures in stereotyping and prejudice.
- Gaining Direction helps us to focus on the Dawson College shooting by looking at the possible influence of media violence and social identity.

SUPERIOR SERVICE

Service takes on a whole new meaning with McGraw-Hill Ryerson and *Psychology: Frontiers and Applications*. More than just bringing you the textbook, we have consistently raised the bar in terms of innovation and educational research. These investments in learning and the academic community have helped us to understand the needs of students and educators across the country, and allowed us to foster the growth of truly innovative, integrated learning.

*i*Learning Sales Specialist

Your Integrated Learning Sales Specialist is a McGraw-Hill Ryerson representative who has the experience, product knowledge, training, and support to help you assess and integrate any of our products, technology, and services into your course for optimum teaching and learning performance. Whether it's using our test bank software, helping your students improve their grades, or putting your entire course online, your *i*Learning Sales Specialist is there to help you do it. Contact your local *i*Learning Sales Specialist today to learn how to maximize all of McGraw-Hill Ryerson's resources!

*i*Learning Services Program

McGraw-Hill Ryerson offers a unique *i*Services package designed for Canadian faculty. Our mission is to equip providers of higher education with superior tools and resources required for excellence in teaching. For additional information, visit **www.mcgrawhill.ca/highereducation/iservices**.

Teaching, Technology & Learning Conference Series

The educational environment has changed tremendously in recent years, and McGraw-Hill Ryerson continues to be committed to helping you acquire the skills you need to succeed in this new milieu. Our innovative Teaching, Technology & Learning Conference Series brings faculty together from across Canada with 3M Teaching Excellence award winners to share teaching and learn best practices in a collaborative and stimulating environment. Pre-conference workshops on general topics, such as teaching large classes and technology integration, are also offered. We will also work with you at your own institution to customize workshops that best suit the needs of your faculty at your institution.

SUPPLEMENTS

A complete, integrated supplements package supports students and instructors to help them meet their learning and teaching challenges.

For Instructors

Instructor's CD-ROM
Instructor Online Learning Centre (www.mcgrawhill.ca/olc/passer)

These products contain all the necessary instructor supplements, fully adapted to accord with *Psychology: Frontiers and Applications*, Third Canadian Edition.

- **Computerized Test Bank:** A completely revised and expanded test bank is available for this title. Each question has been analyzed to ensure complete accuracy and correlation to the third edition text. Each multiple-choice item is classified by type (factual, conceptual, or applied) and difficulty level, and is keyed to the appropriate page number in the textbook. Test items are also available in Word format (Rich text format). An additional bank of conceptual problems is also available for this text.
- **Instructor's Manual:** A rich collection of lecture leads, learning objectives, in-class demonstrations, case studies, critical thinking questions, and current controversies will make course preparation a snap. This manual also provides many activity suggestions as well as handout and overhead transparency masters to engage students' interest in class material.
- **Microsoft® PowerPoint®** slides accompany each chapter. You may choose basic text-only PowerPoint slides, a standard version that adds images and links, or an extended version that includes McGraw-Hill and Discovery Channel videos, animations and interactivities. In addition, **Dynamic PowerPoints** cover more than 80 core concepts in psychology. They are designed to be incorporated into lectures to help you present concepts more visually and engagingly.
- **Image Bank** includes outstanding tables and figures from the text.

NEW! The integrator

Keyed to the chapters and topics of *Psychology: Frontiers and Applications*, the *i*ntegrator ties together all the elements in your resource package, guiding you to where you'll find corresponding coverage in each of the related support package components—be it the Instructor's Manual, Computerized Test Bank, PowerPoint® slides, or the Online Learning Centre or online *i*Study Guide. Link to the *i*ntegrator via the Online Learning Centre at **www.mcgrawhill.ca/olc/passer**.

eInstruction's Classroom Performance System (CPS)

CPS is a student response system using wireless connectivity. It gives instructors and students immediate feedback from the entire class. The response pads are remote controls that are easy to use and engage students. Please contact your *i*Learning Sales Specialist for more information on how you can integrate CPS into your psychology classroom.

Course Management

Visit **www.mhhe.com/pageout** to create a Web page for your course using our resources. PageOut is the McGraw-Hill Ryerson Web site development centre. This Web page-generation software is free to adopters and is designed to help faculty create an online course, complete with assignments, quizzes, links to relevant Web sites, and more—all in a matter of minutes. In addition, content cartridges are available for course management systems such as WebCT and Blackboard. These platforms provide instructors with user-friendly, flexible teaching tools. Please contact your local McGraw-Hill Ryerson *i*Learning Sales Specialist for details.

Additional Resources

Contact your *i*Learning Sales Specialist for these additional resources to supplement your psychology course:

- In-Class Activities Manual for Instructors of Introductory Psychology
- Taking Sides: Clashing Views on Controversial Psychological Issues, 12th Edition
- Sources: Notable Selections in Psychology

For Students

Online Learning Centre

The Online Learning Centre (**www.mcgrawhill.ca/olc/passer**) provides chapter quizzes, Web links, a link to *i*StudyPsychology, and other study tools.

NEW! *i*StudyPsychology

Available 24/7: Instant feedback so you can study when you want, how you want, and where you want: www.mcgrawhill.ca/olc/passer.This online *i*Study space was developed to help you master the concepts and achieve better grades with all of the learning tools you've come to expect (i.e., multiple-choice and true/false quizzes) plus chapter-by-chapter learning goals, key term reviews, psychology interactivities, videos, and added quizzes, including a diagnostic assessment that points you to the concepts you need to focus on to improve your grades. Pick and choose from all of these features to develop your own personalized study plan. *i*Study offers the best, most convenient way to Interact, Learn, and Succeed.

- **Study to Go: A Mobile Learning Application for Palm and PocketPC**

  Do you use a handheld personal digital assistant (PDA)? McGraw-Hill Ryerson's Study to Go application gives you the opportunity to study any time, anywhere. And it's free for students using *i*StudyPsychology.

Σ-STAT

Σ-STAT is an educational resource designed by Statistics Canada and made available to Canadian educational institutions. Using 450,000 current CANSIM (Canadian Socio-economic Information Management System) Time Series and the most recent—as well as historical—census data, Σ-STAT lets you bring data to life in colourful graphs and maps. Access to Σ-STAT is made available to purchasers of this book, via the Passer Online Learning Centre, by special agreement between McGraw-Hill Ryerson and Statistics Canada. The Online Learning Centre provides additional information.

In-Psych Plus Student CD-ROM

In-Psych Plus sets a new standard for introductory psychology multimedia through its total integration with the textbook and Learning Objectives. The material will guide students to videos, animations, interactive activities, and video clips from the Discovery Channel pertaining to topics in the text. It also includes a pre-test, follow-up discussion questions, and Web resources. In-Psych Plus also includes chapter quizzes, a student research guide, and an interactive timeline that puts events, key figures, and research in psychology in historical perspective. Teachers may choose to test students on any of these items.

ACKNOWLEDGMENTS

Every book, large or small, owes a great deal to the people behind the scenes. They keep the project going, offer support and assistance, and provide sage advice to the authors.

Thanks to David Murray for advice and consultation on the history section; Kang Lee and William Gekoski for their suggestions on the developmental chapter; Ann Muir for assistance in proofreading; and to Sandi Martin, who helped to identify Canadian sources and references. Thanks also to Lesley Atkinson and Bill Cox—your support keeps me sane.

Our heartfelt thanks to all the people at McGraw-Hill Ryerson who have nurtured this book over the past year: Nicole Lukach (publisher, humanities, social sciences, and languages); Joanne Limebeer (supervising editor); Kelly Dickson (managing editor, development); Jeff Snook (national channel manager & custom publisher); Jeff MacLean (director of marketing); Paula Brown (senior production coordinator); Imogen Brian (copy editor); Joanna Cotton (editorial director); and Pat Ferrier (president, higher education).

And finally, a special thanks to Jennifer DiDomenico, Denise Foote, and Suzanne Simpson Millar (developmental editors). You kept us on track, on time, and in focus. We simply could not have done this without you.

M.A., J.M., & D.M.

We also owe special thanks to the distinguished corps of colleagues who reviewed the manuscript of *Psychology: Frontiers and Applications,* Third Canadian Edition. Many of the improvements in the book are the outgrowth of their comments about what they want in an introductory psychology textbook for their courses. In this regard, we sincerely appreciate the time and effort contributed by the following instructors:

Emir Andrews	Memorial University of Newfoundland
Wendy Bourque	St. Thomas University and University of New Brunswick
Annabel Evans	Concordia University College of Alberta
Lynne Honey	Grant MacEwan College
Steve Joordens	University of Toronto Scarborough
Daniel Meegan	University of Guelph
Heather Schellinck	Dalhousie University
Jessica Schroeder	University of Toronto
D.L. Sexton	University of Manitoba
Rhonda Snow	University College of the Fraser Valley
Sally Walters	Capilano College
Andrew Winston	University of Guelph

CHAPTER 1

Psychology: The Science of Behaviour

Perhaps the most fascinating and mysterious universe of all is the one within us.

—Carl Sagan

CHAPTER OUTLINE

The Chapter Outline is your road map to each chapter. Skim the outline *before* reading the chapter to get an overview of the chapter's topic.

The compass icon appears next to the opening story. Throughout the chapter, the icon will mark sections of text that may be relevant to this story.

In the past 30 years, there has been a noticeable change in our planet's weather. Many scientists have argued that *global warming*—the increase in temperature resulting from an excess of carbon dioxide and other greenhouse gases in the atmosphere—is the most serious issue facing humanity today. Consider the following:

- In the last 30 years, the number of Category 4 and 5 hurricanes (winds of over 210 km/h) has doubled. Hurricane Katrina (Category 5), which struck the Gulf Coast in August of 2005, was responsible for 1,336 deaths and damage estimated at $75 billion U.S. In the aftermath of the storm, reaction to the devastation reflected a huge range of human behaviours; there were reports of mercy killings, racial discrimination, heroic acts, and people reaching out to help others. And Canada is not immune to the increase in hurricanes: Hurricane Juan, a Category 2 storm and one of the most powerful hurricanes to ever hit Canada, made landfall in Nova Scotia on Sept. 28, 2003.
- The mountain pine beetle has spread into northern regions of Canada, where it is destroying millions of acres of forest. The beetle population has been controlled in the past by cold winters. But for the last decade, winter temperatures have not been cold enough to kill the beetle.
- Resolute Bay, Nunavut, is the second most-northerly town in Canada (893 km north of the Arctic Circle) and is one of the coldest communities on the planet. However, it is now considerably warmer than it has been for decades. Polar bears are spending more time on land than on the ice floes (where they have access to their main source of food, seals) because they must wait longer for the Arctic Ocean to freeze.

The potential consequences of global warming are catastrophic. Many experts predict that

- Deaths attributable to global warming will hit 300,000 per year by 2030.
- The Arctic Ocean will be ice-free by 2050.
- Sea levels could rise by more than six metres.
- Drought and intense heat waves will become more frequent.
- Over a million species could be extinct by 2050.

Climate scientists now estimate that the Earth is a mere 1 degree Celsius short of the highest temperature it has been in the last million years.

- **What are the issues here?**
- **What do we need to know?**
- **Where can you find the information necessary to answer the questions?**

Try to answer these questions after you read the opening story. When you see the compass icon throughout the chapter, consider which issue it might address, what information is provided, and what else we need to know.

"Down through the ages . . . we have had political, economic and nationalistic revolutions. All of them, as our descendants will discover, are but ripples in an ocean of conservatism—trivial by comparison with the psychological revolution toward which we are so rapidly moving." Huxley (1950)

More than a half century has passed since the English literary master and visionary Aldous Huxley (1950) foresaw an age in which scientific knowledge about mind and behaviour would provide us with greater understanding of ourselves and with powerful tools to improve our lives. We are now in the midst of the psychological revolution that Huxley predicted. On many fronts, important advances are being made in unravelling the mysteries of human behaviour. Like the world in which we live, the face of modern-day psychology constantly changes as new discoveries deepen our knowledge and create new opportunities for the application of psychological science.

Terms in boldface indicate new or important concepts. These terms are defined in the Glossary.

THE NATURE OF PSYCHOLOGY

Psychology is the scientific study of behaviour and the factors that influence it. Psychologists use the term *behaviour* very broadly to refer both to actions that we can observe directly and to inner processes—*mental events*—such as thoughts, feelings, images, and physiological reactions. In their search for the causes of these diverse forms of behaviour, psychologists take into account biological, individual, and environmental factors.

1. Define psychology and indicate what kinds of behaviours it studies.

Each chapter contains 40 to 50 directed questions. Read the question *before* you read the material in the text. After reading the material, try to answer the question.

The science of psychology relates to virtually every aspect of our lives. It explores the nature and causes of our behaviour and feelings, our motives and thoughts. Psychology has also assumed an increasingly important role in solving human problems and promoting the welfare of the inhabitants of this complex and rapidly changing world. As you will discover, psychologists are concerned with an enormous range of questions about behaviour. The following is just a sample of the issues we will be viewing through the window of psychology:

- How do we remember, think, and reason?
- How do drugs alter brain functioning and thereby affect consciousness and behaviour?
- What makes us fall in love?
- How does one's culture influence behaviour?
- What are the causes of aggression, and how can aggression be controlled?
- How do our genes affect our abilities, personality, and behaviour?
- Which child-rearing methods produce psychologically healthy adults?
- Why do we sleep, and what functions do our dreams serve? What brain processes regulate sleep and dreaming?
- What are the causes of mental disorders and addictions, and how can they be treated or prevented?
- To what extent are our actions controlled by unconscious factors?
- Can stress kill? What are effective ways of coping with stress?

This book is your map. Follow us as we explore these and many other questions. Because behaviour is so complex and so personal, its scientific study poses special challenges. As you become familiar with the kinds of evidence necessary to validate scientific conclusions, you can become a better-informed consumer of the many claims made in the name of psychology. For one thing, this course will teach you that many widely held beliefs about behaviour have no basis in fact. Examine the beliefs in Table 1.1. Which ones are actually true? Perhaps even more important than the facts you learn in your psychology course will be the habits of thought that you acquire. As you develop the skills of critical thinking, you will learn to ask several very important questions when told about a new "fact":

- "What exactly are you asking me to believe?"
- "How do you know? What's the evidence?"
- "Are there other possible explanations?"

We want you to leave your introductory psychology course with improved critical thinking skills, and with the ability to analyze behaviour and its causes. These skills will serve you well in many areas of your life.

Psychology as a Basic and Applied Science

As scientists, psychologists employ a variety of research methods for developing and testing theories about behaviour and its causes. A distinction is sometimes made between **basic research**, the quest for knowledge purely for its own sake, and **applied research**, which is designed to solve specific practical problems. In psychology, the goals of basic research are to describe how people behave and to identify the factors that influence or cause a particular type of behaviour. Such research may be carried out in the laboratory or in real-world settings. Applied research often uses principles discovered through basic research to solve practical problems. (Research methods will be discussed more fully in Chapter 2.)

2. How do the goals of basic research and applied research differ?

Let us consider an example of the link between basic and applied research. In the following case a classic research study carried out more than a generation ago

Material in tables and figures can be just as important as the text. Be sure you read these sections.

TABLE 1.1 Widely Held Beliefs about Behaviour: Facts or Fiction?

1. Personality development is primarily influenced by the experiences that are shared by members of a family.
2. Intellectual abilities decline dramatically in old age.
3. The primary reason babies develop love for their parents is that they satisfy biological and safety needs.
4. Most people with exceptionally high IQs are poorly adjusted in other areas of their life.
5. A person who is innocent of a crime has nothing to fear from a lie detector test.
6. Hypnosis is a reliable method for helping people recover unconscious memories of childhood sexual abuse.
7. People who need help in an emergency are more likely to get it if there are many bystanders present than if there is only one.
8. A schizophrenic is a person who has two distinct personalities, hence the term "split personality."
9. In romantic relationships, opposites usually attract.
10. If ordered to do so by an authority who could not punish disobedience, most people would refuse to perform an act that would harm another.
11. Consistent punishment for misbehaviour is the most effective way to make people behave appropriately.
12. People who commit suicide usually have signalled to others their intention to do so.

Note: The first 11 statements are not supported by psychological research. The last statement is supported by research findings.

inspired a more recent educational strategy designed to reduce interracial conflict and increase learning in multicultural schools.

From Robbers Cave to the Jigsaw Classroom

The compass icon indicates that the material here may help us understand the opening story.

How do intergroup hostility and prejudice develop, and what can be done to reduce them? In today's multicultural world, in which religious and ethnic groups often clash with one another, this question has great societal importance. To provide an answer to it, basic research explores the factors that increase and reduce intergroup hostility.

Psychologists conducted one such study at a summer camp for 11-year-old boys in Robbers Cave, Oklahoma (Sherif et al., 1961). When they arrived at the camp, the boys were divided by the researchers into two groups, who chose to call themselves the Eagles and the Rattlers. The Eagles and Rattlers lived in different cabins, but did all other activities together and got along well until the second week, when the experimenters began to pit them against one another in a series of competitive contests. It wasn't long before strong hostility developed between the groups. Group members discriminated against the boys from the other group and would not form friendships with them. The researchers then attempted to reduce the escalating conflict, but soon learned that simply increasing contact between the groups only increased the level of hostility and distrust. Was there anything that could be done to restore harmony?

The researchers finally succeeded in reducing the hostility by placing the children in situations in which the two groups were forced to cooperate with each other to accomplish goals that were important to both groups. These activities included repairing the water supply system, pooling their money to rent a movie, and towing a truck to get it started so that they could all go into town. In each instance, the

Eagles and Rattlers needed each other in order to attain a common goal. Within six days, these cooperative experiences virtually dissolved the boundaries between the groups, and many new friendships developed between the Eagles and Rattlers.

3. How do the Robbers Cave experiment and the jigsaw classroom program illustrate the relation between basic and applied science?

The Robbers Cave study showed that competition could breed hostility and that conflict between groups could be decreased by making the groups dependent upon one another so that they would need to cooperate. Could this principle, derived from basic research, be applied to increase harmony and academic achievement in multiracial schools, where different ethnic groups sometimes compete against one another in much the same way the Eagles and Rattlers did? Years later, in the midst of the stormy desegregation of public schools in Texas, psychologist Elliot Aronson and his co-workers applied the Robbers Cave techniques in a classroom procedure called the **jigsaw program** (Aronson et al., 1978). This program requires children to cooperate with one another rather than compete against each other in order for any of them to succeed. It involves creating multi-ethnic groups of five or six children who are assigned to prepare for an upcoming test on, for example, the life of Pierre Elliott Trudeau. Within the groups, each child is given a "piece" of the total knowledge to be learned. Only one child has information about Trudeau's early childhood, another about his political career, a third about his death, and so on. For the group members to pass the test, they must fit their knowledge "pieces" together as if they were working on a jigsaw puzzle. Each child must teach the others his or her piece of knowledge. Like the children at Robbers Cave, the students soon learn that the only way they can be successful is to work together and help one another. In so doing, they learn to appreciate one another and to feel appreciated by the other group members (Figure 1.1).

FIGURE 1.1

The jigsaw classroom designed by psychologist Elliot Aronson was inspired by basic research that showed how conditions of mutual dependence and cooperation among hostile groups can reduce intergroup hostility. Aronson's applied research intervention had similar effects within racially integrated classrooms.

The effects of the jigsaw technique and other "cooperative learning" programs have been carefully evaluated in hundreds of classrooms, and the results are encouraging (Aronson, 2004; Johnson, 2000). Across racial boundaries, children's liking for one another generally increased, prejudice decreased, and self-esteem as well as school achievement improved. In one study, minority children increased their performance by almost one full letter grade after only two weeks of jigsaw participation (Lucker et al., 1977). Measures of school enjoyment also increased for all ethnic groups.

Cooperative learning programs show how basic research such as the Robbers Cave experiment can be used as a basis for designing an intervention program. We will see many other examples of how basic research provides knowledge that not only satisfies our desire to understand our world, but also can be applied to solve practical problems.

Goals of Psychology

As scientists, psychologists have four basic goals:

1. to *describe* how people and other animals behave
2. to *explain and understand* the causes of these behaviours
3. to *predict* how people and animals will behave under certain conditions
4. to *influence or control* behaviour through knowledge and control of its causes to enhance human welfare

As you will learn in Chapter 2, the scientific goals of understanding, prediction, and control are linked in the following manner: If we understand the causes of a behaviour and know when the causal factors are present or absent, then we should be able to successfully predict when the behaviour will occur. Moreover, if

4. What are the four goals of psychology? How are these goals linked to one another?

5. How were the four goals of scientific psychology illustrated in the Robbers Cave study?

we can control the causes, then we should be able to control the behaviour. For scientists, successful prediction and control are the best ways for us to know whether we truly understand the causes of a behaviour. We should also note, however, that prediction can have important practical uses that do not require a complete understanding of why some behaviour occurs. For example, a psychologist might find that scores on a personality test dependably predict school dropout, without fully understanding the psychological processes involved.

All of these goals were pursued in the basic and applied research examples described above. At Robbers Cave, the researchers carefully observed the behaviour of the boys under certain conditions (description). They believed that competition is one cause of intergroup hostility and discrimination, and that cooperation to achieve common goals could reduce such hostility (understanding). They then tested their understanding by forecasting what would happen if they created conditions that first pitted the Eagles and Rattlers against one another, then forced them to cooperate (prediction). When they imposed these conditions, they first created and then reduced intergroup hostility (influence or control). Later, when Aronson and his coworkers wanted to reduce racial hostility and discrimination within newly integrated schools, they had a scientific basis for predicting what might work, and they were able to successfully apply their understanding in the form of the jigsaw program.

These four goals of description, understanding, prediction, and influence or control are not limited to the world of science. They are also important goals of daily life. On a day-to-day basis, we all ask questions such as "What's happening? What am I (or they) doing?" (description); "Why did she do that?" (understanding or explanation); "What will happen if I do it this way?" (prediction); and "What can I do to make sure things turn out the way I want them to?" (influence or control). In daily life, however, we are often satisfied with our "understanding" if we have a logical explanation that is consistent with what happened in the past. We usually don't go the extra mile to test our understanding more systematically through prediction and control, as scientists do.

In Review

- *Psychology is the scientific study of behaviour. The term* behaviour *refers to actions and responses that can be observed and measured directly as well as mental processes such as thoughts and feelings that must be inferred from directly observable responses.*
- *Basic research is the quest for knowledge for its own sake, whereas applied research involves the application of knowledge derived from basic research to solve practical problems.*
- *The primary goals of psychological science are to describe, explain, predict, and influence behaviour and to apply psychological knowledge to enhance human welfare.*

PERSPECTIVES ON BEHAVIOUR: GUIDES TO UNDERSTANDING AND DISCOVERY

On a hot summer evening, a University of Texas student wrote the following letter:

> I don't really understand myself these days. I am supposed to be an average, reasonable, and intelligent young man. However, lately (I can't recall when it started) I have been the victim of many unusual and irrational thoughts. These thoughts constantly recur, and it requires a tremendous mental effort to

concentrate on useful and progressive tasks. In March when my parents made a physical break I noticed a great deal of stress. I consulted a Dr. Cochrum at the University Health Center and asked him to recommend someone that I could consult with about some psychiatric disorders I felt I had. I talked with a doctor once for about two hours and tried to convey to him my fears that I felt overcome by overwhelming violent impulses. After one session I never saw the doctor again, and since then I have been fighting my mental turmoil alone, and seemingly to no avail. After my death I wish that an autopsy would be performed on me to see if there is any visible physical disorder. I have had some tremendous headaches in the past and have consumed two large bottles of Excedrin in the past three months.

Later that night Charles Whitman killed his wife and mother. The next morning he went to a tower on the University of Texas campus and opened fire on the crowded campus below with a high-powered hunting rifle. In 90 horrifying minutes he killed 14 people, wounded another 24, and even managed to hit an airplane before he himself was killed by police.

FIGURE 1.2

Mass murderer Charles Whitman had no previous history of criminal violence. How can we explain such an apparently irrational act?

6. At what three levels of analysis were possible causes for Charles Whitman's violent outburst explored?

7. What are perspectives on behaviour? Cite four ways in which they can influence psychological science.

School shootings and other acts of apparently senseless violence are all too common in today's world. After the Whitman incident, the first question asked was a familiar one: What caused this mild-mannered young man (Figure 1.2) to explode into violence? Psychologists sought clues in the letter he wrote. Following up on his reference to intense headaches, a postmortem examination was conducted. It revealed a highly malignant tumour in an area of the brain known to be involved in aggressive behaviour. Some experts suggested therefore that Whitman's damaged brain might have predisposed him to violent behaviour. Others focused on the "unusual and irrational thoughts" to which he referred and to his "overwhelming violent impulses." Still others sought the answer in Whitman's previous learning experiences and the culture he grew up in. A study of his past revealed a long history of fascination and rewarding experiences with guns, as well as exposure to a brutally abusive father who often beat his mother and siblings. He also lived in a culture that is renowned for its violent solutions to conflict. Perhaps the environment in which he developed had primed him to solve his problems in a violent manner, particularly when he was overwhelmed by the recent life stresses that he described in his letter. The Whitman case thus illustrates how many potential causes, past and present, could contribute to a given behaviour. In their attempts to understand Whitman's actions, psychologists considered potential causes at three different *levels of analysis:* biological, psychological, and environmental. We shall return to the levels of analysis concept later in the chapter. First, however, we consider the major psychological perspectives that provide an understanding of the specific causal factors that are studied at each level of analysis.

The Importance of Perspectives

Partly because psychology has its roots in such varied disciplines as philosophy, medicine, and the biological and physical sciences, different ways of viewing people and their behaviour make up its intellectual and scientific traditions. These diverse viewpoints, or, as we shall call them, **perspectives**, are vantage points for analyzing behaviour and its biological, psychological, and environmental causes (Figure 1.3). Thinking about a behavioural phenomenon from different perspectives can enrich our understanding of its diverse causes.

If you've ever encountered a person who seems to view the world much differently from the way you do, you know that perspectives make a difference. You may have found that he or she had different notions of why things happen and attached great importance to things you barely noticed. Like our own personal viewpoints, psychological perspectives serve as lenses through which the world of behaviour is viewed, and they reflect and shape our conception of human nature. They also determine which aspects of behaviour we consider important and worthy of study, which questions we ask, and which methods of study we employ. Perspectives on behaviour thereby influence the directions in which psychology develops, what it learns about behaviour, and the kinds of contributions it makes to improving the human condition.

FIGURE 1.3

Youth and beauty? . . . or maturity and wisdom? If you examine this drawing, you will see at various times either a young woman or an old one. The images will alternate as you examine the drawing, particularly if you interpret the dark horizontal line in the lower half of the figure as either a necklace or a mouth. Like many aspects of our experience, what we perceive depends on our perspective at the moment.

Six major perspectives characterize contemporary psychological thought. They are the biological, cognitive, psychodynamic, behavioural, humanistic, and sociocultural perspectives (Figure 1.4). Each attempts to address timeless philosophical questions about human nature, and often builds upon insights achieved by other perspectives. The six perspectives also provide us with a historical framework for tracing the intellectual and scientific traditions that have fostered the development of modern-day psychology.

In science, new viewpoints are the lifeblood of progress. Advances occur as existing beliefs are challenged, a debate ensues, and scientists seek new evidence to resolve the debate. Sometimes, the best-supported elements of the contrasting viewpoints are melded into a new viewpoint, which, in turn, stimulates new understandings when it is later challenged. Thus, as one scientist notes, "Science consists of organizing controversy or, if need be, generating it" (Murphy 1982).

We first consider each of the perspectives individually, focusing on its conceptions of human nature and its viewpoints about causal factors in behaviour. Then, we place its contributions in historical perspective, showing how its influence has contributed to the evolution of psychology.

The Biological Perspective: Brain, Genes, and Behaviour

Humans have long sought to understand the role of biological factors in their behaviour. At the centre of this quest lies a philosophical question that has tested and bested the greatest minds of the ages: the so-called *mind-body problem.* The concept of mind—the inner agent of consciousness and thought—has its roots in antiquity. Yet its very nature has been debated down through the ages. Is it a spiritual entity separate from the body, or is it part of our body's activities?

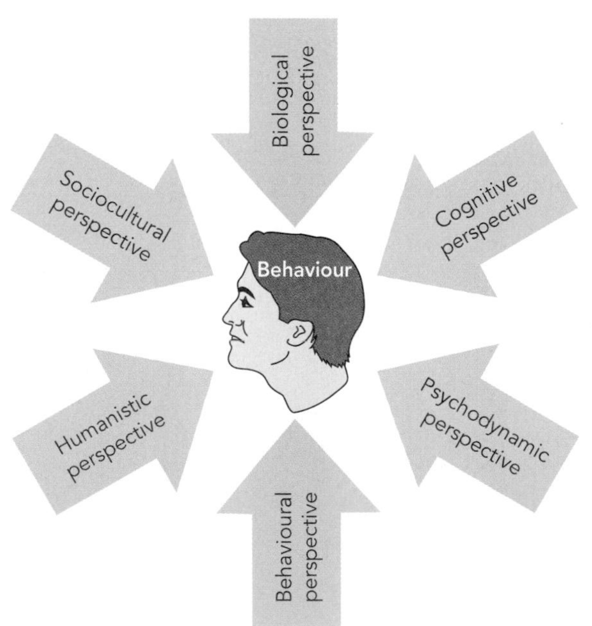

FIGURE 1.4

Six major perspectives guide modern psychology's attempts to understand human behaviour.

The ancient Greeks could not agree on the vital question of how mind and body are related. Pythagoras, Plato, and Hippocrates all believed that the brain is the seat of the mind and the intellect. Aristotle disagreed, believing that the mind is located in the heart. Many of the Greeks as well as other philosophers held a position of **mind–body dualism**, the belief that the mind is a spiritual entity not subject to the physical laws that govern the body. This view implies that no amount of research on the body could ever hope to unravel the mysteries of the mind.

An alternative view of mind-body relations is derived from the Greek word *monos*, meaning "one." **Monism** (in the materialist form) holds that the "mind" is not a separate spiritual entity. Mind and body are one, and mental events are simply a product of physical events. In the modern view, these physical events are electrical and chemical processes occurring in the brain. If this is so, then questions about mental functions *can* be studied scientifically, for we can potentially measure these physical processes. Most modern scientists hold the view that mind and body are one, and many who hold a biological perspective would agree with this somewhat provocative statement by physiological psychologists Richard Thompson and Daniel Robinson:

> . . . answers to the great questions of psychology will ultimately be found in "physiology." Higher organisms, after all, are simply brains with a few minor appendages. All behaviour, all experience, all feeling, indeed all the subject matter of psychology, are nothing more than the outcomes of the activity of the nervous system. (Thompson & Robinson, 1979, p. 449)

In the case of Charles Whitman's murderous behaviour, a biological perspective would attach great importance to the headaches he reported in his letter and the brain tumour found during his autopsy. The **biological perspective** thus focuses on the physical side of human nature. It emphasizes the role of our highly developed brain; the biochemical processes that underlie our every thought, emotion, and action; and the manner in which genetic factors influence the development and behaviour of human organisms.

8. Contrast the positions of dualism and monism as they apply to the "mind-body" problem.

9. What three classes of causal factors does the biological perspective focus on?

The Focus on Neuroscience feature in each chapter highlights how rapidly developing cutting-edge technology is paving the way for groundbreaking imaging studies that give new insights into the workings of the human brain and its relationship to behaviour.

FOCUS ON NEUROSCIENCE

The Neuroscience of Imaging Studies

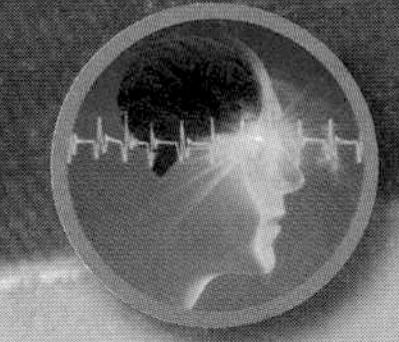

Early attempts to image or map the human brain relied on relatively inaccurate, and, in some cases, subjective, methods. Franz Joseph Gall and his colleague Spurzheim developed the "science" of phrenology in the early 19th century. According to historian E.G. Boring (1950), as a young boy, Gall had noticed a relationship between eye prominence and memory—he believed those with pronounced eyes had superior memory. Gall went on to study the relationship between various mental characteristics and the shape of one's head, producing a number of mental maps based on the bumps and valleys found on the skull. Presumably, the bigger the bump, the more brain tissue underneath and, consequently, the more processing power. Gall's maps are completely inaccurate—language and memory are not reflective of brain tissue behind your eyes. However, the general notion that different functions are mediated by different areas of the brain was an idea whose time had come.

Much of the early work on localization of function involved the examination of patients who had very specific brain injuries that resulted in a very specific mental or behavioural loss (e.g., the case of Phineas Gage discussed in Chapter 3). Upon autopsy, one could examine the nature and extent of the brain injury and relate this to functional loss. However, this method was not very exact and there were relatively few patients to examine. In the laboratory, it was possible to have much more precision. Shepherd Franz and his student Karl Lashley began a series of experiments in the early 1920s designed to investigate the effects of specific tissue loss. Using animal subjects, various brain areas were removed and results were noted. To their surprise, a great deal of cortex could be removed with relatively small losses in function. Many believe that the Franz & Lashley studies are the source of the often-quoted myth that we only use ten percent of our brain (we use it all).

With the development of new technologies, the focus has shifted to imaging the intact brain. Fox (1997) notes that the number of imaging studies is growing at an exponential rate (see Figure 1.5). In the early 1980s, fewer than 15

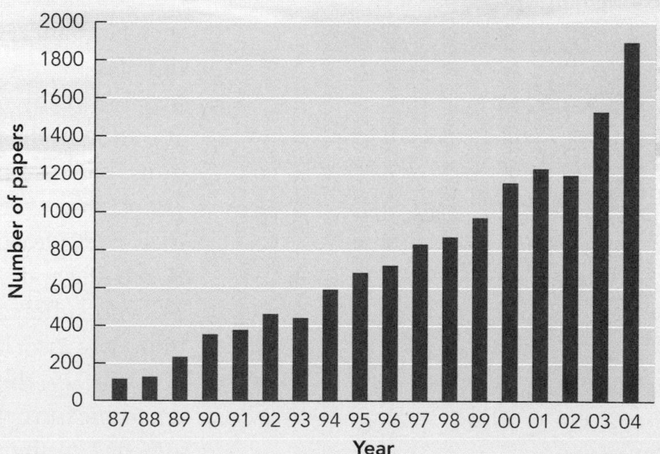

FIGURE 1.5

Growth in imaging abstracts at the annual Society for Neuroscience meeting (adapted from Fox, 1997)

–Continued

imaging papers were presented, on average, at the annual meeting of the Society for Neuroscience. At the 2005 meeting, there were an estimated 30,000 participants who gave a total of 17,040 presentations. Of these, 535 were on fMRI and an additional 210 focused on PET scans. When we consider other conferences and the various journals devoted to neuroscience, literally thousands of new articles on brain imaging are written every year. In every chapter of this text, we will highlight imaging studies in an effort to give a clearer understanding of the human mind.

Discovery of Brain–Behaviour Relations

10. What was the importance of Galvani's discovery for (a) the mind–body problem, and (b) the development of psychology as a science?

Because the biological perspective focuses on processes that are largely invisible to the naked eye, its development has depended on scientific and technological developments. Perhaps the most important discovery for the future science of psychology concerned the electrical nature of nerve conduction. In a landmark experiment in the late 1700s, the Italian scientist Luigi Galvani discovered that the severed leg of a frog would move if an electrical current were applied to it. Galvani's reports were ridiculed by dualist philosophers who believed that all bodily movements were caused by spiritual forces from the soul, but further experiments confirmed Galvani's findings. Soon many experiments on electrical nerve conduction were under way, borne on a wave of excitement about the discovery of "nervous energy." By 1870, researchers at the University of Berlin were applying electrical stimulation directly to the exposed brains of experimental animals. They discovered that stimulation of specific areas on the surface of the brain resulted in movements of particular muscles in the body. Soon they were able to "map" the areas on the brain's surface that controlled movement in various body regions. During this same period, many clinical reports appeared linking damage in specific areas of the brain with behavioural impairments of various kinds. For example, it was found that damage to a region on the left side of the brain resulted in the loss of the ability to understand or produce language.

FIGURE 1.6

Karl Lashley was a pioneer in the field of physiological psychology (behavioural neuroscience). He examined how damage to various brain regions affected rats' ability to learn and remember.

As psychology entered the 20th century, the study of brain-behaviour relations was still in its infancy. Karl Lashley, perhaps the most important figure in the early development of biological psychology in America, was interested in brain mechanisms in learning (Figure 1.6). His approach was to create lesions (damage) in specific brain regions and to study their effects on the learning and memory abilities of experimental animals that had been trained to run mazes. Lashley's research inspired many other attempts to study brain-behaviour relations experimentally and to map the areas of the brain that are involved in specific psychological functions. For example, at McGill University in Montreal, James Olds and Peter Milner (1954) discovered that some areas of the brain were specialized for providing animals with pleasurable sensations. As will be described at the start of Chapter 8, W. B. Scoville and Brenda Milner (1957), in the course of treating a patient named H. M. who suffered from epilepsy, found that damage to some areas of the human brain was associated with severe memory loss.

11. What subsequent technical developments were important in the study of brain–behaviour relations?

In 1929, the invention of the electroencephalogram (EEG) allowed researchers to measure the electrical activity of large areas of the brain through electrodes attached to the scalp. Scientists could now study brain-wave correlates of behaviours and states of consciousness without invading the brain. Yet the EEG is primitive compared to more recent technical tools. For example, tiny microelectrodes now permit the recording of electrical activities of individual brain cells. The electron microscope has made it possible to study formerly invisible brain structures. New computer-based imaging techniques have provided ways of watching the electrochemical activities that are the bases for thought, emotion, and behaviour.

Biochemical research has shown that the brain's electrical activity is controlled by chemical substances released by nerve cells. The role of these *neurotransmitter* substances in both normal and abnormal behaviour is one of the most important areas of current research. As you will see throughout the text, we are on the threshold of many other revolutionary discoveries in brain-behaviour relations.

FIGURE 1.7

Charles Darwin's theory of evolution had a tremendous impact on scientific thought that persists to this day.

Evolution and Behaviour: From Darwin to Evolutionary Psychology

As thinking and acting organisms, we go back a long way—long before our birth. Our species exists today because of our ancestors' ability to adapt, both biologically and behaviourally, to a changing and often hostile environment. Whereas the study of brain functioning often focuses on biological processes that occur in thousandths of a second, another part of the biological perspective focuses on processes that may occur over thousands of generations.

Darwin's evolutionary theory. Charles Darwin (Figure 1.7) casts a giant shadow in the history of scientific thought. In 1859, his book *On the Origin of Species* generated shock waves that are still felt today in debates between creationists and evolutionists. Darwin was not the first to suggest the possibility of evolution in animals, but his theory was the most plausible and best documented. It was vigorously opposed, however, for it seemed to many a denial of philosophical and religious beliefs about the exalted nature of human beings.

Darwin's theory was stimulated by observations he made during a five-year voyage on a British research vessel that explored the coasts of South America, Australia, South Africa, and many South Atlantic and South Pacific islands. Darwin was struck by the many differences between seemingly similar species that lived in different environments. He began to view these differences as ways in which the species had adapted to these environments.

12. What is meant by natural selection? What is its role in physical and behavioural evolution?

In his theory of evolution, Darwin proposed that species evolve over time in response to environmental conditions through a process called natural selection, or "survival of the fittest." **Natural selection** means that any inheritable characteristic that increases the likelihood of survival will be maintained in the species because individuals having the characteristic will be more likely to survive and reproduce. The underlying principle is that members of a given species differ naturally in many ways. Some possess specific traits to a greater extent than others. If any of these traits gives some members a competitive advantage over others, such as increasing their ability to attract mates, escape danger, or acquire food, these members are more likely to survive and pass their genes on to their offspring. In this way, the presence of adaptive traits will increase within the population over generations. In contrast, characteristics that reduce the chances for survival will be eliminated from the species over time because creatures having such characteristics will be less likely to survive (Figure 1.8). Darwin did not know the exact mechanism for the passing on of characteristics. That mechanism was to become evident later in the 19th century when Gregor Mendel's pioneering work on the genetic transmission of characteristics in plants led to the discovery of genes.

FIGURE 1.8

Natural selection pressures result in physical changes. The peppered moth's natural colour is that of the lighter insect. However, over many generations, peppered moths that live in polluted urban areas have become darker because darker insects blend into their grimy environment and are more likely to survive predators and pass their "dark" genes on to their progeny. However, a trip to the countryside to visit their light-coloured relatives could prove fatal for these urban insects.

The characteristics favoured by natural selection are not always positive ones. Sometimes natural selection favours the lesser of two evils. An example is sickle cell disease, a genetically caused blood disorder that is prevalent among people of African descent. Although the long-term effect of the sickle cell gene is to lower life expectancy, it does have one redeeming quality: It offers protection against malaria. Because people having the sickle cell gene were more likely to survive malaria epidemics, the prevalence of sickle cell disorder among African people increased over time (Nascutiu, 1997).

Darwin assumed that the principle of natural selection could be applied to all living things, including human beings. Contrary to a popular misconception, Darwin did *not* propose that humans are the direct descendants of modern apes. Rather, he believed that both human beings and apes branched off from a common ancestor in the distant past.

13. According to evolutionary psychology, how do biological and behavioural evolution influence one another?

Modern evolutionary psychology. **Evolutionary psychology** is an emerging discipline that focuses on the role of evolution in the development of behaviour and mental mechanisms. Psychologists in this field stress that an organism's biology determines its behavioural capabilities, and its behaviour (including its mental abilities) determines whether or not it will survive. In this manner, successful human behaviour evolved along with a changing body (Buss, 2005; Tooby & Cosmides, 1992).

14. According to sociobiology, what is the ultimate importance of evolved social behaviours? On what bases has this position been criticized by other theorists?

The notion that evolutionary pressures have stimulated the development of brain mechanisms that allow us to learn, think, reason, and socialize more effectively is generally accepted today. However, one evolutionary theory (and there are many theories) is more controversial. **Sociobiology** (Wilson, 1980) holds that complex social behaviours are also built into the human species as products of evolution. Sociobiologists argue that natural selection favours behaviours that increase the ability to pass on one's genes to the next generation. These social behaviours include aggression, competition, and dominance in males, and cooperative and nurturing tendencies in females. Indeed, sex differences in reproduction are significant. For example, sociobiologists Martin Daly and Margo Wilson, of McMaster University, note that females have a greater investment in the reproductive process. Women have less opportunity to reproduce (usually only one egg per month, and in Canada, produce only one to two children on average) than males. They also have a greater health risk during pregnancy and delivery, and in Canada, tend to be the primary caregiver after divorce. A major point is that, in the eyes of sociobiologists, one's *genetic* survival (i.e., the transmission of one's genes) is more important than one's own physical survival. This principle can explain certain "altruistic" behaviours, including giving up one's life to save children or relatives. Although such behaviour is hardly in the survival interests of the individual, it serves a higher purpose: It keeps one's genes alive in the gene pool to live on in our descendants (Sober & Wilson, 1998).

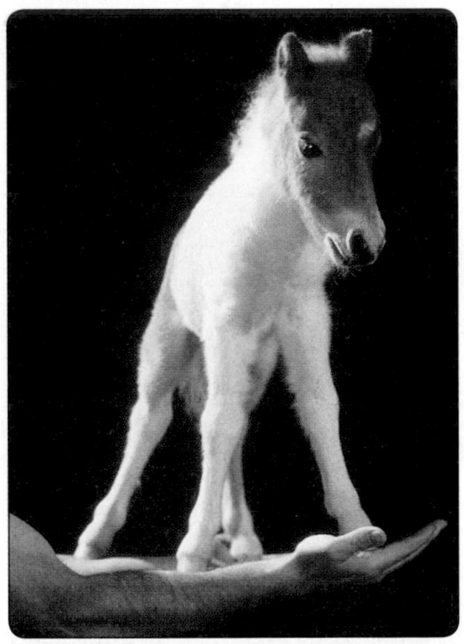

FIGURE 1.9

Selective breeding can produce both physical and behavioural characteristics. This tiny horse was produced by selectively breeding very small horses over a number of generations.

Many critics (e.g., Caporael, 1997) believe that sociobiology overemphasizes innate biological factors at the expense of cultural and social learning factors in explaining complex human social behaviour. Evolutionary theorists with a more cultural orientation suggest that the evolved brain structures that underlie psychological mechanisms (such as the ability to use language) developed in order to enhance adaptation to the demands of social and group living rather than simply to further the survival of one's genes.

Behaviour Genetics

Although scientists sometimes disagree about the role of evolution in the development of the human species, there is no question that our development and behaviour are affected by the genetic blueprint with which we are born (Efran & Greene, 2000; Plomin, 2004; Turkheimer & Waldron, 2000). Psychologists have had a long-standing interest in **behaviour genetics**, the study of how behavioural tendencies are influenced by genetic factors. (See, for example, the pioneering text by Fuller & Thompson, 1960.)

15. What methods do behaviour geneticists use to investigate the role of genetic factors in animal and human behaviour?

Animals can be bred selectively not only for physical traits (Figure 1.9), but also for behavioural traits such as aggression or intelligence. This is done by allowing highly aggressive or very bright males and females to mate with one another over a number of generations. In Thailand, where gambling on fish fights has long been a national pastime, the selective breeding of winners has produced the highly aggressive Siamese fighting fish. The male of this species will instantly attack his own image in a mirror and sometimes engages in fierce fighting contests that last up to six hours.

Human behaviour is also influenced by genetic factors. Identical twins, who result from the splitting of a fertilized egg and therefore have exactly the same genetic makeup, are far more similar to one another on many behavioural traits than are fraternal twins, who result from two different fertilized eggs and therefore differ genetically. This greater degree of similarity is found even when the identical twins have been reared in different homes and dissimilar environments (Bouchard et al., 1990; Plomin & Caspi, 1999; Tellegen et al., 1988). Genetic factors also are implicated in certain brain dysfunctions that produce disturbed behaviour (Gottesman, 1991; Papolos & Lachman, 1994).

The Cognitive Perspective: The Thinking Human

If you were asked what sets humans apart from other species, chances are you would point to our unique mental capabilities. Indeed, the name we immodestly have given to our own species, *Homo sapiens,* is Latin for "wise man."

16. What is the conception of human nature advanced by the cognitive perspective?

A large slice of human nature is captured in our conception of "the thinking human." Derived from the Latin word *cogitare* (to think), the **cognitive perspective** views humans as information processors and problem solvers whose actions are governed by thought and planning. Today's cognitive perspective is concerned with ageless questions about how information is perceived and then organized in our minds, as well as how that information is combined with other contents of the mind to create memories, problem-solving strategies, and creative thoughts. The cognitive perspective causes us to ask how mental processes influence our motives, emotions, and behaviour.

Origins of the Cognitive Perspective

Psychology from its very beginning has been concerned with mental processes. As it developed from its roots in philosophy and medicine, questions concerning the nature of the mind and its relation to the body were foremost in psychology. In the early years, several important schools of psychological thought developed, each of which had its own way of studying mental processes and each of which contributed to today's cognitive perspective. These schools included structuralism, functionalism, and Gestalt psychology.

FIGURE 1.10
Wilhelm Wundt (right) founded the German school of structuralism and established the first laboratory of experimental psychology in 1879 to study the nature of consciousness and the structure of the mind.

Structuralism. Wilhelm Wundt (1832–1920) was a German scientist who wanted to model the study of the mind after the physical and biological sciences. These sciences were analyzing materials with their new scientific tools, such as the microscope and chemical analysis. Wundt therefore founded the first laboratory of experimental psychology at Leipzig in 1879. There he helped train the first generation of scientific psychologists (Figure 1.10). Among these were August Kirschmann and James Baldwin, both of whom were founding members of the Department of Psychology at the University of Toronto, and George Humphrey, who began the tradition of research in experimental psychology at Queen's University at Kingston (Wright & Myers, 1982). One of his students was Edward Titchener, who later established a psychological laboratory in the United States at Cornell University. Like Wundt, Titchener was a kind of mental chemist. He believed that the mind

17. Compare the goals of structuralism and functionalism.

could be studied by breaking it down into its basic components or structures, as a chemist might do in studying a complex chemical compound. Wundt and Titchener's approach was therefore known as **structuralism**, the analysis of the mind in terms of its basic elements.

The structuralists believed that sensations are the basic elements of consciousness, and they set out to study sensations through the method of **introspection** ("looking within"). Participants in their experiments were exposed to all sorts of sensory stimuli—lights, sounds, and tastes—and were trained to describe their inner experiences. Although this method of studying the mind died out after a few decades, the structuralists left an important mark on the infant science of psychology by establishing a scientific tradition for the study of cognition that persists to this day.

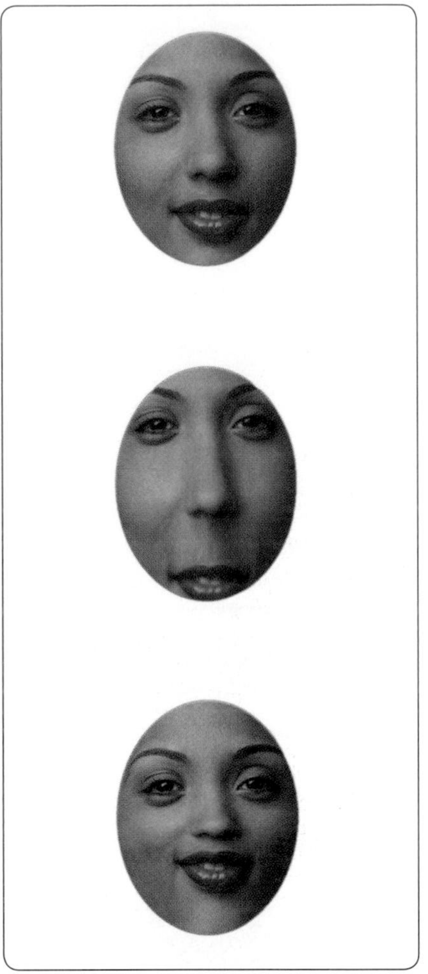

FIGURE 1.11

This illusion illustrates the Gestalt principle that the whole is often greater than the sum of its parts. The three ovals surrounding the faces appear to be of different size, but they are identical (see text). Prove this by measuring the length of each oval. This illusion can be reduced by inverting the page.

Source: Lee & Freire (1999).

Functionalism. In the United States, structuralism eventually gave way to an approach called **functionalism**, which held that psychology should study the *functions*—the whys—of consciousness, rather than its structure—the whats. In part, functionalism was influenced by Darwin's evolutionary theory, which stressed the importance of adaptive behaviour in helping organisms to respond successfully to their environment and survive. Much of the early research on the nature of learning and problem solving in humans and animals was done by functionalists. William James, a leader in the movement, was himself a "big-picture" person who concurrently taught courses in physiology, psychology, and philosophy at Harvard University. James's broad functionalist approach helped widen the scope of psychology to include biological processes, mental processes, and behaviour. Although it no longer exists as a formal school of thought within psychology, the tradition of functionalism endures in modern-day psychology as an emphasis on how the mind processes information and directs behaviour. It is seen also in evolutionary psychology's focus on the origins of adaptive behaviour.

Gestalt psychology. In the 1920s, German scientists again helped to shape psychology through a school of thought known as Gestalt psychology. The word *gestalt* may be translated as "whole" or "organization," and **Gestalt psychology** was concerned with how elements of experience are organized into wholes. The Gestalt approach was the opposite of that taken by the structuralists. Instead of trying to break consciousness down into its basic elements, the Gestalt psychologists argued that our perceptions and other mental processes are organized so that the whole is not only greater than, but also quite different from, the sum of its parts.

As an example, consider the illusion, recently discovered by Queen's psychologists Kang Lee and Alejo Freire (1999), shown in Figure 1.11. Although the oval windows through which you view the three faces are identical, for most people the one in which the internal features of the face are stretched appears longer, and the one in which the features are compressed appears shorter, than the window with the "normal" face. Another interesting point is that facial orientation is important. Slowly turn this page upside down and watch the difference in the size of the oval windows diminish. Gestalt psychologists believed that this tendency to perceive wholes is, like other forms of perceptual organization, built into our nervous system.

18. What does *gestalt* mean? How does this meaning relate to the goals and findings of Gestalt psychology?

Wolfgang Köhler (1887–1967) was one of the leaders of Gestalt psychology. He conducted research with apes and other animals while stranded at a research station in the Canary Islands during World War I. Köhler concluded that the ability to perceive relationships is the essence of what we call intelligence, and he defined **insight** as the sudden perception of a useful relationship or solution to a problem—a kind of "Aha!" experience.

Several examples of insight were demonstrated by Sultan, one of Köhler's chimpanzees. One day, Köhler hung a banana from the top of Sultan's cage, out of the ape's reach. Sultan seemed perplexed at first, but then he looked about his cage, noticed a box in one corner, and placed the box beneath the dangling banana so that he could reach it. Another time, Sultan joined two sticks together to reach a banana that had been placed on the ground outside his cage, a feat that has gone down in history as an act of presumed simian genius (Figure 1.12). Gestalt psychology's demonstrations of insight learning in both animals and humans stimulated new interest in cognitive topics such as perception, problem solving, and intelligence.

FIGURE 1.12

A modern-day counterpart of Sultan demonstrates insight learning by using a series of shorter sticks to pull in a stick that is long enough to reach the delicacy.

In addition to the schools of structuralism, functionalism, and Gestalt psychology, several other prominent theorists exerted a strong influence on the development of the cognitive perspective. Three of these individuals were Jean Piaget, Albert Ellis, and Aaron Beck.

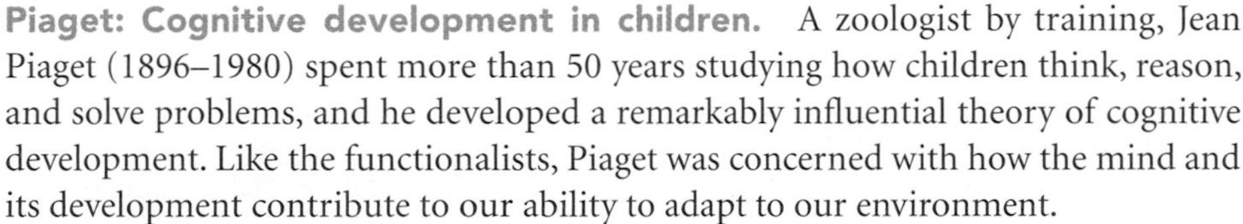

Piaget: Cognitive development in children. A zoologist by training, Jean Piaget (1896–1980) spent more than 50 years studying how children think, reason, and solve problems, and he developed a remarkably influential theory of cognitive development. Like the functionalists, Piaget was concerned with how the mind and its development contribute to our ability to adapt to our environment.

Piaget's primary technique was to carefully observe children as they tried to solve problems. He then tried to imagine how they must have experienced the situation in order to respond as they did (Figure 1.13). As a result of his systematic observations, Piaget concluded that new and specific stages of cognitive development unfold naturally as children mature, and that these abilities cannot be explained by the accumulation of past experiences. Rather, the stages that naturally unfold represent fundamentally different ways of learning about and understanding the world. Interestingly, James Baldwin, who taught at the University of Toronto, identified stages in early development that may have influenced the thinking of Piaget (e.g., Broughton, 1981), whose famous theory on cognitive development is discussed in Chapter 10.

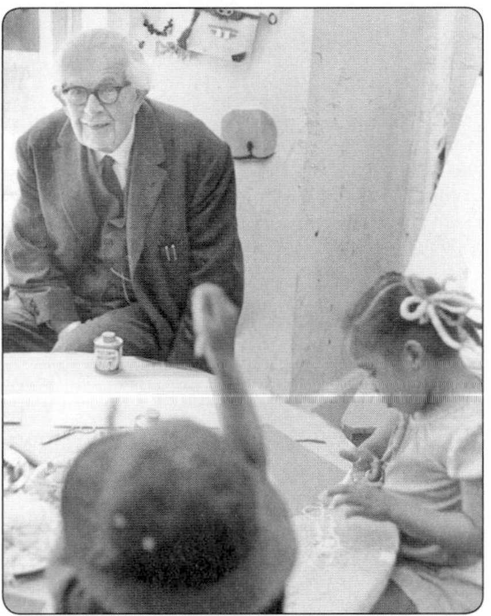

FIGURE 1.13

Jean Piaget was a master of observation. Many of his conclusions about stages of cognitive development came from watching children solve problems and inferring how they must have thought about them to respond as they did.

Cognitive approaches to psychological disorders. The cognitive perspective has strongly influenced our understanding not only of adaptive human thinking, but also of human unhappiness and problems in living. Two prominent psychotherapists, Albert Ellis (1962) and Aaron Beck (1976), led early attempts to understand how mental distortions and irrational thought patterns create emotional problems. Recall, for example, Charles Whitman's reference to his "unusual and irrational thoughts" in the letter written before his murderous rampage. By emphasizing the fact that distress and maladaptive behaviour are caused not by external situations, but by the ways we think about those situations, and by developing ways of helping people to change self-defeating thought habits, Ellis and Beck made notable contributions to the understanding and treatment of clinical disorders.

Modern Cognitive Science

Today's cognitive science has links with computer science, linguistics, biology, and mathematics (Clark & Toribio, 1998; Wagman, 1998). One area of cognitive science, **artificial intelligence**, develops computer models of complex human thought, reasoning, and problem solving (Wagman, 1997). Artificial intelligence researchers reason that by developing computer models that seem to duplicate natural cognitive processes, they will have a better understanding of how humans think. Moreover, by studying the ways experts think about and solve problems, they can develop computerized "expert" systems to lead others along the same cognitive

19. What were the methods used and conclusions reached by Piaget in his studies of cognitive development?

20. How have Beck and Ellis advanced our understanding of emotional problems?

21. What is studied in the cognitive science areas of artificial intelligence and cognitive neuroscience?

paths. For example, there are now computerized medical diagnostic systems that are based upon the thought processes of eminent physicians.

One of the most significant historical figures in the artificial intelligence area was Donald Hebb (1904–1985), a Nova Scotian who taught primarily at McGill University (Klein, 1999). Hebb was an expert on the brain areas in animals that seem to be particularly involved in memory and reasoning. In 1949 he wrote a famous book called *The organization of behaviour: A neuropsychological theory.* Hebb proposed a hypothetical brain structure he called a "cell assembly" to explain how repeated usage is associated with increasing facility in carrying out a particular response (much as practising a musical piece leads to enhanced performance). The cell assembly—a group of brain cells whose connections are assumed to be strengthened with repeated usage—is a fundamental part of computer models of brain function (Adair, Pavio, and Ritchie, 1996). Important research on human memory has also been carried out at the University of Toronto by Fergus I. M. Craik and Endel Tulving, whose work is discussed in Chapter 8.

Cognitive scientists are also interested in how people produce and recognize speech, and how creative solutions to problems are produced. An important melding of the biological and cognitive perspectives has resulted in a new area called *cognitive neuroscience,* in which scientists use sophisticated electrical recording and brain-imaging techniques to eavesdrop on the brain as people engage in mental activities.

Social Constructivism

22. What do social constructivists say about the nature of "reality"?

Social constructivism is a highly influential viewpoint within the cognitive perspective (Gergen, 2000). Its proponents maintain that what we consider "reality" is in large part our own mental creation. According to these theorists, little shared reality exists apart from what groups of people socially construct through the subjective meaning they give to their experiences. Constructivists would maintain, for example, that male and female sex roles are created not by "nature," but by the shared world view that exists within social groups. Likewise, conflicts between groups of people are a product of the differing "realities" that they live. For example, the long-standing conflict between Israelis and Arabs reflects radically different conceptions of God's plan for them, of what is right and what is wrong, and differing historical interpretations and understandings (Rouhana & Bar-Tal, 1998). These two groups, though coexisting in the same places, live in entirely different subjective worlds.

Even highly similar groups from the same culture can be led by their needs and emotions to construct different versions of the same reality. One example is shown in our first *Research Foundations.*

The Research Foundations feature in each chapter presents a classic study in some detail.

RESEARCH FOUNDATIONS

The Social Construction of Reality: They Saw a Game

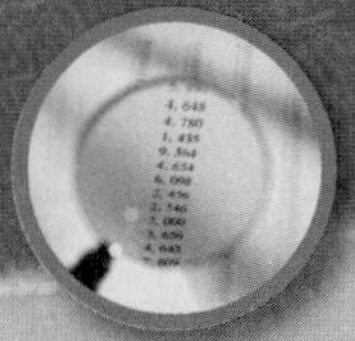

Background

Important beginnings of what is now termed the "cognitive revolution" occurred in the late 1940s and early 1950s as research demonstrated how people's motives, values, and beliefs can strongly affect their perceptions. One such demonstration occurred after a football game between Dartmouth and Princeton. From the opening kickoff, it was clear that the heated rivalry between the two schools was going to result in a very rough game. Tempers flared frequently, and the officials had difficulty maintaining control of the game. In the second quarter, Princeton's All-American running back, Dick

Kazmaier, was led from the field with a concussion and a broken nose. Later in the game, a Dartmouth player was carried from the field with a broken leg. Several other players on both sides suffered serious injuries.

After the game, the air was filled with accusations. Princeton coaches, officials, and fans accused Dartmouth of deliberately trying to maim Kazmaier. In turn, Dartmouth supporters accused Princeton of flagrantly dirty football. Charges and countercharges were exchanged for several weeks, and the heated controversy attracted national attention.

Fortunately, a few of the people at the two institutions were still talking to one another without snarling. Psychologists Albert Hastorf of Dartmouth and Hadley Cantril of Princeton were struck by the violent disagreements over what had actually occurred during the game. It was almost as if the fans had been in two different stadiums that day. Their curiosity aroused, Hastorf and Cantril decided to collaborate on a study of these perceptions.

Method

Dartmouth and Princeton undergraduates participated in the study, which had two phases. In the first phase, 163 Dartmouth students and 161 Princeton students completed a questionnaire concerning their beliefs about what had happened during the game. Next, 48 Dartmouth students and 49 Princeton students were shown a film of the game and were asked to tally any instances of rule infractions, unnecessary roughness, or dirty play that they saw.

Results

The first questionnaire reflected the differing opinions of students from the two schools. When asked who started the rough play, 86 percent of the Princeton students, but only 36 percent of Dartmouth students said that Dartmouth started it. Fifty-five percent of the Princeton students were convinced that Dartmouth had purposely tried to maim Kazmaier, compared to only 10 percent of the Dartmouth students. Equally striking were the results derived from the viewing of the game film. As shown in Figure 1.14, Dartmouth students saw both teams make about the same number of infractions. Princeton fans, however, saw the Dartmouth team make twice as many infractions as the Princeton team did. Compared to the Dartmouth fans, they also detected twice the number of infractions committed by Dartmouth. Even on the not-so-instant replay, students from the two schools continued to see "different" games.

Critical Discussion

This simple but elegant little study illustrates nicely how people's preconceptions and identification with a particular group can influence perceptions and beliefs. Even in the face of "objective" reality as represented by the game film they watched, Dartmouth and Princeton students mentally constructed differing realities through their own perceptions. The study also shows how phenomena from the "real world" can be brought into a laboratory setting and studied under controlled conditions.

"They Saw a Game" and other studies comprising what was termed the "new look" in perception research gave impetus to the cognitive revolution that was soon to occur in psychology. They demonstrated that a psychology based only on external stimuli and responses leaves the person who interprets and thinks about those stimuli out of the causal equation. In the cognitive view, people are less what their experiences make them than what they make of their experiences. Thinking clearly matters.

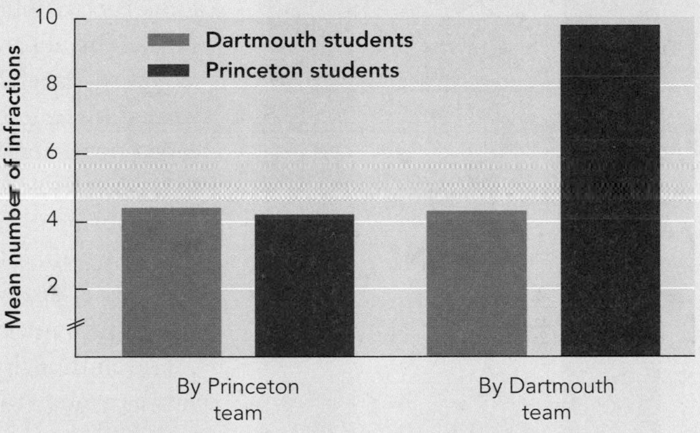

FIGURE 1.14

Average number of infractions detected by Dartmouth and Princeton students while watching the game film.

(Data from Hastorf & Cantril, 1954.)

Source: Albert Hastorf and Hadley Cantril (1954). They saw a game: A case study. *Journal of Abnormal and Social Psychology, 49,* 129–134.[1]

[1]The citation system used in psychology lists the authors, year of publication, title, journal or book, volume number of the journal, and page numbers.

The Psychodynamic Perspective: The Forces Within

> I don't know why I did it. . . . Often in my life, I have done things I had decided not to do. Something—whatever that may be—goes into action; "it" goes to the woman I don't want to see anymore, "it" makes the remark to the boss that costs me my head, "it" keeps on smoking when I have decided to quit, and then quits smoking just when I've accepted the fact that I'm a smoker and always will be. (Schlink, 1997, p. 20)

23. What causal factors are the focus of the psychodynamic perspective?

Have you ever felt mystified about why you did something that seemed "out of character"? If so, you are not alone, for each of us is a unique person with an individual pattern of traits, emotions, motives, and inner conflicts.

The **psychodynamic perspective** searches for the causes of behaviour within the workings of our personality, emphasizing the role of unconscious processes and unresolved conflicts from the past. The first and most influential psychodynamic theory was Sigmund Freud's theory of psychoanalysis.

Psychoanalysis: Freud's Great Challenge

FIGURE 1.15
For more than 50 years, Sigmund Freud probed the hidden recesses of the human mind.

Although the shadowy underworld of hidden motives and meanings has enticed thinkers throughout history, humans traditionally have viewed themselves as creatures ruled by reason and conscious thought. But late in the 19th century, as the aftershocks produced by Darwin's evolutionary theory were still being felt throughout the intellectual world, Sigmund Freud (1856–1939) mounted a second and equally shocking assault on the prevailing conception of human beings as rational, civilized creatures. Unlike Darwin, however, Freud emphasized the role of complex psychological forces in controlling human behaviour (Figure 1.15). He called the theory that he developed psychoanalysis—the analysis of internal unconscious psychological forces.

As a young Viennese medical student in the early 1880s, Freud was intensely interested in the workings of the brain (Miller, 1991). He began to focus his attention on the treatment of **hysteria**, a psychological disorder in which physical symptoms such as blindness, pain, or paralysis develop without any apparent organic cause. This disorder was erroneously thought to be specific to women, hence the diagnostic label derived from the Greek word *hystera*, which means "womb." Freud treated hysterical women, first by using hypnosis, and later by using a technique called free association, in which the patient was to say whatever came to mind and to let one association lead freely to another, even if the order did not seem logical or rational. To Freud's surprise, his female patients consistently reported and relived painful and long-"forgotten" childhood sexual experiences. After reliving these experiences, Freud reported, the patients' symptoms often showed considerable improvement.

24. What observations convinced Freud of the importance of unconscious and childhood determinants of adult behaviour?

Even though Freud was the product of a Victorian culture that regarded sexuality as a taboo topic, he at first believed the reports of sexual abuse given by his clients. Later, perhaps in response to cries of outrage from the medical and scientific communities that threatened to ruin his career, he concluded that, in all likelihood, most of these childhood sexual experiences had never actually occurred. Freud was now faced with the problem of explaining how the "reliving" of events that had never actually occurred could abolish the symptoms of hysteria. He became convinced that his patients were prompted to create these fantasies by a compelling and unsatisfied sexual drive that is a universal aspect of human nature. (It might be noted that Freud's argument is based on the assumption that people cannot always tell the difference between memory representations of real as opposed to imagined events; in 1981, Rita Anderson of Memorial University in Newfoundland provided an early experimental demonstration that Freud's assumption was valid.)

Freud observed also that sexual material often emerged in dreams and in slips of the tongue (so-called "Freudian slips"). These observations, plus an intensive period of self-analysis, led Freud to propose that much of human behaviour is influenced by forces of which we are unaware (he termed them unconscious forces). Prior to Freud's time, many philosophers and psychologists had suggested that humans were influenced by forces of which they were unaware; the Canadian historian of psychology Henry F. Ellenberger (1970) has written an authoritative account of pre-Freudian ideas about the unconscious. Freud claimed that we have inborn sexual and aggressive drives, and he believed that our adult personality is strongly influenced by early childhood experiences and by the ways in which we cope with the internal forces that govern our behaviour as we grow up.

25. In what sense, according to Freud, is the human in continuous internal conflict?

Freud speculated that because early sexual desires and needs are punished, we learn to fear them and become anxious when we are aware of their presence. Consequently, to cope with our anxiety, we develop psychological techniques called defence mechanisms. One of the most important defence mechanisms is **repression**, which protects us by keeping anxiety-arousing impulses, feelings, and memories in the unconscious depths of the mind. There they remain as sources of energy, continually striving for release. All behaviour, whether it is normal or abnormal, is a reflection of the never-ending and largely unconscious internal struggle between the conflicting psychological forces of the impulses and the defences. This ongoing psychological struggle between conflicting energy forces is dynamic in nature, hence the term *psychodynamic.* To explain Charles Whitman's shooting rampage, Freud would surely point to the "overwhelming violent impulses" to which Whitman referred in his letter, explaining that these impulses exploded into action when the defences that held them in check finally shattered in the face of unbearable life stresses.

Freud wrote numerous works of great psychological and literary significance, but he was not a conventional scientist. Freud was opposed to any attempts to explore psychoanalytic theory through laboratory research, believing that his clinical observations and personal self-analysis were far more valid "data" (Rosenzweig, 1992). Many contemporary psychologists view Freud's theory as difficult to test. Nevertheless, Freud's ideas have stimulated considerable psychological research on topics as diverse as dreams, the effects of child-rearing practices, memory, aggression, sex roles, moral development, defence mechanisms, psychological disorders, and psychological treatment. In one scholarly analysis of research based on Freud's ideas, Seymour Fisher and Roger Greenberg (1995) surveyed more than 3,000 studies in the scientific literature. Some of Freud's ideas were supported by subsequent research, whereas others were unsupported or directly contradicted. But even when psychoanalytic theory was not supported, the research it inspired has led to many important discoveries and helped stimulate the development of new theories. Psychoanalytic theory may be the best example of the truism that a theorist doesn't have to be "right" about everything (or even about most things) in order to make a notable scientific contribution.

Current Developments

26. What influence does Freud's theory have on contemporary psychology?

Psychodynamic concepts derived from Freud's psychoanalytic theory continue to have an influence within both academic and applied psychology. The American Psychoanalytic Association was founded by Ernest Jones in Toronto in 1911. Among clinical psychologists in U.S. academic and applied settings, 20 to 30 percent report their orientation as being psychodynamic, and many other practitioners say that they make use of psychodynamic concepts in understanding and treating clinical disorders (Mayne et al., 1994; Norcross et al., 1995). Psychoanalysis continues to be a major force in European psychology, and most major cities in the United States, Canada, and Europe have psychoanalytic training institutes. Psychoanalysis played a dominant part in the operations of the American Psychiatric Association in the years between about 1940 and 1960, as noted by the Canadian historian of psychiatry Edward Shorter (1998). Some of its methods and concepts are now being integrated with other forms of treatment to provide more effective ways of helping people change maladaptive behaviour patterns (Wachtel, 1997). Indeed, some authors (e.g., Shorter, 2003) predict a revival of interest in the careful study of psychopathology.

Links with psychodynamic concepts can be found within other areas of psychological science. For example, scientists working within the biological perspective have identified brain mechanisms that can produce emotional reactions of which we are consciously unaware (LeDoux, 2000). Freud, who was himself trained within the biological perspective, clearly recognized the importance of studying behaviour with different methods and from several vantage points when he wrote, "Let the biologists go as far as they can, and let us go as far as we can. One day the two will meet" (Freud, 1900, p. 276).

Some of Freud's ideas about mental events are also helping to stimulate new theoretical advances and research within the cognitive perspective (Bucci, 1997; Erdelyi, 1995). Cognitive scientists have shown that many aspects of information processing occur outside of our awareness (Wegner, 2000). Moreover, mental events that lie beyond the focus of our awareness, such as our self-concept and social stereotypes, can influence our thoughts, feelings, and behaviours. Thus, while Freud's vision of the unconscious mind as a seething cauldron of painful memories and destructive impulses is not accepted by most contemporary psychological scientists, the concept of a kinder, gentler unconscious endures, as does the notion that many of our behaviours are triggered by subconscious processes (Bargh & Chartrand, 1999; Kirsch & Lynn, 1999; Westen, 1998).

The Behavioural Perspective: The Power of the Environment

27. What are the important causal factors in behaviour within the behavioural perspective? How was this school of thought influenced by British empiricism?

The **behavioural perspective** focuses on the role of the external environment in shaping and governing our actions. From this perspective, people's behaviour is jointly determined by learned habits fashioned by their previous life experiences and by stimuli in their immediate environment. Particular emphasis is placed on the effect of rewards and punishment in shaping behaviour (Rachlin, 1995).

Origins of the Behavioural Perspective

The behavioural perspective is rooted in a seventeenth-century school of philosophy known as **British empiricism**, which held that all ideas and knowledge are gained empirically—that is, through the senses. According to John Locke (1632–1704), one of the early empiricists, the human mind is initially "white paper void of all characters, without any ideas: How comes it to be furnished? To this I answer, in one word, from experience" (*An Essay Concerning Human Understanding*, 1690). Human beings are born as a *tabula rasa*—a blank tablet—and then shaped by their environment. Empiricism also maintained that observation is a more valid approach to knowledge than is reason. To empiricists, seeing was believing, whereas reasoning was fraught with the potential for error. This idea has been enormously influential in the development of science, whose methods are rooted in empirical observation. Among the pioneers in the observational study of the behaviour of newborn puppies and kittens was Wesley Mills (1898), who taught physiology at McGill University.

In the early 1900s, Ivan Pavlov, a Russian physiologist, reported experiments that demonstrated "involuntary" learning in dogs. Pavlov showed that dogs would learn to salivate to the sound of a "new" stimulus, such as a tone, if that stimulus were paired a number of times with the appearance of food. In the United States, meanwhile, researchers were studying more complex forms of learning in both animals and humans. Learning was to be the medium through which experience made its mark on Locke's "white paper void of all characters."

FIGURE 1.16
John B. Watson founded the school of behaviourism in the 1920s.

Behaviourism

In the 1920s, **behaviourism**, a school of thought that emphasizes environmental control of behaviour through learning, emerged as an outspoken alternative to the cognitive and psychodynamic perspectives. John B. Watson (1878–1958) was the leader of the new movement (Figure 1.16). Watson strongly opposed the "mentalism" of the structuralists, functionalists, and psychoanalysts. He argued that the proper subject matter of psychology was observable behaviour, not unobservable inner consciousness. Human beings, he said, are products of their conditioning experiences, and their behaviour can be controlled completely by manipulating their environment. So passionately did Watson hold this position that in 1924 he issued the following challenge:

> Give me a dozen healthy infants, well-formed, and my own specialized world to bring them up in and I'll guarantee you to take any one of them at random and train him to become any type of specialist I might select—doctor, lawyer, artist, merchant-chief and, yes, even beggar-man and thief, regardless of his talents, penchants, tendencies, abilities, vocations, and race of his ancestors. (p. 82)

Clearly, the behaviourists' approach of examining behaviour strictly from the "outside" differs a great deal from our usual approach to understanding our inner selves. This approach is spoofed in the tongue-in-cheek story of the radical behaviourist who, after making love, turned to his partner and said, "That was great for you. How was it for me?"

Because behaviourists believe that we are who we are because of what we learn, they devoted their efforts to discovering the laws that govern learning and performance. Behaviourists believed that the same basic principles of learning apply to all organisms, and their research with both humans and animals led to many discoveries and applications of these principles. Many would argue that the discovery of the laws of learning was the greatest contribution made by American psychology in the first half of the 20th century.

The leading modern figure in behaviourism was B. F. Skinner (1904–1990) of Harvard University (Figure 1.17). Although Skinner did not deny that mental events, images, and feelings occur within us, he maintained that these are themselves behaviours and not causes. "No account of what is happening inside the human body, no matter how complete, will explain the origins of human behaviour," he insisted (Skinner, 1989, p. 18). For Skinner, there was no room for the "mind" or unobservable "mental events" in a scientific account of the causes of human behaviour. Indeed, Skinner believed that a focus on inner factors would lead psychology astray by diverting attention from the real causes of behaviour, which reside in the outer world. He insisted that "A person does not act upon the world, the world acts upon him" (Skinner, 1971, p. 211).

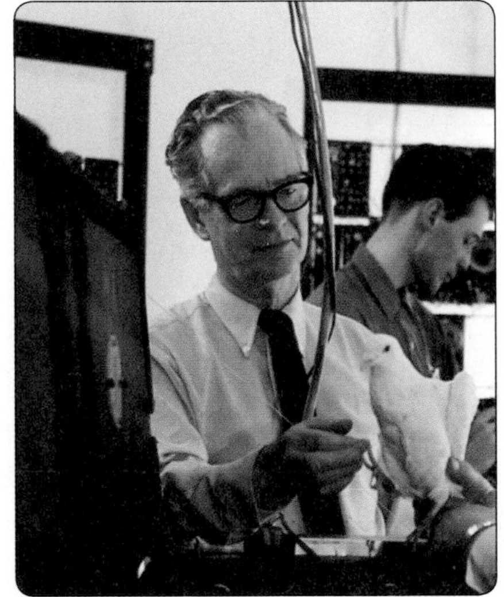

FIGURE 1.17
B. F. Skinner was a major figure in modern behaviourism.

As expressed eloquently in his novel, *Walden Two* (Skinner, 1948), Skinner believed that the power of the environment could be harnessed for good or for evil. If human beings are to be changed, indeed saved, Skinner maintained, we must manipulate the environment that controls behaviour through its pattern of rewards and punishments. Skinner believed that large-scale control over human behaviour is possible today, but that the chief barrier to creating a better world through "social

FIGURE 1.18

Albert Bandura has played a key role in merging the cognitive and behavioural perspectives into cognitive behaviourism.

28. What is cognitive behaviourism? How does it differ from radical behaviourism?

engineering" is an outmoded conception of people as free agents. Needless to say, this was a highly controversial position. Skinner's view was considered extreme by many psychologists, but he was esteemed for his scientific contributions to the study of learning, for the force of his intellect, and for focusing attention on the power of environmental forces and how they could be used to enhance human welfare. In the 1960s, behaviourism inspired powerful techniques of behaviour change that were known collectively as **behaviour modification**. These techniques continue today (e.g., University of Manitoba's Garry Martin and Joseph Pear's (1999) *Behaviour Modification: What is it and how to do it*) to be effective in altering problem behaviours and increasing the frequency of positive behaviours through alterations in environmental factors that control the behaviours. Overall, however, the influence of radical behaviourism waned after the 1970s, when it was overtaken by the cognitive revolution (Robins et al., 1999).

Cognitive Behaviourism

How does the behaviouristic picture of humans as reactors to the environment square with the cognitive perspective's image of the human as thinker? Are we willing to ignore the mental processes that we ourselves experience, or declare them off limits for scientific purposes because we cannot observe them directly? For many behaviourists, the answer was no. That answer stimulated an important recent development within the behavioural perspective known as cognitive behaviourism. **Cognitive behaviourism** is an attempt to bridge the gap between the behavioural and cognitive perspectives and to combine them in a more comprehensive theory (Cervone & Shoda, 1999).

A leading cognitive behaviourist is Albert Bandura (Figure 1.18), who was born in Alberta, received his B.A. from the University of British Columbia in 1949, and Ph.D. from the University of Iowa in 1952. Since 1953 he has taught at Stanford University, where he promotes the view that the environment exerts its effects on behaviour not by automatically "stamping in" or "stamping out" behaviours, as Watson or Skinner maintained, but rather by affecting our thoughts. In this view, learning experiences and the environment affect our behaviour by giving us the *information* we need to behave effectively (Bandura, 1969, 1999).

Cognitive behaviourists also stress that we can learn new behaviours by observing the actions of others and storing this information in memory. We can then imitate and reproduce these behaviours when we believe they will work for us. Finally, these theorists maintain that our mental abilities allow us to control our own behaviour and thereby influence our environment. Control therefore goes both ways, from environment to person and from person to environment.

The Humanistic Perspective: Freedom and Self-Actualization

29. How does the humanistic conception of human nature and motivation differ from that advanced by psychoanalysis and behaviourism?

As noted earlier, Freud's theory acted as a lightning rod. So did the tenets of radical behaviourism. Many rejected the images of humans being controlled by destructive and unconscious forces or by the external environment, and they offered competing images of human nature. The **humanistic perspective** arose largely out of philosophical schools that emphasize free will, innate tendencies toward growth, and the attempt to find ultimate meaning in one's existence (Moss, 1998). Like psychoanalytic theorists, humanistic theorists emphasize the role of internal personality processes, but in contrast to the psychoanalytic emphasis on unconscious determinants of behaviour, humanists stress the importance of conscious motives, freedom, and choice. Humanistic theorists believe that in every human being there is an active force toward growth and **self-actualization**, the reaching of one's individual potential (Figure 1.19). When the human personality unfolds in a benign and supportive environment that allows these creative forces free rein, the positive inner nature of a person emerges. Human misery and pathology, in contrast, are fostered by environments that frustrate the innate tendencies toward self-actualization. In sharp contrast to the image of humans ruled by unconscious dynamics or external stimuli, humanistic theorists such as Rollo May (1961) and Carl Rogers (1983) insist that our existence and its meaning are squarely in our own hands, for we alone can decide what our attitudes and behaviours will be.

FIGURE 1.19

The humanistic perspective emphasizes the human ability to surmount obstacles in our drive toward self-actualization.

Although few of the humanistic thinkers were themselves scientists, many important areas of scientific research have been inspired by the humanistic perspective. For example, research on the self-concept has been one of the most active areas of personality research for the past two decades (Brown, 1998). Much of this research combines concepts from the cognitive perspective with formulations of the self derived from Carl Rogers's (1959) humanistic theory of self-functioning. Rogers was also a pioneer in the scientific study of psychotherapy. In the 1940s and 1950s, his research group was the first to make audio recordings of counselling sessions and subject the recordings to systematic analysis. This research helped identify important therapeutic processes that led to constructive change in clients (Rogers, 1966).

Questions about the ultimate meaning of life and death are a critically important part of our existence, and of the humanistic perspective. According to **terror management theory**, an innate desire for continued life, combined with the uniquely human awareness of the inevitability of death, creates an anxiety called existential terror (Becker, 1973; Kastenbaum, 2000). Current research inspired by this theory addresses how people defend themselves against this anxiety (Greenberg et al., 1997; Pysczynski, et al., 1999; Solomon et al., 1991). To defend its members against the terror, each culture establishes its own "world view." This cultural construction of reality, which often includes some notion of an afterlife, confers a sense of order, permanence, and stability on life, and establishes standards for attaining "a sense of personal value and some hope of literally or symbolically transcending death" (Pysczynski et al., 1999, p. 836).

30. How does terror management theory draw on humanistic concepts? What are some of its major findings?

Terror management theorists believe that in order to allay death-related anxiety, people are motivated to support and defend their cultural world view (often expressed in the form of religious precepts) and to live up to its standards of value. Research inspired by terror management theory has supported two of its most important hypotheses. First, people who see themselves as living up to their culture's values—of living a "good life"—score higher on measures of self-esteem and report lower death anxiety. Second, reminders of their own mortality cause people to be more attracted to people who share and uphold their world view and to react with increased hostility to those who challenge or disagree with their beliefs and values (Greenberg, 1997; Pysczynski, et al., 1999). Terror management theory is thus a current example of how humanistic ideas continue to stimulate psychological theory and research.

The Sociocultural Perspective: The Embedded Human

Every person has his or her individual learning history, but each of us is also embedded in a larger culture that helps shape who we are. How has your own culture influenced your values, your ways of thinking and behaving, your very conception of reality? Such questions, which psychologists of a generation ago might have left to anthropologists, assume increasing importance as technology and emigration shrink the world, and our everyday environment becomes increasingly diverse and multicultural. The **sociocultural perspective** focuses on the manner in which culture is transmitted to its members and on the similarities and differences that occur among people from diverse cultures (Valsiner, 2000).

31. Define culture and norms. What functions does a culture serve?

Culture refers to the enduring values, beliefs, behaviours, and traditions that are shared by a large group of people and are passed on from one generation to the next (Brislin, 1993). The definition of the word "culture" (by nationality, ethnic minority, indigenous populations, etc.) is very complex, as noted by one of the founders of Cross Cultural Psychology, John Berry (1992) of Queen's University. All cultural groups do develop their own social norms. **Norms** are rules that specify what is acceptable and expected behaviour for members of that group. They may involve rules for how to dress, to respond to people higher in status, to behave during religious ceremonies, or to act as a woman in that culture. The fact that norms can differ widely from culture to culture—and even at different times within the same culture—introduces another environmental factor that must be considered if we are to understand the causes of behaviour.

Humans seem to have an inherent need to develop cultures. Cultures introduce order and a particular world view into a social system, thus creating predictability, guidelines for thought and behaviour, and a kind of map for living our lives. As suggested by terror management theory, described earlier, the world view helps us to "understand" many of the unknowns of our existence and thereby reduces some of the anxieties of human existence (Becker, 1973). Culture also provides an expression of a people's way of being through art, literature, and the development of knowledge.

Cultural Learning and Diversity

In 1935, anthropologist Margaret Mead published an account of three tribes in New Guinea that showed striking differences in "normal" behaviour among men and women. Among the Arapesh, both men and women were uncommonly kind, sympathetic, and cooperative. For men to behave aggressively was almost unheard of. The Mundugumor were quite different. Both men and women were expected to be fierce and aggressive, even vicious. A third tribe, the Tchambuli, exhibited a reversal of traditional Western sex roles. The women were boisterous, shaved their heads, and took responsibility for going out and obtaining the tribe's food. The men, in turn, spent their days focusing on their art, their hairstyles, and gossiping about the women (Mead, 1935). Mead's observations provided a graphic illustration of how cultural expectations and learning experiences can affect behaviour.

32. Contrast individualistic and collectivistic societies.

Cultures differ from one another in many ways, but one of the most important differences from a psychological perspective is the extent to which they emphasize individualism versus collectivism (Markus & Kitayama, 1991; Triandis, 1989). Most industrialized cultures of northern Europe and North America promote **individualism**, an emphasis on personal goals and a self-identity based primarily on one's own attributes and achievements. In contrast, many cultures in Asia, Africa, and South America nurture **collectivism**, in which individual goals are subordinated to those of the group, and personal identity is defined largely by the ties that bind one to family and other social groups.

Japan and the United States provide examples of cultures that differ significantly on the individualism-collectivism dimension (Kagitcibasi, 1997). The United States is an inherently individualistic culture, whereas Japan's culture is far more collectivist in nature. This difference is created by social learning experiences that begin in childhood and continue thereafter in the form of social customs. For example, observational studies in Japanese and American schools have shown that Japanese children work more often as part of a group having a common assignment, whereas American children are more likely to work alone on individual projects and assignments (White, 1987). Moreover, even when American children are working in groups, American teachers are far more likely than Japanese teachers to direct their comments to individuals rather than to the group as a whole (Hamilton et al., 1991). Cultural learning experiences like these undoubtedly reflect and also reinforce cultural norms (Lamal, 1991). At many points in this book, we shall discover how the cultural environment can affect the entire spectrum of human behaviour. In the *Research Frontiers* feature that follows, we discuss current conceptions of how culture and biology combine to influence behaviour.

This feature presents a discussion of current and future directions in psychological theory and research.

RESEARCH FRONTIERS

Culture, Language, and Behaviour

The behavioural and sociocultural perspectives emphasize the role of the environment in the development of behaviour. They tell us that we are moulded by our unique learning histories and shaped by the culture into which we are born. Our learning and cultural experiences influence not only our behaviour, but also how we view ourselves (i.e., our "cultural identity") and the world. The behavioural perspective seems straightforward—our behaviour is shaped by learning. But just how does culture influence our behaviour?

Many researchers have argued that language and culture are intimately related (e.g., Vygotsky, 1962). In the most extreme version of this approach, Whorf (1956) suggested that language influences thought and cognition directly. According to Whorf, the language we use literally changes the way we think about the world. We can only make cognitive distinctions among things we encounter if we have a means to describe them. For example, Whorf suggested that a culture using a language without a past tense (such as the Hopi Indians of the United States) would have difficulty remembering past events.

The idea that culture, through language, *determines* how we think is a bit overstated, as various authors have suggested (e.g., Rosch, 1973). Nonetheless there are clear influences of

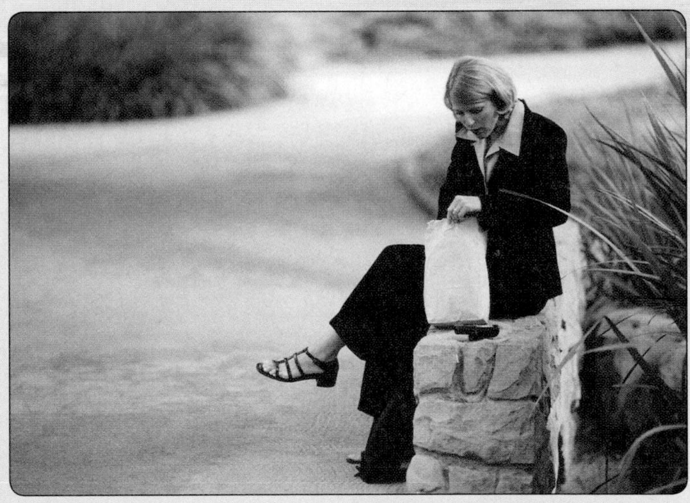

FIGURE 1.20

Culture and language influence cognition. The value that Chinese culture places on relationships and the contrasting value North American culture places on autonomy are reflected in the Chinese and English languages, and in turn in the way their respective speakers think and categorize concepts.

–Continued

both culture and language on cognition and behaviour. Consider some recent work by Li-Jun Ji at Queen's University. Ji and colleagues (Ji, Zhang, & Nisbett, 2004) recruited Chinese students at Hong Kong University and Beijing University. All students were bilingual—they spoke both English and Chinese. They were presented with two different sorting tasks. Each involved looking at sets of three words (e.g., teacher, doctor, homework) and deciding which two were most closely related. One task was presented in English, and the other in Chinese. Note that there are two ways to group the three words: either by category (teacher, doctor) or by relationship (teacher, homework).

A comparison group of European-American students at the University of Michigan (English only) had been tested in an earlier study. The results indicated very different sorting strategies by the European-American students compared to the Chinese students. At Michigan, the students sorted by category, more or less ignoring the possible relationships. The Chinese students used the opposite strategy. Their sorts reflected the relationships among the words, rather than category membership. This was the case regardless of the testing language for the Chinese students, although the students from Beijing were more likely to use relationship sorts when the test language was Chinese. Most likely, the difference between the Hong Kong students and Beijing students reflects the age at which English is learned. For the Hong Kong students, English is learned much earlier, often in conjunction with formal language training. This would result in a shared internal representational system for both languages.

Thus, according to Ji et al. (2004), culture influences these cognitive sorting patterns, independent of language. How is this possible? They suggest that the value of relationships is reinforced much more strongly in Chinese culture compared to North American culture. Chinese people pay more attention to the social environment than do their American counterparts, who value autonomy (e.g., Ji, Schwartz, & Nisbett, 2000). These values are reflected in both the family and school environments and become an integral part of how the world is perceived. The influence of language is to "fine-tune" these preferences, but language can not overcome the influence of culture.

The Perspectives in Historical Context

Today, psychology stands at a scientific crossroads formed by the six perspectives on behaviour. As we have seen, the perspectives provide us with differing conceptions of human nature, they focus on different causes of behaviour, and they sometimes use different methods in their attempt to understand these causes. Table 1.2 summarizes these themes.

Having considered the six perspectives on behaviour individually, let us pull these diverse threads together and trace their historical impact on the development of today's psychology. As an experimental science, psychology began with a cognitive focus in 1879 when Wilhelm Wundt founded the school of structuralism in Germany and used the method of introspection to study the contents of the mind. Near the end of the 19th century, functionalism began to flourish in the United States as Harvard's William James and other pioneers explored cognitive processes such as thinking, memory, and the self-concept. At about the same time, a very different conception of mental life appeared in the person of Sigmund Freud, and psychology became both a laboratory science and a clinical enterprise dedicated to understanding and treating psychological disorders. The psychodynamic perspective dominated clinical thinking and practice for nearly 50 years before being gradually overtaken by behavioural, humanistic, and cognitive approaches to personality and psychological treatment.

The 1920s were a period of dramatic change for psychology. Sparked by Ivan Pavlov's earlier research on "automatic" learning in dogs and John Watson's stimulus-response analysis of behaviour, the new school of behaviourism became a powerful force in American psychology. Its insistence that the only suitable matter for scientific study is externally observable stimuli and responses resonated with many who wanted psychology to model itself on the physical and biological sciences. Led by B. F. Skinner, behaviourism's emphasis on the objective study of learning remained at the forefront of psychological thought into the 1960s. For many years, mentalistic concepts were considered "soft" and non-scientific, and few psychologists would even dare to use the word "mind" in their scientific writings. David

TABLE 1.2 Comparison of Six Major Perspectives on Human Behaviour

	Biological	Cognitive	Psychodynamic	Behavioural	Humanistic	Sociocultural
Conception of human nature	The human animal	The human as thinker and information processor	The human as controlled by inner forces and conflicts	The human as a reactor to the environment	The human as free agent, seeking self-actualization and personal meaning	The human as a social being embedded in a culture
Major causal factors in behaviour	Genetic and evolutionary factors; brain and biochemical processes	Thought, anticipations, planning, perception, and memory processes	Unconscious motives, conflicts, and defences; early childhood experiences and unresolved conflicts	Past learning experiences and the stimuli and behavioural consequences that exist in the current environment	Free will, choice, and innate drive toward self-actualization; search for personal meaning of existence	Social forces, including norms, social interactions, and group processes in one's culture and social environment
Predominant focus and methods of discovery	Study of brain-behaviour relations; role of hormones and biochemical factors on behaviour; behaviour genetics research	Study of cognitive processes, usually under highly controlled laboratory conditions	Intensive observations of personality processes in clinical settings; some laboratory research on personality processes	Study of learning processes in both laboratory and real-world settings, with an emphasis on precise observation of stimuli and responses	Study of meaning, values, and purpose in life; study of self-concept, and its role in thought, emotion, and behaviour	Comparisons of the behaviours and mental processes of people in different cultures; effects of culturally acquired personal characteristics on behaviour

Murray (1995) at Queen's University observed that "... not only I but hundreds of graduate students in the 1960s were afraid to write words like 'image,' 'consciousness' and even 'memory' or 'memories' (we were supposed to talk about 'responses' rather than 'memories')."

33. In what sense has psychology come "full circle" from its early focus on mental events?

The mid-1960s witnessed the beginning of the so called "cognitive revolution" and a reawakening of interest in mental events. One of the pioneers of the revival of interest in mental imagery was Allan Paivio (1971) of the University of Western Ontario. Studies like "They Saw a Game" (*Research Foundations*) helped lay the groundwork for a new interest in how people's mental processes and motives influence their constructions of reality. Even behaviourists saw a need to incorporate cognitive concepts into their theories, and cognitive-behavioural theories eventually pushed radical behaviourism into the background. The advent of the computer inspired new models of the mind based on information-processing concepts. By the end of the 20th century, psychology in many ways had come full circle from its cognitive origins, now armed with far more sophisticated methods for investigating mental events. On another front, a new appreciation for the role of culture in thinking and behaviour has created the thriving area of cross-cultural psychology and an influential socio-cultural perspective.

Biological psychology has always been a prominent part of the field, but its influence has dramatically increased with the development of new tools of discovery, such as computer-based brain-imaging methods. Psychologists no longer need to infer what must be going on inside the brain, as the structuralists had to. They can now "watch" mental events occur as particular brain areas light up during brain-imaging sessions. These advances have resulted in new interactions between the perspectives. One example, described earlier, is cognitive neuroscience, in which scientists representing the biological and cognitive perspectives are joining forces to discover the brain processes that underlie many kinds of mental phenomena.

In Review

- *Several perspectives have shaped psychology's scientific growth. Each perspective views human nature differently and focuses on different causes of behaviour.*
- *With roots in physiology, medicine, and Darwin's theory of evolution, the* biological perspective *examines how bodily functions regulate behaviour. Physiological psychologists study brain processes and other physiological functions that underlie our behaviour, sensory experiences, emotions, and thoughts. Behaviour geneticists study how behaviour is influenced by our genetic inheritance. Evolutionary psychologists examine behaviour in terms of its adaptive functions and seek to explain how evolution has biologically predisposed modern humans toward certain ways of behaving.*
- *Psychology's intellectual roots lie in philosophy, biology, and medicine. In the late 1800s, Wundt and James helped found psychology.* Structuralism, *which examined the basic components of consciousness, and* functionalism, *which focused on the purposes of consciousness, were psychology's two earliest schools of thought.*
- *The* cognitive perspective *views humans as information processors who think, judge, and solve problems. Its roots lie in the early schools of structuralism, functionalism, and Gestalt psychology. Piaget's work on cognitive development, the study of linguistics, and the advent of computers sparked new interest in mental processes. Research in artificial intelligence develops computer models of human thought, whereas cognitive neuroscience studies brain processes that underlie mental activity. Social constructivism maintains that much of what we call reality is a creation of our own mental processes.*
- *The* psychodynamic perspective *calls attention to unconscious motives, conflicts, and defence mechanisms that influence our personality and behaviour. Freud's psychoanalytic theory emphasized unconscious sexual and aggressive impulses and early childhood experiences that shape personality.*
- *With roots in 18th-century British empiricism, the* behavioural perspective *emphasizes how the external environment and learning shape behaviour. Behaviourists such as Watson and Skinner believed that psychology should only study observable stimuli and responses, not unobservable mental processes. They argued that to change behaviour, the key is to modify the environment. Behaviourists discovered basic laws of learning through controlled research with laboratory animals and successfully applied these principles to enhance human welfare.*
- *Humanists reject the notion that people are controlled by unconscious forces or merely react to environmental stimuli. Instead, the* humanistic perspective *emphasizes personal freedom and choice, psychological growth, and self-actualization.*
- *The* sociocultural perspective *examines how the social environment and cultural learning influence our behaviour and thoughts. Cultural psychologists study how culture is transmitted to its members and examine similarities and differences among people from various cultures. An orientation toward individualism versus collectivism represents one of many ways in which cultures vary.*

INTEGRATING THE PERSPECTIVES: THREE LEVELS OF ANALYSIS

34. What three levels of analysis allow us to incorporate causal factors suggested by each of the perspectives?

One way to simplify what the various perspectives bring to our understanding of human behaviour is to realize that behaviour always involves a biopsychological person acting within an environment. The behaviour that results is a reflection of both the characteristics of the person and the features of the environment. Taking these factors into account provides us with a useful framework for approaching the study of behaviour. As noted earlier in the chapter, the various perspectives contribute to three potential **levels of analysis** for describing various aspects of behaviour and classifying causal factors: biological, psychological, and environmental (Figure 1.21).

Everything psychological is at the same time biological, reflecting the activities of the physiological processes that underlie behaviour. Thus we can analyze behaviour and its causes in terms of how brain processes, hormones, and genetic factors contribute to it. This is the *biological level of analysis.* Yet the biological level of analysis cannot tell us everything. To know that certain kinds of thinking and emotions are associated with electrochemical activity in particular brain regions does not tell us what those thoughts and feelings are, how they fit together, and how the person experiences them. To answer such questions, we must move to a different level of analysis, namely, the *psychological level of analysis.* Here, we can take a cognitive perspective and analyze the role of thought, memory, planning, and problem solving in the behaviour of interest. The psychodynamic and humanistic perspectives also lead us to the psychological level of analysis, and beckon us to take account of the motivational, emotional, and personality processes that influence how people respond to their environment.

Finally, an understanding of behaviour requires that we take account of the environment, past and present, personal and cultural, that helps shape and stimulate our behaviours. Thus the behavioural and sociocultural perspectives focus our attention on a third level of analysis, the *environmental level of analysis.*

The concept of levels of analysis helps simplify matters somewhat, but a full understanding of a behaviour may move us back and forth from one level of analysis to another. For example, when we are describing the features of a particular culture, such as the religious values that it conveys to its members, we are operating at the environmental level of analysis. However, once people have been exposed to that culture and taken on those beliefs as their own, they become characteristics of the person and would now be viewed from the psychological level of analysis. Similarly, we might describe a family environment as physically abusive, but the personality traits that result (such as the tendency for a child exposed to that environment to become an aggressive person) will probably move us to the psychological level of analysis. Or, if we're interested in how that child's physiology has been altered by the abusive environment, we may move to a biological level of analysis.

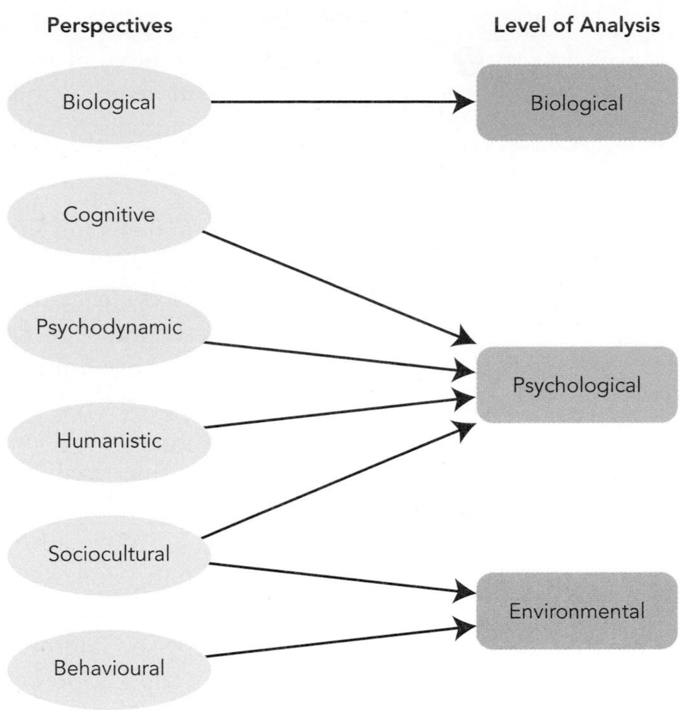

FIGURE 1.21

Each of the six perspectives on behaviour focuses primary attention on one of three levels of analysis, emphasizing the role of biological, psychological, or environmental causal factors.

An Example: Understanding Depression

To appreciate how the biological, psychological, and environmental levels of analysis can help us to understand an important behaviour, let us briefly summarize what is known about one of the most commonly experienced psychological problems in our culture, namely, depression.

Most of us have probably experienced feelings of sadness, grief, or "the blues" at some time in our lives. These feelings, often accompanied by biological reactions such as loss of appetite and sleep difficulties, are usually normal responses to negative events or meaningful losses that we have experienced. However, when these emotional responses remain intense over a long time period, and when they are accompanied by thoughts of hopelessness and an inability to experience pleasure, we have crossed the boundary between a normal reaction and clinical depression (Rubin, 2000).

Depression has sometimes been referred to as the "common cold" of emotional disturbances because it is experienced by so many people. Even if we consider only severe depressive disorders, studies indicate that one in four women and one in eight men in the United States can expect to experience a major depression during their lifetime (Satcher, 2000).

35. What does the biological level of analysis tell us about the causes of depression?

Let's begin at the biological level of analysis. First, genetic factors appear to be involved in at least some cases (Papolos & Lachman, 1994). In one study, relatives of people who had developed a major depression before age 20 were eight times more likely to eventually become depressed than were relatives of non-depressed people (Weissman et al., 1984).

Depression is also related to biochemical factors and sleep/wakefulness rhythms in the brain. Of special interest are certain chemicals, known as neurotransmitters, that are involved in the transmission of nerve impulses within the brain. One line of evidence that these substances are important is the fact that the most effective antidepressant drugs seem to operate by restoring a normal balance of these neurotransmitters (Roland, 1997). Also, researchers have found disruptions in biological rhythms that underlie sleep and dreaming in the brain waves of depressed people (Buysse et al., 1997; Farina et al., 2003). If the "depressive" brain rhythm is interfered with by waking depressed people when it is occurring, they feel less depressed afterward (Berger et al., 1997).

36. What kinds of psychological causal factors have been identified in depression?

Moving from a biological to a psychological level of analysis provides additional understanding of depression and its causes. For example, many studies have shown that depression is associated with a particular thinking style in which the person interprets events in a pessimistic way (Beck, 2002; Seligman & Isaacowitz, 2000). Depressed people can find the black cloud that surrounds every silver lining. They tend to blame themselves for negative things that occur, while taking no personal credit for the good things that happen in their lives, and they generally feel that the world, the self, and the future are bleak and hopeless (Beck, 1991). The Canadian psychologist Norman Endler (1982) has provided an autobiographical account of what he himself felt like during a period of clinical depression.

Are some personality patterns more prone to depression than others? Many psychodynamic theorists believe that severe losses or rejections in childhood help to create a personality style that causes people to overreact to future losses, setting the stage for later depression. In support of this notion, studies of depressed patients show that they are more likely than non-depressed people to have experienced the loss of a parent through death or separation during childhood (Bowlby, 2000; Brown & Harris, 1978). Depression is also related to childhood histories of abuse, parental rejection, and family discord (Hammen, 1991). People who have been subjected to severe loss and neglect may develop pessimistic personalities that predispose them to slide into depression in the face of later life stresses.

37. Which causal factors in depression are seen at the environmental level of analysis?

Finally, the environmental level of analysis reveals several factors that play a major role in depression. According to the behavioural view, depression is a reaction to a non-rewarding environment. A vicious cycle begins when the environment provides fewer rewards for the person. As depression intensifies, such people feel so bad that they stop doing the things that ordinarily give them pleasure, a pattern that decreases environmental rewards still further. To make matters worse, depressed people complain a good deal, seek excessive reassurance and support from others, and generally become less likeable. These behaviours eventually begin to alienate others and cause them to shy away from the depressed person. The net result is a worsening environment with fewer rewards, a reduction in support from others, and the unhappiness and hopeless pessimism that characterize chronic depression (Lewinsohn et al., 1985; Nezlek et al., 2000).

The sociocultural environment also affects depression. Although depression is found in virtually all cultures, both its symptom pattern and its causes may reflect cultural differences. For example, feelings of guilt and personal inadequacy seem to predominate in North American and western European countries, whereas bodily symptoms of fatigue, loss of appetite, and sleep difficulties are more often reported in Latin, Chinese, and African cultures (Brislin, 1993; Lopez & Guarnaccia, 2000). Cross-cultural studies also have shown that in developed countries such as the United States and other Western nations, women are about twice as likely as men to report feeling depressed, whereas no such sex difference is found in developing countries (Culbertson, 1997; Nolen-Hoeksema, 2006). In Canada, the rate is somewhat lower (about 8 percent), (Health Canada, 2002). Why should this be? At present, we do not have the answer, but we must wonder what it is about more technologically advanced cultures that would produce a sex difference that does not show up in developing countries.

38. What is meant by the interaction of causal factors?

Figure 1.22 summarizes causal factors in depression that are supported by theory and research. Although these causal factors are organized into three classes (biological, psychological, and environmental), we should keep two important points in mind. First, the specific causes of depression may not only differ from case to case, but they can also combine or *interact* with one another in ways that vary according to the person and the situation. **Interaction** means that the presence or strength of one factor can influence the effects of other factors. For example, a person who has a strong biological predisposition to depression may become depressed when faced with a relatively minor setback in life that would barely phase a second person who does not have that predisposition. This second person might require a catastrophic loss in order to become depressed. In this instance, strength of biological predisposition and intensity of life stress would combine, or interact, to influence behaviour. Just as boiling water softens celery and hardens an egg, the same environment can affect two different people in very different ways.

Summary of Major Themes

39. Summarize six important themes in contemporary psychology.

We have now surveyed the six major perspectives that shape psychological thought and the levels of analysis at which behaviour is studied. What has our excursion shown us about the science of psychology and its subject matter? The following principles are widely accepted by psychologists and are seen repeatedly as we explore the realm of behaviour:

- As a science, *psychology is empirical*, meaning that it favours direct observation over pure intuition or reasoning as a means of attaining knowledge

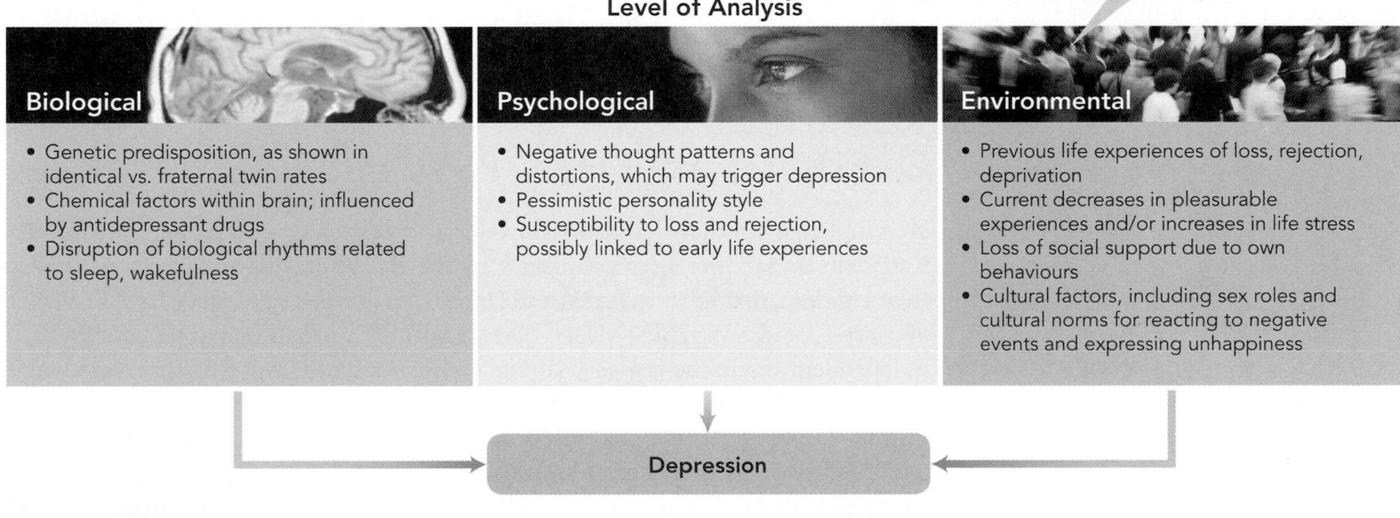

This feature will appear from time to time to help you compare and contrast levels of analysis.
Level of Analysis
Biological
• Genetic predisposition, as shown in identical vs. fraternal twin rates
• Chemical factors within brain; influenced by antidepressant drugs
• Disruption of biological rhythms related to sleep, wakefulness
Psychological
• Negative thought patterns and distortions, which may trigger depression
• Pessimistic personality style
• Susceptibility to loss and rejection, possibly linked to early life experiences
Environmental
• Previous life experiences of loss, rejection, deprivation
• Current decreases in pleasurable experiences and/or increases in life stress
• Loss of social support due to own behaviours
• Cultural factors, including sex roles and cultural norms for reacting to negative events and expressing unhappiness
Depression

FIGURE 1.22
Understanding the causes of behaviour: biological, psychological, and environmental factors in depression.

about behaviour. In Chapter 2 and throughout the book, we study the empirical methods that are used to observe behaviour and identify its causes.

- Though committed to an objective study of behaviour, psychologists recognize that *our experience of the world is subjective* and that we respond to a psychological reality created by our own thought processes, motives, and expectations. Many of these influences operate beyond our conscious awareness.
- As our levels of analysis theme shows us, *behaviour is determined by multiple causal factors* that can interact with one another in complex ways. This increases the challenge of understanding behaviour.
- *Nature and nurture* not only combine to shape our behaviour, but also influence one another. Our biological endowment helps determine the kinds of experiences we can have, and biological processes are, in turn, influenced by our experiences.
- Behaviour is a means of adapting to environmental demands, and *psychological capacities have evolved* during each species' history because they facilitated adaptation and survival.
- Behaviour and mental processes are strongly affected by the *cultural environment* in which they develop. In an increasingly multicultural world, there is a growing need to understand and appreciate the role of cultural factors in behaviour.

In Review

- *Factors that influence behaviour can be organized into three broad levels of analysis. The biological level of analysis focuses on brain processes, hormonal and genetic influences, and evolutionary adaptations that underlie behaviour. The psychological level of analysis examines mental processes and psychological motives, and how they influence behaviour. The environmental level of analysis calls attention to physical and social stimuli, including cultural factors, that shape our behaviour and thoughts.*
- *To understand behaviour, we often move back and forth between these levels of analysis. For example, when as children we are first exposed to cultural norms, those norms reflect a characteristic of our environment. However, once we adopt norms as our own, they become a part of our worldview and now represent the psychological level of analysis.*
- *Biological, psychological, and environmental factors contribute to the development of depression. These factors can also interact to influence a given behaviour. It may take only a mild setback to trigger depression in a person who has a strong biological predisposition toward depression, whereas a person who does not have such a biological predisposition may become depressed only after suffering a severe setback.*

FIELDS WITHIN PSYCHOLOGY

We will begin with a brief history of Canadian psychology. As shown in Table 1.3, Canadian universities were established by the British in the mid-1800s to educate their children, first in Nova Scotia and Upper Canada, and later, in the early 1900s, in Western Canada (Wright & Myers, 1982). The table also shows that psychology as an independent discipline is a very young science. Courses in psychology were taught in the early 1900s at all of the universities listed in the table, generally as part of Philosophy Departments (e.g., at Queens until 1948). The earliest independent Psychology Department was created at McGill University in 1924. Other universities taught psychology in combined "Philosophy and Psychology" Departments from the 1930s until the late 1950s (e.g., McMaster University; University of Alberta; University of

British Columbia). In the 1960s the number of graduate departments in psychology in Canada more than doubled; among the universities that developed graduate schools in that decade were Laval, Carleton, York, Waterloo, Calgary, Simon Fraser, and Victoria (see Wright & Myers, 1982).

TABLE 1.3 **A Brief History of Canadian Psychology Departments: Dates of the founding of the 12 Canadian universities with doctoral programs in psychology developed before 1960 (derived from data presented in Wright & Myers, 1982).**

University	Date Founded	Date Psychology Department Established
Dalhousie University	1838	1948
Queen's University	1841	1948
McGill University	1843	1924
University of Toronto	1850	1926
University of Ottawa	1866	1963
University of Manitoba	1877	1936
University of Western Ontario	1878	1931
McMaster University	1887	1958
University of Alberta	1908	1959
University of Saskatchewan	1908	1947
University of British Columbia	1915	1958
Université de Montréal	1919	1942

Modern-day psychology in Canada and the U.S.A. is a sprawling intellectual domain that stretches from the borders of medicine and the biological sciences to those of the social sciences and philosophy. Figure 1.23 shows psychology's position in the family of modern sciences. Because of the enormous breadth of psychology's subject matter, no psychologist can be an expert in all aspects of behaviour, just as no physician can be an expert in all areas of medicine. As in other scholarly disciplines, areas of specialization have emerged within psychology. Some of the major specialty areas are described in Table 1.4.

To many people, the term psychologist evokes the image of a "therapist" or "counsellor." Many psychologists are, in fact, clinical psychologists who diagnose and treat people with psychological problems in clinics, hospitals, and in private practice. But there are many other types of psychologists who have no connection with therapy in any form. These psychologists work as basic or applied researchers in their chosen subfield. Even within clinical psychology there are scientists who spend most of their time doing research on the causes of mental disorders and the effects of various kinds of treatment.

A career in most of the subfields described in Table 1.4 requires a doctoral degree based on four to six years of training beyond the bachelor's degree. Graduate training in psychology includes broad exposure to the theories and body of knowledge in the field, concentrated study in one or more of the subfields, and extensive training in research methods. In some areas, such as clinical, counselling, school, and industrial-organizational psychology, an additional year or more of supervised practical experience in a hospital, clinic, school, or workplace setting is generally required. Note, however, that psychologists who perform mental-health services are not the same as psychiatrists. Psychiatrists are medical doctors who receive additional specialized training in diagnosing and treating mental disorders.

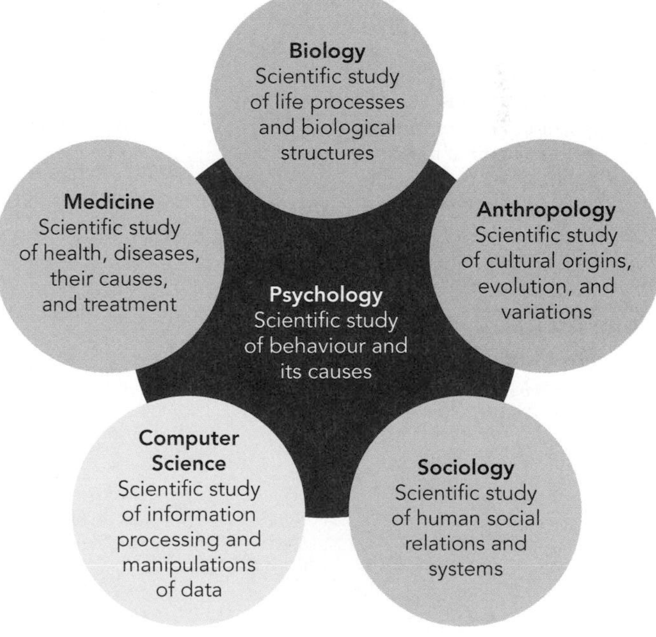

FIGURE 1.23
As the study of behaviour and its causes, psychology draws from and overlaps with many other scientific disciplines.

The American Psychological Association (APA), founded in 1892, is the largest individual psychological association in the world. Its 155,000 members and 55 divisions represent not only the subfields shown in Table 1.4 but also areas that focus on psychology's relation to the arts, religion, the military, the environment, sports, social issues, the law, and the media (APA, 2003). The American Psychology Society (APS), a newer organization consisting primarily of researchers, has grown to 12,000 members in just two decades (APS, 2003). Both APA and APS have international members in dozens of countries.

The actual number of psychologists in the different sub-areas of psychology in Canada is unknown. According to the Canadian Psychological Association's (CPA)

TABLE 1.4 **Major Specialty Areas Within Psychology**

Specialty	Major Focus
Animal behaviour (comparative)	Study of nonhuman species in natural or laboratory environments; includes genetics, brain processes, social behaviour, evolutionary processes
Behavioural neuroscience	Examination of brain and hormonal processes that underlie behaviour; behaviour genetics and evolutionary psychology are sometimes grouped under behavioural neuroscience
Clinical	Diagnosis and treatment of psychological disorders; research on causes of disorders and treatment effectiveness
Cognitive	Study of mental processes such as memory, problem solving, planning, consciousness, and language (psycholinguistics)
Counselling	Consultation with clients on issues of personal adjustment; vocational and career planning; interest and aptitude testing
Cultural/Cross-cultural	Study of cultural transmission, psychological similarities and differences among people from different cultures
Developmental	Study of physical, mental, emotional, and social development across the entire life span
Educational	Study of psychological aspects of the educational process; curriculum and instructional research; teacher training
Experimental	Research (typically laboratory experiments, often with nonhumans) on basic processes such as learning, perception, and motivation
Industrial/Organizational	Examination of behaviour in work settings; study of factors related to employee morale and performance; development of tests to select job applicants; development of machines and tasks to fit human capabilities
Personality	Study of individual differences in personality and their effects on behaviour; development of personality tests
Social	Examination of how the social environment—the presence of other people—influences an individual's behaviour, thoughts, and feelings
Quantitative	Measurement issues and data analysis; development of mathematical models of behaviour

Annual Report for 2004, there are 5123 members (this includes 1159 graduate students) in 23 different sections. Although CPA is the national Canadian organization for psychologists, created by 38 psychologists in 1939, many psychologists do not belong to CPA. We do know that there are over 11,000 clinical psychologists in Canada, according to a recent CPA survey, with the largest number, per capita, in Quebec. There are also many non-clinical psychologists with Master's and Ph.D. degrees working in school, university, hospital, industrial, and other settings who need to be counted.

?

40. Describe three important principles of effective time management.

Besides the fascinating subject matter of psychology, the rich variety of career options and work settings available to the well-trained professional attracts many people to a career in psychology. Figure 1.24 shows some of the major settings in which psychologists in the U.S.A. work (we should expect similar Canadian statis-

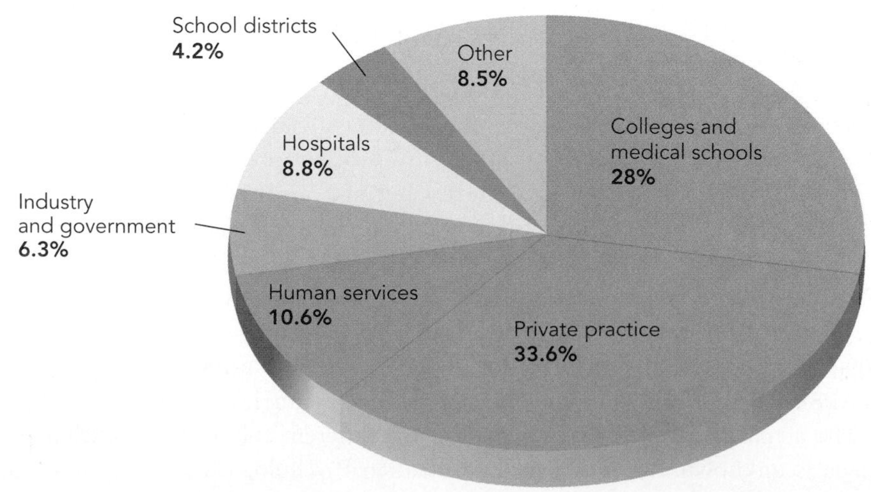

FIGURE 1.24

Work settings of psychologists.

Source: Adapted from data in table, American Psychological Association Research Office, 2001.

tics). Many psychologists teach, engage in research, or apply psychological principles and techniques to help solve personal or social problems. (See the Online Learning Centre for a more detailed discussion of careers in psychology.)

Psychologists in all of the areas shown in Table 1.4 engage in basic research and applied work. Some do one or the other, some do both. As we shall see throughout the book, psychological principles discovered through basic psychological research can be applied to many areas of our lives and to the solution of important social problems. For example, research on learning and memory conducted within the areas of educational and experimental psychology has provided practical guidelines that can enhance your academic performance. Our first *Psychological Applications* feature provides some research-based pointers that can help you to be more successful in your coursework.

41. What does educational psychology research tell us about the effects of directed questions on retention of information? Why do they have these effects?

42. What kinds of strategies are used by test-wise students when they take tests?

This feature will demonstrate how principles from basic research can be applied to everyday life.

PSYCHOLOGICAL APPLICATIONS

Academic Performance Enhancement Strategies

Four classes of strategies—time management, study skills, test-preparation strategies, and test-taking skills—are particularly useful for increasing your learning and academic performance, both in this course and throughout your educational experience.

Effective Time Management

University life imposes conflicting demands that can challenge even the most organized student. However, if you manage your time efficiently, you can allocate the time needed for study and have a clear conscience when it's time for recreational activities and relaxation.

First, it is essential to develop a written schedule. You have exactly 168 hours in every week, no more, no less. A written schedule forces you to decide how you are going to allocate your time to meet particular course demands and increases your commitment to the plan. Begin your master schedule by writing in all of your class meetings and other responsibilities, such as your job schedule. Then block in definite study times, taking into account how long you can study efficiently at one time and avoiding times when you are likely to be tired. Try to distribute your study times throughout the week. If possible, schedule some of your study times immediately before enjoyable activities so that you can use these as rewards for studying.

Once your study times are set, you are ready to apply the time management principle of *prioritizing* (Lakein, 1973). We all tend to work on routine or simple tasks while putting off the most demanding ones until we "have more time." Unfortunately, this can result in never getting to the major tasks (such as a term paper or a major reading assignment) until it is too late to devote sufficient time to them. Prioritizing means asking yourself weekly or even daily, "What is the most important thing to get done?" Do that task first, then move to the second most important, and so on.

Often the large or important task is too big to complete all at once. Time management experts tell us to break down the large task into smaller ones that can be completed at specific times (Haynes, 1987). Also, define each task in terms of a specific but realistic goal (e.g., number of pages to be read or amount of material to be studied). Achieving these goals is rewarding, and such success strengthens your study skills and increases your feelings of mastery.

Like any other skill, time management requires practice. The important tasks are (1) creating written schedules, (2) prioritizing, and (3) constantly monitoring your progress so you can modify your weekly schedule as necessary. The effort put into time management is more than repaid. Working smart can be as important as working hard.

Studying More Effectively

Once you have planned your study time, you will want to use that time most effectively. *Where* you study can make a difference. Choose a place where you can concentrate and where there are no distracting influences. Most students can study better in a quiet library than in front of a TV or in the middle of a Student Union cafeteria. According to a principle of learning that we study in Chapter 7, an excellent practice is to choose a quiet place where you do *nothing* but study. In time, that place will become associated with study behaviours, and it will be easier to study there (Watson & Tharp, 1998).

How you study is vital to your academic success. Rather than simply reading material and passively letting it soak in, you must engage in an active learning process to study most effectively. Psychological research confirms the value of

–Continued

an active approach to learning (Glaser & Bassok, 1989). For example, when you read a chapter in a textbook, don't just start reading from the beginning. First, look over the chapter outline. Then go to the end of the chapter and read the chapter summary, which reviews the chapter's main points. You then will have a good idea of the information you are going to be processing.

The Directed Questions Method

One of the most effective study methods we've encountered in our many years of teaching psychology is what we've termed the Directed Questions Method. It is an active learning procedure that requires you to prepare questions about the material you are reading. Research has shown that responding to questions promotes better recall (Moreland et al., 1997; Pauk & Fiore, 2000). In a major review of the scientific literature on learning aids, Richard Hamilton (1985) reviewed 35 different experimental studies in which the use of "adjunct questions" was compared with control conditions in which participants simply read textual material. He found that using questions like ours resulted in a superiority of about 20 percent in the retention of material. With our own students over the years, this approach has proven so successful that we chose to make it an integral learning tool in this text in the form of the directed questions found in the margins. These questions cover major facts and concepts you should know. Our directed questions can be supplemented by additional questions of your own. These questions will be an invaluable study aid when you prepare for tests. Here's how the directed questions method works.

As you read the material in a textbook, compose a question about each important point that is made. This forces you to actively identify what is being communicated. Put the number of the question in the margin next to the place where the answer is found. Do the same thing for your lecture notes. You can now study from your lists of questions and mentally recite the answers to yourself, referring back to your text and lecture notes to make sure that you are answering them correctly. The questions are written in such a way that they serve as a stimulus or prompt for the correct response, resulting in thorough learning.

The directed questions method has two other benefits. Research shows that there is almost no relation between what students think they know and how well they actually perform on tests (Glenberg et al., 1987; Pressley et al., 1987). However, the specific questions that you prepare in the Directed Questions Method allow you to appraise your current level of mastery. Second, the method can reduce test anxiety. You are likely to go into a test more confident, and such confidence tends to enhance performance (Bandura, 1997). Active learning using a method such as directed questions requires more effort than passive reading does, but it results in more facts being absorbed and principles understood (Estes & Vaughn, 1985).

Preparing for Tests

Bunker Hunt, a Texas oil billionaire, was once asked what advice he would give to someone who wanted to be successful. He answered, "First, decide exactly what you want. Second, decide what it's going to take to get it. Third, decide if you're willing to pay the price. Then, pay the price."

Introductory psychology is not an easy course. In fact, it is often a very demanding one because of the sheer amount of material that is covered and the many new concepts that must be mastered. Many students who take the course are relatively new to university and don't realize that the price to be paid for success far exceeds the demands that existed in high school. Moreover, many students are not aware of how hard high achievers actually work. In one study, students in an introductory psychology class were asked to record the number of hours outside class that they devoted to the course over a period of several weeks. When the students who were failing the course were compared with those who were getting A grades, the researchers found that the failing students were spending only one-third as many hours studying as were the A students (who were spending about two hours of active study for every hour spent in class). Yet the failing students *thought* they were studying as much as anyone else in the class, and many were mystified that they were not doing as well as their high-achieving peers (Watson & Tharp, 1998).

The time management and study strategies we've discussed can be very helpful when preparing for tests. First, the written study schedule helps you allocate sufficient study time, distribute your learning of the material over time, and avoid the need to cram at the last minute. Cramming, or *massed learning*, is a less effective way to study because it is fatiguing and taxes your memory abilities. Moreover, it often increases test anxiety, which can interfere with both the learning process and with actual test performance (Sarason & Sarason, 1990). The ideal situation as you near an exam is to have a solid familiarity with the material through previous study and to use the time before the test to reinforce and refine what you already know at a more general level. The Directed Questions approach can pay big dividends in the final days before an exam if you've paid the price required to prepare them.

Test-Taking Strategies

Some students are more effective test takers than others. They know how to take advantage of the kind of test they are taking (e.g., multiple-choice or essay format) to maximize their performance. Such skills are called *test-wiseness* (Fagley, 1987). Here are some of the strategies that test-wise students use (Millman et al., 1965):

1. Because you have a time limit in which to complete the test, use the time wisely. Check your progress occasionally to make sure that you are on track. Answer the questions you know first (and, in the case of essay exams, the ones that count for the most points). Do not get

bogged down on a question you find difficult to answer. Mark it and come back to it later.

2. On essay exams, organize your answer before you begin writing. Make a rough outline of the points you want to make. On essay exams, try to cover all of the critical points in enough detail to communicate what you know without needless verbiage.
3. On a test in an introductory psychology course, you are likely to have multiple-choice questions. As you read each multiple-choice question, try to answer it without looking at the alternatives. Then look at the answer options. If you find your answer among the alternatives, that alternative is probably the correct one. Nonetheless, read all the other alternatives to make sure that you choose the best one.
4. A widely held belief among both professors and students is that one should not change answers on multiple-choice tests because the first guess is most likely to be correct. Psychologists have checked out this belief and have found it to be untrue. Ludy Benjamin and his colleagues (1984) reviewed 20 different studies that investigated the consequences of changing answers. The results are summarized in Figure 1.25. As you can see, changing an answer is far more likely to result in a wrong answer becoming a correct one than vice versa. Another study showed that, on average, three points are gained for each point lost because of changing answers (Geiger, 1991). Therefore, don't be reluctant to change an answer if you are fairly sure that another alternative is better. At the same time, don't out-think yourself by attaching some esoteric meaning to an alternative so that it could *possibly* be correct. Most multiple-choice alternatives are fairly straightforward and are not meant to trick you.
5. Many multiple-choice items have one or two alternatives that you can rule out immediately. Eliminate them first, then choose your answer from the remaining alternatives, which are likely to have at least a grain of truth in them.
6. Some questions have "all of the above" as an alternative. If one of the other three or four alternatives is clearly incorrect, eliminate this option; if you are sure at least two of the other alternatives are correct but are not sure about the third, choose "all of the above."

The performance enhancement skills of time management, study skills, test-preparation strategies, and test-wiseness can help you improve your academic performance. Remember, however, that such skills are not acquired overnight; they require effort and practice. Psychology is an ideal course in which to acquire or refine them because the subject matter (learning, memory, problem solving, motivation, etc.) often pertains to the very principles you are perfecting. Some of the *Psychological Applications* features in other chapters also may help you enhance your academic performance. These include the following:

- systematic goal-setting strategies (see Chapter 12)
- self-control of behaviour (see Chapter 7)
- improving memory (see Chapter 8)
- coping with stress—including test anxiety (see Chapter 15)

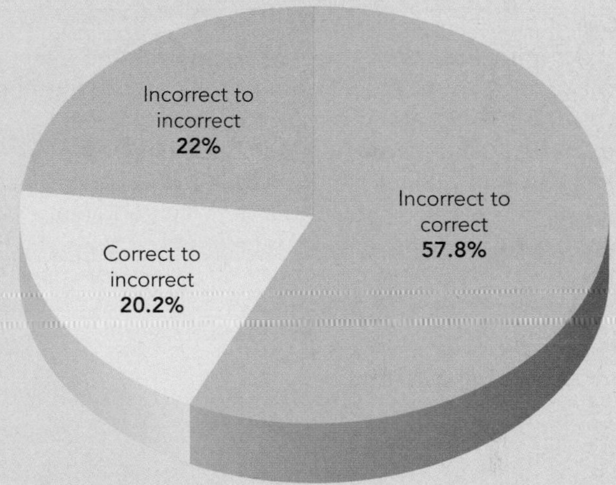

FIGURE 1.25

Combined results of 20 studies on the effects of changing answers on multiple-choice examinations contradict the widespread belief that one's first chosen answer is most likely to be correct and therefore should not be changed.

(Data from Benjamin et al., 1984)

In Review

- *Psychologists specialize in numerous subfields and work in many settings. Their professional activities include teaching, research, clinical work, and application of psychological principles to solve personal and social problems.*
- *Psychologists today conduct research and provide services around the globe.*
- *You can use principles derived from psychological science to enhance your learning and increase your likelihood of performing well on tests. These include time management principles, strategies for studying more effectively, test-preparation strategies, and techniques for taking tests.*

GAINING DIRECTION

This feature takes you back to the opening story and presents some possible answers to the questions posed.

What are the issues?

The opening scenario for Chapter 1 deals with global warming. At first, this may seem like a topic more appropriate for an environmental science text. But as we consider the issue more carefully, we realize that many of the technological solutions are already available. We "simply" need to cut back on emissions. *How* we accomplish this is the real question. What are people's attitudes and beliefs about the environment? Might someone believe that we should reduce our carbon footprint, but still engage in activities that warm the planet? How do we change these attitudes and beliefs? Following Hurricane Katrina in 2005, there were reports of discrimination and violence. Why should this result from a natural disaster? Shouldn't we expect people to pull together and help one another? How do people cope with all of the stress? How will the world respond to more frequent disasters resulting in more and more loss of life?

As you integrate the opening story with the material in the chapters, try to identify the various psychological principles that could help in our understanding of these issues. The issues outlined above are some that *we* identified—you might come up with many others. This is not only acceptable, but exactly what you should do. Note that additional issues require additional answers to the next two sections.

What do we need to know?

How do people form attitudes?
How do we change attitudes?
What are the causes of violence?
Are we naturally helpful or violent?
What factors influence responses to emergencies?
Is intergroup discrimination heightened by conflict?
How do we cope with stress?
How can psychological theory help us to understand events in the "real world"?

Where can you find the information to answer these questions?

Look back at the icons in this chapter. What psychological principles (or research) are presented that may help us to understand some of the issues? Consider the Research Foundations box. The classic research by Hastorf & Cantril (1954) demonstrates that our perception of events and the groups involved depends on our own group membership. We see the behaviour of others (the outgroup) as more hostile than that of our own group (the ingroup). Might this apply to other beliefs as well? For example, might we see our own group as inherently "good" and others as "bad"? If so, then things that happen to others (e.g., drought, plague) might be seen as being "deserved." After all, "bad" people should receive negative outcomes in life. Are there theories or perspectives presented in the chapter that address some of the issues outlined above?

⊙ KEY TERMS AND CONCEPTS*

applied research (5)
artificial intelligence (17)
basic research (5)
behaviour genetics (14)
behaviour modification (24)
behavioural perspective (22)
behaviourism (23)
biological perspective (11)
British empiricism (22)
cognitive behaviourism (24)
cognitive perspective (15)
collectivism (26)
culture (26)
evolutionary psychology (14)
functionalism (16)
Gestalt psychology (16)
humanistic perspective (24)
hysteria (21)
individualism (26)
insight (16)
interaction (33)
introspection (16)
jigsaw program (7)
levels of analysis (30)
mind-body dualism (10)
monism (10)
natural selection (13)
norms (26)
perspectives (9)
psychodynamic perspective (20)
psychology (4)
repression (21)
self-actualization (25)
social constructivism (18)
sociobiology (14)
sociocultural perspective (26)
structuralism (16)
terror management theory (25)

*Each term has been boldfaced in the text on the page indicated in parentheses.

⊙ DO YOU WANT TO ELEVATE YOUR GRADES?

For additional resources and interactive quizzing, visit the book's Online Learning Centre at **www.mcgrawhill.ca/olc/passer**.

CHAPTER 2

Studying Behaviour Scientifically

I have no special talents. I am only passionately curious.
—Albert Einstein

CHAPTER OUTLINE

Post-traumatic stress disorder is an anxiety-based psychological problem that many people experience following an extremely stressful event (e.g., rape, kidnapping, war). A variety of treatments are employed for this disorder (e.g., desensitization, cognitive restructuring, anti-anxiety medication, etc.), but a new treatment is now being used by therapists from Los Angeles to Toronto. Eye Movement Desensitization and Reprocessing (EMDR) involves having clients focus on the distressing problem while sequencing their eye movements to an external stimulus such as a moving light source. The therapist guides the client through the session (about 90 minutes), encouraging him or her to let the thoughts enter into consciousness and to keep pairing these thoughts with the various eye movements. The client may or may not actually discuss the problem during a session.

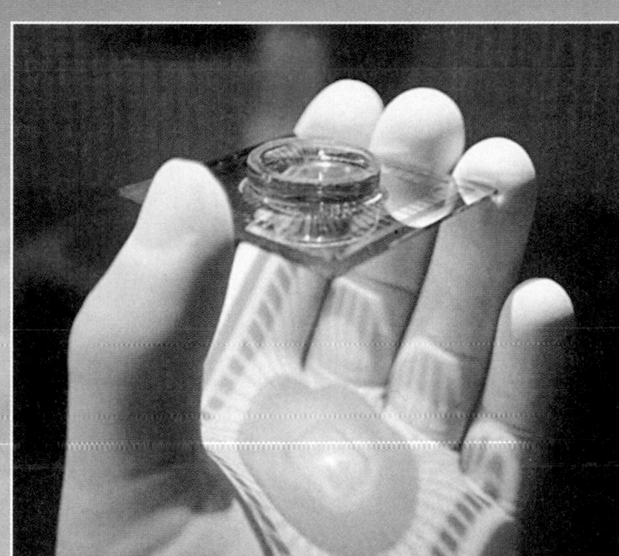

The EMDR Institute has trained over 30,000 therapists, with over 1,000 registered in Canada.

- **What are the issues here?**
- **What do we need to know?**
- **Where can we find the information to answer these questions?**

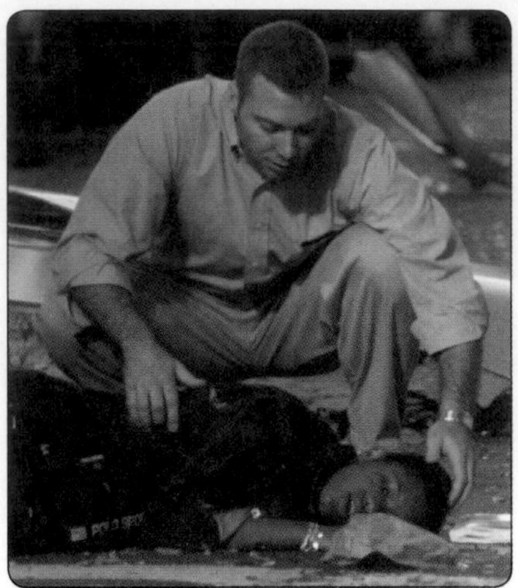

FIGURE 2.1
What determines whether a bystander will help a victim?

Heroic Acts: Jeff Selinger, a bus driver from Halifax, Nova Scotia, saw a car crash into a telephone pole and catch fire. He stopped his bus and ran with his fire extinguisher to free an elderly man who was trapped by his seatbelt inside his smoke-filled car. Ignoring the threat of an explosion, he freed the man and carried him to safety. Years earlier Selinger saved a man and his pets from a burning house.

Bystander apathy: In March of 1964 a young woman named Kitty Genovese was stabbed repeatedly and raped by a knife-wielding assailant as she returned from work to her New York City apartment. The 3 A.M. attack lasted about 30 minutes, during which time her screams and pleas for help were heard by 38 of her neighbours. Many went to their windows to find out what was happening. Yet nobody assisted her, and by the time anyone called the police, she had died. On May 12, 2001, Katerine, a 17-year-old Canadian girl, was severely beaten and left half-naked in a parking lot near a west-end subway station in Montreal. Katerine remained there in a coma for hours, ignored by pedestrians who blithely walked past the girl. Even more upsetting was that employees working at a call centre, Sitel Canada, next to the parking lot, could see Katerine from their windows. When several employees wanted to call 911 and to go to the girl's assistance, they were told not to do so by their supervisor. Katerine remained in a coma for months, and when the police published her photo and pleaded for help from bystanders, no one came forward. Sitel Canada did eventually fire the supervisor.

⊙ SCIENTIFIC PRINCIPLES IN PSYCHOLOGY

Science is about discovery. At its core, science simply is an approach to asking and answering questions about the universe around us. Certainly there are many ways to learn about the world around us—through philosophy, religious faith, art, common sense, and so on. What distinguishes science from these approaches is a general process guided by certain principles—the scientific method. The scientific method was used by physicists and chemists for several centuries to make great progress in determining the laws for the physical sciences. Psychologists took much longer to adopt the scientific method for behavioural science because the subject matter is not as tangible as that in the physical sciences. Calculating the speed of a thrown ball by measuring the time and distance is much easier than measuring a person's intelligence. In this chapter we explore in detail the principles and methods that form the foundation of psychological science.

Scientific Attitudes

Curiosity, skepticism, and *open-mindedness* are driving forces behind scientific inquiry. Like a child who constantly asks "Why?" the good scientist has an insatiable curiosity. And like a master detective, the good scientist is an incurable skeptic. Each claim is met with the reply "Show me your evidence," and even when a mystery appears to be solved the good scientist asks, "Might there be a better explanation?" Scientists also must remain open-minded to conclusions that are supported by facts, even if those conclusions refute their own beliefs.

Following the Kitty Genovese murder, two psychology professors in New York City, John Darley of New York University and Bibb Latané of Columbia University, met for dinner. Like everyone else, they wondered how 38 people could witness a criminal act and not even call the police. But their curiosity was piqued so strongly that they decided to investigate further. Darley and Latané were skeptical of the "bystander apathy" explanation, based on "moral decay" or "dehumanization produced by the urban environment," offered by social commentators. They believed it was unlikely that every one of the 38 bystanders could have been apathetic. As social psychologists, they knew that the immediate environment powerfully influences behaviour, even though people may be unaware of this influence. They noted that the bystanders could see that other neighbours had turned on their lights and were looking out their windows. Each bystander might have been concerned about Kitty Genovese's plight but assumed that someone else surely would help or call the police.

Darley and Latané reasoned that the presence of multiple bystanders produced a *diffusion of responsibility*, a psychological state in which each person feels decreased personal responsibility for intervening. To test their explanation, they performed several experiments that have become classics in social psychology. However, as Darley and Latané set out to gather evidence, they had to remain open-minded to the possibility that the findings would not support their point of view.

1. What key scientific attitudes did Darley and Latané display?

2. How does Darley and Latané's research illustrate the basic steps of the scientific process?

3. What is a hypothesis?

Gathering Evidence: Steps in the Scientific Process

Science involves a continuous interplay between observing and explaining events. Figure 2.2 shows the steps through which the gathering of scientific evidence often proceeds. Curiosity sparks the first step: Scientists observe something noteworthy and ask a question about it. For Darley and Latané, the initial observation was that nobody helped Kitty Genovese, and the question became "Why?"

Next, scientists formulate a testable hypothesis. A **hypothesis** is a tentative explanation or prediction about some phenomenon. To develop a hypothesis, scientists gather clues and logically analyze them. Noting that many bystanders had been present, and recognizing that each one probably knew that others were watching, Darley and Latané combined these clues to arrive at a hypothesis: A diffusion of responsibility reduced the likelihood that any one bystander would feel responsible for helping.

Casual observers might stop here, satisfied that they now understand why the bystanders did not help. But the scientist knows that the hypothesis is tentative and must be tested. To do this, the hypothesis is translated into a specific prediction that often takes the form of an "If—Then" statement. Thus the diffusion of responsibility hypothesis becomes the following: IF an emergency occurs, THEN the greater the number of bystanders, the less likely any one bystander will be to intervene.

The third step of scientific inquiry is to test the hypothesis by gathering evidence. Scientists do this by conducting research. Darley and Latané (1968) carefully created an "emergency" in their experimental laboratory and observed people's responses. The participants were undergraduates who were told that they would be discussing "personal problems faced by normal university students." They were informed that, to ensure privacy, they would be seated in separate rooms, they would communicate through an intercom system, and the experimenter would not listen to their conversation. Participants would take turns speaking for several rounds. In each round, a participant would have two minutes to speak, during which time the others would be unable to interrupt or be heard, because their microphones would be turned off.

As the discussion began over the intercom, a speaker described his difficulties adjusting to university life and disclosed that he suffered from seizures. During the next round of conversation, this same speaker began to gasp and stammer, saying:

1. Initial Observation/Question
Kitty Genovese incident. Why did no one help?
2. Form Hypothesis
IF multiple bystanders are present, THEN a diffusion of responsibility will decrease each bystander's likelihood of intervening.
3. Test Hypothesis (conduct research)
• Create "emergency" in controlled setting. • Manipulate perceived number of bystanders. • Measure helping.
4. Analyze Data
Helping decreases as the perceived number of bystanders increases. The hypothesis is supported. (If data do not support the hypothesis, revise and retest.)
5. Further Research and Theory Building
Additional studies support the hypothesis. A Theory of Social Impact is developed based on these and other findings.
6. New Hypothesis Derived from Theory
The theory is tested directly by deriving a new hypothesis and conducting new research.

FIGURE 2.2

This sequence represents one common path to scientific understanding. In other cases, scientists begin with an observation/question and proceed directly to research without testing hypotheses or trying to build theories.

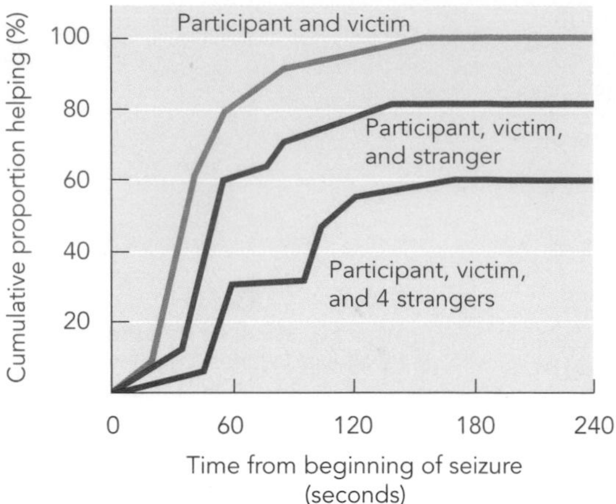

FIGURE 2.3

Some participants believed that they were alone with a student who presumably was having a seizure. Others believed that either one or four more bystanders were present. Participants who believed they were alone with the victim were more likely to intervene, and did so more quickly.

Adapted from data from Darley & Latané, 1968.

"... Could somebody-er-er—help ... [choking sounds] ... I'm gonna die-er-er—I'm gonna die-er—help ... seizure" [chokes, then silence] (Darley & Latané, 1968, p. 379).

Unbeknownst to the participants, they actually were listening to an audio tape recording. This ensured that all of them were exposed to the identical "emergency." To test how the number of bystanders influences helping, Darley and Latané manipulated the number of other people that each participant believed to be present and listening over the intercom. On a random basis, some participants were told that they were alone with the victim; in a second condition, participants were led to believe there was another listener present. In a third condition, they believed that four other listeners were present. The participants believed that the seizure was real and serious. But did they help?

At the fourth step of scientific inquiry, researchers analyze the information (called *data*) they collect and draw tentative conclusions. Darley and Latané measured the percentage of participants who left their room to go to the victim or find help, and the speed with which they acted. Figure 2.3 shows that 80 percent of the participants who thought they were alone with the victim helped within the first minute of the seizure and 100 percent helped within three minutes. As the number of presumed bystanders increased, the proportion who helped decreased, and those who did help took longer to respond. Darley and Latané concluded that the findings supported the diffusion of responsibility hypothesis. Their results also demonstrate how scientific research can contradict common sense adages such as "There's safety in numbers." As you will see throughout this book, many common sense beliefs have not survived the cutting edge of psychological research.

We have described four steps in gathering scientific evidence: asking a question, forming a hypothesis, conducting research, and drawing conclusions based on data analysis. However, the process of inquiry does not end here.

4. What is a theory? How does it differ from a hypothesis?

At the fifth step scientists conduct more research and, as additional evidence comes in, they attempt to build theories. A **theory** is a set of formal statements that explains how and why certain events are related to one another. Theories are broader than hypotheses, and in psychology theories typically specify lawful relations between certain behaviours and their causes. For example, to establish that diffusion of responsibility occurred across a range of situations, researchers conducted nearly 50 additional experiments in laboratories and natural settings, the vast majority of which supported the initial findings (Latané & Nida, 1981). Latané (1981) combined the principle of diffusion of responsibility with other principles of group behaviour to develop a Theory of Social Impact, which he then used to explain a variety of human social behaviours.

Finally, at the sixth step, the theory is used to develop new hypotheses, which are then tested by conducting additional research and gathering new evidence. In this manner the scientific process becomes self-correcting. If research consistently supports the hypotheses derived from the theory, our confidence in the theory becomes stronger. If the predictions made by the theory are not supported, then it will need to be modified or, ultimately, discarded.

Two Approaches to Understanding Behaviour

Humans have a strong desire to understand why things happen. To psychologists, such understanding means being able to specify the *causes* of behaviour, the conditions responsible for its occurrence. Why do scientists favour the step-by-step approach to understanding described above over the approach typically involved in everyday common sense: hindsight (after-the-fact) understanding?

Hindsight Understanding

Danish philosopher Søren Kierkegaard stated: "Life is lived forwards, but understood backwards." Perhaps the most common method we use to try to understand behaviour in our everyday life is after-the-fact ("hindsight") reasoning. Indeed, when you report the results of some of the research described in this book, you might hear the comment: "Big deal—I knew that all along." However, there is a problem in using hindsight explanations based on common sense and folk knowledge to understand behaviour. For example, suppose two highschool sweethearts promised each other undying love before going off to different universities and when they came home for the holidays they broke up. The well-known proverb, "Out of sight, out of mind," can explain this result. But, suppose, instead, the opposite happened. When the sweethearts came home, they were more in love than ever and got married. The proverb "Absence makes the heart grow fonder" explains this result. So which proverb is true; or, are there other reasons for their behaviour—e.g., the break-up occurred when sweethearts met new partners at university?

5. Explain the major drawback of hindsight understanding.

The main problem with relying solely on hindsight reasoning is that related past events can be explained in many creative, reasonable, and sometimes contradictory, ways. There is no sure way to determine which—if any—of the alternatives is correct. Despite this problem, hindsight reasoning can provide valuable insights and is often the foundation on which further scientific inquiry is built. For example, Darley and Latané's diffusion of responsibility explanation was initially based on after-the-fact reasoning about the Kitty Genovese murder.

Understanding through Prediction, Control, and Theory Building

Whenever possible, scientists prefer to test their understanding of "what causes what" more directly. If we understand the causes of a given behaviour, then we should be able to predict the conditions under which that behaviour will occur in the future. Furthermore, if we can control those conditions (e.g., in the laboratory), then we should be able to produce that behaviour.

6. What approach to understanding do scientists prefer? Why?

7. Describe the characteristics of a good theory.

Darley and Latané's research illustrates this approach. To test their causal explanation for why bystanders failed to help Kitty Genovese, Darley and Latané predicted that a greater number of bystanders present during an emergency would reduce individual helping. Next they created a laboratory setting to produce this result. They staged an emergency, controlled participants' beliefs about the number of bystanders present, and carefully structured the environment so that each participant could not tell whether the other "bystanders" were taking action (as was the case in the Kitty Genovese murder). Their prediction was supported. Understanding through prediction and control is a scientific alternative to after-the-fact understanding.

Theory development is the strongest test of scientific understanding because good theories generate an *integrated network of predictions.* A good theory has several important characteristics:

- It incorporates existing facts and observations within a single broad framework. In other words, it organizes information in a meaningful way.
- It is testable. It generates new hypotheses—new specific predictions—whose accuracy or inaccuracy can be evaluated by gathering new evidence (Figure 2.4).
- The predictions made by the theory are supported by the findings of new research.
- It conforms to the *law of parsimony:* If two theories can explain and predict the same phenomena equally well, the simpler theory is the preferred one.

"IT MAY VERY WELL BRING ABOUT IMMORTALITY, BUT IT WILL TAKE FOREVER TO TEST IT."

FIGURE 2.4

Is the scientist's claim of discovering an "eternal life potion" a testable hypothesis? Yes, because it is possible to show the hypothesis to be false. If people drink it but still die, then we have refuted the hypothesis. Therefore it is testable. It is, however, impossible to absolutely prove true. Even after living for a million years, a person who drank the potion could die the next day.

8. Why are operational definitions important?

Even when a theory is supported by many successful predictions, it is never regarded as an absolute truth. It is always possible that some future observation will contradict it, or that a newer and more accurate theory will take its place. If this happens, scientists do not wring their hands in despair. Disproving established theories frequently opens up exciting new frontiers for investigation. The displacement of old beliefs and theoretical frameworks by new ones is the essence of science (Klahr & Simon, 1999).

Finally, although scientists use prediction as a test of "understanding," this does *not* mean that prediction *requires* understanding. Based on experience, a child can predict that thunder will follow lightning without knowing why it does so. Our primeval ancestors undoubtedly could predict that eating certain plants would make them sick, without understanding principles of human physiology. But prediction based on understanding (i.e., "theory building") has important advantages: It satisfies our curiosity, increases knowledge, and generates principles that can be applied to new situations that we have not yet directly experienced.

Defining and Measuring Variables

Psychologists study variables and the relations among them. A **variable**, quite simply, is any characteristic that can differ. Gender is a variable: Some people are female, others male. People's age, ethnicity, school grades, and typing speed are variables, as are national daily ice cream consumption rates and stock market prices.

Many variables represent non-material concepts, such as *memory, personality, intelligence, stress, learning, and motivation.* Such terms may have different meanings for different people. Unless two people share a common definition of what "intelligence" or "stress" means, they cannot be sure that they are talking about the same thing when they discuss these concepts. When scientists conduct research, they resolve this problem by operationally defining concepts. An **operational definition** defines a variable in terms of the specific procedures used to produce or measure it. In essence, operational definitions *translate an abstract term into something observable and measurable.*

For example, to examine whether six months of regular exercise reduces stress, we must first decide upon definitions of "regular exercise" and "stress." We could operationally define "regular exercise" in many ways, such as taking a daily three-kilometre walk or engaging in 30 minutes of vigorous physical activity four times a week. We can operationally define "stress" as people's questionnaire rating of how tense they feel, their level of muscle tension, or frequency of fidgeting (e.g., nail biting, foot tapping). As a researcher, you would use your knowledge about exercise and stress to identify operational definitions that seem most appropriate.

Consider another example. As you may know all too well, taking exams can be stressful. Suppose that we want to study the relation between exam stress and academic performance among university students. How might you operationally define "exam stress" at a biological, psychological, and environmental level of analysis? Think about this, and then see Figure 2.5.

Of course, operational definitions don't solve every problem. Just as you and a friend may disagree about what constitutes a great movie, other scientists may not agree with our definitions of regular exercise and stress. Even so, the key point is that operational definitions let other scientists know exactly what we mean by those terms.

To define a concept operationally, we must be able to measure it. Measurement is challenging because psychologists study incredibly varied and complex processes. Some processes are directly observable, but others are not. Fortunately, psychologists have numerous measurement techniques at their disposal (Figure 2.6).

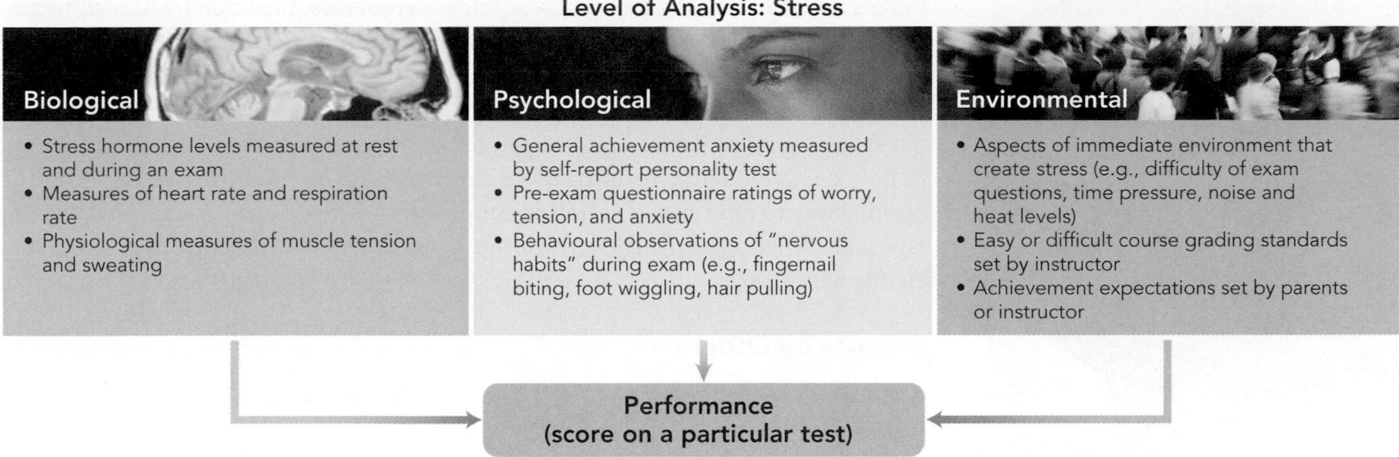

Level of Analysis: Stress
Biological
• Stress hormone levels measured at rest and during an exam
• Measures of heart rate and respiration rate
• Physiological measures of muscle tension and sweating
Psychological
• General achievement anxiety measured by self-report personality test
• Pre-exam questionnaire ratings of worry, tension, and anxiety
• Behavioural observations of "nervous habits" during exam (e.g., fingernail biting, foot wiggling, hair pulling)
Environmental
• Aspects of immediate environment that create stress (e.g., difficulty of exam questions, time pressure, noise and heat levels)
• Easy or difficult course grading standards set by instructor
• Achievement expectations set by parents or instructor
Performance
(score on a particular test)

FIGURE 2.5

Understanding the causes of behaviour: When studying the effects of exam stress on academic performance, the concept of "exam stress" can be operationally defined at the biological, psychological, and environmental levels of analysis.

Self-Report Measures

Self-report measures ask people to report on their own knowledge, beliefs, feelings, experiences, or behaviour. This information can be gathered in several ways, such as interviews, questionnaires, or specially designed psychological tests. The accuracy of self-report measures hinges on people's ability and willingness to respond honestly. Especially when research questions focus on sensitive topics, such as sexual habits and drug use, participants' self-reports may be distorted by a *social desirability bias:* the tendency of participants to give an answer that gives a good impression rather than one that reflects how they truly feel or behave. University of British Columbia researcher, Delroy Paulhus (1991), suggests that one can minimize this bias by wording questions in such a way that social desirability is not relevant or, in cases where this is not possible, by guaranteeing respondents anonymity/confidentiality so that they can respond honestly without fear of future consequences (e.g., questions involving taking drugs, having unsafe sex, etc.).

A variety of methods exist to index socially desirable response biases in individuals, such as self-report questionnaires that measure the degree to which individuals exaggerate their positive and minimize their negative qualities. These measures presume respondents give honest responses. An alternative is the Over-Claiming Questionnaire (OCQ) developed by Paulhus, Harms, Bruce, and Lysy (2003); respondents rate their familiarity with a large number of items, of which 20% (e.g., "cholarine") don't exist. The social desirability bias is high when respondents confidently claim familiarity with a large number of non-existent items.

In interviews, the accuracy of self-reports also can be influenced by the interviewer's behaviour. Nowhere is this issue more explosive than in cases of child sexual abuse. According to Statistics Canada's reports in 2004/6 entitled "Family Violence in Canada: A Statistical Profile" (www.statcan.ca; catalogue #85-224-XIE200400085, p. 15), a disproportionately high number of assaults reported to 94 police departments were against children and youth (over 25,000 cases accounting for 24%), with a high percentage being sexual assaults (8,800 cases), which were four times more likely for girls than boys (ibid., 2006, p. 31). In the United States, over 100,000 substantiated cases a year are reported and in both countries, many cases go unreported (e.g., U.S. Department of Health and Human Services, 1999). Yet some allegations are found to be false. In most cases there is no clear-cut medical evidence, so the accuracy of the child's testimony becomes paramount (Bruck et al., 1998).

Some therapists and police investigators use suggestive (biased) interview techniques to "draw out" allegations of sexual abuse from children who initially deny it,

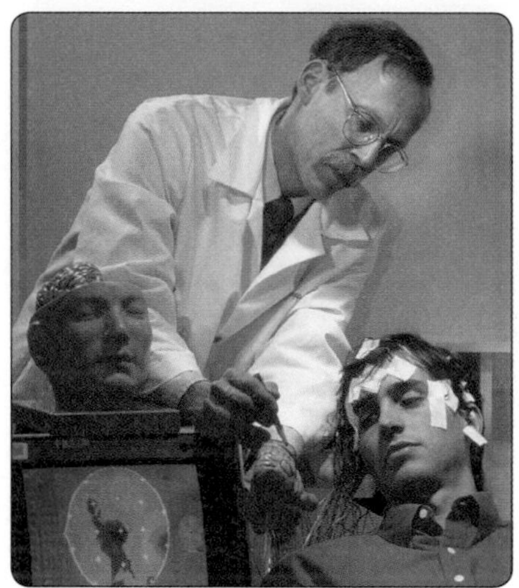

FIGURE 2.6

(a) Self-report, (b) physiological, and (c) behavioural measures are important scientific tools for psychologists.

9. Describe the major ways psychologists measure behaviour, and a limitation of each.

but presumably are reluctant to discuss their experience. Research by American and Canadian psychologists shows that suggestive questions that are repeated can cause some children to falsely report, and even come to believe, that fictitious events are real (Bruck et al., 1995; Ceci & Huffman, 1997). Furthermore, even in non-biased interviews, some children report suggested events that are false (Erdmann, Volbert, & Bohm, 2004). These results raise a hornet's nest of controversy regarding the optimal way to interview children about potential sexual abuse (Bruck et al., 2000), especially when eye-witness verification of the events is missing (Bruck, Ceci, & Hembrooke, 2002).

Reports by Others

We also can learn about someone's behaviour by obtaining reports made by other people. Parents, spouses, and teachers who know a person can provide useful information about him or her. University students might be asked to rate their roommates' personality traits, and job supervisors might be asked to rate a worker's competence and motivation. As with self-reports, researchers try to maximize participants' honesty in reporting about other people.

Physiological Measures

Although psychologists frequently depend on participants' self-reports to measure subjective experiences, there are other ways to measure what is happening "inside" a person. Scientists are able to measure many aspects of physiological functioning, ranging from heart rate, blood pressure, respiration rate, and hormonal secretions, to electrical and biochemical processes in the brain. Physiological measures have long been the mainstay of researchers working within the biological perspective, but these measures have become increasingly important in many areas of psychology.

Physiological responses can have their own interpretive problems, the main one being that we don't always understand what they mean. For example, if a person shows increased heart rate and brain activity in a particular situation, what emotion or thought is being expressed? The links between specific patterns of physiological activity and particular mental events are far from being completely understood.

Behavioural Observations

A fourth measurement approach is to observe people's overt (i.e., directly visible) behaviours in either real-life or laboratory settings. For example, in the bystander apathy study discussed previously, Darley and Latané measured how long it took participants to go and help the "person in distress." Psychologists often need to develop coding systems made up of specific behaviour categories to measure such diverse behaviours as people's facial expressions, parent-child interactions, and marital communications (Ekman & Friesen, 1987). Once a coding system is developed, observers are rigorously trained to use it in exactly the same way so that their measurements will be *reliable,* which means that they are consistent. If two observers watching the same behaviours repeatedly disagree in their coding, then the data are unreliable and of little use.

Psychologists sometimes gather information about people's overt behaviour by using **archival measures**, which are already-existing records or documents. For example, researchers comparing different programs designed to reduce drunk driving could use police arrest records to measure the frequency of "drunk driving."

Humans and other animals may behave differently when they know they are being observed, resulting in an unrepresentative (i.e., atypical) sample of behaviour. To counter this problem, researchers in natural environments may camouflage themselves or use *unobtrusive measures,* which record behaviour in a way that keeps participants unaware that they are being observed (Lee, 2000; Webb et al., 1966). For example, researchers from the Centers for Disease Control assessed the effects of a "safer sex" program by counting the number of used condoms that turned up in a Baltimore sewage treatment plant before and after the program (no one promised that science would always be glamorous).

10. What is unobtrusive measurement?

In sum, psychologists can measure behaviour in many ways, each with advantages and disadvantages. To gain greater confidence in their findings, researchers may use several types of measures within a single study.

In Review

- *Curiosity, skepticism, and open-mindedness are key scientific attitudes. The scientific process proceeds through several steps: (1) asking questions based on some type of observation; (2) formulating a tentative explanation and a testable hypothesis; (3) conducting research to test the hypothesis; (4) analyzing the data and drawing a tentative conclusion; (5) building a theory; and (6) using the theory to generate new hypotheses, which are tested by more research.*
- *In everyday life we typically use hindsight (after-the-fact understanding) to explain behaviour. This approach is flawed because there may be countless possible explanations and no way to ascertain which is correct. Psychologists prefer to test their understanding through prediction, control, and building theories about the causes of behaviour.*
- *A good theory organizes known facts, gives rise to additional hypotheses that are testable, is supported by the findings of new research, and is parsimonious.*
- *An operational definition defines a concept or variable in terms of the specific procedures used to produce or measure it.*
- *Psychologists assess behaviour by obtaining participants' self-reports, gathering reports from others who know the participants, directly observing behaviour, and measuring physiological responses.*

METHODS OF RESEARCH

Like detectives searching for clues to solve a case, psychologists conduct research to gather evidence about behaviour and its causes. The research method chosen depends upon the problem being studied, the investigator's objectives, and ethical principles. In this section, the three research methods described are: **descriptive methods**, which involve recording observations or surveys; **correlational methods**, which involve measuring the strength of an association between two or more events; and **experimental methods**, which involve manipulations to establish cause and effect relationships between two or more events.

Descriptive Research: Recording Events

The most basic goal of science is to describe phenomena. In psychology, **descriptive research** seeks to identify how humans and other animals behave, particularly in natural settings. It provides information about the diversity of behaviour, can be used to test hypotheses, and may yield clues about potential cause-effect relationships that are later tested experimentally. Case studies, naturalistic observation, and surveys are common descriptive methods.

Case Studies: Treating Cases of Failure to Thrive (Starvation) in Human Infants

11. What is a case study? Identify its advantages.

A **case study** is an in-depth analysis of an individual, group, or event. By studying a single case in great detail the researcher typically hopes to discover principles of behaviour that are true for people or situations in general. Data may be gathered through observation, interviews, psychological tests, physiological recordings, and task performance. Archival data may be examined when a case study focuses on people or events from the past.

Case studies have several advantages. They can be a vibrant source of new ideas and hypotheses that subsequently may be examined using more controlled research methods. Case studies have provided important insight into diverse topics such as brain functioning, child development, mental disorders, and cultural influences.

One advantage is that when a rare phenomenon occurs, the case study method enables scientists to study it intensively and collect a large amount of data. See the Focus on Neuroscience box for some examples.

A second advantage is that a case study may challenge the validity of a theory or widely held scientific belief. For example, suppose a theory proposed that, for humans to learn language, they *must* be exposed to a language-rich environment sometime during their childhood. By finding a single contradictory case—a person who was not exposed to language during childhood but later learned to speak normally—this proposition would be shown to be incorrect and the theory would have to be modified.

A third advantage of a case study is that it can illustrate effective intervention programs developed by clinical psychologists to treat special populations. For example, normally human weight gain is very rapid following birth; if an infant stops growing or loses weight, this can have a long-term negative impact on the child's physical and intellectual development. When medical causes are ruled out, this "failure-to-thrive" is related to poverty and parenting problems. One group at risk for neglect is mothers with intellectual disabilities. Researchers at Surrey Place Centre in Toronto developed an intervention program to train mothers with low scores on IQ tests who had failure-to-thrive infants in nutrition and feeding techniques (Feldman, Garrick, & Case, 1997). Their procedure, based on the behaviourist theory discussed in Chapter 1, involved three components. The child's weight (the dependent variable discussed later) was recorded by the child's physician for several weeks to diagnose failure to thrive; this is the *Baseline*. Next, the *Treatment* consisted of six weeks of weekly parental instruction on feeding and nutrition, along with ongoing medical advice and supervision. Finally, in the *Follow-up* the child's weight was measured several times over the next three years. The results are shown in Figure 2.7, in which the child's weight, relative to the weight of the lightest 5 percent of children of each age (i.e., the 5th percentile—at a level that can define failure-to-thrive) is plotted for the three components of the study. Clearly, this child failed to gain weight during the Baseline, rapidly gained weight to a safe level during the brief Treatment, and continued to thrive for the next few years during the Follow-up, suggesting that the treatment program was very effective.

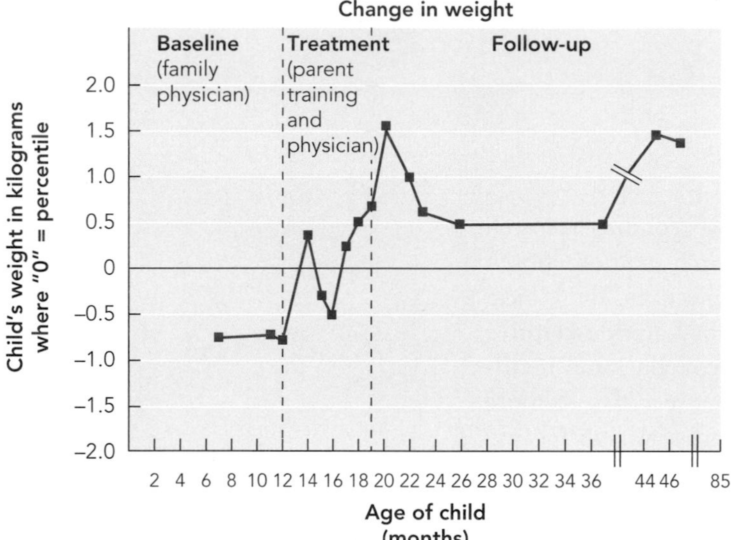

FIGURE 2.7

An example of a case study of a failure-to-thrive infant who stopped growing shortly after birth. Weight on the Y-axis is given in kilograms relative to the 5th percentile (95% of the infants of that age are above the horizontal line at "0" on the Y-axis). During the baseline, the infant was 0.8 Kg below the 5th percentile, but gained weight rapidly to a safe level when the parent received training in feeding and nutrition (Treatment) and remained at a normal weight for the next few years (Follow-up).

Figure adapted from Feldman et al., 1997.

Case studies have several limitations. First, they are a poor method for determining cause-effect relations. In our failure-to-thrive case study the treatment may have caused the infant's weight gain; alternatively, some other change in the mother's and infant's lives could have been responsible, or the symptoms may have ended simply because of the passage of time. Although in this study we cannot prove which explanation is correct, the researchers also measured other behaviours presumed to be

FOCUS ON NEUROSCIENCE

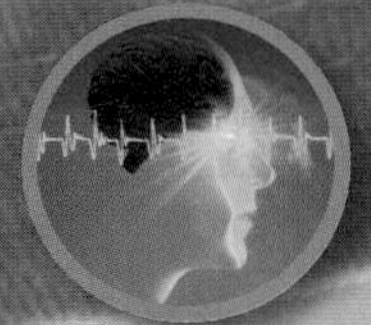

The Neuroscience of the Human Brain at Work

Neuroscientists use various techniques to identify localization of behavioral function in specific areas of the brain. The case study method has been used to test patients with damage to a specific area(s) of the brain to uncover which of their abilities are preserved and which are lost, in an attempt to identify the functions of different brain structures (e.g., see Chapter 3; classic study of Phineas Gage). A modern example is the work of Mel Goodale, at the University of Western Ontario, in the 1990s. Goodale and Milner (1992) studied a patient (D.F.) who suffered damage to one cortical visual processing area ("ventral stream") and left another cortical visual area ("dorsal stream") intact following carbon monoxide poisoning. When D.F. was shown objects (e.g., a rod), she couldn't identify them or their shape or their orientation (i.e., she lost visual object perception). But when D.F. was asked to grab the rod presented in different orientations and positions, she showed normal anticipatory hand opening, rotated her hand into the correct orientation, accurately reached out and grabbed the rod (i.e., she retained normal visually guided reaching). The case study of D.F. provided compelling evidence from purely behavioural data that object perception and action are processed independently by the dorsal and ventral streams, respectively.

As discussed in Chapter 1, recent advances in brain imaging technology have allowed neuroscientists to monitor neural activity in the intact brain of a person during mental or physical tasks (e.g., Talbot, 2003). PET and fMRI scans actually measure changes in local blood flow or oxygen content, which have been shown to reflect local neural activity (Logothetis et al, 2001). Brain imaging technology has been used to map the neural activity of clinical patients with psychiatric disorders (schizophrenia, Alzheimer's disease) and patients suffering from brain damage (e.g., Thompson et al, 2000; Partain, 2006), as well as exploring the development of normal and abnormal brain functions. Using imaging techniques, scientists have identifed neural pathways involved in various mental operations, emotional regulation, language perception and production, and visual perception and action. For example, James, Culham, Humphrey, Milner, and Goodale (2003) used fMRI scans to measure the activation level in D.F.'s ventral and dorsal streams during both object recognition tests and object-directed grasping tasks. As predicted from the behavioural results, D.F.'s loss of form perception was associated with absent/abnormal ventral-stream activation while her dorsal stream regions showed normal activation during object grasping tasks. Finally, Valyear, Culham, Sharif, Westwood, and Goodale (2006) used fMRI to study the activity in the normal human brain and found the predicted differential dorsal and ventral stream activation during the performance of object identity versus object orientation tasks. Clearly brain imaging technology gives neuroscientists a powerful tool to study localization of function.

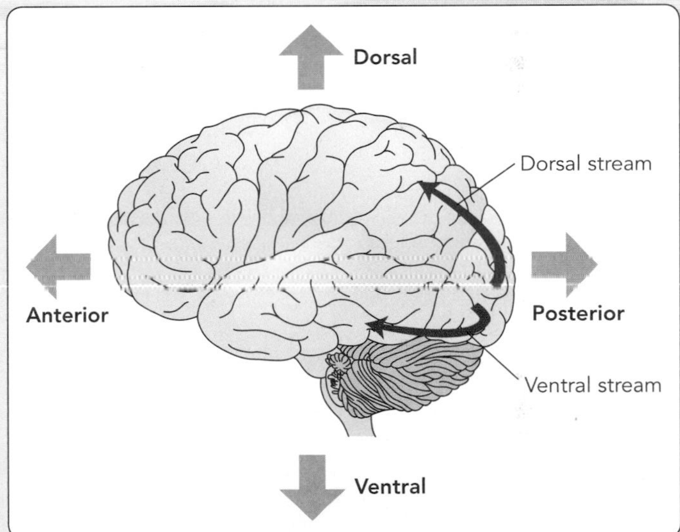

Navigating the brain. When discussing anatomy, we often use the standard terminology shown here. Thus, the dorsal visual stream runs along the upper surface of the cortex; the ventral stream runs along the bottom surface. In addition we often use the term "medial" to describe a structure toward the centre of the brain, and "lateral" to indicate one toward the outer surface.

related to the treatment and expected to change at the same time as the target behaviour. In our example, the mother's performance on tests assessing her knowledge of feeding and nutrition improved in conjunction with the child's weight gain, providing evidence that the treatment was responsible for the infant's increased weight.

A second potential drawback concerns the generalization of the findings: Will the principles uncovered in a case study hold true for other people or in other situations? The question of generalization pertains to all research methods, but drawing broad conclusions from one or several case studies can be particularly risky. The key issue is the degree to which the case under study is representative of other people or situations. In the failure to thrive case study, perhaps the treatment was only beneficial for that particular mother. However, this case study prompted subsequent case studies (another form of a multiple baseline procedure—i.e., multiple baselines with other infants and mothers) that showed similar improvement in infant weight gain as mothers improved their feeding and nutritional skills. Finally, these examples prompted studies with larger groups of infants that also demonstrated the effectiveness of this treatment. To establish the generalization of a general principle (e.g., maternal education can reduce instances of failure-to-thrive), investigators must conduct more case studies, use other research methods, and test a variety of cultural groups.

12. What are the major limitations of case studies?

A third drawback is the possible lack of objectivity in the way the researcher gathers and interprets the data. This is not a serious issue in our failure-to-thrive example because weight measures are relatively objective, although errors can be made that favour our expectations. In fact, measurement bias (also called observer bias) can occur in any type of research, and case studies can be particularly worrisome because they often are based largely on the subjective impressions of the researcher. In science, a skeptical attitude requires that, whenever possible, claims based on case studies be followed up by more comprehensive research methods before they are accepted. In everyday life we should adopt a similar skeptical view. When encountering claims based on case examples or anecdotes, keep in mind that the case may be atypical, consider whether the person making the claim may be biased or have an ulterior motive, and try to seek out other evidence to support or refute the claim.

Naturalistic Observation: Bullying and Victimization in Canadian Public Schools

13. What is naturalistic observation, and what is its major advantage?

In **naturalistic observation**, the researcher observes behaviour as it occurs in a natural setting. Naturalistic observation is used extensively to study animal behaviour. An example of animal observational research is British researcher Jane Goodall's (1986) famous observation of African chimpanzees in the wild (Figure 2.8). She and others discovered that chimpanzees display a variety of behaviours, such as making and using tools, that were formerly believed to lie only within the domain of human capabilities. Christopher Boesch (1995) reported that wild African chimpanzees use a "hammer/ anvil" tool technique. A chimp places a nut on a hard surface (the anvil), and then hammers it several times with a dead branch or stone until it cracks. Some nuts with hard woody shells are tricky to open, and it may take several years for chimps to perfect their hammering. Especially fascinating is Boesch's observation that mothers seem intentionally to teach their young how to use this technique. While this type of observational research is important, it takes many hours, sometimes months or years, before the human observer is able to observe chimps without interfering with their natural activities (i.e., to become "invisible" observers). When used with a human population, naturalist observation can help to sort out conflicting self-reports as illustrated in the following *Research Foundations* box.

FIGURE 2.8

Researcher Jane Goodall uses naturalistic observation to study the behaviour of wild chimpanzees.

14. What problems can occur when conducting naturalistic observations?

Like case studies, naturalistic observation does not permit causal conclusions about the relations between variables. In the real world, many variables simultaneously influence behaviour, and they cannot be disentangled with this research technique. There also is the possibility of bias in the way that researchers interpret the behaviours they observe. Finally, researchers must try to avoid influencing the participants being studied. Even the mere presence of a human observer may disrupt a person's or animal's behaviour, at least initially. As time passes, people and other animals adapt and typically ignore the presence of an observer.

RESEARCH FOUNDATIONS

Studies of Bullying in Canadian Schools

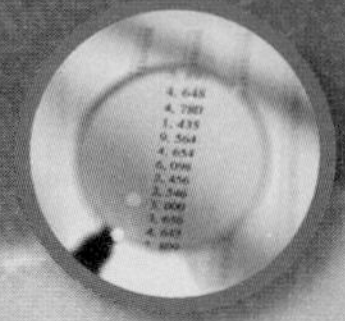

Natural observations are used frequently to study human behaviour. For example, Debra Pepler (York University) and Wendy Craig (Queen's University) studied bullying in school-aged children and adolescents. First, Pepler, Craig, Zeigler, and Charach (1993) measured the incidence of bullying using a self-report survey. Children reported that bullying was unpleasant to watch (88%), they wouldn't join in (70–80%), and they would intervene to help the victim (~50%). However, self-reports may not accurately reflect what children actually do. Pepler and Craig (1995) recorded elementary-aged children on the playground during their school recess using a remote video camera and wireless microphones attached to each child. Despite their knowledge (and consent) that they were being recorded, they appeared to ignore the equipment and engaged in normal play activities. In fact, only one "target" child's microphone (a bully's) was turned on during recess. The video and audio recordings of each bullying episode were coded by several highly trained observers who recorded events leading up to aggressive acts and peer involvements in bullying and victimization. The behavioural observations contradicted the children's self-report data from the first study. Peers actually participated with the bully in 85 percent of the instances! Sometimes peers just watched and/or verbally encouraged the bully's actions, but in almost 50 percent of the instances, they actively participated with the bully. Peers only helped victims in 13 percent of the cases. Surprisingly, although staff members were present 23 percent of the time, they only intervened 4 percent of the time. In further studies, Craig, Pepler, and Atlas (2000) discovered that bullying was approximately twice as frequent in the playground as in the classroom. Finally, Pepler, Craig, et al. (2006) described the developmental course of bullying in children from grades 6 through 12 using self reports. Boys reported more bullying than girls, and bullying incidence peaked for boys in grade 8 and for girls in grade 9, being lowest at the end of high school. Pepler and Craig are now examining intervention procedures designed to reduce bullying.

Survey Research: Does Your Own Personality Match the Canadian National Character?

In **survey research**, information about a topic is obtained by administering questionnaires or interviews to many people about their attitudes, opinions, and behaviour. For example, Terracciano et al. (2005) addressed the following question: Does the stereotypical "national character" of a culture match the averaged personality characteristics (neuroticism, extraversion, openness to experience, agreeableness, and conscientiousness) of individual members of that culture? Eighty-six researchers administered two questionnaires (one measured "national character"; the other measured the respondent's own personality) to individuals from 49 cultures around the world, including university students at York (by L.E. Ayearst), UBC (by D.L. Paulhus), and the University of Winnipeg (by P.D. Trapnell). For each culture, there was a consensus on its national character. However, the national character personality profile was significantly different from the averaged personality scores of individual members on the same characteristics. To illustrate, the national characters of the Canadian and U.S. samples were similar for neuroticism (e.g., anxiety, hostility, depression, impulsiveness) and agreeableness (e.g., altruism, compliance, modesty); but the averaged individuals' ratings on themselves were much higher for agreeableness and much lower on neuroticism for Canadians than for the U.S. respondents, and both profiles were significantly different from their respective national characters. Terracciano et al. concluded that while the cultural stereotype of a national character may define national identity, it does not reflect the actual, assessed personality traits of members of that culture.

Terracciano et al. only surveyed a total of 3989 adults. So how is it possible to obtain accurate estimates of the stereotypic national character of various cultures?

Two key concepts in survey research are "population" and "sample." A **population** consists of all the individuals about whom we are interested in drawing a conclusion. Sometimes it is possible to survey every member of the population. If a professor only wants to learn about the national character of the 50 students in her Introductory Psychology class, then her students are the population and a questionnaire can be given to every one of them. But, Terracciano et al. wanted to know the stereotypic national character and actual personality characteristics of adult populations in 49 cultures. Clearly, it would be impossible to study everyone. Therefore, they surveyed a **sample**, i.e., a subset of individuals drawn from the larger population of interest.

To draw valid conclusions about a population from the results of a single survey, the sample must be representative: A **representative sample** is one that reflects the important characteristics of the population (Figure 2.9). A sample composed of 80 percent males would not represent the student body where only 50 percent of the students are men. Typically, researchers first divide the population into subgroups based on characteristics such as gender or ethnic identity. Suppose the population is 55 percent female. In this case, 55 percent of the spaces in the sample would be allocated to women and 45 percent to men. Where possible, researchers determine quotas for their "representative sample" using national census data. **Random sampling** is then used to select individuals in each subgroup to be in the survey. In truly random sampling, it is critical that every member of the population has an equal probability of being chosen to participate in the survey.

15. Explain what representative sampling is, and why survey researchers use it.

16. What are some advantages and disadvantages of survey research?

When a representative sample is surveyed, we can be confident (though never completely certain) that the findings closely portray the population as a whole. This is the strongest advantage of survey research. Modern political opinion polls use such excellent sampling procedures that, just prior to elections, they can reasonably predict from a sample of one to two thousand people how a national election is going to turn out.

In contrast, unrepresentative samples can produce distorted results. Other things being equal, large samples are better than small ones, but it is better to have a

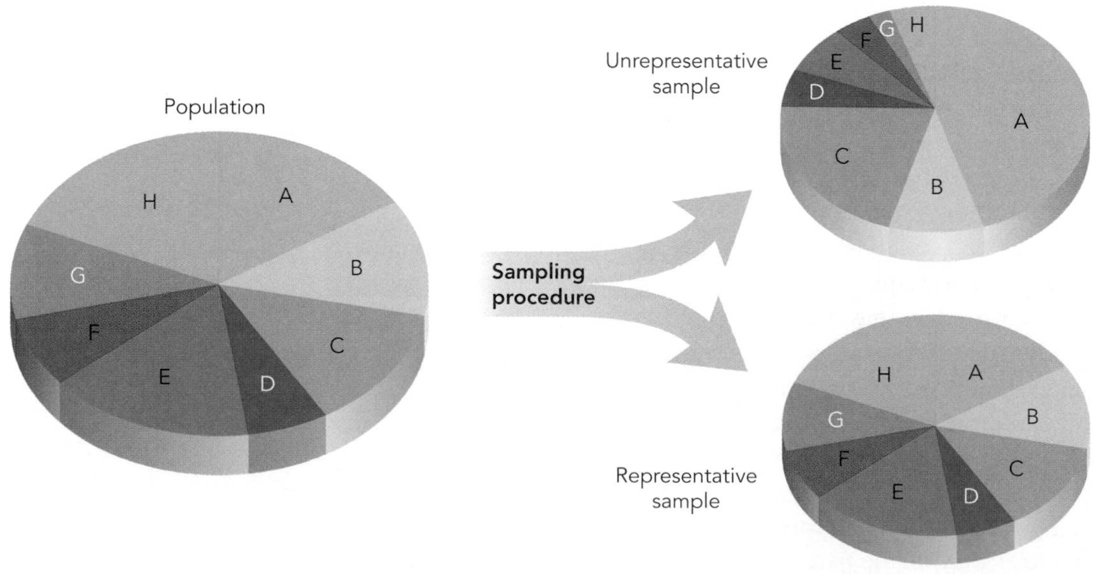

FIGURE 2.9

A representative sample possesses the important characteristics of the population in the same proportions. Data from a representative sample are more likely to generalize to the larger population than data from an unrepresentative sample.

smaller representative sample than a larger, unrepresentative one. A classic example was a mail survey of almost two million voters by *Literary Digest* magazine in 1936 that predicted that the U.S. Republican presidential candidate, Alf Landon, would easily defeat Democratic candidate Franklin Roosevelt. When the election took place, Roosevelt won by a landslide!

How could a prediction based on two million people be wrong? The answer is that the sample selected for the poll was unrepresentative of the population that voted in the election. Names were chosen from telephone directories, automobile registration lists, and magazine subscription lists. In 1936, poorer Americans often did not have telephones or cars, and were less likely to afford magazine subscriptions. Thus the sample under-represented poorer socio-economic groups and over-represented wealthier people. Bad sample. Bad prediction. The magazine went out of business shortly thereafter. In sum, always consider the nature of the sample when interpreting survey results.

Perhaps the largest advance in survey technology followed the World Wide Web revolution in the 1990s that produced a massive electronic interconnection of people around the world on the Internet. Internet computer technology has allowed psychologists to collect questionnaire data from thousands of subjects quickly and at virtually no cost compared to paper-based questionnaires and telephone surveys (see Kraut, et al, 2004). For example, Nosek, Banaji, and Greenwald (2002) measured attitudes toward and stereotypes of social groups of over 1.5 million "drop-in" respondents at their Web site over a period of three-and-a-half years. They recruited respondents through news media, links from other Internet sites and search engines, and word of mouth. Of course, there are problems with Internet questionnaires. Researchers have less control over data quality; respondents can lie about their age, identity and gender; and their anonymity permits frivolous or malicious responding. Also, there is a risk of sample bias because, unlike randomly dialling telephone numbers, there is no method for randomly sampling the population of Internet users. Kraut et al. noted that Internet users in 2002 were more likely than the general U.S. population to be young, white, and to have children. Gosling, Vazire, Srivastava, and John (2004) evaluated these concerns by comparing personality questionnaire data from over 360,000 Internet respondents with that from 510 publications where traditional questionnaires were used. Gosling et al. acknowledged that Internet samples are not without flaws. However, they did find that while their Internet sample was not representative of the general population, it did vary in socioeconomic status, geographic region, age, and gender to a greater extent than the undergraduate psychology student samples used in many questionnaire studies. Moreover, the Internet survey results were comparable to the results of paper-based questionnaire surveys, suggesting that the Internet can be a useful research tool.

We have avoided discussing the details of statistical procedures for analyzing descriptive data in this chapter and focused on the design of studies. We did illustrate the use of graphs to summarize one case study result (Figure 2.7) and to describe sampling issues (the pie graphs in Figure 2.9). Also, percentage differences among groups were noted from surveys on bullying and elsewhere in the chapter. The student is referred to Appendix A for additional examples of descriptive statistics and a comprehensive introduction to statistical methods relevant to survey results and group observations. Appendix A describes measures of the central tendencies to summarize test scores and observations for groups (e.g., group averages) and measures for describing variations in individual scores within a group (e.g., the range of scores), as well as examples of graphic summaries in the form of histograms and pie graphs (including a bystander study example).

There are three major drawbacks to surveys. First, unrepresentative samples can lead to faulty generalizations about how an entire population would respond. In our Canadian bullying example, some school officials argued that Pepler and Craig's data only reflected bad behaviour in certain, "bad" schools; although subsequent research did not support this speculation, it is important to sample from many different types of schools across Canada to establish the generality of the bullying findings. Second, surveys rely on participants' self-reports (indeed, all self-report techniques), which are based on the assumptions that people know themselves and do not lie. Survey data can be distorted by factors such as social desirability bias, interviewer bias, or people's inaccurate perceptions of their own behaviour, as was the case with our bullying example. Finally, survey data cannot be used to draw conclusions about cause and effect.

In Review

- *The goal of descriptive research is to identify how organisms behave, particularly in natural settings. Case studies involve the detailed study of a person, group, or event. Case studies often suggest important ideas for further research, but they are a poor method for establishing cause-effect relations.*
- *Naturalistic observation gathers information about behaviour in real-life settings. It often yields rich descriptions of behaviour and allows the examination of relations between variables. Researchers must be careful to avoid influencing the participants being observed and to interpret their observations objectively.*
- *Surveys involve administering questionnaires or interviews to many people. Most surveys study a subset of people (a sample) that is randomly drawn from the larger population of people the researcher is interested in. A major advantage of surveys is that representative samples allow for reasonably accurate estimates of the opinions or behaviours of the entire population. Unrepresentative samples, however, can lead to inaccurate estimates. Survey results also can be distorted by interviewer bias or biases in the way participants report about themselves.*

Correlational Research: Measuring Associations between Events

17. Explain the main goal of correlational research and how it is achieved.

What factors distinguish happily married couples from those headed for divorce? Do first-born versus later-born children differ in personality? Is monetary wealth related to happiness? Does maternal alcohol consumption during pregnancy have a negative impact on child development? These and countless other psychological questions ask about associations between naturally occurring events or variables. To examine such relationships, scientists typically conduct **correlational research**, which in its simplest form has three components:

1. The researcher *measures one variable (X),* such as monetary wealth.
2. The researcher *measures a second variable (Y),* such as happiness.
3. The researcher *determines statistically whether* X *and* Y *are related.*

Keep in mind that correlational research involves measuring variables, *not manipulating them.*

18. Why are we unable to draw causal conclusions from correlational findings?

Naturalistic observation and surveys are often used not only to describe events, but also to study associations between variables. For example, Boesch found that the approach used by adult chimps to teach the hammer/anvil technique depended upon the age of the pupil (Boesch, 1991). We might conduct a sleep survey to test hypotheses about how sleep difficulties are associated with people's age and self-reported lifestyle habits. Other types of studies also fall under the correlational umbrella, as the following example illustrates.

A Correlational Study: Parenting Styles and Children's Adjustment

In 1951, Robert Sears, Eleanor Maccoby, and Harry Levin (1957) began a landmark study of parenting styles. At the time, child psychologists and the media advocated strictness and discipline as the preferred approach to raising well-adjusted children. During interviews with 379 mothers of 5-year-old children in the Boston area, Sears and his co-workers asked the mothers how they and their husbands behaved in certain child-rearing situations. The researchers were especially interested in a variable called "parental warmth." Warm parents express affection and positive regard for their children, whereas cold parents tend to be disapproving, emotionless, or punitive. Sears, Maccoby, and Levin also asked questions about the children's behaviour, and then examined whether this behaviour was related to parental warmth.

Contrary to the popular wisdom of that era, the findings suggested that children who had warmer mothers were better adjusted (Figure 2.10a). Maternal coldness was related to a variety of children's problems, including bed-wetting, feeding problems, and aggression. It is tempting to conclude from these findings that parental warmth influences the degree to which children are well-adjusted. Unfortunately, correlational research does not allow us to draw such a conclusion.

First, consider the positive relation between parental warmth and children's adjustment when they were five years old. As the researchers pointed out, the direction of causality could be just the opposite. Perhaps parents behaved warmly *in response to* the fact that their children were less aggressive, more affectionate and sociable, and generally easier to raise. In other words, children's positive or negative characteristics may have caused the warm or cold parenting style. In correlational research, you must consider the possibility that variable *X* (parental warmth) has caused variable *Y* (children's adjustment), that *Y* has caused *X*, or that both variables have influenced each other. This interpretive problem is called the *bi-directional (two-way) causality problem* (Figure 2.10b).

To make matters worse, we have another problem. Perhaps the relation between parental warmth and childhood adjustment is artificial, or what scientists call "spurious" ("spurious" means "not genuine"). That is, it may look like parental warmth and childhood adjustment are related, but in fact, neither has any causal effect on the other. In the parenting example, a third variable, *Z*, may really be the reason why some parents are warmer than others, and also be the reason why some children are better adjusted than others. For example, *Z* might be a "genetic predisposition." Genetic factors that partially determine personality might cause some parents to be more sociable, less irritable, and warmer. The same genetic predispositions are passed on to their children, causing them to become more sociable, less irritable, and better adjusted. Therefore it looks like parental warmth and child adjustment are related, but in reality this is only because a third factor is causing differences in both parental warmth and children's adjustment. This interpretive problem is called the "*third-variable problem*": *Z* is responsible for what looks like a relation between *X* and *Y* (Figure 2.10c). As *Z* varies it causes *X* to change. As *Z* varies it also causes *Y* to change. The net result is that *X* and *Y* change in unison, but this is caused by *Z*—not by any direct effect of *X* or *Y* on each other.

To test your understanding, identify the third variable (*Z*) that explains the following relation: Nationally, as the amount of ice cream consumed each day (*X*) increases, the number of drownings per day (*Y*) also tends to increase. The answer appears in the margin on page 61.

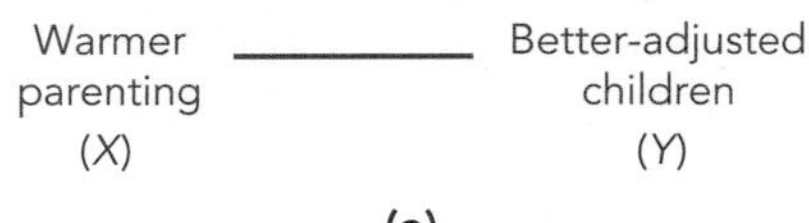

(a)
Parental Warmth and Children's Adjustment Are Correlated

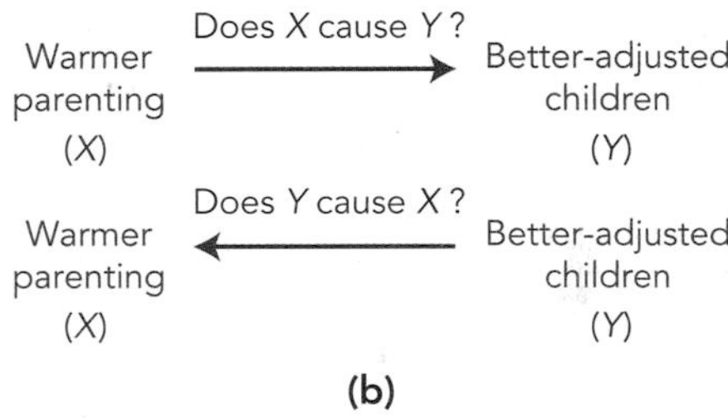

(b)
Bidirectionality Problem

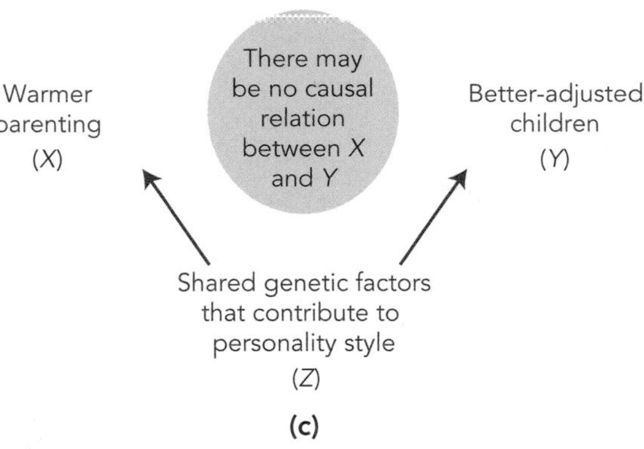

(c)
Third-Variable Problem

FIGURE 2.10

(a) Parents who act more warmly toward their children have better adjusted children. But why does this association occur? (b) Parental warmth could enhance children's adjustment or, conversely, better-adjusted children may stimulate warmer behaviours from their parents. This is the bi-directional causality problem. (c) There may be no causal relation between parental warmth and children's adjustment. Other variables, such as a genetic predisposition, may be part of the true common origin of both parental warmth and children's adjustment. This is the "third-variable" problem.

In sum, the major disadvantage of correlational research is that *correlation does not demonstrate causation.* If *X* and *Y* are correlated, this might mean that *X* causes *Y*, *Y* causes *X*, some third factor (*Z*) causes them both, or any combination of the above. In almost every case, the correlational method cannot provide the information needed to determine which of these possibilities is correct. The pages of history are filled with erroneous conclusions about causality drawn on the basis of correlational data. At one time, medical authorities concluded that "general paresis" (a fatal deterioration of the brain actually caused by syphilis) was caused by seawater because this malady occurred so often among sailors. We invite you to speculate on the real causal factor.

The Correlation Coefficient

19. How do positive and negative correlations differ?

A **correlation coefficient** is a statistic that indicates the direction and strength of the association between two variables. Variables can be correlated either positively or negatively. A **positive correlation** means that higher scores on one variable are associated with higher scores on a second variable. Thus parental warmth and childhood adjustment are positively correlated: Higher levels of warmth are associated with higher levels of adjustment. People's height is positively correlated with their weight: Overall, taller people tend to weigh more.

A **negative correlation** occurs when higher scores on one variable are associated with lower scores on a second variable. Job turnover and job satisfaction are negatively correlated: Workers who have *higher* rates of turnover (e.g., quitting, being fired) tend to be *less* satisfied with their jobs. For people who suffer from a condition called seasonal affective disorder, depression is negatively correlated with the amount of monthly daylight. These individuals have *more* symptoms of depression in months when there is *less* daylight.

20. How is a correlation coefficient interpreted?

Correlation coefficients range from values of +1.00 to −1.00. The plus or minus sign tells you the *direction* of a correlation (i.e., whether the variables are positively or negatively correlated). The absolute value of the statistic tells you the *strength* of the correlation. The closer the correlation is to +1.00 or −1.00, the more strongly the two variables are related. Therefore a correlation of −.59 indicates a stronger association between *X* and *Y* than does a correlation of +.37. A zero correlation means that *X* and *Y* are not related statistically. As scores on *X* increase or decrease, scores on *Y* do not change in any orderly fashion. Figure 2.11 shows how the correlation between two variables can be depicted on a graph called a **scatterplot.** As noted for descriptive statistics, details of how to derive a correlation coefficient are not covered in this chapter. Students are referred to Appendix A, which gives a more detailed discussion of the statistical derivation of the correlation, and

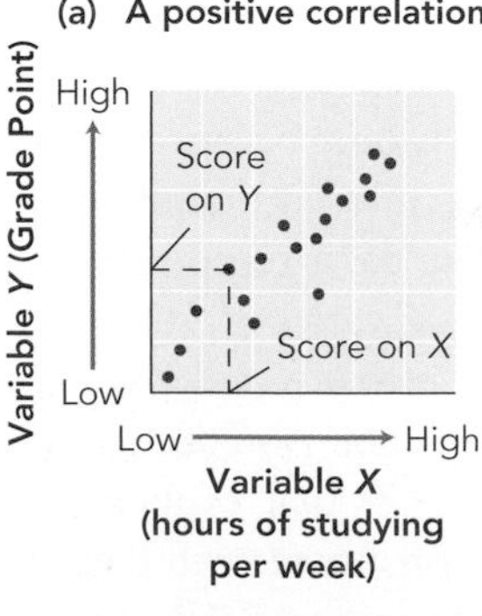

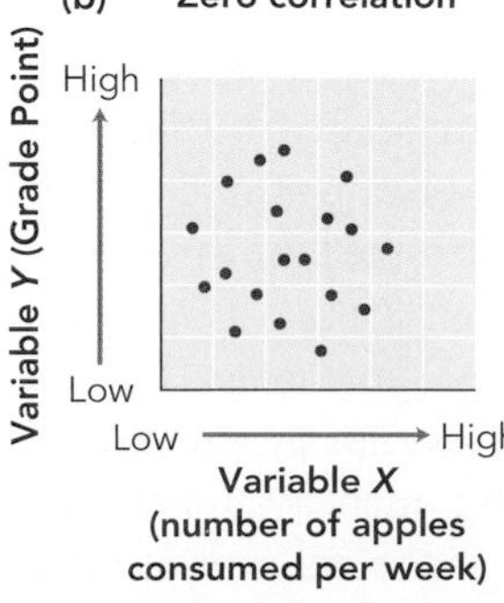

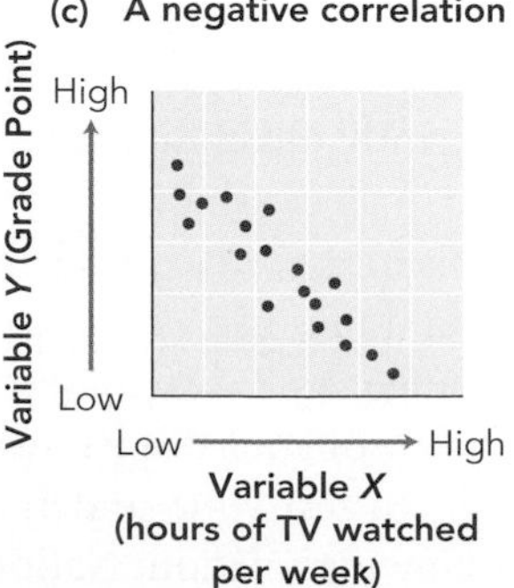

FIGURE 2.11

A scatterplot depicts the correlation between variables. The horizontal axis represents variable X, the vertical axis variable Y. Each data point represents a specific pair of X and Y scores, such as the number of hours a week a student studies (X) and that student's grade point average (Y). The three scatterplots show (a) a strong positive correlation, (b) a zero correlation (0.00), and (c) a strong negative correlation, for hypothetical sets of data.

to the formula for the product-moment correlation coefficient and examples in Table A.4.

Correlation as a Basis for Prediction

21. Explain how correlational research can be used to predict behaviour.

You might wonder why scientists conduct correlational research if the data do not permit clear cause-effect conclusions. One benefit is that correlational research identifies associations in real-world contexts that subsequently can be studied under controlled laboratory conditions. Another benefit is that some questions cannot be studied with experiments, but can be examined correlationally. For practical or ethical reasons, we cannot experimentally manipulate how religious people are or how much alcohol pregnant mothers consume. But we can measure these variables and determine if they are associated with other factors, such as helping behaviour and fetal brain damage, respectively.

Ice cream and drownings. Correlation does not demonstrate causation. It is unlikely that mass national ice cream consumption causes individuals to drown, or that drownings cause the public to eat more ice cream. Rather, as we move from winter into summer and days get hotter, people eat more ice cream. Because more people also go swimming, more drownings occur. Variable Z is average daytime temperature.

Perhaps the most important benefit is that correlational data allow us to make predictions. If two variables are correlated, either positively or negatively, knowing the score of one variable helps us to predict (within certain limits) the score on the other variable. For example, students' high school grades help admissions officers predict how well students are likely to do in first year university, as illustrated by the made-up data pictured in the scatterplot in Figure 2.12. This figure shows a clear overall trend: higher high school grade point averages (GPAs) are *moderately* associated with higher first-year university grade averages (i.e., the relationship is far from perfect). Some students with high grades in high school ended up with average or poor university grades, while others with lower high school GPAs excelled in their first year at university. A perfect correlation would mean that, for this set of data, if we knew a student's high school GPA, we could predict exactly what her or his first-year university grade average would be. Nevertheless, even a moderate correlation between high school and university academic performance is useful to university admissions officers, particularly when grades are used along with other variables—such as student awards and involvement in extracurricular activities—that also help predict university performance. Remember, we are *not* saying that high school grades cause better first-year performance, only that they help predict it.

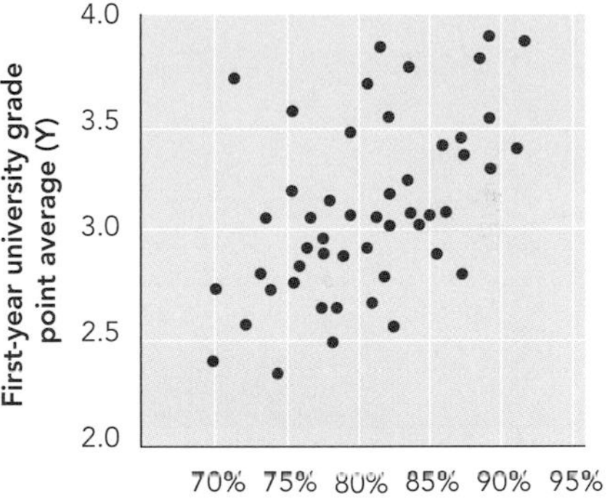

FIGURE 2.12

Data for a hypothetical sample of 50 students. The horizontal axis represents variable X, the students' high school grade point average (GPA). The vertical axis represents variable Y, the same students' first year university GPA. Variables X and Y are moderately correlated because, while most students who had high school grades also had high university grades, there were a number of cases in which high grades in high school were followed by low university grades and vice versa.

Businesses, government, and military organizations spend millions of dollars developing screening tests that correlate with job performance and therefore help predict how well applicants will do on the job. Insurance premiums are based on correlational data. In a sense, your insurance company is betting you that you will not demolish your car, become seriously ill, or die before you are statistically "supposed to," based on how these factors correlate with people's age, marital status, driving history, and so on. Because insurers' predictions are based on sound correlational data, the odds are solidly in their favour. If you doubt this, notice who owns some of the largest and newest buildings in your community.

In Review

- *Correlational research measures the association between naturally occurring variables. A positive correlation means that higher scores on one variable are associated with higher scores on a second variable. A negative correlation occurs when higher scores on one variable are associated with lower scores on a second variable.*
- *Causal conclusions cannot be drawn from correlational data. Variable X may cause Y, Y may cause X, or some third variable (Z) may be the true cause of both X and Y. Nevertheless, if two variables are correlated, then knowing the scores of one variable will help predict the scores of the other.*

Experiments: Examining Cause and Effect

In contrast to descriptive and correlational methods, experiments are a powerful tool for examining cause-and-effect relations. For psychologists, experimentation is the most direct method for testing explanations of why phenomena occur.

The Logic of Experimentation

22. Describe the logic of experimentation.

Suppose we want to determine whether noise influences students' ability to learn new information. Each student is placed alone in a room, has 30 minutes to study five pages of textbook material, and then takes a 10-item multiple-choice test. In its simplest form, an **experiment** has three essential characteristics:

1. The researcher *manipulates one variable.* In this case, the researcher manipulates (i.e., controls) the amount of noise in the room. Some students are exposed to a tape recording of street noise, while for others the room is kept quiet. These would represent the groups or "conditions" of the experiment (i.e., noise condition, no noise condition).
2. The researcher *measures whether this manipulation produces changes in a second variable.* In our example, the researcher uses the multiple-choice test to measure whether the amount of learning differs in the noise versus no noise conditions.
3. The researcher *attempts to control for extraneous factors* that might influence the outcome of the experiment. For example, we would not want one group to do better because they had easier textbook material or test questions. So all the participants will read the same textbook pages and take the same test. Similarly, room temperature and lighting will be kept constant, and the researcher will be friendly to everyone.

The logic behind this approach is straightforward. You begin with equivalent groups of people. You treat them equally in all respects except for one variable that is of particular interest (in this case, noise). You isolate this variable and manipulate it (creating the presence or absence of noise). You then measure how the groups respond (in this case, the amount they learn). If the groups respond differently, then the most plausible explanation is that these differences were caused by the variable that you manipulated (Figure 2.13).

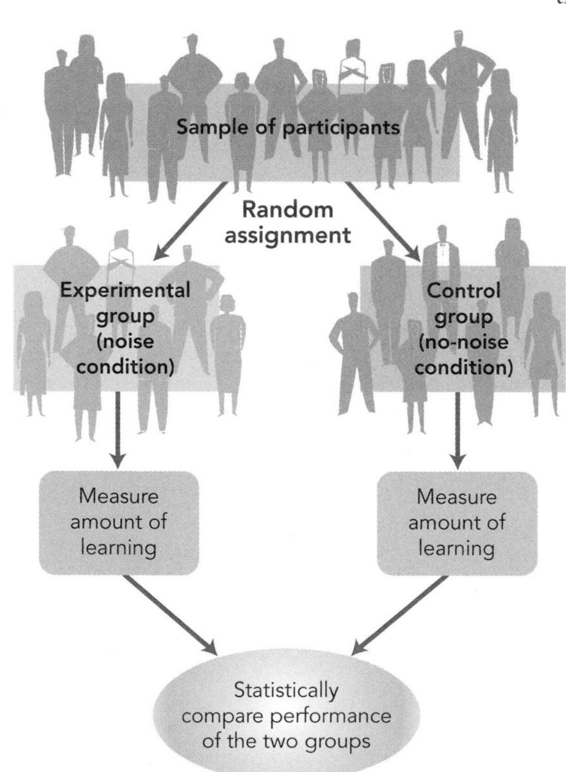

FIGURE 2.13

The logic of designing an experiment. The experimenter manipulates the amount of noise to which participants are exposed, measures their learning, and attempts to treat them equally in every other way. This creates an experimental group and a control group.

Independent and Dependent Variables

The term **independent variable** refers to the factor that is *manipulated* by the experimenter. In our example, noise is the independent variable. The **dependent variable** is the factor that is *measured* by the experimenter and may be influenced by the independent variable. In this experiment, the amount of learning is the dependent variable.

An easy way to keep this distinction clear is to remember that the dependent variable *depends upon* the independent variable. Presumably, students' learning will depend upon whether they were in a noisy or quiet room. The independent variable is the *cause,* and the dependent variable is the *effect.*

We have described the independent and dependent variables at a general level, but recall that when doing research we also must operationally define our variables. "Noise" could mean many things, from the roar of a jet plane to the quiet but annoying drip of a faucet. Learning could mean anything from memorizing a list of words to acquiring the skill to ride a bicycle. In our experiment, we could operationally define our independent and dependent variables as follows:

	Independent Variable (Cause)	Dependent Variable (Effect)
General level	Noise	Learning
Operational level	Listening to a tape of street sounds at 60dB for 30 minutes	Number of multiple-choice questions based on five pages of text answered correctly

23. What are independent and dependent variables? How are they related?

If asked what the dependent variable in our experiment is, we can state that it is learning, or instead reply that it is the number of multiple-choice questions answered correctly. Both answers are correct. They are just describing the dependent variable at different levels of specificity. Our noise experiment thus far has only one dependent variable, but we could have many. For example, we could measure how quickly participants read the material, how many answers they change, their stress during the task, and so on. In this manner, we gain more knowledge about how people are affected by noise.

To test your understanding, think back to the Darley and Latané experiment on bystander helping in an emergency. Can you identify the independent and dependent variables? The answer appears in the margin on this page.

Experimental and Control Groups

24. Why are control groups important?

The terms "experimental group" and "control group" are often used when discussing experiments. An **experimental group** is the group that receives a treatment or an "active level" of the independent variable. A **control group** is not exposed to the treatment, it receives a zero-level of the independent variable. The purpose of the control group is to provide a standard of behaviour to which our experimental group can be compared. The participants exposed to noise represent the experimental group (also called the "experimental condition"), and the participants in the quiet room represent the control group (or "control condition"). To take another hypothetical example, how would we design an experiment to assess the causal relationship between maternal alcohol consumption and children's school performance? We could randomly assign mothers to either a treatment group, in which they were required to drink a heavy dose of alcohol each day of their pregnancy, or a no-alcohol group in which they were required to refrain from consuming any alcohol during their pregnancy. Needless to say, we have neither the power nor the ethical right to conduct such a study. Instead, researchers try to evaluate causal effects by using animals as experimental subjects; in the example described below, pregnant guinea pigs were assigned randomly to either an experimental (drinking alcohol) or a control (sober) group, and their offspring were tested on problem-solving tasks designed to reflect animal intelligence.

Experiments often include several experimental groups plus a control group. In our study on noise, we could play the tape of street noise at three different volume levels, creating high noise, moderate noise, and low noise experimental conditions. The no-noise condition would still represent the control group (zero-level of noise). In the hypothetical alcohol experiment, each guinea pig could be assigned to either a low, medium, or high alcohol consumption group. In the guinea pig example, there were actually two control groups—water and sugar-water controls, the latter group matching the experimental group for caloric intake during the

Helping in an emergency. The independent variable in the Darley and Latané experiment was the number of other bystanders presumed to be present (0, 1, or 4). The dependent variables were the percentage of participants who aided the victim and the speed of response.

mother's pregnancy. Finally, in some experiments, the concept of a control group may not apply. In a "taste test" experiment in which participants taste and rate how much they like Coca-Cola and Pepsi-Cola, each drink represents an experimental condition and we simply make a direct comparison between them.

Two Basic Ways to Design an Experiment

One common way to design an experiment is to have different participants in each condition. If you participated in the noise experiment, you would be in either the experimental group or the control group, but not both.

Suppose that the noise group performs substantially worse on the multiple-choice test than the no-noise group. Further, let's assume that the two groups are treated equally in every important way you can think of (e.g., room temperature, experimenter friendliness). Before concluding that the noise caused poorer learning, we must address a key question: How can we be sure that the noise group would not have done worse than the no-noise group anyway, even if they had not been exposed to noise? Perhaps the students in the noise group were, on average, less intelligent, poorer readers, or more anxious than the students in the no-noise group. Maybe one of these factors—and nothing to do with the noise at all—was the reason why they performed more poorly.

25. Why do researchers randomly assign participants to the conditions in an experiment?

To deal with this issue researchers typically use **random assignment**, a procedure in which each participant has an equal likelihood of being assigned to any one group within an experiment. Thus you would have a 50 percent chance of being in the noise group, a 50 percent chance of being in the no-noise group, and that determination would be made randomly. This procedure does not eliminate the fact that participants differ from one another in important ways. Instead, random assignment *balances* these differences across the various conditions of the experiment. It increases our confidence that, at the start of an experiment, participants in the various conditions are equivalent overall.

26. Identify an alternative to using random assignment in experiments.

A second way to design experiments is to expose each participant to all the conditions. We could measure how much the same people learn when exposed to noise and when the room is quiet. By doing so, factors such as the participants' intelligence, reading ability, and general anxiety are held constant across the no-noise and noise conditions, and, therefore, we can rule them out as alternative explanations for any results we obtain. However, this approach creates problems if not used properly.

For one thing, it would make little sense to have our participants read the same text material and take the same multiple-choice questions twice. Instead, we would develop two equally difficult reading tasks, and participants would perform each task only once. Most importantly, suppose that every participant were exposed to the no-noise condition first. If they then learned more poorly in the noise condition, what would be the cause? The noise? Perhaps. But it could be that participants were bored or fatigued by the time they performed the second task. A procedure called *counterbalancing* avoids this problem: The order of conditions is varied so that no condition has an advantage relative to the others. Half the participants would be exposed to the no-noise condition first and the noise condition second. For the remaining participants this order would be reversed.

Manipulating One Independent Variable: Effects of Fetal Alcohol Exposure on Intellectual Development

We know that there is a relationship in humans between maternal consumption of alcohol during pregnancy and childhood learning problems (Archibald, Fennema-

Notestine, Gamst, Riley, Mattson, & Jernigan, 2001; Mattson, Goodman, Caine, Delis, & Riley, 1999). However, as noted above, we can't randomly assign pregnant mothers to experimental or control groups, so researchers are using animal models to establish a causal relationship between fetal alcohol exposure and later neurological and behavioural deficits. One example is an experiment conducted by psychologist Hans Dringenberg and his colleagues in Pharmacology and Toxicology at Queen's University. They (e.g., Richardson, Byrnes, Brien, Reynolds, & Dringenberg, 2002) studied guinea pigs because of their long pregnancy and, like humans, the significant amount of brain growth that occurs before they are born.

27. Identify the independent and dependent variables in Richardson et al.'s experiment.

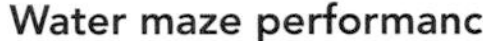

Pregnant guinea pigs were randomly divided into three groups (the independent variable): Each day during pregnancy (lasting from 2 to 67 days gestation; birth on day 68) the *experimental* group received a dose of alcohol, a *control* group received an equal amount of water, while *another control* group received sugar water that matched the caloric intake of the experimental group. In all other respects the pregnant guinea pigs were treated equally. The babies were kept with their mothers following birth until weaning. At about 50 days of age (similar to human young adults), their intellectual ability was assessed using a water maze task. This task was chosen because performance on it is affected by brain damage to the hippocampus, a brain area that is involved in learning and memory for both humans and guinea pigs (also an area of brain damage in humans who experienced severe prenatal exposure to alcohol, according to Archibald et al., 2001). Each day the guinea pigs were placed in a water pool, with opaque water, and had to swim around until they found a hidden platform (always in the same location). They were given eight trials per day for five days, and the time it took for them to escape onto the platform was measured to index their learning and memory abilities (the dependent measure). The results were dramatic. As shown in Figure 2.14, the escape time on the last training day (5th day) for the alcohol group was much (significantly) longer than that for the two control groups; i.e., a learning deficit was present.

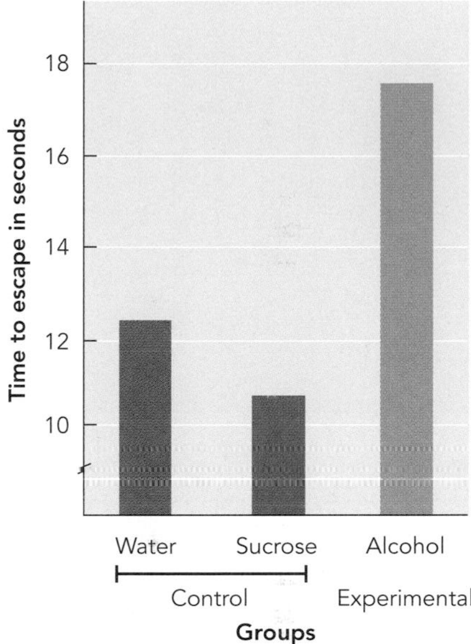

FIGURE 2.14

Performance on a water maze test of spatial memory (see text for details) of offspring of guinea pig mothers that were randomly assigned to consume alcohol, water, or sugar water during pregnancy.

Data provided by Hans Dringenberg, personal communication.

This experiment establishes a causal relationship between maternal alcohol consumption and intellectual development in offspring. However, its application to humans is limited by several factors. First, the daily alcohol dose for the guinea pigs was equivalent to about 12 beers per day for humans—we need to know how the size of the learning deficit changes as a function of dose level. Second, guinea pig results may not generalize to humans; but, a clever experiment by Hamilton, Kodituwakku, Sutherland, and Savage (2003) suggests they might. Hamilton et al. tested human adolescents with and without Fetal Alcohol Syndrome (FAS) on their ability to "swim" to a hidden platform using a computerized (*virtual*) Morris water task. The FAS group took twice as long to find the "hidden platform" and made 10 times more directional errors along the way, compared to the non-FAS group. Other limitations to our ability to generalize findings from animal research will be discussed in future chapters.

Manipulating Two Independent Variables: Effects of Alcohol and Expectations on Sexual Arousal

As noted in Chapter 1, behaviour is complex and has multiple causes. To better capture this complexity, researchers often examine several causal factors within a single experiment by manipulating two or more independent variables simultaneously. The separate influence of each variable on behaviour can then be examined, and researchers also can determine whether particular combinations of variables produce unique effects.

Consider the widely held belief that alcohol is a sexual stimulant, and that a few drinks can lower sexual inhibitions and increase sexual attraction toward someone

28. Why do researchers manipulate two independent variables in the same experiment?

else. Many men and women report that alcohol enhances their sexual arousal, and people who have been drinking are viewed by others as more responsive to sexual advances (George et al., 2000; Norris, 1994). Why might alcohol influence sexual arousal? Perhaps its chemical properties directly influence sexual arousal, or maybe the cause is psychological. That is, if people simply *believe* that alcohol will enhance their sexual arousal, then perhaps this expectation by itself can bring about increased sexual responsiveness.

How can a researcher separate the purely physiological effects of drinking from the psychological ones in order to test this possibility? The answer emerged in the form of an ingenious experimental procedure developed several decades ago (Marlatt et al., 1973; Rohsenow & Marlatt, 1981). The researchers created two drinks that people could not tell apart by taste, one with tonic water and a squirt of lime juice, and the other with vodka added to this mix. Then they designed an experiment with two independent variables. The first variable was whether participants received the alcoholic drink or the non-alcoholic drink. The second variable manipulated participants' expectations. They were told either that their drink contained alcohol or that it didn't.

As Figure 2.15a shows, when these two independent variables are combined within the same experiment, four different conditions are created. Condition 1 is *expect alcohol/receive alcohol.* This is the normal state of affairs when people drink; they expect that they are drinking alcohol and actually are. Changes in sexual arousal that occur in this condition could reflect either the chemical effects of alcohol, psychological expectations, or a combination of both. Condition 2 is *expect no alcohol/receive alcohol.* This condition assesses physiological effects alone. Because

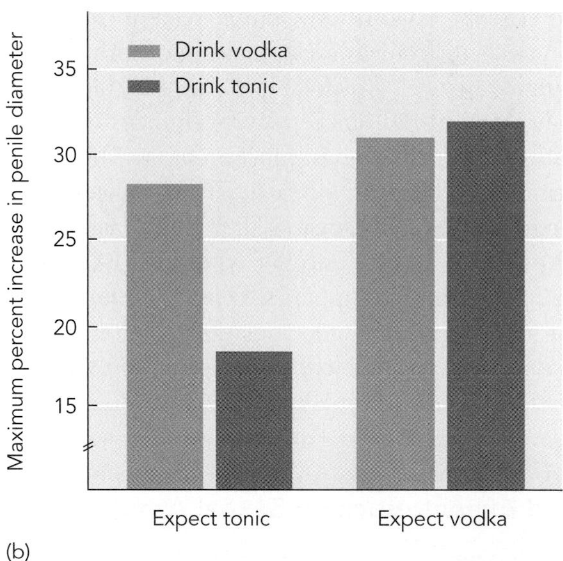

FIGURE 2.15

(a) Simultaneously manipulating two independent variables—participant's expectation and actual drink content—creates four conditions in this design. (b) In one experiment, male participants in these four conditions were shown sexually explicit films. A device that recorded changes in the size of each man's penis measured the dependent variable, sexual arousal. Regardless of what they actually drank, men who believed they had consumed alcohol showed more sexual arousal than men who believed they had not consumed alcohol. Among men who believed they drank alcohol, those who drank only tonic were just as aroused as those who actually drank alcohol.

Data adapted from Wilson & Lawson, 1976.

participants believe they are not receiving alcohol, changes in sexual arousal presumably would be due to alcohol's chemical effects. Condition 3 is *expect alcohol/ receive no alcohol.* Because no alcohol is consumed, changes in sexual arousal would have to be caused by participants' expectations about drinking alcohol. Finally, Condition 4 is *expect no alcohol/receive no alcohol.* This condition creates a control group having neither alcohol nor alcohol expectations.

Participants in the four conditions are then shown identical sexually stimulating materials (e.g., slides or films), or are led to anticipate that they will be viewing such materials. Their sexual arousal is assessed by self-report ratings on questionnaires and by physiological measures.

Most experiments have studied male participants. (In part, this is due to researchers' interest in the issue of alcohol consumption and rape, which overwhelmingly is committed by men (Testa, 2002). We will examine the findings with women shortly.) In which conditions shown in Figure 2.15a would you predict that men would be most aroused when exposed to sexual stimuli? Overall, as Figure 2.15b shows, participants who are led to believe that they have consumed low to moderate doses of alcohol—regardless of whether they actually drink alcohol—feel more aroused and show greater physiological arousal to sexual stimuli than participants who believe that they have consumed only tonic water (placebo)—called the *placebo effect* (Crowe and George, 1989). According to Canadian researchers, Michael Seto and Howard Barbaree (1995), among men, the placebo effect—the mere expectation that one is drinking alcohol—also produces more intense sexual fantasies, lower sexual inhibitions, and greater interest in viewing scenes of sexual violence.

Thus, at low to moderate doses that produce blood alcohol levels of about .04 or less, men's expectations and beliefs about alcohol contribute significantly to the enhanced sexual arousal that they experience. At higher doses, the chemical effects of alcohol take over and decrease—yes, decrease—men's sexual arousal (Kelly, 2001). This occurs because alcohol is a depressant drug; it suppresses neural activity. As blood alcohol levels increase, men typically take longer to reach orgasm, report that orgasms are less intense and less pleasurable, and may be unable to reach orgasm.

This research illustrates how studying several independent variables simultaneously can help unravel some of the complexity of behaviour. It also reinforces one of our main themes: Behaviour (in this case, sexual arousal) results from an interplay of factors that are psychological (beliefs and expectations), environmental (the presence of sexual stimuli), and physiological (chemical effects of alcohol at certain doses).

Finally, not all of the effects of alcohol on sexual behaviour are negative, and placebo effects are not always present. For example, in a study by Tara MacDonald at Queen's University, Geoffrey Fong and Mark Zanna at the University of Waterloo, and Alanna Martineau at San Diego State University (2000), the effects of alcohol on the intentions of young males to engage in sexual risk-taking behaviour were measured. Men were randomly assigned to one of three groups: intoxicated (.08% blood alcohol level), sober, or placebo (drank a non-alcoholic drink that smelled like alcohol). After viewing a videotape depicting a date in which the man and woman progressed to the point just before they engaged in intercourse, the men answered questions about how they would react to having unprotected sex (no condom) with the woman. The second variable manipulated was the presence of either impelling cues encouraging unprotected sex (i.e., the woman says she is on the pill and won't get pregnant and she is believable) versus inhibiting cues (the

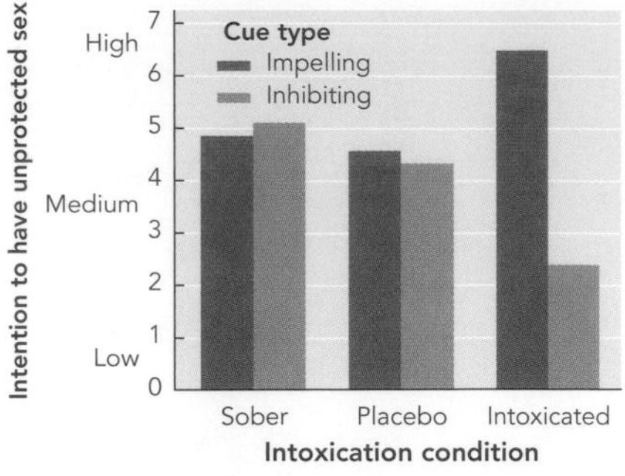

FIGURE 2.16

Male university students' average score on a subjective scale of likelihood of engaging in unprotected sex (i.e., without a condom) when they put themselves in the place of a male shown in a videotape that depicted interaction between a couple, leading up to the point of having sex after they consumed alcohol, a non-alcoholic drink that smelled like alcohol (placebo control), or remained sober. A second variable was either impelling (low-risk) or inhibiting (high-risk) cues for not using a condom. Clearly, unprotected sex was equally likely for the sober and placebo controls, irrespective of cue type, but intoxicated males were more likely to have unprotected sex when they thought it was safe and less likely when they thought it was risky.

Data taken from MacDonald et al., 2000.

woman says she is on the pill but the man can't be certain she is telling the truth). MacDonald and colleagues found that the intentions of engaging in risky behaviour depended on the nature of the cues. As shown in Figure 2.16, both the placebo and sober control groups had a similar intention to engage in unprotected sex, regardless of the cue conditions (i.e., no placebo effect on the cue condition). By contrast, intoxicated men responded differently depending on the cue condition. If they thought having sex would be relatively safe (i.e., "impelling" cues condition), they reported a stronger intention to engage in unprotected sex than controls; if the cues were "inhibiting" (i.e., high-risk), they reported a weaker intention to have unprotected sex than controls.

At this point a note on statistical tests is needed. In Figure 2.16, the difference between the group average scores for the impelling cue versus inhibiting cues groups in the intoxicated condition looks very large; by contrast, the differences in average scores for two cue groups in both the sober and placebo conditions look small. In fact, the difference in performance of the cue groups in the intoxicated condition was "significant," while the differences for the other two groups were not. Formal statistical tests take into account both the difference in group averages and the variations in individual test scores within each group (i.e., standard deviations). It must be emphasized that without a formal statistical test even apparently large differences between average scores for different groups shown in graphs may not be statistically significant if large variation in scores within each group exist. A detailed discussion of these statistics is presented in the section on "Inferential Statistics and Hypothesis Testing" in Appendix A.

Experimental versus Descriptive/Correlational Approaches

29. What are three major differences between the experimental and descriptive/correlational approaches?

There are three major ways in which experiments differ from descriptive and correlational approaches. First, in an experiment the researcher *manipulates* one or more (independent) variables and measures their effect on other (dependent) variables; in descriptive/correlational research all variables are *measured.* Second, whereas most experiments take place in the laboratory, descriptive and correlational research programs typically are conducted in more natural contexts. Third, in descriptive and correlational research, investigators cannot keep extraneous factors constant in the way that they can in experiments.

The net result is that descriptive and correlational approaches are not well suited for examining cause-effect relations, which is a serious limitation. Nevertheless, these methods shine in uncovering exciting new phenomena and in stimulating hypotheses for further research (Klahr & Simon, 1999). And like experiments, they are used to test hypotheses, build new theories, and help confirm or refute existing theories. Table 2.1 summarizes the key features, advantages, and disadvantages of these various research methods.

In Review

- *A well-designed experiment is the best way to examine cause-effect relations. Experiments have three essential characteristics: (1) one or more variables are manipulated; (2) their effects on other variables are measured; and (3) extraneous factors are eliminated or reduced so that cause-effect conclusions can be drawn.*
- *Each variable manipulated by the experimenter is an independent variable. Variables that are measured are dependent variables. The independent variable is viewed as the cause, the dependent variable as the effect. The experimental group receives a treatment or an active level of the independent variable, whereas*

the control group does not. The behaviour of the control group sets a standard against which the behaviour of the experimental group can be compared.

- *In some experiments different participants are randomly assigned to each condition, creating experimental and control groups that are equivalent at the start of the study. In other experiments the same participants are exposed to all the conditions, but the order in which the conditions are presented is counterbalanced.*
- *Researchers often examine several causal factors within a single experiment by simultaneously manipulating two or more independent variables. They examine the separate influence of each variable on behaviour and determine whether particular combinations of variables produce distinct effects.*

TABLE 2.1 An Overview of Research Methods

Method	Primary Feature	Main Advantages	Main Disadvantages
Case studies	An individual, group, or event is examined in detail, often using several techniques (observations, interviews, psychological tests).	Provides rich descriptive information, often suggesting hypotheses for further study. Can study rare phenomena in depth.	Poor method for establishing cause-effect relations. The person or event may not be representative. Often relies heavily on the researcher's subjective interpretations.
Naturalistic observation	Behaviour is observed in the setting in which it naturally occurs.	Can provide detailed information about the nature, frequency, and context of naturally occurring behaviours.	Poor method for establishing cause-effect relations. Observer's presence, if known, may influence participants' behaviour.
Surveys	Questions or tests are administered to a sample drawn from a larger population.	A properly selected, representative sample typically yields accurate information about the broader population.	Unrepresentative samples can provide misleading information about the population. Interviewer bias and social desirability bias can distort the findings.
Correlational studies	Variables are measured and the strength of the association between them is calculated. Naturalistic observation and surveys also are often used to examine associations between variables.	Correlation allows prediction. May help establish how well findings from experiments generalize to more natural settings. Can examine issues that cannot be studied ethically or practically in experiments.	Correlation does not imply causation, due to bidirectionality problem and third-variable problem.
Experiments	Independent variables are manipulated and their effects on dependent variables are measured.	Optimal method for examining cause-effect relations. Ability to control extraneous factors helps rule out alternative explanations.	As described in the text below, confounding of variables, demand characteristics, placebo effects, and experimenter expectancies can threaten the validity of causal conclusions.

THREATS TO THE VALIDITY OF RESEARCH

30. Explain why confounding decreases the internal validity of experiments.

Although the experimental approach is a powerful tool for examining causality, it is not infallible. Researchers must avoid several sources of error that can lead to erroneous conclusions. As a general concept, **validity** refers to how well an experimental procedure actually tests what it is designed to test. Here, we will discuss two general classes of validity: internal and external validity. **Internal validity** represents the degree to which an experiment supports clear causal conclusions. If an experiment is well designed and properly conducted, we can be confident that the independent variable really was the cause of differences in the dependent variable. Such an experiment would have "high internal validity." For example, because Darley and Latané's bystander experiment was conducted carefully and had proper controls, it had high internal validity. We can be confident that it was the presence of multiple bystanders (and not some other factor) that caused participants to help the seizure victim less often and more slowly. But if an experiment contains important flaws—such as those described below—we no longer can be sure what caused the differences in the dependent variable. In this event, an experiment would have "low internal validity."

Confounding of Variables

To introduce the concept of "confounding," consider an experiment on the "Mozart" Effect. In 1993, Rauscher, Shaw, and Ky tested university students who were randomly assigned to one of three groups. The experimental group listened to 10 minutes of a Mozart sonata (an up-tempo, "happy sounding" piece of music); one control group listened to 10 minutes of relaxation instructions; the other control group listened to silence. The Mozart group performed much better on a subsequent test of spatial abilities than the two control groups. This led the popular press to conclude that listening to music makes you smarter (e.g., see *www.mozarteffect.com*). What is wrong with this conclusion? Stated differently, can you identify another major factor that could have produced these results? Perhaps the reason students performed better on the spatial task after listening to music was that they were in a better mood or had a higher arousal level from having had an enjoyable experience—both factors differed between experimental and control groups. The two variables, like strands of a rope, were intertwined or linked together: Both the independent variable (music versus no music) and another variable, mood (happy, excited versus neutral, bored) varied between groups.

Mozart effect

Average paper folding score

16 15 14 13 12 11 10 9 8

Music

Silence

Mozart Albinoni

Music group

FIGURE 2.17

The Mozart Effect—music enhancing performance on a cognitive task (paper folding), relative to silent controls. This is a two-factor study in which two music groups, a Mozart (happy piece) versus an Albinoni (sad piece), and silent controls are compared. The enhanced performance is likely due to the happy mood induction, rather than Mozart's music per se (see text for details).

William Thompson, at York University, and Glenn Schellenberg and Gabriela Husain, at the University of Toronto (2001), tested for this suspected confound by assigning university students to either a Mozart Sonata (happy music) or an Albinoni Adagio (sad music) group. Half of each music group heard 10 minutes of the music, while the other half sat in silence (control groups), at the end of which everyone was given the standard spatial abilities task (paper-folding and cutting). The results, shown in Figure 2.17, replicated the Mozart effect—those hearing Mozart performed better than those who heard silence. However, the Mozart group also did better than the Albinoni group that performed similarly to the silent control group. Clearly, improved spatial ability was not simply due to listening to music, per se. Ratings of subjective enjoyment, positive mood, and arousal were also measured, and they were higher for those who heard Mozart rather than Albinoni. Thompson et al. used a mathematical adjustment to statistically "equate" the groups on mood/arousal/enjoyment and found that the difference between the Mozart and Albinoni groups' performance on the spatial task disappeared. Thus, they concluded that the Mozart effect is an artifact of arousal and positive mood.

Confounding of variables means that two variables are intertwined in such a way that we cannot determine which one has influenced a dependent variable. In the initial experiment on the Mozart effect, the mood level for the experimental and control group varied along with listening to Mozart or silence. The mood level is called a "confound" or a "confounding variable."

	Group 1	Group 2	Group 3
Independent variable (presence of music)	Mozart	Silence	Relaxation
Confounding variable (mood/joy/activity level)	High	Low	Low

An essential point to remember is that this confounding of variables prevents one from drawing clear causal conclusions, and therefore it ruins the internal validity of the experiment. The simplest way to eliminate this problem is to keep the mood level constant across the different music conditions. If this were done—that is, if we used music by Handel and other composers, all of which induced a joyful, aroused mood, then we would expect that all the music groups would do better on spatial tests than the silent controls.

Confounding is a key reason why causal conclusions cannot be drawn from correlational research. Earlier we described the "third-variable problem." When variables *X* and *Y* (e.g., parental warmth and children's adjustment) are correlated, many other *Z* variables (e.g., genetic or environmental factors) may be mixed up with either *X* or *Y*, so we cannot tell what has caused what. Thus the "third variable," *Z*, really is just another type of confounding variable.

Demand Characteristics

31. What are demand characteristics? Why do they lower the internal validity of experiments?

When we enter unfamiliar situations, it is natural for us to search for clues about how we are expected to act. **Demand characteristics** are cues that participants pick up about the hypothesis of a study or about how they are supposed to behave (Orne, 1962). Consider the experiments on alcohol and sexual arousal discussed earlier. In one condition participants are told that they are drinking alcohol, but in reality are given non-alcoholic drinks. Suppose that after a few drinks a participant does not feel intoxicated and concludes that the drinks were non-alcoholic. The participant might think, "Hmm. They told me the drinks were alcoholic, yet I don't feel a thing. Now they're showing me a sex film. Maybe they're just trying to make me think I drank alcohol, to see if I'll be more aroused."

At this point the film, the researchers' statement that the drinks were alcoholic, and the participant's feeling of not being intoxicated have become cues—demand characteristics—that have tipped off the participant about the hypothesis being tested. This damages the internal validity of the experiment because it can distort participants' true response tendencies (Orne, 1962). In some cases participants may intentionally attempt to foil the experimenter's hypothesis, but most people are eager to be "good participants" and may try to give the experimenter the results they think she or he wants (Figure 2.18). In either case, the participant is no longer behaving naturally.

S. Harris
"WHAT IT COMES DOWN TO IS YOU HAVE TO FIND OUT WHAT REACTION THEY'RE LOOKING FOR, AND YOU GIVE THEM THAT REACTION."

FIGURE 2.18

Demand characteristics provide participants with clues about how they "should" behave during a study. This may cause participants to alter their natural responses, thereby ruining the internal validity of the experiment.

Skilled researchers try to anticipate demand characteristics and design studies to avoid them. For example, participants given non-alcoholic drinks can be convinced that they have consumed moderate to high amounts of alcohol (MacDonald et al., 2000). People who actually consume alcohol but are told by experimenters they received a non-alcoholic drink only believe the experimenters if they received relatively low doses (Lyvers & Maltzman, 1991; Seto & Barbaree, 1995). At higher doses, when people feel drunk, they no longer believe the experimenter; but, experimenter credibility can be maintained if the experimenter attributes their feelings of drunkenness to a bogus, non-alcoholic drug (Epps, Monk, Savage, & Marlatt, 1998). The widespread familiarity with alcohol makes designing effective placebo conditions more difficult than in medical studies of unfamiliar drug effects (Testa et al., 2006).

Placebo Effects

32. Explain how the "placebo effect" can cloud the interpretation of research results.

In medical research, the term **placebo** refers to an inactive or inert substance. In experiments testing the effectiveness of new drugs for treating diseases, one group

FIGURE 2.19

Throughout history, placebo effects have fostered the commercial success of many products that had no proven physiological benefit. Herbal medicines are one of today's "health crazes." Do they really work? If so, is it because of placebo effects or the herbs' chemical properties? The best way to answer this question is through experiments that include placebo control groups.

of patients—the treatment group—receives pills containing the actual drug being investigated. A second group of patients, called a placebo control group, receives pills that do not contain the drug; they contain only inactive or inert substances that will not alter the body's physiology. Typically, patients who volunteer for this research are informed that their pills may contain either the true drug or a placebo, but they are not told specifically which type of pill they are receiving.

The rationale for this procedure is simple. Physicians have known for decades that patients' symptoms may improve solely because they *expect* that the drug will help them. Thus, if 40 percent of patients receiving the actual drug improve, but 37 percent of the placebo-control patients show similar improvement, then we have evidence of a strong **placebo effect**: People receiving a treatment show a change in behaviour because of their expectations, not because the treatment itself had any specific benefit (Ray, 2000; Figure 2.19).

Placebo effects decrease internal validity by providing an alternative explanation as to why responses change after exposure to an independent variable. For example, if patients improve after undergoing psychotherapy, is this due to the therapy itself, or is it a placebo effect? In the failure-to-thrive case we discussed earlier, the infant's weight gain may have been a placebo effect—caused by the increase in attention the infant received from the researchers, rather than because of the mother's training in feeding and nutritional skills. Similarly, suppose that business managers feel more confident after taking a leadership training program, or that anxious people become more relaxed after learning how to meditate. By carefully designing experiments to include placebo control conditions, researchers can determine whether behaviour change truly is caused by the various interventions, or whether a placebo effect might have played a role.

Experimenter Expectancy Effects

33. Why do experimenter expectancy effects lower the internal validity of experiments?

Participants are not the only ones who develop expectations about how an experiment is supposed to come out. Researchers typically have a strong commitment to the hypothesis they are testing. In psychology, the term **experimenter expectancy effects** refers to subtle and unintentional ways in which experimenters influence their participants to respond in a manner that is consistent with the experimenter's hypothesis. Although this type of bias historically has been called "experimenter" expectancy effects, it also can occur in correlational and descriptive research in which hypotheses are being tested.

Hundreds of studies demonstrate that, in both human and animal research, if people expect to obtain certain results they are more likely to do so (Rosenthal, 1994). Scientists can take several steps to avoid experimenter expectancy effects. For example, researchers who interact with participants in a study are often "kept *blind* to" (i.e., not told about) the hypothesis or the specific condition to which a participant has been assigned. This makes it less likely that these researchers will develop expectations about how participants "should" behave.

34. How do researchers minimize experimenter expectancy effects?

In experiments, the **double-blind procedure** is a powerful technique for simultaneously minimizing participant placebo effects and experimenter expectancy effects. Both the participant and experimenter are kept "blind" as to which experimental condition the participant is in. This procedure is almost always used in research testing drug effects. Each participant receives either a real drug or a placebo, but does not know which. People who interact with participants (e.g., who dispense the drugs or measure participants' behaviour) also are kept unaware of which participants receive the drug or placebo. This minimizes the likelihood that experimenters will react differently to the two groups of participants, and also reduces the chance that participants' own expectations will influence the outcome of the experiment (Figure 2.20).

"IT WAS MORE OF A 'TRIPLE-BLIND' TEST. THE PATIENTS DIDN'T KNOW WHICH ONES WERE GETTING THE REAL DRUG, THE DOCTORS DIDN'T KNOW, AND I'M AFRAID, NOBODY KNEW"

FIGURE 2.20

Although the double-blind technique is a powerful tool for controlling participants' and researchers' expectations, scientists try to avoid the infamous "triple-blind procedure."

35. How does external validity differ from internal validity?

Replicating and Generalizing the Findings

Let's return for a moment to our hypothetical experiment on noise and learning. Suppose we find that students perform more poorly when learning a task in a noisy room than in a quiet room. Assume that we have designed our experiment properly, eliminated potential flaws, and achieved high internal validity. Thus we are reasonably confident that it was the noise, and not some other factor, that caused the poorer performance.

There remains, however, another important set of questions that we must ask. If this experiment were repeated in other laboratories, would we obtain the same finding? What if the participants were children, or full-time working adults not in university? Would noise impair learning and performance in real-world settings, such as schools, factories, and businesses? Would the results be the same if we examined other types of noise and used other types of learning tasks?

These questions all focus on another important type of validity, known as external validity. **External validity** is the degree to which the results of a study can be generalized to other people, settings, and conditions. It is important to remember that in experiments and most other research, judgments about external validity do not focus on the exact responses of the participants. For example, in our noise experiment, the fact that students in the noisy versus quiet rooms might have answered exactly 48 percent versus 83 percent of the questions correctly is not the issue. Rather, what we are concerned about is the external validity of the basic *underlying principle of behaviour:* Does noise decrease learning?

Ultimately, to determine whether our tentative conclusion that noise impairs learning has external validity, either we or other scientists will need to replicate our experiment. **Replication** is the process of repeating a study to determine whether the original findings can be duplicated. If other scientists successfully replicate our findings, we become more confident in our original conclusion that noise impairs learning. There is just one problem. If every replication uses the same type of participants (i.e., university students), same type of noise (i.e., street noise), and measures learning in the same way (i.e., reading comprehension), we still won't know whether the noise-learning relation would hold true in different types of situations. Thus, attempts to replicate original findings are particularly valuable when the researcher adds something new to the equation.

For example, researchers in Canada, Israel, Japan, and the United States attempted to replicate Darley and Latané's (1968) findings on bystander helping behaviour. Some experiments were performed in laboratories with students and others took place in real-life settings such as subways, liquor stores, and the workplace. The number of bystanders who were present varied across different experiments, and different types of helping behaviour were measured. Women and men were studied. Over a few dozen replications, the vast majority confirmed the original finding (Latané and Nida, 1981).

What happens when research findings fail to replicate? On the one hand, such failures often lead to important discoveries. For example, we have seen that men's belief that they have consumed a few alcoholic drinks (even if the drinks are non-alcoholic) increases their sexual arousal to explicit sexual materials. But replications with women yield a different finding. Women's expectation of having consumed a few alcoholic drinks does *not* increase their sexual responsiveness (Crowe & George, 1989; Norris, 1994). Scientists currently are exploring why this gender difference occurs.

On the other hand, when new studies consistently fail to replicate the original results of earlier research, this suggests that the original study may have been flawed or that the finding was a fluke. If so, the scientific process has done its job and prevented us from getting caught in a blind alley. Ultimately, the accountability for the results of experiments rests with individual researchers and the scientific and academic community, a self-policing professional group. Psychologists are expected to use the highest standards for gathering their data, and to hold their original data in trust for a "reasonable period" so that members of the research community can access it "on a reasonable basis" (from Queen's University ethics policy, *www.queensu.ca/secretariat/senate/policies/resethic.html*, p. 1). Our Research Frontiers feature highlights why replication is such an important component of the scientific process.

In Review

- *An experiment has high internal validity when it is designed well and permits clear causal conclusions. Confounding occurs when the independent variable becomes mixed up with an uncontrolled variable. This ruins internal validity because we can no longer tell which variable caused the changes in the dependent variable.*
- *Internal validity is weakened by (1) demand characteristics, which are cues that tip off participants as to how they should behave; (2) placebo effects, in which the mere expectation of receiving a treatment produces a change in behaviour; and (3) experimenter expectancy effects, which are the subtle ways a researcher's behaviour influences participants to behave in a manner consistent with the hypothesis being tested. The double-blind procedure prevents placebo effects and experimenter expectancy effects from biasing research results.*
- *External validity is the degree to which the findings of a study can be generalized to other people, settings, and conditions. By replicating (repeating) a study under both similar and dissimilar circumstances, researchers can examine its external validity.*

RESEARCH FRONTIERS

Science, Psychics, and the Paranormal

Do you believe in "psychic" (paranormal or psi) phenomena? Surveys around the world (e.g., America, Brazil, Great Britain, India, New Zealand, and Sweden) reveal widespread public belief in the paranormal (Newport & Strausberg, 2001; Zangari & Machado, 1996). In a 2005 Gallup Poll, 73 percent of American adults stated that they believe in *at least 1 of the following 10* paranormal phenomena: "extra sensory perception (ESP—41% of the respondents acknowledged belief in this item), haunted houses (37%), ghosts (32%), [mental] telepathy (31%), clairvoyance (26%), astrology (25%), communication with the dead (21%), witches (21%), reincarnation (20%), and channelling spiritual entities (9%)" (Musella, 2005, p. 5). See Fig. 2.21. Where do you stand?

Adopting a scientific attitude means approaching the question of the existence of paranormal phenomena with open-minded skepticism; that is, we should apply rigorous standards of evaluation, as we do to all phenomena (Cardeña et al., 2000). The ability of independent investigators to replicate initial research findings is one of those standards. Placed under controlled conditions in well-designed experiments and replications, claim after claim of psychic ability has evaporated. Consider claims of dermo-optical perception (DOP), which refers to the ability to use the skin (mainly on the forehead) as a visual sensor and therefore to be able to see while blindfolded. In early studies, people who claimed DOP were discovered to be peeking through their blindfolds. In 1996, medical researchers from two respected Paris laboratories presented evidence to support the existence of DOP. Yet when a subsequent team of French scientists (including psychologists and physicists) employed more rigorous procedures, they found no evidence of DOP (Benski et al., 1998).

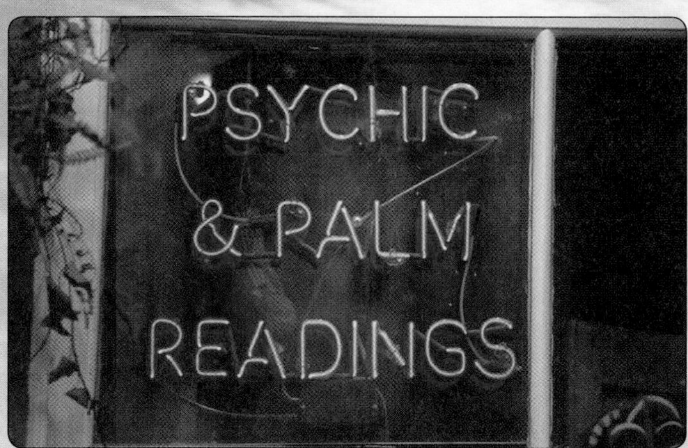

FIGURE 2.21

Many people believe in the paranormal despite an overwhelming lack of reliable scientific evidence. Psychic readings, psychic hotlines, and popular science-fiction TV shows and movies dramatizing paranormal events illustrate the public's fascination.

Over a decade ago Bem & Honorton (1994) published a review in a major psychological journal of 11 studies of mental telepathy which used the "ganzfeld" procedure. A participant (the "receiver") listens to a hissing sound while viewing red light through translucent goggles. Parapsychologists believe this procedure makes the receiver more sensitive to mental telepathy signals. In another shielded room, the "sender" concentrates on one of four different visual forms presented in random order. Combining the results of these studies, receivers reported the correct form on 32 percent of the trials, a statistically significant increase above the chance level of 25 percent.

Does the ganzfeld procedure provide the first solid evidence of a psychic (psi) phenomenon? While most studies had many rigorous controls, scientists have pointed out methodological flaws in the original ganzfeld studies (e.g., receivers might have been able to detect subtle cues on the cards handled by the sender; Hyman, 1994). Several parapsychology researchers have reported successful psi replications (e.g., Parker, 2000). However, when Milton and Wiseman (1999) analyzed 30 psi studies conducted by seven independent laboratories, they concluded that "the ganzfeld technique does not at present offer a replicable method for producing ESP in the laboratory" (p. 387). The scientific debate rages on (e.g., Milton & Wiseman, 2001; Storm & Ertel, 2001). It will only be settled when independent experimenters, using methodologically stringent conditions, are able to replicate the phenomenon.

The Committee for the Scientific Investigation of Claims of the Paranormal, formed in 1976, consists of psychologists, other scientists, philosophers, and magicians who are expert in the art of fakery. To conclude that a phenomenon is psychic, the committee requires that currently known natural physical or psychological explanations be ruled out. To date, it has not judged any psychic claims to be valid.

What about paranormal demonstrations by self-proclaimed psychics, such as using mental powers to bend spoons? Over 30 years ago, James Randi—a magician and expert in the art of psychic fraud—began offering $10,000 to anyone who could demonstrate paranormal ability under his scrutiny. The offer is up to $1,000,000, and still no one has collected. Predictions made by leading psychics in national newspapers also yield dismal results (Emery Jr., 2001). Accuracy rates range between 1 percent and 4 percent (Blodgett, 1986).

Critical thinking requires us to have a reasoned skepticism that demands solid scientific evidence, but not a blind skepticism that rejects the unknown as impossible. In our opinion, at present there is no generally accepted scientific evidence to support the existence of paranormal phenomena. Research continues, and while the burden of proof lies with those who believe in the paranormal, evaluations of their claims should be based on scientific evidence rather than on preconceived positive or negative expectations.

ETHICAL PRINCIPLES IN HUMAN AND ANIMAL RESEARCH

Psychologists sometimes walk an ethical tightrope when they study important problems, weighing the knowledge and possible applications to be gained against potential risks to which research participants may be exposed. Investigators are obliged to adhere to a set of ethical standards based on both government regulations and guidelines developed by national psychological organizations.

Ethical Standards in Human Research

In Canada much university research is funded by one of three national government agencies: the Canadian Institutes of Health Research (CIHR) and the Natural Sciences and Engineering (NSERC) and the Social Sciences and Humanities (SSHRC) Research Councils. These three agencies developed a "tri-council policy

FIGURE 2.22

Ethical standards are designed to protect the welfare of both human and animal subjects in psychological research.

for ethical conduct for research involving humans" which universities must follow if they receive funding from any of the three councils. Universities are required to have ethics review boards (ERBs) which review the ethical issues involved in every research proposal (Figure 2.22). If a proposed study is considered ethically questionable, or if the rights of participants are not sufficiently protected, the methods must be modified or the research cannot be conducted. The ERBs ensure that human participants have given informed consent, are ensured privacy and confidentiality, and that the guidelines are followed for research involving aboriginal peoples, human genetics, embryos and fetuses, and human tissue. Details are found at the SSHRC website [http://www.sshrc.ca/web/about/policies/PAS_e.pdf].

The Canadian Psychological Association (CPA) has published the "Canadian Code of Ethics for Psychologists" (2000, 3rd Edition) on the CPA web site (www.cpa.ca; search "Ethics"), which covers the behaviour of psychologists engaged in research, direct service, teaching, administration, legal cases (e.g., as expert witnesses), or any other role related to the discipline of psychology. It lists four basic principles that should be followed, including respect for the dignity of persons, responsible caring, integrity in relationships, and responsibility to society. Psychologists must:

- protect and promote the welfare of participants;
- avoid doing harm to participants;
- not carry out any studies unless the probable benefit is proportionately greater than the risk;
- explain all aspects of the procedure and ensure that they are understood. Oral or written consent is usually required and assurance is given that one can withdraw from the study without penalty. For those not able to give true informed consent (e.g., children, seriously disturbed mental patients), consent must be obtained from their parents or guardians;
- take all reasonable steps to ensure that consent is not given under coercion; and
- ensure privacy and confidentiality.

36. Describe the major ethical issues in human research and how participants' rights are protected.

37. Why does some research involve deception? What ethical principle does deception violate?

The use of *incomplete disclosure, or deception*, that occurs when participants are misled about the nature of a study, is highly controversial. Consider the Darley and Latané (1968) bystander experiment. Participants were not told that the study was going to examine how they would respond to an emergency, nor were they informed that the procedures (someone presumably having a seizure) might cause them stress. Instead, they were misled to expect a group discussion about the problems of university students. Proponents of deception research argue that, when studying certain types of behaviours, deception is the only way to obtain natural, spontaneous responses from participants. In other words, Darley and Latané's participants had to believe that the emergency was significant and real.

Incomplete disclosure obviously violates the principle of **informed consent**. Guidelines currently permit incomplete disclosure under limited circumstances and only when no other feasible alternative is available. The study must have scientific, educational, or applied benefits that clearly outweigh the ethical costs of deceiving participants. When incomplete disclosure is used, participants must be told the true purpose of the study in a debriefing period at the end of the experiment. The vast majority of psychological studies do not involve incomplete disclosure, and deception research has decreased in recent decades (Nicks et al., 1997). Still, many scientists oppose the use of deception under any circumstance, and the debate continues (Korn, 1998; Ortmann & Hertwig, 1997).

As noted earlier, survey research on the Internet is becoming increasingly popular. Also, given the public nature of Internet forums, researchers can conduct observational studies by joining virtual communities to record and analyze dialogues between participants (e.g., joining hate groups or therapeutic online groups). Internet researchers must take special care to ensure that the data are valid, privacy and confidentiality are maintained, informed consent is obtained, and proper debriefings are conducted (Pittenger, 2003). Pittenger recommends that researchers avoid deceptive manipulations unless the benefits clearly outweigh any risks. When deception is used (e.g., posting false comments designed to evoke reactions from members of a virtual hate group), researchers must ensure that valid informed consent is obtained and that participants are properly debriefed. Debriefing can be difficult however, because Internet respondents can drop out at any point in the study. Despite such ethical challenges the research opportunities available through use of the Internet make efforts to overcome them worth it.

Finally, it should be noted that participants generally enjoy participating in psychological research. In a survey of several thousand introductory psychology students at Queen's University, 93 percent reported that their experiences as research participants were pleasant and informative.

Ethical Standards in Animal Research

38. What are the justifications for, and criticisms of, research in which animals are harmed?

Psychologists study the behaviour of non-human species for both theoretical and practical reasons. They believe that it is morally wrong to subject animals to needless suffering. But, they do not agree with the head of the American Anti-Vivisection Society, who maintains that animals should never be used in research "which is not for the benefit of the animals involved" (Goodman, 1982, p. 61). Scientists point to important medical and psychological advances made possible by animal research (Baldwin, 1993). For example, had Pasteur not subjected some dogs to suffering, he could not have developed the rabies vaccine which has saved the lives of countless animals as well as humans. They ask, "Does the prospect of finding a cure for cancer or identifying the causes of psychological disorders justify exposing some animals to harm?"

Although animal research has declined slightly in recent years, the ethical questions remain as vexing as ever (Petrinovich, 1999; Plous, 1996a). In fact, most animal research is not intrusive or cruel, but sometimes animals are tested in studies considered too hazardous for humans, such as in medical research (e.g., the study of prenatal effects of maternal alcohol consumption discussed earlier). According to a poll at 50 U.S. colleges and universities (Plous & Herzog, 2000), most animal researchers favoured protection under the U.S. federal government's Animal Welfare Act for primates, dogs, and cats (99% agreed); rats and mice (74%); and birds (68%). In Canada, both CPA and federal government codes of ethics state that experimental animals should not be subjected to pain, stress, or privation unless there is no alternative procedure available and the goal is justified by prospective scientific or educational merit. This determination, however, is not always easy to make. For example, should researchers be allowed to inject a chemical into an animal's brain in order to learn whether a specific chemical imbalance ultimately might impair memory in humans? People of good will can disagree.

In Canada, the tri-council granting agency requires university ERBs to review and approve all animal research proposals. Most ERBs follow the rules set down by the Canadian Council on Animal Care in its *Guide to the care and use of experimental animals, Vol. 1* (1993). This manual instructs researchers to provide humane care and treatment, minimize pain and discomfort, and avoid unnecessary use of experimental animals. What is most encouraging is that animal welfare in research is receiving the careful attention it deserves.

In Review

- *Psychological research follows extensive ethical guidelines. In human research, key issues are the use of informed consent, the participants' right to privacy, the degree of risk, and the use of deception.*
- *Ethical guidelines require that animals be treated humanely and that the risks to which they are exposed be justified by the potential importance of the research. As in human research, before animal research can be conducted it must reviewed and approved, often by ethics review boards that include nonscientists.*

CRITICAL THINKING IN SCIENCE AND EVERYDAY LIFE

In today's world we are exposed to a great deal of scientific information, not just in school, but also in the popular media. To be an informed consumer you must be able to critically evaluate research and identify features that limit the validity of conclusions. Critical thinking skills can also help you avoid being misled by claims made in everyday life, such as those in advertisements. Thus, enhancing your critical thinking skills may be one of the most important benefits you will derive from your psychology course. That is why these first two chapters have focused on how psychologists think about and study behaviour.

39. As a critical thinker, what questions should you ask when someone makes a claim or assertion?

As critical thinkers, we must be open-minded and able to tolerate uncertainty. It may be comforting to have the conviction that we possess "truth," but a stubborn refusal to consider other viewpoints or evidence will not serve us well in the long run. At the same time, we should recognize that our beliefs and emotions can act as psychological blinders that allow us to accept inadequate evidence uncritically, especially when this evidence supports our current views. This does not mean that we should be so skeptical of everything that we believe nothing. Rather, we need to balance open-mindedness with a healthy skepticism, and evaluate evidence for what it is worth.

PSYCHOLOGICAL APPLICATIONS

Evaluating Claims in Research and Everyday Life

To give you an opportunity to practise critical thinking skills, we present brief descriptions of a research study, an advertisement, and a newspaper article. Have some fun and see if you agree with the claims made. In each case, you can facilitate critical thinking by asking yourself the following questions:

1. What claim is being made?
2. What evidence is being presented to support this claim?
3. What is the quality of the evidence? Are there any other plausible explanations for the conclusions being drawn?
4. What additional evidence would be needed to reach a clearer conclusion?
5. At present, what is the most reasonable conclusion to draw?

Example 1: A Lot of Bull

Deep inside the brain of humans and other mammals is a structure called the caudate nucleus. Years ago, a prominent researcher hypothesized that this part of the brain is responsible for turning off aggressive behaviour. The scientist was so confident in his hypothesis that he bet his life on it. A microelectrode was implanted inside the caudate nucleus of a large, aggressive bull. The researcher stood before the bull and, like a Spanish matador, waved a cape to incite the bull to charge. As the bull thundered toward him, the researcher pressed a button on a radio transmitter that he held in his other hand. This sent a signal that caused the microelectrode to electrically stimulate the bull's caudate nucleus. Suddenly, the bull broke off its charge and stopped. Each time this sequence was repeated the bull stopped its charge. The researcher concluded that the caudate nucleus was indeed the "aggression-off" centre of the brain.

You can assume that stimulating the caudate nucleus caused the bull to stop charging. But does this demonstrate that the caudate nucleus is an aggressive-off centre? Write down your criticisms and check your critical thinking against the points raised at the end of this feature. (For a hint, read on. Perhaps stimulating the caudate nucleus produced intense pain, and that is why the bull ended its attack. What other bodily functions might the caudate nucleus help regulate that would cause the bull to stop charging?)

Example 2: Vacations and Burglaries

A newspaper advertisement appeared many times in several American cities. The headline "While You're on Vacation, Burglars Go to Work" is followed by this statement: "According to FBI statistics, over 26 percent of home burglaries take place between Memorial Day and Labor Day" (U.S. holidays in late May and early September). The ad then offers a special summer sale price for installation of a home security system. In sum, the ad implies that burglaries are particularly likely to occur while people are away on summer vacation. How do you feel about this claim and its supporting evidence?

Example 3: Will Staying up Late Cause You to Forget What You Have Studied?

The headline of a newspaper article reads: "Best Way to Retain Complex Information? Sleep on It, Researcher Says." The article begins: "Students who study hard Monday through Friday and then party all night on weekends may lose much of what they learned during the week, according to a sleep researcher." The researcher is then quoted as saying: "It appears skewing the sleep cycle by just two hours can have this effect. Watching a long, late movie the night following a class and then sleeping in the next morning will make it so you're not learning what you thought. You'll not lose it all—just about 30 percent."

Next the experiment is described. Participants were university students who were taught a complex logic game. Afterward they were assigned to one of four sleep conditions for the night: Students in the control condition were allowed to have a normal night's sleep. Those in Condition 2 were not allowed to have any sleep. In Conditions 3 and 4, students were awakened only when they went into a particular stage (phase) of sleep (we'll learn about sleep stages in Chapter 6). A week later everyone was tested again. Participants in Conditions 3 and 4 performed 30 percent worse than the other two groups.

Think about the claims reported in the first paragraph above. Then examine the experimental conditions. Does anything seem wrong to you?

Critical Analyses of the Studies

Analysis 1: A Lot of Bull

Perhaps the caudate nucleus plays a role in vision, memory, or movement, and stimulating it momentarily caused the bull either to become blind, to forget what it was doing, or to alter its movement. Perhaps the bull simply became dizzy. These are all possible explanations for why the bull stopped charging. In fact, the caudate nucleus helps to regulate movement; it is *not* an aggression-off centre in the brain.

Analysis 2: Vacations and Burglaries

First, how much is "over 26 percent"? We don't know for sure, but can assume that it is less than 27 percent, because it would be to the advertiser's advantage to state the highest number possible. The key problem is the Memorial Day to Labor Day time period, which typically represents between 26 and 29 percent of the days of the year. Therefore about 26 percent of burglaries occur during about 26 percent of the year. Wow! Technically the ad is correct: Burglars do go to work in the summer while you're on vacation. But the ad also may mislead people. Burglars seem to be just as busy at other times of the year.

Analysis 3: Staying up Late

It could be true that going to bed and waking up later than usual might cause you to forget more of what you study. However, the article does not provide evidence for this claim. Look at the four experimental conditions carefully. Not one involved participants' getting a normal *amount* of sleep, but merely delaying when they went to bed and got up. The conditions examined only the effects of getting no sleep or losing certain types of sleep. When reading newspaper or magazine articles, look beyond the headlines and think about whether the claims are truly supported by the evidence.

Were you able to pick out some flaws? Critical thinking requires practice and you will get better at it if you keep asking the five critical thinking questions listed earlier.

In Review

- *Critical thinking is an important life skill. However, we should also be open-minded to ideas that are supported by solid evidence, even when they conflict with our preconceptions.*
- *There is no generally accepted, replicable scientific evidence to support the existence of paranormal phenomena. Even the ganzfeld procedure, initially supported by several highly controlled experiments, is controversial because it has often failed to replicate.*
- *In science and everyday life, critical thinking can prevent us from developing false impressions about how the world operates and from being duped in everyday life by unsubstantiated claims.*

GAINING DIRECTION

What are the Issues?

In this chapter, we are introduced to a therapy known as Eye Movement Desensitization and Reprocessing (EMDR). The procedure involves a sequencing of the client's eye movements to moving lights while discussing emotionally troubling thoughts. There are over 30,000 registered EMDR therapists, but is this an appropriate type of therapy? How would we know? What are the guidelines (if any) for establishing an intervention treatment as scientific? Does EMDR meet these guidelines? If not, are we looking at a scientific treatment or something more pseudo-scientific?

What do we need to know?

What is the scientific process for studying psychological phenomena?
Is EMDR based on any type of scientific theory?
Is there any research support for EMDR?
How do we evaluate the research support?
Have any potential problems with EMDR been addressed?

Where can we find the information to answer these questions?

Look back over the chapter and identify the components of the scientific method. Does EMDR satisfy the requirements? Is there a theory behind EMDR? If so, what hypotheses might we formulate about EMDR and how it works? We would need to test these hypotheses in some kind of research study. What are the various research methods available? Which one(s) should we use? We might also examine published research on EMDR (check the links on the Online Learning Centre). How would you evaluate these studies? Do they support the hypotheses? Finally, we should consider whether or not there are any pitfalls or artifacts associated with the research. Are there other possible explanations for the findings?

KEY TERMS AND CONCEPTS*

archival measures (51)
case study (52)
confounding of variables (70)
control group (63)
correlation coefficient (60)
correlational methods (51)
correlational research (58)
demand characteristics (71)
dependent variable (62)
descriptive methods (51)
descriptive research (51)
double-blind procedure (72)
experiment (62)
experimental group (63)
experimental methods (51)
experimenter expectancy effects (72)
external validity (73)
hypothesis (45)
independent variable (62)
informed consent (76)
internal validity (69)
naturalistic observation (54)
negative correlation (60)
operational definition (48)
placebo (71)
placebo effect (72)
population (56)
positive correlation (60)
random assignment (64)
random sampling (56)
replication (73)
representative sample (56)
sample (56)
scatterplot (60)
survey research (55)
theory (46)
validity (69)
variable (48)

*Each term has been boldfaced in the text on the page indicated in parentheses.

DO YOU WANT TO ELEVATE YOUR GRADES?

For additional resources and interactive quizzing, visit the book's Online Learning Centre at **www.mcgrawhill.ca/olc/passer**.

CHAPTER 3

Biological Foundations of Behaviour

The brain is the last and grandest biological frontier, the most complex thing we have yet discovered in our universe. It contains hundreds of billions of cells interlinked through trillions of connections. The brain boggles the mind.

—James Watson

CHAPTER OUTLINE

Dr. P. was a musician of distinction, well known for many years as a singer, and then, at the local School of Music as a teacher. It was here, in relation to his students, that certain strange problems were first observed. I had stopped at a florist on my way to his apartment and bought myself an extravagant red rose for my buttonhole. Now I removed this and handed it to him. "About 6 inches in length," he commented. "A convoluted red form with a linear green attachment." "Yes," I said encouragingly, "and what do you think it is?" "Not easy to say." He seemed perplexed. "It lacks the simple symmetry of the Platonic solids, although it may have a higher symmetry of its own . . . I think this could be an inflorescence or flower." "Could be?" I queried. "Could be," he confirmed.

. . . He also appeared to have decided that the examination was over and started to look around for his hat. He reached out his hand and took hold of his wife's head, tried to lift it off, to put it on. He had apparently mistaken his wife for a hat!

—Oliver Sacks (1987), The Man Who Mistook His Wife for a Hat

- **What are the issues here?**
- **What do we need to know?**
- **Where can we find the information necessary to answer the questions?**

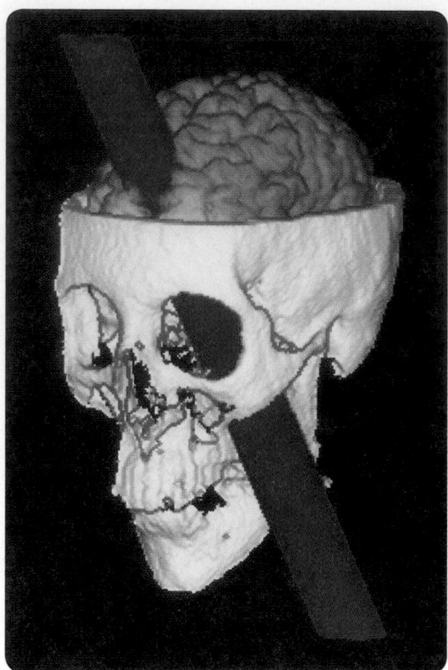

FIGURE 3.1

The brain damage suffered by Phineas Gage seemed to change him into a new person.

The year was 1848. As the Vermont winter approached, a railroad construction crew hurried to complete its work on a new track. They could not know that they were about to witness one of the most celebrated incidents in the annals of neuroscience.

As a blasting crew prepared its charges, the dynamite accidentally exploded. A spike more than a metre long and weighing almost six kilograms was propelled through the face and head of Phineas Gage, a 25-year-old foreman. The spike entered through the left cheek, passed through the brain, and emerged through the top of the skull (Figure 3.1). Dr. J. M. Harlow, who treated Gage, described the incident:

> The patient was thrown upon his back by the explosion, and gave a few convulsive motions of the extremities, but spoke in a few minutes. He . . . seemed perfectly conscious, but was becoming exhausted from the hemorrhage, . . . the blood pouring from the top of his head. . . . He bore his sufferings with firmness, and directed my attention to the hole in his cheek, saying, "the iron entered there and passed through my head." (Harlow, 1868, pp. 330–332)

Miraculously, Gage survived. Or did he?

> His physical health is good, and I am inclined to say that he has recovered. Has no pain in his head, but says it has a queer feeling that he is not able to describe. . . . His contractors, who regarded him as the most efficient and capable foreman in their employ previous to his injury, considered the change in his mind so marked that they could not give him his place again. The equilibrium or balance, so to speak, between his intellectual faculties and animal propensities, seems to have been destroyed. He is fitful, irreverent, indulging at times in the grossest profanity (which was not previously his custom), manifesting but little deference for his fellows, impatient of restraint or advice when it conflicts with his desires . . . devising many plans of future operations, which are no sooner arranged than they are abandoned in turn for others. . . . His mind is radically changed, so decidedly that his friends and acquaintances say that he is "no longer Gage." (Harlow, 1868, pp. 339–340)

As the tragic accident to Phineas Gage shows us, biological and psychological processes are intimately related. Physical damage to Gage's brain changed his thinking and behaviour so radically that a psychologically different person emerged.

In this chapter we explore three interrelated biological systems. The nervous system is the master control network of nerve cells whose activities underlie your every thought, feeling, and behaviour. The endocrine system of glands influences many behaviours through the activities of hormones. The immune system, the body's defence network, is the site of some of the most profound recent discoveries of so-called psychological-biological interactions.

⊙ THE NEURAL BASES OF BEHAVIOUR

The brain is a grapefruit-size mass of tissue that feels like jelly and looks like a greyish gnarled walnut. One of the true marvels of nature, it has been termed "our three-pound universe" (Hooper & Teresi, 1986). To understand how the brain controls our experience and behaviour, we must first understand how its individual cells function and how they communicate with one another.

Neurons

Specialized cells called **neurons** are the basic building blocks of the nervous system. These nerve cells are linked together in circuits, not unlike the electrical circuits in a computer. At birth your brain contained about 100 billion neurons (Bloom, 2000; Kolb & Whishaw, 1989). To put this number in perspective, if each neuron were a centimetre long and they were placed end to end, the resulting chain would circle the earth more than 24 times.

1. Name the three main parts of the neuron and describe their functions.

Each neuron has three main parts: a cell body, dendrites, and an axon (see Figure 3.2). The cell body or *soma,* contains the biochemical structures needed to keep the neuron alive, and its nucleus carries the genetic information that determines how the cell develops and functions. Emerging from the cell body are branchlike fibres called **dendrites** (from the Greek word meaning "tree"). These specialized receiving units are like antennas that collect messages from neighbouring neurons and send them on to the cell body. There the incoming information is combined and processed. The many branches of the dendrites can receive input from 1,000 or more neighbouring neurons. The surface of the cell body also has receptor areas that can be directly stimulated by other neurons. Extending from one side of the cell body is a single **axon**, which conducts electrical impulses away from the cell body to other neurons, muscles, or glands. The axon branches out at its end to form a number of *axon terminals*—as many as several hundred in some cases. Each axon may connect with dendritic branches from numerous neurons, making it possible for a single neuron to pass messages to as many as 50,000 other neurons (Kolb & Whishaw, 2003). Given the structure of the dendrites and axons, it is easy to see how there can be trillions of interconnections in the brain, making it capable of performing the complex psychological activities that are of interest to psychologists.

2. Which structural characteristics permit the many possible interconnections among neurons?

Neurons can vary greatly in size and shape. More than 200 different types of neurons have been viewed through electron microscopes (Nolte, 1998). A neuron with its cell body in your spinal cord may have an axon that extends almost a metre to one of your fingertips, equivalent in scale to a basketball attached to a cord six and a half kilometres long; a neuron in your brain may be less than a millimetre

3. How do glial cells differ from neurons? What three functions do they have in the nervous system?

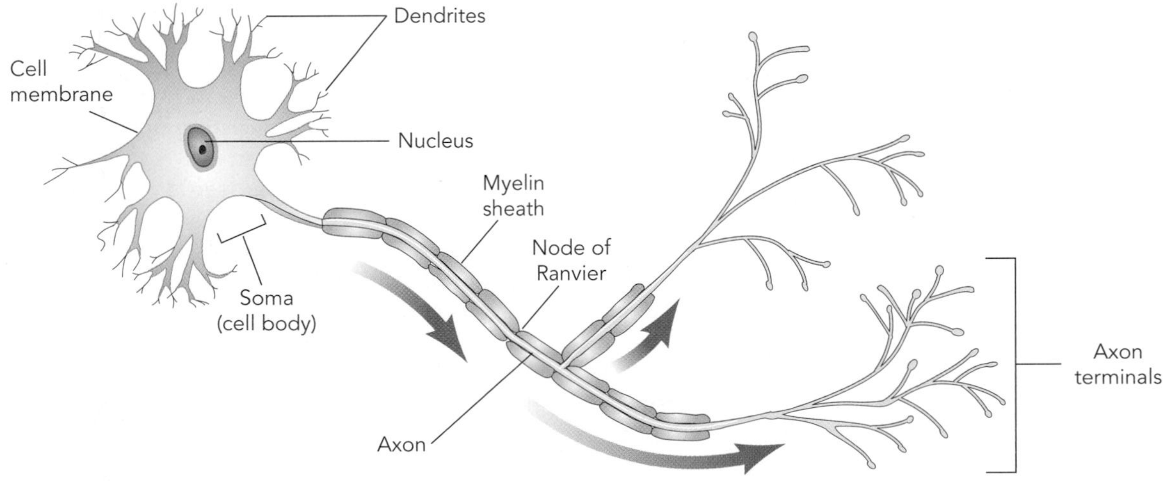

FIGURE 3.2

Structural elements of a typical neuron. Stimulation received by the dendrites or soma (cell body) may trigger a nerve impulse, which travels down the axon to stimulate other neurons, muscles, or glands. Some axons have a fatty myelin sheath interrupted at intervals by the nodes of Ranvier. The myelin sheath helps increase the speed of nerve conduction.

long. Regardless of their shape or size, neurons have been exquisitely sculpted by nature to perform their function of receiving, processing, and sending messages.

Neurons are supported in their functions by *glial cells* (from the Greek word for *glue*). Glial cells surround neurons and hold them in place. Glial cells also manufacture nutrient chemicals that neurons need, form the myelin sheath around some axons, and absorb toxins and waste materials that might damage neurons. During prenatal brain development, as new neurons are being formed through cell division, glial cells send out long fibres that guide newly divided neurons to their targeted place in the brain (Filogamo, 1998). Within the nervous system, glial cells outnumber neurons about ten to one.

Another function of glial cells is to protect the brain from toxins. Many foreign substances can pass from the circulation into the different organs of the body, but cannot pass from the blood into the brain. A specialized barrier, the **blood-brain barrier**, prevents many substances, including a wide range of toxins, from entering the brain. The walls of the blood vessels within the brain contain smaller gaps than elsewhere in the body, and they are also covered by a specialized type of glial cell (Cserr & Bundgaard, 1986). Together, the smaller gaps and glial cells keep many foreign substances from gaining access to the brain. Recent research has found evidence for much more complex glial function, discussed in the Research Frontiers section in this chapter.

RESEARCH FRONTIERS

Gliotransmission?

Within the brain there are both neurons, discussed through much of this chapter, and glial cells, described above. A specific type of glial cell has the important role of providing myelin along the axons of some types of neurons, but otherwise glial cells have been characterized as having rather mundane housekeeping tasks within the nervous system: they clear waste, provide structural support, and help to supply nutrients to the important neurons. That is, glial cells provide important backstage support and custodial services, but neurons, with their complex integrative functions, are the stars. Currently, a radical reevaluation of this scenario is underway. Although our understanding of the emerging issues is still rudimentary, recent research suggests that glial cells may serve functions that are as complex and critical for information processing as are the functions of neurons (see reviews by Haydon, 2001; Todd, Serrano, Lacaille, & Robitaille, 2006; Zhang & Haydon, 2005).

Beginning about 10 years ago, research findings began to appear that indicated that a type of glial cell called an astrocyte may be capable of more complex actions. It was found that glial cells could show changes in their electrical characteristics, especially in levels of positively charged calcium ions, that they contained a range of chemical transmitters, and that they even possessed receptors for various neurotransmitters (Robitaille, 1998; Todd et al., 2006; Zhang & Haydon, 2005). Glial cells seemed to possess a range of mechanisms that could be used for communication, but were these mechanisms used in this way?

Glial cells are known to extend processes, or branches, that wrap around synapses forming what has been called a tripartite, or three-part, synapse (Haydon, 2001). The tripartite synapse is composed of the axon terminal of one neuron, the postsynaptic membrane of another neuron, and a glial process (see Figure 3.3). Such tripartite synapses are widespread in the peripheral nervous system and within the brain. For example, within the hippocampus, a structure linked to memory, as we will discuss later (see p. 108), almost 60 percent of synapses are tripartite synapses (Ventura & Harris, 1999). Traditionally, the presence of the glial cell at the synapse was thought to fit with its role in helping to clear neurotransmitter once the neurons had finished communicating. That is, the glial cell served essentially a housekeeping role.

In 1998 Richard Robitaille of the Université de Montréal reported the results of a technically difficult yet elegant study. Robitaille tested whether or not synaptic activity influenced the glial cell, and if so, did the glial cell then act back on the synapse to modulate neuronal activity. Robitaille studied the neuromuscular junction, the synapse between a motor neuron and a muscle cell. As in the brain, the processes of glial cells cover synapses at the neuromuscular junction; here the tripartite synapse includes the axon terminal, receptive area

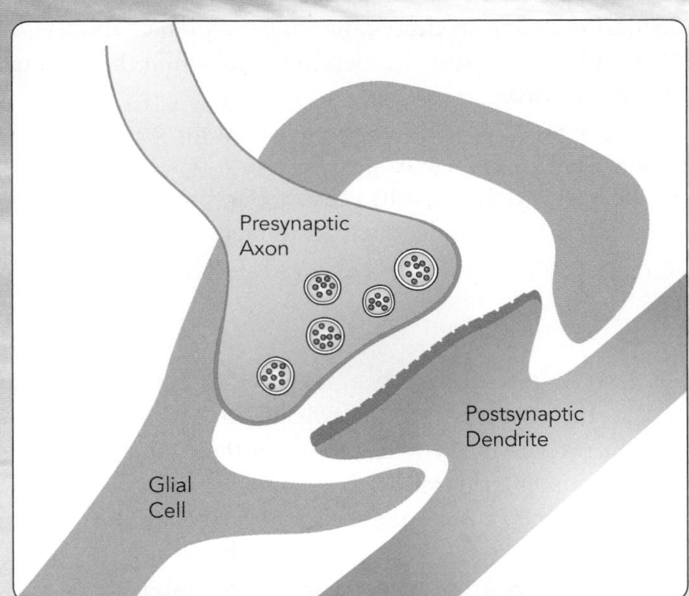

FIGURE 3.3

Schematic of a tripartite synapse. A process of a glial cell surrounds the synapse involving the axon terminal of the presynaptic neuron and dendrite of the postsynaptic neuron. The glial cell has the potential to monitor activity, such as the release of neurotransmitter, at the neuronal synapse and modulate that activity (Haydon, 2001).

of the muscle, and the glial process. Robitaille isolated individual neuromuscular synapses from the frog neuromuscular junction in a way that kept the synapse intact and functional. He also developed a technique to inject drugs directly into the glial cell without damaging the cell and without affecting the other parts of the synapse. Robitaille found that he could modulate synaptic activity by activating or blocking a certain class of proteins within the glial cell (so-called G proteins). For example, if those specific proteins were activated within the glial cell, the amount of neurotransmitter released by the neighbouring axon terminal was reduced. Further tests demonstrated that synaptic activity alone, without drug treatment, was sufficient to change the activity of the glial cell and have the glial cell then modulate transmitter release from the neighbouring axon terminal. That is, the results revealed that glial cells were involved in a synapse-glial-synapse feedback loop, and the feedback loop helped to control the amount of neurotransmitter released at the synapse between the axon terminal and muscle cell.

Recent research from several groups, including Robitaille's group at the Université de Montréal, has found evidence that glial cell-neuron interactions are even involved in the changes in synaptic function that are thought to support learning and memory (Todd et al., 2006). Some of the highest functions within the brain—the abilities to learn and remember—make use of the tripartite synapse. Other research has found evidence that glial cells can communicate not just with neurons, but with each other (Haydon, 2001; Zhang & Haydon, 2005). Currently it is not known what function is served by glial cell-glial cell communication.

Neurons interact with other neurons, neurons and glial cells interact, and glial cells interact with other glial cells. The picture that is emerging suggests two interacting communication systems within the brain, one based on neurons and one based on glial cells. Research on these more complex functions of glial cells is only at the early stages, but already it has offered many surprises. There is a complex system of glial communication and modulation within the brain that was not even anticipated only a few years ago. Not all types of glial cells have been shown to communicate electrically and chemically with other cells. In light of the sheer number of glial cells within the brain (glial cells outnumber neurons by about 10 to 1), the glial-glial and glial-neuron networks appear to be widespread and may be of general importance for normal brain functioning.

Nerve Conduction: An Electrochemical Process

4. What causes the negative resting potential of neurons? When is a neuron said to be in a state of polarization?

Neurons do two important things: They generate electricity and they release chemicals. The electrical properties of neurons have been known for more than a century, but we have only recently begun to understand the chemical processes involved in neural activity. An understanding of how neurons generate electricity requires a brief excursion into chemistry.

Neurons function a bit like batteries in that their own chemical substances are a source of energy. Like other cells, the neuron is surrounded by a cell membrane. This membrane not only protects the inner structures but also operates as a kind of selective filter that allows certain particles in the body fluid around the cell to pass through while refusing passage to other substances.

Neurons are surrounded by a salty liquid environment. This environment's high concentration of sodium carries a positive electrical charge, that is, it has a high concentration of positively charged particles, or ions. Although the inside of the neuron has some positively charged potassium ions, it contains many other ions that carry a negative charge. As a result, the inside of the neuron is electrically negative in relation to the outside, producing an electrical *resting potential* of about –70 millivolts (mV), or –70/1,000 of a volt, across the membrane. When in this resting state, the neuron is said to be *polarized.*

All cells in the body have a similar resting potential. In some animals, specialized organs can combine this tiny voltage to generate very high voltages. For example, electric eels can generate 600 to 700 volts because their muscle tissue cell membranes are arranged so that the small individual cell voltages can be combined to produce one big jolt.

5. What chemical changes cause the process of depolarization that creates graded and action potentials? How do these potentials differ?

The Action Potential

Neurons, like muscle cells, have a unique property among body cells: Sudden and extreme changes can occur in their resting potential voltage. An **action potential**, or nerve impulse, is a sudden reversal in the neuron's membrane voltage, during which the membrane voltage momentarily moves from –70 millivolts (inside) to +40 millivolts (see Figure 3.4). This shift from negative to positive voltage is called **depolarization**.

To understand how this depolarization process occurs, we might liken the release of an action potential to pressing the shutter release button on a camera. When the dendrites or the cell body of a neuron are stimulated by axons from other neurons, small shifts occur in the cell membrane's electrical potential. These changes, called **graded potentials**, are proportional to the amount of incoming stimulation. If the graded potentials are not very strong, the neuron will be partially depolarized, but not enough to generate an action potential. In this sense, a graded potential is like light pressure on the shutter release button of a camera; you can touch the button lightly, even depress it slightly, but the shutter does not release and the flash does not fire. But if the graded potential is large enough to reach the **action potential threshold**, the neuron discharges with an action potential. Unlike the graded potential, which varies in proportion to the intensity of stimulation, the action potential obeys the **all-or-none law**; it either occurs with maximum intensity or it does not occur at all. It is in this sense that triggering an action potential is like using a camera. Unless enough pressure is applied to the shutter release button, the camera will not fire. But once it does, the opening and closing of the shutter and the brightness of the flash have no relation to how hard the button was pressed. Whether you press the shutter release button with just enough force to take a picture or with considerably more pressure, the camera's operation is the same and you take the same picture; pressing the button harder does not make the shutter move faster or make the flash brighter.

Graded potentials change the membrane potential by acting on tiny protein structures in the cell membrane called **ion channels**. Each ion channel allows specific ions to cross the cell membrane and enter or leave the cell. As ion channels for positively charged ions, such as sodium, are opened, positive charge can enter the neuron and make the neuron less negative than it was. This creates a state of partial depolarization that may reach the action potential threshold. The action potential threshold is typically about –55 millivolts, a decrease of only –15 millivolts from the resting potential.

If the graded potentials are sufficiently large, the threshold for an action potential will be reached and the neuron will fire. But what happens when the neuron's membrane reaches its threshold and an action potential is generated? Through a sophisticated series of experiments that won them the 1963 Nobel Prize, British scientists Alan Hodgkin and Andrew Huxley provided the answer. Recall that when

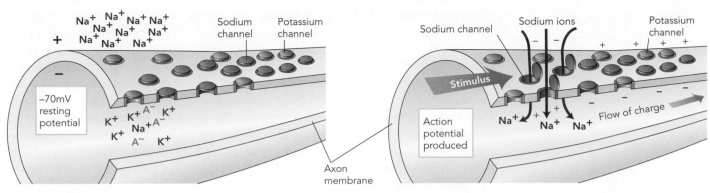

(a) The 10:1 concentration of sodium (Na^+) ions outside the neuron and the negative protein (A^-) ions inside contribute to a resting potential of –70mV.

(b) Sodium channels open and sodium ions flood into the axon. Note that the potassium channels are still closed.

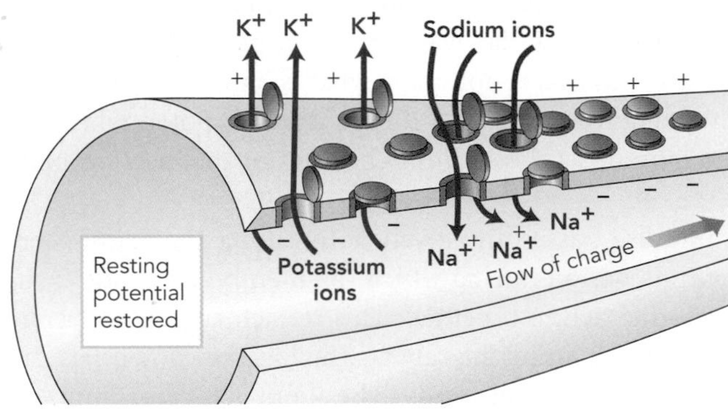

(c) Sodium channels that were open in (b) have now closed and potassium channels behind them are open, allowing potassium ions to exit and restoring the resting potential at that point. Sodium channels are opening at the next point.

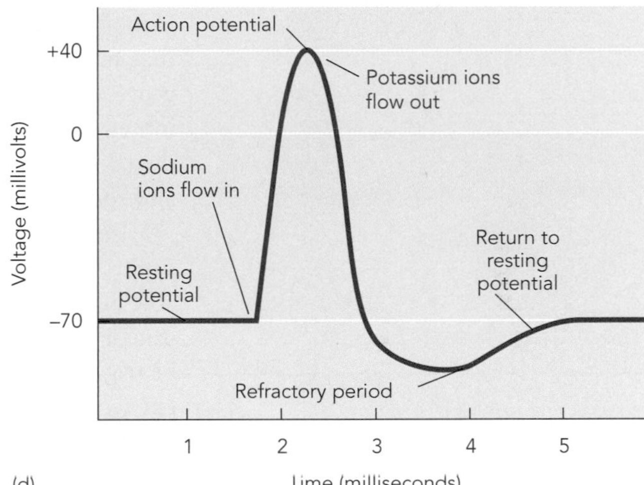

(d)

FIGURE 3.4

From resting potential to action potential. When a neuron is not being stimulated, a difference in electrical charge of about –70 millivolts (mV) exists between the interior and the surface of the neuron. (a) This resting potential is caused by the uneven distribution of positively and negatively charged ions, with a greater concentration of positively charged sodium ions kept outside the cell by closed sodium channels, and the presence of negatively charged protein (A^-) ions inside the cell. In addition, the action of sodium-potassium pumps helps maintain the negative interior by pumping out three sodium (Na^+) ions for every two positively charged potassium (K^+) ions pumped into the cell. (b) Sufficient stimulation of the neuron causes an action potential. Sodium channels open for an instant, and Na^+ ions flood into the axon, reversing the electrical potential from –70 mV to +40 mV. (c) Within a millisecond, the sodium channels close and many K^+ ions flow out of the cell through open potassium channels, helping to restore the interior negative potential. As adjacent sodium channels are opened and the sequence in (b) and (c) is repeated, the action potential moves down the length of the neuron. (d) Shown here are the changes in potential that would be recorded from a particular point on the axon. After a brief refractory period during which the neuron cannot be stimulated, another action potential can follow.

a neuron is at its resting potential, positively charged sodium ions are kept in the salty fluids outside of the cell. When the membrane reaches its threshold for generating an action potential, specific ion channels are activated. Sodium ion channels are usually closed, but when the membrane reaches the threshold for generating an action potential, the sodium ion channels open and positively charged sodium ions flow into the neuron, attracted by the negative electrical force within the cell. This influx of positively charged sodium ions carries positive electrical charge into the interior of the cell, and the interior of the neuron goes from being negative to being more positively charged than the outside of the cell. It is this state of complete depolarization that constitutes the action potential.

The sodium ion channels that opened when the neuron reached its threshold for generating an action potential do not stay open very long, they close in less than a millisecond, less than a thousandth of a second. In order to restore the resting polarity, potassium channels open and the positively charged potassium ions leave the cell. The closing of the sodium channels and opening of the potassium channel, allow the cell's negative resting potential to be restored (Fain, 1999). In a few milliseconds the whole process is over at any given point in the membrane, but the action potential has started a chain reaction "wave" that flows along the membrane as succeeding sodium channels open and the process is repeated. After the action potential, the sodium ions trapped inside the cell are pumped back outside, and the potassium ions that left the neuron during the action potential are pumped back inside the neuron, restoring the normal distribution of ions so that another action potential can occur.

The wavelike quality of the action potential as it moves down the length of the axon is not unlike the human "wave" that occurs in sports stadiums as fans in adjacent seats successively stand up, cheer, raise their arms, and then sit back down. Nobody actually changes position, but the visual and auditory effect is of a "wave" that moves around the stadium. In a similar way, an action potential appears to move along an axon like a wave, but this is not really what is happening. Like fans in neighbouring sections standing in turn, a new, different action potential is produced at each section of membrane as the sodium channels in that section open and sodium ions flow into the cell.

Immediately after an impulse passes any given point along the axon, there occurs a *refractory period*, a time period during which the membrane is not excitable and cannot discharge another action potential. This refractory period, lasting one or two thousandths of a second, limits the rate at which action potentials can be triggered in a neuron. In humans the limit seems to be about 300 nerve impulses per second (Roland, 1997).

If action potentials are always identical to one another, how does the nervous system tell the difference between, for example, a dim light and a bright light, or between a light touch and a hard rub? Such information is communicated in a number of ways. For example, a strong stimulus may increase the *rate* of firing of the individual neuron, or it may increase the *number* of neurons that fire by stimulating additional neurons that fire only in response to high-intensity stimulation. In such ways, information is provided concerning the nature of the stimulus.

The Myelin Sheath

6. What is the nature and importance of the myelin sheath? Which disorder results from inadequate myelinization?

Many axons that transmit information throughout the brain and spinal cord are covered by a tubelike **myelin sheath**, a fatty, whitish insulation layer derived from glial cells during development. The myelin sheath is interrupted at regular intervals by the *nodes of Ranvier*, where the myelin is either extremely thin or absent. The nodes make the myelin sheath look a bit like sausages placed end to end (see Figure 3.2). In unmyelinated axons, the action potential travels down the axon length like a burning fuse. In myelinated axons, electrical conduction can skip from node to node, and these "great leaps" from one gap to another account for high conduction speeds of more than 300 kilometres per hour. But even these high-speed fibres are three million times slower than the speed at which electricity courses through an electric wire. This is why your brain, though vastly more complex than any computer, cannot begin to match it in speed of operation.

The myelin sheath is most commonly found in the nervous systems of higher animals. In many nerve fibres, the myelin sheath is not completely formed until some time after birth. The increased efficiency of neural transmission that results is partly responsible for the gains that infants exhibit in muscular coordination as they grow older (Weyhenmeyer et al., 2000).

The tragic effects of damage to the myelin coating can be seen in people who suffer from *multiple sclerosis*. This progressive disease occurs when the person's own immune system attacks the myelin sheath. Damage to the myelin sheath disrupts the delicate timing of nerve impulses, resulting in jerky, uncoordinated movements and, in the final stages, paralysis.

How Neurons Communicate: Synaptic Transmission

The nervous system operates as a giant communications network, and its action requires the transmission of nerve impulses from one neuron to another. Early in the history of brain research, scientists thought that the tip of the axon made physical contact with the dendrites or cell bodies of other neurons, passing electricity directly from one neuron to the next. Others, such as the famous Spanish anatomist Santiago Ramon y Cajal and British scientist Charles Sherrington, argued that neurons were individual cells that did not make actual physical contact with each other, but communicated at a **synapse**, a functional (but not physical) connection between a neuron and its target. This idea was controversial: How could a neuron influence the functioning of the heart, or a skeletal muscle, or another neuron within the brain if these cells did not actually touch? What carried the message from one neuron to the next? The controversy persisted until the 1920s, when Otto Loewi, in a series of simple but elegant experiments, demonstrated that neurons released chemicals, and it was these chemicals that carried the message from one neuron to the next cell in the circuit (Loewi, 1935; 1960). Otto Loewi won the Nobel Prize for his discovery of chemical neurotransmission. With the advent of the electron microscope, researchers were able to see that there is indeed a tiny gap or space, called the **synaptic cleft**, between the axon terminal of one neuron and the dendrite of the next neuron. This discovery raised new and perplexing questions: If the action potential does not cross the synapse, what does? What carries the message and how does it affect the next neuron in the circuit?

Neurotransmitters

We now know that, in addition to generating electricity, neurons produce **neurotransmitters**, chemical substances that carry messages across the synapse to either excite other neurons or inhibit their firing. This process of chemical communication involves five steps: synthesis, storage, release, binding, and deactivation. In the *synthesis* stage, the chemical molecules are formed inside the neuron. The molecules are then *stored* in chambers called **synaptic vesicles** within the axon terminals. When an action potential comes down the axon, these vesicles move to the surface of the axon terminal and the molecules are *released* into the fluid-filled space between the axon of the sending (presynaptic) neuron and the membrane of the receiving (postsynaptic) neuron. The molecules cross the synaptic space and *bind* (attach themselves) to **receptor sites**—large protein molecules embedded in the receiving neuron's cell membrane. These receptor sites, which look a bit like lily pads when viewed through an electron microscope, have a specially shaped surface that fits a specific transmitter molecule, much like a lock accommodates a single key (Figure 3.5).

Excitation, Inhibition, and Deactivation

7. How do neurotransmitters achieve the processes of excitation and inhibition of postsynaptic neurons?

The binding of a transmitter molecule to the receptor site produces a chemical reaction that can have one of two effects on the postsynaptic neuron. In some cases, the reaction will depolarize (excite) the postsynaptic cell membrane by stimulating the inflow of sodium or other positively charged ions. Neurotransmitters that create depolarization are called *excitatory* transmitters. This stimulation, alone or

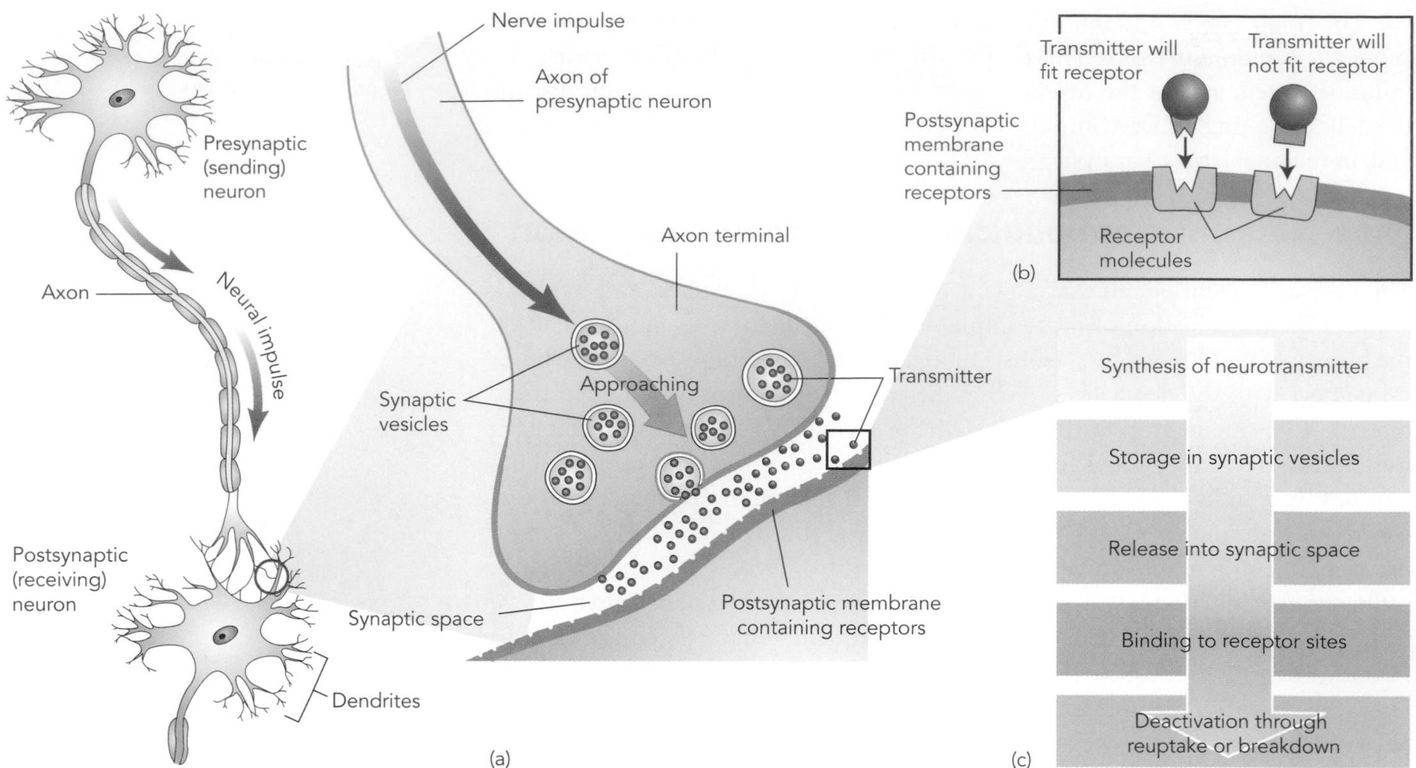

FIGURE 3.5

A synapse between two neurons. The action potential travels to the axon terminals, where it stimulates the release of transmitter molecules from the synaptic vesicles. These molecules travel across the synapse and bind to specially keyed receptor sites on the dendrite of the postsynaptic neuron (a). The lock-and-key nature of neurotransmitters and receptor sites is shown in (b). Only transmitters that fit the receptor will influence membrane potentials. (c) Neurotransmitter activity moves from synthesis to deactivation. If the neurotransmitter has an excitatory effect on the neuron, the chemical reaction creates a graded or an action potential. If the neurotransmitter has an inhibitory effect, the negative potential inside the neuron increases and makes it more difficult to trigger an action potential.

in combination with activity at other excitatory synapses on the dendrites or cell body, may exceed the action potential threshold and cause the postsynaptic neuron to fire an action potential.

In other cases, the chemical reaction created by the docking of a neurotransmitter at its receptor site will *hyperpolarize* the postsynaptic membrane by stimulating ion channels that allow positively charged potassium ions to flow out of the neuron or negatively charged ions, such as chloride, to flow into the neuron. This makes the membrane potential even more negative (e.g., changing it from –70 millivolts to –72 millivolts). Hyperpolarization makes it more difficult for excitatory transmitters at other receptor sites to depolarize the neuron to its action potential threshold of –55 millivolts. Transmitters that create hyperpolarization are thus *inhibitory* in their function (Figure 3.6). A given neurotransmitter can have an excitatory effect on some neurons and an inhibitory influence on others.

Every neuron is constantly bombarded with excitatory and inhibitory neurotransmitters from other neurons, and the interplay of these influences determines whether or not the cell fires an action potential. The action of an inhibitory transmitter from one presynaptic neuron may prevent the postsynaptic neuron from reaching the action potential threshold, even if it is receiving excitatory stimulation from several other neurons at the same time. An exquisite balance between excitatory and inhibitory processes must be maintained if the nervous system is to function properly. The process of inhibition allows a fine-tuning of neural activity and

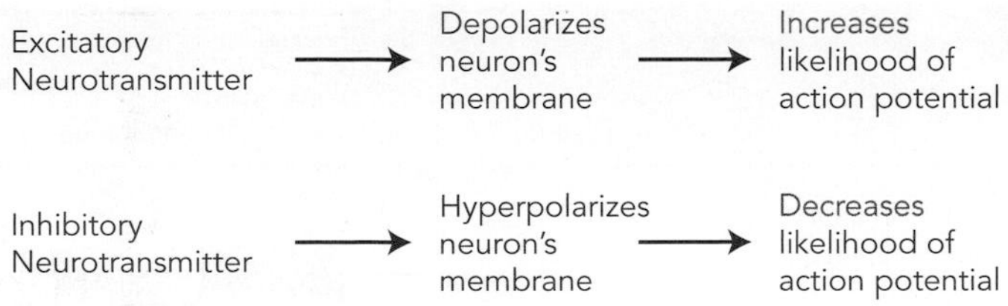

Excitatory Neurotransmitter	→	Depolarizes neuron's membrane	→	Increases likelihood of action potential
Inhibitory Neurotransmitter	→	Hyperpolarizes neuron's membrane	→	Decreases likelihood of action potential

FIGURE 3.6

Neurotransmitters have either excitatory or inhibitory effects on postsynaptic neurons. Excitatory transmitters depolarize the postsynaptic neuron's cell membrane, making it less negative and thereby moving it toward the action potential threshold. Inhibitory neurons hyperpolarize the membrane, making it more negative and therefore more difficult to excite to an action potential.

prevents an uncoordinated discharge of the nervous system, as occurs in a seizure, when large numbers of neurons fire off action potentials in a runaway fashion.

Once a neurotransmitter molecule binds to its receptor, it continues to activate or inhibit the neuron until it is shut off, or *deactivated.* This occurs in two major ways (Fain, 1999). Some transmitter molecules are deactivated by other chemicals located in the synaptic space that break them down into their chemical components. In other instances, the deactivation mechanism is **reuptake**, in which the transmitter molecules are reabsorbed into the presynaptic axon terminal. When the receptor molecule is vacant, the postsynaptic neuron returns to its former resting state, awaiting the next chemical stimulation.

8. Describe two methods by which neurotransmitter molecules are deactivated at the synapse.

Most commonly used, and abused, psychoactive drugs influence one of these steps in chemical neurotransmission. Many drugs target the transmitter's receptor, binding to the receptor in place of the neurotransmitter. Once a molecule of drug has bound to a neurotransmitter receptor, it can have one of two effects: It can either mimic the naturally occurring transmitter, or it can bind to the receptor and have no effect other than denying the transmitter access to its receptor. Opiates such as morphine and codeine, anti-anxiety medications such as Valium, and nicotine are all drugs that act by binding to a specific type of neurotransmitter receptor and mimicking the effects of the natural transmitter. Antipsychotic medications and caffeine are examples of drugs that bind to specific types of neurotransmitter receptors and have no effect other than preventing the transmitter from gaining access to and binding to its receptor. Other drugs alter synaptic transmission by altering how the transmitter is cleared from the synaptic cleft after it has been released. Cocaine and some antidepressants produce their effects by blocking the reuptake of specific transmitters. Other drugs, such as the antidepressant phenelzine act by interfering with a chemical that is responsible for the breakdown of neurotransmitters. A drug's exact psychological effects are determined not by its actions at the synapse, but by which specific chemical transmitter it targets.

Specialized Transmitter Systems

Through the use of chemical transmitters, nature has found an ingenious way of dividing up the brain into systems that are uniquely sensitive to certain messages. There is only one kind of electricity, but there are many shapes that can be assumed by transmitter molecules. Because the various systems in the brain recognize only certain chemical messengers, they are immune to "crosstalk" from other systems. At present, 100 to 150 different substances are known or suspected transmitters in the brain, but there may be hundreds more (Fain, 1999; Wayne & Morris, 1999). Each substance has a specific excitatory or inhibitory effect on certain neurons. Table 3.1 lists several of the more important neurotransmitters that have been linked to psychological phenomena.

Two widespread neurotransmitters are simple amino acids, glutamate, or glutamic acid, and gamma-amino-butyric acid, or GABA. Both glutamate and GABA are found throughout the central nervous system, and hence have some role in mediating virtually all behaviours. Glutamate is excitatory and has a particularly

TABLE 3.1 Some neurotransmitters and their effects

Neurotransmitter	Major Function	Disorders Associated with Malfunctioning
Glutamate (glutamic acid)	Excitatory. Found throughout the brain. Involved in the control of all behaviours, especially important in learning and memory.	
GABA	Inhibitory transmitter; found throughout the brain. Involved in controlling all behaviours, especially important in anxiety and motor control.	Destruction of GABA-producing neurons in Huntington's disease produces tremors and loss of motor control, as well as personality changes.
Acetylcholine (ACh)	Excitatory at synapses involved in muscular movement and memory.	Undersupply produces memory loss in Alzheimer's disease.
Norepinephrine	Excitatory and inhibitory functions at various sites. Involved in neural circuits controlling learning, memory, wakefulness, and eating.	Depression (undersupply)
Serotonin	Inhibitory at most sites. Involved in mood, sleep, eating, and arousal, and may be an important transmitter underlying pleasure and pain.	Depression, sleeping, and eating disorders (undersupply)
Dopamine	Can be inhibitory or excitatory; involved in voluntary movement, emotional arousal, learning, motivation, experiencing pleasure.	Parkinson's disease and depression (undersupply); Schizophrenia (oversupply)

important role in the mechanisms involved in learning and memory. Improving one's memory, however, cannot be as simple as enhancing glutamate activity. Since it has a powerful excitatory effect, over-activation of glutamate will induce seizure activity within the brain, especially within the cerebral cortex. Whereas glutmate has a powerful excitatory effect, GABA is an inhibitory neurotransmitter. GABA is especially important for motor control and for the control of anxiety. For example, many of the drugs commonly used to treat anxiety disorders, the benzodiazepines, act by enhancing GABA activity. A commonly used drug, alcohol, also acts to increase GABA activity, although in a less specific way than the anti-anxiety benzodiazepines. The symptoms of intoxication and alcohol poisoning reflect the progressive inhibition of brain function with increasing GABA-induced inhibition.

9. Describe the roles of (a) acetylcholine, (b) dopamine, (c) serotonin, and (d) endorphins in psychological functions.

Perhaps the best understood neurotransmitter is **acetylcholine (ACh)**, which is involved in memory and in muscle activity. Underproduction of acetylcholine is thought to be an important factor in *Alzheimer's disease,* a degenerative brain disorder involving profound memory impairment that afflicts between 5 and 10 percent of all people over 65 years of age (Ron & David, 1997). Reductions in ACh weaken or deactivate neural circuitry that stores memories.

Acetylcholine is also an excitatory transmitter at the synapses where neurons activate muscle cells (Sherwood, 1991). Drugs that block the action of ACh therefore can prevent muscle activation, resulting in muscular paralysis. One example occurs in *botulism,* a serious type of food poisoning that can result from improperly canned food. The toxin formed by the botulinum bacteria blocks the release of ACh from the axon terminal, resulting in a potentially fatal paralysis of the muscles, including those of the respiratory system. The opposite effect on ACh occurs with the bite of the black widow spider. The spider's venom produces a torrent of ACh, resulting in violent muscle contractions, convulsions, and possible death. Thus, although botulism and black widow venom affect ACh synapses in different ways, they can have equally lethal effects.

Understanding the neurotransmitter dopamine has also had a profound impact on our understanding of several diseases. In Parkinson's disease, one group of dopamine-producing neurons degenerate and die. As dopamine is lost in the affected brain areas, there is a concomitant loss of voluntary motor control. The symptoms of Parkinson's disease are most commonly treated with a drug (L-DOPA) that increases the amount of dopamine within the brain. The treatment of emotionally disturbed people has been revolutionized by the development of psychoactive drugs which operate by either enhancing or inhibiting the actions of transmitters at the synapse. One group of drugs that started the so-called psychiatric revolution of the 1950s and that is still widely used is the antipsychotic drugs. These drugs attach to dopamine receptors and block **dopamine** from having its effects. Such blockade of dopamine is effective in treating symptoms of schizophrenia, including disordered thinking, hallucinations, and delusions (LeMoal, 1999; Robinson, 1997).

Quite a different mechanism occurs in the treatment of depression. Depression involves abnormal sensitivity to **serotonin**, a neurotransmitter that influences mood, eating, sleep, and sexual behaviour. Antidepressant drugs increase serotonin activity in several ways. The drug Prozac blocks the reuptake of serotonin from the synaptic space, allowing serotonin molecules to remain active and exert their mood-altering effects on depressed patients. Other antidepressant drugs work on a different deactivating mechanism. They inhibit the activity of enzymes in the synaptic space that deactivate serotonin by breaking it down into simpler chemicals. In so doing, they prolong serotonin activity at the synapse.

Endorphins are another important family of neurotransmitters. **Endorphins** reduce pain and increase feelings of well-being. They bind to the same receptors as the ones activated by opiate drugs, such as opium and morphine, which produce similar psychological effects. The ability of people to continue to function despite severe injury is due in large part to the release of endorphins and their ability to act as analgesics. It is likely that Phineas Gage was able to sit and chat with his co-workers soon after his accident because of the massive release of pain-killing endorphins triggered by the trauma. We discuss the endorphins in greater detail in Chapter 5.

Most neurotransmitters have their excitatory or inhibitory effects only on specific neurons that have receptors for them. Others, called **neuromodulators**, have a more widespread and generalized influence on synaptic transmission. These substances circulate through the brain and either increase or decrease (i.e., modulate) the sensitivity of thousands, perhaps millions, of neurons to their specific transmitters. Neuromodulators play important roles in functions such as eating, sleep, and stress. Thus some neurotransmitters have very specific effects, whereas others have more general effects on neural activity.

In Review

- *Each neuron has dendrites, which receive nerve impulses from other neurons; a cell body (soma), which controls the vital processes of the cell; and an axon, which conducts nerve impulses to adjacent neurons, muscles, and glands.*
- *Neural transmission is an electrochemical process. The nerve impulse, or action potential, is a brief reversal in the electrical potential of the cell membrane as sodium ions from the surrounding fluid flow into the cell through sodium ion channels, depolarizing the axon's membrane. Graded potentials are proportional to the amount of stimulation being received, whereas action potentials obey the all-or-none law, occuring at full intensity if the action potential threshold of stimulation is reached. The myelin sheath increases the speed of neural transmission.*
- *Passage of the impulse across the synapse is mediated by chemical transmitter substances. Neurons are selective in the neurotransmitters that can stimulate them. Some neurotransmitters excite neurons, whereas others inhibit firing of the postsynaptic neuron.*

THE NERVOUS SYSTEM

10. What are the three major types of neurons? What are their functions?

The nervous system is the body's master control centre. Three major types of neurons carry out the system's input, output, and integration functions. **Sensory neurons** carry input messages from the sense organs to the spinal cord and brain. **Motor neurons** transmit output impulses from the brain and spinal cord to the body's muscles and organs. Finally, there are neurons that link the input and output functions. **Interneurons**, which far outnumber sensory and motor neurons, perform connective or associative functions within the nervous system. For example, interneurons allow us to recognize a tune by linking the sensory input from the song we're hearing with the memory of that song stored elsewhere in the brain. The activity of interneurons makes possible the complexity of our higher mental functions, emotions, and behavioural capabilities.

11. Differentiate between the central nervous system and the peripheral nervous system. What are the two divisions of the peripheral nervous system?

The nervous system can be broken down into several interrelated subsystems (Figure 3.7). The two major divisions are the **central nervous system**, consisting of all the neurons in the brain and spinal cord, and the **peripheral nervous system**, composed of all the neurons that connect the central nervous system with the muscles, glands, and sensory receptors.

The Peripheral Nervous System

The peripheral nervous system contains all the neural structures that lie outside of the brain and spinal cord. Its specialized neurons help carry out the input and output functions that are necessary for us to sense what is going on inside and outside our bodies and to respond with our muscles and glands. The peripheral nervous

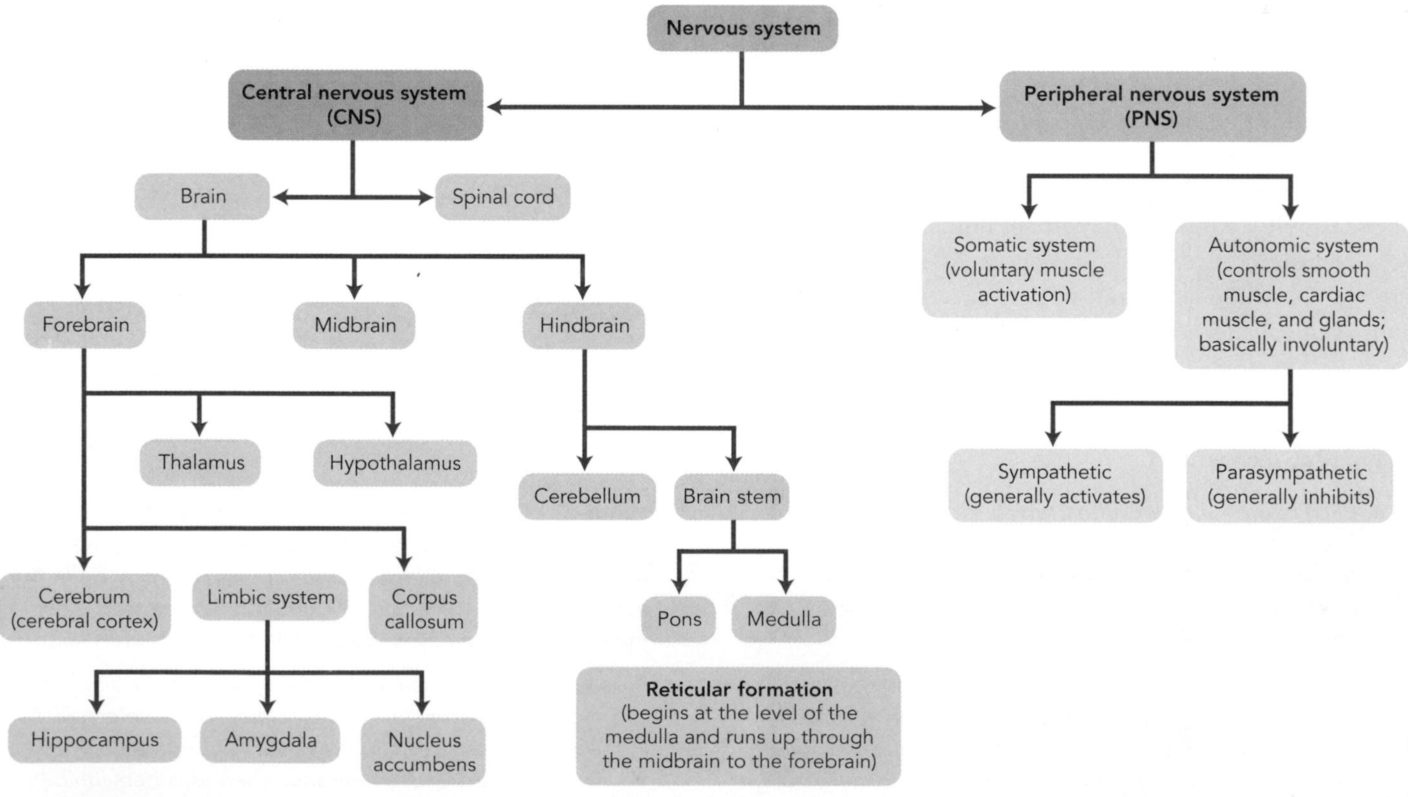

FIGURE 3.7

Structural organization of the nervous system.

system has two major divisions, the somatic nervous system and the autonomic nervous system.

The Somatic Nervous System

The **somatic nervous system** consists of the *sensory neurons* that are specialized to transmit messages from the eyes, ears, and other sensory receptors, and the *motor neurons* that send messages from the brain and spinal cord to the muscles that control our voluntary movements. The axons of sensory neurons group together like the many strands of a rope to form *sensory nerves,* and motor neuron axons combine to form *motor nerves.* (Inside the brain and spinal cord, nerves are called *tracts.*) As you read this page, sensory neurons located in your eyes are sending impulses into a complex network of specialized visual tracts that course through your brain. At the same time, motor neurons are stimulating the eye movements that allow you to scan the lines of type and turn the pages. The somatic system thus allows you to sense and respond to your environment.

The Autonomic Nervous System

12. Describe the two divisions of the autonomic nervous system, as well as their roles in maintaining homeostasis.

The body's internal environment is regulated largely through the activities of the **autonomic nervous system**, which controls the glands and the smooth (involuntary) muscles that form the heart, the blood vessels, and the lining of the stomach and intestines. The autonomic system is largely concerned with involuntary functions, such as respiration, circulation, and digestion, and it is also involved in many aspects of motivation, emotional behaviour, and stress responses. It consists of two subdivisions, the sympathetic nervous system and the parasympathetic nervous system (Figure 3.8). Typically, these two divisions affect the same organ or gland in opposing ways.

The **sympathetic nervous system** has an activation or arousal function, and it tends to act as a total unit. For example, when you encounter a stressful situation, your sympathetic nervous system simultaneously speeds your heart so it can pump more blood to your muscles, dilates your pupils so more light can enter the eye and improve your vision, slows down your digestive system so that blood can be transferred to the muscles, increases your rate of respiration so your body can get more oxygen, and, in general, mobilizes your body to confront the stressor. This is sometimes called the *fight-or-flight response.*

Compared to the sympathetic branch, which tends to act as a unit, the parasympathetic system is far more specific in its opposing actions, affecting one or a few organs at a time. The **parasympathetic nervous system** slows down body processes and maintains a state of tranquility. Thus your sympathetic system speeds up your heart rate; your parasympathetic system slows it down. By working together to maintain equilibrium in our internal organs, the two divisions can maintain *homeostasis,* a delicately balanced or constant internal state. Some acts also require a coordinated sequence of sympathetic and parasympathetic activities. For example, sexual function in the male involves penile erection (through parasympathetic dilation of blood vessels) followed by ejaculation (a primarily sympathetic function) (Masters et al., 1988).

The Central Nervous System

More than any other system in our body, the central nervous system distinguishes us from other creatures. This system contains the spinal cord, which connects most parts of the peripheral nervous system with the brain, and the brain itself.

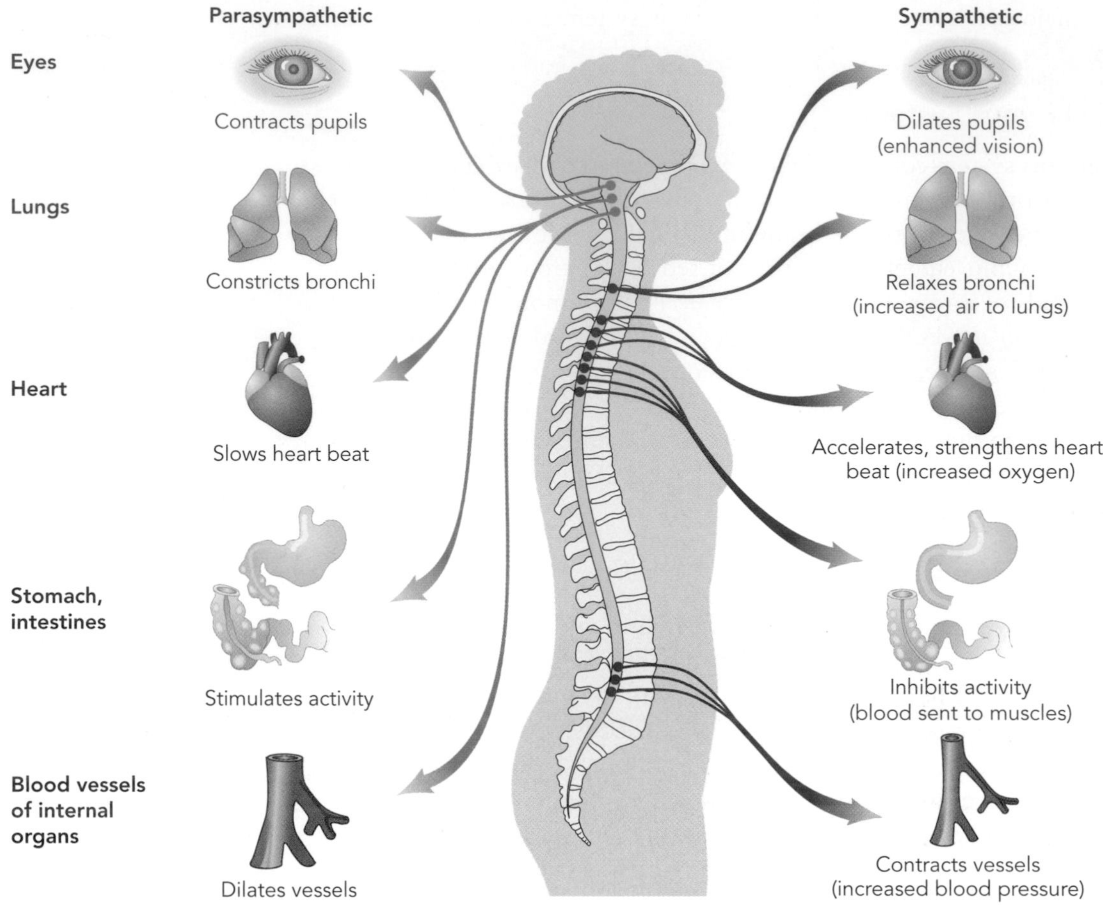

FIGURE 3.8

The sympathetic branch of the autonomic nervous system arouses the body and speeds up its vital processes, whereas the parasympathetic division slows down body processes. The two divisions work together to maintain an equilibrium within the body.

The Spinal Cord

Most nerves enter and leave the central nervous system by way of the spinal cord, a structure that in a human adult is 40 to 45 centimetres long and about two and a half centimetres in diameter. The spinal cord's neurons are protected by the vertebrae (bones of the spine). When the spinal cord is viewed in cross-section (Figure 3.9), its central portion resembles an H, or a butterfly. The H-shaped portion consists largely of grey-coloured neuron cell bodies and their interconnections. Surrounding the grey matter are white-coloured myelinated axons that connect various levels of the spinal cord with each other and with the higher centres of the brain. Entering the back side of the spinal cord along its length are sensory nerves. Motor nerves exit the spinal cord's front side.

13. How do spinal reflexes occur?

Some simple stimulus-response sequences, known as spinal reflexes, can be triggered at the level of the spinal cord without any involvement of the brain. For example, if you touch something hot, sensory receptors in your skin trigger nerve impulses in sensory nerves that flash into your spinal cord and synapse inside with interneurons. The interneurons then excite motor neurons that send impulses to your hand so that it pulls away. Other interneurons simultaneously carry the "Hot!" message up the spinal cord to your brain, but it is a good thing that you don't have to wait for the brain to tell you what to do in such emergencies. Getting messages to and from the brain takes slightly longer, so the spinal cord reflex system significantly reduces reaction time, and, in this case, potential tissue damage.

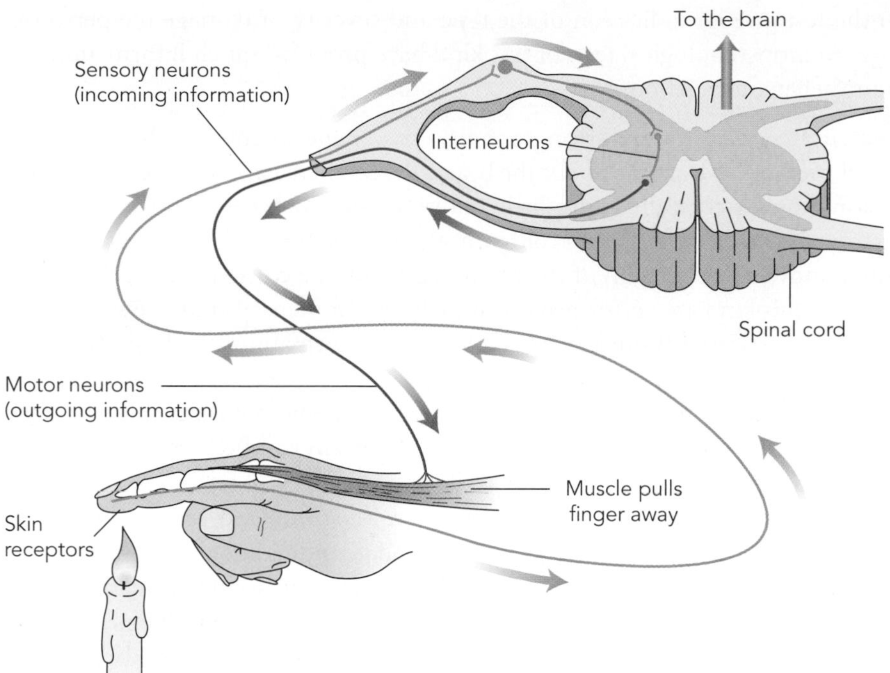

FIGURE 3.9

A cross-section of the spinal cord shows the organization of sensory and motor nerves. Sensory and motor nerves enter and exit the spinal cord on both sides of the spinal column. Interneurons within the H-shaped spinal grey matter can serve a connective function, as shown here, but in many cases, sensory neurons also can synapse directly with motor neurons. At this level of the nervous system, reflex activity is possible without involving the brain.

The Brain

The three pounds of protein, fat, and fluid that you carry around inside your skull is the real "you." It is also the most complex structure in the known universe and the only one that can wonder about itself. As befits this biological marvel, your brain is the most active energy consumer of all your body organs. Although the brain accounts for only about 2 percent of your total body weight, it consumes about 20 percent of the oxygen you use in a resting state (Robinson, 1997). Moreover, the brain never rests; its rate of energy metabolism is relatively constant day and night. In fact, when you dream, the brain's metabolic rate actually increases slightly (Hobson, 1996).

How can this rather nondescript blob of greyish tissue discover the principle of relativity, build the Hubble Telescope, and produce great works of art, music, and literature? Answering such questions requires the ability to study the brain and how it functions. To do so, neuroscientists use a diverse set of tools and procedures.

14. Describe four methods used to study brain-behaviour relations.

Unlocking the Secrets of the Brain

More has been learned in the past three decades about the brain and its role in behaviour than was known in all the preceding ages. This knowledge explosion is due in large part to revolutionary technical advances that have provided scientists with new research tools, as well as to the contributions of psychological research on brain-behaviour relations. Investigators use a variety of methods to study the brain's structures and activities.

Neuropsychological tests. Psychologists have developed a variety of *neuropsychological tests* to measure verbal and non-verbal behaviours that are known to be affected by particular types of brain damage (Lezak, 1995). These tests are used in clinical evaluations of people who may have suffered brain damage through accident or disease. They are also important research tools. For example, Figure 3.10 shows a portion of a Trail Making Test, used to test memory and planning. Scores

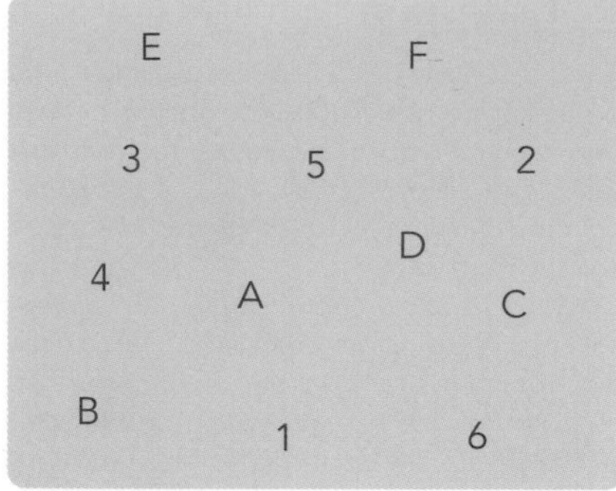

FIGURE 3.10

The Trail Making Test consists of a randomly scattered set of numbers and letters. On this timed test, the patient must connect the numbers and letters consecutively with a continuous line, or "trail" (i.e., A to 1 to B to 2 to C to 3, and so on). People with certain kinds of brain damage have trouble alternating between the numbers and letters because they cannot retain a plan in memory long enough, and poor test performance reflects this deficit.

on the test give an indication of the type and severity of damage the person may have. Neuropsychological tests of this kind have provided much information about brain-behaviour relations.

Destruction and stimulation techniques. Experimental studies are another useful method of learning about the brain. Researchers can produce brain damage (lesions) under carefully controlled conditions in which specific nervous tissue is destroyed with electricity, with cold or heat, or with chemicals. They also can surgically remove some portion of the brain and study the consequences. Most experiments of this kind are performed on animals, but humans also can be studied when accident or disease produces a specific lesion or when abnormal brain tissue must be surgically removed.

An alternative to destroying neurons is stimulating them, which typically produces opposite effects. A specific region of the brain can be stimulated by a mild electric current or by chemicals that excite neurons. Electrodes can be permanently implanted so that the region of interest can be stimulated repeatedly. Some of these electrodes are so tiny that they can stimulate individual neurons. In chemical stimulation studies, a tiny tube is inserted into the brain so that a small amount of the chemical can be delivered directly to the area to be studied. The neurosurgeon Wilder Penfield, of the Montreal Neurological Institute, pioneered brain surgery with an awake, interacting patient. Penfield stimulated specific points of cortex with a mild electrical current in an attempt to map out the functions of the cerebral cortex (see this chapter's *Research Foundations*). Before the advent of modern brain imaging techniques (see below), much of our knowledge of the functions of the human cerebral cortex came from the work pioneered by Wilder Penfield, together with the neuropsychological testing discussed above.

Electrical recording. Because electrodes can record brain activity as well as stimulate it, it is possible also to "eavesdrop" on the electrical conversations occurring within the brain. Neurons' electrical activity can be measured by inserting small electrodes into particular areas of the brain or even into individual neurons.

15. How are CT scans, PET scans, and MRIs produced, and how is each used in brain research?

In addition to measuring individual voices, scientists can tune in to "crowd noise" by placing larger electrodes on the scalp to measure the activity of large groups of neurons with the **electroencephalogram (EEG)** (Figure 3.11a, b). Although the EEG is a rather gross measure that taps the electrical activity of thousands of neurons in many parts of the brain, specific EEG patterns correspond to certain states of consciousness, such as wakefulness and sleep. Clinicians also use the EEG to detect abnormal electrical patterns that signal the presence of brain disorders. Researchers are especially interested in changes in the EEG record that accompany specific psychological events, such as presentation of a sensory stimulus. Changes in the EEG that accompany such events are called event-related potentials (ERPs).

Brain imaging. The newest tools of discovery are imaging techniques that permit neuroscientists to peer into the living brain (Figure 3.11c). The most important of these technological "windows" are CT scans, PET scans, and magnetic resonance imaging (MRI).

Developed in the 1970s, **computerized axial tomography (CT)** scans use X-ray technology to study brain structures (Peyster, 2000). A highly focused beam of X-rays takes pictures of narrow slices of the brain. A computer analyzes the X-rayed slices and creates pictures of the brain's interior from many different angles (Figure 3.11d). Pinpointing where injuries or deterioration have occurred helps clarify relations between brain damage and psychological functioning. CT scans are 100 times more sensitive than standard X-ray procedures, and the tech-

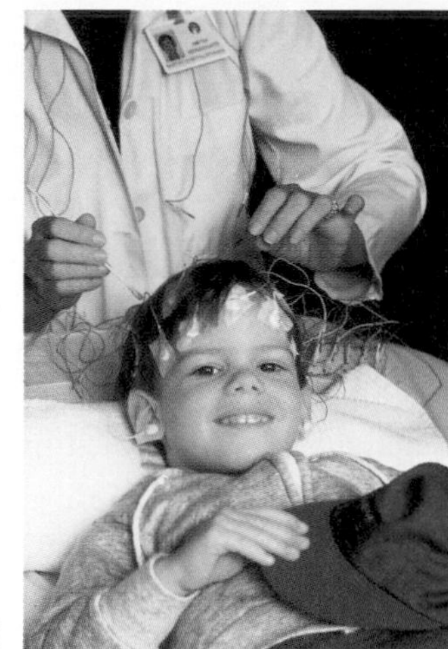

(a)

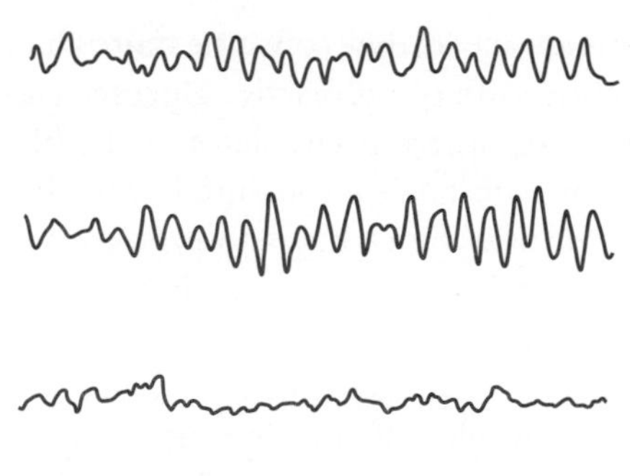

(b)

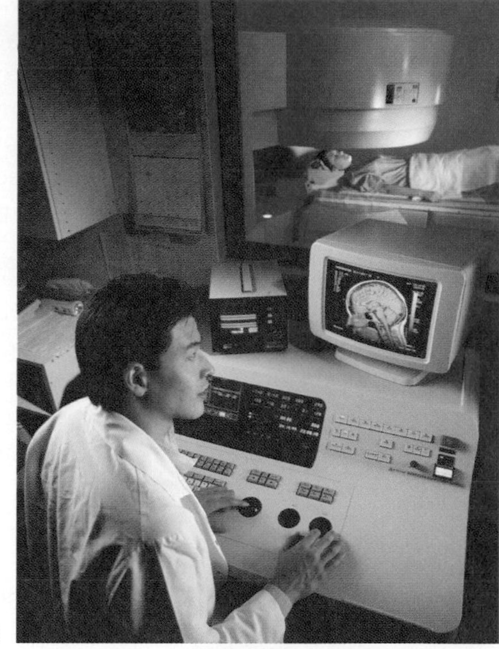

(c)

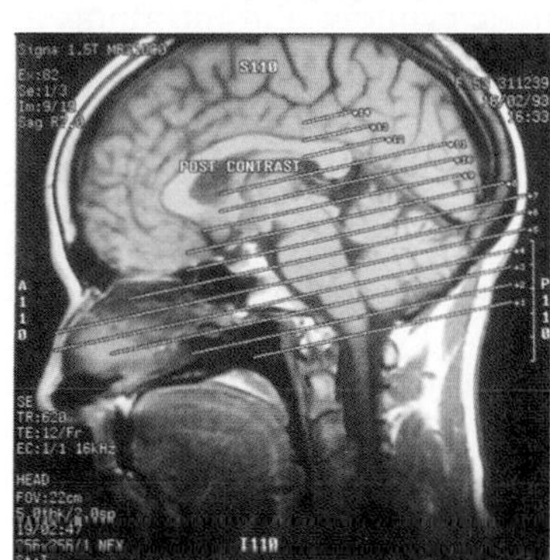

(d)

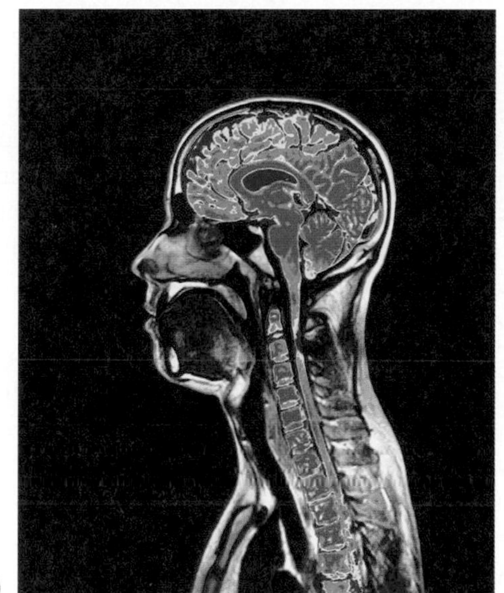

(e)

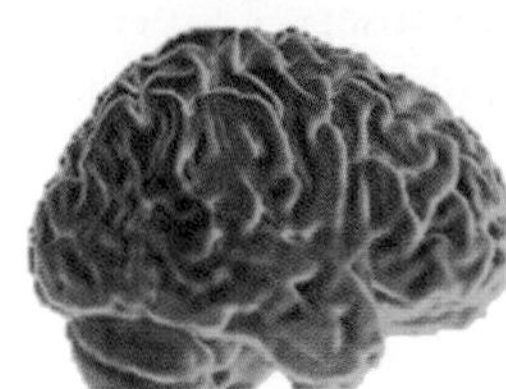

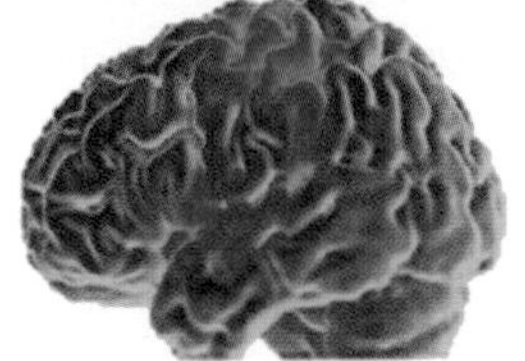

(f)

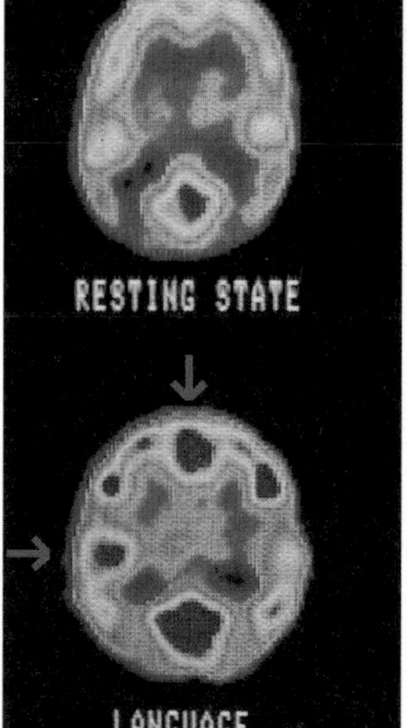

(g)

FIGURE 3.11

Measuring brain activity. (a) The electroencephalogram (EEG) records the activity of large groups of neurons in the brain through a series of electrodes attached to the scalp. (b) The results appear on an EEG readout. (c) Various brain scanning machines, such as the one shown here, produce a number of different images. (d) The CT scan uses narrow beams of X-rays to construct a composite picture of brain structures. (e) MRI scanners produce vivid pictures of brain structures. (f) Functional MRI (fMRI) procedures take images in rapid succession, showing neural activity as it occurs. (g) PET scans record the amount of radioactive substance that collects in various brain regions to assess brain activity.

nological advance was so dramatic that its developers, Allan Cormack and Godfrey Hounsfield, were awarded the 1979 Nobel Prize for Medicine.

Whereas CT scans provide pictures of brain structures, **positron emission tomography (PET)** scans measure brain activity, including metabolism, blood flow, and neurotransmitter activity (Hornak, 2000; Ron & David, 1997). PET is based on the fact that glucose, a natural sugar, is the major nutrient of neurons. Thus, when neurons are active, they consume more glucose. To prepare a patient for a PET scan, a harmless form of radioactive glucose is injected into the bloodstream and travels to the brain, where it circulates in the blood supply. The energy emitted by the radioactive substance is measured by the PET scan, and the data are fed into a computer that uses the readings to produce a colour picture of the brain on a display screen (Figure 3.11c, g). Researchers can tell how active particular neurons are by using the PET scan to measure the amount of radioactive glucose that accumulates in them. If a person is performing a mental reasoning task, for example, a researcher can tell by the glucose concentration pattern which parts of the brain were activated by the task (Raichle, 1994). Using the PET scan, brain activity can be studied in relation to cognitive processes, behaviour, and even forms of mental illness.

Magnetic resonance imaging (MRI) combines features of CT and PET scans and can be used to study both brain structures and brain activity (Chakeres, 2000). MRI creates images based on how atoms in living tissue respond to a magnetic pulse delivered by the device. MRI can make out details one-tenth the size that can be detected by CT scans, and it distinguishes much better between different types of brain tissue (Leondes, 1997). To obtain an MRI, the part of the body to be studied is placed in the hollow core of a long magnetic cylinder and the atoms in the subject's body are exposed to a uniform magnetic field. The field is then altered, and when the magnetic field is shut off, the magnetic energy absorbed by the atoms in the tissue emits a small electrical voltage. The voltage is picked up by detectors and relayed to a computer for analysis. In addition to providing colour images of the tissue, MRI also can tell researchers which chemicals (such as neurotransmitters) are active in the tissue (Figure 3.11e).

The conventional MRI yields pictures taken several minutes apart. A *functional MRI (FMRI)* can produce pictures of blood flow in the brain taken less than a second apart (Baert et al., 1999). Researchers now, quite literally, can watch "live" presentations as different regions of the brain "light up" when subjects are given various types of tasks to perform. Researchers thereby can identify brain regions involved in specific psychological functions (Figure 3.11f).

Advances in brain research have made this area one of the most exciting frontiers of psychology. Driven by its intense desire to "know thyself," the brain is beginning to yield its many secrets. Yet many important questions remain. This should not surprise us, for, as one observer noted, "If the brain were so simple that we could understand it, we would be so simple that we couldn't" (Pugh, 1977).

In Review

- *The nervous system is composed of sensory neurons, motor neurons, and interneurons (associative neurons). Its two major divisions are the central nervous system, consisting of the brain and spinal cord, and the peripheral nervous system. The latter is divided into the somatic system, which has sensory and motor functions, and the autonomic nervous system, which directs the activity of the body's internal organs and glands.*
- *The spinal cord contains sensory neurons and motor neurons. Interneurons inside the spinal cord serve a connective function between the two. Simple stimulus-response connections can occur as spinal reflexes.*
- *The autonomic nervous system consists of sympathetic and parasympathetic divisions. The sympathetic system has an arousal function and tends to act as a unit. The parasympathetic system slows down body processes and is more specific in its actions. Together, the two divisions maintain a state of internal balance, or homeostasis.*
- *Discoveries about brain-behaviour relations are made using techniques such as neuropsychological tests, lesioning and surgical ablation, electrical and chemical stimulation of the brain, electrical recording, and brain-imaging techniques. Recently developed methods for producing computer-generated pictures of structures and processes within the living brain include CT and PET scans and magnetic resonance imaging (MRI).*

RESEARCH FOUNDATIONS

Wilder Penfield and a Cortical Map

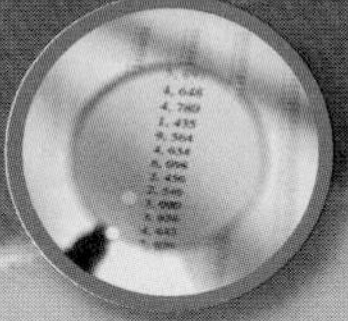

The idea that specific behaviours could be traced to specific brain areas emerged during the nineteenth century. The physiologists Gustav Fritsch and Eduard Hitzig found that electrical stimulation of discrete areas of a dog brain would reliably produce movements. The English neurologist John Hughlings Jackson published a series of papers detailing his observations of the behaviour of patients with brain damage. Paul Broca and Carl Wernicke found that damage to specific parts of the cerebral cortex were associated with specific language deficits. Such seminal work suggested that you could trace different functions, even sophisticated functions such as the ability to produce or comprehend language, to specific brain areas. The brain, it seemed, could be studied and understood much the way any other internal organ could be studied and understood.

Early in the twentieth century, however, progress in understanding brain function within psychology slowed as behaviourism became the dominant orientation. Within psychology, the early and mid-twentieth century saw the work of Edward L. Thorndike, Ivan Pavlov, John B. Watson, and then B.F. Skinner gain prominence. Learning was king; it was learning, not brain structure, that determined what a person would become and do, learning was what turned one person into an artist and another into a thief. Furthermore, the behaviourists argued that psychology, as a science, should study only what was objectively observable: behaviour. According to the behaviourists, you could not tell, figuratively or literally, what was going on inside of someone's head. But then a series of publications by a neurosurgeon rocked the field. The behaviourists had said that you could not study what was going on in the brain, but a neurosurgeon at the Montreal Neurological Institute was doing exactly that. The neurosurgeon Wilder Penfield was studying scientifically the functions of specific areas of the brain with awake and alert surgical patients.

Penfield worked mostly with patients who suffered from severe, uncontrollable epilepsy, and his task as a surgeon was to remove the damaged brain tissue that was responsible for the epileptic seizures. Since there are no pain receptors within the CNS, a patient could have local anesthetics applied to the scalp and remain awake and alert during surgery without experiencing any undue discomfort. With the cooperation of such patients, Penfield explored the effects of small levels of electrical current applied to specific points on the surface of the cerebral cortex (Figure 3.12). Since the patients were fully conscious, they could describe and explain what they experienced during the procedure. Penfield performed brain surgery in this way primarily because the knowledge gained helped to guide his hand as a surgeon. As Penfield wrote, "The patient continued to be in the foreground of my concern, but in the background there was an urge to exploration" (Penfield, 1975, Preface IX).

For many years Penfield systematically explored the effects of brain stimulation over large areas of the cerebral cortex. Much of his early work concentrated on areas surrounding the central sulcus, the large fold separating the frontal cortex and the parietal cortex. Stimulation in front of this fold, in the frontal cortex, produced movement, and the movement produced was reliably related to the specific part of the cortex stimulated. For example, stimulation deep within the fold elicited movement of the toes and feet, while stimulation to the side elicited movement of the face, mouth, or tongue. Stimulation behind the fold, in the parietal cortex, produced no movement, but rather patients reported somatic sensory experiences, such as a light touch, a brush, or an itch. The effects were repeatable and consistent across different patients. Wilder Penfield mapped the body onto the brain and his work produced the first functional maps of the motor cortex and sensory cortex (similar to the ones in Figure 3.17).

If Penfield had mapped only motor cortex and somatosensory cortex, his contribution to understanding the human brain would have been substantial, but Penfield also explored other areas of cortex, as guided by the surgical situation. Here, now, were reports not just of motor control and experiencing sensations of touch, but reports from patients of smelling roses, hearing voices, and recalling memories from

FIGURE 3.12
Internationally renowned Montreal neurologist, Wilder Penfield.

–Continued

their past—experiences likened to déjà vu elicited by mild electrical stimulation of the brain. In describing the reports of one patient, known as D.F., Penfield wrote, "D.F. could hear the instruments playing a melody. I re-stimulated the same point thirty times (!) trying to mislead her, and dictated each response to a stenographer. Each time I re-stimulated, she heard the melody again" (Penfield, 1975, p. 22). Another patient, M.M., reported somatic sensations, such as a tingling in the left thumb in response to stimulation at one point, but in response to stimulation of the temporal lobe there were memories, or parts of memories, "activations of the stream of consciousness from the past" (Penfield, 1975, p. 24). The reports of memories were reliable within the same patient, but less consistent across patients than the motor and somatosensory effects. In a minority of cases, the stimulation elicited unequivocal reports of memories or complex experiences such as hearing music, but in most cases, there was no subjective experience or only something vague and poorly defined.

Wilder Penfield mapped the body onto the brain for motor control and the sense of touch, and provided early tantalizing hints about the functions of the temporal lobes. In the decades since Penfield performed surgery, our interpretation of his results has grown increasingly sophisticated and our tools more elaborate and less invasive, although similar cortical mapping is still used. Our modern understanding of the cerebral cortex, like modern neurosurgery, owes a great deal to the pioneering work of Wilder Penfield.

The Hierarchical Brain: Structures and Behavioural Functions

16. In what sense might the structure of the human brain mirror evolutionary development?

In an evolutionary sense, your brain is far older than you are, for it represents perhaps 500 million years of evolutionary development and fine tuning (Roth, 2000). The human brain can be likened to a living archaeological site, with the more recently developed structures built atop structures from the distant evolutionary past. The structures at the brain's core govern the basic physiological functions, such as breathing and heart rate, that keep us alive. These we share with all other vertebrates (animals having backbones). Built upon these basic structures are newer systems that involve progressively more complex functions—sensing, emoting, wanting, thinking, reasoning. Evolutionary theorists believe that as genetic variation and recombination sculpted these newer structures over time, natural selection favoured their retention because animals who had them were more likely to survive in changing environments. The crowning feature of brain development is the cerebrum, the biological seat of Einstein's scientific genius, Mozart's creativity, Mother Teresa's compassion, and that which makes you a unique human being.

The major structures of the human brain, together with their psychological functions, are shown in Figure 3.13. The brain traditionally has been divided into three major subdivisions: the hindbrain, which is the lowest and most primitive level of the brain; the midbrain, which lies above the hindbrain; and the forebrain.

The Hindbrain

17. Which behavioural functions are controlled by the hindbrain structures, namely, the medulla, the pons, and the cerebellum? What occurs with damage to these structures?

As the spinal cord enters the brain, it enlarges to form the structures that compose the stalklike **brain stem**. Attached to the brain stem is the other major portion of the hindbrain, the cerebellum.

The brain stem: life support systems. The medulla is the first structure encountered after leaving the spinal cord. Well developed at birth, the 3.8 centimetre-long **medulla** plays an important role in vital body functions such as heart rate and respiration. Because of your medulla, these functions occur automatically. Damage to the medulla usually results in death or, at best, the need to be maintained on life support systems. Suppression of medulla activity can occur at high levels of alcohol intoxication, resulting in death by heart or respiratory failure (Blessing, 1997).

The medulla is also a two-way thoroughfare for all the sensory and motor nerve tracts coming up from the spinal cord and descending from the brain. Most

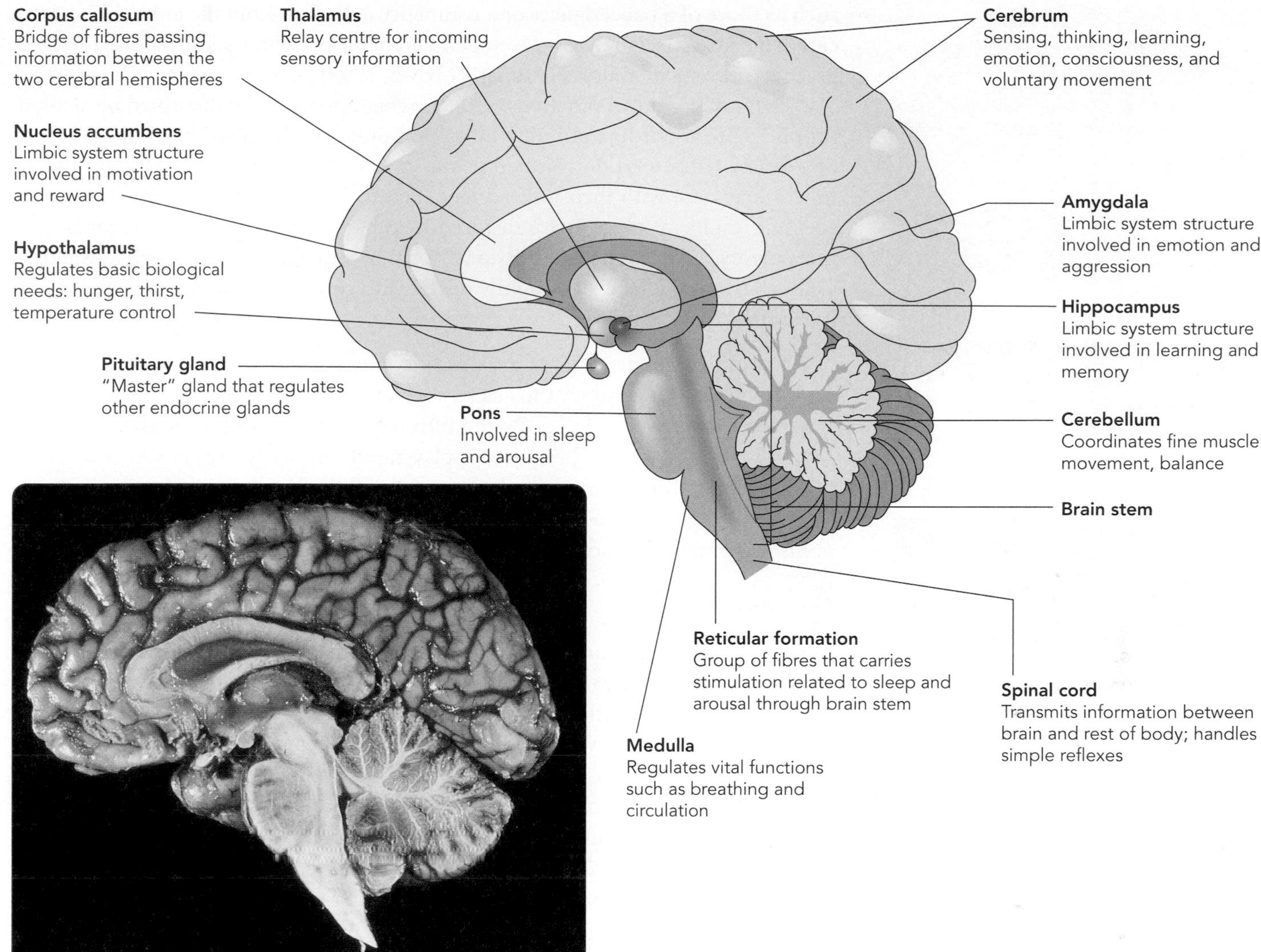
Corpus callosum
Bridge of fibres passing information between the two cerebral hemispheres
Thalamus
Relay centre for incoming sensory information
Cerebrum
Sensing, thinking, learning, emotion, consciousness, and voluntary movement
Nucleus accumbens
Limbic system structure involved in motivation and reward
Amygdala
Limbic system structure involved in emotion and aggression
Hypothalamus
Regulates basic biological needs: hunger, thirst, temperature control
Hippocampus
Limbic system structure involved in learning and memory
Pituitary gland
"Master" gland that regulates other endocrine glands
Pons
Involved in sleep and arousal
Cerebellum
Coordinates fine muscle movement, balance
Brain stem
Reticular formation
Group of fibres that carries stimulation related to sleep and arousal through brain stem
Spinal cord
Transmits information between brain and rest of body; handles simple reflexes
Medulla
Regulates vital functions such as breathing and circulation

FIGURE 3.13

The major structures of the brain and their functions are shown as they would appear if the brain was sectioned at its midline, as in the photo.

of these tracts cross over within the medulla, so the left side of the brain receives sensory input from and exerts motor control over the right side of the body, and the right side of the brain serves the left side of the body. Why this crossover occurs is one of the unsolved mysteries of brain function.

The **pons** (meaning *bridge* in Latin) lies just above the medulla, and it indeed serves as a bridge carrying nerve impulses between higher and lower levels of the nervous system. The pons also has clusters of neurons that help regulate sleep and are involved in dreaming, and it contains motor neurons that control the muscles and glands of the face and neck. Like the medulla, the pons helps to control vital functions, especially respiration, and damage to it can produce death.

The cerebellum: motor coordination centre. The cerebellum ("little brain" in Latin) does indeed look like a miniature brain attached to the rear of the brain stem directly above the pons. Its wrinkled cortex, or covering, consists mainly of grey cell bodies (grey matter). The **cerebellum** is concerned primarily with muscular movement coordination, but it also plays a role in certain types of learning and memory. ← + Balance

Specific motor movements are initiated in higher brain centres, but their timing and coordination depend on the cerebellum (Thatch et al., 1992). The cerebellum regulates complex, rapidly changing movements that require exquisite timing,

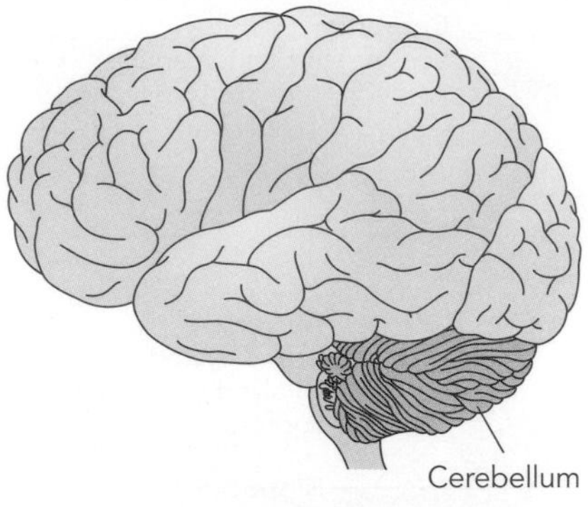

FIGURE 3.14

The movement-control functions of the cerebellum are easily disrupted by alcohol, providing the neural basis for the sobriety tests administered by police.

such as those of a ballet dancer or a competitive diver. Within the animal kingdom, cats have an especially well-developed cerebellum, helping to account for their graceful movement abilities (Altman & Bayer, 1996).

The motor control functions of the cerebellum are easily disrupted by alcohol, producing the coordination difficulties that police look for in their roadside tests of sobriety (Ito, 1984). Intoxicated people may be unable to walk a straight line or touch their nose with their index finger (Figure 3.14). Physical damage to the cerebellum results in severe motor disturbances characterized by jerky, uncoordinated movements, as well as an inability to perform habitual movements such as walking. The behavioural effects of a rapidly developing cerebellar tumour are apparent in the following clinical case:

> Ed could no longer walk a straight line. His gait involved wide separation of his legs. The timing of his steps was jerky and irregular, causing him to lurch from side to side.... By the fifth day he could no longer stand without assistance, and he began to display rapid and jerky eye movements. Ed was admitted to a hospital, where imaging techniques revealed a cerebellar tumor. Surgical removal of the tumor resulted in a marked improvement in his motor coordination. (Gazzaniga et al., 1979)

The Midbrain

Lying just above the hindbrain, the **midbrain** contains clusters of sensory and motor neurons, as well as many sensory and motor fibre tracts that connect higher and lower portions of the nervous system. The sensory portion of the midbrain contains important relay centres for the visual and auditory systems. Here, nerve impulses from the eyes and ears are organized and sent to forebrain structures involved in visual and auditory perception (Kolb & Whishaw, 2003). The midbrain also contains motor neurons that control eye movements. For example, if you see movement out of the corner of your eye, midbrain activity causes your eyes to swing toward the source of the movement in order to identify it.

The reticular formation: the brain's gatekeeper. Buried within the midbrain is a finger-shaped structure that extends from the hindbrain up into the lower portions of the forebrain. This structure receives its name from its resemblance under a microscope to a *reticulum,* or net. The **reticular formation** acts as a kind of sentry, both alerting higher centres of the brain that messages are coming and then either blocking those messages or allowing them to go forward. The reticular formation has an *ascending* part, which sends input to higher regions of the brain to alert it, and a *descending* portion, through which higher brain centres can either admit or block out sensory input.

18. Describe the roles played by the ascending and descending reticular formation. Why is it called the "brain's gatekeeper"?

The reticular formation has attracted a great deal of interest from psychologists because of its central role in consciousness, sleep, and attention. The ascending reticular formation rouses higher centres in the brain, preparing them to receive input from our sense organs. Without reticular stimulation of higher brain regions, sensory messages do not register in conscious awareness even though the nerve impulses may reach the appropriate higher areas of the brain. It is as if the brain is not "awake" enough to notice them. In fact, some general anaesthetics work by deactivating neurons of the ascending reticular formation, producing a state of unconsciousness in which the sensory impulses that ordinarily would be experienced as pain never "register" in the sensory areas of the brain involved in pain perception (Derogatis, 1986).

Sleep, wakefulness, and attention also are affected by the reticular formation. In a classic series of experiments in the late 1940s, researchers discovered that electrical stimulation of different portions of the reticular formation can produce instant sleep in a wakeful cat and sudden wakefulness in a sleeping animal (Moruzzi & Magoun, 1949; Marshall & Magoun, 1997). As you might expect, severe damage to the reticular formation can produce a permanent coma (Roland, 1997).

Attention is an active process in which only important or meaningful sensory inputs get through to our consciousness. Other inputs have to be toned down or completely blocked out or we'd be overwhelmed by stimulation. The descending reticular formation plays an important part in this process, serving as a kind of "gate" through which some inputs are admitted while others are blocked out by signals coming down from higher brain centres (Van Zomeren & Brouwer, 1994). We hope it is operating for you right now, as you focus on these words and "block out" other sights, sounds, and body sensations that could distract you from our messages.

The Forebrain

The most profound biological difference between your brain and that of a lower animal is the size and complexity of your forebrain, or *cerebrum*. The **forebrain** consists of two large cerebral hemispheres, a left side and a right side, that wrap around the brain stem like the two halves of a cut grapefruit might wrap around a spoon. The outer portion of the forebrain has a thin covering, or cortex, and there are a number of important structures buried in the central regions of the hemispheres.

19. What is the role of the thalamus in sensory input, and possibly in thought and perceptual disorders?

The thalamus: the brain's sensory switchboard. The thalamus is located above the midbrain. It resembles two small footballs, one within each cerebral hemisphere. The **thalamus** is an important sensory relay station, sometimes likened to a switchboard that organizes inputs from sense organs and routes them to the appropriate areas of the brain. The visual, auditory, and body senses (balance and equilibrium) all have major relay stations in the thalamus. In each case, nerve tracts from the sensory receptors (e.g., the eyes or the ears) are sent to specific areas of the thalamus. There they synapse with neurons that send the messages on their way to the higher brain regions that create our perceptions (Jones et al., 1997).

Because the thalamus plays such a key role in routing sensory information to higher brain regions, disrupted thalamic functioning can produce a highly confusing world for its victims. In research at the National Institute of Mental Health (NIMH) carried out by Nancy Andreason and her co-workers (1994), MRIs from 39 schizophrenic men were compared to those of 47 normal male volunteers. The brain images showed specific abnormalities in the thalamus of the "schizophrenic" brains. The researchers suggested that malfunctioning in this structure could help to account for the confused thinking and disordered attention that characterize schizophrenic behaviour. Perhaps the thalamus is sending garbled sensory information to the higher regions of the brain. If substantiated by future research, the NIMH discovery may provide increased understanding of this baffling mental disorder.

The basal ganglia: movement Surrounding and enveloping the thalamus is a group of at least five distinct structures that are collectively called the **basal ganglia**. The basal ganglia is critical for voluntary motor control. Whereas the cerebellum is critical for controlling reflexive, automatic, and rapid movements, the basal ganglia plays an important role in the deliberate and voluntary control of movement, especially in initiating voluntary movements. That you can reach out and pick up your coffee mug when you want to indicates that your basal ganglia is functioning. One example that illustrates the role of the basal ganglia is Parkinson's Disease. In Parkinson's Disease, the neurons that supply dopamine to the basal ganglia degenerate and die. Since dopamine is lost from the basal ganglia, the basal ganglia does not function properly, and the ability to initiate voluntary movement is lost. Initially, the signs of Parkinson's Disease are small tremors of the hands and head, but as the basal ganglia loses more and more of its supply of dopamine, the tremors become shaking, then slow and jerky movements, then slow and jerky movements that can be performed only if there is assistance with initiating the movement. There are, for example, many stories from spouses, family, or friends of Parkinson's Disease patients of how the person will stop at a curb or a corner and stay frozen, apparently unable to move, but with a small push to get them started, they will begin walking again. When the basal ganglia has been largely depleted of dopamine and hence does not function, there is complete paralysis. Patients at the advanced stages of Parkinson's Disease cannot move when they want to; they cannot get up from a chair or out of bed or hold a cup or a book. If, however, the movement depends on other, older brain structures, such as the cerebellum, they can perform it.

?

20. What role does the hypothalamus have in motivated behaviour, hunger, pleasure-pain, and hormonal functions?

The hypothalamus: biological drives. The hypothalamus (literally, "under the thalamus") consists of tiny groups of neuron cell bodies that lie at the base of the brain, above the roof of the mouth. The **hypothalamus** plays a major role in controlling many different basic biological drives, including sexual behaviour, temperature regulation, eating, drinking, aggression, and the expression of emotion. Damage to the hypothalamus can disrupt all of these behaviours. For example, destruction of one area of a male's hypothalamus results in a complete loss of sexual behaviour; damage to another portion produces an overwhelming urge to eat that results in extreme obesity. Recently, neuroscientists at the University of Texas Southwestern Medical School found that certain neurons in the hypothalamus manufacture a substance which they called *orexins* (after the Greek word for hunger) that stimulates eating. When they gave orexin to laboratory rats, they ate 8 to 10 times more food than they ordinarily would over a period of hours (Yanagisawa et al., 1998). This discovery holds out the hope that it might be possible to control both undereating (as occurs in some cancer patients) and obesity by producing medicines that either enhance or inhibit orexin activity at the synapses where eating is controlled.

The hypothalamus has important connections with the endocrine system, the body's collection of hormone-producing glands. Through its connection with the pituitary gland (the master gland that exerts control over the other glands of the endocrine system), the hypothalamus directly controls many hormonal secretions that regulate sexual development and behaviour, metabolism, and reactions to stress.

21. What is the possible relation between the hypothalamus and the limbic system regarding emotion and motivation? What roles do the hippocampus and amygdala play in psychological functions?

The limbic system: memory and goal-directed behaviour. As we continue our journey up through the brain, we come to the limbic system, a set of structures lying deep within the cerebral hemispheres. These structures, which are shaped like a wishbone, have an important partnership with the hypothalamus. The **limbic system** helps to coordinate behaviours needed to satisfy motivational and emotional urges that arise in the hypothalamus, and it is also involved in memory. Many instinctive activities in lower animals, such as mating, attacking, feeding, and fleeing from danger appear to be organized by the limbic system (Davis, 1992). Human behaviours are similarly organized into goal-directed sequences. If certain parts of your limbic system were injured, you would be unable to carry out organized sequences of actions to satisfy your needs. A small distraction would make you forget what you had set out to do.

Two key structures in the limbic system are the hippocampus and the amygdala. The **hippocampus** is involved in forming and retrieving memories. Damage to the hippocampus can result in severe memory impairment for recent events, and an inability to transfer information from short-term memory to long-term memory (Scoville & Milner, 1957; Isaacson, 2002). The **amygdala** organizes emotional response patterns, particularly those linked to aggression and fear (LeDoux, 1998). Electrically stimulating certain areas of the amygdala causes animals to snarl and assume aggressive postures (Figure 3.15), whereas stimulation of other areas results in a fearful inability to respond aggressively, even in self-defence. For example, a normally aggressive and hungry cat will cower in fear from a tiny mouse placed in its cage. The amygdala is a key part of a larger control system for anger and fear that also involves other brain regions (Borod, 2000).

An interesting feature of the amygdala is that it can produce emotional responses without the higher centres of the brain "knowing" that we are emotionally aroused. This may provide a possible explanation for clinicians' observations of "unconscious" emotional responses (LeDoux, 1998).

In 1953, James Olds and Peter Milner were conducting an experiment to study the effects of electrical stimulation of the midbrain reticular formation in rats. One of the electrodes missed the target and was mistakenly implanted in the hypothalamus. The investigators noticed that whenever this rat was stimulated, it repeated whatever it had just done, as if it had been rewarded for that behaviour. In a variety of learning situations, other animals with similarly implanted electrodes also learned and performed behaviours in order to receive what was clearly an electrical reward. Some rats would press a lever thousands of times an hour in order to receive the electrical stimulation, and would continue to do so until they dropped from exhaustion. The scientists concluded that they had found the "pleasure centre" in the brain, and that it was in the hypothalamus (Olds, 1958; Olds and Milner, 1954; White & Milner, 1992; Wise, 1996).

Humans who have had electrodes implanted in their brains to search for abnormal brain tissue have reported experiencing pleasure when electrically stimulated in these same brain regions (Heath, 1972). One patient reportedly proposed marriage to the experimenter while being so stimulated. Thus, a misplaced electrode led to a discovery that neural events have important roles in motivation, and suggested that the hypothalamus was the brain area critical for motivation and reward.

Research since that time, however, has changed one important conclusion of Olds and Milner: The brain area critical for reward and motivation is not in the hypothalamus after all. Electrical stimulation applied to the hypothalamus does activate neurons within the hypothalamus, but it also activates axons that are passing through the hypothalamus on their way to other brain areas. More recent research has found that it is a collection of axons that passes through the hypothalamus that is important for the effects of Olds and Milner's electrical simulation, not the neurons of the hypothalamus itself. Electrical stimulation of the hypothalamus activates axons that are going from neuron cell bodies in the midbrain to a limbic structure called the **nucleus accumbens**, and it is the nucleus accumbens that is important for reward and motivation (Wise, 1996; Wise & Rompre,

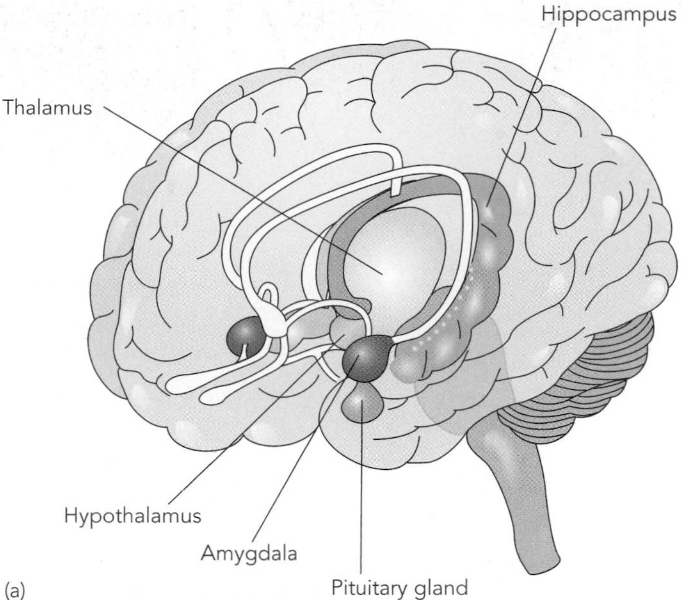

FIGURE 3.15

The limbic system structures are shown in (a). Electrical stimulation of the amygdala, as in (b), can produce an immediate aggressive response.

1989). For example, Roy Wise, of Concordia University in Montreal, has shown that the reward value of electrical stimulation of the hypothalamus can be either amplified or diminished by drugs that enhance or block, respectively, dopamine actions within the nucleus accumbens (Wise, 2004). This brain area, the nucleus accumbens, has also been linked to the rewarding and motivating effects of drugs of abuse. Drugs of abuse such as cocaine, amphetamines, opiates, nicotine, and alcohol, all stimulate the release of dopamine in the nucleus accumbens of the limbic system (LeMoal, 1999; Wise, 1996). Other researchers, such as Alain Gratton of McGill University, have found that naturally occurring rewards such as food, sexually relevant cues, and sexual behaviour also lead to the release of dopamine from axon terminals in the nucleus accumbens (Hernandez & Hoebel, 1988; Mitchell & Gratton, 1991; Phillips, et al., 1992). Interestingly, Alain Gratton has shown that not only do drugs of abuse and preferred foods activate the nucleus accumbens, but that cues that reliably predict the arrival of drugs or food have a similar effect (Gratton & Wise, 1994; Kiyatkin & Gratton, 1994). Thus, Olds and Milner seem to have been correct in arguing that the brain contains a specific area that is critical for motivation and reward, but it is part of the limbic system, not the hypothalamus.

The Cerebral Cortex: Crown of the Brain

The **cerebral cortex**, a two-thirds centimetre-thick sheet of grey (unmyelinated) cells that form the outermost layer of the human brain, is the crowning achievement of brain evolution. Fish and amphibians have no cerebral cortex, and the progression from more primitive to more advanced mammals is marked by a dramatic increase in the proportion of cortical tissue. In humans, the cortex constitutes fully 80 percent of brain tissue (Kolb & Whishaw, 2003).

The cerebral cortex is not essential for physical survival in the way that the brain stem structures are, but it is essential for a human quality of living. How much so is evident in this description of patients who, as a result of an accident during prenatal development, were born without a cerebral cortex:

> Some of these individuals may survive for years, in one case of mine for twenty years. From these cases, it appears that the human [lacking a cortex] sleeps and wakes; . . . reacts to hunger, loud sounds, and crude visual stimuli by movement of eyes, eyelids, and facial muscles; . . . may see and hear, . . . may be able to taste and smell, to reject the unpalatable and accept such food as it likes. . . . [They can] utter crude sounds, can cry and smile, showing displeasure when hungry and pleasure, in a babyish way, when being sung to; [they] may be able to perform spontaneously crude [limb] movements. (Cairns, 1952, p. 109)

Because the cortex is wrinkled and convoluted, like a wadded-up piece of paper, a great amount of cortical tissue is compressed into a relatively small space inside the skull. Perhaps 75 percent of the cortex's total surface area lies within its *fissures,* or canyonlike folds. Three of these fissures are important landmarks. One large fissure runs up the front and along the top of the brain, dividing it into right and left hemispheres. Another major fissure within each hemisphere divides the cerebrum into front and rear halves, and the third fissure runs from front to rear along the side of the brain. On the basis of these landmarks, neurologists have divided each hemisphere into four lobes: **frontal**, **parietal**, **occipital**, and **temporal** (Figure 3.16).

22. What are the four lobes of the brain, and where are they located?

Each of the four cerebral lobes is associated with particular sensory and motor functions (also shown in Figure 3.16). Speech and skeletal motor functions are localized in the frontal lobe. The area governing body sensations is located in the parietal

FIGURE 3.16

Division of the brain into frontal, parietal, occipital, and temporal lobes, and localization of sensory and motor functions in the cortex. The remainder is primarily association cortex, consisting of interneurons involved in complex psychological functions, such as perception and reasoning.

lobe immediately behind the *central fissure*, which separates the frontal and parietal lobes. The brain's visual area is located in the occipital lobe at the back of the brain. Finally, messages from the auditory system are sent to a region in the top of the temporal lobe (Robinson, 1997). The large areas in Figure 3.16 that are not associated with sensory or motor functions (about three-fourths of the cortex) are *association cortex*, involved in mental processes such as thought, memory, and perception.

Most sensory systems send information to specific regions of the cerebral cortex. Motor systems that control the activity of skeletal muscles are situated in other cortical regions. The basic organization of the cortex's sensory and motor areas is quite similar in all mammals, from rats to humans. Let us explore these regions more closely.

23. Differentiate between sensory, motor, and association cortex.

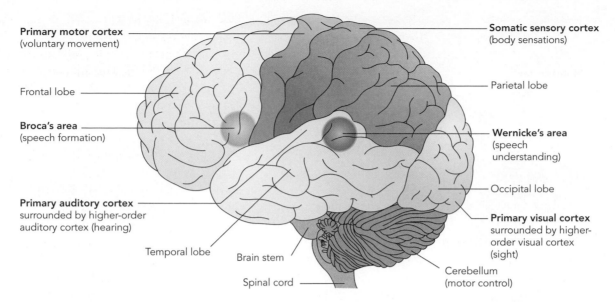

The motor cortex. The **motor cortex**, which controls the 600 or more muscles involved in voluntary body movements, lies at the rear of the frontal lobe adjacent to the central fissure. Each hemisphere governs movement on the opposite side of the body. Thus severe damage to the right motor cortex would produce paralysis in the left side of the body. The left side of Figure 3.17 shows the relative organization of function within the motor cortex. As you can see, specific body areas are represented in different parts of the motor cortex, and the amount of cortex devoted to each area depends on the complexity of the movements that are carried out by the body part. Note, for example, that the amount of cortical tissue devoted to your fingers is far greater than that devoted to your torso, even though your torso is much larger. If we electrically stimulate a particular point on the motor cortex, movements occur in the muscles governed by that part of the cortex.

24. How are the somatic sensory and motor cortexes organized?

The sensory cortex. Specific areas of the cortex receive input from our sensory receptors. With the exception of taste and smell, at least one specific area in the cortex has been identified for each of the senses.

The **somatic sensory cortex** receives sensory input that gives rise to our sensations of heat, touch, cold, and our senses of balance and body movement (kinesthesis). It lies in the parietal lobe just behind the motor cortex, separated from it by the large fissure that divides the frontal lobe from the parietal lobe. As in the case of the motor system, each side of the body sends sensory input to the opposite hemisphere. Like the motor area next to it, the somatic sensory area is basically organized in an upside-down fashion, with the feet being represented near the top of

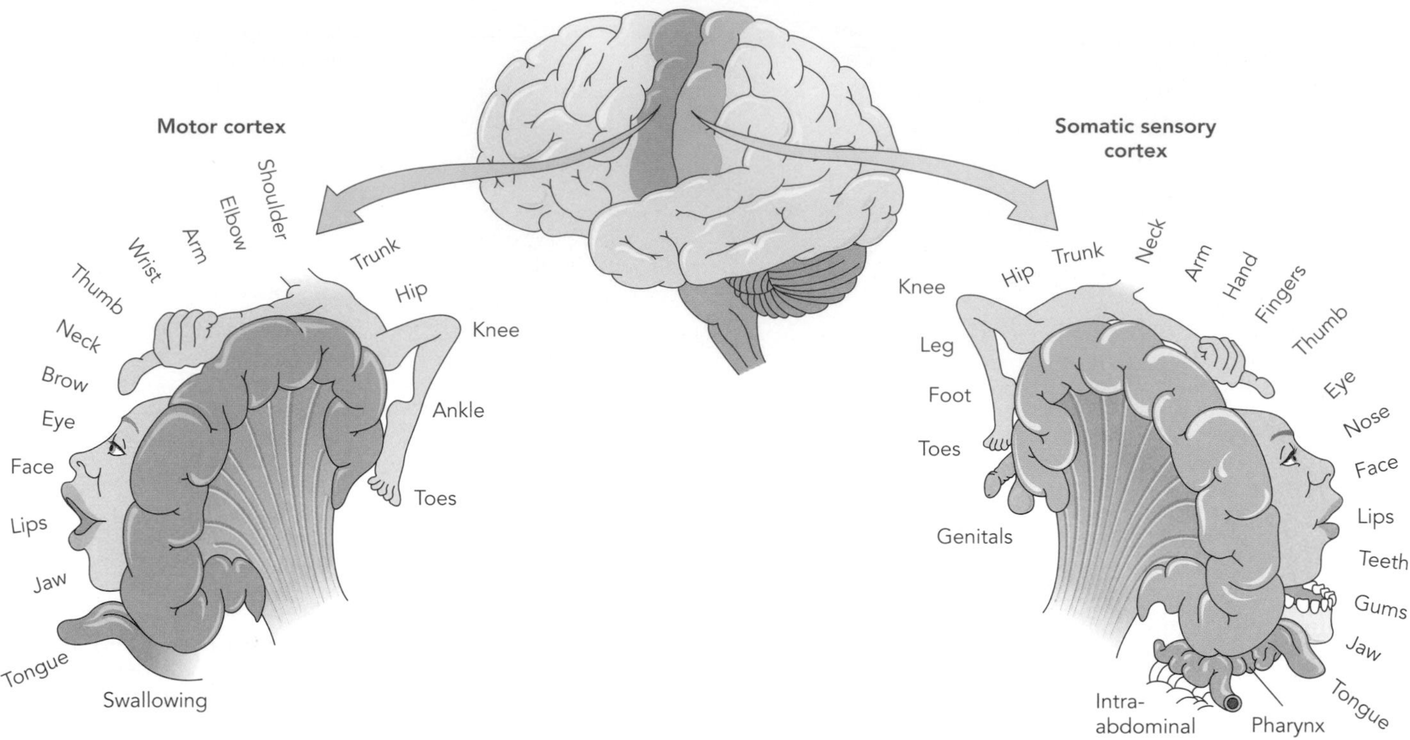

FIGURE 3.17

Both the somatic sensory and the motor cortex are highly specialized so that every site is associated with a particular part of the body. The amount of cortex devoted to each body part is proportional to the sensitivity of that area's motor or sensory functions. Both the sensory and motor cortex are arranged in an upside-down fashion and serve the opposite side of the body.

the brain. Likewise, the amount of cortex devoted to each body area is directly proportional to that region's sensory sensitivity. The organization of the sensory cortex is shown on the right side of Figure 3.17, as is the proportion of cortex devoted to each body area. As far as your sensory cortex is concerned, you are mainly fingers, lips, and tongue. Notice also that the organization of the sensory cortex is such that the body structures it serves lie side by side with those in the motor cortex, an arrangement that enhances sensory-motor interactions in the same body area.

FOCUS ON NEUROSCIENCE

The Neuroscience of the World Around You

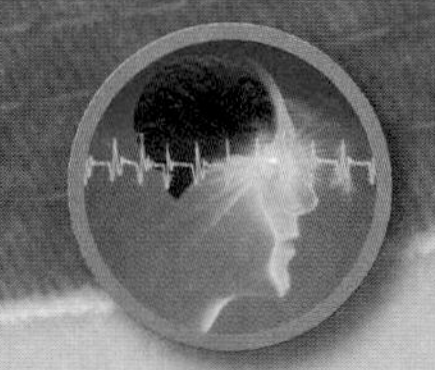

You are sitting at your desk and in front of you there is a bottle of water and a pen. You easily recognize each of these items and have no difficulty picking up the water bottle to have a drink, replacing it, and then picking up the pen to make notes. To do these simple tasks your brain is making a series of complex calculations so that you can recognize what is in front of you and use visual information to guide the shape and movement of your hand. When you reach for your water bottle or pen, you need to reach a specific distance; otherwise you will knock them away or grasp only air. The shape and orientation of your hand also changes. When you reach for the water bottle your hand is shaped so that your thumb will fall along one side of the bottle and your fingers along the other side, with your hand open only slightly larger than the width of the bottle. When you reach for the pen your thumb and fingers are close together and your hand is turned at an angle. We perform such actions many times every day, recognizing objects and reaching the correct distance for them with our hands formed in a way that matches the size and shape of the object. Although this is a simple routine for you, this is not the case for everyone.

In the early 1990s Melvyn Goodale of the University of Western Ontario and his co-workers reported the intriguing case of a woman known as D.F. (Goodale et al., 1991; Goodale & Milner, 1992). D.F. did not consciously recognize objects and when shown even simple objects she could not describe their size, shape, or orientation. Indeed, D.F. had no subjective experience of seeing and considered herself blind. When D.F. was asked to reach for and pick up these objects, however, she was as accurate as normal subjects. How could she pick up something that she was not aware of seeing? Such intriguing findings, together with the results of early imaging studies, led Goodale and colleagues to propose that visual information is divided into two paths, or streams, within the human cortex, and that each stream serves a different function. They proposed that when visual information leaves the primary visual cortex of the occipital lobe it goes in two directions. One stream travels upwards towards and into the parietal lobe. They called this the dorsal stream because this is towards the top, or dorsal, part of the brain. Visual information also travels from the visual cortex along the lower, or ventral, part of the cortex into the temporal lobe, the ventral stream (see Figure 3.18). D.F., they argued, could use visual information to guide her movements because that stream was intact, but did not have the conscious experience of seeing because that stream was not intact.

A recent study by Kenneth Valyear, Jodi Culham, and Melvyn Goodale of the University of Western Ontario together with Nadder Sharif of McGill University and David Westwood of Dalhousie University illustrates the different functions of the dorsal and ventral streams (Valyear, Culham, Sharif, Westwood, & Goodale, 2006). They used functional magnetic resonance imaging (fMRI) to measure brain activity when participants were presented with pairs of shapes. Participants first saw a picture of an everyday object and then, after a brief delay, they saw the same picture, the same object rotated to point in a different direction, a new object aligned like the first, or a new object in a new orientation (see Figure 3.18). As participants looked at these objects, measures of brain activity were obtained using fMRI. That is, they measured changes in brain activity related to recognizing a new object versus changes in activity elicited by having to process spatial orientation to an already seen object or to something new. Consistent with earlier studies, such as the case of D.F., they found that areas within the dorsal stream increased their activity in response to a change in object orientation while areas within the ventral stream increased their activity only when the identity of the object changed. When you move your water bottle the dorsal stream becomes active to process the change, and you use information from the dorsal stream to guide your movements. The ventral stream allows you to recognize an object, but does not process information about where that object is or how it is oriented. For the ventral stream, a water bottle is a water bottle regardless of how it is moved or rotated.

Seeing, recognizing, and then interacting with the objects around you is a seemingly simple task and it is one that you perform with no conscious effort. To recognize and reach for your water bottle, however, requires processing of visual information in two separate ways. Processing within the dorsal stream informs you of the size and orientation of the object and you use this information to guide movements, such as grasping the object. Processing within the ventral stream allows you to recognize the object and provides the conscious experience of seeing.

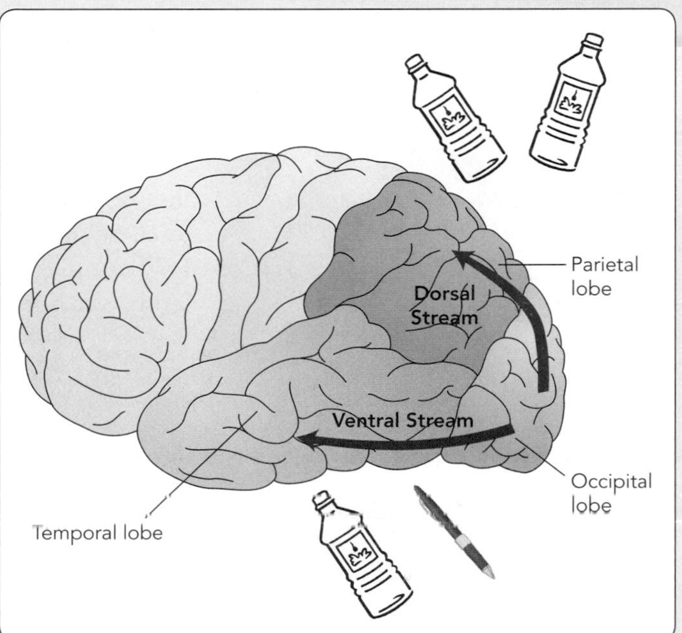

FIGURE 3.18

Information from the primary visual cortex in the occipital lobe travels along the dorsal stream to the parietal lobe. The dorsal stream provides a representation of an object's size and orientation in space and this helps to guide movements directed towards the object. The dorsal stream becomes active if orientation changes, whether the person is viewing the same object or a different object. Visual information also travels along the ventral stream to the temporal lobe. The ventral stream serves functions related to object recognition. The ventral stream becomes active when a new object is shown, regardless of its orientation.

The senses of hearing and sight are well represented in the cortex. The auditory area lies on the surface of the temporal lobe at the side of each hemisphere. Each ear sends messages to the auditory areas of both hemispheres, so the loss of one temporal lobe has little effect on hearing. The major sensory area for vision lies at the rear of the occipital lobe. Here messages from the visual receptors are analyzed, integrated, and translated into sight. As in the auditory system, each eye sends input to both hemispheres.

Within each sensory area, neurons respond to particular aspects of the sensory stimulus; they are tuned in to specific aspects of the environment. Thus certain cells in the visual cortex fire only when we look at a particular kind of stimulus, such as a vertical line or a corner (Hubel & Wiesel, 1979). In the auditory cortex, some neurons fire only in response to high tones, whereas others respond only to tones having some other specific frequency. Many of these single-cell responses are present at birth, suggesting that we are "pre-wired" to perceive many aspects of our sensory environment (Shair et al., 1991). Nonetheless, the sensory cortex, like other parts of the brain, is also sensitive to experience. For example, when people learn to read Braille, the area in the sensory cortex that receives input from the fingertips increases in size, making the person more sensitive to the tiny sets of raised dots (Pool, 1994).

The representation of the body along the somatosensory cortex shown in Figure 3-17 has the head oriented with the top of the face towards the top of the cortex and the chin lower down the side of the cortex. Philip Servos of Wilfrid Laurier University, together with colleagues at the University of California and the Robarts Research Institute of the University of Western Ontario, have provided evidence that this well-known representation may be wrong. Using fMRI measurements, Servos and colleagues found that stimulation of the chin increased activity within the somatosensory cortex towards the top of the head, while stimulation of the forehead increased activity near the lower part of the somatosensory cortex (Servis, Engel, Gati, & Menon, 1999). That is, the representation of the face in the somatosensory cortex may be upside down, with the chin towards the top. This would better align the head with the rest of the body since an upside-down representation of the head within the somatosensory cortex would place the chin nearer the neck and shoulders.

25. Where are Wernicke's and Broca's areas? How are they involved in speech?

Speech comprehension and production. Two specific areas that govern the understanding and production of speech are also located in the cortex (Figure 3.19). **Wernicke's area** in the temporal lobe is involved in language comprehension. The area is named for Carl Wernicke, who in 1874 discovered that damage to this cortical region left patients unable to understand written or spoken speech. **Broca's area** in the frontal lobe is necessary for normal speech production. The neural circuits in and around Broca's area are important for the ability to perform the sequences of fine motor movements needed to speak, and are involved in the abilities to use grammar and find the correct word (Saffrar, Schwartz, & Martin, 1980; Damasio, 1989). Its discoverer, Paul Broca, found that damage to this frontal area left patients with the ability to comprehend speech but not to express themselves in words or sentences. These two speech areas normally work in concert when you are conversing with another person. They allow you to comprehend what the other person is saying and to express your own thoughts (Werker & Tees, 1992). In this example, input is sent from the ears to the auditory cortex and is routed to Wernicke's area for comprehension. When you decide to reply, nerve impulses are sent from Wernicke's area to Broca's area, and impulses passed on from Broca's area to the motor cortex result in the mouthing of a verbal response. This sequence illustrates a key action principle of brain functioning: Even relatively simple acts usually involve the coordinated action of several brain regions.

Broca's area Formulates a speech response and stimulates motor cortex
Motor cortex Stimulates muscles that produce speech
Wernicke's area Processes incoming speech and comprehends it

FIGURE 3.19

Cortical areas involved in language. Wernicke's area is important in the comprehension of spoken or written speech. Broca's area is involved in the production of speech, and the motor cortex stimulates the speech production muscles.

Association cortex. **Association cortex**, found within all lobes of the cerebral cortex, is critically involved in the highest level of mental functions, including perception, language, and thought. These areas are sometimes referred to as "silent areas" because electrically stimulating them does not give rise to either sensory experiences or motor responses. This fact has probably helped promote the widely cited myth that most humans use only 10 percent of their brain power. Nothing could be farther from the truth.

26. What is the role of association cortex, the "silent areas"?

Damage to specific parts of the association cortex causes disruption or loss of functions such as speech, understanding, thinking, and problem solving. As we might expect, since the association cortex is involved in higher mental processes, the amount of association cortex increases dramatically as we move up the brain ladder from lower animals to human beings. It constitutes about 75 percent of the human cerebral cortex and accounts for humans' superior cognitive abilities. Our mass of association cortex has been described by one scientist as "evolution's missing link" (Skoyles, 1997). He suggests that its mental flexibility and learning capacity have allowed us to upgrade our cognitive skills and to acquire new mental skills specific to our human way of life, such as reading and mathematics, more quickly than could have occurred through natural selection alone. Pioneering work on how such activity is represented within the cortex was done by D.O. Hebb of McGill University (see Figure 3-20).

The importance of association cortex is demonstrated in people who suffer from *agnosia*, the inability to identify familiar objects. One such case is described by the neurologist Oliver Sacks (1985) in the opening to this chapter. Dr. P. had suffered brain damage that left him unable to relate the information sent to the visual cortex to information stored in other cortical areas that concerned the nature of objects. The associative neurons responsible for linking the two types of information no longer served him.

27. Describe the role of the frontal cortex in higher mental (including "executive") functions

The frontal lobes: the human difference. Some neuroscientists have suggested that the entire period of human evolutionary existence could well be termed the "age of the frontal lobe" (Krasnegor et al., 1997). This mass of cortex residing behind our eyes and forehead hardly exists in mammals such as mice and rats. The frontal lobes constitute about 3.5 percent of the cerebral cortex in the cat, 7 percent in the dog, and 17 percent in the chimpanzee. In a human, the frontal lobes constitute 29 percent of the cortex. The site of such human qualities as self-awareness, planning, initiative, and responsibility, the frontal lobes are in some respects the most mysterious and least understood part of the brain.

Much of what we know about the frontal lobes comes from detailed studies of patients who have experienced brain damage, such as the pioneering studies performed by Brenda Milner of McGill University. Frontal lobe damage results not so much in a loss of intellectual abilities as in a loss of the ability to plan and carry out a sequence of actions, and judge the order in which a series of events has occurred or will occur in the future (Milner, Petrides, & Smith, 1985).

The frontal cortex is also involved in emotional experience. In people with normal brains, PET scans show increased activity in the frontal cortex when these people are experiencing feelings of happiness, sadness, or disgust (Lane et al., 1997). In contrast, patients with frontal lobe damage often exhibit attitudes of apathy and lack of concern. They literally don't seem to care about anything.

A region of the frontal lobe known as the prefrontal cortex has received increasing attention in recent years. The **prefrontal cortex**, located just behind the forehead, is the seat of the so-called executive functions. *Executive functions*, mental abilities involving goal setting, judgment, strategic planning, and impulse control, allow people to direct their behaviour in an adaptive fashion. Deficits in executive functions seem to underlie a number of problem behaviours. People with

(a)

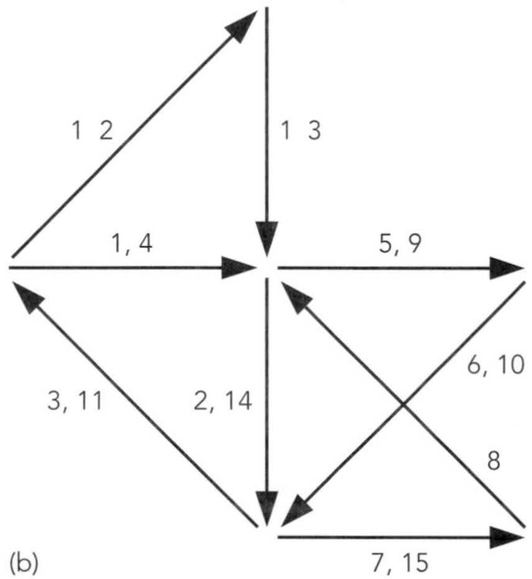

(b)

FIGURE 3.20

Donald Olding Hebb (1904–1985) was one of the towering figures in psychology and neuroscience during the twentieth century. A native of Chester, Nova Scotia, Hebb received his undergraduate education at Dalhousie University and his Ph.D. at Harvard. After brief periods at the Montreal Neurological Institute, Queen's University, and the Yerkes Laboratory of Primate Biology, Hebb accepted a position at McGill University where he published an enormously influential book, The Organization of Behavior: A Neuropsychological Theory *(1949). Among Hebb's many contributions, he is best remembered and still frequently cited for his work on how learning, memory, and thought arise from activity within the cerebral cortex. Hebb proposed a mechanism for learning and memory (now called the Hebb synapse), an explanation of how groups of neurons formed circuits based on use (cell assemblies), and the idea that thought is the sequential activation of cell-assemblies. The lower part (b) of the figure, above, shows a schematic of Hebb's cell-assembly from his book* The Organization of Behavior: A Neuropsychological Theory *(1949).*

prefrontal cortex disorders seem oblivious to the future consequences of their actions and seem to be governed only by immediate consequences (Bechara et al., 1994). As you may have guessed by now, Phineas Gage, the railroad foreman described in our chapter-opening case, suffered massive frontal lobe damage when the spike tore through his brain (see Figure 3.1). Thereafter he exhibited classic symptoms of disturbed executive functions, becoming behaviourally impulsive and losing his capacity for future planning.

A more ominous manifestation of prefrontal dysfunction was discovered by Adrian Raine and his co-workers (1997). Using brain-imaging techniques, the researchers studied 41 violent murderers who had pleaded not guilty by reason of insanity. The murderers' PET scans showed clear evidence of reduced activity in the prefrontal cortex. Their murderous acts, which were often random and impulsive in nature, showed parallel evidence of failure in executive functions such as judgment, foresight, and impulse control. Raine suggested that people with similar prefrontal dysfunction may have a neural predisposition to impulsive violence.

During the 1940s and 1950s many thousands of psychiatric patients who suffered from disturbed and violently emotional behaviour were subjected to operations called *prefrontal lobotomies* (Shorter, 1998). The operation was performed by inserting an instrument with sharp edges into the brain, then wiggling it back and forth to sever the nerve tracts that connected the frontal lobes with the subcortical regions connected with emotion. The calming effect was so dramatic that Egas Moniz, the developer of the technique, was awarded a Nobel Prize. However, the devastating side effects on mental functions that occurred as the executive functions were destroyed were equally dramatic, and the development of antipsychotic drugs resulted in the abandonment of this form of "treatment."

Hemispheric Lateralization: The Left and Right Brains

The left and right cerebral hemispheres are connected by a broad white band of myelinated nerve fibres. The **corpus callosum** is a neural bridge that acts as a major communication link between the two hemispheres and allows them to function as a single unit. Despite the fact that they normally act in concert, however, there are important differences between the psychological functions that are represented in the two cerebral hemispheres. **Lateralization** refers to the relatively greater localization of a function in one hemisphere or the other.

Medical studies of patients who suffered various types of brain damage provided the first clues that certain complex psychological functions were lateralized on one side of the brain or the other. The deficits observed in people with damage to either the left or right hemisphere suggested that for most people, verbal abilities and speech are localized in the left hemisphere, as are mathematical and logical abilities (Springer, 1997).

When Broca's or Wernicke's speech areas are damaged, the result is **aphasia**, the partial or total loss of the ability to communicate. Depending on the location of the damage, the problem may lie in recognizing the meaning of words, in communicating verbally with others, or in both functions. C. Scott Moss, a clinical psychologist who became aphasic in both ways for a time as a result of a left hemisphere stroke, described what it was like for him.

> I recollect trying to read the headlines of the *Chicago Tribune* but they didn't make any sense to me at all. I didn't have any difficulty focusing; it was simply that the words, individually or in combination, didn't have meaning, and even more amazing, I was only a trifle bothered by that fact. . . . I think part of the explanation was that I had [also] lost the ability to engage in self-talk.

In other words, I didn't have the ability to think about the future—to worry, or anticipate or perceive it—at least not with words. (Moss, 1972, pp. 4–5)

28. What is hemispheric lateralization, and what do we know about the functions that are concentrated in the left and right hemispheres?

When the right hemisphere is damaged, the clinical picture is quite different. Language functions are not ordinarily affected, but the person has great difficulty in performing tasks that demand the ability to perceive spatial relations. A patient may have a hard time recognizing faces and may even forget a well-travelled route or, as in the case of Dr. P., mistake his wife for a hat (Sacks, 1985). It appears that mental imagery, musical and artistic abilities, and the ability to perceive and understand spatial relationships are primarily right-hemisphere functions (Ornstein, 1997).

Even among individuals who have not experienced any brain damage and who do not have a history of abnormal brain function, the lateralization of function can be detected. Doreen Kimura, of the University of Western Ontario, has compared the abilities of the right and left hemispheres to quickly recognize letters, words, faces, and music (Kimura, 1973). It is possible to present stimuli such as words or music, for example, in such a way that the information arrives first in one hemisphere. If the brain is intact, as it was for Kimura's subjects, the information is quickly and efficiently transferred to the other hemisphere, but this does mean that the hemisphere that received the information first has a head start on processing that information. Subtle differences in the abilities of the two hemispheres can be detected by precisely measuring the speed and accuracy of subjects when the information is provided to one hemisphere and then the other. Verbal stimuli such as letters and words are identified more quickly and accurately when they are presented in such a way that the information goes first to the left hemisphere. Recognizing faces or melodies is faster and more accurate if that information goes first to the right hemisphere. The right hemisphere, for example, was 20 percent better than the left hemisphere at quickly recognizing melodies, whereas the left hemisphere was 20 percent better than the right at quickly recognizing letters (Kimura, 1973). That is, the two hemispheres are specialized for dealing with specific types of information. Although the corpus callosum provides rapid and efficient transfer of information between the two hemispheres, this specialization can be detected by careful and exact experimentation even among normal volunteer subjects.

The two hemispheres differ not only in the cognitive functions that reside there, but also in their links with particular types of emotions. EEG studies have shown that the right hemisphere is relatively more active when negative emotions such as sadness and anger are being experienced. Positive emotions such as joy and happiness are accompanied by relatively greater left-hemisphere activation (Marshall & Fox, 2000).

29. What roles have (a) the corpus callosum and (b) the optic chiasm played in "split-brain" research? Is it reasonable to speak of separate "right" and "left" brains in normal people?

The split brain: two minds in one body? Despite the lateralization of specific functions in the two cerebral hemispheres, the brain normally functions as a unified whole because the two hemispheres communicate with one another through the corpus callosum. But what would happen if this communication link between the two hemispheres were cut? Would we, in effect, produce two different and largely independent minds in the same person? A series of Nobel Prize-winning studies by Roger Sperry (1970) and his associates addressed this question.

Like many scientific advances, this discovery resulted from natural human misfortune. Some patients suffer from a form of epilepsy in which a seizure that begins as an uncontrolled electrical discharge of neurons on one side of the brain spreads to the other hemisphere. Years ago, neurosurgeons found that by cutting the nerve fibres of the corpus callosum, they could prevent the seizure from spreading to the other hemisphere. Moreover, the operation did not seem to disrupt other major psychological functions. Sperry's studies of patients who had had such operations

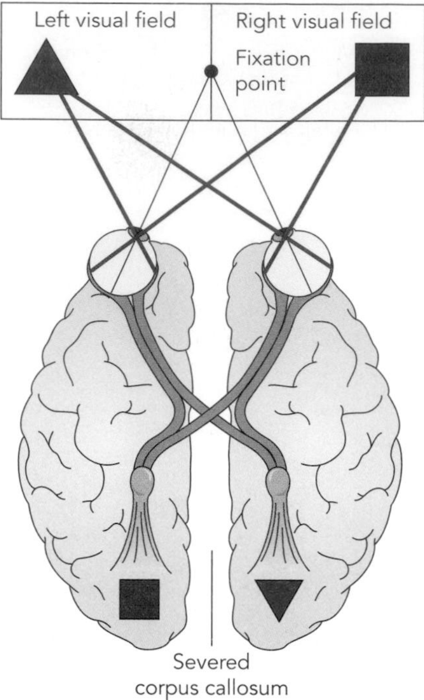

FIGURE 3.21

The visual system's anatomy made studies of split-brain subjects possible. Images entering the eye are reversed by the lens. Optic nerve fibres from the inner portion of the retina (toward the nose) cross over at the optic chiasm, whereas the fibres from the outer portion of the retina do not. As a result, the right side of each eye's visual field projects to the visual cortex of the left hemisphere, whereas the left visual field projects to the right hemisphere. When the corpus callosum is cut, the two hemispheres no longer communicate with each other. By presenting stimuli to either side of the visual fixation point, researchers can control which hemisphere receives the information.

involved some ingenious ways to test the functions of the two hemispheres after the corpus callosum was cut.

Split-brain research was made possible by the way in which our visual input to the brain is "wired." To illustrate, extend your two hands straight out in front of you, separated by about one foot. Now focus on the point between them. You will find that you can still see both hands in your peripheral vision, and that you have a unified view of the scene. Therefore, it might surprise you to know that your left hand is being "seen" only by your right hemisphere and your right hand only by your left hemisphere. To see how this occurs, examine Figure 3.21, which shows that some of the fibres of the optic nerve from each eye cross over at the *optic chiasm* and travel to the opposite brain hemisphere. Fibres that transmit messages from the right side of the visual field project to the left hemisphere; fibres from the visual field's left half project to the right hemisphere. Despite this arrangement, we experience a unified visual world (as you did when you looked at your hands) rather than two half-worlds because the hemispheres' visual areas are normally connected by the corpus callosum. When the corpus callosum is cut, however, visual input to one hemisphere can be restricted by projecting the stimulus to either the right side of the visual field (in which case the image goes only to the left hemisphere) or to the left side of the visual field, which sends it to the right hemisphere.

In Sperry's experiments, split-brain patients basically did what you did with your hands: They focused on a fixation point, a dot on the centre of a screen, while slides containing visual stimuli (words, pictures, and so on) were flashed to the right or left side of the fixation point (Figure 3.22).

Sperry found that when words were flashed to the right side of the visual field, resulting in their being sent to the language-rich left hemisphere, subjects could describe verbally what they had seen. They also could write what they had seen with their right hand (which is controlled by the left hemisphere). However, if words were flashed to the left side of the visual field and sent on to the right hemisphere, the subjects could not describe what they had read on the screen. This pattern of findings indicated that the right hemisphere does not have well-developed language abilities.

The inability to describe stimuli verbally did not mean, however, that the right hemisphere was incapable of recognizing them. If a picture of an object (e.g., a hairbrush) were flashed to the right hemisphere, and the left hand (controlled by the right hemisphere) were allowed to feel many different objects behind the screen, the person's hand would immediately select the brush and hold it up (Figure 3.22c). As long as the person continued to hold the brush in the left hand, sending sensory input about the object to the "non-verbal" right hemisphere, the person was unable to name it. However, if the brush were transferred to the right hand, the person could immediately name it. In other words, until the object was transferred to the right hand, the left hemisphere had no knowledge of what the right hemisphere was experiencing.

Later research showed the right hemisphere's definite superiority over the left in the recognition of patterns. In one study, three split-brain patients were presented with photographs of similar-looking faces, projected onto either the left or right visual fields. On each trial, they were asked to select the photo they had just seen from a set of 10 cards. On this task, the spatially oriented right hemisphere was far more accurate than the linguistic left hemisphere in correctly identifying the photos (Figure 3.23). Apparently the faces were too similar to one another to be differentiated easily by left-hemisphere -verbal descriptions, but the spatial abilities of the right hemisphere could differentiate between them (Gazzaniga & Smylie, 1983).

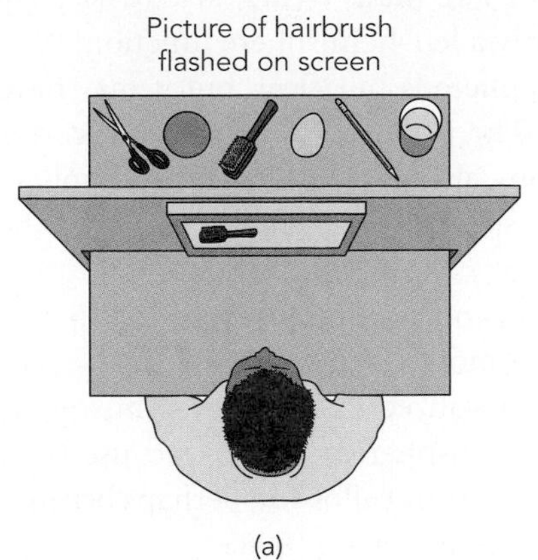

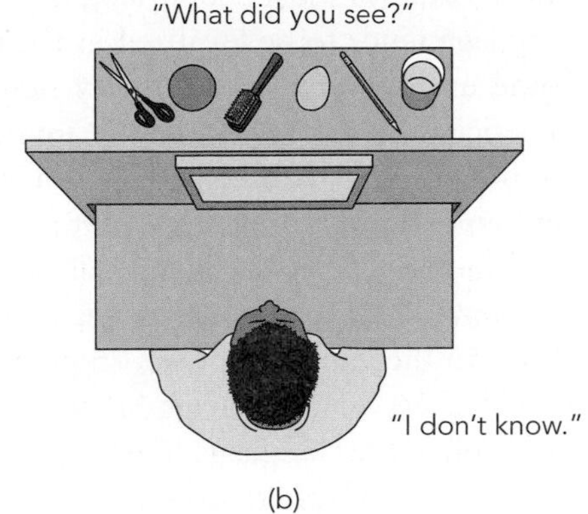

FIGURE 3.22

A split-brain patient focuses on the fixation point in the centre of the screen. In (a), a picture of a hairbrush is briefly projected onto the left side of the visual field, thus sending the information to the right hemisphere. In (b), the patient is asked to state verbally what she saw. She cannot name the object. In (c), she is asked to select the object she saw, and is able to find it with her left hand. If the object were transferred to her right hand, or if the word were flashed to the right side of the visual field, the information would be sent to the language-rich left hemisphere, and she would be able to name the object.

Some psychologists have suggested that what we call the conscious self resides in the left hemisphere, because consciousness is based on our ability to verbalize about the past and present. Is the right hemisphere, then, an unconscious (nonverbal) mind? Yes, these psychologists answer, except when it communicates with the left hemisphere across the corpus callosum (Ornstein, 1997). But when the connections between the two hemispheres are cut, each hemisphere, in a sense, can have a "mind of its own," as this example shows.

> One split brain patient learned to use Scrabble letters to communicate from his right hemisphere using his left hand. To test the dual-mind hypothesis, researchers asked the two hemispheres the same questions—and found that the answers often disagreed. For example, when asked what occupation he would prefer, the left hemisphere responded verbally, "a draftsman." But the right hemisphere used the Scrabble pieces to spell out, "race car driver." (LeDoux and others, 1977)

Keep in mind that in daily life, the split-brain patients could function adequately because they had learned to compensate for their disconnected hemispheres. For example, they could scan the visual environment so that visual input from both the left and right visual fields got into both hemispheres. The "split-mind" phenomena shown in the laboratory appeared because the patients were tested under experimental conditions that were specifically designed to isolate the functions of the two hemispheres. Nonetheless, the results of split-brain research were so dramatic that they led some people (and even some scientists) to promote a conception of brain functions as being highly localized and restricted to one hemisphere or the other. Even today, we hear about "right brain" education programs and the untapped potential that they can release. Certainly, there is some degree of localization of brain functions, but a far more important principle is that in the normal brain, most functions involve many areas of the brain working together. The brain is an exquisitely integrated system, not a collection of localized functions.

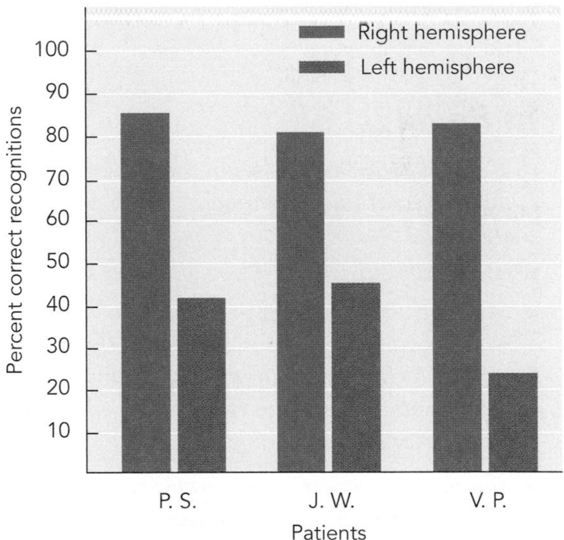

FIGURE 3.23

Facial recognition accuracy by the left and right hemispheres of three split-brain patients, showing greater accuracy when information is flashed to the right hemisphere, which has stronger pattern-recognition abilities.

Data from Gazzaniga & Smylie, 1983

30. How is language lateralized in the brain? Are there sex differences?

Hemispheric lateralization of language. For many years, scientists have known that for most people language is primarily a left-hemisphere function. Why language tends to be localized in the left hemisphere is not clear, but it may have some undiscovered evolutionary significance. The brain of the chimpanzee, our genetically closest relative in the animal kingdom, also has a larger left hemisphere in the region that corresponds with Wernicke's speech comprehension area in the human brain (Gannon et al., 1998).

About 90 percent of people are right-handed, and among this majority, 95 percent have left hemisphere language dominance. Among left-handers, half have language in the left hemisphere, 25 percent have it localized in the right hemisphere, and the rest have language functions in both hemispheres. Those who use both hemispheres for language functions have a larger corpus callosum, perhaps because more interhemispheric communication is required (Springer, 1998).

Left-hemisphere lateralization is the case not only for spoken and written language, but also for non-verbal kinds of language, such as sign language. PET scans of neural activity show that, just as hearing people process speech with their left hemisphere, deaf people use the left hemisphere to decipher sign language. Likewise, a left-hemisphere stroke affects their ability to understand or produce sign language (Corina et al., 1992).

Realize, however, that even if your left hemisphere is dominant for language, this does not mean that your right hemisphere lacks language ability. PET scan studies measuring cerebral blood flow in the brains of normal people indicate that both hemispheres are involved in speaking, reading, and listening (Leondes, 1997; Raichle, 1994). One notable finding, however, is that males and females may differ in the extent to which certain language functions are lateralized, or located, on one side of the brain. Brain imaging studies indicate that during a language task men show greater left hemisphere activation, while women show activity in both hemispheres (Clements et al., 2006).

In Review

- *The human brain consists of the hindbrain, the midbrain, and the forebrain, an organization that reflects the evolution of increasingly more complex brain structures related to behavioural capabilities.*
- *Major structures within the hindbrain include the medulla, which monitors and controls vital body functions; the pons, which contains important groups of sensory and motor neurons; and the cerebellum, which is concerned with motor coordination.*
- *The midbrain contains important sensory and motor neurons, as well as many sensory and motor tracts connecting higher and lower parts of the nervous system. The reticular formation plays a vital role in consciousness, attention, and sleep. Activity of the ascending reticular formation excites higher areas of the brain and prepares them to respond to stimulation. The descending reticular formation acts as a gate, determining which stimuli get through to enter into consciousness.*
- *The forebrain consists of two cerebral hemispheres and a number of subcortical structures. The cerebral hemispheres are connected by the corpus callosum.*
- *The thalamus acts as a switchboard through which impulses originating in sense organs are routed to the appropriate sensory projection areas. The hypothalamus plays a major role in supporting many different biological drives. The limbic system seems to be involved in organizing the behaviours involved in motivation and emotion.*
- *The cerebral cortex is divided into frontal, parietal, occipital, and temporal lobes. Some areas of the cerebral cortex receive sensory input, some control motor functions, and others (the association cortex) are involved in higher mental processes in humans. The frontal lobes are particularly important in such executive functions as planning, voluntary behaviour, and self-awareness.*

- *Although the two cerebral hemispheres ordinarily work in coordination with one another, they appear to have different functions and abilities. Studies of split-brain patients who have had the corpus callosum cut indicate that the left hemisphere commands language and mathematical abilities, whereas the right hemisphere has well-developed spatial abilities, but a generally limited ability to communicate through speech. However, recent findings indicate that language functions are less lateralized in women than in men. Positive emotions are believed to be linked to relatively greater left-hemisphere activation and negative ones to relatively greater right-hemisphere involvement. Despite hemispheric localization, however, most behaviours involve interactions between both hemispheres; the brain operates as a system.*

Plasticity in the Brain: The Role of Experience and the Recovery of Function

Learn to walk, acquire speech, begin to read, fall in love, and your brain changes in a way that makes you a different person than you were before. Learning and practising a mental or physical skill may change the size or number of brain areas involved and alter the neural pathways used in the skill (Posner et al., 1997). This process of brain alteration begins in the womb and continues throughout life. It is governed in important ways by genetic factors, but also is strongly influenced by the environment.

31. What is neural plasticity? How do age, environment, and behaviour affect plasticity?

Neural plasticity refers to the ability of neurons to change in structure and function (Kolb & Whishaw, 1998). Two aspects of neural plasticity—the effects of early experience on brain development and recovery from brain damage—are at the forefront of current research, such as the work of Kolb and Whishaw at the University of Lethbridge.

The role of early experience. Brain development is programmed by complex commands from our genes, but how these genetic commands express themselves can be powerfully affected by the environment in which we develop, including the environment we are exposed to in the womb (Filogamo, 1998). Consider the following research findings:

- For the fetus in the womb, exposure to high levels of alcohol ingested by the pregnant mother can disrupt brain development and produce the lifelong mental and behavioural damage seen in fetal alcohol syndrome (Streissguth et al., 1990).
- The brains of rat pups raised in a stimulating early environment containing lots of playmates and toys weighed more, had larger neurons and more dendritic branches, and greater concentrations of acetylcholine, the neurotransmitter involved in motor control and in memory (Rosenzweig, 1984).
- Prematurely born human infants who were caressed and massaged on a regular basis showed faster neurological development than did those given normal care and human contact (Field et al., 1986).
- MRI recordings revealed that experienced string musicians who do elaborate movements on the strings with their left hands had a larger right-hemisphere somatosensory area devoted to these fingers than did non-musicians. The corresponding left-hemisphere (right-hand) cortical areas of the musicians and non-musicians did not differ. The earlier in life the musicians had started playing their instruments, the more cortical change had occurred (Ebert et al., 1995).
- Cultural factors may affect brain development as well. For example, the Chinese language uses complex pictorial images (rather than words) to

represent objects or concepts. Because pictorial stimuli are processed in the right hemisphere, we might expect less left-hemisphere lateralization of language among speakers of Chinese than among people who speak English or other alphabet-based languages. There is evidence to support this hypothesis in the areas of reading and writing (Tzeng et al., 1979).

In a sense, your brain goes through its own personal "evolutionary" process as it adapts to and is moulded by your individual environment during the course of your life. Once again we can appreciate the many ways in which biology and experience continually interact.

Recovery of function after injury. When an injury results in the destruction of brain tissue, other neurons must take over the lost functions of the dead neurons if recovery is to occur. At times the brain shows an amazing plasticity and recovery of function, as the following case illustrates:

> Jimmy was a healthy and normal 5-year-old child who awoke one day unable to speak and slightly paralyzed on the right side of his body. A blood vessel in his left temporal lobe had ruptured and an area of the brain "downstream" from the site of the stroke had died when its blood supply was cut off. For Jimmy's father, it was like reliving a nightmare. His own grandfather had also suffered a left hemisphere stroke (late in life). The elderly man never recovered his speech and he remained partially paralyzed until his eventual death. But for Jimmy, the story had a happier ending. Within three months, Jimmy was again speaking normally, and his paralysis had disappeared completely. He was ready to resume the life of a normal 5-year-old. All that remained of his ordeal was a frightening memory. (Gazzaniga et al., 1979)

Neural reorganization had occurred in Jimmy's brain, allowing other neurons to take over the functions of those that had died. The outcomes for Jimmy and his grandfather also illustrate an important general principle: Brain damage suffered early in life is less devastating than damage suffered as an adult (Blosser, 2000).

The brain is clearly capable of greater plasticity early in life. In one study, researchers took neurons from the visual cortex of cats and then raised the neurons in a culture containing the nutrients needed for survival. They found that the neurons could survive and create new synapses with other neurons in the culture quite well if they were taken from kittens who were two to four weeks old, but not if they were obtained from older animals (Schoop et al., 1997).

32. Why do children typically show better recovery of function after brain injury?

Studies using the electron microscope may explain why such plasticity is possible early in life. The one- to two-year-old child has about 50 percent more brain synapses than mature adults do (Huttenlocher, 1979). This greater availability of synapses may help to explain why children can recover from brain damage more quickly and completely than adults. But, sadly, the days of synaptic riches don't last forever. Unused or weaker synapses deteriorate with age so that the brain loses some of its plasticity (Huttenlocher, 2002). Moreover, cell death is programmed into every neuron by its genes, and what some neuroscientists refer to as the neuron's "suicide apparatus" is activated by a lack of stimulation from other neurons and by many other unknown factors (Milligan & Schwartz, 1997). As a result, adults actually have fewer synapses in the brain than do children, despite their more advanced cognitive and motor capabilities.

Yet even adults can maintain or recover some functions after neuron death (Varney & Roberts, 1999). When nerve tissue is destroyed or neurons die as part of the aging process, surviving neurons can restore functioning by modifying themselves either structurally or biochemically. They can alter their structure by sprouting enlarged networks of dendrites or by extending axons from surviving neurons to form new synapses (Shepherd, 1997). Surviving neurons may also make up for the loss by increasing the volume of neurotransmitters they release (Robinson, 1997). Finally, recent research findings have begun to challenge the long-standing assumption of brain scientists that dead neurons cannot be replaced in the mature brain (McMillan et al., 1999). The development of new cells *(neurogenesis)* has been demonstrated in the brains of rodents and primates within the hippocampus, which is involved in memory. In 1998, evidence for the birth of new cells in the human adult hippocampus appeared (Eriksson et al., 1998). Then, in what could be a landmark scientific discovery, psychologist Elizabeth Gould and her Princeton co-workers (1999) provided the first evidence of neurogenesis in the cerebral cortex of a primate. Using complex chemical and microscopic analysis techniques with adult macaque monkeys, Gould's team tracked newly developed neurons from their birthplace in subcortical tissue. The immature neurons migrated upward along myelinated nerve tracts into the association areas of the cerebral cortex, where they sprouted axons and extended them toward existing neurons. The researchers speculated that these new neurons may be involved in higher-order mental functions, such as complex learning and memory. If similar results are found in humans, whose brain structures and functions are similar to those of primates, new light could be shed on brain mechanisms of information storage and plasticity. It is even possible that degenerative mental disorders such as Alzheimer's disease represent a failure or decline in a previously unknown process of neuron regeneration in the mature brain.

Behavioural and lifestyle measures also can help preserve brain functioning. In elderly people, for example, continued intellectual stimulation and activity seem to preserve synapses and their resulting cognitive functions, adding support to physiological psychologist David Krech's statement that "Those who live by their wits die with their wits" (Krech, 1978).

Basic research on naturally occurring recovery processes is leading to new ways to help the brain heal itself. These efforts are the focus of this chapter's *Psychological Applications.*

33. How are axon repair, brain grafts, and neural stem cell injections being used to improve the functioning of damaged brains? What kinds of ethical issues arise in the use of these procedures?

PSYCHOLOGICAL APPLICATIONS

Healing the Nervous System

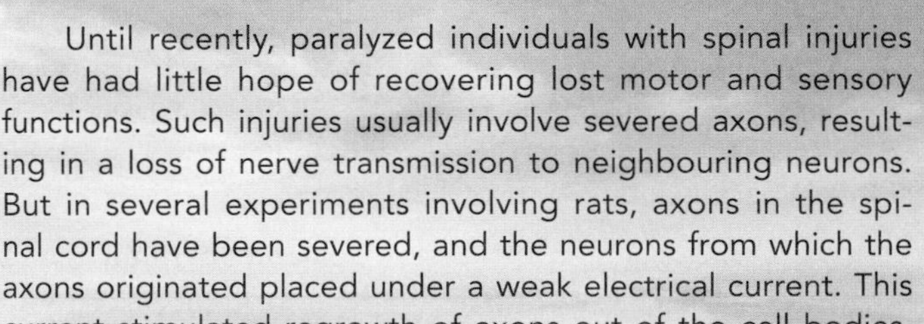

Neurological disorders take a frightening psychological toll on their victims, who often lose basic cognitive, sensory, and motor functions and can suffer devastating emotional and social consequences. Although severed fingers and toes can be reattached and regain their functions, the same has not been true in the damaged spinal cord and brain. Until recently, it was thought that dead neurons were impossible to replace. Now, however, hope for victims of neurological disease or injuries has been rekindled by the discovery that damaged neurons can be repaired (Solso, 1999).

Until recently, paralyzed individuals with spinal injuries have had little hope of recovering lost motor and sensory functions. Such injuries usually involve severed axons, resulting in a loss of nerve transmission to neighbouring neurons. But in several experiments involving rats, axons in the spinal cord have been severed, and the neurons from which the axons originated placed under a weak electrical current. This current stimulated regrowth of axons out of the cell bodies. The axons grew over the injury to seek their pre-damage

–Continued

positions on the other side of the cut. Other studies have used chemical methods to stimulate axon development, including the implantation of cells that produce *nerve growth factor*, a substance that helps stimulate and guide the growth of axons. In many cases, surviving neurons responded by sprouting axons that grew toward the graft and repaired the damaged tract (Joosten, 1997). Researchers are also investigating the therapeutic use of nerve growth factors, or of enhancing the endogenous production of nerve growth factors in treating degenerative diseases such as Huntington's disease (Dunbar, Sandstrom, Rossignol & Lescaudron, 2006).

As we saw earlier, Parkinson's disease is a progressive brain disorder caused by a loss of the dopamine supplied to the basal ganglia.

Might it be possible to transplant healthy neural tissue into diseased areas of the brain so as to produce the missing dopamine and restore neurological function? Successes with animal implants have stimulated experiments with human patients. Scientists have taken advantage of the fact that one of the substances produced by the adrenal glands is dopamine. They have taken dopamine-producing cells from patients' own adrenal glands (to avoid rejection of the transplant) and implanted them into the subcortical brain region affected by Parkinson's disease. The results have been variable, with dramatic improvement occurring in some cases, and no improvement at all in others. In one of the successes reported by a team of Mexican scientists, a patient who had been confined to a wheelchair was out playing soccer with his son 10 months after the surgery (Madrazo et al., 1987).

Dopamine-producing human fetal tissue seems to be even better for transplants than a patient's own adrenal tissue, because fetal tissue tends to secrete more dopamine and is more likely to survive and "take hold" in the damaged area. Such tissue is sometimes available as a result of miscarriages. In one study, six patients who had received fetal tissue transplants were followed up for periods of up to six years. After 8 to 12 months, PET scans showed that the transplanted tissue had survived and was producing significant amounts of dopamine. As a result, the patients required less L-DOPA over time, and one patient was able to be taken off the drug altogether after 32 months. Significant improvement in motor function was observed in four of the six patients (Wenning et al., 1997). Researchers working with laboratory animals have reported success in using neural transplants to treat epilepsy and even strokes (Blank, 1999).

As brain grafting takes us into a new era in which we may be able to physically modify the brain, new ethical and legal questions have become topics for debate (Gold, 1997; Sauer, 1998). What do you think about the following issues?

- Is it possible that increased demand for fetal tissue may provide a profitable market for the "harvesting" of needlessly aborted fetuses? Could the prospect of financial gain encourage some women to become pregnant with the intention of aborting the fetus and selling the tissue? Is it the parents' tissue to sell? (Gold, 1998)
- Suppose the daughter of a Parkinson's patient asked to be artificially inseminated with her father's sperm so that she could later have an abortion, thereby producing a supply of fetal tissue for implantation in his brain with a reduced likelihood of tissue rejection because of genetic similarity. Aside from the moral issue concerning the premeditated abortion, would the insemination constitute incest?
- Suppose a brain graft from another person results in a genetically based change in personality and a penchant for anti-social behaviour. Is the person legally responsible for his or her subsequent acts? In fact, because of the genetic change, is he or she still the same person?

Such issues are now being debated by medical ethicists. One revolutionary technique involves the transplantation into the brain of **neural stem cells**, immature "uncommitted" cells that can mature into any type of neuron or glial cell needed by the brain (Gage & Christen, 1997). These cells, found in both the developing and adult nervous system, can be put into a liquid medium and injected directly into the brain. Once in the brain, they can travel to any of its regions, especially developing or degenerating areas. There they can detect defective or genetically impaired cells and develop into healthy forms of the defective cells.

Researchers at Harvard Medical School demonstrated the potential value of stem cell transplantation (Yandava et al., 1999). They worked with a strain of mice called "shiverers" who have a genetic defect that prevents their glial cells from producing the insulating myelin sheath on axons. Within three weeks after birth, the animals begin to develop severe tremors similar to those seen in multiple sclerosis, a human disease produced by insufficient myelin. Using a neural stem cell culture grown from cells removed 13 years ago from the brain of a newborn mouse, the researchers injected stem cells directly into the brains of randomly selected shiverers. A control group of shiverers did not receive the cells. In the injected rats, the stem cells apparently detected the defective gene and converted themselves into the myelin-producing cells. They then began to produce the missing myelin throughout the brain, and some of the mice developed myelin sheaths that could not be distinguished from those of normal mice. About 60 percent of the experimental group mice behaved like normal mice, showing no signs of the motor disturbances that accompany insufficient myelination. Others showed greatly reduced motor symptoms. All of the control animals became shiverers.

The fact that transplanted stem cells apparently can go anywhere in the brain and become any kind of cell suggests the possibility of revolutionary treatments for diseases involving widespread neural degeneration and dysfunction, such as Alzheimer's, multiple sclerosis, strokes, mental disorders, and genetically based birth defects, all of which have serious psychological consequences. Much more research is needed, but at long last we may be on the threshold of being able to heal the damaged brain and restore lost psychological functions.

In Review

- Neural plasticity refers to the ability of neurons to change in structure and functions. Environmental factors, particularly early in life, have notable effects on brain development.
- A person's ability to recover from brain damage depends on several factors. Other things being equal, recovery is greatest early in life and declines with age.
- When neurons die, surviving neurons can sprout enlarged dendritic networks and extend axons to form new synapses. Neurons can also increase the amount of neurotransmitter substance they release so that they are more sensitive to stimulation. Recent findings suggest that the brains of mature primates and humans are capable of producing new neurons.
- Current advances in the treatment of neurological disorders include experiments on neuron regeneration, the grafting of nerve tissue that produces dopamine in the brains of Parkinson's disease patients, and the injection of neural stem cells into the brain, where they find and replace diseased or dead neurons.

NERVOUS SYSTEM INTERACTIONS WITH THE ENDOCRINE AND IMMUNE SYSTEMS

The nervous system interacts with two other communication systems within the body, namely, the endocrine and immune systems. These interactions have major influences on behaviour and on psychological and physical well-being.

Interactions with the Endocrine System

The **endocrine system** consists of numerous glands distributed throughout the body. The locations of the endocrine glands within the human body and a list of their functions are presented in Figure 3.24.

34. How does the endocrine system differ from the nervous system as a communications network?

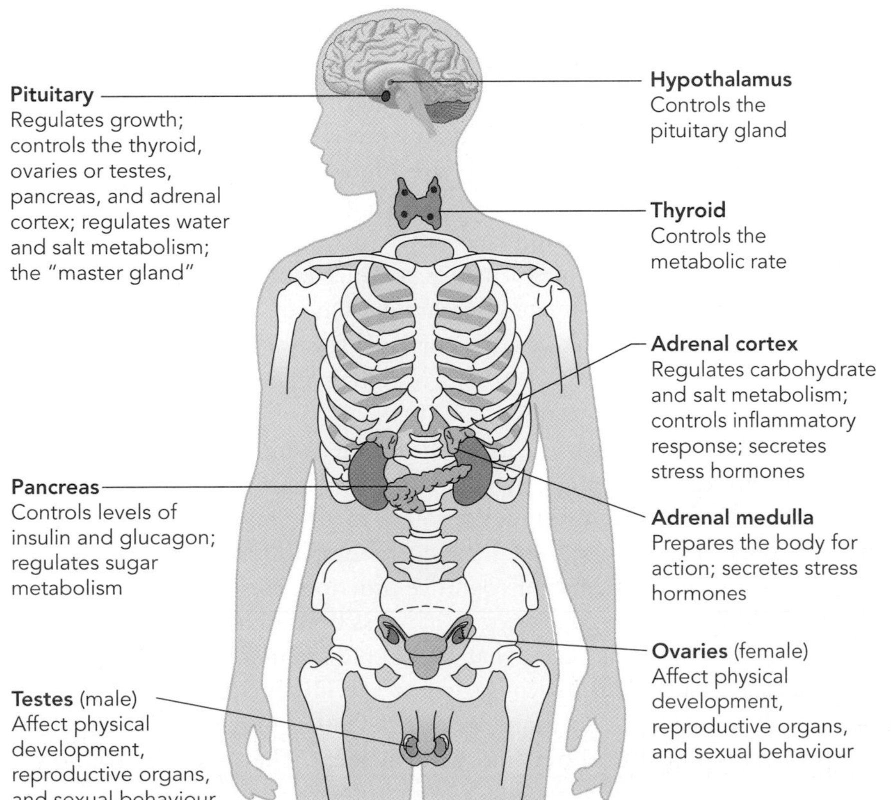
Pituitary
Regulates growth; controls the thyroid, ovaries or testes, pancreas, and adrenal cortex; regulates water and salt metabolism; the "master gland"
Hypothalamus
Controls the pituitary gland
Thyroid
Controls the metabolic rate
Adrenal cortex
Regulates carbohydrate and salt metabolism; controls inflammatory response; secretes stress hormones
Pancreas
Controls levels of insulin and glucagon; regulates sugar metabolism
Adrenal medulla
Prepares the body for action; secretes stress hormones
Ovaries (female)
Affect physical development, reproductive organs, and sexual behaviour
Testes (male)
Affect physical development, reproductive organs, and sexual behaviour

FIGURE 3.24

The glands that compose the endocrine system and the effects of their hormones on bodily functions. The hypothalamus affects the endocrine system by stimulating the pituitary gland.

Like the nervous system, the endocrine system's function is to convey information from one area of the body to another. Rather than using nerve impulses, however, the endocrine system conveys information in the form of **hormones**, chemical messengers that are secreted from its glands into the bloodstream. Just as neurons have receptors for certain neurotransmitters, cells in the body (including neurons) have receptor molecules that respond to specific hormones from the endocrine glands. Many of the hormones secreted by these glands affect psychological development and functioning (Becker et al., 1992). For example, the genetically programmed secretion of sex hormones within the human fetus during the early months following conception affects not only the development of male or female sex organs, but also the development of sex differences in the brain that influence behavioural functions throughout life (Schmidt & Rubinow, 1997). One example may be the sex differences in lateralization of language described earlier.

35. What are some ways in which the nervous and endocrine systems affect each other?

Endocrine messages can affect the nervous system, and mental processes within the brain can, in turn, affect endocrine functioning. For example, negative thoughts about a stressful situation can quickly trigger the secretion of stress hormones within the body (Borod, 2000). In many cultures, there are reports of "voodoo death," cases in which an otherwise healthy person dies after they have been cursed. Can we now account for such inexplicable deaths? One possibility is through the interaction of the brain and the endocrine system. Many years ago, the physiologist Walter Cannon (1942) suggested a possible mechanism, drawing upon his own research on severe stress responses in animals and quoting eyewitness reports by cultural anthropologists of deaths by "black magic." Cannon noted that in cases of death by "black magic," the victim of the curse invariably believed (as did family, friends, and enemies) that he or she was doomed, a conviction that was unquestioned within the victim's culture. He speculated that the victim's beliefs triggered a profound stress response that included a torrent of stress hormones released by the endocrine system. Cannon's research had shown that one effect of such massive endocrine activation was a rapid and potentially fatal drop in blood pressure. He noted that normal autopsy procedures would not detect this mechanism of death, making it appear that there was no natural cause and supporting the belief in death by curse. Cannon's hypothesis is a plausible alternative to supernatural explanations, and is consistent with the results of stress research.

36. What physiological explanation did Cannon offer for death by "black magic"?

Of special interest to psychologists are the **adrenal glands**, twin structures located on top of the kidneys. The adrenal glands produce and secrete about 50 different hormones that regulate many different metabolic processes within the brain and the body. Among the hormones produced and secreted by the adrenal glands are the stress hormones cited by Cannon. One of the most important hormones released by the adrenal cortex is **cortisol**. Together, the hormones secreted by the adrenal glands mobilize the body's resources, allowing the person to function despite the stressful conditions.

The stress hormones, such as cortisol, have potent and long-lasting effects, and their actions are especially important in cases of prolonged stress or frequently repeated stress. To function during stress you have to secrete the stress-related hormones. Prolonged exposure to these same hormones, however, can have important consequences for the brain and for cognitive function. For example, if young animals are exposed to prolonged elevations of stress hormones, they show deterioration of the hippocampus similar to that seen in old animals (Landfield et al., 1978, 1981). Michael Meaney and his colleagues at McGill University have found that elevated levels of this stress hormone are associated not only with deterioration of the hippocampus, but also with memory impairment. They have also found that a history of efficient stress recovery, and so less exposure of the brain to stress-related hormones, is associated with preservation of the hippocampus and of memory in old age (Meaney, Aitken, Bhatnagar, Van Berkel, Sapolsky, 1988; Meaney, Mitchell, Aitken, Bhatnagar, Bodnoff, Sarrieau, 1991). That is, high levels of this stress hormone lead to deterioration of the hippocampus and memory function, but a history of low exposure can leave an old animal relatively unscathed by the passage of time.

If high levels of stress-related hormones are detrimental, can anything protect us from the inevitable stresses of life? Michael Meaney and colleagues found that if rat pups were given additional stimulation (daily handling) during the first week of life, they showed faster recovery from stress during adulthood (Meaney, et al., 1988). Similarly, work with non-human primates has found that mild early life stress strengthens emotional, cognitive, and hormonal resistance to stressors later in life (Parker, Buckmaster, Justus, Schatzberg, & Lyons, 2005). That is, mild stresses early in life may serve to inoculate the individual against subsequent stressors. Recent research has found that the additional stimulation can be applied by the mother, not just imposed by an experimenter. Subtle differences in maternal behaviour, such as differences in grooming by the mother, can lead to enhanced ability to recover from stress during adulthood (Caldji, Diorio, & Meaney, 2000; Meaney, 2003). Interestingly, female rat pups who received the additional early stimulation themselves show differences in maternal behaviour when they eventually become mothers, and the differences are such that their pups also grow to recover from stress more efficiently and behave differently as mothers (Bredy, Weaver, Champagne, & Meaney, 2001). That is, once an animal has received the type of early stimulation that enhances their stress-recovery, concomitant changes in maternal behaviour allow this to be passed from generation to generation. Are there comparable phenomena among humans? Michael Meaney is extending this research to human children and the impact that socio-economic status, maternal behaviour, and early stimulation can have on a person's ability to recover from stress. Although early in this research program, results indicate that early experience among humans has an impact on stress hormone levels and the efficiency with which a person recovers from stress (Lupien, King, & Meaney, 2001; Meaney, 2003).

The nervous system transmits information rapidly, with the speed of nerve impulses. The endocrine system is much slower, because delivery of its messages depends on the rate of blood flow. On the other hand, hormones travel throughout the body in the bloodstream and can reach billions of individual cells. Thus, when the brain has important information to transmit, it has the choice of sending it directly in the form of nerve impulses to a relatively small number of neurons or indirectly by means of hormones to a large number of cells. Often both communication networks are used, resulting in both immediate and prolonged stimulation.

Interactions Involving the Immune System

37. In what ways does the immune system have sensory, response, and memory capabilities?

38. How does under- or overreactivity to internal or external antigens give rise to four varieties of immune dysfunction?

The nervous and endocrine systems interact not only with one another, but also with the immune system. A normal, healthy immune system is a wonder of nature. At this moment, microscopic soldiers patrol every part of your body. They are on a search-and-destroy mission, seeking out biological invaders that could disable or kill you. Programmed into this legion of tiny defenders is an innate ability to recognize which substances belong to the body and which are foreigners that must be destroyed. Such recognition occurs because foreign substances known as **antigens**

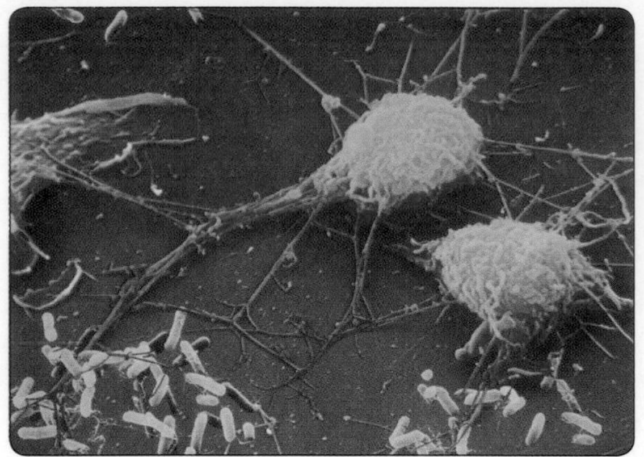

FIGURE 3.25

An immune system cell reaches out to capture bacteria, shown here in yellow. The bacteria that have already been pulled to the surface of the cell will be engulfed and devoured.

(meaning *anti*body *gen*erators) trigger a biochemical response from the immune system. Bacteria, viruses, abnormal cells, and many chemical molecules with antigenic properties start the wars that rage inside our bodies every moment of every day (Figure 3.25).

The immune system has a remarkable memory. Once it has encountered one of the millions of different antigens that enter the body, it will recognize the antigen immediately in the future and will produce the biochemical weapons, or antibodies, needed to destroy it (Nossal & Hall, 1995). This is why we can develop vaccines to protect animals and people from some diseases, and why we normally catch diseases such as mumps and chicken pox only once in our lives. Unfortunately, though the memory may be perfect, our body's defences may not be. Some bacteria and viruses evolve so rapidly that they can change just enough over time to slip past the sentinels in our immune system and give us this year's cold or flu.

39. What evidence exists that the immune and nervous systems communicate with and affect each other?

40. Which psychosocial factors have been shown to influence immune functioning?

41. What can be done to enhance immune functioning?

Antigens can originate externally (a flu virus or pollen) or internally (a cancerous tumour). Problems arise when the immune system has either an underactive or an overactive response (Figure 3.26). An *underactive* immune system response to external antigens is dramatically illustrated in acquired immune deficiency syndrome (AIDS). One class of immune cells, *helper T cells*, issues "calls to action," mobilizing antigen-killing cells in the immune system. The human immunodeficiency virus (HIV) attacks the helper T cells and disables them. As a result, the individual's immune system doesn't get the order to attack and kill invaders. This leaves the body defenceless against virtually anything that can infect humans: bacteria, viruses of all kinds, fungi, and protozoa. Underreaction can also occur in response to an internal antigen. This is what occurs in cancer. Abnormal body cells are allowed to proliferate, resulting in the formation of tumours.

An *overactive* response to an external antigen presents problems in the form of an allergy. For example, in its violent reaction to an allergen, an asthmatic's immune system releases a torrent of histamine, a chemical that causes critical breathing muscles around the bronchial tubes to contract, leaving the asthmatic person wheezing and gasping for air.

Another type of overactive response, an **autoimmune reaction**, results when the immune system mistakenly identifies part of the body as an enemy and attacks it. For example, in rheumatoid arthritis, the immune system attacks connective tissue in the joints, causing inflammation, pain, and loss of flexibility. In diabetes, immune cells attack cells in the pancreas that produce the hormone insulin, which regulates blood sugar level. As a result the diabetic person may experience abnormally high blood sugar that can damage other organs, or drops in blood sugar that can result in a coma.

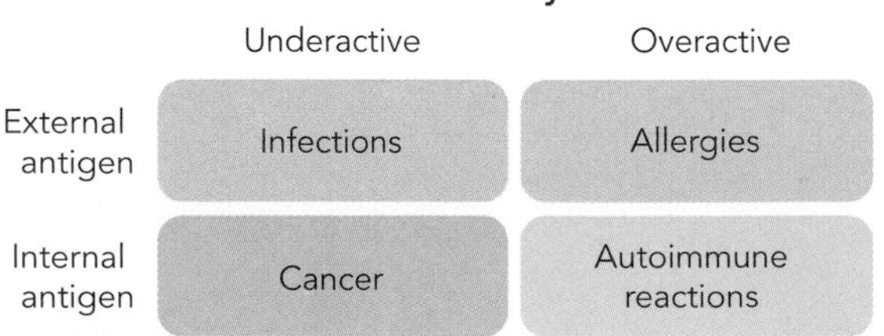

FIGURE 3.26

Disorders of the immune system created by under- or overreaction to either internal or external antigens.

The immune system, like the nervous system, has an exquisite capacity to receive, interpret, and respond to specific forms of stimulation. It senses, learns, remembers, and reacts; in other words, it behaves. Despite these similarities, research on the nervous and immune systems proceeded along independent paths for many years, with only a few visionaries, such as Carleton University's Hymie Anisman and Candace Pert of Georgetown University, suggesting that the two systems might be able to communicate and influence each others' activities. They were right. We now know that the nervous, endocrine, and immune systems are all parts of a communication network that so completely underlies our every mental, emotional, and physical action that neuroscientist Candace Pert has dubbed this network "body-mind" (Pert, 1986).

Pieces of this communication puzzle began to fall into place as a result of several key discoveries. The first was that selective electrical stimulation or destruction of certain areas of the hypothalamus and cerebral cortex resulted in almost instantaneous increases or decreases in immune-system activity. Conversely, activation of the immune system by injecting antigens into the body resulted in increased electrical activity in several brain regions (Saphier, 1992). Clearly, the nervous and immune systems were communicating with and influencing one another.

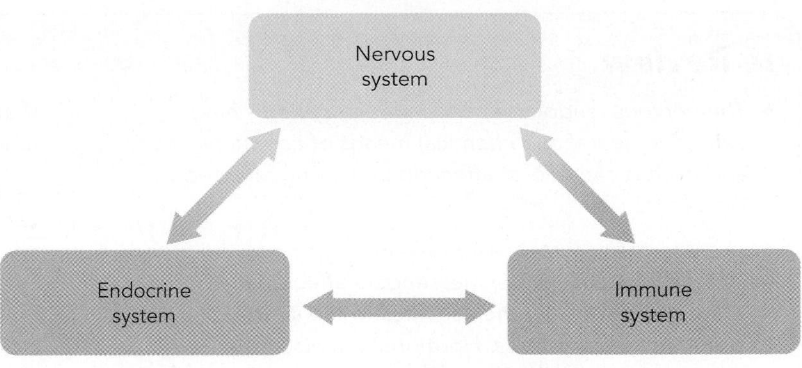

FIGURE 3.27

The nervous, endocrine, and immune systems are part of a complex communication system in which each can affect and be affected by the others. This fact accounts for many of the so-called "body-mind" interactions that are the focus of current interest in psychology.

Later research showed that the nervous and immune systems are chemically connected as well. Immune system cells contain receptors keyed to specific neurotransmitter substances, meaning that the action of immune cells can be directly influenced by chemical messengers from the brain (Maier & Watkins, 1999). An equally startling discovery was that immune cells can actually produce hormones and neurotransmitters, allowing them to directly influence the brain and endocrine system glands. The immune system is therefore not only a response system, but also a giant sensory system. It responds to antigens by sending chemical messengers that affect neurotransmitter activity in the brain and the autonomic nervous system. The brain, in turn, responds with a cascade of chemical and neural signals to both the immune cells and to the endocrine glands and organs of the body (Felton & Maida, 2000; Lu, Song, Ravidran, Merali & Anisman, 1998). In sum, the brain, endocrine glands, and immune system form a complete communication loop, with each system influencing and being influenced by every other (Figure 3.27).

The immune system is clearly affected by a host of factors. As shown in Figure 3.28, these factors can be examined at biological, psychological, and environmental levels of analysis.

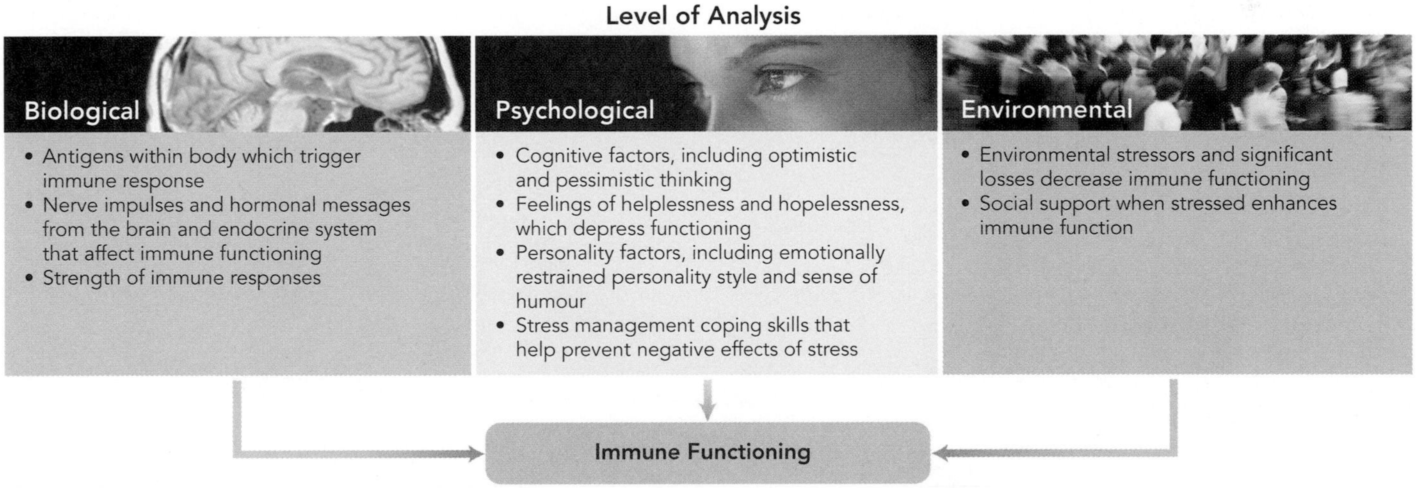

Level of Analysis

Biological	Psychological	Environmental
• Antigens within body which trigger immune response • Nerve impulses and hormonal messages from the brain and endocrine system that affect immune functioning • Strength of immune responses	• Cognitive factors, including optimistic and pessimistic thinking • Feelings of helplessness and hopelessness, which depress functioning • Personality factors, including emotionally restrained personality style and sense of humour • Stress management coping skills that help prevent negative effects of stress	• Environmental stressors and significant losses decrease immune functioning • Social support when stressed enhances immune function

Immune Functioning

FIGURE 3.28

Understanding the causes of behaviour: factors influencing immune functions.

In Review

- *The nervous, endocrine, and immune systems have extensive neural and chemical means of communication, and each is capable of affecting and being affected by the others.*
- *The endocrine system secretes hormones into the bloodstream. These chemical messengers affect many body processes, including the activities of the central and autonomic nervous systems. Hormonal effects in the womb may produce brain differences in males and females that influence sex differences in certain psychological functions.*
- *As a behaving entity, the immune system has the capacity to sense, to interpret, and to respond to specific forms of stimulation. Immune system disorders can occur because of either an underactive or an overactive immune system. Allergic reactions and autoimmune conditions are caused by overactivity; cancer and AIDS result from underactivity.*

GAINING DIRECTION

What are the issues?

This chapter began with a passage from Dr. Oliver Sacks in his 1987 book, *The Man Who Mistook His Wife for a Hat.* It would appear that the patient, Dr. P., is not capable of describing his sensory experiences, nor is he able to distinguish between his wife's head and his hat! Yet he seems otherwise normal. Is this possible? To explain Dr. P. and his behaviour we need to examine normal brain functioning, especially the processing of sensory information. Dr. P. was suffering from a form of sensory agnosia. His processing of the sensory information was intact—the problem was one of interpretation. He "saw" the various stimuli, but was not able to make sense of them. Dr. P.'s problems began as an inability to recognize faces, a disorder known as prosopagnosia.

What do we need to know?

How does the brain process sensory information?
What is the role of the association cortex?
How does one acquire the ability to identify objects?
How does one lose the ability to identify objects?
What is visual agnosia?

Where can we find the information to answer these questions?

We need to examine the organization and function of the cortex. In particular we should look at the role of the primary projection areas. Is there a particular area responsible for visual processing? What would happen if you damaged this area? In addition to the primary projection areas, the cortex contains a number of association areas. Is there a visual association area? What would happen if this area was damaged? Are there other areas involved in object recognition? Can we identify a specific cause of Dr. P.'s problem? As you consider these issues, think about the relationship between the function of a particular cortical area and its location. Are they related?

KEY TERMS AND CONCEPTS*

acetylcholine (ACh) (94)
action potential (88)
action potential threshold (88)
adrenal glands (126)
all-or-none law (88)
amygdala (109)
antigen (127)
aphasia (116)
association cortex (114)
autoimmune reaction (128)
autonomic nervous system (97)
axon (85)
basal ganglia (107)
blood-brain barrier (86)
brain stem (104)
Broca's area (114)
central nervous system (96)
cerebellum (105)
cerebral cortex (110)
computerized axial tomography (CT) scan (100)
corpus callosum (116)
cortisol (126)
dendrites (85)
depolarization (88)
dopamine (95)
electroencephalogram (EEG) (100)
endocrine system (125)
endorphins (95)
forebrain (107)
frontal lobe (110)
graded potential (88)
hippocampus (108)
hormones (126)
hypothalamus (108)
interneurons (96)
ion channels (88)
lateralization (116)
limbic system (108)
magnetic resonance imaging (MRI) (102)
medulla (104)
midbrain (106)
motor cortex (111)
motor neurons (96)
myelin sheath (90)
neural stem cells (124)
neural plasticity (121)
neuromodulators (95)
neurons (85)
neurotransmitter (91)
nucleus accumbens (109)
occipital lobe (110)
parasympathetic nervous system (97)
parietal lobe (110)
peripheral nervous system (96)
pons (105)
positron emission tomography (PET) scan (101)
prefrontal cortex (115)
receptor sites (91)
reticular formation (106)
reuptake (93)
sensory neurons (96)
serotonin (95)
somatic nervous system (97)
somatic sensory cortex (111)
sympathetic nervous system (97)
synapse (91)
synaptic cleft (91)
synaptic vesicles (91)
temporal lobe (110)
thalamus (107)
Wernicke's area (114)

*Each term has been boldfaced in the text on the page indicated in parentheses.

DO YOU WANT TO ELEVATE YOUR GRADES?

For additional resources and interactive quizzing, visit the book's Online Learning Centre at **www.mcgrawhill.ca/olc/passer**.

CHAPTER 4

Genes, Evolution, and Behaviour

Psychology will be based on a new foundation.
—Charles Darwin, 1859

CHAPTER OUTLINE

Identical twins Jim Springer and Jim Lewis met for the first time when they were 39 years old. They discovered each other through a landmark University of Minnesota study of twins who had been separated shortly after birth and raised by different adoptive parents. Although they had been raised in different families, the two Jims found that they had many things in common. Both had married twice and each had a son named James. Both men smoked—and even smoked the same brand of cigarette—and both preferred Miller Lite beer. Both worked as volunteers for their local police departments as part-time sheriffs, favoured poodles as pets, suffered from the same kind of headache symptoms when under stress, and bit their fingernails. Both Jims did woodworking as a hobby, and they were the only people in their respective neighbourhoods to have built a circular bench around a tree in their yard. When given a series of psychological tests, they were strikingly similar in their pattern of personality traits.

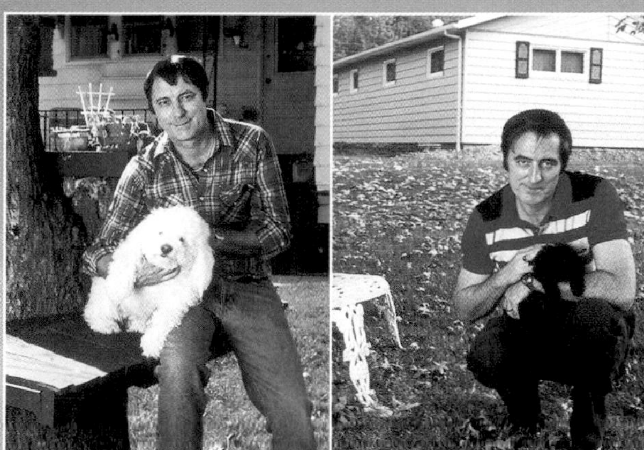

- **What are the issues here?**
- **What do we need to know?**
- **Where can we find the information necessary to answer the questions?**

GENETIC INFLUENCES

Our physical development, including the development of the nervous system, is in large part directed by an elaborate genetic blueprint passed on to us by our parents. These biological characteristics set limits on our behavioural capabilities. However, our genetic endowment combines with environmental forces to determine our behaviour. Nature or nurture is not an appropriate dichotomy; it should be nature *and* nurture. Modern scientists realize that asking whether a particular behaviour is caused by genetic or environmental factors makes no more sense than asking if a triangle is formed by its sides or its corners. Instead, psychologists working in the field of behaviour genetics study the ways in which favourable or unfavourable environmental conditions can affect the genetically inherited potential of an organism.

Chromosomes and Genes

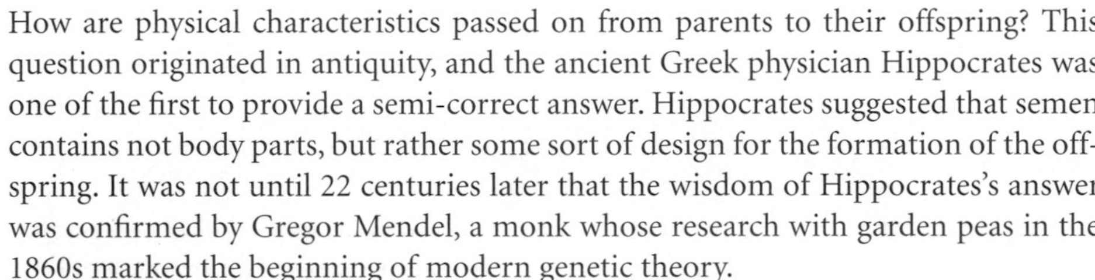

How are physical characteristics passed on from parents to their offspring? This question originated in antiquity, and the ancient Greek physician Hippocrates was one of the first to provide a semi-correct answer. Hippocrates suggested that semen contains not body parts, but rather some sort of design for the formation of the offspring. It was not until 22 centuries later that the wisdom of Hippocrates's answer was confirmed by Gregor Mendel, a monk whose research with garden peas in the 1860s marked the beginning of modern genetic theory.

Mendel showed that heredity involves the passing on of specific organic factors, not a simple blending of the parents' characteristics. These specific factors might produce visible characteristics in the offspring, or they might simply be carried for possible transmission to another generation. In any case, the offspring of one set of parents do not all inherit the same traits, as is evident in the differences we see between brothers and sisters.

?
1. Differentiate between genotype and phenotype.

Early in the 20th century, geneticists made the important distinction between **genotype**, the specific genetic makeup of the individual, and **phenotype**, the observable characteristics produced by that genetic endowment. A person's genotype is like the commands in a computer software program. Some of the directives are used on one occasion, some on another. Some are never used at all, either because they are contradicted by other genetic directives or because the environment never calls them forth. Thus genotypes are present from conception and never change, but phenotypes can be affected by other genes and by the environment. For example, geneticists have discovered that chickens have retained the genetic code for teeth (Kollar & Fischer, 1980). Yet because the code is prevented from being expressed, "hens' teeth" remains an expression for scarcity.

The union of two cells, the egg from the mother and the sperm from the father, is the beginning of a new individual. Like all other cells in the body, the egg and sperm carry within them the material of heredity in the form of rodlike units called chromosomes. A **chromosome** is a tightly coiled molecule of *deoxyribonucleic acid (DNA)* that is partly covered by protein. The DNA portion of the chromosome carries the hereditary blueprint in units called **genes** (Figure 4.1). The many genes carried on each chromosome are like a giant computer file of information about your characteristics, potentials, and limitations. Every moment of every day, the strands of DNA silently transmit their detailed instructions for cellular functioning.

2. How does genetic transmission occur from parents to offspring?

In humans, every cell in the body except one type has 46 chromosomes. The exception is the sex cell (the egg or sperm), which has only 23. At conception, the 23 chromosomes from the egg combine with the 23 from the sperm to form a new cell containing 46 chromosomes. The genes within each chromosome also occur

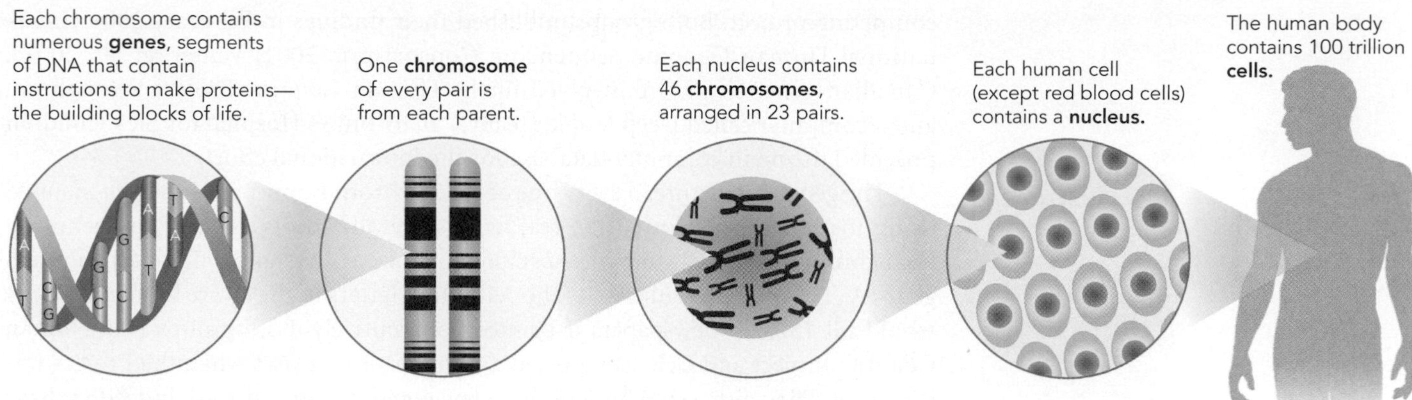

Each chromosome contains numerous **genes**, segments of DNA that contain instructions to make proteins—the building blocks of life.
One **chromosome** of every pair is from each parent.
Each nucleus contains 46 **chromosomes**, arranged in 23 pairs.
Each human cell (except red blood cells) contains a **nucleus.**
The human body contains 100 trillion **cells.**

FIGURE 4.1

The ladder of life. Chromosomes consist of two long, twisted strands of DNA, the chemical that carries genetic information in the form of specific sequences of the substances adenine, thymine, guanine, and cytosine (A, T, G, and C). Every cell in the body (with the exception of red blood cells) carries within its nucleus 23 pairs of chromosomes, each containing numerous genes that regulate every aspect of cellular functioning.

in pairs, so that the offspring receives one of each gene pair from each parent. It is estimated that the union of sperm and egg can result in about 70 trillion potential genotypes, accounting for the great diversity in characteristics even in siblings.

Genes affect our body's development and functioning through one general mechanism: genes code for the production of proteins. The estimated 70,000 different types of proteins found in a human (Wahlsten, 1999) control the structure of individual cells and all of the chemical reactions that go on within those cells, whether they are reactions necessary to sustain the life of the cell or are changes induced only periodically by experience or maturation. Each individual gene carries the code for a specific protein, and when that gene is activated, the cell produces the specified protein. At different points in development, in response to different metabolic demands, or in response to different environmental factors, a gene may be activated and a protein produced or an already active gene may be "turned off" and the levels of a specific protein will then decrease. As the protein levels within a neuron change, there is a corresponding change in the function of that neuron and of the neural circuits in which it participates.

Dominant, Recessive, and Polygenic Effects

3. Compare dominant, recessive, and polygenic influences on phenotypic characteristics.

Genotype and phenotype are not identical, because some genes are dominant and some are recessive. If a gene in the pair received from the mother and father is **dominant**, the particular characteristic that it controls will be displayed; if the gene is **recessive**, the characteristic will not show up *unless* the partner gene inherited from the other parent is also recessive. In humans, for example, brown eyes and dark hair are dominant over blue eyes and light hair. Thus a child will have blue eyes only if both parents have contributed genes for blue eyes. Even if their traits remain hidden, however, recessive genes can be passed on to offspring.

In a great many instances, a number of gene pairs combine their influences to create a single phenotypic trait. This is known as **polygenic transmission**, and it complicates the straightforward picture that would occur if all characteristics were determined by one pair of genes. It also magnifies the number of possible variations in a trait that can occur.

Mapping the Genetic Code

In 1990 geneticists began the Human Genome Project and in 2001 the genetic map was published, two years ahead of schedule. The mapping of the human genetic code was done by the International Human Genome Sequencing Consortium, which involved scientists from around the world. During the last three years of the project, the American biotechnology firm Celera Genomics launched a competing project. Both groups published their findings in February 2001 (International Human Genome Sequencing Consortium, 2001; Venter, et al., 2001). Canadian geneticists were involved in the Human Genome Project throughout, and a computer called Deep Maple (really!) at Toronto's Hospital for Sick Children provided the main computer database for the international effort.

The genetic structure in every one of the 23 chromosome pairs has been mapped using methods that allowed the researchers literally to disassemble the genes on each chromosome and study the specific sequence of substances that occur in each gene (A, T, G, and C; Figure 4.1). The 3.1 billion letters in the entire human genome would fill 152,000 newspapers if printed consecutively. Both groups (the Human Genome Project and Celera) reported a number of surprises when the Project was complete. They discovered humans have fewer genes than expected; indeed we have about the same number as a fruit fly, and they found that approximately 200 human genes may have arisen from genes that bacteria inserted into our early ancestors. As research continues to explore the functions of those 3.1 billion genes, a new understanding of our genetic makeup may lead to the development of effective new medical treatments, to a revolution in how therapeutic drugs are developed, and to a whole new understanding of what makes a human and where we came from.

Genetic Engineering: The Edge of Creation

4. Describe the methods used in recombinant DNA research.

Advances in molecular biology enable scientists not only to map the human genome, but also to duplicate and modify the structures of genes themselves (Aldridge, 1998). In **recombinant DNA procedures**, researchers use certain enzymes to cut the long thread-like molecules of genetic DNA into pieces, combine them with DNA from another organism, and insert them into a host organism, such as a bacterium. Inside the host, the new DNA combination continues to divide and produce many copies of itself.

This procedure has been used to produce *human growth hormone,* which is very difficult to obtain naturally in large enough quantities to use for therapeutic purposes. In one study, the availability of growth hormone produced through recombinant procedures made it possible to treat 121 children of abnormally short stature who were deficient in the hormone. As a result of their treatment, the children achieved adolescent heights that were only slightly below average, and far beyond what would have been possible without the treatment (Blethen et al., 1997). The positive social and psychological consequences that could occur for the children who received such treatments have interested many psychologists in the application of recombinant technology.

Molecular biologists have developed methods for inserting new genetic material into viruses that can infiltrate neurons and modify their genetic structure. These methods are now becoming part of the tool kit of physiological psychologists who wish to study genetic influences on behaviour. Recent gene-modification research by psychologists has focused on processes such as learning, memory, emotion, and motivation (Wahlsten, 1999). One procedure done with animals (typically, mice) is to alter a specific gene in a way that prevents it from carrying out its normal function. This is called a **gene knockout** procedure because that particular function of the gene is eliminated. The effects on behaviour are then observed. For example, psychologists may insert genetic material that will prevent neurons from responding to a particular neurotransmitter, then measure whether the animal's ability to learn or remember is affected. This can help psychologists determine the importance of particular transmitter substances in relation to the behaviours of interest (Thomas & Palmiter, 1997). In a recent study Holmes, Dennis, and Jacqueline (2003) used mice with a knockout for the mechanism involved in the reuptake

5. What is the knockout procedure and how is it used by psychologists to study behaviour?

of the neurotransmitter serotonin (see Chapter 3). Loss of the serotonin reuptake mechanism results in serotonin remaining in the synapse after its release and a consequent alteration in the activity of serotonin-releasing neurons and serotonin receptors. These mice showed increased anxiety-like behaviour and an exaggerated stress response, offering a parallel with human anxiety and depression.

Although a powerful tool, great care needs to be used when interpreting the outcome of gene knockout studies. Very few behaviours are controlled by a single gene. Thus the disruption of a behaviour after a gene knockout may help to identify one of the genes involved in the behaviour, but this does not mean that one gene is wholly responsible for the behaviour. It is also important to note that knocking out a single gene may disrupt a wide range of functions. Many of the substances found in the body do many different things in different areas of the brain and body. Nonetheless, gene-modification techniques may one day enable us to alter genes that contribute to psychological disorders such as schizophrenia.

Genetic engineering gives humans potential control over the processes of heredity and evolution. But these revolutionary techniques also give birth to a host of ethical and moral issues (Reiss & Straughan, 1998; Stephenson, 1998). How and when, if ever, should these techniques be used? To prevent genetic disorders? To propogate desirable human characteristics? To duplicate or clone exceptional people? What are the social and environmental consequences of using genetic engineering to greatly extend the healthy lifespan of people? Questions like these are already the topic of intense discussion as scientific and technological advances carry us toward uncharted genetic frontiers.

In Review

- *Heredity potential is carried within the DNA portion of the 23 pairs of chromosomes in units called genes. Genotype and phenotype are not identical because some genes are dominant while others are recessive. Many characteristics are polygenic in origin, i.e., influenced by interactions of multiple genes.*
- *Genes influence the development, structure, and function of our body, including our brain, by controlling the production of proteins.*
- *Genetic engineering allows scientists to duplicate and alter genetic material or, potentially, to repair dysfunctional genes.*

Behaviour Genetics Techniques

6. What is the percentage of genetic resemblance between parents and children, identical and fraternal twins, brothers and sisters, and grandparents and grandchildren?

Knowledge of the principles of genetic transmission tells us how genetically similar people are, depending on their degree of relatedness to one another. Recall that children get half of their genetic material from each parent. Thus the probability of sharing any particular gene with one of your parents is 50 percent, or .50. Brothers and sisters also have a probability of .50 of sharing the same gene with one another, since they get their genetic material from the same parents. And what about grandparents? Here, the probability of a shared gene is .25 because, for example, your maternal grandmother passed half of her genes on to your mother, who passed half of hers on to you. Thus the likelihood that you inherited one of your grandmother's genes is .50 × .50, or .25. The probability of sharing a gene is also .25 for half-siblings, who share half their genes with their biological parent, but none with the other parent. An adopted child has no genes in common with his or her adoptive parents, nor do unrelated people share genes in common.

Behaviour geneticists are interested in studying how hereditary and environmental factors combine to influence psychological characteristics. One important question is

the potential role of genetic factors in accounting for differences between people. The extent to which variation in a particular characteristic within a group can be attributed to genetic factors is estimated statistically by a **heritability coefficient**. It is easy to confuse two terms in this discussion. *Heredity* means the passage of characteristics from parents to offspring by way of genes; *heritability* means how much of the variation in a characteristic within a population can be attributed to genetic differences.

It is important to note that heritability refers to differences, or variance, in the trait across individuals and not to the trait itself. If a characteristic such as weight has a heritability coefficient of .60, this does not mean that 60 percent of my body weight is due to my genes and 40 percent is due to my environment. If you look around at the other students in your psychology class, you will see a range of body weights. The heritability coefficient is a way of estimating how much of that variation is attributable to genetic factors. Furthermore, heritability applies only to differences *within* a group, not to differences *between* groups. Consider the range of weights apparent within your psychology class, and now think of a different group, such as a group of individuals from a traditional hunter-gatherer society. Differences in body weight between your class and the hunter-gatherer group are most likely attributable to differences in the environment, such as differences in the availability of high sugar and high fat foods and the amount of physical exercise. You could calculate a heritability coefficient for each group and obtain estimates for the importance of genetic factors in explaining individual differences within each group, but this cannot be used to explain differences between groups. This point is widely misunderstood and misreported in the popular media.

In considering heritability estimates, like those shown in Table 4.1, it is important to know what group was studied (the heritability estimates shown in Table 4.1 were obtained from studies of mostly middle-class North Americans). Why does knowing the group matter? If, for example, you were to obtain a heritability coefficient for intelligence from a group of highly advantaged children, those with plentiful resources, enrichment, and educational support, you would find a heritability coefficient with a high value. On the other hand, if you studied children with diverse backgrounds, those from impoverished up to privileged homes, you would find a heritability coefficient with a much lower value. How can the same characteristic, intelligence, have two very different heritability coefficients? Remember that the heritability coefficient is a statistical estimate of how much of the variability within a group is due to genetic factors. For the group of children from advantaged backgrounds, environmental factors that influence intelligence would be very similar from one individual to the next and so unable to explain individual differences. If the variation in intelligence within this group cannot be accounted for by the environment, then it could be due to genetic factors and the heritability coefficient would estimate a high value. Within the second group that included children from a wide range of backgrounds, more of the differences can be attributed to differences in the environment and hence the heritability estimate would be low.

Knowing the level of genetic similarity in family members and relatives provides a basis for estimating the relative contributions of heredity and environment to a physical or psychological characteristic (Plomin, 1997). If a characteristic has higher **concordance**, or co-occurrence, in people who are more highly related to one another, this points to a possible genetic contribution, particularly if the people have lived in different environments.

One research method based on this principle is the **adoption study**, in which a person who was adopted early in life is compared on some characteristic both with the biological parents, with whom the person shares genetic endowment, and with the adoptive parents, with whom no genes are shared. If the adopted person is more

TABLE 4.1 Heritability Estimates for Various Human Characteristics

Trait	Heritability Estimate
Height	.80
Weight	.60
Intelligence (IQ)	.50–.70
School achievement	.40
Personality	
Extraversion	.36
Conscientiousness	.28
Agreeableness	.28
Emotional stability	.31
Temperament	
Emotional reactivity	.40
Activity level	.25
Sociability	.25
Impulsivity	.45

SOURCES: Bouchard et al., 1990; Dunn & Plomin, 1990; Tellegen et al., 1988.

similar to the biological parents than to the adoptive parents, a genetic influence is suggested. If greater similarity is shown with the adoptive parents, environmental factors are probably more important. In one study of genetic factors in schizophrenia, Seymour Kety and co-workers (1978) identified formerly adopted children who were diagnosed with the disorder later in life. They then examined the backgrounds of the biological and adoptive parents and relatives to determine the rate of schizophrenia in the two sets of families. The researchers found that 12 percent of biological family members also had been diagnosed with schizophrenia, compared to a concordance rate of only 3 percent of adoptive family members, suggesting a hereditary link.

7. How are adoption and twin studies used to achieve heritability estimates? What have such studies shown?

Twin studies are one of the more powerful techniques used in behaviour genetics. *Monozygotic* (identical) twins develop from the same fertilized egg, so they are genetically identical (Figure 4.2). Approximately 1 in 250 births produces identical twins. *Dizygotic* (fraternal) twins develop from two fertilized eggs, so they share 50 percent of their genetic endowment, like any other set of brothers and sisters. They occur once in 125 births.

8. Why are studies of twins raised together and apart especially informative? What findings have occurred in such studies?

Twins are usually raised in the same familial environment. Thus we can compare concordance rates or behavioural similarity in samples of identical and fraternal twins, assuming that, if the identical twins are far more similar to one another than are the fraternal twins, a genetic factor is likely to be involved. Of course, it is always possible that, because identical twins are more similar to one another in appearance than are fraternal twins, they might be treated more alike and therefore share a more similar environment. This environmental factor could partially account for greater behavioural similarity in identical twins. To rule out this environmental explanation for greater psychological similarity, behaviour geneticists have adopted an even more elegant research method. Sometimes they are able to find and compare sets of identical and fraternal twins who were separated very early in life and raised in *different* environments (Lykken, Bouchard, McGue, & Tellegen, 1993). This design permits a better basis for evaluating the respective contributions of genes and environment.

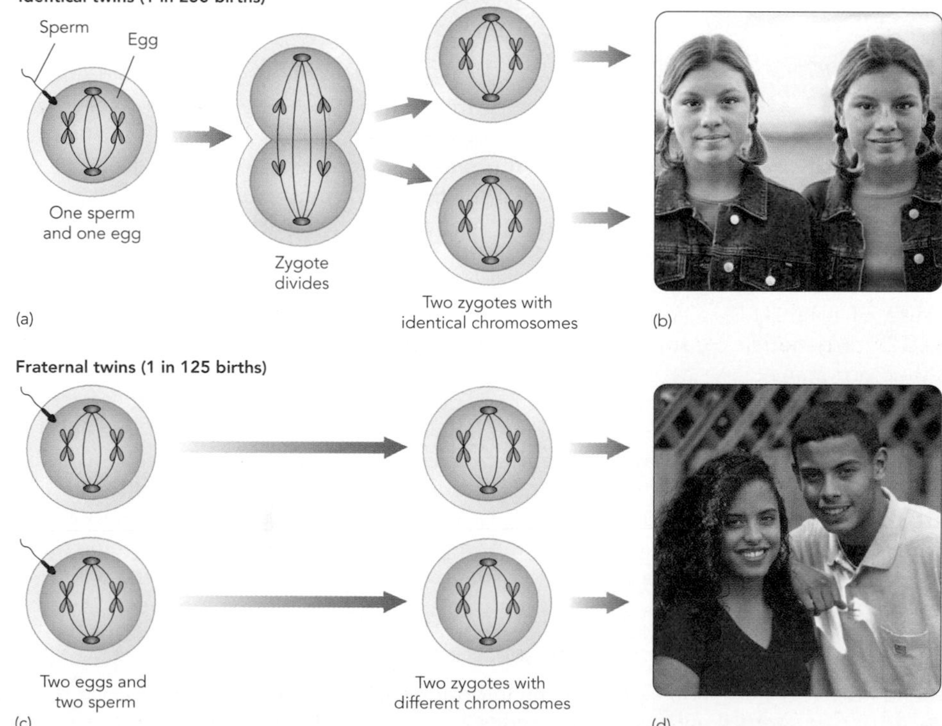

FIGURE 4.2

Identical (monozygotic) twins come from a single egg and sperm as a result of a division of the zygote. They have all of their genes in common. Fraternal (dizygotic) twins result from two eggs fertilized by two sperm. As a result, they share only half of their genes.

PSYCHOLOGICAL APPLICATIONS

Genetic Counselling

You are 18 years old and have just learned that one of your parents has been diagnosed with Huntington's disease. Huntington's disease is a degenerative condition that is invariably fatal, typically 5 to 15 years after the first emergence of symptoms. The symptoms usually appear between the ages of 30 and 45. Huntington's disease is caused by a single dominant gene, so your chance of having Huntington's disease is 50 percent. Your parent's diagnosis will have an enormous impact on your family and your family's future; you know your parent will now live less than 15 years and the last part of this period, when they are in the late stages of Huntington's disease, will be spent in a hospital. And what about you? There is a test to detect the presence of the Huntington's disease gene. Do you want to know if you will develop Huntington's disease when you are in your thirties or early forties? How will knowing, or not knowing, influence your decision to marry and start a family of your own? What about your career plans and life goals?

Genetic counsellors help people deal with such issues. Genetic counselling is a health care service that provides counselling, support, and medical information about genetic disorders and risks. A genetic counsellor provides information on the inheritance of illnesses; addresses the concerns of patients, their families, and their health care providers; and supports patients and their families dealing with illness.

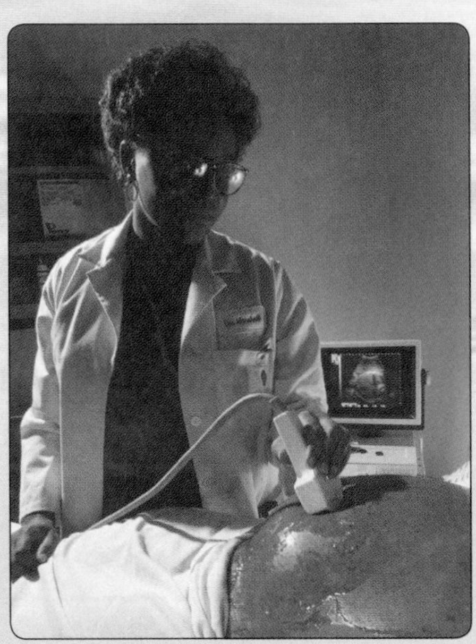

FIGURE 4.3

A genetic counsellor works with other health care professionals, such as obstetricians, to provide advice and support to a couple for whom pregnancy presents special risks because the unborn child may be affected by a genetic disorder.

The goal of genetic counselling is to assist the individual in making decisions about their own or their family's health care. With the completion of the mapping of the human genome in 2001 the role of genetic counselling has increased in scope and importance. Clients may seek advice from a genetic counsellor because they have a disorder or because of a family member's illness, couples with a child affected by a genetic disorder may seek advice as they plan another pregnancy, couples who are planning their first pregnancy may want to understand their future child's disease susceptibility, especially if they are planning a pregnancy late in life, or currently healthy clients may seek advice about lifestyle changes if they are at risk for a disease or disorder. Genetic counselling is useful at all stages of life, from newborns undergoing screening, to teenagers or young adults being tested for disease susceptibility, to middle aged or older adults seeking lifestyle changes appropriate to their genetic predispositions.

Genetic counsellors are specially trained to work with individual patients and with the medical team involved in the patient's health care. A genetic counsellor has training in obtaining and communicating medical information and will help the patient and patient's family understand the medical facts, the way that heredity contributes to the disorder, and the impact of available treatments. Genetic counsellors are also involved in explaining and coordinating appropriate tests, and many work together with scientists and medical doctors in interpreting test results. That is, the genetic counsellor's role is to help the patient and the patient's family gather and understand pertinent information, and to assist them during what is often a difficult and traumatic time. Genetic counsellors provide support and counselling to families, serve as patient advocates, and refer individuals and families to support services. They also serve as educators and resource people for other health care professionals and for the general public. Genetic counsellors work in clinics and hospitals, but many now also work in locations other than the traditional hospital setting. Genetic counsellors work in the fields of education, administration, policy-making, and biotechnology.

The Canadian Association of Genetic Counsellors was formed in 1987. Genetic counselling in Canada is provided by individuals trained specifically as genetic counsellors, or by nurses with additional training in genetic counselling. Currently, three Canadian universities offer accredited graduate programs in genetic counselling—McGill University, the University of British Columbia, and the University of Toronto. An accredited genetic counsellor has a Master of Science degree in genetic counselling. Students entering these programs have a variety of undergraduate backgrounds, most commonly an undergraduate degree in biology, psychology, or social work. Genetic counsellors usually work as part of a team, typically with a geneticist, physicians, and health care professionals from other specialties such as oncologists, obstetricians, dieticians, social workers, and nurses (see Figure 4.3).

For someone faced with the dilemmas associated with the risk of a genetic disorder, or for whom a genetic disorder has been confirmed, such as the parent, family, and child in the opening paragraph, genetic counselling offers often invaluable assistance and support. For the 18-year-old described in the opening paragraph, the decision of whether or not to be tested for Huntington's disease is personal, but the expertise and support offered by genetic counselling can be invaluable in coming to an informed and appropriate decision.

Both adoption and twin studies have led behavioural geneticists to conclude that many psychological characteristics, including intelligence, personality traits, and certain psychological disorders, have a notable genetic contribution. Adoptive children frequently are found to be more similar to their biological parents than to their adoptive parents, and identical twins tend to be more similar to one another on many traits than are fraternal twins, even when they have been reared in different environments (Loehlin, 1992; Lykken et al., 1992; Plomin, 1997). Figure 4.4 shows the results of one such comparison. Three groups of twins—identical twins reared together and apart, and fraternal twins reared together—completed personality tests of extraversion (sociability, liveliness, impulsiveness) and neuroticism (moodiness, anxiousness, and irritability). The higher correlation coefficients reveal that the identical twins are more similar to one another than are the fraternal twins, and that the degree of similarity in identical twins on the trait of neuroticism is almost as great when they are reared in different environments as when they are reared together (Loehlin, 1992).

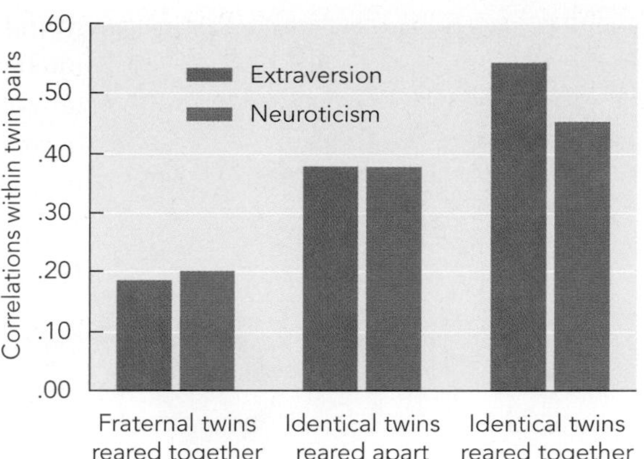

FIGURE 4.4

Degree of similarity on personality measures of extraversion and neuroticism of 24,000 pairs of twins who were reared together and apart.

Data from Loehlin, 1992.

On the other hand, behaviour genetics studies also have demonstrated that environmental factors interact with genetic endowment in important ways. For example, one adoption study compared the criminal records of men who were adopted at an early age with the criminal records of their biological fathers and their adoptive fathers. A low incidence of criminal behaviour was found in the sons whose biological fathers had no criminal record, even when the adoptive fathers who reared them had criminal records. In contrast, the criminal behaviour of sons whose biological fathers had criminal records was very high, even when their adoptive fathers had no criminal records. This pattern clearly points to a genetic component in criminality. But one additional finding deserves our attention: The level of criminality was highest of all for those sons whose biological and adoptive fathers *both* had criminal records, suggesting a combined impact of genetic and environmental factors (Cloninger & Gottesman, 1987). In this case, heredity and environment combined to create a double whammy for society. This finding underscores the conclusion that genetic and environmental factors almost always interact with one another to influence behaviour.

In Review

- *The field of behaviour genetics studies contributions of genetic and environmental factors in psychological traits and behaviours. The major research methods used in attempts to disentangle heredity and environmental factors are adoption and twin studies. The most useful research strategy in this area is the study of identical and fraternal twins who were separated in early life and raised in different environments.*
- *Behaviour genetics techniques allow a heritability coefficient to be determined for different characteristics. The heritability coefficient indicates the extent to which variation in a particular characteristic can be attributed to genetic factors.*

GENETIC INFLUENCES ON BEHAVIOUR

9. What evidence supports a genetic contribution to intelligence, and how much IQ group variation is accounted for?

Our unique characteristics as individuals arise from the combination of our learning experiences and the environment in which we behave acting upon a substrate provided by our genetic makeup. All of our behaviours reflect the interaction between genes and the environment. The best known and most fully explored (although still incomplete) studies of the genes-environment interaction comes from studies of intelligence and personality. Indeed, our growing understanding of intelligence has helped to elucidate how favourable and unfavourable environmental conditions act upon genetically determined potential. Studies of personality have helped to illustrate how opportunities provided by the environment influence the expression of genetically based differences.

Heredity, Environment, and Intelligence

One of the most controversial questions in the history of psychology is the question: To what extent are differences in intelligence due to genetic factors, and to what extent does environment determine differences in intelligence? From the time of Galton in the nineteenth century, this question has been at the centre of controversy and, at times, bitter debate. Proponents on each side of this debate have marshalled strong arguments and sound supporting data, but can both sides be right?

Let's first examine the genetic argument. Suppose that intelligence is totally determined by genes. (No psychologist today would maintain that it is, but examining the extreme view can be instructive.) In that case, any two individuals with exactly the same genes would have identical test scores, so the correlation between the test scores of identical (monozygotic) twins would be +1.00. Nonidentical brothers and sisters (including fraternal twins, who result from two fertilized eggs) share only half their genes. Therefore the correlation between the test scores of fraternal twins and other siblings should be substantially lower. Extending the argument, the correlation between a parent's test scores and his or her children's scores should be about the same as that between siblings, because a child inherits only half of his or her genes from each parent.

What do the actual data look like? Table 4.2 summarizes the results from many studies. As you can see, the correlations between the test scores of identical twins are substantially higher than any other correlations. Identical twins separated early in life and reared apart are of special interest because they have identical genes but experienced different environments. The correlation for identical twins raised apart is nearly as high as that for identical twins reared together, and higher than that for nonidentical twins raised together (Bouchard et al., 1990). Moreover, as Table 4.2 shows, IQs of adopted children correlate as highly with their biological parents' IQ as with the IQs of the adoptive parents who reared them. The pattern is quite clear: The more genes people have in common, the more similar they are in IQ. This is very strong evidence that genes play a significant role in intelligence (Petrill, 2003).

Notice, however, that the figure for identical twins raised together is higher than the figure for identical twins raised apart. The same is true for other types of siblings raised together and raised apart. This rules out an entirely genetic explanation. Although one's genotype seems to be an important factor in determining intelligence test scores, it probably accounts for only 50 to 70 percent of the IQ variation between people in the United States (Bouchard et al., 1990; Plomin, 1997). Thus environment, too, contributes significantly to intelligence. Obviously, then, the question with which this section began is too simplistic. The real question should be, "How do heredity and environment *interact* to affect intelligence?"

TABLE 4.2 Correlations in Intelligence among People Who Differ in Genetic Similarity and Who Live Together or Apart

Relationship	Percentage of Shared Genes	Correlation of IQ Scores
Identical twins reared together	100	.86
Identical twins reared apart	100	.75
Nonidentical twins reared together	50	.57
Siblings reared together	50	.45
Siblings reared apart	50	.21
Biological parent–offspring reared by parent	50	.36
Biological parent–offspring not reared by parent	50	.20
Cousins	25	.25
Adopted child-adoptive parent	0	.19
Adopted children reared together	0	.02

SOURCES: Based on Bouchard & McGue, 1981; Bouchard et al., 1990; Scarr, 1992.

FOCUS ON NEUROSCIENCE

The Neuroscience and Genetics of Dyslexia

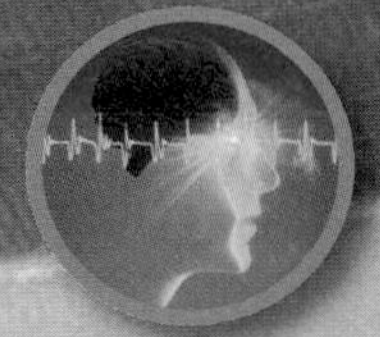

Dyslexia is defined as difficulty learning to read which cannot be explained by general intellectual impairment, educational opportunity, or sensory deficits. Dyslexia represents a meeting of an evolved behaviour, language, and a cultural invention—literacy (Pennington & Olson, 2005). Although first identified and studied more than a century ago, our understanding of dyslexia has increased dramatically within the past decade as both functional brain imaging and behavioural and molecular genetics studies have investigated this disorder.

Dyslexia was first described in the mid-1890s and reports that dyslexia tended to run in families began to appear as early as 1905 (Pennington & Olson, 2005). The early studies of the genetics of dyslexia, however, suffered from a number of methodological flaws and it is difficult to draw any firm conclusions from this early research. More recently, large, methodologically sound studies of reading ability among family members of those with dyslexia have contributed to our understanding of the genetics of dyslexia. In one large study of children identified as having difficulty reading, DeFries and colleagues found strong evidence for a familial transmission of dyslexia (DeFries, Singer, Foch, & Lewitter, 1978). Compared to the relatives of children whose reading ability was within the normal range, the relatives of children identified as having reading difficulties were significantly more likely to also have problems reading. These results have been confirmed by numerous studies, and current evidence indicates that genetic factors are very important in the development of dyslexia, especially among individuals with both a high IQ and dyslexia (Davis, Knopik, Olson, Wadsworth, & DeFries, 2001; Pennington & Olson, 2005). Twin studies also indicate a strong genetic component, with heritability estimates ranging from 0.5 to as high as 0.93 (DeFries, Fulker, & LaBuda, 1987; Petryshen et al., 2001). Behaviour genetics research on dyslexia has found that there is a genetic contribution to the entire range of reading ability, not only to dyslexia. That is, variations in reading skill, including dyslexia, are, in part, heritable. The next question is to determine what gene or genes contribute to the heritability of dyslexia.

Drs. Tracey Petryshen and Bonnie Kaplan of the University of Calgary and their colleagues at the University of Calgary and the University of British Columbia, have been among the leaders in the search for the genetic components of dyslexia (e.g., Petryshen, et al., 2001; Tzenova, Kaplan, Petryshen, & Field, 2004). In one study of 100 Canadian families tested for reading ability, they evaluated potential genetic linkages and found that two measures of dyslexia in particular showed strong evidence of genetic linkage (Tzenova, et al., 2004). These two measures were spelling and phonological coding (the ability to translate letters and syllables into sounds). Their research found a specific dyslexia susceptibility gene on chromosome 6; a finding that has been confirmed by at least four independent research groups (see Pennington & Olson, 2005). Research in behavioural and molecular genetics has found that there are at least six loci, one on each of chromosomes 1, 2, 3, 6, 15, and 18, that influence reading ability. It is interesting to note that none of these gene locations are on the X chromosome. It is popularly reported that dyslexia is a sex-linked disorder, appearing more commonly among males than females, but the evidence does not support this often reported idea. The widely reported male susceptibility to dyslexia is mostly a selection artifact and if corrected for selection biases, there is only a small preponderance of males (1.5:1 male:female), not the three or four time greater rate among males that is sometimes reported (Pennington & Olson, 2005).

If there are genes that influence one's susceptibility to dyslexia, the question is what do these genes do? The functions of the specific genes associated with dyslexia are not yet known, although several intriguing possibilities are currently being explored. The linkage to chromosome 6, the best replicated finding for dyslexia, implicates genes that code for several different substances that are important in brain development. That is, the alleles associated with dyslexia may act to cause subtle changes in brain development.

If the gene variants associated with dyslexia influence brain development and later brain function, then there should be differences in brain activity between those with dyslexia and those reading within the normal range when these individuals are reading. An important challenge with this research, however, is separating the different processes that are involved when reading aloud. When you read aloud you necessarily involve visual sensory processes to see the written words, the cognitive abilities used in reading itself, and then the motor demands of saying the word. Some of the potential confounds could be avoided by asking participants to read silently, but then the researchers would not know if the word was read correctly, or even if the participants had read the word at all. In this research it is also difficult to separate the abnormal processing that underlies dyslexia (i.e., the cause of the reading disorder) from differences that are due to performance deficits (i.e., the consequences of dyslexia).

The results of research on dyslexia using brain imaging techniques such as PET scans and fMRI have found many different brain areas that are involved in reading aloud. Although the results form these studies do not always agree, activity in two brain areas has been found consistently to differ in those with dyslexia and controls during reading. Dyslexics have been found to show less activation than controls in two areas of the left temporal lobe—the left inferior temporal cortex and

–Continued

the middle temporal cortex (see Figure 4.5; Price & McCrory, 2005). Reduced temporal lobe activity has been reported when participants with dyslexia were reading aloud or silently, when making decisions about word or syllable sounds, and when making decisions about word meanings. Furthermore, the level of activation within these areas of the left temporal lobe correlates positively with reading ability across a wide range of reading skill, not only with dyslexia (Price & McCrory, 2005). Whether dyslexia represents activation within these areas falling below some minimum threshold necessary for reading within the normal range, or whether dyslexia affects other, yet unidentified brain areas, is currently under debate (Price & McCrory, 2005).

The results of behaviour genetics studies of dyslexia have found evidence for important heritable components. The results of molecular genetics research have identified six different genetic locations that represent risk factors for the development of dyslexia and the potential gene products of these loci include factors that are involved in brain development. The results of brain imaging studies suggest that differences in the activity of the left temporal lobe are associated with reading ability. There are no large differences in brain activity associated with dyslexia or evidence of brain abnormalities; there are only subtle differences in the activation of neural systems involved in reading between dyslexics and controls. Although there is still a great deal to learn about dyslexia, progress is being made using the tools available in genetics and neuroscience and as our understanding of dyslexia increases it will inform more effective and efficient means of intervention.

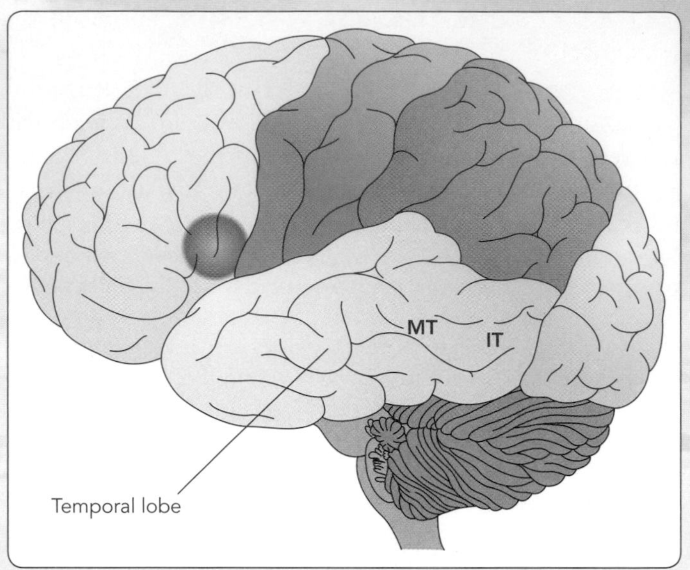

FIGURE 4.5

Brain imaging research has found two areas in which the levels of activation during reading differ consistently between those with dyslexia and those who read within the normal range. These areas are both within the left temporal lobe: the inferior temporal (shown as IT) and the middle temporal (MT) areas. Activity within the IT and MT areas of the left temporal lobe have been found to be lower among dyslexics, and research indicates that the level of activation within these areas correlates with reading ability across a range of reading skill.

Biological Reaction Range, Environment, and Intelligence

10. How does the concept of reaction range illustrate the interaction between heredity and environment?

The concept of reaction range contributes to our understanding of genetic-environmental interactions. The **reaction range** *for a genetically influenced trait is the range of possibilities—the upper and lower limits—that the genetic code allows.* Thus, to say that intelligence is genetically influenced does not mean that intelligence is fixed at birth. Instead, it means that an individual inherits a range for potential intelligence that has upper and lower limits. Environmental effects will then determine where the person falls within these genetically determined boundaries. Each of us has a range of intellectual potential that is jointly influenced by two factors: our genetic inheritance and the opportunities our environment provides for acquiring intellectual skills. The diverse abilities measured by intelligence tests are undoubtedly influenced by large numbers of interacting genes, and different combinations seem to underlie specific abilities (Luciano et al., 2001).

At present, genetic reaction ranges cannot be measured directly, and we do not know if their sizes differ from one person to another. But studies of IQ gains associated with environmental enrichment and adoption programs suggest that the ranges could be as large as 15 to 20 points on the IQ scale (Dunn & Plomin, 1990). If this is indeed the case, then the influence of environmental factors on intelligence would be highly significant.

Some practical implications of the reaction range concept are illustrated in Figure 4.6. First, consider persons B and H. They have identical reaction ranges, but B develops in a very deprived environment and H in an enriched environment with many cultural and educational advantages. Person H is able to realize her innate potential and has an IQ that is 20 points higher than person B's. Now compare persons C and I. Person C actually has greater intellectual potential than person I, but ends up with a lower IQ as a result of living in an environment that does not allow that potential to develop. Finally, note person G, who was born with high genetic endowment and reared in an enriched environment. His IQ of 110 is lower than we would expect, suggesting that he did not take advantage of either his biological capacity or his environmental advantages. This serves to reminds us that intellectual growth depends not only on genetic endowment and environmental advantage but also on interests, motivation, and other personal characteristics that affect how much we "apply ourselves," or take advantage of our gifts and opportunities.

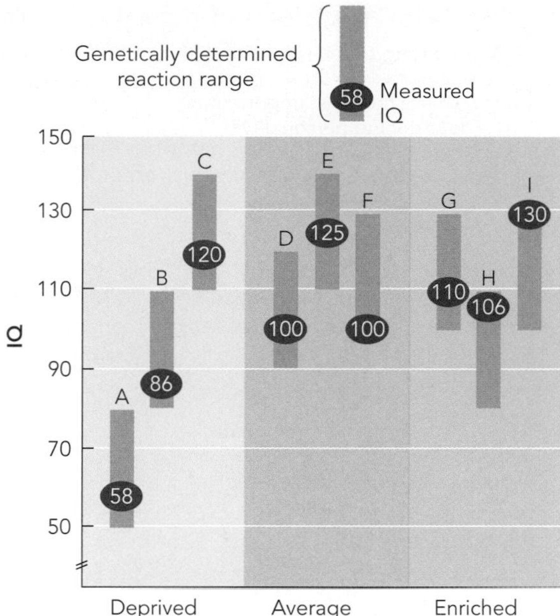

FIGURE 4.6

Reaction ranges, environment, and intelligence. Genetic endowment is believed to create a reaction range within which environment exerts its effects. Enriched environments are expected to allow a person's intelligence to develop to the upper region of his or her reaction range, whereas deprived environments may limit intelligence to the lower portion of the range. The reaction range may cover as much as 15 to 20 points on the IQ scale.

Behaviour Genetics and Personality

Increasingly, personality theorists are working to trace differences in personality characteristics to specific differences in brain activity. Hans Eysenck was one of the first modern personality theorists to suggest a biological basis for major personality traits. Eysenck argued that personality differences could be traced to differences in brain development or function. The personality dimension extraversion-introversion, for example, was argued to reflect differences in brain arousal (Eysenck, 1967). If such personality differences can be traced to specific aspects of brain development or function, then at least some genetic component would be expected.

Since Eysenck's pioneering work, other research has indeed found evidence for specific genetic components of some personality characteristics. For example, a relationship between neuroticism and a gene allele that increases the action of the neurotransmitter serotonin has been reported (Lesch et al., 1996), as has a relationship between novelty seeking and a single gene allele that decreases the action of the neurotransmitter dopamine (Benjamin et al., 1996). The research investigating specific genes and personality characteristics such as novelty seeking or extraversion is controversial, and current findings, although suggestive, are controversial. Clearly this research assumes that there is a genetic component to personality, but one may ask: how good is the evidence that a genetic component to personality even exists?

11. Apart from genetic makeup, how else are monozygotic twins similar or the same?

As discussed earlier, twin studies are particularly informative for studying the role of genetic factors because they compare the degree of resemblance between two individuals who are genetically identical, monozygotic twins, and two who are not, dizygotic twins (Rowe, 1999). As noted briefly under the section "Behaviour Genetics Techniques," across many psychological characteristics, identical twins are more similar to one another than are dizygotic twins, suggesting a role for genetics. The issue, however, is complicated by the possibility that identical twins may also have more similar experiences than fraternal twins. Because identical twins are more similar than fraternal twins in appearance, size, and physical characteristics, others may treat them more similarly. Indeed, some parents even dress identical twins in the same clothes, making it almost impossible for the twins to be treated differently within many contexts (Figure 4.7). Even someone who knows the twins may confuse one for the other. One of us is married to an identical twin. Although she and her sister did not dress alike or even wear their hair the same, from childhood to adulthood her grandparents called her by her own name about half of the time and by her twin's name about half of the time.

FIGURE 4.7

Identical twins may be more similar because people treat them similarly, influenced by their identical appearance, size, and even clothing.

12. According to the results of the Minnesota Twin Study, what factors were the most important in determining personality?

13. How might genes influence the tendency to enjoy reading or participating in organized sports?

The ideal approach would be to compare personality traits in identical and fraternal twins who either were raised together or reared apart. If identical twins who were reared in different environments, by different adoptive families, are as similar as those reared together, a powerful argument could be made for the role of genetic factors. Moreover, this research design would allow us to divide the total variation among individuals on each personality trait into three components: (1) variation attributable to genetic factors; (2) variation due to a shared family environment among those reared together; and (3) variation attributable to other factors, such as unique individual experiences. The relative influence of these sources of variation can be estimated by comparing personality test correlations among four groups of twins: identical twins reared together, identical twins reared apart, fraternal twins reared together, and fraternal twins reared apart (Plomin & Caspi, 1999; Scarr, 1992).

Several studies have used this powerful research design to assess the genetic contribution to a range of personality traits (Lykken et al., 1993; Pederson et al., 1988; Rhee, Waldman, 2002; Tellegen et al., 1988; Yamagata et al., 2006). These studies have shown that identical twins are far more similar in personality traits than are fraternal twins, and it makes little difference whether they were reared together or in different adoptive families. Contrary to what many personality psychologists had expected, family environment had little influence on personality differences in these studies.

One of the best known and largest of these studies was conducted by Lykken, Tellegen, and colleagues at the University of Minnesota. The so-called Minnesota Twin Study (in reference to the university and the participants, not the baseball team) assessed more than 400 pairs of twins, including Jim and Jim who we met at the start of this chapter. For those twins who were separated and reared apart, the median age of separation was 2.5 months, demonstrating relatively little shared experience within the same family environment. The results of this study are shown in Table 4.3. The four types of twin pairs completed measures of 14 different personality traits. Genetic factors accounted for 39 to 58 percent of the variation among people in personality trait scores. Surprisingly the degree of resemblance did not differ much whether the twin pair were reared together or apart, showing that general features of the family environment, such as emotional climate and degree of affluence, accounted for little or no variation in any of the traits. The absence of important effects of family environment, however, does not mean that experience does not matter. The individuals' unique experience, such as school experiences, social interactions, and individual learning experiences, was an important factor and accounted for 36 to 56 percent of the variation in individual personality traits. Even within the same family, individual children have different experiences while growing up, and it is this collection of unique experiences that help to shape personality.

More recently, collaborative work by Tony Vernon at the University of Western Ontario and Kerry Jang at the University of British Columbia and their colleagues

TABLE 4.3 **Estimates of the Percentages of Group Variance in 14 Personality Traits Attributable to Genetic and Environmental Factors**

Trait	Genetic	Familial Environment	Unique Environment
Well-being	.48	.13	.39
Social-potency	.54	.10	.36
Achievement	.39	.11	.50
Social closeness	.40	.19	.41
Stress reaction	.53	.00	.47
Alienation	.45	.11	.54
Aggression	.44	.00	.56
Control	.44	.00	.56
Harm avoidance	.55	.00	.45
Traditionalism	.45	.12	.43
Absorption	.50	.03	.47
Positive emotionality	.40	.22	.38
Negative emotionality	.55	.02	.43
Constraint	.58	.00	.42

*NOTE: The variance estimates are based on a comparison of the degree of personality similarity in identical and fraternal twins who were reared together or apart.
SOURCE: Data from Tellegen et al., 1988.

has demonstrated a genetic basis for a variety of personality and social dimensions. For example, Olson, Vernon, Harris, and Jang (2001) have shown that attitudes have an inherited component. They surveyed over 300 pairs of identical and fraternal twins on a wide variety of attitudinal and personality measures. Results indicated a significant genetic influence on 26 of 30 attitudinal measures and on 18 of 20 personality items. The highest heritability coefficients (all greater than 0.5) were found for attitudes towards reading books, abortion without restriction, playing organized sports, riding roller coasters, and the death penalty. A factor analysis revealed that, in general, attitudes towards preservation of life, equality, and athleticism had the highest genetic component. A "roller coaster gene" may sound like an absurd suggestion, but, as the authors cautioned, a direct and simple relationship between genes and attitudes is very unlikely. A more plausible explanation is that certain inherited factors (e.g., physical characteristics such as muscle coordination) may predispose individuals to prefer certain activities. For example, it is extremely unlikely that there is a "roller coaster gene" that accounts for the results. Genes do, however, control the development and function of physical characteristics such as the development and functioning of the vestibular system, the inner ear, and other structures that give us our sense of balance. If your genetic makeup has resulted in a vestibular system that is easily disrupted, with the consequent feelings of dizziness and nausea, you will not enjoy riding on roller coasters. On the other hand, if your vestibular system developed in a way that makes it more robust and less easily perturbed, that thrilling ride at the fair may give you exciting sensations of speed and movement without making you feel dizzy and nauseous (Figure 4.8).

FIGURE 4.8

Genetic contribution to roller-coaster appreciation may be as simple as how genes develop one's sense of balance.

Genetic influence has also been reported for a tendency to abuse alcohol (Jang, Vernon, & Livesley, 2000), a variety of personality disorder dimensions (Jang, Livesley, & Vernon, 1998; Ni et al., 2006), seasonal mood changes (Jang, Lam, Livesley, & Vernon, 1997), anxiety, and novelty seeking (Vormfelde, et al., 2006). It should be noted that, while there is a genetic component to these personality characteristics, the contribution of the environment, including the individual's unique experiences, is equally important (Plomin, Asbury & Dunn, 2001; Vernon, Jang, Harris, & McCarthy, 1997).

In Review

- *The more genetically similar two individuals, the higher the correlation between their IQ scores. The correlation between even genetically identical individuals, however, is not perfect, indicating an important role for the environment.*
- *Genetic factors contribute a reaction range for intelligence. Where within that range intelligence does develop depends on environmental factors.*
- *Identical twins are more alike than fraternal twins across a wide range of personality characteristics, indicating an important genetic component in personality traits. Together with genetic factors, an individual's unique experiences are important for personality; family environment has little impact.*
- *Genetic factors relevant for personality interact with the environment by predisposing an individual toward particular types of activities because of genetically influenced differences in brain activity, or other physical characteristics.*

EVOLUTION AND BEHAVIOUR

In the misty forests and verdant grasslands of past eons, our early human ancestors faced many environmental challenges as they struggled to survive. If even one of your ancestors had not behaved adaptively enough to survive and reproduce, he or she would not have passed on his or her genes and you would not be here to contemplate your existence. In this sense, each of us is an evolutionary success story. As descendants of those successful forebears, we carry within us genes that contributed to their adaptive and reproductive success. The vast majority of genes we share in common with all other humans create the "human nature" that makes us like all other people. We enter the world with inborn biological mechanisms that enable and predispose us to behave, to feel, and even to think in certain ways.

The field of *evolutionary psychology* seeks to understand how behavioural abilities and tendencies have evolved over the course of millions of years in response to environmental demands. No behaviour by any organism can occur in the absence of **biologically based mechanisms** that receive input from the environment, process the information, and respond to it (Tooby & Cosmides, 1992). Until its closing in May 2000, the Canadian Centre for Wolf Research had allowed detailed studies of a wolf pack over a period of 25 years. Many behaviours shown by these intelligent and highly social animals illustrate the interaction between environmental demands, behaviour, and the biological mechanisms that support behaviour. For example, the most important part of a wolf's life is its pack; a solitary wolf cannot survive for long in the wild. Dr. F. H. Harrington, of Mount Saint Vincent University, has argued that the famous wolf howl functions both as long-distance communication between pack members as they hunt over large distances and as a way to maintain separation from adjacent, and competing, wolf packs (Harrington, 2000). The wolf's environment and the evolved behavioural and biological responses to that environment, such as the wolf howl and the biological mechanisms that allow the wolf to howl and respond to the howls of others, have allowed the wolf to survive.

In humans, these inborn mechanisms allow us to, among other things, learn, remember, speak a language, perceive certain aspects of our environment at birth, respond with universal emotions, and bond with other humans. Evolutionary psychologists also believe that important aspects of social behaviour, such as aggression, altruism, sex roles, protecting kin, and mate selection, are the products of evolved mechanisms. They are quick to point out that no behaviour as such ever evolves; what evolves are genetically produced physical structures that interact with the demands of the environment to produce a behaviour.

Evolution of Adaptive Mechanisms

Evolution

14. Define evolution and explain how genetic variation and natural selection produce adaptations.

Evolution is a change over time in the frequency with which particular genes—and the characteristics they produce—occur within an interbreeding population. As particular genes become more or less frequent in a population, so do the characteristics they influence. Some genetic variations arise in a population through *mutations,* random events and accidents in gene reproduction during the division of cells. If mutations occur in the cells that become sperm and egg cells, the altered genes will be passed on to offspring. Mutations help create variation within a population's physical characteristics. It is this variation that makes evolution possible.

Long before Charles Darwin published his theory of evolution in 1859, people knew that animals and plants could be changed over time by breeding members of a species that shared desired traits. Although Darwin knew nothing about genes, he knew that *something* must be passed on to the next generation through reproduction in order for evolution to occur. Darwin's landmark contribution was in specifying the process by which species change over time as they adapt to environmental demands.

Cartoon by Don Wright, © 2001.

Natural Selection

Just as plant and animal breeders "select" for certain characteristics, so, too, does nature. According to Darwin's principle of **natural selection**, characteristics that increase the likelihood of survival and ability to reproduce within a particular environment will be more likely to be preserved in the population and therefore will become more common in the species over time. As environmental changes produce new and different demands, some different characteristics may contribute to survival and the ability to pass on one's genes (Barrow, 2003). In this way, natural selection acts as a set of filters, allowing certain characteristics of survivors to become more common and those of nonsurvivors to become less common and, perhaps, even extinct over time. The filters also allow "neutral" variations that neither facilitate nor impede fitness to pass through and be preserved in a population. These neutral variations, sometimes called *evolutionary noise,* could conceivably become important in meeting some future environmental demand. For example, people differ in their ability to tolerate radiation (Vral et al., 2002). In today's world, these variations are of limited importance, but they could clearly affect survivability if a future nuclear war were to increase levels of radioactivity around the world. As those who could tolerate higher levels of radiation survived and those who could not perished, the genetic basis for radiation tolerance would become increasingly more common in the human species. Thus, for natural selection to work, there must be individual variation in a relevant species characteristic.

Adaptations

The products of natural selection are called adaptations. **Adaptations** allow organisms to meet recurring environmental challenges to their survival, thereby increasing their reproductive ability. In the final analysis, the name of the natural selection game is to pass on one's genes, either personally or through kin who share at least some of them. Some evolutionary psychologists believe this is why animals and humans may risk or even sacrifice their lives to protect their kin.

Let us apply these concepts to human evolution. We begin with the notion that an organism's biology determines its behavioural capabilities, and its behaviour (including its mental abilities) determines whether or not it will survive. In this manner, successful human behaviour evolved along with a changing body (Buss, 1995; Tooby & Cosmides, 1992).

One theory is that, when dwindling vegetation in some parts of the world forced apelike animals from the trees and required that they hunt for food on open, grassy plains, chances for survival were greater for those who were capable of *bipedal locomotion* (walking on two legs), thereby freeing the hands to use weapons that could kill at a distance (Lewin, 1998). By freeing the hands, bipedalism fostered the development and use of tools and weapons, and hunting in groups encouraged social organization. Social organization required the development of specialized social roles (such as "hunter and protector" in the male and "nurturer of children" in the female). It also favoured the development of language, which enhanced social communication and the transmission of knowledge. Our ancestors' emerging social organization provides an example of how changes contribute to evolutionary development. Social roles emerged as a result of biological predispositions, selection pressures (e.g., women who were sensitive to the needs of their young children likely had more of their children survive, men who provided for their children had more of their children survive) and emerging social organization. The social roles and social organization, shaped by evolutionary processes, themselves become selection pressures that help to shape the species as it continues to evolve.

Tool use, bipedal locomotion, and social organization put new selection pressures on many parts of the body. These included the teeth, the hands, and the pelvis, all of which changed over time in response to the new dietary and behavioural demands. But the greatest pressure was placed on the brain structures involved in the abilities most critical to the emerging way of life: attention, memory, language, and thought. These mental abilities became important to survival in an environment that required the ability to learn quickly and to solve problems. In the evolutionary progression from *Australopithecus* (an early human ancestor who lived about 4 million years ago) through *Homo erectus* (1.6 million to 100,000 years ago) to the human subspecies Neanderthal of 75,000 years ago, the brain tripled in size, and the most dramatic growth occurred in the parts of the brain that are the seat of the higher mental processes (Figure 4.9). Thus, evolved changes in behaviour seem to have contributed to the development of the brain, just as the growth of the brain contributed to evolving human behaviour.

Surprisingly, perhaps, today's human brain does not differ much from the Stone Age brain of our ancient ancestors. In fact, Neanderthal had a slightly larger brain. Yet the fact that we perform mental activities that could not have been imagined in those ancient times tells us that human capabilities are not solely determined by the brain; cultural evolution is also important in the development of

Australopithecus
(4 million years ago)

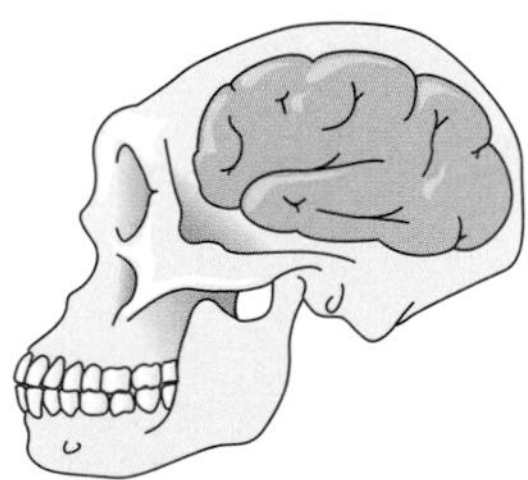

The brain capacity ranges from 450 to 650 cubic centimetres (cc).

Homo erectus
(1.6 million to 100,000 years ago)

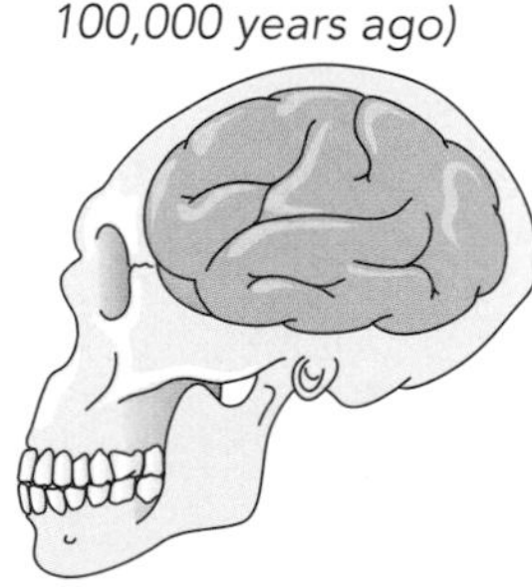

Further development of skull and jaw are evident and brain capacity is 900 cc.

Neanderthal
(75,000 years ago)

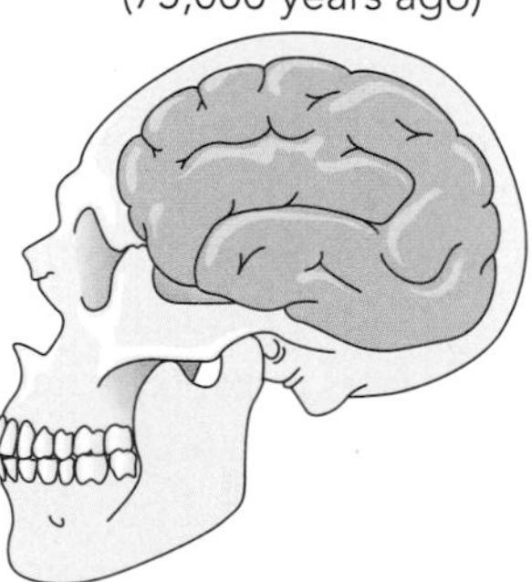

The human skull has now taken shape: the skull case has elongated to hold a complex brain of 1,450 cc.

Homo sapiens

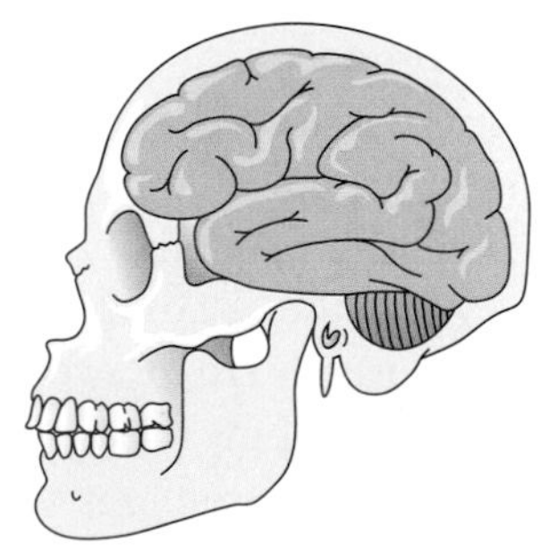

The deeply convoluted brain reflects growth in areas concerned with higher mental processes.

FIGURE 4.9

The human brain evolved over a period of several million years. The greatest growth occurred in those areas concerned with the higher mental processes, particularly attention, memory, thought, and language.

adaptations. From an evolutionary perspective, culture provides important environmental input to evolutionary mechanisms.

Some evolved biological mechanisms allow broad adaptations, such as the ability to learn a language, repeat behaviours that are rewarded and suppress those that are punished, reason logically, and imagine future events. Others are considered to be **domain-specific adaptations**, designed to solve a particular problem, such as selecting a suitable mate, choosing safe foods to eat, avoiding certain environmental hazards (snakes, cliff edges, spiders), detecting cheating and deception in others, and forming cooperative alliances with other people. Domain-specific mechanisms suggest that the human mind is not a general, all-purpose problem solver but rather a collection of specialized and somewhat independent *modules* that evolved to handle specific adaptive problems. As we shall see throughout the book, this modular approach to brain/mind functioning helps us understand many aspects of consciousness, problem solving, emotion, personality, and behaviour.

An Evolutionary Snapshot of Human Nature

15. Describe examples of human behaviour that suggest innate evolved mechanisms. Differentiate between remote and proximate causal factors.

Evolutionary psychologists suggest that the essence of human nature is the adaptations that have evolved through natural selection to solve problems specific to the human environment. We now consider a sampling of common aspects of human behaviour that will be discussed in greater detail throughout the book.

- Infants are born with an innate ability to acquire any language spoken in the world. The specific language(s) learned depends on which ones they are exposed to. Deaf children have a similar innate ability to acquire any sign language, and their language acquisition pattern parallels the learning of spoken language. Language is central to human thought and communication.
- Newborns are prewired to perceive specific stimuli. For example, they are more responsive to pictures of human faces than to pictures of the same facial features arranged in a random pattern (Fantz, 1961). They are also able to discriminate the odour of their mother's milk from that of other women (McFarlane, 1975). Both adaptations improve human bonding with caregivers.
- At one week of age, human infants show primitive mathematical skills, successfully discriminating between two and three objects. These abilities improve with age in the absence of any training. The brain seems designed to make "greater than" and "less than" judgments, which are clearly important in decision making (Geary, 1995).
- According to Robert Hogan (1983), establishing cooperative relationships with a group was critical to the human species' survival and reproductive success. Thus, humans seem to have a need to belong and strongly fear being ostracized from the group. Social anxiety (fear of social disapproval) may be an adaptive mechanism to protect against doing things that will prompt group rejection (Baumeister & Tice, 1990).
- As we will see in Chapter 10, there is much evidence for a set of basic emotions that are universally recognized (Ekman, 1973). Smiling, for example, is a universal expression of happiness and goodwill that typically evokes positive reactions from others (Figure 4.10). Emotions are important means of social communication that evoke psychological mechanisms in others (Ketelaar, 1995).

FIGURE 4.10

The human smile seems to be a universal expression of positive emotion and is universally perceived that way. Evolutionary psychologists believe that expressions of basic emotions are hard-wired biological mechanisms that have adaptive value as methods of communication.

In Review

- *Evolutionary psychology focuses on biologically based mechanisms sculpted by evolutionary forces as solutions to the problems of adaptation faced by species. Some of these genetically based mechanisms are general (e.g., the ability to learn), but many are domain-specific (e.g., mate selection).*
- *Evolution involves a change over time in the frequency with which specific genes occur within an interbreeding population. Evolution represents an interaction between biological and environmental factors in both its original and later influences on behaviour.*
- *The cornerstone of Darwin's theory of evolution is the principle of natural selection, which posits that biologically based characteristics that contribute to survival and reproductive success increase in the population over time because those who lack the characteristic are less likely to pass on their genes.*

Evolutionary Psychology

As is clear from the quotation that opens this chapter, Charles Darwin expected that an evolutionary analysis would be applied to behaviour, including human behaviour, and not just anatomy. Darwin himself wrote about human emotions and other behaviours, and some early psychologists, such as William James, continued that theme. Despite this long history, it is only recently that evolutionary psychology has become a major, and growing, perspective within psychology. An evolutionary analysis is being applied across a growing range of behaviours from traditional areas of evolutionary analysis such as mating patterns, to personality traits and even consciousness (Bridgeman, 2003). Whatever the specific topic, an evolutionary psychologist thinks about behaviour in terms of functions and how those functions contribute to the success and adaptability of the individual.

Personality

Behaviour genetics researchers attempt to understand how biological factors contribute to differences between individuals on personality traits. An approach called **evolutionary personality theory** (Buss, 1999) asks an even more basic question: Where did the traits come from in the first place?

A current theory of personality argues that there are a limited number of basic dimensions to human personality. These basic personality traits have been argued to be found universally across all humans. Why should we find these traits so consistently in cultures around the world? According to David Buss, an evolutionary personality theorist, they exist in humans because they have helped us achieve two overriding goals: physical survival and reproduction of the species (Buss, 1999). Traits such as extraversion and emotional stability were helpful in attaining positions of dominance and mate selection. Conscientiousness and agreeableness might be particularly important to group survival, as well as in reproduction and the care of children. Finally, because openness to experience may be the basis for problem solving and creative activities that could affect the ultimate survival of the species, there has always been a need for intelligent and creative people. Thus evolutionary theorists regard basic personality traits as having been sculpted by natural selection pressures until they became part of human nature. They may also reflect the ways in which we are biologically prepared to think about and discriminate between people. Lewis Goldberg (1981) suggests that over the course of evolution, people have had to ask five basic questions when they interact with another person. In order of importance, these questions have survival and reproductive implications:

16. According to evolutionary theorists, what is the origin of the basic personality traits?

1. Is Person X active and dominant or passive and submissive? Can I dominate X or will I have to submit to X?
2. Is Person X agreeable and friendly, or hostile and uncooperative?
3. Can I count on X? Is X conscientious and dependable?
4. Is X sane (stable, rational, predictable) or crazy (unstable, unpredictable, possibly dangerous)?
5. How smart is X, and how quickly can X learn and adapt?

Not surprisingly, according to Goldberg, these questions map onto five basic personality traits. He believes that this is why factor analyses of trait ratings reveal the same five traits consistently across very diverse cultures. One issue that could arise from considering human personality from an evolutionary analysis is the range of human personality. If extraversion and openness to experience are adaptive and selected for, why, then, are we not all extraverted and open to new experiences? Extraversion is adaptive in some situations, but introversion can also be adaptive in some situations and in some social roles. Similarly, openness to experience is adaptive in many situations and social roles, but not all. One of the reasons that humankind has been so successful is that we are a high adaptable social species. In different times, in different environments, within different social roles, the range of personality characteristics that we can display has allowed us to adapt and thrive.

Mating Systems and Parental Investment

The task facing any species is to insure not only the survival of the current generation but also the survival of the next generation. Of the possible strategies that have evolved to solve this task, at one extreme are species that produce an extremely large number of offspring and offer little or no care but enough of the young survive to continue the species. Many types of fish as well as other animals take this approach. Large numbers of eggs are laid, but many eggs are lost to predation and only a tiny proportion of hatchlings survive to adulthood. At the other extreme are species that produce few offspring, but offer care and protection until the offspring are self-sufficient and capable of surviving on their own. The evolution of many animals, including humans, led to this later approach. Humans and most other mammals

17. What is meant by parental investment?

18. How does the idea of parental investment explain differences in physical size between the sexes?

invest a great deal in a small number of offspring to protect and sustain the next generation in an environment with limited resources and danger of predation (Figure 4.11). From this basic dichotomy—little investment in many offspring versus large investment in few offspring—there are also differences between the sexes because of what females and males each contribute to reproduction. That is, one difference across species is in **parental investment**. Parental investment refers to the time, effort, energy, and risk associated with caring successfully for each offspring.

In one of the most influential papers in modern evolutionary theory, Robert Trivers (1972) described a theory in which he used sex differences in parental investment to explain different mating systems. An offspring of a sexually reproducing species has two parents, but the two parents do not necessarily make equal parental investment. Trivers argued that if parental investment is unequal, the parent who invests most in offspring will be more vigorously competed for and will be more discriminating when choosing a mate. One source of sex difference in parental investment is the simple fact of biology that male and female reproductive cells, or gametes, differ. Female mammals produce relatively few large, nutrient rich gametes, that is, ova or eggs. Males produce many, small, mobile gametes, the sperm. Investment continues to diverge during the nine months of human gestation, then delivery, and then breast feeding (which can last up to four years in some human societies; Shostach, 1981). Although some components of parental investment can vary, there is, at the core, a sex difference due to the biological differences between male and female roles in reproduction.

If females of a species have high parental investment and necessary male parental investment is low, Trivers's theory predicts that polygyny would be most common. Female investment is high, so females will be competed for, and necessary male investment is low, so males can maximize their fitness by producing many offspring with many different females. Most mammals are polygynous, a mating system in which one male may mate with many females (**polygyny** means literally poly-: many; -gyn-: females). Such a system should lead to larger and stronger males since increased size and strength would confer an advantage in male-male competition. In general, it is true that the more polygynous the species, the greater the difference in size between males and females, with the males of the species larger than the females (Figure 4.12). The female, on the other hand, should be discriminating in choice of mate. She can produce a limited number of offspring, and each is a large investment. A poor choice by the female has important consequences: lower reproductive success; risk to her health; fewer of her children will survive to reproductive age; and opportunities for more successful matings missed.

If both female and male investment is high, then Trivers's analysis would predict a **monogamous mating system**. Equal, or approximately equal, parental investment would be expected if it is unlikely that a single parent can successful raise the offspring (Dewsbury, 1988). Natural selection would favour genes that lead to parents staying together, at least until the young are self-sufficient. One reason that many species of birds (approximately 90 percent; Lack, 1968) are monogamous is that it is almost impossible for a single parent to successfully care for young. The eggs must be incubated, and the eggs and the flightless hatchlings need constant protection from predators. A lone parent faces the dilemma of staying at the nest to care for and protect eggs and hatchlings or leaving the nest to find food. A second parent that can share in incubation, protection, and foraging is an enormous advantage. If parental investment is high among both females and males, competition for a mate is not limited to one sex and monogamous species should show few sex differences in size and strength. Monogamous species show little sexual dimorphism in size or strength.

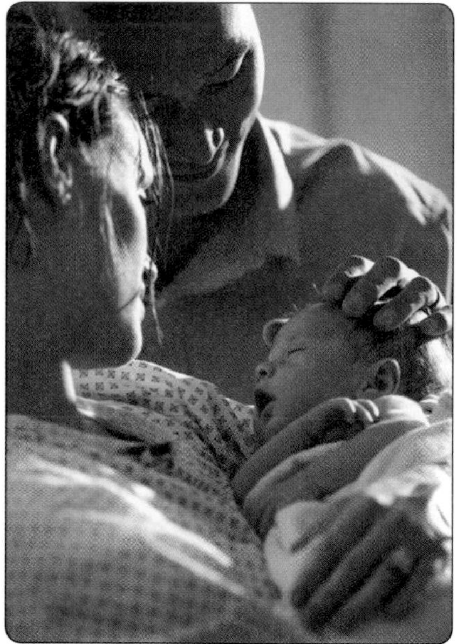

FIGURE 4.11

Some animals, such as the sea turtles shown here, produce enough offspring that even without protection or care enough will survive to adulthood to continue the species. Other species, such as humans, produce few young but offer extensive care until the offspring are self-sufficient.

Of other possible mating systems, **polyandry**, in which one female mates with many males, is rare among mammals but occurs in some species of fish and insects, as well as in a small number of bird species. Within polyandrous species, it is the females who compete with each other for access to males. Consistent with a parental investment analysis, the females of polyandrous species are larger, stronger, more active, and more aggressive than the males of the species.

The final mating system is one of **polygynandry**, or promiscuity, in which all members of the group mate with all other members of the group. Polygynandry is found among some primates such as chimpanzees (Goodall, 1986) and is especially clear among bonobo chimps (Wrangham, 1993). For a highly social species such as bonobos, polygynandry is one possible way to reduce competition for a mate, and may help bonobos be the most peaceful of all primates.

For humans, modern birth control techniques have altered much of the selective pressures for specific mating patterns based on parental investment in reproduction. But it needs to be remembered that human sexual psychology evolved over millions of years to cope with the pressures of adapting to the environment millennia before the advent of birth control. It is still the case that the human female has the greater necessary parental investment. But beyond the necessary minimal parental investment dictated by our reproductive physiology, it is clear that there is the potential for both men and women to invest in children and that parental investment by the male does have an impact on the likelihood that the young will thrive. Even within human societies that are nominally polygynous, and the few putatively polyandrous societies, many young adults find a single partner and stay together for prolonged periods, and even throughout life (Wilson & Daly, 1992).

FIGURE 4.12

Among polygynous species, such as the elephant seals shown here, natural selection has favoured large males but there has been no such selection pressure on females. If the species is monogamous, both sexes compete for mates, so there is no selection pressure for one sex to become significantly larger than the other.

19. What mating system described by Trivers fits with your experience of human society?

Mate Preference

As discussed above, the theory of parental investment predicts that there will be competition for the sex with the highest parental investment. It also predicts that the sex with the greater parental investment will be more discriminating when selecting a mate. Evolutionary psychologists have argued that the most common and powerful mate preferences are all preferences that make the most sense from an evolutionary perspective. The results of a worldwide study of mate preferences, for example, found considerable overlap between what men and women look for in a mate, but also reported differences (Figure 4.13). Both men and women rate

20. How are male and female mate preferences similar? How are they different?

FIGURE 4.13

Culture determines many details about how we live our lives, such as what is appropriate wedding attire. There is surprising consistency across cultures, however, in what men and women each look for in a mate.

mutual attraction, dependability, and emotional stability, respectively, as the three most important characteristics (Buss et al., 1990). Beyond these similarities, men place somewhat greater value on physical attractiveness and good health; women place greater value on a mate's earning potential, status, and ambitiousness (Buss et al., 1990; Toro-Morn & Sprecher, 2003) (see the Research Foundations box).

Women also prefer older men as potential mates. Averaged over all cultures, women preferred men who were about three and a half years older. The actual worldwide average age difference between brides and grooms is three years, and in every culture studied, grooms were older, on average, than brides. That is, the actual marriage decisions of women match their expressed preferences. Evolutionarily this preference makes sense: Young adult males rarely have the respect, status, and access to resources that are achieved by older, more established males. Male physical strength increases into young adulthood and peaks in the late twenties and early thirties. Males in traditional hunter-gatherer societies have their peak access to resources in their late twenties, when status and physical strength are high, or later in life, when accumulated experience, skill, wisdom, and social status confer advantages, not when they are entering adulthood. Even within modern North American society, income changes with age. For example, according to the 2001 Canadian census, males between 15 and 24 years of age had an average annual income of $11,342; for those between 25 and 34, it was $34,797; and for men between 35 and 44, it was $46,528 (Statistics Canada, *2001 Census of Canada*).

Together with the woman's preference for a slightly older mate, women also show a preference for symmetrical faces and other signs of physical health (Thornhill & Gangestad, 2006). A symmetrical face is especially valued by women. Males who have a symmetrical face are judged to be more attractive by women, and such men have more sexual partners during their lifetime (Buss, 1999; Thornhill & Moeller, 1997). A symmetrical face is a sign that the person is free of parasites or has a genetic resistance to parasites, and has had a healthy and normal physical development.

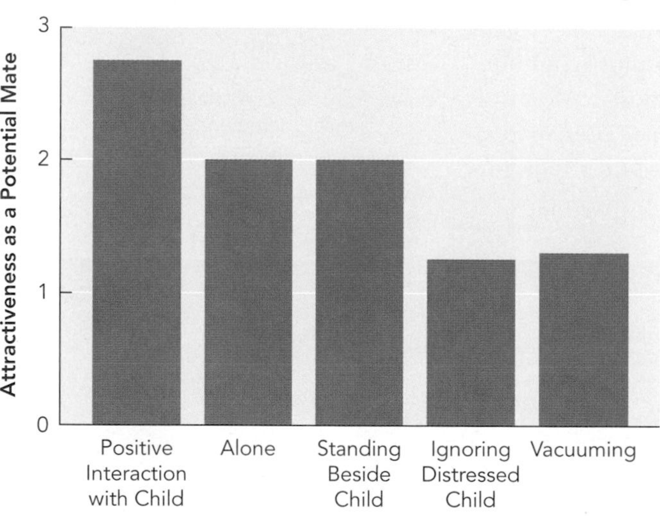

FIGURE 4.14

When rating males on attractiveness as potential mates, evidence of parental investment, such as positive emotional interactions with a young child, increases attractiveness ratings while evidence of low investment, such as ignoring a distressed child, decreases attractiveness.

Adapted from Buss, 1999.

Given the large parental investment by women, and the added advantage to their children conferred by a mate who contributes to the care and rearing of those children, one would expect that women would prefer a mate who has demonstrated a willingness to contribute to a child's well-being. An interesting study by Peggy La Cerra (Buss, 1999) assessed whether women might have evolved a preference for men who show signs of high parental investment. La Cerra showed female undergraduate students pictures of males in one of five conditions: (1) standing alone; (2) smiling and playing with an 18-month old child; (3) ignoring a crying child; (4) with a child, but in an emotionally neutral pose with no male-child interaction; and (5) doing housework (vacuuming). The same set of males was shown in all conditions, so different ratings across the five conditions could not be due to the actual physical attractiveness of the men. Female undergraduates saw a series of 240 slides and then rated the males on a series of criteria, including how attractive the man was as a potential mate (see Figure 4.14). Women rated men who were interacting positively with the child the highest as a potential mate, and the man ignoring the crying child was rated the lowest. But it was not simply that the man interacting with the child portrayed an acceptable domestic scene; the man cleaning house was actually rated as less attractive than the man standing alone or the man and child shown in an emotionally neutral pose. That is, male attractiveness was enhanced by signs of parental investment and decreased by indifference toward a child in distress.

RESEARCH FOUNDATIONS

Gender Differences in the Ideal Mate

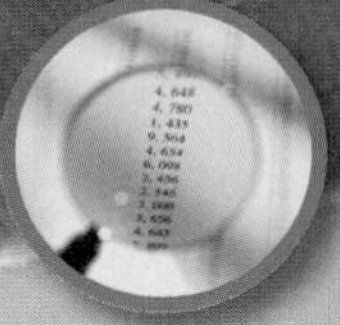

Background

How can we test the hypothesis that across millennia, evolution has shaped the psyche of men and women to be different? Evolutionary psychologist David Buss proposes that, as a start, we can examine whether gender differences in mate preferences are consistent across cultures. If they are, this would be consistent with the argument that men and women follow different, biologically based mating strategies that have developed during our evolutionary history. Buss hypothesized that across cultures

- Men will prefer younger women because such women have greater reproductive capacity;
- Men will value signs of physical health and fertility, such as attractiveness, more than women; and
- Women will place greater value than men on a potential mate's earning potential since such resources provide survival advantages for women and their children.

Method

A team of 50 scientists administered questionnaires to women and men from 37 cultures around the world. Although not randomly selected, the sample of 10,047 participants was ethnically, religiously, and socio-economically diverse. Participants reported the ideal age for marriage for themselves and their spouse, rank-ordered 13 different qualities from least to most desirable in a mate, and performed a separate rating of the importance of 18 mate qualities.

Results and Interpretation

In every culture, men preferred younger women. Overall, men reported that the ideal age for marriage was 27.5 for men and 24.8 for women, a difference of 2.7 years. Women preferred older males, and actually preferred a slightly larger age difference; on average, women reported that the ideal age for men to marry was 28.8 and for women 25.4 years, a difference of 3.4 years. In every one of the 37 cultures, men valued physical attractiveness of a mate more than women did. In 36 of the 37 cultures, women valued a mate's earning potential more than men did. Buss concluded that the results strongly supported the predictions based on evolutionary theory. Table 4.4 shows the study's overall results.

TABLE 4.4 What Do You Look For in a Mate?

Women and men from 37 cultures rated each characteristic on a 4-point scale. From top to bottom, the numbers represent the order (rank) and the most to least highly rated characteristic, for Buss's worldwide sample. How would you rate their importance?

	Preferred by			Preferred by	
Characteristic	Women	Men	Characteristic	Women	Men
Mutual attraction/love	1	1	Refinement	10	9
Dependable character	2	2	Similar education	11	14
Emotional stability/maturity	3	3	Good financial prospect	12	13
Pleasing disposition	4	4	Good looks	13	10
Education/intelligence	5	6	Social status	14	15
Sociability	6	7	Good cook/housekeeper	15	12
Good health	7	5	Similar religion	16	17
Desire for home/children	8	8	Similar politics	17	18
Ambitious	9	11	Chastity	18	16

Data from Buss et al., 1990.

–*Continued*

Conclusions

Buss's research provides evidence of remarkable cross-cultural consistency in gender differences in mate preferences. Buss interprets the cross-cultural consistency as evidence that men and women follow different, biologically based mating strategies. Buss's conclusions have stimulated considerable debate, and some have argued that the cross-cultural consistency may reflect other factors, such as gender inequality (Wood & Eagly, 2000), and not our evolutionary past. It is important to note that there are many similarities in female and male mate preferences, and there are important differences in mate preferences cross-culturally. Indeed, as Buss wrote, "there may be more similarity between men and women from the same culture than between men and men or women and women from different cultures" (p. 17).

Source: Buss, David M. (1989) Sex differences in human mate preferences: Evolutionary hypotheses tested in 37 cultures. *Behavioral and Brain Sciences*, 12, 1-49.

Interestingly, in parallel tests with male participants shown pictures of females in similar situations, it made no difference what the woman was doing. Whether the woman was interacting with a child, ignoring a crying child, standing alone, standing unemotionally next to a child, or vacuuming had no effect: men's attractiveness ratings were the same across all conditions. Such findings among contemporary North American university students are exactly what one would predict based on a parental investment analysis of mate preference.

21. Why do women and men find a symmetrical face attractive?

Male mate preferences have also been explored within an evolutionary perspective. Men tend to prefer women who display signs of youth, such as clear smooth skin, and signs of physical health, such as a symmetrical face (Buss, 1989, 1999; Thornhill & Gangestad, 2006). Males show a preference for a range of other characteristics that are also associated with youth such as animated facial expressions, high energy level, and a bouncy youthful gait (Symons, 1995). The interpretation from an evolutionary perspective is clear: males have evolved to value those characteristics that are associated with youth—and hence future reproductive potential—and with health. Remember that reproductive success is not confined to sex; reproductive success depends on the ability of the woman to remain in good health during pregnancy, to successfully carry the pregnancy to term, to have the energy and physical health to nurse the child, and to be able to care for and nurture the child until the child can eventually care for itself.

22. Why do women in all cultures tend to marry older men?

Together with a strong male preference for signs of a woman's youth and health, research has also found a surprising degree of cross-cultural consistency in male rating of female physical attractiveness. For example, in one study (Cunningham et al., 1995) males of different races judged the attractiveness of women's faces shown in photographs. The photographs were of women of different ethnic groups, including Asian, Hispanic, Black, and White women. The average correlation in the attractiveness ratings between males of different racial groups was +.95, a tremendously high correlation in psychological research. That is, males of all races agreed in their ratings of the photographs. Familiarity with or exposure to Western culture or to the culture of the model shown in the photograph did not influence attractiveness ratings. Similar cross-cultural consensus in attractiveness ratings have been reported by others studying many different ethnic and cultural groups (e.g., Jones, 1996; Buss, 1999; Jackson, 1992). The preference for other characteristics, such as a specific waist-to-hip ratio, has also been shown to be consistent cross-culturally (Singh, 1993).

For mate preferences to evolve they must have had an impact on actual mating. Furthermore, although women's preferences powerfully control actual mating, the mate preferences between the sexes should at least be compatible. A clear example of the compatibility of mate preferences is the worldwide preference of women for older men and men for younger women. The impact of these preferences on actual mating is demonstrated by the worldwide prevalence of brides who are younger than grooms.

Altruism

Despite competition for mates, preferred foods, and safe places to sleep, social animals also help one another. There are two broad categories of helping: cooperation and altruism. **Cooperation** refers to situations in which one individual helps another and in so doing also gains some advantage themselves. When you and your friends work together on a project, you all benefit from each others' efforts and expertise. The adaptive value of cooperation is clear. As a species developed the behavioural repertoire that supported cooperation, groups of individuals became capable of accomplishing more than any individual could accomplish alone. Social animals benefit from cooperation in many activities, from finding food, to dealing with predators, to protecting their home territory, to caring for young. Many of the benefits of being a social species are based on cooperation.

23. What is the difference between cooperation and altruism?

Different from cooperation are acts of altruism. **Altruism** occurs when one individual helps another, but in so doing they accrue some cost. For example, when a bird emits a call to warn of a predator, the warning helps other members of the flock but puts the signaller in greater danger since they have advertised their location to the predator. In a series of classic studies, Sherman (1977) demonstrated that ground squirrels who sounded predator alarms to warn others of their colony were indeed at greater risk (Figure 4.15). Predators (weasels, badgers, coyotes) stalked and killed alarm callers at a far higher rate than noncallers. On the surface, altruism may not appear to make evolutionary sense: by engaging in altruism an individual decreases the likelihood that they will survive.

FIGURE 4.15

This female ground squirrel has spotted a predator and is sounding an alarm call to warn other squirrels of the danger. In sounding an alarm, this female ground squirrel helps others of her colony, but places herself at increased risk of being found and killed by the predator.

There are two important theories of altruism. The first, the **kin selection theory** of altruism argues that altruism developed to increase the survival of relatives (Hamilton, 1964). Many animals evolved living in small groups in which there was at least some degree of genetic relatedness across many group members. Even in large mixed groups, some members of the groups will be genetically related; there may be siblings, offspring, aunts or uncles, and other family members within the group. In showing altruism, one individual may perish, but if this increases the likelihood that genetically related individuals survive, the genes that support altruism will be selected for and spread through more and more members of the species across generations. The kin selection theory predicts that we should direct more acts of altruism towards relatives than toward non-relatives. From squirrels (Sherman, 1977) to chimpanzees (Goodall, 1986) to humans (Burnstein et al., 1994), there is evidence that supports the contention that altruism is more likely to be shown toward kin than nonkin. As shown in Figure 4.16, as the degree of genetic relatedness decreases from .5 (e.g., siblings, parents) to .25 (e.g., half-siblings, aunts, uncles, nieces, nephews) to .125 (e.g., cousins, children of half-siblings), there is a concomitant decrease in altruism (Essock-Vitale & McGuire, 1985; Burnstein et al., 1994).

24. Combining the kin selection and reciprocity theories of altruism, who are you the most likely to help? Who are you the least likely to help?

The second of the evolutionary theories of altruism is the **theory of reciprocal altruism**. This theory argues that altruism is, in essence, long-term cooperation (Trivers, 1971; Cosmides & Tooby, 1992). That is, one individual may help another, but that assistance will be reciprocated at some time in the future. If this theory of reciprocal altruism is correct, then social animals should remember who has helped them in the past and should help those individuals. Furthermore, they should not offer further assistance to individuals who have failed to reciprocate. It also requires a relatively stable social group; transient members are unlikely to be present to offer

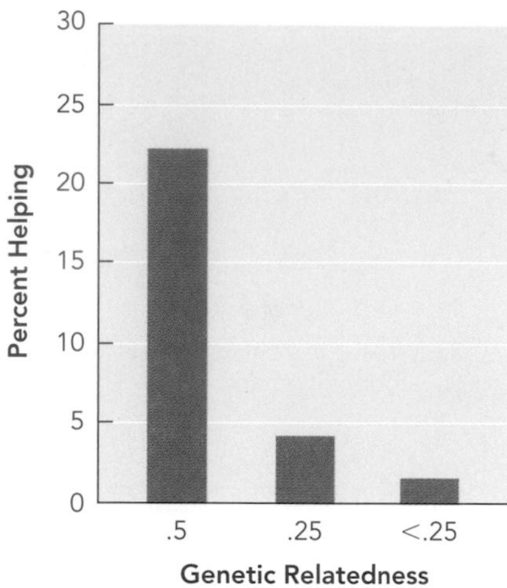

FIGURE 4.16

In a study of 300 adult women, 2,520 instances of receiving help and 2,651 instances of giving help were analyzed. The likelihood of giving and receiving help decreased as degree of genetic relatedness decreased.

Adapted from Essock-Vitale & McGuire, 1985.

assistance at some later date (Figure 4.16). We have all experienced reciprocal altruism. If you help your roommates move, you expect that, in the future, they will come to your assistance when you move; if you have gone out of your way to pick up friends after work, you expect that they would do likewise when you need a ride. A large part of gossip is a public inventory of favours owed and repaid, and a public account of who is and who is not reliable for reciprocating (Barkow, 1992). Such reciprocal altruism between unrelated individuals has been observed in other social primates, such as chimpanzees (de Waal, 1982) and bonobos (Parish, 1996).

These two theories of altruism, kin selection and reciprocity, are not incompatible. Kin selection theory offers an explanation of why we are more likely to act altruistically towards genetically related individuals, and why the likelihood of altruism decreases in an orderly way as genetic relatedness decreases. Reciprocity theory offers an explanation of why we also offer assistance to and request assistance from non-kin. However, as the tragic fate of Kitty Genovese illustrates (discussed in Chapter 2), altruism does not always occur. One of the challenges in the study of altruism is to identify what environmental factors increase and decrease the likelihood that we will engage in acts of altruism.

Aggression

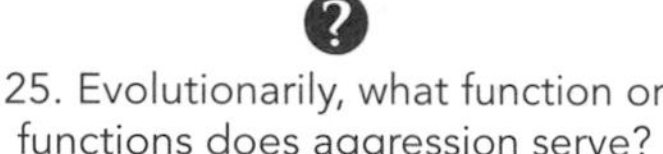

25. Evolutionarily, what function or functions does aggression serve?

One of the problems facing any animal is that the most valued resources are in limited supply. There are not enough of the best things to eat, safest places to shelter from predators, safest and most comfortable places to sleep, or most desirable mates. One possible solution to this problem is for animals to compete with each other or a group to compete with another group to determine who has access to the resource. That is, evolutionarily, aggression may have developed as a means to protect one's mate, young, territory, or food, to co-opt other's resources, or to gain access to unclaimed resources. In many species of birds, for example, a male will attack other males of his species that approach his mate or his nest during the mating season. Fighting to protect one's territory or to usurp the territory and resources of others has been reported among a wide range of species, including lions, macaques, birds, and chimpanzees (Wilson, 1980; Goodall, 1986).

An important source of intra-species aggression is competition for a mate. The rocks of the Galapagos Islands are densely populated by iguanas, and during mating there is a constant display of aggression with ritualized fighting and submissive postures by the losers (Eibl-Eibesfeldt, 1998). Everyone is familiar with film footage of male rams, moose, or elk engaged in aggressive displays and physical confrontations during the mating season (Figure 4.18). Competition for a mate can be intense, and once a male and female have partnered, aggression may be used to protect one's mate from other suitors and the threat of sexual infidelity. Among humans, one of the most common causes of homicide is sexual jealousy, most frequently two men fighting about a woman (Daly, Wilson, & Weghorst, 1982). Less extreme forms of aggression also occur within the context of winning or protecting a mate, and aggression may be used to inflict some cost on rivals. For example, both men and women belittle same-sex rivals, attempting to make their rivals appear less desirable (Buss & Dedden, 1990).

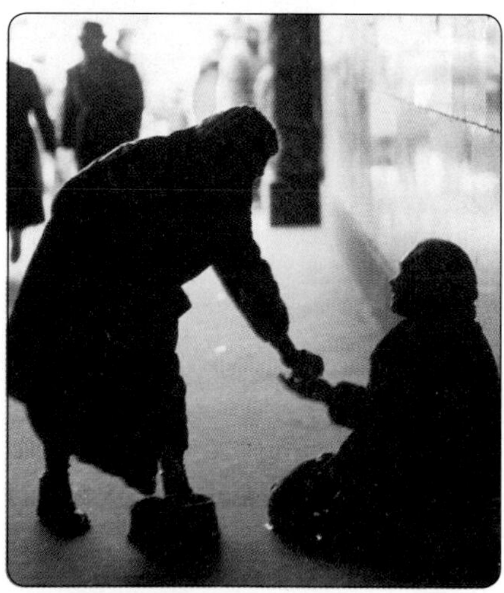

FIGURE 4.17

An act of altruism.

As animals evolved larger, more complex brains and more sophisticated mental functions, an important change occurred in competition: animals acquired the ability to recognize others and to remember past encounters. Unlike the constantly head-butting iguanas, birds and mammals could remember the outcome of a past conflict with another animal. Instead of having to compete anew each time there were resources to allocate or protect, social animals developed dominance hierarchies. Once a dominance hierarchy is established, and provided it is unchallenged, members of the group can determine access to resources without unnecessary, energy-expensive and dangerous aggressive encounters. Hierarchies are established in the initial encounters between animals if the group is being formed or if a new member joins the group. Among social primates, such as chimpanzees, the dominant male is invariably physically large and experienced. Dominance position among primates is not, however, simply a matter of overt aggressiveness (Figure 4.19). The dominant male owes his position as much to his ability to form social alliances with other males, usually relatives, as it does to outright aggression (Goodall, 1971).

FIGURE 4.18
Male rams butting heads is an example of aggression that has developed evolutionarily.

Within a group of social animals, aggression may occur in forming dominance hierarchies and if an animal challenges another in an attempt to better their position in the hierarchy. The dominance hierarchy, however, functions as much to decrease the amount of aggression within the group as it does to provide a context for aggression. Apart from settling order of access to resources in a way that avoids unnecessarily repeated conflict, there may be deliberate quelling of aggression. For example, dominant male chimpanzees, spider monkeys, and macaques have been observed to use their position to stop fighting among subordinates (Wilson, 1980).

26. Which members of a group are usually the most aggressive? Why?

In some contexts, then, aggression appears to make evolutionary sense: it functions to divide limited resources among a group, and those who are most skilled in physical confrontation or in forming social alliances, depending on the situation and species, gain the most. Those physical and behavioural attributes that contribute to success should then be selected for and become more widespread within the species.

There is also, however, a pattern of aggression that has been observed only among chimpanzees and humans. Chimpanzees and humans form male coalitions to attack others as a group. For example, a member of Jane Goodall's Gombe team observed a group of eight young male chimpanzees form a fighting party that ventured into the territory of a neighbouring chimpanzee troop. Once there, they found a lone male chimpanzee, then surrounded and attacked it. The attacking chimpanzees acted cooperatively. One male pinned the victim to the ground while the others attacked, biting and hitting the victim until it was badly injured and bleeding. The badly wounded victim disappeared soon after, presumably having died of its wounds (Wrangham & Peterson, 1996). The fighting party observed by the Gombe team did not occupy any additional territory or gain any tangible benefit from having killed the other chimpanzee, although the actions of the group may have been related to establishing rank and status among the males of the fighting party. Of the 4,000 species of mammals, and more than 10 million animal species in total, only two, humans and chimpanzees, form coalitions that have the express purpose of engaging in acts of lethal aggression against members of their own species who occupy neighbouring territories (Figure 4.20). For humans, history is full of descriptions of such coalitions and the aggression of gangs and invading armies.

FIGURE 4.19
After establishing a dominance hierarchy, primates do not need to rely on aggressive behaviour to maintain dominant status.

Such acts of aggression, by lone attackers or organized cooperative groups, are difficult to explain from any perspective, and traditional explanations, such as an aggression instinct or a drive to be aggressive, are clearly inadequate. How-

FIGURE 4.20

The Oka Crisis confrontation between First Nations people and the Canadian Army featured this famous picture of an aggressive face-to-face showdown.

ever, the point is that many species, including chimpanzees and humans, evolved mechanisms that supported aggressive behaviours. The immediate situation, the environmental cues confronting the individual or the group, can activate those mechanisms, whether such activation is related to the competition functions of aggression or is an aberrant display. The rich evolutionary history of species such as chimpanzees and humans has provided much behavioural flexibility, and that flexibility has great adaptive value. It does, however, also allow behaviours to occur in ways that become less rigidly tied to the original functions. The display of aggression is not invariant or inevitable as some early, simplistic instinct theories suggested, but rather is exquisitely sensitive to contextual cues. A male chimpanzee or human may live their entire lifetime without ever displaying overt aggression. Their evolutionary adaptations have provided the physical and psychological mechanisms that make them capable of displaying aggression, but it requires the appropriate eliciting stimuli for the expression of the behavioural potential.

In Review

- *Parental investment refers to the time, effort, energy, and risk associated with caring successfully for each offspring. The sex that makes the greater parental investment will be more vigorously competed for and will be more discriminating when choosing a mate. Parental investment and the reproductive physiology of a species, together with environmental factors, have influenced the development of that species' mating system(s).*
- *Cross-culturally, women tend to prefer males who show signs of willingness to invest in children, physical health, earning potential, status, and ambitiousness. Consistent male preferences include physical attractiveness, good health, and younger women.*
- *Social species engage in acts of cooperation, in which all involved gain some benefit, and in acts of altruism, in which others benefit but the altruistic individual incurs some risk.*
- *Animals, including humans, are more likely to show altruism towards genetically related individuals than toward non-kin, the kin selection theory of altruism. Altruism among non-kin may contribute to the fitness of the individual by making it more likely that others will act altruistically toward them in the future, the theory of reciprocal altruism.*
- *Aggression may serve functions related to protection of and allocation of resources, and establishing a position in a social dominance hierarchy. Among mammals, including all human cultures that have been studied, males, especially young males, are the most aggressive since they are the group members that most actively compete.*

RESEARCH FRONTIERS

Inequality, Competition, and Murder

Martin Daly and Margo Wilson of McMaster University have applied an evolutionary analysis to what seems a modern, urban problem: homicide. They have analyzed murder statistics from many different jurisdictions, and among widely different cultures, and have found great consistency. Most murders are committed by young males against competing young males. For example, Daly and Wilson found that for homicides committed over a 15-year period in Chicago (1965–1980), 86 percent of homicides were committed by men. Of these, 80 percent of the murder victims were also male. Daly and Wilson have been particularly interested in such same-sex homicides since differences in homicide rates between regions or nations is mostly attributable to differences in same-sex homicides among unrelated males. In Canada between 1974 and 1988, there were 2,965 same-sex homicides involving men, but only 175 female same-sex homicides. That is, 94 percent of these Canadian same-sex homicides involve males. Similar proportions were found wherever Wilson and Daly, and others, looked, whether it was in American cities such as Chicago, Detroit, or Miami; in Scotland, England, Denmark, India, or Kenya; or among traditional hunter-gatherer cultures such as the !Kung San of Botswana: male-male homicides account for the large majority of same-sex murders, typically between 93 and 100 percent of same-sex murders. It is the number of these competitive killings in which both murderer and victim are unrelated males that vary most from region to region and nation to nation (Daly & Wilson, 1985).

Attempts by psychologists, criminologists, and sociologists in explaining the variation in national and regional homicide rates have not been particularly successful. One group of explanations attempted to attribute differences in homicide rates to factors such as wealth or education level. Such explanations, however, have been unconvincing; correlations between income and homicide rates are poor. The prevalence of same-sex homicides cannot be adequately explained by unemployment rates, energy consumption per capita (an indicator of economic development), gross domestic product (GDP), proportion of urban to rural dwellers, literacy rates, or education levels (Krohn, 1976; Messner, 1982).

Daly and Wilson have applied an evolutionary analysis to this problem. They argued that aggression arises most often in situations of competition over limited resources, and among all of the social primates it is the young adult males who are the most competitive and aggressive. If there is limited access to resources, there may also be disparity in acquisition or distribution of those resources. That is, some individuals may gain sufficient access while others are left with little or nothing. Daly and Wilson contend that it is the disparity in resource acquisition that fuels particularly intense competition, and it is in those situations in which competition may escalate to the point of murder. Clearly many murders occur in contexts that are competitive, such as robbery, sexual jealousy or sexual rivalry, or competition over status (Daly & Wilson, 1988). That is, competition based on sex, status, or access to limited materials, such as food or preferred possessions, becomes increasingly frequent and vigorous the greater the disparity between the haves and the have-nots.

Daly and Wilson have found that the ratio of the highest household income to the lowest (a measure of income inequality) shows a significant positive correlation with homicide rates. Using data from Statistics Canada, Daly and Wilson assessed how well this ratio predicted provincial homicide rates. Across a period of 15 years, from 1981 to 1996, the correlation between income inequality and homicide rates in the Canadian provinces and territories is +.845, a large and statistically significant correlation. The correlation between median income (a commonly used measure of overall wealth) and homicide rate is not statistically significant. That is, average or total wealth does not predict homicide rates, but the degree of disparity in wealth does. "When rewards are inequitably distributed and those at the bottom of the resource distribution feel that they have little to lose by engaging in reckless or dangerous behaviour, escalated tactics of social competition, including violent tactics, become attractive" (Daly, Wilson, & Vasdev, 2001, p. 220). The analysis of homicide rates from Canadian and American cities (Table 4.5 breaks down Canadian homicides in 2004 by province and territory), American states, and other countries is consistent with the argument that inequality in resource distribution is important in the level of lethal aggressive competition. Income inequality is a better predictor of regional and national homicide rates than any other measure that has been assessed, including unemployment rate, economic development, or absolute level of wealth.

Daly and Wilson have argued that competition for resources is for us, as it is for all social species, an important cause of aggression, and the greater the disparity in resources within the group the greater the competition that should emerge. Competition for contested resources occurs most commonly among young males competing with other young males. If our social structure permits, or even promotes, great disparity in wealth, then competition, including lethal competition, will become more common.

TABLE 4.5 Homicides in Canadian Provinces and Territories in 2004

	Number of Homicides	Rate per 100,000 People
Newfoundland and Labrador	2	0.39
Prince Edward Island	0	0.00
Nova Scotia	13	1.39
New Brunswick	7	0.93
Quebec	111	1.47
Ontario	187	1.51
Manitoba	50	4.27
Saskatchewan	39	3.92
Alberta	86	2.69
British Columbia[1]	112	2.67
Yukon	7	22.43
Northwest Territories	4	9.34
Nunavut	4	13.49
Canada	**622**	**1.95**

[1]Includes 5 homicides from previous years that were reported by police in 2004.
SOURCE: Statistics Canada.

Sources: Daly, M. & Wilson, M. (1988) Homicide. New York: Aldine de Gruyter; Daly, M, Wilson, M., & Vasdev, S. (2001). Income inequality and homicide rates in Canada and the United States. *Canadian Journal of Criminology,* 43, 219-236.

HOW NOT TO THINK ABOUT BEHAVIOUR GENETICS AND EVOLUTIONARY PSYCHOLOGY

27. What is wrong with the idea that genes always have an effect?

Genetic and evolutionary analyses of human behaviours have frequently been misunderstood and, occasionally, even distorted and misused. When considering behaviour genetics and evolutionary psychology, there are some common sources of error and misunderstanding, and it is important to avoid these pitfalls.

Genetic Determinism

A major source of misunderstanding of genetic and evolutionary explanations is that such explanations imply that if something is found to be genetic, then it cannot be changed. There is sometimes the erroneous view that genes have invariant and unavoidable effects, so-called **genetic determinism**. If intelligence, personality traits, mate preferences, or aggression have genetic bases, they are therefore unalterable. This flawed understanding leads to arguments such as, if someone has a gene for alcoholism then they will inevitably become an alcoholic; if humans have an evolutionary history to engage in aggressive competition, then there is nothing that can be done about assaults, murder, or war. Genetic determinism is not supported by genetic or evolutionary explanations, and indeed behaviour genetics and evolutionary psychology argue strongly against such a view.

The discovery that early-onset diabetes is inherited did not result in medical science abandoning diabetics because nothing could be done for a genetic disorder. Rather, the discovery allowed scientists to stop looking for a nonexistent viral or bacterial cause, and research and resources could go to understanding the genetic basis and to the business of compensating for the missing enzyme. With increased understanding of the genetic basis of early-onset diabetes, it changed from a diagnosis of a slow lingering death to a treatable condition. The expectation is that as our understanding of human genetics advances it will be possible to develop successful treatments for a range of diseases. One reason for the Human Genome Project has been that whether there is a genetic cause for a disease, such as for Alzheimer's disease, or a genetic predisposition, such as for breast cancer, if we know what gene products are involved, then effective treatments can be developed. An understanding of genetics has led to such successes. The best-known example is phenylketonuria. Phenylketonuria was once an important cause of mental and physical degeneration and death among children, but the discovery of the recessive gene that causes it led directly to a wholly successful treatment.

It is important to remember that genes work through the environment. For example, genes may have a role in setting reaction range for intelligence, but it is the environment that determines where within that range an individual develops. And the reaction range may be substantial; research suggests that the reaction range for intelligence, for example, is as much as 15 to 20 IQ points. That is enough to move an individual's IQ from average to superior, or from borderline to average. Similarly, aggression may have served important functions during mammalian evolution but as the work of Daly and Wilson elegantly demonstrates, environmental and cultural factors are critically important in determining the occurrence of aggression. As our understanding of aggression develops, what we learn is not that the display of aggression is invariant and inevitable; we learn what environmental factors elicit and amplify aggressive behaviours and this information suggests things that we can change. We cannot change our evolutionary history, but we can, for example, change income inequality.

As the noted social learning theorist Albert Bandura wrote, "Human nature is characterized by a vast potentiality that can be fashioned by direct and observational experience into a variety of forms within biological limits" (Bandura, 1986, p. 21). Modern behaviour genetics and evolutionary psychology agrees, and is in pursuit of understanding those "biological limits" and the interaction between our biology and experience.

Social Darwinism

28. Why does the idea that some members of society are genetically better than others not make sense from an evolutionary perspective?

Very soon after Darwin published *On the Origin of Species*, some ideas began to be distorted and misapplied. One of the most lasting and detrimental distortions led to what came to be called **social Darwinism**. It was argued that if the more fit are more successful, then those on the top rungs of the social and economic ladder must be most fit of all. This simplistic distortion of Darwin's theory resulted in the now famous phrase, "survival of the fittest." That phrase comes from the philosopher Herbert Spencer (1879), not from Charles Darwin. It implies that the fittest have the right to suppress the less fit and distorts Darwin's insight that it is not mere survival, but reproduction that defines biological fitness. Spencer's phrase was adopted by the socially dominant to justify their positions and their exploitation of others.

Such social Darwinism, as well as its even more distorted cousin, eugenics, assumes that the genes of one group are in some measurable way better than the genes of another group. Every human being is the product of an equally long, equally successful series of reproductions; as a species we do not have members who have longer or "better" evolutionary pedigrees. Currently valued traits are mixed with those less valued and with those that had their real value in the environment we faced millennia ago. As discussed earlier a range of traits, such as personality characteristics, may all be adaptive depending on place, time, and social role. All of these traits, whether good, bad, or indifferent, will be reshuffled for the next generation by sexual reproduction. If some trait had been good for humans, if it had indeed provided superior fitness, that trait would have spread throughout the population by the mechanisms described earlier in this chapter. We are each the product of millions of years of hominid evolution, and expressions of social Darwinism reflect, at best, a distorted and woefully simplistic misunderstanding of evolutionary theory.

Defending the Status Quo

29. Think of examples in which an evolutionary analysis suggests social or political changes.

Another set of objections to behaviour genetics and evolutionary psychology, related to the misguided social Darwinism, is the accusation that evolutionary analyses of human behaviour legitimize the status quo. The argument goes that if genetics and our evolutionary history have resulted in the presence of a trait or behaviour, it is "natural" and "right" in some way, and so we should not attempt to change it. If evolution has led to young adult males forming fighting coalitions, then there is no sense in trying to convince nations to disarm, or warring factions to talk peace; this fallacy argues that the status quo of standing armies and street gangs is somehow legitimized by evolutionary theory and everything is as it should be. The error of these views is similar to that of genetic determinism and social Darwinism. Genes work only in environments, and it is only by understanding our genes and our evolutionary inheritance that we can change our environments in a reasonable and appropriate way to better our quality of life. An understanding of same-sex murder, for example, far from supporting the status quo calls out for attempts to redress inequality.

The status quo arguments become particularly heated, even bitter, when discussing sex differences, such as male-female differences in mate preferences. An evolutionary approach accepts that environment, culture, and unique personal experiences all matter a great deal, and takes the perspective that an evolutionary analysis can be particularly fruitful in disentangling the relative roles of environment, learning, and the very real fact that we have physical brains controlled by the products of our genes and which have evolved over millions of years. The argument that a genetic or evolutionary analysis simply legitimizes the status quo ignores the fact that evolutionary analysis expects variation between individuals and across groups; variation and unexpected variation is what allows evolution.

A similarly flawed argument is that if something appears in nature, it is somehow then morally right. It has become popular for proponents of some idea to find an example of what they think is a comparable behaviour occurring in the "natural" world and use that example to justify their behaviour or support their cause. Curiously, it is often those at the two extreme ends of the social and political spectrum who attempt to use nature to justify a social or political system or some socially atypical behaviour. To use "nature" as a standard of what is ethically and morally correct is logically indefensible. Nature is neither moral nor just nor ethical except as we apply those cultural standards to what we observe. There is also the obvious problem that given the incredible diversity of environments and the range of adaptations that have arisen through natural selection, you can find examples of behaviours that are superficially incompatible but that make sense given that species' evolutionary history and ecological niche. That some species show altruism and cooperation—or infanticide and cannibalism—does not justify the existence of these behaviours in any moral sense.

In Review

- *Genetic determinism assumes that if a characteristic is genetically based then it is invariant and unalterable. This view ignores the fact that genes and the environment constantly and necessarily interact.*
- *Social Darwinism arose from a poor understanding of the principles of natural selection and has been used to justify the exploitation of others. Social Darwinism confuses the Darwinian idea of fitness and the time course of changing adaptations with the erroneous idea that there is some genetic superiority of individual members.*
- *Although genetic and evolutionary arguments have been used to justify the status quo as "right" or "moral," such arguments ignore the fact that natural selection is neither "moral" nor "just." The real perspective in evolutionary psychology, as in much of psychology, is for increased understanding so that appropriate changes can be made to better quality of life. An evolutionary analysis suggests environmental interventions as it attempts to explain human behaviour.*

GAINING DIRECTION

What are the issues?

Is it possible that something as complex as personality has a genetic component? If so, then we would expect twins to show striking similarities in both physical characteristics and in personality traits. This expectation is demonstrated dramatically in studies of twins who were separated at birth and later reunited. Such is the case with Jim Lewis and Jim Springer. Both were married twice and had a son named James. Both had the same habits and hobbies. They even liked the same brand of cigarettes and beer. Yet they did not meet each other until they were 39 years old. How do we account for this remarkable similarity? Is there a gene for choice of hobbies? Beer preference? Is genetics the factor that accounts for the similarity between the two brothers? If it is not genetics, how can we explain the similarity?

What do we need to know?

How are traits passed from one generation to the next?
What affect do nature and nurture have on development?
Are complex traits inherited in humans?
Can personality have a genetic or biological component?
Why should we be interested in twins?

Where can you find the information necessary to answer these questions?

To answer these questions, we must begin by looking at the basics. How do we inherit simple traits such as eye colour? Does the same mechanism underlie more complex behaviour patterns? How about traits such as intelligence or neatness? To answer these questions for humans, we turn to investigations of twins. If we can compare identical twins (who share 100% of their genetic material) who have been raised in separate environments (thus reducing any effects of nurture), we can get a pretty good estimate of the effects of genetics on complex human behaviours. This is exactly what Bouchard and his colleagues have done at the University of Minnesota. In every case, there is a remarkable degree of similarity. You should consider whether or not there are other plausible explanations for this observed similarity, and how complex traits could be inherited.

KEY TERMS AND CONCEPTS*

adaptations (149)
adoption study (138)
altruism (159)
biologically based mechanisms (148)
chromosome (134)
concordance (138)
cooperation (159)
domain-specific adaptations (151)
dominant gene (135)
evolution (148)
evolutionary personality theory (152)
gene knockout (136)
genes (134)
genetic determinism (164)
genotype (134)
heritability coefficient (138)
kin selection (159)
monogamous mating system (154)
natural selection (149)
parental investment (154)
phenotype (134)
polyandry (155)
polygenic transmission (135)
polygynandry (155)
polygyny (154)
reaction range (144)
recessive gene (135)
recombinant DNA procedures (136)
social Darwinism (165)
theory of reciprocal altruism (159)
twin studies (139)

*Each term has been boldfaced in the text on the page indicated in parentheses.

DO YOU WANT TO ELEVATE YOUR GRADES?

For additional resources and interactive quizzing, visit the book's Online Learning Centre at **www.mcgrawhill.ca/olc/passer**.

CHAPTER 5

Sensation and Perception

All our knowledge has its origins in our perceptions.
—Leonardo da Vinci

CHAPTER OUTLINE

In August 1933, three reporters for the *St. John Telegraph* travelled to Moncton to investigate reports of a mysterious hill where cars ran uphill on their own. This was not the first time such stories had emerged. As early as 1880, area farmers noted that horses seemed to be straining with a loaded cart even though they appeared to be going downhill. If the carts were unhitched at the bottom of the hill, they would roll uphill on their own, as would barrels or bales! It was as if some mysterious magnetic force were pulling these items uphill.

The three reporters were skeptical and spent the morning looking for the hill with strange magnetic powers. Indeed, they stopped at the bottom of every hill in and around Moncton waiting to see their 1931 Ford Roadster roll uphill. After hours of frustrating searching they stopped at the base of Lutes Mountain and got out of the car to stretch. To their surprise, the roadster calmly rolled uphill away from them.

There are at least six magnetic or gravity hills in Canada and hundreds around the world. Not a single site has any unusual magnetic field.

- **What are the issues here?**
- **What do we need to know?**
- **Where can we find the information to answer these questions?**

Helen Keller (*left*) "hears" her teacher Anne Sullivan by reading Sullivan's lips with her fingers.

Source: AP/Wide World Photos Helen Keller/ Anne Sullivan

> Sometimes, it is true, a sense of isolation enfolds me like a cold mist as I sit alone and wait at life's shut gate. Beyond, there is light, and music, and sweet companionship; but I may not enter. Fate, silent, pitiless, bars the way. . . . Silence sits immense upon my soul. (Keller, 1955, p. 62)

So wrote Helen Keller, deprived of both vision and hearing by an acute illness when she was 19 months old. For those of us who take for granted the use of these senses, it is hard to imagine what it would be like to sink into a dark and silent universe, cut off from all sight and sound. Helen Keller was saved from this abyss by her teacher, Anne Sullivan, who taught and communicated with her by tapping signs onto the little girl's palm. One day, Sullivan tapped "water" onto Helen's palm as she placed the child's hand under the gushing spout of a pump.

> That living word awakened my soul, gave it light, hope, joy, set it free! That was because I saw everything with a strange new sight that had come to me. . . . It would have been difficult to find a happier child than I was. (p. 103)

Helen Keller went on to write her celebrated book, *The Story of My Life,* while an undergraduate at Radcliffe College, and she became an inspiration and advocate for people with disabilities.

Nature gives us a marvellous set of sensory contacts with our world. If our sense organs are not defective, we experience light waves as brightnesses and colours, air vibrations as sounds, chemical substances as odours or tastes, and so on. However, such is not the case for people with a rare and mysterious condition called **synaesthesia**, which means, quite literally, "mixing of the senses" (Cytowic, 2002; Harrison & Baron-Cohen, 1997). They may experience sounds as colours or tastes as touch sensations that have different shapes. Women are more likely to be synaesthetes than men (1 in 1,150 vs. 1 in 7,150, respectively; Rice et al., 2005). Interestingly, Maurer and her colleague (Maurer & Mondloch, 2006) have suggested that we are all born synaesthetic—the neural pathways of infants are fairly undifferentiated and lead to cross-modal perceptions.

The Russian psychologist A. R. Luria (1968) studied a highly successful writer and musician whose life was a perpetual stream of mixed-up sensations. On one occasion, Luria asked him to report on his experiences while listening to electronically generated musical tones. To a medium-pitch tone, the man experienced a brown strip with red edges, together with a sweet and sour flavour. A very high-pitched tone evoked the following sensation: "It looks something like a fireworks tinged with a pink-red hue. The strip of colour feels rough and unpleasant, and it has an ugly taste—rather like that of a briny pickle. . . . You could hurt your hand on this."

Sensation

Stimulus is received by sensory receptors

↓

Receptors translate stimulus properties into nerve impulses (transduction)

↓

Feature detectors analyze stimulus features

↓

Stimulus features are reconstructed into neural representation

↓

Neural representation is compared with previously stored information in brain

↓

Matching process results in recognition and interpretation of stimuli

Perception

FIGURE 5.1

Sensory and perceptual processes proceed from the reception and translation of physical energies into nerve impulses to the active process by which the brain receives the nerve impulses, organizes and confers meaning on them, and constructs a perceptual experience.

1. Describe the five stages that constitute the process of sensory processing and perception of information.

Sensory-impaired people such as those who experience synaesthesia provide glimpses into different aspects of how we "sense" and "understand" our world. These processes, previewed in Figure 5.1, begin when specific types of stimuli activate specialized sensory receptors. Whether the stimulus is light, sound waves, a chemical molecule, or pressure, your sensory receptors must translate this information into the only language your nervous system understands—the language of nerve impulses. Once this translation occurs, specialized neurons break down and analyze the specific features of the stimuli. At the next stage, these numerous stimulus "pieces" are reconstructed into a neural representation that is then compared with previously stored information, such as our knowledge of what particular objects look, smell, or feel like. This matching of a new stimulus with our internal storehouse of knowledge allows us to recognize the stimulus and give it meaning. We then consciously experience a perception.

In some ways, sensation and perception blend together so completely that they are difficult to separate, for the stimulation we receive through our sense organs is instantaneously organized and transformed into the experiences that we refer to as perceptions. Nevertheless, psychologists do distinguish between them. **Sensation** is the stimulus-detection process by which our sense organs respond to and translate environmental stimuli into nerve impulses that are sent to the brain. **Perception**—making "sense" of what our senses tell us—is the active process of organizing this stimulus input and giving it meaning (Pashler & Yantis, 2002).

2. How do psychologists differentiate between sensation and perception?

Because perception is an active and creative process, the same sensory input may be perceived in different ways at different times. For example, read the two sets of symbols in Figure 5.2. The middle symbols in both sets of curved lines are exactly the same and they send identical input to your brain, but you probably perceive them differently. Your interpretation, or perception, of the characters is influenced by their *context*—that is, by the characters that preceded and followed them, and by your learned expectation of what normally follows the letter A and the number 12. This is a simple illustration of how perception takes us a step beyond sensation.

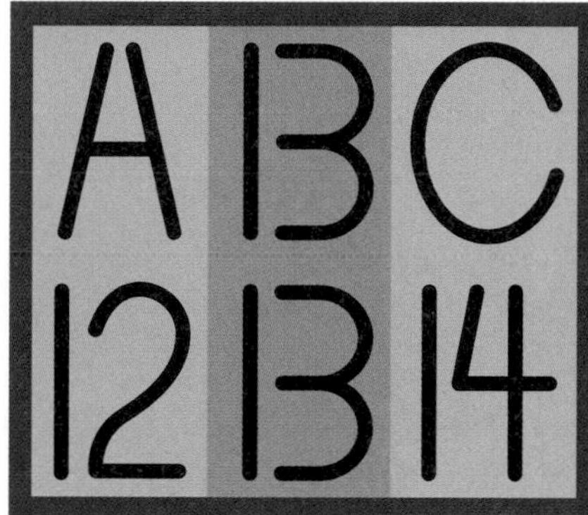

FIGURE 5.2

Quickly read these two lines of symbols out loud. Did your perception of the middle symbol in each line depend on the symbols that surrounded it?

SENSORY PROCESSES

Locked within the silent, dark recesses of your skull, your brain cannot "understand" light waves, sound waves, or the other forms of energy that make up the language of the environment. Contact with the outer world is possible only because certain neurons have developed into specialized sensory receptors that can transform these energy forms into the code language of nerve impulses.

As a starting point, we might ask: How many senses are there? Certainly there appear to be more than the five classical senses with which we are familiar: vision, audition (hearing), touch, gustation (taste), and olfaction (smell). For example, there are senses that provide information about balance and body position. Also, the sense of touch can be subdivided into separate senses of pressure, pain, and temperature. Receptors deep within the brain monitor the chemical composition of our blood. The immune system also has sensory functions that allow it to detect foreign invaders and to receive stimulation from the brain (Nossal & Hall, 1995).

Like those of other organisms, human sensory systems are designed to extract from the environment the information that we need to function and survive. Although our survival does not depend upon having eyes like eagles or owls, noses like bloodhounds, or ears as sensitive as those of the worm-hunting robin, we do have specialized sensors that can detect many different kinds of stimuli with considerable sensitivity. The scientific area of **psychophysics**, which studies relations between the physical characteristics of stimuli and sensory capabilities, is concerned with two kinds of sensitivity. The first concerns the absolute limits of sensitivity. For example, what is the softest sound or the weakest salt solution that humans can detect? The second kind of sensitivity has to do with differences between stimuli. What is the smallest difference in brightness that we can detect? How much difference must there be in two tones before we can tell that they are not identical?

3. What two kinds of sensory capabilities are studied by psychophysics researchers?

Stimulus Detection: The Absolute Threshold

4. What is the absolute threshold, and how is it technically defined and measured?

How intense must a stimulus be before we can detect its presence? Researchers answer this question by systematically presenting stimuli of varying intensities and asking people whether they can detect them. Because we are often unsure of whether we have actually sensed very faint stimuli, researchers designate the **absolute threshold** as the lowest intensity at which a stimulus can be detected correctly 50 percent

TABLE 5.1 Some Approximate Absolute Thresholds for Various Senses

Sense Modality	Absolute Threshold
Vision	Candle flame seen at approximately 50 km on a clear, dark night
Hearing	Tick of a watch under quiet conditions at approximately six metres
Taste	1 teaspoon of sugar in approximately 7.5 litres of water
Smell	One drop of perfume diffused into the entire volume of a large apartment
Touch	Wing of a fly or bee falling on your cheek from a distance of one centimetre

SOURCE: Based on Galanter, 1962.

of the time. Thus the *lower* the absolute threshold, the *greater* the sensitivity. From studies of absolute thresholds, the general limits of human sensitivity for the five major senses can be estimated. Some examples are presented in Table 5.1. As you can see, many of our senses are surprisingly sensitive. Yet some other species have absolute thresholds that seem incredible by comparison. For example, a female silkworm moth that is ready to mate needs to release 2.8 billionths of a gram of an attractant chemical molecule per second to attract every male silkworm moth within a radius of 1.6 kilometres.

Signal Detection Theory

I can remember lying in bed as a child after seeing a horror movie, straining my ears to detect any unusual sound that might signal the presence of a monster in the house. My vigilance caused me to detect faint and ominous sounds that probably would have gone unnoticed had I seen a comedy or a western earlier in the evening. Perhaps you have had a similar experience.

At one time it was assumed that each person had a more or less fixed level of sensitivity for each sense. But psychologists who study stimulus detection found that people's apparent sensitivity can fluctuate quite a bit. They concluded that the concept of a fixed absolute threshold is inaccurate because there is no single point on the intensity scale that separates non-detection from detection of a stimulus. There is instead a range of uncertainty, and people set their own **decision criterion**, a standard of how certain they must be that a stimulus is present before they will say they detect it. The decision criterion can also change from time to time, depending on such factors as fatigue, expectation, and the potential significance of the stimulus. **Signal detection theory** is concerned with the factors that influence sensory judgments.

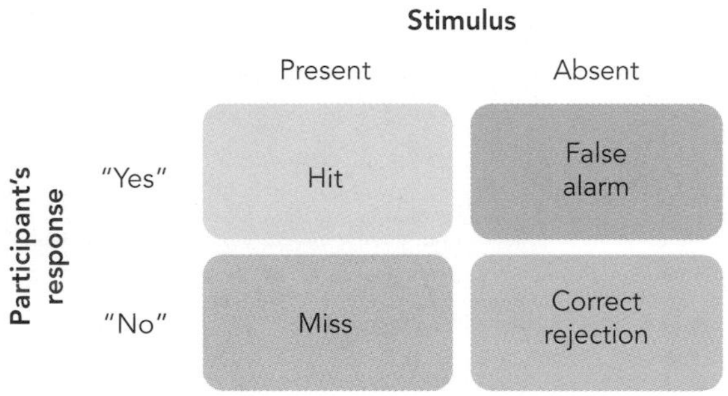

		Stimulus: Present	Stimulus: Absent
Participant's response	"Yes"	Hit	False alarm
	"No"	Miss	Correct rejection

FIGURE 5.3

This matrix shows the four possible outcomes in a signal detection experiment in which participants decide whether a stimulus has been presented or not presented. The percentages of responses that fall within each category can be affected both by characteristics of the participants and by the nature of the situation.

5. Why do signal detection theorists view stimulus detection as a decision? What are the four possible outcomes of such a decision?

6. What kinds of personal and situational factors influence signal detection decision criteria?

In a typical signal detection experiment, participants are told that after a warning light appears, a barely perceptible tone may or may not be presented. Their task is to tell the experimenter whether they heard the tone. Under these conditions, there are four possible outcomes, as shown in Figure 5.3. When the tone is in fact presented, the participant may say "yes" (a hit) or "no" (a miss). When no tone is presented, the participant may also say "yes" (a false alarm) or "no" (a correct rejection).

At low stimulus intensities, both the participant's and the situation's characteristics influence the decision criterion (Methot & Huitema, 1998; Pitz & Sachs, 1984). Bold participants who frequently say "yes" have more hits, but they also have more false alarms than do conservative participants. Participants also can be influenced to become bolder or more conservative by manipulating the rewards and costs for giving correct or incorrect responses. Increasing the rewards for hits or the costs for misses results in lower detection thresholds (more "yes" responses at low intensities). Thus a Navy radar operator may be more likely to notice a faint blip on her screen during a wartime mission, when a miss might have disastrous consequences, than during a peacetime voyage. Conversely, like physicians who will not perform a risky medical procedure without strong evidence to support their diagnosis, participants become more conservative in their "yes" responses as costs for false alarms are increased, resulting in higher detection thresholds (Irwin & McCarthy, 1998). Signal detection research shows us that perception is, in part, a decision.

FOCUS ON NEUROSCIENCE

The Neuroscience of Subliminal Perception and Prosopagnosia

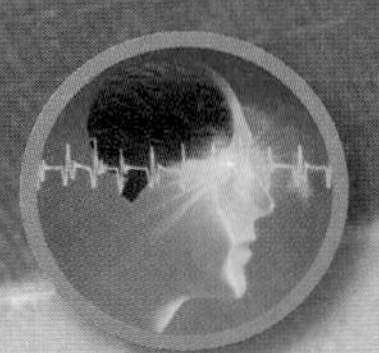

Background

A **subliminal stimulus** is one that is so weak or brief that, although it is received by the senses, it cannot be perceived consciously—the stimulus is well below the absolute threshold. There is little question that subliminal stimuli can register in the nervous system (Kihlstrom, 1990; MacLeod, 1998; Merikle & Daneman, 1998). But can such stimuli affect attitudes and behaviour without our knowing it? The answer appears to be yes—to a limited extent.

In the late 1950s, James Vicary, a public-relations executive, arranged to have subliminal messages flashed on a theatre screen during a movie. The messages urged the audience to "drink Coca-Cola" and "eat popcorn." Vicary's claim that the subliminal messages increased popcorn sales by 50 percent and soft drink sales by 18 percent aroused a public furor. Consumers and scientists feared possible abuse of subliminal messages to covertly influence the buying habits of consumers, and even to achieve mind control and brainwashing. The National Association of Broadcasters reacted by outlawing subliminal messages on American television.

The outcries were, in large part, false alarms. Several attempts to reproduce Vicary's results under controlled conditions failed, and many other studies conducted in laboratory settings, on television and radio, and in movie theatres indicated that there is little reason to be seriously concerned about significant or widespread control of consumer behaviour through subliminal stimulation (Dixon, 1981; Drukin, 1998). Ironically, Vicary admitted years later that his study was a hoax, designed to revive his floundering advertising agency. Nonetheless, his false report stimulated a great deal of useful research on the power of subliminal stimuli to influence behaviour. As far as consumer behaviour is concerned, the conclusion is that persuasive stimuli above the absolute threshold are far more influential than subliminal attempts to sneak into our subconscious mind, perhaps because we are more certain to "get the message."

Though consumer behaviour cannot be controlled subliminally, can such stimuli affect more subtle phenomena, such as attitudes? Here the effects are stronger (Arndt et al., 1997; Greenwald & Benaji, 1995). In one study, Jon Krosnick (1992) showed participants nine slides of a particular person and then measured their attitudes toward the target person. For half of the participants, each photograph was immediately preceded by an unpleasant picture (e.g., a face on fire) that was presented subliminally. The remaining participants were shown pleasant subliminal stimuli, such as smiling babies. Participants shown the associated unpleasant subliminal stimuli expressed somewhat negative attitudes toward the person, indicating a process of subconscious attitude conditioning, whereas those who saw the positive subliminal stimuli did not.

Evidence consistent with subliminal perception can be seen when examining patients who have very specific types of brain damage. For example, individuals with **prosopagnosia** are unable to recognize familiar faces. In essence, they have a type of visual agnosia that is specific for faces. Such individuals typically have cortical damage in areas involved with object perception. In some cases, they may be aware that they are looking at a face, but they cannot tell you who the individual is. Nonetheless, they may be able to categorize the visual stimulus as a face, and some patients can correctly "guess" who the face belongs to. How can this happen if the stimuli cannot be perceived?

Consider the following study by Steeves, Culham, Duchaine, Pratesi, Valyear, Schindler, Humphrey, Milner, & Goodale (2006). Steeves et al. studied patient D.F., a 47-year-old woman who suffered brain damage at age 34 from accidental carbon monoxide poisoning. D.F. has a great deal of difficulty recognizing the size, shape, and orientation of objects, but she is able to perceive colour. Thus, she is often able to recognize objects (e.g., an orange versus a tomato) based on colour and texture information alone. Similarly, people may be identified by non-facial cues such as clothing choice, voice pitch, etc. Earlier studies using fMRI imaging (Culham, 2004; James et al., 2003) had identified specific lesions in D.F.'s cortex. In particular, damage was observed in the lateral occipital area (LOA) in both hemispheres. The LOA has been associated with object perception in the intact cortex. D.F. and three control participants with no brain damage were shown a series of face and object stimuli while imaging with fMRI. Activation was examined in the LOA and in a second area associated with facial processing: the fusiform gyrus. Here we find the Fusiform Facial Area (FFA), a brain region specifically associated with facial perception.

For all participants, including D.F., there was greater brain activation in the FFA when viewing faces than when viewing scenes. However, the control participants showed greater activation in the LOA as well when viewing faces. This area was damaged in D.F. Despite this damage, D.F. was able to accurately categorize the stimuli as faces versus objects 95 percent of the time. In a second test, D.F. was shown a series of 30 images (5 faces and 25 objects) and asked to describe what they were. All five faces were accurately identified as a face, but not one of the objects was correctly described. In a

–Continued

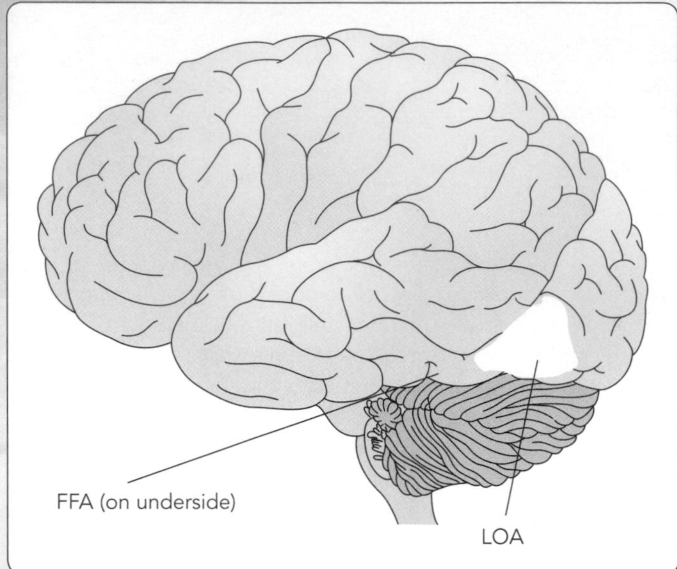

Approximate locations of the lateral occipital area (LOA) and the fusiform facial area (FFA). The FFA is actually on the underside or ventral surface of the cortex.

third test, all participants were shown a series of 60 famous individuals (e.g., John F. Kennedy, Princess Diana) and asked to name them or to provide information about the individual if they could not come up with the name. The controls correctly identified 93 percent of the images; D.F. could not identify a single one.

There are three points we should take away from this study. First, it would appear that higher-order facial recognition is a complex process involving several brain regions including the LOA and the FFA, in addition to the primary visual cortex. Nonetheless, an individual such as D.F. can glean a certain amount of information about visual stimuli even when one of these areas is severely damaged. It is likely that D.F. uses certain heuristic rules to "identify" faces (e.g., elongated oval targets with skin tone are likely to be faces) even though she is not really aware that the stimulus is, in fact, a face. Second, this research emphasizes the importance of the case study to investigate psychological phenomena. D.F. is a unique individual who provides an extraordinary opportunity to examine the role of brain regions in visual processing. In addition, the combination of behavioural testing and fMRI imaging allows the researchers to precisely identify the regions and deficits involved with this disorder.

Finally, the study highlights the subtle manner in which subliminal stimuli may have an effect. Philip Merikle and his colleagues (e.g., Merikle & Skanes, 1992; Merikle et al., 2001) have argued that the effect is one of biasing perception—subliminal cues can bias what we perceive at a conscious level and may alter our conscious experience of those stimuli. In a recent study, Todorov & Bargh (2002) demonstrated that subliminal presentations of aggressively toned words cause people to judge the ambiguous behaviours of others as more aggressive and to increase their own tendency to behave more aggressively. We may not be consciously aware of stimuli, but perhaps like D.F. aspects of the stimuli are processed at a different level and available for us to use in subsequent decisions.

The Difference Threshold

7. What is the technical definition of a difference threshold? How does Weber's law help us compare jnd sensitivities in the various senses?

8. What accounts for sensory adaptation? Of what survival value is adaptation?

Distinguishing between stimuli can sometimes be as important as detecting stimuli in the first place. When we try to match the colours of paints or clothing, very subtle differences can be quite important. Likewise, a slight variation in taste might signal that food is tainted or spoiled. Professional wine tasters and piano tuners make their livings by being able to make very slight discriminations between stimuli.

The **difference threshold** is defined as the smallest difference between two stimuli that people can perceive 50 percent of the time. The difference threshold is sometimes called the *just noticeable difference (jnd)*. Fortunately, as the German physiologist Ernst Weber (pronounced Veh-ber) discovered in the 1830s, there is some degree of lawfulness in the range of sensitivities within our sensory systems. **Weber's law** states that the difference threshold, or jnd, is directly proportional to the magnitude of the stimulus with which the comparison is being made, and can be expressed as a *Weber fraction*. For example, the jnd value for weights is a Weber fraction of approximately 1/50 (Teghtsoonian, 1971). This means that if you lift a weight of 50 grams, a comparison weight must weigh at least 51 grams in order for you to be able to judge it as heavier. If the weight were 500 grams, a second weight would have to weigh at least 510 grams (i.e., 1/50 = 10 g/500 g) for you to discriminate between them.

Although Weber's law breaks down at extremely high and low intensities of stimulation,[1] it holds up reasonably well within the most frequently encountered range, therefore providing a reasonable barometer of our abilities to discern differences in the various sensory modalities. Table 5.2 lists Weber fractions for the various senses. The smaller the fraction, the greater the sensitivity to differences. As highly visual creatures, humans show greater sensitivity in their visual sense than they do in, for example, their sense of smell. Undoubtedly, many creatures who depend upon their sense of smell to track their prey would show quite a different order of sensitivity. Weber fractions also show that humans are highly sensitive to differences in the pitch of sounds, but far less sensitive to loudness differences.

TABLE 5.2 **Weber Fractions for Various Sensory Modalities**

Sensory Modality	Weber Fraction
Audition (tonal pitch)	1/333
Vision (brightness, white light)	1/60
Kinesthesis (lifted weights)	1/50
Pain (heat produced)	1/30
Audition (loudness)	1/20
Touch (pressure applied to skin)	1/7
Smell (India rubber)	1/4
Taste (salt concentration)	1/3

SOURCES: Geldard, 1962; Teghtsoonian, 1971.

Sensory Adaptation

Because changes in our environment are often most newsworthy, sensory systems are finely attuned to *changes* in stimulation. Sensory neurons are engineered to respond to a constant stimulus by *decreasing* their activity, and the diminishing sensitivity to an unchanging stimulus is called **sensory adaptation.**

Adaptation (sometimes called *habituation*) is a part of everyday experience. After a while, monotonous background sounds are largely unheard. The feel of your wristwatch against your skin recedes from awareness. If you dive into a swimming pool, the water may feel cold at first because your body's temperature sensors respond to the change in temperature. With time, however, you become used to the water temperature.

Adaptation occurs in all sensory modalities, including vision. Indeed, were it not for tiny involuntary eye movements that keep images moving about the retina, stationary objects would simply fade from sight if we stared at them (Martinez-Conde, MacKnik, & Hubel, 2004). In an ingenious demonstration of this variety of adaptation, R. M. Pritchard (1961) attached a tiny projector to a contact lens worn by the participant (Figure 5.4a). This procedure guaranteed that visual images presented through the projector would maintain a constant position on the retina, even when the eye moved. When a stabilized image was projected through the lens onto the retina, participants reported that the image appeared in its entirety for a time, then began to vanish and reappear as parts of the original stimulus (Figure 5.4b).

Although sensory adaptation may reduce our overall sensitivity, it is adaptive, because it frees our senses from the constant and the mundane to pick up informative changes in the environment. Such changes may turn out to be important to our well-being or survival.

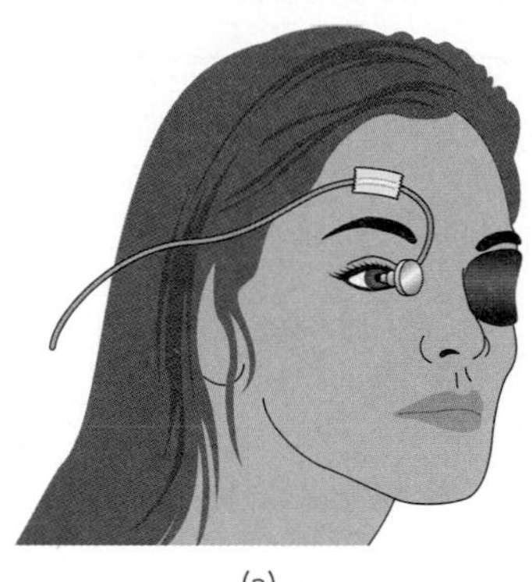

(a)

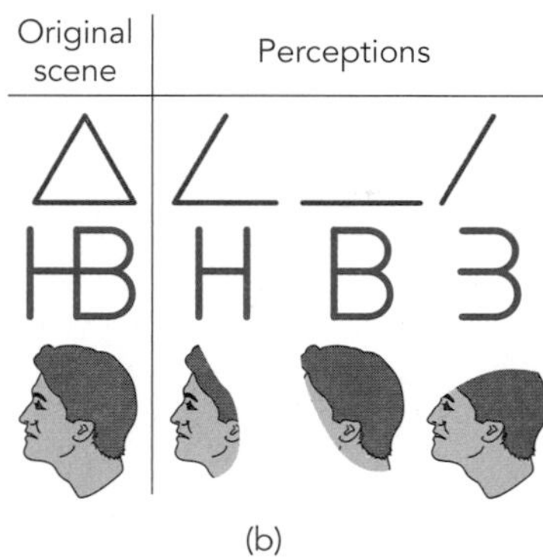

(b)

FIGURE 5.4

(a) To create a stabilized retinal image, a person wears a contact lens to which a tiny projector has been attached. Despite eye movements, images will be cast on the same region of the retina. (b) Under these conditions, the stabilized image is clear at first, then begins to fade and reappear in meaningful segments as the receptors fatigue and recover.

Adapted from Pritchard, 1961.

[1]This breakdown led Gustav Fechner to develop his own, more general, law in 1851. Fechner's Law states that perceived sensation is proportional to the logarithm of physical stimulus intensity.

In Review

- Sensation refers to the activities by which our sense organs receive and transmit information, whereas perception involves the brain's processing and interpretation of the information.
- Psychophysics is the scientific study of how the physical properties of stimuli are related to sensory experiences. Sensory sensitivity is concerned in part with the limits of stimulus detectability (absolute threshold) and the ability to discriminate between stimuli (difference threshold). The absolute threshold is the intensity at which a stimulus is detected 50 percent of the time. Signal detection theory is concerned with factors that influence decisions about whether or not a stimulus is present.
- Research indicates that subliminal stimuli, which are not consciously perceived, can influence perceptions and behaviour in subtle ways, but not strongly enough to justify concerns about the subconscious control of behaviour through subliminal messages. The use of subliminal self-help materials sometimes results in positive behaviour changes that may be a product of expectancy factors rather than the subliminal messages themselves.
- The difference threshold, or just noticeable difference (jnd), is the amount by which two stimuli must differ for them to be perceived as different 50 percent of the time. Studies of the jnd led to Weber's law, which states that the jnd is proportional to the intensity of the original stimulus and is constant within a given sense modality.
- Sensory systems are particularly responsive to changes in stimulation, and adaptation occurs in response to unchanging stimuli.

THE SENSORY SYSTEMS

Vision

The normal stimulus for vision is electromagnetic energy, or light waves, which are measured in *nanometres* (nm, or one billionth of a metre). In addition to that tiny portion that humans can perceive, the electromagnetic spectrum includes X-rays, television and radio signals, and infrared and ultraviolet rays (Figure 5.5). Bees are able to "see" ultraviolet light, and rattlesnakes can detect infrared energy. Our visual system is sensitive only to wavelengths extending from about 700 nm (red) down to about 400 nm (blue-violet). (You can remember the order of the spectrum, from higher wavelengths to lower ones, with the name ROY G. BIV—red, orange, yellow, green, blue, indigo, and violet.)

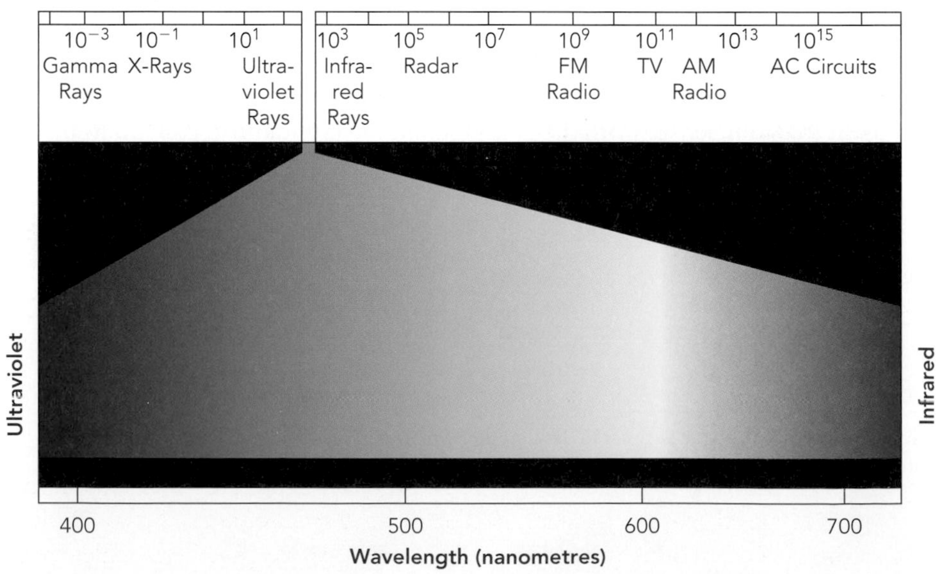

FIGURE 5.5

The full spectrum of electromagnetic radiation. Only the narrow band between 400 and 700 nanometres (nm) is visible to the human eye. One nanometre = 1,000,000,000th of a metre.

Iris
Cornea
Pupil
Lens
Ciliary muscles
Retina
Fovea
Optic nerve to the brain
Blind spot (optic disk)

(a)

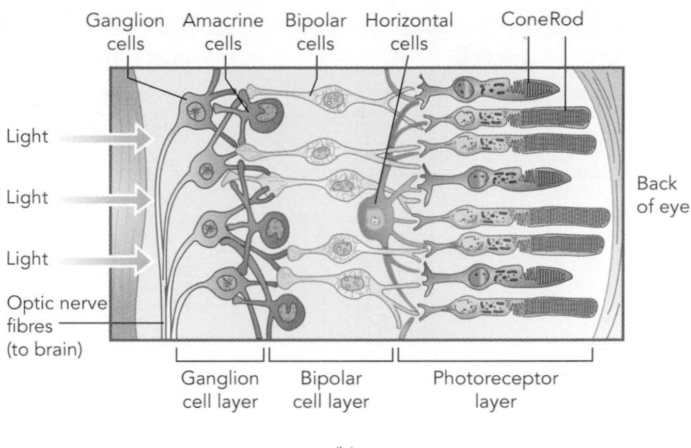

(b)

FIGURE 5.6

(a) This cross-section shows the major parts of the human eye. The iris regulates the size of the pupil. The ciliary muscles regulate the shape of the lens. The image entering the eye is reversed by the lens and cast on the retina, which contains the photoreceptor cells. The optic disk, where the optic nerve exits the eye, has no receptors and produces a "blind spot" as demonstrated in Figure 5.7. (b) Photoreceptor connections in the retina. The rods and cones synapse with bipolar cells, which in turn synapse with ganglion cells, whose axons form the optic nerve. The horizontal and amacrine cells allow sideways integration of retinal activity across areas of the retina.

The Human Eye

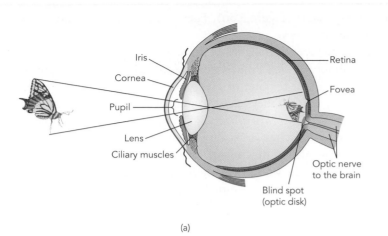

Light waves enter the eye through the *cornea,* a transparent protective structure at the front of the eye (Figure 5.6). Behind the cornea is the *pupil,* an adjustable opening that can dilate or constrict to control the amount of light that enters the eye. The pupil's size is controlled by muscles in the coloured *iris* that surrounds the pupil. Low levels of illumination cause the pupil to dilate, letting more light into the eye to improve optical clarity; bright light triggers constriction of the pupil.

Behind the pupil is the **lens**, an elastic structure that becomes thinner to focus on distant objects and thicker to focus on nearby objects. Just as the lens of a camera focuses an image on a photosensitive material (film), so the lens of the eye focuses the visual image on the light-sensitive **retina**, a multi-layered tissue at the rear of the fluid-filled eyeball. As seen in Figure 5.6a, the lens reverses the image from right to left and top to bottom when it is projected upon the retina, but the brain reconstructs the visual input into the image that we perceive.

The ability to see clearly depends on the lens's ability to focus the image directly onto the retina (Pedrotti & Pedrotti, 1997). If you have good vision for nearby objects but have difficulty seeing faraway objects, you probably suffer from **myopia** (nearsightedness). In nearsighted people, the lens focuses the visual image *in front of* the retina (too near the lens), resulting in a blurred image for faraway objects. This condition generally occurs becase the eyeball is longer (front to back) than normal. In contrast, some people have excellent distance vision but have difficulty seeing close-up objects clearly. **Hyperopia** (farsightedness) occurs when the lens does not thicken enough and the image is therefore focused on a point *behind* the retina (too far from the lens). The aging process typically causes the eyeball to become shorter over time, contributing to the development of hyperopia and the need for many middle-aged people to acquire reading glasses (after complaining that their arms are not long enough to read newspapers and telephone books). Ironically, this age-related shortening of the eyeball often improves the vision of myopic people, for, as the retina moves closer to the lens, it approaches the point where the "nearsighted" lens is projecting the image (Orr, 1998). Eyeglasses and contact lenses are designed to correct for the natural lens's inability to focus the visual image directly onto the retina.

9. How does the lens affect visual acuity, and how does its dysfunction cause the visual problems of myopia and hyperopia?

Photoreceptors: The Rods and Cones

The retina, a multi-layered screen that lines the back surface of the eyeball and contains specialized sensory neurons, is actually an extension of the brain (Bullier, 2002). The retina contains two types of light-sensitive receptor cells, called rods

10. How are the rods and cones distributed in the retina, and how do they contribute to brightness perception, colour vision, and visual acuity?

and cones because of their shapes (Figure 5.6b). There are about 120 million rods and 6 million cones in the human eye.

The **rods**, which function best in dim light, are primarily black-and-white brightness receptors. They are about 500 times more sensitive to light than are the cones, but they do not give rise to colour sensations. The retinas of some night creatures, such as the owl, contain only rods, so they have exceptional vision in very dim light but no colour vision during the day (Dossenbach & Dossenbach, 1998). The **cones**, which are colour receptors, function best in bright illumination. Some creatures that are active only during the day, such as the the pigeon and the chipmunk, have only cones in their retinas, so they see the world in living colour but have very poor night vision (Dossenbach & Dossenbach, 1998). Animals that are active during both day and night, as humans are, have a mixture of rods and cones. In humans, rods are found throughout the retina except in the **fovea**, a small area in the centre of the retina that contains only cones. Cones decrease in concentration as one moves away from the centre of the retina, and the periphery of the retina contains mainly rods.

Rods and cones send their messages to the brain via two additional layers of cells. **Bipolar cells** have synaptic connections with the rods and cones. The bipolar cells, in turn, synapse with a layer of about one million **ganglion cells**, whose axons are collected into a bundle to form the **optic nerve**. Thus input from more than 126 million rods and cones is eventually funnelled into only 1 million traffic lanes leading out of the retina toward higher visual centres. Figure 5.6b shows how the rods and cones are connected to the bipolar and ganglion cells. One interesting aspect of these connections is the fact that the rods and cones not only form the *rear* layer of the retina, but their light-sensitive ends actually point *away from* the direction of the entering light so that they receive only a fraction of the light energy that enters the eye. Furthermore, the manner in which the rods and cones are connected to the bipolar cells accounts for both the greater importance of rods in dim light and our greater ability to see fine detail in bright illumination, when the cones are most active. Typically, many rods are connected to the same bipolar cell. They therefore can combine or "funnel" their individual electrical messages to the bipolar cell, where the additive effect of the many signals may be enough to fire it. That is why we can more easily detect a faint stimulus, such as a dim star, if we look slightly to one side so that its image falls not on the fovea but on the peripheral portion of the retina, where the rods are packed most densely.

Like the rods, the cones that lie in the periphery of the retina also share bipolar cells. In the fovea, however, the densely packed cones each have their own "private line" to a single bipolar cell. As a result, our **visual acuity**, or ability to see fine detail, is greatest when the visual image projects directly onto the fovea. Such focusing results in the firing of a large number of cones and their private-line bipolar cells. Some birds of prey, such as eagles and hawks, are blessed with not one, but two foveas in each eye, contributing to a visual acuity that allows them to see small prey on the ground as they soar thousands of feet above the earth (Tucker, 2000).

FIGURE 5.7

Close your left eye and, from a distance of about 30 centimetres, focus steadily on the dot with your right eye as you slowly move the book toward your face. At some point the image of the X will cross your optic disk (blind spot) and disappear. It will reappear after it crosses the blind spot. Note how the checkerboard remains wholly visible even though part of it falls on the blind spot. Your perceptual system "fills in" the missing information.

The optic nerve formed by the axons of the ganglion cells exits through the back of the eye not far from the fovea, producing a *blind spot*, where there are no photoreceptors. You can demonstrate the existence of your blind spot by following the directions for the demonstration in Figure 5.7. Ordinarily, we are unaware of the blind spot because our perceptual system "fills in" the missing part of the visual field (Rolls & Deco, 2002).

Visual Transduction: From Light to Nerve Impulses

The process whereby the characteristics of a stimulus are converted into nerve impulses is called **transduction**. Rods and cones translate light waves into nerve impulses through the action of protein molecules called **photopigments** (Stryer, 1987; Wolken, 1995). The absorption of light by these molecules produces a chemical reaction that changes the rate of neurotransmitter release at the receptor's synapse with the bipolar cells (Burns & Arshavsky, 2005). The greater the change in transmitter release, the stronger the signal passed on to the bipolar cell and, in turn, to the ganglion cells whose axons form the optic nerve. If nerve responses are triggered at each of the three levels (rod or cone, bipolar cell, and ganglion cell), the message is instantaneously on its way to the visual relay station in the thalamus, and then on to the visual cortex of the brain.

11. What is transduction, and how does this process occur in the photoreceptors of the eye?

Brightness Vision and Dark Adaptation

As noted earlier, rods are far more sensitive than cones under conditions of low illumination. Nonetheless, the brightness sensitivity of both the rods and the cones depends in part on the wavelength of the light. Research has shown that rods have a much greater brightness sensitivity than cones throughout the colour spectrum *except* at the red end, where rods are relatively insensitive. Cones are most sensitive to low illumination in the greenish-yellow range of the spectrum. These findings have prompted many cities to change the colour of their fire engines from the traditional red (which rods are insensitive to) to yellow-green in order to increase the vehicles' visibility to both rods and cones in dim lighting. Similarly, airport landing lights are often blue because this wavelength is picked up particularly well by the rods during night vision, when the cones are relatively inoperative.

12. How is brightness sensitivity in rods and cones affected by the colour spectrum?

Although the rods are by nature sensitive to low illumination, they are not always ready to fulfill their function. Perhaps you have had the embarrassing experience of entering a movie theatre from bright sunlight, groping around in the darkness, and finally sitting down in someone's lap. Although one can meet interesting people this way, most of us prefer to stand in the rear of the theatre until our eyes adapt to the dimly lit interior.

13. What is the physiological basis for dark adaptation? What are the two components of the dark adaptation curve?

Dark adaptation is the progressive improvement in brightness sensitivity that occurs over time under conditions of low illumination. After absorbing light, a photoreceptor is depleted of its pigment molecules for a period of time. If the eye has been exposed to conditions of high illumination, such as bright sunlight, a substantial amount of photopigment will be depleted. During the process of dark adaptation, the photopigment molecules are regenerated, and the receptor's sensitivity increases greatly.

Vision researchers have plotted the course of dark adaptation as people move from conditions of bright light into darkness (Carpenter & Robson, 1999). By focusing light flashes of varying wavelengths and brightness on the fovea, which contains only cones, or on the periphery of the retina, where rods reside, they discovered the two-part curve shown in Figure 5.8. The first part of the curve is due to dark adaptation of the cones. As you can see, the cones gradually become sensitive to fainter lights as time passes, but after about 5 to 10 minutes in the dark, their sensitivity has reached its maximum. The rods, whose photopigments regenerate more slowly, do not reach their maximum sensitivity for about half an hour. It is estimated that after complete adaptation, rods are able to detect light intensities only 1/10,000 as great as those that could be detected before dark adaptation began (Stryer, 1987).

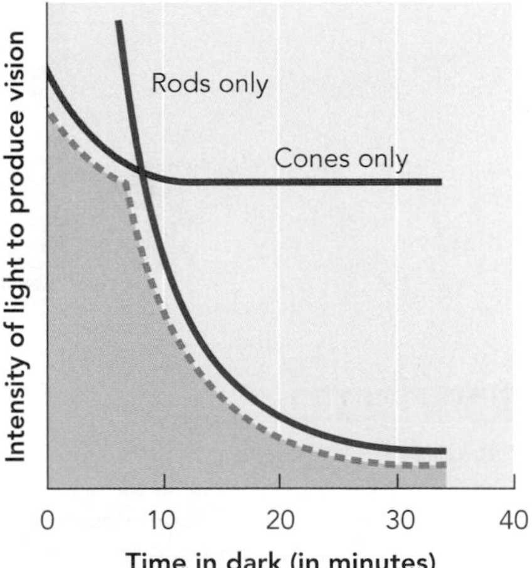

FIGURE 5.8

The course of dark adaptation is graphed over time. The curve has two parts, one for the cones and one for the rods. The cones adapt completely in about 10 minutes, whereas the rods continue to increase their sensitivity for another 20 minutes.

During World War II, psychologists familiar with the facts about dark adaptation provided a method for enhancing night vision in pilots who needed to take off at a moment's notice and see their targets under conditions of low illumination. Knowing that the rods are important in night vision and relatively insensitive to red wavelengths, they suggested that fighter pilots either wear goggles with red

FIGURE 5.9

Working in red light keeps the rods in a state of dark adaptation because rods are quite insensitive to that wavelength. Therefore they retain high levels of photopigment and remain sensitive to low illumination.

lenses or work in rooms lit only by red lights while waiting to be called for a mission. Because red light stimulates only the cones, the rods remain in a state of dark adaptation, ready for immediate service in the dark. That highly practical principle continues to be useful to this day (Figure 5.9).

Colour Vision

We are blessed with a world rich in colour. The majesty of a glowing sunset, the rich blues and greens of a tropical bay, the brilliant colours of fall foliage all produce visual delights for us. Human vision is finely attuned to colour; our difference thresholds for light wavelengths are so small that we are able to distinguish an estimated 7.5 million hue variations (Backhaus et al., 1998). Historically, two different theories of colour vision have tried to explain how this occurs.

14. Describe the Young-Helmholtz trichromatic theory of colour vision. What kinds of evidence support this theory, and what two phenomena challenge it?

15. Describe the opponent-process theory. What evidence supports it?

16. How does the dual-process theory of colour vision combine the trichromatic and opponent-process theories?

The trichromatic theory. Around 1800, it was discovered that any colour in the visible spectrum can be produced by some combination of the wavelengths that correspond to the colours blue, green, and red in what is known as *additive colour mixture* (Figure 5.10a). This fact was the basis of an important trichromatic (three-colour) theory of colour vision advanced by Thomas Young, an English physicist, and Hermann von Helmholtz, a German physiologist. According to the Young-Helmholtz **trichromatic theory**, there are three types of colour receptors in the retina. Although all cones can be stimulated by most wavelengths to varying degrees, individual cones are most sensitive to wavelengths that correspond to either blue, green, or red (Figure 5.11). Presumably, each of these receptor classes sends messages to the brain, based on the extent to which they are activated by the light energy's wavelength. The visual system then combines the signals to recreate the original hue. If all three cones are equally activated, a pure white colour is produced.

Although the Young-Helmholtz theory was consistent with the laws of additive colour mixture, there are several facts that did not fit the theory. For example, according to the theory, yellow is produced by activity of red and green receptors. Yet certain people with red-green colour blindness are able to experience yellow.

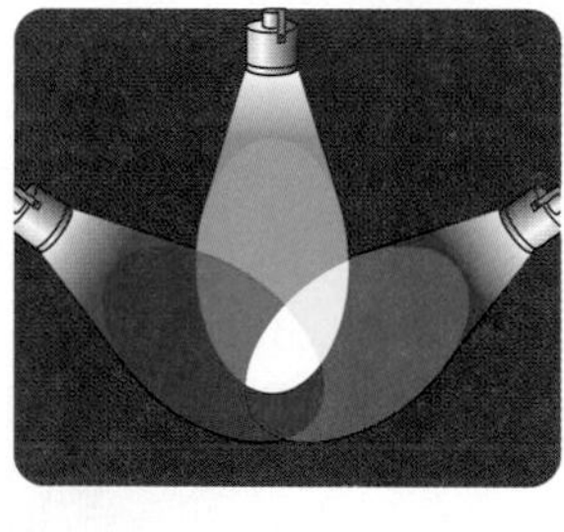

(a)

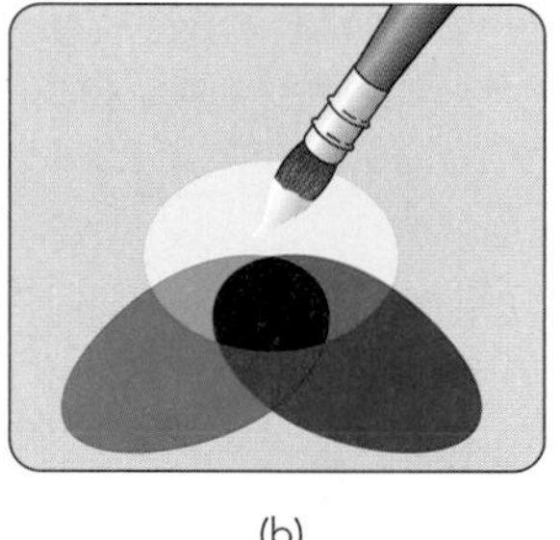

(b)

FIGURE 5.10

Additive and subtractive colour mixture are different processes. (a) Additive colour mixture. A beam of light of a specific wavelength directed onto a white surface is perceived as the colour that corresponds to that wavelength on the visible spectrum. If beams of light that fall at certain points within the red, green, or blue colour range are directed together onto the surface in the correct proportions, a combined or additive mixture of wavelengths will result and any colour in the visible spectrum can be produced (including white at the point where all three colours intersect). The Young-Helmholtz trichromatic theory of colour vision assumes that colour perception results from the additive mixture of impulses from cones that are sensitive to red, blue, and green (see text). (b) Subtractive colour mixture. Mixing pigments or paints produces new colours by subtraction—that is, by removing (i.e., absorbing) other wavelengths. Paints absorb (subtract) colours different from themselves while reflecting their own colour. For example, blue paint mainly absorbs wavelengths that correspond to non-blue hues. Mixing blue paint with yellow paint (which absorbs wavelengths other than yellow) will produce a subtractive mixture that emits wavelengths between yellow and blue (i.e., green). Theoretically, certain wavelengths of the three primary colours of red, yellow (not green, as in additive mixture), and blue can produce the whole spectrum of colours by subtractive mixture. Thus, in additive colour mixture, the primary colours are red, blue, and green; in subtractive colour mixture, they are red, yellow, and blue.

This finding suggested to other scientists that there must be a different means of perceiving yellow. A second phenomenon that posed problems for the trichromatic theory was the colour *afterimage,* in which an image in a different colour appears after a colour stimulus has been viewed steadily and then withdrawn. To experience one yourself, stare steadily at the object in Figure 5.12 for a full minute, then shift your gaze to a blank white space. Trichromatic theory cannot account for what you'll see.

Opponent-process theory. A second influential colour theory, formulated by Ewald Hering in 1870, also assumed that there are three types of cones. Hering's **opponent-process theory** proposed that each of the three cone types responds to *two* different wavelengths. One type responds to red *or* green, another to blue *or* yellow, and a third to black *or* white. For example, a red-green cone responds with one chemical reaction to a green stimulus and with its other chemical reaction (opponent process) to a red stimulus (Figure 5.11). You have experienced one of the phenomena that supports the existence of opponent processes if you did the exercise in Figure 5.12. The colour afterimage you saw in the blank space contains the colours specified by opponent-process theory: The black portion of the flag appeared as white, and the green portion "turned" red. According to opponent-process theory, as you stared at the black and green colours, the neural processes that register these colours became fatigued. Then when you cast your gaze on the white surface, which reflects all wavelengths, a "rebound" opponent reaction occurred as each receptor responded with its opposing white or red reactions.

Dual processes in colour transduction. Which theory—the trichromatic theory or the opponent-process theory—is correct? Two centuries of research have yielded a win-win verdict for both sets of theorists. Today's **dual-process theory** combines the trichromatic and opponent-process theories to account for the colour transduction process (Backhaus et al., 1998).

Trichromatic theorists such as Young and Helmholtz were right about the cones. The cones do indeed contain one of three different protein photopigments that are most sensitive to wavelengths roughly corresponding to the colours blue, red, and green (Abramov & Gordon, 1994). Different ratios of activity in the red-, blue-, and green-sensitive cones can produce a pattern of neural activity that corresponds to any hue in the spectrum (Backhaus et al., 1998). This process is similar to that which occurs on your television screen, where colour pictures (including white hues) are produced by activating combinations of tiny red, green, and blue dots in a process of additive colour mixture.

Hering's opponent-process theory was also partly correct, but opponent processes do not occur at the level of the cones, as he maintained. When researchers began to use microelectrodes to record from single cells in the visual system, they discovered that certain ganglion cells in the retina, as well as some neurons in visual relay stations and the visual cotrex, respond in an opponent-process fashion by altering their rate of firing (DeValois & DeValois, 1993). For example, if a red light is shone on the retina, an opponent-process ganglion cell may respond with a high rate of firing, but a green light will cause the same cell to fire at a very low rate. Other neurons respond in a similar opponent fashion to blue and yellow stimuli. The red-green opponent processes are triggered directly by input from the red- or green-sensitive cones in the retina (Figure 5.13). The blue-yellow opponent process is a bit more complex. Activity of blue-sensitive cones directly stimulates the "blue" process farther along in the visual system. And

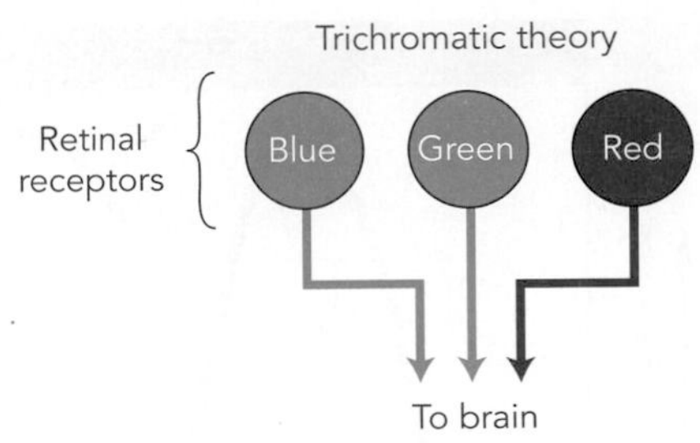

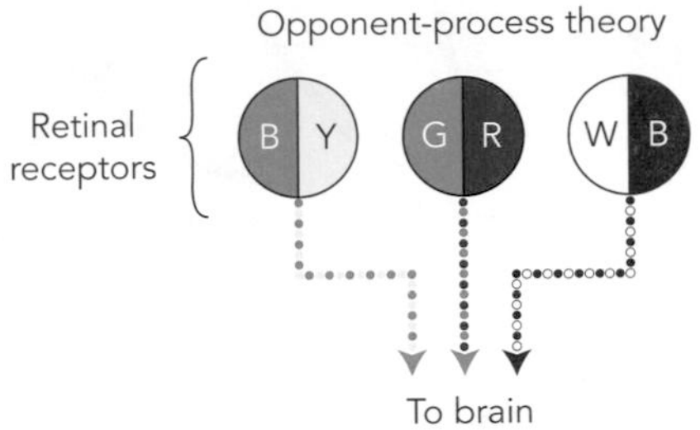

FIGURE 5.11

Two classic theories of colour vision. The Young-Helmholtz trichromatic theory proposed three different receptors, one for blue, one for red, and one for green. The ratio of activity in the three types of cones in response to a stimulus yields our experience of colour. Hering's opponent-process theory also assumed that there are three different receptors: one for yellow-blue, one for red-green, and one for black-white. Each of the receptors can function in two possible ways, depending on the wavelength of the stimulus. Again, the pattern of activity in the receptors yields our perception of the hue.

FIGURE 5.12

Negative colour afterimages demonstrate opponent processes occurring somewhere in the visual system. Stare steadily at the black dot in the centre of the flag for about a minute, then shift your gaze to a blank, white page. The opponent colours should appear.

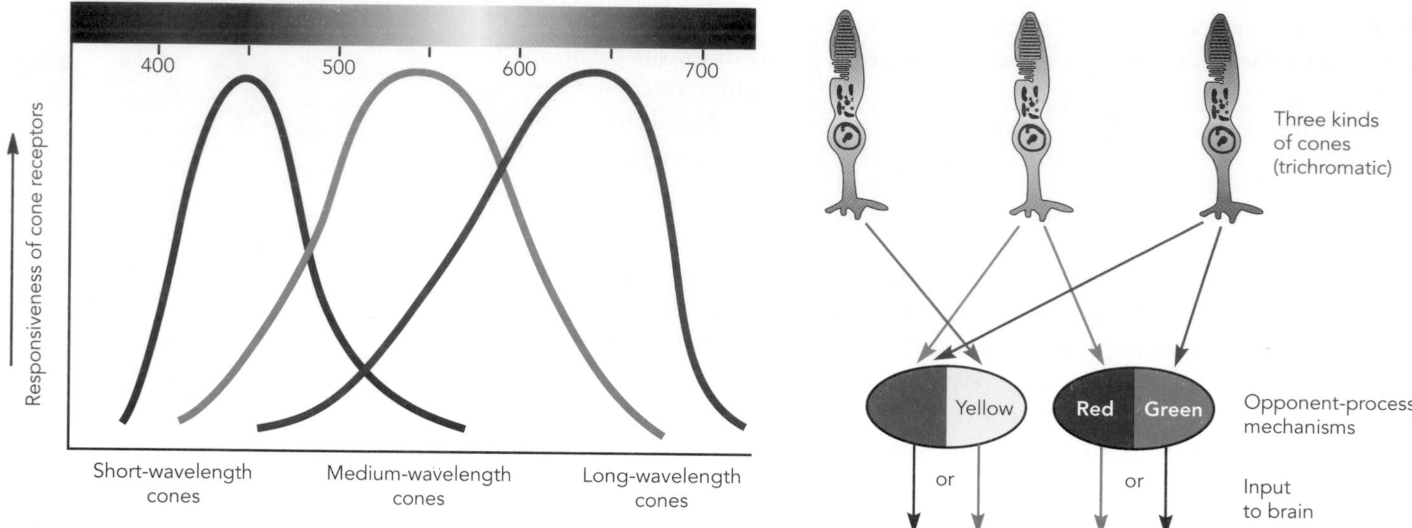

FIGURE 5.13

Colour vision involves both trichromatic and opponent processes that occur at different places in the visual system. Consistent with trichromatic theory, three types of cones are maximally sensitive to short (blue), medium (green), and long (red) wavelengths, respectively. However, opponent processes occur further along in the visual system, as opponent cells in the retina, visual relay stations, and the visual cortex respond differentially to red versus green, blue versus yellow, and black versus white stimuli. Shown here are the inputs from the cones that produce the red-green and blue-yellow opponent processes.

yellow? The yellow opponent process is triggered not by a "yellow-sensitive" cone, as Hering proposed, but rather by simultaneous input from the red- and green-sensitive cones (Abramov & Gordon, 1994).

Colour-deficient vision. People with normal colour vision are referred to as *trichromats.* They are sensitive to all three systems: red-green, yellow-blue, and black-white. However, about 7 percent of the male population and 1 percent of the female population have a deficiency in the red-green system, the yellow-blue system, or both. This deficiency is caused by an absence of hue-sensitive photopigment in certain cone types. A *dichromat* is a person who is colour-blind in only one of the systems (red-green or yellow-blue). A *monochromat* is sensitive only to the black-white system and is totally colour-blind. Most colour-deficient people are dichromats and have their deficiency in the red-green system. Tests of colour-blindness typically contain sets of coloured dots such as those in Figure 5.14. Depending on the type of deficit, a colour-blind person cannot discern certain numbers embedded in the circles.

17. What are the two major types of colour-blindness? How are they tested?

Analysis and Reconstruction of Visual Scenes

Once the transformation of light energy to nerve impulses occurs, the process of combining the messages received from the photoreceptors into the perception of a visual scene begins. As you read this page, nerve impulses from countless neurons are

FIGURE 5.14

These dotted figures are used to test for colour-deficient vision. The first one tests for yellow-blue colour-blindness, the second one for red-green colour-blindness. Because the dots in the picture are of equal brightness, colour is the only available cue for perceiving the numbers in the chips.

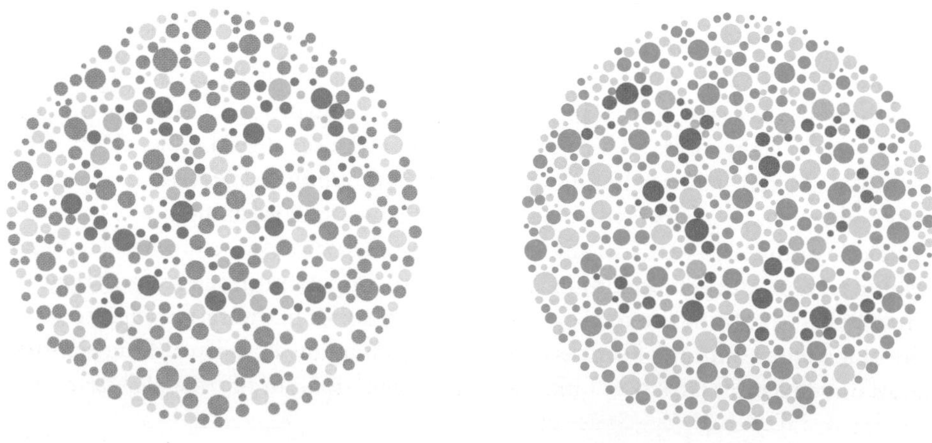

being analyzed and the visual image that you perceive is being reconstructed. Moreover, you know what these black squiggles on the page "mean." How does this occur?

Feature detectors. From the retina, the optic nerve sends nerve impulses to a visual relay station in the thalamus, the brain's sensory switchboard. From there, the input is routed to various parts of the cortex, particularly the **primary visual cortex** in the occipital lobe at the rear of the brain. Microelectrode studies have shown that there is a point-to-point correspondence between tiny regions of the retina and groups of neurons in the visual cortex. As you might expect, the fovea, where the one-to-one synapses of cones with bipolar cells produces high visual acuity, is represented by a disproportionately large area of the visual cortex. Somewhat more surprising is the fact that there is more than one cortical "map" of the retina; there are at least 10 duplicate mappings. Perhaps this is nature's insurance policy against damage to any one of them, or perhaps the duplicate maps are somehow involved in the integration of visual input.

Groups of neurons within the primary visual cortex are organized to receive and integrate sensory nerve impulses originating in specific regions of the retina. Some of these cells are known as **feature detectors**. They fire selectively in response to stimuli that have specific characteristics (Kanwisher, 1998). Discovery of these feature detectors won David Hubel and Torsten Wiesel of Harvard University the 1981 Nobel Prize. Using tiny electrodes to record the activity of individual cells of the visual cortex of animals (Figure 5.15), Hubel and Wiesel found that certain neurons fired most frequently when lines of certain orientations were presented. One neuron might fire most frequently when a horizontal line was presented; another neuron would fire most frequently to a line of a slightly different orientation, and so on "around the clock." For example, a letter "A" could be constructed from the response of feature detectors that responded to three different line orientations: /, \, and —.

FIGURE 5.15

A partially anaesthetized monkey views an image projected onto the screen while an electrode embedded in its visual cortex records the activity of a single neuron. This research by Hubel and Wiesel led to the discovery of feature detectors that analyze visual stimulus features such as contours and shapes, movement, and colour.

18. What kinds of feature detectors exist in the visual system? What is meant by parallel processing of sensory information?

The discovery of feature detectors revolutionized vision research. Since then, scientists have found cells that respond most strongly to bars, slits, and edges in certain positions. Within the cortex, this information is integrated and analyzed by successively more complex feature detector systems to produce our perception of objects (Palmer, 2002). This process is illustrated by the illusion shown in Figure 5.16.

Other classes of feature detectors respond to colour, to depth, or to movement (Livingstone & Hubel, 1994; Smith, Snowdon, & Milne, 1995). These feature detector "modules" subdivide a visual scene into its component dimensions and process them simultaneously. Thus, as a red, white, and green beach ball sails toward you, separate but overlapping modules within the brain simultaneously analyze its colours, shape, distance, and movement by engaging in **parallel processing** of the information and constructing a unified image of its properties (Tarr & Vuong, 2002). In addition, brief, high-frequency "bursts" of firing in sensory neurons may function as feature detectors and can signal the occurrence of important stimuli in the sensory field (Marsat & Pollack, 2006).

FIGURE 5.16

Is the white triangle "real"? It appears to be, because feature detectors that analyze the contours of the pie-shaped circles analyze the corners, and the brain fills in the "missing" lines. The contours are illusory, but they appear real. See what happens to the triangle if you cover up one or two of the circles.

Visual association processes. The final stages in the process of constructing a visual representation occur when the information analyzed and recombined by the primary visual cortex is routed to other cortical regions known as the **visual association cortex**. Here successively more complex features of the visual scene are combined and interpreted in light of our memories and knowledge. If all goes correctly, a process that began with nerve impulses from the rods and cones now ends with us "recognizing" the beach ball for what it "is" and catching it. Quite another conscious experience and response probably would occur if we interpreted the oncoming object as a water balloon.

In Review

- *The senses may be classified in terms of the energy to which they respond. Through the process of transduction, these energy forms are transformed into the common language of nerve impulses.*
- *The normal stimulus for vision is electromagnetic energy, or light waves. Light-sensitive visual receptor cells are located in the retina. The rods are brightness receptors, and the less numerous cones are colour receptors. Light energy striking the retina is converted into nerve impulses by chemical reactions in the photopigments of the rods and cones. Dark adaptation involves the gradual regeneration of photo pigments that have been depleted by brighter illumination.*
- *Colour vision is a two-stage process having both trichromatic and opponent-process components. The first stage involves the reactions of cones that are maximally sensitive to red, green, and blue wavelengths. In the second stage, colour information from the cones is coded through an opponent-process mechanism further along in the visual system.*
- *Visual stimuli are analyzed by feature detectors in the primary visual cortex, and the stimulus elements are reconstructed and interpreted in light of input from the visual association cortex.*

Audition

The stimuli for our sense of hearing are sound waves, a form of mechanical energy. What we call sound is actually pressure waves in air, water, or some other conducting medium. When a stereo's volume is high enough, you can actually see cloth speaker covers moving in and out. The resulting vibrations cause successive waves of compression and expansion among the air molecules surrounding the source of the sound. These sound waves have two characteristics: frequency and amplitude (Figure 5.17).

19. What are the two physical characteristics of sound waves, and which auditory qualities do these characteristics produce?

Frequency is the number of sound waves, or cycles, per second. The **hertz (Hz)** is the technical measure of cycles per second; one Hz equals one cycle per second. The sound waves' frequency is related to the pitch that we perceive; the higher the frequency (Hz), the higher the perceived pitch. Humans are capable of detecting sound frequencies from 20 Hz up to 20,000 Hz (about 12,000 Hz in older people). Most common sounds are in the lower frequencies. Among musical instruments, the piano can play the widest range of frequencies, from 27.5 Hz at the low end of the keyboard to 4,186 Hz at the high end. An operatic soprano's voice, in comparison, has a range of only 250 Hz to 1,100 Hz (Aiello, 1994).

Amplitude refers to the vertical size of the sound waves—that is, to the amount of compression and expansion of the molecules in the conducting medium. The sound wave's amplitude is the primary determinant of the sound's perceived loudness. Differences in amplitude are expressed as **decibels (db)**, a measure of the physical pressures that occur at the eardrum. The absolute threshold for hearing is arbitrarily designated as 0 db, and each increase of 10 db represents a tenfold increase in loudness. Table 5.3 shows various common sounds scaled in decibels.

Auditory Transduction: From Pressure Waves to Nerve Impulses

20. Describe how the middle and inner ear structures are involved in the auditory transduction process.

The transduction system of the ear is made up of tiny bones, membranes, and liquid-filled tubes designed to translate pressure waves into nerve impulses (Figure 5.18). Sound waves travel into an auditory canal leading to the eardrum, a movable membrane that vibrates in response to the sound waves. Beyond the eardrum is the middle ear, a cavity housing three tiny bones (the smallest in the body, in fact). The vibrating activity of these bones—the *hammer* (malleus), *anvil* (incus), and *stirrup* (stapes)—amplifies the sound waves more than 30 times. The first bone, the ham-

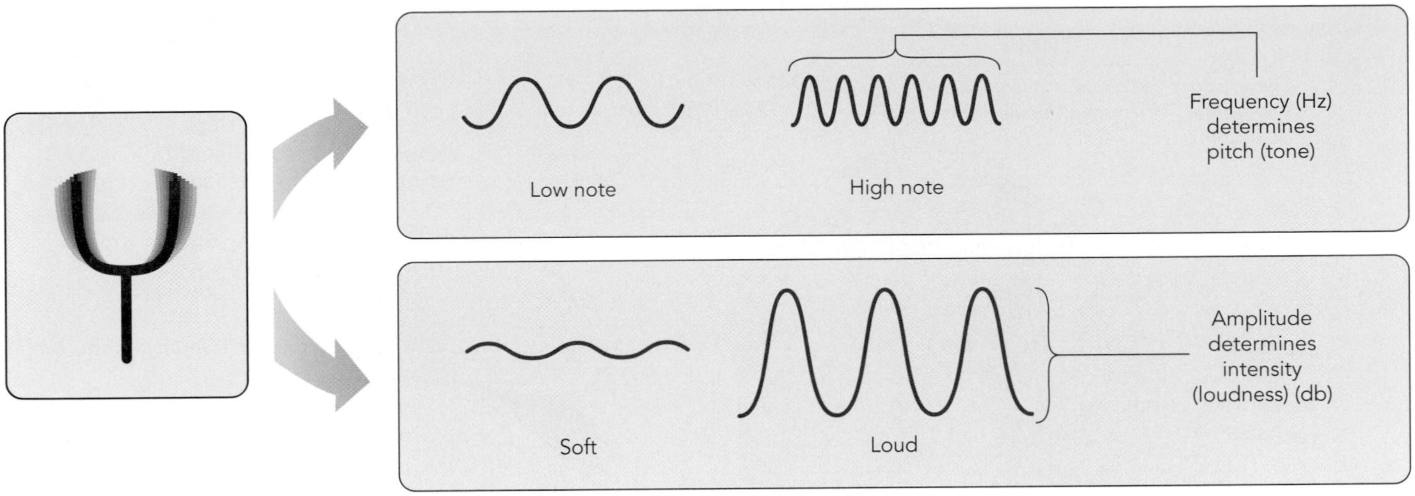

FIGURE 5.17

Sound waves are a form of mechanical energy. As the tuning fork vibrates, it produces successive waves of compression and expansion of air molecules. The number of maximum compressions per second (cycles per second) is its frequency, measured in hertz (Hz). The height of the wave above zero air pressure represents the sound's amplitude. Frequency determines pitch; amplitude determines loudness, measured in decibels (db).

mer, is attached firmly to the eardrum, and the stirrup is attached to another membrane, the *oval window,* which forms the boundary between the middle ear and the inner ear. The inner ear contains the **cochlea**, a coiled, snail-shaped tube about 3.5 cm in length that is filled with fluid and contains the **basilar membrane**, a sheet of tissue that runs its length. Resting on the basilar membrane is the **organ of Corti**, which contains thousands of tiny hair cells that are the actual sound receptors. The tips of the hair cells are attached to another membrane that overhangs the basilar membrane along the entire length of the cochlea. The hair cells synapse with the neurons of the auditory nerve which, in turn, sends impulses via an auditory relay station in the thalamus to the auditory cortex, which is located in the temporal lobe.

TABLE 5.3 **Decibel Scaling of Common Sounds**

Level in Decibels (db)	Common Sounds	Threshold Levels
140	Jet fighter taking off at approximately 25 metres from plane	Potential damage to auditory system
130	Boiler shop	
120	Rock band	Human pain threshold
110	Trumpet automobile horn at approximately one metre	
100	Crosscut saw at position of operator	
90	Train whistle at 150 metres	Hearing damage with prolonged exposure
80		
70	Inside automobile in city	
60	Downtown city street (Toronto)	
50	Restaurant	
40	Classroom	
30	Hospital room	
20	Recording studio	Threshold of hearing (young men)
10		
0		Minimum threshold of hearing

The decibel scale relates a physical quantity—sound intensity—to the human perception of that quantity—sound loudness. It is a logarithmic scale—that is, each increment of 10 db represents a tenfold increase in loudness. The table indicates the decibel ranges of some common sounds as well as thresholds for hearing, hearing damage, and pain. Prolonged exposure at 150 db causes death in laboratory rats.

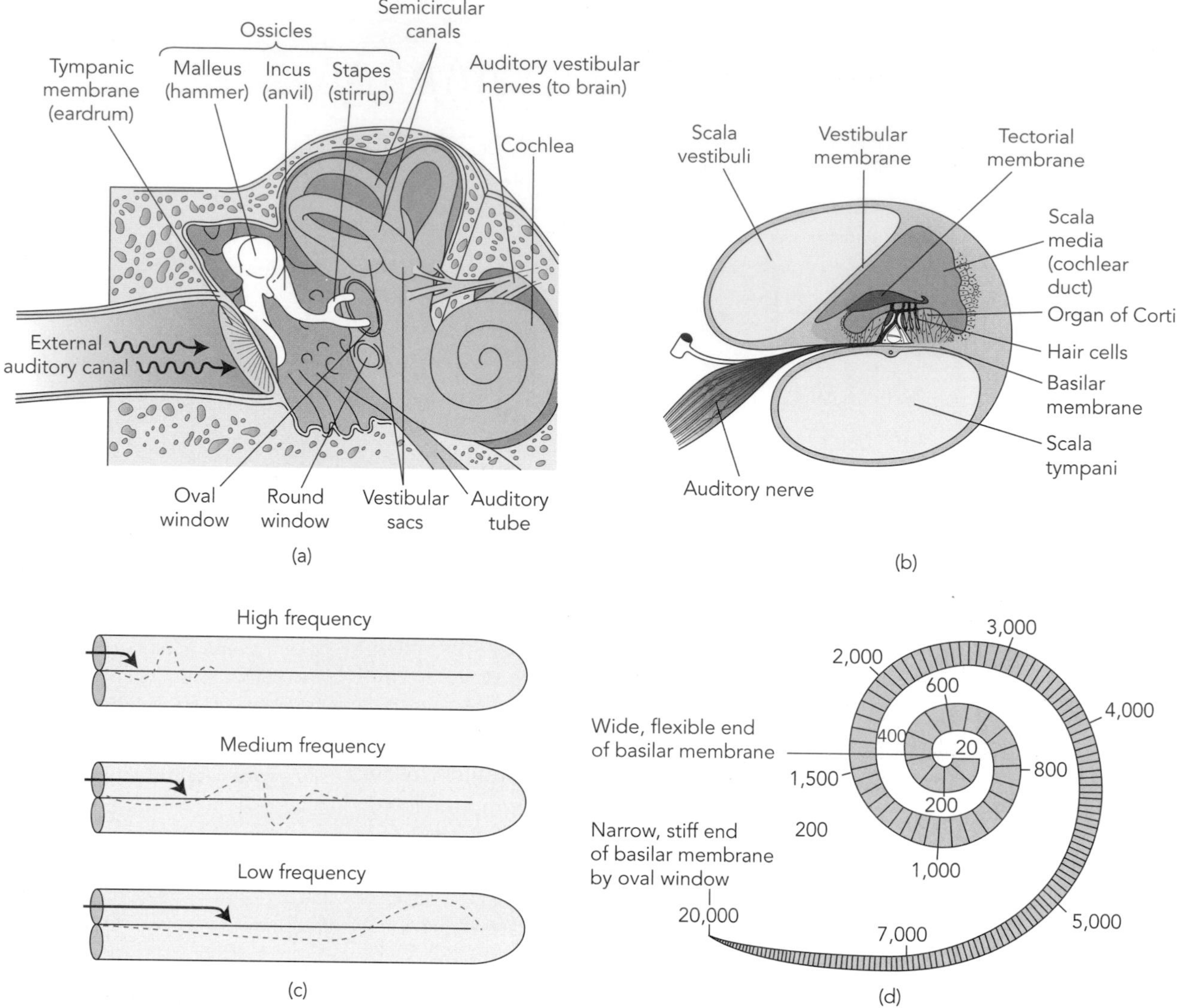

FIGURE 5.18

A cross-section of the ear (a) shows the structures that transmit sound waves from the auditory canal to the cochlea. There sound waves are translated into fluid waves that stimulate hair cells in the organ of Corti (b). The resulting nerve impulses reach the brain via the auditory nerve. The semicircular and vestibular sacs of the inner ear contain sense organs for equilibrium. In (c), the fluid waves created by different sound frequencies are shown, and (d) shows the frequencies that maximally stimulate different areas of the basilar membrane. High-frequency waves peak quickly and stimulate the membrane close to the oval window.

When sound waves strike the eardrum, pressure created at the oval window by the hammer, anvil, and stirrup of the middle ear sets the fluid inside the cochlea into motion. The fluid waves that result vibrate the basilar membrane and the membrane above it, causing a bending of the hair cells in the organ of Corti (Figure 5.18b). This bending of the hair cells triggers a release of neurotransmitter substance into the synaptic space between the hair cells and the neurons of the auditory nerve, resulting in nerve impulses that are sent to the brain. Within the auditory cortex, located in the temporal lobe, are feature detector neurons that respond to specific kinds of auditory input, much as occurs in the visual system (Goldstein, 1998).

Coding of Pitch and Loudness

The auditory system transforms the sensory qualities of loudness and pitch into the language of nerve impulses. In the case of loudness, high-amplitude sound waves cause the hair cells to bend more and release more neurotransmitter substance at the point where they synapse with auditory nerve cells, resulting in a higher rate of firing within the auditory nerve. In addition, certain receptor neurons have higher thresholds than others, so that they will fire only when considerable bending of the hair cells occurs in response to an intense sound. Thus loudness is coded in terms of both the rate of firing in the axons of the auditory nerve and in terms of which specific hair cells are sending messages (Carney, 2002).

The coding of pitch also involves two different processes, one for frequencies below about 1,000 Hz (approximately the midpoint of the piano keyboard) and another for higher frequencies. Historically, as in the case of colour vision, two competing theories were advanced to account for pitch perception. According to the **frequency theory** of pitch perception, nerve impulses sent to the brain match the frequency of the sound wave. Thus a 30 Hz (cycles per second) sound wave from a piano should send 30 volleys of nerve impulses per second to the brain. Unfortunately, frequency theory encounters a major problem. Because neurons are limited in their rate of firing, individual impulses or volleys of impulses fired by groups of neurons cannot produce high enough frequencies of firing to match sound wave frequencies above 1,000 Hz. How then do we perceive higher frequencies, such as a 4,000 Hz note from the same piano?

21. Describe the frequency and place theories of pitch perception. In what sense are both theories correct?

Experiments conducted by Georg von Bekesy (1957) uncovered a second mechanism for coding pitch and earned him the 1961 Nobel Prize. Bekesy cut tiny holes in the cochleas of guinea pigs and human cadavers and observed through a microscope what happened inside the fluid-filled cochlea when he stimulated the eardrum with tones of varying frequencies. He found that high-frequency sounds produced an abrupt wave that peaked close to the oval window, whereas lower-frequency vibrations produced a slower fluid wave that peaked farther down the cochlear canal (Figure 5.18c). Bekesy's observations supported a **place theory** of pitch perception, suggesting that the specific point in the cochlea where the fluid wave peaks and most strongly bends the hair cells serves as a frequency coding cue (Figure 5.18d). Later it was found that, similar to the manner in which the retina is "mapped" onto the visual cortex, the auditory cortex has a tonal frequency "map" that corresponds to specific areas of the cochlea. By analyzing the specific location of the cochlea from which auditory nerve impulses are being received, the brain can code pitches such as our 4,000 Hz piano note (Carney, 2002).

22. How does the structure of the auditory system permit humans to localize sounds? What sensory information is used by the brain in localization?

Thus, like trichromatic and opponent-process theories of colour vision, which were once thought to contradict each another, frequency and place theories of pitch transduction have both proved to be applicable in their own ways. At low frequencies, frequency theory holds true; at higher frequencies, place theory provides the mechanism for coding the pitch of a sound.

Sound Localization

Have you ever wondered why you have two ears, one located on each side of your head? As is usually the case in nature's designs, there is a good reason. Our very survival may depend upon our ability to locate objects that emit sounds. The two ears play a crucial role in *sound localization.* The nervous system uses information concerning the time and intensity differences of sounds arriving at the two ears to locate the source of sounds in space (Luck & Vecera, 2002).

Sounds arrive first and loudest at the ear closest to the sound. When the source of the sound is directly in front of us, the sound wave reaches both ears at the same time and at the same intensity, so the source is perceived as being straight ahead. Our binaural (two-eared) ability to localize sounds is amazingly sensitive. For example, a sound 3 degrees to the right arrives at the right ear only 300 millionths of a second before it arrives at the left ear, and yet we can tell which direction the sound is coming from (Yin & Kuwada, 1984). But, as Figure 5.19 shows, there is always room for improvement.

FIGURE 5.19

This device, used in the late 1800s by sailors to increase their ability to locate sounds while navigating in thick fog, assisted in two ways. First, because the two ear receptors were much larger than human ears, they could capture more sound waves. More importantly, the wide spacing between the receptors increased the time difference between the sound's arrival at the two human ears, thus increasing directional sensitivity.

Nature's design often bests even human ingenuity. For example, the barn owl comes equipped with ears that are exquisitely tailored for pinpoint localization of its prey during night hunting. Its right ear is directed slightly upward, its left ear slightly downward. This allows it to localize sounds precisely in both the vertical and horizontal planes, and thereby to zero in on its prey with deadly accuracy.

Hearing Loss

If you had to make the unwelcome choice of being blind or being deaf, which impairment would you choose? When asked this question, most of our students say that they would rather be deaf. Yet hearing loss can have more devastating social consequences than blindness does (Fletcher, 1995). Helen Keller, who was both blind and deaf, considered deafness to be more socially debilitating. She wrote, "Blindness cuts people off from things. Deafness cuts people off from people."

In Canada alone, almost three million people (approximately 10% of the population) suffer from some form of hearing loss. On a North American basis, the figure is closer to 23 million. Of these, 90 percent were born with normal hearing (Fletcher, 1995). They suffer from two major types of hearing loss. **Conduction deafness** is caused by problems involving the mechanical system that transmits sound waves to the cochlea. For example, a punctured eardrum or a loss of function in the tiny bones of the middle ear can reduce the ear's capacity to transmit vibrations. Use of a hearing aid, which amplifies the sounds entering the ear, may correct many cases of conduction deafness.

23. What are the two varieties of deafness, and how do they differ in their physical bases and in possible treatment?

Nerve deafness is an entirely different matter. It is caused by damaged receptors within the inner ear or damage to the auditory nerve itself, and it cannot be helped by a hearing aid. Although aging and disease can produce nerve deafness, exposure to loud sounds is a leading cause of nerve deafness. Repeated exposure to loud sounds of a particular frequency (as might be produced by a machine in a factory) eventually can cause workers to lose hair cells at a particular point on the basilar membrane, thereby causing hearing loss for that frequency.

Extremely loud music can take a serious toll on young people's hearing (West & Evans, 1990). Figure 5.20 shows the devastating results of a guinea pig's exposure to a sound level approximating that of loud rock music heard through earphones. As Table 5.3 shows, even brief exposure to sounds exceeding 140 db can cause irreversible damage to the transducers in the middle and inner ears, and so can more continuous sounds at lower decibel levels. In 1986, the music at a rock concert conducted by The Who reached 120 db at a distance approximately 50 metres from the speakers. This earned The Who a place in the *Guinness Book of Records* for the all-time loudest concert, but inflicted severe and permanent damage to many of the concert's spectators (Troufexis, 1990). The Who's guitarist, Pete Townshend,

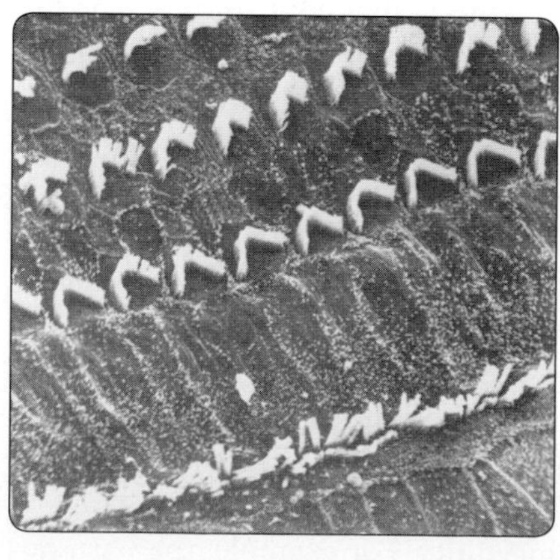

(a)

(b)

FIGURE 5.20

Exposure to loud sounds can destroy auditory receptors in the inner ear. These pictures, taken through an electron microscope, show the hair cells of a guinea pig before (a) and after (b) exposure to 24 hours of noise comparable to that of a loud rock concert.

Micrographs by Robert E. Preston, courtesy of Professor J. E. Hawkins, Kresge Hearing Research Institute, University of Michigan.

eventually suffered severe hearing loss from this prolonged noise exposure. The Canadian Hearing Society recommends that you protect your hearing by listening to music at safe levels (i.e., below 85 db). On a standard portable CD player, a volume setting of four or five will generate this level of intensity.

Although hearing aids can do little to remedy such problems, measures can be taken to prevent damage in people who are exposed to hazardous noise in the workplace (e.g., the use of noise-dampening ear protectors or noise-cancelling headphones).

24. Describe the sensory principles that are applied to create sensory prosthetics for visually and hearing impaired people.

RESEARCH FRONTIERS

Sensory Prosthetics: "Eyes" for the Blind, "Ears" for the Hearing Impaired

Millions of people suffer from blindness and deafness, living in sightless or soundless worlds. Psychological research on the workings of the sensory systems, coupled with technical advances in bioengineering, is being used to produce *sensory prosthetic devices.* These devices produce sensory input that can substitute, to some extent, for what cannot be provided by the normal sensory receptors.

One device, known as a Sonicguide, provides new "eyes" by applying principles of auditory localization (Kay, 1982). The Sonicguide works on the same principle as echolocation, the sensory tool used by bats to navigate in total darkness. The headset contains a transmitter that emits high-frequency sound waves beyond the range of human hearing. These waves bounce back from objects in the environment and are transformed by the Sonicguide into sounds that can be heard through the earphones. Different sound qualities match specific features of external objects, and the wearer must learn to interpret the sonic messages. For example, the sound's pitch tells the person how far away the object is; a low pitch signals a nearby object and the pitch becomes higher with increasing distance. The loudness of the sound tells how large the object is, and the clarity of the sound (ranging from a staticlike sound to a clear tone) signals the texture of the object, from very rough to very smooth. Finally, the auditory localization principle described earlier tells the person where the object is located in the environment by means of differences in the intensity of the sounds that arrive at the two ears.

In the first laboratory tests of the Sonicguide, psychologists Stuart Aitken and T. G. R. Bower (1982) used the apparatus with six blind babies who ranged in age from 5 to 16 months. In his first Sonicguide session with the youngest baby, Bower swung an object on a string until it lightly tapped the baby's nose. After only two presentations, the baby rotated both eyes inward toward his nose as the object approached, and outward as the object swung away. On the seventh trial, the baby reached out with his hand and blocked the object before it reached his face. The blind infant also began to follow the object with his eyes and head when it was moved on a right-left plane in front of him.

Aitken and Bower reported that within hours or days, the older babies using the Sonicguide could reach for objects, walk or crawl through doorways, and listen to the movement of their hands and arms as they moved them about. They also suggested that reaching for objects, recognizing favourite toys, and reaching out to be picked up when mother (but not someone else) approached seemed to occur on the same developmental timetable as in sighted children. They concluded that blind infants can extract the same information from sonic cues as sighted babies do from visual cues, and that this was particularly effective for the young infants. Subsequent long-term longitudinal studies of infants and children by University of Western Ontario researcher Keith Humphrey and his co-workers (Humphrey, Dodwell, Muir, & Humphrey, 1988) and others failed to confirm that infants would immediately use the Sonicguide. In fact, young infants required lengthy training sessions before using the aid effectively to reach and walk. By contrast, 10-year-olds rapidly learned to find large objects handed to them and to navigate through specially constructed obstacle courses (i.e., child mazes) and crowded school corridors; some even played hide-and-seek. The Sonicguide is now being used by visually impaired children in schools and other natural settings in the U.S.A. (e.g., Hill et al., 1995).

The Seeing Tongue

Paul Bach-y-Rita, professor of rehabilitative medicine and biomedical engineering at the University of Wisconsin Medical School, has developed a tactile tongue-based, electrical input sensor as a substitute for visual input (Bach-y-Rita, 2004). The tongue seems an unlikely substitute for the eye, hidden as it is in the dark recess of the mouth. Yet in many ways it may be the second-best organ for providing detailed input, for it is

–*Continued*

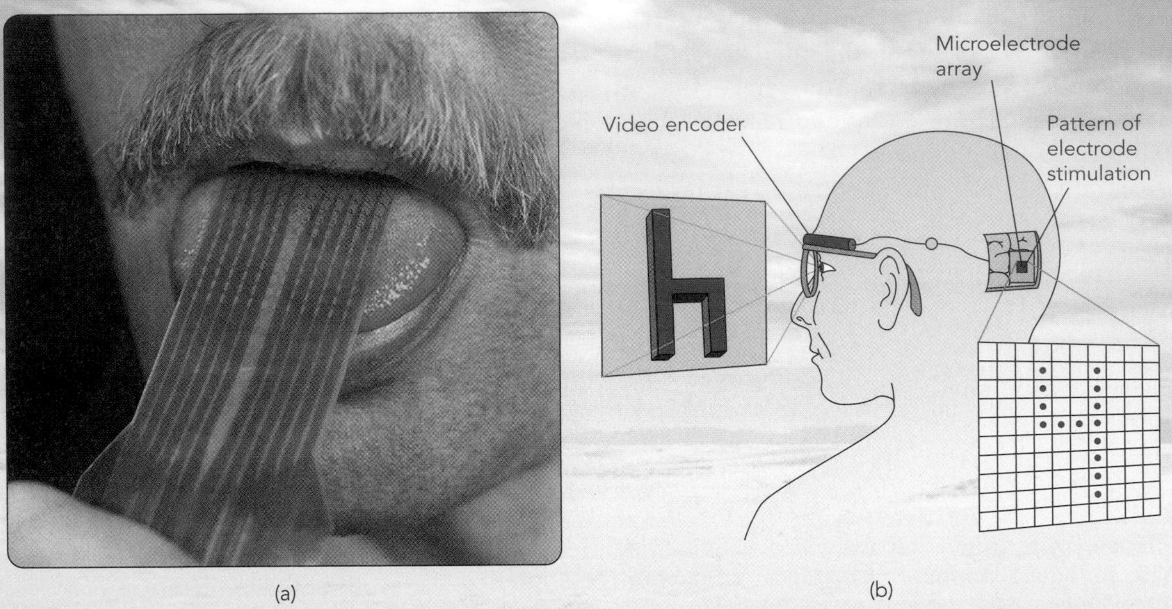

FIGURE 5.21

Two approaches to providing artificial vision for the blind. (a) Bach-y-Rita's device converts digitized stimuli from a camera to a matrix of electrical impulses to route spatial information through the tongue to the brain. (b) Tiny electrodes implanted into individual neurons in the visual cortex produce patterns of phosphenes that correspond to the visual scene observed through the video camera and encoder. Note how the cortical image is reversed as in normal visual input.

densely packed with tactile receptors, thus allowing the transmission of high-resolution data. Moreover, its moist surface is a good conducting medium for electricity, meaning that minimum voltage is required to stimulate the receptors.

The researchers have built an experimental prototype of a device that eventually will be small enough to be invisibly attached directly to the teeth. The current stimulator, shown in Figure 5.21a, receives digital data from a camera and provides patterns of stimulation to the tongue through a 144-electrode array. The array can transmit shapes that correspond to the main features of the visual stimulus. Initial trials with blindfolded sighted and blind people show that with about 9 hours of training, users can "read" the letters of a Snellen eye chart with an acuity of 20/430, a modest but noteworthy beginning (Simpaio et al., 2001). Kupers & Ptito (2004) have further demonstrated that congenitally blind subjects who were trained for a week with the tongue sensor were able to perform a visual discrimination task. In addition, PET scans revealed increased activity in the visual cortex when using the device. Apparently, cross-modal plasticity was still possible in the brains of these individuals who had been blind since birth. With continued development, a miniature camera in an eyeglass will transmit wireless data to a more densely packed electrode array attached to a dental retainer. Bach-y-Rita believes the device also might have both military and civilian applications. For example, it could help soldiers locate objects in pitch-black environments, such as caves, where night-vision devices are useless; it could also aid firefighters as they search smoke-filled buildings for people to rescue.

A different approach to a visual prosthesis is being perfected at the University of Utah, where researchers have developed a device to stimulate the visual cortex directly (Normann, 1995). When cells in the visual cortex are stimulated electrically, discrete flashes of light called *phosphenes* are experienced by both sighted and blind people. Because sensory neurons in the visual cortex are arranged in a manner that corresponds to the organization of the retina, a specific pattern of stimulation applied to individual neurons in the cortex can form a phosphene pattern that conforms to the shapes of letters or objects. The detail or acuity of the pattern depends on the area of the visual cortex that is stimulated (the portion receiving input from the densely packed fovea produces greatest acuity) and on the number of stimulating electrodes in the array.

Building on this approach, researchers have developed the device shown in Figure 5.21b. The Utah Intracortical Electrode Array consists of a silicon strip containing thousands of tiny stimulating electrodes that penetrate directly into individual neurons in the visual cortex, where they can stimulate phosphene patterns. Eventually, a tiny television camera mounted in specially designed eyeglasses will provide visual information to a microcomputer that will analyze the scene and then send the appropriate patterns of electrical stimulation through the implanted electrodes to produce corresponding phosphene patterns in the visual cortex. The researchers already have shown that sighted participants who wore darkened goggles that produce phosphenelike patterns of light flashes can learn quickly to navigate through complex environments and are able to read text at about two-thirds their normal rate (Normann et al., 1996, 1998). Blind people who had the stimulating electrodes implanted in their visual cortex have also been able to learn a kind of "cortical Braille" for reading purposes. Although still experimental, a commercially available intracortical prosthetic device should be available in the near future (Normann et al., 1998).

The hearing impaired also have been assisted by the development of prosthetic devices. Many have been helped by the *cochlear implant,* a device that can restore hearing in people suffering from nerve deafness. The cochlear implant does not amplify sound like a conventional hearing aid, since people with nerve deafness cannot be helped by mere sound amplification. Instead, the device sorts out useful sounds and converts them into electrical impulses, bypassing the disabled hair cells in the cochlea and stimulating the auditory nerve directly. With a cochlear implant, patients can hear everyday sounds such as sirens, and many of them can understand speech (Meyer et al., 1998; Parkinson et al., 1998). Nonetheless, sounds tend to be muffled, and people who expect currently developed cochlear implants to restore normal hearing invariably are disappointed. Improved speech perception is negatively correlated with age at implementation (e.g., Wu & Yang, 2003); thus, it is important to treat congenitally deaf children as early as possible.

Sensory prosthetics illustrate the ways in which knowledge about sensory phenomena such as phosphenes, the organization of the visual cortex, auditory localization, and the place theory of frequency coding can provide the information needed to take advantage of new technological advances. Yet, even with all our present ingenuity, prosthetic devices are not substitutes for our normal sensory systems, a fact that should increase our appreciation for what nature has given us.

Taste and Smell: The Chemical Senses

25. Describe the stimuli and the receptors involved in gustation and olfaction. Why do researchers sometimes refer to a "common chemical sense"?

Gustation (taste) and **olfaction** (smell) are chemical senses because their receptors are sensitive to chemical molecules rather than to some form of energy. These senses are so intertwined that some scientists refer to a "common chemical sense" (Beauchamp & Bartoshuk, 1997). Enjoying a good meal usually depends on the simultaneous activity of taste and odour receptors, as becomes apparent when we have a stuffy nose and our food tastes bland. People who lose their sense of smell typically believe they have lost their sense of taste as well (Bartoshuk, 1993).

Gustation: The Sense of Taste

People who fancy themselves gourmets are frequently surprised to learn that their sense of taste responds to only four qualities: sweet, sour, salty, and bitter. Every other taste experience combines these qualities and those of other senses, such as smell, temperature, and touch. For example, part of the "taste" of popcorn includes its texture, its crunchiness, and its odour.

Taste buds are chemical receptors concentrated along the edges and back surface of the tongue. Humans have about 9,000 taste buds, each consisting of several receptor cells arranged like the segments of an orange (Figure 5.22). A small number of receptors also are found in the roof and back of the mouth, so that even people without a tongue can taste substances. Hairlike structures project from the top of each cell into the taste pore, an opening to the outside surface of the tongue. When a substance is taken into the mouth, it interacts with saliva to form a chemical solution that flows into the taste pore and stimulates the receptor cells. A "taste" results from complex patterns of neural activity produced by the four types of taste receptors (Bartoshuk, 1998; Halpern, 2002).

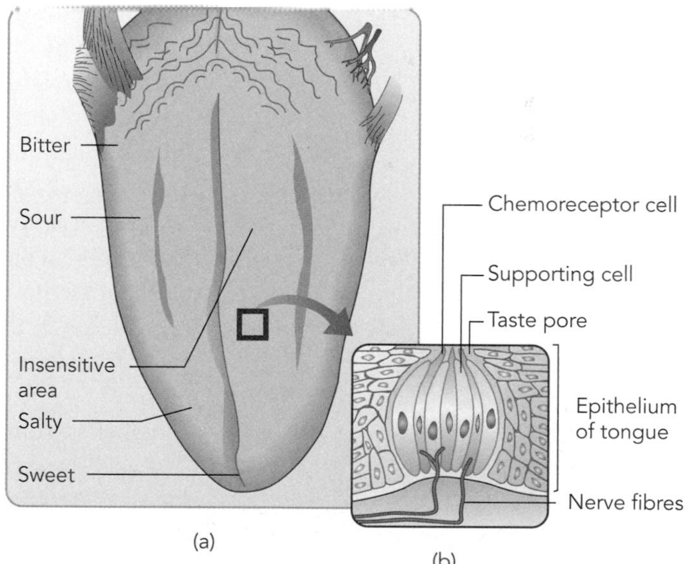

FIGURE 5.22

The receptors for taste are specialized cells located in the tongue's taste buds. The tongue's 9,000 taste buds are grouped in different areas according to the taste sensation they produce. The centre of the tongue is relatively insensitive to the chemical molecules that constitute gustatory stimuli.

The sense of taste not only provides us with pleasure, but also has adaptive significance in discriminating between nutrients and toxins (Scott, 1992). Our response to some taste qualities is innate. For example, newborn infants respond positively to sugar water placed on the tongue and negatively to bitter substances such as quinine (Davidson & Fox, 1988). Many poisonous substances in nature have bitter tastes, so this emotional response seems to be "hardwired" into our physiology (Hoebel, 1997). In nature, sweet substances are more likely to occur in nutritious foods. Unfortunately, many humans now live in an environment different from the food-scarce environment in which preferences for sweet substances may have evolved (Scott & Giza, 1993). As a result, people in affluent countries overconsume sweet foods that are good for us only in small quantities.

Olfaction: The Sense of Smell

Humans are visually oriented creatures, but the sense of smell (olfaction) is of great importance for many species. Bloodhounds, for example, have poor eyesight, but an exquisitely developed olfactory sense that is about two million times more sensitive than ours (Thomas, 1974). A bloodhound can detect a person's scent in a footprint that is four days old, something no human could do. Yet people who are deprived of other senses often develop a highly sensitive olfactory sense. Helen Keller, though blind and deaf, exhibited a remarkable ability to "smell" her environment. With uncanny accuracy, she could tell when a storm was brewing by detecting subtle odour changes in the air. She could also identify people (even those who bathed regularly and did not wear perfumes or colognes) by their distinctive odours (Keller, 1955).

The receptors for smell are long cells that project through the lining of the upper part of the nasal cavity and into the mucous membrane. Humans have about 40 million olfactory receptors, dogs about 1 billion. Unfortunately, our ability to discriminate between different odours is not well understood. The most popular current theory is that olfactory receptors recognize diverse odours individually rather than by mixing the activity of a smaller number of basic receptors, as occurs in taste (Bartoshuk & Beauchamp, 1994). Olfactory receptors have receptor structures that resemble neurotransmitter binding sites on neurons. Any of the thousands of potential odour molecules can lock into sites that are tailored to fit them (Buck & Axel, 1991; Pernollet, Sanz, & Briand, 2006).

The social and sexual behaviour of animals is more strongly regulated by olfaction than is human behaviour (Alcock, 2006). For example, most of us find other ways to mark our territories, such as by erecting fences or spreading belongings over the table we are using in the library. Whether humans have special olfactory systems involved in the regulation of sexual and reproductive behaviour is a matter of some debate, but most researchers believe that there is no overwhelming evidence to support this. Nonetheless, some researchers believe that **pheromones**, chemical signals found in natural body scents, may affect human behaviour in subtle ways (Bartoshuk & Beauchamp, 1994; Monti-Bloch & Grosser, 1991; Rako & Friebely, 2004). One interesting but puzzling observation, known as **menstrual synchrony**, is the tendency of women who live together or are close friends to become more similar in their menstrual cycles. Psychologist Martha McClintock (1971) tested 135 university women and found that, during the course of an academic year, roommates moved from a mean of 8.5 days apart in their periods to 4.9 days apart. Another study of 51 women who worked together showed that close friends had menstrual onsets averaging 3.5 to 4.3 days apart, whereas those who were not close friends had onsets that averaged 8 to 9 days apart (Weller et al., 1999). Are pheromones responsible for synchrony? In experiments conducted at the Monell Chemical Senses Center in Philadelphia, 10 women with

26. What is menstrual synchrony, and what evidence is there that pheromones are involved?

regular cycles were daubed under the nose every few days with underarm secretions collected from other women. After three months, the participants' cycles began to coincide with the sweat donors' cycles. A control group of women who were daubed with an alcohol solution rather than sweat showed no menstrual synchrony with a partner (Preti et al., 1986). In other studies, however, menstrual synchrony was not found for cohabitating lesbian couples or for Bedouin women who spent most of their time together, indicating that prolonged and very intensive contact may not be conducive to menstrual synchrony (Weller & Weller, 1997, 1998).

As anyone who has owned a dog or cat in heat could attest, odours strongly affect the sexual attractiveness of animals. On the other hand, there is no solid evidence to justify the recent rise in commercial sales of "pheromone substances" to humans who wish to become sexually irresistible. At this point, we would conclude that a good personality is a better bet than a good pheromone.

The Skin and Body Senses

The skin and body senses include the senses of touch, kinesthesis (muscle movement), and equilibrium. The last two are called body senses because they inform us of the body's position and movement. They tell us, for example, if we are running or standing still, lying down, or sitting up.

The Tactile Senses

Touch is important to us in many ways. Sensitivity to extreme temperatures and pain enables us to avoid external danger and alerts us to disorders within our bodies. Tactile sensations are also a source of many of life's pleasures, including sexual orgasm. A lack of tactile contact with a caretaking adult retards physical, social, and emotional development (Harlow, 1958), and physically massaging newborn babies enhances their development (Cigales et al., 1997; Field et al., 1996; Canfield, 2006).

27. What four tactile sensations are humans sensitive to? How are these sensations localized, and how are phantom limb sensations produced?

Humans are sensitive to at least four tactile sensations: pressure (touch), pain, warmth, and cold. These sensations are conveyed by receptors in the skin and in our internal organs. Mixtures of these four sensations form the basis for all other common skin sensations, such as itch.

Considering the importance of our skin senses, surprisingly little is known about how they work. The skin, a multi-layered elastic structure that covers 90 cm^2 and weighs between 2.7 and 4.5 kilograms, is the largest organ in our body. It contains a variety of receptor structures, but their role in specific sensations is less clear than for the other senses. Many sensations probably depend upon specific patterns of activity in the various receptors (Goldstein, 2002). We do know that primary receptors for pain and temperature are *free nerve endings,* simple nerve cells beneath the skin's surface that resemble the bare branches of a tree in winter (Gracely et al., 2002). Nerve fibres situated at the base of hair follicles are receptors for touch and light pressure (Heller & Schiff, 1991).

The brain can locate sensations because skin receptors send their messages to the point in the somatosensory cortex that corresponds to the area of the body where the receptor is located. The amount of cortex devoted to each area of the body is related to that part's sensitivity. Our fingers, lips, and tongue are well represented, accounting for their extreme sensitivity to stimulation.

Sometimes the brain "locates" sensations that cannot possibly be present. This occurs in the puzzling *phantom limb* phenomenon, in which amputees experience vivid sensations coming from the missing limb (Warga, 1987). Apparently, an irritation of the nerves that used to originate in the limb fools the brain into interpret-

FIGURE 5.23

Kinesthesis and the vestibular sense are especially well developed in some people, and essential for performing feats like this one.

ing the resulting nerve impulses as real sensations. Joel Katz and Ronald Melzack (1990) studied 68 amputees who insisted that they experienced pain from the amputated limb that was as vivid and "real" as any pain they had ever experienced. This pain was not merely a recollection of what pain used to feel like in the phantom limb; it was actually experienced in the present. The phantom limb phenomenon can be quite maddening: Imagine having an intense itch that you never can scratch, or an ache you cannot rub. When amputees are fitted with prosthetic limbs and begin using them, phantom pain tends to disappear (Gracely et al., 2002).

The Body Senses

We would be totally unable to coordinate our body movements were it not for the sense of **kinesthesis**, which provides us with feedback about our muscles' and joints' positions and movements. The receptors are nerve endings in the muscles, tendons, and joints. The information this sense gives us is the basis for making coordinated movements. Cooperating with kinesthesis is the **vestibular sense**, the sense of body orientation or equilibrium (Figure 5.23). The vestibular receptors are located in the *vestibular apparatus* of the inner ear (see Figure 5.18). One part of the equilibrium system consists of three *semicircular canals*, which contain the receptors for head movement. Each canal lies in a different plane: left/right, backward/forward, or up/down. These canals are filled with fluid and lined with hairlike cells that function as receptors. When the head moves, the fluid in the appropriate canal shifts, stimulating the hair cells and sending messages to the brain. The semicircular canals respond only to acceleration and deceleration; when a constant speed is reached (no matter how high), the fluid and the hair cells return to their normal resting state. That's why takeoffs and landings give a sense of movement, whereas flying at 800 km/h on a cruising airliner does not. Located at the base of the semicircular canals, the *vestibular sacs* also contain hair cells that respond to the position of the body and tell us whether we are upright or tilted at an angle. These structures constitute the second part of the body-sense system.

In Review

- *Sound waves, the stimuli for audition, have two characteristics: frequency, measured in terms of cycles per second or hertz (Hz), and amplitude, measured in terms of decibels (db). Frequency is related to pitch, amplitude to loudness. The receptors for hearing are hair cells in the organ of Corti of the inner ear.*
- *Loudness is coded in terms of the number and types of auditory nerve fibres that fire. Pitch is coded in two ways. Low-frequency tones are coded in terms of corresponding numbers of nerve impulses in individual receptors or by volleys of impulses from a number of receptors. Frequencies above 4,000 Hz are coded according to the region of the basilar membrane that is displaced most by the fluid wave in the cochlear canal.*
- *Hearing loss may result from conduction deafness, produced by problems involving the structures of the inner ear that transmit vibrations to the cochlea, or from nerve deafness, in which the receptors of the inner ear or the auditory nerve are damaged.*
- *Principles derived from the study of sensory processes have been applied in developing sensory prosthetics for the blind and the hearing impaired. Examples include the Sonicguide, a device that provides visual information through tactile stimulation of the tongue, direct electrical stimulation of the visual cortex, and cochlear inplants.*
- *The receptors for taste and smell respond to chemical molecules. Taste buds are responsive to four basic qualities: sweet, sour, salty, and bitter. The receptors for smell (olfaction) are long cells in the upper nasal cavity. Natural body odours produced by pheromones appear to account for a menstrual synchrony that sometimes occurs among women who are in frequent contact.*
- *The skin and body senses include touch, kinesthesis, and equilibrium. Receptors in the skin and body tissues are sensitive to touch, pain, warmth, and cold. Kinesthesis functions by means of nerve endings in the muscles, tendons, and joints. The sense organs for equilibrium are in the vestibular apparatus of the inner ear.*

PERCEPTION: THE CREATION OF EXPERIENCE

Sensory systems provide the raw materials from which experiences are formed. Our sense organs do not select what we will be aware of or how we will experience it; they merely transmit as much information as they can through our nervous system. Yet our experiences are not simply a one-to-one reflection of what is "out there." Different people may experience the same sensory information in radically different ways, because perception is an active, creative process in which raw sensory data are organized and given meaning.

To create our perceptions, the brain carries out two different kinds of processing functions (Figure 5.24). In **bottom-up processing**, the system takes in individual elements of the stimulus and then combines them into a unified perception. Your visual system operates in a bottom-up fashion as you read; its feature detectors analyze the elements in each letter of every word, then recombine them into your visual perception of the letters and words. In **top-down processing**, sensory information is interpreted in the light of existing knowledge, concepts, ideas, and expectations. Top-down processing is occurring as you interpret the words and sentences constructed by the bottom-up process. Here you make use of "higher-order" knowledge, including what you have learned about the meaning of words and sentence construction. Indeed, a given sentence may even convey a different personal meaning to you than to another person if you relate its content to some unique personal experience. Top-down processing accounts for many psychological influences on perception, such as the roles played by our motives, expectations, previous experiences, and cultural learning.

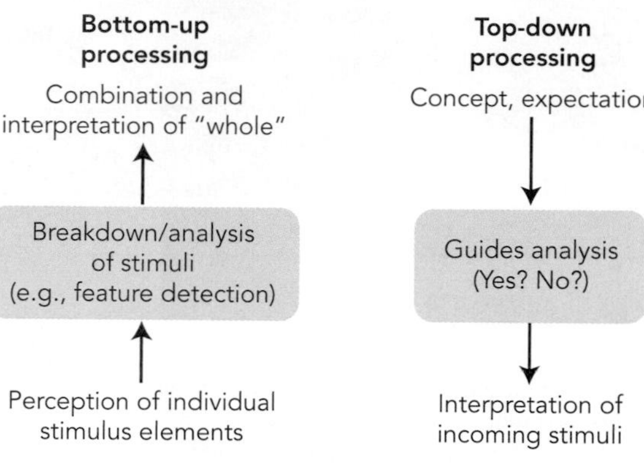

FIGURE 5.24
Bottom-up perceptual processing builds from an analysis of individual stimulus features to a unified perception. Top-down processing begins with a perceptual whole, such as an expectation or an image of an object, and then determines the degree of "fit" with the stimulus features.

Perception Is Selective: The Role of Attention

As you read these words, 100 million sensory messages may be clamouring for your attention. Only a few of these messages register in awareness; the rest you perceive either dimly or not at all. But you can shift your attention to one of those "unregistered" stimuli at any time. (For example, how does the big toe of your right foot feel right now?) Attention, then, involves two processes of selection: (1) focusing on certain stimuli, and (2) filtering out other incoming information (Luck & Vecera, 2002).

These processes have been studied experimentally through a technique called **shadowing**. Participants wear earphones and listen simultaneously to two messages, one sent through each earphone. They are asked to repeat (or "shadow") one of the messages word for word as they listen. Most participants can do this quite successfully, but only at the cost of not remembering what the other message was about. Shadowing experiments demonstrate that we *cannot* attend completely to more than one thing at a time. But we can shift our attention rapidly back and forth between the two messages, drawing on our general knowledge to fill in the gaps (Bonnel & Hafter, 1998; Sperling, 1984).

28. Differentiate between bottom-up and top-down processing of sensory information.

29. What two complementary processes occur in attention?

30. Describe the results of shadowing experiments in relation to attentional capabilities.

Environmental and Personal Factors in Attention

Attention is strongly affected by both the nature of the stimulus and by personal factors. Stimulus characteristics that attract our attention include intensity, novelty, movement, contrast, and repetition. Advertisers use these properties in their commercials and packaging (Figure 5.25).

31. What stimulus and personal characteristics influence attention?

Internal factors, such as our motives and interests, act as powerful filters and influence which stimuli in our environment we will notice. For example, when

FIGURE 5.25

Advertisers are adept at using attention-attracting stimulus characteristics in their advertisements. Personal characteristics are also important. What kinds of individuals do you suppose would be most attentive to this ad?

we are hungry, we are especially sensitive to food-related cues. A botanist walking through a park is especially attentive to the plants; a landscape architect attends primarily to the layout of the park.

People are especially attentive to stimuli that might represent a threat to their well-being, a tendency that clearly would have biological survival value (Bargh, 1984; Izard, 1989). Christine and Ranald Hansen (1988) presented slides showing groups of nine people. In half of the pictures, all of the people looked either angry or happy. In the other half, there was one discrepant face, either an angry face in a happy crowd or a happy face in an angry crowd. Participants were asked to judge as quickly as possible whether there was a discrepant face in the crowd, then press "yes" or "no" buttons attached to electrical timers. The dependent variable was the length of time required to make this judgment, measured in milliseconds (thousandths of a second). The results, summarized in Figure 5.26, showed that participants were much faster at detecting a single angry face in an otherwise happy crowd than at finding a happy face in an angry crowd. It was as if the angry face, which the experimenters assumed to have threat value, "jumped out" of the crowd when the stimuli were scanned. Swedish psychologist Ulf Dimberg (1997) believes that humans are biologically programmed to detect threatening faces, and he has shown via high-speed photography that emotional facial responses to such stimuli occur in observers within one-third of a second. Attentional processes are thus based both on innate biological factors and on past experiences that make certain stimuli important or meaningful to us.

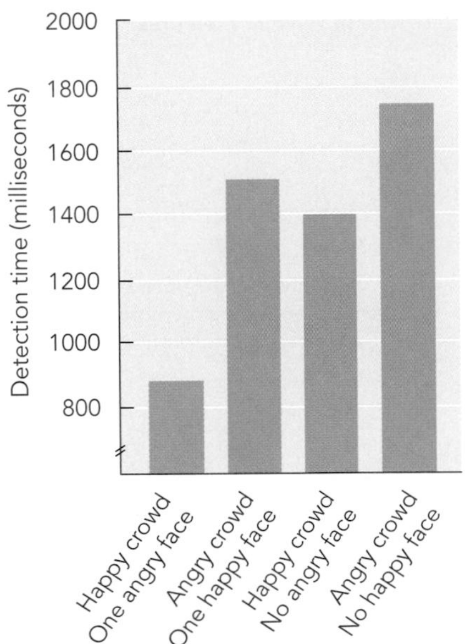

FIGURE 5.26

Perceptual vigilance to threatening stimuli is shown in the finding that people required less time to detect an angry face in a happy crowd than to detect a happy face in an angry crowd or to determine if there was any discrepant face in a happy or an angry crowd.

Data from Hansen & Hansen, 1988.

Perceptions Have Organization and Structure

Have you ever stopped to wonder why we perceive the visual world as being composed of distinct objects? After all, the information sent by the retina reflects nothing but an array of varying intensities and frequencies of light energy. The light rays reflected from different parts of a single object have no more natural "belongingness" to one another than those coming from two different objects. Yet we perceive scenes as involving separate objects, such as trees, buildings, and people. These perceptions must be a product of an organization imposed by our nervous system. This top-down process of perceptual organization occurs so automatically that we take it for granted. But Dr. Richard, a prominent psychologist who suffered brain damage in an accident, no longer does.

> There was nothing wrong with his eyes, yet the input he received from them was not put together correctly. Dr. Richard reported that if he saw a person, he sometimes would perceive the separate parts of the person as not belonging together in a single body. But if all the parts moved in the same direction, Dr. Richard then saw them as one complete person. At other times, he would perceive people in crowds wearing the same colour clothes as "going together" rather than as separate people. He also had difficulty putting sights and sounds together. Sometimes, the movement of the lips did not correspond to the sounds he heard, as if he were watching a badly dubbed foreign movie. Dr. Richard's experience of his environment was thus disjointed and fragmented. . . . (Sacks, 1986, p. 76)

Synaesthesia, in which stimuli in one sensory modality give rise to perceptions in other modalities, is an even more radical departure from ordinary perceptual experience. What, then, are the processes by which sensory nonsense becomes perceptual sense?

Gestalt Principles of Perceptual Organization

Early in the twentieth century, psychologists from the German school of Gestalt psychology set out to discover how we organize the separate parts of our perceptual field into a unified and meaningful whole. *Gestalt* is the German term for "pattern," "shape," or "form." Gestalt theorists were early champions of top-down processing, arguing that the wholes we perceive are often more than (and frequently different from) the sum of their parts.

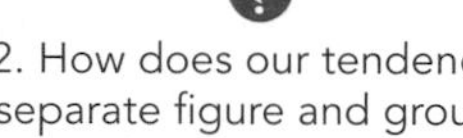

32. How does our tendency to separate figure and ground contribute to perception?

The Gestalt theorists emphasized the importance of **figure-ground relations**. We tend to organize stimuli into a central or foreground figure and a background. In vision, the central figure is usually in front of or on top of what we perceive as background. It has a distinct shape and is more striking in our perceptions and memory than the background. We perceive borders or contours wherever there is a distinct change in the colour or brightness of a visual scene, but we interpret these contours as part of the figure rather than background. Likewise, instrumental music is heard as a melody (figure) surrounded by other chords or harmonies (ground).

Separating figure from ground can be a challenging task (Figure 5.27), yet our perceptual systems usually are equal to the task. At times, however, what's figure and what's ground is not completely obvious, and the same stimulus may give rise to two different perceptions. Consider Figure 5.28, for example. If you examine it for a while, two alternating but equally plausible perceptions will emerge, one based on the inner portion and the other formed by the two outer portions. When the alternative perception (figure) occurs, what was previously the figure becomes the background.

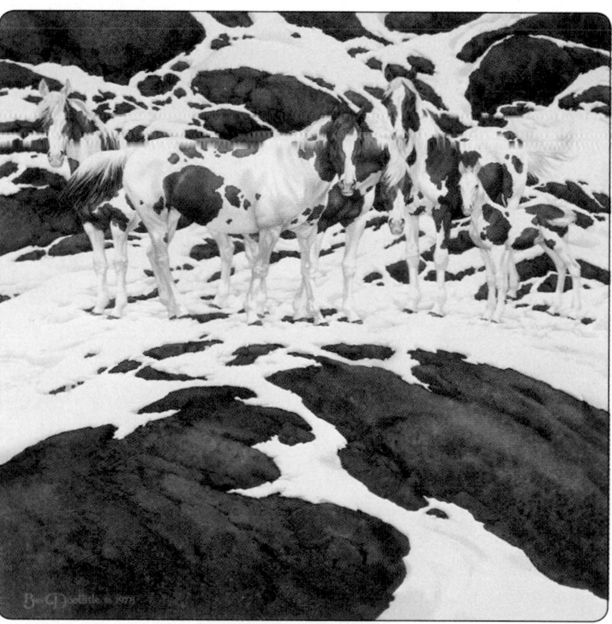

FIGURE 5.27

Figure-ground relations are important in perceptual organization. Here the artist Bev Doolittle has created great similarity between figure and ground in this representation of natural camouflage, yet enough figural cues remain to permit most people to detect the ponies.

Source: Pintos, Bev Doolittle, 1979. The Greenwich Workshop, Trumbull, Conn.

In addition to figure-ground relations, the Gestalt psychologists were interested in how separate stimuli come to be perceived as parts of larger wholes. They suggested that people group and interpret stimuli in accordance with four **Gestalt laws of perceptual organization**: similarity, proximity, closure, and continuity. These organizing principles are illustrated in Figure 5.29.

What was your perception of Figure 5.29a? Did you perceive 15 unrelated dots, or did you view the stimulus as two triangles formed by different-sized dots? If you saw triangles, your perception obeyed the Gestalt *law of similarity,* which says that when parts of a configuration are perceived as similar, they will be perceived as belonging together. The *law of proximity* says that elements that are near one another are likely to be perceived as part of the same configuration. Thus most people perceive Figure 5.29b as three sets of lines rather than as six separate lines. Illustrated in Figure 5.29c is the *law of closure,* which states that people tend to close the open edges of a figure or fill in gaps in an incomplete figure, so that their identification of the form (in this case, a circle) is more complete than what is actually there. Finally, the *law of continuity* holds that people link individual elements together so that they form a continuous line or pattern that makes sense. Thus Figure 5.29d is far more likely to be seen as combining components

FIGURE 5.28

This reversible figure illustrates alternating figure-ground relations. It can be seen as a vase or as two people facing each another. Whichever percept exists at the moment is seen as figure against background.

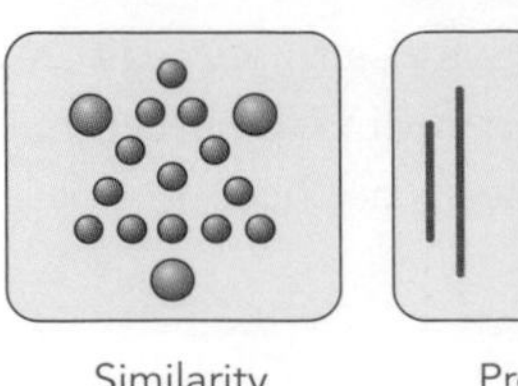

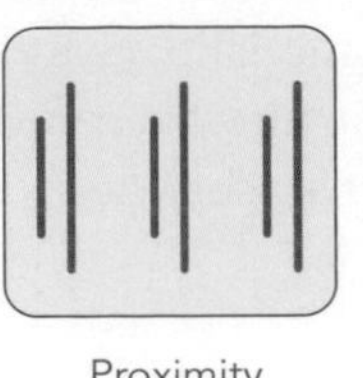

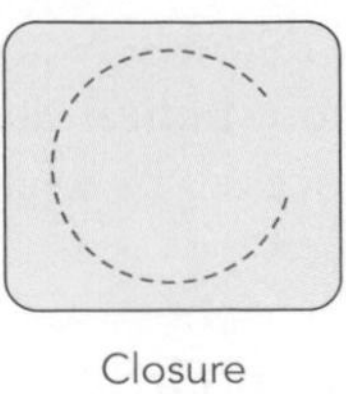

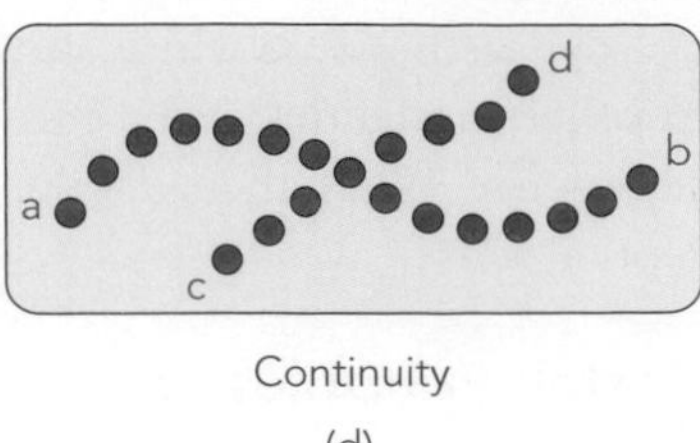

FIGURE 5.29

Among the Gestalt principles for perceptual organization are the laws of similarity (a), proximity (b), closure (c), and continuity (d). Each principle causes us to organize stimuli into "wholes" that are greater than the sum of their parts.

(ab and cd) than (ad and cb), which have poor continuity. Or consider Fraser's spiral, shown in Figure 5.30, which is not really a spiral at all! (To demonstrate, trace one of the circles with a pencil.) We perceive the concentric circles as a spiral because, to our nervous system, a spiral gives better continuity between individual elements than does a set of circles. The spiral is created by us, not by the stimulus.

33. Define and give examples of the four Gestalt laws of perceptual organization.

Perception Involves Hypothesis Testing

"Recognizing" a stimulus implies that we have a **perceptual schema**—a mental representation or image—to compare it with. Our schemas contain the critical features of objects, events, and other perceptual phenomena (Wade & Swanston, 2001). They allow us to classify and identify sensory input in a top-down fashion.

Imagine, for example, that a person approaches you and calls out your name. Who is this person? If the stimuli match your inner representation of your best friend's appearance and voice closely enough, you identify the person as your friend (McAdams & Drake, 2002). Many political cartoonists have an uncanny ability to capture the most noteworthy facial features of famous people, so that we can easily recognize the person represented by even the simplest line sketch.

Perception is, in this sense, an attempt to make sense of stimulus input, to search for the "best" interpretation of sensory information we can arrive at, based on our knowledge and experience. Likening the process to the scientific enterprise described in Chapter 2, Richard L. Gregory (1966) suggested that each of our perceptions is essentially a hypothesis about the nature of the object or, more generally, the meaning of the sensory information. The perceptual system actively searches its gigantic library of internal schemas for the interpretation that best fits the sensory data.

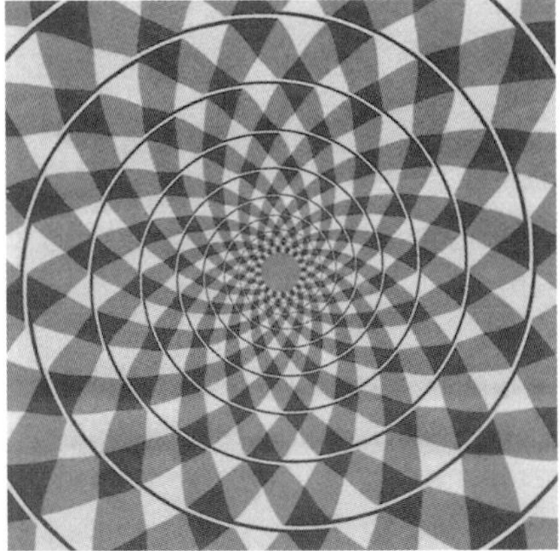

FIGURE 5.30

Fraser's spiral illustrates the Gestalt law of continuity. If you follow any part of the "spiral" with your finger, you will find that it is not really a spiral at all, but a series of concentric circles. The "spiral" is created by your nervous system because that perception is more consistent with continuity of the individual elements.

An example of how effortlessly our perceptual systems build up descriptions or hypotheses that best fit the available evidence is found in the comic strips created by Gustave Verbeek in the early 1900s. The Sunday *New York Herald* told Verbeek that his comic strip had to be restricted to six panels. Verbeek wanted 12 panels, so he ingeniously created 12-panel cartoons in only six panels by drawing pictures like that shown in Figure 5.31a. The reader viewed the first six panels, then turned the newspaper upside down. Try this yourself, and you will find that a bird story becomes a fish story! The point is that you do not simply see an upside-down bird, even though the physical stimuli remain exactly the same. You see a radically different picture because the new stimulus closely matches another of your perceptual schemas.

In some instances, sensory information fits two different internal representations, and there is not enough information to permanently rule out one of them in favour of the other. For example, examine the Necker cube, shown in Figure 5.31b.

If you stare at the cube for a while, you will find that it changes before your eyes as your nervous system "tries out" a new perceptual hypothesis.

34. In what sense is perception a kind of hypothesis testing? What is the role of perceptual schemas in this process?

Perception Is Influenced by Expectations: Perceptual Sets

On July 3, 1988, the warship USS Vincennes was engaged in a pitched battle with several speedy Iranian gunboats. Suddenly, the *Vincennes*'s advanced radar system detected an aircraft taking off from a military/civilian airfield in Iran and heading straight toward the American vessel. Radar operators identified the plane as an Iranian F-14 fighter, known to carry lethal air-to-surface missiles used earlier in a damaging attack on another U.S. warship. Repeated requests to the plane to identify itself yielded no response. The plane was now only 16 kilometres from the ship and, according to the crewmen watching on radar, descending toward the *Vincennes* on an attack course. A final warning evoked no response, and the *Vincennes*'s captain gave the command to fire on the plane. Two surface-to-air missiles streaked into the sky. Moments later, all that remained of the plane was a shower of flaming debris.

The jubilation and relief of the *Vincennes*'s crew was short-lived. Soon the awful truth was known: The plane they had shot down was not an attacking F-14 warplane. Instead, it was a commercial airliner carrying 290 passengers, all of whom died when the aircraft was destroyed. Moreover, videotape recordings of the electronic information that the crew had used to identify the plane and its flight pattern showed conclusively that the aircraft was not an F-14 and that it had actually been climbing rather than descending toward the ship.

How could such a tragic error have been made by a well-trained and experienced crew with access to the world's most sophisticated radar equipment? At a Congressional hearing on the incident, several prominent perception researchers reconstructed the psychological environment that could have caused the radar operators' eyes to "lie."

Clearly, the situation was stressful and dangerous. The *Vincennes* was already under attack by Iranian gunboats, and other attacks could be expected. It was easy for the radar operators, observing a plane taking off from a military field and heading toward the ship, to interpret this as the possible prelude to an air attack. The *Vincennes*'s crew was determined to avoid the fate of the other American warship, producing a high level of vigilance to any stimuli that suggested an impending attack. Fear and expectation thus created a psychological context within which the sensory input from the computer system was interpreted in a top-down fashion. The perception that the aircraft was a warplane and that it was descending toward the ship fit the crew's expectations and fears, and it became the "reality" that they experienced. They had a **perceptual set**—a readiness to perceive stimuli in a particular way. Sometimes believing is seeing.

Perceptual sets influence our social perceptions as well, as psychologist Harold Kelly (1950) demonstrated the day he invited a guest lecturer into his class. Half of the students in the class were given a set of introductory notes that described the guest as "industrious, critical, practical, determined and a rather *cold* person" (italics ours). The other half were given notes that described the visitor as "industrious, critical, practical, determined and a rather *warm* person." After the class, the students rated the guest lecturer and his presentation. Those who received the *cold* description interacted very little with him and later rated the guest lecturer as unhappy and irritable during the lecture. But those who got the *warm* description rated him as happy and good natured during the lecture, and they took part

(a)

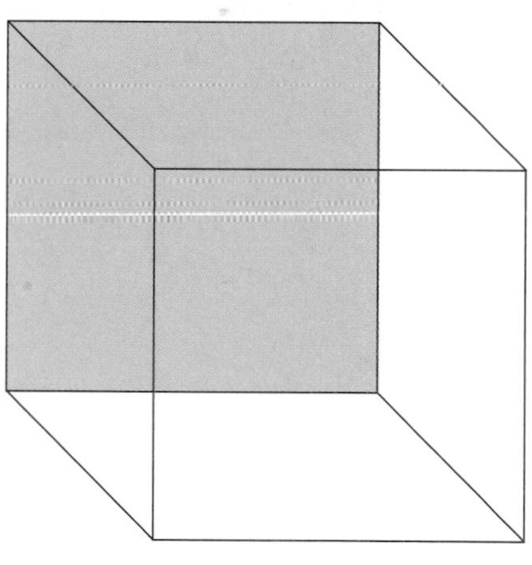

(b)

FIGURE 5.31

Two examples of how the same stimulus can give rise to different perceptions are found in the comic strips of Gustave Verbeek (a) and the Necker cube (b). To produce the reversals, turn the comic strip panel upside down and stare at the cube. The front of the cube will suddenly become the back, and it will appear that the cube is being viewed from a different angle.

35. What is a perceptual set? What factors can create such sets? How did the *Vincennes* incident illustrate this concept? How is it involved in perceiving people?

actively in the class discussion. They also rated his presentation more favourably. All of the students had seen and heard the *same lecturer*, or had they? It seems they perceived what they expected to, as did the football spectators in the classic study by Hastrof and Cantril discussed in Chapter 1.

Stimuli Are Recognizable under Changing Conditions: Perceptual Constancies

?
36. What are the nature and adaptive value of perceptual constancies?

When a door swings open, it casts a different image on our retina, but we still perceive it as a door. Our perceptual hypothesis remains the same. Were it not for **perceptual constancies** that allow us to recognize familiar stimuli under varying conditions, we would have literally to rediscover what something is each time it appeared under different conditions. Thus you can recognize a tune even if it is played in a different octave, as long as the relations among its notes are maintained. You can detect the flavour of a particular spice even when it occurs in foods having very different tastes.

In vision, several constancies are important. *Shape constancy* allows us to recognize people and other objects from many different angles, as in the case of the swinging door. Perhaps you have had the experience of sitting up front and off to one side of the screen in a crowded movie theatre. At first, the picture probably looked distorted, but after a while your visual system corrected for the distortion, and objects on the screen looked normal again.

Because of *brightness constancy*, the relative brightness of objects remains the same under different conditions of illumination, such as full sunlight and shade. Brightness constancy occurs because the ratio of light intensity between an object and its surroundings usually is constant. The actual brightness of the light that illuminates the objects does not matter, as long as the same light intensity illuminates both an object and its surroundings.

When we take off in an airplane, we know that the cars on the highway below are not shrinking and becoming the size of ants. *Size constancy* is the perception that the size of objects remains relatively constant even though images on our retina change in size with variations in distance. Thus a man who is judged to be 180 centimetres tall when standing two metres away is not perceived to be 90 centimetres tall at a distance of four metres, even though the size of his image on the retina is reduced to half its original size (Figure 5.32).

FIGURE 5.32
Size constancy based on distance cues causes us to perceive the person in the background as being of normal size. When the same stimulus is seen in the absence of the distance cues, size constancy breaks down.

In Review

- *Perception involves both bottom-up processing, in which individual stimulus fragments are combined into a perception, and top-down processing, in which existing knowledge and perceptual schemas are applied to interpret stimuli.*
- *Attention is an active process in which we focus on certain stimuli while blocking out other stimuli. We cannot attend completely to more than one thing at a time, but we are capable of rapid attentional shifts. Attentional processes are affected by the nature of the stimulus and by personal factors such as motives and interests. The perceptual system appears to be especially vigilant to stimuli that denote threat or danger.*
- *The Gestalt psychologists identified a number of principles of perceptual organization, including figure-ground relations and the laws of similarity, proximity, closure, and continuity. R. L. Gregory suggested that perception is essentially a hypothesis about what a stimulus is, based on previous experience and the nature of the stimulus.*
- *Perceptual sets involve a readiness to perceive stimuli in certain ways, based on our expectations, assumptions, motivations, and current emotional state.*
- *Perceptual constancies allow us to recognize familiar stimuli under changing conditions. In the visual realm, there are three constancies: shape, brightness, and size.*

PERCEPTION OF DEPTH, DISTANCE, AND MOVEMENT

The ability to adapt to a spatial world requires that we make fine distinctions involving distances and the movement of objects within the environment. Humans are capable of great precision in making such judgments. Consider, for example, the perceptual task faced by a batter in the sport of baseball (Figure 5.33). A fastball thrown by a pitcher at 90 mph from 18 metres will reach the batter who is trying to hit it in about 42/100 of a second. A curveball thrown at 80 mph will reach the hitting zone in 47/100 of a second, a difference of only 5/100 of a second (but a world of difference for timing and hitting the pitch). Within the first two metres of a ball's flight from the pitcher's hand (an interval of about 25/1,000 of a second), the batter must correctly judge the speed, type, and location of the pitch. If any of the judgments is in error, the hitter will be unable to hit a fair ball (Adair, 1990). The perceptual demands of such a task are imposing indeed (as are the salaries earned by those who can perform this task consistently). How does the visual perception system make such judgments?

FIGURE 5.33

The demands faced by a batter in judging the speed, distance, and movements of a pitched baseball within thousandths of a second underscore the capabilities of the visual perceptual system.

Depth and Distance Perception

One of the more intriguing aspects of visual perception is our ability to perceive depth. The retina receives information in only two dimensions (length and width), but the brain translates these cues into three-dimensional perceptions. It does this by using both **monocular cues** (which require only one eye) and **binocular cues** (which require both eyes).

Monocular Depth Cues

37. Identify eight monocular cues for distance and depth.

Judging the relative distances of objects is one important key to perceiving depth. Because artists paint their portraits on a flat canvas, they depend upon a variety of monocular cues to create perceptions of depth in their pictures. One such cue is patterns of *light and shadow*. The Dutch artist M. C. Escher skilfully used light and shadow to create the three-dimensional effect shown in Figure 5.34. The depth effect is as powerful if you close one eye as it is when you use both. Another, *linear perspective*, refers to the perception that parallel lines converge or angle toward one another as they recede into the distance. Thus, if you look down railroad tracks,

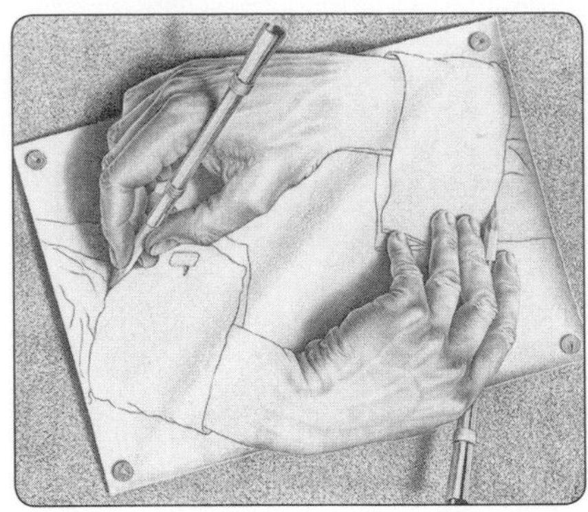

FIGURE 5.34

Patterns of light and shadow can serve as monocular depth cues, as shown in Drawing Hands by M. C. Escher.

they appear to angle toward one another with increased distance, and we use this as a depth cue. The same occurs with the edges of a highway or the sides of an elevator shaft. *Interposition,* in which objects closer to us may cut off part of our view of more distant objects, provides another cue for distance and depth.

An object's *height in the horizontal plane* provides another source of information. For example, a ship eight kilometres offshore appears in a higher plane and closer to the horizon than does one that is only one kilometre from shore. *Texture* is a fifth cue, because the texture or grain of an object appears finer as distance increases. Likewise, *clarity* can be an important cue for judging distance; we can see nearby hills more clearly than ones that are far away, especially on hazy days. *Relative size* is yet another basis for distance judgments. If we see two objects that we know to be of similar size, then the one that looks smaller will be judged to be farther away. A final monocular cue is *motion parallax,* which tells us that if we are moving, nearby objects appear to move faster in the opposite direction than do far-away ones. All of these cues provide us with information that we can use to make judgments about distance and, therefore, about depth.

The artist Raphael Sanzio was a master at using monocular depth and distance cues. *The School of Athens,* shown in Figure 5.35, illustrates seven of the monocular cues described above.

FIGURE 5.35

The School of Athens, *by Raphael Sanzio, illustrates seven monocular depth cues. (1) Linear perspective is produced by the converging lines of the corridor in the background. (2) The arches and the people in the background are smaller than those in front (relative size). (3) The back of the floor is in a higher horizontal plane than the foreground. (4, 5) The objects in the background are less detailed than the closer ones (texture and clarity). (6) Light and shadow are used to create depth. (7) The arches and people in the front of the painting cut off parts of the corridor behind them (interposition).*

Binocular Disparity

The most dramatic perceptions of depth arise with binocular depth cues, which require the use of both eyes. For an interesting binocular effect, hold your two index fingers about 15 centimetres in front of your eyes with their tips about two and a half centimetres apart. Focus on your fingers first, then focus beyond them across the room. The two different views will produce a "third" finger between the other two. This "finger sausage" will disappear if you close either eye.

Many of us are familiar with the delightful depth experiences provided by View Master slides and 3-D movies watched through special glasses. These devices make use of the principle of **binocular disparity**, in which each eye sees a slightly different image. Within the brain, the visual input from the two eyes is analyzed by feature detectors that are attuned to depth (Howard, 2002; Livingstone & Hubel, 1994). Some of the feature detectors respond only to stimuli that are either in front of or behind the point we are fixing our gaze upon. The responses of these depth-sensitive neurons are integrated to produce our perception of depth (Goldstein, 2002).

A second binocular distance cue, **convergence**, is produced by feedback from the muscles that turn your eyes inward to view a near object. You can experience this cue by holding a finger about 30 centimetres in front of your face, then moving it slowly toward you. Messages sent to your brain by the eye muscles provide it with a depth cue.

Perception of Movement

The perception of movement is a complex process that requires the brain to integrate information from several different senses. Try this demonstration: Hold your pen in front of your face. Now, while holding your head still, move the pen back and forth. You will perceive the pen moving. Now hold the pen still and move your head back and forth at the same rate of speed. In both cases, the image of the pen moved across your retina in about the same way. But when you moved your head, your brain took into account input from your kinesthetic and vestibular systems and "concluded" that you were moving but the pen was not.

38. Describe two binocular cues.

The primary cue for perceiving motion is the movement of the stimulus across the retina. Under optimal conditions, a retinal image need move only about one-fifth the diameter of a single cone for us to detect movement (Nakayama & Tyler, 1981). The relative movement of an object against a structured background is also a movement cue (Gibson, 1979). For example, if you fixate on a bird in flight, the relative motion of the bird against its background is a strong cue for perceiving speed of movement.

39. What is the primary cue for motion perception? How is stroboscopic movement used in motion pictures and television?

The illusion of smooth motion can be produced if we arrange for the sequential appearance of two or more stimuli. Gestalt psychologist Max Wertheimer (1912) demonstrated this in his studies of **stroboscopic movement**, illusory movement produced when a light is briefly flashed in darkness and then, a few milliseconds later, another light is flashed nearby. If the timing is just right, the first light seems to move from one place to the other in a manner indistinguishable from real movement.

Stroboscopic movement (termed the *phi phenomenon* by Wertheimer) has been used commercially in numerous ways. For example, we have all seen the strings of successively illuminated lights on theatre marquees that seem to move endlessly around the border or that spell out messages in a "moving" script. Stroboscopic movement is also the principle behind motion pictures, which consist of a series of still photographs, or frames, that are projected onto a screen in rapid succession with dark intervals in between (Figure 5.36). The rate at which the frames are projected is critical to our perception of smooth movement. Early movies, such as the "silent" films of the 1920s, projected the "stills" at only 16 frames per second, and the movements appeared fast and jerky. Today the usual speed is 24 frames per second, which more accurately produces an illusion of smooth movement.

FIGURE 5.36

Stroboscopic movement is produced in moving pictures as a series of still photographs projected at a rate of 24 per second.

ILLUSIONS: FALSE PERCEPTUAL HYPOTHESES

Our knowledge of perceptual schemas, hypotheses, sets, and constancies allows us to understand some interesting perceptual experiences known as illusions. **Illusions** are compelling but incorrect perceptions. They can be understood as erroneous perceptual hypotheses about the nature of the stimulus. Illusions are not only intriguing and sometimes delightful visual experiences, but they also provide important information about how our perceptual processes work under normal conditions.

40. In what sense is an illusion a false perceptual hypothesis? In what ways are constancies and context involved in producing visual illusions?

(a)

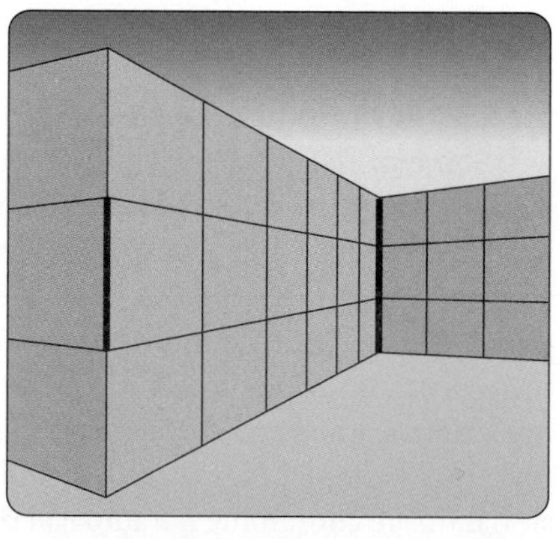

(b)

FIGURE 5.37

The Ponzo illusion. Which lines in (a) and (b) are longer? Measure them and see. The distance cues provided by the converging railroad tracks and walls affect size perception and disrupt size constancy.

(a)

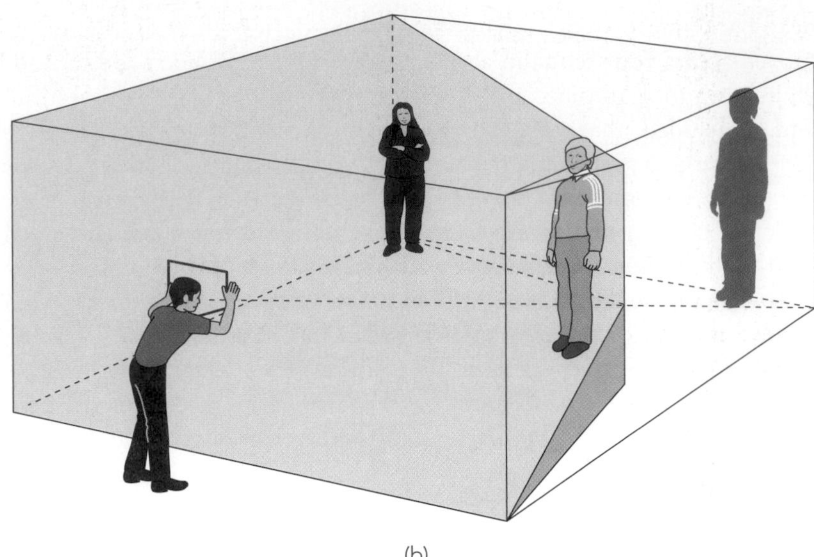

(b)

FIGURE 5.38

The Ames Room (a) produces a striking size perception because it is designed to appear rectangular. However, as (b) shows, the room is actually trapezoidal in shape, and the figure on the left is actually much farther away from the viewer than the one on the right, making it appear smaller.

Ironically, most visual illusions can be attributed to perceptual constancies that ordinarily help us to perceive more accurately (Frisby, 1980). For example, size constancy results in part from our ability to use distance cues to judge the size of objects. But distance cues sometimes may fool us. In the Ponzo illusion, shown in Figure 5.37, the depth cues of linear perspective (the tracks converging) and height in the horizontal plane provide distance cues that make the upper bar appear farther away than the lower bar. Because it seems farther away, the perceptual system concludes that the bar in the background must be larger than the bar in the foreground, despite the fact that the two bars cast retinal images of the same size. The same occurs in the vertical arrangement seen in Figure 5.37b.

Distance cues can be manipulated to create other size illusions. One occurs in a room constructed by Adelbert Ames. Viewed through a peephole with one eye, the scene presents a startling size reversal (Figure 5.38a). Our perceptual system assumes that the room has a normal rectangular shape because, in fact, most rooms do. Monocular depth cues do not allow us to see that, in reality, the left corner of the room is twice as far away as the right corner (Figure 5.38b). As a result, size constancy breaks down, and we base our judgment of size on the sizes of the retinal images cast by the two people.

The study of perceptual constancies shows that our perceptual hypotheses are strongly influenced by the *context*, or surroundings, in which a stimulus occurs. Figure 5.39 shows some examples of how context can produce illusory perceptions.

Some of the most intriguing perceptual distortions are produced when monocular depth cues are manipulated to produce a figure or scene whose individual parts make sense, but whose overall organization is "impossible" in terms of our existing perceptual schemas. Figure 5.40 shows three impossible figures. In each case, our brains extract information about depth from the individual features of the objects, but when this information is put together and matched with our existing schemas, the percept that results simply doesn't make sense. The "devil's tuning fork," for example (Figure 5.40c), could not exist in our universe. It is a two-dimensional image containing paradoxical depth cues. Your brain, however, automatically interprets it as a three-dimensional object and matches it with its internal schema

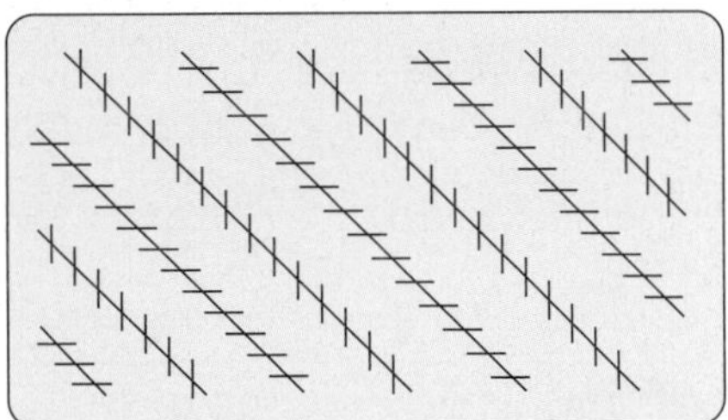

The long lines are actually parallel, but the small lines make them appear crooked.

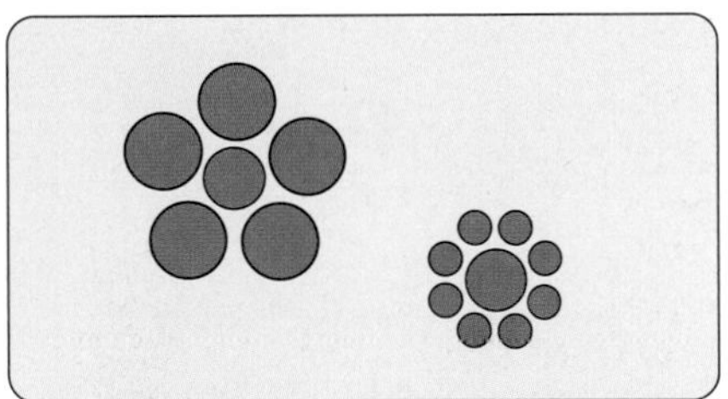

Which inner circle is larger? Check and see.

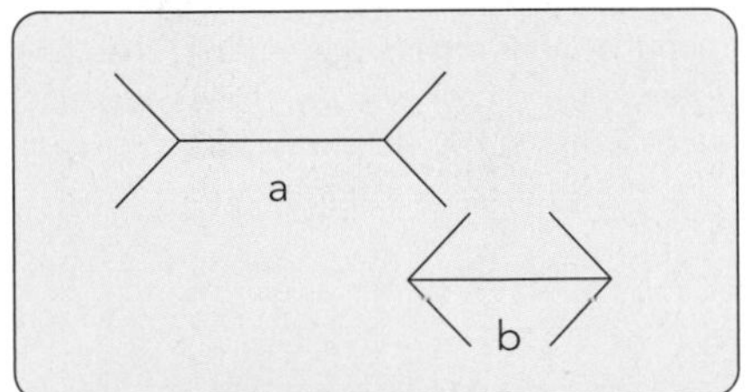

The Müller-Lyer illusion. Which line, a or b, is longer? Compare them with a ruler.

FIGURE 5.39

Context-produced geometric illusions.

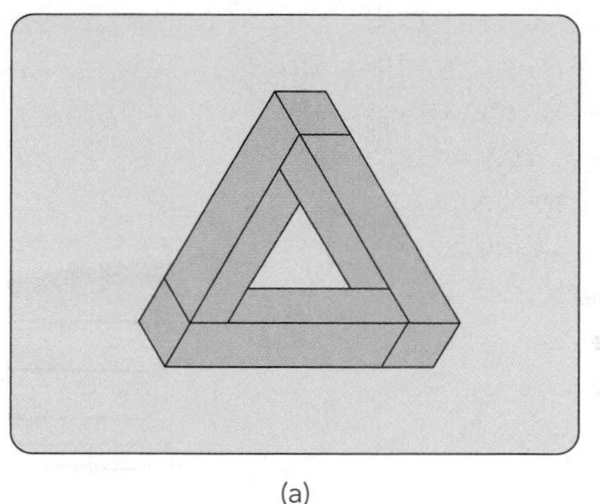
(a)

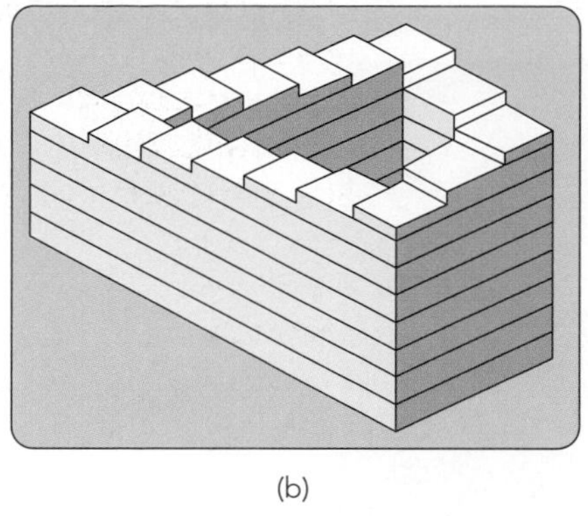
(b)

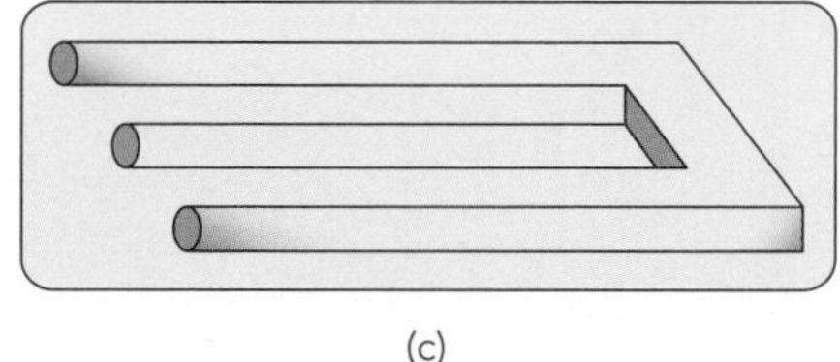
(c)

FIGURE 5.40
Monocular depth cues are cleverly manipulated to produce an impossible triangle, a never-ending staircase, and the "devil's tuning fork."

of a fork, a bad fit indeed. The never-ending staircase (Figure 5.40b) provides another compelling example of an impossible scene that seems perfectly reasonable when we focus only on its individual elements.

Illusions are not only personally and scientifically interesting, but they can have important real-life implications. Our *Psychological Applications* box describes one scientist's search for an illusion having life-and-death implications.

PSYCHOLOGICAL APPLICATIONS

Stalking a Deadly Illusion

Background

When the Boeing Company introduced the 727 jet airliner in the mid-1960s, it was the latest word in aviation technology. The plane performed well in test flights, but four fatal crashes soon after it was placed in service raised fears that there might be some fatal flaw in its design.

The first accident occurred as a 727 made its approach to Chicago over Lake Michigan on a clear night. The plane plunged into the lake 30 kilometres offshore. About a month later, another 727 glided in over the Ohio River to land in Cincinnati. Unaccountably, it struck the ground about two and a quarter metres below the runway elevation and burst into flames. The third accident occurred as an aircraft approached Salt Lake City over dark land. The lights of the city twinkled in the distance, but the plane made too rapid a descent and crashed short of the runway. Months later, a Japanese airliner approached Tokyo at night. The flight ended tragically as the plane, its landing gear not yet lowered, struck the waters of Tokyo Bay 10 kilometres from the runway.

Analysis of these four accidents, as well as others, suggested a common pattern. All occurred at night under clear weather conditions, so that the pilots were operating under visual flight rules rather than performing instrument landings. In each instance, the plane was approaching city lights over dark areas of water or land. In all cases, the lights in the background sloped upward to varying degrees. Finally, all of the planes crashed short of the runway. These observations led a Boeing psychologist, Conrad L. Kraft, to suspect that the cause of the crashes might be pilot error based on some sort of visual illusion.

Method

To test this possibility, Boeing engineers constructed an apparatus to simulate night landings (Figure 5.41). It consisted of a cockpit and a miniature lighted "city" named Nightertown. The city moved toward the cockpit on computer-controlled rollers, and it could be tilted to simulate various terrain slopes. The pilot could control simulated air speed and the rate of climb and descent, and the Nightertown scene was controlled by the pilot's responses just as a true visual scene would be.

The participants were 12 experienced Boeing flight instructors who made virtual reality "landings" at Nightertown under systematically varied conditions created by the computerized simulator. All of their landings were visual landings in order to test whether a visual illusion was occurring. Every

–Continued

FIGURE 5.41

Conrad Kraft, a Boeing psychologist, created an apparatus to study how visual cues can affect the simulated landings of airline pilots. Pilots approached Nightertown in a simulated cockpit. The computer-controlled city could be tilted to reproduce the illusion thought to be responsible for fatal air crashes.

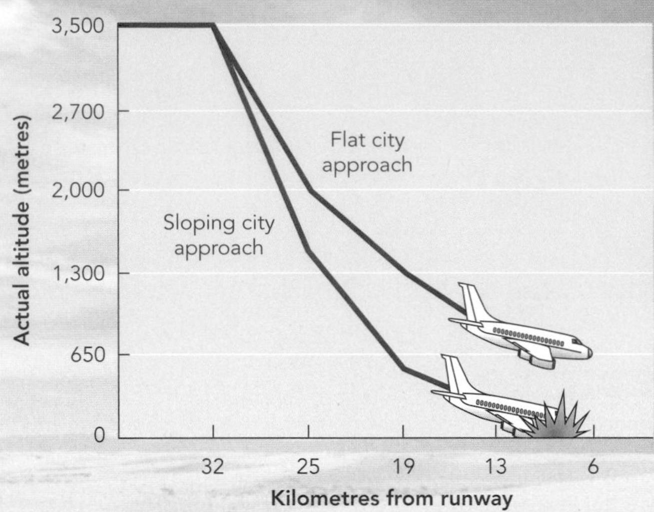

FIGURE 5.42

The illusion caused by upward-sloping city lights caused even highly experienced pilots to overestimate their altitude, and 11 of the 12 flight instructors "crashed" short of the runway. When the lights were flat, all the pilots made perfect approaches.

Data from Kraft, 1978.

aspect of their approach and the manner in which they controlled the aircraft was measured precisely.

Results

The landings made by the flight instructors were nearly flawless until Kraft duplicated the conditions of the fatal crashes by having the pilots approach an upward-sloping distant city over a dark area. When this occurred, the pilots were unable to detect the upward slope, assumed that the background city was flat, and consistently overestimated their altitude. On a normal landing, the preferred altitude at 7.25 kilometres from the runway is about 378 metres. As Figure 5.42 shows, the pilots approached at about this altitude when the simulated city was in a flat position. But when it was sloped upward, 11 of the 12 experienced pilot instructors crashed about 7.25 kilometres short of the runway.

Critical Analysis

This study shows the value of being able to study behaviour under highly controlled conditions and with precise measurements. By simulating the conditions under which the fatal crashes had occurred, Kraft identified the visual illusion that was the source of pilot error. He showed that the perceptual hypotheses of the flight instructors, like those of the pilots involved in the real crashes, were tragically incorrect. It would have been ironic if one of the finest jetliners ever built had been removed from service because of presumed mechanical defects while other less capable aircraft remained in service.

Kraft's research not only saved the 727 from months, and perhaps years, of needless mechanical analysis but, more importantly, it identified a potentially deadly illusion and the precise conditions under which it occurred. On the basis of Kraft's findings, Boeing recommended that pilots attend carefully to their instruments when landing at night, even under perfect weather conditions. Today commercial airline pilots are required to make instrument landings not only at night, but also during the day.

Source: Conrad L. Kraft (1978). A psychophysical contribution to air safety: Simulator studies of illusions in night visual approaches. In H. L. Pick, Jr., H. W. Leibowitz, J. E. Singer, A. Steinschneider, & H. W. Stevenson (Eds.), *Psychology: From research to practice*. New York: Plenum.

In Review

- *Monocular cues to judge distance include linear perspective, relative size, height in the horizontal plane, texture, and clarity. These distance cues also help us judge depth. Depth perception also occurs throughthe monocular cues of light and shadow patterns, interposition, and motion parallax.*

- *Binocular disparity occurs as slightly different images are viewed by each eye and acted on by feature detectors for depth. Convergence of the eyes provides a second binocular cue.*
- *The basis for perception of movement is absolute movement of a stimulus across the retina or relative movement of an object in relation to its background. Stroboscopic movement is illusory.*
- *Illusions are erroneous perceptions. They may be regarded as incorrect perceptual hypotheses. Perceptual constancies help produce a variety of context-produced illusions.*

EXPERIENCE, CRITICAL PERIODS, AND PERCEPTUAL DEVELOPMENT

Development of sensory and perceptual systems results from the interplay of biological and experiential factors. Genes program biological development, but this development is also influenced by environmental experiences. For example, if you were to be blinded in an accident and later learned to read Braille, the area of the somatosensory cortex that is devoted to the fingertips would enlarge over time as it "borrowed" other neurons to increase its sensitivity (Pool, 1994). By the time they are old enough to crawl, children placed on a *visual cliff* formed by a glass-covered table that suddenly drops off beneath the glass ordinarily will not venture "over the edge" (Figure 5.43). This aversion may result from the interaction of innate depth perception abilities and previous experience (Gibson & Walk, 1960).

FIGURE 5.43

Eleanor Gibson and Richard Walk constructed this "visual cliff" with a glass-covered drop-off to determine whether crawling infants and newborn animals can perceive depth. Even when coaxed by their mothers, infants refuse to venture onto the glass over the cliff. Newborn animals also avoid the cliff.

What might a lifetime of experience in a limited environment do to perceptual abilities that seem innate? The Ba Mbuti pygmies, who live in the rain forests of central Africa, spend their lives in a closed-in green world of densely packed trees without open spaces. The anthropologist C. M. Turnbull (1961) once brought a man named Kenge out of the forest to the edge of a vast plain. A herd of buffalo grazed in the distance. To Turnbull's surprise, Kenge remarked that he had never seen insects of that kind. When told that they were buffalo, not insects, he was deeply offended and felt that Turnbull was insulting his intelligence. To prove his point, Turnbull drove Kenge in his jeep toward the animals. Kenge's eyes widened in amazement as the "insects" grew into buffalo before his eyes. To explain his perceptual experience to himself, he concluded that witchcraft was being used to fool him. Kenge's misperception occurred as a failure in size constancy. Having lived in an environment without open spaces, he had no experience in judging the size of objects at great distances.

As noted earlier, when light passes through the lens of the eye, the image projected on the retina is reversed, so that right is left and up is down. What would happen if you were to wear a special set of glasses that undid this natural reversal of the visual image and created a world like that in Figure 5.44? In 1896, perception researcher George Stratton did just that, possibly becoming the first human ever to have a right-side-up image on his retina while standing upright. Reversing how nature and a lifetime of experience had fashioned his perceptual system at first disoriented Stratton. The ground and his feet were now "up" and he had to put on his hat from the bottom up. He had to reach to his left to touch something he saw on his right. Stratton suffered from nausea and couldn't eat or get around for several days. Gradually, however, he adapted to his inverted world, and by the end of eight days, he was able successfully to reach for objects and walk around. Years later,

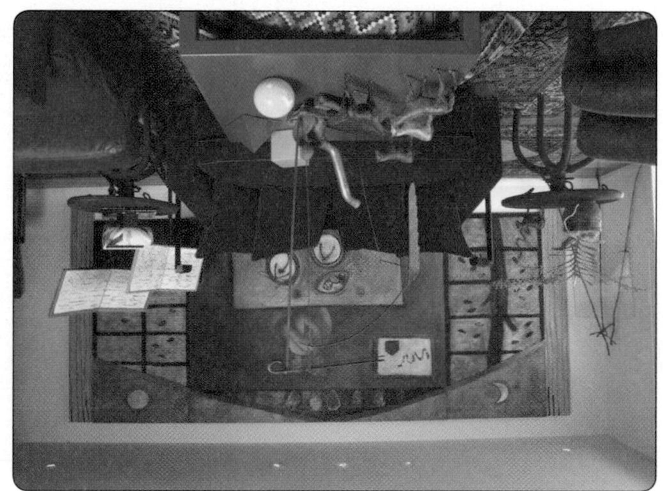

FIGURE 5.44

Inverted vision would create a world that looks like this. Adaptation to such a world is possible, but challenging.

people who wore inverting lenses for longer periods of time did the same. Some were able to ski down mountain slopes or ride motorcycles while wearing the lenses, even though their visual world remained "upside down" and never became normal for them. When they removed the inverting lenses, they initially had some problems, but soon readapted to the normal visual world (Dolezal, 1982).

Cross-Cultural Research on Perception

As far as we know, humans normally come into the world with the same perceptual abilities. However, from that point, the culture one grows up in helps determine the kinds of perceptual learning experiences people have. Cross-cultural research can help identify which aspects of perception occur in all people, regardless of their culture, as well as perceptual differences that result from cultural experiences (Deregowski & Kinnear, 1997). Athough there are far more perceptual similarities than differences in the peoples of the world, the differences that do exist show us that perception can indeed be influenced by experience.

41. What evidence is there that cultural factors can influence picture interpretations, constancies, and susceptibility to illusions?

Consider the perception of a picture, which depends on both the nature of the picture and characteristics of the perceiver. In Figure 5.45a, what is the object above the woman's head? Most North Americans and Europeans reply instantly, "A window." They also tend to see the family sitting inside a dwelling. But when the same picture was shown to East Africans, nearly all perceived the object as a basket or box that the woman is balancing on her head. To them, the family is also outside, sitting under a tree (Gregory & Gombrich, 1973). These interpretations are more consistent with their cultural experiences.

In our earlier discussion of monocular depth cues, we used paintings such as those in Figure 5.35 to illustrate monocular depth perception. In Western culture, we have constant exposure to two-dimensional pictures that our perceptual system effortlessly turns into three-dimensional perceptions. Do people who grow up in cultures in which they are not exposed to pictures have the same perceptions? When presented with the picture in Figure 5.45b and asked which animal the hunter was about to shoot, tribal African people answered that he was about to kill the "baby elephant." They did not use the monocular cues that cause Westerners to

(a)

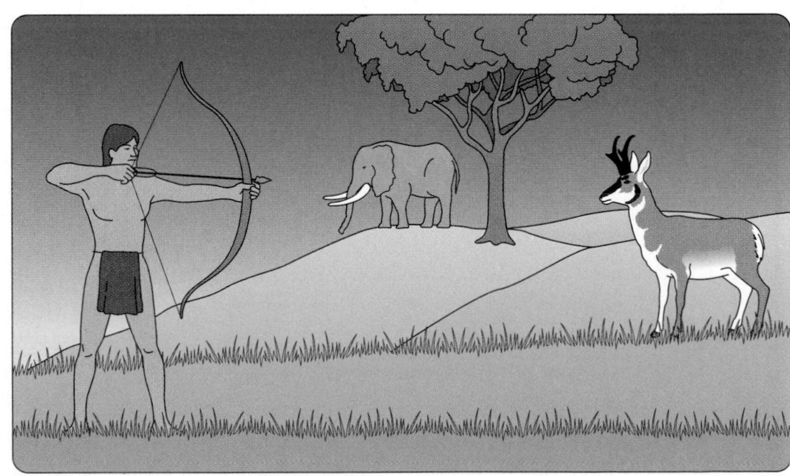

(b)

FIGURE 5.45

(a) What is the object above the woman's head? East Africans had a far different answer than did North Americans. (b) Cultural differences also occurred when people were asked which animal the archer was about to shoot.

(a) Adapted from Gregory & Gombrich, 1973; (b) Adapted from Hudson, 1960.

perceive the man as hunting the antelope and to view the elephant as an adult animal in the distance (Hudson, 1960).

Illusions occur when one of our common perceptual hypotheses is in error. Earlier, we showed you the Müller-Lyer illusion (see Figure 5.39) in which a line appears longer when the V-shaped lines at its ends radiate outward than when they face inward. Westerners are very susceptible to this illusion. They have learned that in their "carpentered" environment, which has many corners and square shapes, inward-facing lines occur when corners are closer, outward-facing lines when they are farther away (Figure 5.46). But when people from other cultures who live in more rounded environments are shown the Müller-Lyer stimuli, they are more likely to correctly perceive the lines as equal in length (Segall et al., 1966). They do not fall prey to a perceptual hypothesis that normally is correct in an environment like ours that is filled with sharp corners, but is wrong when applied to the lines in the Müller-Lyer illusion (Deregowski & Kinnear, 1997).

Cultural learning affects perceptions in other modalities as well. Our perceptions of tastes, odours, and textures are strongly influenced by our cultural experiences. A taste that might produce nausea in one culture may be considered delicious in another. The taste and gritty texture experienced as you chew a large raw insect or the rubbery texture of a fish eye may appeal far less to you than it would to a person from a culture in which that is a staple food.

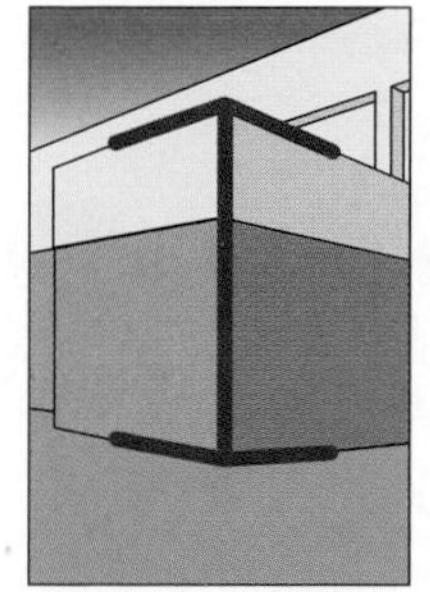
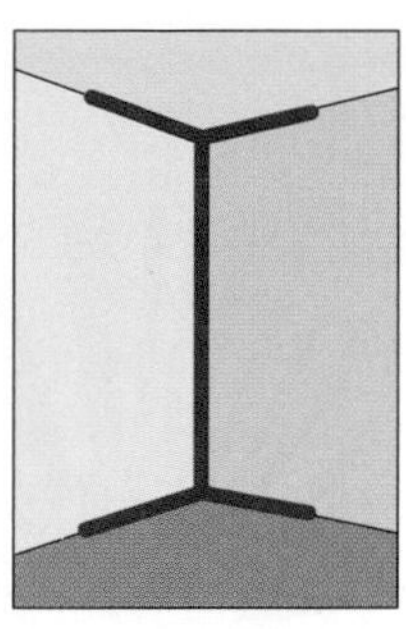

FIGURE 5.46

Perceptual experiences within our "carpentered" environment makes us susceptible to the Müller-Lyer illusion, which appears here in vertical form. Again, the vertical lines are the same physical length.

42. How do animal studies of restricted stimulation and human studies of restored vision illustrate the important role of critical periods for perceptual development?

RESEARCH FOUNDATIONS

Critical Periods: The Role of Early Experience

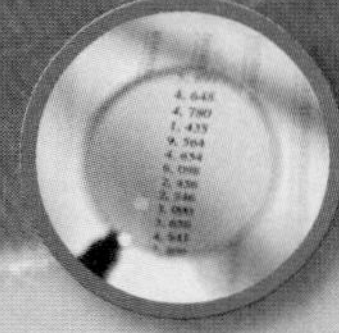

Background

Our discussion of cultural factors in perception suggests that experience is critical to the development of perceptual abilities. For some aspects of perception, there are also **critical periods** during which certain kinds of experiences must occur if perceptual abilities and the brain mechanisms that underlie them are to develop normally. If the critical period passes without the experience occurring, it is too late to undo the deficit that results. How can we find out what the critical period is? Under normal circumstances, young organisms experience the environment into which they are born. Thus, we must arrange for the environmental experience to be absent. This is the basic methodology behind a **deprivation experiment**, such as the one by Blakemore and Cooper (1970) described below.

Method

Recall that the visual cortex has feature detectors composed of neurons that respond only to lines at particular angles. What would happen if newborn animals grew up in a world in which they saw some angles, but not others? British researchers Colin Blakemore and Grahame Cooper (1970) created such a world for newborn kittens. At birth, the kittens were housed in a dark room. At about two weeks of age, the kittens spent five hours each day in specially designed round chambers that had either high contrast vertical or horizontal stripes on the walls. Figure 5.47a shows one of the kittens in a vertically striped chamber. A special collar prevented the kittens from seeing their own bodies while they were in the chamber, guaranteeing that they saw nothing but the stripes. At five months of age, the kittens were no longer exposed to the vertical or horizontal environment. Instead, they spent several hours each week in a well-lit furnished room. The remainder of the time was spent in the dark.

Results

The kittens quickly adapted to this "normal" environment and could easily navigate around the room. However, the kittens seemed to be "blind" to orientations that were perpendicular to the stripes in the special chambers. For example, a kitten raised in the horizontal environment would walk into vertical table legs. The cat would visually track a pencil held in a horizontal position, but showed no interest when the pencil was rotated to vertical. Blakemore and Cooper then proceeded to record from feature detector cells in the visual cortex using bars of light at various orientations as the stimuli. The results for animals raised in the vertical environment are shown in Figure 5.47b. As you can see, these kittens had no cells that fired in response to horizontal stimuli, resulting in visual impairment. As you might expect, the animals raised in the horizontally striped environment showed the opposite effects. They had no feature detectors for ver-

–Continued

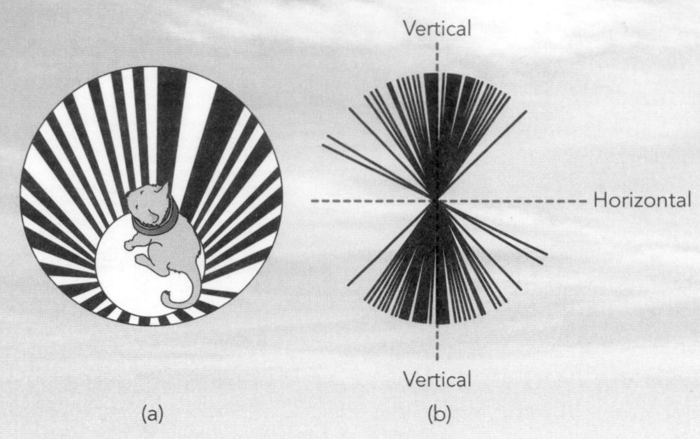

FIGURE 5.47

Kittens raised in a vertically striped chamber such as the one shown in (a) lacked cortical cells that fire in response to horizontal stimuli. The perceptual "holes" are easily seen in (b), which shows the orientation angles that resulted in evoked potentials from feature detectors.

Adapted from Blakemore & Cooper, 1970.

tical stimuli. Thus, the cortical neurons of both groups of kittens developed in accordance with the stimulus features of their environment. Blakemore and Cooper note that almost every cell examined showed this orientation specificity—there were no large areas of inactive cortex. The cells had adapted to their new environment rather than simply degenerating.

Critical Discussion

The type of cortical change found by Blakemore and Cooper seems to be permanent. Using behavioural tests, Muir and Mitchell (1975) have demonstrated that kittens raised in a vertically striped chamber were able to discriminate vertical test patterns as well as kittens raised in a normal environment. However, their ability to "see" horizontal patterns was quite diminished, and showed no improvement whatsoever even after 30 months of exposure to a normal environment. Other cells in the cortex were not able to compensate for the loss.

Should we expect similar findings in humans? Daphne Maurer and her colleagues (e.g., Maurer & Lewis, 2001) have studied a number of children at the Hospital for Sick Children in Toronto who were born with cataracts and, consequently, were deprived of normal visual input. Upon surgical correction, these children were tested for visual acuity (the ability to distinguish patterns, gratings, or letters at various distances). Maurer found that upon correction, visual acuity of the children is about the same as that of newborns. Acuity does improve over time, but some effects of the early deprivation linger (e.g., sensitivity to fine detail). Apparently, the cortices of the children were influenced by the degraded visual input and the cells simply cannot function in the normal way. Maurer notes that the critical period for visual acuity in humans seems to be from about birth until 10 years of age. A child born with cataracts that were not corrected before age 10 would show serious deficiencies in visual acuity.

Some perceptual abilities are influenced more than others by restricted stimulation. For example, monkeys, chimpanzees, and kittens have been raised in an environment devoid of shapes. Such animals distinguish differences in size, brightness, and colour almost as well as normally reared animals do. On the other hand, for the rest of their lives they perform poorly on more complex tasks, such as distinguishing different types of objects and geometric shapes (Riesen, 1965).

Restored Sensory Capacity

Suppose it had been possible to restore Helen Keller's vision when she reached adulthood. What would she have seen? Could she have perceived visually the things that she had learned to identify through her other senses?

Unfortunately, it was not possible to provide Helen Keller with the miracle of restored vision. However, scientists have studied the experiences of other visually impaired people who acquired the ability to see later in life. For example, people born with cataracts grow up in a visual world without form. The clouded lenses of their eyes permit them to perceive light, but not patterns or shapes. One such person was Virgil, who had been almost totally blind since childhood. He read Braille, enjoyed listening to sports on the radio and conversing with other people, and had adjusted quite well to his disability. At the urging of his fiancée, Virgil agreed to undergo surgery to remove his thick cataracts. The day after the surgery, his bandages were removed. Neurologist Oliver Sacks recounts what happened next.

> There was light, there was colour, all mixed up, meaningless, a blur. Then out of the blur came a voice that said, "Well?" Then, and only then . . . did he finally realize that this chaos of light and shadow was a face—and, indeed, the face of his surgeon. . . . His retina and optic nerve were active, transmitting impulses, but his brain could make no sense of them. (Sacks, 1993, p. 62)

Virgil never was able to adjust to his new visual world. He had to touch objects in order to identify them. He had to be led through his own house and quickly would become disoriented if he deviated from his path. Eventually, Virgil lost his sight once again. This time, however, he regarded his blindness as a gift, a release from a sighted world that had become bewildering to him.

Virgil's experiences are characteristic of people who have their vision restored later in life. A German physician, von Senden (1960), compiled data on patients born with cataracts who were tested soon after their cataracts were surgically removed in adulthood. These people were immediately able to perceive figure-ground relations, to scan objects visually, and to follow moving targets with their eyes, indicating that such abilities are innate. However, they could not visually identify objects, such as eating utensils, that were familiar through touch, nor were they able to distinguish simple geometric figures without counting the corners or tracing the figures with their fingers.

After several weeks of training, the patients were able to identify simple objects by sight, but their perceptual constancies were very poor. Often they were unable to recognize the same shape in another colour, even though they could discriminate between colours. Years later, some patients could identify only a few of the faces of people they knew well. Many also had great difficulty judging distances. Apparently, no amount of subsequent experience could make up for their lack of visual experience during the critical period of childhood.

All of these lines of evidence—cross-cultural perceptual differences, animal studies involving visual deprivation, and observations of congenitally impaired people whose vision has been restored—suggest that biological and experiential factors interact in complex ways. Some of our perceptual abilities are at least partially present at birth, but experience plays an important role in their normal development. How innate and experiential factors interact promises to be a continued focus of perception research. Thus perception is very much a biopsychological process whose mysteries are best explored by examining them from biological, psychological, and environmental levels of analysis (see Figure 5.48).

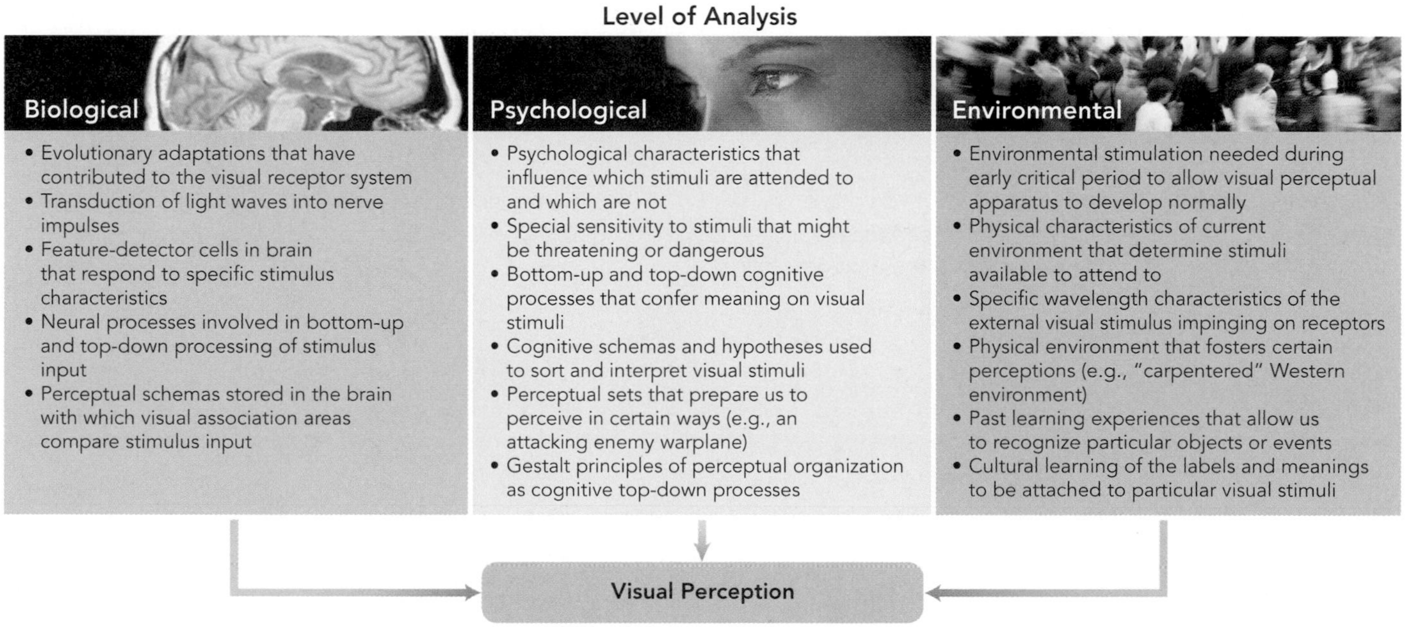

Level of Analysis

Biological	Psychological	Environmental
• Evolutionary adaptations that have contributed to the visual receptor system • Transduction of light waves into nerve impulses • Feature-detector cells in brain that respond to specific stimulus characteristics • Neural processes involved in bottom-up and top-down processing of stimulus input • Perceptual schemas stored in the brain with which visual association areas compare stimulus input	• Psychological characteristics that influence which stimuli are attended to and which are not • Special sensitivity to stimuli that might be threatening or dangerous • Bottom-up and top-down cognitive processes that confer meaning on visual stimuli • Cognitive schemas and hypotheses used to sort and interpret visual stimuli • Perceptual sets that prepare us to perceive in certain ways (e.g., an attacking enemy warplane) • Gestalt principles of perceptual organization as cognitive top-down processes	• Environmental stimulation needed during early critical period to allow visual perceptual apparatus to develop normally • Physical characteristics of current environment that determine stimuli available to attend to • Specific wavelength characteristics of the external visual stimulus impinging on receptors • Physical environment that fosters certain perceptions (e.g., "carpentered" Western environment) • Past learning experiences that allow us to recognize particular objects or events • Cultural learning of the labels and meanings to be attached to particular visual stimuli

Visual Perception

FIGURE 5.48

Understanding Behaviour: biological, psychological, and environmental factors in visual perception.

In Review

- *Perceptual development involves both physical maturation and learning. Some perceptual abilities are innate or develop shortly after birth, whereas others require particular experiences early in life in order to develop.*
- *Cultural factors can influence certain aspects of perception, including picture perception and susceptibility to illusions. However, many aspects of perception seem constant across cultures.*
- *Visual deprivation studies, manipulation of visual input, and studies of restored vision have shown that the normal biological development of the perceptual system depends on certain sensory experiences at early periods of development.*

GAINING DIRECTION

What are the issues?

The opening scenario describes Moncton's "Magnetic Hill." At first it seems that the phenomenon cannot possibly be true. How can cars roll uphill? However, if you've ever visited the site or watched a bus roll uphill on video (check out the link below), you become intrigued. How can this be happening? We know that there are no magnetic or supernatural forces involved, so what gives rise to this perception? There must be something about the geography of the hill or the way we see it that "misleads" our perceptual experience. What are the factors that help us to perceive "up" from "down"? Are these cues available at Magnetic Hill? This scenario deals with image processing, Gestalt rules, and one of the most basic questions regarding perception—how do we construct reality from sensory experience?

http://www.travelvideo.tv/videos/newbrunswick/magnetichillvideo.html

What do we need to know?

How do we separate figure from ground?
What are the Gestalt rules of perception?
How do we perceive depth?
Can our expectations drive perceptual experience?
Can we be "fooled" by erroneous cues in the environment?

Where can you find the information necessary to answer these questions?

A number of the chapter icons point to perceptual processes that influence how we see the world. We need to understand how we construct perception and then locate objects within this perceptual world. So-called magnetic or gravity hills are the result of an optical illusion. Typically, the hill is located in a wooded area where the horizon is obscured. Without access to the horizon, we have to use other cues to determine the lay of the land. Are the trees straight or angled? Does the shading suggest a hill or a valley? What does our sense of balance tell us? As we combine this information, it is likely that we come to believe that we are at the bottom of a hill when, in fact, we are standing at the top of the rise. Thus, a vehicle appears to roll uphill when it actually is rolling downhill. If you were to look at the water in the creek at the side of the road, you would see that it appears to run uphill as well, suggesting that the slope is not as you perceive it.

KEY TERMS AND CONCEPTS*

absolute threshold (171)
amplitude (184)
basilar membrane (185)
binocular cues (201)
binocular disparity (202)
bipolar cells (178)
bottom-up processing (195)
cochlea (185)
conduction deafness (188)
cones (178)
convergence (202)
critical periods (209)
dark adaptation (179)
decibels (db) (184)
decision criterion (172)
deprivation experiment (209)
difference threshold (174)
dual-process theory (181)
feature detectors (183)
figure-ground relations (197)
fovea (178)
frequency (184)
frequency theory (187)
ganglion cells (178)
Gestalt laws (197)
gustation (191)
hertz (Hz) (184)
hyperopia (177)
illusions (203)
kinesthesis (194)
lens (176)
menstrual synchrony (192)
monocular cues (201)
myopia (176)
nerve deafness (188)
olfaction (191)
opponent-process theory (181)
optic nerve (178)
organ of Corti (185)
parallel processing (183)
perception (171)
perceptual constancies (200)
perceptual schema (198)
perceptual set (199)
pheromones (192)
photopigments (179)
place theory (187)
primary visual cortex (183)
psychophysics (171)
retina (176)
rods (178)
sensation (171)
sensory adaptation (175)
shadowing (195)
signal detection theory (172)
stroboscopic movement (203)
subliminal stimulus (173)
synesthesia (170)
taste buds (191)
top-down processing (195)
transduction (178)
trichromatic theory (180)
vestibular sense (194)
visual acuity (178)
visual association cortex (183)
Weber's law (174)

*Each term has been boldfaced in the text on the page indicated in parentheses.

DO YOU WANT TO ELEVATE YOUR GRADES?

For additional resources and interactive quizzing, visit the book's Online Learning Centre at **www.mcgrawhill.ca/olc/passer**.

CHAPTER 6

States of Consciousness

Our normal waking consciousness is but one special type of consciousness, whilst all about it, parted from it by the filmiest of screens, there lie potential forms of consciousness entirely different.
—William James

CHAPTER OUTLINE

In the early morning of May 24, 1987, Ken Parks left his home in the Toronto area and drove 23 kilometres to the house where his in-laws lived. He then proceeded to kill his mother-in-law with a kitchen knife and seriously injure his father-in-law. Mr. Parks then drove to a nearby police station where he turned himself in, telling police that he had, in fact, just killed two people.

At the trial, Parks entered a plea of "not guilty," arguing that he was completely unaware of what had happened because he was sleepwalking at the time. He claimed he had always been a deep sleeper and that his family suffered from a variety of sleep disorders. In addition, the previous year had been particularly stressful for him and his personal life had suffered greatly.

After hearing all the evidence (including expert testimony), the jury acquitted Mr. Parks on the charge of first degree murder and later on a charge of second degree murder. The trial judge also handed down a not guilty verdict on a charge of attempted murder. All acquittals were upheld by the appeal court.

- **What are the issues here?**
- **What do we need to know?**
- **Where can we find the information to answer these questions?**

One autumn afternoon in 1943, Swiss chemist Albert Hofmann became unable to concentrate and noticed that his laboratory assistants were changing shape. He went home to bed, experiencing vivid dreams with intense colours. The next day, Hofmann concluded that a chemical he synthesized had been absorbed through his skin. Curious, he put a tiny bit on his tongue and soon felt like he was splitting into two people. Hofmann's alarmed assistants took him home, where his strange experiences continued:

> The dizziness . . . became so strong at times that I . . . had to lie down on a sofa. . . . Everything in the room spun around and the familiar objects and pieces of furniture assumed grotesque, mostly threatening forms. . . . The neighbour woman who brought me milk . . . She was no longer Mrs. R., but rather a malevolent insidious witch with a coloured mask. Even worse . . . were the alterations that I perceived in myself, in my inner being. . . . A demon had invaded me and had taken possession of my body, mind and soul. (Hofmann, 1980, p. 58)

So it was that Albert Hofmann accidentally discovered the striking alterations in consciousness that can be produced by a dose of lysergic acid diethylamide (LSD) no larger than the tip of a pin.

Although Hofmann's experience is unusual, it is not as far removed from our normal existence as we might think. We all drift into and out of various states of consciousness. By *state of consciousness*, psychologists mean a pattern of subjective experience, a way of experiencing internal and external events. You will also encounter the phrase *altered state of consciousness*, which refers to variations from our normal waking state. While daydreaming or passing from wakefulness to sleep we may experience vivid images that rival Hofmann's hallucinations, and our nighttime dreams can seem just as real and emotionally charged as his drug-induced perceptions.

1. Describe some basic characteristics of consciousness.

We also experience divisions of awareness. Consider this: Why don't you fall out of bed at night? You are not consciously aware of major postural shifts while soundly asleep, yet a part of you somehow knows where the edge of the bed is. Similarly, have you ever "spaced out" while driving, deeply engrossed in thought? Suddenly you snap out of it, with no memory of the kilometres just driven. While you were consciously focused inward, some part of you kept track of the road and controlled your responses at the wheel.

Philosopher David Chalmers (1995) notes that "Conscious experience is at once the most familiar thing in the world and the most mysterious." As we shall see, its mysteries span a range from normal waking states to sleep and dreams, drug-induced experiences, hypnosis, and beyond. When psychology was founded in the late 1800s, its "Great Project" was to scientifically unravel some of the puzzles of consciousness (Natsoulas, 1999). This interest waned during behaviourism's dominance in the mid-twentieth century, but resurgence of the cognitive and biological perspectives has sparked new research, forcing us to rethink long-standing conceptions about the mind (Figure 6.1).

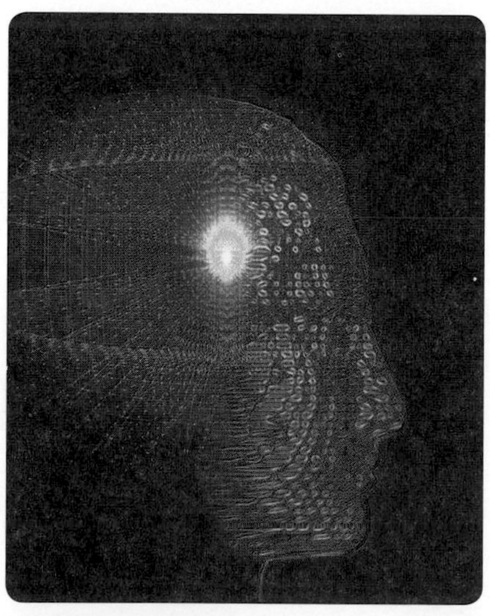

FIGURE 6.1

The mysteries of consciousness have intrigued scholars for ages.

THE PUZZLE OF CONSCIOUSNESS

What is consciousness, and how does it arise? In psychology, **consciousness** often is defined as our moment-to-moment awareness of ourselves and our environment. Among its characteristics, consciousness is:

- *subjective and private.* Other people cannot directly know what reality is for you, nor can you enter directly into their experience. As the author Charles

Dickens observed, "Every human creature is constituted to be that profound secret and mystery to every other."

- *dynamic (ever-changing).* We drift in and out of various states throughout each day. Although the stimuli of which we are aware constantly change, we typically experience consciousness as a continuously flowing "stream" of mental activity, rather than as disjointed perceptions and thoughts (James, 1890/1950).
- *self-reflective and central to our sense of self.* The mind is aware of its own consciousness. Thus, no matter what your awareness is focused on—a lovely sunset or an itch on your back—you can reflect upon the fact that "*you*" are the one who is conscious of it.

Finally, consciousness is *intimately connected with the process of selective attention,* as discussed in Chapter 5. William James noted that ". . . the mind is at every stage a theatre of simultaneous possibilities. Consciousness consists in . . . the selection of some, and the suppression of the rest by the . . . agency of Attention" (1879, p. 13). Selective attention focuses conscious awareness on some stimuli to the exclusion of others. If the mind is a theatre of mental activity, then consciousness reflects whatever is illuminated at the moment—the "bright spot on the stage"—and selective attention is the "spotlight" or mechanism behind it (Baars, 1997).

FIGURE 6.2

Gordon Gallup (1970) exposed four chimps to a mirror. By day three they used it to inspect hard-to-see parts of their own bodies and began making odd faces at themselves in the mirror. To further test whether the chimps knew the mirror image was their own reflection, Gordon anaesthetized them and put a red mark on their faces. Later, with no mirror, the chimps rarely touched the red mark. But upon seeing it when a mirror was introduced, they touched the red spot on their face almost 30 times in 30 minutes, suggesting that the chimps had some self-awareness. Using a similar test in which a red rouge mark is placed on the tip of the infant's nose, researchers find that infants begin to recognize themselves in a mirror around 18 months of age.

Measuring States of Consciousness

Scientists who study consciousness must find ways to operationally define private inner states in terms of measurable responses. The most common measure is *self-report,* in which people describe their inner experiences. Self-reports offer the most direct insight into a person's subjective experiences, but they are not always verifiable. In contrast, *physiological measures* establish the correspondence between bodily states and mental processes. For example, EEG recordings of brain activity help identify different stages of sleep throughout the night. Physiological measures are objective, but cannot tell us what a person is experiencing subjectively. *Behavioural measures* also are used, including performance on special tasks such as the *rouge test* (Figure 6.2). Behavioural measures are objective, but we still must infer the person's (or chimp's) state of mind.

2. How do psychologists measure states of consciousness?

Levels of Consciousness: Psychodynamic and Cognitive Perspectives

A century ago Sigmund Freud (1900/1953) proposed that the human mind consists of three levels of awareness. The *conscious* mind contains thoughts, perceptions, and other mental events of which we are currently aware. *Preconscious* mental events are outside current awareness, but can easily be recalled under certain conditions. For instance, you may not have thought about a childhood friend for years, but when someone mentions your friend's name, you become aware of pleasant memories. *Unconscious* events cannot be brought into conscious awareness under ordinary circumstances. Some unconscious content—such as unacceptable urges and desires stemming from instinctive sexual and aggressive drives, traumatic memories, and threatening emotional conflict—is kept out of conscious awareness because it would arouse anxiety, guilt, or other negative emotions.

3. Explain Freud's three-level model of consciousness.

Behaviourists roundly criticized Freud's model. After all, they sought to explain behaviour without invoking *conscious* mental processes, much less unconscious ones. Cognitive psychologists and many contemporary psychodynamic psychologists also take issue with specific aspects of Freud's model, which we describe more fully in Chapter 12. As psychodynamic psychologist Drew Westen (1998, p. 333) notes, "Many aspects of Freudian theory are indeed out of date, and they should be. Freud died in 1939, and he has been slow to undertake further revisions."

On a broad level, however, research strongly supports Freud's general premise: Nonconscious processes influence behaviour (Dimberg et al., 2000; Westen, 1998). Studies of *placebo effects* (see Chapter 2), *split-brain patients* (see Chapter 3), *subliminal perception* (see Chapter 5), and phenomena that you will encounter in upcoming chapters all indicate that mental processes can affect our behaviour without conscious awareness (Kirsch & Lynn, 1999).

The Cognitive Unconscious

4. How do cognitive psychologists view the unconscious?

Cognitive psychologists reject the notion of an unconscious mind driven by instinctive urges and repressed conflicts. Rather, they view conscious and unconscious mental life as complementary forms of information processing. As Daniel Reisberg (1997, p. 601) notes, unconscious mental activity is "not an adversary to the conscious mind. Instead, the cognitive unconscious functions as a sophisticated support service, working in harmony with our conscious thoughts." To illustrate, consider how we perform everyday tasks.

? 5. What is automatic processing, and why is it important?

Controlled versus automatic processing. Many activities, such as planning a vacation or studying, involve **controlled (effortful) processing**, the voluntary use of attention and conscious effort. Other activities involve **automatic processing** and can be performed with little or no conscious effort. Automatic processing occurs most often when we carry out routine actions or well-learned tasks, particularly under constant or familiar circumstances (Ouellette & Wood, 1998). Learning to type, drive, and eat with utensils all involve controlled processing; you have to pay a lot of attention to what you are doing. With practice, they become more automatic. Through years of practice, typists, athletes, and musicians program themselves to execute highly complex skills with a minimum of conscious thought.

Ellen Langer (1989) points out that automatic processing has a key disadvantage: It can reduce our chances of finding new ways to approach problems. Controlled processing requires effort and therefore is slower than automatic processing, but it is more flexible and open to change. Still, automatic processing offers speed and economy of effort, and in everyday life most actions may be processed this way (Bargh & Chartrand, 1999). In fact, many well-learned behaviours seem performed best when our mind is on "autopilot," with controlled processing taking a backseat. The famous baseball player, Yogi Berra, captured this idea in his classic statement that "You can't think and hit at the same time." At tasks ranging from golf putting to video games, experiments suggest that too much self-focused thinking can hurt task performance and cause people to "choke" under pressure (Baumeister, 1984; Lewis & Linder, 1997).

FIGURE 6.3

Provincial, territorial, and federal governments have all expressed concern about the increased risk posed by the use of cellular phones while driving. On April 1, 2003, it became illegal in Newfoundland and Labrador to use a hand-held cellular phone while driving. Currently no other Canadian jurisdictions ban the use of cell phones while driving, although some jurisdictions are considering legislation and Transport Canada continues to monitor the situation. According to some researchers, even hands-free phone conversations are associated with impaired attention and an increased risk of accidents.

Divided attention. Automatic processing also facilitates **divided attention**, the ability to perform more than one activity at the same time. We can talk while we walk, type as we read, eat while watching TV, and so on. Without the capacity to divide attention, every act would require our full attention and quickly overwhelm our mental capacity. Yet divided attention has limits, and is more difficult when tasks require similar mental resources (Reisberg, 1997). For example, the shadowing experiments described in Chapter 5 indicate that we cannot attend fully to separate messages delivered simultaneously through two earphones.

Although divided attention is wonderfully adaptive most of the time, it can have serious negative consequences in certain situations (Figure 6.3). For example, some studies have found that collision rates triple or quadruple when people talk on the telephone while driving; they are more likely to speed, drive on the wrong side of the road, run off the road, hit fixed objects, and overturn their cars (Redelmeier & Tibshirani, 1997; Violanti & Marshall, 1996). While engaged in a cell phone conversation, drivers leave less space between their car and the car in front of them and, especially during long conversations, drive faster (Rosenbloom, 2006). Even the use of a hands-free cell phone has an impact: braking is delayed, the degree of braking is reduced, and anticipation of upcoming events is degraded (Treffner & Barrett, 2004), all of which are changes that would be expected to increase the chance of an accident.

The Emotional Unconscious

6. Can nonconscious processes influence emotional responses?

Some modern psychodynamic views incorporate information-processing concepts from cognitive psychology, but strongly emphasize that emotional and motivational processes also operate unconsciously and influence behaviour (Gillett, 1997; Westen, 1998). At times, these hidden processes can cause us to feel and act in ways that mystify us or that we cannot explain. Consider the famous case of a 47-year-old amnesia patient who could not remember new personal experiences. One day, as Swiss psychologist Edouard Claparède (1911) shook this woman's hand, he intentionally pricked her hand with a pin hidden between his fingers. Later, Claparède extended his hand toward hers again. The woman could not consciously remember the pinprick, but despite her amnesia, she suddenly withdrew her hand. Apparently, a nonconscious memory of her painful past experience influenced her behaviour.

In the past 15 years an explosion of research—much of it by cognitive, social, physiological, and clinical psychologists—has strengthened the view that unconscious processes can have an emotional and motivational flavour (Epstein, 1994; LeDoux, 2000; Westen, 1998). For example, have you ever been in a bad or good mood, and unsure of why you were feeling that way? Perhaps, as Bargh and Chartrand (1999) propose, it is because you were influenced by events in your environment of which you were not consciously aware.

In one study, Chartrand and Bargh (2000) *subliminally* presented university students with nouns that were either strongly negative (e.g., cancer, cockroach), mildly negative (e.g., Monday, worm), mildly positive (e.g., parade, clown), or strongly positive (e.g., friends, music). Later, students rated their mood on standard psychological inventories. Although they were not consciously aware of seeing the nouns, those shown the strongly negative words displayed the saddest mood, whereas those who had seen the strongly positive words reported the happiest mood. In Chapter 10 we explore other aspects of the modern "emotional unconscious."

The Modular Mind

7. According to the modular model of mind, how does consciousness arise?

Given these findings, how shall we view the human mind? Freud's theory challenged the traditional view that the mind is a single "entity" or process. Today a growing number of models also challenge this traditional view and propose that the mind is a collection of largely separate but interacting *modules* (Epstein, 1999; Estes, 1991; Gazzaniga, 1985). These modules are information-processing subsystems or "networks" within the brain that perform tasks related to sensation, perception, memory, problem solving, emotion, motor behaviour, and so on. The various modules process information in parallel—that is, simultaneously and largely independently. However, the output from one module can provide input for another, as when information recalled from memory becomes input to the problem-solving and motor modules that allow you to write down answers during a math exam.

According to this perspective, our subjective experience of consciousness arises from the integrated activity of the various modules, somewhat akin to listening to a choir sing. We are aware of the integrated, harmonious sound of the choir rather than the voice of each individual member. As we now see, many factors can influence the activity of these modules and, in so doing, alter our state of consciousness.

In Review

- *Consciousness refers to our moment-to-moment awareness of ourselves and the environment. It is subjective, dynamic, self-reflective, and central to our sense of identity. Selective attention focuses conscious awareness on some stimuli to the exclusion of others.*
- *Scientists use self-report, physiological, and behavioural measures to operationally define states of consciousness.*
- *Freud believed that the mind has conscious, preconscious, and unconscious levels. He viewed the unconscious as a reservoir of unacceptable desires and repressed experiences. Cognitive psychologists view the unconscious as an information-processing system.*
- *Controlled processing typically is required for learning new tasks. Automatic processing makes divided attention possible, enabling us to perform several tasks at once. Research on subliminal perception and other topics suggests that emotional and motivational processes also can operate nonconsciously and influence behaviour.*
- *Many theorists propose that the mind consists of separate but interacting information processing modules. Our subjective experience of "unitary" consciousness arises from the integrated output of these modules.*

CIRCADIAN RHYTHMS: OUR DAILY BIOLOGICAL CLOCKS

Consciousness is our moment-to-moment awareness of ourselves and our environment (see pp. 216, 217). One way in which psychologists study consciousness is by studying variations in the state of consciousness; by studying how awareness of self and the external world changes. One very straightforward way in which our state of consciousness changes is that it varies depending on the time of day.

Like other animals, humans have adapted to a world with a 24-hour day-night cycle. Every 24 hours our body temperature, certain hormonal secretions, and other bodily functions undergo a rhythmic change that affects our mental alertness and readies our passage back and forth between states of wakefulness and sleep (Figure 6.4). These daily biological cycles are called **circadian rhythms** (from the Latin *circa*, "around," and *dia*, "day").

Keeping Time: Brain and Environment

8. How do the brain and environment regulate circadian rhythms?

Most circadian rhythms are regulated by the brain's **suprachiasmatic nuclei (SCN)**, located in the hypothalamus, shown in Figure 6.5 (Miller et al., 1996; Albrecht, 2004). Work by Martin Ralph, of the University of Toronto (Ralph, et al., 1990, Ralph et al., 1993) has confirmed that the SCN is indeed the brain's clock. Ralph transplanted normal, healthy SCN neurons into the hypothalamus of animals

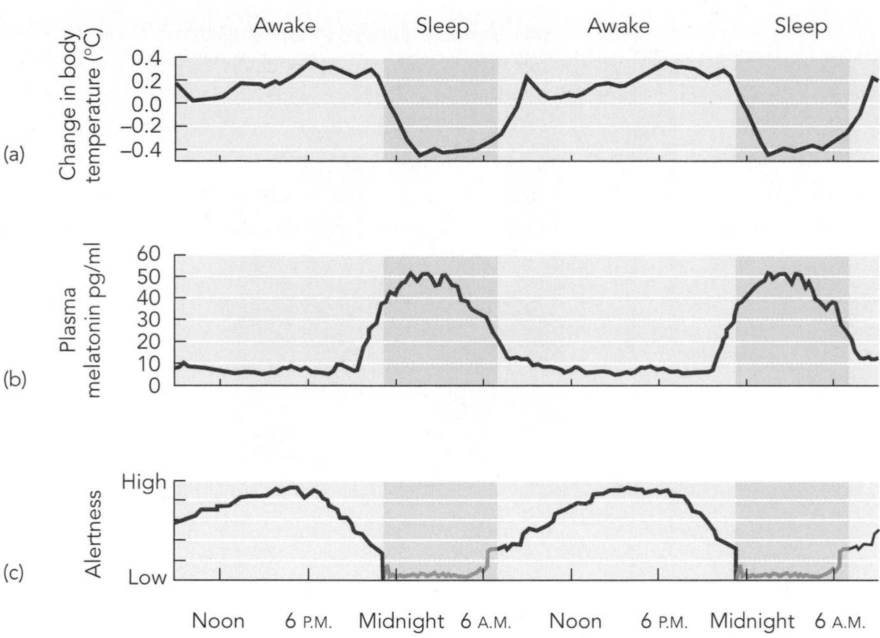

FIGURE 6.4

Changes in our core body temperature, levels of melatonin in our blood, and degree of alertness/sleepiness follow a cyclical 24-hour pattern called a circadian rhythm. Humans also have longer and shorter biological cycles, such as the 28-day female menstrual cycle and a roughly 90-minute brain activity cycle during sleep.

Adapted from Monk et al., 1996.

whose own SCN had been destroyed. The transplanted SCN neurons restored circadian rhythms to the animals that had lacked a healthy SCN (Ralph et al., 1990). SCN neurons have a genetically programmed cycle of activity and inactivity, functioning like a "biological clock." They link to the tiny pineal gland, which secretes **melatonin**, a hormone that has a relaxing effect on the body. SCN neurons become active during daytime and reduce the pineal gland's secretion of melatonin, raising your body temperature and heightening alertness. At night SCN neurons are inactive, allowing melatonin levels to increase and promoting relaxation and sleepiness (Zhdanova & Wurtman, 1997).

Our circadian clock is biological, but environmental factors such as the day-night cycle help keep SCN neurons on a 24-hour schedule (Lewy et al., 1998; Wever, 1979). Your eyes have neural connections to the SCN. After a night's sleep, the light of day increases SCN activity and helps reset your 24-hour biological clock. What would happen if you lived in the dark, or in a laboratory or underground cave without clocks, and could not tell whether it was day or night outside? Most people drift into a longer "natural" cycle of about 24.2 to 24.8 hours, called a *free-running circadian rhythm* (Hillman et al., 1994; Shanahan et al., 1999; Wever, 1989). Amazingly, SCN neurons exhibit this longer cycle of firing even when they are surgically removed from the brain and kept alive in a dish containing nutrients (Gillette, 1986; Schibler, 2006).

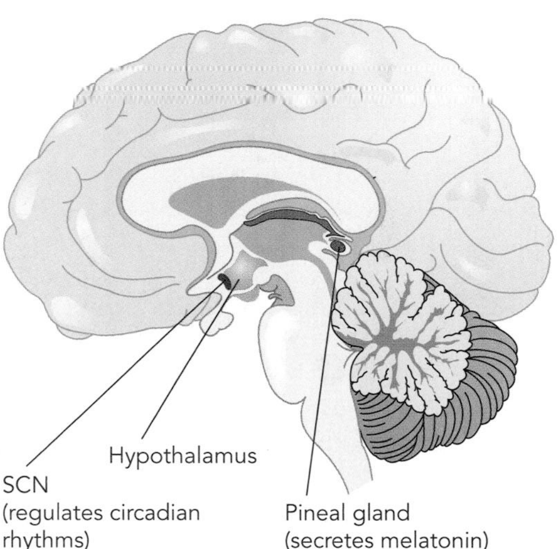

FIGURE 6.5

The suprachiasmatic nuclei (SCN) are the brain's master circadian clock. Neurons in the SCN have a genetically programmed cycle of activity and inactivity, but daylight and darkness help regulate this cycle. The optic nerve links our eyes to the SCN, and SCN activity affects the pineal gland's secretion of melatonin. In turn, melatonin influences other brain systems governing alertness and sleepiness.

Because their free-running circadian rhythm is desynchronized (out of sync) with the 24-hour day-night cycle, participants in these "isolation studies" tend to go to bed and wake up later each day. They do not realize it, but within a few weeks they may be going to bed at noon and awakening at midnight. Blind children and adults whose eyes are completely insensitive to light also may experience free-running circadian rhythms (Sack & Lewy, 1997). When they try to force their sleep-wake cycle into the 24-hour world by going to bed at fixed times, blind people often experience insomnia, other sleep problems, and daytime fatigue.

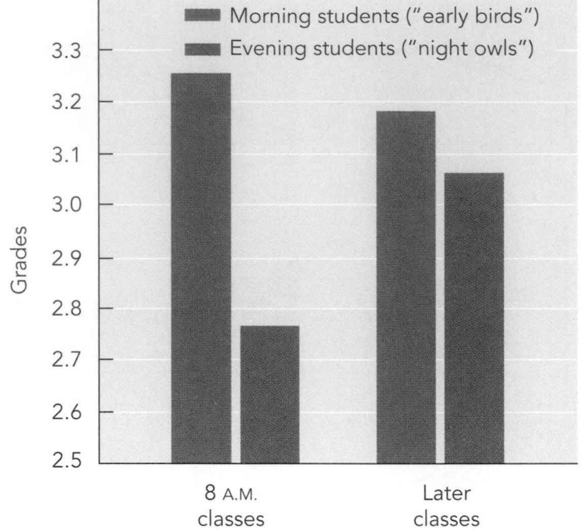

FIGURE 6.6

In a study of 454 University of Kansas students, "night owls" struggled in their 8 A.M. classes, as compared to "early birds." In later classes the two groups performed more similarly. Stated differently, early birds did slightly better in their earliest class than in later classes, whereas night owls did better in their later rather than their earliest classes.

Data from Guthrie et al., 1995.

Early Birds and Night Owls

9. What are free-running circadian rhythms?

Circadian rhythms influence our tendency to be a "morning person" or a "night person" (Duffy et al., 2001). Compared to night people, morning people go to bed and rise earlier, and their body temperature, blood pressure, and alertness peak earlier in the day. Studies around the globe indicate that "morningness" is more common among older adults, whereas more night people are found among 18- to 30-year-olds (Ishikara et al., 1992).

In university, morning people are more likely to take very early classes than are night people and, as Figure 6.6 shows, they perform better than night people in early morning (8 A.M.) classes. Experimenters also find that early birds tend to perform best on some mental tasks in the morning, whereas night owls perform best in the late afternoon or evening (Gordon, 1997; Natale & Lorenzetti, 1997).

Environmental Disruptions of Circadian Rhythms

10. Explain how SAD, jet lag, and night shiftwork involve circadian disruptions.

Gradual and sudden environmental changes can disrupt our circadian rhythms. **Seasonal affective disorder (SAD)** is a cyclic tendency to become psychologically depressed during certain months of the year. Symptoms typically begin in fall or winter, which usher in shorter periods of daylight, and then lift in spring (Rosenthal & Wehr, 1987; Sohn & Lam, 2005). Many experts believe that the circadian rhythms of SAD sufferers may be particularly sensitive to light, so as sunrises occur later in winter, the daily "onset" time of their circadian clocks may be pushed back to an unusual degree (Avery et al., 1997; Teicher et al., 1997). In late fall and winter, when many people must arise for work and school in darkness, SAD sufferers are still in "sleepiness" mode long after the morning alarm clock sounds (Figure 6.7).

Jet lag is a sudden circadian disruption caused by flying across several time zones in one day. Flying east, you "lose" hours from the day; flying west, the travel day becomes longer than 24 hours. Jet lag often causes insomnia, decreased alertness, and poorer performance until the body readjusts. It is a significant concern for

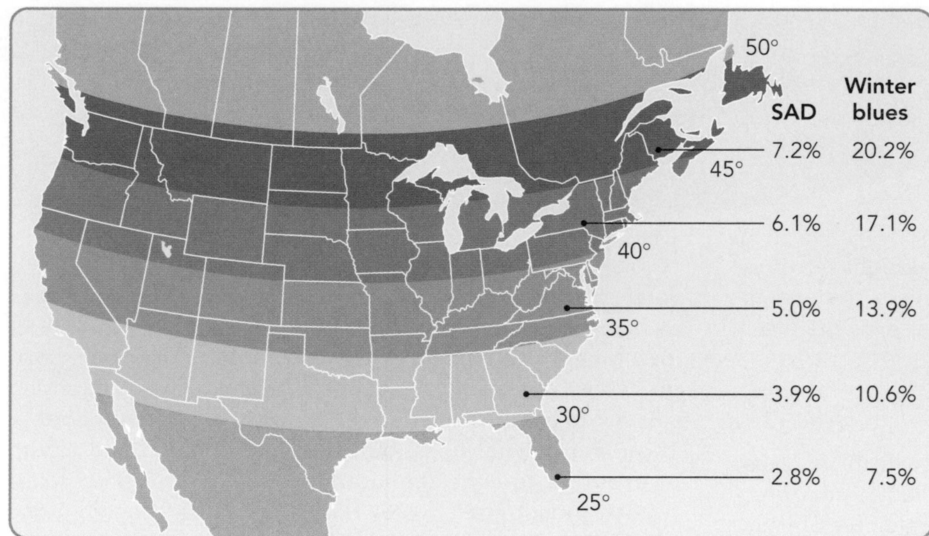

FIGURE 6.7

The latitude puzzle. In North America, the prevalence of winter SAD and milder depression ("winter blues") increases at more northerly latitudes, where the hours of daylight diminish more severely in late fall and winter. SAD and "winter blues" rates of 9.2% and 19.1%, respectively, have been found in Fairbanks, Alaska (64° latitude). Yet European studies report lower winter SAD rates and a weaker SAD–latitude relation. In fact, most studies in Sweden, Norway, Finland, and Iceland (roughly 55° to 70° latitude) report winter SAD rates similar to those in the southern United States (Mersch et al., 1999). At present, the reason for this discrepancy is debated.

businesspeople, athletes, airline crews, and others who frequently travel across many time zones (Ariznavarreta et al., 2002). The body naturally adjusts about one hour or less per day to time zone changes. Typically, people adjust faster when flying west, presumably because lengthening the travel day is more compatible with our natural free-running circadian cycle (Kimble, 1992).

The most problematic circadian disruption for society is caused by *night shiftwork.* Adjusting to an inverted night-day world can be difficult. Night shiftworkers often drive home in morning daylight, making it harder to reset their biological clocks. On days off they often fall back into a day-night schedule to spend daytime with family, which disrupts their hard-earned circadian adjustments.

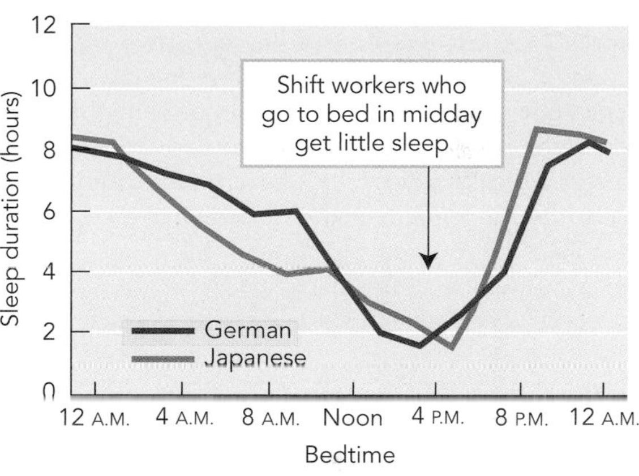

FIGURE 6.8

When night workers try to go to bed in midday, they get little sleep. These data are based on 2,322 German shiftworkers (purple line) and 3,240 Japanese shiftworkers (green line) who recorded their bedtimes and length of sleep.

(From Monk et al., 1996.)

Our biological clocks promote sleepiness in the early morning hours (Akerstedt, 1988). Combined with fatigue from poor daytime sleep, this can be a recipe for disaster. Job performance errors, fatal traffic accidents, and engineering and industrial disasters peak between midnight and 6:00 A.M. (Akerstedt et al., 2001). On-the-job sleepiness is a major concern among nighttime long-distance truck and bus drivers, locomotive engineers, airline crews, and medical doctors and nurses (Quera-Salva et al., 1997).

Some people adjust to night work, but others never do. They become fatigued, stressed, and more accident prone on and off the job. You can see in Figure 6.8 that, overall, nightworkers who try to go to bed during the middle of the day get frightfully little sleep.

One might wonder if it takes large changes in our schedules to disrupt our circadian rhythms, or if smaller changes can also have an impact on our behaviour and our well-being. Stanley Coren, of the University of British Columbia, analyzed reports of all accidental deaths in the U.S. over a three-year period. Interestingly, he found that the springtime shift to Daylight Savings Time, when we all lose an hour's sleep and have to make a small adjustment to our circadian rhythms, produced a short-lived increase in the likelihood of accidental death (Coren, 1996).

Rotating shiftwork. A forward rotating schedule takes advantage of the body's free-running circadian rhythms. When work shifts change, it is easier to extend the "waking day" than to compress it.

11. How is exposure to light used to treat circadian disruptions?

PSYCHOLOGICAL APPLICATIONS

Combatting Winter Depression, Jet Lag, and Night Shiftwork Disruptions

Circadian research has provided important insight into the nature of consciousness. It also has led to several treatments for circadian disruptions affecting millions of people.

Controlling Exposure to Light

Treating SAD

Many experts believe that *phototherapy,* which involves properly timed exposure to bright artificial light, is the best treatment for SAD (Lewy et al., 1998b). Several hours of daily phototherapy can shift circadian rhythms by as much as two or three hours per day (Shanahan et al., 1999). Timo Partonen (1994) found that, during Finland's short winter days, phototherapy for just one hour a day over two weeks significantly reduced SAD sufferers' depression. In *dawn simulation,* artificial light gradually intensifies to normal light levels over the course of one to two hours in the early morning, which helps to reset the circadian clock to an earlier time. The fact that phototherapy effectively treats SAD is the strongest evidence that SAD is triggered by winter's lack of sunlight, rather than its colder temperatures (Figure 6.9).

Reducing Jet Lag

When you fly east across time zones, your body's internal clock "falls behind" the time at your destination. Exposure to outdoor light *in the morning*—and avoiding light late in the day—moves the circadian clock forward and helps it "catch up" to local time. (Think of morning light as "jump starting" your circadian clock at a time when you would be asleep back at home.) Flying west, your body clock moves "ahead" of local time, so to reduce jet lag you want to delay your circadian cycles. Avoiding bright light in the morning and exposing yourself to light *in the afternoon or early evening* will do this. These are general rules, but the specific timing and length of exposure to light depend on the number of time zones crossed (Houpt et al., 1996). For jet travellers, spending time outside (even on cloudy days) is the easiest way to get the needed exposure to light. However, several hotels now offer rooms equipped with phototherapy systems to speed up their guests' recovery from jet lag.

FIGURE 6.9

For many people, the depression accompanying seasonal affective disorder can be reduced by daily exposure to bright fluorescent lights.

Adjusting to Nightwork

Many night employees work indoors, where the artificial light is too weak to shift their circadian rhythms toward a night-day schedule. Circadian adjustment can be increased by having very bright indoor lighting at the workplace, keeping bedrooms dark and quiet to foster daytime sleep, and maintaining a schedule of daytime sleep even during days off (Boulos, 1998).

Melatonin Treatment: Uses and Cautions

Melatonin levels in the brain can be manipulated directly by oral doses. Depending on when it is taken, oral melatonin can shift some circadian cycles forward or backward by as much as 30 to 60 minutes per day of use (Zhdanova et al., 1997). Melatonin treatment has been used with some success to alleviate SAD, decrease jet lag, and help employees adapt to night shiftwork (Arendt et al., 1997).

The availability of melatonin varies in different jurisdictions. Melatonin is not legally available in Canada without a prescription, although it does sometimes appear on store shelves as part of the so-called "grey market." In some countries, such as the United States, it is sold over the counter as a dietary supplement. Tablet doses are often three milligrams, producing melatonin levels in the blood that are more than 10 times the normal concentration (Sack et al., 1997). In contrast, doses of 0.1 to 0.5 milligrams used in research produce blood concentrations more typical of normal levels and are sufficient to produce circadian shifts.

In research, melatonin use is supervised. Taking melatonin at the wrong time can backfire and make circadian adjustments more difficult. Daytime use may decrease alertness. Experts are also concerned that millions of people are using melatonin tablets as a nightly sleeping aid, even though possible side effects of long-term use have not been adequately studied (Arendt, 2005; Sack et al., 1998; Zhdanova & Wurtman, 1997).

Regulating Activity Schedules

Some animal and human studies suggest that properly timed physical exercise can help shift the circadian clock (Eastman et al., 1995; Sinclair & Mistlberger, 1997). To reduce jet lag, you can also begin resynchronizing your biological clock to the new time zone in advance. To do so, adjust your sleep and eating schedules one hour per day, starting several days before you leave. Schedule management also applies to night shiftwork. For workers on rotating shifts, circadian disruptions can be reduced significantly by a *forward rotating shift schedule*—moving from day to evening to night shifts—rather than a schedule that rotates backward from day to night to evening shifts (Czeisler et al., 1982; Knauth, 1996). Can you hypothesize why this is the case? For the answer, see the margin note on page 223.

In Review

- *Circadian rhythms are 24-hour biological cycles that help regulate many bodily processes. The suprachiasmatic nuclei (SCN) are the brain's master circadian clock. Environmental factors, such as the day-night cycle, help to reset our daily clocks to a 24-hour schedule.*
- *Circadian rhythms influence whether we are a "morning person" or a "night person."*
- *Seasonal affective disorder (SAD), jet lag, and night shiftwork involve environmental disruptions of circadian rhythms. Treatments for circadian disruptions include controlling exposure to light, oral melatonin, and regulating daily activity schedules.*

SLEEP AND DREAMING

Our circadian rhythms do not regulate sleep directly. Rather, by decreasing nighttime alertness they promote a readiness for sleep and help determine the optimal time period when we can sleep most soundly (Sack et al., 1998). We spend approximately one-third of our lives asleep, and it is easy to understand why this state of altered consciousness has mystified humans for ages. Each night we seem to relinquish conscious control of our thoughts and actions, enter a world of dreams, toss about and possibly mutter or talk, but remember little of it upon awakening. Yet sleep is a behaviour that, like others, can be studied scientifically at biological, psychological, and environmental levels.

Stages of Sleep

12. What brain-wave patterns distinguish the first four stages of sleep?

Just as waking consciousness involves different states of alertness and awareness, so does sleep. Approximately every 90 minutes while asleep, we cycle through different stages in which our brain activity and other physiological responses change in a generally predictable way (Kleitman, 1963; Dement, 1974).

As Figure 6.10 shows, sleep research often is carried out in specially equipped laboratories in which sleepers' physiological responses are recorded. EEG recordings of your brain's electrical activity show a pattern of **beta waves** when you are awake and alert. Beta waves have a high frequency (of about 15 to 30 cycles per second, or *cps*) but a low "amplitude" or height (Figure 6.11). As you close your eyes, feeling relaxed and drowsy, your brain waves slow down and **alpha waves** occur at about 8 to 12 cps.

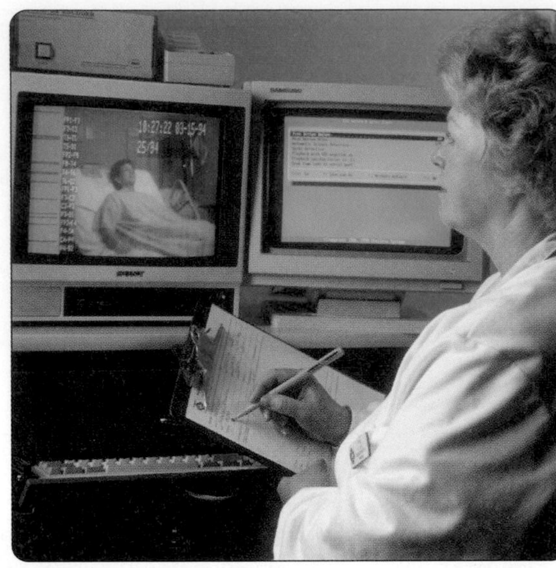

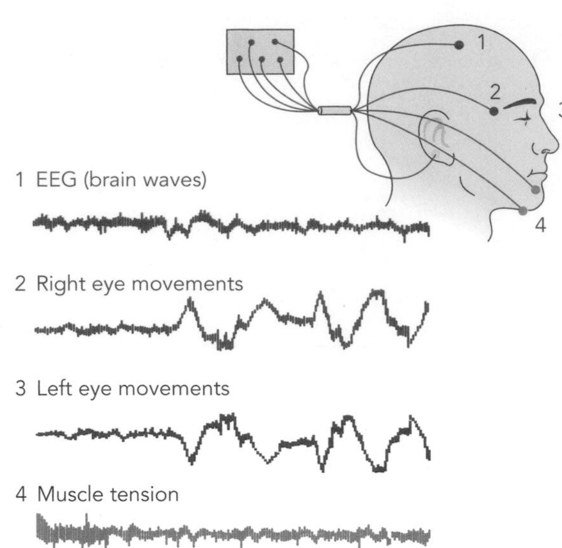

FIGURE 6.10

In a modern sleep laboratory, people sleep while their physiological responses are monitored. Electrodes attached to the scalp area record the person's EEG brain-wave patterns. Electrodes attached beside the eyes record eye movements during sleep. Muscle tension is recorded, and a neutral electrode is attached to the ear.

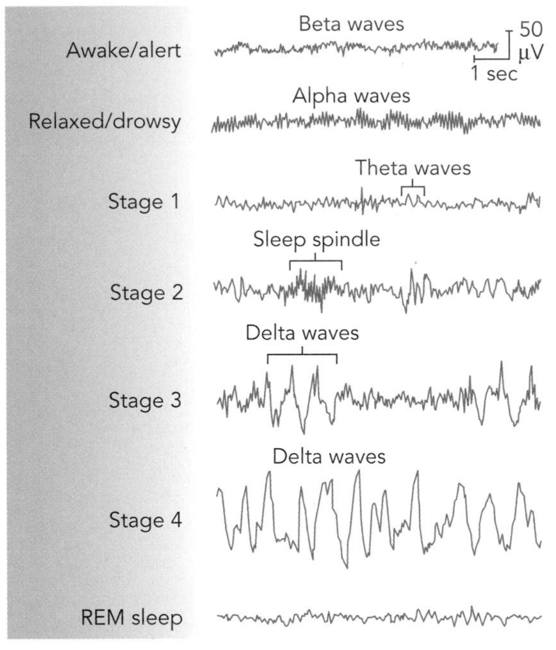

FIGURE 6.11

Changing patterns of brain-wave activity help define the various stages of sleep. Note that brain waves become slower and larger as sleep deepens, and that the general pattern of REM sleep is similar to that of stage 1.

(Adapted from Dement, 1978; Hauri, 1982.)

13. Describe some major characteristics of REM sleep.

Stage 1 through Stage 4

As sleep begins, your brain-wave pattern becomes more irregular, and slower *theta waves* (3.5 to 7.5 cps) increase. You are now in *stage 1,* a form of light sleep from which you can easily be awakened. You will probably spend just a few minutes (or less) in stage 1, during which time some people experience images and sudden body jerks. As sleep becomes deeper, *sleep spindles*—periodic one- to two-second bursts of rapid brain-wave activity (12 to 15 cps)—begin to appear. Sleep spindles indicate that you are now in *stage 2* (Figure 6.11). Your muscles are more relaxed, breathing and heart rate are slower, and you are harder to awaken.

Sleep deepens as you move into *stage 3,* marked by the regular appearance of very slow (0.5 to 2 cps) and large **delta waves.** As time passes they occur more often, and when delta waves *dominate* the EEG pattern this indicates that you have reached *stage 4.* Together, stage 3 and stage 4 are often referred to as **slow-wave sleep.** Your body is relaxed, activity in various parts of your brain has decreased, and you are hard to awaken. After 20 to 30 minutes of stage 4 sleep, your EEG pattern changes as you go "back through" stages 3 and 2, spending a little time in each. Overall, within 60 to 90 minutes of going to sleep, you will have completed a cycle of stages 1-2-3-4-3-2. At this point, a remarkably different sleep stage ensues.

REM Sleep

In 1953, sleep researchers Eugene Aserinsky and Nathaniel Kleitman of the University of Chicago struck scientific gold: They identified a sleep stage unlike the rest. Every half minute or so, bursts of muscular activity caused the sleepers' eyeballs to vigorously move back and forth beneath their closed eyelids. Because of these *rapid eye movements* (REMs), this stage was called **REM sleep.** When Aserinsky and Kleitman awakened sleepers from REM periods, they discovered that a dream was almost always reported. Even people who swore they "never had dreams" recalled them when awakened during REM. At last, science had a window through which to examine dreaming more closely. Wait for a REM period, awaken the sleeper, and catch a dream.

During REM sleep physiological arousal may increase to daytime levels. Heart rate quickens, breathing becomes more rapid and irregular, and brain-wave activity resembles that of active wakefulness. Men have penile erections and women experience vaginal lubrication. Because most dreams do not have sexual content, this REM-induced genital arousal is *not* a response to sexual imagery.

The brain also sends signals, making it more difficult for voluntary muscles to contract. As a result, muscles in the arms, legs, and torso lose tone and become relaxed. These muscles may twitch, but in effect you are "paralyzed" and unable to move. This state is called *REM sleep paralysis,* and because of it REM sleep is sometimes called *paradoxical sleep:* Your body is highly aroused, yet it looks like you are sleeping peacefully because there is so little movement.

REM sleep is often thought to be the only sleep stage in which we dream or even experience mental activity, but that is not correct. We also experience mental activity during non-REM sleep. REM dreams have their well-known storylike quality, with vivid sensory and motor elements and the perception of reality. When you are in a REM dream, you have the experience of sensing people, objects and places, of moving and behaving, of witnessing and participating in a series of real, if bizarre, events. When subjects are awakened from non-REM sleep, they often will report some type of mental activity (Foulkes, 1985). The non-REM dream is shorter than a REM dream (Stickgold et al., 1994). The non-REM dream is also less storylike, lacking the vivid sensory and motor experiences of a REM dream. The non-REM dream is often fixed and unmoving, resembling a tableau more than a story with a plot. Apart from non-REM dreams, mental activity that occurs during non-REM sleep also may resemble daytime thoughts, although in comparison to waking thoughts they are simple and jumbled. Indeed, some of the mental activity that occurs during non-REM sleep has even been referred to as *sleep thoughts* because of the closer resemblance to daytime thinking than to REM dreams (Foulkes, 1985).

Each cycle through the sleep stages takes about 90 minutes. Figure 6.12 shows that, as the hours pass, stage 4 and stage 3 drop out and REM periods become longer.

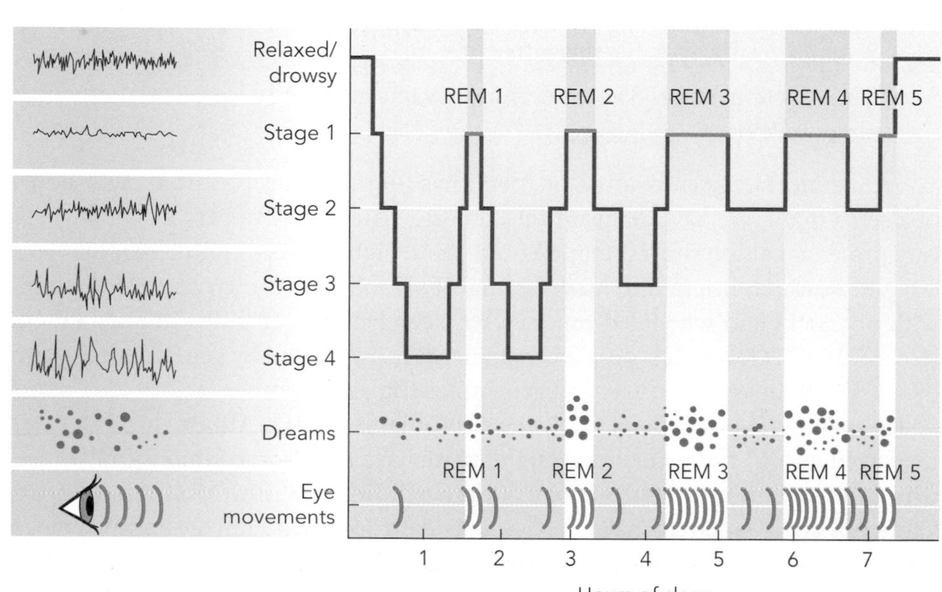

FIGURE 6.12

This graph shows a record of a night's sleep. The REM stages are shown in blue. People typically average four to five REM periods during the night, and these tend to become longer as the night wears on.

Getting a Night's Sleep: Brain and Environment

14. What brain areas help regulate sleep onset and REM sleep?

The brain steers our nightly passage into and through sleep, but it does not contain a single "sleep centre." Different aspects of the sleep cycle, such as falling asleep, REM sleep, and slow-wave sleep, are controlled by different brain mechanisms. Moreover, falling asleep is not just a matter of "turning off" the brain systems that regulate wakefulness. There are separate systems that "turn on" and actively promote sleep.

Areas at the base of the forebrain (called the *basal forebrain*) and within the brain stem are particularly important in regulating our falling asleep (McGinty & Sterman, 1968; Szymusiak, 1995). A different brain stem area—where the reticular formation passes through the pons—plays a key role in initiating REM sleep (Hobson et al., 1998). This region contains "REM-sleep On" neurons that periodically activate other brain systems, each of which controls a different aspect of REM sleep, such as the eye movements, muscular paralysis, and genital arousal.

Sleep is biologically regulated, but the environment plays a role as well. The change of seasons affects sleep; in fall and winter, most people sleep about 15 to 60 minutes longer per night (Campbell, 1993). Shiftwork, jet lag, stress at work and school, and nighttime noise can decrease sleep quality (Bronzaft et al., 1998). In fact, although many people report sleeping well in noisy environments, experiments reveal that noise affects us even while we sleep through it. Noise may increase our arousal and heart rate, decrease time in deep slow-wave sleep, and increase our time in less restful light sleep (Pollak, 1991).

How Much Do We Sleep?

15. How do sleep patterns change as we age?

The question seems simple enough, as does the answer for many of us: not enough! In reality, the issue is complex. Figure 6.13 reveals that there are substantial differences in how much people sleep at various ages. Newborn infants average 16 hours of sleep a day, and almost half of their sleep time is in REM. But as we age, three important changes occur:

- We sleep less. On average, 15- to 24-year-olds average 8½ hours of sleep per day, and elderly adults average just under 6 hours.
- REM sleep decreases dramatically during infancy and early childhood, but remains relatively stable thereafter.
- Time spent in stages 3 and 4 declines. By late adulthood we get relatively little slow-wave sleep.

A parent, caregiver, relative, or friend has told you that you need eight hours of sleep a night. We have all heard this, but is it true? Many researchers and health care professionals do suggest that we need about eight hours of uninterrupted sleep a night. Research has found, however, that if we follow our own natural rhythms, with no clocks and scheduled routines, we sleep between 10 and 12 hours a night (Coren, 1996). How much sleep a person needs is influenced by genetic factors, and by work schedules, stress, age, and general health, among other factors (de Castro, 2002; Heath, 1990; Partinen et al., 1983; Williams, 2001). Although most of us may need 8 to 10 hours of sleep a night, there have been some famous individuals who functioned well on surprisingly little sleep: British Prime Ministers Winston Churchill and Margaret Thatcher, U.S. President John F. Kennedy, and Napoleon Bonaparte all reportedly slept between 3 and 5.5 hours a night (Sharkley, 1993).

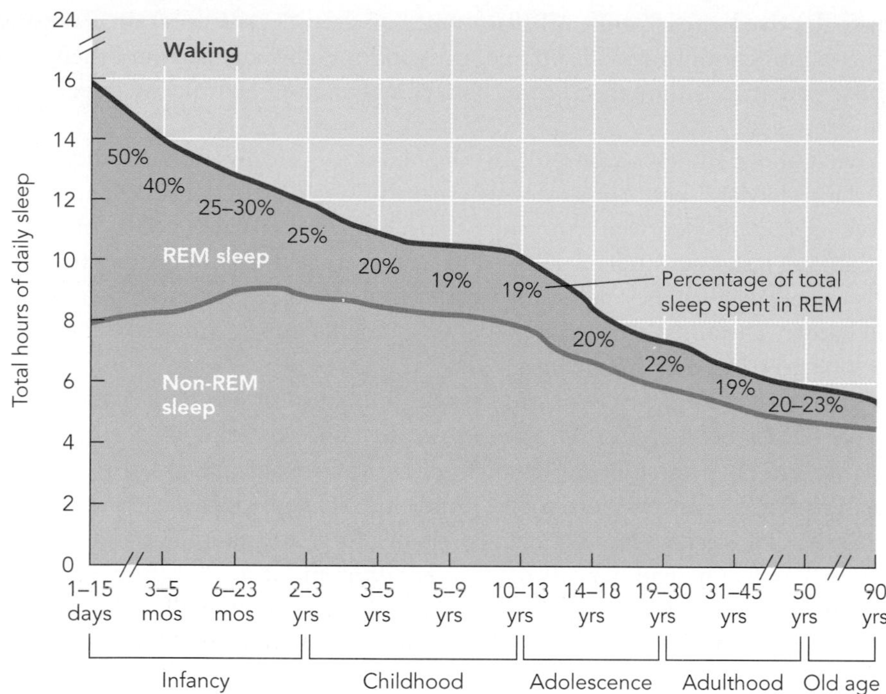

FIGURE 6.13

The percentage of sleep time in REM and non-REM sleep changes with age. Average daily sleep time decreases over the lifespan, and most of the decrease in non-REM sleep is due to decreasing delta sleep (stages 3 and 4). REM sleep time decreases throughout childhood and then is relatively stable through adulthood.

Data from Hartmann, 1977.

Whether we need 8 or 10 hours of sleep a night, how much time do we actually spend sleeping? According to Statistics Canada, men in Canada sleep an average of 8.0 hours a night while women get slightly more sleep, averaging 8.2 hours a night (Williams, 2001). These figures, however, conceal large individual differences. Although we average about 8 hours of sleep a night, 15 percent of Canadians 15 years old and older sleep less than 6.5 hours a night (Williams, 2001). We will also sacrifice our sleep when we are busy; almost half of us (48% of men and 45% of women) cut back on sleep when pressed for time (Williams, 2001).

Sleep Deprivation

16. How do different types of sleep deprivation affect mood and performance?

Sleep deprivation is a way of life for many university students, and they are not alone. Almost half of North Americans sacrifice some sleep to accomplish more work (National Sleep Foundation, 2000). Millions more lose sleep due to disorders.

Psychologists study sleep deprivation for its practical significance and to gain insight into why we need to sleep. June Pilcher and Allen Huffcutt (1996) of Bradley University meta-analyzed 19 sleep deprivation studies in which participants underwent either *short-term total sleep deprivation* (up to 45 hours without sleep), *long-term total sleep deprivation* (more than 45 hours without sleep), or *partial deprivation* (being allowed to sleep no more than five hours per night for one or more consecutive nights). Participants' self-reported mood (e.g., irritability, disorientation) and responses on mental tasks (e.g., ability to concentrate, logical reasoning, word memory) and physical tasks (e.g., manual dexterity, treadmill walking) were measured.

What would you predict? Would all types of deprivation affect behaviour, and which behaviours would be affected the most? Combining across the different types of deprivation and behaviour, the results were remarkable: The "average" sleep-deprived person functioned only as well as someone in the bottom 9 percent of non-deprived participants. All three types of sleep deprivation had a negative impact on functioning. Mood suffered most, followed by cognitive and then physical performance, although *all three* behaviours showed significant impairment from sleep loss.

What about students who pull all-nighters or drastically cut back their sleep, and claim they still perform as well as ever? Pilcher & Walters (1997) found that university students deprived of one night's sleep performed more poorly on a critical-thinking task than students allowed to sleep. Yet sleep-deprived students incorrectly perceived that they performed better and felt that they concentrated and tried harder. The authors concluded that the students underestimated the negative effects of sleep loss on performance.

Most total sleep deprivation studies with humans last less than five days, but 17-year-old Randy Gardner set a world record (since broken) by staying awake for 11 days as his project for a 1964 high school science fair in San Diego. Grateful sleep researchers received permission to study him (Gulevisch et al., 1966). At times during the first few days Randy became irritable, forgetful, nauseous, and intensely tired. By day five he had periods of disorientation and distorted thinking. In the last four days he developed finger tremors and slurred speech. Still, in his final day without sleep he beat sleep researcher William Dement 100 consecutive times at a pinball-type game.

When Randy finally went to bed, he slept almost 15 hours the first night, and then returned to his normal amount of sleep within a week. In general, it takes several nights to recover from extended total sleep deprivation, and we do not make up all the sleep time that we have lost.

Why Do We Sleep?

17. Explain the restoration and evolutionary theories of sleep.

Given that we spend almost a third of our lives sleeping, it must serve an important purpose. According to the **restoration model**, sleep recharges our run-down bodies and allows us to recover from physical and mental fatigue (Hess, 1965). Sleep deprivation and night shiftwork studies strongly support this view: We need sleep to function at our emotional, mental, and physical best. In fact, we may need sleep to live. Laboratory rats deprived of all sleep usually die within a few weeks, and scientists are trying to pinpoint the physiological causes (Constantine et al., 1996; Cirelli et al., 1999).

If the restoration model is correct, activities that increase daily wear on the body should increase sleep. Evidence is mildly supportive. A study of 18- to 26-year-old ultramarathon runners found that they slept much longer and spent a greater percentage of time in slow-wave sleep on the two nights following their 92-kilometre run (Shapiro et al., 1981). For the rest of us mere mortals, a meta-analysis of 38 studies found that we tend to sleep longer by only about 10 minutes on days we have exercised (Youngstedt et al., 1997).

The biggest challenge is determining exactly what it is that "gets restored" in our bodies while we sleep. Are vital chemicals depleted during the day and replenished at night? Does waking activity produce toxins that are purged during sleep? If so, how do these chemical changes regulate sleep? We do not have precise answers, but some researchers believe that a cellular waste product called *adenosine* may play a role (Mendelson, 2000; Rail, 1980). Like a car's exhaust emissions, adenosine is produced as cells consume fuel. As adenosine accumulates, it influences brain systems that decrease alertness and promote sleep, signalling the body to slow down because too much cellular fuel has been burned. Interestingly, caffeine has a molecular structure similar to adenosine's. It fits into adenosine receptor sites but doesn't stimulate them. This blocks the action of adenosine, prevents it from signalling the brain to "slow down," and increases alertness.

Evolutionary/circadian sleep models emphasize that sleep's main purpose is to increase a species' chances of survival in relation to its environmental demands (Webb, 1974). Our prehistoric ancestors had little to gain and much to lose by being active at night. Hunting, food gathering, and travelling were accomplished more easily and safely during daylight. Leaving the protection of one's shelter at night would have served little purpose other than to become dinner for nighttime predators.

In the course of evolution each species developed a circadian sleep-wake pattern that was adaptive in terms of whether it was predator or prey, its food requirements, and its methods of defence from attack. For small prey animals such as mice and squirrels, who reside in burrows or trees safely away from predators, spending a lot of time asleep is adaptive. For large prey animals such as horses, deer, and zebras, who sleep in relatively exposed environments and whose safety from predators depends on running away, spending a lot of time asleep would be hazardous. Sleep may have evolved also as a mechanism for conserving energy (Berger & Phillips, 1995; Horne, 1977). Our body's overall metabolic rate during sleep is about 10 to 25 percent slower than during waking rest (McGinty, 1993). The restoration and evolutionary theories highlight complementary functions of sleep, and both contribute to a two-factor model of why we sleep (Borbely, 1984; Webb, 1994).

Do specific sleep stages have special functions? To answer this question, imagine volunteering for a sleep deprivation study in which we awaken you only when you enter REM sleep; you can sleep through the other sleep stages. In this situation, two things will happen (beyond any unpleasant looks you may give us). First, on successive nights, we will have to awaken you more often, because your brain will be fighting back to get REM sleep (Figure 6.14a). Second, when the study ends, for the first few nights you probably will experience a *REM-rebound effect*, a tendency to increase the amount of REM sleep after being deprived of it (Figure 6.14b). REM-rebound occurs in many species, including humans (Rechtschaffen et al., 1999).

Results such as those shown in Figure 6.14 suggest that we need to have REM sleep. Several theories have proposed that REM sleep is vital for mental functioning, especially for processes related to learning and memory consolidation (Walker, 2005; Walker & Stickgold, 2006). As we saw earlier (see page 226), your brain is as active during REM sleep as it is during alert wakefulness. The high level of brain activity during REM sleep may help to strengthen the neural circuits involved in remembering important information from the preceding day (Maquet et al., 2000; Smith, 1996; Smith & Rose, 1997; Walker & Stickgold, 2006). Studies of REM sleep and learning among both humans (e.g., Maquet et al., 2000; Smith & Lapp, 1991) and animals (e.g., Smith & Rose, 1997) support the idea that REM sleep and learning are related, although exactly how REM sleep, memory, and learning are related is an ongoing area of research (see the Research Frontiers section in this chapter).

18. What evidence supports or contradicts the hypothesis that REM sleep serves a special function?

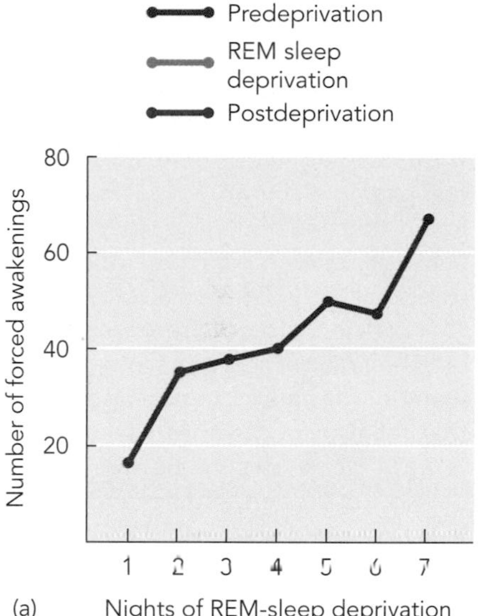

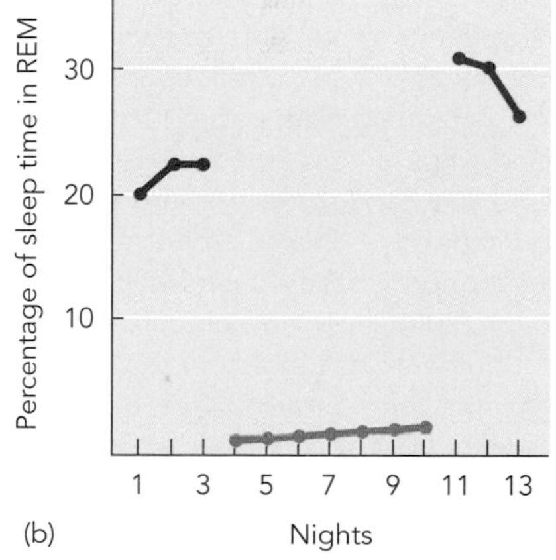

FIGURE 6.14

(a) In REM-sleep deprivation studies, participants start to go into REM periods more times with each passing night, as the brain tries to get REM sleep. (b) After REM deprivation ends, the sleeper spends more time than usual in REM sleep for a few nights. This is the REM-rebound effect.

Data from Agnew & Webb, 1967.

Sleep Disorders

The mechanisms involved in sleep are complex and can go wrong in a variety of ways. A staggering one-half to two-thirds of North American adults feel that they have some type of sleep problem (National Sleep Foundation, 2000).

RESEARCH FRONTIERS

To Sleep, To Dream, Perchance to Learn

More than two hundred years ago, David Hartley suggested that dreaming might alter the strength of associations within the brain, and hence affect memory (Walker & Stickgold, 2006). Early in the twentieth century researchers began to test theories of memory and found that memory performance was better following a night of sleep than after the same amount of time awake (Walker, 2005; Walker & Stickgold, 2006). These early researchers, however, concluded that sleep itself did not facilitate memory; they argued that the benefit of a night's sleep came only from the fact that sleep provides a period free from distractions that interfere with memory formation. Interest in a specific role for sleep in learning and memory was rekindled with a series of research findings in the 1990s. For example, David Koulack of the University of Manitoba found that four hours of sleep improved the performance of university students on a memory task more than four hours of waking activity did (Koulack, 1997).

Carlyle Smith, of Trent University in Peterborough, is one of the leading researchers into the role of sleep in learning and memory formation. In an important early study, Smith found that following Christmas examinations there was an increase in REM sleep and in the number of rapid eye movements during REM sleep among university seniors as compared to baseline measures from the same subjects and control subjects (Smith & Lapp, 1991). In a more recent study, Carlyle Smith and colleagues studied changes in REM sleep after subjects were trained in two different tasks, a mirror tracing task and the Towers of Hanoi puzzle. In the mirror tracing task participants trace different shapes while being able to see their hand only as a reflection in a mirror. To solve the Towers of Hanoi puzzle, participants must move a set of different sized rings across three pegs following a strict set of rules (e.g., you cannot place a large ring on top of a smaller ring, you can move only one ring at a time; see p. 372 for a fuller description of the Towers of Hanoi puzzle) (Smith, Nixon & Nader, 2004). Control subjects spent the evenings in the sleep lab, but were not exposed to these two tasks. Performance in both the mirror tracing task and the Towers of Hanoi puzzle are expected to improve with practice and participants did indeed show improvements when tested the day after training. For example, the number of errors in the mirror tracing task dropped by approximately half on the retest.

Participants who learned the tasks showed an increase in the number of rapid eye movements during REM sleep after training as compared to their baseline night (see Figure 6-15a). Control subjects did not show any change in the number of eye movements across nights. There was also a change in what is called REM density, the total number of eye movements divided by the total amount of time spent in REM sleep. As compared to the baseline night, subjects who received training in the two tasks showed an increase in REM density but control subjects did not. There was also a significant positive correlation between REM density on the post-training night and the degree of improvement in performing each task; participants who showed the best learning also showed the largest changes in their REM sleep. That is, several measures of REM sleep increased following learning, and there was a significant positive relationship between how much REM sleep changed and how well subjects learned. The total amount of time in REM sleep did not change in this study, although this has been reported in some other research (Smith & Lapp, 1991; Walker, 2005; Walker & Stickgold, 2006).

If REM sleep does change with learning, one might expect that selectively depriving someone of REM sleep might interfere with learning. Although not always reported, a number of studies have found poor learning after REM deprivation, even when retesting is delayed until well after recovery from the period of deprivation. Using human participants, a classic study by Karni et al. (1994) found that REM deprivation prevented the expected improvement in performance when subjects were tested the day after training. The participants in this study were given training in a perceptual task in which they were to identify the shape of a small target against a background with a similar texture. For example, subjects had to find three small diagonal lines against a background of horizontal lines of the same length and thickness. After practising this task, subjects were allowed a normal night sleep, deprived of REM sleep, or deprived of deep sleep (stages 3 and 4 sleep). Subjects who had normal sleep showed an improvement in their performance when tested the next day, as did subjects who were deprived of deep sleep. REM sleep deprivation, however, prevented this improvement in performance (see Figure 6-15b).

If REM sleep is involved in learning and memory, what is it about REM sleep that is important? Research using both animals and humans has compared brain activity during initial learning experiences and brain activity during different sleep stages. In rats, patterns of neuronal activity that occurred during waking, active exploration reappeared during subsequent sleep. In humans, imaging studies have found that patterns of brain activity seen during daytime training are repeated during subsequent periods of REM sleep (Maquet et al., 2000; Walker, 2005; Walker & Stickgold, 2006). During sleep the brain appears to "replay" the same pattern of activity that was elicited during the earlier waking practice. Furthermore, the extent of learning during daytime practice is correlated with the amount of reactivation during REM sleep (Peigneux

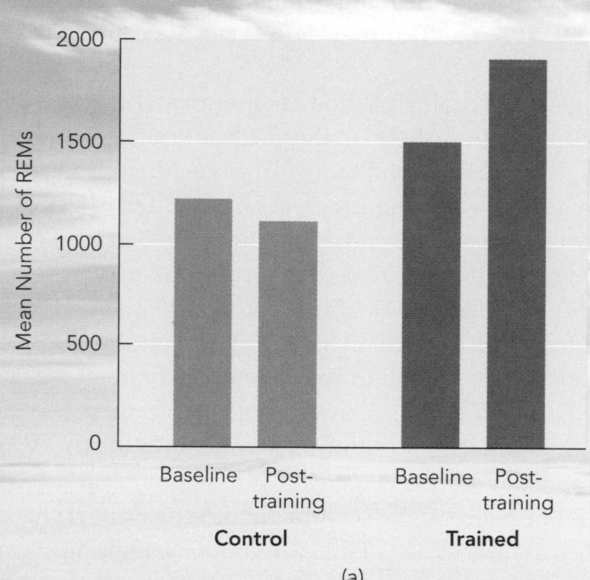

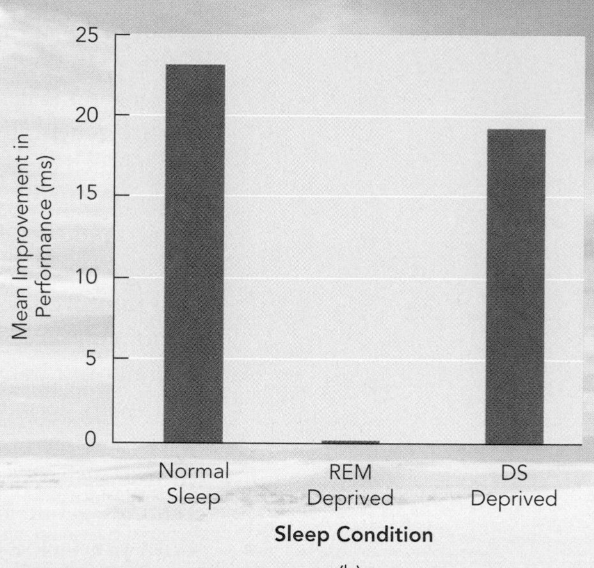

FIGURE 6.15

(a) The mean number of rapid eye movements (REMs) during REM sleep on the night prior to training in the mirror tracing and Towers of Hanoi puzzle tasks (Baseline) and during the night after training (Post-training). Subjects who had practised these tasks (Trained) showed a significant increase in the number of rapid eye movements, whereas subjects engaged in control activities (Control) did not. Adapted from Smith et al., 2004. (b) The results of the study by Karni et al. (1994) showing improvements in a perceptual task when training and testing were separated by an uninterrupted night's sleep (Normal) or by a night with no deep sleep (stages 3 and 4 sleep; DS Deprived), but not after a night during which subjects were selectively deprived of REM sleep (REM Deprived). Adapted from Karni et al., 1994.

et al., 2003). Although a number of studies have found this relationship between learning and REM sleep changes and similar patterns of brain activity during learning and during REM sleep, some studies have found a relationship between learning and slow-wave sleep, rather than REM sleep (Peigneux et al., 2004). Why the results of many studies indicate a relationship between memory formation and REM sleep, while some indicate a relationship to slow-wave sleep is not clear. The discrepancy may relate to the specific types of stimuli used, the specific memory processes involved, or to some other set of methodological factors.

Recent research findings present convincing evidence that sleep is intimately involved in learning and memory, although we do not yet fully understand which sleep stages are involved with which types of learning and memory. REM sleep is clearly important for at least some forms of learning and memory, while some evidence suggests that stage 2 sleep or stages 3 and 4 sleep may be necessary for other types of memory formation (Walker, 2005; Walker & Stickgold, 2006). There is much to discover in this rapidly developing area of research, but one thing is very clear: if you want to optimize learning and memory formation, you need to get a good night's sleep.

Insomnia

19. What is insomnia and how is it treated?

True or False: Someone who falls asleep easily can still have insomnia. The statement is true, because **insomnia** refers to chronic difficulty in falling asleep, staying asleep, or experiencing restful sleep. Trouble falling asleep is most common among young adults, and difficulty staying asleep is most common among older adults. If you occasionally have trouble getting a good night's sleep, don't worry: almost everyone does. True insomniacs' sleep troubles are frequent and persistent.

Insomnia is the most common sleep disorder, experienced by approximately 10 to 40 percent of the population of various countries. Many insomniacs overestimate how much sleep they lose and how long it takes them to fall asleep: 20 minutes may seem like an hour. Certain people, called *pseudoinsomniacs,* complain of insomnia, but sleep normally when examined in the laboratory (Schneider, 1985).

Despite a sound night of sleep, some pseudoinsomniacs awaken in the morning and claim that their insomnia was so bad that they didn't get any sleep at all (McCall & Edinger, 1992)!

Insomnia has biological, psychological, and environmental causes. Some people are genetically predisposed to insomnia, and medical conditions, mental disorders such as anxiety and depression, and many drugs can disrupt sleep (Lydic & Biebuyck, 1989). So can general worrying, stress at home and work, poor lifestyle habits, and circadian disruptions such as jet lag and night shiftwork.

Psychologists have pioneered many non-drug treatments to reduce insomnia and improve sleep quality (Bootzin, 1979; Haynes et al., 1975; Lacks, 1983). One treatment, called *stimulus control,* is based on learning principles. It involves conditioning your body to associate the stimuli in your sleep environment (such as your bed) with sleep, rather than with waking activities and sleeplessness. For example, if you are having sleep difficulties, do not study, do homework, watch TV, or snack in your bedroom. Use your bed only for sleeping. If you cannot fall asleep within 10 minutes, get up and leave the bedroom for a period of time. Do something relaxing until you feel sleepy, then return to bed. Table 6.1 contains additional guidelines from sleep experts for reducing insomnia and achieving better sleep (Bootzin & Rider, 1997; Hryshko et al., 2000).

Narcolepsy

Some people suffer not from an inability to sleep, but from an inability to stay awake. **Narcolepsy** involves extreme daytime sleepiness and sudden, uncontrollable sleep attacks that may last from less than a minute to an hour. No matter how much narcoleptics rest at night, sleep attacks may occur at any time. About 1 out of every 1,000 people is narcoleptic (Mignot, 1998).

When a sleep attack occurs, narcoleptics may go right into a REM stage, and some have intense, dreamlike visual images and sounds (Parkes et al., 1995). Narcoleptics also may experience attacks of cataplexy, a sudden loss of muscle tone often triggered by laughter, excitement, and other strong emotions. In severe cases, the

TABLE 6.1 How to Improve the Quality of Your Sleep

- Maintain a regular sleep-wake pattern to establish a stable circadian rhythm.
- Get the amount of sleep you need during the week and avoid sleeping in on weekends, since doing so will disrupt your sleep rhythm. Even if you sleep poorly or not at all one night, try to maintain your regular schedule the next.
- If you have trouble falling asleep at night, then avoid napping if possible. Evening naps should be avoided especially because they will make you less sleepy when you go to bed.
- Do not eat a lot before going to sleep. If you must eat something, have a light snack, and preferably one that contains L-tryptophan. L-tryptophan is an amino acid that helps the brain produce serotonin, and it can have a sedating effect. It is found in milk and other dairy foods.
- Avoid stimulants. This includes not just tobacco products and coffee, but also soft drinks and chocolate (sorry), both of which contain caffeine. It can take the body four to five hours to reduce the amount of caffeine in the bloodstream by 50 percent.
- Avoid alcohol and sleeping pills. As a depressant, alcohol may make it easier to go to sleep, but it disrupts the sleep cycle and interferes with REM sleep. Sleeping pills also impair REM sleep and constant use can lead to dependence and insomnia.
- Try to go to bed in a relaxed state. Muscular relaxation techniques and meditation can reduce tension, remove worrisome thoughts, and help induce sleep.
- Avoid physical exercise before bedtime because it is too stimulating. If you are unable to fall asleep, do not use exercise to try and wear yourself out.
- If you are having sleep difficulties, avoid performing non-sleep activities in your bedroom. This will condition your body to associate bedroom stimuli with sleep.

Sleep experts recommend a variety of procedures to reduce insomnia and improve the general quality of sleep (Bootzin & Rider, 1997; Hauri, 1997; Hryshko et al., 2000; Lundh, 1998).

knees buckle and the person collapses, conscious but unable to move for anywhere from a few seconds to a few minutes. Cataplexy is an abnormal version of the normal muscular paralysis that takes place during nighttime REM sleep, and many experts view narcolepsy as a disorder in which REM sleep intrudes into waking consciousness.

Narcolepsy can be devastating. Narcoleptics may be discriminated against when seeking jobs and mistakenly viewed as lazy at work (Kryger et al., 2002). They report a lowered quality of life and are more prone to accidents. In a large study, 75 percent of narcoleptics reported falling asleep while driving, in contrast to 12 percent of the non-narcoleptic comparison group (Cohen et al., 1992).

What causes narcolepsy? In humans, if one identical twin is narcoleptic, the other twin has a 30 percent chance of developing it (Mignot, 1998). Narcolepsy also can be selectively bred in dogs (Figure 6.16). Thus, experts believe that a genetic predisposition combines with still unknown environmental factors to cause narcolepsy (Stanford Center for Narcolepsy, 2000). At present there is no cure, but stimulant drugs often reduce daytime sleepiness, and antidepressant drugs (which suppress REM sleep) can decrease attacks of cataplexy (Fry, 1998). Daytime naps help some narcoleptics feel more alert, but their positive effects last for only a few hours.

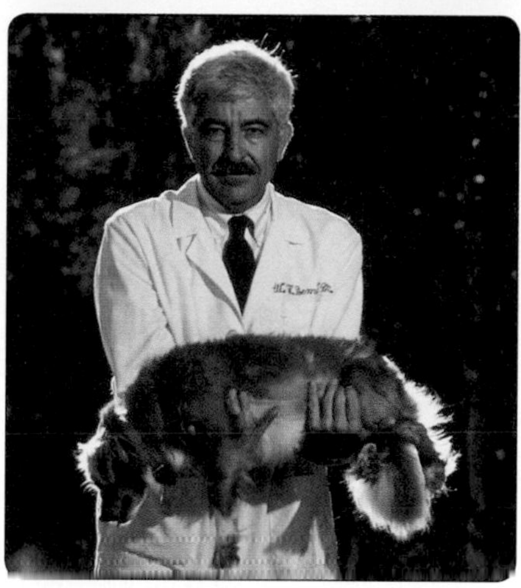

FIGURE 6.16

This dog lapses suddenly from alert wakefulness into a limp sleep while being held by sleep researcher William Dement. Narcolepsy occurs naturally in some dogs, and, by using selective breeding, researchers at Stanford's Sleep Disorders Center have established a colony of narcoleptic canines.

REM-Sleep Behaviour Disorder

Kaku Kimura and his colleagues in Japan (1997) report the case of a 72-year-old woman who, during a night's observation in a sleep laboratory, repeatedly talked, sang, and moved her hands and legs during REM sleep. One singing episode lasted three minutes. She was experiencing **REM-sleep behaviour disorder (RBD)**, in which the loss of muscle tone that causes normal REM sleep paralysis is absent (Olson et al., 2000; Paprrigopoulos, 2005). If awakened, RBD patients often report dream content that matches their behaviour, as if they were acting out their dreams (Dyken et al., 1995). Unfortunately, the consequences of RBD can be severe:

> . . . a 67-year-old man . . . was awakened one night by his wife's yelling as he was choking her. He was dreaming of breaking the neck of a deer he had just knocked down. This patient had tied himself to his bed with a rope at night for 6 years as a protective measure, owing to repeated episodes of jumping from the bed and colliding with furniture and walls. (Schenck et al., 1989, p. 1169)

RBD sleepers may kick violently, throw punches, or get out of bed and move about wildly, leaving the bedroom in a shambles. Many RBD patients seen in sleep clinics have injured themselves while sleeping, and almost half have injured their sleeping partners (Schenck, 1993). Some researchers propose that brain abnormalities may prevent signals that normally inhibit movement during REM from being sent, but at present the causes of RBD are unknown (Zambelis et al., 2002).

20. Describe the major symptoms of narcolepsy and RBD.

Sleepwalking

Sleepwalking typically occurs during a stage 3 or stage 4 period of slow-wave sleep (Guilleminault et al., 2001). Sleepwalkers often have blank stares, are unresponsive to other people, but seem vaguely conscious of the environment as they navigate around furniture, go to the bathroom, or find something to eat. Sleepwalkers often return to bed and awaken in the morning with no memory of the event. About 10 to 30 percent of children sleepwalk at least once, but less than 5 percent of adults do. If you did not sleepwalk as a child, the odds are less than one percent that you will do so as an adult (Hublin et al., 1997). Sleepwalkers can injure themselves accidentally, such as by falling down stairs or wandering out of their home.

A tendency to sleepwalk may be inherited, and daytime stress, alcohol, and certain illnesses and medications also increase sleepwalking (Hublin et al., 2001). Various treatments may be used, including psychotherapy, hypnosis, drugs, and routinely awakening children before the time they typically sleepwalk (Frank et al., 1997). But the most common "treatment" simply is to wait for children to outgrow it while creating a safe home environment so that the sleepwalker does not get injured. Contrary to common belief, awakening sleepwalkers is not harmful, although they may be confused for a few minutes.

Nightmares and Night Terrors

Nightmares are frightening dreams, and virtually everyone has them. Like all dreams, they occur more often during REM sleep and in the hours before we arise. Physiological arousal during nightmares is similar to levels experienced during pleasant dreams.

21. Identify the major differences between nightmares and night terrors.

Night terrors (also called "sleep terrors") are more intense than nightmares. The sleeper, usually a child, suddenly sits up and seems to awaken, letting out a blood-curdling scream. Terrified and aroused to a near-panic state, the person might thrash about in bed or flee to another room, as if trying to escape from something. Come morning, the person often has no memory of the episode. If brought to full consciousness during an episode—which is hard to do—the person may report images or a vague sense of having been choked, crushed, attacked, or exposed to some other type of danger (Fisher et al., 1974).

Unlike nightmares, night terrors are most common during deep sleep (stages 3 and 4) and involve greatly elevated physiological arousal; heart rate may double or triple. Up to six percent of children, but only one or two percent of adults, experience night terrors (Ohayon et al., 1999). In most childhood cases, treatment is simply to wait for the night terrors to diminish with age.

The Nature of Dreams

Traditional aboriginal peoples of Australia speak of The Dreaming. They view dreaming as a "parallel reality" connecting them to the spiritual world and a collective unconscious linked to their ancestral past (Dawson, 1993). The Dreaming involves stories of creation and beliefs that are passed on orally to educate each successive generation, and it defines their personal and cultural identities. Dreams also are a central guiding force in other cultures, such as the Senoi of Malaysia, who believe that events in dreaming and waking life influence one another (Greenleaf, 1973).

Although Western societies attach less importance to dreams than do many cultures, dreams remain a source of endless curiosity. Some Westerners view them as symbolic and informative, and dreams have long been the subject of art, literature, theatre, and cinema. Psychologists study dreaming not only to learn about consciousness, but also because dreaming is a universal mental activity among humans (Foulkes, 1996).

When Do We Dream?

Mental activity occurs throughout the sleep cycle. When Jason Rowley and his colleagues (1998) awakened sleepers merely 45 seconds after sleep onset, participants reported visual images about 25 percent of the time. As this *hypnagogic state* (the transitional state from wakefulness through early stage 2 sleep) continued, mental activity became more dreamlike (Figure 6.17). In general, between 15 to 40 percent of sleepers report dreamlike activity when awakened within six minutes of falling asleep.

22. When do we dream the most? Why?

Research shows that we dream most when the brain is most active (Antrobus, 1991, 1995). Brain activity is higher during REM sleep than non-REM sleep, and we dream more during REM. When awakened from REM sleep, people report a dream about 80 percent, versus 15 to 50 percent of the time for non-REM sleep (Dement, 1978; Foulkes, 1962; Rowley et al., 1998). Brain activity also is higher in the final hours of sleep than it is during the earlier hours, thanks to our circadian sleep-wake cycle preparing us to rise for a new day. Thus we dream more in the last few hours of both REM and non-REM sleep than during the same stages earlier in the night.

What Do We Dream About?

Much of our knowledge about dream content derives from 35 years of research using a coding system developed by Calvin Hall and Robert Van de Castle (1966). Analyzing 1,000 dream reports (mostly from university students), they found that dreams are not nearly as strange as they are stereotyped to be. Most take place in familiar settings and often involve people we know. Certainly, some dreams are bizarre, but they often leave a lasting impression that biases our perception of what most dreams are like. As a case in point, have you ever dreamt that you were flying (under your own power, without a plane!)? Between a third and a half of university students say they have. Yet a study of 635 actual dream reports found only one dream that included flying (Snyder, 1970). This suggests that dreams about flying are quite *un*common, but because they are so striking many people can recall having such a dream at least once.

Given the stereotype of "blissful dreaming," it may surprise you that most dreams contain some negative content (Domhoff, 1999). Hall and Van de Castle (1966) found that 80 percent of dream reports involved negative emotions, almost half contained aggressive acts, and a third involved some type of misfortune. They also found that women dreamt almost equally about male and female characters, whereas about two-thirds of men's dream characters were male. Although the reason for this gender difference is not clear, a similar pattern has been found across several cultures and among teenagers and preadolescents (Avila-White et al., 1999; Hall, 1984).

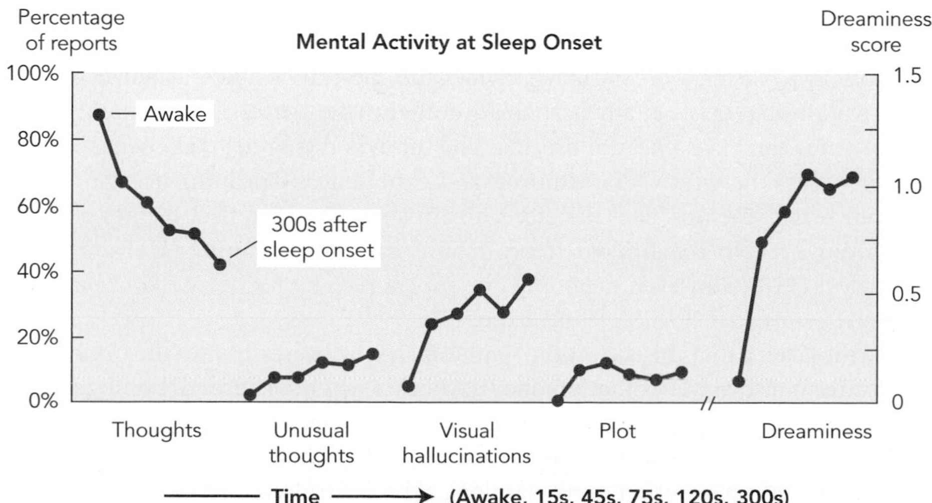

FIGURE 6.17

The mental activity of 11 male and female undergraduates was measured by self-report while awake and then 15, 45, 75, 120, and 300 seconds after sleep onset. Students slept at home, were awakened by computer, and the time of awakenings varied across different nights. In total, 477 reports of mental activity were collected. In general, after sleep onset normal "waking-type" thoughts decreased, unusual thoughts and visual hallucinations (images that seemed "real") increased, and mental activity was more "dreamy." Unlike many REM dreams, however, mental activity after sleep onset rarely had a plot (e.g., a "storyline").

Adapted from Rowley et al., 1998.

Our cultural background, life experiences, and current concerns shape dream content. For example, Palestinian children living in violent regions of the Gaza Strip dream about persecution and aggression more often than their peers living in non-violent areas (Punamaeki & Joustie, 1998). Pregnant women have dreams with many pregnancy themes. Overall, it appears that up to 50 percent of our dreams contain some content reflecting the experiences of our most recent day (Botman & Crovitz, 1992; Harlow & Roll, 1992).

Why Do We Dream?

23. According to the Freudian and activation-synthesis theories, why do we dream?

Speculation about why we dream and whether dreams have special meaning has intrigued humankind for ages. Most scientific dream theories arise from the psychoanalytic, physiological, and cognitive perspectives.

Freud's psychoanalytic theory. Sigmund Freud (1900/1953) believed that the main purpose of dreaming is **wish fulfillment**, the gratification of our unconscious desires and needs. These desires include sexual and aggressive urges that are too unacceptable to be consciously acknowledged and fulfilled in real life. Freud distinguished between a dream's *manifest content*—the "surface" story that the dreamer reports—and its *latent content,* which is its disguised psychological meaning. Thus a dream about being with a stranger on a train that goes through a tunnel (manifest content) might represent a hidden desire for sexual intercourse with a "forbidden" partner (latent content).

Although Freud sparked great interest in dreams and laid the groundwork for other dream theories, many contemporary researchers reject the postulates of his theory. They conclude, for example, that there is little evidence that dreams have disguised meaning or that their general purpose is to satisfy forbidden, unconscious needs and conflicts (Domhoff, 1999; Fisher & Greenberg, 1996). Dream analysis has been criticized as highly subjective: The same dream can be interpreted differently to fit the particular analyst's point of view.

Activation-synthesis theory. Is it possible that dreams serve no special purpose? In 1977, J. Allan Hobson and Robert McCarley proposed a physiological theory of dreaming. When we are awake, neural circuits in our brain are activated by sensory input—sights, sounds, tastes, and so on. The cerebral cortex interprets these patterns of neural activation, producing meaningful perceptions. According to the **activation-synthesis theory**, during REM sleep the brain stem bombards our higher brain centres with random neural activity (the *activation* component). Because we are asleep, this neural activity does not match any external sensory events, but our cerebral cortex continues to perform its job of interpretation. It does this by creating a dream that provides the "best fit" to the particular pattern of activation that exists at any particular moment (the *synthesis* component). This accounts for the bizarreness of dreams: The brain is trying to "make sense" out of *random* neural activity. Our memories and experiences can influence the stories that our brain develops, and, therefore, dream content may reflect themes pertaining to our lives. In this limited sense, dreams can have meaning (Hobson, 1988; McCarley, 1998). However, dreaming does not serve any particular *function*—it is merely *a by-product of REM neural activity.*

Critics claim that the activation-synthesis theory overestimates the bizarreness of dreams. It also assumes that unique REM brain activity causes dreaming, ignoring the fact that dreaming occurs during Non-REM sleep (Domhoff, 1999; Solms, 2002). Nevertheless, the theory has supporters and has helped revolutionize dream research by calling attention to a physiological basis for dreaming.

24. Describe the main assumption of cognitive-process dream theory. What evidence supports it?

Cognitive approaches. According to **problem-solving dream models**, dreams can help us find creative solutions to our problems and conflicts because they are not constrained by reality (Cartwright et al., 1977). Based on research with men and women undergoing divorce, Rosalind Cartwright (1991, p. 3) notes that those who dream "... with strong feelings, and who incorporate the stressor directly into their dreams, appear to 'work through' their depression more successfully than those who do not." But critics point out that, just because a problem shows up in a dream, this does not mean that the dream involved an attempt to solve it. We also may think about our dreams after awakening and obtain new insight, but this also is not the same as solving problems *while* dreaming (Squier & Domhoff, 1998).

Cognitive-process dream theories focus on the *process* of how we dream (Antrobus, 1991; Foulkes, 1982). Based on the modular model of consciousness, these theories propose that dreaming and waking thought are produced by the same mental systems in the brain. Consider that when three- and four-year-old children are awakened from REM sleep, they rarely report dreams, whereas eight- and nine-year-olds display some features of adult dreaming (Foulkes, 1982). Why should this be? According to David Foulkes (1999), it is because dreaming requires imagery skills and other cognitive abilities that young children have not yet developed sufficiently in waking life. As children's mental abilities develop with age, so does their ability to dream.

Research indicates far greater similarity between dreaming and waking mental activity than was traditionally believed (Domhoff, 1999). Consider that one reason many dreams appear bizarre is that their content shifts rapidly (Antrobus, 1991). "I was dreaming about an exam *and all of a sudden*, the next thing I knew, I was in Hawaii on the beach." (Don't we wish.) Yet if you reflect on the contents of your waking thoughts—your stream of consciousness—you will realize that they also shift suddenly. In fact, about half of REM dream reports involve rapid content shifts. But when people are awake and placed in the same environmental conditions as sleepers (a dark, quiet room), about 90 percent of their reports involve rapid content shifts (Antrobus, 1991). Thus, rapid shifting of attention is a *process* common to dreaming and waking mental activity.

Toward integration. Although there currently is no agreed-upon model of dreaming, some theorists have begun to integrate concepts from cognitive, biological, and modern psychodynamic perspectives. For example, John Antrobus (1991) has developed a model to explain how our sleeping brain creates dreams. As Figure 6.18 shows, it incorporates findings on sleep physiology with the cognitive principle of modular consciousness.

Seymour Epstein (1999) also views the unconscious mind as an information processor that weaves input from different brain modules into a coherent story while we dream. He de-emphasizes Freud's notion of wish fulfillment, but adopts the psychodynamic view that the unconscious mind involves emotional and motivational processes as well as cognitive ones. As Epstein (1999, p. 76) notes, in dreams these emotional themes may simply be "... extensions of everyday waking thought, rather than disguised expressions of ... unconscious conflict." Thus dreams are woven together by an unconscious mind that, in part, is emotionally driven. Notice that Antrobus's model in Figure 6.18 includes emotional modules.

Though in need of more testing, these integrative models may signal the future of dream theorizing. As we described earlier, evidence is growing rapidly that unconscious cognitive, emotional, and motivational processes influence our waking life. These models extend this view to sleeping mental life.

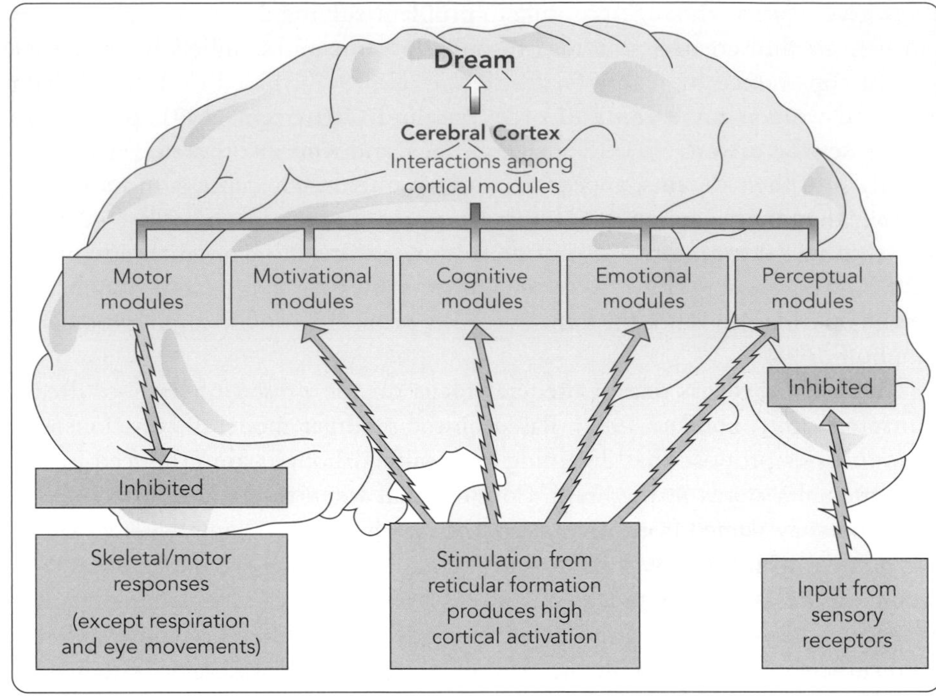

FIGURE 6.18

Antrobus's (1991) theory proposes that during REM sleep, the reticular formation stimulates various modules in the cortex. These modules interact, as they do during waking mental activity. The perceptual modules produce images that then are interpreted by the cognitive modules. Emotional modules may overlay an "emotional theme" to the dream, which stimulates the perceptual modules to produce additional images consistent with the theme. Because external sensory input is restricted, the brain attempts to provide the "best fit" interpretations of these internally generated images. Motor modules are active, but their output is blocked by REM muscular paralysis. This theory places greater emphasis than activation-synthesis theory on interactions between brain modules and proposes other mechanisms for Non-REM dreams.

25. Does daydreaming serve any function? How similar are daydreams and night dreams?

Daydreams and Waking Fantasies

Our dreams and fantasy lives are not restricted to the nocturnal realm. Daydreams are a significant part of waking consciousness, providing stimulation during periods of boredom and letting us experience positive emotions (Singer, 1997). In *The Secret Life of Walter Mitty,* author James Thurber portrayed Walter Mitty as a person who transformed his humdrum existence into an exhilarating fantasy world of adventure and personal fulfillment. Like the fictional Mitty, people who have a **fantasy-prone personality** often live in a vivid, rich fantasy world that they control. They constitute about two to four percent of the population, and most are female. In one study, about three-quarters of fantasy-prone people were able to achieve sexual orgasm merely by fantasizing about sexual activity, and all could experience fantasies "as real as real" in each of the five senses (Wilson & Barber, 1984).

Daydreams typically involve greater visual imagery than other forms of waking mental activity, but tend to be less vivid, emotional, and bizarre than nighttime dreams (Antonietti & Colombo, 1997; Kunzendorf et al., 1997). Their content often reflects personal concerns. In one study, university students listed their major daily issues and kept a daydream diary for two weeks. Nearly two-thirds of their daydreams focused on current concerns (Gold & Reilly, 1985–1986). There is also a surprising degree of similarity in the themes of daydreams and nighttime dreams, suggesting once again that nocturnal dreams may be an extension of daytime mental activity, sometimes reflecting current concerns in the person's life (Beck, 2002).

In Review

- *EEG measurements of brain activity indicate five main stages of sleep. Stages 1 and 2 are lighter sleep, and stages 3 and 4 are deeper, slow-wave sleep. High physiological arousal and periods of rapid eye movements characterize the fifth stage, REM sleep. Several brain regions, including the brain stem, regulate sleep.*

- *The amount we sleep nightly changes as we age. Genetic, psychological, and environmental factors affect our sleep patterns and sleep length.*
- *Sleep deprivation negatively affects mood, mental performance, and physical performance. The restoration model proposes that we sleep to recover from accumulated physical and mental fatigue. Evolutionary/circadian models state that species evolved unique waking-sleeping cycles that maximized their chances of survival.*
- *Insomnia is the most common sleep disorder, but less common disorders such as narcolepsy and REM-sleep behaviour disorder can have extremely serious consequences. Sleepwalking typically occurs during slow-wave sleep, whereas nightmares occur most often during REM sleep. Night terrors create a near-panic state of arousal, typically occur in slow-wave sleep, and are most common among children.*
- *Dreams occur throughout sleep but are most common during REM periods. Unpleasant dreams are common, and there are gender differences in dream content. Our cultural background, current concerns, and recent events influence what we dream about.*
- *Freud proposed that dreams fulfill unconscious wishes that show up in disguised form within our dreams. Activation-synthesis theory regards dreaming as the brain's attempt to "fit" a story to random neural activity. Cognitive-process theories emphasize that dreaming and waking thought are produced by the same mental systems.*
- *Daydreams and nocturnal dreams often share similar themes. People with fantasy-prone personalities have especially vivid daydreams.*

DRUGS AND ALTERED CONSCIOUSNESS

Like sleep and dreaming, drug-induced alterations in consciousness have mystified humans for ages. Three millennia ago the Aztecs considered hallucinogenic mushrooms to be a sacred substance for communicating with the spirit world (Diaz, 1997). Ancient peoples also attributed "magical" healing powers to drugs and used them recreationally for their mind-altering effects. Today, drugs are a cornerstone of medical practice and, as Figure 6.19 shows, psychoactive drugs are a pervasive part of social life. They alter consciousness by modifying brain chemistry, but drug effects also are influenced by psychological, environmental, and cultural factors (Stewart, 2002).

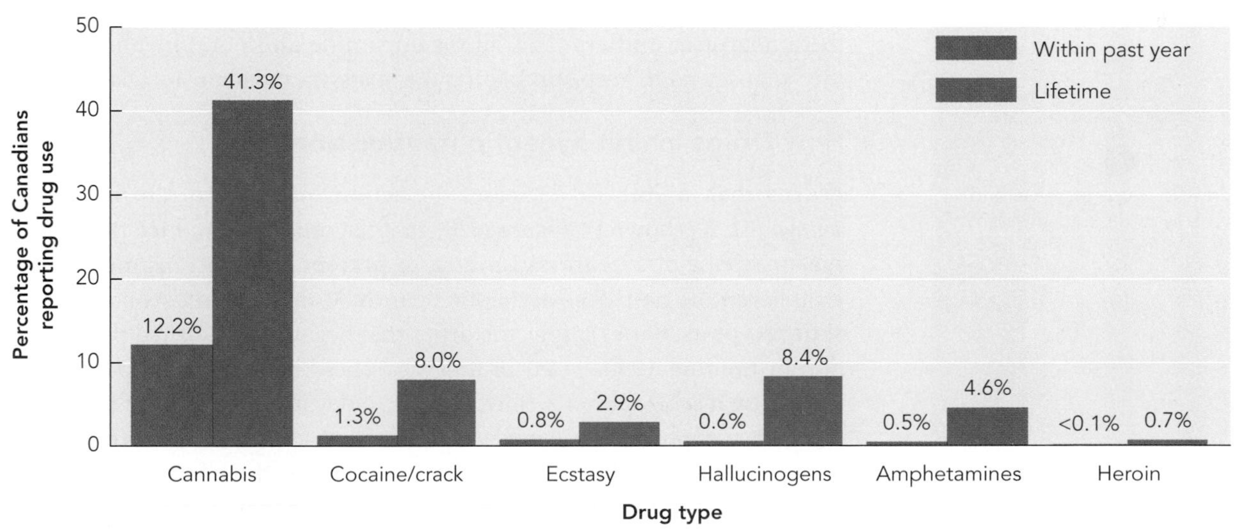

FIGURE 6.19

Past year and lifetime use of illicit drugs by Canadians ages 15 or older. The data include one-time use and are based on the Canadian Community Health Survey (CCHS).

Adapted from Tjepkema, 2004.

Drugs and the Brain

Like any cell, a neuron essentially is a fragile bag of chemicals, and it takes a delicate chemical balancing act for neurons to function properly. Drugs work their way into the bloodstream and are carried throughout the brain by an extensive network of small blood vessels, called *capillaries.* As we saw in Chapter 3, these capillaries contain a **blood-brain barrier**, a special lining of tightly packed cells that lets vital nutrients pass through so that neurons can function. The blood-brain barrier screens out many foreign substances, but some, including a variety of drugs, manage to pass through. Once inside, they alter consciousness by facilitating or inhibiting synaptic transmission (Heckers & Konradi, 2000; Julien, 2005).

Recall from Chapter 3 that synaptic transmission involves several basic steps. First, neurotransmitters are synthesized inside the presynaptic (sending) neuron and stored in vesicles. Next, neurotransmitters are released into the synapse, where they bind with and stimulate receptor sites on the postsynaptic (receiving) neuron. Finally, neurotransmitter molecules are deactivated by enzymes or by reuptake. Psychoactive drugs act by influencing one or more of these steps in synaptic transmission.

How Drugs Facilitate Synaptic Transmission

An *agonist* is a drug that increases the activity of a neurotransmitter. Figure 6.20 shows that an agonist may enhance the production, storage, or release of a neurotransmitter; activate the postsynaptic receptor (or make it easier for the neurotransmitter to stimulate their receptors); or prevent the neurotransmitter from being deactivated. Consider two examples. Opiates (such as morphine, codeine, or oxycodone) are effective pain relievers. Opiates have this action by binding to and activating receptors that normally receive endorphins, a neurotransmitter that plays a major role in pain relief. An example of a psychoactive drug that acts in different ways are the amphetamines. Amphetamines are powerful stimulants and they have this effect by amplifying the actions of the neurotransmitters dopamine and norepinephrine. Amphetamines cause neurons to release dopamine and norepinephrine, even if the neurons are not firing. Amphetamines also block the reuptake of these neurotransmitters. This allows dopamine and norepinephrine to remain in the synapse and to keep stimulating the postsynaptic neuron (Diaz, 1997).

26. How do drugs increase and decrease synaptic transmission?

How Drugs Inhibit Synaptic Transmission

A drug that inhibits or decreases the actions of a neurotransmitter is called an *antagonist.* As shown in Figure 6.20, an antagonist may reduce the synthesis, storage, or release of a neurotransmitter, or prevent a neurotransmitter from binding to its receptors on the postsynaptic neuron. Many antagonists act on the postsynaptic receptors. For example, the drugs that began the so-called psychiatric revolution of the mid-1950s acted in this way. These drugs, the antipsychotics, are still used to treat schizophrenia, one of the most devastating forms of psychosis (we will discuss schizophrenia in detail later in this book). Antipsychotics bind to dopamine receptors, but once bound they have no effect on the postsynaptic neuron. What they accomplish is that by occupying the receptor they prevent the neurotransmitter dopamine from binding and acting on the postsynaptic neuron. That is, with schizophrenia there is too much dopamine activity and if dopamine receptors are blocked by an antipsychotic, dopamine activity decreases towards normal levels and many of the symptoms of schizophrenia improve.

(a) **Synthesis, storage, release** (b) **Binding** (c) **Reuptake**

Agonistic drugs

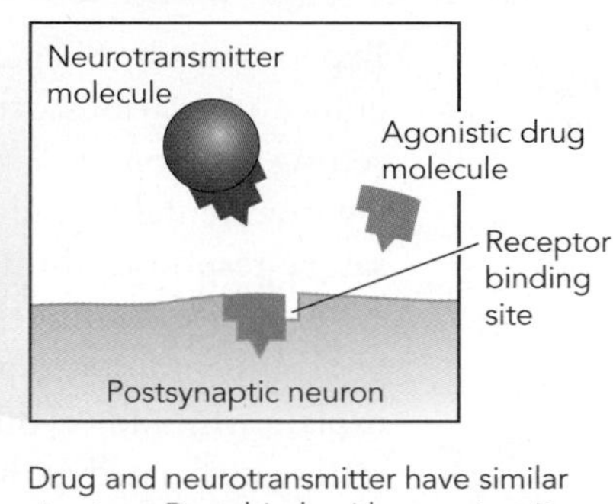

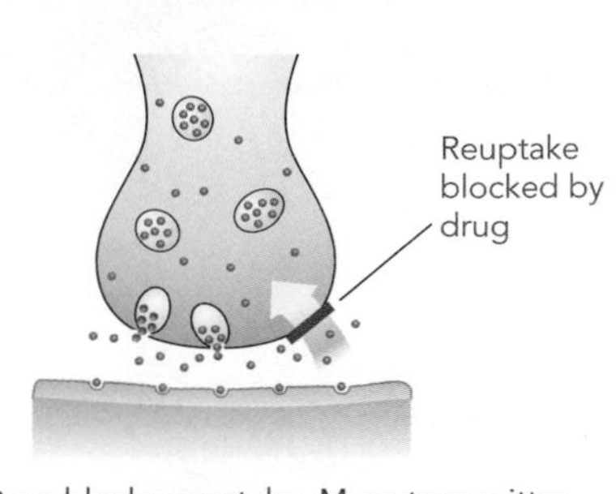

Drug causes neuron to synthesize more transmitter molecules, store them more safely, or release them.

Drug and neurotransmitter have similar structure. Drug binds with receptor site and activates it.

Drug blocks reuptake. More transmitter molecules remain in synapse, available to activate receptor sites.

Antagonistic drugs

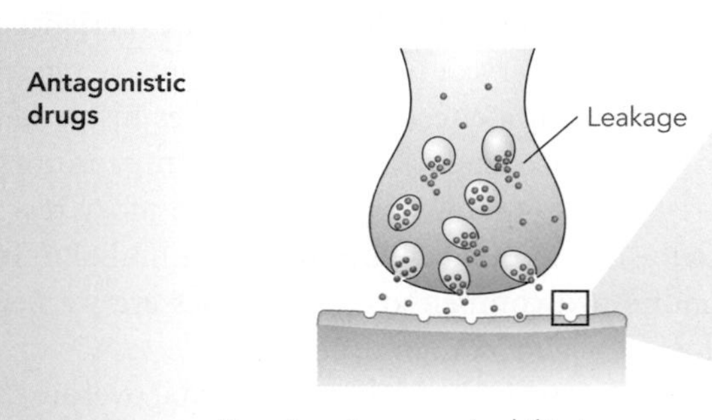

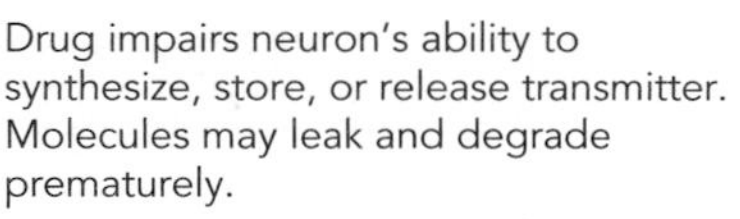

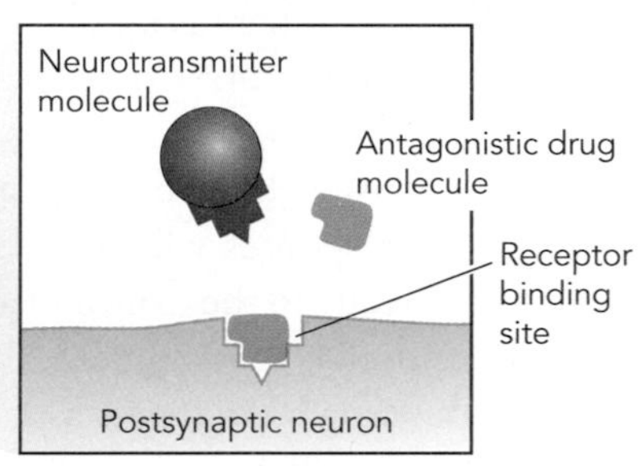

Drug impairs neuron's ability to synthesize, store, or release transmitter. Molecules may leak and degrade prematurely.

Drug binds with receptor site but is not similar enough to transmitter to activate site. Blocks transmitter from activating site.

FIGURE 6.20

(a) Agonists cause neurons to synthesize more neurotransmitter molecules, store them more safely, or release them. In contrast, antagonists impair neurons' ability to synthesize, store, or release neurotransmitters. (b) Agonists and neurotransmitters have similar molecular structure. The drug binds with the receptor site and activates it. In contrast, the antagonist binds with the receptor site but is not similar enough to the neurotransmitter to activate the site. This prevents the real neurotransmitter from binding with and activating the site. (c) The agonist blocks reuptake of the neurotransmitter into the presynaptic neuron. More neurotransmitter molecules remain in the synapse, and are available to activate the postsynaptic neuron.

Tolerance and Withdrawal

27. What is the relation between tolerance, compensatory responses, and withdrawal?

When a drug is used repeatedly, the intensity of effects produced by the same dosage level may decrease over time. This decreasing responsivity to a drug is called **tolerance**. As tolerance develops, the person must take increasingly larger doses to achieve the same physical and psychological effects. Tolerance stems from the body's attempt to maintain a state of optimal physiological balance, called *homeostasis.* If a drug changes bodily functioning in a certain way, say by increasing heart rate, the brain will try to adjust for this imbalance by producing **compensatory responses**, which are reactions opposite to that of the drug (e.g., reactions that decrease heart rate). In effect, compensatory responses represent the body's way of fighting the invasion of drugs.

What happens when drug tolerance develops and the person suddenly stops using the drug? The body's compensatory responses may continue and, no longer balanced out by the drug's effects, the person may experience strong reactions opposite to those produced by the drug. This occurrence of compensatory responses after discontinued drug use is known as **withdrawal** (Diaz, 1997). For example, in the absence of alcohol's sedating and relaxing effects, the chronic drinker may experience increased heart rate, anxiety, and hypertension.

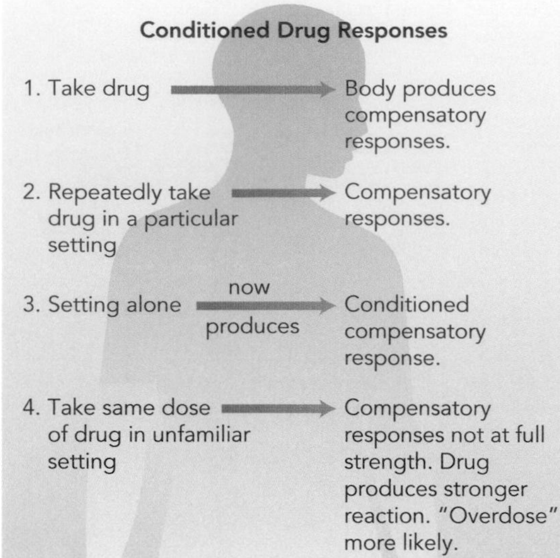

Conditioned Drug Responses
1. Take drug
Body produces compensatory responses.
2. Repeatedly take drug in a particular setting
Compensatory responses.
3. Setting alone
now produces
Conditioned compensatory response.
4. Take same dose of drug in unfamiliar setting
Compensatory responses not at full strength. Drug produces stronger reaction. "Overdose" more likely.

FIGURE 6.21

Environmental stimuli that are repeatedly paired with the use of a drug can acquire the ability to trigger compensatory responses on their own.

Learning, Drug Tolerance, and Overdose

Experiments by Shep. Siegel of McMaster University have shown that tolerance for various drugs partly depends on the familiarity of the drug setting (Larson & Siegel, 1998; Siegel, 1984). Figure 6.21 illustrates how environmental stimuli associated with drug use begin to elicit compensatory responses through a learning process called *classical conditioning.* As drug use continues, the physical setting triggers progressively stronger compensatory responses, increasing the user's tolerance. This helps to explain why addicts often experience increased cravings when they enter a setting associated with drug use. The environmental stimuli trigger compensatory responses, which, without drugs to mask their effect, cause the user to feel withdrawal symptoms (Pilla et al., 1999).

There is a hidden danger in this process, particularly for experienced drug users. Compensatory responses serve a protective function by physiologically countering part of the drug's effects. If a user takes his or her usual high dose in a familiar environment, the body's compensatory responses will be at full strength—a combination of compensatory reactions directly to the drug and also to the conditioned environmental stimuli. But in an *unfamiliar* environment, the conditioned compensatory responses are weaker, and the drug has a stronger physiological net effect than usual.

Siegel (1984) interviewed heroin addicts who experienced near-fatal overdoses. He found that in most cases they *had not* taken a dose larger than their customary one. However, in 70 percent of the cases they *had* injected themselves in unfamiliar environments. Siegel concluded that the addicts were not protected by their usual compensatory responses, resulting in an "overdose" reaction.

Myths about Drug Addiction and Dependence

28. Describe some myths about drug dependence.

Drug addiction, which is formally called **substance dependence**, represents a maladaptive pattern of substance use that causes a person significant distress or substantially impairs that person's life. Substance dependence is diagnosed as occurring with *physiological dependence* if drug tolerance or withdrawal symptoms have developed. You probably have heard the term *psychological dependence* used to describe situations in which people strongly crave a drug because of its pleasurable effects, even though they are not physiologically dependent. However, this is not a diagnostic term, and many drug experts feel it is misleading. They note that such cravings do have a physical basis because they are rooted in patterns of brain activity (Diaz, 1997).

Several misconceptions surround the issue of substance dependence:

Myth 1: Drug tolerance always leads to significant withdrawal. It often does, but not always. Tolerance develops to marijuana and hallucinogens, such as LSD, yet at typical doses withdrawal symptoms are mild (O'Brien, 1997).

Myth 2: Physiological dependence is the major cause of drug addiction. The image of a shaking alcoholic or "heroin junkie" desperately searching for a drink or "fix" contributes to the perception that the motivation to avoid or end withdrawal symptoms is the primary cause of addiction. Certainly, this contributes to drug dependence. But consider these points:

- People become highly dependent on some drugs, such as cocaine, that produce only mild withdrawal (Diaz, 1997). The pleasurable effects of these drugs—often produced by boosting *dopamine* activity—play a powerful role in drug dependence (Everitt et al., 1999).

- Many drug users who quit and make it through withdrawal eventually start using again, even though they are no longer physiologically dependent.
- Drug dependence is influenced by many factors beyond a drug's chemical effects, including genetic predisposition, personality traits, religious beliefs, peer influence, and cultural norms (Marlatt & VandenBos, 1997).

Depressants

Depressants decrease nervous system activity. In moderate doses, they reduce feelings of tension and anxiety, and produce a state of relaxed euphoria. In extremely high doses, depressants can slow down vital life processes to the point of death.

Alcohol

29. Explain how alcohol affects the brain.

Alcohol is the most widely used recreational drug in numerous countries. According to a 1995 national survey by Health Canada, 72 percent of Canadians ages 15 and over said they drank in the past year. Among Canadian university students, more than 90 percent report drinking. Each year Canadians spend more than $15 billion on alcohol, not counting alcohol that is made at home or imported (legally or illegally) by individuals. Tolerance to alcohol develops gradually and can lead to physiological dependence. Almost one in ten Canadians reported having problems with their drinking.

Alcohol increases the activity of gamma-aminobutyric acid (GABA), the main inhibitory neurotransmitter in the brain (Korpi, 1994). By increasing the action of an *inhibitory* neurotransmitter, alcohol dampens down neural firing. Alcohol also decreases the activity of glutamate, a major *excitatory* neurotransmitter (Gonzales & Jaworski, 1997). This further depresses neural firing. Why then do many people report getting a "high" from alcohol and initially seem livelier? The answer is that the neural slowdown depresses the action of inhibitory control centres in the cerebral cortex, so the person literally becomes "less inhibited" and feels euphoric. At higher doses, the brain's control centres become increasingly disrupted, thinking and physical coordination become disorganized, and fatigue and psychological depression may occur (Table 6.2).

Thus alcohol's subjective effects seem to have an initial "upper" phase from the release of inhibitions, followed by a "downer" phase as brain centres become increasingly depressed (Marlatt, 1987). But both phases result from alcohol's action as a nervous system *depressant*. Unfortunately, some people respond to the

TABLE 6.2 Behavioural Effects of Alcohol

BAL	Hours to Leave Body	Behavioural Effects
.03	1	Decreased alertness, impaired reaction time in some people
.05	2	Decreased alertness, impaired judgment and reaction time, feeling of relaxation, release of inhibitions
.10	4	Severely impaired reaction time, motor function, and judgment; less caution
.15	10	Gross intoxication; impairments worsen
.25	?	Extreme sensory and motor impairment, staggering
.30	?	Stuporous but conscious, cannot comprehend immediate environment
.40	?	Lethal in over 50 percent of cases

FIGURE 6.22

Relation between blood-alcohol level and risk of having an auto accident. At .08 to 0.10, the legal definition of intoxication in most American states and Canadian provinces, the risk is six times greater than at 0.00, and the risk climbs to 25 times higher at a BAL of 0.15.

Based on National Safety Council, 1992.

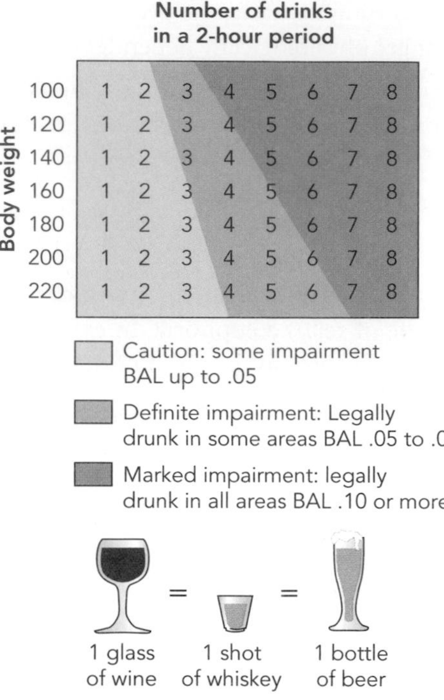

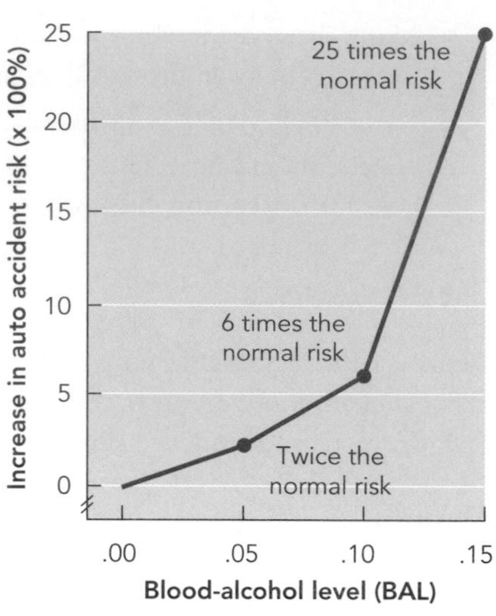

"downer" phase by drinking even more alcohol in the hope that it will make them feel "high" again, a self-defeating strategy if ever there was one.

The *blood-alcohol level (BAL)* is a measure of alcohol concentration in the body. Elevated BAL is linked to risky and harmful behaviours, such as having unprotected sex (Leigh & Stall, 1993). About 40 percent of American and Canadian traffic accident deaths involve alcohol (National Highway Traffic Safety Administration, 2000). As the BAL increases, reaction time, eye-hand coordination, and decision making are impaired (Figure 6.22).

?

30. How does being intoxicated affect decisions about drinking and driving?

Why do intoxicated people often act in risky ways that they wouldn't when sober? It is not simply a matter of lowered inhibitions; alcohol also reduces cognitive capacity. Intoxicated people display what Claude Steele and Robert Josephs (1990) termed **alcohol myopia**, a "shortsightedness" in thinking caused by the inability to pay attention to as much information as sober people. Drinkers start to concentrate only on those aspects of the situation (called *cues*) that stand out. As a result, in the absence of strong cautionary cues (such as warnings) to inhibit risky behaviour, drinkers do not think about the long-term consequences of their actions as carefully as when they are sober (MacDonald et al., 2000). Our *Research Foundations* illustrates this effect.

RESEARCH FOUNDATIONS

Drinking and Driving: Decision Making in Altered States

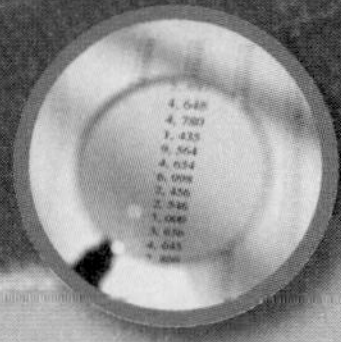

Background

Most people have very negative attitudes about drunk driving and say they would not do it. They realize that the cons (e.g., risk of accident, injury, death, and police arrest) far outweigh the pros (e.g., avoiding cab fare, not leaving one's car behind). Why then do so many people decide to drive after they become intoxicated?

Tara MacDonald and her colleagues at the University of Waterloo examined how alcohol myopia affects decisions about drinking and driving. The authors reasoned that when intoxicated people decide whether to drive, they may focus on the pros or the cons, but do not have the capacity to focus on both. If some aspect of the situation that favours driving (a "facilitating cue") is made salient and captures the intoxicated person's attention (e.g., "It will only be for a short distance"), she or he will latch on to it and fail to consider the cons. But in general situations that do not contain facilitating cues, intoxicated people's feelings about driving should remain as negative as when they were sober.

Based on alcohol myopia principles, the authors made two predictions. First, intoxicated and sober people will have *equally* negative *general* attitudes and intentions toward drinking and driving. Second, intoxicated people will have less negative attitudes and greater intentions to drive than sober people in situations in which a facilitating cue or special circumstance is made salient.

Method

Laboratory Experiment

Fifty-seven male introductory psychology students, all regular drinkers who owned cars, participated. They were randomly assigned to either the sober condition, in which they received no alcohol, or the alcohol condition, in which they received three alcoholic drinks within an hour (the average BAL was .074 percent, just below the .08 percent legal driving limit in Ontario).

Participants then completed a "drinking and driving questionnaire." Some items asked about *general* attitudes and intentions (e.g., "I will drink and drive the next time that I am out at a party or bar with friends"). Other items contained a *facilitating cue*, a special circumstance that suggested a possible reason for drinking and driving ("If I only had a short distance to drive home . . . If my friends tried to persuade me to drink and drive . . . I would drive while intoxicated"). Participants rated each item on a nine-point scale (1 = strongly disagree; 9 = strongly agree).

Party/Bar Diary Study

Fifty-one male and female university students recorded a telephone diary while at a party or bar where they were going to drink alcohol. Some were randomly assigned to record the diary when they first arrived, and others recorded it just before they left. To record the diary, participants opened up a packet containing the same drinking and driving questionnaire described above, called a number on the packet, and recorded their responses on the researchers' answering machine. Based on participants' descriptions of how much alcohol they had consumed, the researchers estimated their BAL and identified two groups: sober participants (average BAL = .01), and intoxicated participants (average BAL = .11).

Results

The findings from both studies supported the predictions. Sober participants and intoxicated participants both expressed negative general attitudes about drinking and driving, and indicated they would not drive when intoxicated. But when the questions presented a facilitating cue, intoxicated participants expressed more favourable attitudes and a greater intention to drive than sober participants (Figure 6.23).

Critical Analysis

This study illustrates nicely how a person's physiological state (sober vs. intoxicated) and an environmental factor (general situation vs. special circumstance) interact to influence psychological functioning (attitudes and decision making). However, before accepting the researchers' claim that alcohol myopia caused the changes in intoxicated participants' responses, we need to think critically about other possible explanations for the results. The authors anticipated two other reasons why people might drive when drunk. First, perhaps drinkers do not realize how intoxicated they are. Second, perhaps intoxicated people overestimate their driving ability, a belief called *drunken invincibility.*

The authors tested and ruled out these explanations. Intoxicated participants believed they were *more* intoxicated than they actually were and estimated that they would drive *more poorly* than the average person. The authors also conducted a placebo control experiment in which some

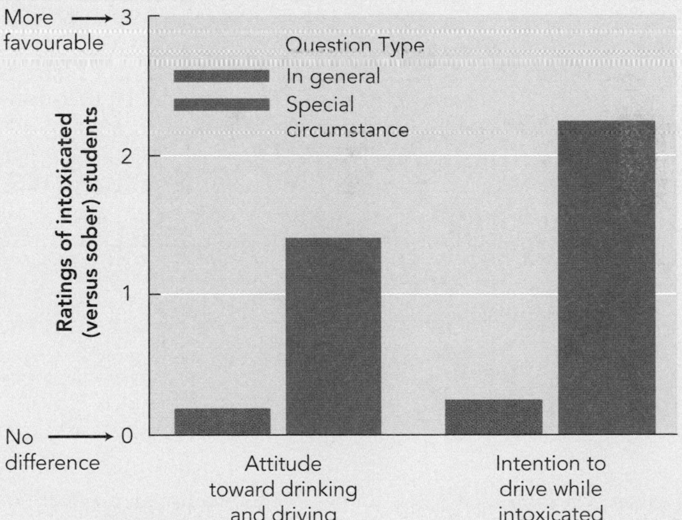

FIGURE 6.23

When general attitudes and intentions toward drinking and driving are measured, intoxicated and sober participants have similarly negative reactions. But when situations involving special circumstances (facilitating cues) are presented, intoxicated participants have less negative attitudes and intentions about drinking and driving than do sober participants.

From MacDonald et al., 1995.

–Continued

participants were convincingly misled to believe they were intoxicated. Results showed that the alcohol myopia effect occurred only for participants who truly had consumed alcohol, and was not caused by participants' expectations.

The party/bar study examined decision making in a real-life but uncontrolled drinking situation, and therefore we cannot draw clear causal conclusions from it. The laboratory experiment examined behaviour in an artificial but controlled setting, permitting clearer causal conclusions. Because the authors conducted both types of research and obtained consistent findings, we can be more confident in their conclusions and the external validity (generalizability) of the findings.

Source: Tara K. MacDonald, Mark P. Zanna, & Geoffrey T. Fong, (1995). Decision making in altered states: Effects of alcohol on attitudes toward drinking and driving. *Journal of Personality and Social Psychology, 68,* 973–985.

Barbiturates and Tranquilizers

Physicians frequently prescribe barbiturates ("sleeping pills") and tranquilizers (anti-anxiety drugs, such as Valium) as sedatives and relaxants. Like alcohol, the vast majority of these drugs depress the nervous system by increasing the activity of the inhibitory neurotransmitter GABA (Diaz, 1997; Ito et al., 1996).

Mild doses of barbiturates are effective as sleeping pills, but they are highly addictive. As tolerance builds, addicts may take as many as 50 sleeping pills a day. At high doses, barbiturates trigger initial excitation, followed by slurred speech, loss of coordination, depression, and severe memory impairment. Overdoses, particularly when taken with alcohol, may cause unconsciousness, coma, and death. Sudden withdrawal after heavy use can cause death, so several months of gradual withdrawal may be needed before addicts lose their physiological dependence.

Barbiturates and tranquilizers are widely overused, and nearly 90 million tranquilizer prescriptions are filled each year (Anthony et al., 1997). Many people mistakenly regard Valium as harmless, but it is not. Tolerance and physiological dependence can occur. Users often don't recognize that they have become dependent until they try to stop and experience serious withdrawal symptoms, such as anxiety, insomnia, and possibly seizures.

Stimulants

31. How do stimulants affect brain functioning? Why does heavy use lead to a "crash"?

Stimulants increase neural firing and arouse the nervous system. They increase blood pressure, respiration, heart rate, and overall alertness. They also can boost mood, produce euphoria, and heighten irritability.

Amphetamines

Amphetamines—popularly known as speed, uppers, and bennies—are powerful stimulants. They are prescribed to reduce appetite and fatigue, decrease the need for sleep, and sometimes, to reduce depression. Unfortunately, they are widely overused to boost energy and mood (Anthony et al., 1997).

Amphetamines increase dopamine and norepinephrine activity. Tolerance develops and users may crave their pleasurable effects. Eventually, many heavy users start injecting large quantities, producing a sudden surge of energy and a rush of intense pleasure. With frequent injections they may remain awake continuously for as long as a week, their bodily systems racing at breakneck speed. Injecting amphetamines greatly increases blood pressure and can lead to heart failure and cerebral hemorrhage (stroke); repeated high doses may cause brain damage (Diaz, 1997).

In schizophrenia, hallucinations and delusions are associated with excess dopamine activity. Imagine what happens when the brain's dopamine activity is artificially increased well beyond normal levels by continuous, heavy amphetamine use: It can cause schizophrenia-like hallucinations and paranoid delusions, a reaction called **amphetamine psychosis** (Lynn, 1971). There is an inevitable "crash" when heavy users stop taking the drug. They may sleep for one or two days, waking up depressed, exhausted, and irritable. This crash occurs because neurons' norepinephrine and dopamine supplies have become depleted. Amphetamines tax the body heavily, and addicts have a short life expectancy. This kind of speed kills, too.

One form of amphetamine is crystal methamphetamine, commonly referred to as "crystal meth." Crystal methamphetamine comes in clear, slightly white or blue-white crystals, hence the street names of "ice," "crystal," and "glass." Crystal methamphetamine is inhaled or smoked and is a particularly potent form of amphetamine. Abuse of crystal methamphetamine has become widespread because of its long-lasting effects, its potency, and because it is relatively easy to make from commonly available ingredients. Crystal methamphetamine causes irritability, insomnia, loss of REM sleep, hyperactivity, confusion, hallucinations, anxiety, paranoia, and increased aggression. It has a powerful impact on the cardiovascular system, increases heart rate and blood pressure, and greatly increases the risk of stroke and heart attack. In high doses, methamphetamine also leads to hypothermia (a drop in core body temperature) and convulsions and can be fatal. Methamphetamine users often show pronounced tooth decay and lose their teeth abnormally quickly, a condition known as "meth mouth." Long-term use leads to heart, liver, kidney, and lung damage.

Another drug that has been popular in recent years, and continues to increase in popularity, belongs to this class. MDMA (3, 4-**m**ethylene**d**ioxy**m**eth**a**mphetamine), commonly called **ecstasy**, is a derivative of amphetamine. Ecstasy acts on several neurotransmitters, including dopamine, but primarily alters serotonin functioning by causing the release of serotonin and blocking its reuptake (Parrott, 2002). MDMA was first synthesized by the Merck drug company in 1914, but it was not developed or researched and was little known until the 1960s when it began to appear on the drug scene (McKim, 2000). Although MDMA was once considered to be a safe drug for enhancing awareness of emotions and sensations (Siegel, 1986), important adverse effects have become apparent. MDMA produces both acute, reversible cognitive deficits and long-term cognitive impairment, especially on language tasks, such as tests of verbal fluency (Bhattachary & Powell, 2001). MDMA has also been found to cause deficits in memory and attention, and to cause sleep disturbances, sexual dysfunction, and impaired immune responses (Parrott, 2006). MDMA also increases body temperature (Freedman, Johanson, & Tancer, 2005), and the metabolic and physical distress from the change in body temperature may be important in amplifying MDMA's effects in hot environmental conditions or when use occurs during high levels of physical activity, such as dancing. It also has been found that MDMA has neurotoxic effects; that is, it acts as a toxin, or poison, that specifically damages neurons. As shown in Figure 6.24, MDMA can deplete the brain of the neurotransmitter serotonin, an effect that has been linked to suicidal depression and even sudden death (McKim, 2000).

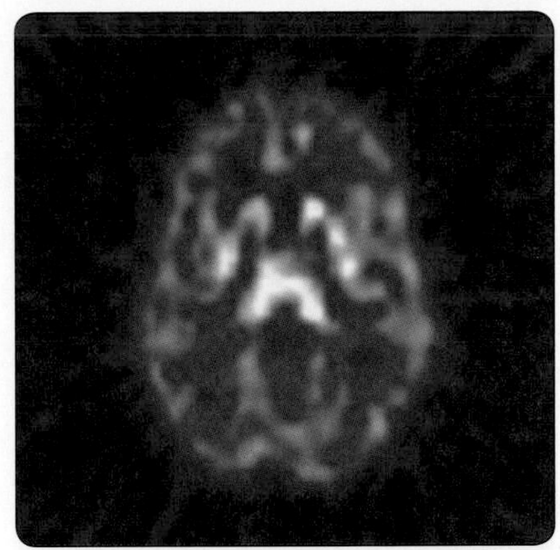

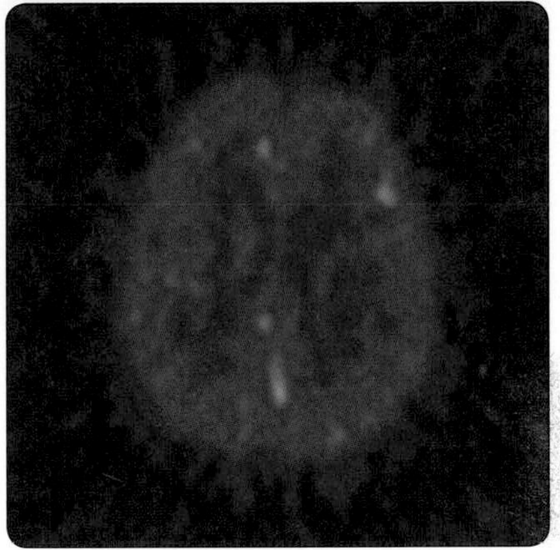

FIGURE 6.24

The top PET-scan image shows the brain of a person who never used ecstasy. The bottom image shows the brain of a person who used ecstasy 70 times or more over a period of at least 1.5 years but who stopped using the drug for several weeks before these images were taken. Areas of lighter colour indicate a higher density of special proteins (called transporters) necessary for normal serotonin reuptake. The darker image of the brain on the bottom suggests that there is damage to the serotonin reuptake system.

Source: McCann et al., 1998.

Cocaine

Cocaine is a powder derived from the coca plant, which grows mainly in western South America. Usually inhaled or injected, it produces excitation, a sense of increased muscular strength, and euphoria. Like amphetamines, cocaine increases the activity of norepinephrine and dopamine, but it does so in only one major way: It blocks their reuptake.

FIGURE 6.25
When Coca-Cola was first produced there was a clear reason why it relieved fatigue. It contained cocaine.

At various times in history, cocaine has been hailed as a wonder drug and branded as a menace. It was once widely used as a local anaesthetic in eye, nose, and throat surgery. Novocaine, a synthetic form of cocaine, is still used in dentistry as an anaesthetic. Due to its stimulating effects, cocaine found its way into potions and tonics sold to the public to enhance health and emotional well-being. In 1885, John Pemberton mixed cocaine with the kola nut and syrup and developed a soda fountain drink that has become one of the icons of American beverages (Figure 6.25).

In large doses, cocaine can produce fever, vomiting, convulsions, hallucinations, and paranoid delusions. A severe depressive crash may occur after a cocaine high, particularly with repeated doses. *Crack* is a chemically converted form of cocaine that can be smoked, and its effects are faster, more intense, and more dangerous. Overdoses of crack cocaine can cause sudden death from cardiorespiratory arrest (Ruttenber et al., 1997).

Tolerance develops to many of cocaine's effects, but withdrawal symptoms are mild and the potential for physiological dependence is low. However, cocaine users often develop strong cravings for the drug and the abuse potential is very high.

Opiates

32. Describe the two effects of opiates.

33. What is the greatest danger of hallucinogens?

Opium is a product of the opium poppy, a plant grown in hot, dry climates. Drugs derived from opium such as morphine, codeine, and heroin, are called **opiates**. Opiates have two major effects. First, they provide pain relief. Second, they cause mood changes, which may include intense euphoria. The opiate oxycodone (sold under several different names such as OxyContin® and Percocet®) dramatically illustrates these two effects; oxycodone is a powerful pain killer and it rapidly became a widely abused drug because of its mood-altering effects. Opiates bind to and stimulate receptors normally activated by endorphins, thereby producing pain relief. Opiates also increase dopamine activity, which may be one reason they induce euphoria (Bardo, 1998).

Experienced heroin users feel an intense, pleasurable "rush" within several minutes of an injection. For a time, users feel peaceful and non-aggressive, as if they are "on top of the world" with no concerns. Heroin users, however, often pay a substantial price for these transient pleasures. High doses can greatly reduce a person's breathing rate and may lead to coma. Overdoses can cause death. Only 2 percent of North Americans have used heroin, but nearly 25 percent of those who use it become addicted to it (Anthony et al., 1997). Withdrawal symptoms are traumatic, as illustrated by the following description from a former addict:

> It's like a terrible case of flu. Your joints move involuntarily. That's where the phrase "kick the habit" comes from. You jerk and twitch and you just can't control it. You throw up. You can't control your bowels either and this goes on for four or five days afterwards. You can't sleep and you cough up blood, because . . . you can't eat and that's all there is to cough up.

Hallucinogens

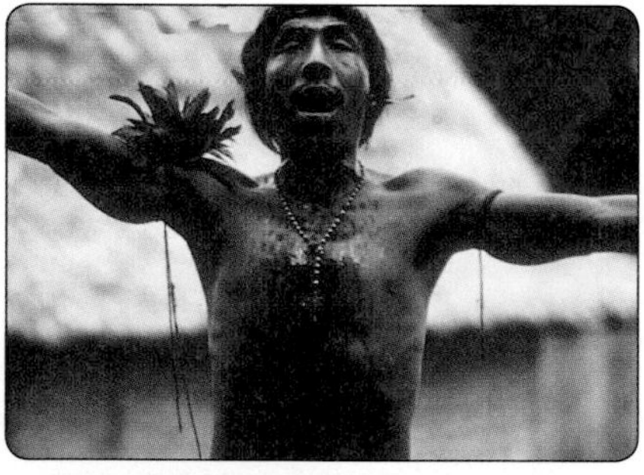

FIGURE 6.26
In some cultures, powerful hallucinogenic drugs are thought to have spiritual powers. Under the influence of peyote, this modern Indian shaman prepares to conduct a religious ceremony.

Hallucinogens are powerful mind-altering drugs that produce hallucinations. Many are derived from natural sources; mescaline comes from the peyote cactus and psilocybin from mushrooms. Natural hallucinogens have been considered sacred in many tribal cultures because of their ability to produce "unearthly" states of consciousness and contact with spiritual forces (Figure 6.26). Other hallucinogens, such as LSD and phencyclidine ("Angel Dust"), are synthetic.

About 10 percent of North Americans have used hallucinogenic drugs (Anthony et al., 1997). Hallucinogens usually distort or intensify sensory experience and can blur the boundaries between reality and fantasy. Users may speak of seeing sounds and hearing colours, of mystical experiences and insights, and of feeling exhilarated. They also may have violent outbursts, experience paranoia and panic, and have flashbacks after the "trip" has ended. The mental effects of hallucinogens are always unpredictable, even when they are taken repeatedly. This unpredictability constitutes their greatest danger.

Lysergic acid diethylamide (LSD) is a powerful hallucinogen. Also known as "acid," LSD causes a flooding of excitation in the nervous system. A dose of pure LSD no larger than the tip of a pin can affect a user for 8 to 16 hours. Tolerance develops rapidly, but decreases quickly. Although chronic use does not appear to produce withdrawal symptoms, about five percent of Americans have developed a dependence on LSD or other hallucinogens (Anthony et al., 1997).

We do not know how LSD produces hallucinations. Part of the LSD molecule has a shape similar to serotonin and, overall, it decreases serotonin activity. During normal sleep, decreased serotonin activity in parts of the brain stem allows REM-On neurons to become active and initiate REM sleep, with its high level of dreaming. For decades, researchers have speculated that LSD's inhibiting action on serotonin allows dreamlike altered perceptions and hallucinations to emerge (Trulson & Jacobs, 1979).

Marijuana

34. Explain three myths about marijuana.

Marijuana is a product of the hemp plant (*Cannabis sativa*). Some experts classify it as a hallucinogen, others as a sedative, and some feel it belongs in its own category (Diaz, 1997). Marijuana is the most widely used illicit drug in Canada. Although estimates vary, most suggest that about a third of all Canadians have used marijuana at least once (Canadian Community Epidemiology Network on Drug Use, 2001; Centre for Addiction and Mental Health, 2001). Among some groups, use is even higher; almost 40 percent of high school students report having used marijuana within the past year (Patton, Brown, Broszeit, & Dhaliwal, 2001).

THC (tetrahydrocannabinol) is marijuana's major active ingredient, and it binds to receptors on neurons throughout the brain. You might wonder, as scientists have, why the brain would have specific receptor sites for a "foreign" substance like marijuana. The answer is that the brain produces its own THC-like substances, called *cannabinoids* (Devane et al., 1992; Stella et al., 1997). With chronic use, THC may increase GABA activity, which slows down neural activity and produces relaxing effects (Diaz, 1997). THC also increases dopamine activity, which may account for some of its pleasurable subjective effects (Ameri, 1999). Recent attempts to legalize marijuana use for medical purposes have stirred up waves of political controversy (Gottfried, 2000) (Figure 6.27).

FIGURE 6.27

The legal status of marijuana has long been a topic of debate in Canada. The use of marijuana has been legalized for certain medical purposes, such as helping cancer patients reduce some of the negative side effects (e.g., nausea) of chemotherapy. Further decriminalization of marijuana is hotly debated.

Certain myths exist about marijuana. One is that chronic use causes people to become unmotivated and apathetic toward everything, a condition called *amotivational syndrome*. Another myth is that marijuana causes people to start using more dangerous drugs. Neither statement is supported by good scientific evidence (Diaz, 1997). A third myth is that using marijuana has no significant dangers. This also is untrue. Marijuana smoke contains more cancer-causing substances than does tobacco smoke. At high doses, users may experience negative changes in mood, sensory distortions, and feelings of panic and anxiety. Marijuana can impair reaction time, thinking, memory, and learning (Smiley, 1986). Research clearly shows that driving under the influence of marijuana (even "social doses") can be hazardous (Robbe, 1998).

Repeated marijuana use produces tolerance. At typical doses, some chronic users may experience mild withdrawal symptoms, such as restlessness. But users of chronically high doses who suddenly stop may experience nausea and vomiting, sleep disruptions, and irritability. About 10 percent of marijuana users develop dependence (Anthony et al., 1997).

From Genes to Culture: Determinants of Drug Effects

35. What evidence supports the hypothesis that genetic factors influence drug reactions?

Table 6.3 summarizes some typical drug effects, but a user's reaction depends on more than the drug's chemical structure. Other biological, psychological, and environmental factors can influence the drug experience (Stewart, 2002).

At the biological level, animal research indicates that genetic factors influence sensitivity and tolerance to drug effects. This has been examined most extensively with alcohol. Rats and mice can be genetically bred to inherit a strong preference for drinking alcohol instead of water (He et al., 1997; Whitney et al., 1970). Even in their first exposure to alcohol, these rats show greater tolerance than normal rats (Gatto et al., 1986). The degree to which mice experience seizures during alcohol withdrawal also can be increased or decreased through controlled breeding (Crabbe et al., 1986).

In human research, three types of correlational evidence are intriguing. First, identical twins have a higher concordance rate for alcoholism than do fraternal twins (Heath et al., 1997). Second, scientists have identified a particular gene that is found more often among alcoholics and their children than among non-alcoholics and their offspring (Hill et al., 1998; Noble, 1998). No one is proposing that this gene "causes" alcoholism. Rather, it may influence how the brain responds to

TABLE 6.3 **Effects of Some Major Drugs**

Class	Typical Effects	Overdose Effects
DEPRESSANTS		
Alcohol	Relaxation, lowered inhibition, depressed/impaired physical and psychological functioning	Disorientation, unconsciousness, possible death at extreme doses
Barbiturates/ Tranquilizers	Tension reduction, depressed reflexes and impaired motor functioning, induced sleep	Shallow breathing, clammy skin, weak and rapid pulse, coma, possible death
STIMULANTS		
Amphetamines Cocaine Ecstacy	Increased alertness, pulse, and blood pressure; elevated mood; suppressed appetite; sleeplessness	Agitation, hallucinations, paranoid delusions, convulsions, heart failure, possible death
OPIATES		
Opium Morphine Heroin Oxycodone	Euphoria, pain relief, drowsiness, impaired motor and psychological functioning	Shallow breathing, convulsions, coma, possible death
HALLUCINOGENS		
LSD Mescaline Psilocybin	Hallucinations and "visions," distorted time perception, loss of reality contact, nausea, restlessness, risk of panic	Psychotic reactions (delusions, paranoia), panic that may lead to behaviour causing injury
MARIJUANA	Mild euphoria, relaxation, enhanced sensory experience, increased appetite, impaired memory and reaction time	Fatigue, anxiety, disorientation, sensory distortions, and possible psychotic reactions

alcohol. Many scientists find compelling evidence for a genetic role in determining responsiveness to alcohol (Li, 2000).

Third, people who grow up with alcoholic versus non-alcoholic parents respond differently to drinking alcohol under laboratory conditions. Offspring of alcoholic parents typically display faster hormonal and psychological reactions as blood-alcohol level rises, but these responses drop off more quickly as blood-alcohol levels decrease (Newlin & Thomson, 1997). Compared to other people, they must drink more alcohol over the course of a few hours to maintain their feeling of intoxication. Growing up with alcoholic parents includes both genetic and social learning components. Animal studies have found that cross-fostered rat pups raised by an alcohol-consuming mother consume more alcohol than rat pups raised by mothers who do not drink alcohol (Honey & Galef, 2004). Animals, including humans, learn what to eat and drink, in part, by cues provided by the parents. Thus, the children of alcoholic parents could be at an increased risk of abusing alcohol for two reasons: genetic factors and exposure to a parent who abuses alcohol. Twin and adoption studies, however, have found that alcohol abuse among adoptees is correlated with alcohol abuse in their biological parents but not their adoptive parents (Cloninger et a., 1995; Heath, 1995; Heath et al., 2002).

36. Describe how environmental and psychological factors influence drug reactions.

At the environmental level, the physical and social setting in which a drug is taken can strongly influence a user's reactions. As noted earlier, compensatory physiological responses to a drug can become associated with, and ultimately triggered by, environmental stimuli in the drug setting. The behaviour of other people who are sharing the drug experience provides important cues about how to respond, and a hostile environment may increase the chances of a "bad trip" with drugs such as LSD (Palfai & Jankiewicz, 1991).

Cultural learning also affects how people respond to a drug (Weil, 1986). In many Western cultures, increased aggressiveness and sexual promiscuity are commonly associated with drunken excess. In contrast, members of the Camba culture of Bolivia customarily drink large quantities of a 178-proof beverage, remaining cordial and non-aggressive between episodes of passing out (MacAndrew & Edgerton, 1969). In the 1700s, Tahitians introduced to alcohol by European sailors reacted at first with pleasant relaxation when intoxicated, but after witnessing the violent aggressiveness exhibited by drunken sailors, they too began behaving aggressively (MacAndrew & Edgerton, 1969).

Cultural factors also affect drug consumption. Traditionally, American Navajo Indians do not consider drinking any amount of alcohol to be normal, whereas drinking wine or beer is central to social life and cultural identity in some parts of the world (Tanaka-Matsumi & Draguns, 1997). In some cultures, hallucinogenic drugs are feared and outlawed, whereas in others they are used in medicinal or religious contexts to provide new types of awareness and to seek advice from spirits (Beardsley & Pedersen, 1997). In many countries, drug use varies across ethnic groups. Black and Hispanic Americans, for example, are less likely ever to have used alcohol, cocaine, marijuana, and hallucinogens than their White peers (Department of Health and Human Services, 1998).

Finally, at the psychological level, people's beliefs and expectancies can influence drug reactions (George et al., 2000). Experiments show that people may behave as if "drunk" if they simply think they have consumed alcohol, but actually have not (Marlatt & Rohsenow, 1980). If a person's fellow drinkers are happy and gregarious, he or she may expect to respond in the same way. The cultural norm that a hallucinogen will enable contact with spirits provides the user with a powerful belief system and expectation that can shape the nature of the hallucinations and overall emotional reaction to the experience. As we learned in Chapter 5, we

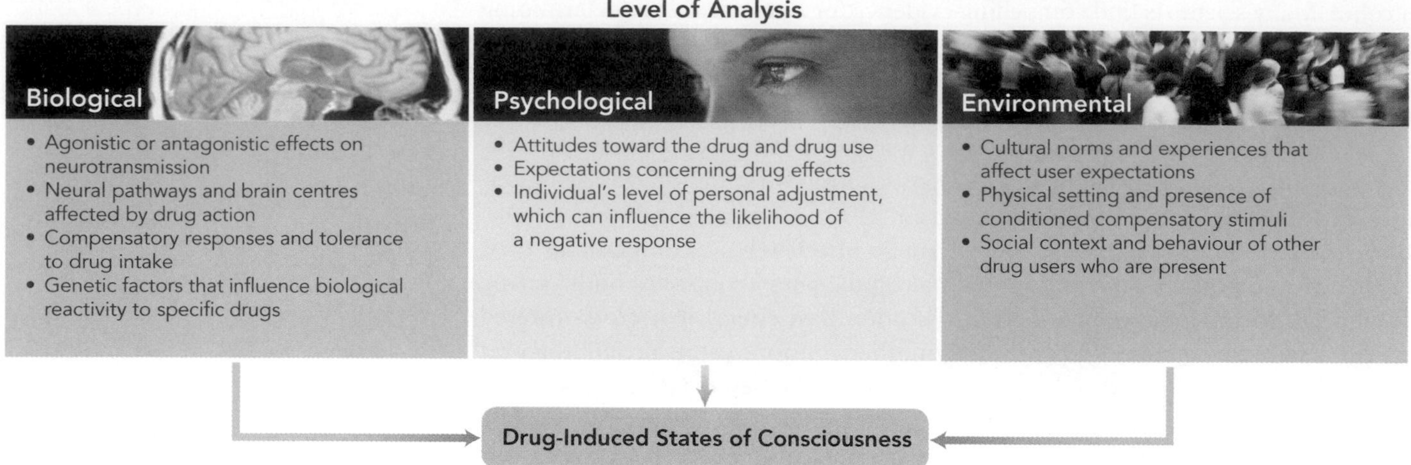

Level of Analysis
Biological
• Agonistic or antagonistic effects on neurotransmission
• Neural pathways and brain centres affected by drug action
• Compensatory responses and tolerance to drug intake
• Genetic factors that influence biological reactivity to specific drugs
Psychological
• Attitudes toward the drug and drug use
• Expectations concerning drug effects
• Individual's level of personal adjustment, which can influence the likelihood of a negative response
Environmental
• Cultural norms and experiences that affect user expectations
• Physical setting and presence of conditioned compensatory stimuli
• Social context and behaviour of other drug users who are present
Drug-Induced States of Consciousness

FIGURE 6.28

Understanding the causes of behaviour: factors influencing drug effects.

often perceive what we expect to perceive, and this applies to drugs; expectations powerfully influence the effects of a psychoactive drug.

Personality factors also influence drug reactions and usage. People who have difficulty adjusting to life's demands or whose contact with reality is marginal may be particularly vulnerable to severe and negative drug reactions and to drug addiction (Ray & Ksir, 1987). Chronic drug use among young people often is associated with a sense of meaninglessness and lack of direction in life (Newcomb & Harlow, 1986). Figure 6.28 illustrates some of the biological, environmental, and psychological factors that may determine drug experiences.

In Review

- *Drugs alter consciousness by modifying neurotransmitter activity. Agonists increase such activity, whereas antagonists decrease it.*
- *Tolerance develops when the body produces compensatory responses to counteract a drug's effects. When drug use is stopped, compensatory responses continue and produce withdrawal symptoms. Substance dependence represents a maladaptive pattern of substance use that causes a person significant distress or substantially impairs that person's life. It can occur with or without physiological dependence.*
- *Depressants decrease neural activity. The subjective "high" and liveliness associated with low alcohol doses occur because alcohol depresses the activity of inhibitory brain centres. Drinking contributes to poor decision making.*
- *Stimulants increase arousal and boost mood by enhancing dopamine and norepinephrine activity. Repeated use depletes these neurotransmitters and can cause a severe depressive "crash" after the drug wears off.*
- *Opiates increase endorphin activity, producing pain relief and mood changes that may include euphoria. Opiates are important in medicine but are highly addictive.*
- *Hallucinogens, such as LSD, powerfully distort sensory experience and can blur the line between reality and fantasy. The effects of hallucinogens are always unpredictable.*
- *THC, the main active ingredient in marijuana, produces relaxation and a sense of well-being at low doses, but can cause anxiety and sensory distortion at higher doses. Marijuana can impair thinking and reflexes, and its smoke contains carcinogens.*
- *A drug's effect depends on its chemical actions, the physical and social setting, cultural norms, learning, and the user's genetic predispositions, expectations, and personality.*

FOCUS ON NEUROSCIENCE

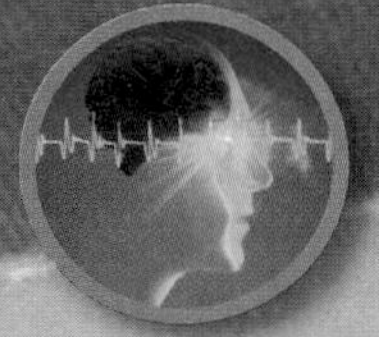

The Neuroscience of Meditation

A widely known but poorly understood state that represents an altered state of consciousness is the one achieved during meditation. **Meditation** is used to refer to a wide range of different practices that self-regulate attention, the mind, and, in some cases, physiological responses. The processes used in meditation are thought to be related to those used to induce hypnosis or relaxation (Cahn & Polich, 2006).

The many different techniques used in meditation can be broadly classified as belonging to one of two types—mindfulness and concentrative (Andresen, 2000). Mindfulness methods involve allowing thoughts, feelings, sensations, and other mental events to flow without analysis or judgment. One adopts the role of an attentive but indifferent observer, allowing mental events to come and go without effort or deliberate consideration (Kabat-Zinn, 2003). Mindfulness meditative techniques include the traditions of Zen and Vipassana meditation. The other broad group of techniques, the concentrative practices, involve focusing one's attention on a specific mental or sensory stimulus. When using a concentrative technique the meditator will focus on a single sensory or mental event such as a repeated sound, a real or imagined image, a bodily sensation (such as breathing), or a statement. Forms of meditation that follow the concentrative approach include Buddhist Samatha meditation, which focuses on breathing, and meditative styles that focus on a statement such as a mantra, or on a prayer or Bible passage in some Christian meditative traditions (Cahn & Polich, 2006). It is important to note that both types of approach, mindfulness and concentrative, involve a deliberate manipulation of attention. In mindfulness practices attention is kept open, nonjudgmental, and receptive and no single mental event is allowed to become one's focus. Concentrative practices, on the other hand, involve a deliberate narrowing of attention so that a single sound, sensation, or thought becomes the sole focus of one's attention.

Whatever approach they use, practised meditators report that meditation can lead to a profound alteration in consciousness. There are both changes in consciousness during meditation and lasting changes that may persist outside of the meditative state. During meditation, practitioners report a deep sense of calm and peacefulness, a slowing or complete cessation of the mind's internal dialogue, heightened perception, absorption in the moment, and a merging of conscious awareness with the object of meditation (Wallace, 1999). Some of the lasting effects, those that may be reported even when not meditating, include a sense of calmness, heightened sensory awareness, and a shift in the experience of self. The shift in sense of self is often reported to involve a blurring of the distinction between the self and what the self is observing; sense of self shifts from being centred on the body to a more expansive sense of self that is not centred on the body (Travis et al., 2002).

Studies of the effects of meditation on brain activity began more than 50 years ago when early researchers obtained EEG records during meditation. The results of these early studies, however, were inconsistent and many of these studies suffered from a number of methodological problems (Cahn & Polich, 2006). Recently, imaging techniques such as PET, SPECT, and fMRI and more rigorous methodology have been used to explore meditation (Figure 6.29). Although the

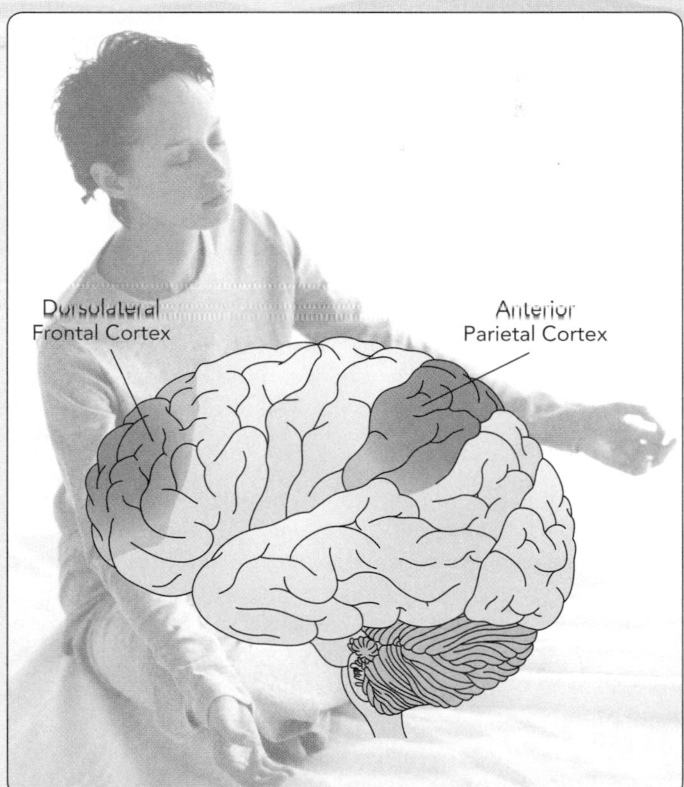

FIGURE 6.29

Although there are many different traditions and techniques used in meditation, all involve a deliberate self-regulation of attention and lead to similar alterations in the state of consciousness. Imaging studies, such as research using fMRI, have begun to describe the neurophysiological changes that occur during a meditative state.

–Continued

results of these more recent studies are not always consistent, some interesting patterns are emerging.

Research on meditation is complicated by a number of factors. Non-meditators can rarely keep themselves physically immobile as long as practised meditators and so brain changes related to movement and the deliberate inhibition of movement may differ between meditators and non-meditators. There are also obvious difficulties in quantifying self-experience, especially of the type that may be achieved during meditation, and in the development of adequate control activities for non-meditation recordings. Despite these challenges, some of the emerging imaging results are compatible with our current understanding of the brain (Cahn & Polich, 2006). For example, PET studies have found that if meditation involves visual imagery, it is accompanied by an increase in activity within the occipital cortex. If meditation focuses attention on bodily sensations, then it is accompanied by activation of the parietal cortex. As we discovered in Chapter 3, the occipital cortex is involved in vision and the somatosensory cortex of the parietal lobe is involved in the representation of bodily sensations. Whether you are currently processing a "real" visual image that is in front of you or imagining a visual stimulus as part of a meditative routine, your occipital cortex is activated. But what of changes in brain state that are specific to a meditative state of consciousness?

An interesting study with Tibetan Buddhist meditators used the SPECT imaging technique (Newberg, et al., 2001). Scans were obtained at baseline and after meditators indicated that they had entered the deepest level of meditation (after about one hour). Compared to baseline, deep meditation was accompanied by increased activity in the cingulate gyrus, two specific areas within the frontal cortex (orbital frontal and dorsolateral prefrontal), the midbrain, and the thalamus.

The results of research using fMRI have focused on some of the same areas that emerged as sites of interest in studies using PET and SPECT. For example, a study with practitioners of Kundalini yoga, which involves both concentration on a statement, or mantra, and heightened awareness of breathing, found that meditation was accompanied by increased activity within the cingulate cortex, areas within the frontal cortex and the parietal cortex, and within the basal ganglia, midbrain, and the hippocampus (Lazar et al., 2000). Changes in brain activity became more pronounced as the meditative state progressed.

Comparing meditators using a mindfulness approach (Vipassana) and a mantra-based, concentrative approach (Kundalini) during meditation and during several control procedures, research has found both commonalities and subtle differences between the different approaches to meditation (Cahn & Polich, 2006). Both groups of meditators showed activation of the cingulate cortex, frontal cortex, and parietal cortex during meditation when compared to control tasks. Areas that differed between the two approaches appear to be those related to autonomic and physiological processes, such as midbrain areas. Remember that one technique involved deliberate attention to and regulation of breathing (Kundalini) and one did not (Vipassana). Changes in midbrain activity in this and previously mentioned studies may be related to changes in autonomic nervous system activity and to the control of functions such as breathing (Cahn & Polich, 2006).

Research using participants practised in other meditative techniques, such as Zen meditation, have similarly found changes within areas of the frontal cortex, cingulate cortex, and basal ganglia during meditation (e.g., Ritskes, et al., 2003; Baerentsen, 2001), although the nature of the changes has not always been consistent (see Cahn & Polich, 2006). It is important to note that two of the areas most commonly found to change with meditation, the cingulate cortex and areas within the frontal cortex, have functions that are consistent with the subjective reports of meditation. The cingulate cortex is thought to be related to attentional focus and the areas of interest within the frontal cortex have been related to emotions, especially feelings of peace and love, and to attention (Cahn & Polich, 2006). Although less studied, other meditation traditions, such as some Christian meditative practices that involve reading a Bible passage or reciting a prayer, have found similar patterns of activation within the frontal and parietal cortices, although changes in the cingulate cortex have not been identified with these meditation techniques (Cahn & Polich, 2006).

Neuroimaging studies of meditation have begun to demonstrate some consistency in brain states that accompany the meditative state. During meditation, brain activity changes within areas of the frontal cortex, parietal cortex, and cingulate cortex. Meditation can involve a profound change in sense of self, in one's relationship to the world, in sensory awareness, and in attentional focus; that is, a profound change in one's state of consciousness. Meditation offers techniques in which the individual intentionally alters consciousness without outside or artificial means, such as perception-altering drugs. The changes in brain activity that accompany changes in consciousness during meditation offer a unique tool to study our awareness of ourselves and our world.

⊙ HYPNOSIS

In 18th-century Vienna, physician Anton Mesmer gained fame by using magnetized objects to cure physical and psychological afflictions. He claimed that illness was caused by blockages of an invisible bodily fluid that obeyed the laws of magnetism, and that his technique of *animal magnetism* (later named *mesmerism* in his honour) would restore the fluid's normal flow. A scientific commission discredited mesmerism, but its use continued. Decades later, Scottish surgeon James Braid investigated the fact that mesmerized patients often went into a "trance" in which they seemed oblivious to their surroundings. He concluded that mesmerism was a state of "nervous sleep" produced by concentrated attention, and renamed it "hypnosis," after Hypnos, the Greek god of sleep.

The Scientific Study of Hypnosis

Hypnosis is a state of heightened suggestibility in which some people are able to experience imagined test suggestions as if they were real. Hypnosis draws great interest because many therapists use it in treating mental disorders. In the United States, about 25 percent of psychology Ph.D. programs offer a course in hypnosis (Walling et al., 1998). Basic scientists explore hypnosis to determine its nature, assess whether it is a unique state of altered consciousness, and put its claims to rigorous experimental test (Hull, 1933; Kirsch, 1999).

Hypnotic induction is the process by which one person (a researcher or hypnotist) leads another person (the subject) into hypnosis. A hypnotist may invite the subject to sit down, relax, gaze at an object on the wall, and then in a quiet voice suggest that the subject's eyes are becoming heavy and tired. The goal is to relax the subject and increase her or his concentration. Contrary to popular belief, people cannot be hypnotized against their will. Even when people want to be hypnotized, they differ in how "susceptible" (i.e., responsive) they are to hypnotic suggestion. **Hypnotic susceptibility scales** contain a standard series of pass/fail suggestions that are read to a subject after a hypnotic induction (Table 6.4). The subject's score is based on the number of "passes." About 10 percent of subjects are completely non-responsive, 10 percent pass all or nearly all of the items, and the rest fall in between (Hilgard, 1977).

Hypnotic susceptibility is a stable characteristic. In one study, Stanford students differed by no more than one point on a 12-item scale when tested 25 years later (Piccione et al., 1989). Hypnotic susceptibility can be enhanced by increasing people's expectation that they have the ability to be hypnotized (Spanos et al., 1991; Vickery & Kirsch, 1991).

Hypnotic Behaviours and Experiences

It is widely claimed that hypnotized people experience substantial alteration in psychological functioning and behaviour. Let's examine some of these claims.

TABLE 6.4 **Sample Test Items from the Stanford Hypnotic Susceptibility Scale, Form C**

Item	Suggested Behaviour	Criterion for Passing
Arm lowering	Right arm is held out; subject is told arm will become heavy and drop.	Arm is lowered at least 15 centimetres in 10 seconds.
Moving hands apart	With hands extended and close together, subject is asked to imagine a force pushing them apart.	Hands are 15 or more centimetres apart in 10 seconds.
Mosquito hallucination	It is suggested that a mosquito is buzzing nearby and lands on the subject.	Any grimace or acknowledgment of the mosquito.
Posthypnotic amnesia	Subject is awakened and asked to recall suggestions after being told under hypnosis that she will not remember.	Three or fewer items recalled before subject is told, "Now you can remember everything."

37. In what sense is hypnotic behaviour "involuntary"? Does hypnosis have a unique power to coerce people against their will?

Involuntary Control and Behaving against One's Will

Hypnotized people *subjectively experience* their actions to be involuntary (Kirsch & Lynn, 1998; Woody & Sadler, 1998). For example, look at the second test item in Table 6.4. To hypnotized subjects, it really feels like their hands *are* being pushed apart by some mysterious force, rather than by any conscious control of bodily movements.

If behaviour seems involuntary under hypnosis, then can a hypnotist make people perform acts that are harmful to themselves or others? Martin Orne and Frederick Evans (1965) found that hypnotized subjects could be induced to dip their hands briefly in a foaming solution they were told was acid and then throw the "acid" in another person's face. This might appear to be a striking example of the power of hypnosis to get people to act "against their will." However, Orne and Evans tested a control group of subjects who were asked simply to pretend that they were hypnotized. These subjects were just as likely as hypnotized subjects to put their hand in the acid or throw it at someone.

In Chapter 16 you will learn about experiments in which researchers induced hundreds of "normal" adults to keep giving what they believed were extremely painful electric shocks to an innocent man with a heart condition who begged them to stop (Milgram, 1974). Not a single one of these participants was hypnotized; they were simply following the researcher's orders. Hypnosis does not involve any unique power to get people to behave "against their will." An authority figure in a legitimate context can induce people to commit highly "out of character" and dangerous acts, whether they are hypnotized or not.

38. Can non-hypnotized people produce the same physiological reactions and feats displayed by hypnotized people?

Physiological Effects and Physical Feats

Hypnosis can have striking physiological effects. Consider a classic experiment involving 13 people who were strongly allergic to the toxic leaves of a certain tree (Ikemi & Nakagawa, 1962). Five of them were hypnotized, blindfolded, and told that a leaf from a harmless tree to which they were not allergic was touching one of their arms. In fact, the leaf really was toxic, but four out of the five hypnotized people had no allergic reaction! Next, the other arm of each hypnotized person was rubbed with a leaf from a harmless tree, but he or she was told falsely that the leaf was toxic. All five people responded to the harmless leaf with allergic reactions!

These findings are impressive, but we must also consider the reactions of the eight non-hypnotized control participants. When blindfolded and exposed to a toxic leaf, but misled to believe that it was harmless, seven out of the eight non-hypnotized persons did not show an allergic response. Conversely, when their arm was rubbed with a harmless leaf but they were told falsely it was toxic, every one of them had an allergic reaction. In short, the non-hypnotized people responded the same way as the hypnotized subjects.

Under hypnosis, nearsighted people can see more clearly, warts can be cured, and stomach acidity can be increased. However, well-controlled studies show that non-hypnotized subjects can exhibit these same responses (Spanos & Chaves, 1988). As we saw when discussing placebo effects in Chapter 2, beliefs and expectations can produce real physiological effects.

Stage hypnotists often get an audience member to perform an amazing physical feat, such as the "human plank" (Figure 6.30). A subject, usually male, is hypnotized and lies outstretched between two chairs. He is told that his body is rigid, and another person stands on his chest. The audience attributes this feat to the "hypnotic trance." What they don't know is that an average man suspended in this manner can support at least 130 kilograms on his chest with little discomfort and no need of a hypnotic trance.

FIGURE 6.30

The "human plank" demonstration, a favourite of stage hypnotists, seems to demonstrate the power of the hypnotic trance. Most of the audience is unaware that the average man suspended in this manner can support a person on his chest without hypnosis. In the photo, The Amazing Kreskin, a professional magician, demonstrates this fact with a group of unhypnotized men.

Pain Tolerance

39. Does hypnosis produce pain relief? Is this a placebo effect?

Scottish surgeon James Esdaile performed more than 300 major operations in the mid-1800s using hypnosis as the sole anaesthetic (Figure 6.31). Joseph Barber (1977), a noted hypnotherapist, needed an average of only 11 minutes to hypnotically produce *analgesia* (an absence of pain) in 99 out of 100 dental patients. Experiments confirm that hypnosis often increases pain tolerance, and that this is not due to a placebo effect (Farthing et al., 1997; Spanos & Katsanis, 1989). For patients who experience chronic pain, hypnosis can produce relief that persists for months or even years (Barber, 1998). But research also shows that non-hypnotic psychological techniques, such as mental imagery, also can reduce pain (Weisenberg, 1998).

We do not know exactly how hypnosis produces its pain-killing effects. Brain imaging studies have found that hypnosis modifies activity in brain areas involved in processing painful stimuli. Nonhypnotic techniques, such as visual imagery and distractions, can, however, also alter activity in these brain areas and reduce the feeling of pain (Petrovic & Ingvar, 2002).

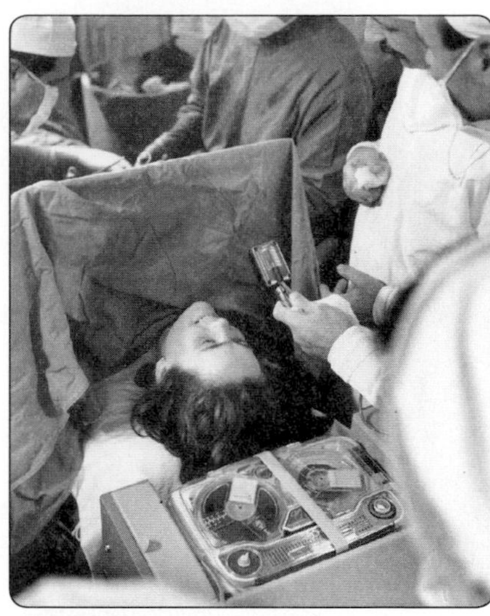

FIGURE 6.31

This patient is having her appendix removed with hypnosis as the sole anaesthetic. Her verbal reports that she feels no pain are being tape recorded.

Hypnosis and Memory

You may have seen TV shows or movies in which hypnotized people are given a suggestion that they will not remember something, either during the session itself (*hypnotic amnesia*), or after "coming out" of hypnosis (*post-hypnotic amnesia*). A "reversal cue" also is given, such as a phrase ("You will now remember everything") that ends the amnesia once the person hears it. Is this Hollywood fiction?

In one interesting case, a math teacher was given a hypnotic suggestion that he would be unable to recall the number six during the session. The teacher mistakenly interpreted the suggestion as including *post*-hypnotic amnesia. Can you imagine someone trying to teach math while being unable to recall the number six! Indeed, it proved difficult, until the hypnotist reversed the amnesia suggestion at a later session.

More extensive research indicates that about 25 percent of hypnotized university students can be led to experience amnesia (Kirsch & Lynn, 1998). Though researchers agree that hypnotic and post-hypnotic amnesia occur, they dispute the causes. Some feel it results from voluntary attempts to avoid thinking about certain information, and others believe it is caused by an altered state of consciousness or weakening of normal memory systems (Kihlstrom, 1985, 1998; Spanos, 1986).

Theories of Hypnosis

Hypnos may have been the Greek god of sleep, but hypnosis definitely is *not* sleep. Moreover, experts still debate whether hypnosis produces a unique pattern of physiological activity (Bauer & McCanne, 1980; Dixon & Laurence, 1992; Woody & Sadler, 1998). What then is hypnosis, and how does it produce its effects?

Dissociation Theories: Hypnosis as Divided Consciousness

Several influential researchers, such as Ken Bowers of the University of Waterloo and Ernest Hilgard of Stanford University, proposed **dissociation theories** that view hypnosis as an altered state involving a division ("dissociation") of consciousness (Bowers, 1983; Bowers, 1992; Kihlstrom, 1984). For example, Hilgard (1977, 1991) proposed that hypnosis creates a *division of awareness* in which the person simultaneously experiences two streams of consciousness that are cut off from one another. One stream responds to the hypnotist's suggestions, while the second stream—the part of consciousness that monitors behaviour—remains in the

40. According to the dissociation theory of hypnosis, why do hypnotic behaviours seem involuntary?

background but is aware of everything that goes on. Metaphorically, Hilgard refers to this second "part" of consciousness as the *hidden observer.*

Suppose a hypnotized subject is given a suggestion that she will not feel pain. Her arm is lowered into a tub of ice-cold water for 45 seconds and every few seconds she reports the amount of pain. In contrast to unhypnotized subjects, who find this experience moderately painful, she probably will report feeling little pain. But suppose the procedure were done differently. Before lowering the subject's arm, the hypnotist says, "Perhaps there is another part of you that is more aware than your hypnotized part. If so, would that part of you report the amount of pain." In this case, the subject's other stream of consciousness, the "hidden observer," will report a higher level of pain (Figure 6.32).

For Hilgard, this dissociation explains why behaviours that occur under hypnosis seem involuntary or automatic. Given the suggestion that "your arm will start to feel lighter and will begin to rise," the subject intentionally raises the arm, but only the hidden observer is aware of this. The main stream of consciousness that responds to the command is blocked from this awareness, and thus perceives that the arm is rising all by itself.

Social Cognitive Theories: Roles and Expectations

41. According to social cognitive theories of hypnosis, why do hypnotic behaviours seem involuntary?

Nicholas Spanos of Carleton University was one of the leading proponents of a very different view of hypnosis. To Spanos and others, hypnosis does not represent a special state of dissociated consciousness (Kirsch & Lynn, 1998; Sarbin & Coe, 1972; Spanos, 1991). In general, **social cognitive theories** propose that hypnotic experiences result from expectations of people who are motivated to take on the role of being "hypnotized." Most people believe that hypnosis involves a trancelike appearance, responsiveness to suggestion, and a loss of self-consciousness. People motivated to conform to this role and who expect to succeed in it develop a perceptual set—a readiness to respond to the hypnotist's suggestions and to perceive hypnotic experiences as real and "involuntary."

In a classic study, Martin Orne (1959) illustrated the importance of expectations about hypnosis. During a classroom demonstration, university students

(a)

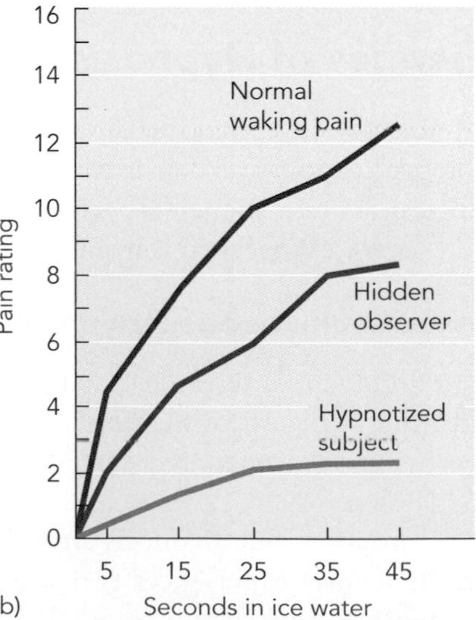

(b)

FIGURE 6.32

(a) This hypnotized subject's hand is immersed in painfully cold ice water. Placing his hand on her shoulder, Ernest Hilgard contacts her dissociated "hidden observer." (b) Pain intensity ratings given by a subject when she is not hypnotized, by the subject under hypnosis, and by the hidden observer in the same hypnotic state. The hidden observer reports more pain than the hypnotized subject, but less pain than the subject when she is not hypnotized.

Data from Hilgard, 1977.

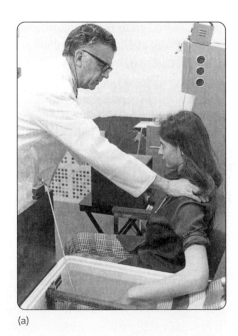

were told that hypnotized people frequently exhibit spontaneous stiffening of the muscles in the dominant hand. Actually, this rarely occurs. An accomplice of the lecturer pretended to be hypnotized and, sure enough, he "spontaneously" exhibited hand stiffness. When students who had seen the demonstration were later hypnotized, 55 percent of them exhibited stiffening of the hand without any suggestion from the hypnotist. Control group participants saw a demonstration that did not mention or display hand stiffening. Not one of these students exhibited hand stiffening when they were hypnotized.

Does social cognitive theory imply that people are faking or play-acting when they are hypnotized? Not at all. Role theorists emphasize that, when people immerse themselves in the hypnotic role, their responses are completely "real." Recall from the chapter on perception that perceptual sets strongly influence how the brain organizes sensory information. Often we literally "see" what we expect to see. According to social cognitive theory, many of the effects of hypnosis represent an extension of this basic principle. The hypnotized subject whose arm "automatically" rises in response to a suggestion genuinely perceives the behaviour to be involuntary because this is what the subject expects, and because attention is focused externally on the hypnotist and hypnotic suggestion.

Can the debate about hypnosis be resolved? Some psychologists believe the dissociation and social cognitive viewpoints can be integrated into a comprehensive theory (Kihlstrom, 1998; Woody & Sadler, 1998). Others disagree, saying it is time to discard some ideas of dissociation theory (Kirsch & Lynn, 1998). The only sure bet is that hypnosis will remain a controversial topic for some time to come.

In Review

- *Hypnosis involves an increased receptiveness to suggestion. Hypnotic susceptibility scales measure people's responsiveness to hypnosis.*
- *Hypnotized people subjectively experience their actions to be involuntary, but hypnosis has no unique power to make people behave "against their will." In experiments, hypnotized and unhypnotized people are equally likely to show striking physiological reactions and perform "amazing" physical feats. Hypnosis increases pain tolerance, but other psychological techniques also can reduce pain.*
- *Some people can be led to experience hypnotic and post-hypnotic amnesia.*
- *Dissociation theories view hypnosis as an altered state of divided consciousness. Hilgard proposes that one stream of consciousness responds to the hypnotist's suggestions, while another stream (the hidden observer) stays in the background and is fully aware of everything going on. Social cognitive role theories state that hypnotic experiences occur because people have strong beliefs and expectations about hypnosis and are highly motivated to enter a hypnotized "role." People's actions are sincere, but not the result of divided consciousness.*

SOME FINAL THOUGHTS

We have seen that consciousness can be studied scientifically at biological, psychological, and environmental levels. In so doing, we have learned that altered states are not as divorced from "normal" waking consciousness as had previously been thought. In a way, we all experience dissociated consciousness in the form of divided attention, and dreaming shares much in common with waking thought processes. As you learned in Chapter 1, expectations powerfully affect everyday waking perception. Now we see that our expectations and beliefs influence hypnotic and drug-induced experiences.

Consider the behaviour of the following participant in the *Research Foundations* experiment on drinking and driving. This university student consumed three non-alcoholic drinks, but through taste and smell cues was convincingly led to believe that they were alcoholic. Prior to taking a Breathalyzer test, he estimated his blood-alcohol level to be .07, just below the .08 legal driving limit where he lived. He felt he was almost drunk! When told the drinks were non-alcoholic, he argued that there had to be a mistake. When shown his true Breathalyzer result of .000, he claimed it was rigged and refused to drive home until the effects of his "drinks" wore off (MacDonald et al., 1995)!

Clearly, we have a remarkable capacity to alter our own state of consciousness without being aware that we are responsible for causing the change. In fact, might this capacity to alter consciousness underlie dissociative identity disorder (DID)? Social-cognitive theorists propose that, as with hypnosis, DID is a state in which people become deeply enmeshed in a role and sincerely come to perceive themselves as having multiple identities (Lilienfeld et al., 1999; Spanos, 1991). In contrast, dissociation theorists believe that DID represents a state of divided consciousness that usually develops as a protective reaction to extreme childhood trauma, such as prolonged sexual abuse (Gleaves, 1996; Putnam, 1998). Add to this mix the fact that some people intentionally fake DID, and you have an intriguing controversy that we explore in Chapter 13.

Along with the study of perception, probing the mysteries of conscious experience goes to the heart of understanding the subjective nature of "reality." On this matter, the century-old words of William James remain pertinent today:

> Our normal waking consciousness is but one special type of consciousness, whilst all about it, parted from it by the filmiest of screens, there lie potential forms of consciousness entirely different. . . . No account of the universe in its totality can be final which leaves these other forms of consciousness quite disregarded." (James, 1902, p. 298)

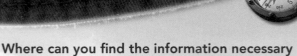

GAINING DIRECTION

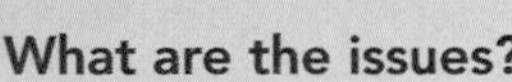

What are the issues?

The story of Ken Parks is intriguing. Mr. Parks killed his mother-in-law and attempted to kill his father-in-law. His defence appealed to a family history of sleep disorders and argued that he was, in fact, sleepwalking at the time. The jury dismissed all charges. Can an individual commit acts that are totally out of their awareness? Can an individual act out a dream or nightmare? If so, who is to be held accountable for these actions? In puzzling through these issues, we need to assess just what goes on during sleep.

What do we need to know?

What is consciousness?
What happens during sleep?
How do we explain sleepwalking?
Can you act out your dreams?
Can an individual perform an unconscious action that is "against their will"?

Where can you find the information necessary to answer these questions?

As you review the chapter, there are several critical pieces of information to assess. First, look at the material on the stages of sleep. What happens as you fall to sleep? Carefully examine the different stages and determine what is likely to happen at each stage. Second, consider the material on sleep disorders. When does sleepwalking typically occur? Is this the same stage as dreaming? If Ken Parks was not acting out a dream, what was happening in this situation? You should also consider what aspects of the evidence make this story more plausible. For example, is the report of sleep disorders within Parks' family of any use? You might look for reports of similar cases in the media. As you consider other cases, try to identify the factors that are similar (or different) to the Parks' case and why this may have resulted in a different verdict.

KEY TERMS AND CONCEPTS*

activation-synthesis theory (238)
alcohol myopia (246)
alpha waves (225)
amphetamine psychosis (249)
automatic processing (218)
beta waves (225)
blood-brain barrier (242)
circadian rhythms (220)
cognitive-process dream theory (239)
compensatory responses (243)
consciousness (216)
controlled (effortful) processing (218)
delta waves (226)
depressants (245)
dissociation theory (of hypnosis) (259)
divided attention (218)
ecstasy (MDMA) (249)
evolutionary/circadian sleep models (231)
fantasy-prone personality (240)
hallucinogens (250)
hypnosis (257)
hypnotic susceptibility scale (257)
insomnia (233)
meditation (255)
melatonin (220)
narcolepsy (234)
night terrors (236)
opiates (250)
problem-solving dream model (239)
REM sleep (226)
REM-sleep behaviour disorder (RBD) (235)
restoration model (230)
seasonal affective disorder (SAD) (222)
slow-wave sleep (226)
social cognitive theory (of hypnosis) (260)
stimulants (248)
substance dependence (244)
suprachiasmatic nuclei (SCN) (220)
THC (tetrahydrocannabinol) (251)
tolerance (243)
wish fulfillment (238)
withdrawal (243)

*Each term has been boldfaced in the text on the page indicated in parentheses.

DO YOU WANT TO ELEVATE YOUR GRADES?

For additional resources and interactive quizzing, visit the book's Online Learning Centre at **www.mcgrawhill.ca/olc/passer**.

CHAPTER 7

Learning and Adaptation: The Role of Experience

A man who carries a cat by the tail learns something he can learn in no other way.
—Mark Twain

CHAPTER OUTLINE

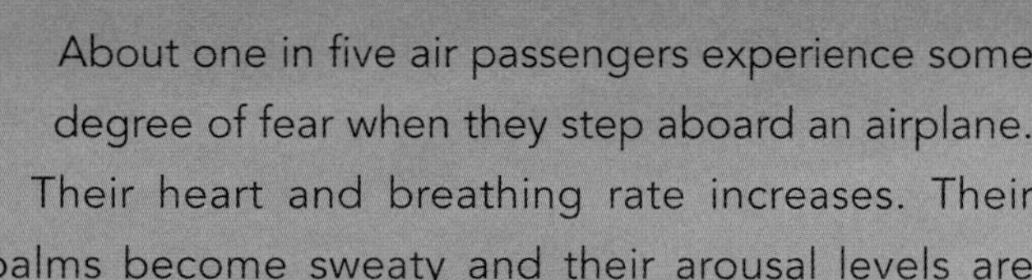

About one in five air passengers experience some degree of fear when they step aboard an airplane. Their heart and breathing rate increases. Their palms become sweaty and their arousal levels are high. For 3 percent of air travellers, the arousal is so high that they are in a state of panic, even when sitting in the airport parking lot. These individuals have aviophobia. The fear and panic stems from a variety of sources: media reports, unusual sounds aboard the aircraft, turbulence, and a general loss of control. Some take to driving all the way across Canada to avoid air travel completely.

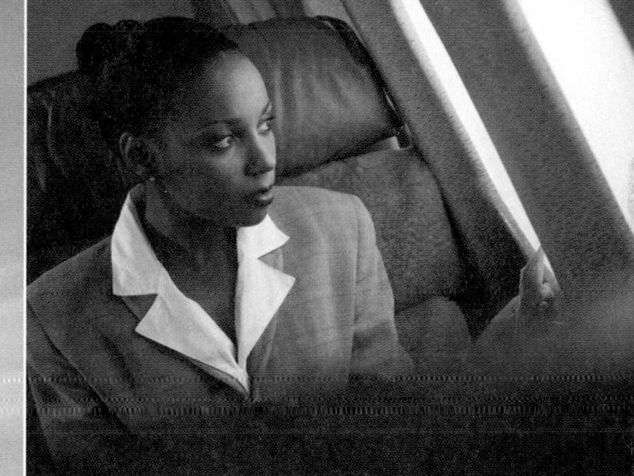

In an effort to overcome this problem, people have turned to drugs, hypnosis, and audio self-help tapes. The tapes have limited success, hypnosis works for some, and drugs, while reducing anxiety, do not really cure the problem. But recently, a new program run by Marc-Antoine Plourde of Montreal is showing a lot of promise. Plourde, a captain with Air Canada, runs the DePlour Training Centre where individuals can sign up for a two-day course to reduce their fear. The course involves seminars on pilot training, aircraft design, and maintenance; a ride in a flight simulator; plus a graduation "liberty flight" from Montreal to Toronto. Together with a licensed therapist, Plourde explains the science of flight and the psychology of fear. During a demonstration of aircraft design, Plourde uses a model of an Airbus A330 to show how the wings are engineered to bend. However, he bends them a little too much (on purpose), breaking off the wing much to the astonishment (and shock) of the participants. Their worst fear realized, Plourde explains how this could not happen in the real world.

Does the program work? Plourde claims a 94 percent satisfaction rate and notes that only 4 of 500 people have failed to take the liberty flight. Apparently, dealing with the emotional anxiety is more important than stressing airplane safety. As Captain Tom Bunn who runs a similar program in the U.S. notes, "People tell us that they know that flying is safer than driving, but my car doesn't fall 30,000 feet from the sky."

- **What are the issues here?**
- **What do we need to know?**
- **Where can we find the information to answer these questions?**

A young woman—we will call her Emily—has a debilitating fear of snakes. Although she never has to see a real snake, her snake phobia is so severe that anything that is at all snakelike elicits a strong and aversive emotional reaction. Finally, Emily seeks treatment for her snake phobia from a psychotherapist. She tells the therapist that her fear of snakes started when she was a young girl, only four years old. She was at a park with her family and while she was playing she saw a snake. She ran to her parents' car and jumped inside, closing the door behind her. She closed the door in such haste that the car door slammed on her hand, causing severe pain and resulting in a long series of visits to the doctor. Before this incident she was wary of snakes, and maybe even a little afraid of them, but after this incident, a full phobia of snakes developed. Emily's snake phobia persisted throughout childhood and adolescence and into adulthood, at which time she sought treatment. To help Emily, the therapist used a highly successful procedure based, in part, on principles of behaviour discovered in laboratory investigations of salivating dogs.

Reflect for a moment on how much of your behaviour is learned: telling time, getting dressed, driving, reading, using money, playing sports, and so on. Beyond such skills, learning affects our emotional reactions, perceptions, and physiological responses. Through experience, we learn to think, act, and feel in ways that contribute richly to our individual identity.

Learning is a process by which experience produces a relatively enduring change in an organism's behaviour or capabilities. The term *capabilities* highlights a distinction made by many theorists: "knowing how," or learning, versus "doing," or performance. For example, experience may provide us with immediate knowledge (e.g., the boys "learned" how to apply a choke-hold when they watched TV on Sunday), but in science we must *measure* learning by actual changes in performance (e.g., two days later, they began applying choke-holds to each other).

⊙ ADAPTING TO THE ENVIRONMENT

From the moment we are born, we encounter changing environments, each with its unique challenges. Some challenges affect survival, such as acquiring food and shelter. Others do not, such as deciding where to go on a date. But no matter the challenge, learning makes it possible for us to adapt to it. In fact, we can view learning as a process of *personal adaptation* to the ever-changing circumstances of our lives.

How Do We Learn? The Search for Mechanisms

1. Historically, how have behaviourists and ethologists differed in their study of learning?

2. Explain the concept of adaptive significance.

For a long time, the study of learning proceeded along two largely separate paths, guided by two different perspectives on behaviour: behaviourism and ethology (Bolles & Beecher, 1988). Within psychology, behaviourists focused on *how* organisms learn, examining the processes by which experience influences behaviour. Behaviourists assumed that there are laws of learning that apply to virtually all organisms. For example, each species they studied—whether birds, reptiles, rats, monkeys, or humans—responded in predictable ways to patterns of reward or punishment.

Behaviourists treated the organism as a *tabula rasa,* or blank tablet, upon which learning experiences were inscribed. Most of their research was conducted with non-human species in controlled laboratory settings. Behaviourists explained learning solely in terms of directly observable events and avoided speculating about an organism's unobservable "mental state."

Why Do We Learn? The Search for Functions

While behaviourism flourished in America, a specialty area called ethology arose in Europe within the discipline of biology (Lorenz, 1937; Tinbergen, 1951). *Ethology* focused on animal behaviour within the natural environment. Ethologists viewed the organism as anything but a blank tablet, arguing that because of evolution every species comes into the world biologically prepared to act in certain ways. They focused on the *functions* of behaviour, particularly its **adaptive significance**: How does a behaviour influence an organism's chances for survival and reproduction in its natural environment?

Consider how newly hatched herring gulls "beg" for food by pecking at a red mark on their parents' bills. Parents respond by regurgitating food, which the chick ingests. Seeing the red mark and long shape of the parent's bill automatically triggers the chick's pecking. This behaviour is so strongly "prewired" that chicks will peck just as much at long inanimate models or objects with red dots or stripes (Figure 7.1). Ethologists call this instinctive behaviour a **fixed action pattern**: an unlearned response automatically triggered by a particular stimulus.

As ethological research grew, two things soon became clear. First, some fixed action patterns could be modified by experience. Unlike newly hatched chicks, older chicks have learned what an adult gull looks like and will not peck at inanimate objects unless they resemble the head of an adult (Hailman, 1967). Second, in many cases what appeared to be "instinctive" behaviour actually involved learning. Ethologists noted striking differences among species, not so much in how they learned, but in what they learned in order to survive.

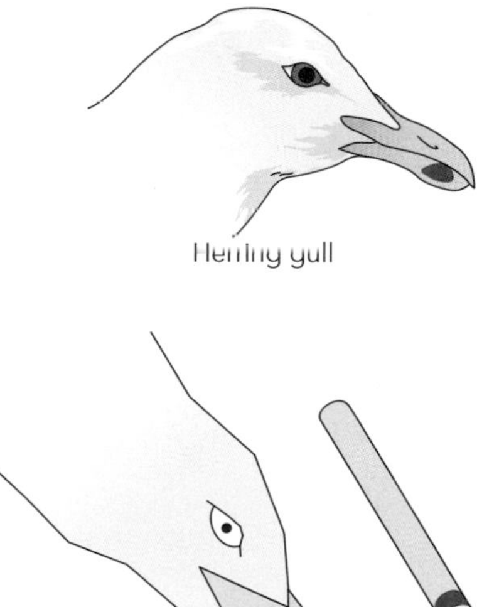

FIGURE 7.1

A newborn herring gull chick will peck most frequently at objects that are long and have red markings, even if they are inanimate models or do not look like an adult gull's bill. This fixed action pattern is present from birth and does not require learning. The stimuli that trigger a fixed action pattern are called "releaser stimuli."

Based on Hailman, 1967.

Consider the indigo bunting, a beautiful songbird that migrates during autumn nights from eastern North America to Central America. It navigates by flying "away from" the North Star, which by virtue of being directly over the North Pole, is the only star in the Northern Hemisphere that maintains a fixed compass position as the earth rotates on its axis. In spring, the bunting migrates north at night by flying "toward" the North Star. Were the bird to navigate by any other star, it would fly increasingly off course, because all other stars move across the night sky.

Navigating by the North Star would seem to be a fixed action pattern, as if birds instinctively know where "north" is. To test this idea, Stephen Emlen (1975) raised indigo buntings in a planetarium with either a true sky (with the North Star as the stationary star) or a false sky (in which a star in a different portion of the sky was the only one that remained stationary). In the fall, the birds became restless in their cages because it was time to migrate. As expected, the buntings raised with a true sky moved away from the North Star. But the other group moved away from the "false" stationary star, indicating that environmental changes could modify the bunting's navigational behaviour. Emlen concluded that the bunting is genetically prewired to navigate by a fixed star, but it has to learn which specific star is stationary through observation and experience.

Crossroads of Learning: Biology, Cognition, and Culture

3. What role does the environment play in *personal* and *species* adaptation?

The separate paths of behaviourism and ethology have increasingly converged in recent decades, reminding us that the environment shapes behaviour in two fundamental ways: through *personal adaptation* and through *species adaptation*. Personal adaptation occurs through the laws of learning that the behaviourists examined, and it results from our interactions with immediate and past environments (Dukas, 1998; Hollis, 1997). When you drive or go out on a date, your behaviour is influenced by the immediate environment (traffic, your date's smiles) and by capabilities you have acquired through experience (driving skills and social skills).

The environment also plays a role in species adaptation. Through the process of evolution, environmental conditions faced by each species help shape its biology. This does not occur directly—learning, for example, does *not* modify an organism's genes—and, therefore, learned behaviours are not passed down genetically from one generation to the next. But through natural selection, genetically based features that enhance a species' ability to adapt to the environment, and thus to survive and reproduce, are more likely to be passed on to the next generation. Eventually, as characteristics influenced by those genes become more common, they become a part of a species' very "nature."

For an individual, and a species, to survive, the ability to learn is a powerful tool. Species that can learn have the potential to adapt to changing environmental conditions or expand into new and different environments. Consider humans; our powerful learning capabilities allow us to adapt to a wide range of environments and we have successfully spread across all of the land mass of the planet earth, from tropical rainforests to equatorial deserts to the frozen tundra of the far north. Although the learned behaviours themselves are not passed across generations by the genes, the ability to learn is. The brain structure and function that allows learning are under genetic control.

Theorists propose that in response to environmental demands faced by our ancestors over millions of years, the human brain acquired the capacity to perform psychological functions that have adaptive value and enable us to learn (Cosmides & Tooby, 2000). In essence, we have become prewired to learn. Of course, to varying degrees, so have other species. Because all organisms face some common adaptive challenges, we might expect some similarity in their "library" of learning mechanisms (Roitblat & von Ferson, 1992). What are these common adaptive challenges? Every organism's environment is full of events, and the organism must learn:

- which events are, or are not, important to its survival and well-being;
- which stimuli signal that an important event is about to occur; and
- whether its responses will produce positive or negative consequences.

As we will see, each learning mechanism examined in this chapter helps us respond to one or more of these adaptive challenges. Although many learning mechanisms are common across a wide range of species, each species' evolutionary history and ecological niche place constraints on the learning that can occur. After exploring the basic forms of learning, we will return to the issue of constraints on learning.

The resurgence of the *cognitive perspective* and emergence of *cross-cultural psychology* also have expanded our understanding of learning. Cognitive psychologists have continued to challenge the behaviourist assumption that learning does not involve mental processes (Bandura, 1965; Dickinson, 1997). We will return to this issue later in this chapter. And as we have seen and will continue to explore in upcoming chapters, cross-cultural research highlights the vast impact of culture on what we learn—from social customs (*norms*) and beliefs to our most basic perceptions of the world and ourselves (Figure 7.2; Super & Harkness, 1997). This is not surprising, given that learning represents adaptation to the environment, and culture is the human-made part of our environment (Herskovits, 1948). Yet the learning mechanisms that foster this adaptation are universal among humans and, in some cases, occur across countless species.

FIGURE 7.2

People in different cultures learn different behaviours in order to adapt to their environment. The skills that most urbanized people have learned to acquire food—navigating around a supermarket and using money—would have little adaptive value in some cultures.

Habituation

Imagine that you are sitting alone in a quiet laboratory room. Suddenly, a loud sound occurs and you instantly become startled. Your body jerks slightly, you become aroused, and you look toward the source of the sound. Over time, as the sound occurs again and again, your startle response diminishes and eventually you ignore it. Similarly, studying at the library, you initially may be distracted by a student who is coughing frequently or tapping a pen. As time passes, you no longer notice it.

Habituation is a decrease in the strength of response to a repeated stimulus. It may be the simplest form of learning and occurs across species ranging from humans to dragonflies and sea snails (Carew & Kandel, 1973; Manning, 1967). Touch the skin of a sea snail in a certain location, and it will reflexively contract its gill. With repeated touches, this response habituates. Habituation serves a key adaptive function. If an organism responded to every stimulus in its environment, it would rapidly become overwhelmed and exhausted. By learning not to respond to uneventful familiar stimuli, organisms conserve energy and can attend to other stimuli that are important. Habituation also plays an important role in enabling scientists to study behaviour.

4. What is habituation, and what is its adaptive significance?

Habituation is different from sensory adaptation, which we discussed in Chapter 5. Sensory adaptation refers to a decreased sensory response to a continuously present stimulus. For example, when you enter a bakery you notice the smell of freshly baked bread, but if you stay in the bakery your olfactory system adapts and the smell becomes less and less noticeable. Habituation, on the other hand, is a simple form of learning that occurs within the central nervous system, not within the sensory neurons. You may habituate to a stimulus, but that sensory information is still available if it becomes relevant. For example, you may habituate to the sound of wind and rustling leaves outside of your window at night. The sounds have been presented frequently with no important consequences, and you no longer notice them. If, however, there is an unexpected noise, you may suddenly become keenly aware of all of those night-time sounds that a few seconds ago had shown habituation.

In Review

- *Learning is a process by which experience produces a relatively enduring change in an organism's behaviour or capabilities. Learning is measured by changes in performance.*
- *Learning involves adapting to the environment. Historically, behaviourists focused on the processes by which organisms learn, and ethologists focused on the adaptive significance of learning. Today these two perspectives have crossed paths, and more attention is paid also to how mental processes and cultural environments influence learning.*
- *Habituation is a decrease in the strength of a response to a repeated stimulus. It may be the simplest form of learning.*
- *Habituation allows organisms to attend to other stimuli that are more important.*

CLASSICAL CONDITIONING: ASSOCIATING ONE STIMULUS WITH ANOTHER

Life is full of interesting associations. Do you ever hear songs on the radio or find yourself in places that instantly make you feel good because they're connected to special times you've had? When you smell the aroma of popcorn or freshly baked cookies, does it make your mouth water or stomach growl? These examples illustrate a learning process called **classical conditioning**, in which an organism learns to associate two stimuli (e.g., a song and a pleasant event), such that one stimulus (the song) comes to produce a response (feeling happy) that originally was produced only by the other stimulus (the pleasurable event).

Like habituation, classical conditioning is a basic form of learning that occurs in mammals, birds, reptiles, fish, and even sea snails (Kandel & Hawkins, 1992). But unlike habituation, classical conditioning involves *learning an association* between stimuli. Its discovery dates back to the late 1800s and an odd twist of fate.

Pavlov's Pioneering Research

In the 1860s, Ivan Pavlov was studying theology in a Russian seminary and preparing for the priesthood when his career plans unexpectedly changed. A new government policy allowed the translation of Western scientific publications into Russian. Before long, Pavlov read Darwin's theory of evolution and other works, sparking a strong interest in the sciences (Windholz, 1997). Pavlov became a renowned physiologist, conducting research on digestion in dogs that won him the Nobel Prize in 1904.

To study digestion, Pavlov presented various types of food to dogs and measured their natural salivary response (Figure 7.3). But as often occurs in science, Pavlov was about to make an accidental but important discovery through astute observation. He noticed that with repeated testing, the dogs began to salivate *before* the food was presented, such as when they heard the footsteps of the approaching experimenter.

Further study confirmed Pavlov's observation. Dogs have a natural reflex to salivate to food, but not to tones. Yet when a tone or other stimulus that ordinarily did not cause salivation was presented just before food powder was squirted directly into a dog's mouth, the sound of the tone alone soon made the dog salivate. Pavlov's (1923–1928) research team rigorously studied this process for decades,

(a)

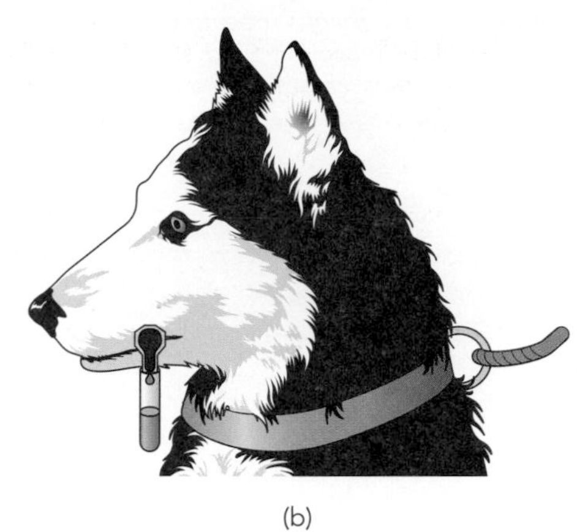

(b)

FIGURE 7.3

(a) Ivan Pavlov (the man with the white beard) is shown here with colleagues and one of his canine subjects. (b) In his early research, Pavlov measured salivation using a simple device similar to the one shown here. In later research, a collection tube was inserted directly into the salivary gland.

and this type of learning by association came to be called *classical* or *Pavlovian* conditioning. Many psychologists regard Pavlov's discovery as "among the most important in the history of psychology" (Dewsbury, 1997). But why all the fuss about dogs salivating to tones?

This question raises a widely misunderstood point about basic scientific research. As noted in Chapter 2, *what is paramount is the underlying principle being demonstrated, not the specific findings.* Even Pavlov viewed the salivary glands as relatively insignificant organs, but he recognized his discovery. Here was a basic learning process that performs a key adaptive function; classical conditioning alerts organisms to stimuli that signal the impending arrival of an important event. And, Pavlov noted, if salivation could be conditioned, so might other bodily processes, including those affecting susceptibility to disease and mental disorders.

Basic Principles

What factors influence the acquisition and persistence of conditioned responses? Let us examine some basic principles of conditioning.

Acquisition

Acquisition refers to the period during which a response is being learned. Suppose we wish to condition a dog to salivate to a tone. Sounding the tone initially may cause the dog to perk up its ears and stare at us oddly, but not to salivate. At this time, the tone is a *neutral stimulus* because it does not elicit (i.e., trigger) the salivation response (Figure 7.4). Now, if we place food in the dog's mouth, the dog will salivate. This salivation response to food is reflexive—it's what dogs do by nature. Because no learning is required for the food to produce salivation, the food is called an **unconditioned stimulus (UCS)** and salivation is an **unconditioned response (UCR)**. Next the tone and the food are paired—each pairing is called a *learning trial.* After several learning trials, when the tone is presented by itself, the dog

5. How do you create a conditioned salivation response in a dog?

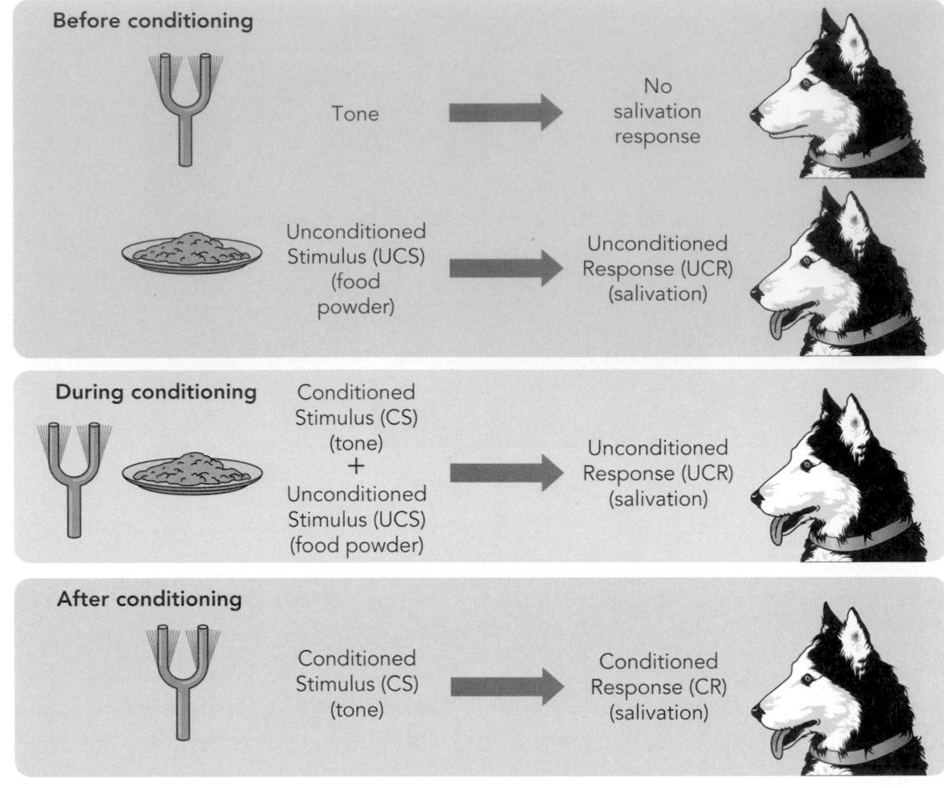
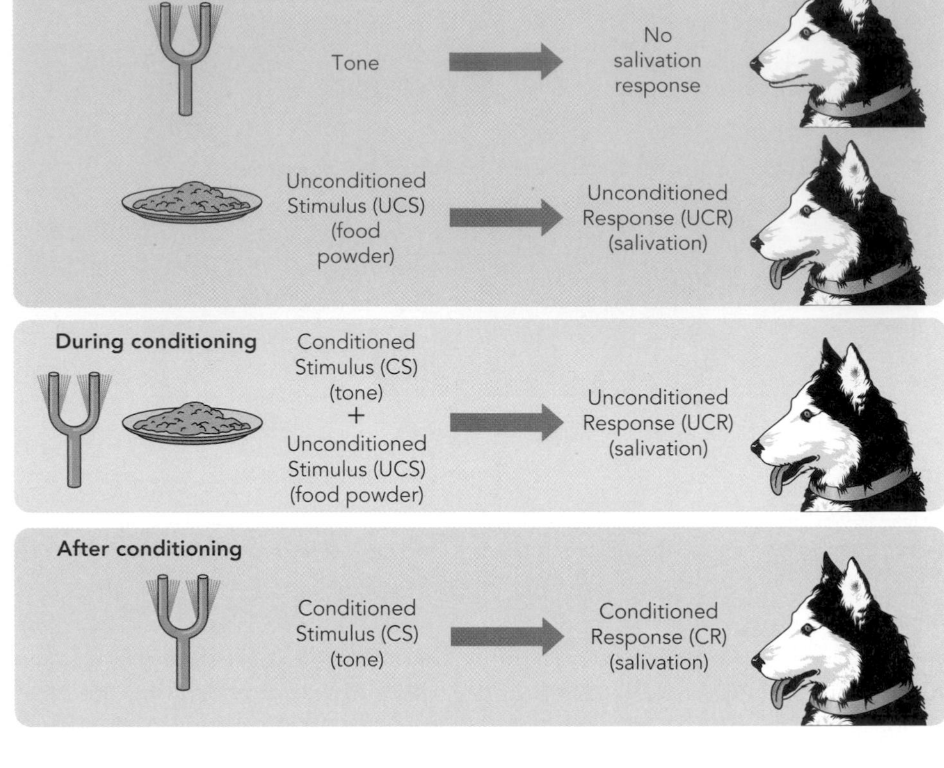

FIGURE 7.4

In classical conditioning, after a neutral stimulus such as a tone is repeatedly associated with food (unconditioned stimulus), the tone becomes capable of eliciting a salivation response.

salivates even though there is no food. Through association, the tone has become a **conditioned stimulus (CS)** and salivation has become a **conditioned response (CR)**. Table 7.1 offers a quick reference to these classical conditioning terms.

Notice that we have two terms for salivation: UCR and CR. When the dog salivates to food, this UCR is a *natural, unlearned (unconditioned) reflex.* But when it salivates to a tone, this CR represents a *learned (conditioned) response.*

6. Under what circumstances are CRs typically acquired most quickly?

During acquisition, a CS typically must be paired multiple times with a UCS to establish a strong CR (Figure 7.5). Pavlov also found that a tone became a CS more rapidly when it was followed by greater amounts of food. Indeed, when the UCS is intense and aversive—such as an electric shock or a traumatic event—conditioning may require only one CS-UCS pairing (Richard et al., 2000; Mahoney & Ayres, 1976). Emily's snake phobia illustrates this *one-trial (single-trial) learning.* In Emily's example, a stimulus (seeing a snake) became a CS after only one pairing with an intense UCS (the extremely painful experience of having the car door slammed on

TABLE 7.1 **A Quick Guide to Classical Conditioning**

Term	Abbreviation	Description	Example
Un**c**onditioned **S**timulus	UCS	A stimulus that innately elicits a response	Food
Conditioned **S**timulus	CS	A stimulus that gains value through learning	The sight of your favourite restaurant
Un**c**onditioned **R**esponse	UCR	A reflexive, unlearned response to an innately important stimulus	Salivation in response to food
Conditioned **R**esponse	CR	A response elicited by a stimulus whose importance depends on past learning	Feeling hungry when you see your favourite restaurant

FIGURE 7.5

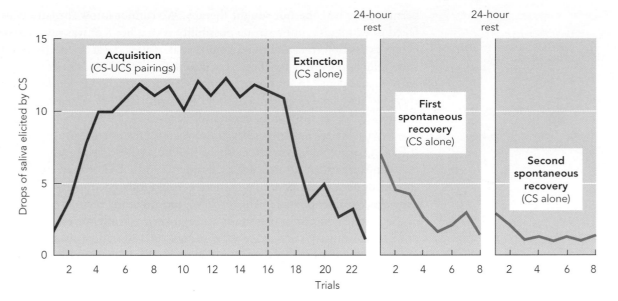

The strength of the CR (salivation) increases during the acquisition phase as the CS (tone) and the UCS (food) are paired on each trial. During the extinction phase, only the CS is presented, and the strength of the CR decreases and finally disappears. After a rest period following extinction, presentation of the CS elicits a weaker CR (spontaneous recovery) that extinguishes more quickly than before.

her hand). Fear was the UCR, and it became a CR triggered by the sight of snakes (Figure 7.6).

The sequence and time interval of the CS-UCS pairing also affect conditioning. Learning usually occurs most quickly with *forward short-delay pairing:* The CS (tone) appears first and is still present when the UCS (food) appears. In *forward trace pairing*, the tone would come on and off, and afterward the food would be presented. In forward pairing, it is often optimal for the CS to appear no more than two or three seconds before the UCS (Klein & Mowrer, 1989). Forward pairing has adaptive value because the CS signals the impending arrival of the UCS. Typically, presenting the CS and UCS at the same time (*simultaneous pairing*) produces less rapid conditioning, and learning is slowest, or does not occur at all, when the CS is presented after the UCS (*backward pairing*).

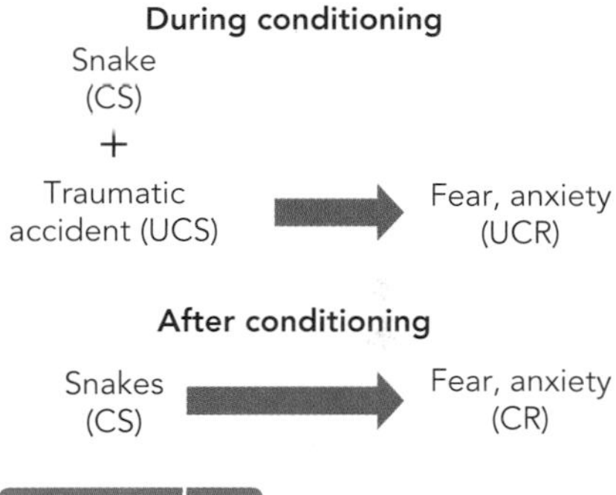

FIGURE 7.6

It is likely that Emily's phobia of snakes was acquired through classical conditioning.

To summarize, classical conditioning usually is strongest when there are repeated CS-UCS pairings, the UCS is more intense, the sequence involves forward pairing, and the time interval between the CS and UCS is short.

Extinction and Spontaneous Recovery

If the function of classical conditioning is to help organisms adapt to their environment, there must be a way of eliminating the CR when it is no longer appropriate. Fortunately, there is. If the CS is presented repeatedly in the absence of the UCS, the CR weakens and eventually disappears. This process is called **extinction**, and each presentation of the CS without the UCS is called an *extinction trial.* When Pavlov repeatedly presented the tone without the food, the dogs eventually stopped salivating to the tone (Figure 7.5). Occasional re-pairings of the CS (e.g., tone) and the UCS (e.g., food) usually are required to maintain a CR.

In some situations, a CR seems to persist for a long time without such CS-UCS "booster" sessions (Edwards, 1962). For example, Emily's fear of snakes persisted for years despite the fact she had no similar accidents, and may have lasted permanently had she not sought therapy. We cannot know for sure why her fear failed to extinguish, but a strong possibility is that her fear was not exposed to sufficient extinction trials. If Emily avoided snakes after the accident, there would have been little opportunity for the CS (snakes) to occur without the presentation of the UCS (an accident). In short, *the key ingredient to extinction is not the mere passage of time, but repeated presentation of the CS without the UCS.* Without exposure to the CS, the CR will be difficult to extinguish.

7. Explain the key factor in producing extinction of a CR.

Even when a CR extinguishes, this does not mean that all traces of it are erased. If Emily, the young lady with the snake phobia, is presented repeatedly with snakes (CS exposure) with no aversive consequences (no UCS), then her snake phobia should undergo extinction. Later, however, if Emily encounters a snake, she may experience fear once again. This is called **spontaneous recovery**, which is defined as the reappearance of a previously extinguished CR after a rest period, and without new learning trials. As Figure 7.5 shows, the spontaneously recovered CR usually is weaker than the initial CR and extinguishes more rapidly in the absence of the UCS. The phenomenon of spontaneous recovery is why practical applications of extinction, such as treatment of phobias or other anxiety disorders, require multiple sessions. The abnormal CR, such as fear, may appear to have undergone extinction, but it will return in the future. With each set of extinction trials the CR is progressively weakened and with sufficient extinction training spontaneous recovery is weak enough that it is not a problem.

Generalization and Discrimination

8. Explain the adaptive significance of stimulus generalization and discrimination.

Thus far we have explained Emily's snake phobia as a case of one-trial conditioning in which seeing a snake was paired with a traumatic experience. But why would Emily fear other snakes, or even anything that was at all snakelike, when it was one specific snake that was present just before her accident?

Pavlov found that once a CR is acquired, the organism often responds not only to the original CS, but also to stimuli that are similar to it. The greater the stimulus similarity, the greater the chance that a CR will occur. A dog that salivates to a medium-pitched tone is more likely to salivate to a new tone slightly different in pitch, than to a low- or high-pitched tone. Learning theorists call this **stimulus generalization**: Stimuli similar to the initial CS elicit a CR (Figure 7.7).

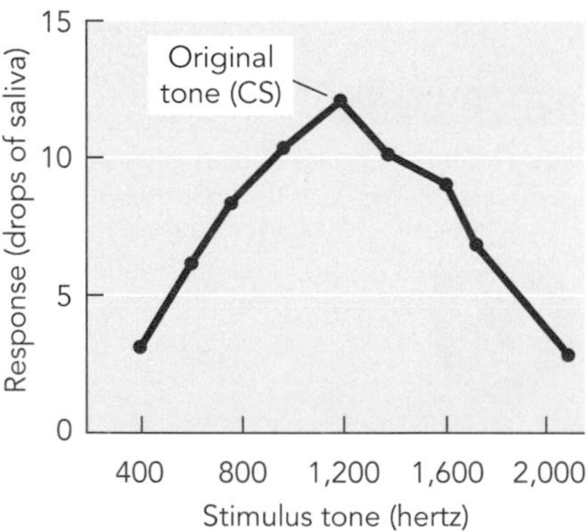

FIGURE 7.7

A stimulus generalization curve. An animal will salivate most strongly to the CS that was originally paired with the UCS. Progressively weaker conditioned responses occur as stimuli become less similar to the CS, as seen here with tones of lower or higher frequencies (pitch).

Stimulus generalization serves critical adaptive functions. An animal that ignores the sound of rustling bushes and then is attacked by a hidden predator will become alarmed by the sound of a rustling bush in the future (assuming it escapes). If stimulus generalization did not occur, then the next time the animal heard rustling it would become alarmed only if the sound were identical to that preceding the earlier attack. This has little value to the animal's survival. Through stimulus generalization, the animal develops an alarm response to a range of rustling sounds. Some will be false alarms, but safe is better than sorry.

To prevent stimulus generalization from running amok, organisms must be able to *discriminate* (i.e., detect) differences between stimuli. An animal that becomes alarmed at every sound it hears will exhaust itself from stress. It must learn to distinguish irrelevant sounds from those that may signal danger. In classical conditioning, **discrimination** is demonstrated when a CR (such as an alarm reaction) occurs to one stimulus (a sound) but not to others. Emily's fear of snakes was widespread, but it did not occur when she saw other animals.

As another example, when my mother was a girl, a large, rabid dog bit her several times. From that painful moment on, she was extremely afraid of dogs. Many years later, when my brother wanted a dog, my mother would have none of it. But he pleaded endlessly. How could we satisfy my brother's wish, yet not trigger my mother's fear? The solution was to get a dog as dissimilar as possible to the large dog that bit her, in hopes that my mother's fear would display stimulus discrimination. So we adopted a tiny Chihuahua puppy—and the plan was half-successful. My mother was not afraid, and adored the dog. But my brother's fondness for big dogs failed to generalize to Chihuahuas, and he was repeatedly observed muttering something like "yippity oversized rat."

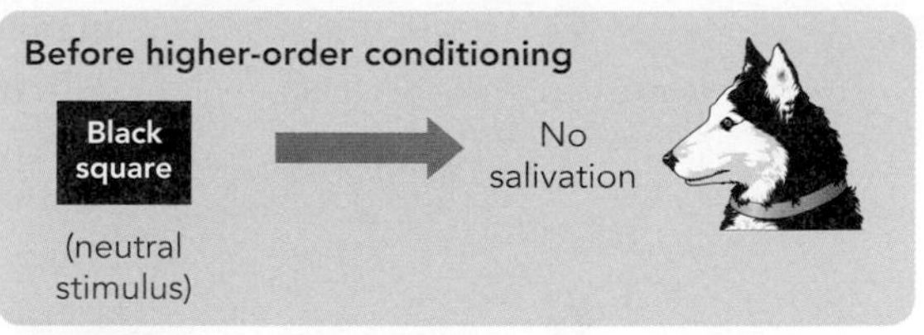

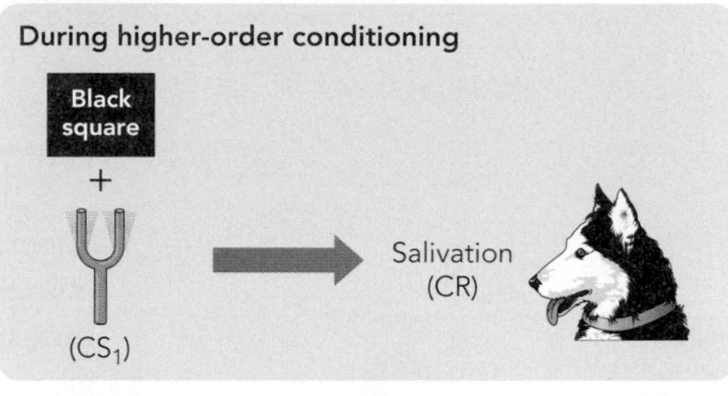

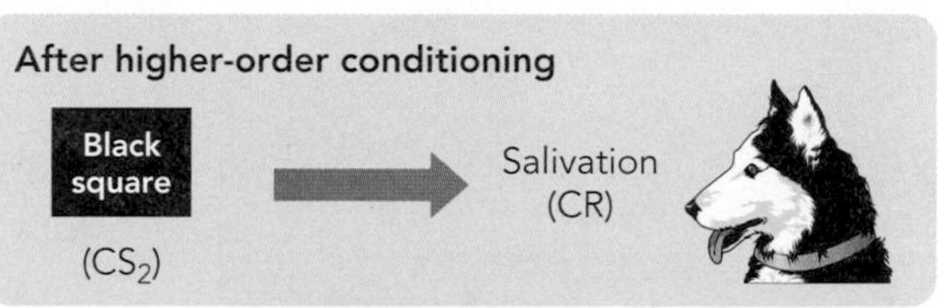

FIGURE 7.8

Once a tone has become a conditioned stimulus that triggers salivation, we can now use it to condition a salivation response to a new neutral stimulus—a black square. The tone is the CS_1. The black square becomes the CS_2.

Higher-Order Conditioning

Imagine that we have exposed a dog to repeated tone-food pairings, and the tone is now a well-established CS that elicits a strong salivation response. Next, suppose that we present a neutral stimulus, such as a black square, and the dog does not salivate. Now we present the black square just prior to sounding the tone, but do not present any food. After repeated square-tone pairings, the square will become a CS and elicit salivation by itself (Figure 7.8). This process, discovered by Pavlov, is called **higher-order conditioning**: A neutral stimulus becomes a CS after being paired with an already established CS. Typically, a higher-order CS produces a CR that is weaker and extinguishes more rapidly than the original CR. The dog will salivate less to the black square than to the tone, and its response to the square will extinguish sooner.

Higher-order conditioning greatly expands the influence of conditioned stimuli and can affect what we come to value, like, fear, or dislike (Gewirtz & Davis, 1998; Mowrer et al., 1988). For example, political candidates try to get us to like them by associating themselves with patriotic symbols, cuddly babies, admired athletes and civic leaders, and other conditioned stimuli that already trigger positive emotional reactions among voters.

Applications of Classical Conditioning

9. Explain the process of higher-order conditioning.

Pavlov's belief that salivation was merely the tip of the classical conditioning iceberg has proven correct. Conditioning principles discovered in laboratory research—much of it with non-human species—help us understand diverse human behaviours and problems.

Acquiring and Overcoming Fear

Pavlov's discoveries enabled early American behaviourists to challenge Freud's psychoanalytic view of the causes of anxiety disorders, such as phobias. To explain Emily's snake phobia, no Freudian assumptions about hidden unconscious conflicts or repressed traumas are needed. Instead, the behaviourist view is that snakes have become a fear-triggering CS due to one-trial pairing with the UCS (injury to her hand) and stimulus generalization.

Does this explanation seem reasonable? It may, but it suffers from a serious limitation: Almost any explanation can seem plausible when it is provided *after* some event occurs. So behaviourists John B. Watson and Rosalie Rayner (1920) set out to obtain stronger evidence that fear could be conditioned. They studied an 11-month-old infant named Albert. One day, as Albert played in a hospital room, Watson and Rayner showed him a white rat. Albert displayed no sign of fear. Later, knowing that Albert *was* afraid of loud noises, they hit a steel bar with a hammer, making a loud noise as they showed Albert the rat. The noise scared Albert and

10. How does classical conditioning explain fear acquisition?

11. How is classical conditioning used in society to increase or decrease our arousal/attraction to stimuli?

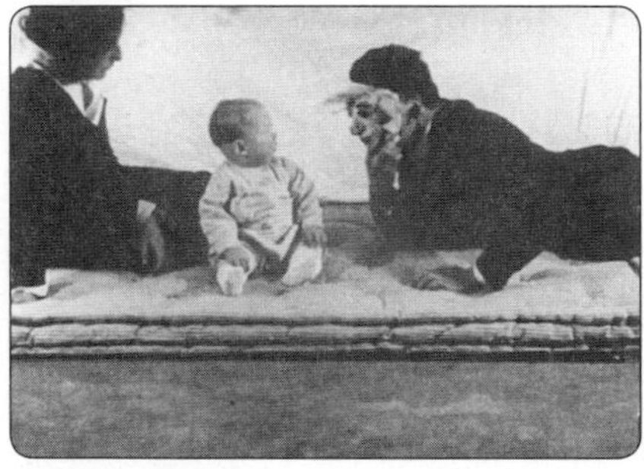

FIGURE 7.9

John Watson and Rosalie Rayner examine how little Albert reacts to a furry mask.

TABLE 7.2 Using Exposure Training to Reduce Fear

This table lists 10 of the 17 steps used by Mary Cover Jones to eliminate Peter's fear of rabbits.

Step No.	Peter's Progress
1	Rabbit anywhere in room triggers fear
2	Rabbit four metres away tolerated
4	Rabbit one metre away tolerated
5	Rabbit close in cage tolerated
6	Rabbit free in room tolerated
8	Rabbit touched when free in room
10	Rabbit allowed on tray of high chair
12	Holds rabbit on lap
16	Fondles rabbit affectionately
17	Lets rabbit nibble his fingers

Adapted from Jones (1924).

made him cry. After several rat-noise pairings, the sight of the white rat alone made Albert cry.

To examine stimulus discrimination and generalization, Watson and Rayner exposed Albert to other test stimuli several days later. Albert displayed no fear when shown coloured blocks, but furry white or grey objects, such as a rabbit and a bearded Santa Claus mask, made him cry (Figure 7.9). By the time Albert left the hospital, he had not been exposed to any treatment designed to extinguish his fear. Unfortunately, we do not know what became of Albert after that. (Had ethics review boards been in existence in the 1920s—they were not—would you have approved this study, and if so, under what conditions or precautions?)

Two other sources of evidence suggest that at least some fears are conditioned. Laboratory experiments convincingly show that animals become afraid of neutral stimuli that are paired with electric shock (Ayres, 1998; Monti & Smith, 1976). In humans, behavioural treatments partially based on classical conditioning principles are among the most effective psychotherapies for phobias (Wolpe, 1997). The key assumption is that if phobias are learned, they can be "unlearned."

In 1924, psychologist Mary Cover Jones successfully treated a boy named Peter, who had a strong fear of rabbits. Jones, who acknowledged Watson and Rayner's work, gradually extinguished Peter's fear using the procedure shown in Table 7.2. Her approach was a forerunner of current behaviour therapies, discussed in Chapter 14. In a nutshell, they are called **exposure therapies** because their basic goal is to expose the phobic patient to the feared stimulus (CS) without any UCS, allowing extinction to occur.

Mental imagery, real-life situations, or both can be used to present the phobic stimulus. In one approach, called *systematic desensitization*, the patient learns muscular relaxation techniques and then is gradually exposed to the fear-provoking stimulus (Wolpe, 1958, 1997). Another approach, sometimes called *flooding*, immediately exposes the person to the phobic stimulus (Spiegler & Guevremont, 1998; Nesbitt, 1973). In Emily's case, her therapist extinguished the snake phobia in six sessions of flooding. As Emily's initially strong anxiety decreased, she was able to see and even touch a real snake. Exposure therapies are highly effective and represent one of behaviourism's important applied legacies. See the Psychological Applications box for a new variant of exposure therapy.

Conditioned Attraction and Aversion

Much of what attracts and pleasurably arouses us is influenced by classical conditioning. Consider sexual arousal. The comment, "It really turns me on when you wear that," reflects how a clothing outfit or scent of a partner's cologne can become a conditioned stimulus for arousal. Experiments show that pairing a neutral odour with pleasing physical massage increases people's attraction to that smell (Baeyens et al., 1996), and that people become more sexually aroused to various stimuli after those CSs have been paired with sexually arousing UCSs (Rachman & Hodgson, 1968). Experiments with fish, birds, and rats confirm that originally neutral stimuli can trigger sexual arousal after they have been paired with a naturally arousing UCS (Domjan et al., 1989; Hollis, 1997).

Classical conditioning also can decrease our arousal and attraction to stimuli. This principle is used in **aversion therapy**, which attempts to condition an aversion (a repulsion) to a stimulus that triggers unwanted behaviour by pairing it with a noxious UCS. To reduce an alcoholic's attraction to alcohol, the patient is given a drug that induces severe nausea when alcohol is consumed (Nathan, 1985). Aversion therapies yield mixed results, often producing short-term changes that extinguish over time.

PSYCHOLOGICAL APPLICATIONS

Learning, Virtual Reality, and Therapy

The most widely accepted theory for the acquisition of anxiety disorders such as phobias is that these disorders are acquired through classical conditioning. Exposure to an environmental stimulus (CS) is paired with an aversive event (UCS), and as a result the originally neutral stimulus comes to elicit an emotional reaction of anxiety or fear (CR). For example, as discussed earlier (see page 266), Emily's snake phobia began because she saw a snake (CS) then had her hand painfully injured by the car door (UCS). If we acquire anxiety disorders through conditioning, then conditioning procedures may be effective at treating these anxiety disorders. The most commonly used and most effective therapies for anxiety disorders such as specific phobias are based on a classical conditioning model.

These therapeutic approaches have been classified as exposure treatments because they all involve exposure to the phobic stimulus without aversive consequences. From studies of classical conditioning we know that if a CS is presented repeatedly without any biologically important following event, the learned response will gradually diminish in strength and may eventually disappear. As discussed earlier, this is the process of extinction; with extinction training the CS loses its value and the learned response (CR) is progressively weakened. The traditional exposure therapy approaches have involved presenting the client with either the real, phobic stimulus (give Emily a real snake), or exposure to a series of stimuli that gradually get closer to, and more like, the phobic stimulus. For example, you may show Emily a cartoon picture of a not very realistic snake, then gradually work toward the presentation of a realistic model snake, to the eventual presentation of a real snake in close proximity. Such procedures, especially when combined with relaxation training, are very effective at treating anxiety disorders such as snake and spider phobias, fear of flying, and public speaking anxiety. Exposure therapy with gradual introduction of the phobic stimulus is the treatment of choice for specific phobias (Antony & Swinson, 2000; Garcia-Palacios, et al., 2002; Marks, 1987). In a variant of exposure therapy, the client imagines exposure to the feared stimulus or situation rather than confronting the real thing. Clinical research has found that although imaginal exposure can be successful, real world exposure (referred to as *in vivo* exposure) is superior (Krijn et al., 2004).

Although exposure therapy is very successful, a surprising number of individuals with phobias do not seek treatment. Some estimates are that as many as 40% of individuals with a specific phobia never seek treatment and the phobia continues to needlessly generate anxiety and disrupt their lives (Garcia-Palacios, et al., 2002). Individuals with a phobia often avoid treatment because they fear having to confront the phobic stimulus, even though they know that the therapy will help them overcome that fear.

Recent advances in computer and video technology have presented an innovative approach to treating anxiety disorders: the use of virtual reality (VR). VR uses real-time computer graphics and high resolution 3-D visual displays, body tracking, sound, and, in some cases, other types of sensory input (e.g., tactile stimulation) to immerse clients in a computer-generated world. The power of VR comes from the perception of the user that they are really there, really within the computer generated world. The therapist guides, via their computer, what happens within the client's virtual world (see Figure 7.10). If you can overcome your fear of snakes, public speaking, or heights with exposure therapy, can that exposure take place in a virtual world? If VR is effective, it would make it more practical to apply exposure therapy in some cases (e.g., fear of flying, fear of heights). This may also be a more appealing therapy for individuals who have avoided or abandoned therapy because exposure to the real stimulus generates such intense fear or is impractical. If you have a fear of flying, you may not have to arrange to actually go up in an airplane (with the expense and inconvenience that involves); you may be able to simply put on a VR helmet.

Apart from presenting virtual stimuli within a virtual world, exposure therapy using VR progresses like any other graded exposure therapy. The initial stimulus or situation is only remotely like the fear-inducing stimulus, and as the client is able to confront the situation without anxiety it is gradually moved closer and closer to the phobic situation.

One study of the effectiveness of VR to treat phobias involved clients with a spider phobia (Garcia-Palacios, et al., 2002). Clients in this study had to meet a series of criteria, including the full diagnostic criteria for a specific phobia established by the American Psychiatric Association (DSM-IV, the American Psychiatric Association, 1994; see Chapter 13 for additional information on the DSM and clinical diagnosis). During treatment, clients donned a VR helmet and visited a virtual kitchen. Gradually over a series of trials, clients received increasing exposure to a virtual spider. For example, they initially saw a virtual spider at a distance, later they came within arm's reach of a virtual spider, and eventually they were to touch the virtual spider. The goal of the VR exposure was to have the client hold a furry virtual tarantula within their cyber-kitchen and report low levels of anxiety. In a clever and creative twist, tactile feedback was provided by having the client's real hand explore a model spider while their virtual hand explored the cyber-spider. Across the course of this study, members of a waiting list control group showed no

–Continued

The intended "punishments" failed because they actually reinforced Pascal with what he wanted most: attention. The psychologist instructed Mrs. Adams to use a procedure called *time out,* which is short for "time out from positive reinforcement." When Pascal misbehaved, Mrs. Adams deprived him of attention, either by ignoring him or by placing him in another room for a specific period of time. She also began to reinforce Pascal's desirable behaviours by paying attention to him. Soon thereafter, Pascal was no longer a rascal.

Positive Punishment

Like reinforcement, punishment comes in two forms. One involves actively *applying* aversive stimuli, such as painful slaps, electric shock, and verbal reprimands. This is **positive punishment**, also called aversive punishment. A response is *weakened* by the subsequent *presentation* of a stimulus. Spanking or scolding a child for misbehaving are obvious examples, but so is a child's touching a hot stovetop burner. The pain delivered by the burner makes it less likely that the child will touch it in the future. Positive punishment often is subtle. A teenager wears a new blouse, her close friends halfheartedly say "Uh-huh, nice," but their facial expressions betray dislike and the student stops wearing the outfit.

Positive punishment often produces rapid results, an important consideration when it is necessary to stop a particularly dangerous behaviour, such as an animal or person attacking someone. Sometimes electric shocks are applied to stop the self-destructive behaviours of profoundly disturbed children who injure themselves by banging their heads on sharp objects or biting themselves (Matson & Gardner, 1991). The shock is presented immediately after each self-injurious response begins. In one case, a severely disturbed girl with a six-year history of banging her head against sharp objects stopped after she received only 15 shocks (Lovaas, 1977).

20. Describe some disadvantages of using positive punishment to control behaviour.

Though positive punishment often works, it has important limitations. Punishment suppresses behaviour, but does not cause the organism to forget how to make the response. Moreover, this suppression may not generalize to other relevant situations, as when scolded children refrain from using "bad language" only when their parents are present. (Analogously, reinforced behaviours also may fail to generalize, as when a child reinforced for saying "thank you" does so only when a parent is present.)

Unlike reinforcement, punishment arouses negative emotions, such as fear and anger, that can produce dislike and avoidance of the person delivering the punishment. Positive physical punishment also may set a bad example. It amounts to control by aggression and can send a message to the recipient that such aggression is appropriate and effective.

Do physically punished children learn such a lesson? Correlational research finds that toddlers and children whose parents use physical punishment display more aggression in daycare centres and at school than do otherwise similar children who are not physically punished (George & Main, 1979; Hart et al., 1998; Stormshak et al., 2000). Although correlation does not demonstrate causation, controlled experiments indicate that children can learn aggressive behaviours by watching adult models (Bandura, 1965). In sum, positive punishment has its place, but many psychologists recommend against this form of behaviour control unless other alternatives are not feasible.

Negative Punishment

The legendary baseball umpire Bill Klem once called a batter out on a close third strike. The enraged batter flung his bat high into the air and whirled around to argue the call. Klem whipped off his mask, stared at the batter, and said, "If that bat comes down, it'll cost you 100 bucks."

Monetary fines, loss of privileges, and "groundings" represent attempts to punish behaviour by taking away something that an organism desires or finds satisfying ("that'll cost you"). In **negative punishment**, a response is *weakened* by the subsequent *removal* of a stimulus (see Figure 7.15). Negative punishment is sometimes referred to as response cost.

Negative punishment may seem similar to "time out" (operant extinction) because both processes weaken behaviour by depriving the individual of something he or she desires. But there is a key difference. If you recall Pascal the Rascal, "time out" meant depriving him of the specific stimulus (attention) that was reinforcing his misbehaviour in the first place. Negative punishment would have involved depriving him of other stimuli that he desired (perhaps "no TV"), but which did not cause him to act out in the first place.

Negative punishment has two distinct advantages over positive punishment. First, although it may arouse temporary frustration or anger, it is less likely to create strong fear or even hatred of the punishing agent (Pazulinec et al., 1983). Second, the punishing agent is not modelling physical aggression, so there is less opportunity for learning of aggression through imitation.

When parents use negative punishment to punish children's behaviour, the withheld reinforcer should be some prized object or activity, rather than love. Withholding love and rejecting the child can damage the child's self-concept (Brown, 1998). The same principle applies to using positive punishment. Communicate dislike for the *behaviour*, not for the child. Finally, punishment teaches the recipient what *not* to do, but does not guarantee that desirable behaviour will appear in its place. Desirable alternative responses should be strengthened directly through positive reinforcement.

Immediate versus Delayed Consequences

21. Why would a fine or ticket, payable later, not be very effective for changing behaviour?

In general, reinforcement or punishment that occurs immediately after a behaviour has a stronger effect than when it is delayed (Commons et al., 1984). Training animals typically requires very quick reinforcement so that they associate the correct response—rather than some subsequent behaviour—with the satisfying outcome.

The timing of consequences may have less influence on human behaviour because we are able to imagine future consequences and weigh them against more immediate ones. This often confronts us with interesting dilemmas. If you could have $100 right now, or $200 a year from now, which would you choose? This decision involves **delay of gratification**, the ability to forego an immediate but smaller reward for a delayed but more satisfying outcome (Mischel et al., 1972, 1989). Do I spend my income as I get it, buying things I want right now? Or, do I save up to buy a special item I want very much?

Individuals vary in their ability to delay gratification, a capacity that typically develops in the preschool years (Metcalfe & Mischel, 1999). Interestingly, young children who display less ability to delay gratification show poorer adjustment and have more difficulty coping with stress and frustration when they become adolescents. The inability to delay gratification also may play a role in behaviours such as chronic drinking, smoking, and even criminal acts (Brown, 1998).

Chronic drug use, for example, is difficult for many people to overcome because the immediate gratifying consequences override the delayed benefits of *not* performing the behaviour (e.g., being healthier, living longer). With some drugs, such as cocaine, use is positively reinforced by feelings of pleasure that seem to result from enhanced dopamine activity (Pilla et al., 1999). With other drugs, powerful negative reinforcers play a key role. Chronic cigarette smokers experience increased tension as the level of nicotine in their blood drops after their last cigarette. When they smoke again, tension is reduced. Thus smoking is negatively reinforced by the removal of unpleasant tension. Given that the typical chronic smoker inhales about 60,000 cigarette puffs a year (Parrott, 1999), this adds up to a lot of negative reinforcement.

Shaping and Chaining: Taking One Step at a Time

Mark is a four-year-old preschooler. He doesn't play much with other children, rarely engages in physical activity, and during outdoor recess spends most of his time sitting in the sandbox. His teachers and parents would like him to be more active. How can we use operant conditioning to change Mark's behaviour?

22. How might you shape a child who never cleans up his room to do so?

First, we need to operationally define our goal. What exactly do we mean by "being active"? For starters, let's define it as "playing on the monkey bars." Second, we need to select a positive reinforcer, which in Mark's case will be "attention." Finally, all we need to do is reinforce Mark when he is playing on the monkey bars. The problem is, we will be waiting a long time, because he rarely displays such behaviour.

Fortunately, Skinner developed a powerful procedure, called *shaping*, for overcoming this problem. We begin by reinforcing Mark with attention every time he stands up in the sandbox. This is the first approximation toward our final goal. Once this response is established, we now reinforce him only if he stands up and walks out of the sandbox toward the monkey bars. This is the *second approximation*. Then we might reinforce him only when he stands next to the bars, and finally only when he is on the bars and moving. This process, called **shaping**, involves reinforcing successive approximations toward a final response. This technique also is called the *method of successive approximations*. Using a shaping procedure similar to the one just described, it took researchers little time to start Mark playing on monkey bars (Johnston et al., 1966).

Even when behaviours might reasonably be learned through trial and error—such as a rat learning to press a lever for food—shaping speeds up the process. By reinforcing successive approximations, such as standing near the lever, raising a front paw, touching the lever, and finally depressing the lever, acquisition time is drastically reduced.

Another procedure, **chaining**, is used to develop a *sequence* (chain) of responses by reinforcing each response with the opportunity to perform the next response. For example, suppose that a rat has learned to press a lever when a light is on to receive food. Next we place a bell nearby. By accident, the rat eventually bumps into and rings the bell, which turns on the light. Seeing the light, the rat runs to and presses the lever. Over time, the rat will learn to ring the bell because this response is reinforced by turning on the light, which provides the opportunity to press the lever for food. As in this example, chaining usually begins with the final response in the sequence and works backward toward the first response (Catania, 1998). Figure 7.17 shows another example.

The amazing feats you see animals perform on TV, in the movies, or at circuses and theme parks, are developed through shaping and chaining. So is the behaviour of animals who assist people with disabilities. Humans learn many complex behaviours this way. For example, specific musical, athletic, and academic skills often are shaped by starting with a basic, simplified operation and reinforcing progressively closer approximations to the final response.

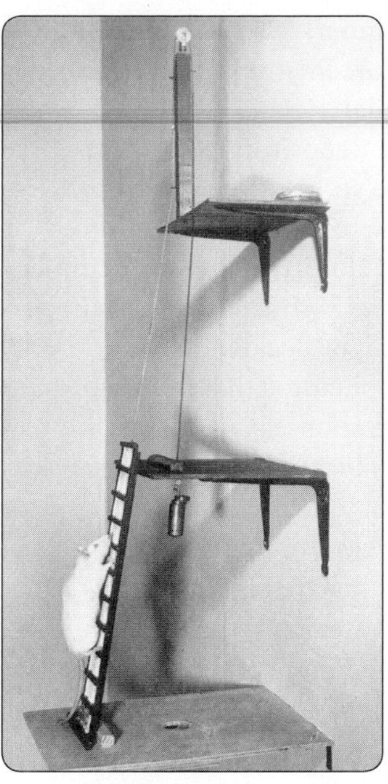

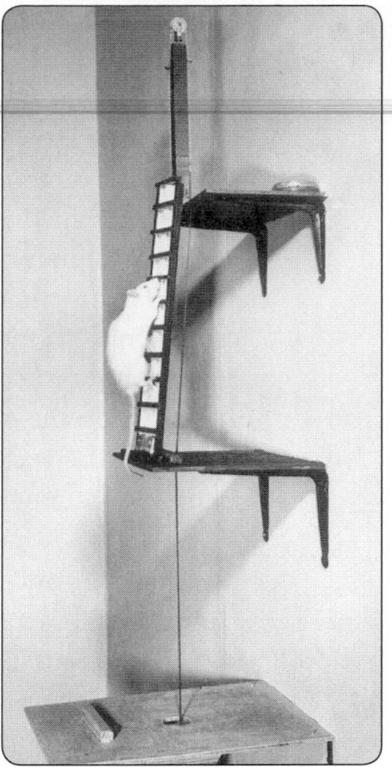

FIGURE 7.17

Through chaining this rat has learned to climb a ladder to reach a string, pull on the string to raise the ladder, then climb the ladder again to reach food at the top. Typically, you begin this training with the last step in the chain. Then, working backward, each prior step in the chain is reinforced by the opportunity to perform the next step.

Generalization and Discrimination

As in classical conditioning, operant responses may generalize to similar antecedent situations. A dog taught to "Sit" by its owner will likely start sitting when other people give the command. A young child who touches a hot stovetop burner learns to avoid touching not only that burner, but other hot burners as well. Thus, in **operant generalization**, an operant response occurs to a new antecedent stimulus or situation that is similar to the original one.

Through experience, we also learn to discriminate between antecedent conditions. Children learn to raid the cookie jar only when the parents are not in the kitchen. We learn to board busses and trains marked by specific symbols (79: Express) and avoid otherwise identical vehicles with different symbols (78: Local). **Operant discrimination** means that an operant response will occur to one antecedent stimulus but not to another. As already discussed, these antecedent stimuli—parent's presence or absence, bus markings—are called *discriminative stimuli.* When discriminative stimuli influence a behaviour, that behaviour is said to be under *stimulus control.* For example, the sight of a police car exerts stimulus control over most people's driving behaviour.

23. What are some examples of discriminative stimuli in your own life?

The concept of operant discrimination gives science a powerful tool for examining the perceptual and cognitive abilities of infants and non-human species (Berg & Boswell, 1998; Lashley, 1930). We can't ask infants and animals to tell us if they can distinguish between different colours, sounds, shapes, faces, and so on. But by using a procedure called *operant discrimination training,* we can teach an organism that making a response (e.g., pressing a lever) when a discriminative stimulus is present (e.g., a red light is on) produces food or some other positive consequence. Now all we have to do is change the colour of the light and not reinforce any response when that light is on. If the organism learns to respond to one colour and not the other, we infer that it can discriminate between them.

Schedules of Reinforcement

24. Describe four major schedules of partial reinforcement and their effects on behaviour.

In daily life, reinforcement comes in different patterns and frequencies. These patterns, called schedules of reinforcement, have strong and predictable effects on learning, extinction, and performance (Ferster & Skinner, 1957). The most basic distinction is between continuous and partial reinforcement. On a **continuous reinforcement** schedule, every response of a particular type is reinforced. Every press of the lever results in food pellets. Every toonie deposit in the pop machine results in a can of cool bubbly drink (at least, we hope so). With **partial reinforcement**, also called *intermittent reinforcement,* only some responses are reinforced.

Partial reinforcement schedules can be categorized along two important dimensions. The first is ratio versus interval schedules. On *ratio schedules,* a certain percentage of responses is reinforced. For example, we might decide to reinforce only 50 percent of the rat's lever presses with food. The key factor is that ratio schedules are based on the number of correct responses. More responses . . . more reinforcement. (In the workplace, this is called *pay for performance.*) On *interval schedules,* a certain amount of time must elapse between reinforcements, regardless of how many correct responses might occur during that interval. We might reinforce lever pressing only once per minute, no matter whether the rat presses the lever 5, 10, or 60 times. The key factor is that interval schedules are based on the passage of time.

The second dimension is fixed versus variable schedules. With a *fixed schedule,* reinforcement always occurs after a fixed number of responses or after a fixed time interval. With a *variable schedule,* the required number of responses or the time interval varies at random around an average. Combining these two dimensions creates four types of reinforcement schedules.

Fixed-Ratio Schedule

On a **fixed-ratio (FR) schedule**, reinforcement is given after a fixed number of responses. For example, FR-3 means that reinforcement occurs after every third response, regardless of how long it takes for those responses to occur.

If I told you that you would receive $1 every three times you pressed a lever, would you work hard? Skinner found that fixed-ratio schedules produce high rates of responding. That is one reason why some businesses prefer paying employees' wages based on a set number of items produced. Experiments conducted with several types of tasks confirm that such fixed-ratio "piecework" schedules result in greater work output than hourly wages (Pritchard et al., 1980). If the ratio is gradually increased over time, many responses can be obtained with relatively few reinforcements. Pigeons in a Skinner box have been known to wear down their beaks pecking a disc on an FR-20,000 schedule (one reinforcer per 20,000 responses). Some labour unions fight against the use of piecework wage systems, believing that they tempt employees to work to exhaustion.

FR schedules have a second characteristic effect. As shown in Figure 7.18, the organism often pauses briefly after each reinforcement, perhaps because the next response (or responses) is never reinforced.

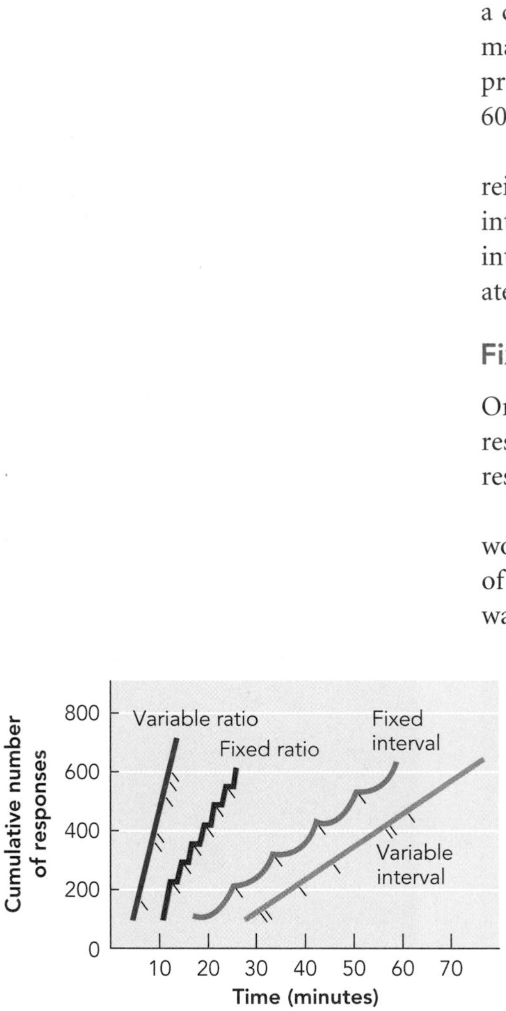

FIGURE 7.18

Each type of positive reinforcement schedule produces a typical cumulative response curve. The hash marks indicate the delivery of a reinforcer. Ratio schedules produce a high rate of responding, as shown in the steep slopes of the curves. Variable schedules produce a steadier rate of responding. Notice the prominent scallops in the fixed interval schedule; the subject learns to stop responding until the time interval for the next reinforcement approaches.

Variable-Ratio Schedule

On a **variable-ratio (VR) schedule**, reinforcement is given after a variable number of correct responses, all centred around an average. A VR-3 schedule means that, *on average,* three responses are required for reinforcement. For example, for the first 12 responses, reinforcement might occur after responses 2, 3, 6, and 11.

VR schedules, like FR schedules, produce a high rate of responding. But because the occurrence of reinforcement is less predictable on a VR schedule, there is less pausing after reinforcement. After all, the next response *might* be reinforced. Instead, there is a relatively high, steady rate of responding, as shown in Figure 7.18. VR schedules also are highly resistant to extinction, because the organism learns that long periods of no-payoff eventually will be followed by reinforcement. Thus VR schedules can be physically taxing, and both humans and other species may continue to respond to the point of exhaustion.

Gambling activities are maintained by VR schedules (Figure 7.19). A gambler, for example, may play a slot machine programmed to pay off an *average* of every 20 pulls (a VR-20 schedule). After eight pulls, our gambler receives a 10-coin payoff. After five more pulls, a 15-coin jackpot. But then, after 40 more attempts, nothing, and our gambler is now down 28 coins. He's frustrated but "hooked" by the VR schedule. The next attempt just may be the one that pays off, so our gambler plays again . . . and again.

FIGURE 7.19

Gambling is reinforced on a variable-ratio schedule. It is ratio, because the frequency of reinforcement is based on the amount of performance. On average, you will receive more payoffs when you pull the slot machine 100 times than when you play only 10 times. It is variable, because you never know when the next jackpot may occur.

Fixed-Interval Schedule

On a **fixed-interval (FI) schedule**, the first correct response that occurs after a fixed time interval is reinforced. Suppose a rat is pressing a lever on an FI-3 (minute) schedule. After a lever press is reinforced, for the next three minutes it makes no difference how many more times the rat responds. There will be no further reinforcement. Once these three minutes elapse, the next lever-press is reinforced. The FI schedule's characteristic response pattern is shown in Figure 7.18. After each reinforcement, you see a substantial pause, followed by increased responding as the time interval passes.

You probably encounter FI schedules in university. Many instructors give exams at equal (or nearly equal) intervals, perhaps one exam every two, three, or four weeks. If you are like many students, your study behaviour may resemble the pattern shown in Figure 7.18, reflecting relatively little studying during the period immediately following each exam, and a great deal of "cramming" just before the test. This uneven performance rate is typical of FI schedules.

Variable-Interval Schedule

On a **variable-interval (VI) schedule**, reinforcement is given for the first response that occurs after a variable time interval. A VI-3 schedule means that, *on average*, there is a three-minute interval between opportunities to obtain reinforcement. Sometimes, responses only a few seconds apart may be reinforced; at other times the interval may be many minutes. As Figure 7.18 shows, because the availability of reinforcement is less predictable than with an FI schedule, the VI schedule produces a steadier response rate.

"Pop quizzes" represent a VI schedule. A course might average a quiz every one or two weeks, but their unpredictable timing likely will produce a steadier approach to studying than regularly scheduled quizzes. Other examples of VI schedules include random drug testing of athletes and roadside speed traps. These activities reinforce desired behaviours (staying drug-free, driving within the speed limit) by appearing at unpredictable intervals. Of course, they also punish undesired behaviours with suspensions and fines!

Partial Reinforcement, Learning, and Extinction

Reinforcement schedules significantly influence the rate of learning and extinction. Continuous reinforcement produces more rapid learning than partial reinforcement because the association between behaviour and its consequences is easier to perceive. However, continuously reinforced responses also extinguish more rapidly, because the shift to no reinforcement is sudden and easier to perceive.

25. Are variable or fixed schedules more resistant to extinction? Why?

Partial reinforcement produces behaviour that is learned more slowly but is more resistant to extinction, especially if the behaviour is reinforced on a *variable* schedule. If reinforcement has been unpredictable in the past, it takes longer to learn that it is gone forever. Most people do not continue to drop coins into a candy or pop machine that doesn't deliver, because vending machines are supposed to operate on a continuous schedule. But it would take many pulls of a slot machine to recognize that it had stopped paying off completely. Similarly, when the response of pecking a key is reinforced on a VR schedule, a pigeon may continue to peck over 100,000 times after reinforcement has ended (Skinner, 1953).

To sum up, the best way to promote fast learning and high resistance to extinction is to begin reinforcing the desired behaviour on a continuous schedule until the behaviour is well established. Then shift to a partial (preferably variable) schedule that is gradually made more demanding. This is what was done with four-year-old Mark. Reinforcement for playing on the monkey bars gradually was reduced so that, eventually, maintaining his behaviour required only occasional attention from his teachers (Johnston et al., 1966). Once partial reinforcement is used, variable schedules generally produce *steadier* rates of responding than fixed schedules, and ratio schedules typically produce *higher* rates of responding than interval schedules (Ferster & Skinner, 1957).

Escape and Avoidance Conditioning

26. Describe the role of negative reinforcement in escape and avoidance conditioning.

Behaviour often involves escaping from or avoiding unpleasant situations. Simple escape situations include taking medications to relieve pain and putting on more clothes when we are cold. Examples of avoidance include putting on lotion to avoid sunburn and obeying traffic laws to avoid tickets. The examples are endless.

In **escape conditioning**, organisms learn a response to terminate an aversive stimulus. Escape behaviours are acquired and maintained through negative reinforcement. Putting on a sweater is negatively *reinforced* by the desirable consequence that I no longer shiver. Taking two aspirin is negatively *reinforced* by the reduction of headache pain. In **avoidance conditioning**, the organism learns a response to avoid an aversive stimulus. We learn to dress warmly before going outside to avoid feeling cold.

Escape and avoidance conditioning can be demonstrated experimentally (Zhulkov et al., 1999; Solomon & Wynne, 1953). For example, an animal is placed in a shuttlebox, a rectangular chamber divided into two compartments and connected by a doorway (Figure 7.20). The floor is a grid through which electric shock can be delivered to either compartment. When shock is turned on in the animal's compartment, it attempts to escape. Eventually, it runs through the door and into the other compartment. When shock is delivered to that compartment, it can escape by running back to the original side. Running through the door removes the shock, which negatively *reinforces* this escape behaviour. Over a few trials, the animal learns to escape as soon as the shock is administered.

To study avoidance conditioning experimentally, researchers introduce a warning signal, such as a light, that precedes the shock by a few seconds. After a few trials, the animal learns that the light signals impending shock. It runs to the other compartment as soon as it sees the light, and thereby avoids being shocked. As discussed in this chapter's Focus on Neuroscience box, we are discovering more about learning with warning signals.

FIGURE 7.20

The shuttlebox is used to study escape and avoidance learning.

Once this avoidance response is learned, it often is hard to extinguish. This is puzzling, because the animal no longer experiences any shock after the light is turned on. We saw the same situation with Emily's snake phobia. She continued to avoid snakes and anything resembling a snake even though the intense pain from her accident was no longer experienced.

According to one model, the **two-factor theory of avoidance learning**, classical *and* operant conditioning are involved in avoidance learning (Mowrer, 1947; Rescorla & Solomon, 1967). For our rat, the warning light initially is a neutral stimulus paired with shock (UCS). Through classical conditioning, the light becomes a CS that elicits fear. Now operant conditioning takes over. Fleeing from the light is *negatively reinforced* by the termination of fear. This strengthens and maintains the avoidance response. Now, if we permanently turn off the shock, the avoidance response prevents extinction from taking place. Seeing the light come on, the animal will not "hang around" long enough to learn that the shock no longer occurs.

In a similar fashion, Emily's fear of snakes was classically conditioned. The mere sight of a snake (like the light for the rat) elicits fear and she flees, thereby avoiding any further exposure to the snake. This avoidance is negatively reinforced by fear reduction, so it remains strong (Figure 7.21). Extinction is difficult because Emily doesn't give herself the opportunity to be exposed to snakes without then experiencing physical pain and trauma. This is why exposure therapies for phobias are effective. By preventing avoidance responses, they provide the key ingredient for extinction: exposure to the CS in the absence of the UCS.

Two-factor theory helps us understand how many avoidance behaviours develop (Levis, 1989; Plaud & Plaud, 1998). However, it has trouble explaining some aspects of avoidance, such as why people and other animals develop phobic avoidance to some stimuli (e.g., snakes) much more easily than to others (e.g., squirrels). Modern research shows that our biological predispositions, thinking patterns, and ability to learn through observation also regulate our avoidance responses (Mineka & Zinbarg, 1998).

Factor 1: Classical conditioning of fear

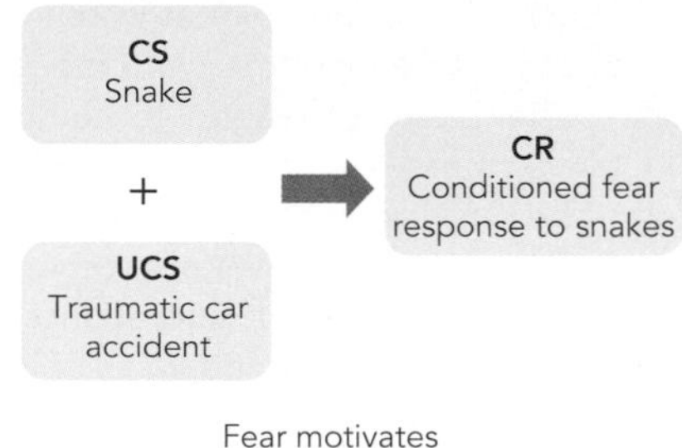

Fear motivates

Factor 2: Operant conditioning of avoidance

Avoidance of snakes is negatively reinforced

FIGURE 7.21

The two-factor theory of avoidance learning would account for Emily's snake phobia in terms of two sets of learning processes: classical conditioning of a fear response, and the negative reinforcement of avoidance of snakes through fear reduction.

FOCUS ON NEUROSCIENCE

The Neuroscience of Fear Conditioning

Of all the different types of environmental stimuli that we need to learn about, potential dangers in our environment are especially important. Regardless of species, individuals need to learn what stimuli pose a danger and, hopefully, learn to predict when danger is imminent. If you can learn to predict approaching danger and learn what is immediately dangerous, your chance of living a long, healthy, and injury-free life is obviously enhanced. The ability to appropriately perceive, assess, learn about, and respond to signals that predict danger is critical for survival across species. As discussed elsewhere (see Chapter 3), evidence from a number of sources has indicated that the amygdala is critical for assessing, learning about, and reacting to cues that predict danger. For example, animals with damage to their amygdala fail to learn a response that allows them to avoid a painful or aversive stimulus (LeDoux, 2000).

Recent imaging technology, such as fMRI, has been used to explore the neural substrates that mediate human learning about danger signals. In an example of classical conditioning, the conditional stimulus (CS) is paired with an aversive unconditional stimulus (UCS) such as electric shock. With repeated presentations of the CS-UCS pair, the CS alone comes to elicit a behavioural response (CR). Learning that a stimulus predicts an aversive event provides an opportunity for preparatory responses or avoidance of the aversive event entirely. Conditioning with an aversive UCS can produce a range of learned responses, or CRs, that include physiological changes such as changes in heart rate, muscle tension, and skin conductance (a measure of sympathetic nervous system activity), and emotional responses, especially anxiety or fear. Since the expected conditioned emotional response in such situations is anxiety or fear, this scenario is often referred to as fear conditioning.

A recent fMRI study with human participants examined the role of the amygdala in fear conditioning (Cheng, Knight, Smith, & Helmstetter, 2006). Participants in this study were exposed to a visual cue CS that predicted arrival of the UCS or to a visual cue that predicted that the UCS would not be delivered (CS-). The UCS was an electric shock applied to the side of the ankle. Each participant adjusted the intensity of

–Continued

the shock UCS to the point at which they judged it to be painful, but tolerable. Together with measuring brain activity using fMRI, Cheng and colleagues obtained measures of skin conductance to assess activation of the sympathetic nervous system. The CS+ presentations (the CS that had been followed by UCS), but not the CS- presentations (the cue that predicted a period free of shock) led to an increase in skin conductance indicating that the learning was sufficiently potent to activate the sympathetic nervous system and influence functions such as sweat gland activity. Analysis of the fMRI scans revealed a cluster of activation in the right amygdala on CS+ trials, but not on CS- trials (Figure 7.22). That is, the right amygdala became active when participants were presented with a visual cue that predicted the arrival of painful electric shock to their ankle, but not with a visual cue that predicted a safe period. Cheng et al. (2006) found similar results in a second experiment using a different group of participants.

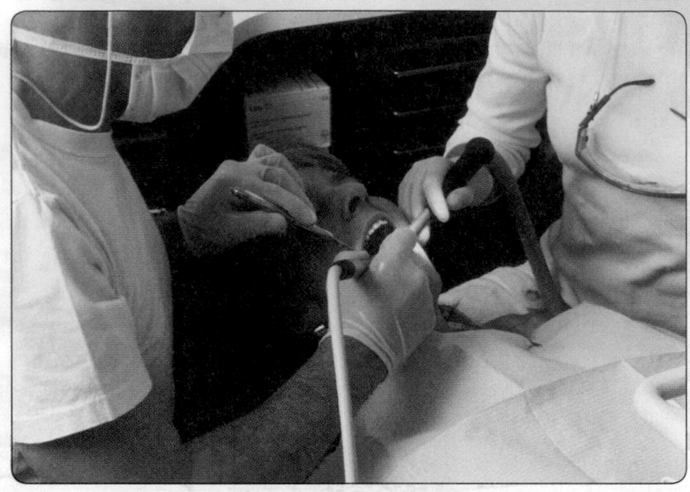

FIGURE 7.22

If looking at this picture makes you feel anxious, even fearful, neuroimaging studies indicate that the level of activity in your right amygdala has increased.

Imaging results, such as those reported by Cheng et al. (2006), and others (e.g., Morris, Büchel, & Dolan, 2001; Phelps et al., 2001) are consistent with other information about the functions of the amygdala (LeDoux, 2000), and indicate that it is indeed involved in learning about environmental cues that predict dangerous or aversive events. Studies of fear conditioning help us understand the acquisition of normal emotional responses. These studies are also important for our understanding of exaggerated or abnormal emotional responses. It is adaptive to learn to be anxious, even fearful, around stimuli that have accurately predicted danger in the past. In some situations, however, the mechanisms of fear conditioning may lead to inappropriate or maladaptive changes.

One situation in which fear conditioning may lead to maladaptive responses is one in which your learned anxiety or fear is misdirected or unfounded. For example, an inappropriate CS may become associated with an aversive UCS and the individual will develop a phobia to a stimulus or situation that does not pose any real danger (see pages 275, 276, and the Psychological Applications feature on page 277). Fear conditioning may be maladaptive in another type of situation: one in which the individual is exposed to an extremely traumatic event. An individual who experiences or witnesses a severe emotionally traumatic event can develop posttraumatic stress disorder (PTSD). The main symptoms of PTSD are re-experiencing the traumatic event (e.g., flashbacks), avoiding situations or cues that remind the individual of the traumatic event, and chronically heightened physiological arousal. PTSD can be considered an example of extreme or exaggerated fear learning, and a fear conditioning perspective is considered to be a useful and appropriate model for explaining the development of PTSD (Rauch, Shin, & Phelps et al., 2006).

Neuroimaging studies have examined changes in brain activity among individuals suffering from PTSD. These studies have compared PTSD patients experiencing active symptoms (e.g., flashbacks, high levels of anxiety) to controls, as well as assessing how brain activity changes for PTSD patients as symptoms are induced by the use of scripts and imagery. An early imaging study of PTSD using PET scans found a number of changes in brain activity; especially interesting were increased activity within the right amygdala and decreased activity within areas of the frontal cortex (Rauch et al., 1996). The results of more recent studies using fMRI have also found evidence for amygdala and frontal involvement in PTSD. One interesting study performed by Rauch and colleagues (Rauch et al., 2006) found that when presented with frightening faces, PTSD patients showed greater activation within the right amygdala and lower frontal activity than did trauma-exposed participants who had not developed PTSD. The extent of amygdala activation correlated positively with symptom severity among PTSD patients, a finding that has been replicated in several other studies (see Rauch et al., 2006). The lower activity within the frontal cortex has also been found across several studies (Rauch et al., 2006). The model that is emerging from these imaging studies is, in part, that the decreased activity within the frontal cortex represents a loss of cortical control over the amygdala. When an individual with PTSD is presented with a fear-inducing stimulus, the amygdala is unchecked by higher mental processes and becomes over-active. Similarly, when a PTSD patient is exposed to a stimulus associated with the past trauma, the overly reactive and over-active right amygdala leads to the extreme emotional and physiological response.

Consistent with older studies of fear conditioning, recent neuroimaging research among healthy volunteers has found that activity within the right amygdala is associated with fear conditioning (e.g., Cheng et al., 2006). Among individuals exposed to a severe emotional trauma who later develop PTSD, higher level cortical control is weakened and the right amygdala over-reacts and anxiety disorders develop (Rauch et al., 2006). Based on older animal research and on the more recently conducted neuroimaging studies, the right amygdala appears to be critically involved in our ability to learn about environmental cues associated with potential dangers in our world.

Applications of Operant Conditioning

Skinner was passionate about applying operant principles to enhance human welfare. In his best-selling books *Walden Two* (1948) and *Beyond Freedom and Dignity* (1971), Skinner set forth his utopian vision of how a "technology of behaviour" based on positive reinforcement could put an end to war, deteriorating education, and other social problems. To his critics, Skinner's ideas conjured up images of people being manipulated like rats, of "Big Brother" (government) controlling its citizens. But Skinner's point was that social influence is a natural part of human existence. Parents and children influence each other, as do employees and employers, teachers and students, friends, roommates, and romantic partners. We smile and say "please" to increase the chance someone will do us a favour. In Skinner's view, individual and societal problems are created by the all-too-common *haphazard* use of reinforcement and overreliance on punishment.

Training Animals

27. How has operant animal training helped humans?

Through shaping and chaining, animals can learn to perform some truly remarkable behaviours. Some are trained to be television, movie, or circus performers, while others learn to assist people who are blind or have other disabilities (Figure 7.23). Law enforcement and military organizations also rely on operantly trained animals. Police dogs assist officers on routine patrol, and other dogs learn to use their sense of smell to help locate hidden bombs, illegal drugs, and missing persons. The U.S. Navy trains sea lions to dive and retrieve sunken test weapons, and dolphins learn to patrol waters around nuclear submarine bases and search for underwater intruders (Morrison, 1988). Operantly trained dolphins also patrolled the waters around some U.S. ships during the Vietnam and Persian Gulf wars.

Some applications push the boundaries of ingenuity, such as using pigeons to assist in air-sea rescue. Pigeons have sharp long-distance visual acuity and a wide field of vision. Years ago, the U.S. Coast Guard put these abilities to good use by training pigeons to peck a key whenever they saw an orange object (Simmons, 1981). Orange, of course, is the international colour of life jackets. Three trained pigeons were then placed in a glass dome mounted underneath the search-and-rescue helicopter. Each pigeon had a different view outside, but together, they covered the entire 360° visual field. When a pigeon spotted an orange object in the ocean, it pecked a key connected to a particular directional signal in the cockpit. Depending on which pigeon was pecking at any moment, the pilot maintained or altered course and was guided to the victim's location.

FIGURE 7.23

Because of injuries suffered in an accident, this woman cannot move her arms or legs. The monkey has been operantly trained to assist her with basic chores, such as eating.

All of these applications involve training animals to enhance human welfare, but operant conditioning also benefits animals' lives. It is the cornerstone of formal pet training, which with dogs typically includes numerous commands (e.g., "Heel," "Stay") that help keep them away from traffic and other hazards.

Human Applications: Education, the Workplace, and Beyond

Walk into your local computer store and you likely will find shelves of educational software, teaching everything from geography and math to foreign languages. The effectiveness of such computerized instruction rests on two key principles championed by Skinner: *immediate performance feedback* and *self-paced learning.*

Skinner was deeply concerned about the inefficiency of traditional instructional methods (1961, 1989). Decades ago, long before the advent of personal computers, he developed mechanical teaching machines. Each machine presented material, quizzed the student, and provided immediate feedback. Students who did not learn the material the first time could repeat steps. Those who did could advance their machine to the next set of information. Today personal computers are helping Skinner's vision become an educational reality. *Computer-assisted instruction (CAI)* also is found in business, industry, and the military (Parchman et al., 2000).

Skinner's work also heightened societal attention to the broad issue of "motivation" and reinforcing desired behaviour. A key behaviourist assumption is that poor performance should not be attributed to "laziness" or a "bad attitude." Instead, we should assume that the *environment* is not providing the proper consequences to reinforce the desired behaviour. Incentive systems—from stock options to bonuses for meeting performance goals—are now common in business and professional sports. **Token economies**, in which desirable behaviours are quickly reinforced with "tokens" (e.g., points, gold stars) that are later turned in for tangible rewards (e.g., prizes, recreational time), have been used to enhance academic and work performance. In one study, a token economy reduced the number of work injuries among open-pit mine workers (Fox et al., 1987). Miners received stamp awards for making safety suggestions and avoiding injuries, and they lost stamps for unsafe behaviours. Stamps were later traded in for tangible reinforcers. The program cost money, but far less than the cost of worker absenteeism due to accidents.

28. In what broad ways has operant conditioning directly enhanced human welfare?

At work, motivating employees is a key managerial function, and many major companies invest heavily in training programs designed to enhance managers' effectiveness in reinforcing desired worker behaviour (Saari et al., 1988). Similarly, numerous youth sport organizations require coaches to take training programs that teach how to reinforce young athletes effectively (Smith & Smoll, 1997).

Finally, Skinner's work gave rise to a field called **applied behaviour analysis** (also known as *behaviour modification*), which combines a behavioural approach with the scientific method to solve individual and societal problems (Kazdin, 1975; Martin & Pear, 1999; Pierce & Epling, 1999). Essentially, a program (usually based on positive reinforcement) is designed and implemented to change behaviour, and its effectiveness is objectively measured by gathering data before and after the program is in place.

Applied behaviour analysis has been used to reduce an array of behaviour problems. Two interesting examples come from the work of Ron Van Houten of Mount Saint Vincent University. Van Houten used the principles of applied behaviour analysis to increase safety at stop signs (Van Houten & Retting, 2001). Van Houten was able to increase the percentage of vehicles coming to a complete stop before entering the intersection from 55 percent to 77 percent, and to decrease the instances of vehicles coming to a sudden stop because of a vehicle unsafely entering the intersection from an average of 4 occurrences per observation session to only 1.4 per session. Van Houten has also reported a program that significantly increased seat belt use (Wells, Malenfant, Williams, & Van Houten, 2000). Other applications have improved students' academic performance and social skills, enhanced elite athletic performance, and reduced unsportsmanlike behaviour (Hughes et al., 1998). Workplace applications include increasing employee productivity, reducing injuries and accidents, enhancing the job interview skills of unemployed adults, and increasing energy conservation (Staats et al., 2000).

In Review

- *Thorndike's law of effect states that responses followed by satisfying consequences will be strengthened, whereas those followed by unsatisfying consequences will be weakened.*
- *B. F. Skinner analyzed operant conditioning in terms of relations between antecedents, behaviours, and consequences. Antecedents that signal the likely consequences of particular behaviours in a given situation are called discriminative stimuli.*

- *Operant behaviours are emitted (under voluntary control), whereas classically conditioned responses are elicited (reflexive). Classically conditioned responses are influenced by what happens before the behaviour (i.e., by the CS-UCS pairing), whereas operant behaviours are influenced by consequences that occur after the behaviour.*
- *Reinforcement occurs when a response is strengthened by an outcome (a reinforcer) that follows it. With positive reinforcement, a response is followed by the presentation of a positive stimulus, so the response becomes stronger. With negative reinforcement, a response is followed by the removal of an aversive stimulus, so again, the response becomes stronger.*
- *Operant extinction is the weakening and eventual disappearance of a response because it no longer is reinforced.*
- *Punishment occurs when a response is weakened by an outcome (a punisher) that follows it. With positive punishment, a behaviour is followed by the presentation of an aversive stimulus, and the behaviour becomes weaker. With negative punishment, a behaviour is followed by the removal of a positive stimulus, and the behaviour becomes weaker.*
- *Shaping, which uses the method of successive approximations, involves the reinforcement of behaviours that increasingly resemble the final desired behaviour.*
- *When behaviour changes in one situation due to reinforcement or punishment, and then this new response carries over to similar situations, this is called operant generalization. In contrast, when an operant response is made to one discriminative stimulus but not to another, this is called operant discrimination.*
- *On a continuous reinforcement schedule every response is reinforced. Partial reinforcement may occur on a ratio schedule, in which a certain percentage of responses are reinforced, or on an interval schedule, in which a certain amount of time must pass before a response gets reinforced. In general, ratio schedules produce higher rates of performance than interval schedules.*
- *On fixed ratio and interval schedules, reinforcement always occurs after a fixed number of correct responses or a fixed time interval. On variable schedules, the required number of responses or interval of time varies around some average.*
- *Learning occurs most rapidly under continuous reinforcement, but partial schedules produce behaviours that are more resistant to extinction.*
- *Escape and avoidance conditioning result from negative reinforcement. According to two-factor theory, fear is created through classical conditioning. This fear motivates escape and avoidance, which is then negatively reinforced by fear reduction.*
- *Animals are operantly trained to perform in entertainment industries and to assist disabled people, the police, and the military. Human applications include teaching machines, computerized instruction, token economies, and applied behaviour analysis.*

BIOLOGY AND LEARNING

Behaviourists never suggested that a rat could learn to fly, but for decades they assumed that they could condition virtually any behaviour an organism was physically capable of performing. Yet evidence mounted that "conditioned" animals did not always respond as they were supposed to. The behaviourist assumption was wrong because it ignored a key principle discussed at the outset of this chapter: Behaviour is influenced by an organism's evolutionary history (Crawford & Anderson, 1989).

Martin Seligman's (1970) concept of "preparedness" captures this idea. **Preparedness** means that, through evolution, animals are biologically "prewired" to easily learn behaviours related to their survival as a species. Behaviours contrary to an organism's natural tendencies are learned slowly, if at all. Let's consider some examples.

29. How do learned taste aversions illustrate the concept of preparedness?

Constraints on Classical Conditioning: Learned Taste Aversions

Imagine eating or drinking something, then becoming sick to your stomach and throwing up. Perhaps it is food poisoning. Or perhaps, like cancer patients, it is chemotherapy that makes you ill. Pairing the smell and taste of food (CS) with a toxin or some illness producing agent (UCS) can produce a CR called **conditioned taste aversion**: The taste and smell of the food now disgusts and repulses us (Garcia et al., 1985). It may even make us feel queasy, and we learn to avoid it. Cancer patients may develop aversions to foods they eat before treatment even though they know that the food did not cause their post-treatment stomach illness. Pairing food with nausea creates an aversion involuntarily.

Psychologist John Garcia pioneered numerous taste aversion experiments that challenged two basic assumptions of classical conditioning. First, behaviourists had assumed that the CS-UCS time interval had to be relatively short, usually within a few seconds. Garcia showed that animals learned taste aversions even though the food (CS) was consumed up to several hours—or even a day—before they became ill (UCR).

Second, in a classic experiment, Garcia illustrated how biological preparedness influences learned aversions (Garcia & Koelling, 1966). Whenever rats licked a drinking tube they were simultaneously exposed to three neutral stimuli: sweet-tasting water, a bright light, and a buzzer (Figure 7.24). In one condition, half the rats were exposed to X-rays (UCS) upon drinking the water, which later made them ill (UCR). Would the rats develop an aversion to all three neutral stimuli? No, they avoided the sweet water, but not the light or buzzer. Why did only the sweet taste become a CS? Because rats are biologically primed to form taste-illness associations, which means that in nature they most easily identify poisonous or "bad" food by its taste (or smell). Sounds and lights in nature don't make rats sick.

When rats in a second condition licked the tube, the light, buzzer, and sweet taste were all paired with an electric shock. Would the rats learn to fear all three neutral stimuli? No, they avoided the light and buzzer, but kept drinking the sweet water. This also makes adaptive sense. In nature, sights and sounds—but not how food and drink taste—signal fear-provoking situations (e.g., a cat about to pounce). The same principle applies in humans. When a food makes us violently sick, we may develop an aversion to it, but not to the friends we ate with. Furthermore, seeing the food again may repulse us, but not make us afraid.

Stage 1: All Rats
When rats touch the drinking tube, sweet water is delivered and a light and buzzer turn on.

Stage 2
Illness condition

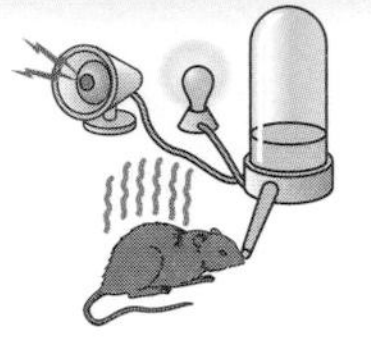

Group 1 rats get nauseating x-rays when they drink.
Fear condition

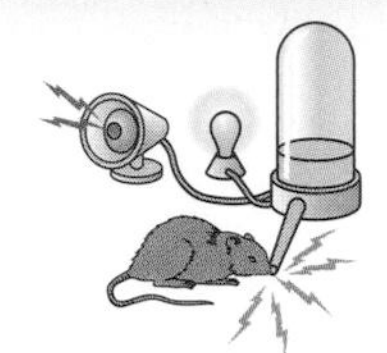

Group 2 rats get electric shocks when they drink.
Stage 3

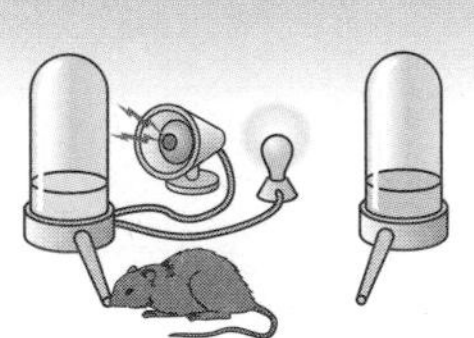

Group 1 rats avoid the sweet water and prefer the plain water with the light and buzzer.
Group 2 rats still drink the sweet water, but avoid the plain water with the light and buzzer.

FIGURE 7.24

Biological preparedness in classical conditioning. This figure illustrates the design and main results of Garcia and Koelling's (1966) aversion experiment.

Psychologists have applied their knowledge of conditioned aversions to save animals' lives. To prevent coyotes from killing ranchers' sheep, Carl Gustavson and his colleagues laced pieces of meat with lithium chloride, a nausea-inducing drug (Gustavson et al., 1974). The meat was wrapped in sheep hide and left out for coyotes to eat. The coyotes ate it, became ill, developed an aversion to the meat, and became less likely to kill sheep. This saved the lives of sheep and also of the coyotes who otherwise would have been shot by ranchers. As part of wildlife management, researchers also have created conditioned aversions to various foods in other species, such as raccoons, wolves, and baboons (Gustavson & Gustavson, 1985). For an intriguing example of nature's own "wildlife management" based on learned taste aversions, see Figure 7.25.

As mentioned earlier in this section, a serious problem that can occur with patients receiving chemotherapy is that chemotherapy makes many patients extremely nauseous. Patients undergoing chemotherapy are thus exposed to the necessary conditions for the development of conditioned aversions: a CS (taste and smell of food at mealtime) is later followed by nausea, in this instance caused not by food but by the cancer treatment (Bovbjerg, 2006; Hickok, Roscoe, & Morrow, 2001; Stockhorst, Steingrueber, & Klosterhalfen, 2006). A patient receiving chemotherapy for cancer risks the gradual elimination of more and more items from their diet as they accumulate more and more conditioned aversions. This is especially important among children who do not have as long a learning history about foods as do adults. Although it may not be possible to completely prevent the development of conditioned taste aversions, it is possible to direct how they form. Darla Broberg and Ilene Bernstein (1987) gave child cancer patients unusual tasting candy before their chemotherapy treatments. The candy, with its novel and unusual flavour, became the "scapegoat" for the children's taste aversions, protecting them from developing aversions to their normal foods.

FIGURE 7.25

This blue jay has never eaten a monarch butterfly before, and doesn't pass up an easy meal. Soon toxins in the butterfly cause food poisoning. The jay feels discomfort, vomits, and develops a conditioned aversion triggered by the sight of the monarch's brightly patterned wings. From now on, it will leave monarchs alone.

Photos courtesy of Lincoln P. Brower.

Are We Biologically Prepared to Fear Certain Things?

Seligman (1971) proposed that humans, like other animals, are biologically prepared to acquire certain fears more readily than others. Case studies of phobic patients support this idea. The case that started this chapter, Emily and her snake phobia, originally presented by the British psychologist Isaac Marks (1977), provides an example of this idea. Remember that Emily saw a snake and then had her hand slammed in a car door. Although it was a car that injured her, Emily developed a lasting phobia not of cars or car doors, but of snakes. A similar case was reported by Larsen (1965). An 18-year old woman was a passenger in a car that was involved in an accident. She was looking through a magazine and, just by chance, happened to be looking at a picture of a snake at the moment of the accident. This woman developed a phobia of snakes, not of cars, magazines, or photographs in general.

Numerous experiments by Arne Öhman and his Swedish research team provide evidence of preparedness (Öhman et al., 1978; Öhman & Soares, 1998). In this research, various CSs were paired with electric shock (UCS), and participants' physiological responses were measured when the CSs were subsequently presented alone. People who received shocks each time pictures of snakes, spiders, or angry faces were flashed on a screen quickly acquired conditioned fear responses to these stimuli, even when the pictures were displayed too briefly to be consciously perceived. But participants who received shocks while looking at slides of flowers, houses, berries, or happy faces displayed much weaker fear conditioning.

Humans develop phobias to many stimuli, but most often we fear things that seem to have greater evolutionary significance: snakes, spiders, other animals, and dangerous places. Although there are cases of it occurring, people rarely develop phobias to the things that really do injure, maim, and kill people in today's world; phobias to cars, cigarettes, knives, and guns are rare. Is this the result of evolution-based preparedness, or might it be due to learning experiences within our own lifetime? Through cultural transmission of knowledge, perhaps we come to expect that some stimuli can be dangerous, making us "cognitively" rather than "biologically" prepared to acquire certain fears. The role of cognitive factors in human fear conditioning continues to be examined (Davey, 1995), but one thing is clear: As with taste aversions and sexual arousal, fear can be conditioned much more easily to some stimuli than to others.

30. How has knowledge of learned taste aversions been applied to help animals?

Constraints on Operant Conditioning: Animals That "Won't Shape Up"

Two of B. F. Skinner's students, Keller and Marian Breland, became renowned animal trainers. They used shaping and chaining to train thousands of animals for circuses, advertising agencies, television, and the movies. Training usually was successful, but not always. Sometimes the animals simply refused to behave according to the "laws" of operant conditioning (Breland & Breland, 1961, 1966).

On one occasion, the Brelands tried to train a chicken to play baseball. The game was arranged so that a small ball would roll toward home plate and the chicken would pull a chain to swing a small metal bat. If the ball was hit, a bell would ring and the chicken would run to first base to get its food. The Brelands easily trained the chicken to pull the chain that swung the bat, and to run to first base when it heard the bell. But when the ball was introduced into the game, utter chaos occurred. Whenever the chicken hit the ball, instead of running to first base to collect its food reinforcement, it chased the ball all over the playing field, pecking furiously at it, and flapping its wings. Try as they might, the Brelands could not extinguish these behaviours. End of training, and end of the chicken's baseball career. In this and many other examples, animals simply refused to "shape up."

31. What evidence led the Brelands to propose the concept of instinctive drift?

The Brelands found that once a particular stimulus came to represent food, animals began to act as if it *were* food. The chicken pecked at the ball as if it were something to eat. In another example, raccoons kept on rubbing their tokens as if they were "washing" real food. In the raccoon's case, they had successfully performed the learned response of dropping a token in a box several times, but their "washing behaviour" was so deeply rooted in their evolutionary history that it simply overrode the conditioning procedure. The Brelands called this **instinctive drift**: a conditioned response "drifts back" toward instinctive behaviour. People who adopt wild animals as pets, or who train them for circuses, face some personal risk no matter how hard they try to domesticate these animals. An acquaintance of ours once rescued a cuddly baby raccoon and raised it lovingly for nearly a year, at which time the raccoon unexpectedly reverted to its more instinctive, aggressive behaviour. Our friend, now known as "Ole Three-Fingers," returned his pet to the wild.

Experiments confirm that operant learning is constrained by biology. It is relatively easy to train a pigeon to peck a novel object (such as a disc on a wall) for food reinforcers, because pigeons come into the world biologically primed to peck for food. Training a pigeon to peck an object to escape from electric shock is more difficult, because in their natural environment pigeons do not escape from danger by pecking; they fly away. As another example, wild rats trained to press a lever for food often will drift back to instinctive behaviours of scratching and biting the lever (Powell & Curley, 1976).

Learning and the Brain

32. How do biology and learning influence each other?

Biology and learning are deeply intertwined. Clearly, biology determines our ability to learn. The concepts of preparedness and instinctive drift illustrate how organisms are biologically predisposed to learn some associations more easily than others. Neuroscientists have found that certain brain regions, such as the nucleus accumbens, and certain neurotransmitters, such as dopamine, play a key role in regulating the ability to experience reward (Olds, 1958; Rolls, 2000). Human medical patients report pleasure when specific areas of their hypothalamus are electrically stimulated, and rats will repeatedly press a lever to receive a similar electrical reward.

Yet, no single part of the brain "controls" learning. For example, the cerebellum plays an important role in acquiring classically conditioned movements—such as conditioned eyeblink responses—whereas the amygdala is centrally involved in acquiring classically conditioned fears (Gabrieli, 1998; LeDoux, 1992; Thompson, 1985). We examine the brain mechanisms underlying learning more closely when discussing memory in the next chapter (without memory, we could not learn from experience).

Biology affects learning, but experience and learning environments also influence our biological functioning (Wachs, 2000). Compared to their littermates who grow up in standard cages, young animals who are exposed to enriched environments—with toys and greater opportunities to learn—develop heavier brains with more dendrites and synapses, and with greater concentrations of various neurotransmitters (Rosenzweig, 1984). In turn, this increased brain development subsequently enables animals to perform better on learning and cognitive tasks (Meaney et al., 1991). Experiments with humans find that infants who regularly receive stimulating "touch sessions" develop more mature movement patterns, are less stressed, and perform better on cognitive tests than infants who do not receive these sessions (Field, 2000).

In late adulthood, continued exposure to stimulating environments seems to slow down the decline in human brain functioning, as measured by better performance on intellectual and perceptual tasks (Goldstein et al., 1997; Schaie, 1998). In a sense then, every day you are alive your brain continues its own "personal evolution," its neural networks and patterns of activity affected not only by your genetic endowment, but as Figure 7.26 shows, by your experiences as well.

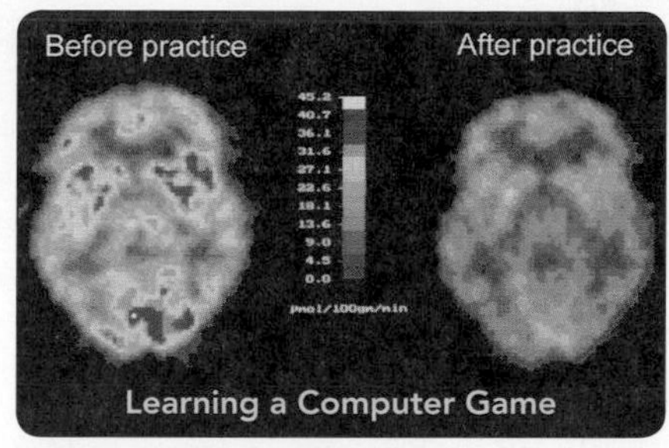

FIGURE 7.26

While learning a computer game, the brain of a novice player is highly active and uses a lot of energy, as indicated by the large yellow and red areas in the left PET scan. As the right scan shows, energy consumption decreases with experience.

In Review

- *An animal's evolutionary history prepares it to learn certain associations more easily than others. This principle is called biological preparedness, and it illustrates that there are biological constraints on learning.*
- *Humans show faster fear conditioning to CSs that have evolutionary significance, suggesting that we are biologically prepared to acquire specific kinds of phobias.*
- *It is difficult to operantly condition animals to perform behaviours that are contrary to their evolved natural tendencies. Such conditioned behaviours often are abandoned in favour of a more natural response, a concept called instinctive drift.*
- *Various brain regions and chemicals regulate learning. Environmental experiences affect brain development and functioning, which in turn influence our future ability to learn.*

COGNITION AND LEARNING

Early behaviourists believed that learning involves the relatively automatic formation of bonds between stimuli and responses. In classical conditioning, the CS elicits the CR: tone → salivation. In operant conditioning, a discriminative stimulus leads to an emitted response: Light comes on → a hungry rat presses the lever to obtain food. This behaviourist orientation came to be known as *S-R (stimulus-response) psychology.* Behaviourists opposed explanations of learning that went beyond observable stimuli and responses. They did not deny that people had thoughts and feelings, but argued that behaviour could be explained without referring to such mentalistic concepts (Skinner, 1953, 1990).

Behaviourism guided much learning research from the early 1900s through the 1960s, and it remains influential today (Reid & Staddon, 1998; Leighland, 2000). But even in psychology's early days, some learning theorists argued that in between stimulus (S) and response (R) there was something else: the organism's (O) mental representation of the world. This came to be known as the *S-O-R,* or *cognitive model* of learning. Today the cognitive perspective represents an important force in learning theory (Hollis, 1997).

FIGURE 7.27

Sultan seemed to study the hanging bananas that were out reach. After looking around, he suddenly grabbed some crates, stacked them, and obtained his tasty reward.

Insight and Cognitive Maps

In the 1920s, German psychologist Wolfgang Köhler (1925) challenged Thorndike's behaviourist assumption that animals learn to perform tasks only by trial-and-error learning. Köhler exposed chimpanzees to novel learning tasks and concluded that they were able to learn by **insight**, the sudden perception of a useful relationship that helps to solve a problem. Figure 7.27 shows how one of his apes solved the problem of how to reach bananas that were dangling beyond reach. Köhler emphasized that the apes often spent time staring at the bananas and available tools, as if they were contemplating the problem, after which the solution suddenly appeared.

Behaviourists argued that such "insight" was merely a combination of previously reinforced and shaped responses (Epstein, 1984). To make their point, they trained pigeons to perform supposedly "insightful" behaviours, such as pushing a platform under some tiny toy bananas, then standing on the platform to peck at the bananas. But just because pigeons must be shaped, does this imply that shaping was responsible for the apes' solutions? Although the debate over animal insight continues, Köhler's work helped place the cognitive learning viewpoint on the map.

Another cognitive pioneer, learning theorist Edward Tolman of the University of California, Berkeley, studied spatial learning in rats. Look at the maze in Figure 7.28a. A rat runs to an open circular table, continues across, and follows the only path available to a goal box containing food. After 12 trials, the rat easily negotiates the maze. Next, the maze is changed. The rat runs its usual route and reaches a dead-end (Figure 7.28b). What will the rat do?

Tolman found that rats returned to the table, briefly explored most of the 18 new paths for just a few centimetres, and then chose one. By far, the largest number—36 percent—chose the fourth path to the right of their original route, which took them to about 10 centimetres in front of where the goal box had been. In short, the rats behaved as you would, given your advantage of seeing the maps in Figure 7.28.

Tolman (1948) argued that reinforcement theory could not explain this behaviour, but that he could: The rats had developed a mental representation of the maze layout—a **cognitive map**. The concept of cognitive maps supported Tolman's belief that learning does not merely "stamp in" stimulus-response connections. Rather, learning provides *knowledge*, and, based on their knowledge, organisms develop an *expectancy*, a cognitive representation of "what leads to what."

Behaviourists disagreed with Tolman's interpretations and developed non-cognitive models to explain how organisms learn their way around (Hull, 1943; Reid & Staddon, 1998). Still, an explosion of research on spatial learning offers much support for the concept of cognitive maps in humans and other animals (Jacobs et al., 1998). Most importantly, Tolman's concept of expectancy remains a cornerstone of today's cognitive approaches to both classical and operant conditioning.

Cognition in Classical Conditioning

Early American behaviourists believed that classical conditioning created a direct reflexlike connection between the CS (tone) and CR (salivation). Interestingly, Pavlov held a different view, proposing that a neural bond is formed between the CS and the UCS. Thus the tone triggers an association with meat, which then triggers the reflexive salivation response.

Cognitive learning theorists also believe that classical conditioning forms a CS-UCS link. In cognitive terminology, the link is an expectancy that the CS will be followed by the UCS (Bolles, 1979; Hollis, 1997). This *expectancy model* states that the most important factor in classical conditioning is *not* how often the CS and the UCS are paired, but *how well the CS predicts (i.e., signals) the appearance of the UCS* (Rescorla & Wagner, 1972).

Robert Rescorla (1968) of Yale University demonstrated this principle in an experiment on fear conditioning. Rats in one condition received electric shocks (UCS), and each shock was preceded by a tone. As usual, the tone soon became a CS that elicited a fear response when presented alone. In a second condition, rats received the same number of tone-shock pairings as the first group, but they also received as many shocks that were not preceded by the tone. Would the tone become a CS for fear? According to traditional learning theory, the answer should be "yes," because the number of tone-shock pairings was the same as in the first group. But the expectancy model predicts "no," because the tone does not reliably predict when the shock will occur. The results supported Rescorla's hypothesis: The tone did not elicit a fear response for the second group.

CS-UCS inconsistency also explains why we don't become conditioned to all the neutral stimuli that are present just before a UCS appears. For example, when Pavlov's dogs were presented with tone-food pairings, there was light in the room. Why didn't the dogs learn to salivate whenever they saw light? Or imagine a doctor testing your "knee-jerk reflex." Many of us jerk slightly at the mere sight of that little rubber mallet moving toward our knee. Why doesn't this response occur to other stimuli that are present just before the hammer strikes, such as the sight of a physician sitting on a stool?

The key is that when Pavlov's dogs' room was lit, they often were not receiving food. And most of the time physicians sit on stools, they are not about to tap our knees. From a cognitive viewpoint, these neutral stimuli do not consistently predict the arrival of the UCS, dramatically reducing the chance that they will become a CS. This is highly adaptive; if it were not the case, you and I (along with Pavlov's dogs) would be twitching, salivating, blinking, and exhibiting all sorts of embarrassing reflexive responses to so many stimuli that it would be difficult to function.

Other types of evidence support this cognitive model over a simple CS-UCS pairing model. For example, recall that *forward pairing* (CS followed by UCS) typically produces the strongest learning, *simultaneous pairing* produces weaker learning, and *backward pairing* (UCS followed by CS) produces the weakest or no learning. This makes sense, based on the expectancy model. In forward tone-food pairing, the tone predicts the imminent arrival of the UCS; it is a signal that something meaningful is about happen. With simultaneous pairing, the tone has less value as a signal because the food arrives at the same time. And in backward pairing, the tone has no predictive value because the food has already arrived.

Learning theorists continue to test other models of classical conditioning (Giftakis & Tait, 1998; Schmajuk & Nestor, 1998; Tait & Saladin, 1986), but the expectancy model has been highly influential (Siegel & Allan, 1996). In sum, there is good evidence that cognition plays a role in classical conditioning.

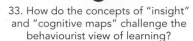

33. How do the concepts of "insight" and "cognitive maps" challenge the behaviourist view of learning?

34. Provide evidence that supports the "expectancy model" of classical conditioning.

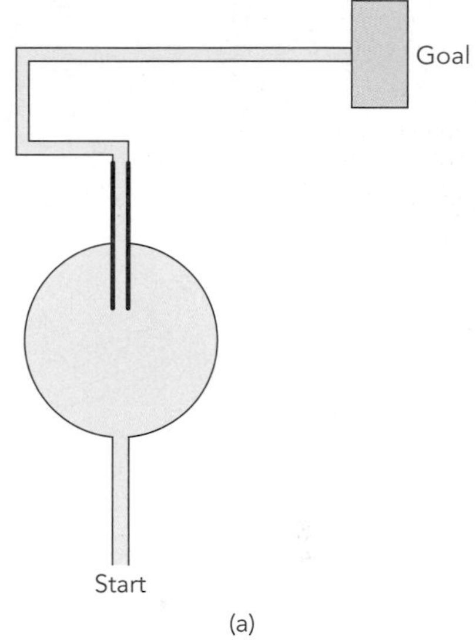

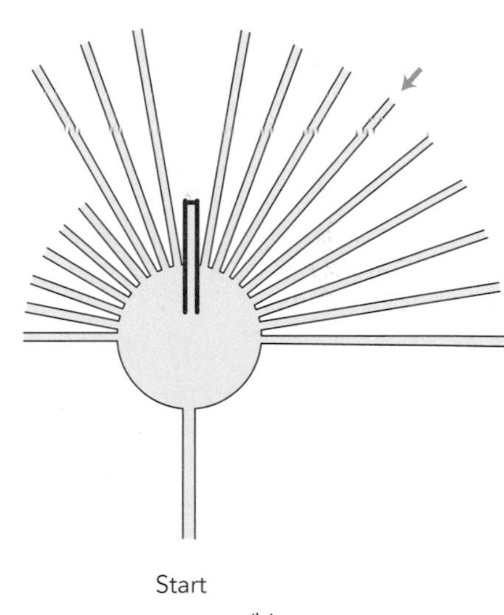

FIGURE 7.28

Rats first learned to run the simple maze shown in (a). When the maze was switched (b), many rats chose the fourth path to the right of the original route. Tolman proposed that the rats had developed a cognitive map of the maze.

Adapted from Tolman, 1948.

Cognition in Operant Conditioning

Cognitive theorists point to a variety of evidence to support their claim that mental processes also play a key role in operant conditioning. We'll examine three issues here.

The Role of Awareness

Cognitive theorists emphasize that organisms develop an *awareness* or *expectancy* of the relations between their responses and probable consequences. Many of

35. What role does awareness play in operant conditioning?

Tolman's rats acted as if they were aware that running through one alternate path or the other would produce the best consequence, once they learned that their primary route was blocked. Similarly, suppose you are in an experiment in which your task is to make up a sentence and tell it to me. As you speak, I say "good" or "mmm-hmm" every time your sentence contains a noun that refers to humans (e.g., boy, woman, people). We go through this process for 10 sentences, and I measure whether your usage of human nouns changes. In the actual experiment, only those participants who received praise *and* who became aware of the reinforcement contingency increased their usage of human nouns (Spielberger & DeNike, 1966). Those who received praise but remained unaware of why it was given performed no differently than a control group receiving no praise.

"Boy, have I got this guy conditioned! Every time I press the bar down, he drops in a piece of food."

FIGURE 7.29

Perception versus reality.

From a cognitive perspective, the concept of "awareness" implies that the best predictor of behaviour is the *perceived* contingency, not the actual one (Figure 7.29). In many instances the two are identical, but sometimes people perceive contingencies that do not actually exist. One example is superstitious behaviour. In cognitive terms, the organism misperceives that a specific behaviour (e.g., not walking under ladders, holding on to a "good luck" charm) produces good consequences or helps avoid bad ones.

Another example of a misperceived contingency sometimes occurs with punishment. As the following tongue-in-cheek anecdote illustrates, the person delivering punishment may be attempting to suppress one behaviour, but the recipient perceives that the punishment is directed at another behaviour:

> A psychologist reported that a frustrated mother once contacted him for assistance in the reduction of swearing behaviour on the part of her two young sons. A behaviour therapist, the psychologist recommended that she use punishment techniques. He told her that it was important to use immediate and severe punishment each and every time the swearing occurred. To maximize the impact of that punishment, he also recommended that she try to use each child as an example for the other—that is, punish him in front of his brother.
>
> Enthusiastic over this advice, the mother returned home. At breakfast the next morning, she sat down ready and raring to modify behaviour. The older son opened the conversation by requesting that she "pass the [expletive deleted] Cheerios." With lightning fury, the mother lunged across the table and hit her son—sent both him and his chair sprawling to the floor. Pleased with her skilful execution of behavioural principles, the mother turned to her somewhat bewildered younger son. "Well, what will you have?" He paused a moment, glanced at his supine brother, and answered, "You can bet your sweet ass it isn't Cheerios!" (Mahoney, 1980, pp. 136–137)

Latent Learning

Tolman's research, described in Figure 7.28, suggested that rats developed cognitive maps when they were reinforced with food for running the maze. Tolman also believed that cognitive maps could be learned without reinforcement, posing an even greater challenge to the behaviourist viewpoint. In one experiment, three groups of rats were run in a complex maze (Tolman & Honzik, 1930). Rats in Group 1 found food each time they reached the goal box. Rats in Group 2 found the goal box empty each time they reached it. The third group of rats found no

?

36. How does latent learning challenge the behaviourist view of learning?

food at the end of the maze for the first 10 days, but did find food in the goal box starting on the 11th day.

The results are shown in Figure 7.30, and the key finding is this: On Day 11, the rats in Group 3 discovered food in the goal box for the first time. By the very next day, they were performing just as well as the Group 1 rats who had been reinforced all along. What could explain this large, sudden performance improvement? According to Tolman, during Days 1 to 10, the Group 3 rats were learning the spatial layout of the maze as they wandered about. They were not being reinforced by food, but they gained knowledge and developed their cognitive maps. This learning remained "latent" (hidden) until the rats discovered a good reason on Day 11 to get to the goal box quickly, and then it immediately was manifested in performance the next day. Tolman's experiments supported the concept of **latent learning**, which refers to learning that occurs but is not demonstrated until there is an incentive to perform (Blodgett, 1929). In short, like Tolman's rats, we may "learn how" to do something (gain knowledge), but not display that knowledge outwardly (performance) until some future time.

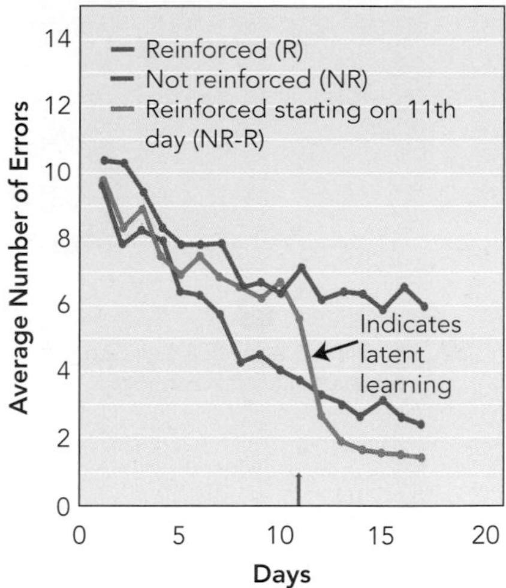

FIGURE 7.30

Tolman's demonstration of latent learning. Rats had one trial in the maze per day. Group NR received no reinforcement in the maze at any time. Group R was reinforced with food every time they reached the end of the maze. The critical group (NR-R) had food reward introduced on the 11th day. Their immediate performance improvement suggested that they had learned the maze prior to the introduction of reinforcement.

(Tolman & Honzik, 1930)

Self-Evaluations as Reinforcers and Punishers

Students called him "Holy Hubert," and he visited my campus for over 10 years. His fire-and-brimstone exhortations to repent and avoid damnation often evoked amused smiles, loud insults, and ridicule. One could hardly imagine less positive consequences for an evangelist. One day, I asked Hubert why he continued to preach when students' responses were so negative. He answered, "I don't care what they say. When I know I'm doing the Lord's work, I feel so good that they could hang me for all I care."

Hubert's persistence in the face of adversity illustrates that external reinforcement and punishment are not the only consequences controlling behaviour. If they were, how could we account for the actions of people who resist temptation when there is no chance of discovery and punishment? We often feel pride for doing something, even if others do not know or approve of our deeds. In this sense, virtue is indeed its own reward. We also may disapprove of ourselves for failing to live up to our own standards. These *cognitive self-evaluations* represent important internal reinforcers and punishers (Bandura, 1986; Cervone, 1992).

Our internal standards develop in many ways. As part of our *socialization* into society, parents, teachers, and other people set standards for our behaviour, reinforcing us when we meet their expectations and disapproving of us when we don't. Eventually we may adopt (i.e., internalize) their standards. Once we develop self-evaluative standards, our actions can be influenced by external and internal consequences.

In Review

- *Köhler's early research on animal insight and Tolman's pioneering research on cognitive maps indicated that cognitive factors play a role in learning. Tolman emphasized that learning is based on knowledge and an expectation of "what leads to what."*
- *Cognitive interpretations of classical conditioning propose that what is learned is an expectancy that the CS will be followed by the UCS.*
- *Cognitive theorists view operant conditioning as the development of an expectancy that certain behaviours will produce certain consequences under certain conditions. Tolman's research on latent learning indicates that "knowledge" and "performance" are conceptually distinct, and that learning can occur without reinforcement.*
- *In humans, internal self-evaluations (e.g., pride and shame) can function as reinforcers and punishers.*

OBSERVATIONAL LEARNING: WHEN OTHERS PAVE THE WAY

37. What is the adaptive significance of observational learning?

How did you learn to write, drive a car, and make a peanut butter and jelly sandwich? Reinforcement certainly was involved, but so was **observational learning**, the learning that occurs by observing the behaviour of a model. Teachers, parents, and peers help us learn by modelling academic skills. Coaches and music teachers demonstrate motor skills. Through observation, we learn that peanut butter is spread across a piece of bread, rather than piled up in the centre. In the time-honoured apprenticeship system, a novice watches and learns from a master.

Observational learning can be highly adaptive. By observing others, an organism can learn which events are important, which stimuli signal that such events are about to occur, and which responses are likely to produce positive or negative consequences. Animals learn what to eat, where to find food, and even how to eat by watching other animals (Galef & Giraldeau, 2001). B. G. Galef, at McMaster University, has found that rats can learn food aversions (Galef & Whiskin, 2000) and food preferences (Galef & Whiskin, 2001) by observing other rats. Observation of other animals can even influence mating among Japanese quail (White & Galef, 1999; White & Galef, 2000), or which other animals one can reasonably pick a fight with among hens (Hogue et al., 1996). Monkeys may learn adaptive fears—such as a fear of snakes—by observing other monkeys' reactions (Mineka & Hamida, 1998).

Our capacity to learn by observation, which is also called *modelling*, far outstrips that of other creatures. It saves us enormous time and effort, and helps us bypass the potentially time-consuming and dangerous process of trial and error. We do not want each new generation of medical surgeons, airline pilots, and firefighters to learn their craft only through trial and error. Beyond such skill acquisition, what makes observational learning so important is that we also learn fears, prejudices, likes and dislikes, and social behaviours by watching others (Bandura, 1977; Hendy & Raudenbush, 2000). Lockwood and Kunda (1997), at the University of Waterloo, found that highly successful models can inspire us and boost our self-image when we view their achievements as attainable and relevant. Through observation we may learn desirable and adaptive responses, or, if we choose models who display prejudicial, antisocial, aggressive, or violent actions, we may acquire undesirable behaviours.

Models, of course, differ in many ways. We are more likely to imitate those who are competent, likable, and have higher status or social power (Brewer & Wann, 1998; Brody & Stoneman, 1985). Our reasons for observing behaviour also differ. Imagine observing a model, knowing that you will be trying to imitate the behaviour later on. Now imagine observing a model, knowing that you will not be asked to imitate the behaviour. An experiment using PET scans suggests that brain regions involved in planning are more active when we watch models with the intent of imitating their behaviour (Decety et al., 1997).

FIGURE 7.31

In Bandura's experiment, most children who watched an aggressive model attack a Bobo model later imitated that behaviour. These photos show only one of several specific actions that the children spontaneously imitated.

The Modelling Process

Alberta native and UBC alumnus Albert Bandura (1977), who helped pioneer the scientific study of observational learning, views it as a cognitive process involving four basic steps: *attention, retention, reproduction,* and *motivation.* First, we must pay attention to the model's behaviour. Second, we must retain that information in memory so that it can be recalled at a later time. Third, we must be physically capable of reproducing the model's behaviour, or something similar to it. And fourth, we must be motivated to display the behaviour.

38. Explain how Bandura's experiment illustrates the distinction between learning and performance.

The fourth step, motivation, highlights the important distinction between *learning* and *performance*. Recall that we defined learning as a change in an organism's behaviour *or capabilities* based on experience. Research shows that observation alone is enough to learn a behaviour, but future performance depends on the consequences that we expect (Bandura, 1989). Tolman's work on latent learning and Bandura's research on modelling demonstrate that knowledge and the capability to perform a behaviour can be acquired at one time, but not be displayed until a later time.

Bandura (1965) demonstrated this point in a classic experiment. Children watched a film in which a model acted aggressively toward a "Bobo doll" (a plastic, inflatable clown), punching, kicking, and hitting it with a mallet. One group saw the model rewarded with praise and candy, a second group saw the model reprimanded for aggression, and a third group saw no consequences for the model. After the film, each child was placed in a room with various toys, including a Bobo doll (Figure 7.31).

Children who saw the model punished performed fewer aggressive actions toward Bobo than did children in the other two groups. Does this mean that the first group failed to learn how to respond aggressively? To find out, the experimenter later offered the children attractive prizes if they could do what the model had done. All of the children quickly reproduced the model's aggressive responses.

Do these findings generalize to the real world? This research helped stir a societal controversy that was brewing in the 1960s and which continues to this day: What effect does viewing media violence have on our attitudes and behaviour? We discuss this issue more fully in Chapter 16. In brief, despite some scientific disagreement, the weight of laboratory experiments and real-world correlational studies strongly suggests that viewing media violence has these effects (Eron, 2000; Huesmann, 1997; Smith & Donnerstein, 1998):

39. Evaluate the internal and external validity of the *Lassie* experiment.

- it decreases concerns about the suffering of victims,
- it habituates us (reduces our sensitivity) to the sight of violence, and
- it provides aggressive models that increase the likelihood of aggression.

If watching aggressive models on television can enhance our aggression, can watching "pro-social" models (models who do good deeds) increase our tendency to help others? The following *Research Foundations* examines this question.

RESEARCH FOUNDATIONS

Lessons from Lassie: Can Watching TV Increase Helping Behaviour?

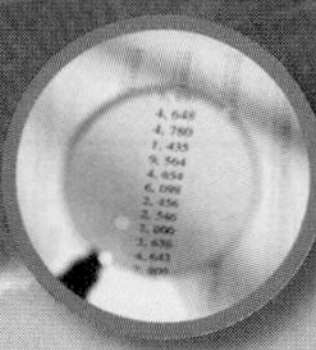

Background

This experiment by Joyce Sprafkin and her colleagues represents one of the earliest attempts to examine whether children behave more helpfully after watching pro-social models on TV. It is the first controlled experiment to do so using a general "entertainment" program from the major TV networks. The authors also examined whether a specific act of helping

–Continued

You are about to meet H.M., a 27-year-old man who recently had most of his hippocampus and surrounding brain tissue surgically removed to reduce his severe epileptic seizures. The operation succeeded, but it unexpectedly has left H.M. with *amnesia,* or memory loss.

When you first meet H.M. he might appear normal, for he is bright and has retained good language and social skills. Perhaps to your surprise, he can discuss his childhood, teens, and early twenties, for those memories are intact. H.M. has forgotten some events that occurred within the two years prior to surgery, but for the most part, his amnesia has not robbed him of his past. Rather, as of age 27, it is about to rob him of his future.

H.M. has lost the ability to form new memories that he can consciously recall. Typically, once an experience or fact leaves his immediate train of thought, he cannot remember it. Spend the day with H.M., depart and return minutes later, and he will not recall having met you. He forgets that he has recently eaten and reads magazines over and over as if he has never seen them before. A favourite uncle has died, but H.M. cannot remember. Thus, every time H.M. asks how his uncle is, he experiences shock and grief as though it were the first time he learned of his uncle's death.

H.M.'s surgery actually took place in 1953, and he has been studied extensively by Brenda Milner at the Montreal Neurological Institute. Researchers have followed his case for over 40 years (Corkin, 2002; MacKay, 2006; Scoville & Milner, 1957). No matter how many years pass, H.M.'s memory for events contains little after 1953. He cannot consciously remember new facts, nor retain the meaning of words that have entered the English language since his operation. He once guessed, for example, that "biodegradable" meant "two grades."

Memory refers to the processes that allow us to record and later retrieve experiences and information. As H.M.'s case illustrates, memory is precious and complex. What prevents H.M. from recalling new experiences, while leaving most of his pre-1953 memories intact? Why is it, as Figure 8.1 shows, that H.M. can learn and remember how to perform new tasks, yet swear each time he encounters these tasks that he has never seen them before? In this chapter, we explore these and other fascinating questions about memory.

MEMORY AS INFORMATION PROCESSING

1. In what ways is memory like an information-processing system?

Psychological research on memory has a rich tradition, dating back to late 19th-century Europe, when Hermann Ebbinghaus (1885) studied the rate at which new information is forgotten and Sir Francis Galton (1883) investigated people's memories for personal events. Decades later, the cognitive revolution within North American psychology and the advent of computers ushered in a metaphor that has influenced memory research since the 1960s: the mind as a processing system that encodes, stores, and retrieves information (Bower, 2000).

Encoding refers to getting information into the system by translating it into a neural code that your brain processes. This is a little like what happens when you type on a computer keyboard, as your keystrokes are translated into an electrical code that the computer can understand and process. **Storage** involves retaining information over time. Once in the system, information must be filed away and saved, as happens when a computer stores information on a hard drive. Finally, there must be a way to pull information out of storage when we want to use it, a process called **retrieval**. On a computer, retrieval occurs when you give a software

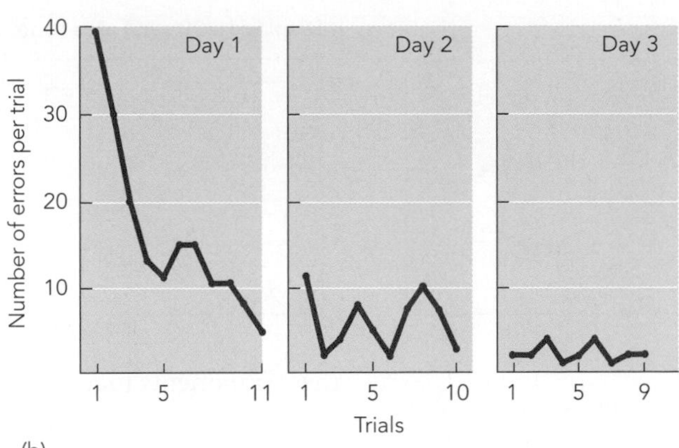

FIGURE 8.1

(a) On this complex task, participants trace a pattern while looking at its mirror image, which shows their hand moving in the direction opposite to its actual movement. (b) H.M.'s performance rapidly improved over time, indicating that he had retained a memory of how to perform the task. Yet, each time he performed it, he stated that he had never seen the task before, and had to have the instructions re-explained.

Adapted from Milner, 1965.

command (e.g., "Open File") that transfers information from the hard drive back to the screen where you can view it. Keep in mind, however, that this analogy between human and computer is crude. For one thing, we routinely forget and distort information, and may "remember" events that never occurred (Morris et al., 2006; Pickrell et al., 2003). Human memory is highly dynamic, and its complexity cannot be fully captured by any existing information-processing model.

Encoding, storage, and retrieval represent what our memory system does with information, and they could not take place without memory having some type of organization or structure. Thus, before exploring these processes in more detail, let us examine some basic components of memory.

A Three-Component Model

Our encounter with H.M. suggests an interesting possibility regarding how memory might be organized. If you told H.M. your name or read him a series of numbers, he could recall it for a short time. Yet he could not form a lasting memory; once his train of thought changed, that information would be lost forever. Could it be, as William James (1890) suggested long ago, that memory has distinct yet interacting components, one temporary and the other more long-lasting?

The model shown in Figure 8.2 incorporates this assumption. Originally developed by Richard Atkinson and Richard Shiffrin (1968), and subsequently modified, it proposes that memory has three major components: sensory memory, short-term or "working" memory, and long-term memory. The model does not assume that each component corresponds to a specific structure within the brain. Rather,

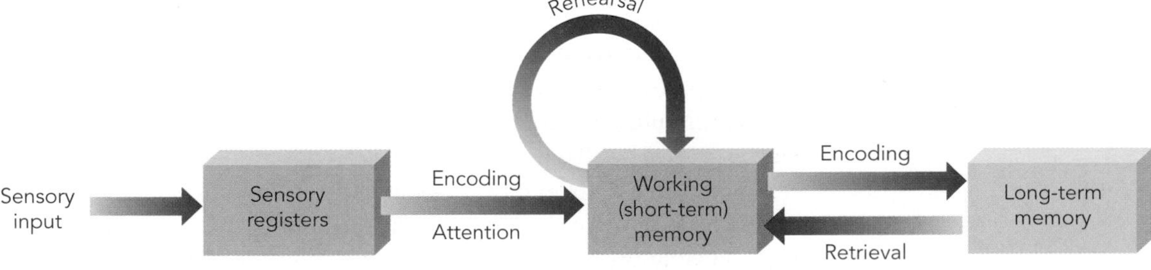

FIGURE 8.2

In this model, memory has three major components: (1) sensory registers, which detect and briefly hold incoming sensory information; (2) working memory, which processes certain information received from the sensory registers and information retrieved from long-term memory; and (3) long-term memory, which stores information for longer periods of time.

Adapted from Atkinson & Shiffrin, 1968.

Fixation

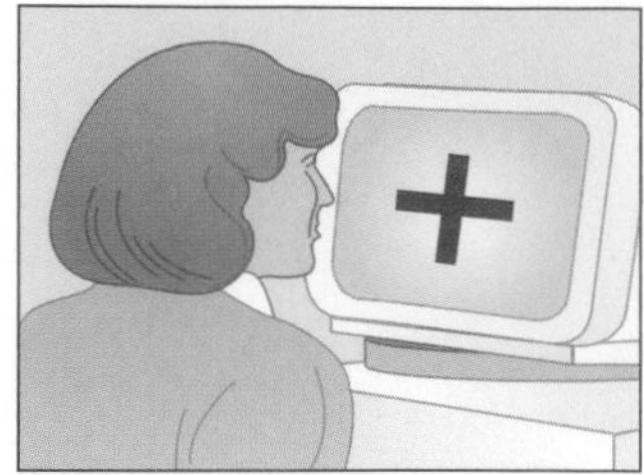

Display (1/20 sec.) plus tone

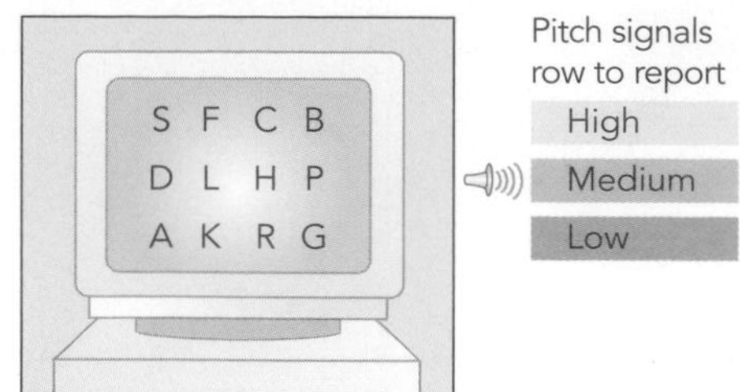

Report

FIGURE 8.3

After a participant fixates on a screen, a matrix of letters is flashed for 1/20 of a second. In one condition, participants do not hear any tone and must immediately report as many letters as they can. In another condition, a high-, medium-, or low-pitched tone signals the participant to report either the top, middle, or bottom row. If the tone occurs immediately, participants typically can report three or all four letters, no matter which row is signalled.

2. What is sensory memory? How did Sperling assess the duration of iconic memory?

3. Describe the limitations of short-term memory, and how they can be overcome.

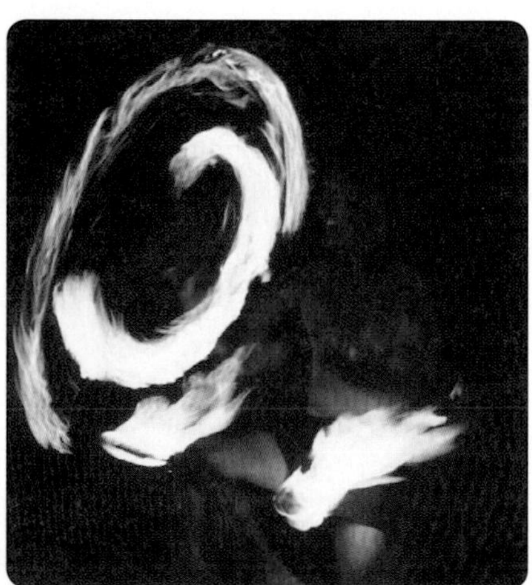

FIGURE 8.4

The arc of light that you see traced by a fiery baton, or the lingering flash that you see after observing a lightning bolt, results from the brief duration of information in iconic memory. Due to a slow camera shutter speed, this photo captures more arcs of light than you could actually see: Because your iconic memory stores complete information for only a fraction of a second, the image would quickly vanish.

the components may involve interrelated neural sites, and memory researchers use these terms in a more abstract sense.

Sensory Memory

Sensory memory holds incoming sensory information just long enough for it to be recognized. It is composed of different subsystems, called *sensory registers,* which are the initial information processors. Our visual sensory register is called the *iconic store,* and in 1960 George Sperling conducted a classic experiment to assess how long it stores information (see Research Foundations). As Figure 8.3 illustrates, the time course for visual sensory memory is very brief. Indeed, it is difficult, perhaps impossible, to retain complete information in purely visual form for more than a fraction of a second. See Figure 8.4. (Barsalou, 1992).

The auditory sensory register, called the *echoic store,* is studied by asking participants to recall different sets of numbers or letters that are simultaneously presented to their left and right ears via headphones. Echoic memory lasts longer than iconic memory. A nearly complete echoic trace may last about two seconds and a partial trace may linger for several more (Winkler et al., 2002).

Short-Term/Working Memory

Because our attentional capabilities are limited, most information in sensory memory simply fades away. But through selective attention, a small portion enters **short-term memory**, which holds the information that we are conscious of at any given time. Short-term memory also is referred to as **working memory**, because it consciously processes, codes, and "works on" information (Atkinson & Shiffrin, 1968; Baddeley, 1986).

Mental representations. Once information leaves sensory memory, it must be represented by some type of code if it is to be retained in short-term and eventually long-term memory. For example, the words that someone just spoke to you ("please buy some gum") or the phone number that you just looked up must somehow become represented in your mind. Such *mental representations,* or memory codes, can take various forms (Jackendoff, 1996). We may try to form a mental image (visual encoding), code something by sound (phonological encoding), or focus on the meaning of a stimulus (semantic encoding). For physical actions, such as learning sports or playing musical instruments, we code patterns of movement (motor encoding).

Note that the form of a memory code often does not correspond to the form of the original stimulus. For example, as you read these words (visual stimuli) you probably are not storing images of the way the letters look. Rather, you likely are forming phonological codes (saying the words silently to yourself) and, as you think about the material, semantic codes that represent their meaning. When people are presented with lists of words or letters and asked to recall them immediately, the errors that they make often are phonetic. They might recall a V instead of a B because of the similarity in how the letters sound (Conrad, 1964). Likewise,

RESEARCH FOUNDATIONS

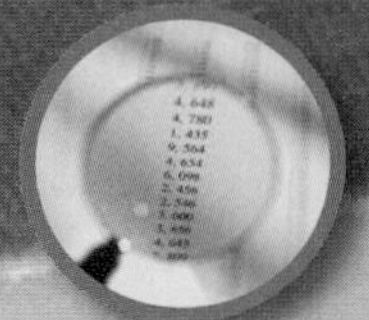

In Search of the Icon

How does information from some sensory input get translated into memory? Are we able to attend to all of the information or is only some of it available? These questions were of central importance in Sperling's pioneering work on iconic memory.

Sperling (1960) had participants view matrices of letters such as the one shown in Fig. 8.3. The matrix was presented for a very brief time (about 50 milliseconds). When asked to report what they had seen, participants could only correctly identify 4.5 letters (typically from the first row) on average. Even if the presentation time was increased to 500 milliseconds or the number of letters was reduced, the results remained the same. Thus, it would appear that the memory span for a visual stimulus was quite limited—only about 33 percent of the display could be reported.

Sperling devised a method of **partial report** to demonstrate that much more information was actually available. The same matrices were presented, but when the visual stimulus was removed a tone was presented. For a high-pitched tone, participants were to report the letters in the first row. If the tone was low-pitched, the bottom row was to be reported. A medium-pitched tone called for a report of the middle row. Results indicated that approximately 75 to 90 percent of the letters could be correctly reported, regardless of the line they appeared in. Since the pitch of the tone was determined randomly, participants could not predict which line they needed to attend to until the stimulus display was gone. Sperling argued that some kind of memory trace must remain after the visual stimulus is removed. This trace is very short-lived (less than 1 second), but is available for scanning and, thus, any line in the matrix can be accurately recalled. However, when asked for a total report (recall as many letters as possible without the tone cue), the trace has faded by the time one line is reported.

This memory trace (referred to as an **icon**, Neisser, 1967) is a purely visual representation of the stimulus array. It is subject to interference by additional visual information, and its strength is affected by visual factors such as contrast, intensity, etc. This notion of a sensory storage mechanism was quickly integrated into many models of memory and Sperling's 1960 paper remains one of the most cited studies in psychology.

given word lists such as (1) *man, mad, cap, can, map;* (2) *old, late, thin, wet, hot;* and (3) *big, huge, broad, long, tall,* people become most confused recalling the first list, in which the words sound similar (Baddeley, 1966). Such findings suggest that phonological codes play an important role in short-term memory.

Capacity and duration. Short-term memory can hold only a limited amount of information at a time. Depending upon the stimulus, such as numbers, letters, or words, most people can hold no more than five to nine meaningful items in short-term memory, leading George Miller (1956) to set the capacity limit at "the magical number seven, plus or minus two." To demonstrate this, try administering the *digit-span task* in Table 8.1 to some people you know.

If our short-term memory capacity is so limited, how can we remember and understand sentences as we read? To answer this, read the line of letters below (about one per second), then cover it up and write down as many letters as you can remember, *in the order presented.*

B I R C Y K A E U Q S A S A W T I

Did you have trouble remembering even half of these 17 letters in order? Now we rearrange (reverse) the letters and again ask you to write them down in order. Here are the 17 letters: "It was a squeaky crib." No doubt, you find this task much easier. The limit on short-term memory capacity concerns the number of meaningful *units* that can be recalled, and the original 17 letters have been combined into five meaningful units (words). Combining individual items into larger units of meaning is called **chunking**, and it can greatly aid recall.

Short-term memory is limited in duration as well as capacity. Have you ever experienced rapid forgetting, such as being introduced to someone, starting a conversation, and then suddenly realizing that you don't have the foggiest idea what

TABLE 8.1 Digit-Span Test

Directions: Starting with the top sequence, read these numbers at a steady rate of one per second. Immediately after saying the last number in each series, signal the person to recall the numbers in order. Most people can recall a maximum sequence of five to nine digits.

8 3 5 2

4 3 9 3 1

7 1 4 9 3 7

5 4 6 9 2 3 6

1 5 2 4 8 5 8 4

9 3 2 6 5 8 2 1 4

6 8 1 3 1 9 4 7 3 5

4 2 4 6 9 5 2 1 7 4 3

3 7 9 8 4 6 1 7 2 4 9 5

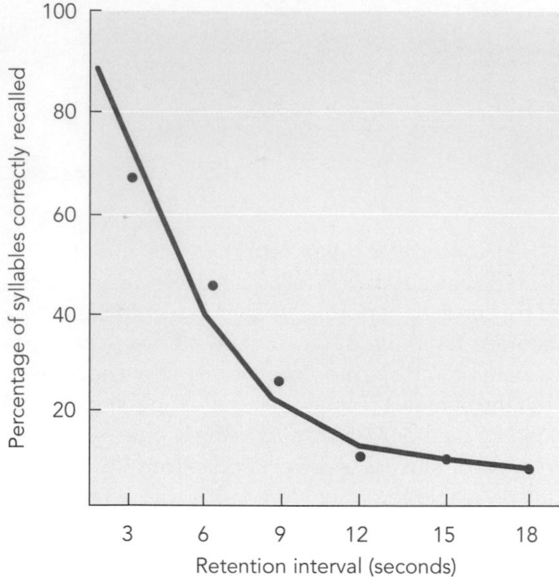

FIGURE 8.5

Participants who were prevented from rehearsing three-letter syllables in working memory showed almost no recall of the letters within 18 seconds, illustrating the rapid forgetting of information in short-term memory.

Based on Peterson & Peterson, 1959.

her or his name was? Without rehearsal, the "shelf-life" of information in short-term memory is indeed short, perhaps lasting about 20 seconds. Lloyd and Margaret Peterson (1959) demonstrated this by presenting participants with three-letter syllables (all consonants), such as BSX, followed by a three-digit number, such as 140. Upon seeing the number, participants counted backward by threes, which prevented them from rehearsing the letters. As Figure 8.5 indicates, after counting backward for as little as 18 seconds, few syllables were recalled.

By rehearsing information we can extend its duration in short-term memory indefinitely. This occurs when you look up a telephone number and keep saying it to yourself, either out loud or silently, while waiting to use a phone. This simple repetition of information is called **maintenance rehearsal**. In contrast, **elaborative rehearsal** involves focusing on the meaning of information or relating it to other things we already know. Thus you could rehearse the term "iconic memory" by thinking about examples of iconic memory in your own life. Both types of rehearsal keep information active in short-term memory, but elaborative rehearsal is more effective in transferring information into long-term memory, which is our more permanent memory store (Gardiner et al., 1994; Mäntylä, 1986).

Putting short-term memory "to work." Picture the seemingly endless stacks of a library (representing long-term memory), and a tiny "loading platform" (representing short-term memory) outside the building. New books (pieces of information) rapidly arrive and, because there isn't enough space, knock other ones off the platform. According to the original three-stage model, items that remain on the short-term loading dock long enough—such as through maintenance rehearsal—eventually get transferred into the long-term library.

4. Why do researchers refer to short-term memory as "working memory"?

The original three-stage model of memory focused on short-term memory primarily as a loading platform or holding station for information along the route from sensory to long-term memory. Many cognitive scientists now reject this view of short-term memory as too passive and too sequential. Instead, they view short-term memory as a *working memory*—a "mental workspace" that actively and simultaneously processes different types of information and supports other cognitive functions, such as problem solving and planning. Metaphorically, rather than a loading platform, working memory "is instead more like the office of a busy librarian, who is energetically categorizing, cataloging, and cross-referencing new material" (Reisberg, 1997, p. 139).

To illustrate how working memory stores information, processes it, and supports problem solving, add the numbers 27 and 46 "in your head." Your working memory stores the numbers, calls up information from long-term memory on "how to add," keeps track of the interim steps (7 + 6 = 13, carry the 1), and coordinates these mental processes.

5. Identify three components of working memory.

One model, proposed by Alan Baddeley (1986, 1998; Repous & Baddeley, 2006), divides working memory into three components. First, we maintain some information in an *auditory working memory* (the "phonological loop"), such as when you repeat a phone number, name, or new vocabulary terms to yourself mentally. A second component, *visual-spatial working memory* (the "visuo-spatial sketchpad"), allows us to temporarily store and manipulate images and spatial information, as when forming mental "maps" of the route to some destination. Finally, a control process, called the *central executive,* directs the action. It decides how much attention to allocate to mental imagery and auditory rehearsal, calls up information from long-term memory, and integrates the input. Research suggests that the prefrontal cortex, the seat of "executive functions" described in Chapter 3, is heavily involved in directing the processing of information in working memory (Nelson et al., 2000; Tsujimoto et al., 2004)).

Long-Term Memory

As already noted, **long-term memory** is our vast library of more durable stored memories. Perhaps there have been times in your life, such as periods of intensive study during finals, when you have felt as if "the library is full," with no room for storing so much as one more new fact inside your brain. In reality, barring brain damage, we remain capable of forming new long-term memories until we die. And, as far as we know, long-term storage capacity essentially is unlimited. Once formed, a long-term memory can endure for up to a lifetime (Bahrick et al., 1994).

Are short-term and long-term memory really distinct? Case studies of amnesia victims such as H.M. support this distinction, but another source of evidence comes from laboratory experiments in which participants with normal memory learn lists of words. Suppose that we present you with a series of unrelated words, one word at a time. The list might contain 10, 15, 20, or even 30 items. Immediately after the last word is presented, you will recall as many words as you can, in any order you wish. As Figure 8.6 illustrates, most experiments find that words at the end and beginning of the list are the easiest to recall. This U-shaped pattern is called the **serial position effect**, meaning that recall is influenced by a word's position in a series of items. The serial position effect has two components, a *primacy effect*, reflecting the superior recall of early words, and a *recency effect*, representing the superior recall of the most recent words.

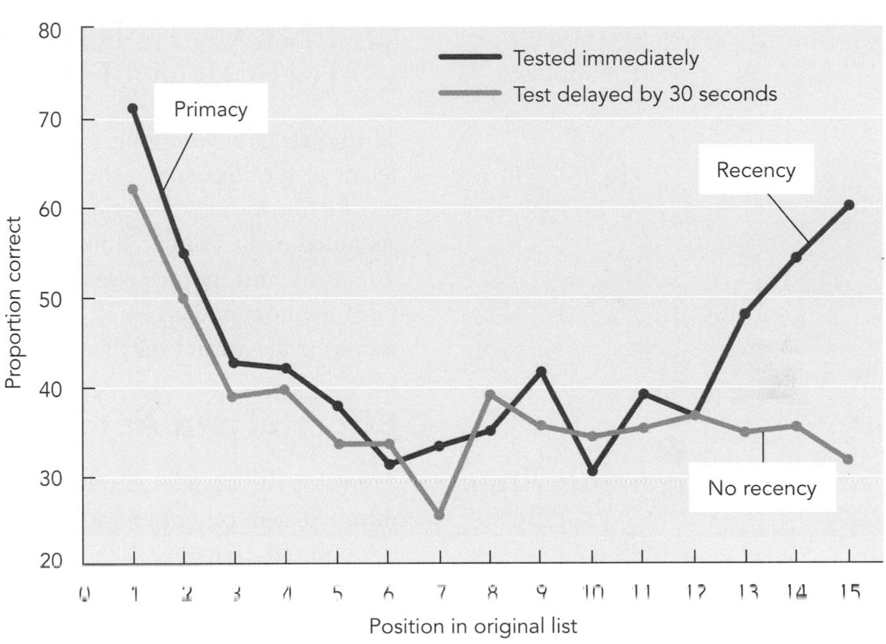

FIGURE 8.6

Immediate recall of word lists produces a serial position curve, in which primacy and recency effects are both evident. However, even a short delay of 30 seconds in recall (during which rehearsal is prevented) eliminates the recency effect, indicating that the later items in the word list have disappeared from short-term memory.

Adapted from Glanzer & Cunitz, 1966.

What causes the primacy effect? According to the three-stage model, as the first few words enter short-term memory, we can quickly rehearse them and transfer them into long-term memory. However, as the list gets longer, short-term memory rapidly fills up, and there are too many words to keep repeating before the next word arrives. Therefore, beyond the first few words, we cannot rehearse the items and they are less likely to get transferred into long-term memory. If this hypothesis is correct, then the primacy effect should disappear if we can prevent people from rehearsing the early words, say by presenting the list at a faster rate. Indeed, this is what happens (Glanzer, 1972).

6. What is the serial position effect? Under what conditions do primacy and recency effects occur?

As for the recency effect, the last few words have the benefit of not being "bumped out" of short-term memory by any new information. Thus, if we try to recall the list immediately, all we have to do is "read out" the last words while they linger in short-term memory. In sum, according to the three-stage model, the primacy effect is due to the transfer of early words into long-term memory, whereas the recency effect is due to short-term memory.

If this explanation is correct, then we should be able to wipe out the recency effect—but not the primacy effect—by eliminating the last words from short-term memory. This happens when the recall test is delayed, even for as little as 15

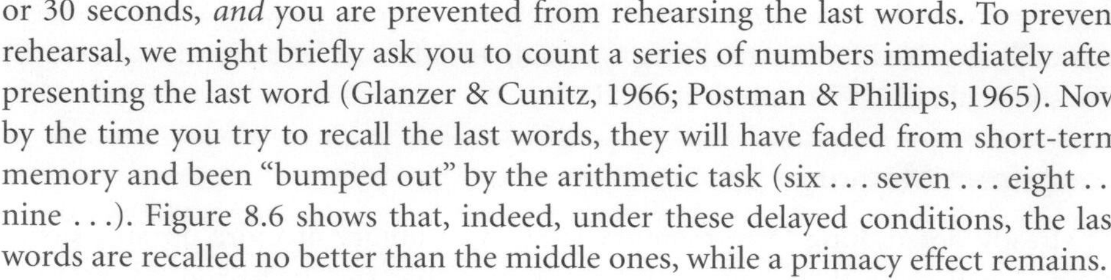

or 30 seconds, *and* you are prevented from rehearsing the last words. To prevent rehearsal, we might briefly ask you to count a series of numbers immediately after presenting the last word (Glanzer & Cunitz, 1966; Postman & Phillips, 1965). Now by the time you try to recall the last words, they will have faded from short-term memory and been "bumped out" by the arithmetic task (six . . . seven . . . eight . . . nine . . .). Figure 8.6 shows that, indeed, under these delayed conditions, the last words are recalled no better than the middle ones, while a primacy effect remains.

7. According to the three-component model, why do primacy and recency effects occur?

Having examined some of the basic components of memory, let us now explore more fully how information is encoded into long-term memory, how it is stored, and factors that affect our ability to retrieve it.

ENCODING: ENTERING INFORMATION

The holdings of your long-term memory, like those of a library, must be organized in terms of specific codes if the information is to be available when you wish to retrieve it. In a library, new material is assigned a call number before it is placed in storage. As noted earlier, our "call numbers" come in various forms—semantic, visual, phonological, and motor codes—that later enable us to activate information in long-term memory and access it. The more effectively we encode material into long-term memory, the greater the likelihood of retrieving it (Van Overschelde et al., 2005).

Effortful and Automatic Processing

8. Provide some examples of effortful and automatic processing in your own life.

Think of the parade of information that you have to remember: names, phone numbers, computer passwords, and mountains of schoolwork on which you expect to be tested. Learning such information involves *effortful processing,* encoding that is initiated intentionally and requires conscious attention (Hasher & Zacks, 1979). Rehearsing, making lists, and taking class notes illustrate effortful processing.

In contrast, have you ever been unable to answer an exam question, and said to yourself "Why can't I answer this? I can even picture the diagram; it was on the upper portion of the left page!" Here incidental information about the diagram's location on the page (that you were not trying to learn) appears to have been transferred into long-term memory through *automatic processing,* encoding that occurs without intention and requires minimal attention.

Information about the frequency, spatial location, sequence, and timing of events often is encoded automatically (Hasher & Zacks, 1984; Mangels, 1997). For example, if I ask you what you did yesterday, you probably will have little trouble remembering your sequence of activities, despite the fact that you never had to sit down and intentionally memorize this information. Some processes (e.g., reading) are so automatic that we have difficulty switching to a more effortful style.

Levels of Processing: When Deeper Is Better

9. Explain the concept of "depth of processing."

Imagine that you are participating in a laboratory experiment, and are about to be shown a list of words, one at a time. Each word will be followed by a question, and all you have to do is answer "yes" or "no." Here are three examples:

1. POTATO "Is the word in capital letters?"
2. horse "Does the word rhyme with course?"
3. TABLE "Does the word fit in the sentence, 'The man peeled the _____'?"

Each question requires effort, but differs from the others in an important way. The first question requires superficial *structural encoding,* since you only have to notice how the word looks. Question 2 requires a little more effort. You must engage in *phonological* (also called *phonemic) encoding* by sounding out the word to yourself and then judging whether it matches the sound of another word. The last question requires *semantic encoding* because you must pay attention to what the word means.

In this experiment, every word shown to you will be followed by a question similar to one of these. Unexpectedly, you will then be given a memory test. Which group of words will be recognized most easily: those processed structurally, phonologically, or semantically?

According to the **levels of processing** concept developed by Fergus Craik and Robert Lockhart (1972) of the University of Toronto, the more deeply we process information, the better it will be remembered. In the study above, semantic encoding involves the deepest processing because it requires us to focus on the *meaning* of information. Merely perceiving the structural properties of the words (e.g., capitalized vs. lowercase) involves shallow processing, and phonemically encoding words is intermediate. You can see in Figure 8.7 that the results of a study conducted by Craik and Endel Tulving (1975) in Toronto support the value of deeper, semantic encoding.

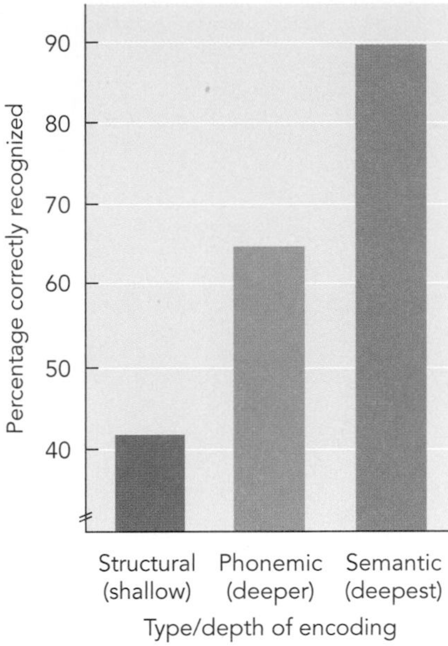

FIGURE 8.7

Depth of processing facilitates memory. Participants were shown words and asked questions that required superficial structural processing of a word, somewhat deeper phonemic processing, or deeper semantic processing. Depth of processing increased later recognition of the words in a larger list.

Data from Craik & Tulving, 1975.

Although many experiments have replicated this finding (Gabrieli et al., 1996), at times the concept of "depth of processing" can be difficult to measure. Suppose that some randomly assigned students study a chapter by creating hierarchical outlines and notes. A second group creates flash cards, jumbles them up, and rehearses them. Which study method represents deeper processing? If the first group performs better on a test, should we assume that they must have processed the information more deeply? To do so, warns Alan Baddeley (1990), is to fall into a trap of circular reasoning. Then again, there are situations in which few would argue with at least a broad distinction between shallow and deep processing. Here is one of them.

Exposure and Rehearsal

Years ago a student came into my office after failing the first exam in introductory psychology. He told me he had been to all the lectures, completed the chapters ahead of time, and reread each chapter twice more just before the exam. Yet when I looked through his textbook, not a word or sentence had been underlined or highlighted. I asked if he took notes as he read or paused to reflect on the information, and he said "No." Instead, he read each chapter quickly, much like a novel, and assumed that merely by looking at everything three times the information would somehow "sink in."

Unfortunately, this student's approach stood little chance of success. To learn factual and conceptual information presented in most academic or job settings, we need to employ effortful, deep processing. Simple repeated exposure to a stimulus without stopping to think about it represents shallow processing. To demonstrate this, try drawing from memory a picture of a Canadian penny, accurately locating all the markings. Few of our students can do this. Thus, even thousands of shallow exposures to a stimulus do not guarantee long-term retention (Jones, 1990; Nickerson & Adams, 1979).

10. How effectively do maintenance and elaborative rehearsal process information into long-term memory?

Rehearsal goes beyond mere exposure because we are thinking about the information. Of course, not all thinking is created equal, and neither is all rehearsal. As noted earlier, *maintenance rehearsal* involves simple repetition, as when silently repeating an unfamiliar phone number while waiting to use the phone. Maintenance rehearsal is most useful for keeping information active in short-term, working memory, and it may help transfer some information into long-term memory (Naveh & Jonides, 1984; Wixted, 1991). However, it is an inefficient method for bringing about long-term transfer.

In contrast, *elaborative rehearsal* focuses on the meaning of information—we *elaborate* on the material in some way. Organizing information, thinking about how it applies to our own lives, and relating it to concepts or examples we already know illustrate such elaboration. According to Craik and Lockhart (1972), elaborative rehearsal involves deeper processing than maintenance rehearsal and should be more effective in transferring information into long-term memory. In contexts as varied as university students learning word-lists to sixth-graders learning CPR (cardiopulmonary resuscitation), experiments support the greater effectiveness of elaborative rehearsal (Gardiner et al, 1994; Mäntylä, 1986; Rivera-Tovar & Jones, 1990). Even thinking about examples of concepts that other people provide for us facilitates later recall (Palmere et al., 1983).

Organization and Imagery

Dining at the restaurant where J.C. is a waiter can be an awe-inspiring experience. Perhaps you would like a filet mignon, medium-rare, with a baked potato, and Thousand Island dressing on your salad? Whatever you choose, it represents only one of over 500 possible options that can be ordered (seven entrees × five serving temperatures × three side dishes × five choices of salad dressing). Yet you and 20 or so of your best friends can place your selections with J.C., and he will remember them perfectly without writing them down. How does he do it?

Psychologists K. Anders Ericsson and Peter Polson (1988), who studied J.C., found that he invented an overall organizational scheme to aid his memory. He divided his customers' orders into four categories (entrees, temperatures, side dish, dressing) and then used a different system to encode the orders in each category. For example, he represented dressings by their initial letter, so orders of Thousand Island, oil and vinegar, blue cheese, and oil and vinegar would become TOBO.

Imposing organization on a set of stimuli is an excellent way to enhance memory. An organizational scheme can enhance the meaningfulness of information and also serve as a cue that helps trigger our memory for the information it represents, just as the word *TOBO* jogs J.C.'s memory of the four orders of salad.

Hierarchies and Chunking

11. Why do hierarchies, chunking, mnemonic devices, and imagery enhance memory?

Organizing material in a *hierarchy* takes advantage of the principle that memory is enhanced by associations between concepts. Gordon Bower and his co-workers (1969) demonstrated this experimentally by presenting some participants with a logically organized list of words, based on a hierarchical tree like the one in Figure 8.8a. Other participants received the same words placed randomly within the tree. As Figure 8.8b shows, participants presented with a meaningful hierarchy remembered more than three times as many words.

Notice that the hierarchy in Figure 8.8a does not reduce the amount of information to be remembered. With or without it, there are the same number of words to learn. Rather, a logical hierarchy enhances our *understanding* of how these diverse elements are related, and as we proceed from top to bottom, each category can serve as a cue that triggers our memory for the associated items below it. Because the hierarchy has a visual organization, there also is a greater possibility of using imagery as a supplemental memory code.

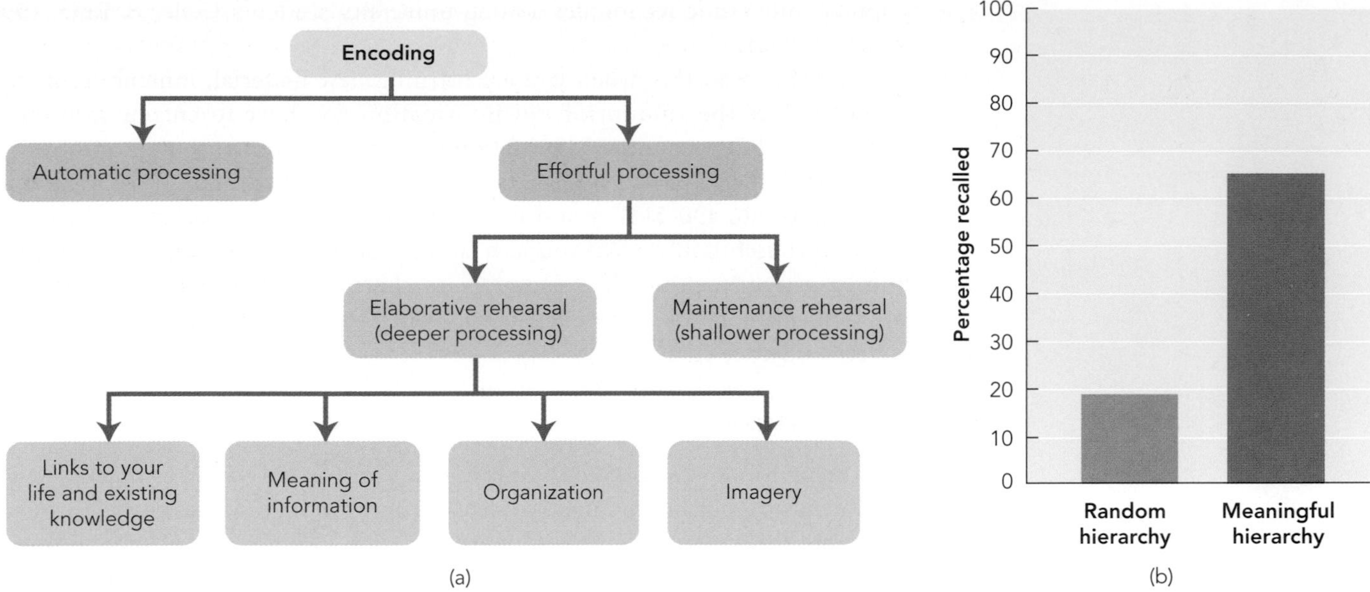

FIGURE 8.8

Words presented in a logically organized hierarchical structure (a) are remembered better than the same words placed randomly in a similar-looking structure (b).

Bower et al., 1969.

Chunking refers to combining individual items into a larger unit of meaning, and it widens the information-processing bottleneck caused by the limited capacity of short-term memory (Gobet et al., 2001; Miller, 1956). To refresh your memory, read the line of letters below to yourself (about one per second) and try to recall as many as you can, in the same sequence.

C T V Y M C A I B M K G B F B I

If you remembered four to eight of the letters in order, you did quite well. Now we can reorganize these sixteen individual bits of information into five larger, more meaningful chunks: CTV, YMCA, IBM, KGB, and FBI. This rearrangement is easier to keep active in short-term memory and, should you be so motivated, to rehearse and transfer into long-term memory. A common example of chunking in everyday life is the way we encode and later retrieve phone numbers from long-term memory. Thus, if you periodically call someone who lives far away, you probably encode the number as a set of three chunks (e.g., 905-430-5147) rather than as ten individual numbers.

Mnemonic Devices

The search for memory aids dates back thousands of years. In fact, the term "mnemonics" (ne-mon'-iks), which refers to "the art of improving memory," derives from the name Mnemosyne, the Greek goddess of memory. A mnemonic device is any type of memory aid. Hierarchies and chunking represent two types of mnemonic devices. So do acronyms, which combine one or more letters (usually the first letter) from each piece of information you wish to remember. For example, many students learn the acronyms HOMES and ROY G. BIV to help remember the names of the five Great Lakes of North America (Huron, Ontario, Michigan, Erie, Superior) and the hues in the visible spectrum—the "colours of the rainbow" (red, orange, yellow, green, blue, indigo, violet). Acronyms are one of the most popular mnemonic techniques among university students (Soler & Ruiz, 1996; Manolo, 2002).

Keep in mind that when you are learning new material, mnemonic devices do not reduce the amount of *raw* information you have to encode into memory. Rather, they reorganize information into more meaningful units and provide extra cues to help retrieve information from long-term memory. When chunking seven digits into 430-5147, you still have to encode seven digits. And the acronym HOMES is useful only when you have also encoded the names of the Great Lakes into long-term memory. Thus some researchers argue that acronyms—DAM—*d*on't *a*id *m*emory, or at least do so only when you are already familiar with the material (Carney et al., 1981, 1994).

Visual Imagery

How many windows are there in your home? Can you tell me, in as much detail as possible, what your bedroom looked like during your high school years? To answer these questions, you might try to construct and scan a series of mental images in your working memory, based on information that you draw out of long-term memory.

Allan Paivio (1969) proposes that information is stored in long-term memory in two forms: verbal codes and nonverbal (typically visual) codes. According to his **dual coding theory**, *encoding information using both codes enhances memory*, because the odds improve that at least one of the codes will be available later to support recall. In short, two codes are better than one, though dual coding is harder to use with some types of stimuli than others. Try to construct a mental image for each of the following: (1) fire truck, (2) lightbulb. Now construct an image for these words: (1) jealousy, (2) knowledge. You probably found the second task more difficult, because the latter words represent abstract concepts rather than concrete objects (Sadoski et al., 1997). Abstract concepts are easier to encode semantically than visually.

Memory improvement books often recommend using imagery to dual-code information, and research supports this approach (Tye, 1991). The ancient Greeks developed an effective and well-known imagery technique called the *method of loci* (loci is Latin for "places"). To use this technique, imagine a physical environment with a sequence of distinct landmarks, such as the rooms in a house or places on your campus. In one psychology class, students rapidly learned to use the 40 locations on the Monopoly game board as their visual reference (Schoen, 1996).

To remember a list of items or concepts, take an imaginary stroll through this environment and form an image linking each place with an item or concept. To remember the three components of working memory, you might imagine walking into the president's office at your school (executive control system), then watching a band rehearsal in your gym (phonological loop), and finally visiting an art class (visuo-spatial sketchpad). Many studies support the method of loci's effectiveness (Crovitz, 1971; Roediger, 1980).

How Prior Knowledge Shapes Encoding

Long-term memory is densely populated with semantic codes that represent the meaning of information. Typically, when we read, listen to someone speak, or experience some other event, we do not precisely record every word, sentence, or moment. Rather, we form a mental representation that captures the essential meaning or gist of that event. For example, in the two preceding paragraphs we described the method of loci. Can you recall those paragraphs word for word? More likely, what you have encoded is the gist—the general theme—that the method of loci involves forming images that link items to places.

Schemas: Our Mental Organizers

12. What is a schema? Explain how schemas influence encoding.

The themes that we extract from events and store in memory are often organized around schemas. A **schema** (plural: *schemas,* or *schemata*) is a "mental framework"—an organized pattern of thought about some aspect of the world, such as a class of people, events, situations, or objects (Bartlett, 1932; Koriat et al., 2000). We form schemas through experience, and they can strongly influence the way we encode material in memory. To demonstrate this, read the following paragraph:

> The procedure is actually quite simple. First you arrange things into different groups. Of course, one pile may be sufficient depending on how much there is to do. If you have to go somewhere else due to lack of facilities, that is the next step; otherwise you are pretty well set. It is important not to overdo things. That is, it is better to do too few things at once than too many. In the short run this might not seem important, but complications can easily arise. A mistake can be expensive as well. . . . After the procedure is completed, one arranges the materials into different groups again. Then they can be put into their appropriate places. Eventually they will be used once more, and the whole cycle will have to be repeated. However, that is part of life. (Bransford & Johnson, 1972, p. 722)

Asked to recall as much as you can of the preceding paragraph, you would probably have difficulty remembering much of it. Certainly, participants in the original experiment did. However, suppose we tell you that the paragraph is about a common activity: washing clothes. Now if you read the material again, you will find that the abstract and seemingly unrelated ideas suddenly make sense. Your schema—your mental framework for "washing clothes"—helps you organize these ideas and recall a great deal more.

This example illustrates that how we perceive a stimulus shapes the way we mentally represent it in memory. Essentially, schemas create a perceptual set, which is a readiness to perceive—*to organize and interpret*—information in a certain way.

Schemas and Expert Knowledge

13. In what sense are schemas and expert knowledge related?

When people who have never learned to "read notes" look at a musical score, they see an uninterpretable mass of information. In contrast, musicians see organized patterns that they can easily encode, eventually learning to play a piece "from memory." In music as in other fields, acquiring *expert knowledge* can be viewed as a process of developing schemas—mental frameworks—that help encode information into meaningful patterns.

William Chase and Herbert Simon (1973) demonstrated the relation between expertise, schemas, and encoding in an intriguing study. Three chess players—an expert ("master"), an intermediate player, and a beginner—were allowed to look at a chess board containing about 25 pieces for only 5 seconds. Then they looked away and, on an empty board, attempted to reconstruct the placement of the pieces from memory. This was repeated over several trials, each with a different arrangement of pieces. On some trials, the chess pieces were arranged in *meaningful positions* that actually might occur in game situations. With only a 5-second glance, the expert typically recalled 16 pieces, the intermediate player 8, and the novice only 4. What may surprise you is that, when the pieces were in *random positions,* there was no difference in recall between the three players. They each did poorly, accurately recalling only two or three pieces.

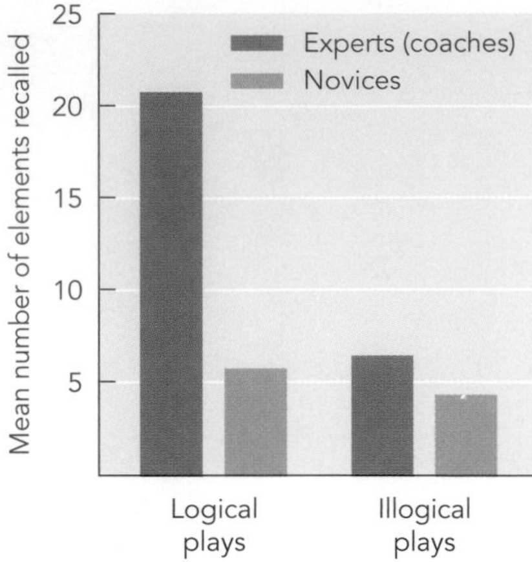

FIGURE 8.9

Diagrams of football plays were shown to football coaches (experts) and people who had played football, but were not coaches (novices). Coaches, allowed to see each play for just five seconds, displayed excellent memory—but only when the plays were logical. Their well-developed football schemas were of little use when the patterns of Xs and Os were illogical. The findings are very similar to those obtained when expert and novice chess players tried to reproduce meaningful and random arrangements of chess pieces.

Data from Garland & Barry, 1991.

How would you explain these results? We have to reject the conclusion that the expert had better overall memory than the other players, because he performed no better than they did with the random arrangements. But the concepts of schemas and chunking do explain the findings (Chase & Simon, 1973; Gobet & Simon, 1998). When the chess pieces were arranged in meaningful positions, the expert could apply well-developed schemas to recognize patterns and group pieces together. For example, he would treat as a unit all pieces that were positioned to attack the king. The intermediate player and especially the novice, who did not have well-developed chess schemas, could not construct the chunks and had to try to memorize the position of each piece. However, if the pieces were not in positions that would occur in a real game, they were no more meaningful to the expert than to the other players. In this case, the expert lost the advantage of schemas and had to approach the task on a piece-by-piece basis just as the other players did. Similarly, football coaches show much better recall than novices do after looking at diagrams of football plays (patterns of Xs and Os), but only when the plays are logical (Figure 8.9).

You may not be an advanced chess player, but there are many areas in which you possess expert knowledge. You have used language for most of your life and have years of experience about how the world works. As the washing machine example illustrates, your own "expert schemas" strongly influence what you encode and remember.

STORAGE: RETAINING INFORMATION

After information is encoded, how is it organized and stored in long-term memory? Consider the following statements, indicating as quickly as possible whether each is true or false:

1. A raccoon has wings.
2. Moscow is in Russia.
3. A bat is a fish.
4. Coca-Cola is green.
5. An apple is a fruit.
6. Some fire engines are red.

Chances are, you were able to respond to each statement almost instantaneously. Considering their diversity, it is remarkable that you could access the information so quickly. The fact that we are able to perform such tasks routinely—that we can recall an incredible wealth of information at a moment's notice—has influenced many cognitive models of how knowledge is stored and organized in memory.

Memory as a Network

We noted earlier that memory is enhanced by elaborative rehearsal, which involves forming associations between new information and other items already in memory. The general principle that memory involves associations goes to the heart of the network approach.

Associative Networks

14. Explain the concepts of associative networks and priming.

One group of theories proposes that memory can be represented as an **associative network**, a massive network of associated ideas and concepts (Collins & Loftus,

1975). Figure 8.10 shows what a small portion of such a network might be like. In this network, each concept or unit of information—fire engine, red, and so on—is represented by a *node* somewhat akin to each knot in a huge fishing net. The lines in this network represent associations between concepts, with shorter lines indicating stronger associations. For simplicity, Figure 8.10 shows only a few connections extending from each node, but there could be hundreds or more. Notice that items within the same category—types of flowers, types of fruits, colours, and so on—generally have the strongest associations and therefore tend to be clustered closer together.

Alan Collins and Elizabeth Loftus (1975) theorize that when people think about a concept, such as "fire engine," there is a *spreading activation* of related concepts throughout the network. For example, when you think about a "fire engine" related concepts such as "truck," "fire," and "red" should be partially activated as well. The term **priming** refers to the activation of one concept (or one unit of information) by another. Thus "fire engine" primes the node for "red," making it more likely that our memory for this colour will be accessed (Chwilla & Kolk, 2002).

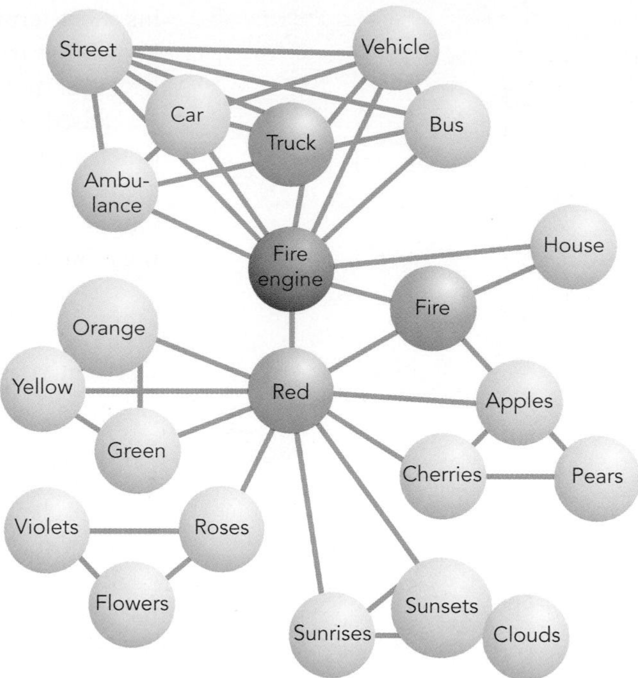

FIGURE 8.10

A network of concepts in semantic memory. The lines in the semantic network represent associations between concepts, with shorter lines indicating stronger associations.

Adapted from A. M. Collins and E. F. Loftus, 1975.

For an interesting three-dimensional look at an associative network, check out the visual thesaurus at *www.visualthesaurus.com*.

The notion that memory stores information in an associative network provides one possible explanation for why "hints" and mnemonic devices help stimulate our recall (Reisberg, 1997). For example, when I ask "Name the colours of the rainbow," the nodes for "colour" and "rainbow" jointly activate the node for ROY G. BIV, which in turn primes our recall for "red," "orange," and so forth.

Neural Networks

The neural network approach provides a different and increasingly popular model of memory and cognition (Chappell & Humphreys, 1994; McLelland & Rumelhart, 1985). A neural network has nodes that are linked to one another, but these nodes are physical in nature and do not contain individual units of information. There is no single node for "red," for "fire engine," and so on. Instead, each node is more like a small information-processing unit. As an analogy, some proponents would say: Think of each neuron in your brain as a node. A neuron processes inputs and sends outputs to other neurons, but as far as we know, the concepts of "red," or "fire engine," or your mental image of an elephant are not stored within any single neuron.

15. How do neural network models differ from associative network models?

Where, then, is the concept "red" stored? In a **neural network**, each concept is represented by a particular *pattern* or *set of nodes* that becomes activated simultaneously. When node 4 is activated simultaneously (i.e., in parallel) with nodes 9 and 42, the concept "red" might come to mind. But when node 4 is simultaneously activated with nodes 75 and 690, another concept enters our thoughts. Looking across the entire network, as a multitude of nodes *distributed* throughout the brain fire in *parallel* at each instant and spread their activation to other nodes, concepts and information are retrieved and thoughts arise. For this reason, neural network models are often called *parallel distributed processing models*, and researchers in a wide variety of areas have shown much interest in these constructs (Tryon, 2002).

Types of Long-Term Memory

16. Use the concepts of declarative versus procedural memory, and explicit versus implicit memory, to explain the pattern of H.M.'s amnesia.

Think back to the nature of H.M.'s amnesia. Since his brain operation, H.M. has been unable to consciously recall new facts or personal experiences once they leave his short-term memory. Each time he meets you he will believe it is the first time. Yet with practice, H.M. learned new tasks even though he would never remember having seen them before (Milner, 1965).

Based on research with amnesia patients, brain-imaging studies, and animal experiments, many cognitive scientists believe that we possess several long-term memory systems that interact with one another (Squire & Zola-Morgan, 1991; Tulving, 2002.) This view is consistent with the concept, described in Chapter 6, that the mind involves distinct yet interrelated modules.

Declarative and Procedural Memory

Declarative memory involves factual knowledge, and includes two subcategories (Figure 8.11). **Episodic memory** is our store of factual knowledge concerning personal experiences: when, where, and what happened in the *episodes* of our lives. My recollection that I ate pizza last night is an episodic memory. **Semantic memory** represents general factual knowledge about the world and language, including memory for words and concepts. You know that Mt. Everest is the world's tallest peak, and that $e = mc^2$. Episodic and semantic memories are called *declarative* because, to demonstrate our knowledge, we typically have to "declare it"—we tell other people what we know.

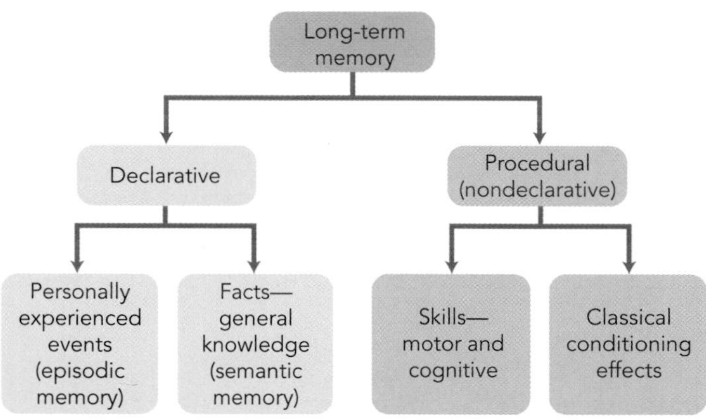

FIGURE 8.11

Some theorists propose that we have separate but interacting declarative and procedural memory systems. Episodic and semantic memories are declarative; their contents can be verbalized. Procedural memory is non-declarative; its contents cannot readily be verbalized.

H.M.'s brain damage severely impaired both components of his declarative memory, but this is not always the case. Some brain-injured children with amnesia cannot remember their daily personal experiences but can retain general factual knowledge, enabling them to learn language and attend mainstream schools (Vargha-Khadem et al., 1997).

In contrast to declarative memory, whose contents are verbalized, **procedural memory** (non-declarative memory) is reflected in skills and actions. One component of procedural memory consists of *skills* that are expressed by "doing things" in particular situations, such as typing, riding a bicycle, or playing a musical instrument. *Classically conditioned responses* also reflect procedural memory (Gabrieli, 1998). After a tone was repeatedly paired with a puff of air blown toward H.M.'s eye, he began to blink involuntarily to the tone alone (Woodruff-Pak, 1993). Although H.M. could not recall undergoing this procedure, his brain stored a memory for the association between the tone and the air puff, affecting his actions (he blinked) when subsequently exposed to the tone alone.

Explicit and Implicit Memory

Many researchers distinguish between explicit and implicit memory. **Explicit memory** involves conscious or intentional memory retrieval, as when you consciously recognize or recall something (Graf & Schacter, 1985). *Recognition* requires us to decide whether a stimulus is familiar, as when an eyewitness is asked to pick out a suspect from a police lineup, or students take multiple-choice tests. In recognition tasks, the "target" stimuli (possible suspects or answers) are provided for you. *Recall* involves spontaneous memory retrieval, in the sense that you must retrieve the target stimuli or information on your own. This occurs when you are briefly shown a list of words and then asked to recall them. With *cued recall,* hints are given to stimulate memory. If you cannot recall the word "hat" from the list, we might say, "It rhymes with 'bat.'" In academics, essay, short-answer, and fill-in-the-blank questions involve recall or cued recall.

Implicit memory occurs when memory influences our behaviour without conscious awareness. H.M. was able to remember how to perform the mirror-tracing task, although he had no conscious awareness of having learned it. His memory for the task (in this case, procedural memory) was implicit. In Chapter 6 we encountered another amnesia patient, whose hand Edouard Claparède (1911) intentionally pricked with a pin during a handshake. Shortly thereafter she could not consciously recall this incident, but despite her amnesia, she showed implicit memory of their encounter by withdrawing her hand when Claparède offered to shake it again.

17. Describe some ways to measure explicit and implicit memory.

In less dramatic ways, all of us demonstrate memory without conscious awareness. Riding a bicycle, driving, or performing any well-learned skill provides a common example. You may be consciously thinking about an upcoming school test or last night's party, while your implicit, procedural memory enables you to keep executing the skill.

Priming tasks provide another example. You might read a list of words (one word per second) that includes "kitchen," "moon," and "defend." Later—even a year later—you are rapidly shown many word stems, some of which might be KIT_____ , MO_____ , and DE_____ , and are asked to complete each stem to form a word. You are not aware that this is a memory test. Compared to people not given the original list of words, you will be more likely to complete the stems with words on the original list (e.g., MOon, rather than MOther). The word stems have activated or "primed" your stored mental representations of these words—the information is still in your memory—even though you may be unable to consciously recall the original words (Schacter, 1992; Sloman et al., 1988).

In Review

- *Memory involves three main processes (encoding, storage, and retrieval) and three main components (sensory memory, short-term/working memory, and long-term memory).*
- *Sensory memory briefly holds incoming sensory information. Some information reaches working memory and long-term memory, where it is mentally represented by phonological, visual, semantic, or motor codes.*
- *Short-term/working memory actively processes information and supports other cognitive functions. It has auditory, visuo-spatial, and executive (coordinating) components. Long-term memory stores enormous amounts of information for up to a lifetime. Studies of amnesia patients and research on the serial position effect support the distinction between short- and long-term memory.*
- *Effortful processing involves intentional encoding and conscious attention. Automatic processing occurs without intention and requires minimal effort.*
- *Deep processing enhances memory. Elaborative rehearsal provides deeper processing than maintenance rehearsal. Hierarchies, chunking, dual-coding by adding visual imagery, and other mnemonic devices facilitate deeper encoding.*
- *Schemas are mental frameworks that shape how we encode information. As we become experts in any given field, we develop schemas that allow us to encode information into memory more efficiently.*
- *Associative network models view long-term memory as a network of associated nodes, with each node representing a concept or unit of information. Neural network models propose that each piece of information in memory is represented not by a single node but by multiple nodes distributed throughout the brain. Each memory is represented by a unique pattern of simultaneously activated nodes.*
- *Declarative long-term memories involve factual knowledge and include episodic memories (knowledge concerning personal experiences) and semantic memories (facts about the world and language). In contrast, procedural memory is reflected in skills and actions. Explicit memory involves conscious or intentional memory retrieval, whereas implicit memory occurs when memory influences our behaviour without conscious awareness.*

◉ RETRIEVAL: ACCESSING INFORMATION

Storing information is useless without the ability to retrieve it. Imagine looking for a specific title in a library, searching book by book because items are placed onto shelves without call numbers. In contrast, if we have a call number and the book is shelved correctly, we can easily gain access to it.

A **retrieval cue** is any stimulus, whether internal or external, that stimulates the activation of information stored in long-term memory. If I ask you, "Have you seen Sally today?" the word *Sally* is intended to serve as a retrieval cue. Likewise, seeing a yearbook picture of a high school classmate can act as a retrieval cue that triggers memories of that person. *Priming* is a good example of how a retrieval cue ("fire engine," "MO_____") can trigger associated elements ("red," "MOon") in memory, presumably via a process of spreading activation.

The Value of Multiple and Self-Generated Cues

18. Why does having multiple, self-generated retrieval cues enhance recall?

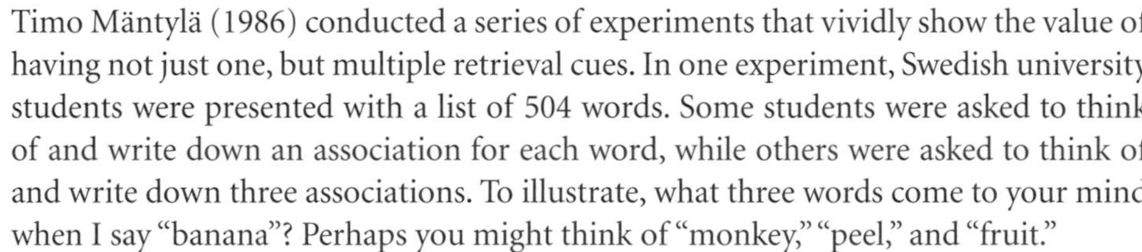

Timo Mäntylä (1986) conducted a series of experiments that vividly show the value of having not just one, but multiple retrieval cues. In one experiment, Swedish university students were presented with a list of 504 words. Some students were asked to think of and write down an association for each word, while others were asked to think of and write down three associations. To illustrate, what three words come to your mind when I say "banana"? Perhaps you might think of "monkey," "peel," and "fruit."

The students had no idea that their memory for these words would be tested, and once the association task was completed, they were given an unexpected immediate recall test for 252 of the words. For some words, students were first shown the one or three associations that they had previously generated. As a control, for other words they were first shown one or three associations that *another* participant had generated. Then they were asked to recall the original word.

The results were astounding. When the associations (i.e., retrieval cues) were self-generated, students shown one cue correctly recalled 61 percent of the words, and those shown three cues correctly recalled 91 percent. In contrast, when students were shown cues that someone else had generated, recall with one cue dropped to 11 percent and with three cues to 55 percent. Finally, when given another surprise recall test one week later on the remaining words, students still remembered 65 percent of the words when they were first provided with three self-generated retrieval cues, far better than any other condition.

In seven experiments, Mäntylä consistently found that having multiple, self-generated retrieval cues was the most effective approach to maximizing recall (Mäntylä, 1986; Mäntylä & Nilsson, 1988). Why might this be? On the encoding side of the equation, generating our own associations involves deeper, more elaborative rehearsal than does being presented with associations generated by someone else. Similarly, generating three associations involves deeper processing than thinking of only one. On the retrieval side, these self-generated associations become cues that have personal meaning. And with multiple cues, if one fails, another may activate the memory. The implication for studying academic material is clear. Think about the material, and draw one or preferably more links to items you already have in memory.

The Value of Distinctiveness

There is a quick exercise that you can perform to demonstrate a simple point. A list of words appears below. Say each word silently to yourself (about one per second), then when you see the word *WRITE,* look away and jot down as many words as you can recall, in any order. Here are the words: *robin, eagle, nest, crow, feather, goose, owl, tomato, rooster, fly, sparrow, nightingale, chirp, hawk, pigeon, WRITE.*

Recall that in the serial position effect, words in the middle of a list usually are recalled less well. Yet, if you are like 95 percent of our students, you will have recalled the word "*tomato,*" which occurred in the middle. In this list, tomato is distinctive. It stands out from the crowd (or at least, from the flock) and catches our attention. Upon retrieval, it is less likely to become "blended in" with all the other words. In general, distinctive stimuli are better remembered than non-distinctive ones (Ghetti et al., 2002; Hirshman & Jackson, 1997). This principle also applies to the events of our lives. In one study, university students were asked to list their three clearest memories (Rubin & Kozin, 1984). Distinctive events such as weddings, romantic encounters, births and deaths, vacations, and accidents were among the most frequently recalled.

Can we enhance the memorability of non-distinctive stimuli by associating them with other stimuli that help make them distinctive? According to Mäntylä (1986), this is a key reason why students who generated their own three-word associations were able to remember almost all of the 500 words on their list. Associating each word with three others helped form a distinctive, personally meaningful set of cues. Thus, when studying, one way to increase your recall when all the material "starts looking alike" is to make it distinctive by associating it with other information that is personally meaningful to you.

FIGURE 8.12

A flashbulb memory is a recollection that seems so vivid and clear that we can picture it as if it were a snapshot of a moment in time.

Flashbulb Memory: Fogging Up the Picture?

Do you recall what you were doing when you heard that Princess Diana had been killed in a car crash? Do you remember where you were at 9 A.M. on the morning of September 11, 2001? Like others of our generation, we can vividly recall the moment about 40 years ago when we heard that President John F. Kennedy had been assassinated.

Flashbulb memories are recollections that seem so vivid, so clear, that we can picture them as if they were a "snapshot" of a moment in time (Figure 8.12). They are most likely to occur for distinctive, positive or negative events that evoke strong emotional reactions and which are repeatedly recalled in conversations with other people (Brown & Kulik, 1977).

19. Do flashbulb memories always provide an accurate picture? Describe some evidence.

Because flashbulb memories are vivid and easily recalled, we are confident of their accuracy. But are they accurate? The day after the space shuttle *Challenger* blew up shortly after take-off, Ulric Neisser and Nicole Harsch (1993) asked university students to describe how they learned of the accident, where they were, and so on. Reinterviewed three years later, about half of them remembered some details correctly, but recalled other details inaccurately. A fourth of the students completely misremembered all the major details, and were astonished by how inaccurate their memories were after reading their original descriptions.

For a captivated public that followed the 1995 O. J. Simpson murder trial, the jury's verdict seemed to be an unforgettable moment. Was it? Three days after Simpson's acquittal, university undergraduates were asked how, when, with whom, and where they had learned of the verdict (Schmolck et al., 2000). Students also reported whether they agreed with the verdict and how emotional they felt about it. When some students' memory was retested 15 months later, only 10 percent made major mistakes in recalling the event. Over time, however, the flashbulb seemed to fade. Among other students retested 32 months after the verdict, 43 percent misremembered major details. Memory accuracy was not related to whether students originally had agreed or disagreed with the verdict, but those who reported a stronger emotional reaction in 1995 displayed better memory 32 months later. Perhaps most striking, among those students with grossly inaccurate recall, 61 percent were highly confident of their memories.

In the seventh week after the 9/11 terrorist attacks, psychologist Kathy Pezdek (2002) asked 569 students attending college in New York City (Manhattan), Southern California, and Hawaii to complete a memory questionnaire. One item asked, "On September 11, did you see the videotape on television of the first plane striking the first tower." Overall, 73 percent of the students said yes. Yet this was impossible, because the videotape of the first plane crashing was not broadcast until after September 11. Moreover, students who incorrectly responded yes were more confident in their memory than the students who correctly said no! Similarly, after Princess Diana died, a study in England found that 44 percent of participants said that they had seen a videotape on the TV news showing the crash take place. No such tape was ever shown; in fact, it is highly doubtful that such a tape even exists, yet they were as confident in their memory as participants who said they never saw such a tape (Ost et al., 2002).

Memory researchers have studied the relation between confidence and accuracy with children and adults, inside and outside the laboratory, and for many types of events. Overall, confidence and accuracy are weakly related (Busey et al., 2000). People accurately recall many events—even after years pass— and typically are very confident when they do. But people often swear by inaccurate memories too. Even for a distinctive event, a memory can feel "like it just happened yesterday" when, in truth, it's foggy.

Context, State, and Mood Effects on Memory

20. Explain how context-dependent and state-dependent memory illustrate the encoding specificity principle.

Years ago, two Swedish researchers reported the case of a young woman who was raped while out for a jog (Christianson & Nilsson, 1989). When found by a passerby, she was in shock and could not remember the assault. Over the next three months the police took her back to the crime scene several times. Although she could not recall the rape, she became emotionally aroused, suggesting implicit memory of the event. While jogging one day shortly thereafter, she consciously recalled the rape.

Because this is a case study, we cannot be sure what caused her memory to return. One possibility, the **encoding specificity principle**, states that memory is enhanced when conditions present during retrieval match those that were present during encoding (Tulving & Thompson, 1973). This occurs because stimuli associated with an event may become encoded as part of the memory and later serve as retrieval cues.

Context-Dependent Memory: Returning to the Scene

Applying the encoding specificity principle to *external* cues leads us to **context-dependent memory**: It typically is easier to remember something in the same environment in which it was acquired. Thus, upon returning to your elementary school or old neighbourhood, sights and sounds may trigger memories of teachers, classmates, and friends. As with the Swedish jogger, police detectives may take an eyewitness or crime victim back to the crime scene, hoping to stimulate the person's memory.

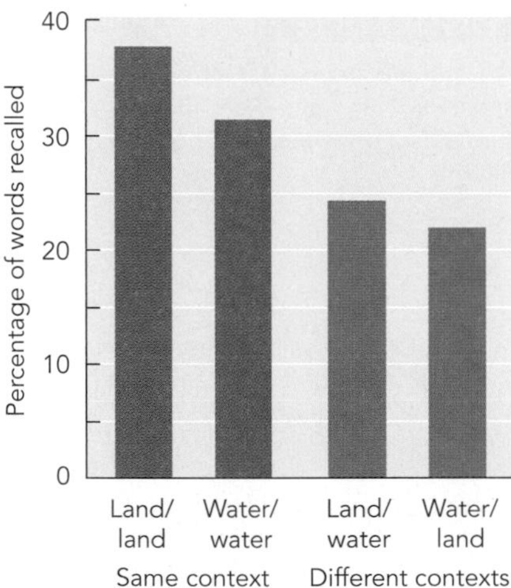

FIGURE 8.13

Context-dependent memory. Scuba divers who learned lists of words while underwater later recalled them better while underwater, whereas words learned on land were recalled better on land. Recall was poorer when the learning and testing environments were mismatched.

Data from Godden & Baddely, 1975.

In a classic experiment, Duncan Godden and Alan Baddeley (1975) asked scuba divers to learn some lists of words underwater and some on dry land. As Figure 8.13 shows, when the divers were later retested in the two environments, lists learned underwater were recalled better underwater and those learned on land were better recalled while on land. Similarly, when randomly assigned university students studied material in either a quiet or noisy room, they later displayed better memory on short-answer and multiple-choice questions when tested in a corresponding (quiet or noisy) environment (Grant et al., 1998). Thus, if you take exams in quiet environments, try to study in a quiet environment.

State-Dependent Memory: Arousal, Drugs, and Mood

Moving from external to internal cues, the concept of **state-dependent memory** proposes that our ability to retrieve information is greater when our *internal* state at the time of retrieval matches our original state during learning. The Swedish jogger who was raped consciously remembered her assault for the first time while jogging. In her case, both context-dependent cues (similar environment) and state-dependent cues (arousal while jogging) may have stimulated her memory.

Diverse experiments support this effect. Many students at the campus gym read course materials while exercising on a bicycle, treadmill, or stairclimber machine. Christopher Miles and Elinor Hardman (1998) found that material learned while we are aroused during aerobic exercise is later recalled more effectively if we are once again aerobically aroused, rather than at rest. Conversely, material learned at rest is better recalled at rest.

Many drugs produce physiological effects that directly impair memory, but state-dependency is another reason why events experienced in a drug state may be difficult to recall later while in a drug-free state (Figure 8.14). Experiments examining alcohol, marijuana, amphetamines, barbiturates, nicotine, caffeine, antihistamines, and other drugs have often found that information recall is poorer when there is a mismatch between the person's state during learning and testing (Carter & Cassaday, 1998; Eich et al., 1975; Peters & McGee, 1982). This *does not* mean, by the way, that drugs improve memory during initial learning.

Does state-dependent memory extend to mood states? Is material learned while in a happy mood or a sad mood better recalled when we are in that mood again? Inconsistent findings suggest that such *mood dependent memory* is not a reliable phenomenon, although researchers continue to study whether it might occur under certain conditions (Ryan & Eich, 2000). Instead, there is more consistent evidence of **mood-congruent recall**: We tend to recall information or events that are congruent with our current mood (Teasdale & Fogarty, 1979; Fiedler, 2000). When happy we are more likely to remember positive events, and when sad we tend to remember negative events. This helps perpetuate our mood and may be one factor that maintains depression once people have entered a depressed state (Pyszczynski et al., 1991).

Clearly, many factors affect how we encode, store, and retrieve information. Our *Psychological Applications* feature highlights some principles that are particularly relevant to helping you improve your memory.

FIGURE 8.14

State-dependent memory. In the film City Lights, a drunken millionaire befriends and spends the evening partying with Charlie Chaplin after Chaplin saves his life. The next day, in a sober state, the millionaire doesn't remember Chaplin and considers him an unwanted pest. After getting drunk again, he remembers Chaplin and treats him like a good buddy.

21. Identify practical principles of encoding and retrieval that can be used to enhance memory.

PSYCHOLOGICAL APPLICATIONS

Improving Memory and Academic Learning

Memory enhancement strategies fall into three broad categories (Park et al., 1990; Soler & Ruiz, 1996):

- *external aids,* such as shopping lists, notes, appointment calendars, and placing objects (such as keys) in the same location;
- *general memory strategies,* such as organizing and rehearsing information; and
- *formal mnemonic techniques,* such as acronyms and other systems that take training to be used effectively.

–*Continued*

Overall, memory researchers most strongly recommend using external aids and general strategies to enhance memory (Park et al., 1990; Moe & De Benji, 2005). Of course, in situations such as "closed-book" exams, using external aids may land you in the Dean's office! The following sound psychological principles can best enhance memory.

Use Elaborative Rehearsal to Process Information Deeply

Elaborative rehearsal—focusing on the meaning of information—enhances deep processing and memory (Gabrieli et al., 1996). Put simply, *if you are trying to commit information to memory, make sure that you understand what it means.* You may feel that we're daffy for stating such an obvious point, but let us ask you this: Do you always seek assistance when you encounter material that you have trouble understanding? Unfortunately, some students who find material confusing simply try to rote memorize it, an approach that usually fails. The "directed questions" that appear in this book's margins can help you process the course material more deeply, and also serve as good retrieval cues.

Link New Information to Examples and Items Already in Memory

Once you understand the material, process it more deeply by associating it with information you already know. This creates memory "hooks" onto which you can hang new information. Because you already have many memorable life experiences, *make new information personally meaningful* by relating it to your life.

Pay attention to examples, even if they are unrelated to your own experience. In one study, participants read a 32-paragraph essay about a fictitious African nation. Each paragraph presented a topic sentence stating a main theme along with zero, one, two, or three examples illustrating that theme. The greater the number of examples, the better the participants recalled the themes (Palmere et al., 1983).

Organize Information

Organizing information keeps you actively thinking about the material and makes it more meaningful. Before reading a chapter, look at the outline to determine how the material is logically developed. When studying, take notes from a chapter and use outlining to organize the information. This hierarchical structure forces you to arrange main ideas above subordinate ones and becomes an additional retrieval cue that facilitates recall (Bower et al., 1969).

Overlearn the Material

Overlearning refers to continued rehearsal past the point of initial learning, and it significantly improves performance on memory tasks (Driskell et al., 1992). In general, the greater the amount of overlearning, the greater the benefit. Moreover, much of this memory boost persists for weeks after overlearning ends. In short, just as elite athletes keep practising their skills, you should continue to rehearse material after you have first learned it.

Distribute Learning over Time

You have finished the readings and organized your notes for an upcoming test. Now it's time to study and review. Are you better off with *massed practice,* a marathon session of highly concentrated learning, or with *distributed practice,* several shorter sessions spread out over a few days? Research suggests that you will retain more information with distributed practice (Smith & Rothkopf, 1984; Underwood, 1970). It can reduce fatigue and anxiety, both of which impair learning.

Minimize Interference

Interference, as we soon will discuss more fully, occurs when one piece of information encoded in memory impairs our ability to remember some other piece of information. Distributed practice is effective because the rest periods between study sessions reduce interference from competing material. However, when studying for several exams on the same or consecutive days, there really are few rest periods. There is no simple solution to this problem. Suppose you have a psychology exam on Thursday and a sociology exam on Friday. Try to arrange several sessions of distributed practice for each exam over the preceding week. On Wednesday, limit your studying to psychology if possible. Once your psychology exam is over, turn your attention to your second test. This way, the final study period for each course will occur as close as possible to test time and minimize interference from other cognitive activities.

Studying before you go to sleep may enhance retention by temporarily minimizing interference, but, most of all, a typical university course load illustrates why overlearning is so important. Realistically, interference cannot be avoided, so study the material beyond the point where you feel you have learned it.

Use Imagery

Among formal mnemonic techniques, memory researchers view imagery as the most valuable (Park et al., 1990). As dual-coding theory predicts, images provide a splendid second "cognitive hook" on which to hang and retrieve information (Paivio, 1969, 1995). Instead of writing down customers' orders, some restaurant waiters and waitresses form images, such as visualizing a man who has ordered a margarita turning light green. As one waitress remarked, "After a while, customers start looking like drinks" (Bennett, 1983, p. 165). Perhaps an image of a camera flashbulb with a big red X through it will help you remember that flashbulb memories often are less accurate than people think they are. In sum, although there may not be any "magic" or effortless way to enhance memory, psychological research has established numerous principles that you can use to your advantage.

FORGETTING

Some very bright people are legendary for their memory failures, or "absentmindedness." The eminent French writer Voltaire began a passionate letter "My Dear Hortense" and ended it "Farewell, my dear Adele." The splendid absentmindedness of Canon Sawyer, an English nobleman, once led him, while welcoming a visitor at the railroad station, to board the departing train and disappear (Bryan, 1986). Indeed, how we forget is nearly as interesting a scientific question as how we remember.

FIGURE 8.15

Hermann Ebbinghaus was a pioneering memory researcher.

The Course of Forgetting

German psychologist Hermann Ebbinghaus (1885/1964) pioneered the study of forgetting by testing only one person—himself (Figure 8.15). He created over 2,000 *nonsense syllables*, meaningless letter combinations (e.g., *biv, zaj, xew*), to study memory with minimal influence from prior learning, as would happen if he used actual words. A dedicated scientist, in one study Ebbinghaus spent over 14,000 practice repetitions trying to memorize 420 lists of nonsense syllables.

Ebbinghaus typically measured memory by using a method called *relearning* and computing a savings percentage. For example, if it initially took him 20 trials to learn a list, but only half as many trials to relearn it a week later, then the savings percentage was 50 percent. In one series of studies, he retested his memory at various time intervals after mastering several lists of nonsense syllables. As Figure 8.16a shows, forgetting occurred rapidly at first and slowed noticeably thereafter.

22. Describe Ebbinghaus's "forgetting curve" and factors that contributed to his rapid, substantial forgetting.

Perhaps you are dismayed by this finding, which suggests that we quickly forget most of what we learn. Ebbinghaus, however, studied so many lists that his ability to distinguish between them undoubtedly suffered. If you learned just one or a few lists of syllables, the general shape of your forgetting curve might resemble Ebbinghaus's over the first 24 hours, but the amount you forget would likely be much less. Moreover, when material is meaningful (unlike nonsense syllables), we are likely to retain more of it for a longer time.

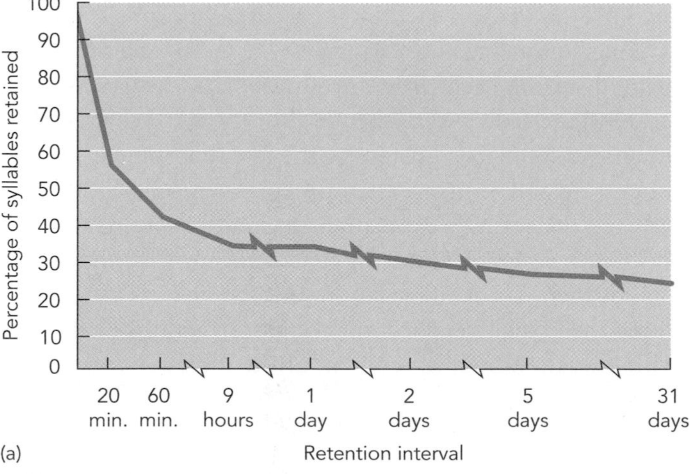

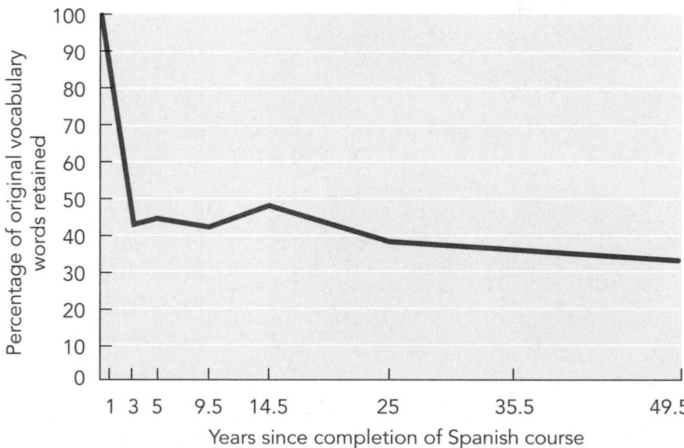

FIGURE 8.16

(a) Hermann Ebbinghaus's forgetting curve shows a rapid loss of memory for nonsense syllables at first, then a more gradual decline. The rapid decline is probably due to the meaningless nature of the nonsense syllables. (b) The forgetting of vocabulary from high school Spanish language classes follows a similar curve, except that the time frame is in years, not days.

Data from (a) Ebbinghaus (1964) and (b) Bahrick (1984).

Consider the forgetting curve shown in Figure 8.16b, based on a study examining the vocabulary retention of people who had studied Spanish in school anywhere from 3 to 50 years earlier and then rarely used it (Bahrick, 1984). Once again, forgetting occurred more rapidly at first, then more slowly as time passed. Notice, however, that we are now employing a time frame of years rather than hours and days as Ebbinghaus did. Similarly, in another study, first and second year university students accurately recalled 73 percent of their grades from their last year in high school, and their recall for grades from earlier years was almost as good (Bahrick et al., 1996). Of course, although participants in these studies retained considerable information over time, their memory was far from perfect.

Why Do We Forget?

Given that some memories last a lifetime, why do we forget so much? Researchers have proposed several explanations for normal memory loss, emphasizing difficulties in encoding, storage, and retrieval.

Encoding Failure

23. Identify encoding, storage, retrieval, and motivational processes that have been hypothesized to contribute to forgetting.

If memory is in some respects like a giant library, then one reason we do not remember information is that the book was never put on the shelf. Many memory failures result not from "forgetting" information that we once knew well, but from failing to encode the information into long-term memory in the first place. Much of what we sense is not processed deeply enough to commit to memory, which is understandable given the flood of stimuli that enter the sensory registers every day.

We noted earlier that few people can draw a penny (or other coin) from memory, with accurate detail. Even when the task is made easier by requiring only recognition, as in Figure 8.17, most people cannot identify the correct coin (Jones, 1990; Nickerson & Adams, 1979). The details of a coin's appearance are not meaningful to most of us, so we do not encode them no matter how often we see coins in our daily lives.

FIGURE 8.17

Which of the coins pictured here corresponds to a real penny? Most people have difficulty choosing the correct one because they have never bothered to encode all of the features of a real penny. Which representation of the penny is correct? The answer is in the margin on page 337.

Adapted from Nickerson & Adams, 1982.

At other times, we may notice information but fail to encode it deeply because we turn our attention to something else. Brad Bushman and Angelica Bonacci (2002) randomly assigned 328 adults to watch either a sexually explicit, violent, or neutral TV program. Nine commercial advertisements (e.g., for snacks, cereal, laundry detergent) appeared during each program. Immediately afterward and again a day later, the researchers tested viewers' memory for the ads. When analyzing their findings, Bushman and Bonnaci adjusted for the fact that some of the TV programs were more interesting and arousing than others. Even so, at both time periods, viewers who watched the sexually explicit and violent programs remembered the fewest number of ads. Several factors might account for this, and, as the researchers proposed, one of them is encoding failure: All the viewers clearly saw the ads, but those watching the sexually explicit and violent programs likely were the most preoccupied with thoughts about the content of the shows.

Decay of the Memory Trace

Turning from encoding to storage, one early explanation for forgetting was **decay theory**, which proposed that with time and disuse the physical memory trace in the nervous system fades away. Decay theory soon fell into disfavour because scientists could not identify what physical memory traces were, where they were located, or how physical decay could be measured. In recent decades, however, scientists have begun to unravel some of the ways that neural circuits change when a long-term memory is formed. This research has sparked new interest in examining how these changes might decay over time (Villarreal et al., 2002).

Decay theory's prediction that the longer the interval of disuse between learning and recall, the less would be recalled, was also problematic. When participants learn a list of words or a set of visual patterns and are retested at two different times, they sometimes recall *more* material during the second testing than during the first. This phenomenon, called *reminiscence,* seems inconsistent with the concept that a memory trace decays over time (Greene, 1992; Klimesch, 1979).

Interference, Retrieval Failure, and the Tip-of-the-Tongue

According to *interference theory,* we forget information because other items in long-term memory impair our ability to retrieve it (Postman & Underwood, 1973). Many cognitive psychologists view interference as a major cause of forgetting (Anderson & Neely, 1996).

Figure 8.18 illustrates two major types of interference. **Proactive interference** occurs when material learned in the past interferes with recall of newer material. Suppose that Charles changes residences, acquires a new phone number, and memorizes it. That night he sees a friend who asks for his new number. When Charles tries to recall it, he can remember only two or three digits, and instead keeps remembering the digits of his old phone number. Memory of his old phone number is interfering with his ability to retrieve the new one.

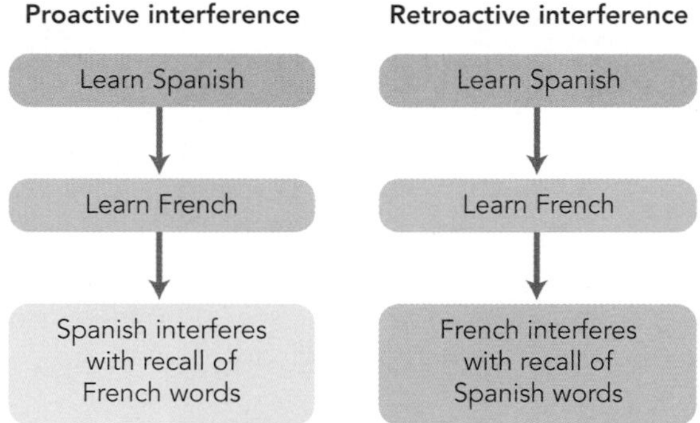

FIGURE 8.18

Interference is a major cause of forgetting. With proactive interference, older memories interfere with the retrieval of newer ones. With retroactive interference, newer memories interfere with the retrieval of older ones.

Retroactive interference occurs in the opposite direction. Here newly acquired information interferes with the ability to recall information learned at an earlier time (Tulving & Psotka, 1971). Suppose Charles has now had his new phone number for several months, and recalls it perfectly each time. If we ask him, "What was your old phone number?" Charles may have trouble remembering it, perhaps mixing up the digits with his new number. In general, the more similar two sets of information are, the more likely it is that interference will occur. You would probably experience little interference in recalling highly dissimilar material, such as French vocabulary and mathematical formulas.

Some researchers believe that interference is caused by competition among retrieval cues (Anderson & Neely, 1996; Runquist, 1975). When different memories become associated with similar or identical retrieval cues, confusion can result and accessing a cue may "call up" the wrong memory. Retrieval failure also can occur because we have too few retrieval cues or the cues may be too weak (Tulving & Psotka, 1971).

Almost all of us have experienced the so-called *tip-of-the-tongue (TOT) phenomenon,* in which we cannot recall a fact or name (a target word), but feel that we are on the verge of recalling it. Often we keep recalling an incorrect word that sounds similar to or resembles the target word. TOT states are common, perhaps occurring on average about once a week (Brown, 1991). Eventually, we retrieve the correct answer about half the time, and when we cannot, we often recall related information that makes us feel "I really do know the answer" (Brown, 1991; Riefer et al., 1995).

Do TOT states always reflect a retrieval problem? In one experiment, Bennett Schwartz (1998) asked university students a series of general factual questions, some of which actually had no correct answer. Yet when asked these impossible questions, all students claimed at least once that the answer was on the tip of their tongue. In short, some TOT experiences seem to be illusory. Rather than retrieval failure, perhaps we never knew the answer to begin with (Lampinen & Schwartz, 2000).

Motivated Forgetting

Psychodynamic theorists and other psychologists suggest yet another reason for some forgetting. They maintain that motivational processes, such as **repression**, may protect us by blocking the recall of anxiety-arousing memories (Singer, 1990, 1999).

During therapy sessions Sigmund Freud often observed that his patients remembered traumatic or anxiety-arousing events that had long seemed "forgotten." For example, one of his patients suddenly remembered with great shame that while standing beside her sister's coffin, she had thought, "Now my brother-in-law is free to marry me." Freud concluded that the thought had been so shocking and anxiety arousing that the woman had *repressed* it—pushed it down into her unconscious mind—there to remain until it was uncovered years later during psychoanalysis.

The concept of motivated forgetting is controversial. Some evidence supports it, and other evidence does not (Bonanno & Kaltman, 2000; Weinberger, 1990). People certainly do forget unpleasant events (and pleasant ones as well), but it has been difficult to demonstrate experimentally that a process akin to "repression" is the cause of such memory loss (Holmes, 1990; Schooler & Eich, 2000). We will return to this topic shortly.

Amnesia

24. Describe the nature and some possible causes of retrograde, anterograde, and infantile amnesia.

The most dramatic instances of forgetting occur in amnesia, which takes several forms. **Retrograde amnesia** represents memory loss for events that occurred *prior to* the onset of amnesia. For example, H.M. suffered mild memory loss for events in his life that had occurred during the year or two *before* his operation. A football player who is "knocked out" in a concussion, regains consciousness, and cannot remember the events just before being hit, is experiencing retrograde amnesia.

Anterograde amnesia refers to memory loss for events that occur *after* the initial onset of amnesia. H.M.'s brain operation, and particularly the removal of much of his hippocampus, produced severe anterograde amnesia and robbed him of the ability to consciously remember new experiences and facts. The woman whose hand was pinpricked by Claparède during a handshake also experienced anterograde amnesia; moments later she could not consciously remember the episode. Unlike H.M., her anterograde amnesia was caused by *Korsakoff's syndrome*, which can result from chronic alcoholism and may also cause severe retrograde amnesia (Kopelman et al., 1999).

Alzheimer's disease, which affects millions, mostly elderly adults, produces severe retrograde and anterograde amnesia. This memory loss may be due to a decline in the operation of several neurotransmitter systems, especially the *acetylcholine* system (Kimble, 1992). Acetylcholine plays a key role in synaptic transmission in several brain areas involved in memory.

Finally, there is one type of amnesia that all of us experience: an inability to remember personal experiences from the first few years of our lives. This memory loss for early experiences is called **infantile amnesia** (also known as *childhood amnesia*). Our memories of childhood typically do not include events that occurred before the age of three or four, although some adults can partially recall major events that happened when they were as young as two years of age (Crawley & Eacott, 2006; Usher & Neisser, 1993). Major events might be the birth of a sibling, hospitalization, or a death in the family.

This does not mean that infants and preschool children don't form long-term memories. They clearly do. Newborns retain memories for sensory information (e.g., they can distinguish between the sound of their mother's versus another woman's voice) and can remember behaviours that produce rewards (DeCasper & Fifer, 1980). But we are not able to consciously recall the events of our infancy and earliest childhood. Indeed, even 9- and 10-year-old children have difficulty remembering the faces of their preschool classmates (Newcombe & Fox, 1994).

What causes infantile amnesia? One possibility is that brain regions responsible for encoding long-term memories are still immature in the first years after birth. Another hypothesis is that we do not encode our early experiences deeply, and fail to form rich retrieval cues for them. For example, older children are more likely than younger children to spontaneously discuss, and thus rehearse, their recent experiences (Fivush & Nelson, 2004; Nelson & Fivush, 2004). Additionally, because infants and very young children lack a clear self-concept, they do not have a personal frame of reference around which to organize rich memories (Howe & Courage, 1993; Harley & Reese, 1999).

Forgetting to Do Things: Prospective Memory

Have you ever forgotten to mail a letter, turn off the oven, keep an appointment, or purchase something at the market? In contrast to *retrospective memory,* which refers to memory for past events, **prospective memory** concerns remembering to perform an activity in the future (Meacham & Singer, 1977). That people forget to do things as often as they do is interesting, because prospective memories typically involve little content (Baddeley, 1990). Often we need only recall that we must perform some event-based task ("Remember, on your way out, mail the letter") or time-based task ("Remember, take your medication at 4 P.M."). Successful prospective memory, however, draws upon other cognitive abilities, such as planning and allocating attention while performing other tasks (Marsh et al., 1998). The frontal lobes, which direct these executive processes, appear to be centrally involved in prospective memory (McDaniel et al., 1999).

Correct change? In Figure 8.17, penny "D" is the actual penny.

Are people with better retrospective memory less likely to be forgetful on prospective memory tasks? Some findings suggest not, at least when retrospective memory is measured explicitly by recall and recognition tasks (McDaniel & Einstein, 1993). In one experiment, researchers assessed participants' retrospective memory ability by having them recall lists of words (Wilkins & Baddeley, 1978). Next, participants performed a prospective, simulated pill-taking task by carrying around a small box with a button. Four times a day at a specified time they had to remember to press the button, which time-stamped their response. Overall, participants who performed better on the word-recall task did not display better memory on the simulated pill-taking task.

During adulthood, do we become increasingly absentminded about remembering to do things, as a common stereotype suggests? Numerous laboratory experiments support this view (Vogels et al., 2002). Typically, participants perform a task that requires their ongoing attention while trying to remember to signal the experimenter at certain time intervals or whenever specific events take place. Older adults generally display poorer prospective memory, especially when signalling is time-based. However, when prospective memory is tested outside the laboratory using tasks such as simulated pill-taking, healthy adults in their sixties to eighties often perform as well as or better than adults in their twenties (Rendell & Thomson, 1993, 1999; Henry et al., 2004; Phillips et al., 2006). Perhaps older adults are more motivated to remember in such situations or rely more on a standard routine (Anderson & Craik, 2000). In sum, prospective memory—like other areas of memory—is far from simple.

In Review

- *Retrieval cues activate information stored in long-term memory. Memory retrieval is more likely to occur when we have multiple cues, self-generated cues, and distinctive cues.*
- *We experience flashbulb memories as vivid and clear "snapshots" of an event and are confident of their accuracy. However, over time many flashbulb memories become inaccurate. Overall, memory accuracy and memory confidence are only weakly related.*
- *The encoding specificity principle states that memory is enhanced when cues present during retrieval match those that were present during encoding. Typically it is easier to remember a stimulus when we are in the same environment (context-dependent memory) or same internal state (state-dependent memory) as when the stimulus was originally encoded. One exception is mood states, where we tend to recall information or events that are congruent with our current mood.*
- *Forgetting tends to be most rapid relatively soon after initial learning, but the time frame and degree of forgetting can vary widely depending on many factors.*
- *Due to encoding failure, we often cannot recall information because we never entered it into long-term memory in the first place.*
- *Decay theory proposes that physical memory traces in long-term memory deteriorate with disuse over time, but evidence of reminiscence contradicts this view.*
- *Proactive interference occurs when material learned in the past interferes with recall of newer material. Retroactive interference occurs when newly acquired information interferes with the ability to recall information learned at an earlier time.*
- *Psychodynamic theorists propose that we may forget anxiety-arousing material through repression, an unconscious process of motivated forgetting.*
- *Retrograde amnesia represents memory loss for events that occurred prior to the onset of amnesia. Anterograde amnesia refers to memory loss for events that occur after the initial onset of amnesia. Infantile amnesia is our inability to remember personal experiences from the first few years of our lives.*
- *Whereas retrospective memory refers to memory for past events, prospective memory refers to our ability to remember to perform some activity in the future.*

MEMORY AS A CONSTRUCTIVE PROCESS

Retrieving information from long-term memory is not like viewing a taped replay on a video cassette recorder. Usually, our memories of things past are incomplete and sketchy. In such situations we may literally *construct* (or as some researchers prefer to say, *reconstruct*) a memory by piecing together bits of stored information in a way that intuitively "makes sense," and which therefore seems real and accurate (Schacter & Curran, 2000; Garoff-Eaton et al., 2006). Memory construction can be amusing at times, but it also can have serious personal and societal consequences.

Memory Distortion and Schemas

A classic experiment by Sir Frederick Bartlett (1932) provides an excellent illustration of memory construction. Bartlett asked residents of Cambridge, England, to read and then retell stories months, or in some cases years, later. One story, "The War of the Ghosts," is a Pacific Northwest Indian tale about a man on a seal-hunting trip who meets a group of warriors and goes on a raid with them. During the raid, he discovers that his companions are ghosts; subsequently, he dies a supernatural death.

25. How do Bartlett's research and studies of boundary extension illustrate memory construction?

Bartlett's participants, however, were twentieth-century residents of England, not eighteenth-century Native Americans. When these English participants retold the story, they reconstructed it in a way that made sense to them. For example, one participant retold the story 20 hours after reading it. The story was shorter and the plot had changed significantly. Now the hero was fishing rather than hunting seals, the word "boat" was substituted for "canoe" and most importantly the enemy—not the war party—is described as ghosts. Bartlett found that the longer the time interval between the reading and retelling of the story, the more the story changed to fit English culture.

Earlier we described how schemas (such as the concept "washing clothes") shape encoding. Bartlett, who coined the term *schema*, believed that people have generalized ideas (schemas) about how events happen and that they use these ideas to organize and reconstruct their memories. In reading "The War of the Ghosts," our pre-existing schemas no doubt affect how we encode the story, but they also influence how we "fill in the gaps" and reconstruct the story when we later recall it.

In general, the use of appropriate schemas improves memory by helping us organize information as we encode and retrieve it. Remember that, whether we are a chess player, coach, musician, or simply an experienced user of language, schemas are a key component of "expert knowledge." But schemas can exert a cognitive price. Fitting information into our schemas is sometimes like trying to squeeze a square peg into a round hole, requiring us to reshape and distort information so that it "makes sense" and fits in with pre-existing assumptions about the world.

Advertisers often exploit people's tendency to elaborate and change their memories, thereby skirting laws against false advertising. Consider the following commercial for the mouthwash Listerine.

> "Wouldn't it be great," asks the mother, "if you could make him coldproof? Well, you can't. Nothing can do that. [Boy sneezes.] But there is something you can do that may help. Have him gargle with Listerine antiseptic. Listerine can't promise to keep him cold-free, but it may help him fight off colds. During the cold-catching season, have him gargle twice a day with full-strength Listerine. Watch his diet, see he gets plenty of sleep, and there's a good chance he'll have fewer colds, milder colds, this year." (Anderson, 1980, p. 203)

This commercial, with the name of the product changed to *Gargoil*, (alas, not Gargoyle) was used in a memory experiment (Harris, 1977). When participants were asked to recall the commercial, they agreed with the statement "Gargoil antiseptic helps prevent colds," even though the commercial *did not* say that. (The advertisement said it *may* help.) Participants elaborated on what the ad said when they reconstructed it in their memories. Undoubtedly, this is what the advertisers hoped would happen.

Memory construction extends, quite literally, to how we visualize the world (Intraub, 2002). As Figure 8.19 illustrates, when university students look at photographs that have a main object within a scene, and then draw the pictures from memory, they consistently display *boundary extension*, remembering a scene as more expansive—as being "wider-angle"—than it really was (Intraub et al., 1996, 1998). In real life, objects occur against an expansive background, creating a schema for how we expect scenes to look. Thus, when remembering close-up images, our schemas lead us to "see beyond the edge" and retrieve a broader scene, not the one we saw.

(a)

(b)

FIGURE 8.19

Boundary extension. (a) What you see. (b) What you remember. Helene Intraub and her colleagues (1996) have found that when people briefly look at close-up pictures, such as this one of a teddy bear, and then draw the pictures from memory, they unknowingly convert the image into a "wider-angle scene" in which the size of the main object (e.g., the teddy bear) shrinks. This effect is less likely to occur if the original picture already is a wide-angle scene.

Images courtesy of Helene Intraub.

The Misinformation Effect and Eyewitness Testimony

If memories are constructed, then information that occurs *after* an event may shape that construction process. This **misinformation effect**, the distortion of a memory

(a)

(b)

FIGURE 8.20

Seven eyewitnesses to armed robberies committed by Ronald Clouser (a) mistakenly identified Father Bernard Pagano (b) as the robber, probably as a result of information from police that influenced their memory reconstructions.

United Press International.

by misleading post-event information, has been investigated most thoroughly in relation to mistaken eyewitness testimony. In fact, mistaken eyewitness identification is the source of more wrongful convictions in both Canada and the U.S. than all other sources together (Yarmey, 2001). In one celebrated case, Father Bernard Pagano, a Roman Catholic priest, was positively identified by seven eyewitnesses as the perpetrator of a series of armed robberies in the Wilmington, Delaware, area. He was saved from almost certain conviction when the true robber, dubbed the "gentleman bandit" because of his politeness and concern for his victims, confessed to the crimes. You can see in Figure 8.20 that there was little physical resemblance between the two men.

Two pieces of information may have affected the witnesses' memory. First, the gentlemanly and concerned manner of the robber is consistent with the schema many people have of priests. All else being equal, we will tend to make decisions in line with our schemas. Indeed, there is a high degree of consistency in the schemas that people have for "good-guys" and "bad-guys" in eyewitness situations (Yarmey, 1993). Second, before presenting pictures of suspects to the eyewitnesses, the police let it be known that the suspect might be a priest. Father Pagano was the only suspect wearing a clerical collar, and the witnesses' memories may have been strongly affected by this information (Rodgers, 1982; Tversky & Tuchin, 1989).

The misinformation effect can be subtle, produced by changing a single word while questioning an eyewitness. Imagine that after you witness a two-car crash, a police officer takes your statement and simply asks you, "About how fast were the cars going when they smashed into each other?" In one experiment, university students viewed a brief film of a car accident and then judged how fast the cars were going. Their judgments varied by almost 25 percent, depending upon how the question was asked (Loftus & Palmer, 1974). The recalled speed became progressively slower when the words *smashed into* (65.3 km/h) were changed to *collided with* (62.9 km/h), *bumped* (61.0 km/h), *hit* (54.4 km/h), and *contacted* (50.9 km/h).

Confusing the Source

Misinformation effects also occur because of **source confusion**, our tendency to recall something or recognize it as familiar, but to forget where we encountered it. Suppose an eyewitness to a crime looks through a series of mugshots and reports that none of the individuals is the perpetrator. Several days later, the eyewitness is brought back to view a lineup and is asked to identify the person who committed the crime. In reality, none of the people in the lineup did, but one suspect was pictured in a mugshot that the eyewitness had seen days ago. "That's the person," says the eyewitness. Source confusion (also called *source amnesia* or *source misattribution*) occurred because the eyewitness recognized that individual's face as familiar, but failed to remember that this familiarity stemmed from the mugshot. Instead, the witness mistakenly assumed that he or she saw the familiar-looking suspect committing the crime.

26. Explain how source confusion contributes to misinformation effects.

In an experimental analog to this situation, 29 percent of participants who witnessed a staged event and later viewed mugshots misidentified *innocent* suspects as having been involved in the event because of source confusion (Brown et al., 1977). Source confusion also occurs when participants are exposed to several misleading statements about an event that they have witnessed (Zaragoza & Mitchell, 1996; Dalton & Doneman, 2006). They eventually forget that the source of the misinformation (e.g., that a bare-handed thief wore gloves) was a statement made by someone else, and come to believe it was part of what they saw while witnessing the event.

Does post-event information permanently alter a witness's original memory, so that the original memory can never again be retrieved? Researchers debate the answer, but all agree that eyewitness reports can be influenced by post-event information. Results like these have raised concern about the reliability of eyewitness testimony not only from adults, but also from children in cases of alleged physical and sexual abuse. We explore this issue in our *Research Frontiers* feature.

?

27. Are younger and older children equally susceptible to misinformation effects, and equally accurate in recalling traumatic events? Describe some evidence.

RESEARCH FRONTIERS

How Accurate Are Young Children's Memories?

Research on the accuracy of children's memory has grown dramatically in the past 15 years. This interest stems from at least three factors. First, basic researchers seek to understand how memory capabilities develop with age. Second, misinformation experiments with adults raise the question of whether children's memory is as malleable. Third, society's increasing sensitivity to the tragedy of child abuse raises legal and scientific debate about the possible overreporting (false reporting) and underreporting of abuse (Ceci et al., 2000).

In cases of alleged sexual abuse there often is no conclusive corroborating medical evidence (sexual abuse often does not involve intercourse) and the child usually is the only witness (Bruck et al., 1998). If the charges are true, the thought of failing to convict the abuser and returning the child to an environment in which the abuse might continue is frightening. Conversely, if the charges are false, the consequences of convicting an innocent person are equally distressing. Thus the accuracy and believability of children's recall is of paramount concern (London et al., 2005).

Children's Susceptibility to Suggestive Questioning

As with adults, misinformation experiments indicate that a single instance of suggestive questioning can distort children's memory. Moreover, among children and adults, suggestive questioning most often leads to false memories when it is repeated (Ceci et al., 1994; Zaragoza & Mitchell, 1996). In both situations, young children typically are more susceptible to misleading suggestions than older children (Ceci et al., 2000; Templeton, & Wicox, 2000).

In one experiment by Michelle Leichtman and Stephen Ceci (1995), three- to six-year-old children were told about a man named Sam Stone. During interviews over several weeks, some children were repeatedly told stories that portrayed Sam as clumsy. Later, "Sam" visited the children's classroom, was introduced to them, and behaved innocuously. In class the next day, the children were shown a ripped book and soiled teddy bear, things that Sam clearly had not done. Over the next 10 weeks children were interviewed several times and some were asked suggestive questions about Sam (e.g., "When Sam Stone tore the book, did he do it on purpose or was he being silly?"). Two weeks later a new interviewer asked all the children to describe Sam's visit to the classroom.

Children who only heard suggestive stories about Sam *before* his classroom appearance, and those who only were asked suggestive questions *after* his appearance, made more false reports about Sam's behaviour than a control group receiving neither type of suggestive treatment. Moreover, children who received both types of misinformation made the highest number of false reports, and younger children were much more likely to do so. One child stated that after soaking the teddy bear in the bath, Sam smeared it with a crayon.

Many researchers believe that these findings have troubling implications. In many cases in which abuse allegations are investigated, the child initially offers no statements about being abused, or denies it if questioned. Over time and with repeated suggestive questioning during therapy or police investigation, the child may acknowledge having been abused, may later deny it again, and then admit it once more (Olafson & Lederman, 2006).

Accurate versus False Reports: Can We Tell Them Apart?

Can adults, even trained professionals, distinguish between children's accurate and false reports of personal events? The answer appears to be "no," at least when false reports arise after repeated, suggestive questioning. When judges, mental-health professionals, social workers, and prosecutors were shown videotapes of the children's reports in the Leichtman and Ceci (1995) experiment, they could not reliably tell which were true and which were false. The false reports were often judged as highly credible, perhaps because many children who make such false reports are not intentionally lying. Rather, like adults in misinformation experiments, they believe that what they are remembering is accurate (Bruck et al., 1998).

–*Continued*

Children's Memory for Traumatic Events

Some researchers have moved outside the laboratory to study children's memory for naturally occurring events that involve traumatic physical touch, such as medical examinations. Gail Goodman and her colleagues (1994) obtained permission to study 46 children who, because of health problems, underwent a painful medical procedure involving forced genital contact (a catheter had to be inserted through the urethra, and liquid was infused into each child's bladder). About two weeks later, the children's memory of the procedure was tested.

The children's free recall was assessed first using general questions (e.g., "Tell me everything you can remember about what happened."). Then they were asked non-leading questions that did not present any inaccurate information (e.g., "Was the doctor a man or a woman?"), and misleading questions that contained false information (e.g., "Didn't the doctor look in your ears when he gave you that test?"). The results showed that misleading questions did not influence children's memories for this particular traumatic event. However, although the oldest children correctly answered 82 percent of both non-leading and misleading questions, the youngest children answered only 48 percent accurately. Overall, children who underwent multiple operations did not have more accurate memories than did children who had only one operation. Still, although the youngest children misremembered many details of the situation, all of them remembered something. There was no evidence of memory repression, at least of this experience.

Conclusions

From the standpoint of basic science, it appears that young children remember a great deal, but like adults, they also misremember, and seem more susceptible to misinformation effects. On the applied side, mental-health and legal professionals are now paying greater attention to how children's admissions of abuse are elicited, and training programs are helping practitioners minimize suggestive inter-viewing techniques (Ceci et al., 2000; Sternberg et al., 2002). For researchers, the applied goal is not to discredit children's allegations of abuse. On the contrary, the hope is that by minimizing the risk of false allegations, non-suggestive interviewing will elicit allegations judged as even more compelling, thereby helping to ensure that justice is done.

Other Factors in Eyewitness Testimony

Misinformation effects are one source of inaccuracy in eyewitness testimony, but there are other factors that may come into play as well. Imagine that a fight breaks out in a bar. An eyewitness insists that it was George who started the fight, not Paul. What are some possible sources of inaccuracy in this situation?

We might expect alcohol to be a factor. After people have been drinking, their memory for events may be less than accurate. Compared to people who have not consumed alcohol, a blood-alcohol level of 0.10 resulted in less information being recalled from a staged theft, and more inaccurate identifications one week later (Yuille & Tollestrup, 1990). The effects of marijuana are much less pronounced (Yuille et al., 1998), and seem limited to a slight decrease in information recalled directly after an incident. One's ability to identify a possible perpetrator depends as well on the kind of information we have available. Identifications based on voice alone ("earwitness" identification) tend to be less accurate than those based on both visual and auditory cues, or on visual cues alone (Yarmey, 1993). Finally, we should note that, while men and women are equally inaccurate in their identifications, men tend to be more confident in their decisions (Yarmey & Yarmey, 1997).

28. Do people ever forget traumatic personal events? Why are recovered memories and repression controversial topics?

The "Recovered Memory" Controversy: Repression or Reconstruction?

In 1997 a woman from Illinois settled a lawsuit against two psychiatrists and their hospital for $10.6 million. She alleged that her psychiatrists used hypnosis, drugs, and other treatments that led her to develop false memories of having been a high priestess in an abusive satanic cult. That same year, criminal charges were brought against a group of Houston mental-health professionals, alleging that they "used techniques commonly associated with mind control and brainwashing" with seven patients, creating false memories of having been abused in a satanic cult (*APA Monitor*, December 1997, p. 9). Yet, only years earlier, there had been a wave of cases in which adults—usually in the course of psychotherapy—began to remember long-forgotten childhood abuse and sued their parents, other family members, and former teachers for the alleged trauma (Figure 8.21).

The debate over the validity of "recovered memories" of childhood trauma has escalated the long-running scientific controversy over Freud's concept of repression (Brown, 2000; Loftus et al., 2000). This controversy can be broken down into two issues, though, unfortunately, they are often intertwined. First, when a recovered memory of sexual abuse occurs, is it accurate? Second, if the abuse really happened, what caused the memory to be forgotten for so long—repression, or some other psychological process? For the person having the memory, the alleged abuser, and the legal system, accuracy is what matters most. For researchers and therapists, both issues are important.

Let's briefly examine the second issue. Many scientists and therapists question Freud's concept of repression. Repression implies a special psychological mechanism that actively pushes traumatic memories into the unconscious mind, and we have already noted that researchers have had difficulty demonstrating it experimentally. Elizabeth Loftus (1998) and other researchers propose that recovered memories of childhood abuse should not be taken as automatic evidence of repression. Alternative explanations include the possibility that the memory loss occurred because of ordinary (non-motivated) sources of forgetting, or because the victim intentionally avoided thinking about the abuse or reinterpreted the trauma to make it less upsetting (Epstein & Bottoms, 2002). In contrast, other researchers and many therapists believe, based primarily on numerous case studies, that repression is a valid concept (Karon, 2002). This controversy will not be resolved soon.

What about the more basic question? Is it possible that someone could forget their childhood sexual abuse, by whatever psychological mechanism, and then recover that memory as an adult? We know that memory loss can occur following a psychological trauma. Trauma victims may report not remembering the event at all or may report partial memory loss and confusion. Amnesia without obvious signs of brain damage has been reported among survivors of natural disasters, children who witnessed the violent death of a parent, victims of rape, and combat veterans (Arrigo & Pezdek, 1997; Epstein & Bottoms, 2002). In cases of child sexual abuse, some victims do not recall their trauma when they are adults (Williams, 1994; Kluft, 1999). Moreover, laboratory experiments indicate that a mentally shocking event (e.g., viewing a sudden, violent film scene) can produce retrograde amnesia for information presented just before the shocking event occurred (Loftus & Burns, 1982).

In some cases it appears that accurate memories can indeed return after decades of post-trauma forgetting (Arrigo & Pezdek, 1997; Kluft, 1999). Yet memory loss after psychological trauma usually is far shorter, with memory returning over weeks, months, or perhaps a few years. In many cases of trauma the victim's primary problem is not memory loss, but rather an *inability* to forget, which may involve recurrent nightmares and flashbacks (Ross et al., 1989). Experiments with adults and children also indicate that false memories of personal events can be created ("implanted") by suggestive questioning or comments, or merely by having someone imagine that the event took place (Laney & Loftus, 2005; Bruck et al., 1998; Loftus & Pickrell, 1995). Many memory researchers are concerned that in "recovered memory therapy," therapists repeatedly suggest the possibility of abuse to people who already are emotionally vulnerable. Given everything psychology has taught us about forgetting, constructive memory, and the "fogging up" of even flashbulb memories, they argue that it is naive to take the accuracy of recovered memories of long-past events at face value.

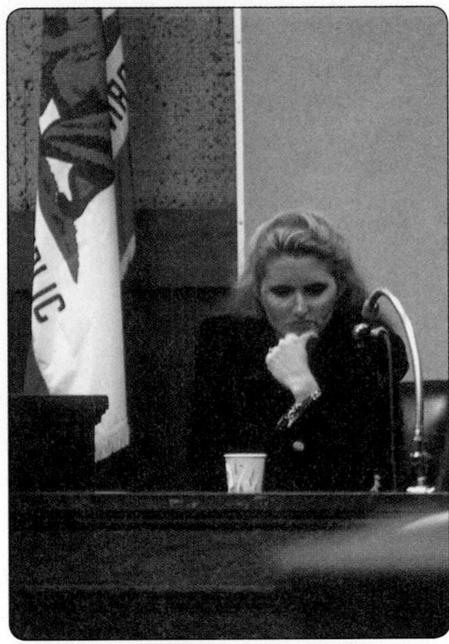

FIGURE 8.21

In a famous 1990 repressed memory case, George Franklin was convicted of murdering Susan Nason, an eight-year-old girl killed in 1969. Franklin's 28-year-old daughter Eileen (shown above), who had been Susan's childhood friend, provided the key evidence. During therapy, Eileen recovered memories of her father sexually assaulting and killing Susan. A judge overturned the conviction after learning that Eileen's memories had been recovered under hypnosis. All of the details about the case that Eileen recalled had been published in the newspapers, creating the possibility of source confusion in her memory. Eileen also had other recovered memories that were proven to be untrue, such as those of her father killing two other girls.

The message from science is not that all claims of recovered traumatic memories should be dismissed. Rather, it is to urge caution in unconditionally accepting those memories, particularly in cases where suggestive techniques are used to recover the memories (Brandon et al., 1998; Gothard & Ivker, 2000; Prout & Dobson, 1998). Some day it may be possible scientifically to separate true memories from false ones. Researchers have begun to examine whether some types of true versus false memories are associated with different patterns of brain activity, and true memories often are described in greater detail than false ones. But at present, these findings cannot be used to determine reliably whether any individual memory is true or false (Pickrell et al., 2003).

In Review

- *Our schemas may cause us to remember events not as they actually occurred but in ways that fit with our pre-existing concepts about the world.*
- *At times we may recall information that never occurred. Schemas, spreading activation, and priming are some of the reasons why this occurs.*
- *Misinformation effects occur when our memory is distorted by misleading postevent information, and they often occur because of source confusion—our tendency to recall something or recognize it as familiar but to forget where we encountered it.*
- *Like adults, children experience misinformation effects. Vulnerability is greatest among younger children and when suggestive questions are asked repeatedly. Experts cannot reliably tell when children are reporting accurate versus sincerely believed false memories.*
- *Psychologists debate whether recovered memories of child abuse are accurate and whether they are forgotten through repression or other psychological processes. Concern about the possibility of false memory has led many experts to urge caution in unconditionally accepting the validity of recovered memories.*

THE BIOLOGY OF MEMORY

Since the early 1900s, the scientific quest to determine the biological basis of memory has taken some remarkable twists and turns. Karl Lashley, a pioneering physiological psychologist, spent decades searching for the *engram*—the physical "memory trace" that presumably was stored somewhere in the brain when a memory was formed. Lashley (1950) trained animals to perform various tasks, such as running mazes, and later removed or damaged (lesioned) specific regions of their cortex to see if they would forget how to perform the task. No matter what small area was lesioned, the animals' memory remained intact. Large lesions affected memory, but even then, it didn't seem to matter where the lesion was made. Lashley never found the engram, and concluded that a memory is stored throughout the brain.

Other research initially suggested that, indeed, engrams exist. While performing neurosurgery, Wilder Penfield and his colleagues (1963) at the Montreal Neurological Institute electrically stimulated specific sites on the cerebral cortex of patients who were under local anaesthesia and fully conscious. Penfield reported that the stimulation sometimes triggered patients' memories. One patient reported seeing the office in which she had worked a long time ago, with a man leaning on her desk, pencil in hand. Unfortunately, when other researchers reviewed Penfield's data, they concluded that such instances were rare and probably involved inaccurate, "reconstructed" images (Loftus & Loftus, 1980). For example, people sometimes reported memories of being in places where, in fact, they had never been.

Perhaps most striking was James McConnell's (1962) discovery of "memory transfer." He classically conditioned flatworms to a light that was paired with an electric shock, eventually causing the worms to contract to the light alone. Next he chopped them up and fed a chemical from their cells, RNA (ribonucleic acid), to a sample of untrained worms. Amazingly, the new worms showed some conditioning to the light. This suggested that RNA might be a chemical engram, a "memory molecule" that stored experiences. Some scientists found memory transfer effects with rats, mice, and goldfish, but others were unable to replicate these findings. Controversy ensued, and McConnell gave up on the idea (Rilling, 1996). Yet, despite the inevitable "dead ends," neuroscientists have made considerable progress in understanding the biological bases of memory.

Where in the Brain Are Memories Formed?

Scientists rely on three approaches to map the "geography" of memory (Gabrieli, 1998). In *human lesion studies,* they examine memory loss following naturally occurring damage (e.g., from disease or accidents) to different parts of the brain. In *non-human animal lesion experiments,* researchers damage a specific part of the brain and observe how memory is affected. Finally, *brain-imaging studies* examine the healthy brain as participants perform various memory tasks. Together, these lines of research reveal that memory involves many interacting brain regions, several of which are shown in Figure 8.22.

29. What three approaches do scientists use to study the brain regions involved in memory?

The Hippocampus and Cerebral Cortex

30. What major roles do the hippocampus, cerebral cortex, thalamus, amygdala, and cerebellum play in memory?

The pioneering work of Brenda Milner at McGill University led to the conclusion that the hippocampus and its adjacent tissue help to encode and retrieve long-term declarative memories (Milner, 1965; Rolls, 2000; Scoville & Milner, 1957). Like H.M., most patients with hippocampal damage retain short-term memory, but cannot form new, explicit long-term memories of personal experiences and facts (Milner, 1965; Squire & Zola-Morgan, 1991). For example, one patient could recall the names of U.S. presidents elected before his brain injury occurred, but not the names of presidents elected after his injury (Squire, 1987).

The hippocampus does not seem to be the site where long-term memories are permanently stored, which is why H.M. retained his long-term memories acquired

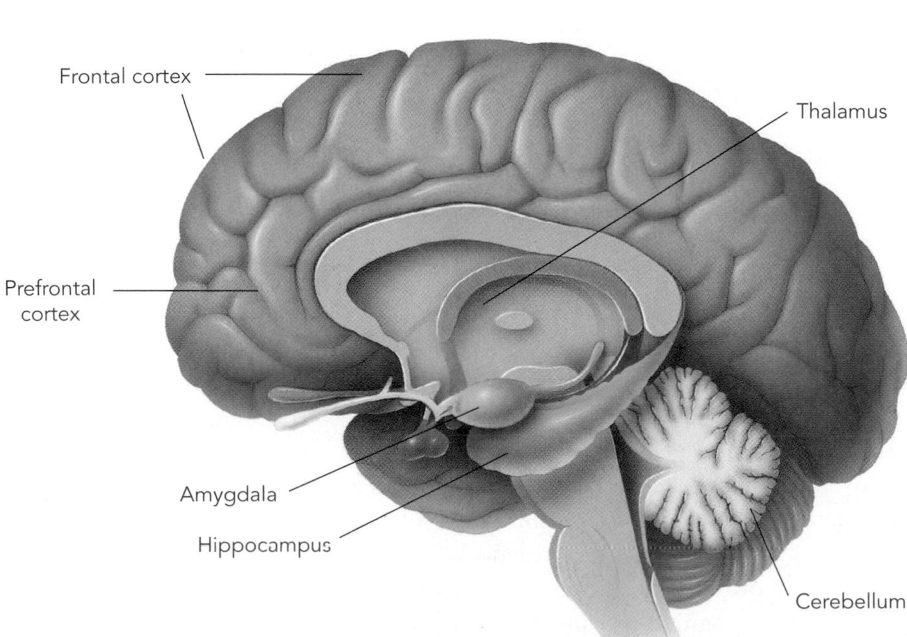

FIGURE 8.22
Many areas of the brain, such as the regions shown here, play key roles in memory.

earlier in life. Rather, it seems to be an "encoding station" that helps to convert short-term memories into more permanent ones. Brain-imaging studies show that specific hippocampal regions become highly active during encoding and retrieval (Lepage et al., 1998; Tulving et al., 1994).

The cerebral cortex plays a vital role in encoding by processing information from the sensory registers. The diverse components of an experience—where something happened, what the scene or people looked like, sounds we heard, the meaning of events or information, and so on—may be processed in different regions of the cortex and then gradually "bound" together in the hippocampus (Squire & Zola-Morgan 1991). This hypothetical and gradual "binding" process is called **memory consolidation**, and it may involve the creation of codes that allow information to be transferred from short-term memory into long-term memory. Neuroscience researchers have reported some fascinating results concerning the way consolidation might occur at the level of the synapse (see Figure 8.23).

The cerebral cortex also appears to store semantic memories across wide-ranging sites. As John Gabrieli (1998, p. 94) notes, "knowledge in any domain [e.g., for pictures or words] . . . is distributed over a specific, but extensive, neural network that often extends over several lobes." Similarly, the various components of an episodic memory are stored across wide areas of the cortex (Greenberg et al., 2005; Schacter et al., 1998; Squire, 1992). Yet we retrieve and reintegrate these components as a "unified memory," thanks to their previous consolidation in the hippocampus.

Finally, brain-imaging studies suggest that the frontal lobes—especially the prefrontal cortex—play a central role in carrying out the functions of working memory (van Asselen, et al., 2006; Nelson et al., 2000; Cabeza & Nyberg, 2000). In one experiment, John Gabrieli and his colleagues (1996) used functional MRI imaging to study brain activity during shallow and deep processing. In the shallow (structural) processing task, young adults identified whether each word was capitalized or lowercase. The deep (semantic) processing task required them to pay attention to the meaning of the words by identifying whether a word referred to an abstract concept (e.g., trust, love) or a concrete object (e.g., chair, book). As Figure 8.24 shows, the researchers found that deep processing increased brain activation in specific regions of the left prefrontal cortex and, consistent with prior research, led to better recall.

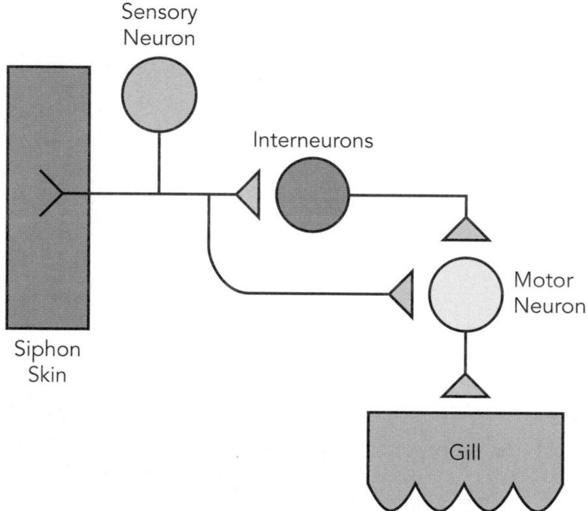

FIGURE 8.23

The 2000 Nobel Prize in physiology or medicine was awarded jointly to Arvid Carlsson, Paul Greengard, and Eric Kandel for their work on signalling within the nervous system. Eric Kandel's Nobel Prize was for his pioneering research on learning-induced changes that occur within and between neurons. For the past 30 years, Eric Kandel has studied learning in the sea slug (aplysia). This animal has a simple nervous system of about 20,000 neurons (compared to our 100 billion), and this allowed Kandel and co-workers to trace which neurons change as a result of learning. Once the critical neurons were identified, it then was possible to study how these neurons changed, and what inter- and intra-cellular messengers triggered learning-induced changes. Many of the same mechanisms studied in marine molluscs such as aplysia, and in insects such as the honeybee and fruit fly, have been found to be important for learning and memory in mammals.

The Thalamus and Amygdala

Damage to the thalamus can produce severe amnesia, although we are not sure why this happens (Gabrieli, 1998). In a famous case, a young U.S. Air Force technician named N.A. was injured in a freak accident (Squire, 1987). While his roommate was practising thrusts with a miniature fencing foil, N.A. suddenly turned around in his seat and was stabbed through the right nostril, piercing his brain and damaging a portion of his thalamus. The damage permanently limited his ability to form new declarative memories (Cohen & Squire, 1981). He also could not recall events from the two-year period prior to the accident, but over time this retrograde amnesia improved. In many cases, however, thalamic damage results in permanent, extensive anterograde and retrograde amnesia. Following a car accident in 1988, Terry Evanshen, former CFL star receiver awoke from a coma to find that his memory of everything prior to the accident had vanished. He could not remember how to speak, did not recognize his wife or daughters, and had no recollection of anything from the past 40 years. Terry had to re-learn everything all over again.

The amygdala seems to encode emotionally arousing and disturbing aspects of events (Gabrieli, 1998; LaBar & Phelps, 1998). In laboratory experiments, most people remember emotionally arousing stimuli (film clips, slides) better than neutral ones. But damage to the amygdala eliminates much of this "memory advantage" from arousing stimuli (LaBar & Phelps, 1998). In addition, for humans and other animals, damage to the amygdala impairs the ability to form conditioned fear responses (Amorapanth et al., 2000; LeDoux, 1992). For example, if a light is paired with electric shock, animals with amygdala damage will not develop a typical fear response to the light alone.

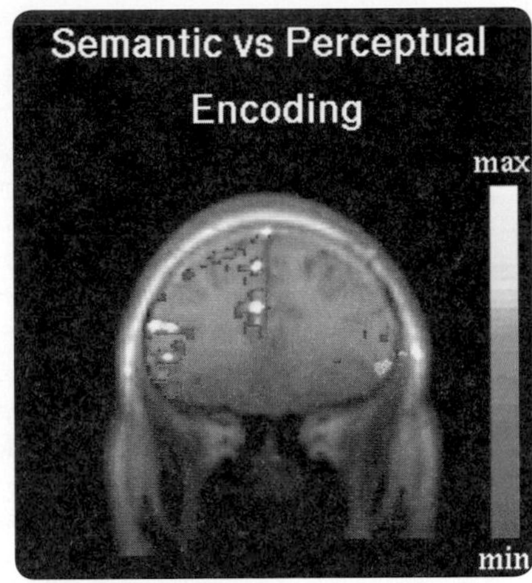

FIGURE 8.24

Four of the participants in this experiment performed shallow (i.e., perceptual/structural) encoding and deep (semantic) encoding tasks while undergoing functional magnetic resonance imaging (fMRI). Activity in a section of their prefrontal cortex was imaged every 1.5 seconds, yielding a total of 224 images per participant. The results, shown here for one participant, revealed that semantic encoding was accompanied by greater neural activity in specific regions of the left prefrontal cortex.

Photo courtesy of John Gabrieli.

The Cerebellum

Along with several other parts of the brain, the cerebellum plays an important role in the formation of procedural memories (Gabrieli, 1998; Sanes et al., 1990). This helps explain why H.M., whose cerebellum was not damaged by the operation, showed improved performance at various hand-eye coordination tasks (such as mirror-tracing) even though he was unable to consciously remember having performed the tasks.

Focusing on another type of procedural memory, Richard Thompson and his co-workers established a classically conditioned eyeblink response in rabbits by pairing a tone (CS) with a puff of air to the eye (UCS). As the rabbits learned the conditioned response, electrical recordings revealed increased electrical activity in the cerebellum (Thompson, 1985; Thompson & Steinmetz, 1992). Later, Thompson found that removing a tiny portion of the cerebellum completely abolished the memory for the *conditioned* eyeblink, but did not affect a general (unconditioned) eyeblink response. Similarly, eyeblink conditioning fails to work with human patients who have damaged cerebellums (Green & Woodruff, 2000).

FOCUS ON NEUROSCIENCE

The Neuroscience of Retrieving Accurate and Fabricated Memories

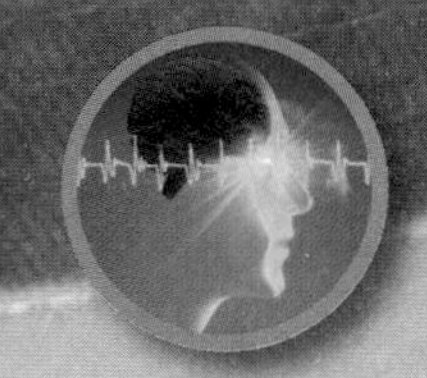

On Sept. 19, 1961, Betty and Barney Hill were driving back to New Hampshire from Montreal. Along the way, they claim that they saw a UFO and were subsequently abducted and physically examined by aliens. This seems a fantastic story, but is there any way to verify the details?

Daniel Schacter and his colleagues have investigated these claims along with more mundane recollections for true and fabricated memories. Slotnick and Schacter (2004) had participants view a series of 144 shapes. Their task was to remember each shape and its location on the screen. Later they examined sets of "old" shapes (those shown earlier), related but not viewed shapes ("lures"), and completely new shapes while undergoing fMRI. A distinct sensory signature was associated with the correct identification of the shapes—activity in the primary visual cortex (areas 17 and 18). Correct responses also produced activity in later visual areas (visual association area and visual-temporal lobe), as did incorrect answers. The authors attribute this differential activity to a type of implicit memory and as such, we may not be consciously aware that we have accurately identified a target.

But what of more emotionally laden information? Kensinger and Schacter (2005a) have argued that the successful retrieval of memories that have an emotional component may be associated with limbic system activity. Participants were shown the names of both neutral (e.g., frog) and emotional (e.g., snake) targets and asked to form an image of each. Half of the words were presented with a photo of the target. During the test phase (fMRI scan), participants were shown the target names and asked if that target had been presented with a photo. Results indicated that activity in the hippocampus was related to accurate recall of both emotional and

—Continued

neutral targets. This should be expected given the role of the hippocampus in memory. However, for the emotional targets, there was also activity in the amygdala and regions of the frontal lobes (e.g., the orbitofrontal cortex). Thus, retrieval of emotional memories seems to be related to activity in brain regions thought to be involved in emotion. The accuracy of these retrieved memories is moderated by activity in other brain areas. For example, increased activity in the anterior cingulate was related to more retrieval errors for emotional items (Kensinger & Schacter, 2005b). Interestingly, arousing items with a negative tone tend to be remembered with a great deal of contextual information and are less prone to retrieval errors than neutral information (Kensinger & Schacter, 2006). Different types of information may involve other brain regions as well. For example, one's ability to retrieve verbal information is related to the amount of activity in the left prefrontal and temporal lobes during encoding (Wagner et al., 1998).

Perhaps we could use scans to determine the veracity of information such as that reported by Betty Hill. We would expect that an accurate recovered memory for a negative, arousing event would be associated with increased activity in the amygdala and oribtofrontal cortex plus decreased activity in the cingulate. While this study remains to be conducted, Schacter and his colleagues (Clancy et al., 2002) have examined retrieval in people who actually do believe that they have been abducted by aliens. Individuals reporting recovered memories of alien abduction exhibited false recall and recognition in a lab situation. Schacter suggests that these false memories are generated by faulty source monitoring—an incorrect attribution as to where and how the memory was acquired. As fragments of real memories (perhaps from movies, media reports, etc.) are pieced together, the actual source of these fragments is forgotten or "overwritten." Thus, the recovered memory seems very real to the individual, but in fact, it never happened.

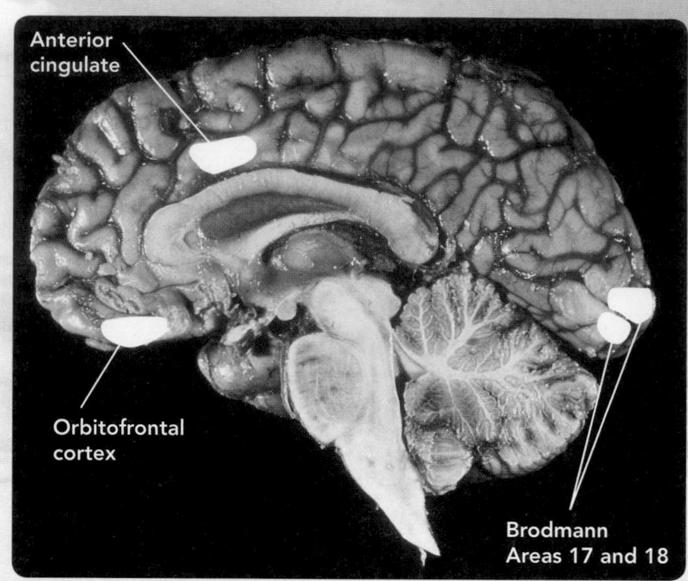

Areas involved in the recall of accurate and fabricated memories.

TABLE 8.2 "S."'s Memory Matrix

"S." memorized this 50-digit matrix in 3 minutes and recalled it in 40 seconds. He recalled it in any pattern that Luria requested, such as the second column from bottom to top (30 seconds) and a zig-zag pattern (35 seconds) shown here by the italicized numbers.

6	6	8	0
5	*4*	3	2
1	6	*8*	4
7	9	3	*5*
4	2	*3*	7
3	*8*	9	1
1	0	0	2
3	*4*	5	1
2	7	*6*	8
1	9	2	*6*
2	9	*6*	7
5	*5*	2	0
	0	1	

Adapted from Ericsson & Chase, 1982.

EXCEPTIONAL MEMORY

H.M. became famous for his extraordinary forgetting. In contrast, some people (called *mnemonists*) display extraordinary remembering. The distinguished Italian conductor Arturo Toscanini reputedly could recall from memory each note for every instrument in 250 symphonies, as well as the music and lyrics for 100 operas (Marek, 1982). Russian newspaper reporter S. V. Shereshevski had a remarkable capacity to remember numbers, mathematical formulas, nonsense syllables, sounds, and poems in foreign languages. At one point, psychologist Aleksandr Luria (1968), who studied "S." for decades, presented him with the 50-digit matrix shown in Table 8.2. "S." took only three minutes to learn it, could rapidly recall the digits in any direction—up, down, left, right, and zigzag—and could recite them years later. In 1981, former psychology major Rajan Mahevedan set a world record by reciting from memory the first 31,811 digits of pi (π).

31. According to some researchers, what basic memory principles account for exceptional memory? Do you agree with this position?

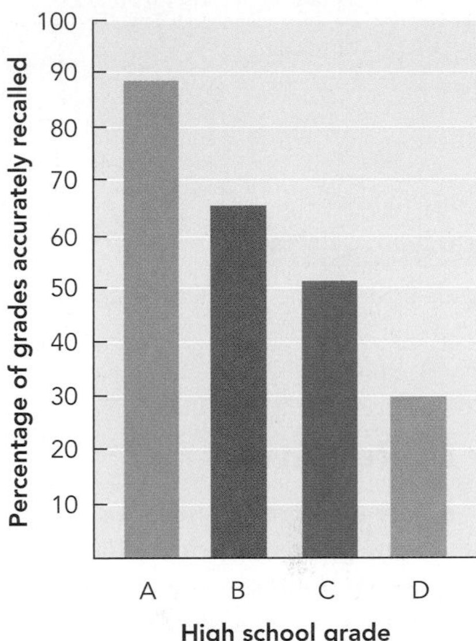

FIGURE 8.25

The lower the grade, the smaller the percentage of students who accurately recalled it. Almost all recall "errors" for grades of B, C, and D overestimated how well the student did.

Bahrick et al., 1996.

A Final Thought: The "Curse" of Exceptional Memory

There is one obvious sense in which normal forgetting is a blessing, for it can dull the unpleasant experiences of the past. All of us forget most of the details of daily life, both positive and negative ones, although the scales are not necessarily balanced. As Figure 8.25 shows, when university students in one study recalled their high school grades, the worse the grade, the less often students remembered it accurately (Bahrick et al., 1996). In addition, errors were positively biased; Bs were misremembered as As, Cs as Bs, and Ds as Cs. That is, students tended to reconstruct their academic past through slightly rosy glasses.

There is another, more important way in which it pays to forget. Most of us would like at times (especially around final exam periods) to have a photographic long-term memory from which we could retrieve everything we ever saw, heard, or learned. We seldom stop to think what a curse this could be. Luria (1968) describes how "S." was tyrannized by his seeming inability to forget meaningless information. Almost any retrieval cue might unleash a flood of trivial memories that dominated "S."'s consciousness and made it difficult for him to concentrate or think abstractly. If you had a photographic memory, you would be paralyzed trying to answer a question as simple as "What does a dog look like." Instead of easily generating a dog's abstract qualities (four legs; wagging tail; tendency to seek out foul, smelly objects), you would be mired in images of every dog your ever saw and of how different they actually looked (Reisberg, 1997). In short, we should appreciate just how wonderfully our memory system is balanced between the adaptiveness of remembering and the benefits of forgetting. Figure 8.26 highlights some of the biological, psychological, and environmental factors that cause us to forget.

32. In what ways is "forgetting" adaptive? How might perfect memory be a burden?

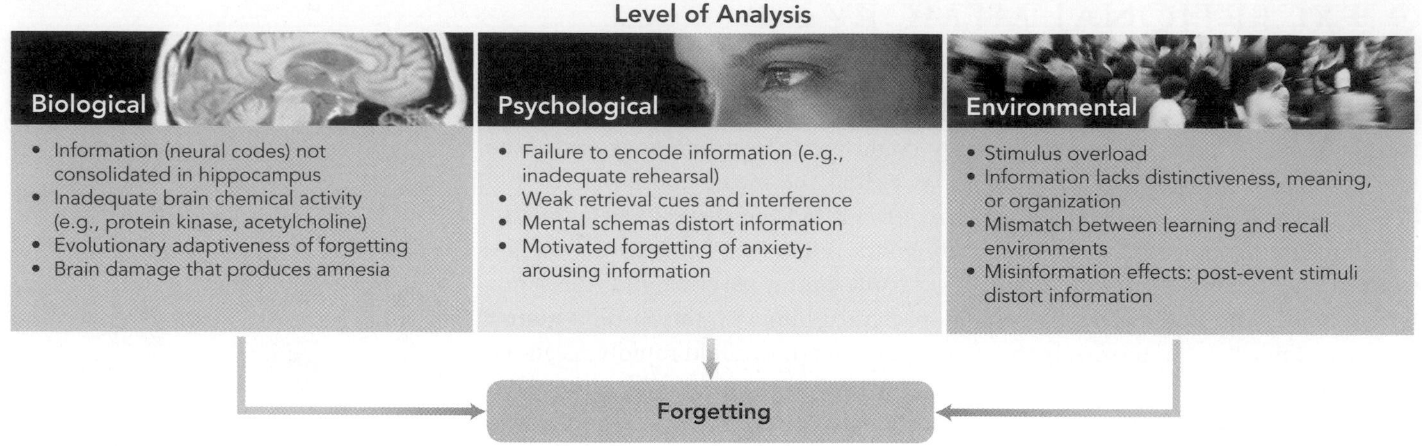

Level of Analysis
Biological
• Information (neural codes) not consolidated in hippocampus
• Inadequate brain chemical activity (e.g., protein kinase, acetylcholine)
• Evolutionary adaptiveness of forgetting
• Brain damage that produces amnesia
Psychological
• Failure to encode information (e.g., inadequate rehearsal)
• Weak retrieval cues and interference
• Mental schemas distort information
• Motivated forgetting of anxiety-arousing information
Environmental
• Stimulus overload
• Information lacks distinctiveness, meaning, or organization
• Mismatch between learning and recall environments
• Misinformation effects: post-event stimuli distort information
Forgetting

FIGURE 8.26

Understanding the causes of behaviour: factors that cause forgetting.

In Review

- *Memory involves numerous interacting brain regions. Sensory memory depends on input from our sensory systems and sensory areas of the cortex that initially process this information.*
- *Working memory involves a network of brain regions. The frontal lobes play a key role in performing the executive functions of working memory.*
- *The hippocampus helps consolidate long-term declarative memories. The cerebral cortex stores declarative memories across distributed sites.*
- *The amygdala encodes emotionally arousing aspects of events, and the cerebellum helps form procedural memories. Damage to the thalamus can produce severe amnesia.*
- *Research with sea snails and studies of long-term potentiation in other species indicate that as memories form, complex chemical and structural changes occur in neurons that enhance synaptic efficiency.*
- *People who display exceptional memory are called mnemonists. Researchers debate whether mnemonists have unique memory abilities, or instead employ basic memory skills to an extraordinary degree.*
- *Although people sometimes wish for a perfect memory, our memory system strikes a highly adaptive balance between the benefits of remembering and benefits of forgetting.*

GAINING DIRECTION

What are the issues?

The story of Michael Kliman highlights the challenges of recovered memory. Kliman was originally convicted of sexual abuse on the basis of recovered memories—events that the victim recalled years later when she was in therapy. How can we be sure that these memories were accurate? Might they have been influenced by the therapy sessions? A Freudian interpretation would suggest that the memories had been repressed by the trauma and could only be visited later with the help of therapy. Is this a valid interpretation? Do we, in fact, encode everything that happens to us, but stumble when we try to recall? As with the scenario in Chapter 6, legal implications of psychological phenomena play a role in this story.

What do we need to know?

How does memory work?
What is the effect of stress on memory?
Can memories be repressed?
Can repressed or forgotten memories be recalled?
What is the "normal" route to forgetting?
Is recall perfectly accurate, or do we embellish incomplete memories?
How might a therapist influence a victim's memory?
What do experts suggest about the accuracy of recovered memories?

Where can you find the information necessary to answer these questions?

Look back at the compass icons in this chapter. You will find reference to the three-component model of memory, factors that result in maintaining memory (encoding), the influence of schemas, processes involved in retrieval and forgetting, and the construction of memory. Pay careful attention to the section on recovered memory and repression. The issue of recovered memory is very controversial, and we need to be aware of the processes that might be involved.

KEY TERMS AND CONCEPTS*

anterograde amnesia (336)
associative network (324)
chunking (315)
context-dependent memory (330)
decay theory (334)
declarative memory (326)
dual coding theory (322)
elaborative rehearsal (316)
encoding (312)
encoding specificity principle (330)
episodic memory (326)
explicit memory (326)
flashbulb memories (329)
icon (315)
implicit memory (327)
infantile amnesia (336)
levels of processing (319)
long-term memory (317)
maintenance rehearsal (316)
memory (312)
memory consolidation (346)
misinformation effect (339)
mood-congruent recall (331)
neural network (325)
overlearning (332)
partial report (315)
priming (325)
proactive interference (335)
procedural memory (326)
prospective memory (337)
repression (336)
retrieval (312)
retrieval cue (328)
retroactive interference (335)
retrograde amnesia (336)
schema (323)
semantic memory (326)
sensory memory (314)
serial position effect (317)
short-term memory (314)
source confusion (339)
state-dependent memory (331)
storage (312)
working memory (314)

*Each term has been boldfaced in the text on the page indicated in parentheses.

DO YOU WANT TO ELEVATE YOUR GRADES?

For additional resources and interactive quizzing, visit the book's Online Learning Centre at **www.mcgrawhill.ca/olc/passer**.

CHAPTER 9

Thought, Language, and Intelligence

"A moment's insight is sometimes worth a life's experience."
—Oliver Wendell Holmes

CHAPTER OUTLINE

In the 1988 Oscar-winning movie Rain Man, the inspiration for Dustin Hoffman's character was Kim Peek. When Kim came into this world on November 11, 1951, he was born without a corpus callosum, and a damaged cerebellum. Although he did not walk until the age of four, he began to demonstrate some special abilities early in his life. By 20 months of age, he was able to memorize every book read to him—in a single reading. By the time he was three years old, he could use the dictionary, look up words alphabetically, pronounce them correctly, and remember the definition. Today, Kim can tell you practically anything about world history, geography, sports, movies, and literature. In all, his expertise spans 14 different content areas. He has read and memorized over 7,600 books and, knowing your birthday, can tell you without hesitation on what day of the week you will turn 65 years old.

Kim has autism and his tested IQ is over two standard deviations below normal.

- **What are the issues here?**
- **What do we need to know?**
- **Where can we find the information necessary to answer the questions?**

For the crew and passengers of United Airlines Flight 118, the skies over Hawaii were about to become the scene of a terrifying test of human resourcefulness, with survival at stake. On a routine flight 20,000 feet above the Pacific Ocean, with an explosive popping of rivets and a shriek of tearing metal, part of the surface of the plane suddenly ripped away from the rest of the aircraft, leaving the flight deck and forward passenger compartments exposed to the air. Inside, terrified passengers and flight attendants hung on for dear life as gale-force winds swirled through the cabin and the plane threatened to spin out of control.

The sudden change in the aerodynamics of the plane meant that it could not be flown normally. The captain, an experienced pilot, needed to develop a mental model of the plane in its altered form to keep it from plunging into the ocean. Thanks to his experience and knowledge of the principles by which the aircraft normally responded to its controls, the captain quickly recognized what needed to be done, formulated a plan for doing it, and then executed the appropriate actions. Unable to communicate with one another verbally because of the noise from the engines and the wind, the captain and the first officer used hand signals to coordinate their activities. Through perfect teamwork, they landed the aircraft safely at an airfield, a feat labelled by one aeronautical engineer as "astonishing."

1. What are mental representations? How are they involved in thinking and communicating?

Though human beings are physically puny and defenceless in comparison to some other species, we dominate the world because we think better and communicate more effectively than other animals do. Humans have remarkable abilities to create "mental representations" of the world and to manipulate them through language, thinking, reasoning, and problem solving (Simon, 1990). **Mental representations** take a variety of forms, including images, ideas, concepts, and principles. You are engaged in some of these mental activities at this very moment. To the extent that we are communicating effectively via the written word, mental representations are being transferred from our minds to yours through the medium of language. The process of education is all about transferring ideas and skills from mind to mind.

LANGUAGE

According to anthropologists who have studied the skulls of prehistoric humans, the brain probably achieved its present form some 50,000 years ago (Pearson, 1998; Pilbeam, 1984). Why then did it take another 35,000 years before lifelike paintings began to appear on cave walls, and another 12,000 years for humans to develop a way to store knowledge outside the brain in the form of writing (Kottak, 2000; Rose, 1973)? These time lags tell us that human thought and behaviour depend on more than the physical structure of the brain. Although the structure of the brain may not have changed much in the last 50,000 years, human cognitive skills clearly have.

Language, which various scientists have labelled "the jewel in the crown of cognition" (Pinker, 2000) and "the human essence" (Chomsky, 1972), may well be the most important of these cognitive skills. Evolutionary theorists believe that language evolved as humans gathered to form larger social units. The ability to form cooperative social systems, develop social customs, communicate thoughts to others, create divisions of labour, and pass on knowledge and wisdom were made easier by the development of language (Bjorklund & Pelligrini, 2002; Kottak, 2000). Given the enormous adaptive value of language for the emerging human way of life, it is not surprising that there developed in the human brain an inborn capacity to acquire any of the thousands of languages that are spoken in the world (Figure 9.1).

S. Harris
"GOT IDEA. TALK BETTER. COMBINE WORDS. MAKE SENTENCES."

FIGURE 9.1

According to many theorists, including Noam Chomsky and B. F. Skinner, the development of language was a major milestone in human evolution.

The Nature and Structure of Language

Language consists of a system of symbols and rules for combining these symbols in ways that can produce an almost infinite number of possible messages or meanings. This definition implies three critical properties that are essential to any language.

2. Define three properties common to any human language.

First, language is *symbolic.* It uses sounds, written signs, or gestures to refer to objects, events, ideas, and feelings. Language allows communicators to form and then transfer mental representations to the mind of another person. Thus you can tell another person about your house, what you did last week, your plans after graduation, how you feel about your current life situation, and the meaning of the word *cognition.* The linguistic feature of **displacement** refers to the fact that past, future, and imaginary events and objects that are not physically present can be symbolically represented and communicated through the medium of language. Language thus helps free us from being restricted to the present.

Second, language has a *structure,* with rules that govern how symbols can be combined to create meaningful communication units. Thus, if I ask you if *zpflrovc* is an English word, you will almost certainly say that it is not. Why? Because it violates rules of the English language that *z* is not to be followed by *pf* and that five consonants are not to be combined. Likewise, you would not consider the string of words "Bananas have sale for I no" an appropriate English sentence. You may not be able to verbalize the formal rules of English that are violated in these examples, but you know them implicitly because they are part of the language you speak.

Third, language is *generative.* This means that its symbols can be combined to generate an almost infinite number of messages that can have novel meaning. Thus you can create and understand a sentence such as "Who put the nightingale under my strudel?" even though you are unlikely to have heard anything like it before. Indeed, in reading that sentence, you may already have formed a mental representation (most likely, an image) of that unlikely scene, illustrating the concept of displacement.

Surface and Deep Structure

Psycholinguists, who study the psychological properties of language and the underlying mechanisms that produce it, describe language as having both a surface structure and a deep structure. The **surface structure** consists of the way symbols are combined within a given language. The rules for such combination are called the **syntax** (rules of grammar) of a language. Thus the word *zpflrovc* and the "banana" sentence described above violate English syntax.

3. Differentiate between surface structure and deep structure.

Deep structure refers to the underlying meaning of the combined symbols. The rules for connecting the symbols to what they represent are known as **semantics**. To distinguish surface structure from deep structure, consider the following sentences:

1. Eloise ran over the attacking pit bull with her Big Wheel.
2. The Big Wheel driven by Eloise ran over the attacking pit bull.
3. The police must stop drinking after midnight.

The first two sentences have different surface structures, but share the same deep structure. In other words, they have different syntax but similar semantic meaning. Either way, the pit bull got it. The third sentence is ambiguous and can have two different deep structures, one relating to police duties, the other to their personal conduct. The rules for surface structure and deep structure are both stored in long-term memory. However, when we recall something, we are likely to retrieve deep structure (meaning) rather than the specific words. That's why, as you may have experienced to your sorrow on essay examinations, you can sometimes "under-

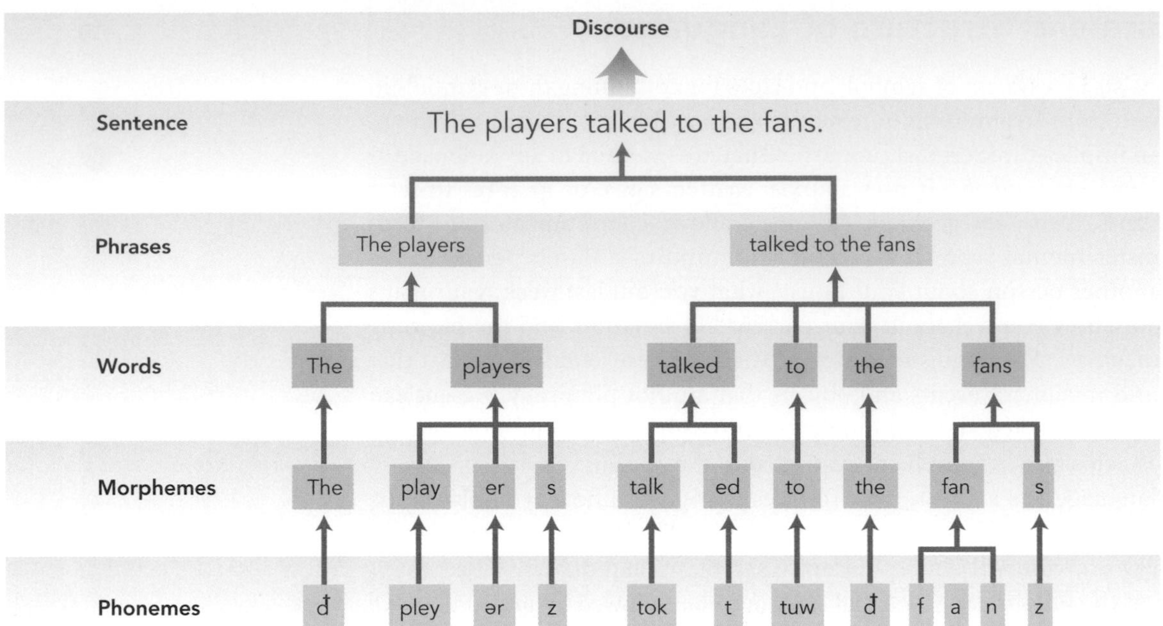

FIGURE 9.2

Human language is structured hierarchically, with phonemes being the most basic unit. The line of phonemes contains symbols used by linguists to denote particular sounds.

stand" a concept without being able to reproduce the precise definition. Or you can recall what someone said without being able to reconstruct the exact sentences.

In considering the formal structure of language, we can retreat to an even more elemental level and consider the basic building blocks that are combined into the symbols that convey meaning.

Language from the Bottom Up

4. What are phonemes and morphemes? Where do they fit in the hierarchy of language?

Human languages have a hierarchical structure. The lowest rung on the ladder is the phoneme. **Phonemes** are the smallest units of sound that are recognized as separate in a given language. English uses about 46 phonemes, consisting of the various vowel and consonant sounds, as well as certain letter combinations such as *th* and *sh*. Thus the sounds *h, a,* and *t* can be combined to form the three-phoneme word *hat.*

Humans are capable of producing several hundred phonemes, including clicking sounds used in some African languages, but no language uses all of these sounds. The world's languages vary considerably in phonemes, some employing as few as 15 and others more than 80, although most use 40 to 50.

At the next level of the hierarchy, phonemes are combined into **morphemes**, the smallest units of meaning in a language. Thus *hat, sick,* and *tel* are all morphemes, as are prefixes and suffixes such as *-ed, un-, -ous,* and *pre-*. The suffix *-ous* is formed from two phonemes, *uh* and *s*. In every language, syntax rules determine how phonemes can be combined into morphemes. English's 46 phonemes can be combined into more than 100,000 morphemes.

Morphemes, in turn, are the stuff of which words are formed. English morphemes can be combined into nearly half a million words, words into countless phrases, and phrases into an almost infinite number of sentences. Thus, from the humble phoneme to the elegant sentence, we have a five-step language hierarchy (Figure 9.2).

Acquiring a Language

Language acquisition is one of the most striking events in human cognitive development. Many language experts believe that humans are born linguists, inheriting a biological readiness to recognize and eventually produce the sounds and structure of whatever language they are exposed to (Chomsky, 1965; Lieberman, 1984).

Biological Foundations

5. What scientific evidence supports the notion that human language has a biological basis?

Several facts suggest a biological basis for language acquisition. First, human children, despite their limited thinking skills, begin to master language early in life without any formal instruction. Moreover, despite their differences at the phoneme level, all adult languages throughout the world—including sign languages for the deaf that have developed independently in different parts of the world—seem to have a common underlying deep structure (Anderson & Lightfoot, 1999). Language acquisition (see Table 9.1) thus represents the unfolding of a biologically primed process within a learning environment as part of the more general growth of cognitive capacities in the developing human (Aitchison, 1996; Chomsky, 1987).

6. What findings indicate that learning interacts with biology to affect language development? What evidence exists for a sensitive period?

Whether born in Toronto, Taiwan, or Tanzania, between one and about three months of age, infants vocalize the entire range of phonemes found in the world's languages. This stage of language acquisition is called cooing because of the coo-like sounds infants make when they are happy. At about six months of age, however, they begin to make the sounds of their native tongue and to discard those of other languages. At this age, children also begin to lose the ability to perceive differences in the sounds of other languages (Werker & Tees, 1984; 2002). For example, Japanese children lose the ability to distinguish between the *r* and *l* sounds because their language does not make this distinction, but children exposed to English can discriminate these sounds at an early age. During this stage of language development, called babbling, a young child's vocalizations gradually become more and more similar to the language to which they are exposed. Interestingly, Laura Pettito, at McGill University, found that deaf children exposed to a sign language begin to babble with their hands just as hearing children begin to babble vocally (Pettito & Marentette, 1991). With exposure to language, children also extract the complex rules of syntax, not just the sounds of the language. For example, as Japanese-speaking children learn to put the object before the verb ("Sadahara the ball threw"), English-speaking children are learning that the verb comes before the object ("John threw the ball"). The striking similarities in language acquisition across language groups led the noted linguist Noam Chomsky (1987) to liken our language acquisition capacity to a huge electrical panel with banks of linguistic switches that are thrown as children hear the words and syntax of their native language.

Some linguists are convinced that there is a *sensitive period* during which language is most easily learned. This period typically extends from infancy to puberty (Lenneberg, 1967). Support for a sensitive period comes from studies of children who lived by themselves in the wild or were isolated from human contact by disturbed parents. One such child was found when she was six years old. She immediately received language training and seemed to develop normal language abilities (Brown, 1958). In contrast, language-deprived children who were found when they were past puberty seemed unable to acquire normal language skills, despite extensive training (Clarke & Clarke, 2000; Curtiss, 1977). Support for a sensitive period also comes from cases of brain damage. Recovery of language is rare if the damage occurs after puberty, but if the damage occurs at an earlier age, there is a good chance that language will recover (Lenneberg, 1967).

The importance of early language exposure applies to any language, not just spoken language. Because sign languages share the deep structure characteristics of spoken languages, deaf children who learn sign language before puberty develop normal linguistic and cognitive abilities even though they never hear a spoken word (Marschark & Mayer, 1998). In contrast, deaf people who are not exposed to sign language before the age of 12 show a distinct language-learning deficit even at 30 years of age (Meier, 1991).

Sex differences. Language functions are distributed in diverse areas of the brain, but the regions shown in Figure 9.3 are especially significant. As discussed in Chapter

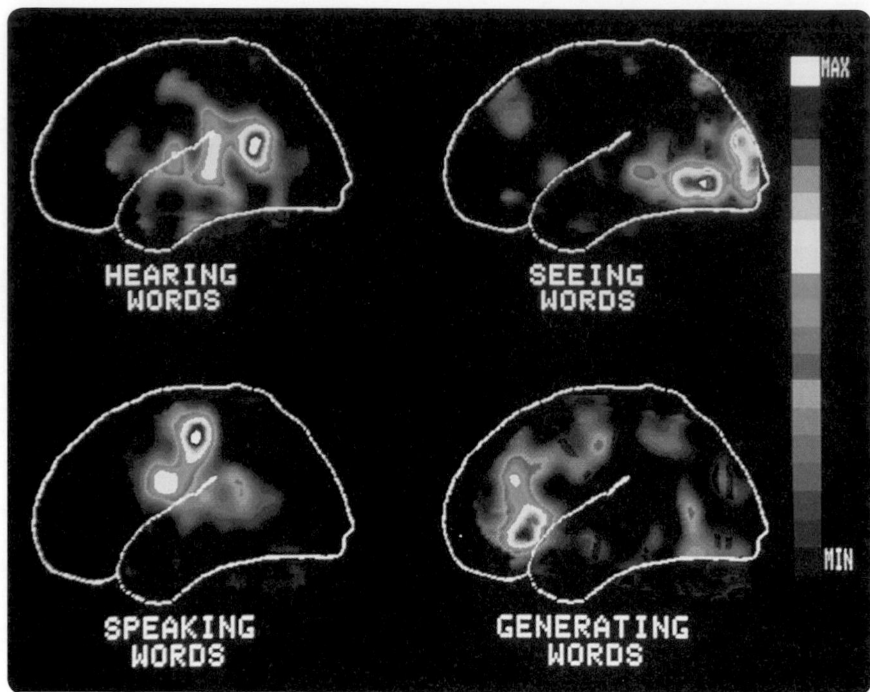

FIGURE 9.3

Different brain areas are involved in various aspects of language. Regions of white, red, and yellow show the greatest activity. Broca's area, located in the frontal lobe below the motor cortex, is important in speech production (generating words). Wernicke's area, in the temporal lobe, is important in speech comprehension (hearing words). Damage to these areas can produce aphasia, a disruption in speech comprehension and/or production.

3, Broca's area, located in the left hemisphere's frontal lobe, is involved in speech production (lower right brain scan). Wernicke's area, in the rear portion of the temporal lobe, is involved in speech comprehension (upper left scan). People with damage in one or both areas suffer from *aphasia*, a disruption in speech comprehension and/or production. The visual area is also involved in recognizing written words.

Years ago, scientists noted that men who suffer left hemisphere strokes are more likely than women to show severe aphasic symptoms. In female stroke victims with left hemisphere damage, language functions are more likely to be spared, suggesting that more of their language function is shared with the right hemisphere.

Recent brain imaging research by Susan Rossell and co-workers (2002) supports this hypothesis. In their study, men and women engaged in a language task in which words and nonwords were presented on each side of a computer screen. Participants had to identify which was the real word as quickly as possible by pressing one of two computer keys. Functional MRIs (fMRIs) were recorded during the task and during a nonlanguage control task. As the reversed image (see caption) in Figure 9.4 shows, men exhibited left-hemisphere activation (red areas) during the language task, whereas women's brain activation occurred in both the left and right hemispheres. Maximum activation occurred in regions corresponding to Broca's and Wernicke's areas. Neural systems involved in at least some aspects of language seem to be organized differently in women than in men, but the reasons for the differences are not yet known (Gleason & Ely, 2002; Sommer et al., 2004).

7. Describe how biological, maturational, and social learning factors are involved in language acquisition. What sex difference exists in language functions within the brain?

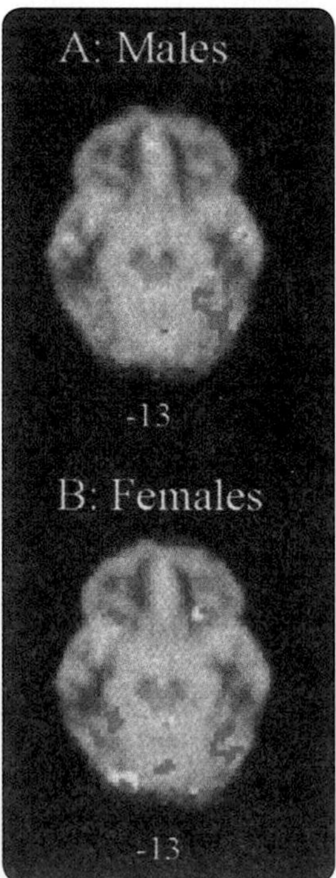

FIGURE 9.4

Sex differences in brain activation during a language task as shown by fMRI. Activation is shown in the red areas. The image is reversed, as if taken from below the brain, so that the activation in males is actually in the left hemisphere. Females' activation patterns are distributed in corresponding areas of both hemispheres, indicating less lateralization of language functions. The yellow activation patterns occurred in response to a nonlanguage control task.

Source: Rossell et al., 2002.

Social Learning Processes

Social learning plays a central role in acquiring a language (Kramsch, 2003). Early on, mothers and fathers maintain their children's interest and attract their attention by conversing with them in what has been termed *motherese,* a high-pitched intonation that seems to be used all over the world (Fernald et al., 1989). Parents also teach their children words by pointing out objects and naming them, by reading aloud to them, and by responding to the never-ending question, "What dat?" (Figure 9.5).

The behaviourist B. F. Skinner (1957, 1985) developed an operant conditioning explanation for language acquisition. His basic premise was that children's language development is strongly governed by adults' reinforcing appropriate language and non-reinforcing of inappropriate verbalization. However, most modern psycholinguists doubt that operant learning principles alone can account for language development. For one thing, children learn too much too fast. By 30 months of age they already have learned several hundred words. By age six, children are learning an average of more than 15 words per day, and their vocabularies have grown to between 8,000 and 14,000 words (Carey, 1977; Smith, 1926). Moreover, observational studies have shown that parents typically do *not* correct their children's grammar as language skills are developing. Rather, parents' corrections focus primarily on the "truth value" (or deep structure) of what the child is trying to communicate. Thus, they are less likely to correct a young child's statement that "I have two foots" than they are to correct one who says, "I have three feet," even though the latter statement is grammatically correct. As this point also shows, much of children's language is very different from that of their parents, and thus can't be explained simply as an imitative process. Certainly, social learning is crucial, but it seems unlikely that it is the sole factor in acquiring a language.

As biological factors (including the maturation of speech-production mechanisms) and experiential factors combine their influences, language acquisition proceeds according to a developmental timetable that is common to all cultures. As shown in Table 9.1, children progress from reflexive crying at birth through stages of cooing, babbling, and one-word utterances. By the second year of life, children are uttering two-word sentences, called **telegraphic speech**, that consist of a noun and a verb ("Want cookie"). In the short span of five years, an initially non-verbal creature has come to understand and produce a complex language.

FIGURE 9.5

Language development depends not only on the brain's biological programming device but also on exposure to one's language. Childhood is an important sensitive period for such exposure.

Bilingualism: Learning a Second Language

For those of us labouring to learn a second language, there are models to inspire us. M. D. Berlitz, inventor of the system for teaching languages that bears his name, spoke 58 of them. Sir John Bowring, once the British governor of Hong Kong, could speak 100 languages and read 100 more. And some sort of record must be held by Benjamin Schulze (1699–1760), who could recite the Lord's Prayer in 215 languages (Bryan, 1986). Somewhat more modestly, roughly 16 percent of the Canadian population can speak both official languages, French and English

8. What factors affect the learning of a second language and its effects on thinking?

TABLE 9.1 Course of Normal Language Development in Children

Age	Speech Characteristics
1–3 months	Infants can distinguish speech from non-speech sounds, and they prefer speech sounds (phonemes); undifferentiated crying gives way to cooing when happy.
4–6 months	Babbling sounds begin to occur. These contain sounds from virtually every language. Child vocalizes in response to verbalizations of others.
7–11 months	Babbling sounds narrow to include only the phonemes heard in the languages spoken by others in the environment. Child moves tongue with vocalizations ("lalling"). Child discriminates between some words without understanding their meaning and begins to imitate word sounds heard from others.
12 months	First recognizable words typically spoken as one-word utterances to name familiar people and objects (e.g., *da-da* or *block*).
12–18 months	Child increases knowledge of word meanings and begins to use single words to express whole phrases or requests (e.g., *out* to express a desire to get out of the crib); primarily uses nouns.
18–24 months	Vocabulary expands to 50–100 words. First rudimentary sentences appear, usually consisting of two words (e.g., *more milk*) with little or no use of articles (*the, a*), conjunctions (*and*), or auxiliary verbs (*can, will*). This condensed, or telegraphic speech, is characteristic of first sentences throughout the world.
2–4 years	Vocabulary expands rapidly at the rate of several hundred words every six months. Two-word sentences give way to longer sentences that, though often grammatically incorrect, exhibit basic language syntax. Child begins to express concepts with words and to use language to describe imaginary objects and ideas. Sentences become more correct syntactically.
4–5 years	Most children have learned the basic grammatical rules for combining nouns, adjectives, articles, conjunctions, and verbs into meaningful sentences.

A second language is learned best and spoken most fluently when it is learned during the sensitive period of childhood. Much of the evidence argues that the vocabulary of a language can be learned at any age, but mastery of the syntax, or grammar, depends on early acquisition (Bialystok, 2001). After about the age of seven, mastery of English grammar, for example, becomes progressively more difficult (Johnson & Newport, 1989; 1991). One concern with the early learning of multiple languages is that children will confuse the two languages. Young bilingual children do sometimes mix their two languages, but as McGill University's Fred Genesee has shown, children begin to differentiate their two languages by two years of age, perhaps younger, and such code mixing is not a lasting or important source of confusion (Nicoladis & Genesee, 1997).

The study of bilingualism has special importance in Canada with our two official languages and policy of multiculturalism. During the past 40 years, the study of second language learning has often focused on the Canadian development and practice of French-immersion programs in the educational system. The idea of French immersion programs originated with a group of English-speaking parents in St. Lambert, Quebec. The parents wanted their children to acquire proficiency in French so that they would be able to function in the majority language of the province and also to improve relationships with francophone Quebecers (Genesee & Gandara, 1999). This group of parents began to work with Wally Lambert, a psychologist at McGill University, and a French immersion program was developed. The first French immersion class in Canada opened in September 1965. From these modest beginnings, the French immersion program has grown tremendously; more than 300,000 Canadian students are now enrolled in immersion programs (Genesee & Gandara, 1999).

Some of the early research on bilingualism suggested that having to learn two vocabularies and sets of grammar put bilingual speakers at a disadvantage. Lambert (Lambert, 1992; Lambert et al., 1993), however, found quite the opposite. When matched on background variables, bilingual speakers scored at least as well as monolinguals on performance tests. More recent research has found that bilingual children actually show superior cognitive processing when compared to their monolingual peers. On average, French immersion students outperform monolingual students in reading (Allen, 2004). Ellen Bialystok, at York University, has found that bilingual children better understand the symbolic nature of print, even before they can read (Bialystok, 1997), and show enhanced performance on tasks that require control of attention (Bialystok, 1998). Positive correlates of bilingualism, such as greater flexibility in thinking and better performance on standardized intelligence tests, have been discovered in a number of countries, including Switzerland and South Africa, as well as in Canada. For children who are entering into a new language group, such as the children of recent immigrants, research has found that non-English-speaking immigrant children perform best in bilingual educational settings in which they are taught in both their native language and in English. Compared to similar children who are placed in English-only classrooms, those in bilingual classes are less likely to drop out of school and they develop higher self-esteem, achieve better academic performance, and have better English fluency (Thomas & Collier, 1997).

When a second language is learned, is it represented in the same part of the brain as the first language? Again, the answer may depend on how early in life the new language is acquired and how well it is learned. At the University of Milan, Daniela Perani and her co-workers (1998) used PET scans to measure cortical activation patterns in the brains of bilingual Italians as they listened to stories read aloud in Italian and in English. People who were highly proficient in English and who had learned the second language before the age of 10 showed representation of the two languages in the same cortical areas. The two languages had, in a sense, become one, as was suggested by the fluent participants' ability to use the languages interchangeably. In contrast, Italians who had learned English later in life and were less fluent in English than in their native language showed brain activity in different areas than those activated by native language stories when they read stories in English, indicating different patterns of language processing. Such people also were less able to switch rapidly back and forth from one language to the other.

Linguistic Influences on Thinking

9. Define the linguistic relativity hypothesis and evaluate its validity. How does language influence thought?

Despite the fact that many politicians prove on a daily basis that a well-developed larynx bears little relation to the capacity for sound thinking, a relation between language and thinking has long been assumed. The linguist Benjamin Lee Whorf (1956) took an extreme position on this matter, contending in his **linguistic relativity hypothesis** that language not only influences, but also *determines* what we are capable of thinking. For example, he suggested that people reared in a culture whose language lacks a past tense, such as the Hopi Indians of the United States, would have difficulty remembering past events.

In the hindsight provided by nearly a half century of research, Whorf's position clearly was overstated. For example, if the linguistic relativity hypothesis were correct, then people whose cultures have only a few words for colours should have greater difficulty in perceiving the spectrum of colours than do people whose languages have many different colour words. To test this proposition, Eleanor Rosch (1973) studied the Dani of New Guinea, who have only two colour words in their language, one for bright, warm colours, the other for cool, dark ones. She found that, contrary to what strict linguistic determinism would suggest, the Dani could discriminate among and remember a wide assortment of hues in much the same manner as can speakers of the English language, which contains many colour names.

Today most linguists do not agree with Whorf that language *determines* how we think. They would say instead that language can *influence* how we think, how efficiently we can categorize our experiences, and perhaps how much detail we attend to in our daily experience (Hunt & Agnoli, 1991). Language also can colour our perceptions and the conclusions we draw. Consider, for example, the ability of sexist language to evoke gender stereotypes. Thirty years ago, it was conventional to use the male pronoun *he* to refer to people in general: "As *man* masters *his* thoughts and feelings, *he* will attain new heights." Does such language make any difference? Indeed it does, at least to people who have now become accustomed to gender-neutral language. In one study, university students read one of the following two statements about psychology:

a. "The psychologist believes in the dignity and worth of the individual human being. He is committed to increasing man's understanding of himself and others."

b. "Psychologists believe in the dignity and worth of the individual human being. They are committed to increasing people's understanding of themselves and others."

The students then were asked to rate the attractiveness of a career in psychology for men and women. Students who had read the first statement rated psychology as a less attractive profession for women than did those who read the second statement, written in gender-neutral language (Briere & Lanktree, 1983). Apparently, statement *a* implied that psychology is a male profession. In such ways, language can help create and maintain stereotypes.

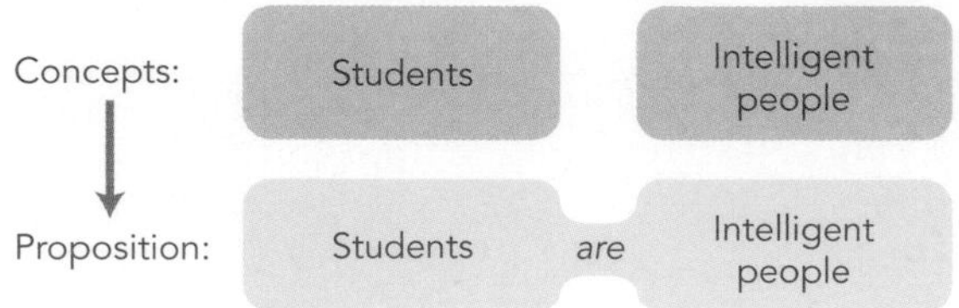

FIGURE 9.6

Concepts are the building blocks of thinking and reasoning. They can be combined into propositions to create both simple and complex thoughts, and the propositions serve as the basis for reasoning.

The fact that language influences what and how we think is of major importance, since, as we have seen, how we encode information affects perception and memory in important ways. As their vocabularies expand, children become capable of thinking in more sophisticated ways. The power of language to influence thinking makes vocabulary development a critical part of the educational process in any field. For example, the vocabulary you are learning in this course provides new concepts that will influence how you think about your own and others' behaviour in the future.

Language not only influences how we think, but also how well we think in certain domains. For example, English-speaking children consistently score lower than children from Asian countries in mathematical skills such as counting, addition, and subtraction (Geary, 1995). One reason may be the words and symbols the languages use to represent numbers. Asian languages make it far easier to learn the base 10 number system, particularly the numbers between 10 and 100. For example, in Chinese, the number 11 is "ten one," 13 is "ten three," and 46 is "four ten six." In contrast, English speakers struggle with such words as "eleven," "twelve," and "thirteen," which bear little conceptual relation to a base-10 mode of thinking. Regardless of their counting proficiency, North American and British children fail to grasp the base 10 system by age 5, whereas many Chinese children do, enabling them to do addition and subtraction with greater ease (Miller & Stigler, 1987). In this manner, the English language hampers the development of skills in using numbers, whereas Asian languages facilitate the development of mathematical skills.

10. Describe three major modes of thought.

Thinking may be considered the internal "language of the mind," but it actually includes a wide range of mental activities. One mode of thought takes the form of verbal sentences that we seem to "hear" in our minds. This is called **propositional thought** because it expresses a proposition, or statement. Another thought mode, **imaginal thought**, consists of images that we can "see," "hear," or "feel" in our mind. There also is a third mode, **motoric thought**, which relates to mental representations of motor movements, such as throwing an object. All three of these modes of thinking enter into our abilities to reason, solve problems, and engage in many forms of "intelligent" behaviour.

Concepts and Propositions

11. What are propositions, and how are they formed?

Much of our thinking occurs in the form of **propositions**, statements that express facts. "University students are intelligent people" is a proposition. All propositions consist of concepts combined in a particular way. Typically, one concept is a *subject* and another is a *predicate* (Figure 9.6). **Concepts** are basic units of semantic memory—mental categories into which we place objects, activities, abstractions (such as "liberal" and "conservative," for example), and events that have essential features in common (Medin et al., 2000). Every psychological term you are learning in this course is a concept. Concepts can be acquired through explicit instruction or by our own observation of similarities and differences among various objects and events.

12. What are concepts, and what is the role of prototypes in concept formation?

Many concepts are difficult to define explicitly. For example, you are quite familiar with the concept "vegetable," yet you might be hard-pressed to come up with an explicit definition of what a vegetable is. However, you can quickly think of a good example of a vegetable. According to Eleanor Rosch (1977), many concepts are defined by **prototypes**—the most typical and familiar members of the class. Rosch suggests that we often decide which category something belongs to by its degree of resemblance to the prototype (Figure 9.7).

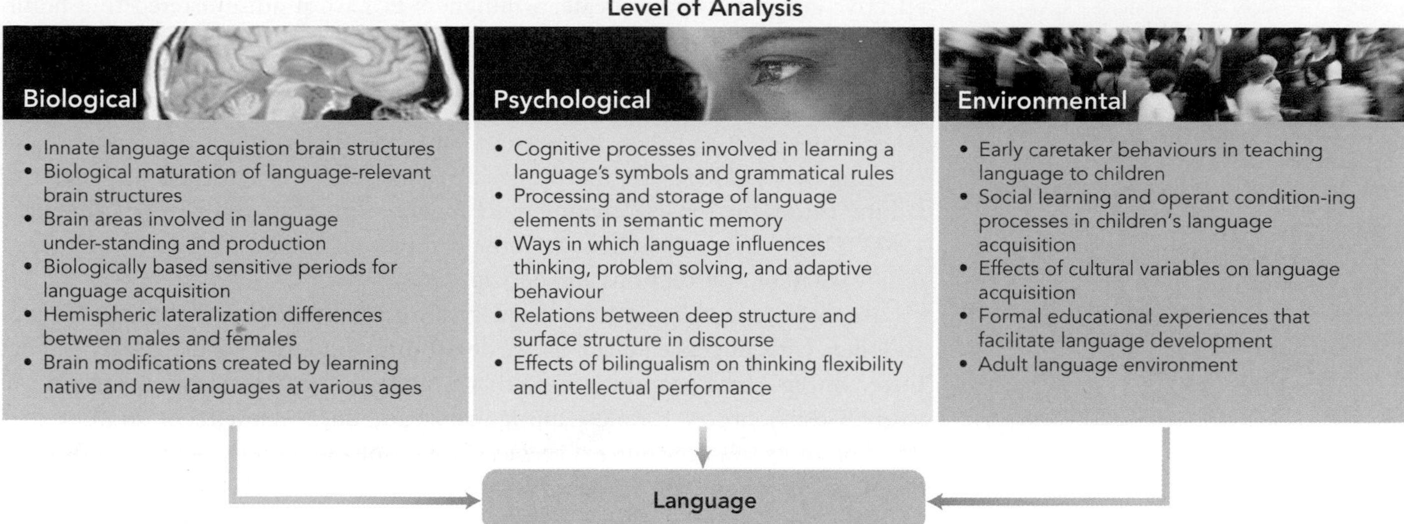

Level of Analysis
Biological
• Innate language acquistion brain structures
• Biological maturation of language-relevant brain structures
• Brain areas involved in language under-standing and production
• Biologically based sensitive periods for language acquisition
• Hemispheric lateralization differences between males and females
• Brain modifications created by learning native and new languages at various ages
Psychological
• Cognitive processes involved in learning a language's symbols and grammatical rules
• Processing and storage of language elements in semantic memory
• Ways in which language influences thinking, problem solving, and adaptive behaviour
• Relations between deep structure and surface structure in discourse
• Effects of bilingualism on thinking flexibility and intellectual performance
Environmental
• Early caretaker behaviours in teaching language to children
• Social learning and operant condition-ing processes in children's language acquisition
• Effects of cultural variables on language acquisition
• Formal educational experiences that facilitate language development
• Adult language environment
Language

FIGURE 9.7

Understanding Behaviour: Language analyzed at biological, psychological, and environmental levels of analysis.

Consider the following questions:

1. Is a sparrow a bird?
2. Is a penguin a bird?
3. Is a bat a bird?

According to the prototype view, you should have come to a quicker decision on the first question than on the last two. Why? Because a sparrow fits most people's "bird" prototype better than does a penguin (which is a bird, though it lacks some essential prototypic features, such as the ability to fly) or a bat (which is not a bird, even though it does fly). Experiments measuring speed of "yes" and "no" responses to the questions above have found that, indeed, it does take most people longer to decide whether penguins or bats are birds (Rips, 1997).

The use of prototypes is perhaps the most elementary method of forming concepts. It requires *only* that we note similarities among objects. Thus, children's early concepts are based on prototypes of the objects and people they encounter personally. They then decide if new objects they encounter are similar enough to the prototype to be a "Mommy," a "cookie," a "doggie," and so on (Smith & Zarate, 1992). Because prototypes may differ as a result of personal experience, there is considerable room for arbitrariness and individual difference in prototypic concepts. Thus one person's concept of a "political radical" may differ sharply from another's.

How we state propositions about a problem or decision can influence how we try to solve the problem, reason through to a decision, or make a judgment (Anderson, 1991). For example, assume that a loved one has received a cancer diagnosis. You are told about a new experimental treatment that removes cancerous cells in successful cases. Would it make a difference to you if you were told that the treatment had a "50 percent success rate" as opposed to a "50 percent failure rate"?

Research suggests that these two propositions for representing the potential outcomes of the treatment, though logically equivalent, are not at all equivalent psychologically. Participants in an experiment who were told that the treatment had a 50 percent success rate judged the treatment to be significantly more

13. What evidence supports the position that animals can exhibit true language? What evidence is used to dispute that position?

effective and expressed a greater willingness to have it administered to a family member than did participants who were told that it had a 50 percent failure rate (Kahneman & Tversky, 1979). Representing outcomes in terms of positives or negatives has this effect because people tend to assign greater costs to negative outcomes (such as losing $100) than they assign value to an equivalent positive outcome (earning $100). Therefore, the proposition that "there is a 50 percent chance of failure" causes the "50–50" treatment to appear more risky (Tversky & Kahneman, 1981). Thus differences in how we verbally represent choices and goals can make a difference in our perceptions and decisions.

As we have seen, we acquire language during childhood with exceptional ease, and then, with language to help us, we define our world using concepts. We arrange these concepts into propositions so that we can then make statements about our world. Clearly, however, we use our language and our statements to do more than describe ourselves and our experiences; much of our mental activity is directed at solving problems. We are faced with a myriad of problem-solving tasks in our everyday life, whether it is that question on the calculus quiz, how to find our way to a new restaurant, or how to unfreeze our computer without losing all of our work. With the background of language, concepts, and propositions, we now turn to how we use these capabilities in reasoning and problem solving.

RESEARCH FRONTIERS

Can Animals Acquire Language?

Language use has often been considered *the* uniquely human ability. Indeed, the famous linguist Noam Chomsky referred to language as the "human essence." Yet many nonhuman species communicate effectively with other members of their flock, herd, colony, or group. For example, many avian species have special calls to warn of predators, attract a mate, or warn others away from their nest or foraging areas (Alcock, 2005). Many species communicate, but can they communicate with language? Research with apes provides the most controversial challenge to the view that only humans are capable of language.

Early research attempted to teach chimpanzees to speak, but it was quickly realized that chimps lack the vocal apparatus to produce the subtly different sounds required by a spoken language. In 1966, Allen and Beatrice Gardner took a very different approach: they began to teach American Sign Language (ASL) to a 10-month-old chimp named Washoe (Gardner & Gardner, 1969). By the age of five, Washoe had learnt more than 160 signs, and the Gardners reported that Washoe would, at times, combine signs in novel ways. Other researchers seemed to replicate this early success. Lana, another chimp, was taught to use lexigrams, visual symbols on a keyboard (Rumbaugh, 1977); Chantek, an orangutan, also learnt to use symbols (Miles et al., 1996); and Koko the gorilla learned more than 600 signs (Bonvillian & Paterson, 1997).

Successes in teaching apes to communicate with language, however, were not uniform. Terrace and colleagues (Terrace, 1979) attempted to teach sign language to a chimp named Nim Chimpsky (a play on the name of linguist Noam Chomsky). After early optimism and many years of training, Terrace concluded that Nim Chimpsky had not learnt language. He found that when Nim produced what appeared to be sentences, it was either simple imitation of a trainer's signs or it was a case of "running on" with his hands, producing long streams of unconnected signs until he got what he wanted. Unlike human use of language and the acquisition of sentences by young children, as Nim's sentences got longer they did not convey any more information.

The success of the Gardners and the failure of Terrace added to the controversy. Terrace's training methods were criticized. The Gardners and others were criticized for inadequately controlling for operant conditioning and for less than rigorous data collection. Then a series of well-controlled tests with a bonobo ape named Kanzi attracted attention (Figure 9.8a). With only informal training, Kanzi learnt the meaning of about 80 geometric symbols (Figure 9.8b) over 1½ years and began to produce two and three symbol sequences. For example, Kanzi created the combinations "person chase Kanzi," "Kanzi chase person," and "person chase person" to designate who should chase whom during play. Kanzi seemed to be sensitive to syntax, and seemed to respond correctly to language at a level typical of a 2½- to 3-year-old child (Savage-Rumbaugh et al., 1993).

The debate continues today. Proponents argue that apes have demonstrated rudimentary language skills (Savage-Rumbaugh et al., 1986; Beran et al., 1998). Others have argued that the apes are displaying only imitation and operant conditioning, and to infer language from what the apes have demonstrated requires unwarranted assumptions about what is going on inside the apes' minds. Recall that language is symbolic, structured, and generative. Clearly apes have been able to acquire a small "vocabulary" of several hundred signs or symbols. As for structure and generativity, the evidence is mixed and controversial. There are examples in which apes are sensitive to syntax and examples of complete insensitivity to syntax. However the debate is eventually resolved, it is important to remember that we acquire language with incredible ease during childhood and use it spontaneously and continuously throughout our lives. The evidence for language among nonhuman species is limited and controversial, and even the most ardent supporters agree that ape linguistic capabilities are, at best, on a par with those of a young child.

(a)

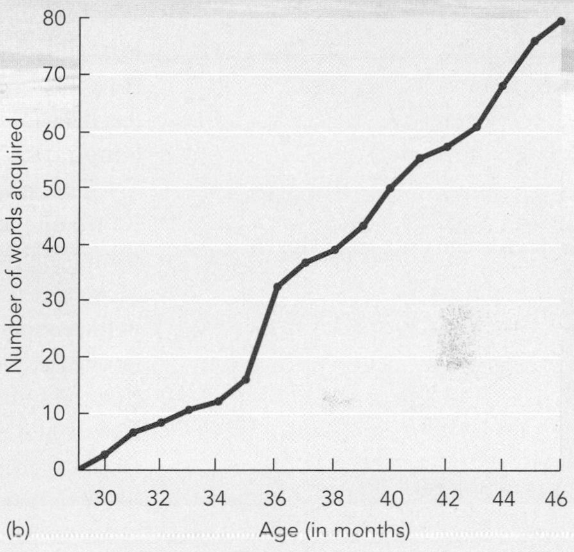

(b)

FIGURE 9.8

(a) Kanzi, a bonobo chimpanzee, communicates using complex symbols with his trainer, psychologist Sue Savage-Rumbaugh. Kanzi uses the symbols to signify objects and qualities. (b) This figure shows the rate of Kanzi's symbol acquisition over 17 months of informal training.

Adapted from Savage-Rumbaugh et al., 1986.

In Review

- *Human language is symbolic, structured, and generative. The surface structure of a language refers to how symbols are combined; the deep structure refers to the underlying meaning of the symbols. Language elements are arranged hierarchically from the phoneme to morphemes, and on to words, phrases, and sentences.*
- *In infancy, babies emit all the phonemes that exist in the languages of the world. At about six months of age, babbling sounds narrow to include only the languages spoken by others in the environment. By ages four to five, most children have learned the basic grammatical rules for combining words into meaningful sentences.*
- *Language development seems to depend heavily on innate mechanisms that permit the learning and production of language, provided that the child is exposed to an appropriate linguistic environment. There may be a sensitive period for exposure to language that extends from early childhood to puberty. Thereafter normal linguistic development does not occur.*
- *When both languages are well learned, bilingualism has been shown to have positive influences on cognitive performance. A second language is most easily mastered and fluently spoken if it is learned during the sensitive period of childhood.*
- *Language does not appear to determine thought, but it does influence what and how effectively people think. Expansion of vocabulary allows people to encode and process information in more sophisticated ways.*

- *Concepts are classes that share certain characteristics. Many concepts are based on prototypes, the most typical and familiar members of a class. How much something resembles the prototype determines whether the concept is applied to it. Propositional thought involves the use of concepts in the form of statements having subjects and predicates.*
- *The issue of whether animals can acquire human language is controversial. Animals clearly can communicate. There is little doubt that apes are capable of learning, combining, and communicating symbols at a level similar to that of a young child, but skeptics question whether they can learn syntax and generate novel ideas.*

REASONING AND PROBLEM SOLVING

What is "intelligent" thinking? Certainly, it involves the ability to reason and think logically. Such thinking helps us acquire knowledge, make sound decisions, and solve problems. Cognitive scientists believe that our capacity for logical thinking has been honed by evolutionary forces because of its adaptive value (Eisenstadt & Simon, 1997; Rips, 1997).

The most primitive way of solving problems is through trial and error, in which we try one solution after another in the real world until the problem is solved. Reasoning helps us avoid the hazards and time-consuming efforts of trial and error. Most of the time, people solve problems by developing solutions in their minds before applying them in the external world. For example, if you decide to build a bookcase, you are unlikely to nail or screw boards together at random in the hope that the finished product will serve your purposes. Instead, you will develop mental representations to guide your efforts. These likely will include a visual image of the finished product as well as general principles for successful construction, which are likely to be expressed in linguistic terms (e.g., "Build from the bottom up").

Reasoning

14. Distinguish between deductive reasoning and inductive reasoning. Why is deductive reasoning seen as the stronger form of reasoning?

Two types of reasoning underlie many of our attempts to make decisions and solve problems (Figure 9.9). In **deductive reasoning**, we reason from the "top down," that is, from general principles to a conclusion about a specific case. People reason deductively when they begin with a set of premises (propositions assumed to be true) and determine what they imply about a specific situation. Deductive reasoning is the basis of formal mathematics and logic. Logicians regard it as the stronger and more valid form of reasoning because the conclusion *cannot be false* if the premises (factual statements) are true. More formally, the underlying deductive principle may be stated: Given a proposition, *if X then Y*, if *X* occurs, then you can infer *Y*. Thus to use the classic deductive argument, called a syllogism,

if all humans are mortal (first premise), and
if Socrates is a human (second premise),
then Socrates must be mortal (conclusion).

15. How is a combination of inductive and deductive reasoning involved in scientific activity?

In **inductive reasoning**, we reason in a "bottom-up" fashion, starting with specific facts and trying to develop a general principle (Figure 9.9). For example, scientists use induction when they discover general principles, or laws, as a result of observing a number of specific instances of a phenomenon. If enough apples fall on our heads, we may conclude that there exists a general force that pulls objects toward the earth. Likewise, after Ivan Pavlov observed a number of instances in which the dogs began to salivate when approached by the experimenter who fed them, he began to think in terms of a general principle that later was formalized as classical conditioning.

An important difference between deductive and inductive reasoning lies in the certainty of the results. Deductive conclusions are certain to be correct, *if* the premises are true, but inductive reasoning leads to likelihood rather than certainty. Even if we reason inductively in a flawless manner, the possibility of error always remains because some new observation may disprove our conclusion.

In both daily life and in science, inductive and deductive reasoning may be used at different points in problem solving and decision making. For example, psychologists often make informal observations that cause them to construct an initial explanation for a particular behavioural phenomenon (such as the failure of many bystanders to help in emergencies). But they know that the explanation they have derived through inductive reasoning from specific observations could be wrong, even if it is consistent with all the known facts. Therefore they move to a deductive process in which they design experiments to formally test specific *if–then* hypotheses. If the results of these experimental tests do *not* support their hypotheses, they conclude that their explanation or theory cannot be correct and must be revised or discarded. This latter process is known formally as the *hypothetico-deductive* approach to scientific theory building.

Deductive Reasoning
(general principles to specific case)

General principles, assumed universally true

Assess "fit" to specific instance

Conclusion regarding individual case

Inductive Reasoning
(specific facts to general principle)

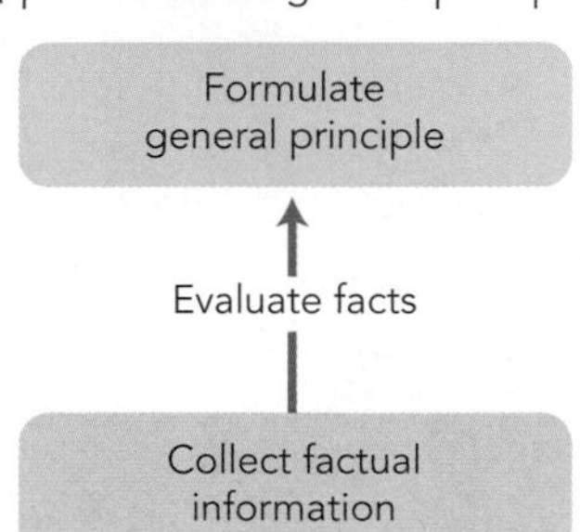

FIGURE 9.9
Comparing deductive and inductive reasoning.

Stumbling Blocks in Reasoning

The ability to reason effectively is a key factor in critical thinking, in making sound decisions, and in solving problems. Unfortunately, several factors may prevent us from selecting the information needed to draw sound conclusions.

Distraction by irrelevant information. Distinguishing relevant from irrelevant information at times can be challenging. Consider, for example, the following problem. As you solve it, analyze the mental steps you take, and do not read on until you have decided on an answer.

> Your drawer contains 19 black socks and 13 blue socks. Without turning on the light, how many socks do you have to pull out of the drawer to be sure you have a complete set?

As you solved the problem, what information entered into your reasoning? Did you take into account the fact that there were 19 black socks and 13 blue ones? If so, you're like many of Robert Sternberg's (1988) Yale University students who did the same thing, thereby making the problem much more difficult than it should be. In this case, all that matters is how many *colours* of socks there are. It doesn't matter if there are a thousand socks of each colour; once you have selected any three of them, you are bound to have at least two of the same colour. People often fail to solve problems because they simply don't focus on the *relevant* information. Instead, they take into account irrelevant information that leads them astray.

Failure to apply deductive rules. Even when people have learned to use general problem-solving methods, such as formal logic and mathematical formulas, they tend to think of them as methods to be used only in certain situations and may fail to apply them to new problems. For example, all of us have encountered arithmetic-progression problems, in which a variable is set at an initial value and then is increased by a constant amount per interval for a number of intervals. An example is "If your car were going 50 km/h and you increased your speed by 8 km/h every minute for 7 consecutive minutes, how fast would you be going at the end?" The appropriate formula is $Y = B + (a)D$, where Y is the correct answer, B is the

16. Summarize three factors that can interfere with the correct application of deductive reasoning. What is meant by belief bias?

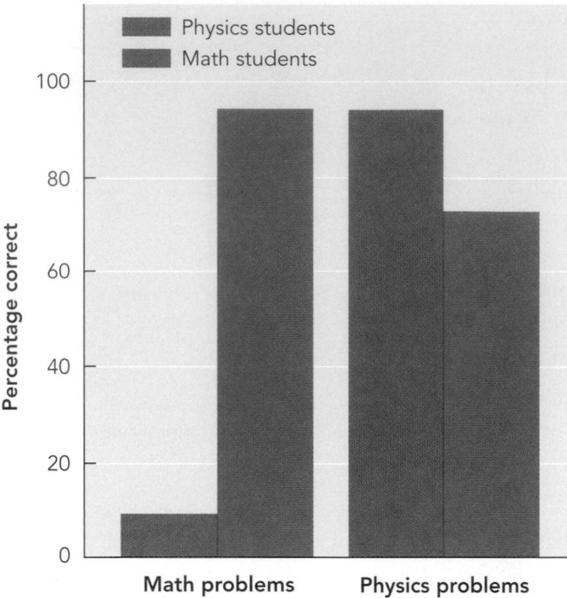

FIGURE 9.10

Percentage of arithmetic-progression problems solved by students who were trained to use the same equations, either as a type of mathematics or as a tool in solving physics problems. The specificity of the physics students' previous use apparently interfered with their ability to generalize what they knew to the mathematics problems.

Data from Bassok & Holyoak, 1989.

original value, D is the amount added, and (a) is the number of times it is added, providing a Y of 106 km/h in this case.

Both mathematics and physics students learn this formula for solving such problems. However, students in physics classes learn to solve arithmetic-progression problems only as they apply to physics, whereas students in mathematics classes solve arithmetic-progression problems drawn from a variety of areas. What happens if physics students are presented with arithmetic-progression problems from a mathematics class and mathematic students are given similar problems used in the physics class? Will math and physics students be equally adept at "plugging in" the correct problem-solving method?

Figure 9.10 shows the results of one experiment (Bassok & Holyoak, 1989). The mathematics students, who had practised recognizing when to use the $Y = B + (a)D$ problem-solving method in different situations, quickly applied it to the physics problems. In contrast, the physics students failed to apply their knowledge in the novel math situations. Sometimes, knowledge is not enough; one must have the wisdom to know when and how to apply the knowledge.

Belief bias. **Belief bias** is the tendency to abandon logical rules in favour of our own personal beliefs. To illustrate, let us consider an experiment in which university students were asked to judge whether conclusions followed logically from syllogisms such as the following:

All things that are smoked are good for one's health.

Cigarettes are smoked.

Therefore cigarettes are good for one's health.

What do you think? Is the logic correct? Actually, it is. If we accept (for the moment) that the premises are true, then the conclusion *does* follow logically from the premises. Yet students frequently claimed that the conclusion was not *logically correct* because they disagreed with the first premise that all things smoked are good for the health. In this case, their beliefs about the harmful effects of smoking got in the way of their logic. When the same syllogisms were presented with nonsense words such as *ramadians* substituted for cigarettes, the errors in logic were markedly reduced (Markowitz & Nantel, 1989). Incidentally, we agree that the conclusion that cigarettes are good for one's health is factually false. However, it is false because the major premise is false, not because the logic is faulty. Unfortunately, many people confuse factual correctness with logical correctness. The two are not at all the same.

Problem Solving

Humans have an unmatched ability to solve problems and to adapt to the challenges of their world. People can systematically use inductive and deductive reasoning to solve problems. Such problem solving proceeds through four stages (Figure 9.11). How well we carry out each of these stages determines our success in solving the problem.

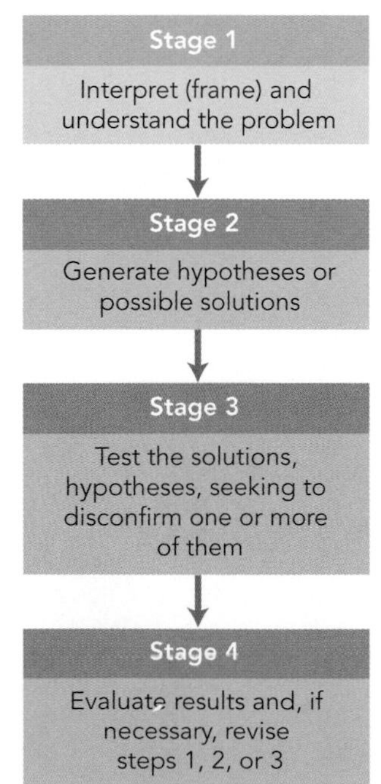

FIGURE 9.11

Stages of problem solving.

Understanding, or Framing, the Problem

Most of us have had the experience of feeling totally frustrated in our attempts to solve a problem. We may even think that the problem is unsolvable. Then someone suggests a new way of looking at the problem, and the solution suddenly becomes obvious. How we mentally represent, or *frame*, a problem can make a huge difference. Consider the problem illustrated in Figure 9.12.

> Train A leaves Winnipeg for its 50-km trip to St. Boniface at a constant speed of 25 km/h. At the same time, Train B leaves St. Boniface, bound for Winnipeg at the same speed of 25 km/h. An energetic crow leaves Winnipeg at the same time as Train A, flying above the tracks toward St. Boniface at a speed of 60 km/h. When the crow encounters Train B, it turns and flies back to Train A, then instantly reverses its direction and flies back to Train B. The supercharged bird continues this sequence until Trains A and B meet midway between Winnipeg and St. Boniface. Try to solve this problem before reading on: *What is the total distance the bird will have travelled in its excursions between Trains A and B?*

FIGURE 9.12

The crow and the trains problem described in the text. (The answer appears on p. 398.) Adapted from Posner, 1973.

Many people approach the problem as a distance problem, which is quite natural because the question was stated in terms of distance. They try to compute how far the bird will fly during each segment of its flight between Trains A and B, sometimes filling up several pages with computations in the process. But suppose you approach the problem by asking *how long* it will take the trains to meet? The crow will have flown the same period of time at 60 km/h. Now that you have reframed it as a time problem, the problem becomes much easier to solve. (You can check your solution against the answer given on page 398.)

17. Describe the four stages of problem solving.

18. How does the Crow and Trains problem demonstrate the role of framing?

As you can see, our initial understanding of a problem is a key step toward a successful solution. If we frame a problem poorly, we can easily be led into a maze of blind alleys and ineffective solutions. If we frame it optimally, we have at least a chance of generating an effective solution.

Generating Potential Solutions

Once we have interpreted the problem, we can begin to formulate potential solutions or explanations. Ideally, we might proceed in the following fashion:

1. Determine which procedures and explanations will be considered.
2. Determine which of these solutions are consistent with the evidence that has so far been observed. Rule out any solutions that do not fit the evidence.

Testing the Solutions

Consider the possible solutions that remain. If the solution requires you to choose between specific explanations, ask if there is any test that would give one result if one explanation were true and another result if a different explanation were true. If so, make that test and evaluate the explanations again in light of the evidence from that test. This is essentially what scientists do when they design experiments.

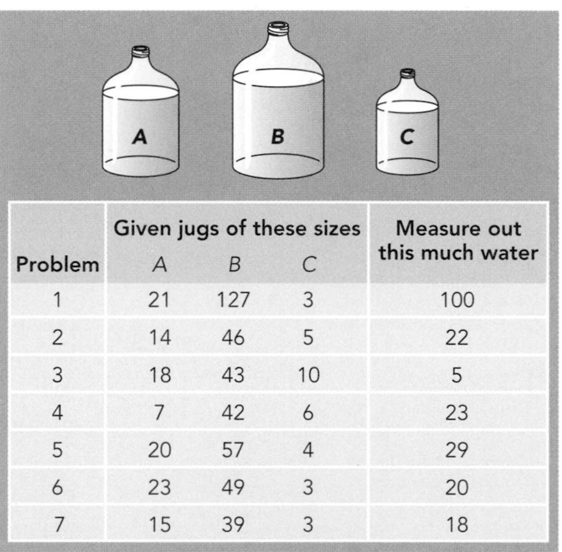

Problem	Given jugs of these sizes A	B	C	Measure out this much water
1	21	127	3	100
2	14	46	5	22
3	18	43	10	5
4	7	42	6	23
5	20	57	4	29
6	23	49	3	20
7	15	39	3	18

FIGURE 9.13

Luchins's water jars problems. Using containers A, B, and C with the capacities shown in the table, how would you measure out the volumes indicated in the right-hand column? You may discover a general problem-solving formula that fits all seven problems.

Let us consider a common problem that can arise in the process of discovering and applying solutions to problems. Figure 9.13 shows a series of seven problems that we invite you to solve. Here is the first of those problems:

> Suppose you have a 21-cup jug, a 127-cup jug, and a 3-cup jug. Drawing and discarding as much water as you like, how would you measure out exactly 100 cups of water?

FIGURE 9.14

Experienced snowboarders learn schemas for various types of snow, and the discriminations made possible by these schemas can affect planning and decision making. This boarder might approach a slope covered with "powder" differently than one covered with "corn" because of their different effects on the board and potentially on the boarder's physical well-being.

19. Which problem-solving pitfall is revealed by Luchins's water jars problems?

20. What are problem-solving schemas? How do they relate to expertise, and to the strengths and weaknesses of human memory?

This problem is followed by the remaining six problems in Figure 9.13. Try to solve all of them in order and write your calculations before reading on. Does a common solution emerge? If so, see if you can specify what it is.

As you worked the problems, you probably discovered that they are all solvable by the same formula, namely $B - A - (2 \times C) =$ desired amount—for example, in Problem 1, $127 - 21 - (2 \times 3) = 100$. If you discovered this, it gave you a logical formula that you could apply to the rest of the problems. And it worked, didn't it? However, by applying the successful formula used on Problems 1 through 5 to Problems 6 and 7, you may have missed even easier solutions for these last two problems, namely $A - C$ for Problem 6 and $A + C$ for Problem 7.

Abraham Luchins (1942) developed the water jars problems to demonstrate the manner in which a **mental set**—the tendency to stick to solutions that have worked in the past—can result in less effective problem solving. Luchins found that most people who worked on Problems 6 and 7 were blinded by the mental set they had developed by working the first five problems. In contrast, people who had not worked on Problems 1 through 5 almost always applied the simple solutions to Problems 6 and 7. Studies of mental set show how easy it is to become rigidly fixated on one particular approach if we enjoy some degree of success with that approach.

Evaluating Results

The final stage of problem solving is to evaluate the solutions. As we saw in the water jars problems, even solutions that prove successful may not be the easiest or the best. Thus, after solving a problem, we should ask ourselves, "Would there have been an easier or more effective way to accomplish the same objective?" This can lead to the development of additional problem-solving principles that may be applicable to future problems.

Problem-Solving Schemas

In solving problems, people often learn to employ shortcut problem-solving methods that apply to specific situations (Johnson-Laird, 1997; Rips, 1994). **Problem-solving schemas** can be likened to mental blueprints, or step-by-step scripts for selecting information and solving specialized classes of problems. We have all learned a great many of them, from schemas for cooking dinner or getting acquainted with a person we've just met to schemas for studying and mastering academic course content. Once they are mastered, we seem to "know what to do" without having to engage in step-by-step formal problem-solving procedures.

Schemas help explain what it means to be an expert (Figure 9.14). For example, masters and grand masters in chess far exceed the playing ability of even the brightest novices. They can glance at a chess board and quickly plan strategies and make adjustments in the heat of competition. The world's best players can store in memory as many as 50,000 board configurations, together with the locations of each of the individual pieces (Chase & Simon, 1973). For years, world chess champion Gary Kasparov's sophisticated schemas enabled him to regularly defeat chess-playing computers that used logical rules, even those capable of logically analyzing up to 100,000 moves per second. It took Deep Blue, a 1273 kg behemoth capable of "thinking" at a rate of 200 million positions and 200,000 moves per second, to finally defeat the schemas within Kasparov's 1.4 kg brain (Figure 9.15).

Expert athletic coaches, surgeons, military leaders, and political consultants all rely on the schemas they have developed with experience. Planning military strategy, chess playing, running a political campaign, and piloting aircraft are very different activities. Nevertheless, researchers have found that there is a common factor underlying expertise: Experts have developed a great many schemas to guide problem solving in their field, and they are much better than novices at recognizing when each schema should be applied (Bedard & Chi, 1992). Applying the correct mental blueprint provides a proven route to solving problems quickly and effectively.

Consider what this difference in schema application means in terms of what we know about human memory. As we learned in Chapter 8, human long-term memory is quite good, and that is where schemas reside. Because they rely on learned schemas, experts depend on their spacious long-term memory. They can quickly analyze a problem, select the retrieval cues needed to pull the appropriate schema from memory, and apply it to solve the problem at hand. In contrast, novices who haven't yet learned specialized schemas must use general problem-solving methods that force them to solve problems in working memory, on the space-limited "blackboard of the mind" (Newell & Simon, 1972). In so doing, they tax their working memories—the weakest link in the human mind.

FIGURE 9.15

Chess master Gary Kasparov has developed chess schemas that make him a worthy opponent for even the most sophisticated computers, including IBM's Deep Blue.

The development of expertise is accompanied by alterations in brain functioning that increase processing efficiency. This occurs even in animals. Thus, as macaque monkeys in one study became experts in categorizing objects, recordings from individual feature-detector neurons in the brain revealed quicker and stronger activity in the specific neurons that responded to the stimulus features of importance in categorizing the stimuli (Sigala & Logothetis, 2002). These feature detectors were referred to as "expert neurons" (Hasegawa & Myashita, 2002).

Algorithms and Heuristics

21. Differentiate between an algorithm and a heuristic.

Algorithms and heuristics are two important strategies for problem solving. **Algorithms** are formulas or procedures that automatically generate correct solutions. Mathematical and chemical formulas are algorithms; if you use them correctly, you will always get the correct answer. Another algorithm is that if the letters of a word are scrambled in random order to produce an anagram like *teralbay,* then the word can be discovered by a process in which the letters are recombined in all possible combinations.

As this last example illustrates, using algorithms can at times be very time-consuming. In this case, the eight letters can be rearranged in no fewer than 40,320 different ways, and applying the algorithm might significantly delay your finishing this chapter. Therefore we may decide to use some more general rule-of-thumb strategy, such as trying out only consonants in the first and last positions, because we know that more words begin and end in consonants than begin and end in vowels. When we adopt rule-of-thumb approaches like this, we are using heuristics.

Heuristics are general problem-solving strategies that we apply to certain classes of situations. They are mental shortcuts that may or may not provide correct solutions. In using heuristics, we typically compare the present facts with some concept or schema that seems applicable to the present situation.

Means-ends analysis is one example of a heuristic (Newell & Simon, 1972). In using this strategy, we identify differences between the present situation and one's desired state, or goal, and then make changes that will reduce these differences. Assume, for example, that you have a 30-page paper due at the end of the term and have not yet begun working on it. The present situation is zero pages written; the desired end state is a 30-page paper. What, specifically, needs to be done to reduce that discrepancy, and how are you going to do it?

22. Describe two commonly used problem-solving heuristics.

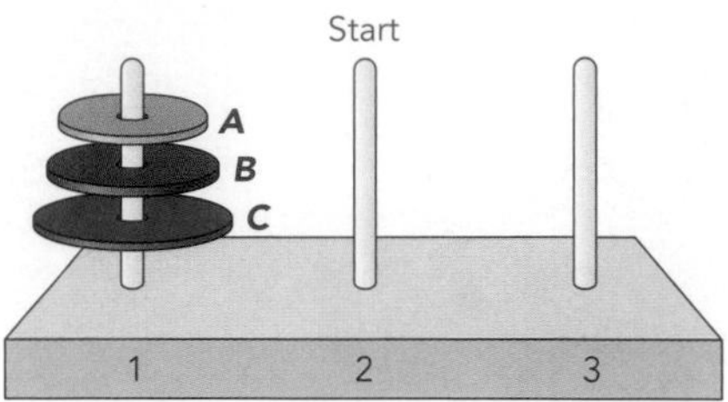

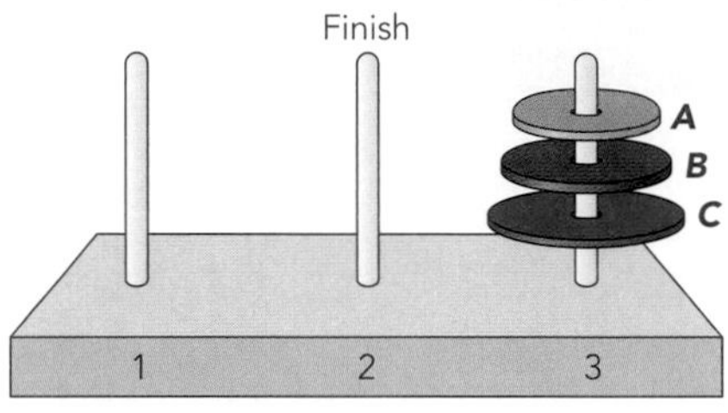

FIGURE 9.16

The Tower of Hanoi problem. The object is to move the rings one at a time from peg 1 to peg 3 in the smallest number of moves possible. (It can be done in seven moves.) Only the top ring on a peg can be moved, and a large ring can never be placed on top of a smaller one. (The answer appears on p. 398)

Means-ends analysis often involves the use of another heuristic, known as **subgoal analysis**. People can attack a large problem by formulating subgoals, or intermediate steps toward a solution. For example, it is unlikely that you can write a 30-page paper at one sitting. Instead, your expertise as a student likely will lead you to break this big task down into subgoals, such as (a) choosing a topic; (b) doing library and Internet research on the topic to get the facts you need; (c) organizing the facts within a general outline of the paper; (d) writing a first draft, or specific sections of the paper; (e) reorganizing and refining the first draft, and so on. In so doing, a huge task becomes a series of smaller and more manageable tasks, each with a subgoal that leads you toward the ultimate goal of a quality 30-page paper.

The value of setting subgoals can be seen in the Tower of Hanoi problem, depicted in Figure 9.16. The ultimate goal for this problem is to move all three rings on peg 1 to peg 3 using no more than seven moves. There are, however, two restrictions. First, only the top ring on a peg can be moved. Second, a ring must never be placed above a smaller ring. Can you solve this challenging problem? It can be done in seven steps.

Breaking this task into subgoals helps us solve the problem. The first subgoal is to get ring C to the bottom of peg 3. The second subgoal is to get ring B over to peg 3. With these two subgoals accomplished, the final subgoal of getting ring A to peg 3 is quite easy. The solution requires planning (hypothesis formation), checking, and revising hypotheses—all processes discussed previously. The correct seven-step sequence of moves is presented on page 398.

Heuristics enter not only into problem-solving strategies, but also into judgments and decisions. As we shall see, they also can contribute to errors in judgment.

Uncertainty, Heuristics, and Decision Making

Few decisions in everyday life can be made with the absolute certainty that comes from applying some mathematical formula. Typically, the best we can hope for is a decision that has a high probability of a positive outcome. Because we seldom know what the exact probabilities are (e.g., how likely it is that the stock market will be up or down when you need your money at a specific time in the future, or how probable it is that a new dating relationship will become permanent), we tend to apply certain heuristics to form judgments of likelihood.

In daily life, we routinely make decisions about what other people are like. Suppose, for example, you are given the following description of a young woman:

> Linda is 31 years old, single, outspoken, and very bright. She majored in philosophy. As a student, she was deeply concerned with issues of discrimination and social justice, and participated in anti-nuclear demonstrations.

Now rate the likelihood that each of the following hypotheses is true. Use 1 to indicate the most likely statement, 8 to indicate the least likely statement, and any number between 2 and 7 to indicate the likelihood of the second most likely statement.

_______ A Linda is active in the feminist movement.

_______ B Linda is a bank teller.

_______ C Linda is active in the feminist movement and is a bank teller.

This problem was used in a series of experiments conducted by cognitive psychologists Amos Tversky and Daniel Kahneman to study the role of heuristics in judgment and decision making. Kahneman and Tversky (1980, 1982) showed that certain heuristics underlie much of our inductive decision making (drawing conclusions from facts), and that their misuse results in many of our thinking errors. Let us examine how that occurs.

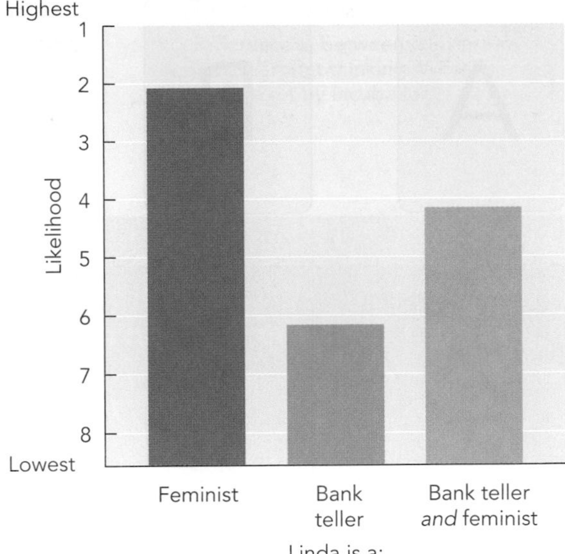

FIGURE 9.17

Mean likelihood judgments made by students on the basis of the description of Linda cited in the text.

Data from Tversky & Kahneman, 1982.

The representativeness heuristic. "What does it look [or seem] like?" This is probably the first task faced by our perceptual system when it processes incoming stimuli. Earlier, we discussed the importance of prototypes in concept formation. We use the **representativeness heuristic** to infer how closely something or someone fits our prototype for a particular concept, or class, and therefore how likely it is to be a member of that class. In essence, we are asking, "How likely is it that this [person, object, event] *represents* that class?" Sometimes, our use of representativeness can cause us to make decisions that fly in the face of logic.

For example, what was your order of likelihood judgments concerning Linda? Figure 9.17 shows the mean likelihood estimates that university students attached to each statement (a low number indicating greater likelihood). First of all, there is a clear tendency to favour Hypothesis A (Linda is a feminist). This is not surprising; the description of her does sound like a feminist. However, the significant finding is that Hypothesis C (Linda is a feminist bank teller) was favoured over Hypothesis B (Linda is a bank teller). But this cannot possibly be correct. Why not? Because everyone who is both a feminist and a bank teller is also "just" a bank teller. Furthermore, there are many bank tellers who are not feminists, and Linda could be one of them. Stated differently, any person is more likely to be just a bank teller than to be a bank teller *and* a feminist—or for that matter, a bank teller and anything else. People who say that Hypothesis C is more likely than Hypothesis B (and about 85 percent of participants given this problem do so) violate the logical principle that the combination of two events cannot be more likely than either event alone.

23. Describe the representativeness heuristic and indicate how it applies to people's response to the Linda problem.

Tversky and Kahneman believe that the reason people make this sort of error is that they confuse representativeness with probability. Linda represents our prototype for a feminist bank teller better than she fits our prototype for a bank teller. Therefore the former is (we erroneously think) more likely than the latter. Notice how this argument fits with the ideas about memory discussed in Chapter 8. The description of Linda as "outspoken" and "concerned with issues of discrimination and social justice" serves a priming function, activating the elements in memory that are associated with the concept of *feminist*, so it is hard to think of Linda without thinking of a feminist. On the other hand, there is nothing in Linda's description that would activate the concept of bank teller. Thus, if Linda is to be a bank teller at all, we think she must be a feminist bank teller.

The availability heuristic. Another heuristic that can sometimes lead us astray is the **availability heuristic**, which causes us to base judgments and decisions on the availability of information in memory. We tend to remember events that are most important and significant to us. Usually that principle serves us well, keeping important information at the forefront of our memories, ready to be applied. But, if something comes easily to mind, we may exaggerate the likelihood that it could occur. For example, a recent memorable event, such as the terrorist bombing of an airliner, is readily accessible to memory and can increase people's belief that they could suffer a similar fate (Fiske & Taylor, 1991). After the terrorist hijackings of September 11, 2001, airline bookings and tourism declined dramatically within the United States for a significant period. Demand for office space in landmark high-rise buildings also declined, and many businesses sought space in less conspicuous suburban settings. Similarly, the year after Steven Spielberg's movie *Jaws* provided graphic images of a great white shark devouring swimmers at New

24. How does the availability heuristic influence judgments of likelihood or probability?

28. What two assumptions did Alfred Binet make in developing his measure of intelligence?

In developing his tests, Binet made two assumptions about intelligence. The first was that mental abilities develop with age. The second was that the rate at which people gain mental competence is a characteristic of the person and is fairly constant over time. If this is true, then a child who is less competent than expected at age 5 should also be lagging at age 10.

To develop a measure of mental skills, Binet asked experienced teachers what sorts of problems children could solve at ages three, four, five, and so on, up through the school years. He then used their answers to develop a "standardized interview" in which an adult examiner posed a series of questions to a child to determine whether the child was performing at the correct mental level for his or her age (Table 9.2). The result of the testing was a score called the **mental age**. For instance, if a child of 8 could solve problems at the level of the average 10-year-old, the child would be said to have a mental age of 10. For the French school system, the practical implication was that educational attainment could be enhanced if placement in school were based at least in part on the child's mental age. An eight-year-old child with a mental age of six could hardly be expected to cope with the academic demands of a normal classroom for eight-year-olds.

The concept of mental age was subsequently expanded by the German psychologist William Stern to provide a relative score—a common yardstick of intellectual attainment—for people of different chronological ages. Stern's **intelligence quotient**, or **IQ**, was originally based on the ratio of mental age to chronological age, according to the formula:

29. What was Stern's original IQ ratio? Why was it abandoned, and what replaced it?

$$IQ = (\text{Mental age}/\text{chronological age}) \times 100.$$

Thus a child who was performing at exactly his or her age level would have an IQ of 100. In our previous example, the child with a mental age of 10 and a chronological age of 8 would have an IQ of (10/8) × 100 = 125. A 12-year-old with a mental age of 16 would also have an IQ of 125, so the two children would be comparable in intelligence even though their ages differed.

TABLE 9.2 Sample Problems from the Stanford-Binet Intelligence Test that Should be Answered Correctly at Particular Ages

Age 3—Child should be able to:	Point to objects that serve various functions such as "goes on your feet." Name pictures of objects such as *chair, flag.* Repeat a list of two words or digits—e.g., *car, dog.*
Age 4—Child should be able to:	Discriminate visual forms such as squares, circles, and triangles. Define words such as *ball* and *bat.* Repeat 10-word sentences. Count up to four objects. Solve problems such as "In daytime it is light; at night it is . . ."
Age 6—Child should be able to:	State the differences between similar items such as a *bird* and a *dog.* Count up to nine blocks. Solve analogies such as "An inch is short; a mile is . . ."
Age 9—Child should be able to:	Solve verbal problems such as "Tell me a number that rhymes with tree." Solve simple arithmetic problems such as "If I buy 4 cents worth of candy and give the storekeeper 10 cents, how much money will I get back? Repeat four digits in reverse order.
Age 12—Child should be able to:	Define words such as *skill* and *muzzle.* Repeat five digits in reverse order. Solve verbal absurdities such as "One day we saw several icebergs that had been entirely melted by the warmth of the Gulf Stream. What is foolish about that?"

Source: Terman & Merrill, 1972.

Today's tests no longer use the concept of mental age. One problem is that increases in mental age begin to slow down dramatically at about age 16. Because many of the skills measured by intelligence tests are learned by that age through normal life experiences and schooling, mental age works pretty well for children, but not for adults. A 40-year-old cannot be expected to have twice the level of mental skill of a 20-year-old. (Indeed, some 20-year-olds seem convinced that the opposite is the case.) A second problem is that some intellectual skills show an actual decline at advanced ages rather than the growth assumed by the concept of mental age. Finally, a notable discovery by New Zealand researcher James Flynn (1987, 1998) suggests that much of the world's population is scoring progressively higher on intelligence tests. This "rising curve" phenomenon has produced IQ increases of 28 points in North America since 1910 and a similar increase in Britain since 1942. Whether this increase is due to better nutrition, richer learning environments, or some unknown factor is unclear at this time (Neisser et al., 1998). What is clear, however, is that the intelligence score distribution has to be recalibrated upward if the average IQ is to remain at 100, the traditional midpoint of the intelligence range. To deal with these problems, today's intelligence tests provide an "IQ" score that is not a quotient at all, but, rather, is based on a person's performance relative to the scores of a large sample of other people his or her age. This score is known as **deviation IQ** and represents how much standardized distance (or deviation) a score is above or below the mean for that particular sample.

The Stanford-Binet and Wechsler Scales

Lewis Terman, a professor at Stanford University, revised Binet's test for use in the United States, translating it into English and rewriting some of its items so that they were relevant to American culture. Terman's revision became known as the Stanford-Binet test. By the mid-1920s, it had been widely accepted in North America. The Stanford-Binet contained mostly verbal items, and yielded a single IQ score.

Somewhat later, a major competitor to the Stanford-Binet emerged in the form of the Wechsler scales. Psychologist David Wechsler believed that intelligence should be measured as a group of distinct but related verbal and non-verbal abilities. He therefore developed intelligence tests for adults and for children that measured a range of intellectual skills. In 1939, the Wechsler Adult Intelligence Scale (WAIS) appeared, followed by the Wechsler Intelligence Scale for Children (WISC) in 1955, and the Wechsler Preschool and Primary Scale of Intelligence (WPPSI) in 1967. Like the Stanford-Binet, the Wechsler scales are regularly revised. Today the Wechsler tests (WAIS-III and WISC-III) are the most widely used individually administered intelligence tests in the United States (Groth-Marnat, 2003).

The Wechsler scales consist of a series of subtests that fall into two classes: Verbal Tests and Performance Tests (Figure 9.22). A psychologist therefore can plot a profile of the scores on each of the subtests to assess a person's pattern of intellectual strengths and weaknesses. The test yields three different summary scores: a Verbal IQ based on the sum of the Verbal subscales; a Performance IQ based on the Performance subscales; and a Full-Scale IQ based on all of the scales. For some purposes, it is useful to examine differences between the Verbal IQ and the Performance IQ. For example, a person from an impoverished environment with little formal schooling might score higher on the Performance scales than on the Verbal scales, suggesting that the overall IQ might be an underestimate of intellectual potential. Sometimes, too, various types of brain damage are reflected in large discrepancies between certain subtest scores (Goldstein, 2000).

Sample Items for the Wechsler Adult Intelligence Scale (WAIS)

Subtest	Description	Example
Verbal scale		
Information	Taps general range of knowledge	On what continent is Italy?
Comprehension	Tests understanding of social conventions and ability to evaluate past experience	Why are children required to go to school?
Arithmetic	Tests arithmetic reasoning through verbal problems	How many hours will it take to drive 150 kilometres at 50 kilometres per hour?
Digit span	Tests attention and rote memory by orally presenting series of digits to be repeated forward or backward	Repeat the following numbers backward: 7 3 5 1 6 8
Vocabulary	Tests ability to define increasingly difficult words	What does "formidable" mean?
Performance scale		
Digit symbol	Tests speed of learning through timed coding tasks in which numbers must be associated with drawings of various shapes	Shown: 1 2 3 4 ○ □ △ ◇ Fill in appropriate symbol: 1 4 3 2 __ __ __ __
Picture completion	Tests visual alertness and visual memory through presentation of an incompletely drawn figure; the missing part must be discovered and named	What is missing in this picture? 
Block design	Tests ability to perceive and analyze patterns by presenting designs that must be copied with blocks	Assemble blocks to match this design: 
Picture arrangement	Tests understanding of social situations through a series of comic-strip-type pictures that must be arranged in the right sequence to tell a story	Put the pictures in the correct order: 1 2 3 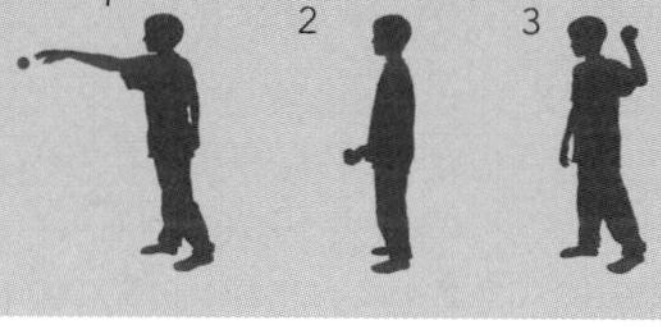

FIGURE 9.22

Sample items resembling those found on the subscales of the Wechsler Adult Intelligence Scale.

A newer version of the Stanford-Binet published in 1986 is also designed to measure more specific mental functions. It consists of 15 subtests designed to measure four areas of intellectual functioning: verbal reasoning, abstract/visual reasoning, quantitative reasoning, and short-term memory (Thorndike et al., 1986). A score similar to an IQ can be computed for each of the four intellectual domains, for any combination of them, or for the test as a whole.

Group Tests of Aptitude and Achievement

Intelligence tests such as the Stanford-Binet and the Wechsler scales are administered to an individual by a trained tester. They typically take as long as two hours to administer and therefore are impractical for large-scale screening purposes. Group tests of intelligence can be used to obtain IQ scores from groups of people at the same time, using written questions rather than the verbal ones asked by an examiner using a test like the Wechsler. Group tests such as the Lorge-Thorndike Intelligence Test and the Otis-Lennon School Ability Test are routinely used by many school districts, and you may very well have taken one of these tests during your school years.

Other group tests do not provide IQ scores, but measure specific mental skills. These include the Scholastic Aptitude Test (SAT), widely used to select college applicants in the United States; the Graduate Record Examination (GRE), used to select applicants for post-graduate study; the Medical College Admission Test (MCAT); and the Law School Aptitude Test (LSAT).

30. What is the distinction between achievement and aptitude tests? What controversy exists concerning their respective values for measuring mental skills?

Using written tests for selection purposes highlights an issue that Binet faced and that continues to plague test developers today. Should we test a person's abstract "aptitude for learning," or should we test what a person already knows? Consider an example. In selecting applicants for university, we could give students either an **achievement test** designed to find out how much they have learned in high school, or we could present them with an **aptitude test** containing novel puzzlelike problems that presumably go beyond prior learning and are thought to measure the applicant's potential for future learning and performance.

The argument for achievement testing is that it is usually a good predictor of future performance in a similar situation. The argument against achievement testing is that it assumes that everyone has had the same opportunity to learn the material being tested. In the university selection example, if there are marked differences in the quality of the high schools the applicants have attended, a person's test score could depend on whether that person went to a good school rather than on his or her ability to learn in university.

The argument for aptitude testing is that it is "fairer," since aptitude tests are supposed to depend less on prior knowledge than on a person's ability to react to the problems presented on the test. The argument against aptitude testing is that it is difficult to construct a test that is independent of prior learning. When such a test is constructed, it may require an "ability to deal with puzzles" that is not relevant to success in situations other than the test itself.

In fact, most intelligence tests measure a combination of aptitude and achievement, reflecting both native ability and previous learning. This fact has raised major scientific and social issues concerning the meaning of test scores and the usefulness of the measures for describing mental competence and predicting performance in non-test situations.

Scientific Standards for Psychological Tests

A **psychological test** is a method for measuring individual differences related to some psychological concept, or construct, based on a sample of relevant behaviour in a scientifically designed and controlled situation. In the case of intelligence testing, intelligence is the construct in question. To design a test, we need to decide which specific behaviours serve as indicators or reflections of intellectual abilities. Then we need to devise test items that allow us to assess individual differences in those behaviours. We will, of course, need evidence that our sample of items (a sample, because we can't ask every conceivable question) actually measures the abilities we are assessing. As in designing an experiment (see Chapter 2), we will want to collect that "sample of relevant behaviour" under standard conditions, attempting to control for other factors that could influence responses to the items. To understand how psychologists meet these requirements, we must examine three key measurement concepts: reliability, validity, and standardization.

Reliability

31. Define reliability and describe three different kinds of reliability that apply to psychological tests.

Reliability refers to consistency of measurement, and consistency can take several forms (Table 9.3). One is consistency over time. If you step on your bathroom scale

TABLE 9.3 Types of Reliability and Validity in Psychological Testing

Types of Reliability	Meaning and Critical Questions
Test-retest reliability	Are scores on the measure stable over time?
Internal consistency	Do all of the items on the measure seem to be measuring the same thing, as indicated by high correlations among them?
Interjudge reliability	Do different raters or scorers agree on their scoring or observations?
Types of Validity	
Construct validity	To what extent is the test actually measuring the construct of interest (e.g., intelligence)?
Content validity	Do the questions or test items relate to all aspects of the construct being measured?
Predictive validity	Do scores on the test predict some present or future behaviour or outcome assumed to be affected by the construct being measured?

five times in a row, you should expect it to register the same weight each time (unless you have a very unusual metabolism). Likewise, if we assume that intelligence is a relatively stable trait (which virtually all psychologists do), then scores on our measure should be stable, or consistent, over time. Where psychological tests are concerned, this type of measurement consistency is defined as **test-retest reliability**, and is assessed by administering the measure to the same group of participants on two separate occasions and correlating the two sets of scores.

After about age 7, scores on intelligence tests show considerable stability, even over many years (Gregory, 1999). Over a short interval (2 to 12 weeks) the test-retest correlation of adult IQs on the WAIS is .96, or nearly perfect (Wechsler, 1997). Correlations between IQs at age 9 and age 40 are in the .70 to .80 range (McCall, 1977), indicating a high degree of stability. Thus *relative to her age group,* a person who achieves an above-average IQ at age 9 is very likely also to be above the average for 40-year-olds when she reaches that age. Even during childhood, when children's cognitive skills are developing rapidly, IQs are quite stable. In one large-scale study, test-retest correlations of .87, .87, and .91 were found for Wechsler Verbal, Performance, and Full-Scale IQs, respectively, over an interval of nearly three years (Canivez & Watkins, 1998).

Another form of reliability, **internal consistency**, has to do with consistency of measurement *within* the test itself. If a test is internally consistent, all of the items within a test are measuring the same thing. For example, the items on the Vocabulary subtest of the Wechsler test all correlate highly with one another.

Finally, **interjudge reliability** refers to consistency of measurement when different people score the same test. Ideally, two different psychologists who independently score the same test would assign exactly the same scores. To attain high interjudge reliability, the scoring instructions must be so explicit that trained professionals will use the scoring system in the same way.

Validity

Validity refers to how well a test actually measures what it is designed to measure. As in the case of reliability, there are several types of validity (Table 9.3).

32. Define validity and distinguish between construct, content, and predictive (criterion-related) validity.

Is this test actually measuring intelligence, or is it measuring something else? Such a question addresses the issue of **construct validity**. If an intelligence test had perfect construct validity, individual differences in IQs would be due to differences in intelligence and nothing else. This ideal is never attained, for other factors such as motivation and educational background also influence test scores.

Two other kinds of validity contribute to construct validity. **Content validity** refers to whether the items on a test measure all the knowledge or skills that are assumed to comprise the construct of interest. For example, if we want the Arithmetic subtest of the WAIS-III to measure general mathematical reasoning skills, we would not want that subtest to have only addition problems; we would want the items to sample other relevant mathematical abilities as well.

33. How well do intelligence tests predict academic and job performance?

If an intelligence test is valid, the IQ it yields should allow us to predict other behaviours that are assumed to be influenced by intelligence, such as school grades or job performance. These outcome measures are called *criterion* measures.

Predictive validity is defined by how highly test scores correlate with, or can predict, criterion measures. Thus we could determine how well your IQ predicts your current or future university grades.

Intelligence tests were originally developed to predict academic and other forms of achievement. How well do they do so? Correlations of IQ with school grades are in the +.60 range for high school students and in the +.30 to +.50 range for university students (Aiken, 1999). In general, then, people who score well on the tests tend to do well academically. Likewise, university admission tests used in the United States (such as the SAT) do predict grades in university, with correlations slightly below +.50 (Willingham et al., 1990). This correlation, which is about the same magnitude as the correlation between people's height and weight, is high enough to justify using the tests for screening purposes, but low enough to suggest the use of other predictors (such as high school grades) in combination with SAT scores. After all, would you let a tailor design a $600 suit of clothes on the basis of your height alone?

Intelligence test scores also predict military and job performance, yielding correlations of +.20 to +.50 with various measures of job performance across different occupations (Hartigan & Wigdor, 1989; Hunter & Hunter, 1984). Generally, intelligence tests are better at predicting academic success (which requires the kinds of cognitive skills they measure) than job success, which may require other skills as well. However, they are far from perfect predictors in any achievement domain. In many performance settings, including university, a certain level of intellectual ability is needed to survive, but for people who have that requisite level, other factors, such as motivation and work habits, may assume greater importance.

FIGURE 9.23

When administering intelligence tests, psychologists use consistently applied instructions and procedures in order to create a standardized testing environment.

Standardization and Norms

The third measurement requirement, **standardization**, has two facets. The first has to do with creating a well-controlled, or *standardized*, environment for administering the intelligence test so that other uncontrolled factors will not influence scores. Tests such as the Stanford-Binet and Wechsler scales have very detailed instructions that must be closely adhered to, even to the point of reading the instructions and items to the person being tested (Figure 9.23).

34. What are the two meanings of the term standardization?

The second aspect of standardization is especially important in providing a meaningful IQ score. It involves the collection of **norms**, or test results derived from a large sample that represents particular age segments of the population. These normative scores provide a basis for interpreting a given individual's score, just as the distribution of scores in a course exam allows you to determine how well you did relative to your classmates.

When norms are collected for mental skills (and for many other human characteristics), the scores usually form a bell-shaped curve known as a **normal distribution**, with most scores clustering around the centre of the curve. On intelligence tests, the centre of the distribution for each age group from childhood to late adulthood is assigned an IQ score of 100. Because the normal distribution has known statistical properties, we can specify what percentage of the population will score higher than a given score. Thus, as Figure 9.24 shows, an IQ score of 100 cuts the distribution in half, with an equal percentage of the population scoring above and below this midpoint. The farther we move in either direction from this average score of 100, the fewer people attain the higher or lower scores. The figure also shows the percentage of people who score above certain IQ levels. On modern intelligence tests, this method of assigning an IQ score has replaced the original formula of mental age divided by chronological age.

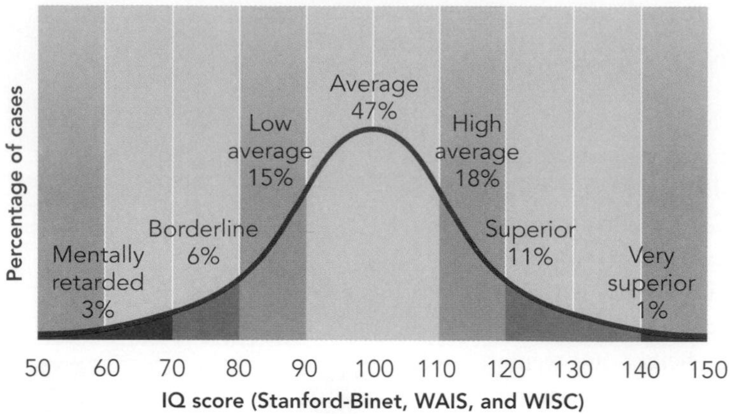

FIGURE 9.24

When administered to large groups of people, intelligence tests yield a normal, or bell-shaped, distribution of IQ scores that has known statistical properties. The mean of the distribution is set at 100. It is possible to specify for any given score what percentage of the standardization group achieved higher or lower scores. Common descriptive labels are shown relative to the bell-shaped distribution. The range of scores from 90 to 110 is labelled average and includes nearly half of the population.

The relative nature of the IQ has important implications for interpreting the meaning of intelligence test scores. Consider two people, one with an IQ of 150 and another with an IQ of 75. Because the scores are computed relative to a population norm, it makes no sense whatsoever to say that the first person is "twice as intelligent" as the second. What can be said is that in a random sample of 100 people we would expect only 1 person to have a score higher than 150, while 95 people would have a score higher than 75.

The Nature of Intelligence

Two major approaches have been taken to studying intelligence. The *psychometric approach* attempts to map the structure of intellect and to specify the kinds of mental ability that underlie test performance. Is intelligence a single dimension of general mental competence, or is it a loose collection of very specific abilities? A second approach, the *cognitive processes approach,* studies the specific thought processes that underlie mental competencies.

35. Differentiate between the psychometric and cognitive psychology approaches to intelligence.

The Psychometric Approach: The Structure of Intellect

Psychometrics is the statistical study of psychological tests. Thus standardization, reliability, and validity are all psychometric concepts. The psychometric approach to intelligence tries to identify and measure the abilities that underlie individual differences in performance on intelligence tests. In essence, the psychometric approach tries to produce a measurement-based map of the mind.

One of the major tools used by psychometric researchers is **factor analysis**, which analyzes patterns of correlations between test scores in order to discover clusters of measures that correlate highly with one another but not with measures in other clusters. When such clusters, or factors, are found, the investigator tries to decide what common underlying ability accounts for the high correlations. For example, if we were to find that four different tests were highly correlated with one another and that the tests all required subjects to solve mathematical problems, we might conclude that the underlying factor is "mathematical reasoning ability." If another cluster of correlated tests all required the ability to define and use words, we might conclude that the underlying intellectual factor is "verbal ability."

Psychometric theorists disagree on the nature of intelligence. Some believe that intelligence is a single global mental capability that cuts across all of what we would call "thinking." At the other extreme are those who regard intelligence not as a unitary trait, but as a set of specific abilities to do different types of thinking.

36. What kinds of evidence gave rise to the *g* factor and specific mental abilities conceptions of intelligence?

The *g* factor: intelligence as general mental capacity. The psychometric argument for intelligence as a general ability was first advanced by the British psychologist Charles Spearman (1923), who pioneered the use of factor analysis. He observed that school grades in very different subjects, such as English and mathematics, were almost always positively correlated, but that the correlations were not perfect. Spearman found the same to be true for different types of Binet intelligence test items, such as vocabulary questions, arithmetic reasoning problems, and the ability to construct puzzles.

Faced with this pattern of results, Spearman concluded that intellectual performance is determined partly by "general intelligence" (usually indicated by the symbol *g*), and partly by whatever special abilities might be required to perform that particular task. Spearman contended that since the general factor—the *g* factor—was so important on virtually all tasks, it constituted the most important aspect of intelligence. For instance, Spearman would argue that your performance in a mathematics course would depend mainly on your general intelligence, but also on your specific ability to learn mathematics. Today, many theorists continue to believe that the *g* factor is the core of what we call intelligence (Jensen, 1998).

TABLE 9.4 Thurstone's Primary Mental Abilities

Ability Name	Description
S—Space	Reasoning about visual scenes
V—Verbal comprehension	Understanding verbal statements
W—Word fluency	Producing verbal statements
N—Number facility	Dealing with numbers
P—Perceptual speed	Recognizing visual patterns
M—Rote memory	Memorization
R—Reasoning	Dealing with novel problems

Intelligence as specific mental abilities. Spearman's conclusion concerning the *g* factor was soon challenged by L.L. Thurstone of the University of Chicago. Whereas Spearman had been impressed by the fact that scores on different mental tasks are correlated, Thurstone was impressed by the fact that the correlations are far from perfect. Thurstone concluded that human mental performance depends not on a general factor, but rather on seven distinct abilities, which he called **primary mental abilities** (Table 9.4). Contesting Spearman's position, Thurstone maintained that performance on any mental task is more influenced by the specific abilities relevant to that task than by any underlying *g* factor. Following Thurstone's lead, other investigators claimed to have found even more factors. One prominent theorist maintained that there are over one hundred distinct and measurable mental abilities (Guilford, 1967, 1998).

Despite the lack of agreement as to whether intelligence is best conceived of as a single ability that is applicable in many settings or as a set of specialized abilities, there are some trends that are found in almost every population. The clearest of these is a distinction between the ability to deal with verbal information and the ability to solve spatial-visual problems, such as the one shown in Figure 9.25. These appear to be two relatively distinct abilities. Mathematical reasoning is more strongly related to spatial-visual reasoning than it is to verbal reasoning (Hunt, 1997).

37. Differentiate between crystallized and fluid intelligence. How is their utilization related to age?

Crystallized and fluid intelligence. Current knowledge about the nature of mental abilities suggests a position intermediate between Spearman's general intelligence and Thurstone's separate factors of the mind (Hunt, 1997). This position, originally developed by Raymond Cattell (1971) and subsequently extended by John Horn (1985), accounts for the facts quite well. Horn and Cattell break down Spearman's general intelligence into two correlated (around .50) but distinct abilities (Figure 9.26). **Crystallized intelligence** is the ability to apply previously acquired knowledge to current problems. Vocabulary and information tests are good measures of crystallized intelligence. Crystallized intelligence depends in large part on the ability to retrieve information and previously learned problem-solving schemas from long-term memory (Hunt, 1997).

Cattell and Horn's second general factor is **fluid intelligence**, defined as the ability to deal with novel problem-solving situations for which personal experience does not provide a solution. It involves inductive reasoning and creative problem-solving skills such as those discussed earlier in the chapter. The four-card, Tower of Hanoi, and nine-dot problems you worked on earlier in the chapter are fluid intelligence tasks. Fluid intelligence requires the ability to reason abstractly, think logically, and manage information in working (short-term) memory so that

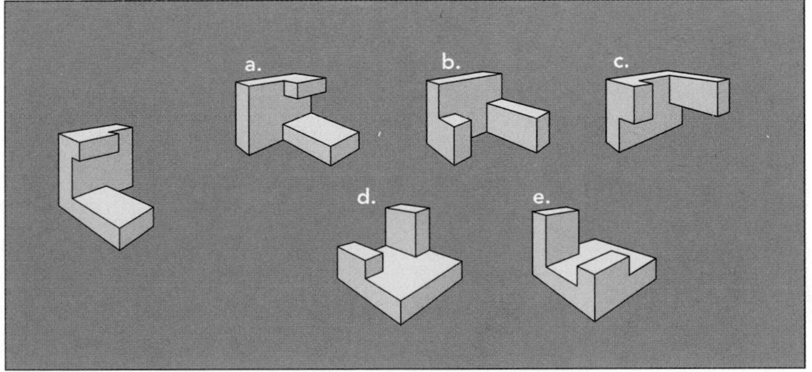

FIGURE 9.25
Spatial-visual skills are assessed with problems like this one. Which of the five objects on the right is the same as the object on the left? (The answer appears on p. 398.)

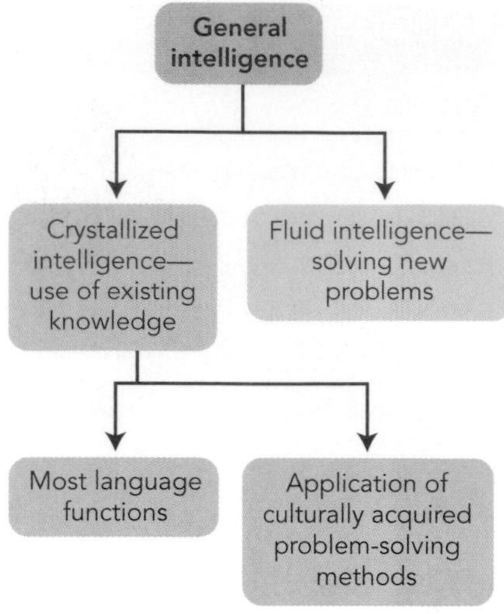

FIGURE 9.26

The structure of general intelligence, according to Cattell and Horn, includes an important distinction between crystallized and fluid intelligence.

new problems can be solved on the "blackboard of the mind" (Hunt, 1997). Thus long-term memory contributes strongly to crystallized intelligence and working memory to fluid intelligence.

Cattell and Horn argue that over our life span we progress from using fluid intelligence to depending more on crystallized intelligence. This makes sense in terms of problem-solving schemas, discussed earlier. Early in life, we encounter many problems for the first time, so fluid intelligence is needed to figure out solutions. As experience makes us more "expert," we have less need to approach each situation as a new problem. We simply call up the appropriate information and schemas from long-term memory and use them. Now we are being served by our crystallized intelligence.

Reflecting the "wisdom" of experience, performance on tests of crystallized intelligence improves or remains stable well into late adulthood. In contrast, performance on tests of fluid intelligence begins to decline as people enter late adulthood (Schaie, 1994, 1998). Thus the issue of whether intelligence declines in old age depends on whether you are talking about crystallized or fluid intelligence (Cattell, 1998). The fact that age affects the two forms of intelligence differently is additional evidence that they represent different classes of mental abilities (Weinert & Hany, 2003).

38. What types of competencies are represented in Gardner's theory of multiple intelligences?

Multiple intelligences: beyond mental competencies. All the conceptions of intelligence discussed so far view intelligence in terms of *mental* competence. Yet, if we regard intelligence as the ability to adapt to environmental demands, a broader conception beckons. Some psychologists suggest that intelligence may be conceived more broadly as relatively independent *intelligences* that relate to different adaptive demands. Harvard psychologist Howard Gardner (1983) is one of the strongest proponents of this view. Gardner has advanced a theory of multiple intelligences that defines six distinct varieties of intelligence: (1) linguistic; (2) mathematical; (3) visual-spatial; (4) musical (the ability to perceive pitch and rhythm); (5) body-kinesthetic (the ability to control body movements and skilfully manipulate objects, as might be personified in a great ballerina, athlete, or skilled surgeon); and (6) personal (understanding of ourselves and others).

The first three abilities are measured by existing intelligence tests, but the other three are not. Indeed, some of Gardner's critics insist that these abilities are not really part of intelligence. However, Gardner replies that the form of intelligence that is most highly valued within a given culture depends on the adaptive requirements of that culture. In Gardner's view, the abilities exhibited by Albert Einstein, Tiger Woods, and a "street-smart" gang leader exemplify different forms of intelligence that are highly adaptive within their respective environments (Figure 9.27). Gardner further believes that these six classes of abilities require the functioning of separate but interacting modules in the brain. He bases his argument on studies of brain damage, which often leaves some abilities devastated while sparing others, and on the characteristics of **savants.** These people are intellectually disabled in a general sense, yet they exhibit striking skills in specific areas, such as the ability to memorize hundreds of television commercials word-for-word after hearing them only once, or the ability to mentally compute mathematical problems such as the square root of 2,349,867 × 43,978. A *g* factor alone would not allow for these specific areas of extraordinary ability. Gardner's approach is provocative, but remains controversial because it goes far beyond traditional conceptions of intelligence as mental skills.

39. Describe the five abilities that constitute emotional intelligence.

Emotional intelligence. Another form of adaptive ability that is attracting the attention of psychologists relates to the emotional realm. **Emotional intelligence** involves the ability to read others' emotions accurately, to respond to them appro-

FIGURE 9.27

According to Howard Gardner, these people's abilities exemplify forms of intelligence that are not measured by traditional intelligence tests. Avril Lavigne possesses high musical intelligence, whereas Sidney Crosby and Oprah Winfrey exhibit high bodily-kinesthetic and interpersonal intelligence, respectively.

priately, to motivate oneself, to be aware of one's own emotions, and to regulate and control one's own emotional responses (Epstein, 1998; Mayer & Salovey, 1997). Proponents of emotional intelligence point to the important adaptive advantages of skills in managing the emotional challenges of daily life. Emotionally intelligent people, they suggest, form stronger emotional bonds with others, enjoy greater success in careers, marriage, and childrearing, modulate their own emotions so as to avoid strong depression, anger, or anxiety, and work more effectively toward long-term goals by being able to control impulses for immediate gratification. In the end, those high in emotional intelligence may enjoy more success in life than do others who surpass them in mental intelligence (Salovey et al., 1997).

Table 9.5 shows sample items from one recently developed measure of emotional intelligence. Scores on this measure were unrelated to cognitive measures, but did predict higher university grades. In accord with predictions, psychotherapists achieved higher emotional intelligence scores, on average, than did non-professionals, and women scored higher on the measure than did men (Schutte et al., 1998).

Critics of non-cognitive forms of intelligence are concerned that the concept of intelligence is being stretched too far from its original focus on mental ability (e.g., Cooper, 1998). Proponents respond that if we regard intelligence as adaptive abilities, we should not limit ourselves to the purely cognitive realms of human ability. This debate promises to continue into the future.

TABLE 9.5 Sample Items from a Test of Emotional Intelligence

I am aware of the non-verbal messages I send to others.
I help other people feel better when they're down.
I have control over my emotions.
I easily recognize my emotions as I experience them.
I motivate myself by imagining a good outcome to tasks I take on.
I know why my emotions change.

Note: Items are answered on a 5-point scale ranging from 1, *strongly disagree,* to 5, *strongly agree.*

Source: Schutte et al., 1998.

Cognitive Process Approaches: Processes Underlying Intelligent Thinking

Psychometric theories of intelligence are statistically sophisticated ways of describing *how* people differ from one another. What psychometric theories don't explain is *why* people vary in these ways. **Cognitive process theories** try to do so by relating the types of individual variation described in the psychometric approach to the cognitive skills presented in the first part of the chapter. Recall that this was the logic behind Galton's early attempts to relate thinking ability to speed of reaction and sensory acuity.

Sternberg's triarchic theory. Robert Sternberg (1998) is a leading proponent of the cognitive processes approach to intelligence. His **triarchic theory of intelligence** addresses both the psychological processes involved in intelligent behaviour and the diverse forms that intelligence can take. Sternberg's theory divides the

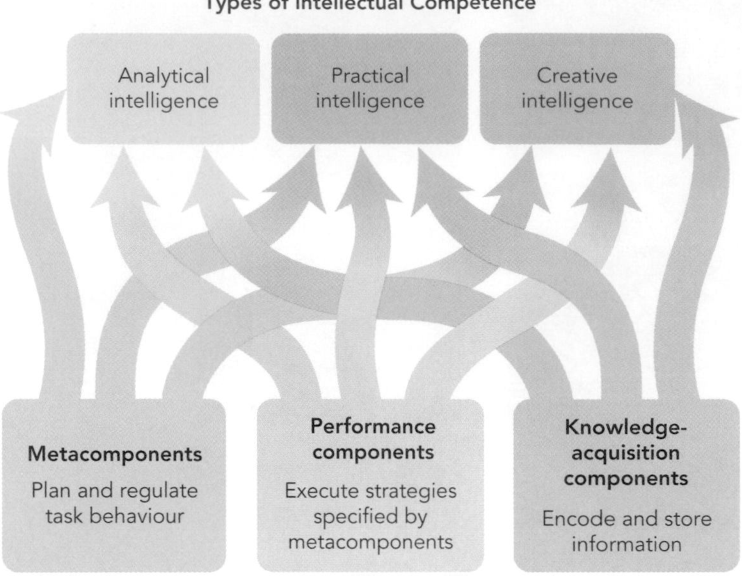

FIGURE 9.28

Sternberg's theory of intelligence deals with the specific cognitive processes assumed to underlie intelligent behaviour, and it illustrates the current interest of cognitive psychology in underlying processes.

40. What are the three levels of psychological processes that underlie intelligence in Sternberg's triarchic theory? What are the three different kinds of "intelligence"?

cognitive processes that contribute to intelligent behaviour into three specific classes: metacomponents, performance components, and knowledge acquisition components (Figure 9.28).

Metacomponents are the higher-order processes used to plan and regulate task performance. They include the problem-solving skills discussed earlier in the chapter: identifying problems, formulating hypotheses and strategies, testing them logically, and evaluating performance feedback. Sternberg believes that metacomponents are the fundamental sources of individual differences in fluid intelligence. He finds that intelligent people spend more time framing problems and developing strategies than do less intelligent people, who have a tendency to plunge right in without sufficient forethought.

The second-level components, **performance components**, are the actual mental processes used to perform the task. They include perceptual processing, retrieving appropriate memories and schemas from long-term memory, and making responses. The third-level components are **knowledge-acquisition components**, which allow us to learn from our experience, store information in memory, and combine new insight with previously acquired information. These abilities underlie individual differences in crystallized intelligence. Thus Sternberg's theory addresses the processes that underlie the important distinction made by Cattell and Horn between fluid and crystallized intelligence.

Sternberg's theory also addresses intelligent behaviour as it relates to the individual's culture and environment. Sternberg (1986, 1998) suggests that environmental demands may call for three different manifestations of intelligence, and that people differ in their intellectual strengths in these areas:

1. *Analytical* intelligence involves the kinds of academically oriented problem-solving skills assessed by traditional intelligence tests.
2. *Practical* intelligence refers to the skills needed to cope with everyday demands and to manage oneself and other people effectively. Emotional intelligence would fall within this category.
3. *Creative* intelligence is the mental skills needed to deal adaptively with novel problems.

Sternberg has shown that these forms of intelligence, while having a modest underlying *g* factor, are distinct from one another. Consider, for example, the relation between academic and practical skills. In one study, Kenyan adolescents were given one set of tests measuring traditional academic knowledge and another set measuring their knowledge of natural herbal medicines used to treat illnesses, a kind of knowledge viewed by villagers as important to their survival. The results indicated that the practical intelligence measure of herbal knowledge was unrelated to (and sometimes negatively correlated with) the academic measures (Sternberg et al., 2001).

Sternberg believes that educational programs should teach all three classes of skills, not just the analytical/academic skills. In studies with elementary school children, he and his colleagues have shown that a curriculum that also teaches practical and creative skills results in greater mastery of course material than does a traditional, analytic, memory-based approach to learning course content (Sternberg et al., 1998). As Sternberg's work illustrates, cognitive science is leading us in a new direction in which the focus is on understanding and enhancing the mental processes that underlie intelligent behaviour.

Galton resurrected: intelligence and neural efficiency. The scientific study of intelligence began in part with Sir Francis Galton's attempts to develop measures of nervous system efficiency that might underlie mental skills. As noted earlier, these attempts fell into disfavour because scores on his measures were unrelated to one another and to external criteria of success. As tools for directly measuring brain functions become more sophisticated, however, Galton's legacy lives on in current attempts to relate neural measures to IQ (e.g., Posthuma et al., 2001; 2002).

41. What evidence is there that intelligence might involve neural efficiency?

Two types of evidence suggest that this line of research may bear fruit. The first comes from electrophysiological studies of brain responses to visual and auditory stimuli. Modest relations have been shown between traditionally measured IQ and both the nature and speed of the brain's electrical response to stimuli. These electrical responses may reflect the speed and efficiency of information processing in the brain (Barrett & Eysenck, 1992; Caryl, 1994).

The second line of evidence comes from studies of brain metabolism. PET scans of people's brains taken while they engage in problem-solving tasks have shown lower levels of glucose consumption in people of high intelligence, suggesting that their brains are working more efficiently and expending less energy (Haier et al., 1993). Whether these findings herald a new way of measuring intelligence is an unanswered question. The proof of this pudding will be in the ability of such measures to predict external achievement criteria, as traditional intelligence tests do.

FOCUS ON NEUROSCIENCE

The Neuroscience of Brain Size: Is Bigger Better?

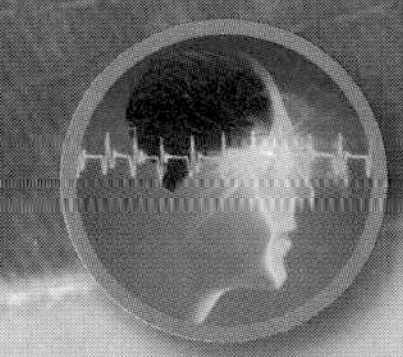

The brain is clearly the locus of intellectual activities. As noted in Chapter 3, evolutionary evidence indicates a progressive increase in brain size as humanoid species evolved over the ages. Particularly evident is growth in the parts of the brain involved in higher mental functions, especially the cerebral cortex and frontal lobes (Kolb & Whishaw, 2001). Not suprisingly, therefore, scientists have entertained the hypothesis that within a given species, individual differences in brain size might be related to intellectual competency.

One intriguing way of testing this hypothesis might be to study the brains of dead geniuses to see if they differ from the brains of less brilliant people and, if so, how. Consider, for example, Albert Einstein's brain. After Albert Einstein's death in 1955, a Missouri physician removed and preserved his brain. The brain has undergone several analyses by neuroscientists over the years. Based on your knowledge of brain functions, what differences would you expect to find?

Perhaps Einstein's brain should be larger than average, at least in the areas related to his notable abilities. The examinations have shown that Einstein's brain was not larger than average overall; it was actually smaller than average in some regions. But it was indeed bigger in some ways. His parietal lobes were densely packed with both neurons and glial cells (which produce nutrients for neurons and support them). As a result, his parietal lobes were about 15 percent wider than normal. So densely was this brain area packed that some major fissures were no longer visible. Significantly, this area of the brain is involved in mathematical thinking and visual-spatial functions—precisely the kinds of abilities that seemed to underlie his creative genius (Witelson et al., 1999; 2006).

These findings are intriguing, but are you ready to conclude that the larger your brain is, the more intelligent you're likely to be? If so, consider these points: Women and men have virtually identical mean IQs, but women's brains are smaller on average (Ankney, 1992). Other research, beginning with Galton's, indicates that brain size is pretty much unrelated to intelligence. It's not how large your brain is but how efficiently it functions, and it is the efficiency question that drives today's research.

–Continued

The size of certain brain areas may indeed result in more efficiency on certain types of tasks. Haier et al. (2005) have shown that there are different amounts of white and grey matter devoted to intelligence in men and women. In general, men have about 6.5 times as much grey matter (related to general intelligence) as women do, but women have almost 10 times the amount of white matter. Thus, it would appear that males have greater information processing capacity, but women have superior connectivity. This could well explain reported sex differences in cognitive abilities (see the Research Foundations box). In addition, the areas related to general intelligence tended to be more centralized (e.g., in the frontal lobe) in women than in men. These anatomical differences would appear to occur early in biological development (Schmithorst & Holland, 2007).

In Review

- *The psychometric approach to intelligence attempts to map the structure of intellect and establish how many different classes of mental ability underlie test performance. A newer approach, the cognitive processes approach, focuses on the specific thought processes that underlie mental competencies.*
- *Spearman believed that intelligence is determined both by specific cognitive abilities and by a general intelligence (g) factor that constitutes the core of intelligence. Thurstone disagreed, viewing intelligence as a set of specific abilities. Thurstone's position is best supported by observed distinctions between verbal and visual-spatial abilities.*
- *Cattell and Horn have differentiated between crystallized intelligence, the ability to apply previously learned knowledge to current problems, and fluid intelligence, the ability to deal with novel problem-solving situations for which personal experience does not provide a solution. They argue that over our life span, we show a progressive shift from using fluid intelligence to using crystallized intelligence as we attain wisdom.*
- *Gardner and Sternberg maintain that there are distinct forms of intelligence beyond the traditional concept. Emotional intelligence refers to people's ability to read and respond appropriately to others' emotions, to motivate themselves, and to be aware of and in control of their emotions.*
- *Cognitive process theories of intelligence have focused on the elementary information-processing abilities that contribute to intelligence. Sternberg's triarchic theory of intelligence includes a components subtheory that addresses the specific cognitive processes that underlie intelligent behaviour. Recent physiological evidence suggests that the brains of intelligent people may function more efficiently.*

Influences on Intelligence

Cultural and Group Differences in Intelligence

> We know that you highly esteem the kind of learning taught in those colleges. . . . But you, who are wise, must know that different nations have different conceptions of things: and you will not therefore take it amiss, if our ideas of this kind of education happen not to be the same with yours. We have had some experience of it; several of our young people were formerly brought up at the colleges of the Northern provinces; they were instructed in all your sciences; but, when they came back to us, they were bad runners, ignorant of every means of living in the woods, unable to bear either cold or hunger, knew neither how to build a cabin, take a deer, nor kill an enemy, spoke our language imperfectly, were therefore neither fit for hunters, warriors, nor counselors; they were totally good for nothing. . . . We are, however not the less obligated by your kind offer, though we decline accepting it; and to show our grateful sense of it, if the gentlemen of Virginia will send us a dozen of their sons, we will take care of their education, instruct them in all we know, and make men of them. (A Native American leader quoted in Benjamin Franklin's *Remarks Concerning the Savage of North America* [1784]).

This response to a well-intentioned offer by colonists to provide Native American children with access to White educational opportunities reminds us that if we view intelligence as adaptive behaviour, people in other cultures might have an entirely different conception concerning which behaviours are "intelligent" ones. Thus intelligence is in some respects a cultural construction, based on the adaptive demands that confront a culture and the behaviours that are required to cope with those demands. Consider, for example, what the items on an intelligence test constructed within that Native American culture might be like. Undoubtedly, they would bear little resemblance to Wechsler intelligence test items.

Ethnic group differences. Some of the most controversial debates in psychology have concerned the existence and meaning of ethnic and racial group differences in intelligence. Discussions of intellectual differences between ethnic groups (and between men and women) touch on deeply held notions of social equality. Consider the case of J. Philippe Rushton at the University of Western Ontario. Rushton (1995) suggested that on over 60 measures ranging from intelligence to brain size to a host of physical and social variables there was a consistent pattern: Individuals of East Asian descent scored the "highest," those of African descent scored the "lowest," and Caucasians fell in the middle. There was an immediate flurry of political activity following his announcement of these findings at a conference. Rushton was investigated by both the Ontario Provincial Police and the Ontario Human Rights Commission. The Premier called for his dismissal, and the university was forced to cancel all classes taught by Rushton due to safety considerations. Over the past decade, there have been many supporters of Rushton's right to publish articles on these matters, while many others have argued that the work encourages hatred and, consequently, violates the Ontario Human Rights code.

Are there consistent differences in intelligence among various ethnic and national groups? The data are mixed. Some national comparisons indicate that Japanese children have the highest mean IQ in the world (Hunt, 1995; Lynn, 1982). Their mean score of 111 places 77 percent of Japanese children above the mean scores of North American and European children. In addition, reports from a number of surveys indicate that East Asian populations score the highest on a variety of intelligence tests (e.g., Herrnstein & Murray, 1994; Lynn & Vanhanen, 2002). Other authors (e.g., Flynn, 1991) suggest that the mean IQ for Japanese children is more modest (between 101 and 105); some report no difference at all between Asian and North American samples (Stevenson et al., 1995).

42. What differences are found in the average IQ between ethnic groups in the United States?

Within the United States, there are reports of significant ethnic group differences in school grades and standardized tests of achievement with Asian-Americans scoring higher than other groups and African-Americans scoring the lowest. Does this reflect actual differences in intelligence? Asian-Americans test somewhat above the White norms, especially on tests related to visual-spatial and mathematical reasoning. Flynn (1991) reports that Asian-Americans actually score slightly below the mean of 100 for Whites. African-Americans score, on average, 12 to 15 IQ points below the White American average (Jencks et al, 1998). This, of course, does not mean that all Whites test lower than all Asians, or that all Blacks test lower than the other ethnic groups; in all groups, some individuals score at the highest levels. Nonetheless, the average group differences may be large enough to have practical consequences. The unanswered question is where these differences come from (see Fish, 2002). For example, many anthropologists and geneticists would argue that the concept of "race" is no longer a meaningful scientific category. There may be genetic influences in intelligence, but it is not possible to attribute these to race or ethnic group per se.

43. How well do intelligence tests predict the performance of different ethnic groups?

Keep in mind that these findings apply to test scores, which are the standard operational definition of the construct we call intelligence. Concerns have been expressed that these tests underestimate the mental competence of minority group members because the tests are culturally biased, based on Euro-American White culture. But defenders of the tests point out that racial differences appear throughout intelligence tests, not just on those items that would, on their face, appear to be culturally biased (Jensen, 1980, 1998). Second, they point out that intelligence test scores predict the performance of minority group members as well as they predict White performance (Barrett & Depinet, 1991; Hartigan & Wigdor, 1989). For example, even though African-Americans as a group score lower than Whites, the tests predict academic and occupational performance equally well for both racial groups, indicating that they are measuring relevant mental skills (Hunt, 1995).

The next dispute about racial differences is a rather different one. The nature–nurture argument tentatively accepts the differences in measures of mental abilities as being real and then asks why they exist. Consider the differences between White Americans and African-Americans. On the nurture side, there is no question that a higher proportion of African-American than White children in the United States are raised and schooled in environments that do not optimize the development of cognitive skills. However, social changes over the past 25 years have provided African-Americans with greater access to educational and vocational opportunities and have coincided with a reduction in the IQ difference between African-Americans and White Americans (Jencks et al., 1998). These shrinking ethnic differences also extend to reading and mathematics achievement tests in grades 1 through 12, as well as to scores on the SAT (Block, 2002). People who are impressed by this decreasing test gap tend to attribute racial differences to environmental differences that can be changed (Grigorenko, 2003; Nisbett, 1998). Meredith Phillips and her co-workers (1998) analyzed a wide range of family environment factors in relation to intellectual differences between five- and six-year-old African-American and White children. They concluded that family environment factors alone could account for about two-thirds of the test score gap. Figure 9.29 provides an agricultural analogue of how an environment could produce group differences, even for a genetically affected variable.

44. Are IQ differences between Blacks and White increasing or decreasing? What does this imply?

The key role played by the cultural environment also may be illustrated by a historical example involving a different minority group. Early in the twentieth century, the average Italian-American child had an IQ of 87, about the same as the average

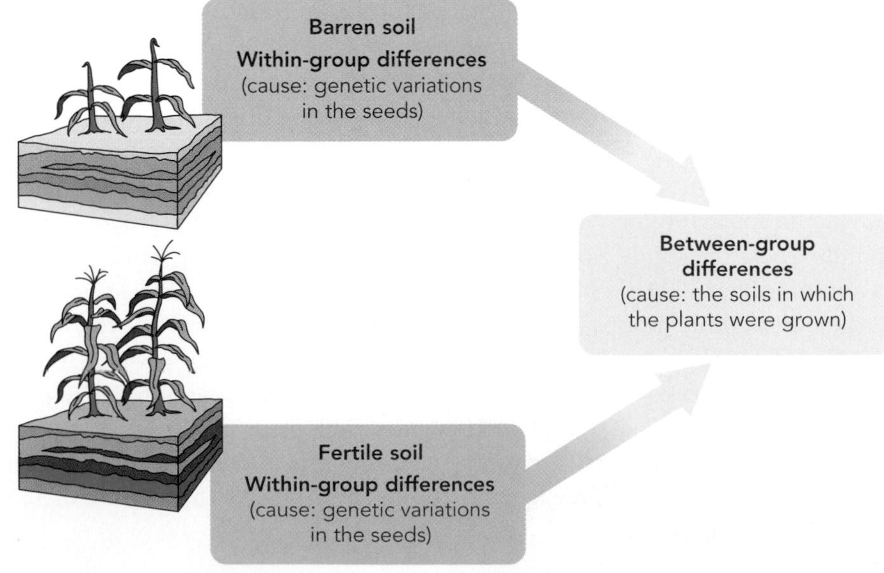

FIGURE 9.29

The interaction of heredity and environment is shown in this agricultural analogy. Seeds planted in a fertile field will produce, on average, larger plants than those planted in poor soil. This between-groups variability is attributable to environment. Within each field, however, plants also will differ in size as a result of genetic factors. Applied to intelligence, this analogy indicates how between-group differences could result from environmental factors despite the fact that intelligence has a strong genetic component.

score of African-Americans today. Henry Goddard (1917), a leading hereditarian researcher of the time, concluded that 79 percent of Italian-American immigrants were "feeble minded" and posed a danger to the gene pool of the United States. Today the average Italian-American student obtains an above-average IQ (Ceci, 1996). Obviously, genetic changes could not produce a result of this size in such a short time. Cultural assimilation and educational and economic opportunity seem much more reasonable explanations for this pronounced increase in test scores.

Another factor worth noting is a tendency, even among some scientists, to overemphasize genetic differences between groups. Indeed, when measured directly, gene differences tend to be greater *within* any given racial group than they are between racial groups (Block, 2002). For example, both Blacks and Whites exhibit greater genetic variation among themselves than exists between the average Black and the average White.

The differential between the mean intelligence test scores of Blacks and Whites (about one standard deviation, although it may be diminishing) does not result from any obvious biases in test construction and administration, nor does it simply reflect differences in socio-economic status. Explanations based on factors of caste and culture may be appropriate, but so far have little direct empirical support. There is certainly no support for a genetic interpretation. At present, no one knows what causes this differential.

45. What are the major differences between men and women in cognitive skills? What biological and environmental factors might be responsible for them?

Sex differences in cognitive abilities. Men and women differ in physical attributes and reproductive function. They also differ in their abilities to perform certain types of intellectual tasks. The gender differences lie not in levels of general intelligence but, rather, in the patterns of cognitive skills that men and women exhibit. These ability differences have been reported quite consistently by researchers (Halpern, 2000; Hampson & Kimura, 1992).

Figure 9.30 summarizes the most consistent differences, though most of them are relatively small. Men, on average, tend to outperform women slightly on certain

Problem-solving tasks favouring women

Women tend to perform better than men on tests of perceptual speed, in which people must rapidly identify matching items—for example, pairing the house on the far left with its twin.

On some tests of ideational fluency, for example those in which people must list objects that are the same colour, and on tests of verbal fluency, for example those in which participants must list words that begin with the same letter, women also outperform men.

L _ _ _	Limp, Livery, Love, Laser, Liquid, Low, Like, Lag, Live, Lug, Light, Lift, Liver, Lime, Leg, Load, Lap, Lucid . . .

Problem-solving tasks favouring men

Men tend to perform better than women on certain spatial tasks. They do well on tests that involve mentally rotating an object or manipulating it in some fashion such as choosing which of the three objects at right is the same as the one on the left.

Men also are more accurate than women in target-directed motor skills, such as guiding or intercepting projectiles.

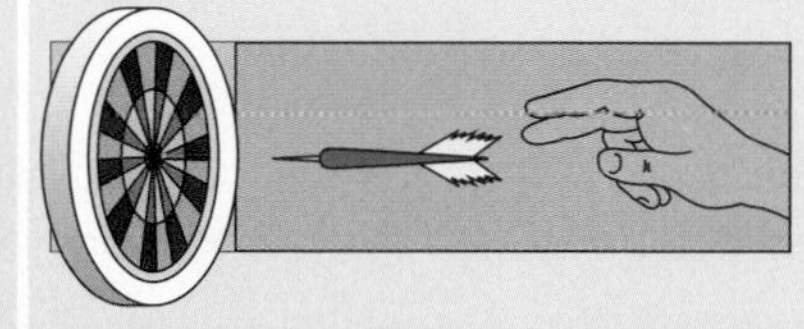

FIGURE 9.30

Gender differences in cognitive abilities reported in the scientific literature.

Source: Kimura, 1992; reprinted by permision.

spatial tasks; they are more accurate in target-directed skills, such as throwing and catching objects; and they tend to perform slightly better on tests of mathematical reasoning. Women, on average, perform better on tests of perceptual speed, verbal fluency, mathematical calculation, and precise manual tasks requiring fine motor coordination (Collins & Kimura, 1997). Keep in mind, however, that men and women also vary considerably among themselves in all of these skills, and the performance distributions of males and females overlap considerably.

Explanations for these gender differences have emphasized both biological and environmental factors. The environmental explanations typically focus on the socialization experiences that males and females have as they grow up, especially the kinds of sex-typed activities that boys and girls are steered toward (Crawford & Chaffin, 1997). Until relatively recently, for example, boys were far more likely to play sports that involve throwing and catching balls, which might help account for their general superiority in this ability.

Biological explanations have increasingly focused on the effects of hormones on the developing brain (Halpern & Tan, 2001). These influences begin shortly after conception when, during a critical period, the sex hormones establish sexual differentiation. The hormonal effects go far beyond reproductive characteristics, however. They also alter brain organization and appear to extend to a variety of behavioural differences between men and women, including aggression and problem-solving approaches (Nelson & Luciana, 2001). One intriguing finding is that fluctuations in women's hormonal levels during the menstrual cycle are related to fluctuations in task performance. This research is discussed in the Research Foundations box.

RESEARCH FOUNDATIONS

Effects of Hormonal Fluctuations on Perceptual and Motor Skills

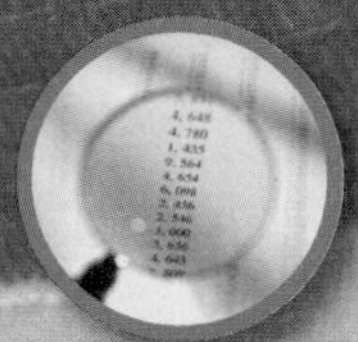

Background

Gonadal steroids have been shown to influence sex-linked behaviour in a variety of nonhuman species (e.g., Hines & Gorsky, 1985). Much of this work has focused on reproduction, but other behaviours (such as bird song) may be influenced as well. Could some of the sex differences in cognitive abilities among humans also be influenced by hormonal fluctuation? This intriguing question is addressed in the following study by Hampson & Kimura (1988).

Method

Thirty-four women with regular, spontaneous menstrual cycles were recruited for the study. The average age of the participants was 24.65 years and most (32) were right-handed. All participants were tested twice, approximately six weeks apart. For each woman, one testing session was scheduled during menstruation (day 3, 4, or 5). At this time, levels of estrogen and progesterone are low. The second testing session took place when levels of estrogen and progesterone were much higher—seven days before the onset of menstruation (the midluteal phase). Order of testing was counterbalanced across all participants.

At each of the sessions, the women completed a battery of cognitive and motor tests. These tests included the portable Rod-and-Frame test (Oltman, 1968; Witkin et al., 1962) and three tests of manual coordination. The Rod-and-Frame test requires the participant to align a rod to the true vertical position when it is presented against a tilted background. Typically, men are more accurate at this test than women are. The manual coordination tests included finger tapping (tapping a telegraph key with the index finger), pegboard assembly (inserting pegs into a board to assemble various targets), and a test of manual sequencing in which participants first learn a series of movements and are then tested under speeded conditions. The women also completed a mood inventory prior to each session.

Results

The women were significantly less accurate on the Rod-and-Frame task during the midluteal phase than during menstrua-

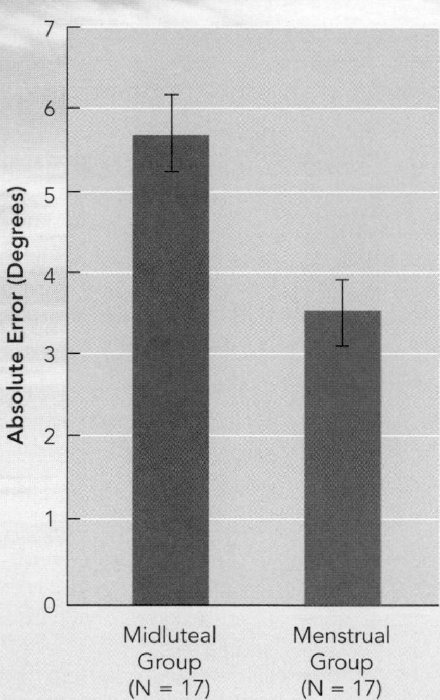

FIGURE 9.31
Rod-and-Frame performance.

tion (see Figure 9.31) The rod was set more degrees off true vertical when levels of estrogen and progesterone were high. In contrast, performance on the manual coordination tasks was better during the midluteal phase than during menstruation. Participants assembled more peg components, required less time on the speeded manual coordination task, and achieved higher accuracy during the midluteal phase. The mood inventory revealed no significant differences in affect for the two sessions. Thus, mood cannot account for any of the observed differences.

In a separate study, results were obtained for a group of women who were on oral contraceptives. Their performance on speeded tasks was even better than that of the miduteal group. This result could be expected given the elevated levels of estrogen and progestin from the oral contraceptives.

Critical Analysis

The women in this study performed differently at different phases of their menstrual cycles. When levels of estrogen and progesterone were high (midluteal phase), the women performed the tasks faster and with greater accuracy. However, when these hormonal levels were lower (during menstruation), performance declined. It is interesting to note that the size of the performance difference due to these hormonal fluctuations is about 70 percent of the reported difference between men and women on these tasks.

Kimura has also demonstrated that there are reliable differences in these skills based on sexual orientation (Hall & Kimura, 2005). On a throw-to-target task, heterosexual men outperformed heterosexual women, but gay men were less accurate than heterosexual men, and lesbian women were more accurate than heterosexual women. These results held when sports history and hand strength were controlled. Whether these observed differences in motor skills based on sexual orientation reflect biological underpinnings remains a subject for further research.

Extremes of Intelligence

Because of the many genetic and environmental influences on intelligence, there are individuals at both ends of the intelligence distribution who have exceptional mental abilities. At the low end are those labelled mentally retarded or cognitively disabled; at the upper end are the intellectually gifted.

The Cognitively Disabled

Approximately 3 to 5 percent of the North American population, or about 10 million people, are classified as mentally retarded, or cognitively disabled. The American Psychiatric Association has devised a four-level classification system that characterizes cognitive disability as mild, moderate, severe, and profound on the basis of IQ scores. Table 9.6 describes these classifications. As you can see, the vast majority are mildly disabled, obtaining IQs between about 50 and 70. Most of the mildly disabled are capable of living in the mainstream of society, given appropriate support. They are capable of marrying and holding jobs. Progressively greater environmental support is needed as we move toward the profoundly disabled range, in which institutional care is usually required.

46. What are the behavioural capabilities of mildly disabled people?

Mildly disabled children can attend school, but they have difficulty with tasks requiring reading, writing, memory, and mathematical computation. Many of their

TABLE 9.6 **Adaptive Capabilities of Cognitively Challenged People Over the Life Span**

Category	Percentage of Retarded Population	Characteristics from Birth to Adulthood: Birth through Five	Six through Twenty	Twenty-one and Over
Mild 50–70 IQ	85%	Often not noticed as delayed by casual observer, but is slower to walk, feed him- or herself, and talk than most children.	Can acquire practical skills and master reading and arithmetic to a third- to sixth-grade level with special education. Can be guided toward social conformity.	Can usually achieve adequate social, vocational, and self-maintenance skills; may need occasional guidance and support when under unusual social or economic stress.
Moderate 35–50 IQ	10%	Noticeable delays in motor development, especially in speech; responds to training in various self-help activities.	Can learn simple communication, elementary health and safety habits, and simple manual skills; does not progress in functional reading or arithmetic.	Can perform simple tasks under sheltered conditions; participate in simple recreation; can travel alone in familiar places; usually incapable of self-maintenance.
Severe 20–35 IQ	4%	Marked delay in motor development; little or no communication skill; may respond to training in elementary self-help, such as self-feeding.	Usually walks, barring specific disability; has some understanding of speech and some response; can profit from systematic habit training.	Can conform to daily routines and repetitive activities; need continuing direction and supervision in protective environment.
Profound below 20 IQ	1%	Gross disability; minimal capacity for functioning in sensorimotor areas; needs nursing care.	Obvious delays in all areas of development; shows basic emotional responses; may respond to skilful training in use of legs, hands, and jaws; needs close supervision.	May walk, need nursing care, have primitive speech; usually benefit from regular physical activity; incapable of self-maintenance.

Source: American Pyschiatric Associaton, 1994.

difficulties result from poorly developed problem-solving strategies. They often have difficulty with reasoning, planning, and evaluating feedback from their efforts (Molfese & Molfese, 2002).

Cognitive disability has a variety of causes, some genetic, some due to other biological factors, and some environmental. About 25 percent of cases have known biological causes. More than 100 different genetic causes of retardation have been identified (Shaffer, 1996). For example, Down syndrome, which is characterized by mild to severe mental retardation, is caused by an abnormal division of the 21st chromosome pair. Other genetic disorders such as Fragile-X syndrome (a disorder that takes its name from damage to the X sex chromosome) and phenylketonuria (PKU) result in increased risk of cognitive disability. Retardation also can be caused by accidents at birth, such as severe deprivation of oxygen (anoxia), and by diseases contracted from the mother during pregnancy, such as syphilis and fetal alcohol syndrome. Despite this range of potential biological causes, however, 75 to 80 percent of cases lack a clear biological cause. These cases may be due to undetectable brain damage, extreme environmental deprivation, or a combination of the two.

In the United States, federal law requires that cognitively disabled children, who were formerly segregated into special education classes, be given individualized instruction in the "least restrictive environment." This has resulted in a practice called *mainstreaming*, or inclusion programs, which allows many cognitively challenged children to attend school in regular classrooms and to experience a more normal peer environment (Gaylord-Ross, 1990). Although not embodied in Canadian federal law, similar practices are followed by all of the provinces. Each provincial education act outlines a policy of inclusion—exceptional students (whether disadvantaged or gifted) must be integrated into the regular classroom.

The Intellectually Gifted

47. What did Terman's longitudinal study of gifted children reveal about their success as adults?

Gifted individuals have a higher than normal IQ (120 or above) and show superior abilities in a particular area. Quite often, children will display giftedness in one area (e.g., art), but in others (e.g., math), their talents are average. Winner (1996) has suggested that gifted children are very alert, curious, persistent, and full of energy. They tend to begin speaking and walking earlier, read almost obsessively, and demonstrate superior memory. Abstract reasoning is good, but strangely, their handwriting is poor. The gifted child has a good sense of humour and prefers older children for playmates.

Like children at the other end of the competence continuum, gifted children often need special educational opportunities. They may become bored in regular classrooms and even drop out of school if they are not sufficiently challenged (Fetterman, 1988). In a recent study conducted at the University of Calgary, Lupart and Pyryt (1996) estimated that approximately 21 percent of a sample of 373 gifted students were actually underachieving in school. The authors suggest that their estimates are low and that the actual number is closer to 40 or 50 percent.

Like the cognitively disabled, the gifted are often the victims of stereotypes that depict them as eccentric and socially maladjusted. One of the first studies to challenge this stereotype was conducted by Lewis Terman, who helped develop the Stanford-Binet test. He identified some 1,500 California children who had an average IQ of 150 and began an extensive study of them that has continued for over 70 years. Terman and other researchers found these children to be above average not only in intelligence but also in height, weight, strength, physical health, emotional adjustment, and social maturity. They continued to exhibit high levels of adjustment throughout their adolescent and adult years. By midlife, they had authored 92 books, 2,200 scientific articles, and 235 patents. Their marriages tended to be happy and successful, and they seemed well adjusted psychologically. In essence, the gifted children became gifted and happy adults (Sears, 1977).

It would be a mistake to assume that high intelligence alone will result in the kind of eminence that we term "genius." To make enduring contributions to one's field, people are likely to need, in addition to high intelligence, exceptionally good creative problem-solving skills and high motivation to develop their gifts and to perform at an extraordinary level (Renzulli, 1986).

As we have seen, intelligent thinking and behaviour have many causal factors. Some of these factors are summarized in Figure 9.32.

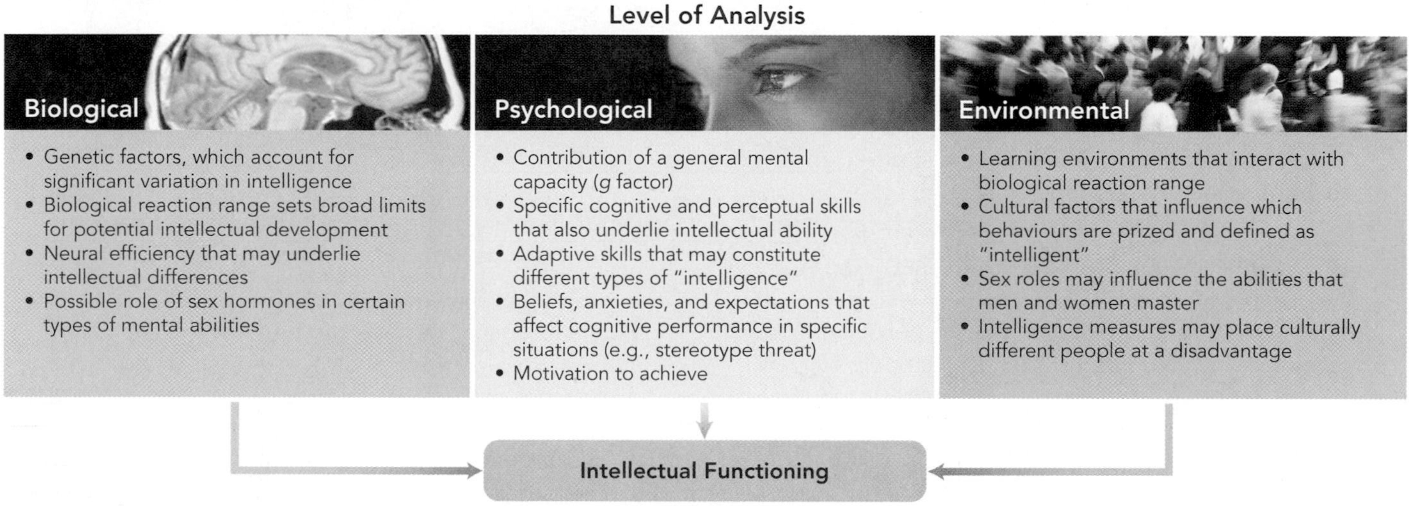

Level of Analysis

Biological	Psychological	Environmental
• Genetic factors, which account for significant variation in intelligence • Biological reaction range sets broad limits for potential intellectual development • Neural efficiency that may underlie intellectual differences • Possible role of sex hormones in certain types of mental abilities	• Contribution of a general mental capacity (*g* factor) • Specific cognitive and perceptual skills that also underlie intellectual ability • Adaptive skills that may constitute different types of "intelligence" • Beliefs, anxieties, and expectations that affect cognitive performance in specific situations (e.g., stereotype threat) • Motivation to achieve	• Learning environments that interact with biological reaction range • Cultural factors that influence which behaviours are prized and defined as "intelligent" • Sex roles may influence the abilities that men and women master • Intelligence measures may place culturally different people at a disadvantage

→ **Intellectual Functioning**

FIGURE 9.32

Understanding the causes of behaviour: factors that influence intellectual functioning.

In Review

- *Cultural and ethnic differences in intelligence exist (though they may be narrowing), but the relative contributions of genetic and environmental factors are still in question. Evidence exists supporting both genetic and environmental determinants of IQ at the individual level, but on the whole, there is no support for a genetic source of ethnic group differences in intelligence.*
- *Although the differences are not large, men tend as a group to score higher than women on certain spatial and mathematical reasoning tasks. Women perform slightly better than men on tests of perceptual speed, verbal fluency, mathematical calculation, and fine motor coordination. Both environmental and biological bases of such differences have been suggested.*
- *Cognitive disability can be caused by a number of factors. Biological causes are identified in only about 25 percent of cases. Cognitive disability can range from mild to profound. The vast majority of disabled individuals are able to function in the mainstream of society, given appropriate support.*
- *People with exceptionally high IQs are sometimes believed to have a higher frequency of social and psychological problems than do people of normal intelligence, but most adjust adequately. Lewis Terman's longitudinal study of gifted children indicated that these individuals, as a group, tended to be well adjusted and to have happy and productive adulthoods. Other personality, motivational, and environmental factors—combined with their high intelligence—also contributed to their success.*

Answers to Problems in Text

Figure 9.12 Winnipeg and St. Boniface are 50 km apart. The trains are travelling at the same speed (25 kph). Hence, they will meet at the halfway point, which is 25 km, after one hour of travel time. Since the crow is flying at 60 kph, it will have flown a total of 60 km when the trains meet.

Figure 9.16 Sequence of moves: **A** to **3**, **B** to **2**, **A** to **2**, **C** to **3**, **A** to **1**, **B** to **3**, **A** to **3**.

Figure 9.19 Here are two solutions to the nine dot problem. Both require you to "think outside the box."

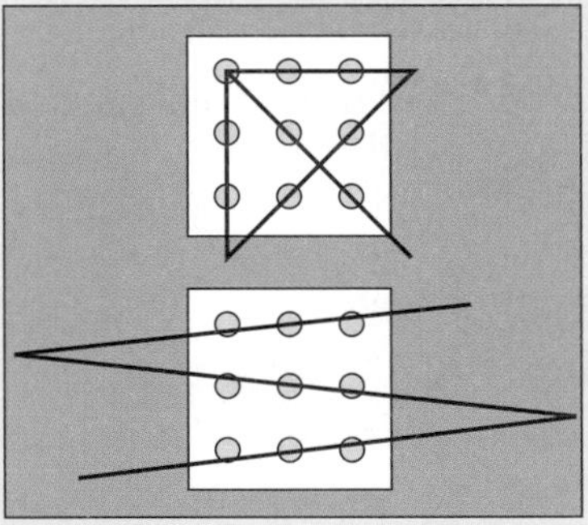

Figure 9.20 Solution to the candlestick problem:

Figure 9.25 Object **b** is identical.

GAINING DIRECTION

What are the issues?

The opening story describes the case of Kim Peek—the individual on whom Dustin Hoffman's character in the film *Rain Man* was based. Kim has savant syndrome. He can perform a number of extraordinary mental feats (such as counting), but his measured IQ is below normal. How can this be? If intelligence is a single entity, then Kim should not be able to perform lightning-fast calculations and still test below normal in intelligence. Alternatively, the way we measure intelligence might be flawed—it fails to account for Kim's abilities. But perhaps intelligence is more than a single entity. Perhaps there are many ways to demonstrate intelligent behaviour. We also may want to address the issue of autism because there is a relationship between autism and savant syndrome.

What do we need to know?

What is intelligence?
Are there competing theories of intelligent behaviour?
How do we measure intelligence?
Is the measurement of intelligence biased in any fashion?
What can savants do?
What causes savant syndrome?

Where can you find the information necessary to answer these questions?

You should have a look at the various theories of intelligence, paying particular attention to how intelligence is defined and how it is measured. How can you account for Kim's abilities? Do you need to consider the issue of multiple intelligences? Is it possible that some kind of measurement error could be involved? Information on autism and on savant syndrome would be very useful. Two excellent Internet resources are Autism Treatment Services Canada (*www.autism.ca*) and Dr. Darold Treffert's site on savant syndrome (*www.wisconsinmedicalsociety.org/savant*).

KEY TERMS AND CONCEPTS*

achievement test (381)
algorithm (371)
aptitude test (381)
availability heuristic (373)
belief bias (368)
cognitive process theories (387)
concept (362)
confirmation bias (374)
construct validity (382)
content validity (382)
crystallized intelligence (385)
deductive reasoning (366)
deep structure (355)
deviation IQ (379)
displacement (355)
divergent thinking (375)
emotional intelligence (386)
factor analysis (384)
fluid intelligence (385)
functional fixedness (375)
heuristics (371)
imaginal thought (362)
incubation (375)
inductive reasoning (366)
intelligence (377)
intelligence quotient (IQ) (378)
interjudge reliability (382)
internal consistency (382)
knowledge-acquisition components (388)
language (355)
linguistic relativity hypothesis (361)
means-ends analysis (371)
mental representations (354)
mental age (378)
mental set (370)
metacomponents (388)
morpheme (356)
motoric thought (362)
normal distribution (383)
norms (383)
performance components (388)
phoneme (356)
predictive validity (383)
primary mental abilities (385)
problem-solving schemas (370)
proposition (362)
propositional thought (362)
prototype (362)
psychological test (381)
psychometrics (384)
reliability (381)
representativeness heuristic (373)
savant (386)
semantics (355)
standardization (383)
subgoal analysis (372)
surface structure (355)
syntax (355)
telegraphic speech (359)
test-retest reliability (382)
triarchic theory of intelligence (387)
validity (382)

*Each term has been boldfaced in the text on the page indicated in parentheses.

DO YOU WANT TO ELEVATE YOUR GRADES?

For additional resources and interactive quizzing, visit the book's Online Learning Centre at **www.mcgrawhill.ca/olc/passer**.

CHAPTER 10

Motivation and Emotion

One can never consent to creep when one feels an impulse to soar.
—Helen Keller

CHAPTER OUTLINE

Dr. Larry Farwell, a former member of the Harvard Medical School, has developed a new technique for determining guilt or innocence. "Brain Fingerprinting" involves the monitoring of brain waves to determine whether or not a suspect has details of a crime or other information stored in the brain. Suspects are shown words or images that would be accessible only to someone who was actually at the scene of the crime. By monitoring brain waves, the investigator can determine whether or not the suspect recognizes these images.

Dr. Farwell's testimony was instrumental in exonerating Terry Harrington, a convicted murderer who was serving a life sentence in Iowa. Brain Fingerprinting revealed that the information in Harrington's brain did not match the details of the crime but, in fact, were consistent with his alibi. Unlike polygraph examinations, Brain Fingerprinting has been ruled admissible in U.S. courts.

- **What are the issues here?**
- **What do we need to know?**
- **Where can we find the information necessary to answer the questions?**

Sara gained 7 kg during her first year of university, thanks to late night pizza-and-beer parties. She dieted and returned to her normal weight of 52 kg. Proud of her success, 155-cm Sara continued dieting and lost 11 more kg. Her menstrual period stopped, but she was so afraid of gaining weight that she could not bring herself to eat normally. Finally, weighing 37 kg, she was hospitalized and began psychotherapy. Lisa also gained weight during her freshman year and felt like a "big fat failure." Then she began to eat lightly during the day, but binge at night on pizza and cookies. After bingeing she waited for the laxatives to kick in—the fifty laxatives she usually ate along with ten diet pills during the prior breakfast. Lisa sought help after a laxative-consuming friend suffered a heart attack at age twenty (Hubbard et al., 1999).

The term "motivation" often triggers images of people who persevere to attain their dreams and stretch the boundaries of human achievement. But to psychologists, motivational issues are broader. What motivates eating, sexual behaviour, thrill seeking, and affiliation? **Motivation** is a process that influences the direction, persistence, and vigour of goal-directed behaviour. The word *motivation* derives from the Latin term meaning "to move," and psychologists who study motivation identify factors that move us toward our goals, whether they be obtaining food, a mate, success, or even peace and quiet.

◉ PERSPECTIVES ON MOTIVATION

Psychology's diverse theoretical perspectives view motivation through different lenses. Let's examine some of their basic motivational concepts.

Instinct Theory and Evolutionary Psychology

1. According to evolutionary psychologists, how does the concept of adaptive significance help us understand human motivation?

Darwin's theory of evolution inspired early psychological views that instincts motivate much of our behaviour. An **instinct** is an inherited predisposition to behave in a specific and predictable way when exposed to a particular stimulus. Instincts have a genetic basis, are found universally among all members of the species, do not depend on learning, and have survival value for the organism. William James (1890) proposed about three dozen human instincts, and by the 1920s, researchers had proposed thousands (Atkinson, 1964).

Human instinct theories faded because there was little evidence to support them and they often relied on circular reasoning. Why are people greedy? Because greed is an instinct. How do we know that greed is an instinct? Because people are greedy. This explains nothing. Today scientists examine hereditary contributions to human motivation more productively. By conducting twin and adoption studies, behaviour geneticists seek to establish how strongly heredity accounts for differences among people in many aspects of motivated behaviour, such as tendencies to be outgoing or anti-social (Neiderhiser et al., 1999) and even, as studied by James Olson of the University of Western Ontario, attitudes towards reading books, playing organized sports, and riding roller coasters (Olson, Vernon, Harris, and Jang, 2001).

Modern evolutionary psychologists propose that many "psychological" motives have evolutionary underpinnings that are expressed through the actions of genes (Buss, 2000; Palmer & Palmer, 2002). From this perspective, the *adaptive significance* of behaviour is a key to understanding motivation. For example, why are we such social creatures? Presumably, affiliation produced survival advantages—such as shared resources and protection against predators—that afforded our ancestors a greater opportunity to pass their genes on to successive generations. Over the ages the genes of "affiliative people" made up an increasing part of the human gene pool, and we became biologically predisposed to be social rather than reclusive.

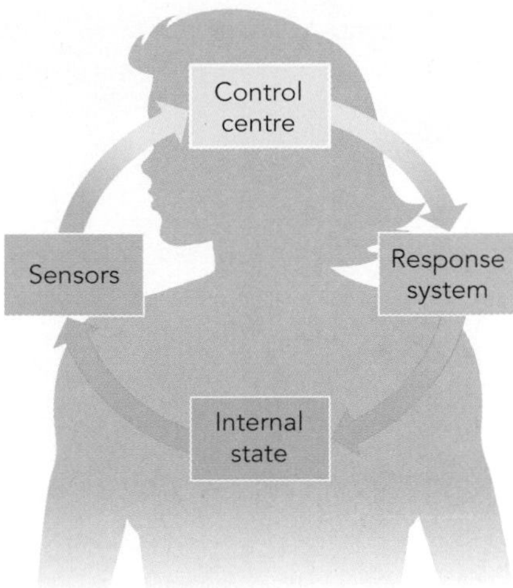

FIGURE 10.1
Your body's internal environment is regulated by homeostatic mechanisms. Sensors detect bodily changes and send this information to a control centre, which in turn regulates a response system that restores bodily equilibrium.

Homeostasis and Drive Theory

Your body's biological systems are delicately balanced to ensure survival. For example, when you are hot your body automatically tries to cool itself by perspiring. When you are cold your body generates warmth by shivering. In 1932, Walter Cannon proposed the concept of **homeostasis**, a state of internal physiological equilibrium that the body strives to maintain.

Maintaining homeostasis requires a sensory mechanism for detecting changes in the internal environment, a response system that can restore equilibrium, and a control centre that receives information from the sensors and activates the response system (Figure 10.1). The control centre functions somewhat like the thermostat in a furnace or air-conditioning unit. Once the thermostat is set at a fixed temperature, or *set point,* the sensors detect significant temperature changes in either direction. The control unit responds by turning on the furnace or air conditioner until the sensor indicates that the set point temperature has been restored, and then turns it off. Homeostatic regulation also can involve learned behaviours. When we're hot we not only perspire, but also may seek a shady place or deliciously cool drink.

According to Clark Hull's (1943, 1951) influential **drive theory** of motivation, physiological disruptions to homeostasis produce *drives,* states of internal tension that motivate an organism to behave in ways that reduce this tension. Drives such as hunger and thirst arise from tissue deficits (e.g., lack of food and water) and provide a source of energy that pushes an organism into action. Hull, a prominent learning theorist, proposed that reducing drives is the ultimate goal of motivated behaviour.

2. How are homeostatic and drive concepts of motivation related?

Homeostatic models currently are applied to many aspects of motivation, such as the regulation of hunger, thirst, body temperature, weight, and sleep (Woods & Seeley, 2002). Drive theory is, however, less influential than in the past. For one thing, people often behave in ways that seem to increase rather than reduce states of arousal, as when people skip meals in order to diet or flock to tension-generating horror movies.

Incentive and Expectancy Theories

3. According to expectancy X value theory, why might people respond differently to the same incentive?

Whereas drives are viewed as internal factors that "push" organisms into action, **incentives** represent environmental stimuli that "pull" an organism toward a goal. To a student, a good grade can be an incentive for studying.

Incentive theories focus attention on external stimuli that motivate behaviour, though historically the concepts of incentives and drives were often linked. Clark Hull (1943, 1951) argued that all reinforcement involves some kind of biological drive reduction (e.g., food is an incentive because it reduces the drive of hunger), but this view is no longer held. Modern incentive theory emphasizes the "pull" of external stimuli and how stimuli with high incentive value can motivate behaviour, even in the absence of biological need. We have all had the experience of finishing a meal, and hence having no biological need for more food, but quite happily eating dessert when someone places our favourite cake or pie on the table. In this situation, behaviour is motivated not by biological need, but by the incentive value of the external stimulus (the dessert). Incentive theories of motivation have also been powerfully applied to the study of drug abuse (Stewart, 2000; Stewart & Wise, 1992). An incentive theory of drug use argues that seeking and administering a drug is motivated by the positive incentive value of the drug's effect. Heroin users, for example, will find and inject heroin because the drug makes them feel good, not because of a biological heroin drive or a desire to escape withdrawal.

Why is it, however, that people often respond differently to the same incentive? In part to address such questions, expectancy theories of motivation include the value of incentives, but take a cognitive perspective. Incentive theories typically have had more in common with classical conditioning (e.g., Stewart, 2000) than with cognition, but expectancy theory has broken from this tradition and given a larger role to cognition. Consider James, Lenora, and Harrison, students in a calculus class who have similar math aptitude. Yet James studies hard in hopes of getting an A, whereas Lenora and Harrison put in just enough effort to pass with a C.

According to the cognitive perspective, the answer lies in their thoughts about this situation. One cognitive approach, called **expectancy × value theory**, proposes that goal-directed behaviour is jointly determined by two factors: the strength of the person's expectation that particular behaviours will lead to a goal, and the value the individual places on that goal—often called *incentive value* (Brehm & Self, 1989). These two factors are multiplied, producing the following equation: *Motivation = expectancy × incentive value.* James works hard because he believes that the more you study the greater the probability of getting an A, and he values an A highly. Lenora also believes that studying hard will lead to an A, but getting an A holds little value for her in this course. In contrast, Harrison values an A, but believes that because the tests are tricky, studying hard is unlikely to produce a high grade.

Can external incentives ever decrease motivation? Many cognitive theorists distinguish between **extrinsic motivation**, performing an activity to obtain an external reward or to avoid punishment, and **intrinsic motivation**, performing an activity for its own sake—because you find it enjoyable or stimulating. According to *the overjustification hypothesis,* giving people extrinsic rewards to perform activities that they intrinsically enjoy may "overjustify" that behaviour and reduce intrinsic motivation (Lepper et al., 1974). In essence, if we begin to perceive that we are performing for the extrinsic rewards rather than for enjoyment, the rewards will turn "play" into "work," and it might be difficult to return to "play" if those rewards were to cease.

Overall, research indicates that extrinsic rewards reduce intrinsic motivation most strongly when they are tangible (e.g., prizes or money, rather than praise), given merely for performing a task (regardless of how well), and when the performer expects rewards to be offered (Deci et al., 1999). But, when extrinsic rewards such as praise are perceived as *informative*—as a means of positive feedback rather than as an attempt to control behaviour—they can increase feelings of competence and intrinsic motivation.

Psychodynamic and Humanistic Theories

The psychodynamic and humanistic perspectives view motivation within a broader context of personality development and functioning, but take radically different approaches. Freud's (1923) psychoanalytic theory highlighted the motivational underworld. To Freud, much of our behaviour results from a never-ending battle between unconscious impulses struggling for release and psychological defences used to keep them under control. Energy from these unconscious motives—especially from instinctive sexual and aggressive drives—is often disguised and expressed through socially acceptable behaviours. Thus hidden aggressive impulses may fuel one's career as a trial attorney, businessperson, or athlete.

Although research offers little support for Freud's "dual-instinct" model, his work stimulated other psychodynamic theories that highlighted different needs, such as needs for self-esteem and relatedness to other people (Adler, 1927; Kohut,

1977). Today's diverse psychodynamic theories continue to emphasize that, along with conscious mental processes, unconscious motives and tensions guide how we act and feel (Westen, 1998). Experiments in cognitive psychology and neuroscience increasingly support this view; although, as discussed in Chapter 6, cognitive models of the unconscious differ markedly from psychodynamic ones (Bargh & Chartrand, 1999; Wenzlaff & Wegner, 2000). The nature of the unconscious within psychodynamic theory and the influence of cognitive and perceptual processes outside of conscious awareness share no real common ground.

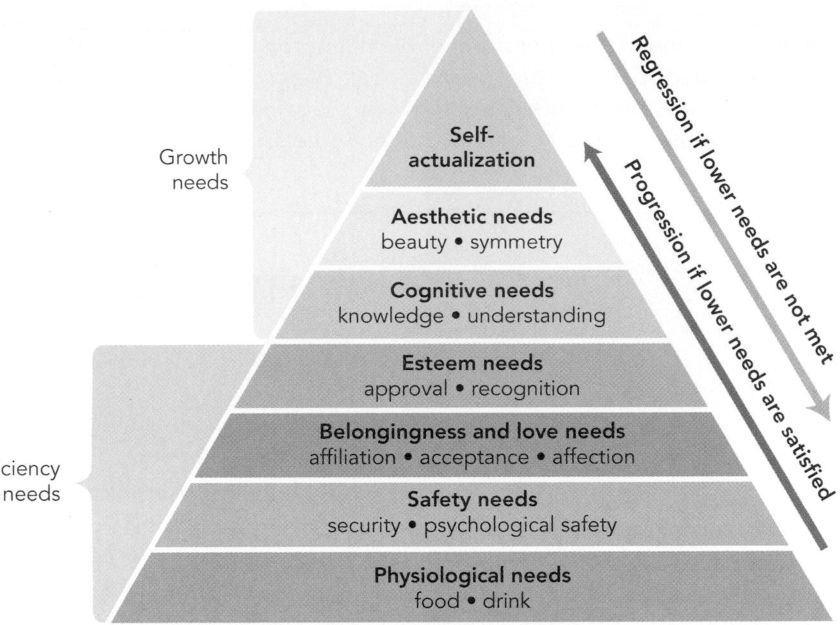

FIGURE 10.2

Maslow proposed that needs are arranged in a hierarchy. After meeting our more basic needs, we experience need progression *and focus on needs at the next level. If a need at a lower level is no longer satisfied, we experience* need regression *and focus once again on meeting that lower-level need. Critics wonder whether people might focus on belonging, love, esteem, and higher-level needs even when their physiological and safety needs are not met. What do you think?*

Humanist Abraham Maslow believed that psychology's other perspectives ignored a key motive: our striving for personal growth. Maslow (1954) distinguished between *deficiency needs,* which are concerned with physical and social survival, and *growth needs,* which are uniquely human and motivate us to develop our potential. He proposed the concept of a **need hierarchy**, a progression of needs containing deficiency needs at the bottom and growth needs at the top (Figure 10.2). Once our basic physiological needs are satisfied, we focus on our needs for safety and security. After these needs are met, we turn our attention to needs at the next highest level, and so on. **Self-actualization** represents the need to fulfill our potential, and it is the ultimate human motive. To echo an army recruiting slogan, self-actualization is striving to "be all that you can be."

Critics question the validity of Maslow's need hierarchy and believe that the concept of "self-actualization" is vague (Heylighen, 1992). How does the hierarchy explain why prisoners of war endure torture rather than betray their comrades, or why millions of women live in constant hunger in order to be thin? Still, the model draws valuable attention to the human desire for growth, incorporates a wide range of psychological and biological motives, and has influenced thinking in such diverse fields as philosophy, education, and business (Muchinsky, 2000).

4. Explain Maslow's concept of a need hierarchy. Do you agree with this model?

In sum, each of these theoretical approaches raises provocative questions about human motivation and has strong proponents and critics, just as some perspectives no doubt resonate more than others with your own views about motivation. Taken together, they underscore the complexity of behaviour and the value of studying it from multiple levels of analysis. We begin that analysis with one of our most basic motives: hunger.

In Review

- *Motivation is a process that influences the direction, vigour, and persistence of behaviour. Evolutionary psychologists propose that in our ancestral past, motivational tendencies that had adaptive significance were more likely to be passed from one generation to the next, eventually evolving into genetically based predispositions to act in certain ways.*
- *Homeostatic models view motivation as an attempt to maintain equilibrium in bodily systems. Drive theories propose that tissue deficits create drives, such as hunger, that motivate or "push" an organism from within to reduce the deficit and restore homeostasis.*

- *Incentive theories emphasize the role of environmental factors that "pull" people toward a goal. The cognitive expectancy X value theory explains why the same incentive may motivate some people, but not others.*
- *Psychodynamic theories emphasize that unconscious motives and mental processes guide much of our behaviour. Humanist Abraham Maslow proposed that needs exist in a hierarchy, from basic biological needs to the ultimate need for self-actualization.*

HUNGER AND WEIGHT REGULATION

If you could give up all food forever and satisfy your hunger and nutritional needs with a daily pill, would you? Eating is a necessity, but for many people it also is one of life's delicious pleasures. Thus, while biology provides a "push" to eat, the anticipated and actual good taste of food offers a powerful "pull" (Bolles, 1980). Indeed, numerous biological, psychological, and environmental factors regulate our food intake.

The Physiology of Hunger

Eating and digestion supply the body with the fuel it needs to function and survive. **Metabolism** is the body's rate of energy (or caloric) utilization, and about two-thirds of the energy we normally use goes to support *basal metabolism,* the resting, continuous metabolic work of body cells. Several mechanisms attempt to keep the body in energy homeostasis by regulating food intake (Kennedy, 1953; Woods & Seeley, 2002). There are "short-term" signals that start meals by producing hunger and stop food intake by producing *satiety* (the state in which we no longer feel hungry as a result of eating). Your body also monitors "long-term" signals based on how much body fat you have. These signals adjust appetite and metabolism to compensate for times when you overeat or eat too little in the short term.

Before we describe some of these signals, consider three points. First, many of us believe that hunger occurs when we begin to "run low on energy," and that we feel "full" when immediate energy supplies are restored (Assanand et al., 1998). Your body does monitor its immediate energy supplies, but this information interacts with other signals to regulate food intake. Thus hunger is not necessarily linked to immediate energy needs (Pinel, 1997; Woods et al., 1998). Second, homeostatic mechanisms are designed to *prevent* you from "running low" on energy in the first place. In evolutionary terms, an organism that does not eat until its energy supply starts to become low (in any absolute sense) would be at a serious survival disadvantage.

Finally, many researchers believe that there is a *set point*—an internal physiological standard—around which body weight (or more accurately, our fat mass) is regulated (Powley & Keesey, 1970). This view holds that if we overeat or eat too little, homeostatic mechanisms will return us close to our original weight. The set point concept is well ingrained in popular culture, but some researchers, such as John Pinel at the University of British Columbia, believe it is flawed (Pinel, 1997; Pinel, Assanand, & Lehman, 2000). They propose that, as we gain or lose weight, homeostatic mechanisms kick in and make it harder to keep gaining or losing weight, but do not necessarily return us to our original weight. Over time, we may "settle in" at a new weight.

Signals That Start and Terminate a Meal

5. Describe some physiological signals that initiate hunger.

Is hunger produced by those familiar muscular contractions ("hunger pangs") of an empty stomach? In an early experiment, A. L. Washburn showcased a unique scientific talent: He swallowed a balloon. When it reached his stomach the balloon

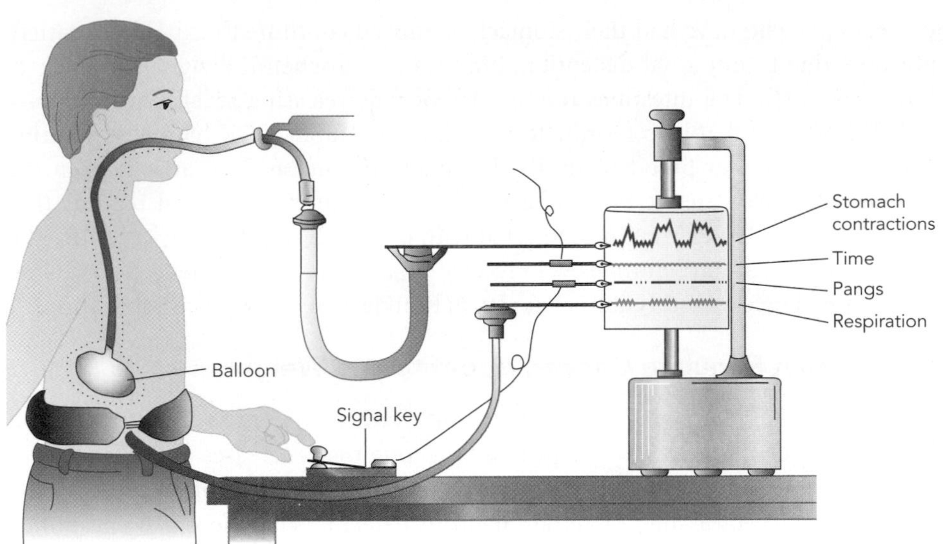

FIGURE 10.3

A. L. Washburn swallowed a balloon and inflated it in his stomach. A machine recorded stomach contractions by amplifying changes in the pressure on the balloon, and Washburn pressed a telegraph key every time he felt a hunger pang. Hunger pangs occurred when the stomach contracted.

Based on Cannon and Washburn, 1912.

was inflated and hooked up to an amplifying device to record his stomach contractions. Washburn then pressed a key every time he felt hungry (Figure 10.3). The findings revealed that Washburn's stomach contractions did indeed *correspond* to subjective feelings of hunger (Cannon & Washburn, 1912). But did they *cause* the "experience" of hunger?

Surprisingly, other research indicates that "hunger pangs" do not depend on an empty stomach, or any stomach at all! Animals display hunger and satiety even if all nerves from their stomach to their brain are cut, and people who have had their stomach surgically removed for medical reasons continue to feel hungry and "full" (Brown & Wallace, 1980). Thus, other signals must help trigger hunger.

When you eat, digestive enzymes break food down into various nutrients. One key nutrient is **glucose**, a simple sugar that is the body's (and especially the brain's) major source of immediately usable fuel. After a meal, some glucose is transported into cells to provide energy, but a large portion is transferred to your liver and fat cells, where it is converted into other nutrients and stored for later use. Sensors in the hypothalamus and liver monitor blood glucose concentrations. When blood glucose levels decrease, the liver responds by converting stored nutrients back into glucose. This produces a drop-rise glucose pattern.

6. What physiological signals cause us to stop eating?

L. Arthur Campfield and his colleagues have found that humans and rats display a temporary drop-rise glucose pattern prior to experiencing hunger (Campfield & Smith, 1990; Campfield et al., 1996). This occurs not only when glucose levels fall and rise naturally (by about 10 percent), but also when they are manipulated experimentally. The meaning of this drop-rise pattern is not certain, but it may contain information that helps the brain regulate hunger (Campfield, 1997). See Table 10.1.

As we eat, several bodily signals combine and ultimately cause us to end our meal. *Stomach and intestinal distention* are "satiety signals" (Stricker & Verbalis, 1987). The walls of these organs stretch as food fills them up, sending nerve signals to the brain. This does not mean that the stomach literally has to be "full" for us to feel satiated. Nutritionally rich food seems to produce satiety more quickly than an equal volume of less nutritious food, suggesting that some satiety signals respond to food content.

TABLE 10.1 **Some of the signals that control eating by increasing or decreasing hunger.**

Signal	Source	Effect
Glucose	blood glucose levels monitored by hypothalamus, liver	drop-rise pattern increases hunger
CCK	released into bloodstream by intestines	decreases hunger
Leptin	secreted into bloodstream by fat cells	decreases hunger
Neuropeptide Y	secreted by neurons within the PVN of the hypothalamus	increases hunger

Patients who have had their stomachs removed continue to experience satiety not only due to intestinal distention, but also due to chemical signals (Collier & Johnson, 2004). The intestines respond to food by releasing several hormones—called peptides—that help terminate a meal. For example, **CCK (cholecystokinin)** is released into your bloodstream by the small intestine as food arrives from the stomach. It travels to the brain and stimulates receptors in several regions that decrease eating. Hungry animals injected with CCK will stop feeding or reduce the size of their meals, and humans who receive small doses of peptides report feeling full after eating less food (Gibbs et al., 1973; Konkle et al., 2000). See Table 10.1.

Signals That Regulate General Appetite and Weight

7. Explain how leptin regulates appetite. How did scientists learn about leptin's role?

Fat cells are not passive storage sites for fat. Rather, they actively regulate food intake and weight by secreting **leptin**, a hormone that decreases appetite (Halaas et al., 1995). As we gain fat, more leptin is secreted into the blood and reaches the brain, where receptor sites on certain neurons detect it. These leptin signals influence neural pathways to decrease appetite and increase energy expenditure (Woods et al., 1998, 2000). See Table 10.1.

Leptin is a "background" signal. It does not make us feel "full" like CCK and other satiety signals that respond directly to food intake during a meal. Instead, leptin may regulate appetite by increasing the potency of these other signals (Woods & Seeley, 2002). Thus, as we gain fat and secrete more leptin, we tend to eat less because these mealtime satiety factors make us feel full sooner. As we lose fat and secrete less leptin, it takes more food and a greater accumulation of satiety signals to make us feel full. In essence, high leptin levels may tell the brain "There is plenty of fat tissue, so it's time to eat less."

FIGURE 10.4

The mouse on the top has an ob gene mutation. Its fat cells fail to produce leptin, and it becomes obese. Leptin injections help these mice return to normal weight.

Evidence for leptin's important role grew out of research with genetically obese mice (Coleman, 1978; Zhang et al., 1994) (see Figure 10.4). A gene called the *ob* gene (*ob* = obesity) normally directs fat cells to produce leptin, but mice with an *ob* gene mutation lack leptin. As they gain weight, their brains do not receive this "curb your appetite" signal, and the mice overeat and become obese. Daily leptin injections reduce their appetite and increase their energy expenditure, and the mice become thinner. Another strain of obese mice produces ample leptin, but because of a mutation in a different gene (the *db* gene), their brain receptors are insensitive to leptin (Chen et al., 1996; Halaas et al., 1995). The "curb your appetite" signal is there, but they can't detect it, and become obese. Injecting these mice with leptin does not reduce their food intake and weight.

Are these specific *ob* and *db* gene mutations a major source of human obesity? Probably not, for both genetic conditions seem to be rare in humans (Clement, 1999). However, when they do occur, these conditions are associated with extreme obesity, suggesting the importance of normal leptin functioning in human weight regulation. Might leptin injections be the "magic bullet" that would help most obese people lose weight? Unfortunately, there is reason for doubt, because obese people already have ample leptin in their blood due to their fat mass (Jequier & Tappy, 1999; Ravussin & Gautier, 1999). For currently unknown reasons, their brains appear to be insensitive to that information.

Brain Mechanisms

8. What evidence suggested that the LH and VMH were hunger "on" and "off" centres? What evidence suggests otherwise?

Many parts of the brain—ranging from the primitive brain stem to the lofty cerebral cortex—play a role in regulating hunger and eating (Logue, 1991). But is there a "master control centre"? Early experiments pointed to two regions in the hypothalamus (Stellar, 1954). Areas near the side, called the *lateral hypothalamus (LH)*, seemed to be a "hunger on" centre (Figure 10.5). Electrically stimulating a rat's LH causes it to start eating, and lesioning (damaging or destroying) the LH causes it to refuse to eat, even to the point of starvation (Anand & Brobeck, 1951).

In contrast, structures in the lower-middle area, called the *ventromedial hypothalamus* (VMH), seemed to be a "hunger off" centre. Electrically stimulating the VMH caused even a hungry rat to stop eating, and lesioning the VMH produced gluttons who ate frequently and doubled or tripled their body weight (Hetherington & Ranson, 1942). Medical case studies of people with damage to these hypothalamic areas also found that normal weight regulation was disrupted (Gazzaniga et al., 1979).

As scientists explored further, they learned that, although the LH and VMH played a role in hunger regulation, they were not really "hunger on" and "hunger off" centres (Pinel, 1997; Schwartz, 1984). For example, rats with LH damage stop eating and lose weight in part because they develop trouble swallowing and digesting, and they become generally unresponsive to external stimuli, not just to food. Moreover, axons from many brain areas funnel into the hypothalamus and then fan out again upon leaving it. Cutting these nerve tracts anywhere along their path—not just within the hypothalamus—duplicates some of the effects of the LH and VMH lesions (Schwartz, 1984).

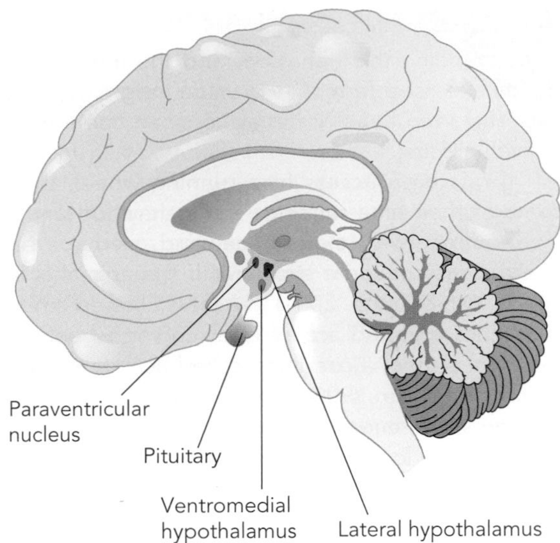

FIGURE 10.5

Various structures within the hypothalamus play a role in regulating hunger, thirst, sexual arousal, and body temperature. The lateral hypothalamus (LH), ventromedial hypothalamus (VMH), and paraventricular nucleus (PVN) are involved in hunger regulation.

Researchers are examining how various neural circuits within the hypothalamus regulate food intake. Many pathways involve the **paraventricular nucleus (PVN)**, a cluster of neurons packed with receptor sites for various transmitters that stimulate or reduce appetite (Figure 10.5). The PVN appears to integrate several different short-term and long-term signals that influence metabolic and digestive processes (Berthoud, 2002). One transmitter, *neuropeptide Y*, is a powerful appetite stimulant (Leibowitz, 1992). Rats in one experiment quickly became obese when they received three daily injections of neuropeptide Y into their PVN for 10 days. Their food intake doubled, their fat mass tripled, and their total body weight increased sixfold (Stanley et al., 1986).

A fascinating finding about leptin and the PVN in rats may help explain why we become so hungry when trying to lose weight. When leptin reaches the hypothalamus, it seems to *inhibit* the activity of neurons that release neuropeptide Y into the PVN, and therefore appetite is reduced. But when rats lose fat, less leptin is secreted and therefore neuropeptide Y neurons become more active, increasing appetite (Woods & Seeley, 2002). See Table 10.1.

RESEARCH FRONTIERS

Excessive Exercise: Activity Anorexia

At any one time, in any situation, we have a variety of behaviours we can choose from. We choose one behaviour from a range of possibilities, and as the situation changes we may switch from our previous behaviour to doing something new. Motivated behaviours such as exercise, playing video games, gambling, or eating occur as part of a range of activities in one's life, and under normal circumstances do not pose any undue threat to the individual. In some situations, however, these behaviours may become problematic. If an individual devotes excessive amounts of time and effort to their chosen activity, their behaviour can create a range of social, psychological, and health problems. One such activity that has been studied experimentally in nonhumans is wheel running by rats.

–Continued

(a)

(b)

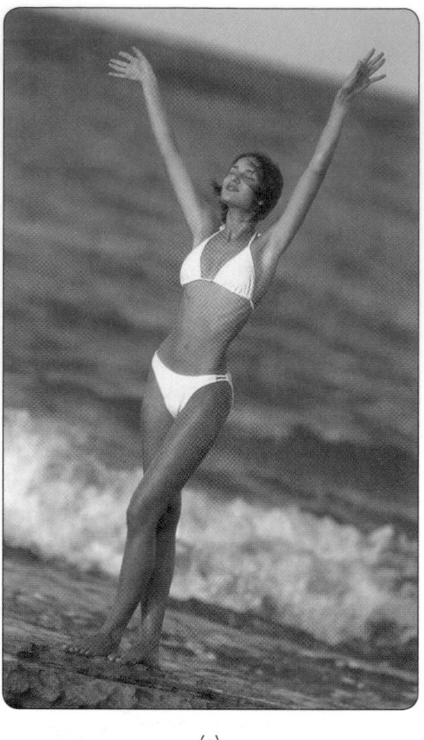

(c)

FIGURE 10.7

Throughout much of Western history, a full-bodied woman's figure was esteemed. This is illustrated by (a) Peter Paul Rubens's 17th-century painting, The Three Graces, *and by (b) actress Lillian Russell, who represented the American ideal of feminine beauty a century ago. In recent decades, the norm of "thin = attractive" has evolved, as illustrated (c) by this contemporary swimsuit model.*

hungry. Conversely, countless dieters intentionally restrict their food intake even though they *are* hungry.

Especially for women, such food restriction often stems from social pressures to conform to cultural standards of beauty (Figure 10.7). Studies of *Playboy* magazine centrefolds, beauty pageant contestants, and fashion models indicate a clear trend toward a thinner, leaner, and increasingly unrealistic "ideal" female body shape between the 1950s and 1990s (Owen & Laurel-Seller, 2000). Correspondingly, relative to men, over the past 50 years, women have become increasingly dissatisfied with their body image (Feingold & Mazzella, 1998).

A classic study by April Fallon and Paul Rozin (1985) suggests an additional reason why this is so. University women overestimated how thin they needed to be to conform to men's preferences, whereas men overestimated how bulky they should be to conform to women's preferences (Figure 10.8). Women also perceived their body shape as heavier than ideal, whereas men viewed their body shape as close to ideal. As Fallon and Rozin noted, "Overall, men's perceptions serve to keep them satisfied with their figures, whereas women's perceptions place pressure on them to lose weight" (1985, p. 102).

People who perceive themselves as heavy tend to have lower self-esteem, but this relation is stronger among women than men (Miller & Downey, 1999). According to Barbara Fredrickson and Tomi Ann Roberts's (1997) *objectification theory,* Western culture teaches women to view their bodies as objects, much as external observers would. This increases body shame and anxiety, which in turn leads to eating restriction and even eating disorders (Fredrickson et al., 1998). Laboratory experiments suggest that women do indeed restrict eating to restore self-esteem. In one experiment, university women ate less food in the presence of a desirable versus undesirable male, particularly when their feelings of femininity had been publicly threatened beforehand (Mori et al., 1987).

The norms that "thin = attractive" and "you can never be too thin" are strongly ingrained by adolescence and have a powerful impact even early in adolescence. As

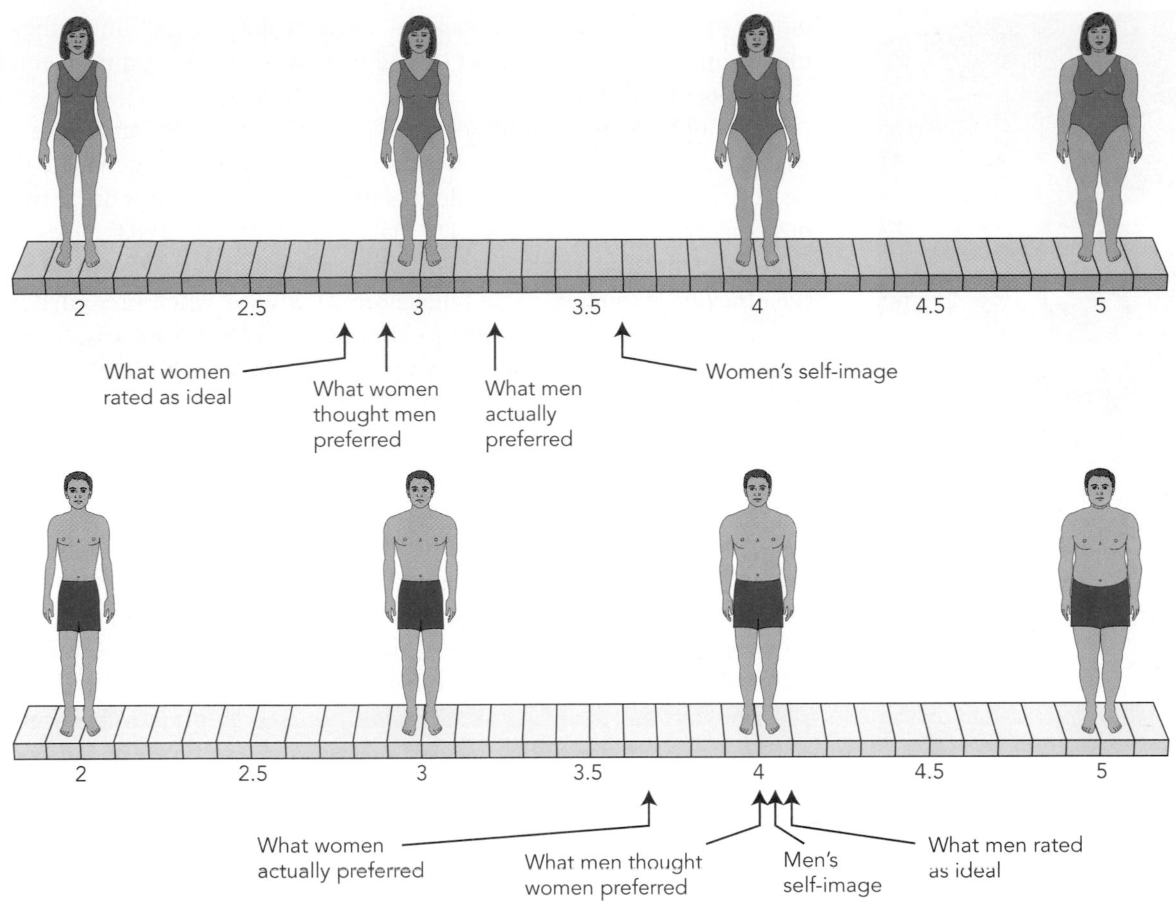

FIGURE 10.8

University women overestimated how thin they needed to be to conform to men's preferences and viewed their own body shape as heavier than ideal. In contrast, men overestimated how bulky they should be to conform to women's preferences and viewed their body shape as close to ideal.

Data from Fallon & Rozin, 1985.

early as the eighth grade, many girls have adopted the belief that they have to be thin to be popular with boys (Nichter & Vuckovic, 1994; Halpern et al., 1999). Such social pressures and beliefs can lead to a high level of dissatisfaction with one's own body. As few as one in five adolescent and young adult females report being happy with their weight, even when body weight is within a normal, healthy range (Halpern et al., 1999; Huon et al., 2002; Kenardy et al., 2001).

Environmental and Cultural Factors

Although not very sensitive to manipulation of biological variables such as overfeeding, underfeeding, or changes in the caloric density of the diet, people are very sensitive to changes in environmental stimuli, such as portion size, the number of people present during a meal, the amount that others eat, and the variety of foods available (Levitsky, 2005). We will consider a few of the most important environmental variables that influence how much we eat.

10. Identify several environmental and cultural factors that influence eating.

Food availability is the most obvious environmental regulator of eating. For millions of people who live in poverty or famine-ravaged regions, food scarcity limits consumption. In contrast, abundant low-cost food (including high-fat foods) in many countries contributes to a high rate of obesity among children and adults (Wadden et al., 2002).

Food taste and variety powerfully regulate eating. Good-tasting food positively reinforces eating and increases food consumption, but during a meal and from meal to meal, we can become "tired of eating the same thing" and terminate a meal more quickly (Rolls et al., 1981). In contrast, food variety increases consumption, which you know all too well if you attend buffet meals. Rats also seem to enjoy a

FIGURE 10.9

Cultural upbringing strongly affects food preferences. Would you like to eat these insect-topped appetizers? Not interested? Perhaps you would prefer some other insects, reptiles, camel eyes, or dog—all delicacies in other cultures.

buffet, or what technically is called a *cafeteria diet.* At each meal they may focus mostly on one type of food, but overall they eat more when their menu has variety (Rogers & Blundell, 1984).

Through classical conditioning we learn to associate the smell and sight of food with its taste, and these food cues can trigger hunger. Eating may be the last thing on your mind until your nose detects the sensuous aroma wafting from a bakery, pizzeria, or popcorn machine. Dr. Harvey Weingarten (1983), then at McMaster University, demonstrated that rats who have eaten recently and are not hungry (i.e., they have food available but ignore it) will eat when presented with sounds and lights that they have learned to associate with food. Similarly, does the musical jingle of the neighbourhood ice cream truck tweak your hunger?

Many other environmental stimuli affect food intake. We typically eat more when dining with other people rather than alone, in part because meals take longer (de Castro, 2002). Cultural norms influence when, how, and what we eat. In countries such as Spain and Greece, people often begin dinner in the late evening (say, around 9 P.M.), by which time most North Americans have finished their supper. And although we like variety, we usually feel most comfortable selecting from among familiar foods and often have difficulty "getting past" our squeamish thoughts about unfamiliar dishes (Figure 10.9). Figure 10.10 summarizes several factors that help to regulate hunger and eating.

Obesity

The heaviest known man and woman in recorded history, both Americans, weighed 636 kg and 545 kg at their respective peaks in 1978 and 1987 (*Guinness Book,* 2000). (After hospitalization and dieting, the man lost 418 kg over 16 months, and the woman lost 417 kg over 7 years.) Health Canada guidelines suggest that a body mass index (BMI, the ratio of weight to height—kg/m^2) between 25 and 29.9 is considered overweight, and a BMI over 30 is considered obese. In June 2004, Health Canada reported that 33 percent of adult Canadians are overweight and 15 percent are obese. Among Canadian children, almost 20 percent are overweight and 8 percent are obese. Not only does obesity pose a health risk, even children evaluate the obese negatively (LeBow, 1988). However, Michael LeBow of the University of Manitoba found that Canadian children (LeBow, 1988) and adolescents (LeBow et al., 1989) do not disparage obesity to the extent their American counterparts do.

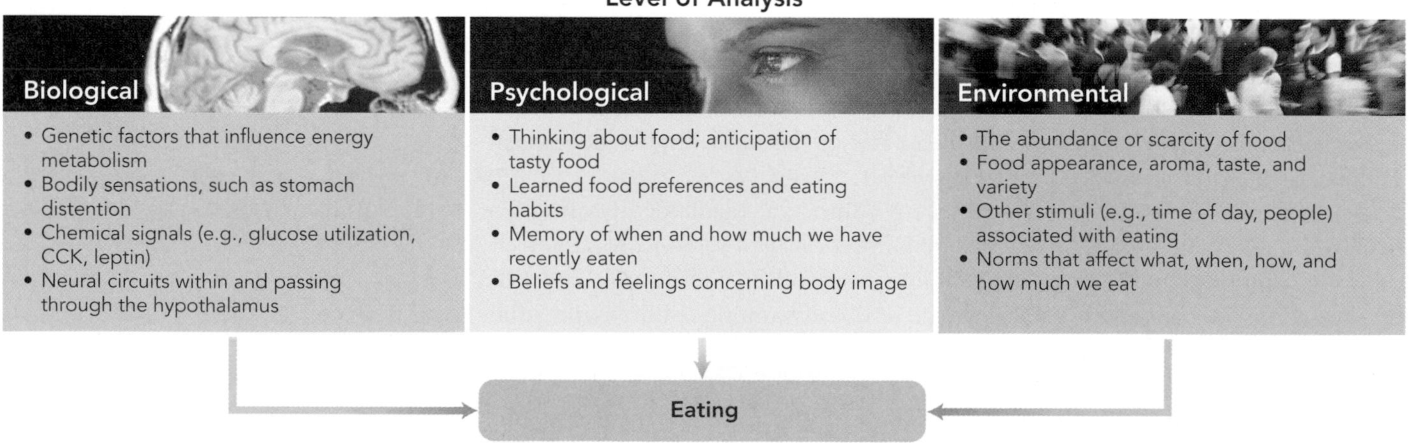

Level of Analysis
Biological
• Genetic factors that influence energy metabolism
• Bodily sensations, such as stomach distention
• Chemical signals (e.g., glucose utilization, CCK, leptin)
• Neural circuits within and passing through the hypothalamus
Psychological
• Thinking about food; anticipation of tasty food
• Learned food preferences and eating habits
• Memory of when and how much we have recently eaten
• Beliefs and feelings concerning body image
Environmental
• The abundance or scarcity of food
• Food appearance, aroma, taste, and variety
• Other stimuli (e.g., time of day, people) associated with eating
• Norms that affect what, when, how, and how much we eat
Eating

FIGURE 10.10

Understanding the causes of behaviour: factors that regulate hunger and eating.

Obesity is often blamed on a lack of willpower, a weak character, or emotional disturbances, but research does not consistently find such psychological differences between obese and non-obese people (Faith et al., 2002). Some scientists hypothesize that obese people eat to cope with stress, or that they react more strongly than non-obese people to food cues, such as the aroma and appearance of food (Schachter, 1968). But again, evidence that these factors cause obesity is mixed (Greeno & Wing, 1994).

Genes and Environment

Do you know people who seem to gain weight easily, and other envied souls who eat even more food without adding weight? Data from over 25,000 pairs of twins and 50,000 other biological and adoptive family members point to heredity as one source of such differences. Heredity influences our basal metabolic rate and tendency to store energy as either fat or lean tissue (Bouchard et al., 1990). Overall, genetic factors appear to account for about 40 to 70 percent of the variation in body mass among women and among men (Maes et al., 1997; Comuzzie & Allison, 1998). Identical twins reared apart are about as similar in body mass as identical twins reared together, and adopted children resemble their biological parents more closely than their adoptive parents (Stunkard et al., 1990). And yes, obese people are more likely than non-obese people to have parents and grandparents who are obese (Noble, 1997).

11. What evidence suggests a genetic role in obesity? How does obesity among the Pima Indians illustrate a gene–environment interaction?

Over 200 genes have been identified as possible contributors to human obesity, and in most cases it is the combined effect of a subset of genes—rather than "single-gene" variations—that produces an increased risk (Comuzzie & Allison, 1998). However, although heredity affects our susceptibility to obesity, so does the environment. Genes have not changed much in recent decades, but obesity rates in Canada and the United States have increased significantly. According to experts such as James Hill and John Peters (1998), the culprits are:

- an abundance of inexpensive, tasty, high-fat foods available almost everywhere;
- a cultural emphasis on "getting the best value," which contributes to the "supersizing" of menu items; and
- technological advances that decrease the need for daily physical activity and encourage a sedentary lifestyle.

The Pima Indians of Arizona provide a striking example of how genes and environment interact to produce obesity. Despite the fact that the Pimas are genetically predisposed to obesity and diabetes, both conditions were rare among tribe members before the 20th century (Savage & Bennett, 1992). Their native diet and way of life prevented their genetic predisposition from expressing itself. But, particularly among Pimas born after World War II, obesity rates increased dramatically as they adopted a Westernized diet and sedentary lifestyle (Price et al., 1993; Esparza et al., 2000). Today they have one of the highest rates of obesity (and diabetes) in the world. In contrast, Pimas living in northwest Mexico, who still eat a more traditional diet and perform more physical labour, have an obesity rate much lower than that of their Arizonan counterparts (Ravussin et al., 1994).

Dieting and Weight Loss

12. Why is it especially hard for obese people to lose weight? Are diets doomed to fail?

Unfortunately, being fat primes people to stay fat, in part by altering body chemistry and energy expenditure (Logue, 1991). For example, obese people generally have higher levels of insulin (a hormone secreted by the pancreas) than people of normal weight, which increases the conversion of glucose into fat. Substantial weight gain also makes it harder to exercise vigorously, and dieting slows basal metabolism because the body responds to food deprivation with decreased energy expenditure. Along with a genetic predisposition to obesity, these factors cause many obese people to maintain excess weight with fewer calories than people who are gaining the same weight for the first time. In contrast to earlier reports, however, there is no consistent evidence that the body's energy-saving metabolic slowdown becomes more pronounced with each weight loss attempt (Brownell & Rodin, 1994, National Task Force, 1994). Thus, whether repeated "*yo-yo dieting*" makes it more difficult to lose weight is debatable.

Are diets doomed to fail? The common adage that "95 percent of people who lose weight regain it within a few years" evolved from just one study decades ago. According to Albert Strunkard, one of the researchers, 100 obese patients were "just given a diet and sent on their way. That was state of the art in 1959." (Fritsch, 1999). Certainly, achieving weight loss is not easy, and combining healthy eating (reduced energy input) with exercise (increased energy output) has a greater chance of success than dieting alone. But in truth, we do not have good estimates of weight-loss success rates, partly because people who succeed (or fail) on their own without going to clinics or treatment programs are rarely heard from (Schachter, 1982). For example, the National Weight Control Registry (2000) has a database of over 2,000 successful, long-term dieters who, on average, have lost about 27 kg and kept it off for about five years. About half of these participants did so on their own, without any type of formal program.

Health concerns motivate some dieters, but psychological and social concerns are the primary motivators for many others. Many *non-obese* adolescent girls and women diet, including those of average and below-average weight (Halpern et al., 1999; Miller et al., 2000).

PSYCHOLOGICAL APPLICATIONS

The Battle to Control Eating and Weight

Many people, especially high school and university students, are concerned about their weight. Many adolescent females with average and even below average body fat diet (Halpern et al., 1999; Kenardy et al., 2001). Our body size and shape, or, more accurately, our perception of our body size and shape forms an important part of our self-image. How we perceive our own body and how closely that matches our ideal is an important issue for many (look back at Figure 10.8). Can what we have learned about hunger help us in our battle to control our girth? Many different factors control hunger, and what we know about their influences and interactions can indeed be put to use.

As discussed previously, having an "empty" stomach does contribute to feelings of hunger and having a "full" stomach is one of the satiety signals. But it is not just the sheer mass of food in the stomach that helps us feel full and slows our eating. Acting through mechanisms that are not yet well understood, what is in the stomach also matters. Nutritionally rich food makes us feel fuller than an equal volume of food with little or no nutritive value. Nutritionally rich food is lower in fats and calories than nutritionally empty food, and it will make you feel fuller faster.

The incentive value of the foods in front of us is also important. An attractive buffet display of many different foods will increase food consumption. High incentive foods increase eating even in the complete absence of physiological need. We certainly do not want to isolate ourselves in a sterile and boring environment, but knowing that such cues have a powerful impact can help us to control them. Do not ask to see the dessert tray, with its array of attractive, high incentive delicacies, unless you plan to eat one.

Cues that predict the arrival of food, such as the smell of popcorn, the sight of your favourite restaurant, or the sound of a steak sizzling on a barbecue can all make us feel hungry, even when we do not need food. Controlling the response to such food cues is not simply a matter of willpower. The smell, sight, and even sound of a favourite food can stimulate the release of the hormone insulin (Rodin, 1978, 1981). Insulin stimulates the transfer of glucose from the blood into the cells of the body, and an increase in insulin leads to a rapid drop in blood glucose levels. Secretion of insulin is associated with increased hunger (Rodin, et al., 1985). When you identify that sound as a barbecuing steak, insulin levels go up and that potently stimulates feelings of hunger. If you can, avoid such cues. For example, do not stop and look in the window of that bakery or chocolatier unless you want to be hungry. We know how such cues work and we cannot prevent them from working, so the available option is to control our exposure to such cues.

If you eat a small amount of food before a meal, will you eat more or less of the main meal? You might expect that the small amount of food will decrease meal size since your stomach now has food in it and is no longer empty; that the pre-meal snack has "ruined your appetite." Unfortunately, it does not work that way. If you eat a small amount of food before the main meal, that is, eat an appetizer, you will eat more of the following meal. An appetizer is aptly named as it does indeed increase your appetite. Appetizers work for at least two reasons. One is that an appetizer provides more variety in the meal and food variety increases consumption. The second reason is that if the appetizer stimulates insulin secretion, as it should, the increase in blood insulin levels and subsequent drop in blood glucose levels are powerful hunger cues. If you are visiting a fine restaurant and want to enjoy every possible mouthful, go ahead and have that appetizer. However, if you want to control the amount of food that you consume, do not have an appetizer or small snack close to mealtime; it will only make you feel hungrier and increase the amount of food that you eat.

Eat when you are hungry. Although we tend to attribute our eating to hunger, we often eat out of habit. Although we are not hungry, we snack while watching T.V., while watching sports, while talking with friends, and when reading. To make matters worse, these snacks are often high fat, high calorie foods such as chips, peanuts, or donuts. Do not put that bowl of chips on the table beside your favourite reading or T.V. chair.

You can lose weight by consuming a constant number of calories and increasing energy expenditure (i.e., exercising) or you can lose weight by decreasing the number of calories that you consume without changing your energy expenditure. It is important to know, however, that weight loss through exercise is not the same as weight loss through dieting. If weight is lost because of an increase in exercise, that weight is subsequently regained much more slowly than if the weight is lost because of dietary restriction (Wainwright et al., 1990). Weight loss through diet is due to a loss of both lean body mass and fat, whereas weight loss through exercise is due to a loss of fat. If weight is lost through exercise, there is a consequent increase in the ratio of muscle to fat (since only fat is lost), and that generally leads to an increase in basal metabolic rate (VanItallie & Kissileff, 1990). The heightened basal metabolism will help to burn calories, even when you are not exercising.

We go to great lengths, sometimes tragically unhealthy ones, to control our weight. The study of hunger has demonstrated that many different factors contribute to the control of appetite and weight. Some, such as our genetic endowment, are beyond our control, but others, such as exposure to food-related cues, types of food eaten, and how we arrange our meals, are within our control, and they can have a dramatic effect on how much food we eat, without resorting to the current fad diet.

In Review

- *The body monitors several chemicals involved in energy utilization. Changing patterns of glucose usage provide one signal that helps initiate hunger. Upon eating, hormones such as CCK are released into the bloodstream and signal the brain to stop eating. Fat cells release leptin, which acts as a long-term signal that helps to regulate appetite. The hypothalamus and other brain regions play a role in hunger regulation.*
- *The expected good taste of food motivates eating, and the thought of food can trigger hunger. Our memory, attitudes, habits, and psychological needs affect our food intake.*
- *The availability, taste, and variety of food powerfully regulate eating. Through classical conditioning, neutral stimuli can acquire the capacity to trigger hunger. Cultural norms affect our food preferences and eating habits.*
- *Heredity and the environment affect our susceptibility to becoming obese. Homeostatic mechanisms make it difficult to lose substantial weight.*

⊙ SEXUAL MOTIVATION

Why do people have sex? If you are thinking, "Isn't it obvious?" let's take a look. Sex often is described as a biological "reproductive drive," yet people usually do not have sex to conceive children. Moreover, a drive to reproduce does not explain why people masturbate, have oral sex, use birth control, and have sex into their seventies and eighties. Pleasure, then, must be the key. Evolution has shaped our physiology so that sex feels good; periodically this leads to childbirth, and our genes are passed on. But consider the following:

- In a study asking adolescents why they have sex, both genders cited peer pressure far more often than "sexual gratification" (Stark, 1989).
- In the 1920s, British sex researcher Helena Wright found that most women she surveyed viewed sex as an unenjoyable marital duty (Kelly, 2001).
- Many women find their first sexual intercourse disappointing (Sprecher et al., 1995). Some sex researchers call this reaction "Peggy Lee syndrome," named for a singer who had a hit song entitled, "Is That All There Is?" (Hyde & DeLamater, 2000).
- About 10 percent of American men and 20 percent of women report that sex is not pleasurable (Laumann et al., 1994).

In reality, people engage in sex for a host of noble and not so noble reasons: to reproduce, obtain and give pleasure, express love, foster intimacy, build one's ego, fulfill one's "duty," conform to peer pressure, get over a broken relationship, and for millions of people worldwide, to earn money (Byer et al., 1999).

Sexual Behaviour: Patterns and Changes

Because most people are reluctant to let researchers into their bedrooms, scientists typically learn about people's sexual activities by conducting surveys. Alfred Kinsey and his colleagues (1948, 1953) at Indiana University conducted the first large-scale American sex surveys in the late 1930s. One of the best and more recent U.S. surveys, based on a nationally representative sample of 18- to 59-year-olds, found that about 70 percent of this age group have sex with a partner at least a few times per month (Figure 10.11; Laumann et al., 1994; Michael et al., 1994). Overall, single adults who cohabit (are not married but live with a sexual partner) are the most sexually active, followed by married adults. Single adults who do not cohabit are the least active.

The survey also found that, although men and women have sex with a partner about equally often, men masturbate and fantasize about sex more often than women do. About 25 percent of men and 10 percent of women masturbate one or more times per week, and 60 percent of men and 40 percent of women report masturbating at least once a year. The common belief that adults masturbate simply because they do not have a sex partner is *false:* 85 percent of men and 45 percent of women with regular sex partners masturbate at least once a year.

Overall, males tend to have their first sexual intercourse experience one to two years earlier than females (CDC, 1976), but by the end of high school, similar proportions of males and females have had sexual intercourse at least once, and a high proportion of high school-aged youth are sexually active. For example, in 2002 Health Canada reported that 23 percent of grade 9 males and 19 percent of grade 9 females had engaged in sexual intercourse; by grade 11, 40 percent of males and 46 percent of females had engaged in sexual intercourse (Canadian Youth, Sexual

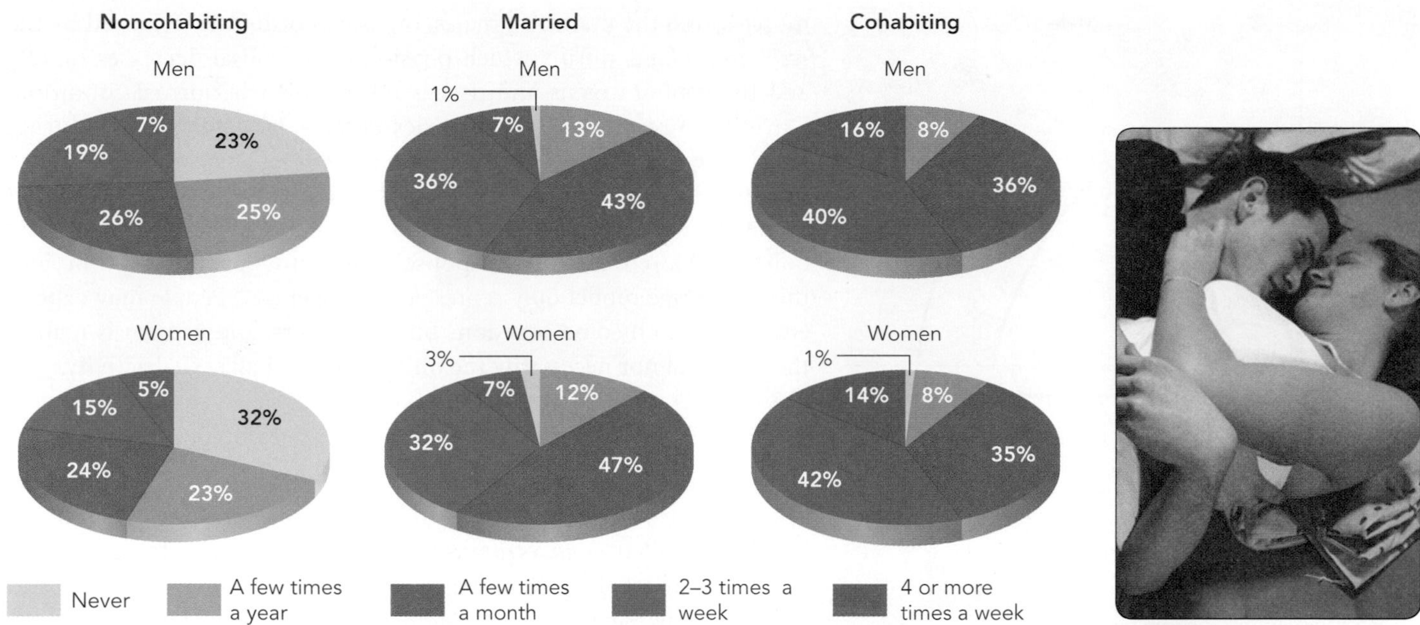

FIGURE 10.11

Frequency of sex over the past 12 months by gender and marital status among adult men and women.

Source: Adapted from Michael et al., 1994.

Health and HIV/AIDS Study, Health Canada, 2004). Premarital intercourse has become more common in many countries over the past half-century. Changing social norms, a trend toward sexual activity at a younger age, and a tendency to delay marriage have all contributed to an increase in premarital sex.

Some findings suggest, however, that these premarital trends may be levelling off and possibly reversing (CDC, 1997). This may be a response to an increased cultural emphasis on the depth of relationships (Wade & Cirese, 1992) and to the crisis concerning AIDs and other sexually transmitted diseases (STDs). According to the World Health Organization, about 360,000 people worldwide contract an STD each day, yielding 125 million new cases each year (Alexander, 1996.)

The Physiology of Sex

In 1953, William Masters and Virginia Johnson began a landmark study in which they examined the sexual responses of 694 men and women under laboratory conditions. In total, they physiologically monitored about 10,000 sexual episodes in which volunteers masturbated, had intercourse, and performed other sexual activities. By putting a camera into a transparent penis-shaped case, Masters and Johnson were able to film vaginal reactions during simulated intercourse.

The Sexual Response Cycle

13. Explain the stages of the sexual response cycle.

Masters and Johnson (1966) concluded that most people go through a four-stage **sexual response cycle** when sexually aroused (Figure 10.12). During the *excitement phase*, arousal builds rapidly. Blood flow increases to arteries in and around the genital organs, nipples, and women's breasts, pooling and causing these body areas to swell (this process is called *vasocongestion*). The penis and clitoris begin to become erect, the vagina becomes lubricated, and muscle tension increases throughout the body. In the *plateau phase*, respiration, heart rate, vasocongestion, and muscle tension continue to build until there is enough muscle tension to trigger orgasm.

During the *orgasm phase* in males, rhythmic contractions of internal organs and muscle tissue surrounding the urethra project semen out of the penis. In females, orgasm involves rhythmic contractions of the outer third of the vagina, surrounding

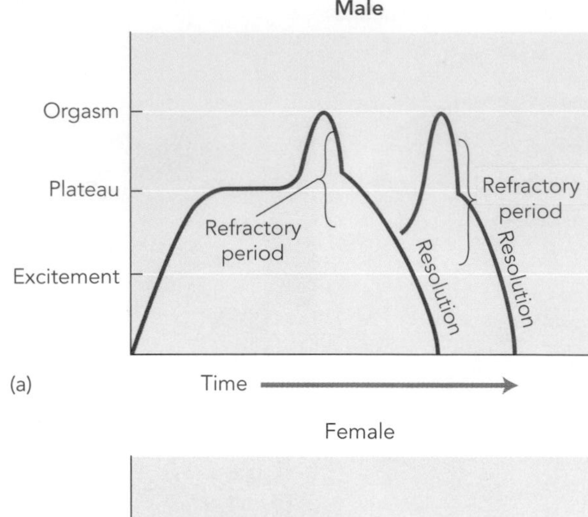

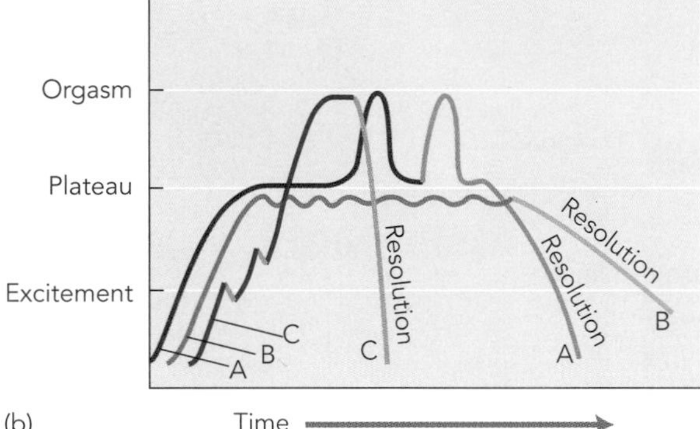

FIGURE 10.12

Masters and Johnson discovered a four-stage pattern of sexual response. (a) In males, there is a refractory period after orgasm during which no further response is possible. (b) In females, pattern "a" represents one or more orgasms followed by resolution, pattern "b" shows a plateau stage with no orgasm, and pattern "c" shows an orgasm with no preceding plateau stage.

Based on Masters & Johnson, 1966.

14. Describe the organizational and activational effects of sex hormones. How do the activational effects differ in humans versus non-humans?

muscles, and the uterus. In males, orgasm is ordinarily followed by the *resolution phase,* during which physiological arousal decreases rapidly and the genital organs and tissues return to their normal condition. During the resolution phase, males enter a *refractory period* during which they are temporarily incapable of another orgasm. Females may have two or more successive orgasms before the onset of the resolution phase, but Masters and Johnson reported that most women experienced only one. Moreover, sexual response varies across people and time, and this four-stage model only represents an "average." People may experience orgasm on some occasions but not others, and orgasm is neither the only goal nor necessarily the ultimate goal of all sexual activity.

Hormonal Influences

As with hunger, the hypothalamus plays a key role in sexual motivation. It controls the pituitary gland, which regulates the secretion of hormones called *gonadotropins* into the bloodstream. In turn, these hormones affect the rate at which the *gonads* (testes in the male and ovaries in the female) secrete *androgens,* the so-called "masculine" sex hormones such as testosterone, and *estrogens,* the so-called "feminine" sex hormones such as estradiol. Note that, despite these labels, both men and women produce androgens and estrogens.

Sex hormones have *organizational effects* that direct the development of male and female sex characteristics (Breedlove, 1992; Byer et al., 1999). In the womb, male and female embryos form a primitive gonad that has the potential to develop into either testes or ovaries. If genetically male, the embryo forms testes about eight weeks after conception. Then, as the testes release sex hormones during a key period of prenatal development, there typically is sufficient androgen activity to produce a male pattern of genital, reproductive, brain, and other organ development. Years later, as part of this pattern, the hypothalamus stimulates an increased release of sex hormones from the testes when the male reaches puberty. In contrast, a genetically female embryo does not form testes and, in the absence of sufficient androgen activity during this prenatal period, a female pattern of development ensues. As part of this pattern, at puberty the hypothalamus stimulates the release of sex hormones from the ovaries on a cyclical basis that regulates the female menstrual cycle.

Sex hormones also have *activational effects* that stimulate sexual desire and behaviour. The activational effects of the sex hormones begin at puberty, when the individual's gonads begin to secrete sex hormones. Mature males have a relatively constant secretion of sex hormones, and their readiness for sex is largely governed by the presence of environmental stimuli (e.g., a receptive female). In contrast, hormone secretions in female animals follow an "estrus" cycle, and they are sexually receptive only during periods of high estrogen secretion (i.e., when they are "in heat"). Sex hormones also influence human sexual desire, as when the hormonal surge of puberty results in increased sexual motivation for most people. But in humans, normal short-term hormonal fluctuations have relatively little effect on sexual arousability (Morrell et al., 1984). Women may experience high sexual desire at any time during their menstrual cycle.

In men and women, androgens—rather than estrogens—appear to have the primary influence on sexual desire (Alexander & Sherwin, 1993; Kelly, 2001). However, desire does not go up and down like a yo-yo as blood levels of sex hormones change. Rather, a baseline level of certain hormones, such as testosterone, appears necessary to maintain sexual desire. Women who have had their androgen-producing organs (ovaries, adrenal glands) removed for medical reasons experience a gradual loss of sexual desire that can be reversed by administering sex hormones (Kaplan & Owett, 1993; Sherwin & Gelfand, 1988). Similarly, most men who are castrated (have their testes removed) experience a gradual decrease of sexual desire. But, particularly if the man is sexually experienced, sexual responsiveness declines more slowly than sexual desire. In some cases, men continue to have sexual intercourse for years after they have been castrated (Hyde & DeLamater, 2000). This is one reason why castrating sex offenders is not a guaranteed method of preventing future rapes.

The Psychology of Sex

15. What psychological factors stimulate and inhibit sexual functioning?

Sexual arousal involves more than physiological responses. It typically begins with desire and a sexual stimulus that is perceived positively (Walen & Roth, 1987). Such stimuli can even be imaginary.

Sexual Fantasy

Sexual fantasy is an important component of many people's lives. Among 18- to 59-year-old American adults, about half of men and a fifth of women fantasize about sex at least once a day (Laumann et al., 1994). Fantasy illustrates how mental processes can affect physiological functioning. Indeed, sexual fantasies alone may trigger genital erection and orgasm in some people, and are often used to enhance arousal during masturbation (Byrne & Osland, 2000).

Most men and women also fantasize at least occasionally during sexual intercourse (Leitenberg & Henning, 1995), as comedian Rodney Dangerfield acknowledged with his quip, "Last time I tried to make love to my wife nothing was happening, so I said to her, 'What's the matter, you can't think of anybody either?'" However, in contrast to what Dangerfield's joke implies, sexual fantasy typically is not a response to dissatisfaction with one's partner. Rather, people who are more sexually active also tend to fantasize more (Kelly, 2001).

Desire, Arousal, and Sexual Dysfunction

Psychological factors not only can trigger sexual arousal, but also inhibit it. A person may be anticipating an evening of lovemaking, or be engaged in sexual activity, and then become "turned off" by something a partner does. Many people who are physiologically capable of becoming sexually aroused simply do not have the desire. About one in three women and one in six men report that they lack an interest in sex (Laumann et al., 1994).

Other people desire sex, but have difficulty becoming or staying aroused. Stress, fatigue, and anger at one's partner can lead to temporary arousal problems. *Sexual dysfunction* refers to chronic, impaired sexual functioning that distresses a person. It may result from injuries, diseases, and drug effects, but some causes are psychological. About 10 percent of men report difficulty maintaining an erection, and about 20 percent of women have difficulty lubricating and becoming aroused (Laumann et al., 1994). Performance anxiety can cause both types of problems, and arousal difficulties also may be a psychological consequence of sexual assault or childhood sexual abuse (Byers et al., 1999).

Cultural and Environmental Influences

16. How do cultural norms and environmental stimuli influence sexual behaviour?

The psychological meaning of sex depends strongly upon cultural contexts and learning. For example, some religions discourage or prohibit premarital sex, extramarital sex, and public dress and behaviour that arouses sexual desire (Figure 10.13). In turn, most people who view themselves as very religious believe it is important to bring their sexual practices into harmony with their religious beliefs (Janus & Janus, 1993).

Cultural Norms

Anyone who doubts culture's power to shape the expression of human sexuality need only examine sexual customs around the globe. Consider that childhood sexuality is suppressed in our culture, but is permitted and even encouraged in others. In the Marquesas Islands of French Polynesia, families sleep together in one room and children have ample opportunity to observe sexual activity. When a baby boy is distressed, Marquesan parents may masturbate the child. Boys and girls begin to masturbate at age two or three, and most engage in casual homosexual contacts during their youth. When they reach adolescence, an adult of the opposite sex instructs them in sexual techniques and has intercourse with them (Suggs, 1962).

Although North Americans are less sexually permissive than the Marquesans, they are not as repressive as the inhabitants of Inis Beag, an island off the coast of Ireland. Sex is a taboo topic among these people and nudity is abhorred. Only infants are allowed to be completely naked. The genders are separated from early childhood until marriage, and during marital sex both partners keep their underwear on. Sexual revulsion is so intense that dogs and other animals are often beaten if they are caught licking their genitals. In contrast to Marquesan women, who customarily experience orgasm in sexual interactions, orgasm among the women of Inis Beag is rare and viewed as abnormal (Messenger, 1971). Clearly, what is considered proper, moral, and desirable varies enormously across cultures.

FIGURE 10.13

Habits of dress that many people take for granted in some societies, such as wearing tank tops, short-sleeve shirts, and shorts, are unacceptable in other cultures because they would be considered sexually provocative.

Arousing Environmental Stimuli

The environment affects sexuality not only through cultural experiences, but also by providing sexually arousing stimuli. A lover's caress can trigger sexual desire in an instant. So too can watching a partner undress, which ranks second only to vaginal intercourse as the sexual activity that most men and women find appealing (Laumann et al., 1994).

Erotic portrayals of sex can trigger arousal and sexual behaviour as long as people perceive those stimuli positively (Davis & Bauserman, 1993). In one study, Julia Heiman (1975) measured the genital arousal and self-reported arousal of sexually experienced university students as they listened to tape recordings of erotic and nonerotic stories from popular novels. Women and men experienced sexual arousal to descriptions of explicit sex, but not to descriptions devoid of sexual content (romantic or general conversations). Both genders showed the strongest arousal when erotic stories focused on the female character, and when she was the one who initiated sex.

Pornography, Sexual Violence, and Sexual Attitudes

By today's standards, depictions of sex in popular novels are a tame form of erotica. Sexually explicit magazines and movies, telephone sex lines, nude dance clubs, and Internet "cyberporn" constitute a multi-billion-dollar pornography industry. Most pornography consumers are men, though about one-third of people who have purchased or rented X-rated video tapes are women (Laumann et al., 1994).

Given the appalling incidence of sexual assault in some countries, the public and scientists alike have asked whether exposure to pornography fosters sexual violence against women. Twenty percent of 15- to 44-year-old North American women report that they have experienced forced sexual intercourse at least once during their lives, and about 25 to 30 percent of female university students have experienced some type of sexual assault (CDC, 1997; Koss, 1988). Contrary to a common belief, as Figure 10.14 shows, most rapes are *not* committed by strangers (Laumann et al., 1994).

Two psychological viewpoints are especially relevant to predicting pornography's effects. According to *social learning theory*, people learn through observation. Many pornographic materials model "rape myths"; that sex is impersonal, that men are entitled to sex when they want it, and that women enjoy being dominated and coerced into sex (Burton, 1980; Malamuth, 1998). Men who view such materials should become more likely to treat women as objects and sexually aggress toward them. In contrast, Freud and other psychoanalysts advocated a *catharsis principle*, which states that as inborn aggressive and sexual impulses build up, actions that release this tension provide a "catharsis" that temporarily returns us to a more balanced physiological state. Thus, viewing pornography—especially materials that contain aggressive or violent content—should provide people with a safe "outlet" for releasing sexual and aggressive tensions, and should decrease sexually aggressive behaviour toward women.

Correlational studies of real-world sexual violence do not clearly support either viewpoint. For example, although some sex offenders use pornography to arouse themselves in preparation for a crime, overall, they do not report having been exposed to pornography at a younger age or to a substantially larger degree than males in general (Bauserman, 1996). More broadly, some countries with high rape rates have little pornography, whereas others have a great deal. In some countries, pornography is widely available but rape rates are low (Bauserman, 1996).

To isolate pornography's possible effects on behaviour, controlled experiments are needed. In one such experiment, Edward Donnerstein and Leonard Berkowitz (1981) randomly divided male university students into four groups. Group 1 saw a non-sexual film of a talk show. Group 2 watched a sexually explicit film in which a young couple made consensual love. Groups 3 and 4 watched explicit depictions of a woman being sexually assaulted by two men. In one film (Group 3)—a "rape myth" version—the woman resisted at first but then became a willing sexual participant. In the other film (Group 4), she was shown resisting and then suffering during the entire experience.

Next, in a supposedly unrelated second experiment, these male participants interacted with a woman (actually, an accomplice of the experimenter). During this interaction, she intentionally angered half of the participants. Later the men were given the opportunity to aggress against her by giving her electric shocks as punishment for errors made on a learning task she was performing. As Figure 10.15 shows, watching the "rape myth" film (Group 3) increased the aggression of both angered and non-angered men. Further, *for angered men*, aggression increased even when they saw the rape depiction showing the woman suffering (Group 4). This heightened aggression was specifically directed toward women; in a related experiment, viewing these rape depictions increased men's aggression toward a female confederate, but *not* toward a male confederate.

Based on over two dozen experiments, researchers still debate whether non-violent sexually explicit materials increase men's aggression toward women, but the clearest and strongest effects emerge for violent pornography (Allen et al., 1995; Byrne & Osland 2000; Donnerstein & Malamuth, 1997). At least temporarily, such

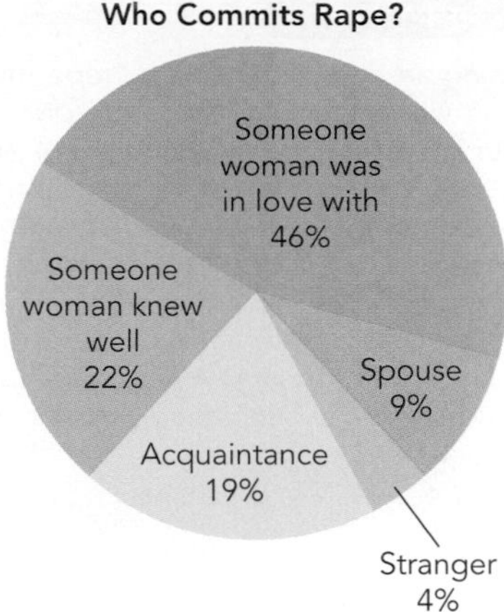

FIGURE 10.14

In one study of 18- to 59-year-old women who had been victims of forced sex, the offender was typically someone the victim knew (Laumann et al., 1994). Another study of university women (Koss et al., 1988) found similar results: the rape offender was a boyfriend or other steady date in 31% of attacks; non-romantic acquaintance in 26%; casual date in 22%; stranger in 11%; and family member, including spouse, in 9% of attacks.

Data from Edward O. Laumann, Robert T. Michael, and Gina Kolata.

17. According to social learning and catharsis principles, how should viewing pornography affect sexual aggression? What does research find?

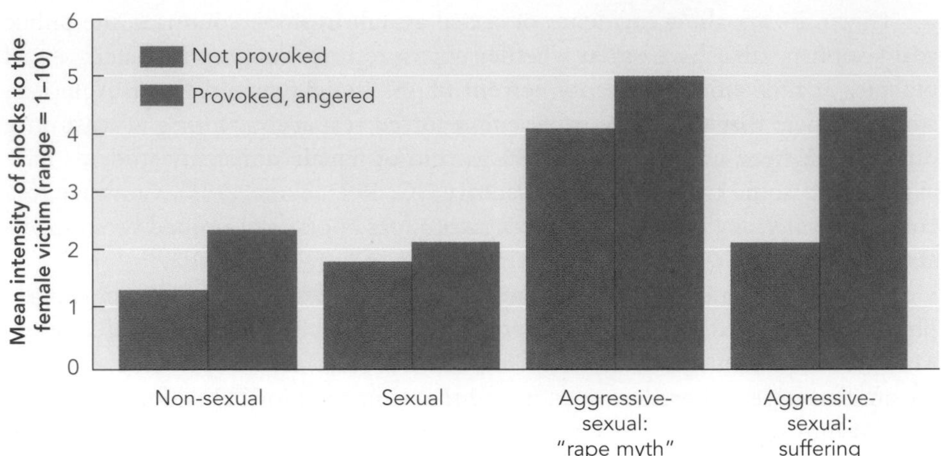

FIGURE 10.15

Viewing an aggressive-sexual "rape myth" film in which the victim did not appear to suffer increased the aggression of both angered and non-angered male participants toward a woman. After seeing an aggressive-sexual film in which the female victim did appear to suffer, only angered men showed substantially higher aggression toward a woman. A sexually explicit film without violent content did not increase later aggression.

Data from Donnerstein & Berkowitz, 1981.

films seem to increase men's aggressive behaviour toward women. Pornography also promotes a view that sex is impersonal and decreases viewers' satisfaction with their own sexual partners (Donnerstein & Malamuth, 1997; Zillmann, 1994). In combination with a hostile attitude toward women, the belief that sex is impersonal contributes to rape (Malamuth, 1998). Incarcerated rapists and students who have admitted committing date rape both display an impersonal orientation to sex.

18. Do you believe that research findings should influence societal decisions about pornography? Why or why not?

Should violent pornography, or all pornography, be banned? This is a moral and political question that goes beyond what the data can answer. Like everyone else, researchers have personal values, and some take a strong stand on this issue. In an encouraging vein, research also shows that providing men with realistic information about sexual assault can lead them to reject rape myths (Linz & Donnerstein, 1989). Strong messages against coercive sexual practices may promote attitudes that help reduce sexual crimes against women.

Sexual Orientation

19. Why is the issue of defining sexual orientation complicated?

Sexual orientation refers to one's emotional and erotic preference for partners of a particular sex (Byer et al., 1999). On one level, defining sexual orientation seems simple: Heterosexuals prefer opposite-sex partners, homosexuals prefer same-sex partners, and bisexuals are sexually attracted to members of both sexes. So how would you classify the sexual orientation of the following 25-year-olds?

- Earl is attracted to and has sex only with men, and views himself as homosexual.
- Susan feels sexually attracted to men and women, but has had sex only with men and thinks of herself as heterosexual.
- Larry has had sex with other men twice since puberty, yet isn't attracted to men and views himself as heterosexual.

Prevalence of Different Sexual Orientations

For decades, researchers viewed sexual orientation as a single dimension ranging from "exclusively heterosexual" to "exclusively homosexual," with "equally heterosexual and homosexual" at the midpoint (Kinsey 1948). But this concept is simplistic, and modern researchers propose that sexual orientation has three dimensions: *self-identity, sexual attraction,* and *actual sexual behaviour* (Kelly, 2001).

Figure 10.16 shows that about three percent of North American men and one percent of women identify themselves as homosexual or bisexual, but higher percentages report same-gender attraction and at least one same-gender sexual experience (Laumann et al., 1994). National surveys in England and France report slightly lower rates of same-gender sexual activity (Johnson et al., 1992).

Overall, 10 percent of North American men and 9 percent of women answered affirmatively to at least one of the items in Figure 10.16. Of this group, roughly half report same-gender attraction but have never had same-gender sex and do not think of themselves as homosexual. In contrast, almost all individuals who have a homosexual or bisexual self-identity also report same-gender attraction and same-gender sexual activity.

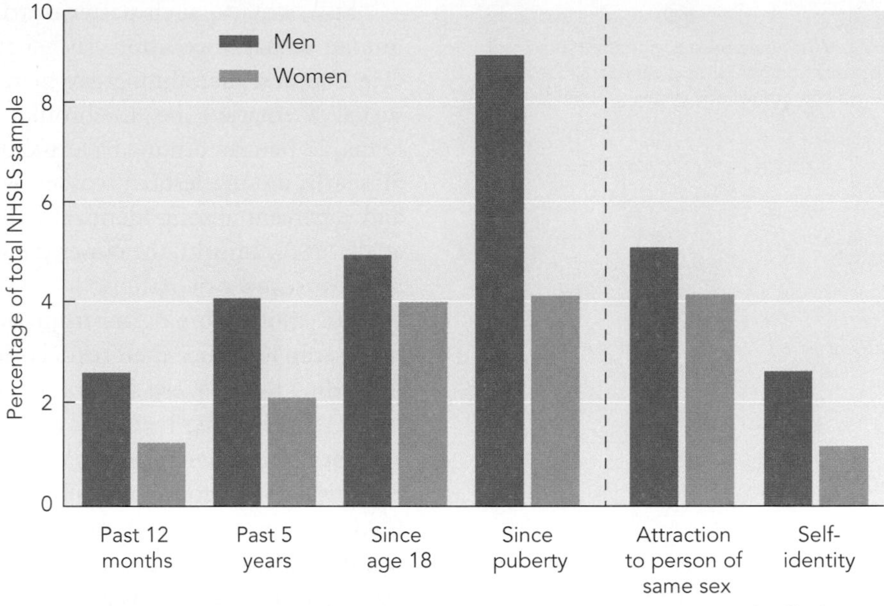

FIGURE 10.16

More men and women report same-sex attraction and same-sex activity than view themselves as homosexual or bisexual.

Adapted from Michael et al., 1994.

Determinants of Sexual Orientation

During the twentieth century, theory after theory about the origins of sexual orientation fell by the scientific wayside. An early and unsupported biological theory was that homosexual and heterosexual males differ in their adult levels of sex hormones. One psychodynamic view proposed that male homosexuality develops when boys grow up with a weak, ineffectual father and identify with a domineering or seductive mother. Another hypothesized that being sexually seduced by an adult homosexual caused children to divert their sex drive toward members of their own sex. Behaviourists suggested that homosexuality was a conditioned response, developed by associating adolescent sexual urges with the presence of same-sex peers.

20. What do you believe determines sexual orientation? Does your belief correspond to theories that have been rejected?

These early theories took a scientific beating. In an extensive study of nearly 1,000 homosexual and over 500 heterosexual men and women in the San Francisco area, Alan Bell and his colleagues (1981) asked participants more than 200 questions about their childhood, adolescence, and adulthood. They searched in vain for a common pattern of early experiences that might suggest clues about the determinants of sexual orientation, and concluded:

> No particular phenomenon of family life can be singled out, on the basis of our findings, as especially consequential for either homosexual or heterosexual development. . . . What we seem to have identified . . . is a pattern of feelings and reactions within the child that cannot be traced back to a single social or psychological root. (pp. 191–192)

Overall, there was one notable pattern: Even in childhood, homosexual men and women felt that they were somehow different from their same-sex peers and were more likely to engage in gender-non-conforming behaviours. Similarly, a cross-cultural study found that, compared to heterosexual women, homosexual women in Brazil, Peru, the Phillipines, and the United States were about twice as likely during childhood to be considered tomboys, to engage in pretend play with men's clothes or other items, and to be interested in boys' toys (Whitam & Mathy, 1991).

21. What evidence suggests that sexual orientation has biological roots? Describe the limitations of this evidence.

Still, why do such patterns arise? At present, many researchers believe that human sexual orientation has genetic roots. J. Michael Bailey and Richard Pillard (1991) found that among gay men who had a brother, the concordance rates for sexual orientation (i.e., the brother was gay also) were 52 percent among identical twins, 22 percent among fraternal twins, and 11 percent among adoptive brothers. Similarly, among lesbian women with sisters, the concordance rates were 48, 16, and 6 percent among identical twins, fraternal twins, and adopted sisters (Bailey et al., 1993). In sum, the closer the genetic relatedness, the higher the concordance rates for sexual orientation.

On another biological front, altering animals' prenatal exposure to sex hormones can influence their sexual orientation (Collaer & Hines, 1995; Money, 1987). According to one view, the brain develops a neural pattern that predisposes organisms to prefer either female or male sex partners, depending upon whether prenatal sex hormone activity follows a masculine or feminine path (Ellis & Ames, 1987). Scientists do not conduct similar experiments with humans, but some women have used medications during pregnancy that altered fetal exposure to sex hormones. Additionally, in rare cases some genetically male fetuses are insensitive to their own androgen secretions and some female fetuses experience an atypical buildup of androgens. Several studies of these individuals suggest a relation between their prenatal sex hormone exposure and adulthood sexual orientation (Dessens et al., 1999; Williams et al., 2000).

These findings are intriguing, but the human research is correlational, and many investigators believe that there is no clear evidence that prenatal sex hormones directly affect human sexual orientation (Byne, 1997; Doell, 1995). For example, male fetuses who have androgen insensitivity develop the external anatomy of females and typically are raised as girls, and socialization could account for their sexual orientation.

What about environmental influences? Despite identical genes, in about half the cases in which one identical twin is homosexual, the other is heterosexual. Thus several biological factors, or a biological predisposition and socialization experiences, may combine to determine our sexual orientation (Money, 1987). At present, we do not know what those factors are. It is also possible, argues Daryl Bem (1996), that heredity affects sexual orientation only indirectly by influencing children's basic personality style. He proposes that different personality styles steer children toward different socialization experiences, which then play the key role in determining sexual orientation. Finally, there may be multiple paths toward developing a sexual orientation, and the paths for men and women may differ (Byne, 1997; Peplau et al., 1998). Although much more research is needed to examine these models, one point is clear. No matter what our sexual orientation, close relationships provide us with much more than the mere opportunity for sexual expression.

In Review

- *The last half century has witnessed changing patterns of sexual activity, such as an increase in premarital sex.*
- *During sexual intercourse people often experience a four-stage physiological response pattern consisting of excitement, plateau, orgasm, and resolution.*
- *Sex hormones have organizational effects that guide the prenatal development of internal and external organs along either a male or female pattern. Sex hormones also have activational effects that influence sexual desire.*
- *Sexual fantasy can trigger arousal, whereas stress and psychological difficulties can interfere with sexual arousal. Cultural norms determine the sexual practices and beliefs that are considered moral, proper, and desirable.*

- *Environmental stimuli affect sexual desire. Viewing sexual violence reinforces men's belief in rape myths and increases men's aggression toward women, at least temporarily.*
- *Sexual orientation involves dimensions of self-identity, sexual attraction, and actual sexual behaviour. No single biological, social, or psychological factor—and no specific combination of causes—has been clearly identified as the cause of sexual orientation.*

ACHIEVEMENT MOTIVATION

Extraordinary accomplishments vividly demonstrate the desire to achieve. As a university student, you are keenly aware of society's emphasis on achievement, and you know that some people seek out and thrive on challenges, whereas others do not. In the 1950s, David McClelland, John Atkinson, and their associates (1953) began to explore these individual differences in **need for achievement**, which represents the desire to accomplish tasks and attain standards of excellence. They viewed the need for achievement as a relatively stable personality characteristic that energizes and guides our achievement behaviour.

Motivation for Success: The Thrill of Victory

People can strive to succeed for two radically different reasons. The first is a positively oriented *motive for success* and the second is a negatively oriented motivation to avoid failure, more commonly called *fear of failure.* McClelland and his colleagues (1953) measured the motive for success by showing participants a series of pictures like the one in Figure 10.17 and asking them to make up a story about each one. Other researchers use psychological tests that ask participants about their own achievement behaviour (Elliot & Church, 1997).

People who have a strong motive for success are attracted to the "thrill of victory" that comes about from mastering skills or outperforming other people. Andrew Elliot and Marcy Church (1997) report that university students with a high motivation for success focus on *mastery goals* and *performance-approach goals.* Mastery goals reflect intrinsic motivation and include "I want to learn as much as possible from this class" and "I prefer course material that arouses my curiosity, even if it is difficult to learn." Students who view mastery as important study hard, think about the material deeply, and display better long-term retention than their peers. In contrast, performance-approach goals involve social comparison, such as "I am motivated by the thought of outperforming my peers in this class." Striving to outperform classmates also leads to high effort and predicts somewhat higher course grades (Elliot & Church, 1997; Elliot et al., 1999).

FIGURE 10.17

Pictures like this are used to elicit stories that are scored for the motive to succeed. Which of the following two stories, written by different people, reflects a stronger motive to succeed? (1) This young man is sitting in school, but he is dreaming about the day when he will become a doctor. He . . . will study and work harder than anyone else. He goes on to become one of the top medical researchers in the world. (2) The boy is daydreaming about how much he hates being in school. . . . He would like to run away from home and just take it easy on a tropical island. However, he is doomed to be in the rat race the rest of his life.

Fear of Failure: The Agony of Defeat

Fear of failure usually is measured by psychological tests that ask people to report how much anxiety they experience in achievement situations. People with a high fear of failure show an interesting pattern of achievement goals (Elliot & Church, 1997; Elliot & McGregor, 1999). They tend to adopt *performance-approach goals* in which it is important to outperform peers, but they also have strong *performance-avoidance goals* (e.g., "My fear of performing poorly in this class is often what motivates me").

Common sense might suggest that a strong motive for success combined with a strong fear of failure might lead a person to perform better on challenging tasks than someone who is motivated only by a desire for success. But this is not the case. The worry associated with fear of failure and performance-avoidance goals impairs task performance. Anxiety makes it difficult to process information effectively and attend to the task requirements, and performance deteriorates (Sarason & Sarason, 1990). In sports, this is the athlete who "chokes" under pressure (Smith et al., 1996).

Achievement Needs and Situational Factors

People with a strong need for achievement—particularly those who score high on motivation for success and low on fear of failure—are ambitious and persist longer after encountering difficulty than do people with a low need for achievement. University students with high achievement motivation (which researchers call *need achievement*) tend to seek out and enter more prestigious occupations (Heckhausen, 1991). But this striving for success does not apply equally to all situations.

22. How do people with high versus low achievement needs differ in the difficulty of tasks they select? Explain why this occurs.

In the laboratory and the workplace, high-need achievers generally do not outperform individuals with low achievement motivation when conditions are relaxed and tasks are easy. But when tasks are challenging or the importance of doing well is stressed, high-need achievers outshine low-need achievers (McClelland, 1989). Competitive situations decrease low-need achievers' task enjoyment, but are music to the ears of high-need achievers (Epstein & Harackiewicz, 1992). In general, high-need achievers are most likely to strive hard for success when:

- they perceive themselves as personally responsible for the outcome;
- they perceive some risk of not succeeding; and
- there is an opportunity to receive performance feedback (Koester & McClelland, 1990).

What would you predict? When given a choice of performing a task that is very easy (a high probability of success), moderately difficult (a 40 to 60 percent probability of success), or very difficult (a low probability of success), which task will high-need achievers choose? Contrary to what you might expect, they prefer intermediate rather than extremely high or low risks (Atkinson & Birch, 1978). On a ring-toss task, they tend at first to select an intermediate distance to toss the ring at the peg. This distance is the most challenging because the outcome—success versus failure—*is most uncertain.* People with a high fear of failure are more likely to choose tasks that are easy (where success is almost assured) or very difficult (where success is not expected).

The key to understanding this behaviour is to recognize that it is the individual's *perception* of task uncertainty that counts. For most of us, the probability of successfully climbing Mt. Everest is virtually zero. But to highly trained mountaineers, the task is neither impossible nor easy. Decades ago, sociologist and mountain climber Dick Emerson (1966) joined a Mt. Everest expedition. He predicted that the climbers' communications with one another would strike a balance between optimistic and pessimistic comments about reaching their goal to keep their perceived chance of success–failure at 50–50, thereby maintaining maximum motivation. Not only did Emerson find such a pattern when he monitored the climbers' spontaneous communications, but he also tested this hypothesis by randomly making optimistic or pessimistic statements to individual members of the climbing team. Most of the time, the climbers' replies were opposite to Emerson's, thereby "balancing out" their interaction and maintaining a perception that the climb had an intermediate chance of success.

Family and Cultural Influences

23. How do cultural factors influence the expression of achievement needs?

High need for achievement develops when parents encourage and reward achievement, but do not punish failure (Koestner & McClelland, 1990). Conversely, fear of failure seems to develop when successful achievement is taken for granted by parents, but failure is punished. Therefore the child learns to dread the possibility of failing (Weiner, 1992). Providing children with a cognitively stimulating home environment that has many opportunities for learning fosters their intrinsic motivation to perform academic tasks (Gottfried et al., 1998).

Individualistic cultures, such as those in North America and much of Europe, tend to stress personal achievement. In cultures that nurture collectivism, such as those in China and Japan, achievement motivation more strongly reflects a desire to fit into the family and social group, meet its expectations, and work for its goals (Markus & Kitayama, 1999). Chinese high school students, for example, typically care more about meeting their parents' expectations of academic success than do American students (Chen & Lan, 2006).

These cultural differences, however, do not portray a black-and-white picture. As Sushila Niles (1998) found in comparing the achievement goals of Sri Lankans (collectivistic) and Anglo-Australians (individualistic), both groups supported the concept of individual responsibility and a strong work ethic. As expected, Sri Lankans' achievement goals were more group and family oriented than those of the Australians, but they also reported important individual goals. Conversely, the Australians held some group-oriented goals, particularly as concerns the family.

The relation between cultural values and achievement motivation also is suggested by the correspondence between the amount of achievement imagery in children's storybooks and measures of national accomplishment. Presumably, the level of concern for achievement in children's books reflects the motivational level of the adults in the country at that time, as well as the values that are being transmitted to children. In one study, achievement motivation scores based on the content of second- and fourth-grade schoolbooks corresponded closely to the number of patents issued per million population in the United States between 1810 and 1950 (Figure 10.18; de Charms & Moeller, 1962).

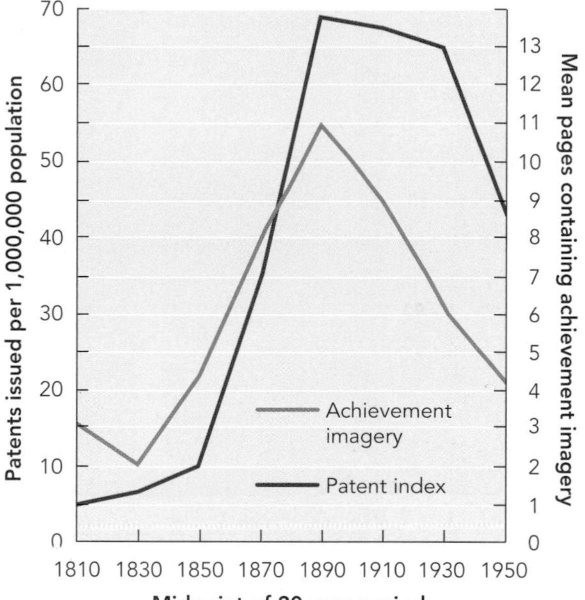

FIGURE 10.18

Relation between achievement imagery found in children's stories and number of patents per million population issued in the United States between 1810 and 1950.

From deCharms & Moeller, 1962.

In Review

- *People who have a high motivation for success are attracted to the thrill of victory. They value mastery and social comparision. People who have a high fear of failure experience anxiety in achievement settings. They are motivated by social comparison and a fear of performing poorly.*
- *High-need achievers seek moderately difficult tasks that are challenging but attainable. Low-need achievers are more likely to choose easy tasks in which success is assured or very difficult tasks in which success is not expected. Child-rearing and cultural factors influence our level and expression of achievement motivation.*

MOTIVATION IN THE WORKPLACE

The workplace is one of life's most important achievement arenas. You may devote forty to fifty years of your life to a career, and you probably desire that that work be motivating and satisfying. Motivation also is vital to organizations. To succeed, an organization needs workers who are motivated to join it and perform their jobs well (Steers & Porter, 1991).

Why Do People Work?

24. In the workplace, are most people motivated primarily by money? Explain.

The earliest theory of work motivation, advanced by Frederick Taylor (1911), held that workers are motivated almost entirely by money. This view may characterize some workers, but research indicates that many more view personal accomplishment as the most important job attribute. Opportunities for mastery, growth, and satisfying interpersonal relationships are key motivators for many employees (Buckingham & Coffman, 1999; McGregor, 1960).

25. How strongly is job satisfaction related to job productivity? Do you have any ideas why this might be?

Cultural factors influence work motivation. In collectivistic Japan, traditional business organizations adopt a concept of *Kaizen* (continuous improvement), encouraging workers to develop skills and increase productivity (Berry, 1998). Companies assume responsibility for their employees' welfare, promote them slowly, and are willing to retain them for life (Ouichi, 1981). The company becomes integral to the workers' identity and workers are strongly motivated by loyalty to their managers and the organization (Misumi, 1985).

Job Satisfaction and Performance

If we tell you that satisfied employees perform much better than unsatisfied employees, this conclusion seems so obvious that you may wonder why researchers bother to study it. There is just one problem: It is not true. Major research reviews have found that *job productivity* (making more sales, building better products, and so on) and job satisfaction are only weakly related (Brayfield & Crockett, 1955; Iaffaldano & Muchinsky, 1985). At present, there is no agreed-upon theory to explain why this relation is so weak. *Absenteeism* and *turnover* (leaving the organization) are other important aspects of job performance. Dissatisfied workers tend to be absent slightly more often than satisfied workers and, especially when the job market is good, they are somewhat more likely to quit their current job (Aamodt, 1996; Gerhart, 1990).

Enhancing Work Motivation

Given the high cost of poor productivity, absenteeism, and turnover to organizations, industrial/organizational (I/O) psychologists have designed many programs to enhance employee motivation and performance.

Enriching and Redesigning Jobs

Job enrichment programs, reflecting Maslow's humanistic theory, attempt to increase intrinsic motivation by making jobs more fulfilling and providing workers with opportunities for growth. A job is most intrinsically motivating and satisfying when it provides (Hackman and Lawler, 1971):

- *skill variety.* A variety of tasks must be performed, requiring many talents and skills.
- *task identity.* A "whole" product is completed from beginning to end.
- *task significance.* Tasks have an impact on the lives or work of other people.

- *autonomy.* The worker has some freedom to determine work procedures and schedules.
- *job feedback.* The job provides clear feedback about performance effectiveness.

26. Describe three types of programs that psychologists have designed to enhance work motivation. What major perspectives do these programs rest upon?

Job enrichment has promoted better work outcomes in manufacturing plants, white-collar and police organizations, and other work settings (van der Vegt et al., 1998). At a truck assembly plant owned by Volvo in Sweden, job enrichment improved performance, lowered absenteeism, and reduced turnover (Wexley & Yukl, 1977). Production teams of five to twelve workers replaced assembly lines (which were low on all five core job dimensions). Team members elected their own coordinator, decided task distribution, managed their own quality control, and could vary their work as long as they met production standards.

Modifying External Incentives

Learning theory predicts that performance will increase when reinforcers are made contingent on productivity. Union National Bank instituted a program in which it paid workers for the number of customers served and new accounts opened. As a result, employees' take-home pay increased by 25 percent and the bank's profits doubled (Aamodt, 1991). Another program reduced tardiness and absenteeism among industrial workers in an unusual way. Every day, each worker who arrived on time was dealt a card from a poker deck. At the end of the week, the worker with the best five-card poker hand (and who therefore had to be on time every day) won a $20 prize (Pedalino & Gamboa, 1974)!

Money is not the only external incentive than modifies performance. The Emory Air Freight Corporation used praise and recognition to reinforce desired employee behaviours, and a large department store improved the performance of its salespeople by reinforcing them with "time off" for desired behaviours (Luthans et al., 1981).

Goal-Setting and Management by Objectives

Goal setting is a powerful motivational technique that has increased employee productivity in almost every study conducted, and **management by objectives (MBO)** combines goal setting with employee participation and feedback (Locke & Latham, 1990). These approaches reflect the cognitive assumption that motivation is maximized when people pursue valued goals that they perceive as attainable. Effective goal setting involves developing specific goals (rather than general goals or "do your best goals") that are challenging yet attainable (rather than easy) *and* planning a clear strategy for achieving them (Locke, 1996).

Employee participation is the second component of MBO. Employees meet at least once a year with their managers to develop employee goals and plan how to attain them. Goals may focus on individual or group performance. Participation is designed to increase employees' acceptance of the goals and enhance the likelihood that goals will be attained. The third MBO component, *objective feedback*, is essential to effective goal setting (Locke & Latham, 1990; Wilk & Resmon, 1998). It provides opportunities to recognize success and, when goals are not met, it encourages a search for new methods to reach them.

Robert Rodgers and John Hunter (1991) meta-analyzed 70 studies that tested MBO in different organizations. Productivity increased in 97 percent of the studies, but the amount of improvement depended strongly upon whether top management actively supported the program. Even well-planned motivation programs will be less effective when an organization is not highly committed to them.

In Review

- *For most workers, opportunities for accomplishment and growth are stronger motivators than money. Dissatisfied workers are higher in absenteeism and job turnover than satisfied employees, but job satisfaction is correlated weakly with job productivity.*
- *Job enrichment programs attempt to increase employees' motivation by making work tasks more intrinsically motivating. Incentive programs make external reinforcers contingent on certain types of performance. Goal-setting programs set challenging goals and plan a strategy to reach them. Management by objectives includes goal setting, employee participation, and objective performance feedback.*

MOTIVATIONAL CONFLICT

27. Explain three main types of motivational conflict. Can you think of examples from your own life?

Motivational goals sometimes conflict with one another. Achievement and affiliation motives may clash, for example, when we have to choose between studying for an exam and attending a party. This conflict places us in a motivational bind that can affect our well-being. Kurt Lewin (1935) described such conflicts in terms of two opposing tendencies: approach and avoidance. When something attracts us, we tend to approach it; when something repels us, we tend to avoid it. Different combinations of approach and avoidance tendencies can produce three basic types of conflict.

Approach-approach conflict involves opposition between two attractive alternatives. Selecting one means losing the other. Conflict is at its greatest when both alternatives, such as a choice between two desirable career paths, are equally attractive and important. The reverse dilemma is **avoidance-avoidance conflict,** in which a person faces two undesirable alternatives (Figure 10.19). Do I spend all week studying boring material for my test, or do I skip studying and fail the exam?

Approach-avoidance conflict involves being attracted to and repelled by *the same goal.* These are sometimes the most difficult conflicts to resolve. A fourth-year university student, thinking of changing majors, is attracted to job opportunities in this new major but is repelled by the possibility of a fifth year of classes. Seeing a person on a bench hold out some food, a squirrel is motivated by hunger to approach and by fear to keep its distance.

In approach-avoidance relationships the tendency to approach a desired goal and the desire to avoid it both grow stronger as we get nearer to the goal (Miller, 1944). A critical factor, however, is that the avoidance tendency usually increases in strength faster than does the approach tendency (Figure 10.20). Thus, at first we may be attracted to a goal and only slightly repelled by its drawbacks. As we get closer to it, the negative aspects become more dominant. We may stop and then retreat, approach again, and continue to vacillate in a state of conflict.

Another issue that can trigger a motivational conflict comes from the fact that some consequences are in the future. For example, this evening you may be faced with the choice of writing the essay that is due in two weeks or watching your favourite television show. That is, you have an immediate incentive (the TV show that is about to start) and a delayed incentive (your mark from a well-written essay). Your choice this evening will be different than it will be when there are only two days left to finish the essay (I hope). The value of an incentive, such as getting a good mark, decreases with a delay. This phenomenon is called **delay discounting** (Mischel et

"C'mon, c'mon—it's either one or the other."

FIGURE 10.19

An unfortunate avoidance-avoidance conflict.

al., 1972). Delay discounting refers to the decrease (or discount) in the value of a future incentive. The further away in time, the greater the decrease in the value. We discussed immediate versus delayed consequences and delay of gratification in Chapter 7, and many of those considerations apply here. Motivational conflicts can ensue as we are faced with various delays in achieving a goal, such as between an immediate, small reward and a delayed, large reward. The value of a future reward will change as the time one has to wait for it decreases; as we approach the availability of a reward, its incentive value increases. The motivation to study for your Introductory Psychology test is stronger if the test is tomorrow than if the test is next month. Research on self-control, delay discounting, and delay of gratification has examined factors that influence the relative preference for a small, immediate reward over a larger, delayed reward and how our motivational state varies as we are faced with positive incentives of different sizes and different availabilities (for reviews, see Ainslie, 2001; Rachlin, 2000).

Some methods of coping with motivational conflict can be maladaptive. Of these, *defensive avoidance* may be the most common (Janis and Mann, 1977). Here, the decision maker procrastinates and generally avoids coming to grips with the decision. We see in Chapter 13 that psychodynamic models often focus on unconscious ways in which people resolve such conflicts.

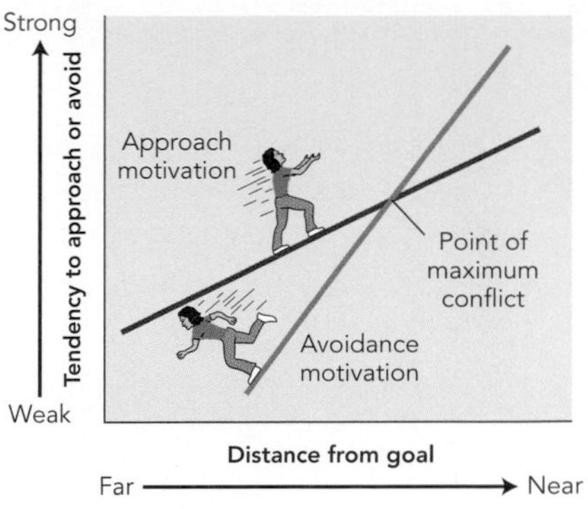

FIGURE 10.20

According to Neal Miller (1944), the tendency to approach and the tendency to avoid grow stronger as one moves closer to the goal. However, the tendency to avoid increases faster than the tendency to approach. Maximum conflict is experienced where the two gradients cross, because at this point the opposing motives are equal in strength.

In Review

- *Motivational goals may conflict with one another. Approach-approach conflicts occur when a person has to select between two attractive alternatives. Avoidance-avoidance goals involve choosing between two undesirable alternatives.*
- *Approach-avoidance conflicts occur when we are attracted to, and repelled by, the same goal. As we approach the goal, the avoidance tendency usually increases in strength more rapidly than the approach tendency.*

THE NATURE AND FUNCTIONS OF EMOTION

Life without emotion would be bland and empty. Our subjective experience of love, anger, joy, fear, and other emotions energize and add colour to our lives. Emotions can foster happiness and well-being, or they can contribute to psychological and physical dysfunction. Modern psychology's focus on the study of emotion echoes a timeless fascination—expressed in songs, paintings, stories, poems, and scholarly treatises—with human emotions.

28. What is an emotion?

Emotions are positive or negative feeling (affect) states consisting of a pattern of cognitive, physiological, and behavioural reactions to events that have relevance to important goals or motives. The events in question may be external situations, such as seeing an oncoming car swerving into your lane, or a group of laughing, smiling friends walking toward you. They may be internal thoughts, memories, or images, such as remembering the look and sound of someone special that you just met, or thinking about a coming exam.

The concepts of motivation and emotion have always been closely linked, and the dividing line between them is not always clear (Carlson & Hatfield, 1992; Edwards, 1998). One reason is that motivation and emotion both involve states of arousal, and they both can trigger patterns of action (e.g., flight in the case of fear and attack in the case of anger). Indeed, the terms *moti*vation and *emoti*on are both derived from the Latin word *movere,* "to move." The link between motivation and emotion involves more than a common linguistic root, however. Emotion theorist Richard Lazarus (2006) believes that there is *always* a link between motives and emotions, because we react emotionally only when our motives and goals are gratified, threatened, or frustrated. Emotional reactions are especially strong when an experience is pertinent to goals that are very important to us (Figure 10.21).

How then shall we distinguish between motivation and emotion? One way is to place them within a stimulus-response framework. Some theorists suggest that motives operate as internal *stimuli* that energize and direct behaviour toward some goal or incentive, whereas emotions are basically reactions, or *responses,* to events that relate to important goals (Mandler, 1984; Scherer, 1988).

The Adaptive Value of Emotion

29. How are emotions related to motivation?

Like other psychological processes, emotions have important adaptive functions. First, they signal that something important is happening, and they direct our attention to that event. In an evolutionary sense, some emotions are part of an emergency arousal system that increases the chances of survival by energizing, directing, and sustaining adaptive behaviours. Probably the most basic of these behavioural tendencies, seen in virtually all species, is fighting or fleeing when confronted by threat or danger. The physiological arousal that is so central to the emotions of anger and fear energizes and intensifies such behaviours.

FIGURE 10.21

The intimate relations between motivation and emotion are seen in the strong emotional responses that can occur when important goals are either attained or lost.

Barbara Fredrickson (1998) suggests that positive and negative emotions have different adaptive functions. Negative emotions have been sculpted by evolutionary survival pressures to *narrow* attention and action tendencies so that the organism can respond to a threatening situation with a focused set of responses. An animal threatened with attack should selectively attend to attack-relevant stimuli and respond by either fighting or fleeing.

What good, then, are positive emotions? Fredrickson suggests that, unlike negative emotions, positive emotions usually arise under conditions of safety and goal attainment, in which high physiological arousal is not needed. Rather than narrowing attention and behaviour tendencies, positive emotions such as interest, joy, contentment, and love actually *broaden* our thinking and behaviour so that we explore, consider new ideas, try out new ways to achieve goals, play, and savour what we have. These activities help individuals to build new resources, some of which are intellectual (gaining new knowledge and insight), some physical (finding new ways to complete tasks, or new physical skills), and some social (building and strengthening relationships). Fredrickson believes that in these ways, positive emotions also are highly adaptive for humans.

Emotions are also a form of social communication. By providing observable information about our internal states and intentions, emotions influence how other people behave toward us (Isaacs, 1998). Consider, for example, the effects of a baby's crying or smiling on adults. Parents and other adults report feeling irritated, annoyed, disturbed, distressed, sympathetic, or unhappy when babies cry, and they become more physiologically aroused themselves (Frodi et al., 1978). Parents and other adults generally respond to crying infants with caretaking responses that have obvious survival value for the infant. Positive emotions also pay off for babies. A smiling infant is likely to increase parents' feelings of love and caring, thereby increasing the likelihood that the child's biological and emotional needs will be satisfied.

Emotional messages begin to have an impact early in life. Within one to three days after birth, human infants respond to another infant's crying with crying of their own. Children who are less than a year old respond with negative affect to vocal expressions of fear by their mother (Mumme et al., 1996), and by two years of age they react to their mother's real or simulated signs of distress with efforts to help or comfort her (Sagi & Hoffman, 1976; Zahn-Waxler et al., 1979, 1992). Adults' expressions of sadness and distress also evoke concern, empathy, and helping behaviour from others (Izard, 1989).

30. What are the adaptive functions of positive and negative emotions?

31. In what ways are emotions modes of communication?

In Review

- *An emotion is a positive or negative feeling (or affective state) consisting of a pattern of cognitive, physiological, and behavioural reactions to events that have relevance to important goals or motives. Negative emotional responses are a central feature of the stress response.*
- *Emotions further our well-being in several ways: by rousing us to action, by helping us communicate with others, and by eliciting empathy and help. Negative emotions narrow attention and behaviours, whereas positive thoughts tend to broaden our thinking and behaviour.*

The Nature of Emotion

Psychologist James Averill (1980) found more than 550 words in the English language that refer to various positive and negative emotional states. We surely do not have 550 different emotions, but the emotions we do have share four common features.

32. Name the four major components of emotions, including the two classes of behavioural responses.

- First, emotions are responses to external or internal eliciting stimuli.
- Second, emotional responses result from our interpretation or **cognitive appraisal** of these stimuli, which gives the situation its perceived meaning and significance.
- Third, our *bodies respond physiologically* to our appraisal. We may become physically "stirred up," as in fear, joy, or anger, or we may experience decreased arousal, as in contentment or depression.
- Fourth, emotions include *behaviour tendencies.* Some are *expressive behaviours* (e.g., exhibiting surprise, smiling with joy, or crying). Others are *instrumental behaviours,* ways of doing something about the stimulus that aroused the emotion (e.g., studying for an anxiety-arousing test, fighting back in self-defence, or running away).

Figure 10.22 illustrates the general relations among these four emotional components. For example, an insulting remark from another person (eliciting stimulus) may evoke a cognitive appraisal that one has been unfairly demeaned, an increase in physiological arousal, a clenching of jaw and fists (expressive behaviour), and a verbal attack on the other person (instrumental behaviour). As the two-way arrows indicate, these emotional components can influence one another. Cognition can trigger physiological changes and expressive behaviour which, in turn, can affect what we think about the situation and about ourselves (Forgas, 2000).

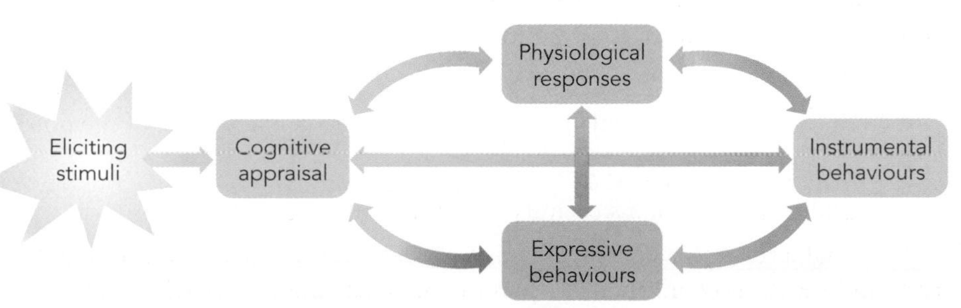

FIGURE 10.22

Components of emotion, showing the relations between eliciting stimuli, cognitive appraisal processes, physiological arousal, expressive behaviours, and instrumental behaviours. Note the reciprocal (two-way) causal relations that are thought to exist among the appraisal, physiological arousal, and expressive behaviour components.

Emotion is a dynamic ongoing *process*. Thus any of its four elements can change rapidly as the situation and our responses to it influence one another. For example, as anger begins to escalate during a disagreement, you might choose to make a conciliatory response that evokes a positive reaction or apology from the other person, helps defuse the situation, and reduces your negative appraisal of the other person and your level of emotional arousal. This dynamic, ever-changing property of emotional reactions makes them a challenging "moving target" for scientific study.

Eliciting Stimuli

33. In what sense can eliciting stimuli be external or internal? What are the roles of biological and learning factors?

Emotions do not occur in a vacuum. They are responses to situations, people, objects, or events. We become angry *at* something or someone; fearful or proud *of* something; in love *with* someone. Moreover, the stimuli that trigger cognitive appraisals and emotional responses are not always external; they can be internal stimuli, such as mental images and memories. Most of us can work up a state of anger simply by recalling or imagining a painful injustice or insult from the past, or evoke warm feelings by recalling significant positive experiences.

Innate biological factors help determine which stimuli have the greatest potential to arouse emotions. Newborn infants come equipped with the capacity to respond emotionally with either interest or distress to events in their environment (Davidson & Fox, 1988; Galati & Lavelli, 1997). Adults, too, may be biologically primed to experience emotions in response to certain stimuli that have evolutionary significance. As discussed in Chapter 7, fear responses can be classically conditioned more easily to pictures of snakes and spiders than to more innocuous stimuli, such as flowers, when these stimuli are paired with mild electric shocks (Hygge & Öhman, 1978).

34. How can learning influence emotion?

Learning also influences the ability of particular objects or people to arouse emotions. Previous experiences can make certain people or situations eliciting stimuli for emotions. In Chapter 7 we encountered Little Albert who had learnt a fear of white rats and other white furry objects. The mere sight of one's lover can evoke feelings of passion, and the sight of a disliked person an instantaneous feeling of revulsion that seems almost reflexive in nature. On the broadest level, cultures have different standards for defining the good, the bad, and the ugly, and these standards affect how eliciting stimuli will be appraised and responded to emotionally. Physical features that provoke sexual arousal and feelings of infatuation in one culture, such as ornamental facial scars or a bone through the nose, may elicit feelings of disgust in another. In Western societies, recent increases in the popularity and acceptability of body piercing and tattoos illustrate how quickly cultural standards can change.

The Cognitive Component

You are walking across campus with a group of people from one of your classes when you encounter a person you met at a party the previous night and to whom you are attracted. The person looks at you as you warmly say "Hello," responds with a blank stare, and then turns away without responding. Which emotions would the following thoughts trigger in you?

- "Oh no! What a total put-down. What do my classmates think of me now?"
- "What a jerk, ignoring me like that."
- "Just like always. I'll never find anyone who likes me."
- "What a relief! Now I won't be distracted from my usual 50-hour study week and my thimble collection."

Embarrassed? Angry? Depressed? Relieved? As you think, so shall you feel.

Cognitions are involved in virtually every aspect of emotion. They can evoke emotional responses, they are part of our subjective experience of the emotion, and they influence how we express our emotions and act on them. A situation may evoke pleasure or distress, depending on how we appraise it. For example, sexual stimulation may elicit anger, fear, or disgust instead of pleasure if it is deemed inappropriate or unwanted.

35. How do cognitive appraisals enter into emotion? Do they need to involve conscious thought?

Appraisal processes. Emotions are always responses to our perceptions of the eliciting stimuli. While all perceptions involve attaching meaning to sensory stimuli, the appraisals involved in emotion are especially evaluative and personal; they relate to what we think is desirable or undesirable for us or for the people we care about (Lazarus, 2006).

Often we are not consciously aware of the appraisals that underlie emotional responses (Bargh & Chartrand, 1999; Cacioppo & Gardner, 1999). Some appraisals involve little more than an almost automatic interpretation of sensory input (Lazarus, 2006; Zajonc, 1984). Your emotional reaction to the sight of a milk truck bearing down upon you would probably not require an extended contemplation of the impending outcomes. More likely, you'd reflexively jump out of the way and experience an instantaneous fear response.

Infants who have no formal language obviously experience emotion, providing further evidence of the role of primitive appraisals. As our cognitive abilities develop, however, appraisals are more likely to become tied to language, whether or not we are consciously aware of the actual appraisals (Izard & Malatesta, 1987). Indeed, many language-based appraisals become so habitual that they run off in a subconscious shorthand with little or no awareness on our part (Bargh, 1997; Beck, 1976). We often fail to appreciate how arbitrary can be our interpretations of "the way things are." To us, they're simply "reality," but someone else may appraise the same situation in a manner that creates an entirely different "reality" and triggers a different emotional response.

FIGURE 10.23

Differences in appraisal can trigger entirely different emotional reactions, as in this instance. What kinds of appraisals are likely occurring in these people?

The idea that emotional reactions are triggered by cognitive appraisals rather than external situations helps to account for the fact that different people (or even the same person at different times) can have very different emotional reactions to the same object, situation, or person (Figure 10.23). Statements such as "I have a new attitude toward her now" or "I've decided what's really important in life" reflect changes in appraisals of certain situations or people.

36. What evidence exists for (a) universal and (b) culturally determined appraisals? Provide examples of each.

Culture and appraisal. Like theorists who study the situations that elicit emotion in various cultures, those who study cognitive appraisal have looked for cross-cultural similarities and differences in the thoughts and perceptions that precede emotions (Scherer, 1984; Smith & Ellsworth, 1985). Respondents in a variety of cultures have been asked to recall events that evoked certain emotions, then to answer questions about how they appraised or interpreted the situations. In one study conducted in 27 different countries, the researchers found strong cross-cultural similarities in the types of appraisals that evoked joy, fear, anger, sadness, disgust, shame, and guilt (Wallbott & Scherer, 1988). In another cross-cultural study comparing American and Asian people in Japan and Hong Kong, Robert Mauro and his co-workers (1992) found that Americans reported feeling happiness, pride, and hope more frequently than did the Japanese. The Japanese, in turn, reported more frequent feelings of shame and regret than did people from Hong Kong. Nonetheless, whenever any of these emotions did occur, similar appraisals were involved, regardless of the culture.

Despite these cross-cultural commonalities in appraisal, the same type of situation also can evoke different appraisals and resulting emotional reactions, depending on one's culture. Consider, for example, the circumstance of "being alone." For Tahitians, being alone is appraised as an opportunity for bad spirits to bother a person, and fear is the most common emotional response. In the close-knit Utku Inuit, an Eskimo culture, being alone signifies social rejection and isolation, triggering sadness and loneliness. In Western cultures, being alone may at times represent a welcome respite from the frantic pace of daily life, evoking contentment and happiness (Mesquita et al., 1997). Thus, where appraisals are concerned, there seem to be certain universals, but also some degree of cultural diversity in some of the more subtle aspects of interpreting situations (Mesquita et al., 1997; Scherer, 1998).

The Physiological Component

One of the first things we notice is the bodily changes that occur when our feelings are "stirred up." Many parts of the body are involved in emotional arousal, but certain brain regions, the autonomic nervous system, and the endocrine system play especially significant roles.

Brain structures and neurotransmitters. The brain's involvement in emotion is complex, and many aspects are not well understood. It is clear, however, that emotions involve important interactions between cortical and subcortical areas (Borod, 2000; Edwards, 1998).

37. Which subcortical and cortical structures are involved in emotion? How does LeDoux's theory explain unconscious emotional phenomena?

Subcortical structures, such as the hypothalamus, the amygdala, the hippocampus, and other limbic system structures play major roles in emotion (Figure 10.24). If animals are electrically stimulated in specific areas of the limbic system, they will growl at and attack anything that approaches them. Destroying the same sites produces an absence of aggression, even if the animal is provoked or attacked (Sotres-Bayon, Cain & LeDoux, 2006). Other areas of the limbic system show the opposite pattern: lack of emotion when they are stimulated and unrestrained emotion when they are removed (Thompson, 1988).

The cerebral cortex has many connections with the hypothalamus and limbic system, allowing constant communication between cortical and subcortical regions. Cognitive appraisal processes surely involve activities in the cortex, where the mechanisms for language and complex thought reside. Moreover, the ability to regulate emotion depends heavily on the executive functions of the *prefrontal cortex*, which lies immediately behind the forehead (Gross, 1998).

Groundbreaking research and theorizing by psychologist Joseph LeDoux (1986, 2000, 2006) has revealed important links between the cortex and the limbic system. As shown in Figure 10.24, the key brain structures in this model are the thalamus, which routes sensory input to various parts of the brain, the amygdala, which helps coordinate and trigger physiological and behavioural responses to emotion-arousing situations, and the cortex, where sensory input is organized as perceptions and evaluated by the "thinking" or linguistic part of the brain. LeDoux's key discovery was that the thalamus sends messages along two independent neural pathways, one travelling to the cortex and the other directly to the amygdala. This means that the amygdala can receive direct input from the senses and generate emotional reactions before the cerebral cortex has had time to fully interpret what is causing the reaction. LeDoux suggests that this primitive mechanism (which is the only emotional mechanism in species such as birds and reptiles) has survival value because it enables the organism to react with great speed. Shortly afterward, the cerebral cortex responds with a more carefully processed cognitive interpretation of the situation. This may be what occurs when a hiker sees an object that looks like a snake and jumps out of the way, only to realize an instant later that the object is a rope.

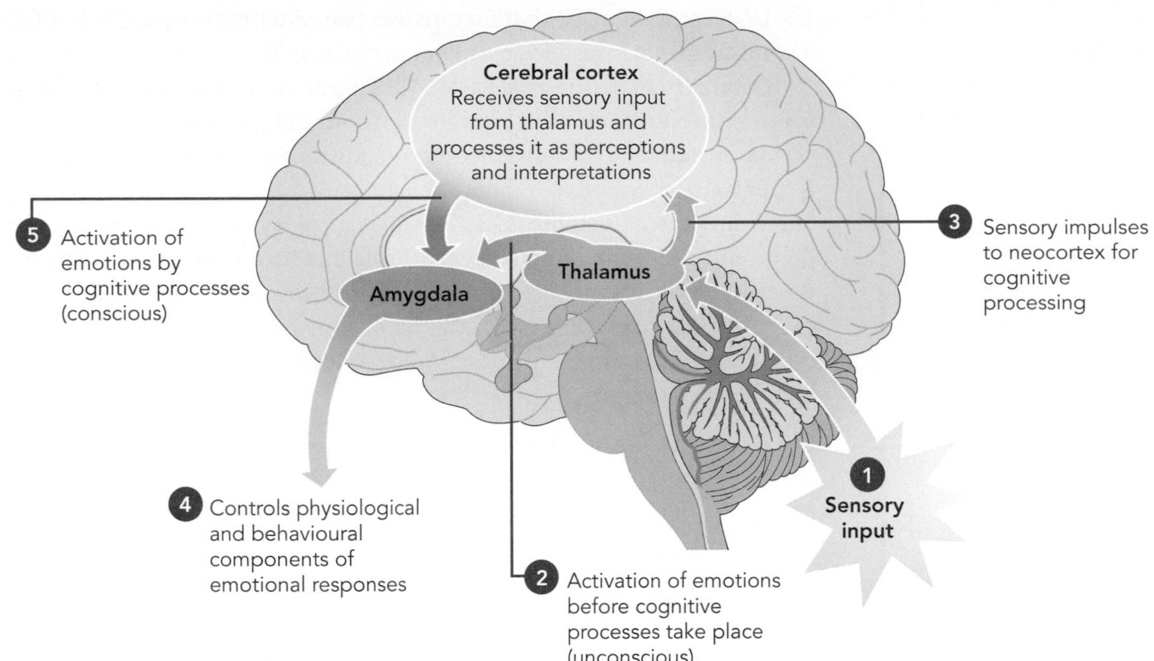

FIGURE 10.24

Parallel neural processes may produce conscious and unconscious emotional responses at about the same time. LeDoux's research suggests that sensory input to the thalamus can be routed directly to the amygdala in the limbic system, producing an "unconscious" emotional response before cognitive responses evoked by the other pathway to the cortex can occur

The existence of a dual system for emotional processing may help explain some puzzling aspects of our emotional lives. For example, most of us have had the experience of suddenly feeling emotional without understanding why. LeDoux (2000) also suggests that people are capable of having two simultaneous emotional reactions to the same event, a conscious one occurring as a result of cortical activity and an unconscious one triggered by the amygdala. This might help explain instances in which people are puzzled by behavioural reactions that seem to be at odds with the emotion they are consciously experiencing: "I don't know why I came across as being angry. I felt very warm and friendly."

Many of our emotional responses are based on previous learning experiences. LeDoux (1989) has shown that the amygdala can indeed learn on its own, providing a possible mechanism for "unconscious" emotional memories. First, he surgically removed the visual cortex of rats so that visual stimuli could not be processed in the cortex. Then, using a classical conditioning procedure, he paired a light with electric shock. Although the rat's visual cortex couldn't "see" the light, the rats developed a conditioned fear response to this CS, indicating that the amygdala learned to fear it.

38. What experimental and clinical evidence supports the role of the amygdala in emotional learning?

Studies with humans suggest emotional processing by the amygdala without conscious awareness. British scientists measured neural activity in the amygdala while participants viewed pictures of faces. Some of the faces had been previously paired with an aversive noise to establish a conditioned negative emotional response to them. Even when the faces were presented in such a manner that the participants could not consciously report their presence, brain recordings showed that the amygdala in the right (non-verbal) hemisphere reacted to the aversively conditioned faces, but not to the non-conditioned faces (Morris et al., 1998).

Research with brain-damaged patients suggests different neural bases for conscious awareness and emotional responses. Two limbic system structures that have been studied are the hippocampus, which is involved in forming memories, and the amygdala. Patients with damage to their hippocampus suffer memory impairment. They can develop a classically conditioned emotional response even though they cannot consciously learn the connection between the CS and the UCS. In contrast, people with no hippocampal damage, but a damaged amygdala, can describe the

39. Which neurotransmitters are involved in specific emotional responses?

CS-UCS contingency ("that picture was paired with the shock"), but fail to develop a conditioned fear response (Bechara et al., 1995).

Neuroscientist Candace Pert (1997) argues that, because all of the neural structures involved in emotion operate biochemically, it is the ebbs and flows of various neurotransmitter substances that activate the emotional programs residing in the brain. For example, dopamine activity appears to underlie some pleasurable emotions, and endorphins may also play a role (Panksepp, 1998; Robinson, 1997). Serotonin and norepinephrine play a role in anger. Despite these linkages, however, it seems unlikely that specific brain substances will be found to produce specific emotions on their own. When the final story of the brain and emotion can at last be told, it will undoubtedly describe complex interactions between brain chemicals and neural structures.

Hemispheric activation and emotion. Years ago in Italy, psychiatrists treated clinically depressed patients with electroshock treatments to either the right or the left hemisphere. The electric current temporarily disrupted activity in the hemisphere to which it was applied. With the left hemisphere knocked out (forcing the right hemisphere to take charge), patients had what physicians termed a "catastrophic" reaction, wailing and crying until the shock effects wore off. When shock was applied to the right hemisphere, allowing the left hemisphere to dominate, the patients reacted quite differently. They seemed unconcerned, happy, and sometimes even euphoric. A similar pattern of emotions was noted in patients in whom one hemisphere had been damaged by lesions or strokes. Left hemisphere damage, particularly in the frontal lobe, accentuated negative emotions such as depression; right frontal damage was linked to indifference or euphoria (Gainotti, 1972).

40. What clinical and research evidence is there to support a "left-right" theory of hemispheric activation differences for positive and negative emotions?

These findings suggest that left-hemisphere activation might underlie certain positive emotions, and right-hemisphere functioning negative ones (Sutton, 2002). To test this proposition, Richard Davidson and Nathan Fox obtained EEG measures of frontal lobe activity as people experienced various emotions (Davidson & Fox, 1988; Fox & Davidson, 1991). They found that when people felt positive emotions by recalling pleasurable experiences or watching a happy film, the left hemisphere was relatively more active than the right. But when sadness or other negative emotions were evoked, the right hemisphere became relatively more active. This pattern seems to be innate. Infants only three to four days old showed a similar pattern of hemispheric activation when given sucrose solutions, which evoke positive reactions, or a citric acid solution, which apparently disgusts them (Davidson & Fox, 1988).

People differ in their tendency to experience positive or negative emotions (see the Focus on Neuroscience box on p. 446). Individual differences in typical or *resting* hemispheric activation, measured under emotionally neutral conditions, seem related to this tendency. Davidson and Fox (1989) found that human infants with resting right-hemisphere dominance were more likely to become upset and cry if their mothers left the room than were those with left-hemisphere dominance (Figure 10.25). In adults, a higher resting level of right-hemisphere EEG activity appears to be a risk factor for the later development of adult depressive disorders (Marshall & Fox, 2000; Tomarken & Keener, 1998).

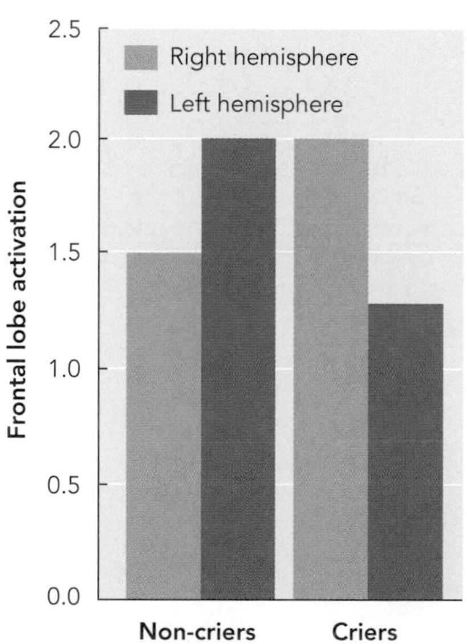

FIGURE 10.25

Resting activation in the left and right frontal hemispheres differs in infants who later reacted with distress or no distress when their mothers left. The criers showed relatively greater right-hemisphere activation, the non-criers greater left-hemisphere activation.

Data from Davidson & Fox, 1989.

Autonomic and hormonal processes. You are afraid. Your heart starts to beat faster. Blood is drawn from your stomach to your muscles, and digestion slows to a crawl. You breathe harder and faster to get more energy-sustaining oxygen. Your blood sugar level increases, producing more nutrients for your muscles. The pupils of your eyes dilate to let in more light so you can see the danger better. Your skin perspires to keep you cool and to flush out waste products created by extra exertion. Your muscles tense, ready for action.

Some theorists call this state of arousal the *fight-or-flight response*. It is produced by the sympathetic branch of the autonomic nervous system and by hormones from the endocrine system. The sympathetic nervous system produces arousal within a few seconds by directly stimulating the organs and muscles of the body. Meanwhile, the endocrine system pumps epinephrine, cortisol, and other stress hormones into the bloodstream. These hormones produce physiological effects like those triggered by the sympathetic nervous system, but their effects are longer lasting and can keep the body aroused for a considerable length of time.

41. How are the sympathetic and endocrine systems involved in emotion? Do different emotions have different patterns of autonomic arousal?

Do different emotions produce different patterns of arousal? Many investigators conclude that complex and subtle emotions such as jealousy and tenderness do not involve distinct patterns of arousal (Panksepp, 1998). On the other hand, autonomic patterns do show subtle differences in certain basic emotions, such as anger and fear (Levenson, 1992). For example, heart rate speeds up in both fear and anger, but there are differences in where the blood gets pumped (Ekman et al., 1983). Anger causes more blood to flow to the hands and feet, whereas fear reduces blood flow to these areas (providing a scientific basis for the colloquial expression "cold feet"). But whether people can detect such subtle physiological differences in a manner that would allow them to identify and label their emotions is an unanswered question.

42. What considerations and research evidence challenge the validity of the "lie detector"? What kinds of errors are most likely?

We cannot easily control autonomic nervous system activation with exposure to emotion-evoking stimuli. This simple observation led to the idea that changes in physiological arousal might tell us whether someone is lying or telling the truth. The rationale is that when someone lies, they should become anxious and that increase in anxiety will be reflected in physiological responses such as increases in heart rate, respiration, and skin conductance (which increases due to sweat gland activity). On the other hand, if they are answering honestly, then no change in physiological arousal would be expected. The instrument used to measure such changes is the **polygraph**, the famous, or infamous, "lie detector" (Figure 10.26). Although controversial, research findings support the contention that the lie detector can be fooled by someone who manages to remain calm while lying, or by someone who is experiencing fear, anxiety, or lack of confidence while telling the truth. Research has found an especially high rate of false positives, identifying an innocent person as guilty, with polygraph tests (Lykken, 1981, 1984; Honts & Perry, 1992).

(a)

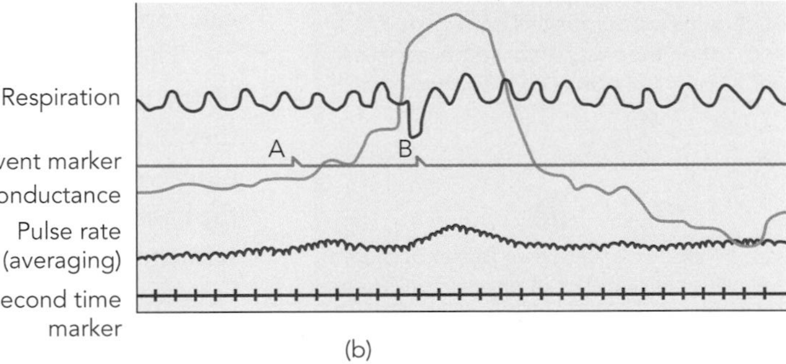

(b)

FIGURE 10.26

The polygraph (a) records physiological changes (b) that are part of emotional responses. Between points A and B, an emotionally loaded question was asked. Within two seconds, the effects of the question were visible in the subject's respiration, skin conductance, and pulse rate. Does this mean he was lying?

The Behavioural Component

So far, we have examined the situational, cognitive, and physiological components of emotion. We now turn to the directly observable behaviours that are part of emotional responses.

Expressive behaviours. Although we can never directly experience another person's feelings, we can often infer that someone is angry, sad, fearful, or happy on the basis of his or her emotional displays, or **expressive behaviours**. When exposed to slides showing angry or happy faces, university students responded with subtle facial muscle responses that denote displeasure or pleasure within 1/3 of a second (Dinberg & Thunberg, 1998). Sometimes, too, others' emotional displays can evoke similar emotional responses in us, a process known as **empathy**. Perhaps you have found yourself experiencing the same emotion as the central character while reading a novel or viewing a movie. Professional actors sometimes find that they become so immersed in the expressive behaviours of a character they are playing that the boundaries

FIGURE 10.27

Similarities among species in the expression of certain basic emotions convinced Darwin and other theorists that some expressive behaviours have an evolutionary origin.

43. What evidence exists for fundamental emotional patterns of expression? How do they fit into an emotional hierarchy?

between self and role begin to fade. Kirk Douglas reported one such experience when he played Vincent Van Gogh in *Lust for Life*:

> I was close to getting lost in the character of Van Gogh . . . I felt myself going over the line, into the skin of Van Gogh. . . . Sometimes I had to stop myself from reaching my hand up and touching my ear to find out if it was actually there. It was a frightening experience. That way lies madness . . . I could never play him again. (Lehman-Haupt, 1988, p. 10)

Evolution and emotional expression. Where do emotional expressions come from? In his classic work, *The Expression of Emotions in Man and Animals* (1872–1965), Charles Darwin argued that emotional displays are products of evolution, and that they developed because they contributed to species survival. Darwin emphasized the basic similarity of emotional expression in animals and humans. For example, both wolves and humans bare their teeth when they are angry (Figure 10.27). As Darwin explained it, this behaviour makes the animal look more ferocious, and thus decreases its chances of being attacked and perhaps killed in a fight. Darwin did not maintain that all forms of emotional expression are innate, but he believed that many of them are.

Like Darwin, modern evolutionary theorists stress the adaptive value of emotional expression (Izard, 1984; Plutchik, 1994; Tomkins, 1991). Two key findings suggest that humans have innate, or **fundamental emotional patterns**. First, the expressions of certain emotions (e.g., rage and terror) are similar across a variety of cultures, suggesting that certain expressive behaviour patterns are wired into the nervous system. Second, children who are blind from birth seem to express these basic emotions in the same ways that sighted children do, ruling out the possibility that they are learned solely through observation (Eibl-Eibesfeldt, 1973). The fundamental emotional patterns proposed by three leading evolutionary theorists are shown in Table 10.2. Other emotions are seen as resulting from some combination of these innate emotions. The evolutionary view does *not* assume that all emotional expressions are innate, nor does it deny that innate emotional expressions can be modified or inhibited as a result of social learning.

Emotions can be organized in terms of a hierarchy ranging from the most universal expressions to the more subtle subordinate categories (Fischer et al., 1990). Positive and negative affect, expressed as interest and distress, are the most basic categories, the most universal, and the first to manifest themselves after birth.

The basic emotions described by evolutionary theorists appear at the second level of the hierarchy. These basic emotions are assumed to apply across all cultures, but they appear later in a child's development than do the positive and negative affect observed in infants. The third level consists of more subtle emotions derived from the basic emotions. These emotions and the ways they are expressed are more heavily influenced by cultural learning. For example, distinctions are made in Western cultures between many different varieties of love, including passionate love, friendship love, parental love, possessive love, and infatuation (Lee, 1988; Sternberg, 1988). In contrast, only two forms of love are distinguished in India: mother love and erotic love (Lynch, 1990). Children learn these cultural distinctions much later in their development.

Facial expression of emotion. Most of us are fairly confident in our ability to "read" the emotions of others. Although many parts of the body can communicate feelings, we tend to concentrate on what the face tells us. Most lower animals have relatively few facial muscles, so their facial expressions are limited. Only monkeys, apes, and humans have enough well-developed facial muscles to produce a large number of expressions.

Interest in studying facial expressions was spurred by the development of sophisticated measuring procedures, such as the Facial Action Coding System (FACS). Developed by Paul Ekman and Wallace Friesen (1987), the FACS requires a trained observer to dissect an observed expression in terms of all the muscular actions that produced it. The system is so complex that it takes about 100 minutes to score each minute of observed facial expression (Ekman et al., 1988).

Common lore has it that the eyes are particularly good sources of information about what is being felt: "if looks could kill"; "the look of love"; "her eyes twinkled with amusement." Research tells us, however, that other parts of the face are at least as important, if not more so. In fact, it appears that different emotions are expressed through different parts of the face.

TABLE 10.2 Fundamental or Primary Innate Emotions Proposed by Three Leading Evolutionary Theorists

Carroll Izard	Silvan Tomkins	Robert Plutchik
Anger	Anger	Anger
Fear	Fear	Fear
Joy	Joy	Enjoyment
Disgust	Disgust	Disgust
Interest	Interest	Anticipation
Surprise	Surprise	Surprise
Contempt	Contempt	
Shame	Shame	
	Sadness	Sadness
	Distress	
Guilt		
		Acceptance

Source: Based on Izard, 1984; Tomkins, 1991; and Plutchik, 1991.

In one experiment, judges first agreed on the emotions being expressed in a set of 32 posed facial photographs. Each photograph was then cut into three parts, a brow-forehead part, an eyes part, and a mouth part. People were then asked to rate these partial photos in terms of six basic emotions: anger, fear, happiness, surprise, sadness, and disgust. The results showed that different parts of the face provided the best cues for recognizing the various emotions. The eyes provided the most important cues for fear and sadness, but the mouth was the major cue for happiness and disgust, and the forehead was the best indicator of surprise. Anger appeared to be a more complex emotion, requiring information from all facial areas to be recognized accurately (Boucher & Ekman, 1975).

44. What results concerning emotional perception, sex differences, and universal expressions of emotion have been found using the FACS?

Although facial expressions can be valuable cues for judging emotion, even people within the same culture may learn to express the same emotions differently. Thus some people have learned to appear very calm when they are angry. Fortunately, we usually know something about the situation to which the person is reacting, and this often is an important basis for judging emotions. For example, if a woman is crying, is she crying because of sadness or because of happiness? A background showing her being declared the winner of a lottery will result in a different emotional judgment than one showing her at a graveside. Many experiments have shown that people's accuracy and agreement in labelling emotions from pictures is considerably higher when the pictures show a background situation (Ekman & Davidson, 1994).

Across many cultures, women have generally proven to be more accurate judges of emotional expressions than men (Ekman, 1982; Zuckerman, 1976). Perhaps the ability to accurately read emotions has greater adaptive significance for women, whose traditional role within many cultures has been to care for others and attend to their needs (Buss, 1991). This ability may also result from cultural encouragement for women to be sensitive to others' emotions and to express their feelings openly. Men who work in professions that emphasize these skills, such as psychotherapy, drama, and art, are as accurate as women in judging emotions, suggesting that these skills can be learned (Rosenthal et al., 1974).

What of Darwin's claim that certain facial expressions are universal indicators of specific emotions? Modern researchers have approached this question by determining the extent to which people in different cultures agree on the emotions being expressed in facial photographs (Ekman, 1973; Russell et al., 1997). The results of one such study are shown in Figure 10.28. You can see that there is

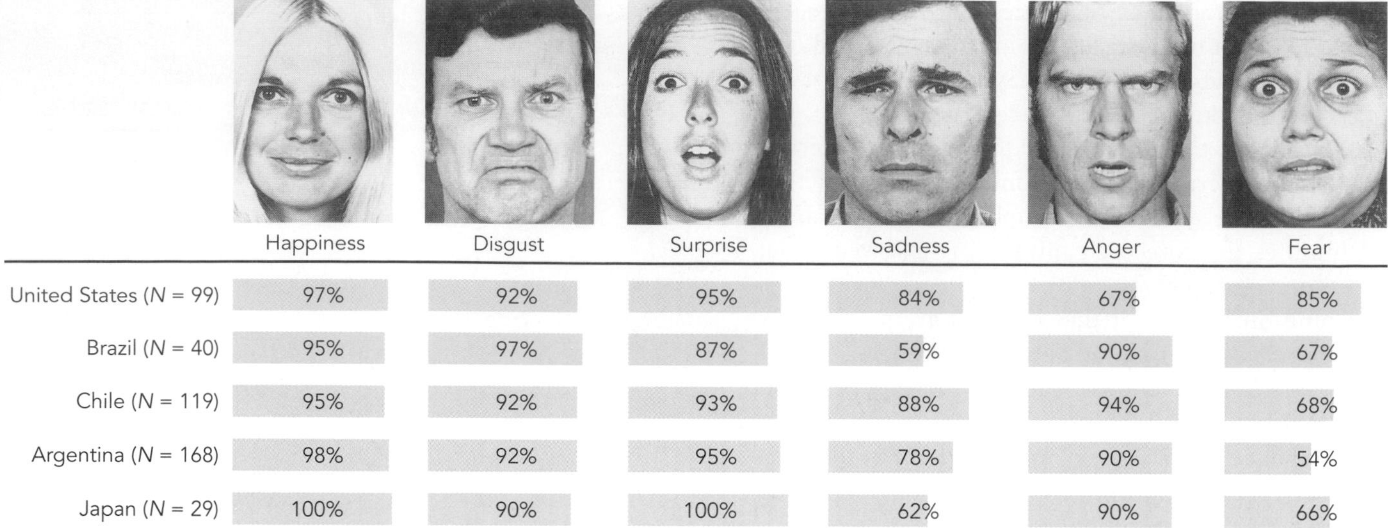

	Happiness	Disgust	Surprise	Sadness	Anger	Fear
United States (*N* = 99)	97%	92%	95%	84%	67%	85%
Brazil (*N* = 40)	95%	97%	87%	59%	90%	67%
Chile (*N* = 119)	95%	92%	93%	88%	94%	68%
Argentina (*N* = 168)	98%	92%	95%	78%	90%	54%
Japan (*N* = 29)	100%	90%	100%	62%	90%	66%

FIGURE 10.28

Percentage of agreement in judgments of facial expressions of emotion by people in five different cultures.

Source: Ekman, 1973.

generally high agreement on these photos of basic emotions, but also some cultural variation. Other researchers have found levels of agreement ranging from 40 to 70 percent across a variety of cultures, well above chance but still far from perfect (Russell, 1994).

In an interesting study of facial expressions, Matsumoto and Willingham (2006) analyzed the facial expressions of medal winners in the judo competition at the 2004 Olympic Summer Games, held in Athens, Greece. Using photographic and videotaped records, they analyzed the facial expressions of winners immediately after completing the medal-winning match and again later when they received their medals. Matsumoto and Willingham used the FACS coding system developed by Elman and Friesen (see page 443) to score the facial expressions of 84 winning athletes from 35 countries. Their results support the argument that the facial expressions displayed spontaneously in an emotion-evoking situation can be considered to be universal.

45. What are cultural display rules? How do they affect emotional behaviour?

Cultural display rules. The norms for emotional expression within a given culture are called **display rules**. Certain gestures, body postures, and physical movements can convey vastly different meanings in different cultures. For example, using the familiar upright thumb gesture while hitchhiking in certain regions of Greece and Sardinia could result in decidedly negative consequences, such as tire tracks on one's body. In those regions, an upright thumb is the equivalent of a raised middle finger in North America (Morris et al., 1979). Likewise, spitting on someone is a sign of contempt in most cultures. Yet the Masai tribe of Africa traditionally considered being spat on a great compliment, particularly if the person doing the spitting is a member of the opposite sex (Thomson, 1887). One can only imagine what a Masai singles bar would be like.

Do emotional expressions differ across cultures in the same way that gestures do? To some extent they do, since the display rules of a particular culture dictate *when* and *how* particular emotions are to be expressed. In the Orissa culture of India, sticking out one's tongue is the display rule for expressing feelings of shame (Menon & Schweder, 1994). Some Asian cultures, such as the Japanese, are more subdued in their expression of emotion in public settings than are Europeans and Americans (Mesquita et al., 1997). Within the Utku Inuit Eskimo culture, the expression of anger is nearly absent. The only exceptions occur toward individuals who have been ostracized by the community and toward dogs, who are the frequent targets of vented aggression (Briggs, 1970). A number of emotion theorists, including Silvan Tomkins (1991), Paul Ekman (1994), and Carroll Izard (1989), conclude that innate biological factors and cultural display rules combine to shape emotional expression.

Instrumental behaviours. Emotional responses are often "calls to action," requiring some sort of response to the situation that aroused the emotion. A highly anxious student must find some way to cope with an impending test. A mother angered by her child's behaviour must find a non-destructive way to get her point across. These are **instrumental behaviours**, directed at achieving some goal.

Batja Mesquita, Nico Frijda, and Klaus Scherer (1997) analyzed cross-cultural studies and concluded that instrumental actions fall into five broad categories: moving toward others (e.g., love), moving away from others (fear, revulsion), moving against others (anger), helplessness, and submission. Within each of these broad categories, many different goal-directed behaviours can occur. Whether an instrumental behaviour will be successful depends on the appropriateness of the response to the situation, the skill with which it is carried out, and the level of emotional arousal that accompanies the behaviours.

46. How do level of arousal and task complexity combine to affect task performance?

People often assume that high emotional arousal enhances task performance, as when athletes try to "psych themselves up" for competition. Yet, as students who have experienced extreme anxiety during tests could testify, high emotional arousal can also interfere with performance. In many situations, the relation between emotional arousal and performance seems to take the shape of an upside-down, or inverted, U. As physiological arousal increases up to some optimal level, performance improves. But beyond that optimal level, further increases in arousal impair performance. It is thus possible to be either too "flat" or too "high" to perform well.

The relation between arousal and performance depends not only on arousal level, but also on task complexity (Yerkes & Dodson, 1908). Task complexity involves how complicated the task is, how much precision is required to do the task, and how well the task has been learned. Generally speaking, as task complexity *increases*, the optimal level of arousal for maximum performance *decreases*. Thus even a moderate level of arousal can disrupt performance on a highly complex task.

Figure 10.29 illustrates these two principles. Note that the inverted U relation applies for all three tasks and that the more complex the task, the lower is the optimal arousal level. One other feature of Figure 10.29 is worth noting: Performance drops off less at high levels of arousal for the simple task than for the others. In fact, even the highest levels of arousal can enhance performance of very simple tasks, such as running or lifting something. This fact may account for seemingly "superhuman" feats we hear about occasionally, such as one incident in which a highly distraught 46 kg mother lifted up the front end of a truck to free her child, who was trapped under one of its wheels (*Honolulu Star-Bulletin*, January 6, 1980).

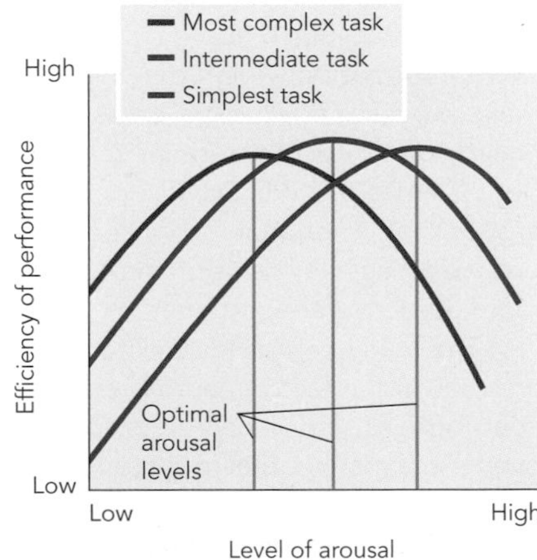

FIGURE 10.29

The relation between arousal and performance often takes the form of an inverted U, with performance declining above and below an optimal arousal level. However, the more difficult or complex a task is, the lower is the optimal level of arousal for performing it.

For complex tasks, the relation between arousal and performance is different. High emotionality can interfere with the ability to attend to and process information effectively. Thus people may underachieve on intelligence test items that require complicated mental processing if they are too anxious, and the performance of air traffic control officers can suffer in highly stressful circumstances (Joslyn & Hunt, 1998; Pierce et al., 1998). On physical tasks, muscle tension can interfere with the skilful execution of complex movements. For example, in the sport of golf, which requires precise and complex movements, the optimal level of arousal should be quite low. Robert Weinberg and Marvin Genuchi (1980) studied the effects of anxiety on performance during an intercollegiate golf tournament. Before the tournament began, they administered a questionnaire to identify players who were low, moderate, or high in performance anxiety. Although the three groups of golfers were similar in ability and performed equally well during practice rounds, their golf scores differed sharply during the anxiety-arousing tournament rounds. On the first day of competition, the average performance of golfers in the low-anxiety group was five strokes better than the performance of those in the high-anxiety group. On the pressure-packed last day of the tournament, this difference rose to nearly seven strokes. The moderate-anxiety group had intermediate scores.

FOCUS ON NEUROSCIENCE

The Neuroscience of Affective Style

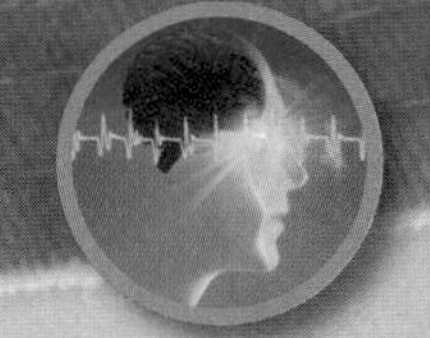

A new area within neuroscience developed late in the twentieth century. Dr. Richard Davidson, one of the area's most important founders, has called it *affective neuroscience*. Affective neuroscience is concerned with how emotion is represented in the brain, with how to explore the components of emotion in a way that is consistent with the neural basis of emotion, and, importantly, with individual differences in affective style (Davidson, 2003). Affective style refers to the observation that the same event can elicit very different emotional reactions among different individuals. We can all remember situations in which the emotional reactions of those present ranged from aversive to neutral to positive. For example, have you ever seen someone trip and fall? It is likely that among the witnesses, some laughed, some were concerned and serious, and some did not react at all. Affective neuroscience is interested in understanding this difference.

An important theme in affective neuroscience is that emotions exert a powerful, adaptive influence on decision making. When you decide what course to take, who to ask out on a date, or what job to apply for, you do not just collect the relevant information, weigh the various pros and cons, and then make a reasoned, logical decision. Our decisions are influenced, often even determined, on the basis of what "feels" right (Damasio, 1995; Davidson, 2003). Affective neuroscience argues that emotional responses interact with other cognitive processes, such as decision making, in a way that can promote rapid, effective adaptation.

The study of individual differences in affective style is one area in which affective neuroscience is making important, novel contributions. Individuals tend to react to emotion-provoking events in a manner that is consistent across time and across situations. You probably know someone who is generally happy, someone who typically shows negative emotions, and someone who is generally calm and rarely shows strong emotional reactions. These individuals differ in their affective style. Questions posed by affective neuroscience are why do these individuals show differing styles, and does this difference reflect differences within the brain? Davidson has suggested that affective style includes a collection of individual differences. These differences include: the threshold at which an emotional response is generated; the magnitude of the response; how quickly the emotional response peaks; the duration of the emotional response; and the time for the emotional response to dissipate (Davidson, 1998, 2000, 2003). All of these contribute to an individual's affective style. An understanding of affective style will help us to understand individual difference; it is also important for understanding an individual's risk of developing some types of psychopathology, such as a mood or anxiety disorder.

Early research in this area using both infants and adults found that there are large individual differences in baseline (resting) activity within the prefrontal cortex, and, interestingly, individual differences in whether the left prefrontal cortex or the right prefrontal cortex shows higher levels of activation while at rest (see Davidson, 2003). Davidson refers to this difference between greater left or greater right prefrontal activity as prefrontal asymmetry in activation. Davidson and Fox (1989) found that even at rest, 10-month old infants differed in their prefrontal asymmetry. Infants who showed greater activity in their right prefrontal cortex than in their left prefrontal were more likely to cry in response to maternal separation than infants who showed greater left prefrontal activity. These early studies suggested that the difference between left and right prefrontal activity, the prefrontal asymmetry in activation, was associated with different affective styles (see Figure 10.30). If the asymmetry in prefrontal cortex activity is related to affective style, then one would expect such asymmetry to be stable across time. Results have been consistent with this prediction; prefrontal asymmetry does appear to be reliable and stable over time (Tomarken, Davidson, Wheeler & Kinney, 1992; Hagemann, Naumann, Thayer, and Bartussek, 2002).

Davidson and colleagues tested whether individuals who show greater left prefrontal activity would show more positive affect, whereas individuals who show relatively more right prefrontal activity would experience more negative affect. They have tested subjects using measures of positive and negative affect (e.g., the trait version of the Positive and Negative Affect Scales, the PANAS, Watson, Clark & Tellegren, 1988) and measures of behavioural inhibition versus behavioural activation (the BIS/BAS scales, Carver & White, 1994). Subjects

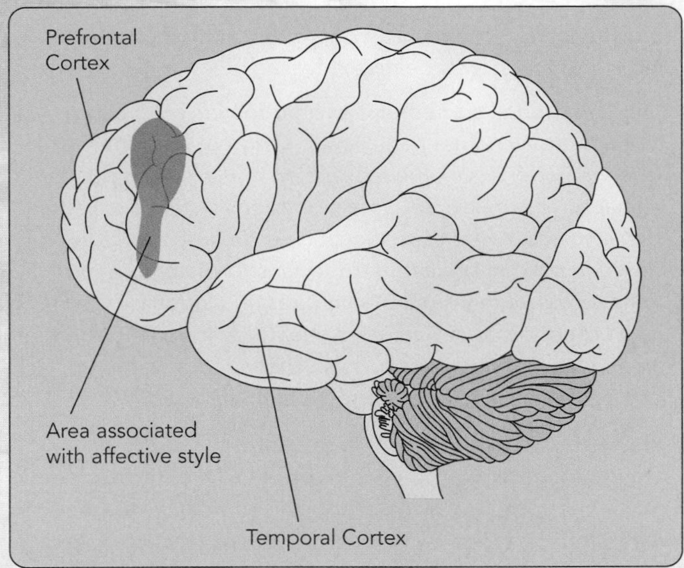

FIGURE 10.30

The shaded area within the prefrontal cortex corresponds to the area found by Davidson and colleagues to show the greatest left–right differences in activation, both at rest and in response to emotion-provoking stimuli. Whether an individual shows greater left or greater right prefrontal activation is associated with that individual showing greater positive or greater negative affect (adapted from Davidson, 2003).

who reported more positive affect and greater behavioural activation were found to show greater left than right prefrontal activity. Subjects who reported more negative affect and greater behavioural inhibition were found to show greater right than left prefrontal activity (see Davidson, 2003). That is, subjects whose left prefrontal cortex is more active have a positive affective style, while subjects whose right prefrontal cortex is more active have a negative affective style.

Apart from the relationship between resting prefrontal activation asymmetry and affect, Davidson and colleagues also tested for a relationship between prefrontal asymmetry and the reaction to an emotion-evoking stimulus, even with baseline differences removed statistically (Wheeler, Davidson & Tomarken, 1993). If the stimulus, film clips showing emotionally powerful scenes, elicited more left frontal activation than right prefrontal activation, subjects reported stronger positive affect than negative affect. If, on the other hand, the film clips elicited stronger right than left prefrontal activation, subjects reported stronger negative affect than positive affect. That is, the side of the prefrontal cortex that showed the greatest response to an emotion-evoking stimulus predicted whether subjects would respond with stronger negative or positive affect.

Events that generate a negative emotional response are also expected to generate a stress response. If an event generates an emotional response of fear or sadness, one would expect an accompanying stress response. If individuals with greater right prefrontal activation show stronger negative emotional responses, do they show greater stress responses? Davidson and colleagues have assessed the relationship between prefrontal activation asymmetry and different measures of the stress response, including measurements of immune function and the levels of stress-related hormones. For example, Davidson and colleagues (Davidson et al., 1999) measured immune system activity among individuals for whom they had also measured prefrontal asymmetry. Stress is known to suppress the immune system, and stress-induced suppression of immune system activity can have important health consequences. (We will discuss the stress response and the impact of stress on health and well-being in Chapter 16.) Individuals who show greater right prefrontal activity have lower immune system activity than do left prefrontal individuals, as measured by natural killer cell (NK) activity. They also show a greater stress-induced inhibition of immune function, and a muted response to an immune challenge (less antibody production to influenza vaccine) (Davidson et al., 1999). Other measures of the stress response show a similar relationship to prefrontal activation asymmetry (Davidson, 2003). That is, a negative affective style, right prefrontal dominance, lower immune function, and a heightened stress response occur together.

Although still early in its development, affective neuroscience has begun to explain differences in affective style, and to show how such individual differences are related to differences in brain function. Other studies in affective neuroscience are exploring how such differences may be related to the development of psychopathology, such as depression; how we regulate our emotions; and how changes in the prefrontal cortex and the amygdala may relate to experience-induced changes in emotions. Affective neuroscience is also beginning to explore emotionally positive events and characteristics such as the neural correlates of well-being (Urry et al., 2004).

In Review

- *The primary components of emotion are the eliciting stimuli, cognitive appraisals, physiological arousal, and expressive and instrumental behaviours. Individual differences in personality and motivation affect the experience and expression of emotion, as do cultural factors.*
- *Although innate factors can affect the eliciting properties of certain stimuli, learning can also play an important role in determining the arousal properties of stimuli.*
- *The cognitive component of emotional experience involves the evaluative and personal appraisal of the*

eliciting stimuli. The ability of thoughts to elicit emotional arousal has been demonstrated clinically and in experimental research. Cross-cultural research indicates considerable agreement across cultures in the appraisals that evoke basic emotions, but also some degree of variation in more complex appraisals.

- *Our physiological responses in emotion are produced by the hypothalamus, the limbic system, and the cortex, and by the autonomic and endocrine systems. There appear to be two systems for emotional behaviour, one involving conscious processing by the cortex, the other unconscious processing by the amygdala.*
- *Recent studies suggest that negative emotions reflect greater relative activation of the right hemisphere, whereas positive emotions are related to relatively greater activation in the left hemisphere.*
- *The validity of the polygraph as a "lie detector" has been questioned largely because of the difficulty of establishing which emotion is being expressed.*
- *The behavioural component of emotion includes expressive and instrumental behaviours. Different parts of the face are important in the expression of various emotions. The accuracy of people's interpretations of these expressions increases when situational cues are also available. Based in part on similarities in facial expression of emotions across widely separate cultures, evolutionary theorists propose that certain fundamental emotional patterns are innate. They agree, however, that cultural learning can influence emotional expression in important ways.*
- *Research on the relation between arousal and performance suggests that there is an optimal level of arousal for the performance of any task. This optimal level varies with the complexity or difficulty of the task; complex tasks have lower optimal arousal levels.*

INTERACTIONS AMONG THE COMPONENTS OF EMOTION

Emotions involve complex interactions among eliciting stimuli, thoughts, physiological responses, and behaviours. For more than 100 years, theorists and researchers have explored the nature of these interactions.

The James-Lange Somatic Theory

47. Compare the James-Lange (somatic) and Cannon-Bard explanations for emotional perception and labelling.

In 1890, the eminent psychologist William James ignited considerable controversy with this counterintuitive statement:

> Common sense says . . . we meet a bear, are frightened, and run; we are insulted by a rival, are angry, and strike. The hypothesis here to be defended says that this order of sequence is incorrect . . . and that the more rational statement is that we feel sorry *because* we cry, angry *because* we strike, afraid *because* we tremble. (James, 1890–1950, p. 451, italics ours)

At about the same time that James advanced his theory, a Danish psychologist named Carl Lange reached a similar conclusion, so the theory was attributed to both men. Today, the *James-Lange theory* lives on as the **somatic theory of emotion** (Papanicolaou, 1989). To proponents of this theory, body informs mind; our physiological reactions determine our emotions. We know we are afraid or in love only because our bodily reactions tell us so.

The Cannon-Bard Theory

It wasn't long before the James-Lange theory was challenged. In 1927, the physiologist Walter Cannon fired back. He pointed out that people's bodies do *not* respond instantaneously to an emotional stimulus; several seconds may pass before signs of physiological arousal appear. Yet people typically experience the emotion immediately. This would be impossible according to the James-Lange theory. Cannon and his colleague L. L. Bard concluded that cognition must be involved as well.

The *Cannon-Bard theory* proposed that, when we encounter an emotion-arousing situation, the thalamus simultaneously sends sensory messages to the cerebral cortex *and* to the body's internal organs. The message to the cortex produces the experience of emotion, and the one to the internal organs produces the physiological arousal. Thus neither cognition nor arousal causes the other; they are independent responses to stimulation from the thalamus. The James-Lange and Cannon-Bard theories are compared in Figure 10.31.

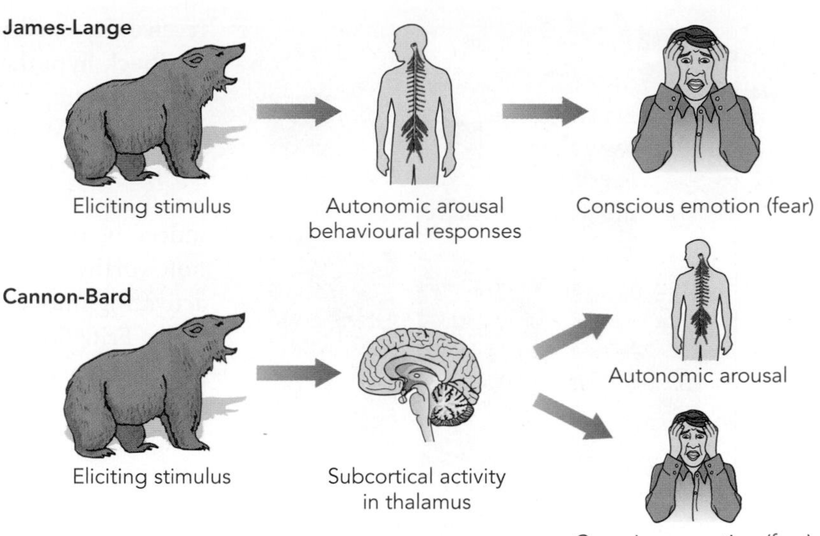

FIGURE 10.31

Two early theories of emotion continue to influence current-day theorizing. The James-Lange theory holds that the experience of emotion is caused by somatic feedback and physiological arousal. According to the Cannon-Bard theory, the thalamus receives sensory input and simultaneously stimulates physiological responses and cognitive awareness.

The Role of Autonomic Feedback

The James-Lange and Cannon-Bard theories differ on one critical point. According to the James-Lange theory, feedback from the body's reactions to eliciting stimuli tells the brain that we are experiencing an emotion. Without such feedback, there would be no emotional response. In contrast, the Cannon-Bard theory maintains that experiencing emotion results from signals sent from the thalamus to the cortex, not from bodily feedback. Is there any situation that would provide a test of whether bodily feedback is necessary?

In fact, there is. What if organisms were deprived of sensory feedback from their internal organs so that they never knew when these organs were aroused? Would they be devoid of emotional reactions? To answer this question, Cannon (1929) carried out experiments with animals in which he severed the nerves that provide feedback from the internal organs to the brain. He found that even after surgery, the animals still exhibited emotional responses, supporting his theory over that of James and Lange.

48. How does research on animals and people deprived of sensory feedback bear on the validity of the James-Lange and Cannon-Bard theories?

But perhaps people are different from other species. Obviously, Cannon's animal experiments could never be replicated with people, but nature provides a tragic parallel. Like Cannon's animals, people whose spinal cords have been severed in accidents receive no sensory feedback from body areas below the injury. Given this fact, what are their emotional lives like? To find out, Kathleen Chwalisz, Ed Diener, and Dennis Gallagher (1988) administered self-report measures of emotional experience to people who had sustained spinal injuries. For comparative purposes, the same measures were administered to individuals having physical handicaps that did not affect sensory feedback, and to a group of non-handicapped people.

As shown in Figure 10.32, the people with spinal cord injuries did not differ from the other two groups in the reported intensity of either their positive or negative emotions. Indeed, some reported that they frequently experienced very intense emotions—sometimes more intense than those they had experienced before their injury. Moreover, people with upper and lower spinal cord injuries—who differed in the amount of bodily feedback they could receive—did not differ in the intensity of their emotions. These results, like those of Cannon's animal studies, appear to cast doubt on the claim that arousal feedback from the body is absolutely necessary for people to experience intense emotion. But let us take this issue one step further.

The Facial Feedback Hypothesis

49. What is the facial feedback hypothesis? What research evidence supports it? What might be the role of vascular feedback?

Arousal feedback is not the only kind of bodily feedback the somatic theory considers important. Facial muscles involved in emotional displays also feed messages to the brain, and these muscles are active even in patients with spinal injuries who may

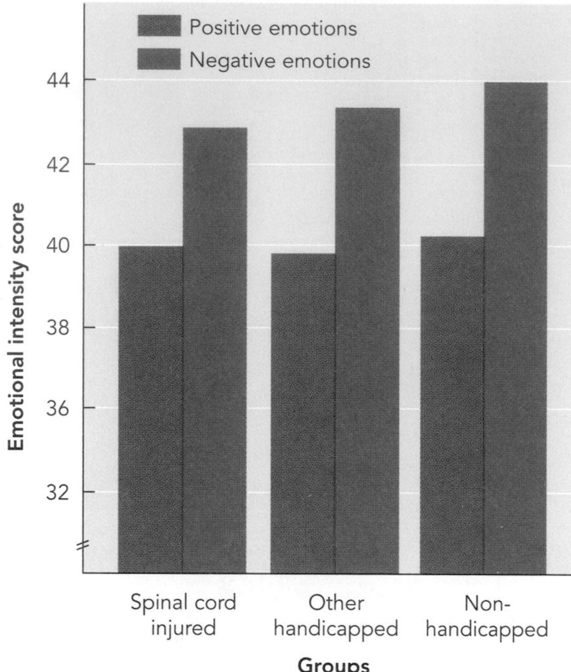

FIGURE 10.32

Intensity of positive and negative emotions reported by people with spinal cord injuries, by handicapped people with no spinal damage, and by non-handicapped people. The lack of differences casts doubt on the assertion that feedback from physiological arousal is essential for the experiencing of normal emotional responses.

Data from Chwalisz et al., 1988.

receive no sensory input from below the neck. According to the **facial feedback hypothesis**, this feedback to the brain might play a key role in determining the nature and intensity of emotion that we experience, as the James-Lange theory would suggest (Adelmann & Zajonc, 1989; McIntosh et al., 1997; Soussignan, 2002).

Research shows that positive or negative emotional responses can indeed be triggered by contraction of specific facial muscles. Especially noteworthy are studies in which participants do not know that they are activating muscles used in specific emotional expressions. In one such study, Fritz Strack and his co-workers (1988) found that when participants held pens in their teeth, activating muscles used in smiling (Figure 10.33a), they rated themselves as feeling more pleasant than when they held the pens with their lips (Figure 10.33b), which activates muscles involved in frowning. Participants also rated cartoons as funnier while holding pens in their teeth and activating the "happy muscles" than while holding pens with their lips (Figure 10.33c). In another study, Robert Zajonc and his colleagues compared the subjective experiences of subjects who pronounced different sounds, such as *eee* and *ooh*. Saying the *eee* sound, which activates muscles used in smiling, was associated with more pleasant feelings than saying the *ooh* sound, which activates muscles involved in negative facial expressions (Zajonc et al., 1989). Perhaps photographers should force us to say "cheese" not only when they take our picture, but also later when they show us proofs that not even our mothers could love.

How might facial feedback trigger emotional experience? According to the **vascular theory of emotional feedback** (McIntosh et al., 1997; Zajonc, 1985), tensing facial muscles alters the temperature of blood entering the brain by controlling the volume of air inhaled through the nose. Cooling the blood increases positive affect,

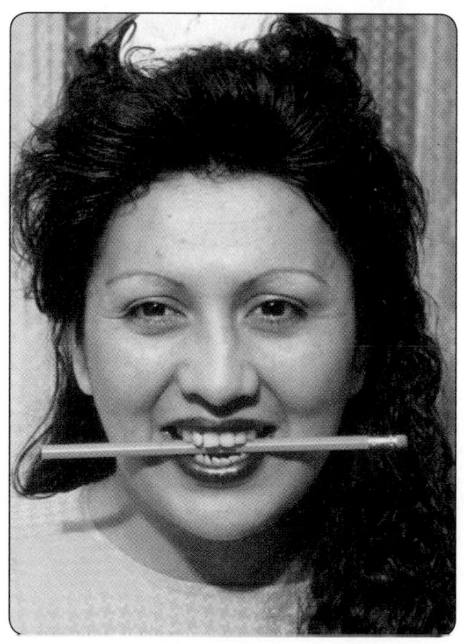

(a)

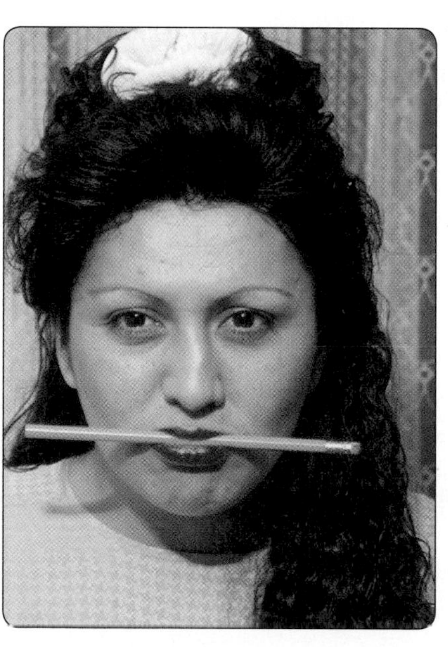

(b)

Mean funniness rating of cartoons
6
5
4
3
2
1
0
Lips
Teeth
Position of pencil

(c)

FIGURE 10.33

Holding a pen in the teeth (a) so as to activate the muscles used in smiling evokes more pleasant feelings than holding the pen in one's lips (b), which activates muscles used in frowning. This finding (c) provides support for the facial feedback hypothesis.

Data from Strack et al., 1988.

whereas warming it produces negative affect, perhaps by influencing the release of different neurotransmitters in the brain. Proponents of this theory have shown that activating the muscles involved in smiling not only cools the blood supply to the forehead as more air is inhaled through the nostrils, but also increases pleasant feelings. Conversely, activating the muscles involved in negative facial expressions reduces air flow, raises forehead temperature as the blood supply warms, and evokes negative affect (McIntosh et al., 1997). Perhaps the vascular theory can help to explain how body influences mind in the experiencing of emotions.

Cognitive-Affective Theories

Nowhere are mind-body interactions more obvious than in the emotions, where thinking and feeling are intimately connected. Cognitive-affective theories focus on the ways in which cognitions and physiological responses interact. Historically, Richard Lazarus and Stanley Schachter have been major figures in this approach.

Lazarus strongly emphasizes the link between cognitive appraisal and arousal, insisting that all emotional responses require some sort of appraisal, whether we are aware of that appraisal or not.

> The fundamental premise is that in order to survive, animals (humans particularly) are constructed biologically to be constantly evaluating (appraising) their relationship with the environment with respect to significance for well-being. . . . If a person (or animal) appraises his or her relationship with the environment in a particular way, then a specific emotion, which is tied to the appraisal, always results; and if two persons make the same appraisal, then they will experience the same emotion regardless of the actual circumstances. (Lazarus, 1991, p. 825)

It is worth emphasizing a key difference between the Cannon-Bard and the cognitive-affective theories of emotion. According to the Cannon-Bard theory of emotion, when you encounter a specific environmental cue, a matching emotion is triggered. That is, which emotion you experience is importantly determined by what is in the environment. For example, the sight of a bear triggers fear or hearing an insult triggers anger. The cognitive-affective theories, however, argue that what matters is how you appraise, or interpret, environmental stimuli. The sight of a bear can elicit fear, but if the bear is perceived as an impressive and noble animal, the emotion may be awe. Similarly, hearing an insult may trigger anger, but that same comment may be interpreted as a cutting and valid personal criticism and trigger sadness, or it may be interpreted as sarcasm and elicit happiness and laughter. That is, for Lazarus and Schachter, what matters is not what environmental cue confronts you, what matters is your appraisal. For Cannon and Bard, a specific stimulus would be expected to consistently trigger the same emotion, whereas for Lazarus and Schachter it would trigger the same emotion only if the appraisal was the same; a stimulus could trigger as many different emotions as there are different appraisals.

As noted earlier, the appraisal itself need not be a conscious thought; it may be some automatic perception that does not enter conscious awareness. Once the appraisal has triggered the arousal response, arousal cues may feed back into the ongoing appraisal process. Thus, if you feel yourself becoming aroused in the presence of another person, you may begin to appraise the person as more desirable and attractive than before.

Like Lazarus, Stanley Schachter emphasized the link between cognition and arousal, and he developed the best known of the cognitive-affective theories of emotion. He was intrigued with the question of how we know both *what* we are

Schachter's Theory

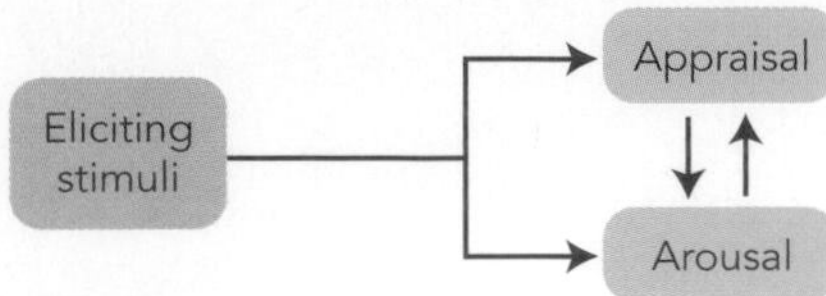

FIGURE 10.34

Stanley Schachter's two-factor theory focuses on the interactive role of cognition and arousal. Schachter emphasized the role of appraisals of the environment in our labelling of the emotions we experience.

50. According to Schachter, what influences perceptions of emotional intensity? What tells us which emotion we are experiencing?

51. How did Lazarus and co-workers show that appraisals influence level of arousal? How did Schachter and Wheeler show that arousal level can affect appraisals?

feeling and *how strongly* we are feeling it. Schachter's **two-factor theory of emotion**, also called the Schachter-Singer theory of emotion, states that arousal and cognitive labelling based on situational cues are the critical ingredients in emotional experience. The intensity of physiological arousal tells us *how strongly* we are feeling something, but situational cues give us the information we need in order to tell us *what* we are feeling—fear, anger, love, or some other emotion (Schachter, 1966). Lazarus would agree, viewing these cues as an important determinant of the appraisal process (Figure 10.34). Thus both view situation, cognition, and arousal as highly interrelated.

A classic, and creative, test of Schachter's two-factor theory was performed by Dutton and Aron of the University of British Columbia (Dutton & Aron, 1974). Dutton and Aron arranged for either a male or a female research assistant to approach males who were crossing two different bridges and ask them to participate in a study of creativity. Participants were asked to complete a short questionnaire and write a short story based on a picture shown to them by the research assistant. The participants were then told that they could contact the research assistant if they had any questions and were given the researcher's name and phone number. The participants were recruited on one of two different bridges. One was the Capilano Canyon Suspension Bridge, a 137-metre-long suspension bridge 70 metres above a section of rapids. The other was a wide, sturdy cedar bridge only 3 metres above a small stream. Dutton and Aron reasoned that, if Schachter was correct, when males crossed the swaying, anxiety-provoking suspension bridge and met the attractive female research assistant they would attribute their arousal to the female research assistant. The results supported a cognitive-appraisal theory. Participants who had crossed the suspension bridge included more sexual imagery in their stories and were more likely to later call the female research assistant than participants who had crossed the low, sturdy cedar bridge (Figure 10.35). For participants met by the male research assistant, it did not matter which bridge they crossed, sexual imagery and later behaviour were similar between bridges. Two classic experiments performed by Lazarus and Schachter that also explored the links between cognition and arousal are described in the *Research Foundations* section.

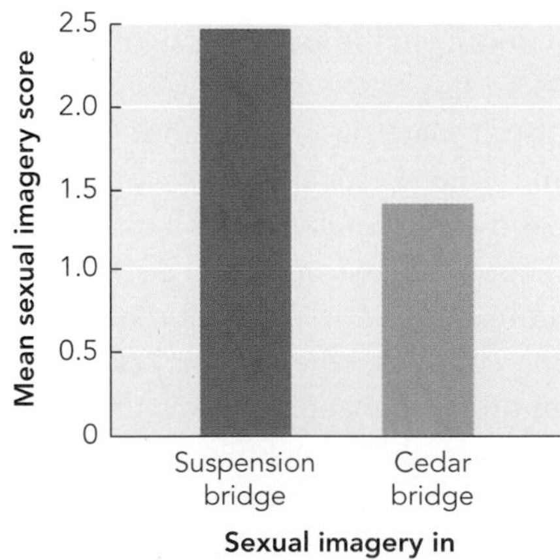

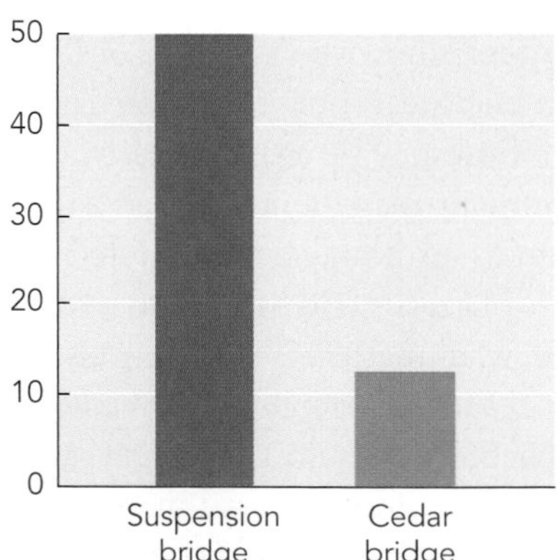

FIGURE 10.35

Results from Dutton and Aron's classic 1974 experiment in the Capilano Canyon. Male participants who experienced increased arousal from crossing a suspension bridge included more sexual imagery in their stories and were more likely to later call the research assistant attributed this arousal to the female research assistant.

RESEARCH FOUNDATIONS

Cognition-Arousal Relations

Manipulating Appraisal to Influence Arousal

Introduction

Richard Lazarus and his University of California colleagues examined how differences in cognitive appraisal can influence physiological arousal. To do so, they needed to measure physiological arousal in response to visual stimuli that were held constant for all participants, while influencing the manner in which these eliciting stimuli were appraised. If people in different appraisal conditions showed different arousal responses to the same eliciting stimuli, it would support the notion that arousal is influenced by appraisal.

Method

The researchers monitored university students' physiological responses while they watched an anthropology film, *Subincision in the Arunta,* which depicts in graphic detail an aboriginal puberty rite during which the penises of adolescent boys are cut with a jagged flint knife. The film typically elicits a high level of physiological arousal in viewers (and, according to the researchers, many leg-crossing responses in males). The dependent variable, measured by recording electrodes attached to the participants' palms, was changes in electrical skin conductance caused by sweat gland activity.

To study the effects of participants' appraisal of the filmed visual stimuli on arousal, the researchers experimentally varied the film's soundtrack. Four different soundtrack conditions were used to manipulate the independent variable:

- A *trauma* soundtrack emphasized the pain suffered by the boys, the danger of infection, the jaggedness of the flint knife, and other unpleasant aspects of the operation.
- A *denial* soundtrack was just the opposite; it denied that the operation was excessively painful or traumatic and emphasized that the boys looked forward to entering adulthood by undergoing the rite and demonstrating their bravery.
- The *intellectualization* soundtrack, also designed to produce a more benign appraisal, ignored the emotional elements of the scenes altogether and focused on the traditions and history of the tribe.
- In a *silent* control condition, the film was shown without any soundtrack at all, leaving viewers to make their own appraisals.

Results

As shown in Figure 10.36, the soundtracks produced markedly different levels of arousal. As predicted, the trauma soundtrack resulted in the highest arousal, followed by the silent film condition, which likely evoked dire appraisals as well. The denial and intellectualization soundtracks, designed to create more benign appraisals, resulted in much lower levels of arousal. This classic study supported Lazarus's contention that appraisal can influence arousal.

Manipulating Arousal to Influence Appraisal

Introduction

Is the reverse also true? Can level of arousal influence people's appraisal of an eliciting stimulus? To test this hypothesis, one must cause people to experience different levels of arousal without knowing the true reason. The level of arousal should then be attributed to whatever eliciting stimuli are present in the situation.

Method

In Stanley Schachter's laboratory at Columbia University, participants were told they were in a study involving the effects of a new vitamin called suproxin on visual perception. The researchers directly manipulated level of physiological arousal by injecting participants with one of three difference substances. In one condition, participants received epinephrine,

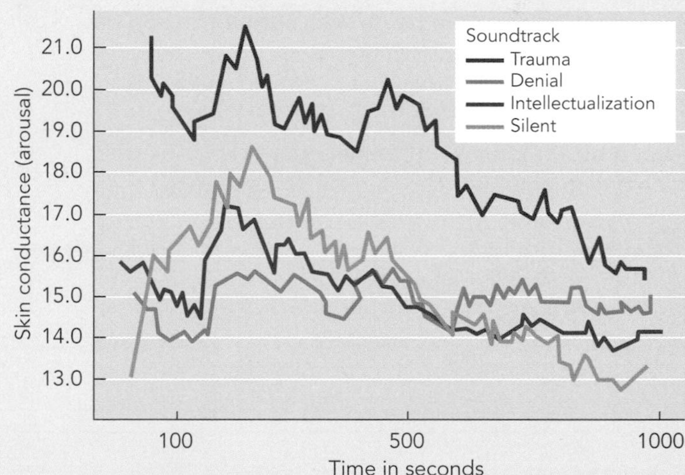

FIGURE 10.36

Appraisal influences arousal. Participants who viewed a film showing a tribal subincision rite in vivid detail exhibited different levels of physiological arousal, depending on the soundtrack that accompanied the film.
Data from Speisman, et al., 1964.

–Continued

a drug that increases arousal. In a second experimental condition, participants received a tranquilizer drug that would decrease arousal. A placebo control group received a saline injection that would have no effects on arousal. The experimenters told all participants that the suproxin injection would have no side effects (when, in fact, the epinephrine and tranquilizer would begin to have immediate and opposite effects on arousal). Then, while presumably waiting for the vitamin to take effect, the participants were shown a short movie "to provide continuous black-and-white stimulation to the eyes." The movie was a comedy that included a slapstick chase scene. The experimenters hypothesized that the participants in the two drug conditions would attribute their heightened or lowered level of arousal to the funniness (or lack thereof) of the film, because they would know of no other reason why they should feel as they did.

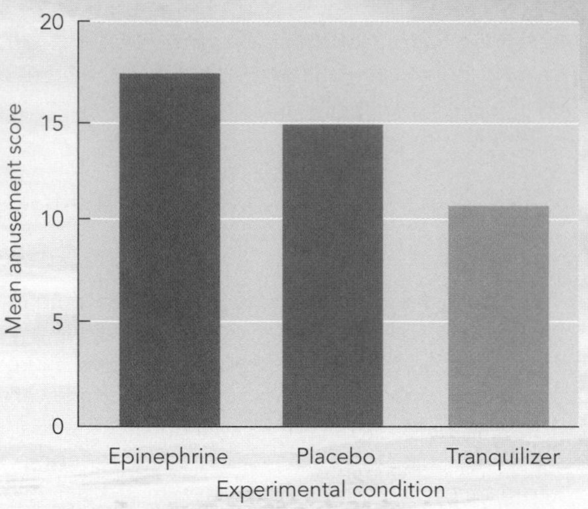

FIGURE 10.37

Arousal influences appraisal. Participants were injected with either epinephrine, a tranquilizer, or a placebo to affect arousal and then were shown a humorous film. The amount of amusement they displayed varied with their state of arousal.

Data from Schachter & Wheeler, 1962.

Results

Participants were observed from behind a one-way mirror while they watched the movie. The observers, who were unaware of which participants had received which injections, recorded how frequently the participants smiled, grinned, laughed, threw up their hands, slapped their legs, or doubled over with laughter. These behaviours were combined into an "amusement score" that served as the dependent variable measure of how funny the participants found the film to be.

It appears that arousal cues can indeed influence one's appraisal of the situation. As Figure 10.37 shows, the results supported the experimenters' hypothesis that level of arousal would influence participants' appraisal of the film. The aroused participants in the epinephrine group found the film funnier than the tranquilized participants did, and the placebo control group fell in the middle. Thus a person injected with epinephrine might think, "Here I am watching this film and getting all excited. This film's really funny!"

Critical Discussion

These two studies were among the first to experimentally manipulate appraisal and arousal so as to study their effects on one another. In the first study, even though it was not possible to completely control for participants' own tendencies to appraise situations in certain ways, the four soundtrack conditions did have effects on the arousal responses of participants as they watched the subincision film. When Schachter and Wheeler turned Lazarus's procedure around and manipulated arousal levels with the stimulant and tranquilizing drugs, they found the expected differences in appraisal of the films. Moreover, they were able to measure these differences in terms of observable behaviour.

Taken together, these two studies show that appraisal influences arousal and that arousal can influence appraisal, demonstrating the two-way causal relation between cognition and arousal shown in the model of emotion originally presented in Figure 10.22 (p. 435).

Sources: Joseph Speisman, Richard Lazarus, Arnold Mordkoff, and Les Davison, 1964. Experimental reduction of stress based on ego-defense theory. *Journal of Abnormal and Social Psychology, 68,* 367–380.

Stanley Schachter and Ladd Wheeler, 1962. Epinephrine, chlorpromazine, and amusement. *Journal of Abnormal and Social Psychology, 65,* 121–128.

In Review

- *Several past and present theories posit causal relations among emotional components. The James-Lange/somatic theory maintains that we first become aroused and then judge what we are feeling. The Cannon-Bard theory proposes that arousal and cognition are simultaneously triggered by the thalamus. Cognitive appraisal theory states that appraisals trigger emotional arousal. According to Schachter's two-factor theory, arousal tells us how strongly we feel, while cognitions derived from situational cues help us to label the specific emotion.*

- *The facial feedback hypothesis, derived from the James-Lange/somatic theory, states that feedback from the facial muscles associated with innate emotional displays affects cognitive and physiological processes. Recent evidence supplies support for the theory.*
- *Because of the two-way relations between the cognitive and physiological components of emotion, it is possible to manipulate appraisals and thereby influence the level of arousal. Arousal changes can also affect appraisal of the eliciting stimuli.*

GAINING DIRECTION

What are the issues?

The opening scenario for Chapter 10 deals with a new approach to forensic neurology called "Brain Fingerprinting." The basic idea is to present details of a crime to a suspect and then monitor the suspect's brain waves. The developers argue that familiar information generates a very specific response pattern (known as *P300*). Such a pattern is not emitted for new information. Issues surrounding this scenario range from the specifics of brain wave patterns, to the reliability of testing, to the use of such a technology in court.

What do we need to know?

How reliable and valid is Brain Fingerprinting?
What is P300?
How are brain waves measured?
Is this procedure any different from polygraph testing?
What happens when someone is lying?

Where can you find the information necessary to answer these questions?

You should begin by reviewing the information on polygraph testing. What specifically is measured by the polygraph, and what does Brain Fingerprinting assess? Is Brain Fingerprinting a more reliable method? Why? You will probably want to look back at Chapter 2 and consider what type of information constitutes a valid scientific claim. As a general background source, look for information on lying and deception. A leading authority in this area is Dr. Paul Ekman at the University of California Medical School, San Francisco.

KEY TERMS AND CONCEPTS*

approach-approach conflict (432)
approach-avoidance conflict (432)
avoidance-avoidance conflict (432)
CCK (cholecystokinin) (408)
cognitive appraisal (435)
delay discounting (432)
display rules (444)
drive theory (403)
emotion (433)
empathy (441)
expectancy × value theory (404)
expressive behaviours (441)
extrinsic motivation (404)
facial feedback hypothesis (450)
fundamental emotional patterns (442)
glucose (407)
homeostasis (403)
incentive (403)
instinct (402)
instrumental behaviours (445)
intrinsic motivation (404)
job enrichment (430)
leptin (408)
management by objectives (MBO) (431)
metabolism (406)
motivation (402)
need for achievement (427)
need hierarchy (405)
paraventricular nucleus (PVN) (409)
polygraph (441)
self-actualization (405)
sexual orientation (424)
sexual response cycle (419)
somatic theory of emotions (448)
two-factor theory of emotion (452)
vascular theory of emotional feedback (450)

*Each term has been boldfaced in the text on the page indicated in parentheses.

DO YOU WANT TO ELEVATE YOUR GRADES?

For additional resources and interactive quizzing, visit the book's Online Learning Centre at **www.mcgrawhill.ca/olc/passer**.

CHAPTER 11

Development over the Life Span

There are only two lasting bequests we can hope to give our children. One of these is roots; the other, wings.

—Hodding Carter

CHAPTER OUTLINE

Tattoo shops are busy these days. However, the clientele are no longer predominantly in their 20s; rather they are 40- and 50-year-olds. According to Toronto tattoo artist Raven Rowanchilde (Canadian Press, July 2000), older clients know what they're looking for. They are often "marking something very significant, they want their tattoos to reflect who they are—to identify them. . . When you are younger you are so preoccupied with stuff, but in your 50s you have done all that and there is more time for reflection on age-old cosmic questions . . . 'Who am I? Why am I here?' "

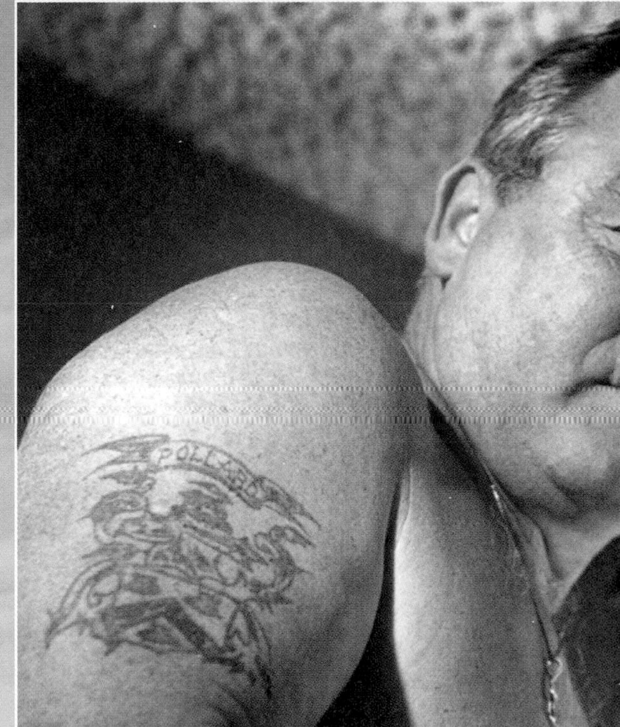

At 50, people often look back on their lives, searching for a new meaning, a new symbol. Larry Pollard of Windsor, Ontario, felt that he might have been experiencing a mid-life crisis when he had his family crest tattooed on his arm. He chose the crest because it was meaningful, a reflection of his historical roots.

Pollard also traded in his family minivan for a sportier Grand Prix.

- **What are the issues here?**
- **What do we need to know?**
- **Where can we find the information to answer these questions?**

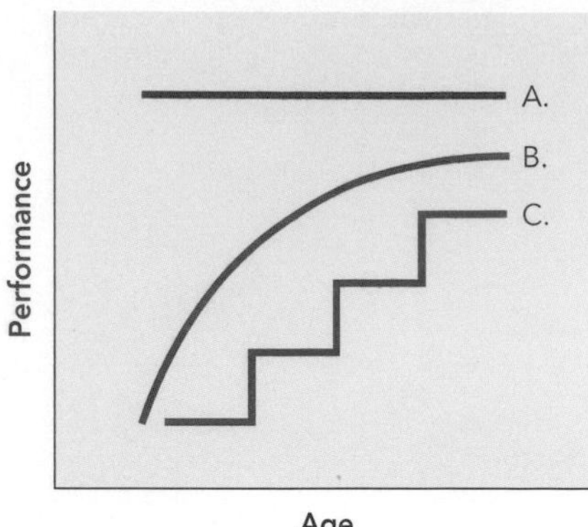

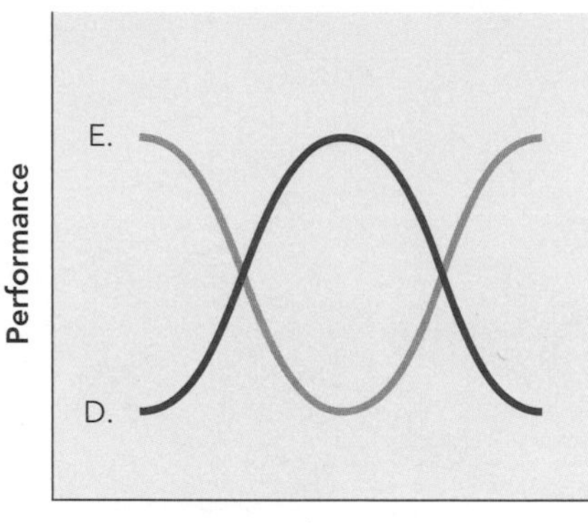

FIGURE 11.1

Five different developmental functions (changes with age) representing: (A) abilities present at birth that remain constant across the life span; (B) abilities not present or immature at birth that mature gradually over age; (C) abilities that emerge in stages; (D) abilities that emerge after birth, peak, and then disappear with age; (E) abilities present early in life that disappear temporarily and re-emerge later. Examples are given in the text.

In 1799 three hunters discovered a remarkable child living in the forests of Aveyron, France. Likely abandoned at a young age, he grew up isolated from human contact, foraging for food and surviving naked in the wild. About 12 years old, he easily climbed trees, ate nuts and roots, scratched and bit people who interfered with him, and made few sounds. He could walk upright, yet ran quickly on all fours. Some regarded him as half-human, half-beast, and they called him the "Wild Boy of Aveyron" (Itard, 1894/1962).

Several medical experts concluded that the boy was incurably "mentally deficient," but others disagreed, noting that it took intelligence to survive in the wild. They argued that special education and care would enable the child to flower into a normal, civilized adult. In Paris, the boy was placed under the care of a prominent young physician, Jean-Marc Itard, who named him Victor and diligently supervised his training.

Victor initially was unresponsive to stimuli that most people find aversive. Unfazed, he would stick his hand into boiling kitchen water to grab food or eagerly roll around half-naked on the cold winter ground. Eventually, he learned to sense temperature differences, dress himself, and perform other self-care behaviours. Victor's emotional responses, which at first fluctuated without reason, began to fit the situation. He laughed in playful situations, shed tears over someone's death, and displayed some signs of affection toward Itard. Victor learned to read and write some words, communicate basic needs, and perform simple tasks.

Although Victor changed in important ways, his progress slowed considerably. He never learned to speak, and after five years of education his cognitive, emotional, and social development remained limited. Pessimism over further progress grew and the "project" ended. Victor was moved nearby and cared for by a woman for the rest of his life.

At the time, people expected Victor's case study to help answer an intense debate about the role of "nature versus nurture" in shaping who we are. But it raised more questions than it answered. Was Victor a normal, inherently noble infant who became harmed by his childhood isolation, or was he born "mentally deficient"?

Modern research tells us that, although unfavourable environments can significantly impair development, some children exposed to extreme adversity are highly resilient and thrive later in life (Masten & Coatsworth, 1998). Although we cannot pinpoint the causes of Victor's stunted development and failure to recover, this famous case highlights a broader issue: Just how does the miracle of human development unfold, and what conditions are required for normal growth?

MAJOR ISSUES AND METHODS

Developmental psychology examines changes in our biological, physical, psychological, and behavioural processes as we age. Four broad issues guide much developmental research.

1. Describe four broad issues that guide developmental research.

- *Nature and nurture.* To what extent is our development the product of heredity (nature) or the product of environment (nurture)? How do nature and nurture interact?
- *Critical and sensitive periods.* Are some experiences especially important at particular ages? A **critical period** is an age range in which certain experiences *must occur* for development to proceed normally or along a certain path. A **sensitive period** is an *optimal* age range for certain experiences, but if those experiences occur at another time, normal development will still be possible.

- *Continuity versus discontinuity.* Is development continuous and gradual, as when a sapling slowly grows into a tree? Or is it discontinuous, progressing through qualitatively distinct *stages,* as when a creeping caterpillar emerges from its cocoon as a soaring butterfly?
- *Stability versus change.* Do our characteristics remain consistent as we age?

Developmental psychologists address these issues by plotting (describing) developmental functions that portray how different processes change with age (Slater & Muir, 1999). Five developmental functions with different shapes shown in Figure 11.1 are:

(A) No change—an ability present at or before birth that remains relatively constant across the lifespan (e.g., the ability to discriminate high- from low-pitched sounds, or to see objects as distinct from their background—figure-ground perception).

(B) Continuous change (continuity)—an ability not present, or very immature, at birth that develops gradually over months or years and then remains constant over age (e.g., certain types of intelligence).

(C) Stages (discontinuity)—an ability that progresses in stages, with relatively rapid shifts from a lower level of performance to a higher level (e.g., in motor development, the shift from rolling to crawling to standing to walking; in cognitive development, the shift from nonverbal thought to symbolic thinking involving words).

(D) Inverted U-Shaped function—an ability that emerges after birth, peaks, and disappears with age (e.g., separation anxiety; visual acuity across the lifespan).

(E) U-Shaped function—an ability that is present early in life, disappears temporarily, and re-emerges later (e.g., newborns turning towards off-centred sound and stepping with support).

2. Explain how cross-sectional, longitudinal, and sequential designs differ.

The developmental psychologist's job is to describe these functions and explain their existence.

Developmental psychologists often use special research designs (Figure 11.2) to plot these age functions. Suppose we wish to study how intellectual abilities change from age 10 to age 60. Using a **cross-sectional design** we would compare people of different ages at the same point in time. Thus we could administer intellectual tasks to 10-, 20-, 30-, 40-, 50-, and 60-year-olds. We would test each person only once and compare how well the different age groups perform. The cross-sectional design is widely used because data from many age groups can be collected relatively quickly, but a key drawback is that the different age groups, called *cohorts,* grew up in different historical periods. Thus, if 60-year-olds have poorer intellectual abilities than 20-year-olds, is this due to aging per se or to environmental differences, such as poorer nutrition or medical care or less education, growing up in the 1940s versus the 1980s?

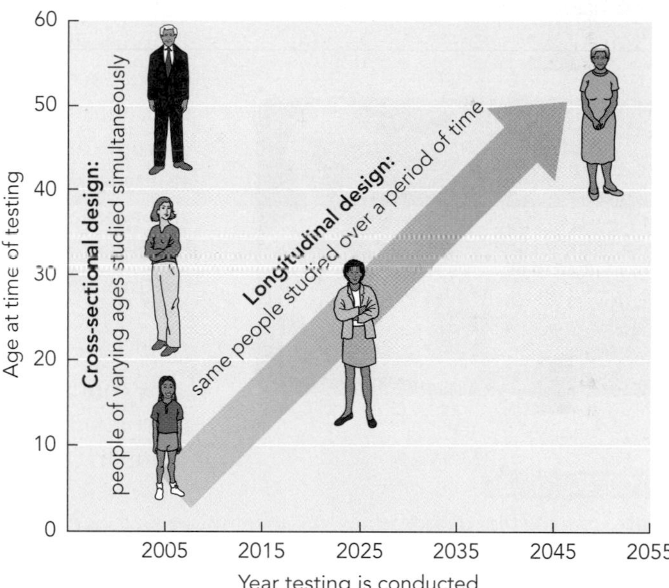

FIGURE 11.2

Using a cross-sectional design we would test different age groups in the year 2000 and compare their performance. Using a longitudinal design, we would test one age group and then retest them every 10 years until age 60. Using a sequential design (there are many types), we might test 10- through 60-year-olds in the year 2000 and then retest them every 10 years until age 60. Suppose that in the year 2000 the 60-year-olds perform worse than younger adults. Also suppose that, as the 10- through 50-year-olds age, their performance worsens at age 60. We are now more confident that this decline, replicated over different age cohorts, represents a true effect of aging.

To avoid this problem a **longitudinal design** repeatedly tests the same cohort as it grows older. We could test a sample of 10-year-olds this month and then retest them every 10 years, up to age 60. Now everyone is exposed to the same historical time frame. Unfortunately, this design is time consuming and, as years pass, our sample may shrink substantially as people move, drop out of the study, or die. Furthermore, suppose we find that intelligence declines at age 60. Is this really

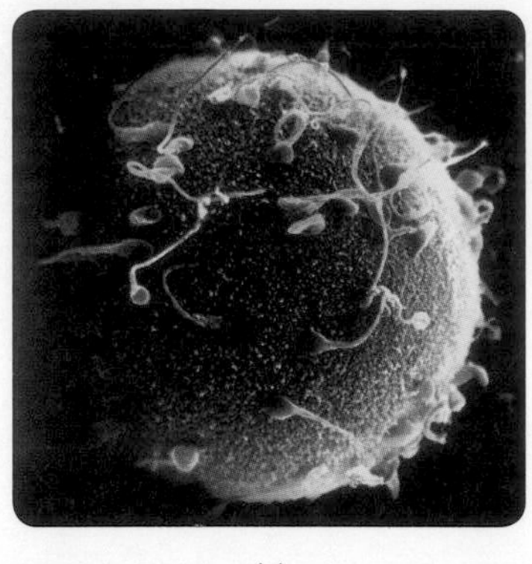

(a)

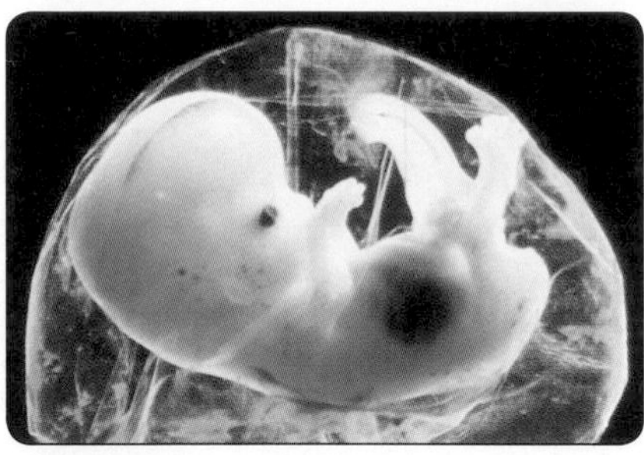

(b)

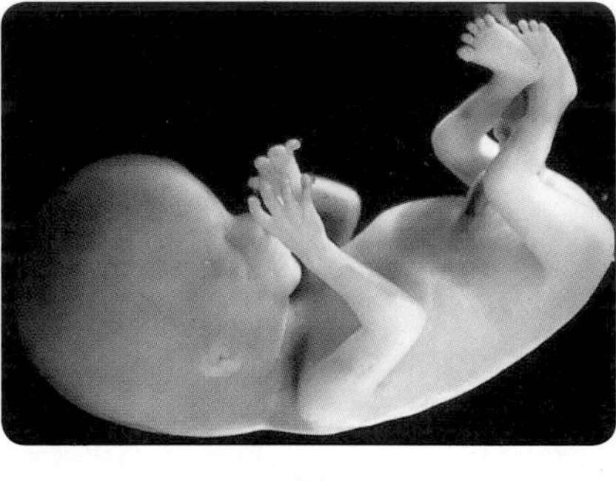

(c)

FIGURE 11.3

These remarkable photos show (a) the moment of conception, as one of many sperm cells fertilizes the ovum, (b) the embryo at six to seven weeks, and (c) the fetus at three months of age.

due to aging or to developmental experiences unique to our particular cohort? Researchers can answer this question by using a *sequential design* that combines the cross-sectional and longitudinal approaches. That is, we can repeatedly test *several* age cohorts as they grow older and determine whether they follow a similar developmental pattern. This design is the most comprehensive, but also the most time consuming and costly.

These research approaches provide much of our knowledge about human development, which we now explore from conception through death. We begin with the *prenatal period*, approximately 266 days during which we develop from a single-cell organism barely larger than a pinhead into a wondrously complex newborn human.

○ PRENATAL DEVELOPMENT

Prenatal development consists of three stages (Figure 11.3) of physical growth. The *germinal stage* constitutes approximately the first two weeks of development, beginning when one sperm fertilizes a female egg (ovum). This fertilized egg is called a **zygote**. Through repeated cell division the zygote becomes a mass of cells that attaches to the mother's uterus about 10 to 14 days after conception.

The *embryonic stage* extends from the end of the second week through the eighth week after conception, and the cell mass now is called an **embryo**. Two life-support structures, the placenta and umbilical cord, develop at the start of this stage. Located on the uterine wall, the *placenta* contains membranes that allow nutrients to pass from the mother's blood to the umbilical cord. In turn, the *umbilical cord* contains blood vessels that carry these nutrients and oxygen to the embryo, and waste products back from the embryo to the mother. Supplied with nutrients, embryonic cells divide rapidly and become specialized. Bodily organs and systems begin to form, and by week eight the heart of the two-centimetre-long embryo is beating, the brain is forming, and facial features such as eyes can be recognized.

At the ninth week after conception, the embryo is called a **fetus**. During this *fetal stage,* which lasts until birth, muscles become stronger and other bodily systems continue to develop. At about 24 weeks the eyes open, and by 28 weeks the fetus attains the *age of viability,* meaning that it is likely to survive outside the womb in case of premature birth (Hetherington, Locke, & Parke, 1999).

Genetics and Sex Determination

3. What determines the sex of a child?

Throughout history many women have been blamed and belittled for failing to give birth to a male heir. Ironically, any father who feels a need to "lay blame" should look in the mirror, for his genetic contribution determines the sex of the baby. Recall from Chapter 3 that a female's egg cells and a male's sperm cells each have only 23 chromosomes. At conception an egg and sperm unite to form the zygote, which now contains the full set of 23 *pairs* found in other human cells. The 23rd pair of chromosomes determines the baby's sex. A genetic female's 23rd pair contains two X chromosomes (XX), so called because of their shape (Figure 11.4). Because women carry only X chromosomes, the 23rd chromosome in the egg is always an X. A genetic male's 23rd pair contains an X and a Y chromosome (XY). Thus the 23rd chromosome in the sperm is an X in about half of the cases and a Y in the other half. The Y chromosome contains a specific gene, known as the *TDF gene,* that triggers male sexual development. The union of an egg with a sperm cell having a Y chromosome results in an XY combination and therefore a boy. A sperm containing an X chromosome produces an XX combination and so a baby girl.

How does the Y chromosome determine our sex characteristics? If a Y chromosome is present, its *TDF* gene initiates the development of testes at roughly six to eight weeks after conception. In fact, the term *TDF* stands for "testis-determining factor." Once formed, the testes secrete sex hormones called androgens that continue to direct a male pattern of organ development. If the *TDF* gene is not present, as happens with an XX pair on the 23rd chromosome, testes do not form and—in the absence of sufficient androgen activity during this prenatal *critical period*—an inherent female pattern of organ development ensues (Hyde & DeLamater, 2000).

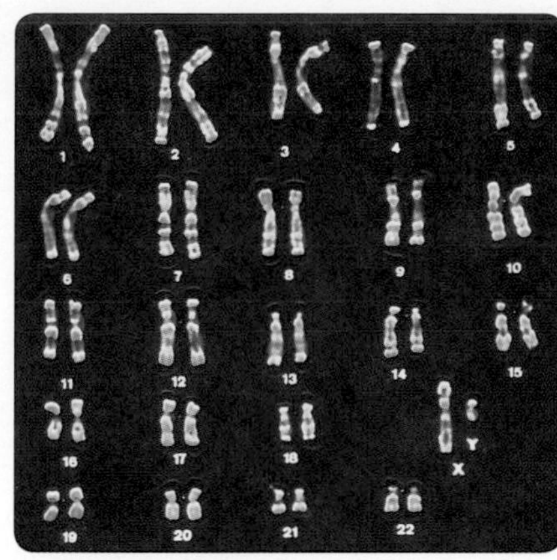

FIGURE 11.4

Most human cells contain 23 pairs of chromosomes. Each pair consists of one chromosome from each parent. The 23rd pair determines a person's sex. In males, the 23rd pair, which is shown in the lower right area of the photo, consists of an X chromosome and a Y chromosome. In females, the 23rd pair contains two X chromosomes.

Environmental Influences

Our genetic blueprint sets forth a path of prenatal development, but nature and nurture become intertwined to influence physical and behavioural development even before we are born. For example, because the embryo and fetus receive their nutrients from the mother, severe maternal malnutrition is associated with a greater risk of miscarriage, premature birth, stillbirth, smaller birth size, and impaired prenatal brain development (Read, 1982).

Teratogens (the root word in Greek means "malformed") are environmental agents that cause abnormal prenatal development. The placenta prevents many dangerous substances from reaching the embryo and fetus, but some harmful chemical molecules and diseases (e.g., German measles; untreated syphilis, HIV infections) do pass through and can result in brain damage, blindness, deafness, infections and even fetal death in some children, depending on the virus (Vander Zanden, 1997). Stress hormones also can cross the placenta; prolonged maternal stress is associated with increased risk of premature birth, infant irritability, and attention deficits (Weinstock, 1997). Mercury, lead, radiation, and many other environmental toxins also produce birth defects, as do some drugs. Nicotine is a teratogen, and maternal smoking (and fathers' second hand smoke) does increase the risk of miscarriage, premature birth, and low birth weight (Wakefield et al., 1998). More severe effects are found in babies of pregnant mothers who regularly used heroin or cocaine during pregnancy—they are often born addicted and go through withdrawal after birth. Many show deficits in cognitive functioning and attention as newborns (see Potter, Zelazo, Stack & Papageorgiou, 2000, discussed below) and throughout infancy (Mayes, Cicchetti, Suddhasatta, Zhang, & Heping, 2003).

4. How do STDs, alcohol, and other drugs affect prenatal development? Identify other broad classes of teratogens.

Perhaps the most widely studied teratogen is alcohol—its abuse during pregnancy can have devastating effects on fetal/infant development. Remember our discussion in Chapter 2 about the negative effects of prenatal exposure to alcohol on humans and guinea pigs? **Fetal Alcohol Syndrome** (FAS) consists of a group of abnormalities resulting from prenatal exposure to maternal alcohol consumption which include facial abnormalities, small malformed brains (Figure 11.5), and small stature (Streissguth et al., 1998). Psychological symptoms of FAS include intellectual (IQ) and fine and gross motor impairments and poor adaptive functioning (deficits in communication and social skills) (Wacha & Obrzut, 2007). One study found 40 percent of FAS children had

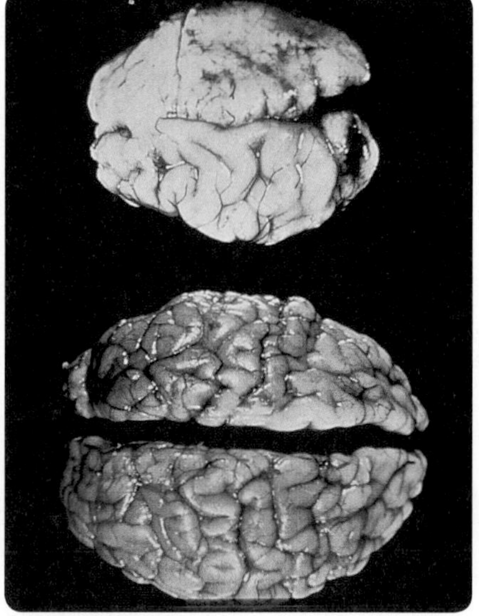

FIGURE 11.5

Children who suffer from fetal alcohol syndrome (FAS) not only look different (left), but have brains that are underdeveloped compared with those of normal children (right).

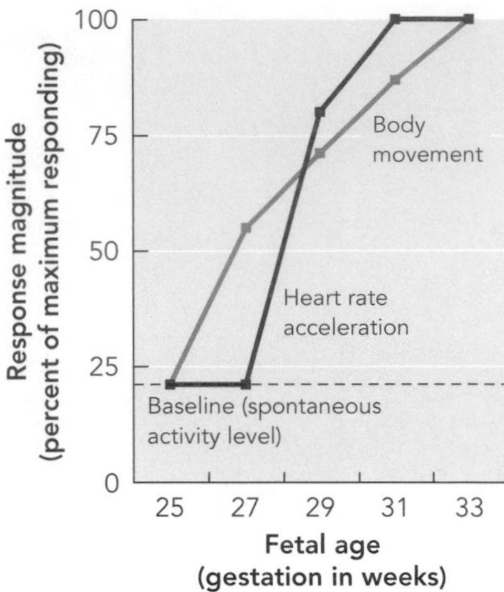

FIGURE 11.6

Schematic results adapted from Kisilevsky et al., (1992, Figures 5 & 6) showing different development functions for the onset of reliable fetal responses to vibration: for body movements, beginning at 27 weeks gestational age (GA) and increasing gradually to 33 weeks GA; for heart rate accelerations, a sudden response onset at 29 weeks GA.

Adapted from Kisilevsky et al., 1992.

attention deficit hyperactivity disorder (Burd, Cotsonas-Hassler, & Martsolf, 2003). FAS has been identified as a major cause of mental retardation in Western countries. About one-third to one-half of infants born to alcoholic mothers have FAS, but even "social drinking" or an episode of binge-drinking increases the risk of prenatal damage and long-term cognitive impairment (Larroque & Kaminski, 1998). Although Canadian statistics on the prevalence of FAS as a function of alcohol consumed by Canadian mothers were not found, in parts of the Canadian Northwest Territories, where drinking is common, FAS is also common (in one of every three births; Baron, Earhard, & Ozier, 2001).

Given this information, some politicians have suggested making drinking during pregnancy illegal, while others recommend educational prevention. However, it must be emphasized that not all fetuses exposed to alcohol in the womb have FAS; some show no symptoms, others display only some or milder forms of these deficits, which include impaired executive functioning (problems with higher level attention, learning, planning, abstract thought and organizational skills). This less severe pattern of symptoms has been called Fetal Alcohol Effects (FAE) (Streissguth et al., 1998). The threshold level of alcohol exposure needed to produce FAS/FAE is unknown. We do know that the children at greatest risk for FAS are those exposed to heavy maternal alcohol consumption throughout pregnancy (Wacha & Obrzut, 2007). Also, O'Leary (2004) suggests that the most damaging effects of alcohol exposure occur during sensitive periods of fetal brain growth, around the end of the first month and during the last two months of pregnancy. Given that we don't know the absolutely safe level of alcohol consumption during pregnancy, women are best advised to avoid drinking any alcohol while pregnant.

Some mothers have noted that during the latter third of their pregnancy fetal movements increased when they heard a loud sound or were listening to loud music. Their observations have been verified by researchers who measured fetal body movements and heart rate changes with ultrasound technology. Queen's University researchers, Kisilevsky & Muir (1991) found that relatively loud sounds elicited reliable increases in fetal heart rate and body movements during the third trimester of pregnancy. Even greater responses at earlier fetal ages can be elicited by vibroacoustic stimulation. Kisilevsky, Muir, & Low (1992) used both longitudinal and cross-sectional designs to compare changes in heart rate and body movements of fetuses of different ages elicited by a vibrator, placed on the mother's abdomen, when it was turned on (experimental trials) or remained off (control trials). As shown in Figure 11.6, reliable fetal body movements were first elicited around 27 weeks after conception (fetal age) and increased with fetal age. By contrast, heart rate acceleration responses were elicited in almost all fetuses beginning at 29 weeks fetal age, and responses remained high until birth. These data illustrate that different response measures relate to different developmental functions, which leads to conflicting estimates of fetal sensory development.

(a)

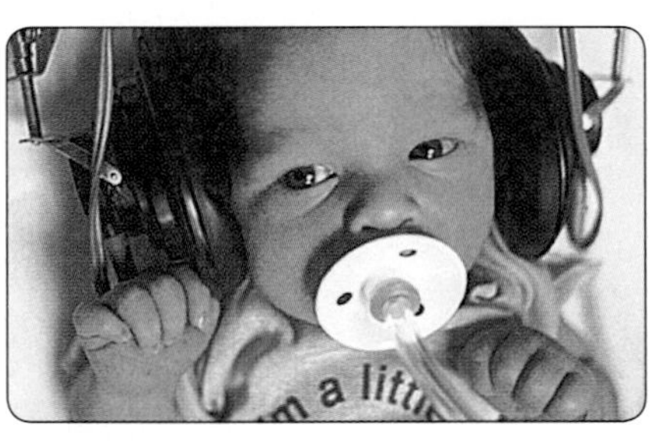

(b)

FIGURE 11.7

Can the fetus learn? (a) Twice a day during their last six weeks of pregnancy, mothers read out loud the same passage of a nursery rhyme from Dr. Seuss's story, The Cat in the Hat. *(b) Two or three days after birth, newborns were able to turn on a recording of their mother reading either the* Cat in the Hat *rhyme or an unfamiliar rhyme by sucking on a sensor-equipped nipple at different rates. Compared to infants in a control condition, these newborns more often altered their sucking rate on a sensor-equipped nipple in whichever direction (faster or slower) selected the familiar rhyme (DeCasper & Spence, 1986).*

Fetuses also learn—they stop responding to repeated presentations of vibroacoustic and auditory stimuli, reflecting short-term memory (Kisilevsky & Muir, 1991). They also have a long-term memory for sounds they hear repeatedly during fetal development. As Figure 11.7 describes, newborns seem to prefer sounds that become familiar to them during their last months of fetal development (e.g., mothers' voices over strangers' voices), during which time they can hear sounds transmitted through the womb (DeCasper & Spence, 1986). They even listen to TV. Peter Hepper (1988) found that moms who were "addicted" to watching the Australian soap opera *Neighbours* every day had infants who stopped crying and remained silent when Hepper played them the soap opera's theme song; infants of "non-addicted" moms were unaffected by the same song. Fetuses also learn about odours from their pregnant mother's diet. The newborns of mothers who habitually consumed anise-flavoured foods and drinks also preferred anise odours, while those of non-anise consuming mothers responded either neutrally or showed aversion to anise odours (Soussignan & Schaal, 2005). Clearly, nature and nurture interact throughout pregnancy.

In Review

- *Developmental psychology studies the process of aging. Questions about the influence of nature and nuture, the existence of critical and sensitive periods, continuity versus discontinuity, and stability versus change have played a major role in guiding much developmental research.*
- *Cross-sectional designs compare people of different age groups at a single point in time. A longitudinal design repeatedly tests the same age group as it grows older. A sequential design tests several groups at one point in time and then again when they are older.*
- *Prenatal development involves the zygote, embryonic, and fetal stages.*
- *The 23rd chromosome in a mother's egg cell always is an X chromosome. If the 23rd chromosome in the father's sperm cell is an X, the child will be genetically female (XX); if a Y, the child will be born genetically male (XY). Maternal malnutrition, stress, illness, drug use, and environmental toxins can cause abnormal prenatal development.*
- *Behavioural responses and learning begin during the fetal stage.*

INFANCY AND CHILDHOOD

Studying infants poses interesting challenges. During research studies, infants may start to fuss, cry, drool, spit up, soil their diapers, or simply fall asleep! The experimental context must be designed to keep the infant alert and "on task," a difficult job because infants are easily overwhelmed by novel, highly stimulating environments and rapidly become bored by bland environments; optimal test settings are difficult to achieve and change with age during the first year of life. Finally, because infants can't describe their experiences, researchers must find clever ways to use those responses that infants can make, such as sucking and looking, to draw inferences about their capabilities and preferences.

The Amazing Newborn

William James (1890) suggested that the newborn's world is a "buzzing, blooming confusion"—that is, that they are passive, disorganized, and have an empty mind. This view is no longer tenable, given our knowledge of prenatal sensory-motor development; the tactile, auditory, and chemical perceptual systems have been stimulated and are operating at birth. By contrast, the visual system receives little fetal stimulation, making it a candidate for identifying innate capacities.

Newborn Sensation and Perception

Daphne and Charlie Maurer (1988) at McMaster University noted that newborn vision is limited by poor acuity (objects' details are blurred; see Figure 11.8), a lack of coordinated eye movements (i.e., they see double), and "tunnel vision" (i.e.,

(a)

(b)

(c)

FIGURE 11.8

Seeing through an infant's eyes. These three images approximate the visual acuity of an infant at (a) age 1 month, (b) 3 months, and (c) 12 months.

a very small visual field compared to adults). Despite this, within minutes after birth, when newborns are held properly in a dimly lit, quiet room (to eliminate distractions) they will turn to face off-centred visual (e.g., red balls) targets. They also turn toward auditory (e.g., rattles or voices sounded opposite one ear) and tactile (e.g., touching the cheek) targets (Muir, Humphrey, & Humphrey, 1994) and odours (e.g., MacFarlane, 1975; Soussignan, Schaal, Marlier, & Jiang, 1997). Thus, newborns orient to significant stimuli in their environment, the most important being their mother's face, voice, and smell. This system optimizes the newborn's access to food, warmth, and social stimulation provided by caregivers.

5. How can scientists measure a newborn's sensory capabilities and perceptual preferences? What are some of those preferences?

Extensive work has been done on newborn visual perception, following from Robert Fantz's (1961) development of the *preferential looking procedure.* Fantz placed infants on their backs, showed them two or more stimuli at the same time, filmed their eyes to record how long they looked at each stimulus, and discovered that newborns have visual preferences. They look longer at patterned rather than non-patterned targets and prefer complex patterns—such as realistic or scrambled drawings of a human face—to simpler patterns (Figure 11.9). They even appear to prefer their mother's face over a stranger's face relatively soon after birth (e.g., Bushnell, Sai, & Mullin, 1989), although this preference may be based on the mother's hairline rather than her face, since the preference disappeared when the women's hairlines were covered by a scarf (Pascalis, de Schonen, Morton, Deruell, & Fabre-Grenet, 1995). This makes sense, given the newborn's poor visual acuity, as measured by the visual preference procedure (Courage and Adams, 1990). When gratings (black and white vertical stripes) are paired with an equally bright grey field, and the side of the grating and size of the stripes are varied across trials, infants look longer at the grating when the stripes are wide. As the stripe width is reduced, at some point their preference disappears, defining their resolution threshold. Newborn acuity, estimated using this technique, is about 20/800, or 40 times worse than normal adult acuity of 20/20 (Maurer & Lewis, 2001).

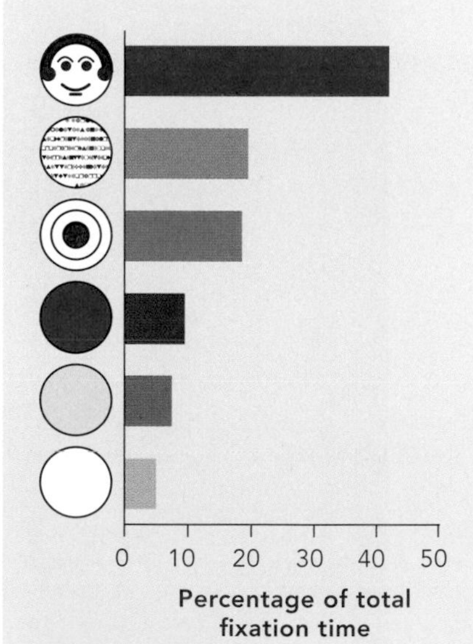

FIGURE 11.9

Whether two days old or two to three months old, infants preferred to look at complex patterns rather than simple patterns or solid colours.

Based on R. L. Frantz, 1961.

It is also possible to establish a new visual preference in newborns using the *visual habituation procedure*—the same stimulus is presented repeatedly until infant looking time declines (usually by 50%). When a novel stimulus is presented, infants usually look longer at the novel rather than the familiar stimulus. This is evidence that infants have a memory and that they discriminate between familiar and novel stimuli. Memorial University researchers Russell Adams and Mary Courage (1998) habituated newborns to white lights, and found that they recovered visual interest when they viewed lights of similar intensities but different dominant wavelengths of 545 nm, 585 nm, and 659 nm (adults see these as green, yellow, and red hues, respectively), suggesting that newborns see in colour. Newborns also show shape and size constancies (see descriptions in Chapter 5); they remain bored after being habituated to an object that is presented in a different orientation or at a different distance (Slater, 2000).

The use of habituation and other test procedures demonstrate that infants are born with the capacity to recognize, respond to, and remember their primary caretakers and to learn other important information about significant events in their environment.

Newborn Learning

Philip Zelazo and colleagues at McGill (e.g., Swain, I., Zelazo, P. R., & Clifton, R., 1993) habituated two-day-olds head-turning toward an off-centred, recorded speech sound (e.g., "Tinder"). After about 16 presentations, infants stopped turning to face the now familiar sound. They were not simply fatigued because: (1) by the end of habituation, many infants were turning away from the sound, perhaps trying to avoid it; (2) they readily turned toward a novel sound (e.g., "Beagle"), indicating that they could discriminate between some adult speech sounds; and (3) partial habituation to the sound lasted for at least 24 hours, reflecting the operation of long-term memory. Zelazo's group has used these tests to identify information-processing problems in high-risk infants (e.g., Down syndrome & premature infants—Zelazo, Weiss, Papageorgiou, & Laplante, 1989, and cocaine babies—Potter et al. 2000, mentioned above). Finally, using the habituation procedure, Barbara Morrongiello at the University of Guelph (Morrongiello, Fenwick, & Chance, 1998) and others (Slater, 2000) have shown that newborns rapidly learn to associate particular sounds with particular objects.

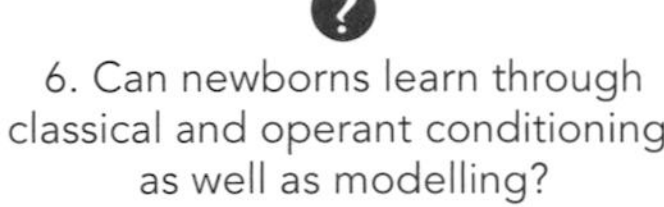
6. Can newborns learn through classical and operant conditioning, as well as modelling?

Newborns also rapidly acquire classically conditioned responses. Blass, Ganchrow, & Steiner (1984) followed a touch on newborns' foreheads (the CS) with the delivery of milk to their mouths (the UCS). After a few pairings, newborns turned toward the food source and puckered their lips (the UCR) during the CS. When the food was withheld during extinction, they cried, reflecting that they were upset when learned expectancies were violated. Through operant conditioning, newborns learn that they can "make things happen." In DeCasper and Fifer's (1980) classic study, three-day-olds learned to suck a plastic nipple with a certain pattern of bursts in order to activate a tape recorder playing their mother's voice (see Figure 11.7). Finally, Meltzoff and Moore (1977) discovered that newborns will imitate adult facial expressions, as shown in Figure 11.10 in which Andrew Meltzoff elicits tongue protrusions from a newborn. Many (e.g., Kugiumutzakis, Kokkinaki, Makrodimitraki, and Vitalaki, 2005), but not all, researchers have replicated Meltzoff and Moore's findings. What function does this very early presocial behaviour serve? Some developmentalists suggest that tongue protrusion is not true imitation but merely a reflexive response released by any large, high-contrast, round target (resembling the mother's nipple); but, Meltzoff and Moore (2000) also reported selective imitation of mouth opening and lip protrusion. They suggest that this innate ability helps infants recognize people and engage them in social exchange. Kugiumutzakis et al. tracked imitation of facial expressions and vocalizations from birth to 10 months of age and observed that infants displayed strong emotions (e.g., pleasure) during all imitation exchanges; they suggest this socio-emotional engagement facilitates the infant's development of thought, self-awareness, and language.

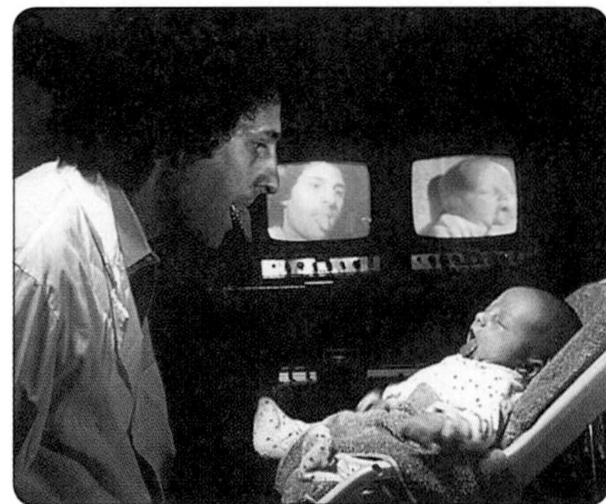

FIGURE 11.10

Young infants have been found to reproduce tongue protrusion after watching an adult model. Here researcher Andrew Meltzoff models the behaviour and records an infant's response.

Sensory-Perceptual Development

Newborns' crude sensory-perceptual abilities improve rapidly. Their visual field in each eye expands to almost adult size by six months of age, while grating

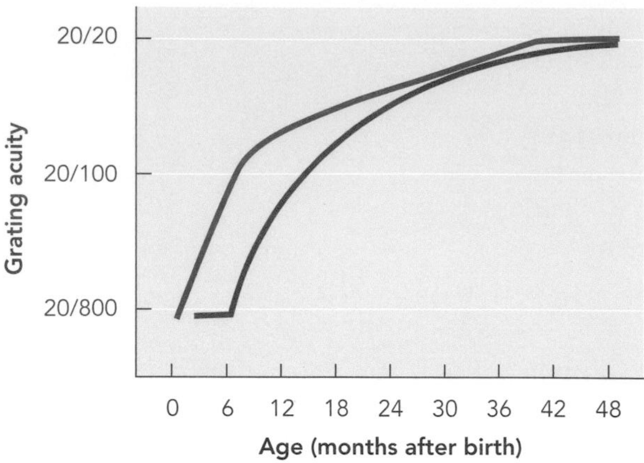

FIGURE 11.11

The normal developmental function for visual acuity (the blue line) consists of a rapid improvement in grating acuity during the first year of life followed by a more gradual improvement during the next few years until adult levels are reached by three to four years of age. The critical/sensitive period for damage to visual acuity as a consequence of early visual deprivation lasts for the first 10 years of life in humans. Although acuity may be damaged following early visual deprivation, the effect is partially reversible when vision is restored. This point is illustrated by the results of a case study of an infant born with cataracts (red line). For this infant, grating acuity was still at the newborn level when the cataracts were removed at about six months of age, after which grating acuity rapidly improved to almost normal levels. Although grating acuity becomes almost normal for such visually deprived infants, other aspects of their visual perception remain abnormal.

Adapted from Maurer & Lewis, 2001.

acuity improves in a continuous developmental function from 20/800 at birth to 20/100 by six months of age, and then progresses more slowly until it reaches adult levels by about four years of age (Maurer & Lewis, 2001). This continuous developmental function is shown in Figure 11.11. Researchers, using visual habituation and preference procedures, have shown that by three to four months of age, infants discriminate between patterns made up of subjective contours (Ghim, 1990) such as the one shown in Chapter 5; their pattern perception is organized according to Gestalt principles (e.g., closure and proximity shown in Chapter 5; Quinn, Brown, & Streppa, 1997); and they discriminate internal features of schematic faces (Maurer & Barrera, 1981). However, some Gestalt principles are used more easily than others by young infants to perceive abstract patterns (Quinn & Bhatt, 2006). Different aspects of pattern perception appear to emerge as infants age in a step-like fashion (stage), although they may be present at birth but are masked by poor visual acuity or insensitive behavioural tests.

Not all perceptual developmental functions show improvement with age during infancy. For example, a U-shaped function exists for sound localization—the remarkable ability of newborns to turn toward sounds at birth disappears in the second month of life and returns again at four to five months of age (Muir et al., 1994). Possible reasons for this drop in responding include a lack of practice, being captured by visual targets, and temporary inhibition as the cortical structures mature and take control of subcortically driven reflexes. Other examples of U-shaped functions are discussed below.

Auditory pattern perception is also relatively advanced in young infants, who can detect tiny changes in adult speech sounds that differentiate one word from another (called phonemes) by one to two months of age. Janet Werker (1989) and co-workers at the University of British Columbia found that six-month-olds rapidly learned to turn their heads to receive a visual reward (a toy that lights up) whenever they heard one repeated phoneme (the "b" sound in "bah") change to another (the "d" in "dah"). They were equally good at detecting changes in phonemes not found in their parents' language (e.g., two ways to pronounce a "t" sound in Hindi) that their mothers could not detect. The infants lost this latter ability by 12 months of age, as they began to speak words in their native language, demonstrating an early case of "use it or lose it." This is an example of a U-shaped function since adults could learn to discriminate these non-native phonemes after extensive training.

In the first half-year of life, infants appear to perceive music as adults do, according to the research of Laurel Trainor (McMaster University) and colleagues. For example, six-month-olds will look longer to hear a pitch change in tones that adults find pleasant (or consonant) than to hear a pitch change that adults rate as unpleasant (or dissonant) (Trainor & Heinmiller, 1998; also, see Trainor, Tsang, & Cheung, 2002). Masataka (2007) hypothesized that this primitive early musical appreciation reflects an early stage in the evolution of our communication system composed of melodies (also found in non-human primates) rather than words.

To summarize, the sensory-perceptual processes that are exercised in the uterus, as well as vision, all operate at some level at birth, and most improve rapidly during the first year of life. Other perceptual abilities appear rather suddenly several months after birth. Finally, a few perceptual responses decline temporarily or disappear during the first year of life. The reasons for the U-shaped functions are not fully understood. Similar U-shaped functions also exist for several motor skills discussed next.

Physical, Motor, and Brain Development

Our bodies and movement (motor) skills develop rapidly during infancy and childhood. On average, by our first birthday body weight triples, height increases by 50 percent, and we are standing easily and learning to walk. **Maturation** is the genetically programmed biological process that governs our growth.

Physical and motor development follow several biological principles. The **cephalocaudal principle** reflects the tendency for development to proceed in a head-to-foot direction. Thus the head of a fetus or infant is disproportionately large, because physical growth concentrates on the head and proceeds toward the lower part of the body (Figure 11.12). The **proximodistal principle** states that development begins along the innermost parts of the body and continues toward the outermost parts. Thus a fetus's arms develop before its hands and fingers, and at birth infants can control their shoulders, but not their arm or hand muscles.

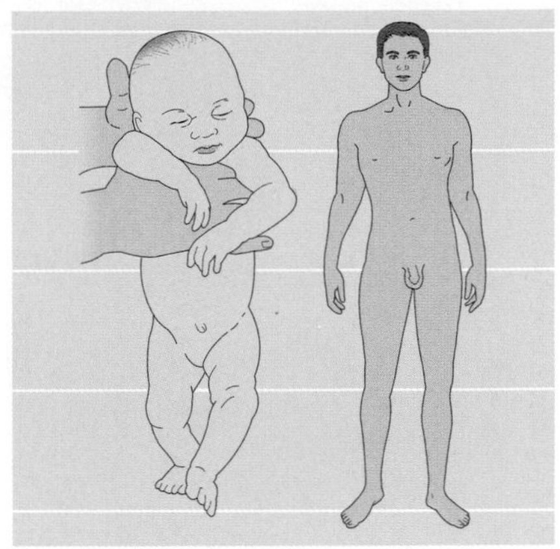

FIGURE 11.12

The cephalocaudal principle. Compared to adults, a newborn's head is disproportionately large relative to the rest of the body, reflecting the tendency for development to proceed in a head-to-foot direction. In a fetus, the head represents an even greater proportion of the body (look carefully at Figure 11.3c).

7. Explain how nature and nurture jointly influence physical growth and motor development during infancy.

No organ in the human body develops more rapidly and dramatically than the brain (Kolb, 1989). Still, at birth the newborn's brain is far from mature, and is only about 25 percent of its eventual adult weight. By six months, however, the brain already is 50 percent of its adult weight. What makes the brain heavier? Cells become larger, many axons develop an insulating myelin sheath, and as Figure 11.13 shows, neural networks that form the basis for cognitive and motor skills develop rapidly.

From the embryonic stage through childhood, brain maturation occurs in an orderly fashion. The first areas to develop and mature, such as the brain stem, lie deep within the brain and regulate basic survival functions such as heartbeat and breathing. The last areas to mature include the association areas of the frontal cortex, which are vital to our highest-level cognitive functions such as thinking and language.

The rapid rate of growth during infancy and early childhood slows in later childhood. Five-year-olds' brains have reached almost 90 percent of adult size, and are closer to adult weight than any other part of the body (Tanner, 1978). Although the size of the brain increases little between the ages of 5 and 10 years, its maturation continues. New synapses form, the association areas of the cerebral cortex mature, and the cerebral hemispheres become more highly specialized.

Motor development tends to follow a regular, stage-like sequence, as illustrated by examples of North American motor-scale norms shown in Figure 11.14. A major point is that infants vary in the age at which they acquire a particular skill, but the sequence in which each skill appears is similar across infants. However, this figure leaves out the so-called **"reflexes"**—defined as automatic, "inborn" behaviours elicited by specific stimuli—present at birth. Some, such as breathing, the rooting reflex, and sucking have clear adaptive value; together, they regulate the infant's ability to feed. Other reflexes have less obvious adaptive significance, but illustrate the degree to which many complex motor acts are developed in the uterus. For example, some newborns will crawl when placed prone on a surface and "swim" when placed in water (don't do this without supervision). They grasp objects with their hands and feet, and some even appear to "walk" (lift each leg in alternation) when held upright with their feet touching a surface. The famous behaviourist, John Watson, made a film of many of these reflexes in the early 1900s. Generally, healthy reflexes indicate normal neurological maturity at birth.

We now know that some motor skills follow a U-shaped developmental function. For example, the newborn stepping reflex (and others) usually drops out after one to two months and reappears around 12 months of age when North American infants attempt to walk. It turns out that this motor skill is hidden, not lost. Thelen,

At birth

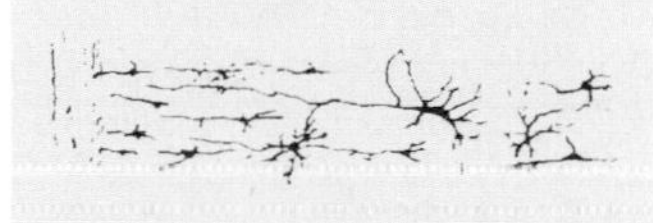

1 month

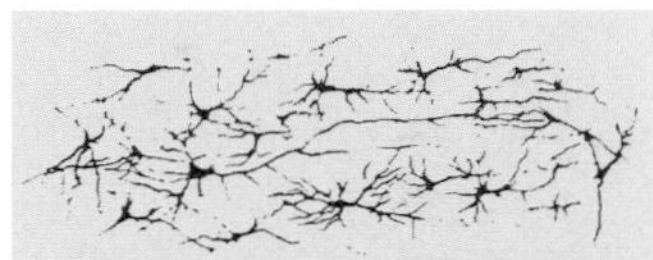

3 months

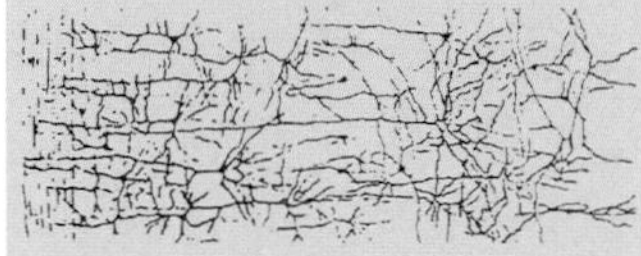

15 months

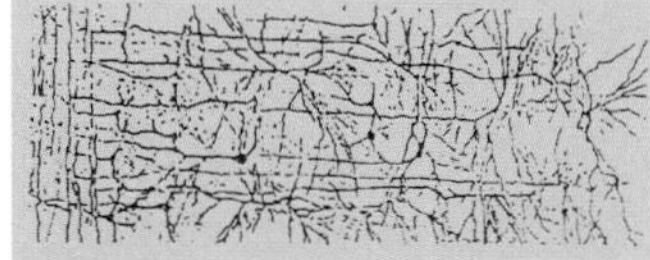

24 months

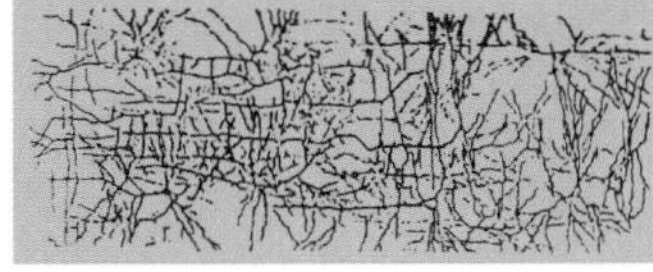

FIGURE 11.13

Increases in the density of neural networks during early development are apparent in these drawings of tissue from the human cerebral cortex.

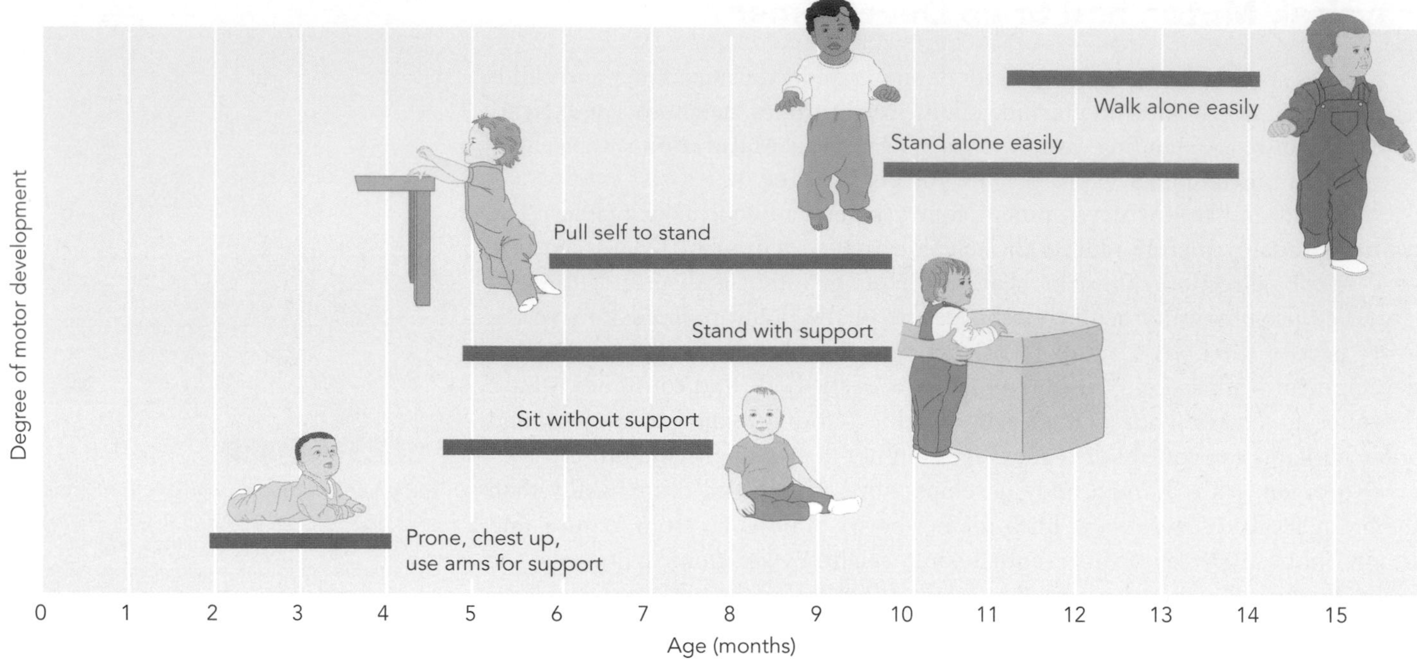

FIGURE 11.14

Infant motor development occurs in an orderly sequence, but the age at which abilities emerge varies across children. The left end of each bar represents the age by which 25 percent of children exhibit the skill; the right end represents the age by which 90 percent have mastered it.

Fisher, and Ridley-Johnson (1984) suspected that, as the legs grew heavier, the slower developing leg muscles were not able to lift them; when they held babies in water, where the buoyancy lightened the load, alternate stepping reappeared.

Environmental and Cultural Influences

Although physical and motor development are guided by genetic programs (i.e., maturation), they are also influenced by experience. Diet is an obvious example. Chronic, severe malnutrition not only stunts general growth and brain development, but also is a major source of infant death worldwide (Pelletier & Frongillo, 2003).

Physical touch and environmental enrichment also affect growth in infancy. Properly nourished newborn rats show stunted development if they are deprived of normal physical contact with their mothers, but vigorously stroking the rats with a brush helps maintain normal physical growth (Kuhn & Schanberg, 1998). Premature and full-term human infants who are regularly massaged gain weight more rapidly and show faster neurological development (Field, 2002). Rats raised in an enriched environment develop heavier brains, larger neurons, more synaptic connections, and greater amounts of acetylcholine, a brain neurotransmitter that enhances learning (Rosenzweig & Bennett, 1996). Finally, as discussed in Chapter 5, visual deprivation during the first few months of life (during the sensitive period) can permanently damage a cat's visual acuity. Visual deprivation early in life, due to cataracts, can also damage human visual abilities, as described in the *Research Frontiers* box on the next page.

Clearly, experience plays a critical role in the development of sensory, perceptual, motor, and physical development. Our discussion of physical growth and perceptual-motor development reinforces three points that apply across the realm of human development:

- *Biology sets limits on environmental influences.* The best nutrition will not enable most people to grow seven feet tall, and no infant can be toilet-trained before the nerve fibres that help regulate bladder control have matured biologically.

- *Environmental influences can be powerful.* Nurturing environments foster physical, sensory-motor, and psychological growth, while impoverished environments can stunt growth.
- *Biological and environmental factors interact.* Enriched environments enhance brain development. In turn, brain development facilitates our ability to learn and benefit from environmental experiences.

RESEARCH FRONTIERS

Effects of Early Experience on Human Perceptual-Motor Abilities

Experience has a major effect on the acquisition of complex motor skills acquired by toddlers and children (see Figure 11.15). For example, the U-shaped function for stepping has been altered experimentally by Philip R. Zelazo's group at McGill. Beginning at six weeks of age, experimental groups received three minutes of daily practice either sitting or stepping. For each group the targeted behaviour increased dramatically, relative to the no-practice control group (Zelazo, Zelazo, Cohen & Zelazo, 1993). With long-term practice, infants walked about two months earlier than controls (Zelazo, Zelazo & Kolb, 1972). Cross-cultural studies tell a similar story. Compared to North Americans, infants, when raised in cultures in which parents restrict walking experience, walk later (e.g., Ache infants from Paragua around age two; Kaplan & Dove, 1987) and in cultures in which parents exercise walking, infants walk sooner (e.g., Kipsigis infants from Kenya at about 10 months; Super, 1976).

Experience also plays a critical role in visual development. Maurer and Lewis (2001) summarized the results of their long-term longitudinal study of infants born with congenital cataracts (opaque lens preventing pattern vision) in one or both eyes who were treated at the Hospital for Sick Children in Toronto. All were optically corrected between one week and nine months of age. Lewis and Maurer tested their visual acuity (using the preferential looking test described above) within minutes after the operation, and repeatedly over a number of years. Visual acuity was at newborn levels immediately after the operation, irrespective of the infant's age, and improved very quickly (by a factor of four within an hour), reaching normal levels by 12 months of age. The results of one case study are shown in Figure 11.11.

Sleeper Effects: If Maurer and Lewis had stopped follow-up testing at that point, they would have concluded that there was no negative impact from early visual deprivation; the visual system was kept intact by non-patterned light experience until it received patterned visual input, after which it rapidly recovered normal vision. However, Maurer and her colleagues continued to test these children's (and the non-visually deprived control group) grating acuity until they were 14 years of age. She also added new tests of more complex visual perception (e.g., face perception). Significant "sleeper effects" (permanent effects in visual information processes not functioning at the time of deprivation that emerge long after the early deprivation is corrected) were found. Infants with early binocular deprivation during their first year of life displayed a permanent loss of acuity for very fine gratings that normally mature around six years of age (Maurer, Ellemberg & Lewis, (2006). Furthermore, visually deprived children were deficient in complex, configural visual pattern perception (e.g., deprived children failed to detect changes in spacing of internal features of pictures of faces that were obvious to the non-deprived children) (Maurer, Mondloch & Lewis, 2007). Maurer et al suggest that disruptions in early visual experience with crude images (gratings with broad stripes) failed to set up a neural structure that would be refined later in development to mediate more complex visual pattern perception. Finally, while the most devastating impact on later visual processing appears to occur following even short periods of visual deprivation in the first year of life, the sensitive/critical period for visual deprivation effects extends until about 10 years of age—cataracts that form any time before 10 years of age, if left unattended, can cause some lasting damage, while cataracts that form after 10 years produce no permanent deficits when vision is restored (Maurer & Lewis, 2001).

FIGURE 11.15

At the Parker Ranch in Hawaii, this two-year-old is learning to ride a horse and use a lasso.

In Review

- *Newborns have poor sensory acuity, but they can distinguish between different visual patterns, speech sounds, odours, and tastes. They display perceptual preferences, learn through classical and operant conditioning, and may have a primitive capacity for imitation.*
- *Sensory, perceptual, and motor abilities have several different developmental functions. Most rapidly improve during the first year of life. Some newborn perceptual-motor responses temporarily decline during the first few months after birth and then recover during the first year of life.*
- *The cephalocaudal principle reflects the tendency for development to proceed in a head-to-foot direction. The proximodistal principle states that development begins along the innermost parts of the body and continues toward the outermost parts.*
- *Experience is critical for normal development; without pattern vision, acuity stalls at the newborn level, but recovers to a large extent when vision is restored, although permanent deficits remain if the deprivation occurs during the sensitive/critical period.*

Cognitive Development

What are the thought processes of a child like, and how do they change with age? Swiss psychologist Jean Piaget (1926, 1977) spent over 50 years exploring these questions, and his ideas have influenced generations of developmental researchers (De Vries et al., 2000).

Piaget's Stage Model

8. Describe assimilation and accommodation. How are they related to cognitive development?

Early in his career Piaget worked for French psychologist Alfred Binet, the pioneer of intelligence testing. Piaget became intrigued by the patterns of errors children made on test questions, with children of the same age often making similar mistakes. He came to believe that the key issue in understanding how children think was not whether they got the right answers, but *how* they arrived at their answers.

Piaget relied on observational research, carefully watching children and listening to them reason as they tried to solve problems. He proposed that children's thinking changes *qualitatively* with age, and that it differs from the way adults think. Piaget believed that cognitive development results from an interplay of maturation and experience, and he viewed children as natural-born "scientists" who actively explore and seek to understand their world.

To achieve this understanding, the brain builds **schemas**, which are organized patterns of thought and action. Think of a schema as an "internal framework" that guides our interaction with the world. For example, infants are born with a sucking reflex that provides a primitive framework—a schema—for interacting with physical objects. To the infant, the world is meant to be sucked. In a sense, sucking is a basic way in which the infant "knows" the world. Similarly, when a child says "doggie" to describe the family pet, this word reflects an underlying schema—a concept or framework—that the child is using to understand this particular experience.

Cognitive development occurs as we acquire new schemas, and as our existing schemas become more complex. According to Piaget, two key processes are involved. **Assimilation** is the process by which new experiences are incorporated into existing schemas. For example, when a young infant encounters a new object—a small plastic toy, a blanket, a doll—she will try to suck it. She tries to "fit" this new experience into a schema that she already has: Objects are suckable. Similarly, a child who sees a horse for the first time may exclaim "big doggie." After all, the horse has four legs and a tail, so the child tries to make sense of this new experience by applying her familiar schema: "doggie."

Accommodation is the process by which new experiences cause existing schemas to change. As the infant tries to suck different objects, she will eventually encounter ones that are too big to go into her mouth or that taste bad. Similarly, the child who calls a horse a "big doggie" eventually will realize that this "big doggie" doesn't bark, sit, fetch, or otherwise behave like a dog. This imbalance or *disequilibrium* between existing schemas and new experiences ultimately forces those schemas to change. Thus the infant's "suckability" schema will become more complex; some objects are suckable, some are not. The child's "doggie" schema also will change, and she will begin to develop new schemas for "horsey," "kitty," and so on. This may not seem earth-shaking to us, but to them, their understanding of the world has changed fundamentally. Every time a schema is modified it helps create a better balance, an *equilibrium*, between the environment and the child's understanding of it.

Cognitive growth thus involves a give-and-take between trying to understand new experiences in terms of what we already know (assimilation), and having to modify our thinking when new experiences don't fit into our current schemas (accommodation). As Table 11.1 shows, Piaget charted four major stages of cognitive growth.

TABLE 11.1 Piaget's Model of Cognitive Development

Stage	Age (years)	Major Characteristics
Sensorimotor	Birth to 2	• Infant understands world through sensory and motor experiences • Achieves object permanence • Emergence of symbolic thought
Preoperational	2–7	• Symbolic thinking; child uses words and images to represent objects and experiences; pretend play • Thinking displays egocentrism, irreversibility, and centration
Concrete operational	7–12	• Child can think logically about concrete events • Grasps concepts of conservation and serial ordering
Formal operational	12 on	• Adolescent can think more logically, abstractly, and flexibly • Can form hypotheses and test them systematically

Sensorimotor stage. In the **sensorimotor stage**, which lasts from birth to about age two, infants understand their world primarily through sensory experiences and physical (motor) interactions with objects. Their reflexes are the earliest schemas that guide thought and action, but as sensory and motor capabilities increase, babies begin to explore their surroundings. Eventually, they realize that they can "make things happen": They bang spoons, take objects apart, and find amazing ways to get themselves into trouble. One 18-month-old peeled sheets of latex paint from a nursery wall, proudly proclaiming the guiding schema to his shocked parents: "Band-Aid!"

9. How do infants develop cognitively during the sensorimotor stage?

For young infants, said Piaget, "out of sight" literally means "out of mind." If you hide six-month-old Cindy's favourite toy from view she will not search for it, just as if the toy no longer existed (Figure 11.16); but, around eight months, she will pull back the blanket and retrieve the hidden toy. According to Piaget, the infant now has **object permanence**—the ability to understand that an object continues to exist even when it disappears from sight. This major developmental milestone frees the child from immediate sensory experience by allowing the child to be conscious of invisible objects and past experiences as she plans a response to current events.

Infants begin to acquire language after age one, and toward the end of the sensorimotor period they use words increasingly to represent objects, needs, and actions. Thus, in the space of two years, infants have grown into planful thinkers who can form simple concepts, solve some problems mentally, and communicate their thoughts to others.

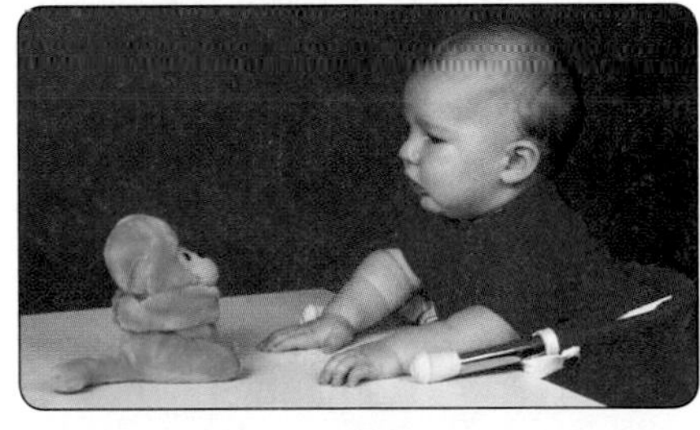

(a)

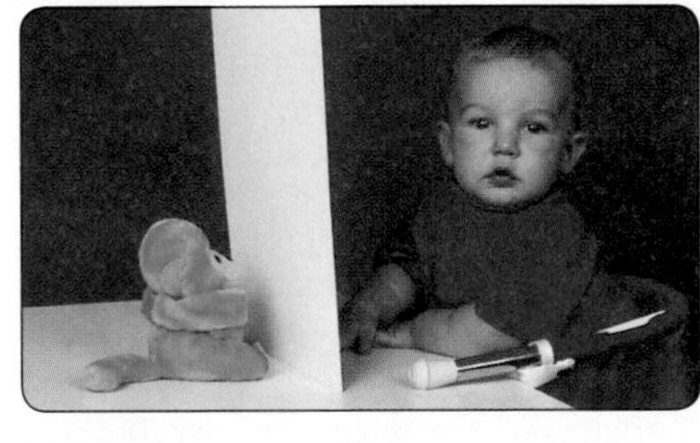

(b)

FIGURE 11.16

During the early sensorimotor period a baby will reach for a visible toy (a), but not for one that has been hidden from view while the infant watches (b). According to Piaget, the child lacks the concept of object permanence; when something is out of sight, it ceases to exist.

Preoperational stage. Children enter the **preoperational stage** around age two: They represent the world symbolically through words and mental images, but do not yet understand basic mental operations or rules. Rapid language development helps children label objects and represent simple concepts, such as that two objects can be "the same" or "different." Children become capable of thinking about the past ("yesterday") and future ("tomorrow," "soon"), they become better at anticipating the consequences of their actions, and symbolic thinking enables them to engage in "make-believe," otherwise known as *pretend play*.

(a)

(b)

(c)

Conservation of number

Initial equality

Now, which row has more objects?

(d)

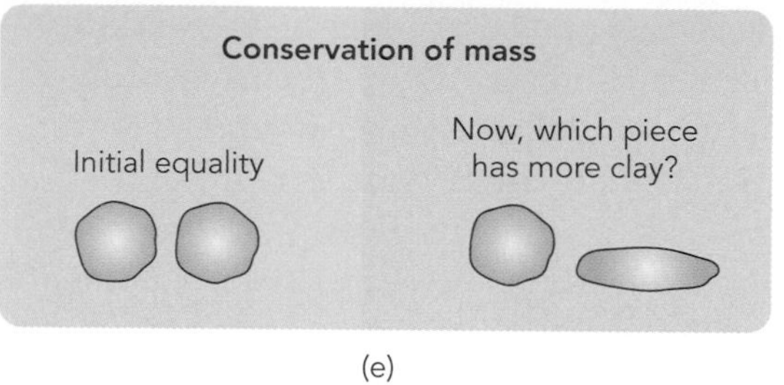

(e)

FIGURE 11.17

(a, b, c) Conservation of volume. At the end of this sequence (from left to right), when the preoperational child is asked which beaker contains more liquid, he points to the taller one. (d) Conservation of number. *Two rows with an equal number of objects are aligned. After one row is spread out, preoperational children will say that it has more objects than the other row. (e)* Conservation of mass. *Preoperational children watch as one of two identically sized clay balls is rolled into a new shape. They typically will say that it now has more clay.*

10. Identify some achievements and limitations of children's thinking in the preoperational stage.

FIGURE 11.18

Piaget used the three-mountain problem to illustrate the egocentrism of young children. Suppose that a preoperational child named Ted is looking at the mountains just as you are. Another child, Susan, is standing at the opposite (far) side of the table. Ted is asked what Susan sees. Because Ted is able to see the road, he will mistakenly say that Susan also can see it, indicating that he has failed to recognize Susan's perspective as different from his own.

Despite these advances, their cognitive abilities still have important limitations. According to Piaget, the preoperational child does not understand the concept of **conservation**, the principle that basic properties of objects, such as their volume, mass, or quantity stay the same (are "conserved") even though their outward appearance may change (Figure 11.17). For example, suppose we have two short, wide beakers containing equal amounts of liquid. To many people's surprise, when the liquid from one is poured into a tall, narrow beaker, a four-year-old often will say that the taller glass now has more liquid.

Whereas you understand that the water can be poured back into the short beaker to return to the original state of affairs, the child's thinking displays *irreversibility:* It is difficult for him to mentally reverse an action. You also pay attention to height and width, recognizing that the water is "taller" because the beaker is narrower. But the child exhibits *centration*, focusing (centring) on only one aspect of the situation. Usually, this is the most striking feature, such as the height of the water. Centration also contributes to young preoperational children's more general tendency to be deceived by striking but false appearances.

Preoperational children often display *animism*, attributing lifelike qualities to physical objects and natural events. When it rains "the sky is crying" and stars twinkle at night "because they're winking at you." Their thinking also reflects **egocentrism**, difficulty in viewing the world from someone else's perspective. By "egocentrism" Piaget did not mean "selfishness." Rather, children at this stage believe that other people perceive things in the same way they do (Figure 11.18).

Concrete operational stage. In the **concrete operational stage**, which Piaget believed lasts from about ages 7 to 12, children can perform basic mental operations concerning problems that involve tangible (i.e., "concrete") objects and situations. Because they now grasp the concept of reversibility and display less centration, these children easily solve the water-beaker task and other conservation problems that baffled them as preschoolers.

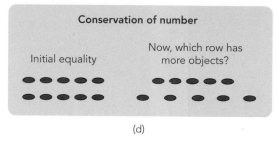

Unlike younger children, concrete operational children grasp the concept of serial ordering and can easily arrange a set of objects along various dimensions, such as from "shortest" to "tallest." These children also can form mental representations of a series of actions. For example, a concrete operational child can draw a map showing the route to get to school. A preoperational child might be able to lead you to school, but would have difficulty representing the route symbolically.

When concrete operational children confront problems that are hypothetical or require abstract reasoning, however, they often have difficulty or show rigid types of thinking. To demonstrate this, ask a few nine-year-olds: "If you could have a third eye, where on your body would you put it? Draw a picture." Then ask them to explain their reason. David Shaffer (1989) reports that nine-year-olds typically draw a row of three eyes across their face. Their thinking is concrete, bound by the reality that eyes appear on the face, and their justifications often are unsophisticated (e.g., ". . . so I could see you better"). Many find the task silly because "Nobody has three eyes" (Shaffer, 1989, p. 324).

11. How does thinking change during the concrete and formal operational stages?

Formal operational stage. Piaget's model ends with the **formal operational stage**, in which individuals are able to think logically and systematically about both concrete and abstract problems, form hypotheses, and test them in a thoughtful way. Formal thinking begins around ages 11 to 12 and increases through adolescence (Ward & Overton, 1990).

Children entering this stage begin to think more flexibly when tackling hypothetical problems, such as "brain-teasers," and typically enjoy the challenge. Shaffer (1989) reports that 12-year-olds provide more creative answers and better justifications to the "third-eye problem" than do 9-year-old concrete thinkers. One child placed the eye on the palm of his hands so that he could use it to ". . . see around corners. . . ." Another placed it on top of his head, so that he could "revolve the eye to look in all directions." Formal operational children loved this hypothetical task and begged their teacher for more. We will return to this stage when discussing adolescence.

Assessment of Piaget's Theory: Stages, Ages, and Culture

Piaget considered his stages of cognitive development to be universal. Tests of children in diverse cultures around the world on Piaget's cognitive tasks have shown that *the general cognitive abilities associated with Piaget's four stages appear to occur in the same order across cultures,* according to John Berry at Queen's University (Berry, Poortinger, Segall & Dasen, 2002). For example, children understand object permanence (stage 1) before symbolic thinking blooms (stage 2), and formal operational thinking (stage 4), although not as common as Piaget suggested, always emerges after concrete reasoning develops (stage 3). However, contrary to Piaget's universality principle, researchers have also found that *culture influences cognitive development.* Piaget's Western perspective equated "cognitive development" with scientific-logical thinking, but many cultures do not share this view. As David Matsumoto and Philip Hull note:

> Different societies value and reward different skills and behaviours. . . . Many cultures . . . consider cognitive development to be more relational, involving the thinking skills and processes to engage in successful interpersonal contexts. (Matsumoto & Hull, 1994, p. 105)

Compared to Westerners, people from underdeveloped countries or tribal societies often appear to show a large "age-delay" or to achieve less success in solving Piaget's concrete and formal operational tasks. But these differences shrink or disappear when culturally appropriate tasks are chosen, when researchers speak the native language, or when children receive special training or formal schooling (Jahoda, 1983).

12. In what major ways does research support and contradict Piaget's basic ideas?

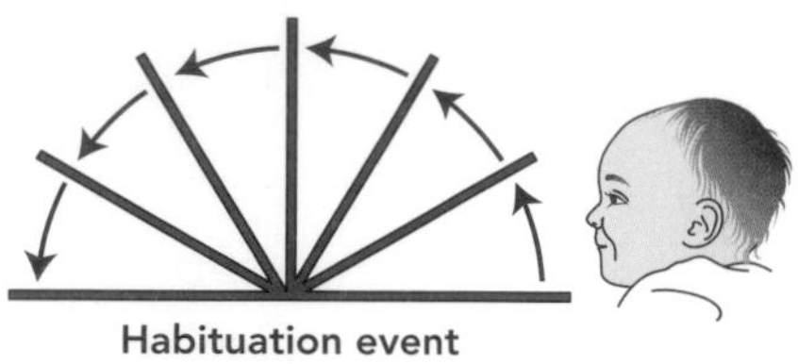

Habituation event
(a)

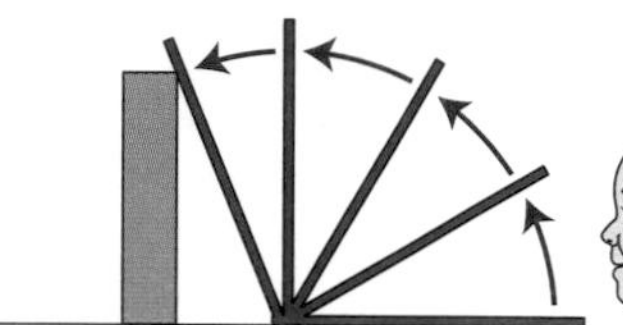

Possible event
(b)

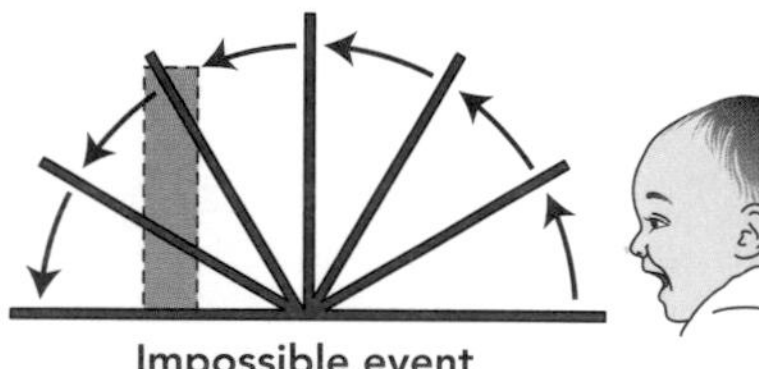

Impossible event
(c)

FIGURE 11.19

(a) Habituation. *Renée Baillargeon (1987) repeatedly exposes young infants to a screen that slowly rotates 180 degrees. Eventually, they habituate and become bored. Then the infants watch as a box is placed in the screen's path. (b)* Possible event. *The screen rotates, conceals the infant's view of the box, and then stops as the box blocks it. (c)* Impossible event. *The screen rotates, conceals the view of the box, and continues a full 180 degrees because the box is secretly removed. Infants stare longer at the "impossible" than at the "possible" event, as if they are surprised that the box did not stop the screen. This can only happen, reasons Baillargeon, if the infants understand that the box continues to exist even when concealed from view (i.e., object permanence).*

Adapted from Baillargeon, 1987.

New research continues to challenge some of Piaget's ideas. With the invention of new, more sensitive testing procedures, evidence is accumulating to show that infants and children acquire many cognitive skills at younger ages than Piaget had postulated (Aguiar & Baillargeon, 2002). In her classic experiment, Baillargeon (1987) demonstrated that four-month-olds displayed a basic grasp of object permanence when they were tested on special tasks that did not require them to physically search for a hidden object (see details in Figure 11.19). Using a similar procedure, Luo & Baillargeon (2007) have shown that four-month-olds treat inanimate, self-propelled objects (e.g., a moving box) as though they are alive, with goals and desires, much as adults do. Also, young children have been found to make fewer conservation errors and show less egocentric thinking when they are tested on tasks that are more familiar to them, or that depend less on language than the tasks invented by Piaget (Borke, 1975).

Another problem is that *cognitive development within each stage seems to proceed inconsistently.* A child may perform at the preoperational level on some tasks, yet solve other tasks at a concrete operational level (Dasen, 1975; Siegler, 1981; Marini & Case, 1994). This problem goes to the heart of the continuity-discontinuity debate. If development proceeds in qualitatively distinct stages, then a child at a given stage should *not* show large inconsistencies in solving conceptually similar tasks.

So what are we to conclude? While modern research reveals a number of problems with his theory, Piaget did revolutionize our thinking about children's cognitive development. His work continues to guide many researchers, called *neo-Piagetians*, who continue to modify his theory to account for some of the issues discussed above (Flavell, Miller & Miller, 1993).

Vygotsky: The Social Context of Cognitive Development

Whereas Piaget focused mainly on children's independent exploration of the physical world, Russian psychologist Lev Vygotsky (1935–1978) emphasized that children also live in a *social* world, and that cognitive development occurs in a socio-cultural context. In all types of daily interactions, including fantasy play, adults and older peers stimulate children's cognitive growth and provide them with knowledge about the world.

To illustrate a key aspect of Vygotsky's approach, suppose that five-year-olds Ray and Juanita have similar scores on cognitive tests, and that neither child can solve Piaget's conservation problems. However, with guidance from a parent, teacher, or older sibling, Juanita "gets it" and can now solve these problems. Ray, even with assistance, just doesn't understand. Were these two children really at the same cognitive level to begin with? Vygotsky says no, introducing a concept called the **zone of proximal development**: *the difference between what a child can do independently, and what the child can do with assistance from adults or more advanced peers.*

13. What is the "zone of proximal development" and why is it important?

14. Describe how information-processing capabilities improve during childhood. How is this relevant to the continuity-discontinuity debate?

Why is the zone of proximal development important? For one thing, it helps us recognize "those functions that have not yet matured but are in the process of maturation . . ." (Vygotsky, 1935–1978, p. 86). In other words, it gives us an idea of what children may soon be able to do on their own. Second, this concept emphasizes that people can provide experiences and feedback that "move" a child's cognitive development forward within limits (the "zone") dictated by the child's level of biological maturation. For example, when parents work with a child on scientific tasks, they may push the child's understanding further along by using age-appropriate but cognitively demanding speech (e.g., introducing scientific concepts and terms) than by using only simpler speech (Tenenbaum & Leaper, 2003).

Having older siblings around the house may stimulate a younger child's cognitive development, as long as the child is biologically ready for the input. In one study of two- to six-year-old English and Japanese children, those over age three who grew up with older brothers and sisters performed better on a cognitive task than children who grew up alone or with younger brothers and sisters (Ruffman et al., 1998). However, two- to three-year-olds performed poorly on the task regardless of how many older or younger siblings they had. The task was simply beyond their current cognitive capacity.

Information-Processing Approaches

Many researchers believe that cognitive development is best examined within an information-processing framework. For example, young children may be unable to solve conservation problems because they pay insufficient attention to the task, don't search for key information, or are unable to hold enough pieces of information simultaneously in memory (Siegler, 1996).

Consider children's *information-search strategies.* Look at the two houses in Figure 11.20. Are they identical or different? This visual scanning task is easy for you or me, but not for young children. Elaine Vurpillot (1968) recorded the eye movements of 3- to 10-year-olds while they examined these and other sets of houses. Older children methodically scanned the houses, but preschoolers often looked at only a few windows and failed to compare each window in the house on the left to the corresponding window in the house on the right. In short, preschoolers were less able to search systematically for relevant details. Preschoolers also have problems with cognitive flexibility and selective attention—aspects of executive function that improve with age. Philip Zelazo (University of Toronto) and colleagues (e.g., Zelazo et al., 2003) demonstrated this by using a card sorting task. They asked children to sort a set of cards, each containing a coloured shape, into piles according to a colour rule (piles of green, red, etc.). Then they asked the children to sort the same set of cards according to a shape rule (e.g., rabbits, boats, etc.).

While most preschoolers easily solved the first task, using *either* colour or shape rules, they failed when asked to switch rules, showing their lack of cognitive flexibility, compared to school-aged children. Mueller, Zelazo, Leone, and Hood (2004) suggested that the preschoolers' problem with this task was due to immature selective attention. Their performance improved when they were prompted by, for example, labelling the correct colour during the task.

Information-processing speed also improves during childhood, as Robert Kail's (1991) review of 72 studies shows in Figure 11.21. Notice that processing speed improves continuously and that the relatively rapid rate of change between ages 8 to about 12 slows during adolescence.

Memory capabilities expand significantly during childhood. When it comes to organizing information and using strategies to improve memory, preschoolers fall far short of school-aged children. John Flavell (1970) gave children lists of words or numbers to remember. Preschoolers rarely used rehearsal spontaneously, whereas 8- to 10-year-olds often could be heard rehearsing words or numbers under their breath. Similarly, young children do not make effective use of "chunking," an organizational strategy for grouping related objects or words (Brown et al., 1983).

Metacognition refers to an awareness of one's own cognitive processes. Older children display greater awareness of their own mental processes than do younger children (Flavell, 1985). For example, older children are better at judging how well they understand material for a test or directions to someone's house. In turn, this can help them decide whether they need to study more or ask for a map.

FIGURE 11.20

Stimuli used by Vurpillot to assess visual inspection through filmed eye movements. Preschoolers fail to scan the pictures systematically, which often leads them to claim that the two houses are identical.

Based on Vurpillot, 1968.

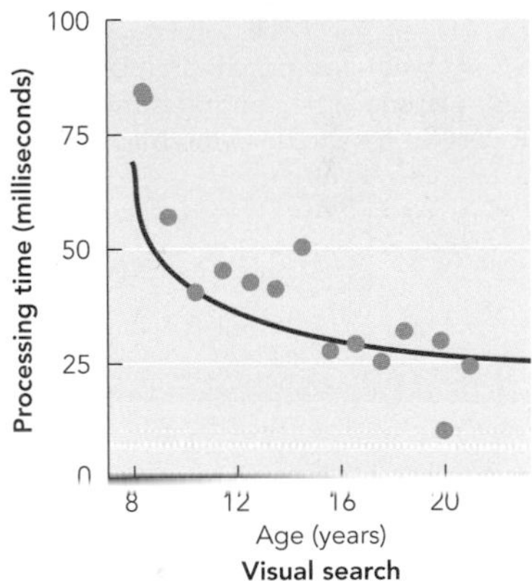

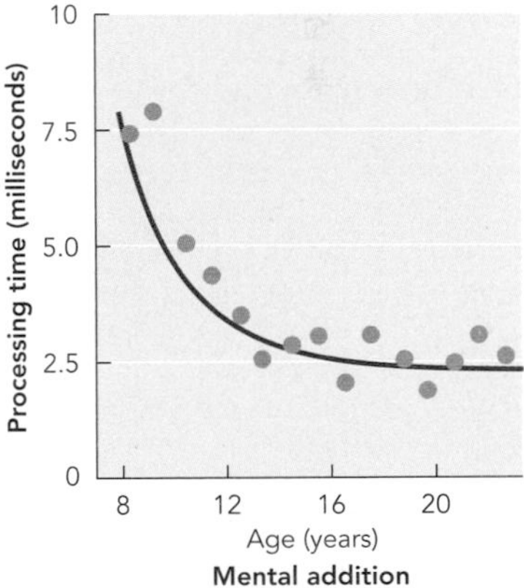

FIGURE 11.21

These two graphs show how information processing speed for visual search and mental addition tasks becomes faster with age. The relatively rapid rate of change between ages 8 to about 12 slows during adolescence. A similar non-linear pattern also occurs in name retrieval, mental rotation, and other cognitive tasks.

Data from Kail (1988, 1991).

Many researchers who adopt an information-processing approach believe that cognitive development is a continuous, gradual process in which the same set of processing abilities becomes more efficient over time. They reject the notion of stages.

Neo-Piagetian theorists, by contrast, believe that children also acquire new modes of processing information as they age (Flavell et al., 1993). Some argue that development involves both discontinuity (stages) *and* continuity. For example, Susan Gathercole (1998) suggests that memory capabilities change qualitatively (i.e., new abilities emerge) between infancy and age seven, but then undergo only gradual quantitative improvements through adolescence. The late Robbie Case (1944–2000), from the University of Toronto, offered a more elaborate, integrative view. He related the continuous growth in working memory, computational facility, and task-specific knowledge to both major shifts in reasoning ability, similar to advances through Piaget's stages, and more minor shifts. Case (1996) outlined how the network of "central conceptual structures" (mental blueprints or plans used to solve various sets of problems, similar to Piaget's mental schemas) that process the relationships between events and objects become more abstract, complex, and flexible with age. Case offered empirical support for his theory, but the debate is far from resolved.

Theory of Mind: Children's Understanding of Mental States

15. At what age do children begin to understand other people's thinking? How have researchers established this?

The term **theory of mind** refers to a person's beliefs about how the "mind" works, and what others are thinking about. Adults assume the mind exists, that it consists of various mental states such as knowledge, feelings, desires, intentions, etc., and that these states are related to a person's actions (Lee & Homer, 1999). They use these assumptions to explain and predict their own and other people's behaviour. According to Piaget, children under six or seven years of age have a very limited understanding of how the mind works, and thus have difficulty inferring what others are thinking. Indeed, this is what Piaget's concept of egocentrism is all about: not being able to understand how someone else perceives a situation. But consider the following story:

> Susie puts a candy bar inside a green box on the table, and then she goes away. Then her mother takes the candy bar out of the box and puts it inside a red bag on the bed. Susie doesn't see her mother do this. Later, Susie comes back and wants to get her candy because she is hungry. Where will Susie look for her candy bar?

Most two- and three-year-olds indicate that Susie will look in the red bag, as if she had the same knowledge that they have. Piaget would not be surprised. But most four-year-olds say she will choose the green box, recognizing that Susie does not have the information they do (see Astington & Gopnik, 1991). Thus, at some level, they comprehend that Susie's mental state—her "mind"—is different from theirs. Using culturally equivalent examples, studies with young children from African tribal societies, Canada, China, Japan, the United Kingdom, and the United States obtain similar findings (Avis & Harris, 1991; Ruffman et al., 1998). Finally, when Hala, Chandler, and Fritz (1991) asked three-year-olds who failed the false-belief question (where Susie "thought" the candy was), 75 percent answered correctly, indicating they understood that deceptive strategies lead others into false beliefs.

Lying and deception reflect the operation of a theory of mind; they imply an understanding that one can instill a false belief into another person's mind. In a classic American study, Lewis, Stranger, and Sullivan (1989) told three-year-olds not to peek at a toy when the adult left the room. Most peeked, and when the adult returned and asked them if they had peeked, about one-third of the peekers lied.

Lewis (1993) obtained similar results in Japan. Victoria Talwar (McGill) and Kang Lee (U. of Toronto) (2002) tested three- to seven-year-olds, and found that across age, about 80 percent of children peeked. About one-third of the three-year-olds said they had not peeked, while about 80 percent of the older children lied—and did so convincingly (neither parents nor strangers could tell if a child was telling a lie when they reviewed the child's videotaped answer). Even police and customs officers, who were trained in lie-detection, failed to discriminate between lie- and truth-tellers (Leach, Talwar, Lee, Bala, & Lindsay, 2004). It is noteworthy that the liars (77%) in Talwar and Lee's study found it difficult to conceal their lie in follow-up questions—some even named the toy they had "never seen." These results may have important implications for the use of child eyewitness testimony in legal cases.

In early word-learning studies, infants make inferences about the adult's knowledge, intentions, and perspective by 1½ to 2 years of age. Dare Baldwin's (1993) classic work shows that, at this age, infants will attach a novel word to a novel object only if the adult looks in the direction of the object while saying "it's a modi." This is true even if the object is hidden from the infant's view in a bucket, as long as the adult says the word while looking into the bucket. By four years of age, children become more sophisticated; they attached the word the adult used while looking at the object only if the adult appeared knowledgeable rather than uncertain about the object's name (Sabbagh & Baldwin, 2001). Overall, it appears that children understand some aspects of other people's thinking by three to four years of age, well before Piaget proposed (Ritblatt, 2000).

Moral Development

All societies have norms of moral conduct, and a major goal of socialization is to help children recognize "right" from "wrong" and become moral adults. Sigmund Freud (1935) believed that children develop a moral conscience (i.e., they *internalize* society's moral norms) by identifying with their parents. B. F. Skinner (1971) proposed that we learn which behaviours and values are "good" and "bad" through their association with reinforcement and punishment. And Piaget (1932) viewed moral development as a cognitive process in which children pass from a simple stage of believing that actions are good or bad because adults say so, to a more complex stage of believing that morality involves subjective judgments about fairness.

Kohlberg's Stage Model

Drawing upon Piaget's model of cognitive development, Lawrence Kohlberg (1963, 1984) developed a highly influential theory of moral reasoning. He presented children, adolescents, and adults with hypothetical moral dilemmas such as the following:

> Heinz's wife was dying from cancer. A rare drug might save her, but the druggist who made the drug for $200 would not sell it for less than $2,000. Heinz tried hard, but he could only raise $1,000. The druggist refused to give Heinz the drug for that price even though Heinz promised to pay the rest later. So Heinz broke into the store to steal the drug. What do you think? Should Heinz have stolen the drug? Why or why not?

Kohlberg was interested not in whether people agreed or disagreed with Heinz's behaviour, but in the reasons for their judgment. He analyzed responses to various moral dilemmas and concluded that there are three main levels of moral reasoning, with two substages within each level (Table 11.2).

16. How do preconventional, conventional, and postconventional moral reasoning differ?

TABLE 11.2 Kohlberg's Stages of Moral Reasoning

Level of Moral Reasoning	Basis for Judging What Is Moral
Level 1: Preconventional	Actual or anticipated punishment and rewards, rather than internalized values
Stage 1: Punishment/obedience orientation	Obeying rules and avoiding punishment
Stage 2: Instrumental/hedonistic orientation	Self-interest and gaining rewards
Level 2: Conventional	Conformity to the expectations of social groups; person adopts other people's values
Stage 3: Good child orientation	Gaining approval and maintaining good relations with others
Stage 4: Law and order orientation	Doing one's duty, showing respect for authority, and maintaining social order
Level 3: Postconventional	Moral principles that are well thought out and part of one's belief and value system
Stage 5: Social contract orientation	General principles agreed upon by society that foster community welfare and individual rights; recognition that society can decide to modify laws that lose their social utility
Stage 6: Universal ethical principles	Abstract ethical principles based on justice and equality; following one's conscience

Source: Based on Kohlberg, 1963, 1984.

17. What aspects of Kohlberg's model have been supported? What are its limitations?

Preconventional moral reasoning is based on anticipated punishments or rewards. Consider reasons given for stealing the drug. In stage 1, children focus on punishment: "Heinz should steal the drug because, if he lets his wife die he'll get into trouble." In stage 2, morality is judged by anticipated rewards and doing what is in the person's own interest: "Heinz should steal the drug because that way he'll still have his wife with him."

Conventional moral reasoning is based on conformity to social expectations, laws, and duties. In stage 3, conformity stems from the desire to gain people's approval: "People will think that Heinz is bad if he doesn't steal the drug to save his wife." In stage 4, children believe that laws and duties must be obeyed simply because rules are meant to be followed. Thus: "Heinz should steal the drug because it's his duty to take care of his wife."

Postconventional moral reasoning is based on well thought out, general moral principles. Stage 5 involves recognizing the importance of societal laws, but also taking individual rights into account. Thus "Stealing breaks the law, but what Heinz did was reasonable because he saved a life." In stage 6, morality is based on abstract, ethical principles of justice that are viewed as universal. For example, "Saving life comes before financial gain, even if the person is a stranger. The law in this case is unjust, and stealing the drug is the morally right thing to do."

Kohlberg believed that progress in moral reasoning depends upon general cognitive maturation and the opportunity to confront moral issues, particularly when such issues can be discussed with someone who is at a higher stage of development. Moral education programs based on Kohlberg's theory have been applied in schools, prisons, and with at-risk youth (Higgins, 1991).

Culture, Gender, and Moral Reasoning

Researchers have studied moral reasoning throughout North, Central, and South America, Africa, Asia, Europe, and India (Colby et al., 1983; Eckensberger & Zimba, 1997). Overall, findings indicate that:

- As we age from childhood through adolescence, moral reasoning changes from preconventional to conventional levels (Figure 11.22).

- Even in adulthood, postconventional reasoning is relatively uncommon, though its frequency varies across cultures.
- Levels are not skipped. Preconventional reasoning occurs before conventional reasoning, and when it occurs, postconventional reasoning is last to emerge.
- A person's moral judgments do not always reflect the same level or stage within levels.

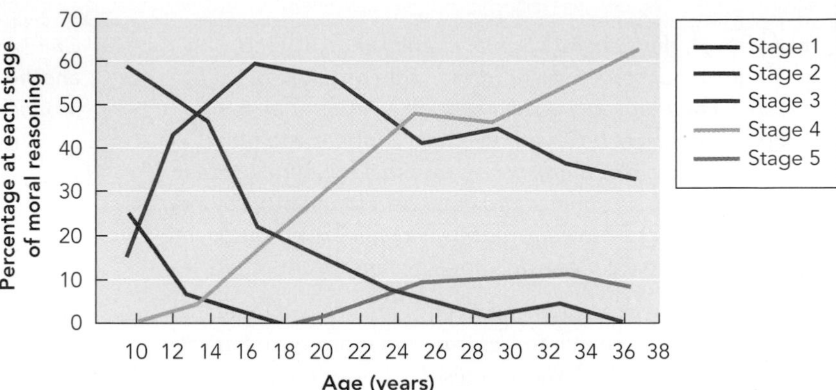

FIGURE 11.22

In this study based on Kohlberg's model, 58 American boys responded to moral dilemmas over more than 20 years. As they aged, preconventional morality (stages 1 and 2) decreased and conventional morality (stages 3 and 4) took precedence during adolescence. Postconventional moral reasoning was not common at any age.

Based on Colby et al., 1983.

Research using Kohlberg's tasks also finds that postconventional reasoning occurs more often among people from Westernized, formally educated, and middle- or upper-class backgrounds than among people in developing countries. Critics, however, claim that the theory has a Western cultural bias. Fairness and justice are Kohlberg's postconventional ideals, but in many cultures the highest moral values focus on principles that do not fit easily into Kohlberg's model: benevolence, non-violence, respect for all animal life, protecting the souls of dead ancestors from harm, respect for the elderly, and collective harmony (Eckensberger & Zimba, 1997). Critics charge that when people respond to Kohlberg's moral dilemmas, answers that involve such concepts are often "scored" as reflecting a lower level of reasoning than they should be.

Another criticism concerns gender bias. Carol Gilligan (1982) argued that Kohlberg's emphasis on "justice" primarily reflects a male perspective. She claimed that highly moral women place greater value than men do on caring and responsibility for others' welfare. Overall, however, evidence of such gender bias is mixed, and most cross-cultural studies find that females and males display similar levels of moral reasoning (Eckensberger & Zimba, 1997). Females use justice reasoning when the situation calls for it, and males use reasoning based on caring and relationships when appropriate (Friedman et al., 1987; Walker, 1987). Nevertheless, Gilligan's analysis reinforces the key point that high-level moral reasoning can be based on values other than "justice" (Gump et al., 2000).

Critics also charge that the model focuses too heavily on moral thinking and not enough on moral behaviour. We cannot assume, for example, that people at more advanced stages in Kohlberg's model always behave more morally (Richards et al., 1992). Remember, what determines someone's stage of reasoning is not whether they feel that stealing or other actions are right or wrong, but the types of justification given for their belief. Furthermore, moral behaviour may vary across situations: Cheating, honesty, or altruism in academic situations may not predict similar behaviours elsewhere. In general, moral behaviour is more consistent across situations and is tied more strongly to moral beliefs in adulthood than in childhood (Blasi, 1980).

In sum, research relating culture and gender to moral behaviour reminds us of an important point: Moral development is not just a cognitive process. It has a behavioural component, it overlaps with other aspects of personality development, and it occurs within a social context (Killen et al., 2000).

In Review

- *According to Piaget, cognitive development depends on processes of assimilation and accommodation, and occurs in four stages: sensorimotor, preoperational, concrete operational, and formal operational.*

- *Although the general cognitive abilities associated with Piaget's four stages occur in the same order across cultures, children acquire many cognitive skills at an earlier age than Piaget believed. Vygotsky emphasized that cognitive development occurs in a socio-cultural context. Each child has a zone of proximal development, reflecting the difference between what a child can do independently and what the child can do with assistance from others.*
- *Information-processing capacities improve with age. Older children search for information more systematically, process it more quickly, and display better memory.*
- *Children begin to develop a theory of mind (beliefs about another person's knowledge, feelings, intentions, etc.) around three to four years of age.*
- *Kohlberg proposed that moral reasoning proceeds through three levels. Preconventional moral judgments are based on anticipated rewards and punishments. Conventional morality is based on conformity to social expectations, laws, and duties. Postconventional moral judgments are based on well thought out moral principles. Critics argue that the model contains cultural and gender biases.*

Personality and Social Development

Children grow not only physically and mentally, but also socially and emotionally. They form attachments and relationships, and each child displays a unique *personality*—a distinctive yet somewhat consistent pattern of thinking, feeling, and behaving. Sigmund Freud (1933, 1964) believed that adult personality is largely established during the first five years of life. Research does not support this view, but it does support Freud's general point that childhood is a special period of personality and social development.

Erikson's Psychosocial Theory

18. What does Erikson's model imply about the stability of personality?

Psychoanalytic psychologist Erik Erikson (1963, 1968) believed that personality develops through confronting a series of eight major **psychosocial stages**, each of which involves a different "crisis" (i.e., conflict) over how we view ourselves in relation to other people and the world. Each crisis is present throughout life, but takes on special importance during a particular age period. As Table 11.3 shows, four crises occur in infancy and childhood:

TABLE 11.3 Erikson's Psychosocial Stages

Age (years)	Major Psychosocial Crisis
First year	Basic trust vs. basic mistrust
1–2	Autonomy vs. shame and doubt
3–5	Initiative vs. guilt
6–12	Industry vs. inferiority
12–20	Identity vs. role confusion
20–40	Intimacy vs. isolation
40–65	Generativity vs. stagnation
65+	Integrity vs. despair

- *Basic trust versus basic mistrust.* During the first year of life we depend totally on our parents or other caretakers. How adequately our needs are met, and how much love and attention we receive, determine whether we develop a basic trust or basic mistrust of the world.
- *Autonomy versus shame and doubt.* During the next two years, children become ready to separate themselves from their parents and exercise their individuality. If parents unduly restrict children or make harsh demands during toilet training, children develop shame and doubt about their abilities and later lack the courage to be independent.
- *Initiative versus guilt.* From age three through age five, children display great curiosity about the world. If they are allowed freedom to explore and receive answers to their questions, they develop a sense of initiative. If they are held back or punished, they develop guilt about their desires and suppress their curiosity.
- *Industry versus inferiority.* From age six until puberty, the child's life expands into school and peer activities. Children who experience pride and encouragement in mastering tasks develop "industry"—a striving to achieve. Repeated failure and lack of praise for trying leads to a sense of inferiority.

Although critics argue that Erikson's model lacks detail and question its "stage" approach, the model successfully captures several major issues that developing children confront. Because each stage of life creates new opportunities, personality is not fixed in childhood. Yet, as Erikson proposed and as some research supports, successfully resolving each crisis helps prepare us to meet the next (Hazen & Durrett, 1982; Kahn et al., 1985). Like the early chapters of a novel, themes that emerge in childhood help set the stage for the unfolding story of our lives.

19. Does infants' temperament predict their childhood behaviour? Does children's temperament predict their adult functioning?

Do the roots of adult personality truly reside in childhood? Our Research Foundations feature examines another approach to this issue.

RESEARCH FOUNDATIONS

Were You a Shy Baby or a Fussy Baby? Does Infant Temperament Predict Adult Functioning?

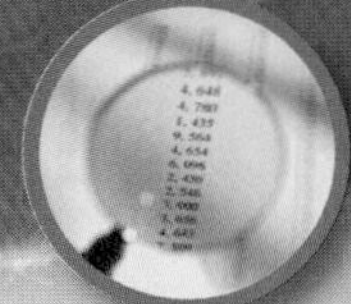

Infants differ from one another at birth in terms of their **temperament**, a biologically based general style of emotional and behavioural reactions to the environment. Some very young infants are calm and happy, while others are irritable and fussy; some are active, others inactive; some are sociable, while others are shy. Within any age group, people differ in temperament (Shiner, 1998). Here we consider whether people actually are born with a temperament that remains relatively constant across their lifespan.

In a classic, 10-year longitudinal study, Alexander Thomas and Stella Chess (1977, 1986) used parental reports about various aspects of their babies' behaviour to classify infants into three general temperament categories: *easy*—regular sleeping and feeding patterns, positive reactions to novel situations, playful, and tolerant of frustrations; *difficult*—irritable, irregular eating and sleeping patterns, and negative reactions to novelty; and *slow to warm up*—low activity, mild reactions, and slow to adapt to novel situations. They reported that infant temperament remained relatively stable over time, and that the difficult group had the highest incidence of emotional and behavioural problems. While their work was praised by many, it was criticized for not verifying parental reports with more objective, behavioural observations of infants and by limiting temperament to only three categories.

Subsequent research showed that temperament is only weakly to moderately stable during infancy (e.g., Plomin et al., 1993; Carnicero et al., 2000); temperament remains stable across all ages for some infants and changes for others. Consider *shyness*, which is part of the more general temperament style called *behavioural inhibition*. Inhibited infants are quiet and timid, and when they are exposed to novel people, places, objects, and sounds they become more physiologically aroused, show more fear and anxiety, and try harder to avoid contact with these novel stimuli. Uninhibited infants are more sociable, verbal, and spontaneous. Kagan and colleagues (1988) found between 20 to 25 percent of infants could be called inhibited, and that they remained so throughout infancy. In longitudinal studies, Kagan (1989) found that categorizing infants as inhibited or uninhibited failed to predict how shy or outgoing they were at 7½ years of age. However, the most extreme groups in each category (the top 15 percent) were stable. These highly uninhibited infants became sociable and talkative children, while extremely inhibited infants became quiet, cautious, socially avoidant children (Kagan, 1989).

Louis Schmidt at McMaster University and colleagues (Schmidt, Fox, Rubin, Hu & Hamer, 2002) conducted a four-year longitudinal study of several hundred infants representing a normal population and identified a similar percentage of infants who were extremely shy or extremely uninhibited at 9 months of age and who remained shy or "exuberant" at 14 months and 48 months of age. Schmidt and colleagues also conducted a molecular genetic analysis of the four-year-olds' cheek cells to look for relationships between genetic markers and maternal reports of shy versus aggressive behaviours. They found that those classified as aggressive had a very different genetic profile for the dopamine receptor gene (DRD4) than those classified as non-aggressive. This gene marker has been found in children with attention deficits (Schmidt, Fox, Perez-Edgar, Hu & Hamer, 2001), but Schmidt's study (Schmidt et al., 2002) is the first to relate this genetic marker to a temperament category in normally developing preschool children.

Finally, researchers have conducted lengthy longitudinal studies to find out whether temperament characteristics identified in children predict their adult temperaments. For example, in the United States and Sweden, inhibited 8- to 12-year-old boys are more likely than noninhibited peers to delay marriage and fatherhood as adults, possibly reflecting their avoidance of new relationships (Caspi et al., 1988; Kerr, 1996), while shy American girls are more likely to quit work and become homemakers after marriage. In an impressive study, Newman et al. (1997) used a 90-minute observation to classify the temperaments of 961 three-year-old New Zealanders, who were then re-assessed at age 21. Adults classified as "undercontrolled" (i.e., irritable, impulsive, inattentive) at three years of age were more antisocial (more family/romantic conflicts, job losses), while "inhibited" three-year-olds had fewer adult relationships, compared with adults who

–*Continued*

had been "well-adjusted" three-year-olds. Attempts to relate certain temperament characteristics to adult psychopathology—such as the characteristic of childhood behavioural inhibition (similar to extreme shyness)—with later anxiety disorders have had some degree of success (Tincas, Benga & Fox, 2006).

To summarize, while there is evidence that very strong temperament traits can be relatively stable over age, and that some traits may have genetic markers, predicting how any individual infant or child will turn out as an adult is very difficult. Many factors influence development, and even during childhood strong temperaments often mellow (e.g., Pfeifer et al., 2002). Furthermore, temperament classifications vary depending on context (level of environmental stress) and observers (parents versus trained observers) (e.g., Hane, Fox, Polak-Toste, Ghera & Gunner, 2006). Given these considerations, it is remarkable that Newman et al. were able to use a mere 90 minutes of observing three-year-olds to predict (albeit modestly) different patterns of adult adjustment 18 years later.

Attachment

20. How does imprinting illustrate the concept of critical periods?

21. How did Harlow demonstrate the importance of contact comfort?

Imagine a single-file procession of ducklings following you around campus and everywhere you go, as if you were their mother. For this to happen, we need only isolate the ducklings after they hatch and then expose them to you at a certain time. If they later encounter their real parents, the ducklings will ignore them and continue to follow you. If the only moving object the ducklings see for their first 24 hours is a model duck or ball, they will faithfully follow that object as they grow up (Hess, 1959).

German ethologist Konrad Lorenz (1937) called this sudden, biologically primed form of attachment **imprinting** (Figure 11.23a). It occurs in some species of birds, including ducks, chickens, and geese, and in a few mammals, such as shrews. Imprinting illustrates the concept of *critical periods.* In mallard ducklings, for example, the strongest imprinting takes place within a day after hatching, and by 2½ days the capacity to imprint is lost (Hess, 1959). Thus, depending on the species, offspring *must* be exposed to parents within hours or days after entering the world in order to attach to them.

Attachment refers to the strong emotional bond that develops between children and their primary caregivers (Figure 11.23b). Human infants do not automatically imprint on a caregiver the way that ducklings do, and there is not an immediate post-birth critical period when contact is required for infant-caregiver bonding. Instead, the first few years of life seem to be a *sensitive period* when we most easily form a first attachment to caregivers, a bond that enhances our social and personality adjustment later in life (Sroufe, 2002). Although it may be more difficult, a strong first attachment to caregivers still can be formed later in childhood.

(a)

(b)

FIGURE 11.23

(a) When they were hatchlings, Canadian wildlife sculptor Bill Lishman imprinted these Canada geese to the sight of his ultralight airplane. Although they have now matured, the ultralight still represents "mother" to the geese, and they follow it in flight. (b) In humans, infant-caretaker attachment is more complex and forms over a much longer period.

The attachment process. For decades, people assumed that infant-caregiver bonding resulted primarily from the mother's role in satisfying the infant's need for nourishment. Harry Harlow (1958) tested this notion by separating infant rhesus monkeys from their biological mothers shortly after birth. Each infant was raised in a cage with two artificial, "surrogate" mothers. One was a bare wire cylinder with a feeding bottle attached to its "chest." The other was a wire cylinder covered with soft terry cloth, without a feeding bottle (Figure 11.24).

Faced with this choice, the infant monkeys became attached to the cloth mother. When they were exposed to frightening situations or removed from their cages and later returned, the infants ran to the terry cloth figure and clung tightly to it. They even maintained contact with the cloth mother while feeding from the wire mother's bottle. Thus Harlow showed that *contact comfort*—body contact with a comforting object—is more important in fostering attachment than the provision of nourishment.

22. According to Bowlby, what are the phases of attachment in infancy?

Around the same time, other researchers studied human attachment in Africa, Europe, and North America (Ainsworth, 1967; Bowlby, 1958). Based on this work, British psychoanalyst John Bowlby (1969) proposed that attachment during infancy develops in three phases:

- *Indiscriminate attachment behaviour.* Newborns cry, vocalize, and smile, and they emit these behaviours toward everyone. In turn, these behaviours evoke caregiving from adults.
- *Discriminate attachment behaviour.* Around three months of age, infants direct their attachment behaviours more toward familiar, regular caregivers than toward strangers.
- *Specific attachment behaviour.* By seven or eight months of age, infants develop their first meaningful attachment to specific caregivers. Infants smile more at these caregivers, hold out their arms to be picked up by them, and want to be in their presence. The caregiver becomes a "secure base" from which the infant can crawl about and explore the environment.

FIGURE 11.24

Infant monkeys reared from birth with a cloth-covered surrogate clung to it as they would a real mother, and they preferred to remain in contact with the terry cloth mother even though the wire mother satisfied nutritional needs.

From Harlow, 1958.

As an infant's attachment becomes more focused, two types of anxiety occur. **Stranger anxiety**, distress over contact with unfamiliar people, emerges around age six or seven months, and ends by 18 months of age. **Separation anxiety**, distress over being separated from a primary caregiver, typically begins a little later, peaks around age 12 to 16 months, and disappears between two and three years of age. Both forms of anxiety show a similar pattern across many cultures (Figure 11.25); note that both examples are inverted U-shaped functions.

Some theorists propose that these responses may stem from infants' increasing cognitive abilities (Kagan, 1972). For example, although newborns may distinguish their mother from a female stranger based on different hair styles, they don't have well-formed schemas for people that enable them to distinguish strangers from non-strangers. As these schemas develop, stranger anxiety emerges. Others suggest that stranger and separation anxiety are adaptive reactions shaped over the course of evolution (Bowlby, 1973). At an age when infants master crawling and then learn to walk, fear of strangers and of separation help prevent infants from wandering beyond the sight of their caretakers, especially in unfamiliar situations.

Around age three to four, as children's cognitive and verbal skills grow, they develop a better understanding of their attachment relationships. According to Bowlby (1969), a stage of *goal-corrected partnership* emerges in which children and caregivers can describe their wishes and feelings to each other, and their relationship can be maintained whether they are together or apart.

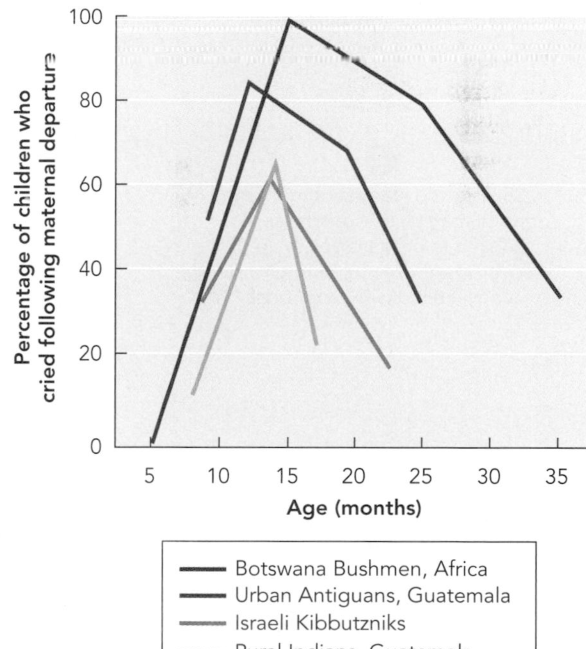

FIGURE 11.25

The rise and fall of separation anxiety in infancy shows a similar pattern across cultures.

Based on Kagan et al., 1978.

Variations in attachment. Infants progress through similar attachment stages, but they develop different types of attachment with their caretakers. Canadian psychologist Mary Ainsworth (1913–1999) worked briefly with John Bowlby in the 1950s. Later, she and her colleagues (1978) developed a standard procedure, the famous **Strange Situation Test (SST)**, for examining infant attachment. The infant, typically a 12- to 18-month-old, first plays with toys in the mother's presence. Then a stranger enters the room and interacts with the child. Soon the mother leaves the child with the stranger. Later the stranger leaves and the child is alone. Finally, the mother returns.

The infant's behaviour throughout the SST is scored to classify infants into one of three categories. In the mother's presence, *securely attached* infants explore

23. Does separation anxiety follow a similar pattern across cultures? What is the adaptive value of separation anxiety?

the playroom and react positively to strangers (Ainsworth et al., 1978). They are distressed when she leaves and happily greet her when she returns. In contrast, there are two types of *insecurely attached* infants. *Anxious-resistant* infants are fearful when the mother is present, demand her attention, and are highly distressed when she leaves. They are not soothed when she returns and may angrily resist her attempts at contact. *Anxious-avoidant* infants show few signs of attachment and seldom cry when the mother leaves. They don't seek contact when she returns, but won't resist contact if the mother initiates it.

Across most cultures studied, about one-half to three-quarters of infants are securely attached. Correlational studies find that mothers of U.S. (Ainsworth et al., 1978) and Canadian (Pederson, Gleason, Moran & Bento, 1998) infants classified as secure in the SST are rated as more consistently responsive and sensitive to their babies' needs during the first year than those classified as insecure.

Attachment and later behaviour. Most researchers believe that early attachment has a long-term influence on children's adjustment (Ainsworth & Bowlby, 1991; Goldberg, 1991). Elementary school children who are securely attached as infants seem better adjusted socially, have higher self-esteem, and are better behaved in school. In contrast, those who are insecurely attached as infants are more likely to have behavioural problems in school, be overly aggressive, and show attention-seeking behaviour in the classroom (Ainsworth, 1989). This research lends credence to Erikson's view that establishing a stable, trusting relationship with a caregiver is an important component of early social development.

Attachment Deprivation

24. What is the "strange situation"? Describe the styles of attachment identified by this procedure.

If infants and young children are deprived of a stable attachment with a caregiver, how do they fare in the long run?

Isolate monkeys and children. Harry Harlow studied this issue under controlled conditions. After rearing "isolate" monkeys either alone or with artificial surrogate mothers, Harlow returned them to the monkey colony at six months of age. Exposed to other monkeys, the isolates were indifferent, terrified, or aggressive. When they became adults, these monkeys could not copulate normally. Some female isolates were artificially inseminated, and as parents they were highly abusive toward their first-borns (Harlow & Suomi, 1970). Clearly, having being raised without attachment to a real, interactive caregiver produced long-term social impairment.

25. How do studies of monkey and human child isolates, and of children in orphanages, help us discover whether attachment involves critical or sensitive periods?

What of isolate human children? Victor, the Wild Boy of Aveyron, was abandoned early in life and lived alone in a forest in Aveyron, France, until about 12 years of age. He was severely impaired after his isolation and showed only limited recovery after intensive remedial training (Itard, 1962). But was it a lack of human contact that severely stunted Victor's development, or was it brain damage, possibly present from birth? And if severe isolation was the cause, could its negative effects possibly be reversed?

26. Why might Victor's recovery have been so limited, compared to that of the Czech twins?

In the 1960s, in Czechoslovakia, twin boys were forced by their father and stepmother to live in extreme isolation beginning at 18 months of age. The twins were discovered at age seven years, emotionally and socially retarded, with the cognitive development of a three-year-old and speech skills of a two-year-old. Jarmila Koluchova (1972, 1991) studied the boys for over 20 years, and found that they became happy, sociable, and firmly attached to their foster family. Their IQ increased to normal levels and they became well-adjusted adolescents and young adults.

Why the difference? In case studies such as these, we can only speculate. Unlike Victor, the twins had each other's company, though this cannot explain why "single" isolate children have recovered. The twins' isolation ended—and their rehabilitation began—at a younger age, when the brain's neural plasticity is greater (Victor was older). Moreover, in their first year of recovery, the twins were well cared for in a home that allowed them to interact with younger, non-threatening preschool children. Harlow's monkey research demonstrated the value of this "younger companion."

Children raised in orphanages. Developmentalists have studied orphans to address the question of whether it is necessary to have a primary attachment figure during the hypothesized sensitive period, in the first year of life. An impressive Canadian study was initiated after the overthrow of Ceausescu in 1989, when thousands of Romanian orphans were discovered who were reared in state-run orphanages under deplorable conditions, including the absence of a primary attachment figure. Elinor Ames and her colleagues at Simon Fraser University, and Kim Chisholm, now at St. Francis Xavier University, conducted a longitudinal study of a large group of Romanian orphans adopted into Canadian homes (see Chisholm, 1998). They compared three groups matched for age and sex: early (adopted before four months of age) and late (adopted after at least eight months in an orphanage) Romanian adoptees, and Canadian-born, non-adoptees. After about one year with the adopted family, the late-adopted orphans were more insecurely attached than the two comparison groups, according to a parental report attachment scale. After two years, the three groups did not differ on the parental report attachment scale; but, when attachment was assessed using a separation-reunion procedure, compared to the other two groups, the late-adoptees displayed more insecure attachment behaviours that were related to more behaviour problems, lower IQ scores, and more parental stress. The late-adoptees also showed more indiscriminately friendly behaviour, indicating a possible lack of specific attachment.

Of course, negative factors other than a lack of a sensitive, early attachment figure may have contributed to the attachment and other problems shown by the Romanian late-adopted children. Barbara Tizard and Jill Hodges (1978) studied children raised in stimulating, high-quality orphanages. The nurses were attentive, but high staff turnover prevented children from forming a stable bond with any caregiver. In this case, the vast majority adopted between ages two to eight years formed healthy attachments with their adoptive parents. However, in adolescence, many had difficulty forming peer relationships because they appeared to need "too much attention" (Hodges & Tizard, 1989). Although being adopted at a later age increases the risk of adjustment problems during the teen years, the vast majority of adopted children—especially those raised in two-parent families—are normally adjusted and differ little from children raised by their biological parents (Miller et al., 2000).

In sum, it appears that infancy is a sensitive (not critical) period in which an initial attachment to caregivers forms most easily and facilitates subsequent development. Prolonged attachment deprivation creates long-term developmental risks, but when deprived children are placed in a nurturing environment at a young enough age, most become attached to their caretakers and grow into well-adjusted adults. It should be noted that, although unfavourable environments can significantly impair development, some children exposed to extreme adversity are highly resilient and thrive in later life (Masten & Coatsworth, 2001).

FIGURE 11.26

Today, many preschoolers are cared for during the day by someone other than a parent.

The Daycare Controversy

27. Does daycare impair infants' attachment? Does it seem to have long-term effects on children?

As a child, were you in daycare? Approximately 60 percent of both American (Scarr, 1998a) and Canadian (Canadian Council of Social Development, 1997) preschoolers are cared for during the day by someone other than a parent (Figure 11.26), and most who enter daycare do so before age one. High-quality daycare provides a stimulating environment with well-trained caretakers, few children per caretaker, and low staff turnover, whereas poor daycare does the opposite. But in either case, many parents worry about how daycare will affect their child's development. Thirty years of research—mostly in North America, Sweden, and other European countries—suggests some surprising conclusions.

- *Attachment.* Overall, as measured by the *strange situation procedure,* daycare *does not* seem to disrupt infants' attachment to their parents, even when daycare begins in early infancy and occurs for many hours a week (National Institute of Child Health and Human Development/NICHD, 1997; Scarr, 1998a). However, if several negative factors combine—daycare is poor, the child spends many hours there, parents are not sensitive to the child at home, and the child has multiple daycare arrangements—the risk of insecure attachment increases.
- *Other parent-child interactions.* Compared to families not using daycare, infants and toddlers in daycare are slightly less engaged and sociable toward their mothers when tested during a play situation, and their mothers are slightly less sensitive (e.g., less supportive, more intrusive) toward them (NICHD, 1999). But there is no relation between these patterns and children's attachment to their mother.
- *Long-term effects.* Infants and preschoolers from low-income families who receive high-quality daycare tend to be better adjusted socially and perform better in elementary school than their peers who either receive poor-quality daycare or do not attend daycare (Scarr, 1998). For infants and preschoolers from middle- and upper-income homes, their daycare experience—regardless of quality—seems to have little carry-over effect to their elementary school years. Rather, the quality of their family experience is more important in predicting social adjustment and academic performance in school.

28. In the short and long term, how do children generally respond to parental divorce? What factors enhance their adjustment to divorce and remarriage?

This last point is underscored in a study of *after-school care* (Vandell & Ramanan, 1991). Among 390 third- through fifth-graders who either attended adult-supervised after-school programs, cared for themselves, or were cared for by their mothers, the type of after-school care was a less important predictor of children's psychological adjustment than was the quality of their relationship with their families. Margaret McKim at the University of Saskatchewan and co-workers in Ontario (McKim, Cramer, Stuart & O'Connor, 1999) conducted a short-term longitudinal study of infants ranging in age from 2 to 30 months who were tested prior to and for 6 months following their entry into out-of-home care, including another woman's home or a daycare centre, and a group with home care for an equivalent time. She found that age of entry into out-of-home care and type and quality of care were not related to the infants' security of attachment. However, infants with less sensitive mothers who also employed extensive out-of-home care were least secure.

Concerns about disrupted parent-child relations also surface when parents divorce. Our *Psychological Applications* feature, later in this chapter, examines this societally important issue.

Styles of Parenting

29. What parenting styles are associated with the most and least positive child outcomes?

Beyond the issues of divorce and remarriage, how do different child-rearing practices affect children's development in general? After studying how parents interacted with their preschool children, Diana Baumrind (1967) identified two key dimensions of parental behaviour. The first is *warmth versus hostility.* Warm parents communicate love and caring for the child, and respond with greater sensitivity and empathy to the child's feelings. Hostile parents express rejection and behave as if they did not care about the child. The second dimension is *restrictiveness versus permissiveness.* Parents differ in the extent to which they make and enforce rules, place demands on children, and discipline children. As Figure 11.27 shows, combining these dimensions yields four parenting styles that are associated with different patterns of child development (Maccoby & Martin, 1983).

Authoritative parents are controlling but warm. They establish clear rules, consistently enforce them, and reward children's compliance with warmth and affection. They communicate high expectations, caring, and support. This style is associated with the most positive childhood outcomes (Baumrind, 1991). Children with authoritative parents tend to have higher self-esteem, are higher achievers in school, have fewer conduct problems, and are more considerate of others.

Authoritarian parents also exert control over their children, but do so within a cold, unresponsive, or rejecting relationship. Their children tend to have lower self-esteem, be less popular with peers, and perform more poorly in school than children with authoritative parents (Dornbusch et al., 1987).

Indulgent parents have warm and caring relationships with their children, but do not provide the guidance and discipline that helps children learn responsibility and concern for others. Their children tend to be more immature and self-centred (Patterson, 1982).

Neglectful parents provide neither warmth nor rules and guidance. Their children are most likely to be insecurely attached, have low achievement motivation and disturbed relationships with peers and adults at school, and to be impulsive and aggressive. Neglectful parenting is associated with the most negative developmental outcomes (Ainsworth, 1989).

Do these findings extend to adolescence? Laurence Steinberg and his colleagues (1994) studied several thousand high school students in California and Wisconsin. Consistent with earlier research, they found that authoritative parenting generally was associated with the most positive developmental outcomes among adolescents, and neglectful parenting was associated with the poorest outcomes. Many of the findings held true across African-, Asian-, Caucasian-, and Hispanic-American students (Lamborn et al., 1991).

A note of caution concerning the interpretation of both the parenting and attachment studies we have reviewed is necessary, because most of the research is correlational and thus does not specify the causal factors. Keep in mind that parent-child influences are bidirectional. Children who have an irritable, hostile, and difficult temperament tend to elicit harsher and less warm parenting behaviours and have less secure attachment. Moreover, parents do not mould their children's personality and behaviour like lumps of clay. Parenting makes a difference, but the way children "turn out" depends on interactions among their inherited characteristics, parental behaviours, and other environmental experiences (Collins et al., 2000). For example, schizophrenia is a serious mental disorder that has a strong genetic component. In one study, biologically "at-risk" children (i.e., they had schizophrenic biological parents) placed into good adoptive homes were no more likely to develop various mental disorders in adulthood than adopted children who were not at biological risk (Tienari et al., 1994). But, when the adoptive family environment was dysfunctional, the "at-risk" children later developed significantly more disorders than the children who were not at risk.

Richard Tremblay and his colleagues (1995) at the University of Montreal and McGill University used a bi-directional model of parent-child relationships to design an intervention program and long-term follow-up study for children at risk of delinquency. Over 300 Montreal kindergarten boys, identified by their teachers

	Warmth/ acceptance	Hostility/ rejection
Restrictive	**Authoritative** Demanding, but caring; good child-parent communication	**Authoritarian** Assertion of parental power without warmth
Permissive	**Indulgent** Warm toward child, but lax in setting limits	**Neglectful** Indifferent and uninvolved with child

FIGURE 11.27

The combination of two basic dimensions of parental behaviour (warmth-hostility and restrictiveness-permissiveness) yields four different styles of child rearing.

Based on Maccoby & Martin, 1983.

as being disruptive, were randomly assigned to treatment or control groups. The treatment group received a two-year program of parent training in the home and social skills training during lunch hours at school. Parents were trained in reading and monitoring their children's behaviour, the use of positive reinforcement of pro-social behaviour and non-abusive discipline techniques, and family crisis management techniques. The children were assessed yearly until they were 15 years old. Tremblay et al. found that children in the treatment group were more likely than controls to remain in the regular, age-appropriate classroom during elementary school years, and reported less delinquent behaviours between 10 and 15 years of age. Clearly, parenting styles can alter the path of children at risk of teenage delinquency.

PSYCHOLOGICAL APPLICATIONS

Understanding How Divorce and Remarriage Affect Children

Divorce is more common than it was 30 years ago. According to Statistics Canada data for 2003, almost 40 percent of marriages will end in divorce by the 30th wedding anniversary; and many legally married couples are separated. Family break-ups create a stressful life transition for both parents and children. Also, most parents remarry, which leads to a second major transition for children as they become part of a stepfamily (16 percent of married partners were previously divorced). Recent research tells us how these major life events affect children.

How Does Divorce Affect Children?

Many children report that parental divorce is one of the most painful experiences of their lives. In the short term, they may experience anxiety, fear, anger, confusion, and depression; regress to immature forms of behaviour; and develop behaviour problems at school. In the long term, it should be emphasized that most children of divorce turn out just fine. However, as a group, compared with children from intact families, greater percentages experience (i.e., are at risk for) a variety of difficulties, including academic problems, troubled relationships with family members and peers, low self-esteem, and depression (Reifman et al., 2001). As adolescents, children of divorced parents are more likely to disengage themselves from their family (or stepfamily), spending as little time at home as possible. They also are more likely to drop out of school, be unemployed, use drugs, have sex at an earlier age, and become unmarried teen parents. In adulthood, they display poorer problem-solving skills during marital interactions, experience more marital conflict, and have a higher divorce rate (Teachman, 2002).

Most of these problems tend to cluster together into an overall pattern of "maladjustment." Hetherington and her co-workers (1998) estimate that about 20 to 25 percent of children in divorced families, versus 10 percent of children in nondivorced families, experience this cluster of problems. This is a significantly elevated risk for maladjustment, but still, most children of divorced parents do not experience these long-term effects. Rather they grow up to be normally adjusted adults. Moreover, children's age at the time of divorce is only weakly related to how well they ultimately cope.

Should Parents Stay Together "For the Sake of the Child"?

Many parents considering divorce wonder whether they should stay together for the child's sake. The answer depends on the amount of conflict present in the marriage. Reviewing 92 studies, Amato and Keith (1991) found that children living with married but contentious parents had poorer school achievement, lower self-esteem, and more behaviour problems than children from divorced families and children from intact families with low parental conflict. When divorce ends a highly conflicted marriage, children's psychological adjustment typically benefits in the long run. But many unhappy marriages do not involve extensive conflict, and in those cases divorce usually puts children at greater risk for maladjustment (Amato & Booth, 2001).

How Can Divorced Parents Help Their Children?

The major factor affecting a child's adjustment to divorce is the quality of life within the postdivorce family, and it often takes a few years for divorced parents and children to redevelop stable family relationships. The period during and after divorce can intensify parents' anger and conflicts. By fighting over their children or trying to enlist them in loyalty battles, parents can damage their children's well-being. In contrast, cooperative and amicable parental behaviours can cushion the negative effects of divorce during this rocky transition

(Hetherington & Stanley-Hagan, 2002). By remaining emotionally close to the children, the parent who does not have custody (usually the father) can help them adjust to living with the custodial parent (Marsiglio et al., 2000). For children, the lasting problems of divorce often lie in a disruption of parenting that follows marital breakdown, in lingering conflicts between parents, in economic hardships that parents—especially mothers—often experience after divorce, and in other factors that impair parents' ability to stabilize their own lives.

How Do Children Respond to Remarriage and Stepfamilies?

Loving stepfamilies in which children develop close relationships with their new step-parent and step-siblings are to be admired, because it is more difficult to make a stepfamily function well than a nondivorced family. When one or both spouses bring children from a previous marriage with them, the odds of remarriage ending in divorce may increase by as much as 50 percent (Tzeng & Mare, 1995).

Forming a stepfamily requires new adaptations, temporarily disrupts children's relationships with the remarried custodial parent, and typically increases children's short-term problem behaviours (Hetherington & Stanley-Hagan, 2002). It can take several years for parents and children to adjust to their new roles within the stepfamily. In general, young adolescents seem to have the most difficulty coping with the transition into a stepfamily.

In remarriages, children may be hostile and reject the stepparent, especially when the stepparent attempts to be a strong disciplinarian. Research suggests that children usually adjust better to living in a stepfamily when: (1) the custodial parent is warm but firm and has primary responsibility for discipline, and (2) the stepparent is warm toward the child but supports the custodial parent's authority (Bray & Berger, 1993).

Gender Identity and Socialization

30. How does socialization shape children's beliefs about gender?

Parents also play a role in helping children develop a **gender identity**, a sense of "femaleness" or "maleness" that becomes a central aspect of our personal identity. Infants display some knowledge about gender. For example, Poulin-Dubois and her colleagues (1994; 1998) at Concordia University presented infants with pairs of male and female pictures, along with a male *or* female vocal recording. Infants at 9 and 12 months, looked longer at the female picture when it was matched to the female voice, and, by 18 months, at both male and female gender-matched pictures. Between two and three years of age, most children develop a basic gender identity; they can label themselves (and others) as being either a boy or girl, but their understanding of gender is still fragile. Just as young children often report that a cat wearing a dog mask has suddenly become a dog, they may believe that a boy wearing a dress is a "girl" and that a girl can grow up and become a man. **Gender constancy**, which is the understanding that being male or female is a permanent part of a person, develops around age six to seven (Szkrybalo & Ruble, 1999).

As gender identity develops, children also acquire **sex-role stereotypes**, which are beliefs about the types of characteristics and behaviours that are appropriate for boys and girls to possess. **Socialization**, which refers to the process by which we acquire the beliefs, values, and behaviours of a group, plays a key role in shaping our gender identity and sex-role stereotypes. Every group, including our family and cultural groups, has norms that set standards for expected and accepted behaviour. Through socialization, we ultimately internalize these expectations and standards, and they become part of our identity (Valsiner & Lawrence, 1997). Sex-role stereotypes are no exception.

Sex-typing involves treating others differently based on whether they are female or male. From infancy onward, girls and boys are viewed and treated differently (Figure 11.28). Fathers use more physical and verbal prohibition with their 12-month-old sons than with their daughters, and they steer their sons away from activities that are considered stereotypically feminine (Snow et al., 1983). Even when their sons and daughters display equal interest and aptitude in science, fathers and mothers are more likely to believe that sons have the greater interest and will

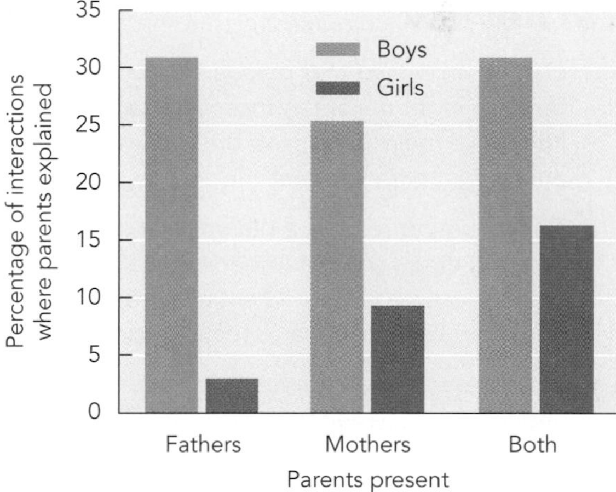

FIGURE 11.28

Fathers and mothers provided more explanations to their one- to eight-year-old sons than to their daughters while engaged with science exhibits at a children's museum. Similar results were obtained regardless of the children's age.

Adapted from Crowley et al., 2001.

FIGURE 11.29

In subtle and not so subtle ways, cultures socialize most female and male children in gender-stereotypic ways.

find science easier (Tenenbaum & Leaper, 2002). Indeed, as Figure 11.28 shows, when parents interact with their one- to eight-year-olds at science exhibits in a children's museum, they are much more likely to explain the exhibits to their sons than to their daughters—even though the children rarely ask for such explanations (Crowley et al., 2001).

Sex-role stereotypes also are transmitted through observational learning and operant conditioning (Figure 11.29). Children observe parents, other adults, peers, and television and movie characters, and often attempt to emulate what they see (Bandura, 1965). In ways both obvious and subtle, others approve of us and reinforce our behaviour when we meet their expectations, and disapprove of us when we don't. In turn, this influences the way children think about gender. Some children as young as two or three years of age display sex-role stereotypes in their ability to identify objects, such as hammers and brooms, as "belonging with" one gender or the other (Fagot et al., 1992). By age seven or eight, stereotyped thinking is firmly in place; children believe that boys and girls possess different personality traits and should hold different occupations as adults (Miller & Budd, 1999).

As children make the transition to adolescence and enter junior high school, they generally display more flexible thinking about gender. Some come to believe that traditionally masculine and feminine traits can be blended within a single person—what is called an *androgynous* gender identity—as when a person is both assertive and compassionate. During the remaining junior high and high school years some adolescents maintain this view. Overall, however, stereotypes about men's and women's psychological traits seem to become a little more rigid, and most people continue to adhere to relatively traditional beliefs (Alfieri et al., 1996).

In Review

- *Erikson proposed that personality development proceeds through eight major psychosocial stages. Each stage involves a major crisis, and the way we resolve it influences our ability to meet the challenges of the next stage.*
- *Temperament reflects a biologically based pattern of reacting emotionally and behaviourally to the environment. Extreme temperamental styles in infancy and childhood can predict some aspects of functioning years later.*
- *Infant-caretaker attachment develops in three phases, and infants experience periods of stranger and separation anxiety. Secure attachment is associated with better developmental outcomes in childhood and adolescence than insecure attachment. For most children, daycare does not disrupt attachment.*
- *Parenting styles vary along dimensions of warmth-hostility and restrictiveness-permissiveness. The children of authoritative parents generally display the best developmental outcomes. Gender identity begins to form early in childhood, and socialization influences children's acquisition of sex-role stereotypes.*

ADOLESCENCE

We call it Sunrise Dance. It's the biggest ceremony of the White Mountain Apache—when a girl passes from childhood to womanhood. . . . On Friday evening Godmother dressed me . . . Saturday is like an endurance test. Men begin prayer chants at dawn. Godmother tells me to dance. . . . When the time comes for running, I go fast around a sacred cane. . . . Next, my father pours candies and corn kernels over me to protect me from famine. My Godfather directs my dancing on Sunday. . . . Godfather paints me. . . . On Monday there is more visiting and blessing. (Quintero, 1980, pp. 262–271)

FIGURE 11.30

A White Mountain Apache girl participates in the Sunrise Dance, a four-day ceremony that initiates her into womanhood.

In some cultures, ceremonies such as the Sunrise Dance represent *rites of passage* that mark a transition from childhood to adulthood status (Figure 11.30). But what of *adolescence,* the well-known period between childhood and adulthood? Alice Schlegel and Herbert Barry (1991) found that among almost 200 non-industrial societies worldwide, nearly all recognize some type of transition period between childhood and adulthood. Yet in many societies this period is brief and is not marked by a special term analogous to "adolescence."

As we know it, the lengthy period called "adolescence" is largely an invention of eighteenth- to twentieth-century Western culture (Valsiner & Lawrence, 1997). In pre-industrial times, biological maturity was a major criterion for adult status. In many cultures, for example, girls were expected to marry once they became capable of bearing children. But, as the Industrial Revolution brought new technology and a need for more schooling, recognition of adult status was delayed and the long transition period we call adolescence evolved.

Physical Development

31. Describe some factors that influence adolescents' psychological reactions to experiencing puberty.

Adolescence begins at **puberty**, a period of rapid maturation in which the person becomes capable of sexual reproduction. The brain's hypothalamus signals the pituitary gland to increase its hormonal secretions. This stimulates other glands and physical growth throughout the body, speeding up maturation of the *primary sex characteristics* (the sex organs involved in reproduction). Hormonal changes also produce *secondary sex characteristics* (non-reproductive physical features, such as breasts in girls, and facial hair in boys).

The pubertal landmark in girls is *menarche*, the first menstrual flow. For boys, it is the production of sperm and the first ejaculation. In North America and Europe, these events occur most often around age 12 or 13 for girls, and 14 for boys, but variations occur across people, cultures, and lifestyles. In parts of New Guinea, 50 percent of girls have their first menstrual period after they turn 17 (Roche, 1979). Girls who participate in high-level figure skating, gymnastics, and ballet often experience delayed menarche, possibly as a result of restricting their diet and exercising vigorously (Warren, 1992). Puberty is a biological process, but it can be affected by environmental factors (Graber et al., 1995).

The physical changes of puberty have psychological consequences. For one thing, hormones that steer puberty also can affect mood and behaviour (Buchanan et al., 1992). But there is a social component too. Did your parents and peers react to you differently as you matured? Did your self-image change? In one study, African- and Caucasian-American girls whose mothers were supportive and helped them prepare for menarche ended up feeling most positive about it (Scott et al., 1989).

Psychological reactions to puberty are influenced by whether it occurs early or late. Overall, early maturation tends to be associated with more positive outcomes for boys than for girls. Early maturing boys acquire physical strength and size, facilitating their success in athletics and other physical activities that contribute to a male's popularity and positive body image (Sigelman & Shaffer, 1991).

In contrast, early maturing girls are more likely to develop eating disorders, smoke, drink, have problems in school, and experience psychological distress than girls who mature later (Ge et al., 1996). Some early-maturing girls welcome their mature appearance, but others develop a negative body image and feel they are too fat (Peterson, 1987). However, it is not simply the absolute timing of puberty that

32. Discuss how adolescents' reasoning abilities change, and the ways in which their thinking is egocentric.

matters, but also the individual's *perception* of whether maturation is occurring too early or too late (Lerner, 1987).

Cognitive Development

Cognitive changes during adolescence can be as dramatic as physical ones. Many teenagers acquire a new maturity that enables them to reason abstractly and reflect more deeply on their own and others' thoughts.

Abstract Reasoning Abilities

Piaget (1926, 1970) proposed that the final stage of cognitive development, *formal operational thinking,* is attained during adolescence. Adolescents can more easily contemplate abstract and hypothetical issues, ranging from scientific problems to questions about social justice and the meaning of life (Figure 11.31). They reason more flexibly and creatively than concrete thinkers, and use both the deductive and inductive problem-solving methods described in Chapter 9.

FIGURE 11.31
When adolescents attain formal operational thought, they can use deductive reasoning to solve scientific problems systematically.

Consider the "pendulum problem" in Figure 11.32. Which variable(s)—length of string, weight of object, how hard it is pushed, and release point (height in the arc)—influence(s) how quickly the pendulum oscillates? This problem is best solved by forming and testing an organized set of deductive hypotheses (e.g., "*If* string length is a factor, *then* the swing time with a short versus long string should differ"). Concrete operational children find this task difficult (Inhelder & Piaget, 1958). For example, when they adjust the string length they often adjust the weight as well, making it impossible to draw a conclusion about either variable. In contrast, adolescents think more systematically and manipulate each variable while holding the others constant. However, the application of formal operational thought is not uniform across tasks, challenging the generality of Piaget's stage concept. For example, neo-Piagetians Zopito Marini (Brock) and Robbie Case (University of Toronto) (1993) tested adolescents between 9 and 19 years of age on two types of reasoning: One involved a mathematical analysis of the operation of a balance beam and the other a social analysis of the behaviour of a character in a story. While two-thirds of the group performed at the same reasoning level on the two tasks, the other one-third was more advanced on one task.

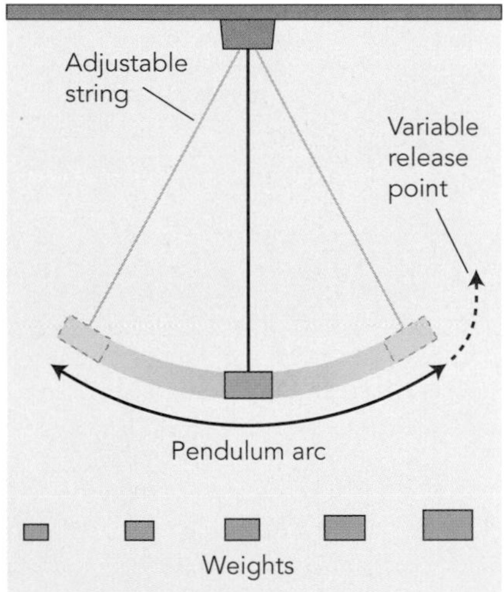

FIGURE 11.32
The materials for the pendulum problem used by Inhelder and Piaget include an adjustable string and a set of weights. The problem is to determine what factors influence how long it takes the pendulum to move through its arc. String length is the only relevant factor: The shorter the string, the less time it takes the pendulum to swing back and forth.

Adapted from B. Inhelder & J. Piaget, 1958.

The capacity for abstract reasoning increases substantially during adolescence (Chapell & Overton, 1998). Furthermore, task performance differs for different types of reasoning, and partly depends on formal schooling and exposure to scientific-abstract tasks. Even with schooling, however, many teens and adults struggle at formal operational tasks. Some people frequently use abstract reasoning, but others rarely do.

Social Thinking

Adolescent thinking can be highly self-focused, particularly in the earlier teenage years. David Elkind (1967) proposes that such **adolescent egocentrism** has two main parts. First, adolescents overestimate the uniqueness of their feelings and experiences, which is called the *personal fable.* Examples would be "My parents can't possibly understand how I really feel," and "Nobody's ever felt love as deeply as ours." Second, many adolescents feel that they are always "on stage" and that "Everybody's going to notice" how they look and what they do. Elkind calls this oversensitivity to social evaluation the *imaginary audience.*

Adolescents who think more egocentrically tend to be more depressed and are more likely to underestimate the negative consequences of risky behaviours, such as sex without contraception, drunk driving, or using psychoactive drugs (Baron

& Hanna, 1990). In short, "They don't know me . . . I can handle it." Yet some researchers believe that adolescent egocentrism is an outgrowth of the search for individuality and independence (Vartanian, 2000). Thus, it may be as much a social phenomenon as a cognitive one.

Social and Personality Development

G. Stanley Hall (1904), the first psychologist to study adolescence, viewed it as a time of "storm and stress." As they cross the bridge between childhood and adulthood, adolescents may grapple with issues concerning parental and peer relations, career goals, gender roles and ethnicity, sexuality, drug use, politics, and religion. Although some adults recall adolescence as a period of conflict and alienation, others find it to be a positive, relatively carefree period of life (Arnett, 1999).

The Search for Identity

"Who am I?" "What do I believe in?" "How do I want to live my life?" Erik Erikson (1968) proposed that questions such as these reflect the pivotal crisis of adolescent personality development, which he termed *identity versus role confusion* (see Table 11.3, p. 480). Erikson believed that an adolescent's "identity crisis" (a term he coined) can be resolved positively, leading to a stable sense of identity, or can end negatively, leading to confusion over one's identity and values.

33. Identify some of the different ways that adolescents approach the challenge of establishing an identity.

James Marcia (1966, 1994) built upon Erikson's work. He interviewed adolescents and young adults, and found many adolescents in a condition or "status" that Marica called *identity diffusion:* They have not yet gone through an identity crisis, and remain uncommitted to a coherent set of values or roles. Some may be unconcerned or cynical about identity issues. Other adolescents are in *foreclosure,* adopting an identity without first going through a crisis. For example, an adolescent may automatically adopt peer group or parental values without giving them much thought.

In contrast, two other groups experience an identity crisis. Adolescents in a status of *moratorium* are currently experiencing a crisis, but have not resolved it. They want to establish a clear identity, but are unsure which way to go. Those in *identity achievement* have gone through a crisis and successfully resolved it. They have adopted a coherent set of values and are pursuing goals to which they are committed.

Figure 11.33 shows that most young adolescents are in identity diffusion or foreclosure; they have not experienced an identity crisis. But, with age, many identity-diffused teens think more deeply about who they are and most teens in foreclosure reconsider their prematurely adopted values. They experience an identity crisis, and more than half successfully resolve it by young adulthood.

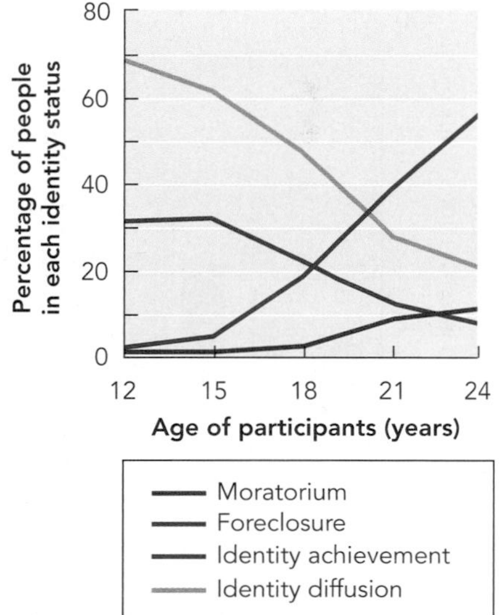

FIGURE 11.33

Based on interviews in one study, this graph shows the percentage of participants in each of Marcia's four identity statuses at various ages. These data suggest that most young people attain identity a few years later than Erikson suggested.

Adapted from P. W. Meilman, 1979.

Although we have discussed "identity" as a single concept, our sense of identity actually has multiple components (Camilleri & Malewska-Peyre, 1997). These include:

- our gender, ethnicity, and other attributes by which we define ourselves as members of social groups ("daughter," "student," "athlete");
- how we view our personality and other characteristics ("shy," "friendly"); and
- our goals and values pertaining to areas we view as important, such as family and peer relations, career, religion, and so forth.

Typically, we achieve a stable identity regarding some of these components before others (Skorikov & Vondracek, 1998). And, even after an identity crisis has been resolved, changing situations may trigger new crises and cause us to reevaluate prior goals and values.

Finally, culture plays an important role in identity formation, one that goes beyond the simple idea that we view ourselves as belonging to certain cultural groups. Our cultural upbringing influences the very way we view concepts such as "self" and "identity." Having grown up in an individualistic culture, my sense of identity assumes that "I" am an autonomous individual with clear boundaries separating me from other people. But in collectivistic cultures, the concept of "self" traditionally is based more strongly on the interdependence and connectedness between people (Kagitçibasi, 1997; Kurman, 2001). Thus the question "Who am I" is more likely to be answered in ways that reflect a person's relationships with family members, friends, and others.

Relationships with Parents

34. To what extent are parent-teen relationships characterized by "storm and stress"?

Research around the world has examined teenagers' relationships with their parents, and it appears that "storm and stress" is the exception rather than the rule. In a national survey conducted during the socially turbulent 1970s, 56 percent of American teenagers reported getting along "very well" with their parents, and 41 percent reported getting along "fairly well" (Gallup, 1988). More recently, a study of over 600 Dutch teenagers found little evidence of conflicting tastes and negative relationships with parents (Van Wel, 1994). Judith Smetana and Cheryl Gaines (1999) reported that, among 51 African-American middle-class families, conflict between parents and young teens centred around routine issues such as chores, neatness, and bedtime. Though moderately frequent, conflict usually was mild in intensity.

In a larger project, Andrew Fuligni (1998) studied 1,341 female and male American students in sixth, eighth, and tenth grades. They came from immigrant and native-born families of Mexican, Chinese, Filipino, and European ancestry. Fuligni found that, among all four ethnic groups:

- Adolescents agreed with their parents' right to "make the rules," but more for some issues than others (Figure 11.34).
- Older adolescents felt it was less appropriate for parents to make the rules.
- Girls believed their parents would "grant them autonomy" at a later age than boys did.

So what about actual conflict with parents?

- Overall, there was somewhat more conflict with mothers than fathers, *but:*
- Regardless of adolescents' gender, ethnic group, or age, conflict was low with *both* mothers and fathers.

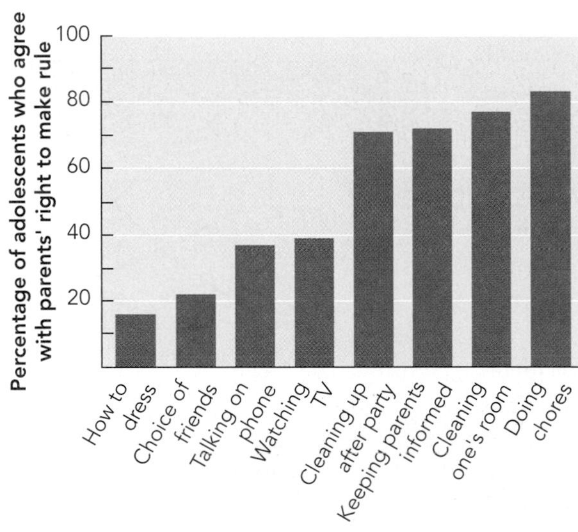

FIGURE 11.34

Using a questionnaire developed by Judy Smetana (1988), Andrew Fuligni (1998) found that the percentage of teenagers who agree that their parents have the right to "make the rules" depends on the particular issue.

Data courtesy of Andrew Fuligni.

Of course, some parents and teenagers do struggle a lot, and parent-teen conflict is correlated with other signs of distress. Chuansheng Chen and colleagues (1998) studied 600 seventh- and eighth-graders from America (European- and Chinese-Americans), Taiwan, and Beijing, China. Parent-teen conflict generally was low in each cultural group, but young teens who reported more conflict had higher levels of school misconduct (e.g., cheating, skipping school) and more anti-social behaviour (e.g., getting into fistfights, damaging property). Teens who report more conflict with parents also report greater hopelessness, lower self-esteem, and less life satisfaction (Shek, 1998). Although parent-teen conflict may contribute to teens' psychological problems, we should remember that it also is likely to be caused by such problems. Indeed, Hastings and Grusec (1997) found that conflict between Canadian teens and their parents was reduced when the parents accurately perceived their teens' cognitions and affect.

Peer and Friendship Relationships

35. How do peer relationships change during adolescence?

Peer relationships increase in importance during the adolescent years. From Alabama to the Arctic, teens like to spend time "hanging out" with their friends. According to some studies, adolescents spend more time with peers than doing almost any other activity, and they tend to identify more with peers than with adults (Csikszentmihalyi & Larson, 1984). But this pattern may be stronger in Canada and the United States than in Europe or Asia, where teens generally place a relatively stronger emphasis on family relationships (Chen et al., 1998).

Adolescent friendships typically are more intimate than those at previous ages, involving a greater sharing of problems and better mutual understanding (Hunter & Youniss, 1982). Perhaps one reason intimacy with peers increases is that, in choosing best friends, adolescents (like older adults) tend to select peers who are similar to themselves (Iervolino et al., 2002). This increase in peer intimacy seems to fit with another shift in peer interactions that occurs over the high school years: The amount of time spent in groups decreases, and time spent with individual friends increases.

Peer relationships also play a part in the process of separating from parents and establishing one's own identity. Because they help satisfy the adolescent's needs for intimacy, approval, and belonging, peers can strongly influence a teenager's values and behaviours. For some adolescents, peer pressure increases the risk of misconduct, such as cheating, skipping school, damaging property, or disobeying parental rules about smoking and drinking. Fortunately, peer pressure *against* committing misdeeds typically has an even stronger effect in inhibiting misconduct, and closeness to parents is an added buffer that helps many teenagers resist peer pressure to do misdeeds (Brown et al., 1986; Chen et al., 1998). And despite increased peer influence on dress, hairstyles, and attitudes toward other people, parental influence remains high on issues of politics and religion, morality, and career decisions (Bachman et al., 1987). And of course not all adolescent behaviour can be blamed on peers or parents (e.g., aggressive behaviour may have a genetic component; Guo, 2006).

FOCUS ON NEUROSCIENCE

The Neuroscience of the Teenage Brain

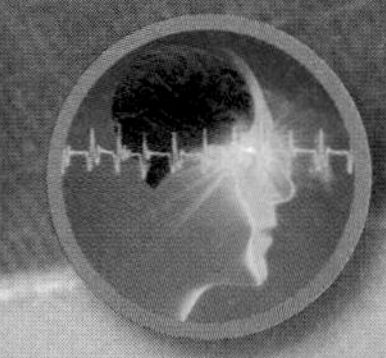

During adolescence, increases in impulsive behaviour, poor judgment (e.g., reckless driving) and social anxiety (e.g., emotional upset when snubbed by a classmate) are commonly observed by parents and other adults. Can this "emotional turmoil" be explained by environmental factors involved with "coming of age"? Or do these differences in information processing reflect, in part, the biological maturation process of brain structures in adolescents? Recent advances in neuroimaging technology are allowing neuroscientists to address this question and are providing some interesting findings (Packard, 2007).

Brain maturation clearly occurs during adolescence. The brain of a 9-year-old is very different from that of a 15-year-old. Longitudinal studies using MRI techniques summarized by Giedd (2004) have shown that brain activity in children differs from that in adolescents, which in turn differs from that in adults. Cortical white matter (neurons with axons insulated by white myelin sheaths that increase speed and integrity of impulse transmission) increases linearly in areas of the frontal cortex (important for controlling impulses and abstract thought) which continue to mature into the early 20s. In contrast, non-myelinated grey matter in the frontal lobes peaks at around 11 years of age for girls and a year later for boys, presumably reflecting the pruning of unnecessary cells by maturation and experience.

Giedd notes that the link between changes in the brain and behaviour is not yet well understood, but cutting-edge research by Harvard's Deborah Yurgelun-Todd and her colleagues reveal some provocative links. In a study on increases in social anxiety, she studied the relationship between brain maturation and emotional responses to threat-related emotional stimulation. Yurgelun-Todd and Killgore (2006) measured prefrontal cortical

–Continued

brain activity (using functional MRI) in male and female adolescents (8 to 15 years of age) while they viewed faces expressing fear versus faces expressing happiness. They found that frontal activation to fear faces increased with age while no change was noted for happy faces. So, maturation of threat-related emotional processing in adolescence is related to increases in prefrontal functional activity.

There also is a link between increased speed and integrity of frontal brain activation by the corpus callosum (see Chapter 3) and response inhibition and cognition during adolescence. This structure changes significantly during adolescence, increasing in area by 10 percent within a two-year period (White and Nelson, 2004). Children with attention deficit/hyperactivity disorder (ADHD), who perform poorly on tasks requiring response inhibition, appear to have smaller than normal right anterior white matter in the corpus callosum (Giedd, Blumenthal, Molloy & Castellanos, 2001). Silveri, Rohan, Pimentel, Gruber, Rosso, et. al. (2006) studied the relationship between maturational changes in frontal lobe activation and behavioural impulse control and response inhibition in 12-year-old girls and boys without ADHD or other known pathologies. They used an MRI procedure that measured the integrity and speed of neural transmission by the white matter in the corpus callosum. Impulse control was evaluated with a questionnaire designed to measure emotional intelligence. Response inhibition was measured using the Stroop Colour-Word Interference test; people take longer to name the ink colours (show inhibition) when colour names differ from ink colours (e.g., RED printed in green) than when they match (RED printed in red). Silveri et al. found a significant relationship between increases in the degree of white matter integrity and both impulse and inhibitory control scores.

To summarize, ground-breaking imaging research has established a link between various aspects of brain maturation and behavioural changes during adolescence. Does this mean that adolescent "emotional turmoil" is simply a product of brain maturation? Yurgelun-Todd pointed out in her interview with Erika Packard (2007) that while "there are neurobiological components to teen behaviour (this) doesn't discount the effects of environmental or social factors, nor does it absolve teenagers of accountability" (Packard, p. 22) for their behaviour. At this point neuroscientists are only beginning to determine which parts of the brain become more active during adolescence. Such information does not specify the neurological mechanisms underlying changes in adolescent behaviour. Furthermore, this correlational research suffers from the methodological limitations we discussed in Chapter 2 when we try to make causal inferences from correlational findings. We can't specify the direction of cause and effect or the possible influences of third factors. For example, maturation of another neural structure might drive changes in both transmission integrity of cortical white matter and emotional reactions to social stimuli, impulsivity, and inhibitory control. Perhaps experimental studies with adolescent animals will help us determine causal relationships between brain maturation and social-emotional behaviour.

In Review

- *In Western cultures, puberty marks the onset of adolescence. Generally, early maturation is a more positive experience for boys than it is for girls.*
- *Abstract thinking capabilities increase during adolescence, but young adolescents often show egocentrism in their social thinking. The search for identity is a key task of adolescence. With age, teens who have not experienced an identity crisis become more likely to do so, and most resolve it successfully.*
- *Divorce disrupts children's psychological adjustment in the short term and, for some children and adolescents, is associated with a long-term pattern of maladjustment.*
- *During adolescence, peer relationships become more important and intimate. Most teens maintain good relations with their parents.*

⊙ ADULTHOOD

It was a grand birthday party. Jeanne Calment was born in France 10 years after the American Civil War. By age 60, she had lived through a world war and the invention of the radio, telephone, motion picture, automobile, and airplane. Still to come was another world war, television, space flight, computers, the Internet, and riding a bicycle until age 100. Yes, her 120th birthday was grand indeed. When a reporter asked how her future looked, Jeanne replied with a wry sense of humour, "Very brief" (Figure 11.35).

Older adults are the fastest-growing segment of the population in many countries, including Canada. In 2006, according to Statistics Canada, a record 13.7 percent of the total population was over 65. By contrast, there was a record low of only 17.7 percent under 15 years of age. Furthermore, the age group between 55 and 64 which will soon retire is at a record high of 3,700,000! Most developmental theorists have studied changes that occur between birth and adolescence. However, developmental change occurs continuously from conception until we die. Here, we examine some of the physical, cognitive, and social changes that occur during young (roughly 20 to 40 years), middle (40 to 60 years), and late adulthood (60 years and over). Aging research is particularly difficult because we study age spans as large as 60 years. This leads most researchers to use cross-sectional designs to describe age functions which can result in cohort effects such as those described at the beginning of this chapter and below in the section on intellectual decline with age (e.g., is the decline due to aging or group differences in educational level?). In general, when we observe any drop in performance as a function of age, it is difficult to disentangle age effects from disease, lack of use, drug abuse, and other potentially confounding factors.

FIGURE 11.35

Jeanne Louise Calment of Arles, France, was born in 1875 and died in 1997 at the age of 122. Calment's life is the longest that has been verified.

Physical Development

Young adults are at the peak of their physical, sexual, and perceptual functioning. Maximum muscle strength in the legs, arms, and other parts of the body is reached at age 25 to 30. Vision, hearing, reaction time, and coordination are at peak levels in the early to mid-twenties (Hayslip & Panek, 2002). Although many physical capacities decline in the mid-thirties, the changes aren't noticeable until years later.

36. What are some of the major bodily changes that occur from early through late adulthood?

Physical status typically declines at mid-life (Troll, 1985). The developmental function for various aspects of vision (e.g., acuity, colour vision) shows a decline with age (Kline, 1994). For example, the active visual field that expanded in the first six months of life begins to shrink in the 20s; and by late adulthood this "tunnel vision" interferes with tasks such as driving, in which a quick reaction to peripheral input is important. Allison Sekuler at McMaster University and her colleagues (Sekuler, Bennett & Mamelak, 2000) studied this aging effect, and discovered that for older adults the problem was not a shrinking visual field per se, but rather their difficulty with tasks requiring them to divide their attention between central and peripheral targets, especially in a cluttered scene.

Muscles become weaker and stiffer, especially among sedentary people. After age 40 the *basal metabolic rate*, the rate at which the resting body converts food into energy, slows and produces a tendency to gain weight. The efficiency of oxygen consumption decreases, and it is harder for middle-aged adults to maintain the physical endurance needed for sustained exercise. Around age 50 women's ovaries stop producing estrogen; they lose their fertility, and experience *menopause*, the end of menstruation. Men remain capable of fathering children, but their fertility gradually declines in middle age.

Despite this decline, many middle-aged adults are in excellent health and vigorously active. Growing experience in job and recreational skills can offset much of the age-related decline. From climbing mountains to running marathons, they may achieve physical goals well beyond those attained by many younger adults.

The physical changes of middle adulthood become more pronounced in late adulthood. About 80 percent of a young adult's body consists of so-called lean body mass (muscles, organs, and bone), and the remaining 20 percent consists of fatty tissue. By age 70, the balance between lean and fat body mass may be 50–50. Bones lose calcium, becoming more brittle and slower to heal, and hardened ligaments make movements stiffer and slower (Weg, 1983). At age 90 the brain of a healthy adult has lost 5 to 10 percent of its early adult weight, due to the normal loss of neurons that occurs as we grow older (Whitbourne, 1985). But with regular

(a)

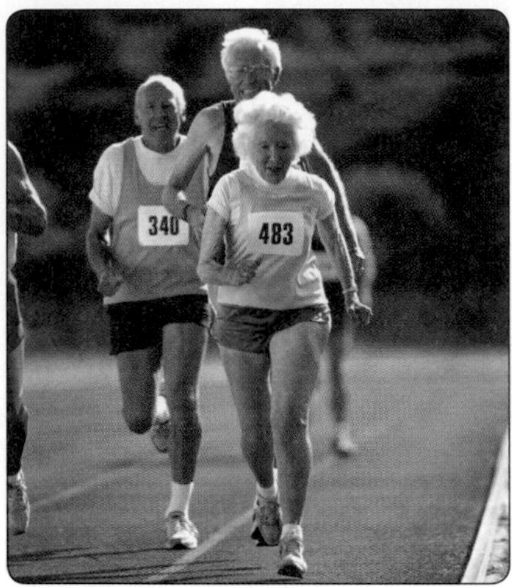

(b)

FIGURE 11.36

Many older adults maintain a physically active lifestyle.

exercise, good nutrition, the right attitude, and barring major disease, many adults maintain physical vigour and an active lifestyle well into old age (Figure 11.36).

Cognitive Development

Piaget believed that formal operational thinking was the fourth and final stage of cognitive development. He argued that adults do not develop new modes of thinking; rather, they simply use formal operations in new and more complex ways.

Several theorists disagree, proposing a fifth stage of cognitive development called **post-formal thought**, in which people can reason logically about opposing points of view and accept contradictions and irreconcilable differences (Rakfeldt et al., 1996; Lampont & Richards, 2003). Post-formal thinkers also realize that, from social behaviour to ethics and politics, life involves many interacting factors (Kramer, 1983). When reasoning about social problems, post-formal thinkers engage in complex thought and are more likely to acknowledge opposing points of view and see both sides of a disagreement as having legitimate arguments.

Information Processing and Memory

Many people assume that cognitive functioning declines throughout middle and late adulthood. Fergus Craik and his colleagues at the University of Toronto, and others, show that this is true in some ways, but not others (e.g., Craik & Salthouse, 2000). For example:

- *Perceptual speed* (reaction time) declines steadily after the mid-thirties. Thus it takes older adults longer to visually identify and evaluate stimuli (Scialfa & Joffe, 1997) and to remember the item's context (source memory), especially under time pressure (Benjamin & Craik, 2001). While it has been tempting to blame the drop in performance in many abilities to a drop in speed of processing, this hypothesis is under debate (Hartley, 2006).
- *Memory for new factual information* declines during adulthood. Compared to younger adults, older adults find it harder to remember new series of numbers, names and faces of unfamiliar people, map directions, and directions for using new prescription drugs (Morrell et al., 1989).
- *Spatial memory* declines with age, according to Concordia's Cooney & Arbuckle (1997) and Kessels & Postma (2006). For example, Uttl & Graf (1993) measured memory for the location of objects in an office setting or a museum and found that spatial memory remains constant in adulthood and begins to decline in the sixties.
- *Recall* declines more strongly than recognition, because recall requires more processing resources (Craik & McDowd, 1998; Arbuckle, Gold, et al., 1992).

?

37. Discuss how information-processing abilities and memory change throughout adulthood.

On the other hand, certain types of verbal memory show less decline with aging. Thus the ability to repeat just-heard sentences decreases more slowly than the ability to repeat single, unrelated words. Healthy elderly adults also do well in recalling personal events and recognizing *familiar* stimuli from long ago, such as the faces of high school classmates (Bahrick et al., 1975).

Intellectual Changes

How do our intellectual abilities change in adulthood? The conclusion from early research seemed clear: After 30 we were "over the hill." When the IQ scores of different age groups were compared in cross-sectional studies, they began to decline noticeably, beginning between ages 30 and 40 (Doppelt & Wallace, 1955).

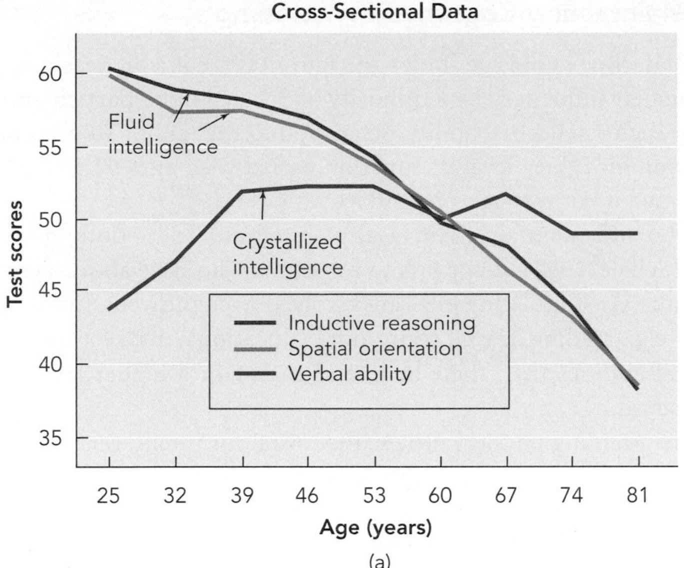

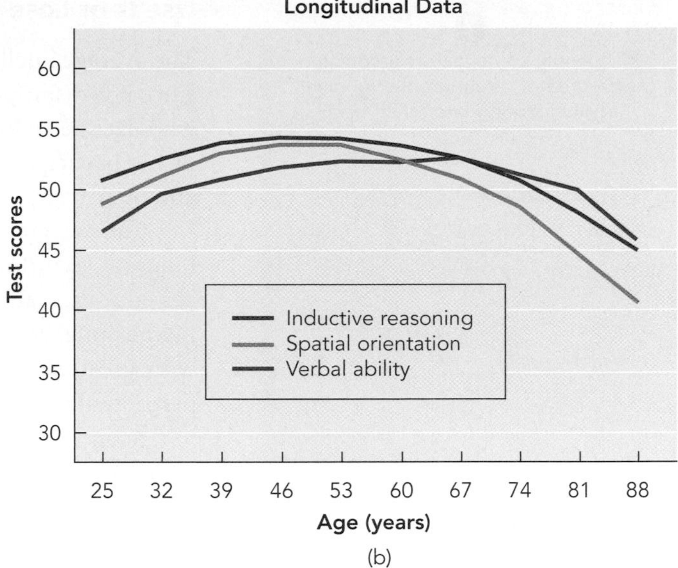

FIGURE 11.37

(a) Cross-sectional data indicate that fluid abilities (reasoning and spatial task performance) begin to decline in young adulthood, whereas crystallized intelligence (verbal ability) begins to decline in late adulthood. However, (b) longitudinal data from the same study indicate that both fluid and crystallized intelligence remain fairly stable through young and middle adulthood and do not decline significantly until late adulthood. The longitudinal and cross-sectional data are consistent in showing that crystallized abilities decline at a later age than fluid abilities.

Adapted from Schaie, 1994.

Researchers made a breakthrough when they examined separate intellectual abilities rather than overall IQ. They studied *fluid intelligence,* which reflects the ability to perform mental operations (such as abstract reasoning, solving logic problems, and mentally rotating objects), and *crystallized intelligence,* which reflects the accumulation of verbal skills and factual knowledge (Horn & Cattell, 1966). *Cross-sectional* research comparing different age groups typically found that fluid intelligence began to decline steadily in young adulthood, whereas crystallized intelligence peaked during middle adulthood and then began to decline in late adulthood (Figure 11.37a).

Some researchers wondered whether this early decline in fluid abilities was really a function of aging or the result of different experiences encountered by the various age generations. The older groups may have had less exposure to scientific problem solving in school, or may have had jobs requiring less use of abstract intellectual skills. Such factors could have artificially depressed the scores of older adults.

38. How do intellectual abilities change with age? To what extent does the answer depend on the research design used?

To answer this question, K. Warner Schaie of Pennsylvania State University and his co-workers (Schaie, 1994, 1998) began a study in 1956 that has now involved about 5,000 adults. This study uses a sequential design that includes both longitudinal and cross-sectional components. The *longitudinal data* do not support an early decline in either fluid or crystallized intelligence. Rather, most abilities are relatively stable (or even increase slightly) throughout young and middle adulthood, and do not begin to decline reliably until late adulthood (Figure 11.37b). But both the cross-sectional and longitudinal data add further support to the previously established finding that certain fluid intellectual abilities (such as reasoning and spatial ability) begin to decline at a somewhat earlier age than crystallized intelligence (such as verbal abilities). On average, verbal abilities at ages 25 and 88 were similar.

Age-related intellectual declines are partly due to poorer perceptual speed, memory, vision, and hearing (Fristoe et al., 1997). Thus we find a bigger intellectual decline during old age when test questions call for quick responses (i.e., "*timed tests*") than when they involve unlimited or ample time ("*untimed tests*"). This decrease in intellectual speed shows up in various real-world tasks, such as learning to use a computer. But, although 75- to 89-year-olds may take longer to acquire computer skills and need more assistance than their 60- to 74-year-old counterparts, the key is that many retain the intellectual capacity to learn (Echt et al., 1998).

39. Identify some factors associated with greater retention of cognitive abilities during late adulthood.

Use It or Lose It? Maintaining Cognitive Functioning

The average intellectual decline in old age shown in Figure 11.37b is a bit deceiving, since it is disproportionately influenced by a minority of Schaie's older participants who declined a lot. For each intellectual ability, Schaie found that about 70 percent of his participants *maintained* their level of functioning between ages 67 and 74, and 65 percent maintained it between ages 74 and 81.

Can we predict who will maintain their level of intellectual functioning the longest? According to (Schaie, 1994), it appears to be people who have above-average education and cognitively stimulating jobs, are involved in cognitively stimulating personal activities (e.g., reading, travel, continuing education), marry a spouse with greater intellectual abilities than their own, and maintain a higher level of perceptual processing speed.

As in the case of maintaining physical fitness, the moral for intellectual fitness appears to be "use it or lose it" (Clarkson-Smith & Hartley, 1990). Singh-Manous, Hillsdon, Brunner, and Marmot (2005) conducted a longitudinal study on 10,308 civil servants beginning in the mid-1980s, when they were 34 to 55 years of age. Their physical activity was assessed 5 years later and again, along with cognitive function, after 10 years. Low physical activity levels were associated with cognitive decline, especially in fluid intelligence. Evidence from animal experiments (Churchill, et al, 2002) and from human cross-sectional studies (Allmer, 2005; Newson & Kemps, 2006) suggest that regular physical exercise and perceptual-motor activities help preserve cognitive abilities in late adulthood. Maintenance of cognitive function also is positively influenced by cognitive exercise. Arbuckle, et al. (1992) studied over 300 Canadian World War II veterans and found that greater intellectual activity (along with more education and better health) was related to less intellectual decline with age. Hultsch, Hertzog, Small, and Dixon (1999) measured the intellectual engagement and cognitive performance of 250 Canadians between 55 and 86 years of age three times over six years. Again, the degree of intellectually engaging everyday activity was related to maintaining high cognitive function.

Of course, cause and effect relationships are not determined by correlational studies. Intellectual and physical activities could act as a buffer against declining cognition, or high-functioning individuals could continue to lead active lives until old age limited their activities. In an experiment, Dutch researchers randomly assigned some elderly adults (ages 69 to 90 years) to play the video game "Super Tetris" for five hours a week for five weeks (Goldstein et al., 1997). This challenging game requires progressively faster perceptual-motor responses at each new level. Compared to a non-playing control group, the Tetris players improved their reaction time on a standard psychological test.

Remaining intellectually and physically active may help slow the decline with age of some cognitive functions. With age we also accumulate knowledge that can lead to "wisdom" (Erikson, Erikson & Kiunick, 1986).

40. Does theory of mind research support the notion that elderly adults are "older but wiser"?

Older but Wiser?

Anthropologist Peter Collings (2001) notes that, as in many cultures, the Inuit living in the Arctic of Western Canada accord their elders special status and great respect. Young and old Inuit alike regard wisdom as a key component of aging successfully, and it largely reflects "the individual's function as a repository of cultural knowledge and his or her involvement in community life by interacting with younger people and talking to them, teaching them about 'traditional' cultural values" (p. 146).

But does age bring greater wisdom? Baltes and Staudinger (2000) defined wisdom as having a basic knowledge about human nature and social relationships; having procedural knowledge to make decisions, give good advice, and handle conflicts; understanding past, present, and future aspects of relationships between family, friends, and people at work; and being able to deal with uncertainty, given that the future can't be fully known. Baltes and Staudinger (and Pasupathi et al., 2001) measured "wisdom" by presenting people of different ages with various life problems such as, "A 15-year-old girl wants to get married right away; an adult realizes that she hasn't achieved major goals." Participants were asked what the girl should do, and their answers were scored by experts, blind to their ages, according to how well they fit the definition of wisdom. Baltes and Staudinger found that wisdom scores rose steadily from age 13 to 25 and then remained relatively stable through age 75. Similar results were obtained by Happe, Winner, and Brownell (1998), who tested participants' abilities to infer what people must have been thinking to have committed various acts, or to predict how people would behave based on what they must have been thinking (i.e., theory-of-mind tests). Young adults (average age of 21 years) gave good responses, while older adults (average age of 73 years) displayed superior social reasoning.

Of course, all of these studies are cross-sectional and do not answer the question of whether people actually become wiser as they age. Only longitudinal and sequential studies can answer that, but in certain respects, older populations are at least as wise as younger ones, based on group averages. Clearly some older adults, even in their eighties, may display greater wisdom than many young adults, but stereotyping the elderly as "wise" is just as inappropriate as stereotyping them as "senile." Erikson et al. (1986) pointed out that old age brings the potential for wisdom, and, as the Inuit acknowledge, not everyone ages successfully.

Social and Personality Development

Adults follow a great diversity of life paths. As Bernice Neugarten notes, "If you look at people's lives, they're like the spreading of a fan. The longer they live, the greater the differences between them" (Neugarten & Hall, 1980, p. 78). Yet all adults confront the biological realities of aging. Most are also influenced by a ticking **social clock**, a set of cultural norms concerning the optimal age range for work, marriage, parenthood, and other major life experiences to occur (Neugarten, 1979).

Stages and Critical Events

41. According to Erikson, what are the three major developmental challenges of adulthood?

Many researchers view adult social development as a progression through age-related stages (Levinson, 1990; Vaillant, 1977). According to Erik Erikson (1980), whose model we introduced earlier, *intimacy versus isolation* is the major developmental challenge of young adulthood (ages 20 to 40). Intimacy is the ability to open oneself to another person and to form close relationships. This is the period of adulthood when many people form close adult friendships, fall in love, and marry.

Middle adulthood (ages 40 to 60) brings with it the issue of *generativity versus stagnation*. Through their careers, volunteer work, raising children, or involvement in religious and political activities, people achieve generativity by doing things for others, exercising leadership, and making the world a better place. Certainly, many young adults make such contributions to society, but generativity typically becomes a more central issue later in adulthood (Strough et al., 1996).

Late adulthood (over 60) accentuates the final crisis, *integrity versus despair*. Older adults review their life and evaluate its meaning. If the major crises of earlier stages have been successfully resolved, the person experiences integrity: a sense of completeness and fulfillment. Older adults who have not achieved positive outcomes at earlier stages may experience despair, regretting that they cannot relive their lives in a more fulfilling way.

Consistent with Erikson's model, many of our goals vary in importance as we age, and successfully resolving certain life tasks may contribute to mastering others (McAdams & de St. Aubin, 1998). But critics caution that we should avoid viewing early, middle, and late adulthood as strict "stages" or dividing lines in which one life task takes over while others fade away. For example, "intimacy" goals may be as important in middle adulthood as in early adulthood (Sheldon & Kasser, 2001).

Another way to view adult social development is through the major life events that people experience. Sigmund Freud once defined psychological adjustment as "the ability to love and work" (1935, p. 112), and research confirms that many key life events revolve around these two themes (Holmes & Rahe, 1967).

Marriage and Family

The vast majority of adults marry at some point in their lives. Most expect a great deal from marriage, including satisfaction of social, emotional, and sexual needs. Although many couples realize these goals, a high divorce rate in many countries indicates that happiness is by no means an automatic outcome. Successful marriages are characterized by emotional closeness and physical intimacy, positive communication and problem-solving, agreement on basic values and expectations, and a willingness to accept and support changes in the partner (Gottman & Levenson, 1992).

Cohabitation. Some people in committed relationships cohabit—that is, live together without being married. According to the Statistics Canada 2001 census (*www.statcan.ca*), in the total population over 15 years of age, 9 percent cohabited in a "common-law" relationship. If we look at family breakdowns, 71 percent were married couples, 14 percent were common-law relationships, and the other 15 percent were single-parent families. While these statistics apply to couples that cohabit as a permanent alternative to marriage, many more do so as a "trial marriage" to determine if they are compatible before tying the knot. In Sweden, premarital cohabitation appears to be the norm among newlyweds (Duvander, 1999).

Not all premarital cohabitation leads to marriage; Manning and Smock (2002) found that the probability of cohabiters expecting to marry depended in part on the socioeconomic status of the man. One might expect trial marriages to eliminate unstable relationships and thus result in less divorce for those who do marry. Instead, national surveys in several countries (e.g., Bennett et al., 1988; Bumpass & Sweet, 1988), including Canada (Hall & Zhao, 1995), consistently show that premarital cohabitation is associated with a higher risk of marital discord and subsequent divorce. This relation, however, does not appear to be causal. Rather, couples who cohabit before marriage differ psychologically from couples who don't cohabit first. For example, premarital cohabiters tend to be less religious and report less commitment to marriage as an institution, and some are ambivalent about whether to marry. Taken together, these, and other, pre-existing factors could increase the risk of divorce even if these couples had not cohabited. When researchers limited their analyses to cohabiting couples who start out with a strong orientation toward marriage (e.g., living together only after being engaged), the risk of divorce was no higher, and the quality of marital relations was no poorer, than for couples not cohabiting prior to marriage (Kline et al, 2004; Stanley, Rhoades & Markman, 2006).

What's love got to do with it? Culture and marriage. Suppose someone had all the qualities you desired in a mate, but you didn't love the person. Would you still marry him or her? Robert Levine and his colleagues (1995) posed this question to 1,163 university students from 11 countries. Table 11.4 shows that in five Western countries, 80 percent or more of women and men said they would not marry such a person. But in the least economically developed Eastern countries of

TABLE 11.4 Love and Marriage

If someone had all the other qualities you desired, would you marry this person if you were not in love with him/her?

	Percentage*	
Country	No	Yes
India	24	49
Thailand	34	19
Pakistan	39	50
Philippines	64	11
Japan	64	2
Hong Kong	78	6
Australia	80	5
Mexico	83	10
England	84	7
Brazil	86	4
United States	86	4

*The remaining students selected "Undecided" as their response.

Source: Adapted from Levine et al., 1995.

India, Pakistan, and Thailand, only 24 to 39 percent said "No." In fact, half of the Indian and Pakistani students said they would marry someone they didn't love, versus only four percent of American students. There were few gender differences, but on the individualism-collectivism dimension, students from collectivistic countries were less likely to believe that love is a prerequisite to marriage.

Do these results surprise you? In many cultures, marriages are "arranged" by family members. To some extent, the notion that romantic love is a prerequisite to marriage is a well-ingrained but culture-bound norm.

42. How does marital satisfaction typically change over time? What major events are associated with these changes?

Marital satisfaction, parenthood, and the empty nest. On average, marital satisfaction declines in the first few years after the knot is tied (Glenn, 1998; VanLaningham, Johnson, & Amato, 2001). This does not mean, however, that most couples are unhappy. They are still satisfied, just less than they were. In a sense, the honeymoon is over.

The birth of a first baby represents a major change in the way couples spend their time. For many couples, marital satisfaction decreases in the year or two after their first child is born (Cowan & Cowan, 1988, 2000; Shapiro et al., 2000). Compared to husbands, wives are more likely to leave their outside job, spend more time parenting, and feel that their spouse is not helping enough. Disagreement over the division of labour and parenting is a major contributor to the drop in marital satisfaction (Belsky & Hsieh, 1998).

Over a broader age period, many cross-sectional studies suggest a U-shaped relation between marital satisfaction and progression through various major life events. The percentage of couples reporting that they are "very satisfied" in their marriage typically is highest before or just as the first child is born, drops during the child-rearing years, and increases in the years after all the children have left home (Orbuch et al., 1996; Rollins & Feldman, 1970). Several longitudinal studies did not find this late adulthood rebound in marital satisfaction (Glenn, 1998; VanLaningham et al., 2001; Vaillant & Vaillant, 1993), but this research challenges a myth about the so-called "empty nest" years after the last grown child leaves home. Contrary to popular stereotypes, most middle-aged couples do not become significantly depressed or suffer a crisis when their children leave (Ward & Spitze, 2004). Spouses maintain meaningful relationships with their children, but have more time to spend with each other and to pursue leisure activities.

Despite the stresses that accompany marriage and parenthood, married people are happier; have lower rates of chronic illness, depression, and stress; and live longer than unmarried adults (Shumaker & Hill, 1991; Verbrugge, 1979). Moreover, although raising children is demanding, parents often report that "having children" is one of best things that has ever happened in their lives. The knowledge that many married couples experience a drop in marital satisfaction over time can help newlyweds establish more realistic expectations, and perhaps encourage couples to take a more active role in maintaining a satisfying relationship.

Attachment revisited. Before we leave marriage and parenthood, note that, according to attachment theory, security of attachment influences the relationships adults form with their partner and their children. Adults' security of attachment with their mothers has been classified using interviews (e.g., Benoit & Parker, 1994) and questionnaires (e.g., Webster, 1997). The proportions of secure, avoidant, and resistant attachment styles are similar for adults and infants, at least for Canadian and American samples, and adult attachment styles are related to social relationships (Goldberg, 1991). For example, a disproportionate number of adults with various behavioural problems (including criminal behaviour; e.g., Wand, Hudson & Marshall, 1996) have a history of insecure attachment. Diane Benoit and Kevin

Parker (1994) conducted a longitudinal study on 96 Canadian infants, their mothers, and their grandmothers. They found 88 percent agreement in attachment classification of mothers and their infants, and 65 percent agreement across the three generations, much greater than expected by chance. Benoit and Parker's results suggest that the patterns of attachment are passed on from one generation to the next. However, as noted in the parenting section above, this research is correlational; one cannot conclude that insecure maternal attachment causes poor social relationships and parenting and anti-social behaviour—difficult temperaments, poverty, and other factors may be the causal agents.

Establishing a Career

43. Describe some major differences between women and men's typical career paths.

One of the first questions a new acquaintance typically asks is, "What do you do?" A career not only helps us earn a living, but also defines part of our identity and allows us to express "who we are" (Super, 1981). Work provides an outlet for achievement and feelings of success, gives us structure, counteracts boredom, and is a significant source of social interaction (Berry, 1998). A 14-country study suggests that having satisfying interpersonal relationships at work is particularly important in collectivistic countries (Hui et al., 1995).

According to Donald Super (1957), a pioneer in the field of vocational psychology, in childhood and through our mid-twenties we first enter a *growth stage* of career interests in which we form initial impressions about the types of jobs we like or dislike, followed by a more earnest *exploration stage* in which we form tentative ideas about a preferred career and pursue the necessary education or training. During their first two years in university, however, most students cannot accurately predict their future occupations, and many change their majors during university. Two of your authors (Passer and Smith) did; neither of them entered university intending to become a psychologist.

From their mid-twenties to mid-forties, people often enter an *establishment phase* during which they begin to make their mark. Initially, they may experience some job instability. After university, for example, many people are likely to change careers at least once (Holland, 1985). Careers tend to become more stable by the end of this period, and people enter a *maintenance stage* that continues through the rest of middle adulthood and into late adulthood. In general, older workers tend to be more satisfied with their jobs than younger workers, but there are also developmental changes in what workers view as most important (Berry, 1998). Younger workers are more interested in salary and advancement, but in middle adulthood, job security becomes more important (Krausz, 1982). Finally, during the *decline stage*, one's investment in work tends to decrease, and we eventually retire.

Though useful as a general model, people's career paths may vary quite a bit, and this is especially true for women. Nora Keating and Barbara Jeffrey (1983) traced the work histories of women who had retired from lengthy, non-professional careers. Most who never married had a continuous, non-delayed career, but all of the married women experienced career gaps or postponed a career until their thirties for family reasons. Similarly, Joy Schneer and Frieda Reitman (1995, 1997) found that, among students who obtained an M.B.A. (Master of Business Administration) degree and then pursued managerial careers, women were more likely than men to experience work gaps by mid-career. Such work gaps tend to retard professional advancement and salary level.

Childbirth is one of the major causes of work gaps for women. About 75 percent of women who hold outside jobs become pregnant during their working years, and over half return to work within a year (Muchinsky, 1997). Career gaps also occur when adults must leave the workforce temporarily to care for their elderly parents. As in raising children, women disproportionately fill this eldercare role. Not surprisingly, married women in the workforce experience greater *interrole conflict* than married men, as they try to juggle the demands of career and family (Berry, 1998). But, as children grow up and leave home, this conflict decreases. During middle adulthood, women who work outside the home report higher self-esteem, better physical health, and less psychological distress than homemakers do (Frankenhaeuser et al., 1991). Indeed, after raising a family, many women enter the workforce for the first time, reinvigorate an earlier career, or return to university in preparation for a new one.

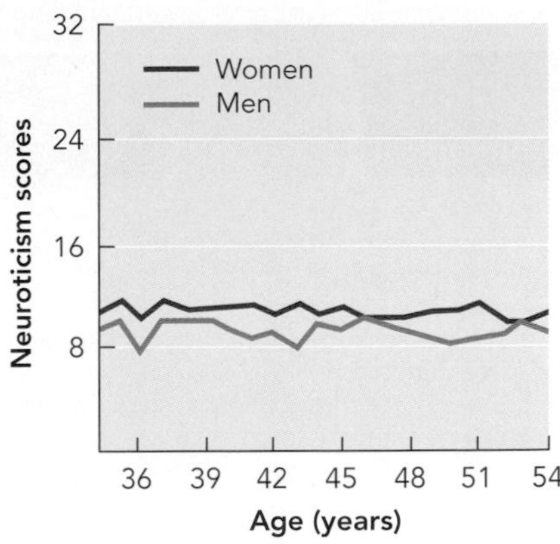

FIGURE 11.38

In a national health survey of over 10,000 men and women, the percentage of individuals measured to have "emotional instability" remained steady between the ages of 33 and 54.

From McCrae & Costa, 1990.

Mid-life Crisis: Fact or Fiction?

Popular wisdom holds that, along the developmental path of career and family, people hit a massive pothole called "mid-life crisis." Is it true? Daniel Levinson and his co-workers (1978, 1986) longitudinally studied 85 men and women and found that many experienced a turbulent mid-life transition between the ages of 40 and 45. They began to focus on their mortality and realized that some of their life's dreams pertaining to career, family, and relationships would not come true.

Critics note that Levinson's sample was small and non-representative. In fact, there is considerable evidence that the notion of a full-blown, turmoil-filled mid-life crisis is largely a myth. Research conducted around the world shows that happiness and life satisfaction generally are unrelated to age (Diener et al., 1999). In one study of adolescents and people in young, middle, and late adulthood from eight Western European countries, about 80 percent of each age group reported they were "satisfied" or "very satisfied" with their lives (Ingelhart & Rabier, 1986). Moreover, people in their forties *do not* have higher rates of divorce, suicide, depression, feelings of meaninglessness, or emotional instability than younger or older adults (Figure 11.38; McCrae & Costa, 1990).

44. Is mid-life crisis a myth? Discuss the evidence.

In sum, adults surely experience conflict, disappointment, frustration, and worry as they enter mid-life, but so do people of all ages. As Erikson emphasized, there are major goals to achieve, crises to resolve, and rewards to experience in every phase of life.

Retirement and the Golden Years

Retirement is an important milestone in life. Some adults view it as a reminder that they are growing older, but many look forward to leisure time, volunteer work, and other opportunities they were unable to pursue during their careers. Most retired people do not become more anxious, depressed, or lonely due to retirement, although those who have strong work values are most apt to miss their jobs (Hardy & Quadagno, 1995).

45. Does retirement cause psychological problems for most retirees? Under what conditions are such problems most likely?

The decision to retire or keep working typically involves many factors, such as feelings about the job, leisure interests, one's physical health, and family relationships (Shultz et al., 1998). In one study, workers were more likely to choose retirement if their marriage was satisfying and their spouse was not working (Reitzes et al., 1998). In this case, retirement meant an opportunity to spend more time with a loved one.

Some people, of course, do not have the luxury to choose their work status. They may be forced into retirement or feel compelled to keep working for economic reasons, and this has an important impact on well-being. Whether in their fifties or seventies, adults who are working or retired because this is what *they* prefer report higher life satisfaction and better physical and mental health than adults who are involuntarily working or retired (Shultz et al., 1998).

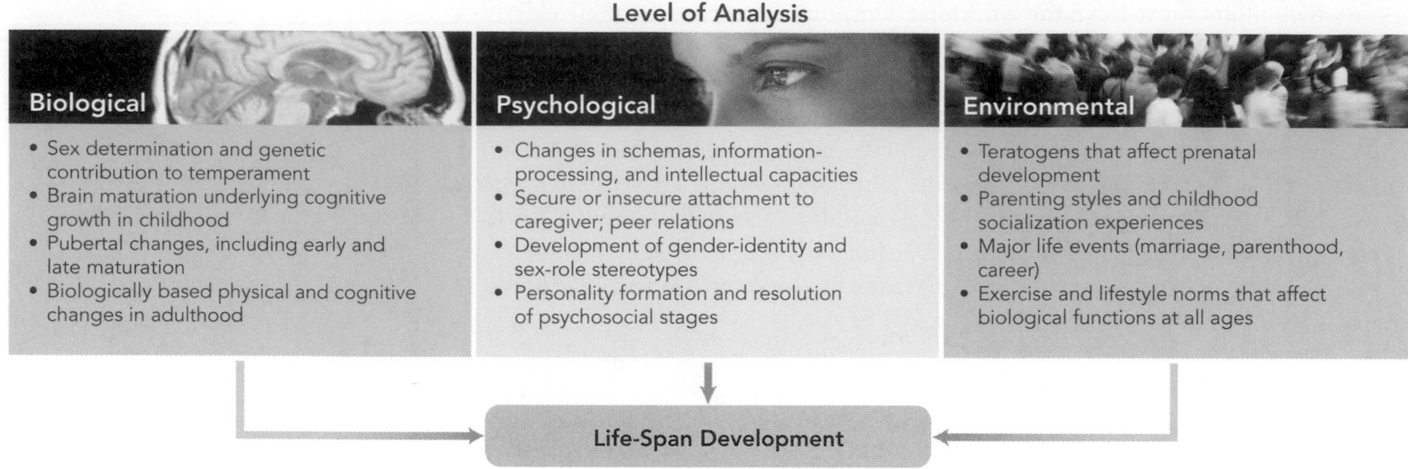

Level of Analysis
Biological
• Sex determination and genetic contribution to temperament
• Brain maturation underlying cognitive growth in childhood
• Pubertal changes, including early and late maturation
• Biologically based physical and cognitive changes in adulthood
Psychological
• Changes in schemas, information-processing, and intellectual capacities
• Secure or insecure attachment to caregiver; peer relations
• Development of gender-identity and sex-role stereotypes
• Personality formation and resolution of psychosocial stages
Environmental
• Teratogens that affect prenatal development
• Parenting styles and childhood socialization experiences
• Major life events (marriage, parenthood, career)
• Exercise and lifestyle norms that affect biological functions at all ages
Life-Span Development

FIGURE 11.39

Understanding the causes of behaviour: factors that influence life-span development.

46. Why is it incorrect to say that there is a "normal" or "proper" way to confront death?

Death and Dying

All of us eventually face death. Like other aspects of life-span development summarized in Figure 11.39, death can be viewed at several levels; it is an inevitable biological process, but one with important psychological and environmental components.

In her pioneering work on dying, Elisabeth Kübler-Ross (1969) found that terminally ill patients often experienced five stages as they coped with impending death. *Denial* typically came first, as the person refused to accept that the illness was terminal. Next, denial often gave way to *anger* and then to *bargaining*, such as "Lord, please let me live long enough to see my grandchild." *Depression* ushered in the fourth stage, as patients began to grieve. Finally, many experienced *acceptance* and a resigned sense of peacefulness.

It is essential to keep in mind that these stages do not represent a "normal" or "correct" way to face death, and that terminally ill patients' reactions may not typify those of people facing death under other circumstances (Doka, 1995). Even among terminally ill patients, some move back and forth between stages, do not experience all the stages, or look forward to death (Schulz & Aderman, 1980). Nevertheless, Kübler-Ross's work spurred interest in understanding and helping people cope with death, and this may be her most enduring legacy.

As Figure 11.40 illustrates, beliefs and customs concerning death vary across cultures and individuals (Seale, 1998). To some, death means the complete end of one's existence. Others believe in reincarnation or that the soul enters an afterlife. Death also means different things to people of different ages (Cicirelli, 1998). Older adults typically have lost more friends and loved ones, and have thought more about their own deaths than have younger people. Understandably, the elderly are more accepting of their own deaths than any other age group (Kalish & Reynolds, 1977). In the midst of a fatal heart attack, one 81-year-old man reassuringly told his family, "It's my time. It's been a good life." We should all wish for this blessing of a fulfilled life's journey.

FIGURE 11.40

Many cultures honour a person's death with a ceremony that involves family, friends, and the wider community. In some cultures this is traditionally a sombre occasion; in others it is a more joyous celebration.

In Review

- *Young adults are at the peak of their physical capabilities. Information-processing speed declines steadily after reaching one's thirties. Longitudinal data show that many intellectual abilities do not begin to decline reliably until late adulthood. Cross-sectional studies suggest that wisdom increases with age.*
- *Erikson proposed that intimacy versus isolation, generativity versus stagnation, and integrity versus despair are the main crises of early, middle, and late adulthood.*
- *Premarital cohabitation is associated with a higher risk of marital divorce, though this does not appear to be a causal relation. For many couples marital satisfaction*

tends to decline in the years following the birth of children, but increases later in adulthood. Adult-mother attachment styles are related to social relationships and may be passed on from one generation to the next.

- *Work serves important psychological and social functions. Overall, women experience more career gaps and their career paths are more variable than men's. Most adults do not experience a full-blown "mid-life crisis." Similarly, most retired people do not become more anxious, depressed, or lonely due to retirement.*
- *Many terminally ill patients experience similar psychological reactions as they cope with their impending death, but beliefs and feelings about death vary with culture and age, and there is no "normal" way to approach death.*

GAINING DIRECTION

What are the issues?

The term "mid-life crisis" is familiar to most people. But what exactly is this crisis (if it exists)? The suggestion in the opening scenario is that we continue to develop well after our mid-teens. Larry Pollard was looking for new meaning in his life, so he had his family crest tattooed on his arm (he also bought a new sports car). Why do we question our lives at 40 or 50 years of age? Do we question anything before this? Why do we need to define who we are? These issues are addressed through a consideration of lifespan development.

What do we need to know?

How do children develop physically?
How do children develop socially?
Are there stages in life when we question our beliefs or self-image?
How do we address any inconsistencies in our self-image?
Is there a "mid-life crisis"?
Are there other crises in our development?

Where can you find the information necessary to answer these questions?

As you look over this chapter, there are a number of topics that you should explore. First, you should examine the various theories on social development (e.g., theories by Erikson, Levenson, and Marcia). What do these theories suggest about the resolution of crises? Are they particular to a specific developmental stage, or do they occur throughout the lifespan? What might you expect to be going on in Larry Pollard's life? You may want to consider some of the material on attachment and satisfaction, and whether personality tends to be fixed or changeable as we grow older.

KEY TERMS AND CONCEPTS*

*Each term has been boldfaced in the text on the page indicated in parentheses.

DO YOU WANT TO ELEVATE YOUR GRADES?

For additional resources and interactive quizzing, visit the book's Online Learning Centre at **www.mcgrawhill.ca/olc/passer**.

CHAPTER 12

Personality

Much of our lives is spent in trying to understand others and in wishing others understood us better than they do.
—Gordon Allport

CHAPTER OUTLINE

Aquarius (Jan. 20-Feb. 18). Those born under the 11th sign of the zodiac tend to have a strong social conscience and want to make the world a better place. They are visionary, progressive, and humanitarian. Famous Aquarians include Galileo, Charles Darwin, Paul Newman, and Oprah Winfrey. There are two distinct personality types: one shy and gentle and the other exuberant and lively. Both types have strong convictions and seek the truth. While they have the ability to see both sides of an argument, they leave no question as to which side they favour. Aquarians are intelligent, logical, refined, frank, and idealistic. Their desire for truth and knowledge makes the Aquarian ideally suited to be a scientist or historian. The progressive trait may find an outlet in poetry, broadcasting, or teaching. In general, Aquarians value friendship and strive to give as much as possible.

Other famous Aquarians include Benedict Arnold, Eva Braun, and Don Cherry.

- **What are the issues here?**
- **What do we need to know?**
- **Where can we find the information necessary to answer the questions?**

Bathed in the early spring sunlight, three university women sat on their front porch. Donna spoke first. "I'm not sure how much longer I can take Julia's moodiness. She jumped down my throat again the other day when I asked her to turn down her stereo. She seems to have all this anger inside that gets directed at us for no real reason. At first she seemed really nice, but now I regret the day she moved in with us."

"I talked to someone who knew her in middle school and high school," replied Kim. "He told me Julia was always tough to get close to. Her sister's the same way. Maybe it's the family genes, or maybe she was just raised as a spoiled brat. The strange thing is that she can be totally different in other situations. She's friendly and nice when we go to parties or when she's in a large group of people where things are pretty superficial. It's when you try to get close to her that she goes into attack mode. That's what Brad said, too, when he broke up with her."

Ellen had been listening closely. "You know, I think that deep down, Julia has a pretty negative self-image that she covers over by being arrogant. I wonder if she really understands what she's doing. I wouldn't be surprised if she's been hurt in the past and is really scared of letting her guard down. Maybe if we can just hang in with her a little longer, she can relax her defences. I think I've seen that start to happen a bit."

Why does Julia act as she does? Do the roots of her behaviour lie in "the family genes"? Did overindulgent parents turn her into "a spoiled brat"? Or has she been "deeply hurt" in the past, leaving lots of unresolved anger that bubbles over and gets directed at others inappropriately? Does Julia indeed have a negative self-concept, and are her behaviours really an unconscious defence to keep people from getting close enough to hurt her? How is she able to be such a different person in different situations? Can she change in meaningful ways? As we shall see in this chapter, Donna's, Kim's, and Ellen's hypotheses are similar to those that might be advanced by various personality theorists who try to understand human individuality and the reasons people behave as they do.

WHAT IS PERSONALITY?

1. What two common observations give rise to the concept of personality?

The concept of personality arises from the fascinating spectrum of human individuality. We observe that people differ meaningfully in the ways they customarily think, feel, and act. As one group of theorists noted, each of us is in certain respects like *all other* people, like *some other* people, and like *no other* person who has lived in the past or will exist in the future (Kluckhohn & Murray, 1953).

The concept of personality also rests on the observation that people seem to behave somewhat consistently over time and across different situations. From this perceived consistency comes the notion of "personality traits" that characterize individuals' customary ways of responding to their world. Although only modest stability is found from childhood personality to adult personality, consistency becomes greater as we enter adulthood (Caspi & Roberts, 1999). Nonetheless, even in adulthood, there remains a capacity for meaningful personality change (Lewis, 1999). Combining these notions of individuality and consistency, we can define **personality** as the distinctive and relatively enduring ways of thinking, feeling, and acting that characterize a person's responses to life situations.

The thoughts, feelings, and actions that are seen as reflecting an individual's personality typically have three characteristics. First, they are seen as components of identity that distinguish that person from other people. Second, the behaviours are viewed as being caused primarily by internal rather than environmental factors.

Third, the person's behaviours seem to "fit together" in a meaningful fashion, suggesting an inner personality that guides and directs behaviour (Figure 12.1).

Perhaps more than any other topic, the study of personality has been guided by the psychodynamic, humanistic, biological, behavioural, cognitive, and socio-cultural perspectives. These perspectives provide different conceptions of what personality is and how it functions. As one pair of observers noted, "It seems hard to believe that all the theorists are talking about the same creature, who is now angelic and now depraved, now a black-box robot shaped by reinforcers and now a shaper of its own destiny, now devious . . . and now hardheadedly oriented to solid reality" (Stone & Church, 1968). Yet this very diversity arises from the fact that the theorists have their own personalities that influence how they perceive and understand themselves and their world. No doubt you will find some of the theories more in accord with your own life views than others. But for personality psychologists, their subjective "truth" is less important than their *usefulness* as scientific theories. As discussed in Chapter 2, a theory is scientifically useful to the extent that it (1) provides a comprehensive framework within which known facts can be incorporated, (2) allows us to predict future events with some precision, and (3) stimulates the discovery of new knowledge. We will evaluate each of the theories we describe in terms of these scientific standards.

Behaviours
Components of identity
Perceived internal cause
Perceived organization and structure
Attributed to
Personality

FIGURE 12.1
Perceived characteristics of behaviours that are seen as reflecting an individual's personality.

2. What three standards are used to evaluate the usefulness of a personality theory?

THE PSYCHODYNAMIC PERSPECTIVE

Psychodynamic theorists look for the causes of behaviour in a dynamic interplay of inner forces that often conflict with one another. They also focus on unconscious determinants of behaviour. Sigmund Freud's psychoanalytic theory was the first and most influential of these theories, and his ideas continue to influence Western thought today.

Freud's Psychoanalytic Theory

3. Which clinical phenomena convinced Freud of the power of the unconscious mind?

Freud (1856–1939) spent most of his life in Vienna, where he attended medical school with the intention of becoming a medical researcher concentrating on brain functioning (Figure 12.2). A pivotal event in his life occurred when he was awarded a fellowship to study in Paris with the famous French neurologist Jean Charcot. Charcot was treating patients who suffered from a disorder called *conversion hysteria* in which physical symptoms such as paralysis and blindness appeared suddenly and with no apparent physical cause. Freud's experiences in treating these patients convinced him that their symptoms were related to painful memories and feelings that seemed to have been repressed, or pushed out of awareness. When his patients were able to re-experience these traumatic memories and unacceptable feelings, which were often sexual or aggressive in nature, their physical symptoms often disappeared or improved markedly.

These observations convinced Freud that an unconscious part of the mind exerts great influence on behaviour. He began to experiment with various techniques to access the unconscious mind, including hypnosis, free association (saying whatever comes to mind, no matter how trivial or embarrassing), and dream analysis. In an attempt to relieve painful bouts of depression he was experiencing, Freud conducted an extensive self-analysis based on his own dreams. Freud's work

FIGURE 12.2
Sigmund Freud is shown here with his daughter Anna, who also became an influential psychoanalytic theorist.

on dream analysis culminated in the publication of his book *The Interpretation of Dreams* in 1900. The book sold only 600 copies in its first six years, but his revolutionary ideas began to attract followers. His theory also provoked scathing criticism from a Victorian society that was not ready to regard people as seething cauldrons of sexual and aggressive impulses.

Freud based his theory on careful clinical observation and constantly sought to expand it. Over time, psychoanalysis became a theory of personality, an approach to studying the mind, and a method for treating psychological disorders.

Psychic Energy and Mental Events

4. How did hydraulic systems of his time contribute to Freud's psychodynamic concepts?

Inspired by the hydraulic models of 19th-century physics, which emphasized exchanges and releases of physical energy, Freud considered personality to be an energy system, somewhat like the steam engines of his day. According to Freud, instinctual drives generate **psychic energy**, which powers the mind and constantly presses for either direct or indirect release. For example, a buildup of energy from sexual drives might be discharged directly in the form of sexual activity, or indirectly through such diverse behaviours as sexual fantasies, farming, or painting.

Mental events may be *conscious, preconscious,* or *unconscious.* The conscious mind consists of mental events that we are presently aware of. The preconscious contains memories, thoughts, feelings, and images that we are unaware of at the moment but that can be called into conscious awareness. Memories of your sixteenth birthday reside in your preconscious mind. If mention of your sixteenth birthday resulted in you thinking about it, that prompt triggered the movement of those memories from your preconscious to your conscious mind. Because we are aware of their contents, we are likely to see the conscious and preconscious areas of the mind as the most prominent. Freud, however, believed that these areas are dwarfed in both size and importance by the unconscious mind, a dynamic realm of wishes, feelings, and impulses that lies beyond our awareness. Only when impulses from the unconscious are discharged some way, such as in dreams, slips of the tongue, or some disguised behaviour, does the unconscious reveal itself.

The Structure of Personality

Freud divided personality into three separate but interacting structures: id, ego, and superego. The **id** exists totally within the unconscious mind (Figure 12.3). It is the innermost core of the personality, the only structure present at birth, and the source of all psychic energy. The id has no direct contact with reality and functions in a totally irrational manner. Operating according to the **pleasure principle**, it seeks immediate gratification or release, regardless of rational considerations and environmental realities. Its dictum: "Want . . . take!"

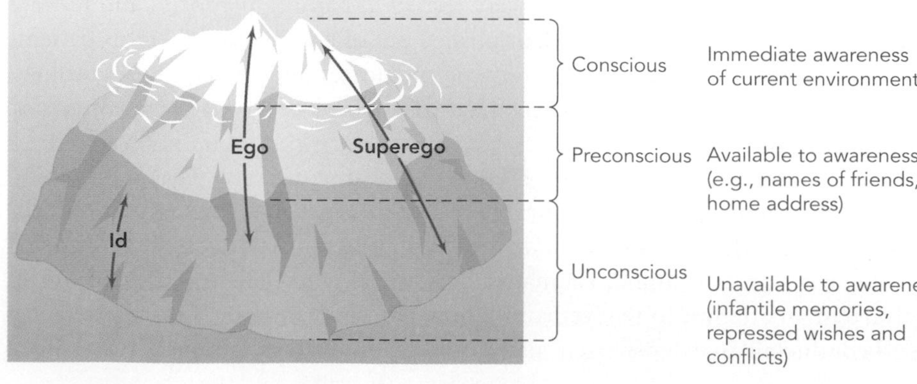

FIGURE 12.3

Freud's own representation of his three-part conception of personality shows the relation of the id, ego, and superego to the conscious, preconscious, and unconscious areas of the mind. Note how relatively small the conscious portion of the mind is compared with the unconscious.

Source: Adapted from Smith, 1998.

The id cannot directly satisfy itself by obtaining what it needs from the environment because it has no contact with the outer world. Therefore, in the course of development, a new structure develops that has direct contact with reality. The **ego** functions primarily at a conscious level, and it operates according to the **reality principle**. It tests reality to decide when and under what conditions the id can safely discharge its impulses and satisfy its needs.

5. Discuss the roles of the pleasure principle, the reality principle, and identification in relation to Freud's three personality structures.

The last personality structure to develop is the **superego**, the moral arm of the personality. According to Freud, the superego developed by the age of four or five, and was the repository for the values and ideals of society. These ideals are internalized by the child through identification with his or her parents, and by explicit training about what is "right," what is "wrong," and how the child "should" be. With the development of the superego, self-control takes over from the external controls of rewards and punishments. Like the ego, the superego strives to control the instincts of the id, particularly the sexual and aggressive impulses that are condemned by society. Whereas the ego tries to delay gratification until conditions are safe and appropriate, the superego, in its quest for perfection, tries to block gratification permanently. For the superego, moralistic goals take precedence over realistic ones, regardless of the potential cost to the individual. Thus the superego might cause a person to experience intense guilt over sexual activity even within marriage because it has internalized the idea that sex is "dirty."

With the development of the superego, the ego is squarely in the eye of a psychic storm. It must achieve compromise between the demands of the id, the constraints of the superego, and the demands of reality. This balancing act has earned the ego the title "executive of the personality."

6. Why is the ego sometimes referred to as the "executive of the personality"?

Conflict, Anxiety, and Defence

The dynamics of personality involve a never-ending struggle between the id trying to discharge its instinctive energies and the opposing forces generated by the ego and superego. Observable behaviour often represents compromises between motives, needs, impulses, and defences. When the ego confronts impulses that threaten to get out of control or is faced with dangers from the environment, anxiety results. Like physical pain, anxiety serves as a danger signal and motivates the ego to deal with the problem at hand. In many instances, the anxiety can be reduced through realistic coping behaviours, as when a person who is extremely angry at someone works out the problem through rational discussion. However, when realistic strategies are ineffective in reducing anxiety, the ego may resort to **defence mechanisms** that deny or distort reality. Some of the defence mechanisms permit the release of impulses from the id in disguised forms that will not conflict with the limits imposed by the external world or with the prohibitions of the superego. The major defence mechanisms are described in Table 12.1.

7. How and why do defence mechanisms develop? What specific forms do they take?

Psychoanalysts believe that repression is the primary means by which the ego "keeps the lid on the id." In **repression**, the ego uses some of its energy to prevent anxiety-arousing memories, feelings, and impulses from entering consciousness. Repressed thoughts and wishes remain in the unconscious, striving for release, but they may be expressed indirectly, as in slips of the tongue or in dreams. They may even be channelled into socially desirable behaviours through the defence mechanism of **sublimation**, completely masking the forbidden underlying impulses. For example, hostile impulses may find expression in tracking down criminals or being a successful trial lawyer. Although Freud described several defence mechanisms, his primary interest was in repression. His daughter Anna Freud, also a psychoanalyst, extended his ideas and described many of the defence mechanisms shown in Table 12.1.

TABLE 12.1 **Psychoanalytic Ego Defence Mechanisms**

Defence Mechanism	Description	Example
Repression	An active defensive process through which anxiety-arousing impulses or memories are pushed into the unconscious mind.	A person who was sexually abused in childhood develops amnesia for the event.
Denial	A person refuses to acknowledge anxiety-arousing aspects of the environment. The denial may involve either the emotions connected with the event or the event itself.	A man who is told he has terminal cancer refuses to consider the possibility that he will not recover.
Displacement	An unacceptable or dangerous impulse is repressed, then directed at a safer substitute target.	A man who is harassed by his boss experiences no anger at work, then goes home and abuses his wife and children.
Intellectualization	The emotion connected with an upsetting event is repressed, and the situation is dealt with as an intellectually interesting event.	A person who has been rejected in an important relationship talks in a highly rational manner about the "interesting unpredictability of love relationships."
Projection	An unacceptable impulse is repressed, then attributed to (projected onto) other people.	A woman with strong repressed desires to have an affair continually accuses her husband of being unfaithful to her.
Rationalization	A person constructs a false but plausible explanation or excuse for an anxiety-arousing behaviour or event that has already occurred.	A student caught cheating on an exam justifies the act by pointing out that the professor's tests are unfair and, besides, everybody else was cheating, too.
Reaction formation	An anxiety-arousing impulse is repressed, and its psychic energy finds release in an exaggerated expression of the opposite behaviour.	A mother who harbours feelings of hatred for her child represses them and becomes overprotective of the child.
Sublimation	A repressed impulse is released in the form of a socially acceptable or even admired behaviour.	A man with strong hostile impulses becomes an investigative reporter who ruins political careers with his stories.

Defence mechanisms operate unconsciously, so people are usually unaware that they are using self-deception to ward off anxiety. Freud argued that excessive reliance on defence mechanisms, with their denial or distortion of reality, was a primary cause of maladaptive or dysfunctional behaviour.

Psychosexual Development

8. What happens if there is deprivation during a stage of psychosexual development?

Freud's clinical experiences convinced him that personality is powerfully moulded by experiences in the first years of life. He proposed that children pass through a series of psychosexual stages during which the id's pleasure-seeking tendencies are focused on specific pleasure-sensitive areas of the body called *erogenous zones* (see Table 12.2). Potential deprivations or overindulgences can arise during any of these stages, resulting in *fixation,* a state of arrested psychosexual development in which instincts are focused on a particular psychic theme. Freud's theory of psychosexual development is the most controversial part of his work. Many theorists reject Freud's assertions about childhood sexuality as well as the notion of specific psychosexual stages in the development of personality. Although there is evidence that childhood experiences, such as emotional attachments, do indeed influence the development of personality (Westen, Nakash, Thomas & Bradley, 2006), there is little to support the idea that personality development unfolds in the manner theorized by Freud.

Research on Psychoanalytic Theory

Freud was committed to testing his ideas through case studies and clinical observations. He believed that careful observations of everyday behaviour and clinical phenomena were the best source of evidence. He opposed experimental research, believing that the complex phenomena he had identified could not be studied under controlled conditions (Rosenzweig, 1992). Most modern psychologists do not believe that clinical observations are sufficient proof of a theory, although they do acknowledge the difficulty of studying psychoanalytic concepts under controlled laboratory conditions (Carver & Scheier, 2000; Mischel, 1999). A major shortcoming of psychoanalytic theory is that many of its concepts are ambiguous and difficult to operationally define and measure (Westen & Gabbard, 1999). How, for example, can we measure the strength of an individual's id impulses or study processes that are by definition unconscious and inaccessible to the person?

Cognitive psychologists have developed methods to identify and measure nonconscious processing of information, and a growing body of research has shown that much of our moment-to-moment mental and emotional life does occur outside our awareness (Bargh & Chartrand, 1999; Kirsch & Lynn, 1999). On the biological front, cognitive neuroscience has provided methods for tapping into mental processes as they occur by measuring brain activity (D'Esposito, 2003). Although some researchers are using these tools to test hypotheses derived from Freudian theory with greater scientific precision, there is relatively little current research attempting to assess psychoanalytic theory.

TABLE 12.2 Freud's Stages of Psychosexual Development

Stage	Approximate Age	Erogenous Zone	Key Task
Oral	0–2	Mouth	Weaning
Anal	2–3	Anus	Toilet training
Phallic	4–6	Genitals	Resolving Oedipus complex
Latency	7–puberty	None	Developing social relationships
Genital	puberty on	Genitals	Developing mature social and sexual relationships

According to Freud's theory of Psychosexual Development, we develop our personality as we pass through a series of discrete developmental stages, each defined by an erogenous zone, a bodily source of pleasure. If there is either excessive or inadequate gratification at a particular stage, fixation at that stage occurs and adult personality is affected.

Evaluating Psychoanalytic Theory

Although it has profoundly influenced popular culture, psychology, psychiatry, and other fields, psychoanalytic theory has often been criticized on scientific grounds. One reason is that many of its specific propositions have not held up under the scrutiny of research (Fisher & Greenberg, 1996). Another major problem with psychoanalytic theory is that it is hard to test, not because it doesn't explain enough, but because it often explains too much to allow clear-cut behavioural predictions (Meehl, 1995). For example, suppose we predict on the basis of psychoanalytic theory that participants in an experimental condition will behave aggressively, and they behave instead in a loving manner. Is the theory wrong, or is the aggression being masked by the defence mechanism called reaction formation (which produces exaggerated behaviours that are the opposite of the impulse)? The difficulty in making clear-cut behavioural predictions means that some psychoanalytic hypotheses are untestable. Science, including the science of human behaviour, progresses by the development of theories and the rigorous testing of hypotheses based on those theories. Many personality theorists have rejected psychoanalytic theory on the grounds that it cannot be tested.

9. Why is it difficult to test psychoanalytic theory? What is the current status of unconscious processes and psychosexual development?

Freud's emphasis on the unconscious was scorned by a Victorian society that emphasized rationality and was condemned as unscientific by generations of personality psychologists with a behaviourist orientation. Research over the past 20 years, however, has vindicated Freud's belief in unconscious events by showing that nonconscious mental and emotional phenomena do indeed occur and can powerfully affect our behaviour (Bargh & Chartrand, 1999; Erdelyi, 1995). On the other hand, the nonconscious processes that have been experimentally demonstrated are far different from those proposed by Freud (Kihlstrom, 1999). Accepted nonconscious mental processes, such as automatic processing (see Chapter 9), are very different from the types of phenomena that Freud placed in the unconscious mind. Rather than a seething cauldron of forbidden wishes and desires, current research is unearthing what one theorist described as "a kinder, gentler unconscious" (Greenwald, 1992).

10. Explain how neoanalytic theorists Adler and Jung departed from Freudian theory. What is the focus of the object relations approach?

FIGURE 12.4

In Alfred Adler's theory, people have an inborn social interest that can cause them to put society's welfare above their interests. Mother Teresa's selfless service to others is one striking example.

Freud's Legacy: Neoanalytic and Object Relations Approaches

Freud's ideas were so revolutionary that they generated disagreement even within his circle of disciples. *Neoanalysts* were psychoanalysts who disagreed with certain aspects of Freud's thinking and developed their own theories. Among them were Alfred Adler, Karen Horney, Erik Erickson, and Carl Jung. The neoanalysts believed that Freud did not give social and cultural factors a sufficiently important role in the development and dynamics of personality. In particular, they believed that he stressed infantile sexuality too much (Kurzweil, 1989). The second major criticism was that Freud laid too much emphasis on the events of childhood as determinants of adult personality. Neoanalytic theorists agreed that childhood experiences are important, but some of them, such as Erik Erikson, believed that personality development continues throughout the life span as individuals confront challenges that are specific to particular phases in their lives.

In contrast to Freud's assertion that behaviour is motivated by inborn sexual and aggressive instincts and drives, Alfred Adler (1870–1937) insisted that humans are inherently social beings who are motivated by *social interest,* the desire to advance the welfare of others. They care about others, co-operate with them, and place general social welfare above selfish personal interests (Figure 12.4). In contrast, Freud seemed to view people as savage animals caged by the bars of civilization. Perhaps influenced by his own struggles to overcome childhood illnesses and accidents, Adler also postulated a general motive of *striving for superiority,* which drives people to compensate for real or imagined defects in themselves (the *inferiority complex*) and to strive to be ever more competent in life.

Like Adler, Carl Jung (1875–1961) was Freud's friend and associate before he broke away and developed his own theory of **analytic psychology**. Jung expanded Freud's notion of the unconscious in unique directions. For example, he believed that humans possess not only a *personal unconscious* based on their life experiences, but also a *collective unconscious* that consists of memories accumulated throughout the entire history of the human race. These memories are represented by **archetypes**, inherited tendencies to interpret experience in certain ways. Archetypes find expression in symbols, myths, and beliefs that appear across many cultures, such as the image of a god, an evil force, the hero, the good mother, and the quest for self-unity and completeness.

Following Freud's death in 1939, a new psychodynamic emphasis known as object relations became highly influential. **Object relations** theorists, including Melanie Klein (1991), Otto Kernberg (1976), Margaret Mahler (1968), and Heinz Kohut (1975), focus on the images or mental representations that people form of themselves and other people as a result of early experience with caregivers. Whether realistic or distorted, these internal representations of important adults—for example, of the mother as kind or malevolent, the father as protective or abusive—become lenses, or "working models" through which later social interactions are viewed, and these relational themes exert an unconscious influence on a person's relationships throughout life (Westen, 1998). People who have difficulties forming and maintaining intimate relationships tend to mentally represent themselves and others in negative ways, expecting painful interaction and attributing malevolence or rejection to others (Kernberg, 1984; Nigg et al., 1992). These working models often create self-fulfilling prophesies, influencing the recurring relationships people form with others.

John Bowlby's (1969, 2000) attachment theory, discussed in Chapter 11, is an outgrowth of the object relations approach. Correlational research relating early attachment experiences to later adult relationships is yielding provocative results

TABLE 12.3 **Attachment Styles in Adult Relationships**

Question: Which of the following best describes your feelings?*

A. I find it relatively easy to get close to others and am comfortable depending on them and having them depend on me. I don't often worry about being abandoned or about someone getting too close to me.

B. I am somewhat uncomfortable being close to others; I find it difficult to trust them completely, difficult to allow myself to depend on them. I am nervous when anyone gets too close, and often, love partners want me to be more intimate than I feel comfortable being.

C. I find that others are reluctant to get as close as I would like. I often worry that my partner doesn't really love me or won't want to stay with me. I want to merge completely with another person, and this desire sometimes scares people away.

*The first type of attachment style is described as "secure," the second as "avoidant," and the third as "anxious/ambivalent."

Source: Shaver et al., 1988.

(Lewis, 1999). For example, university students with a history of positive early attachments tend to have longer and more satisfying romances (Shaver & Clark, 1996). In contrast, child-abusing parents often have mental representations of their own parents as punitive, rejecting, and abusive (van Iizendoorn, 1995). Table 12.3 shows descriptive statements that characterize people who manifest secure, avoidant, and anxious-ambivalent adult attachment styles. The lasting impact of attachment patterns is also apparent in the finding that some forms of early attachment are associated with personality disorders among both adolescents and adults (Westen, Nakash, Thomas & Bradley, 2006). Today a large proportion of psychodynamic theorists and clinicians claim to rely more heavily on object relations concepts than on classical psychoanalytic theory (Aron, 1996; Westen et al., 2006). The concepts in object relations theories are also easier to define and measure, making them more amenable to research.

In Review

- *Freud's psychoanalytic theory views personality as an energy system. Personality dynamics involve modifications and exchanges of energy within this system. Mental events may be conscious, preconscious, or unconscious.*
- *Freud divided the personality into three structures: id, ego, and superego. The id is irrational and seeks immediate instinctual gratification on the basis of the pleasure principle. The ego operates on the reality principle, which requires it to test reality and to mediate between the demands of the id, the superego, and reality. The superego is the moral arm of the personality.*
- *The dynamics of personality involve a continuous conflict between impulses of the id and counterforces of the ego and superego. When dangerous id impulses threaten to get out of control or when danger from the environment threatens, the result is anxiety. To deal with threat, the ego may develop defence mechanisms, which are used to ward off anxiety and permit instinctual gratification in disguised forms.*
- *Freud's psychosexual theory of personality development held that adult personality is basically moulded by how children deal with instinctual sexual urges.*
- *Neoanalytic theorists modified and extended Freud's ideas in important ways, stressing social and cultural factors in personality development. Modern object relations theorists focus on the mental representations that people form of themselves, others, and relationships.*

THE HUMANISTIC PERSPECTIVE

11. What is self-actualization? How does this concept conflict with Freud's conception of human nature?

Humanistic theories were in part a reaction to Freud's conception of the human as being driven by "those half-tamed demons that inhabit the human beast" (Freud, 1900, p. 202). Instead, humanists embrace a positive view that affirms the inherent dignity and goodness of the human spirit. They emphasize the central role of conscious experience, as well as the individual's creative potential and inborn striving for **self-actualization**, the total realization of one's human potential (Figure 12.5). As described in Chapter 10, humanist Abraham Maslow considered self-actualization to be the ultimate human need and the highest expression of human nature.

FIGURE 12.5

The motivations underlying behaviour are much different for humanistic theorists than they are for Freudians. In the view of humanistic theorists such as Maslow and Rogers, creative and artistic accomplishments like this one are a product not of intrapsychic conflict and sublimation, but an expression of an innate tendency toward self-actualization.

Carl Rogers's Self Theory

Carl Rogers (1902–1987) was one of the most influential humanistic theorists. In contrast to Freud, Rogers believed that our behaviour is not a reaction to unconscious conflicts, but a response to our immediate conscious experience of self and environment (Rogers, 1951). He believed that the forces that direct behaviour are within us and that, when they are not distorted or blocked by our environment, they can be trusted to direct us toward self-actualization.

The Self

The central concept in Rogers's theory is the **self**, an organized, consistent set of perceptions of and beliefs about oneself (Rogers, 1959). Once formed, the self plays a powerful role in guiding our perceptions and directing our behaviour.

Rogers theorized that, at the beginning of their lives, children cannot distinguish between themselves and their environment. As they interact with their world, children begin to distinguish between the "me" and the "not-me." The self-concept continues to develop in response to our life experience, though many aspects of it remain quite stable over time.

12. Describe the roles of self-consistency and congruence in Rogers's self theory. How do these concepts relate to adjustment?

Once the self-concept is established, there is a tendency to maintain it, for it helps us to understand ourselves in relation to the world. We therefore have needs for **self-consistency** (an absence of conflict among self-perceptions) and **congruence** (consistency between self-perceptions and experience). Any experience we have that is inconsistent with our self-concept, including our perceptions of our own behaviour, evokes **threat** and anxiety. Well-adjusted individuals can respond to threat adaptively by modifying the self-concept so that the experiences are congruent with the self. But other people choose to deny or distort their experiences to remove the incongruence, a strategy that can lead to what Rogers termed "problems in living."

Suppose that an important aspect of a young man's self-concept is the belief that he is so charming and handsome that every woman finds him irresistible. He meets a young woman whom he finds very attractive but who shows a total lack of interest in him. This incongruence between his self-concept and his experience produces threat and anxiety because his basic view of himself is challenged. He could react adaptively by modifying his self-concept to acknowledge that he is not, after all, irresistible to *all* women. On the other hand, he might resolve the incongruence by distorting reality. He might deny the woman's lack of interest ("She's just playing hard to get"), or he might distort his perception of the woman ("She would have to be crazy not to appreciate how special I am—thank heaven I found out in time").

The self-consistency knife can cut in both directions, however. At the other extreme, consider a young man who believes that he is totally unattractive to women. If a desirable woman expresses interest, he might appropriately revise his self-concept in a positive direction. But it is often as difficult for people with negative self-concepts to accept success as it is for those with unrealistically positive self-concepts to accept failure (Rogers, 1959). Thus he might find it necessary to give a congruent explanation. ("She's just trying to be nice. She doesn't really like me.") Such interpretations will allow the young man to maintain his negative image of himself.

To preserve their self-image, people not only interpret situations in self-congruent ways, but they also behave in ways that will lead others to respond to them in a self-confirming fashion (Brown, 1997). As Rogers frequently noted, people are pushed by self-consistency needs to behave in accord with their self-concept (Figure 12.6).

"I can't say I like the looks of that bunch."

FIGURE 12.6

Tendencies to behave in accordance with one's self-concept at times can have ominous implications.

According to Rogers, the degree of congruence between self-concept and experience helps define one's level of adjustment. The more inflexible people's self-concepts are, the less open they will be to their experience and the more maladjusted they will become (Figure 12.7a). If there is a significant degree of incongruence between self and experience, and the experiences are forceful enough, the defences used to deny and distort reality may collapse, resulting in extreme anxiety and a temporary disorganization of the self-concept.

The Need for Positive Regard

13. How do conditions of worth develop and how can they hinder adjustment?

Rogers believed that we are born with an innate **need for positive regard**—that is, for acceptance, sympathy, and love from others. Rogers viewed positive regard as essential for healthy development. Ideally, positive regard received from the parents is unconditional—that is, independent of how the child behaves. **Unconditional positive regard** communicates that the child is inherently worthy of love. *Conditional positive regard,* on the other hand, is dependent on how the child behaves. In the extreme case, love and acceptance are given to the child *only* when the child behaves as the parents want.

People need positive regard not only from others but also from themselves. We all want to feel good about ourselves. Thus a **need for positive self-regard** also develops. Lack of unconditional positive regard from parents and other significant people in the past teaches people that they are worthy of approval and love only when they meet certain standards. This fosters the development of **conditions of worth** that dictate when we approve or disapprove of ourselves. A child who has experienced parental approval when behaving in a friendly fashion, but disapproval whenever she became angry or aggressive, may come to disapprove of her own "angry" feelings, even when they are justified. She may, therefore, come to deny in herself all feelings of anger and struggle to preserve a self-image of being totally loving. Rogers believed that conditions of worth can tyrannize people and cause major incongruence between self and experience, together with a need to deny or distort important aspects of experience. Conditions of worth are similar to the "shoulds" that populate Freud's superego.

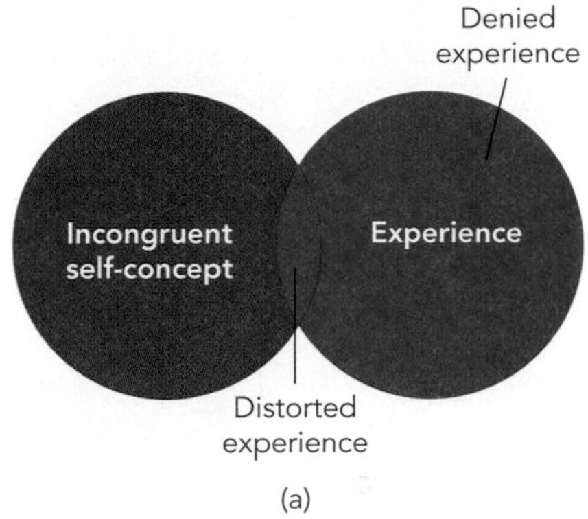

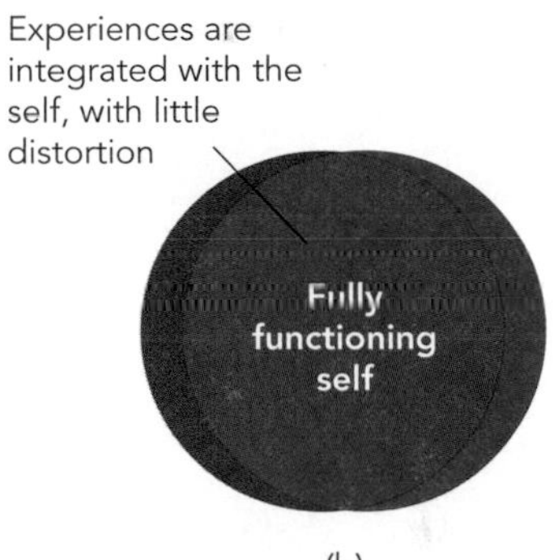

FIGURE 12.7

Rogers defined psychological adjustment in terms of the degree of congruence between self-concept and experience. Maladjustment (a) occurs when a person faced with incongruities between self and experience distorts or denies reality in order to make it consistent with the self-concept. In contrast, extremely well-adjusted, or fully functioning, people integrate experiences into the self with minimal distortion (b), so they are able to profit fully from their experiences.

Source: After Rogers, 1951.

Fully Functioning Persons

Toward the end of his career, Rogers became particularly interested in people who had achieved self-actualization. As Rogers viewed them, **fully functioning persons** do not hide behind masks or adopt artificial roles. They feel a sense of inner freedom, self-determination, and choice in the direction of their growth. They have no fear of behaving spontaneously, freely, and creatively. Because they are fairly free of conditions of worth, they can accept inner and outer experiences as they are, without modifying them defensively to suit a rigid self-concept or the expectations of others. Thus a fully functioning unmarried woman would be able to state quite frankly that her career is more important to her than a role as wife and mother *if* she truly felt that way, and to act comfortably on those feelings. In a sense, she could be true to herself (Figure 12.7b).

Research on the Self

By giving the self a central place in his theory, Rogers helped stimulate a great deal of research on the self-concept (Brown, 1997; Robins et al., 1999). Two topics at the forefront are: (1) the development of self-esteem and its effects on behaviour, and (2) the roles played by self-enhancement and self-consistency motives.

Self-Esteem

Self-esteem (how positively or negatively we feel about ourselves) is a very important aspect of personal well-being, happiness, and adjustment (Brown, 1998;

14. How do differences in self-esteem affect behaviour? What conditions affect the development of self-esteem?

Diener, 2000). Self-esteem is related to many positive behaviours and life outcomes. People with high self-esteem are less susceptible to social pressure, have fewer interpersonal problems, are happier with their lives, achieve at a higher and more persistent level, and are more capable of forming satisfying love relationships (Baumeister, 1999). In contrast, people with a poor self-image are more prone to psychological problems such as anxiety and depression, to physical illness, and to poor social relationships and underachievement (Heimpel et al., 2002). Men and women do not differ in overall level of self-esteem (Feingold, 1994; Maccoby & Jacklin, 1974).

What conditions foster the development of high self-esteem? Children develop higher self-esteem when their parents communicate unconditional acceptance and love, establish clear guidelines for behaviour, and reinforce compliance while giving the child freedom to make decisions and express opinions within those guidelines (Coopersmith, 1957; Harrington et al., 1987). One study showed that when low self-esteem children were exposed to highly supportive youth sport coaches who gave them much positive reinforcement and encouragement, the children's self-esteem increased significantly over the course of the sport season (Smoll et al., 1993). Apparently, the positive feedback caused the children to revise their self-concepts in a positive direction.

The value of high self-esteem has been well publicized and has led to a range of self-help books, educational programs, child-rearing manuals, and other resources meant to help people elevate their feelings of self-worth. But is high self-esteem always beneficial? Unstable or unrealistically high self-esteem may be even more dangerous to the individual and to society than low self-esteem. When unstable or inflated self-esteem is threatened, individuals may react aggressively, even violently, to protect their self-esteem (Baumeister, Smart & Boden, 1996). Indeed, the higher one's self-esteem, the greater the vulnerability to ego threats (Baumeister et al., 1996). Recently, it has been recognized that the pursuit of self-esteem can also be a source of problems. When you attempt some new task, such as learning to snowboard, tackle a new and challenging university course, or join a band, do you do it to master the task? Or do you do it because success will enhance your self-esteem and validate your abilities? If the goal is enhanced self-esteem, achieving your goal imparts a feeling of worth and value, but the emotional benefits may only be temporary (Crocker & Park, 2004). Furthermore, a failure when the goal is enhanced self-esteem is more damaging to the individual than a failure when the goal is to master the task (Crocker, 2002; Crocker & Park, 2004). If the goal is enhanced self-esteem, people feel particularly challenged to succeed and may react to threats or perceived threats in ways that are destructive or self-destructive. When the pursuit of self-esteem is successful it does have emotional benefits, but the pursuit of self-esteem can also have costs, such as decreasing learning and leading to poor self-regulation and poor mental and physical health (Baumeister & Leary, 1995; Crocker, 2002; Deci & Ryan, 2000).

Self-Verification and Self-Enhancement Motives

Rogers proposed that people are motivated to preserve their self-concept by maintaining self-consistency and congruence. Modern researchers call this need **self-verification**, and it has received considerable research support. In one study, researchers measured university students' self-concepts. In a later experiment, the students interacted with other participants and received fake feedback from them in the form of adjectives that were either consistent or inconsistent with their self-concept. Later, when the students were asked to recall and identify the adjectives that had been attributed to them, they showed greater recall for the consistent adjectives, suggesting that people selectively attend to and recall self-consistent information (Suinn et al., 1962).

15. Define self-verification and self-enhancement. What research evidence is there to support these processes?

Self-verification needs are also expressed in people's tendency to seek out self-confirming relationships. One study found that if people with firmly held negative self-views marry spouses who appraise them favourably, they tend eventually to withdraw from the marriage. Such people are more likely to remain with spouses who agree with the negative image they have of themselves. In contrast, people with positive self-concepts prefer spouses who share their positive view of themselves (Swann et al., 1992).

Rogers also suggested that people have a need to regard themselves positively, and research confirms a strong and pervasive tendency to gain and preserve a positive self-image. These processes are known as **self-enhancement** (Brown, 1998; Swann, 1996). Several self-enhancement strategies have been identified. For example, people show a marked tendency to attribute their successes to their own abilities and effort, but to attribute their failures to environmental factors. Furthermore, most people rate themselves as better than average on virtually any socially desirable characteristic that is subjective in nature (Steele & Baumeister, 1999). The vast majority of businesspeople and politicians rate themselves as more ethical than the average. In defiance of mathematical possibility, about 80 percent of high-school students rate themselves in the top 10 percent in their ability to get along with others. Even people who have been hospitalized after causing auto accidents rate themselves as more skilful than the average driver (Pyszczyncki & Greenberg, 1987). Indeed, as evidence on self-serving biases in self-perception continues to accumulate, researchers are concluding that positive illusions of this sort are the rule rather than the exception in well-adjusted people and that these self-enhancement tendencies, or "positive illusions," contribute to their psychological well-being (Taylor & Brown, 1988; Taylor et al., 2000).

16. What cultural and gender differences have been found in self-concept research?

Culture, Gender, and the Self

Culture provides a learning context in which the self develops. Individualistic cultures such as those in North America and northern Europe place an emphasis on independence and personal attainment, whereas collectivistic cultures such as those found in many parts of Asia, Africa, and South America emphasize connectedness between people and the achievement of group goals (Cross & Markus, 1999; Triandis, 1989). What kinds of self-concept differences would you predict in people from these two types of cultures?

In one study, American and Japanese university students were given a self-concept questionnaire on which they listed their five most important attributes. The researchers then classified each statement according to whether it referred to a personal attribute (e.g., I am honest; I am smart), a social identity (e.g., I am an oldest son; I am a student), or something else, such as a physical trait. As Figure 12.8 shows, the Americans were far more likely than the Japanese to list personal traits, abilities, or dispositions, whereas the Japanese more frequently described themselves in social identity terms. Thus the social embeddedness of the collectivist Japanese culture was reflected in their self-perceptions, as was cultural individualism in the Americans' self-concepts (Cousins, 1989).

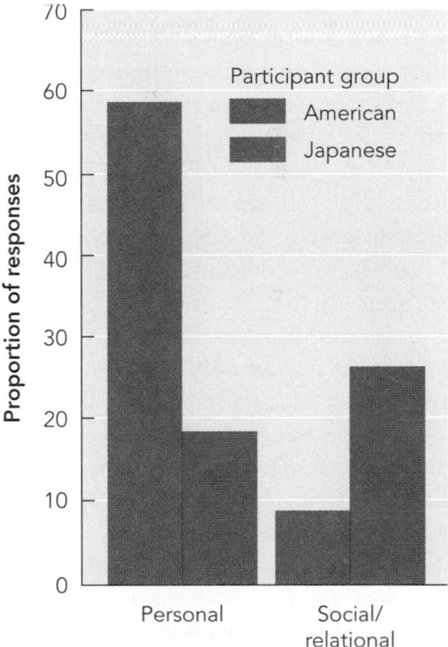

FIGURE 12.8

Cultural differences in the self-concept. Percentages of personal identity and social/relational self-attributes given by Japanese and American university students as key aspects of their self-concept.

Data from Cousins, 1989.

Gender-role socialization provides us with **gender schemas**, organized mental structures that contain our understanding of the attributes and behaviours that are appropriate and expected for males and females (Bem, 1981). Within a given culture, gender schemas tell us what the typical man or woman "should" be like. In Western cultures, men tend to prize attributes related to achievement, emotional strength, athleticism, and self-sufficiency, whereas women especially prize interpersonal competencies, kindness, and helpfulness to others (Beyer, 1990; Brown, 1998; Marsh, 1990). In a sense, men in Western cultures tend to develop more of an individualistic self-concept, emphasizing achievement and separateness from others, whereas women's self-concepts tend to be more collectivistic, emphasizing their social connectedness with others (Watkins et al., 2003; Bresnahan et al., 2005). Nonetheless, we should keep in mind that significant individual differences exist within each gender group, with many women being highly individualistic and many men collectivistic (Brown, 1998).

RESEARCH FRONTIERS

Stressed by Success

If you had a bad day—say you did poorly on an exam or an anticipated social event turned into a disappointment—would you engage in a behaviour that you knew would improve your mood and make you feel better? Conversely, if you'd experienced a meaningful success in your life—perhaps you did much better than anticipated on an exam, or were praised by someone important to you—would you now savour that success, or do you immediately begin to anticipate problems, thus dampening your good mood and becoming anxious? You might expect that if people knew how to make themselves feel better after a setback, they would do so. Similarly, you might expect that successes are savoured, at least for a while, before we again worry about the future. Research by Joanne Wood and Sara A. Heimpel of the University of Waterloo, and their colleagues, has found that this is not always true. Whether success makes a person feel good or anxious, and whether or not someone acts to improve a bad mood depends importantly on their self-esteem.

Earlier work had argued that self-esteem differences had an important impact after failures but not after successes (Blaine & Crocker, 1993). Wood, Heimpel, Newby-Clark, and Ross (2005), however, proposed that individuals who are low in self-esteem do not enjoy success the way that those high in self-esteem enjoy success. Perhaps counter-intuitively, they suggested that whereas success helps to bolster the self-esteem of those already high in self-esteem, success generates self-doubt and anxiety among those low in self-esteem (Heimpel, Wood, Marshall & Brown, 2002; Wood, Heimpel & Michela, 2003; Wood et al., 2005). Consistent with their argument is the surprising finding that positive life events are associated with better physical health among those with high self-esteem, but with more illness, not less, among those with low self-esteem (Brown & McGill, 1989). (As we will discover in the discussion of stress and health in chapter 15, a person's reaction to stress has a powerful impact on their physical health.)

In an interesting series of studies Wood, Heimpel, and colleagues (Wood et al., 2005) tested reactions to success among individuals who had either low self-esteem or high self-esteem, as determined by an earlier measure of self-esteem. Those whose self-esteem score was in the lower third were placed in the low self-esteem group, while high self-esteem participants were from those who scored in the top third. Half of the high self-esteem and half of the low self-esteem participants were assigned to receive successes and half were placed in a neutral condition. Participants were given a series of simple cognitive tasks, such as composing sentences that contained specific words and doing simple arithmetic, and received either positive feedback or no comments. The positive feedback, the success condition, was designed to create the belief that the participant's performance had been exceptionally good. Participants in the neutral condition received no feedback and the test session was conducted in a way that would minimize any perception that they were being evaluated. After creating a success or neutral situation, participants' anxiety and mood were assessed. Low and high self-esteem participants in the neutral condition did not differ in measures of anxiety. After a successful performance, however, the low self-esteem participants reported significantly more anxiety than did the high self-esteem participants (see Figure 12.9). That is, subjects low in self-esteem did not have their self-esteem improve when told that they had done very well; instead such comments made them anxious.

In a related study Wood and colleagues (Wood et al., 2005) assessed participants' expectations and thoughts about themselves. After completing a series of simple cognitive tasks in the success or neutral condition, current thoughts about self and expectations about an expected second testing phase were collected. Participants were also asked to provide a detailed description of a past event from their own experience. Those with high self-esteem had higher expectations about their performance in a coming test and expressed more positive thoughts about themselves after being told that they had performed extremely well. When told that they had performed exceptionally well, participants with low self-esteem did not then generate high expectations for the coming test or think well of themselves. Low self-esteem participants also showed more anxiety after a success than did high self-esteem participants. That is, high and low self-esteem participants did not differ in their expectations or self-relevant thoughts in the neutral condition, but they did differ in the success condition: success increased positive thoughts about self for those who already had high self-esteem, but not for those with low self-esteem. Interestingly, the memories described by those with

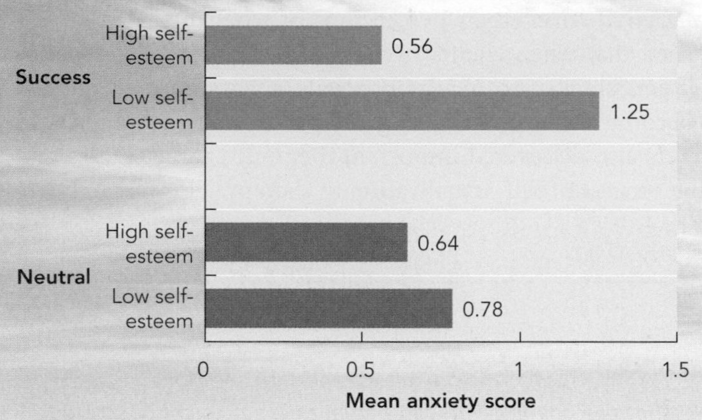

FIGURE 12.9

Mean composite anxiety score for participants with low or high self-esteem after completion of a series of simple cognitive tasks with encouraging and positive feedback (Success) or after completion of the cognitive tasks in a neutral setting (Neutral). Higher anxiety scores indicate greater anxiety, such as reports of feeling tense or trembling and self-reported anxiety. Although differences in self-esteem were not related to anxiety in the neutral setting, those with low self-esteem experienced significantly more anxiety after a success. Adapted from Wood et al., 2005.

low self-esteem became less positive after a success. That is, across the different measures, those with high self-esteem benefited from a success but those with low self-esteem did not gain any benefit as assessed by measures of anxiety, anticipated future performance or the types of memories that they recalled. Indeed, success had a negative impact on those with low self-esteem.

Even when people are asked to daydream about an emotionally positive event in the future, such as falling in love or doing very well on an important exam, differences between those with low self-esteem and those with high self-esteem are apparent. When imagining a future positive event, everyone reports anticipated happiness, but those with low self-esteem also anticipate feeling anxious as a result of an imagined future success (Wood et al., 2005).

Earlier work by these researchers had found that self-esteem also had an impact on how people act to regulate their mood. In response to failure, participants with low self-esteem were less likely to express a desire to improve their mood than were participants with high self-esteem. Although those with low self-esteem knew what to do to improve their mood (e.g., watch a comedy), they did not engage in these behaviours when in a negative mood (Heimpel et al., 2002). After experiencing a positive event in their own lives, people with low self-esteem reported more dampening of their good mood. They reported that they deliberately thought about things that would calm their excitement, that would make them feel less good about themselves and their success, or that would distract them from the success (Wood et al., 2003).

Earlier research had focused on the impact of failure on self-esteem. The argument was that those with low self-esteem are especially damaged by failure and that this exaggerated impact of failure perpetuated their low self-esteem (Blaine & Crocker, 1993). Newer research, such as that by Joanne Wood, Sara Heimpel, and colleagues has shown that those with low self-esteem also react differently to success. Success increases their anxiety and that robs the experience of success of much of its positive impact. Even when people with low self-esteem know what to do to improve their mood, they are less likely to do it. Without acting to improve their mood, without enjoying a good mood, and with success bringing doubt and anxiety, people with low self-esteem can rob their positive life experiences of all joy.

Evaluating Humanistic Theories

Humanistic theorists focus on the individual's subjective experiences. What matters most is how people view themselves and the world (Nye, 1996). Some critics believe that the humanistic view relies too much on individuals' reports of their personal experiences. For example, psychoanalytic theorists maintain that accepting what a person says at face value may easily lead to erroneous conclusions because of the always-present influence of unconscious factors. Some critics also believe that it is impossible to define an individual's actualizing tendency except in terms of the behaviour that it supposedly produces. This would be an example of circular reasoning: "Why did the person achieve such success? Because of self-actualization." "How do we know self-actualization was at work? Because the person achieved great success."

Though humanism may indeed seem non-scientific to some, Carl Rogers (1959) dedicated himself to developing a theory whose concepts could be measured and whose laws could be tested. One of his most notable contributions was a series of groundbreaking studies on the process of self-growth that can occur in psychotherapy. To assess the effectiveness of psychotherapy, Rogers and his co-workers measured the discrepancy between clients' *ideal selves* (how they would like to be) and their *perceived selves* (their perceptions of what they are actually like). The studies revealed that when clients first enter therapy, the discrepancy typically is large, but it gets smaller as therapy proceeds, suggesting that therapy may help the client to become more self-accepting and perhaps also more realistic. Rogers and his co-workers also discovered important therapist characteristics that either aid or impede the process of self-actualization in therapy. This research will be described in Chapter 14.

In Review

- *Humanistic theories emphasize the subjective experiences of the individual and thus deal with perceptual and cognitive processes. Self-actualization is viewed as an innate positive force that leads people to realize their positive potential, if not thwarted by the environment.*
- *Carl Rogers's theory attaches central importance to the role of the self. Experiences that are incongruous with the established self-concept produce threat and may result in a denial or distortion of reality. Conditional positive regard may result in realistic conditions of worth that can conflict with self-actualization. Rogers described a number of characteristics of the fully functioning person.*
- *Rogers's theory helped stimulate a great deal of research on the self-concept, including studies on the origins and effects of differences in self-esteem, self-enhancement and self-verification motives, and cultural and gender contributions to the self-concept.*

TRAIT AND BIOLOGICAL PERSPECTIVES

How do people differ in personality? The goals of trait theorists are to describe the basic classes of behaviour that define personality, to devise ways of measuring individual differences in personality traits, and to use these measures to understand and predict a person's behaviour.

The starting point for the trait researcher is identifying the behaviours that define a particular trait. But here we have an embarrassment of riches. Years ago, the trait theorist Gordon Allport went through the English dictionary and painstakingly recorded all of the words that could be used to describe personal traits. The result: a gigantic list of 17,953 words (Allport & Odbert, 1936). Obviously, it would be impractical if not impossible to describe people in terms of where they fall on some 18,000 dimensions. The trait theorist's goal is to condense all of these behavioural descriptors into a manageable number of basic traits that can capture personal individuality.

17. In what way is factor analysis based on correlation, and how is it used to identify personality traits?

Two major approaches have been taken to define what Allport (1937) called "the building blocks of personality." One approach is to propose traits (e.g., "dominance," "friendliness," or "self-esteem") on the basis of intuition or a theory of personality. A more systematic approach uses the statistical tool of **factor analysis** to identify clusters of specific behaviours that are correlated with one another so highly that they can be viewed as reflecting a basic dimension, or trait, on which people vary. For example, you might find that most people who are socially reserved also avoid parties, like quiet activities, and enjoy being alone. At the other end of the spectrum are people who are very talkative and sociable, like parties and excitement, dislike solitary activities such as reading, and constantly seek out new acquaintances. These behavioural patterns define a general factor or dimension that we might label *introversion-extraversion* (or simply *extraversion*). At one end of the dimension are highly introverted behaviours, and at the other end are highly

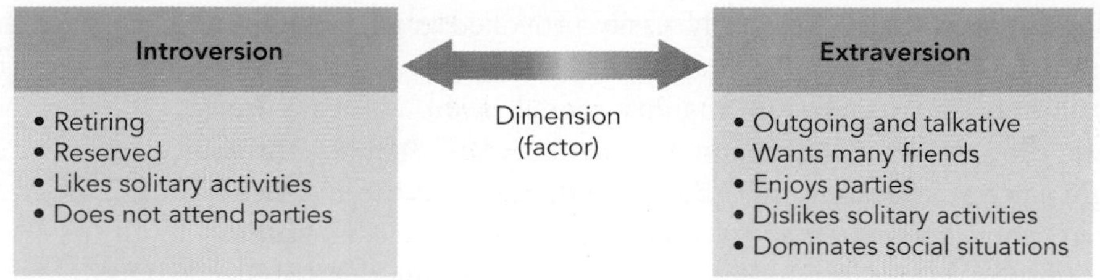

FIGURE 12.10

Factor analysis allows researchers to reduce many behaviours to a smaller number of basic dimensions, or factors. A factor consists of behaviours that are highly correlated with one another and therefore are assumed to have common psychological meaning. Here, we see the kinds of behaviours that might fall on the two ends of the introversion-extraversion dimension. The two groups of behaviours are negatively correlated with one another.

extraverted behaviours (Figure 12.10). Presumably, each of us could be placed at some point along this dimension in terms of our customary behaviour patterns. In fact, as we shall see, factor analytic studies have found introversion-extraversion to be a major dimension of personality.

Cattell's Sixteen Personality Factors

If you were asked to describe and compare every person you know, how many different traits would it take to do the job? This is where trait theorists begin to part company. Because factor analysis can be used and interpreted in different ways, trait theorists have cut up the personality pie into smaller or larger pieces. For example, the pioneering trait theorist Raymond B. Cattell (1965, 1990) asked thousands of people to rate themselves on numerous behavioural characteristics and also obtained ratings from people who knew the participants well. When he subjected this mass of data to factor analysis, he identified 16 basic behaviour clusters, or factors. These personality dimensions are shown in Figure 12.11. Using this information, Cattell developed a widely used personality test called the 16 Personality Factor Questionnaire (16PF) to measure individual differences on each of the dimensions and provide a comprehensive personality description. He was able to develop personality profiles not only for individuals, but also for groups of people. For example, Figure 12.11 compares average scores obtained by creative artists and Olympic athletes.

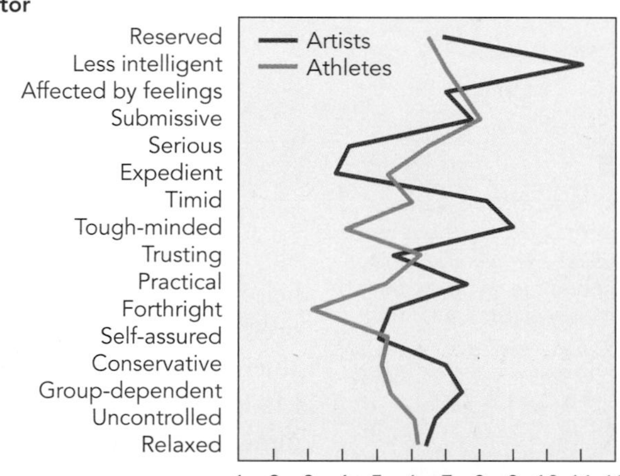

FIGURE 12.11

Cattell identified 16 basic personality traits through factor analysis. Here we see personality profiles (mean scores) for Olympic athletes and creative artists on the 16PF, the test developed by Cattell to measure the traits.

Based on data from Cattell, 1965.

Eysenck's Extraversion-Stability Model

Among traits theorists, some, like Cattell, proposed a large number of basic traits. At the other extreme was the British psychologist Hans Eysenck (1916–1997) who proposed surprisingly few basic traits (Figure 12.12a). In his original theory, Eysenck proposed only two basic dimensions, although he later added a third (Eysenck 1967, 1991). Eysenck called his original basic dimensions of personality Introversion-Extraversion and Stability-Instability (which he first referred to as Stability-Neuroticism). Eysenck argued that personality within the normal range could be understood with only two basic dimensions.

Extraversion reflects the tendency to be sociable, active, and willing to take risks; the Introversion end of the scale represents a tendency toward social inhibition, passivity, and caution. The Stability-Instability dimension represents a continuum from high emotional stability and poise at the Stability end, to moodiness,

(a)

Unstable
Moody
Touchy
Anxious
Restless
Rigid
Aggressive
Sober
Excitable
Pessimistic
Changeable
Reserved
Impulsive
Unsociable
Optimistic
Quiet
Active
Introverted
Extraverted
Passive
Sociable
Careful
Outgoing
Thoughtful
Talkative
Peaceful
Responsive
Controlled
Easygoing
Reliable
Lively
Even-tempered
Carefree
Calm
Leadership
Stable

(b)

FIGURE 12.12

According to Hans Eysenck (a), various combinations of two major dimensions of personality, Introversion-Extraversion and Stability-Instability, combine to form the more specific traits shown in (b).

From H. J. Eysenck, The Biological Basis of Personality, Figure 12, 1967. Courtesy of Charles C Thomas, Publisher, Ltd., Springfield, Illinois.

a tendency to worry excessively, easily provoked guilt feelings, and anxiety at the Instability end.

Eysenck's Extraversion-Stability model is shown in Figure 12.12b. The two basic dimensions, Extraversion-Introversion and Stability-Instability, intersect at right angles, indicating that these two dimensions are independent, or uncorrelated. Thus, knowing how extraverted a person is tells us nothing about her level of emotional stability; she could fall anywhere along the Stability-Instability continuum. The secondary traits shown around the periphery of the circle reflect various combinations or mixtures of the two primary dimensions. Thus, someone who scores high on emotional stability and high on extraversion is a carefree, lively person who tends to be well-adjusted and to seek leadership roles. In contrast, someone who scores high on instability (neuroticism) and high on extraversion tends to be touchy, aggressive, and restless. With even subtle variations along one or both dimensions, different combinations of these two basic dimensions can produce very diverse personality patterns.

Although Eysenck continued to emphasize these two "supertraits," he added a third dimension to his theory of personality (Eysenck 1991, 1993). Eysenck called this third factor Psychoticism-Self Control. Unfortunately, the choice of the name Psychoticism evokes an image of pathology, but scoring high on this scale does not mean that someone is at risk for later development of psychosis (Eysenck, 1993). By Psychoticism, Eysenck meant someone who was creative and had a tendency toward nonconformity, impulsivity, and social deviance.

The Five Factor Model

Other trait theorists argued that Cattell's 16 dimensions may be more than are needed and that Eysenck's two or three may be too few. Their factor analytic studies suggest to them that five "higher-order" factors, each including several of Cattell's more specific factors, are all that are needed to capture the basic structure of personality (Digman, 1990; McCrae & Costa, 2003). These theorists also believe that these "Big Five" factors may be universal to the human species, since the same five factors have been found consistently in trait ratings within diverse North American, Asian, Hispanic, and European cultures (John & Srivastava, 1999; Trull & Geary, 1997).

The Big Five factors are shown in Table 12.4. (The acronym OCEAN—for Openness, Conscientiousness, Extraversion, Agreeableness, and Neuroticism—may help you remember them.) Two of the five factors, Extraversion and Neuroticism, overlap with Eysenck's theory, and two other factors, Conscientiousness and Agreeableness, are similar to Eysenck's Psychoticism factor. Proponents of the Five Factor Model believe that when a person is placed at a specific point on each of these five dimensions by means of a psychological test, behaviour ratings, or direct observations of behaviour, the essence of his or her personality is captured (McCrae & Costa, 2003).

18. What does *OCEAN* stand for in the Five Factor model?

What do you think about that conclusion? Your reaction may be one of skepticism, since it seems that there *must* be more to individuality than can be captured by only five dimensions. However, we should remember that, as discussed in Chapter 5, the incredible number of colours that humans can discriminate is based on the activity patterns of only three types of cones. Thus the many variations that can occur from the blending of five personality dimensions could account for enormous variation in the pattern of people's behavioural tendencies.

Traits and Behaviour Prediction

Trait theorists try not only to describe the basic structure of personality, but also to predict real-life behaviour on the basis of a person's traits. Even if a limited number of general traits such as the Big Five seem adequate to describe important features of personality, it is entirely possible that a larger number of specific traits such as Cattell's would be more likely to capture nuances of behaviour within particular situations and therefore would be better for predictive purposes.

To address this issue, Bryan Mershon and Richard Gorsuch (1988) used scores derived from the 16PF test to predict real-life outcomes such as choice of occupation, job performance and promotions, marijuana smoking, and the development of psychological disorders. They scored the 187 items of the 16PF in two different ways. First, they calculated scores for each of Cattell's 16 factors. Then they scored the test for broader factors that corresponded to the Big Five. Finally, they determined which set of scores did a better job of predicting the various behaviours.

Mershon and Gorsuch found that, although the Big Five factors were able to predict the behaviours to a moderate degree, the 16 factors were far superior in their ability to predict specific behaviours. In fact, on average, they did about twice as well, though different combinations of the 16 scores were most strongly correlated with each of the various behaviours. Thus it appears that broad traits such as the Big Five and Eysenck's "big two" may do an adequate job of predicting behaviour across a whole range of situations, much as a wide-beamed floodlight illuminates a large area. However, like a narrowly focused and intense spotlight, specific traits such as Cattell's may do better in specific situations that call for the behaviours measured by the narrower traits.

TABLE 12.4 The Big Five Personality Factors and Their Lower-order Traits

Big Five Factors	Lower-Order Traits
Openness	Artistically sensitive vs. artistically insensitive
	Intellectual vs. unreflective, narrow
	Polished, refined vs. crude, boorish
	Imaginative vs. simple, direct
Conscientiousness	Fussy, tidy vs. careless
	Responsible vs. undependable
	Scrupulous vs. unscrupulous
	Persevering vs. quitting, fickle
Extraversion	Talkative vs. silent
	Frank, open vs. secretive
	Adventurous vs. cautious
	Sociable vs. reclusive
Agreeableness	Good-natured vs. irritable
	Not jealous vs. jealous
	Mild, gentle vs. headstrong
	Co-operative vs. negativistic
Neuroticism	Poised vs. nervous, tense
	Calm vs. anxious
	Composed vs. excitable
	Emotionally stable vs. moody, unstable

19. What are the predictive advantages of (a) broad general traits and (b) narrow, specific ones? What's the research evidence?

Biological Foundations of Personality Traits

Both nature and nurture influence the development of personality traits, but their contributions differ depending on the trait in question (Plomin & Caspi, 1999). Biological explanations for personality differences focus on three levels. Some researchers search for differences in the functioning of the nervous system (Pickering & Gray, 1999). As discussed in Chapter 4, there is evidence that genes make an important contribution to personality. Some psychologists have also used evolutionary principles to explain why these traits exist among humans (Buss, 1999; and see Chapter 4). In considering the biological perspective for personality, keep in mind the role of behaviour genetics and the evolutionary explanations that we explored earlier.

20. In Eysenck's theory, what are the biological bases for individual differences in Extraversion and Stability?

Hans Eysenck (1967) was one of the first modern theorists to suggest a biological basis for major personality traits. He linked Introversion-Extraversion and Stability-Instability to differences in individuals' normal patterns of arousal within the brain. He started with the notion that there is an optimal, or preferred, level of biological arousal in the brain. Eysenck believed that extreme introverts are chronically *overaroused;* their brains are too electrically active, so they try to minimize stimulation and reduce arousal to get down to their optimal arousal level, or "comfort zone." In contrast, the brains of extreme extraverts are chronically *underaroused,* so they need powerful or frequent stimulation to achieve an optimal level of cortical arousal and excitation. The extravert thus seeks social contact and physical arousal, likes parties, takes chances, is assertive, and readily suffers from boredom.

Whereas Introversion-Extraversion reflects a person's customary level of cortical arousal, Stability-Instability represents the suddenness with which shifts in autonomics nervous system arousal occur. Unstable people have hair-trigger nervous systems that show large and sudden shifts in arousal, whereas stable people show smaller and more gradual shifts (Pickering & Gray, 1999). Eysenck also called this stability dimension Neuroticism because he found that people with extremely unstable nervous systems are more likely to experience emotional problems that require clinical attention.

Eysenck believed that the arousal patterns that underlie Introversion-Extraversion and Stability-Instability have genetic bases. As we learned in Chapter 4, a growing body of evidence supports his view. Eysenck believed that, although personality is strongly influenced by life experiences, the ways people respond to those experiences may be at least partly programmed by biological factors.

Other personality researchers continue attempts to link personality traits to biological foundations. For example, Cloninger has attempted to link three broad personality traits—novelty-seeking, harm avoidance, and reward dependence—to differences in the functioning of specific neurotransmitter systems (Cloninger, 1986, 1987). Novelty-seeking, for example, is related to levels of the neurotransmitter dopamine and dopamine's role in activating behaviour. This approach has been used to explore the foundations of personality within the normal range and to explain behaviours such as substance abuse (Berman, Ozkaragoz, Young & Noble, 2002). Examples of recent investigations into the biological foundations of personality traits are presented in this chapter's Neuroscience feature (p. 530).

The Stability of Personality Traits

21. How does research evidence bear on the assumption of stability across time and across situations?

Because traits are defined as enduring behavioural predispositions, they should show some degree of stability over time and across situations. As far as stability over time is concerned, the research literature shows evidence of both stability and change (Caspi & Roberts, 1999). Some personality dimensions tend to be more stable than others. For example, introversion-extraversion, as well as temperamental traits such as emotionality and activity level, tend to be quite stable from childhood into adulthood and across the adult years (Eysenck, 1990; McCrae & Costa, 1990; Zuckerman, 2005).

Certain habits of thought may also be fairly stable. One is our tendency to think optimistically or pessimistically. Melanie Burns and Martin Seligman (1989) coded diaries and letters that elderly people had written approximately 50 years earlier for the tendency to respond either optimistically or pessimistically to life events. The elderly people also completed a questionnaire that measured their current optimistic-pessimistic tendencies. Although little consistency over time was shown for dealing optimistically or pessimistically with positive events, Burns and Seligman found a stable tendency to respond with optimism or pessimism to negative life events. The authors suggested that this tendency to be pessimistic might constitute an enduring risk factor for depression, low achievement, and physical illness, and they are presently studying such linkages. Table 12.5 contains items from the Life Orientation Test (Scheier & Carver, 1985), used by personality researchers to measure the disposition to be optimistic or pessimistic.

When it comes to stability of behaviour across situations, personality again shows both a degree of stability and some capacity for change (Mischel & Shoda, 1999). Because behaviour always results from a person interacting with a situation, we would be foolish to expect people to behave in the same manner from situation to situation. Even on a trait so central as honesty, people can show considerable behavioural variability across situations. In a classic study, Hugh Hartshorne and Mark May (1928) tested the honesty of thousands of children. The children were given opportunities to lie, steal, and cheat in a number of different settings—at home, in school, at a party, and in an athletic contest. The rather surprising finding was that "lying, cheating and stealing as measured by the test situations in this study are only very loosely related. . . . Most children will deceive in certain situations but not in others" (p. 411). More than a half-century later, Walter Mischel (1984) reported similar findings for university students on the trait of "conscientiousness." A student might be highly conscientious in one situation (e.g., coming to work on time) without being conscientious in another (turning in class assignments on time).

TABLE 12.5 Sample Items From a Trait Measure of Optimism-Pessimism*

1. In uncertain times, I usually expect the best.
2. Overall, I expect more good things to happen to me than bad.
3. If something can go wrong for me, it will.
4. I rarely count on good things happening to me.

*Items on the Life Orientation Test are answered on a five-point scale ranging from strongly disagree to strongly agree.

Source: Scheier & Carver, 1985.

Three factors make it difficult to predict on the basis of personality traits how people will behave in particular situations. First, personality traits interact with other traits as well as with characteristics of different situations. This melding accounts for the incredible richness we see in personality, but it also poses a challenge to psychologists who want to predict behaviour. When two or more traits, such as honesty, dominance, and agreeableness, influence a behaviour in a particular situation, our ability to predict on the basis of only one of the traits is bound to be quite limited (Ahadi & Diener, 1989).

22. What three factors make it difficult to predict behaviour on the basis of individual personality traits?

Second, the degree of consistency across situations is influenced by how important a given trait is for the person. A person for whom honesty is a central component of the self-concept may show considerable stability across situations in honest behaviours because feelings of self-worth may be linked to living up to moral standards regardless of the circumstances (Kenrick & Funder, 1991).

Third, people differ in their tendency to tailor their behaviour to what is called for by the situation. This personality trait is called **self-monitoring** (Table 12.6). People who are high in self-monitoring are very attentive to situational cues and adapt their behaviour to what they think would be most appropriate. Extreme self-monitors resemble behavioural chameleons who act very differently in different situations. Low self-monitors, on the other hand, tend to act primarily in terms of their internal beliefs and attitudes rather than the demands of the situation. The saying "What you see is what you get" applies well to low self-monitors, and such people show greater consistency across situations than do high self-monitors (Snyder, 1987).

TABLE 12.6 Sample Items From the Self-Monitoring Scale*

1. In different situations and with different people, I often act like very different persons.
2. I am not always the person I appear to be.
3. I have trouble changing my behaviour to suit different people and different situations.
4. I would not change my opinion (or the way I do things) in order to please someone or win their favour.

*Items 1 and 2 are keyed *true,* and items 3 and 4 *false* for self-monitoring.

Source: Snyder, 1974.

According to some trait theorists, the stability and distinctiveness that we see in personality do not come from the fact that we behave the same way in every situation. Rather, they result from our exhibiting an *average* amount of extraversion, emotional stability, agreeableness, honesty, and other traits across many different situations (Epstein, 1983; Kenrick & Funder, 1988). Nonetheless, if they wish to understand more about these interactions between personality traits, situations, and behaviour, personality researchers need to define the relevant characteristics of both the person and the situation (Shoda & Mischel, 2000).

FOCUS ON NEUROSCIENCE

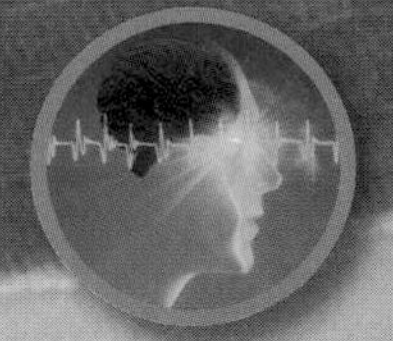

The Neuroscience of the Big Five

The Five Factor Model of personality has gained widespread support among personality theorists and researchers (see the section on the Five Factor model beginning on page 526). One criticism of the Five Factor Model, however, has been that it labels aspects of personality but does not explain them. If a person is imaginative, sensitive, curious, creative and intellectual, a Five Factor personality theorist would say that they are high in the personality trait "Openness." But does saying that someone is high in Openness explain *why* they behave the way that they do? Some have argued that if the Five Factor Model is to move beyond a "descriptive taxonomy" (DeYoung, Peterson & Higgins, 2005, p. 826) it must include an explanation of the causes of individual differences in personality traits and why those traits even appear. Personality theorists such as Hans Eysenck began to examine the basis of personality traits from a neurobiological and behavioural genetics perspective forty years ago (e.g., Eysenck, 1967), but this research has been limited until recently. Modern imaging techniques and recent neuropsychological testing are now being used to explore the neurobiological bases of Extraversion, Agreeableness, Emotional Stability, Conscientiousness, and Openness—the Big Five. The hope is that we will one day be able to say *why* someone shows the personality trait Openness, not just that they show the set of behaviours that are, collectively, called Openness.

In an interesting recent study Deckersbach and colleagues (Deckersbach et al., 2006) examined the association between activity within a number of different brain regions and the personality traits of Extraversion and Neuroticism (one end of the Emotional Stability—Neuroticism dimension, see page 527). Individuals who score high on Extraversion can be described as behaviourally and socially active (see page 525). Those high in Extraversion also report more positive emotions than do those low in Extraversion. A person who scores high in Neuroticism tends to worry, to be rather anxious and apprehensive, and to easily have feelings of guilt (page 526). Using information from the clinical neuropsychology literature to guide their investigation, Deckersbach and colleagues focused on different regions within the frontal cortex, limbic system and midbrain. Normal healthy volunteers completed the NEO Five-Factor Inventory, a commonly used personality inventory designed to assess the Big Five personality factors. To measure brain activity, they measured regional brain glucose metabolism with a PET scan while the participants were awake and alert but not engaged in any specific mental tasks. These researchers found a significant negative correlation between Neuroticism scores and activity within the left insular cortex (an area deep within the temporal lobe) and the left superior temporal gyrus, the top border of the temporal lobe (Figure 12.13). There was a positive correlation between the personality trait Extraversion and areas within the left and the right orbitofrontal cortex of the frontal cortex (Figure 12.13), along the medial, or middle, part of the orbitofrontal cortex. No correlations were found between Extraversion or Neuroticism and activity within the other brain structures that were assessed, including several limbic system structures and other areas of the frontal cortex. That is, NEO scores on the Neuroticism scales were correlated with activity in parts of the temporal lobe (the insular cortex and superior temporal gyrus). The measure of Extraversion was associated with activity within a specific region of the frontal cortex.

Together with exploring the relationship between brain activity and personality factors among normal, healthy individuals, such results have implications for our understanding of personality traits as risk factors for abnormal or dysfunctional behaviour. The medial part of the orbitofrontal cortex and the insular cortex are brain regions that have been associated with several different psychiatric and psychological disorders. For example, the insular cortex, associated with Neuroticism in the study by Deckersbach and colleagues, has been implicated in post-traumatic stress disorder (Liberzon, et al., 1999) and some phobias (Wright et al., 2003). The area of the frontal cortex linked to Extraversion by Deckersbach is believed to play a role in inhibitory functions such as constraining

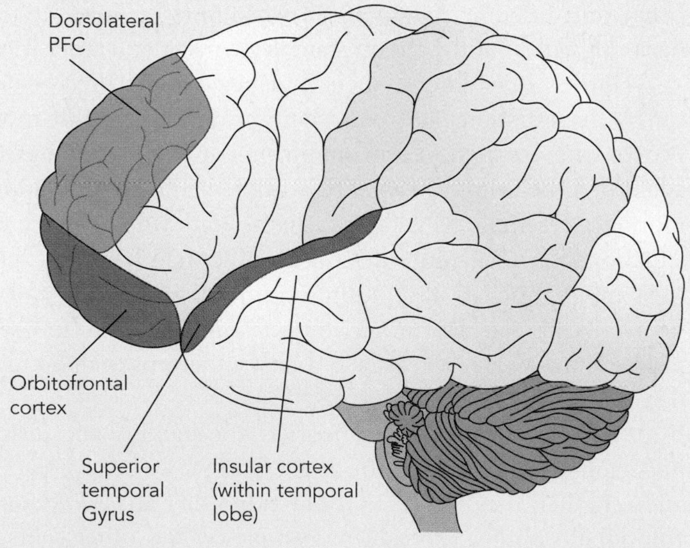

FIGURE 12.13

Activity within the superior temporal gyrus and insular cortex (buried within the temporal lobe) has been associated with the personality trait Neuroticism. The orbitofrontal cortex, especially the medial part, has been linked to Extraversion, and the dorsolateral PFC to Openness.

impulsive acts, including impulsive acts of aggression (Davidson, Putnam & Larson 2000).

Other researchers have examined different members of the Big Five, including Openness, the least understood of the personality traits (see page 527). Colin DeYoung and Jordan Peterson of the University of Toronto together with Daniel Higgins of Harvard University have analyzed the personality trait of Openness using a neuropsychological approach (DeYoung et al., 2005). DeYoung and colleagues argued that Openness includes two key components: "a motivational component, having to do with interest in novelty and complexity, and a cognitive component, having to do with the manner in which information is processed and organized." (DeYoung et al., 2005, p. 828). These considerations suggested an involvement of the prefrontal cortex (PFC), an area of the brain known to be involved in higher cognitive functions and to also be part of a circuit important for motivation, a circuit that links the PFC with structures within the midbrain and the nucleus accumbens of the limbic system (see the discussion of the limbic system and goal-directed behaviour in Chapter 3). Within the PFC, one particular region has been associated with cognitive functions that are consistent with the personality trait Openness. This region of the PFC, the dorsolateral PFC, is involved in functions that allow the conscious manipulation of information when one plans, considers different strategies, deals with complex information, and deals with novelty. There is also evidence linking the dorsolateral PFC with intelligence, and Openness is associated with behaving in an "intellectual" way. Indeed, Openness is sometimes referred to as "Openness/Intellect" (DeYoung et al., 2005). Imaging studies have shown that the dorsolateral PFC is preferentially activated during tasks that require use of general intelligence (Duncan et al., 2000).

DeYoung, Peterson, and Higgins (2005) tested 175 male and female university students on two personality tests designed to assess the Big Five personality traits, a battery of seven separate neuropsychological tests that are associated with dorsolateral PFC function, and two tests of general intelligence. Scores from the seven different tests of PFC function were combined into a single composite PFC score as an index of dorsolateral PFC function. DeYoung and colleagues found that the personality trait Openness correlated significantly with the measure of PFC function and with the measures of intelligence. None of the other Big Five personality traits, including Extraversion, correlated significantly with either the PFC score or the measures of intelligence. Extraversion has been thought to be closely related to Openness and some theorists have argued that Extraversion and Openness together form a higher order trait that has been called Plasticity (see Digman, 1997; DeYoung, Peterson & Higgins, 2002), but these results suggest that the two are separable at the neurobiological level.

The results of the neuropsychological testing done by DeYoung and colleagues indicate that the dorsolateral PFC is one brain region involved in the personality trait Openness, although it is unlikely that a characteristic as rich and complex as Openness is determined by a single brain region, even one as complex as the dorsolateral PFC. These results, however, will help to guide continuing studies of one of the least understood of the Big Five personality factors.

Research associating the Big Five personality factors with activity in specific brain regions, such as the two studies outlined above, is still at its early stages and much is still to be discovered. Early results, however, suggest that each of the main dimensions of personality may have their own brain circuitry. These studies are a critical first step in exploring how individual differences in personality are represented within the brain and will lead to a fuller understanding of how genetic factors, maturation and brain development, experience, and the environment interact to make you, you.

Evaluating the Trait Approach

Despite differences of opinion concerning the nature and number of basic personality dimensions, trait theorists have made an important contribution by focusing attention on the value of identifying, classifying, and measuring stable, enduring personality dispositions. Several challenges confront trait theorists, however. More attention must be paid to how traits interact with one another to affect various behaviours if we are to capture the true complexity of personality (Ahadi & Diener, 1989; Choca et al., 1992; Smith et al., 1990). All too often, researchers try to make specific predictions on the basis of a single measured personality trait without taking into account other personality factors that also might influence the behaviour in question. This approach sells short the complexity of personality.

23. Describe Type A, Type B, and Type C personalities, as well as the risk factors inherent in the Type A and Type C patterns.

In evaluating the trait perspective, we must remember the distinction between description and explanation. To say that someone is outgoing and fun-loving *because* she is high in extraversion is merely to describe the behaviour with a trait name, not to explain the inner disposition and how it operates. Traditionally, the trait perspective has been more concerned with describing the structure of

24. How do differences in optimism-pessimism and conscientiousness relate to health and longevity?

personality, measuring individual differences in personality traits, and predicting behaviour than with understanding the psychological processes that produce the traits (McAdams, 1992). Eysenck's theory of brain arousal is a notable exception, since it attempts to explain the biological bases for behavioural differences produced by extraversion and stability.

The next crucial task for trait theorists is to understand how biological, psychodynamic, cognitive, and environmental factors combine to determine personality, and how these personality dispositions affect behaviour and well-being.

In Review

- *Trait theorists try to identify and measure the basic dimensions of personality. They disagree concerning the number of traits needed to adequately describe personality. Cattell suggested 16 basic traits; other theorists insist that as few as five may be adequate. Eysenck posits three major dimensions, including extraversion and stability. Prediction studies indicate that a larger number of more specific traits may be superior for prediction of behaviour in specific situations.*
- *Traits have not proved to be highly consistent across situations, and they also vary in stability over time. Individuals differ in their self-monitoring tendencies, and this variable influences the amount of cross-situational consistency they exhibit in social situations. Traits interact not only with situations but also with one another, thereby producing inconsistency.*
- *Biological perspectives on traits focus on differences in the nervous system, the contribution of genetic factors, and the possible role of evolution in the development of universal human traits and ways of perceiving behaviour. Introversion-Extraversion, for example, has been linked to a person's level of brain arousal.*
- *Researchers are exploring relations between personality factors and health. Evidence exists for a Type A personality that is a risk factor in coronary heart disease, a Type C cancer-prone pattern, and for the roles of optimism and conscientiousness in promoting health and longevity.*

⊙ SOCIAL COGNITIVE THEORIES

25. How does reciprocal determinism apply to an individual's personality pattern? Specify the two-way causal links.

The psychology of learning has great relevance for understanding personality. Many behaviours ascribed to personality are acquired through classical conditioning, operant conditioning, and modelling (Bandura, 1999). However, the learner is not simply a passive reactor to environmental forces. Instead, as the cognitive perspective tells us, the human is a perceiver, a thinker, and a planner who mentally interprets events, thinks about the past, anticipates the future, and decides how to behave. Whatever effects the environment has are filtered through these cognitive processes and are influenced—even changed—by them. **Social cognitive** theorists such as Julian Rotter (1954, 1966), Albert Bandura (l986, 1999), and Walter Mischel (1973, 1999) have combined the behavioural and cognitive perspectives into an approach to personality that stresses the interaction of a thinking human with a social environment that provides learning experiences.

To understand behaviour, psychodynamic, humanistic, and trait theorists emphasize internal, personal causes of behaviour, such as unconscious conflicts, self-actualization tendencies, and personality traits. In a sense, they account for behaviour from "the inside out." In contrast, radical behaviourists emphasize environmental causes and view humans as reactors to external events (Parker et al., 1998). To them, behaviour is to be explained from "the outside in." Social-cognitive theorists take an intermediate position, focusing on both internal and external factors. They believe that the debate about whether behaviour is more strongly influenced by personal factors or by the person's environment is basically a meaningless one. Instead, according to the social cognitive principle of **reciprocal determinism**

(Bandura, 1978), the person, the person's behaviour, and the environment all influence one another in a pattern of two-way causal links (Figure 12.14).

Julian Rotter: Expectancy, Reinforcement Value, and Locus of Control

In 1954, Julian Rotter (whose name is pronounced like "motor") laid the foundation for today's social cognitive approaches. According to Rotter, the likelihood that we will engage in a particular behaviour in a given situation is influenced by two factors: expectancy and reinforcement value. *Expectancy* is our perception of how likely it is that certain consequences will occur if we engage in a particular behaviour within a specific situation. *Reinforcement value* is basically how much we desire or dread the outcome that we expect the behaviour to produce. Thus a student who strongly values academic success and expects that studying will result in high grades is quite likely to study. Note that this approach makes use of reinforcement, a central behaviourist concept, but views its effects within a cognitive framework that emphasizes how we think about our behaviour and its expected outcomes.

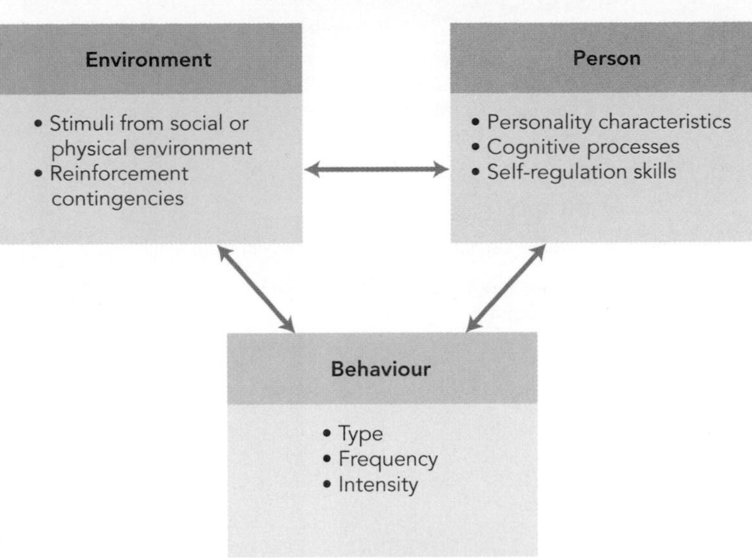

FIGURE 12.14
The social cognitive concept of reciprocal determinism states that the characteristics of the person, the person's be-haviour, and the environment all affect one another in reciprocal, or two-way causal relations.

Locus of Control

One of Rotter's most influential concepts is **internal-external locus of control**, an expectancy concerning the degree of personal control we have in our lives. People with an internal locus of control believe that life outcomes are largely under personal control and depend on their own behaviour (Figure 12.15). In contrast, people with an *external* locus of control believe that their fate has less to do with their own efforts than with the influence of external factors, such as luck, chance, and powerful others. Table 12.7 contains items from Rotter's (1966) Internal-External (I-E) Scale, used to measure individual differences in locus of control.

Locus of control is a highly researched personality variable (Steptoe & Wardle, 2001). Quite consistently, people with an internal locus of control behave in a more self-determined fashion (Burger, 2000). In the 1960s, for example, African-Americans who actively participated in the civil rights movement were more internal on the I-E Scale than were those who did not (Rotter, 1966). Internal university students achieve better grades than do external students of equal academic ability, probably because they link their studying to degree of success and work harder. Internals are more likely to actively seek out the information needed to succeed in a given situation (Ingold, 1989). Interpersonally, internals tend to be independent but co-operative in their dealings with others and are more resistant to social influence, whereas externals tend to give in to high-status people whom they see as powerful others. Internals are more likely than externals to engage in health-promoting behaviours, such as exercising regularly, maintaining a healthy diet, using seat belts, and abstaining from smoking (Steptoe & Wardle, 2001; Wallston, 1993).

Internal locus of control is positively related to self-esteem and feelings of personal effectiveness, and internals tend to cope with stress in a more active and problem-focused manner than do externals (Jennings, 1990). They are also less likely to experience psychological maladjustment in the form of depression or

26. Define Rotter's concepts of expectancy and reinforcement value and explain how they jointly influence behaviour.

27. Describe Rotter's concept of locus of control and how it affects behaviour.

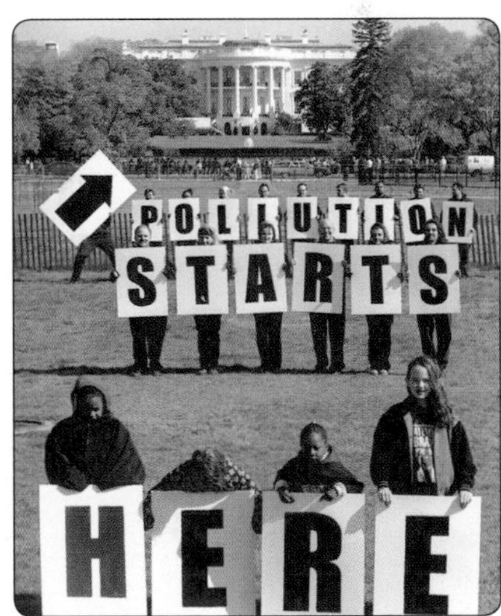

FIGURE 12.15
Research shows that people with an internal locus of control are more likely to take an active role in social change movements.

TABLE 12.7 Sample Items From Rotter's Internal-External Scale

Choose statement a or b

1a. Many times I feel that I have little influence over the things that happen to me.

1b. It is impossible for me to believe that chance or luck plays an important part in my life.

2a. The average citizen can have an influence in government decisions.

2b. The world is run by the few people in power and there isn't much the little guy can do about it.

3a. In the long run, people get the respect they deserve in this world.

3b. Unfortunately, an individual's worth often passes unrecognized no matter how hard one tries.

Note: 1b, 2a, and 3a are the internal alternatives.

Source: Rotter, 1966.

anxiety (Hoffart & Martinson, 1991). Locus of control is called a *generalized expectancy* because it is thought to apply across many life domains as a general world view. Recent research has begun to explore the biological bases of locus of control. De Brabander and Declerck (2004), for example, have reported an association between the neurotransmitter dopamine and locus of control. Their results indicate that increased dopamine metabolism is associated with an external locus of control.

Albert Bandura: Social Learning and Self-Efficacy

Albert Bandura has made major contributions to the development of the social cognitive approach. His early studies of modelling, described in Chapter 7, helped to meld the psychology of learning with the cognitive perspective. Bandura's social learning analyses of aggression, moral behaviour, and behavioural self-control demonstrated the wide applicability of the social cognitive approach (Bandura, 1973, 1988, 1991). His concept of human agency is central to the Social Cognitive Perspective (see the Research Foundations insert on p. 535 in this chapter). Perhaps his most influential contribution, however, is his theory and research on the development of self-efficacy.

Self-Efficacy

28. Define self-efficacy. What four sources of information influence efficacy beliefs?

According to Bandura (1997), a key factor in the way people regulate their lives is their sense of **self-efficacy**, their beliefs concerning their ability to perform the behaviours needed to achieve desired outcomes. People whose self-efficacy is high have confidence in their ability to do what it takes to overcome obstacles and achieve their goals.

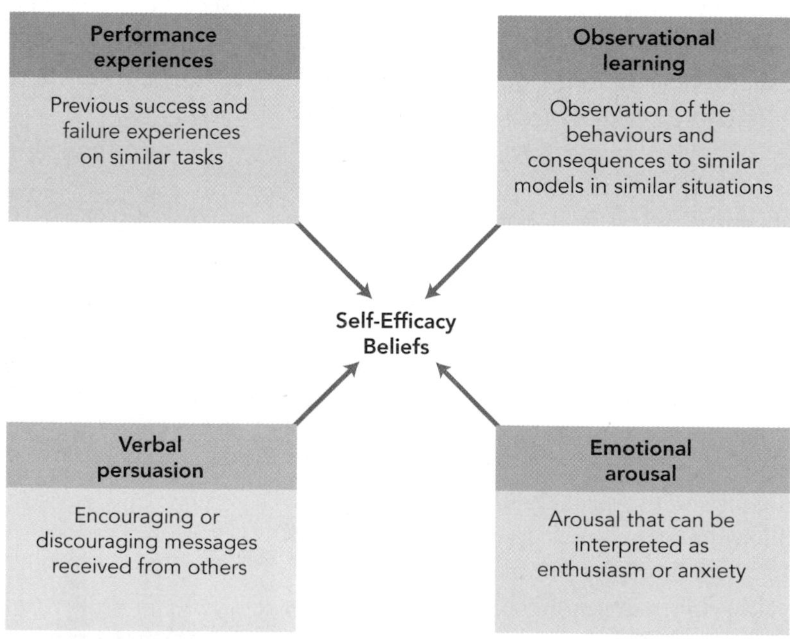

FIGURE 12.16

Four classes of information that affect self-efficacy beliefs.

After Bandura, 1997.

A good deal of research has been done on the factors that create differences in self-efficacy (Figure 12.16). Four important determinants have been identified (Bandura, 1997; Maddux, 1999). The most important is our previous *performance attainments* in similar situations. Such experiences shape our beliefs about our capabilities. For example, as shown in Figure 12.17, university women who felt that they had mastered the martial arts and emotional control skills taught in a physical self-defence training program showed dramatic increases in their belief that they could escape from or disable a potential assailant or rapist (Weitlauf et al., 2000). Bandura stresses that self-efficacy beliefs are always specific to particular situations. Thus we may have high self-efficacy in some situations and low self-efficacy in others. For example, the women who mastered the physical self-defence skills did not feel more generally capable in all areas of their lives, despite their enhanced self-defence efficacy.

A second source of information comes from *observational learning*—that is, observing others' behaviours and their outcomes. If you observe a person similar to

(a)

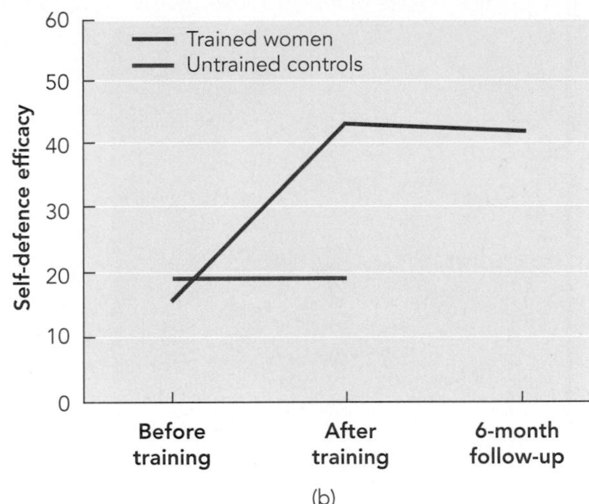

(b)

FIGURE 12.17

Physical self-defence training (a) has dramatic effects on women's self-efficacy to perform the behaviours needed to defend themselves (b). The physical defence self-efficacy scores in this study could extend from 6 to 60.

Based on data from Weitlauf et al., 2000.

yourself accomplish a particular goal, then you are likely to believe that if you perform those same behaviours, you will also succeed. A striking example of how powerful such expectations can be comes from the world of sports. At one time, physiologists insisted that it was physically impossible for a human being to run a mile in less than four minutes, and no one in the history of track and field had ever done it. When the Englishman Roger Bannister broke the four-minute barrier in 1954, that limiting belief was shattered. The impact on other runners' performance was immediate and dramatic. In the year following Bannister's accomplishment, 37 other runners broke the barrier, and the year after that, nearly 300 runners did the "impossible." Apparently, a great many people came to believe that "if he can do it, so can I."

RESEARCH FOUNDATIONS

Albert Bandura, Human Agency, and the Social Cognitive Perspective

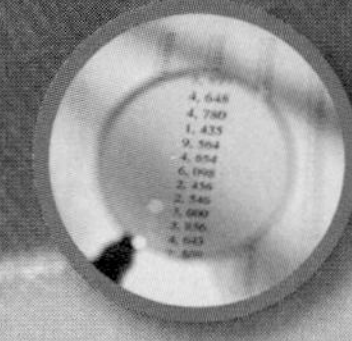

Albert Bandura's research and theory has been critical in establishing, popularizing, and expanding the Social Cognitive Perspective in psychology. His research is known as rigorous and creative, his theoretical writing as clear, carefully argued and based on a solid empirical foundation. Albert Bandura (Figure 12.18) is widely considered one of the most influential of all psychologists and was selected as the most influential psychologist of the modern era by the American Psychological Association. These are lofty heights for someone born in the small northern Alberta town of Mundare (population 715). Bandura received his undergraduate degree from the University of British Columbia and his graduate training at the University of Iowa. In 1953 he joined the faculty of Stanford University in California and he has spent his academic career there.

Bandura laid much of the foundation of the Social Cognitive perspective and his research and theories about human agency, self-efficacy (see pages 534 and 535), observational learning (see Chapter 7), and reciprocal determinism (page 533) continue to be widely influential. Bandura began his career when behaviourism was the dominant perspective in psychology. He argued, however, that our behaviour is not controlled simply by stimuli in our environment and the immediate consequences of our behaviour. Bandura wrote, "If actions were performed only on behalf of anticipated external rewards and punishments, people would behave like weather vanes, constantly shifting direction to conform to whatever influence happened to impinge upon them at the moment" (Bandura, 2001, p. 7).

A concept central to Bandura's work, and to Social Cognitive theory, is the idea of human agency, that humans are active agents in their own lives and are self-reflective and self-regulatory. Human agency is a process, not a trait or

–Continued

FIGURE 12.18
The research and theories of Albert Bandura have been instrumental in establishing the Social Cognitive perspective in psychology.

characteristic, and includes four aspects: intentionality, forethought, self-reactiveness, and self-reflectiveness. By intentionality, Bandura argued that we plan, modify our plans, and act with intention. We also show forethought; we anticipate outcomes, set goals, and actively choose behaviours relevant to those goals. Self-reactiveness refers to the process of motivating and regulating our own actions, the processes that we use when we modify our goals, monitor our progress towards those goals, and, when necessary, change strategies. With self-reflectiveness we think about and evaluate our own motivations, values, and goals, (Bandura, 2001).

In a classic study that laid some of the early foundation for Bandura's agentic perspective (and was important for his work on observational learning), Bandura and Carol Kupers tested seven- to nine-year old children in a bowling game (Bandura & Kupers, 1964). Each child could reward him- or herself with candy (M&Ms) for their performance in the bowling game, and it was left to the child to decide when and how much candy he or she should receive. Before their turn at the bowling game, some of the children watched an adult or another nine-year-old bowl and reward themselves verbally and with candy for their performance. The models differed in the standard that they used to determine if they should reward themselves or not. Some children watched a model who made positive statements about self and took candy only when they scored 20 points or more out of a possible 30 points. Other children saw a model take candy as a reward for scores as low as 10 points. The children were then allowed to bowl, and reward themselves when they thought it appropriate. Scoring of the bowling game was fixed so that all of the children achieved the same pattern of scores across the different bowling attempts. There was one group of children in a control condition and they bowled and rewarded themselves without the experience of first watching a model. One might expect that offering children candy and the authority to determine when they should take candy would result in the children obtaining as much of the candy as possible. I can picture a child rolling the bowling ball and, before it even strikes the pins, taking a handful of M&Ms from the candy bowl. But that was not how the children behaved.

If the children saw an adult or peer model, the criteria used by the model had a powerful impact on the child's own criteria for self-reinforcement (Figure 12.19). Children who saw a model with a high performance standard themselves adopted a more stringent performance criterion for self-reinforcement than did the children who watched a model with a low standard. Children in the control condition took candy independently of their performance in the bowling game. Based on these findings Bandura and Kupers argued that although externally applied reinforcements are clearly important, self-administered reinforcement and punishment may be particularly important in governing behaviour. In the bowling experiment children could set any criteria they wanted, but they adopted a criterion that they had observed and applied it to their own behaviour, even if doing so meant that they received less candy.

Bandura and Kupers wrote, "people typically make self-reinforcement contingent on their performing certain classes of responses which they have come to value as an index of personal merit. They often set themselves relatively explicit criteria of achievement, failure to meet which is considered undeserving of self-reward and may elicit self-denial or even

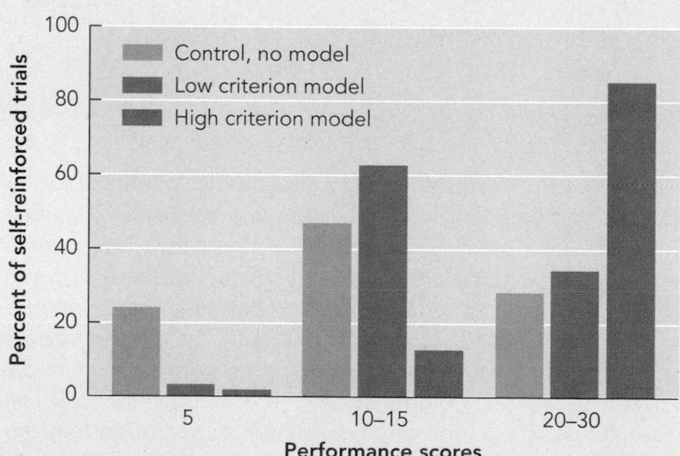

FIGURE 12.19
Percentage of trials in which children took candy as a reward for their performance in a bowling game. Children who previously watched a model with a high criterion for self-reinforcement only rewarded themselves for similarly high levels of performance (highest score obtained was 30 points). Children who had watched a model with a lower criterion for self-reward reinforced themselves for lower levels of performance. Adapted from Bandura and Kupers, 1964.

self-punitive responses; on the other hand, they tend to reward themselves generously on those occasions when they attain their self-imposed standards" (Bandura & Kupers, 1964, p. 1). If you think about this I am sure that you can identify examples from your own life. All of us have had occasions when we met our goal on a test, exam, or other challenge and followed this success with a night off from working, buying ourselves a treat, or some other act of self-reinforcement. We have also had the experience of not meeting our performance standard and so not self-reinforcing. Indeed when we fail to meet our own self-imposed standards we may engage in some self-punitive behaviour such as negative verbal comments about self or denying ourselves an activity ("I didn't do well enough on that test to allow myself a camping trip/shopping trip/movie night/party this weekend").

Children not only adopt performance criteria that they have seen modelled, but models can also influence a particularly difficult decision: forgoing a reward that is available now for a larger reward that will be available at some time in the future. Bandura and Walter Mischel, his colleague at Stanford, found that children would sacrifice a small immediately available reward in favour of a delayed but more valuable reward if they saw a model behave in this way (Bandura & Mischel, 1965). That is, behaviour was controlled not by the immediacy of a reward in front of the child but by the behaviour they saw modelled by others, even when that meant delaying reward to a future time. These early studies of the social origins of a child's self-motivation and self-regulation provided new and experimentally testable alternatives to older conditioning explanations, explanations based on the subconscious, and to personality trait theories.

If a child is going to adopt specific performance criteria, even when doing so means less reward, and is willing to sacrifice an immediate reward for a better reward sometime in the future, that child is acting in accordance with the concept of human agency as outlined by Bandura. Bandura has argued that much of our behaviour, and especially our social behaviour, is guided by the process of human agency, not by the learning phenomenon explored by Pavlov, Watson, and Skinner, not by the repressed urges of a Freudian subconscious, and not by personality type or trait. We plan, act with intention, anticipate outcomes, set goals, actively choose behaviours, and regulate our own actions. How we engage in these processes is set in part by our learning history, including past models, and by our reciprocal interactions with others in our environment.

Third, self-efficacy can be increased or decreased by *verbal persuasion*. The messages we get from other people who affirm our abilities or downgrade them affect our efficacy beliefs. Thus inspirational teachers who convey high standards and a "you can do it" conviction can inspire their students to great accomplishments.

Finally, high *emotional arousal* that is interpreted as anxiety or fatigue tends to decrease self-efficacy. On the other hand, if we find ourselves able to control negative arousal, it may enhance efficacy beliefs and subsequent performance. For example, test-anxious students who mastered relaxation skills showed increases in their belief that they could remain relaxed and focused during tests, and their performance on tests increased as well (Smith, 1989).

Efficacy beliefs are strong predictors of future performance and accomplishment (Bandura, 1997). They become a kind of self-fulfilling prophesy. In the words of Henry Ford, "Whether you believe you can do something or you believe you can't, you're probably right."

29. Summarize six principles of effective goal setting.

PSYCHOLOGICAL APPLICATIONS

Increasing Self-Efficacy through Systematic Goal Setting

Because positive self-efficacy beliefs are consistently related to success in behaving effectively and achieving goals, Bandura and other social cognitive theorists have been strongly interested in practical measures for enhancing self-efficacy. When people are successful and when they attribute their success to their own competencies (internal locus of control), their self-efficacy increases and assists them in subsequent

–Continued

goal-directed efforts (Maddux, 1999). Moreover, successful people usually have mastered the skills involved in setting challenging and realistic goals, figuring out what they need to do on a day-by-day basis to achieve them, and making the commitment to do what is required. As they achieve each goal they have set, they become more skilful and increase their sense of personal efficacy (Bandura, 1997).

Not all goal-setting procedures are created equal, and it is important to apply the principles that make goal-setting programs most effective (Locke & Latham, 1990). Here are some research-derived guidelines for effective goal setting:

1. **Set specific, behavioural, and measurable goals.** The first step in changing some aspect of your life is to set a goal. The kind of goal you set is very important, because certain kinds of goals encourage us to work harder, enjoy success, and increase self-efficacy.

   Specific and fairly narrow goals have been shown to be far more effective than general "do your best" goals (Locke & Latham, 1990). A goal such as "improving my tennis game" is less likely to be helpful than "increasing the percentage of serves I put in play by 20 percent." The latter goal refers to a specific behaviour that you can focus on and measure.

   One of the most important aspects of goal setting is systematically measuring progress toward the goal. This was shown in a study by Bandura and Daniel Cervone (1983) in which participants worked on a strenuous bicycle-pedalling task over a number of trials. Two independent variables were manipulated: (a) whether the participants were given specific improvement goals, and (b) whether the participants were given feedback about their performance on the previous trial. A control condition got neither goals nor feedback and provided a basis for evaluating the effects of goals and feedback, alone or in combination. The dependent variable was the speed and power with which the participants pedalled.

   As shown in Figure 12.20, simply having goals was not enough, nor was feedback effective by itself. The participants who had both goals and feedback showed by far the greatest improvement. This shows how important it is to find a way to measure your progress toward the goal so that you get performance feedback and can see your improvement. Visible movement toward realistic goals builds self-efficacy.

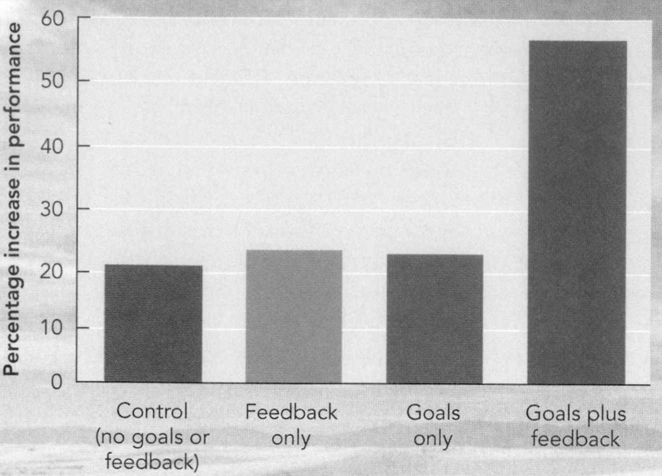

FIGURE 12.20

The effects of improvement goals and performance feedback on performance improvement on a grueling bicycling task. Clearly, the combination of explicit goals and performance feedback resulted in the greatest improvement in performance.

Data from Bandura & Cervone, 1983.

2. **Set performance, not outcome, goals.** Many of our goals relate to outcomes in the future, such as "getting an A in this course." You are more likely to achieve such goals if you use the means-ends heuristic discussed in Chapter 9 and think about the specific things you must do to achieve that outcome goal. Performance goals (what one has to do) work better than outcome goals because they keep the focus on the necessary behaviours. A performance goal might be "read the book and outline the lecture notes for one hour each day." Achieving this performance goal can also be measured quickly and repeatedly, giving you constant feedback. Many people focus on outcome goals and forget what has to be done on a day-to-day basis to achieve them. It has been said that there are three kinds of people in this world: those who make things happen, those who wait for things to happen, and those who wonder what happened. Make sure you're someone who makes things happen.
3. **Set difficult but realistic goals.** Moderately difficult goals challenge and motivate us and give us a sense of hope. When reached, they increase self-efficacy. Easy goals do not provide a sense of accomplishment, and extremely difficult goals do not provide the success experiences you need to increase self-efficacy.
4. **Set positive, not negative, goals.** Chapter 7 discussed the advantages of positive reinforcement over punishment. Working toward positive goals, such as "getting a B," is better than avoiding a negative consequence, as in "not flunking." Again, positive goals keep you focused on the positive steps that you need to take to achieve them.
5. **Set short-range as well as long-term goals.** Short-range goals are important because they provide the opportunity for immediate mastery experiences, and they keep you working positively. A long-term goal such as "graduating with honours" can easily be broken into a series of subgoals that you can be working toward right now. Short-term goals are like the steps on a staircase leading to the long-term goal. As they are accomplished, they not only provide mastery experiences but

also lead you toward your ultimate goal. In reaching any goal, "divide and conquer" is a cliché that works.

6. **Set definite time spans for achievement.** It is said that the road to hell is paved with good intentions. To keep a goal-setting program on track, it is important to specify the dates by which specific performance goals or subgoals will be met, together with the behaviours needed to attain them in that time span.

Goal setting is a motivational technique that has resulted in remarkable improvement in productivity in many work, social, and academic settings (Locke & Latham, 1990). Moreover, for purposes of increasing self-efficacy, it has the added advantage of providing the repeated mastery experiences that are the most powerful sources of efficacy information.

Evaluating Social Cognitive Theories

A strength of the social-cognitive approach is its strong scientific base. It brings together two perspectives, the behavioural and the cognitive, that have strong research traditions. The constructs of social cognitive theory can be defined, measured, and researched with considerable precision. As a result, the social cognitive approach has advanced our understanding of how processes within the person and characteristics of the situation interact with one another to influence behaviour. Another strength is its ability to translate insights derived from other perspectives into cognitive-behavioural concepts (Carver & Scheier, 2000; Mischel et al., 2004).

Social cognitive theory also helps resolve an apparent contradiction between the central assumption that personality produces stability in behaviour and research findings that people's behaviour is not very consistent across different situations. Social cognitive theory suggests that the inconsistency of a person's behaviour across situations is actually a manifestation of a stable underlying cognitive-affective personality structure that reacts to certain features of situations.

We have seen that the various perspectives focus on different determinants of personality. Figure 12.21 summarizes the determinants stressed by the various theories at the biological, psychological, and environmental levels of analysis.

Level of Analysis

Biological	Psychological	Environmental
• Personality differences shaped by evolutionary factors (evolutionary personality theory) • Genetic bases for individual differences and temperament (behaviour genetics) • Individual differences in customary level of cortical arousal and suddenness with which autonomic shifts occur (Eysenck)	• Psychodynamic processes involving impulse, defence, unconscious conflicts, and psychosexual factors (Freud) • Processes involving the self-concept and striving for self-actualization (Rogers) • Personality dispositions to act, think, and feel in particular ways (trait theorists) • Cognitive social learning variables that interact with situational factors (Bandura, Rotter)	• Early psychosexual learning experiences (psychodynamic theories) • Environmental factors that support or stifle self-actualization (humanistic theorists) • Past social learning experiences and current environmental factors that interact with social cognitive person variables (social cognitive theorists)

→ **Personality Differences**

FIGURE 12.21

Understanding the causes of behaviour: personality differences.

In Review

- *Social cognitive theories are concerned with how social relationships, learning mechanisms, and cognitive processes jointly contribute to behaviour. A key concept is reciprocal determinism, relating to two-way causal relations between personal characteristics, behaviour, and the environment.*
- *Rotter's theory viewed behaviour as influenced by expectancies and the reinforcement value of potential outcomes. His concept of locus of control is a generalized belief in the extent to which we can control the outcomes in our life.*
- *Bandura's concept of self-efficacy relates to our self-perceived ability to carry out the behaviours necessary to achieve goals in a particular situation.*

PERSONALITY ASSESSMENT

30. Cite six methods that can be used to measure personality variables.

If we were to introduce you to a woman you have never met and give you one week to provide a complete personality description of her, what would you do?

Chances are, you would seek information in a variety of ways. You might start by interviewing the woman and finding out as much as you could about her. Based on your knowledge of the theories we have discussed, what questions would you ask? Would you ask about early childhood experiences and dreams? About how she sees herself and others? Would you be interested in the kinds of traits embodied in the Big Five or in Eysenck's dimension of Introversion-Extraversion? Would you want to know how the woman customarily feels and responds in various situations? Your answers to these questions and your other assessment decisions would in some sense reflect your own theory of what is important in describing personality.

You probably would not be content simply to interview the woman. You may also decide to interview other people who know her well and get their views of what she is like. You might even ask them to rate her on a variety of traits, such as those found in Cattell's model of personality or in the Five Factor model, and you could ask the person you are studying to rate herself on the same measures to see if her self-concept agrees with how others see her.

Finally, you may decide that it would be useful to actually observe how the woman behaves in a variety of situations. You would want to observe her in such a way that you got as "natural" and characteristic a sample of her behaviour as possible. This information, together with that obtained from the person and from those who know her best, may provide a reasonable basis for a personality description.

Figure 12.22 shows the major methods that psychologists use to assess personality characteristics. As you can see, they use some of the same methods you might have chosen: the interview; trait ratings and behaviour reports; and behavioural assessment, or direct observation and measurement of the person's behaviour. In addition, they have developed several types of psychological tests, including objective self-report measures and "projective" tests that ask respondents to interpret ambiguous stimuli, such as inkblots or pictures. Finally, physiological measures can be used to measure various aspects of personality, such as emotional reactivity or levels of cortical arousal.

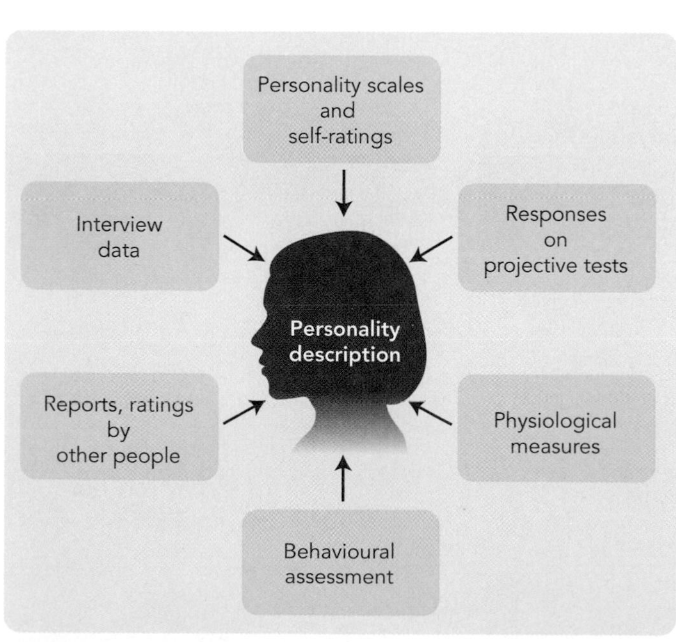

FIGURE 12.22
Measurement approaches used to assess personality.

The task of devising valid and useful personality measures is anything but simple, and it has taxed the ingenuity of psychologists for nearly a century. To be useful from either a scientific or a practical perspective, personality tests must conform to the standards of reliability and validity discussed in Chapter 9. *Reliability*, or consistency of measurement, takes several forms. A test that measures a stable personality trait should yield similar scores when administered to the same individuals at different times (test-retest reliability). Another aspect of reliability is that different professionals should score and interpret the test in the same way (interjudge or inter-rater reliability). *Validity* refers to the most important question of all: Is the test actually measuring the personality variable that it is intended to measure? A valid test allows us to predict behaviour that is influenced by the personality variable being measured. Research on test reliability and validity is an important activity of personality psychologists, and good measures of personality are an absolute must for scientific research on personality and for ethical clinical application (Domino & Domino, 2006).

Interviews

Interviews are one of the oldest methods of assessment. Long before the invention of writing, people undoubtedly made judgments about others by observing them and talking with them. Interviewers can obtain information about a person's thoughts, feelings, and other internal states, as well as information about current and past relationships, experiences, and behaviour.

31. What is a structured interview? What are its advantages over informal approaches?

Structured interviews, frequently used to collect research data or to make a psychiatric diagnosis, contain a set of specific questions that are administered to every participant. An attempt is made to create a standardized situation so that interviewees' responses to more-or-less identical stimuli can be interpreted and compared.

Good interviewers do not limit their attention to what an interviewee says; they also look at how she or he says it. They note interviewees' general appearance and grooming, their voice and speech patterns, the content of their statements, and their facial expressions and posture. Sometimes, attitudes that are not expressed verbally can be inferred from behaviour, as in this instance:

> During the interview she held her small son on her lap. The child began to play with his genitals. The mother, without looking directly at the child, moved his hand away and held it securely for a while. . . . Later in the interview the mother was asked what she ordinarily did when the child masturbated. She replied that he never did this—he was a very "good" boy. She was evidently entirely unconscious of what had transpired in the very presence of the interviewer. (Maccoby & Maccoby, 1954, p. 484)

The interview is valuable for the direct personal contact it provides, but it has some limitations. First, characteristics of the interviewer may affect how the person responds in ways that can affect the validity of the information. The validity of information obtained in an interview also depends on the interviewee's desire to co-operate, to respond honestly, and to report accurately what the interviewer is trying to assess. Some interview data may be valid, others invalid.

Despite its limitations, the face-to-face interview is essential for certain purposes. A clinical psychologist needs to observe and converse with someone who is being considered for admission to a mental hospital. Interviews are often used in research.

Behavioural Assessment

32. How are behavioural assessments designed, and what three questions are they designed to answer?

Personality psychologists sometimes can observe the behaviours they are interested in rather than asking people about them. In **behavioural assessment**, psychologists devise an explicit coding system that contains the behavioural categories of

FIGURE 12.23

In remote behaviour sampling, a computerized device resembling a cell phone is used to collect responses from participants—such as ratings of their mood at a certain time—as they live their daily lives.

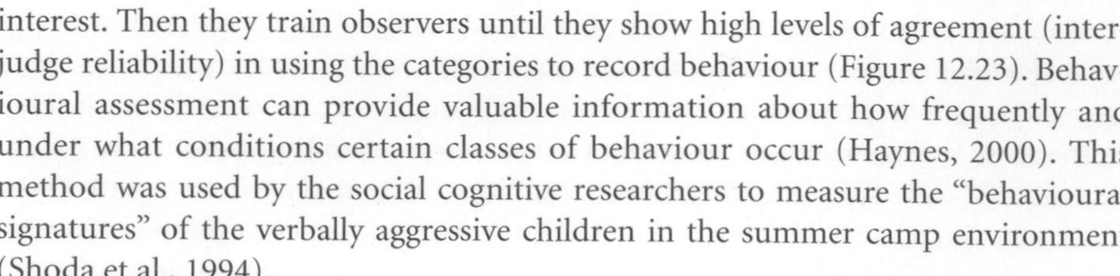

interest. Then they train observers until they show high levels of agreement (interjudge reliability) in using the categories to record behaviour (Figure 12.23). Behavioural assessment can provide valuable information about how frequently and under what conditions certain classes of behaviour occur (Haynes, 2000). This method was used by the social cognitive researchers to measure the "behavioural signatures" of the verbally aggressive children in the summer camp environment (Shoda et al., 1994).

Behavioural assessment requires precision in defining the behaviours of interest and the conditions under which they occur. For example, observers studying a young child who is having problems in school do not simply say "Jerry is disruptive." Instead, they try to answer the question, "What, specifically, does Jerry do that causes disruption?" Once they have identified Jerry's specific behaviours, the next questions are, "How often and under what conditions does the disruptive behaviour occur?" and "What kinds of outcomes do the behaviours produce?" Answers to these questions can be particularly important, not only in measuring differences in people's personality characteristics, but also in identifying potential situational causes of their behaviour (Greene & Ollendick, 2000).

Remote Behaviour Sampling

33. Describe remote behavioural sampling procedures and the types of reports that can be collected.

It is not practical or possible for behavioural assessors to follow people around from situation to situation on a daily basis. In addition, assessors are frequently interested in unobservable events, such as emotional reactions and thinking patterns, that may shed considerable light on personality functioning. Through **remote behaviour sampling**, researchers and clinicians can collect samples of behaviour from respondents as they live their daily lives. A tiny computerized device carried by respondents pages them at randomly determined times of the day. When the "beeper" sounds, respondents record their current thoughts, feelings, or behaviours, depending on what the researcher or therapist is assessing (Csikszentmihalyi, 1990; Singer, 1988; Stone et al., 2000). Respondents also may report on the kind of situation they are in so that situation-behaviour interactions can be examined. The data can either be stored in the computer or transmitted directly to the assessor.

Remote sampling procedures can be used over weeks or even months to collect a large behaviour sample across many situations. This approach to personality assessment holds great promise, since it enables researchers and clinicians to detect patterns of personal functioning that might not be revealed by other methods.

Personality Scales

Personality scales, or inventories, are widely used for assessing personality in both research and clinical work. Personality scales are termed *objective* measures because they include standard sets of questions, usually in a true-false or rating scale format, that are scored using an agreed-upon scoring key (Nezami & Butcher, 2000). Their advantages include the ability to collect data from many people at the same time, the fact that all people respond to the same items, and ease of scoring. Their major disadvantage is the possibility that some people will choose not to answer the items truthfully, in which case their scores will not be valid reflections of the trait being measured. To combat this threat to validity, some widely used tests have special *validity scales* that detect tendencies to respond in a socially desirable manner or to present an overly negative image of oneself.

34. Contrast the rational and empirical approaches to personality test development. Give an example of a test developed by each approach.

The items on personality scales are developed in two major ways. In the **rational approach**, items are based on the theorist's conception of the personality trait to be measured. For example, to develop a measure of introversion-extraversion, we might ask ourselves what introverts and extraverts would be likely to say about themselves, then write items that capture those kinds of self-descriptions (e.g., "I love to be at large social gatherings" or "I'm very content to spend time by myself"). One frequently used measure developed using the rational approach is the NEO-PI, which measures the Big Five personality traits of Openness, Conscientiousness, Extraversion, Agreeableness, and Neuroticism (Costa & McCrae, 1992).

In a second approach to personality test development, known as the **empirical approach,** items are chosen not because their content seems relevant to the trait on rational grounds, but because previous research has shown that the items were answered differently by groups of people known to differ in the personality characteristic of interest. The empirical approach was used to develop the **Minnesota Multiphasic Personality Inventory** (**MMPI**; Hathaway & McKinley, 1983), the most widely used personality inventory. Developed in the 1940s, the MMPI was originally designed to provide an objective basis for psychiatric diagnosis. Its 567 true-false items consist of statements that were answered differently by groups of patients who were diagnosed as having specific psychiatric disorders (e.g., hysteria, paranoia, and schizophrenia) than they were by a non-psychiatric comparison sample of "normal" people. The items vary widely in content; some are concerned with attitudes and emotions, others relate to overt behaviour and symptoms, and still others refer to the person's life history.

The revised MMPI-2, like the original, has ten clinical scales and three validity scales (Table 12.8). The validity scales are used to detect tendencies to present either an overly positive picture or to exaggerate the degree of psychological disturbance. The clinical scales were originally intended to measure severe personality deviations such as schizophrenia, depression, and psychopathic personality, and they do. In addition, however, the pattern or *configuration* of scores obtained on the various scales also reveals important aspects of personality functioning in people

TABLE 12.8 **The Validity and Clinical Scales of the Minnesota Multiphasic Personality Inventory-2 (MMPI-2) and the Behavioural Characteristics Associated with High Scores on the Scales.**

Scale	Abbreviation	Behavioural Correlates
Validity scales		
Lie	L	Lies or is highly conventional
Frequency	F	Exaggerates complaints, answers haphazardly
Correction	K	Denies problems
Clinical scales		
Hypochondriasis	Hs	Expresses bodily concerns and complaints
Depression	D	Is depressed, pessimistic, guilty
Hysteria	Hy	Reacts to stress with physical symptoms, lacks insight into negative feelings
Psychopathic Deviate	Pd	Is impulsive, in conflict with the law, involved in stormy relationships
Masculinity-Femininity	Mf	Has interests characteristic of the opposite sex
Paranoia	Pa	Is suspicious, resentful
Psychasthenia	Pt	Is anxious, worried, high-strung
Schizophrenia	Sc	Is confused, disorganized, disoriented, and withdrawing from others
Hypomania	Ma	Is energetic, active, restless
Social Introversion	Si	Is introverted, with little social contact

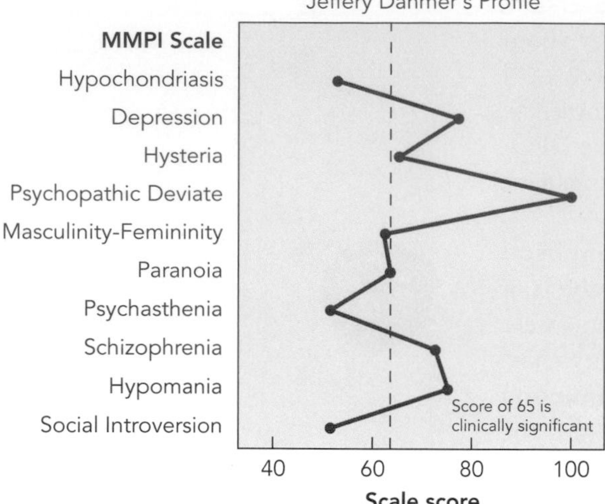

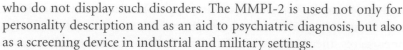

FIGURE 12.24

The MMPI profile of convicted mass murderer Jeffrey Dahmer reflects his severe psychological disturbance and is consistent with his pattern of unrestrained and vicious victimization of others. Scores greater than the dotted line are considered clinically significant.

Caldwell Report, 1994.

who do not display such disorders. The MMPI-2 is used not only for personality description and as an aid to psychiatric diagnosis, but also as a screening device in industrial and military settings.

Responses on the MMPI-2 are scored and then plotted on a graph, or profile sheet, that reflects the degree to which the individual's responses resemble those of the psychiatric groups. Figure 12.24 shows the MMPI profile of mass murderer Jeffrey Dahmer, who mutilated and dismembered his victims, sometimes eating their body parts. According to MMPI expert Alex B. Caldwell (1994), several aspects of this profile are consistent with his bizarre and destructive behaviour. The extraordinarily high score on the Psychopathic Deviate scale reflects an extreme anti-social impulsiveness coupled with a total lack of capacity for compassion and empathy. His victims in all likelihood were regarded as little more than objects to satisfy his perverse needs. Caldwell viewed the profile as reflecting Dahmer's sense of being fated or doomed to repeat his acts until he was caught (the high Depression score), together with an absence of fear that, in normal people, might inhibit murderous behaviour [the low Psychasthenia (anxiety) score]. Although the profile clearly indicates his high level of psychological disturbance (a normal score on each scale is 50), it also reflects an ability to mask his pathology and put up the normal facade that for years fooled law enforcement officials.

Projective Tests

35. What is the assumption underlying projective tests? Describe two widely used projective tests.

Freud and other psychodynamic theorists emphasized the importance of unconscious factors in understanding behaviour. By definition, however, people are unaware of unconscious dynamics, so they cannot report them to interviewers or on questionnaires such as the NEO-PI or the MMPI. Therefore other methods were needed to assess them. The assumption underlying **projective tests** is that, when a person is presented with an ambiguous stimulus whose meaning is not clear, the interpretation attached to the stimulus will have to come partly from within. The person's interpretation thus may reflect the "projection" of inner needs, feelings, and ways of viewing the world onto the stimulus.

Rorschach Inkblots

The Rorschach test consists of 10 inkblots. The person being tested is shown each one in succession and asked, "What does this look like? What might it be?" (Figure 12.25). After responding, the person is asked what specific feature of the inkblot (e.g., its shape or its colour) caused it to be seen in that manner. Examiners write down the responses word for word. They also carefully note subjects' behaviour during testing, including gestures, mannerisms, and expressed attitudes. They categorize and score responses in terms of the kinds of objects reported, the features attended to (e.g., the whole blot, coloured portions, tiny details), and the emotional tone associated with particular types of responses (Erdberg, 2000).

Interpretations made by Rorschach examiners are often based on what the responses seem to symbolize. For example, people who see peering eyes and threatening figures in the inkblots are likely to be viewed as projecting their own paranoid fears and suspicions onto the stimuli. A problem is that different examiners may interpret the same response very differently, producing unreliability between examiners. In an attempt to minimize clinician subjectivity in interpreting Rorschach responses, John Exner (Exner & Erdberg, 2005) developed a Comprehensive

System with specific coding categories and scoring criteria. Although this system created greater uniformity in scoring, the usefulness of the test for predicting behaviour is still hotly debated (e.g., Dawes, 1994; Wood, Nezworski, Lilienfield & Garb, 2003). A recent meta-analysis, however, did find good test-retest stability when the Comprehensive System scoring was used (Gronnerod, 2003), and others, such as the University of Windsor's Stephen Hibbard, have presented evidence that the Rorschach is clinically useful (Hibbard, 2003). Many psychodynamic clinicians maintain their faith in the usefulness of the Rorschach, insisting that they find it useful for gaining insight into unconscious processes.

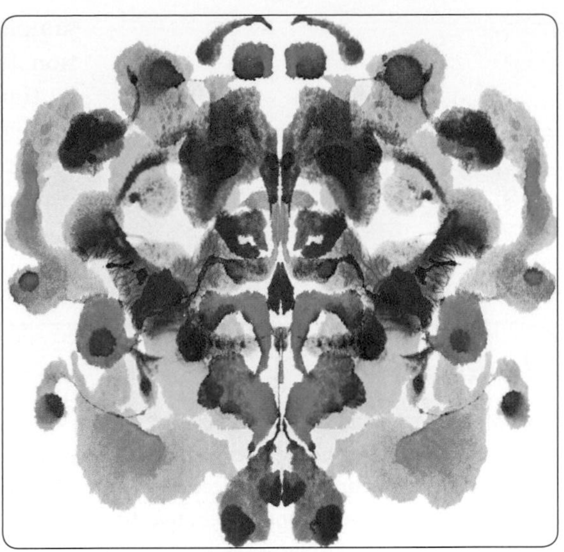

FIGURE 12.25

During a Rorschach test administration, the person being tested is shown a series of inkblots similar to this one and is asked to indicate what each resembles and what feature of the stimulus (for example, its shape or its colour) makes it appear that way.

Thematic Apperception Test

The Thematic Apperception Test (TAT) consists of a series of pictures derived from paintings, drawings, and magazine illustrations. Although the pictures are more ambiguous than most photographs (Figure 12.26), they are less ambiguous than the Rorschach inkblots. Respondents are asked to describe what is going on in each scene, what has led up to the current situation, what the characters are thinking and feeling, and what the outcome of the situation will be. The stories are analyzed for recurrent themes that are assumed to reflect important aspects of the respondent's personality. These might include the kinds of relationships depicted in the stories, the types of motives and feelings that are attributed to the characters, whether positive or negative outcomes occur, and factors that produce such outcomes, such as personal weakness or forces in the environment.

The TAT, like the Rorschach, has the problem of non-standardized or subjective interpretation of responses, which can result in different interpretations of the same stories. Since not everyone can be right, the possibility of erroneous interpretations is obvious. Stephen Hibbard (Hibbard, 2003) and others (e.g., Atkinson, 1958) have found that, where specific systems have been developed to score stories, the TAT has proven to be a useful and valid test. As discussed in Chapter 10, this method is used by researchers to measure motivational variables such as the needs for achievement, affiliation, and power. The TAT appears to provide a more valid measure of these needs than do objective self-report measures of the same motives, showing stronger relations with motivated behaviour (Ferguson, 2000; McClelland, 1988). Despite such exceptions, however, objective measures of personality have generally been found to have better reliability and validity than projective measures (Nezami & Butcher, 2000; Groth-Marnat, 2003).

FIGURE 12.26

A picture from the Thematic Apperception Test. Subjects are asked to make up a story about the picture, covering specific questions such as those listed in the text. These stories are analyzed for recurrent themes that are assumed to reflect significant aspects of personality.

Personality Theory and Personality Assessment

Personality assessment is intimately related to theory. Theories provide us with a framework that specifies how thoughts, feelings, and bodily processes relate to one another and to behaviour. Assessment provides tools for measuring personality variables and testing the theory. A clinician's or researcher's theoretical perspective therefore influences which assessment approach he or she is likely to use.

Projective techniques are favoured by psychodynamic theorists who believe that people's responses to tests such as the Rorschach and TAT reveal unconscious processes. Humanistic theorists favour self-report measures of the self-concept and personal aspirations (Wylie, 1989). Social cognitive researchers use behavioural assessments and ask people to rate their expectations about what will happen in the future and how well they will do in particular situations. Remote behaviour

36. What kinds of personality measures are favoured within the various perspectives?

sampling is also useful in studying interactions between the person and the situation. Paper-and-pencil inventories such as the MMPI and the NEO-PI are favoured by trait theorists who want to measure specific personality traits, and by behaviour geneticists who want to estimate genetic contributions to traits through twin or adoption studies. Researchers interested in biological processes that underlie personality functioning, such as emotional reactivity or brain processes, use physiological measures. All of these assessment methods have their place in studying personality and can help illuminate important aspects of individuality.

In Review

- *Methods used by psychologists to assess personality include the interview, behavioural assessment, remote behaviour sampling, physiological measures, objective personality scales, and projective tests.*
- *The major approaches to constructing personality scales are the rational approach, in which items are written on an intuitive basis, and the empirical approach, in which items that discriminate between groups known to differ on the trait of interest are chosen. The MMPI-2 is the best-known test developed with the empirical approach. The NEO-PI, developed via the rational approach, measures individual differences in the Big Five factors.*
- *Projective tests present ambiguous stimuli to subjects. It is assumed that interpretations of such stimuli give clues to important internal processes. The Rorschach inkblot test and the Thematic Apperception Test are the most commonly used projective tests.*

GAINING DIRECTION

What are the issues?

How can you assess personality? We are faced with such assessments in the media all the time—horoscopes are readily available in the daily paper. But how can a horoscope capture personality? For that matter, what is personality anyway? Some theories discuss crisis or decision points required for "proper" development. Others focus on the achievement of developmental goals for particular purposes. Thus, it would seem that personality is the result of interacting with a demanding environment using the resources that nature has given us. But just how does this result in a stable set of characteristics that we call personality? Is it really determined by the stars...or might there be other forces (which we may or may not be aware of) at work?

What do we need to know?

What is personality?
How is personality acquired?
How do we measure personality?
Is there any evidence for consistent personality traits?
What happens when a person fails to develop personality in a "normal" fashion?
Is personality stable across the life span?

Where can you find the information necessary to answer these questions?

Look back at the compass icons in this chapter. There are many theories of personality (e.g., Freud's Psychodynamic theory, Roger's Self theory, the Trait Approach, etc.) and you should be familiar with each of them. What do each of these theories say about "normal" development? How would you explain a particular personality type? Note how we measure personality (e.g., using a scale) and compare this to how a horoscope is constructed. Which method has more validity?

KEY TERMS AND CONCEPTS*

analytic psychology (516)
archetypes (516)
behavioural assessment (541)
conditions of worth (519)
congruence (518)
defence mechanisms (513)
ego (512)
empirical approach (543)
factor analysis (524)
fully functioning persons (519)
gender schema (521)
id (512)
internal-external locus of control (533)
Minnesota Multiphasic Personality Inventory (MMPI) (543)
need for positive regard (519)
need for positive self-regard (519)
object relations theories (516)
personality (510)
pleasure principle (512)
projective tests (544)
psychic energy (512)
rational approach (542)
reality principle (513)
reciprocal determinism (532)
remote behaviour sampling (542)
repression (513)
self (518)
self-actualization (517)
self-consistency (518)
self-efficacy (534)
self-enhancement (521)
self-esteem (519)
self-monitoring (529)
self-verification (520)
social cognitive theory (532)
sublimation (513)
superego (513)
threat (518)
unconditional positive regard (519)

*Each term has been boldfaced in the text on the page indicated in parentheses.

DO YOU WANT TO ELEVATE YOUR GRADES?

For additional resources and interactive quizzing, visit the book's Online Learning Centre at **www.mcgrawhill.ca/olc/passer.**

CHAPTER 13

Psychological Disorders

How come when we talk to God we're praying, but when God talks to us we're schizophrenic?

—Lily Tomlin

CHAPTER OUTLINE

At 9:00 P.M. on the evening of May 30, 1998, Kimberly Brooks and Monique Ishikawa were killed when their car was hit from behind by Julia Campagna. Brooks and Ishikawa were stopped at the Peace Arch border crossing when Campagna's Grand Am crashed into them at a speed estimated to be nearly 160 km/h. Campagna was charged with two counts of dangerous driving causing death, but pleaded not guilty by reason of temporary insanity. She said that she was suffering from psychotic delusions as the result of taking the diet drug Xenadrine. Apparently she thought that her car was an airplane and that she heard the voice of hockey star Joe Nieuwendyk on the radio asking her to speed to Canada and conceive his child. Prosecutors agreed with expert testimony that a temporary psychosis might result from such drugs. The judge found Campagna to be "not criminally responsible by reason of mental illness." Two days later, the judge also ruled that Campagna posed no threat to society and since the psychosis was temporary, she was released from custody.

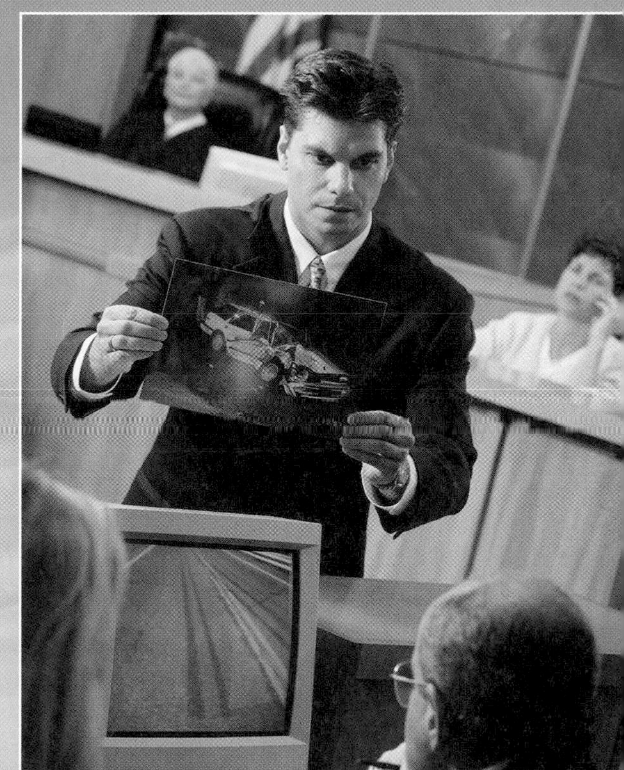

- **What are the issues here?**
- **What do we need to know?**
- **Where can we find the information necessary to answer the questions?**

Mark has been depressed for several years, but things are even worse now. He feels totally inadequate and inferior. The future looks hopeless, and he cannot sleep at night. During the day, he can barely function, and his moods alternate between deadening depression and intense anxiety. A friend has suggested that he seek professional counselling, but Mark is convinced that he has slipped too deeply into the black hole of despair to ever feel good again. He wonders how long he wants to go on living in his private hell.

Sarah was walking across campus the first time it happened. Suddenly, her heart began pounding and skipping beats. She grew weak and shaky, began sweating profusely, and felt an indescribable sense of impending doom. She was sure she was either going to die or become insane on the spot. Gathering all her strength, she made it to her dormitory room and began to feel better. Now, after several such incidents while on campus, she is afraid to leave her dorm.

These people could very well live in your city, on your campus, or in your neighbourhood. In December 1999, a comprehensive report summarizing the results of hundreds of mental health studies (Satcher, 1999) concluded:

- At any given point in time, 22 percent of the population suffers from a diagnosable mental disorder.
- Nearly half of all North Americans between the ages of 15 and 54 will experience a psychological disorder at some time in their lives.
- Psychological disorders are the second leading cause of disability, after heart disease.
- Medications used to treat anxiety and depression are among the most frequently prescribed drugs in North America.
- One adolescent commits suicide every 90 seconds.
- Each year, more than a million students withdraw from university because of emotional problems.
- One in four North Americans will have a substance abuse disorder during his or her lifetime. The loss to North American businesses is over $120 billion annually, much of which stems from the sharp decline in job productivity.

These cold statistics, startling though they may be, cannot possibly capture the intense suffering that they reflect. They cannot communicate the confusion and terror felt by the schizophrenic patient whose psychological world is disintegrating, the intense personal misery of a depressed person who is sinking into a quagmire of hopelessness, or the suffering endured by the families and friends of those who have psychological disorders.

This chapter is therefore not just about the problems of "someone else." Even if you do not at some point in your life experience a psychological disorder, statistics suggest that a family member, friend, or acquaintance almost surely will.

⊙ HISTORICAL PERSPECTIVES ON PSYCHOLOGICAL DISORDERS

The pages of history are filled with accounts of prominent people who suffered from psychological disorders. Tamerlane, the 14th-century Mongol conquerer of much of central Asia and Europe, was particularly fond of building pyramids out of human skulls. One of his creations reportedly contained 40,000 of them. The

FIGURE 13.1

Abraham Lincoln and Winston Churchill suffered from severe depression during their lifetimes. Billionaire Howard Hughes had a debilitating obsessive-compulsive disorder involving fears of contamination that kept him isolated and bedridden for many years.

18th-century French philosopher Jean-Jacques Rousseau developed marked paranoid symptoms in the latter part of his life and was obsessed with fears of secret enemies. During the time he was composing his requiem, Mozart was convinced he was being poisoned. Winston Churchill periodically suffered from severe depression, referring to it as his "black dog" (Figure 13.1).

These dysfunctional behaviours did not go unnoticed. Human society has explained and responded to abnormal behaviour in different ways at different times, based on its values and assumptions about human life and behaviour. At various times, psychological disorders have been viewed as the work of demons, as physical diseases, as the result of psychological conflicts, as learned maladaptive behaviours, and as a product of the ways in which we perceive our world.

The Demonological View

1. Describe the demonological perspective on abnormal behaviour and its implications for dealing with deviant behaviour.

The belief that abnormal behaviour is caused by supernatural forces goes back to the ancient Chinese, Egyptians, and Hebrews, all of whom attributed deviance to the work of the devil. One ancient "treatment" was based on the notion that bizarre behaviour reflected an evil spirit's attempt to escape from a person's body. In order to "release" the spirit, a procedure called *trephination* was carried out. A sharp tool was used to chisel a hole in the skull about two centimetres in diameter (Figure 13.2). It seems likely that in many cases, this procedure did indeed result in the elimination of abnormal behaviours, as well as all others.

In Medieval Europe, the demonological model of abnormality reigned supreme. Religious dogma held that disturbed people either were possessed involuntarily by the devil or had voluntarily made a pact with the forces of darkness (Figure 13.3). The killing of witches was justified on theological grounds, and various "diagnostic" tests were devised. One test was to bind a woman's hands and feet and throw her into a lake or pond. Based on the notion that impurities float to the surface, a woman who sank and drowned was declared pure (which undoubtedly was of great consolation to the victim). Of course, a woman who floated was in *real* trouble. During the sixteenth and seventeenth centuries, it is estimated that more than 100,000 people with psychological disorders were identified as witches, hunted down, and executed.

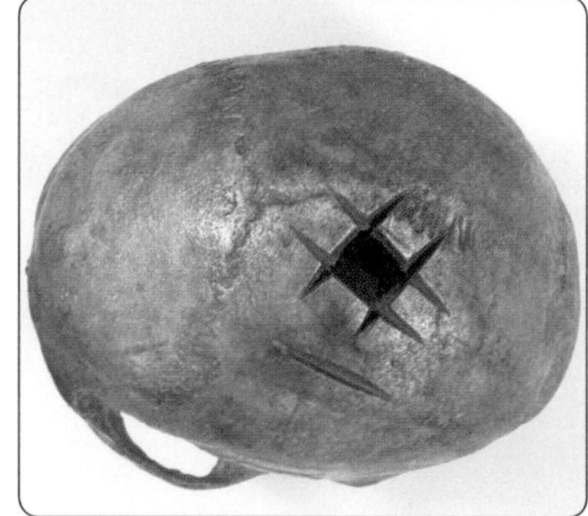

FIGURE 13.2

An early treatment for disordered behaviour was trephination, in which a hole was chiselled through the skull to release the evil spirit thought to be causing the abnormal behaviour. Some people survived the operation but many died from it.

Early Biological Views

About the 5th century B.C., the Greek physician Hippocrates suggested that mental illnesses are diseases just like physical disorders. He insisted that people with

FIGURE 13.3

This painting by Francisco Jose Goya reflects the widespread belief that disordered people were possessed by the devil. Sabbath portrays the weekly gathering of Satan and the witches he possessed.

2. What was the historical importance of discovering the cause of general paresis?

3. What concepts are used by the psychodynamic, behavioural, cognitive, humanistic, and socio-cultural perspectives to explain abnormal behaviour?

disordered behaviour were sick, not possessed by evil spirits. Hippocrates believed that the site of illness was the brain, which he saw as the organ of the mind. Hippocrates was the first to suggest that a mental or behavioural disorder could be caused by a physical dysfunction, a belief that now is reflected in the biological perspective on psychological disorders.

By the 1800s, attempts were being made to extend medical diagnoses to mental disorders, which were increasingly being viewed as biological disorders. The biological emphasis was given impetus by the discovery that *general paresis,* a disorder characterized in its advanced stages by mental deterioration and bizarre behaviour, resulted from massive brain deterioration caused by syphilis. This was a breakthrough, the first demonstration that a psychological disorder was linked to an underlying physical malady.

Psychological Perspectives

In the early 1900s, Sigmund Freud's theory of psychoanalysis emerged as a new way of viewing deviant behaviour. Freud was convinced that psychological disorders are caused by unresolved conflicts from childhood that make the person vulnerable to certain kinds of life events. These situations arouse anxiety, and the person tries to cope with the anxiety by using defence mechanisms such as repression, projection, reaction formation, and displacement. Inappropriate or extreme use of the defence mechanisms results in maladaptive patterns of behaviour. Some disorders, such as obsessions, phobias, and depression that do not involve a loss of contact with reality were called *neuroses.* Freud thought that in some instances, however, the anxiety caused by these unresolved conflicts may become so great that the person can no longer deal with reality and withdraws from it. These more severe disorders, such as schizophrenia, were called *psychoses.*

The behavioural perspective views disordered behaviours not as a reflection of internal psychodynamics and unconscious conflicts, but rather as learned responses that, like normal behaviours, are learned through classical conditioning, operant conditioning, and modelling. The behavioural perspective has profoundly influenced our understanding of how environmental factors help shape abnormal behaviour.

Cognitive theorists emphasize the important role played by people's thoughts and perceptions about themselves and the environment. Aaron Beck and other cognitive researchers have identified maladaptive and self-defeating thought patterns that are linked to a number of different disorders, such as depression and anxiety. From this perspective, the key to understanding many maladaptive behaviours is to isolate the specific thought patterns, beliefs, and attitudes that underlie them.

The humanistic perspective views abnormality as the result of environmental forces that frustrate or pervert people's inherent self-actualization tendencies and search for meaning in life. Conditions of worth imposed by parents and others can result in the development of a negative self-concept and the need to deny or distort important aspects of experience. If experience, including one's inner feelings, becomes so incongruous with the self-concept that it arouses severe threat, a breakdown or disorganization of the self may occur.

In recent years, the socio-cultural perspective has had a major impact on the study of psychological disorders (Lopez & Guarnaccia, 2000; Tanaka-Matsumi & Draguns, 1997). Increasingly, it is apparent that psychological disorders cannot be totally understood without taking into account the cultural context in which they occur and the cultural factors that influence the forms they take. (Lopez, 2002; Kealey, 2005).

Today's Vulnerability-Stress Model

Biological, psychological, and environmental/socio-cultural factors play important roles in the psychological disorders. How these complex factors interact in a given disorder, or even in a particular individual who exhibits that disorder, can vary. One useful way to think about the causal factors is in terms of the relation between vulnerabilities and stress (Figure 13.4). According to the **vulnerability-stress model**, each and every one of us has some degree of vulnerability (ranging from very low to very high) to developing a given psychological disorder. The **vulnerability**, or predisposition, can have a biological basis, such as our genotype, a brain malfunction, or a hormonal factor. It could also arise from a personality factor, such as low self-esteem or extreme pessimism, or from previous environmental factors, such as poverty or a severe trauma or loss earlier in life. Likewise, cultural factors can create vulnerability to certain kinds of disorders (Ingram & Price, 2001).

But vulnerability is only part of the equation. In most instances, a predisposition creates a disorder only when a **stressor**—some recent or current event that requires a person to cope—combines with a vulnerability to trigger the appearance of the disorder (van Praag, 2004). Thus a person who has a genetic predisposition to depression or who suffered a traumatic loss of parents early in life may be primed to develop a depressive disorder *if* faced with the stress of another loss later in life. The biological, psychological, and environmental levels of analysis have all contributed to the vulnerability-stress model and to our understanding of behaviour disorders and how they develop.

Vulnerability factors
- Genetic factors
- Biological characteristics
- Psychological traits
- Previous maladaptive learning
- Low social support

Stressors
- Economic adversity
- Environmental trauma
- Interpersonal stresses or losses
- Occupational setbacks or demands

Current vulnerability | **Currently experienced stress**

Psychological disorders

FIGURE 13.4

The vulnerability-stress model views behaviour disorders as resulting from an interaction between personal vulnerability factors and life stressors. Personal vulnerability factors contribute to maladaptive efforts to cope with life's challenges.

4. How does the vulnerability-stress model illustrate person-situation interactions?

DEFINING AND CLASSIFYING PSYCHOLOGICAL DISORDERS

So far, we have discussed historical and contemporary accounts of abnormal behaviour without actually defining what is meant by the term. Defining what is normal and what is abnormal is not as easy as it may at first appear.

What Is "Abnormal"?

Judgments about where the line between normal and abnormal should be drawn differ depending on the time and the culture. In the 1940s, a woman who decided to forsake marriage and children in favour of a career in engineering would have been seen by many segments of society, including some psychologists and psychiatrists, as deviant and possibly in need of psychotherapy. Today most people would regard the woman's choice as a valid one. In certain Hispanic cultures, a woman who loses a loved one exhibits a range of symptoms that would merit a diagnosis of major depression in the United States. However, in Ecuador, she would be viewed not as psychologically disturbed, but as suffering from *susto,* or "soul loss," a normal bereavement pattern that quickly subsides after a mourning ritual designed to help the person deal with the loss (Goleman, 1995).

Abnormality is, in the final analysis, a social construction (Neimeyer & Raskin, 2000). As such, it can be affected by value judgments and political agendas. In the 1840s, for example, a census commissioned by Senator John Calhoun of South Carolina concluded that 1 in every 14 former slaves in the state of Maine "is either an idiot, or lunatic" (Gamwell & Tomes, 1995). In contrast, the census identified almost

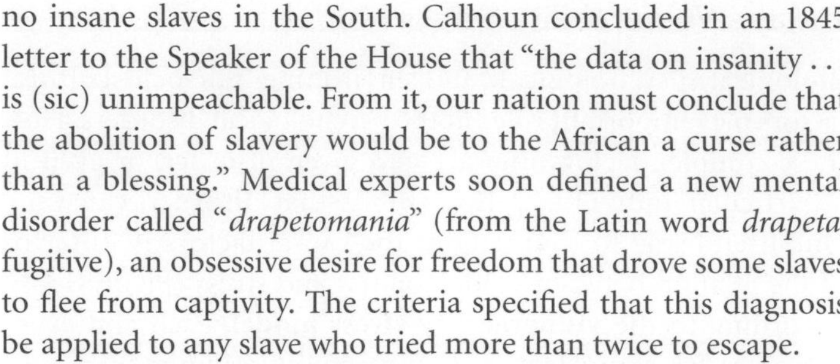

no insane slaves in the South. Calhoun concluded in an 1845 letter to the Speaker of the House that "the data on insanity . . . is (sic) unimpeachable. From it, our nation must conclude that the abolition of slavery would be to the African a curse rather than a blessing." Medical experts soon defined a new mental disorder called "*drapetomania*" (from the Latin word *drapeta,* fugitive), an obsessive desire for freedom that drove some slaves to flee from captivity. The criteria specified that this diagnosis be applied to any slave who tried more than twice to escape.

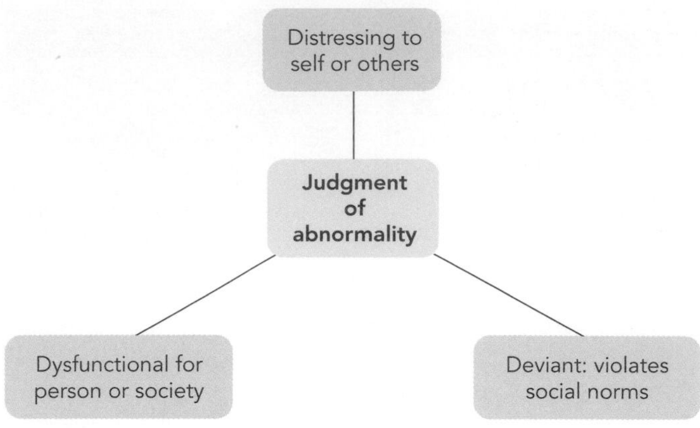

FIGURE 13.5

Whether a behaviour is or is not considered abnormal involves a social judgment made on the basis of the "three Ds."

5. Cite the "three Ds" that typically underlie judgments that behaviour is abnormal.

More recently, a spirited political battle was fought over the proposed inclusion of *self-defeating/masochistic personality disorder* in the psychiatric diagnostic system. The diagnosis was to be applied to people who repeatedly involve themselves in hurtful circumstances and relationships. Critics vigorously protested that this label would be applied to many women who remained in abusive relationships, thereby shifting the responsibility from the abuser to the woman's "personality disorder." Following years of debate, the critics prevailed and this category was not included in the diagnostic system despite many clinicians' reports that they frequently encounter such individuals in their practices (Widiger, 1995).

Despite the arbitrariness introduced by time, place, and value judgments, there are certain criteria that seem to govern decisions about abnormality. These are sometimes referred to as the "three Ds," and one or more of them seem to apply to virtually any behaviour regarded as abnormal (Figure 13.5).

First, we are likely to label behaviours as abnormal if they are intensely *distressing* to the individual. People may be viewed as having a psychological disorder when they are inordinately anxious, depressed, dissatisfied, or otherwise seriously upset about themselves or about life circumstances, particularly if they seem to have little control over these reactions. On the other hand, personal distress is neither necessary nor sufficient to define abnormality. For example, some seriously disturbed mental patients are so out of contact with reality that they seem to experience little distress, and yet their bizarre behaviours are considered very abnormal. Conversely, almost all of us experience suffering as a part of our lives. Nonetheless, when such suffering is disproportionate to the situation, or too long-lasting, it may be viewed as abnormal.

Most behaviours that are labelled abnormal are *dysfunctional* either for the individual or for society. Behaviours that interfere with a person's ability to work and to experience satisfying relationships with other people are likely to be seen as maladaptive and self-defeating, especially if an individual seems unable to control such behaviours. Sometimes, behaviours are labelled abnormal because they interfere with the well-being of society. But even here, the standards are not cut and dried. For example, is a political terrorist who plants a bomb in a public market psychologically disturbed, a criminal, or a patriot?

The third criterion for abnormality is based on society's judgments of the *deviance* of a given behaviour. As we have seen, conduct within every society is regulated by norms, behavioural rules that specify how people are expected to behave. Some norms are explicitly codified as laws, and violation of these norms defines criminal behaviour. Other norms, however, are far less explicit. For example, it is generally expected in our culture that one should not carry on animated conversations with people who are not present and should not face the rear of the elevator staring intently into the eyes of one's fellow passengers. (You might try engaging in the latter behaviour if you want to see an elevator empty out quickly.) People are likely to be viewed as psychologically disturbed if they violate these unstated norms, especially if the violations cannot be attributed to environmental causes and if they make others uncomfortable.

To summarize, both personal and social judgments of behaviour enter into judgments of what is abnormal. Nonetheless, as a working definition, we might define **abnormal behaviour** as behaviour that is personally distressful, personally dysfunctional, and/or so culturally deviant that other people judge it to be inappropriate or maladaptive.

6. What is meant by reliability and validity of diagnostic classification systems?

Diagnosing Psychological Disorders

7. How do the five axes of DSM-IV describe an individual's abnormal behaviour and factors that may contribute to it or predict its future course?

Classification is a necessary first step toward introducing order into discussions of the nature, causes, and treatment of psychological disorders. To be scientifically and practically useful, however, a classification system has to meet standards of reliability and validity. **Reliability** means that clinicians using the system should show high levels of agreement in their diagnostic decisions. Because professionals with different types and amounts of training—including psychologists, psychiatrists, social workers, and general physicians—make diagnostic decisions, the system should be couched in terms of observable behaviours that can be reliably detected and should minimize subjective judgments (American Psychiatric Association, 1994). **Validity** means that the diagnostic categories should accurately capture the essential features of the various disorders. Thus, if research and clinical observations show that a given disorder has four behavioural characteristics, the diagnostic category for that disorder should also have those four features. Moreover, the diagnostic categories should allow us to differentiate one psychological disorder from another.

The *Diagnostic and Statistical Manual of Mental Disorders, Fourth Edition* (DSM-IV), is the most widely used diagnostic classification system in North America (although in much of Europe, a different classification system—the *International Statistical Classification of Diseases*—is often used). For each of its more than 350 diagnostic categories, DSM-IV contains detailed lists of observable behaviours that must be present in order for a diagnosis to be made. Table 13.1 samples the range of major DSM-IV categories.

The DSM-IV allows diagnostic information to be represented along five dimensions, or axes, that take both the person and his or her life situation into account. Axis I, the primary diagnosis, represents the person's primary clinical symptoms. Axis II reflects long-standing personality or developmental disorders, such as ingrained, inflexible aspects of personality, that could influence the person's behaviour and response to treatment. Axis III notes any physical conditions that might be relevant, such as high blood pressure. Reflecting the vulnerability-stress model discussed earlier, the clinician also rates the intensity of environmental stressors in the person's recent life on Axis IV, and the person's coping resources as reflected in recent adaptive functioning on Axis V. Figure 13.6 shows how the axes are represented in a DSM-IV diagnosis.

TABLE 13.1 A Sample of Major Diagnostic Categories in DSM-IV

1. Anxiety disorders
   Intense, frequent, or inappropriate anxiety, but no loss of reality contact; includes phobias, generalized anxiety reactions, panic disorders, obsessive-compulsive disorders, and post-traumatic stress disorders
2. Mood (affective) disorders
   Marked disturbances of mood, including depression and mania (extreme elation and excitement)
3. Somatoform disorders
   Physical symptoms, such as blindness, paralysis, or pain, that have no physical basis and are assumed to be caused by psychological factors; also, excessive preoccupation and worry about health (hypochondriasis)
4. Dissociative disorders
   Psychologically caused problems of consciousness and self-identification, including amnesia and multiple personalities (dissociative identity disorder)
5. Schizophrenic and other psychotic disorders
   Severe disorders of thinking, perception, and emotion that involve loss of contact with reality and disordered behaviour
6. Substance abuse disorders
   Personal and social problems associated with the use of psychoactive substances, such as alcohol, heroin, or other drugs
7. Sexual and gender identity disorders
   Inability to function sexually or enjoy sexuality (sexual dysfunctions); deviant sexual behaviours, such as child molestation and arousal by inappropriate objects (fetishes); strong discomfort with one's gender accompanied by the desire to be a member of the other sex
8. Eating disorders
   Includes anorexia nervosa (self-starvation) and bulimia nervosa (patterns of bingeing and purging)
9. Personality disorders
   Rigid, stable, and maladaptive personality patterns, such as anti-social, dependent, paranoid, and narcissistic disorders

Source: Derived from American Psychiatric Association, 1994.

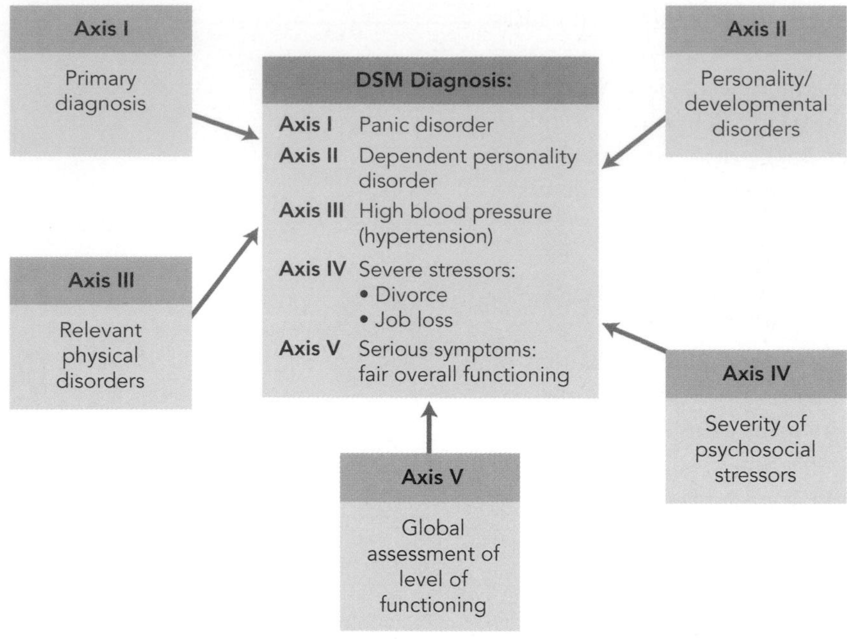

FIGURE 13.6

The DSM-IV uses a five-axis system to arrive at a comprehensive diagnosis that takes into account not only deviant behaviours, but also other relevant personal and environmental factors.

Although the reliability and validity of DSM-IV are still being evaluated, it appears that the highly specific behavioural criteria in the DSM-IV categories have improved Axis I reliability over earlier versions (Brown et al., 2001). On the other hand, the criteria are sometimes so strict that many people don't fit into the categories. Moreover, debate continues over the validity of some of the categories. Especially problematic are the Axis II personality disorders, which overlap extensively with one another and with Axis I disorders (Beutler & Malik, 2002). As many as half of all people who receive a specific personality disorder diagnosis could easily be classified differently (Morey, 1988). Such overlap reduces both reliability and validity. Although this state of affairs has led some to call for a complete revision of the personality disorder categories and, perhaps, their abandonment (Trull & McCrae, 2002), many other categories of DSM-IV appear to be diagnostically useful and reliable. An important goal in the development of the next version of the DSM is to develop categories with less overlap (Helzer & Hudziak, 2002).

Critical Issues in Diagnostic Labelling

Beyond their clinical and scientific utility, diagnostic labels can have important personal, social, and legal consequences for the people who receive them.

Social and Personal Implications

8. What effects does psychiatric labelling have on social- and self-perceptions?

Once a diagnostic label is attached to a person, it becomes all too easy to accept the label as an accurate description of the *individual* rather than of the *behaviour.* It then becomes difficult to look at the person's behaviour objectively, without preconceptions about how he or she will act. It also is likely to affect how we will interact with that person. Consider for a moment what your reaction might be if you were informed that your new next-door neighbour had been diagnosed as a "sexual psychopath." It would be surprising indeed if this label did not influence your perceptions and interactions with that person, whether or not the label was accurate. We discuss this in the following Research Foundations feature.

RESEARCH FOUNDATIONS

On Being Sane in Insane Places

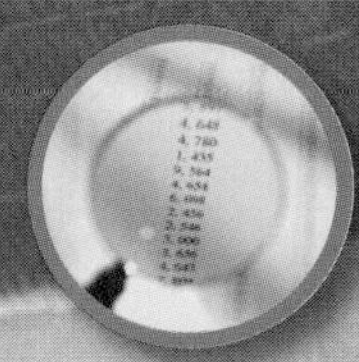

How do we come to know when someone is "insane"? For that matter, can we tell when someone is "normal"? Of course, we could administer a battery of tests and use the classification system from DSM-IV. But what if someone were to simply walk into a treatment facility complaining that they heard voices—would they perhaps be viewed as suffering from a mental disorder? The implications of such behaviour were examined in this classic study by Davis Rosenhan (1973).

Rosenhan arranged for eight "pseudopatients" (five men and three women) to present themselves at the admissions desk of 12 mental hospitals across the United States. Most were older, and they came from a variety of backgrounds (three psychologists, a psychiatrist, a pediatrician, a painter, and a housewife, plus Rosenhan himself). All were sane. The pseudopatient arrived at admissions complaining of hearing voices. If asked about the voices, the pseudopatient indicated that the message was unclear, but contained the words "hollow," "empty," and "thud." The voice was not familiar, but of the same sex as the pseudopatient. Nothing further was ever said about the symptoms or about hearing voices. If questioned by any member of the staff, the pseudopatients gave accurate details from their own life history and indicated that they no longer heard voices. They participated in all aspects of the hospital environment as directed by the staff. Each person was to appear as "normal" as possible and to convince the staff that they should be released.

All eight pseudopatients were admitted to hospital with a diagnosis of schizophrenia, and upon discharge the diagnosis of "schizophrenia in remission" was indicated. Not a single member of staff at any of the hospitals realized that these patients were, in fact, perfectly sane. Interestingly, many of the patients at the various hospitals did see through the ruse, often commenting that the pseudopatient was not a real patient—that he or she was probably a journalist or a professor. The average stay at the hospital was 19 days, with a range from 7 to 52 days.

After hearing about some of these results, many hospitals claimed that such an error would never happen at their institution. So Rosenhan arranged the following demonstration. The staff at a large teaching and research hospital was told that sometime during the next three months, one or more pseudopatients would present themselves at the admission desk. The staff were asked to rate each new patient during this time frame and indicate the likelihood that the patient was a fake. During the three-month period, 193 patients were admitted. Of these, 41 were determined with a high degree of confidence by at least one staff member to be pseudopatients. Nineteen were rated as suspect by at least one staff member and a psychiatrist. Not a single person was, in fact, a pseudopatient—all were real.

Beyond the issues of simply failing to detect both sanity and insanity, it is interesting to note how the staff responded to the pseudopatients. Once labelled as "schizophrenic," every behaviour performed by these individuals was viewed as consistent with this label. For example, the pseudopatients kept journals during their stay. This journal writing was interpreted as symptomatic of paranoid delusions. Details of family history were reinterpreted in a manner consistent with the diagnosis. Rosenhan concludes that we must be cautious in both using and interpreting the labels we place on others.

Although the results of this experiment are compelling, we must remember that the staff at the various hospitals were responding with the best interests of the pseudopatients in mind. As Spritzer (1975) has noted, it would have been unprofessional of them to respond in any other fashion. Nonetheless, Rosenhan's demonstration points out the difficulty of deciding just what is "normal." It should be noted that the Canadian Mental Health Act would prohibit the lengthy institutional stays reported by Rosenhan (1973). If a psychiatrist determines upon interview that you are a danger to yourself or society, you may be held involuntarily for up to 72 hours. You must be reassessed within that time. If the psychiatrist still believes that you are a threat, you can be held for an additional two weeks, after which there must be another assessment. The pseudopatients in the Rosenhan study would likely have been discharged within the first three days.

Diagnostic labels may also play a role in creating or worsening psychological disorders (Matorin, 2002). When people become aware that a psychiatric label has been applied to them, they may accept the new identity implied by the label and develop the expected role and outlook. Because psychiatric labels often carry degrading and stigmatizing implications, the effects on morale and self-esteem can be devastating. Moreover, a person may despair of ever changing, and therefore give up attempts to deal with life circumstances that may be responsible for the problems. In this way, the expectations that accompany a label may result in a self-fulfilling prophecy, in which expectation becomes reality.

Legal Consequences

9. Differentiate between the legal concepts of competency and insanity. What is the current burden of proof in insanity hearings?

Psychiatric diagnoses also have important legal consequences. Individuals judged to be dangerous to themselves or others may be involuntarily committed to mental institutions under certain circumstances. When so committed, they lose some of their civil rights and may be detained indefinitely if their behaviour does not improve.

The law tries to take into account the mental status of individuals accused of crimes. Two particularly important legal concepts are competency and insanity. **Competency** refers to a defendant's state of mind at the time of a judicial hearing (not at the time the crime was committed). A defendant judged to be too disturbed

FIGURE 13.7

Both John Hinckley (top), who shot Ronald Reagan and his press secretary, and the mass murderer Jeffrey Dahmer (bottom) pleaded not guilty by reason of insanity. Hinckley won his plea, whereas Dahmer's was rejected. These cases focused considerable attention on the insanity defence.

to understand the nature of the legal proceedings may be labelled as *not competent to stand trial* and institutionalized until judged competent.

Insanity, a far more controversial issue, relates to the presumed state of mind of the defendant at the time the crime was committed. Defendants may be declared *not guilty by reason of insanity* if they are judged to have been so severely impaired during the commission of a crime that they lacked the capacity either to appreciate the wrongfulness of their acts or to control their conduct. In 1992, Canada officially changed this verdict to *not criminally responsible on account of mental disorder (NCRMD)*. It is important to understand that insanity is a legal term, not a psychological one.

The insanity defence has long been hotly debated. The acquittal of John Hinckley, who attempted to assassinate President Ronald Reagan in 1981, created an uproar (Figure 13.7). Twelve years later, Jeffrey Dahmer, accused of the grisly murders and mutilations of 15 men, also entered a plea of not guilty by reason of insanity. The defence contended that no sane person could have committed the shocking acts that Dahmer freely admitted, which included storing and eating victims' body parts. As you saw in Chapter 12 (p. 521), psychological test results also indicated severe psychological disturbance. Yet the insanity plea was rejected, and Dahmer was found guilty.

Both defendants clearly had serious mental disorders. Why the different verdicts? An important change had occurred in the legal requirement for proving sanity or insanity. At the time Hinckley was tried, the law required the prosecution to prove that Hinckley was *sane*. They could not do so beyond a reasonable doubt, and Hinckley was acquitted. Partly in response to Hinckley's acquittal, the law was changed, and the burden of proof was shifted to the defence. Dahmer's attorneys were not able to prove that their client was *insane* at the time he committed his crimes, so Dahmer was convicted of murder.

To balance punishment for crimes with concern about a defendant's mental status and possible need for treatment, the verdict of NCRMD requires that the defendant be institutionalized for treatment. When the defendant is judged to be no longer a risk to society, the individual would be gradually reintroduced to the community.

"Do I Have That Disorder?"

Having considered issues of diagnosis, we now move to a description of the disorders themselves. First, however, you should be aware of a common phenomenon that in medical education is termed "medical students' disease." When people read descriptions of disorders, whether physical or psychological, they often see some of those symptoms or characteristics in themselves. In the case of psychological disorders, this is quite understandable. We all experience problems in living at various times, and we may react to them in ways that bear similarities to the behaviours you will be reading about. Seeing such a similarity does not necessarily mean that you have the disorder. On the other hand, if you find that maladaptive behaviours such as those described in this chapter are interfering with your happiness or personal effectiveness, then you should not hesitate to seek help in changing these behaviours. Some guidelines for doing so are presented in Chapter 14 (p. 636).

In Review

- *Abnormality is largely a social judgment. Behaviour that is judged to reflect a psychological disorder typically is (1) distressing to the person or to other people; (2) dysfunctional, maladaptive, or self-defeating; and/or (3) socially deviant in a way that arouses discomfort in others and cannot be attributed to environmental causes.*
- *The major psychiatric classification system in North America is the DSM-IV, which describes the current status of the individual using five different dimensions, or axes, that capture personal and environmental factors. Reliability (diagnostic agreement) and validity are important issues in diagnostic classification systems.*

- *Among the important issues in psychiatric diagnosis are the potential negative effects of labelling on social perceptions and self-perceptions. Legal implications of competency and insanity judgments are also receiving attention. Competency to stand trial means that the individual is in sufficient contact with reality to understand the legal proceedings. Insanity refers to an inability to appreciate the wrongfulness of one's act and control one's behaviour at the time the crime was committed.*

ANXIETY DISORDERS

10. Describe the three components of anxiety.

All of us have experienced anxiety, the state of tension and apprehension that is a natural response to perceived threat. But in **anxiety disorders**, the frequency and intensity of anxiety responses are out of proportion to the situations that trigger them, and the anxiety interferes with daily life.

Anxiety responses have four components: (1) a *subjective-emotional* component, including feelings of tension and apprehension; (2) a *cognitive* component, including subjective feelings of apprehension, a sense of impending danger, and a feeling of inability to cope; (3) *physiological* responses, including increased heart rate and blood pressure, muscle tension, rapid breathing, nausea, dry mouth, diarrhea, and frequent urination; and (4) *behavioural* responses, such as avoidance of certain situations and impaired task performance (Noyes & Hoehn-Saric, 1999; Barlow, 2002; Figure 13.8).

Anxiety disorders take a number of different forms, including phobic disorders, generalized anxiety disorders, panic disorders, post-traumatic stress disorders (discussed in Chapter 15), and obsessive-compulsive disorders. Large-scale population studies indicate that anxiety disorders are the most prevalent of all psychological disorders in North America, affecting 17.6 percent of the population during their lifetimes (Kessler et al., 1994; Robins & Regier, 1991; Satcher, 1999). Figure 13.9 shows lifetime prevalence rates for various anxiety disorders. All of the anxiety disorders tend to occur more frequently in females than in males.

Phobic Disorder

Laura's fear of the water dates back to her childhood. She recalled her mother, who had a similar fear, vividly describing an incident in which one of her own childhood friends had drowned at a school picnic. Laura's fear of water intensified after she breathed in some water and panicked when she was

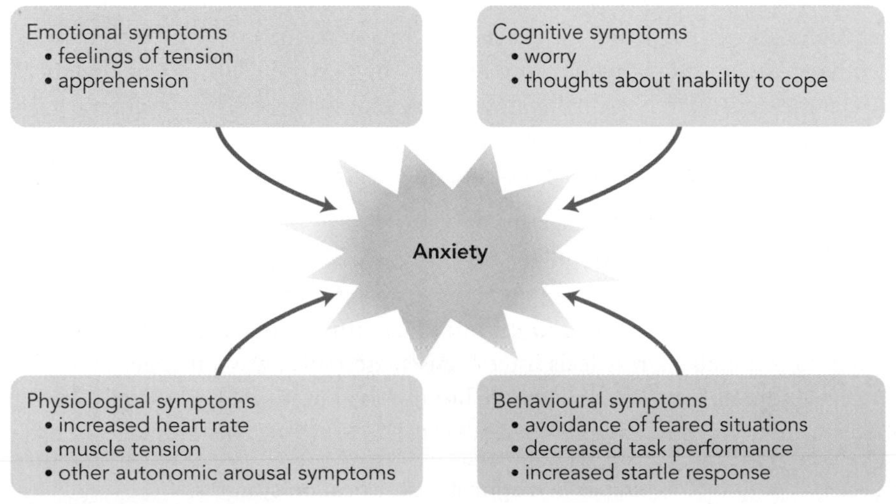

FIGURE 13.8

Anxiety consists of subjective-emotional, cognitive, physiological, and behavioural components.

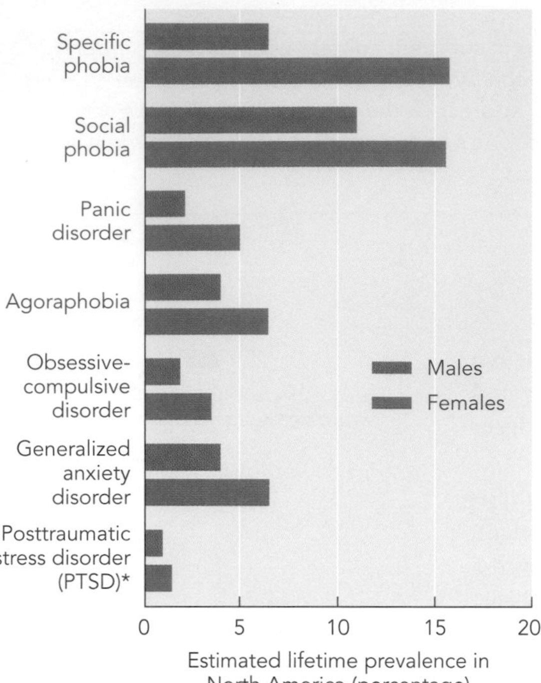

FIGURE 13.9

Lifetime prevalence rates for the anxiety disorders in men and women. All of the disorders occur more frequently in women.

Sources: Based on Kessler et al., 1994; Robins & Regier, 1991.

11. What is a phobia, and what are the three major types?

FIGURE 13.10

Many people suffer from a fear of flying. One famous figure is John Madden, formerly a professional football coach and currently a television analyst, who travels to his weekly assignments (sometimes separated by thousands of kilometres) in a specially equipped motor home.

"dunked" by a playmate at a swimming pool. She floundered and was sure she was going to drown until a lifeguard pulled her to safety. For the past 15 years, Laura has avoided outings that would take her into deep water. Although she knows how to swim, she dreads the thought of going swimming. She makes excuses to avoid boating trips and once turned down a free trip to Hawaii because of the anxiety she knew she would experience flying over the ocean.

Phobias are strong and irrational fears of certain objects or situations. The word was originally derived from *Phobos*, the Greek god of fear, whose likeness was painted on masks and shields to frighten enemies in battle. Today's phobic fights a different kind of battle, with fears of a less realistic, but no less intense nature.

People with phobias realize that their fears are out of all proportion to the danger involved, but they feel helpless to deal with these fears. Instead, they make strenuous efforts to avoid the phobic situation or object. Among the most common phobias in Western society are **agoraphobia**, a fear of open and public places, **social phobias** (excessive fear of situations in which the person might be evaluated and possibly embarrassed), and **specific phobias**, such as fears of dogs, snakes, spiders, airplanes, elevators, enclosed spaces, water, injections, illness, or death. Phobias can develop at any point in life, but many of them develop during childhood, adolescence, and early adulthood. Once phobias develop, they seldom go away on their own, and they may broaden and intensify over time (Stein & Hollander, 2002).

The degree of impairment produced by a phobia depends in part on how often the phobic stimulus is encountered in the individual's normal round of activities. For example, fear of flying is a common phobia that occurs in some 25 million North Americans (Bruce & Sanderson, 1998). An airplane phobia may be a relatively minor inconvenience for a person who never needs to travel by air, but it may be a debilitating condition for an executive who has to travel frequently. Some people simply refuse to fly even at great personal inconvenience (Figure 13.10).

Generalized Anxiety Disorder

On initial assessment, Dr. N, who is manifestly tense, complains of never being entirely free of a sense of impending disaster, although he cannot further specify the nature of this anticipated catastrophe. He notes a number of signs of autonomic hyperarousal that he experiences on virtually a daily basis, emphasizing in particular excessive sweating, which has become a source of embarrassment. He is medicating himself for persistent attacks of diarrhea. He complains of an inability to attain a refreshing level of sleep even on those rare occasions when he can count on a few uninterrupted off-duty hours, and his very few waking "leisure" hours are filled with restless irritability. (Carson et al., 1988, p. 195)

Dr. N is suffering from a **generalized anxiety disorder**, a chronic state of diffuse, or "free-floating," anxiety that is not attached to specific situations or objects. In such cases, the anxiety may last for months on end, with the signs almost continuously present. Emotionally, Dr. N feels jittery, tense, and constantly on edge. Cognitively, he expects something awful to happen, but doesn't know what. Physically, he experiences a mild chronic emergency reaction. Dr. N sweats, his stomach is usually upset, he has diarrhea, and so forth.

As we might expect, this disorder can interfere markedly with daily functioning, even if the symptoms are not continually present for the six months required for a formal diagnosis (Kessler & Wittchen, 2002). The person may find it hard to concentrate, to make decisions, and to remember commitments. One large-scale study found that five percent of people between the ages of 15 and 45 reported having experienced the symptoms of generalized anxiety disorder. Onset tends to occur in childhood and adolescence (Wittchen et al., 1994).

12. How does a generalized anxiety disorder differ from a phobic disorder? From a panic disorder?

Panic Disorder

13. What occurs in a panic disorder, and how do these experiences frequently result in development of agoraphobia?

In contrast to generalized anxiety disorder, which involves chronic tension and anxiety, **panic disorders** occur suddenly and unpredictably, and they are much more intense. The symptoms of panic attacks can be terrifying. As in the case of Sarah, the university student described at the beginning of the chapter, it is not unusual for victims to feel that they are dying (Ballenger, 2000).

In most cases, panic attacks occur out of the blue and in the absence of any identifiable stimulus. It is this unpredictable quality that makes panic attacks so mysterious and terrifying to their victims. Many people with panic attacks develop *agoraphobia,* a fear of public places, because of their fear that they will have an attack in public. In extreme cases, they may fear leaving the familiar setting of the home, and agoraphobics have been known to be housebound for years at a time because of their "fear of fear" (Milrod et al., 1997). This case shows the development of an agoraphobic pattern:

> As the attacks continued, Ms. Watson began to dread going out of the house alone. She feared that while out she would have an attack and would be stranded and helpless. She stopped riding the subway to work out of fear she might be trapped in a car between stops when an attack struck, preferring instead to walk the 20 blocks between her home and work. Social and recreational activities, previously frequent and enjoyed, were severely curtailed because an attack might occur. (Adapted from Spitzer et al., 1983)

Panic disorders with or without agoraphobia tend to appear in late adolescence or early adulthood and affect about 3.5 percent of the population (Kessler et al., 1994). Even more common are occasional panic attacks. In one survey of Canadian students, 34 percent reported having had at least one unexpected panic attack within the previous year, usually during periods of extreme stress (Norton et al., 1985). Under DSM-IV criteria, these students would *not* be diagnosed as having a panic disorder unless they developed an inordinate fear of having future attacks.

Obsessive-Compulsive Disorder (OCD)

> A thirty-eight-year-old mother of one child had been obsessed by fears of contamination during her entire adult life. Literally hundreds of times a day, thoughts of being infected by germs would occur to her. Once she began to think that either she or her child might become infected, she could not dismiss the thought. The constant concern about infection resulted in a series of washing and cleaning rituals that took up most of her day. Her child was confined to one room only, which the woman tried to keep entirely free of germs by scrubbing it—floor to ceiling—several times a day. Moreover, she opened and closed all doors with her feet, in order to avoid contaminating her own hands. (Rachman & Hodgson, 1980)

14. Differentiate between obsessions and compulsions. How are they typically related to one another?

This woman was diagnosed as having an **obsessive-compulsive disorder**. Such disorders usually consist of two components, one cognitive, the other behavioural, although either can occur alone. **Obsessions** are repetitive and unwelcome thoughts, images, or impulses that invade consciousness, are often abhorrent to the person, and are very difficult to dismiss or control. This mother was tyrannized by thoughts and images of contamination. **Compulsions** are repetitive behavioural responses—such as the woman's cleaning rituals—that can be resisted only with great difficulty. Compulsions are often responses to obsessive thoughts, and function to reduce the anxiety associated with the thoughts (De Silva & Rachman, 1998). Once the mother had performed her compulsive cleanliness acts, she was relatively free from anxiety, at least until the thoughts of contamination intruded once more.

Behavioural compulsions are extremely difficult to control. They often involve checking things repeatedly, cleaning, and repeating tasks endlessly. If the person does not perform the compulsive act, he or she may experience tremendous anxiety, perhaps even a panic attack. Like phobic avoidance responses, compulsions appear to reduce anxiety and to be strengthened through a process of negative reinforcement because they allow a person to avoid anxiety (Jenicke, 1998).

Recent studies have found the lifetime prevalence of obsessive-compulsive disorder in the United States and Canada to be about 2.5 per 100 people. Onset typically occurs in the twenties (Robins & Regier, 1991; Weissman et al., 1994). We examine some of the brain mechanisms involved in OCD in this chapter's Focus on Neuroscience.

FOCUS ON NEUROSCIENCE

The Neuroscience of Obsessive-Compulsive Disorder

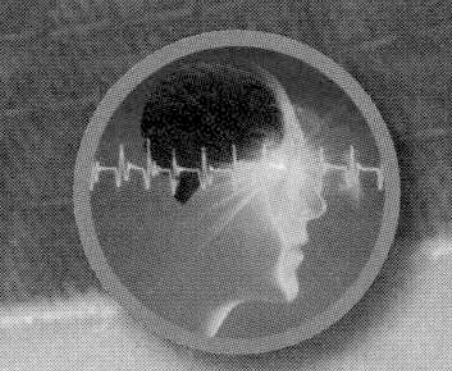

Obsessive-compulsive disorder (OCD) can be debilitating. The behavioural compulsions are difficult to control and may result in physical damage to the individual. For example, excessive hand washing may result in severe skin abrasions. Why do people engage in such potentially damaging behaviours?

Neuroimaging (fMRI, PET and CT) has helped to shed light on two underlying neural circuits involved in OCD. In a recent review, Friedlander & Desrocher (2006) examine the data on both models. The executive dysfunction model (e.g., Rapoport, 1991) suggests that the underlying problem lies in impulse control and behavioural inhibition. The modulatory control model (e.g., Saxena et al., 1998) posits a different mechanism, reflecting lack of control of socially appropriate behaviours. According to the executive dysfunction model, the problem is an inability to inhibit behaviours viewed as inappropriate for a particular situation. Friedlander & Desrocher (2006) suggest that this model would predict altered activity in the prefrontal cortex (in particular, regions to the back and the side of the prefrontal cortex). However, they also suggest that the caudate nucleus (a major structure in the basal ganglia) should be involved, since it is richly connected to the prefrontal cortex and helps regulate limbic system activity, especially with respect to the completion of behaviours. However, the findings seem to be mixed, with

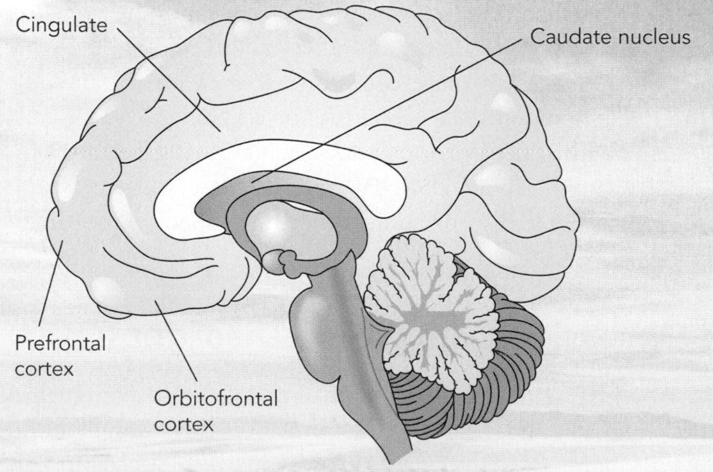

FIGURE 13.11

Areas involved in Obsessive-compulsive disorder. Research indicates that obsessions are likely generated through an orbitalfrontal-cingulate pathway, while compulsions involve a prefrontal-caudate-thalamus circuit.

several showing increased volume of the caudate, and others showing a decrease or no difference (e.g., Baxter et al., 1988; Robinson et al., 1995; Szeszeko et al., 2004). Furthermore, the involvement of the prefrontal cortex is more likely to be seen in adults than in children. The data are more consistent regarding activity in the thalamus, which serves as a major relay station for incoming information. For example, using PET scans, Perani et al. (1995) report that thalamic abnormality is directly related to OCD symptom severity.

More compelling support is found for the modulatory control model. In general, the evidence (e.g., Sawle et al., 1991) supports increased metabolism in the orbitofrontal (the prefrontal lobe directly behind the eyes) and medial (toward the middle) prefrontal cortex. These areas have been implicated in the control of socially appropriate behaviours and motivation. If these areas do not function properly, the individual may display a variety of inappropriate, impulsive behaviours, and may fixate on one aspect of the environment. Friedlander & Desrocher (2006) suggest that dysfunction in the orbitofrontal cortex and associated areas may be responsible for the generation and persistence of obsessive thought. Abnormalities were also observed in the cingulate gyrus, which is connected to both the frontal lobes and the limbic system.

These imaging studies suggest the involvement of two separate pathways contributing to OCD. Friedlander & Desrocher (2006) argue that the executive dysfunction model is best equipped to explain compulsions, and that the neural wiring should be found in the prefrontal-caudate-thalamus circuit (Figure 13.11). The modulatory control model is focused on obsessions, and the underlying pathway involves the orbitofrontal cortex and the cingulate. Early identification of abnormalities in either route may help with the timing of effective treatment for OCD.

Causal Factors in Anxiety Disorders

Anxiety is a complex phenomenon having biological, psychological, and environmental causes. Within the vulnerability-stress model presented earlier, any of these factors can create predispositions to respond to stressors with an anxiety disorder.

Biological Factors

15. What evidence is there for a genetic predisposition to anxiety disorders? What form might the vulnerability factor take?

Genetic factors may create a vulnerability to anxiety disorders (Blackwood, 2000). David Barlow (2002) suggests that such vulnerability may take the form of an autonomic nervous system that overreacts to perceived threat, creating high levels of physiological arousal. Hereditary factors may cause overreactivity of neurotransmitter systems involved in emotional responses (Mineka et al., 1998). Other evidence suggests that trauma-produced overactivity in the emotional systems of the right hemisphere (whose activity underlies negative emotional states) may produce vulnerability to PTSD (Schore, 2002). Indeed, when experiencing the anxiety associated with PTSD, it is primarily the right hemisphere that is activated (Lanius et al., 2004).

Studies of identical and fraternal twins raised together and apart provide important clues to the importance of genetic causes. Identical twins are far more similar to one another in scores on psychological tests that measure anxiety than are fraternal twins, even when the identical twins were separated early in life and raised in different families. Heritability estimates indicate that about 50 to 60 percent of the variation in anxiety scores can be attributed to genetic factors, with the remaining 40 to 50 percent attributable to individuals' life experiences (Blackwood, 2000; Tellegen et al., 1988). As far as clinical levels of anxiety are concerned, identical twins have a concordance rate (if one twin has it, so does the other) of about 40 percent for anxiety disorders, compared to a 4 percent concordance rate in fraternal twins (Carey & Gottesman, 1981). Although such findings indicate a genetic predisposition, the concordance rate even in identical twins is far from 100 percent, indicating the importance of psychological and environmental factors.

16. How might GABA be related to anxiety disorders? How might the biochemical factor in panic disorder be different?

The search for biological processes associated with anxiety disorders has focused on several neurotransmitters in the brain. One such transmitter is *GABA (gama-aminobutyric acid)*. GABA is an inhibitory transmitter that reduces neural activity in the amygdala and other brain structures that stimulate physiological arousal. Some researchers believe that abnormally low levels of inhibitory GABA activity in these arousal areas may cause some people to have highly reactive nervous systems that quickly produce anxiety responses in response to stressors (Bremner, 2000). Such people might also be more susceptible to classically conditioned phobias because they already have a strong unconditioned arousal response in place, ready to be conditioned to new stimuli. In support of this hypothesis, brain scans showed that patients with a history of panic attacks had a 22 percent lower concentration of GABA in the occipital cortex than age-matched controls without panic disorder (Goddard et al., 2001). Other transmitter systems may also be involved in the anxiety disorders.

17. What factors might produce the sex difference seen in the prevalence of anxiety disorders?

As noted earlier, women exhibit anxiety disorders more often than men do (Leibenluft, 1999). In a large epidemiological study of adolescents, Peter Lewinsohn and co-workers (1998) found that this sex difference emerges as early as seven years of age. The contributing role of biological factors is suggested by Lewinsohn's finding that, even when 11 psychosocial factors (including negative life events, self-esteem, and social support) that differentiated males from females were controlled for statistically, the large sex difference remained.

Such findings suggest a sex-linked biological predisposition for anxiety disorders, but social conditions that give women less power and personal control may also contribute (Kessler et al., 1994; Craske, 2003). As in other instances of sex differences, it seems likely that biological, psychological, and environmental factors combine in complex ways.

Finally, we should recall the possible role of evolutionary factors in predisposing people to fear certain types of stimuli that might have had survival significance in the past, such as snakes, spiders, storms, and heights. As discussed in Chapter 6, evolutionary theorists believe that **biological preparedness** makes it easier for us to learn to fear certain stimuli, and may explain why phobias seem to centre on certain classes of "primal" stimuli and not on more dangerous modern ones, such as guns and electrical power stations (Oehman, 1993).

Psychological Factors

18. How does psychoanalytic theory explain the development of anxiety disorders?

Psychodynamic theories. Anxiety is a central feature of psychoanalytic conceptions of abnormal behaviour. According to Freud, **neurotic anxiety** occurs when unacceptable impulses threaten to overwhelm the ego's defences and explode into action. How the ego's defence mechanisms deal with neurotic anxiety determines the form of the anxiety disorder. Freud believed that in phobic disorders, neurotic anxiety is displaced onto some external stimulus that has symbolic significance in relation to the underlying conflict. For example, in one of Freud's most celebrated cases, a little boy named Hans suddenly developed a fear of horses and the possibility of being bitten. To Freud, the phobia resulted from the boy's unresolved Oedipus complex. The powerful horse represented Hans's father, and the fear of being bitten symbolized Hans's unconscious fear of being castrated by his father if he acted on his sexual desire for his mother.

Obsessions and compulsions are also ways of handling anxiety. According to Freud, the obsession is symbolically related to, but less terrifying than, the underlying impulse. A compulsion is a way of "taking back," or undoing, one's unacceptable urges, as when obsessive thoughts about dirt and compulsive handwashing are used to deal with one's "dirty" sexual impulses. Finally, generalized anxiety and panic attacks are thought to occur when one's defences are not strong enough to control or contain anxiety, but are strong enough to hide the underlying conflict.

Although psychoanalytic theory has stimulated considerable thinking about the causes and treatment of anxiety disorders, the notion of anxiety disorder symptoms as symbolic expressions of underlying conflicts has not received much research support (Fisher & Greenberg, 1996). Cognitive and behavioural approaches are far more influential today in guiding research on anxiety disorders and their treatment.

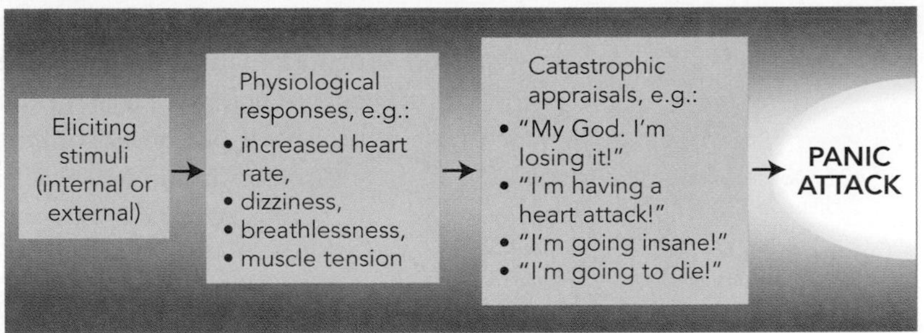

FIGURE 13.12

Current cognitive explanations of panic attacks depict a process in which normal manifestations of anxiety are appraised catastrophically, ultimately resulting in a full-blown panic attack.

Cognitive factors. Cognitive theorists stress the role of maladaptive thought patterns and beliefs in anxiety disorders. Anxiety-disordered people "catastrophize" about demands and magnify them into threats. They anticipate that the worst will happen and feel powerless to cope effectively (Clark, 1988; Mineka et al., 1998). Edna Foa and co-workers (1996) asked social phobics (1) how likely it was that they would embarrass themselves in a social situation and (2) how serious and costly the consequences of performing poorly would be for them. Compared to non-phobics, the social phobics judged both the likelihood and the costs to be much higher. Interestingly, these judgments were restricted to social situations. The social phobics did not differ in their likelihood and cost judgments in non-social situations.

Cognitive processes also play an important role in panic disorders. According to David Barlow (2002), panic attacks are triggered by exaggerated misinterpretations of normal anxiety symptoms, such as heart palpitations, dizziness, and breathlessness. The panic-disordered person appraises these as signs that a heart attack or a psychological loss of control is about to occur, and these catastrophic appraisals create even more anxiety until the process spirals out of control, producing a full-blown state of panic (Figure 13.12). Helping panic patients to replace such "mortal danger" appraisals with more benign interpretations of their bodily symptoms (e.g., "It's only a bit of anxiety, not a heart attack") results in a marked reduction in panic attacks (Barlow, 1997; Craske, 1999).

19. How do cognitive factors enter into anxiety disorders, particularly panic disorder? What research supports these explanations?

Anxiety as a learned response. From the behavioural perspective, anxiety disorders result from emotional conditioning (Öhman, 2000; Rachman, 1998). Some fears are acquired as a result of traumatic experiences that produce a classically conditioned fear response. For example, a person who has a traumatic fall from a high place may develop a fear of heights (a CR) because the high place (CS) was associated with the pain and trauma of the fall (UCS).

20. Explain anxiety disorders in terms of classical conditioning, negative reinforcement, and observational learning.

Classical conditioning cannot be the whole story, however, because many phobics have never had a traumatic experience with the phobic object or situation that they now fear (Bruce & Sanderson, 1998; Menzies & Clarke, 1995). Most people who are afraid to fly have never been in an air crash themselves. So how did they learn their fear? Clearly, phobias also can be acquired through observational learning. For example, televised images of air crashes can evoke high levels of fear in some people. Yet most people do not develop phobias under these conditions, so there must be still more going on. It may be that biological dispositions and cognitive factors help determine whether a person develops a phobia by observing a traumatic event. Thus, if a person has a biological disposition toward intense fear, and if the person comes to believe that "sooner or later, the same thing will happen to me," the likelihood of developing a phobia on the basis of observational learning may increase.

Once anxiety is learned, it may be triggered either by cues from the environment or by internal cues, such as thoughts and images (Pitman et al., 2000). In the case of phobic reactions, the cues tend to be external ones relating to the feared object or situation. In panic disorders, on the other hand, the anxiety-arousing cues tend to be internal ones, such as bodily sensations (e.g., one's heart rate) or mental images (such as the image of collapsing and having a seizure in a public place) (Craske, 1999).

People are highly motivated to avoid or escape anxiety because it is such an unpleasant emotional state. Here is where operant conditioning enters the picture. Behaviours that are successful in reducing anxiety, such as compulsions or phobic avoidance responses, are strengthened through a process of negative reinforcement.

Thus the obsessive-compulsive mother's scrubbing ritual reduces anxiety about contamination, and the water phobic's avoidance of swimming prevents her from experiencing anxiety. Unfortunately, successful avoidance prolongs the problem because it prevents extinction of the learned anxiety response, which would occur eventually if these people exposed themselves to the feared stimuli enough times.

21. Describe four culture-bound disorders that involve anxiety.

Sociocultural Factors

Social and cultural factors also play a role in the development of anxiety disorders (Lopez & Guarnaccia, 2000). The role of culture is most dramatically shown in **culture-bound disorders** that occur only in certain places. *Koro* is a Southeast Asian anxiety disorder in which a man fears that his penis is going to retract into his abdomen and kill him. Another culture-specific disorder, found in Japan, is a social phobia called *Taijin Kyofushu* (Tanaka-Matsumi, 1979). People with this disorder are pathologically fearful of offending others by emitting offensive odours, blushing, staring inappropriately, or having a blemish or improper facial expression. Taijin Kyofushu has been attributed to the Japanese cultural value of extreme interpersonal sensitivity and to cultural prohibitions against expressing negative emotions (Kleinknecht et al., 1997; Russell, 1989; Ono et al., 2001; Torwin et al., 2004).

Several culture-bound anxiety-based disorders occur in the United States. *Windigo* is an anxiety disorder found among certain North American Indians. Persons with Windigo are fearful of being possessed by monsters who will turn them into homicidal cannibals. A more familiar culturally based anxiety occurs in *anorexia nervosa.* Though formally classified as an eating disorder, anorexia nervosa has a strong phobic component, namely the fear of getting fat. This eating disorder is found almost exclusively in developed countries, in which the emphasis on being thin has become a cultural obsession (Becker et al., 1999).

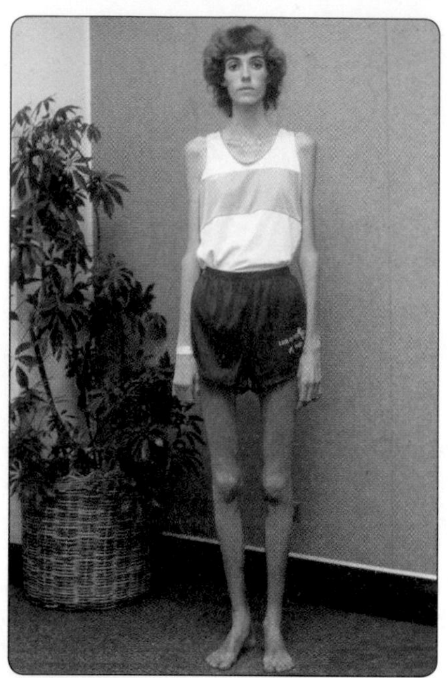

FIGURE 13.13

Anorexia nervosa is a potentially life threatening disorder in which people virtually starve themselves to be thin. This anorexic woman returned to normal weight after therapy.

Eating Disorders

Victims of **anorexia nervosa** have an intense fear of being fat and severely restrict their food intake to the point of self-starvation. Despite looking emaciated and weighing less than 85 percent of what would be expected for their age, anorexics continue to view themselves as fat (Figure 13.13). They often crave food, but have what amounts to an eating phobia that can be life threatening. About 90 percent of anorexics are female, mostly adolescents and young adults (Becker et al., 1999). Anorexia causes menstruation to stop, strains the heart, produces bone loss, and increases the risk of death (Neumäker, 2000). In 1982, the death of a famous singer, Karen Carpenter, was attributed to heart strain caused by her anorexia.

People who suffer from **bulimia nervosa** are overly concerned with becoming fat, but instead of self-starvation they binge eat and then purge the food, usually by inducing vomiting or using laxatives. Bulimics often consume 2,000 to 4,000 calories during binges, and in some cases may consume 20,000 calories per day (Crandall, 1989; Geracioti et al., 1995). About 90 percent of bulimics are female.

Although most bulimics are of normal body weight, repeated purging can produce severe physical consequences, including gastric problems and badly eroded teeth. Some surveys indicate that up to 10 percent of university women exhibit symptoms of bulimia, although its general prevalence among North American women is 1 to 3 percent—compared to 0.5 percent for anorexia (Becker et al., 1999; Walsh & Devlin, 1998).

Causes of Anorexia and Bulimia

What motivates people to develop such abnormal eating patterns? The answer—as with general eating regulation—seems to lie in a combination of environmental, psychological, and biological factors. Anorexia and bulimia are more common in industrialized cultures in which beauty is equated with "thinness." Indeed, as found by Cheryl Thomas of the University of Windsor, many women who immigrate to Western countries are at risk of developing eating disorders (Geller & Thomas, 1999). Variations in beauty norms among different ethnic groups also may help explain why, in North America, eating disorders are more common among Whites than Blacks (Zhang & Snowden, 1999). Consistent with objectification theory, a study of 16- to 21-year-old female university students suggests that a cultural emphasis on viewing one's body as an object contributes to eating disorders (Noll & Fredrickson, 1998).

22. Describe some of the symptoms and causes of anorexia and bulimia.

Cultural norms alone cannot account for eating disorders, because only a small percentage of women within a particular culture are anorexic or bulimic. Some researchers believe that personality factors are another piece of the puzzle. Anorexics often are perfectionists—high achievers who often strive to live up to lofty self-standards, including distorted standards concerning an acceptably thin body (Garfinkel & Garner, 1982). In one study, Monique Smeets (1999) showed anorexic and normal women a "morphing movie" in which a woman's thin body transforms into an obese one. When asked to judge the transition points at which the body changes from "thin" to "normal," "fat," and "obese," anorexics set harsher standards (e.g., lower weight levels to meet the transition point) for their own *and* other women's bodies.

For anorexics, losing weight becomes a battle for success and control: "Me versus food, and I'm going to win." Their perfectionism and need for control may stem partly from their upbringing (Chan & Ma, 2002). Anorexics describe their parents as disapproving and as setting abnormally high achievement standards, and they report more stressful events related to their parents than do non-anorexics (Waller & Hartley, 1994).

A different pattern emerges for bulimics, who tend to be depressed and anxious, exhibit low impulse control, and seem to lack a stable sense of personal identity and self-sufficiency (Strober & Humphrey, 1987). Bingeing is often triggered by life stress, and guilt and self-contempt follow it. The purging may be a means of reducing depression and anxiety triggered by the bingeing (Waters et al., 2001).

On the biological side, genetic factors may create a predisposition toward eating disorders. Concordance rates for eating disorders are higher among identical twins than fraternal twins, and higher among first-degree relatives than second- or third-degree relatives (Kortegaard et al., 2001). Anorexics and bulimics exhibit abnormal activity of serotonin and other body chemicals that help regulate eating (Bruch, 1973; Walsh & Devlin, 1998). However, because the findings are correlational, it is not clear whether these chemical abnormalities help cause eating disorders, or are a reaction to self-starvation and binge-purge eating.

Many researchers believe that these physiological changes initially are a *response* to abnormal eating patterns, but once started, they *perpetuate* eating and digestive irregularities (Walsh & Devlin, 1998). For example, because leptin is secreted by fat cells and anorexics have low fat mass, the amount of leptin circulating in their bloodstream is abnormally low (Mantzoros et al., 1997). But when anorexics begin to eat more, their leptin levels rebound more quickly than their weight gain. Because leptin is a signal that reduces appetite, this leptin rebound may make it more difficult for anorexics to keep gaining weight (Walsh & Devlin, 1998). Similarly, stomach acids expelled into the mouth during vomiting cause bulimics to lose taste sensitivity, making the normally unpleasant taste of vomit more tolerable (Rodin et al., 1990). This helps to perpetuate bulimics' willingness to keep purging in this manner.

Treating eating disorders is difficult and may take years, but with professional help about half of anorexics and bulimics fully recover (Becker et al., 1999; Walsh & Devlin, 1998). Others are able to eat more normally, but maintain their preoccupation with weight.

In Review

- *Anxiety involves four components: (1) subjective-emotional feelings of tension and discomfort; (2) cognitive processes involving worry, perceptions of threat, and lack of control; (3) excessive physiological arousal; and (4) behaviours that reflect the anxious state and often are designed to escape or avoid the feared object or situation.*
- *Anxiety disorders include phobic disorder (an irrational fear of a specific object or situation), generalized anxiety disorder (recurrent anxiety reactions that are difficult to link to specific environmental stimuli), panic disorder, obsessive-compulsive disorder (which involves uncontrollable and unwelcome thoughts and repetitive behaviours), and post-traumatic stress disorder.*
- *Biological factors in anxiety disorders include both genetic and biochemical processes, possibly involving the action of neurotransmitters, such as GABA, within parts of the brain that control emotional arousal.*
- *Psychoanalytic theorists believe that neurotic anxiety results from the inability of the ego's defences to deal with internal psychological conflicts. The cognitive perspective stresses the role of cognitive distortions, including the tendencies to magnify the degree of threat and danger and, in the case of panic disorder, to misinterpret normal anxiety symptoms in ways that can evoke panic.*
- *The behavioural perspective views anxiety asa learned response established through classical conditioning or vicarious learning. The avoidance responses in phobias and compulsive disorders are seen as operant responses that are negatively reinforced through anxiety reduction.*
- *Sociocultural factors are also involved in anxiety disorders, as illustrated by certain culture-bound anxiety disorders. The greater prevalence of anxiety disorders in women has been explained in both biological and sociocultural terms.*
- *Anorexia and bulimia are eating disorders that have serious physical consequences, occur more often in cultures that value thinness, and are associated with different psychological profiles and childhood patterns of family interaction.*

MOOD (AFFECTIVE) DISORDERS

Another set of emotion-based disorders are the **mood disorders**, which involve depression and mania (excessive excitement). Together with anxiety disorders, mood disorders are the most frequently experienced psychological disorders (Kessler et al., 1994; Robins & Regier, 1991).

Depression

Almost everyone has experienced depression, at least in its milder and more temporary forms. Loss and pain are inevitable parts of life, and when they occur, most of us feel blue, sad, discouraged, apathetic, and passive. The future looks bleak, and some of the zest goes out of living. Such reactions are normal; at any given point in time, 25 to 30 percent of university undergraduates are experiencing mild depression (Seligman, 1991). These feelings usually fade away after the event has passed or as the person becomes accustomed to the new situation. In clinical depression, however, the frequency, intensity, and duration of depressive symptoms are out of proportion to the person's life situation (Oatley & Jenkins, 1992). Thus some people may respond to a minor setback or loss with an intense **major depression** that leaves them unable to function effectively in their lives. Mark, the young man described at the beginning of the chapter, typifies a major depression. Other people exhibit a less intense form of depression called **dysthymia** that has less dramatic effects on personal and occupational functioning. Dysthymia is, however, a more chronic and long-lasting form of misery, occurring for years on end with intervals of normal mood that never last more than a few weeks or months.

23. Differentiate between major depression and dysthymia.

24. Describe the four classes of symptoms that characterize (a) depression and (b) mania.

Although depression is primarily a disorder of mood, there are three other types of symptoms: cognitive symptoms, motivational symptoms, and somatic (physical) symptoms (Figure 13.14).

The *negative mood state* is the core feature of depression. When depressed people are asked how they feel, they most commonly report sadness, misery, and loneliness. Whereas people with anxiety disorders retain their capacity to experience pleasure, depressed people lose it (Mineka et al., 1998). Activities that used to bring satisfaction and happiness feel dull and flat. Even biological pleasures, such as eating and sex, lose their appeal.

Cognitive symptoms are also a central part of depression. Depressed people have difficulty concentrating and making decisions. They usually have low self-esteem, believing that they are inferior, inadequate, and incompetent. When setbacks occur in their lives, depressed people tend to blame themselves; when failure has not yet occurred, they expect that it will and that it will be caused by their own inadequacies. Depressed people almost always view the future with great pessimism and hopelessness (Clark et al., 1999).

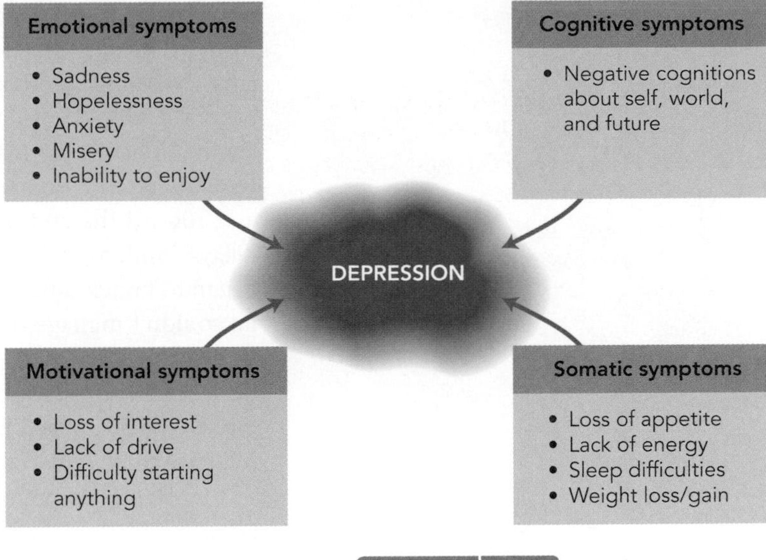

FIGURE 13.14

Depression includes emotional, cognitive, motivational, and somatic features.

Motivational symptoms in depression involve an inability to get started and to perform behaviours that might produce pleasure or accomplishment. A depressed student may be unable to get out of bed in the morning, let alone go to class or study. Everything seems too much of an effort. In extreme depressive reactions, the person may have to be prodded out of bed, clothed, and fed. In some cases of severe depression, movements slow down and the person walks or talks slowly and with excruciating effort.

Somatic (bodily) symptoms often include loss of appetite and weight loss in moderate and severe depression. Sleep disturbances, particularly insomnia, commonly occur. Sleep disturbance and weight loss lead to fatigue and weakness, which tend to add to the depressed feelings. Depressed people also may lose sexual desire and responsiveness. In mild depression, weight gain sometimes occurs as a person eats compulsively.

Bipolar Disorder

When a person experiences only depression, the disorder is called unipolar depression. In a **bipolar disorder**, depression (which is usually the dominant state) alternates with periods of **mania**, a state of highly excited mood and behaviour that is quite the opposite of depression. In a manic state, mood is euphoric and cognitions are grandiose. The person believes there are no limits to what can be accomplished and does not recognize the negative consequences that may ensue if grandiose plans are acted upon. At a motivational level, manic behaviour is hyperactive. The manic person engages in frenetic activity, be it in work, in sexual relationships, or elsewhere. The 19th-century composer Robert Schumann produced 27 works during one manic year, but his productivity ground to a halt when he sank back into the depressive phase of his bipolar disorder (Jamison, 1995).

In a manic state, speech is often rapid or pressured, as if the person must say as many words as possible in the time allotted. With all this flurry of activity comes a greatly lessened need for sleep. Manic people may go for several days without sleeping, until exhaustion inevitably sets in and the mania slows down. The following case illustrates a manic episode:

> Robert B, a 56-year-old dentist, awoke one morning with the idea that he was the most gifted dental surgeon in his tri-state area; his mission then was

to provide service for as many persons as possible so that they could benefit from his talents. Consequently, he decided to enlarge his two-chair practice to a 20-chair one, and his plan was to reconstruct his two dental offices into 20 booths so that he could simultaneously attend to as many patients. That very day he drew up the plans for this arrangement and telephoned a number of remodellers and invited them to submit bids for the work.

Toward the end of that day he became irritated with the "interminable delays" and, after he attended to his last patient, rolled up his sleeves and began to knock down the walls of his dental offices. When he discovered that he couldn't manage this chore with the sledgehammer he had purchased for this purpose earlier, he became frustrated and proceeded to smash his more destructible tools, washbasins, and X-ray equipment. He justified this behaviour in his own mind by saying, "This junk is not suitable for the likes of me; it'll have to be replaced anyway."

He was in perpetual motion and his speech was "overexcited." When Robert was later admitted to a hospital, he could not sit in his chair; instead he paced the office floor like a caged animal. (Kleinmuntz, 1980, pp. 309–310)

Prevalence and Course of Mood Disorders

25. How prevalent is depression in men and women? Why the difference? What is its course if left untreated, and its likelihood of recurrence?

Epidemiological studies suggest that, at this moment, about one in twenty North Americans is severely depressed (Satcher, 1999). Statistically, your chances of having a depressive episode of clinical proportions at least once in your lifetime is about one in five (Hamilton, 1989). No age group is exempt from depression. It appears in infants as young as six months who have been separated from their mothers for prolonged periods. The rate of depressive symptoms in children and adolescents is as high as the adult rate (Essau & Petermann, 1999).

Data from numerous studies indicate that depression is on the rise in young groups, with the onset of depression increasing dramatically in 15- to 19-year-olds (Burke et al., 1991). People born after 1960 are 10 times more likely to experience depression than are their grandparents, even though their grandparents have lived much longer (Seligman, 1989). The reasons for this striking increase are not totally clear, but we will consider one possible explanation later. (Costello et al., 2006; Lewinson et al., 1993)

The prevalence of depressive disorders is similar across socio-economic and ethnic groups, but there is a major sex difference in our culture. Though men and women do not differ in prevalence of bipolar disorder, women appear to be about twice as likely as men to suffer unipolar depression (Figure 13.15). Biological theories suggest that genetic factors, biochemical differences in the nervous system, or the monthly premenstrual depression that many women experience could increase vulnerability to depressive disorders (Donaldson, 1998). In contrast, environmental theories focus on possible cultural causes. One suggestion is that the traditional sex role expectation for females in Western cultures is to be passive and dependent in the face of stress or loss and to focus on their feelings, whereas men are more likely to distract themselves through activities such as physical activity and drinking (Nolen-Hoeksema et al., 1994).

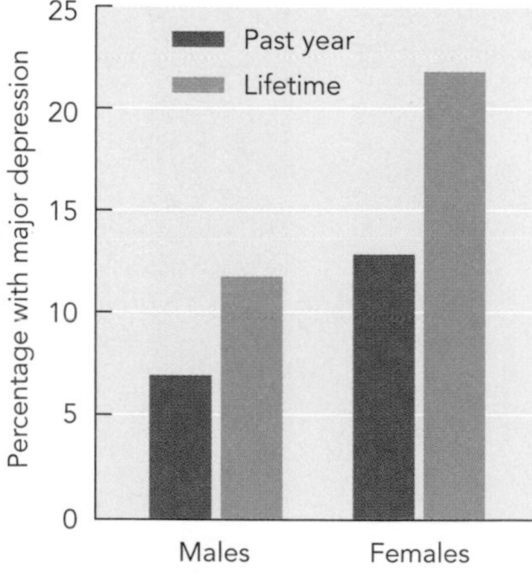

FIGURE 13.15

Prevalence rates for major depression in men and women.

Data from Kessler et al., 1994.

Most people who suffer depressive episodes never seek treatment. What is likely to happen to such people? Perhaps the one positive thing that can be said about depression is that it usually dissipates with time. After the initial episode, which typically comes on suddenly after a stressful experience, depression typically lasts an average of 5 to 10 months when untreated (Tollefson, 1993).

Once a depressive episode has occurred, one of three patterns may follow. In perhaps half of all cases, depression will never recur. Many other cases show a second pattern: recovery with recurrence. On average, these people will remain symptom-free for perhaps three years before experiencing another depressive episode of about the same severity and duration. The time interval between subsequent episodes of depression tends to become shorter over the years (Rubin, 2000). Finally, about 10 percent of people who have a major depressive episode will not recover and will remain chronically depressed (Figure 13.16).

Manic episodes, though less common than depressive reactions, are far more likely to recur. Fewer than one percent of the population experience mania, but more than 90 percent of those who do have a recurrence (American Psychiatric Association, 1994; Kessler et al., 1994).

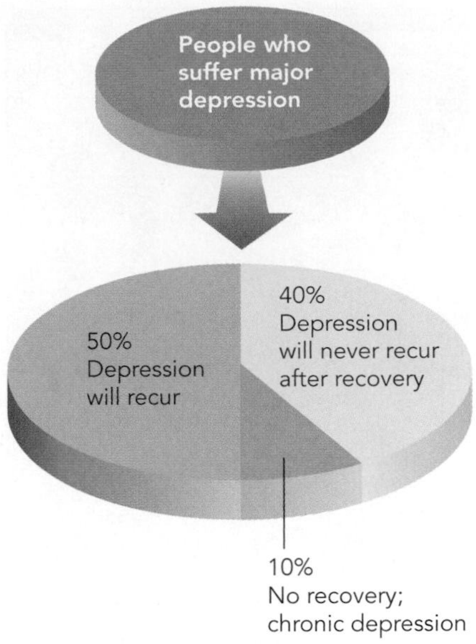

FIGURE 13.16

Course of outcome following a major depressive episode. About 40 percent never have a recurrence, perhaps 50 percent do have a recurrence, and about 10 percent suffer chronic (ever-present) depression.

Causal Factors in Mood Disorders

Biological Factors

Both genetic and neurochemical factors have been linked to depression (Donaldson, 1998). Genetic factors surface in both twin and adoption studies. Identical twins have a concordance rate of about 67 percent for experiencing clinical depression, compared to a rate of only 15 percent for fraternal twins (Gershon et al., 1989). Among adopted people who developed depression, biological relatives were found to be eight times more likely than adoptive relatives to also suffer from depression (Wender et al., 1986). What is likely inherited is a predisposition to develop a depressive disorder, given certain kinds of environmental factors such as significant losses and low social support (Barondes, 1999).

26. What evidence exists for a genetic factor in depression?

Research also has focused on the possible role of brain chemistry in depression. One influential theory holds that depression is a disorder of motivation caused by underactivity in a family of neurotransmitters that includes norepinephrine, dopamine, and serotonin (Davidson, 1998). These transmitters play important roles in several brain regions known to be important sites for experiencing reward and pleasure. When neural transmission decreases in these brain regions, the result is the lack of pleasure and loss of motivation that characterizes depression (Donaldson, 1998; White & Milner, 1992). In support of this theory, several highly effective antidepressant drugs operate by increasing the activity of these neurotransmitters, thereby increasing stimulation of the neural systems that underlie positive mood and goal-directed behaviour (Sen et al., 1999). A study by Lescia Tremblay and co-workers (2002) tested the amount of reward experienced by depressed patients when these centres were activated by a stimulant drug, reasoning that an enhanced pleasure response would reflect a normally underactive reward system. Severely depressed individuals showed a much stronger pleasure response to the drug, supporting the hypothesis of a "pleasure deficit" in the brain.

27. What biochemical processes might underlie depression? Mania?

Bipolar disorder, in which depression alternates with less frequent periods of mania, has been studied primarily at the biological level because it appears to have a stronger genetic basis than does unipolar depression (Young & Joffe, 1997). Among both men and women, the lifetime risk of developing a bipolar disorder is just below one percent. Yet about 50 percent of patients with bipolar disorder have a parent, grandparent, or child with the disorder (Barondes, 1999; Rubin, 2000). The concordance rate for bipolar disorder is five times higher in identical twins than in fraternal twins, suggesting a genetic link.

Manic disorders may stem from an *overproduction* of the same neurotransmitters that are underactive in depression. This might explain the symptom picture

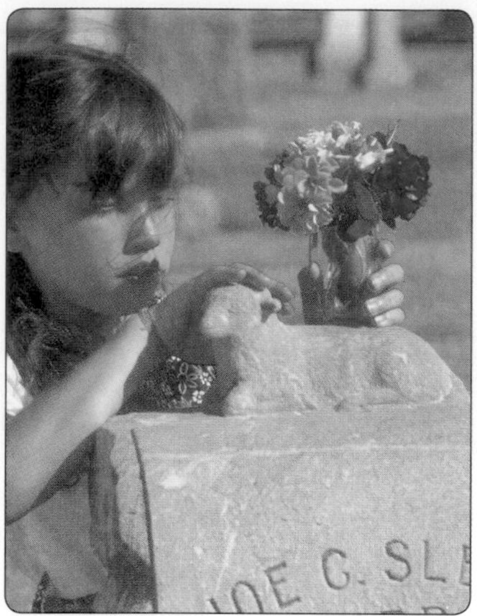

FIGURE 13.17

Early catastrophic losses are thought by psychoanalysts to increase vulnerability to later depressive disorders.

that is quite the opposite of that seen in depression. Significantly, lithium chloride, the drug most frequently used to calm manic disorders, works by decreasing the activity of these transmitters in the brain's motivational/pleasure activation system (LeMoal, 1999; Robinson, 1997).

Psychological Factors

Biological factors seem to increase vulnerability to certain types of psychological and environmental events that then can trigger the disorders. Other perspectives specify what those events might be.

Personality-based vulnerability. Psychoanalysts Karl Abraham (1911) and Sigmund Freud (1917) believed that early traumatic losses or rejections create vulnerability for later depression by triggering a grieving and rage process that becomes part of the individual's personality (Figure 13.17). Subsequent losses and rejection reactivate the original loss and cause a reaction not only to the current event, but also to the unresolved loss from the past.

Were he alive today, Freud would surely point to research by British sociologists George Brown and Terrill Harris (1978) to support his theory of early loss. Brown and Harris interviewed women in London and found that the rate of depression among women who had lost their mothers before age 11 and who had also experienced a severe recent loss was almost three times higher than the rate of depression among women who had experienced a similar recent loss but had not lost their mothers before age 11. Other research has shown that death of the father while a child is young is also associated with a greatly increased risk of later depression (Barnes & Prosen, 1985; Bowlby, 2000).

28. What evidence is there to support the notion that early losses create a risk factor for later depression?

The humanistic perspective also addresses causes of depression. In attempting to explain the dramatic increase in depression among people born after 1960, Martin Seligman (1989) has suggested that the "me" generation, with its overemphasis on individuality and personal control, has sown the seeds for its own depression. Because people define their self-worth in terms of individual attainment and have lesser commitment to traditional values of family, religion, and the common good, they are likely to react much more strongly to failure, to view negative events as reflecting their own inadequacies, and to experience a sense of meaninglessness in their lives.

29. How does Seligman explain the dramatic increase in depression among people born after 1960?

Cognitive processes. According to Aaron Beck (1976), depressed people victimize themselves through their own beliefs that they are defective, worthless, and inadequate. They also believe that whatever happens to them is bad, and that negative things will continue happening because of their personal defects (Clark et al., 1989). This **depressive cognitive triad** of negative thoughts concerning (1) the world, (2) oneself, and (3) the future seems to pop into consciousness automatically, and many depressed people report that they cannot control or suppress the negative thoughts (Wenzlaff et al., 1988). Depressed people also tend to recall most of their failures and few of their successes, and they tend to focus much of their attention on their perceived inadequacies (Haaga et al., 1991; Clark et al., 1999). Such thoughts trigger depressed affect.

30. Describe (a) the cognitive triad and (b) the depressive attributional pattern described by Beck.

As noted in the discussion of self-enhancement tendencies in Chapter 12, most people tend to take personal credit for the good outcomes in their lives and to blame their misfortunes on factors outside of themselves, thereby maintaining and enhancing their self-esteem. According to Beck, depressed people do exactly the opposite: They interpret successes or other positive events as being due to factors outside the self, while attributing negative outcomes to personal factors

(Figure 13.18). Beck believes that this **depressive attributional pattern** of taking no credit for successes but blaming themselves for failures maintains depressed people's low self-esteem and their belief that they are worthless failures. Quite literally, they can't win!

Another prominent cognitive account of depression, **learned helplessness theory**, holds that depression occurs when people expect that bad events will occur and that there is nothing they can do to prevent or cope with them (Abramson et al., 1978; Seligman & Isaacowitz, 2000). The depressive attributional pattern described above plays a central role in the learned helplessness model, but learned helplessness theorists take it a step further by specifying what the negative attributions for failure are like. They suggest that chronic and intense depression occurs as the result of negative attributions for failure that are *personal* ("It's all *my* fault"), *stable* ("I'll *always* be this way"), and *global* ("I'm a *total* loser"). Thus people who attribute negative events in their lives to factors such as low intelligence, physical repulsiveness, or an unlovable personality tend to believe that their personal defects will render them helpless to avoid negative events in the future, and therefore they are at significantly greater risk of depression.

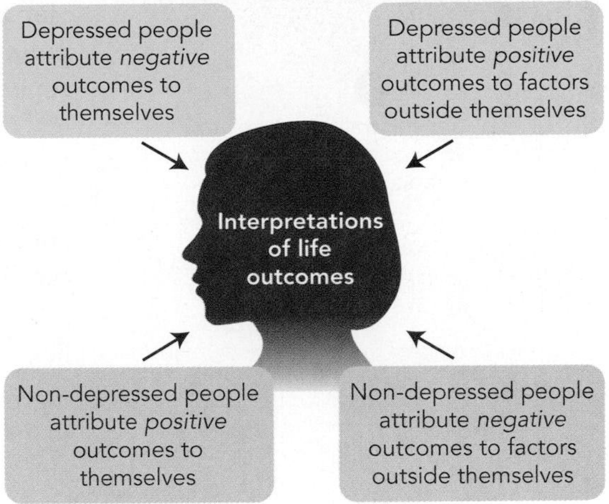
Depressive attributional pattern
Depressed people attribute *negative* outcomes to themselves
Depressed people attribute *positive* outcomes to factors outside themselves
Interpretations of life outcomes
Non-depressed people attribute *positive* outcomes to themselves
Non-depressed people attribute *negative* outcomes to factors outside themselves
Self-enhancement attributional pattern (non-depressed people)

FIGURE 13.18

Cognitive theorists believe that the attributional patterns of depressed people are the opposite of the self-enhancing patterns that characterize non-depressed people.

31. According to learned helplessness theory, what kinds of attributions trigger depression?

32. How does Lewinsohn's learning theory explain the spiralling downward course that occurs in severe depression?

Learning and environmental factors. Peter Lewinsohn and his colleagues (1985) believe that depression is usually triggered by a loss, some other punishing event, or by a drastic decrease in the amount of positive reinforcement that the person receives from her or his environment (Figure 13.19). As the depression begins to take hold, people stop performing behaviours that previously provided reinforcement, such as hobbies and socializing. Moreover, depressed people tend to make those who come in contact with them feel anxious, depressed, and hostile (Joiner & Coyne, 1999). Eventually, these other people begin to lose patience, failing to understand why the person doesn't "snap out of it." This diminishes social support still further, and may eventually cause depressed people to be abandoned by those who are most important to them (Nezlek et al., 2000).

Behavioural theorists believe that to begin feeling better, depressed people must break this vicious cycle by initially forcing themselves to engage in behaviours that are likely to produce some degree of pleasure. Eventually, positive reinforcement produced by these behaviours will begin to counteract the depressive affect, undermine the sense of helplessness that characterizes depression, and increase feelings of personal control over the environment.

Environmental factors may also help explain why depression tends to run in families. Constance Hammen (1991) studied the family histories of depressed people and concluded that children of depressed parents often experience poor parenting and many stressful experiences as they grow up. As a result, they may fail to develop good coping skills and a positive self-concept. They therefore are vulnerable later in life to stressful events that can trigger depressive reactions. This conclusion is supported by findings that children of depressed parents exhibit a significantly higher incidence of depression and other disorders as adolescents and young adults (Lieb et al., 2002; Halligan et al., 2007).

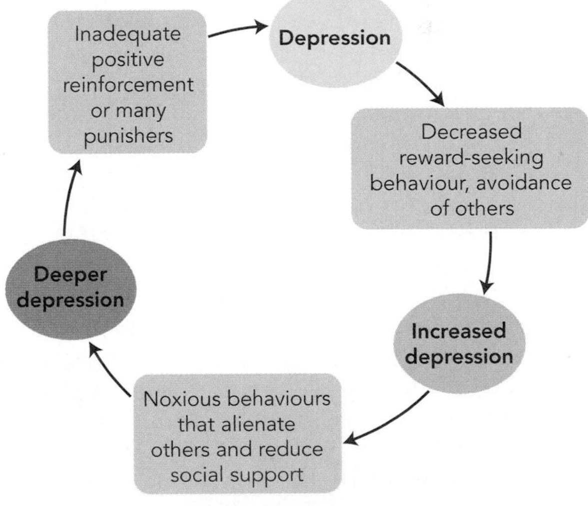
Inadequate positive reinforcement or many punishers
Depression
Decreased reward-seeking behaviour, avoidance of others
Increased depression
Noxious behaviours that alienate others and reduce social support
Deeper depression

FIGURE 13.19

Lewinsohn's behavioural model of depression focuses on the environmental causes and effects of depression. Depression results from loss of positive reinforcement and produces further decline in reinforcement and social support in a vicious-cycle fashion.

Sociocultural Factors

Although depression is found in virtually all cultures, its prevalence, symptom pattern, and causes reflect cultural variation (Lopez & Guarnaccia, 2000). For example, compared to Western nations, the prevalence of depressive disorders is far lower in Hong Kong and Taiwan, where strong connections to family and other groups help reduce the negative impact of loss and disappointments and provide strong social support when they occur (Tseng et al., 1990).

33. How are cultural factors related to the prevalence, manifestation, and sex differences in depression?

Cultural factors also can affect the ways in which depression is manifested. Feelings of guilt and personal inadequacy seem to predominate in North American and western European countries, whereas somatic symptoms of fatigue, loss of appetite, and sleep difficulties are more often reported in Latin, Chinese, and African cultures (Manson, 1994).

Finally, cultural factors may influence who develops depression. As noted earlier, women are about twice as likely as men to report feeling depressed in technologically advanced countries such as Canada, the United States, and other Western nations. Yet this sex difference is not found in developing countries (Culbertson, 1997; Nolen-Hoeksema, 1990). At present, we do not know why this pattern occurs, but attempts are under way to learn more about how the cultural environment influences the development of depression.

34. What is the relation between depression and suicide? What are the major motives and risk factors for suicide? Describe four practical guidelines for helping a suicidal person.

At one time or another, many depressed people consider suicide as a way to escape from the unhappiness of their lives. We now examine suicide, its causes, and what can be done to prevent this tragic event.

PSYCHOLOGICAL APPLICATIONS

Understanding and Preventing Suicide

Suicide is defined as the wilful taking of one's own life. The World Health Organization estimates that nearly 500,000 people worldwide commit suicide annually, about 1.4 per minute. Nearly 3,500 suicides a year are recorded in Canada, and there are up to 100 times as many attempts. Suicide is the second most common cause of death, surpassed only by accidents, for those in the 15–24 age bracket (Suicide Information and Education Centre, 1996). In 1993, there were 400 more recorded suicides than motor vehicle deaths. In North America, suicide rates for 15- to 24-year-olds have tripled since 1960 (National Centre for Health Statistics, 1995; Figure 13.20). In Canada, the suicide rate for 15- to 19-year-olds (12.9 per 100,000 population) is now similar to the rate for adults (15.8 per 100,000 population) (Statistics Canada, 2002).

Women make about three times as many suicide attempts as men, but men are three times more likely to actually kill themselves. These differences may be due to (a) a higher incidence of depression in women and (b) men's choice of more lethal methods, such as shooting themselves or jumping off buildings. The suicide rate for both men and women is higher among those who have been divorced or widowed. Women who commit suicide have a relatively greater tendency to be motivated by failure in love relationships, whereas men have a greater tendency to be motivated by failure in their occupations (Shneidman, 1976). A history of sexual or physical abuse significantly increases the likelihood of later suicide attempts (Fergusson & Lynskey, 1997; Garnefski & Arends, 1998).

Depression is one of the strongest predictors of suicide. About 15 percent of clinically depressed individuals eventually will kill themselves, a rate that is 22 to 36 times higher than the suicide rate for the general population. An estimated 80 percent of suicidal people are significantly depressed. It is noteworthy, however, that suicide does not usually occur when depression is deepest. Instead, suicide often occurs unexpectedly as a depressed person seems to be emerging from depression and feeling better. The lifting of depression may provide the energy needed to complete the suicidal act, without affecting the person's underlying sense of hopelessness and despair.

Motives for Suicide

There appear to be two fundamental motivations for suicide: the desire to end one's life and the desire to manipulate and coerce other people into doing what the suicidal person wants (Beck et al., 1979). Those who wish to end their lives basically have given up. They see no other way to deal with intolerable emotional distress, and in death they see an end to their problems. In one report, 56 percent of suicide attempts were classified as having been motivated by the desire to die (Beck,

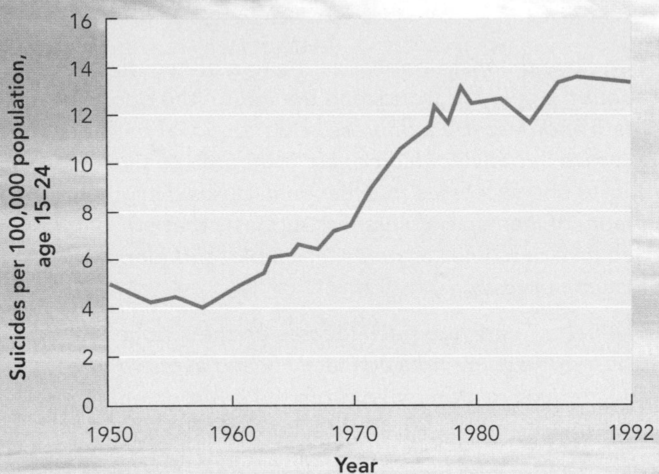

FIGURE 13.20

Suicide rate per 100,000 persons aged 15 to 24, from 1950 to 1992.
Data from National Centre for Health Statistics, 1998.

1976). These attempts were accompanied by high levels of depression and hopelessness, and they tended to be more lethal than other suicide attempts.

The second primary motivation for suicide is manipulation of others. Many *parasuicides* (suicide attempts that do not end in death) are cries for help or attempts to coerce people into meeting one's needs. Trying to prevent a lover from ending a relationship or trying to dramatize one's suffering are manipulative motives. Manipulative suicide attempters tend to use less lethal means (such as drug overdoses or wrist-slashing) and to make sure help is available. In the report cited earlier (Beck, 1976), 13 percent of the suicide attempts were classified as manipulative. The remaining 31 percent combined the two types of motivation. A small minority of suicides result from altruistic decisions to sacrifice one's life for the survival of others. Examples are the soldier who dives on a hand grenade to save comrades or a mother who elects to give birth rather than aborting her baby, knowing that she will die in the process.

Warning Signs for Suicide

The best predictor of suicide attempts in both men and women is a verbal or behavioural threat to commit suicide, and such threats should always be taken seriously. One of the most destructive myths about suicide is that people who talk openly about suicide don't actually carry out the act. Yet research shows that a high proportion of suicide attempts—perhaps 80 percent—are preceded by some kind of warning (Bagley & Ramsay, 1997; Chiles & Strossahl, 1995). Sometimes the warning is an explicit statement of intent, such as "I don't want to go on living" or "I won't be a burden much longer." Other times, the warnings are more subtle, as when a person expresses hopelessness about the future, withdraws from others or from favourite activities, gives away treasured possessions, or takes unusual risks. Other important risk factors are a history of previous suicide attempts and a detailed plan that involves a lethal method (Chiles & Strossahl, 1995; Shneidman, 1998).

Suicide Prevention

Much has been learned about the dynamics and prevention of suicide as a result of scientific research. These findings provide guidelines for preventing this tragic answer to life's problems. For example, another myth about suicide is that broaching the topic with a potentially suicidal person may prompt the person to carry out the act. In truth, the best first step if you suspect that someone may be suicidal is to ask the person directly whether he or she is considering suicide: "Have you thought about hurting yourself, or ending your life?" If the person responds affirmatively, try to find out if he or she has a plan or a timetable in mind. Do not be hesitant to approach the person. *Diffusion of responsibility* (discussed in Chapters 2 and 12) could result in your assuming that someone else is helping a potentially suicidal person, when in fact no one is (Kalafat et al., 1993). Your ultimate goal should be to help the person to receive assistance from a qualified professional as soon as possible, not to treat the person yourself. Nonetheless, you can take some immediate steps that may be helpful.

Many suicidal people feel alone in their misery. It is important to provide social support and empathy at this critical juncture. An expression of genuine concern can pave the way for other potentially helpful interventions (Barnett & Porter, 1998). For example, a frank discussion of the problem that is foremost in the person's life can be helpful. Suicidal people often feel totally overwhelmed by life, and focusing on a specific problem may help the person realize that it is not unsolvable and need not cloud his or her total perception of life.

When people are distressed and hopeless, their time orientation tends to narrow, and they have difficulty seeing beyond their current distress. Try to help the person see his or her present situation within a wider time perspective and to consider positive possibilities that might exist in the future. In particular, discuss reasons for continuing to live, and focus on any doubts the person might have about electing suicide. For example, if the person indicates that his or her family will suffer greatly from the suicide, adopt this as one of your arguments for a different solution to the problem. Many suicidal people would like to feel that they do not have to commit suicide. Capitalize on such feelings.

If a person is suicidal, stay with him or her and seek professional assistance. Most cities have suicide prevention centres that offer 24-hour services, including telephone and direct counselling. These centres usually are listed under *suicide* or *crisis* in the phone book.

In Review

- *Mood disorders include several depressive disorders and bipolar disorder, in which intermittent periods of mania (intense mood and behaviour activation) occur. Depression has four sets of symptoms: emotional, cognitive, motivational, and somatic. The symptoms of negative emotions and thoughts, loss of motivation, and behavioural slowness are reversed in mania.*
- *Both genetic and neurochemical factors have been linked to depression. One prominent biochemical theory links depression to an underactivity of neurotransmitters (norepinephrine, dopamine, and serotonin) that activate brain areas involved in pleasure and positive motivation. Drugs that relieve depression increase the activity of these transmitters. Bipolar disorder seems to have an even stronger genetic component than unipolar depression does.*
- *Psychoanalytic theorists view depression asa long-term consequence of traumatic losses and rejections early in life that create a personality vulnerability pattern.*
- *Cognitive theorists emphasize the role of negative beliefs about the self, the world, and the future (the depressive triad) and describe a depressive attributional pattern in which negative outcomes are attributed to personal causes and successes to situational causes. Seligman's theory of learned helplessness suggests that attributing negative outcomes to personal, stable, and global causes fosters depression.*
- *The behavioural approach focuses on the vicious cycle in which depression-induced inactivity and aversive behaviours reduce reinforcement from the environment and thereby increase depression still further.*
- *Manipulation and a desire to escape distress are the two major motives for suicide. The risk for suicide increases if the person is depressed and has a lethal plan and a past history of parasuicide.*

SOMATOFORM DISORDERS

35. Describe three varieties of somatoform disorders. What causal factors might be involved in somatoform disorders?

Somatoform disorders involve physical complaints or disabilities that suggest a medical problem, but which have no known biological cause and are not produced voluntarily by the person (Finell, 1997). In **hypochondriasis**, people become unduly alarmed about any physical symptom they detect, and are convinced that they have or are about to have a serious illness. People with **pain disorder** experience intense pain that either is out of proportion to whatever medical condition they might have or for which no physical basis can be found. Somatoform disorders differ from *psychophysiological disorders*, in which psychological factors cause or contribute to a real medical condition, such as an ulcer, asthma, hypertension (chronic high blood pressure), or a cardiac problem.

Perhaps the most fascinating of the somatoform disorders is **conversion disorder**, in which serious neurological symptoms, such as paralysis, loss of sensation, or blindness suddenly occur. People with conversion disorders often exhibit *la belle indifference*, a strange lack of concern about their symptom and its implications (Pajer, 2000). In some cases, the complaint itself is physiologically impossible. An example is the so-called *glove anaesthesia*, in which a person loses all sensation below the wrist. As Figure 13.21 shows, the hand is served by nerves that also provide sensory input above the hand, making glove anaesthesia physiologically impossible.

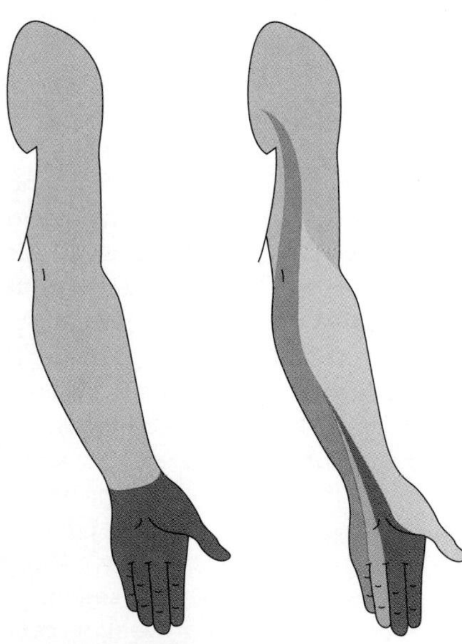

FIGURE 13.21

Glove anaesthesia is a conversion disorder in which all feeling is lost below the wrist. The skin areas served by nerves in the arm make this symptom physiologically impossible.

Conversion disorders are relatively rare, occurring in about 3 in 1,000 North Americans during peacetime (American Psychiatric Association, 1994), but such disorders occur more frequently under wartime conditions (Slavney, 1990). Thus a soldier about to return to the trauma of combat may suddenly develop blindness or paralysis for which no physical cause can be found.

Although "psychogenic blindness" is quite rare in the general population, researchers have discovered the largest known civilian group of people in the world having trauma-induced blindness. They are Cambodian refugees who escaped from their country and settled in Long Beach, California. These survivors of the "killing fields" of Cambodia were subjected to unspeakable horror at the hands of the Khmer Rouge in the years following the Vietnam War (Cooke, 1991). More than 150 of them are functionally blind, even though their eyes appear intact and electrophysiological monitoring shows that visual stimuli "register" in their visual cortex (Figure 13.22). The doctors who studied this remarkable group are convinced that they are not faking blindness. Many of the victims reported that their blindness occurred suddenly after witnessing traumatic scenes of murder. Were the sights from the outer world so painful that in these people, the visual system involuntarily shut down? An intriguing but as yet unanswered question is how cultural factors might have affected the development of this response to trauma.

FIGURE 13.22

A physician examines one of the Cambodian refugees who appear to be suffering from psychologically induced blindness. There is nothing wrong with their eyes, but they cannot see.

To Freud, such symptoms were a symbolic expression of an underlying conflict that aroused so much anxiety that the ego kept the conflict in the unconscious by converting the anxiety into a physical symptom that in some way symbolized the conflict. Contemporary psychodynamic theorists continue to accept this explanation (Fisher & Greenberg, 1996). In one of Freud's cases, a young woman who was forced to take care of her hostile, verbally abusive, and unappreciative father suddenly developed paralysis in her arm. According to Freud, this occurred when her repressed hostile impulses threatened to break through and cause her to strike him using that arm (Freud, 1935).

A predisposition to somatoform disorders may involve a combination of biological and psychological vulnerabilities. Somatoform disorders tend to run in families, though it is not clear whether this reflects the role of genetic factors, environmental learning and social reinforcement for bodily symptoms, or both (Trimble, 2003). Other theorists have suggested that some people may experience internal sensations more vividly than others, or may focus more attention on them (Barsky, 1992). If this results in a person being self-absorbed in his or her own body sensations, it could set the stage for increased apprehension about the body. Somatoform patients are also very suggestible (Roelofs et al., 2002). The incidence of somatoform disorders tends to be much higher in cultures that discourage open discussion of emotions or that stigmatize psychological disorders (Tanaka-Matsumi & Draguns, 1997). In such settings, somatic symptoms may be the only acceptable outlet for emotional distress. The same may occur in people who are so emotionally constricted that they cannot acknowledge their emotions or communicate them to others verbally (Traue & Deighton, 2000).

DISSOCIATIVE DISORDERS

Ordinarily, personality has unity and coherence, and the many facets of the self are integrated so that people act, think, and feel with some degree of consistency. Memory plays a critical role in this integration, for it connects past with present and provides a sense of personal identity that extends over time. **Dissociative disorders** involve a breakdown of this normal integration, resulting in significant alterations in memory or identity. Three forms that such disorders can take are psychogenic amnesia, psychogenic fugue, and dissociative personality disorder.

36. What is the central feature of dissociative disorders? Describe the three major types of dissociative disorders.

In **psychogenic amnesia**, a person responds to a stressful event with extensive but selective memory loss. Some people can remember nothing about their past. Others can no longer recall specific events, people, places, or objects, although other contents of memory, such as language and cognitive or motor skills remain intact.

Psychogenic fugue is a more profound dissociative disorder in which a person loses all sense of personal identity, gives up his or her customary life, wanders to a new faraway location, and establishes a new identity. Usually, the fugue is triggered by a highly stressful event or trauma, and it may last from a few hours or days to several years. Some adolescent runaways have been found to be in a fugue state, and married fugue victims may wed someone else and start a new career (Loewenstein, 1991). Typically, the fugue ends when the person suddenly recovers his or her original identity and "wakes up," mystified and distressed at being in a strange place under strange circumstances.

Dissociative identity disorder (DID), formerly called *multiple personality disorder,* is the most striking and widely publicized of the dissociative disorders; it is also the most controversial. Several celebrated cases of DID have been dramatized in books and movies, such as *Sybil* and *The Three Faces of Eve.* In this disorder, two or more separate personalities coexist in the same person. A primary, or *host personality* appears more often than the others (called *alters*), but each personality has its own integrated set of memories and behaviours. The personalities may or may not know about the existence of the others. They also can differ in age and gender, with one being male, another female. The personalities can differ not only mentally and behaviourally but also physiologically, as in the following case.

A 38-year-old woman named Margaret was admitted to a hospital with paralysis of her legs following a minor car accident. During the course of her interview the woman, a member of an ultrareligious sect, reported that she sometimes heard a strange voice inside her threatening to "take over completely." The physician suggested that she let the voice "take over." Here is his report of what happened:

> The woman closed her eyes, clenched her fists, and grimaced for a few moments during which she was out of contact with those in the room. Suddenly she opened her eyes and one was in the presence of another person. Her name, she said, was "Harriet." Whereas Margaret had been paralyzed, and complained of fatigue, headache, and backache, Harriet felt well and she at once proceeded to walk around the room unaided. She spoke scornfully of Margaret's religiousness, her invalidism, and her puritanical life, professing that she herself liked to drink and "go partying" but that Margaret was always going to church and reading the Bible. . . . At length, at the interviewer's suggestion, Harriet reluctantly agreed to "bring Margaret back" and after more grimacing and fist clenching, Margaret reappeared paralyzed, complaining of her headache and backache, and completely amnesic for the brief period of Harriet's release from her prison. (Nemiah, 1978, pp. 179–180)

37. How does the trauma-dissociation theory account for the development of DID?

According to **trauma-dissociation theory**, the development of new personalities occurs in response to severe stress. For a vast majority of patients, this begins to occur in early childhood, frequently in response to physical or sexual abuse. Frank Putnam (1989) studied the life histories of 100 diagnosed DID cases and found that 97 of them reported severe abuse and trauma in early and middle childhood, a time when children's identities are not well established and it is quite easy for them to dissociate. Putnam believes that, in response to the trauma and their helplessness to resist it, children may engage in something akin to self-hypnosis and dissociate from reality. They create a new alternate identity to detach themselves from the trauma, to transfer what is happening to someone else who can handle it, and to blunt the pain. Over time, it is theorized, the protective functions served by the new personality remain separate in the form of an alternate personality, rather than being integrated into the host personality (Meyer & Osborne, 1987; Putnam, 1989).

38. On what grounds have critics questioned the validity of DID, and what explanations do they offer instead?

Dissociative identity disorder has become a controversial topic, and some question its very existence. We now consider some of the reasons why.

RESEARCH FRONTIERS

Dissociative Identity Disorder: A Clinical and Scientific Puzzle

Scientists at the National Institute of Mental Health (NIMH) in Washington, D.C., have studied more than 150 cases of DID (Putnam, 1989, 1998). In many cases, they were able to study the physiological responses of the patients when different personalities were active. The results of these studies suggest that the alternate selves may be different in both mind and body. If Eve had three faces, she may also have had three voices, three memory systems, and, in a limited sense, three biological response systems.

Prior to the NIMH studies, physicians and mental-health workers had frequently reported dramatic physical differences between the alternate personalities of DID patients. The differences include physical health differences, voice changes, and even changes in right- and left-handedness. Some patients had severe allergies when one personality was present, but no allergies when the others were active. One patient nearly died of a violent allergic reaction to a bee sting. A week later, when an alternate personality was active, another sting produced no reaction. Female patients frequently have different menstrual cycles for each female personality; one patient had three periods per month. Other patients need eyeglasses with different prescriptions for different personalities; one may be farsighted, another nearsighted (Miller et al., 1991). Epileptic patients with DID often have their seizures in one personality but not another (Drake et al., 1988).

Physiological studies of DID patients under controlled laboratory conditions have also shown differences between the various personalities (Atchison & McFarlane, 1994). Indeed, the responses of the various personalities frequently appear as different as if they had come from different people (Figure 13.23). For example, Christine Ludlow did computerized spectral analyses ("voice prints") of audio recordings made by alternate personalities, and found that the voices were quite distinct from one another (Putnam, 1984). Using electrical recording and brain-scanning techniques to study brain differences associated with alternate personalities, Frank Putnam (1984) found that cerebral blood-flow patterns differed between the personalities. Moreover, Putnam found shifts in EEG measures of hemispheric dominance when the individual had right-handed and left-handed personalities. When a left-handed personality appeared, the right hemisphere became more active. In another study, ophthalmologists found shifts in visual acuity and eye-muscle balance as DID patients shifted from one personality to another. Such changes did not occur among control subjects who were asked to simulate another personality (Miller et al., 1991).

As dramatic as these physiological differences between DID alters might appear, they are not universally accepted by critics, who correctly point out that many of the observations are based on uncontrolled case studies. Could the average person asked to role play separate personalities exhibit such differences as well? Indeed there is some evidence that EEG differences can be produced by such role playing in normal individuals (Coons et al., 1982), but so far none of the other more exotic physiological phenomena described above has been shown in role-playing controls (Gleaves, 1996). In

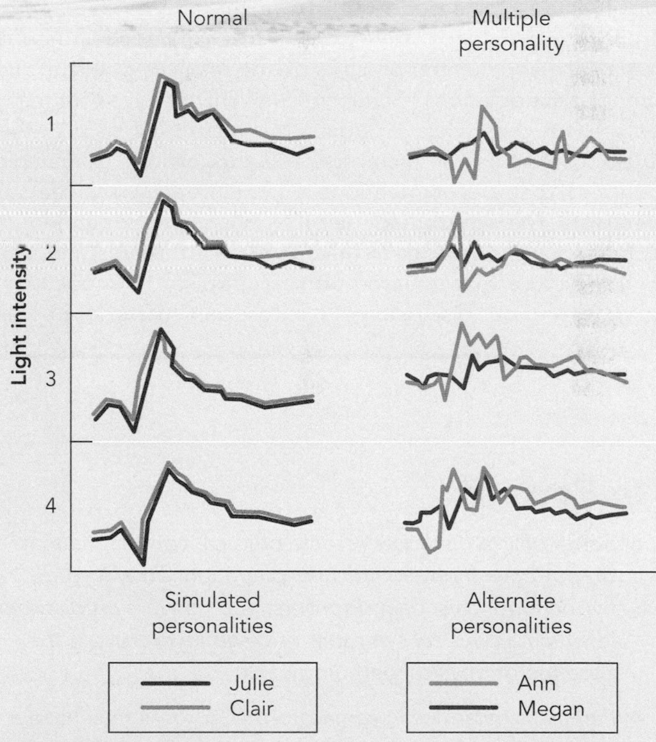

FIGURE 13.23

Comparisons of evoked potentials of a DID patient (Ann and her alternate personality, Megan) and a control participant (Julie) simulating a second personality (Clair) to four levels of visual stimulation. The DID patient's EEG records differed more from one another.

Adapted from Putnam, 1984.

–*Continued*

some studies, such as the visual acuity and eye muscle study described above, role players have been unable to produce the responses shown by DID patients. Nonetheless, it is clear that additional controlled studies of physiological alterations are needed.

Some critics consider the notion of multiple personalities to be nothing more than science fiction, and they dispute the existence of DID as a valid clinical disorder (Beahrs, 1994; Spanos, 1994; Piper & Merslay, 2004ab). Troubling to many psychologists and legal experts is a tendency for some people who have committed serious crimes to disclaim personal responsibility on the grounds that they are DID victims and that one of the alternative personalities committed the crime (Beahrs, 1994). Other critics wonder if DID is, in reality, a therapist-produced phenomenon. They point out that, prior to 1970, only about 100 cases of what was then called multiple personality disorder had been reported worldwide. Even today, it is virtually unknown in many cultures, including Japan (Takahashi, 1990). But, after the disorder was highly publicized in the book and movie *Sybil*, many additional cases began to be reported by therapists, until they numbered in the tens of thousands by the mid-1990s. The number of alternate personalities also increased from two or three to an average of about fifteen (Spanos, 1994). Could this dramatic increase in prevalence and number of alters be the result of publicity and therapist expectations? Some critics of DID believe that many features of the cases, including the memories of previous abuse, could be false memories and suggestions of multiple identities that are unintentionally implanted by overzealous therapists. The widespread use of hypnosis in the treatment of suspected DID only adds to the danger of a therapist-induced clinical picture that is based on susceptibility to suggestion. As we saw in our discussion of hypnosis in Chapter 6, people can become so immersed in an imagined role that it becomes quite real to them, and they act accordingly (Spanos, 1996).

In some instances, clients have filed lawsuits against therapists, charging them with creating the disorder in them. In one bizarre case, a Wisconsin woman and her insurance company successfully sued a psychiatrist who used hypnosis to allegedly unearth 120 different personalities in her, including Satan and a duck, then billed the insurance company at the higher group therapy rate on the grounds that he was treating multiple people! The woman charged the therapist with implanting false memories of sexual abuse, rape, being pushed into an open grave, and aborting a baby. She maintained that she had never had any of the memories before beginning therapy and that the false memories caused nightmares, flashbacks, suicidal impulses, and, eventually, the need for hospitalization (*Associated Press*, December 12, 1997). Such extreme instances, which by no means typify the efforts of ethical therapists to help their clients, serve to fuel the concerns of critics.

Is DID real? Suppose it were to be convincingly demonstrated in experimental studies that role playing by average people can produce all of the DID phenomena described at the beginning of this feature. Would this prove that true dissociation does not occur in *any* of the cases seen by mental-health workers? Not at all, supporters maintain, any more than a compelling depiction of a schizophrenic person by a skilled actor such as Jack Nicholson would prove that all cases of schizophrenia involve nothing more than acting. The controversy that swirls around DID may help fuel continued investigation of the cognitive and physiological phenomena that are seen in DID. Such research may advance our understanding of factors that can produce dramatic alterations in memory, physiological responses, and behaviour.

In Review

- *Somatoform disorders involve physical complaints that do not have a physiological explanation. They include hypochondriasis, pain disorders, and conversion disorders in which a physical symptom or disability occurs in the absence of physical pathology.*
- *Familial similarities in somatoform disorders may have a biological basis, or they may be the result of environmental shaping through attention and sympathy. Somatoform patients may be highly vigilant and reactive to somatic symptoms. Such disorders tend to occur with greater frequency in cultures that discourage open expression of negative emotions.*
- *Dissociative disorders involve losses of memory and personal identity. The major dissociative disorders are psychogenic amnesia, psychogenic fugue, and dissociative identity disorder (DID).*
- *The trauma-dissociation theory holds that DID emerges when children dissociate to defend themselves from severe physical or sexual abuse. This model has been challenged by other theorists who believe that multiple personalities result from role immersion and therapist suggestion.*

SCHIZOPHRENIA

Of all the psychological disorders, schizophrenia is the most serious and, in many ways, the most puzzling and difficult to treat (Hogarty, 2003). Despite many theories of schizophrenia and thousands of research studies, a complete understanding of this disorder continues to elude us.

Schizophrenia is a psychotic disorder that involves severe disturbances in thinking, speech, perception, emotion, and behaviour (Herz & Marder, 2002). The term *schizophrenia* was introduced by the Swiss psychiatrist Eugen Bleuler in 1911. Literally, the term means "split mind," which often has led people to confuse schizophrenia with dissociative identity disorder or with a Dr. Jekyll–Mr. Hyde phenomenon. But multiple personality is not what Bleuler had in mind when he coined the term. Instead, Bleuler intended to suggest that certain psychological functions, such as thought, language, and emotion, which are joined together in normal people, are somehow split apart or disconnected in schizophrenia.

39. What is meant by the term schizophrenia? What are the major cognitive, behavioural, emotional, and perceptual features of these disorders?

Characteristics of Schizophrenia

A diagnosis of schizophrenia requires evidence that a person misinterprets reality and exhibits disordered attention, thought, or perception. In addition, withdrawal from social interaction is common, communication is strange or inappropriate, personal grooming may be neglected, and behaviour may become disorganized (American Psychiatric Association, 1994).

The schizophrenic thought disorder sometimes includes delusions (Nadelson & Reinburg, 1999). **Delusions** are false beliefs that are sustained in the face of evidence that normally would be sufficient to destroy them. A schizophrenic person may believe that his brain is being turned to glass by ray guns operated by his enemies from outer space, or that Jesus Christ is a special agent of his. The first is a *delusion of persecution,* the second a *delusion of grandeur.*

Several aspects of thought disorder were described by a schizophrenic during a period of recovery:

> The most wearing aspect of schizophrenia is the fierce battle that goes on inside my head in which conflicts become unresolvable. I am so ambivalent that my mind can divide on a subject, and those two parts subdivide over and over until my mind feels like it is in pieces, and I am totally disorganized. At other times, I feel like I am trapped inside my head, banging against its walls, trying desperately to escape while my lips can utter only nonsense. (*New York Times,* March 18, 1986, p. C12)

Perceptual disorganization and disordered thought become more pronounced as people progress into a schizophrenic condition. What the world might come to look like from inside the schizophrenic mind is illustrated in art by patients during periods of disturbance (Figure 13.24). Some experience **hallucinations**, false perceptions that have a compelling sense of reality. Auditory hallucinations (typically voices speaking to the patient) are most common, although visual and tactile hallucinations may also occur. This patient describes his hallucinations:

> Recently, my mind has played tricks on me, creating The People inside my head who sometimes come out to haunt me and torment me. They surround me in rooms, hide behind trees and under the snow outside. They taunt me and scream at me and devise plans to break my spirit. The voices come and go, but The People are always there, always real. (*New York Times,* March 18, 1986, p. C12)

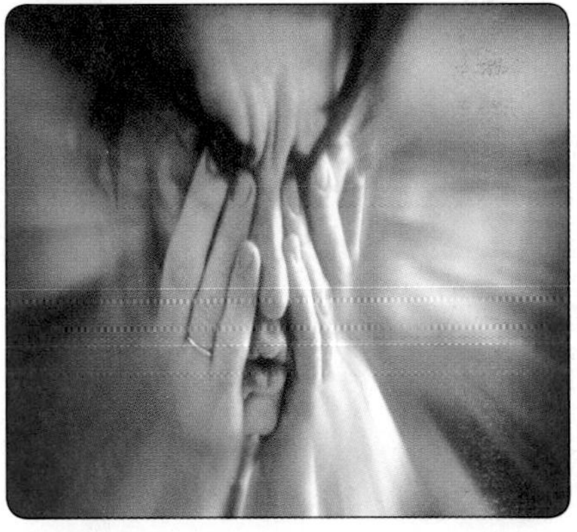

(a)

(b)

FIGURE 13.24

(a) Patients diagnosed with schizophrenia are tormented by bizarre and intrusive thoughts and images. (b) This picture, drawn by a patient diagnosed with schizophrenia, may offer insights into his subjective world.

The language of schizophrenic patients is often disorganized, and can contain strange words.

> I am here from a foreign university . . . and you have to have a "plausity" of all acts of amendment to go through for the children's code . . . and it is no mental disturbance or "putenance" . . . it is an "amorition" law . . . it is like their "privatilinia." (Vetter, 1969, p. 189)

Patients' language sometimes contains word associations that are based on rhymes or other associations rather than meaning. Consider the following conversation between a psychologist and a hospitalized schizophrenic:

> After two weeks, the psychologist said to him: "As you say, you are wired precisely wrong. But why won't you let me see the diagram?" Carl answered: "Never, ever will you find the lever, the eternalever that will sever me forever with my real, seal, deal, heel. It is not on my shoe, not even on the sole. It walks away." (Rosenhan & Seligman, 1989, p. 369)

Emotions can be affected in a number of ways. Many people with schizophrenia have *blunted affect,* manifesting less sadness, joy, and anger than most people. Others have *flat affect,* showing almost no emotion at all. Their voices are monotonous, their faces impassive. *Inappropriate affect* can also occur, as in the following case:

> The psychologist noted that Carl "smiles when he is uncomfortable, and smiles more when in pain. He cries during television comedies. He seems angry when justice is done, frightened when someone compliments him, and roars with laughter on reading that a young child was burned in a tragic fire." (Rosenhan & Seligman, 1989, p. 369)

?
40. Describe the four major types of schizophrenic disorders.

Subtypes of Schizophrenia

Schizophrenia has cognitive, emotional, and behavioural facets that can vary widely from case to case. DSM-IV differentiates among four major subtypes of schizophrenia:

FIGURE 13.25

The woman pictured here exhibits catatonic rigidity. She might hold this position for several hours.

- **Paranoid type.** The most prominent features in paranoid schizophrenics are delusions of persecution, in which people believe that others mean to harm them, and delusions of grandeur, in which they believe they are enormously important. Suspicion, anxiety, or anger may accompany the delusions, and hallucinations may also occur in this subtype.
- **Disorganized type.** The central features are confusion and incoherence, together with severe deterioration of adaptive behaviour. Thought disorganization often is so extreme that it is difficult to communicate with them. Their behaviour often appears silly and childlike, and their emotional responses are highly inappropriate. These people are usually unable to function on their own.
- **Catatonic type.** The catatonic subtype shows striking motor disturbances, ranging from muscular rigidity to random or repetitive movements. Catatonics sometimes alternate between stuporous states in which they seem oblivious to reality and agitated excitement during which they can be dangerous to others. While in a stuporous state, they may exhibit a *waxy flexibility* in which their limbs can be moulded by another person into grotesque positions that they will then maintain for hours (Figure 13.25).
- **Undifferentiated type.** This category is for people who exhibit some of the symptoms and thought disorders of the above categories but do not have enough of the specific criteria to be diagnosed in those categories.

In addition to these formal DSM-IV categories, many mental-health workers and researchers categorize schizophrenic reactions into two main categories on the basis of two classes of symptoms. **Type I schizophrenia** is characterized by a predominance of **positive symptoms**, such as delusions, hallucinations, and disordered speech and thinking. These symptoms are called *positive* because they represent pathological extremes of normal processes. **Type II schizophrenia** features **negative symptoms**—an absence of normal reactions—such as lack of emotional expression, loss of motivation, and an absence of normal speech (Herz & Marder, 2002).

The distinction between positive and negative symptom subtypes seems to be an important one. Researchers have found differences in brain function between schizophrenics having positive symptoms and those with primarily negative symptoms (Gur et al., 1998; Zakzanis, 1998). The subtypes also show differences in life history and prognosis. Negative symptoms are likely to be associated with a long history of poor functioning prior to hospitalization and with a poor outcome following treatment (McGlaskan & Fenton, 1992). In contrast, positive symptoms, especially those associated with a diagnosis of paranoid schizophrenia, are associated with good functioning prior to breakdown and a better prognosis for eventual recovery, particularly if the symptoms came on suddenly and were preceded by a history of relatively good adjustment (Fenton & McGlaskan, 1991a, 1991b).

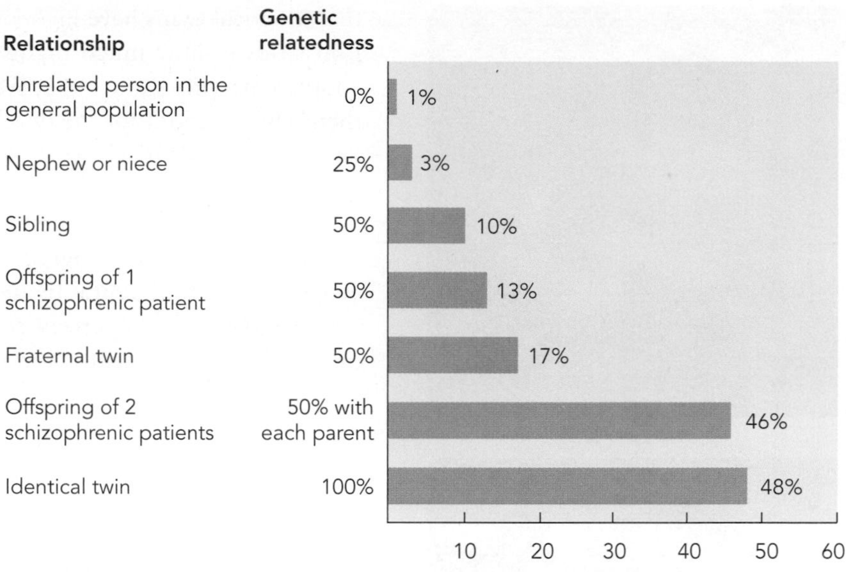

FIGURE 13.26

The degree of risk for developing schizophrenia in one's lifetime correlates highly with the degree of genetic relationship with someone who has that disorder. These data summarize the results of 40 concordance studies conducted in many countries.

Based on data from Gottesman, 1991.

Schizophrenia afflicts only one to two percent of the population, yet schizophrenic patients occupy about half of all psychiatric hospital beds (Satcher, 1999). Many others, such as Eddie, the man described at the beginning of the chapter, barely function as homeless "street people" in large cities (Herman et al., 1998). About 10 percent of people with schizophrenia remain permanently impaired, and 65 percent show intermittent periods of normal functioning. The other 25 percent recover from the disorder (American Psychiatric Association, 1994). Schizophrenia affects equal numbers of males and females, but it appears earlier in males, frequently between the ages of 15 and 30 (Jeste & Heaton, 1994).

41. Distinguish between Type I and Type II schizophrenia. How are positive and negative symptoms related to past history and future prognosis?

Causal Factors in Schizophrenia

Because of the seriousness of the disorder and the many years of anguish and incapacitation that its victims are likely to experience, schizophrenia is perhaps the most widely researched of the psychological disorders. There is a growing consensus that schizophrenia results from a biologically based vulnerability factor that is set into motion by psychological and environmental events (Fowles, 1992; Gottesman, 1991; Green, 1998).

42. Describe the evidence for genetic and neurological factors in schizophrenia.

Biological Factors

Strong evidence exists for a genetic predisposition to schizophrenia, though the specific genes involved and their roles in creating the disposition are still unknown (Franzek & Beckmann, 1999). As Figure 13.26 shows, the closer the biological relationship to a person diagnosed with schizophrenia, the greater the risk for developing the disorder during one's lifetime (Gottesman, 1991). Twin studies show

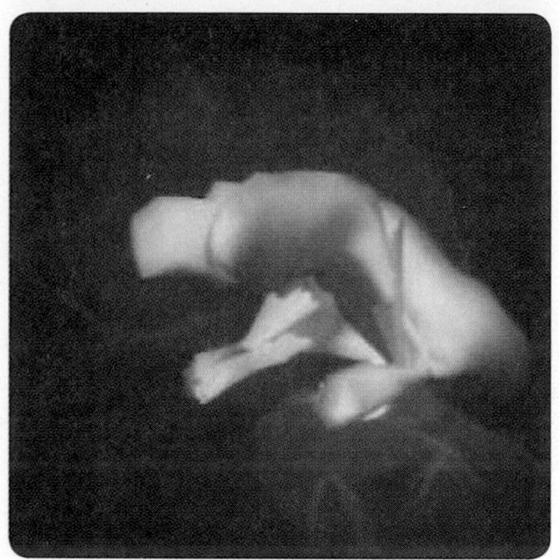

FIGURE 13.27

Schizophrenia and the brain. One difference between the brains of schizophrenics and nonschizophrenics is enlarged ventricles (the butterfly-shaped spaces seen in the middle of the MRIs) in the schizophrenic brain (bottom). Findings like these support the position that brain abnormalities play a role in schizophrenia.

that identical twins have higher concordance rates than fraternal twins, and adoption studies show much higher concordance with biological parents than with adoptive parents (Kety, 1988; Wahlberg et al., 1997). But, again, genetics do not by themselves account for the development of schizophrenia. If they did, the concordance rate in identical twins would be 100 percent, not 48 percent (Ingraham & Kety, 2000).

Brain scans have indicated a number of structural abnormalities in the brains of schizophrenic patients (Figure 13.27). According to the neurodegenerative hypothesis, destruction of neural tissue can cause schizophrenia (Weinberger & McClure, 2002). First, 20 to 35 percent show mild to moderate *brain atrophy,* a general loss or deterioration of neurons in the cerebral cortex and limbic system (Jernigan et al., 1991). The atrophy is centred in brain regions that influence cognitive processes and emotion, which may help explain the thought disorders and inappropriate emotion that are seen in such patients. Likewise, the thalamus, which collects and routes sensory input to various parts of the brain, shows MRI abnormalities. This may help account for the disordered attention and perception reported by schizophrenic patients whose cerebral cortex may be getting garbled or unfiltered information from the thalamus (Andreason, 1994). All of these structural differences are more common in patients who exhibit the Type II negative-symptom pattern (Herz & Marder, 2002). As we have seen, these patients have a poorer chance of recovery than those with the Type I positive-symptom pattern.

Dopamine, a major excitatory transmitter substance, may play a key role in schizophrenia. The **dopamine hypothesis** states that the symptoms of schizophrenia—particularly positive symptoms—are produced by overactivity of the dopamine system in areas of the brain that regulate emotional expression, motivated behaviour, and cognitive functioning (White & Milner, 1992). People diagnosed with schizophrenia have more dopamine receptors on neuron membranes than do non-schizophrenics, and these receptors seem to be overreactive to dopamine stimulation (Black et al., 1988; Wong et al., 1986). Additional support comes from the finding that the effectiveness of antipsychotic drugs used to treat schizophrenia is directly related to their effectiveness in reducing dopamine-produced synaptic activity (Creese et al., 1976; Green, 1997). Other neurotransmitter systems are probably involved in this complex disorder as well.

The biological findings concerning schizophrenia are intriguing. What is not clear is whether they cause the disorder or are caused by it. Future research is almost certain to reveal other biological bases for the complex disorders of schizophrenia.

Psychological Factors

Freud and other psychoanalytic thinkers viewed schizophrenia as a retreat from unbearable stress and conflict. For Freud, schizophrenia represented an extreme example of the defence mechanism of **regression**, in which a person retreats to an earlier and more secure (even infantile) stage of psychosocial development in the face of overwhelming anxiety. Other psychodynamic thinkers, focusing on the interpersonal withdrawal that is an important feature of schizophrenia, view the disorder as a retreat from an interpersonal world that has become too stressful to deal with. Although Freud's regression explanation has not received much direct research support (Fisher & Greenberg, 1996), the belief that life stress is a causal factor is generally accepted today (Crook & Copolov, 2000).

?

43. What is the dopamine hypothesis? What evidence supports it?

Cognitive theorists believe that schizophrenics have a defect in the attentional mechanism that filters out irrelevant stimuli, so that they are overwhelmed by both internal and external stimuli. Thus sensory input becomes a chaotic flood, and irrelevant thoughts and images flash into consciousness. The stimulus overload produces distractability, thought disorganization, and the sense of being overwhelmed by disconnected thoughts and ideas. As one schizophrenic noted, "Everything seems to come pouring in at once . . . I can't seem to keep anything out" (Carson et al., 1988, p. 329). The recent MRI findings of thalamic abnormalities described above may help explain how this stimulus overload could occur through malfunction of the brain's "switchboard." Schizophrenic thought processes may be linked to deficits in the executive functions of the frontal lobe (Kerns & Berenbaum, 2002 & 2003). In one study, schizophrenic patients pressed a key to signal the experimenter when they were hearing voices or experiencing a strange visual experience. PET scans performed at these times showed that the auditory or visual areas of the cortex were highly active, but there was no activity in the prefrontal cortex, whose functioning helps us distinguish reality from fantasy (Silbersweig et al., 1995).

44. What concepts do (a) psychoanalytic and (b) cognitive theorists use to explain the symptoms of schizophrenia?

Environmental Factors

Stressful life events seem to play an important role in the emergence of schizophrenic behaviour. These events tend to cluster in the two or three weeks preceding the "break" when the acute signs of the disorder appear (Day et al., 1987). Stressful life events seem to interact with biological or personality vulnerability factors. A highly vulnerable person may require little in the way of life stress to reach the breaking point (Fowles, 1992; van Praag, 2004).

45. How successful have researchers been in identifying family factors that cause schizophrenia? What role does expressed emotion play as a family variable?

Family dynamics have long been a prime suspect in the origins of schizophrenia, but the search for parent or family characteristics that might cause the disorder has been largely unsuccessful. Significantly, children of biologically normal parents who are raised by schizophrenic adoptive parents do not show an increased risk of developing schizophrenia (Kety, 1988). Although persons with schizophrenia often come from families with problems, the nature and seriousness of those problems are not different from those of families in which non-schizophrenics are raised.

This does not mean that family dynamics are not important; rather, it may mean that a biological vulnerability factor must be present if stressful familial events are to cause their damage. Indeed, there is evidence that this vulnerability factor may appear early in life. In one study, researchers analyzed home movies showing children who were later to develop schizophrenic behaviours, as well as movies of their non-schizophrenic brothers and sisters. Even at these early ages—sometimes as young as two years of age—preschizophrenic children tended to show more odd and uncoordinated movements and less emotional expressiveness, especially for positive emotions (Grimes & Walker, 1994). These behavioural oddities may reflect not only a vulnerability factor, but may also help to create environmental stress by evoking negative reactions from others.

46. Contrast the social causation and social drift hypotheses concerning social class and the prevalence of schizophrenia.

Although researchers have had difficulty pinpointing family factors that contribute to the *initial* appearance of schizophrenia, one consistent finding is that previously hospitalized schizophrenics are more likely to relapse if they return to a home environment that is high in a factor called **expressed emotion** (Vaughn & Leff, 1976). Expressed emotion involves high levels of *criticism* ("All you do is sit in front of that TV"), *hostility* ("We're getting sick and tired of your craziness") and *overinvolvement* ("You're not going out unless I go with you"). One review of 26 studies showed that within 9 to 12 months of their return home, an average relapse rate of 48 percent occurred in patients whose families were high in expressed emotion, compared to a relapse rate of 21 percent when families were low in this factor (Kavanaugh, 1992). Before we conclude that high expressed emotion causes patients to relapse, however, we should note a finding from another study in which researchers videotaped actual interactions involving patients and their families

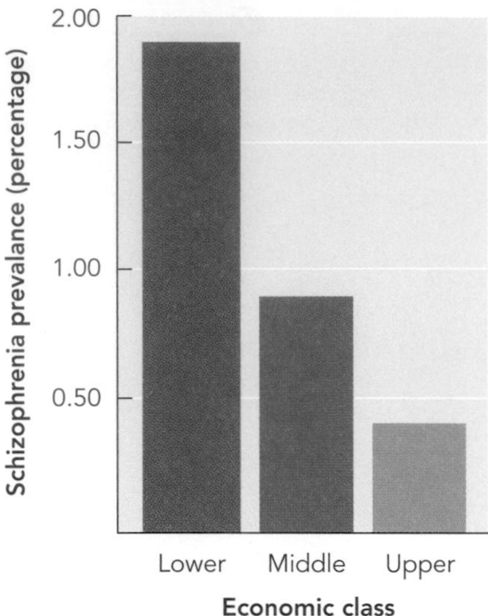

FIGURE 13.28

Relation between economic status and the prevalence of schizophrenia. Is economic status a cause or an effect of schizophrenia?

Based on data from Keith et al., 1991.

(Rosenfarb et al., 1995). Analyses of the videotapes revealed that families high in expressed emotion did indeed make more negative comments to patients when they engaged in strange behaviours, but they also showed that the patients in these families engaged in about four times as many strange and disruptive behaviours, clouding the issue of what causes what. Thus high expressed emotion may be either a cause of or a response to patients' disordered behaviours.

Sociocultural Factors

Sociocultural factors are undoubtedly linked to schizophrenia (Murray et al., 2003). Many studies have found that the prevalence of schizophrenia is highest in lower socio-economic populations (Figure 13.28). Why is this? Is poverty a cause of schizophrenia, or is it an effect of the disorder? Two theories give opposite answers. The *social causation hypothesis* attributes the higher prevalence of schizophrenia to the higher levels of stress that low-income people experience, particularly within urban environments. In contrast, the *social drift hypothesis* proposes that, as people develop schizophrenia, their personal and occupational functioning deteriorates, so that they drift down the socio-economic ladder into poverty and migrate to low-cost urban environments. Perhaps social causation and social drift are both at work, since the factors that link poverty, social and environmental stressors, and schizophrenia are undoubtedly complex (Figure 13.29).

In contrast to most of the disorders we have described so far, schizophrenia may be a "culture-free" disorder. A worldwide epidemiological study sponsored by the World Health Organization indicated that the prevalence of schizophrenia is not dramatically different throughout the world (Jablensky et al., 1992). On the other hand, researchers have found that the likelihood of *recovery* is greater in developing countries than in developed nations such as the United States and Canada. This may reflect a stronger community orientation and greater social support extended to disturbed people in developing countries (Tanaka-Matsumi & Draguns, 1997).

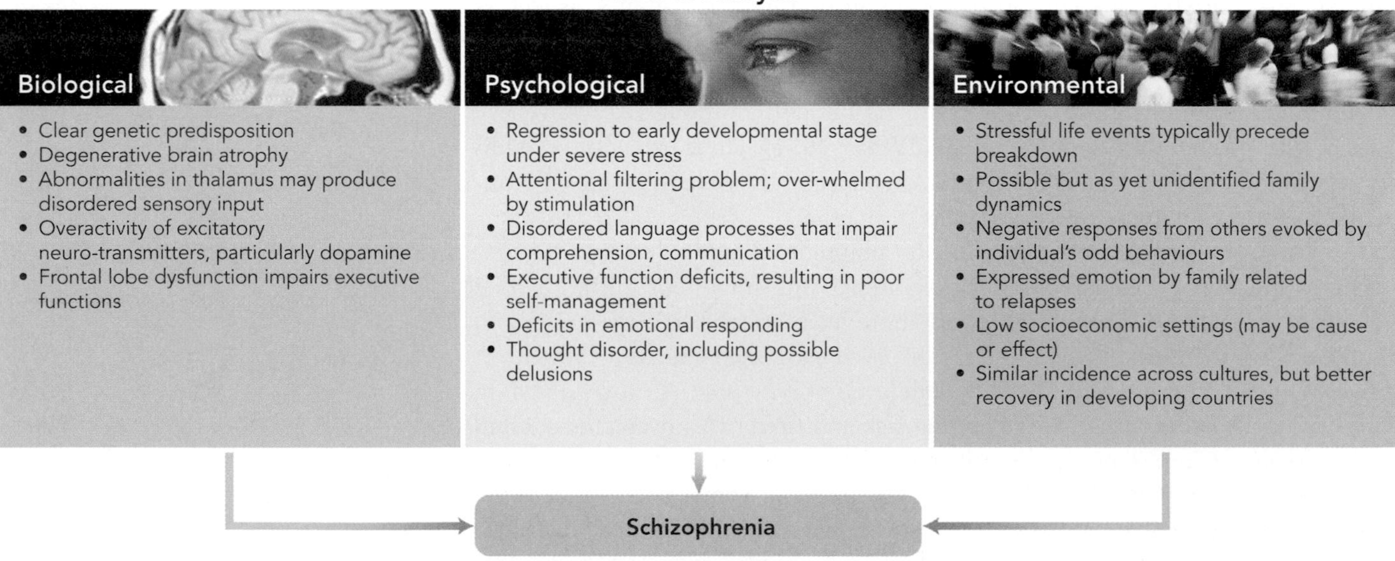

FIGURE 13.29

Understanding behaviour: Biological, psychological, and environmental factors in schizophrenia.

In Review

- *Schizophrenia is a psychotic disorder featuring disordered thinking and language; poor contact with reality; flat, blunted, or inappropriate emotion; and disordered behaviour. The cognitive portion of the disorder can involve delusions (false beliefs) or hallucinations (false perceptions).*
- *Schizophrenias have been categorized in a number of ways. The DSM-IV lists four subtypes: paranoid, disorganized, catatonic, and undifferentiated. Another categorization is based on the nature of the symptoms: a positive versus negative. Positive symptoms, such as delusions or hallucinations, predict a better outcome than negative symptoms, such as lack of emotional expression.*
- *There is strong evidence for a genetic predisposition to schizophrenia that makes some people particularly vulnerable to stressful life events. The dopamine hypothesis states that schizophrenia involves overactivity of the dopamine system, resulting in too much stimulation.*
- *Psychoanalytic theorists regard schizophrenia as a profound regression to a primitive stage of psychosocial development in response to unbearable stress, particularly within the family. Stressful life events do often precede a schizophrenic episode, but researchers have not been successful in identifying a family pattern related to the onset of schizophrenia. However, negative expressed emotion is a family variable related to relapse among formerly hospitalized schizophrenic individuals.*
- *Cognitive theorists focus on the thought disorder that is central to schizophrenia. One idea is that people with schizophrenia have a defect in their attentional filters, so that they are overwhelmed by internal and external stimuli and become disorganized. Deficiencies may also exist in the executive functions needed to organize behaviour.*

PERSONALITY DISORDERS

People diagnosed with **personality disorders** exhibit stable, ingrained, inflexible, and maladaptive ways of thinking, feeling, and behaving. When they encounter situations in which their typical behaviour patterns do not work, unresolved conflicts tend to re-emerge, they are likely to intensify their inappropriate ways of coping, and their emotional controls may break down (Millon et al., 1998).

Table 13.2 briefly describes the 10 personality disorders in Axis II of DSM-IV. The disorders are divided into three clusters that capture important commonalities: dramatic and impulsive behaviours; anxiety and fearfulness; or odd and eccentric behaviours. We focus here on the personality disorder that has received the greatest attention from clinicians and researchers over the years, namely, anti-social personality disorder.

Anti-social Personality Disorder

In the past, individuals with anti-social personality disorder have been referred to as *psychopaths* or *sociopaths*. As Robert Hare of the University of British Columbia describes in his book *Without Conscience: The Disturbing World Of The Psychopaths Among Us* (2001), they are among the most interpersonally destructive and emotionally harmful individuals. Males outnumber females three to one in this diagnostic group (American Psychiatric Association, 1994).

47. Describe the major characteristics of the anti-social personality disorder.

People with anti-social personality disorder seem to lack a conscience. In the nineteenth century, they were sometimes referred to as "moral imbeciles." They exhibit little anxiety or guilt and tend to be impulsive and unable to delay gratification of their needs. They also exhibit a lack of emotional attachment to other people, as suggested in this report by a man diagnosed as having an anti-social personality:

> When I was in high school my best friend got leukemia and died and I went to his funeral. Everybody else was crying . . . (but) . . . I suddenly realized I

TABLE 13.2 **DSM-IV Axis II Personality Disorders and Their Major Features**

Disorder	Major Features
Dramatic/impulsive Cluster	
Anti-social personality disorder	Severe irresponsible and anti-social behaviour beginning in childhood and continuing past age 18; impulsive need gratification and lack of empathy for others; often highly manipulative and seem to lack conscience
Histrionic personality disorder	Excessive, dramatic emotional reactions and attention seeking; often sexually provocative; highly impressionable and suggestible; out of touch with negative feelings
Narcissistic personality disorder	Grandiose fantasies or behaviour, lack of empathy, and oversensitivity to evaluation; constant need for admiration from others; proud self-display
Borderline personality disorder	Pattern of severe instability of self-image, interpersonal relationships, and emotions, often expressing alternating extremes of love and hatred toward the same person; high frequency of manipulative suicidal behaviour
Anxious/fearful Cluster	
Avoidant personality disorder	Extreme social discomfort and timidity; feelings of inadequacy and fearfulness of being negatively evaluated
Dependent personality disorder	Extreme submissive and dependent behaviour; fears of separation from those who satisfy dependency needs
Obsessive-compulsive personality disorder	Extreme perfectionism, orderliness, and inflexibility; preoccupied with mental and interpersonal control
Odd/eccentric cluster	
Schizoid personality disorder	Indifference to social relationships and a restricted range of experiencing and expressing emotions
Schizotypal personality disorder	Odd thoughts, appearance, and behaviour, and extreme discomfort in social situations
Paranoid personality disorder	An unwarranted tendency to interpret the behaviour of other people as threatening, exploiting, or harmful

Source: Abstracted from DSM-IV Axis II, American Psychiatric Association, 1994.

wasn't feeling anything at all. . . . That night I thought about it some more and found I wouldn't miss my mother and father if they died and that I wasn't too nuts about my brothers and sisters for that matter. I figured there wasn't anybody I really cared for but, then, I didn't need any of them anyway so I rolled over and went to sleep. (McNeil, 1967, p. 87)

Lack of the capacity to care about others can make anti-social individuals a danger to society (Black, 1999; Hare, 2001). For example, murderers Charles Manson, Paul Bernardo, and Jeffrey Dahmer failed to show any remorse for their serial murders or sympathy for their victims (Figure 13.30). Although anti-social individuals often verbalize feelings and commitments with great sincerity, their behaviours indicate otherwise. They often appear very intelligent and charming, and they have the ability to rationalize their inappropriate behaviour so that it appears reasonable and justifiable. Consequently, they are often virtuosos at manipulating others and talking their way out of trouble. One researcher who wanted to study non-incarcerated anti-social personalities quickly attracted 25 of them from the Boston area with the following classified ad:

FIGURE 13.30

The murderer Paul Bernardo exhibited many features of the anti-social personality, including a charismatic personality and an ability to injure others without remorse or guilt.

Wanted: Charming, aggressive, carefree people who are impulsively irresponsible but are good at handling people and at looking after Number One. Send name, address, phone, and short biography proving how interesting you are to . . . (Widom, 1983, p. 72)

People with anti-social personalities also display a perplexing failure to respond to punishment. Because of their lack of anxiety, punishment does not deter them from engaging in self-defeating or illegal acts again and again. As a result some of them develop imposing prison records.

To be diagnosed as having an anti-social personality disorder, a person must be at least 18 years of age. However, the diagnostic criteria also require substantial evidence of anti-social behaviour before the age of 15, including such acts as habitual lying, early and aggressive sexual behaviour, excessive drinking, theft, vandalism, and chronic rule violations at home and school. Thus anti-social personality disorder is the culmination of a behaviour pattern that typically begins in childhood (Kernberg, 2000).

Causal Factors

Biological Factors

Biological research on the anti-social personality disorder has focused on both genetic and physiological factors. A genetic factor is indicated by consistently higher rates of concordance for anti-social behaviour among identical twins than among fraternal twins (Rutter, 1997). Adoption studies suggest a similar conclusion. In one study, researchers compared the criminal records of men who had been adopted early in life with those of their biological fathers and their adoptive fathers. Men whose biological fathers had no criminal record showed a low incidence of criminal behaviour themselves, even if their adoptive fathers were criminal offenders. In contrast, the criminality rate was nearly twice as high if the biological father had a criminal record and the adoptive father did not, clearly suggesting the operation of genetic factors. However, the rate of criminality in the sons was greater still when both the biological *and* the adoptive fathers were criminals. These sons probably inherited a tendency toward criminality from their biological fathers and learned criminal behaviours from their adoptive fathers, showing the additive influences of genetic and environmental factors (Cloninger & Gottesman, 1989).

48. How are biological factors implicated in the anti-social personality disorder?

How might genetic factors predispose individuals to engage in anti-social behaviour? One clue might lie in the relative absence of anxiety and guilt that seems to underlie many of the behaviours in the anti-social disorder. Many researchers have suggested that the physiological basis for the disorder might lie in some dysfunction in brain structures that govern emotional arousal and behavioural inhibition, resulting in a chronically under-aroused state that impairs avoidance learning, causes boredom and a search for excitement, and fosters behavioural impulsiveness (Arnett, 1997; Ishikawa et al., 2001; Raine et al., 2003). Support comes from MRI findings that individuals diagnosed with the disorder have subtle neurological deficits in the prefrontal lobes, the seat of executive functions such as planning, reasoning, and behavioural inhibition, and that these neurological deficits are associated with reduced autonomic activity (Raine et al., 2000). Recently, Ross and co-workers at the University of British Columbia reported that, based on functional MRI studies, the limbic input to the frontal cortex was weaker in criminal psychopaths than in criminal non-psychopaths and non-criminal control subjects (Kiehl et al., 2001). Thus it appears, as long suspected, that anti-social individuals may indeed be "wired" differently at a neurological level.

Psychological and Environmental Factors

Psychodynamic theorists regard anti-social personalities as people without a conscience. Psychoanalytic theorists suggest that such people lack anxiety and guilt

49. How are classical conditioning and modelling concepts used to account for the development of anti-social personality disorder?

because they did not develop an adequate superego (Gabbard, 1990). In the absence of a well-developed superego, the restraints on the id are reduced, resulting in impulsive and hedonistic behaviour. The failure to develop a strong superego is thought to result from inadequate identification with appropriate adult figures because these figures were either physically or psychologically unavailable to the child (Kernberg, 2000).

Like some biological theories, learning explanations suggest that persons with the disorder lack impulse control because of impaired ability to develop conditioned fear responses when punished. This results in a deficit in avoidance learning. Hans Eysenck (1964) maintained that developing a conscience depends on the ability to learn fear and avoidance responses through classical conditioning, and people who fail to do so will be less able to inhibit their behaviour. In accord with this hypothesis, Adrian Raine and co-workers (1996) did a 14-year follow-up of males who had been subjected at age 15 to a classical conditioning procedure in which a soft tone was used as the CS and a loud, aversive tone as the UCS. The conditioned fear response was the participant's skin conductance response when the CS occurred after a number of pairings with the loud UCS. The researchers found that men who had accumulated a criminal record by age 29 showed much poorer emotional conditioning at age 15 than had those with no criminal record.

Learning through modelling may also play an important role. Many anti-social individuals come from homes in which parents exhibit a good deal of aggression and are inattentive to their children's needs (Rutter, 1997). Such parents provide role models for both aggressive behaviour and disregard for the needs of others. Another important environmental factor is exposure to deviant peers. Children who become anti-social often learn some of their deviant behaviour from peer groups who both model anti-social behaviour and reinforce it with social approval (Bandura, 1997). Combined with a possible genetic predisposition for anti-social behaviour, such environmental factors surely would encourage the development of deviant behaviour patterns.

Cognitive theorists believe that another deficit in anti-social personalities is their consistent failure to think about or anticipate the long-term negative consequences of their acts. As a result, they behave impulsively, thinking only of what they want at that moment (Bandura, 1997).

Though people with anti-social personality disorders often lack the capacity to form intimate and caring relationships, they frequently do marry, though such individuals may be among a troubling population, namely men who abuse their wives physically and emotionally.

In Review

- *Personality disorders are rigid, maladaptive patterns of behaviour that characterize an individual's behaviour over a long time. They fall on Axis II of DSM-IV. Personality disorders can contribute to the development of Axis I disorders and reduce the chances of recovery from those disorders.*
- *Antisocial personality disorder is the most studied of the Axis II disorders. It is characterized by an egocentric and manipulative tendency toward immediate self-gratification, a lack of empathy for others, a tendency to act out impulsively, and a failure to profit from punishment.*
- *Research on antisocial personality disorder suggests that genetic and physiological factors that result in underarousal may contribute to the disorder's causes. Psychoanalysts view the disorder as a failure to develop a superego, which might otherwise restrain the individual's impulsive self-gratification. Learning explanations focus on the failure of punishment to inhibit maladaptive behaviours and exposure to aggressive, uncaring models. It seems likely that there is a genetic predisposition that increases the risk of antisocial behaviour, especially if the person is exposed to deviant models.*

DISORDERS OF CHILDHOOD AND OLD AGE

Although we often tend to think of "the mentally ill" as young to middle-aged adults, the reality is that psychological disorders can occur at any point in the life span. Mental health professionals have observed symptoms resembling clinical depression in infants, and older children exhibit a wide range of problem behaviours (Mash & Barkley, 2003). Elderly adults can experience any of the disorders discussed in this chapter; in fact, people over age 65 are at greater risk for depression, and commit suicide in proportionately higher numbers, than any other age group (American Psychiatric Association, 2000). In addition, changes in brain functioning associated with the aging process or disease can create a state of deteriorated cognitive functioning known as *dementia.*

Childhood Disorders

Because emotional and social development occurs at different rates in individual children, it is often more difficult to diagnose a child with a behaviour disorder than it is with an adult. An adult who has frequent, violent temper tantrums is likely to be judged as having a problem—but what about a 5-year-old who behaves in the same way? Does this behaviour reflect a disorder, or is the child simply lagging in emotion-regulation skills? Children are also less able than adults to verbalize their feelings and thought processes, creating additional problems in judging the internal causes of their behaviour.

Epidemiological studies indicate that psychological disorders are relatively common between infancy and age 17 (Mash & Barkley, 2003). In one study of several thousand children between the ages of 2 and 5, researchers diagnosed over 20 percent of the children with a DSM-IV disorder and considered half of them to be significantly affected by their symptoms (Lavigne et al., 1996). Similar levels of incidence and impairment exist in children between the ages of 9 and 17 (Satcher, 1999). Other studies show that only about 40 percent of children with psychological disorders receive professional attention, and only half of this group is seen by qualified mental health professionals (Satcher, 1999). In contrast, 74 percent of children with physical handicaps receive professional treatment (U.S. Office of Behavior Technology, 1990). Failure to treat childhood behaviour disorders not only results in needless distress for children and families, but such disorders tend to continue into adulthood as psychological problems. In one New Zealand study, 4 in 5 adults with diagnosed DSM disorders also had histories of childhood or adolescent problems that met DSM criteria (Newman et al., 1996).

Externalizing Disorders

50. Compare the types, causes, and consequences of internalizing and externalizing disorders in children.

Externalizing disorders are directed toward the environment in the form of behaviours that are disruptive and often aggressive. In **attention-deficit/hyperactivity disorder (ADHD)**, problems may take the form of attentional difficulties, hyperactivity-impulsivity, or a combination of the two that results in impaired functioning. Ratings by teachers and parents indicate that 7 to 10 percent of North American children meet DSM criteria for the disorder, making ADHD the most common childhood disorder. The disorder occurs at least four times more frequently in boys than in girls; boys are more likely to exhibit aggressive and impulsive behaviours, whereas girls are more likely to be primarily inattentive. Some professionals believe that the diagnosis is applied too liberally, since normal children also exhibit the

FIGURE 13.31

A history of rule breaking and aggressive behaviour in childhood may predict the development of a clinically significant conduct disorder.

behaviours in question. They worry that some children may be inappropriately labelled and medicated (Carlson, 2000).

It may be tempting to assume that children routinely "outgrow" ADHD, but follow-up studies of individuals diagnosed with the disorder suggest that in 50 to 80 percent the problems persist into adolescence and, for 30 to 50 percent, into adulthood (Biederman, 1998). Overall, adults with ADHD have more occupational, family, emotional, and interpersonal problems.

Despite many years of research, the precise causes of ADHD are unknown. Genetic factors are probably involved, as concordance is higher in identical than fraternal twins. In adoption studies of ADHD children, the children's biological parents are more likely to have ADHD than the adoptive parents (Smalley et al., 2000). Experts have long suspected that the disorder has a biological basis, but EEG studies of electrical brain activity and imaging studies of brain structures and neurotransmitters have failed to reveal consistent differences between people with ADHD and control groups (Green, 1999). This may be due to the fact that ADHD is a multifaceted disorder with several subcategories of biological patterns. Environmental factors are also involved, perhaps in complex combinations with biological factors.

Two other externalizing disorders have features in common with the hyperactive-impulsive component of ADHD. Children with **oppositional defiant disorder (ODD)** consistently behave in a disobedient, defiant, and hostile manner that interferes with the child's functioning and interpersonal relationships (Figure 13.31; McMahon & Forehand, 2004). Unlike ADHD, the incidence of ODD does not differ for boys and girls, and the diagnosis is most likely to be applied during adolescence. ODD is more common in children with at least one parent having a history of ODD, antisocial behaviour, mood disorder, or substance abuse. Both genetic and social learning factors may produce ODD in children. Serious marital conflict and harsh parental discipline are often associated with ODD.

In a small number of cases, ODD leads to a more severe pattern of misbehaviour. Children with **conduct disorder** violate important social norms and show disregard for the rights of others. They exhibit a persistent pattern of behaviour that may cause or threaten harm to other people and animals. They lie and steal and may commit serious rule violations. Boys are much more likely to receive this diagnosis than are girls. The incidence of the disorder in boys peaks at about age 10 and then declines, whereas girls are more likely diagnosed in their mid-teens. Conduct disorder is associated with poverty, family stress, and antisocial behaviour in parents (McMahon & Forehand, 2004).

Internalizing Disorders

Unlike externalizing disorders, internalizing disorders are easy to overlook because the behaviours are not disruptive to others. **Internalizing disorders** involve maladaptive thoughts and emotions. They include anxiety and mood disorders. About 13 percent of children between the ages of 9 and 17 have a diagnosable anxiety disorder, and 9 percent have a mood disorder (Satcher, 1999).

Childhood internalizing disorders may take a toll on self-esteem and self-efficacy and interfere with the development of effective coping and interpersonal skills. In addition, having an anxiety or depressive disorder as a child increases the likelihood of similar problems as an adult (Kovacs & Devlin, 1998). This may be due to a genetically caused deficit in emotional regulation, the development of thinking styles that foster anxiety or depression, or classical conditioning of severe anxiety responses that persist into adulthood (as in the case of some childhood phobias).

Childhood anxiety disorders may take any of the forms discussed earlier in the chapter, including phobias, generalized anxiety disorder, panic disorder, and obsessive-compulsive disorder. Of the anxiety disorders, *separation anxiety disorder*, in which children experience anxiety or panic when separated from their caregivers or familiar environment, is the only DSM-IV category that is specific to children. The causal factors for these anxiety and mood disorders appear to be the same as those discussed for adult disorders.

Dementia in Old Age

I fear I am not in my perfect mind.

Methinks I should know you, and know this man; Yet I am doubtful, for I am mainly ignorant

What place this is, and all the skill I have

Remembers not these garments; nor I know not

Where I did lodge last night.

(Shakespeare, *King Lear*, Act IV, Scene 7)

In his characterization of the elderly King Lear, William Shakespeare captured the onset of **dementia**, the gradual loss of cognitive abilities that accompanies brain deterioration and interferes with normal functioning. In people with dementia, a progressive atrophy, or degeneration, of brain tissue occurs as a result of disease or injury. Depending on the cause, dementia can occur at any point in the life span, but elderly people are at greater risk than the general population. More than a dozen types and causes of dementia exist, the most common being Alzheimer's disease, Parkinson's disease, Huntington's disease, and Creutzfeldt-Jakob disease. Complications from high blood pressure and stroke may also be causes.

Regardless of the specific diagnosis, when dementia begins after age 65, it is labelled *senile dementia.* A large Canadian study indicated an overall rate of senile dementia of about 8 percent, and a female-to-male ratio of about 2 to 1. The prevalence rates were 2.4 percent between ages 65 and 74, 11 percent for those between 75 and 84, and 34.5 percent for those 85 and older (Costa, 1996). More than half of those over 65 living in institutions had dementia.

The onset of dementia is typically gradual, as is the appearance of symptoms. Memory impairment, poor judgment, confusion, language problems, and disorientation may appear gradually or sporadically. Memory for recent events is particularly affected, and the person may seem to live in the past because those memories are largely intact.

It is important to recognize that simple forgetfulness is not necessarily a symptom of dementia. Individuals who are developing dementia typically have episodes of distress because they feel confused; they may make nonsensical remarks, lose the procedural ability to perform familiar tasks, or even undergo marked personality change. Over half the cases diagnosed as senile dementia show various combinations of depression, anxiety, agitation, paranoid reactions, and disordered thinking that may resemble schizophrenia (American Psychiatric Association, 1994).

Alzheimer's disease is the leading cause of dementia in the elderly, accounting for about 60 percent of senile dementias. The disorder is caused by deterioration in the frontal and temporal lobes of the brain, including the hippocampus, a subcortical structure involved in memory. Medical and mental health professionals typically diagnose Alzheimer's by observing and interviewing the patient, but a postmortem microscopic examination of brain tissue is necessary to determine whether the patient had the tangled clumps of neurons and patches of disintegrating nerve cell branches called plaques that characterize the disease. A key to Alzheimer's disease is the destruction of cells that produce acetylcholine, a neurotransmitter that is critically involved in the neural processes underlying memory. One focus of current research is the development of drugs that might prevent the destruction of acetylcholine, enhance acetylcholine production, or directly stimulate acetylcholine receptors.

As people live longer lives, finding a cure for Alzheimer's disease and other forms of senile dementia becomes more urgent. Until then, many of us can expect our own family members to become Alzheimer's patients. Being a caregiver or watching the disease develop in a loved one is a painful and frustrating experience. In the advanced stages of the disease, the patient may not recognize even close family members. In addition, he or she may lose the ability to speak, walk, and control bladder and bowel functions. People with Alzheimer's also experience considerable stress as they feel their minds slipping away and their environment becoming more confusing.

In Review

- *Psychological disorders can occur at any point in the life span, and epidemiological data show that both children and aged people are at high risk for a variety of disorders. Moreover, many childhood disorders are precursors for psychological disorders in adulthood.*
- *Childhood disorders are divided into externalizing disorders, characterized by inattentive, disruptive, or aggressive behaviour; and internalizing disorders, typically characterized by anxiety or depression. Attention-deficit/hyperactivity disorder, oppositional defiant disorder, and conduct disorder are externalizing disorders.*
- *Cognitive deterioration, or dementia, can occur at any point in life but is especially prevalent in old age. Alzheimer's disease accounts for more than half of senile dementias. Other diseases, brain damage, and strokes also produce dementias.*

GAINING DIRECTION

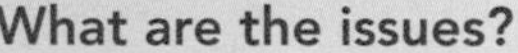

What are the issues?

What does it mean to be "insane"? Can this state be induced on a temporary basis? These questions are of considerable importance in a trial such as the one described in this chapter. Julia Campagna killed Kimberly Brooks and Monique Ishikawa when her car slammed into theirs at a border crossing. Julia claimed that she was suffering from delusions because of the diet drug Xenadrine. She thought that her car was an airplane and that she had to speed to Canada to conceive Joe Nieuwendyk's child. Is it possible to become psychotic by taking a drug? Do you have to be predisposed to a disorder? How long will a state of "temporary insanity" last? How long does any mental disorder last? How can you hear voices that are not really there?

What do we need to know?

What is the cause of mental disorders?
What are the various types of mental disorders?
What is a psychotic delusion?
Can delusions be drug-induced?
If disorders can be drug-induced, what is happening in the nervous system?
How does the legal system treat "temporary insanity"?
How could we be sure that this temporary state would not happen again?

Where can you find the information necessary to answer these questions?

We need to start by looking at the various types of mental disorders. In some cases, the symptoms would include delusions (e.g., schizophrenia); in others, there would be specific thought disorders (e.g., phobias). If delusions are present, what kind of biochemical reactions might be happening? For example, in schizophrenia, the problem results from too much dopamine in various neural systems. Can drugs result in an oversupply of dopamine? In fact, they can. You may recall from Chapter 6 that hallucinogenic drugs (e.g., LSD) produce similar symptoms and work in a similar fashion. Perhaps Xenadrine works in this way as well. You should check the Web for information on the action of Xenadrine (which is a combination of ephedra, caffeine, and aspirin). In addition, look for news stories on lawsuits related to the Campagna case. You should note that the legal definition of "insanity" differs in Canada and the United States.

Since the original ruling in 1999 on criminal charges, two lawsuits have been filed in civil court related to this case—one by the parents of Monique Ishikawa and the other by Julia Campagna herself. Both seek damages from Cytodyne Technologies and General Nutrition—respectively, the maker and supplier of Xenadrine.

KEY TERMS AND CONCEPTS*

abnormal behaviour (555)
agoraphobia (560)
Alzheimer's disease (593)
anorexia nervosa (566)
anxiety disorders (559)
attention-deficit/hyperactivity disorder (ADHD) (591)
biological preparedness (564)
bipolar disorder (569)
bulimia nervosa (566)
catatonic schizophrenia (582)
competency (legal) (557)
compulsion (562)
conduct disorder (592)
conversion disorder (576)
culture-bound disorders (566)
delusions (581)
dementia (593)
depressive attributional pattern (573)
depressive cognitive triad (572)
disorganized schizophrenia (582)
dissociative disorders (577)
dissociative identity disorder (DID) (578)
dopamine hypothesis (584)
dysthymia (568)
expressed emotion (585)
externalizing disorders (591)
generalized anxiety disorder (560)
hallucinations (581)
hypochondriasis (576)
insanity (legal) (558)
internalizing disorders (592)
learned helplessness theory (573)
major depression (568)
mania (569)
mood disorders (568)
negative symptoms (583)
neurotic anxiety (564)
obsession (562)
obsessive-compulsive disorder (562)
oppositional defiant disorder (ODD) (592)
pain disorder (576)
panic disorder (561)
paranoid schizophrenia (582)
personality disorder (587)
phobias (560)
positive symptoms (583)
psychogenic amnesia (577)
psychogenic fugue (577)
regression (584)
reliability (diagnosis) (555)
schizophrenia (581)
social phobia (560)
somatoform disorder (576)
specific phobia (560)
stressor (553)
suicide (574)
trauma-dissociation theory (578)
Type I schizophrenia (583)
Type II schizophrenia (583)
undifferentiated schizophrenia (582)
validity (diagnosis) (555)
vulnerability (553)
vulnerability-stress model (553)

*Each term has been boldfaced in the text on the page indicated in parentheses.

DO YOU WANT TO ELEVATE YOUR GRADES?

For additional resources and interactive quizzing, visit the book's Online Learning Centre at **www.mcgrawhill.ca/olc/passer**.

CHAPTER 14

Treatment of Psychological Disorders

It is a process, a thing-in-itself, an experience, a relationship, a dynamic.
—Carl Rogers

CHAPTER OUTLINE

In March 1980, eight former patients of Dr. Ewen Cameron sued the CIA and the Canadian government, alleging that Cameron had subjected them to "mind-control" experiments funded by the CIA. The experiments allegedly had been conducted in the late 1950s and early 1960s as part of Cameron's controversial treatment known as "deep sleep" or "depatterning" therapy. This treatment involved administering a large dose of barbiturates to the patient, which resulted in a drug-induced coma. While unconscious, the patient was given a series of powerful electric shocks—up to five or six per day at twenty times the rated maximum safe intensity. This would be followed by a variety of tape-recorded messages played to the patient. Dr. Cameron was an eminent psychiatrist and founder of the Department of Psychiatry at McGill. He was president of the American Psychiatric Association and the World Psychiatric Association, and was well-respected by his colleagues. He argued that the treatments were necessary in order to "erase" the patients' thoughts and to "rebuild" their personality. However, many patients stated that they did not know they were receiving electric shocks or messages and that the treatments resulted in massive memory loss.

The case was settled out of court in 1988 when the U.S. Department of Justice agreed to pay the plaintiffs $750,000 so long as the case was never discussed in public again.

- **What are the issues here?**
- **What do we need to know?**
- **Where can we find the information necessary to answer these questions?**

I fought my way through Harvard in the midst of psychosis and "spaciness."... There is no doubt in my mind that therapy helped me get through school. ... For so long I wondered why my therapist insisted on talking about my relationship with him. He was not my problem; the problem was my life—my past, my fears, what I was going to do tomorrow, how I would handle things, sometimes just how to survive. ... I took a long time, but finally I saw why it was important to explore my relationship with my therapist—it was the first real relationship I had ever had: that is, the first I felt safe enough to invest myself in. I rationalized that it was all right because I would learn from this relationship how to relate to other people and maybe even one day leave behind the isolation of my own world. ... I often felt at odds with my therapist until I could see that he was a real person and he related to me and I to him, not only as patient and therapist, but as human beings. Eventually I began to feel that I too was a person, not just an outsider looking in on the world.

Medication or superficial support is not a substitute for the feeling that one is understood by another human being. For me, the greatest gift came the day I realized that my therapist really had stood by me for years and that he would continue to stand by me and help me achieve what I wanted to achieve. With that realization, my viability as a person began to grow. ("A Recovering Patient," 1986, pp. 68–70)

1. What two therapeutic elements combine in the treatment of behaviour disorders?

In this poignant account, written by a person who had suffered from schizophrenia for much of her life, we see that even in this most serious of behaviour disorders, humans can reach out and help one another. This chapter explores the many approaches that are being taken to treat psychological disorders, as well as the critical issue of their effectiveness. Although first-person reports such as that offered by the "recovering patient" suggest that many people derive considerable benefit from psychotherapy, psychologists demand much more in the way of evidence. Nearly 40 years of research on psychological treatments has taught us that the question of efficacy, or treatment outcome, is a tremendously complex one that has no simple answers. Yet, as we shall see, much has been learned about the effectiveness of these various therapeutic approaches and about the factors that influence treatment outcome.

THE HELPING RELATIONSHIP

The basic goal of all treatment approaches is to help people change maladaptive, self-defeating thoughts, feelings, and behaviour patterns so that they can live happier and more productive lives. As the remarks of the "recovering patient" suggest, the relationship between the client and the person providing help is a prime ingredient of therapeutic success (Binder & Strupp, 1997; Norcross, 2003; Safran & Christopher, 2000). Within that helping relationship, therapists use a variety of treatment techniques to promote positive change in the client. These techniques vary widely, depending on the therapists' own theories of cause and change, and they may range from biomedical approaches (such as administering psychoactive drugs) to a wide range of psychological treatments. Both of these elements, relationship and techniques, are important to the success of the treatment enterprise (see Figure 14.1).

A majority of people with mental health problems first seek help not from mental health professionals, but from family members, physicians, members of the clergy, acquaintances, or self-help groups (Seligman, 1995). Often, however, these sources of psychological support are not enough, and distressed people are increasingly seeking help from professional counsellors and therapists. Surveys indicate that nearly 30 percent of North Americans have sought psychological counselling from professionals at some point in their lives, a dramatic rise from the 13 percent who had done so in the mid-1950s (Gaylin, 2000; Meredith, 1986). These people receive treatment from mental health professionals who fall into several categories.

Counselling and clinical psychologists make up one group. These psychologists, who typically hold a Ph.D. (Doctor of Philosophy) or Psy.D. (Doctor of Psychology) degree, have received five or more years of intensive training and supervision in a variety of psychotherapeutic techniques as well as training in research and psychological assessment techniques. The Psy.D. is not currently offered at Canadian universities, but a number of American schools do have this degree program. A second group, *psychiatrists,* are medical doctors who specialize in psychotherapy and in biomedical treatments, such as drug therapy.

In addition to psychologists and psychiatrists, a number of other professionals provide treatment. These professionals typically receive master's degrees based on two years of highly focused and practical training. They include *psychiatric social workers,* who often work in community agencies; *marriage and family counsellors,* who specialize in problems arising from family relations; *pastoral counsellors,* who tend to focus on spiritual issues; and *abuse counsellors,* who work with substance and sexual abusers and their victims.

Having previewed the nature of therapy and those who provide it, we now consider the therapeutic approaches that have developed within the major perspectives on human behaviour. Figure 14.2 provides an overview of the therapies we will consider.

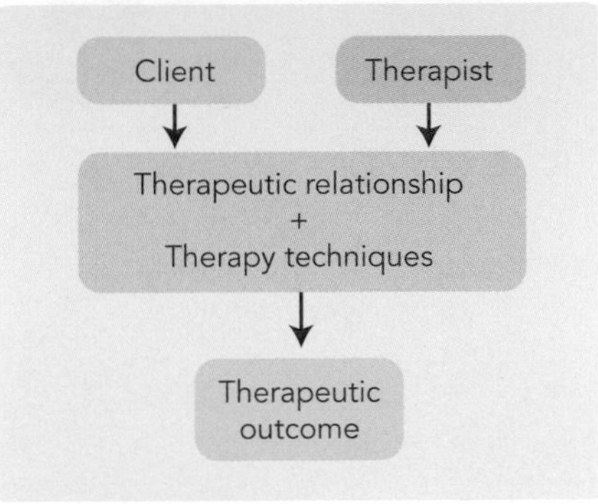

FIGURE 14.1

The process of therapy involves a relationship between a client and a therapist who applies the techniques dictated by his or her approach to treatment.

PSYCHODYNAMIC THERAPIES

The psychodynamic approach to psychotherapy focuses on internal conflict and unconscious factors that underlie maladaptive behaviour. The historical roots of psychodynamic approaches are to be found in Sigmund Freud's development of

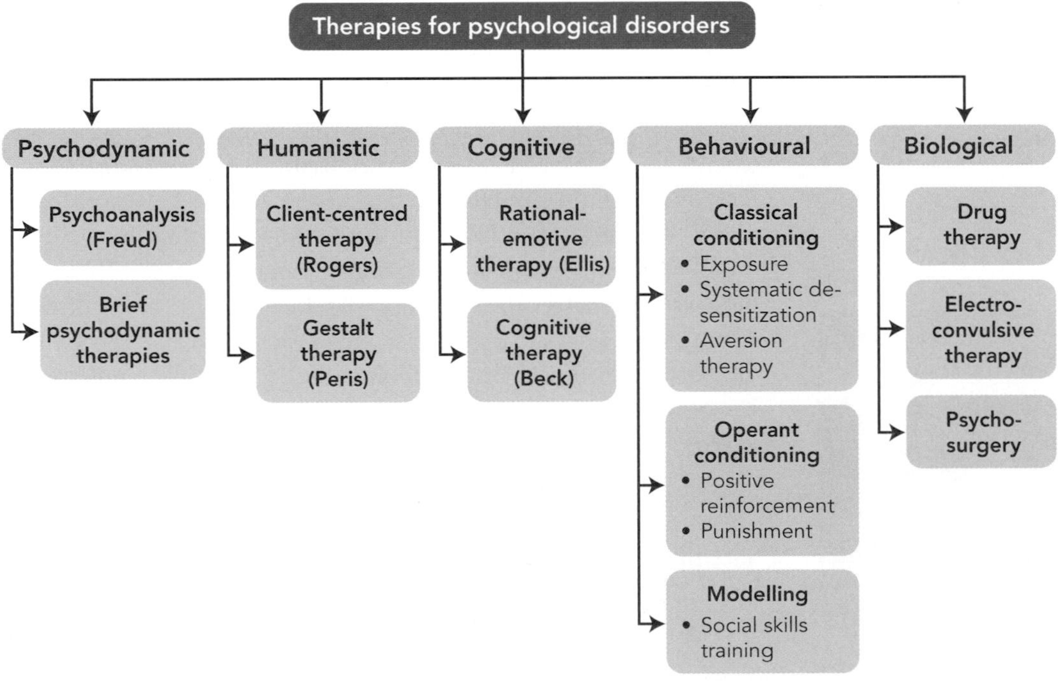

FIGURE 14.2

An overview of the major treatment approaches to the behaviour disorders, organized according to five major perspectives on behaviour.

psychoanalysis. The term *psychoanalysis* refers not only to Freud's theory of personality, but also to the specific approach to treatment that he developed. Although both the theory and the techniques of therapy were later modified by his followers and by those who defected to pursue rival approaches, the psychodynamic principles underlying Freud's approach continue to exert a major influence today.

Psychoanalysis

The goal of psychoanalysis is to help clients achieve **insight**, the conscious awareness of the psychodynamics that underlie their problems. Such awareness permits clients to adjust their behaviour to their current life situations, rather than continuing to repeat the old maladaptive routines learned in childhood. Analysts believe that, as the client repeatedly encounters and deals with buried emotions, motives, and conflicts both within and outside of therapy, the psychic energy that was previously devoted to keeping the unconscious conflict under control can be released and redirected to more adaptive ways of living.

2. What is the major therapeutic goal in psychoanalysis?

Free Association

3. How are free association and dream analysis used in psychoanalysis?

Freud believed that mental events are meaningfully associated with one another, so that clues to the contents of the unconscious are to be found in the constant stream of thoughts, memories, images, and feelings we experience. In his technique of **free association**, Freud asked his clients to recline on a couch and to report verbally without censorship any thoughts, feelings, or images that entered awareness. Freud sat out of sight behind the client so that the client's thought processes would be determined primarily by internal factors (Figure 14.3).

The analyst does not expect that free association necessarily will lead directly to unconscious material, but rather that it will provide clues concerning important themes or issues. For example, a client's stream of thoughts may suddenly stop after she has mentioned her father, suggesting the possibility that she was approaching a "loaded" topic that activated repressive defences.

Dream Interpretation

Psychoanalysts believe that dreams express impulses, fantasies, and wishes that the client's defences keep in the unconscious during waking hours. Even in dreams, which Freud termed "the royal road to the unconscious," defensive processes usually disguise the threatening material to protect the dreamer from the anxiety that the material might evoke. In dream interpretation, the analyst tries to help the client search for the unconscious material contained in the dreams. One means of doing so is to ask the client to free associate to each element of the dream and to help the client arrive at an understanding of what the symbols in the dream really represent (Figure 14.4).

FIGURE 14.3

In classical Freudian psychoanalysis the client reclines on a couch, with the analyst sitting out of the client's view.

Resistance

Although clients come to therapists for help, they also have a strong unconscious investment in maintaining the status quo. After all, their problems result from the fact that certain unconscious conflicts are so painful that the ego has resorted to maladaptive defensive patterns to deal with them. These avoidance patterns emerge in the course of therapy as **resistance**, defensive manoeuvres that hinder the process of therapy. Resistance can be manifested in many different ways. A client may experience difficulty in free-associating, may come late or "forget about" a therapy appointment, or may avoid talking about certain topics. Resistance is a sign that anxiety-arousing sensitive material is being approached. An important task of analysis is to explore the reasons for resistance, both to promote insight and to guard against the ultimate resistance: the client's decision to drop out of therapy prematurely.

Transference

As noted earlier, the analyst sits out of view of the client and reveals nothing to the client about himself or herself. Nonetheless, clients will eventually begin to project onto the "blank screen" of the therapist important perceptions and feelings related to their underlying conflicts. **Transference** occurs when the client responds irrationally to the analyst as if he or she were an important figure from the client's past. Transference is considered a most important process in psychoanalysis, for it brings out into the open repressed feelings and maladaptive behaviour patterns that the therapist can point out to the client.

Transference takes two basic forms. *Positive transference* occurs when a client transfers feelings of intense affection, dependency, or love to the analyst, whereas *negative transference* involves irrational expressions of anger, hatred, or disappointment. Analysts believe that until transference reactions are analyzed and resolved, there can be no full resolution of the client's problems. In the following excerpt from a psychoanalytic session, a client traces her transference reaction to its source and then recognizes the operation of similar reactions in other relationships.

"HAVE A COUPLE OF DREAMS, AND CALL ME IN THE MORNING."

FIGURE 14.4

Dream analysis is a central technique in psychoanalysis.

© 2003 by Sidney Harris.

4. How do resistance and transference reflect underlying conflicts?

Client: I don't want to like you. I'd rather not like you.

Therapist: I wonder why?

Client: I feel I'll be hurt. Liking you will expose me to being hurt.

Therapist: But how do you feel about me?

Client: I don't know. I have conflicting emotions about you. Sometimes I like you too much and sometimes I get mad at you for no reason. I often can't think of you, even picture you. . . . Yes, I don't want to like you. If I do, I won't be able to help myself. I'll get hurt. But why do I feel or insist that I'm in love with you?

Therapist: Are you?

Client: Yes. And I feel so guilty and upset about it. At night I think of you and get sexual feelings and it frightens me.

Therapist: Do I remind you of anyone?

Client: Yes. (Pause) There are things about you that remind me of my brother. (Laughs) I realize this is silly.

Therapist: Mmhmm.

Client: My brother Harry, the one I had the sex experiences with when I was little. He made me do things I didn't want to. I let him fool with me because he made me feel sorry for him.

Therapist: Do you have any of the same feelings toward me?

Client: It's not that I expect that anything will really happen, but I just don't want to have feelings for you. . . . I know it's the same thing. I'm afraid of you taking advantage of me. If I tell you I like you, that means you'll make me do what you want.

Therapist: Just like Harry made you do what he wanted.

Client: Yes. I didn't want to let him do what he did, but I couldn't help myself. I hated myself. That's why. I know it now because there is no reason why I should feel you are the same way. That's why I act that way with other people too. . . . I don't like to have people get too close to me.

the relationship that develops between client and therapist, and he began to focus his attention on the kind of therapeutic environment that seemed most effective in fostering self-exploration and personal growth (Bozarth et al., 2002). Rogers's research and experiences as a therapist identified three important and interrelated therapist attributes:

1. **Unconditional positive regard** is communicated when therapists show clients that they genuinely care about and accept them, without judgment or evaluation. The therapist also communicates a sense of trust in clients' ability to work through their problems. In part, this sense of trust is communicated in the therapist's refusal to offer advice or guidance.
2. **Empathy**, the willingness and ability to view the world through the client's eyes, is a second vital factor. In a good therapeutic relationship, the therapist comes to sense the feelings and meanings experienced by the client and communicates this understanding to the client. The therapist does this by *reflecting* back to the client what he or she is communicating—perhaps by rephrasing something the client has just said in a way that captures the meaning and emotion involved.

8. Define the three important therapist attributes described by Rogers.

3. **Genuineness** is the third important therapist attribute. There must be consistency between the way the therapist feels and the way he or she behaves. A therapist must be open enough to honestly express feelings, whether positive or negative. In the case of negative feelings, this may seem to be contradictory to the attribute of unconditional positive regard, but that is not necessarily the case. Indeed, the most striking demonstration of both attributes occurs when a therapist can express displeasure with a client's behaviour and at the same time communicate acceptance of the client as a person. For example, a therapist might say, "I feel frustrated with the way you handled that situation because I want things to work out better than that for you."

Rogers believed that when therapists can express these three critical therapeutic attributes, they create a situation in which the client feels accepted, understood, and free to explore basic attitudes and feelings without fear of being judged or rejected. Within such a relationship, clients experience the courage and freedom to grow.

These therapeutic attitudes are exhibited in the following excerpt from one of Rogers's therapy sessions:

Client: I cannot be the kind of person I want to be. I guess maybe I haven't the guts or the strength to kill myself, and if someone else would relieve me of the responsibility or I would be in an accident, I—just don't want to live.

Rogers: At the present time things look so black that you can't see much point in living. (Note the use of empathic reflection and the absence of any criticism.)

Client: Yes, I wish I'd never started this therapy. I was happy when I was living in my dream world. There I could be the kind of person I wanted to be. But now there is such a wide, wide gap between my ideal and what I am. . . . (Notice how the client responds to reflection with more information.)

Rogers: It's really tough digging into this like you are and at times the shelter of your dream world looks more attractive and comfortable. (Reflection.)

Client: My dream world or suicide. . . . So I don't see why I should waste your time coming in twice a week—I'm not worth it—what do you think?

Rogers: It's up to you. . . . It isn't wasting my time. I'd be glad to see you whenever you come, but it's how you feel about it. . . . (Note the genuineness in stating an honest desire to see the client and the unconditional positive regard in trusting her capacity and responsibility for choice.)

Client: You're not going to suggest that I come in oftener? You're not alarmed and think I ought to come in every day until I get out of this?

Rogers: I believe you're able to make your own decision. I'll see you whenever you want to come. (Trust and positive regard.)

Client: (Note of awe in her voice.) I don't believe you are alarmed about—I see—I may be afraid of myself but you aren't afraid for me. (She experiences the therapist's confidence in her.)

Rogers: You say you may be afraid of yourself and are wondering why I don't seem to be afraid for you. (Reflection.)

Client: You have more confidence in me than I have. I'll see you next week, maybe. (Based on Rogers, 1951, p. 49)

[The client did not attempt suicide.]

Rogers believed that, as clients experience a constructive therapeutic relationship, they exhibit increased self-acceptance, greater self-awareness, enhanced self-reliance, increased comfort with other relationships, and improved life functioning (Rogers, 1959). Research does indicate that therapists' characteristics have a strong effect on the outcome of psychotherapy. Therapy is most likely to be successful when the therapist is perceived as genuine, warm, and empathic (Bohart & Greenberg, 1997; Sachse & Elliott, 2002).

Gestalt Therapy

9. How is gestalt therapy derived from gestalt psychology principles?

Frederick S. (Fritz) Perls, a European psychoanalyst who was trained in Gestalt psychology, developed another humanistic approach to treatment. As noted in Chapter 5, the term *gestalt* ("organized whole") refers to perceptual principles through which people actively organize stimulus elements into meaningful "whole" patterns. Ordinarily, in whatever we perceive, whether external stimuli, ideas, or emotions, we concentrate on only part of our whole experience—the figure—while largely ignoring the background against which the figure appears. For people who have psychological difficulties, that background includes important feelings, wishes, and thoughts that are blocked from ordinary awareness because they would evoke anxiety. Gestalt therapy's goal is to bring them into immediate awareness so that the client can be "whole" once again.

Gestalt therapy is often carried out in groups, and Gestalt therapists have developed a variety of imaginative techniques to help clients "get in touch with their inner selves." These methods are much more active and dramatic than client-centred approaches, and sometimes even confrontational in nature. Therapists often ask clients to role-play different aspects of themselves so that they may directly experience their inner dynamics. In the *empty-chair technique,* a client may be asked to imagine his mother sitting in the chair, then carry on a conversation in which he alternatively role-plays his mother and himself, changing chairs for each role and honestly telling her how he feels about important issues in their relationship. These techniques can evoke powerful feelings and make clients aware of unresolved issues that affect other relationships in their lives as well.

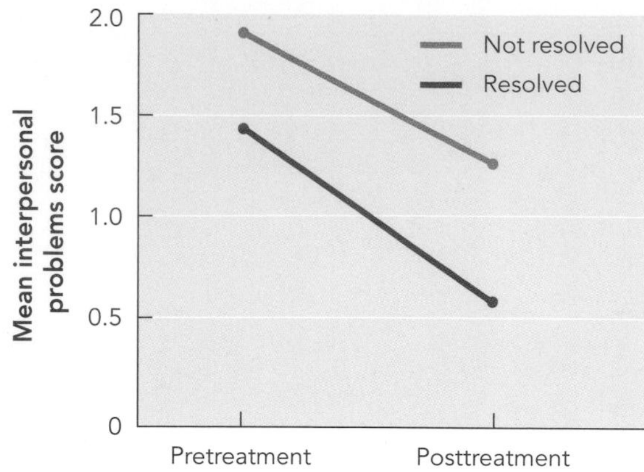

FIGURE 14.7

Use of the Gestalt therapy empty-chair technique to facilitate the resolution of unfinished business with significant others. Those clients judged to have achieved a full resolution of the past conflicts over the course of treatment showed a significant reduction in scores on a self-report measure of current interpersonal difficulties.

Source: Based on Greenberg & Malcolm, 2002.

Despite their common commitment to humanistic principles, Rogers and Perls differed sharply in their attitudes toward doing research on humanistic therapies. Rogers was committed to research that would help identify the factors that contribute to therapeutic success. He was a pioneer in tape-recording therapy sessions and analyzing them to study what went on in therapy (Rogers & Dymond, 1954). In contrast, Perls had a strongly antiscientific attitude that kept him and his followers from doing systematic research on the effectiveness of Gestalt therapy. As a result, the influence of the Gestalt movement began to wane following Perls's death in 1970. More recently, however, some clinical researchers have begun assessing the effects of Gestalt techniques.

In one recent study, Leslie Greenberg and Wanda Malcolm (2002) tested the effects of the empty-chair technique in helping clients resolve "unfinished business" with significant others in their past lives. The clients were seen for 12 to 14 hourly sessions. One client was a submissive middle-aged man who had felt humiliated and emotionally rejected by his mother's hurtful teasing and public humiliation of him as a child. Here is an sample of the client's (C) empty-chair statements to his mother (M) over several sessions:

> *C:* You were self-centered and you didn't care too much about me and the way I was brought up as far as my emotions go.
>
> *M:* (as client occupies her chair) What are you talking about? What do you mean? I gave you the best years of my life. Somebody had to look after you. I did the best I could.
>
> *C:* I was hurt so much. I carry that. I lost some of that warmth inside me. It affects the way I have relationships. The way I relate to myself. The way I feel about myself. All these years I thought I was a joke. This is what I carry (crying). I'm ashamed of myself.
>
> *M:* Yes, I know I did some of those things you said. And I could have been a better mother, but I guess I was young. I was still a child myself. I couldn't give you the emotional stability you wanted. . . . I'm sorry that it had an effect on you.
>
> *C:* As a little boy I couldn't tell you "Stop it. Don't do it. Keep away." But I can tell you now that I resent you for it and I won't forgive you. . . . I'm not going to dance around you any more. I'm going to stand up for myself. I think it's about time. (p. 408)

Greenberg and Malcolm then had clinicians listen to tapes of these sessions. The clinicians judged 13 of 32 clients to have completely resolved their unfinished business, as evidenced by affirmation of the self as worthwhile and either an increased understanding, empathy, or forgiveness of the other person or the ability to hold the other accountable for wrongdoing. Compared to those who did not reach complete resolution, resolved clients expressed more intense emotions during the empty-chair exercise and had significantly better treatment outcomes on measures ofpsychological distress, self-esteem, and improvement in interpersonal problems. Figure 14.7 shows pre- and posttreatment scores on a measure of interpersonal problems for the resolved and unresolved clients. Although both groups showed therapeutic gains, only those shown by the resolved group were statistically significant. Paivio & Greenberg (1995) have also demonstrated that the empty-chair exercise is more effective than simply receiving information about resolving "unfinished business." Today, the empty-chair exercise is one of several Gestalt techniques being incorporated into non-humanistic therapies as well (Cain & Seeman, 2002; A. Lazarus, 1995).

In Review

- *Humanistic psychotherapies attempt to liberate the client's natural tendency toward self-actualization by establishing a growth-inducing therapeutic relationship.*
- *Rogers's client-centred therapy emphasizes the importance of three therapist characteristics: unconditional positive regard, empathy, and genuineness.*
- *The goal of Gestalt therapy is to remove blockages to clients' awareness of the wholeness of immediate experience by making them more aware of their feelings and the ways in which they interact with others.*

COGNITIVE THERAPIES

As we have seen, many behaviour disorders involve maladaptive ways of thinking about oneself and the world. Cognitive approaches to psychotherapy focus on the role of irrational and self-defeating thought patterns, and therapists who employ this approach try to help clients discover and change the cognitions that underlie their problems.

10. What do ABCD stand for in rational-emotive therapy, and how is this model used in therapy?

In contrast to psychoanalysts, cognitive therapists do not emphasize the importance of unconscious psychodynamic processes. They do, however, point out that, because our habitual thought patterns are so well-practised and ingrained, they tend to "run off" almost automatically, so that we may be only minimally aware of them and simply may accept them as reflecting "reality" (Clark et al., 1999). Thus clients often need help in identifying the beliefs, ideas, and self-statements that trigger maladaptive emotions and behaviours. Once identified, these cognitions can be challenged and, with practice and effort, changed. Since there is a focus on both thoughts and behaviours, this type of therapy is often referred to as Cognitive-Behaviour Therapy (CBT). Albert Ellis and Aaron Beck are the most influential figures in the cognitive approach to therapy.

Ellis's Rational-Emotive Therapy

Ellis's theory of emotional disturbance and his rational-emotive therapy are embodied in his ABCD model (Figure 14.8).

- *A* stands for the *activating event* that seems to trigger the emotion.
- *B* stands for the *belief system* that underlies the way in which a person appraises the event.
- *C* stands for the emotional and behavioural *consequences* of that appraisal.
- *D* is the key to changing maladaptive emotions and behaviours: *disputing*, or challenging, an erroneous belief system.

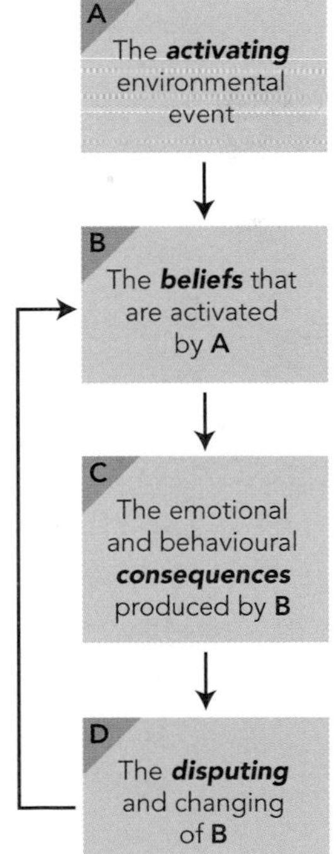

FIGURE 14.8

Albert Ellis's ABCD model describes his theory of the cause—and cure—of maladaptive emotional responses and behaviours. In therapy, the goal is to discover, dispute, and change the client's maladaptive beliefs.

Ellis (Figure 14.9) points out that people are accustomed to viewing their emotions (*C*s) as being caused directly by events (*A*s). Thus a young man who is turned down for a date may feel rejected and depressed. However, Ellis would insist that the woman's refusal is *not* the true reason for the emotional reaction. Rather, that reaction is caused by the young man's irrational belief that "to be a worthwhile person, I must be loved and accepted by virtually everyone, especially those I consider important." If the young man does not want to feel depressed and rejected, this belief must be countered and replaced by a more rational interpretation (e.g., "It would have been nice if she had accepted my invitation, but I don't need to turn it into a catastrophe and believe that no one will ever care about me.").

FIGURE 14.9

"The essence of effective therapy according to rational-emotive therapy is full tolerance of people as individuals combined with a ruthless campaign against their self-defeating ideas. . . . These can be easily elicited and demolished by any scientist worth his or her salt; and the rational-emotive therapist is exactly that: an exposing and nonsense-annihilating scientist."—Albert Ellis

Rational-emotive therapists introduce clients to common irrational ideas (Table 14.1) and then train them to ferret out the particular ideas that underlie their maladaptive emotional responses. Clients are given homework assignments to help them analyze and change self-statements. They also may be asked to place themselves in challenging situations and practise control over their emotions by using the new self-statements. For example, a shy person might be required to go to a party and practise rational thoughts that counteract social anxiety. By learning and practising cognitive coping responses, clients eventually can modify underlying belief systems in ways that enhance well-being (Dryden, 2002).

Beck's Cognitive Therapy

Like Ellis, Aaron Beck's goal is to point out errors of thinking and logic that underlie emotional disturbance and to help clients identify and reprogram their overlearned "automatic" thought patterns (Figure 14.10). In treating depressed clients, a first step is to help clients realize that their thoughts, not the situation, cause their maladaptive emotional reactions. This sets the stage for identifying and changing the maladaptive thoughts.

Client: I get depressed when things go wrong. Like when I fail a test.

Beck: How can failing a test make you depressed?

Client: Well, if I fail, I'll never get into law school.

Beck: So failing a test means a lot to you. But if failing a test could drive people into clinical depression, wouldn't you expect everyone who failed a test to have a depression? Did everyone who failed get depressed enough to require treatment?

Client: No, but it depends on how important the test was to the person.

Beck: Right, and who decides the importance?

Client: I do.

Beck: Now what did failing mean?

TABLE 14.1 **Irrational Ideas that Cause Disturbance, and Alternatives that Might be Offered by a Rational-Emotive Therapist**

Irrational Belief	Rational Alternative
It is a dire necessity that I be loved and approved of by virtually everyone for everything I do.	Although we might prefer approval to disapproval, our self-worth need not depend on the love and approval of others. Self-respect is more important than giving up one's individuality to buy the approval of others.
I must be thoroughly competent and achieving to be worthwhile. To fail is to be a *failure*.	As imperfect and fallible human beings, we are bound to fail from time to time. We can control only effort; we have incomplete control over outcome. We are better off focusing on the process of doing rather than on demands that we do well.
It is terrible, awful, and catastrophic when things are not the way I demand that they be.	Stop catastrophizing and turning an annoyance or irritation into a major crisis. Who are we to demand that things be different from what they are? When we turn our preferences into dire necessities, we set ourselves up for needless distress. We had best learn to change those things we can control and accept those that we can't control (and be wise enough to know the difference).
Human misery is externally caused and forced on one by other people and events.	Human misery is produced not by external factors, but rather by what we tell ourselves about those events. We feel as we think, and most of our misery is needlessly self-inflicted by irrational habits of thinking.
Because something deeply affected me in the past, it must continue to do so.	We hold ourselves prisoner to the past because we continue to believe philosophies and ideas learned in the past. If they are still troubling us today, it is because we are still propagandizing ourselves with irrational nonsense. We *can* control how we think in the here and now and thereby liberate ourselves from the "scars" of the past.

Client: (Tearful) That I couldn't get into law school.

Beck: And what does that mean to you?

Client: That I'm just not smart enough.

Beck: Anything else?

Client: That I can never be happy.

Beck: And how do those thoughts make you feel?

Client: Very unhappy.

Beck: So it is the *meaning* (italics added) of failing a test that makes you very unhappy. In fact, believing that you can never be happy is a powerful factor in producing unhappiness. So you get yourself into a trap—by definition, failure to get into law school equals "I can never be happy." (Based on Beck et al., 1979, pp. 145–146)

FIGURE 14.10

"The formula for treatment may be stated in simple terms: The therapist helps the patient to identify his warped thinking and to learn more realistic ways to formulate his experience."—Aaron Beck

Beck's contributions to the understanding and treatment of depression have made his cognitive therapy a psychological treatment of choice for that disorder (Moorey, 2003). More recently, cognitive therapy has been extended to the treatment of anger and anxiety disorders, with equally encouraging results (Craske, 1999; Rush, 1998). For example, Donald Meichenbaum's work (e.g., Meichenbaum, 1991) on **self-instructional training** has been very influential in treatments related to stress and coping. As we shall see, cognitive therapy is also being combined with other therapeutic techniques to form highly effective treatment "packages" for certain disorders (Hollon et al., 1991).

FOCUS ON NEUROSCIENCE

The Neuroscience of Treating Unipolar Depression

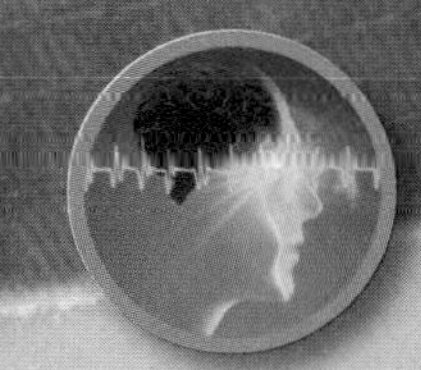

Cognitive Behaviour Therapy (CBT) is viewed as the treatment of choice for unipolar depression (Kuyken, Dalglish, & Holden, 2007). The goal of this approach is to identify maladaptive thoughts and behaviours and through therapy, help the patient to think more rationally. But what changes are going on in the brain while this is happening?

As discussed in Chapter 13, depression may stem from the underactivity of certain neurotransmitters such as norepinephrine, dopamine, and serotonin (collectively known as the monoamines). Drug treatments for depression target these monoamines, resulting in higher levels of the neurotransmitters in specific brain areas. Working with a group of depressed patients, Kennedy et al. (2001) report increased activity (via PET scan) in much of the prefrontal cortex, parietal cortex, and the cingulate cortex (area above the corpus callosum) following six weeks of treatment with the antidepressant drug Paxil. This increased activity reflects a return to "normal" levels and further illustrates the involvement of the cortex and limbic system in depression. Would we expect similar changes using a talking therapy?

In a study also using PET (Meyer et al., 2004), no global differences were found between patients with and without major depression. But for the depressed group, reduced serotonin transport was observed for those who expressed higher levels of dysfunctional beliefs. Thus, it would appear that maladaptive thoughts are related to lower levels of serotonin and consequently, CBT should be a very effective treatment. Indeed, changes in brain function can be noted following a course of CBT treatment. Goldapple et al. (2004) have demonstrated that those patients who were successfully treated with CBT showed a change in function (as measured by PET) in both the limbic system and the cortex. Compared to a group of patients treated with paroxetine (Paxil), there were specific changes for CBT in both the frontal cortex and the hippocampus. So it would appear that talking therapy can alter brain function in much the same way that drug treatments do.

The agenda for DSM-V as it is being developed calls for paying increased attention to the biological underpinnings of various psychological disorders (Phillips, 2007). To this end,

–Continued

various researchers are trying to develop screening tests for disorders based on neuroimaging. Siegle et al. (2006) presented a series of emotional words to both a group of unmedicated, unipolar patients and a comparison group of individuals who had never experienced depression. All participants rated the personal relevance of these words while undergoing an fMRI scan. Following this task, the depressed group received 16 sessions of CBT. Those participants who reacted with low levels of activity in the cingulate cortex and high levels in the amygdala when processing negative emotional words showed the most improvement after CBT. Seigle et al. (2006) note that the cingulate cortex is involved in the regulation of activity in the limbic system. Thus, depressed individuals showing this lack of regulation are precisely those who will benefit from CBT since CBT will help them to regain emotional control.

BEHAVIOUR THERAPIES

In the 1960s, behavioural approaches emerged as a dramatic departure from the assumptions and methods that characterized psychoanalytic and humanistic therapies. The new practitioners of behaviour therapy denied the importance of inner dynamics. Instead, they insisted that (1) behaviour disorders are learned in the same ways normal behaviours are, and (2) these maladaptive behaviours can be unlearned by application of principles derived from research on classical conditioning and operant conditioning. Behaviourists demonstrated that these learning procedures could be applied to change the behaviours of schizophrenics, to effectively treat anxiety disorders, and to modify many child and adult behaviour problems that seemed resistant to traditional therapy approaches (Hersen, 2002).

11. Which disorders have responded most favourably to Beck's cognitive therapy? What is the focus of the therapy in these disorders?

In Chapter 7, we described three important learning mechanisms: classical conditioning, operant conditioning, and modelling. We now consider therapy techniques based on each of these forms of learning.

Classical Conditioning Treatments

Classical conditioning procedures have been used in two major ways. First, they have been used to reduce, or decondition, anxiety responses. Second, they have been used in attempts to condition new anxiety responses to a particular class of stimuli, such as alcoholic beverages or inappropriate sexual objects. The most commonly used classical conditioning procedures are exposure therapies, systematic desensitization, and aversion therapy.

Exposure: An Extinction Approach

12. What are the classical and operant conditioning procedures used in exposure therapy? How was this procedure used to treat agoraphobics?

From a behavioural point of view, phobias and other fears result from classically conditioned emotional responses (e.g., Rachman, 1991). The conditioning experience is assumed to involve a pairing of the phobic object (the neutral stimulus) with an aversive unconditioned stimulus (UCS). As a result, the phobic stimulus becomes a conditioned stimulus (CS) that elicits the conditioned response (CR) of anxiety. According to the two-factor learning theory discussed in Chapter 7, avoidance responses to the phobic situation are then reinforced by anxiety reduction (operant conditioning based on negative reinforcement). Thus a person who is injured in an automobile accident may find herself afraid to ride in a car. Moreover, each time she avoids exposure to cars, her avoidance response is strengthened through anxiety reduction.

According to this formulation, the most direct way to reduce the fear is through a process of classical extinction of the anxiety response. This requires **exposure** to the feared CS in the absence of the UCS while using **response prevention** to keep the operant avoidance response from occurring. This is the theoretical basis for the exposure approach (Marks, 1991; Zinbarg et al., 1992). The client may be exposed to real-life stimuli (a treatment known as **flooding**; Figure 14.11) or may be asked to imagine scenes involving the stimuli (referred to as **implosion therapy**). Of course, these stimuli will evoke considerable anxiety, but the anxiety will extinguish in time if the person remains in the presence of the CS and the UCS does not occur.

Exposure has proved to be a highly effective technique for extinguishing anxiety responses in both animals and humans (Bruce & Sanderson, 1998; Spiegler & Guevremont, 2003). In one study, agoraphobics who feared leaving the safety of their homes and going into public places were treated. The researchers used an exposure therapy that required these clients to confront feared situations such as driving alone and going into crowded shopping centres. Both before and after the exposure therapy, each client was assessed on a series of real-life performance tasks. For example, an agoraphobic who feared being in public might be asked to go and stand in a long checkout line in a crowded supermarket. Before exposure treatment began, the phobics were able to pass only 27 percent of these performance tasks. At the end of treatment, they were able to perform 71 percent of the tasks. Moreover, this degree of improvement was maintained or even increased at follow-ups ranging from three months to two years (Williams et al., 1989). These are extremely encouraging results, since agoraphobics are difficult to treat with non-behavioural methods. An additional advantage is that clients can administer exposure treatment to themselves under a therapist's direction, with high success rates (Marks, 1991). Stanley Rachman at the University of British Columbia also reports success using behavioural methods for the treatment of obsessive-compulsive disorder (Rachman, Hodgson, & Marks, 1997). Patients who were rated as "moderately incapacitated" were helped effectively with a treatment based on flooding.

FIGURE 14.11

A behaviour therapist guides and supports a client with a dog phobia during an in vivo exposure therapy session. As a result of exposure, the man's anxiety will extinguish and he will be able to interact more comfortably with this animal and with other dogs.

Systematic Desensitization: A Counterconditioning Approach

In 1958, Joseph Wolpe introduced **systematic desensitization**, a new learning-based treatment for anxiety disorders. Wolpe also presented impressive outcome data for 100 phobics he had treated with the technique. Systematic desensitization remains a widely used treatment today. In many controlled studies, its success rate in treating a wide range of phobic disorders has been 80 percent or better (Rachman, 2000; Spiegler & Guevremont, 2003).

Wolpe viewed anxiety as a classically conditioned emotional response. His goal was to eliminate the anxiety by using a procedure called **counterconditioning**, in which a new response that is incompatible with anxiety is conditioned to the anxiety-arousing CS.

The first step in systematic desensitization is to train the client in the skill of voluntary muscle relaxation. Next the client is helped to construct a **stimulus hierarchy** of 10 to 15 scenes relating to the fear. The hierarchy is carefully arranged in roughly equal steps from low-anxiety scenes to high-anxiety ones. Table 14.2 shows a stimulus hierarchy that was used in treating a university student with high test anxiety.

In the desensitization sessions, the therapist deeply relaxes the client and then asks the client to vividly imagine the first scene in the hierarchy (the least anxiety-arousing one) for several seconds. The client can't be

TABLE 14.2 **A Stimulus Hierarchy Used in the Systematic Desensitization Treatment of a Test-Anxious University Student**

Scene 1.	Hearing about someone else who has a test
Scene 2.	Instructor announcing that a test will be given in three weeks
Scene 3.	Instructor reminding class that there will be a test in two weeks
Scene 4.	Overhearing classmates talk about studying for the test, which will occur in one week
Scene 5.	Instructor reminding class of what it will be tested on in two days
Scene 6.	Leaving class the day before the exam
Scene 7.	Studying the night before the exam
Scene 8.	Getting up the morning of the exam
Scene 9.	Walking toward the building where the exam will be given
Scene 10.	Walking into the testing room
Scene 11.	Instructor walking into room with tests
Scene 12.	Tests being passed out
Scene 13.	Reading the test questions
Scene 14.	Watching others finish the test
Scene 15.	Seeing a question I can't answer
Scene 16.	Instructor waiting for me to finish the test

13. How does systematic desensitization differ from exposure in terms of its (a) underlying principle and (b) specific techniques?

both relaxed and anxious at the same time, so if the relaxation is strong enough, it replaces anxiety as the CR to that stimulus—the counterconditioning process. When the client can imagine that scene for increasingly longer periods without experiencing anxiety, the therapist proceeds to the next scene. Once low-arousal scenes have been deconditioned, some of the total anxiety has been reduced, and the person is now able to imagine more anxiety-arousing ones without becoming anxious. Desensitization also can be accomplished through carefully controlled exposure to a hierarchy of real-life situations (**in vivo desensitization**). For example, an individual with a height phobia might actually stand on a step stool and, eventually, walk across a suspension bridge while voluntarily relaxed, rather than simply imagining the scenes. Both desensitization approaches are highly effective in reducing anxiety (Hersen, 2003).

Although both exposure therapy based on extinction and systematic desensitization are very effective in reducing fear responses, systematic desensitization is sometimes preferred because the client will experience far less anxiety during the treatment. On the other hand, exposure often reduces anxiety more quickly than does systematic desensitization (Bruce & Sanderson, 1998).

14. How does classical conditioning underlie aversion therapy? What additional training can enhance its effectiveness?

Aversion Therapy

For some clients, the therapeutic goal is not to reduce anxiety, but to actually condition it to a particular stimulus so as to reduce deviant approach behaviours. In **aversion therapy**, the therapist pairs a stimulus that is attractive to a person and that stimulates deviant or self-defeating behaviour (the CS) with a noxious UCS in an attempt to condition an aversion to the CS. For example, aversion treatment for alcoholics may involve injecting the client with a nausea-producing drug, then having him or her drink alcohol (the CS) as nausea (the UCS) develops. Similarly, pedophiles (child molesters) have undergone treatment in which strong electric shock is paired with slides showing children similar to those the offenders sexually abused (Figure 14.12). To measure the effects of the treatment on males, readings from a physiological recording device that measures penile blood volume responses to the slides can be compared before and after treatment (Sandler, 1986).

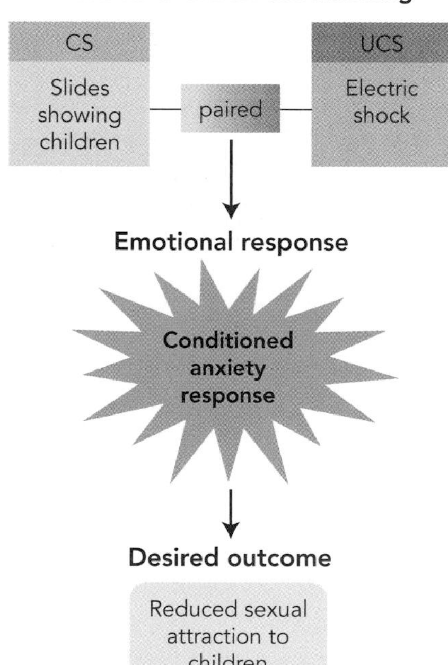

FIGURE 14.12

The classical conditioning that occurs in aversion therapy is illustrated in the treatment of a pedophile who receives electric shocks when pictures of children are presented. The goal of the treatment is the development of a conditioned anxiety response that reduces the sexual attractiveness of children.

Aversion therapies have been applied to a range of disorders with variable results. In one study of 278 alcoholics who underwent aversion therapy, 190 (63 percent) were still abstinent a year after treatment ended. Three years later, a third of the patients were still abstinent, an impressive result given the traditionally high relapse rate of chronic alcoholics (Wiens & Menustik, 1983). Unfortunately, however, treatment effects from aversion therapies often fail to generalize from the treatment setting to the real world. Some experts believe that aversion therapy is most likely to succeed if it is part of a more comprehensive treatment program in which the client also learns specific coping skills for avoiding relapses (Marlatt & Gordon, 1985).

Operant Conditioning Treatments

The term **behaviour modification** refers to treatment techniques that involve the application of operant conditioning procedures in an attempt to increase or decrease a specific behaviour. These techniques may use any of the operant procedures for manipulating the environment that were discussed in Chapter 7: positive reinforcement, extinction, negative reinforcement, or punishment. The focus in behaviour modification is on externally observable behaviours, and measurement of the behaviours targeted for change occurs throughout the treatment program. This measurement allows the therapist to track the progress of the treatment program and to make modifications if behaviour change begins to lag.

Behaviour modification techniques have been applied successfully to many different behaviour disorders. They have yielded particularly impressive results when applied to populations that are difficult to treat with more traditional therapies, such as chronic hospitalized schizophrenics, profoundly disturbed children, and mentally retarded individuals (Ayllon & Azrin, 1968; DeRubeis & Crits-Christoph, 1998; Lovaas, 1977). We now consider the use of positive reinforcement and punishment in two of these populations.

15. How do token economies work, and what evidence exists for their effectiveness?

Positive Reinforcement

One of the dangers of long-term psychiatric hospitalization is the gradual loss of social, personal-care, and occupational skills needed to survive outside the hospital. Such deterioration is common among chronic schizophrenic patients who have been hospitalized for an extended period. Verbal psychotherapies have had very limited success in rebuilding such skills.

In the 1960s, Teodoro Ayllon and Nathan Azrin (1968) introduced a revolutionary approach to the behavioural treatment of hospitalized schizophrenics. The **token economy** is a system for strengthening desired behaviours—such as personal grooming, appropriate social responses, housekeeping behaviours, working on assigned jobs, and participation in vocational training programs—through the systematic application of positive reinforcement. Rather than giving tangible reinforcers, such as food or grounds privileges, a kind of "menu" is derived in which a specified number of plastic tokens is given for performance of each desired behaviour. The tokens can be redeemed by the patients for a wide range of tangible reinforcers, such as a private room, exclusive rental of a radio or television set, selection of personal furniture, freedom to leave the ward and walk around the grounds, recreational activities, and items from the hospital commissary. The long-term goal of token economy programs is to get the desired behaviours started with tangible reinforcers until they eventually come under the control of social reinforcers and self-reinforcement processes (such as self-pride), which will be needed to maintain them in the world outside the hospital. When this begins to occur, the tokens can be phased out and the desired behaviours continue to occur (Kazdin, 2003).

Token economy programs have proven highly effective with some of the most challenging populations. Figure 14.13 shows how quickly the introduction of a token economy increased the work behaviour of chronic schizophrenic patients who were supposedly too disturbed to engage in a work-retraining program (Ayllon & Azrin, 1965). In another study, a token economy program was carried out over a four-year period with severely disturbed schizophrenic patients who had been hospitalized an average of more than 17 years. During the course of the program, 98 percent of the patients from the behavioural treatment program were able to be released from the hospital (most to shelter-care facilities in the community), compared to only 45 percent of a control group that received the normal hospital treatments (Paul & Lentz, 1977). Token economies have also been applied successfully within business, school, prison, and home environments to increase desirable behaviours (Sullivan & O'Leary, 1990).

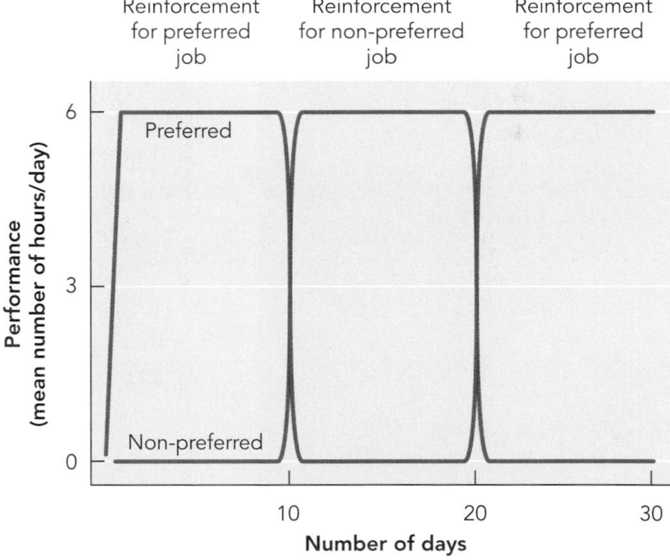

FIGURE 14.13

Average number of hours hospitalized schizophrenic patients worked per day on a job they preferred and a job they did not prefer when tokens were used as reinforcement. Notice how quickly and how strongly their behaviour was influenced by the reinforcement contingency.

Data from Ayllon & Azrin, 1965.

Therapeutic Use of Punishment

In the view of most psychologists, punishment is the least preferred way to control behaviour because of its aversive qualities and the potential negative side effects

16. Under what conditions is punishment used as a behaviour modification technique? What evidence is there for its effectiveness?

described in Chapter 7 (p. 286). Therefore before deciding to use punishment as a therapeutic technique, therapists ask themselves two important questions: (1) Are there alternative, less painful approaches that might be effective? (2) Is the behaviour to be eliminated sufficiently injurious to the individual or to society to justify the severity of the punishment?

Sometimes, the answers to these questions lead to a decision to use punishment. For example, some of the most startling self-destructive behaviours imaginable occur in certain severely disturbed autistic children. Such children may strike themselves repeatedly, bang their heads on sharp objects, bite or tear pieces of flesh from their bodies, or engage in other self-mutilating behaviours. O. Ivar Lovaas (1977), a UCLA psychologist who pioneered the use of operant conditioning techniques in the treatment of such children, successfully eliminated such behaviours with a limited number of contingent electric shocks. One seven-year-old boy had been self-injurious for five years and had to be kept in physical restraints. During one 90-minute period when his restraints were removed, he struck himself more than 3,000 times. With the consent of his parents, shock electrodes were attached to the boy and he was given a painful electric shock each time he struck himself. Only 12 shocks were needed to virtually eliminate the self-destructive behaviour. In another case, 15 shocks eliminated self-destructive behaviour in a severely disturbed girl with a history of banging her head against objects. Punishment is never employed without consent of the client or the client's legal guardian in the event that the client is mentally incompetent to give consent.

Modelling and Social Skills Training

Modelling is one of the most important and effective learning processes in humans, and modelling procedures have been used to treat a variety of behavioural problems. One of the most widely used applications is designed to teach clients social skills that they lack.

17. How is modelling used in social skills training? How is self-efficacy involved in its effectiveness?

In **social skills training**, clients learn new skills by observing and then imitating a model who performs a socially skilful behaviour. In the following example, a therapist served as a model for his client, a socially anxious university student who had great difficulty asking women for dates. The client began by pretending to ask for a date over the telephone:

> *Client:* By the way (pause), I don't suppose you want to go out Saturday night?
>
> *Therapist:* Up to actually asking for the date you were very good. However, if I were the girl, I might have been offended when you said, "By the way." It's like asking her out is pretty casual. Also, the way you posed the question, you are kind of suggesting to her that she doesn't want to go out with you. Pretend for the moment I'm you. Now, how does this sound: '*There's a movie at the Varsity Theatre that I want to see. If you don't have other plans, I'd very much like to take you.*'
>
> *Client:* That sounded good. Like you were sure of yourself and like the girl, too.
>
> *Therapist:* Why don't you try it? (Masters et al., 1988, p. 100)

Social skills training has been used with many populations, including individuals who have minor deficits in social skills, delinquents who need to learn how to resist negative peer pressures, and even hospitalized schizophrenic patients who need to learn social skills in order to function adaptively outside the hospital. It is often used in conjunction with other psychological or biological treatments to "jump start" new adaptive behaviours that then can be strengthened by natural reinforcers in the client's everyday environment.

Research demonstrates that a key factor underlying the effectiveness of social skills training is increased self-efficacy. When clients come to believe that they are capable of performing the desired behaviours, they succeed in doing so (Bandura, 1997; Maddux, 1999). Observing successful models also increases self-efficacy by encouraging the view, "If she can do that, so can I."

INTEGRATING AND COMBINING THERAPIES

18. What is eclecticism? Give an example of an integration of therapies.

We have now surveyed a variety of therapeutic orientations. To an increasing extent, clinicians are becoming **eclectic**, combining treatments and making use of whatever orientations and therapeutic techniques seem appropriate to the particular client they are treating (Lazarus, 1995; Snyder & Ingram, 2000). For example, many therapists now label themselves *cognitive-behavioural therapists* because their techniques include elements of both perspectives. In recent years, Albert Ellis and other rational-emotive therapists have renamed their technique *rational-emotive behaviour therapy* (Dryden, 2002). In part, this tendency reflects a responsiveness to research findings that certain approaches to therapy are well suited to some problems and ill suited for others. For example, Gestalt techniques are highly effective for helping people to discover underlying feelings, but a behavioural approach would be the treatment of choice for treating a phobia, and cognitive therapy is highly effective for depression. A therapist could choose to use any combination of techniques in a case having multiple problems. Also prompting the move toward eclecticism is the fact that modern therapists are being trained in a variety of perspectives and therapeutic approaches, so that they emerge as professionals with a wider range of therapeutic competencies (Norcross, 1991; Compropoulos, 2000). One national survey of eclectic therapists revealed that 72 percent included psychodynamic principles within their version of treatment, 54 percent included cognitive approaches, 45 percent used behavioural techniques, and a smaller percentage used various humanistic techniques (Jensen et al., 1990).

The move toward eclecticism has resulted in some integration that would have been unthinkable 30 years ago. For example, **psychodynamic behaviour therapy**, developed by Paul Wachtel (1997), involves an integration of psychoanalysis and behaviour therapy. These would appear to be strange bedfellows indeed, but Wachtel, originally trained as a psychoanalyst, has skilfully blended them into an approach that seems capable of being applied to a wide range of problems. For example, consider a highly submissive man who is unaware of unresolved anger that has contributed to the development of an ulcer. Wachtel might treat this client with psychodynamic techniques to help him achieve insight into his unconscious anger and its origins in his early life. Having achieved such insight, the irrational aspects of his anger may disappear, but he may still find himself unable to be assertive even when it would be appropriate. At this point, psychoanalysis has reached its limits of therapeutic effectiveness and the therapist might switch to a behavioural social skills training program to allow the person to develop and practise the needed assertiveness skills.

19. Which specific attributes of VR make it potentially useful in therapy? What evidence is there that VR can work therapeutically?

The search for more effective therapy techniques has resulted not only in a tendency to combine various therapeutic approaches, but also in a search for new technologies. Our *Research Frontiers* feature focuses on attempts to use the high-tech capabilities of virtual reality as a therapy tool.

RESEARCH FRONTIERS

Virtual Reality as a Therapeutic Technique

Almost all therapeutic perspectives are based on the assumption that therapy outcomes are likely to be most favourable if clients are able to vividly experience or re-experience important environmental, emotional, and relationship elements that underlie their problems. **Virtual reality (VR)** involves the use of computer technology to create highly realistic "virtual environments" that simulate actual experience so vividly that they evoke many of the same reactions that a comparable real-world environment would create. Observers typically wear helmets containing two small video monitors (one for each eye) attached to a high-speed computer. The image to each eye is slightly different to produce binocular depth perception cues that result in a 3-D image. With the aid of position-tracking devices, the computer monitors the person's physical movements and adjusts the images and sounds accordingly. Observers thus have a vivid experience of *presence* in a "different place" when navigating through the virtual world. This power to immerse the user in a simulated environment derives not so much from the realism of the displays as from the fact that perception and action are integrated as they are in real life (North et al., 2002).

Several other aspects of VR heighten its potential usefulness as a therapy tool. VR is highly flexible and programmable, allowing a therapist to present a variety of controlled situations and monitor their effects on a client. Scenes can easily be changed, depending on the actions of the client. Moreover, the therapist can don his or her own helmet and accompany the client into the virtual world, experiencing exactly what the client does and providing input to the client at appropriate moments. These shared experiences in the virtual world could enable clients to overcome old problems, experiment with new social roles, and learn new skills with the guidance of the therapist.

VR's use in psychotherapy is in its infancy, but it has already been applied to a variety of problems (Hoffman et al., 2001; Rothbaum et al., 2000). Most of these applications have been in the treatment of phobias and PTSD, where VR allows clients to interact with feared stimuli or situations while undergoing exposure or systematic desensitization therapy. For example, researchers have produced simulations of heights (e.g., a virtual elevator that could produce the sensations of being at various heights under different conditions, such as with or without walls, inside or on the outside of a building). Compared to a no-treatment control group of height phobics, those who received a seven-session VR graded exposure treatment showed a significant reduction in anxiety and less avoidance of heights. Over a third of the VR participants spontaneously exposed themselves to heights after the treatment, including one who rode up 72 stories in a glass-walled elevator (Rothbaum et al., 1995). VR therapy has also been applied successfully to fear of flying by taking the client on trips, accompanied by the therapist, in a virtual Apache helicopter that takes off and flies over the airport and city (Klein, 1999; North et al., 1997).

A case study by Albert Carlin, Hunter Hoffman, and Suzanne Weghorst (1997) provides an example of how several sensory modalities can be combined to immerse people in a virtual environment. The client was a 37-year-old woman with a debilitating spider phobia that had interfered with her life for 20 years. At the time she entered treatment, any encounter with a spider or a spider web evoked panic, weeping, and shame about her "out of control" fear. She took elaborate precautions to avoid spiders, including fumigating and vacuuming her car before entering it, sealing her bedroom door and windows with duct tape each night, placing each piece of her clothing in a separate plastic bag immediately after washing or ironing it, and avoiding the outdoors where she might encounter a spider. Even viewing photographs or drawings of spiders evoked anxiety.

Over a period of 12 weekly sessions, VR was used to create a "virtual kitchen" in which the client had encounters with either a small black spider in a web or a large brown virtual spider with a furry texture. Using a computer mouse to move about the 3-D virtual kitchen and a glove that operated her

FIGURE 14.14

Virtual reality (VR) was used to treat this spider phobic. The client views a virtual "spiderworld" inside the helmet. Psychologist Hunter Hoffman brings a virtual spider (shown on monitor) closer by slowly moving the VR position sensor in his right hand closer to the client's face. The sensor also can be attached to a furry toy spider to increase stimulus exposure.

Courtesy of Hunter Hoffman; photo by Mary Levin, University of Washington.

"virtual hand" inside the scene, the client exposed herself to spider experiences that gradually increased in intensity (Figure 14.14). When she opened a cupboard in the kitchen, she might encounter a spider that would crawl toward her. The spiders were preprogrammed to jump into the air when touched, swing toward her in their webs, and engage in other frightening behaviours. Later in treatment, when she began touching the large hairy brown spider with her virtual hand, another sensory modality was brought into the virtual world in the form of a palm-sized replica of a fur-covered Guyana bird-eating tarantula. When the client reached out with her virtual hand to touch the brown spider, her real hand encountered the furry tarantula, and any movement of the toy spider caused a similar movement of the virtual spider. These experiences, which evoked considerable anxiety at first, resulted in a dramatic reduction in spider anxiety both within the virtual world and in her real-life environment. Her ritualistic avoidance behaviours disappeared and she was able to stand over a spider that she encountered in her home for 20 minutes, to crush another one, and to go camping for the first time since adolescence. A controlled experimental study has since confirmed the effectiveness of the VR treatment for spider phobics (Hoffman et al., 2000).

The promising results achieved so far point to the need for systematic studies of VR therapy to explore several questions. Is it more effective than exposure through imagination or in real life? Is it cost effective in terms of computer and programming costs and number of therapy sessions needed? Up to now, most VR applications have depicted physical aspects of the environment. Can it be extended to social situations in which a client might be able to have realistic interaction with significant virtual others from the client's past or present life? Could it be used in aversion therapies to classically condition negative emotional responses to depictions of children, in the case of pedophiliacs, or to alcohol, in the case of alcoholics? Rizzo has maintained that VR is quite effective in the treatment of a variety of problems, from occupational rehabilitation to post-traumatic stress disorder (e.g., Rizzo & Kim, 2005). However, the effectiveness may not extend to other psychological disorders.

In Review

- *Cognitive and behaviour therapies are among the most popular and effective approaches to psychological treatment.*
- *Ellis's rational-emotive therapy and Beck's cognitive therapy focus on discovering and changing maladaptive beliefs and logical errors of thinking that underlie maladaptive emotional responses and behaviours.*
- *Behavioural treatments based on classical conditioning are directed at modifying emotional responses. Exposure to a CS and prevention of avoidance responses promote extinction. Exposure may be provided in vivo (real life), through imagination, or through virtual reality (VR) technology.*
- *Systematic desensitization is designed to countercondition a response to anxiety-arousing stimuli that is incompatible with anxiety, such as relaxation. Aversion therapy is used to establish a conditioned aversion response to an inappropriate stimulus that attracts the client.*
- *Operant procedures have been applied successfully in many behaviour modification programs. The token economy is a positive reinforcement program designed to strengthen adaptive behaviours. Punishment has been used to reduce self-destructive behaviours in disturbed children.*
- *Modelling is an important component of social skills training programs, which help clients learn and rehearse more effective social behaviours.*
- *Psychotherapy today shows a growing trend toward eclecticism—the combination of perspectives and techniques from several different therapies. There is also a movement to develop more effective therapies by combining different forms of therapy into new therapeutic techniques.*

CULTURAL AND GENDER ISSUES IN PSYCHOTHERAPY

Psychological treatments reflect the cultural context in which they develop. Within the dominant cultures of western Europe and North America, personal problems are seen as originating within people in the form of dysfunctional thinking, conflict, and stress responses. People are assumed capable of expressing their feelings and taking personal responsibility for improving themselves. We can easily see these values and assumptions reflected in the therapies we have discussed.

Psychodynamic, humanistic, and cognitive treatments all focus on changing these internal factors.

These values are not shared by all cultures and ethnic groups, however. For example, people from some Asian cultures might view the "therapeutic" expression of hostility toward one's parents as unthinkable (Hall & Okazaki, 2003). Likewise, the suggestion that assertiveness training would be helpful in competing more successfully with others and standing up for one's rights might be appalling to a person from a highly collectivistic culture (Cooper & Denner, 1998). Given diverse cultural norms and values, we should not be surprised that some individuals from non-Western cultures view psychotherapy as a totally inappropriate, and even shameful, option for the solution of their problems in living (Foulks et al., 1995).

Cultural Factors in Treatment Utilization

Although overall rates of psychopathology do not differ greatly between ethnic groups, utilization of mental health services is far less for minority groups than it is for the majority White population (Wang et al., 2002; Lai, 1995). Even when minorities do seek out mental-health services, they often fail to stay in treatment. As a result, many problems that could benefit from psychological treatment go untreated (Sue, 1998; Wang et al., 2002). The growing cultural diversity in North America (Toronto was recently named the most culturally diverse city in the world) has important implications for the practice of psychotherapy, and researchers are trying to identify the barriers to psychological treatment and what can be done to lower them.

20. What factors serve as barriers to therapy for ethnic minorities?

Psychologists Derald Sue and David Sue (1999) have identified several of these barriers. One of them is a cultural norm against turning to professionals outside one's own culture for help. Instead, the family, clergy, acupuncturists, herbalists, and folk healers are looked to for assistance. Moreover, many minority members have a history of frustrating experiences with White bureaucracies that makes them unwilling to approach a hospital or mental-health centre. There may also be language barriers.

Sometimes, access to treatment is a major problem. Because many minority groups suffer high rates of unemployment and poverty, they may not be able to afford therapy. In addition, many community mental-health agencies and professional therapists may be located outside the areas in which the underserved populations live.

But, according to Stanley Sue and Nolan Zane (1987; Griner & Smith, 2006), the biggest problem of all is that there are too few skilled counsellors who can provide culturally responsive forms of treatment. Therapists often have little familiarity with the cultural backgrounds and personal characteristics of ethnic groups other than their own. Sometimes they operate on the basis of inaccurate stereotypes. This can result in unrealistic and possibly inappropriate goals and expectations on the part of the therapist, as well as great difficulty in establishing the positive relationship that has been shown to be a powerful factor in therapeutic success.

What can be done to increase the access of culturally diverse groups to psychological treatment? One answer is to take therapy to the people. Studies have shown that establishing mental health service agencies in minority population areas increases utilization of mental health services, particularly if agencies are staffed by culturally skilled counsellors (S. Sue, 1998). Another solution might be to train more therapists from these ethnic groups. Stanley Sue and his co-workers (1991) found that dropout rates were reduced and the number of therapy sessions increased when clients saw ethnically similar therapists. However, for clients who elect to remain in therapy, it has *not* been demonstrated that treatment outcomes are better for clients who are seen by therapists from their own ethnic group. What seems more important than ethnic match is that the therapist and client form a good relationship and share similar viewpoints regarding goals for treatment and preferred means for resolving problems (Figure 14.15).

Stanley Sue (1998) suggests that **culturally competent therapists** are able to use knowledge about the client's culture to achieve a broad understanding of the client. At the same time, they are attentive to how the client may differ from the cultural stereotype, thereby balancing cultural understanding with the individual characteristics and needs of the client. They also are able to introduce *culture-specific elements* into the therapy. Thus a therapist might draw upon some of the techniques used by folk healers within that culture (e.g., prayer or a specific ritual) to effect changes in the client. Obviously, this would require a good working knowledge of the culture from which the client comes, plus a willingness to take advantage of what "works" in that culture (Mishne, 2002).

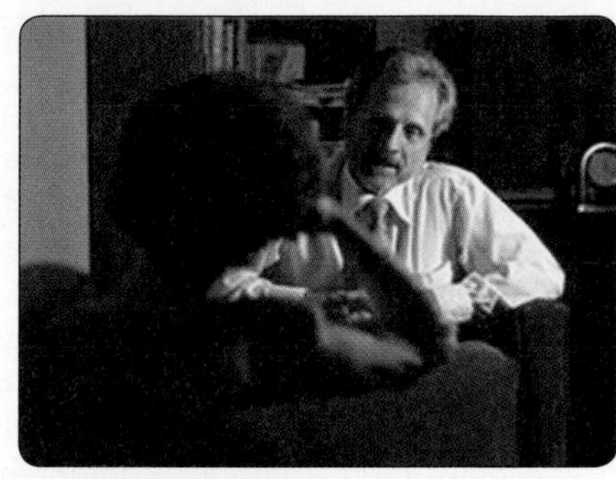

FIGURE 14.15

Research suggests that the outcome of therapy with minority populations is affected more by the cultural sensitivity and competency of the therapist than it is by the ethnic similarity of therapist and client.

Can therapists be trained to be more culturally sensitive? Indeed they can. In one study, experienced African-American and White therapists were assigned to either a four-hour cultural sensitivity training program or to a control condition that received no training. The therapists then treated African-American clients from the community, and the outcome of therapy was carefully assessed. The results showed that exposure to the ethnic training was more important to therapeutic outcome than whether the therapist was African-American or White. Clients rated the therapists who had received training (whether African-American or White) as having greater empathy and expertise, and these clients also attended more therapy sessions (Wade & Bernstein, 1991). Thus it appears that cultural sensitivity can be acquired and used to enhance the process of therapy for members of minority cultures.

21. What skills are found in culturally competent therapists?

Gender Issues in Therapy

Even within the same culture, the lives of men and women can differ in many ways, as can the life demands they are called upon to cope with. As we saw in Chapter 13, psychological disorders, particularly those involving anxiety and depression, occur more frequently among women in Western cultures. This may reflect the impact of specific stressors that women face, such as poverty (women are overrepresented below the poverty level), lack of opportunity fostered by sexism, strains created by the demanding multiple roles of mother, worker, and spouse among married women, and the violence and histories of abuse that many have been subjected to. In many instances, psychological problems arise not so much from internal problems and conflicts as from oppressive elements in the family, social, and political worlds. As women strive for more egalitarian relationships with men and for equal opportunity to develop their potential, they often meet external barriers that are deeply embedded in their culture's traditional sex roles (Worell & Remer, 2003).

In the eyes of many therapists, it may be more important to focus on what can be done to change women's life circumstances than to help them adapt to sex-role expectations that constrain them (Brown, 1994). It is important for both men and women therapists to support people in making choices that meet their needs, whether it be a man who wishes to stay at home and care for children or a woman who wants a career in the military. Consistent with the research on cultural similarity between therapist and client, research on therapy with women clients indicates that it is not necessary that women be treated by female therapists. Rather, what seems important is the therapist's sensitivity to gender issues (Worell & Remer, 2003).

In Review

- Research has shown that members of minority groups underutilize mental health services. Barriers include lack of access to therapists who can provide culturally responsive forms of treatment. More important to outcome than a cultural match is a therapist who can understand the client's cultural background and share viewpoints on therapy goals and the means used to achieve them. Culturally competent therapists take into account both cultural and individual factors to understand and treat the client.
- For female clients, the most helpful therapist is one who is aware of oppressive environmental conditions and is willing to support life goals that do not necessarily conform to gender expectations. Whether the therapist is a man or a woman seems less important to outcome than gender sensitivity.

EVALUATING PSYCHOTHERAPIES

Given the human suffering created by psychological disorders, the effects of psychotherapy have both personal and societal implications. Practising clinicians and clinical researchers want to know which approaches are most effective, what kinds of problems are best treated with each approach, and what "active ingredients" of each treatment produce its effects.

22. What is the "specificity question" in psychotherapy research?

Today the basic question "Does psychotherapy work?" is viewed as a gross oversimplification of a much more involved question known as the **specificity question**: "Which types of therapy, administered by which kinds of therapists to which kinds of clients having which kinds of problems, produce which kinds of effects?" After nearly a half century of psychotherapy research involving many hundreds of studies, this complex question still is not fully answered (Snyder & Ingram, 2000). Nonetheless, for many reasons, this question demands answers. Selecting and administering the most appropriate kind of intervention is vital in human terms. It is also important for economic reasons. Billions of dollars are spent each year on psychological treatments, and an increasing share of these costs is being paid by so-called third parties, such as insurance companies, health maintenance organizations, and government agencies. As the costs rise, those who bear the financial burden increase their demands for accountability and for demonstration that the treatments are useful.

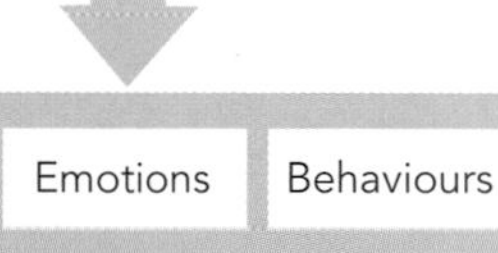

FIGURE 14.16

The measures used to assess the outcome of psychotherapy may come from a variety of data sources, and they may measure different aspects of the client's functioning.

Designing good psychotherapy research is one of the most challenging tasks in all of psychology because there are many variables that cannot be completely controlled. In contrast to laboratory studies, in which the experimental conditions can be highly standardized, therapist-client interactions are by their nature infinitely varied. Another difficulty involves measuring the effects of psychotherapy. Figure 14.16 shows some of the typical ways of measuring change. These measures differ in the outcome variable assessed (emotions, thoughts, or behaviours) and in the source of the data (the client, the therapist, or other informants). Which measures of change are most important or valid? A behaviourist will insist that direct observations of behaviour are the best measures, whereas a psychodynamic therapist may be most interested in how clients feel and how much insight they have achieved into the childhood roots of their problems. A humanistic therapist may place the greatest stock in self-concept changes. What if one set of measures indicates improvement, another indicates no change, and a third suggests that the client is worse off than before treatment? How should we evaluate the effects of the therapy? These are just a few of the vexing issues that can arise in psychotherapy research.

23. What types of measures are used to assess the outcome of therapy?

Psychotherapy Research Methods

In the 1930s and 1940s, individual case studies provided most of the psychotherapy outcome data. Indeed, Freud and other psychoanalysts opposed the use of experimental methods to evaluate psychoanalysis, insisting that case studies left no doubt regarding its effectiveness (Fisher & Greenberg, 1996; Rosenzweig, 1992). They assumed that without therapy, patients would not improve, and they saw plenty of people who did improve in analysis.

24. Describe Eysenck's challenge to therapy effectiveness and the data on which it was based.

In 1952, British psychologist Hans Eysenck mounted a frontal assault on this assumption. Using recovery data from insurance companies on people who applied for disability because of psychological problems, Eysenck (1952) concluded that the rate of **spontaneous remission**—symptom reduction in the absence of any treatment—was as high as the success rates reported by psychotherapists. He therefore concluded that troubled people who receive psychotherapy are no more likely to improve than are those who go untreated. He also pointed out, quite correctly, that virtually all of the existing outcome data were based on therapists' evaluations of their clients' improvement, and he suggested that these evaluations could be biased by therapists' needs to see themselves as competent and successful.

Eysenck's conclusions sparked intense debate—even outrage—among clinicians, and it now appears that his conclusions were overly pessimistic. More importantly, Eysenck's challenge stimulated a vigorous increase in research on psychotherapy and the development of more sophisticated methods for evaluating treatment outcomes. Fifty years and many hundreds of studies later, we have reached the point where the American Psychological Association's Division of Clinical Psychology has taken the lead in reviewing all of this research to identify *empirically validated therapies* that research shows to be effective for specific disorders (APA Task Force on Psychological Intervention Guidelines, 1995; DeRubeis & Crits-Christoph, 1998; Kazdin & Weisz, 2003).

What Is a Good Psychotherapy Research Design?

25. Summarize desirable standards for designing psychotherapy research studies with regard to design, treatment standardization, and follow-up.

For many of the reasons discussed in Chapter 2, in which we discussed experimental methods and their value in drawing conclusions about causality, most psychotherapy researchers favour **randomized clinical trials** involving participants who have well-defined psychological disorders and are similar on other variables that might affect response to treatment (age and ethnic status, for example). These individuals are randomly assigned either to an experimental condition that gets the treatment or to a control condition (Kazdin, 2003). The control group may be either a no-treatment condition or (even better) a **placebo control group** that gets an intervention that is not expected to work, but that controls for client expectations of improvement because clients are being seen by a therapist and think they're getting an effective treatment. (Clients in the control group, whether it be a no-treatment or placebo condition, are often given the real treatment later for ethical reasons.)

Another control condition, which avoids the ethical dilemma of withholding or delaying treatment for some people, involves randomly assigning participants to either the treatment being studied or to another kind of treatment that has proven effective for that disorder. If the treatment being tested in the experimental condition is equally or more effective than the established treatment, the new therapy is deemed effective. Sometimes, the design of a study involves a group in which the treatment is combined with another intervention such as a drug treatment. It is then possible to see if the group that received the drug *plus* therapy does better than the groups that got only the drug or only the therapy (Hollon, 1996).

To *standardize* the treatment, much as one would do in a laboratory experiment, the APA treatment evaluation group recommends that there be a manual containing procedures that the therapists have to follow exactly, and that therapists' compliance with these procedures be evaluated by observing them or taping their sessions. Some therapists, particularly those who do psychodynamic or humanistic therapies, object to this requirement on the grounds that every therapy case they see is different in its course, client characteristics, and procedures used. As a result, most of the current empirically validated therapies are cognitive-behavioural in nature, because these therapies are more often "manualized" into a step-by-step procedure that therapists can apply in a uniform manner. However, there is a movement toward standardizing even psychodynamically oriented therapies so that they can be evaluated more effectively (Crits-Christoph, 1992; Weissman & Markowitz, 1994).

In evaluating the treatment, at least some of the measures of improvement should be behavioural in nature. Interviewers or observers should not know what condition the clients were in so as to minimize experimenter bias in evaluating change during interviews or behavioural observations following treatment.

Finally, researchers should collect follow-up data. This is extremely important, for we want to know not only how the treatment conditions differ at the end of the clinical trial, but also how lasting the effects are. For example, in some studies comparing psychotherapy for depression with the effects of antidepressant drugs, the drug treatment effects occurred more quickly and were stronger at the end of the treatment period, suggesting a superiority for drug therapy. But follow-up data showed psychotherapy ultimately to be more effective, with fewer relapses into depression because clients had learned specific psychological skills that they could apply after therapy ended (Hollon & Beck, 1994; Weissman & Markowitz, 1994).

?

26. How is meta-analysis used to assess therapy effects? What have meta-analyses shown about overall effectiveness and the effects of different forms of therapy?

Meta-Analysis: A Look at the Big Picture

As discussed in Chapter 2, the technique of **meta-analysis** allows researchers to combine the results of many studies to arrive at an overall conclusion. In the psychotherapy research literature they can compute an **effect size statistic** that represents a common measure of treatment effectiveness. The effect size tells researchers what percentage of clients who have received therapy had a more favourable outcome than that of the average control client who did not receive the treatment.

In 1977, Mary Ann Smith and Gene Glass used meta-analysis to combine the effects of 375 studies of psychotherapy involving 25,000 clients and 25,000 control participants. These studies differed in many ways, but they all compared a treatment condition with a control condition. The results indicated that the average therapy client had a more favourable outcome than 75 percent of the untreated cases. Smith and Glass therefore disputed Eysenck's earlier conclusion, maintaining that therapy does indeed have positive effects beyond spontaneous remission. More recent meta-analyses support this conclusion. Robert Grissom (1997) found that, across a large number of studies, clients who received therapy were likely to have a more favourable outcome than 70 percent of those in no-treatment control conditions and 66 percent of those in placebo conditions.

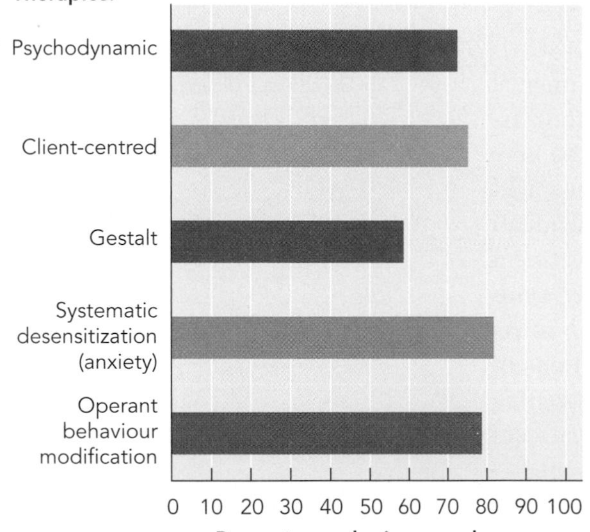

FIGURE 14.17

This meta-analysis of 375 studies of psychotherapy outcome yielded effectiveness data on various types of psychotherapy. The bars indicate the percentage of treated clients who improved more than the average control client.

Data from Smith & Glass, 1977.

What about differences among therapies? Smith and Glass broke down their meta-analysis in terms of many of the therapies described in this chapter. As shown in Figure 14.17, psychodynamic, client-centred, and behavioural approaches were quite similar in their effectiveness, and all of them seemed to yield somewhat more positive effects than Gestalt therapy. A more recent meta-analysis of brief psychodynamic therapy outcome studies supports a similar conclusion: That form of therapy yielded significantly better outcomes than did no-treatment or placebo control conditions, but did not differ in effectiveness from other forms of therapy with which it was compared (Anderson & Lambert, 1997). This finding of similar efficacy for widely differing therapies has been termed the **dodo bird verdict**, after the dodo bird's statement in *Alice in Wonderland* that "Everybody has won and all must have prizes" (Luborsky et al., 2002). Other researchers challenge this conclusion, maintaining that lumping together studies involving different kinds of clinical problems may mask *differential effectiveness,* i.e., the fact that specific therapies might be highly effective for treating some clinical disorders but not others (Beutler, 2002; Westen & Morrison, 2001).

The very definition of therapy "success" is a topic of debate. How much do clients have to improve in order to have a successful outcome? Is therapy successful if deeply depressed clients show a statistically significant decrease in self-report scores of depression following therapy but their scores still fall within the clinically depressed range? According to Neil Jacobson and co-workers (1996), **clinical significance** would require that at the end of therapy, clients' depression scores fall within the range for nondepressed people. This is, of course, a more stringent definition of therapeutic success than the one used in most meta-analyses (i.e., greater positive change in a treatment group than in a control group of similarly depressed clients) and would undoubtedly indicate lower levels of therapeutic success for most treatments.

In evaluating the results of meta-analyses, we should remember that the studies lumped together in a meta-analysis may differ in many ways, including the nature and severity of the problems that were treated, the outcome measures that were used, and the quality of the methodology. Psychotherapy researchers point out that combining good studies with less adequate ones can produce misleading results (Kazdin, 2003; Matt & Navarro, 1997). When studies that meet rigorous research standards are compared in meta-analyses with less rigorous studies, the rigorous studies tend to yield more favourable outcomes for therapy conditions (Matt & Navarro, 1997). Apparently, the rigorous methods used in such studies allow effective therapies to show their true effects.

Factors Affecting the Outcome of Therapy

27. What client variables are important to treatment outcome?

Clearly, not everyone who enters therapy profits from it. There is even evidence that some clients—-perhaps 10 percent—may get worse as a result of treatment (Binder & Strupp, 1997; Lambert et al., 1986). What then are the factors that influence treatment outcome? Three sets of factors have been the focus of research designed to answer this question, namely, client variables, therapist variables, and technique variables (Figure 14.18).

As far as client variables are concerned, three important factors are an openness to therapy, self-relatedness, and the nature of the problem. **Openness** involves clients' general willingness to invest themselves in therapy and take the risks required to change themselves. **Self-relatedness** refers to their ability to experience and understand internal states such as thoughts and emotions, to be attuned to the processes that go on in their relationship with their therapist, and to be able to apply what they learn in therapy to their lives outside of treatment (Howard et al., 1993). The third important client factor is the nature of the problem and its degree of "fit" with the therapy being used. For example, specific problems such as phobias may respond best to a behavioural anxiety-reduction treatment such as systematic desensitization or exposure, whereas a more global problem, such as a search for self-discovery and greater meaning in life, may respond better to a psychodynamic, cognitive, or humanistic approach.

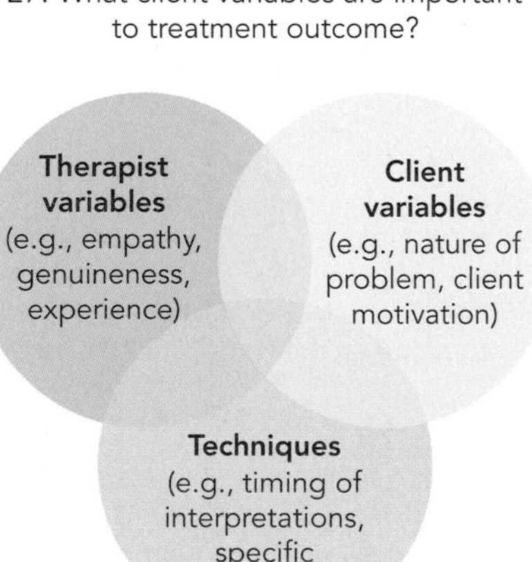

FIGURE 14.18

Research on factors that influence therapy outcome has focused on three sets of interacting variables: client factors, therapist factors, and technique factors.

28. Which therapist factors affect treatment outcome?

A second important determinant of therapy outcome is the quality of the relationship that the therapist is able to establish with the client (Teyber & McClure, 2000). Carl Rogers's emphasis on the importance of therapist qualities such as empathy, unconditional acceptance of the client as a person, and genuineness has been borne out in a great many studies (Beutler et al., 1994; Norcross, 2003). The establishment of an empathic, trusting, and caring relationship forms the foundation upon which the specific techniques employed by the therapist can have their most beneficial effects. When therapists do not manifest these behaviours, the effects of therapy are not simply null; clients can actually get worse. For example, hostile interchanges between therapist and client can contribute to a *deterioration effect* in therapy (Binder & Strupp, 1997).

We do not mean to imply that as long as a therapist has a good relationship with a client, it does not matter what therapy techniques are used or how they are used. It does matter. Therapists must be skilled in what they do. For example, a large-scale study at the University of Pennsylvania revealed that the correctness of the interpretations made by psychoanalytic therapists, as measured by expert ratings, was related to more positive treatment outcome (Crits-Christoph et al., 1988). Likewise, in a detailed analysis of the audiotaped therapy sessions of 21 psychotherapists, Enrico Jones and co-workers (1988) found that the most effective therapists adjusted their techniques to the specific needs of their clients. They concluded that "general relationship factors, such as therapeutic alliance, are closely bound with the skillful selection and application of psychotherapeutic techniques" (p. 55). If therapy is to be effective, clients must remain in treatment long enough for the therapeutic relationship and techniques to have their effects. For this reason, new research is focusing on the **dose-response effect**, the relation between the amount of treatment received and the quality of the outcome. One recent review of 29 randomized controlled clinical trials primarily involving cognitive and behavioural treatments found that between 58 and 67 percent of clients showed clinically significant improvement within an average of 13 sessions (Hansen et al., 2002). These rates are quite consistent with those typically found in research settings. The reviewers then turned to what occurs in the "real world" of clinical practice, examining the treatment records of 6,072 clients seen in a variety of naturalistic settings, including employee assistance programs, community and university counselling centres, and health maintenance organizations. Here they found that the average number of treatment sessions given was fewer than five, and the rate of improvement in this sample was only about 20 percent. These results suggest that many clients seen in these naturalistic settings do not remain in therapy long enough to realize its potential benefits. One possible reason is that many insurance plans limit their coverage to a number of treatment sessions that is too low to expect meaningful improvement.

29. Define and give examples of common factors in psychotherapy.

Despite dramatic differences in the techniques they employ, various therapies tend to enjoy similar success rates, probably because people who differ on the client variables are lumped together. This finding has led many experts to search for **common factors** shared by these diverse forms of therapy that might contribute to their success. These common factors include the following:

- faith in the therapist and a belief on the part of clients that they are receiving help;
- a plausible explanation for their problems, and an alternative way of looking at themselves and their problems;
- a protective setting in which clients can experience and express their deepest feelings within a supportive relationship;

- an opportunity to practise new behaviours; and
- increased optimism and self-efficacy.

The complexities of psychotherapy pose a formidable challenge for clinical researchers. Our *Research Foundations* describes one notable attempt to assess client perceptions of treatment outcome.

30. What were the major findings of the *CR* survey? On what bases were its conclusions criticized?

RESEARCH FOUNDATIONS

The Effectiveness of Psychotherapy: Feedback from the Consumer

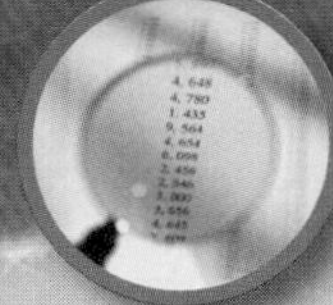

Background

Martin Seligman (1995) drew a distinction between two important questions about psychotherapy and its effects. The first is **efficacy**, a scientific term referring to whether a therapy can produce positive outcomes exceeding those in appropriate control conditions. Efficacy is best demonstrated in experimental clinical trials, in which the form of therapy and the nature of the clinical problems are controlled. The second is **effectiveness**, meaning the outcomes that psychotherapy has in the real-life settings of clinical practice, in which clients are free to pursue any kind of treatment they wish and the nature of the treatment is left uncontrolled. Seligman (1995) argued that highly controlled efficacy studies may not provide a true indication of psychotherapy's effectiveness in "real-life" clinical practice. He therefore assisted the periodical *Consumer Reports (CR)* in a large-scale survey of its readership to assess consumers' evaluations of their treatment experiences and the professionals they worked with.

Method

Each year, *CR* sends questionnaires to over four million of its subscribers on which they rate various products and services. One form of the 1994 annual survey, mailed to 184,000 randomly selected subscribers, contained a section on stress and mental health. Readers were asked to complete the mental health section if they had sought help for emotional problems in the past three years. A total of 22,000 readers responded to the questionnaire—a 13 percent response rate that is typical of *CR* surveys. Of these, 35 percent reported that they had a mental-health problem, and 40 percent of this latter group (approximately 2,900 respondents) reported that they had sought professional help from a psychologist, psychiatrist, social worker, or marriage counsellor. The respondents were asked to indicate the nature of the problem(s) for which they sought therapy, how much they improved as a result of treatment, and how satisfied they were with the treatment they received.

Results

Clients most frequently sought treatment for depression, followed by marital and sexual problems, anxiety, and family or social problems. Forty-three percent said they were feeling either "very poorly" or "poorly" when they began therapy, and 44 percent reported feeling "so-so." As shown in Figure 14.19, the majority of clients said they had improved as a result of treatment and were satisfied with their therapist. Those who were in treatment longer than six months said that they improved more than did those who were treated less than six months, even when the nature and severity of their problem were held constant. No overall outcome differences were found among mental health professionals, but clients were less satisfied with marriage counsellors than with psychologists, psychiatrists, or social workers. As in the meta-analyses described earlier, the *CR* survey found no effectiveness differences between the various types of psychotherapy the clients said they had received.

Critical Discussion

Seligman concluded that "*CR* has provided empirical validation of the effectiveness of therapy" (1995, p. 974). Furthermore, he concluded that the survey method used in this study might actually have provided data that are more representative of "real-life" outcomes than data yielded by highly controlled clinical trials.

Given what you've learned about psychotherapy research, do you agree with Seligman's conclusions? Can you think of any aspects of the *CR* methods that might limit your ability to conclude that psychotherapy is effective?

Seligman's conclusions were strongly contested on scientific grounds, and the American Psychological Association devoted an entire issue of its flagship publication (*American Psychologist*, November, 1996) to reactions from leading psychotherapy researchers. Here are some of the issues they raised:

–*Continued*

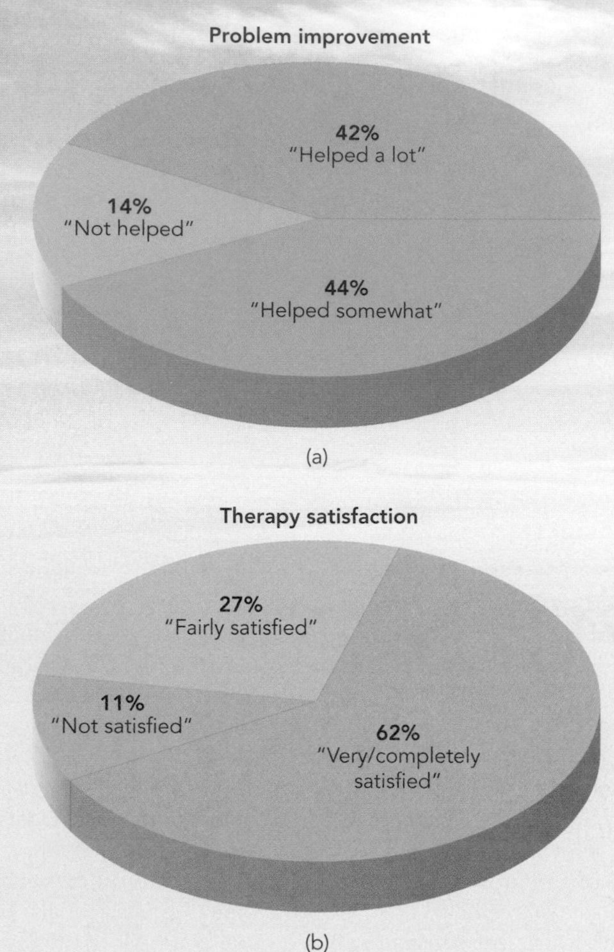

FIGURE 14.19

Ratings of (a) self-perceived improvement and (b) satisfaction with therapy outcome made by about 2,900 subscribers of Consumer Reports *who had been in psychotherapy for the treatment of psychological disorders.*

Data from Consumer Reports, 1995.

1. Consider the nature of the sample. Only 1.6 percent of the original 184,000 people contacted described their therapy experience. Is it possible that among the other 98.4 percent are a significant percentage of people who had been in therapy with unfavourable results and chose not to share their experiences? If so, the effectiveness of therapy could be exaggerated in this self-selected sample.
2. What about the nature and quality of the data? We have only global after-the-fact reports from clients. There is no way to corroborate respondents' reports with other sources of data. How do we know that they are not biased by memory distortions or affected by cognitive dissonance ("If I spent that much time and money, I must have gotten better"). A dissonance effect could also account for the apparent superiority of long-term therapy, in which more time and money were expended, as well as the tendency to return the questionnaire and share the success story.
3. What has this study told us about the more important specificity question? We don't know if some matches of clinical problems with specific forms of therapy yielded better outcomes than others. In fact, we can't even be sure what kinds of therapy were administered, because respondents didn't describe their treatment in detail.
4. How about the absence of a control group? Can we rule out spontaneous remission of symptoms? As we saw in Chapter 13, many mental-health problems (e.g., depression and anxiety) fluctuate or improve with time. People who are assessed at their low points, when they are most likely to seek therapy, are almost certain to improve, with or without therapy (Mintz et al., 1996). Could this factor alone explain the respondents' perceptions that they had improved? As Seligman himself conceded:

> Because there are no control groups, the *CR* . . . study cannot tell us directly whether talking to sympathetic friends or merely letting time pass would have produced just as much improvement as treatment by a mental-health professional. (1995, p. 972)

We chose to feature this study because it illustrates how difficult it can be to draw causal conclusions from studies that lack the precision of randomized clinical trials that are designed to control for all of the above factors. It may be that Seligman's conclusions are indeed correct, but we simply can't be sure when there are so many alternative explanations for the results.

Sources: *Consumer Reports* (1995, November). Mental health: Does therapy help? 734–739. Martin E. P. Seligman (1995). The effectiveness of psychotherapy: The Consumer Reports study. *American Psychologist, 50,* 965–974.

In Review

- *Eysenck challenged the effectiveness of psychotherapy and stimulated the use of increasingly more sophisticated research methods to evaluate the outcomes of various therapies. The randomized clinical trial is the most powerful approach to researching the effects of therapy, and a number of standards have been established for conducting psychotherapy research.*

- *Meta-analysis is a method for combining the results of many studies into an effect size statistic. Meta-analyses of treatment outcome studies found more improvement in therapy clients than in 70 to 75 percent of control clients and little difference in effectiveness among various therapies (the so-called dodo bird verdict). The Consumer Reports study of client self-report suggested high levels of client satisfaction.*
- *Three sets of interacting factors affect the outcome of treatment: client characteristics (including the nature of the problem), therapist characteristics, and therapy techniques.*
- *Client variables that contribute to therapy success include openness, self-relatedness, and a good match between the nature of the problem and the kind of therapy being received.*
- *A crucial factor in the success of various therapies is the quality of the relationship that the therapist establishes with the client. The three therapist characteristics suggested by Rogers—empathy, unconditional positive regard, and genuineness—are particularly important.*
- *Factors common to many therapies, such as faith in the therapist, a protected environment for self-exploration, and the ability to try out new behaviours, contribute to therapeutic outcome.*

BIOLOGICAL APPROACHES TO TREATMENT

In the previous chapter, we found that biological factors play an important role in many psychological disorders. Thus a direct biological approach designed to alter the brain's functioning is an alternative (or an addition) to psychological treatment.

Drug Therapies

Drug therapies are the most commonly used biological interventions. Discoveries in the field of psychopharmacology (the study of how drugs affect cognitions, emotions, and behaviour) have revolutionized the treatment of the entire range of behaviour disorders. Each year, more than 200 million prescriptions are filled for drugs that affect mood, thought, and behaviour (Lieberman, 1998; Lieberman & Tasman, 2006). The most commonly prescribed drugs fall into three major categories: anti-anxiety drugs, antidepressant drugs, and antipsychotic drugs.

Anti-anxiety Drugs

31. How do anti-anxiety drugs achieve their effects? Do they have any drawbacks?

Surveys have shown that more than 15 percent of Americans between the ages of 18 and 74 use anti-anxiety or tranquilizing drugs such as Valium, Xanax, and BuSpar. Health Canada (1997) reports that only about 4 percent of Canadians were prescribed tranquilizers, but there are large regional differences: 6.8 percent in Quebec and only 3.2 percent in the prairie provinces. These drugs are designed to reduce anxiety as much as possible without affecting alertness or concentration. Sometimes anti-anxiety drugs are used in combination with other therapies to help clients cope successfully with problematic situations (Stahl, 2000). A temporary reduction in anxiety resulting from the use of a drug may allow a client to enter anxiety-arousing situations and learn to cope more effectively with them.

One drawback of anti-anxiety drugs is psychological and physical dependence that can result from their long-term use. As with any other addictive drug, people who have developed physiological dependence on tranquilizers may experience characteristic withdrawal symptoms, such as intense anxiety, nausea, and restlessness when they stop taking them (Lieberman, 1998). Another problem is that anxiety symptoms often return when people stop taking the drugs.

A newer anti-anxiety drug, *buspirone* (BuSpar), is slow acting, has fewer fatiguing side effects, and seems to have less potential for abuse. It has proven effective in the treatment of generalized anxiety and post-traumatic stress disorder (Lieberman, 1998; Stahl, 2000). Like the other anti-anxiety drugs, BuSpar works by slowing down excitatory synaptic activity in the nervous system. One mechanism for doing so is by enhancing the postsynaptic activity of GABA, an inhibitory transmitter that reduces neural activity in areas of the brain associated with emotional arousal (Gorman, 2002; Pies, 2005).

Antidepressant Drugs

32. How do the three classes of antidepressant drugs achieve their effects biologically? How effective are they compared/combined with therapy?

Antidepressant drugs fall into three major categories: tricyclics (trade names Elavil, Tofranil); *monoamine oxidase (MAO) inhibitors* (Nardil, Parnate); and *selective serotonin reuptake inhibitors, or SSRIs* (Prozac, Zoloft, Paxil). The first two classes increase the activity of the excitatory neurotransmitters norepinephrine and serotonin, whose lowered level of activity in brain regions involved in positive emotion and motivation is related to depression. The tricyclics work by preventing reuptake of the excitatory transmitters into the presynaptic neurons, allowing them to continue stimulating postsynaptic neurons. The MAO inhibitors reduce the activity of monoamine oxidase, an enzyme that breaks down the neurotransmitters in the synapse.

MAO inhibitors have more severe side effects than the tricyclics. They can cause dangerous elevations in blood pressure when taken with certain foods, such as cheeses and some types of wine. Many patients have abandoned their antidepressant medications because of severe side effects. The SSRIs were designed to decrease side effects by increasing the activity of just one transmitter, serotonin (Marangell, 2002). Like the other antidepressants, however, SSRIs do have side effects. For example, about 30 percent of patients on Prozac report nervousness, insomnia, sweating, joint pain, or sexual dysfunction (Hellerstein et al., 1993). Nonetheless, the SSRIs are gradually replacing the tricyclics because, in addition to milder side effects, they reduce depressive symptoms more rapidly and also reduce anxiety symptoms, including panic disorder, obsessive-compulsive behaviours, and social phobia (Lickey & Gordon, 1991; Lieberman, 1998). Figure 14.20 shows how the SSRIs produce their effects. A great deal of attention has been drawn to the possible relationship between SSRI usage and suicide. Indeed, warnings have been placed on the packaging of these antidepressants cautioning patients about the risk of suicidal thoughts, particularly in children. Jureidini et al. (2004) report that the data from various clinical trials is conflicting. In a large meta-analysis of clinical trial data, the authors point out that the effectiveness of SSRIs is considerably less than we would like. In addition, adverse effects (such as suicidal thoughts) may be vastly underestimated. In contrast, Khan et al. (2003) argue that we should look at actual suicides and not just increased risk. They examined the FDA summary reports for controlled clinical trials of nine antidepressants. Of the 48,277 patients who participated in the trials, 77 committed suicide. The rates were comparable for SSRIs (e.g. Prozac) and standard antidepressants (e.g., Welbutrin). Goldberg (2006) reports that suicide rates for children are actually lower for those on high levels of SSRIs. More research is needed to assess this question.

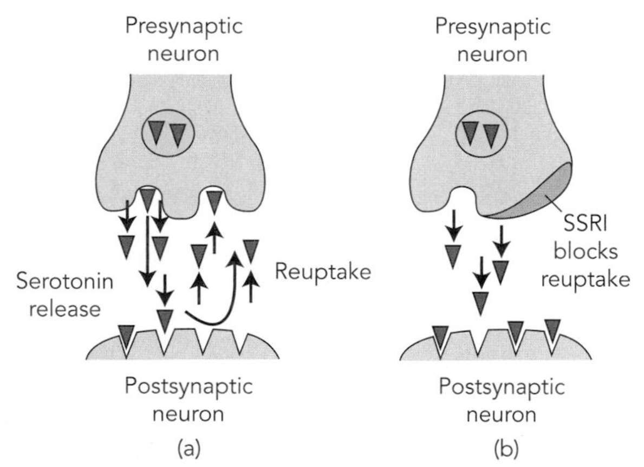

FIGURE 14.20

Serotonin activity is low in many depressed clients. When a presynaptic neuron releases serotonin into the synaptic space, a pumplike reuptake mechanism begins to pull neurotransmitter molecules back into the "sending" neuron, limiting the stimulation of the postsynaptic neuron (a). By blocking the reuptake of serotonin into the presynaptic neuron (b), the selective serotonin reuptake inhibitors (SSRIs) allow serotonin to continue its stimulation of postsynaptic neurons.

Increasingly, depression researchers are studying the effects of combining drugs and psychotherapy. A meta-analysis of such studies revealed that recovery rates for psychotherapy and the combined treatments did not differ for less severely depressed people. However, the combination of psychotherapy and drug treatment yielded the best recovery rates in more severe cases of depression (Thase et al., 1997).

Antipsychotic Drugs

Perhaps the most dramatic effects of drug therapy have occurred in the treatment of severely disordered people, permitting many of them to function outside of the hospital setting (Shorter, 1998). As shown in Figure 14.21, a sharp decline in the number of in-patients in public mental hospitals has occurred since 1955, when antipsychotic drugs were first introduced on a wide scale.

33. What is tardive dyskinesia, and how is it caused?

The revolution in drug therapy for severe psychological disorders began when it was accidentally discovered that reserpine, a drug derived from the root of the snakeroot plant, calmed psychotic patients. This discovery resulted in the development of synthetic antipsychotic drugs (also called *major tranquilizers*) used today to treat schizophrenic disorders. The primary effect of the major tranquilizers is to decrease the action of dopamine, the neurotransmitter whose overactivity is thought to be involved in schizophrenia (Schatzberg et al., 2005). These drugs have dramatic effects in reducing positive symptoms, such as hallucinations and delusions. However, they have little effect on negative symptoms, such as apathy and withdrawal. Antipsychotic drugs are now so widely used that nearly all schizophrenic patients living in the United States, Canada, and western Europe have received them at one time or another. Because patients often relapse very quickly if they stop taking the drugs, it is common practice to recommend that the medication be continued indefinitely once the individual has returned to the community (Carpenter & Heinrichs, 1983).

Although antipsychotic drugs have allowed many patients to be released from hospitals and reduced the need for padded cells, straitjackets, and other restraints that were used to control the behaviour of hospitalized patients, these drugs can produce a severe movement disorder known as **tardive dyskinesia** (Kane, 2006). Uncontrollable and grotesque movements of the face and tongue are especially prominent in this disorder, and sometimes the patient's arms and legs flail uncontrollably. Tardive dyskinesia can be more debilitating than the psychotic symptoms that prompted the drug treatment, and it appears to be irreversible once it develops (Barnes, 1994). One study found that within four years of beginning antipsychotic medications, 18.5 percent of young adults and 31 percent of those over 55 developed tardive dyskenesia symptoms (Saltz et al., 1991).

Researchers are working to develop new drugs that can control schizophrenic symptoms without producing side effects, such as the devastating symptoms of tardive dyskinesia. A new drug called *clozapine* (Clozaril) reduces not only positive symptoms, but also negative ones, and it appears not to produce tardive dyskenesia (Lieberman, 1998). Unfortunately, it produces a fatal blood disease in one to two percent of people who take it, requiring expensive weekly blood tests for patients who use the medication. Haas et al. (2007) examined the data for all patients taking clozapine between 1993 and 2003. In this group, 116 developed the infection and 12 died. Typically, onset of the disease is early in treatment and young people are most likely to be adversely affected.

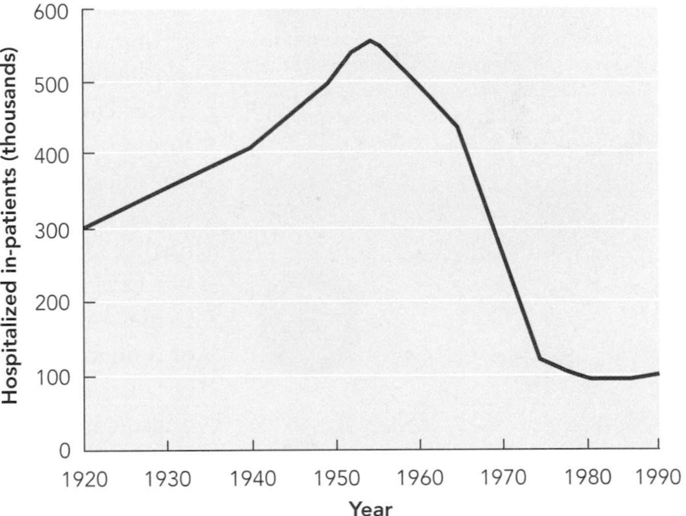

FIGURE 14.21

Antipsychotic drugs have revolutionized the treatment of severely disturbed individuals, allowing many of them to leave mental hospitals. Note the decline in hospitalized in-patients that occurred following the introduction of antipsychotic drugs in the mid-1950s.

Source: National Institute of Mental Health, 1992.

Antipsychotic drugs often can be used effectively in conjunction with psychotherapy. For example, drugs may be used to bring psychotic symptoms under control so that other approaches such as social skills training, family therapy, and group therapy can be applied to maintain the initial improvement.

Electroconvulsive Therapy

Another biologically based treatment, **electroconvulsive therapy (ECT)**, was based on the observation by a Hungarian physician that schizophrenia and epilepsy rarely occur in the same person. (Apparently, he didn't stop to consider the fact that the probability of epilepsy and any other disorder occurring together is very low.) The physician therefore suggested that seizure induction might be useful in the treatment of schizophrenia. Two Italian physicians, Ugo Cerletti and Lucio Bini, began to treat schizophrenic patients by attaching electrodes to their skulls and inducing a seizure by means of an electric current administered to the brain.

34. Which disorders do and do not respond favourably to ECT?

When ECT was first introduced in the 1930s, it was applied to a wide range of disorders, but later research revealed that it cannot relieve anxiety disorders and it is of questionable value for schizophrenic patients (Herrington & Lader, 1996; Weiner & Coffey, 1988). However, ECT can be useful in treating severe depression, particularly if there is a high risk of suicide. In such cases, the use of antidepressant drugs may be impractical because they likely will take several weeks to begin reducing the depression. In contrast, the effects of ECT can be immediate, and controlled studies indicate that 60 to 70 percent of severely depressed people given ECT improve (Rey & Walter, 1997).

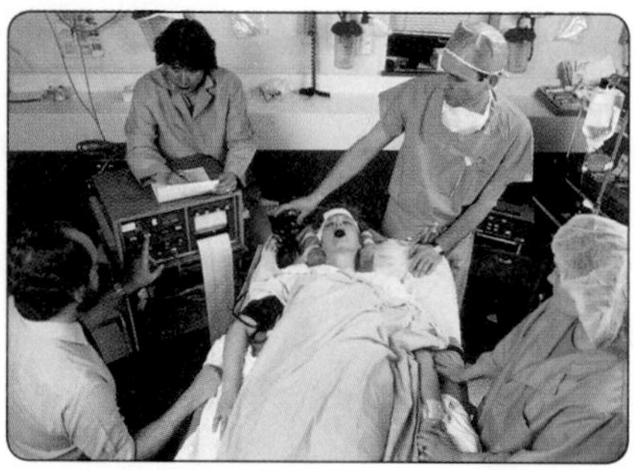

FIGURE 14.22

A severely depressed and possibly suicidal patient is prepared for an ECT session. The patient has been sedated and given a muscle relaxant to minimize limb movements during the brief electrical stimulation of the brain. The rubber object in her mouth prevents her from biting her tongue or damaging her teeth during the convulsion.

Dramatizations of ECT in the mass media sometimes portray a procedure that appears barbaric. In early applications of ECT, a wide-awake patient was strapped to a table, electrodes were attached to the patient's scalp, and roughly 100 volts of electricity was applied to the brain, producing violent convulsions and momentary unconsciousness. Sometimes, the seizures were so violent that patients fractured their arms or legs.

Today, however, the procedure is quite different (Figure 14.22). A patient is first given a sedative and a muscle relaxant to prevent injuries from convulsions. The patient is then placed on a well-padded mattress, and electrodes are attached to his or her scalp. A modified procedure in which electrodes are placed on only one side of the head is often used (Martin, 1986). The duration of the shock is less than a second, causing a seizure of the central nervous system. There is little observable movement in the patient, other than a twitching of the toes and a slight facial grimace. The patient wakes up 10 to 20 minutes after ECT, possibly with a headache, sore muscles, and some confusion. Recently, scientists have been able to calibrate the amount of electric current a patient needs so that treatments can be individualized, and research is being carried out to determine whether certain drugs can further reduce seizure-induced confusion and amnesia.

ECT has many critics, despite its effectiveness in alleviating major depression. Critics note that even when the effects are dramatically positive, the possibility of a depressive relapse is high. Concern has been raised about the safety of ECT because, in some instances, permanent memory loss has been reported, and there is also concern about possibly permanent brain damage when ECT is used repeatedly. Today the number of ECT treatments is limited to less than 10, but in the past, many patients received numerous treatments. One person who suffered a tragic outcome was the author Ernest Hemingway.

> In December 1960, Hemingway underwent 11 shock treatments at the Mayo Clinic in Rochester, Minnesota. Three months later he was back for another series. His friend and biographer, A. E. Hotchner, described him at that time: "Ernest was even more infuriated with these treatments than the previous ones, registering bitter complaints about how his memory was wrecked and how he was ruined as a writer." Hemingway told Hotchner, "What these shock doctors don't know is about writers and such things as remorse and contrition and what they do to them. What is the sense of ruining my head and

erasing my memory, which is my capital, and putting me out of business? It was a brilliant cure but we lost the patient." Shortly afterwards, Hemingway committed suicide. (Friedberg, 1975, pp. 25–26)

Steps have been taken to increase the safety of ECT, and available scientific evidence suggests that today's ECT is a safer treatment than were previous forms. MRI studies of the brains of patients who received brief pulse treatment to both sides of the brain revealed no evidence of brain damage (Coffey et al., 1991). After reviewing both sides of the issue, the American Psychiatric Association (1990) concluded that this therapy should be regarded as a useful procedure for major depression in patients who cannot take or do not respond to medication and has published guidelines for its use.

Psychosurgery

35. What were the rationale and effects of prefrontal lobotomy?

Psychosurgery refers to surgical procedures that remove or destroy brain tissue to change disordered behaviour. It is the least used of the biomedical procedures, but such was not always the case. In the 1930s, before the advent of antipsychotic drugs, Portuguese surgeon Egas Moniz reported that cutting the nerve tracts that connect the frontal lobes with subcortical areas of the brain involved in emotion resulted in a calming of psychotic and uncontrollably violent patients. The operation eliminated emotional input from the limbic system into the areas of the brain connected with executive functions of planning and reasoning. Walter Freeman developed a 10-minute *lobotomy* operation performed by inserting an icepick-like instrument with sharp edges through the eye socket into the brain, then wiggling it back and forth to sever the targeted nerve tracts. During the 1930s and 1940s, tens of thousands of patients—50,000 in the United States alone—underwent the operation. Moniz received a Nobel prize for his contribution (Shorter, 1998).

Initial enthusiasm for lobotomy was soon replaced by a sober recognition that the massive neural damage it caused had severe side effects on mental and emotional functioning, including seizures, stupor, memory and reasoning impairment, and listlessness. With the development of antipsychotic drugs in the 1950s, lobotomies decreased and are hardly ever used today. However, more precise and limited psychosurgery procedures still are used at times in the most extreme cases and when every other avenue has been tried (Pressman, 1998). One procedure called *cingulotomy* involves cutting a small fibre bundle near the corpus callosum that connects the frontal lobes with the limbic system. Cingulotomy has been used successfully in treating severe depressive and obsessive-compulsive disorders that have failed to improve with drug treatment or psychotherapy. However, this more limited procedure also can produce side effects, including seizures (Herrington & Lader, 1996; Pressman, 1998). Appropriately, cingulotomy and other forms of psychosurgery are considered to be last-resort procedures.

Mind, Body, and Therapeutic Interventions

The impact of drug and electroconvulsive therapies on psychological disorders illustrates once again the important interactions between biological and psychological phenomena. In the final analysis, both psychological and biological treatments affect brain functioning in ways that can change disordered thoughts, emotions, and behaviour. Moreover, they may constitute different routes to the same changes, as illustrated in a recent study by Tomas Furmark and co-workers (2002) at Uppsala University in Sweden. The researchers randomly assigned patients with social phobia to nine-week treatments that involved either drug therapy with an SSRI or a course of cognitive and behavioural psychotherapy involving exposure

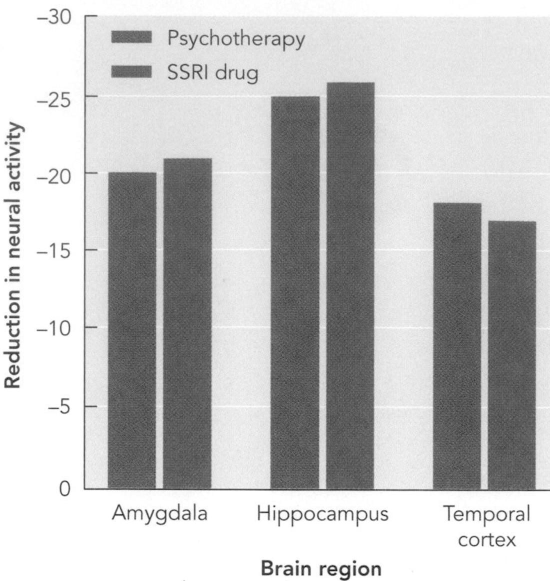

FIGURE 14.23

Effects of psychotherapy and drug therapy on brain activity in clients treated for social phobia. Clients who responded to the treatments with reduced anxiety showed nearly identical changes in PET-scan recordings of neural activity in three areas of the brain whose activation is thought to underlie anxiety.

Source: Based on Furmark et al., 2002.

to feared social situations and cognitive modification of anxiety-arousing thoughts. Before and after treatment, the participants received PET scans while they gave a hastily prepared speech to a group of six to eight persons standing around the scanner bed. They also provided subjective ratings of their anxiety during the procedure. Uniformly high anxiety scores were reported by all participants prior to treatment.

In general, both treatments were effective, although overall the psychological treatment produced a stronger reduction in fear and social phobia symptoms than did the drug treatment. Nonetheless, when the researchers compared the pre- and post-treatment PET scans of those participants who responded to the two treatments with reduced social anxiety, the psychotherapy and drug groups showed basically the same changes in cerebral blood flow from the first speech situation to the second. These changes involved reduced neural activity in an "anxiety circuit" involving the amygdala, the hippocampus, and areas of the temporal cerebral cortex (Figure 14.23).Treatment nonresponders did not show these brain changes. Thus different forms of therapy, whether "psychological" or "biological" in nature, may result in similar changes at a neurological level and, ultimately, at a behavioural level.

An important factor to keep in mind is that drug treatments, however effective they may be in modifying some disordered behaviours in the short term, do not "cure" the disorder. They suppress symptoms, but do not teach the client coping and problem solving skills that might be used to deal with stressful life situations (DeLongis et al., 2000; Nezu et al., 2000). Many therapists believe that one of the major benefits of psychological treatments is their potential not only for helping clients deal with current problems but also for increasing their personal resources so that they might enjoy a higher level of adjustment and life satisfaction in the future (Hollon, 1996).

We have now considered a wide spectrum of approaches to treating abnormal behaviour. Figure 14.24 summarizes the mechanisms for therapeutic change that are emphasized by the various psychological and biological approaches.

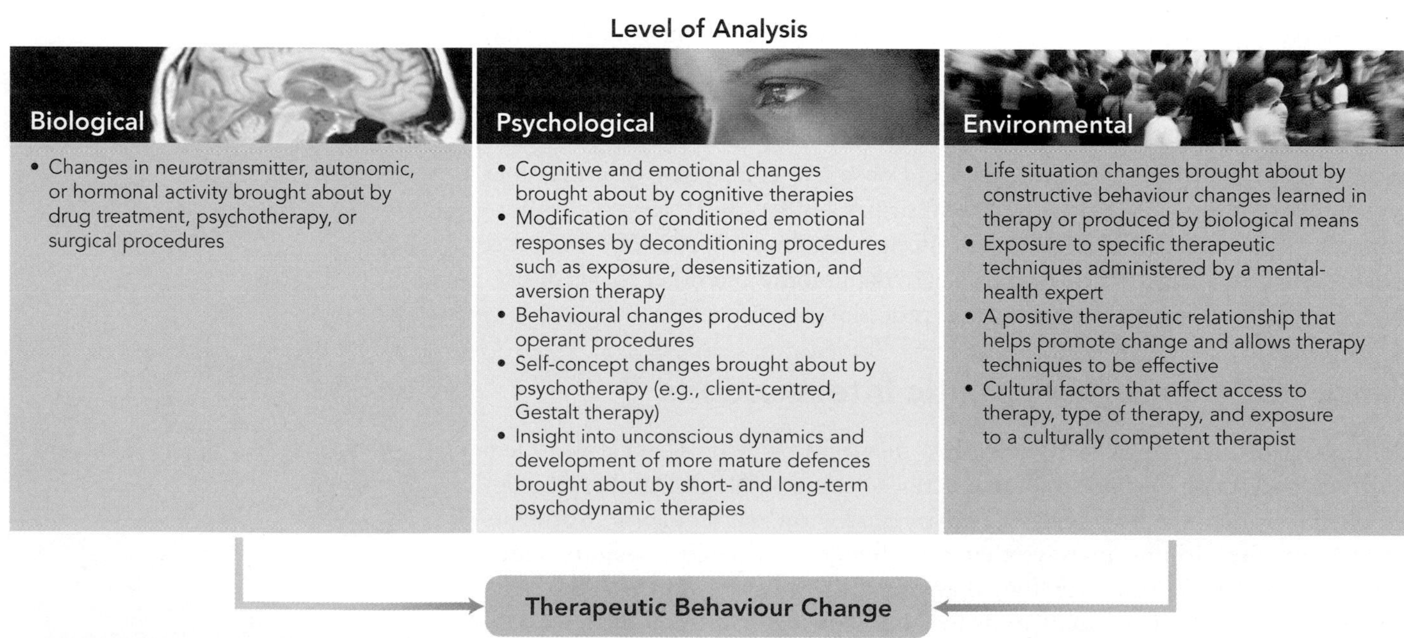

Level of Analysis
Biological
• Changes in neurotransmitter, autonomic, or hormonal activity brought about by drug treatment, psychotherapy, or surgical procedures
Psychological
• Cognitive and emotional changes brought about by cognitive therapies
• Modification of conditioned emotional responses by deconditioning procedures such as exposure, desensitization, and aversion therapy
• Behavioural changes produced by operant procedures
• Self-concept changes brought about by psychotherapy (e.g., client-centred, Gestalt therapy)
• Insight into unconscious dynamics and development of more mature defences brought about by short- and long-term psychodynamic therapies
Environmental
• Life situation changes brought about by constructive behaviour changes learned in therapy or produced by biological means
• Exposure to specific therapeutic techniques administered by a mental-health expert
• A positive therapeutic relationship that helps promote change and allows therapy techniques to be effective
• Cultural factors that affect access to therapy, type of therapy, and exposure to a culturally competent therapist
Therapeutic Behaviour Change

FIGURE 14.24

Understanding the causes of behaviour: mechanisms of therapeutic behaviour change.

In Review

- *Drugs have revolutionized the treatment of many behaviour disorders and have permitted many hospitalized patients to function outside of institutions. Drugs and psychotherapy may be combined to hasten the relief of symptoms while establishing more effective coping responses to deal with the sources of the disorder. Effective drug treatments exist for anxiety, depression, schizophrenia, and mania. Some of these drugs have undesirable side effects and can be addictive. All of them affect neurotransmission within the brain, and they work on specific classes of neurotransmitters.*
- *Electroconvulsive therapy is used less frequently than in the past, and its safety has been increased. It is used primarily to treat severe depression, particularly when a strong threat of suicide exists.*
- *Psychosurgery techniques have become more precise, but they are still generally used only after all other treatment options have failed.*
- *Studies have shown similar alterations of brain functioning in successful treatment, whether the treatment involves drug treatment or psychotherapy.*

PSYCHOLOGICAL DISORDERS AND SOCIETY

Since the days of insane asylums, first established in the sixteenth century to segregate the insane from society, severe behaviour disorders have been treated in institutional settings. This move towards institutionalization was pioneered by Dorothy Dix who travelled throughout Canada and the United States promoting the humane treatment of people with mental disorders. Her pleas did not fall on deaf ears. For example, in 1852, the Nova Scotia legislature enacted a statute founding a provincial asylum for the "proper keeping of lunatics and idiots." The Provincial Hospital for the Insane was constructed and the first patient admitted in 1858. The name was changed to the Nova Scotia Hospital for the Insane in 1900, and parts of the facility still stand today. By the early 1900s most provinces had similar institutions. However, it was readily apparent to mental-health experts that, although there were some high-quality institutions, many public mental hospitals were not fulfilling their intended role as treatment facilities. They were overcrowded, understaffed, and underfinanced. Many of them could provide little more than minimal custodial care and a haven from the stresses and demands of the outer world. Moreover, people who were admitted to such hospitals often sank into a chronic "sick" role in which passive dependence and "crazy" behaviour not only were tolerated, but expected (Goffman, 1961; Scheff, 1966). They lost the self-confidence, motivation, and skills needed to re-enter and adapt to the outside world, and had little chance of surviving outside the hospital.

Deinstitutionalization

36. What is the rationale for deinstitutionalization? What prevents it from achieving its goals?

By the 1960s, the stage was set for a new approach to the treatment of behaviour disorders. Concern about the inadequacies of mental hospitals, together with the ability of antipsychotic drugs to "normalize" patients' behaviour, resulted in a **deinstitutionalization** movement to transfer the primary focus of treatment from the mental institution to the community.

In 1957, the Canadian government passed legislation to partially fund provincial hospital insurance plans, providing for universal health care (Saskatchewan had actually established public health insurance 10 years earlier). However, the plan did not extend to mental institutions. Thus the provinces were forced to find alternative methods to care for those with psychological disorders. Psychiatric units were added to many of the regular hospitals and community services were

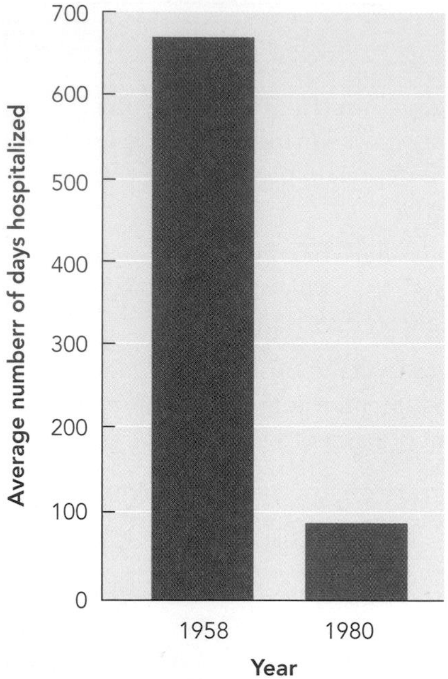

FIGURE 14.25

Average length of psychiatric hospitalization at Veterans Administration Hospitals in 1958 and 1980.

Data from National Institute of Mental Health, 1992.

FIGURE 14.26

The "revolving door" phenomenon created by inadequate funding of community-based treatment facilities has produced a large population of severely disturbed homeless people who live on our nation's streets.

established—both partially covered by federal transfer payments. Community mental health centres are designed to provide comprehensive services to their local communities. Their major function is to provide outpatient psychotherapy and counselling so that clients can remain in their normal social and work environments. For example, the Centre for Addiction and Mental Health in Toronto provides "direct patient care for people with mental health and addiction problems." Many have crisis centres and telephone "hot lines" to respond to emergency situations encountered by people in the community. Finally, community mental health centres provide education and training, and some operate as research facilities.

Combined with the development of effective drug treatments, the impact of deinstitutionalization on the treatment of behaviour disorders has been dramatic. According to the U.S. National Institute of Mental Health, 77.4 percent of all patients were being treated as in-patients in public and private hospitals in 1955. By 1990, the in-patient figure had shrunk to 27.1 percent. As Figure 14.25 indicates, the average length of hospitalization for patients having severe (typically schizophrenic) disorders also has decreased markedly. In Canada, the deinstitutionalization movement resulted in an 80 percent decrease in the number of institutionalized patients.

The concept of community treatment is a good one, since it allows people to remain in their social and work environments and to be treated with minimal disruption of their lives. However, it requires the availability of high-quality mental health care in community clinics, halfway houses, sheltered workshops, and other community facilities. When these facilities are available, deinstitutionalization can work. Unfortunately, however, many communities never were able to fund the needed facilities, and the 1980s saw sharp cutbacks in federal funding of community mental-health centres. As a result, many patients are being released into communities that are ill-prepared to care for their needs. The result is a *revolving door phenomenon* involving repeated rehospitalizations. Nearly three-fourths of all hospital admissions involve formerly hospitalized patients. While in the hospital, they respond well to antipsychotic medication and are soon released back into a community that cannot offer them the care they require. Soon they stop taking their medication. In the absence of treatment, their condition deteriorates to the point where they must be hospitalized, and so the cycle begins again. One result is a growing population of disturbed and homeless people who have nowhere to go for help (Figure 14.26). In some provinces with large urban populations, the largest mental wards exist not in hospitals but on city streets. There are as many as one million homeless people in the United States, and approximately one-third have a severe mental disorder, typically schizophrenia (Torrey, 1997). Estimates in Canada are proportionately similar—approximately 40 to 45 percent of the homeless have been hospitalized for a mental disorder in the past three years (Wasylenski, Goering, Lemire, Lindsey, & Lancee, 1993).

Deinstitutionalization can work only if society has the will to make it work. Time will tell if funding will be provided for the community programs needed to slow the revolving door and provide the help so desperately needed by the many people who are being left without treatment and without hope.

Preventive Mental Health

37. Define the two major approaches to prevention.

Up to now, we have focused entirely on what can be done to help people once they have developed a behaviour disorder. Successful treatment is one way to reduce the toll of human suffering produced by failures to adapt. Another way is to try to *prevent* the development of disorders through psychological intervention. In terms of economic, personal, and societal costs, it may indeed be the case that "an ounce of prevention is worth a pound of cure." If current efforts to enhance personal well-being and to slow the rise of health care costs are to be successful, the prevention of behaviour disorders must be a focal point in social policy (Munoz et al., 1996).

People may become vulnerable to psychological disorders as the result of situational factors, personal factors, or both. Thus prevention can be approached from two perspectives (Figure 14.27). **Situation-focused prevention** is directed at reducing or eliminating the environmental causes of behaviour disorders or at enhancing situational factors that help prevent the development of disorders. Psychologist George Albee (1996), who champions this approach, insists that prevention must focus on efforts to reduce the stresses of unemployment, economic exploitation, discrimination, and poverty. Programs designed to enhance the functioning of families, reduce stress within organizations, provide better educational opportunities for children, and develop a sense of "connection" to other people and the community at large all have the potential to help prevent the development of behaviour disorders (Albee, 1997; Taylor & Wang, 2000).

The personal side of the equation is addressed by **competency-focused prevention**, which is designed to increase personal resources and coping skills. Such programs may focus on strengthening resistance to stress, improving social and vocational competencies, enhancing self-esteem, and helping people to gain the skills needed to build stronger social support systems. One illustrative program, developed by Edna Foa and her co-workers (1995), focused on preventing the development of post-traumatic stress disorder in women who had recently been raped or assaulted.

The victims were randomly assigned to either a treatment condition or to a non-treatment control condition. Over a four-week period, the women in the treatment group underwent an educational program designed to increase their stress management coping skills. They learned about the common psychological reactions to being raped, showing them that their responses were normal, and they emotionally relived their trauma through imagery to defuse their lingering fears through exposure. They also learned stress coping skills such as relaxation, and they went through a cognitive therapy procedure so that they could replace their negative beliefs about themselves and their stress-producing cognitions with more realistic appraisals.

The results of the prevention program are shown in Figure 14.28. The women exposed to the prevention treatment had less severe symptoms at both the 2-month and 5.5-month assessments. Moreover, two months after their trauma, diagnostic interviews with the women in the two groups revealed that 70 percent of the women in the control condition met the DSM-IV criteria for PTSD compared to only 10 percent of the women who had received the prevention program. Thus, for many of the women, an efficient four-hour program prevented what might have been a PTSD disorder that would have created tremendous personal misery and have required a far more expensive and time-consuming course of therapy (Rasmussen & Charney, 2000).

Many mental-health experts believe that more resources need to be focused on prevention so that the occurrence of maladaptive behaviour can be reduced. However, prevention presents its own challenges. For example, we cannot develop an intervention program until we understand the causes of the disorder we want to reduce. Even when causal factors are known, we need also to understand what kinds of interventions might be successful in modifying them. This requires careful research into which types of programs are most effective in preventing which types of problems in which types of people—our old specificity question. Another

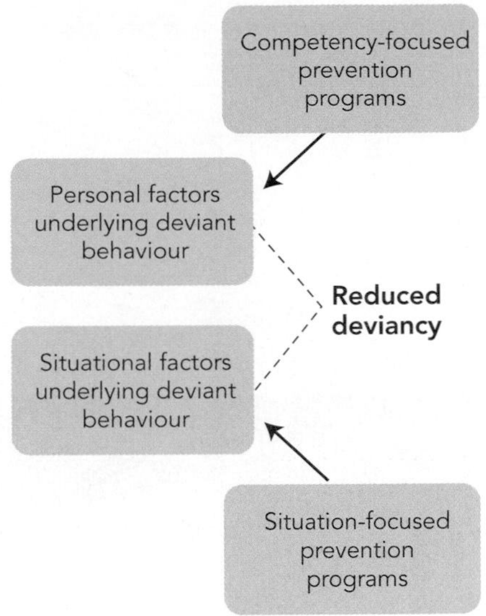

FIGURE 14.27

Two approaches to prevention of psychological disorders, based on the principle that deviant behaviour represents the interaction of personal and situational factors. Situation-focused approaches increase situational protective factors or reduce vulnerability factors in the environment. Competency-focused approaches reduce personal vulnerability factors or strengthen personal competencies and coping skills.

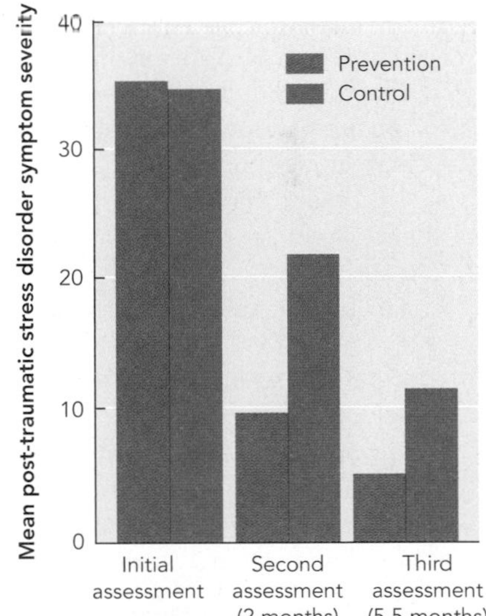

FIGURE 14.28

Results of a competency-based prevention project designed to prevent PTSD in women who were victims of rape and assault. The program, which combined a number of behavioural and cognitive therapy techniques to increase stress management coping skills, sharply reduced the likelihood of developing PTSD.

Based on Foa et al., 1995.

practical problem is that the effects of prevention are not usually immediately obvious. It may take years for their effects to become evident. Moreover, their effects (which usually involve the *absence* of a disorder) can be hard to measure. For these reasons, prevention programs can be difficult to justify when funding priorities are being set, even though the programs may, in the long run, have greater positive impact than programs that focus on treating disorders that have already developed.

Having described the nature and benefits of treatments, we end this chapter with guidelines for seeking and profiting from therapy.

PSYCHOLOGICAL APPLICATIONS

When and Where to Seek Therapy

No one is immune to problems in living. Every day, each of us does the best we can to balance our personal and social resources against the demands created by our life circumstances. We all have certain vulnerabilities, and if environmental demands and our vulnerabilities combine to exceed our resources, we may experience psychological problems for which professional assistance would be helpful. Here are some general guidelines for seeking such help and profiting from it.

First is the issue of when to seek help. In general terms, you should consider seeking professional assistance if any of the following apply:

- You are experiencing serious emotional discomfort, such as feelings of depression or anxiety, that are adversely affecting your personal, work, or family life.
- You are encountering a serious problem or life transition that you feel unable to handle on your own.
- A problem that has interfered with your life or personal happiness in the past is worsening or has suddenly resurfaced.
- You have experienced some traumatic event, either in the past or recently, that you find yourself thinking about, dreaming about, or responding to with negative emotions.
- You are preoccupied with your weight or body image and are taking extreme steps such as bingeing, then purging by vomiting or taking laxatives.
- You have severe and recurring conflicts with other people.
- You hear voices telling you what to do or feel that others are controlling your thoughts.

How does one go about getting help in dealing with psychological problems? Help may be sought at a school counselling centre, at a community agency, the emergency ward at your local hospital, or from a professional in private practice. The counselling centre is often a good place for a student to start, since it can provide either help or an appropriate referral to a reputable mental health professional. If you are at a larger university that has a graduate program in clinical psychology, there may also be a psychology clinic administered by that program.

How expensive is treatment? It is often offered free or at a nominal fee at a campus facility. Most likely, it will be covered in your student fees, but the number of visits may be limited. A community agency may have a sliding fee based on income, and many services are covered by your provincial health plan. Thus financial considerations need not be a barrier to seeking professional assistance. A private practitioner may charge a fee similar to that charged by doctors, dentists, and attorneys, perhaps exceeding $100 per 50-minute session. A prospective client should always ask beforehand about the fee. You should also check into the mental health benefits provided by your health insurance coverage. For example, some provinces may cover the costs if the service is provided by a psychiatrist, but only partially cover the expenses for a psychologist.

In choosing a therapist, what should you look for? It is important that your therapist be fully trained and licensed. Ask the therapist about his or her degree, licence, training, therapeutic orientation, and the problems in which she or he specializes. Remember that there is a difference between a psychiatrist, a psychologist, and a counsellor (see the beginning of this chapter). The requirements for licensing may differ from province to province, and certain terms may not be protected by law (e.g., almost anyone can call themselves a martial therapist). If you are unsure about whom to seek advice from, ask your family doctor for a recommendation or contact the local branch of the Canadian Mental Health Association. You can also check the website of the Canadian Psychological Association (*www.cpa.ca*).

As we've seen, the relationship between client and therapist is of the utmost importance. You will want a therapist who can create a good working relationship with you. Degree of value similarity between you and the therapist can be important. Timothy Kelly and Hans Strupp (1992) found that the most positive therapeutic outcomes were achieved when the client and therapist were neither very similar nor very dissimilar in values. High similarity may result in a failure to explore value-related issues that should be explored, whereas too much dissimilarity may interfere with building a good therapeutic relationship. One exception to this general rule may occur in the area of religious values. Clients who have strong and committed religious values may profit most from a therapy that supports those values and uses them to help change problem behaviours (Probst et al., 1992).

Some clients prefer to work with either a male or female therapist, depending in part on the nature of the personal issues that have caused them to seek counselling. As we have seen, research has shown that personal warmth, sincere concern, and empathy are important therapist characteristics. You should like and feel comfortable with your therapist, and you should feel at ease with the methods the therapist uses. Under no circumstances should your therapeutic relationship involve physical intimacy of any kind, and if a therapist were ever to make inappropriate advances, a client should immediately terminate treatment with that therapist and notify the appropriate professional organization, such as the local psychological or medical association. Such conduct is a serious breach of professional ethics and cannot be condoned under any circumstances.

You and your therapist should have explicit, agreed-on goals for the treatment program. If therapy proceeds well, you will experience beneficial changes that indicate movement toward these goals. It may take some time for these changes to occur, however, since long-standing personal vulnerabilities are not easily changed, and significant change seldom occurs overnight. If you do not see any progress after several months, or if you seem to be functioning less well than before, you should discuss your progress with the therapist. It is possible that the therapist is more satisfied with your progress than you are. However, if you continue to be dissatisfied with your progress or with the therapeutic relationship, you may at some point decide to terminate it. This should not prevent you from seeking help from another therapist.

Entering a helping relationship is a courageous step, and resolving problems in living may involve taking risks and experiencing pain. However, many clients look back on the pain and risks and feel that the process has been a valuable one that has enabled them to live happier lives than they could otherwise have. Here is a reflection by Dr. Sandra L. Harris, a prominent clinical psychologist, on the course of therapy she undertook as a university student:

> When I think about the girl I was in my freshman year at the University of Maryland and the young woman I was when I graduated four years later, it is clear that it was not only the issues Jim and I discussed, but how we talked that made the difference. The intangibles of trust, respect, and caring were at least as important as the active problem solving that transpired in our weekly meetings. It was not a dramatic transformation, rather it was a slight shifting of a path by a few degrees on the compass. Over the years that shift has had a cumulative effect and I walk a very different road than I would have without him. (Harris, 1981, p. 3)

In Review

- *The introduction of drug therapies that normalize disturbed behaviour, as well as concerns about the deterioration of life skills during hospitalization, have helped stimulate a move toward deinstitutionalization—the treatment of people in their communities.*
- *Research has shown that deinstitutionalization can work when adequate community treatment is provided. Unfortunately, many communities have been unable to fund the needed facilities, resulting in a "revolving door" of release and rehospitalization, as well as a new generation of homeless people who live on the streets and do not receive needed treatment.*
- *Prevention programs may be classified as either situation-focused or competency-focused, depending on whether they are directed at changing environmental conditions or personal factors.*

GAINING DIRECTION

What are the issues?

Treatments for many disorders—physical and mental—may seem barbaric. But presumably, a sound reason exists for proceeding with such a treatment. The case presented in this chapter describes a treatment that appears to be similar to electroconvulsive therapy (ECT), but has a number of important differences: the patients are drugged into unconsciousness, a series of strong shocks is administered, tape recorded messages are played to "re-program" the patient, and no one gives consent. What is the psychological rationale for such a treatment? Is there any evidence that this type of therapy works? Must a patient consent to treatment? As with other scenarios, this story has legal implications for both patients and therapists.

What do we need to know?

What are the models for the treatment of psychological disorders?
What is psychotherapy?
Can you "re-program" an individual?
Why would a therapist administer electric shock for treatment?
What are the therapy options?
Are there legal and ethical considerations with respect to treatment?

Where can you find the information necessary to answer these questions?

We should begin by looking at the basic goal requirements for psychotherapy. The techniques will vary, but the goal of any legitimate therapy is to help the patient live a better life. To evaluate Dr. Cameron's "depatterning" therapy, we need to look for information on how and why this treatment may work, and also consider ethical issues and standards. Treatments that "work" are of no use if they are not delivered in an ethical fashion. Cameron's approach seems similar to the delivery of ECT. You should examine how ECT works and whether there are specific disorders for which ECT would be used. Next, look at the "re-programming" aspect. Can you train individuals to think differently? You may want to review at the "Cognitive Therapies" section. These therapies are in no way related to Cameron's approach, but they do suggest that we can get people to "restructure" their thought patterns. Review as well the "Evaluating Psychotherapies" section. Perhaps other factors could explain any apparent success. Finally, consider the ethics. Do patients have to give informed consent for treatment? Always? Did Cameron's work achieve these ethical standards?

KEY TERMS AND CONCEPTS*

aversion therapy (612)
behaviour modification (612)
clinical significance (623)
common factors (624)
competency-focused prevention (635)
counterconditioning (611)
culturally competent therapist (619)
deinstitutionalization (633)
dodo bird verdict (623)
dose-response effect (624)
eclectic (615)
effect size statistic (622)
effectiveness (625)
efficacy (625)
electroconvulsive therapy (ECT) (630)
empathy (604)
exposure (610)
flooding (611)
free association (600)
genuineness (604)
implosion therapy (611)
in vivo desensitization (612)
insight (600)
interpersonal therapy (602)
interpretation (602)
meta-analysis (622)
openness (623)
placebo control group (621)
psychodynamic behaviour therapy (615)
psychosurgery (631)
randomized clinical trial (621)
resistance (600)
response prevention (610)
self-instructional training (609)
self-relatedness (623)
situation-focused prevention (635)
social skills training (614)
specificity question (620)
spontaneous remission (621)
stimulus hierarchy (611)
systematic desensitization (611)
tardive dyskinesia (629)
token economy (613)
transference (601)
unconditional positive regard (604)
virtual reality (VR) (616)

*Each term has been boldfaced in the text on the page indicated in parentheses.

DO YOU WANT TO ELEVATE YOUR GRADES?

For additional resources and interactive quizzing, visit the book's Online Learning Centre at **www.mcgrawhill.ca/olc/passer**.

CHAPTER 15

Stress, Coping, and Health

Life is largely a process of adaptation to the circumstances in which we exist.
—Hans Selye

CHAPTER OUTLINE

Multiple sclerosis (MS) is a neurological disorder that is thought to arise from an autoimmune reaction. The body's immune system begins to attack and break down the myelin sheath surrounding axons. The de-myelinated neuron can no longer transmit action potentials efficiently. This results in symptoms ranging from weakness and a lack of coordination in mild cases to severe speech problems and paralysis in the more extreme form.

The milder version (Relapse Remitting Multiple Sclerosis, or RRMS) is more common; symptoms flare up and then ease over a period of several days. Chronic MS is much more debilitating. The symptoms simply get worse over time and never relapse. MS is not terminal, but it does lead to a shorter life expectancy. We do not yet know what causes MS. There is a certain genetic predisposition, but environmental triggers are necessary. Implicated in the onset of MS and the cycling in RRMS are diet, stress, trauma, and lack of sunshine.

Canadians have the highest rate of MS in the world (about 1 in 500). Three new cases are diagnosed every day.

- **What are the issues here?**
- **What do we need to know?**
- **Where can we find the information necessary to answer the questions?**

Priscilla, now 15, had anything but an idyllic childhood. She grew up in an impoverished inner city home with an alcoholic father who sexually abused her and her younger sister. Her mother was hospitalized twice with "nervous breakdowns." When Priscilla was seven years of age, her father called his family together in the living room and told them, "You drove me to this." He then put a gun to his head and committed suicide as his wife and children watched in horror. From that time on, Priscilla had to work after school to help support the family. Her mother became increasingly disturbed and sometimes beat her.

Considering her background, we might expect Priscilla to be an unhappy, maladjusted child, her emotional life dominated by anxiety, anger, and depression. Instead, she grew into a delightful and popular young woman who was emotionally well adjusted, president of her high school class, a talented singer, and an honour student.

Children like Priscilla have been termed "invulnerable" or "resilient" youngsters (Garmezy, 1983; Masten & Coatsworth, 1998; Masten, 2001). What allows resilient people to rise above extraordinarily stressful environments, while other individuals blessed with more benign life histories collapse under the weight of less severe stresses? The answer will show us that our psychological and physical well-being depends on complex interactions among environmental demands, the personal and environmental resources that we have to deal with them, and the individual vulnerabilities that make us susceptible to certain kinds of demands.

THE NATURE OF STRESS

1. Describe three ways that theorists have defined the term "stress."

Psychologists have viewed stress in three different ways: as a stimulus, as a response, and as an organism-environment interaction. Some define stress in terms of eliciting stimuli, or events that place strong demands on us. These situations are termed **stressors**. We use the term stress in this "stimulus" fashion when we make statements such as, "There's all kinds of stress in my life right now. I have three exams next week, I lost my backpack, and my car just broke down."

Stress has also been viewed as a *response* having cognitive, physiological, and behavioural components (Keyse, 2000). Thus a person might say, "I'm feeling all stressed out. I'm tensed up, I can't concentrate because I'm really worried, and I've been flying off the handle all week." The presence of negative emotions is an important feature of the stress response and links the study of stress with the field of emotion (Zautra, 2003).

A third way of thinking about stress combines the stimulus and response definitions into a more inclusive model. Here stress is viewed as a *person-situation interaction*, or, more formally, as a *transaction* between the organism and the environment (Lazarus, 1991, 1998). The transactional conception of stress forms the basis for the model shown in Figure 15.1 and will guide our discussion of stress. From this perspective, **stress** is a pattern of cognitive appraisals, physiological responses, and behavioural tendencies that occurs in response to a perceived imbalance between situational demands and the resources needed to cope with them. You will recognize this as an adaptation of the general model of emotion presented in Chapter 10.

Stressors

Stressors are specific kinds of eliciting stimuli. Whether physical or psychological, they place demands on us that endanger well-being, requiring us to adapt in some

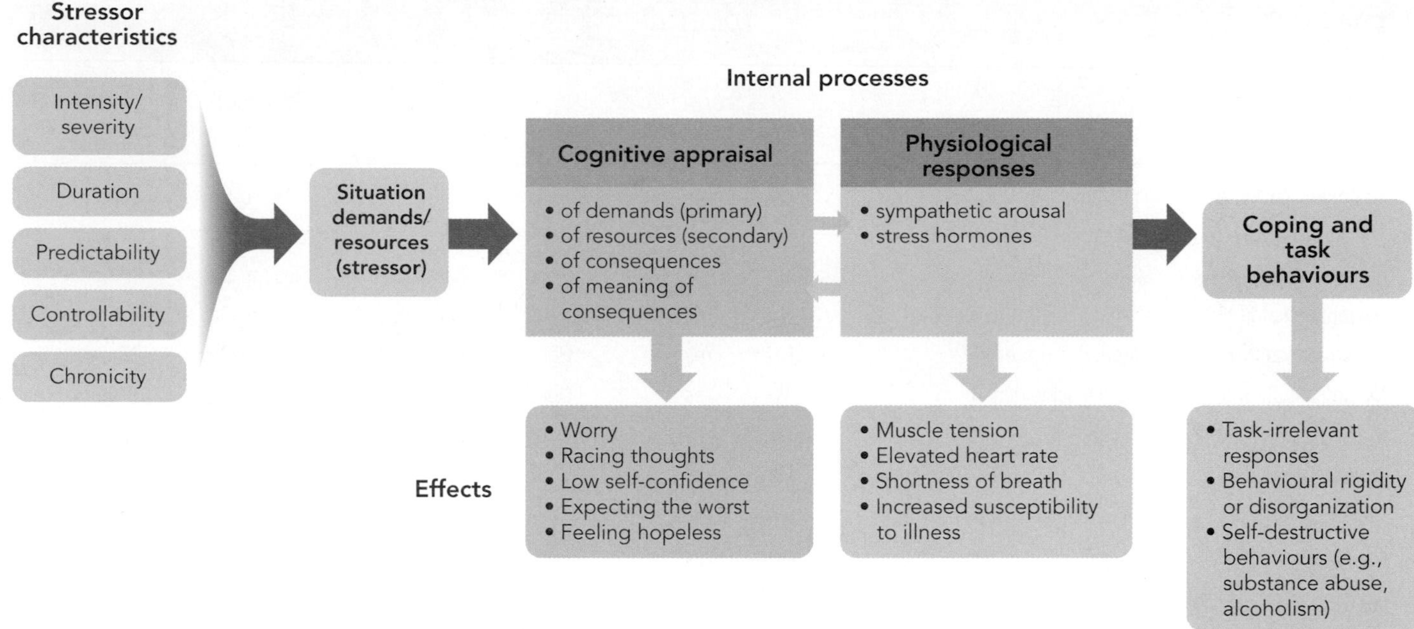

FIGURE 15.1

Stress involves complex interactions among situational factors, cognitive appraisal processes, physiological responses, and behavioural attempts to cope with the situational demands. Stressor characteristics that increase stress responses are shown. The lower panels show potential cognitive, physiological, and behavioural stress responses that can interfere with well-being.

manner. The greater the imbalance between demands and resources, the more stressful a situation is likely to be. Stressors can range in severity from *microstressors*—the daily hassles and everyday annoyances we encounter at school, on the job, and in our family relations—to very severe stressors. *Catastrophic events* often occur unexpectedly and typically affect large numbers of people. They include such events as natural disasters, acts of war, and concentration camp confinement (Figure 15.2). *Major negative events* such as being the victim of a major crime or sexual abuse, the death or loss of a loved one, an academic or career failure, or a major illness, also require major adaptation. As we shall see, all three classes of stressors can have a significant negative impact on psychological and physical well-being (Baum et al., 2000).

In addition to intensity or severity, several other characteristics of stressors have been identified as important and are listed in Figure 15.1. In general, events over which the person has little or no control, which occur suddenly and unpredictably, and which impact a person over a long period of time seem to take the greatest toll on physical and psychological well-being (Lazarus & Folkman, 1984; Taylor, 1999).

FIGURE 15.2

Stressful life events can vary from catastrophic ones to microstressors, or "daily hassles." Both classes of stressor take their toll on physical and psychological well-being.

Measuring Stressful Life Events

Sometimes it is possible to verify the life events a person has experienced. We may know that a person has lived through a natural disaster or lost a loved one to death. In other cases, researchers must rely on people's self-reports. To study linkages between life events and well-being, researchers have devised **life event scales** to quantify the amount of life stress that a person has experienced over a given period of time (e.g., the last six months or the past two years). The life event scale shown in Table 15.1 asks people to indicate not only whether a particular event occurred, but also their appraisal of whether the event was a positive or a negative one, and whether it was a major event (defined as having a significant and long-term impact on the person's life) or a "day-to-day" event (Smith et al., 1990). Moreover, addi-

TABLE 15.1 Sample Items from a Self-report Measure of Positive and Negative Life Events

Experience	Happened in Last Six Months?		Good or Bad?		"Day-to-day" or "Major"	
Parents discover something you didn't want them to know	No	Yes	Good	Bad	Day-to-Day	Major
Pressures or expectation by parents	No	Yes	Good	Bad	Day-to-Day	Major
Receiving a gift	No	Yes	Good	Bad	Day-to-Day	Major
Having plans fall through (not going on a trip, etc.)	No	Yes	Good	Bad	Day-to-Day	Major
Losing job (quitting, getting fired, laid off, etc.)	No	Yes	Good	Bad	Day-to-Day	Major
Making honour roll or other school achievement	No	Yes	Good	Bad	Day-to-Day	Major
Making love or sexual intercourse	No	Yes	Good	Bad	Day-to-Day	Major
Something good happens to a friend	No	Yes	Good	Bad	Day-to-Day	Major
Work hassles (rude customers, unpleasant jobs, etc.)	No	Yes	Good	Bad	Day-to-Day	Major
Death of a friend or family member	No	Yes	Good	Bad	Day-to-Day	Major

Source: Scale used in Smith et al., 1990.

tional information can be obtained. For example, respondents might be asked to rate the predictability, controllability, and duration of each event they experienced, permitting an analysis of these factors as well. Life event scales have been widely used in life stress research (see the *Research Foundations* box). Like other self-report measures, however, they are subject to possible distortion and failures of recall.

Some early theorists believed that any life event that requires adaptation, whether negative or positive in nature, is a stressor (Holmes & Rahe, 1967; Selye, 1956). Because later research showed that only negative life changes consistently predicted adverse health and behavioural outcomes, most modern researchers now define stress in terms of negative life changes only (Cohen et al., 1995; Lazarus, 1998). Indeed, positive life events sometimes counter or even cancel out the negative impact of negative events (Thoits, 1983).

The Stress Response

2. What four types of appraisal occur in response to a potential stressor? How do these correspond to primary and secondary appraisal?

We respond to situations as we perceive them. The starting point for the stress response is, therefore, our appraisal of the situation and of its implications for us. As Figure 15.1 indicates, four aspects of the appraisal process are of particular significance:

1. appraisal of the *demands* of the situation (primary appraisal);
2. appraisal of the *resources* available to cope with it (secondary appraisal);
3. judgments of what the *consequences* of the situation could be; and
4. appraisal of the *personal meaning*, that is, what the outcome might imply about us.

Let us apply these appraisal steps to a real-life situation. You are about to have an important job interview. According to Richard Lazarus (1991), you will first engage in a **primary appraisal** of this situation as being either benign, neutral/irrelevant, or threatening in terms of its demands (how difficult an interview it will be) and its significance for your well-being (how badly you want or need the job). At the same time, you will be appraising your perceived ability to cope with the situation, that is, the resources available to deal with it. Lazarus calls this resource-appraisal step **secondary appraisal**. Coping resources include your knowledge and abilities, your verbal skills, and your social resources, such as people who will give you emotional support and encouragement. If you believe that the demands of the interview greatly exceed your resources, you will likely experience stress. Primary and secondary appraisal correspond to aspects 1 and 2 above, respectively.

You will also take into account the *potential consequences* of failing to cope successfully with the situation, including both the seriousness of the consequences and the likelihood that they will occur. Will you be able to pay your tuition if you perform poorly and don't get the job? How likely is it that you will fail? Appraising the consequences of failing as very costly and very likely to occur increases the perceived stressfulness of the situation.

Finally, the *psychological meaning of the consequences* may be related to your basic beliefs about yourself or the world. Certain beliefs or personal standards can make people vulnerable to particular types of situational demands. For example, if your feelings of self-worth depend on how successful you are in situations like this one, you may regard doing poorly during the interview as evidence that you are a worthless failure.

Distortions and mistaken appraisals can occur at any of the four points in the appraisal process, causing inappropriate stress responses. People may overestimate the seriousness of the situation, they may underestimate their own resources, they may exaggerate the seriousness of the consequences and the likelihood that they will occur, or they may have irrational self-beliefs that confer inappropriate meaning on the consequences (e.g., "If I don't succeed at this, it means I am and always will be a total loser"). The fact that appraisal patterns can differ from person to person in so many ways helps us understand why there can be so much individual variation in the way people respond to the same event or situation, and it also helps us understand why some people are particularly vulnerable to certain types of demands.

As soon as we make appraisals, the body responds to them (Borod, 2000; Tomaka et al., 1997). Although appraisals begin the process, appraisals and physiological responses mutually affect one another, since autonomic and somatic feedback can affect our reappraisals of how stressful a situation is and whether our resources are sufficient to cope with it. Thus, if you find yourself trembling as you enter the interview room, you may appraise the situation as even more threatening than you did initially.

Chronic Stress and the GAS

3. Describe the three stages of Selye's GAS.

Endocrinologist Hans Selye, of the University of Montreal, was a pioneer in studying the body's response to stress (Selye, 1976). He described a physiological response pattern to strong and prolonged stressors that he called the **general adaptation syndrome (GAS)**. The GAS consists of three phases: alarm reaction, resistance, and exhaustion (Figure 15.3).

In response to a physical or psychological stressor, animals exhibit a rapid increase in physiological arousal. This *alarm reaction* occurs because of the sudden activation of the sympathetic nervous system and the release of stress hormones by the endocrine system. As you will recall from Chapter 3, the sympathetic nervous system has an activating effect on the smooth muscles, organs, and glands of the body. Sympathetic nervous system activation, for example, leads to an increase in heart rate and respiration, dilates the pupils, and slows digestion. This alarm reaction helps the body deal with the source of the stress. The slowing of digestion leads to blood being diverted from the digestive system to muscle. The increased heart

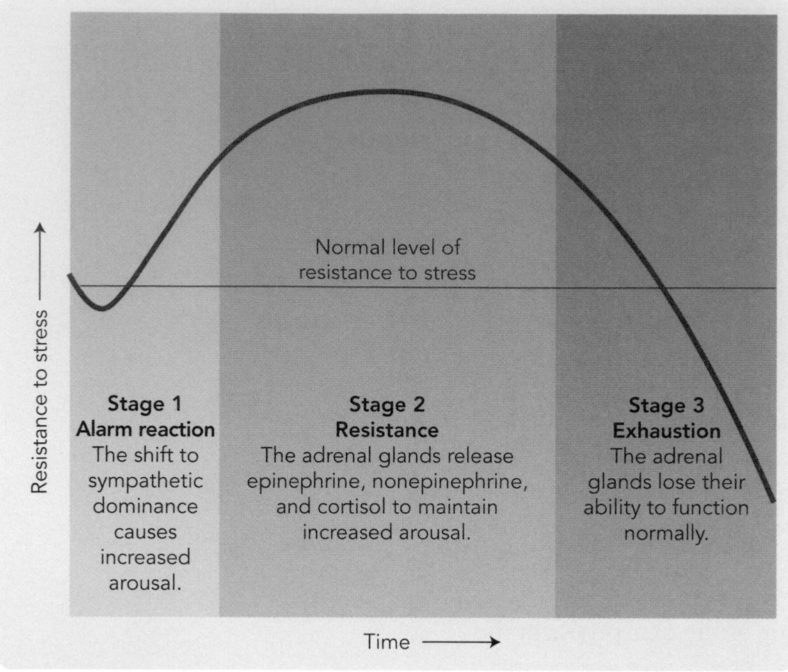
Normal level of
resistance to stress
Resistance to stress
Stage 1
Alarm reaction
The shift to
sympathetic
dominance
causes
increased
arousal.
Stage 2
Resistance
The adrenal glands release
epinephrine, nonepinephrine,
and cortisol to maintain
increased arousal.
Stage 3
Exhaustion
The adrenal
glands lose their
ability to function
normally.
Time

FIGURE 15.3

Hans Selye described the general adaptation syndrome. When a person is exposed to a stressor, the alarm reaction mobilizes the body's resources. During the stage of resistance, stress hormones maintain the body's defensive changes, and the body signs characteristic of the alarm reaction virtually disappear. But, if the stress persists over a long time, the body's resources become depleted and exhaustion occurs; the organism can no longer cope and is highly vulnerable to breakdown.

(Selye, 1976.)

rate and respiration means that the extra blood arriving at your skeletal muscles contains extra oxygen. Pupil dilation makes our eyes more sensitive to light and enhances vision.

There is also an endocrine, or hormonal, stress response. Perception of a threat leads a cascade of messages from the hypothalamus within the brain to the pituitary gland at the base of the brain, and then from the pituitary gland to the adrenal glands (you may want to refer back to Figure 3.23). The adrenal glands produce a number of different hormones, but during a period of stress the most important is cortisol. Cortisol triggers an increase in blood sugars, in part by acting on the liver. Thus the extra blood arriving at your skeletal muscles contains additional sugar along with the additional oxygen. Cortisol also suppresses the immune system (Chiapelli, 2000). If you are injured, this action of cortisol suppresses inflammation so that injured tissues do not swell. The powerful anti-inflammatory effects of cortisol are well demonstrated by the use of cortisone, which the body converts to cortisol, to treat the joint inflammation of tennis elbow, bursitis, and some cases of arthritis.

Sympathetic nervous system activation and the hormonal response help you deal with the stressor. The stress response has been characterized as the "fight or flight" response, and in many ways that is an apt description. Your ability to confront the source of stress ("fight") or retreat from it ("flight") is enhanced by the stress response. You are more sensitive to visual stimuli, movement is faster and stronger, and injury is less likely to generate movement-limiting swelling; your body is primed and ready to act.

The alarm reaction stage cannot last indefinitely, however, and the body's natural tendency to maintain the stable internal state of homeostasis results in parasympathetic nervous system activity. The parasympathetic nervous system functions to reduce arousal. Despite attempts to return to homeostasis, if the stressor continues, the stress response also continues, although sympathetic nervous system activity is partially muted by the opposing parasympathetic nervous system. With continued exposure to stress, the body remains on red alert and enters the second stage, resistance.

During the stage of *resistance*, the body's resources continue to be mobilized so that the person can function despite the presence of the stressor. Resistance can last for a relatively long time, but the body's resources are being depleted. How long the stage of resistance can last depends on the severity of the stress, the individual's general health, available support (such as social support), and other factors. Elevation of heart rate and respiration, suppression of digestion, suppression of the immune system, and changes in blood sugar levels cannot continue indefinitely without exhausting the body. Eventually, remaining bodily resources are no longer sufficient and the stage of resistance comes to an end.

If the stressor is intense and persists for too long, the body may reach the stage of *exhaustion*, in which the body's resources are dangerously depleted. It is during the stage of exhaustion that there is increased vulnerability to disease and, in extreme cases, collapse and even death (Hancock & Desmond, 2000). When a person leaves the stage of resistance and enters the stage of exhaustion is again determined by a number of factors, especially the severity of the stress, the person's ability to cope with stress, and their general health. The more severe the stress, however, the sooner you expect to reach the stage of exhaustion. Selye argued that whichever system of the body is the weakest will be the first to be affected during the stage of exhaustion. If, because of maturational, genetic, or experiential factors, a person's cardiovascular system is at risk, then that will be the first system to break down during the stage of exhaustion. If, on the other hand, a person's immune system is weak, then that person may develop diseases related to immune system dysfunction or show evidence of weakened immune function.

A mild form of this process is familiar to students who deal with periods of stress, such as during the end of an academic term. You continue to function despite the stress of term-end deadlines and final exams (resistance), only to become ill when the stressors end and the vacation begins.

In Review

- *Stress has been viewed by various theorists as a stimulus; as a response having cognitive, physiological, and behavioural components; and as a person-situation interaction, i.e., a transaction between the person and the environment.*
- *A transactional model of stress specifies interactions among situational factors, cognitive appraisal processes, physiological responses, and behavioural attempts to cope. This model by its nature predicts individual differences in response to stressors.*
- *Stressors are events that place physical or psychological demands on organisms. The stressfulness of a situation is defined by the balance between demands and resources. Life events can vary in terms of how positive or negative they are, as well as in predictability, controllability, chronicity, and other dimensions that affect their impact.*
- *Cognitive appraisal processes play an essential role in people's responses to stressors. People appraise the nature of the demands, the resources available to deal with them, their possible consequences, and the personal meaning of these consequences. Distortions at any of these levels can result in inappropriate stress responses.*
- *The physiological response to stressors is mediated by the autonomic and endocrine systems, and involves a pattern of arousal that mobilizes the body to deal with the stressor.*
- *Selye described a general adaptation syndrome (GAS) that describes the changes that occur during chronic stress. The changes progress through the three stages of alarm reaction, during which the stress response is activated; resistance, during which bodily resources are mobilized to allow you to function despite the stress; and exhaustion, during which resources are depleted and stress-induced illness occurs.*

STRESS AND HEALTH

Selye's work inspired a generation of medical and psychological researchers to explore the effects of stress on both physical and psychological well-being. As we shall now see, stress can result in physical and psychological deterioration. One conclusion is that a physical mobilization system sculpted by evolution to help organisms deal with life-threatening *physical* stressors may not be as adaptive for dealing with the *psychological* stressors we face in modern life. As noted by one medical authority, "Stone Age physiological and biochemical responses to emotion have become inappropriate in a Space Age setting, and can pave the way to psychosomatic diseases" (Carruthers, 1981, p. 239).

Stress and Psychological Well-Being

Effects of stress on psychological well-being are clearest and most dramatic among people who have experienced catastrophic life events. Anthony Rubonis and Leonard Bickman (1991) surveyed the results of 52 studies of catastrophic floods,

hurricanes, and fires. In the wake of natural disasters, they found an average increase of 17 percent in rates of psychological disorders such as anxiety and depression.

Some stressors are so traumatic that they can have a strong and long-lasting psychological impact. More than 50 years after the horror of the Holocaust, psychological scars remain for Jewish survivors of the Nazi concentration camps (Nadler & Ben-Shushan, 1989; Valent, 2000; Zahava & Ginzburg, 1998). Many survivors are still troubled by high levels of anxiety and recurrent nightmares about their traumatic experiences. Children who lost their parents and siblings continue to experience sudden fears that something terrible will happen to their spouses or children whenever they are out of sight. Depression and crying spells are also common, as are feelings of insecurity and difficulties in forming close relationships. As one researcher reported, "child survivors (now in their 50s and 60s) . . . despite their outward normalcy, remain entrapped in this survival mode" (Valent, 1998, p. 751).

Long-lasting psychological symptoms have also been found among American soldiers who experienced trauma during the Vietnam War. Paula Schnurr and her co-workers (1998) found a significantly greater number of stress symptoms in traumatized servicemen than in veterans from the same era who did not experience combat or non-combat trauma. (See the section on post-traumatic stress disorder on p. 649).

4. What are the characteristics of the rape trauma syndrome?

Women who experience the trauma of rape sometimes find that its aftermath can be nearly as stressful as the incident itself. Many victims experience a reaction known as the **rape trauma syndrome** (Burgess & Holmstrom, 1974). For months or even years after the rape, victims may feel nervous and may fear another attack by the rapist. Many victims change their place of residence but continue to have nightmares and to be frightened when they are alone, outdoors, or in crowds. Victims frequently report decreased enjoyment of sexual activity long after the rape, even when their ability to have orgasms is not affected (Feeny & Foa, 2000; Holmes & St. Lawrence, 1983). In one long-term study of rape victims, one-fourth of the women felt that they had not recovered psychologically six years after the rape (Meyer & Taylor, 1986).

5. Describe three possible causal paths between self-reported stress and distress.

Fortunately, the majority of stressors that people experience are not as severe as concentration camp confinement, combat, or rape. How do more typical but less serious stressors affect psychological well-being? To answer this question, researchers have examined the relation between self-reported life events and measures of psychological well-being. Findings consistently show that, the more negative life events people report on measures such as the one shown in Table 15.1, the more likely they are also to report symptoms of psychological distress (Holahan & Moos, 1990; Monroe & Peterman, 1988). We might therefore be tempted to conclude that "stress causes distress." This causal interpretation is shown in path 1 in Figure 15.4, but it may not be accurate because the data are correlational in nature and other causal interpretations are possible. For example, path 2 reverses the first causal interpretation, suggesting that people's levels of distress may influence their reporting of negative life events. That is, distressed people may be more likely to remember negative things that have happened to them. Or they may tend to view more events as negative, resulting in higher negative life change scores. Psychological distress also might cause more negative events to occur in people's lives because of their own behaviour. For example, distressed people tend to evoke negative reactions from others (Coyne et al., 1991; Joiner et al., 1992).

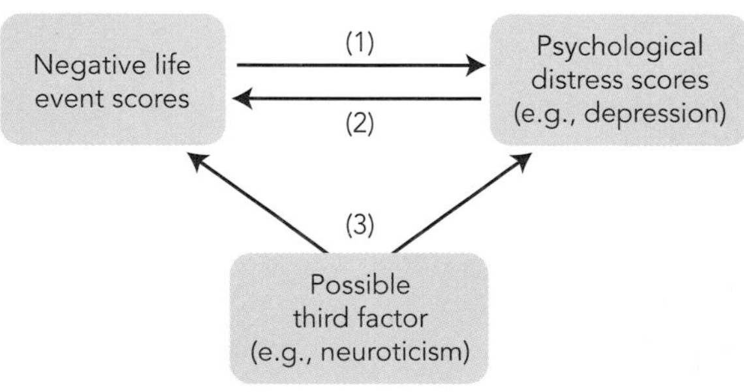

FIGURE 15.4

Statistical relations between stressful life events and psychological distress may reflect a number of different causal relations: (1) stressful life events may cause distress; (2) distress may cause higher stressful life event scores; or (3) a third factor, such as neuroticism, may cause both distress and high negative life change scores.

A third causal possibility, shown in path 3, is that a third variable causes both negative life events and psychological distress. The personality trait of **neuroticism** might be one such factor. People who are high in neuroticism have a heightened tendency to experience negative emotions and to get themselves into stressful situations through their maladaptive behaviours (Eysenck, 1989; Suls et al., 1998). In one longitudinal study of Dutch adults, Johan Ormel and Tamar Wohlfarth (1991) found that initial scores on a neuroticism scale were related positively to both the number of stressful events and the amount of psychological distress reported over the next six years. Thus we are again reminded that stressful life events are part of a network of causal relations that involve ongoing transactions between people and situations. It appears that stressful life events can function as both cause and effect (Cohen & Edwards, 1989; Suls et al., 1998).

Post-Traumatic Stress Disorder (PTSD)

Canadian General Roméo Dallaire was in charge of the United Nations peacekeeping force for Rwanda in 1993 and 1994 during the genocide in that country. After being released from the Canadian Armed Forces in 2000 for medical reasons, Roméo Dallaire began speaking engagements about his experiences, chronicled in his book *Shake Hands With the Devil*, published in 2003. Roméo Dallaire is now a federal senator representing Quebec, he has been appointed an Officer of the Order of Canada, received Canada's Pearson Peace Medal, the Legion of Merit from the U.S. government, and has been presented with at least 10 honorary degrees from Canadian and American universities. Dallaire is a Fellow at the Carr Center for Human Rights Policy, Harvard University and is a Senior Fellow at the Montreal Institute for Genocide and Human Rights Studies. He has been the subject of a CBC documentary and a PBS special, and was the model for the UN colonel portrayed by Nick Nolte in the 2004 movie Hotel Rwanda.

How could such a man be found intoxicated under a park bench in Hull, Quebec in June 2000? When found he was barely conscious and slipping into a coma due to the mixture of alcohol and anti-depressants in his system. Like many who have experienced extreme trauma, Dallaire blamed himself for what had happened, in his case for the world's failure to halt the brutal murders that occurred during the genocide in Rwanda. Senator Roméo Dallaire is not alone, but he is Canada's most famous example of a person who suffered from post-traumatic stress disorder.

As discussed earlier in this chapter, exposure to stress can have serious consequences. Post-traumatic stress disorder (PTSD) represents what can happen to victims of extreme stress and trauma. PTSD is a severe anxiety disorder that is caused by exposure to traumatic life events, to severe stress. Four major groups of symptoms occur with PTSD:

- severe anxiety, physiological arousal (the stress response), and distress
- painful uncontrollable reliving of the event(s) in flashbacks, dreams, and fantasies (Pitman et al., 2000)
- emotional numbing and avoidance of stimuli associated with the trauma
- intense "survivor guilt" in instances where others were killed but the individual survived (Valent, 2000).

Some individuals with PTSD also show self-destructive and impulsive behaviour.

6. Describe four common features of PTSD.

The study of PTSD arose in part from studies of soldiers who had witnessed the horrors of an active war zone. One study found that the incidence of PTSD was seven times greater for Vietnam veterans who had spent significant time in combat and were wounded than it was for other Vietnam-era veterans (Centers for Disease Control [CDC], 1988). Another study found that within 12 months of combat

FIGURE 15.5

The devastation and loss of life caused by the 2004 Indian Ocean tsunami traumatized millions of people in 11 countries. One effect of the trauma was the development of post-traumatic stress disorder in many people, particularly those who were personally affected by the destruction.

exposure, 27.8 percent of veterans developed PTSD (Prigerson et al., 2002). Civilian victims of war are even more likely to develop PTSD than are soldiers. Amy Ai and colleagues (2002) found that 60.5 percent of the refugees from the bloody civil war in Kosovo showed PTSD. Traumas caused by human perpetrators, such as war, rape, assault, and torture, tend to cause more severe PTSD than do natural disasters (O'Donohue & Elliot, 1992). Following exposure to a severe trauma, women are more likely to develop PTSD than are men. Although anyone can develop PTSD if they are exposed to a sufficiently severe trauma, the likelihood of developing PTSD is influenced by the victim's social support, the presence of significant childhood stresses, personality factors, coping strategies, and preexisting psychological conditions (American Psychiatric Association, 1994). However, if the trauma is sufficiently severe, such as the genocide helplessly witnessed by Dallaire or the trauma suffered by the victims of violent rape, the likelihood of developing PTSD is high regardless of the presence of mitigating factors.

Terrorist acts can be a powerful trigger for the development of PTSD (Figure 15.5). Interviews with more than a thousand adult residents of Manhattan found that 7.5 percent manifested symptoms consistent with PTSD in the five to eight weeks following the September 11, 2001, destruction of the World Trade Center. Among those living closest to the World Trade Center, the rate of PTSD was 20 percent (Galea et al., 2002). PTSD does not necessarily develop immediately after the trauma. Although PTSD usually develops within three months, in some cases it can be many months or even years before PTSD fully emerges (American Psychiatric Association, 1994; Meyer & Taylor, 1986).

The severe problems caused by PTSD can also increase later vulnerability to other disorders. One study found that women who had developed PTSD had double the risk of developing alcohol-related problems in the future (Bresalau et al., 1997). The unpredictability of who will develop PTSD, the severity of PTSD, and the ensuing problems caused by PTSD all highlight the importance of prompt and careful post-trauma intervention (Sorenson, 2002). If post-trauma intervention is available for the victims of rape or torture they can be spared one of the most severe stress-related disorders. If post-trauma intervention had been available for Roméo Dallaire when he returned from the horrors in Rwanda, his many years of suffering could have been prevented.

Stress and Illness

Stress can combine with other physical and psychological factors to influence the entire spectrum of physical illness, from the common cold to cancer, heart disease, diabetes, and sudden death (Marsland et al., 2002; Segerstrom & Miller, 2004; Dougall & Baum, 2000). Sometimes the effects are immediate. On the day of the 1994 Los Angeles earthquake, the number of sudden deaths due to heart attacks in that city increased from an average of 35.7 per day during the 7 previous days to 101 fatalities (Leor et al., 1996). Other effects of major stressors on physical well-being are less immediate but no less severe. Within a month following the death of a spouse, bereaved widowers and widows begin to show a higher mortality rate than married people of the same age who have not lost a spouse (Kaprio et al., 1987). Sklar and Anisman (1981), of Carleton University, found that stressful life events also increased the risk of developing cancer.

Statistics Canada (Health Reports, February 2004) reported that adults who experienced high stress during 1994–95 were at increased risk of developing chronic health conditions by 2000–01. The chronic health conditions included arthritis and rheumatism, bronchitis or emphysema, and stomach or intestinal ulcers. For men, the risk of heart disease was also increased; for women, the risk of asthma and migraines was increased. Each additional stressor reported during 1994–95 increased the chance of reporting a chronic health problem six years later by 6 percent among men and by 8 percent among women. For someone experiencing several different stressors, the increased risk of developing a chronic health problem quickly becomes substantial. For example, experiencing just three lasting stressors—such as financial worries, difficulties in a relationship, and problems at work or school—increase the risk of developing a chronic health condition by 18 percent among males and by 24 percent among females.

7. What are some of the delayed effects of stress?

A traumatic life event can worsen an already existing medical condition, as in the case of a seven-year-old African-American girl with sickle-cell anemia.

> This little girl was bused to a new elementary school in a white neighborhood. . . . She and other black children were met with cries by angry whites to "go back to where you belong!" The little girl was quite upset by the incident. After some time at the school she went to the principal's office crying and complaining of chest pains. She died later that day in the hospital, apparently from a sickle-cell crisis brought on by stress. As she died, she kept repeating "go back where you belong." (Friedman & DiMatteo, 1989, p. 169)

8. By what physiological and behavioural mechanisms can stress contribute to illness?

Linkages between long-term stress and illness are not surprising, for physiological responses to stressors can directly harm other body systems. For example, the secretion of stress hormones by the adrenal gland is an important part of the stress response. These hormones affect the activity of the heart, and excessive secretions can damage the lining of the arteries. By reducing fat metabolism, the stress hormones also can contribute to the fatty blockages in arteries that cause heart attacks and strokes (Kimble, 1992; Willenberg et al., 2000).

Stress also can trigger illness by causing a breakdown in immune system functioning (Maier & Watkins, 1999; Marsland et al., 2000; Segerstrom & Miller, 2004). Janice Kiecolt-Glaser and her co-workers (1998) brought 90 newly married couples into a laboratory and asked them to discuss areas of conflict in their relationship. They coded the couples' behaviour during the discussions and measured their physiological and immune responses. Among those couples whose interactions became hostile during the conflict discussions, measurable decreases in immune function occurred within 24 hours (Figure 15.6). Similar results were observed in an older sample of 31 couples who had been married an average of 42 years. In this older sample, one of the immune functions that decreased after hostile interchanges helps protect against influenza and pneumonia, leading causes of death in elderly people.

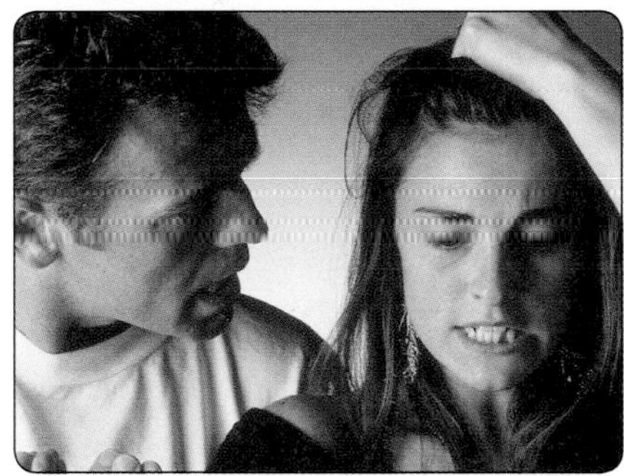

FIGURE 15.6

Research has shown that the stress produced by marital conflict can produce a decrease in immune function.

An important aspect of the stress response is the secretion of cortisol by the adrenal glands. As we saw in Chapter 3, cortisol and related hormones can have profound effects on the brain, especially if cortisol levels are elevated for prolonged periods, such as in cases of chronic stress. Michael Meaney (of McGill University) and others have shown that exposure of the hippocampus to prolonged elevations of stress-related hormones causes deterioration of the hippocampus and accompanying memory impairment (Landfield et al., 1978; Meaney et al., 1988; Meaney et al., 1991). Even short duration exposure to stress-related hormones affects the hippocampus. A stressor lasting only a few hours can release sufficient stress hormone to induce structural changes in the hippocampus that last for a month or even longer (McEwen, 2000).

Stress also can contribute to health breakdown by causing people to behave in ways that increase the risk of illness. For example, people with adult-onset diabetes frequently can control their disease by means of medication and diet. When under stress, however, diabetics are less likely to regulate their diets and take their medication, resulting in an increased risk of serious medical consequences (Brantley & Garrett, 1993). People are more likely to quit exercising when under stress, even if the primary reason they began exercising in the first place was to reduce stress (Stetson et al., 1997). Stress may also lead to smoking, alcohol and drug use, sleep loss, undereating and overeating, and other health-compromising behaviours.

In Review

- *Measures of both major negative life events and microstressors are associated with negative psychological outcomes. Causal links may be difficult to identify in the relation between negative life events and psychological distress.*
- *Life stress can decrease immune function, worsen pre-existing medical conditions, and increase the risk of illness and death.*

VULNERABILITY AND PROTECTIVE FACTORS

9. Differentiate between vulnerability and protective factors, and give examples of each.

Some individuals seem able to tolerate extremely demanding stressors over a long period of time; others appear to quickly fall prey to even relatively minor stressors. **Vulnerability factors** increase people's susceptibility to stressful events. They include lack of a support network, poor coping skills, tendencies to become anxious or pessimistic, and other factors that reduce stress resistance. In contrast, **protective factors** are environmental or personal resources that help people cope more effectively with stressful events. They include social support, coping skills, and personality factors such as optimism.

Social Support

10. What evidence exists that social support is a protective factor? In what ways can it protect against stressful events?

11. Can disclosing upsetting experiences to others enhance well-being? Cite relevant data.

Social support is one of the most important environmental resources that people can have (Wills & Filer, 2000; Suls & Wallston, 2003). The knowledge that we can rely on others for help and support in a time of crisis helps blunt the impact of stress (Figure 15.7). In contrast, social isolation is an important vulnerability factor. Studies carried out in the United States, Finland, and Sweden carefully tracked the well-being of some 37,000 people for up to 12 years. Even after taking into account medical risk factors such as age, smoking, high blood pressure, high cholesterol levels, obesity, and lack of physical exercise, the researchers found that people with weak social ties were twice as likely to die during the period of the study as those with strong ties (House et al., 1988). The relation between social isolation and poor health was stronger for men than for women.

FIGURE 15.7

Social support is one of the strongest protective factors against stress.

One way that social support protects against stress is by enhancing immune system functioning. Robert Baron and his co-workers (1990) studied distressed people whose spouses were being treated for cancer. The participants agreed to be injected with an antigen so that their immune responses could be measured. As Figure 15.8 shows, the immune systems of the spouses who rated themselves high in social support produced more immune cells, particularly at high levels of the antigens, than did the immune systems of those who indicated lower social support in their lives. These results may help explain why people who have high levels of social support are more disease-resistant when they are under stress (House et al., 1988). Many other studies show that social support decreases psychological distress in people who are dealing with stressful life events of all kinds (Holahan & Moos, 1986, 1990; Rodin & Salovey, 1989; Schwarzer, 1998).

Why is social support such a strong protective factor? One possibility is that people who feel that they are part of a social system experience a greater sense of identity and meaning in their lives, which in turn results in greater psychological well-being (S. Cohen, 1988; Rodin & Salovey, 1989). Social networks also reduce exposure to other risk factors, such as loneliness, and having the backing of others can increase feelings of control over stressors. Finally, true friends can apply social pressure to prevent people from coping with stressors in maladaptive ways (e.g., through alcohol or drug use). Any of these buffering effects can help to counteract the impact of stressful life events.

A series of studies conducted by James Pennebaker (1995, 1997) suggests the importance of having someone to talk to about upsetting experiences. University students talked about traumas they had experienced to an experimenter in an adjoining room, or they tape recorded or wrote about them. Many tearfully recounted incidents of personal failure, family tragedies, shattered relationships, sexual or physical abuse, or traumatic accidents. Participants in a control group were asked to talk or write about trivial everyday matters. At the end of the session, blood samples taken from the students indicated enhanced immune functioning in those who had purged themselves of negative emotions, but not in those who had not. Moreover, the students who had disclosed the traumatic incidents had 50 percent fewer visits to the campus health centre over the next six months than the control group. In another study, Pennebaker invited 33 Holocaust survivors to talk about their horrible ordeal. Many discussed their traumatic experiences in greater detail than ever before and even showed friends and families videotapes of the Holocaust. Those who were the most disclosing had the most improved health 14 months later. Pennebaker's results are intriguing but controversial, and more research is needed to determine when emotional "purging" is helpful and whether there are circumstances when it is not. Likewise, because participants in these studies could choose to purge their emotions or not, it is possible that some other factor, such as a personality trait, contributes to both the emotional disclosure and the health consequences. See the Focus on Neuroscience box in this chapter for more about social support.

Returning to the case of Priscilla described earlier, how was she able to overcome her traumatic childhood—the abuse, the suicide of her father, the absence of a mother? Studies of resilient children like Priscilla have repeatedly highlighted the role of social support in helping blunt the impact of the terrible stressors they experienced in their daily lives (Garbarino, 1995; Garmezy, 1983; Masten & Coatsworth, 1998; Werner & Smith, 1982; see Table 15.2). Summarizing the findings of her 30-year longitudinal study of resilient children, psychologist Emmy Werner noted, "Without exception, all of the children who thrived had at least one person that provided them with consistent emotional support—a grandmother, an older sister, a teacher or a neighbor" (*New York Times,* October 13, 1987, p. C11). For Priscilla, that person was a schoolteacher who cared enough to befriend and encourage her during her childhood years.

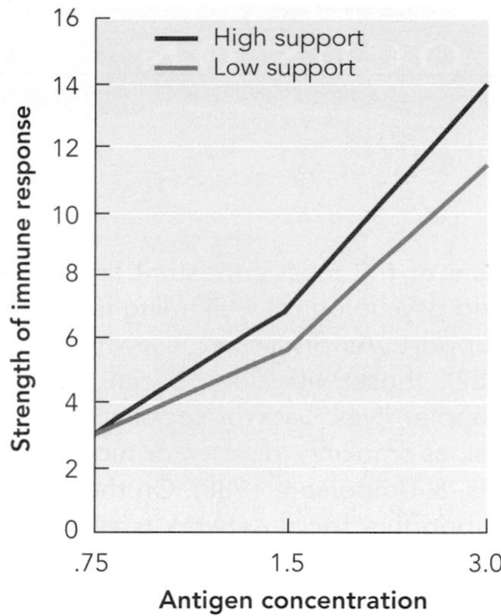

FIGURE 15.8

Relation of social support to immune function in spouses of cancer patients. Immune cell activity in response to antigens was greater in spouses high in social support, particularly at high antigen levels that place people at increased risk.

Data from Baron et al., 1990.

12. What environmental factors make some children highly resistant to stressful environments?

TABLE 15.2 Personal and Environmental Factors That Contribute to Stress-Resilience in Children

Source	Characteristic
Individual	Good intellectual functioning
	Appealing, sociable, easygoing disposition
	Self-efficacy, self-confidence, high self-esteem
	Talents
	Faith
Family	Close relationship to caring parent figure
	Authoritative parenting: warmth, structure, high expectations
	Socio-economic advantages
	Connections to extended supportive family networks
Extrafamilial context	Bonds to pro-social adults outside the family
	Connections to pro-social organizations
	Attending effective schools

Source: Masten & Coatsworth, 1998, p. 212.

anger, distrust, and antagonism seems particularly important (Barefoot et al., 1989; Miller, 2000). This aspect of the Type A pattern is likely to alienate others, produce conflict, and reduce the amount of social support they receive. As was discussed earlier (see page 652) social support is powerfully related to physical and emotional health, so anything that acts to decrease social support is a powerful risk factor for illness. Adding to the risk equation is the tendency of Type A people to overreact physiologically to events that arouse anger, a biological factor that may contribute to their tendency to develop heart disease (Fichera & Andreassi, 1998; Taylor, 1999).

16. Describe Type A, Type B, and Type C personalities.

Quite a different personality style, known as the **Type C** pattern, may be a risk factor for cancer (Eysenck, 1994; Sanderman & Ranchor-Adelita, 1997). Type Cs are almost the mirror image of the Type A pattern. They are highly sociable and "nice" people who are very inhibited in expressing negative emotions. Their tendency to bottle up such emotions, particularly anger and anxiety, seems to get in the way of active coping, and they tend to feel helpless and hopeless in the face of severe stress. The emotional inhibitions may take a toll on their bodies as well. In one large-scale European study that extended over 10 years, people with the Type C pattern were far more likely than others to develop cancer (Eysenck & Grossarth-Maricek, 1991). Once diagnosed with cancer, patients who continue to suppress their negative emotions are less likely to survive the disease (Salovey et al., 2000; Sanderman & Ranchor-Adelita, 1997). In contrast, those who learn to release negative emotions are more likely to survive. In Eysenck's (1994) longitudinal study, those Type C people who became more emotionally expressive had only a 4 percent death rate from cancer over the next 13 years, compared to a 43 percent cancer mortality rate in the most extreme Type C group. Other research also shows that bottling up negative feelings can be hazardous to one's health (Traue & Deighton, 2000).

17. What is it about Type A and C patterns that increase an individual's risk for health problems?

Among the Big Five personality factors that we discussed in Chapter 12, conscientiousness seems to have the strongest links to physical health and longevity. In one study, a large group of children were followed for over 70 years. Those children who were judged by their parents and teachers to be highly conscientious at age 11 have lived significantly longer and are about 30 percent less likely to die in any given year (Friedman et al., 1995). Conscientious people were less likely to engage in risky behaviours, and therefore less likely to die from violent deaths in accidents or fights. They were also less likely to smoke and drink to excess and more likely to exercise regularly, eat a balanced diet, have regular physicals, and follow medical prescriptions when ill. Thus the effects of being carefree and careless add up during one's life and can be quite harmful in the end.

18. Which personality factor is most strongly linked to good health?

Considerable evidence exists that personality plays a role in health and longevity (Contrada et al., 1999). Researchers continue to explore links between personality and health, and their findings may shed important light on psychological processes that can affect physical well-being.

Finding Meaning in Stressful Life Events

19. In what ways do spiritual and religious beliefs affect the response to stressful events?

Humanistic theorists emphasize the human need to find meaning in one's life, and the psychological benefits of doing so (May, 1961; Watson & Greenberg, 1998; Yalom, 1980). Some people find personal meaning through spiritual beliefs, which can be a great source of comfort in the face of crises. Daniel McIntosh and co-workers (1993) studied 124 parents who had lost their babies to sudden infant death syndrome. They found that religious beliefs that helped the grieving parents find some higher meaning in their loss were related to greater well-being and less distress 18 months later. In another study, researchers studied people who recently had lost a family member to death. In following up with the survivors over a period

Level of Analysis

Biological	Psychological	Environmental
• Physiological responses of autonomic and endocrine systems to situational stressors • Stress effects on immune system • Individual differences in emotional reactivity to stressors	• Cognitive appraisal of environmental demands, resources, potential consequences, and personal meaning of consequences • Personality factors, such as optimism and hardiness, that affect responses to stressors • Coping strategies and skill with which they are applied • Self-efficacy and expectations of available social support	• Number and nature of the stressful events • Availability of social support • Cultural factors that teach one how to respond to stressors

Stress

FIGURE 15.11

Understanding the causes of behaviour: stress and its effects.

of 18 months, the researchers discovered that people who were able to find meaning in the loss experienced less distress during the first year. Finding a sense of meaning from their own process of coping with the loss (e.g., by growing spiritually) had even longer-term positive effects (Davis et al., 1998).

Religious beliefs can be a two-edged sword, however. They can either decrease or increase stress, depending on their nature and the type of stressor to which they are applied. In one study of medically ill elderly adults, poorer physical and psychological adjustment occurred in patients who viewed God as punishing them, saw themselves as the victims of demonic forces, expressed anger toward God, clergy, or church members, or questioned their faith (Koenig et al., 1998). Religious beliefs may have positive effects in dealing with some types of stressors, but not with others. Such beliefs seem to help people cope more effectively with losses, illnesses, and personal setbacks. In contrast, they can increase the negative impact of other stressors such as marital problems and abuse, perhaps by inducing guilt or placing internal pressures on individuals to remain in the stressful relationship (Strawbridge et al., 1998).

As we now have seen, a variety of biological, cognitive, and environmental factors influences stress and its effects on us. Figure 15.11 summarizes these important influences.

Physiological Reactivity

Responses of the autonomic and endocrine systems appear to underlie many of the negative psychological and health consequences of stress (McEwen, 2001). The fact that people differ widely in the pattern and intensity of their physiological responses makes people more or less vulnerable to stressors. As we saw in Chapter 12, people high in neuroticism, who tend to have intense and prolonged autonomic responses, seem more vulnerable to stress than are people low in this personality factor (Eysenck, 1990; Snyder, 2001).

20. Describe the physiological toughness endocrine pattern.

Physiological toughness, a particular stress hormone pattern, appears to be a protective factor (Dienstbier, 1989). **Physiological toughness** involves relations between two classes of hormones secreted by the adrenal glands in the face of stress. Both *catecholamines* (which include epinephrine and norepinephrine) and *corticosteroids* (particularly cortisol) mobilize the body's fight-or-flight response

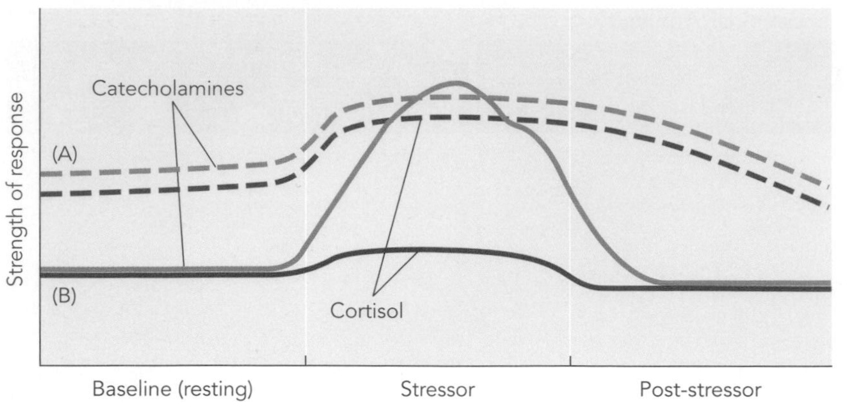

FIGURE 15.12

Hormonal patterns of response to stress. When a stressor occurs, a typical response (pattern A) is a strong, long-lasting rise in corticosteroid (cortisol) and catecholamine (epinephrine, norepinephrine) hormones. In physiologically tough individuals, however, cortisol secretion remains low, and there is a strong catecholamine response followed by a quick return to baseline (pattern B). This response, as well as low baseline levels of the hormones involved, seems to protect the body from damage.

in the face of stressors, but they have somewhat different effects on the body. Cortisol's arousal effects last much longer and seem to be more damaging than those produced by the catecholamines (unless the catecholamines are secreted at high levels over a long period of time). For example, cortisol reduces immune system functioning and helps create fatty deposits in the arteries that lead to heart disease. In contrast, catecholamine secretion increases immune system functioning (Taylor, 2003).

Physiological toughness consists of (1) a low resting level of cortisol, low levels of cortisol secretion in response to stressors, and a quick return to baseline level of cortisol after the stress is over; and (2) a low resting level of catecholamines but a quick and strong catecholamine response when the stressor occurs, followed by a quick decline in catecholamine secretion and arousal when the stressor is over (Figure 15.12). This hormonal pattern seems to provide maximum short-term mobilization of resources needed to deal with the stressor but prevents the eventual depletion of catecholamines and the wear and tear on the body that Selye identified with the exhaustion phase of GAS (Dienstbier, 1989). Increased vulnerability to bodily breakdowns occurs when the person responds to stress with high levels of cortisol instead of catecholamines. The fact that physical exercise entails catecholamine-produced arousal may help account for exercise's health-enhancing effects and its ability to promote physiological toughness and stress resistance (Ehrman, 2003; Morgan, 1997).

RESEARCH FRONTIERS

Stress and Working Memory

You are on your way to class, and you are thinking about the questions that you will ask the instructor and the answers that you will have ready for when you are asked. But along the way something happens, perhaps someone cuts you off in traffic, you see an accident, you have an argument with a friend, or you hear some disturbing news on the radio. That is, on route to class you experience an acute, or short-lived, uncontrollable stressor. You arrive at class disorganized and distracted, and you find it difficult to concentrate. What *were* those questions you were going to ask? Your planned questions and your answers to anticipated questions are gone and what parts of them that you do remember do not make sense.

You sit down to write the exam. You are well prepared and know the material; this should go well. It is, however, an important examination, and you feel stressed because the mark will have a substantial impact on your course grade. You look at the examination questions and you draw blanks. Who *was* the leading proponent of the functionalist perspective in psychology? You know the answer, but cannot bring it to mind. You know how to solve that statistics question—you have done many similar practice questions—but sitting in the examination hall you just cannot seem to get the steps straight (Figure 15.13).

We have all had experiences similar to the scenarios in the opening two paragraphs. When stressed, our ability to plan and organize our behaviour, to maintain concentration, and to make full use of working memory is compromised. Despite knowing the material our performance is poor during the stress, but only during the stress. Once the stress is over, we remember that illusive piece of information or realize what we should have said. The study of the effects of stress on the brain is beginning to explain how this happens.

Even mild to moderate levels of stress can impair our ability to plan, organize our behaviour, maintain concentration, and use working memory. Many of the cognitive impairments that appear as a result of acute stress are similar to the impairments that occur with dysfunction of the frontal cortex. Indeed, moderate uncontrollable stress has been shown to impair the function of the frontal cortex in humans, monkeys, and rats (Arnsten & Goldman-Rakic, 1998).

A recent report by Amy Arnsten and co-workers (Birnbaum, et al., 2004), has helped to elucidate what stress is doing to interfere with the frontal cortex. Arnsten and colleagues trained both rats and monkeys in tasks that required the animals to maintain spatial information in working memory, inhibit competing responses, and sustain attention despite the presence of distractions. All of these are functions of the frontal cortex. They also trained the animals in a simple discrimination task, one that does not require working memory. They found that activation of a specific substance, called PKC (protein kinase C), within the neurons of the frontal cortex impaired the animals' ability to perform the working memory task, but left intact the ability to perform the simpler discrimination task. This substance is normally activated within the neurons of the frontal cortex, as in neurons elsewhere in the brain, but stress can lead to an excess of this substance. Too much PKC interfered with the ability of the frontal cortex to process information appropriately and compromised working memory. The researchers were able to block this chemical within the frontal cortex and blocking the chemical overactivation prevented the impairment in working memory. Other results, such as recording the electrical activity of individual neurons within the frontal cortex, supplied supporting evidence. Neurons that normally were active during a working memory task were not active if PKC production was too high. Behavioural and biochemical evidence and electrical recordings all supported the conclusion that excess PKC within the frontal cortex interferes with working memory. Blocking or limiting the activation of PKC can prevent the cognitive impairments.

FIGURE 15.13

Even mild to moderate levels of stress can interfere with the functioning of the frontal cortex, and impair working memory, concentration, and problem solving.

That is, if stress causes too great an activation of a specific substance within the frontal cortex, then neurons within the frontal cortex do not work appropriately and the functions of the frontal cortex, including working memory, behavioural regulation, concentration, and planning, are disrupted. These findings support the widely experienced phenomenon that acute stress can impair working memory and problem solving. This specific neurochemical effect of stress helps to explain why practiced problem solving can be so easily disrupted by stress, why we think of the things that we should have done and said after the stressful interview is over, or why stress may cause a performer to lose concentration and perform far below the level they demonstrated in rehearsal. The study of stress and the frontal cortex is also beginning to shed light on more serious problems. For example, children in a stressful home environment sometimes exhibit behaviours similar to those that occur with disorders of the frontal cortex, such as ADHD, but they may really be showing the temporary effects of acute stress on the frontal cortex (Arnsten, 1998). Several disorders, including bipolar disorder (Ellicott, et al., 1990) and schizophrenia (Mazure, 1995) include symptoms of frontal cortex dysfunction and both of these disorders are known to be worsened by stress. Arnsten and colleagues have begun to shed light upon one mechanism that may explain stress-induced impairments in our cognitive abilities.

Source: Birnbaum, S. G., Yuan, P. X., Wang, M., Vijayraghavan, S., Bloom, A. K., Davis, D. J., Gobeske, K. T., Sweatt, J. D., Manji, H. K., & Arnsten, A. F. T. (2004). Protein kinase C overactivity impairs prefrontal cortical regulation of working memory. *Science, 306*, 882–884.

In Review

- *Social support is an important protective factor for people who are confronting stressors. Such support has both direct and buffering effects that help people cope with stress.*
- *Hardiness is a protective factor against stress. Hardy individuals are characterized by commitment, feelings of personal control, and a tendency to perceive stressful situations as a challenge. Other cognitive protective factors are self-efficacy and optimism. Spiritual beliefs often help people cope more effectively with stressful life events, but certain religious beliefs are negatively related to adjustment.*
- *Individual differences in physiological reactivity also affect well-being. People who exhibit strong and prolonged arousal responses are more susceptible to negative psychological and health effects. Physiological toughness refers to a stress hormone pattern that involves (1) a low resting level of cortisol and low levels of cortisol secretion in response to stressors and (2) a quick, strong catecholamine response when the stressor occurs, followed by a quick decline in arousal when the stressor is over.*

COPING WITH STRESS

> My courage sank, and with each succeeding minute it became less possible to resist this horror. My cue came, and on I went to that stage where I knew with grim certainty I would not be capable of remaining more than a few minutes. . . . I took one pace forward and stopped abruptly. My voice had started to fade, my throat closed up and the audience was beginning to go giddily round. (Aaron, 1986, p. 24)

This account of "stage fright" was given not by a novice actor in his first play, but by Sir Laurence Olivier, considered by many to be the greatest actor of his generation. Few people were aware that for most of his career, Olivier experienced a private hell before every performance. His audiences saw only what happened once he stepped onto the stage: another flawless performance. Olivier had a remarkable ability to purge the terror from his mind, relax his body, and concentrate fully on his role once showtime arrived (Aaron, 1986).

21. Define and give an example of the three major classes of coping strategies.

Although there are countless ways people might respond to a stressor, coping strategies can be divided into the three broad classes shown in Figure 15.14. (Carver et al., 1989; Folkman & Lazarus, 1988; Smith et al., 1999). **Problem-focused coping** strategies attempt to confront and deal directly with the demands of the situation, or to change the situation so that it is no longer stressful. Examples include studying for a test, going directly to another person to work out a misunderstanding, and signing up for a course in time management in order to deal with time pressures.

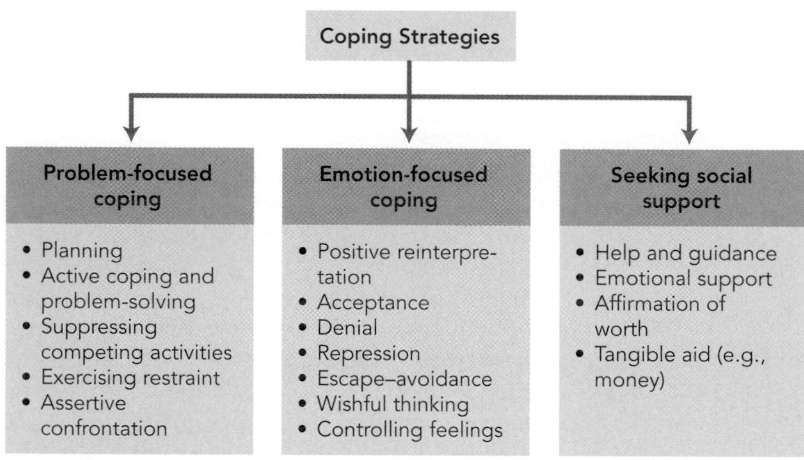

FIGURE 15.14

Coping strategies fall into three general categories: (1) problem-focused coping, consisting of active attempts to respond to situational demands; (2) emotion-focused coping, directed at minimizing emotional distress; and (3) seeking or accepting social support.

Rather than dealing directly with the stressful situation, **emotion-focused coping** strategies attempt to manage the emotional responses that result from it. As Figure 15.14 shows, some forms of emotion-focused coping involve appraising the situation in a manner that minimizes its emotional impact. A person might deal with the stress from an interpersonal conflict by denying that any problem exists. Other forms involve avoidance or acceptance of the stressful situation. Thus a student might decide to deal with anxiety about an upcoming test by going to a party and forgetting about it. Informed that he has a terminal illness, a man might simply accept grim reality, realizing that there is nothing that can be done to change the situation.

A third class of coping strategies involves **seeking social support**, that is, turning to others for assistance and emotional support in times of stress. Thus the man with the terminal illness might choose to join a support group for the terminally ill, and the student might seek help in preparing for the test.

Effectiveness of Coping Strategies

Which of the three general classes of coping strategies would you expect to be most generally effective? Whenever we ask this question in our classes, the majority of students vote for problem-focused coping. This response is understandable, since many people approach problems with the attitude that if something needs fixing, we should fix it.

What does the research literature say? Charles Holahan and Rudolf Moos (1990) studied coping patterns and psychological outcomes in more than 400 California adults over a one-year period. They found that problem-focused coping methods and seeking social support were associated with favourable adjustment to stressors. In contrast, emotion-focused strategies that involved avoiding feelings or taking things out on other people predicted depression and poorer adjustment. Other studies have yielded similar results. In both children and adults, and across many different types of stressors, emotion-focused strategies that involve avoidance, denial, and wishful thinking seem to be related to less effective adaptation (Aldwin, 1994). On the other hand, there are adaptive emotion-focused strategies, such as identifying and changing irrational negative thinking and learning relaxation skills to control arousal. These emotion-focused methods can reduce stress responses without avoiding or distorting reality, and can be effective ways of dealing with stress (DeLongis, 2000; Meichenbaum, 1985).

Controllability and Coping Efficacy

Despite the evidence generally favouring problem-solving coping, attempts to change the situation are not always the most adaptive way to cope with a stressor. When we cannot influence or modify a situation, problem-focused coping may do us little good, and could even make things worse. In such cases emotion-focused coping may be the most adaptive approach we can take, since, even if we cannot master the situation, we may be able to prevent or control maladaptive emotional responses to it (Auerbach, 1989; Taylor, 1991). Of course, reliance on emotion-focused coping is likely to be maladaptive if it prevents us from acting to change situations in which we actually *do* have control.

22. How does controllability influence the effectiveness of coping strategies?

Thomas Strantz and Stephen Auerbach (1988) demonstrated the effectiveness of emotion-focused coping in adapting to a stressful situation with limited personal control. As part of a training program conducted by the Federal Bureau of Investigation, airline employees who might be future victims of hijackings volunteered to participate in an exercise in which they were abducted by FBI agents posing as terrorists and held hostage for four days under very realistic and stressful conditions.

Before their abduction, the employees were assigned randomly to two experimental conditions and a control condition. In one condition, employees were trained in problem-focused techniques that hostages can use to actively deal with and modify the situation. They were shown how to interact with captors and to maintain a facade of dignity and composure through appearance and behaviour. They also learned ways of supporting one another non-verbally and communicating with one another through the use of the prisoner-of-war tap code.

Training for the second experimental group focused on the emotional reactions the hostages would likely experience and techniques they could use to minimize their stress responses. These emotion-focused techniques included deep breathing, muscular relaxation, stopping unwanted thoughts, and generating pleasant fantasies. Hostages in the control condition were given no coping skills training.

At various points during their captivity, all of the hostages completed self-report measures of emotional distress and psychiatric symptoms. In addition, the adaptiveness of their behaviour was coded by trained observers. The hostage groups trained in either problem-focused or emotion-focused strategies fared better than the untrained employees on both the self-report and the behavioural measures. However, employees who had received emotion-focused training adapted better to the largely uncontrollable conditions of captivity than did those who had received problem-focused coping instruction (Figure 15.15).

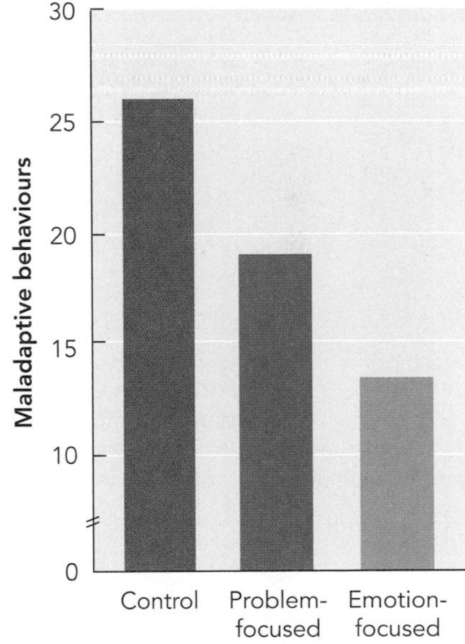

FIGURE 15.15

Behavioural ratings of adjustment to the stress of captivity by airline personnel given instruction in problem- or emotion-focused coping techniques prior to their abduction by FBI agents posing as terrorists. The control group received no coping skills instruction. Higher scores indicated more disturbed behaviours.

Data from Strantz & Auerbach, 1988.

The important principle is that no coping strategy or technique is equally effective in all situations. Instead, effectiveness depends on the characteristics of the situation, the appropriateness of the technique, and the skill with which it is carried out. People are likely to adapt most effectively to the stresses of life if they have mastered a variety of coping techniques and know how and when to apply them most effectively. The importance of controllability in the choice of techniques recalls the wisdom in the theologian Reinhold Niebuhr's famous prayer that asks for the courage to change those things that can be changed, the forbearance to accept those that cannot be changed, and the wisdom to discern the difference.

Bottling Up Feelings: The Costs of Constraint

You can probably think of several people in your life who differ greatly in how they express their negative emotions in response to stress. While constantly venting strong negative feelings may not be a good way to make friends and influence people, an inability to express negative feelings can also have its costs (remember our earlier discussion of Type C personalities). Some studies have reported relations between cancer development and the use of denial or repressive coping strategies, but others have not (McKenna et al., 1999). In one long-term European study, people who were experiencing high stress levels but were too emotionally restrained to express negative feelings, even when appropriate, had a significantly higher likelihood of developing cancer than did highly stressed people who were not so emotionally restrained. Seeking to reduce this potential vulnerability factor, the researchers designed a treatment program to help stress-ridden but emotionally constrained people who had not yet developed cancer. The program focused on teaching participants how to express their emotions in an adaptive fashion and on building stress-coping skills to manage their feelings without bottling them up. A control group of similar people did not receive the training. Thirteen years later, a follow-up study revealed that 90 percent of the trained participants were still alive, whereas 62 percent of the control group participants had died from cancer and other ailments (Eysenck, 1994; Eysenck & Grossarth-Marticek, 1991).

The question of whether there is indeed a "cancer-prone personality" remains a topic of scientific study and debate (Suls & Wallston, 2003; Taylor, 2003). Nonetheless, in the eyes of many researchers, there is enough evidence to suggest that severe emotional constraint can have negative effects on health.

Gender, Culture, and Coping

23. How do gender and cultural factors affect the tendency to use particular coping strategies?

Many factors, including gender roles and culture, influence our tendency to favour one coping strategy over another. Although men and women both use problem-focused coping, men are more likely to favour it as the first strategy they use when they confront a stressor (Matud, 2004; Tamres, Janicki, & Helgeson, 2002). On the other hand, women, who tend to have larger support networks and higher needs for affiliation than men, are more likely than men to seek social support (Billings & Moos, 1984; Schwarzer, 1998). Women also are somewhat more likely than men to report using emotion-focused coping (Carver et al., 1989; Pearlin & Schooler, 1978). This general pattern of coping preferences is consistent with the socialization that boys and girls traditionally experience. In most cultures, boys are pushed to be more independent, assertive, and self-sufficient, whereas girls are expected to be more emotionally expressive, supportive, and dependent (Chaplin, Cole, & Zahn-Waxler, 2005; Tsai, et al., 2007).

Cultural differences in coping have also been found. North Americans and Europeans show a tendency to use problem-focused coping more than do Asian and Hispanic peoples (Essau & Trommsdorff, 1996; Tsai, Levenson, & McCoy,

2007). The latter two groups tend to favour greater use of emotion-focused coping and social support. Asians also show a greater tendency to avoid the stressful situation, particularly interpersonal stressors, reflecting their culture's emphasis on interpersonal harmony (Elliot, Chirkov, Kim, & Sheldon, 2001).

PSYCHOLOGICAL APPLICATIONS

Stress Management

As we have seen, stress can exact a devastating toll on a person's psychological and physical well-being. The model shown in Figure 15.1 suggests that we can reduce the impact of stress by modifying any of its major components. We can change the situation that elicits a stress response, modify our cognitive appraisal, control the physiological responses, or learn more effective coping strategies. Many stress management training programs focus on teaching people to modify ways of thinking that trigger inappropriate emotional responses and to use relaxation to control their physiological responses.

Cognitive appraisal plays a critical role in generating the stress response. This has led psychologists such as Lazarus and Ellis to argue that the most effective means of regulating stress is by controlling how we think about potentially stressful situations and how we think about ourselves. Our thinking can turn minor events and inconveniences into major stressors. For example, we tell ourselves that we *must* succeed in order to be worthy; that we *must* be approved of by others; that it is terrible, even catastrophic, when life, other people, or even we do not meet our expectations (Ellis, 1962). Such thoughts generate unnecessary anxiety, despair, and even anger and potently activate the stress response. The techniques of cognitive restructuring are used to systematically detect, challenge, and replace such irrational ideas with healthy ways of thinking. The practice of cognitive restructuring can follow a number of procedures, but central to the idea is to become aware of and challenge how we interpret events. For example, if an event elicits anxiety, what automatic and reflexive thoughts elicit the stress response? Once you have identified unhealthy thoughts, what healthy and rational interpretations can you apply to the situation? As we become more practiced in interpreting events in a healthy way, low-stress interpretations become easier and more automatic and replace the unhealthy, stress-evoking thoughts.

Another approach to changing the way we think is with self-instructional training. In self-instructional training, people learn to talk to themselves and guide their behaviour in ways that help them cope more effectively (Meichenbaum, 1985). Adaptive self-statements can be applied to all stages of the coping process, from preparing for the stressor, to confronting and handling the stressor, to evaluating and encouraging self-reinforcement once the stressor is over (see Table 15.3). For example, while preparing for a potentially stressful event a person may be taught to make statements such as, "What do I have to do?" or "I can work out a plan to deal with this." While confronting a stressor, such as a difficult examination, the person may have statements such as, "I can do this, just take it one question at a time" or "Take a deep breathe, relax."

TABLE 15.3 Self-Instructional Training: Examples of Adaptive Self-Statements That Can Be Applied at Various Stages of the Coping Process

Phase of Coping Process	Self-Statements
Preparing for the stressor	• What do I have to do? • I can work out a plan to deal with it. • Remember, stick to the issues and don't take it personally. • Stop worrying. Worrying won't help anything.
Confronting and handling the stressor	• As long as I keep my cool, I'm in control of the situation. • I can meet this challenge. This tenseness is just a cue to use my coping techniques. • Don't think about stress, just about what I have to do. • Take a deep breath and relax. Ah, good.
Coping with the feeling of being overwhelmed	• Keep my focus on the present. What is it I have to do? • Relax and slow things down. • Don't try to eliminate stress totally; just keep it manageable. • Let's take the issue point by point.
Evaluation and self-reinforcement	• OK, what worked and what didn't? • I handled it pretty well. • It didn't work, but that's OK. I'll do better next time. • Way to go! You did it!

Source: Adapted from Meichenbaum, 1985.

–Continued

Coping skills training also includes relaxation training. Relaxation and arousal are incompatible; you cannot be relaxed and show the stress response simultaneously. There are a variety of relaxation techniques, but one of the most commonly used involves tensing and then relaxing all of the major muscle groups, one muscle group at a time. The release of tension from the muscles is paired with a trigger word, such as "Relax," and the exhalation (relaxing) phase of the breathing cycle. The goal is to condition relaxation to the trigger word and to exhalation so that a state of relaxation can be achieved rapidly in stressful situations by exhaling and saying the trigger word. Such somatic relaxation training is a cornerstone of most stress-management programs. Relaxation achieved through the use of meditation is also effective at decreasing stress (Figure 15.16). Meditation not only relaxes the body, but also produces cognitive relaxation, a peaceful, mind-clearing state. Although both somatic relaxation and meditation are effective, somatic relaxation has the advantage that, once trained, it can be applied at any time during a stressor, whereas meditation is best done in a quiet, private space.

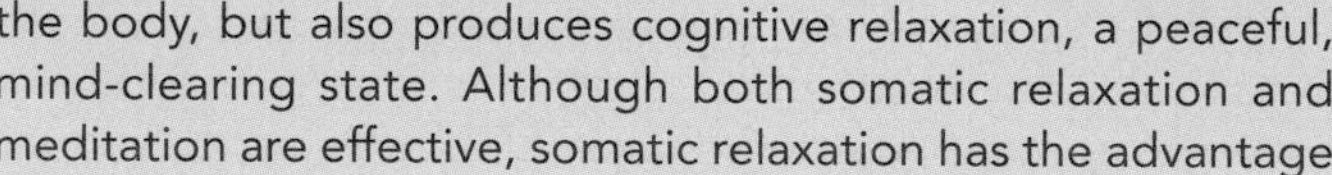

FIGURE 15.16
Relaxing through meditation is effective at decreasing stress.

When busy and stressed many of us cut meals to a minimum, eating something quick while working rather than spending time to prepare and eat a proper meal. We also tend to surrender leisure activities and exercise. We have a hard time justifying that game of squash, jog, or bicycle ride when there are many high priority tasks waiting to be done. It is, however, especially important to look after your lifestyle needs when stressed. If you compromise your health with too little sleep, no physical exercise, and poor nutrition, you will be less able to deal with the stressor. Physical health, with important contributions from nutritious meals and exercise, is an important tool in your battle against stress. Get enough sleep, take the time to eat properly, and maintain at least some leisure activities and exercise. These lifestyle factors are even more important when you are stressed and busy than at other times, but unfortunately they are often the first to suffer when times are busy.

In Review

- *Three major ways of coping with stressors are problem-focused coping, emotion-focused coping, and seeking social support.*
- *Problem-focused coping and seeking social support generally relate better to adjustment than emotion-focused coping. However, the outcome of a coping strategy depends on its appropriateness to the situation and the skill with which it is carried out. In situations involving low personal control, emotion-focused coping may be the most appropriate and effective strategy.*
- *Stress management also can be accomplished through coping skills training. Cognitive restructuring and self-instructional training can be used to develop cognitive coping responses, and relaxation training can be used to develop greater control of physiological arousal.*

HEALTH PROMOTION AND ILLNESS PREVENTION

24. What changes have occurred in the major causes of death during the 20th century? How do these changes suggest the potential contributions of health psychology?

In 1979, the Surgeon General of the United States issued a report entitled Healthy People (U.S. Public Health Service, 1979). The report concluded that improvements in health are more likely to result from efforts to prevent disease and promote health than from new drugs and medical technologies.

That conclusion is borne out by comparing the leading modern causes of death in North America to those in 1900. As Figure 15.17 indicates, the leading culprits in Canada have changed from influenza, pneumonia, tuberculosis, and gastroenteritis to heart disease, cancer, and stroke. The major killers of the early 1900s have been largely controlled by medical advances. In contrast, the death rate has doubled for heart disease and tripled for cancer since 1900. As shown in Table 15.4, these diseases and today's other killers are strongly influenced by behavioural factors. Health authorities estimate that half the early mortality (deaths occurring prior to the life expectancy age within a culture) from the 10 leading causes of death can be traced to cigarette smoking, excessive alcohol consumption, insufficient exercise, poor dietary habits, use of illicit drugs, failure to adhere to doctors' instructions, and other self-defeating behaviours, such as risky sex practices and failure to wear auto seat belts (Centers for Disease Control; 1994; Taylor, 2003).

Recognition of the crucial role that behaviour plays in health maintenance has added impetus to the field of **health psychology**, which studies psychological and behavioural factors in the prevention and treatment of illness and in the maintenance of health (see the Research Foundations section in this chapter). Research by psychologists has helped identify many of the psychological and social causes of risky health behaviours, and the clear need for lifestyle interventions has spurred attempts around the world to promote positive changes in such behaviours (Suls & Wallston, 2003; Taylor, 2003). This effort is also driven by attempts to contain rising medical costs. Total health care costs in Canada have risen from $37 billion in 1984 to over $121 billion in 2003 (Canadian Institutes for Health Information, 2007). That equates to $3,839 per person for health care costs in Canada in 2003 (the last year full data is currently available). With Canada's aging population, health care costs are expected to continue to increase. Prevention of illness by modifying people's health behaviour before they ever become ill has the potential to result in both financial savings and the avoidance of illness-produced human distress.

Health-related behaviours fall into two main categories. **Health-enhancing behaviours** serve to maintain or increase health. Such behaviours include exercise, healthy dietary habits, safe sexual practices, regular medical checkups, and breast and testicular self-examination. **Health-compromising behaviours** are those that promote the development of illness. They include smoking, fatty diets, a sedentary lifestyle, and unprotected sexual activity. Psychologists have developed programs that are focused on both categories.

How People Change: The Transtheoretical Model

In order to increase health-enhancing behaviours and reduce health-impairing ones, we need to understand the processes that underlie

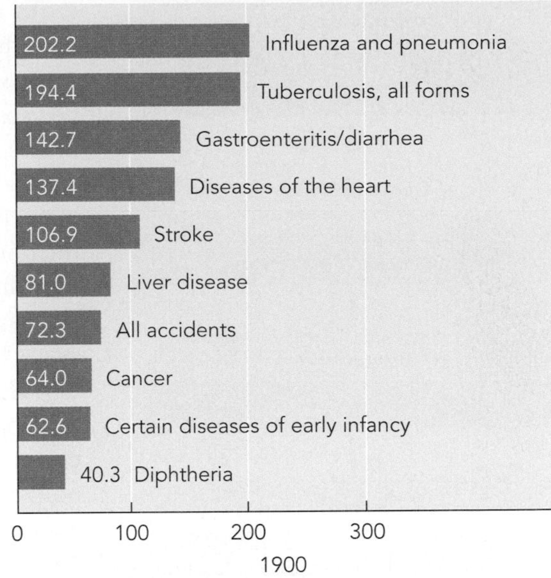

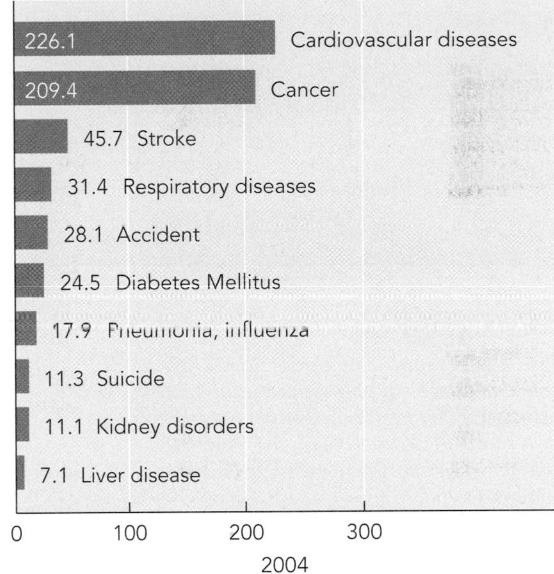

FIGURE 15.17

Causes of death in North America in 1900 (upper panel) and in Canada in 2004 (lower panel). Modern causes of death are far more attributable to health-endangering behaviours than has been the case in the past.

Sources: Based on data from Sexton, 1979; Murphy, 2000; Centers for Disease Control, 2002a; Mortality: Summary List of Causes 2004, Health Statistics Division, Statistics Canada, 2007.

TABLE 15.4 **Behavioural Risk Factors for the Leading Causes of Death in North America**

Disease	Risk Factors
Heart disease	Tobacco, obesity, elevated blood pressure, cholesterol, sedentary lifestyle
Cancer	Tobacco, improper diet, alcohol, environmental exposure
Cerebrovascular disease (stroke)	Tobacco, elevated blood pressure, cholesterol, sedentary lifestyle
Accidental injuries	Safety belt non-use, alcohol, home hazards
Chronic lung disease	Tobacco, environmental exposure

Source: Based on McGinnis, 1994.

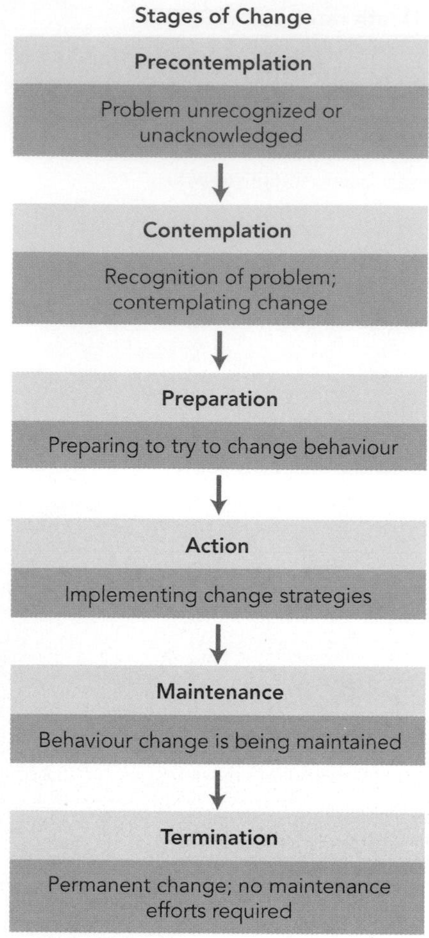

FIGURE 15.18

The transtheoretical model identifies a series of phases through which people pass as they modify their behaviour. People may move up and down through the stages several times before they reach the final stage of termination.

Source: Prochaska et al., 1998.

25. What are the two major categories of health-related behaviours? Give an example of each type.

26. Describe the transtheoretical model and the rationale for stage-matched interventions.

behaviour change in general. In the 1980s, psychologists James Prochaska and Carlo DiClemente began to study the process that occurs as people modify their thoughts, feelings, and behaviours in positive ways, either on their own or with professional help. Their research resulted in a **transtheoretical model** that identified six major stages in the change process (DiClemente, 2003; Prochaska & DiClemente, 1984). The model, shown in Figure 15.18, does not assume that people go through the stages in a smooth sequence. Longitudinal studies have shown that many people move forward and backward through the stages as they try to change their behaviour over time, and many people make repeated efforts to change before they finally succeed (Davidson, 1998; Burkholder, Evers, Burbank, & Riebe, 2002). It is assumed, however, that failure at a given stage is likely to occur if the previous stages have not been mastered.

The first stage is *precontemplation.* In this stage, people have no desire to change their behaviour. Often they don't perceive themselves as having a problem, or they deny that their behaviour has negative consequences. For example, public opinion polls suggest that there may be as many as 10 million people in the United States who still refuse to believe that smoking leads to premature death (Prochaska et al., 1994). Some precontemplators who do perceive a problem feel powerless to change their behaviour, so they have no inclination to try.

Some precontemplators move on to the stage of *contemplation.* Here the person perceives a problem or the desirability of a behaviour change but has not yet decided to take action. Thus some smokers are well aware of the health risks of their habit, yet they are not ready to make a decision to quit. Until the perceived benefits of changing outweigh the costs or effort involved, contemplators will not take action.

In the *preparation* stage, people have decided that they want to change their behaviour but have not actively begun to do so. Typically, they are developing a plan to take action within the next month to accomplish the change. People in this stage have often begun making small changes, such as reducing the number of cigarettes they are smoking or identifying conditions that affect the behaviour they want to change.

In the *action* stage, people actively begin to modify their behaviour and their environment. For example, they stop smoking altogether. Success at this stage hinges on the behaviour control skills necessary to carry out the plan of action. The action stage requires the greatest commitment of effort and energy.

If the person has been successful in avoiding relapse and has controlled the target behaviour for six months, he or she is in the stage of *maintenance.* This does not mean that the struggle is over. Many people lapse back into their former behaviour pattern at various times, as would be expected when one is trying to change deeply ingrained habits. The big challenge is not to give up when a lapse occurs and abandon the change program. It typically takes smokers three to five cycles through the action stage before they finally beat the habit, and New Year's resolutions are typically made for five or more consecutive years before they are finally carried out successfully (Prochaska et al., 1994; Schachter, 1982). The message is clear: If at first you don't succeed, don't give up. Instead, acquire the behavioural skills you need in order to succeed.

The final stage, *termination,* occurs when the change in behaviour is so ingrained and under personal control that the original problem behaviour will never return. It is the ultimate goal for all people who seek change.

The transtheoretical model is important because it helps us understand how people change and it has important applied implications. For example, we know that different intervention procedures are needed for people at various stages. Psychologists have therefore developed ways of determining what stage people are in so that they can apply *stage-matched interventions* designed to move the person toward the action, maintenance, and termination stages. Precontemplators need consciousness-raising information that finally convinces them that there is a problem, as well as social support to change (De Vries et al., 1998). Contemplators often need a "wakeup" emotional experience that increases their motivation to change or causes them to reevaluate themselves in relation to the behaviour. For example, a serious auto accident while intoxicated may finally convince a problem drinker that this behaviour has to change. In the preparation stage, the person needs to develop a specific plan (ideally based on the goal-setting procedures described in Chapter 12) and have the skills to carry it out before action is likely to be successful. Only when the person is ready for the action stage are change techniques, however powerful, likely to have their intended effect.

RESEARCH FOUNDATIONS

Life Events, Illness, and the Emergence of Health Psychology

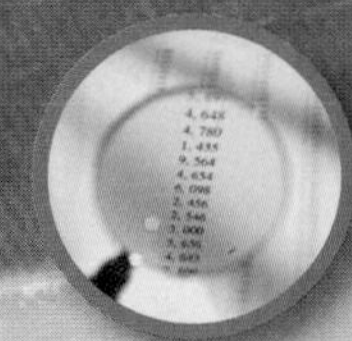

"Over 99 per cent of us are born healthy and made sick as a result of personal misbehavior and environmental conditions" (Knowles, 1977, p. 58).

During the 1960s and '70s, evidence began to accumulate that psychological factors were critically involved in physical health. By the late 1970s research had been published on the behavioural treatment or management of pain, enuresis, migraine headache, sexual dysfunction, essential hypertension, presurgery apprehension and postsurgery recovery, alcohol abuse, and obesity. Evidence supporting the importance of psychological factors in the development of coronary heart disease, hypertension, and a variety of stress-related medical disorders had also appeared (Matarazzo, 1980). The importance of this work and its growth as an area for study and clinical practice was formally recognized in 1978 when the American Psychological Association created a new division, Health Psychology (Division 38). The type of research and clinical practice that is now included under health psychology had been done prior to 1978, but it had been done under many names and was not formally recognized as a separate specialty. What we now call health psychology was sometimes called behavioural medicine, behavioural health, psychosomatic medicine, health psychology, medical psychology, or was subsumed under the more general clinical psychology (Matarazzo, 1980). (A distinction between behavioural medicine and health psychology is sometimes still made based on how great an emphasis there is on medical practice versus psychology.)

According to Joseph Matarazzo, one of the key figures in the founding of health psychology, "*Health psychology* is the aggregate of the specific educational, scientific, and professional contributions of the discipline of psychology to the promotion and maintenance of health, the prevention and treatment of illness, and the identification of etiologic and diagnostic correlates of health, illness, and related dysfunction" (Matarazzo, 1980, page 815).

An important research program in the development of health psychology was Holmes, Rahe, and Masuda's work on the impact of life events on physical health. In 1967 Thomas Holmes and Richard Rahe published a research report on the relationship between life changes, stress, and illness that had a lasting impact in psychology and in medicine. Commenting on Holmes and Rahe's research, two of the most influential stress researchers of the time wrote, "Probably no recent and ongoing program of research on stress and illness has had the degree of impact on psychosomatic medicine as the one initiated by Holmes and Rahe (1967) ..." (Monat & Lazarus, 1977, p. 13). The idea that life events, stress, and illness are linked is now widely accepted, but few acknowledged this idea when Holmes and Rahe first published their work on illness and life changes. Illness was seen as purely medical, a bodily malfunction caused by disease; stress and lifestyle were psychological concerns and therefore within a different realm. Holmes and Rahe built a convincing, if at times controversial, bridge between medicine and psychology.

Earlier studies had reported a link between stress and illness, but there was disagreement over what type of stress was involved, and even what constituted a stress. Holmes and Rahe argued that life changes, ranging from a vacation to the loss of a loved one, are stressful because they force changes in the way we live our lives. In response to a life change you may have to meet new people and establish new friendships,

–*Continued*

TABLE 15.5 Sample Items and Their Life Change Units (LCU) from the Social Readjustment Rating Scale (Holmes & Rahe, 1967).

Rank	Life Event	LCU
1	Death of a spouse	100
3	Marital separation	65
6	Personal injury or illness	53
7	Marriage	50
13	Sex difficulties	39
17	Death of a close friend	37
25	Outstanding personal achievement	28
27	Begin or end school	26
33	Change in schools	20
41	Vacation	13
43	Minor violations of the law	11

change your daily routine, change your life goals, or experience loneliness and the loss of shared activities; that is, you experience some social readjustment. They argued that life events requiring social readjustment were especially important and attempted to quantify the impact of different life events.

Holmes and Rahe presented questionnaires to 394 participants. The questionnaire contained 43 items Holmes and Rahe selected based on their clinical experience, items that all necessitated some social readjustment. One item, marriage, was arbitrarily given a score of 500 and participants were asked to rate the impact of the other 42 items relative to marriage and to assign a proportionally larger or smaller number based on how intense and prolonged the readjustment relative to marriage. All of the subjects' ratings were averaged and then standardized to a 100 point scale (that is, in the final version marriage had a value of 50 points). Holmes and Rahe referred to the points as Life Change Units. The higher the number of Life Change Units assigned to an event, the greater the required social readjustment. To check for consistency in the ratings, Holmes and Rahe divided the sample into subgroups and compared ratings between different subgroups. They divided the sample by sex, age, marital status, educational level, socioeconomic status, religious affiliation, and ethnicity. For all of the subgroup comparisons the correlations were very high; all of the correlation coefficients were above +.9, indicating a very high level of agreement among the participants. The end result was the Social Readjustment Rating Scale (SRRS; see Table 15.5 for examples from the SRRS).

Holmes and Rahe's SRRS was used as a tool for studying the relationship between stress and illness and the results supported Holmes and Rahe's contention that there was a relationship between the stress of life changes and illness. For example, Holmes and Masuda (1974) reported that the more Life Change Units a person had accumulated during the past 12 months, the greater the likelihood that they developed a physical illness of sufficient seriousness that they sought medical attention (Figure 15.19).

The SRRS was criticized because it included both emotionally positive (e.g., vacation) and emotionally negative (e.g., injury) events, and included both events within a person's control (e.g., marriage) and events outside the individual's control (e.g., death of a friend). The SRRS has also been criticized because it does not consider the interpretation of an event and we now know that cognitive appraisal is critically important in these situations. For example, "change in number of family get-togethers" has a score of 15, but whether this is an increase or a decrease in the frequency of family get-togethers and what you think of those family get-togethers is not considered. A decrease in the number of family get-togethers may be negative and stressful for someone who relishes such events with a close-knit family, but the same decrease may be a welcome relief for someone who does not get along well with his or her relatives.

Despite such shortcomings, the SRRS was a breakthrough in the study of the relationship between psychological factors and illness. The work by Holmes, Rahe and colleagues provided a dramatic, controversial example of how adjusting to life changes can impact a person's physical health. Together with its impact on our understanding of the risks for the development of physical illness, research on the SRRS made an important contribution to the development of health psychology.

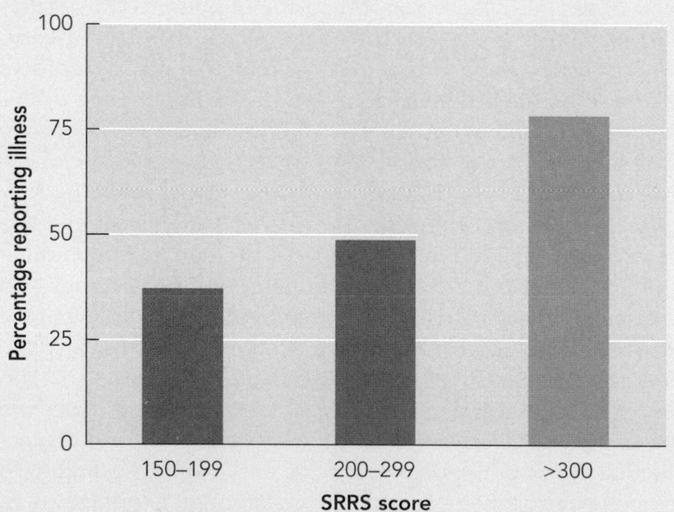

FIGURE 15.19

The more life changes an individual has experienced during the past year (SRRS score), the more likely they are to develop an illness serious enough to seek medical attention. Adapted from Holmes and Masuda, 1974.

Increasing Behaviours That Enhance Health

During the 1970s, the role of behaviour in maintaining health and living longer became evident as researchers began to study the effects of lifestyle. Figure 15.20 shows the results of one longitudinal study of nearly 7,000 adults. The researchers studied the relation of seven good-health practices to life expectancy. These included sleeping seven to eight hours per day, eating breakfast, not smoking, rarely eating between meals, being at or near one's prescribed body weight, engaging in regular physical activity, and drinking only small to moderate amounts of alcohol. For men and women alike, these behaviours predicted a longer life. A higher mortality rate among those with poor health practices began to appear in men between the ages of 45 and 64 and in women between 55 and 64 (Belloc, 1973). Let's examine some of these health-enhancing behaviours and what can be done to encourage them.

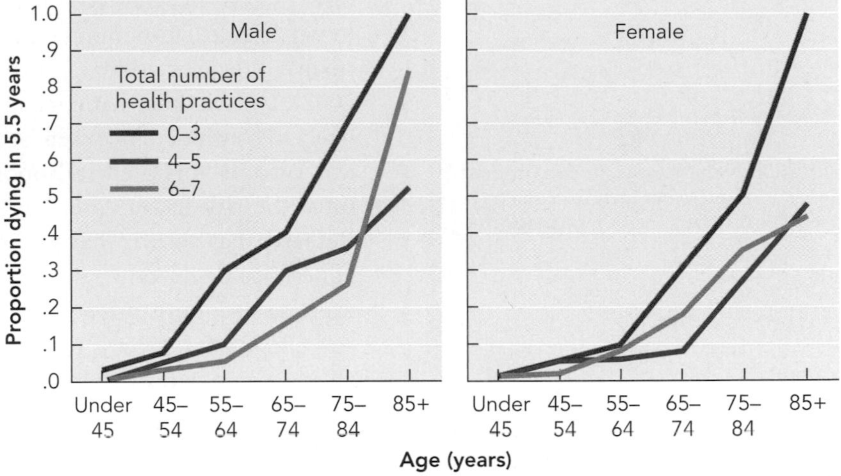

FIGURE 15.20

Relation between the number of positive health practices and longevity in men and women. Those who adhered to few of the health practices experienced earlier mortality, with the pattern appearing earlier for men than for women.

Source: Adapted from Belloc, 1973.

Exercise

The couch potato lives! (But apparently, not as long.) A sedentary lifestyle is a significant risk factor for a variety of health problems, including coronary heart disease, diabetes and obesity (Rodin & Salovey, 1989; Taylor, 2003). Despite this widely publicized fact, about 70 percent of North Americans are inactive (Baum et al., 1997; Ehrman, 2003). Inactivity has helped double the rate of obesity since 1900, despite a 10 percent decrease in daily caloric intake over the same period (Friedman & DiMatteo, 1989).

Aerobic exercise is sustained activity, such as jogging, swimming, and bicycling, that elevates the heart rate and increases the body's need for oxygen. This kind of exercise has many physiological benefits. In a well-conditioned person, the heart beats more slowly and efficiently, oxygen is better utilized, cholesterol levels may be reduced, faster adaptation to stressors occurs, and more calories are burned (Baum & Posluszny, 1999; deGeus, 2000).

Exercise is associated with both physical health and longevity (Figures 15.20 and 15.21). A study that followed 17,000 Harvard undergraduates into middle age revealed that death rates were one-quarter to one-third lower among moderate exercisers than among those in a less active group. Surprisingly, perhaps, very high levels of exercise were not associated with enhanced health; instead, moderate exercise (burning 2,000 to 3,500 calories per week) on a regular basis produced the best health benefits (Paffenbarger et al., 1986). Performing at 70 to 85 percent of maximal heart rate non-stop for 15 minutes three times a week is related to reduced risk for coronary heart disease (Dishman, 1982). Most experts suggest that a regular (three times per week) program of aerobic exercise performed at 60 to 85 percent maximal heart rate for 20 to 60 minutes per session has a host of health benefits.

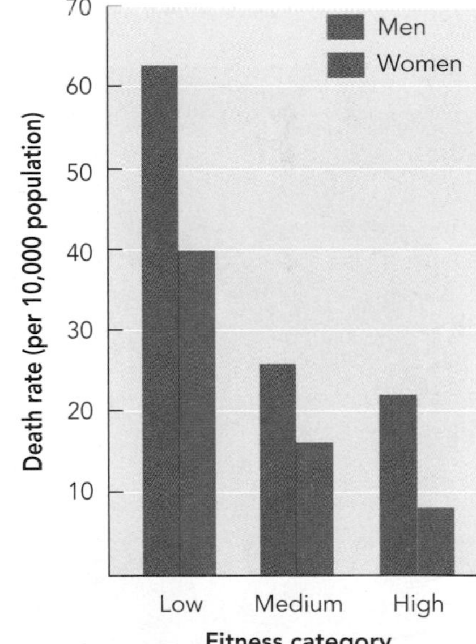

FIGURE 15.21

Aerobic exercise is an important health-enhancing behaviour, contributing to physical well-being. Significantly higher death rates occur for both men and women who are low in physical fitness.

Based on Blair et al., 1989.

Findings like these have inspired behavioural interventions designed to promote regular exercise. Typically, these programs have an educational component that provides information on the benefits of regular exercise and the best ways to exercise. They may also include other components of behaviour change, such as goal setting, writing explicit contracts that specify an exercise regimen, monitoring

27. What is aerobic exercise? What evidence is there that it promotes health and longevity?

28. How large are exercise dropout rates? What factors predict dropout and compliance?

one's exercise behaviour on a daily basis, and increasing social support by choosing an exercise partner or group.

Despite the demonstrated benefits of regular exercise, people have a strong tendency either to avoid doing it or to discontinue it after a short period. When employers offer exercise programs to their employees, it is uncommon for more than 30 percent to participate. Dropout rates of 50 percent within six months are quite typical in virtually all the exercise programs that have been studied (Dishman, 1988; Chenoweth, 2002). On the other hand, people who are able to persist for three to six months are likely to continue, since exercise becomes a healthy habit (McAuley, 1992).

What factors predict dropout? This is an important research question, because, once the risk factors are identified, measures can be taken to counteract them. Research has shown that general attitudes toward physical fitness do *not* predict adherence or dropout; the attitudes of dropouts and people who adhere to their exercise programs are equally favourable (Suls & Wallston, 2003). However, low self-efficacy for success in exercising regularly ("I can't do this"), Type A personality ("Sorry, too busy to exercise"), inflated estimates of current physical fitness ("I'm already in great shape from walking from my couch to the refrigerator"), and inactive leisure-time pursuits (such as watching television and walking to the refrigerator) all predict dropout (Martin & Dubbert, 1985; Wilcox & Storandt, 1996). The strongest social-environmental factor related to dropout is lack of social support from friends, family, or other exercisers (Ehrman, 2003).

Psychologists have been able to increase compliance by helping exercisers identify these impediments and prepare specific strategies to deal with them before they occur (Rosen, 2000; Simkin & Gross, 1994). For example, a person who anticipates feeling "too tired" to work out at the end of the day might prepare a set of self-statements about how much better she will feel after exercising. If she is not receiving social support and encouragement from others, she could also arrange for a pleasurable activity after exercise so as to positively reinforce her exercising (Courneya, 1995).

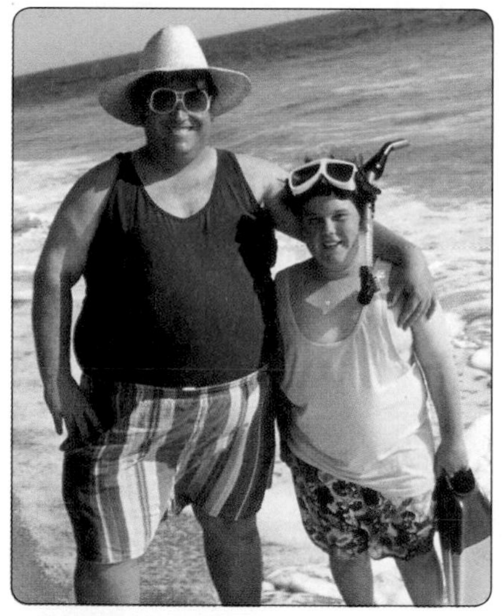

FIGURE 15.22

An alarmingly large percentage of North American adults and children are overweight, increasing health risks. Family-based interventions are directed at modifying bad dietary habits, such as high-fat diets.

Weight Control

According to Statistics Canada (2000), 48 percent of Canadians aged 20 to 64 are overweight and nearly 15 percent are obese (30 percent in the United States), defined as being more than 20 percent overweight (Figure 15.22). Since 1980, the average North American adult's body weight has increased by about 3.6 kg, with the upward trend continuing (Suls & Wallston, 2003; Taylor, 1999). A significant proportion of children (13.7 percent) and adolescents (11.5 percent) are obese (Buet & Harris, 1994). Statistics Canada reports a 500 percent increase in childhood obesity between 1980 and 2004.

Obesity is a risk factor for a variety of chronic diseases, such as cardiovascular disease, kidney disease, and diabetes (Baum & Posluszny, 1999). Women who are 30 percent overweight are more than three times more likely to develop heart disease than normal weight women (Manson et al., 1990). For reasons yet unknown, fat that is localized in the abdomen is a far greater risk factor for cardiovascular disease, diabetes, and cancer than is excessive fat in the hips, thighs, or buttocks (Taylor, 2003). The accumulation of abdominal fat is increased by **yo-yo dieting** that results in big up-and-down weight fluctuations. Such dieting markedly increases the risk of dying from cardiovascular disease, an excellent reason to avoid this practice (Hafen & Hoeger, 1998; Rodin et al., 1990).

Behavioural intervention for weight loss usually begins with a period of self-monitoring in which clients keep careful records of what they eat, how much they eat, and under what circumstances. This is designed to make them more aware of their eating habits and to identify situational factors (antecedents) that affect their eating. They then are taught to take control of those antecedents. For example, they make low-calorie foods such as raw vegetables freely available, while limiting high-calorie foods in the house. Stimulus control techniques are then used, such as confining eating to one location in the house and eating only at certain times of the day. Because overeaters tend to wolf down their food and overload their stomachs, clients also learn to slow down their eating by putting down eating utensils until the food is chewed and swallowed, and by pausing between mouthfuls. These behaviours reduce food intake and allow clients to pay attention to how full they are. They are told to savour each mouthful of food. The goal is to eat less, but enjoy it more. Finally, they chart the amount of food they eat to provide constant feedback, and they arrange to reinforce themselves for successful performance. These behavioural practices are combined with nutritional and attitudinal guidelines. Table 15.6 shows specific guidelines from a highly successful weight-reduction program developed by Yale psychologist Kelly Brownell (1994).

TABLE 15.6 A Sample of Effective Behavioural Weight Control Techniques

Keep an eating diary	Keep problem foods out of sight
Examine your eating patterns	Serve and eat one portion at a time
Prevent automatic eating	Use gradual shaping for behaviour change
Examine triggers for eating	Distinguish hunger from cravings
Do nothing else while eating	Focus on behaviour, not weight loss
Eat in one place	Cope positively with slips, lapses
Put fork down between bites	Keep an exercise diary
Pause during the meal	Understand benefits of exercise
Shop on a full stomach	Know calorie values of various exercise activities
Buy foods that require preparation	Program exercise activity

Source: After Brownell, 1994.

Research shows that the addition of an exercise program increases the positive effects of the behavioural eating control program (Jeffery & Wing, 1995; Wadden et al., 1997). High levels of physical activity are associated with initial weight loss and maintenance of the weight loss, and physical activity adds to the effectiveness of other weight loss methods, such as dietary change. Many people are able to attain gradual weight loss of about one kg per week for up to 20 weeks, and to keep the weight off over two years, whereas others are less successful (Jackson et al., 1999; Taylor, 2003).

29. Why is yo-yo dieting an undesirable practice?

Teaching people how to control their health-related programs can have dramatic benefits even for those who are already afflicted with serious illnesses. William Haskell and co-workers (1994) randomly divided a sample of patients suffering from coronary artery disease into two groups. Both groups received the usual high-quality medical care from their physicians at Stanford University Medical School. In addition, the experimental group received a behavioural self-regulation program that targeted health factors such as smoking, exercise, weight, nutrition, and medication adherence.

30. What are the major behaviour-change techniques used in behavioural weight control programs?

A four-year follow-up revealed dramatic results. Those receiving the usual medical care showed either no improvement or a worsening of their condition, and their health habits had not improved. In contrast, those who also received the behavioural self-regulation program showed significant positive changes in their health habits. They reduced their intake of dietary fat, lowered their bad (LDL) cholesterol and raised their good (HDL) cholesterol, increased their exercise, and raised their cardiovascular capacity. The program also influenced the progression of the disease, as the self-management group had 47 percent less buildup of blockage material on artery walls. During the four-year follow-up period, 45 percent of the control patients either died or had nonfatal heart attacks or other cardiac emergencies, compared with only 24 percent in the behaviour self-regulation group. This study, like the others we've discussed, demonstrates the value of psychologically based health-promotion efforts.

Reducing Behaviours That Impair Health

We now turn our attention to several types of health-impairing behaviours. We begin with a class of behaviours that two decades ago was not considered a major health threat. Although a number of serious diseases can be transmitted through sexual contact, the majority of them can be successfully treated. In the early 1980s, however, a mysterious and lethal sexually transmitted disease emerged.

On June 5, 1981, the Centers for Disease Control reported the first case of acquired immune deficiency syndrome (AIDS). In the two decades that followed, AIDS grew from an unknown disease into a devastating worldwide epidemic for which there is currently no medical cure. According to the World Health Organization (2002), about 16,000 new infections occur each day. Worldwide, 1 in every 100 adults ages 15 to 49 is infected with the AIDS virus, and the disease has claimed the lives of nearly 20 million people. Of the 3 million people who died from AIDS in 2001, 37 percent were women and 20 percent were children. Worldwide, only 5 to 10 percent of the cases presently occur in homosexual men (the population typically identified with the affliction), and women now make up half of all HIV cases (United Nations, 2002). In the early 2000s, the rates of infection began to rise again among homosexual men in North America, Europe, and Australia due to increases in risky sexual behaviour (CDC, 2003). In 2004, AIDS accounted for 420 deaths in Canada, making the mortality rate from AIDS a larger killer than accidental drowning, fire, meningitis, or salmonella poisoning (Statistics Canada, 2007). The AIDS epidemic threatens to overwhelm the world's health-care financing and delivery systems.

31. What is the scope of the worldwide AIDS crisis?

AIDS is caused by the *human immunodeficiency virus (HIV)*, which cripples the immune system by killing cells that coordinate the body's attack against invading viruses, bacteria, and tumours, which become the actual killers. Because the AIDS virus changes rapidly, vaccines at present are ineffective in preventing its spread. Moreover, the incubation period between initial infection and the appearance of the disease may be as long as 10 years, meaning that an infected person unknowingly may pass the virus on to many other people. The major modes of transmission are direct exposure to infected semen, vaginal fluids, and blood through either homosexual or heterosexual contact, the sharing of infected needles in intravenous drug use, and exposure to infected blood through transfusion or in the womb.

Prevention Programs

32. Summarize the four features of most AIDS prevention projects, and the outcomes of a program directed at homosexual men. How do cultural factors influence outcomes?

In the absence of a vaccine, the only existing means of controlling the AIDS epidemic is changing the high-risk behaviours that transmit the virus. In this respect, AIDS is as much a psychological problem as a medical one. In recent years, principles derived from educational psychology, social psychology, and the psychology of learning have been applied in designing and carrying out prevention programs. Such programs typically are designed to (1) educate people concerning the risks that attend certain behaviours, such as having sex without using a condom; (2) motivate people to change their behaviour and convince them that they can do so; (3) provide specific guidelines for changing the risky behaviours and teach the skills needed for change; and (4) give support and encouragement for the desired changes (O'Leary et al., 2001).

Early AIDS interventions were directed at homosexual men, who were originally the major at-risk group. In this population, a major mechanism of HIV transmission is anal intercourse without use of a condom. In one early prevention study (Kelly & St. Lawrence, 1989), 42 homosexual men went through a program that provided them with information about the risks accompanying unprotected intercourse, helped them develop and rehearse strategies for avoiding high-risk situations (such as sexual relations with strangers), and taught them how to be more assertive in refusing to engage in high-risk behaviours such as sexual relations without a condom. Another group of 43 homosexual men also completed the program after serving as an initial control group.

Both groups were assessed before and after the first group went through the program, and then were followed for eight months after completion of the program to assess long-term behaviour changes. As shown in Figure 15.23, the intervention program resulted in substantial and lasting changes in the use of condoms during sexual activity. Similar programs are now being conducted with adolescent populations, in which unprotected heterosexual intercourse is resulting in a surge of new infections (Jemmott et al., 1998). Another target for intervention is heterosexual women, who not only are the fastest-rising segment of the HIV population, but who also have the potential to infect their babies (Stevens & Bogart, 1999).

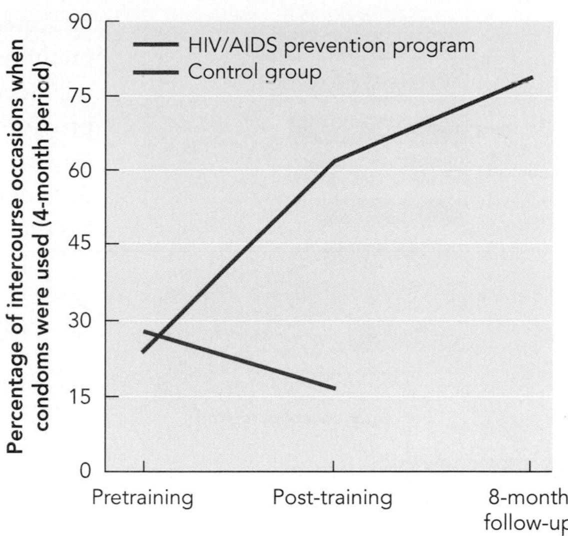

FIGURE 15.23

Effects of an HIV/AIDS prevention program for homosexual men on their use of condoms during sexual activity. The program educated the men on the risks involved in sexual behaviours (especially unprotected sex), promoted use of condoms, and taught them coping skills to deal with high-risk situations.

Data from Kelly et al., 1989.

Even when something as urgent as AIDS prevention is involved, research has shown that the success of prevention programs depends on the extent to which the individual's social system supports the desired changes. When the use of condoms runs contrary to the values of an individual or cultural group, people may continue to engage in high-risk behaviours even though they have been informed of the dangers involved (Herdt & Lindenbaum, 1992; Huff et al., 1999). Likewise, within both homosexual and heterosexual populations, and particularly among adolescents and young adults, many individuals continue to have an irrational sense of invulnerability to infection, and this belief contributes to a failure to engage in safe sexual practices (Kelly, 2001). Counteracting these barriers to safe sexual behaviour is a major challenge for health psychologists.

33. What cultural and belief factors promote unsafe sexual behaviour?

One promising approach to cultural attitude change was inspired by Albert Bandura's social-cognitive theory. It involves the use of modelling procedures to change attitudes and behaviour in some of the poorest and most hopeless parts of the world (Bandura, 2000). The strategy is to produce highly engaging "entertainment-education" radio dramas to increase awareness and counteract false beliefs. In Tanzania, for example, many people erroneously believe that AIDS is transmitted by mosquitoes and that using a condom while having sex could actually cause the disease.

In 1993, a new radio serial began in parts of that country. It was based on Bandura's findings that people learn from role models whose behaviour they admire, and it was designed to have a compelling story line whose purpose was to encourage protected sex and to reduce soaring population growth. The program features three types of characters: positive role models whose behaviours have positive consequences, negative role models whose behaviours lead to disaster, and transitional models who start out behaving negatively and then change for the better and enjoy positive outcomes. For example, one soap opera character is a long-distance truck driver who has unprotected sex with multiple partners. His long-suffering wife finally leaves him and, with help from the community, establishes a business to support herself and her children. The promiscuous husband eventually develops AIDS and dies an agonizing death, while the woman becomes a successful businesswoman.

The program attracted many thousands of listeners in the regions where it was broadcast. Within two years, evaluations of the program showed that listeners were more likely to believe that unprotected sex could result in HIV infection. They also discussed AIDS more among themselves, reduced their number of sexual partners,

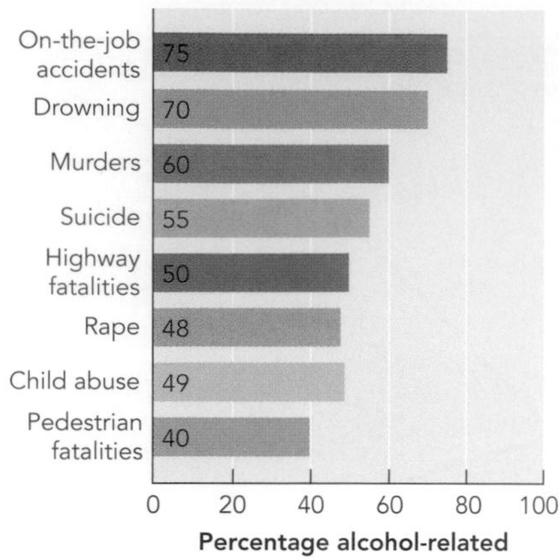

FIGURE 15.24

Societal costs of alcohol abuse, showing the percentage of common negative events that are alcohol-related.

Data from Carroll et al., 1993.

increased condom use, developed more positive attitudes toward family-planning methods and a later age for women to marry, and desired smaller families. Control regions of Tanzania where the program was not aired showed no changes until the program was aired there, after which changes in their attitudes and behaviours also occurred (Rogers et al., 1996). Similar programs are now being aired in other developing countries. This social-cognitive approach may someday be referred to as "the theory that saved a million lives."

COMBATTING SUBSTANCE ABUSE

Substance abuse exacts a fearsome toll on society. In May, 1994, the Canadian Centre on Substance Abuse (CCSA) organized an International Symposium, *the Economic and Social Costs of Substance Abuse.* Their report was the first time that the costs of the use of alcohol, tobacco, and illicit drugs were calculated for Canada, and stands as the most detailed report of its kind for Canada. In their report Single, Robson, Zie, and Rehm (1996) estimated that 6,701 Canadians lost their lives as a result of alcohol consumption in 1992. Most alcohol-related deaths were from traffic accidents involving an impaired driver, followed by alcoholic liver cirrhosis and alcohol-related suicides. Apart from being a critical factor in so many deaths, alcohol was a major factor in 86,076 hospitalizations in Canada during 1992. Alcohol abuse affects not just the drinker: for every person who has a problem with alcohol, an average of four other people's lives are adversely affected on a daily basis (Levinthal, 2005). There are an estimated 640,000 Canadians with alcohol dependence (The Daily, Sept. 3, 2003, Statistics Canada). The conclusion is clearly that a shocking number of Canadians have their daily lives disrupted in some way by alcohol. The economic costs of alcohol abuse are substantial. In 1992, alcohol abuse accounted for more than $7.5 billion in costs, almost three percent of Canada's total Gross Domestic Product for the year. The economic costs of alcohol use come from lost productivity ($4.1 billion), law enforcement ($1.36 billion) and direct health care costs ($1.3 billion).

Other varieties of substance abuse also have adverse effects. Tobacco use damages both smokers and those who breathe their second-hand smoke. Smoking ranks as the single largest cause of preventable death, killing more than half a million North Americans each year (American Cancer Society, 2000). Tobacco use and illicit drugs also have a major economic impact, with the economic costs of tobacco use estimated at $9.6 billion and illicit drugs at $1.4 billion in 1992 (Single et al., 1996). Together with the economic costs, alcohol and drug use has a social cost (Figure 15.24). Estimates from the 1999 General Social Survey (Statistics Canada, 2004) indicate that in approximately half of physical (51%) and sexual (48%) assaults, there is evidence that the incident was related to the perpetrator's use of alcohol or illicit drugs. Moreover, substance abuse is highly associated with psychological disorders, often being part of a larger pattern of maladjustment in both adolescents and adults (Miller, 1997).

Psychological Approaches to Treatment and Prevention

A variety of psychological principles discussed in earlier chapters has been applied to the treatment of substance abuse (Marlatt & Witkiewitz, 2002; Taylor, 2003; Prochaska et al., 1998). Disappointing results from traditional psychotherapy, such as long-term psychodynamic approaches, and limited effectiveness of biological treatments, pointed the way to cognitive-behavioural approaches, which have proven to be more cost-effective and successful in reducing abuse (Institute of Medicine, 1990; Marlatt et al., 1998; Miller et al., 1995).

Motivational Interviewing

34. What are the major goals and techniques in motivational interviewing?

If smokers, problem drinkers, drug abusers, and others who practice self-defeating behaviours are to change, they must increase their awareness of their problems, have a desire to take action, and believe that they can change (Miller & Rollnick, 2002; Miller, 1996). Rather than confronting the person with his or her problem (which often drives away people who need help), the technique of **motivational interviewing** leads the person to his or her own conclusion by asking questions that focus on discrepancies between the current state of affairs and the individual's ideal self-image, desired behaviours, and desired outcomes. Focusing on these discrepancies may help motivate change. Consider the following exchange:

Client: I really don't believe I have a drinking problem.

Counsellor: You're the best judge of that. May I ask how many drinks you have a day?

Client: Oh, it varies. Probably five or six.

Counsellor: Is that about what you'd like to be drinking?

Client: Well, I'd probably be better off if I cut down a little—maybe to three or four.

Counsellor: How would that be helpful to you?

Client: Well, I could study better and reduce the arguments with my roommate. I can get pretty nasty when I'm buzzed. I hate being nasty. I'm not that kind of person. Our relationship is going downhill, and I'd hate to lose a friend.

Counsellor: Well, you know, you don't have to have a big problem in order to want to make a change. I'm sure you could do so if you really want to.

Client: I can see that I'd be more the person I want to be if I worked on this.

Counsellor: And I'd be happy to help you make your change.

Following a client's decision to pursue behaviour change, the counsellor helps the client set specific goals and select from a menu of behaviour-change strategies the ones he or she would like to employ. Thereafter the counsellor provides feedback and support for the client's efforts.

Motivational interviewing has proven to be an effective and low-cost treatment approach for substance abusers (Miller & Rollnick, 2002). In one large-scale study of alcohol abuse patients, a four-session motivational interviewing intervention proved to be as effective as a twelve-session program modelled on Alcoholics Anonymous (Project MATCH Research Group, 1997).

Multimodal Treatment Approaches

35. What kinds of behaviour-change procedures are employed in multimodal treatments for substance abuse?

All substance-abuse behaviours are resistant to change, and for good reason. Some people may be more vulnerable than others because of genetic factors (Crabbe, 2002). Craving, caused by either psychological need or physical dependence, is a huge barrier to overcome. Negative emotions, such as anxiety, irritability, or depression, that are temporary results of abstinence cause many who quit successfully to have relapses. Past conditioning may create stimuli that trigger the behaviour in certain common situations. For example, coffee drinking or social situations are linked with smoking for many individuals, thus encouraging lapses in behavioural control when those stimuli are present. The numerous factors that encourage smoking, drinking, or drug abuse make these behaviours very hard to change.

Psychologists are therefore willing to combine anything that has proven effective into what they hope will be a more powerful behaviour-change "package" to apply when people are ready to make a change. These **multimodal treatments** often include biological measures (for example, the use of nicotine patches to help smokers who are trying to quit), together with psychological measures such as the following:

- Aversion therapy, in which the undesired behaviour is associated with an aversive stimulus, such as electric shock or a nausea- producing drug, in an attempt to create a negative emotional response to the currently pleasurable substance;
- Relaxation and stress-management training, which help the person adapt to and deal with stressful situations;
- Self-monitoring procedures that help the person identify the antecedents and consequences of the abuse behaviours;
- Coping and social skills training for dealing with high-risk situations that trigger abuse;
- Marital and family counselling to reduce conflicts and increase social support for change; and
- Positive reinforcement procedures to strengthen change.

This broad-based multimodal approach appears to produce favourable outcomes for many people who have substance addictions. For example, in one of the more successful multimodal treatment outcome studies, 427 alcoholic patients were followed for 12 to 20 months after completing an inpatient program that included aversion therapy (using a drug that produces nausea when alcohol is consumed), personal counselling, and coping skills training. Follow-up assessments revealed that 65 percent were totally abstinent for one year after treatment. The best outcome occurred in cases where urges to drink had been eliminated (presumably by aversion therapy) and alternate coping skills were increased through the use of cognitive-behavioural techniques such as those just described (Smith & Frawley, 1993). Despite these encouraging results, typical treatment results are less favourable: Long-term maintenance of behaviour changes often occurs in fewer than 30 percent of treated individuals, whether the target behaviour is smoking, drinking, or some other substance abuse (Ockene et al., 2001). The goal of many researchers is therefore to develop increasingly more effective treatment packages.

36. How severe is the problem of relapse in substance abuse treatment?

Relapse Prevention

High dropout rates are a major problem in treating substance abuse. For example, the Alcoholics Anonymous (AA) program seems to be moderately effective in reducing drinking if people remain in the program and adhere to its procedures (Morgenstern et al., 1997). Yet only 10 percent of those who begin the AA program remain in it, become abstinent, and remain abstinent for a year (Tonigan et al., 1996). As we've already noted, aversion therapy programs such as Antabuse treatment suffer from the same dropout problem. Overall, fewer than 30 percent of treated alcoholics remain improved one year after treatment, and 80 percent of people who quit smoking relapse within a year (Baker et al., 1987; Baum et al., 1997). Virtually every behaviour change program has the same problem, even New Year's resolutions.

FIGURE 15.25

A model of relapse prevention. Relapse is most likely to occur as a result of inadequate coping skills for dealing with high-risk situations, a focus on anticipated positive effects of substance use, and a resulting abstinence violation effect that causes the person to feel incapable of successful change and to abandon attempts at behaviour control.

Source: Marlatt & Gordon, 1985.

These self-initiated change attempts are maintained for more than four months by only 40 to 45 percent of people (Marlatt & Kaplan, 1972; Norcross et al., 1989).

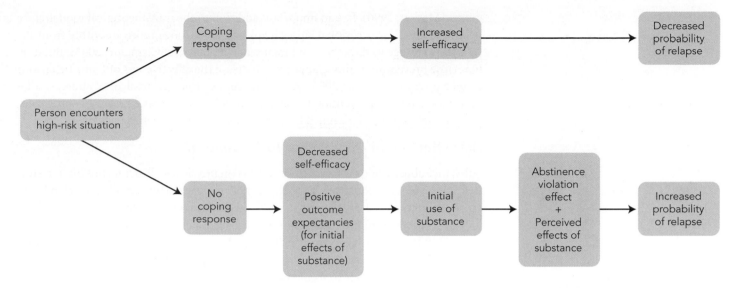

Why do people relapse into their problem behaviours, and what can be done to prevent relapse? Research on these questions led G. Alan Marlatt and Judith Gordon (1985) to develop the model of relapse shown in Figure 15.25, together with an intervention known as *relapse prevention.* Research with substance abusers showed that most **relapses** (a return to the undesirable behaviour pattern) tended to occur after the person had suffered a **lapse** (a one-time "slip") when confronted with a high-risk situation. High-risk situations included stressful events, interpersonal conflicts, social pressure to perform the undesirable behaviour, being in the company of other individuals using the substance, and experiencing negative emotions (Marlatt, 1996).

37. What is the difference between a lapse and a relapse? How does the abstinence violation effect contribute to relapse?

Increased likelihood of relapse occurred when people had not developed strong enough coping skills to deal successfully with the high-risk situation. Consequently, they felt a lack of self-efficacy for resisting the temptation, or they allowed expected positive benefits (such as enjoyment of the substance or anticipated stress reduction) to prompt their decision to perform the undesirable behaviour. A lapse would then occur, followed by a critically important reaction called the **abstinence violation effect**: The person became upset and self-blaming over the failure to remain abstinent and viewed the lapse as proof that he or she would never be strong enough to resist temptation. This self-blaming sense of hopelessness placed people at great risk of abandoning all attempts to change, and in many cases a total relapse would occur. In contrast, people with sufficient coping skills who confront high-risk situations feel confident in their ability to handle them and are far less likely to relapse, even if they slip once in a while.

Relapse prevention strategies involve teaching people that a lapse means nothing more than the fact that they have encountered a situation that exceeded their current coping skills. Moreover, the episode has given them valuable information about the specific situational, cognitive, and emotional antecedents that they must learn to handle more effectively. When they master the needed skills, they will be better able to resist high-risk situations. Attention is then directed at learning and practising the required skills so that self-efficacy improves. The continuing focus is on "progress, not perfection."

38. How does relapse prevention treatment attempt to keep lapses from becoming a relapse? How effective is this approach?

Relapse prevention, which was developed from a research-based theory of why people relapse, is increasingly being incorporated into many behaviour change programs (Marlatt, 1996). It is an important addition to the transtheoretical model, since being prepared for occasional lapses helps people to move more smoothly from the preparation stage to the action and maintenance stages (DiClemente, 2003). Building in relapse prevention training appears to increase the effectiveness of many behaviour change programs (Taylor, 2003). As a stand-alone approach to alcohol abuse, studies have shown relapse prevention to have an overall effectiveness equal to AA programs, even though it is usually a much briefer intervention (Ouimette et al., 1997).

Harm Reduction Approaches to Prevention

39. What is a harm reduction approach, and how does it differ from an abstinence-based one?

Substance abuse not only has negative effects on physical well-being, but often results in other severe consequences, such as self-defeating sexual and aggressive behaviours. **Harm reduction** is a prevention strategy that is designed not to eliminate a behaviour, but rather to reduce the harmful effects of a behaviour when it occurs (MacCoun, 1998; Weingardt & Marlatt, 1998). In the area of drug abuse, harm reduction approaches include needle and syringe exchange programs to reduce the spread of HIV infections. Another example is methadone maintenance programs for heroin addicts that are targeted at reducing their need to engage in criminal activity to feed their heroin habit. The reasoning is that, even if an addictive behaviour cannot be eliminated, it is possible to modify how often and under what conditions it occurs and thereby to minimize its harmful effects on the person and society.

TABLE 15.7 **Percentage of Binge-Drinking University Students Who Reported Drinking-Related Problems**

Problem	Percentage
Missed a class	61%
Forgot where they were or what they did	54%
Engaged in unplanned sex	41%
Got hurt	23%
Had unprotected sex	22%
Damaged property	22%
Got into trouble with campus or local police	11%
Had five or more alcohol-related problems in school year	47%

Source: Data from Wechsler et al., 1994.

Many university students fail to realize the extent to which they place themselves in harm's way through their use of alcohol. In one national study carried out by the Harvard School of Public Health, binge drinking was defined as having more than four (for women) or five (for men) drinks at a time on at least three occasions during the previous two weeks (Wechsler et al., 1994). Data from 18,000 students at 140 U.S. universities revealed that 50 percent of the males and 40 percent of the women met this bingeing criterion, yet fewer than one percent saw themselves as having an alcohol problem. However, the dangerous consequences of their drinking became clear when binge drinkers were asked about alcohol-related problems (Table 15.7). Frequent binge drinkers were seven to ten times more likely than moderate drinkers to engage in unplanned and unprotected intercourse, to suffer injuries, to drive under the influence of alcohol, to damage property, and to get into trouble with the police. At schools with the highest alcohol consumption rates, non-drinkers and moderate drinkers were two to three times more likely to report physical assault, sexual harassment, destruction of their property, and interruption of their sleep and studying by heavy drinkers. Some university women (obviously, sound sleepers) complained that they woke up Sunday after Sunday to find a strange man in bed with their roommate (and all too frequently, the heavy-drinking roommate didn't know him either).

40. How serious are the consequences of heavy drinking among university students?

Previous attempts to convince heavy-drinking university students to abstain from alcohol have met with limited success (Marlatt, 1998). Typically, it seems, problem drinkers laugh all the way to the liquor store after being told to simply stop drinking. As a result, a new generation of intervention programs is focused on helping drinkers control how much and under what conditions they drink so as to reduce harmful consequences to themselves and others. In one harm reduction project carried out at a large U.S. university, incoming freshmen were screened for alcohol problems before they arrived on campus (Marlatt et al., 1998). Once on campus, those identified as problem drinkers were randomly assigned to either an intervention condition or to a no-treatment control condition. Over the next two years, the students in both conditions regularly reported on their alcohol consumption and alcohol-related problems. People who knew them well also furnished reports, and high agreement between the two sources of data indicated that the students were being truthful and accurate. Students' degree of alcohol dependence (craving for alcohol and withdrawal symptoms when not drinking) was assessed through psychological tests and interviews.

The brief intervention, occurring in the winter of the freshman year, was based on the motivational interviewing approach described earlier. The goal was to prevent or reduce harmful consequences of drinking by increasing motivation to make constructive changes, rather than to stop students' drinking. Clinical psychologists met with each student individually for one session. The interviewer reviewed the drinking data submitted by the student over the previous academic term and gave individualized feedback in graphic form. The graph compared the student's drinking rates with university student averages, which were invariably much lower. This feedback actually surprised many students. Because most of their friends drank as much as they did, they thought the same was true for university students in general. Potential risks for heavy drinkers (such as those shown in Table 15.4) were pointed out. The psychologists also told the students about the physiological effects of alcohol, including the biphasic effect described in Chapter 6 (an initial stimulating effect followed by a depressive one) to show that the expectation that "drinking more will make me feel better" is incorrect. Environmental risk factors, such as being in a fraternity or sorority or having heavy-drinking friends, were also discussed when relevant.

The interviewers were never confrontational, but instead helped students to evaluate their situation ("What do you make of this? Are you surprised?"), to think about present and possible future problems ("Would you be worried about something like this happening to you? What impact would it have on your life?"), and to consider the possibility of change. Specific goals of behaviour change were left to the student and not imposed by the interviewer. Later, during the winter of their second year in university, students in the intervention condition were mailed individualized feedback on their self-reported drinking data and alcohol related problems over the previous year so that they could evaluate possible changes in their situations.

Did this very brief program have positive effects on the at-risk students? At the end of two years, the students in the intervention group were drinking less than were the students in the control condition, but still nearly 80 percent more than the average university student. However, only 11 percent of the intervention students were judged to be alcohol-dependent, compared to 27 percent in the control group. Although they continued to have more alcohol-related problems than did a comparison group of average university students, the intervention group had far fewer alcohol-related problems than did the untreated high-risk group (Figure 15.26). Thus, despite the lack of an explicit focus on reducing drinking, the brief one-session intervention had significant positive effects. In particular, students learned to moderate their drinking when in potentially hazardous situations, thereby reducing harmful consequences.

Changing health-related and substance abuse behaviours is challenging. That is why advances from theory development and research are such important foundations for interventions, and why program evaluations provide important information on how to make them better. Moreover, given the widespread nature of health-endangering behaviours, even modest increases in success are socially significant. For example, an estimated 18 million people try to quit smoking each year (Wetter et al., 1998). Even if an improved intervention results in an increase of only 10 percent in the success rate, this translates into 1.8 million additional people (plus those affected by their second-hand smoke) whose health and life expectancy are positively affected.

41. What methods and outcomes occurred in Marlatt et al.'s alcohol harm reduction study with high-risk university students?

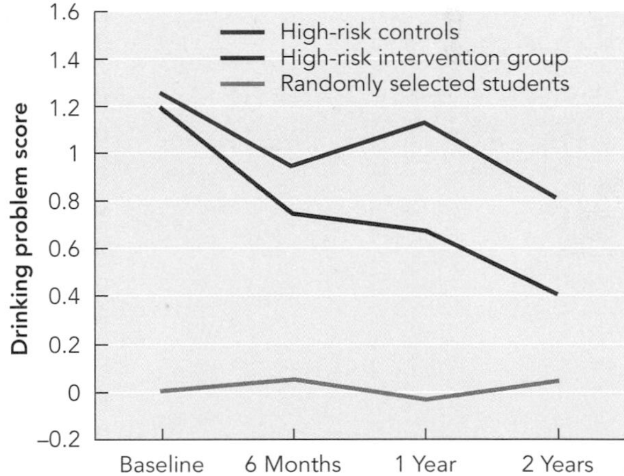

FIGURE 15.26

Effects of a brief harm reduction intervention based on motivational interviewing. One year and two years after the intervention, high-risk drinkers who underwent the program still reported more alcohol-related problems than the average university student, but fewer than the high-risk drinkers in the control group.

Data from Marlatt et al., 1998.

In Review

- *The transtheoretical model identifies six stages through which people may move during the process of successful long-term behavioural change: precontemplation, contemplation, preparation, action, maintenance, and termination. The model has inspired stage-matched interventions focused on the individual's current stage, with the intent of moving the person to the action, maintenance, and termination stages.*
- *Exercise is an important health-enhancing behaviour that affects both physical and psychological well-being. Numerous behavioural interventions have been developed to promote exercise, but many people fail to adhere to exercise programs. One factor that influences adherence is social support. People who are able to stick with it for three to six months have a better chance of adhering thereafter.*
- *About a third of the North American population is obese, as are one in six children and adolescents. Behavioural weight-control programs feature self-monitoring, stimulus control procedures, and eating procedures designed to help people eat less but enjoy it more. The addition of an exercise program to weight-control procedures enhances weight loss.*
- *Because HIV infection is caused by high-risk sexual and drug-abuse behaviours (e.g., sharing needles), a prevention approach is essential. Behavioural changes have been accomplished in homosexual populations, and efforts are centring on high-risk heterosexual populations, such as teenagers. Cultural factors sometimes conflict with safe sex practices, increasing the challenges of reducing health-endangering behaviours.*
- *Substance abuse is highly associated with other disorders and is often part of a larger pattern of maladjustment. Multimodal treatments combine a number of techniques, including aversion training, stress-management and coping-skills training, and positive reinforcement for change. A promising new approach is motivational interviewing, a nonconfrontational procedure designed to engage the person's own motivation to change self-defeating behaviours.*
- *Relapse prevention is designed to keep lapses from becoming relapses by building effective coping skills to deal with high-risk situations and countering the abstinence violation effect when lapses occur. This approach enhances the effects of many behaviour-change programs.*
- *Harm-reduction approaches attempt to reduce the negative consequences that a behaviour produces rather than to focus on stopping the behaviour itself. Examples include needle exchange programs for drug addicts and programs designed to reduce the destructive consequences of binge drinking in university students.*

PAIN AND PAIN MANAGEMENT

In this chapter we have discussed stress, coping, health, and substance abuse; all of which have clear links with pain and pain management. Pain can be both a source of stress and a reaction to stress. For example, if someone is experiencing severe pain, the pain itself can act as a stressor and activate all of the stress-related mechanisms we discussed earlier in this chapter. Stress can also cause pain. Many of us have had the experience of being so psychologically stressed by interpersonal problems, public speaking, a job interview, or an important examination that we experience actual physical pain, such as a headache or abdominal pains. For example, the first time that I stood in front of an audience to talk about my research, I had both a headache and a sore stomach; you may have experienced the same when giving an in-class oral presentation. Pain management is also an important topic in health psychology. Half of all adults in North America suffer from back pain and 10 percent from severe headaches (Baum et al., 1997). Pain is a significant feature of many illnesses, and some form of pain is responsible for a staggering 80 percent of all medical complaints in North America and Europe (Salovey et al., 2000).

Pain, however, serves an important survival function. It acts as a warning signal when the body is being threatened or has suffered damage. If your knee begins to hurt as you sit reading this chapter it is a warning that you are putting too much pressure on that joint and you should shift your body position to avoid damage to your knee. Pain can trigger a variety of behavioural reactions that help us cope with the threat, whether the reaction is shifting your posture to redistribute the pressure on your joints or going to see a doctor. Pain tells us that something is wrong and that we need to react; its extreme unpleasantness insures that we will react.

On the surface, pain may seem a purely sensory phenomenon and you may wonder why it is of interest to psychologists (and why it is in "the stress chapter" and not in Chapter 5, Sensation and Perception). When we examine it more carefully, however, we see that pain is a complex phenomenon that involves the operation of numerous psychological processes, and that it is inextricably linked to stress, health, and coping. For example, as studied by Ronald Melzack of McGill University, it is possible for people to experience excruciating pain in the absence of any real tissue damage (Melzack, 1998), or they may suffer severe physical injury but experience no pain (e.g., Fordyce, 1998). For all other sensory systems our perception of the sensory information can vary, but only within a limited range. If someone flashes a light in your eyes, you will see it. But whether or not your flu shot hurt depends on many factors such as whether or not you expected it to hurt, not just on the skill of the nurse wielding the needle. Pain is a sensory phenomenon but, as we will explore in the following sections, it is also much more.

Biological Mechanisms of Pain

With the exception of the brain, bones, hair, nails, and nonliving parts of the teeth, pain receptors are found in all body tissues. Nerve endings in the skin and internal organs respond to intense mechanical, thermal, or chemical stimulation, and then send nerve impulses into the spinal cord, where sensory tracts carry pain information to the brain. Once in the brain, the sensory information about pain intensity and location is relayed by the thalamus to the somatosensory and frontal areas of the cerebral cortex (Zubieta & Stohler, 2002). Other tracts from the thalamus direct nerve impulses to the limbic system, which is involved in motivation and emotion. These tracts seem to control the emotional component of pain (Melzack, 1998). Thus pain has both a sensory and an emotional component. *Suffering* occurs when both painful sensations and a negative emotional response are present (Fordyce, 1988; Turk, 2001).

?

42. How does gate control theory explain pain perception and control?

Gate Control Theory

Gate control theory, developed by McGill University psychologist Ronald Melzack and physiologist Patrick Wall (1982), was a major advance in the study of pain. **Gate control theory** proposes that the experience of pain results from the opening and closing of "gating mechanisms" in the nervous system. Briefly, sensations from two types of sensory fibres enter the spinal cord, where they can activate neurons that travel up toward the brain regions responsible for our perception of pain. Some of the sensory fibres are very thin in diameter, whereas others are thicker. The thin fibres carry sharp-pain impulses; the thick fibres convey dull-pain and touch information. Whether we experience pain depends partly on the ratio of thin-to-thick fibre transmission. Relatively high levels of thin-fibre activity open a system of spinal cord "gates" and allow the nerve impulses to travel toward the brain, whereas thick-fibre activity closes the gates.

It follows, then, that our perception of pain can be decreased by increasing thick-fibre nerve impulses. This explains why rubbing a bruise or scratching an itch, both of which stimulate primarily thick fibres, produces relief. Gate control theorists also suggest that acupuncture achieves its pain-relieving effects because the acupuncture needles stimulate mostly thick fibres, thereby closing the pain gates (Figure 15.27).

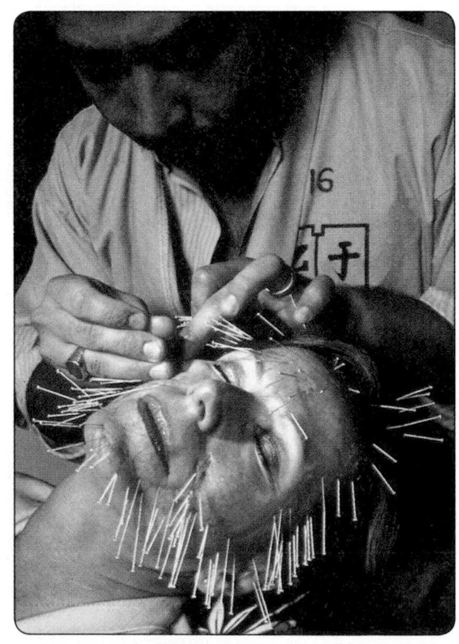

FIGURE 15.27

Acupuncture is a proven pain-reduction procedure. Gate control theory attributes its effects to the stimulation of thick sensory fibres. There is also evidence that acupuncture stimulates endorphin release.

From a psychological perspective, perhaps the most intriguing feature of gate control theory is that nerve impulses in fibres descending from the brain can also influence the spinal gates, thereby increasing or decreasing the flow of "pain" stimulation to the brain. This *central control mechanism* allows thoughts, emotions, and beliefs to influence the experience of pain and helps explain why pain is a psychological phenomenon as well as a physical one. Gate control theory has been valuable in suggesting techniques for pain control and in stimulating research on psychological factors in pain (Turk & Melzack, 2001).

The Endorphins

In 1680 an English physician wrote, "Among the remedies which it has pleased Almighty God to give man to relieve his suffering, none is so universal and so efficacious as opium" (quoted in Snyder, 1977). Opiates (such as opium, morphine, and heroin) have been used for centuries to relieve pain, and they strongly affect the brain's pain and pleasure systems. In the 1970s, scientists discovered that opiates produce their effects by locking into specific receptor sites in brain regions associated with pain perception.

43. How do endorphins influence pain perception and physical well-being?

But why would the brain have built-in receptors for opiates unless there was some natural chemical in the brain for the receptor to receive? Later research disclosed what had to be true: The nervous system has its own built-in analgesics (painkillers) with opiate-like properties. These natural opiates were named **endorphins** (meaning endogenous, or internally produced, morphines). Endorphins exert some of their pain-killing effects by inhibiting the release of neurotransmitters involved in the synaptic transmission of pain impulses from the spinal cord to the brain (Fessler, 1989). Some endorphins are enormously potent. One of the brain endorphins isolated by scientists is more than 200 times more powerful than morphine (Franklin, 1987). Endorphins are of great interest to psychologists because they may help explain how psychological factors "in the head" can have such strong effects on pain and suffering.

In 2001, John-Kar Zubieta and co-workers published a landmark study that showed the endorphins in action within the brain. They injected a radioactive form of an endorphin into volunteer participants, then stimulated them with painful injections of salt water into the jaw muscles. Brain scans allowed the researchers to see which areas of the brain "lit up" from endorphin activity and to relate this activity to pain reports given by the participants every 15 seconds. The scans revealed a surge of endorphin activity within several brain regions, including the thalamus (the sensory "switchboard"), the amygdala (an emotion centre), and a sensory area of the cortex. As the endorphin surge continued over 20 minutes of pain stimulation, participants reported decreased sensory and emotional ratings of pain.

Two other findings were noteworthy. First, people differed in their pain experiences despite identical pain stimulation. Second, these differences were linked to variations in (1) the number of opioid receptors the participants had for the endorphins to bind to and (2) their own ability to release endorphins. Thus biological as well as psychological factors seem to underlie differences in people's ability to tolerate pain (Zubieta et al., 2001).

Acupuncture is a pain-reduction technique that may ultimately be understood in terms of endorphin mechanisms. Injections of *naloxone,* a drug that counteracts the effects of endorphins, greatly decrease the pain-reducing effects of acupuncture (Oleson, 2002). This suggests that acupuncture normally releases endorphins.

Another phenomenon attributable to endorphins is **stress-induced analgesia**, a reduction in—or absence of—perceived pain that occurs under stressful conditions. For example, research has shown that about 65 percent of soldiers wounded during combat report having felt no pain at the time of their injury (Warga, 1987). Likewise, people involved in accidents are sometimes unaware of serious injuries until the crisis is over. This analgesic response could be highly adaptive. In a life-threatening situation, fight-or-flight defensive behaviour must be given immediate priority over normal responses to pain, which typically involve immobility. By reducing or preventing pain sensations through the mechanism of endorphin release, stress-induced analgesia helps suppress these pain-related behaviours so that the person or animal can get on with the actions that are needed for immediate survival, such as fleeing, fighting, or getting help (Fanselow, 1991). As an example, consider the report of a man who was so severely bitten during an attack by a grizzly bear that he required more than 200 stitches:

> I had read the week before about someone who was killed and eaten by a grizzly bear. So I was thinking that this bear was going to eat me unless I got away. I did not have time for pain. I was fighting for my life. It was not until the next day that I started feeling pain and fear. (Kolb & Whishaw, 2001, p. 386)

The release of endorphins seems to be part of the body's natural response to stress, but we may pay a price for this temporary relief from pain. It appears that chronically high levels of endorphin release help block the activity of immune system cells that recognize and selectively kill tumour cells. This may be one way in which stress makes us more susceptible to serious illnesses such as cancer (Shavit, 1990).

Cultural and Psychological Influences on Pain

As a complex perception, pain is influenced by numerous factors. Cultural learning, meanings attributed to pain, beliefs, and personality factors all affect our experiences of pain.

Cultural Factors

Our interpretation of pain impulses sent to the brain depends in part on our experiences and beliefs, and both of these factors are influenced by the culture in which we develop (Rollman, 1998; 2003a). Consider, for example, the experience of childbirth. This event is widely perceived as a painful ordeal in Western cultures, and many women express considerable anxiety about going through it (Blechman & Brownell, 1998). Yet in some cultures, women show virtually no distress during childbirth. Indeed, in one culture studied by anthropologists, it was customary for the woman's husband to get into bed and groan as if he were in great pain while the woman calmly gave birth to the child. The husband stayed in bed with the baby to recover from his terrible ordeal while the mother returned to work in the fields almost immediately (Kroeber, 1948).

44. How do cultural factors influence pain experience and behaviour?

Are there any general sex differences in pain perception? Women and girls report pain more frequently than men and boys, and are more often treated for pain-related disorders. While a number of studies in the animal literature suggest a biological base for this difference (e.g., Turner et al, 2003), we must be cautious when considering humans (Negus et al., 2004). Any human sex differences in pain perception are most likely due to both biological and psychosocial factors (Myers et al., 2003; Rollman, 2003b).

45. How do cognitive and personality factors affect people's responses to pain stimuli?

Certain societies in India practise an unusual hook-hanging ritual. A holy person, chosen to bless children and crops, travels from village to village on a special ceremonial cart. Large steel hooks, attached by ropes to the top of the cart, are shoved under the skin and muscles on each side of the holy person's back. At the climax of the ceremony, he leaps from the cart and swings free, hanging only by the hooks embedded in his back (Figure 15.28). Incredibly, though hanging from the hooks with his entire body weight, the celebrant shows no evidence of pain during the ritual; on the contrary, he appears to be in a state of ecstasy. When the hooks are removed, the wounds heal rapidly and are scarcely visible within two weeks (Kosambi, 1967).

FIGURE 15.28

Illustration of a hook-hanging ceremony practised in remote villages in India. After blessing all the children and farm fields in a village, the celebrant leaps from the cart and hangs suspended by the hooks in a state of ecstasy, showing no sign of pain.

Source: Based on Kosambi, 1967.

Although ethnic groups do not appear to differ in their ability to discriminate among pain stimuli, members of different cultural groups may differ greatly in their interpretation of pain and the amount of suffering they experience (Rollman, 1998; Zatzick & Dimsdale, 1990). In the Indian hook-hanging ceremony, for example, the religious meanings attached to the act seem to transform the interpretations and meaning of the sensory input from the hooks. Likewise, childbearing mothers in cultures where the pain of childbirth is not feared do not attach strong negative emotions to the associated sensations, and they therefore suffer far less.

The role of cultural factors in pain perception is found even within modern Western subcultures. In a study done in Massachusetts, researchers studied pain perception in 372 medical patients who represented six different ethnic groups: "Old Americans" (at least third-generation U.S.-born Caucasians who identified with no ethnic group except "Americans"), Hispanic Americans, Italian Americans, Irish Americans, French Canadians, and Polish Americans. All of the patients suffered from chronic pain conditions that had persisted for at least three months and were beyond the point of healing. The patients completed self-report measures about their pain experiences.

The ethnic groups did not differ overall in type of physical affliction, how long they had had it, or the kinds of treatments and medications they were receiving. They did differ, however, in the pain levels they reported, and these differences were associated with different attitudes and beliefs about their pain. The Hispanic American and Italian American patients believed most strongly that they had no control over their pain, reported feeling worried and angry about it, and believed that they would be unhappy as long as they experienced it. They also believed that it is appropriate to express one's pain openly. These two ethnic groups reported the highest levels of pain and suffering. In contrast, the Old American and Polish American patients felt it best to suppress the outward expression of pain, reported feeling less upset about their pain sensations, and believed that they had greater personal control over their lives. These attitudinal differences were associated with much lower levels of reported suffering (Bates et al., 1993).

Meanings and Beliefs

Differences exist not only between cultural groups but also within them, as physician Henry Beecher (1959) observed while working at Anzio Beachhead in World War II and later at Massachusetts General Hospital. At Anzio, Beecher found that only about 25 percent of the severely wounded soldiers he observed required pain medication, compared with 80 percent of civilian men who had received similarly serious "wounds" from surgeons at Massachusetts General. Why the difference? Beecher concluded that for the soldiers, the wounds had a fundamentally positive meaning: They spelled evacuation from the war zone and a socially acceptable "ticket back home" to their loved ones. For the civilian surgical patients, on the other hand, the operations meant a major life disruption and possible complications. The different meanings attributed to the pain stimuli resulted in very different levels of suffering and, consequently, different needs for pain relief.

Perhaps nowhere is the influence of belief on pain perception more evident than in the effects of **placebos**, substances that have no medicinal value but are thought by the patient to be helpful (Shapiro & Shapiro, 1997). In one classic study by Henry Beecher (1959), either a placebo or a morphine injection was given to 122 surgical patients who were suffering postoperative pain. All were told they were receiving pain medication. Of those who received morphine, 67 percent reported relief, but 42 percent of those given placebos reported equal relief. More recent medical studies of placebo effects have yielded even higher rates of pain relief, as high as 100 percent in some studies (Turner et al., 1994). However, it is also clear that placebos work only if people *believe* they are going to work. Research using PET-scan technology at the Karolinska Institute in Sweden indicates that given a positive belief in the placebo's effectiveness, the brain sends messages that result in the release of endorphins to reduce pain (Petrovic et al., 2002).

Where pain is concerned, the statement "I can control it" may be more than an idle boast or an empty reassurance. In one experiment, patients suffering from the prolonged pain of a bone-marrow transplant were randomly assigned to one of two conditions. One group was allowed to directly control the amount of pain medication that they received intravenously. The other patients were given prescribed amounts of the same medication by the hospital staff (and told they could request additional medication if needed). The patients who had direct control over their medication not only rated their pain as less intense but also gave themselves less pain medication (Zucker et al., 1998). As in the case of placebo effects, beliefs about personal control apparently exert their effects by increasing endorphin release. Naloxone injections, which counteract endorphin activity, sharply reduce the ability of people to endure intensely painful stimuli, no matter how high their confidence in their pain tolerance (Bandura et al., 1987).

Personality Factors and Social Support

Beginning with Sigmund Freud, personality theorists have suggested that emotional and personality factors can play a role in experiencing and responding to pain. Pain and suffering can be a way of attaining certain goals. For some bitter and deprived people, pain can be a way of dramatizing their unhappiness; eliciting caring, sympathy, or guilt from others; or gaining favours. Pain may also be a way of escaping from or avoiding threatening situations. For example, an athlete who dreads the possibility of failing may avoid the feared competition by experiencing severe pain that prevents participation. This coping process can occur at a subconscious level that is different from consciously faking being hurt (May & Sieb, 1987).

People who have the personality trait of *neuroticism,* the tendency to experience negative emotions such as anxiety and depression, report higher levels of physical pain, both in relation to medical conditions and in controlled laboratory administrations of painful stimuli such as heat, cold, electrical shock, or pressure (Turner & Aaron, 2001). In contrast, personality styles that include optimism and a sense of personal control over one's life are associated with lower pain perception and less suffering (Pellino & Ward, 1998). Moreover, patients with chronic pain conditions who are able to simply accept the pain rather than bemoaning their fate and responding emotionally to it have less disability, better social adjustment, and higher work performance (McCracken, 1998). Thus it seems clear that psychological factors play important roles in pain perception and adaptation.

Further evidence that one's emotional state and social support network are associated with one's experience of pain comes from a study by Carmen Alonso and Christopher Coe (2001). In a sample of 184 university women, the researchers found that self-reported depression and anxiety were strongly associated with ratings of menstrual pain. More significantly, perhaps, the greatest pain and distress occurred in women who had recently lost a significant source of social support.

The fact that psychological processes are so central to the experience of pain has stimulated many health psychologists to research methods that can be used to control or reduce pain and suffering. The following section highlights work on this new frontier.

Psychological Techniques for Controlling Pain and Suffering

We all occasionally experience physical pain, and for some people, pain is a never-ending nightmare. In recent years, psychological pain-control strategies have received increasing attention from health psychologists (Turk, 2001).

Cognitive Strategies

Recent attention has focused on two classes of cognitive strategies known as *dissociation* and *association.* A *dissociative strategy* involves dissociating, or distracting, oneself from the painful sensory input. This can be done in a variety of ways: by directing your attention to some other feature of the external situation, by vividly imagining a pleasurable experience, or by repeating a word or thought to yourself. Research has shown that dissociative strategies are most effective when they require a great deal of concentration or mental activity, thereby directing attention away from the painful stimuli.

If you are a recreational jogger or a long-distance runner, you may be familiar with the discomfort of extending yourself. Endurance running seems an ideal real-life task to use in the study of cognitive strategies. William Morgan and co-workers (1983) gave this simple dissociate strategy to participants who were running on a treadmill to exhaustion: "Focus your attention on a spot in front of you on the treadmill and say 'Down' each time your right foot comes down on the treadmill." A control group also ran the treadmill but did not receive the strategy. Although the two groups did not differ physiologically while running the treadmill, the mental-strategy group was able to tolerate the discomfort of treadmill running 32 percent longer than the control group.

A more dramatic, high-tech dissociative strategy is being tested in the burn centre at the Harborview Medical Center in Seattle, Washington. There children and adults with burns covering up to 60 percent of their bodies are donning virtual-reality goggles during the often agonizing processes of wound cleansing and physical therapy. The goggles take patients into a visually compelling world of shapes and colours. Pain ratings are significantly lower when these patients are immersed in virtual reality than when they are in a nondistracted condition (Hoffman et al., 2001).

Associative strategies are just the opposite of dissociative ones. Here you focus your attention on the physical sensations and study them in a detached and unemotional fashion, taking care not to label them as painful or difficult to tolerate. It appears that when pain is intense, associative strategies become more effective than dissociative ones (McCaul & Malott, 1984). There seems to be a point at which pain stimuli become too intense to ignore and dissociative strategies become ineffective.

Thus one strategy is to use dissociation as long as possible and then shift to an associative mode when the pain becomes too intense to permit distraction.

Combined dissociative and associative strategies can be quite effective in dealing with acute pain. In one study, participants' pain tolerance was tested by measuring how long they could keep their hand immersed in ice water. One group of participants was then trained and practised a number of dissociative coping strategies (such as attention diversion and the use of distracting imagery) and associative strategies (such as imagining that the hand immersed in the ice water was detached from the body and focusing nonemotionally on the pain sensations). Two control groups equated in initial pain tolerance were given either no strategies or a placebo "pain reducer." Then their ice-water pain tolerance was tested a second time. As shown in Figure 15.29, the cognitive skills training resulted in a large increase in pain tolerance (Bandura et al., 1987).

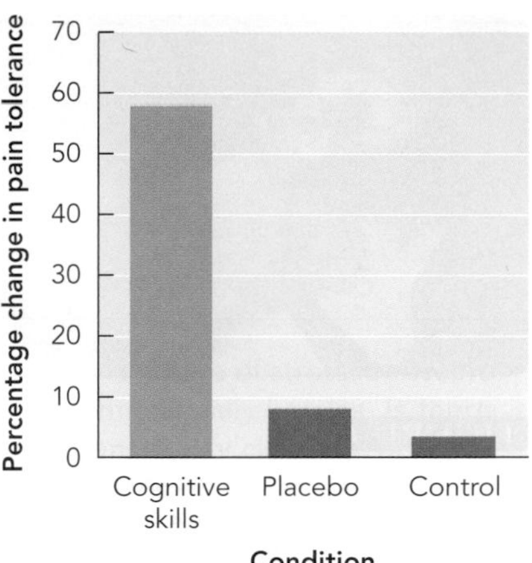

FIGURE 15.29

Increases in pain tolerance (ice water hand-immersion task) shown by a cognitive-skills training group, a placebo condition, and a control group that repeated the task with no intervention.

Source: Based on Bandura et al., 1987.

Hospital Interventions: Giving Patients Informational Control

Having relevant information about a challenging environment and event is also a kind of cognitive control, since it tells us what to expect. In the medical setting of the past, doctors typically gave patients no more information than "needed" about the medical procedure and its aftermath. However, psychological research on how certain types of information reduce anxiety and contribute to positive medical outcomes has ushered in a new era in many medical settings.

Imagine that you're in the hospital for major surgery. You know that this surgical procedure entails risk and that your recovery will be painful. What kinds of information would help you cope and recuperate more easily?

You might profit from *sensory information* about what you will feel after the operation. Knowing, for example, that patients often have shooting pains in their stomach after the surgery could prevent surprise or fear if it occurred to you. You would see the pain as a normal consequence of the surgery and the recovery process rather than as a sign of danger.

Second, *procedural information* on the surgery itself would help you understand what exactly is going to be done and why. You might be shown a model of the body part to demonstrate what will be done in the surgery, or you may see a video describing the procedure. This kind of information would give you a sense of predictability and control and reassure you that precautions were being taken to anticipate and reduce possible hazards.

Third, you could profit from *coping guidance* about handling the pain or other complications from the surgery. For example, you might learn breathing exercises designed to reduce pain by helping you relax (Tollison et al., 2002). You might also be taught some of the cognitive strategies previously described to get through sieges of acute pain during the recovery process.

Informational interventions have proved helpful in many medical settings. Surgical patients show better courses of recovery and require less pain medication than those treated in a traditional fashion (Faust, 1991). Such interventions have proven particularly successful in decreasing distress in hospitalized children, who are likely to find major medical procedures particularly frightening (Christopherson & Mortweet, 2001).

A Key Behavioural Strategy: Becoming Active Again

Recovering patients who avoid activity and become overly protective of an injured body part are at risk for developing a chronic pain condition (Turk, 2001). It is important to return to activity after an injury as soon as the healing process will

person's behaviour say something about her or him, or is it caused by the situation? Other factors, however, also affect how we form and maintain impressions.

Primacy versus Recency: Are First Impressions More Important?

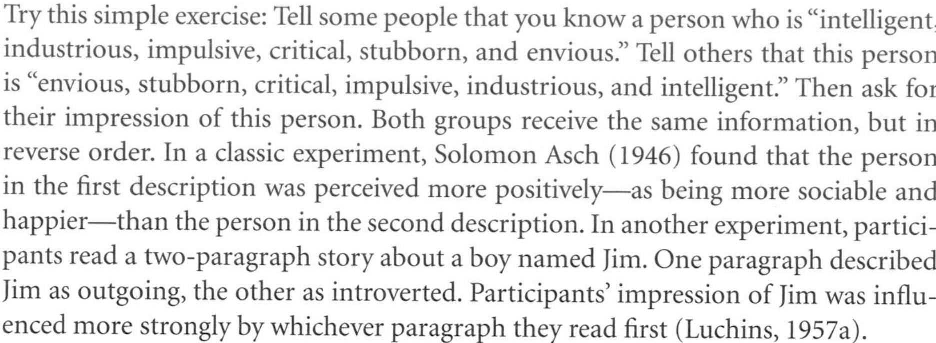

Try this simple exercise: Tell some people that you know a person who is "intelligent, industrious, impulsive, critical, stubborn, and envious." Tell others that this person is "envious, stubborn, critical, impulsive, industrious, and intelligent." Then ask for their impression of this person. Both groups receive the same information, but in reverse order. In a classic experiment, Solomon Asch (1946) found that the person in the first description was perceived more positively—as being more sociable and happier—than the person in the second description. In another experiment, participants read a two-paragraph story about a boy named Jim. One paragraph described Jim as outgoing, the other as introverted. Participants' impression of Jim was influenced more strongly by whichever paragraph they read first (Luchins, 1957a).

3. Why do primacy effects occur in impression formation? How can they be reduced?

When forming impressions, the **primacy effect** refers to our tendency to attach more importance to the initial information that we learn about a person. New information can change our opinion, but it has to "work harder" to overcome that initial impression for two reasons. First, we tend to be most alert to information we receive first. Second, initial information may shape how we perceive subsequent information. Imagine a student and an athlete who, respectively, get off to a great start in class or in training camp. The teacher and the coach attribute high ability to these people, but, suppose that as time goes on, performance declines. To maintain their positive initial impression, the teacher and coach need only attribute the performance decline to fatigue, a drop in motivation, or a string of bad breaks.

Primacy is the general rule of thumb in impression formation, especially for people who dislike ambiguity and uncertainty (Kruglanski & Webster, 1996). We seem to have a remarkable capacity for forming snap judgments based on small amounts of initial information, and some evolutionary psychologists propose that evaluating stimuli quickly (such as rapidly distinguishing friend from foe) was adaptive for our survival (Krebs & Denton, 1997). But we are not slaves to primacy. Primacy effects decrease—and *recency effects* (giving greater weight to the most recent information) may occur—when we are asked to avoid making snap judgments, are reminded to carefully consider the evidence, and are made to feel accountable for our judgments (Luchins, 1957b; Webster et al., 1996).

Mental Sets and Schemas: Seeing What We Expect to See

Imagine that we are going to a party and I tell you that the host, George, is a distant, aloof, cold person. You meet him and try to make pleasant conversation. George doesn't say much in response to your questions, avoids eye contact, and doesn't ask you about your life. A bit later, you say to me, "You were right, he's really a cold fish." Now let's roll back this scene. Suppose that I had described George as nice, but extremely shy. Later, when you try to make conversation, he doesn't say much, avoids eye contact, and doesn't ask you about your life. You say to me, "You were right, he's really shy." Same behaviour, different impression. This example reminds us of a key perceptual principle highlighted in Chapter 5. Whether perceiving objects or people, the same stimulus can be "seen" in different ways. Our mental *set,* which is a readiness to perceive the world in a particular way, powerfully shapes how we interpret a stimulus (see Figure 5.2).

What creates our mental sets? One important factor that we have encountered throughout the book is *schemas,* mental frameworks that help us organize and interpret information. By telling you that our host is "cold," "shy," or "distracted," I activate a set of concepts and expectations (your schema) for how such a person is likely to behave. Although the host's behaviour can be interpreted in multiple ways, you "fit" his behaviour into the particular schema that is already activated.

4. How do mental sets shape the way we perceive people? How do stereotypes create mental sets?

A **stereotype**, which is a generalized belief about a group or category of people, represents a powerful type of schema. In one experiment, participants watched a videotape of a nine-year-old girl named Hannah and were asked to judge her academic potential. Half of the participants were told that Hannah came from an upper-middle-class environment and that her parents had white-collar careers. Other participants were told that Hannah came from a poor neighbourhood and that her parents were blue-collar workers. On the videotape, Hannah performed at an average level, answering some difficult questions and missing some others. Although all participants saw the same performance, those who thought Hannah came from an affluent setting rated her higher in ability than did those who thought she came from a disadvantaged background (Darley & Gross, 1983). In a real sense, participants' stereotypes about blue-collar and white-collar workers created a mental set that biased their perception of Hannah's subsequent behaviour.

Self-Fulfilling Prophecies: Creating What We Expect to See

5. Explain how our incorrect expectations can become self-fulfilling.

Seeing what we expect to see is only one way we confirm our initial expectations and impressions. A **self-fulfilling prophecy** occurs usually without conscious awareness, when people's erroneous expectations lead them to act toward others in a way that brings about the expected behaviours, thereby confirming the original impression. Returning to our "party" example, if you expect the host to be cold and aloof, your behaviour toward him may change in subtle ways. You make conversation, but perhaps smile less, stand further away, or give up a little earlier than you would have, had I told you he was a great guy. His reserved response, in part, could be a reaction to *your* behaviour (Figure 16.6).

Self-fulfilling prophecies have since been demonstrated in hundreds of studies across different countries and settings, including schools, business organizations, the military, sports, and dating and marital relationships (Eden & Greenberg, 2003; Meissner & Kassin, 2004; McNatt, 2000; Rosenthal, 1991; Snyder, 2001). In interacting with others, our initial, unfounded expectations can influence how we behave toward them, thereby shaping their behaviour in a way that ultimately confirms our expectations.

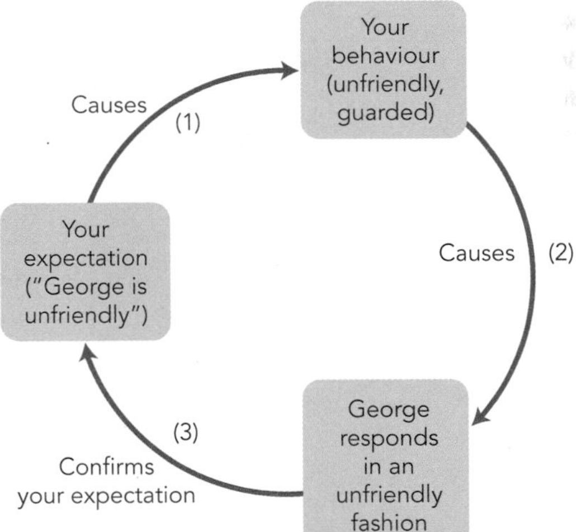

FIGURE 16.6

The self-fulfilling prophecy begins when a false expectation that we have about someone else influences how we treat that person. Next, influenced by our behaviour, the person responds in a particular way. Finally, we interpret the person's behaviour as evidence that our expectation was correct all along—unaware of the role that we played in shaping the person's behaviour.

Attitudes and Attitude Change

In 1935, Gordon Allport called attitude "social psychology's most indispensable concept" (p. 798). Our attitudes help define our identity, guide our actions, and influence how we judge people (Maio & Olson, 2000). Indeed, attitudes help steer the course of world events, from political elections to war to the latest fashion craze.

An **attitude** is a positive or negative evaluative reaction toward a stimulus, such as a person, action, object, or concept (Tesser & Shaffer, 1990). Whether disagreeing with a governmental policy or agreeing with a movie review, you are expressing evaluative reactions. Sometimes, as shown in Figure 16.7, our attitudes are supported by an extensive personal belief and value system.

Do Our Attitudes Influence Our Behaviour?

If we tell you that, according to research, people's attitudes strongly guide their behaviour, you might reply "So what? That's just common sense." But consider a

Reduces social discomfort
Eases studying
Friends dislike smoking
Smoking cigarettes
Health risks
Roommate dislikes smoking
Expensive
Makes you smell bad

FIGURE 16.7

The components of a person's attitude toward smoking. Around the attitude object (smoking) are beliefs related to smoking. The plus and minus signs show the positive or negative value the person associates with each belief. The minus sign in the centre indicates the resulting overall negative attitude toward smoking cigarettes.

Adapted from Sears et al., 1985.

classic study by Richard LaPiere (1934). In the 1930s he toured the United States with a young Chinese couple, stopping at 251 restaurants, hotels, and other establishments. At the time, prejudice against Asians was widespread, yet the couple—who often entered the establishment before LaPiere did—was refused service only once. Later LaPiere wrote to all the places they had visited, asking if they would provide service to Chinese patrons. More than 90 percent of those who responded stated they would not. In a similar study, Page (1999) reported that landlords in Windsor and London, Ontario, were less likely to want to rent to a potential tenant if that person identified himself or herself on the phone as an individual with AIDS.

In LaPiere's study we cannot be sure that the people who expressed negative attitudes in the survey were the same individuals who, months earlier, had actually served the Chinese couple. Yet the discrepancy between stated prejudicial attitudes and non-discriminatory behaviour seemed so overwhelming that it called into question the "common-sense" assumption of attitude-behaviour consistency. Better-controlled studies found similar results, and in a 1969 research review, Allen Wicker concluded that there was little evidence that attitudes predict behaviour.

6. Why did LaPiere's study raise doubts about attitude-behaviour consistency?

After this wake-up call psychologists explored the attitude-behaviour link in greater detail, leading Stephan Kraus (1995) to conclude in a more recent review that, overall, attitudes predict behaviour to a modest degree. Most importantly, we now understand three factors that help to explain why the attitude-behaviour relationship is strong in some cases, but weak in others.

First, attitudes influence behaviour more strongly when counteracting situational factors are weak. Financial incentives, conformity and obedience pressures, deindividuation, groupthink, and other conditions may lead people to behave in ways that are at odds with their inner convictions. According to the **theory of planned behaviour** and similar models (Ajzen, 1991; Fishbein, 1980), our intention to engage in a behaviour is strongest when we have a positive attitude toward that behaviour, when *subjective norms* (our perceptions of what other people think we should do) support our attitudes, and when we believe that the behaviour is under our control. Based on this approach researchers have successfully predicted numerous behaviours, including whether people will undergo breast cancer screenings, become smokers, use condoms, attend church, donate blood, and seek out therapy (Courneya et al., 1999; Armitage, 2005; Elliot et al., 2007; Yardley & Donovan-Hall, 2007; Rutter, 2000; Blanchard et al., 2002).

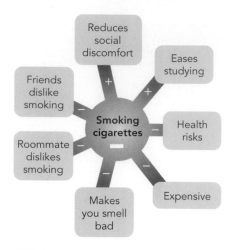

7. Discuss three broad conditions under which attitudes best predict behaviour.

Second, *attitudes have a greater influence on behaviour when we are aware of them and when they are strongly held.* Sometimes we seem to act "without thinking," out of impulse or habit. Attitude-behaviour consistency increases when people consciously think about their attitudes before acting (Powell & Fazio, 1984; White et al., 2002). In addition, attitudes are stronger and more predictive of behaviour when they are formed through direct personal experience, rather than through second-hand, indirect information (Millar & Millar, 1996).

Third, *general attitudes are better at predicting general classes of behaviour, and specific attitudes are better at predicting specific behaviours.* For example, Martin Fishbein and Icek Ajzen (1974) found almost no relation between people's general attitudes toward religion and 70 specific religious behaviours (such as the frequency of praying before meals or attending services). However, when they combined the 70 specific behaviours into a single "global index" of religious behaviour, the relation between general religious attitudes and overall religious behaviour was substantial. Similarly, Zanna, Olson, & Fazio (1980) found a general composite index of over 90 separate religious behaviours (referred to as a multiple-act behavioural criterion) was reasonably correlated with general attitudes ($r = 0.54$), whereas the correlation with specific behaviours was quite low ($r = .09$ to $.38$).

Does Our Behaviour Influence Our Attitudes?

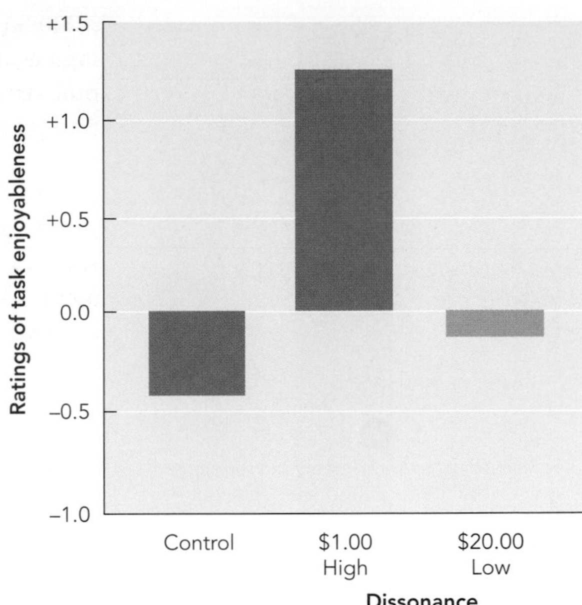

FIGURE 16.8

Participants lied to a fellow student by saying that a boring task was interesting. Those offered \$1 to lie later rated the task most positively. Presumably, they reduced their cognitive dissonance about lying by convincing themselves that the task was interesting after all. Participants offered \$20 had an external justification to lie, experienced little dissonance, and therefore did not need to convince themselves that the task was enjoyable. They and control participants who had not lied rated the task less favourably than did the \$1 group.

Based on Festinger & Carlsmith, 1959.

As we have just seen, under the proper conditions people's attitudes guide their behaviour. But attitude-behaviour consistency is not a one-way street: We also come to develop attitudes that are consistent with the way we behave. In the Stanford Prison Study, as the guards slipped into their roles and began mistreating the prisoners, they began to view the prisoners as little more than animals. Why should this be?

Self-justification. Imagine that you volunteer for an experiment, arrive at the laboratory, and perform two extremely boring tasks, emptying and filling a tray with spools over and over, and repeatedly turning 48 pegs stuck into holes. After 60 minutes of the laboratory equivalent of being bitten to death by ducks, the experimenter enters, thanks you for participating, and asks for your help. You are told that it is important for the next student to begin the study with a "positive attitude" about the tasks, and that all you have to do is tell the student that the boring tasks are interesting. Depending upon the condition to which you have been randomly assigned, the experimenter offers to pay you either \$1 or \$20 for, essentially, lying to the next participant. To help out, you agree to do so. Afterward, you go to the psychology department's main office to collect your money and fill out a "routine form" that asks how much you enjoyed the tasks in the experiment.

Make a prediction: Comparing participants who received \$1 and those who received \$20 with a control group that simply rated the boring tasks without telling any lie beforehand, which of the three groups rated the task most positively? Why?

Common sense might suggest that participants paid \$20 would feel happiest about the experiment and rate the task most highly. However, as Figure 16.8 shows, and as Leon Festinger and J. Merrill Carlsmith (1959) predicted, participants who were paid \$1 gave the most positive ratings. Indeed, they actually rated the boring tasks as slightly enjoyable!

According to Festinger's (1957) **theory of cognitive dissonance**, people strive for consistency in their cognitions. When two or more cognitions contradict one another (such as "I am a truthful person" and "I just told another student that those boring tasks were interesting"), the person experiences an uncomfortable state of tension that Festinger calls *cognitive dissonance,* and becomes motivated to reduce this dissonance.

The theory predicts that, in order to reduce dissonance and restore a state of cognitive consistency, people will change one of their cognitions or add new cognitions. Participants who received \$20 could justify their behaviour by adding a new cognition "Who wouldn't tell a little lie for \$20?"—and there was little reason for them to change their attitude toward the boring tasks. Those who had lied for only \$1 could not use this trivial monetary gain to justify their behaviour. But, if they could convince themselves that the tasks were actually enjoyable, then they wouldn't have lied after all! In short, they changed their attitude about the task to bring it more into line with how they had behaved.

8. What causes cognitive dissonance, and how can it produce attitude change?

Behaviour that is inconsistent with our attitude is called *counterattitudinal* behaviour, and it produces dissonance only if we perceive that our actions were freely chosen, rather than coerced. Dissonance is maximized when the behaviour threatens our sense of self-worth or produces negative consequences that were foreseeable (Stone & Cooper, 2001; Petty & Wegener, 1998; Steele, 1988).

Dissonance, however, does not always lead to attitude change. People can reduce dissonance by rationalizing that their attitude or their behaviour wasn't important, by finding external justification, or by making other excuses (Buunk & Dijkstra, 2001; Stalder & Baron, 1998; Gosling et al., 2006). In surveys of over

3,300 Scandinavian adolescents and adults, people who drank alcohol despite having negative attitudes toward drinking often emphasized that "Other people drink more than I do." As researcher Klaus Mäkelä (1997) noted, the general rationalization seemed to be "I may not be perfect, but other people are still worse."

Despite the many ways to reduce dissonance, the theory has successfully inspired researchers to change people's attitudes by inducing them to engage in counterattitudinal behaviours. For example, university students who agree to write essays advocating positions opposite to their own (such as supporting a tuition increase) often shift their attitudes in the direction of the essay they have produced (Croyle & Cooper, 1983; Stalder & Baron, 1998). Mediators in labour disputes occasionally use this principle by asking company executives and labour leaders to switch roles for a time and present each other's arguments.

9. According to self-perception theory, why does counterattitudinal behaviour produce attitude change?

Self-perception. If we observe someone campaigning for a political candidate, we likely will assume that this person has a positive attitude toward the candidate. If we see someone exerting great effort to achieve a goal, we will judge, logically, that the goal is important to that person. In short, we infer what other people's attitudes "must be" by watching how they behave. According to Daryl Bem's (1972) **self-perception theory**, we make inferences about our own attitudes in much the same way: by observing how *we* behave. Knowing that, for very little external justification ($1), you have told a fellow student that the boring experimental tasks are enjoyable, you logically conclude that "deep down" you *must* feel that the tasks were at least somewhat enjoyable. In Bem's view, your attitude is not produced by a mysterious concept called "cognitive dissonance." Rather, you simply observe how you have acted, and infer how you *must* have felt to have behaved in this fashion.

10. What evidence supports dissonance theory? What evidence favours self-perception theory?

Self-perception theory and cognitive dissonance theory both predict that counterattitudinal behaviour will produce attitude change. How can we determine which theory more accurately explains the reason behind such attitude change? One key difference is that dissonance theory assumes that we experience heightened physiological arousal (tension produced by dissonance) when we engage in counterattitudinal behaviour. Do we? At least in some instances, it appears so (Elliot & Devine, 1994). In one study, university students consumed an unpleasant-tasting drink and then were asked to write a sentence stating that they liked the taste. Students who were given a high degree of choice about whether to write this counterattitudinal statement showed higher arousal and greater attitude change than participants who were told simply to generate such arguments (Harmon-Jones et al., 1996).

Moreover, if unpleasant arousal motivates attitude change, then factors that reduce arousal should reduce attitude change. When research participants experience arousal from dissonance-producing behaviours but are led to believe that their arousal is a side effect caused by a pill (which in reality is a placebo), they do not change their attitudes to be more in line with their behaviour (Cooper, 1998; Zanna & Cooper, 1974). The pill gives participants an external justification (albeit a false one) for their arousal.

These and other findings indicate that dissonance theory better explains why people change their views after behaving in ways that openly contradict their clearly defined attitudes, particularly when such behaviours threaten one's self-image. However, in situations in which counterattitudinal behaviour does not threaten one's self-worth and we have weak attitudes to begin with, such behaviour is less likely to create significant arousal—yet people still may alter their attitudes to be more consistent with the way they have behaved. In this case, self-perception theory may provide the better explanation. Thus, both dissonance theory and self-perception theory appear to be correct, but under different circumstances (Fazio et al., 1977; Tesser & Shaffer, 1990). Both theories, however, agree that *our behaviours can influence our attitudes.*

Persuasion

Whether through political speeches, advertisements, or discussions with family and friends, persuasion is a fact of everyday life (Maio & Olson, 2000). Persuasion involves a *communicator* who delivers a *message* through a *channel* (e.g., in writing, verbally, or visually) to an *audience* within a surrounding *context* (e.g., a cultural setting) (Petty & Cacioppo, 1986). Here, we briefly examine three components that have been studied extensively.

11. Identify communicator and message characteristics that increase persuasiveness.

The communicator. **Communicator credibility**—how believable the communicator is—often is the key to effective persuasion. In fact, audience members who do not enjoy thinking deeply about issues may pay little attention to the content of a message and simply go along with the opinions of a highly credible source (Chaiken & Maheswaran, 1994). Credibility has two major components: *expertise* and *trustworthiness.* The most effective persuader is one who appears both to be an expert and to be presenting the truth in an unbiased manner (Hovland et al., 1953), as well as one who advocates a point of view contrary to his or her own self-interest (Petty et al., 2001). Perceived expertise may be particularly important when the issue is complex (Cooper et al., 1996; Cooper & Neuhaus, 2000).

Communicators who are physically attractive, likable, and similar to us (such as in interests or goals) also may persuade us more effectively, which is why advertisers spend millions of dollars hiring likable, attractive stars to promote their products. But the positive impact of communicator characteristics—including credibility—tends to dissipate with time *if* we remember the message, but forget the messenger (Chaiken, 1987).

The message. In trying to persuade someone, is it more effective to present only your side of the issue, or also to present the opposition's arguments and then refute them? A meta-analysis indicates that, overall, the *two-sided refutational approach* is more effective (Allen, 1991). Especially when an audience initially disagrees with a message or is aware that there are two sides to the issue, a two-sided message will be perceived as less biased.

In stating your position to an audience that disagrees with you, should you "go for broke" and present extreme arguments, hoping that the audience will compromise by moving toward your position? Or should you present a position that is only moderately discrepant with their viewpoint? A highly credible communicator can afford to present a more discrepant viewpoint than a low-credibility communicator (Aronson et al., 1963), but in general, a *moderate degree of discrepancy* is more effective (Bochner & Insko, 1966).

Messages that attempt to persuade by arousing fear, such as those in Figure 16.9, can be effective under certain conditions (Wood, 2000). Overall, fear arousal works best when the message evokes *moderate fear*, and provides people with effective, feasible (i.e., low-cost) ways to reduce the threat (Johnson, 1991; Witte & Allen, 2000). If the message is too frightening, people may reduce their anxiety by simply denying the message or the communicator's credibility.

12. Describe the central and peripheral routes to persuasion. For whom is the central route more likely to be effective?

The audience. A message loaded with logical arguments and facts may prove highly persuasive to some people, yet fall flat on its face with others. According to Richard Petty and John Cacioppo (1986), there are two basic routes to persuasion. The **central route to persuasion** occurs when people think carefully about the message and are influenced because they find the arguments compelling. The **peripheral route to persuasion** occurs when people do not scrutinize the message, but are influenced mostly by other factors, such as a speaker's attractiveness or a message's emotional appeal. Attitude change that results from the central route tends to have a deeper foundation, lasts longer, and predicts future behaviour more successfully.

Under what conditions will we follow the central route? Petty and Cacioppo (1986) suggest that we tend to process a message more closely when it is personally relevant—when it actually will affect us in some way. Typically, high personal relevance or high involvement with an issue will result in central processing. But this is not always the case. One reason is that people differ in their *need for cognition.* Some enjoy analyzing issues; others prefer not to spend much mental effort (Cacioppo et al., 1983, 1996). People who have a high need for cognition tend to follow the central route to persuasion. In forming attitudes about consumer products, for example, they are influenced by information about product characteristics (Wood & Swait, 2002). In contrast, people with a low need for cognition are more strongly influenced by peripheral cues, such as the attractiveness of the person who endorses the product (Haugtvedt et al., 1992).

Sorrentino and his colleagues at the University of Western Ontario (e.g., Sorrentino, Bobocel, Gitta, Olson, & Hewitt, 1988) have reported also that people differ in their approach to new information. Those who are uncertainty-oriented look for information, particularly in situations that are new and unpredictable. In contrast, certainty-oriented individuals avoid such situations, particularly when the information is self-relevant. Thus, uncertainty-oriented people follow the central route when issues are personally relevant, but those who are certainty-oriented do not. In fact, they are more likely to rely on peripheral information when the information is self-relevant, and are more influenced by factors such as speaker attractiveness or expertise.

In Review

- *Consistency, distinctiveness, and consensus information jointly influence whether we make a personal or situational attribution for a particular act.*
- *The fundamental attribution error is the tendency to attribute other people's behaviour to personal factors while underestimating the role of situational factors. The self-serving bias is the tendency to attribute one's successes to personal factors and one's failures to situational factors.*
- *Although our impressions of people may change over time, our first impression generally carries extra weight. Stereotypes and schemas create mental sets that powerfully shape our impressions.*
- *Through self-fulfilling prophecies, our initially false expectations shape the way we act toward someone. In turn, this person responds to our behaviour in a way that confirms our initially false belief.*
- *Attitudes are evaluative judgments. They predict behaviour best when situational influences are weak, when the attitude is strong, and when we consciously think about our attitude.*
- *Our behaviour also influences our attitudes. Counterattitudinal behaviour is most likely to create cognitive dissonance when the behaviour is freely chosen and has negative implications for our sense of self-worth or produces foreseeable negative consequences.*
- *To reduce dissonance, we may change our attitude to become more consistent with how we have behaved. In situations where our attitudes are weak and counterattitudinal behaviour doesn't threaten our self-worth, we may change our attitudes through self-perception.*
- *Communicator, message, and audience characteristics influence the effectiveness of persuasion. Communicator credibility is highest when the communicator is perceived as expert and trustworthy. Fear-arousing communications may be effective if they arouse moderate to strong fear and suggest how to avoid the feared result. The central route to persuasion works best with listeners who have a high need for cognition; for those with a low cognition need, the peripheral route works better.*

SOCIAL INFLUENCE

Patricia, a novice piano player, makes more mistakes after her parents enter the room to listen to her practise. Shawn donates money to a charity after seeing his co-workers contribute. A guard at Abu Ghraib mistreats prisoners in much the same way as the student "guards" in Zimbardo's Stanford Prison Study. These diverse situations share one basic ingredient: They all involve social influence.

The Mere Presence of Others

13. Under what conditions does the mere presence of other people enhance or impair performance? Why?

Norman Triplett (1898) helped launch the field of social psychology by testing a deceptively simple hypothesis: The presence of others energizes performance. Triplett, who loved bicycle racing, analyzed the records of numerous competitions. In some races, cyclists performed individually against the clock; in other races of similar distance, they performed together in a "pack." As Triplett predicted, cyclists' average speed per mile was much faster in group races than in individual races. Next, in a laboratory experiment, Triplett had children perform a simple physical task as rapidly as they could, either alone or in the presence of another child (called a *coactor*) who independently performed the same task. Again, performance improved when people were in each other's presence (Triplett, 1898).

Many early studies replicated this finding; the *mere presence* of coactors or a passive, silent audience enhanced performance. Even ants carried more dirt when in the presence of other ants (Chen, 1937). Yet, other experiments found that performance on learning tasks worsened when coactors or an audience were present.

In 1965, Robert Zajonc proposed a theory to explain this seeming paradox. First, the mere physical presence of another person (or member of the same species) increases our arousal. Second, as arousal increases, we become more likely to perform whatever behaviour happens to be our *dominant response* (i.e., our most typical response) to that specific situation. When a task is difficult and complex, and we are first trying to learn it, our dominant response is to make errors. Therefore, performing in front of an audience or with coactors should impair performance. But when a task either is simple or is complex but well learned, our dominant response usually is to perform the task correctly. In these situations, performing in the presence of others enhances performance (Figure 16.9). This phenomenon is called **social facilitation**, an increased tendency to perform one's dominant response in the mere presence of others (Blascovich et al., 1999).

Social facilitation occurs in species ranging from cockroaches and fruit flies to rats and hens (Duncan et al., 1998; Thomas et al., 2002). Meta-analyzing the results of 241 studies involving almost 24,000 participants, Charles Bond and Linda Titus (1983) found that social facilitation produced small but reliable effects on human

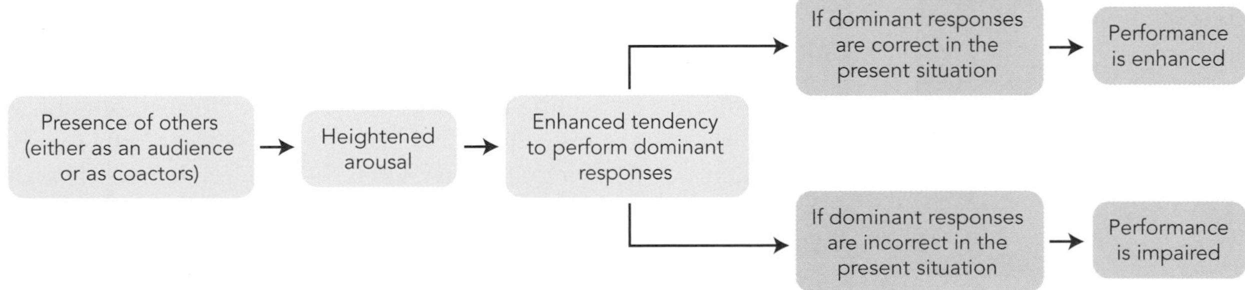

FIGURE 16.9

Social facilitation of dominant responses. Whether this pool player's performance improves or worsens when other people are watching depends on whether she is highly skilled or a novice (Michaels et al., 1982). Zajonc's (1965) theory of social facilitation proposes that the presence of other people increases our arousal, which then makes us more likely to perform our dominant responses. If a dominant response (e.g., stroking the pool cue in a particular way) happens to be correct—as typically occurs on simple tasks or complex tasks that have been mastered—then performance will be enhanced. But if a dominant response is incorrect—as often occurs when a novice is trying to learn a complex task—then the presence of other people most likely will impair performance.

performance. In one study, James Michaels and his colleagues (1982) identified pairs of pool players who had either above average or below average skill. Then four observers (researchers) sauntered over to the pool tables at the student union building to watch the players. As predicted, the presence of an audience improved the performance of the accomplished players (whose dominant responses were assumed to be correct), but worsened the performance of the less skilled players (whose dominant responses were assumed to be incorrect). Social facilitation may be the most basic of all social influence processes, and it has an important practical implication: When learning complex tasks, minimize the presence of other people.

Social Norms: The Rules of the Game

Years ago a professor we knew gave his class an unusual assignment: Without doing anything illegal, they were to violate some "unspoken rule" of social behaviour and observe people's reactions. One student licked her plate clean at a formal dinner, receiving cold stares from other guests. Another boarded a city bus, sat down next to the only other passenger, and said "Hi." The passenger sat up stiffly and stared out the window. The assignment ended when a third student entered class—attired only in a thin coat of oil.

14. How do norms and roles guide our behaviour?

Social norms are shared expectations about how people should think, feel, and behave, and they are the cement that binds social systems together (Morris et al., 2001). Some norms are formal laws and regulations, but many are implicit and unspoken. As the "break-a-norm" examples illustrate, such norms powerfully regulate daily behaviour without our conscious awareness; we take them for granted—until they are violated.

A **social role** consists of a set of norms that characterizes how people in a given social position ought to behave. The roles of "university student," "professor," "police officer," and "spouse" carry different sets of behaviour expectations. Because we may wear many hats in our daily life, *role conflict* can occur when the norms accompanying different roles clash. University students who hold jobs or who have children often experience role conflict as they try to juggle the competing demands of school, work, and parenthood.

Norms and roles can influence behaviour so strongly that they compel a person to act uncharacteristically. The guards in the Stanford Prison Study were well-adjusted students, yet norms related to the role of "guard" and to concepts of "crime and punishment" seemed to override their values, leading to dehumanizing treatment of the prisoners.

FIGURE 16.10

The evolution of norms across time and cultures. The Academy Award-winning movie Million Dollar Baby *portrayed an aspiring professional female boxer—an activity that women would be barred from in many countries, and that women were barred from decades ago in America.*

Culture and Norm Formation

Social norms lose invisibility not only when they are violated, but also when we examine behaviour across cultures and historical periods. In doing so, we see that social customs we take for granted as "*normal*"—from gender roles to sexual practices and views of love and marriage—are merely arbitrary (Figure 16.10). Norms regulate even such subtle aspects of social behaviour as the amount of *personal space* that we prefer when interacting with people (Li, 2001; Li & Li, 2007). For example, Japanese sit farther apart when conversing than Venezuelans do, and Americans prefer an intermediate distance (Sussman & Rosenfeld, 1982). Italians and Greeks are more likely to touch while interacting than are Europeans from more northern regions (Remland et al., 1995).

Indeed, it is difficult to imagine any society, organization, or social group functioning well without norms. In a classic experiment, Muzafer Sherif (1935) found that even randomly created groups develop norms. The task involved an optical illusion called the *autokinetic effect:* When people stare at a dot of light projected onto a screen in a dark room, they begin to perceive the dot as moving, even though it really is stationary. When Sherif tested university students individually over several trials, each student perceived the light moving a different amount, from a few centimetres to almost 30 centimetres.

Later, the students were randomly placed into groups of three and made further judgments. As the members within each group heard one another's judgments over several sessions, their judgments converged and a group norm evolved. The participants did not explicitly communicate or "decide" to develop a group norm; it just happened. Moreover, just as norms vary across cultures, the norm that evolved for how far the dot of light moved varied from group to group, and it was not the simple average of the original judgments (Figure 16.11). When participants were retested *individually* a year later, their judgments continued to reflect their group's norm (Rohrer et al., 1954).

Sherif's finding has been replicated in other countries and with different types of tasks (Khoury, 1985). Whether at a cultural level or in small random groups, humans placed together seem to develop common standards for behaviour and judgment.

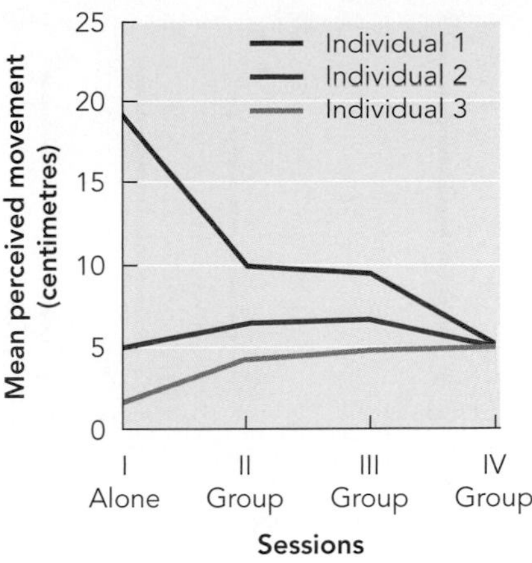

FIGURE 16.11

In Sherif's experiments, individuals' autokinetic judgments made alone (Session I) began to converge when they were made in the presence of two other participants (Sessions II, III, IV). Each mean is based on 100 judgments per session. These data are from one of the three-person groups.

Based on Sherif, 1935.

Conformity and Obedience

Norms can influence behaviour only if people conform to them. Without *conformity*—the adjustment of individual behaviours, attitudes, and beliefs to a group standard—we would have social chaos. It is no accident, therefore, that all social systems exert overt and subtle pressures on their members to conform.

Why Do People Conform?

Psychologically, our desire to understand the world and respond to it effectively provides one basic motive for conforming (Biener & Boudreau, 1991). As Figure 16.12 illustrates, at times we follow the opinions or behaviour of other people because we believe they have accurate knowledge and what they are doing is "right." This is called **informational social influence**. We also may conform to obtain rewards that come from being accepted by other people, while at the same time avoiding their rejection. This is called **normative social influence** (Deutsch & Gerard, 1955).

15. Explain the difference between informational and normative social influence.

Solomon Asch's (1951, 1956) landmark conformity experiments illustrated both types of influence. In the experimental condition, groups of university students performed several trials of a simple visual task, shown in Figure 16.13. Only one member of the group, however, actually was a participant. The rest were accomplices (called "confederates") of the experimenter. Group members sat around a table and were called on in order. The real participant sat next to last. According to plan, every confederate intentionally gave the same wrong answer on some trials. Imagine, for example, that the first member says "Line 1." (You think to yourself, "Huh?"). Then the next four members also say "Line 1." (You wonder, "Can this really be?"). Now it is your turn.

Would anybody conform to the group's incorrect judgments? Asch found that one-quarter of the participants never conformed, one-quarter conformed frequently, and the rest conformed once or a few times. Overall, participants conformed 37 percent of the time, compared to a mere 1 percent error rate in a control condition in which people judged the lines by themselves. This conformity rate stunned many scientists since the task was very easy and the confederates did not overtly pressure participants to conform.

"Well, heck! If all you smart cookies agree, who am I to dissent?"

FIGURE 16.12

Often we conform to a majority because we believe that their opinion "must be right."

During debriefing discussions with the experimenter after the task was over, many participants said they were puzzled by the difference between their own and

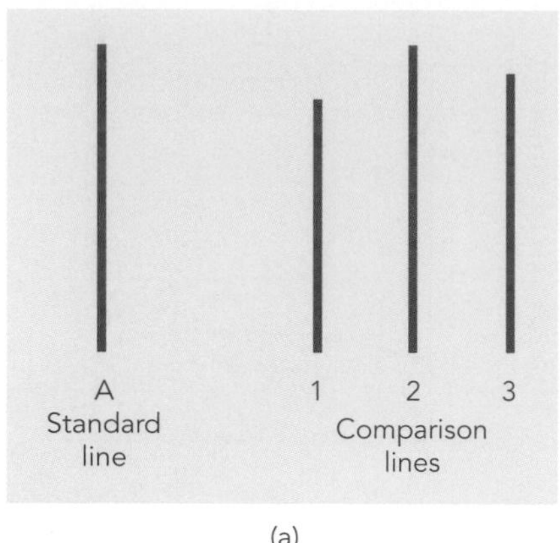

(a)

(b)

FIGURE 16.13

(a) In Asch's (1956) conformity experiments, students were asked to judge which of three comparison lines was the same length as the standard line. They performed this task for eighteen trials, using a different set of standard and comparison lines each time. (b) Upon hearing other group members unanimously say that "Line 1" is the correct match, the participant wonders whether his own judgment (Line 2) is correct.

the group's perceptions. Some felt that the group was wrong, but went along to avoid "making waves" and possible rejection. This behaviour reflects normative social influence. After several trials, other participants succumbed to informational social influence and began to doubt their eyesight and judgment.

Factors That Affect Conformity

Asch demonstrated that complex social behaviour could be studied scientifically under controlled conditions. In subsequent experiments he manipulated different independent variables and measured their effects on conformity. Consider two examples:

- *Group size.* Conformity increased from about 5 to 35 percent as group size increased from one to four or five confederates, but, contrary to common sense, further increases in group size did not increase conformity. Participants were just as likely to conform when there were four or five confederates giving incorrect answers as when there were ten or fifteen.
- *Presence of a dissenter.* When one confederate (according to plan) disagreed with the others, this greatly reduced real participants' conformity. Even when the dissenter gave an incorrect answer (e.g., the majority said "Line 3" and the dissenter said "Line 1"), participants made many fewer errors. The key is that, when someone else dissents, this person serves as a model for remaining independent from the group.

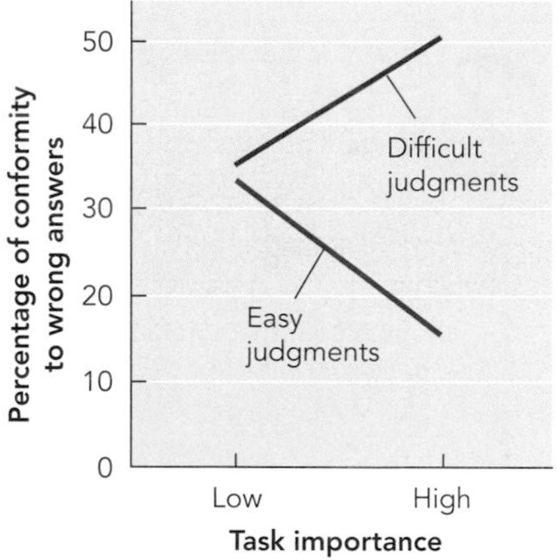

FIGURE 16.14

In this experiment, university students made a series of eyewitness memory judgments. For each judgment, one participant and two accomplices were shown a slide of a person. Next they had to pick out that person from a second slide showing four people. The second slide was presented for 5 seconds (easy task) or 0.5 seconds (hard task), and the accomplices intentionally gave wrong answers on some trials. Participants were told that the task was important (including a possible $20 prize for high accuracy) or unimportant. The high incentive decreased conformity on the easy task, but increased conformity when the task was difficult.

Based on Baron et al., 1996.

Would Asch's participants have conformed less if the task had been made more important to them, say, by offering a financial incentive for giving correct answers? As Figure 16.14 shows, when the correct answer is obvious (the task is easy, as was Asch's), conformity decreases when the consequences of going along with the group's erroneous judgment are made more costly (Baron et al., 1996). But, when we are less sure of the right way to behave (the task is hard), conformity increases as the stakes become higher.

Reviewing 97 conformity experiments conducted in the United States from 1951 to 1990, Rod Bond and Peter Smith (1996) found that the overall level of conformity has decreased slightly over recent decades. Around the globe, conformity tends to be greater among research participants from collectivist cultures, in which group harmony is valued more highly than in individualistic cultures. Overall, gender differences in conformity have been weak or non-existent (Bond & Smith, 1996; Eagly & Carli, 1981).

Minority Influence

Although majority influence is powerful, in some cases a minority of the group's members may influence the majority's behaviour (Clark, 2001). Serge Moscovici (1985) proposes that, to maximize its influence, the minority must be highly committed to its point of view, remain independent in the face of majority pressure, and be consistent over time, yet appear to keep an open mind. Dissenting information presented by the minority may cause majority members to change their view, at least on a private level (Maass & Clark, 1984). In reviewing almost a hundred studies, Wendy Wood and her colleagues (1994) found that minority influence is strongest when it maintains a highly consistent position over time. However, if the minority appears too unreasonable, deviant, or negative, it may cause the majority to become entrenched or lead some people to shift their attitudes even further away from the minority's position.

16. Identify some situational factors that influence people's degree of conformity.

Obedience to Authority

Like conformity to a group, obedience to an authority figure is inherently neither good nor bad. As an airplane passenger, you would not be amused if the co-pilot disregarded the pilot's commands simply because he or she "didn't feel like obeying," putting the flight and your life at risk. Without obedience, society would face chaos.

But obedience can also produce tragic results. After World War II, the famous Nuremberg trials were held to judge Nazi war criminals who had slaughtered millions of innocent people in concentration camps. In many instances, the defence offered by the defendants was that they had "only followed orders." In the massacre of men, women, and children at My Lai during the Vietnam War, American soldiers accused of atrocities gave the same explanation. No doubt we will hear the cry "I was just following orders" again as accountability is judged for more recent mass atrocities in Kosovo, Rwanda, and elsewhere around the globe.

17. Under what conditions is the minority most likely to influence the majority?

18. Describe Milgram's obedience experiment. Do you believe the results would be similar today? Why or why not?

Just as the Nuremberg court did, many of us reject justifications based on obedience to authority as mere rationalizations, secure in our conviction that we would behave more humanely in such situations. But would we? Let's consider the answers provided by Stanley Milgram in our *Research Foundations* feature.

RESEARCH FOUNDATIONS

The Dilemma of Obedience: When Conscience Confronts Malevolent Authority

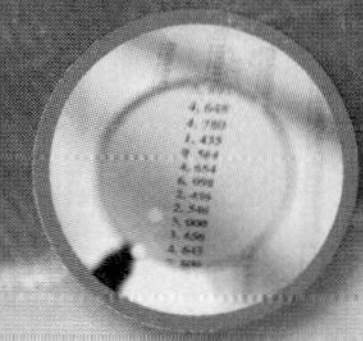

Stanley Milgram wanted to examine conformity in a more powerful situation than Asch had. Rather than have participants judge lines, Milgram thought about testing whether people would conform to group pressure and give electric shocks to a protesting victim. But he realized that a control condition was needed to measure how much shock people would give without group pressure. Here the experimenter would instruct each participant to give the shocks. As he thought about it, Milgram wondered: Would ordinary citizens obey such malevolent orders? How far would they go? At that moment, Milgram shifted his focus from conformity to obedience. Fuelled by his desire to better understand the horrors and lessons of the Holocaust, Milgram conducted 18 obedience experiments between 1960 and 1963 (Milgram, 1974).

The following experiment was conducted twice, first with 40 men and then with 40 women. Participants ranged in age from 20 to 50 years and represented a cross-section of occupations and educational backgrounds.

In the laboratory each participant met a middle-aged man who was introduced as another participant, but who actually was a confederate. They were told that the experiment examined the effects of punishment on memory. Then, through a supposedly random draw (it was rigged), the real participant became the *teacher* and the confederate became the *learner*. The teacher presented a series of memory problems to the learner through a two-way intercom system. Each time the learner made an error the teacher was instructed to administer an electric shock, using a machine that had 30 switches, beginning with 15 volts and increasing step-by-step to 450 volts. As the teacher watched, the learner was strapped into a chair in an adjoining room and hooked up to wires from the shock generator (Figure 16.15). The learner expressed concern about the shock and mentioned he had a slight heart problem.

Returning to the main room, the experimenter gave the teacher a sample shock (45 volts) and then ordered the experiment to begin. Unbeknownst to the teacher, the learner actually did *not* receive any shock and intentionally committed many errors. The learner made verbal protests that were standardized on a tape recorder, so that they were the same for all participants.

As the learner's errors mounted the teacher increased the shock. If the teacher balked at continuing, the experimenter issued one or more escalating commands, such as "Please continue," "You must continue," and "You have no other choice." At 75 volts the learner moaned when the teacher threw the switch. At 150 volts the learner's reaction was "Ugh!!! Experimenter! That's all. Get me out of here. I told

–*Continued*

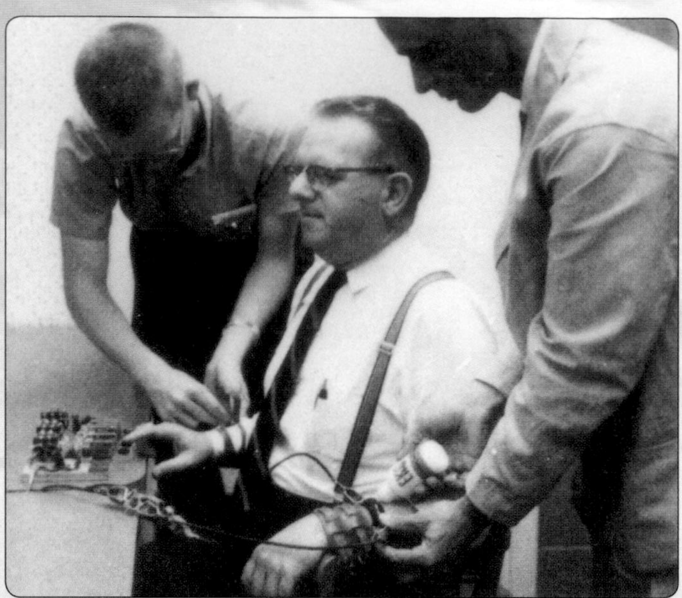

FIGURE 16.15

The participant (teacher) saw the learner being strapped into the chair.

you I had heart trouble. My heart's starting to bother me now. Get me out of here, please . . . I refuse to go on. Let me out." Beyond 200 volts he emitted agonized screams every time a shock was delivered, yelling "Let me out! Let me out!" At 300 volts the learner refused to answer and continued screaming to be let out. At 345 volts and beyond, there was only silence. Full obedience was operationally defined as continuing to the maximum shock level of 450 volts.

Participants wrestled with a dilemma: Should they continue to hurt this innocent person, as the experimenter commanded, or should they stop the learner's pain by openly disobeying? Most participants became stressed. Some trembled, sweated, laughed nervously, or in a few cases, experienced convulsions. But would they obey? Make a prediction: What percentage of people obeyed to 450 volts, and were there any gender differences?

When Milgram asked psychiatrists, professors, university students, and middle-class adults to predict the outcome, they estimated a one percent obedience rate. Indeed, most participants balked or protested at one time or another and said they would not continue. But ultimately, 26 of the 40 men and an identical 26 of 40 women (65 percent) obeyed to the end (Figure 16.16).

Milgram's research has generated controversy for decades (Blass, 2000). On one level, its ethics were harshly criticized (Baumrind, 1964): Participants were deceived, exposed to substantial stress, and risked long-lasting negative effects to their self-image. Milgram countered that the research was so socially significant as to warrant the deception, that participants were carefully debriefed afterward, and that psychiatric follow-ups of a sample of obedient participants suggested no long-term ill effects. Weighing the costs and benefits, do you believe that this research was justified?

Researchers also debate why obedience was high, but many agree with Milgram's view that participants psychologically transferred much of the "responsibility" for the teacher's fate to the experimenter (Blass & Schmitt, 2001). While administering the shock, some participants stated that they "were not responsible" for what happened. Others asked, "Who is responsible if something happens to the learner?" When the experimenter replied, "I am responsible," participants felt greater freedom to continue. Yet they were the ones flipping the switch.

Would similar results occur today? We suspect so. For 25 years after Milgram's research, experiments in different countries; in "real-world" settings; and with children, adolescents, and adults yielded depressingly consistent results (Miller, 1986). In the 1980s, Dutch researchers Wim Meeus and Quinten Raaijmakers (1986, 1995) conducted 19 obedience studies. In one, 92 percent of male and female participants completely obeyed an experimenter's orders to repeatedly disrupt the performance of a job applicant (actually a confederate) taking a very important job screening test. The applicant pleaded to no avail with participants to stop.

How would you have responded? Almost all of our own students say they would have disobeyed. So suppose we conduct the experiment today, but with real electric shock and with you as the learner. The teacher will be a randomly selected student from your class. Are you confident that this student will disobey? Few of our students express such confidence. In short, virtually all of us are confident that *we* would not obey, but we are not so sure about other people—and in turn they are not so sure about *us*.

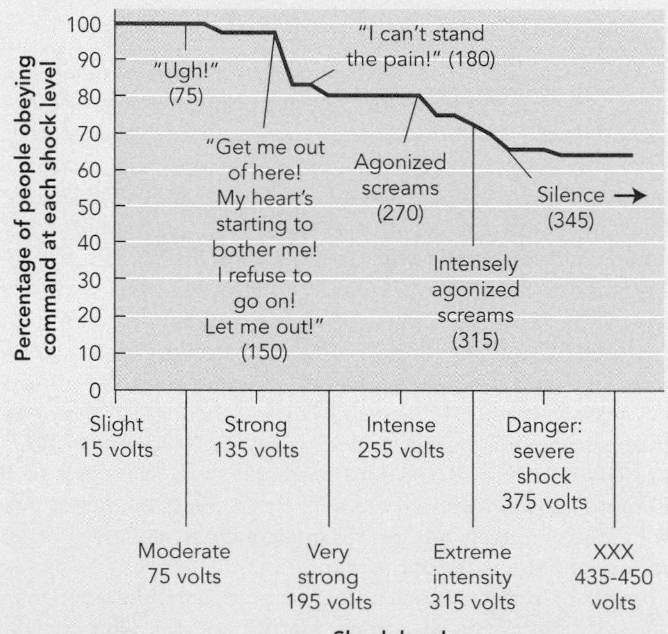

FIGURE 16.16

This graph shows the percentage of male participants who continued to shock the learner through various voltage levels. The pattern for women was similar.

Source: Based on Milgram, 1974.

Factors That Influence Destructive Obedience

19. What situational factors increase obedience?

By changing various aspects of the experimental situation, Milgram and other researchers obtained obedience rates ranging from zero to over 90 percent.

- *Remoteness of the victim.* Obedience was greater when the learner was out of sight. When the teacher and learner were placed in the same room, obedience dropped to 40 percent. Furthermore, when the teacher had to make physical contact and force the learner's hand onto a "shock plate," obedience dropped to 30 percent (Figure 16.17).
- *Closeness and legitimacy of the authority figure.* Obedience was highest when the authority figure was close and perceived as legitimate. When the experimenter left the scene and gave orders by phone, or when an "ordinary person" (a confederate) took over and gave the orders, obedience dropped to about 20 percent.
- *Cog in a wheel.* When another "participant" (actually a confederate) flipped the shock switch and real participants only had to perform another aspect of the task, 93 percent obeyed. In short, *obedience increases when someone else does the "dirty work."* In contrast, when Harvey Tilker (1970) made participants feel fully responsible for the learner's welfare, not a single person obeyed to the end.
- *Personal characteristics.* Milgram compared the political orientation, religious affiliation, occupations, education, length of military service, and psychological characteristics of obedient versus disobedient participants. Differences were weak or non-existent. Likewise, gender was not consistently related to obedience rates (Milgram, 1974; Shanab & Yahya, 1977).

FIGURE 16.17

In one of Milgram's studies (Touch Proximity), the teacher was ordered to physically force the learner's hand onto a shock plate after the learner refused to continue. Here, 30 percent of participants obeyed fully to 450 volts. Although touch proximity strongly reduced obedience, the fact that a significant minority still obeyed raises considerable concern.

Lessons Learned: From the Holocaust to Airline Safety

What lessons shall we draw from this research? Certainly, it is *not* that people are apathetic or evil. Participants became stressed precisely because they did care about the learner's welfare. Neither is the lesson that we are sheep. If we were, obedience would be high across all situations, which is not the case. Rather, Milgram sums up a key lesson as follows:

> ". . . it would be a mistake . . . to make the simple-minded statement that kindly and good persons disobey while those who are cruel do not . .. often, it is not so much the kind of person a man is as the kind of situation in which he finds himself that determines how he will act." (Milgram, 1974, p. 205)

In other words, by arranging the situation appropriately, most people—ordinary, decent citizens—can be induced to follow orders from an authority figure they perceive as legitimate, even when doing so contributes to harming innocent people. The applicability of this principle to the Holocaust and other atrocities seems clear (Saltzman, 2000). During the Holocaust, obedience was made easier because most of the personnel working at the concentration camps were cogs in a horrendous wheel: They didn't pull the switch to flood the chambers with gas, but instead performed other tasks. Their victims also were "remote" at the moment of their murder. Furthermore, to lessen concentration camp workers' feeling of responsibility, Hitler's subordinate Heinrich Himmler told them in manipulative speeches that only he and Hitler were personally responsible for what took place (Davidowicz, 1975).

Does obedience research suggest that we are not responsible for following orders? This is a moral and legal question, not a scientific one. But this research should heighten our sense of responsibility and awareness of the pitfalls of blind obedience and prevent us from being so smug or naive as to feel that such events "could never happen here."

FIGURE 16.18

On September 2, 1998, Swiss Air flight 111, carrying 215 passengers and 14 crew members, crashed off the coast of Peggy's Cove, Nova Scotia. Indications arose later that there was a disagreement between the pilot and co-pilot, in which the co-pilot acquiesced.

Increased sensitivity to the power of obedience pressures also has concrete applications. As an airline passenger, there are times when you would want the co-pilot to challenge a pilot's commands, such as when the pilot's actions pose a clear threat to flight safety. But, traditionally, co-pilots have been reluctant to do this (National Transportation Safety Board, 1979). Actual cockpit recordings and flight simulator experiments suggest that several jetliner crashes might have been prevented had co-pilots been more assertive in taking over control or questioning pilots' decisions (Foushee, 1984; Helmreich, 1997). For example, there were reports of disagreement between the pilot and co-pilot on the ill-fated Swiss Air 111 (Figure 16.18).

Detecting and Resisting Compliance Techniques

From telemarketers and salespeople to TV and Internet advertisements, would-be persuaders often come armed with special *compliance techniques:* strategies that may manipulate you into saying yes when you really want to say no. By learning to identify these techniques, you will be in a better position to resist them.

The powerful **norm of reciprocity** involves the expectation that when others treat us well, we should respond in kind. Thus to get you to comply with a request, I can do something nice for you now—such as an unsolicited favour—in hopes that you will feel pressure to reciprocate later when I present you with my request (Cialdini, 1988). As Figure 16.19 illustrates, the Hare Krishna Society (a religious group) cleverly used "flower power" to manipulate the norm of reciprocity and raise millions of dollars in donations.

20. Identify four common compliance techniques and explain how they work.

Now consider the **door-in-the-face technique**: A persuader makes a large request, expecting you to reject it (you "slam the door" in the persuader's face), and then presents a smaller request. Telemarketers feast on this technique. Rather than ask you directly for a modest monetary contribution to some organization or cause, they first ask for a much larger contribution, knowing that you will say no. After you politely refuse, they ask for the smaller contribution. In one experiment, after people declined an initial request to donate $25 to a charity, they were more likely to donate $2 than were participants who were directly asked for $2 (Wang et al., 1989). To be effective, the same persuader must make both requests. The persuader "compromises" by making the second, smaller request, so we feel pressure to reciprocate by complying. Refusing the first request also may produce guilt, and complying with the smaller request may help us reduce guilt or feel socially responsible (Tusing & Dillard, 2000).

Using the **foot-in-the-door technique**, a persuader gets you to comply with a small request first (getting the "foot in the door") and later presents a larger request. Imagine receiving an E-mail message from a stranger requesting help. It's a student who needs to collect data for a class project and asks if you would fill out a 20-minute online questionnaire about your dietary habits. Would you do it? In an experiment with French college students, 44 percent complied (Guéguen, 2002). Now let's turn to a different condition of this experiment. Imagine receiving an E-mail from a stranger who asks for simple advice about a word processing program. It takes less than a minute to reply, and you do (as did all the participants in this condition of the experiment). Once the person gets the foot in the door, a second E-mail appears minutes later, asking if you would help with a class project by filling out a dietary questionnaire. In this condition many more students—76 percent—complied. Although hypotheses abound, researchers are not sure why the foot-in-the-door technique is effective.

FIGURE 16.19

In the 1970s, members of the Hare Krishna Society approached passersby and gave them a small flower. If a passerby refused, the member said "Please. It is a gift for you." Reluctantly, people often accepted. Then the member asked for a donation. People felt pressure to reciprocate, donated money, and often threw the flower away.

With a final technique, **lowballing**, a persuader gets you to commit to some action and then—before you actually perform the behaviour—he or she increases the "cost" of that same behaviour. Imagine negotiating to buy a used car for $8,000, a "great price." The salesperson says, "I need to confirm this with my manager," comes back shortly, and states, "I'm afraid my manager says the price is too low. But you can have the car for only $400 more. It's still a great price." At this point, you are more likely to go through with the deal than you would have been, had the "real" $8,400 price been set at the outset.

Both lowballing and the foot-in-the-door technique involve moving from a smaller request to a larger, more costly one. But with the foot-in-the-door approach, the smaller and larger requests often involve different acts (e.g., giving advice, filling out a questionnaire) and the larger request is made after you finish complying with the smaller request. In lowballing, the stakes for the *same behaviour* are raised after you commit to it but *before* you consummate the behaviour. Having made a commitment, you may find it easier to rationalize the added costs or may feel obligated to the person to whom you made the commitment.

By recognizing when compliance techniques are being used to manipulate your behaviour, you are in a better position to resist them. Consider the norm of reciprocity. Robert Cialdini (1988), an expert on influence techniques, suggests that the key is not to resist the initial gift or favour; instead, accept the unsolicited "favour," but if the person then asks you for a favour in return, recognize this as a manipulative technique. As Cialdini notes, "The rule says that favors are to be met with favors; it does not require that tricks be met with favors" (1988, p. 53). Similarly, if a telemarketer asks you to agree to a large request and then after you decline immediately asks for a smaller commitment, respond by thinking or even saying, "I see; the door-in-the-face technique." Of course, you can still choose to comply if you believe it is the right thing to do. The goal is not to automatically reject every social influence attempt but to avoid feeling coerced into doing something you don't want to do.

Crowd Behaviour and Deindividuation

21. Describe deindividuation and how conditions in the Stanford Prison Study may have fostered it.

Years ago in New York City, a handyman sat perched on a ledge for an hour while a crowd of nearly 500 people on the street below shouted at him to jump. Fortunately, police managed to rescue the man. New York is hardly alone, as Australian psychologist Leon Mann (1981) found when he analyzed newspaper reports of 21 cases in which crowds were present when a person threatened to jump off a building. In 10 cases, the crowd had encouraged the person to jump.

What could prompt people to encourage distraught human beings to end their lives? In the nineteenth century, French physician Gustave LeBon (1895) suggested that the anonymity that exists in mobs leads to a loss of personal identity and a weakening of restraints that prompt people to engage in behaviours they would not perform as individuals. This condition is called **deindividuation**, a loss of individuality that leads to disinhibited behaviour (Festinger et al., 1952). The concept of deindividuation has been applied to diverse types of anti-social behaviour, from cheating and stealing to riots by sports fans and acts of genocide (Staub, 1996).

But what is the primary aspect of deindividuation that disinhibits behaviour? Tom Postmes and Russell Spears (1998) meta-analyzed 60 deindividuation studies and determined that *anonymity to outsiders* was the key. Conditions that make an individual less identifiable to people *outside* the group reduce feelings of accountability and, slightly but consistently, increase the risk of anti-social actions. Postmes and Spears suggest that being anonymous to outsiders enhances the individual's tendency to focus on his or her identity with the group and makes the person more responsive to emerging group norms.

Reinforcing the importance of anonymity to outsiders, Mann (1981) found that people were most likely to encourage a potential suicide victim to jump when the crowd was large and it was dark outside. During the Stanford Prison Study, no names were used and guards had to be called "Mr. Correctional Officer." All guards wore identical uniforms and reflecting sunglasses that prevented the prisoners from making direct eye contact. The guards were unaware that their behaviour was being monitored by the experimenters, and anti-social norms evolved from the role of "tough prison guard" adopted by those participants who spontaneously took over leadership roles (Zimbardo et al., 1973). These factors led Zimbardo to conclude that deindividuation was a key factor in the cruelty exhibited by the guards. Reducing anonymity—and thereby increasing public accountability—may be the most basic approach to counteracting deindividuation.

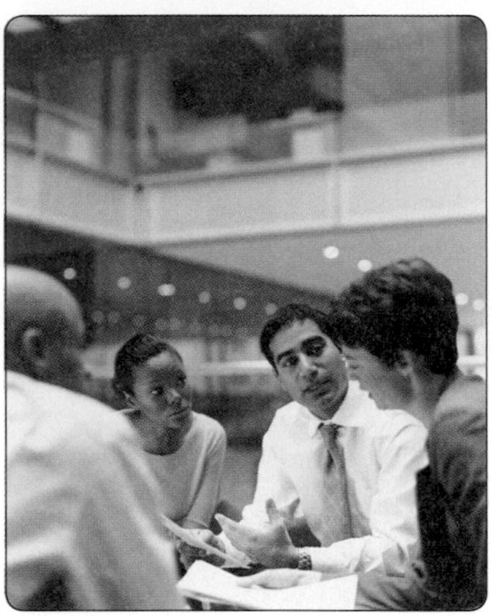

FIGURE 16.20

Whether for recreational, volunteer, or work activities, much of human behaviour occurs in groups.

22. What is social loafing and when is it most likely to occur?

Group Influences on Performance and Decision Making

Much of our behaviour occurs in groups, from family and friendship groups to social clubs, work groups, and athletic teams. People often form groups to make decisions or perform tasks that are too complex or physically demanding to be accomplished by one person (Figure 16.20). We now consider some factors that enhance or interfere with group productivity.

Social Loafing: Failing to Pull Your Own Weight

In 1913, Max Ringelmann, a French agricultural engineer, measured the force that men exerted while pulling on a rope as hard as they could. Individually, the men averaged 63 kilograms (kg) of pull. In groups of three, you might expect a combined pull of about 3×63 kg = 189 kg, and 504 kg for groups of eight. But this isn't what happened. The total pull in three- and eight-man groups was 16 percent and 51 percent below expectations, respectively.

Why did this happen? Perhaps the men didn't coordinate the timing of their pull precisely, and there was a loss of mechanical efficiency. Or perhaps each person exerted less effort when in a group. To resolve this issue, Alan Ingham and his colleagues (1974) led blindfolded participants to believe that they were pulling a rope (connected to a force meter) either alone or in groups of various sizes. In reality, participants were always alone, and therefore any performance drop had to be due to diminished effort. Overall, participants exerted 18 percent less force when they thought they were in a group.

The tendency for people to expend less individual effort when working in a group than when working alone is called **social loafing**. In contrast to social facilitation experiments, in which a person performs a task individually (in front of an audience or with a coactor) and *does not pool* her or his effort with anyone, social loafing involves collective performance. Thus, contrary to what common sense might tell you, when university students and high school cheerleaders are asked to be as loud as possible, they individually clap, shout, and cheer *less* loudly when performing as a group than when they are alone (Hardy & Latané, 1986).

Social loafing also occurs on cognitive tasks, such as when people have to evaluate written materials, make decisions in simulated juries, and monitor the concentration of gases in the air (Hoeksema et al., 1998). Why does social loafing occur? Steven Karau and Kipling Williams (1993, 2001) propose a *collective effort model:* On a collective task, people will put forth effort only to the extent that they expect their effort to contribute to obtaining a valued goal. In support of this model, their meta-analysis of 78 social loafing studies revealed that social loafing is *more* likely to occur when:

- people believe that individual performance within the group is not being monitored;
- the task (goal) has less value or meaning to the person;

- the group is less important to the person; and
- the task is simple and the person's input is redundant with that of other group members.

Fatigue also seems to increase social loafing. By having participants work on various cognitive tasks for 20 hours without sleep, Dutch researchers demonstrated that we are more likely to "skate by" on other group members' shoulders when we are tired (Hoeksema et al., 1998). Social loafing also depends on gender and culture (Karau & Williams, 1993). It occurs more strongly in all-male groups than in all-female or mixed-sex groups, possibly because women may be more concerned about group outcomes than men. Participants from individualistic cultures (Canada and the United States) exhibit more social loafing than people from collectivistic cultures (China, Japan, Taiwan), in which group goals are especially valued.

Social loafing suggests that, in terms of group performance, "the whole is less than the sum of its parts." But this is not always the case. Social loafing may disappear when individual performance is monitored or when members highly value their group or the task goal (Karau & Hart, 1998). In fact, to achieve a highly desired goal, some members may engage in *social compensation:* They will work harder in a group than alone if they expect that their colleagues either don't have enough ability or will slack off (Hart et al., 2001).

Group Polarization: Going to Extremes

23. Identify two causes of group polarization.

Groups are often called upon to make key decisions. Governments, educational institutions, and corporations frequently develop policies through committees. The fate of defendants often rests in the hands of juries. Such decisions are often entrusted to groups because they are assumed to be more conservative than individuals and less likely to "go off the deep end." Is this assumption correct? It is, as long as the group is generally conservative to begin with. In such cases, the group's final opinion or attitude likely will be even *more conservative.* But, if the group members lean toward a more liberal or risky viewpoint to begin with, the group's decision will tend to become *more liberal or riskier.* This principle is called **group polarization**: When a group of like-minded people discusses an issue, whether face to face or through e-mail, the "average" opinion of group members tends to become more extreme (Liu & Latané, 1998; Moscovici & Zavalloni, 1969).

Why does group polarization occur? One reason, reflecting *normative social influence,* is that individuals who are attracted to a group may be motivated to adopt a more extreme position in order to gain the group's approval. A second reason, reflecting *informational social influence,* is that during group discussions people hear arguments supporting their positions that they had not previously considered. These new arguments tend to make the initial positions seem even more valid (Sia et al., 2002).

Groupthink: Suspending Critical Thinking

After the U.S. military ignored warning signs of imminent attack by Japan in 1941, the fleet at Pearl Harbor was destroyed in a "surprise" attack. In 1961, President Kennedy and his advisors launched the doomed Bay of Pigs invasion of Cuba. In 1972, five men broke into Democratic Party offices at the Watergate hotel, and the following cover-up forced President Nixon to resign. According to Yale social psychologist Irving Janis (1983), the decision makers involved in each of these historical blunders fell victim to a process called **groupthink**, the tendency for group members to suspend critical thinking because they are striving to seek agreement.

Janis developed the concept of groupthink, shown in Figure 16.21, after analyzing historical accounts of group deliberations that resulted in disas-

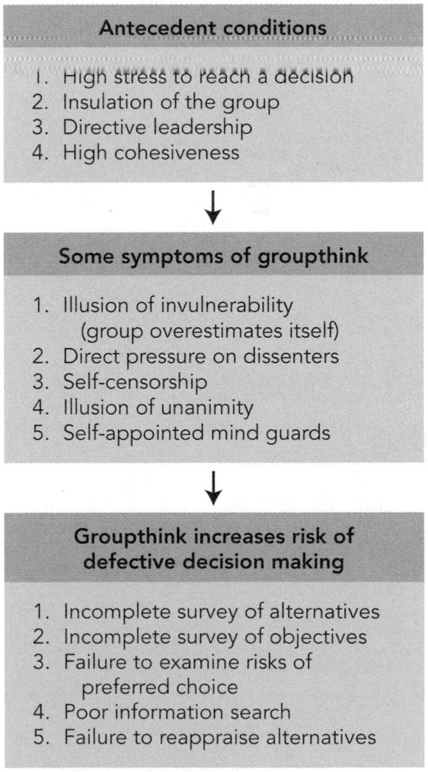

Antecedent conditions

1. High stress to reach a decision
2. Insulation of the group
3. Directive leadership
4. High cohesiveness

Some symptoms of groupthink

1. Illusion of invulnerability (group overestimates itself)
2. Direct pressure on dissenters
3. Self-censorship
4. Illusion of unanimity
5. Self-appointed mind guards

Groupthink increases risk of defective decision making

1. Incomplete survey of alternatives
2. Incomplete survey of objectives
3. Failure to examine risks of preferred choice
4. Poor information search
5. Failure to reappraise alternatives

FIGURE 16.21

Antecedents, symptoms, and negative effects of groupthink on decision making.

Adapted from I. L. Janis, 1983.

trous decisions. He proposed that groupthink is most likely to occur when a group:

- is under *high stress* to reach a decision;
- is *insulated* from outside input;
- has a *directive leader* who promotes her or his personal agenda; and
- has *high cohesion*, reflecting a spirit of closeness and ability to work well together.

24. What are some causes, symptoms, and consequences of groupthink?

Under these conditions, the group is so committed to reaching a consensus, while remaining loyal and agreeable, that members suspend their critical judgment.

Various symptoms signal that groupthink is at work. For example, group members who express doubt are faced with *direct pressure* to stop "rocking the boat." Some members serve as *mind guards* by preventing negative information from reaching the group. Ultimately, members display *self-censorship* and withhold their doubts, creating a potentially disastrous *illusion of unanimity* in which each member comes to believe that "everyone else seems to agree with the decision" (Figure 16.22).

Many aspects of groupthink were present during the decision process leading up to the fatal launch of the space shuttle *Challenger* in 1986 (Esser & Lindoerfer, 1995; Moorhead et al., 1991). The engineers who designed the rocket boosters had strongly opposed the launch, fearing that subfreezing weather would make rubber seals too brittle to contain hot gases from the rocket. NASA, however, was under great stress, and leadership was directive. This shuttle mission was to be historic, carrying America's first civilian into space. There had been several delays and NASA did not want another one. To foster an illusion of unanimity, a key NASA executive polled only management officials, excluding the engineers from the final decision-making process (Magnuson, 1986). Thanks to mind guarding, the NASA official who gave the final go-ahead was never informed of the concerns expressed by the engineers.

In the days leading up to the fiery disintegration of the space shuttle *Columbia* as it reentered earth's atmosphere in 2003, engineers, supervisors, and some NASA officials intensely debated whether *Columbia*'s left wing had sustained damage due to a mishap during launch. But as the Columbia Accident Investigation Board found, tragically, "dangerous aspects of NASA's 1986 culture... remained unchanged" (2003, p. 198). For example, stress was high, key managers were isolated from outside expert opinion, and a "need to produce consensus at each level" filtered out dissenting information on safety risks (p. 198).

(a)

(b)

FIGURE 16.22

(a) The illusion of unanimity occurs when group members collectively fail to speak their true minds. (b) This illusion contributed to the ill-fated decision to launch the space shuttle Challenger on January 28, 1986. The Challenger exploded shortly after takeoff, killing all the astronauts on board.

Can groupthink be prevented? Janis suggests that the leader should remain impartial during discussions, regularly encourage critical thinking, bring in outsiders to offer their opinions, and divide the larger group into subgroups—to see if each subgroup independently reaches the same decision. Of course, even groups that display poor decision-making procedures may still end up making a correct decision, or at least may "get away" with a bad one (Raven, 1998). Conversely, critical debate does not guarantee a positive outcome, but it does enhance the odds.

In Review

- *A social norm is a shared rule or expectation about how group members should think, feel, and behave. A social role is a set of norms that defines a particular position in a social system.*
- *People conform to a group because of informational social influence and normative social influence. The size of the majority and the presence or absence of dissenters influence the degree of conformity. Minority influence is strongest when the minority maintains a consistent position over time but does not appear too deviant.*
- *Milgram's obedience research raised strong ethical concerns and found unexpectedly high percentages of people willing to obey destructive orders. Such obedience is stronger when the victim is remote and when the authority figure is close by, legitimate, and assumes responsibility for what happens.*
- *People often use special techniques to get us to comply with their requests. These compliance techniques include the norm of reciprocity, the door-in-the-face technique, the foot-in-the-door technique, and lowballing.*
- *Social loafing occurs when people exert less individual effort when working as a group than when working alone. Social loafing decreases when the goal or group membership is valued highly and when people's performance within the group can be individually monitored.*
- *When the members of a decision-making group initially share the same conservative or liberal viewpoint, the group's final decision often reflects a polarization effect and becomes more extreme than the average opinion of the individual members.*
- *Cohesive decision-making groups that have directive leaders, are under high stress, and are insulated from outside input, may display groupthink, a suspension of critical thinking to maintain cohesion and loyalty to the leader's viewpoint.*
- *Deindividuation is a temporary lowering of restraints that can occur when a person is immersed in a group. Anonymity to outsiders appears to be the key factor in producing deindividuation.*

SOCIAL RELATIONS

Our relations with other people take many forms. Here we explore four types of social interaction that help define who we are, both individually and collectively: attraction, prejudice, altruism, and aggression.

Affiliation and Interpersonal Attraction

What makes your life meaningful? To many people, close relationships are one key. Abraham Maslow (1954) viewed belongingness and love as basic psychological needs, and considerable research indicates that ". . . the need to belong is a powerful, fundamental, and extremely pervasive motivation" (Baumeister & Leary, 1995, p. 497).

Why Do We Affiliate?

Humans are social beings, and affiliate in many ways (Figure 16.23). Some theorists argue that, over the course of evolution, individuals whose biological makeup predisposed them to affiliate were more likely to survive and reproduce than those who were reclusive. By affording greater access to sexual mates, more protection from predators, an efficient division of labour, and the passing of knowledge across

25. According to evolutionary and social comparison viewpoints, why are humans such social creatures?

FIGURE 16.23

Affiliation brings us companionship, intimacy, love, and also basic social contact. To satisfy these desires we form friendships, interact with family members, join groups, converse with strangers, and flock together in crowds.

generations, a socially oriented lifestyle had considerable adaptive value (Flinn, 1997; Kottak, 2000).

Craig Hill (1987) suggests that, psychologically, we affiliate for four basic reasons: to obtain positive stimulation, to receive emotional support, to gain attention, and to permit social comparison. **Social comparison** involves comparing our beliefs, feelings, and behaviours to those of other people. This helps us determine whether our responses are "normal," and enables us to judge the level of our cognitive and physical abilities (Festinger, 1954).

People differ in how strongly they desire to affiliate. In one study, university students who scored high on a personality test of *need for affiliation* made more friends during the semester than did students who scored low (Byrne & Greendlinger, 1989). In another study, high school students wore beepers over a one-week period. They were signalled approximately every two hours, and then recorded their thoughts and activities. Participants with high need for affiliation were more likely than their peers to report they were thinking about friends and wishing they could be with people (Wong & Csikszentmihalyi, 1991).

People with high need for affiliation also show a stronger *psychological sense of community*—the feeling of being part of a larger collective, of being engaged with others in pursuing common goals (Burroughs & Eby, 1998). People with a strong sense of community are more likely to engage in extracurricular school activities and to keep abreast of local and national news (Davidson & Cotter, 1997). Clearly, our desire to feel connected can express itself in many ways.

26. How does fear influence affiliation?

Many situational factors affect our tendency to affiliate. For example, fear-inducing situations increase our desire to be with others (Schachter, 1959). During emergencies, as in the aftermath of earthquakes, floods, and hurricanes, many people find themselves bonding to strangers (Humphriss, 1989). When afraid, we prefer to be with people who have been through the feared situation we are facing. This way, we can gauge the normalcy of our reactions and learn information about what to expect. In one study, hospital patients awaiting open-heart surgery expressed a stronger desire to have a roommate who already had been through the surgery than a preoperative roommate like themselves (Kulik & Mahler, 1989). And, when such patients were assigned to postoperative rather than preoperative roommates, they became less anxious and later recovered from surgery more quickly (Kulik et al., 1996).

Initial Attraction

Attraction is the first phase of most friendships and romantic relationships. What causes us to "connect" with some people, but not others?

27. How and why does proximity influence affiliation and attraction?

Proximity and mere exposure: "Haven't I seen you somewhere?" People cannot develop a relationship unless they first meet, and proximity (nearness) is the best predictor of who will cross paths with whom. Movies such as Sleepless in Seattle and *You've Got Mail* spotlight "long-distance" encounters, but, in reality, we interact most with people who are physically closer (Latané et al., 1995). Residents in married-student apartments are more likely to form friendships with other residents who live close by; students placed in assigned classroom seats are more likely to become friends with students seated nearby; and many adults meet their spouse or current dating partner at school, work, or place of worship (Festinger et al., 1950; Michael et al., 1994).

Proximity increases the chance of frequent encounters, and over 200 experiments provide evidence of a **mere exposure effect**: Repeated exposure to a stimulus typically increases our liking for it. No matter the stimuli—university classmates, photographs of faces, random geometric shapes, foreign words, and so on—so long as they are not unpleasant and we are not oversaturated, exposure generally enhances liking (Monahan et al., 2000; Winograd et al., 1999).

Similarity: birds of a feather. When it comes to attraction, folk wisdom covers all the bases. On the one hand, "opposites attract." On the other, "birds of a feather flock together." So which is it? The evidence is overwhelming: People most often are attracted to others who are similar to themselves (Byrne, 1997). For psychological attributes, similarity of attitudes, beliefs, and values seems to matter the most (Buss, 1985).

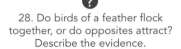

28. Do birds of a feather flock together, or do opposites attract? Describe the evidence.

In the laboratory, university students' degree of liking for a stranger can be predicted very accurately simply by knowing the proportion of similar attitudes that they share (Byrne, 1997; Byrne & Nelson, 1965). This similarity-attraction relationship has been found across many groups, including people in Mexico, India, and Japan who ranged from fourth-graders to retirees. Outside the laboratory, Donn Byrne and his colleagues (1970) matched university students on a brief 30-minute date, pairing people with partners who had either highly similar or dissimilar attitudes. Students were more attracted to similar partners, talked with them more during the rest of the semester, and had a stronger desire to date them. One reason we like people with similar attitudes is that they validate our view of the world.

So like mismatched roommates Felix Unger (an uptight neatnik) and Oscar Madison (a carefree slob) in the classic movie *The Odd Couple*, do opposites ever attract? At times, of course. But much more often, opposites repel (Krueger & Caspi, 1993; Rosenbaum, 1986). When choosing potential friends or mates, we typically screen out people who are dissimilar to us. And, when dissimilar people do form relationships, they tend not to last as long (Byrne, 1997). As Diane Felmlee (1998) found, dissimilarity increases the risk of "fatal attractions": We initially find some characteristic of another person appealing, but over time we come to dislike it. In short, what is intriguing and different today may repel us tomorrow!

Physical attractiveness: spellbound by beauty. It may be shallow and in many ways unfair, but most people seem drawn to beauty like moths to a flame (Figure 16.24). In many studies, when men and women rate the desirability of hypothetical short-term dating partners, their judgments are influenced most strongly by how good-looking the person is (Wiederman & Dubois, 1998). When faced with a potential dating partner who is attractive rather than unattractive, women and men are more likely to misrepresent their personal qualities in a way that makes them appear more similar to the potential date (Rowatt et al., 1999). And, when Donn Byrne (1970) matched university students on an actual brief date, students rated physically attractive partners more desirable and were more interested in dating them.

FIGURE 16.24

Hey, good lookin'! The way that both sexes initially judge someone is influenced by that person's attractiveness and other physical features. We are not alone. Many species, such as these Frigate birds (male on the right), have evolved distinct features and ritualized mating displays to attract a potential mate's attention.

In a classic study, Elaine Walster and her colleagues (1966) randomly paired over 700 first-year University of Minnesota students on blind dates for a "Welcome Week" dance. Earlier, the researchers had given all the participants a battery of personality, intelligence, and social skills tests, and had other students rate each participant's physical attractiveness. During an intermission at the dance, students rated how desirable they found their partner. Did any of the psychological characteristics predict who would like whom? No. Only one factor did. Women and men who dated physically attractive partners liked them more and had a stronger desire to date them again. Similarly, among 100 homosexual men who researchers paired together for a date, men's liking for their partner and desire to date him again were most strongly influenced by the partner's physical attractiveness (Sergios & Cody, 1986).

What motivates our desire to affiliate with attractive people? One factor may be the widespread stereotype that "what is beautiful is good"; we often assume that attractive people have more positive personality characteristics than unattractive people (Dion et al., 1972; Feingold, 1992). The popular media reinforce this stereotype. Analyzing five decades of top-grossing Hollywood movies, Stephen Smith and his colleagues (1999) found that good-looking male and female characters were portrayed as more intelligent, moral, and sociable than less attractive characters. Because we are often judged by the company we keep, we also may prefer to associate with attractive people in order to buttress our self-esteem. Self-conscious people, who are highly concerned about how they come across to others, are especially likely to gravitate toward attractive people (Richardson, 1991; Snyder et al., 1985).

29. Identify two factors that may underlie the desire to affiliate more with attractive people.

Lest you conclude that beauty is the key to happiness, we should note that physical attractiveness during the university years is unrelated to life satisfaction in middle age (Kaner, 1995). And physically attractive people do not necessarily have the highest levels of self-esteem (Major et al., 1984). Beauty is sometimes linked with self-doubt, because highly attractive individuals may attribute the positive responses of others solely to their "surface" beauty rather than to their inner personal qualities.

Although we are attracted to "beautiful people," we are most likely to have a dating partner or spouse whose level of physical attractiveness is similar to our own—a **matching effect** (Feingold, 1988). In this case, "birds of equally attractive feathers flock together." One reason for this is that the most attractive people may match up first and be "taken," then the next most attractive, and so on (Kalick & Hamilton, 1988). Another factor is that, to lessen the risk of rejection, some people may refrain from approaching potential dating partners who are more attractive than they are (Huston, 1973). Among dating couples, those who are best matched on attractiveness are most likely to fall deeply in love, and couples who eventually marry are more similar in attractiveness than dating couples in general (White, 1980).

Close relationships: as attraction deepens. People may share an initial attraction, but have different goals regarding what form they want a relationship to take. Compared to women, men show more interest in short-term mating (e.g., dating without developing a committed relationship) and perceive short-term mates as more desirable (Wiederman & Dubois, 1998). Men typically have more permissive attitudes than women about both casual and premarital sex, and have more sexual partners over their lifetime (Clark & Hatfield, 1989; Hyde and Oliver, 2000). Women—even those who have permissive attitudes about premarital sex—are more likely than men to want partners who make an emotional investment in the relationship.

What Do Men and Women Seek in a Mate?

30. Describe some gender differences in mate preferences.

Whether initial attraction leads to a close relationship also depends on the degree to which each partner perceives the other to have desired characteristics. But what do women and men want in a mate? Men typically prefer younger women, whereas women prefer older men. In terms of personal qualities, men and women show considerable overall agreement, but some gender differences also emerge. In Chapter 4, we addressed this question in terms of an evolutionary perspective on attraction. Supporting this perspective, we found that men place greater value on a potential mate being physically attractive and possessing good domestic skills, whereas women place greater value on a potential mate's earning potential, status, and ambitiousness.

31. How do social structure models explain gender differences in mate preferences?

Social-cultural perspectives. Many scientists challenge evolutionary psychologists' explanations for human mating patterns and other social behaviours (Scher, 1999; Lynn, 1989). Adaptive behaviour patterns may have been passed from parents to children not through genes, but through learning. In addition, **social structure theory** proposes that men and women display different mating preferences because society directs them into different social roles (Eagly & Wood, 1999). Even in this day and age, women generally have less power, lower wages, and less access to resources than men do. In two-income marriages, women are more likely to be the partner who switches to part-time work or a full-time homemaker role after childbirth. Thus society's division of labour still tends to socialize men into the "breadwinner" role and women into the "homemaker" role.

It makes sense, then, for women to seek men who will be successful wage earners, and for men to seek mates who can fulfill the domestic worker role. An older male–younger female age gap is favourable because older men are likely to be further along in earning power, and younger women are more economically dependent, and this conforms to our cultural expectations of marital roles. This division-of-labour hypothesis does not address directly why men emphasize a mate's physical attractiveness more than women, but Alice Eagly and Wendy Wood (1999) speculate that attractiveness is viewed as part of what women "exchange" in return for a male's earning capacity.

32. According to social penetration and social exchange theories, what factors influence whether a relationship will deepen, be satisfying, and continue?

Social penetration and social exchange. How do close relationships grow? According to **social penetration theory**, relationships progress as interactions between people become *broader*, involving more areas of their lives, and *deeper*, involving more intimate and personally meaningful areas (Altman & Taylor, 1973). Partners may share activities, other experiences, or physical intimacy, but *self-disclosure*—the sharing of innermost thoughts and feelings—plays a key role in fostering close relationships (Dindia, 2002). In friendships, dating relationships, and marriages, more extensive and intimate self-disclosure is associated with greater emotional involvement and relationship satisfaction (Hendrick, 1989; Miller, 1990). This relation is reciprocal. Self-disclosure fosters intimacy and trust, and intimacy and trust encourage self-disclosure.

According to John Thibaut and Harold Kelley's (1959) **social exchange theory**, the course of a relationship also is governed by rewards and costs that the partners experience. Rewards include companionship, emotional support, and the satisfaction of other needs. Costs may include effort spent to maintain the relationship, arguments and conflict, and so forth. The overall *outcome* (rewards minus costs) in a relationship can be positive or negative.

Outcomes are evaluated against two standards (Figure 16.25). The first, called the *comparison level*, is the outcome that a person has grown to expect in relationships, and it influences the person's *satisfaction* with the present relationship. Outcomes that meet or exceed the comparison level are satisfying; those that fall below this standard are unsatisfying. The second standard, called the *comparison level for alternatives*, focuses on potential alternatives to the relationship, and it influences the person's degree of *commitment* (Floyd & Wasner, 1994; Honeycutt, 1995). Thus a person may leave a satisfying relationship if something even better is available, or may remain committed to a relationship that is unsatisfying because the alternatives seem even worse.

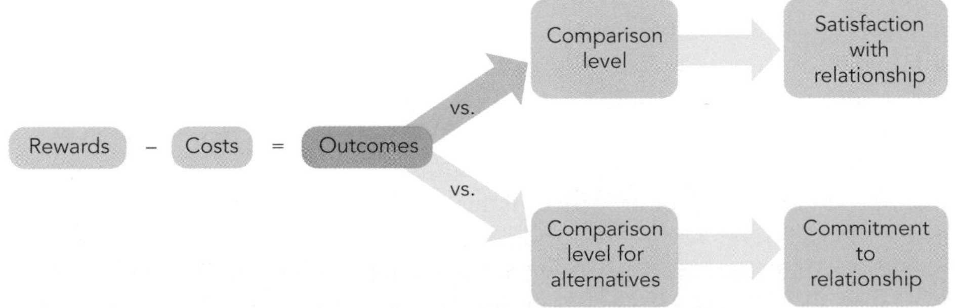

FIGURE 16.25
According to Thibaut and Kelley's social exchange theory, rewards minus costs equals the outcome of a relationship. Comparing our outcomes with two standards, the comparison level and the comparison level for alternatives, determines our satisfaction and commitment in the relationship, respectively.

Love

33. How does Sternberg's model expand upon the passionate-companionate love distinction?

Love must be a powerful motive if it indeed "makes the world go round," but which type of love does this? In his book, *The Art of Loving,* psychoanalyst Erich Fromm (1956) identified five fundamental types of love: parental love, erotic (sexual) love, self-love, love for humanity, and love of God. Restricting ourselves to friendships and romantic relationships, poet Elizabeth Barrett Browning's insight, "How do I love thee? Let me count the ways" is most applicable.

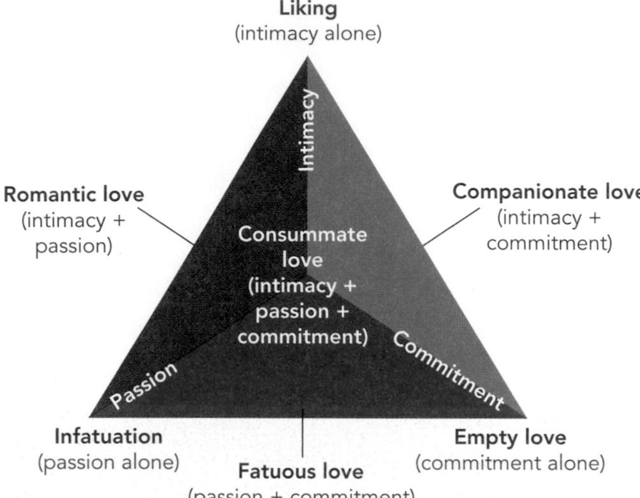

FIGURE 16.26

According to Sternberg, different types of love involve varying combinations of intimacy, commitment, and passion. Consummate love involves the presence of all three factors, whereas non-love represents the absence of all three.

Types of Love

Passionate love involves intense emotion, arousal, and yearning for the partner (Hatfield, 1988). We may ride an emotional roller coaster that ranges from ecstasy when the partner is present to heartsickness when the person is absent. **Companionate love** involves affection, deep caring about the partner's well-being, and a commitment to "being there" for the other (Caspi & Herbener, 1990; Hatfield, 1988). Both types of love contribute to satisfaction in long-term romantic relationships (Sprecher & Regan, 1998). In general, passionate love is less stable and declines more quickly over time than companionate love, but this does not mean that the flames of passionate love inevitably are extinguished (Tucker & Aron, 1993).

The distinction between passionate and companionate love is one of psychology's most basic. However, Robert Sternberg (1988, 1997) proposes a three-component **triangular theory of love** that focuses on *intimacy* (closeness, sharing, and valuing one's partner), *commitment* (the decision to remain in the relationship), and *passion* (feelings of romance, physical attraction, and sexual desire). Research suggests that these three qualities do a good job of capturing the way people commonly think about love (Aron & Westbay, 1996).

Figure 16.26 shows that different combinations of these components characterize seven types of love (plus "non-love," which is the absence of all three). Sternberg proposes that the ultimate form of love between people—*consummate love*—occurs when intimacy, passion, and commitment are all present.

The Cognitive-Arousal Model: Why Does My Heart Pound?

?

34. Explain how transfer of excitation can influence our feelings of love.

Our culture believes in the concept of love, and we are exposed to love themes from childhood. Woman meets Prince Charming; they fall in love, get married, and live happily ever after. By adolescence, we are eagerly awaiting the glories of love.

According to the **cognitive-arousal model of love**, the passionate component of love has interacting cognitive and physiological components (Berscheid, 1984; Hatfield & Rapson, 1987). Primed with our beliefs and expectations about love, when we experience high arousal in the presence of someone whom we perceive as attractive and desirable, we may conclude that we must be "falling in love." This model suggests that emotional arousal actually caused by some other factor may sometimes be misinterpreted as love. This phenomenon is known as **transfer of excitation**: arousal due to one source is perceived ("misattributed") as being due to another source (Zillmann, 1984).

Consider an experiment by Donald Dutton and Arthur Aron (1974). An experimenter—either a male or attractive young female—approached male participants as they crossed over one of two bridges just north of Vancouver. The "arousing" bridge was the Capilano Suspension Bridge, a narrow 150-metre-long structure that wobbles and sways on cables 76 metres above a deep ravine and river. The "non-arousing" bridge was broader, sturdier, and much lower over the same river. Participants were asked to write stories in response to a series of pictures, after which the experimenter offered his or her name and phone number to the participant and told him to call if he wanted more information about the study. When the researchers analyzed the stories, they found sexual themes only in the stories of participants who had encountered the female experimenter on the suspension bridge. This group also made the most follow-up calls to the experimenter.

Dutton and Aron (1974) concluded that men's sexual attraction toward the woman was increased by the arousal produced by being on the suspension bridge, and a meta-analysis of over 30 experiments supports this model (Foster et al., 1998). When we are in the presence of someone we find attractive, other sources of arousal—whether a wobbly bridge, physical exercise, or a frightening movie—increase our sexual attraction even if we recognize those outside sources. If we are not aware of these sources, our attraction increases even more.

Of course, for close relationships to develop and endure, they need more than passion alone. Intimacy, self-disclosure, and commitment provide a basis for the trust and friendship that sustain and increase love. As our *Psychological Applications* feature highlights, other behaviours also help to make close relationships successful.

35. Based on marital research, give some advice to a newlywed couple about behaviours that will help keep their relationship strong.

PSYCHOLOGICAL APPLICATIONS

Making Close Relationships Work: Lessons from Psychological Research

Close relationships go through good times and bad, persisting or dissolving over time. Consider marriage. Though highly intimate, this union often is fragile. In North America, about half of first marriages end in divorce, and the failure rate for second marriages is higher. How can people make their close relationships more satisfying and stable? Recent research on marriage suggests several answers that also may be applied to dating relationships and friendships.

For decades, most marital research simply asked people about their marriages. But as Figure 16.27 shows, researchers are now bringing couples into laboratories to videotape their interactions and to chart their facial and physiological responses as they discuss emotionally charged issues (Gottman et al., 1999; Kiecolt-Glaser et al., 1998). Rather than focusing only on unhappy couples to find out what is going wrong in their relationships, researchers also are studying happy couples to discover the secrets of their success.

Using these methods and new marital interview techniques, psychologists have predicted whether marriages will last or dissolve with impressive accuracy (Carrière et al., 2000). In one laboratory study, John Gottman and his co-workers (1998) collected behavioural and physiological data from 130 newlywed couples as they discussed areas of marital conflict (e.g., in-laws, finances, sex) during the first six months of their marriage. Six years later, participants reported being happily married, unhappily married, or divorced. Using data collected while the couples were newlyweds, the researchers predicted which marriages would end in divorce with 83 percent accuracy, and the degree of marital satisfaction in still-married couples with 80 percent accuracy.

FIGURE 16.27
In John Gottman's "love lab," married couples (husband visible in rear) are filmed while interacting. Facial expressions, actions, heart rate, breathing rate, perspiration, fidgeting, and other responses are measured.

–*Continued*

Surprisingly, the amount of anger expressed by husbands and wives in their laboratory interactions predicted neither stability nor happiness six years later. Instead, the crucial factor was the manner in which couples dealt with their anger. Particularly important were four behaviours that Gottman (1994) calls "The Four Horsemen of the Apocalypse": *criticism, contempt, defensiveness,* and *stonewalling* (listener withdrawal and non-responsiveness).

Couples headed for unhappiness or divorce often exhibit these behaviours while discussing conflict, thereby escalating their conflict and negative emotions. When the wife criticizes the husband, he often stonewalls and withdraws from her attempts to reach some resolution. Her resulting frustration leads to stronger emotional displays and criticism, and the interaction degenerates into exchanges of contempt in which the partners tear down each other. Once this negative cycle develops, even positive overtures by one spouse are likely to evoke a negative response from the other (Margolin & Wampold, 1981).

Happily married couples experience conflict and anger too, but do not allow the spiral of negativity to get out of control. Instead, they make frequent "repair attempts" to resolve their differences in a spirit of mutual respect and support. Gottman and his co-workers (1998) found that in happy marriages, the wife often introduced the conflict topic in a softened or low-intensity manner, rather than with sarcasm, criticism, and strong emotion. Next a key factor occurred: The husband responded to the issues she raised in a concerned and respectful manner that de-escalated negative emotion. A husband who turns off the television and listens to his wife, or who says, "I can see you're upset, so let's work this out," demonstrates that her concerns are important to him. In happy marriages, after the husbands' responsiveness de-escalated the conflict, couples tended to "soothe" one another (and themselves) with positive comments and humour, resulting in more emotionally positive interchanges and lowered physiological arousal.

Happily married partners also make the effort to get to know each other's psychological world—their fears and dreams, philosophy of life, attitudes, and values—and they continually update their knowledge. This "love map," as Gottman calls it, allows each partner to be more responsive to the other's needs and to navigate around relationship roadblocks (Gottman, 1998; Gottman & De Claire, 2002). Such behaviour contributes to an essential aspect of happy marriages: a deep and intimate friendship between the partners. Gottman (1994) notes that the lessons of happy marriages can be applied to other types of close relationships. Affirmative answers to the questions in Table 16.1 suggest that such relationships are on solid psychological ground.

TABLE 16.1 **How Strong is Your Relationship?**

Answer each question True (T) or False (F):		
I can tell you about some of my partner's dreams.	T	F
We just love talking to each other.	T	F
My partner is one of my best friends.	T	F
My partner listens respectfully, even when we disagree.	T	F
We generally mesh well on basic values and goals in life.	T	F
I feel that my partner knows me pretty well.	T	F

The greater the number of "True" answers, the stronger your relationship. (Courtesy of John Gottman.)

Prejudice and Discrimination

Walk into a party, classroom, job interview—any social situation—and just by looking at your body build people will start to form an impression of you (Crandall et al., 2001). If they perceive you as "fat," for example, you may be judged as less likable, as having poorer will power and social skills, and as being more unhappy with yourself than your non-fat peers (Crandall & Martinez, 1996; Carr & Friedman, 2007).

Attractiveness matters too. Both children and adults tend to form less favourable impressions of people who are less attractive. They expect them to have less desirable personality traits and to achieve less success and happiness in life, even though correlational studies typically find that such variables are unrelated or only weakly related to attractiveness and other facial features (Dion et al., 1972; Zebrowitz et al., 1996).

Perhaps above all, ethnicity and gender matter. They are likely to be the first characteristics someone notices about you, and like so many other personal qualities, can be the basis for prejudice and discrimination (Fiske, 2002). **Prejudice** refers to a negative attitude toward people based on their membership in a group. Thus we *prejudge* people—dislike them or hold negative beliefs about them—simply because they are female or male, belong to one ethnic group or religion rather than to another, are "gay" or "straight," and so on. **Discrimination** refers to overt behaviour: It involves treating people unfairly based on the group to which they belong.

Overt and Covert Prejudice: Have Times Changed?

Even in this day and age, overt prejudice and discrimination are in abundant supply. Armed conflicts based on ethnic or religious divisions continue across the globe; supremacist groups and hate crimes persist (Figure 16.28); and people's race, gender, religion, and sexual orientation spark unfair treatment (Herek, 2000). In some ways, however, the most blatant forms of prejudice and discrimination have decreased in many countries. Racial segregation is no longer sanctioned by government policy in the United States and South Africa, and opinion polls indicate that fewer people express prejudiced attitudes toward other ethnic groups than was the case decades ago (Newport, 1999, March 1, March 29).

FIGURE 16.28

Prejudice reveals itself in many subtle and not-so-subtle forms.

Although prejudiced attitudes truly seem to have faded a bit, in many ways modern racism, sexism, and other forms of prejudice have gone underground and are more difficult to detect (Dovidio et al., 2005; Dovidio et al., 1997; Sigall & Page, 1971). Many people consciously hide their prejudices, expressing them only when they feel it is safe or socially appropriate. In other cases people may honestly believe that they are not prejudiced, but still show bias when tested in sophisticated ways (Fazio et al., 1995).

36. How do psychologists use reaction time tasks to detect people's covert prejudice?

To measure covert prejudice, Anthony Greenwald and his co-workers (1998) developed an *implicit association test* in which a series of word-pairs, such as "black—pleasant" and "white—pleasant" are flashed on a computer screen. As soon as you see each pair, your task is to press a computer key as quickly as you can, and this represents your reaction time. The principle underlying this test is that people react more quickly when they perceive that the two words in each pair are associated with one another (i.e., the words "fit" together) than when they don't fit together. Thus, without conscious control, a person prejudiced against Blacks will react more slowly to the "black—pleasant" pair than to the "white—pleasant" pair. The larger the discrepancy in reaction times, the stronger are the person's underlying negative attitudes. Greenwald and his associates found large reaction time differences of this kind even among White males who claimed in response to standard questions—to have no prejudice toward Blacks. Likewise, Japanese and Koreans, whose nations have a history of conflict, react differently toward pairs such as "Japanese—pleasant" and "Korean—pleasant."

Prejudiced attitudes may surface when we are cued to think in negative ways. Esses & Zanna (1995) had students listen to music that put them in either a good, bad, or neutral mood. They then generated a set of traits for a variety of ethnic groups (e.g., English Canadians, Pakistanis, etc.) and rated how positive or negative they felt each trait was. The data indicated that English Canadian students rated other ethnic groups more negatively when they were in a bad mood, but not when they were in a good mood. Thus, the way we are feeling can influence how we think about others. Recent research has attempted to identify the neural basis for these reactions. We examine this work more closely in the Focus on Neuroscience box in this chapter.

FOCUS ON NEUROSCIENCE

The Neuroscience of Stereotyping

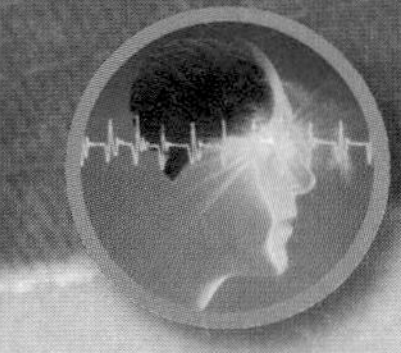

Researchers wanting to study stereotyping acknowledge that modern versions of prejudice are more covert, more implicit than they were in the past (e.g., Esses & Hodson, 2006; Greenwald, 1998). Rather than directly indicating that a particular group is disliked, prejudice is more likely to show up as

–*Continued*

increased reaction time when the names of targeted groups are paired with positively-toned adjectives (e.g., Black-pleasant). What neural circuits might we expect to be involved in this kind of reaction?

Recent work has focused on the amygdala. Activity in the amygdala can reflect a quick assessment of the potential threat posed by an emotionally laden stimulus (Adolphs et al., 1994). Thus, if an individual perceives an out-group member as threatening, we should observe heightened amygdala activity. This result has been reported by several researchers (e.g., Cunningham et al., 2004; Eberhart, 2005) in studies where participants simply look at faces of in-group and out-group members. Indeed, amygdala activation can be observed even when the target face is presented subliminally (Cunningham et al., 2004) and the strength of activation is correlated with measures of implicit racism (Phelps et al., 2000).

Which facial features might trigger such a response? While there are many possible features to examine (e.g., size of nose, straightness of hair, etc.), one that seems an obvious candidate is skin tone. Variations in skin tone are related to perceptions of favourability (lighter skin tones are preferred) even by same-race judges (e.g., Maddox & Gray, 2002). Perhaps looking at skin tone itself will activate the amygdala. Ronquillo et al. (2007) presented photographs of both Black and White faces to participants (White males) while being scanned with fMRI. The faces had been colour adjusted using Photoshop so that participants saw both light-toned and dark-toned versions of each face. Their task was simply to decide whether the individual presented was older or younger than 24 years. Consistent with previous findings, greater activity was observed in the amygdala for Black faces than for White faces. However, the dark-toned White face resulted in as much activity as observed with the Black faces (see Figure 16.29). There was a nonsignificant decrease observed for the light-toned Black faces.

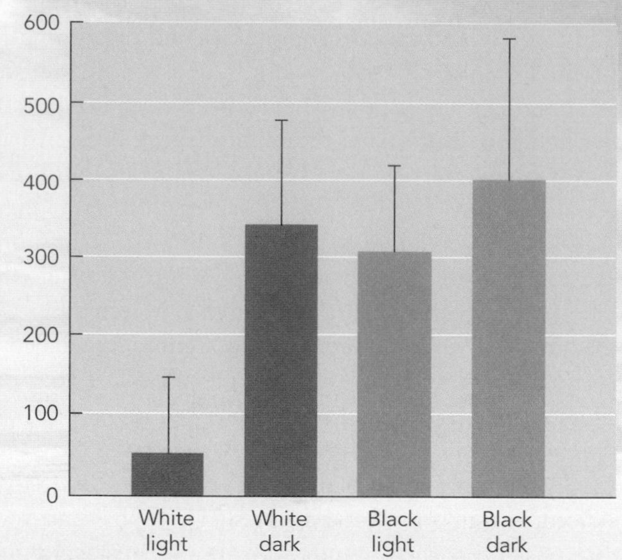

FIGURE 16.29

Amygdala activity in response to Black and White faces (after Ronquillo et al., 2007).

Ronquillo et al. (2007) suggest that these subtle differences are the bases of stereotype formation. Phenotypic features such as dark skin tone are detected at the level of the amygdala and in a largely automatic fashion result in stereotypic bias. We are likely to have a negative-affective response to individuals who possess this feature, regardless of their group membership.

37. Identify cognitive processes that foster prejudice.

Cognitive Roots of Prejudice

Whether overt or subtle, prejudice and discrimination are caused by a constellation of factors, including historical and cultural norms that legitimize differential treatment of various groups. Here, we examine several cognitive and motivational causes of prejudice.

Categorization and us-them thinking. To organize and simplify our world, we have a normal perceptual tendency to categorize objects and people. At times, this helps us react to the environment quickly and to predict others' behaviour (Ito & Cacioppo, 2000). But our automatic tendency to categorize people also helps to lay a foundation for prejudice (Dovidio et al., 1997; Glick & Fiske, 1999).

Categorization leads to the perception of "in-groups" and "out-groups," groups to which we do and do not belong, respectively. In turn, in-group versus out-group distinctions spawn two common biases. First, we display *in-group favouritism*, a tendency to favour in-group members and attribute more positive qualities to "us" than to "them." In-group favouritism emerges in laboratory experiments across the globe, even when participants are assigned to temporary groups based on the flip of a coin or some trivial characteristic (Reichl, 1997; Tajfel, 1971). *Out-group derogation* reflects a tendency to attribute more negative qualities to "them" than to "us." Although people may display both biases, especially when they feel threatened, in-group favouritism is usually the stronger of the two (Hewstone et al., 2002).

Second, people display an *out-group homogeneity bias*. They generally view members of out-groups as being more similar to one another than are members of in-groups (Du et al., 2003; Brauer, 2001). In other words, we perceive that "they are all alike," but recognize that "we are diverse" (Linville & Jones, 1980). The mere fact that we identify people as "Asian," "Hispanic," "Black," and "White" reflects such a bias, because each of these ethnic categories contains many subgroups. In one study, Anglo-American university students were less likely to distinguish among "Hispanic" subgroups than were Cuban-American, Mexican-American, and Puerto Rican-American university students (Huddy & Virtanen, 1995). But just like Anglo students, the Cuban-, Mexican-, and Puerto Rican-American students also engaged in us-them thinking: They saw their own subgroup as distinct from the others, but did not differentiate between the other two Hispanic subgroups.

38. How can people maintain their stereotypes in the face of contradictory information?

Stereotypes and attributional distortions. Categorization and in-group biases lead us to respond quickly to out-group members based on perceived group characteristics—stereotypes—rather than based on their individual characteristics. Recall that merely labelling Hannah's parents as "blue-collar" or "white-collar" created a mental set that shaped how people perceived her behaviour (Darley & Gross, 1983). Similarly, 73 percent of White university students who observed a videotape of a Black man shoving a White man perceived the behaviour as "violent," but when the tape showed a White man shoving a Black man, only 13 percent of students saw it as violent (Duncan, 1976). Figure 16.30 illustrates how racial and gender stereotypes affect our perceptions.

What happens when we encounter individual members of out-groups whose behaviour clearly contradicts our stereotypes? One possibility is that we may change our stereotype; but someone who is motivated to hold on to their prejudiced belief can "explain away" discrepant behaviour in several ways. For example, the out-group member may be seen as an "exceptional case" or as having succeeded at a task not because of high ability, but due to tremendous effort, good luck, or special advantage (Pettigrew, 1979). People who stereotype women as passive and dependent may respond to a strong and assertive woman by placing her in a special subcategory, such as "feminist," thereby leaving the general stereotype intact.

Motivational Roots of Prejudice

39. According to realistic conflict theory and social identity theory, what are the motivational roots of prejudice?

People's well-ingrained ways of perceiving the world—categorizing, forming in-groups and out-groups, and so forth—appear to set the wheels of prejudice in motion, but motivational factors affect how fast those wheels spin.

Competition and conflict. According to **realistic conflict theory**, competition for limited resources fosters prejudice. In the United States and Europe, hostility toward minority groups increases when economic conditions worsen (Green et al., 1998; Catalano et al., 2002; Hovland & Sears, 1940; Pettigrew & Meertens, 1995). Originally, it was believed that a threat to one's personal welfare was the prime motivator of prejudice, but research suggests that prejudice is triggered more strongly by a *perceived threat to one's in-group* (Tajfel & Turner, 2004). As the Robbers Cave summer camp experiment illustrated in Chapter 1, competition between groups often breeds hostility and derogation of the out-group (Sherif et al., 1961). Likewise, among Whites, prejudice toward Blacks is not related to personal resource gains and losses, but to the belief that White people as a group are in danger of being overtaken (Bobo, 1988).

(a)

(b)

FIGURE 16.30

(a) Who is holding the razor knife? Allport and Postman (1947) showed this picture to one person, who then told another, who then told another, and so forth. Typically, by the sixth telling, the Black man was erroneously described as holding the razor. (b) Which person contributes most strongly to this research team? When the drawing shows an all-male group, all-female group, or mixed-sex group with a male at the head of the table (seat 3), participants say that the person in seat 3 is the strongest member. But in this mixed-gender drawing, most male and female participants do not pick the woman in seat 3. Instead, they pick one of the two men (Porter & Geis, 1981).

Enhancing self-esteem. According to **social identity theory**, prejudice stems from a need to enhance our self-esteem. Some experiments find that people express more prejudice after their self-esteem is threatened (such as by receiving negative feedback about their abilities), and that the opportunity to derogate others helps to restore self-esteem (Fein & Spencer, 1997). Self-esteem, however, is based on two components: a personal identity and a "group" identity that reflects membership in various groups (Tajfel & Turner, 1986). We can raise self-esteem by associating ourselves with our in-group's accomplishments, and, conversely, threats to the in-group threaten our self-esteem. Our group identity thus creates a tendency to take pride in one's in-group while also derogating out-groups (Perdue et al., 1990). Compared to relatively unprejudiced people, prejudiced individuals show greater concern with accurately determining who is an in-group versus out-group member (Blascovich et al., 1997).

How Prejudice Confirms Itself

40. Discuss how self-fulfilling prophecies and stereotype threat perpetuate prejudice.

Self-fulfilling prophecies are one of the most invisible yet damaging ways of maintaining prejudiced beliefs. A classic experiment by Carl Word and his colleagues (1974) illustrates this point. The researchers began with the premise—supported by research at the time—that Whites held several negative stereotypes of Blacks. In the experiment, White male university students interviewed White and Black high school students who were seeking admission into a special group. The participants used a fixed set of interview questions provided by the experimenter. Unknown to them, each applicant was an "accomplice" who had been trained to respond in a standard way to the questions. The findings indicated that these White participants sat farther away, conducted shorter interviews, and made more speech errors when the applicants were Black. In short, their behaviour was discriminatory.

But this is only half the picture. In a second experiment—a job interview simulation—White male undergraduates served as *job applicants*. Through random assignment they were treated either as the White applicants had been treated in the first experiment, or as the Black applicants had been treated. In other words, for half the participants, the interviewer sat farther away, held a shorter interview, and made more speech errors. The findings revealed that White participants who were treated more negatively performed worse during the job interview, were less composed, made more speech errors, and rated the interviewer as less friendly. In short, these experiments suggest that an interviewer's negative stereotypes can lead to discriminatory treatment during a job interview, and this discriminatory behaviour can cause the applicant to perform more poorly—ultimately confirming the interviewer's initial stereotype.

Stanford psychologist Claude Steele (1997) has demonstrated another debilitating way that prejudice ends up "confirming itself." As described in Chapter 9, his concept of **stereotype threat** proposes that stereotypes create a fear and self-consciousness among stereotyped group members that they will "live up" to other people's stereotypes. For example, in a study comparing female and male college students who major in various fields, women majoring in the traditionally "male" fields of math, science, and engineering reported the highest level of stereotype threat (Steele et al., 2002). They were more likely to feel that they (as well as other women in their major) had been targets of sex discrimination and that because of their gender, other people (including their professors) expected them to have less ability and do more poorly. Stereotype threat can occur even if the group members do not accept the stereotype themselves. Given the stereotype that "Blacks are not as intelligent as Whites," Black university students who take a difficult test perform more poorly than White students when the test is described as "an intelligence test." But Blacks perform as well as Whites when the items are described merely as being a "laboratory task." Stereotypes that Whites are inferior to Asians in math, and that women are inferior to men in math, produce analogous results. When a difficult standardized math test is given in situations that activate these stereotypes, Whites and women perform more poorly than when the test is presented in a more neutral way (Aronson et al., 1999; Spencer et al., 1999).

Reducing Prejudice

Psychologists are interested not only in the causes of prejudice but also in identifying ways to reduce it. With some success, they have implemented many techniques aimed at changing the way people categorize one another and think about in-groups and out-groups (Hewstone et al., 2002).

The best-known approaches to prejudice reduction are based on a principle called **equal status contact**: Prejudice between people is most likely to be reduced when they (1) engage in sustained close contact, (2) have equal status, (3) work to achieve a common goal that requires cooperation, and (4) are supported by broader social norms (Allport, 1954).

In 1954, the United States Supreme Court handed down a momentous decision in the case of *Brown v. Board of Education*, ruling that school segregation based solely on race violates the constitutional rights of racial minorities. Providing key testimony, several psychologists stated that segregation contributed to racial prejudice and hostility.

Did school desegregation reduce prejudice? Walter Stephan (1990) reviewed more than 80 evaluation studies of desegregation programs and concluded that increasing direct contact through desegregation did not, in and of itself, consistently reduce racial prejudice. Indeed, some studies found that prejudice increased after desegregation.

Why weren't the results more positive? First, the condition of equal status contact was often not met, and contact when status is unequal serves only to perpetuate both groups' negative stereotypes of one another. Second, in many integrated school situations, close and personal contact between group members did

FIGURE 16.31

Like these rescue workers, many people seek out careers or join volunteer organizations that allow them to help other people.

not occur. Black and White students were sometimes placed in different "learning tracks" that minimized in-class contact, and they tended to associate only with members of their own ethnic group outside of class. Third, classroom experiences focused on individual rather than cooperative learning. And finally, intergroup contact was often not supported by broader social norms. In the early years of desegregation, many White politicians, parents, teachers, and school officials militantly opposed school integration.

When intergroup contact takes place under proper conditions, however, prejudice often decreases (Pettigrew & Tropp, 2000). In school settings, *cooperative learning programs* (such as the "jigsaw classroom" program described in Chapter 1) place children into multiracial learning groups. Contact is close and sustained, each child is accorded equal status, and each has responsibility for learning and then teaching other group members one piece of the information that is needed for the group to succeed in its assignment (Aronson et al., 1978). Overall, such programs reduce prejudice and promote appreciation of ethnic group differences (Johnson, 2000).

Beyond equal status contact, cooperative learning programs enable children to forge a common group identity, much as athletes on a team or members of a military unit form a group identity. Adopting a common identity is another factor that helps reduce prejudice among group members (Dovidio et al., 2000).

Pro-social Behaviour: Helping Others

Helping behaviour comes in many forms, from heroic acts of bravery and charitable donations to tutoring a classmate or returning a lost wallet. It characterizes the entire being of people such as Mother Teresa, who devoted her life to the world's poor. Acts of violence often grab the news headlines, but we should not lose sight of the mountains of good deeds performed around the world each day (Figure 16.31).

Why Do People Help?

41. According to sociobiologists, what is the evolutionary basis of helping behaviour?

What motivates pro-social behaviour? The debate over this question has practical consequences and profound implications for our conception of human nature. In Chapter 4, we considered the evolutionary principle of kin selection. Let's examine some more environmental explanations.

Social learning and cultural influences. Socialization, modelling, and reinforcement play a key role in fostering pro-social behaviour and attitudes (Eisenberg & Mussen, 1989; Janoski et al., 1998). Beginning in childhood, we are exposed to helpful models and taught pro-social norms. Recall from Chapter 7 that children were more likely to place several dogs' welfare above their own if they had first seen adults rescue a puppy on a TV program (Sprafkin et al., 1975). A survey of nearly 200 studies suggests that television programs that model acts of kindness and helping have a strong positive effect on viewers' pro-social behaviour (Hearold, 1986).

Two social norms are especially relevant to helping behaviour (De Cremer & van Lange, 2001; Miller et al., 1990). First, the *norm of reciprocity* states that we should reciprocate when others treat us kindly. Second, the *norm of social responsibility* states that people should help others and contribute to the welfare of society. We are reinforced with approval when we adhere to these norms, receive disapproval when we do not, and observe that other people receive praise for conforming to these norms. Eventually, we internalize pro-social norms and values as our own, enabling powerful *self-reinforcers* such as pride, self-praise, and feelings of satisfaction to maintain pro-social behaviours even when external reinforcement is absent.

42. How do social norms, self-reinforcers, and empathy influence helping behaviour?

Studies in Europe, Asia, and North America confirm that socialization matters (Eisenberg & Valiente, 2002). Children are more likely to act pro-socially when they have been raised by parents who have high moral standards, who are warm and supportive, and who encourage their children to develop empathy and "put themselves in other people's shoes" (Janssens & Dekovic, 1997; Krevans & Gibbs, 1996). However, there also are cross-cultural differences in beliefs about when and why we should help (Eckensberger & Zimba, 1997). Joan Miller and her colleagues (1990) found that Hindu children and adults in India believe that one has a moral obligation to help friends and strangers, whether their need is serious or mild. In contrast, when a person's need for assistance is mild, American children and adults feel less obligated to help and view helping as more of a choice.

Empathy and altruism. Are all pro-social acts, regardless of how noble they appear, ultimately motivated by self-reinforcement, or do we have a capacity for *altruism,* the desire to aid another without concern for oneself? According to C. Daniel Batson's **empathy-altruism hypothesis**, altruism does exist, and it is produced by *empathy,* the ability to put oneself in the place of another and to share what that person is experiencing (Batson, 1991; Batson et al., 2002).

In one study, female students' empathy for another female participant (actually an accomplice) was increased or decreased by leading them to believe that her values were either similar or dissimilar to their own (Batson et al., 1981). Then, by a rigged coin flip, the accomplice was selected to receive supposedly painful electric shocks while performing a task, while the real participant acted as an observer. When the experiment began, the accomplice expressed great fear of the shocks. At this point, the participant was told that she could leave after watching only two shock trials or, if she wished, could change places with the woman, thereby saving her from the trauma of being shocked. Consistent with the empathy-altruism hypothesis, Figure 16.32 shows that high empathy participants were much more likely to voluntarily change places.

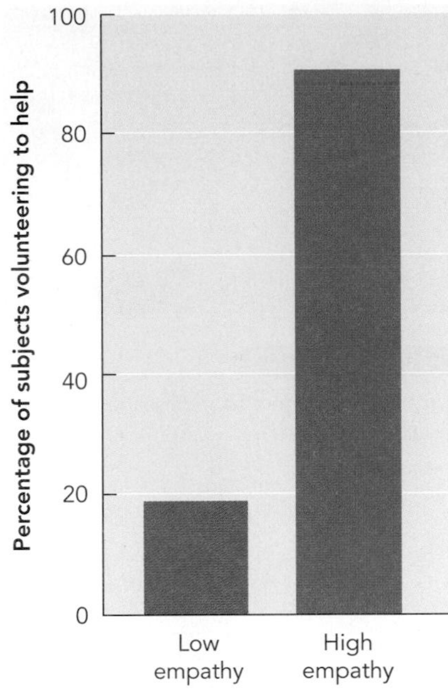

FIGURE 16.32

Compared to women in a low-empathy condition, women who were led to feel high empathy for a fellow research participant were more likely to volunteer to receive electric shocks in her place.

Data from Batson et al., 1981.

As critical thinkers, we need to ask whether participants exchanged places not by virtue of empathy, but because they would have felt guilty for not doing so. Or perhaps, as the **negative state relief model** proposes, high empathy causes us to feel distress when we learn of others' suffering, so by helping them we reduce *our own* personal distress—a self-focused goal, not an altruistic one (Cialdini et al., 1987). Indeed, there are many reasons for acts of helping, but Batson's research suggests that at least some pro-social behaviour is motivated by unselfish goals and not by the reduction of guilt, sadness, or one's own distress (Batson et al., 1997). Other researchers are not convinced, however, and the larger philosophical debate as to whether people are ever truly altruistic rages on (Cialdini et al., 1997).

When Do People Help?

Ordinary citizens often go to great lengths to help strangers, but, as the infamous Kitty Genovese murder illustrates, at times bystanders fail to assist victims who are clearly in distress (Figure 16.33). What influences whether a bystander will intervene?

43. Identify two key ways (two stages of intervention) in which the presence of other bystanders often inhibits people from responding to an emergency.

Bibb Latané and John Darley (1970) view bystander intervention as a five-step process (Figure 16.34). First, a bystander will not help unless she or he notices the situation. Imagine that as you walk along a street, you hear two people yelling and then hear a single scream coming from inside a house. You've noticed the situation, but now what? In everyday life, many social situations are ambiguous, and step 2 involves deciding whether this is an emergency. Is someone really in danger? To answer this question, we often engage in *social comparison:* We look around to see how other people are responding. You might say to yourself, "No one else seems

FIGURE 16.33

Why do bystanders sometimes fail to assist a person in need?

concerned, so it mustn't be anything too serious." In Kitty Genovese's murder, some bystanders mistakenly thought that because nobody else intervened they were merely witnessing a "lover's quarrel" that didn't warrant their "butting in" (Darley & Latané, 1968).

Laboratory experiments confirm the importance of social comparison. In one classic study, participants were filling out a questionnaire when smoke started to pour into the room from underneath a locked side door (Latané & Darley, 1968). Among those who were alone, three-quarters left the room to report the smoke. But when three participants were in the room together, only 38 percent of the groups reported the smoke. Astonishingly, most groups kept working while the room filled with smoke. Each person looked around, saw that nobody else was doing anything, and became convinced that the smoke didn't represent an emergency!

If you conclude that a situation is an emergency, then you move to the next step: assuming responsibility to intervene. If you are the only person to hear someone screaming, then responsibility for helping falls squarely on you. But if others are present, there may be a *diffusion of responsibility*—"If I don't help, someone else will"—and if each bystander has this thought, the victim won't receive help. In the Kitty Genovese murder, many bystanders who *did* interpret the incident as an emergency failed to intervene because they were certain that someone must already have called the police (Darley & Latané, 1968). Similarly, in a experiment in which university students were isolated in individual cubicles and listened to another student who indicated he was having a seizure, participants were less likely to assist the seizure victim if they believed that other bystanders were present (Darley & Latané, 1968).

If you take responsibility, whether you actually intervene still depends on a fourth factor, your *self-efficacy* (confidence) in dealing with the situation. Sometimes we fail to help because we don't know how or believe that our help won't be effective. In one survey, 269 university students and faculty indicated they had witnessed a public episode of child abuse, yet only a quarter reported that they had intervened (Christy & Voigt, 1994). Of those who intervened, 71 percent said that they had been certain about what to do. Among those who did not intervene, 80 percent said they were *not* certain about what action to take.

1. Notice an event? — No / Yes ↓
2. Interpret as an emergency? — No / Yes ↓
3. Assume responsibility for helping? — No / Yes ↓
4. Know how to help? — No / Yes ↓
5. Decide to help — No / Yes ↓

Help victim | No help given

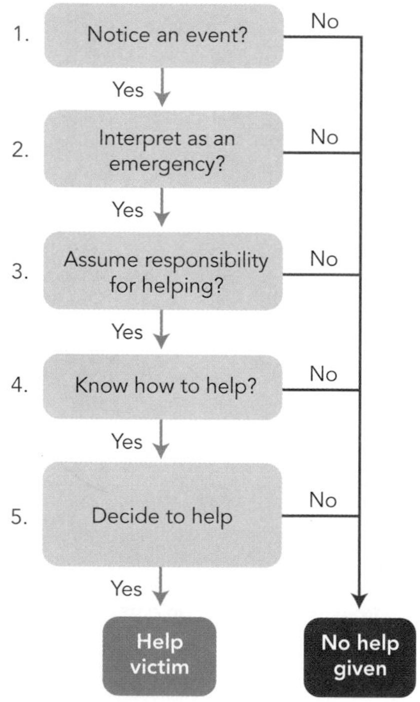

FIGURE 16.34

Bystander intervention in an emergency situation can be viewed as a five-step process. If the answer at each step is "yes," help is given.

Based on Latané & Darley, 1970.

Finally, a bystander might decide not to intervene because of the perceived costs (Dovidio et al., 1991). Potential costs include not only possible physical danger, but also negative social consequences, such as "appearing foolish" by trying to help inappropriately.

As this model indicates, the common sense adage "there is safety in numbers" is not always true when it comes to receiving help. Many experiments find a **bystander effect**: The presence of multiple bystanders inhibits each person's tendency to help, largely due to social comparison or diffusion of responsibility. This inhibition is more likely to occur when the bystanders are strangers rather than friends (Latané & Rodin, 1969). Markey (2000) reports that the bystander effect occurs even when communicating over the Web. A general request for help ("Can anyone tell me how to look at someone's profile?") was sent to 200 chat groups over a 30-day period. Assistance came more slowly from larger chat groups than from smaller ones.

Beyond the bystander effect, other factors also help to explain why people may be helpful on some occasions but not on others. First, we are more likely to help when we are in a *good mood* (Salovey et al., 1991). Ironically, *pre-existing guilt*—feeling guilty about something we have recently done—also increases helping (Regan et al., 1972). Apparently, assisting others eases our guilt, even when the two actions are unrelated. Observing a *helpful role model,* such as someone assisting a stranded motorist or donating blood, increases pro-social behaviour (Sarason et al., 1991). Finally, we help more when there is a lack of time pressure and we are *not in a hurry.*

Whom Do We Help?

44. Who are we most likely to help? How might the belief in a just world inhibit us from helping?

Some people are more likely to receive help than others. Three prominent factors are:

- *Similarity.* Perceiving that a person is similar to us increases our willingness to provide help. The similarity may be in dress, attitudes, nationality, or other characteristics (Dovidio, 1984), and it may make it easier for us to identify with the victim's plight.
- *Gender.* Women are more likely to receive help than men *if* the bystander is male (Eagly & Crowley, 1986). Women and men are equally likely to be helped by female bystanders.
- *Perceived responsibility.* People are more likely to receive help when their need for aid is viewed as being caused by factors beyond their control (Blader & Tyler, 2002; Weiner, 1996). Thus people who are homeless because of a natural disaster are more likely to receive help than those who are perceived as being homeless because they are unwilling to work.

Because our attributions regarding why a person needs help can be inaccurate, this last factor—perceived responsibility—can take an odd twist. Ironically, one factor that can lead attributions astray is a belief that the world is a just place. The **just world hypothesis** (Lerner, 1980) holds that, because people want to view the world as fair, they perceive that people get what they deserve and deserve what they get. This belief may lead some people to conclude that victims of rape, AIDS, and other misfortunes somehow *deserve* their fate (Ford et al., 1998; Wyer et al., 1985). This irrational blaming of victims may reduce people's feelings of responsibility to help.

Increasing Pro-social Behaviour

Can pro-social behaviour be increased? "Mandatory volunteerism" is one approach used in some high schools, universities, and businesses. Obviously, the students and workers who are required to donate their time to charitable organizations provide a valuable service, but do these programs increase participants' intrinsic volunteerism later in life? Unfortunately, research results are mixed (Janoski et al., 1998; Stukas, 1999). The outcome probably depends on the personal rewards that volunteers experience and their increased awareness of human needs.

Another approach, consistent with social learning theory, is to expose people to pro-social models. Psychologists used pro-social modelling as part of a nationwide program to increase blood donations (Sarason et al., 1991). Students in 66 high schools watched an audiovisual program showing high-school donors giving blood. Compared to a control condition presented with a standard appeal from the local blood bank, the pro-social video increased blood donations by 17 percent.

Research suggests that developing feelings of empathy and connectedness with others also may make people more likely to help (Eisenberg, 2000). Margaret Clark and her co-workers (1987) found that people who felt a greater sense of connectedness to their communities were more likely to experience a need to be socially responsible and to help others.

Finally, simply learning about factors that hinder bystander intervention may increase the tendency to help someone in distress. Arthur Beaman and his co-workers (1978) exposed some university students to information about the *bystander effect.* Control participants did not receive this information. Two weeks later, more than half of the students who had learned about the bystander effect provided aid to the victim of an accident (staged by the researchers), compared to only about one-fourth of the control group participants.

Aggression: Harming Others

We love. We nurture. We help. But as current events and the history of humankind attest, we also harm. In humans, *aggression* represents any form of behaviour that is intended to harm another person, and it can be analyzed at biological, environmental, and psychological levels.

Biological Factors in Aggression

45. What evidence supports a genetic role in aggression?

Is aggression rooted in heredity? From bulls, roosters, and dogs to laboratory mice and rats, animals can be selectively bred over generations to be more or less aggressive (Lagerspetz et al., 1968). In some species, such as the stickleback fish shown in Figure 16.35, certain aggressive behaviours represent a fixed-action pattern that is reflexively triggered by specific environmental stimuli. Humans do not display such rigid, reflexive aggressive responses, but behaviour geneticists argue that heredity partly determines why some people are more aggressive than others. Identical twins are more similar in their aggressive behaviour patterns than are fraternal twins, even when the identical twins are raised in different homes with presumably different social environments (Bouchard et al., 1990; Coccaro et al., 1997; Beatty et al., 2002). Sociobiologists propose that a genetic predisposition toward aggression can be traced to evolutionary adaptation (see Chapter 4). As in non-humans, aggression at the proper time helped our ancestors compete successfully for mates, food, and shelter, defend territory, and survive against attack. This increased the odds that such individuals would pass their genes on to the next generation (Rushton, 1989).

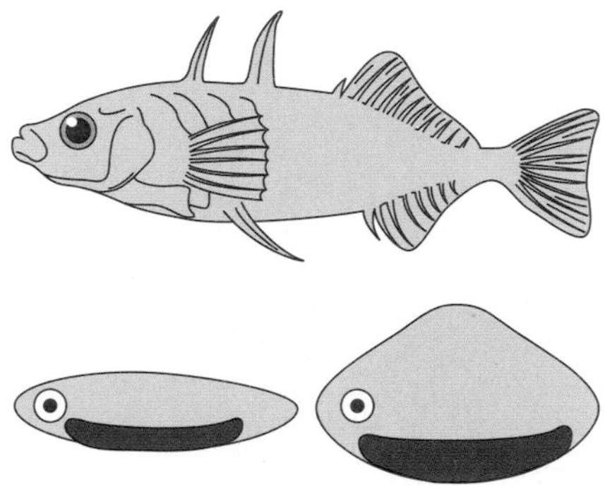

FIGURE 16.35

During the mating season the male stickleback fish develops a red belly. The sight of another red-bellied male—a potential rival for a mate—reflexively triggers an attack by the first male. The key releaser stimulus for this fixed action pattern is the red marking. A male stickleback will not attack a realistic-looking male model that has no red belly, but will attack unrealistic fish models that have this red marking.

Based on Tinbergen, 1951.

The search for biological causes of aggression also has led researchers deep within the brain, to the *hypothalamus, amygdala,* and other subcortical structures (Flynn, 1975; Siegel et al., 1999). Electrically stimulate certain neural pathways in a cat's hypothalamus, and it will arch its back and attack. Surgically destroy areas of the amygdala—an approach that sometimes has been used with violent human criminals—and in many species defensive aggression will decrease (Aggleton, 1993). There is, however, no single brain structure that "turns on" and "turns off" aggression. Different types of aggression—defending oneself, defending one's offspring, predatory aggression, establishing dominance, and so forth—may involve different neural circuits (Siegel et al., 1999).

46. Describe some brain regions and body chemicals that play a role in aggression.

Aggression also involves activity of the *frontal lobes*, and the important role that the frontal lobes play in impulse control (Hawkins & Trobst, 2000). Adrian Raine and his colleagues (1998) examined the brain functioning of 24 adults who had murdered someone, either out of emotional, momentary impulse, or as a planned predatory act. PET scans revealed that both groups of murderers showed more subcortical activity than a control group of non-murderers, but the impulsive murderers also had lower frontal lobe activity. Deficient frontal lobe activity may make it more difficult to regulate aggressive impulses generated by subcortical brain regions (Raine, 2002).

Just as there is no single brain centre for aggression, there is no one "aggression chemical." In humans and other animals, however, atypically low levels of *serotonin* activity may play a role in impulsive aggression, as when people lash out from emotional rage (Siegel et al., 1999; Siever et al., 1999; Moore et al., 2002). When a drug designed to boost serotonin activity is administered to men who physically abuse their partners and also to psychiatric patients who have difficulty controlling aggressive impulses, both groups show a relatively weak response to the drug (Rosenbaum et al., 1997).

And what about the sex hormone *testosterone*, which is found in males and also in females (though in smaller amounts)? In many species of mammals, higher testosterone levels contribute to greater *social aggression:* unprovoked aggressive acts that are designed to establish a dominance hierarchy among members of the same species. Injecting adult males with testosterone increases social aggression, whereas castration decreases it. But in humans and other primates, the association between testosterone and aggression is weaker and less consistent (Pinel, 1997; O'Connor et al., 2002).

Aversive Environmental Stimuli: Beyond Frustration

Aggression is influenced not only by biology, but also by our present environment and past learning experiences (Eron, 2000; Rotton & Cohn, 2000). Frustration, which occurs when some stimulus or event interferes with our progress toward a goal, often contributes to aggression. In 1939, several leading psychologists proposed the **frustration-aggression hypothesis**, stating that (1) frustration inevitably leads to aggression, and (2) all aggression is the result of frustration (Dollard et al., 1939).

Both of these sweeping assertions have since been disproved. From human infants to adults, frustration does increase the risk of verbal or physical aggression (Calkins & Johnson, 1998). At the workplace, it contributes to acts of employee hostility, theft, and sabotage (Spector, 1997). But people do not always respond to frustration by aggressing. Instead, they may exhibit despair, resignation, or non-aggressive ways of dealing with conflict (Björkqvist, 1997).

47. Identify some major types of environmental stimuli that increase the risk of aggression.

The second postulate is false as well. Aggression can be increased not only by frustration, but also by exposure to a wide range of aversive stimuli (Berkowitz, 1990). For example, *painful stimuli* can trigger irritability and aggression in humans and other animals. *Provocation* is another stimulus to aggress. Experiments with university students confirm that we often retaliate against someone who insults us or causes us physical harm (Ohbuchi & Kambara, 1985). In other species, even animals that are normally passive and prefer to flee when attacked will fight if they become cornered (Enquist & Leimar, 1990).

Crowding can trigger aggression in many species. In humans, when people feel crowded and believe they have little control over the situation, they report greater stress, have higher levels of stress hormones, and tolerate frustration more poorly (Fleming et al., 1987). For some motorists, increasingly congested roads and being trapped in inescapable traffic jams set the stage for high stress and aggressive acts of "road rage" (Figure 16.36).

Heat also increases the risk of aggression (Anderson, 2001; Bushman et al., 2005). Assaults, rapes, family disturbances, and riots increase in summer months. These correlational findings are supported by several controlled experiments. In one, Dutch police officers were exposed to two temperature conditions (27° and 21° C/80.6° and 69.8° F) and shown firearm-training videotapes portraying interactions with crime suspects (Vrij et al., 1994). When the temperature was hotter, police perceived suspects as more threatening and responded with greater aggression.

Learning to Aggress: Reinforcement and Modelling

Aggression, like other behaviours, is influenced by learning (Anderson & Bushman, 2002). Non-aggressive animals can be trained to become vicious aggressors if conditions are arranged so that they are consistently victorious in fights with weaker animals. Conversely, if conditions are arranged so that an animal is defeated in its early battles, it becomes submissive. The younger an animal is when it first suffers repeated defeats, the more submissively it will react to attacks by other animals (Zillmann, 1979).

FIGURE 16.36
Increasingly crowded roads and stressed drivers have made road rage an international problem.

Reward affects human aggression in much the same way. In one study of four-year-old nursery-school children, the investigators recorded a total of 2,583 aggressive acts and their consequences. Children became increasingly aggressive

48. Discuss how reinforcement and modelling contribute to aggression.

when their aggressive behaviour produced positive outcomes for them (as when an aggressive act resulted in another child's giving up a desired toy). Children whose aggressive behaviour was unsuccessful or who experienced unpleasant consequences were less likely to be aggressive in the future (Patterson et al., 1967). Unfortunately, about 80 percent of the aggressive behaviours were rewarding for the aggressor.

Aggression also can be learned by observing others (Huesmann, 1997). As Albert Bandura's (1965) famous "Bobo doll" experiments clearly demonstrated, children learn "how to aggress" even when they witness an aggressive model being punished (Chapter 7). Later, if the punishing agent is not present, or if rewards are available for aggressing, children may reproduce the model's actions. Correlational studies, while not establishing cause and effect, find that aggressive and delinquent children tend to have parents who frequently model aggressive behaviour (Bandura, 1973; Stormshak et al., 2000).

Psychological Factors in Aggression

49. How do cognitive factors determine whether we will respond to a stimulus aggressively?

Numerous psychological factors influence whether we behave aggressively in a particular situation (Anderson & Bushman, 2002). From gang violence to "road rage" and war, people may employ several types of *self-justification* to make it psychologically easier to aggress toward others (Schlenker & Weigold, 1992; Lanier, 2001). Aggressors may blame the victim for imagined wrongs, thereby convincing themselves that the victim "deserves it." They may minimize the seriousness of their own aggression by believing that other people's acts are even more repulsive, or by displacing responsibility. They may also "dehumanize" their victims by stripping them of human qualitites and regarding them as objects or animals, as the guard in the Stanford Prison Study did when he began to view the prisoners as "cattle."

Perceived intent, empathy, and emotional regulation. Other cognitive factors, such as the *attribution of intentionality,* affect how we respond to provocation. When we perceive that someone's negative behaviour toward us was intended or controllable, we are more likely to become angry and retaliate (Betancourt & Blair, 1992; Graham et al., 1992). Unfortunately, people who are generally angry and aggressive tend to perceive others as having greater hostile intent, which may contribute to a vicious cycle of aggression (Epps & Kendall, 1995).

Our degree of *empathy* for someone also influences how we react to provocation. When someone offends us and then apologizes, the likelihood that we will forgive her/him depends, in part, on how well we can understand her/his viewpoint (McCullough et al., 1997). And even when we don't forgive, whether we respond to provocation calmly or lash out depends on our *ability to regulate our emotions.* Some children and adults seem to be more physiologically reactive to provocation than others, and reduced frontal lobe activity may impair the ability to control aggressive impulses (Raine et al., 1998). But cultural norms and cognitive factors also influence how we regulate our emotions and manage conflict (Bjoerkqvist, 1997). Thus, when non-violent married men listen to audiotaped interactions designed to induce anger, they respond with more anger-controlling thoughts than do men with a history of domestic abuse (Eckhardt & Kassinove, 1998).

Psychodynamic processes. Sigmund Freud believed that human aggression is instinctive, a view shared by the famous ethologist Konrad Lorenz (1966) and some modern psychodynamic thinkers (Raphling, 1998). Freud proposed that, in a never-ending cycle, aggressive impulses build up over time, eventually have to be released, and then build up again. His principle of **catharsis** stated that performing an act of aggression discharges aggressive energy and *temporarily* reduces our impulse to aggress. But how does one do this in a world in which violence is discouraged and punished? One method of releasing aggressive impulses is to channel them into socially acceptable "aggressive" behaviours, such as participating in verbal debates, vigorous exercise, competitive sports, hunting, and so forth. Another approach is to discharge aggressive impulses *vicariously* by watching and identifying with other people who behave aggressively.

If people cannot express their aggressive impulses in direct or disguised forms, will the unreleased pressures build up to an explosion point? In some cases, seemingly meek or unassertive people commit shocking and brutal crimes. These individuals, whom psychologist Edwin Megargee (1966) describes as having *overcontrolled hostility,* show little immediate reaction to provocation. Instead, they bottle up their anger and, over time, the pressure to aggress builds up. At a critical point, they erupt into violence. Often the provocation that triggers their destructive outburst is trivial. For example, one 10-year-old boy with no previous history of aggression stabbed his sister more than 80 times with an ice pick after she changed the channel during his favourite television show. After the aggressive outburst, such people revert to their former passive, unassertive state (Quinsey et al., 1983).

Cases of overcontrolled hostility are consistent with the concept of catharsis, but other research results are not. For example, when people are aroused by just-completed vigorous physical exercise, it is easier—not harder—to provoke them to aggression (Bushman, 2002). Psychodynamic theory also predicts that viewing violent pornography should help people discharge aggressive impulses, but, as noted in Chapter 10, this is not what happens. After watching scenes of rape and sexual coercion, men act *more* aggressively toward women (Donnerstein & Berkowitz, 1981). And what about watching violent movies and television programs? Do these activities help people "blow off steam," as some stars in the entertainment industry claim?

Media Violence: Catharsis versus Social Learning

Many movies, as well as fiction and non-fiction television programs, are saturated with violence. Analyzing 6,000 hours of American TV programming from 1994 to 1997, researchers found that 60 percent of shows contained acts of violence (National Television Violence Study, 1998). On premium cable channels, the figure was 92 percent. Canadian network programming is just as bad. While there is a Canadian content requirement, the networks are reasonably free to acquire programming from around the globe. The result is television that is every bit as violent as the U.S. networks. Signorielli et al. (1982) report that roughly 80 percent of the shows on Canadian networks contain some kind of violence. This figure rises to 94 percent when we consider only "children's" programming (e.g., Saturday morning cartoons). Various authors have suggested that the average child will witness over 8,000 murders by the time she/he completes elementary school.

50. According to the catharsis and social learning viewpoints, what role does media violence play in regulating human aggression?

According to psychodynamic theory, movie and TV violence should be a cathartic pot of gold. But social learning theorists argue that, by providing numerous aggressive models—including many who are reinforced—media violence is more likely to increase viewers' aggressive behaviour than to reduce it. From a social learning perspective, it is particularly disturbing that (National Television Violence Study, 1998):

- Forty percent of violent incidents on television were initiated by "good guys" whom viewers were likely to perceive as attractive role models and identify with.

- About 75 percent of violent scenes contained no remorse or penalty for violence, and the "bad guys" went unpunished in 40 percent of the programs.
- Only 15 percent of TV programs portrayed long-term negative consequences of violence.

Headline-making "copycat" acts of violence clearly illustrate social learning effects. Still, hundreds of millions of people view media violence, and such horrendous acts thankfully are rare. What, then, are the more general effects of media violence on aggression? Over the past 30 years, hundreds of experiments and correlational studies have shed light on the "catharsis versus social learning" debate.

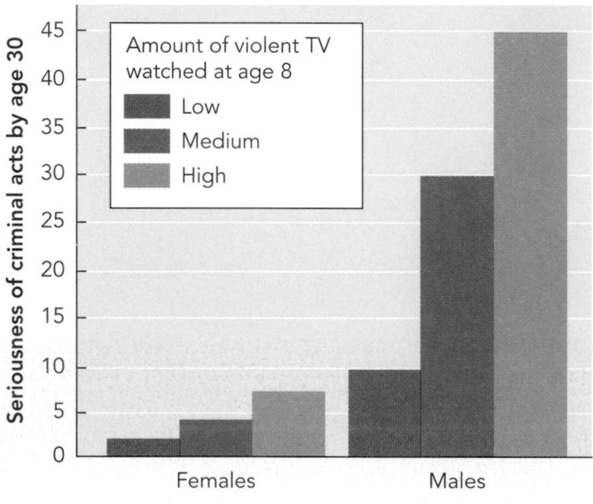

FIGURE 16.37

Children who watched more violent television at age eight committed more serious criminal behaviour by age 30. Although criminal behaviour is higher overall for males than for females, the general pattern of results is the same. These findings are correlational (can you think of alternative explanations for this TV-crime relation?), but, in conjunction with controlled experiments, the weight of evidence convinces most experts that viewing media violence has psychological consequences.

Data from Eron, 1987.

To most experts, the verdict is clear: The preponderance of evidence favours the social learning view (Eron, 2000; Johnson et al., 2002; Smith & Donnerstein, 1998). Exposure to television and movie violence is related to the tendency of both children and adults to behave aggressively (Huesmann et al., 2003).

For example, using data collected over 22 years, Leonard Eron (1987) found that American children who had watched greater amounts of television violence at age eight were more likely to have committed serious criminal activity by age 30 (Figure 16.37). In Finland, Vappu Viemeroe (1996) found that boys and girls who had watched more violent TV when they were seven to nine years old were more likely to have been arrested by their mid-twenties. In Belgium, Jacque Leyens and his colleagues (1975) went into a facility for high-school-age juvenile delinquents and held a special "movie week" in which they showed different groups of boys either violent or non-violent movies each night. The result: Among boys who watched the violent films, physical and verbal aggression increased.

Media violence appears to exert its effects through multiple avenues (Huesman, 1997; National Television Violence Study, 1998):

- Viewers learn new aggressive behaviours through modelling.
- Viewers come to believe that aggression usually is rewarded, or at least, is rarely punished.
- Viewers become desensitized to the sight and thought of violence, and to the suffering of victims.
- Viewers' fear of becoming a target of crime or violence increases.

51. Based on research, how does media violence affect people's behaviour and attitudes?

52. According to learning principles, how might violent video games teach people to behave aggressively? Does evidence support this view?

Before you become completely disillusioned and toss out your television, there are some qualifications that we should consider. First of all, some people are more influenced by TV violence than others. For example, Eron (1987) notes that boys tend to be more susceptible to media violence effects than girls (see Figure 16.37 again). In addition, aggressive behaviour does not occur in a vacuum—in most cases some kind of negative stimulus (e.g., insult, provocation, extreme heat, high arousal level, etc.) must be present. Finally, the highest level of aggression is observed when the cues present in the television program are similar to those encountered in the actual situation. Wendy Josephson (1997) at the University of Winnipeg asked boys in the second or third grade to watch either a violent or non-violent program. Both shows were action-oriented, but the violent show involved a lot of gunplay between a police SWAT team and gang members. The SWAT team kept in constant communication with each other using walkie-talkies. After watching the program, the boys were asked to play a game of floor hockey while observers coded their behaviour for aggression. However, before starting the match the players were "interviewed" by the experimenter in a manner similar to pre-game interviews at actual hockey games. For some of the boys, the experimenter used a microphone and for others, a walkie-talkie.

The highest level of aggression was found in the boys who watched the violent program and who were interviewed with a walkie-talkie. The lowest level was reported for those who watched the non-violent show. Apparently the presence of the aggressive cue (the walkie-talkie) stimulated more aggression because of its association with the violence in the film clip. Similar results of increased aggression following exposure to aggressive cues have been reported in both laboratory (e.g., Berkowitz & LePage, 1967) and field settings (e.g., Boyanowski & Griffiths, 1982).

Beyond movies and TV, the question of whether violent video games promote aggression also has raised public and scientific concern (Figure 16.38). In July 2000, the St. Louis County (Missouri) Council passed an ordinance to penalize businesses that allow people under the age of 18 to play violent video games without parental consent (Jurkowitz, 2002). This decision has since been overturned by a U.S. federal appeals court, but it still highlights the issue of video game violence. What does science have to say?

FIGURE 16.38

Do children who play graphically violent video games become desensitized to violence and more likely to behave aggressively toward other people?

RESEARCH FRONTIERS

Do Violent Video Games Promote Aggression?

Sociologist Tracy Dietz (1998) examined 33 popular video games marketed by Nintendo and Sega (two major manufacturers). Almost half involved direct aggression toward other characters, and one-fifth included violence toward women. Especially in some arcade games, players use realistic "guns" to kill human or human-like characters, whose deaths are graphically portrayed. Successful aggression is rewarded. The more targets you kill, the more points you score and the longer the game plays on.

Do violent video games stimulate aggression, or even prime some children and adolescents to kill? Few people believe that such games are the primary cause of shootings such as the highly publicized 1999 Columbine High School murders in Littleton, Colorado, but 58 percent feel that the federal government should do more to regulate video game violence (Newport, 1999, May 10). Clearly, both the public and scientists are concerned.

Video Games as Target Practice: Conditioning and Desensitization?

To psychologist David Grossman of Arkansas State University, the issue of media and video game violence has special meaning. He lives in Jonesboro, where in March 1998 an 11- and 13-year-old boy staged a false fire alarm, lured classmates out of school, then fatally shot four girls and a teacher and wounded 10 other people. Three years earlier, before a shocking string of similar schoolground killings across the United States, Grossman (1995) published *On Killing: The Psychological Cost of Learning to Kill in War and Society.* His major point: In order to kill, we must learn to overcome a natural inhibition *against* killing members of our own species. And, he argues, violent video games can be a powerful disinhibitor and teacher.

Grossman, a retired U.S. Army officer, points to a history of warfare in which soldiers have been reluctant to kill the enemy face-to-face. In World War II, the U.S. Army found that, for every 100 soldiers who had a clear shot at the enemy, only 15 percent fired at their target: a 15 percent "kill rate." To counteract this situation, the army trained soldiers by using operant and classical conditioning principles. A "shooting" response was gradually shaped via increasingly realistic target practice, progressing from bull's-eye targets to human silhouettes and "pop-up" human figures, and finally to video combat simulations. Over time, soldiers became desensitized to shooting at human forms and, by the Korean and Vietnam

–Continued

Wars, the kill rates increased to 55 and 90 percent, respectively. For over 20 years, police and other law enforcement agencies also have conditioned their personnel to shoot—and to discern when not to shoot—by using video simulations (Cummins, 1999, March 2).

Experiments on Video Game Violence

Does evidence support Grossman's view that video games can be training grounds for violence? Unfortunately, there are relatively few experiments, they focus on short-term effects, and some (particularly in the 1980s) involve "violent" video games that are tame by today's standards.

In one of the best studies to date, Roland Irwin and Alan Gross (1995) of the University of Mississippi randomly assigned 60 seven- and eight-year-old boys to play either a violent or non-violent Nintendo video game for 20 minutes. In the violent game, *Double Dragon,* the player assumes the role of a martial arts hero who kicks, punches, and uses a rope or chain to whip and defeat ruthless street gang members. In the non-violent game, *Excitebike,* the player races a motorcycle against the clock.

After playing one of the games, each child engaged in a 10-minute "free-play" period with another boy (an accomplice). Next, as each participant competed against this boy on a task for a prize, the boy (according to plan) cheated. Observers who were blind to each child's video game condition coded the participants' behaviour during both the free-play period and the frustrating event. Compared to participants who had played *Excitebike,* those who played *Double Dragon* displayed more physical and verbal aggression toward inanimate objects (e.g., toys), more verbal aggression toward the other boy during the free-play period, and more physical aggression toward the other boy during the frustrating competition.

Let us think critically about this result. Did *Double Dragon's* violent *content* increase participants' aggression, or was it simply a more exciting game? If so, perhaps it was only *greater arousal* that led to more aggression. To help decide between these two alternatives, Irwin and Gross measured participants' heart rates both before and during the video game play. The result: no heart rate differences between the two video game conditions, strengthening the conclusion that the aggressive content of the violent game was the key factor.

To date, of four studies (including this one) employing this procedure, three have found that children's aggression while playing with peers increases immediately after playing violent video games (Bensley & Van Eenwyk, 2001). More recently, Bruce Bartholow and Craig Anderson (2002) found that among college students, briefly playing a violent video game (*Mortal Kombat*) increased women's and especially men's aggressive behaviour toward a female student (actually a confederate) who had earlier aggressed against them.

The Big Picture

Three extensive reviews of experiments and real-world correlational studies on violent video games suggest that

- for both sexes, there is a weak but positive relation between playing violent video games and increased aggressive behaviour;
- the relation between playing video games and aggression is strongest for games that involve violent fantasy action;
- evidence does not support the catharsis hypothesis that playing violent video games will decrease people's aggression by letting them "blow off steam"; and
- we cannot draw conclusions about long-term consequences because research has focused on the short-term effects of playing video games (Anderson & Bushman, 2001; Bensley & Van Eenwyk, 2001; Sherry, 2001).

Are these findings cause for worry? We know how the video game industry feels (this is no surprise), but how do you interpret the evidence?

Clearly, the overwhelming majority of children and adults who play violent video games do not go out and assault or kill people. But aggression comes in many forms, physical and verbal, obvious and subtle. It is also noteworthy that the more recent studies, examining participants who are exposed to more graphically violent video games, find stronger effects than older studies (Sherry, 2001). Still, continued research focusing on long-term effects is needed to pinpoint how strongly children and adults are affected by a world full of *Mortal Kombat* and *Doom.*

In closing, Figure 16.39 highlights some of the biological, psychological, and environmental factors that contribute to human aggression.

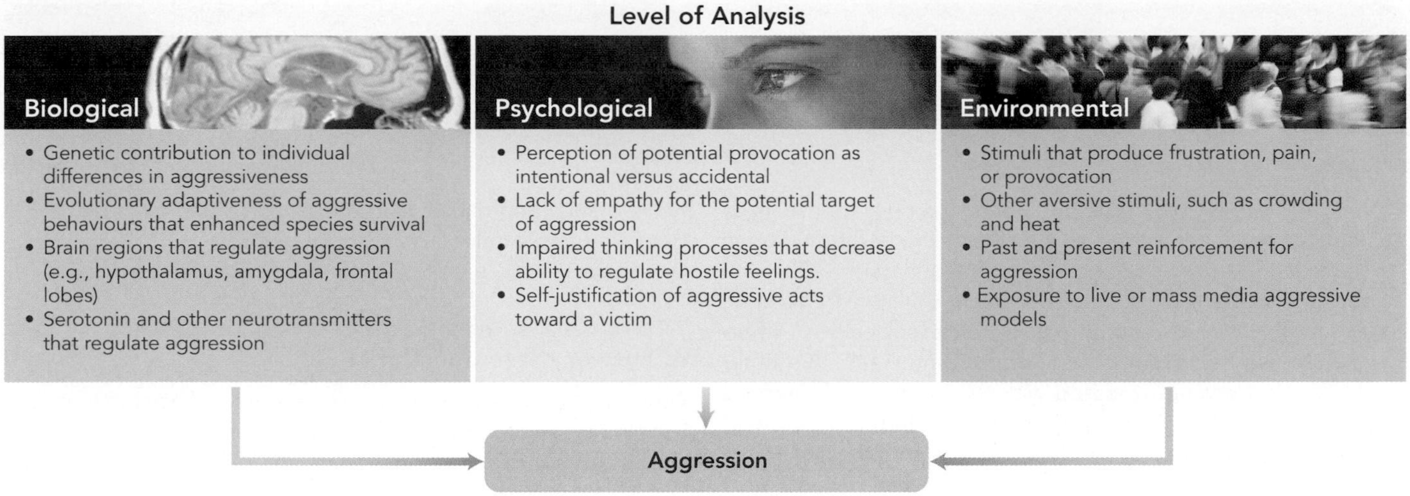

Level of Analysis

Biological	Psychological	Environmental
• Genetic contribution to individual differences in aggressiveness • Evolutionary adaptiveness of aggressive behaviours that enhanced species survival • Brain regions that regulate aggression (e.g., hypothalamus, amygdala, frontal lobes) • Serotonin and other neurotransmitters that regulate aggression	• Perception of potential provocation as intentional versus accidental • Lack of empathy for the potential target of aggression • Impaired thinking processes that decrease ability to regulate hostile feelings. • Self-justification of aggressive acts toward a victim	• Stimuli that produce frustration, pain, or provocation • Other aversive stimuli, such as crowding and heat • Past and present reinforcement for aggression • Exposure to live or mass media aggressive models

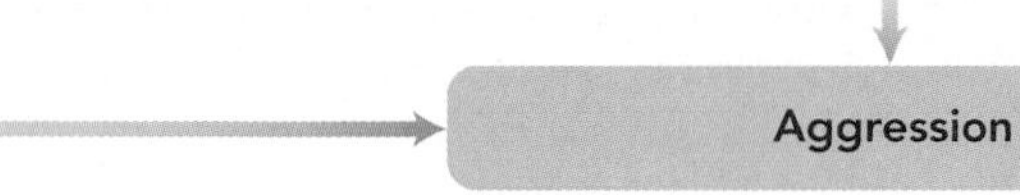

Aggression

FIGURE 16.39

Understanding the causes of behaviour: why do people aggress?

In Review

- *Proximity, mere exposure, similarity of attitudes, and physical attractiveness typically enhance our attraction toward someone. Relationships deepen as partners self-disclose and exchanges between them become more intimate and broader. Social exchange theory analyzes relationships in terms of the rewards and costs experienced by each partner.*
- *The qualities that people find most attractive in a mate vary somewhat across cultures. Evolutionary theorists propose that gender difference in mate preferences reflect inherited biological tendencies, whereas sociocultural theorists believe that these differences result from socialization and gender inequities in economic opportunities.*
- *Partners are more likely to remain happily married when they understand each other and deal with conflicts by de-escalating their emotions and providing mutual support.*
- *Overt prejudice has decreased in some ways, but people may hide their prejudice or be unaware of subtle prejudices they harbour.*
- *Prejudice stems partly from our tendency to perceive in-groups and out-groups. People typically display in-group favouritism and an out-group homogeneity bias. Perceived threats to one's in-group and a need to enhance one's self-esteem can motivate prejudice.*
- *Prejudice often is reduced when in-group and out-group members work closely together, with equal status, on tasks involving common goals and under conditions of broader institutional support.*
- *Some theorists propose that through kin selection and reciprocal altruism, evolution has helped shape a genetic predisposition toward prosocial behaviour among humans. Social learning theorists emphasize how social norms, modelling, and reinforcement shape prosocial attitudes and behaviour.*
- *The presence of multiple bystanders may decrease bystander intervention through social comparison processes and a diffusion of responsibility for helping. We are most likely to help others when we perceive that they are similar to us and are not responsible for their plight.*
- *Prosocial behaviour can be increased by enhancing people's feelings of empathy for victims and providing prosocial models.*
- *Heredity influences the strength of an organism's tendency to aggress. The hypothalamus, amygdala, and frontal lobes play especially important roles in certain types of aggression.*
- *Provocation, heat, crowding, and stimuli that cause frustration or pain increase the risk of aggression. Learning experiences help shape a tendency to behave more or less aggressively. People are more likely to aggress when they find ways to justify and rationalize their aggressive behaviour, perceive provocation as intentional, and have little empathy for others.*
- *Most research supports the social learning theory prediction that watching movie and TV violence, and playing video games, increase the risk that children and adults will act aggressively.*

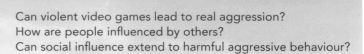

GAINING DIRECTION

What are the issues?

Among all the events of the past years, the ones that seem to have the greatest impact on the millennial generation involve disasters and mass shootings (e.g., the tsunami of 2004, the shooting at Dawson College). Kimveer Gill, much like Eric Harris and Dylan Klebold, was best described as "different." He was into Goth culture, and did not really like other people. He became obsessed with 9/11 conspiracy theories and the Columbine massacre. Months before the shooting at Dawson College, he cut off all ties with his friends. Like Harris and Klebold, he liked violent video games and hated almost everything that was "normal." Goth culture was where he found his identity. His online profile lists as his number one dislike, "the world and everything in it." How do people decide which groups to affiliate with? What happens when you feel rejected from the majority group? Does a culture of fantasy violence lead to actual violence? Do people copy the behaviours of others?

What do we need to know?

What is social identity?
Why do we conform to group norms?
How does the group affect the individual?
Can violent video games lead to real aggression?
How are people influenced by others?
Can social influence extend to harmful aggressive behaviour?

Where can you find the information necessary to answer these questions?

A good place to start is with the section on social influence. People respond to group norms (real or imagined) all the time. We often view this as positive (e.g., complying with laws), but in some situations, conformity can result in behaviours that are not consistent with one's true beliefs. If you feel rejected from one group, you may adopt the norms of another and over time, come to believe them. Such behaviour can be harmful, as demonstrated in Stanley Milgram's classic work on obedience. But how might we come to adopt such beliefs? Review the section on dissonance theory. Festinger reminds us that we may come to hold "false" beliefs as our own in order to justify our behaviour. Finally, look at the material regarding media influences on aggression. If an individual is predisposed to aggression because they are angry, upset, or frustrated, media portrayals of aggression (e.g., TV, movies, video games) can fuel these feelings and result in actual violence.

KEY TERMS AND CONCEPTS*

attitude (699)
attribution (694)
bystander effect (732)
catharsis (736)
central route to persuasion (703)
cognitive-arousal model of love (722)
companionate love (722)
communicator credibility (703)
deindividuation (713)
discrimination (724)
door-in-the-face technique (712)
empathy-altruism hypothesis (731)
equal status contact (729)
foot-in-the-door technique (712)
frustration-aggression hypothesis (735)
fundamental attribution error (696)
group polarization (715)
groupthink (715)
informational social influence (707)
just world hypothesis (733)
lowballing (712)
matching effect (720)
mere exposure effect (718)
negative state relief model (731)
norm of reciprocity (712)
normative social influence (707)
passionate love (722)
peripheral route to persuasion (703)
prejudice (724)
primacy effect (698)
realistic conflict theory (727)
self-fulfilling prophecy (699)
self-perception theory (702)
self-serving bias (697)
social comparison (718)
social exchange theory (721)
social facilitation (705)
social identity theory (728)
social loafing (714)
social norm (706)
social penetration theory (721)
social role (706)
social structure theory (720)
stereotype (699)
stereotype threat (729)
theory of cognitive dissonance (701)
theory of planned behaviour (700)
transfer of excitation (722)
triangular theory of love (722)

*Each term has been boldfaced in the text on the page indicated in parentheses.

DO YOU WANT TO ELEVATE YOUR GRADES?

For additional resources and interactive quizzing, visit the book's Online Learning Centre at **www.mcgrawhill.ca/olc/passer**.

Appendix
Statistics in Psychology

At various points throughout the text we have briefly described statistical procedures to help you understand the information being presented. This appendix discusses statistics in greater detail and focuses on the concepts underlying these procedures. Our goal is to help you understand how psychologists use statistics in their research.

For some students, the prospect of studying statistics evokes visions of complex higher mathematics. You will find, however, that if you can add, subtract, multiply, and divide, you can easily perform basic statistical operations.

DESCRIPTIVE STATISTICS

Psychological research often involves a large number of measurements. Typically, it is difficult to make sense of the data merely by examining the individual scores of each participant. **Descriptive statistics** summarize and describe the characteristics of a set (also called a *distribution*) of scores.

To summarize a set of scores, we might first construct a **frequency distribution,** which shows how many participants received each score. For example, suppose that 50 university students took a 32-item psychological test that measured their level of self-esteem. The frequency distribution in Table A.1 tells us that two participants had scores of 30, 31, or 32; one had a score of 27, 28, or 29; eleven had scores of 15, 16, or 17; and so on. Note that the researcher chose to use *intervals* of three points (e.g., 30–32) rather than to show the number (frequency) of participants who obtained each of the 33 possible (0–32) scores. She could have done the latter if she had wished to break down the scores even further. The number of intervals chosen is somewhat arbitrary, but frequency distributions often contain 10 to 12 categories.

This frequency distribution tells us at a glance about certain characteristics of the data, such as whether scores tend to cluster in one region of the distribution or are scattered throughout. We can easily convert these data into a **histogram,** which is a graph of a frequency distribution. Typically, the scores (or in this case, score intervals) are plotted along the horizontal axis (i.e., *x-axis,* or *abscissa*), and the frequencies are plotted on the vertical axis (i.e., *y-axis,* or *ordinate*). This produces a column or bar above each score or score interval that shows how frequently the score occurred. Figure A.1 represents a histogram of the self-esteem scores for our sample of 50 university students.

TABLE A.1 **Frequency Distribution of Self-Esteem Scores**

Self-Esteem Scores	Frequency
30–32	2
27–29	1
24–26	4
21–23	6
18–20	9
15–17	11
12–14	8
9–11	3
6–8	4
3–5	1
0–2	1

Measures of Central Tendency

Frequency distributions and histograms give us a general picture of how scores are distributed. **Measures of central tendency** describe a distribution in terms of a single statistic that is in some way "typical" of the sample as a whole. There are three commonly used measures of central tendency: the *mode,* the *mean,* and the *median.* For example, Table A.2 shows the salaries of the 10 employees who work at Honest Al's Savings and Loan Corporation. Our task is to arrive at a single number that somehow typifies the salaries of the group as a whole.

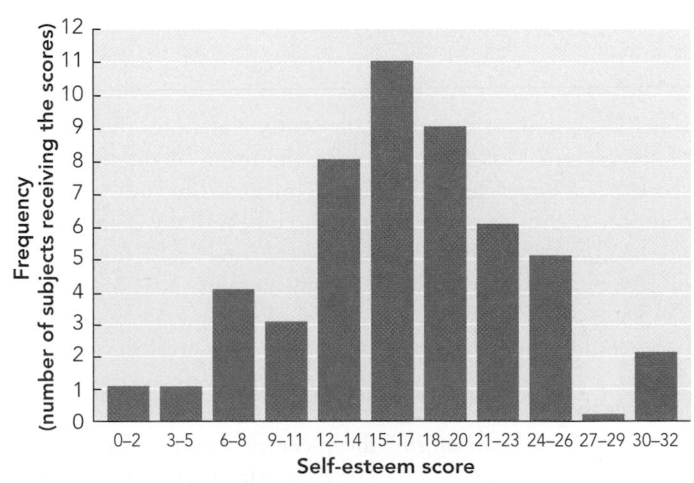

FIGURE A.1
A histogram of the self-esteem distribution shown in Table A.1.

TABLE A.2 **Annual Salaries of 10 Employees**

Employee	Annual Salary (X)
1. Honest Al	\$205,000
2. Honest Al's mother	205,000
3. Johnson	20,000
4. Hussein	19,500
5. Jones	19,000
6. Chen	18,000
7. Brown	17,500
8. Chu	17,000
9. Mullins	16,500
10. Watson	16,000
$N = 10$	$\Sigma X = \$553{,}500$

Mode = The score that occurs most often—in this case, \$205,000.

Mean = The arithmetic average, computed by the following formula:

$$M = \frac{\Sigma X}{N} = \frac{553{,}500}{10} = 55{,}350$$

Median = The point above and below which there is an equal number of scores. In this case, because there is an even number of scores, the median is midway between the 5th- and 6th-ranked salaries—that is, \$18,500.

The **mode** is the most frequently occurring score in a distribution. At Honest Al's, the modal salary is \$205,000, because it is the only salary received by more than one person. Although the mode is easy to identify in a distribution, it is not always the most representative score, particularly if it falls far from the centre of the distribution. Clearly, \$205,000 is not the "typical" salary of the 10 employees, because 8 of them receive \$20,000 or less.

The most commonly used measure of central tendency, the **mean,** represents the arithmetic average of a set of scores. The mean is calculated by adding up all the scores and dividing by the number of scores. The statistical formula for computing the mean is:

$$M = \frac{\Sigma X}{N}$$

X is the symbol for an individual score, N denotes the number of scores, and M is the symbol for the mean of the individual scores. The Greek letter Σ (sigma) means "the sum." Thus to compute the mean of the salaries at Honest Al's, we simply add up the individual salaries and divide the total by 10, the number of salaries. As Table A.2 shows, the mean salary at Honest Al's is \$55,350.

Would you be tempted to go to work at Honest Al's if, during a job interview, Al told you that "our average salary is \$55,350 per year"? Your negative answer to this question illustrates a shortcoming of the mean as a measure of central tendency. The mean can be strongly affected by one or more extremely high or low scores that are not representative of the group as a whole. In this case, the high salaries of Honest Al and his mother increased the mean to a figure more than twice as great as the salary of the next highest paid employee (i.e., Johnson). Thus we cannot consider the mean to be representative of the salaries of Honest Al's employees.

Our third measure of central tendency, the **median,** is the point that divides the distribution in half when the individual scores are arranged in order from lowest to highest. In other words, half of the remaining scores lie above the median and half below it. If there is an odd number of scores, there will be one score that is exactly in the middle. If there were 11 salaries in Table A.2, the sixth-ranked score would be the median, because 5 scores would fall above and 5 below. In a distribution having an even number of scores, the median is halfway between the two middle scores. In our salary distribution, the median is the point halfway between employee 5 (\$19,000) and employee 6 (\$18,000), or \$18,500.

The median has an important property that the mean does not have: It is unaffected by extreme scores. Whether Honest Al makes \$205,000 or \$500,000, the median remains the same. Therefore the median is more representative of the group as a whole in instances when there are very extreme scores. In Honest Al's case, the median figure of \$18,500 is more representative of the "typical" employee's salary than is the mean figure of \$55,350 or the modal figure of \$205,000. The median, however, can fail to capture important information. For example, suppose that employee 3 (Johnson) and employee 4 (Hussein) each received an \$80,000 raise. In this case the median would not change, because the "middle score" would still be the midpoint between employees 5 (Jones) and 6 (Chen). The mean, however, would increase to \$71,350 (\$713,500/10) and reflect the fact that Honest Al is being more generous in paying some of his employees.

Measures of Variability

Measures of central tendency provide us with a single score that typifies the distribution. But to describe a distribution adequately, we need to know more. One key question concerns the amount of variability, or spread, that exists among scores. Do they tend to cluster closely about the mean, or do they vary widely? **Measures of variability** provide information about the spread of scores in a distribution.

The **range,** which is the difference between the highest and the lowest score in a distribution, is the simplest but least informative measure of variability. At Honest Al's, the range is $\$205{,}000 - \$16{,}000 = \$189{,}000$. As another example, if we have a distribution of 20 IQ scores and the highest IQ is 150 and the lowest is 70, then the range is $150 - 70 = 80$. But suppose the other 18 people all have IQs of 110. If we knew only the range of scores, we might be led to believe that the scores in this distribution vary far more than they actually do. Thus it would be more useful to know how much, on average, each IQ score varies or deviates from the mean of the distribution.

To do this we first create a *deviation score* (represented by a lowercase x) that measures the distance between each score (X) and the mean (M). To provide a simple example, suppose we have two distributions, A and B, each composed of 10 scores. Looking at the "X (score)" column in Table A.3 for each distribution, you can see that although each distribution has a mean of 10, the scores in distribution B are more spread out than

TABLE A.3 Computation of the Variance and Standard Deviation for Two Distributions of Scores with Identical Means ($M = 10$)

	Distribution A			Distribution B	
X (score)	$X - M = x$	x^2	X (score)	$X - M = x$	x^2
12	+2	4	18	+8	64
12	+2	4	18	+8	64
11	+1	1	15	+5	25
11	+1	1	15	+5	25
10	0	0	10	0	0
10	0	0	10	0	0
9	−1	1	5	−5	25
9	−1	1	5	−5	25
8	−2	4	2	−8	64
8	−2	4	2	−8	64
$\Sigma X = 100$	$\Sigma x = 0$	$\Sigma x^2 = 20$	$\Sigma X = 100$	$\Sigma x = 0$	$\Sigma x^2 = 356$
$N = 10$			$N = 10$		
$M = 10.00$			$M = 10.00$		

x (deviation) $= X - M$

Distribution A: variance $= \frac{\Sigma x^2}{N} = \frac{20}{10} = 2.00$

SD (standard deviation) $= \sqrt{2.00} = 1.414$

Distribution B: variance $= \frac{\Sigma x^2}{N} = \frac{356}{10} = 35.6$

$SD = \sqrt{35.6} = 5.967$

in distribution A. Now for each score we compute how much it differs from the mean (i.e., $x = X - M$). At this stage, you might think that to measure the variability of each distribution we need only add up its deviation scores and then compute the average deviation. But we have a problem. Even though distribution B is more spread out than distribution A, adding up the deviation scores for each distribution yields a sum of zero ($\Sigma x = 0$). In fact, the sum of deviation scores for any distribution will always add up to zero.

To avoid this problem we must get rid of the plus and minus signs that end up cancelling each other out. As the rightmost column under each distribution in Table A.3 shows, we achieve this goal by taking each deviation score, squaring it, and then adding up these squared deviation scores. This produces a sum of 20 for distribution A and 356 for distribution B. Now we divide by 10 (i.e., the number of scores in each distribution) to find the average squared deviation. This statistic, called the **variance,** is the average of the squared deviation scores about the mean. You can see that the variance for distribution B (35.6) is considerably greater than the variance for distribution A (2.00), reflecting the greater spread of the scores in B.

The most popular measure of variability, the **standard deviation (SD),** is the square root of the variance. Because we had to square the deviation scores to compute the variance, we now return to the original scale of measurement by taking the square root of the variance. Thus the standard deviation describes variability in the same units of measurement as the original data. You can see in Table A.3 that the standard deviation from the mean of distribution B (5.967) is more than four times greater than the standard deviation from the mean of distribution A (1.414).

THE NORMAL CURVE

The **normal curve** is a symmetrical bell-shaped curve that represents a theoretical distribution of scores in the population. In the normal curve, 50 percent of the cases fall on each side of the mean, and the median and mode have the same value as the mean. Figure A.2 shows that in a normal curve, as we move away from the mean the frequency of each score steadily decreases. The normal curve is important because many variables in the population—weight, height, IQ, and anxiety, to name a few—are distributed in a way that approximates the normal curve. Thus a few people are extremely tall or short, a greater number of people are moderately tall or short, and most are close to average in height.

The normal curve has several key properties. The most important of these is that the standard deviation can be used to divide the normal curve into areas containing known percentages of the population. In a normal curve, about two-thirds of the scores fall within plus or minus 1 standard deviation of the mean; about 95 percent of cases fall within plus or minus 2 standard deviations; and nearly all of the cases fall between 3 standard deviations above and 3 standard deviations below the mean. Therefore if we know that a psychological characteristic or any other variable is normally distributed, then we can deduce more information about it. For example, IQ scores

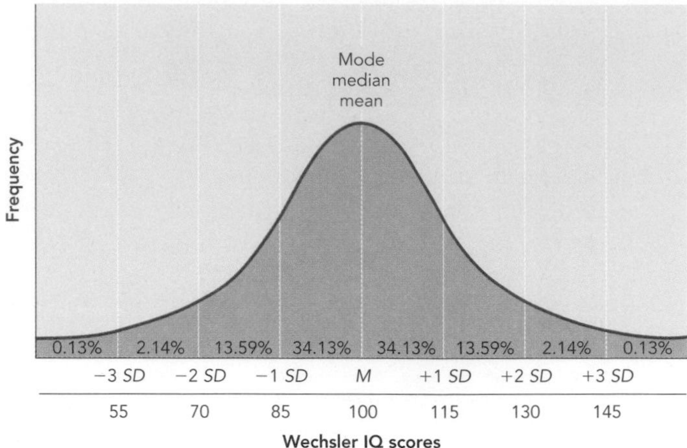

FIGURE A.2

The normal curve, showing the percentage of cases falling within each area of the normal distribution and also showing Wechsler IQ scores that correspond to standard deviation (SD) units.

as measured by the Wechsler intelligence tests (see Chapter 9) are normally distributed with a mean of 100 and a standard deviation of 15. Knowing this, we can use our knowledge of the normal curve to answer questions like these:

1. What percentage of people have IQs between 70 and 130? (Approximately 95 percent. These scores are −2 SD and +2 SD from the mean, respectively. As Figure A.2 shows, this area below the curve includes 13.59 + 34.13 + 34.13 + 13.59 percent of the cases, or 95.44 percent.)
2. My IQ is 115, so where does that place me? (115 is +1 SD above the mean, so as Figure A.2 shows, about 16 percent of the population will have a higher IQ, and 84 percent will have a lower IQ. That is, the area to the right of +1 SD represents 13.59 + 2.14 + 0.13 percent of the cases, or 15.86 percent.)
3. What is the probability that a person selected at random from the population will have an IQ of 145 or more? (About one eighth of 1 percent. This probability corresponds to the area under the curve beyond +3 SD, or 0.13 percent.)

These examples point to a major use of the normal curve: It allows us to estimate the probability that a given event will occur. Indeed, the statistical tests we describe next are methods for arriving at probability statements based on the assumption that the variables being investigated are normally distributed.

STATISTICAL METHODS FOR DATA ANALYSIS

Given a set of data for any single variable, such as the scores of a sample of people on a self-esteem test, we use descriptive statistics to summarize the characteristics of those data. But psychologists do more than describe variables individually. They seek to explain and predict behaviour by examining how variables are *related* to one another. The following statistical methods are used to analyze relations among variables and draw inferences about the meaning of those relations.

Accounting for Variance in Behaviour

Behaviour varies. It varies between individuals (e.g., some people are more aggressive or helpful than others), and it varies for the same individual across time and situations (a person may perform a task well under some conditions but more poorly under other circumstances). Explaining why variations in behaviour occur (i.e., accounting for variance) is a central goal of psychological science.

As an example, suppose we want to examine how the number of bystanders present during an emergency influences the speed with which they assist a person in distress. In this instance, the number of bystanders is the independent variable, and the speed of helping is the dependent variable. We conduct an experiment, randomly assign participants to different conditions (one, two, or four bystanders present), and find that, overall, bystanders who were alone responded most quickly and groups of four responded most slowly. We also find that the speed of response varied even within each condition; for example, among those bystanders who were alone, some simply responded more quickly than others. Maybe they were in a better mood, had more altruistic personalities, and so on.

In any experiment, the total amount of variation in people's behaviour (e.g., speed of helping) may be divided into two components: the amount of *variance accounted for* by the differences in the independent variable(s) being manipulated (e.g., being placed alone or with other bystanders) and the amount of variance that is left over and therefore must be due to other factors (e.g., participants' mood, personality). Thus

Total variance	=	Variance accounted for (due to independent variables)	+	Variance not accounted for (due to random, unmeasured, or uncontrolled factors)

In our experiment, suppose a statistical analysis reveals that 20 percent of the total variance in the speed with which participants helped a person in distress can be accounted for by our independent variable—the number of other bystanders present. Figure A.3 shows this schematically. The other 80 percent of the variance in speed of helping is due to other factors that were not controlled in the experiment. Some of these other factors, which are random and beyond the control of the experimenter, produce what is called *error variance.* For example, some participants may have been momentarily bored or preoccupied with personal problems and thus responded more slowly than they otherwise would have. The rest of the unexplained variance results from factors that systematically affect the speed of helping but which the researcher either does not know about or were not controlled for in the experiment. Such variables may include the participants' personality characteristics or mood, the victim's gender, the nature of the emergency, and so forth. In future research, we might introduce additional independent variables, such as manipulating (i.e., creating) an environment that puts

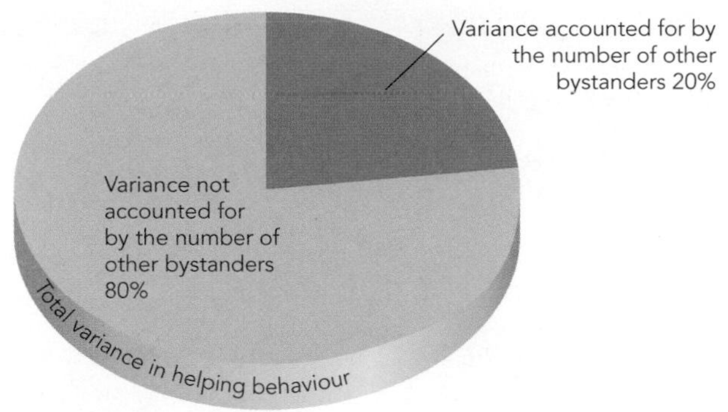

FIGURE A.3

The total amount of variation in the dependent variable (speed of responding to another person in distress) is represented within the circle. The total variance may be divided into one portion accounted for by the independent variable (number of bystanders) and another portion not accounted for by the independent variable.

bystanders in a good or bad mood just prior to the emergency. By studying other independent variables, we attempt to increase the amount of variance accounted for, thereby increasing the size of the "accounted for" area in Figure A.3. Perhaps we will find that by knowing both the number of bystanders present and the participants' mood, we can now account for 35 percent of the variance in people's speed of helping.

From this perspective, understanding and/or predicting behaviour involves isolating factors that account for behavioural variance. The more important a particular variable is, the more variance it helps us account for. To be sure, we can never completely eliminate the random factors that produce error variance. But as scientific research proceeds, the goal is to discover new variables that account for additional portions of the total variance in people's behaviour.

Correlational Methods

The concept of *variance accounted for* applies not only to experiments but also to correlational studies. As discussed in Chapter 2, correlational research does not involve manipulating independent variables. Rather, it involves measuring two or more variables and determining whether changes in one variable are associated with changes in the other. Suppose that we administer two psychological tests—one measuring self-esteem and the other measuring depression—to 200 adults. On each test we will find that the scores vary: Some people will have higher self-esteem than others, and some will be more depressed than others. The question is this: Is there a relation between the variance in self-esteem scores and the variance in depression scores? Stated differently, as self-esteem scores (variable X) become higher or lower (i.e., as they move further away from the mean of X), do depression scores (variable Y) tend to become either higher or lower (i.e., move away from the mean of Y) in a systematic manner?

The Correlation Coefficient

Relations between variables can differ in *direction* (positive or negative) and in *strength.* To illustrate, imagine that we have a sample of six people, with scores on two variables (X and Y) for each person. Table A.4 shows five hypothetical sets of X and Y scores for these six people. In set A the relation between variables X and Y is positive in direction. That is, higher scores on variable X are associated with higher scores on Y, and lower scores on X are associated with lower scores on Y. In contrast, set E reveals a negative relation. Here, higher scores on X are associated with lower Y scores, and vice versa. In set C the pairs of X and Y scores bear no clear relation to each other: They are not correlated. As scores on X change, scores on Y do not change in any consistent manner. Thus in sets A, C, and E, we see three different types of relations—positive, none, and negative.

TABLE A.4 Five Data Sets Illustrating Various Relations That May Exist between Two Variables

	Set A		Set B		Set C		Set D		Set E	
Participant	*X*	*Y*	*X*	*Y*	*X*	*Y*	*X*	*Y*	*X*	*Y*
1	1	2	1	4	1	5	1	6	1	12
2	2	4	2	5	2	8	2	8	2	10
3	3	6	3	2	3	6	3	10	3	8
4	4	8	4	10	4	2	4	4	4	6
5	5	10	5	6	5	6	5	2	5	4
6	6	12	6	8	6	7	6	1	6	2
$N = 6$	$r = +1.00$		$r = +.58$		$r = .00$		$r = -.75$		$r = -1.00$	

Each set consists of the scores of six people on two variables, X and Y. The product–moment correlation coefficient (r) has been computed for each set. The computational formula for r is as follows:

$$r = \frac{N(\Sigma X_i Y_i) - (\Sigma X_i)(\Sigma Y_i)}{\sqrt{[N(\Sigma X_i^2) - (\Sigma X_i)^2]\,[N(\Sigma Y_i^2) - (\Sigma Y_i)^2]}}$$

Where X_i = Each person's score on variable X; ΣX_i = sum of Xs

Y_i = Each person's score on variable Y; ΣY_i = sum of Ys

N = Total number of people

To illustrate how relations between variables differ in strength, let us compare set A with set B. In set A, there is a perfect positive relation between X and Y: As each X score increases by a constant amount (in this case, by 1), each Y score also increases by a constant amount (in this case, by 2). In set B, individuals having higher X scores also tend to have higher Y scores, but this positive relation is not as consistent as in Set A. For example, in set B participant 3 has a higher X score than participant 2 yet a lower Y score. Likewise, compare set E with set D. Set E displays a perfect negative relation: As each X score increases by a constant amount, each Y score decreases by a constant amount. In set D, the negative relation between X and Y is not as consistent and thus is not as strong.

The **Pearson product-moment correlation coefficient** is a statistic that reflects the direction and strength of the relation between two variables. The correlation coefficient (designated r) can range in magnitude from -1.00 to $+1.00$. If $r = +1.00$, this reflects a perfect positive relation between X and Y scores, as in set A of Table A.4. A correlation coefficient of -1.00 signifies a perfect negative relation, as in set E. Correlations close to 0.00 indicate no systematic relation between the variables, as in set C.

In actual research, a correlation of -1.00 or $+1.00$ is rare; psychological variables tend to be imperfectly correlated with one another. More typically, correlation coefficients might resemble those in sets B ($r = +.58$) and D ($r = -.75$). Remember that it is the magnitude of the correlation coefficient and not its sign (direction) that indicates the degree to which two variables are related to one another. Thus X and Y are more strongly related in set D ($r = -.75$) than in set B ($r = +.58$), even though the correlation in set D is negative.

How shall we interpret a correlation coefficient? A correlation of +.50, for example, *does not* mean that X and Y are 50 percent related. Rather, squaring the correlation coefficient (r^2) indicates the amount of variance that the two variables share or have in common. Stated another way, r^2 tells us how much of the variance in one measure can be accounted for by differences in the other measure. For example, suppose we obtain a correlation of +.50 between scores on a mechanical aptitude test and grades in a university engineering course. As illustrated in Figure A.4, squaring the correlation coefficient ($+.50^2 = .25$) tells us that 25 percent of the total variance in course grades can be accounted for by differences in mechanical aptitude scores. Obviously, the more highly two variables are correlated, the more common variance they share. If the two variables in Figure A.4 correlated +.70, the area of overlap would include about half of each circle, because $(+.70)^2 = .49$. Finally, if two variables are perfectly correlated, the two circles in Figure A.4 would overlap completely.

Recall from Chapter 2 that a correlation between two variables does not allow us to conclude that one caused the other. We know only that they are statistically related to one another. If variables X and Y are correlated, it is possible that X causes Y or that Y causes X—or that both X and Y are caused by some third variable, Z.

Correlation and Prediction

If two variables are correlated and we know an individual's score on one variable, then this information will help us estimate his or her score on the other variable. *The more highly two variables are correlated, the more accurate our predictions will be.* In fact, if two variables are perfectly correlated—if their variance overlaps completely—we can make precise predictions. For example, in set A of Table A.4, once we know a person's score on X, we can accurately predict that $Y = 2X$. (Conversely, if we know Y, we can predict that $X = .5Y$.) In statistical prediction based on correlation, we are thus taking advantage of lawful relations among variables to predict to the individual case.

There are many practical applications for predictions based on correlational analysis. Industrial-organizational psychologists, for example, often help organizations develop aptitude tests that correlate with on-the-job performance. Personnel managers can therefore use job applicants' test scores to predict which applicants are most likely to perform well. The more highly a *predictor variable* (e.g., aptitude test scores) is correlated with the *criterion variable* (e.g., job performance), the more accurate the selection decisions will be.

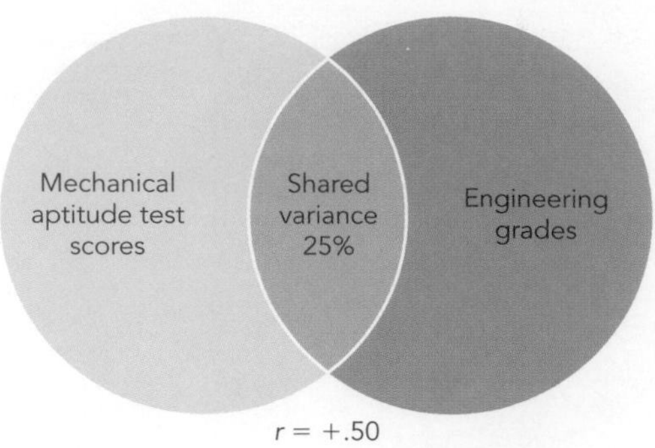

FIGURE A.4

Squaring the correlation coefficient provides an estimate of the amount of variance shared by two variables. In this instance, r = .50, indicating that 25 percent of the variance in engineering grades in this sample can be accounted for by individual differences in mechanical aptitude.

Factor Analysis

Within a single study, researchers may measure many variables and examine the correlations among them. For example, suppose we want to determine the mental abilities that people possess. Are there dozens of different mental abilities, or are there are only a few basic ones that influence performance across diverse tasks? If so, what is the nature of these abilities? To answer such questions, let us assume that a psychologist administers 40 different performance tests to hundreds of participants and correlates all of the test scores with one another. He reasons that if several tests are correlated highly with one another—if performance scores on these tests "cluster," or "hang together"—then these tests are probably measuring the same underlying or basic mental ability. Further, if the tests within a cluster or group correlate highly with one another but are not correlated with tests in other clusters, then these various test clusters probably reflect different and distinct mental abilities. Thus the psychologist hopes to determine the number of test clusters and to use this information to infer the nature of the underlying abilities.

When the sets of scores for the 40 tests are correlated with one another (N = the number of tests or variables), our psychologist will end up with 780 correlations—that is, $[N \times (N - 1)]/2$, or $[40 \times 39]/2$ correlations—to examine. Obviously, with so many correlations, trying to determine visually which tests cluster together (while not clustering with other tests) is a hopeless task. Fortunately, a statistical technique called **factor analysis** reduces a large number of correlations among many measures to a smaller number of clusters, with each cluster containing variables that correlate highly with one another. Today, computers can analyze the patterns of correlations and perform a factor analysis in a few seconds. The term *factor* refers to the underlying characteristic that presumably accounts for why the measures within each cluster are linked together.

Factor analysis is complex, and for purposes of this discussion, we need not be concerned with its mathematical basis. Our interest is in how psychologists use it as a research tool, so consider a simple example. Let us assume that Table A.5 shows the correlations among only 6 of the 40 measures. Such a table is called a *correlation matrix*. The correlation coefficients of 1.00 along the diagonal of the matrix reflect the obvious fact that each variable correlates perfectly with itself. Because the bottom half of the matrix contains the same correlations as the top, we need concern ourselves only with the upper half.

Examining Table A.5 reveals two clusters of tests. Tests 1, 2, and 3 correlate strongly with one another. Likewise, tests 4, 5, and 6 correlate strongly with one another. Notice also that tests 1, 2, and 3 have low correlations with tests 4, 5, and 6, which indicates that the two clusters are measuring different things. But just what do these two clusters of tests measure? Factor analysis cannot answer this question directly; it can only identify the clusters for us. Now it is up to the psychologist to examine the nature of the tests in each cluster and decide what the underlying factors might be. Suppose that test 1 measures vocabulary, test 2 measures reading comprehension, and test 3 requires participants to fill in sentences having missing words. Because all three tasks involve the use of words, the psychologist might decide to name the underlying factor "verbal ability" or perhaps "word fluency." What matters in Table A.5 is that we have reduced 6 variables and 15 correlations to two underlying factors. In our complete example, with 40 tests and 780 correlations, a typical factor analysis might identify between two to six factors. In psychology, where researchers often attempt to identify basic dimensions of behaviour, factor analysis is a valuable tool.

TABLE A.5 Intercorrelations among Six Ability Tests

Test	1	2	3	4	5	6
1	1.00	.84	.71	.04	.11	−.07
2		1.00	.79	.12	.01	.00
3			1.00	−.05	.12	.08
4				1.00	.69	.74
5					1.00	.92
6						1.00

Inferential Statistics and Hypothesis Testing

Regardless of the type of research, psychologists rarely have access to the entire population of people they are interested in. Instead, they must be satisfied with studying relatively small samples of participants. Thus 80 introductory psychology students might participate in an experiment on bystander helping, and 400 adults recruited through newspaper advertisements might participate in a correlational study examining the relation between self-esteem and depression. On the basis of the results obtained from such samples, researchers seek to generalize their conclusions to the population as a whole.

In experiments, we are typically interested in overall differences between the various conditions. Suppose we find that participants randomly assigned to be alone help a victim more quickly than participants assigned to groups of two or four bystanders. Before concluding that the independent variable (number of bystanders) truly influenced the dependent variable (speed of helping), we must first ask whether this difference is "real" or is merely a "chance" finding. In other words, because our data are based only on a particular sample of people in each condition, how do we know that similar results would have occurred if we had tested other samples? Perhaps for one reason or another the participants we tested were not truly representative of the populations from which they were drawn. Perhaps, despite random assignment, participants assigned to be alone happened by chance to have more highly altruistic personalities than participants in the other conditions, and this (rather than "being alone") is the reason they helped more quickly.

Inferential statistics tell us how confident we can be in drawing conclusions or inferences about a population based on findings obtained from a sample. Thus if we observe differences in an experiment between experimental and control groups or find that there is a correlation between two variables, we use inferential statitistics to determine the likelihood that these results occurred by chance alone and thus do not reflect a genuine difference in the population from which the sample is drawn. When researchers analyze their data and conclude that a correlation or a difference in behaviour between groups in an experiment is "statistically significant," the term **statistical significance** means that it is unlikely that the particular finding occurred by chance alone. Psychologists typically consider a result to be statistically significant only if it could have occurred by chance alone less than 5 times in 100.

The logic underlying tests of statistical significance is related to our previous discussion of the normal curve and its statistical properties. Determining statistical significance is in many ways similar to the IQ problem presented earlier in the appendix: If IQ is normally distributed with a mean of 100 and a standard deviation of 15, what is the likelihood of randomly selecting a person with an IQ of 145? To answer that question, all we had to do was to determine what proportion of cases are three standard deviations above the mean in a normal distribution. We found that proportion to be about one tenth of 1 percent. Thus we would expect to randomly select a person with an IQ that high about 1 in 1,000 times—pretty small odds. With this example in mind, let us consider the logic of statistical inference in greater detail.

Suppose we are interested in the effects of a stress-management program on the academic performance of first-year university students who are high in test anxiety. We hypothesize that learning to control anxiety during tests will result in better performance. We randomly assign 40 students who have received high scores on a self-report measure of test anxiety to either an experimental group (20 participants) that participates in a stress-management program for test anxiety, or to a control group (20 participants) that receives no guidance or treatment. All of the students take the same required courses, and at the end of the academic year we compare the mean grade point averages of the two groups. On a 0.0 (F) to 4.0 (A) scale, we find that the experimental group (training program condition) obtains a mean grade point of 3.17 and the control group has a mean grade point of 2.61. Thus the difference between the two groups is 3.17 − 2.61 = +0.56 grade points. How can we decide whether this difference between the two samples reflects a difference in the respective populations (i.e., all high-test-anxious students who might participate in a stress-management program and all who do not)?

If we repeated our experiment several times with different high-anxiety participants, we would find that the means for the two samples would vary in each experiment. For example, the next three times we performed the study the means might be 2.94 (experimental) versus 2.77 (control), 3.34 versus 2.31, and 2.89 versus 2.83, yielding differences between the groups of 0.17, 1.03, and 0.06, respectively. By repeating the experiment a great many times, we could create a distribution of experimental versus control difference scores, and mathematical theory tells us that this distribution would be a *normal* distribution. This gives us the key. Because we have a normal distribution, just as we previously assessed the exact likelihood of randomly selecting a person with an IQ of 145, we can now determine the likelihood of randomly obtaining a difference of any particular size between our sample means. But to do this, we must first know what the mean and standard deviation of our distribution of differences are. As we've seen, one way to determine these values would be to perform our experiment a large number of times. But, fortunately, we can estimate these values on the basis of a single experiment and thereby avoid the need for many replications.

To do this, we use an approach to statistical analysis that involves testing the **null hypothesis**, which states that any observed differences between the samples are due to chance. We begin by assuming that the null hypothesis is true—that there is no real difference, for example, in grade point average between the populations of trained and untrained test-anxious students. If the null hypothesis is true, then if we repeated our experiment a great many times, we would expect the mean of our distribution of difference scores to be zero. Therefore, the normal distribution of difference scores would cluster around this mean of zero. The standard deviation of this normal distribution can be estimated from the standard deviations of the two samples, although the mathematics need not concern us here.

In our hypothetical experiment, we obtained grade point means of 3.17 for the experimental group and 2.61 for the control group, a difference of +0.56. Let us now suppose that the standard deviation of our distribution of differences between means was estimated on the basis of our samples to be .25. Thus our obtained difference of +0.56 is slightly more than 2 SD above the mean (0) of the null hypothesis distribution. From the properties of the normal curve, we know that more than 95 percent of the cases fall in the area of the curve between −2 SD and +2 SD. Thus, *if the null hypothesis were true,* we would expect a difference in means as large as .56 (either above or below zero) less than 5 percent of the time on the basis of chance factors. This probability level meets the criterion for statistical significance described earlier. In view of this fact, we would reject the null hypothesis and conclude that there is a real difference in grade point average in the two populations. Thus our experimental hypothesis that the stress-management program resulted in a higher level of academic performance would be supported.

Note that we used the term *supported,* not *proven,* because we are making an inference based on a probability statement. There is, after all, some possibility (though less than 5 percent) that the null hypothesis is true and this really was a chance finding. Note also that this statistical analysis does not tell us why the stress-management group performed better (e.g., Did they perform better due to the program's content or the mere attention they received?). This is one reason why repeating or replicating research studies is so valuable. If another study—particularly one with more control groups—also yields statistically significant results, we can have more confidence that the difference we obtained reflects a real relation between the independent and dependent variables. But no matter how many times we repeat the experiment, we shall never move from the world of probability into the world of absolute truth.

⊙ KEY TERMS AND CONCEPTS*

descriptive statistics (744)
factor analysis (750)
frequency distribution (744)
histogram (744)
inferential statistics (751)
mean (744)
measures of central tendency (744)
measures of variability (746)
median (745)
mode (744)
normal curve (747)
null hypothesis (752)
Pearson product-moment correlation coefficient (749)
range (746)
standard deviation (SD) (746)
statistical significance (751)
variance (746)

*Each term has been boldfaced in the text on the page indicated in parentheses.

Credits

Chapter 1

Page 3, © NASA/Jeff Schmaltz, MODIS Land Rapid Response Team; Page 7, © Gabe Palmer/Corbis; Page 9, © Bettmann/Corbis; Page 11, Fox P.T., Parsons L.M., and Lancaster J.L. Beyond the single study: function/location metanalysis in cognitive neuroimaging. *Current Opinion in Neurobiology*, 8(2):178–87, (1998); Page 12, © Archives of the History of American Psychology; Page 13 (top), © Granger Collection; Page 13 (bottom), © Michael W. Tweedie/Photo Researchers; Page 14, © Thomas Nebbia/Woodfin Camp & Associates; Page 15, © Erich Lessing/Art Resource; Page 17 (top), © Yerkes National Primate Research Center, Emory University; Page 17 (bottom), © Anderson/Monkmeyer; Page 20, © Bettmann/Corbis; Page 23 (top), © Culver Pictures, Inc.; Page 23 (bottom), © Falk/Monkmeyer; Page 24, Courtesy of Stanford News Service; Page 25, Steven E. Sutton/Duomo; Page 27 (left), © Ron Stroud; Page 27 (right), © Steve Mason/Getty Images.

Chapter 2

Page 43, © Steven Potter; Page 44, © Allan Tannenbaum/Gamma; Page 48, Copyright © 2004 by Sidney Harris. ScienceCartoonsPlus.com. Reprinted with permission.; Page 50 (top), Jose Luis Pelaez, Inc./Corbis; Page 50 (middle), © Richard T. Nowitz/Photo Researchers; Page 50 (bottom), © Spencer Grant/PhotoEdit; Page 54, © Karl Ammann/Corbis; Page 71, Copyright © by Sidney Harris. ScienceCartoonsPlus.com. Reprinted with permission.; Page 72, © Carolyn A. McKeone/Photo Researchers, Inc.; Page 73, Copyright © 2000 by Sidney Harris. ScienceCartoonsPlus.com.; Page 75, © Brad Rickerby/AGE Fotostock; Page 76 (top), © Annabella Bluesky/Photo Researchers, Inc.; Page 76 (bottom), © Volker Steger/Photo Researchers, Inc.

Chapter 3

Page 83, © PhotoDisk/Getty Images; Page 84, From: Damasio, H., Grabowski, T., Frank, R., Galaburda, A.M., Damasio, A.R.: The Return of Phineas Gage: Clues about the brain from the skull of a famous patient. *Science*, 264:1102–1105, 1994. Departments of Neurology and Image Analysis Facility, University of Iowa.; Page 87, Haydon, P.G. (2001). Glia: Listening and talking to the synapse. *Nature Reviews, Neuroscience*. 2, 185–193.; Page 101 (a) and (b), © Larry Mulvehill/Science Source/Photo Researchers, Inc.; Page 101 (d), © Richard Price/Getty; Page 101 (e), © Lester Lefkowitz/Corbis; Page 101 (f), © Dr. Scott T. Grafton/Visuals Unlimited; Page 101 (g), Can McCoy/Rainbow; Page 103, CP Archive Photo; Page 105, © Martin M. Rotker/Science Source/Photo Researchers; Page 106, © Richard Hutchings/Corbis; Page 109, © Karl Ammann/Corbis; Page 116 (a), McGill University Archives, Photographic Collection. PN000387 – Portrait: Donald O. Hebb, Professor of Psychology; Page 116 (b), Hebb, 1949. *The Organization of Behavior: A Neuropschological Theory*.; Page 128, © Manfred Kage/Peter Arnold, Inc.

Chapter 4

Page 134 (both), © Michael Nichols/Magnum; Page 139 (b), © L. Clarke/Corbis; Page 139 (d), © Jim Whitmer; Page 140, © Richard T. Nowitz/Corbis/Magma; Page 145, © Royalty-Free/Corbis; Page 147, © Purestock/Getty Images; Page 149, Cartoon by Don Wright, © 2001.; Page 152 (left), © Ryan McVay/Getty; Page 152 (middle), © David Bartruff/Stock Boston; Page 152 (right), © Owen Franken/Corbis; Page 154 (top), © Image Source/PunchStock; Page 154 (bottom), Rubberball Productions/Getty Images; Page 155 (top), © Corbis/Magma; Page 155 (far left), © Lindsay Hebberd/Corbis/Magma; Page 155 (middle left), © Natalie Fobes/Corbis/Magma; Page 155 (middle right), © Kerstin Geier; Gallo Images/Corbis/Magma; Page 155 (far right), Courtesy of John Mitchell; Page 156, Thinkstock/Royalty Free/Getty Images; Page 159, © Richard R. Hansen/Photo Researchers; Page 160, © Peter Turnley/Corbis/Magma; Page 161 (top), © W. Perry Conway/Corbis/Magma; Page 161 (bottom), © Randy Wells/CorbisS/Magma, Page 162, Shaney Komulainen/CP; Page 163, Statistics Canada.

Chapter 5

Page 169, Library and Archives Canada/J.R. Warren collection/Accession 1977-036; Page 170, © AP/Wide World Photos Helen Keller/Anne Sullivan; Page 175, Adapted from Pritchard, 1961; Page 180, © Matthew McVay/Stone; Page 183, Fritz Goro, *Life Magazine* © Time, Inc.; Page 187, © Culver Pictures; Page 188, Micrographs by Robert E. Preston, courtesy of Professor J.E. Hawkins, Kresge Hearing Research Institute, University of Michigan; Page190, Courtesy of the Department of Veterans Affairs; Page 194, © Gavin Smith/FSP/Liaison Agency; Page 196, © Bill Aron/PhotoEdit; Page 197, © Crockett Photography and Design, Appears with photo: *Pintos*, Bev Doolittle, 1979. The Greenwich Workshop, Trumbull, CT; Page 200 (both), © Jeffrey Grosscup; Page 201, © Shaun Best/Reuters/Corbis; Page 202 (top), © 1948 M.C. Escher Foundation/Baarn-Holland, All Rights Reserved; Page 202 (bottom), *School of Athens* by Raphael. Scala/Art Resource, NY; Page 203, © Holway & Lobel Globus/Stock Market; Page 204 (a), © Baron Wolman/Woodfin Camp & Associates; Page 206, © Dawson Jones/Stock Boston; Page 207 (top), © Enrico Ferorelli; Page 207 (bottom), © K Rice/RobertStock.

Chapter 6

Page 215, © Erik Christensen/GNM/CP; Page 216, © Imtek Imagineering/Masterfile; Page 217, Photo by Donna T. Biershwale, courtesy of UL Lafayette Institute of Cognitive Science; Page 218, PhotoDisc Blue/Royalty Free/Getty Images; Page 224, © Najlah Feanny/Stock Boston; Page 226, © Ed Young/Photo Researchers, Inc.; Page 235 (both), © Louis Psihoyos/Matrix; Page 249 (both), © Dr. G.A. Ricaurte, Johns Hopkins University School of Medicine. Reprinted with permission from Elsevier Science (*The Lancet*. 1998, Vol. 352. pp. 1433–1437); Page 250 (top), The Advertising Archive, Ltd.; Page 250 (bottom), © Claudia Andujar/Photo Researchers; Page 251, © Tony Caldwell/CP/OTTS; Page 258, © AP/Wide World Photos; Page 259, © Bettmann/Corbis; Page 260, Courtesy, News and Publications Service, Stanford University.

Chapter 7

Page 265, Royalty-Free/Corbis; Page 269 (top), © Oan Connell. The Image Works; Page 269 (bottom), © George Houlton/Photo Researchers, Inc.; Page 271, © Bettmann/Corbis; Page 276, Courtesy of Professor Benjamin Harris; Page 279, Susan Van Etten/Photo Edit; Page 282, © Nina Leen, *Life Magazine*; Page 285, © Comstock/PictureQuest; Page 289 (all), Rogert W. Kelley, *Life Magazine* © Time, Inc.; Page 291, © Nicolas Le Corre/Gamma; Page 294, © Andrew Wakeford/Getty Images; Page 295, © Luc Marescot/Gamma; Page 299 (both), © Lincoln P. Brower; Page 301, © Monte S. Buchsbaum, M.D., Mt. Sinai School of Medicine, New York, NY; Page 302 (all), © Superstock; Page 304, Cartoon by H. Mazzeo and P. Ganler, 1951. Reprinted with permission of Jester of Columbia; Page 306, © Courtesy Albert Bandura, Stanford University.

Chapter 8

Page 311, © Doug Menuez/PhotoDisc; Page 314, © Mark Gibson/Gibson Stock Photography; Page 329, © Peter C. Brandt/Getty Images; Page 331, Photofest; Page 333, © Bettmann/Corbis; Page 334, Adapted from Nickerson & Adams, 1982; Page 339, Images courtesy of Helene Intraub; Page 340 (both), © Bettmann/Corbis; Page 343, © Shahn-Kermani/Liaison Agency; Page 347, Photo courtesy of John Gabrieli.

Chapter 9

Page 353, Courtesy of Fran and Kim Peek; Page 354, © 2002 by Sidney Harris; Page 358 (top), Marcus Raichle, Washington University, St. Louis, McDonnell Centre for High Brain Function; Page 358 (bottom), Sex differences....*Brain and Language*,

80, 97–105, Fig. 1, p. 102, "Rossell, S.L. et al. (2002). Sex differences in functional brain activation during a lexical visual field task. *Brain and Language*. Copyright © 2003 Elsevier Science (USA). All rights reserved."; Page 359, © Simon Marcus/Corbis; Page 365, Courtesy of Sue Savage-Rumbaugh; Page 370, © Ross Woodhall/Getty; Page 371, © AP/Wide World Photos; Page 377 (top), Sir Francis Galton Hulton Archive/Getty Images; Page 377 (bottom), Bettmann/Corbis; Page 383, © Laura Dwight/Photo Edit, Inc.; Page 387 (left), AP/Stephen Chemin; Page 387 (middle), CP/Larry MacDougal; Page 387 (right), © George Burns/Harpo Productions/ Getty Images

Chapter 10

Page 401, © Michael L. Abramson/Woodfin Camp & Associates; Page 408, Copyright 1995 Amgen Inc.; Page 412, © ImageState; Page 419, © Cheryl Maeder/Corbis; Page 422 (top), © David Young-Wolff/Photo Edit; Page 422 (bottom), © Milner Moshe/Corbis Sygma; Page 427, © Irvington Publishers; Page 432, The Farside ©1985 Far-Works, Inc. Used by Permission. All rights reserved.; Page 434 (top), Paul Chiasson/CP; Page 434 (bottom), © Jed Jacobson/Allsport/Getty; Page 437, © Kwame Zikomo/SuperStock; Page 441, © Michael L. Abramson/Woodfin Camp & Associates; Page 442 (top), © Thomas Kitchen & Victoria Hurst; Page 442 (bottom), The Beauty Archive/eStock Photo; Page 444, © P. Ekman and W.V. Friesan, "Pictures of Facial Affect." Consulting Psychologists Press, Palo Alto, CA, 1976; Page 450 (a) and (b), © Tony Freeman/PhotoEdit.

Chapter 11

Page 457, Stringer/CP; Page 460 (a), © David M. Phillips/The Population Council/Photo Researchers; Page 460 (b), © Biophoto Associaties/Photo Researchers; Page 460 (c), © John Watney Photo Library/Photo Researchers; Page 461 (top), © CNRI/SPL/Photo Researchers; Page 461 (bottom left), © George Setinmetz; Page 461 (bottom right), © Streissguth, A.P., & Little, R.E. (1994). "Unit 5: Alcohol, Pregnancy and the Fetal Alcohol Syndrome; Second Edition" of the Project Cork Institute Medical School Curriculum (slide lecture series) on Biomedical Education: Alcohol Use and Its Medical Consequences, produced by Dartmouth Medical School; Page 462 (a), © Michael Siluk; Page 462 (b), © Dr. Melanie Spence, University of Texas, Dallas; Page 464, © Dr. Charles A. Nelson; Page 465, © Enrico Ferorelli; Page 469, © Steven Raymer/National Geographic Image Collection; Page 471 (a) and (b), Tony Freeman/Photo Edit; Page 472 (a) to (c), Tony Freeman/Photo Edit; Page 482 (a), © Carroll E. Izard; Page 482 (b), © Myrleen Ferguson/Photo Edit; Page 483, © Harlow Primate Laboratory, University of Wisconsin; Page 485, Liquidlibrary/Jupiterimages; Page 490 (left), © SuperStock Inc.; Page 490 (right), © LWA-JDC/Corbis; Page 491, © Bill Gillette/Stock Boston; Page 492, © Bob Daemmrich/Stock Boston LLC; Page 497, © Fonlupt Gilles/Gamma; Page 498 (a), © George Shelley/Masterfile; Page 498 (b), © Ken Fisher/ Getty Images; Page 506, © Reuters/Corbis.

Chapter 12

Page 509, CP Photo/Tom Hanson; Page 511, © Corbis; Page 516, © PhotoEdit; Page 517, © Greg Mancuso/Stock Boston; Page 518, © The New Yorker Collection 1971. Dana Fradon from cartoonbank.com. All Rights Reserved; Page 526 (a), © Randy J. Larsen, 1987; Page 533, AFP/Corbis; Page 535 (a), © Spencer Bank/PhotoEdit; Page 536, Courtesy of Stanford News Service; Page 542, © Wei Yan/Masterfile; Page 545 (top), This image is not from the original series of the Rorschach®-Test. Printed with the permission of Verlag Hans Huber, Hogrefe AG, Bern. Rorschach is a worldwide registered trademark.; Page 545 (bottom), Reprinted by permission of the publisher from Henry A. Murray, *Thematic Apperception Test*, Plate 12F. Cambridge, MA: Harvard University Press. Copyright © 1943 by the President and Fellows of Harvard College, Copyright © 1971 by Henry A. Murray.

Chapter 13

Page 549, Corbis Royalty Free; Page 551 (top three), © Bettmann/Corbis; Page 551 (bottom), © Kjell Sandved/Visuals Unlimited, Inc.; Page 552, © *Witches' Sabbath: The He-Goat*, 1978 Museo Lazaro Galdiano, Madrid, Spain; Page 558 (top), © Bettmann/Corbis; Page 558 (bottom), © Wide World Photos; Page 560, © AP/Wide World Photos; Page 566 (both), © William Thompson/Index Stock Imagery; Page 572, © Alan Oddie/Photo Edit; Page 577, © Steve Smith; Page 581 (a), © Tom & Dee Ann McCarthy/Corbis; Page 581 (b), © Bettmann/ Corbis; Page 582, © Grunnitus/Monkmeyer; Page 584, © Nancy C. Andreason; The National Institute of Mental Health; Page 588, © Phil Snell/CP; Page 592, © Pixland/PunchStock.

Chapter 14

Page 597, © TRSUN/CP photo; Page 599, © David Buffington/PhotoDisc/Getty; Page 600, © Bruce Ayres/Stone/Getty; Page 601, © 2003 by Sydney Harris; Page 603, Courtesy Natalie Rogers; Page 608, © Courtesy Dr. Albert Ellis; Page 609, © Courtesy Dr. Aaron T. Beck; Page 611, © Geri Engberg/The Image Works; Page 616, © Courtesy Hunter Hoffman; photo by Mary Levin, University of Washington; Page 619, © Ed Lallo/Index Stock; Page 629, © Michael Newman/Photo Edit; Page 630, © Will & Dent McIntyre/Photo Researchers; Page 634, © David Young-Wolff/PhotoEdit.

Chapter 15

Page 641, © Comstock/Corbis; Page 643 (top), © David Hamilton/Getty; Page 643 (bottom), © PhotoDisc Blue/Getty; Page 650, © Arko Datta/ Reuters/Corbis; Page 651, © Oscar Burriel/Latin Stock/SPL/Photo Researchers; Page 652, © Jennie Woodcock; Reflections Photolibrary/Corbis; Page 661, © Stockbyte/Getty Images; Page 666, © PhotoAlto/PunchStock; Page 672, © Bruce Ayres/ Stone; Page 683, © J.P. Laffont/Corbis-Sygma; Page 686, Based on Kosambi, 1967; Page 690, © Ronnie Kaufman/Corbis.

Chapter 16

Page 693, © CP Photo/Peter McCabe; Page 695, © Bruce Ayres/Getty; Page 696, Kobal Collection; Page 705, © PhotoAlto/SuperStock; Page 706, © Merie W. Wallace/Warner Bros/Bureau LACollections/Corbis; Page 707, © The New Yorker Collection 1972. J.B. Handelsman from cartoonbank.com. All Rights Reserved; Page 708 (a) and (b), © William Vandivert, *Scientific American*, November 1955, Vol. 193, Issue 5, pp. 31–35; Page 710, © 1965 by Stanley Milgram. From the film *Obedience*, distributed by Penn State, Media Sales; Page 711, © 1965 by Stanley Milgram. From the film *Obedience*, distributed by Penn State, Media Sales; Page 712 (top), © STRJOH/Jonathan Hayward/CP; Page 712 (bottom), © Owen Franken/Stock Boston LLC; Page 714 (top), © Ryan McVay/Getty Images; Page 714 (bottom), © Digital Vision/Getty Images; Page 716 (a), © The New Yorker Collection 1979. Henry Martin from cartoonbank.com. All Rights Reserved; Page 716 (b), © NASA; Page 718, © Brand X Pictures/PunchStock; Page 719 (top), © Richard Lord/PhotoEdit; Page 719 (bottom), © Sid Bahrt/ Photo Researchers; Page 723, © Andrew Brusso; Page 725, © Royalty-Free/Corbis; Page 728 (a), Allport, G.W. & Postman, L. (1947). *The Psychology of Rumor*. Copyright © 1947 Henry Holt & Company. Copyright © Graphic Presentation Services; Page 730, © Das Fotoarchiv GmBH/Peter Arnold, Inc.; Page 732, © Viviane Moos/Corbis; Page 735, © Keith Brofsky/Getty Images; Page 739, © Johnathan Nourok/PhotoEdit.

Glossary

A

abnormal behaviour behaviour that is personally distressful, personally dysfunctional, and/or so culturally deviant that other people judge it to be inappropriate or maladaptive

absolute threshold the lowest intensity at which a stimulus can be detected correctly 50 percent of the time

accommodation (cognitive development) the process by which new experiences cause existing schemas to change

accommodation (vision) the process whereby the lens changes shape in order to focus objects at varying distances onto the retina

acetylcholine (ACh) an excitatory neurotransmitter that operates at synapses with muscles and is also the transmitter in some neural networks involved in memory

achievement test a measure of an individual's degree of accomplishment in a particular subject or task based on a relatively standardized set of experiences

action potential a nerve impulse resulting from the depolarization of an axon's cell membrane

action potential threshold the intensity of stimulation (excitatory minus inhibitory) needed to produce an action potential

activation-synthesis theory the theory that dreams represent the brain's attempt to interpret random patterns of neural activation triggered by the brain stem during REM sleep

activity anorexia a condition in which a rat given limited access to food and unlimited access to a running wheel eventually comes to choose running over eating; considered by many researchers to be an animal model of the human eating disorder *anorexia nervosa*

adaptations allow organisms to meet recurring environmental challenges to their survival, thereby increasing their reproductive ability

adaptive significance the manner in which a particular behaviour enhances an organism's chances of survival and reproduction

adolescent egocentrism highly self-focused thinking, particularly in the earlier teenage years

adoption studies a research method in behaviour genetics in which adopted people are compared on some characteristic with both their biological and adoptive parents in an attempt to determine how strong a genetic component the characteristic might have

adrenal glands endocrine glands that release stress hormones, including epinephrine and norepinephrine

aerobic exercise sustained activity that elevates the heart rate and body's need for oxygen

affect an alternate term for feelings and emotions

affective neuroscience the study of how emotion is represented in the brain in a way that is consistent with the neural basis of emotion and with individual differences in affective style

affective styles different emotional reactions among different individuals to the same event

agoraphobia a phobia centred around open spaces and public places

alcohol myopia when intoxicated, a "short-sightedness" in thinking (a failure to consider consequences) caused by an inability to pay attention to as much information as when sober

algorithm procedures, such as mathematical formulas, that automatically generate correct solutions to problems

alleles the two genes, one on each chromosome, that control the same trait

all-or-none law the fact that an action potential is not proportional to the intensity of stimulation; a neuron either fires with maximum intensity or it does not fire (compare with graded potential)

alpha waves a brain-wave pattern of 8 to 12 cycles per second that is characteristic of humans in a relaxed waking state

altruism occurs when one individual helps another, but in so doing accrues some cost

Alzheimer's disease the leading cause of dementia in the elderly, accounting for about 60 percent of senile dementias

amphetamine psychosis schizophrenia-like hallucinations and delusions that occur when the brain's dopamine activity is artificially increased far beyond normal levels by continuous, heavy amphetamine use

amplitude the vertical size of the sound wave, which gives rise to the perception of loudness and is measured in terms of decibels

amygdala a limbic system structure that helps organize emotional response patterns

analytic psychology Jung's expansion of Freud's notion of the unconscious; Jung believed that humans possess not only a personal unconscious based on their life experiences, but also a collective unconscious that consists of memories accumulated throughout the entire history of the human race

androgens so-called "male" sex hormones

anorexia nervosa an eating disorder involving a severe and sometimes fatal restriction of food intake

anterograde amnesia memory loss for events that occur after the initial onset of amnesia

anticipatory nausea and vomiting (ANV) classically conditioned nausea and vomiting that occur when cancer patients are exposed to stimuli associated with their treatment

antigens literally, antibody generators, or foreign substances that activate the cells of the immune system

anxiety an emotional state characterized by apprehension accompanied by physiological arousal and fearful behaviour

anxiety disorders a group of behaviour disorders in which anxiety and associated maladaptive behaviours are the core of the disturbance

aphasia the loss of ability to understand speech (receptive aphasia) or to produce it (productive aphasia)

applied behaviour analysis a process (also called behaviour modification) in which operant conditioning is combined with scientific data collection to solve individual and societal problems

applied research research involving the application of scientific knowledge to solve practical problems

approach-approach conflict a conflict in which an individual is simultaneously attracted to two incompatible positive goals

approach-avoidance conflict a conflict in which an individual is simultaneously attracted to and repelled by the same goal

aptitude test a measure of a person's ability to profit from further training or experience in an occupation or skill; usually based on a measure of skills gained over a person's lifetime rather than during a specific course of study

archetypes innate concepts and memories (e.g., God, the hero; the good mother); memories that reside in the collective unconscious (Jung)

artificial intelligence the field within cognitive science that attempts to develop computer simulations of human mental processes

assimilation in cognitive development, the process by which new experiences are incorporated into existing schemas

association cortex the areas of the cerebral cortex that do not have sensory or motor functions but are involved in the integration of neural activity that underlies perception, language, and other higher-order mental processes

associative network the view that long-term memory is organized as a massive network of associated ideas and concepts

attachment the strong emotional bond that develops between children and their primary caregivers

attention-deficit/hyperactivity disorder (ADHD) disorder in which problems may take the form of attentional difficulties, hyperactivity-impulsivity, or a combination of the two that results in impaired functioning

attitude a positive or negative evaluative reaction toward a stimulus (e.g., toward a person, action, object, or concept)

attributions judgments about the causes of our own and other people's behaviour and outcomes

authoritarian parents caregivers who exert control over their children, but do so within a cold, unresponsive, or rejecting relationship

authoritative parents caregivers who are controlling, but warm; they establish and enforce clear rules within a caring, supportive atmosphere

autoimmune reactions immune disorders in which the immune system mistakenly identifies part of the body as an antigen and attacks it

automatic processing mental activities that occur automatically and require minimal or no conscious control or awareness

autonomic nervous system the branch of the peripheral nervous system that stimulates the body's involuntary muscles (e.g., heart) and internal organs

autonomic response stereotypy individual differences in patterns of physiological responses to emotion-arousing stimuli

availability heuristic a guideline used to make likelihood judgments based on how easily examples of that category of events come to mind, or are "available" in memory

aversion therapy the pairing of a CS that currently evokes a positive but maladaptive response with a noxious UCS in an attempt to condition repulsion toward the CS

avoidance-avoidance conflict a conflict in which an individual must choose between two alternatives, both of which she or he wishes to avoid

avoidance conditioning the conditioning of an organism to perform a response to avoid an undesirable consequence

axon an extension from one side of the neuron cell body that conducts nerve impulses to other neurons, muscles, or glands

B

baseline data measures of behaviour that are gathered before an intervention program is implemented; these provide a standard against which to judge the outcome of a program

basic research research designed to obtain knowledge for its own sake

basilar membrane a membrane that runs the length of the cochlea and contains the organ of Corti and its sound receptor hair cells

behaviour genetics the scientific study of the role of genetic inheritance in behaviour

behaviour modification therapeutic procedures based on operant conditioning principles, such as positive reinforcement, operant extinction, and punishment

behavioural assessment explicit coding system devised by psychologists that contains the behavioural categories of interest

behavioural coping responses behavioural attempts to cope with the demands of a situation

behavioural perspective a view that emphasizes the manner in which the environment and the learning experiences it provides shape and control behaviour

behavioural signatures consistent ways of responding in particular classes of situations

behaviourism school of psychology that emphasizes the role of learning and environmental control over behaviour, and maintains that the proper subject matter of psychology is observable behaviour; John Watson and B. F. Skinner were major figures in behaviourism

belief bias the tendency to abandon logical rules and to form a conclusion based on one's existing beliefs

beta waves a brain-wave pattern of 15 to 30 cycles per second that is characteristic of humans who are in an alert waking state

Big Five personality factors the five personality factors of openness, conscientiousness, extraversion, agreeableness, and neuroticism (OCEAN) that are thought by Five Factor theorists to be the five basic and universal dimensions of personality

binocular depth cues depth cues that require the use of both eyes

binocular disparity the binocular depth cues produced by the projection of slightly different images of an object on the retinas of the two eyes

biological perspective perspective that focuses on the role of biological factors in behaviour, including biochemical and brain processes as well as genetic and evolutionary factors

biological preparedness the notion that evolutionary factors have produced an innate readiness to learn certain associations that have had survival implications in the past

biologically based mechanisms mechanisms that receive input from the environment, process the information, and respond to it

bipolar cells the second layer of retinal cells with which the rods and cones synapse

bipolar disorder mood disorder in which intermittent mania appears against a background of depression

blindsight condition in which patients with damage to the visual cortex are able to respond adaptively to stimuli while maintaining that they cannot see them

blood-brain barrier specialized lining of cells in the brain's blood vessels that screen out foreign substances while letting nutrients pass through to neurons

bottom-up processing perceptual processing that begins with the analysis of individual elements of the stimulus and works up to the brain's integration of them into a unified perception

brain stem the portion of the brain formed by the swelling of the spinal cord as it enters the skull; its structures regulate basic survival functions of the body, such as heart rate and respiration

British empiricism 17th-century school of philosophy championed by John Locke, according to which all the contents of the mind are gained experientially through the senses; this notion was later a cornerstone for the behaviourists' position that we are shaped through our experiences

Broca's area a region of the left frontal lobe involved in speech production

bystander effect the finding that the presence of multiple bystanders inhibits each person's tendency to help, largely due to social comparison or diffusion of responsibility

C

cannaboids natural pain-killing substances in the body that resemble THC, the analgesic agent in marijuana

case study an in-depth analysis of an individual group or event

catatonic type a schizophrenic reaction characterized by alternating stuporous states and agitated excitement during which the person can be quite dangerous

catharsis the discharge of aggressive energy and temporary reduction of the impulse to aggress argued to occur through performing an act of aggression

CCK (cholecystokinin) a peptide that appears to decrease eating and thereby helps regulate food intake

central nervous system portion of the nervous system that includes the brain and the spinal cord

central route to persuasion occurs when people think carefully about a message and are influenced because they find the arguments compelling

cephalocaudal principle the tendency for physical development to proceed in a head-to-foot direction

cerebellum a convoluted hindbrain structure involved in motor coordination and some aspects of learning and memory

cerebral cortex the grey, convoluted outer covering of the brain that is the seat of higher-order sensory, motor, perceptual, and mental processes

chaining an operant conditioning procedure used to develop a sequence (chain) of responses by reinforcing each response with the opportunity to perform the next response

chromosomes tightly coiled strands of deoxyribonucleic acid (DNA) and protein that contain the genes

chunking combining individual items into larger units of meaning

circadian rhythms biological cycles within the body that occur on an approximately 24-hour cycle

classical conditioning a procedure in which a formerly neutral stimulus (the conditioned stimulus) comes to elicit a conditioned response by virtue of being paired with an unconditioned stimulus that naturally elicits a similar response (the unconditioned response)

cochlea a small coil-shaped structure of the inner ear that contains the receptors for sound

cognitive-affective personality system (CAPS) the five personality variables that account for how a given person might respond to a particular situation are organized into this system; the dynamic interplay among these five factors, together with the characteristics of the situation, account for individual differences between people as well as differences in people's behaviour across different situations

cognitive appraisal the process of making judgments about situations, personal capabilities, likely consequences, and the personal meaning of consequences

cognitive-arousal model of love the view that passionate love has interacting cognitive and physiological components

cognitive behaviourism behavioural approach that incorporates cognitive concepts, suggesting that the environment influences our behaviour by affecting our thoughts and giving us information; these cognitive processes allow us to control our behaviour and the environment

cognitive distortions persistent, automatic modes of illogical thinking that tend to evoke depression, anxiety, and other negative emotions

cognitive map a mental representation of the spatial layout of an area

cognitive perspective psychological perspective that views humans as rational information processors and problem solvers, and focuses on the mental processes that influence behaviour

cognitive-process dream theory a theory that focuses on how (rather than why) we dream, and proposes that dreaming and waking thought are produced by the same mental systems in the brain

cognitive process theories approaches to intelligence that analyze the mental processes that underlie intelligent thinking

cognitive restructuring cognitive stress-reduction approach that involves attempts to detect, dispute, and change maladaptive or irrational ideas that trigger negative emotions

collective unconscious Jung's notion of an unconscious that consists of ancestral memories that are innate

collectivism a cultural factor that emphasizes the achievement of the group rather than individual goals and in which personal identity is largely defined by ties to the larger social group (see individualism)

common factors therapeutic elements that are possessed by virtually any type of therapy and which may contribute to the similar positive effects shown by many different treatment approaches

comorbidity the tendency for more than one disorder, such as a mood and an anxiety disorder, to occur together in a given individual

companionate love an affectionate relationship characterized by commitment and caring about the partner's well-being; sometimes contrasted with passionate love, which is more intensely emotional

compensatory response bodily response that opposes a drug's effects and occurs in an attempt to restore homeostasis

competency a legal decision that a defendant is mentally capable of understanding the nature of criminal charges, participating meaningfully in a trial, and consulting with an attorney

competency-focused intervention prevention programs that are designed to enhance the personal resources needed to cope with situations that might otherwise cause psychological disorders

compulsion a repetitive act that the person feels compelled to carry out, often in response to an obsessive thought or image

computerized axial tomography (CT) scan a method of scanning the brain with narrow beams of X-rays that are then analyzed and combined by a computer to provide pictures of brain structures from many different angles

concept a mental category containing similar objects, people, and events

concordance the likelihood that two people share a particular characteristic

concrete operational stage in Piaget's theory, the stage of cognitive development during which children can perform basic mental operations concerning problems that involve tangible (i.e., "concrete") objects and situations

conditioned response (CR) in classical conditioning, a response to a conditioned stimulus; the CR is established by pairing a conditioned stimulus with an unconditioned stimulus that evokes a similar response

conditioned stimulus (CS) a neutral stimulus that comes to evoke a conditioned response after being paired with an unconditioned stimulus

conditioned taste aversion a learned repulsion to a food that formerly was neutral or desired, by virtue of pairing the food with an aversive UCS (e.g., nausea, stomach illness)

conditions of worth internalized standards of self-worth fostered by conditional positive regard from others

conduct disorder disorder in which children violate important social norms and show disregard for the rights of others

conduction deafness hearing loss caused by damage to the mechanical system that conducts sound waves to the cochlea

cones photoreceptors in the retina that function best in bright light and are differentially sensitive to red, green, or blue wavelengths; the retina's colour receptors

confirmation bias the tendency to seek and favour information that reinforces our beliefs rather than to be open to disconfirming information

confounding of variables in an experiment, the intertwining of the independent variable with another, uncontrolled variable; thus, we cannot tell which variable is responsible for changes in the behaviour of interest (i.e., the dependent variable)

congruence consistency between self-perceptions and experience

consciousness our moment-to-moment awareness of ourselves and our environment; consciousness involves selective attention to ongoing thoughts, perceptions, and feelings

conservation the principle that basic properties of objects, such as their mass or quantity, stay the same (are "conserved") even though their outward appearance may change

construct validity the extent to which a test measures the psychological construct (e.g., intelligence, anxiety) that it is purported to measure

contact hypothesis Allport's hypothesis that increasing contact between hostile groups can result in positive attitudinal change

content validity the extent to which test items adequately sample the domain that the test is supposed to measure (e.g., intelligence, mathematical reasoning)

context-dependent memory the phenomenon that it is typically easier to remember something in the same environment in which it was originally learned or experienced

continuous reinforcement schedule a reinforcement schedule in which each correct response is followed by reinforcement

control group in an experiment, the group that is not exposed to the treatment, or which receives a zero level of the independent variable

controlled (effortful) processing mental processing that requires some degree of volitional control and attentiveness

conventional moral reasoning moral judgments that are based on conformity to social expectations, laws, and duties

convergent thinking a form of creative thinking in which the problem is solved by eliminating alternative solutions to converge on the correct one

conversion disorder disorder in which serious neurological symptoms, such as paralysis, loss of sensation, or blindness, suddenly occur

cooperation situations in which one individual helps another and in so doing gains some advantage
cooperative learning programs educational programs that place children of different ethnic groups in a setting in which they need to cooperate and teach one another if the group is to succeed
coping self-efficacy beliefs relating to our ability to deal effectively with a stressful stimulus or situation, including pain
corpus callosum a broad band of white, myelinated fibres that connect the left and right cerebral hemispheres and allow the two hemispheres to communicate with one another
correlation coefficient a statistic that indicates the direction and strength of a relation between two variables
correlational methods research methods that involve measuring the strength of an association between two or more events
correlational research research that measures two or more naturally occurring variables, and examines whether they are statistically related
counterbalancing a procedure in which participants in an experiment are exposed to all the conditions; the order of conditions is varied so that no condition has an advantage relative to the others
counterconditioning the process of conditioning an incompatible response to a particular stimulus in order to eliminate a maladaptive response (e.g., anxiety), as occurs in systematic desensitization
critical period a time period in which exposure to particular kinds of stimulation (e.g., perceptual) is required for normal development to occur
cross-sectional design a research design that simultaneously compares people of different ages at a particular point in time
crystallized intelligence intellectual abilities that depend on a store of information and the acquisition of particular skills (contrast to fluid intelligence)
cultural competence a set of therapeutic skills, including scientific mindedness, the ability to consider both cultural and individual factors, and the capacity to introduce culture-specific elements into therapy with people from minority cultures
culture the enduring values, beliefs, behaviours, and traditions that are shared by a large group of people and passed from one generation to the next
culture-bound disorders behaviour disorders whose specific forms are restricted to one particular cultural context

D

dark adaptation the progressive increase in brightness sensitivity that occurs over time as photopigments regenerate themselves during exposure to low levels of illumination
decay theory the theory that with time and disuse the physical memory trace in the nervous system fades away
deception a procedure in which participants are misled about the purpose or nature of a study
decibel a logarithmic measure of sound intensity
decision criterion in signal detection theory, the potentially changing standard of how certain a person must be that a stimulus is present in order to report its presence
declarative memory our memory for factual knowledge, which is composed of two subcategories: knowledge pertaining to personal experience (episodic memory) and knowledge of general facts and language (semantic memory)
deductive reasoning reasoning from a general principle to a specific case
deep structure a linguistic term that refers to the underlying meaning of a spoken or written sentence; the meanings that make up deep structure are stored as concepts and rules in long-term memory
defence mechanisms unconscious processes by which the ego prevents the expression of anxiety-arousing impulses or allows them to appear in disguised forms
deindividuation a state of increased anonymity in which a person, often as part of a group or crowd, engages in disinhibited behaviour
deinstitutionalization the attempt to move the primary locus of treatment from mental hospitals to the community
delay discounting the decrease in value of a future incentive as a function of its distance in time
delay of gratification the ability to forgo immediate rewards for delayed but more satisfying outcomes
delta waves low-frequency, high-amplitude brain waves that occur in stage 3 sleep and predominate in stage 4 sleep
delusions false beliefs, often involving themes of persecution or grandeur, that are sustained in the face of evidence that normally would be sufficient to destroy them
demand characteristics cues used by research participants to guess the purpose or hypothesis of a study, thereby causing them to alter their behaviour
dementia the gradual loss of cognitive abilities that accompanies brain deterioration and interferes with normal functioning
dendrites small branching fibres that extend from the soma of a neuron and receive messages from adjacent neurons
dependent variable in an experiment, the factor that is measured by the researcher and which presumably is influenced by the independent variable
depolarization the reversal of the resting potential of a neuron's cell membrane that produces the action potential
depressants drugs—including alcohol, barbiturates, and tranquilizers—that reduce neural activity and may decrease feelings of tension and anxiety
depressive attributional pattern the tendency of depressed people to attribute negative outcomes to their own inadequacies and positive ones to factors outside themselves
deprivation experiment method of determining the critical periods during which certain experiences must occur for the related brain mechanisms to develop normally
descriptive method research method that involves recording observations or surveys
descriptive research research in which the main goal is to carefully describe how organisms behave, particularly in natural settings
deterioration effect the tendency of some people to deteriorate rather than improve as a result of therapy
deviation IQ standardized distance (or deviation) a score is above or below the mean for a particular sample
difference threshold the smallest difference between two similar stimuli that people can detect; also termed the just noticeable difference (jnd)
discrimination (classical conditioning) the occurrence of a CR to one stimulus, but not to another stimulus
discrimination (operant conditioning) the ability to respond differentially to stimuli that signal particular consequences
discriminative stimulus an antecedent stimulus that signals the likelihood of certain consequences if a response is made
disorganized type a schizophrenic disorder marked by verbal incoherence, disordered thought processes, disorganized behaviour, and inappropriate emotional responses
displacement the capacity of language to represent objects and conditions that are not physically present
display rules culturally influenced standards for the circumstances and manner in which specific emotions are expressed
dissociation theories (of hypnosis) the view that hypnosis is an altered state involving a division ("dissociation") of consciousness; one theory proposes that the hypnotized person simultaneously experiences two streams of consciousness that are cut off from one another
dissociative disorders disorders which involve a major dissociation of personal identity or memory
dissociative identity disorder (DID) a dissociative disorder in which two or more separate identities or personalities coexist within an individual
divergent thinking a creative form of thinking that involves the generating of novel ideas that diverge from the normal ways of thinking about something
divided attention the ability to perform more than one activity at the same time

domain-specific adaptations adaptations designed to solve a particular problem
dominant gene a gene, which when present, will produce a particular characteristic
door-in-the-face technique a manipulation technique in which a persuader makes a large request, expecting you to reject it, and then presents a smaller request
dopamine an excitatory neurotransmitter whose overactivity may underlie some of the disordered behaviours seen in schizophrenia
dopamine hypothesis view that the symptoms of schizophrenia are produced by overactivity of the dopamine system in areas of the brain that regulate emotional expression, motivated behaviour, and cognitive functioning
double-blind procedure a procedure in which both the participant and the experimenter are kept unaware of the research condition to which the participant has been assigned
downward comparison the act of comparing oneself or one's situation with less positive alternatives
drive theory the theory that physiological disruptions to homeostasis produce states of internal tension (called drives) that motivate an organism to behave in ways that reduce this tension
dual coding theory the theory that, if we encode information using both verbal and imagery codes, the chances improve that at least one of the two codes will be available later to support recall
dual-process theory the modern colour vision theory that posits cones that are sensitive to red, blue, and green and opponent processes at the level of ganglion cells and beyond
dyslexia difficulty learning to read which cannot be explained by general intellectual impairment, educational opportunity, or sensory deficits
dysthymia a depressive mood disorder of moderate intensity that occurs over a long period of time but does not disrupt functioning as a major depression does

E

eclectic an approach to therapy that incorporates principles and procedures from multiple therapies to provide the most suitable therapy for an individual
effect size in meta-analysis, a measure of treatment effectiveness that indicates what percentage of treated clients improves more than the average untreated client
effect size statistic common measure of treatment effectiveness
effectiveness Seligman's term for the outcomes achieved by therapies in real-life, uncontrolled therapy settings
efficacy the extent to which therapy can be shown to achieve positive outcomes in controlled outcome studies
ego the "executive" of the personality that is partly conscious and that mediates between the impulses of the id, the prohibitions of the superego, and the dictates of reality
egocentrism difficulty in viewing the world from someone else's perspective
elaborative rehearsal focusing on the meaning of information or relating it to other things we already know
electroconvulsive therapy (ECT) a biomedical technique involving the application of electrical current to the brain that is used primarily to reduce severe depression
electroencephalograph (EEG) a device used to record the simultaneous activity of many thousands of neurons through electrodes attached to the scalp
embryo scientific term for the prenatal organism during the second week through the eighth week after conception
emotion a pattern of cognitive, physiological, and behavioural responses to situations and events that have relevance to important goals or motives
emotion-focused coping coping strategies directed at minimizing or reducing emotional responses to a stressor
emotional intelligence ability to respond adaptively in the emotional realm by reading and responding appropriately to others' emotions, to be aware of one's own emotions and have the ability to control them, and to delay gratification
empathy the capacity for experiencing the same emotional response being exhibited by another person; in therapy, the ability of a therapist to view the world through the client's eyes and to understand the client's emotions
empathy-altruism hypothesis the theory that pure altruism does exist, and that it is produced by empathy
empirical approach an approach to test construction in which items (regardless of their content) are chosen that differentiate between two groups that are known to differ on a particular personality variable
encoding getting information into the memory system by translating it into a neural code that the brain processes and stores
encoding specificity principle observation that memory is enhanced when conditions present during retrieval match those that were present during encoding
endocrine system the body's system of glands that secrete hormones into the bloodstream and thereby affect many bodily functions
endorphins natural opiate-like substances that are involved in pain reduction
episodic memory our store of factual knowledge concerning personal experience—when, where, and what happened in the episodes of our lives
escape conditioning a form of learning in which the organism learns to perform a behaviour in order to escape from an aversive stimulus
estrogens so-called "female" sex hormones
evolution a change over time in the frequency with which particular genes—and the characteristics they produce—occur within an interbreeding population
evolutionary/circadian sleep models the view that in the course of evolution each species developed an adaptive circadian sleep-wake pattern that increased its chances of survival in relation to its environmental demands
evolutionary personality theory a recently developed attempt to account for personality traits in terms of the evolutionary history of the human species; these traits are thought to develop from processes of natural selection
evolutionary psychology a field of study that focuses on the role of evolutionary processes (especially natural selection) in the development of adaptive psychological mechanisms and social behaviour in humans
expectancy x value theory a cognitive theory that goal-directed behaviour is jointly influenced by 1) the person's expectancy that a particular behaviour will contribute to reaching the goal and 2) how positively or negatively the person values the goal
experiment a research method in which the researcher manipulates an independent variable under controlled conditions and measures whether this produces changes in a dependent variable
experimental group in an experiment, the group that receives a treatment or is exposed to an active level of the independent variable
experimental methods research methods that involve manipulations to establish cause and effect relationships between two or more events
experimenter expectancy effects subtle and unintentional ways in which an experimenter influences participants to behave in a way that will confirm the experimenter's hypothesis
explicit memory conscious or intentional memory retrieval
exposure (therapy) a therapeutic technique designed to extinguish anxiety responses by exposing clients to anxiety-arousing stimuli or situations while preventing escape or avoidance through response prevention
expressed emotion a family interaction pattern involving criticism, hostility, and overinvolvement that is associated with relapse when formerly hospitalized schizophrenic patients return home
expressive behaviours observable behavioural indications of subjectively experienced emotions
external validity the degree to which the results of a study can be generalized to other people, settings, and conditions
externalizing disorders disorders directed toward the environment in the form of behaviours that are disruptive and often aggressive

extinction (classical conditioning) weakening and eventual cessation of a CR caused by the presentation of the CS without the UCS

extinction (operant conditioning) occurs when the absence of reinforcement for a previously reinforced response causes that response to weaken and eventually to stop

extrinsic motivation motivation to perform a behaviour to obtain external rewards and reinforcers, such as money, status, attention, and praise

F

facial feedback hypothesis the notion that somatic feedback from facial muscles provides feedback to the brain and influences emotional experience

factor analysis a statistical technique that permits a researcher to reduce a large number of measures to a small number of clusters or factors; it identifies the clusters of behaviour or test scores that are highly correlated with one another

fantasy-prone personality the tendency of some people to spend much of their waking time living in a vivid, rich fantasy world that they control

feature detectors sensory neurons that respond to particular features of a stimulus, such as its shape, angle, or colour

fetal alcohol syndrome (FAS) a severe group of abnormalities that result from prenatal exposure to alcohol

fetus the scientific term for the prenatal organism from the ninth week after conception until birth

figure-ground relations perceptual organization in which a focal stimulus is perceived as a figure against a background of other stimuli

Five Factor model personality model that categorizes individual differences in personality traits in terms of extraversion, agreeableness, emotional stability, conscientiousness, and openness

fixation a state of arrested development due to unresolved conflict at a particular earlier psychosexual stage

fixed action pattern an unlearned response that is automatically triggered by a simple (releaser) stimulus

fixed-interval schedule a reinforcement schedule in which the first correct response occurring after a constant time interval is reinforced

fixed-ratio schedule a reinforcement schedule in which reinforcement is given after a constant number of correct responses

flashbulb memories recollections that seem so vivid and clear that we can picture them as if they were a "snapshot" of a moment in time

fluid intelligence the ability to deal with novel problem-solving situations for which personal experience does not supply a solution (contrast to crystallized intelligence)

foot-in-the-door technique a manipulation technique in which the persuader gets someone to comply with a small request first and later presents a larger request

forebrain brain structures above the midbrain, including the thalamus, hypothalamus, limbic system, and the cerebral hemispheres; involved in higher-order sensory, motor, and cognitive functions

formal operational stage in Piaget's theory, a period in which individuals are able to think logically and systematically about both concrete and abstract problems, form hypotheses, and test them in a thoughtful way

fovea a small area in the centre of the retina that contains only cones and in which visual acuity is greatest

free association in psychoanalysis, the procedure of verbalizing all thoughts that enter consciousness without censorship

frequency in audition, the number of cycles per second in a sound wave, responsible for the pitch of the sound; the measure of frequency is the hertz (Hz), which equals one cycle per second

frequency theory the theory of pitch perception that holds that the number of nerve impulses sent to the brain by the hair cells of the cochlea corresponds to the frequency of the sound wave; this theory is accurate at low frequencies

frontal lobe the anterior (front) portion of the cerebral hemispheres that includes Broca's speech production area, the motor cortex, and associative cortex involved in planning and problem solving

frustration-aggression hypothesis the view that 1) frustration inevitably leads to aggression, and 2) all aggression is the result of frustration

fully functioning persons Rogers's term for self-actualized people who are free from unrealistic conditions of worth and who exhibit congruence, spontaneity, creativity, and a desire to develop still further

functional fixedness a phenomenon often found in problem-solving tasks in which the customary use of an object interferes with its use in a novel situation

functional magnetic resonance imaging (fMRI) highly detailed imaging technology used to study local neural activity by measuring changes in local blood flow or oxygen content

functionalism an early school of American psychology that focused on the functions of consciousness and behaviour in helping organisms adapt to their environment and satisfy their needs

fundamental attribution error a tendency to underestimate the impact of the situation and overestimate the role of personal factors when explaining other people's behaviour

fundamental emotional patterns basic emotional response patterns that are believed to be innate

G

ganglion cells the third layer of retinal cells with which the bipolar cells synapse and whose axons form the optic nerve

gate control theory theory that proposes that the experience of pain results from the opening and closing of "gating mechanisms" in the nervous system

gender constancy the understanding that being male or female is a permanent part of a person

gender identity the sense of "femaleness" or "maleness" that is an integral part of our identity

gender schemas organized mental structures that contain our understanding of the attributes and behaviours that are appropriate and expected for males and females

gene knockout a procedure that alters a specific gene in a way that prevents it from carrying out its normal function

general adaptation syndrome (GAS) Selye's description of the body's responses to a stressor, which includes successive phases of alarm reaction, resistance, and exhaustion

generalized anxiety disorder a chronic state of diffuse, or "free-floating," anxiety that is not attached to specific situations or objects

genes the biological units of heredity, located on the chromosomes

genetic counselling health care service that provides counselling, support, and medical information about genetic disorders and risks

genetic determinism the view (sometimes erroneous) that genes have invariant and unavoidable effects

genotype the specific genetic makeup of an individual, which may or may not be expressed in the observable phenotype

genuineness the ability of a therapist to honestly express his or her feelings to a client

Gestalt laws of perceptual organization the laws of perceptual organization advanced by the Gestalt psychologists—namely, similarity, proximity, closure, and continuity

Gestalt psychology a German school of psychology that emphasized the natural organization of perceptual elements into wholes, or patterns, as well as the role of insight in problem solving

glial cells cells of the central nervous system that provide physical support for neurons and supply neurons with needed chemicals

gliotransmission communication between glial cells

glove anesthesia a type of conversion symptom in which a person experiences a physiologically unexplainable loss of feeling below the wrist

glucose a simple sugar that is the body's (and especially the brain's) major source of immediately usable fuel

graded potential a change in the electrical potential of a neuron that is proportional to the intensity of the incoming stimulation, but not sufficient to produce an action potential

group polarization the tendency for the "average" opinion of group members to become more extreme when like-minded people discuss an issue

groupthink the tendency of group members to suspend critical thinking because they are motivated to seek agreement

gustation the sense of taste

H

habituation a decrease in the strength of response to a repeated stimulus

hallucinations false perceptions that have a compelling sense of reality

hallucinogens drugs—such as LSD and PCP—that distort or intensify sensory experience and evoke hallucinations and disordered thought processes

hardiness a stress-resistant personality pattern that involves the factors of commitment, control, and challenge

harm reduction a prevention strategy that is designed not to eliminate a problem behaviour, but to reduce its harmful consequences

health-compromising behaviours behaviours, such as poor dietary habits and unprotected sexual activity, that impair health and reduce longevity

health-enhancing behaviours behaviours, such as exercise and good dietary habits, that support and increase health and longevity

health psychology the study of psychological and behavioural factors in the prevention and treatment of illness and in the maintenance of health

heritability coefficient the extent to which the degree of variation in a particular characteristic among a group of people can be attributed to genetic factors

hertz (Hz) the measure of sound wave frequency as cycles per second

heuristics a method of problem solving characterized by quick and easy search procedures

higher-order conditioning in classical conditioning, when a neutral stimulus becomes a CS after it is paired with another CS (rather than with the original UCS)

hippocampus a structure of the limbic system that plays a key role in the formation and storage of memories

homeostasis the maintenance of biological equilibrium, or balance, within the body

hormones chemical substances secreted by the glands of the endocrine system that travel in the bloodstream and affect bodily organs as well as psychological functions and development

hospitalization syndrome the adoption of a chronic sick role and the deterioration of social and vocational skills that can occur as a result of custodial psychiatric hospitalization

humanistic perspective a psychological perspective that emphasizes personal freedom, choice, and self-actualization

hyperopia a visual deficit sometimes called farsightedness in which the lens focuses the image behind the retina, reducing acuity for nearby objects

hypnosis a condition of enhanced suggestibility in which some people are able to experience imagined test suggestions as if they were real

hypnotic susceptibility scale a set of induction procedures and test questions that enable researchers to measure a person's responsiveness to hypnotic suggestion

hypochondriasis a somatoform disorder characterized by an overreaction to physical symptoms and a conviction that one has or is on the verge of a serious illness

hypothalamus a forebrain structure located below the thalamus and above the pituitary gland that controls autonomic and hormonal processes and plays a major role in many aspects of motivation and emotional behaviour

hypothesis a tentative explanation or prediction about some phenomenon

hysteria a psychological disorder studied and treated by Freud in which physical symptoms appear without any apparent underlying organic cause

I

iconic memory sensory storage mechanism in which a purely visual representation of a stimulus array is held as a trace memory (or *icon*)

id the primitive and unconscious part of the personality that contains the instincts

illusions incorrect perceptions based on false perceptual hypotheses that often result from constancies that do not apply to the stimuli in question

imaginal thought a form of thinking that uses images that can be from any sense modality

implicit memory the ability of memory to influence our behaviour without conscious awareness

imprinting in some species, a sudden, biologically primed form of attachment

incentive an environmental stimulus or condition that motivates behaviour

incubation a phenomenon in which the solution to a problem suddenly appears in consciousness after a problem solver has stopped thinking about it for a while

independent variable in an experiment, the factor that is manipulated by the researcher

individualism a cultural characteristic that favours the achievement of the individual over group goals and which is characteristic of many Western nations; self-identity is based primarily on one's own attributes and achievements (see collectivism)

inductive reasoning reasoning that proceeds from a set of specific facts to a general conclusion or principle

indulgent parents caregivers who have warm and caring relationships with their children, but do not provide much guidance and discipline

infantile amnesia an inability to remember personal experiences from the first few years of our lives

informational social influence following the opinions or behaviour of other people because we believe they have accurate knowledge and what they are doing is "right"

informed consent the principle that, prior to agreeing to participate in research, a person should be fully informed about the procedures, risks involved, and the right to withdraw at any time without penalty

insanity a legal decision that a defendant was so severely impaired at the time a crime was committed that he or she was incapable of appreciating the wrongfulness of the act or of controlling his or her behaviour

insight in Gestalt psychology, the sudden perception of a useful relationship or solution to a problem; in psychoanalysis, the conscious awareness of unconscious dynamics that underlie psychological problems

insomnia a sleep disorder involving chronic difficulty in falling asleep, staying asleep, or experiencing restful sleep

instinct an inherited characteristic, common to all members of a species, that automatically produces a particular response when the organism is exposed to a particular stimulus

instinctive drift the tendency for innate behaviours to override a conditioning procedure, thus making it difficult to create or maintain a conditioned response

instrumental behaviours emotional coping behaviours that are directed at achieving the goal or performing the task that is relevant to the emotion

intelligence a concept that refers to individual differences in the ability to acquire knowledge, to think and reason effectively, and to deal adaptively with the environment

intelligence quotient (IQ) originally defined as mental age (MA) divided by chronological age (CA) multiplied by 100 (IQ = (MA/CA) ÷ 100); an IQ of 100 indicates an individual is average for his or her age group. IQ scores are today based on norms derived from people of various ages

interaction in analyzing causal factors, the influence that the presence or strength of one factor can have on other causal factors

interactive problem solving a procedure used in the field of international conflict resolution that brings competing groups together, enables them to share their differing perspectives, and work together to develop solutions that will satisfy both groups' human needs

interjudge reliability the extent to which different observers or scorers agree in their scoring of a particular test or observed behaviour

internal consistency the extent to which items within a psychological test correlate with one another, indicating that they are measuring a common characteristic

internal–external locus of control Rotter's generalized expectancy that one's outcomes are under personal versus external control

internal validity the degree to which an experiment produces clear causal conclusions; internal validity is high when there is no confounding of variables

internalization the process of taking on as one's own the values and moral dictates communicated by parents and society

internalizing disorders disorders, such as anxiety disorders and mood disorders, that involve maladaptive thoughts and emotions

interneurons neurons that are neither sensory nor motor neurons, but perform associative or integrative functions within the nervous system

interpersonal therapy a form of brief therapy that focuses on the client's interpersonal problems and seeks to develop new interpersonal skills

interpretation in psychoanalysis, a statement made by the analyst that is intended to promote insight in the client

interventions systematically applied programs designed to solve a practical problem by changing behaviour

intrinsic motivation the motivation to perform a behaviour simply because one finds it interesting or enjoyable for its own sake

introspection the method of "looking within" and verbally reporting on immediate experience; used by the structuralists to study the contents of the mind

ion channels special protein molecules located on the membrane of a neuron that control the entry and exit of specific ions, such as sodium and potassium

J

jigsaw program an applied research program in which knowledge gained from basic research on factors that increase and decrease intergroup hostility was translated into a cooperative learning program designed to reduce interracial hostility in racially integrated schools

job enrichment an approach to increasing employees' intrinsic motivation by making their jobs more fulfilling and providing them with opportunities for growth

just world hypothesis holds that because people want to view the world as fair, they perceive that people get what they deserve and deserve what they get

K

kin selection the view that organisms are most likely to help others with whom they share the most genes—namely, their offspring and genetic relatives

kinesthesis the body sense that provides feedback on the position and movements of our body parts

knowledge-acquisition components allow us to learn from our experience, store information in memory, and combine new insight with previously acquired information

L

la belle indifference an attitude of indifference to the seriousness of one's symptom shown in some cases of conversion disorder

language a system of symbols and rules for combining them that can produce an almost infinite number of possible messages and meanings

lapse a one-time return to an undesirable behaviour pattern, usually in a high-risk situation

latent learning learning that occurs in the absence of reinforcement, but which is not displayed until reinforcement is later introduced into the situation

lateralization the localization of a function in either the right or left cerebral hemisphere

law of effect Thorndike's concept that a response followed by satisfying consequences will become more likely to occur, whereas a response followed by unsatisfying consequences will become less likely to occur

learned helplessness theory a theory of depression that states that if people are unable to control life events, they develop a state of helplessness that leads to depressive symptoms

learning a relatively enduring change in an organism's behaviour or performance capabilities that occurs as a result of experience

lens the transparent structure behind the pupil that changes its shape to focus images on the retina

leptin a hormone secreted by fat cells that decreases general appetite

levels of analysis an approach to analyzing behavioural phenomena and their causal factors in terms of biological, psychological, and environmental factors

levels of processing the concept that the more deeply we process information, the better it will be remembered

life event scales questionnaires that measure the number (and, sometimes, the intensity) of positive and negative life events that have occurred over a specific period of time

limbic system a group of subcortical structures, including the hippocampus and amygdala, which are involved in organizing many goal-directed and emotional behaviours

linguistic relativity hypothesis the idea, suggested by Benjamin Whorf, that people's language determines the ways in which they perceive and think about their world

longitudinal design research that repeatedly tests the same cohort as it grows older

long-term memory our vast library of durable stored memories

long-term potentiation an enduring increase in synaptic strength that occurs after a neural circuit is rapidly stimulated

lowballing a manipulation technique in which a persuader gets someone to commit to some behaviour and then increases the "cost" of that same behaviour

M

magnetic resonance imaging (MRI) a procedure that produces a highly detailed image of living tissue based on the tissue's response to a magnetic field; can be used to study both structure and, in the case of functional MRI (fMRI), brain functions as they occur

maintenance rehearsal the simple mental repetition of information

major depression a mood disorder characterized by intense depression that interferes markedly with functioning

management by objectives (MBO) an approach to increasing employees' motivation by combining goal-setting with employee participation and feedback

mania a state of intense emotional and behavioural excitement in which a person feels very optimistic and energized

matching effect in romantic relationships, the tendency for partners to have a similar level of physical attractiveness

maturation a genetically programmed, biological process that governs our growth

means-end analysis a heuristic problem-solving device in which people first define a subgoal they hope to achieve (an "end"), compare that subgoal to their present state of knowledge and, if there is discrepancy, try to find the means to reduce the difference

medulla a brain stem structure that controls vital functions, including heartbeat and respiration

melatonin a hormone, secreted by the pineal gland, that has a relaxing effect on the body and promotes readiness for sleep

memory the processes that allow us to record and later retrieve experiences and information

memory consolidation the creation and binding together of neural codes that allow information to be transferred from short-term memory into long-term memory

menstrual synchrony the tendency for some women who live together over time to become more similar to one another in the timing of their menstrual cycles

mental age the mental level (or age) at which a child is performing as determined by a "standardized interview" in which the child responds to a series of questions

mental representations cognitive representations of the world, including images, ideas, concepts, and principles, that are the foundations of thinking and problem solving

mental set the tendency to stick to problem-solving strategies or solutions that have worked in the past

mere exposure effect the tendency to evaluate a stimulus more favourably after repeated exposure to it

meta-analysis a statistical procedure for combining the results of different studies that examine the same topic

metabolism the rate of energy expenditure by the body

metacomponents higher-order processes used to plan and regulate task performance (triarchic theory)

midbrain brain structures above the hindbrain that are involved in sensory and motor functions and in attention and states of consciousness

mind-body dualism the philosophical position that the mind is a non-physical entity that is not subject to physical laws and cannot be reduced to physical processes; body and mind are separate entities

Minnesota Multiphasic Personality Inventory (MMPI) a widely used personality test whose items were developed using the empirical approach and by comparing various kinds of psychiatric patients with normal patients

misinformation effect the distortion of a memory by misleading post-event information

monism the philosophical position that mental events are reducible to physical events in the brain, so that "mind" and body are one and the same

monocular depth cues depth cues that require only one eye; include linear perspective, decreasing size, height in the horizontal plane, texture, clarity, light and shadow, motion parallax, and interposition

monogamy a mating system in which parents stay together, at least until their young are self-sufficient

mood-congruent recall tendency to recall information or events that are congruent with our current mood

mood disorders psychological disorders whose core conditions involve maladaptive mood states, such as depression or mania

morpheme the smallest unit of meaning in a given language; English morphemes include whole words, prefixes, and suffixes; there are over 100,000 English morphemes

motherese a high-pitched intonation that seems to be used by adults with young children all over the world

motivation a process that influences the direction, persistence, and vigour of goal-directed behaviour

motivational interviewing a treatment approach that avoids confrontation and leads clients to their own realization of a problem and to increased motivation to change

motor cortex cortical area in the back of the frontal lobes that controls voluntary movements on the opposite sides of the body

motor neurons specialized neurons that carry neural messages from the brain and spinal cord to the muscles and glands

motoric thought mental representations of motor movements, such as throwing an object

multiculturalism a social-intellectual movement that emphasizes the value of diversity and insists that all groups be treated with equality and respect

multimodal treatment approaches substance abuse interventions that combine a number of treatments, such as aversion therapy and coping skills training

myelin sheath a fatty insulating substance on the axon of some neurons that increases the speed of neural transmission

myopia a visual defect, sometimes called nearsightedness, in which the lens focuses distant images in front of the retina rather than on it

N

naloxone an opiate antagonist drug that interferes with the action of endorphins by occupying the receptor sites tailored for endorphins and morphine, resulting in increased pain perception

narcolepsy a sleep disorder that involves extreme daytime sleepiness and sudden, uncontrollable sleep attacks during waking hours

natural selection the evolutionary process through which characteristics that increase the likelihood of survival are preserved in the gene pool and thereby become more common in a species over time

naturalistic observation a method in which the researcher observes behaviour in a natural setting and tries to avoid influencing the participants being observed

need for achievement the desire to accomplish tasks and attain standards of excellence

need for positive regard (and positive self-regard) an innate need to be positively regarded by others and by oneself

need hierarchy Maslow's view that human needs are arranged in a progression, beginning with deficiency needs and then reaching growth needs

negative affectivity a temperamental disposition to experience negative emotional states, such as anxiety and depression

negative correlation as scores on one variable change, scores on a second variable change in the opposite direction

negative process hostile interchanges between therapist and client that may result in negative therapy outcomes

negative punishment the removal of a (positive) stimulus following an undesired response in order to weaken it (e.g., TV privileges are taken away from a misbehaving child who wants attention)

negative reinforcement a response is strengthened by the subsequent removal of a (noxious) stimulus

negative state relief model the view that empathy does not lead to pure altruism, but instead, that high empathy causes us to feel distress when we learn of others' suffering, so that by helping them we reduce our own personal distress

negative symptoms schizophrenic symptoms that reflect a lack of normal reactions, such as emotions or social behaviours

neglectful parents caregivers who provide neither warmth, nor rules, nor guidance

neoanalytic theorists former followers of Freud, such as Adler and Jung, who developed their own psychodynamic theories that generally deemphasized psychosexual factors in favour of social ones and gave increased emphasis to ego functioning

nerve deafness hearing loss caused by damage to the cochlear receptor cells or to the auditory nerve

neural network a model in which each concept stored in memory is represented by a unique pattern of distributed and simultaneously activated nodes that process information in parallel; also known as a parallel distributed processing model

neural plasticity the ability of neurons to modify their structure and function in response to experiential factors or injury

neuroimaging scanning technologies (fMRI, PET and CT) that allow for detailed observations of neural circuits

neuromodulators neurotransmitter substances that are released by neurons and circulate within the nervous system to affect the sensitivity of many neurons to their natural transmitter substances

neurons nerve cells that constitute the basic building blocks of the nervous system

neuropsychological tests psychological measures that are designed to detect sensory, cognitive, or motor deficits produced by neurological damage

neurotic anxiety in psychoanalytic theory, a state of anxiety that arises when impulses from the id threaten to break through into behaviour

neuroticism a personality trait that involves the tendency to experience high levels of negative affect and to behave in self-defeating ways

neurotransmitters chemical substances that are released from the axons of one neuron, travel across the synaptic space, and bind to specially keyed receptors in another neuron, where they produce a chemical reaction that is either excitatory or inhibitory

night terrors a disorder in which a sleeper—often feeling a strong sense of dread or danger—becomes aroused to a near panic state; the sleeper may suddenly sit up, let out a blood-curdling scream, and thrash about or flee to another room, as if trying to escape

norm of reciprocity the norm that when other people treat us well, we should respond in kind

normal distribution a frequency distribution in the shape of a symmetrical or bell-shaped curve that satisfies certain mathematical conditions deduced from the theory of probability

normative social influence conformity motivated by gaining social acceptance and avoiding social rejection

norms test scores derived from a relevant sample used to evaluate individuals' scores; behavioural "rules"

O

object permanence the recognition that an object continues to exist even when it can no longer be seen

object relations the images or mental representations that people form of themselves and other people as a result of early experience with caregivers

observational learning learning through observing the behaviour of a model

obsession an unwanted and disturbing thought or image that invades consciousness and is very difficult to control

obsessive-compulsive disorder an anxiety disorder characterized by persistent and unwanted thoughts and compulsive behaviours

occipital lobe the rearmost portion of the cerebral cortex that contains the primary visual sensory area

olfaction the sense of smell

openness a willingness to invest oneself in the process of therapy that predicts favourable therapeutic outcomes

operant conditioning a type of learning in which behaviour is modified by its consequences, such as by reinforcement, punishment, and extinction

operant discrimination an operant response occurs when a particular antecedent stimulus is present, but not when another antecedent stimulus is present

operant generalization an operant response occurs to a new antecedent stimulus that is similar to the original antecedent stimulus

operational definition defining a concept or variable in terms of the specific procedures used to produce or measure it

opiates opium and drugs derived from it, such as morphine, codeine, and heroin; opiates provide pain relief and cause mood changes, which may include euphoria

opponent-process theory the theory proposed by Hering that the retina contains three sets of colour receptors that respond differentially to red-green, blue-yellow, and black-white; the opponent processes that result can produce a perception of any hue

oppositional defiant disorder (ODD) disorder in which a child consistently behaves in a disobedient, defiant, and hostile manner that interferes with the child's functioning and interpersonal relationships

optic chiasma the point at which optic nerves cross after leaving the eyes, so that half of each eye's visual field is sent to each hemisphere's visual projection area

organ of Corti structure embedded in the basilar membrane that contains the hair cell receptors for sound

Over-Claiming Questionnaire (OCQ) method used to index socially desirable response biases in individuals

overlearning continued rehearsal past the point of initial learning that significantly improves performance on memory tasks

P

pain disorder a somatoform disorder in which the person's complaints of pain cannot be accounted for in terms of physical damage

panic disorder an anxiety disorder characterized by unpredictable panic attacks and a pervasive fear that another will occur; may also include a resulting agoraphobia

paranoid type a schizophrenic disorder marked by delusional thinking and suspiciousness

parasympathetic nervous system the branch portion of the autonomic nervous system that slows down bodily processes in order to conserve energy and reduce arousal

paraventricular nucleus (PVN) a cluster of neurons in the hippocampus packed with receptor sites for transmitters that stimulate or reduce appetite

parental investment theory the view, based on evolutionary theory, that the gender with a greater investment (higher costs) in producing offspring will be more selective in choosing a mate

parietal lobe the cerebral region behind the frontal lobe that contains the somatic sensory cortex and Wernicke's speech comprehension area

partial reinforcement schedule a schedule in which reinforcement follows some correct responses but not others

partial report method used to measure iconic memory and to demonstrate that memory span for a visual stimulus is longer than suggested by full reporting

passionate love a form of love that involves intense emotional arousal and yearning for one's partner

perception the process of organizing stimulus input and giving it meaning

perceptual constancies the ability to recognize stimulus characteristics—size, colour, and so on, under varying conditions

perceptual schemas internal representations that contain the essential features of an object of perception

perceptual set a readiness to perceive a stimulus in a particular way based on expectations, motives, emotions, or beliefs

performance components the actual mental processes used to perform a task (triarchic theory)

peripheral nervous system all of the neurons that connect the central nervous system with the sensory receptors, the muscles, and the glands

peripheral route to persuasion occurs when people do not scrutinize a message, but are influenced mostly by other factors such as a speaker's attractiveness or a message's emotional appeal

personal unconscious according to Jung, those aspects of the unconscious that arise from the individual's life experience

personality the biologically and environmentally determined characteristics within a person that account for distinctive and relatively enduring patterns of thinking, feeling, and acting

personality disorder stable, inflexible, and maladaptive personality styles

perspective a theoretical vantage point from which to analyze behaviour and its causes

phenotype the observable characteristics produced by one's genetic endowment

pheromones chemical signals found in natural body scents

phobias strong and irrational fears of particular objects or circumstances

phoneme the smallest unit of sound in a language; these are the vowel and consonant sounds that are recognized in any given language; English has 45 phonemes

photopigments protein molecules within the rods and cones whose chemical reactions when absorbing light result in nerve impulses being generated

physiological toughness relations between two classes of hormones secreted by the adrenal glands in the face of stress

place theory the theory of pitch perception that holds that sound frequencies are coded in terms of the portion of the basilar membrane where the fluid wave in the cochlea peaks; this theory accounts for perception of frequencies above 4,000 Hz

placebo an inactive or inert substance that has no medicinal value but is believed by a patient to be helpful

placebo control group a control group that receives an intervention that is assumed to have no therapeutic value

placebo effect a change in behaviour that occurs because of the expectation or belief that one is receiving a treatment

pleasure principle the drive for instant need gratification that is characteristic of the id

polyandry a mating system in which one female mates with many males

polygenic transmission a number of genes working together to create a particular phenotypic characteristic

polygraph a research and clinical instrument that measures a wide array of physiological responses

polygynandry a mating system in which all members of a group mate with all other members of that group

polygyny a mating system in which one male may mate with many females

pons a brain stem structure having sensory and motor tracts whose functions are involved in sleep and dreaming

population in a survey, the entire set of individuals about whom we wish to draw a conclusion

positive affectivity a relatively stable disposition to experience pleasure and positive emotions

positive correlation as scores on one variable change, scores on a second variable change in the same direction

positive punishment occurs when a response is weakened by the subsequent presentation of a (noxious) stimulus

positive reinforcement a response is strengthened by the subsequent presentation of a (positive) stimulus

positive symptoms schizophrenic symptoms such as delusions, hallucinations, and disordered speech and thinking

positron emission tomography (PET) scan a procedure that provides a visual display of the absorption of a radioactive substance by neurons, indicating how actively they are involved as the brain performs a task

postconventional moral reasoning moral judgments are based on a system of internalized, well-thought-out moral principles

postformal thought the ability to reason logically about opposing points of view and to accept contradictions and irreconcilable differences

post-traumatic stress disorder (PTSD) a pattern of distressing symptoms, such as flashbacks, nightmares, avoidance, and anxiety responses that recur after a traumatic experience

preconventional level stage at which moral judgments are based on anticipated punishments or rewards

predictive validity the ability of a test to predict future outcomes (e.g., academic performance) that are influenced by the characteristic measured by the test (e.g., intelligence)

prefrontal cortex the area of the frontal lobe just behind the eyes and forehead that is involved in the executive functions of planning, self-awareness, and responsibility

prejudice a negative attitude toward people based on their membership in a group

preoperational stage in Piaget's model, a stage of cognitive development in which children represent the world symbolically through words and mental images, but do not yet understand basic mental operations or rules

preparedness the notion that evolutionary factors have produced an innate readiness to learn certain associations that have had survival implications in the past

primacy effect (impression formation) our tendency to attach more importance to the initial information that we learn about a person

primary appraisal the initial appraisal of a situation as benign, irrelevant, or threatening; a perception of the severity of demands

primary mental abilities spatial ability, perceptual speed, numerical ability, verbal meaning, memory, verbal fluency, and inductive reasoning; defined by L. L. Thurstone on the basis of his factor analysis of intelligence test items

primary reinforcer a positive reinforcer that satisfies a biological need, such as food or water

primary visual cortex the area of the occipital lobe which receives impulses generated from the retina via the thalamus and analyzes visual input using its feature detectors

priming the activation of one concept (or one unit of information) by another

proactive interference occurs when material learned in the past interferes with recall of newer material

problem-focused coping coping strategies that involve direct attempts to confront and master a stressful situation

problem-solving models (of dreaming) the view that dreams can help us find creative solutions to our problems and conflicts because they are not constrained by reality

problem-solving schemas step-by-step scripts for selecting information and solving specialized classes of problems

procedural memory (non-declarative memory) is reflected in learned skills and actions

program evaluation research research designed to measure the outcomes of an intervention

projective tests tests, such as the Rorschach and the TAT, that present ambiguous stimuli to the subject; the responses are assumed to be based on a projection of internal characteristics of the person onto the stimuli

proposition a statement that expresses an idea in subject-predicate form

prospective memory remembering to perform an activity in the future

protective factors environmental or personal resources that help people fare better in the face of stress

prototype the most typical and familiar members of a class that defines a concept

proximodistal principle the principle that physical development begins along the innermost parts of the body and continues toward the outermost parts

psychic energy generated by instinctual drives, this energy powers the mind and constantly presses for either direct or indirect release

psychodynamic behaviour therapy an integration of psychoanalysis and behaviour therapy

psychodynamic perspective a psychological perspective that focuses on inner personality dynamics, including the role of unconscious impulses and defences, in understanding behaviour

psychogenic amnesia an extensive, but selective memory loss that occurs after a traumatic event

psychogenic fugue a dissociative phenomenon in which a person loses all sense of personal identity and may wander to another place and establish a new identity

psychological risk the degree to which research procedures may expose participants to significant mental or emotional harm

psychological test a method for measuring individual differences related to some psychological construct, based on a sample of relevant behaviour obtained under standardized conditions

psychology the scientific study of behaviour and its causes

psychometrics the study of the statistical properties of psychological tests; the psychometric approach to intelligence focuses on the number and nature of abilities that define intelligence

psychoneuroimmunology (PNI) the field of study that explores relations between psychological and immune functions

psychophysics the study of relations between the physical characteristics of stimuli and the sensory experiences they evoke

psychosocial stages a sequence of eight developmental stages proposed by Erikson, each of which involves a different "crisis" (i.e., conflict) over how we view ourselves

psychosurgery surgical procedures, such as lobotomy or cingulotomy, in which brain tissue involved in a behaviour disorder is removed or destroyed

puberty a period of rapid maturation in which one becomes capable of sexual reproduction

punishment a response is weakened by an outcome that follows it

R

random sampling a method of choosing a sample in which each member of the population has an equal opportunity to be included in the sample

randomized clinical trial a research design that involves the random assignment of clients having specific problems to an experimental (therapy) group or to a control condition so as to draw sound causal conclusions about the therapy's efficacy

rape trauma syndrome a pattern of cognitive, emotional, and behavioural responses that occurs in response to the trauma of being raped

rational-theoretical approach an approach to test construction in which test items are made up on the basis of a theorist's conception of a construct

reaction range the genetically influenced limits within which environmental factors can exert their effects on an organism

realistic conflict theory the theory that competition for limited resources fosters prejudice

reality principle the ego's tendency to take reality into account and to act in a rational fashion in satisfying its needs

receptor sites protein molecules on neurons' dendrites or soma that are specially shaped to accommodate a specific neurotransmitter molecule

recessive gene a gene whose characteristic will be masked by a corresponding dominant gene; its characteristic will be expressed if the correspondent gene is also recessive

reciprocal determinism Bandura's model of two-way causal relations between people, behaviour, and the environment

recombinant DNA procedures gene-splicing procedures that can be used to produce new life forms, such as bacteria that can produce scarce chemical materials such as human growth hormone

reflexes automatic, inborn behaviours triggered by specific stimuli

refractory period the period of time following an action potential during which the neuron cannot be stimulated to produce another nerve impulse

regression a psychoanalytic defence mechanism in which a person retreats back to an earlier stage of development in response to stress

reinforcement the strengthening of a response by an outcome that follows it

relapse a complete return to a previous undesirable behaviour and an abandonment of attempts to change

relapse prevention a treatment approach designed to teach coping skills, increase self-efficacy, and counter the abstinence violation effect and thus reduce the likelihood of relapse

relational aggression negative behaviour that involves spreading of vicious rumours, exclusion from peer groups, and withdrawal from friendships

reliability in psychological testing, the consistency with which a measure assesses a given characteristic, or different observers agree on a given score

REM sleep a recurring sleep stage characterized by rapid eye movements, increased physiological arousal, paralysis of the voluntary muscles, and a high rate of dreaming

REM-sleep behaviour disorder a sleep disorder in which the loss of muscle tone that causes normal REM-sleep paralysis is absent, thereby enabling sleepers to move about—sometimes violently—and seemingly "act out" their dreams

remote behaviour sampling researchers and clinicians collect samples of behaviour from respondents as they live their daily lives

replication the process of repeating a study to determine whether the original findings can be duplicated

representative sample a sample that accurately reflects the important characteristics of the population

representativeness heuristic a guide in estimating the probability that an object or event belongs to a certain category based on the extent to which it represents a prototype of that category

repression the basic defence mechanism that actively keeps anxiety-arousing material in the unconscious

resistance largely unconscious manoeuvres that protect clients from dealing with anxiety-arousing material in therapy

response prevention the prevention of escape or avoidance responses during exposure to an anxiety-arousing CS so that extinction can occur

restoration model the theory that sleep recharges our run-down bodies and allows us to recover from physical and mental fatigue

reticular formation a structure extending from the hindbrain into the midbrain that plays a central role in consciousness and attention, in part by alerting and activating higher brain centres (ascending portion), and by selectively blocking some inputs from admission to higher regions in the brain (descending portion)

retina the light-sensitive back surface of the eye that contains the visual receptors

retrieval the process of accessing information in long-term memory

retrieval cue any stimulus, whether internal or external, that stimulates the activation of information stored in long-term memory

retroactive interference newly acquired information interferes with the ability to recall information learned at an earlier time

retrograde amnesia memory loss for events that occurred prior to the onset of amnesia

reuptake process whereby transmitter substances are taken back into the presynaptic neuron so that they do not continue to stimulate postsynaptic neurons

right to privacy the principle that people's right to have their behaviour considered "private" depends upon the setting, the sensitivity of the behaviour, and the way in which information would be reported

rods visual receptors that function under low levels of illumination and do not give rise to colour sensations

S

sample in a survey, a subset of individuals drawn from the population

savant a person who is intellectually disabled but shows some striking mental ability, such as being able to mentally compute complex mathematical problems

scatterplot a graph commonly used to examine correlational data; each pair of scores on variable X and variable Y is plotted as a single point

schema a "mental framework"—an organized pattern of thought about some aspect of the world, such as a class of people, events, situations, or objects

schizophrenia a psychotic disorder involving serious impairment of attention, thought, language, emotion, and behaviour

seasonal affective disorder (SAD) a disorder in which depressive symptoms appear or worsen during certain seasons of the year (typically, fall and winter) and then improve during the other seasons

secondary appraisal one's judgment of the adequacy of personal resources needed to cope with a stressor

secondary (conditioned) reinforcer a stimulus that acquires reinforcing qualities by being associated with a primary reinforcer

selective serotonin reuptake inhibitors (SSRIs) a class of antidepressant drugs that increase the activity of serotonin by preventing its reuptake into the presynaptic neuron

self in Rogers's theory, an organized, consistent set of perceptions and beliefs about oneself

self-actualization in humanistic theories, an inborn tendency to strive toward the realization of one's full potential

self-consistency an absence of conflict among self-perceptions

self-efficacy the conviction that we can perform the behaviours necessary to produce a desired outcome

self-enhancement processes whereby one enhances positive self-regard

self-esteem how positively or negatively we feel about ourselves

self-evaluative processes the ability of humans to reinforce or punish themselves contingent upon certain behaviours that relate to internal standards

self-fulfilling prophecy when people's erroneous expectations lead them to act in a way that brings about the expected behaviours, thereby confirming the original impression

self-instructional training a cognitive coping approach of giving adaptive self-instructions to oneself at crucial phases of the coping process

self-monitoring a personality trait that reflects people's tendencies to regulate their social behaviour in accord with situational cues as opposed to internal values, attitudes, and needs

self-perception theory the theory that we make inferences about our own attitudes by observing how we behave

self-reinforcement processes self-administered rewards and punishments that are contingent on meeting certain standards for behaviour that are an important basis for self-regulation of behaviour

self-regulation the ability to structure antecedent conditions and behavioural consequences in a way that increases desirable behaviours or reduces undesirable ones

self-relatedness the ability to be flexible to change, to listen carefully to the therapist, and to use constructively what is learned in therapy

self-serving bias the tendency to make relatively more personal attributions for success and situational attributions for failure

self-verification the tendency to try to verify or validate one's existing self-concept—that is, to satisfy congruence needs

semantic memory general factual knowledge about the world and language, including memory for words and concepts

semantics rules for connecting symbols to what they represent

sensation the process by which stimuli are detected, transduced into nerve impulses, and sent to the brain

sensitive period an optimal age range for certain experiences, but if those experiences occur at another time, normal development will still be possible

sensorimotor stage in Piaget's theory, the stage of cognitive development in which children understand their world primarily through sensory experience and physical (motor) interaction with objects

sensory adaptation diminishing sensitivity to an unchanging stimulus with the passage of time as sensory neurons habituate to the stimulation

sensory memory memory processes that retain incoming sensory information just long enough for it to be recognized

sensory neurons specialized neurons that carry messages from the sense organs to the spinal cord and brain

separation anxiety distress experienced by infants when they are separated from a primary caregiver, peaking around age 12 to 16 months

sequential design repeatedly testing several age cohorts as they grow older

serial position effect the finding that recall is influenced by a word's position in a series of items

serotonin a neurotransmitter that seems to underlie positive mood states; underactivity may be a factor in depression

sex-role stereotypes beliefs about the types of characteristics and behaviours that are appropriate for boys versus for girls

sexual orientation a person's emotional and erotic preference for partners of a particular sex

sexual response cycle a physiological response to sexual stimulation that involves stages of excitement, plateau, orgasm, and resolution

shadowing an experimental procedure used in attention research in which a person simultaneously receives two or more messages, is asked to focus on one of them, and then is asked to report on the other messages as well

shaping an operant conditioning procedure in which reinforcement begins with a behaviour that the organism can already perform, and then is made contingent upon behaviours that increasingly approximate the final desired behaviour

short-term memory type of memory that holds the information that we are conscious of at any given time; also called working memory

signal detection theory a theory that assumes that stimulus detection is not based on a fixed absolute threshold, but rather is affected by rewards, punishments, expectations, and motivational factors

situation-focused intervention prevention efforts that focus on altering environmental conditions that are known to promote the development of psychological disorders

Skinner box an experimental chamber in which animals learn to perform operant responses, such as bar presses or pecking responses, so that the learning process can be studied

sleep apnea a disorder characterized by a repeated cycle in which the sleeper stops breathing, momentarily awakens gasping for air, and then returns to sleep

sleeper effects permanent effects in information processes not functioning at the time of deprivation that emerge long after the early deprivation is corrected

slow-wave sleep stages 3 and 4 of sleep, in which the EEG pattern shows large, slow brain waves called delta waves

social clock a set of cultural norms concerning the optimal age range for work, marriage, parenthood, and other major life experiences to occur

social cognitive theory a cognitive-behavioural approach to personality, developed by Albert Bandura and Walter Mischel, that emphasizes the role of social learning, cognitive processes, and self-regulation

social-cognitive theory (of hypnosis) the view that hypnotic experiences occur because people are highly motivated to assume the role of being "hypnotized"

social comparison the act of comparing one's personal attributes, abilities, and opinions to those of other people

social constructivism the position that people construct their reality and beliefs through their cognitions

social Darwinism a distortion of Darwinism that argues if the more fit are more successful, then those at the top of the social and economic ladder must be most fit of all

social desirablity bias tendency of people to exaggerate their positive and minimize their negative qualities

social exchange theory a theory proposing that a social relationship can best be described in terms of exchanges of rewards and costs between the two partners

social facilitation an increased tendency to perform one's dominant response in the mere presence of others

social identity theory the theory that prejudice stems from a need to enhance our self-esteem

social norms shared expectations about how people should think, feel, and behave

social penetration theory a theory proposing that, as a relationship deepens, exchanges (including self-disclosure) become broader and more intimate

social phobia excessive and inappropriate fear of social situations in which a person might be evaluated and possibly embarrassed

Social Readjustment Rating Scale (SRRS) a tool used for studying the relationship between stress and illness

social risk the degree to which research information about individual participants could become known to others and produce negative consequences for the participants

social role a set of norms that characterizes how people in a given social position ought to behave

social skills training a technique in which a client learns more effective social behaviours by observing and imitating a skilful model

social structure theory the theory that men and women behave differently (e.g., expressing different mate preferences) because society directs them into different social and economic roles

socialization the process by which we acquire the beliefs, values, and behaviours of a group

socially toxic environments Garbarino's term for negative settings that involve poverty, violence, lack of intellectual stimulation, and other factors that have harmful effects on children's development

sociobiology an evolutionary theory of social behaviour that emphasizes the role of adaptive behaviour in maintaining one's genes in the species' gene pool

sociocultural perspective a perspective that emphasizes the role of culture and the social environment in understanding commonalities and differences in human behaviour

somatic nervous system the branch of the peripheral nervous system that provides input from the sensory receptors and output to the voluntary muscles of the body

somatic relaxation training a means of voluntarily reducing or preventing high levels of arousal

somatic sensory cortex cortical strips in the front portions of the parietal lobes that receive sensory input from various regions of the body

somatic theory of emotions a modern emotion theory inspired by the James-Lange theory that emphasizes the causal role of bodily responses in the experiencing of emotion

somatoform disorder a disorder in which a person complains of bodily symptoms that cannot be accounted for in terms of actual physical damage or dysfunction

source confusion tendency to recall something or recognize it as familiar, but to forget where it was encountered

specific phobia irrational and excessive fear of specific objects or situations that pose little or no actual threat

specificity question the ultimate question of psychotherapy research: "Which types of therapy, administered by which kinds of therapists to which kinds of clients having which kinds of problems, produce which kinds of effects?"

spinal reflex a simple stimulus-response sequence carried out by sensory input and motor output at the level of the spinal cord without the involvement of higher brain centres

spontaneous recovery in classical conditioning, the reappearance of a previously extinguished conditioned response after a period of time has passed following extinction

spontaneous remission improvements in symptoms in the absence of any therapy

standardization in psychological testing, 1) creating a standard set of procedures for administering a test or making observations, and 2) deriving norms to which an individual's performance can be compared

state-dependent memory theory that our ability to retrieve information is greater when our internal state at the time of retrieval matches our original state during learning

stereotype a generalized belief about a group or category of people

stimulants drugs that stimulate neural activity, resulting in a state of excitement or aroused euphoria

stimulus generalization a CR occurs to stimuli other than the original CS, based on the similarity of these stimuli to the CS

stimulus hierarchy in systematic desensitization, the creation of a series of anxiety-arousing stimuli that are ranked in terms of the amount of anxiety they evoke

storage the retention of information over time

stranger anxiety distress over contact with strangers that typically develops in the first year of infancy and dissipates in the second year

stress a pattern of cognitive appraisals, physiological responses, and behavioural tendencies that occurs in response to a perceived imbalance between situational demands and the resources available to cope with them

stress-induced analgesia a reduction in sensitivity that occurs when endorphins are released under stressful conditions

stressors situations that place demands on organisms that tax or exceed their resources

striving for superiority Adler's notion that people are driven to compensate for intrinsic feelings of inferiority and inadequacy by achievement of personal and social goals

structuralism an early German school of psychology established by Wilhelm Wundt that attempted to study the structure of the mind by breaking it down into its basic components, thought to be sensations

subgoal analysis a problem-solving heuristic in which people attack a large problem by formulating subgoals, or intermediate steps toward a solution

subjective well-being happiness; the overall degree of satisfaction with one's life

sublimation the channelling of unacceptable impulses into socially accepted behaviours, as when aggressive drives are expressed in violent sports

subliminal psychodynamic activation a research technique which uses subliminal stimuli to activate unconscious conflicts and study their effects on behaviour

subliminal stimuli weak stimuli below the perceptual threshold that are not consciously perceived

substance dependence a maladaptive pattern of substance use that causes significant distress or substantially impairs a person life; diagnosed as occurring "with physiological dependence" if drug tolerance or withdrawal symptoms have developed

suicide the wilful taking of one's own life

superego the moral arm of the personality that internalizes the standards and values of society and serves as the person's conscience

suprachiasmatic nuclei (SCN) the brain's master "biological clock," located in the hypothalamus, that regulates most circadian rhythms

surface structure a linguistic term for the words and organization of a spoken or written sentence; two sentences with different surface structure may still mean the same thing

survey research a method in which questionnaires or interviews are used to obtain information about many people

sympathetic nervous system the branch of the autonomic nervous system that has an arousal function on the body's internal organs, speeding up bodily processes and mobilizing the body

synapse the microscopic space between neurons over which the nerve impulse is biochemically transmitted

synaptic vesicles chambers within the axon that contain the neurotransmitter substance

synaesthesia a condition in which stimuli are experienced not only in the normal sensory modality, but in others as well

syntax the rules for the combination of symbols within a given language

systematic desensitization an attempt to eliminate anxiety using counterconditioning, in which a new response that is incompatible with anxiety is conditioned to the anxiety-arousing conditioned stimulus

T

tardive dyskinesia an irreversible motor disorder that can occur as a side effect of certain antipsychotic drugs

target behaviour when trying to modify behaviour, the specific behaviour that is to be changed

taste buds the receptors for taste in the tongue and in the roof and back of the mouth that are sensitive to the qualities of sweet, sour, salty, and bitter

telegraphic speech two-word sentences that consist of a noun and a verb

temperament a biologically based general style of reacting emotionally and behaviourally to the environment

temporal lobe the portion of the cortex that lies below the parietal lobes and is the major site of auditory input to the brain

teratogens environmental (non-genetic) agents that cause abnormal prenatal development

terror management theory a theory that focuses on the ways people defend against the fear of death

test-retest reliability the extent to which scores on a presumably stable characteristic are consistent over time

thalamus a major sensory integration and relay centre in the forebrain, sometimes referred to as the brain's sensory switchboard

THC (tetrahydrocannabinol) the major active ingredient in marijuana

theory a set of formal statements that explain how and why certain events or phenomena are related to one another

theory of cognitive dissonance the theory that people strive to maintain consistency in their beliefs and actions, and that inconsistency creates dissonance—unpleasant arousal that motivates people to restore balance by changing their cognitions

theory of mind beliefs about the "mind" and the ability to understand other people's mental states

theory of planned behaviour view that our intention to engage in a behaviour is strongest when we have a positive attitude toward that behaviour, when subjective norms (our perceptions of what other people think we should do) support our attitudes, and when we believe that the behaviour is under our control

theory of reciprocal altruism view that altruism is long-term cooperation; one individual may help another, but that assistance will be reciprocated at some time in the future

token economy a procedure in which desirable behaviours are reinforced with tokens or points that can later be redeemed for other reinforcers

tolerance a condition in which increasingly larger doses of a drug are required to produce the same level of bodily response; caused by the body's compensatory responses

top-down processing perceptual processing in which existing knowledge, concepts, ideas, or expectations are applied in order to make sense of incoming stimulation

transduction the conversion of one form of energy into another; in sensation, the process whereby physical stimuli are translated into nerve impulses

transfer of excitation a misinterpretation of one's state of arousal that occurs when arousal actually is caused by one source, but the person attributes it to another source

transference the psychoanalytic phenomenon in which a client responds irrationally to the analyst as if the latter were an important person from the client's past who plays an important role in the client's dynamics

transtheoretical model identifies six major stages in the process of how people change: precontemplation, contemplation, preparation, action, maintenance, and termination

trauma-dissociation theory a theory that accounts for the development of dissociative identity disorder in terms of dissociation as a defence against severe childhood abuse or trauma

triangular theory of love the view that various types of love result from different combinations of three core factors: intimacy, commitment, and passion

triarchic theory of intelligence Sternberg's theory of intelligence that distinguishes between analytical, practical, and creative forms of mental ability

trichromatic theory the colour vision theory originally advanced by Young and Helmholtz that there are three types of colour receptors in the retina and that combinations of activation of these receptors can produce perception of any hue in the visible spectrum

twin studies a behaviour genetics method in which identical (monozygotic) and fraternal (dizygotic) twins are compared on some characteristic; this method is particularly informative if the twins have been raised in different environments

two-factor theory of avoidance learning theory that avoidance learning first involves the classical conditioning of fear, followed by learning operant responses that avoid an anticipated aversive stimulus and thus are reinforced by anxiety reduction

two-factor theory of emotion Schachter's theory that the intensity of physiological arousal determines perceived intensity of emotion, whereas the appraisal of environmental cues tells us which emotion we are experiencing

Type I schizophrenia subtype of schizophrenia characterized by a predominance of positive symptoms

Type II schizophrenia subtype of schizophrenia characterized by negative symptoms

Type A personality a behavioural pattern involving a sense of time urgency, pressured behaviour, and hostility that appears to be a risk factor in coronary heart disease

Type B personality a relaxed and agreeable personality type, with little sense of time urgency

Type C personality a personality pattern characterized by inhibition of negative emotions that may be a risk factor in the development of cancer

U

unconditional positive regard a communicated attitude of total and unconditional acceptance of another person that conveys the person's intrinsic worth

unconditioned response (UCR) a response (usually reflexive or innate) that is elicited by a specific stimulus (the UCS) without prior learning

unconditioned stimulus (UCS) a stimulus that elicits a particular reflexive or innate response (the UCR) without prior learning

undifferentiated type a residual category of schizophrenia for people who show some of the symptoms of paranoid, disorganized, and catatonic types, but not enough to be placed in one of those diagnostic categories

unobtrusive measurement recording behaviour in a way that keeps participants unaware that they are being observed

upward comparison comparing oneself or one's current situation to more positive alternatives

V

validity the extent to which a test measures what it is supposed to; the degree to which a diagnostic system's categories contain the core features of the behaviour disorders and permit differentiation among the disorders

variable any characteristic of an organism or situation that can differ

variable-interval schedule a schedule in which reinforcement follows the first correct response that occurs after an average (but variable) time interval following the last reinforced response

variable-ratio schedule a schedule in which reinforcement is based on an average but variable number of responses

vascular theory of emotional feedback the version of the facial feedback hypothesis that attributes facial muscle effects to the warming or cooling of blood that is entering the brain

vestibular sense the sense of body orientation or equilibrium

virtual reality computer-produced virtual environments that produce experiences like those that would be produced by a corresponding real environment

visual acuity the ability to see fine detail

visual association cortex cortical areas in the occipital, parietal, and temporal lobes that analyze visual stimuli sent to the primary visual cortex in relation to stored knowledge and establish the "meaning" of the stimuli

vulnerability a predisposition that can have a biological basis, such as our genotype, a brain malfunction, or a hormonal factor

vulnerability-stress model a model that explains behaviour disorders as resulting from predisposing biological or psychological vulnerability factors that are triggered by a stressor

W

Weber's law the principle that to perceive a difference between two stimuli, the stimuli must differ by a constant percentage or ratio

Wernicke's area an area of the left temporal lobe that is involved in speech comprehension

wish fulfillment in Freudian theory, the partial or complete satisfaction of a psychological need through dreaming or waking fantasy

withdrawal the occurrence of compensatory responses after drug use is discontinued, causing a person to experience physiological reactions opposite to those that had been produced by the drug

working memory a more current name for short-term memory, reflecting the fact that it consciously processes, codes, and "works on" information

Z

zone of proximal development the difference between what a child can do independently, and what the child can do with assistance from adults or more advanced peers

zygote the fertilized egg

References

"A recovering patient" (1986). "Can we talk?" The schizophrenic patient in psychotherapy. *American Journal of Psychiatry, 143,* 68–70.

Aamodt, M. G. (1991). *Applied industrial/organizational psychology.* Belmont, CA: Wadsworth.

Aamodt, M. G. (1996). *Applied industrial/organizational psychology* (2nd ed.). Belmont, CA: Thomson Brooks/Cole Publishing.

Aaron, S. (1986). *Stage fright.* Chicago: University of Chicago Press.

Abraham, K. (1911). Notes on the psychoanalytic investigation and treatment of manic-depressive insanity and allied conditions. In K. Abraham, *Selected Papers of Karl Abraham.* New York: Basic Books, 1968.

Abramson, L. Y., Seligman, M. E., Teasdale, J. D. (1978). Learned helplessness in humans: critique and reformulation. *Journal of Abnormal Psychology, 87*(1), 49–74.

Abramov, I., & Gordon, J. (1994). Color appearance: On seeing red—or yellow, or green, or blue. *Annual Review of Psychology, 45,* 451–485.

Adair, J.G., Paivio, A., & Ritchie, P. (1996). Psychology in Canada. *Annual Review of Psychology, 47,* 341–370.

Adair, R. K. (1990). *The physics of baseball.* New York: Harper & Row.

Adams, G. R., & Fitch, S. A. (1982). Ego stage and identity status development: A cross-sequential analysis. *Journal of Personality and Social Psychology, 43,* 574–583.

Adams, R.J., & Courage, M.L. (1998). Human newborn color vision: measurement with chromatic stimuli varying in excitation purity. *Journal of Experimental Child Psychology, 68,* 22–34.

Adelmann, P. K., & Zajonc, R. B. (1989). Facial efference and the experience of emotion. *Annual Review of Psychology, 40,* 249–280.

Ader, R. (2000). True or false: The placebo effect as seen in drug studies is definitive proof that the mind can bring about clinically relevant changes in the body. *Advances in Mind Body Medicine, 16,* 7–11.

Ader, R. (2001). Psychoneuroimmunology. *Current Directions in Psychological Science, 10,* 94–98.

Ader, R., & Cohen, N. (1975). Behaviorally conditioned immunosuppression. *Psychosomatic Medicine, 37,* 333–340.

Ader, R., & Cohen, N. (1982). Behaviorally conditioned immunosuppression and murine systemic lupus erythematosus. *Science, 215,* 1534–1536.

Ader, R., & Cohen, N. (1990). The influence of conditioning on immune responses. In R. Ader, N. Cohen, & D. L. Felten (Eds.), *Psychoneuroimmunology II.* New York: Academic Press.

Ader, R., Cohen, N., & Felten, D. (1995). Psychoneuroimmunology: Interactions between the nervous system and the immune system. *Lancet, 345,* 99–103.

Adler, A. (1927). *The practice and theory of individual psychology.* New York: Harcourt.

Adler, S. R. (1995). Refugee stress and folk belief: Hmong sudden deaths. *Social Science and Medicine, 40,* 1623–1629.

Adolphs, R., Cahill, L., Schul, R., & Babinsky, R. (1997). Impaired declarative memory for emotional material following bilateral amygdala damage in humans. *Learning and Memory, 4,* 291–300.

Adolphs, R., Tranel, D., Damasio, H., & Damasio, A. (1994). Impaired recognition of emotion in facial expressions following bilateral damage to the human amygdala, *Nature, 372,* 669–72

Aggleton, J. P. (1993). The contribution of the amygdala to normal and abnormal emotional states. *Trends in Neurosciences, 16,* 328–333.

Agnew, H. W. Jr., Webb, W. B., & Williams, R. L. (1967). Comparison of stage four and 1-REM sleep deprivation. *Perceptual and Motor Skills, 24,* 851–858.

Aguiar, A., & Baillargeon, R. (2002). Developments in young infants' reasoning about occluded objects. *Cognitive Psychology, 45,* 267–336.

Ahadi, S., & Diener, E. (1989). Multiple determinants and effect size. *Journal of Personality and Social Psychology, 56,* 398–406.

Ahn, S., Riccio, A., & Ginty, D. G. (2000). Spatial considerations for stimulus-dependent transcription in neurons. *Annual Review of Physiology, 62,* 803–823.

Ai, A. K., Peterson, C., & Ubelhor, D. (2002). War-related trauma and symptoms of posttraumatic stress disorder among adult Kosovar refugees. *Journal of Traumatic Stress, 15,* 157–160.

Aiello, R., Sloboda, J. A. (1994). *Musical perceptions.* Oxford University Press.

Aiken, L. R. (1999). *Psychological testing and assessment.* Needham Heights, MA: Allyn & Bacon.

Ainslie, G. (2001). *Breakdown of will.* New York: Cambridge University Press.

Ainsworth, M. (1989). Attachments beyond infancy. *American Psychologist, 44,* 709–716.

Ainsworth, M. & Bowlby, J. (1991). An etiological approach to personality development. *American Psychologist, 46,* 333–341.

Ainsworth, M., Blehar, M. C., Waters, E., & Wall, S. (1978). *Patterns of attachment: A psychological study of the strange situation.* Hillsdale, NJ: Erlbaum.

Ainsworth, M. D. S. (1967). *Infancy in Uganda: Infant care and the growth of love.* Baltimore: The Johns Hopkins University Press.

Aitchison, J. (1996). *The seeds of speech: Language origin and evolution.* New York: Cambridge University Press.

Aitken, S., & Bower T. G. (1982). Intersensory substitution in the blind. *Journal of Experimental Child Psychology, 33,* 309–323.

Ajzen, I. (1991). The theory of planned behavior. *Organizational Behavior and Human Decision Processes, 50,* 179–211.

Akerstedt, T. (1988). Sleepiness and a consequence of shift work. *Sleep, 11,* 17–34.

Akerstedt, T., Kecklund, G., & Hoerte, L.G. (2001). Night driving, season and the risk of highway accidents. *Sleep: Journal of Sleep and Sleep Disorders Research, 24,* 401–406.

Albee, G. W. (1996). Revolutions and counterrevolutions in prevention. *American Psychologist, 51,* 1130–1133.

Albee, G. W. (1997). Speak no evil? *American Psychologist, 52,* 1143–1144.

Albrecht, U. (2004). The mammalian circadian clock: A network of gene expression. *Frontiers in Bioscience, 9,* 48-55.

Alcock, J. (2005). *Animal behavior: An evolutionary approach* (8th ed.). Sunderland, MA: Sinauer Associates.

Aldridge, S. (1998). *The thread of life: The story of genes and genetic engineering.* New York: Cambridge University Press.

Alexander, G. M., & Sherwin, B. B. (1993). Sex steroids, sexual behavior, and selection attention for erotic stimuli in women using oral contraceptives. *Psychoneuroendocrinology, 18,* 91–102

Alexander, N. (1996). Barriers to sexually transmitted diseases. *Scientific American: Science and Medicine, 3*(2), 32–41.

Alfieri, T., Ruble, D. N., & Higgins, E. T. (1996). Gender stereotypes during adolescence: Developmental changes and the transition to junior high school. *Developmental Psychology, 32,* 1129–1137.

Allen, M. (1991). Meta-analysis comparing the persuasiveness of one-sided and two-sided messages. *Western Journal of Speech Communication, 55,* 390–404.

Allen, M. (2004). Reading achievement of students in French immersion programs. *Education Quarterly Review, 9(4),* 25–30.

Allen, M., D'Alessio, D., & Brezgel, K. (1995). A meta-analysis summarizing the effects of pornography: II. Aggression after exposure. *Human Communication Research,* 22, 258–283.

Allmer, H. (2005). Physical activity and cognitive functioning in aging. *Journal of Public Health, 13*(4), 185–188.

Alloy, L. B., Jacobson, N. S., & Acocella, J. (1999). *Abnormal psychology: Current perspectives.* Boston: McGraw-Hill.

Allport, G. W. (1935). Attitudes. In C. Murchison (Ed.), *Handbook of social psychology.* Worcester, MA: Clark University Press.

Allport, G. W. (1937). *Personality: A psychological interpretation.* New York: Holt, Rinehart & Winston.

Allport, G. W. (1954). *The nature of prejudice.* Reading, MA: Addison-Wesley.

Allport, G. W., & Odbert, H. S. (1936). Trait names: A psycho-lexical study. *Psychological Monographs, 47* (Whole No. 211).

Allport, G. W., & Postman, L. (1947). *The psychology of rumor.* New York: Holt.

Alm, H., & Nilsson, L. (1995). The effects of a mobile telephone task on driver behaviour in a car following situation. *Accident Analysis and Prevention, 27,* 707–715.

Alonso, C., & Coe, C. J. (2001). Disruptions of social relationships accentuate the association between emotional distress and menstrual pain in young women. *Health Psychology, 20,* 411–416.

Altman, I., & Taylor, D. A. (1973). *Social penetration: The development of interpersonal relationships.* New York: Holt, Rinehart & Winston.

Altman, J., & Bayer, S. A. (1996). *Development of the cerebellar system: In relation to its evolution, structure and functions.* Boca Raton, FL: CRC Press.

Alvarado, C. S. (2000). Psi-related experiences. In E. Cardeña, S. J. Lynn, & S. Krippner, (Eds.), *Varieties of anomalous experience: Examining the scientific evidence.* Washington, DC: American Psychological Association.

Amato, P. R. & Booth, A. (2001). The legacy of parents' marital discord: Consequences for children's marital quality. *Journal of Personality and Social Psychology, 81,* 627–638.

Amato, P. R., & Keith, B. (1991). Parental divorce and the well-being of children: A meta-analysis. *Psychological Bulletin,* 110, 26–46.

Amato, P. R., Loomis, L. S., & Booth, A. (1995). Parental divorce, marital conflict, and offspring well-being during early adulthood. *Social Forces, 73,* 895–915.

Ameri, A. (1999). The effects of cannabinoids on the brain. *Progress in Neurobiology,* 58, 315–348.

American Cancer Society (1997). *Smoking facts and figures.* New York: Author.

American Psychiatric Association (1994). *Diagnostic and statistical manual of mental disorders* (4th ed.). Washington, DC: Author.

American Psychological Association Task Force on Psychological Intervention Guidelines (1995). *Template for developing guidelines: Interventions for mental disorders and psychological aspects of physical disorders.* Washington, DC: American Psychological Association.

American Psychological Society. (2003). *History of APS.* Available online: http://www. psychologicalscience. org/about/history.html.

Amorapanth, P., LeDoux, J. E., & Nader, K. (2000). Different lateral amygdala outputs mediate reactions and actions elicited by a fear-arousing stimulus. *Nature Neuroscience, 3,* 74–79.

Anand, B. K., & Brobeck, J. R. (1951). Hypothalamic control of food intake in rats and cats. *Yale Journal of Biology and Medicine, 24,* 123–140.

Andersen, P. A., & Guerrero, L. K. (Eds.) (1998). *Handbook of communication and emotion: Research, theory, applications, and contexts.* San Diego: Academic Press.

Anderson, C. A. (1999). Attributional style, depression, and loneliness: A cross-cultural comparison of American and Chinese students. *Personality and Social Psychology Bulletin, 25,* 482–499.

Anderson, C. A. (2001). Heat and violence. *Current Directions in Psychological Science, 10,* 33–38.

Anderson, C. A., & Anderson, K. B. (1998). Temperature and aggression: Paradox, controversy, and a (fairly) clear picture. In R. G. Geen & E. Donnerstein (Eds.), *Human aggression: Theories, research, and implications for social policy.* San Diego: Academic Press.

Anderson, C. A., & Bushman, B. J. (2001). Effects of violent video games on aggressive behavior, aggressive cognition, aggressive affect, physiological arousal, and prosocial behavior: A meta-analytic review of the scientific literature. *Psychological Science, 2,* 353–359.

Anderson, C. A., & Bushman, B. J. (2002). Human aggression. *Annual Review of Psychology, 15,* 503–514.

Anderson, C. A., & Dill, K. E. (2000). Video games and aggressive thoughts, feelings, and behavior in the laboratory and in life. *Journal of Personality and Social Psychology, 78,* 772–790.

Anderson, E. (1994, May). The code of the streets. *Atlantic Monthly,* pp. 81–94.

Anderson, E. M., & Lambert, M. J. (1995). Short-term dynamically oriented psychotherapy: A review and meta-analysis. *Clinical Psychology Review, 15,* 503–514.

Anderson, J. R. (1980). *Cognitive psychology and its implications.* San Francisco: W. H. Freeman.

Anderson, J. R. (2000). *Cognitive psychology and its implications* (5th ed.). New York: Worth Publishers.

Anderson, J. R. (1991). The adaptative nature of human categorization. *Psychological Review, 98,* 409–429.

Anderson, M. C., & Neely, J. H. (1996). Interference and inhibition in memory retrieval. In E. L. Bjork & R. A. Bjork (Eds), *Memory. Handbook of perception and cognition* (2nd ed). San Diego: Academic Press.

Anderson, N. D., & Craik, F. I. M. (2000). Memory in the aging brain. In E. Tulving & F. I. M. Craik (Eds.), *The Oxford handbook of memory.* New York: Oxford University Press.

Anderson, R.E. (1984). Did I do it or did I only imagine doing it? *Journal of Experimental Psychology: General, 113,* 594–613.

Anderson, S. R., & Lightfoot, D. W. (1999). The human language faculty as an organ. *Annual Review of Physiology, 62,* 697–722.

Andreasen, N. C., Arndt, S., Swayze, V. Cizadlo, T. (1994). Thalamic abnormalities in schizophrenia visualized through magnetic resonance image averaging. *Science, 266,* 294–298.

Andresen, J. (2000). Meditation meets behavioral medicine: The story of experimental research on meditation. *Journal of Consciousness Studies,* 7, 17–73.

Ankney, C. D. (1992). Sex differences in relative brain size: The mismeasure of women, too? *Intelligence, 16,* 329–336.

Antonietti, A., & Colombo, B. (1997). The spontaneous occurrence of mental visualization in thinking. *Imagination, Cognition and Personality, 16,* 415–428.

Antony, M. M., & Swinson, R. P. (2000). Specific phobia. In M. M. Antony, & R. P. Swinson (Eds), *Phobic disorders and panic in adults: A guide to assessment and treatment* (79–104). Washington, DC: American Psychological Association.

Antrobus, J. (1983). REM and NREM sleep reports: Comparison of word frequenciesby cognitive classes. *Psychophysiology, 20,* 562–568.

Antrobus, J. (1991). Dreaming: Cognitive processes during cortical activation and high afferent thresholds. *Psychological Review, 98,* 96–121.

Aponte, H., & Hoffman, L. (1973). The open door. A structural approach to a family with an anorectic child. *Family Process, 12,* 1–44.

Arbuckle, T.Y., Gold, D.P., Andres, D., Schwartzman, A., & Chaikelson, J. (1992). The role of psychosocial context, age, and intelligence in memory performance of older men. *Psychology and Aging, 7,* 25–36.

Archer, J. (1996). Sex differences in social behavior: Are the social role and evolutionary explanations compatible? *American Psychologist, 51,* 909–917.

Archibald, S.L., Fennema-Notestine, C., Gamst, A., Riley, E.P., Mattson, S.N., & Jernigan, T.L. (2001). Brain dysmorphology in individuals with severe prenatal alcohol exposure. *Developmental Medicine & Child Neurology, 43,* 148–154.

Arendt, J. (2005). Melatonin: Characteristics, concerns, and prospects. *Journal of Biological Rhythms, 20,* 291-303.

Arendt, J., Skene, D. J., Middleton, B., Lockley, S. W., & Deacon, S. (1997). Efficacy of melatonin treatment in jet lag, shift work, and blindness. *Journal of Biological Rhythms, 12,* 604–617.

Argyle, M. (1999). Causes and correlates of happiness. In D. Kahneman, E. Diener, & N. Schwarz (Eds.), *Well-being: The foundations of hedonic psychology.* New York: Russell Sage Foundation.

Ariznavarreta, C., Cardinali, D.P., Villanuna, M.A., Granados, B., Martin, M., & Chiesa, J.J. (2002). Circadian rhythms in airline pilots submitted to long-haul transmeridian flights. *Aviation, Space, and Environmental Medicine, 73,* 445–455.

Armitage, C. J. (2005) Can the the theory of planned behavior predict the maintenance of physical activity? *Health Psychology, 24*(3), 235–245.

Armony, J. L., & LeDoux, J. E. (2000). How danger is encoded: Toward a systems, cellular, and computational understanding of cognitive-emotional interactions in fear. In M. S. Gazzaniga (Ed.), *The new cognitive neurosciences* (2nd ed.). Cambridge, MA: MIT Press.

Arnett, J. J. (1999). Adolescent storm and stress, reconsidered. *American Psychologist, 54,* 317–326.

Arnett, P. A. (1997). Autonomic responsivity in psychopaths: A critical review and theoretical proposal. *Clinical Psychology Review, 17,* 903–936.

Arnsten, A. F. T. (1998). The biology of being frazzled. *Science, 280,* 1711–1712.

Arnsten, A. F. T. & Goldman-Rakic, P. S. (1998). Noise stress impairs prefrontal cortical cognitive function in monkeys: Evidence for a hyperdomanergic mechanism. *Archives of General Psychiatry, 55,* 362–369.

Aron, A., & Westbay, L. (1996). Dimensions of the prototype of love. *Journal of Personality and Social Psychology, 70,* 535–551.

Aron, L. (1996). *A meeting of minds: Mutuality in psychoanalysis.* Hillsdale, NJ: Analytic Press.

Aronson, E. (2004). *The jigsaw classroom: Building cooperation in the classroom.* Reading, MA: Good Year Books.

Aronson, E. (2007). *The Social Animal* (10th ed.). New York: Worth Publishers.

Aronson, E., Stephan, C., Sikes, J., Blaney, N., & Snopp, M. (1978). *The jigsaw classroom.* Beverly Hills, CA: Sage Publications.

Aronson, E., Turner, J. A., & Carlsmith, J. M. (1963). Communicator credibility and communicator discrepancy as determinants of opinion change. *Journal of Abnormal and Social Psychology, 67,* 31–36.

Aronson, J., Lustina, M. J., Good, C., Keough, K., Steele, C. M., & Brown, J. (1999). When White men can't do math: Necessary and sufficient factors in stereotype threat. *Journal of Experimental Social Psychology, 35,* 29–46.

Aronson, M., & Hagberg, B. (1998). Neuropsychological disorders in children exposed to alcohol during pregnancy: A follow-up study of 24 children born to alcoholic mothers in Goeteborg, Sweden. *Alcoholism: Clinical and Experimental Research, 22,* 321–324.

Arrigo, J. M., & Pezdek, K. (1997). Lessons from the study of psychogenic amnesia. *Current Directions in Psychological Science, 6,* 148–152.

Asch, S. E. (1946). Forming impressions of personality. *Journal of Abnormal and Social Psychology, 41,* 258–290.

Asch, S. E. (1951). Effects of group pressure upon the modification and distortion of judgment. In Guetzkow, H. (Ed.), *Groups, leadership, and men.* Pittsburgh: Carnegie Press.

Asch, S. E. (1956). Studies of independence and conformity: A minority of one against a unanimous majority. *Psychological Monographs, 70,* 416.

Aserinsky, E., & Kleitman, N. (1953). Regularly occurring periods of ocular motility and concomitant phenomena during sleep. *Science, 118,* 361–375.

Aslin, R. N. (1987). Visual and auditory development in infancy. In J. Osofsky (Ed.), *Handbook of infant development.* New York: Wiley.

Aspy, D.N., Aspy, C. B., & Quimby, P.M. (1993). What doctors can teach teachers about problem-based learning. *Educational Leadership, 50(7),* 22–24.

Assanand, S. P., John, P. J., & Lehman, D. R. (1998). Teaching theories of hunger and eating: Overcoming students' misconceptions. *Teaching of Psychology, 25,* 44–46.

Associated Press (1989, June 25). Best way to retain complex information: Sleep on it, researchers say. *Seattle Times,* p. A9.

Astington, J.W., & Gopnik, A. (1991). Theoretical explanations of children's understanding of the mind. *British Journal of Developmental Psychology, 9,* 7–31.

Atchinson, M., McFarlane, A. C. (1994). A review of dissociation and dissociative disorders. *Australian and New Zealand Journal of Psychiatry, 28*(4), 591–599.

Atkinson, D. (1977). Society and sexes in the Russian past. In D. Atkinson & G. W. Lapidus (Eds.), *Women in Russia.* Stanford, CA: Stanford University Press.

Atkinson, J. W. (1964). *An introduction to motivation.* Princeton, NJ: Van Nostrand.

Atkinson, J. W. (Ed.) (1958). *Motives in fantasy, action, and society.* Princeton, NJ: Van Nostrand.

Atkinson, J. W., & Birch, D. (1978). *An introduction to motivation.* New York: Van Nostrand.

Atkinson, R. C., & Shiffrin, R. M. (1968). Human memory: A proposed system and its control processes. In K. W. Spence & J. T. Spence (Eds.), *Advances in the psychology of learning and motivation: Research and theory* (Vol. 2). New York: Academic Press.

Auerbach, S. M. (1989). Stress management and coping research in the health care setting: An overview and methodological commentary. *Journal of Consulting and Clinical Psychology, 57,* 388–395.

Averill, J. A. (1980). A constructivist view of emotion. In R. Plutchik & H. Kellerman (Eds.), *Emotion: Theory, research and experience* (Vol. 1). New York: Academic Press.

Avery, D. H., Dahl, K., Savage, M. V., & Brengelmann, G. L. (1997). Circadian temperature and cortisol rhythms during a constant routine are phase-delayed in hypersomnic winter depression. *Biological Psychiatry, 41,* 1109–1123.

Avila-White, D., Schneider, A., & Domhoff, G. W. (1999). The most recent dreams of 12–13- year-old boys and girls: A methodological contribution to the study of dream content in teenagers. *Dreaming: Journal of the Association for the Study of Dreams, 9,* 163–171.

Avis, J., & Harris, P. L. (1991). Belief-desire reasoning among Baka children: Evidence for a universal conception of mind. *Child Development, 62,* 460–467.

Ayllon, T., & Azrin, N. H. (1965). The measurement and reinforcement of behavior of psychotics. *Journal of the Experimental Analysis of Behavior, 8,* 357–383.

Ayllon, T., & Azrin, N. H. (1968). *The token economy: A motivational system for therapy and rehabilitation.* New York: Appleton-Century-Crofts.

Ayres, J. J. B. (1998). Fear conditioning and avoidance. In W. T. O'Donohue (Ed.), *Learning and behavior therapy.* Boston: Allyn & Bacon.

Azrin, N. H., & Nunn, R. G. (1973). Habit reversal: A method of eliminating nervous habits and tics. *Behaviour Research and Therapy, 11,* 619–628.

Baars, B. J. (1997). In the theatre of consciousness: Global workspace theory, a rigorous scientific theory of consciousness. *Journal of Consciousness Studies, 4,* 292–309.

Bach-Y-Rita, P. (2004). Coevolution of human potential and converging technologies. New York: New York Academy of Sciences, 83–91.

Bachman, J. G., Johnson, L. D., & O'Malley, P. M. (1987). *Monitoring the future: Questionnaire responses from the nation's high school seniors.* Ann Arbor, MI: Institute for Social Research, University of Michigan.

Backhaus, W. G., Kliegl, R., & Werner, J. S. (Eds.). (1998). *Color vision: Perspectives from different disciplines.* New York: Walter De Gruyter.

Baddeley, A. (1998). Recent developments in working memory. *Current Opinion in Neurobiology, 8,* 234–238.

Baddeley, A. D. (1966). Short-term memory for word sequences as a function of acoustic, semantic, and formal similarity. *Quarterly Journal of Experimental Psychology, 18,* 362–365.

Baddeley, A. D. (1986). *Working memory.* Oxford: Oxford University Press.

Baddeley, A. D. (1990). *Human memory: Theory and practice.* Boston: Allyn & Bacon.

Baddeley, A. D. (1994). The magical number seven: Still magic after all these years? *Psychological Review, 101,* 353–356.

Baddeley, A. D. (2000). Working memory: The interface between memory and cognition. In M. S. Gazzaniga (Ed.), *Cognitive neuroscience: A reader.* Malden, MA: Blackwell.

Baerentsen, K. B. (2001). Onset of meditation explored with fMRI. Neuroimage, 13, S297.

Baeyens, F., Wrzesniewski, A., de-Houwer, J., & Eelen, P. (1996). Toilet rooms, body massages, and smells: Two field studies on human evaluative odor conditioning. *Current Psychology: Developmental, Learning, Personality, & Social, 15,* 77–96.

Bagley, C., & Ramsay, R. (1997). *Suicidal behaviour in adolescents and adults: Research, taxonomy and prevention.* Ashgate, UK: Ashgate.

Bahrick, H. P. (1984). Semantic memory content in permastore: Fifty years of memory for Spanish learned in school. *Journal of Experimental Psychology: General, 113,* 1–29.

Bahrick, H. P., Bahrick, P. O., & Wittlinger, R. P. (1975). Fifty years of memory for names and faces: A cross-sectional approach. *Journal of Experimental Psychology: General, 104,* 54–75.

Bahrick, H. P., Hall, L. K., & Berger, S. A. (1996). Accuracy and distortion in memory for high school grades. *Psychological Science, 7,* 265–271.

Bahrick, H., Hall, L. K., Goggin, J. P. (1998). Fifty years of language maintenance and language dominance in bilingual Hispanic immigrants. *Journal of Experimental Psychology, General, 123,* 264–283.

Bailey, C. H., & Chen, M. (1992). The anatomy of long-term sensitization in *Aplysia:* Morphological insights into learning and memory. In L. R. Squire, N. M. Weinberger, G. Lynch, & J. L. McGaugh (Eds.), *Memory: Organization and locus of change.* New York: Oxford University Press.

Bailey, J. M., & Pillard, R. C. (1991). A genetic study of male sexual orientation. *Archives of General Psychiatry, 48,* 1089–1096.

Bailey, J. M., Pillard, R. C., Neale, M. C., & Agyei, Y. (1993). Heritable factors influence sexual orientation in women. *Archives of General Psychiatry, 50,* 217–223.

Baillargeon, R. (1987). Object permanence in 3 1/2- and 4 1/2-month-old infants. *Developmental Psychology, 23,* 655–664.

Baker, L. H., Cooney, N. L., & Pomerleau, O. F. (1987). Craving for alcohol: Theoretical processes and treatment procedures. In W. M. Cox (Ed.), *Treatment and prevention of alcohol problems: A resource manual.* New York: Academic Press.

Baldwin, D. A. (1993). Early referential understanding: Infants' ability to recognize referential acts for what they are. *Developmental Psychology, 29,* 832–843.

Baldwin, E. (1993). The case for animal research in psychology. *Journal of Social Issues, 49,* 121–131.

Ballenger, J. C. (2000). Panic disorder and agoraphobia. In G. Fink (Ed.), *Encyclopedia of stress.* San Diego: Academic Press.

Baltes, P., & Staudinger, U. M. (2000). Wisdom: A metaheuristic (pragmatic) to orchestrate mind and virtue toward excellence. *American Psychologist, 55,* 122–136.

Bandura, A. (1965). Influence of models' reinforcement contingencies on the acquisition of imitated responses. *Journal of Personality and Social Psychology, 1,* 589–595.

Bandura, A. (1969). *Principles of behavior modification.* New York: Holt, Rinehart & Winston.

Bandura, A. (1973). *Aggression: A social learning analysis.* Englewood Cliffs, NJ: Prentice Hall.

Bandura, A. (1977a). Self-efficacy: Toward a unifying theory of behavioral change. *Psychological Review, 84,* 191–215.

Bandura, A. (1977b). *Social learning theory.* Englewood Cliffs, NJ: Prentice Hall.

Bandura, A. (1986). *Social foundations of thought and action: A social-cognitive theory.* Englewood Cliffs, NJ: Prentice Hall.

Bandura, A. (1988). Mechanisms of moral disengagement in terrorism. In W. Reich (Ed.), *The psychology of terrorism: Behaviors, world-views, states of mind.* New York: Cambridge University Press.

Bandura, A. (1989). Social cognitive theory. *Annals of Child Development, 6,* 3–58.

Bandura, A. (1991). Human agency: The rhetoric and the reality. *American Psychologist, 46,* 157–162.

Bandura, A. (1997). *Self-efficacy: The exercise of control.* New York: W. H. Freeman.

Bandura, A. (2000). Health promotion from the perspective of social cognitive theory. In P. Norman, C. Abraham, & M. Conner (Eds.), *Understanding and changing health and behaviour.* Reading, England: Harwood.

Bandura, A. (2001). Social cognitive theory: An agentic perspective. *Annual Review of Psychology, 52,* 1–26.

Bandura, A., & Cervone, D. (1983). Self-evaluative and self-efficacy mechanisms governing the motivational effects of goal systems. *Journal of Personality and Social Psychology, 45,* 1017–1028.

Bandura, A. and Kupers, C. J. (1964). Transmission of patterns of self-reinforcement through modeling, *Journal of Abnormal and Social Psychology, 69,* 1–9.

Bandura, A. and Mischel, W. (1965). Modification of self-imposed delay of reward through exposure to live and symbolic models. *Journal of Personality and Social Psychology, 2,* 698–705.

Bandura, A., O'Leary, A., Taylor, C. B., Gauthier, J., & Gossard, D. (1987). Perceived self-efficacy and pain control: Opioid and nonopioid mechanisms. *Journal of Personality and Social Psychology, 53,* 563–571.

Bandura, A., Perrig, W. J., Grob, A. (2000). *Control of human behavior, mental processes, and consciousness: Essays in honor of the 60th birthday of August Flammer.* Mahwah, NJ, US: Lawrence Erlbaum Associates.

Bandura, A., & Walters, R. H. (1959). *Adolescent aggression.* New York: Ronald Press.

Banks, W. P., & Krajicek, D. (1991). Perception. *Annual Review of Psychology, 42,* 305–332.

Barbalet, J. M. (1998). *Emotion, social theory and social structure: A macrosociological approach.* New York: Cambridge University Press.

Barber, J. (1977). Rapid induction analgesia. *American Journal of Clinical Hypnosis, 19,* 138–143.

Barber, J. (1998). The mysterious persistence of hypnotic analgesia. *International Journal of Clinical and Experimental Hypnosis, 46,* 28–43.

Bardo, M. T. (1998). Neuropharmacological mechanisms of drug reward: Beyond dopamine in the nucleus accumbens. *Critical Reviews in Neurobiology, 12,* 37–67.

Barefoot, J. C., Dodge, K. A., Peterson, B. L., Dahlstrom, W. G., & Williams, R. B. (1989). The Cook-Medley Hostility Scale: Item content and ability to predict survival. *Psychosomatic Medicine, 51,* 46–57.

Bargh, J. A. (1984). Automatic and conscious processing of social information. In R. S. Wyer & T. K. Srull (Eds.), *Handbook of social cognition* (Vol. 3). Hillsdale, NJ: Erlbaum.

Bargh, J. A. (1997). The automaticity of everyday life. In R. S. Wyer, Jr. (Ed.), *The automaticity of* everyday life: Advances in social cognition (Vol. 10). New York: Guilford Press.

Bargh, J. A., & Chartrand, T. L. (1999). The unbearable automaticity of being. *American Psychologist, 54,* 462–479.

Barkow, J. (1992). Beneath new culture is old psychology: Gossip and social stratification. In J. Barkow, L. Cosmides, & J. Tooby (Eds.), *The adapted mind: Evolutionary psychology and the generation of culture.* London: Oxford University Press.

Barlow, D. H. (1991). Disorders of emotion. *Psychological Inquiry, 2,* 58–71.

Barlow, D. H. (1997). Cognitive-behavioral therapy for panic disorder: Current status. *Journal of Clinical Psychiatry, 58* (Suppl. 2), 32–36.

Barlow, D. H. (2002). *Anxiety and its disorders.* New York: Guilford Press.

Barlow, D. H., & Rapee, R. M. (1991). *Mastering stress: A lifestyle approach.* Dallas: American Health.

Barnes, G. E., & Prosen, H. (1985). Parental death and depression. *Journal of Abnormal Psychology, 94,* 64–69.

Barnes, T. R. (Ed.) (1994). *Antipsychotic drugs and their side effects.* San Diego: Academic Press.

Barnett, J. E., & Porter, J. E. (1998). The suicidal patient: Clinical and risk management strategies. In L. VandeCreek & S. Knapp (Eds.), *Innovations in clinical practice: A source book* (Vol. 16). Sarasota, FL: Professional Resource Press.

Baron, P., & Hanna, J. (1990). Egocentrism and depressive symptomatology in young adults. *Social Behavior and Personality, 18,* 279–285.

Baron, R.A., Earhard, B., & Ozier, M. (2001). *Psychology,* (3rd Canadian ed.). Pearson; Toronto.

Baron, R. S. (1986). Distraction-conflict theory: Progress and problems. In L. Berkowitz (Ed.), *Advances in experimental social psychology* (Vol. 20). New York: Academic Press.

Baron, R. S., Cutrona, C. E., Hicklin, D., Russell, D. W., & Lubaroff, D. M. (1990). Social support and immune responses among spouses of cancer patients. *Journal of Personality and Social Psychology, 59,* 344–352.

Baron, R. S., Vandello, J. A., & Brunsman, B. (1996). The forgotten variable in conformity research: Impact of task importance on social influence. *Journal of Personality and Social Psychology, 71,* 915–927.

Barondes, S. H. (1999). *Mood genes: Hunting for origins of mania and depression.* New York: Oxford University Press.

Barrett, G. V., & Depinet, R. L. (1991). A reconsideration of testing for competence rather than for intelligence. *American Psychologist, 46,* 1012–1024.

Barrett, P. T., & Eysenck, H. J. (1992). Brain evoked potentials and intelligence: The Hendrickson paradigm. *Intelligence, 16,* 361–381.

Barsalou, L. W. (1992). *Cognitive psychology: An overview for cognitive scientists.* Hillsdale, NJ: Erlbaum.

Barsky, A. J. (1992). Amplification, somatization, and the somatoform disorders. *Psychosomatics, 33,* 28–34.

Bartholow, B. D., & Anderson, C. A. (2002). Effects of violent video games on aggressive behavior: Potential sex differences. *Journal of Experimental Social Psychology, 38,* 283–290.

Bartlett, F. C. (1932). *Remembering: A study in experimental and social psychology.* New York: Cambridge University Press.

Bartoshuk, L. M. (1993). The biological basis of food perception and acceptance. *Food Quality and Preference, 4,* 21–32.

Bartoshuk, L. M., & Beauchamp, G. K. (1994). Chemical senses. *Annual Review of Psychology, 45,* 419–449.

Bassok, M., & Holyoak, K. J. (1989). Interdomain transfer between isomorphic topics in algebra and physics. *Journal of Experimental Psychology: Memory, Learning, and Cognition, 15* (1), 153–166.

Bastik, T. (1982). *Intuition: How we think and act.* New York: Wiley.

Bates, M. S., Edwards, W. T., & Anderson, K. O. (1993). Ethnocultural influences on variation in chronic pain perception. *Pain, 52,* 101–112.

Batson, C. D. (1991). *The altruism question: Toward a social-psychological answer.* Hillsdale, NJ: Erlbaum.

Batson, C. D., Ahmad, N., Lishner, D. A., & Tsang, J. A. (2002). Empathy and altruism. In C. R. Snyder & S. J. Lopez (Eds.), *Handbook of positive psychology.* London: Oxford University Press.

Batson, C. D., Duncan, B. D., Ackerman, P., Buckley, T., & Birch, K. (1981). Is empathic emotion a source of altruistic motivation? *Journal of Personality and Social Psychology, 40,* 290–302.

Batson, C. D., Sager, K., Garst, E., & Kang, M. (1997). Is empathy-induced helping due to self-other merging? *Journal of Personality and Social Psychology, 73,* 495–509.

Baudry, M., & Davis, J. L. (Eds.) (1991). *Long-term potentiation: A debate of current issues.* Cambridge, MA: MIT Press.

Bauer, K. E., & McCanne, T. R. (1980). Autonomic and central nervous system responding during hypnosis and simulation of hypnosis. *International Journal of Clinical and Experimental Hypnosis, 28,* 148–163.

Baum, A., & Posluszny, D. M. (1999). Health psychology: Mapping biobehavioral contributions to health and illness. *Annual Review of Psychology, 50,* 137–164.

Baum, A., Krantz, D. S., & Gatchel, R. J. (1997). *An introduction to health psychology* (3rd ed.). Boston: McGraw-Hill.

Baumeister, R. F. (1984). Choking under pressure: Self-consciousness and paradoxical effects of incentives on skillful performance. *Journal of Personality and Social Psychology, 46,* 610–620.

Baumeister, R. F. (1989). The optimal margin of illusion. *Journal of Social and Clinical Psychology, 8,* 176–189.

Baumeister, R. F., & Leary, M. R. (1995). The need to belong: Desire for interpersonal attachments as a fundamental human motivation. *Psychological Bulletin, 117,* 497–529.

Baumeister, R. F., Smart, L. & Boden, J. M. (1996). Relation of threatened egotism to violence and aggression: The dark side of high self-esteem. *Psychological Review, 103,* 5–33.

Baumrind, D. (1964). Some thoughts on ethics of research: After reading Milgram's behavioral study of obedience. *American Psychologist, 19,* 421–423.

Baumrind, D. (1967). Child care practices anteceding three patterns of preschool behavior. *Genetic Psychology Monographs, 75,* 43–88.

Baumrind, D. (1980). New directions in socialization research. *American Psychologist, 35,* 639–652.

Baumrind, D. (1983). Rejoinder to Lewis's reinterpretation of parental firm control effects: Are authoritative families really harmonious? *Psychological Bulletin, 94,* 132–142.

Baumrind, D. (1991). Parenting styles and adolescent development. In J. Brooks-Gunn, R. Lerner, & A. C. Petersen (Eds.), *The encyclopedia of adolescence.* New York: Garland.

Bauserman, R. (1996). Sexual aggression and pornography: A review of correlational research. *Basic and Applied Social Psychology, 18,* 405–427.

Baxter, L. R. (1992). Neuroimaging studies of obsessive compulsive disorder. *Psychiatric Clinics of North America, 15,* 871–884.

Baxter, L.R., Schwartz, J.M., Mazziota, J.C., Phelps, M.E., Pahlm J.J. & B.H. Guze.(1988). Cerebral glucose metabolic rates in nondepressed patients with obsessive-compulsive disorder. *American Journal of Psychiatry, 145*(12), 1560–1563.

Beahrs, J. O. (1994). Dissociative identity disorder: Adaptive deception of self and others. *Bulletin of the American Academy of Psychiatric Law, 22,* 223–237.

Beaman, A. L., Barnes, P. J., Klentz, B., & McQuirk, B. (1978). Increasing helping rates through information dissemination: Teaching pays. *Personality and Social Psychology Bulletin, 4,* 406–411.

Beardsley, L., & Pedersen, P. (1997). Health and culture-centered intervention. In J. W. Berry, M. H. Segall, and C. Kagitáibasi (Eds.), *Handbook of Cross-Cultural Psychology: Social Behavior and Applications* (Vol 1, 2nd ed.). Boston: Allyn & Bacon.

Beatty, M. J., Heisel, A. D., Hall, A. E., Levine, T. R., & La France, B. H. (2002). What can we learn from the study of twins about genetic and environmental influences on interpersonal affiliation, aggressiveness, and social anxiety? A meta-analytic study. *Communication Monographs, 69,* 1–18.

Beauchamp, G. K., & Bartoshuk, L. (Eds.) (1997). *Tasting and smelling.* Philadelphia: Academic Press.

Bechara, A., Damasio, A. R., Damasio, H., & Anderson, S. W. (1994). Insensitivity to future consequences following damage to human prefrontal cortex. *Cognition, 50,* 7–15.

Bechara, A., Tranel, D., et al. (1995). Double dissociation of conditioning and declarative knowledge relative to the amygdala and hippocampus in humans. *Science, 29,* 1115–1118.

Beck, A. P., & Lewis, C. M. (Eds.) (2000). *The process of group psychotherapy: Systems for analyzing change.* Washington, DC: American Psychological Association.

Beck, A. T. (2002). *Cognitive therapy and the emotional disorders.* New York: International Universities Press.

Beck, A. T. (1988). Cognitive approaches to panic disorder: Theory and therapy. In S. Rachman and J. D. Maser (Eds.), *Panic: Psychological perspectives.* Hillsdale, NJ: Erlbaum.

Beck, A. T. (1991). Cognitive therapy: A 30-year retrospective. *American Psychologist, 46,* 368–375.

Beck, A.T. (2002). Cognitive patterns in dreams and daydreams. *Journal of Cognitive Psychotherapy, 16,* 23–28.

Beck, A. T., & Freeman, A. (1990). *Cognitive theory of personality disorders.* New York: Guilford Press.

Beck, A. T., Rush, A. J., Shaw, B. F., & Emery, G. (1979). *Cognitive therapy of depression.* New York: Guilford Press.

Becker, A. E., Grinspoon, S. K., Klibanski, A., & Herzog, D. B. (1999). Current concepts: Eating disorders. *New England Journal of Medicine, 340,* 1092–1098.

Becker, E. (1973). *The denial of death.* New York: Free Press.

Becker, J. B., Breedlove, S. M., & Crews, D. (Eds.) (1992). *Behavioral endocrinology.* Cambridge, MA: MIT Press.

Bedard, J., & Chi, M. T. (1992). Expertise. *Current Directions in Psychological Science, 4,* 135–139.

Bednekoff, P. A., & Balda, R. P. (1996). Observational spatial memory in Clark's nutcrackers and Mexican jays. *Animal Behaviour, 52,* 833–839.

Beecher, H. K. (1959). Generalization from pain of various types and diverse origins. *Science, 130,* 267–268.

Beitman, B. D. (1998). *The psychotherapist's guide to cost containment: How to survive and thrive in an age of managed care.* Newbury Park, CA: Sage Publications.

Bekesy, G. von (1957). The ear. *Scientific American, 230,* 66–78.

Bell, A. P., Weinberg, M. S., & Hammersmith, S. K. (1981). *Sexual preference: Its development in men and women.* Bloomington: Indiana University Press.

Belsky, J., & Hsieh, K. H. (1998). Patterns of marital change during the early childhood years: Parent personality, coparenting, and division-of-labor correlates. *Journal of Family Psychology, 12,* 511–528.

Bem, D. J. (1972). Self-perception theory. In L. Berkowitz (Ed.), *Advances in experimental social psychology* (Vol. 6). New York: Academic Press.

Bem, D. J. (1996). Exotic becomes erotic: A developmental theory of sexual orientation. *Psychological Review, 103,* 320–335.

Bem, D. J., & Honorton, C. (1994). Does psi exist? Replicable evidence for an anomalous process of information transfer. *Psychological Bulletin, 115,* 4–18.

Bem, S. L. (1981). Gender schema theory: A cognitive account of sex typing. *Psychological Review, 88,* 354–364.

Benjamin, A. S., & Craik, F. (2001). Parallel effects of aging and time pressure on memory for source: evidence from the spacing effect. *Memory & Cognition, 29,* 691–697.

Benjamin, J., Li, L., Patterson, C., Greenberg, B. D., Murphy, D. L., & Hamer, D. H. (1996). Population and familial association between the D4 dopamine receptor gene and measures of novelty seeking. *Nature Genetics, 12,* 81–84.

Benjamin, L. S. (2003). *Interpersonal reconstructive therapy: Promoting change in nonresponders.* New York: Guilford Press.

Benjamin, L. T., Cavell, T. A. & Shallenberger, W. R. (1984). Staying with initial answers on objective tests: Is it a myth? *Teaching of Psychology, 11,* 133–141.

Bennett, H. L. (1983). Remembering drink orders: The memory skills of cocktail waitresses. *Human Learning, 2,* 157–169.

Bennett, N. G., Blanc, A. K., & Bloom, D. E. (1988). Commitment and the modern union: Assessing the link between premarital cohabitation and subsequent marital stability. *American Sociological Review, 53,* 127–138.

Benoit, D., & Parker, K. (1994). Stability and transmission of attachment across three generations. *Child Development, 65,* 1444–1456.

Benski, C., & Scientists from CRSSA. (1998). Testing new claims of dermo-optical perception. *Skeptical Inquirer, 22*(1), 21–26.

Bensley, L., & Van Eenwyk, J. (2001). Video games and real life aggression: Review of the literature. *Journal of Adolescent Health, 29,* 244–257.

Bentley, D. R. (2000). The human genome project: An overview. *Medical Research Review, 20,* 189–196.

Benton, A. L. (1994). Neuropsychological assessment. *Annual Review of Psychology, 45,* 1–23.

Beran, M. J., Rumbaugh, D. M., Savage-Rumbaugh, E. S. (1998). Chimpanzee (pan troglodyte) counting in a computerized testing paradigm. *The Psychological Record, 48,* 3–19.

Berg, K. M., & Boswell, A. E. (1998). Infants' detection of increments in low- and high-frequency noise. *Perception and Psychophysics, 60,* 1044–1051.

Bergen, R. K. (1998). *Issues in intimate violence.* Thousand Oaks, CA: Sage Publications.

Berger, M., Vollmann, J., Hohagen, F., & Konig, A. (1997). Sleep deprivation combined with consecutive sleep phase advance as a fast-acting therapy in depression: An open pilot trial in medicated and unmedicated patients. *American Journal of Psychiatry, 154,* 870–872.

Berger, R. J., & Phillips, N. H. (1995). Energy conservation and sleep. *Behavioural Brain Research, 69,* 65–73.

Berkowitz, L. (1972). Social norms, feelings, and other factors affecting helping and altruism. In L. Berkowitz (Ed.), *Advances in experimental social psychology.* New York: Academic Press.

Berkowitz, L. (1990). On the formation and regulation of anger and aggression. *American Psychologist, 45,* 494–503.

Berkowitz, L. (1998). Aggressive personalities. In D. F. Barone, M. Hersen, & V. B. Van Hasselt (Eds.), *Advanced personality.* New York: Plenum.

Berman, S., Ozkaragoz, T., Young, R. M. & Noble, E. P. (2002). D2 dopamine receptor gene polymorphism discriminates two kinds of novelty seeking. *Personality and Individual Differences, 33,* 867–882.

Bernstein, I. L. (1978). Learned taste aversions in children receiving chemotherapy. *Science, 200,* 1302–1303.

Berry, J. W., Poortinga, Y. H., Segall, M. H., & Dasen, P. (2002). *Cross-cultural psychology: Research and applications* (2nd ed.). New York: Cambridge University Press.

Berry, J. W., Segall, M. H., & Kagitáibasi, C. (1997). *Handbook of cross-cultural psychology: Social behavior and applications.* Boston: Allyn & Bacon.

Berry, J., & Ataca, B. (2000). Cultural factors. In G. Fink (Ed.), *Encyclopedia of stress.* San Diego: Academic Press.

Berry, L. M. (1998). *Psychology at work* (2nd ed.). Boston: McGraw-Hill.

Berscheid, E. (1984). *The problem of emotion in close relationships.* New York: Plenum.

Berthoud, H. R. (2002). Multiple neural systems controlling food intake and body weight. *Neuroscience and Biobehavioral Reviews, 26,* 393–428.

Best, D. L., Williams, J. E., Cloud, J. M., Davis, S. W., Robertson, L. S., Edwards, J. R., Giles, H., & Fowles, J. (1977). Development of sex-trait stereotypes among young children in the United States, England, and Ireland. *Child Development, 48,* 1375–1384.

Betancourt, H., & Blair, I. (1992). A cognition (attribution)-emotion model of violence in conflict situations. *Personality and Social Psychology Bulletin, 18,* 343–350.

Beutler, L. E. (2002). The dodo bird is extinct. *Clinical Psychology: Science and Practice, 9,* 30–34.

Beutler, L. E., Machado, P. P., & Neufeldt, S. A. (1994). Therapist variables. In A. E. Bergin & S. L. Garfield (Eds.), *Handbook of psychotherapy and behavior change* (4th ed.). New York: Wiley.

Beutler, L. E., & Malik, M. L. (2002). *Rethinking the DSM: A psychological perspective.* Washington, DC: American Psychological Association.

Beyer, S. (1990). Gender differences in the accuracy of self-evaluations of performance. *Journal of Personality and Social Psychology, 59,* 960–970.

Beyerstein, B. L. (1990). Brainscams: Neuromythologies of the New Age. *International Journal of Mental Health, 19,* 27–36.

Bhattachary, S., & Powell, J. H. (2001). Recreational use of 3,4-methylenedioxymethamphetamine (MDMA) or 'ecstasy': Evidence for cognitive impairments. *Psychological Medicine,* 31, 647–658.

Bialystok, E. (1997). Effects of bilingualism and biliteracy on children's emerging concepts of print. *Developmental Psychology, 33,* 429–440.

Bialystok, E. (1998). The relationship between bilingualism and the development of cognitive processes in problem solving. *Applied Psycholinguistics, 19,* 69–85.

Bialystok, E. (2001). *Bilingualism in development: Language, literacy, & cognition.* New York: Cambridge University Press.

Biederman, J. (1998). Attention-deficit/hyperactive disorder: A life-span perspective. *Journal of Clinical Psychology, 59,* 1–13.

Biener, L., & Boudreau, L. (1991). Social power and influence. In R. M. Baron, W. G. Graziano, & C. Stangor (Eds.), *Social psychology.* Ft. Worth, TX: Holt, Rinehart & Winston.

Billings, A. G., & Moos, R. H. (1981). The role of coping responses and social resources in attenuating the stress of life events. *Journal of Behavioral Medicine, 4,* 139–157.

Billings, A. G., & Moos, R. H. (1984). Coping, stress, and social resources among adults with unipolar depression. *Journal of Personality and Social Psychology, 46,* 877–891.

Binder, J. L., & Strupp, H. H. (1997). "Negative process": A recurrently discovered and underestimated facet of therapeutic process and outcome in the individual psychotherapy of adults. *Clinical Psychology: Science & Practice, 4,* 121–139.

Binet, A. M., & Simon, T. (1905). Methodes nouvelles pour le diagnostic du niveau intellectuel des anormaux. *L'Anee Psychologique, 11,* 191–224.

Birnbaum, S. G., Yuan, P. X., Wang, M., Vijayraghavan, S., Bloom, A. K., Davis, D. J., Gobeske, K. T., Sweatt, J. D., Manji, H. K., & Arnsten, A. F. T. (2004). Protein kinase C overactivity impairs prefrontal cortical regulation of working memory. *Science, 306,* 882–884.

Bjorklund, D. F., & Pellegrini, A. D. (2002). Evolutionary perspectives on social development. In P. K. Smith & C. H. Hart (Eds.), *Blackwell handbook of childhood social development.* Malden, MA: Blackwell.

Björkqvist, K. (1997). The inevitability of conflict, but not of violence: Theoretical considerations on conflict and aggression. In D. P. Fry & K. Björkqvist (Eds.), *Cultural variation in conflict resolution: Alternatives to violence.* Mahwah, NJ: Erlbaum.

Black, D. W. (1999). *Bad boys, bad men: Confronting antisocial personality disorder.* New York: Oxford University Press.

Black, D. W., Yates, W. R., & Andreasen, N. C. (1988). Schizophrenia, schizophreniform disorder, and delusional paranoid disorders. In J. A. Talbott, R. E. Hales, & S. C. Yudofsky (Eds.), *Textbook of psychiatry.* Washington, DC: American Psychiatric Press.

Blackwood, D. (2000). Genetic predispositions to stressful conditions. In G. Fink (Ed.), *Encyclopedia of stress.* San Diego: Academic Press.

Blader, S. L., & Tyler, T. R. (2002). Justice and empathy: What motivates people to help others? In M. Ross & D. T. Miller (Eds.), *The justice motive in everyday life.* New York: Cambridge University Press.

Blaine, B. & Crocker, J. (1993). Self-esteem and self serving biases in reactions to positive and negative events: An integrative review. In R. F. Baumeister (Ed.), *Self-esteem: The puzzle of low self-regard,* 55–85. New York: Plenum Press.

Blakemore, C., & Cooper, G. F. (1970). Development of the brain depends on visual environment. *Nature, 228,* 477–478.

Blanchard, C. M., Courneya, K. S., Rodgers, W. M., Daub, B., Knapik, G. (2002). Determinants of exercise intention and behavior during and after phase 2 cardiac rehabilitation: An application of the theory of planned behavior. *Rehabilitation Psychology, 47,* 308–323.

Blank, R. H. (1999). *Brain policy: How the new neuroscience will change our lives and our politics.* Washington, DC: Georgetown University Press.

Blascovich, J., Mendes, W. B., Hunter, S. B., & Salomon, K. (1999). Social "facilitation" as challenge and threat. *Journal of Personality and Social Psychology, 77,* 68–77.

Blascovich, J., Wyer, N. A., Swart, L. A., & Kibler, J. L. (1997). Racism and racial categorization. *Journal of Personality and Social Psychology, 72,* 1364–1372.

Blasi, A. (1980). Bridging moral cognition and moral action: A critical review of the literature. *Psychological Bulletin, 88,* 1–45.

Blass, E.M., Ganchrow, J.R., & Steiner, J.E. (1984). Classical conditioning in newborn humans 2-48 hours of age. *Infant Behavior and Development, 7,* 223–235.

Blass, T. (1996). Attribution of responsibility and trust in the Milgram obedience experiment. *Journal of Applied Social Psychology, 26,* 1529–1535.

Blass, T. (Ed.) (2000). *Obedience to authority: Current perspectives on the Milgram paradigm.* Mahwah, NJ: Erlbaum.

Blass, T., & Schmitt, C. (2001). The nature of perceived authority in the Milgram paradigm: Two replications. *Current Psychology: Developmental, Learning, Personality, Social, 20,* 115–121.

Blechman, E., & Brownell, K. D. (1998). *Behavioral medicine and women: A comprehensive handbook.* New York: Guilford Press.

Blessing, W. W. (1997). *The lower brainstem and bodily homeostasis.* New York: Oxford University Press.

Blethen, S. L., Baptista, J., Kuntze, J., Foley, T., LaFranchi, S., & Johanson, A. (1997). Adult height in growth hormone (GH)-deficient children treated with biosynthetic GH. The Genentech Growth Study Group. *Journal of Clinical Endocrinology and Metabolism, 82,* 418–420.

Block, L., & Keller, P. (1998). Beyond protection motivation: An integrative theory of health appeals. *Journal of Applied Social Psychology, 28,* 1584–1608.

Block, N. (2002). How heritability misleads about race. In J. M. Fish (Ed.), *Race and intelligence: Separating science from myth.* Mahwah, NJ: Erlbaum.

Blodgett, H. C. (1929). The effect of the introduction of reward on the maze performance of rats. *University of California Publications in Psychology,* 4(8), 114–126.

Blodgett, R. (1986, May). Lost in the stars: Psychics strike out (again). *People Expression,* 32–35.

Bloom, F. E. (1998). *Brain, mind and behavior.* San Francisco: W. H. Freeman.

Bobo, L. (1988). Attitudes toward the black political movement: Trends, meaning, and effects of racial policy preferences. *Social Psychology Quarterly, 51,* 287–302.

Bochner, S., & Insko, C. A. (1966). Communicator discrepancy, source credibility, and opinion change. *Journal of Personality and Social Psychology, 4,* 614–621.

Boesch, C. (1991). Teaching among wild chimpanzees. *Animal Behaviour, 41,* 530–532.

Boesch, C. (1995). Innovation in wild chimpanzees (Pan troglodytes). *International Journal of Primatology, 16,* 1–16.

Bohart, A. C., & Greenberg, L. S. (Eds.) (1997). *Empathy reconsidered: New directions in psychotherapy.* Washington, DC: American Psychological Association.

Bolles, R. C. (1979). *Learning theory* (2nd ed.). New York: Holt, Rinehart & Winston.

Bolles, R. C. (1980). Some functionalistic thought about regulation. In F. M. Toates & T. R. Halliday (Eds.), *Analysis of motivational processes.* London: Academic Press.

Bolles, R. C., & Beecher, M. D. (Eds.) (1988). *Evolution and learning.* Hillsdale, NJ: Erlbaum.

Bonanno, G. A., Kaltman, S., Duberstein, P. R., & Masling, J. M. (2000). The assumed necessity of working through memories of traumatic experiences. In P. R. Duberstein & J. M. Masling (Eds.), *Psychodynamic perspectives on sickness and health.* Washington, DC: American Psychological Association.

Bond, C. F., Jr., & Titus, L. J. (1983). Social facilitation: A meta-analysis of 241 studies. *Psychological Bulletin, 94,* 265–292.

Bond, R., & Smith, P. B. (1996). Culture and conformity: A meta-analysis of studies using Asch's (1952b, 1956) line judgment task. *Psychological Bulletin, 119,* 111–137.

Bonnel, A. M., & Hafter, E. R. (1998). Divided attention between simultaneous auditory and visual signals. *Perception and Psychophysics, 60,* 179–190.

Bonvillian, J. D., & Patterson, F. G. P. (1997). Sign language acquisition and the development of meaning in a lowland gorilla. In C. Mandell & A. McCabe (Eds.), *The problem of meaning: Behavioral and cognitive perspectives.* Amsterdam, Netherlands: North-Holland/Elsevier Science.

Book, H. E. (1997). *How to practice brief psychodynamic psychotherapy: The core conflictual relationship theme method.* Washington, DC: American Psychological Association.

Booth-Kewley, S., & Friedman, H. S. (1987). Psychological predictors of heart disease: A quantitative review. *Psychological Bulletin, 101,* 343–362.

Bootzin, R. R. (1979). Effects of self-control procedures for insomnia. *American Journal of Clinical Biofeedback, 2,* 70–77.

Bootzin, R. R., Rider, S. P., Pressman, M. R., & Orr, W. C. (Eds.) (1997). *Behavioral techniques and biofeedback for insomnia. Understanding sleep: The evaluation and treatment of sleep disorders.* Washington, DC.: American Psychological Association.

Borbely, A. A., Achermann, P., Trachsel, L., & Tobler, I. (1989). Sleep initiation and initial sleep intensity: Interactions of homeostatic and circadian mechanisms. *Journal of Biological Rhythms, 4,* 149–160.

Boring, E. G. (1950). *A history of experimental psychology.* New York: Appleton-Century-Crofts.

Borke, H. (1975). Piaget's mountains revisited: Changes in the egocentric landscape. *Developmental Psychology, 11,* 240–243.

Bornstein, R. F. (1989). Subliminal techniques as propaganda tools: Review and critique. *Journal of Mind and Behavior, 10,* 231–262.

Borod, J. C. (2000). *The neuropsychology of emotion.* New York: Oxford University Press.

Botman, H. I., & Crovitz, H. F. (1989–1990). Dream reports and autobiographical memory. *Imagination, Cognition and Personality, 9,* 213–224.

Bouchard, C., Tremblay, A., Despres, J. P., Nadeau, A., Lupien, P. J., & Theriault, G. (1990). The response to long-term overfeeding in identical twins. *The New England Journal of Medicine, 322,* 1477–1482.

Bouchard, T. J., Lykken, D. T., McGue, M., Segal, N. L., & Tellegen, A. (1990). Sources of human psychological differences: The Minnesota study of twins reared apart. *Science, 250,* 223–228.

Boucher, J. D., & Ekman, P. (1975). Facial areas and emotional information. *Journal of Communication, 25,* 21–29.

Boulos, Z. (1998). Bright light treatment for jet lag and shift work. In R. Lam & W. Raymond (Eds.), *Seasonal affective disorder and beyond: Light treatment for SAD and non-SAD conditions.* Washington, DC: American Psychiatric Press.

Bovbjerg, D. H. (2006). The continuing problem of post chemotherapy nausea and vomiting: Contributions of classical conditioning. *Autonomic Neuroscience: Basic & Clinical, 129,* 92–98.

Bower, G. H. (2000). A brief history of memory research. In E. Tulving and F. I. M. Craik (Eds.), *The Oxford handbook of memory.* New York: Oxford University Press.

Bower, G. H., Clark, M. C., Lesgold, M. A., & Winzenz, D. (1969). Hierarchical retrieval schemes in recall of categorized word lists. *Journal of Verbal Learning and Verbal Behavior, 8,* 323–343.

Bowers, K. S. (1983). *Hypnosis for the seriously curious.* NY: Norton.

Bowers, K. S. (1992). Imagination and dissociation in hypnotic responding. *International Journal of Clinical and Experimental Hypnosis, 40,* 253–275.

Bowlby, J. (1958). The nature of the child's tie to his mother. *International Journal of Psychoanalysis, 39,* 350–373.

Bowlby, J. (1969). *Attachment and loss: Vol. 1. Attachment.* New York: Basic Books.

Bowlby, J. (1973). *Attachment and loss: Vol. 2. Separation: Anxiety and anger.* London: Hogarth.

Bowlby, J. (2000a). *Loss: Sadness and depression.* New York: Basic Books.

Bowlby, J. (2000b). *Separation: Anxiety and anger.* New York: Basic Books.

Bozarth, J. D., Zimring, F. M., & Tausch, R. (2002). Client-centered therapy: The evolution of a revolution. In D. J. Cain (Ed.), *Humanistic psychotherapies: Handbook of research and practice.* Washington, DC: American Psychological Association.

Brandon, S., Boakes, J., Glaser, D., & Green, R. (1998). Recovered memories of childhood sexual abuse: Implications for clinical practice. *British Journal of Psychiatry, 172,* 296–307.

Bransford, J. D., & Johnson, M. K. (1972). Contextual prerequisites for understanding: Some investigations of comprehension and recall. *Journal of Verbal Learning and Verbal-Behavior, 11,* 717–726.

Brantley, P., & Garrett, V. D. (1993). Psychobiological approaches to health and disease. In P. B. Sutker & H. E. Adams (Eds.), *Comprehensive handbook of psychopathology* (2nd ed.). New York: Plenum.

Brauer, M. (2001). Intergroup perception in the social context: The effects of social status and group membership on perceived out group homogeneity and ethnocentrism. *Journal of Experimental Social Psychology, 37,* 15–31.

Bray, J. H., & Berger, S. H. (1993). Developmental Issues in Step Families Research Project: Family relationships and parent-child interactions. *Journal of Family Psychology, 7,* 76–90.

Brayfield, A. H., & Crockett, W. H. (1955). Employee attitudes and employee performance. *Psychological Bulletin, 52,* 396–424.

Bredy, T., Weaver, I., Champagne, F., & Meaney, M. (2001). Stress, maternal care, and neural development in the rat. In C. A. Shaw & J. C. McEachern (Eds.). *Toward a theory of neuroplasticity.* Philadelphia: Psychology Press.

Breedlove, S. M. (1992). Sexual differentiation of brain and behavior. In J. B. Becker, S. M. Breedlove, & D. Crews (Eds.), *Behavioral endocrinology.* Cambridge, MA: MIT Press.

Brehm, J. W., & Self, E. A. (1989). The intensity of motivation. *Annual Review of Psychology, 40,* 109 131.

Breland, K., & Breland, M. (1961). The misbehavior of organisms. *American Psychologist, 16,* 681–684.

Breland, K., & Breland, M. (1966). *Animal behavior.* New York: Macmillan.

Bremner, J. D. (2000). Neurobiology of posttraumatic stress disorder. In G. Fink (Ed.), *Encyclopedia of stress.* San Diego: Academic Press.

Bresnahan, M. J., Levine, T. R., Shearman, S. M., Lee, S. Y., Park, C. Y., & Kiyomiya, T. (2005). A multimethod multitrait validity assessment of self-construal in Japan, Korea, and the United States. *Human Communication Research, 31,* 33–59.

Brewer, K. R., & Wann, D. L. (1998). Observational learning effectiveness as a function of model characteristics: Investigating the importance of social power. *Social Behavior and Personality, 26,* 1–10.

Brickman, P., Coates, D., & Janoff-Bulman (1978). Lottery winners and accident victims: Is happiness relative? *Journal of Personality and Social Psychology, 36,* 917–927.

Bridgeman, B. (2003). *Psychology and evolution: The origins of mind.* Thousand Oaks, CA: Sage Publications.

Brief, A. P., Butcher, A. H., George, J. M., & Link, K. E. (1993). Integrating bottom-up and top-down theories of subjective well being: The case of health. *Journal of Personality and Social Psychology,* 64, 646–653.

Briere, J., & Lanktree, C. (1983). Sex role-related effects of sex bias in language. *Sex Roles, 9,* 625–632.

Brinton, R. D., & Berger, T. W. (2000). Hippocampal neurons. In G. Fink (Ed.), *Encyclopedia of stress.* San Diego: Academic Press.

Brislin, R. (1993). *Understanding culture's influence on behavior.* Fort Worth, TX: Harcourt Brace Jovanovich.

Broberg, D. J., & Bernstein, I. L. (1987). Candy as a scapegoat in the prevention of food aversions in children receiving chemotherapy. *Cancer, 60,* 2344–2347.

Brody, G. H., & Stoneman, Z. (1985). Peer imitation: An examination of status and competence hypotheses. *Journal of Genetic Psychology, 146,* 161–170.

Brody, G. H., Neubaum, E., & Forehand, R. (1988). Serial marriages: A heuristic analysis of an emerging family form. *Psychological Bulletin, 103,* 211–222.

Brody, J. E. (1995, September 14). Even moderate weight gain can be risky, study finds. *New York Times,* A1, A11.

Bronzaft, A. L., Ahern, K. D., McGinn, R., O'Connor, J., & Savino, B. (1998). Aircraft noise: A potential health hazard. *Environment and Behavior, 30,* 101–113.

Brooks-Gunn, J., & Warren, M. P. (1985). Measuring physical status and timing in early adolescence: A developmental perspective. *Journal of Youth and Adolescence, 14,* 163–184.

Broughton, J. (1981). The genetic psychology of James Mark Baldwin. *American Psychologist, 36,* 396–407.

Brown, A. L. (1997). Transforming schools into communities of thinking and learning about serious matters. *American Psychologist, 52,* 399–413.

Brown, A. L., Bransford, J. D., Ferrara, R. A., & Campione, J. C. (1983). Learning, remembering, and understanding. In P. Mussen (Ed.), *Handbook of child psychology: Vol. 3. Cognitive development.* New York: Wiley.

Brown, A. S. (1991). A review of the tip-of-the-tongue experience. *Psychological Bulletin, 109,* 204–223.

Brown, B. B., Clasen, D. R., & Eicher, S. A. (1986). Perceptions of peer pressure, peer conformity dispositions, and self-reported behavior among adolescents. *Developmental Psychology, 22,* 521–530.

Brown, E., Deffenbacher, K., & Sturgill, W. (1977). Memory for faces and the circumstances of encounter. *Journal of Applied Psychology, 62,* 311–318.

Brown, G. W., & Harris, T. O. (1978). *Social origins of depression.* London: Tavistock Press.

Brown, J. A. (1958). Some tests of the decay theory of immediate memory. *Quarterly Journal of Experimental Psychology, 10,* 12–21.

Brown, J. D. (1998). *The self.* Boston: McGraw-Hill.

Brown, J. D., & McGill, K. L. (1989). The cost of good fortune: When positive life events produce negative health consequences. *Journal of Personality and Social Psychology, 57,* 1103–1110.

Brown, J. M. (1998). Self-regulation and the addictive behaviors. In W. R. Miller & N. Heather (Eds.), *Treating addictive behaviors* (2nd ed.). New York: Plenum.

Brown, L. S. (1994). *Subversive dialogues: Theory in feminist therapy.* New York: Basic Books.

Brown, L. S. (2000). The controversy concerning recovered memory of traumatic events. In A. Y. Shalev, R. Yehuda, & A. C. McFarlane (Eds.), *International handbook of human response to trauma.* New York: Kluwer Academic/Plenum.

Brown, N. O. (1959). *Life against death.* New York: Random House.

Brown, R. (1958). How shall a thing be called? *Psychological Review, 65*(1), 14–21.

Brown, R., & Kulik, J. (1977). Flashbulb memories. *Cognition, 5,* 73–99.

Brown, S. L., & Booth, A. (1996). Cohabitation versus marriage: A comparison of relationship quality. *Journal of Marriage and the Family, 58,* 668–678.

Brown, T. A., Di-Nardo, P. A., Lehman, C. L., & Campbell, L. A. (2001). Reliability of DSM-IV anxiety and mood disorders: Implications for the classification of emotional disorders. *Journal of Abnormal Psychology, 110,* 49–58.

Brown, T. S., & Wallace, P. (1980). *Physiological psychology.* New York: Academic Press.

Brownell, K. D. (1994). *The LEARN program for weight control.* Dallas: American Health.

Brownell, K. D., & Rodin, J. (1994). The dieting maelstrom: Is it possible and advisable to lose weight? *American Psychologist, 49,* 781–791.

Bruce, T. J., & Sanderson, W. C. (1998). *Specific phobias: Clinical applications of evidence-based psychotherapy.* Northvale, NJ: Jason Aronson.

Bruch, H. (1973). *Eating disorders: Obesity, anorexia nervosa, and the person within.* New York: Basic Books.

Bruck, M., & Ceci, S. J. (1999). The suggestibility of children's memory. *Annual Review of Psychology, 50,* 419–439.

Bruck, M., Ceci, S. J., & Francoeur, E. (2000). Children's use of anatomically detailed dolls to report genital touching in a medical examination: Developmental and gender comparisons. *Journal of Experimental Psychology: Applied, 6,* 74–83.

Bruck, M., Ceci, S. J., & Hembrooke, H. (1998). Reliability and credibility of young children's reports: From research to policy and practice. *American Psychologist, 53,* 136–151.

Bruck, M. Ceci, S.J., & Hembrooke, H. (2002). The nature of children's true and false narratives. Developmental Review, 22, 520-554.

Bruck, M., Ceci, S. J., Francoeur, E., & Barr, R. (1995). "I hardly cried when I got my shot": Influencing children's reports about a visit to their pediatrician. *Child Development, 66,* 193–208.

Bruederl, J., Diekmann, A., & Engelhardt, H. (1997). Erhoeht eine Probeehe das Scheidungrisiko? Eine empirische Untersuchung mit dem Familiensurvey./ Does a trial marriage increase divorce risk? Empirical study of the Families Survey. *Koelner Zeitschrift fuer Soziologie und Sozialpsychologie, 49,* 205–222.

Bruunk, B., & Gibbons, F. X. (Eds.) (1997). *Health, coping, and well-being: Perspectives from social comparison theory.* Mahwah, NJ: Erlbaum.

Bryan, J., III. (1986). *Hodgepodge: A commonplace book.* New York: Ballantine.

Bryant, R. A., & Harvey, A. G. (2000). *Acute stress disorder: A handbook of theory, assessment, and treatment.* Washington, DC: American Psychological Association.

Bucci, W. (1997). *Psychoanalysis and cognitive science: A multiple code theory.* New York: Guilford Press.

Buchanan, C. M., Eccles, J. S., & Becker, J. B. (1992). Are adolescents the victims of raging hormones? Evidence for activational effects of hormones on moods and behaviors at adolescence. *Psychological Bulletin, 111,* 62–107.

Buck, L., & Axel, R. (1991). A novel multigene family may encode odorant receptors: A molecular basis for odor recognition. *Cell, 65,* 175–187.

Buck, R. & Ginsburg, B. (1991). Spontaneous communication and altruism: The communicative gene hypothesis. In M. S. Clark (Ed.), *Prosocial behavior.* Newbury Park, CA: Sage.

Buckingham, M., & Coffman, C. (1999). *Gallup's discoveries about great managers and great workplaces.* The Workplace Column. [Online]. Available: http://www.gallup. com/poll/managing/grtwrkplc.asp

Buergin, D. (1999). Psychosocial failure to thrive. In U. Eiholzer, F. Haverkamp, & Voss, L. D. (Eds.), *Growth, stature, and psychosocial well-being.* Seattle, WA: Hogrefe & Huber.

Buet, V. I., & Harris, T. (1994). The third national health and nutrition examination survey: Contributing data. *Gerontologist, 34,* 486–490.

Bullier, J. (2002). Neural basis of vision. In H. Pashler & S. Yantis (Eds.), *Steven's handbook of experimental psychology: Vol. 1. Sensation and perception* (3rd ed.). New York: Wiley.

Bumpass, L. L., & Sweet, J. A. (1989). National estimates of cohabitation. *Demography, 26,* 615–625.

Burd, L., Cotsonas-Hassler, T., & Martsolf, J. (2003). Recognition and management of fetal alcohol syndrome. Neurotoxicology and Teratology, 25, 681–688.

Bureau of the Census. (2000). *Statistical abstract of the U.S.* Washington, DC: U.S. Government Printing Office.

Burger, J. M. (1991). Changes in attributions over time: The ephemeral fundamental attribution error. *Social Cognition, 9,* 182–193.

Burger, J. M. (1999). Personality and control. In V. J. Derlega, B. A. Winstead, & W. H. Jones (Eds.), *Personality: Contemporary theory and research.* Chicago: Nelson Hall.

Burger, J. M. (2000). *Personality* (5th ed). Belmont, CA: Wadsworth.

Burger, J. M., & Petty, R. E. (1981). The low-ball compliance technique: Task or person commitment? *Journal of Personality and Social Psychology, 40,* 492–500.

Burger, J. M., Horita, M., Kinoshita, L., Roberts, K., & Vera, C. (1997). Effects of time on the norm of reciprocity. *Basic and Applied Social Psychology, 19,* 91–100.

Burgess, A. W., & Holmstrom, L. I. (1974). Rape trauma syndrome. *American Journal of Psychiatry, 131,* 981–986.

Burke, K. C., Burke, J. D., Rae, D. S., & Regier, D. A. (1991). Comparing age at onset of major depression and other psychiatric disorders by birth cohorts in five U.S. community populations. *Archives of General Psychiatry, 48,* 789–795.

Burkholder, G. J., Evers, K. A., Burbank, P. M., & Riebe, D. (2002). Application of the transtheoretical model to several problem behaviors. In P. M. Burbank and D. Riebe (Eds.). *Promoting exercise and behavior change in older adults: Interventions with the transtheoretical model,* 85–145. New York, NY: Springer Publishing Co.

Burnam, M. A., Hough, R., Escobar, J. I., & Karno, N. (1987). Six months prevalence rates for specific psychiatric disorders among Mexican-American and non-Hispanic whites in Los Angeles. *Archives of General Psychiatry, 44,* 687–694.

Burns, M. E., Arshavsky, V. Y. (2005). Beyond counting photons: Trials and trends in vertebrate visual transduction. *Neuron, 48,* 387–401.

Burns, M. O., & Seligman, M. E. P. (1989). Explanatory style across the life span: Evidence for stability over 52 years. *Journal of Personality and Social Psychology, 56,* 471–477.

Burns, M. O., & Seligman, M. E. P. (1991). Explanatory style, helplessness, and depression. In C. R. Snyder & D. R. Forsyth (Eds.), *Handbook of social and clinical psychology: The health perspective.* New York: Pergamon.

Burnstein, E. (1983). Persuasion as argument processing. In M. Brandstatter, J. H. Davis, & G. Stocker-Kreichgauer (Eds.), *Group decision processes.* London: Academic Press.

Burnstein, E., Crandall, C., & Kitayama, S. (1994). Some neo-Darwinian decision rules for altruism: Weighing cues for inclusive fitness as a function of the biological importance of the decision. *Journal of Personality & Social Psychology, 67,* 773–789.

Burroughs, S. M., & Eby, L. T. (1998). Psychological sense of community at work: A measurement system and explanatory framework. *Journal of Community Psychology, 26,* 509–532.

Burton, J. W. (1969). *Conflict and communication: The use of controlled communication in international relations.* London: Macmillan.

Busey, T. A., Tunnicliff, J. J., Loftus, G. R., & Loftus, E. F. (2000). Accounts of the confidence-accuracy relation in recognition memory. *Psychonomic Bulletin and Review, 7,* 26–48.

Bushman, B. J. (2002). Does venting anger feed or extinguish the flame? Catharsis, rumination, distraction, anger and aggressive responding. *Personality and Social Psychology, 28,* 724–731.

Bushman, B. J., & Bonacci, A. M. (2002). Violence and sex impair memory for television ads. *Journal of Applied Psychology, 87,* 557–564.

Bushman, B. J., Wang, M., Anderson, C. A. (2005). Is the curve relating temperature to aggression linear or curvilinear: Assaults and temperature in Minneapolis reexamined. *Journal of Personality and Social Psychology, 89*(1), 62–65.

Bushnell, I. W. R., Sai, F., & Mullin, J. T. (1989). Neonatal recognition of the mother's face. *British Journal of Developmental Psychology, 7,* 3–15.

Buske-Kirschbaum, A., Kirschbaum, C., & Hellhammer, D. H. (1994). Conditioned modulation of NK cells in humans: Alteration of cell activity and cell number by conditioning protocols. *Psychologische Beitraege, 36,* 100–111.

Buske-Kirschbaum, A., Kirschbaum, C., Stierle, H., & Lehnert, H. (1992). Conditioned increase of natural killer cell activity (NKCA) in humans. *Psychosomatic Medicine, 54,* 123–132.

Buss, D. M. (1985). Human mate selection. *American Scientist, 73,* 47–51.

Buss, D. M. (1989). Sex differences in human mate preferences: Evolutionary hypotheses tested in 37 cultures. *Behavioral and Brain Sciences, 12,* 1–49.

Buss, D. M. (1991). Evolutionary personality theory. *Annual Review of Psychology, 42,* 459–491.

Buss, D. M. (1998). Sexual strategies theory: Historical origins and current status. *Journal of Sex Research, 35,* 19–31.

Buss, D. M. (1999). Human nature and individual differences: The evolution of human personality. In L. A. Pervin & O. P. John (Eds.), *Handbook of personality: Theory and research.* New York: Guilford Press.

Buss, D. M. (2000). *The dangerous passion: Why jealousy is as necessary as love and sex.* New York: Free Press.

Buss, D. M. (2005). Evolutionary psychology: A new paradigm for psychological science. *Psychological Inquiry, 6,* 1–30.

Buss, D. M., Abbott, M., Angleitner, A., & Asherian, A. (1990). International preferences in selecting mates: A study of 37 cultures. *Journal of Cross-Cultural Psychology, 21,* 5–47.

Buss, D. M., & Dedden, L. A. (1990). Derogation of competitors. *Journal of Social and Personal Relationships, 7,* 395–422.

Buunk, B. P., & Dijkstra, P. (2001). Rationalizations and defensive attributions for high-risk sex among heterosexuals. *Patient Education and Counseling, 45,* 127–132.

Buysse, D. J., Frank, E., Lowe, K. K., Cherry, C. R. (1997). Electroencephalographic sleep correlates of episode and vulnerability to recurrence in depression. *Biological Psychiatry, 41,* 406–418.

Byer, C. O., Shainberg, L. W., & Galliano, G. (1999). *Dimensions of human sexuality* (5th ed.). Boston: McGraw-Hill.

Byne, W. (1997). Why we cannot conclude that sexual orientation is primarily a biological phenomenon. *Journal of Homosexuality, 34,* 73–80.

Byrne, D. (1997). An overview (and underview) of research and theory within the attraction paradigm. *Journal of Social and Personal Relationships, 14,* 417–431.

Byrne, D., & Greendlinger, V. (1989). *Need for affiliation as a predictor of classroom friendships.* Unpublished manuscript, State University of New York at Albany.

Byrne, D., & Nelson, D. (1965). Attraction as a linear function of proportion of positive reinforcements. *Journal of Personality and Social Psychology, 1,* 659–663.

Byrne, D., & Osland, J. A. (2000). Sexual fantasy and erotica/pornography: Internal and external imagery. In L. T. Szuchman & F. Muscarella, (Eds). *Psychological perspectives on human sexuality.* New York: Wiley.

Byrne, D., Clore, G. L., & Smeaton, G. (1986). The attraction hypothesis: Do similar attitudes affect anything? *Journal of Personality and Social Psychology, 51,* 1167–1170.

Byrne, D., Ervin, C. R., & Lamberth, J. (1970). Continuity between the experimental study of attraction and real-life computer dating. *Journal of Personality and Social Psychology, 16,* 157–165.

Cabeza, R., & Nyberg, L. (2000). Imaging cognition II: An empirical review of 275 PET and fMRI studies. *Journal of Cognitive Neuroscience, 12,* 1–47.

Cacioppo, J. T., & Gardner, W. L. (1999). Emotion. *Annual Review of Psychology, 50,* 101–124.

Cacioppo, J. T., Petty, R. E., & Morris, K. J. (1983). Effects of need for cognition on message evaluation, recall, and persuasion. *Journal of Personality and Social Psychology, 45,* 805–818.

Cacioppo, J. T., Petty, R. E., Feinstein, J. A., & Jarvis, W. B. G. (1996). Dispositional differences in cognitive motivation: The life and times of individuals varying in need for cognition. *Psychological Bulletin, 119,* 197–253.

Cadieu, N., & Cadieu, J. C. (1998). Is food recognition in an unfamiliar environment a long-term effect of stimulus or local enhancement? A study in the juvenile canary. *Behavioural Processes, 43,* 183–192.

Cahill, L., Babinsky, R., Markowitsch, H. J., & McGaugh, J. L. (1995). The amygdala and emotional memory. *Nature, 377,* 295–296.

Cahn, B. R. & Polich, J. (2006). Meditation states and traits: EEG, ERP, and neuroimaging studies. *Psychological Bulletin, 132,* 180–211.

Cain, D. J., & Seeman, J. (Eds.). (2002). *Humanistic psychotherapies: Handbook of research and practice.* Washington, DC: American Psychological Association.

Cairns, H. (1952). Disturbances of consciousness in lesions of the mid-brain and diencephalon. *Brain, 75,* 107–114.

Caldji, C., Diorio, J., & Meaney, M. J. (2000). Variations in maternal care in infancy regulate the development of stress reactivity. *Biological Psychiatry, 48,* 1164–1174.

Caldwell, A. B. (1994). *The profile of Jeffrey Dahmer* (videotape). Los Angeles: Caldwell Report, Inc.

Calhoun, J. B. (1962). Population density and social pathology. *Scientific American, 206*(2), 139–148.

Calignano, A., LaRana, G., Giuffrida, A., & Peiomelli, D. (1998). Control of pain initiation by endogenous cannabinoids. *Nature, 394,* 277–281.

Calkins, S. D., & Johnson, M. C. (1998). Toddler regulation of distress to frustrating events: Temperamental and maternal correlates. *Infant Behavior and Development, 21,* 379–395.

Camilleri, C., & Malewska-Peyre, H. (1997). Socialization and identity strategies. In J. W. Berry, P. R. Dasen, & T. S. Saraswathi (Eds.), *Handbook of cross-cultural psychology: Basic processes and human development* (2nd ed, Vol. 2). Boston: Allyn & Bacon.

Campbell, S. S. (1993). Seasonal effects on sleep. In M. A. Carskadon (Ed.), *Encyclopedia of sleep and dreaming.* New York: Macmillan.

Campfield, L. A. (1997). Metabolic and hormonal controls of food intake: Highlights of the last 25 years: 1972–1997. *Appetite, 29,* 135–152.

Campfield, L. A., Smith, F. J., & Stricker, E. M. (Eds.) (1990). Systemic factors in the control of food intake: Evidence for patterns as signals. In E. M. Stricker (Ed.), *Neurobiology of food and fluid intake.* New York: Plenum.

Campfield, L. A., Smith, F. J., Rosenbaum, M., & Hirsch, J. (1996). Human eating: Evidence for a physiological basis using a modified paradigm. *Neuroscience and Biobehavioral Reviews, 20,* 133–1137.

Canadian Council on Social Development (1997). *The progress of Canada's children.* Ottawa: Canadian Council on Social Development.

Canadian Institutes for Health Information (2007). *National Health Expenditure Trends, 1975–2007,* Ottawa: CIHI.

Canivez, G. L., & Watkins, M. W. (1998). Long-term stability of the Wechsler Intelligence Scale for Children–Third Edition. *Psychological Assessment, 10,* 285–291.

Cannon, W. B. (1929). *Bodily changes in pain, hunger, fear, and rage.* New York: Appleton-Century.

Cannon, W. B. (1932). *The wisdom of the body.* New York: W. W. Norton.

Cannon, W. B. (1942). "Voodoo" death. *American Anthropologist, 44,* 169–181.

Cannon, W. B., & Washburn, A. L. (1912). An explanation of hunger. *American Journal of Physiology, 29,* 441–454.

Capon, N., & Kuhn, D. (1979). Logical reasoning in the super-market: Adult females' use of proportional reasoning strategy in an everyday context. *Developmental Psychology, 15,* 450–452.

Caporael, L. R. (1997). The evolution of truly social cognition: The core configurations model. *Personality and Social Psychology Review, 1,* 276–298.

Cardeña, E., Lynn, S. J., & Krippner, S. (2000). Introduction: Anomalous experiences in perspective. In E. Cardeña, S. J. Lynn, & S. Krippner (Eds.), *Varieties of anomalous experience: Examining the scientific evidence.* Washington, DC: American Psychological Association.

Carew, T. J., & Kandel, E. R. (1973). Acquisition and retention of long-term habituation in *Aplysia:* Correlation of behavioral and cellular processes. *Science, 182,* 1158–1160.

Carew, T. J., Marcus, E. A., Nolen, T. G., & Rankin, C. H. (1990). The development of learning and memory in *Aplysia.* In J. L. McGaugh, N. M. Weinberger, & G. Lynch (Eds.), *Brain organization and memory: Cells, systems, and circuits.* New York: Oxford University Press.

Carey, F. (1977). The child as a word learner. In M. Halle, J. Bresnan, & G. Miller (Eds.), *Linguistic theory and psychological reality.* Cambridge, MA: MIT Press.

Carlin, A. S., Hoffman, H. G., & Weghorst, S. (1997). Virtual reality and tactile augmentation in the treatment of spider phobia: A case report. *Behaviour Research and Therapy, 35,* 153–158.

Carlson, C. (2000). ADHD is overdiagnosed. In R. L. Atkinson, R. C. Atkinson, E. E. Smith, D. J. Bem, & S. Nolen-Hoeksema, *Hilgard's introduction to psychology* (13th ed.). Ft. Worth, TX: Harcourt Brace.

Carlson, J. G., & Hatfield, E. (1992). *Psychology of emotion.* Ft. Worth, TX: Harcourt Brace Jovanovich.

Carlson, S. M., Moses, L. J., & Hix, H. R. (1998). The role of inhibitory processes in young children's difficulties with deception and false belief. *Child Development, 69,* 672–691.

Carney, L. H. (2002). Neural basis of audition. In H. Pashler & S.Yantis (Eds.), *Steven's handbook of experimental psychology: Vol. 1. Sensation and perception* (3rd ed.). New York: Wiley.

Carney, R. N., Levin, J. R., & Levin, M. E. (1994). Enhancing the psychology of memory by enhancing memory of psychology. *Teaching of Psychology, 21,* 171–174.

Carnicero, J. A. C., Perez-Lopez, J., Salinas, M. D. C. G., & Martinez-Fuentes, M. T. (2000). A longitudinal study of temperament in infancy: Stability and convergence of measures. *European Journal of Personality, 14,* 21–37.

Carpenter, R., & Robson, J. (Eds.) (1999). *Vision research: A practical guide to laboratory methods.* New York: Oxford University Press.

Carpenter, W. T., Jr., & Heinrichs, D. W. (1983). Early intervention, time-limited, targeted pharmacotherapy of schizophrenia. *Schizophrenia Bulletin, 9,* 533–542.

Carr, D., Friedman, M A. (2005). Is obesity stigmatizing? Body weight, perceived discrimination, and psychological well-being in the United States. *Journal of Health and Social Behavior, 46(3),* 244–259.

Carrere, S., Buehlman, K. T., Gottman, J. M., Coan, J. A., & Ruckstuhl, L. (2000). Predicting marital stability and divorce in newlywed couples. *Journal of Family Psychology, 14,* 42–58.

Carruthers, M. (1981). Field studies: Emotion and beta-blockade. In M. J. Christie & P. G. Mellett (Eds.), *Foundations of psychosomatics.* Chichester, England: Wiley.

Carson, R. C., Butcher, J. N., & Coleman, J. C. (1988). *Abnormal psychology and modern life* (8th ed.). Glenview, IL: Scott, Foresman.

Carter, S. J., & Cassaday, H. J. (1998). State dependent retrieval and chlorpheniramine. *Human Psychopharmacology: Clinical and Experimental, 13,* 513–523.

Cartledge, B. (1997). *Mind, brain and the environment.* New York: Oxford University Press.

Cartwright, R. D. (1977). *Night life: Explorations in dreaming.* Englewood Cliffs, NJ: Prentice-Hall.

Cartwright, R. D. (1991). Dreams that work: The relation of dream incorporation to adaptation to stressful events. *Dreaming: Journal of the Association for the Study of Dreams, 1,* 3–9.

Carver, C. S., & Scheier, M. F. (1988). *Perspectives on personality.* Boston: Allyn & Bacon.

Carver, C. S., & Scheier, M. F. (2000). *Perspectives on personality* (4th ed.). Boston: Allyn & Bacon.

Carver, C. S., Scheier, M. F., & Weintraub, J. K. (1989). Assessing coping strategies: A theoretically based approach. *Journal of Personality and Social Psychology, 56,* 267–283.

Carver, C. S., & White, T. L. (1994). Behavioral inhibition, behavioral activation and affective responses to impending reward and punishment: The BIS/BAS scales. *Journal of Personality and Social Psychology, 67,* 319–333.

Caryl, P. G. (1994). Early event-related potentials correlate with inspection time and intelligence. *Intelligence, 18,* 15–46.

Case, R. (1987). The structure and process of intellectual development. *International Journal of Psychology, 22,* 571–607.

Case, R. (1996). Modeling the process of conceptual change in a continuously evolving hierarchical system. *Monographs of the Society for Research in Child Development, 61,* 283–295.

Case, R., Okamoto, Y., Griffin, S., McKeough, A., Bleiker, C., Henderson, B., & Mara, K. (1996). The role of central conceptual structures in the development of children's thought. *Monographs of the Society for Research in Child Development, 61,* (1-2, Serial # 246).

Caspi, A., & Herbener, E. S. (1990). Continuity and change: Assortative marriage and the consistency of personality in adulthood. *Journal of Personality and Social Psychology, 58,* 250–258.

Caspi, A., & Roberts, B. W. (1999). Personality continuity and change across the life course. In L. A. Pervin & O. P. John (Eds.), *Handbook of personality: Theory and research.* New York: Guilford Press.

Caspi, A., Elder, G. H., & Bem, D. J. (1988). Moving away from the world: Life course patterns of shy children. *Developmental Psychology, 24,* 824–831.

Catalano, R., Novaco, R. W., McConnell, W. (2002). Layoffs and violence revisitied. *Aggressive Behavior, 28(3),* 233–247.

Catania, C. A. (1998). *Learning* (4th ed.). Upper Saddle River, NJ: Prentice Hall.

Catchpole, C. K., & Rowell, A. (1993). Song sharing and local dialects in a population of the European wren Troglodytes troglodytes. *Behaviour, 125,* 67–78.

Cattell, R. B. (1965). *The scientific analysis of personality.* Chicago: Aldine.

Cattell, R. B. (1971). *Abilities: Their growth, structure, and action.* Boston: Houghton Mifflin.

Cattell, R. B. (1990). Advances in Cattellian personality theory. In L. A. Pervin (Ed.), *Handbook of personality: Theory and research.* New York: Guilford Press.

Cattell, R. B. (1998). Where is intelligence? Some answers from the triadic theory. In J. J. McArdler, R. W. Woodcock, & et al. (Eds.), *Human cognitive abilities in theory and practice.* Mahwah, NJ: Erlbaum.

Caulfield, R. (2000). Beneficial effects of tactile stimulation on early development. *Early Childhood Education Journal, 27,* 255–257.

Ceci, S. J. (1996). *On intelligence: A bioecological treatise on intellectual development.* Cambridge, MA: Harvard University Press.

Ceci, S. J., & Huffman, M. L. C. (1997). How suggestible are preschool children? Cognitive and social factors. *Journal of the American Academy of Child and Adolescent Psychiatry 36,* 948–958.

Ceci, S. J., Bruck, M., & Battin, D. B. (2000). The suggestibility of children's testimony. In D. F. Bjorklund (Ed.), *False-memory creation in children and adults: Theory, research, and implications.* Mahwah, NJ: Erlbaum.

Ceci, S. J., Loftus, E. F., Leichtman, M. D., & Bruck, M. (1994). The possible role of source misattributions in the creation of false beliefs among preschoolers. *International Journal of Clinical and Experimental Hypnosis, 42,* 304–320.

Centers for Disease Control and Prevention (1994). *Addressing emerging infectious disease threats: A prevention strategy for the United States.* Washington, DC: Author.

Centers for Disease Control and Prevention (1996). *National and international HIV seroprevalence surveys—Summary of results.* Washington, DC: Author.

Centers for Disease Control and Prevention (CDC) (1996, September 27). Youth risk behavior surveillance—United States, 1995. *Morbidity and Mortality Weekly Report, 45*(SS-4). Washington, DC: Author.

Centers for Disease Control and Prevention (CDC) (1997). *Fertility, family planning, and women's health: New data from the 1995 National Survey on Family Growth* (Series 23, No. 19). Washington DC: Author.

Centers for Disease Control and Prevention (CDC) (2002). *Statistics on addictive behaviors.* Atlanta, GA: Author.

Centers for Disease Control and Prevention (CDC) (2003). *HIV/AIDS statistics.* Atlanta, GA: Author.

Cervone, D. (1992). The role of self-referent cognitions in goal-setting, motivation, and performance. In M. Rabinowitz (Ed.), *Applied Cognition.* New York: Ablex.

Cervone, D., & Shoda, Y. (1999). *The coherence of personality: Social-cognitive bases of consistency, variability, and organization.* New York: Guilford Press.

Chaiken, S. (1987). The heuristic model of persuasion. In M. P. Zanna, J. M. Olson, & C. P. Herman (Eds.), *Social influence: The Ontario symposium* (Vol. 5). Hillsdale, NJ: Erlbaum.

Chaiken, S., & Maheswaran, D. (1994). Heuristic processing can bias systematic processing: Effects of source credibility, argument ambiguity, and task importance on attitude judgment. *Journal of Personality and Social Psychology, 66,* 460–473.

Chalmers, D. J. (1995). The puzzle of conscious experience. *Scientific American, 273*(6): 80–86.

Chambless, D. L., & Hollon, S. D. (1998). Defining empirically supported therapies. *Journal of Consulting and Clinical Psychology, 66,* 7–18.

Chan, Z. C. Y. & Ma, J. L. C. (2002). Family themes of food refusal: Disciplining the body and punishing the family. *Health Care for Women International, 23,* 49–58.

Chang, E. C. (1996). Cultural differences in optimism, pessimism, and coping: Predictors of subsequent adjustment in American and Caucasian American college students. *Journal of Counseling Psychology, 43,* 113–123.

Chang, E. C. (1998). Dispositional optimism and primary and secondary appraisal of a stressor: Controlling for confounding influences and relations to coping and psychological and physical adjustment. *Journal of Personality and Social Psychology, 74,* 1109–1120.

Chapell, M. S., & Overton, W. F. (1998). Development of logical reasoning in the context of parental style and test anxiety. *Merrill Palmer Quarterly, 44,* 141–156.

Chaplin, T. M., Cole, P. M. & Zahn-Waxler, C. (2005). Parental socialization of emotion expression: Gender differences and relations to child adjustment. *Emotion, 5,* 80-88.

Chappell, M., & Humphreys, M. S. (1994). An auto-associative neural network for sparse representations: Analysis and application to models of recognition and cued recall. *Psychological Review, 101,* 103–128.

Chartrand, T. L., & Bargh, J. A. (2000). *Consequences of automatic motivation for current mood.* Manuscript in preparation, Ohio State University.

Chartrand, T., Pinckert, S., & Burger, J. M. (1999). When manipulation backfires: The effects of time delay and requester on the foot-in-the-door technique. *Journal of Applied Social Psychology, 29,* 211–221.

Chase, W. G. and Simon, H. A. (1973). Perception in chess. *Cognitive Psychology, 4,* 55–81.

Chen, C., Greenberger, E., Leter, J., Dong, Q., & Guo, M. S. (1998). A cross-cultural study of family and peer correlates of adolescent misconduct. *Developmental Psychology, 34,* 770–781.

Chen, H., Charlat, O., Tartaglia, L. A., Woolf, E. A., Weng, X., & Ellis, S. J. (1996). Evidence that the diabetes gene encodes the leptin receptor: Identification of a mutation in the leptin receptor gene in db/db mice. *Cell, 84,* 491–495.

Chen, H. & Lan, W. (2006). Adolescents' perceptions of their parents; academic expectations: Comparison of American, Chinese-American, and Chinese high school students. *Family Therapy, 33,* 113–118.

Chen, S., English, T., Peng, K. (2006). Self-verification and contextualized self-views. *Personality and Social Psychology Bulletin, 32(7),* 930–942.

Chen, S. C. (1937). Social modification of the activity of ants in nest-building. *Physiological Zoology, 10,* 420–436.

Cheng, D. T., Knight, D. C., Smith, C. N., Helmstetter, F. J. (2006). Human amygdala activity during the expression of fear responses. *Behavioral Neuroscience, 120,* 1187–1195.

Chenoweth, D. (2002). *Evaluating worksite health promotion.* Champaign, IL: Human Kinetics.

Cherlin, A. J., & Furstenberg, F. F. (1994). Stepfamilies in the United States: A reconsideration. *Annual Review of Sociology, 20,* 359–381.

Chi, M. T. H. (1997). Creativity: Shifting across ontological categories flexibly. In T. B. Ward & S. M. Smith (Eds.), *Creative thought: An investigation of conceptual structures and processes.* Washington, DC: American Psychological Association.

Chiappelli, F. (2000). Immune suppression. In G. Fink (Ed.), *Encyclopedia of stress.* San Diego: Academic Press.

Chiles, J. A., & Strosahl, K. D. (1995). *The suicidal patient: Principles of assessment, treatment, and case management.* Washington, DC: American Psychiatric Press.

Chiriboga, D. A. (1989). Mental health at the midpoint: Crisis, challenge, or relief? In S. Hunter & M. Sundel (Eds.), *Midlife myths: Issues, findings, and practice implications.* Newbury Park, CA: Sage Publications.

Chisholm, K. (1998). A three year follow-up of attachment and indiscriminate friendliness in children adopted from Romanian orphanages. *Child Development, 69,* 1092–1106.

Choca, J. P., Shanley, L. A., & Van Denburg, E. (1992). *Interpretive guide to the Millon Clinical Multiaxial Inventory.* Washington, DC: American Psychological Association.

Choi, I., Dalal, R., Kim Prieto, C., & Park, H. (2003). Culture and judgement of causal relevance. *Journal of Personality and Social Psychology, 84,* 46–59.

Chomsky, N. (1965). *Aspects of a theory of syntax.* Cambridge, MA: MIT Press.

Chomsky, N. (1972). *Language and mind.* New York: Harcourt.

Chomsky, N. (1987). Language in a psychological setting. *Sophia Linguistic Working Papers in Linguistics, 22.* Tokyo: Sophia University.

Christianson, S. A., & Nilsson, L. G. (1989). Hysterical amnesia: A case of aversively motivated isolation of memory. In T. Archer & L. G. Nilsson (Eds.), *Aversion, avoidance, and anxiety: Perspectives on aversively motivated behavior.* Hillsdale, NJ: Erlbaum.

Christopherson, E. R., & Mortweet, S. L. (2001). *Treatments that work with children: Empirically supported strategies for managing childhood problems.* Washington, DC: American Psychological Association.

Christy, C. A., & Voigt, H. (1994). Bystander responses to public episodes of child abuse. *Journal of Applied Social Psychology, 24,* 824–847.

Chwalisz, K., Diener, E., & Gallagher, D. (1988). Autonomic arousal feedback and emotional experience: Evidence from the spinal cord injured. *Journal of Personality and Social Psychology, 54,* 820–828.

Churchill, J. D., Galvez, R., Colcombe, S., Swain, R. A., Kramer, A. F. & Greenough, W. T. (2002). Exercise, experience and the aging brain. *Neurobiology of Aging, 23,* 941–955.

Chwilla, D. J., & Kolk, H. H. J. (2002). Three step priming in lexical decision. *Memory and Cognition, 30,* 217–225.

Cialdini, R. B. (1988). *Influence: Science and practice* (2nd ed.). Glenview, IL: Scott, Foresman.

Cialdini, R. B., & Trost, M. R. (1998). Social influence: Social norms, conformity and compliance. In D. T. Gilbert, S. T. Fiske, & G. Lindzey (Eds.), *The handbook of social psychology* (4th ed., Vol. 2). Boston: McGraw-Hill.

Cialdini, R. B., Brown, S. L., Lewis, B. P., & Luce, C. (1997). Reinterpreting the empathy-altruism relationship: When one into one equals oneness. *Journal of Personality and Social Psychology, 73,* 481–494.

Cialdini, R. B., Cacioppo, J. T., Bassett, R., & Miller, J. A. (1978). Lowball procedure for producing compliance: Commitment then cost. *Journal of Personality and Social Psychology, 36,* 463–476.

Cialdini, R. B., Schaller, M., Hoolihan, D., Arps, K., Fultz, J., & Beaman, A. L. (1987). Empathy-based helping: Is it selflessly or selfishly motivated? *Journal of Personality and Social Psychology, 52,* 749–758.

Cialdini, R. B., Vincent, J. E., Lewis, S. K., Catalan, J., Wheeler, D., & Darby, B. L. (1975). Reciprocal concessions procedure for inducing compliance: The door-in-the-face technique. *Journal of Personality and Social Psychology, 31,* 206–215.

Cianelli, S.N., & Fouts, R. S. (1998). Chimpanzee to chimpanzee American Sign Language. *Human Evolution, 13,* 147–159.

Cicirelli, V. G. (1998). Personal meanings of death in relation to fear of death. *Death Studies, 22,* 713–733.

Cigales, M., Field, T., Lundy, B., Cuadra, A., & Hart, S. (1997). Massage enhances recovery from habituation in normal infants. *Infant Behavior and Development, 20,* 29–34.

Cirelli, S. N., Shaw, P. J., Rechtschaffen, A., & Tononi, G. (1999). No evidence of brain cell degeneration after long term sleep deprivation in rats. *Brain Research, 840,* 184–193.

Clancy, S. A., McNally, R. J., Schacter, D. L., Lenzenweger, M. F., & Pitman, R. K. (2002.) Memory distortion in people reporting abduction by aliens. *Journal of Abnormal Psychology, 111*(3), 455–461.

Claparède, E. (1911). Recognition et moiité. *Archives de Psychologies, 11,* 79–90.

Clark, A., & Toribio, J. (1998). *Cognitive architectures in artificial intelligence: The evolution of research.* New York: Garland.

Clark, A., & Toribio, J. (1998). *Consciousness and emotion in cognitive science: Conceptual and empirical issues.* New York: Garland.

Clark, D. A., Beck, A. T., & Alford, B. A. (1999). *Scientific foundations of cognitive theory and therapy of depression.* New York: Wiley.

Clark, D. A., Beck, A. T., & Brown, G. (1989). Cognitive mediation in general psychiatric outpatients. A test of the content-specificity hypothesis. *Journal of Personality and Social Psychology, 56,* 958–964.

Clark, D. M. (1988). A cognitive model of panic attacks. In S. Rachman & J. D. Maser (Eds.), *Panic: Psychological Perspectives.* Hillsdale, NJ: Erlbaum.

Clark, M. S., Ouellette, R., Powell, M. C., & Milberg, S. (1987). Recipient's mood, relationship type, and helping. *Journal of Personality and Social Psychology, 53,* 94–103.

Clark, R. D., III. (2001). Effects of majority defection and multiple minority sources on minority influence. *Group Dynamics, 5,* 57–62.

Clark, R. D., & Hatfield, E. (1989). Gender differences in receptivity to sexual offers. *Journal of Psychology and Human Sexuality, 2,* 39–55.

Clarke, A. M., & Clarke, A. D. B. (2000). *Early experience and the life path.* London: Jessica Kingsley.

Clarkson-Smith, L., & Hartley, A. A. (1990). Structural equation models of relationships between exercise and cognitive abilities. *Psychology and Aging, 5,* 437–446.

Clayton, P. J. (2000). Bereavement. In G. Fink (Ed.), *Encyclopedia of stress.* San Diego: Academic Press.

Cleare, A. J., & Bond, A. J. (1997). Does central serotonergic function correlate inversely with aggression? A study using d-fenfluramine in healthy subjects. *Psychiatry Research, 69,* 89–95.

Clement, K. (1999). Leptin and the genetics of obesity. *Acta paediatrica, 88,* 51–57.

Clements, A. M., Rimrodt, S. L., Abel, J. R., Blankner, J. G., Mostofsky, S. H., Pekar, J. J., Denckla, M. B., and Cutting, L. E. (2006). Sex differences in cerebral laterality of language and visuospatial processing. *Brain and Language, 98,* 150–158.

Cloninger, C. R., Bohman, M., & Sigvardsson, S. (1981). Inheritance of alcohol abuse: Cross-fostering analysis of adopted men. *Archives of General Psychiatry, 38,* 861–868.

Cloninger, C. R., & Gottseman, I. I. (1989). Genetic and environmental factors in antisocial behavior disorders. In S. Mednick, T. Moffitt, & S. Strack (Eds.), *The causes of crime: New biological approaches.* New York: Cambridge University Press.

Cobb, J. M. T., & Steptoe, A. (1998). Psychosocial influences on upper respiratory infectious illness in children. *Journal of Psychosomatic Research, 45*(4), 319–330.

Coccaro, E. F., Bergeman, C. S., Kavoussi, R. J., & Seroczynski, A. D. (1997). Heritability of aggression and irritability: A twin study of the Buss-Durkee aggression scales in adult male subjects. *Biological Psychiatry, 41,* 273–284.

Coffey, C. E., Weiner, R. D., Djang, W. T., et al. (1991). Brain anatomic effects of electroconvulsive therapy: A prospective magnetic resonance imaging study. *Archives of General Psychiatry, 48,* 1013–1020.

Cohen, F. L., Ferrans, C. E., & Eshler, B. (1992). Reported accidents in narcolepsy. *Loss, Grief and Care, 5,* 71–80.

Cohen, N. J., & Squire, L. R. (1981). Retrograde amnesia and remote memory impairment. *Neuropsychologia, 19,* 337–356.

Cohen, S. (1988). Psychosocial models of the role of social support in the etiology of physical disease. *Health Psychology. 7,* 269–297.

Cohen, S., & Edwards, J. R. (1989). Personality characteristics as moderators of the relationship between stress and disorder. In R. W. J. Neufeld (Ed.), *Advances in the investigation of psychological stress.* New York: Wiley.

Cohen, S., & Herbert. T. B. (1996). Health psychology: Psychological factors and physical disease from the perspective of human psychoneuroimmunology. *Annual Review of Psychology, 47,* 113–142.

Cohen, S., Frank, E. D., Doyle, W. J., Skoner, D. P., Rabin, B. S., & Gwaltney, J. M., Jr. (1998). Types of stressors that increase susceptibility to the common cold in healthy adults. *Health Psychology, 17,* 214–223.

Cohen, S., Kessler, R. C., & Gordon, L. U. (1995). *Measuring stress.* New York: Oxford University Press.

Cohen, S., Wills, T. A. (1985). Stress, social support, and the buffering hypothesis. *Psychological Bulletin, 93,* 310–357.

Colby, A., Kohlberg, L., Gibbs, J., & Lieberman, M. (1983). A longitudinal study of moral judgment. *Monographs of the Society for Research in Child Development, 48* (1–2, Serial No. 200).

Coleman, D. L. (1978). Obese and diabetes: Two mutant genes causing diabetes-obesity syndromes in mice. *Diabetologia, 14,* 141–148.

Collaer, M. L., & Hines, M. (1995). Human behavioral sex differences: A role for gonadal hormones during early development? *Psychological Bulletin, 118,* 55–107.

Collier, G. & Johnson, D. F. (2004). The paradox of satiation. *Physiology & Behavior, 82,* 149–153.

Collings, P. (2001). If you got everything, it's good enough: Perspectives on successful aging in a Canadian Inuit community. *Journal of Cross-Cultural Gerontology, 16,* 127–155.

Collins, A. M., & Loftus, E. F. (1975). A spreading activation theory of semantic processing. *Psychological Review, 82,* 407–428.

Collins, D. W., Kimura, D. (1997). A large sex difference on a two dimensional mental rotation task. *Behavioural Neuroscience, 111(4),* 845–849.

Collins, W. A., Maccoby, E. E., Steinberg, L., & Hetherington, E. M. (2000). Contemporary research on parenting: The case for nature and nurture. *American Psychologist, 55,* 218–232.

Commons, M. L., Rachlin, H., & Nevin, J. A. (Eds.) (1984). *Quantitative analyses of behavior: Vol. 5. Reinforcement value: The effect of delay and intervening events.* Cambridge, MA: Ballenger.

Comuzzie, A. G., & Allison, D. B. (1998). The search for human obesity genes. *Science, 280,* 1374–1377.

Conrad, R. (1964). Acoustic confusions in immediate memory. *British Journal of Psychology, 55,* 75–84.

Constantine, M. G., Feng, P. F., Ladany, N., Bergmann, B. M., Inman, A. G., Rechtschaffen, A., & Ponterotto, J. G. (1995). Sleep deprivation in rats with preoptic/anterior hypothalamic lesions. *Brain Research, 703,* 93–99.

Contrada, R. J., Cather, C., & O'Leary, A. (1999). Personality and health: Dispositions and processes in disease susceptibility and adaptation to illness. In L. A. Pervin & O. P. John (Eds.), *Handbook of personality: Theory and research.* New York: Guilford Press.

Cook, S. W. (1985). Experimenting on social issues: The case of school desegregation. *American Psychologist, 40,* 452–460.

Cooke, P. (1991, June 23). They cried until they couldn't see. *New York Times Magazine,* pp. 25, 43.

Cooney, R., & Arbuckle, T. (1997). Age, context, and spatial memory: A neuropsychological approach. *Aging, Neuropsychology, & Cognition, 4,* 249–265.

Coons, P. M., Milstein, V., & Marley, C. (1982). EEG studies of two multiple personalities and a control. *Archives of General Psychiatry, 39,* 823–825.

Cooper, C. R., & Denner, J. (1998). Theories linking culture and psychology: Universal and community-specific processes. *Annual Review of Psychology, 49,* 559–584.

Cooper, J. (1998). Unlearning cognitive dissonance: Toward an understanding of the development of dissonance. *Journal of Experimental Social Psychology, 34,* 562–575.

Cooper, J. Bennett, E. A., & Sukel, H. L. (1996). Complex scientific testimony: How do jurors make decisions? *Law and Human Behavior, 20,* 379–394.

Cooper, J., & Fazio, R. H. (1984). A new look at dissonance theory. In L. Berkowitz (Ed.), *Advances in experimental social psychology* (Vol. 17). New York: Academic Press.

Cooper, J., Neuhaus, I. M. (2000). The "Hired Gun" effect: Assessing the effect of pay, frequency of testifying, and credentials on the perception of expert testimony. *Law and Human Behavior, 24(2),* 149–171.

Coopersmith, S. (1967). *The antecedents of self-esteem.* San Francisco: W. H. Freeman.

Cordova, J. V., Jacobson, N. S., & Christensen, A. (1998). Acceptance versus change interventions in behavioral couple therapy: Impact on couples' in-session communication. *Journal of Marriage and Family Counseling, 24,* 437–455.

Coren, S. (1994). *The intelligence of dogs: canine consciousness and capabilities.* New York: The Free Press.

Coren, S. (1996). Accidental death and the shift to daylight savings time. *Perceptual and Motor Skills, 83,* 921–922.

Coren, S. (1996). *Sleep Thieves.* New York: The Free Press.

Corina, D. P., Poizner, H., Bellugi, U., Feinberg, T., Dowd, D., & O'Grady-Batch, L. (1992). Dissociation between linguistic and nonlinguistic gestural systems: A case for compositionality. *Brain and Language, 43,* 414–447.

Corkin, S. (2002). What's new with the amnesia patient HM? Nature Reviews *Neuroscience, 3(2),* 53-60.

Cosmides, L. & Tooby, J. (1992). Cognitive adaptations for social exchange. In J. Barkow, L. Cosmides, & J. Tooby (Eds.), *The adapted mind: Evolutionary psychology and the generation of culture.* London: Oxford University Press.

Cosmides, L., & Tooby, J. (2002). Unraveling the enigma of human intelligence: Evolutionary psychology and the multimodular mind. In R. J. Sternberg & J. C. Kaufman (Eds.), *The evolution of intelligence.* Mahwah, NJ: Erlbaum.

Costa, L. (1996). Lifespan neuropsychology. *Clinical Neuropsychologist, 10,* 365–374.

Costa, P. T., & McCrae, R. R. (1992). The five-factor model of personality and its relevance to personality disorders. *Journal of Personality Disorders, 6,* 343–359.

Costello, E. J., Erkanli, A., Angold, A. (2006). Is there an epidemic of child or adolescent depression? *Journal of Child Psychology and Psychiatry, 47(2),* 1263–1271.

Cotman, C. W., Brinton, R., Galaburda, G., & McEwen, S. (1987). *The neuro-immune-endocrine connection.* Philadelphia: Lippincott-Raven.

Courage, M.L., & Adams, R.J. (1990). The early development of visual acuity in the binocular and monocular peripheral fields. *Infant Behavior and Development, 13,* 123–128.

Courneya, K. S. (1995). Understanding readiness for regular physical activity in older individuals: An application of the theory of planned behavior. *Health Psychology, 14,* 80–87.

Courneya, K. S., Friedenreich, C. M., Arthur, K., & Bobick, T. M. (1999). Understanding exercise motivation in colorectal cancer patients: A prospective study using the theory of planned behavior. *Rehabilitation Psychology, 44,* 68–84.

Cousins, S. D. (1989). Culture and self-perception in the United States and Japan. *Journal of Personality and Social Psychology, 56,* 124–131.

Cowan, C. P., & Cowan, P. A. (2000). *When partners become parents: The big life change for couples.* Mahwah, NJ: Erlbaum.

Cowan, P. A., & Cowan, C. P. (1988). Changes in marriage during the transition to parenthood: Must we blame the baby? In G. Y. Michaels, W. A. Goldberg, & A. Wendy (Eds.), *The transition to parenthood: Current theory and research. Cambridge studies in social and emotional development.* New York: Cambridge University Press.

Coyne, J. C., Burchill, S. A. L., & Stiles, W. B. (1991). An interactional perspective on depression. In C. R. Snyder & D. R. Forsyth (Eds.), *Handbook of social and clinical psychology: The health perspective.* New York: Pergamon.

Coyle, J. T., Price, D. L., & Delong, M. R. (1983). Alzheimer's disease: A disorder of cortical cholinergic innervation. *Science, 219,* 1184–1190.

Crabbe, J. C. (2002). Genetic contributions to addiction. *Annual Review of Psychology, 53,* 435–462.

Crabbe, J. C., Young, E. R., Tam, B., & Kosobud, A. (1986). Genetic differences in anticonvulsant sensitivity in mouse lines selectively bred for ethanol withdrawal severity. *Journal of Pharmacology and Experimental Therapeutics, 239,* 154–159.

Craig, T. P. (1991). Kin-selection, reciprocal altruism, and information sharing among Maine lobstermen. *Ethology and Sociobiology, 12,* 221–235.

Craig, W. M., Pepler, D., & Atlas, R. (2000). Observations of bullying in the playground and in the classroom. *School Psychology International, 21,* 22–36.

Craik, F. I. M., & McDowd, J. M. (1998). Age differences in recall and recognition. In M. P. Lawton & T. A. Salthouse (Eds.), *Essential papers on the psychology of aging.* New York: University Press.

Craik, F. I. M., & Lockhart, R. S. (1972). Levels of processing: A framework for memory research. *Journal of Verbal Learning and Verbal Behavior, 11,* 671–684.

Craik, F. I. M., & Salthouse, T. A. (Eds.) (2000). *The handbook of aging and cognition.* Mahwah, NJ: Erlbaum.

Craik, F. I. M., & Tulving, E. (1975). Depth of processing and the retention of words in episodic memory. *Journal of Experimental Psychology: General, 104,* 268–294.

Crain, W. M., & Pepler, D. J. (1995). Peer processes in bullying and victimization: An observational study. *Exceptionality Education Canada, 5,* 81–95.

Crandall, C. S., & Martinez, R. (1996). Culture, ideology, and antifat attitudes. *Personality and Social Psychology Bulletin, 22,* 1165–1176.

Crandall, C. S., D'Anello, S., Sakalli, N., Lazarus, E., Wieczorkowska, G., & Feather, N. T. (2001). An Attribution-Value model of prejudice: Anti-fat attitudes in six nations. *Personality and Social Psychology Bulletin, 27,* 30–37.

Craske, M. (1999). *Anxiety disorders: Psychological approaches to theory and treatment.* Boulder, CO: Westview Press.

Craske, M. (2003). *Origins of phobias and anxiety disorders: Why more women than men?* New York: Elsevier Science.

Crawford, C. B., & Anderson, J. L. (1989). Sociobiology: An environmentalist discipline? *American Psychologist, 44,* 1449–1459.

Crawford, M., & Chaffin, R. (1997). The meanings of difference: Cognition in social and cultural context. In P. J. Caplan, and M. Crawford (Eds.), *Gender differences in human cognition. Counterpoints: Cognition, memory, and language.* New York: Oxford University Press.

Crawford, M., Stark, A. C., & Renner, C. H. (1998). The meaning of Ms.: Social assimilation of a gender concept. *Psychology of Women Quarterly, 22,* 197–208.

Crawley, R. A., Scott, M. J. (2006). Memories of early childhood: Qualities of the experience of recollection. *Memory & Cognition, 34(2),* 287–294.

Creese, I., Burd, D. R., & Snyder, S. H. (1976). Dopamine receptor binding predicts clinical and pharmacological potencies of antischizophrenic drugs. *Science, 192,* 481–483.

Crick, N. R., & Bigbee, M. A. (1998). Relational and overt forms of peer victimization: A multiinformant approach. *Journal of Consulting and Clinical Psychology, 66,* 337–347.

Crits-Christoph, P. (1992). The efficacy of brief dynamic psychotherapy: A meta-analysis. *American Journal of Psychiatry, 149,* 151–158.

Crits-Christoph, P., & Mintz, J. (1991). Implications of therapist effects for the design and analysis of comparative studies of psychotherapies. *Journal of Consulting and Clinical Psychology, 59,* 20–26.

Crits-Christoph, P., Cooper, A., & Luborsky, L. (1988). The accuracy of therapists' interpretations and the outcome of dynamic psychotherapy. *Journal of Consulting and Clinical Psychology, 56,* 490–495.

Crocker, J. (2002). Contingencies of self-worth: Implications for self-regulation and psychological vulnerability. *Self and Identity, 1,* 143–149.

Crocker, J. & Park, L. E. (2004). The costly pursuit of self-esteem. *Psychological Bulletin, 130,* 392–414.

Crocker, P. R. E. (1989). A follow-up of cognitive-affective stress management training. *Journal of Sport and Exercise Psychology, 11,* 236–242.

Crook, J. M., & Copolov, D. L. (2000). Schizophrenia. In G. Fink (Ed.), *Encyclopedia of stress.* San Diego: Academic Press.

Cross, S. E., & Markus, H. R. (1999). The cultural constitution of personality. In L. A. Pervin & O. P. John

(Eds.), *Handbook of personality: Theory and research.* New York: Guilford Press.

Cross, S., & Markus, H. (1991). Possible selves across the life span. *Human Development, 34,* 230–255.

Crovitz, H. F. (1971). The capacity of memory loci in artificial memory. *Psychonomic Science, 24,* 187–188.

Crowe, L. C., & George, W. H. (1989). Alcohol and human sexuality: Review and integration. *Psychological Bulletin, 105,* 374–386.

Crowley, K., Callanan, M. A., Tenenbaum, H. R., & Allen, E. (2001). Parents explain more often to boys than to girls during shared scientific thinking. *Psychological Science, 12,* 258–261.

Crowley, R. A., Eacott, M. J. (2006). Memories of early childhood: Qualities of the experience of recollection. *Memory & Cognition, 34(2),* 287–294.

Croyle, R. T., & Cooper, J. (1983). Dissonance arousal: Physiological evidence. *Journal of Personality and Social Psychology, 45,* 782–791.

Csikszentmihalyi, M. (1990). *Flow: The psychology of optimal experience.* New York: Harper & Row.

Csikszentmihalyi, M., & Larson, R. (1984). *Being adolescent: Conflict and growth in the teenage years.* New York: Basic Books.

Culbertson, F. M. (1997). Depression and gender: An international review. *American Psychologist, 52,* 25–31.

Culham, J. (2004). Neuroimaging investigations of visually-guided grasping. Attention and performance XX: Functional brain imaging of human cognition. Oxford: Oxford University Press, 415–436

Cummins, H. J. (1999, March 2). Kids learn to kill like soldiers do, author says. *Seattle Post-Intelligencer,* p. E4.

Cunningham, M. R., Roberts, A. R., Wu, C-H, Barbee, A. P., & Druen, P. B. (1995). "Their ideas of beauty are, on the whole, the same as ours": Consistency and variability in the cross-cultural perception of female attractiveness. *Journal of Personality and Social Psychology, 68,* 261–279.

Cunningham, W.A., Johnson, M.K., Raye, C.L., Gatenby, J.C., Gore, J.C., & Banaji, M.R. (2004). Separate neural components in the processing of black and white faces. *Psychological Science, 15,* 12806-813

Curran, T., & Schacter, D. L. (2000). Amnesia II: Cognitive neuropsychological issues. In M. J. Martha & T. E. Feinberg (Eds.), *Patient-based approaches to cognitive neuroscience. Issues in clinical and cognitive neuropsychology.* Cambridge, MA: MIT Press.

Curtiss, S. (1977). *Genie: A psychological study of a modern day "wild child."* New York: Academic Press.

Cytowic, R. E. (2002). *Synesthesia: A union of the senses* (2nd ed.). Boston: MIT Press.

Czeisler, C. A., Moore, E., Martin, C., & Coleman, R. M. (1982). Rotating shift work schedules that disrupt sleep are improved by applying circadian principles. *Science, 217,* 460–463.

Dalton, A. L., Daneman, M. (2006). Social suggestibility to central peripheral misinformation. *Memory, 14(4),* 468–501.

Daly, M., Wilson, M., & Vasdev, S. (2001). Income inequality and homicide rates in Canada and the United States. *Canadian Journal of Criminology, 43,* 219–236.

Daly, M., Wilson, M., & Weghorst, S.J. (1982). Male sexual jealousy. *Ethology and Sociobiology, 3,* 11–27.

Daly, M., & Wilson, M. (1988). *Homicide.* New York: Aldine de Gruyter.

Daly, M., & Wilson, M. (1999). *The truth about Cinderella: A Darwinian view of parental love.* New Haven, CT: Yale University Press.

Damasio, A. R. (1995). *Descartes' error: Emotion, reason, and the human brain.* New York: Avon Books.

Damasio, H. (1989). Neuroimaging contributions to the understanding of aphasia. In F. Boller and J. Grafman (Eds.), *Handbook of Neuropsychology, Vol. 2.* Amsterdam: Elsevier.

Dantzer, R. (2000). Psychoneuroimmunology. In G. Fink (Ed.), *Encyclopedia of stress.* San Diego: Academic Press.

Dark, K., Peeke, H. V., Ellman, G., & Salfi, M. (1987). Behaviorally conditioned histamine release: Prior stress and conditionability and extinction of the response. *Annals of the New York Academy of Sciences,* 496, 578–582.

Darley, J. M. (1995). Constructive and destructive obedience: A taxonomy of principal-agent relationships. *Journal of Social Issues, 51,* 125–154.

Darley, J. M., & Gross, P. H. (1983). A hypothesis-confirming bias in labeling effects. *Journal of Personality and Social Psychology, 44,* 20–33.

Darley, J. M., & Latane, B. (1968). Bystander intervention in emergencies: Diffusion of responsibility. *Journal of Personality and Social Psychology, 8,* 377–383.

Darwin, C. J., Turvey, M. T., & Crowder, R. G. (1972). An auditory analogue of the Sperling partial report procedures. *Cognitive Psychology, 3,* 255–267.

Darwin, C. R. (1872/1965). *The expression of emotions in man and animals.* Chicago: University of Chicago Press.

Dasen, P. R. (1975). Concrete operational development in Canadian Eskimos. *International Journal of Psychology, 10,* 165–180.

Davey, G. C. L. (1995). Preparedness and phobias: Specific evolved associations or a generalized expectancy bias? *Behavioral and Brain Sciences, 18,* 289–325.

Davidson, R. J. (1988). Cerebral asymmetry, affective style, and psychopathology. In M. Kinsbourne (Ed.), *Cerebral hemisphere function in depression.* Washington, DC: American Psychiatric Press.

Davidson, R. J. (1998). Affective style and affective disorders: Perspectives from affective neuroscience. *Cognition and Emotion, 12,* 307–320.

Davidson, R. J. (1998). *Neuropsychological perspectives on affective and anxiety disorders.* Chicago: Psychology Press.

Davidson, R. J. (2000). Affective style, psychopathology, and resilience: Brain mechanisms and plasticity. *American Psychologist, 55,* 1196–1214.

Davidson, R. J. (2003). Affective neuroscience and psychophysiology: Toward a synthesis. *Psychophysiology, 40,* 655–665.

Davidson, R. J., Coe, C. C., Dolski, I., & Donzella, B. (1999). Individual differences in prefrontal activation asymmetry predict natural killer cell activity at rest and in response to challenge. *Brain, Behavior, and Immunity, 13,* 93–108.

Davidson, R. J., & Fox, N. A. (1988). Cerebral asymmetry and emotion: Developmental and individual differences. In D. L. Molfese & S. J. Segalowitz (Eds.), *Brain lateralization in children: Developmental implications.* New York, Guilford Press.

Davidson, R. J., & Fox, N. A. (1989). Frontal brain asymmetry predicts infants' response to maternal separation. *Journal of Abnormal Psychology, 98,* 127–131.

Davidson, R. J., Marshall, J. R., Tomarken, A. J., & Henriques, J. B. (2000). While a phobic waits: Regional brain electrical and autonomic activity in social phobics during anticipation of public speaking. *Biological Psychiatry 47,* 85–95.

Davidson, R. J., Putnam, K. M., & Larson, C. L. (2000). Dysfunction in the neural circuitry of emotion regulation: A possible prelude to violence. *Science 289,* 591–594.

Davidson, W. B., & Cotter, P. R. (1997). Psychological sense of community and newspaper readership. *Psychological Reports, 80,* 659–665.

Davis, C. G., Nolen, H. S., & Larson, J. (1998). Making sense of loss and benefiting from the experience: Two construals of meaning. *Journal of Personality and Social Psychology, 75,* 561–574.

Davis, C. J., Knopik, V. S., Olson, R. K., Wadsworth, S. J., & DeFries, J. C. (2001). Genetics and environmental influences on rapid naming and reading ability. *Annals of Dyslexia, 51:* 231–247.

Davis, C. M., & Bauserman, R. (1993). Exposure to sexually explicit materials: An attitude change perspective. *Annual Review of Sex Research, 4,* 121–209.

Davis, M. (1992). The role of the amygdala in fear and anxiety. *Annual Review of Neuroscience, 15,* 311–327.

Davis, M., Whalen, P.J. (2001). The amygdala: vigilance and emotion. *Molecular Psychiatry, 6,* 13–34.

Davis, M. H., Luce, C., & Kraus, S. J. (1994). The heritability of characteristics associated with dispositional empathy. *Journal of Personality, 62,* 369–391.

Dawes, R. M. (1994). *House of cards: Psychology and psychotherapy built on myth.* New York: Free Press.

Dawidowicz, L. S. (1975). *The war against the Jews, 1933–1945.* New York: Holt, Rinehart & Winston.

Dawson, W. A. (1993). Aboriginal dreaming. In M. A. Carskadon (Ed.), *Encyclopedia of sleep and dreaming.* New York: Macmillan.

Day, R., et al. (1987). Stressful life events preceding the acute onset of schizophrenia. *Culture, Medicine, and Psychiatry, 11,* 123–205.

De Brabander, B. & Declerck, C. H. (2004). A possible role of central dopamine metabolism associated with individual differences in locus of control. *Personality and Individual Differences, 37,* 735–750.

De Cremer, D., & van Lange, P. A. M. (2001). Why prosocials exhibit greater cooperation than proselfs: The roles of social responsibility and reciprocity. *European Journal of Personality, 15,* 5–18.

De Silva, P., & Rachman, J. (1998). *Obsessive compulsive disorders.* New York: Oxford University Press.

de Waal, F. (1982). *Chimpanzee politics: Power and sex among apes.* Baltimore: John Hopkins University Press.

DeCasper, A. J., & Fifer, W. P. (1980). Of human bonding: Newborns prefer their mothers' voices. *Science, 208*(4448), 1174–1176.

DeCasper, A. J., & Spence, M. J. (1986). Prenatal maternal speech influences newborns' perceptions of speech sounds. *Infant Behavior and Development, 9,* 133–150.

De Castro, J. (2002). The influence of heredity on self-reported sleep patterns in free-living humans. *Physiology & Behavior, 76,* 479–486.

deCastro, J. M. (2002). Age-related changes in the social, psychological, and temporal influences on food intake in free-living, healthy, adult humans. *Journals of Gerontology: Series A. Biological Sciences and Medical Sciences, 57A,* 368–377.

Decety, J., Grezes, J., Costes, N., Perani, D., Jeannerod, M., Procyk, E., Grassi, F., & Fazio, F. (1997). Brain activity during observation of actions: Influence of action content and subject's strategy. *Brain, 120,* 1763–1777.

deCharms, R. C., & Zador, A. (2000). Neural representation and the cortical code. *Annual Review of Neuroscience, 23,* 613–647.

DeCharms, R., & Moeller, G. H. (1962). Values expressed in American children's readers: 1800 to 1950. *Journal of Abnormal and Social Psychology, 64,* 135–142.

Deci, E. L. (1971). Effects of externally mediated rewards on intrinsic motivation. *Journal of Personality and Social Psychology, 18,* 105–115.

Deci, E. L., Koestner, R., & Ryan, R. M. (1999). A meta-analytic review of experiments examining the effects of extrinsic rewards on intrinsic motivation. *Psychological Bulletin, 125,* 627–668.

Deci, E. L., & Ryan, R. M. (2000). The "what" and "why" of goal pursuits: Human needs and the self-determination of behavior. *Psychological Inquiry, 11,* 227–268.

Deckel, A. W., & Fuqua, L. (1998). Effects of serotonergic drugs on lateralized aggression and aggressive displays in *Anolis carolinensis. Behavioural Brain Research, 95,* 227–232.

Deckersbach, T., Miller, K. K., Klibanski, A., Fischman, A., Dougherty, D. D., Blais, M. A., & Herzog, D. B., Rauch, S. L. (2006). Regional cerebral brain metabolism correlates of neuroticism and extraversion. *Depression and Anxiety, 23,* 133–138.

DeFries, J. C., Fulker, D. W., & LaBuda, M. C. (1987). Evidence for a genetic aetiology in reading disability of twins. *Nature,* 329: 537–539.

DeFries, J. C., Singer, S. M., Foch, T. T., & Lewitter, F. I. (1978). Familial nature of reading disability. *British Journal of Psychiatry,* 132: 361–367.

deGeus, E. J. C. (2000). Aerobics in stress reduction. In G. Fink (Ed.), *Encyclopedia of stress.* San Diego: Academic Press.

Dekker, E., & Groen, J. (1956). Reproducible psychogenic attacks of asthma. *Journal of Psychosomatic Research, 1,* 56–67.

DeLongis, A. (2000). Coping skills. In G. Fink (Ed.), *Encyclopedia of stress.* San Diego: Academic Press.

Dement, W. C. (1974). *Some must watch while some must sleep.* San Francisco: W. H. Freeman.

DeMoranville, B. M., Jackson, I., Ader, R., Madden, K. S., Felten, D. L., & Bellinger, D. L. (2000). Endocrine and immune systems. In B. S. Fogel, R. B. Schiffer, & S. M. Rao (Eds.), *Synopsis of neuropsychiatry.* Philadelphia: Lippincott-Raven.

Dennis, W. (1973). *Children of the creche.* New York: Appleton-Century-Crofts.

Department of Health and Human Services (1998). *National Household Survey On Drug Abuse: Population Estimates 1997.* Rockville, MD: Author.

Department of Health and Human Services (1999). *Child maltreatment 1997: Reports from the states to the National Child Abuse and Neglect Data System.* Washington, DC: U.S. Government Printing Office.

Depue, R. A. (1992). *Neurobehavioral systems, personality, and psychopathology.* New York: Springer-Verlag.

Derogatis, L. R. (1986). *Clinical psychopharmacology.* Menlo Park, CA: Addison-Wesley.

DeRubeis, R. J., & Crits-Christoph, P. (1998). Empirically supported individual and group psychological treatments for adult mental disorders. *Journal of Consulting and Clinical Psychology, 66,* 37–52.

Desmond, S. M., Price, J. H., Hallinan, C., & Smith, D. (1989). Black and white adolescents' perceptions of their ideal weight. *Journal of School Health, 59,* 353-358.

D'Esposito, M. D. (2003). *Neurological Foundations of Cognitive Neuroscience.* Boston: MIT Press.

Dessens, A. B., Cohen, K. P. T., Mellenbergh, G. J., van der Poll, N., Koppe, J. G., & Boer, K. (1999). Prenatal exposure to anticonvulsants and psychosexual development. *Archives of Sexual Behavior, 28,* 31–44.

Deutsch, M., & Gerard, H. B. (1955). A study of normative and informational social influence upon individual judgment. *Journal of Abnormal and Social Psychology, 51,* 629–636.

DeValois, R. L., & DeValois, K. K. (1988). *Spatial vision.* New York: Oxford University Press.

Devane, W. A., Hanus, L., Breuer, A., Pertwee, R. G., Stevenson, L. A., & Griffin, G., (1992). Isolation and structure of a brain constituent that binds to the cannabinoid receptor. *Science, 18,* 1946–1949.

DeVries, H., Mudde, A. N., Dijkstra, A., & Willemsen, M. C. (1998). Differential beliefs, perceived social influences, and self-efficacy expectations among smokers in various motivational phases. *Preventive Medicine, 27,* 681–689.

DeVries, R. (1969). Constancy of genetic identity in the years three to six. *Monographs of the Society for Research in Child Development, 34* (Serial No. 127).

DeVries, R., Hildebrandt, C., & Zan, B. (2000). Constructivist early education for moral development. *Early Education and Development, 11,* 9–35.

Dewsbury, D. A. (1988). The comparative psychology of monogamy. In D. W. Leger (Ed.), *Comparative perspectives in modern psychology.* Nebraska Symposium on motivation. Lincoln: University of Nebraska Press.

Dewsbury, D. A. (1997). In celebration of the centennial of Ivan P. Pavlov's (1897/1902). The Work of the Digestive Glands. *American Psychologist, 52,* 933–935.

DeYoung, C. G., Peterson, J. B., & Higgins, D. M. (2002). Higher-order factors of the Big Five predict conformity: Are there neuroses of health? *Personality and Individual Differences, 33,* 533–552.

DeYoung, C. G., Peterson, J. B., & Higgins, D. M. (2005). Sources of openness/intellect: Cognitive and neuropsychological correlates of the fifth factor of personality. *Journal of Personality, 73,* 825–858.

Diaz, J. (1997). *How drugs influence behavior: A neurobehavioral approach.* Upper Saddle River, NJ: Prentice Hall.

Dickinson, A. (1997). Bolles's psychological syllogism. In M. E. Bouton, M. S. Fanselow, & S. Michael (Eds.), *Learning, motivation, and cognition: The functional behaviorism of Robert C. Bolles.* Washington, DC: American Psychological Association.

DiClemente, C. C. (2003). *Addiction and change: How addictions develop and addicted people recover.* New York: Guilford Press.

DiClemente, C. C., & Prochaska, J. C. (1998). Toward a comprehensive, transtheoretical model of change: Stages of change and addictive behaviors. In W. R. Miller & N. Heather (Eds.), *Treating addictive behaviors* (2nd ed.). New York: Plenum.

Diener, E. (2000). Subjective well-being: The science of happiness and a proposal for a national index. *American Psychologist, 55,* 34–43.

Diener, E., & Fujita, F. (1997). Social comparisons and subjective well-being. In B. Bruunk & F. X. Gibbons (Eds.), *Health, coping, and well-being: Perspectives from social comparison theory.* Mahwah, NJ: Erlbaum.

Diener, E., Suh, E., Lucas, R. E., & Smith, H. L. (1999). Subjective well-being: Three decades of progress. *Psychological Bulletin, 125,* 276–302.

Dienstbier, R. A. (1989). Arousal and physiological toughness: Implications for mental and physical health. *Psychological Review, 96,* 84–100.

Dietz, T. L. (1998). An examination of violence and gender role portrayals in video games: Implications for gender socialization and aggressive behavior. *Sex Roles, 38,* 425–442.

Digman, J. M. (1990). Personality structure: Emergence of the five-factor model. *Annual Review of Psychology, 41,* 417–440.

Digman, J. M. (1997). Higher-order factors of the Big Five. *Journal of Personality and Social Psychology, 73,* 1246–1256.

DiLalla, D. L., Carey, G., Gottesman, I. I., & Bouchard, T. J. (1996). Heritability of MMPI personality indicators of psychopathology in twins reared apart. *Journal of Abnormal Psychology, 105,* 491–499.

Dimberg, U. (1997). Psychophysiological reactions to facial expressions. In U. C. Segerstrale, et al. (Eds.), *Nonverbal communication: Where nature meets culture.* Mahwah, NJ: Erlbaum.

Dimberg, U., & Thunberg, M. (1998). Rapid facial reactions to emotional facial expressions. *Scandinavian Journal of Psychology, 39,* 39–46.

Dimberg, U., Thunberg, M., & Elmehed, K. (2000). Unconscious facial reactions to emotional facial expressions. *Psychological Science, 11,* 86–89.

Dindia, K. (2002). Self-disclosure research: Knowledge through meta-analysis. In M. Allen, R. W. Preiss, B. M. Gayle, & N. A. Burrell (Eds.), *Interpersonal communication research: Advances through meta-analysis.* Mahwah, NJ: Erlbaum.

Dion, K. K., Berscheid, E., & Walster, E. (1972). What is beautiful is good. *Journal of Personality and Social Psychology, 24,* 285–290.

Dishion, T. J., McCord, J., & Poulin, F. (1999). When interventions harm: Peer groups and problem behavior. *American-Psychologist, 54,* 755–764.

Dishman, C. (2001). Terrorism, crime and transformation. *Studies in Conflict and Terrorism, 23(1),* 43–58.

Dishman, R. K. (1982). Compliance/adherence in health-related exercise. *Health Psychology, 1,* 237–267.

Dittmann, R. W., Kappes, M. H., & Kappes, M. E. (1993). Cognitive functioning in female patients with 21-hydroxylase deficiency. *European Child and Adolescent Psychiatry, 2,* 34–43.

Dixon, M., & Laurence, J. R. (1992). Two hundred years of hypnosis research: Questions resolved. Questions unanswered. In E.Fromm & M. R. Nash (Eds.), *Contemporary hypnosis research.* New York: Guilford.

Dixon, N. F. (1981). *Preconscious processing.* New York: Wiley.

Dodge, K. A. (1986). A social information processing model of social competence. *Minnesota Symposium on Child Psychology, 18,* 77–125.

Doell, R. G. (1995). Sexuality in the brain. *Journal of Homosexuality, 28,* 345–354.

Doka, K. J. (1995). Coping with life-threatening illness: A task model. *Omega: Journal of Death and Dying, 32,* 111–122.

Dolezal, H. F. (1977). Long-term adaptation to up-down reversing the field of view: Complex changes afforded by optical invariants. *Dissertation Abstracts International, 37*(12-B, Pt 1): 6364–6365.

Dollard, J., Doob, L., Miller, N., Mowrer, O. H., & Sears, R. R. (1939). *Frustration and aggression.* New Haven, CT: Yale University Press.

Domhoff, G. W. (1999). Drawing theoretical implications from descriptive empirical findings on dream content. *Dreaming: Journal of the Association for the Study of Dreams, 9,* 201–210.

Domino, G. (2000). *Psychological testing.* Upper Saddle River, NJ: Prentice Hall.

Domino, G. & Domino, M. L. (2006). *Psychological testing: An introduction,* New York: Cambridge University Press.

Domjan, M., Greene, P., & North, N. C. (1989). Contextual conditioning and the control of copulatory behavior by species-specific sign stimuli in male Japanese quail. *Journal of Experimental Psychology: Animal Behavior Processes, 15,* 147–153.

Domjan, M., O'Vary, D., & Green, P. (1988). Conditioning of appetitive and consummatory sexual behavior in male Japanese quail. *Journal of the Experimental Analysis of Behavior, 50,* 505–519.

Donaldson, D. (1998). *Psychiatric disorders with a biochemical basis.* New York: Parthenon.

Donnerstein, E., & Berkowitz, L. (1981). Victim reactions in aggressive erotic films as a factor in violence against women. *Journal of Personality and Social Psychology, 41,* 710–724.

Donnerstein, E., & Donnerstein, M. (1976). Research on the control of interracial aggression. In R. G. Geen &

E. C. O'Neal (Eds.), *Perspectives on aggression.* New York: Academic Press.

Donnerstein, E., & Malamuth, N. (1997). Pornography: Its consequences on the observer. In L. B. Schlesinger & E. Revitch (Eds.), *Sexual dynamics of anti-social behavior* (2nd ed.). Springfield, IL: Charles C Thomas.

Doppelt, J. E., & Wallace, W. L. (1955). Standardization of the Wechsler Adult Intelligence Scale for older persons. *Journal of Abnormal and Social Psychology, 51,* 312–330.

Dornbusch, S. M., Ritter, P. L., Liederman, P. H., Roberts, D. F., & Fraleigh, M. J. (1987). The relation of parenting style to adolescent school performance. *Child Development, 58,* 1244–1257.

Dossenbach, M., & Dossenbach, H. D. (1998). *All about animal vision.* Chicago: Blackbirch Press.

Dovidio, J. F. (1984). Helping behavior and altruism: An empirical and conceptual overview. In L. Berkowitz (Ed.), *Advances in experimental social psychology* (Vol. 17). New York: Academic Press.

Dovidio, J. F., & Gaertner, S. L. (1997). On the nature of contemporary prejudice: The causes, consequences, and challenges of aversive racism. In J. L. Eberhardt & S. T. Fiske (Eds.), *Racism: The problem and the response.* Thousand Oaks, CA: Sage Publications.

Dovidio, J. , Glick, P., Rudman, L. A. (Eds.) (2005). On the nature of prejudice: Fifty years after Allport. Malden, MA, US: Blackwell Publishing.

Dovidio, J. F., Kawakami, K., & Gaertner, S. L. (2000). Reducing contemporary prejudice: Combatting bias at the individual and intergroup levels. In S. Oskamp (Ed.), *Reducing prejudice and discrimination.* Mahwah, NJ: Erlbaum.

Dovidio, J. F., Kawakami, K., Johnson, C., Johnson, B., & Howard, A. (1997). On the nature of prejudice: Automatic and controlled processes. *Journal of Experimental Social Psychology, 33,* 510–540.

Dovidio, J. F., Piliavin, J. A., Gaertner, S. L., Schroeder, D. A., & Clark, R. D. III. (1991). The arousal cost-reward model and the process of intervention. A review of the evidence. In M. S. Clark (Ed.), *Prosocial behavior. Review of personality and social psychology* (Vol. 12). Newbury Park, CA: Sage Publications.

Downey, G., Freitas, A. L., Michaelis, B., & Khouri, H. (1998). The self-fulfilling prophecy in close relationships: Rejection sensitivity and rejection by romantic partners. *Journal of Personality and Social Psychology, 75,* 545–560.

Drake, M. E., Pakalnis, A., & Denio, L. C. (1988). Differential diagnosis of epilepsy and multiple personality: Clinical and EEG findings in 15 cases. *Neuropsychiatry, Neuropsychology, and Behavioral Neurology, 1,* 131–140.

Draycott, S., & Dabbs, A. (1998). Cognitive dissonance 2: A theoretical grounding of motivational interviewing. *British Journal of Clinical Psychology, 37,* 355–364.

Driskell, J. E., Willis, R. P., & Copper, C. (1992). Effect of overlearning on retention. *Journal of Applied Psychology, 77,* 615–622.

Drukin, K. (1998). Implicit content and implicit processes in mass media use. In K. Kirsner et al. (Eds.), *Implicit and explicit mental processes.* Mahwah, NJ: Erlbaum.

Dryden, W. (Ed.). (2002). *Handbook of individual therapy.* Thousand Oaks, CA: Sage.

Du, X., Liu, Y. Li, Y. (2003). The effect of familiarity on out-group homogenicity. *Psychological Science (China), 26(4),* 625–627.

Duffy, J.F., Rimmer, D.W., & Czeisler, C.A. (2001). Association of intrinsic circadian period with morningness-eveningness, usual wake time, and circadian phase. *Behavioral Neuroscience, 115,* 895–899.

Dukas, R. (1998). Evolutionary ecology of learning. In R. Dukas et al. (Eds.), Cognitive ecology: *The evolutionary ecology of information processing and decision making.* Chicago: University of Chicago Press.

Dunbar, G. L., Sandstrom, M. I., Rossignol, J. and Lescaudron, L. (2006). Neurotrophic enhancers as therapy for behavioural deficits in rodent models of Huntington's Disease: Use of gangliosides, substituted pyrimidines, and mesenchymal stem cells. *Behavioral and Cognitive Neuroscience Reviews, 5,* 63–79.

Duncan, B. L. (1976). Differential social perception and attribution of intergroup violence: Testing the lower limits of stereotyping of blacks. *Journal of Personality and Social Psychology, 34,* 590–598.

Duncan, D. F., Donnelly, J. W., Nicholson, T., & Hees, A. J. (1992). Cultural diversity, superstitions, and pseudoscientific beliefs among allied health students. *College Student Journal, 26,* 525–530.

Duncan, I. J. H., Widowski, T. M., Malleau, A. E., Lindberg, A. C., & Petherick, J. C. (1998). External factors and causation of dustbathing in domestic hens. *Behavioural Processes, 43,* 219–228.

Duncan, J., Seitz, R. J., Kolodny, J., Bor, D., Herzog, H., Ahmed, A., et al. (2000). A neural basis for general intelligence. *Science, 289,* 457–460.

Duncan, R. (1997). *SPECT imaging of the brain.* New York: Kluwer Academic.

Dunn, J., & Plomin, R. (1990). *Separate lives: Why siblings are so different.* New York: Basic Books.

Dutton, D. G., & Aron, A. P. (1974). Some evidence for heightened sexual attraction under conditions of high anxiety. *Journal of Personality and Social Psychology, 30,* 510–517.

Duvander, A. Z. E. (1999). The transition from cohabitation to marriage: A longitudinal study of the propensity to marry in Sweden in the early 1990s. *Journal of Family Issues, 20,* 698–717.

Duvernoy, H. M. (1997). *The human hippocampus: Functional anatomy, vascularization and serial sections with MRI.* New York: Springer-Verlag.

Dyken, M. E., Lin-Dyken, D. C., Seaba, P., & Yamada, T. (1995). Violent sleep-related behavior leading to subdural hemorrhage. *Archives of Neurology, 52,* 318–321.

Eagly, A. H., & Carli, L. L. (1981). Sex of researcher and sex-typed communications as determinants of sex differences in influenceability: A meta-analysis of social influence studies. *Psychological Bulletin, 90,* 1–20.

Eagly, A. H., & Crowley, M. (1986). Gender and helping behavior: A meta-analytic review of the social psychological literature. *Psychological Bulletin, 100,* 283–308.

Eastman, C. I., Hoese, E. K., Youngstedt, S. D., & Liu, L. (1995). Phase-shifting human circadian rhythms with exercise during the night shift. *Physiology and Behavior, 58,* 1287–1291.

Ebbinghaus, H. (1964). *öber das Gedächtnis: Untersuchungen Zur Experimentellen Psychologie (Memory: A contribution to experimental psychology).* (H. A. Ruger & C. E. Bussenius, Trans.). New York: Dover. (Original work published 1885)

Eberhardt, J.L. (2005). Imaging race. *American Psychologist, 60,* 2181-90.

Ebmeier, K. (2000). Cerebral metabolism, brain imaging. In G. Fink (Ed.), *Encyclopedia of stress.* San Diego: Academic Press.

Eccles, J. (1991). Gender-role socialization. In R. M. Baron, W. G. Graziano, & C. Stangor (Eds.), *Social psychology.* Ft. Worth, TX: Holt, Rinehart & Winston.

Echt, K. V., Morrell, R. W., & Park, D. C. (1998). Effects of age and training formats on basic computer skill acquisition in older adults. *Educational Gerontology, 24,* 3–25.

Eckensberger, L. H., & Zimba, R. F. (1997). The development of moral judgment. In J. W. Berry, P. R. Dasen, & T. S. Saraswathi (Eds.), *Handbook of cross-cultural psychology* (2nd ed., Vol. 2). Boston: Allyn & Bacon.

Eckhardt, C. I., & Kassinove, H. (1998). Articulated cognitive distortions and cognitive deficiencies in maritally violent men. *Journal of Cognitive Psychotherapy, 12,* 231–250.

Eden, D. Greenberg, J. (2003) *Organizational behavior: The state of the science* (2nd ed.) (pp. 91–122). Mahwah, NJ: Lawrence Elrbaum Associates Publishers.

Edser, S. J. (2002). Hypnotically facilitated nausea and vomiting associated with chemotherapy: A case study. *Australian Journal of Clinical Hypnotherapy and Hypnosis, 23,* 18–30.

Edwards, A. E. (1962). A demonstration of the long-term retention of a conditioned galvanic skin response. *Psychosomatic Medicine, 24,* 459–463.

Edwards, D. C. (1998). *Motivation and emotion: Evolutionary, physiological, cognitive and social influences.* Thousand Oaks, CA: Sage Publications.

Edwards, K. (1998). The face of time: Temporal cues in facial expressions of emotion. *Psychological Science, 9,* 270–276.

Efran, J. F., & Greene, M. A. (2000). The limits of change: Heredity, environment, and family influence. In W. C. Nichols & M. A. Pace-Nichols (Eds.), *Handbook of family development and intervention.* New York: Wiley.

Ehrman, J. (2003). *Clinical exercise psychology.* Champaign, IL: Human Kinetics.

Eibl-Eibesfeldt, I. (1973). The expressive behavior of the deaf-and-blind children. In M. von Cranach & I. Vine (Eds.), *Social communication and movement.* New York: Academic Press.

Eibl-Eibesfeldt, I. (1998). Us and the others: The familial roots of ethnonationalism. In I. Eibl-Eibesfeldt & F. Salter (Eds.), *Indoctrinability, ideology and warfare.* New York: Berghahn Books.

Eich, J. E., Weingartner, H., Stillman, R. C., & Gillin, J. C. (1975). State-dependent accessibility of retrieval cues in the retention of a categorized list. *Journal of Verbal Learning and Verbal Behavior, 14,* 408–417.

Eichenbaum, H. (1997). How does the brain organize memories. *Science, 277,* 330–332.

Einstein, G. O., McDaniel, M. A., Smith, R., & Shaw, P. (1998). Habitual prospective memory and aging: Remembering instructions and forgetting actions. *Psychological Science, 9,* 284–288.

Eiseley, L. (1946). *The immense journey.* New York: Random House.

Eisenberg, N. (2000). Emotion, regulation, and moral development. *Annual Review of Psychology, 51,* 665–697.

Eisenberg, N., & Mussen, P. H. (1989). *The roots of prosocial behavior in children.* Cambridge, England: Cambridge University Press.

Eisenberg, N., & Valiente, C. (2002). Parenting and children's prosocial and moral development. In M. H. Bornstein (Eds.), *Handbook of parenting: Vol. 5. Practical issues in parenting* (2nd ed.). Mahwah, NJ: Erlbaum.

Eisenberg, N., Shepard, S. A., Fabes, R. A., Murphy, B. C., & Guthrie, I. K. (1998). Shyness and children's emotionality, regulation, and coping: Contemporaneous, longitudinal, and across-context relations. *Child Development, 69,* 767–790.

Eisenberger, N. I., Lieberman, M. D., Williams, K. D. (2003). Does rejection hurt? An fMRI study of social exclusion. *Science, 302,* 290–292.

Eisenberger, N. I., Taylor, S. E., Gable, S. L., Hilmert, C. J., and Lieberman, M. D. (2007). Neural pathways link social support to attenuated neuroendocrine stress responses. *NeuroImage, 35,* 1601–1612.

Eisenstadt, S. A., & Simon, H. A. (1997). Logic and thought. *Minds & Machines, 7,* 365–385.

Ekman, P. (1973). *Darwin and facial expression: A century of research in review.* New York: Academic Press.

Ekman, P. (1999a). Basic emotions. In T. Dalgleish & M. J. Power (Eds.), *Handbook of cognition and emotion.* Chichester, England: Wiley.

Ekman, P. (1999b). Facial expressions. In T. Dalgleish & M. J. Power (Eds.), *Handbook of cognition and emotion.* Chichester, England: Wiley.

Ekman, P., & Davidson, R. (1994). *The nature of emotion: Fundamental questions.* New York: Oxford University Press.

Ekman, P., & Friesen, W. V. (1987). *Facial action coding system.* Palo Alto, CA: Consulting Psychologists Press.

Ekman, P., Davidson, R. J., & Friesen, W. V. (1990). The Duchenne smile: Emotional expression and brain physiology II. *Journal of Personality and Social Psychology, 58,* 342–353.

Ekman, P., et al. (1976). Universal and cultural difference in the judgments of social expressions of emotions. *Journal of Personality and Social Psychology, 53,* 712–717.

Ekman, P., Friesen, W. V., & O'Sullivan, M. (1988). Smiles when lying. *Journal of Personality and Social Psychology, 54,* 414–420.

Ekman, P., Levenson, R. W., & Friesen, W. V. (1983). Autonomic nervous system activity distinguishes among emotions. *Science, 221,* 1208–1210.

Elbert, T., Pantev, C., Wienbruch, C., Rockstroh, B., & Taub, E. (1995). Increased cortical representation of the fingers of the left hand in string players. *Science, 270,* 305–307.

Elkind, D. (1967). Egocentrism in adolescence. *Child Development, 38,* 1025–1034.

Ellenberger, H. F. (1970). *The discovery of the unconscious.* New York: Basic Books.

Ellicott, A., Hammen, C., Gitlin, M., Brown, G., & Jamison, K. (1990). Life events and the course of bipolar disorder. *American Journal of Psychiatry, 147,* 1194–1198.

Elliot, A. J., Chirkov, V. I., Kim, Y., & Sheldon, K. M. (2001). A cross-cultural analysis of avoidance (relative to approach) personal goals. *Psychological Science, 12,* 505-510.

Elliot, A. J., & Church, M. A. (1997). A hierarchical model of approach and avoidance achievement motivation. *Journal of Personality and Social Psychology, 72,* 218–232.

Elliot, A. J., & Devine, P. G. (1994). On the motivational nature of cognitive dissonance: Dissonance as psychological discomfort. *Journal of Personality and Social Psychology, 67,* 382–394.

Elliot, A. J., & McGregor, H. A. (1999). Test anxiety and the hierarchical model of approach and avoidance achievement motivation. *Journal of Personality and Social Psychology, 76,* 628–644.

Elliot, A. J., McGregor, H. A., & Gable, S. (1999). Achievement goals, study strategies, and exam performance: A mediational analysis. *Journal of Educational Psychology, 91,* 549–563.

Elliott, M. A., Armitage, C. J., Baughan, C. J. (2007). Using the theory of planned behaviour to predict observed driving behaviour. *British Journal of Social Psychology, 46*(1), 69–70.

Ellis, A. (1962). *Reason and emotion in psychotherapy.* New York: Lyle Stuart.

Ellis, L., & Ames, M. A. (1987). Neurohormonal functioning and sexual orientation: A theory of homosexuality-heterosexuality. *Psychology Bulletin, 101,* 233–258.

Ellis, N. R., & Hope, R. (1968). Memory processes and the serial position curve. *Journal of Experimental Psychology, 77,* 613–619.

Emerson, R. M. (1966). Mount Everest: A case study of communication feedback and sustained group goal-striving. *Sociometry, 29,* 213–227.

Emery, C. E., Jr. (2001). Cracked crystal balls? Psychics' predictions for past year a litany of prognostive failures. *The Skeptical Inquirer, 25(1),* 7–8.

Emery, R. E. (1982). Interparental conflict and the children of discord and divorce. *Psychological Bulletin, 92,* 310–330.

Emery, R. E., & Laumann-Billings, L. (1998). An overview of the nature, causes, and consequences of abusive family relationships: Toward differentiating maltreatment and violence. *American Psychologist, 53,* 121–135.

Emlen, S. T. (1975, August). The stellar-orientation system of a migratory bird. *Scientific American,* 102–111.

Emler, N. (1998). Sociomoral understanding. In A. Campbell & S. Muncer (Eds.), *The social child.* Hove, England: Psychology Press/Erlbaum.

Endler, N. S. (1982). *Holiday of darkness: A psychologist's personal journey out of his depression.* New York: Wiley.

Enquist, M., & Leimar, O. (1990). The evolution of fatal fighting. *Animal Behaviour, 39,* 1–9.

Epling, W. F., & Pierce, W. D. (1992). *Solving the anorexia puzzle: A scientific approach.* Toronto: Hogrefe & Huber.

Epps, J., & Kendall, P. C. (1995). Hostile attributional bias in adults. *Cognitive Therapy and Research, 19,* 159–178.

Epps, J., Monk, C., Savage, S., & Marlatt, G. A. (1998). Improving credibility of instructions in the balanced placebo design: a misattribution manipulation. *Addictive Behaviors, 23,* 427–435.

Epstein, J. A., & Harackiewicz, J. M. (1992). Winning is not enough: The effects of competition and achievement orientation on intrinsic interest. *Personality and Social Psychology Bulletin, 18,* 128–138.

Epstein, M. A., & Bottoms, B. L. (2002). Explaining the forgetting and recovery of abuse and trauma memories: Possible mechanisms. *Child Maltreatment: Journal of the American Professional Society on the Abuse of Children, 7,* 210–225.

Epstein, R., Kirshnit, C. E., Lanza, R. P., & Rubin, L. C. (1984). "Insight" in the pigeon: Antecedents and determinants of an intelligent performance. *Nature, 308,* 61–62.

Epstein, S. (1983). Aggregation and beyond: Some basic issues on the production of behavior. *Journal of Personality, 51,* 360–392.

Epstein, S. (1994). Integration of the cognitive and the psychodynamic unconscious. *American Psychologist, 49,* 709–724.

Epstein, S. (1998). *Constructive thinking: The key to emotional intelligence.* Westport, CT: Praeger.

Epstein, S. (1999). The interpretation of dreams from the perspective of cognitive experiential self-theory. In J. A. Singer & P. Salovey (Eds.), *At play in the fields of consciousness: Essays in honor of Jerome L. Singer.* Mahwah, NJ: Erlbaum.

Erdberg, P. (2000). Rorschach assessment. In G. Goldstein & M. Hersen (Eds.), *Handbook of psychological assessment* (3rd ed.). New York: Elsevier.

Erdelyi, M. H. (1985). *Psychoanalysis: Freud's cognitive psychology.* New York: W. H. Freeman.

Erdelyi, M. H. (1988). Repression, reconstruction and defense: History and integration of the psychoanalytic and experimental frameworks. In J. Singer (Ed.), *Repression: Defense mechanism and cognitive style.* Chicago: University of Chicago Press.

Erdelyi, M. H. (1995). *Psychoanalysis: Freud's cognitive psychology.* New York: W. H. Freeman.

Erdmann, K., Volbert, R., & Bohm, C. (2004). Children report suggested events even when interviewed in a non-suggestive manner: What are its implications for credibility assessment? *Applied Cognitive Psychology, 18,* 589–611.

Ericsson, K. A., & Polson, P. G. (1988). An experimental analysis of the mechanisms of a memory skill. *Journal of Experimental Psychology: Learning, Memory, and Cognition, 14,* 305–316.

Erikson, E. H. (1950, 1963). *Childhood and society.* New York: W. W. Norton.

Erikson, E. H. (1968). *Identity, youth and crisis.* New York: W. W. Norton.

Erikson, E. H. (1980). *Identity and the life cycle.* New York: W. W. Norton. (Original work published 1959)

Erikson, E. H., Erikson, J. M., & Kivnick, H. Q. (1986). *Vital involvement in old age.* New York: W. W. Norton.

Eriksson, P. S., Perfilieva, E., Bjork-Erikkson, T., Alborn, A. M., Nordborg, C., Peterson, D. A., & Gage, F. H. (1998). Neurogenesis in the adult human hippocampus. *Nature Medicine, 4*(11), 1313–1317.

Eron, L. D. (1987). The development of aggressive behavior from the perspective of a developing behaviorism. *American Psychologist, 42,* 435–442.

Eron, L. D. (2000). A psychological perspective. In V. B. Van Hasselt & M. Hersen (Eds.), *Aggression and violence: An introductory text.* Boston: Allyn & Bacon.

Esparza, J., Fox, C., Harper, I. T., Bennett, P. H., Schulz, L. O., Valencia, M. E., & Ravussin, E. (2000). Daily energy expenditure in Mexican and USA Pima indians: Low physical activity as a possible cause of obesity. *International Journal of Obesity and Related Metabolic Disorders, 24,* 55–59.

Essau, C. A., & Petermann, F. (1999). *Depressive disorders in children and adolescents: Epidemiology, risk factors, and treatment.* Northvale, NJ: Jason Aronson.

Essau, C. A., & Trommsdorff, G. Coping with university-related problems: A cross-cultural comparison. *Journal of Cross-Cultural Psychology, 27,* 315–328.

Esser, J. K. (1998). Alive and well after 25 years: A review of groupthink research. *Organizational Behavior and Human Decision Processes, 73,* 116–141.

Esser, J. K., & Lindoerfer, J. S. (1989). Groupthink and the space shuttle Challenger accident: Toward a quantitative case analysis. *Journal of Behavioral Decision Making, 2,* 167–177.

Esses, V., Dovidio, J., & Hodson, G. (2001). Public Attitudes Toward Immigration in the United States and Canada in Response to the September 11, 2001 "Attack on America" in Unger, R. (Ed), *Terrorism and Its Consequences. Analysis of Social Issues and Public Policy, Society for the Psychological Study of Social Issues,* Blackwell Publishers. [Online]. Available: http://www.asap-spssi.org/default.htm

Esses, V.M., & Hodson, G. (2006). The role of lay perceptions of ethnic prejudice in the maintenance and perpetuation of ethnic bias. *Journal of Social Issues, 62,* 453-56.

Esses, V.M., & Zanna, M.P. (1995). Mood and the expression of ethnic stereotypes. *Journal of Personality and Social Psychology,* 69, 1052–1068.

Essock-Vitale, S. M., & McGuire, M. T. (1985). Women's lives viewed from an evolutionary perspective: II. Patterns of helping. *Ethology and Sociobiology, 6,* 155–173.

Estes, T. H., & Vaughn, J. L. (1985). *Reading and learning in the content classroom: Diagrams and instructional strategies* (3rd ed.). Boston: Allyn & Bacon.

Estes, W. K. (1991). Cognitive architectures from the standpoint of an experimental psychologist. *Annual Review of Psychology, 42,* 1–28.

Everitt, B. J., Parkinson, J. A., Olmstead, M. C., Arroyo, M., Robledo, P., Robbins, T. W. (1999). Associative processes in addiction and reward. The role of amygdala-ventral striatal subsystems. *Annals of the New York Academy of Sciences, 877,* 412–438.

Evers, K. E., Harlow, H. L., Redding, C. A., & LaForge, R. G. (1998). Longitudinal changes in stages of change for condom use in women. *American Journal of Health Promotion, 13,* 19–25.

Exner, J. E. Jr. & Erdberg, P. (2005). *The Rorschach: A comprehensive system* (3rd ed.) *Advanced interpretation, Vol. 2.* Hoboken, NJ: John Wiley & Sons.

Eysenck, H. J. (1952). The effects of psychotherapy: An evaluation. *Journal of Consulting Psychology, 16,* 319–324.

Eysenck, H. J. (1964). *Crime and personality.* Boston: Houghton Mifflin.

Eysenck, H. J. (1967). *The biological basis of personality.* Springfield, IL: Charles C Thomas.

Eysenck, H. J. (1990). Biological dimensions of personality. In L. A. Pervin (Ed.), *Handbook of personality: Theory and research.* New York: Guilford Press.

Eysenck, H. J. (1991). Dimensions of personality: 16, 5, or 3? Criteria for a taxonic paradigm. *Personality and Individual Differences, 12,* 773–790.

Eysenck, H. J. (1993). Creativity and personality: Word association, origence, and psychoticism. *Creativity Research Journal, 7,* 209–216.

Eysenck, H. J. (1994). Cancer, personality, and stress: Prediction and prevention. *Advances in Behaviour Research and Therapy, 16,* 167–215.

Eysenck, H. J., & Grossarth-Marticek, R. (1991). Creative novation behavior therapy as a prophylactic treatment for cancer and coronary heart disease: Part II—Effects of treatment. *Behavior Research and Therapy, 29,* 17–31.

Eysenck, M. W. (1989). Personality, stress arousal, and cognitive processes in stress transactions. In R. W. J. Newfeld (Ed.), *Advances in the investigation of psychological stress.* New York: Wiley.

Eysenck, M. W., & Eysenck, M. C. (1980). Effects of processing depth, distinctiveness, and word frequency on retention. *British Journal of Psychology, 71,* 263–274.

Fagley, N. S. (1987). Positional response bias in multiple-choice tests of learning: Its relation to testwiseness and guessing strategy. *Journal of Educational Psychology, 79,* 95–97.

Fagot, B. I., Leinbach, M. D., & O'Boyle, C. (1992). Gender labeling, gender stereotyping, and parenting behaviors. *Developmental Psychology, 28,* 225–230.

Faith, M. S., Matz, P. E., & Jorge, M. A. (2002). Obesity depression associations in the population. *Journal of Psychosomatic Research, 53,* 935–942.

Fallon, A. E., & Rozin, P. (1985). Sex differences in perceptions of desirable body shape. *Journal of Abnormal Psychology, 94,* 102–105.

Fanselow, M. S. (1991). Analgesia as a response to aversive Pavlovian conditional stimuli: Cognitive and emotional mediators. In M. R. Denny (Ed.), *Fear, avoidance, and phobias: A fundamental analysis.* Hillsdale, NJ: Erlbaum.

Fanselow, M. S. (2000). Amygdala. In G. Fink (Ed.), *Encyclopedia of stress.* San Diego: Academic Press.

Fantz, R. L. (1961, May). The origin of form perception. *Scientific American,* 66–72.

Farina, B., Della marca, A., & Grochocinski, V. J. (2003). Microstructure of sleep in depressed patients according to the cyclic alternating pattern. *Journal of Affective Discord, 77,* 227–235.

Farthing, G. W., Venturino, M., Brown, S. W., & Lazar, J. D. (1997). Internal and external distraction in the control of cold-pressor pain as a function of hypnotizability. *International Journal of Clinical and Experimental Hypnosis, 45,* 433–446.

Faust, J. (1991). Same-day surgery preparation: Reduction of pediatric patient arousal and distress through participant modeling. *Journal of Consulting and Clinical Psychology, 59,* 473–478.

Fawcett, G. M., Heise, L. L., Isita-Espejel, L., & Pick, S. (1999). Changing community responses to wife abuse: A research and demonstration project in Iztacalco, Mexico. *American Psychologist, 54,* 41–49.

Fazio, R. H., Jackson, J. R., Dunton, B. C., & Williams, C. J. (1995). Variability in automatic activation as an unobstrusive measure of racial attitudes: A bona fide pipeline? *Journal of Personality and Social Psychology, 69,* 1013–1027.

Fazio, R. H., Zanna, M. P., & Cooper, J. (1977). Dissonance and self-perception: An integrative view of each theory's proper domain of application. *Journal of Experimental Social Psychology, 13,* 464–479.

Federal Bureau of Investigation (1999). *FBI supplementary homicide reports.* Washington, DC: Author.

Feeny, N. C., & Foa, E. B. (2000). Sexual assault. In G. Fink (Ed.), *Encyclopedia of stress.* San Diego: Academic Press.

Fein, S., & Spencer, S. J. (1997). Prejudice as self-image maintenance: Affirming the self through derogating others. *Journal of Personality and Social Psychology, 73,* 31–44.

Feingold, A. (1988). Matching for attractiveness in romantic partners and same-sex friends: A meta-analysis and theoretical critique. *Psychological Bulletin, 104,* 226–235.

Feingold, A. (1992). Good-looking people are not what we think. *Psychological Bulletin, 11,* 304–341.

Feingold, A. (1994). Gender differences in personality: A meta-analysis. *Psychological Bulletin, 116,* 429–456.

Feingold, A., & Mazzella, R. (1998). Gender differences in body image are increasing. *Psychological Science, 9,* 190–195.

Feist, J., & Brannon, L. (2000). *Health psychology.* Boston: Allyn & Bacon.

Felder, C. C., & Glass, M. (1998). Cannabinoid receptors and their endogenous agonists. *Annual Review of Pharmacology and Toxicology, 38,* 179–200.

Feldman, M.A., Garrick, M., & Case, L. (1997). The effects of parent training on weight gain of non-organic-failure-to-thrive children of parents with intellectual disabilities. *Journal on Developmental Disabilities, 5,* 47–61.

Felmlee, D. H. (1998). "Be careful what you wish for . . .": A quantitative and qualitative investigation of "fatal attractions." *Personal Relationships, 5,* 235–253.

Felton, D. L., & Maida, M. E. (2000). Neuroimmunomodulation. In G. Fink (Ed.), *Encyclopedia of stress.* San Diego: Academic Press.

Feng, A. S., & Ratnam, R. (2000). Neural basis of hearing in real-world situations. *Annual Review of Psychology, 51,* 699–726.

Fenton, W. S., & McGlaskan, T. H. (1991a). Natural history of schizophrenia subtypes: I. Longitudinal study of paranoid, hebephonic, and undifferentiated schizophrenia. *Archives of General Psychiatry, 48,* 969–977.

Fenton, W. S., & McGlaskan, T. H. (1991b). Natural history of schizophrenia subtypes: II. Positive and negative symptoms and long-term course. *Archives of General Psychiatry, 48,* 978–986.

Ferguson, E. D. (1999). *Motivation: A biosocial and cognitive integration of motivation and emotion.* New York: Oxford University Press.

Fergusson, D. M., & Lynskey, M. T. (1997). Physical punishment/maltreatment during childhood and adjustment in young adulthood. *Child Abuse and Neglect, 21,* 617–630.

Fernald, A., Taeschner, T., Dunn, J., Papousek, M., De Boysson-Bardies, B., & Fukui, I. (1989). A cross-cultural study of prosodic modification in mothers' and fathers' speech to preverbal infants. *Journal of Child Language, 16,* 477–501.

Ferster, C. B., & Skinner, B. F. (1957). *Schedules of reinforcement.* Englewood Cliffs, NJ: Prentice-Hall.

Fessler, R. G. (1989). Physiology, anatomy and pharmacology of pain perception. In P. M. Camic & F. D. Brown, (Eds.), *Assessing chronic pain: A multidisciplinary approach.* New York: Springer-Verlag.

Festinger, L. (1954). A theory of social comparison processes. *Human Relations, 2,* 117–140.

Festinger, L. (1957). *A theory of cognitive dissonance.* Stanford, CA: Stanford University Press.

Festinger, L., & Carlsmith, J. M. (1959). Cognitive consequences of forced compliance. *Journal of Abnormal and Social Psychology, 58,* 203–210.

Festinger, L., Pepitone, A., & Newcomb, T. (1952). Some consequences of deindividuation in a group. *Journal of Abnormal and Social Psychology, 47,* 382–389.

Festinger, L., Schachter, S., & Back, K. (1950). *Social pressures in informal groups: A study of a housing community.* New York: Harper.

Fetterman, D. M. (1988). *Excellence and equality: A qualitatively different perspective on gifted and talented education.* Albany, NY: State University of New York Press.

Fichera, L. V., & Andreassi, J. L. (1998). Stress and personality as factors in women's cardiovascular reactivity. *International Journal of Psychophysiology, 28,* 143–155.

Fiedler, K. (2000). Toward an integrative account of affect and cognition phenomena using the BIAS computer algorithm. In J. P. Forgas (Ed.), *Feeling and thinking: The role of affect in social cognition.* New York: Cambridge University Press.

Field, T. (1995). Massage therapy for infants and children. *Journal of Developmental and Behavioral Pediatrics, 16,* 105–111.

Field, T. (2002). Preterm infant massage therapy studies: an American approach. *Seminars in Neonatology, 7,* 487–494.

Field, T. M., Schanberg, S. M., Scafidi, F., Bauer, C. R., Vega-Lahr, N., Garcia, R., Nystrom, J., & Kuhn, C. M. (1986). Tactile/kinesthetic stimulation effects on preterm neonates. *Pediatrics, 77,* 654–658.

Field, T., Grizzle, N., Scafidi, F., Abrams, S., Richardson, S., Kuhn, C., & Schanberg, S. (1996). Massage therapy for infants of depressed mothers. *Infant Behavior and Development, 19,* 107–112.

Field, T., Woodson, R., Cohen, D., Garcia, R., & Greenberg, R. (1983). Discrimination and imitation of facial expressions by term and pre-term neonates. *Infant Behavior and Development, 6,* 485–490.

Filogamo, G. (1998). *Brain plasticity: Development and aging: Advances in neurobiology: plasticity and regeneration.* New York: Plenum.

Finell, J. S. (1997). *Mind-body problems: Psychotherapy with psychosomatic disorders.* Northvale, NJ: Jason Aronson.

Fischer, K. W., Shaver, P. R., & Carnochan, P. (1990). How emotions develop and how they organize development. *Cognition and Emotion, 4,* 81–127.

Fishbein, M. (1980). A theory of reasoned action: Some applications and implications. In H. E. Howe & M. M. Page (Eds.), *Nebraska Symposium on Motivation*

(Vol. 27, 65–116). Lincoln: University of Nebraska Press.

Fishbein, M., & Ajzen, I. (1974). Attitudes toward objects as predictors of single and multiple behavioral criteria. *Psychological Review, 81,* 59–74.

Fisher, C., Kahn E., Edwards, A., Davis, D. M., & Fine, J. (1974). A psychophysiological study of nightmares and night terrors: III. Mental content and recall of stage 4 night terrors. *Journal of Nervous and Mental Disease, 158,* 174–188.

Fisher, S., & Greenberg, R. P. (1996). *Freud scientifically reappraised: Testing the theories and therapy.* New York: Wiley.

Fiske, S. T. (2000). Interdependence reduces stereotyping and prejudice. In S. Oskamp (Ed.), *Reducing prejudice and discrimination.* Mahwah, NJ: Erlbaum.

Fiske, S. T. (2002). What we know about bias and intergroup conflict, the problem of the century. *Current Directions in Psychological Science, 11,* 123–128.

Fiske, S. T., & Taylor, S. E. (1991). *Social cognition* (2nd ed.). New York: McGraw-Hill.

Fivush, R., Nelson, K. (2004). Culture and language in the emergence of autobiographical memory. *Psychological Science, 15(9),* 573–577.

Flavell, J. H. (1970). Developmental studies of mediated behavior. In H. W. Reese and L. P. Lipsett (Eds.), *Advances in child development and behavior* (Vol. 5). New York: Academic Press.

Flavell, J. H., Miller, P. H., and Miller, S. A. (1993). *Cognitive Development* (3rd ed.). Upper Saddle River, NJ: Prentice-Hall.

Flavell, J. H., Green, F. L., & Flavell, E. R. (1990). Developmental changes in young children's knowledge about the mind. *Cognitive Development, 5,* 1–27.

Flegal, K. M., Carroll, M. D., Kuczmarski, R. J., & Johnson, C. L. (1998). Overweight and obesity in the United States: Prevalence and trends, 1960–1994. *International Journal of Obesity Related Metabolic Disorders, 22,* 39–47.

Fleming, I., Baum, A., & Weiss, L. (1987). Social density and perceived control as mediators of crowding stress in high-density residential neighborhoods. *Journal of Personality and Social Psychology, 52,* 899–906.

Flett, G. L., Vredenbrug, K., & Krames, L. (1997). The continuity of depression in clinical and nonclinical samples. *Psychological Bulletin, 121,* 395–416.

Flinn, M. V. (1997). Culture and the evolution of social learning. *Evolution and Human Behavior, 18,* 23–67.

Floyd, F. J., & Wasner, G. H. (1994). Social exchange, equity, and commitment: Structural equation modeling of dating relationships. *Journal of Family Psychology, 8,* 55–73.

Flynn, J. P. (1975). Experimental analysis of aggression and its neural basis. In J. P. Flynn (Ed.), *Advances in behavioral biology, the neurophysiology of aggression.* New York: Academic Press.

Flynn, J. R. (1987). Massive IQ gains in 14 nations. What IQ tests really measure. *Psychological Bulletin, 101*(2), 171–191.

Flynn, J. R. (1998). IQ gains over time: Toward finding the causes. In U. Neisser et al. (Eds.). *The rising curve: Long-term gains in IQ and related measures.* Washington, DC: American Psychological Association.

Flynn, J. R. (1991). *Asian-Americans: Achievement beyond IQ.* Hillsdale, NJ: Erlbaum.

Foa, E. B., Franklin, M., Perry, K., Herbert, J. (2006). Cognitive biases in generalized social phobia. *Journal of Abnormal Psychology, 105(3),* 433–439.

Foa, E. B., & Meadows, E. A. (1997). Psychosocial treatments for posttraumatic stress disorder: A critical review. *Annual Review of Psychology, 48,* 449–480.

Foa, E. B., Hearst-Ikeda, D., & Perry, K. J. (1995). Evaluation of a brief cognitive-behavioral program for the prevention of chronic PTSD in recent assault victims. *Journal of Consulting and Clinical Psychology, 63,* 948–955.

Foa, E. B., Riggs, D. S., & Gershuny, B. S. (1995). Arousal, numbing, and intrusion: Symptom structure of post traumatic stress disorder following assault. *American Journal of Psychology, 152,* 116–120.

Foa, E. B., Steketee, G., & Grayson, J. B. (1985). Imaginal and in vivo exposure: A comparison with obsessive-compulsive checkers. *Behavior Therapy, 16,* 292–302.

Folkman, S., & Lazarus, R. S. (1988). Coping as a mediator of emotion. *Journal of Personality and Social Psychology, 54,* 466–475.

Ford, T. M., Liwag, M., Michelle, G., Foley, L. A. (1998). Perceptions of rape based on sex and sexual orientation of victim. *Journal of Social Behavior and Personality, 13,* 253–262.

Fordyce, W. E. (1988). Pain and suffering: A reappraisal. *American Psychologist, 43,* 276–283.

Forgas, J. P. (Ed.) (2000). *Feeling and thinking: The role of affect in social cognition.* New York: Cambridge University Press.

Foster, C. A., Witcher, B. S., Campbell, W. K., & Green, J. D. (1998). Arousal and attraction: Evidence for automatic and controlled processes. *Journal of Personality and Social Psychology, 74,* 86–101.

Foulkes, D. (1962). Dream reports from different states of sleep. *Journal of Abnormal and Social Psychology, 65,* 14–25.

Foulkes, D. (1982). REM-dream perspectives on the development of affect and cognition. *Psychiatric Journal of the University of Ottawa, 7,* 48–55.

Foulkes, D. (1985). *Dreaming: A cognitive-psychological analysis.* Hillsdale, NJ: Erlbaum.

Foulkes, D. (1996). Dream research: 1953–1993. *Sleep, 19,* 609–624.

Foulkes, D. (1999). *Children's dreaming and the development of consciousness.* Cambridge, MA: Harvard University Press.

Foulks, F. F., Bland, I. J., & Shervington, D. (1995). Psychotherapy across cultures. *Review of Psychiatry, 14,* 511.

Foushee, H. C. (1984). Dyads and triads at 35,000 feet: Factors affecting group process and aircrew performance. *American Psychologist, 39,* 885–893.

Fouts, D. H. (1994). The use of remote video recordings to study the use of American Sign Language by chimpanzees when no humans are present. In R. A. Gardner, B. T. Gardner, A. B. Chiarelli, & F. X. Plooij (Eds.), *The ethological roots of culture.* Dordrecht, Netherlands: Kluwer.

Fouts, R. S. (1972). Use of guidance in teaching sign language to a chimpanzee (Pan troglodytes). *Journal of Comparative and Physiological Psychology, 80,* 515–522.

Fouts, R. S., Fouts, D. H., & Van Cantfort, T. E. (1989). The infant Loulis learns signs from other cross-fostered chimpanzees. In R. A. Gardner, B. T. Gardner, & T. E. Van Cantfort (Eds.), *Teaching sign language to chimpanzees.* Albany, NY: State University of New York Press.

Fowers, B. J., & Richardson, F. C. (1996). Why is multiculturalism good? *American Psychologist, 51,* 609–621.

Fowles, D. C. (1992). Schizophrenia: Diathesis-stress revisited. *Annual Review of Psychology, 43,* 303–336.

Fox, D. K., Hopkins, B. L., & Anger, W. K. (1987). The long-term effects of a token economy on safety performance in open-pit mining. *Journal of Applied Behavior Analysis, 20,* 215–224.

Fox, N. A., & Davidson, R. J. (1991). Hemispheric specialization and attachment behaviors: Developmental processes and individual differences in separation process. In J. L. Gewirtz & W. M. Kurtines (Eds.). *Interactions with attachment.* Hillsdale, NJ: Erlbaum.

Fox, P. T. (1977). The growth of human brain mapping. *Human Brain Mapping, 5,* 1–2.

Frank, N. C., Spirito, A., Stark, L., Owens-Stively, J. (1997). The use of scheduled awakenings to eliminate childhood sleepwalking. *Journal of Pediatric Psychology, 22,* 345–353.

Frankenhaeuser, M., Lundberg, U., & Chesney, M. (1991). *Women, work, and health: Stress and opportunities.* New York: Plenum.

Franklin, J. (1987). *Molecules of the mind: The brave new science of molecular psychology.* New York: Atheneum.

Franzek, E., & Beckmann, H. (1999). *Psychoses of the schizophrenic spectrum in twins: A discussion on the nature-nurture debate in the etiology of "endogenous" psychoses.* New York: Springer-Verlag.

Frazier, K. (Ed.) (1986). *Science confronts the paranormal.* Buffalo, NY: Prometheus Books.

Fredrickson, B. L. (1998). What good are positive emotions? *Review of General Psychology, 2,* 300–319.

Fredrickson, B. L., & Roberts, T. A. (1997). Objectification theory: Toward understanding women's lived experiences and mental health risks. *Psychology of Women Quarterly, 21,* 173–206.

Fredrickson, B. L., Roberts, T. A., Noll, S. M., Quinn, D. M., & Twenge, J. M. (1998). That swimsuit becomes you: Sex differences in self-objectification, restrained eating, and math performance. *Journal of Personality and Social Psychology, 75,* 269–284.

Freedman, J. L., & Fraser, S. C. (1966). Compliance without pressure: The foot-in-the-door technique. *Journal of Personality and Social Psychology, 4,* 195–202.

Freedman, R. R., Johanson, C. E., & Tancer, M. E. (2005). Thermoregulatory effects of 3,4-methylenedioxymethamphetamine (MDMA) in humans. *Psychopharmacology (Berlin) 183,* 248–256.

Freeman, H. (1994). Schizophrenia and city residence. *British Journal of Psychiatry, 164* (Suppl. 23), 39–50.

Freud, S. (1923). *The ego and the id.* New York: W. W. Norton.

Freud, S. (1935). *A general introduction to psychoanalysis.* New York: Washington Square Press.

Freud, S. (1950). Project for a scientific psychology. In J. Strachey (Ed. and Trans.), *The standard edition of the complete works of Sigmund Freud* (Vol. 5). London: Hogarth Press. (Original work published 1893)

Freud, S. (1953). *A general introduction to psychoanalysis.* New York: Perma-books.

Freud, S. (1953). The interpretation of dreams. In J. Strachey (Ed.), *The standard edition of the complete psychological works of Sigmund Freud* (Vols. 4 & 5). London: Hogarth. (Original work published 1900)

Freud, S. (1957). Mourning and melancholia. In J. Strachey (Ed.), *The standard edition of the complete psychological works of Sigmund Freud* (Vol. 14). London: Hogarth. (Original work published 1917)

Freud, S. (1964). *New introductory lectures in psychoanalysis.* New York: Norton. (Original work published 1933)

Friedberg, J. (1975). Let's stop blasting the brain. *Psychology Today, 35,* 18–26.

Friedlander, L., & Desrocher, M. (2006). Neuroimaging studies of obsessive-compulsive disorder in adults and children. *Clinical Psychology Review, 26*(1), 32-49.

Friedman, H. (Ed.) (1991). *Hostility, coping, and health.* Washington, DC: American Psychological Association.

Friedman, H. & DiMatteo, M. R. (1989). *Health psychology.* New York: Prentice Hall.

Friedman, H. S., & Booth-Kewley, S. (1987). The "disease-prone personality": A meta-analytic view of the construct. *American Psychologist, 42,* 539–555.

Friedman, H. S., Tucker, J. S., Schwartz, J. E., Tomlinson-Keasy, C., Wingard, L., & Criqui, M. H. (1995). Psychosocial and behavioral predictors of longevity: The aging and death of the Termites. *American Psychologist, 50,* 69–78.

Friedman, W. J., Robinson, A. B., & Friedman, B. L. (1987). Sex differences in moral judgments? A test of Gilligan's theory. *Psychology of Women Quarterly, 11,* 37–46.

Frisby, J. P. (1980). *Seeing: Illusion, brain, and mind.* Oxford: Oxford University Press.

Fristoe, N. M., Salthouse, T. A., & Woodard, J. L. (1997). Examination of age-related deficits on the Wisconsin Card Sorting Test. *Neuropsychology, 11,* 428–436.

Fritsch, J. (1999, May 25). 95% Regain Lost Weight. Or Do They? *The New York Times,* F7.

Frodi, A. M., et al. (1978). Fathers' and mothers' responses to the faces and cries of normal and premature infants. *Developmental Psychology, 14,* 490–498.

Fromm, E. (1956). *The art of loving.* New York: Harper.

Fry, J. M. (1998). Treatment modalities for narcolepsy. *Neurology, 50* (2, Suppl. 1), S43–S48.

Fuligni, A. J. (1998). Authority, autonomy, and parent-adolescent conflict and cohesion: A study of adolescents from Mexican, Chinese, Filipino, and European backgrounds. *Developmental Psychology, 34,* 782–792.

Fuller, J. L. & Thompson, W.R. (1960). *Behavior Genetics.* New York: Wiley.

Funk, S. C. (1992). Hardiness: A review of theory and research. *Health Psychology 11,* 335–345.

Furmark, T., Tillfors, M., Marteinsdottir, I., Fischer, H., Pissiota, A., Langstroem, B., Fredrikson, M. (2002). Common changes in cerebral blood flow in patients with social phobia treated with citalopram or cognitive-behavioral therapy. *Archives of General Psychiatry, 59,* 425–433.

Gabbard, G. O. (1990). *Psychodynamic psychiatry in clinical practice.* Washington, DC: American Psychiatric Press.

Gabrieli, J. D. E. (1998). Cognitive neuroscience of human memory. *Annual Review of Psychology, 49,* 87–115.

Gabrieli, J. D. E., Desmond, J. E., Demb, J. B., & Wagner, A. D. (1996). Functional magnetic resonance imaging of semantic memory processes in the frontal lobes. *Psychological Science, 7,* 278–283.

Gacsaly, S. A., & Borges, C. A. (1979). The male physique and behavioral expectancies. *Journal of Psychology, 101,* 97–102.

Gaertner, S. L., Dovidio, J. F., Banker, B. S., Houletter, M., Johnson, K. M., & McGlynn, E. A. (2000). Reducing intergroup conflict: From superordinate goals to decategorization, recategorization, and mutual differentiation. *Group Dynamics, 4,* 98–114.

Gainotti, G. (1972). Emotional behavior and hemispheric side of lesion. *Cortex, 8,* 41–55.

Galati, D., & Lavelli, M. (1997). Neonate and infant emotion expression perceived by adults. *Journal of Nonverbal Behavior, 21,* 57–83.

Galavotti, C., Saltzman, L. E., Sauter, S. L., & Sumartojo, E. (1997). Behavioral science activities at the Centers for Disease Control and Prevention: A selected overview of exemplary programs. *American Psychologist, 52,* 154–166.

Galea, S., Ahern, J., Resnick, H., Kilpatrick, D., Bucuvalas, M., Gold, J., & Vlahov, D. (2002). Psychological sequelae of the September 11 terrorist attacks in New York City. *New England Journal of Medicine, 346,* 982–987.

Galef, B. G., Jr. (1985). Social learning in wild Norway rats. In T. D. Johnson & A. T. Pietrewicz (Eds.), *Issues in the ecological study of learning.* Hillsdale, NJ: Erlbaum.

Galef, B. G. Jr., & Giraldeau, L-A. (2001). Social influences on foraging in vertebrates: Causal mechanisms and adaptive functions. *Animal Behaviour, 61,* 3–15.

Galef, B. G. Jr., & Whiskin, E. E. (2000). Demonstration of a socially transmitted flavor aversion in rats. Kuan and Colwill (1997) revisited. *Psychonomic Bulletin and Review, 7,* 631–635.

Galef, B. G. Jr., & Whiskin, E. E. (2001). Interaction of social and individual learning in food preferences of Norway rats. *Animal Behaviour, 62,* 41–46.

Gallo, V., & Chittajallu, R. (2001). Unwrapping glial cells from the synapse: What lies inside? *Science, 292,* 872–873.

Gallup Organization (1988). *America's youth 1977–1988.* Princeton, NJ: Author.

Gallup, G. G., Jr. (1970). Chimpanzees: Self-recognition. *Science, 167*(3914), 86–87.

Gallup, G. G., Jr. (1979). Self-awareness in primates. *American Scientist, 67,* 417–421.

Gallup, G. G., Jr., & Suarez, S. D. (1986). Self-awareness and the emergence of mind in humans and other primates. In J. Suls & A. G. Greenwald (Eds.), *Psychological perspectives on the self* (Vol. 3). Hillsdale, NJ: Erlbaum.

Gallup, G. H., Jr., & Newport, F. (1991, Winter). Belief in paranormal phenomena among adult Americans. *Skeptical Inquirer,* 137–146.

Galton, F. (1869). *Hereditary genius: An inquiry into its laws and consequences.* New York: Appleton.

Galton, F. (1883). *Inquiries into human faculty and its development.* London: Dent.

Gamwell, L., & Tomes, N. (1995). *Madness in America: Cultural and medical perceptions of mental illness before 1914.* Ithaca, NY: Cornell University Press.

Gander, P. H., Nguyen, D., Rosekind, M. R., & Connell, L. J. (1993). Age, circadian rhythms, and sleep loss in flight crews. *Aviation, Space, and Environmental Medicine, 64,* 189–195.

Garbarino, J. (1995). *Raising children in a socially toxic environment.* San Francisco: Jossey-Bass.

Garcia, J., & Koelling, R. A. (1966). The relation of cue to consequence in avoidance learning. *Psychonomic Science, 4,* 123–124.

Garcia, J., Lasiter, P. S., Bermudez, R. F., & Deems, D. A. (1985). A general theory of aversion learning. *Annals of the New York Academy of Sciences, 443,* 8–21.

Garcia-Palacios, A., Hoffman, H., Carlin, A. C., Furness III, T. A., & Botella, C. (2002). Virtual reality in the treatment of spider phobia: a controlled study. *Behaviour Research and Therapy, 40,* 983–993.

Gardiner, J. M., Gawlick, B., & Richardson, K. A. (1994). Maintenance rehearsal affects knowing, not remembering; elaborative rehearsal affects remembering, not knowing. *Psychonomic Bulletin and Review, 1,* 107–110.

Gardner, B. T., & Gardner, R. A. (1975). Evidence for sentence constituents in the early utterances of child and chimpanzee. *Journal of Experimental Psychology: General,* 104, 244–267.

Gardner, B. T., & Gardner, R. A. (1998). Development of phrases in the early utterances of children and cross-fostered chimpanzees. *Human Evolution, 13,* 161–188.

Gardner, H. (1983). *Frames of mind: The theory of multiple intelligences.* New York: Basic Books.

Gardner, R. A., & Gardner, B. T. (1969). Teaching language to a chimpanzee. *Science, 165,* 664–672.

Garfinkel, P. E. (1992). Evidence in support of attitudes to shape and weight as a diagnostic criterion of bulimia nervosa. *International Journal of Eating Disorders, 11,* 321–325.

Garfinkel, P. E., & Garner, D. M. (1982). *Anorexia nervosa: A multidimensional perspective.* New York: Brunner-Mazel.

Garland, D. J., & Barry, J. R. (1991). Cognitive advantage in sport: The nature of perceptual structures. *American Journal of Psychology, 104,* 211–228.

Garmezy, N. (1983). *Stress, coping and development in children.* New York: McGraw-Hill.

Garnefski, N., & Arends, E. (1998). Sexual abuse and adolescent maladjustment: Differences between male and female victims. *Journal of Adolescence, 21,* 99–107.

Garoff-Eaton, R. J., Slotnick, S. D., Schacter, D. L. (2006). Not all false memories are created equal: the neural basis of false recognition. *Cerebral Cortex, 16*(11), 1645–1652.

Gatchel, R. J., & Weisberg, J. N. (2000). *Personality characteristics of patients with pain.* Washington, DC: American Psychological Association.

Gathercole, S. E. (1998). The development of memory. *Journal of Child Psychology and Psychiatry and Allied Disciplines, 39,* 3–27.

Gauci, M., Husband, A. J., Saxarra, H., & King, M. G. (1994). Pavlovian conditioning of nasal tryptase release in human subjects with allergic rhinitis. *Physiology and Behavior, 55,* 823–825.

Gaylord-Ross, R. (1990). *Issues and research in special education.* New York: Teachers College Press.

Gazzaniga, M. S. (1985). *The social brain.* New York: Basic Books.

Gazzaniga, M. S., & Smylie, C. S. (1983). Facial recognition and brain asymmetries: Clues to underlying mechanisms. *Annals of Neurology, 13,* 536–540.

Gazzaniga, M. S., Fendrich, R., & Wessinger, C. M. (1994). Blindsight reconsidered. *Current Directions in Psychological Science, 3,* 93–95.

Gazzaniga, M. S., Steen, D., & Volpe, B. T. (1979). *Functional neuroscience.* New York: Harper & Row.

Ge, X., Conger, R. D., & Elder, G. H., Jr. (1996). Coming of age too early: Pubertal influences on girls' vulnerability to psychological distress. *Child Development, 67,* 3386–3400.

Geary, D. (1995). Reflections of evolution and culture in children's cognition: Implications for mathematical instruction and development. *American Psychologist, 50,* 24–37.

Geiger, M. A. (1991). Changing multiple choice answers: A validation and extension. *College Student Journal, 25,* 181–186.

Geller, G. & Thomas, C. D. (1999). A review of eating disorders in immigrant women: Possible evidence for a culture-change model. *Eating Disorders: The Journal of Treatment and Prevention.* 7: 279–297.

Genesee, F. & Gandara, P. (1999). Bilingual education programs: A cross-national perspective. *Journal of Social Issues, 55,* 665–685.

George, C., & Main, M. (1979). Social interactions of young abused children: Approach, avoidance, and aggression. *Child development, 50,* 306–318.

George, L. (1980). *Role transitions in later life.* Monterey, CA: Brooks/Cole.

George, W. H., Lehman, G. L., Cue, K. L., & Martinez, L. J. (1997). Postdrinking sexual inferences: Evidence for linear rather than curvilinear dosage effects. *Journal of Applied Social Psychology, 27,* 629–648.

George, W. H., Stoner, S. A., Norris, J., Lopez, P. A., & Lehman, G. L. (2000). Alcohol expectancies and sexuality: A self-fulfilling prophecy analysis of dyadic perceptions and behavior. *Journal of Studies on Alcohol, 61,* 168–176.

Geracioti, T. D., Loosen, P. T., Ebert, M. H., & Schmidt, D. (1995). Fasting and postprandial cerebrospinal fluid glucose concentrations in healthy women and in an obese binge eater. *International Journal of Eating Disorders, 18,* 365–369.

Gerben, R., deCraen, A. J. M., DeBoer, A., & Kessels, A. G. H. (1998). Is placebo analgesia mediated by endogenous opioids? A systematic review. *Pain, 76,* 273–275.

Gergen, K. (2000). *An invitation to social constructivism.* Thousand Oaks, CA: Sage Publications.

Gerhart, B. (1990). Voluntary turnover and alternative job opportunities. *Journal of Applied Psychology, 75,* 467–476.

Gershon, E. S., Berrettini, W. H., & Golden, L. E. (1989). Mood disorders: Genetic aspects. In H. I. Kaplan & B. J. Sadock (Eds.), *Comprehensive textbook of psychiatry/V.* Baltimore: Williams & Wilkins.

Gewirtz, J. C., & Davis, M. (1998). Application of Pavlovian higher-order conditioning to the analysis of the neural substrates of fear conditioning. *Neuropharmacology, 37,* 453–459.

Ghetti, S., Qin, J., & Goodman, G. S. (2002). False memories in children and adults: Age, distinctiveness, and subjective experience. *Developmental Psychology, 38,* 705–718.

Ghim, H.R. (1990). Evidence for perceptual organization in infants: Perception of subjective contours by young infants. *Infant Behavior & Development. 13,* 221–248.

Gibbs, J., Young, R. C., & Smith, G. P. (1973). Cholecystokinin decreases food intake in rats. *Journal of Comparative and Physiological Psychology, 84,* 488–495.

Gibson, E. J., & Walk, R. D. (1960). The "visual cliff." *Scientific American, 202,* 64–71.

Gibson, J. J. (1979). *The ecological approach to visual perception.* Boston: Houghton Mifflin.

Giedd, J. N. (2004). Structural magnetic resonance imaging of the adolescent brain. *Annals of the New York Academy of Sciences, 2021,* 77–85.

Giedd, J. N., Blumenthal, J., Molloy, E., & Castellanos, F. X. (2001). Brain imaging of attention deficit/hyperactivity disorder. *Annals of the New York Academy of Sciences, 931,* 33–49.

Giftakis, J. E., & Tait, R. W. (1998). Blocking of the rabbit's classically conditioned nictitating membrane response: Effects of modifications of contextual associative strength. *Learning and Motivation, 29,* 23–48.

Gilbert, D. T., & Malone, P. S. (1995). The correspondence bias. *Psychological Bulletin, 117,* 21–38.

Gilboa-Schechtman, E., & Foa, E. B. (2001). Patterns of recovery from trauma: The use of intraindividual analysis. *Journal of Abnormal Psychology, 110,* 392–400.

Gillespie, M. (1999, April 30). *Americans have very mixed opinions about blame for Littleton shootings.* Gallup News Service. Princeton, NJ: Gallup Organization.

Gillett, E. (1997). Revising Freud's structural theory. *Psychoanalysis and Contemporary Thought, 20,* 471–499.

Gillette, M. U. (1986). The suprachiasmatic nuclei: Circadian phase-shifts induced at the time of hypothalamic slice preparation are preserved in vitro. *Brain Research, 379,* 176–181.

Gilligan, C. (1982). *In a different voice: Psychological theory and women's development.* Cambridge, MA: Harvard University Press.

Glantz, K., Durlach, N. I., Barnett, R. C., & Aviles, W. A. (1996). Virtual reality (VR) for psychotherapy: From the physical to the social environment. *Psychotherapy, 33,* 464–473.

Glanzer, M., & Cunitz, A. R. (1966). Two storage mechanisms in free recall. *Journal of Verbal Learning and Verbal Behavior, 5,* 351–360.

Glaser, R., & Bassok, M. (1989). Learning theory and the study of instruction. *Annual Review of Psychology, 40,* 631–666.

Gleason, J.-B., & Ely, R. (2002). Gender differences in language development. In A. McGillicuddy-De Lisi & R. De Lisi (Eds.), *Biology, society, and behavior: The development of sex differences in cognition. Advances in applied developmental psychology* (Vol. 21). Westport, CT: Ablex Publishing.

Gleaves, D. H. (1996). The sociocognitive model of dissociative identity disorder: A reexamination of the evidence. *Psychological Bulletin, 120,* 42–59.

Glenberg, A. M., Sanocki, T., Epstein, W., & Morris, C. (1987). Enhancing calibration of comprehension. *Journal of Experimental Psychology: General, 116,* 119–136.

Glenn, N. D. (1998). The course of marital success and failure in five American 10-year marriage cohorts. *Journal of Marriage and the Family, 60*(3), 569–576.

Glick, P., & Fiske, S. T. (1999). Gender, power dynamics, and social interaction. In M. M. Ferree, J. Lorber, & B. B. Hess (Eds.), *Revisioning gender. The gender lens.* (Vol. 5). Thousand Oaks, CA: Sage Publications.

Gobet, F., Lane, P. C. R., Croker, S., Cheng, D. C. H., Jones, G., Oliver, L., Pine, J. M. (2001). Chunking mechanisms in human learning. *Trends in Cognitive Sciences, 5*(6), 236–243.

Goddard, A. W., Mason, G. F., Almai, A., et al. (2001). Reductions in occipital cortex GABA levels in panic disorder detected with sup-1H-magnetic resonance spectroscopy. *Archives of General Psychiatry, 58,* 556–561.

Goddard, H. H. (1917). Mental tests and the immigrant. *Journal of Delinquency, 2,* 243–277.

Godden, D. R., & Baddeley, A. D. (1975). Context-dependent memory in two natural environments: On land and under water. *British Journal of Psychology, 66,* 325–332.

Goffman, E. (1961). *Asylums: Essays on the social situation of mental patients and other inmates.* New York: Doubleday.

Gold, E. R. (1997). *Body parts: Property rights and ownership of human biological materials.* Washington, DC: Georgetown University Press.

Gold, S. R., & Reilly, J. P. (1985–1986). Daydreaming, current concerns and personality. *Imagination, Cognition and Personality, 5,* 117–125.

Goldapple, K. Segal, Z., Garson, C. et al. (2004) Modulation of cortical-limbic pathways in major depression: treatment-specific effects of cognitive behavior therapy. *Arch Gen Psychiatry, 61*(1), 34–41.

Goldberg, I. (2006). SSRIs and suicide. *American Journal of Psychiatry, 163*(11), 898–904.

Goldberg, J. L., & Barres, B. A. (2000). The relationship between neuronal survival and regeneration. *Annual Review of Neuroscience, 23,* 579–612.

Goldberg, L. R. (1981). Unconfounding situational attributions from uncertain, neutral, and ambiguous ones: A psychometric analysis of descriptions of oneself and various types of others. *Journal of Personality and Social Psychology, 41,* 517–552.

Goldberg, S. (1991). Recent developments in attachment theory and research. *Canadian Journal of Psychiatry, 36,* 393–400.

Goldstein, B. (2002). *Sensation and perception* (6th ed.). Belmont, CA: Wadsworth.

Goldstein, G. (2000). Comprehensive neuropsychological assessment batteries. In G. Goldstein & M. Hersen (Eds.), *Handbook of psychological assessment* (3rd ed.). New York: Elsevier.

Goldstein, J. H., Cajko, L., Oosterbroek, M., Michielsen, M., Houten, O., & Salverda, F. (1997). Video games and the elderly. *Social Behavior and Personality, 25,* 345–352.

Goleman, D. (1995, December 5). Making room on the couch for culture. *New York Times,* C1, C3.

Gonzales, R. A., Jaworski, J. N. (1997). Alcohol and glutamate. *Alcohol Health and Research World, 21,* 120–127.

Goodale, M.A., & Milner, A.D. (1992). Separate visual pathways for perception and action. *Trends Neuroscience, 15,* 20–25.

Goodale, M. A. et al. (1991). A neurological dissociation between perceiving objects and grasping them. *Nature, 349,* 154-156.

Goodall, J. (1971). *In the shadow of man.* London: William Collins.

Goodall, J. (1986). *The chimpanzees of Gombe: Patterns of behavior.* Cambridge, MA: Harvard University Press.

Goodman, G. S., Quas, J. A., Batterman-Faunce, J. M., Riddlesberger, M. M., & Kuhn, J. (1994). Predictors of accurate and inaccurate memories of traumatic events experienced in childhood. *Consciousness and Cognition: An International Journal, 3,* 269–294.

Goodman, W. (1982, August 9). Of mice, monkeys and men. *Newsweek,* p. 61.

Goody, E. N. (1997). Social intelligence and language: Another rubicon? In A. Whiten, et al. (Eds.), *Machiavellian intelligence II: Extensions and evaluations.* Cambridge: Cambridge University Press.

Gordon, R. A. (1997). The moderation of distinctiveness-based illusory correlation: The impact of circadian variations and personal need for structure. *Journal of Social Psychology, 137,* 514–526.

Gorman, J. M. (2002). Treatment of generalized anxiety disorder. *Journal of Clinical Psychiatry, 63*(Suppl. 8), 17–23.

Gosling, P., Denizeau, M., Oberlé, D. (2006). Denial of Responsibility: A new mode of dissonance reduction. *Journal of Personality and Social Psychology, 90*(5), 722–733.

Gosling, S. D., Vazire, S., Srivastava, S., & John, O. P. (2004). Should we trust web-based studies? A comparative analysis of six preconceptions about Internet questionnaires. *American Psychologist, 59,* 93–104.

Gothard, S. I., & Ivker, N. A. C. (2000). The evolving law of alleged delayed memories of childhood sexual abuse. *Child Maltreatment Journal of the American Professional Society on the Abuse of Children, 5,* 176–189.

Gottesman, I. I. (1991). *Schizophrenia genesis: The origins of madness.* New York: W. H. Freeman.

Gottfried, A. E., Fleming, J. S., & Gottfried, A. W. (1998). Role of cognitively stimulating home environment in children's academic intrinsic motivation: A longitudinal study. *Child Development, 69,* 1448–1460.

Gottfried, T. (2000). *Should drugs be legalized?* Brookfield: Twenty First Century.

Gottman, J. M. (1994). *What predicts divorce? The relationship between marital processes and marital outcomes.* Hillsdale, NJ: Erlbaum.

Gottman, J. M., & DeClaire, J. (2002). *The relationship cure: A five-step guide to strengthening your marriage, family, and friendships.* New York: Three Rivers Press.

Gottman, J. M., & Levinson, R. (1992). Marital processes predictive of later dissolution: Behavior, physiology and health. *Journal of Personality and Social Psychology, 63,* 221–233.

Gottman, J. M., Coan, J., Carrere, S., & Swanson, C. (1998). Predicting marital happiness and stability from newlywed interactions. *Journal of Marriage and the Family, 60,* 5–22.

Gottman, J., Swanson, C., & Murray, J. (1999). The mathematics of marital conflict: Dynamic mathematical nonlinear modeling of newlywed marital interaction. *Journal of Family Psychology, 13,* 3–19.

Gould, E., Reeves, A. J., Graziano, M. S. A., & Gross, C. G. (1999). Neurogenesis in the neocortex of adult primates. *Science* (October 15), 548–552.

Gouze, K. R., & Nadelman, L. (1980). Constancy of gender identity for self and others in children between the ages of three and seven. *Child Development, 51,* 275–278.

Graber, J. A., Brooks-Gunn, J., & Warren, M. (1995). The antecedents of menarcheal age: Heredity, family environment and stressful life events. *Child Development, 66,* 346–359.

Gracely, R. H., Farrell, M. J., & Grant, M. A. B. (2002). Temperature and pain perception. In H. Pashler & S.Yantis, (Eds.), *Steven's handbook of experimental psychology: Vol. 1. Sensation and perception* (3rd ed.). New York: Wiley.

Graf, P., & Schacter, D. L. (1985). Implicit and explicit memory for new associations in normal and amnesic subjects. *Journal of Experimental Psychology: Learning, Memory, and Cognition, 11,* 501–518.

Graham, S., Hudley, C., & Williams, E. (1992). Attributional and emotional determinants of aggression among African-American and Latino young adolescents. *Developmental Psychology, 28,* 731–740.

Grant, H. M., Bredahl, L. C., Clay, J., Ferrie, J., Groves, J. E., McDorman, T. A., & Dark, V. J. (1998). Context-dependent memory for meaningful material: Information for students. *Applied Cognitive Psychology, 12,* 617–623.

Gratton, A. & Wise, R. A. (1994). Drug- and behaviour-associated changes in dopamine-related electrochemical signals during intravenous cocaine self-administration in rats. *Journal of Neuroscience, 14,* 4130–4146.

Green, D. P., Glaser, J., Rich, A. (1998). From lynching to gay bashing: The elusive connection between economic conditions and hate crime. *Journal of Personality and Social Psychology, 75*(1), 82–92.

Green, J. T., & Woodruff-Pak, D. S. (2000). Eyeblink classical conditioning: Hippocampal formation is for neutral stimulus associations as cerebellum is for association-response. *Psychological Bulletin, 126,* 138–158.

Green, M. (1999). Diagnosis of attention-deficit/hyperactivity disorder. *Technical Review Number 3, Publication No. 99-0050.* Rockville, MD: Agency for Health Care Policy and Research.

Green, M. F. (1998). *Schizophrenia from a neurocognitive perspective: Probing the impenetrable darkness.* Needham Heights, MA: Allyn & Bacon.

Greenberg, D. L., Rice, H. J., Cooper, J. J., Cabeza, R., Rubin, D. C., LaBar, K. S. (2005). Co-activation of the amygdala, hippocampus and inferior frontal gyrus during autobiographical memory retrieval. *Neuropsycholigia, 43*(5), 659–674.

Greenberg, J., Solomon, S., & Pyszynski, T. (1997). Terror management theory of self-esteem and cultural worldviews: Empirical assessments and conceptual refinements. In M. P. Zanna (Ed.), *Advances in experimental social psychology* (Vol. 29). San Diego: Academic Press.

Greenberg, L. S., & Malcolm, W. (2002). Resolving unfinished business: Relating process to outcome. *Journal of Consulting and Clinical Psychology, 70,* 406–416.

Greenberg, L. S., & Rice, L. N. (1997). Humanistic approaches to psychotherapy. In P. L. Wachtel & S. B. Messer (Eds.), *Theories of psychotherapy: Origins and evolution.* Washington, DC: American Psychological Association.

Greene, R. L. (1992). *Human memory: Paradigms and paradoxes.* Hillsdale, NJ: Erlbaum.

Greene, R. W., & Ollendick, T. H. (2000). Behavioral assessment of children. In G. Goldstein & M. Hersen (Eds.), *Handbook of psychological assessment* (3rd ed.). New York: Elsevier.

Greenfield, P. M. (1997). Culture as process: Empirical methods for cultural psychology. In J. W. Berry, Y. H. Poortinga, & J. Pandey (Eds.), *Cross-cultural psychology: Theory and method* (2nd ed., Vol. 1). Boston: Allyn & Bacon.

Greenleaf, E. (1973). "Senoi" dream groups. *Psychotherapy:Theory, Research and Practice, 10,* 218–222.

Greeno, C. G., & Wing, R. R. (1994). Stress-induced eating. *Psychological Bulletin, 115,* 444–464.

Greenwald, A. G. (1992). New look 3: Unconscious cognition reclaimed. *American Psychologist, 47,* 766–779.

Greenwald, A. G., McGhee, D. E., & Schwartz, J. (1998). Measuring individual differences in implicit cognition: The implicit association test. *Journal of Personality and Social Psychology, 74,* 1464–1480.

Greenwald, A. G., Spangenberg, E. R., Pratkanis, A. R., & Eskenazi, J. (1991). Double-blind tests of subliminal self-help tapes. *Psychological Science, 2,* 119–122.

Greer, H. S., Morris, T., & Pettingale, K. W. (1979). Psychological response to breast cancer: Effect on outcome. *Lancet, 2,* 785–787.

Gregory, R. J. (1999). *Foundations of intellectual assessment: The WAIS-III and other tests in clinical practice.* Needham-Height, MA, US: Allyn & Bacon.

Gregory, R. L. (1966). *Eye and brain.* New York: McGraw-Hill.

Gregory, R. L., Gombrich, E. H., Eds. (1973). *Illusion in Nature and Art.* London: Duckworth.

Griffiths, M. (1997). Video games and aggression. *Psychologist, 10,* 397–401.

Grigorenko, E. L. (2003). Selected links between nutrition and the mind. In R. J. Sternberg, J. Lautrey, & T. I. Lubart (Eds.), *Models of intelligence: International perspectives.* Washington, DC: American Psychological Association.

Grimes, K., & Walker, E. F. (1994). Childhood emotional expressions, educational attainment, and age at onset of illness in schizophrenia. *Journal of Abnormal Psychology, 103,* 784–790.

Griner, D., Smith, T. (2006). Culturally adapted mental health intervention: A meta-analytic review. Psychotherapy: Theory, Research, Practice, Training. *Special issue: Culture, race, and ethnicity in psychotherapy, 43*(4), 531–548.

Grissom, R. J. (1996). The magical number 7 plus or minus 2: Meta-meta-analysis of the probability of superior outcome in comparisons involving therapy, placebo, and control. *Journal of Consulting and Clinical Psychology, 64,* 973–982.

Gronnerod, C. (2003). Temporal stability in the Rorschach method: A meta-analytic review. *Journal of Personality Assessment, 80,* 272–293.

Gross, J. J. (1999). Emotion and emotion regulation. In L. A. Pervin & O. P. John (Eds.), *Handbook of personality: Theory and research* (2nd ed.). New York: Guilford Press.

Grossman, D. (1995). *On killing: The psychological cost of learning to kill in war and society.* Boston: Little, Brown.

Grossman, R. P., & Till, B. D. (1998). The persistence of classically conditioned brand attitudes. *Journal of Advertising, 27,* 23–31.

Groth-Marnat, G. (2003). *Handbook of psychological assessment (4th edition).* Hoboken, New Jersey: Wiley.

Guéguen, N. (2002). Foot in the door technique and computer mediated communication. *Computers in Human Behavior, 18,* 11–15.

Guilford, J. P. (1959). Three faces of intellect. *American Psychologist, 14,* 469–479.

Guilford, J. P. (1967). *The nature of human intelligence.* New York: McGraw-Hill.

Guilleminault, C. (1987). Obstructive sleep apnea syndrome: A review. *Psychiatric Clinics of North America, 10,* 607–621.

Guilleminault, C., Poyares, D., Abat, F., & Palombini, L. (2001). Sleep and wakefulness in somnambulism: A spectral analysis study. *Journal of Psychosomatic Research, 51,* 411–416.

Guinness book of records (2000). Stamford, CT: Guinness Media.

Gump, L. S., Baker, R. C., & Roll, S. (2000). Cultural and gender differences in moral judgment: A study of Mexican Americans and Anglo-Americans. *Hispanic Journal of Behavioral Sciences, 22,* 78–93.

Guo, G. (2006). Genetic similarity shared by best friends among adolescents. *Twin Research and Human Genetics, 9,* 113–121.

Gur, R. E., Cowell, P., Turetsky, B. I., Gallacher, F., Cannon, T., Bilker, W., & Gur, R. B. (1998). A follow-up magnetic resonance imaging study of schizophrenia: Relationship of neuroanatomical changes to clinical and neurobehavioral measures. *Archives of General Psychiatry, 55,* 145–152.

Gustafson, S. B., & Magnusson, D. (1991). *Female life careers: A pattern approach.* Hillsdale, NJ: Erlbaum.

Gustavson, C. R., & Gustavson, J. C. (1985). Predation control using conditioned food aversion methodology: Theory, practice, and implications. *Annals of the New York Academy of Sciences, 443,* 348–356.

Gustavson, C. R., Garcia, J., Hankins, W. G., & Rusiniak, K. W. (1974). Coyote predation control by aversive conditioning. *Science, 184,* 581–583.

Guthrie, J. P., Ash, R. A., & Bendapudi, V. (1995). Additional validity evidence for a measure of morningness. *Journal of Applied Psychology, 80,* 186–190.

Guze, S. B. (1993). Genetics of Briquet's syndrome and somatization disorder: A review of family, adoption, and twin studies. *Annals of Clinical Psychiatry, 5,* 225–230.

Haaga, D. A. F., Dyck, M. J., & Ernst, D. (1991). Empirical status of cognitive theory of depression. *Psychological Bulletin, 110,* 215–236.

Haas, H., Fink, H., & Hartfelder, G. (1959). Das placeboproblem (translation). *Psychopharmacology Service Center Bulletin, 2,* 1–65. (U.S. Public Health Service.)

Haas, S. J., Hill, R., Krum, H., Liew, D., Tonkin, A., Demos, L., Sephan, K., McNeil, L. (2007). Clozapine-associated myocarditis: A review of 116 cases of suspected myocarditis associated with the use of clozapine in Australia during 1993–2003. *Drug Safety, 30*(1), 47–57.

Hackman, J. R., & Lawler, E. E. (1971). Employee reactions to job characteristics. *Journal of Applied Psychology, 55,* 259–286.

Hafen, B. Q., & Hoeger, W. W. K. (1998). *Wellness: Guidelines for a healthy lifestyle.* Englewood, CO: Morton.

Hagemann, D., Naumann, E., Thayer, J. F., & Bartussek, D. (2002). Does resting electroencephalograph asymmetry reflect a trait? An application of latent state-trait theory. *Journal of Personality and Social Psychology, 82,* 619–641.

Haier, R. J., Jung, R. E., Yeo, R. A., Head, K., Alkire, M. J. (2005). The neuroanatomy of general intelligence: Sex matters. *NeuroImage, 25,* 320–327.

Haier, R. J., Siegel, B. V., Crinella, F. M., & Buchsbaum, M. S. (1993). Biological and psychometric intelligence: Testing an animal model in humans with positron emission tomography. In D. K. Detterman (Ed.), *Individual differences and cognition. Current topics in human intelligence* (Vol. 3). Norwood, NJ: Ablex.

Hailman, J. P. (1967). The ontogeny of an instinct. *Behaviour Supplements, 15,* 1–159.

Hala, S., Chandler, M., & Fritz, A.S. (1991). Fledgling theories of mind: Deception as a marker of three-year-olds' understanding of false belief. *Child Development, 62,* 83–97.

Halaas, J. L., Gajiwala, K. S., Maffei, M., & Cohen, S. L., Chait, B. T., & Rabinowitz, D. (1995). Weight-reducing effects of the plasma protein encoded by the obese gene. *Science, 269,* 543–546.

Hall, C. S. (1984). "A ubiquitous sex difference in dreams" revisited. *Journal of Personality and Social Psychology, 46,* 1109–1117.

Hall, C. S., & Van de Castle, R. (1966). *The content analysis of dreams.* New York: Appleton-Century-Crofts.

Hall, D. R., & Zhao, J. Z. (1995). Cohabitation and divorce in Canada: Testing the selectivity hypothesis. *Journal of Marriage and the Family, 57,* 421–427.

Hall, G. C. N., & Okazaki, S. (2003). *Asian American psychology: The science of lives in context.* Washington, DC: American Psychological Association.

Hall, G. S. (1904). *Adolescence* (Vols. 1 & 2). New York: Appleton-Century-Crofts.

Hall, J.A.Y. & Kimura (1995). Sexual orientation and performance on sexually dimorphic tasks. *Archives of Sexual Behavior, 24,* 395–407.

Halligan, S., Murray, C., Martins, C., Cooper, P. J. (2007). Maternal depression and psychiatric outcomes in adolescent offspring: a 13-year longitudinal study. *Journal of Affective Disorders, 97*(1–3), 145–154.

Halpern, B. (2002). Taste. In H. Pashler & S. Yantis (Eds.). *Steven's handbook of experimental psychology: Vol. 1. Sensation and perception* (3rd ed.). New York: Wiley.

Halpern, C. T., Udry, J. R., Campbell, B., & Suchindran, C. (1999). Effects of body fat on weight concerns, dating, and sexual activity: A longitudinal analysis of Black and White adolescent girls. *Developmental Psychology, 35,* 721–736.

Halpern, D. F. (2000). *Sex differences in cognitive abilities* (3rd ed.). Mahwah, NJ: Erlbaum.

Halpern, D. F., & Tan, U. (2001). Stereotypes and steroids: Using a psychobiosocial model to understand cognitive sex differences. *Brain and Cognition, 45,* 392–414.

Hamer, D. H., & Copeland, P. (1998). *Living with our genes: Why they matter more than you think.* New York: Doubleday.

Hamilton, D. A., Kodituwakku, P., Sutherland, R. J., & Savage, D. D. (2003). Children with fetal alcohol syndrome are imparied at place learning but not cued-navigation in a virtual Morris water task. *Behavioural Brain Research, 143,* 85–94.

Hamilton, R. J. (1985). A framework for the evaluation of the effectiveness of adjunct questions and objectives. *Review of Educational Research, 55,* 47–85.

Hamilton, W. D. (1964). The genetical theory of social behaviour, I, II. *Journal of Theoretical Biology, 12,* 12–45.

Hammen, C. (1991). *Depression runs in families: The social context of risk and resilience in children of depressed mothers.* New York: Springer-Verlag.

Hampson, E., & Kimura, D. (1988). Reciprocal effects of hormonal fluctuations on human motor and perceptual-spatial skills. *Behavioral Neuroscience, 102*(3), 456–459.

Hampson, E., & Kimura, D. (1992). Sex differences and hormonal influences on cognitive function in humans. In J. B. Becker, S. M. Breedlove, & D. Crews (Eds.), *Behavioral endocrinology.* Cambridge, MA: MIT Press.

Hane, A. A., Fox, N. A., Polak-Toste, C., Ghera, M., & Gunner, B. (2006). Contextual basis of maternal perceptions of infant temperament. *Developmental Psychology, 42,* 1077–1088.

Haney, C., & Zimbardo, P. (1998). The past and future of U.S. prison policy: Twenty-five years after the Stanford Prison Experiment. *American Psychologist, 53,* 709–727.

Hansen, C. H., & Hansen, R. D. (1988). Finding the face in the crowd: An anger superiority effect. *Journal of Personality and Social Psychology, 54,* 917–924.

Hansen, N. B., Lambert, M. J., & Forman, E. M. (2002). The psychotherapy dose-response effect and its implications for treatment delivery services. *Clinical Psychology: Science and Practice, 9,* 329–343.

Happé, F. G. E., Winner, E., & Brownell, H. (1998). The getting of wisdom: Theory of mind in old age. *Developmental Psychology, 34,* 358–362.

Hardy, C., & Latané, B. (1986). Social loafing on a cheering task. *Social Science, 71,* 165–172.

Hardy, M. A., & Quadagno, J. (1995). Satisfaction with early retirement: Making choices in the auto industry. *Journals of Gerontology: Psychological Sciences and Social Sciences, 50B,* S217–S228.

Hare, R. D. (1978). Psychopathy and electrodermal responses to nonsignal stimulation. *Biological Psychology, 6,* 237–246.

Hare, R.D. (2001). *Without conscience: The disturbing world of the psychopaths among us.* Guilford Press: New York NY.

Harley, K., & Reese, E. (1999). Origins of autobiographical memory. *Developmental Psychology, 35,* 1338–1348.

Harlow, H. F. (1958). The nature of love. *The American Psychologist, 13,* 673–685.

Harlow, H. F., & Suomi, S. J. (1970). The nature of love-simplified. *American Psychologist, 25,* 161–168.

Harlow, J. M. (1868). Recovery from the passage of an iron bar through the head. *Massachusetts Medical Society, 2,* 327.

Harlow, J., & Roll, S. (1992). Frequency of day residue in dreams of young adults. *Perceptual and Motor Skills, 74,* 832–834.

Harman, R. L. (Ed.) (1990). *Gestalt therapy: Discussions with the masters.* Springfield, IL: Charles C Thomas.

Harmon-Jones, E., Brehm, J. W., Greenberg, J., Simon, L., & Nelson, D. E. (1996). Evidence that the production of aversive consequences is not necessary to create cognitive dissonance. *Journal of Personality and Social Psychology, 70,* 5–16.

Harre, R., & Parrot, W. G. (1996). *Emotion: Social, cultural and physical dimensions.* Thousand Oaks, CA: Sage Publications.

Harrington, D. M., Block, J. H., & Black, J. (1987). Testing aspects of Carl Rogers's theory of creative environments: Child-rearing antecedents of creative potential in young adolescents. *Journal of Personality and Social Psychology, 52,* 851–856.

Harrington, F. H. (2000). What's in a howl? Retrieved from http://www.pbs.org/wgbh/nova/wolves/howl.html, December 14, 2006.

Harris, R. J. (1977). Comprehension of pragmatic implications in advertising. *Journal of Applied Psychology, 62,* 603–608.

Harris, S. L. (1981). A letter from the editor on loss and trust. *The Clinical Psychologist, 34*(3), 3.

Harrison, J. E., & Baron, S. C. (1997). Synaesthesia: A review of psychological theories. In S. C. Baron, J. E. Harrison et al. (Eds.), *Synaesthesia: Classic and contemporary readings.* Oxford: Blackwell.

Hart, C. H., Nelson, D. A., Robinson, C. C., Olsen, S. F., & McNeilly, C. M. K. (1998). Overt and relational aggression in Russian nursery-school-age children: Parenting style and marital linkages. *Developmental Psychology, 34,* 687–697.

Hart, J. W., Bridgett, D. J., & Karau, S. J. (2001). Coworker ability and effort as determinants of individual effort on a collective task. *Group Dynamics, 5,* 181–190.

Hartigan, J. A., & Wigdor, A. K. (Eds.). (1989). *Fairness in employment testing.* Washington, DC: National Academy Press.

Hartley, A. (2006). Changing role of the speed of processing construct in the cognitive psychology of human aging. In Birren, James E. (Ed.); Schaire, K. Warner (Ed.). Handbook of the psychology of aging (6th ed.). (183-207). Amsterdam: Elsevier.

Hartshorne, H., & May, A. (1928). *Studies in the nature of character, Vol. 1: Studies in deceit.* New York: Macmillan.

Harvey, J. H., & Omarzu, J. (1997). Minding the close relationship. *Personality and Social Psychology Review, 1,* 224–240.

Hasegawa, I., & Myashita, Y. (2002). Categorizing the world: Expert neurons look into key features. *Nature: Neuroscience, 5,* 90–91.

Hasher, L., & Zacks, R. T. (1979). Automatic and effortful processes in memory. *Journal of Experimental Psychology: General, 108,* 356–388.

Hasher, L., & Zacks, R. T. (1984). Automatic processing of fundamental information: The case of frequency of occurrence. *American Psychologist, 39,* 1372–1388.

Haskell, W. L., Alderman, E. L., Fair, J. M., et al. (1994). Effects of intensive multiple risk factor reduction on coronary atherosclerosis and clinical cardiac events in men and women with coronary artery disease. *Circulation, 89,* 975–990.

Hastings, P., & Grusec, J.E., (1997). Conflict outcome as a function of parental accuracy in perceiving child cognitions and affect. *Social Development, 6,* 76–90.

Hastorf, A., & Cantril, H. (1954). They saw a game: A case study. *Journal of Abnormal and Social Psychology, 49,* 129–134.

Hatfield, E. (1988). Passionate and companionate love. In R. J. Sternberg & M. L. Barnes (Eds.), *The psychology of love.* New Haven, CT: Yale University Press.

Hatfield, E., & Rapson, R. L. (1987). Passionate love/sexual desire: Can the same paradigm explain both? *Archives of Sexual Behavior, 16,* 259–278.

Hathaway, S. R., & McKinley, J. C. (1983). *The Minnesota Multiphasic Personality Inventory manual.* New York: Psychological Corporation.

Haugtvedt, C. P., Petty, R. E., & Cacioppo, J. T. (1992). Need for cognition and advertising: Understanding the role of personality variables in consumer behavior. *Journal of Consumer Psychology, 1,* 239–260.

Hauri, P. (1982). *The sleep disorders* (2nd ed.). Kalamazoo, MI: Upjohn Corp.

Hauri, P. J. (1997). Can we mix behavioral therapy with hypnotics when treating insomniacs? *Sleep, 20,* 1111–1118.

Hawkins, K. A., & Trobst, K. K. (2000). Frontal lobe dysfunction and aggression: Conceptual issues and research findings. *Aggression and Violent Behavior, 5,* 147–157.

Haydon, P. G. (2001). Glia: Listening and talking to the synapse. *Nature Reviews Neuroscience, 2,* 185–193.

Haynes, S. G., Feinleib, M., and Kannel, W. B. (1980). The relationship of psycho-social factors in coronary heart disease in the Framingham study: Study III: Eight-year incidence of coronary heart disease. *American Journal of Epidemiology, 111,* 37–58.

Haynes, S. N. (1990). Behavioral assessment of adults. In G. Goldstein & M. Hersen (Eds.), *Handbook of psychological assessment.* Elmsford, NY: Pergamon.

Haynes, S. N. (2000). Behavioral assessment of adults. In G. Goldstein & M. Hersen (Eds.), *Handbook of psychological assessment* (3rd ed.). New York: Elsevier.

Haynes, S. N., Price, M. G., & Simons, J. P. (1975). Stimulus control treatment of insomnia. *Journal of*

Behavior Therapy and Experimental Psychiatry, 6, 279–282.

Hayslip, B., & Panek, P. E. (2002). *Adult development and aging.* New York: Harper & Row.

Hazen, N. L., & Durrett, M. E. (1982). Relationship of security of attachment to exploration and cognitive mapping abilities in 2-year-olds. *Developmental Psychology, 18,* 751–759.

He, X. X., Nebert, D. W., Vasiliou, V., Zhu, H., & Shertzer, H. G. (1997). Genetic differences in alcohol drinking preference between inbred strains of mice. *Pharmacogenetics, 7,* 223–233.

Hearold, S. (1986). A synthesis of 1043 effects of television on social behavior. In G. Comstock (Ed.), *Public communications and behavior* (Vol. 1). New York: Academic Press.

Heath, A. C. (1995). Genetic influences on alcoholism risk: A review of adoption and twin studies. *Alcohol Health and Research World, 19,* 166–171.

Heath, A. C., Bucholz, K. K., Madden, P. A. F., Dinwiddie, S. H., Slutske, W. S., & Bierut, L. J. (1997). Genetic and environmental contributions to alcohol dependence risk in a national twin sample: Consistency of findings in women and men. *Psychological Medicine, 27,* 1381–1396.

Heath, A. C., Kendler, K. S., Eaves, L. J., & Martin, N. G. (1990). Evidence for genetic influences on sleep disturbance and sleep pattern in twins. *Sleep, 13,* 318–335.

Heath, A. C., Todorov, A. A., Nelson, E. C., Madden, P. A. F., Bucholz, K. K., and Martin, N. G. (2002). Gene–environment interaction effects on behavioral variation and risk of complex disorders: The example of alcoholism and other psychiatric disorders. *Twins Research, 5:* 30–37.

Heath, R. G. (1972). Pleasure and brain activity in man. *Journal of Nervous and Mental Disease, 154,* 3–18.

Heatherton, T. F., Herman, C. P., & Polivy, J. (1991). Effects of physical threat and ego threat on eating behavior. *Journal of Personality and Social Psychology, 60,* 138–143.

Hebb, D. O. (1949). *The organization of behavior.* New York: Wiley.

Heckers, S., & Konradi, C. (2000). Anatomic and molecular principles of psychopharmacology: A primer for psychiatrists. *Child and Adolescent Psychiatric Clinics of North America, 9,* 1–22.

Heckhausen, H. (1991). *Motivation and action* (2nd ed.). New York: Springer-Verlag.

Heider, F. (1958). *The psychology of interpersonal relations.* New York: Wiley.

Heiman, J. R. (1977). A psychophysiological exploration of sexual arousal patterns in females and males. *Psychophysiology, 14,* 266–274.

Heimpel, S. A., Wood, J. V., Marshall, M. A., & Brown, J. D. (2002). Do people with low self-esteem really want to feel better? Self-esteem differences in motivation to repair negative moods. *Journal of Personality and Social Psychology, 82,* 128–147.

Heller, M. A., & Schiff, W. (Eds.) (1991). *The psychology of touch.* Hillsdale, NJ: Erlbaum.

Hellerstein, D., Yankowitch, P., Rosenthal, J., et al. (1993). A randomized double-blind study of fluoxetine versus placebo in the treatment of dysthymia. *American Journal of Psychiatry, 150,* 1169–1175.

Hellriegel, D., Slocum, J. W., Jr., & Woodman, R. W. (1989). *Organizational behavior* (5th ed.). St. Paul, MN: West.

Helmreich, R. L. (1997, May). Managing human error in aviation. *Scientific American,* 62–67.

Helmreich, R. L., Merritt, A. C., & Wilhelm, J. A. (1999). The evolution of crew resource management training in commercial aviation. *International Journal of Aviation Psychology, 9,* 19–32.

Helzer, J. E., & Hudziak, J. J. (Eds). (2002). *Defining psychopathology in the 21st century: DSM-V and beyond.* Washington, DC: American Psychiatric Publishing.

Hendrick, C. (Ed.) (1989). *Close relationships.* Newbury Park, CA: Sage Publications.

Hendy, H. M., & Raudenbush, B. (2000). Effectiveness of teacher modeling to encourage food acceptance in preschool children. *Appetite, 34,* 61–76.

Henry, J. D., MacLeod, M. S., Phillips, L. H., Crawford, J. P. (2004). A meta-analytical review of prospective memory and aging. *Psychology and Aging, 19*(1), 27–39.

Hepper, P. G. (1988). Fetal "soap" addiction. *The Lancet, 1,* 1347–1348.

Herdt, G., & Lindenbaum, S. (Eds.) (1992). *Social analysis in the time of AIDS.* Newbury Park, CA: Sage Publications.

Herek, G. M. (2000). The psychology of sexual prejudice. *Current Directions in Psychological Science, 9,* 19–22.

Herman, D. B., Susser, E. S., Jandorf, L., Lavelle, J., & Bromet, E. J. (1998). Homelessness among individuals with psychotic disorders hospitalized for the first time: Findings from the Suffolk County Mental Health Project. *American Journal of Psychiatry, 155,* 109–113.

Hernandez, L., & Hoebel, B. G. (1988). Food reward and cocaine increase extracellular dopamine in the nucleus accumbens as measured by microdialysis. *Life Sciences, 42,* 1705–1712.

Herrington, R., & Lader, M. H. (1996). *Biological treatments in psychiatry* (2nd ed.). New York: Oxford University Press.

Herrnstein, R.J. & Murray, C. (1994). *The bell curve: Intelligence and class struggle in American life.* New York: Free Press.

Hersen, M. (2002). *Clinical behavior therapy: Adults and children.* New York: Wiley.

Hersen, M. (2003). *Effective brief therapies.* New York: Academic Press.

Herskovits, M. J. (1948). *Man and his works.* New York: Knopf.

Herz, M., & Marder, S. (2002). *Schizophrenia: A comprehensive text.* New York: Williams & Wilkins.

Herz, R. S., & Cupchik, C. G. (1995). The emotional distinctiveness of odor-evoked memories. *Chemical Senses, 20,* 517–528.

Hess, E. H. (1959). Imprinting. *Science, 130,* 133–141.

Hess, W. R. (1965). Sleep as phenomenon of the integral organism. In: K. Akert, C. Bally, & J. P. Schade (Eds), *Sleep mechanisms.* New York: Elsevier.

Hetherington, A. W., & Ranson, S. W. (1942). The spontaneous activity and food intake of rats with hypothalamic lesions. *American Journal of Physiology, 136,* 609–617.

Hetherington, E. M. (1989). Coping with family transitions: Winners, losers, and survivors. *Child Development, 60,* 1–14.

Hetherington, E. M. (1998). Relevant issues in developmental science: Introduction to the special issue. *American Psychologist, 53,* 93–94.

Hetherington, E. M., Bridges, M., & Insabella, G. M. (1998). What matters? What does not? Five perspectives on the association between marital transitions and children's adjustment. *American Psychologist, 53,* 167–184.

Hetherington, E. M., Parke, R. D., & Locke, V. O. (1999). *Child psychology: A contemporary viewpoint* (5th ed.). Boston: McGraw-Hill.

Hetherington, E. M., & Stanley-Hagan, M. (2002). Parenting in divorced and remarried families. In M. H. Bornstein (Ed.), *Handbook of parenting: Being and becoming a parent* (2nd ed., Vol. 3). Mahwah, NJ: Erlbaum.

Hewstone, M., Rubin, M., & Willis, H. (2002). Intergroup bias. *Annual Review of Psychology, 53,* 575–604.

Heylighen, F. (1992). A cognitive-systemic reconstruction of Maslow's theory of self-actualization. *Behavioral Science, 37,* 39–58.

Hibbard, S. (2003). A critique of Lilienfeld et al.'s (2000) "The scientific status of projective techniques." *Journal of personality Assessment, 80,* 260–271.

Hickok, J. T., Roscoe, J. A., & Morrow, G. R. (2001). The role of patients' expectations in the development of anticipatory nausea related to chemotherapy for cancer. *Journal of Pain and Symptom Management, 22,* 843–850.

Higgins, A. (1991). The Just Community approach to moral education: Evolution of the idea and recent findings. In W. M. Kurtines & J. L. Gerwirtz (Eds.), *Handbook of moral behavior and development,* (Vol. 3). Hillsdale, NJ: Erlbaum.

Hilgard, E. R. (1977). *Divided consciousness: Multiple controls in human thought and action.* New York: Wiley.

Hilgard, E. R. (1991). A neodissociation interpretation of hypnosis. In S. J. Lynn & J. W. Rhue (Eds.), *Theories of hypnosis: Current models and perspectives.* New York: Guilford Press.

Hill, C. A. (1987). Affiliation motivation: People who need people but in different ways. *Journal of Personality and Social Psychology, 52,* 1008–1018.

Hill, J. O., & Peters, J. C. (1998). Environmental contributions to the obesity epidemic. *Science, 280,* 1371–1374.

Hill, M. M., Dodson, B. B., Hill, E. W., & Fox, J. (1995). An infant sonicguide intervention program for a child with a visual disability. *Journal of Visual Impairment and Blindness, 89,* 329–336.

Hill, S. Y., Locke, J., Zezza, N., Kaplan, B., Neiswanger, K., & Steinhauer, S. R. (1998). Genetic association between reduced P300 amplitude and the DRD2 dopamine receptor A1 allele in children at high risk for alcoholism. *Biological Psychiatry, 43,* 40–51.

Hillman, D. C., Siffre, M., Milano, G., & Halberg, F. (1994). Free-running psycho-physiologic circadians and three-month pattern in a woman isolated in a cave. *New Trends in Experimental and Clinical Psychiatry, 10,* 127–133.

Hines, M., Gorski, R. A. (1985). Hormonal influences on the development of neural asymmetries. In D. F. Benson, E. Saidel, (Eds.), *The Dual Brain* (75–96). New York: Guilford Press.

Hirshkowitz, M. (2000). Nightmares. In G. Fink (Ed.), *Encyclopedia of stress.* San Diego: Academic Press.

Hirshman, E., & Jackson, E. (1997). Distinctive perceptual processing and memory. *Journal of Memory and Language, 36,* 2–12.

Hirst, R. A., Lambert D. G., & Notcutt, W. G. (1998). Pharmacology and potential therapeutic uses of cannabis. *British Journal of Anaesthesia, 81,* 77–84.

Hixon, M. D. (1998). Ape language research: A review and behavioral perspective. *Analysis of Verbal Behavior, 15,* 17–39.

Hobson, A. (1988). Psychoanalytic dream theory: A critique based upon modern neurophysiology. In P. Clark & C. Wright (Eds.), *Mind, psychoanalysis and science.* Oxford: Basil Blackwell.

Hobson, J. A. (1996). *Chemistry of conscious states: How the brain changes its mind.* Boston: Little, Brown.

Hobson, J. A., & McCarley, R. W. (1977). The brain as a dream state generator: An activation-synthesis hypothesis of the dream process. *American Journal of Psychiatry, 134,* 1335–1348.

Hobson, J. A., Stickgold, R., Pace, S., & Edward, F. (1998). The neuropsychology of REM sleep dreaming. *Neuroreport: An International Journal for the Rapid Communication of Research in Neuroscience, 9,* R1–R14.

Hodges, J., & Tizard, B. (1989). Social and family relationships of ex-institutional adolescents. *Journal of Child Psychology and Psychiatry, 30,* 77–97.

Hoebel, B. G. (1997). Neuroscience and appetitive behavior research: 25 years. *Appetite, 29,* 119–133.

Hoeksema, V. O., Claudia, Y. D., Gaillard, A. W. K., & Buunk, B. P. (1998). Social loafing under fatigue. *Journal of Personality and Social Psychology, 75,* 1179–1190.

Hoffart, A., & Martinson, E. W. (1991). Mental health locus of control in agoraphobia and depression: A longitudinal study of inpatients. *Psychological Reports, 68,* 1011–1018.

Hoffman, H. G., Patterson, D. R., Canougher, G. J., & Sharar, S. R. (2001). Effectiveness of virtual reality-based pain control with multiple treatments. *Clinical Journal of Pain, 17,* 229–235.

Hofmann, A. (1980). *LSD, my problem child.* New York: McGraw-Hill.

Hogarty, G. E. (2003). *Personal therapy for schizophrenia and related disorders.* New York: Guilford Press.

Hogue, M. E., Beaugrand, J. P., & Lauguee, P. C. (1996). Coherent use of information by hens observing their former dominant defeating or being defeated by a stranger. *Behavioural Processes, 38,* 241–252.

Holahan, C. J., & Moos, R. H. (1986). Personality, coping, and family resources in stress resistance: A longitudinal analysis. *Journal of Personality and Social Psychology 51,* 389–395.

Holahan, C. J., & Moos, R. H. (1990). Life stressors, resistance factors, and improved psychological functioning: An extension of the stress resistance paradigm. *Journal of Personality and Social Psychology, 58,* 909–917.

Holahan, C. J., Moos, R. H., Holahan, C. K., & Cronkite, R. C. (2000). Long-term posttreatment functioning among patients with unipolar depression: An integrative model. *Journal of Consulting and Clinical Psychology, 68,* 226–232.

Holland, J. L. (1985). *Making vocational choices: A theory of vocational personalities and work environments* (2nd ed.). Englewood Cliffs, NJ: Prentice Hall.

Hollis, K. L. (1997). Contemporary research on Pavlovian conditioning: A "new" functional analysis. *American Psychologist, 52,* 956–965.

Hollon, S. D. (1996). The efficacy and effectiveness of psychotherapy relative to medications. *American Psychologist, 51,* 1025–1030.

Hollon, S. D., & Beck, A. T. (1994). Cognitive and cognitive-behavioral therapies. In A. E. Bergin & S. L. Garfield (Eds.), *Handbook of psychotherapy and behavior change.* New York: Wiley.

Hollon, S. D., Shelton, R. C., & Loosen, P. T. (1991). Cognitive therapy and pharmacotherapy for depression. *Journal of Consulting and Clinical Psychology, 59,* 88–99.

Holloway, M. (1991). Rx for addiction. *Scientific American, 264,* 95–103.

Holmes, A., Murphy, D., and Crawley, J. N. (2003). Abnormal behavioral phenotypes of serotonin transporter knockout mice: Parallels with human anxiety and depression. *Biological Psychiatry, 54,* 953–959.

Holmes, D. S. (1990). The evidence for repression: An examination of sixty years of research. In J. L. Singer (Ed.), *Repression and dissociation.* Chicago: University of Chicago Press.

Holmes, M. R., & St.-Lawrence, J. S. (1983). Treatment of rape-induced trauma: Proposed behavioral conceptualization and review of the literature. *Clinical Psychology Review, 3,* 417–433.

Holmes, T. H., & Masuda, M. (1974). Life change and illness susceptibility. In D. S. Dohrenwend & B. P. Dohrenwend (Eds.), *Stressful life events: Their nature and effects.* New York: Wiley.

Holmes, T. H., & Rahe, R. H. (1967). The social readjustment rating scale. *Journal of Psychosomatic Research, 11,* 213–218.

Honey, P. L. & Galef, B. G. Jr. (2004). Long lasting effects of rearing by an ethanol-consuming dam on voluntary ethanol consumption by rats. *Appetite, 43,* 261–268.

Honeycutt, J. M. (1995). Predicting relational trajectory beliefs as a consequence of typicality and necessity ratings of relationship behaviors. *Communication Research Reports, 12,* 3–14.

Honts, C. R., & Perry, M. V. (1992). Polygraph admissibility: Changes and challenges. *Law and Human Behavior, 16,* 357–379.

Honts, C. R., Devitt, M. K., Winbush, M., & Kircher, J. C. (1996). Mental and physical countermeasures reduce the accuracy of the concealed knowledge test. *Psychophysiology, 33,* 84–92.

Hooper, J., & Teresi, M. (1986). *The three-pound universe.* New York: Macmillan.

Hopkins, W. D., & Leavens, D. A. (1998). Hand use and gestural communication in chimpanzees (Pan troglodytes). *Journal of Comparative Psychology, 112,* 95–99.

Horn, J. L. (1985) Remodeling old models of intelligence. In B. B. Wolman (Ed.), *Handbook of intelligence* (257–300). New York: John Wiley & Sons.

Horn, J. L., & Cattell, R. C. (1966). Refinement and test of the theory of fluid and crystallized general intelligences. *Journal of Educational Psychology, 57,* 253–270.

Horne, J. A. (1977). Factors relating to energy conservation during sleep in mammals. *Physiological Psychology, 5,* 403–408.

Horne, S. (1999). Domestic violence in Russia. *American Psychologist, 54,* 55–61.

Houpt, T. A., Boulos, Z., Moore, E., & Martin, C. (1996). MidnightSun: Software for determining light exposure and phase-shifting schedules during global travel. *Physiology and Behavior, 59,* 561–568.

House, J. S., Landis, K. R., & Umberson, D. (1988). Social relationships and health. *Science, 241,* 540–545.

Houston, J. P. (1992). *Fundamentals of learning and memory.* Ft. Worth: Harcourt Brace Jovanovich.

Hovland, C. I., & Sears, R. (1940). Minor studies of aggression: Correlation of lynchings with economic indices. *Journal of Psychology, 9,* 301–310.

Hovland, C. I., Janis, I., and Kelley, H. H. (1953). *Communication and persuasion.* New Haven, CT: Yale University Press.

Howard, I. P. (2002). Depth perception. In H. Pashler & S.Yantis (Eds.), *Steven's handbook of experimental psychology: Vol. 1. Sensation and perception* (3rd ed.). New York: Wiley.

Howard, I. P., & Rogers, B. J. (1995). *Binocular vision and stereopsis.* New York: Oxford University Press.

Howard, K. I., Kopta, S. M., Krause, M. S., & Orlinsky, D. E. (1986). The dose-effect relationship in psychotherapy. *American Psychologist, 41,* 159–164.

Howard, K. I., Lueger, R. J., Maling, M. S., & Martinovich, Z. (1993). A phase model of psychotherapy outcome: Causal mediation of change. *Journal of Consulting and Clinical Psychology, 61,* 678–685.

Howe, Mark L., & Courage, M. L. (1993). On resolving the enigma of infantile amnesia. *Psychological Bulletin, 113,* 305–326.

Hryshko-Mullen, A. S., Broeckl, L. S., Haddock, C. K., & Peterson, A. L. (2000). Behavioral treatment of insomnia: The Wilford Hall Insomnia Program. *Military Medicine, 165,* 200–207.

Hubbard, K., O'Neill, A. M., & Cheakalos, C. (1999, April 12). Out of control. *People,* 52–72.

Hublin, C., Kaprio, J., Partinen, M., Heikkila, K., Koskenvuo, M. (1997). Prevalence and genetics of sleepwalking: A population-based twin study. *Neurology, 48,* 177–181.

Hublin, C., Kaprio, J., Partinen, M., & Koskenvuo, M. (2001). Parasomnias: Co-occurrence and genetics. *Psychiatric Genetics, 11,* 65–70.

Huddy, L., & Birtanen, S. (1995). Subgroup differentiation and subgroup bias among Latinos as a function of familiarity and positive distinctiveness. *Journal of Personality and Social Psychology, 68,* 97–108.

Hudson, W. (1960). Pictorial depth perception in subcultural groups in Africa. *Journal of Social Psychology, 52,* 183–208.

Huesmann, L. R. (1997). Observational learning of violent behavior: Social and biosocial processes. In A. Raine, P. A. Brennan, D. P. Farrington, & S. A. Mednick (Eds.), *Biosocial bases of violence.* New York: Plenum.

Huesmann, L. R., Moise, Titus, J., Podolski, C. L., & Eron, L. D. (2003). Longitudinal relations between children's exposure to TV violence and their aggressive and violent behavior in young adulthood: 1977–1992. *Developmental Psychology, 39,* 201–221.

Huff, R. M., Kline, M. V. (Eds.) (1999). *Promoting health in multicultural populations: A handbook for practitioners.* Thousand Oaks, CA: Sage Publications.

Hughes, C., Lorden, S. W., Scott, S. V., Hwang, B., Derer, K. R., & Rodi, M. S., (1998). *Journal of Applied Behavior Analysis, 31,* 431–446.

Hui, C. H., Yee, C., & Eastman, K. L. (1995). The relationship between individualism-collectivism and job satisfaction. *Applied Psychology: An International Review, 44,* 276–282.

Hull, C. L. (1933). *Hypnosis and suggestibility: An experimental approach.* New York: Appleton-Century.

Hull, C. L. (1943). *Principles of behavior, an introduction to behavior theory.* New York: Appleton-Century.

Hull, C. L. (1951). *Essentials of behavior.* New Haven, CT: Yale University Press.

Hultsch, D.F., Hammer, M., & Small, B.J. (1993). Age differences in cognitive performance in later life: Relationships to self-reported health and activity life style. *Journal of Gerontology, 48,* 1–11.

Hultsch, D. F., Hertzog, C., Small, B., & Dixon, R. A. (1999). Use it or lose it: engaged lifestyle as a buffer of cognitive decline in aging? *Psychology and Aging, 14,* 245–263.

Humphrey, G., Dodwell, P., Muir, D., & Humphrey, D. (1988). Can blind infants and children use sonar sensory aids? *Canadian Journal of Psychology, 42,* 94–119.

Humphriss, N. (1989, November 20). Letters. *Time,* p. 12.

Hunt, E. (1993). A proposal for computer modeling of animal linguistic comprehension. In H. L. Roitblat, L. M. Herman, et al. (Eds.), *Language and communication: Comparative perspectives. Comparative cognition and neuroscience.* Hillsdale, NJ: Erlbaum.

Hunt, E. (1997). The status of the concept of intelligence. *Japanese Psychological Research, 39,* 1–11.

Hunt, E., & Agnoli, F. (1991). The Whorfian hypothesis; A cognitive psychology perspective. *Psychological Review, 98,* 377–389.

Hunt, E., Streissguth, A. P., Kerr, B., & Olson, H. C. (1995). Mothers' alcohol consumption during pregnancy: Effects on spatial-visual reasoning in 14-year-old children. *Psychological Science, 6,* 339–342.

Hunt, E. B. C. (1995). *Will we be smart enough? A cognitive analysis of the coming workforce.* New York: Russell Sage Foundation.

Hunter, F. T., & Youniss, J. (1982). Changes in functions of three relations during adolescence. *Developmental Psychology, 18,* 806–811.

Hunter, J. E., & Hunter, R. F. (1984). Validity and utility of alternative predictors of job performance. *Psychological Bulletin, 96,* 72–98.

Hunter, J. E., & Schmidt, F. L. (1982). Fitting people to jobs: The impact of personnel selection on national productivity. In M. D. Dunnette & E. A. Fleishman (Eds.), *Human performance and productivity: Vol. 1. Human capability assessment.* Hillsdale, NJ: Erlbaum.

Huon, G. F., Mingyi, Q., Oliver, K. & Xiao, G. (2002). A large-scale survey of eating disorder symptomatology among female adolescents in the People's Republic of China. *International Journal of eating Disorders, 32,* 192–205.

Huston, T. L. (1973). Ambiguity of acceptance, social desirability, and dating choice. *Journal of Experimental Social Psychology, 9,* 32–42.

Huttenlocher, P. R. (1979). Synaptic density in human frontal cortex: Developmental changes and effects of aging. *Brain Research, 163,* 195–205.

Huxley, A. (1950). *Science, liberty, and peace.* London: Chato and Winders.

Hyde, J. S., & DeLamater, J. (2000). *Understanding human sexuality* (7th ed.). Boston: McGraw-Hill.

Hyde, J. S., & Oliver, M. B. (2000). Gender differences in sexuality: Results from meta-analysis. In C. B. Travis & J. W. White (Eds.), *Sexuality, society, and feminism.* Washington, DC: American Psychological Association.

Hyman, R. (1994). Anomaly or artifact? Comments on Bem and Honorton. *Psychological Bulletin, 115,* 19–24.

Iaffaldano, M. T., & Muchinsky, P. M. (1985). Job satisfaction and job performance: A meta-analysis. *Psychological Bulletin, 97,* 251–273.

Ichimaru, Y., & Miyamoto, M. (1998). Cardiovascular diseases. *Nippon-Rinsho, 56,* 461–468.

Iervolino, A. C., Pike, A., Manke, B., Reiss, D., Hetherington, E. M., & Plomin, R. (2002). Genetic and environmental influences in adolescent peer socialization: Evidence from two genetically sensitive designs. *Child Development, 73,* 162–174.

Iidaka, T., Anderson, N. D., Kapur, S., Cabeza, R., & Craik, F. I. M. (2000). The effect of divided attention on encoding and retrieval in episodic memory revealed by positron emission tomography. *Journal of Cognitive Neuroscience, 12,* 267–280.

Ikemi, Y., & Nakagawa, A. (1962). A psychosomatic study of contagious dermatitis. *Kyushu Journal of Medical Science, 13,* 335–350.

Ingelhart, R., & Rabier, J. R. (1986). Aspirations adapt to situations—but why are the Belgians so much happier than the French? A cross-cultural study of the quality of life. In F. M. Andrews (Ed.), *Research on the quality of life.* Ann Arbor, MI: Institute for Social Research, University of Michigan.

Ingham, A. G., Levinger, G., Graves, J., & Peckham, V. (1974). The Ringelmann effect: Studies of group size and group performance. *Journal of Experimental Social Psychology, 10,* 371–384.

Ingold, C. H. (1989). Locus of control and use of public information. *Psychological Reports, 64,* 603–607.

Ingraham, L. J., Kety, S. S. (2000). Adoption studies of schizophrenia. *American Journal of Medical Genetics, 97*(1), 18–22.

Ingram, R. E., & Price, J. M. (2001). *Vulnerability to psychopathology: Risk across the lifespan.* New York: Guilford Press.

Inhelder, B., & Piaget, J. (1958). *The growth of logical thinking from childhood to adolescence.* New York: Basic Books.

International Human Genome Sequencing Consortium, 2001. Initial sequencing and analysis of the human genome. *Nature, 409:* 860–921.

Intraub, H. (2002). Anticipatory spatial representation of natural scenes: Momentum without movement? *Visual Cognition, 9,* 93–119.

Intraub, H., Gottesman, C. V., & Bills, A. J. (1998). Effects of perceiving and imagining scenes on memory for pictures. *Journal of Experimental Psychology: Learning, Memory, and Cognition, 24,* 186–201.

Intraub, H., Gottesman, C. V., Willey, E. V., & Zuk, I. J. (1996). Boundary extension for briefly glimpsed photographs: Do common perceptual processes result in unexpected memory distortions? *Journal of Memory and Language, 35,* 118–134.

Ip, M. S. M., Tsang, W. T., Lam, W. K., & Lam, B. (1998). Obstructive sleep apnea syndrome: An experience in Chinese adults in Hong Kong. *Chinese Medical Journal, 111,* 257–260.

Irwin, A. R., & Gross, A. M. (1995). Cognitive tempo, violent video games, and aggressive behavior in young boys. *Journal of Family Violence, 10,* 337–350.

Irwin, J. R., & McCarthy, D. (1998). Psychophysics: Methods and analyses of signal detection. In K. A. Lattal & M. Perone (Eds.), *Handbook of research methods in human operant behavior: Applied clinical psychology.* New York: Plenum.

Irwin, M., Daniels, M., & Weiner, H. (1987). Immune and neuroendocrine changes during bereavement. *Psychiatric Clinics of North America, 10,* 449–465.

Irwin, W., Davidson, R. J., Lowe, M. J., Mock, B. J., Sorenson, J. A. & Turski, P. A. (1996). Human amyg dala activation detected with echo-planar functional magnetic resonance imaging. *Neuroreport: An International Journal for the Rapid Communication of Research in Neuroscience, 7,* 1765–1769.

Isaacs, K. S. (1998). *Uses of emotion: Nature's vital gift.* New York: Praeger.

Ishihara, K., Miyake, S., Miyasita, A., & Miyata, Y. (1992). Morningness-eveningness preference and sleep habits in Japanese office workers of different ages. *Chronobiologia, 19,* 9–16.

Ishikawa, S. L., Raine, A., Lencz, T., Bihrle, S., & Lacasse, L. (2001). Autonomic stress reactivity and executive functions in successful and unsuccessful criminal psychopaths from the community. *Journal of Abnormal Psychology, 110,* 423–432.

Itard, J. M. G. (1962). *The wild boy of Aveyron* (G. Humphrey & M. Humphrey, Trans.). New York: Appleton-Century-Crofts. (Original work published 1894)

Ito, T., Suzuki, T., Wellman, S. E., & Ho, I. K. (1996). Pharmacology of barbiturate tolerance/dependence: GABA-sub(A) receptors and molecular aspects. *Life Sciences, 59,* 169–195.

Ito, T. A., & Cacioppo, J. T. (2000). Electrophysiological evidence of implicit and explicit categorization processes. *Journal of Experimental Social Psychology, 36,* 660–676.

Izard, C. E. (1989). The structure and functions of emotions: Implications for cognition, motivation, and personality. In I. S. Cohen (Ed.), *The G. Stanley Hall lecture series* (Vol. 9). Washington, DC: American Psychological Association.

Izard, C. E., & Malatesta, C. Z. (1987). Perspectives on emotional development: I. Differential emotions theory of early emotional development. In J. D. Osofsky (Ed.), *Handbook of infant development* (2nd ed.). New York: Wiley Interscience.

Jablensky, A., Sartorius, N., Enberg, C., Anker, M., Korten, A., et al. (1992). Schizophrenia: Manifestation, incidence, and course in different cultures: A World Health Organization ten country study. *Psychological Medicine Monograph Supplement 20.* Cambridge, England: Cambridge University Press.

Jackendoff, R. (1996). The architecture of the linguistic-spatial interface. In P. Bloom, M. A. Peterson, L. Nadel, & M. F. Garrett, (Eds.), *Language and space. Language, speech, and communication.* Cambridge, MA: MIT Press.

Jackson, A., Morrow, J., Hill, D., & Dishman, R. (1999). *Physical activity for health and fitness.* Champaign, IL: Human Kinetics.

Jackson, L. A. (1992). *Physical appearance and gender: Sociobiological and sociocultural perspectives.* Albany, NY: State University of New York Press.

Jacobs, W. J., Thomas, K. G. F., Laurance, H. E., & Hadel, L. (1998). Place learning in virtual space: Topographical relations as one dimension of stimulus control. *Learning and Motivation, 29,* 288–308.

Jacobson, N. S., & Christensen, A. (1996). *Integrative couple therapy: Promoting acceptance and change.* New York: W. W. Norton.

Jacobson, N. S., & Gottman, J. M. (1998). *When men batter women: New insights into ending abusive relationships.* New York: Simon & Schuster.

Jacobson, N. S., Christensen, A., Prince, S. E., Cordova, J., & Eldridge, K. (2000). Integrative couple behavior therapy: An acceptance-based, promising new treatment for couple discord. *Journal of Consulting and Clinical Psychology, 68,* 351–355.

Jacobson, N. S., Gottman, J. M., Gortner, E., Berns, S., & Shortt, J. W. (1996). Psychological factors in the longitudinal course of battering: When do the couples split up? When does the abuse decrease? *Violence & Victims, 11,* 371–392.

Jaggar, S. I., Hasnie, F. S., Sellaturay, S., Rice, A. S. (1998). The anti-hyperalgesic actions of the cannabinoid anandamide and the putative CB2 receptor agonist palmitoylethanolamide in visceral and somatic inflammatory pain. *Pain, 76,* 189–199.

Jahoda, G. (1983). European "lag" in the development of an economic concept: A study in Zimbabwe. *British Journal of Developmental Psychology, 1,* 113–120.

Jahoda, M. (1958). *Current concepts of positive mental health.* New York: Basic Books.

James, T. W., Culham, J., Humphrey, G. K., Milner, A. D., and Goodale, M. A. (2003). Ventral occipital lesions impair object recognition but not object-directed grasping: an fMRI study. *Brain, 126,* 2463–2475.

James, W. (1879). Are we automata? *Mind, 4,* 1–22.

James, W. (1902). *The varieties of religious experience: A study in human nature.* New York: Longmans, Green.

James, W. (1950). *Principles of psychology* (Vol. 2). New York: Dover Publications. (Original work published 1890)

Jamison, K. (1995, February). Manic-depressive illness and creativity. *Scientific American,* 63–67.

Jamison, K. R. (1995). *An unquiet mind.* New York: Vantage Books.

Jang, K.L., Lam, R.W., Livesley, W.J., & Vernon, P.A. (1997). Gender differences in the heritability of seasonal mood change. *Psychiatry Research, 70(3),* 145–154.

Jang, K.L., Livesley, W.J., & Vernon, P.A. (1998). A twin study of genetic and environmental contributions to gender differences in traits delineating personality disorder. *European Journal of Personality. 12(5),* 331–344.

Jang, K.L., Vernon, P.A., & Livesley, W.J. (2000). Personality disorder traits, family environment, and alcohol misuse: A multivariate behavioural genetic analysis. *Addiction, 95(6),* 873–888.

Jang, K.L., Vernon, P.A., & Livesley, W.J. (2001). Intra- and extra-familial influences on alcohol and drug misuse: A twin study of genetic-environment correlation. *Addiction, 96(9),* 1307–1318.

Janis, I. L. (1983). *Groupthink: Psychological studies of policy decisions and fiascos* (2nd ed.). Boston: Houghton Mifflin.

Janis, I. L., & Mann, L. (1977). Emergency decision making: A theoretical analysis of responses to disaster warnings. *Journal of Human Stress, 3*(2), 35–48.

Janoski, T., Musick, M., & Wilson, J. (1998). Being volunteered? The impact of social participation and pro-social attitudes on volunteering. *Sociological Forum, 13,* 495–519.

Janssens, Jan M. A. M., & Dekovic, M. (1997). Child rearing, prosocial moral reasoning, and prosocial behaviour. *International Journal of Behavioral Development, 20,* 509–527.

Janssens, R. (1998). Structuring complex concepts. In C. E. Dowling & F. S. Roberts (Eds.), *Recent progress in mathematical psychology: Psychophysics, knowledge, representation, cognition, and measurement.* Mahwah, NJ: Erlbaum.

Janus, S. S., & Janus, C. L. (1993). *The Janus report on sexual behavior.* New York: Wiley.

Jasper, H. H. (1995). A historical perspective: The rise and fall of prefrontal lobotomy. In H. H. Jasper & S. Riggio (Eds.), *Epilepsy and the functional anatomy of the frontal lobe. Advances in neurology* (Vol. 66). New York: Raven Press.

Jeffery, R. W., & Wing, R. R. (1995). Long-term effects of interventions for weight loss using food provisions and money incentives. *Journal of Consulting and Clinical Psychology, 63,* 793–796.

Jeffery, R. W., Epstein, L. H., Wilson, G. T., Drewnowski, A., Stunkard, A. J., & Wing, R. R. (2000). Long-term maintenance of weight loss: Current status. *Health Psychology, 19,* 5–16.

Jemmott, J. B., Jemmott, L. S., & Fong, G. T. (1998). Abstinence and safer sex HIV risk-reduction interventions for African American adolescents. *Journal of the American Medical Association, 279,* 1529–1536.

Jenike, M. A. (1998). *Obsessive-compulsive disorders.* St. Louis: Mosby.

Jennings, B. M. (1990). Stress, locus of control, social support, and psychological symptoms among head nurses. *Research in Nursing and Health, 13,* 393–401.

Jensen, A. R. (1980). *Bias in mental testing.* New York: Free Press.

Jensen, A. R. (1998). The g factor and the design of education. In R. J. Sternberg & W. M. Williams (Eds.), *Intelligence, instruction, and assessment: Theory into practice.* Mahwah, NJ: Erlbaum.

Jensen, J. P., Bergin, A. E., & Greaves, D. W. (1990). The meaning of eclecticism: New survey and analysis of components. *Professional Psychology: Research and Practice, 21,* 124–130.

Jensen, M. P., Turner, J. A., & Romano, J. M. (2001). Changes in beliefs, catastrophizing, and coping are associated with improvement in multidisciplinary pain treatment. *Journal of Consulting and Clinical Psychology, 69,* 655–662.

Jentsch, J. D., Wise, A., Katz, Z., & Roth, R. H. (1998). Alpha-noradrenergic receptor modulation of the phencyclidine- and delta9-tetrahydrocannabinol-induced increases in dopamine utilization in rat prefrontal cortex. *Synapse, 28,* 21–26.

Jepson, C., & Chaiken, S. (1990). Chronic issue-specific fear inhibits systematic processing of persuasive communications. *Journal of Social Behaviors and Personality, 5,* 61–84.

Jequier, E., & Tappy, L. (1999). Regulation of body weight in humans. *Physiological Reviews, 79,* 451–480.

Jernigan, T. L., Zisook, S., Heaton, R. K., Moranville, J. T., Hesselink, J. R., & Braff, D. L. (1991). Magnetic resonance imaging abnormalities in lenticular nuclei and cerebral cortex in schizophrenia. *Archives of General Psychiatry, 48,* 881–890.

Jeste, D., & Heaton, S. (1994). How does late-onset compare with early-onset schizophrenia? *Harvard Mental Health Letter, 49,* 132–139.

Ji, L.J., Schwarz, N., & Nisbett, R. E. (2000). Culture, autobiographical memory, in cross-cultural studies. *Personality and Social Psychology Bulletin, 26*(5), 586-594.

Ji, L.J., Zhang, Z., & Nisbett, R.E. (2004). Is it Culture, or is it language? Examination of language effects in cross-cultural research on categorization. *Journal of Personality and Social Psychology, 87*(1), 57-65.

John, O. P., & Srivastava, S. (1999). The Big Five trait taxonomy: History, measurement, and theoretical perspectives. In L. A. Pervin & O. P. John (Eds.), *Handbook of personality: Theory and research.* New York: Guilford Press.

Johnson, A. M., Wadsworth, J., Wellings, K., & Bradshaw, S. (1992). Sexual lifestyles and HIV risk. *Nature, 360,* 410–412.

Johnson, B. T. (1991). Insights about attitudes: Meta-analytic perspectives. *Personality and Social Psychology Bulletin, 17,* 289–299.

Johnson, D. W. (2000). Cooperative learning processes reduce prejudice. In S. Oskamp (Ed.), *Reducing prejudice and discrimination.* Mahwah, NJ: Erlbaum.

Johnson, J. G., Cohen, P., Smailes, E. M., Kasen, S., & Brook, J. S. (2002). Television viewing and aggressive behavior during adolescence and adulthood. *Science, 295,* 2468–2471.

Johnson, J. S., & Newport, E. L. (1989). Critical period effects on universal properties of language: The influence of maturational state on the acquisition of English as a second language. *Cognitive Psychology, 21*(1), 60.

Johnson, J. S., & Newport, E. L. (1991). Critical period effects on universal properties of language: The status of subjacency in the acquisition of a second language. *Cognition, 39,* 215–258.

Johnson, L. P. N. (1997). An end to the controversy? A reply to Rips. *Minds & Machines, 7,* 425–432.

Johnston, L. D., O'Malley, P. M., & Bachman, J. G. (1999). *National survey results on drug use from the Monitoring the Future Study, 1975–1998* (Vol. 2). U.S. Department of Health and Human Services. Washington, DC: U.S. Government Printing Office.

Johnston, M. S., Kelley, C. S., Harris, F. F., & Wolf, M. M. (1966). An application of reinforcement principles to development of motor skills of a young child. *Child Development, 37,* 379–387.

Johnstone, E. C., Humphreys, M. S., Lang, F. H., et al. (Eds.) (1999). *Schizophrenia: Concepts and clinical management.* New York: Cambridge University Press.

Joiner, T. E., & Coyne, J. C. (Eds.) (1999). *The interactional nature of depression: Advances in interpersonal approaches.* Washington, DC: American Psychological Association.

Joiner, T. E., Alfano, M. S., & Metalsky, G. I. (1992). When depression breeds contempt: Reassurance seeking, self-esteem, and rejection of depressed college students by their roommates. *Journal of Abnormal Psychology, 101,* 165–173.

Jones, D. (1996). *Physical attractiveness and the theory of sexual selection.* Ann Arbor: University of Michigan Press.

Jones, E. E., & Harris, V. A. (1967). The attribution of attitudes. *Journal of Experimental Social Psychology, 3,* 2–24.

Jones, E. G. (2000). Cortical and subcortical contributions to activity-dependent plasticity in primate somatosensory cortex. *Annual Review of Neuroscience, 23,* 1–37.

Jones, E. G., Steriade, M., & McCormick, D. A. (1997). *Thalamus.* New York: Elsevier Science.

Jones, E., Cumming, J. D., & Horowitz, M. J. (1988). Another look at the nonspecific hypothesis of therapeutic effectiveness. *Journal of Consulting and Clinical Psychology, 56,* 48–55.

Jones, G. V. (1990). Misremembering a common object: When left is not right. *Memory and Cognition, 18,* 174–182.

Jones, M. C. (1924). A laboratory study of fear: The case of Peter. *Pedagogical Seminary, 31,* 308–315.

Judge, T. A., Bono, J. E., & Locke, E. A. (2000). Personality and job satisfaction: The mediating role of job characteristics. *Journal of Applied Psychology, 85,* 237–249.

Julien, R. M. (1991). *A primer of drug action* (6th ed.). New York: W. H. Freeman.

Julien, R. M. (2005). *A primer of drug action: A comprehensive guide to the actions, uses and side effects of psychoactive drugs* (10th ed.). New York: Worth Publishers.

Jung, J. (1995). Ethnic group and gender differences in the relationship between personality and coping. *Anxiety, Stress & Coping: An International Journal 8,* 113–126.

Jureidini, J. N., Doecke, C. J., Mansfield, P. R., Haby, M. H., Menkes, D. B., Tomkin, A. L. (2004). Efficacy and safety of antidepressants for children and adolescents. *British Medical Journal, 328,* 879–883.

Jurkowitz, M. (2002, October 2). Appeals court holds key in battle over regulation of violent video games. *Boston Globe,* D1.

Kabat-Zinn, J. (2003). Mindfulness-based interventions in context: Past, present, and future. *Clinical Psychology: Science and Practice, 10,* 144–158.

Kaemingk, K., & Paquette, A. (1999). Effects of prenatal alcohol exposure on neuropsychological functioning. *Developmental Neuropsychology, 15,* 111–140.

Kagan, J. (1972) Do infants think? *Scientific American, 226,* 74–82.

Kagan, J. (1989). Temperamental contributions to social behavior. *American Psychologist, 44,* 668–674.

Kagan, J., & Snidman, N. (1991). Infant predictors of inhibited and uninhibited profiles. *Psychological Science, 2,* 40–44.

Kagan, J., Kearsley, R. B., & Zelazo, P. (1978). *Infancy: Its place in human development.* Cambridge, MA: Harvard University Press.

Kagan, J., Reznick, S., & Snidman, N. (1988). Biological bases of childhood shyness. *Science, 240,* 167–171.

Kagitáibasi, C. (1997). Individualism and collectivism. In J. W. Berry, M. H. Segall, & C. Kagitáibasi (Eds.), *Handbook of cross-cultural psychology* (Vol. 3). Boston: Allyn & Bacon

Kagitáibasi, C., & Poortinga, Y. H. (2000). Cross-cultural psychology: Issues and overarching themes. *Journal of Cross Cultural Psychology, 31,* 129–147.

Kahn, A., Kahn, S., Kolts, R. Brown, W. A. Suicide rates in clinical trials of SSTRs, other antidepressants, and placebo: analysis of FDA report. *American Journal of Psychiatry, 160,* 790–792.

Kahn, S., Zimmerman, G., Csikszentmihalyi, M., & Getzels, J. W. (1985). Relations between identity in young adulthood and intimacy at midlife. *Journal of Personality and Social Psychology, 49,* 1316–1322.

Kahneman, D., & Tversky, A. (1979). Prospect theory: An analysis of decisions under risk. *Econometrica, 47,* 263–291.

Kahneman, D., & Tversky, A. (1982). On the study of statistical intuitions. *Cognition, 11,* 123–141.

Kail, R. (1991). Developmental change in speed of processing during childhood and adolescence. *Psychological Bulletin, 109,* 490–501.

Kalick, S. M., & Hamilton, T. E., III. (1988). Closer look at a matching simulation: Reply to Aron. *Journal of Personality and Social Psychology, 54,* 447–451.

Kalin, N. H., Larson, C., Shelton, S. E., & Davidson, R. R. (1998). Asymmetric frontal brain activity, cortisol, and behavior associated with fearful temperament in rhesus monkeys. *Behavioral Neuroscience, 112,* 286–292.

Kalish, R. A., & Reynolds, D. K. (1977). The role of age in death attitudes. *Death Education, 1,* 205–230.

Kallen, D. J. (1971). Nutrition and society. *Journal of the American Medical Association, 215,* 94–100.

Kandel, E. R., & Hawkins, R. D. (1992). The biological basis of learning and individuality. *Scientific American, 267*(3), 78–87.

Kane, J. M. (Ed.) (1992). *Tardive dyskinesia: A task force report of the American Psychiatric Association.* Washington, DC: American Psychiatric Press.

Kane, J. M. (2006). Tardive Dyskinesia Circa 2006. *American Journal of Psychiatry, 16*(8), 1316–1318.

Kaner, A. (1995). Physical attractiveness and women's lives: Findings from a longitudinal study. *Dissertation Abstracts International: Section B: The Sciences and Engineering, 56,* 2942.

Kanfer, F. H. (1996). Motivation and emotion in behavior therapy. In K. S. Dobson & K. D. Craig (Eds.), *Advances in cognitive-behavioral therapy* (Vol. 2). Thousand Oaks, CA: Sage Publications.

Kanwisher, N. (1998). The modular structure of human visual recognition: Evidence from functional imaging. In M. Sabourin, C. Fergus et al. (Eds.), *Advances in psychological science, Vol. 2: Biological and cognitive aspects.* Hove, England: Psychology Press/Erlbaum (UK), Taylor & Francis.

Kaplan, H. S., & Owett, T. (1993). The female androgen deficiency syndrome. *Journal of Sex and Marital Therapy, 19,* 3–24.

Kaplan, H., & Dove, H. (1987). Infant development among the Ache of eastern Paraguay. *Development Psychology, 23,* 190–198.

Kaprio, J., Koskenvu, M., & Rita, H. (1987). Mortality after bereavement: A prospective study of 95,647 widowed persons. *American Journal of Public Health, 77,* 283–287.

Karau, S. J., & Hart, J. W. (1998). Group cohesiveness and social loafing: Effects of a social interaction manipulation on individual motivation within groups. *Group Dynamics, 2,* 185–191.

Karau, S. J., & Williams, K. D. (1993). Social loafing: A meta-analytic review and theoretical integration. *Journal of Personality and Social Psychology, 65,* 681–706.

Karau, S. J., & Williams, K. D. (2001). Understanding individual motivation in groups: The collective effort model. In M. E. Turner (Ed.), *Groups at work: Theory and research. Applied social research.* Mahwah, NJ: Erlbaum.

Karni, A., Tanne, D., Rubenstein, B. S., Jean J. M., Askenasy, J. J. M., and Sagi, D. (1994). Dependence on REM sleep of overnight improvement of a perceptual skill. *Science, 265,* 679–682.

Karon, B. P. (2002). Psychoanalysis: Legitimate and illegitimate concerns. *Psychoanalytic Psychology 19,* 564–571.

Karper, L. P., & Krystal, J. H. (1997). Pharmacotherapy of violent behavior. In D. M. Stroff, J. Breiling, & J. D. Maser (Eds.), *Handbook of antisocial behavior.* New York: Wiley.

Karremans, J. C., Stroebe, W., Claus, J. (2006). Beyond Vicary's fantasies: The impact of subliminal priming and brand choice. *Journal of Experimental Social Psychology, 42,* 792–798.

Kastenbaum, R. (2000). Death anxiety. In G. Fink (Ed.), *Encyclopedia of stress.* San Diego: Academic Press.

Katz, J., & Melzack, R. (1990). Pain "memories" in phantom limbs: Review and clinical observations. *Pain, 43,* 319–336.

Katz, L. J., & Slomka, G. T. (2000). Achievement testing. In G. Goldstein & M. Hersen (Eds.), *Handbook of psychological assessment* (3rd ed.). New York: Elsevier.

Kay, L. (1982). *Spatial perception through an acoustic sensor.* Christchurch, New Zealand: University of Canterbury Press.

Kayser, J., Tenke, C., Nordby, H., Hammerborg, D., et. al. (1997). Event-related potential (ERP) asymmetries to emotional stimuli in a visual half-field paradigm. *Psychophysiology, 34(4),* 414–426.

Kazdin, A. E. (1975). The impact of applied behavior analysis on diverse areas of research. *Journal of Applied Behavior Analysis, 8,* 213–229.

Kazdin, A. E. (Ed.). (2003). *Methodological issues and strategies in clinical research* (3rd ed.). Washington, DC: American Psychological Association.

Kazdin, A. E., & Weisz, J. R. (2003). *Evidence-based psychotherapies for children and adolescents.* New York: Guilford Press.

Kealy, E. M. (2005). Variations in the experience of schizophrenia: A cross-cultural review. *Journal of Social Work Research and Evaluation, 6(1),* 47–56.

Keating, N., & Jeffrey, B. (1983). Work careers of ever married and never married retired women. *Gerontologist, 23,* 416–421.

Keefe, F. J., Lefebvre, J. C., Maixner, W., Salley, A. N., & Caldwell, D. S. (1997). Self-efficacy for arthritis pain: Relationship to perception of thermal laboratory pain stimuli. *Arthritis Care & Research, 10,* 177–184.

Keller, H. (1955). *The story of my life.* New York: Doubleday.

Kelley, H. H. (1950). The warm-cold variable in first impressions of persons. *Journal of Personality, 18,* 431–439.

Kelley, H. H. (1973). The process of causal attribution. *American Psychologist, 28,* 107–128.

Kellner, R. (1992). *Psychosomatic syndromes and somatic symptoms.* Washington, DC: American Psychiatric Press.

Kelly, G. F. (2001). *Sexuality today: The human perspective* (7th ed). Boston: McGraw-Hill.

Kelly, J. A., St. Lawrence, J. S., & Brasfield, T. L. (1991). Predictors of vulnerability to AIDS risk behavior relapse. *Journal of Consulting and Clinical Psychology, 59,* 163–166.

Kelly, J. A., St. Lawrence, J. S., Hood. H. V., & Brasfield, T. L. (1989). Behavioral intervention to reduce AIDS risk activities. *Journal of Consulting and Clinical Psychology, 57,* 60–67.

Kelly, T. A., & Strupp, H. H. (1992). Patient and therapist values in psychotherapy: Perceived changes, assimilation, similarity, and outcome. *Journal of Consulting and Clinical Psychology, 60,* 34–40.

Kelman, H. C. (1996). Negotiation as interactive problem solving. *International Negotiation, 1,* 99–123.

Kelman, H. C. (1997). Group processes in the resolution of international conflicts: Experiences from the Israeli-Palestinian case. *American Psychologist, 52,* 212–220.

Kenardy, J., Brown, W. J., & Vogt, E. (2001). Dieting and health in young Australian women. *European Eating Disorders Review, 9,* 242–254.

Kendall, D. (1998). *Social problems in a diverse society.* Boston: Allyn & Bacon.

Kennedy, S. H., Evans, K. R., Krüger, S., Mayberg, H. S., Meyer, J. H., McCann, S., Arifuzzman, A. I., Houle, S., & Vaccarino, F. J. (2001). Changes in regional brain glucose metabolism measured with positron emission tomography after paroxetine treatment of major depression. *American Journal of Psychiatry, 158,* 899–905.

Kenrick, D. T., & Funder, D. C. (1988). Profiting from controversy: Lessons from the person-situation debate. *American Psychologist, 43,* 23–34.

Kenrick, D. T., & Funder, D. C. (1991). The person-situation debate: Do personality traits really exist? In N. J. Derlega, B. A. Winstead, & W. H. Jones, (Eds.), *Personality: Contemporary theory and research.* Chicago: Nelson-Hall.

Kensinger, E. & Schacter, D. (2005a). Emotional content and reality monitoring ability: fMRI evidence for the influences of encoding processes. *Neuropsychologia, 43,* 1429–1443.

Kensinger, E. & Schacter, D. (2005b). Memory accuracy versus memory assignment: An fMRI study of reality-monitoring ability. *Journal of Cognitive Neuroscience,* 96–96.

Kensinger, E. A. & Schacter, D. L. (2006). Reality monitoring and memory distortion: effects of negative, arousing content. *Memory & Cognition, 34*(2), 251–260.

Kernberg, O. (1976). *Object relations theory and clinical psychoanalysis.* New York: Jason Aronsen.

Kernberg, O. F. (1984). *Severe personality disorders.* New Haven, CT: Yale University Press.

Kernberg, O. F. (1984). *Severe personality disorders: Psychotherapeutic strategies.* New Haven, CT: Yale University Press.

Kernberg, O. F. (1999). *Personality disorders in children and adolescents.* Poulsbo, WA: H-R Press.

Kerns, J. G., & Berenbaum, H. (2002, 2003). Cognitive impairments associated with formal thought disorder in people with schizophrenia. *Journal of Abnormal Psychology, 111,* 211–224.

Kerns, J. G., Berenbaum, H. (2003). The relationship between formal thought disorder and executive functioning component processes. *Journal of Abnormal Psychology, 112*(3), 339–352.

Kerr, M., Lambert, W. W., & Bem, D. J. (1996). Life course sequelae of childhood shyness in Sweden: Comparison with the United States. *Developmental Psychology, 32,* 1100–1105.

Kessels, R. P. C. & Postma, A. (2006). Object-location memory in ageing and dementia. In T. Vecchi and G. Bottini, (Eds.), *Imagery and Spatial Cognition: Methods, models and cognitive assessment.* (227–243). Amsterdam: John Benjamins Publishing.

Kessler, R. C., McGonagle, K. A., Zhao, S., & Nelson, C. (1994). Lifetime and 12-month prevalence of DSM-III-R psychiatric disorder in the United States: Results from the National Comorbidity Survey. *Archives of General Psychiatry, 51,* 8–19.

Kessler, R. C., & Wittchen, H. U. (2002). Patterns and correlates of generalized anxiety disorder in community samples. *Journal of Clinical Psychiatry, 63*(Suppl. 8), 4–10.

Kety, S. S. (1988). Schizophrenic illness in the families of schizophrenic adoptees: Findings from the Danish national sample. *Schizophrenia Bulletin, 1988; 14,* 217–222.

Kety, S., Rosenthal, D., Wender, P. H., Schulsinger, F., & Jacobson, B. (1978). The biological and adoptive families of adopted individuals who become schizophrenic: Prevalence of mental illness and other characteristics. In L. C. Wynne, R. L. Cromwell, & S. Matthysse (Eds.), *The nature of schizophrenia: New approaches to research and treatment.* New York: Wiley.

Keyes, D. (1982). *The minds of Billy Milligan.* New York: Bantam.

Khan, A. U., & Olson, D. L. (1977). Deconditioning of exercise-induced asthma. *Psychosomatic Medicine, 39,* 382–392.

Khoury, R. M. (1985). Norm formation, social conformity, and the confederating function of humor. *Social Behavior and Personality, 13,* 159–165.

Kiecolt-Glaser, J. K., Glaser, R., Cacioppo, J. T., & Malarkey, W. B. (1998). Marital stress: Immunologic, neuroendocrine, and autonomic correlates. *Annals of the New York Academy of Sciences, 840,* 656–663.

Kiehl, K.A., Smith, A.M., Hare, R.D., Mendrek, A., Foster, B.B., Brink, J., and Liddle, P.F. (2001). Limbic abnormalities in affective processing by criminal psychopaths as revealed by functional magnetic resonance imaging. *Biological Psychiatry, 50,* 677–684.

Kiesler, C. A. (1992). U.S. mental health policy: Doomed to fail. *American Psychologist, 47,* 1077–1082.

Kihlstrom, J. F. (1982). Hypnosis and the dissociation of memory, with special reference to posthypnotic amnesia. *Research Communications in Psychology, Psychiatry and Behavior, 7,* 181–197.

Kihlstrom, J. F. (1985). Posthypnotic amnesia and the dissociation of memory. *Psychology of Learning and Motivation, 19,* 131–178.

Kihlstrom, J. F. (1998). Dissociations and dissociation theory in hypnosis: Comment on Kirsch and Lynn. *Psychological Bulletin, 123,* 186–191.

Kihlstrom, J. F. (1999). The psychological unconscious. In L. A. Pervin & O. P. John (Eds.), *Handbook of personality: Theory and research.* New York: Guilford Press.

Killen, M., Ardila-Rey, R., Barakkatz, M., & Wang, P. L. (2000). Preschool teacher's perceptions about conflict resolution, autonomy, and the group in four countries: United States, Colombia, El Salvador, and Taiwan. *Early Education and Development, 11,* 73–92.

Kim, J., Lim, J. S., & Bhargava, M. (1998). The role of affect in attitude formation: A classical conditioning approach. *Journal of the Academy of Marketing Science, 26,* 143–152.

Kimble, D. P. (1992). *Biological psychology* (2nd ed.). Ft. Worth, TX: Harcourt Brace Jovanovich.

Kimerling, R., Ouimette, P., & Wolfe, J. (2003). *Gender and PTSD.* New York: Guilford Press.

Kimura, D. (1973). The Asymmetry of the human brain. *Scientific American, 228,* 70–78.

Kimura, D., & Hampson, E. (1994). Cognitive pattern in men and women is influenced by fluctuations in sex hormones. *Current Directions in Psychological Science, 3*(2), 57–61.

Kimura, K., Tachibana, N., Aso, T., Kimura, J., & Shibasaki, H. (1997). Subclinical REM sleep behavior disorder in a patient with corticobasal degeneration. *Sleep, 20,* 891–894.

Kinsey, A. C., Pomeroy, W. B., & Martin, C. E. (1948). *Sexual behavior in the human male.* Philadelphia: Saunders.

Kinsey, A. C., Pomeroy, W. B., Martin, C. E., & Gebhard, P. H. (1953). *Sexual behavior in the human female.* Philadelphia: Saunders.

Kirchner, W. H., & Grasser, A. (1998). The significance of odor cues and dance language information for the food search behavior of honeybees (Hymenoptera Apidae). *Journal of Insect Behavior, 11,* 169–178.

KIRO News (1998, January 17). *KIRO evening news.* Seattle, WA.

Kirsch, I. (1999). Clinical hypnosis as a nondeceptive placebo. In I. Kirsch, A. Capafons, B. E. Cardeña, & S. (Eds,)., *Clinical hypnosis and self-regulation: Cognitive behavioral perspectives.* Washington, DC: American Psychological Association.

Kirsch, I., & Lynn, S. J. (1998a). Dissociation theories of hypnosis. *Psychological Bulletin, 123,* 100–115.

Kirsch, I., & Lynn, S. J. (1998b). Social cognitive alternatives to dissociation theories of hypnotic involuntariness. *Review of General Psychology, 2,* 66–80.

Kirsch, I., & Lynn, S. J. (1999). Automaticity in clinical psychology. *American Psychologist, 54,* 504–515.

Kirschbaum, A. K., Krischbaum, C., Stierle, H., & Lehnert, H. (1992). Conditioned increase of natural killer cell activity (NKCA) in humans. *Psychosomatic Medicine, 54,* 123–132.

Kirsh, S. J. (1998). Seeing the world through Mortal Kombat–colored glasses: Violent video games and the development of a short-term hostile attribution bias. *Childhood: A Global Journal of Child Research, 5,* 177–184.

Kisilevsky, B.S., & Muir, D.W. (1991). Human fetal and subsequent newborn responses to sound and vibration. *Infant Behavior & Development, 14,* 1–26.

Kisilevsky, B.S., Muir, D.W., & Low, J.A. (1992). Maturation of human fetal responses to vibroacoustic stimulation. *Child Development, 63,* 1497–1508.

Kiyatkin, E. A. & Gratton, A. (1994). Electrochemical monitoring of extracellular dopamine in nucleus accumbens of rats lever-pressing for food. *Brain Research,* 652, 225–234.

Klahr, D., & Simon, H. A. (1999). Studies of scientific discovery: Complementary approaches and convergent findings. *Psychological Bulletin, 125,* 524–543.

Klein, M. (1975). *The writings of Melanie Klein.* London: Hogarth Press.

Klein, R. M. (1999). The Hebb Legacy. *Canadian Journal of Experimental Psychology, 53,* 1–3.

Klein, S. B., & Mowrer, R. R. (1989). *Contemporary learning theories. Vol I: Pavlovian conditioning and the status of tradition.* Hillsdale, NJ: Erlbaum.

Kleinknecht, R. A., Dinnel, D. L., Kleinknecht, E. E. & Hiruma, N. et al. (1997). Cultural factors in social anxiety: A comparison of social phobia symptoms and Taijin Kyofusho. *Journal of Anxiety Disorders, 2,* 157–177.

Kleinmuntz, B. (1980). *Essentials of abnormal psychology* (2nd ed.). New York: Harper & Row.

Kleitman, N. (1963). *Sleep and wakefulness* (2nd ed.). Chicago: University of Chicago Press.

Klimesch, W. (1979). Reminiscence and visual memory: Implications for the respective kind of the forgetting process. *Psychologische Beitraege, 21,* 40–48.

Kline, D.W. (1994). Optimizing the visibility of displays for older observers. *Experimental Aging Research. Special Issue: Human factors and the aging driver, 20,* 11–23.

Kline, G. H., Stanley, S. M., Markman, H. J., Olmos-Gallo, P. A., St Peters, M., Whitton, S. W., & Prado, L. M. (2004). Timing is everything: pre-engagement cohabitation and increased risk for poor marital outcomes. *Journal of Family Psychology, 18,* 311–318.

Kluckhohn, C., & Murray, H. A. (1953). Personality formation: The determinants. In C. Kluckhohn, H. A. Murray, & D. M. Schneider (Eds.), *Personality in nature, society, and culture.* New York: Alfred A. Knopf.

Kluft, R. P. (1999). True lies, false truths, and naturalistic raw data: Applying clinical research findings to the false memory debate. In L. M. Williams & V. L. Banyard, (Eds), *Trauma and memory.* Thousand Oaks, CA: Sage Publications.

Knauth, P. (1996). Designing better shift systems. *Applied Ergonomics, 27,* 39–44.

Knowles, J. H. (1977). The responsibility of the individual. In J. H. Knowles (Ed.), *Doing better and feeling worse: Health in the United States.* New York: Norton.

Kobasa, S. C., Maddi, S. R., Puccetti, M. C., & Zola, M. A. (1985). Effectiveness of hardiness, exercise and social support as resources against illness. *Journal of Psychosomatic Research, 29,* 525–533.

Koenig, H. G., Pargament, K. L., & Nielsen, J. (1998). Religious coping and health status in medically ill hospitalized older adults. *Journal of Nervous and Mental Disease, 186,* 513–521.

Koestner, R., & McClelland, D. C. (1990). Perspectives on competence motivation. In L. A. Pervin (Ed.), *Handbook of personality theory and research.* New York: Guilford Press.

Kohlberg, L. (1963). The development of children's orientations toward a moral order: I. Sequence in the development of moral thought. *Human Development, 6,* 11–33.

Kohlberg, L. (1984). *The psychology of moral development: Essays on moral development* (Vol. 2). New York: Harper & Row.

Köhler, W. (1925). *The mentality of apes.* New York: Harcourt. (Trans. from the 2nd rev. ed. by Ella Winter)

Kohut, H. (1971). *Analysis of the self.* New York: International Universities Press.

Kohut, H. (1977). *The restoration of self.* New York: International Universities Press.

Kolb, B. (1989). Brain development, plasticity, and behavior. *American Psychologist, 44,* 1203–1212.

Kolb, B., & Whishaw, I. Q. (1989). Plasticity in the neocortex: Mechanisms underlying recovery from early brain damage. *Progress in Neurobiology, 32,* 235–276.

Kolb, B., & Whishaw, I. Q. (1998). Brain plasticity and behavior. *Annual Review of Psychology, 49,* 43–64.

Kolb, B., & Whishaw, I. Q. (2001). *An introduction to brain and behavior.* New York: Worth.

Kolb, B., & Whishaw, I. Q. (2003). *Fundamentals of human neuropsychology* (5th ed.). New York: Worth.

Kollar, E. J., & Fisher, C. (1980). Tooth induction in chick epithelium: Expression of quiescent genes for enamel synthesis. *Science, 207,* 993–995.

Koluchova, J. (1972). Severe deprivation in twins: A case study. *Journal of Child Psychology and Psychiatry, 13,* 107–114.

Koluchova, J. (1991). Severely deprived twins after 22 years of observation. *Studiea Psychologica, 33,* 23–28.

Konkle, A. T. M., Kubela, S. L., & Bielajew, C. (2000). The effects of cholecystokinin on stimulation-induced feeding and self-stimulation. *Behavioural Brain Research, 107,* 145–152.

Kopelman, M. D., Stanhope, N., & Kingsley, D. (1999). Retrograde amnesia in patients with diencephalic, temporal lobe or frontal lesions. *Neuropsychologia, 37,* 939–958.

Koriat, A., Goldsmith, M., & Pansky, A. (2000). Toward a psychology of memory accuracy. *Annual Review of Psychology, 51,* 481–537.

Korn, J. H. (1998). The reality of deception. *American Psychologist, 53,* 805.

Korpi, E. R. (1994). Role of GABA-sub(A) receptors in the actions of alcohol and in alcoholism: Recent advances. *Alcohol and Alcoholism, 29,* 115–129.

Kortegaard, L., Hoerder, K., Joergensen, J., Gillberg, C., & Kyvik, K. O. (2001). A preliminary population-based twin study of self-reported eating disorder. *Psychological Medicine, 31,* 361–365.

Kosambi, D. D. (1967). Living prehistory in India. *Scientific American, 216,* 105.

Koss, M. P., & Ingram, M. (2000). Male partner violence. In G. Fink (Ed.), *Encyclopedia of stress.* San Diego: Academic Press.

Koss, M. P., Gidycz, C. A., & Wisniewski, N. (1987). The scope of rape: Incidence and prevalence of sexual aggression and victimization in a national sample of higher education students. *Journal of Consulting and Clinical Psychology, 55,* 162–170.

Kottak, C. P. (2000). *Cultural anthropology* (8th ed.). Boston: McGraw-Hill.

Koulack, D. (1997). Recognition memory, circadian rhythms, and sleep. *Perceptual and Motor Skills, 85,* 99–104.

Kovacs, M., & Devlin, B. (1998). Internalizing disorders in childhood. *Journal of Child Psychology and Psychiatry, 39,* 47–63.

Kraft, C. L. (1978). A psychophysical contribution to air safety: Simulator studies of visual illusions in night visual approaches. In H. L. Pick, Jr., H. W. Leibowitz, J. E. Singer, A. Steinschneider, & H. W. Stevenson (Eds.), *Psychology: From research to practice.* New York: Plenum.

Kramer, A., Hahn, S. & McAuley, E. (2000). Influence of aerobic fitness on the neurocognitive function of older adults. *Journal of Aging and Physical Activity, 8,* 379–385.

Kramer, D. A. (1983). Post-formal operations? A need for further conceptualization. *Human Development, 26,* 91–105.

Kramsch, C. J. (2003). *Language acquisition and language socialization: Ecological perspectives.* New York: Continuum International Publishing Group.

Krasnegor, N. A., Lyon, G. R., & Goldman, R. P. S. (1997). *Development of the prefrontal cortex: Evolution, neurobiology, and behavior.* Baltimore: Paul H. Brookes.

Kraus, S. J. (1995). Attitudes and the prediction of behavior: A meta-analysis of the empirical literature. *Personality and Social Psychology Bulletin, 21,* 58–75.

Krause, M. A., & Fouts, R. S. (1997). Chimpanzee (Pan troglodytes) pointing: Hand shapes, accuracy, and the role of eye gaze. *Journal of Comparative Psychology, 111,* 330–336.

Krausz, M. (1982). Policies of organizational choice at different vocational life stages. *Vocational Guidance Quarterly, 31,* 60–68.

Kraut, R., Olson, J., Banaji, M., Bruckman, A., Cohen, J., & Cooper, M. (2004). Psychological research online: Report of board of scientific affairs' advisory group on the conduct of research on the internet. *American Psychologist, 59,* 105–117.

Krebs, D. L., & Denton, K. (1997). Social illusions and self-deception: The evolution of biases in person perception. In J. A. Simpson & D. T. Kenrick (Eds.), *Evolutionary social psychology.* Mahwah, NJ: Lawrence Erlbaum.

Krech, D. (1978). Quoted in M. C. Diamond, The aging brain: Some enlightening and optimistic results. *American Scientist, 66,* 66–71.

Krevans, J., & Gibbs, J. C. (1996). Parents' use of inductive discipline: Relations to children's empathy and prosocial behavior. *Child Development, 67,* 3263–3277.

Krijn, M., Emmelkamp, P. M. G., Biemond, R., de Wilde de Ligny, C., Schuemie, M. J., & van der Mast, C. A. P. G. (2004a). Treatment of acrophobia in virtual reality: The role of immersion and presence. *Behaviour Research and Therapy, 42,* 229–239.

Krijn, M., Emmelkamp, P.M.G. Olafsson, R.P. & Biemond, R. (2004b). Virtual reality exposure therapy of anxiety disorders: A review. *Clinical Psychology Review, 24,* 259–281.

Kroeber, A. L. (1948). *Anthropology.* New York: Harcourt Brace Jovanovich.

Krohn, M. D. (1976). Inequality, unemployment and crime: Cross-national data and criminology theories. *Criminology, 24,* 269–295.

Krosnick, J. A., Betz, A. L., Jussim, L. J., & Lynn, A. R. (1992). Subliminal conditioning of attitudes. *Personality and Social Psychology Bulletin, 18,* 152–162.

Krueger, R. F., & Caspi, A. (1993). Personality, arousal, and pleasure: A test of competing models of interpersonal attraction. *Personality and Individual Differences, 14,* 105–111.

Kruglanski, A. W., & Webster, D. M. (1996). Motivated closing of the mind: "Seizing" and "freezing." *Psychological Review, 103,* 263–283.

Kryger, M.H., Walld, R., & Manfreda, J. (2002). Diagnoses received by narcolepsy patients in the year prior to diagnsis by a sleep specialist. *Sleep: Journal of Sleep and Sleep Disorders Research, 25,* 36–41.

Kubler-Ross, E. (1969). *On death and dying.* New York: Macmillan.

Kugiumutzakis, Kokkinaki, Makrodimitraki, and Vitalaki, (2005). Emotions in early mimesis. In Nadel, J. & Muir, D. (Eds.) *Emotional Development: Current and future research directions.* Oxford: Oxford University Press (161–182).

Kuhn, C. M., & Schanberg, S. M. (1998). Responses to maternal separation: Mechanisms and mediators. *International Journal of Developmental Neuroscience, 16,* 261–270.

Kulik, J. A., & Mahler, H. I. M. (1989). Stress and affiliation in a hospital setting: Preoperative roommate preferences. *Personality and Social Psychology Bulletin, 15,* 183–193.

Kulik, J. A., Mahler, H. I. M., & Moore, P. J. (1996). Social comparison and affiliation under threat: Effects of recovery from major surgery. *Journal of Personality and Social Psychology, 66,* 301–309.

Kumar, P., & Dhyani, J. (1996). Marital adjustment: A study of some related factors. *Indian Journal of Clinical Psychology, 23,* 112–116.

Kunzendorf, R. G., Hartmann, E., Cohen, R., & Cutler, J. (1997). Bizarreness of the dreams and daydreams reported by individuals with thin and thick boundaries. *Dreaming: Journal of the Association for the Study of Dreams, 7,* 265–271.

Kupers, R. & Ptito, M. (2004). "Seeing" through the tongue: cross-modal plasticity in the congenitally blind. *International Congress Series, 1270,* 79–84, Elsevier.

Kurdek, L. A. (1999). The nature and predictors of the trajectory of change in marital quality for husbands and wives over the first 10 years of marriage. *Developmental Psychology, 35,* 1283–1296.

Kurman, J. (2001). Self-enhancement: Is it restricted to individualistic cultures? *Personality and Social Psychology Bulletin, 27,* 1705–1716.

Kurzweil, E. (1989). *The Freudians: A comparative perspective.* New Haven, CT: Yale University Press.

Kutter, P. (Ed.) (1995). *Psychoanalysis international: A guide to psychoanalysis throughout the world.* New York: Analytic Press.

Kuyken, W., Dalgleish, T., & Holden, E. R. (2007). Advances in cognitive-behavioural therapy for unipolar depression. *Canadian Journal of Psychiatry, 52,* 5–13.

LaBar, K. S., & Phelps, E. A. (1998). Arousal-mediated memory consolidation: Role of the medial temporal lobe in humans. *Psychological Science, 9,* 490–493.

Lack, D. (1968). *Ecological adaptations for breeding in birds.* London: Methuen.

Lacks, P., Bertelson, A. D., Gans, L., & Kunkel, J. (1983). The effectiveness of three behavioral treatments for different degrees of sleep onset insomnia. *Behavior Therapy, 14,* 593–605.

Lafferty, P., Beutler, L. E., & Crago, M. (1989). Differences between more and less effective psychotherapists: A study of select therapist variables. *Journal of Consulting and Clinical Psychology, 57,* 76–80.

Lagerspetz, K. Y., Tirri, R., & Lagerspetz, K. M. (1968). Neurochemical and endocrinological studies of mice selectively bred for aggressiveness. *Scandinavian Journal of Psychology, 9,* 157–160.

Lai, D. W. L. (1995). *Needs assessment on the Chinese community in Calgary: Final report.* Calgary, AB: Calgary Chinese Community Service Association.

Laing, R. D. (1967). *The politics of experience.* New York: Pantheon Books.

Lakein, A. (1973). *How to get control of your time and your life.* New York: Peter H. Wyden.

Lakin, M. (1998). Carl Rogers and the culture of psychotherapy. In G. A. Kimble & M. Wertheimer (Eds.), *Portraits of pioneers in psychology* (Vol. 3). Washington, DC: American Psychological Association.

Lamal, P. A. (Ed.) (1991). *Behavioral analysis of societies and cultural practices.* Bristol, PA: Hemisphere.

Lambert, M. J., Shapiro, D. A., & Bergin, A. E. (1986). The effectiveness of psychotherapy. In S. L. Garfield & A. E. Bergin (Eds.), *Handbook of psychotherapy and behavior change* (3rd ed.). New York: Wiley.

Lambert, W.E. (1992). Challenging established views on social issues: The power and limitations of research. *American Psychologist,* 47: 533–542.

Lambert, W. E., Genesee, F., Holobow, N., & Chartrand, L. (1993). Bilingual education for majority English-speaking children. *European Journal of Psychology of Education, 8,* 3–22.

Lamble, D., Kauranen, T., Laakso, M., & Summala, H. (1999). Cognitive load and detection thresholds in car following situations: Safety implications for using mobile (cellular) telephones while driving. *Accident Analysis and Prevention, 31,* 617–623.

Lamborn, S. D., Mounts, N. S., Steinberg, L., & Dornbusch, S. M. (1991). Patterns of competence and adjustment among adolescents from authoritative, authoritarian, indulgent, and neglectful families. *Child Development, 62,* 1049–1065.

Lampinen, J. M., Schwartz, R. M. (2000). The impersistence of false memory persistence. *Memory, 8*(6), 393–400.

Lampropoulos, G. K. (2000). Evolving psychotherapy intergration: Eclectic selection and prescriptive applications of common factors in therapy. *Psychotherapy, 37*(4), 285–297.

Lamke, L. K. (1982). The impact of sex-role orientation on self-esteem in early adolescence. *Child Development, 53,* 1530–1535.

Lamport, M. & Richards, F. A. (2003) Four postformal stages. In J. Demick, C. Andreoletti, (Eds.). *Handbook of adult development. The Plenum series in adult development and aging.* (199–219). New York, NY: Kluwer Academic/Plenum.

Landfield, P., Baskin, R. K., & Pitler, T. A. (1981). Brain-aging correlates: Retardation by hormonal-pharmacological treatments. *Science, 214,* 581–583.

Landfield, P., Waymire, J., & Lynch, G. (1978). Hippocampal aging and adrenocorticoids: A quantitative correlation. *Science, 202,* 1098–1101.

Lane, R. D., Reiman, E. M., Ahern, G. L., & Schwartz, G. E. (1997). Neuroanatomical correlates of happiness, sadness, and disgust. *American Journal of Psychiatry, 154,* 926–933.

Laney, C., Loftus, E. F. (2005). Traumatic memories are not necessarily accurate memories. *Canadian Journal of Psychiatry, 50*(13), 823–828.

Langer, E. (1989). *Mindlessness.* Reading, MA: Addison-Wesley.

Langs, R. J. (1996). *The evolution of the emotion-processing mind: With an introduction to mental Darwinism.* New York: International Universal Press.

Lanier, C. A. (2001). Rape accepting attitudes: Precursors to or consequences of forced sex. *Violence Against Women, 7,* 876–885.

Lanius, R. A.,Williamson, P. C., Densmore, M., Boksman, K., Neufeld, R. W., Gati, J. S., & Menon, R. S. (2004). The nature of traumatic memories: a 4-T fMRI functional connectivity analysis. *American Journal of Psychiatry, 161,* 36–44.

Lanning, K. (2001). Reflections on September 11: Lessons from four psychological perspectives. *Analyses of Social Issues and Public Policy, 2002,* 27–34.

LaPiere, R. T. (1934). Attitudes and actions. *Social Forces, 13,* 230–237.

Larimer, M. E., Baer, J. S., Quigley, L. A., Blume, A. W., & Hawkins, E. H. (1998). Harm reduction for alcohol problems: Expanding access to and acceptability of prevention and treatment services. In G. A. Marlatt (Ed.), *Harm reduction: Pragmatic strategies for managing high-risk behaviors.* New York: Guilford Press.

Larroque, B., & Kaminski, M. (1998). Prenatal alcohol exposure and development at preschool age: Main results of a French study. *Alcoholism: Clinical and Experimental Research, 22,* 295–303.

Larson, S. J., & Siegel, S. (1998). Learning and tolerance to the ataxic effect of ethanol. *Pharmacology, Biochemistry and Behavior, 61,* 131–142.

Lashley, K. S. (1930). The mechanism of vision: 1. A method for rapid analysis of pattern-vision in the rat. *Journal of Genetic Psychology, 37,* 453–460.

Lashley, K. S. (1950). In search of the engram. In *Symposium of the Society for Experimental Biology* (Vol. 4). New York: Cambridge University Press.

Laska, M., & Metzker, K. (1998). Food avoidance learning in squirrel monkeys and common marmosets. *Learning and Memory, 5,* 193–203.

Latané, B. (1981). The psychology of social impact. *American Psychologist, 36,* 343–356.

Latané, B., & Darley, J. M. (1968). Group inhibition of bystander intervention in emergencies. *Journal of Personality and Social Psychology, 10,* 215–221.

Latané, B., & Darley, J. M. (1970). *The unresponsive bystander: Why doesn't he help?* New York: Appleton-Century-Crofts.

Latané, B., & Nida, S. (1981). Ten years of research on group size and helping. *Psychological Bulletin, 89,* 308–324.

Latané, B., & Rodin, J. (1969). A lady in distress: Inhibiting effects of friends and strangers on bystander intervention. *Journal of Experimental Social Psychology, 5,* 189–202.

Latané, B., Liu, J. H., Nowak, A., Bonevento, M., & Zheng, L. (1995). Distance matters: Physical space and social impact. *Personality and Social Psychology Bulletin, 21,* 795–805.

Lau, R. R., & Russell, D. (1980). Attribution in the sports pages. *Journal of Personality and Social Psychology, 39,* 29–38.

Laughlin, H. P. (1967). *The neuroses.* Washington, DC: Butterworth.

Laumann, E. O., Gagnon, J. H., Michael, R T., & Michaels, S. (1994). *The social organization of sexuality: Sexual practices in the United States.* Chicago: University of Chicago Press.

Lavigne, J. V., Gibbons, R. D., Christoffel, K. K., & Arend, R. (1996). Prevalence rates and correlates of psychiatric disorders among preschool children. *Journal of the American Academy of Child and Adolescent Psychiatry, 35,* 204–214.

Lawler, K. A., Kline, K. A., Harriman, H. L., & Kelly, K. M. (1999). Stress and illness. In V. J. Derlega, B. A. Winstead, et al. (Eds.), *Personality: Contemporary theory and research* (2nd ed.). Chicago: Nelson-Hall.

Lazar, S. W., Bush, G., Gollub, R. L., Fricchione, G. L., Khalsa, G., & Benson, H. (2000). Functional brain mapping of the relaxation response and meditation. *NeuroReport, 11,* 1581–1585.

Lazarus, A. A. (1995). Multimodal therapy. In R. J. Corsini & D. Wedding (Eds.), *Current psychotherapies* (5th ed.). Itaska, IL: Peacock.

Lazarus, R., Lazarus, B., Campos, J. J., Tennen, R., & Tennen, H. (2006). Emotions and interpersonal relationships: Toward a person-centered conceptualization of emotions and coping. *Journal of Personality. 74,* 9–46

Lazarus, R. S. (1991). Progress on a cognitive-motivational-relational theory of emotion. *American Psychologist, 46,* 819–834.

Lazarus, R. S. (1998). *Fifty years of the research and theory of R. S. Lazarus: An analysis of historical and perennial issues.* Mahwah, NJ: Erlbaum.

Lazarus, R. S., & Folkman, S. (1984). *Stress, appraisal, and coping.* New York: Springer.

Leach, A. M., Talwar, V., Lee, K., Bala, N., & Lindsay, R. C. L. (2004). "Intuitive lie detection" of children's deception by law enforcement officials and university students. *Law and Human Behavior, 28,* 661–685.

Leaper, C., Anderson, K. J., & Sanders, P. (1998). Moderators of gender effects on parents' talk to their children: A meta-analysis. *Developmental Psychology, 34,* 3–27.

LeBon, G. (1895). *Psychologies des foules.* Paris: Oleon.

LeBow, M. D. (1988). Attitudes, perceptions, and practices of Canadian school children towards obesity. *Journal of Obesity and Weight Regulation,* 7: 43–55.

LeBow, M. D., Ness, D., Makarenko, P., & Lam, T. (1989). Attitudes, perceptions and practices of Canadian teenagers towards obesity. *Journal of Obesity and Weight Regulation,* 8: 53–65.

LeDoux, J. E. (1989). Cognitive-emotional interactions in the brain. *Cognition and Emotion, 3,* 267–289.

LeDoux, J. E. (1992). Systems and synapses of emotional memory. In L. R. Squire, N. M. Weinberger, G. Lynch, & J. L. McGaugh (Eds.), *Memory: Organization and locus of change.* New York: Oxford University Press.

LeDoux, J. E. (1996, 1998). *The emotional brain.* New York: Simon & Schuster.

LeDoux, J. E. (2000). Emotion circuits in the brain. *Annual Review of Neuroscience, 23,* 155–184.

LeDoux, J. E., Wilson, D. H., & Gazzaniga, M. S. (1977). A divided mind: Observations on the conscious properties of the separated hemispheres. *Annals of Neurology, 2,* 417–421.

LeDoux, J., & Gorman, J. (2001). A call to action: Overcoming anxiety through active coping. *American Journal of Psychiatry,* 158(12): 1953–1955.

Lee, J. A. (1973). *Colors of love.* Toronto: New Press.

Lee, K. & Freire, A. (1999). Effects of face configuration change on shape perception: A new illusion. *Perception, 28,* 1217–1226.

Lee, R. M. (2000). *Unobtrusive methods in social research.* Buckingham, UK: Open University Press.

Lee, K. & Homer, B. (1999). Children as folk psychologists: The developing understanding of the mind. In A. Slater & D. Muir (Eds.). *The Blackwell Reader in Developmental Psychology.* Oxford: Blackwell.

Lehmann-Haupt, C. (1988, August 4). Books of the times: How an actor found success, and himself. *New York Times,* p. 2.

Leibowitz, S. F. (1992). Hypothalamic neurochemical systems mediate drug effects on food intake. *International Journal of Obesity and Related Metabolic Disorders, 15,* 701A–702A.

Leibowitz, S. F., Xuereb, M., & Kim, T. (1992). Blockade of natural and neuropeptide Y-induced carbohydrate feeding by a receptor antagonist PYX-2. *Neuroreport, 3,* 1023–1026.

Leichtman, M. D., & Ceci, S. J. (1995). The effects of stereotypes and suggestions on preschoolers' reports. *Developmental Psychology, 31,* 568–578.

Leigh, B. C., & Stall, R. (1993). Substance use and risky sexual behavior for exposure to HIV: Issues in methodology, interpretation, and prevention. *American Psychologist, 48,* 1035–1045.

Leigland, S. (2000). On cognitivism and behaviorism. *American Psychologist, 55,* 273–274.

Leitenberg, H., & Henning, K. (1995). Sexual fantasy. *Psychological Bulletin, 117,* 469–496.

LeMoal, H. (1999). *Dopamine and the brain: From neurons to networks.* New York: Academic Press.

Lenneberg, E. H. (1967). *Biological foundations of language.* New York: Wiley.

Leondes, C. T. (1997). *Medical imaging systems techniques and applications: Brain and skeletal systems.* New York: Gordon and Breach.

Lepage, M., Habib, R., & Tulving, E. (1998). Hippocampal PET activations of memory encoding and retrieval: The HIPER model. *Hippocampus, 8,* 313–322.

Lepper, M. R. (1998). A whole much less than the sum of its parts. *American Psychologist, 53,* 675–676.

Lepper, M. R., Greene, D., & Nisbett, R. E. (1973). Undermining children's intrinsic interest with extrinsic reward: A test of the "overjustification" hypothesis. *Journal of Personality and Social Psychology, 28,* 129–137.

Lerner, M. J. (1980). *The belief in a just world: A fundamental delusion.* New York: Plenum.

Lerner, R. M. (1987). A life-span perspective for early adolescence. In R. M. Lerner & T. T. Foch (Eds.), *Biological-psychosocial interactions in early adolescence.* Hillsdale, NJ: Erlbaum.

Lerner, R. M. (1995). *America's youth in crisis: Challenges and options for programs and policies.* Thousand Oaks, CA: Sage Publications.

Lesch, K. P., Bengel, D., Heils, A., Sabol, S.Z., Greenberg, B. D., Petri, S., Benjamin, J., Clemens, R. M., Hamere, D. H., & Murphy, D. L. (1996). Association of anxiety-related traits with a polymorphism in the serotonin transporter gene regulation region. *Science, 274,* 1527–1531.

Lett, B. T., Grant, V. L., Byrne, M. J., and Koh, M. T. (2000). Pairings of a distinctive chamber with the aftereffect of wheel running produce conditioned place preference. *Appetite, 34,* 87–94.

Lett, B. T., Grant, V. L., & Koh, M. Y. (2001). Naloxone attenuates the conditioned place preference induced by wheel running in rats. *Physiology & Behavior, 72,* 355–358.

Lett, B. T., Grant, V. L., Koh, M. T., & Smith, J. F. (2001). Wheel running simultaneously produces conditioned taste aversion and conditioned place preference in rats. *Learning and Motivation 32,* 129–136.

Lett, B. T., Grant, V. L, Koh, M T., & Flynn, G. (2002). Prior experience with wheel running produces cross-tolerance to the rewarding effect of morphine. *Pharmacology, Biochemistry and Behavior, 72,* 101–105.

Levenson, H. (2002). *Concise guide to brief dynamic and interpersonal therapy.* Washington, DC: American Psychiatric Press.

Leventhal, H. (2000). Emotions: Structures and adaptive functions. In G. Fink (Ed.), *Encyclopedia of stress.* San Diego: Academic Press.

Levine, D. S. (2000). *Introduction to neural and cognitive modeling* (2nd ed.). Mahwah, NJ: Lawrence Erlbaum.

Levine, R., Sato, S., Hashimoto, T., & Verma, J. (1995). Love and marriage in eleven cultures. *Journal of Cross-Cultural Psychology, 26,* 554–571.

Levinson, D. J. (1986). A conception of adult development. *American Psychologist, 41*, 3–13.

Levinson, D. J. (1990). A theory of life structure development in adulthood. In C. N. Alexander & E. J. Langer. (Eds.), *Higher stages of human development: Perspectives on adult growth.* New York: Oxford University Press.

Levinson, D. J., Darow, C. N., Klein, E. B., Levinson, M. H., & McKee, B. (1978). *The seasons of a man's life.* New York: Knopf.

Levinthal, C. E. 2005. *Drugs, behavior and modern society* (4th ed.). Aukland, New Zealand, Pearson Education New Zealand.

Levinthal, C. F. (1996). *Drugs, behavior, and modern society.* Boston: Allyn & Bacon.

Levis, D. J. (1989). The case for a return to a two-factor theory of avoidance: The failure of non-fear interpretations. In S. B. Klein, B. Stephen, & R. R. Mowrer (Eds.), *Contemporary learning theories: Pavlovian conditioning and the status of traditional learning theory.* Hillsdale, NJ: Erlbaum.

Levitsky, D. A. (2005). The non-regulation of food intake in humans: Hope for reversing the epidemic of obesity. *Physiology & Behavior, 86*, 623–632.

Levy, S., Marrow, L., Bagley, C., & Lippman, M. (1989). Survival hazards analysis in first recurrent breast cancer patients: Seven-year follow-up. *Psychosomatic Medicine, 50*, 520–528.

Lewin, K. (1935). *A dynamic theory of personality.* New York: McGraw-Hill.

Lewinsohn, P. M., Gotlib, I. H., Lewinsohn, M., Seeley, J. R., & Allen, N. B. (1998). Gender differences in anxiety disorders and anxiety symptoms in adolescents. *Journal of Abnormal Psychology, 107*, 109–117.

Lewinsohn, P. M., Hoberman, H., Teri, L., & Hantzinger, M. (1985). An integrative theory of depression. In S. Reiss & R. Bootzin (Eds.), *Theoretical issues in behavior therapy.* New York: Academic Press.

Lewinsohn, P. M., Hops, H., Roberts, R. E., Seeley, J. R., et al. (1993). Adolescent psychopathology: I. Prevalence and incidence of depression and other DSM-III—R disorders in high school students. *Journal of Abnormal Psychology, 102*, 133–144.

Lewinsohn, P. M., Rohde, P., Seeley, J., R., Fischer, S. A. (1993). Age-cohort changes in the lifetime occurence of depression and other mental disorders. *Journal of Abnormal Psychology, 102*, 110–120.

Lewis, B. P., & Linder, D. E. (1997). Thinking about choking? Attentional processes and paradoxical performance. *Personality and Social Psychology Bulletin, 23*, 937–944.

Lewis, M. (1993). The development of deception. In M.Lewis, & C. Saarni (Eds.), *Lying and deception in everyday life* (pp. 90–105). New York: Guilford Press.

Lewis, M. (1999). On the development of personality. In L. A. Pervin & O. P. John (Eds.), *Handbook of personality: Theory and research.* New York: Guilford Press.

Lewis, M., Stranger, C., & Sullivan, M.W. (1989). Deception in 3 year olds. *Developmental Psychology, 25*, 439–443.

Lewis, T.L., Maurer, D., & Brent, H.P. (1995). The development of grating acuity in children treated for unilateral or bilateral congenital cataract. *Investigative Ophthalmology & Visual Science, 36*, 2080–2095.

Lewy, A. J., Bauer, V. K., Cutler, N. L., Sack, R. L., Ahmed, S., Thomas, K. H., Blood, M. L., & Jackson, J. M. L. (1998). Morning vs evening light treatment of patients with winter depression. *Archives of General Psychiatry, 55*, 890–896.

Lewy, A. J., Sack, R. L., & Cutler, N. L. (1998). Melatonin in circadian phase sleep and mood disorders. In M. Shafii, S. Mohammad, & L. Sharon (Eds.), *Melatonin in psychiatric and neoplastic disorders. Progress in Psychiatry, 55*, Washington, DC: American Psychiatric Press.

Leyens, J. P., Camino, L., Parke, R. D., & Berkowitz, L. (1975). Effects of movie violence on aggression in a field setting as a function of group dominance and cohesion. *Journal of Personality and Social Psychology, 32*, 346–360.

Lezak, M. (1995). *Neuropsychological assessment* (3rd ed.). New York: Oxford Press.

Li, S. (2001). How close is too close? A comparison of proxemic reactions of Singaporean Chinese to male intruders of four ethnicities. *Perceptual and Motor Skills, 93*, 124–126.

Li, S., Li, Y. (2007). How far is far enough?: A measure of information privacy in terms of interpersonal distance. *Environment and Behavior, 39*(3), 317–331.

Li, T. K. (2000). Pharmacogenetics of responses to alcohol and genes that influence alcohol drinking. *Journal of Studies on Alcohol, 61*, 5–12.

Liberzon, I., Taylor, S. F., Amdur, R., Jung, T. D., Chamberlain, K. R., Minoshima, S., Koeppe, R. A., & Fig, L. M. (1999). Brain activation in PTSD in response to trauma-related stimuli. *Biological Psychiatry 45*, 817–826.

Lickey, M. E., & Gordon, B. (1991). *Medicine and mental illness: The use of drugs in psychiatry.* New York: W. H. Freeman.

Lieb, R., Isensee, B., Hoefler, M., Pfister, H., & Wittchen, H. U. (2002). Parental major depression and the risk of depression and other mental disorders in offspring: A prospective-longitudinal community study. *Archives of General Psychiatry, 59*, 365–374.

Lieberman, J., Tasman, A. (2006). *Handbook of Psychiatric Drugs.* New York: John Wiley & Sons.

Lieberman, J. A. (1998). *Psychiatric drugs.* Philadelphia: Saunders.

Lieberman, P. (1984). *The biology and evolution of language.* Cambridge: Harvard University Press.

Linn, R. L. (Ed.) (1989). *Intelligence: Measurement, theory, and public policy.* Urbana, IL: University of Illinois Press.

Linville, P. W., & Jones, E. E. (1980). Polarized appraisals of out-group members. *Journal of Personality and Social Psychology, 38*, 689–703.

Linz, D., & Donnerstein, E. (1989). The effects of countertransformation on the acceptance of rape myths. In D. Zillmann & J. Bryant (Eds.), *Pornography: Research advances and policy considerations.* Hillsdale, NJ: Erlbaum.

Lipsitt, L. P. (1990). Learning processes in the human newborn: Sensitization, habituation, and classical conditioning. *Annals of the New York Academy of Sciences, 608*, 113–127.

Litz, B. T., Orsillo, S. M., Kaloupek, D., & Weathers, F. (2000). Emotional processing in posttraumatic stress disorder. *Journal of Abnormal Psychology, 109*, 26–39.

Liu, J. H., & Latane, B. (1998). Extremitization of attitudes: Does thought- and discussion-induced polarization cumulate? *Basic and Applied Social Psychology, 20*, 103–110.

Livingstone, M., & Hubel, D. (1994). Segregation of form, color, movement, and depth: Anatomy, physiology, and perception. In H. Gutfreund, & G. Toulouse (Eds.), *Biology and computation: A physicist's choice. Advanced series in neuroscience.* Singapore: World Scientific.

Locke, D. C. (1992). *Multicultural understanding: A comprehensive model.* Newbury Park, CA: Sage Publications.

Locke, E. A. (1996). Motivation through conscious goal setting. *Applied and Preventive Psychology, 5*, 117–124.

Locke, E. A., & Latham, G. P. (1990). *A theory of goal setting and task performance.* Englewood Cliffs, NJ: Prentice Hall.

Lockwood, P., & Kunda, Z. (1997). Superstars and me: Predicting the impact of role models on the self. *Journal of Personality and Social Psychology, 73*, 91–103.

Loehlin, J. C. (1992). *Genes and environment in personality development.* Newbury Park, CA: Sage Publications.

Loehlin, J. C., Willerman, L., & Horn, J. M. (1988). Genetics and human behavior. *Annual Review of Psychology, 39*, 101–134.

Loewenstein, R. J. (1991). Psychogenic amnesia and psychogenic fuge: A comprehensive review. In A. Tasman & S. M. Goldfinger (Eds.), *American Psychiatric Press review of psychiatry* (Vol. 10). Washington, DC: American Psychiatric Association.

Loewi, O. (1935). Humoral transmission of nervous impulses. *Nature, 135*, 1082–1083.

Loewi, O. (1960). An autobiographical sketch. *Perspectives in Biology, 4*, 3–25.

Loftus, E. F. (1979) *Eyewitness testimony.* Cambridge, MA: Harvard University Press.

Loftus, E. F., & Burns, T. E. (1982). Mental shock can produce retrograde amnesia. *Memory and Cognition, 10*, 318–323.

Loftus, E. F., & Loftus, G. R. (1980). On the permanence of stored information in the human brain. *American Psychologist, 35*, 409–420.

Loftus, E. F., & Palmer, J. C. (1974). Reconstruction of automobile destruction: An example of the interaction between language and memory. *Journal of Verbal Learning and Verbal Behavior, 13*, 585–589.

Loftus, E. F., & Pickrell, J. E. (1995). The formation of false memories. *Psychiatric Annals, 25*, 720–725.

Logothetis, N. K., Pauls, J., Augath, M., Trinath, T. & Oeltermann, A. (2001). Neurophysiological investigation of the basis of the fMRI signal. *Nature, 412*, 150–157.

Logue, A. W. (1991). *The psychology of eating and drinking* (2nd ed.). New York: W. H. Freeman.

London, K., Bruck, M., Ceci, S. J., Shuman, D. W. (2005). Disclosure of child sexual abuse: What does the research tell us about the ways that children tell? *Psychology, Public Policy and Law, 11*(1), 199–226.

Lopez, S. R. (2002). Teaching culturally informed psychological assessment: conceptual issues and demonstrations. *Journal of Personality Assessment, 79*(7), 226–234.

Lopez, S. R., & Guarnaccia, P. J. (2000). Cultural psychopathology: Uncovering the social world of mental illness. *Annual Review of Psychology, 51*, 571–598.

Lopez-Mendoza, D., Aguilar, B. H., & Swanson, H. H. (1998). Combined effects of gepirone and (1)WAY 100135 on territorial aggression in mice. *Pharmacology, Biochemistry and Behavior, 61*, 1–8.

Lorenz, K. (1937). The companion in the bird's world. *Auk, 54*, 245–273.

Lorenz, K. (1966). *On aggression.* New York: Harcourt Brace Jovanovich.

Louis, W., & Taylor, D. (2001). Understanding the September 11 Terrorist Attack on America: The Role of Intergroup Theories of Normative Influence in Unger, R. (Ed), *Terrorism and Its Consequences. Analysis of Social Issues and Public Policy, Society for the Psychological Study of Social Issues,* Blackwell Publishers. [Online]. Available: http://www.asap-spssi.org/default.htm

Lovaas, O. I. (1977). *The autistic child.* New York: Irvington.

Lubinski, D. (2000). Scientific and social significance of assessing individual differences: "Sinking shafts at a few critical points." *Annual Review of Psychology, 51,* 405–444.

Luborsky, L. (1987). Research can now affect clinical practice: A happy turnaround. *Clinical Psychologist 40,* 56–60.

Luborsky, L., Rosenthal, R., Diguer, L., Andrusyna, T. P., Berman, J. S., Jeffrey, S., Levitt, J. T., Seligman, D. A., & Krause, E. D. (2002). The dodo bird verdict is alive and well—mostly. *Clinical Psychology: Science and Practice, 9,* 2–12.

Luborsky, L., & Crits-Christoph, O. (1998). *Understanding transference: The core conflictual relationship theme method* (2nd ed.). Washington, DC: American Psychological Association.

Luchins, A. (1957a). Primacy-recency in impression formation. In C. Hovland, W. Mandell, E. Campbell, T. Brock, A. Luchins, & A.Cohen (Eds.), *The order of presentation in persuasion.* New Haven, CT: Yale University Press.

Luchins, A. (1957b). Experimental attempts to minimize the impact of first impressions. In C. Hovland, W. Mandell, E. Campbell, T. Brock, A. Luchins, & A. Cohen (Eds.), *The order of presentation in persuasion.* New Haven, CT: Yale University Press.

Luchins, A. J. (1942). Mechanization in problem solving: The effect of Einstellung. *Psychological Monographs, 54,* 6 (Whole No. 248).

Luck, S. J., & Vecera, S. P. (2002). Attention. In H. Pashler & S.Yantis (Eds.), *Steven's handbook of experimental psychology: Vol. 1. Sensation and perception* (3rd ed.). New York: Wiley.

Lucker, W., Rosenfield, D., Sikes, J., & Aronson, E. (1977). Performance in the interdependent classroom: A field study. *American Educational Research Journal, 13,* 115–123.

Lundh, L. G. (1998). Cognitive-behavioural analysis and treatment of insomnia. *Scandinavian Journal of Behaviour Therapy, 27,* 10–29.

Luo, Y. & Baillargeon, R. Can a self-propelled box have a goal? *Psychological Science, 16,* 601–608.

Lupart, J. L., Purt, M. C. (1996). "Hidden gifted" students: underachiever prevalence and profile. *Journal for the Education of the Gifted, 20,* 36–53.

Lupien, S. J., King, S., Meaney, M. J., & McEwen, B. S. (2001). Can poverty get under your skin? Basal cortisol levels and cognitive function in children from low and high socioeconomic status. *Development & Psychopathology, 13,* 653–676.

Lupien, S. J., & Briere, S. (2000). Memory and stress. In G. Fink (Ed.), *Encyclopedia of stress.* San Diego: Academic Press.

Luthans, F., Paul, R., & Baker, D. (1981). An experimental analysis of the impact of contingent reinforcement on salespersons' performance behavior. *Journal of Applied Psychology, 66,* 314–323.

Lydic, R., & Biebuyck, J. F. (Eds.). *Clinical physiology of sleep.* New York: Oxford.

Lykken, D. T. (1984). Polygraph interrogation. *Nature, 307,* 681–684.

Lykken, D. T. (1998). *A tremor in the blood: Uses and abuses of the lie detector.* New York: Plenum.

Lykken, D. T., Bouchard, T. J., McGue, M., & Tellegen, A. (1993). Heritability of interests: A twin study. *Journal of Applied Psychology, 78,* 649–661.

Lykken, D. T., McGue, M., Tellegen, A., & Bouchard, T. J. (1992). Emergenesis: Genetic traits that may not run in families. *American Psychologist, 47,* 1565–1577.

Lykken, D., & Tellegen, A. (1996). Happiness is a stochastic phenomenon. *Psychological Science, 7,* 186–189.

Lynn, E. J. (1971). Amphetamine abuse: A "speed" trap. *Psychiatric Quarterly, 45,* 92–101.

Lynn, M. (1989). Race differences in sexual behavior: A critique of Rushton and Bogaert's evolutionary hypothesis. *Journal of Research in Personality, 23,* 1–6.

Lynn, R. (1982). IQ in Japan and the United States shows a growing disparity. *Nature, 297,* 222–223.

Lynn, R. (1998a). Has the black-white intelligence difference in the United States been narrowing over time? *Personality and Individual Differences, 25,* 999–1002.

Lynn, R. (1998b). The decline of genotypic intelligence. In U. Neisser, et al. (Eds.), *The rising curve: Long-term gains in IQ and related measures.* Washington, DC: American Psychological Association.

Lynn, R. and Vanhanen, T. (2002). *IQ and the Wealth of Nations* Westport, CT: Praeger.

Lytton, H., & Romney, D. M. (1991). Parents' differential socialization of boys and girls: A meta-analysis. *Psychological Bulletin, 109,* 267–296.

Maass, A., & Clark, R. D. III. (1984). Hidden impact of minorities: Fifteen years of minority influence research. *Psychological Bulletin, 95,* 428–450.

MacAndrew, C., & Edgerton, R. B. (1969). *Drunken comportment: A social explanation.* Chicago: Aldine.

Maccoby, E. E. (1988). Gender as a social category. *Developmental Psychology, 24,* 755–765.

Maccoby, E. E., & Jacklin, C. N. (1974). *The psychology of sex differences.* Stanford, CA: Stanford University Press.

Maccoby, E. E., & Maccoby, N. (1954). The interview: A tool of social science. In G. Lindzey (Ed.), *Handbook of social psychology.* Cambridge, MA: Addison-Wesley.

Maccoby, E. E., & Martin, J. A. (1983). Socialization in the context of the family: Parent-child interaction. In E. M. Hetherington (Ed.), *Handbook of child psychology: Socialization, personality, and social development.* New York: Wiley.

MacCoun, R. J. (1998). Toward a psychology of harm reduction. *American Psychologist, 53,* 1199–1208.

MacDonald, T. K., Fong, G. T., Zanna, M. P., & Martineau, A. M. (2000). Alcohol myopia and condom use: Can alcohol intoxication be associated with more prudent behavior? *Journal of Personality and Social Psychology, 78,* 605–619.

MacDonald, T. K., Zanna, M. P., & Fong, G. T. (1995). Decision making in altered states: Effects of alcohol on attitudes toward drinking and driving. *Journal of Personality and Social Psychology, 68,* 973–985.

MacFarlane, J. A. (1975). Olfaction in the development of social preferences in the human neonate. In M. A. Hofer (Ed.), *Parent-infant interaction.* Amersterdam: Elsevier.

MacKay, D. G. (2006). Aging, Memory, and Language in Amnesia. *Hippocampus, 16*(5), 491–494.

MacLeod, C. (1998). Implicit perception: Perceptual processing without awareness. In K. Kirsner, et al. (Eds.), *Implicit and explicit mental processes.* Mahwah, NJ: Erlbaum.

Maddox, K.B. & Gray, S.A. (2002). Cognitive representations of black Americans: Reexploring the role of skin tone. *Personality and Social Psychology Bulletin, 28,* 2250-2259.

Maddux, J. E. (1999). Personal efficacy. In V. J. Derlega, B. A. Winstead, & W. H. Jones (Eds.), *Personality: Contemporary theory and research.* Chicago: Nelson-Hall.

Madraza, I., Drucker-Colin, R., Diaz, V., Martinez-Mata, J., Torres, C., & Becerril, J. J. (1987). Open microsurgical autograph of adrenal medulla to the right candate nucleus in two patients with intractable Parkinson's disease. *New England Journal of Medicine, 316,* 831–834.

Maes, H. H. M., Neale, M. C., & Eaves, L. J. (1997). Genetic and environmental factors in relative body weight and human adiposity. *Behavior Genetics, 27,* 325–351.

Magels, J. A. (1997). Strategic processing and memory for temporal order in patients with frontal lobe lesions. *Neuropsychology, 11,* 207–221.

Magnuson, S. (1986). "A serious deficiency": The Rogers Commission faults NASA's "flawed" decision-making process. *Time* (Intl. Ed.), pp. 40–42.

Mahler, M. (1968). *On human symbiosis and the vicissitudes of individuation: Infantile psychosis.* New York: Basic Books.

Mahoney, M. J. (1980). *Abnormal psychology: Perspectives on human variance.* New York: Harper & Row.

Mahoney, W. J., & Ayres, J. J. (1976). One-trial simultaneous and backward fear conditioning as reflected in conditioned suppression of licking in rats. *Animal Learning and Behavior, 4,* 357–362.

Mai, J. K., Assheuer, J. K., & George, W. (1997). *Atlas of the human brain.* San Diego: Academic Press.

Maier, S. F., Watkins, L. R., & Fleshner, M. (1994). Psychoneuroimmunology: The interface between brain, behavior, and immunity. *American Psychologist, 49,* 1004–1017.

Maio, G. R., & Olson, J. M. (Eds.) (2000). *Why we evaluate: Functions of attitudes.* Mahwah, NJ: Erlbaum.

Major, B., Carrington, P. I., & Carnevale, P. J. D. (1984). Physical attractiveness and self-esteem: Attributions for praise from an other-sex evaluator. *Personality and Social Psychology Bulletin, 10,* 43–50.

Mäkelä, K. (1997). Drinking, the majority fallacy, cognitive dissonance and social pressure. *Addiction, 92,* 729–736.

Malamuth, N. M. (1998). The confluence model as an organizing framework for research on sexually aggressive men: Risk moderators, imagined aggression, and pornography consumption. In R. G. Geen & E. Donnerstein (Eds.), *Human aggression: Theories, research, and implications for social policy.* San Diego: Academic Press.

Malcangi, G. (1997). *Evelyn's hearing.* [Online]. Available: http://www.evelyn.co.uk/hearing.htm

Malott, R. W. (1994). From the tabula rasa to murder, massacre, and genocide. *The ABA International Newsletter, 17*(4), 10.

Mandel, D. R. (2001). Evil and the Instigation of Collective Violence in Unger, R. (Ed), *Terrorism and Its Consequences. Analysis of Social Issues and Public Policy, Society for the Psychological Study of Social Issues,* Blackwell Publishers. [Online]. Available: http://www.asap-spssi.org/default.htm

Mandler, G. (1984). *Mind and body: Psychology of emotion and stress.* New York: W. W. Norton.

Mangels, J. A. (1997). Strategic processing and memory for temporal order in patients with frontal lobe lesions. *Neuropsychology, 11,* 207–221.

Mann, L. (1981). The baiting crowd in episodes of threatened suicide. *Journal of Personality and Social Psychology, 41,* 703–709.

Manning, B. (1967). "Pre-imaginal conditioning" in Drosophila." *Nature, 216,* 338–340.

Manning, W. D. & Smock, P. J. (2002). First comes cohabitation then comes marriage? A research note. *Journal of Family Issues, 23,* 1065–1087.

Manolo, E. (2002). Uses of mnemonics in educational settings: A brief review of selected research. *Psychologia, 45*(2), 69–79.

Manson, S. M. (1994). Culture and depression: Discovering variations in the experience of illness. In W. J. Lonner & R. S. Malpass (Eds.), *Psychology and culture.* Boston: Allyn & Bacon.

Mäntylä, T. (1986). Optimizing cue effectiveness: Recall of 500 and 600 incidentally learned words. *Journal of Experimental Psychology: Learning, Memory, and Cognition, 12,* 66–71.

Mäntylä, T. N., & Nilsson, L. G. (1997). Remembering to remember in adulthood: A population-based study on aging and prospective memory. *Aging, Neuropsychology, and Cognition, 4,* 81–92.

Mäntylä, T., & Nilsson, L. G. (1988). Cue distinctiveness and forgetting: Effectiveness of self-generated retrieval cues in delayed recall. *Journal of Experimental Psychology: Learning, Memory, and Cognition, 14,* 502–509.

Mantzoros, C., Flier, J. S., Lesem, M. D., Brewerton, T. D., & Jimerson, D. C. (1997). Cerebrospinal fluid leptin in anorexia nervosa: Correlation with nutritional status and potential role in resistance to weight gain. *The Journal of Clinical Endocrinology and Metabolism, 82,* 1845–1851.

Manuck, S. F., Flory, J. D., McCaffery, J. M., Matthews, K. A., Mann, J. J., & Muldoon, M. F. (1998). Aggression, impulsivity, and central nervous system serotonergic responsivity in a nonpatient sample. *Neuropsychopharmacology, 19,* 287–299.

Maquet, P., Laureys, S., Peigneux, P., Fuchs, S., Petiau, C., Phillips, C., Aerts, J., Del Fiore, G., Degueldre, C., Meulemans, T., Luxen, A., Franck, G., Van Der Linden, M., & Smith, C. (2000). Experience-dependent changes in cerebral activation during human REM sleep. *Nature Neuroscience, 3,* 831–836.

Marangell, L. B. (2002). *Concise guide to psychopharmacology.* Washington, DC: American Psychiatric Publishing.

Marcia, J. E. (1966). Development and validation of ego identity status. *Journal of Personality and Social Psychology, 3,* 551–558.

Marcia, J. E. (1994). The empirical study of ego identity. In H. A. Bosma, T. L. G. Graafsma, H. D. Grotevant, & D. J. de Levita (Eds.), *Identity and development: An interdisciplinary approach.* Thousand Oaks, CA: Sage Publications.

Marek, G. (1982). Toscanini's memory. In U. Neisser (Ed.), *Memory observed.* San Francisco: W. H. Freeman.

Margolin, G., & Gordis, E. B. (2000). The effects of family and community violence on children. *Annual Review of Psychology, 51,* 445–480.

Margolin, G., & Wampold, B. E. (1981). Sequential analysis of conflict and accord in distressed and nondistressed marital partners. *Journal of Consulting and Clinical Psychology, 49,* 554–567.

Marini, Z.A., & Case, R. (1994). The development of abstract reasoning about the physical and social world. *Child development, 65,* 147–159.

Markey, P. M. (2000). Bystander intervention in computer mediated communication. *Computers in Human Behavior, 16,* 183–188.

Markovitz, H., & Nantel, G. (1989). The belief-bias effect in the production and evaluation of logical conclusions. *Memory and Cognition, 17,* 11–17.

Marks, D., Murray, M., Evans, B., & Willig, C. (2000). *Health psychology: Theory, research, and practice.* Thousand Oaks, CA: Sage Publications.

Marks, I. M. (1977). Phobias and obsessions: Clinical phenomena in search of laboratory models. In J. Maser & M. E. P. Seligman (Eds.), *Psychopathology: Experimental models.* San Francisco: W. H. Freeman.

Marks, I. M. (1987). *Fear, phobias, and rituals: Panic, anxiety, and their disorders.* New York: Oxford University Press.

Marks, I. M. (1991). Self-administered behavioural treatment. *Behavioural Psychotherapy, 19,* 42–46.

Markus, H. R., & Kitayama, S. (1999). Culture and the self: Implications for cognition, emotion, and motivation. In Baumeister, Roy F. (Ed). *The self in social psychology. Key readings in social psychology.* (339–371). New York, NY: Psychology Press.

Markus, H., & Nurius, P. (1986). Possible selves. *American Psychologist. 41,* 954–969.

Marlatt, G. A. (1987). Alcohol, the magic elixir: Stress, expectancy, and the transformation of emotional states. In E. Gottheil, K. A. Druley, S. Pashko, & S. P. Weinstein (Eds.), *Stress and addiction.* New York: Brunner/Mazel.

Marlatt, G. A. (1996). Taxonomy of high-risk situations for alcohol relapse: Evolution and development of a cognitive-behavioral model. *Addiction, 91* (Suppl.), S37–S49.

Marlatt, G. A. (Ed.) (1998). *Harm reduction: Pragmatic strategies for managing high-risk behaviors.* New York: Guilford Press.

Marlatt, G. A. & Witkiewitz, K. (2002). Harm reduction approaches to alcohol use: Health promotion, prevention, and treatment. *Addictive Behaviors, 27,* 867–886.

Marlatt, G. A., & Gordon, J. R. (1985). *Relapse prevention: Maintenance strategies in the treatment of addiction.* New York: Guilford Press.

Marlatt, G. A., & Kaplan, B. E. (1972). Self-initiated attempts to change behavior: A study of New Year's resolutions. *Psychological Reports, 30,* 123–131.

Marlatt, G. A., & VandenBos, G. R. (Eds.) (1997). *Addictive behaviors: Readings on etiology, prevention and treatment.* Washington, DC: American Psychological Association.

Marlatt, G. A., Baer, J. S. et al. (1998). Screening and brief intervention for high-risk college student drinkers: Results from a 2-year follow-up assessment. *Journal of Consulting and Clinical Psychology, 66,* 604–615.

Marlatt, G. A., Demming, B., & Reid, J. B. (1973). Loss of control drinking in alcoholics: An experimental analogue. *Journal of Abnormal Psychology, 81,* 233–241.

Marler, P. (1970). A comparative approach to vocal learning: Song development in white-crowned sparrows. *Journal of Comparative and Physiological Psychology, 71,* 1–25.

Marsat, G., Pollack, G. S. (2006). A Behavioral role for feature detection by sensory bursts. *Journal of Neuroscience, 26,* 10542 10547.

Marschark, M., & Mayer, T. S. (1998). Interactions of language and memory in deaf children and adults. *Scandinavian Journal of Psychology, 39,* 145–148.

Marsella, A. J. (1994, August). *Cross-cultural psychopathology: Foundations, issues, and directions.* Address presented at Annual Meeting of American Psychological Association, Los Angeles.

Marsella, A. J. (1998). Toward a "global-community psychology": Meeting the needs of a changing world. *American Psychologist, 53,* 1282–1291.

Marsh, H. W. (1990). A multidimensional, hierarchical model of self-concept: Theoretical and empirical justification. *Educational Psychology Review, 2,* 77–172.

Marsh, R. L., Hicks, J. L., & Landau, J. D. (1998). An investigation of everyday prospective memory. *Memory and Cognition, 26,* 633–643.

Marshall, L. H., & Magoun, H. W. (1997). *Discoveries in the human brain: Neuroscience prehistory, brain structure, and function.* New York: Humana Press.

Marsiglio, W., Amato, P., Day, R. D., Lamb, M. E. (2000). Scholarship on fatherhood in the 1990s and beyond. *Journal of Marriage and the Family, 62,* 1173–1191.

Marsland, A. L., Bachen, E. A., Cohen, S., Rabin, B., and Manuck, S. (2002). Stress immune reactivity and susceptibility to infectious disease. *Physiology & Behavior, 77,* 711–716.

Martin, G.L. & Pear, J.J. (1999). *Behavior Modification: What is it and how to do it* (6th ed.). Upper Saddle River, NJ: Prentice Hall.

Martin, J. E., & Dubbert, P. M. (1985). Adherence in exercise. In R. I. Terjung (Ed.), *Exercise and sport sciences review* (Vol. 13). New York: Macmillan.

Martin, S. J., Grimwood, P. D., & Morris, G. M. (2000). Synaptic plasticity and memory: An evaluation of the hypothesis. *Annual Review of Neuroscience, 23,* 649–711.

Martinez-Conde, S., Macknik, S. L., Hubel, D. H. (2004). The role of fixational eye movements in visual perception. *Nature Reviews Neuroscience, 5,* 229-240.

Masataka, N. (2007). Music, evolution and language. *Developmental Science, 10,* 35–39.

Mash, E. J., & Barkley, R. A. (2003). *Child psychopathology* (2nd ed.). New York: Guilford Press.

Maslow, A. H. (1954). *Motivation and personality.* New York: Harper.

Maslow, A. H. (1971). *The farther reaches of human nature.* New York: Viking Press.

Masten, A. S. (2001). Ordinary magic: Resilience processes in development. *American Psychologist, 56,* 227–238.

Masten, A. S., & Coatsworth, J. D. (1998). The development of competence in favorable and unfavorable environments: Lessons from research on successful children. *American Psychologist, 53,* 205–220.

Masters, W. H., Johnson, V. E., & Kolodny, R. C. (1988). *Human Sexuality* (3rd ed.). Boston: Little, Brown.

Masters, W., & Johnson, V. (1966). *Human sexual response.* London: Churchill.

Matarazzo, J. D. (1980). Behavioral health and behavioral medicine: Frontiers for a new health psychology. *American Psychologist, 35,* 807-817.

Matorin, S. (2002). Stigma as a barrier to recovery. *Psychiatric Services, 53,* 629–630.

Matson, J. L., & Gardner, W. I. (1991). Behavioral learning theory and current applications to severe behavior problems in persons with mental retardation. *Clinical Psychology Review, 11,* 175–183.

Matsumoto, D. (1994). *People: Psychology from a cultural perspective.* Pacific Grove, CA: Brooks/Cole.

Matsumoto, D., & Hull, P. (1994). Cognitive development and intelligence. In D. Matsumoto (Ed.), *People: Psychology from a cultural perspective,* Pacific Grove, CA: Brooks/Cole.

Matsumoto, D. & Willingham, B. (2006). The thrill of victory and the agony of defeat: Spontaneous expressions of medal winners of the 2004 Athens Olympic Games. *Journal of Personality and Social Psychology, 91,* 568–581.

Matt, G. E., & Navarro, A. M. (1997). What meta-analyses have and have not taught us about psychotherapy effects: A review and future directions. *Clinical Psychology Review, 17,* 1–32.

Mattaini, M. A., Twyman, J. S., Chin, W., & Lee, K. N. (1996). Youth violence. In M. A. Mattaini & B. A. Thyer (Eds.), *Finding solutions to social problems: Behavioral strategies for change.* Washington, DC: American Psychological Association.

Matthews, K. (2000). Depression models. In G. Fink (Ed.), *Encyclopedia of stress.* San Diego: Academic Press.

Mattson, S.N., Goodman, A.M., Caine, C., Delis, D.C., Riley, E.P. (1999). Executive functioning in children with heavy prenatal alcohol exposure. *Alcoholism: Clinical and Experimental Research, 23,* 1808–1815.

Matud, M. P. (2004). Gender differences in stress and coping styles. *Personality and Individual Differences, 37,* 1401-1415.

Maurer, D. Ellemberg, D., & Lewis, T.L. (2006). Repeated measures of contrast sensitivity reveal limits to visual plasticity after early binocular deprivation in humans. *Neuropsychologica, 44,* 2104–2112.

Maurer, D. & Lewis, T.L. (2001). Visual acuity: the role of visual input in inducing postnatal change. *Clinical Neuroscience Research, 1,* 239–247.

Maurer, D., & Barrera, M. (1981). Infants' perception of natural and distorted arrangements of a schematic face. *Child Development, 52,* 196–202.

Maurer, D., & Maurer, C. (1988). *The World of the Newborn.* New York: Basic Books.

Maurer, D., & Mondloch, C. J. (2006). *Processes of change in brain and cognitive development: Attention and performance.* New York: Oxford University Press. pp. 449-471.

Maurer, D., Mondloch, C. J. & Lewis, T. L. (2007). Sleeper effects. *Developmental Science, 10,* 40–47.

Mauro, R., Sato, K., & Tucker, J. (1992). The role of appraisal in human emotions: A cross-cultural study. *Journal of Personality and Social Psychology, 62,* 301–317.

May, J. R., & Sieb, G. E. (1987). Athletic injuries: Psychosocial factors in the onset, sequellae, rehabilitation, and prevention. In J. R. May & M. J. Asken (Eds.), *Sports psychology: The psychological health of the athlete.* New York: PMA Publishing.

May, R. (1961). The emergence of existential psychology. In R. May (Ed.), *Existential psychology.* New York: Random House.

Mayer, J. D., & Salovey, P. (1997). What is emotional intelligence? In P. Salovey & D. J. Sluyter (Eds.), *Emotional development and emotional intelligence: Educational implications.* New York: Basic Books.

Mayes, L. C., Cicchetti, D., Suddhasatta, A., Zhang, H., Hepping (2003). Developmental trajectories of cocaine-and-other-drug-exposed and non-cocaine-exposed children. *Journal of Developmental & Behavioral Pediatrics, 24,* 323–335.

Mayne, T. J., Norcross, J. C., & Sayette, M. A. (1994). Admission requirements, acceptance rates, and financial assistance in clinical psychology programs. *American Psychologist, 49,* 806–811.

Mazure, C. M. (1995). *Does stress cause psychiatric illness.* Washington, DC: American Psychiatric Press.

McAdams, D. P., & deSt., Aubin (Eds.) (1998). *Generativity and adult development: How and why we care for the next generation.* Washington, DC: American Psychological Association.

McAdams, D. T. (1992). The five-factor model in personality: A critical appraisal. *Journal of Personality and Social Psychology, 60,* 329–361.

McAdams, S., & Drake, C. (2002). Auditory perception and cognition. In H. Pashler & S. Yantis (Eds.), *Steven's handbook of experimental psychology: Vol. 1. Sensation and perception* (3rd ed.). New York: Wiley.

McAuley, E. (1992). The role of efficacy cognitions in the prediction of exercise behavior in middle-aged adults. *Journal of Behavioral Medicine, 15,* 65–88.

McCall, R. B. (1977). Childhood IQs as predictors of adult educational and occupational status. *Science, 1977,* 482–483.

McCall, W. V., & Edinger, J. D. (1992). Subjective total insomnia: An example of sleep state misperception. *Sleep, 15,* 71–73.

McCarley, R. W. (1998). Dreams: Disguise of forbidden wishes or transparent reflections of a distinct brain state? In R. M. Bilder & F. F. LeFever (Eds.), *Neuroscience of the mind on the centennial of Freud's Project for a Scientific Psychology: Annals of the New York Academy of Sciences* (Vol. 843). New York: New York Academy of Sciences.

McCarty, R., & Pacek, K. (2000). Alarm phase and general adaptation syndrome. In G. Fink (Ed.), *Encyclopedia of stress.* San Diego: Academic Press.

McCaul, K. D., & Malott, J. J. (1984). Distraction and coping with pain. *Psychological Bulletin, 95,* 516–533.

McCauley, C., & Segal, M. (1989). Terrorist individuals and terrorist groups: The normal psychology of extreme behavior. In J. Groebel & J. H. Goldstein (Eds.), *Terrorism* (pp. 41–64). Seville University Press.

McClelland, D. C. (1989). *Human motivation.* New York: Cambridge University Press.

McClelland, D. C., Atkinson, J. W., Clark, R. A., & Lowell, E. L. (1953). *The achievement motive.* New York, Appleton-Century-Crofts.

McClelland, J. L., & Rumelhart, D. E. (1985). Distributed memory and the representation of general and specific information. *Journal of Experimental Psychology: General, 114,* 159–188.

McClintock, M. K. (1971). Menstrual synchrony and suppression. *Nature, 229,* 244–245.

McConnell, J. V. (1962). Memory transfer through cannibalism in planarians. *Journal of Neuropsychiatry, 3* (Suppl. 1), 542–548.

McCoy, D. F., Roszman, T. L., Miller, J. S., Kelly, K. S., & Titus, M. J. (1986). Some parameters of conditioned immunosuppression. Species difference and CS-US delay. *Physiology and Behavior, 36,* 731–736.

McCracken, L. M. (1998). Learning to live with pain: Acceptance of pain predicts adjustment in persons with chronic pain. *Pain, 74,* 21–27.

McCrae, R. R. & Costa, P. T. (1990). *Personality in adulthood.* New York: The Guildford Press.

McCrae, R. R., & Costa, P. T. (1999). The five-factor model of personality. In L. A. Pervin & O. P. John (Eds.), *Handbook of personality: Theory and research.* New York: Guilford Press.

McCrae, R. R., & Costa, P. T. (2003). *Personality in adulthood: A Five-Factor Theory perspective.* New York: Guilford Press.

McCullough, M. E., Worthington, E. L., Jr., & Rachal, Kenneth C. (1997). Interpersonal forgiving in close relationships. *Journal of Personality and Social Psychology, 73,* 321–336.

McCusker, C. G., & Brown, K. (1990). Alcohol-predictive cues enhance tolerance to and precipitate "craving" for alcohol in social drinkers. *Journal of Studies on Alcohol, 51,* 494–499.

McDaniel, M. A., & Einstein, G. O. (1993). The importance of cue familiarity and cue distinctiveness in prospective memory. *Memory, 1,* 23–41.

McDaniel, M. A., Glisky, E. L., Guynn, M. J., & Routhieaux, B. C. (1999). Prospective memory: A neuropsychological study. *Neuropsychology, 13,* 103–110.

McDermott, P. A., & Weiss, R. V. (1995). A normative typology of healthy, subclinical, and clinical behavior styles among American children and adolescents. *Psychological Assessment, 7,* 162–170.

McEwen, B. S. (2000). Effects of adverse experiences for brain structure and function. *Biological Psychiatry, 48,* 721–731.

McEwen, B. S. (2001). *Coping with the environment: Neural and endocrine mechanisms.* New York: Oxford University Press.

McFarland, P. T., & Christensen, A. (2000). Marital conflict. In G. Fink (Ed.), *Encyclopedia of stress.* San Diego: Academic Press.

McGinty, D. (1993). Energy conservation. In M. A. Carskadon (Ed.), *Encyclopedia of sleep and dreaming.* New York: Macmillan.

McGinty, D. J., & Sterman, M. B. (1968). Sleep suppression after basal forebrain lesions in the cat. *Science, 160,* 1253–1255.

McGlaskan, T. H., & Fenton, W. S. (1992). The positive-negative distinction in schizophrenia: Review of natural history validators. *Archives of General Psychiatry, 49,* 63–72.

McGregor, D. (1960). *The human side of enterprise.* New York: McGraw-Hill.

McGuffin, P., Riley, B., Plomin, R. (2001). Toward Behavioral Genomics. *Science, 291,* 1232–1239.

McIntosh, D. N., Silver, R. C., & Wortman, C. B. (1993). Religion's role in adjustment to a negative life event: Coping with the loss of a child. *Journal of Personality and Social Psychology, 65,* 812–821.

McIntosh, D. N., Zajonc, R. B., Vig, P. S., & Emerick, S. W. (1997). Facial movement, breathing, temperature, and affect: Implications of the vascular theory of emotional efference. *Cognition and Emotion, 11*(2), 171–195.

McKenna, M. C., Zevon, M. A., Corn, B., & Rounds, J. (1999). Psychosocial factors and the development of breast cancer: A meta-analysis. *Health Psychology, 18,* 520–531.

McKim, M. K., Cramer, K. M., Stuart, B., & O'Connor, D. L. (1999). Infant care decisions and attachment security: the Canadian Transition to Child Care study. *Canadian Journal of Behavioural Science, 31,* 92–106.

McKim, W. A. (2000). *Drugs and behavior* (4th ed.). Upper Saddle River, NJ: Prentice Hall, Inc.

McMahon, R. J., & Forehand, R. L. (2004). *Helping the noncompliant child: Family-based treatment for oppositional behavior.* New York: Guilford Press.

McMillan, T. M., Robertson, I. H., & Wilson, B. A. (1999). Neurogenesis after brain injury: Implications for neurorehabilitation. *Neuropsychological Rehabilitation, 9,* 129–133.

McNatt, D. B. (2000). Ancient Pygmalion joins contemporary management: A meta-analysis of the result. *Journal of Applied Psychology, 85,* 314–322.

McNeil, E. B. (1967). *The quiet furies: Man and disorder.* Englewood Cliffs, NJ: Prentice Hall.

Meacham, J. A., & Singer, J. (1977). Incentive effects in prospective memory. *Journal of Psychology, 97,* 191–197.

Mead, M. (1935). *Sex and temperament in three primitive societies.* New York: Morrow.

Meaney, M. J. (2003). Plasticity and health: Social influences on gene expression and neural development. In F. Kessel & P. L. Rosenfield (Eds), *Expanding the boundaries of health and social science: Case studies in interdisciplinary innovation.* London: Oxford University Press.

Meaney, M. J., Aitken, D. H., Bhatnagar, S., Van Berkel, C., & Sapolsky, R. M. (1988). Postnatal handling attenuates the neuroendocrine, anatomical, and cognitive impairments related to the aged hippocampus. *Science, 238,* 766–768.

Meaney, M. J., Mitchell, J. B., Aitken, D. H., Bhatnagar, S., Bodnoff, S. R., & Sarrieau, A. (1991). The effects of neonatal handling on the development of the adrenocortical response to stress: Implications for neuropathology and cognitive deficits in later life. *Psychoneuroendocrinology, 16,* 85–103.

Medin, D. L., & Coley, J. D. (1998). Concepts and categorization. In H. Julian et al. (Eds.), *Perception and cognition at century's end. Handbook of perception and cognition* (2nd ed.). San Diego: Academic Press.

Medin, D. L., Lynch, E. B., & Solomon, K. O. (2000). Are there kinds of concepts? *Annual Review of Psychology, 51,* 121–147.

Meehl, P. E. (1995). "Is psychoanalysis one science, two sciences, or no science at all? A discourse among friendly antagonists": Comment. *Journal of the American Psychoanalytic Association, 43,* 1015–1023.

Meeus, W. H. J., & Raaijmakers, Q. A. W. (1986). Administrative obedience: Carrying out orders to use psychological-administrative violence. *European Journal of Social Psychology, 16,* 311–324.

Meeus, W. H. J., & Raaijmakers, Q. A. W. (1995). Obedience in modern society: The Utrecht studies. *Journal of Social Issues, 51,* 155–175.

Megargee, E. I. (1966). Undercontrolled and overcontrolled personality types in extreme anti-social aggression. *Psychological Monographs, 80* (Whole No. 611).

Mehnert, T., Krauss, H. H., Nadler, R., & Boyd, M. (1990). Correlates of life satisfaction in those with disabling conditions. *Rehabilitation Psychology, 35,* 3–17.

Meichenbaum, D. (1985). *Stress inoculation training.* New York: Pergamon.

Meichenbaum, D. (1991). Evolution of cognitive behavior therapy: Origins, tenets and clinical examples. In J. Zeig (Ed.), *The evolution of psychotherapy, II.* New York: Brunner/Mazel.

Meier, R. P. (1991). Language acquisition by deaf children. *American Scientist, 79,* 61–70.

Meilman, P. W. (1979). Cross-sectional age changes in ego identity status during adolescence. *Developmental Psychology, 15,* 230–231.

Meissner, C. A,. Kassin, S., Lassiter, G. D. (2004). Interrogations, confessions, and entrapment. *Perspectives in law psychology,* Vol. 20 (85–106). New York: Kluwer Academic/Plenum Publishers.

Meltzoff, A. N. (1988). Infant imitation and memory: Nine-month-olds in immediate and deferred tests. *Child Development, 59,* 217–225.

Meltzoff, A. N., & Moore, M. K. (1977). Imitation of facial and manual gestures by human neonates. *Science, 198,* 75–78.

Meltzoff, A. N., & Moore, M. K. (1999). A new foundation for cognitive development in infancy: The birth of the representational infant. In E. K. Scholnick, K. Nelson, S. A. Gelman, & P. H. Miller (Eds.), *Conceptual development: Piaget's legacy.* Mahwah, NJ: Erlbaum.

Meltzoff, A.N., & Moore, M.K. (2000). Resolving the debate about early imitation. In Muir, D., & Slater, A. (Eds.) *Infant Development: The Essential Readings.* (pp. 176–181). Blackwell; Oxford; UK.

Melzack, R. (1998). Pain and stress. Clues toward understanding chronic pain. In M. Sabourin et al. (Eds.), *Advances in psychological science.* Hove, England. Psychology Press/Erlbaum.

Melzack, R., & Wall, P. D. (1982). *The challenge of pain.* New York: Basic Books.

Mendelson, W. B. (2000). Sleep-inducing effects of adenosine microinjections into the medial preoptic area are blocked by flumazenil. *Brain Research, 852,* 479–481.

Menon, U., & Schweder, R. A. (1994). Cultural psychology and the power of shame in Orissa, India. In S. Kitayama & H. Markus (Eds.), *Emotion and culture.* Washington, DC: American Psychological Association.

Menzies, R. G., & Clarke, J. C. (1995). The etiology of acrophobia and its relationship to severity and individual response patterns. *Behaviour Research and Therapy, 33,* 795–803.

Meredith, N. (1986). Testing the talking cure. *Science, 232,* 31–37.

Merikle, P. M., & Daneman, M. (1998). Psychological investigations of unconscious perception. *Journal of Consciousness Studies, 5,* 5–18.

Merikle, P. M., & Rondi, G. J. (1993). Memory for events during anesthesia has not been demonstrated: A psychologist's viewpoint. In Sebel, Peter S., & Bonke, Benno (Eds.). *Memory and awareness in anesthesia.* (476–497). Upper Saddle River, NJ: Prentice-Hall, Inc.

Merikle, P. M., & Skanes, H.E. (1992). Subliminal self-help audiotapes: A search for placebo effects. *Journal of Applied Psychology, 77,* 772–776.

Merikle, P.M., Smilek, D., & Eastwood, J.D. (2001). Perception without awareness: Perspectives from cognitive psychology. *Cognition, 79,* 115–134.

Mersch, P. P. A., Middendorp, H. M., Bouhuys, A. L., Beersma, D. G. M., & van den Hoofdakker, R. H. (1999). Seasonal affective disorder and latitude: A review of the literature. *Journal of Affective Disorders, 53,* 35–48.

Mershon, B., & Gorsuch, R. L. (1988). Number of factors in the personality sphere: Does increase in factors increase predictability of real-life criteria. *Journal of Personality and Social Psychology, 55,* 675–680.

Messenger, J. C. (1971). Sex and repression in an Irish folk community. In D. S. Marshall & R. C. Suggs (Eds.), *Human sexual behavior.* Englewood Cliffs, NJ: Prentice Hall.

Messner, S. F. (1982). Societal development, social equality, and homicide: A cross-national test of a Durkheimian model. *Social Forces, 61,* 225–240.

Metcalfe, J., & Mischel, W. (1999). A hot/cool-system analysis of delay of gratification: Dynamics of willpower. *Psychological Review, 106,* 3–19.

Methot, L. L., & Heuitema, B. E. (1998). Effects of signal probability on individual differences in vigilance. *Human Factors, 40,* 78–90.

Meyer, C. B., & Taylor, S. E. (1986). Adjustment to rape. *Journal of Personality and Social Psychology, 50,* 1226–1234.

Meyer, R. G., & Osborne, Y. H. (1987). *Case studies in abnormal behavior* (2nd ed.). Boston: Allyn & Bacon.

Meyer, J. H., Houie, S. Sagrati, S. et al. (2004). Brain serotonin transporter binding potential measured with carbon 11-labeled DASB positron emission tomgraphy: effects of major depressive episodes and severity of dysfuntional attutides. *Arch Gen Psychiatry, 61*(12) 1271–1279.

Meyer, T. A., Svirsky, M. A., Kirk, K. I., & Miyamoto, R. T. (1998). Improvements in speech perception by children with profound prelingual hearing loss: Effects of device, communication mode, and chronological age. *Journal of Speech, Language, & Hearing Research, 41,* 846–858.

Michael, R. T., Gagnon, J. H., Laumman, E. O., & Kolata, G. (1994). *Sex in America: A definitive survey.* Boston: Little, Brown.

Michaels, J. W., Blommel, J. M., Brocato, R. M., Linkous, R. A., & Rowe, J. S. (1982). Social facilitation and inhibition in a natural setting. *Replications in Social Psychology, 2,* 21–24.

Middlebrooks, J. C., & Green, D. M. (1991). Sound localization by human listeners. *Annual Review of Psychology, 42,* 135–159.

Mignot, E. (1998). Genetic and familial aspects of narcolepsy. *Neurology, 50,* S16–S22.

Miles, C., & Hardman, E. (1998). State dependent memory produced by aerobic exercise. *Ergonomics, 41,* 20–28.

Miles, H. L., Mitchell, R. W., & Harper, S. E. (1996). Simon says: The development of imitation in an enculturated orangutan. In A. E. Russon, K. A. Bard, & A. Kim (Eds.), *Reaching into thought: The minds of the great apes.* Cambridge, England: Cambridge University Press.

Milgram, S. (1974). *Obedience to authority: An experimental view.* New York: Harper & Row.

Millar, M. G., & Millar, K. U. (1996). The effects of direct and indirect experience on affective and cognitive responses and the attitude-behavior relation. *Journal of Experimental Social Psychology, 32,* 561–579.

Miller, A. G. (1986). *The obedience experiments: A case study of controversy in social science.* New York: Praeger.

Miller, B. C., Fan, X., Christensen, M., Grotevant, H. D., & van Dulmen, M. (2000). Comparisons of adopted and nonadopted adolescents in a large, nationally representative sample. *Child Development, 71,* 1458–1473.

Miller, C. T., & Downey, K. T. (1999). A meta-analysis of heavyweight and self-esteem. *Personality and Social Psychology Review, 3,* 68–84.

Miller, G. A. (1956). The magical number seven, plus or minus two: Some limits on our capacity for processing information. *Psychological Review, 63,* 81–97.

Miller, J. D., Morin, L. P., Schwartz, W. J., & Moore, R. Y. (1996). New insights into the mammalian circadian clock. State of the art review. *Sleep, 19,* 641–667.

Miller, J. G. (1984). Culture and the development of everyday social explanation. *Journal of Personality and Social Psychology, 46,* 961–978.

Miller, J. G., Bersoff, D. M., & Harwood, R. L. (1990). Perceptions of social responsibility in India and in the United States: Moral imperatives or personal decisions? *Journal of Personality and Social Psychology, 58,* 33–47.

Miller, K. F., & Stigler, J. F. (1987). Counting in Chinese: Cultural variation in a basic cognitive skill. *Cognitive Development. 2,* 279–305.

Miller, K. J., Gleaves, D. H., Hirsch, T. G., Green, B. A., Snow, A. C., & Corbett, C. C. (2000). Comparisons of body image dimensions by race/ethnicity and gender in a university population. *International Journal of Eating Disorders, 27,* 310–316.

Miller, L. C. (1990). Intimacy and liking: Mutual influence and the role of unique relationships. *Journal of Personality and Social Psychology, 59,* 50–60.

Miller, L. K. (1999). The Savant Syndrome: Intellectual impairment and exceptional skill. *Psychological Bulletin, 125,* 31–46.

Miller, L., & Budd, J. (1999). The development of occupational sex-role stereotypes, occupational preferences and academic subject preferences in children at ages 8, 12, and 16. *Educational Psychology, 19,* 17–35.

Miller, N. E. (1944). Experimental studies of conflict. In J. McV Hunt (Ed.), *Personality and the behavior disorders* (Vol. 1). New York: Ronald Press.

Miller, S. D., Blackburn, T., Scholes, G., White, G. L., & Mamales, N. (1991). Optical differences in multiple personality disorder: A second look. *Journal of Nervous and Mental Disease, 179,* 132–135.

Miller, T. Q. (2000). Type A behavior. In G. Fink (Ed.), *Encyclopedia of stress.* San Diego: Academic Press.

Miller, W. R. (1996). Motivational interviewing: Research, practice, and puzzles. *Addictive Behaviors, 21,* 835–842.

Miller, W. R., & Brown, S. A. (1997). Why psychologists should treat alcohol and drug problems. *American Psychologist, 52,* 1269–1279.

Miller, W. R., & Rollnick, S. (1991). *Motivational interviewing: Preparing people to change addictive behavior.* New York: Guilford Press.

Miller, W. R., & Rollnick, S. (2002). *Motivational interviewing* (2nd ed.). New York: Guilford Press.

Millman, J., Bishop, C. H., & Ebel, R. (1965). An analysis of testwiseness. *Educational and Psychological Measurement, 25,* 707–726.

Millon, T., Simonsen, E., Birket-Smith, M., & Davis, R. D. (Eds). *Psychopathy: Antisocial, criminal and violent behavior.* New York: Guilford Press.

Mills, W. (1898). *The nature and development of animal intelligence.* London: T. Fisher Unwin.

Milner, B. (1965). Memory disturbances after bilateral hippocampal lesions. In P. Milner & S. Glickman (Eds.), *Cognitive processes and the brain.* Princeton, NJ: D. Van Nostrand.

Milner, B. R. (1970). Memory and medial temporal regions of the brain. In K. H. Pribram & D. R. Broadbent (Eds.), *Biology of memory.* Orlando, FL: Academic Press.

Milner, B., Corkin, S., & Teuber, H. L. (1968). Further analysis of the hippocampal syndrome: 14-year follow-up study of H. M. *Neuropsychologia, 6,* 215–234.

Milner, B., Petrides, M., & Smith, M. L. (1985). Frontal lobes and the temporal organization of memory. *Human Neurobiology, 4,* 137–142.

Milrod, B., Busch, F., Cooper, A., & Shapiro, T. (1997). *Manual of panic-focused psychodynamic psychotherapy.* Washington, DC: American Psychiatric Press.

Miltenberger, R. G., Fuqua, R. W., & Woods, D. W. (1998). Applying behavior analysis to clinical problems: Review and analysis of habit reversal. *Journal of Applied Behavior Analysis, 31,* 447–469.

Milton, J., & Wiseman, R. (1999). Does psi exist? Lack of replication of an anomalous process of information transfer. *Psychological Bulletin, 125,* 387–391.

Milton, J., & Wiseman, R. (2001). Does psi exist? Reply to Storm and Ertel. *Psychological Bulletin, 127,* 434–438.

Mineka, S., & Cook, M. (1993). Mechanisms involved in the observational conditioning of fear. *Journal of Experimental Psychology: General, 122,* 23-38.

Mineka, S., & Zinbarg, R. (1998). Experimental approaches to the anxiety and mood disorders. In J. G. Adair, D. Belanger, & K. L. Dion (Eds.), *Advances in psychological science, Vol. 1: Social, personal, and cultural aspects.* Hove, England: Psychology Press/Erlbaum.

Mineka, S., Davidson, M., Cook, M., & Kier, R. (1984). Observational conditioning of snake fear in rhesus monkeys. *Journal of Abnormal Psychology, 93,* 355–372.

Mineka, S., Watson, D., & Clark, L. A. (1998). Comorbidity of anxiety and unipolar mood disorder. *Annual Review of Psychology, 49,* 377–412.

Minuchin, S. (1974). *Families and family therapy.* Cambridge, MA: Harvard University Press.

Mischel, W. (1984). Convergences and challenges in the search for consistency. *American Psychologist, 39,* 351–364.

Mischel, W. (1999). Personality coherence and dispositions in a cognitive-affective processing system (CAPS) approach. In D. Cervone and Y. Shoda (Eds.), *The coherence of personality: Social-cognitive bases of consistency, variability, and organization.* New York: Guilford Press.

Mischel, W., Ebbesen, E. B., & Raskoff, Z. A. (1972). Cognitive and attentional mechanisms in delay of gratification. *Journal of Personality and Social Psychology, 21,* 204–218.

Mischel, W., Shoda, Y., & Rodriguez, M. L. (1989). Delay of gratification in children. *Science, 244*(4907), 933–938.

Mischel, W., Shoda, Y. & Smith, R. E. (2004). *Introduction to personality: Toward an integration.* New York: Wiley.

Mishne, J. (2002). *Multiculturalism and the therapeutic process.* New York: Guilford.

Misumi, J. (1985). *The behavioral science of leadership: An interdisciplinary Japanese research program.* Ann Arbor, MI: University of Michigan Press.

Mitchell, J. B., & Gratton, A. (1994). Involvement of mesolimbic dopamine neurons in sexual behaviors: Implications for the neurobiology of motivation. *Reviews in the Neurosciences,* 5, 317–330.

Moe, A., De Benji, R. (2005). Stressing the efficacy of the loci method. Oral presentation and the subject-generation of the loci pathway with expository passages. *Applied Cognitive Psychology, 19*(1), 95–106.

Molfese, D. L., & Molfese, V. J. (2002). *Developmental variations in learning: Applications to social, executive function, language, and reading skills.* Mahwah, NJ: Erlbaum.

Monahan, J. L., Murphy, S. T., & Zajonc, R. B. (2000). Subliminal mere exposure: Specific, general, and diffuse effects. *Psychological Science, 11,* 462–466.

Monat, A., & Lazarus, R. S. (1977). *Stress and coping.* New York: Columbia University Press.

Money, J. (1987). Sin, sickness or status. *American Psychologist, 42,* 384–399.

Monk, T. H., Folkard, S., Wedderburn, A. I. (1996). Maintaining safety and high performance on shift-work. *Applied Ergonomics, 27,* 17–23.

Monroe, S. M., & Peterman, A. M. (1988). Life stress and psychopathology. In L. H. Cohen (Ed.), *Life events and psychological functioning: Theoretical and methodological issues.* Newbury Park, CA: Sage Publications.

Monti, P. M., & Smith, N. F. (1976). Residual fear of the conditioned stimulus as a function of response prevention after avoidance or classical defensive conditioning in the rat. *Journal of Experimental Psychology: General, 105,* 148–162.

Monti-Bloch, L., Grosser, B. I. (1991). Effect of putative pheromones on the electrical activity of the human vomeronasal organ and olfactory epithelium. *Journal of Steroid Biochemistry and Molecular Biology, 39,* 573–582.

Moon, C., & Fifer, W. P. (1990). Syllables as signals for 2-day-old infants. *Infant Behavior and Development, 13,* 377–390.

Moore, L. P., Moore, J. W., & Hauck, W. E. (1982). Conditioning children's attitudes toward alcohol, smoking, and drugs. *Journal of Experimental Education, 50,* 154–158.

Moore, T. M., Scarpa, A., & Raine, A. (2002). A meta-analysis of serotonin metabolite 5 HIAA and antisocial behavior. *Aggressive Behavior, 28,* 299–316.

Moorey, S. (2003). *Cognitive behaviour therapy for people with cancer.* Oxford, England: Oxford University Press.

Moorhead, G., Ference, R., & Neck, C. P. (1991). Group decision fiascoes continue: Space shuttle Challenger and a revised groupthink framework. *Human Relations, 44,* 539–550.

Moreland, J. L., Dansereau, D. F., & Chmielewski, T. L. (1997). Recall of descriptive information: The roles of presentation format, annotation strategy, and individual differences. *Contemporary Educational Psychology, 22,* 521–533.

Morey, L. C. (1988). Personality disorders in DSM-III and DSM-III-R: Convergence, coverage, and internal consistency. *American Journal of Psychiatry, 145,* 573–577.

Morgan, W. (1997). *Physical activity and mental health.* Philadelphia: Taylor & Francis.

Morgenstern, J., Labouvie, E., McCrady, B. S., Kahler, C. W., & Frey, R. M. (1997). Affiliation with Alcoholics Anonymous after treatment: A study of therapeutic effects and mechanisms of action. *Journal of Consulting and Clinical Psychology, 65,* 768–777.

Mori, D., Chaiken, S., & Pliner, P. (1987). "Eating lightly" and the self-presentation of femininity. *Journal of Personality and Social Psychology, 53,* 693–702.

Morrell, M. J., Dixen, J. M., Carter, C. S., & Davidson, J. M. (1984). The influence of age and cycling status on sexual arousability in women. *American Journal of Obstetrics and Gynecology, 148,* 66–71.

Morrell, R. W., Park, D. C., & Poon, L. W. (1989). Quality of instructions on prescription drug labels: Effects on memory and comprehension in young and old adults. *Gerontologist, 29,* 345–354.

Morris, D., Collett, P., Marsh, P., & O'Shaughnessy, M. (1979). *Gestures.* New York: Stein & Day.

Morris, E. K., Laney, C., Bernstein, D. M., Loftus, E. F. (2006). Susceptibility to memory distortion: How do we decide it has occurred? *American Journal of Psychology, 119*(2), 255–274.

Morris, J. S., Büchel, C., & Dolan, R. J. (2001). Parallel neural responses in amygdala subregions and sensory cortex during implicit fear conditioning. *NeuroImage, 1,* 1044–1052.

Morris, J. S., Oehman, A., & Dolan, R. J. (1998). Conscious and unconscious emotional learning in the human amygdala. *Nature, 393*(6684), 467–470.

Morris, M. W., Podolny, J. M., & Airel, S. (2001). Culture, norms and obligations: Cross national differences in patterns of interpersonal norms and felt obligations toward coworkers. In W. Wosinska, R. B. Cialdini, D. W. Barrett, & J. Reykowski (Eds.), *The practice of social influence in multiple cultures.* Mahwah, NJ: Erlbaum.

Morrison, D. C. (1988). Marine mammals join the navy. *Science, 242,* 1503–1504.

Morrison, D. R., & Coiro, M. J. (1999). Parental conflict and marital disruption: Do children benefit when high-conflict marriages are dissolved? *Journal of Marriage and the Family. 61,* 626–637.

Morrongiello, B.A., Fenwick, K.D., & Chance, G. (1998). Crossmodal learning in newborn infants: inferences about properties of auditory-visual events. *Infant Behavior & Development, 21,* 543–553.

Morrow, G. W., Roscoe, J. A., Kirshner, J. J., Hynes, H. E., & Rosenbluth, R. J. (1998). Anticipatory nausea and vomiting in the era of 5-HT3 antiemetics. *Support Care Cancer, 6,* 244–247.

Morton, J., & Johnson, M. H. (1991). Conspec and Conlern: A two-process theory of infant face recognition. *Psychological Review, 98,* 164–181.

Moscovici, S. (1985). Social influence and conformity. In G. Lindzey & E. Aronson (Eds.), *Handbook of social psychology* (3rd ed.). New York: Random House.

Moscovici, S., & Zavalloni, M. (1969). The group as a polarizer of attitudes. *Journal of Personality and Social Psychology, 12,* 124–135.

Moss, C. S. (1972). *Recovery with aphasia.* Urbana: University of Illinois Press.

Moss, D. (Ed.) (1998). *Humanistic psychology: A historical and biographical sourcebook.* Westport, CT: Greenwood.

Motta, R. W., & Joseph, J. M. (2000). Group intelligence tests. In G. Goldstein & M. Hersen (Eds.), *Handbook of psychological assessment* (3rd ed.). New York: Elsevier.

Mowrer, O. H. (1947). On the dual nature of learning: A reinterpretation of "conditioning" and "problem solving." *Harvard Educational Review, 17,* 102–150.

Muchinsky, P. M. (1997). *Psychology applied to work* (5th ed.). Pacific Grove, CA: Brooks/Cole.

Muchinsky, P. M. (2000). *Psychology applied to work* (6th ed.). Pacific Grove, CA: Brooks/Cole.

Mueller, U., Zelazo, P. D., Leone, T., & Hood, S. (2004). Interference control in a new rule use task: Age-related changes, labeling, and attention. *Child Development, 75,* 1594–1609.

Muir, D., Hains, S. (2004). The U-shaped developmental function for auditory localization. *Journal of Cognition and Development, 1,* 123–130.

Muir, D.W., & Mitchell, D.E. (1975). Behavioural deficits in cats following early selective visual exposure to contours of a single orientation. *Brain Research, 85,* 459–477.

Mullen, B., Anthony, T., Salas, E., & Driskell, J. E. (1994). Group cohesiveness and quality of decision making: An integration of tests of the groupthink hypothesis. *Small Group Research, 25,* 189–204.

Mumme, D. L., Fernald, A., & Herrera, C. (1996). Infants' responses to facial and vocal emotional signals in a social referencing paradigm. *Child Development, 67,* 3229–3237.

Munoz, R. F., Mrazek, P. J., & Haggerty, R. J. (1996). Institute of Medicine Report on Prevention of Mental Disorders: Summary and commentary. *American Psychologist, 51,* 1116–1122.

Murdoch, H. (1984). Maternal rubella: The implications. *AEP Association of Educational Psychologists Journal, 6,* 3–6.

Murray, D. J. (1995). *Gestalt psychology and the cognitive revolution.* Hemel Hempstead, UK: Harvester Wheatsheaf / Prentice Hall.

Murray, J. B. (1995). Evidence for acupuncture's analgesic effectiveness and proposals for the physiological mechanisms involved. *Journal of Psychology, 129,* 443–461.

Murray, R., Jones, P., Van Oss, J., et al. (2003). *The epidemiology of schizophrenia.* New York: Cambridge University Press.

Musella, D. P. (2005). Gallup poll shows that Americans' belief in the paranormal persists. *The Skeptical Inquirer, 29,* 5.

Myers, C. D., Riley III, J. L., & Robinson, M. E. (2003). Psychosocial contributions to sex-correlated differences in pain. *Clinical Journal of Pain, 19(4),* 225–232.

Myers, D. G. (2000). The funds, friends, and faith of happy people. *American Psychologist, 55,* 56–67.

Myers, D. G., & Diener, E. (1995). Who is happy? *Psychological Science, 6,* 10–19.

Na, E. Y., & Loftus, E. F. (1998). Attitudes toward law and prisoners, conservative authoritarianism, attribution, and internal-external locus of control: Korean and American law students and undergraduates. *Journal of Cross Cultural Psychology, 29,* 595–615.

Nadelson, C. C., & Reinburg, C. E. (Eds.) (1999). *Schizophrenia: Losing touch with reality.* Broomall, England: Chelsea House.

Nadler, A., & Ben-Slushan, D. (1989). Forty years later: Long-term consequences of massive traumatization as manifested by holocaust survivors from the city and the Kibbutz. *Journal of Consulting and Clinical Psychology, 57,* 287–293.

Nakayama, K., & Tyler, C. W. (1981). Psychophysical isolation of movement sensitivity by removal of familiar position cues. *Vision Research, 21,* 427–433.

Natale, V., & Lorenzetti, R. (1997). Influences of morningness-eveningness and time of day on narrative comprehension. *Personality and Individual Differences, 23,* 685–690.

Nathan, P. E. (1985). Aversion therapy in the treatment of alcoholism: Success and failure. *Annals of the New York Academy of Sciences, 443,* 357–364.

National Center for Health Statistics (1995). *Healthy people 2000.* Washington, DC: Author.

National Center for Health Statistics (1996). *Health, United States, 1995.* Hyattsville, MD: U.S. Public Health Service.

National Highway Traffic Safety Administration (2000). *Traffic Safety Facts 1998: Alcohol* (DOT HS 808 950). [Online]. PDF file available: http://www.nhtsa.dot.gov/people/ncsa/factshet.html.

National Sleep Foundation (2000). *2000 omnibus sleep in America poll* [Online]. Available: http://www.sleepfoundation.org/publications/2000poll.html#9.

National Task Force on the Prevention and Treatment of Obesity (1994). Weight cycling. *Journal of the American Medical Association, 272,* 1196–1202.

National Television Violence Study (Vol. 3) (1998). Thousand Oaks, CA: Sage Publications. Author.

National Transportation Safety Board (NTSB) (1979, June). *Aircraft accident report* (NTSB-AAR-79-7). Washington. DC: NTSB Bureau of Accident Investigations.

National Weight Control Registry. (2000). [On-line]. Available: http://www.uchsc.edu/nutrition/nwcr.htm

Natsoulas, T. (1999). An ecological and phenomenological perspective on consciousness and perception: Contact with the world at the very heart of the being of consciousness. *Review of General Psychology, 3,* 224–245.

Naveh, B. M., & Jonides, J. (1984). Cognitive load and maintenance rehearsal. *Journal of Verbal Learning and Verbal Behavior, 23,* 494–507.

Nederhof, A. J. (1985). Methods of coping with social desirability bias: A review. *European Journal of Social Psychology, 15,* 263–280.

Negus, S. S., Wurrey, B. A., & Mello, N. K. (2004). Sex differences in thermal nociception and prostaglandin-induced thermal hypersensitivity in rhesus monkeys. *Journal of Pain, 5(2),* 92–103.

Neiderhiser, J. M., Reiss, D., Hetherington, E. M., & Plomin, R. (1999). Relationships between parenting and adolescent adjustment over time: Genetic and environmental contributions. *Developmental Psychology, 35,* 680, 692.

Neimeyer, R. A., & Raskin, J. D. (Eds.) (2000). *Constructions of disorder: Meaning-making frameworks for psychotherapy.* Washington, DC: American Psychological Association.

Neisser, U. (1967). *Cognitive psychology.* New York: Appleton-Century-Crofts.

Neisser, U., & Harsch, N. (1993). Phantom flashbulbs: False recollections of hearing the news about Challenger. In E. Winograd & U. Neisser (Eds.), *Affect and accuracy in recall: Studies of "flashbulb" memories.* New York: Cambridge University Press.

Neisser, U., Boodoo, G., Bouchard, T. J., Boykin, A. W., Brody, N., Ceci, S. J., Halpern, D. F., Loehlin, J. C., Perloff, R., Sternberg, R. J., & Urbina, S. (1996). Intelligence: Knowns and unknowns. *American Psychologist, 51,* 77–101.

Neisser, U., Bouchard, T. J., Jr., Boykin, A. W., Brody, N., Ceci, S. J., Halpern, D. F., Loehlin, J. C., Perloff, R., Sternberg, R. J., & Urbina, S. (1998). Intelligence: Knowns and unknowns. In M. E. Hertzig, E. A. Farber et al. (Eds.), *Annual progress in child psychiatry and child development: 1997.* Bristol, PA: Brunner/Mazel.

Nelson, C. A., & Luciana, M. (Eds.). (2001). *Handbook of developmental cognitive neuroscience.* Cambridge, MA: MIT Press.

Nelson, C. A., Monk, C. S., Lin, J., Carver, L. J., Thomas, K. M., & Truwit, C. L. (2000). Functional neuroanatomy of spatial working memory in children. *Developmental Psychology, 36,* 109–116.

Nelson, F. V., Zimmerman, L., Barnason, S., Nieveen, J., & Schmaderer, M. (1998). The relationship and influence of anxiety on postoperative pain in the coronary artery bypass graft patient. *Journal of Pain and Symptom Management, 15,* 102–109.

Nelson, K. D., Fivush, R. (2004). Culture and language in the emergence of autobiographical memory. *Psychological Science, 15*(9), 573–577

Nemiah, J. C. (1978). Psychoneurotic disorders. In A. M. Nicholi (Ed.), *Harvard guide to modern psychiatry.* Cambridge, MA: Harvard University Press.

Nesbitt, E. B. (1973). An escalator phobia overcome in one session of flooding in vivo. *Journal of Behavior Therapy and Experimental Psychiatry, 4,* 405–406.

Neugarten, B. L. (1979). Time, age, and the life cycle. *American Journal of Psychiatry, 136,* 887–894.

Neugarten, B. L., & Hall, E. (1980, April). Acting one's age: New roles for old. *Psychology Today,* pp. 66–80.

Neumäker, K. J. (2000). Mortality rates and causes of death. *European Eating Disorders Review, 8,* 181–187.

New York Times (1999, January 30). Driver on Long Island saves a woman trapped in her burning car. *New York Times,* p. B2.

Newberg, A., Alavi, A., Baime, M., Pourdehnad, M., Santanna, J., & d'Aquili, E. (2001). The measurement of regional cerebral blood flow during the complex cognitive task of meditation: A preliminary SPECT study. *Psychiatry Research, 106,* 113–122.

Newcomb, M. D., & Harlow, L. L. (1986). Life events and substance use among adolescents: Mediating effects of perceived loss of control and meaninglessness in life. *Journal of Personality and Social Psychology, 51,* 564–577.

Newcombe, N., & Fox, N. A. (1994). Infantile amnesia: Through a glass darkly. *Child Development, 65,* 31–40.

Newell, A., & Simon, H. A. (1972). *Human problem solving.* Englewood Cliffs, NJ: Prentice Hall.

Newlin, D. B., & Thomson, J. B. (1997). Alcohol challenge with sons of alcoholics: A critical review and analysis. In G. A. Marlatt & G. R. VandenBos (Eds.), *Addictive behaviors: Readings on etiology, prevention and treatment.* Washington, DC: American Psychological Association.

Newman, D. L., Caspi, A., Moffitt, T. E., & Silva, P. A. (1997). Antecedents of adult interpersonal functioning: Effects of individual differences in age 3 temperament. *Developmental Psychology, 33,* 206–217.

Newman, D. L., Moffit, T. E., Caspi, A., Silva, P. A., & Stanton, W. R. (1996). Psychiatric disorder in a birth cohort of young adults: Prevalence, comorbidity, clinical significance, and new case incidence from ages 11–21. *Journal of Consulting and Clinical Psychology, 64,* 552–562.

Newport, F. (1999, March 1). *Some change over time in American attitudes towards homosexuality, but negativity remains.* Gallup News Service. Princeton, NJ: Gallup Organization.

Newport, F. (1999, March 29). *Americans today much more accepting of a woman, Black, Catholic, or Jew as president.* Gallup News Service. Princeton, NJ: Gallup Organization.

Newport, F. (1999, May 10). *Media portrayals of violence seen by many as causes of real-life violence.* Gallup News Service. Princeton, NJ. Gallup Organization.

Newport, F., & Strausberg, M. (2001, June). Americans' belief in psychic and paranormal phenomena is up over last decade. *Gallup Poll Monthly,* 14–17.

Newson, R. S. & Kemps, E. B. (2006). Cardiorespiratory fitness as a predictor of successful cognitive ageing. *Journal of Clinical and Experimental Neuropsychology, 28,* 949–967.

Nezami, E., & Butcher, J. N. (2000). Objective personality assessment. In G. Goldstein & M. Hersen (Eds.), *Handbook of psychological assessment* (3rd ed.). New York: Elsevier.

Nezlek, J. B., Hampton, C. P., & Shean, G. (2000). Clinical depression and day-to-day social interaction in a community sample. *Journal of Abnormal Psychology, 109,* 11–19.

Nezu, A. M., Nezu, C. M., & D'Zurilla (2000). Problem-solving skills training. In G. Fink (Ed.), *Encyclopedia of stress.* San Diego: Academic Press.

Ni, X., Chan, K., Bulgin, N., Sicard, T., Bismil, R., McMain, S., & Kennedy, J. L. (2006). Association between serotonin transporter gene and borderline personality disorder. *Journal of Psychiatric Research. 40,* 448–453.

NICHD Early Child Care Research Network (1997). The effects of infant child care on infant-mother attachment security: Results of the NICHD study of early child care. *Child Development, 68,* 860–879.

NICHD Early Child Care Research Network (1999). Child care and mother-child interaction in the first three years of life. *Developmental Psychology, 35,* 1399–1413.

Nichter, M. & Vuckovic, N. (1994). Fat talk: Body image among adolescent girls. In N. Sault (Ed.), *Many mirrors: Body image and social relations.* New Brunswick, NJ: Rutgers University Press.

Nickerson, R. S., & Adams, M. J. (1979). Long term memory for a common object. *Cognitive Psychology, 11,* 287–307.

Nicks, S. D., Korn, J. H., & Mainieri, T. (1997). The rise and fall of deception in social psychology and personality research, 1921 to 1994. *Ethics and Behavior, 7,* 69–77.

Nicoladis, E., & Genesee, F. (1997). Language development in preschool bilingual children. *Journal of Speech-Language Pathology & Audiology, 21,* 258–270.

Nigg, J. T., Lohr, N. E., Westen, D., & Gold, L. J. (1992). Malevolent object representation in borderline personality disorder and major depression. *Journal of Abnormal Psychology, 101,* 61–67.

Niles, S. (1998). Achievement goals and means: A cultural comparison. *Journal of Cross Cultural Psychology, 29,* 656–667.

Nisbett, R. E. (1998). Race, genetics, and IQ. In C. Jencks & M. Phillips et al. (Eds.), *The Black-White test score gap.* Washington DC: Brookings Institution.

Nisbett, R. E., Peng, K., Choi, I., & Norenzayan, A. (2001). Culture and systems of thought: Holistic vs. analytic cognition. *Psychological Review, 108,* 291–310.

Nishith, P., Mechanic, M. B., & Resick, P. A. (2000). Prior interpersonal trauma: The contribution to current PTSD symptoms in female rape victims. *Journal of Abnormal Psychology, 109,* 20–25.

Noble, E. P. (1998). The D2 dopamine receptor gene: A review of association studies in alcoholism and phenotypes. *Alcohol, 16,* 33–45.

Noble, R. E. (1997). The incidence of parental obesity in overweight individuals. *International Journal of Eating Disorders, 22,* 265–271.

Nolen-Hoeksema, S. (2006). *Sex differences in depression.* Stanford, CA: Stanford University Press.

Nolen-Hoeksema, S., & Morrow, J. (1991). A prospective study of depression and post-traumatic stress symptoms following a natural disaster: The 1989 Loma Prieta earthquake. *Journal of Personality and Social Psychology, 61,* 115–121.

Nolen-Hoeksema, S., Parker, L. E., Larson, J. (1994). Ruminative coping with depressed mood following loss. *Journal of Personality and Social Psychology, 67,* 97–107.

Noll, S. M., & Fredrickson, B. L. (1998). A mediational model linking self-objectification, body shame, and disordered eating. *Psychology of Women Quarterly, 22,* 623–636.

Nolte, J. (1998). *The human brain: An introduction to its functional anatomy.* St. Louis: Mosby.

Norcross, J. C. (1991). Prescriptive matching in psychotherapy: An introduction. *Psychotherapy, 28,* 439–443.

Norcross, J. C. (2003). *Psychotherapy relationships that work: Therapist contributions and responsiveness to patients.* New York: Oxford University Press.

Norcross, J. C., Karg-Bray, R. S., & Prochaska, J. O. (1995). *Clinical psychologists in the 1990s.* Unpublished manuscript, University of Scranton.

Norcross, J. C., Ratzin, A. C., & Payne, D. (1989). Ringing in the New Year: The change processes and reported outcomes of resolutions. *Addictive Behaviors, 14,* 205–212.

Normann, R. A. (1995). Visual neuroprosthetics—functional vision for the blind. *IEEE Engineering in Medicine and Biology, 14,* 77–83.

Normann, R. A., Maynard, E. M., Guillory, K. S., & Warren, D. J. (1996). Cortical implants for the blind. *IEEE Spectrum, 33,* 54–59.

Norris, J. (1994). Alcohol and female sexuality: A look at expectancies and risks. *Alcohol Health and Research World, 18,* 197–201.

North, M. M., North, S. M., & Coble, J. R. (1997). Virtual reality therapy for fear of flying. *American Journal of Psychiatry, 154,* 130.

North, M., North, S. M., & Coble, J. R. (2002). Virtual reality therapy: An effective treatment for psychological disorders. In K. M. Stanney (Ed.), *Handbook of virtual environments: Design, implementation, and applications. Human factors and ergonomics.* Mahwah, NJ: Erlbaum.

Norton, G. R., Harrison, B., Haunch, J., & Rhodes, L. (1985). Characteristics of people with infrequent panic attacks. *Abnormal Psychiatry, 94,* 216–221.

Nosek, B. A., Banaji, M. R., & Greenwald, A. G. (2002). Harvesting implicit group attitudes and beliefs from a demonstration web site. *Group Dynamics: Theory, research and practice,* 6, 101–115.

Nossal, C. J. V., & Hall, E. (1995). Choices following antigen entry: Antibody formation or immunologic tolerance? *Annual Review of Immunology, 13,* 171–204.

Novaco, R. (1975). *Anger control.* Lexington, MA: Lexington Books.

Noveck, J. (1997, August 4). Oldest person to ever live dies in France at 122. *Seattle Times,* A2.

Noyes, R., & Hoehn, S. R. (1999). *The anxiety disorders.* New York: Cambridge University Press.

Nyberg, L., Persson, J., Habib, R., Tulving, E., McIntosh, A. R., Cabeza, R., & Houle, S. (2000). Large scale neurocognitive networks underlying episodic memory. *Journal of Cognitive Neuroscience, 12,* 163–173.

Nye, R. D. (1996). *Three psychologies: Perspectives from Freud, Skinner, and Rogers* (4th ed.). Pacific Grove, CA: Brooks/Cole.

O'Brien, C. P. (1997). Recent developments in the pharmacotherapy of substance abuse. In G. A. Marlatt & G. R. VandenBos (Eds.), *Addictive behaviors: Readings on etiology, prevention and treatment.* Washington, DC: American Psychological Association.

O'Connor, D. B., Archer, J., Hair, W. M., & Wu, F. C. W. (2002). Exogenous testosterone, aggression, and mood in eugonadal and hypogonadal men. *Physiology and Behavior, 75,* 557–566.

O'Connor, T. G., Deater, D. K., Fulker, D., Rutter, M., & Plomin, R. (1998). Genotype-environment correlations in late childhood and early adolescence: Antisocial behavioral problems and coercive parenting. *Developmental Psychology, 34,* 970–981.

O'Connor, T. G., Thorpe, K., Dunn, J., & Golding, J. (1999). Parental divorce and adjustment in adulthood: Findings from a community sample. *Journal of Child Psychology and Psychiatry and Allied Disciplines, 40,* 777–789.

O'Donnell, C. R. (1995). Firearm deaths among children and youth. *American Psychologist, 50,* 771–776.

O'Donohue, W., & Elliot, A. (1992). The current status of posttraumatic stress disorder as a diagnostic category: Problems and proposals. *Journal of Traumatic Stress, 5,* 421–439.

O'Keefe, D. J., & Figge, M. (1997). A guilt-based explanation of the door-in-the-face influence strategy. *Human Communication Research, 24,* 64–81.

O'Leary, A., & The National Institute of Mental Health Multisite HIV Prevention Trial Group. (2001). Social-cognitive theory mediators of behavior change in the National Institute of Mental Health Multisite HIV Prevention Trial. *Health Psychology 20,* 369–376.

O'Leary, C. M. (2004). Fetal alcohol syndrome: Diagnosis, epidemiology, and developmental outcomes. *Journal of Paediatric Child Health, 40,* 2–7.

O'Leary, K. D., & Wilson, G. T. (1987). *Behavior therapy: Application and outcome.* Englewood Cliffs, NJ: Prentice Hall.

Oatley, K., & Jenkins, J. M. (1992). Human emotions: Function and dysfunction. *Annual Review of Psychology, 43,* 55–85.

Ockene, J. K., et al. (2001). Relapse and maintenance issues for smoking cessation. *Health Psychology, 19,* 17–31.

Ohayon, M. M., Guilleminault, C., & Priest, R. G. (1999). Night terrors, sleepwalking, and confusional arousals in the general population: Their frequency and relationship to other sleep and mental disorders. *Journal of Clinical Psychiatry, 60,* 268–276.

Ohbuchi, K., & Kambara, T. (1985). Attacker's intent and awareness of outcome, impression management, and retaliation. *Journal of Experimental Social Psychology, 21,* 321–330.

Öhman, A. (1993). Fear and anxiety as emotional phenomena: Clinical phenomenology, evolutionary perspectives, and information-processing mechanisms. In M. Lewis & J. M. Haviland (Eds.), *Handbook of emotions.* New York: Guilford Press.

Öhman, A. (2000). Anxiety. In G. Fink (Ed.), *Encyclopedia of stress.* San Diego: Academic Press.

Öhman, A., & Soares, J. J. F. (1998). Emotional conditioning to masked stimuli: Expectancies for aversive outcomes following nonrecognized fear-relevant stimuli. *Journal of Experimental Psychology: General, 127,* 69–82.

Öhman, A., Fredrikson, M., & Hugdahl, K. (1978). Towards an experimental model for simple phobic reactions. *Behavioural Analysis and Modification, 2,* 97–114.

Okawa, M., Nanami, T., Wada, S., Shimizu, T., & et al. (Eds.) (1987). Four congenitally blind children with circadian sleep-wake rhythm disorder. *Sleep, 10,* 101–110.

Olafson, E., Lederman, C. S. (2006). The state of the debate about children's disclosure patterns in child sexual abuse cases. *Juvenile and Family Court Journal, 57,* 27–40.

Oldenburg, D. (1990, April 3). Hidden messages. *Washington Post,* p. C5.

Oldridge, N. B. (1984). Adherence to adult exercise fitness programs. In J. D. Matarzzo, Sh.M. Weiss, J. A. Herd, N. E. Miller, & St.M. Weiss (Eds.), *Behavioral health: A handbook of health enhancement and disease prevention.* New York: Wiley.

Olds, J. (1956). Pleasure centers in the brain. *Scientific American, 193,* 105–116.

Olds, J. (1958). Self-stimulation of the brain. *Science, 127,* 315–324.

Olds, J., & Milner, P. (1954). Positive reinforcement produced by electrical stimulation of septal area and other regions of rat brain. *Journal of Comparative and Physiological Psychology, 47,* 419–427.

Oleson, T. (2002). Auriculotherapy stimulation for neuro-rehabilitation. *NeuroRehabilitation, 17,* 49–62.

Olness, K., & Ader, R. (1992). Conditioning as an adjunct in the pharmacotherapy of lupus erythematosus. *Journal of Developmental and Behavioral Pediatrics, 13,* 124–125.

Olson, J. M., Vernon, P. A,. Harris, J. A., & Jang, K. L. (2001). The heritability of attitudes: A study of twins. *Journal of Personality and Social Psychology,* 80: 845–860.

Olson, J. M., & Zanna, M. P. (1991). Attitude change and attitude-behavior consistency. In R. M. Baron, W. G.

Graziano, & C. Stangor (Eds.), *Social psychology.* Ft. Worth, TX: Holt, Rinehart & Winston.

Oltman, P. K. (1968). A portable Rod-and-Frame apparatus. *Perceptual and Motor Skills, 26,* 503–506.

Ono, Y., Yoshimura, K., Yamauchi, K., Asai, M., Young, J., Fujihara, S., Kitamura, T. (2001). Taijin Kyofusho in a Japanese community population. *Transcultural Psychiatry, 38*(4), 506–514.

Orbuch, T. L., House, J. S., Mero, R. P., & Webster, P. S. (1996). Marital quality over the life course. *Social Psychology Quarterly, 59,* 162–171.

Ormel, J., & Wohlforth, T. (1991). How neuroticism, long-term difficulties, and life situation change influence psychological distress. *Journal of Personality and Social Psychology, 60,* 744–755.

Orne, M. T. (1959). The nature of hypnosis: Artifact and essence. *Journal of Abnormal and Social Psychology, 58,* 277–299.

Orne, M. T. (1962). On the social psychology of the psychological experiment: With particular reference to demand characteristics and their implications. *American Psychologist, 17,* 776–783.

Orne, M. T., & Evans, F. J. (1965). Social control in the psychological experiment: Antisocial behavior and hypnosis. *Journal of Personality and Social Psychology, 1,* 189–200.

Ornstein, R. (1997). *Right mind.* Ft. Worth, TX: Harcourt Brace.

Orr, A. L. (1998). *Issues in aging and vision: A curriculum.* Washington, DC: American Foundation for the Blind Press.

Ortmann, A., & Hertwig, R. (1997). Is deception acceptable? *American Psychologist, 52,* 746–747.

Osborn, A. F. (1963). *Applied imagination: Principles and procedures for creative problem-solving* (3rd ed.). New York: Scribners.

Ost, J., Vrij, A., Costall, A., & Bull, R. (2002). Crashing memories and reality monitoring: Distinguishing between perceptions, imaginations and false memories. *Applied Cognitive Psychology, 16,* 125–134.

Ost, L. (1987). Age of onset in different phobias. *Journal of Abnormal Psychology, 96,* 223–229.

Ouchi, W. G. (1981). *Theory Z: How American business can meet the Japanese challenge.* Reading, MA: Addison-Wesley.

Ouellette, J. A., & Wood, W. (1998). Habit and intention in everyday life: The multiple processes by which past behavior predicts future behavior. *Psychological Bulletin, 124,* 54–74.

Ouimette, P. C., Finney, J. W., & Moos, R. H. (1997). Twelve-step and cognitive-behavioral treatment for substance abuse: A comparison of treatment effectiveness. *Journal of Consulting and Clinical Psychology, 65,* 230–240.

Owen, P. R. & Laurel-Seller, E. (2000). Weight and shape ideals: Thin is dangerously in. *Journal of Applied Social Psychology, 30,* 979–990.

Ozer, D. J. (1989). Construct validity in personality assessment. In D. M. Buss & N. Cantor (Eds.), *Personality psychology: Recent trends and emerging directions.* New York: Springer-Verlag.

Ozer, E. M., & Bandura, A. (1990). Mechanisms governing empowerment effects: A self-efficacy analysis. *Journal of Personality and Social Psychology, 58,* 472–486.

Packard, E. (2007). That teenage feeling. *Monitor on Psychology, 38,* 20–24.

Paffenbarger, R. S., Jr., Hyde, R. T., Wing, A. L., & Hsieh, C. C. (1986). Physical activity, all-cause mortality, and longevity of college alumni. *New England Journal of Medicine, 314,* 605–613.

Page, S. (1999). Accommodating persons with AIDS: Acceptance and rejection in rental situations. *Journal of Applied Social Psychology, 29, 2,* 261–270.

Paivio, A. (1969). Mental imagery is associative learning and memory. *Psychological Review, 76,* 241–263.

Paivio, A. (1971). *Imagery and verbal processes.* New York: Holt, Rinehart & Winston.

Paivio, A. (1986). *Mental representations: A dual coding approach.* New York: Oxford University Press.

Paivio, A. (1995). Imagery and memory. In M. S. Gazzaniga (Ed.). *The cognitive neurosciences.* Cambridge, MA: MIT Press.

Paivio, S. C., Greenberg, L. S. (1995). Resolving "unfinished business": efficacy of experiential therapy using empty-chair dialogue. *Journal of Consulting and Clinical Psychology, 63,* 419–425.

Pajer, K. (2000a). Antisocial disorders. In G. Fink (Ed.), *Encyclopedia of stress.* San Diego: Academic Press.

Pajer, K. (2000b). Hysteria. In G. Fink (Ed.), *Encyclopedia of stress.* San Diego: Academic Press.

Palfai, T., & Jankiewicz, H. (1991). *Drugs and human behavior.* Dubuque, IA: Wm. C. Brown.

Palmer, C. T. (1991). Kin-selection, reciprocal altruism, and information sharing among Maine lobstermen. *Ethology and Sociobiology, 12,* 221–235.

Palmer, J. A., & Palmer, L. K. (Eds.). (2002). *Evolutionary psychology: The ultimate origins of human behavior* (Vol. 15). Needham Heights, MA.: Allyn & Bacon.

Palmer, S. E. (2002). Perceptual organization in vision. In H. Pashler & S. Yantis (Eds.), *Steven's handbook of experimental psychology: Vol. 1. Sensation and perception* (3rd ed.). New York: Wiley.

Palmere, M., Benton, S. L., Glover, J. A., & Ronning, R. (1983). Elaboration and recall of main ideas in prose. *Journal of Education Psychology, 75,* 898–907.

Panksepp, J. (1998). *Affective neuroscience: The foundations of human and animal emotions.* Oxford, England: Oxford University Press.

Papanicolaou, A. C. (1989). *Emotion: A reconsideration of the somatic theory.* New York: Gordon and Breach.

Paparrigopoulos, T. L. (2005). REM sleep behaviour disorder: Clinical profiles and pathophysiology. *International Review of Psychiatry, 17,* 293–300.

Papolos, D. F., & Lachman, H. M. (1994). *Genetic studies in affective disorders: Overview of basic methods, current directions, and critical research issues.* New York: Wiley.

Parchman, S. W., Ellis, J. A., Christinaz, D., & Vogel, M. (2000). An evaluation of three computer-based instructional strategies in basic electricity and electronics training. *Military Psychology, 12,* 73–87.

Parish, A. R. (1996). Female relationships in bonobos (Pan paniscus). *Human Nature, 7,* 61–96.

Park, D. C., Smith, A. D., & Cavanaugh, J. C. (1990). Metamemories of memory researchers. *Memory and Cognition, 18,* 321–327.

Parker, A. (2000). A review of the ganzfeld work at Gothenburg University. *Journal of the Society for Psychical Research, 64,* 1–15.

Parker, C. R., Bolling, M. Y., & Kohlenberg, R. J. (1998). Operant theory of personality. In D. F. Barone, M. Hersen, & V. B. Van Hasselt (Eds.), *Advanced personality.* New York: Plenum.

Parker, K. J., Buckmaster, C. L., Justus, K. R., Schatzberg, A. F., and Lyons, D. M. (2005). Mild early life stress enhances prefrontal-dependent response inhibition in monkeys. *Biological Psychiatry, 57,* 848–855.

Parkes, J. D., Clift, S. J., Dahlitz, M. J., & Chen, S. Y. (Eds.) (1995). The narcoleptic syndrome. *Journal of Neurology, Neurosurgery and Psychiatry, 59,* 221–224.

Parkin, A. J. (2000). Memory impairment. In G. Fink (Ed.), *Encyclopedia of stress.* San Diego: Academic Press.

Parkinson, A. J., Parkinson, W. S., Tyler, R. S., Lowder, M. W., & Gantz, B. J. (1998). Speech perception performance in experienced cochlear-implant patients receiving the SPEAK processing strategy in the Nucleus Spectra-22 cochlear implant. *Journal of Speech, Language, and Hearing Research, 41,* 1073–1087.

Parrott, A. C. (1999). Does cigarette smoking cause stress? *American Psychologist, 54,* 817–820.

Parrott, A.C. (2002). Human psychopharmacology of Ecstasy (MDMA): A review of 15 years of empirical research. *Human Psychopharmacology Clinical and Experimental, 16,* 557–577.

Parrot, A. C. (2006). MDMA in humans: Factors which affect the neuropsychobiological profiles of recreational ecstasy users, the integrative role of bioenergetic stress. *Journal of Psychopharmacology, 20,* 147–163.

Partain, C. (2006) JMRI Special Issue: Clinical potential of brain mapping using MRI. *Journal of magnetic resonance imaging, 23,* 785–786.

Partonen, T. (1994). Effects of morning light treatment on subjective sleepiness and mood in winter depression. *Journal of Affective Disorders, 30,* 47–56.

Pascalis, O., DeSchoenen, S., Morton, J., & Deruelle, C. (1995). Mother's face recognition by neonates: A replication and an extension. *Infant Behavior and Development, 18,* 79–85.

Pashler, H., & Yantis, S. (Eds.). (2002). *Steven's handbook of experimental psychology: Vol. 1. Sensation and perception* (3rd ed.). New York: Wiley.

Pasupathi, M., Staudinger, U. M., & Baltes, P. B. (2001). Seeds of wisdom: Adolescents' knowledge and judgment about difficult life problems. *Developmental Psychology, 37,* 351–361.

Patrick, C. J., Cuthbert, B. N., & Lang, P. J. (1994). Emotion in the criminal psychopath: Fear image processing. *Journal of Abnormal Psychology, 103,* 523–534.

Patterson, G. R. (1982). *Coercive family processes.* Eugene, OR: Castalia Press.

Patterson, G. R., Littman, R. A., & Bricker, W. (1967). Assertive behavior in children: A step toward a theory of aggression. *Monographs of the Society for Research in Child Development, 32* (Whole No. 5).

Patton, D., Brown, D., Broszeit, B., & Dhaliwal, J. (2001). *Substance use among Manitoba high school students, 2001.* Addictions Foundation of Manitoba.

Pauk, W., & Fiore, J. P. (2000). *Succeed in college!* Boston: Houghton Mifflin.

Paul, G. L., & Lentz, R. J. (1977). *Psychosocial treatment of chronic mental patients: Milieu versus social learning programs.* Cambridge, MA: Harvard University Press.

Paulhus, D.L. (1991). Measurement and control of response bias. In Robinson, J., Shaver, P., & Wrightsman, L. (Eds.) *Measures of personality and social psychological attitudes* (pp. 17–59). Toronto: Academic Press.

Paulhus, D. L., Harms, P. D., Bruce, M. N., & Lysy, D. C. (2003). The over-claiming technique: Measureing self-enhancement independent of ability. *Journal of Personality and Social Psychology, 84,* 890–904.

Pavlov, I. P. (1902). *The work of the digestive glands* (W. H. Thompson, Trans.). London: Griffin. (Original work published 1897)

Pavlov, I. P. (1906). The scientific investigation of the psychical faculties or processes in the higher animals. *Science, 24,* 613–619.

Pavlov, I. P. (1928). *Lectures on conditioned reflexes: Twenty-five years of objective study of the higher nervous activity (behaviour) of animals* (W. H. Gantt, Trans.). New York: International Publishers. (Original work published 1923)

Pearlin, L. I., & Schooler, C. (1978). The structure of coping. *Journal of Health and Social Behavior, 19,* 2–21.

Pearson, R. (1998). *Physical anthropology.* New York: Scott-Townsend.

Pecchinenda, A., & Zoccolotti, P. (1993). Facial expressions as modulators of emotional experiences. *Rassegna di Psicologia, 10(3),* 55–75.

Pedalino, E., & Gamboa, V. U. (1974). Behavior modification and absenteeism: Intervention in one industrial setting. *Journal of Applied Psychology, 59,* 694–698.

Pedersen-Pietersen, L. (1997, January 12). You're sober at last: Now prove it to the boss. *New York Times,* p. F10.

Pederson, D.R., Gleason, K.E., Moran, G., & Bento, S. (1998). Maternal attachment representations, maternal sensitivity, and the infant-mother attachment relationship. *Developmental Psychology, 34,* 925–933.

Pederson, N. L., Plomin, R., McClearn, G. E., & Griberg, L. (1988). Neuroticism, extraversion, and related traits in adult twins reared apart and reared together. *Journal of Personality and Social Psychology, 55,* 950–957.

Pedrotti, F. L., & Pedrotti, L. S. (1997). *Optics and vision.* Englewood Cliffs, NJ: Prentice Hall.

Peigneux, P., Laureys, S., Fuchs, S., Collette, F., Perrin, F., Reggers, J., Phillips, C., Degueldre, C., Del Fiore, G., Aerts, J., Luxen, A. & Maquet, P. (2004). Are spatial memories strengthened in the human hippocampus during Slow Wave Sleep? *Neuron, 44,* 535–545.

Peigneux, P., Laureys, S., Fuchs, S., Destrebecqz, A., Collette, F., Delbeuck, X., Phillips, C., Aerts, J., Del Fiore, G., Degueldre, C., Luxen, A., Cleeremans, A. & Maquet, P. (2003). Learned material content and acquisition level modulate reactivation during post-training rapid-eye-movements sleep. *NeuroImage, 20,* 125–134.

Pelletier, D. L., & Frongillo, E. A. (2003). Changes in child survival are strongly associated with changes in malnutrition in developing countries. *Journal of Nutrition, 133,* 107–119.

Pellino, T. A., & Ward, S. E. (1998). Perceived control mediates the relationship between pain severity and patient satisfaction. *Journal of Pain and Symptom Management, 15,* 110–116.

Penfield, W., & Perot P. (1963). The brain's record of auditory and visual experience. *Brain, 86,* 595–696.

Pennebaker, J. W. (1995). *Emotion, disclosure and health.* Washington, DC: American Psychological Association.

Pennebaker, J. W. (1997). *Opening up: The healing power of expressing emotions.* New York: Guilford Press.

Pennington, B. F. & Olson, R. K. (2005). Genetics of dyslexia. In M. J. Snowling & C. Hulme (Eds.), *The Science of Reading: A Handbook.* Malden, MA: Blackwell Publishing. 453–472.

Peplau, L. A., Garnets, L. D., Spalding, L. R., Conley, T. D., & Veniegas, R. C. (1998). A critique of Bem's "Exotic Becomes Erotic" theory of sexual orientation. *Psychological Review, 105,* 387–394.

Pepler, D. J., & Craig, W. M. (1995). A peek behind the fence: Naturalistic observations of aggressive children with remote audiovisual recording. *Developmental Psychology, 31,* 548–553.

Pepler, D. J., Craig, W. M., Connolly, J. A., Yuile, A., McMaster, L., & Jiang, D. (2006). A developmental perspective on bullying. *Aggressive Behavior, 32,* 376–384.

Pepler, D., Craig, W., & O'Connell, P. (1999). Understanding bullying from a dynamic systems perspective. In A. Slater & D. Muir (Eds). *The Blackwell reader in developmental psychology* (pp. 440–451). Oxford: Blackwell.

Pepler, D.J., Craig, W.M., Ziegler, S., & Charach, A. (1993). A school-based antibullying intervention: Preliminary evaluation. In D. Tattum (Ed.), *Understanding and managing bullying* (pp. 76–91). Heinemann Books.

Perani, D., Colombo, C., Bressi, S., Bonfanti, A., Grassi, F., and S. Scarone et al. (1995). PET study in obsessive–compulsive disorder: A clinical metabolic correlation study after treatment. *British Journal of Psychiatry, 166*(2), 244–250.

Perani, D., Paulesu, E., Galles, N. S., Dupoux, E., & Dehaene, S. (1998). The bilingual brain: Proficiency and age of acquisition of the second language. *Brain, 121,* 1841–1852.

Perdue, C. W., Dovidio, J. F., Gurtman, M. B., & Tyler, R. B. (1990). Us and them: Social categorization and the process of intergroup bias. *Journal of Personality and Social Psychology, 59,* 475–486.

Perls, F. S. (1972). Gestalt therapy. In A. Bry (Ed.), *Inside psychotherapy.* New York: Basic Books.

Perna, F. M., Schneiderman, N., & LaPerriere, A. (1997). Psychological stress, exercise, and immunity. *International Journal of Sports Medicine, 18* (Suppl.), S78–S83.

Pernollet, J. C., Sanz, G., Briand, L. (2006). Olfactory receptors and odour coding. *Comptes Rendus Biologies, 329,* 679–690.

Pert, C. B. (1986). The wisdom of the receptors: Neuropeptides, the emotions, and bodymind. *Advances, 3,* 8–16.

Pert, C. B. (1997). *Molecules of emotion: Why you feel the way you feel.* New York: Simon & Schuster.

Peters, R., & McGee, R. (1982). Cigarette smoking and state-dependent memory. *Psychopharmacology, 76,* 232–235.

Peterson, A. C. (1987). The nature of biological-psychsocial interactions: The sample case of early adolescence. In R. M. Lerner & T. T. Foch (Eds.), *Biological-psychosocial interactions in early adolescence.* Hillsdale, NJ: Erlbaum.

Peterson, C., & Park, C. (1998). Learned helplessness and explanatory style. In D. F. Barone, M. Hersen, & V. B. Van Hasselt (Eds.), *Advanced personality.* New York: Plenum.

Peterson, L. R., & Peterson, M. J. (1959). Short term retention of individual verbal items. *Journal of Experimental Psychology, 58,* 193–198.

Peterson, C., & Seligman, M. E. P. (1987). Explanatory style and illness. *Journal of Personality, 55,* 237–265.

Petitto, J. M., Gariepy, J. L., Gendreau, P. L., Rodriguiz, R., Lewis, M. H., & Lysle, D. T. (1999). Differences in NK cell function in mice bred for high and low aggression: Genetic linkage between complex behavioral and immunological traits? *Brain, Behavior and Immunity, 13,* 175–186.

Petrinovich, L. F. (1999). *Darwinian dominion: Animal welfare and human interests.* Cambridge, MA.: MIT Press.

Petrovic, P., & Ingvar, M. (2002). Imaging cognitive modulation of pain processing. *Pain, 95,* 1–5.

Petrovic, P., Kalso, E., Petersson, M. K., & Ingvarm, M. (2002). Placebo and opioid analgesia: Imaging a shared neuronal network. *Science Express Reports,* 17–22.

Petryshen, T. L., Kaplan, B. J., Liu, M. F., de French, N. S., Tobias, R., Hughes, M. L., & Field, L. L. (2001). Evidence for a susceptibility locus on chromosome 6q influencing phonological coding dyslexia. *American Journal of Medical Genetics (Neuropsychiatric Genetics), 105,* 507–517.

Pettigrew, T. F. (1969). Racially separate or together? *Journal of Social Issues, 25,* 43–69.

Pettigrew, T. F. (1979). The ultimate attribution error: Extending Allport's cognitive analysis of prejudice. *Personality and Social Psychology Bulletin, 55,* 461–476.

Pettigrew, T. F. (1991). Normative theory in intergroup relations: Explaining bad harmony and conflict. *Psychology and Developing Societies, 3,* 3–16.

Pettigrew, T. F., & Meertens, R. W. (1995). Subtle and blatant prejudice in western Europe. *European Journal of Social Psychology, 25,* 57–76.

Pettigrew, T. F., & Tropp, L. R. (2000). Does intergroup contact reduce prejudice: Recent meta-analytic findings. In S. Oskamp (Ed.), *Reducing prejudice and discrimination. The Claremont Symposium on Applied Social Psychology.* Mahwah, NJ: Erlbaum.

Pettito, L. A. & Marentette, P. F. (1991). Babbling in the manual mode: Evidence for the ontogeny of language. *Science, 251,* 1493–1496.

Petty, R. E., & Cacioppo, J. T. (1986). *Communication and persuasion: Central and peripheral routes to attitude change.* New York: Springer-Verlag.

Petty, R. E., & Wegener, D. T. (1998). Attitude change: Multiple roles for persuasion variables. In D. T. Gilbert, S. T. Fiske, & G. Lindzey (Eds.), *The handbook of social psychology* (4th ed., Vol. 1). Boston: McGraw-Hill.

Petty, R. E., Fleming, M. A., Priester, J. R., & Feinstein, A. H. (2001). Individual versus group interest violation: Surprise as a determinant of argument scrutiny and persuasion. *Social Cognition, 19,* 418–442.

Pezdek, K. (2002). *Event memory and autobiographical memory for the events of September 11, 2001.* Manuscript submitted for publication.

Pfeffer, K., Cole, B., & Dada, M. K. (1998). Attributions for youth crime among British and Nigerian primary school children. *Journal of Social Psychology, 138,* 251–253.

Pfefferbaum, B., Nixon, S, Tivis, R., Doughty, D., Pynoos, R., Gurwitch, R., & Foy, D. (2001). Television exposure in children after a terrorist incident. *Psychiatry: Interpersonal and Biological Processes,* 64(3): 202–211.

Pfeifer, M., Goldsmith, H. H., Davidson, R. J., & Rickman, M. (2002). Continuity and change in inhibited and uninhibited children. *Child Development, 73,* 1474–1485.

Phares, E. J. (1992). *Clinical psychology: Concepts, methods, and profession.* Pacific Grove, CA: Brooks/Cole.

Phelps, E. A., O'Connor, K. J., Cunningham, W. A. et al. (2000). Performance on indirect measures of race evaluation predicts amygdala activation. *Journal of Cognitive Neuroscience, 12,* 5729–5738.

Phelps, E. A., O'Connor, K. J., Gatenby, C., Gore, J. C., Grillon, C., & Davis, M. (2001). Activation of the left amygdala to a cognitive representation of fear. *Nature Neuroscience, 4,* 437–441.

Phillips, A. G., Blaha, C. D., Pfaus, J. G., & Blackburn, J. R. (1992). Neurobiological correlates of positive emotional states: Dopamine, anticipation and reward. In Strongman, Ken T. (Ed). *International review of studies on emotion,* Vol. 2. (31–50). New York: John Wiley & Sons.

Phillips, L. H., Kriegiel, M., Martin, M. (2006). Age and planning tasks: The influence of ecological validity. *International Journal of Aging and Human Development, 62(2),* 175–184.

Phillips, M. (2007). The emerging role of neuroimaging in psychiatry: Characterizing treatment-relevant endophenotypes. *American Journal of Psychiatry, 164,* 697–699.

Phillips, M., Brooks, G. J., Duncan, G. J., Klebanov, P., & Crane, J. (1998). Family background, parenting practices, and the Black-White test score gap. In C. Jencks & M. Phillips (Eds.), *The Black-White test score gap.* Washington, DC: Brookings Institution.

Piaget, J. (1926). *The language and thought of the child.* New York: Meridian Books.

Piaget, J. (1932). *The moral judgement of the child.* New York: Harcourt Brace.

Piaget, J. (1970). Piaget's theory. In P. H. Mussen (Ed.), *Carmichael's manual of child psychology* (Vol.1). New York: Wiley.

Piaget, J. (1977). *The development of thought: Equilibration of cognitive structure.* New York: Viking.

Piaget, J., & Inhelder, B. (1956). *The child's conception of space.* London: Routledge & Kegan Paul.

Piccione, C., Hilgard, E. R., & Zimbardo, P. G. (1989). On the degree of measured hypnotizability over a 25-year period. *Journal of Personality and Social Psychology, 56,* 289–295.

Pickering, A. D., & Gray, J. A. (1999). The neuroscience of personality. In L. A. Pervin & O. P. John (Eds.), *Handbook of personality: Theory and research.* New York: Guilford Press.

Pickrell, J. E., Bernstein, D., & Loftus, E. F. (2003). The misinformation effect. In R. Pohl (Ed.), *Cognitive illusions: Fallacies and biases in thinking, judgment, and memory.* London: Psychology Press.

Pierce, G. R., Sarason, B. R., & Sarason, I. G. (1996). *Cognitive interference: Theories, methods, and findings.* Mahwah, NJ: Erlbaum.

Pierce, W. D., & Epling, W. F. (1999). *Behavior analysis and learning* (2nd ed.). Englewood Cliffs, NJ: Prentice-Hall.

Pies, R. W. (2005). *Handbook of essential psychopharmacology (*2nd ed.). Washington, DC: American Psychiatric Press.

Pilbeam, D. (1984). The descent of hominoids and hominids. *Scientific American, 250,* 84–87.

Pilcher, J. J., & Huffcutt, A. J. (1996). Effects of sleep deprivation on performance: A meta-analysis. *Sleep, 19,* 318–326.

Pilcher, J. J., & Walters, A. S. (1997). How sleep deprivation affects psychological variables related to college students' cognitive performance. *Journal of American College Health, 46,* 121–126.

Pilla, M., Perachon, S., Sautel, F., Garrido, F., Mann, A., Wermuth, C. G., Schwartz, J. C., Everitt, B. J., & Sokoloff, P. (1999). Selective inhibition of cocaine-seeking behaviour by a partial dopamine D3 receptor agonist. *Nature, 400,* 371–375.

Pina, P. (1995, December 5). No rest for many weary Americans. *USA Today,* p. D5.

Pinel, J. P. J. (1997). *Biopsychology.* Boston: Allyn & Bacon.

Pinel, J. P., Assanand, S., & Lehman, D. R. (2000). Hunger, eating and ill health. *American Psychologist, 55,* 1105–1116.

Pinker, S. (2000). *Words and rules: The ingredients of language.* New York: Basic Books.

Piper, A., Merskey, H. (2004a). The persistence of folly: a critical examination of Dissociative Identity Disorder. Part I: The excesses of an improbable concept. *Canadian Journal of Psychiatry, 49*(9), 592–600.

Piper, A., Merskey, H. (2004b). The persistence of folly: a critical examination of Dissociative Identity Disorder. Part II: The defence and decline of multiple personality or dissociative identitity disorder. *Canadian Journal of Psychiatry, 49*(10), 678–683.

Pisklakova, M. (1992, Spring). Another perspective on domestic violence. *You and We: The Women's Dialogue,* 22.

Pitman, R. K., Shalev, A. Y., & Orr, S. P. (2000). Posttraumatic stress disorder: Emotion, conditioning, and memory. In M. S. Gazzaniga (Ed.), *The new cognitive neurosciences* (2nd ed.). Cambridge, MA: MIT Press.

Pittenger, D. J. (2003). Internet research: An opportunity to revisit classic ethical problems in behavioral research. *Ethics & Behavior, 13,* 45–60.

Pitz, G. F., & Sachs, N. J. (1984). Judgment and decision: Theory and application. *Annual Review of Psychology, 35,* 139–163.

Plaud, J. J., & Plaud, D. M. (1998). Clinical behavior therapy and the experimental analysis of behavior. *Journal of Clinical Psychology, 54,* 905–921.

Pliner, P., Hart, H., Kohl, J., & Saari, D. (1974). Compliance without pressure: Some further data on the foot-in-the-door technique. *Journal of Experimental Social Psychology, 10,* 17–22.

Plomin, R. (1997). *Behavioral genetics.* New York: St. Martins Press.

Plomin, R. (2004). *Nature And Nurture: An Introduction To Human Behavioral Genetics.* London: Wadsworth Publishing Company.

Plomin, R., Asbury, K., & Dunn, J. (2001). Why are children in the same family so different? Nonshared environment a decade later. *Canadian Journal of Psychiatry, 46,* 225–233.

Plomin, R., & Caspi, A. (1999). Behavior genetics and personality. In L. A. Pervin & O. P. John (Eds.), *Handbook of personality: Theory and research* (2nd ed.). New York: Guilford Press.

Plomin, R., & Rende, R. (1991). Human behavioral genetics. *Annual Review of Psychology, 42,* 161–190.

Plomin, R., De Fries, J. C., & McClearn, G. E. (1990). *Behavior genetics: A primer* (2nd ed.). New York: W. H. Freeman.

Plomin, R., Emde, R. N., Braungart, J. M., & Campos, J. (1993). Genetic change and continuity from fourteen to twenty months: The MacArthur Longitudinal Twin Study. *Child Development, 64,* 1354–1376.

Plous, S. (1996a). Attitudes toward the use of animals in psychological research and education: Results from a national survey of psychologists. *American Psychologist, 51,* 1167–1180.

Plous, S. & Herzog, H. A. (2000). Poll shows researchers favor lab animal protection. *Science,* 290, 711.

Plumert, J. M., & Nichols, W. P. (1996). Parental scaffolding of young children's spatial communication. *Developmental Psychology, 32,* 523–532.

Plutchik, R. (1994). *Psychology of emotion.* Reading, MA: Addison-Wesley.

Polivy, J., & Herman, C. P. (1992). Undieting: A program to help people stop dieting. *International Journal of Eating Disorders, 11,* 261–268.

Pollak, C. P. (1991). The effects of noise on sleep. In T. Fay (Ed.), *Noise and health.* New York: New York Academy of Medicine.

Pollner, M. (1989). Divine relations, social relations, and well-being. *Journal of Health and Social Behavior, 30,* 92–104.

Polster, E., & Polster, M. (1973). *Gestalt therapy integrated: Contours of theory and practice.* New York: Brunner/Mazel.

Pool, G. J., Wood, W., & Leck, K. (1998). The self-esteem motive in social influence: Agreement with valued majorities and disagreement with derogated minorities. *Journal of Personality and Social Psychology, 75,* 967–975.

Pool, R. (1994). *The dynamic brain.* Washington, DC: National Academy Press.

Porkka, H. T., Strecker, R. E., Thakkar, M., & Bjorkun, A. A. (1997). Adenosine: A mediator of the sleep-inducing effects of prolonged wakefulness. *Science, 276,* 1265–1267.

Porter, N. P., & Geis, F. L. (1981). Women and nonverbal leadership cues: When seeing is not believing. In C. Mayo & N. M. Henley (Eds.), *Gender and nonverbal behavior.* New York: Springer-Verlag.

Porter, R. H., & Winberg, J. (1999). Unique salience of maternal breast odors for newborn infants. *Neuroscience and Biobehavioral Reviews, 23,* 439–449.

Post, J (2001). Transcript of the United States versus Usama Bin Laden, et al., United States District Court, New York, N.Y. June 27.

Posthuma, D., Mulder, E. J. C. M., Boomsma, D. I., de Geus, E. J. C. (2002). Genetic analysis of IQ, processing speed and stimulus response in congruency effects. *Biological Psychology, 61*(1-2), 157–182.

Posthuma, D., Neale, M. C., Boomsma, D. I., & de Geus, E. J. C. (2001). Are smarter brains running faster? Heritability of alpha peak frequency, IQ, and their interrelation. *Behavior Genetics, 31,* 567–579.

Postman, L., & Phillips, L. W. (1965). Short-term temporal changes in free recall. *Quarterly Journal of Experimental Psychology, 17,* 132–138.

Postman, L., & Underwood, B. J. (1973). Critical issues in interference theory. *Memory and Cognition, 1,* 19–40.

Postmes, T., & Spears, R. (1998). Deindividuation and antinormative behavior: A meta-analysis. *Psychological Bulletin, 123,* 238–259.

Potter, S.M., Zelazo, P.R., Stack, D.M., & Papgeorgiou, A.N. (2000). Adverse effects of fetal cocaine exposure on neonatal auditory information processing. *Pediatrics, 105, #3.*

Powell, M. C., & Fazio, R. M. (1984). Attitude accessibility as a function of repeated attitudinal expression. *Personality and Social Psychology Bulletin, 10,* 139–148.

Powell, R. W., & Curley, M. (1976). Instinctive drift in nondomesticated rodents. *Bulletin of the Psychonomic Society, 8,* 175–178.

Powley, T. L., & Kessey, R. E. (1970). Relationship of body weight to the lateral hypothalamic feeding syndrome. *Journal of Comparative and Physiological Psychology, 70,* 25–36.

Pratkanis, A. R., Eskenazi, J., & Greenwald, A. G. (1994). What you expect is what you believe (but not necessarily what you get): A test of the effectiveness of subliminal self-help audiotapes. *Basic and Applied Social Psychology, 15,* 251–276.

Pressley, M., Snyder, B. L., Levin, J. R., Murray, H. G., & Ghatala, E. S. (1987). Perceived readiness for examination performance (PREP) produced by initial reading of text and text containing adjunct questions. *Reading Research Quarterly, 22,* 219–236.

Pressman, J. D. (1998). *Last resort: Psychosurgery and the limits of medicine.* New York: Cambridge University Press.

Pressman, S. D. & Cohen, S. (2005). Does positive affect influence heath? *Psychological Bulletin, 131,* 925-971.

Preti, G., Cutler, W. B., Garcia, G. R., Huggins, G. R. & Lawley, J. J. (1986). Human axillary secretions influences women's menstrual cycles: The role of donor extract from females. *Hormones and Behavior, 20,* 473–480.

Price, C. J. & McCrory, E. (2005). Functional brain imaging studies of skilled reading and developmental dyslexia. In. M. J. Snowling & C. Hulme (Eds.), *The Science of Reading: A Handbook.* Malden, MA: Blackwell Publishing. 473–496.

Price, R. A., Charles, M. A., Pettitt, D. J., & Knowler, W. C. (1993). Obesity in Pima Indians: Large increases among post–World War II birth cohorts. *American Journal of Physical Anthropology, 92,* 473–479.

Prigerson, H., Maciejewski, P. K, & Rosenheck, R. A. (2002). Population attributable fractions of psychiatric disorders and behavioral outcomes associated with combat exposure among U.S. men. *American Journal of Public Health, 92*(1), 59–63.

Prilleltensky, I. (1997). Values, assumptions, and practices: Assessing the moral implications of psychological discourse and action. *American Psychologist, 52,* 517–535.

Pritchard, R. D., Hollenback, J., & DeLeo, P. J. (1980). The effects of continuous and partial schedules of reinforcement on effort, performance, and satisfaction. *Organizational Behavior and Human Decision Processes, 25,* 336–353.

Pritchard, R. M. (1961, June). Stabilized images on the retina. *Scientific American,* 72–78.

Probst, L. R., Ostrom, R., Watkins, P., Dean, T., & Mashburn, D. (1992). Comparative efficacy of religious and non-religious cognitive-behavioral therapy for the treatment of clinical depression in religious individuals. *Journal of Consulting and Clinical Psychology, 60,* 94–103.

Prochaska, J. O., Johnson, S., & Lee, P. (1998). The transtheoretical model of behavior change. In S. A. Shumaker & E. B. Schron (Eds.), *The handbook of health behavior change* (2nd ed.). New York: Springer.

Prochaska, J. O., Norcross, J. C., & DiClemente, C. C. (1994). *Changing for good.* New York: Avon Books.

Project MATCH Research Group (1997). Matching alcoholism treatments to client heterogeneity: Project MATCH posttreatment drinking outcomes. *Journal of Studies on Alcohol, 58,* 7–29.

Prout, P. I., & Dobson, K. S. (1998). Recovered memories of childhood sexual abuse: Searching for the middle ground in clinical practice. *Canadian Psychology, 39,* 257–265.

Psychological Perspectives in Unger, R. (Ed), *Terrorism and Its Consequences. Analysis of Social Issues and Public Policy, Society for the Psychological Study of Social Issues,* Blackwell Publishers. [Online]. Available: http://www.asap-spssi.org/default.htm

Ptacek, J. T., Smith, R. E., & Zanas, J. (1992). Gender, appraisal, and coping: A longitudinal analysis. *Journal of Personality, 60,* 747–770.

Pugh, G. E. (1977). *The biological origin of human values.* New York: Basic Books.

Punamaki, R. L., & Joustie, M. (1998). The role of culture, violence, and personal factors affecting dream content. *Journal of Cross-Cultural Psychology, 29,* 320–342.

Putnam, F. W. (1984). The psychophysiologic investigation of multiple personality disorder: A review. *Psychiatric Clinics of North America, 7,* 31–39.

Putnam, F. W. (1989). *Diagnosis and treatment of multiple personality disorder.* New York: Guilford Press.

Putnam, F. W. (1991). Recent research on multiple personality disorder. *Psychiatric Clinics of North America, 14*(3), 489–502.

Putnam, F. W. (1993). Diagnosis and clinical phenomenology of multiple personality disorder: A North American perspective. *Dissociation: Progress in the Dissociative Disorders, 6*(2–3), 80–86.

Putnam, F. W. (1998). *Dissociation in children and adolescents: A developmental perspective.* New York: Guilford Press.

Pyszczynski, T., & Greenberg, J. (1987). Toward an integration of cognitive and motivational perspectives on social inference: A biased hypothesis-testing model. In L. Berkowitz (Ed.), *Advances in experimental social psychology* (Vol. 20). Orlando, FL: Academic Press.

Pyszczynski, T., Hamilton, J. C., Greenberg, J., & Bekker, S. E. (1991). Self-awareness and psychological dysfunction. In C. R. Snyder & D. O. Forsyth (Eds.), *Handbook of social and clinical psychology: The health perspective.* New York: Pergamon.

Quera-Salva, M. A., Guillenminault, C., Claustrat, B. & Defrance, A., et al. (1997). Rapid shift in peak melatonin secretion associated with improved performance in short shift work schedule. *Sleep, 20,* 1145–1150.

Quinn, P. C. & Bhatt, R. S. Are some gestalt principles deployed more readily than others during early development? The case of lightness versus form similarity. *Journal of Experimental Psychology: Human Perception and Performance, 32,* 1221–1230.

Quinn, P.C., Brown, C.R., & Streppa, M.L. (1997). Perceptual organization of complex visual configurations by young infants. *Infant Behavior and Development, 20,* 35–46.

Quinsey, V. L., Maguire, A., & Varney, G. W. (1983). Assertion and overcontrolled hostility among mentally disordered murderers. *Journal of Consulting and Clinical Psychology, 51,* 550–566.

Quintero, N. (1980, February). Coming of age the Apache way. *National Geographic, 157* (2), 262–271. Rachlin, H. (1995). *Introduction to modern behaviorism.* New York: W. H. Freeman.

Rachman, S. (1998). *Anxiety.* Mahwah, NJ: Erlbaum.

Rachman, S. (2000). Joseph Wolpe: Obituary. *American Psychologist, 55,* 431–432.

Rachman, S. J., & Hodgson, R. J. (1980). *Obsessions and compulsions.* Englewood Cliffs, NJ: Prentice Hall.

Rachman, S., Hodgson, R. J. (1968). Experimentally-induced "sexual fetishism": Replication and development. *Psychological Record, 18,* 25–27.

Rachman, S.J. (1991). Neo-conditioning and the classical theory of fear acquisition. *Clinical psychology Review, 11,* 155–173.

Rachman, S.J., Hodgson, R., Marks, I.M. (1997). The treatment of chronic obsessive-compulsive disorder. In D. J. Stein & M.H. Stone (Eds.), *Essential papers on obsessive-compulsive disorder.* New York, New York: New York University press.

Rahe, R. (2000). Acute reactions to combat. In G. Fink (Ed.), *Encyclopedia of stress.* San Diego: Academic Press.

Raichle, M. E. (1994). Images of the mind: Studies with modern imaging techniques. *Annual Review of Psychology, 45,* 333–356.

Rail, T. W. (1980). Central nervous system stimulants: The xanthines. In A. G. Gilman, L. Goodman, & A. Gilman (Eds.), *The pharmacological basis of therapeutics.* New York: Macmillan.

Raine, A., Buchsbaum, M., & LaCasse, L. (1997). Brain abnormalities in murderers indicated by positron tomography. *Biological Psychiatry, 42,* 495–508.

Raine, A., Lencz, T., Bihrle, S., LaCasse, L., & Colletti, P. (2000). Reduced prefrontal gray matter volume and reduced autonomic activity in antisocial personality disorder. *Archives of General Psychiatry, 57,* 119–127.

Raine, A., Lencz, T., Taylor, K., Hellige, J. B., Bihrle, S., Lacarre, L., Lee, M., Ishikawa, S., Colletti, P. (2003). Corpus callosum abnormalities in psychopathic antisocial individuals. *Archives of General Psychiatry, 60*(11), 1134–1142.

Raine, A., Meloy, J. R., Bihrle, S., Stoddard, J., LaCasse, L., & Buchsbaum, M. S. (1998). Reduced prefrontal and increased subcortical brain functioning assessed using positron emission tomography in predatory and affective murderers. *Behavioral Sciences and the Law, 16,* 319–332.

Raine, A., Venables, P. H., & Williams, M. (1996). Better autonomic conditioning and faster electrodermal half-recovery time at age 15 years as possible protective factors against crime at age 29 years. *Developmental Psychology, 32,* 624–630.

Rakfeldt, J., Rybash, J. M., & Roodin, P. A. (1996). Affirmative coping: A marker of success in adult therapeutic intervention. In M. L. Commons, J. Demick, & C. Goldberg (Eds.), *Clinical approaches to adult development.* Norwood, NJ: Ablex.

Rakic, P. (1995). Corticogenesis in human and nonhuman primates. In M. S. Gazzaniga (Ed.), *The cognitive neurosciences.* Cambridge, MA: MIT Press.

Rakic, P. (2002). Neurogenesis in adult primate neocortex: An evaluation of the evidence. *National Review of Neuroscience, 3*(1), 65–71.

Rako, S., Friebely, J. (2004). Pheromonal Influences on Sociosexual Behavior in Postmenopausal Women. *Journal of Sex Research, 41,* 372–380.

Ralph, M. R., Foster, R. G., Davis, F. C., & Menaker, M. (1990). Transplanted suprachiasmatic nucleus determines circadian period. *Science, 247,* 975–978.

Ralph, M. R., Joyner, A. L., & Lehman, M. N. (1993). Culture and transplantation of the mammalian circadian pacemaker. *Journal of Biological Rhythms, 8*(Suppl), S83-S87.

Ramirez, J. C., & Uribe, G. (1993). Mujer y violencia: Un hecho cotidiano [Women and violence: A daily occurrence]. *Salud Publica de Mexico, 35,* 148–160.

Raphling, D. L. (1998). Aggression: Its relation to desire and self-interest. *Journal of the American Psychoanalytic Association, 46,* 797–811.

Rapoport, J.L. (1991). Recent advances in obsessive–compulsive disorder, *Neuropsychopharmacology 5,* 1–10.

Rasenberger, J. (2004, February 8). Kitty: 40 years later. *The New York Times,* 14, p. 1.

Rasmussen, A. M., & Charney, D. S. (2000). Posttraumatic therapy. In G. Fink (Ed.), *Encyclopedia of stress.* San Diego: Academic Press.

Rauch, S. L., Shin, L. M., & Phelps, E. A. (2006). Neurocircuitry models of posttraumatic stress disorder and extinction: Human neuroimaging research—past, present, and future. *Biological Psychiatry, 60,* 376–382.

Rauch, S. L., van der Kolk, B. A., Fisler, R. E., Alpert, N. M., Orr, S. P., Savage, C. R., et al (1996). A symptom provocation study of posttraumatic stress disorder using positron emission tomography and script-driven imagery. *Archives of General Psychiatry, 53,* 380–387.

Rauch, S. L., Whalen, P. J., Shin, L. M., McInerney, S., Macklin, M. L., Lasko, N. B, et al. (2000). Exaggerated amygdala responses to masked facial stimuli in posttraumatic stress disorder: A functional MRI study. *Biological Psychiatry, 47,* 769–776.

Rauscher, F.H., Shaw, G.L., & Ky, K.N. (1993). Music and spatial task performance. *Nature, 365,* 611.

Raven, B. H. (1998). Groupthink, Bay of Pigs, and Watergate reconsidered. *Organizational Behavior and Human Decision Processes, 73,* 352–361.

Ravussin, E., & Gautier, J. F. (1999). Metabolic predictors of weight gain. *International Journal of Obesity and Related Metabolic Disorders, 23* (Suppl 1), 37–41.

Ravussin, E., Valencia, M. E., Esparza, J., Bennett, P. H., & Schulz, L. O. (1994). Effects of a traditional lifestyle on obesity in Pima Indians. *Diabetes Care, 17,* 1067–1074.

Ray, O. S. (1983). *Drugs, society, and human behavior* (3rd ed.). St. Louis: Mosby.

Ray, O. S., & Ksir, C. (1987). *Drugs, society and human behavior* (4th ed.). St. Louis: Mosby.

Ray, W. J. (2000). *Methods: Toward a science of behavior and experience* (6th ed.). Belmont, CA: Wadsworth.

Read, M. S. (1982). Malnutrition and behavior. *Applied Research in Mental Retardation, 3,* 279–291.

Rechtschaffen, A., Bergmann, B. M., Gilliland, M. A., & Bauer, K. (1999). Effects of method, duration, and sleep stage on rebounds from sleep deprivation in the rat. *Sleep, 22,* 11–31.

Redelmeier, D. A., & Tibshirani, R. J. (1997). Association between cellular telephone calls and motor vehicle collisions. *New England Journal of Medicine, 336,* 453–458.

Reeve, J. (1992). *Understanding motivation and emotion.* Ft. Worth, TX: Harcourt Brace Jovanovich.

Regan, D. T., & Fazio, R. (1977). On the consistency between attitudes and behavior: Look to the method of attitude formation. *Journal of Experimental Social Psychology, 13,* 28–45.

Regan, D. T., Williams, M., & Sparling, S. (1972). Voluntary expiation of guilt: A field experiment. *Journal of Personality and Social Psychology, 24,* 42–45.

Reichl, A. J. (1997). Ingroup favouritism and outgroup favouritism in low status minimal groups: Differential responses to status-related and status-unrelated measures. *European Journal of Social Psychology, 27,* 617–633.

Reid, A. K., & Staddon, J. E. F. (1998). A dynamic route finder for the cognitive map. *Psychological Review, 105,* 585–601.

Reifman, A.,Villa, L. C., Amans, J. A., Rethinam, V., & Telesca, T. Y. (2001). Children of divorce in the 1990s: A meta-analysis. *Journal of Divorce and Remarriage, 36,* 27–36.

Reisberg, D. (1997). *Cognition: Exploring the science of the mind.* New York: W. W. Norton.

Reiss, A. J., Jr., & Roth, J. A. (Eds.) (1993). *Understanding and preventing violence: Vol III. Social influences.* Washington, DC: National Academy Press.

Reiss, M., & Straughan, R. (1998). *Improving nature?: The science and ethics of genetic engineering.* New York: Cambridge University Press.

Reitzes, D. C., Mutran, E. J., & Fernandez, M. E. (1998). The decision to retire: A career perspective. *Social Science Quarterly, 79,* 607–619.

Remland, M. S., Jones, T. S., & Brinkman, H. (1995). Interpersonal distance, body orientation, and touch: Effects of culture, gender, and age. *Journal of Social Psychology, 135,* 281–297.

Rendell, P. G., & Thomson, D. M. (1993). The effect of ageing on remembering to remember: An investigation of simulated medication regimens. *Australian Journal on Ageing, 12,* 11–18.

Rendell, P. G., & Thomson, D. M. (1999). Aging and prospective memory: Differences between naturalistic and laboratory tasks. *Journals of Gerontology: Series B: Psychological Sciences and Social Sciences, 54B(4),* 256–269.

Renzulli, J. S. (1986). The three-ring conception of intelligence: A developmental model for creative productivity. In R. J. Sternberg & J. E. Davidson (Eds.), *Conceptions of giftedness.* Cambridge, England: Cambridge University Press.

Repous, G., Baddlely, A. (2006). The multicomponent model of working memory: Explorations in experimental cognitive psychology. *Neuroscience, 139*(1), 5–21.

Reschly, D. J., & Robinson-Zanurtu, C. (2000). Evaluation of aptitudes. In G. Goldstein & M. Hersen (Eds.), *Handbook of psychological assessment* (3rd ed.). New York: Elsevier.

Rescorla, R. A. (1968). Probability of shock in the presence and absence of CS in fear. *Journal of Comparative and Physiological Psychology, 66,* 1–5.

Rescorla, R. A. (1988). Pavlovian conditioning: It's not what you think it is. *American Psychologist, 43,* 151–160.

Rescorla, R. A., & Solomon, R. L. (1967). Two-process learning theory: Relationships between pavlovian conditioning and instrumental learning. *Psychological Review, 74,* 151–182.

Rescorla, R. A., & Wagner, A. R. (1972). A theory of Pavlovian conditioning: Variations in the effectiveness of reinforcement and nonreinforcement. In A. H. Black & W. F. Prokasky (Eds.), *Classical conditioning: II. Current research and theory.* New York: Appleton-Century-Crofts.

Rey, J. M., & Walter, G. (1997). Half a century of ECT use in young people. *American Journal of Psychiatry, 154,* 595–602.

Reznick, J. S., Gibbons, J., Johnson, M. O., & McDonough, P. (1992). Behavioral inhibition in a normative sample. In J. S. Reznick (Ed.), *Perspectives in behavioral inhibition.* Chicago: University of Chicago Press.

Rhee, S. H. & Waldman, I. D. (2002). Genetic and environmental influences on antisocial behavior: A meta-analysis of twin and adoption studies. *Psychological Bulletin, 128,* 490–529.

Rice, M. E. (1997). Violent offender research and implications for the criminal justice system. *American Psychologist, 52,* 414–423.

Rice, M. E., Harris, G. T., & Cormier, C. A. (1992). An evaluation of a maximum security therapeutic community for psychopaths and other mentally disordered offenders. *Law and Human Behavior, 16,* 399–412.

Rich, A. N., Bradshaw, J. L., Mattingley, J. B. (2005). A systematic, large-scale study of synaesthesia: Implications for the role of early experience in lexical-colour associations. *Cognition, 98:* 53–84.

Richard, S., Davies, D. C., & Faure, J. M. (2000). The role of fear in one-trial passive avoidance learning in Japanese quail chicks genetically selected for long or short duration of the tonic immobility reaction. *Behavioural Processes, 48,* 165–170.

Richards, H. C., Bear, G. G., Stewart, A. L., & Norman, A. D. (1992). Moral reasoning and classroom conduct: Evidence of a curvilinear relationship. *Merrill Palmer Quarterly, 38,* 176–190.

Richardson, D. P., Byrnes, M. L., Brien, J. F., Reynolds, J. N., and Dringenberg, H. C. (2001) Impaired water maze acquisition and hippocampal long-term potentiation after chronic prenatal ethanol exposure in the guinea pig. 31st Annual Meeting of the Society for Neuroscience, *Society for Neuroscience Abstracts,* in press.

Richardson, D. R. (1991). Interpersonal attraction and love. In R. M. Baron, W. G. Graziano, & C. Stangor (Eds.), *Social psychology.* Ft. Worth, TX: Holt, Rinehart & Winston.

Riefer, D. M., Keveri, M. K., & Kramer, D. L. F. (1995). Name that tune: Eliciting the tip-of-the-tongue experience using auditory stimuli. *Psychological Reports, 77,* 1379–1390.

Riesen, A. R. (1965). Effects of early deprivation of photic stimulation. In S. Oster & R. Cooke (Eds.), *The biosocial basis of mental retardation.* Baltimore, MD: The Johns Hopkins University Press.

Rilling, M. (1996). The mystery of the vanished citations: James McConnell's forgotten 1960s quest for planarian learning, a biochemical engram, and celebrity. *American Psychologist, 51,* 589–598.

Rips, L. J. (1994). *The psychology of proof: Deductive reasoning in human thinking.* Cambridge, MA: MIT Press.

Rips, L. J. (1997). Goals for a theory of deduction: Reply to Johnson-Laird. *Minds & Machines, 7,* 409–424.

Risold, P.Y., Thompson, R.H., Swanson, L.W., (1997). The structural organization of connections between hypothalamus and cerebral cortex. *Brain Research Reviews, 24,* 197–254.

Ritblatt, S. N. (2000). Children's level of participation in a false-belief task, age, and theory of mind. *Journal of Genetic Psychology, 161,* 53–64.

Ritskes, R., Ritskes-Hoitinga, M., Stodkilde-Jorgensen, H., Baerentsen, K., & Hartman, T. (2003). MRI scanning during Zen meditation: The picture of enlightenment? *Constructivism in the Human Sciences, 8,* 85–90.

Rivera Tovar, L. A., & Jones, R. T. (1990). Effect of elaboration on the acquisition and maintenance of cardiopulmonary resuscitation. *Journal of Pediatric Psychology, 15,* 123–138.

Rizzo, A., & Kim, G.J. (2005). A SWOT analysis of the field of virtual reality rehabilitation and therapy. *Presence: Teleoperators and Virtual Environments, 14*(2), 99–146.

Robbe, H. (1998). Marijuana's impairing effects on driving are moderate when taken alone but severe when combined with alcohol. *Human Psychopharmacology Clinical and Experimental, 13* (Suppl. 2), S70–S78.

Robers, P. J., & Blundell, J. E. (1984). Meal patterns and food selections during the development of obesity in rats fed a cafeteria diet. *Neuroscience and Biobehavioral Reviews, 8,* 441–453.

Robins, L. N. (1966). *Deviant children grow up.* Baltimore: Williams & Wilkins.

Robins, L. N., & Regier, D. A. (Eds.) (1991). *Psychiatric disorders in America: The Epidemiological Catchment Area Study.* New York: Free Press.

Robins, R. W., Gosling, S. D, & Craik, K. H. (1999). An empirical analysis of trends in psychology. *American Psychologist, 54,* 117–128.

Robins, R. W., Norem, J. K., & Cheek, J. M. (1999). Naturalizing the self. In L. A. Pervin & O. P. John (Eds.), *Handbook of personality: Theory and research.* New York: Guilford Press.

Robinson, D. (1997). *Neurobiology.* New York: Springer-Verlag.

Robinson, D., Wu, H., Munne, R., Ashtari, M., Alvir, J. J., Lerner, G., et al. (1995). Reduced caudate nucleus volume in obsessive-compulsive disorder. *Archives of General Psychiatry, 52*(5), 393–398.

Robitaille, R. (1998). Modulation of synaptic efficacy and synaptic depression by glial cells at the frog neuromuscular junction. *Neuron, 21,* 847–855.

Roche, A. F. (1979). Secular trends in human growth, maturation, and development. *Monographs of the Society for Research and Child Development, 44* (3–4, Serial No. 179).

Rodgers, J. E. (1982). The malleable memory of eyewitnesses. *Science Digest, 3,* 32–35.

Rodgers, R., & Hunter, J. E. (1991). Impact of management by objectives on organizational productivity. *Journal of Applied Psychology, 76,* 322–336.

Rodin, J. (1978). Has the distinction between internal versus external control of feeding outlived its usefulness? In G. A. Bray (Ed.), *Recent advances in obesity research* (Vol. 2). London: Newman.

Rodin, J. (1981). Current status of the internal-external hypothesis for obesity: What went wrong? *American Psychologist,* 36: 361–372.

Rodin, J., & Salovey, P. (1989). Health psychology. *Annual Review of Psychology, 40,* 533–579.

Rodin, J., Bartoshuk, L., Peterson, C., & Schank, D. (1990). Bulimia and taste: Possible interactions. *Journal of Abnormal Psychology, 99,* 32–39.

Rodin, J., Wack, J., Ferrannini, E., & Defronzo, R. A. (1985). Effect of insulin and glucose on feeding behavior. *Metabolism,* 34: 826–831.

Roediger, H. L. (1980). The effectiveness of four mnemonics in ordering recall. *Journal of Experimental Psychology: Human Learning and Memory, 6,* 558–567.

Roelofs, K., Hoogduin, K. A. L., Keijsers, G. P. J., Naering, G. W. B, Moene, F. C., & Sandijck, P. (2002). Hypnotic susceptibility in patients with conversion disorder. *Journal of Abnormal Psychology, 111,* 390–395.

Rogers, C. R. (1951). *Client-centered therapy.* Boston: Houghton Mifflin.

Rogers, C. R. (1959). A theory of therapy, personality and interpersonal relationships, as developed in the client-centered framework. In S. Koch (Ed.), *Psychology: A study of a science* (Vol. 3). New York: McGraw-Hill.

Rogers, C. R. (1961). *On becoming a person: A therapist's view of psychotherapy.* Boston: Houghton Mifflin.

Rogers, C. R. (1980). *A way of being.* Boston: Houghton Mifflin.

Rogers, C. R. (Ed.) (1967). *The therapeutic relationship and its impact: A study of psychotherapy with schizophrenics.* Madison, WI: University of Wisconsin Press.

Rogers, C. R., & Dymond, R. F. (1954). *Psychotherapy and personality change: Coordinated studies in the client-centered approach.* Chicago: University of Chicago Press.

Rogers, E. J., Vaughan, P. W., Swalahe, R. M. A., Rao, N., & Sood, S. (1996). *Effects of an entertainment-education radio soap opera on family planning and HIV/AIDS prevention behavior in Tanzania.* Unpublished manuscript, Department of Communication and Journalism, University of New Mexico at Albuquerque.

Rogers, P. J., & Blundell, J. E. (1984). Meal patterns and food selections during the development of obesity in rats fed a cafeteria diet. *Neuroscience and Biobehavioral Reviews, 8,* 441–453.

Rogers, R. W. (1983). Cognitive and psychological processes in fear appeals and attitude change: A revised theory of protection motivation. In J. Cacioppo & R. Petty (Eds.), *Social psychophysiology: A sourcebook.* New York: Guilford Press.

Rohrer, J. H., Baron, S. H., Hoffman, E. L., & Swander, D. V. (1954). The stability of autokinetic judgments. *Journal of Abnormal and Social Psychology, 49,* 595–597.

Rohsenow, D. J., & Marlatt, G. A. (1981). The balanced placebo design: Methodological considerations. *Addictive Behaviors, 6,* 107–122.

Rohsenow, D. J., & Smith, R. E. (1985). Stress management training as a prevention program for heavy social drinkers: Cognitions, affect, drinking, and individual differences. *Addictive Behaviors, 10,* 45–54.

Roitblat, H. L., & von Ferson, L. (1992). Comparative cognition: Representations and processes in learning and memory. *Annual Review of Psychology, 43,* 671–710.

Roland, P. E. (1997). *Brain activation.* New York: Wiley.

Rollin, S. A., Anderson, C. W., Buncher, Robert M., & Frydenberg, E. (Eds.) (1999). Coping in children and adolescents: A prevention model for helping kids avoid or reduce at-risk behaviour. *Learning to cope: Developing as a person in complex societies.* New York: Oxford University Press.

Rollins, B. C., & Feldman, H. (1970). Marital satisfaction over the family life cycle. *Journal of Marriage and the Family, 32,* 20–28.

Rollman, G. (1998). Culture and pain. In S. S. Kazarian, et al. (Eds.), *Cultural clinical psychology: Theory, research, and practice.* New York: Oxford University Press.

Rollman, G. B. (2003a). Ethnocultural variations in the experience of pain. In T. Hadjistavropoulos and K. D. Craig (Eds.), *Pain: Psychological perspectives.* Mahwah, NJ: Erlbaum.

Rollman, G. B. (2003b). Sex makes a difference: Experimental and clinical pain responses. *Clinical Journal of Pain, 19,* 204–207.

Rolls, B. J., Rolls, E. T., Rowe, E. A., & Sweeney, K. (1981). Sensory specific satiety in man. *Physiology and Behavior, 27,* 137–142.

Rolls, E. T. (2000). Memory systems in the brain. *Annual Review of Psychology, 5,* 599–630.

Rolls, E. T., & Deco, G. (2002). *Computational neuroscience of vision.* London: Oxford University Press.

Romanes, G.J. (1888). *Mental Evolution in Man: Origin of Human Faculty.* London: Kegan Paul, Trench.

Romeo, R. D. and McEwen, B. S. (2006). Stress and the adolescent brain. *Annals of the New York Academy of Sciences, 1094,* 202–214.

Ron, M. A., & David, A. S. (1997). *Disorders of brain and mind.* Cambridge, England: Cambridge University Press.

Ronquillo, J., Denson, T. F., Lickel, B., Lu, Z., Nandy, A., Maddox, K. B. (2007). The effects of skin tone on race-related amygdala activity: an fMRI investigation. *Social Cognitive and Affective Neuroscience, 2*(1), 39–44.

Rothbaum, B. O., Hodges, L., Smith, S., Lee, J. H., Prince, L. (2000). A controlled study of virtual reality exposure therapy for the fear of flying. *Journal of Consulting and Clinical Psychology, 68,* 6, 1020–1026.

Rosch, E. (1973). On the internal structure of perceptual and semantic categories. In T. E. Moore (Ed.), *Cognitive development and the acquisition of language.* New York: Academic Press.

Rosch, E. (1977). Human categorization. In N. Warren (Ed.), *Advances in cross-cultural psychology* (Vol. 1). London: Academic Press.

Rose, R. J. (1995). Genes and human behavior. *Annual Review of Psychology, 46,* 625–654.

Rose, S. (1973). *The conscious brain.* New York: Knopf.

Rosen, C. S. (2000). Integrating stage and continuum models to explain processing of exercise messages and exercise initiation among sedentary college students. *Health Psychology, 19,* 172–180.

Rosenbaum, A., Abend, S. S., Gearan, P. J., & Fletcher, K. E. (1997). Serotonergic functioning in partner-abusive men. In A. Raine, P. A. Brennan, D. P. Farrington, & S. A. Mednick (Eds.), *Biosocial bases of violence.* New York: Plenum.

Rosenbaum, M. E. (1986). The repulsion hypothesis: On the ondevelopment of relationships. *Journal of Personality and Social Psychology, 51,* 1156–1166.

Rosenman, R. H., Brand, R. J., Jenkins, C. D., et al. (1975). Coronary heart disease in the Western Collaborative Group Study. *Journal of the American Medical Association, 233,* 872–877.

Rosenberg, M. (1985). Self-concept and psychological well-being in adolescence. In R. L. Leahy (Ed.), *The development of the self.* Orlando, FL: Academic Press.

Rosenbloom, T. (2006). Driving performance while using cell phones: An observational study. *Journal of Safety Research, 37,* 207–212.

Rosenfarb, I. S., Goldstein, M. J., Mintz, J., Nuechterlein, K. H. (1995). Expressed emotion and subclinical psychopathology observable within the transactions between schizophrenic patients and their family members. *Journal of Abnormal Psychology, 104,* 259–267.

Rosenhan, D. (1973). On being sane in insane places. *Science, 179,* 250–258.

Rosenhan, D. L., & Seligman, M. E. P. (1989). *Abnormal psychology* (2nd ed.). New York: W. W. Norton.

Rosenthal, N. E., & Wehr, T. A. (1987). Seasonal affective disorders. *Psychiatric Annals, 17,* 670–674.

Rosenthal, R. (1985). From unconscious experimenter bias to teacher expectancy effects. In J. B. Dusek, V. C. Hall, & W. J. Meyer (Eds.), *Teacher expectancies.* Hillsdale, NJ: Erlbaum.

Rosenthal, R. (1991). Teacher expectancy effects: A brief update 25 years after the Pygmalion experiment. *Journal of Research in Education, 1,* 3–12.

Rosenthal, R. (1994). Interpersonal expectancy effects: A 30-year perspective. *Current Directions in Psychological Science, 3,* 176–179.

Rosenthal, R., Archer, D., DiMatteo, M. R., Koivumaki, J. H., & Rogers, P. L. (1974). Body talk and tone of voice: The language without words. *Psychology Today, 8,* 64–71.

Rosenzweig, M. R. (1984). Experience, memory, and the brain. *American Psychologist, 39,* 365–376.

Rosenzweig, M. R., & Bennett, E. L. (1996). Psychobiology of plasticity: Effects of training and experience on brain and behavior. *Behavioural Brain Research, 78,* 57–65.

Rosenzweig, S. (1992). Freud and experimental psychology: The emergence of idiodynamics. In S. Koch & D. E. Leary (Eds.), *A century of psychology as science.* Washington, DC: American Psychological Association.

Ross, L. (1977). The intuitive psychologist and his shortcomings: Distortions in the attribution process. In L. Berkowitz (Ed.), *Advances in experimental social psychology* (Vol. 10). New York: Academic Press.

Ross, L. (2001). Getting down to fundamentals: Lay dispositionism and the attributes of psychologists. *Psychological Inquiry, 12,* 37–40.

Ross, L., & Nisbett, R. E. (1991). *The person and the situation: Perspectives of social psychology.* New York: McGraw-Hill.

Ross, R. J., Ball, W. A., Sullivan, K. A., & Caroff, S. N. (1989). Sleep disturbance as the hallmark of post-traumatic stress disorder. *American Journal of Psychiatry, 146,* 697–707.

Rossell, S. L., Bullmore, E. T., Williams, S. C. R., et al. (2002). Sex differences in functional brain activation during a lexical visual field task. *Brain and Language, 80,* 97–105.

Rothbaum, B. O., Anderson, P., Zimand, E., Hodges, L., Lang, D., & Wilson, J. (2006). Virtual reality exposure therapy and standard (in vivo) exposure therapy in the treatment of fear of flying. *Behavior Therapy, 37,* 80–90.

Rothbaum, B. O., Hodges, L. F., Kooper, I. R., et al. (1995). Effectiveness of computer-generated (virtual reality) graded exposure in the treatment of acrophobia. *American Journal of Psychiatry, 52,* 626–628.

Rotton, J., & Cohn, E. G. (2000). Violence is a curvilinear function of temperature in Dallas: A replication. *Journal of Personality and Social Psychology, 78,* 1074–1081.

Rouhana, N. N., & Bar-Tal, D. (1998). Psychological dynamics of intractable ethnonational conflicts: The Israeli-Palestinian case. *American Psychologist, 53,* 761–770.

Rousche, P. J., & Normann, R. A. (1998). Chronic recording capability of the Utah intracortical electrode array in cat sensory cortex. *Journal of Neuroscience Methods, 82,* 1–15.

Rowatt, W. C., Cunningham, M. R., & Druen, P. B. (1999). Lying to get a date: The effect of facial physical attractiveness on the willingness to deceive prospective dating partners. *Journal of Social and Personal Relationships, 16,* 209–223.

Rowe, D. C. (1999). Heredity. In V. J. Derlega, B. A. Winstead, & W. H. Jones (Eds.), *Personality: Contemporary theory and research.* Chicago: Nelson-Hall.

Rowley, J. T., Stickgold, R., & Hobson, J. A. (1998). Eyelid movements and mental activity at sleep onset. *Consciousness and Cognition: An International Journal, 7,* 67–84.

Rozin, P., Dow, S., Moscovitch, M., & Rajaram, S. (1998). What causes humans to begin and end a meal? A role for memory for what has been eaten, as evidenced by a study of multiple meal eating in amnesic patients. *Psychological Science, 9,* 392–396.

Rubin, D. C., & Kozin, M. (1984). Vivid memories. *Cognition, 16,* 81–95.

Rubin, R. T. (2000). Depression and manic-depressive illness. In G. Fink (Ed.), *Encyclopedia of stress.* San Diego: Academic Press.

Rubonis, A. V., & Bickman, L. (1991). Psychological impairment in the wake of disaster: The disaster-psychopathology relationship. *Psychological Bulletin, 109,* 384–399.

Ruby, C. (2001). Are Terrorists Mentally Deranged? In Unger, R. (Ed), *Terrorism and Its Consequences. Analysis of Social Issues and Public Policy, Society for the Psychological Study of Social Issues,* Blackwell Publishers. [Online]. Available: http://www.asap-spssi.org/default.htm

Ruffman, R., Perner, J., Naito, M., Parkin, L., & Clements, W. A. (1998). Older (but not younger) siblings facilitate false belief understanding. *Developmental Psychology, 34,* 161–174.

Rugg, M. (1995). La difference vive. *Nature, 373* (16 February), 561.

Rumbaugh, D. M. (1977). *Language Learning by a Chimpanzee: The Lana Project.* New York: Academic Press.

Runge, C. B. (2000). *Clinical MRI.* St. Louis: Harcourt Health Sciences.

Runquist, W. N. (1975). Interference among memory traces. *Memory and Cognition, 3,* 143–159.

Rush, A. J., Crismon, M. L. et al. (1998). Consensus guidelines in the treatment of major depressive disorder. *Journal of Clinical Psychiatry, 59* (Suppl. 20), 73–84.

Rushton, J. P. (1989). Genetic similarity, human altruism, and group selection. *Behavioral and Brain Sciences, 12,* 503–559.

Rushton, J. P. (1995). Asian achievement, brain size, and evolution: comments on A. H. Yee. *Educational Psychology Review, 7*(4), 373–380.

Russell, J. A. (1994). Is there universal recognition of emotion from facial expressions? A review of the cross-cultural studies. *Psychological Bulletin, 115,* 102–141.

Russell, J. C. (1989). Anxiety disorders in Japan: A review of the Japanese literature on Shinkeishitsu and Taijin Kyofushu. *Culture, Medicine, and Psychiatry, 13,* 391–403.

Russell, J., & Fernandez-Dols, J. M. (1994). Is there universal recognition of emotion from facial expression? A review of cross-cultural studies. *Psychological Bulletin, 115,* 102–141.

Russell, M., Dark, K. A., Cummins, R. W., Ellman, G., Callaway, E., & Peeke, H. V. (1984). Learned histamine release. *Science, 225,* 733–734.

Russell, P. A., Deregowski, J. B., & Kinnear, P. R. (1997). Perception and aesthetics. In J. W. Berry & P. R. (Eds.), *Handbook of cross-cultural psychology, Vol. 2: Basic processes and human development* (2nd ed.). Boston: Allyn & Bacon.

Russian Association of Crisis Centers for Women (1995). *Report for the non-governmental forum of the United Nations' fourth world congress on the status of women: Violence against women in Russia.* Moscow: Author.

Ruttenber, A. J., Lawler, H. J., Yin, M., & Wetli, C. V. (1997). Fatal excited delirium following cocaine use: Epidemiologic findings provide new evidence for mechanisms of cocaine toxicity. *Journal of Forensic Sciences, 42,* 25–31.

Rutter, D. R. (2000). Attendance and reattendance for breast cancer screening: A prospective 3-year test of the Theory of Planned Behaviour. *British Journal of Health Psychology, 5,* 1–13.

Rutter, M. L. (1997). Nature-nurture integration: The example of antisocial behavior. *American Psychologist, 52,* 390–398.

Ryan, L., & Eich, E. (2000). Mood dependence and implicit memory. In E. Tulving (Ed)., *Memory, consciousness, and the brain: The Tallinn Conference.* Philadelphia: Psychology Press/Taylor & Francis.

Rys, G. S., & Bear, G. G. (1997). Relational aggression and peer relations: Gender and developmental issues. *Merrill Palmer Quarterly, 43,* 87–106.

Saad, L. (1999, April 23). *Public views Littleton tragedy as sign of deeper problems in country.* Gallup News Service. Princeton, NJ: Gallup Organization.

Saari, L. M., Johnson, T. R., McLaughlin, S. D., & Zimmerle, D. M. (1988). A survey of management training and education practices in U.S. companies. *Personnel Psychology, 41,* 731–743.

Sabbagh, M.A., Baldwin, D.A. (2001). Learning words from knowledgeable versus ignorant speakers: links between preschoolers' theory of mind and semantic development. *Child Development, 72,* 1054–1070.

Sachse, R., & Elliott, R. (2002). Process-outcome research on humanistic therapy variables. In D. J. Cain (Ed.), *Humanistic psychotherapies: Handbook of research and practice.* Washington, DC: American Psychological Association.

Sack, R. L., & Lewy, A. J. (1997). Melatonin as a chronobiotic: Treatment of circadian desynchrony in night workers and the blind. *Journal of Biological Rhythms, 12,* 595–603.

Sack, R. L., Hughes, R. J., Edgar, D. M., & Lewy, A. J. (1997). Sleep-promoting effects of melatonin: At what dose, in whom, under what conditions, and by what mechanisms? *Sleep, 20,* 908–915.

Sack, R. L., Lewy, A. J., & Hughes, R. J. (1998). Use of melatonin for sleep and circadian rhythm disorders. *Annals of Medicine, 30,* 115–121.

Sacks, O. (1985, 1986). *The man who mistook his wife for a hat and other clinical tales.* New York: Summit Books and Simon & Schuster.

Sacks, O. (1993). To see and not to see: a neurologist's notebook. *The New Yorker, 69,* 59.

Sadoski, M., Kealy, W. A., Goetz, E. T., & Paivio, A. (1997). Concreteness and imagery effects in the written composition of definitions. *Journal of Educational Psychology, 89,* 518–526.

Saffran, E. M., Schwartz, M. F., & Marin, O. S. M. (1980). Evidence from aphagia: Isolating the components of a production model. In B. Butterworth (Ed.), *Language Production.* London: Academic Press.

Safran, J.D., & Christopher, J. (2000). *Negotiating the Therapeutic Alliance: A Relational Treatment Guide.* New York: Guilford.

Safran, J. D., & Muran, J. C. (2000). *Negotiating the therapeutic alliance: a relational treatment guide.* New York: Guilford Press.

Sagi, A., & Hoffman, M. L. (1976). Empathic distress in the newborn. *Developmental Psychology, 12,* 175–176.

Salovey, P., Mayer, J. D., & Rosenhan, D. L. (1991). Mood and helping: Mood as a motivator of helping and helping as a regulator of mood. In M. S. Clark (Ed.), *Prosocial behavior* (Vol. 12). Newbury Park, CA: Sage Publications.

Salovey, P., Mayer, J. D., Goldman, S. L., Turvey, C., & Palfai, T. P. (1995). Emotional attention, clarity, and repair: Exploring emotional intelligence using the Trait Meta-Mood Scale. In J. W. Pennebaker, et. al. (Eds.), *Emotion, disclosure and health.* Washington, DC: American Psychological Association.

Salovey, P., Sluyter, D., & Goleman, D. (1997). *Emotional development and emotional intelligence.* New York: Basic Books.

Salovey, P., Rothman, A. J., Detweiler, J. B., & Steward, W. T. (2000). Emotional states and physical health. *American Psychologist, 55,* 110–121.

Salthouse, T. A. (1994). The nature of the influence of speed on adult age differences in cognition. *Developmental Psychology, 30,* 240–259.

Saltz, B., et al. (1991). Prospective study of tardive dyskinesia incidence in the elderly. *Journal of the American Medical Association, 266,* 2402–2406.

Saltzman, A. L. (2000). The role of the obedience experiments in Holocaust studies: The case for renewed visibility. In T. Blass (Ed.), *Obedience to authority: Current perspectives on the Milgram paradigm.* Mahwah, NJ: Erlbaum.

Sampaio, E. (1989). Is there a critical age for using the Sonicguide with blind infants? *Journal of Visual Impairment & Blindness, 82,* 105–108.

Sanderman, R. & Ranchor-Adelita, V. (1997). The predictor status of personality variables: Etiological significance and their role in the course of disease. *European Journal of Personality. 11,* 359–382.

Sanes, J. N., Dimitrov, B., & Hallett, M. (1990). Motor learning in patients with cerebellar dysfunction. *Brain, 113,* 103–120.

Saphier, D. (1992). Electrophysiological studies of the effects of interleukin-1 and interferon on the EEG and pituitary-adrenocortical activity. In J. J. Rothwell & R. D. Dantzer (Eds.), *Interleukin-1 in the brain.* Oxford, England: Pergamon.

Sapse, A. T. (1997). Cortisol, high cortisol diseases, and anticortisol therapy. *Psychoneuroendocrinology, 22,* 3–8.

Sarason, I. G., & Sarason, B. R. (1990). Test anxiety. In H. Leitenberg (Ed.), *Handbook of social and evaluation anxiety.* New York: Plenum.

Sarason, I. G., Sarason, B. R., Pierce, G. R., Shearin, E. N., & Sayers, M. H. (1991). A social learning approach to increasing blood donations. *Journal of Applied Social Psychology, 21,* 896–918.

Sarbin, T. R., & Coe, W. C. (1972). *Hypnosis: A social psychological analysis of influence communication.* New York: Holt, Rinehart and Winston.

Satcher, D. (2000). *Mental health: A report of the Surgeon General.* Washington, DC.: U.S. Department of Health and Human Services.

Satir, V. (1967). *Conjoint family therapy.* Palo Alto, CA: Sciences and Behavior Books.

Sauer, M. V. (1998). *Principles of oocyte and embryo donation.* New York: Springer-Verlag.

Savage, P. J., & Bennett, P. H. (1992). Obesity and diabetes in American Indians and their interrelationships among the Pima Indians of Arizona. In E. W. Haller & L. P. Aitken (Eds.), *Mashkiki: Old medicine nourishing the new. American Indians and Alaska Natives in biomedical research careers.* Lanham, MD: University Press of America.

Savage-Rumbaugh, E. S., McDonald, K., Sevick,, R. A. (1986). Spontaneous symbol acquisition and communicative use by pygmy chimpanzees (pan paniscus). *Journal of Experimental Psychology, General, 115,* 211–235.

Savage-Rumbaugh, E. S., Murphy, J., et al. (1993). Language comprehension in ape and child. *Monographs of the Society for Research in Child Development, 58* (no. 233), 1–254.

Savage-Rumbaugh, E. S., Pate, J. L., Lawson, J., Smith, S. T., & Rosenbaum, S. (1983). Can a chimpanzee make a statement? *Journal of Experimental Psychology, General, 112,* 457–492.

Savage-Rumbaugh, S. (1998). Scientific schizophrenia with regard to the language act. In J. Langer and M. Killen (Eds.), *Piaget, Evolution & Development.* The Jean Piaget Symposium Series. Lawrence Erlbaum Associates.

Sawle, G.V., Hymas, N.F., Lees, A.J., Frackowiak, R.S.J. (1991). Obsessional slowness: Functional studies with positron emission tomography. *Brain 114,* 2191–2202.

Saxena, S., Brody, A. L., Schwartz, J. M., & Baxter, L. R. (1998). Neuroimaging and frontal-subcortical circuitry in obsessive-compulsive disorder. *British Journal of Psychiatry, 173*(35S), 26–37.

Scarr, S. (1992). Developmental theories for the 1990s: Development and individual differences. *Child Development, 63,* 1–19.

Scarr, S. (1998a). American child care today. *American Psychologist, 53,* 95–108.

Scarr, S. (1998b). How do families affect intelligence? Social environmental and behavior genetic predictions. In J. J. McArdle & R. W. Woodcock et al. (Eds.). *Human cognitive abilities in theory and practice.* Mahwah, NJ: Erlbaum.

Schachter, S. (1959). *The psychology of affiliation: Experimental studies of the sources of gregariousness.* Stanford, CA: Stanford University Press.

Schachter, S. (1966). The interaction of cognitive and physiological determinants of emotional state. In C. D. Spielberger (Ed.), *Anxiety and behavior.* New York: Academic Press.

Schachter, S. (1968). Obesity and eating. *Science, 16,* 751–756.

Schachter, S. (1982). Recidivism and self-cure of smoking and obesity. *American Psychologist, 37,* 436–444.

Schachter, S., & Latane, B. (1964). Crime, cognition, and the autonomic nervous system. In D. Levine (Ed.), *Nebraska Symposium on Maturation.* Lincoln: University of Nebraska Press.

Schachter, S., & Wheeler, L. (1962). Epinephrine, chlorpromazine, and amusement. *Journal of Abnormal and Social Psychology, 65,* 121–128.

Schacter, D. L. (1992). Understanding implicit memory: A cognitive neuroscience approach. *American Psychologist, 47,* 559–569.

Schacter, D. L., & Curran, T. (2000). Memory without remembering and remembering without memory: Implicit and false memories. In M. S. Gazzaniga (Ed.), *The new cognitive neurosciences* (2nd ed.). Cambridge, MA: MIT Press.

Schacter, D. L., Norman, K. A., & Koutstaal, W. (1998). The cognitive neuroscience of constructive memory. *Annual Review of Psychology, 49,* 289–318.

Schaeff, C. M., Boness, D. J., & Bowen, W. D. (1999). Female distribution, genetic relatedness, and fostering behaviour in harbour seals, Phoca vitulina. *Animal Behaviour, 57,* 427–434.

Schaie, K. W. (1994). The course of adult intellectual development. *American Psychologist, 49,* 304–313.

Schaie, K. W. (1998). The Seattle Longitudinal Studies of adult intelligence. In M. Lawton & T. A. Salthouse (Eds.), *Essential papers on the psychology of aging.* New York: University Press.

Schatzberg, A. F., Cole, J. O., & DeBattista, C. (2005). *Manual of clinical psychopharmacology.* Washington, DC: American Psychiatric Publishing.

Scheff, T. J. (1966). *Being mentally ill: A sociological theory.* Chicago: Aldine.

Scheier, M. F. (2000). Optimism. In G. Fink (Ed.), *Encyclopedia of stress.* San Diego: Academic Press.

Scheier, M. F., & Carver, C. S. (1985). Optimism, coping, and health: Assessment and implications of generalized outcome expectancies. *Health Psychology, 4,* 219–247.

Schenck, C. H., Milner, D. M., Hurwitz, T. D., & Bundlie, S. R. (1989). A polysomnographic and clinical report on sleep-related injury in 100 adult patients. *American Journal of Psychiatry, 146,* 1166–1173.

Scherer, K. (1984). On the nature and function of emotion: A component process approach. In K. Scherer & P. Ekman (Eds.), *Approaches to emotion.* Hillsdale, NJ: Erlbaum.

Scherer, K. R. (1988). *Facets of emotion: Recent research.* Hillsdale, NJ: Erlbaum.

Scherer, Klaus R. (1999). Appraisal theory. In T. Dalgleish & M. J. Power (Eds.), *Handbook of cognition and emotion.* Chichester, England: Wiley.

Schibler, U. (2006). Circadian time keeping: The daily ups and downs of genes, cells, and organisms. *Progress in Brain Research, 153,* 271–282.

Schlegel, A., & Barry, H. (1991). *Adolescence: An anthropological inquiry.* New York: Free Press.

Schlenker, B. R., & Weigold, M. F. (1992). Interpersonal processes involving impression regulation and management. *Annual Review of Psychology, 43,* 133–168.

Schlink, B. (1997). *The reader.* New York: Random House.

Schmajuk, N. A., & Holland, P. C. (Eds.) (1998). *Occasion setting: Associative learning and cognition in animals.* Washington, DC: American Psychological Association.

Schmajuk, N. A., Lamoureux, J. A., & Holland, P. C. (1998). Occasion setting: A neural network approach. *Psychological Review, 105,* 3-32.

Schmidt, L. A., Fox, N. A., Perez-Edgar, K., Hu, S., & Hamer, D. H. (2001). Association of DRD4 with attention problems in normal childhood development. *Psychiatric Genetics, 11,* 25–29.

Schmidt, L. A., Fox, N. A., Rubin, K. H., Hu, S., & Hamer, D. H. (2002). Molecular genetics of shyness and aggression in preschoolers. *Personality and Individual Differences, 33,* 227–238.

Schmidt, P. J., & Rubinow, D. R. (1997). Neuroregulatory role of gonadal steroids in humans. *Psychopharmacology Bulletin, 33*(2), 219–220.

Schmithorst, V. J., Holland, S. K. (2007). Sex differences in the development of neuroanatomical funtional connectivity underlying intelligence found using Bayesian connectivity analysis. *NeuroImage, 35*(1), 406–419.

Schmolck, H., Buffalo, E. A., & Squire, L. R. (2000). Memory distortions develop over time: Recollections of the O.J. Simpson trial verdict after 15 and 32 months. *Psychological Science, 11,* 39–45.

Schneer, J. A., & Reitman, F. (1995). The impact of gender as managerial careers unfold. *Journal of Vocational Behavior, 47,* 290–315.

Schneer, J. A., & Reitman, F. (1997). The interrupted managerial career path: A longitudinal study of MBAs. *Journal of Vocational Behavior, 51,* 411–434.

Schnurr, P. P., Spiro III, A., Aldwin, C. M., & Stukel, T. A. (1998). Physical symptom trajectories following trauma exposure: Longitudinal findings from the Normative Aging Study. *Journal of Nervous and Mental Disease, 186,* 522–528.

Schoen, L. M. (1996). Monopoly: Board games and mnemonics. *Teaching of Psychology, 23,* 30–32.

Schofeld, J. W., & Wagar, H. A. (1979). Unplanned social learning in an interracial school. In R. Rist (Ed.), *Inside desegregated schools: Taking stock of a great American experiment.* New York: Academic Press.

Schooler, J. W., & Eich, E. (2000). Memory for emotional events. In E. Tulving and F. I. M. Craik (Eds.), *The Oxford handbook of memory.* New York: Oxford University Press.

Schore, A. N. (1996). The experience-dependent maturation of a regulatory system in the orbital prefrontal cortex and the origin of developmental psychopathology. *Development and Psychopathology, 8,* 59–87.

Schore, A. N. (2002). Dysregulation of the right brain: a fundamental mechanism of traumatic attachment and the psychopathogenesis of posttraumatic stress disorder. *Australian and New Zealand Journal of Psychiatry, 36,* 9–30.

Schriever, S. H. (1990). Comparison of beliefs and practices of ethnic Viet and Lao Hmong concerning illness, healing, death and mourning: Implications for hospice care with refugees in Canada. *Journal of Palliative Care, 6,* 42–49.

Schulz, R., & Aderman, D. (1980). Clinical research and the stages of dying. In R. A. Kalish (Ed.), *Death, dying, and transcending.* Farmingdale, New York: Baywood.

Schutte, N. S., Malouff, J. M., Hall, L. E., Haggerty, D. J., Cooper, J. T., Golden, C. J., & Dornheim, L. (1998). Development and validation of a measure of emotional intelligence. *Personality and Individual Differences, 25,* 167–177.

Schwartz, B. L. (1998). Illusory tip-of-the-tongue states. *Memory, 6,* 623–642.

Schwartz, B. L., Travis, D. M., Castro, A. M., & Smith, S. M. (2000). The phenomenology of real and illusory tip-of-the-tongue states. *Memory and Cognition, 28,* 18–27.

Schwartz, R. (1984). Body weight regulation. *University of Washington Medicine, 10,* 16–20.

Schwarzer, R. (1998). Stress and coping from a social-cognitive perspective. *Annals of the New York Academy of Sciences, 851,* 531–537.

Schweder, R. A., & Sullivan, L. (1990). The semiotic subject of cultural psychology. In L. A. Pervin (Ed.), *Handbook of personality: Theory and research.* New York: Guilford Press.

Scialfa, C. T., & Joffe, K. M. (1997). Age differences in feature and conjunction search: Implications for theories of visual search and generalized slowing. *Aging, Neuropsychology, and Cognition, 4,* 227–246.

Scott, C. S., Arthur, D. P., Panizo, M. I., & Owen, R. (1989). Menarche: The Black American experience. *Journal of Adolescent Health Care, 10,* 363, 368.

Scott, T. R. (1992). Taste, feeding, and pleasure. In A. N. Epstein, et al. (Eds.), *Progress in psychobiology and physiological psychology.* San Diego: Academic Press.

Scott, T. R., & Giza, B. K. (1993). Gustatory control of ingestion. In D. A. Booth, et al. (Eds.), *Neurophysiology of ingestion. Pergamon studies in neuroscience.* Oxford, England: Pergamon.

Scoville, W. B., & Milner, B. (1957). Loss of recent memory after bilateral hippocampal lesions. *Journal of Neurology, Neurosurgery, and Psychiatry, 20,* 11–21.

Seale, C. (1998). *Constructing death: The sociology of dying and bereavement.* New York: Cambridge University Press.

Sears, R. R. (1977). Sources of life satisfaction of the Terman gifted men. *American Psychologist, 32,* 119–128.

Sears, R. R., Maccoby, E. E., & Levin, H. (1957). *Patterns of child rearing.* Evanston, IL: Row, Peterson.

Seattle Times (1997, December 11). Paralyzed woman is good Samaritan. *Seattle Times,* p. B3.

Segall, M. H., Campbell, D. T., Herskovits, M. J. (1966). *The Influence of Culture on Visual Perception.* Oxford: Bobbs-Merrill.

Segerstron, S. C. & Miller, G. E. 2004. Psychological stress and the human immune system: A meta-analytic study of 30 years of inquiry. *Psychological Bulletin, 130,* 601-630.

Segerstrom, S. C., Taylor, S. E., Kemeny, M. E., & Fahey, J. L. (1998). Optimism is associated with mood, coping and immune change in response to stress. *Journal of Personality and Social Psychology, 74,* 1646–1655.

Sekuler, A.B., Bennett, P, Mamelak, M. (2000). Effects of aging on the useful field of view. *Experimental aging research, 26,* 103–120.

Seligman, M. E. P. (1970). On the generality of the laws of learning. *Psychological Review, 77,* 406–418.

Seligman, M. E. P. (1971). Phobias and preparedness. *Behavior Therapy, 2,* 307–320.

Seligman, M. E. P. (1975). *Helplessness: On depression, development, and death.* New York: W. H. Freeman.

Seligman, M. E. P. (1989). Research in clinical psychology: Why is there so much depression today? In I. S. Cohen (Ed.), *The G. Stanley Hall lecture series* (Vol. 9). Washington, DC: American Psychological Association.

Seligman, M. E. P. (1991). *Learned optimism.* New York: Knopf.

Seligman, M. E. P. (1995). The effectiveness of psychotherapy: The Consumer Reports study. *American Psychologist, 50,* 965–974.

Seligman, M. E. P., & Csikszentmihalyi, M. (2000). Positive psychology: An introduction. *American Psychologist, 55,* 5–14.

Seligman, M. E. P., & Isaacowitz, D. M. (2000). Learned helplessness. In G. Fink (Ed.), *Encyclopedia of stress.* San Diego: Academic Press.

Selye, H. (1976). *The stress of life.* New York: McGraw-Hill.

Sen, D., Jefferson, J. W., & Greist, J. H. (1999). *Depression and antidepressants: A guide.* Madison, WI: Madison Institute of Medicine.

Senden, M. von (1960). *Space and sight: The perception of space and shape in the congenitally blind before and after operation.* New York: Free Press. (P. Heath, Trans.)

Sergios, P. A., & Cody, J. (1985–1986). Importance of physical attractiveness and social assertiveness skills in male homosexual dating behavior and partner selection. *Journal of Homosexuality, 12,* 71–84.

Servos, P., Engel, S. A., Gati, J. & Menon, R. (1999). fMRI evidence for an inverted face representation in human somatosensory cortex. *NeuroReport, 10,* 1393–1395.

Seto, M. C., & Barbaree, H. E. (1995). The role of alcohol in sexual aggression. *Clinical Psychology Review, 15,* 545–566.

Shaffer, D. R. (1996). *Developmental psychology: Childhood and adolescence* (4th ed.). Belmont, CA: Thompson Brooks/Cole Publishing..

Shair, H. N., Barr, G. A., & Hofer, M. A. (Eds.). (1991). *Developmental psychobiology.* New York: Oxford University Press.

Shallice, T., & Burgess, P. (1991). Higher-order cognitive impairments and frontal-lobe lesions in man. In H. S. Levin, H. M. Eisenberg, & A. L. Benton (Eds.), *Frontal lobe function and dysfunction.* New York. Oxford University Press.

Shanab, M. E., & Yahya, L. A. (1977). A behavioral study of obedience in children. *Journal of Personality and Social Psychology, 35,* 530–536.

Shanahan, T. L., Kronauer, R. E., Duffy, J. F., Williams, G. H., & Czeisler, C. A. (1999). Melatonin rhythm observed throughout a three-cycle bright-light stimulus designed to reset the human circadian pacemaker. *Journal of Biological Rhythms, 14,* 237–253.

Shapiro, A. F., Gottman, J. M., & Carrere, S. (2000). The baby and the marriage: Identifying factors that buffer against decline in marital satisfaction after the first baby arrives. *Journal of Family Psychology, 14,* 59–70.

Shapiro, A. K., & Shapiro, E. (1997). *The powerful placebo: From ancient priest to modern physician.* Baltimore: Johns Hopkins University Press.

Shapiro, C. M., Bortz, R., Mitchell, D., Bartel, P., & Jooste, P. (1981). Slow-wave sleep: A recovery period after exercise. *Science, 214,* 1253–1254.

Shapiro, K. J. (1997). The separate world of animal research. *American Psychologist, 52,* 1250.

Sharkey, K. M. (1993). Short sleepers in history and legend. In M. A. Carskadon (Ed.), *Encyclopedia of sleep and dreaming.* New York: Macmillan.

Sharma, J., Angelucci, A., & Sur, M. (2000). Induction of visual orientation modules in auditory cortex. *Nature, 404,* 841–847.

Sharp, S. (1995). How much does bullying hurt? The effects of bullying on the personal wellbeing and educational progress of secondary aged students. *Educational and Child Psychology, 12,* 81–88.

Shaver, P. R., & Clark, C. L. (1996). Forms of adult romantic attachment and their cognitive and emotional underpinnings. In G. G. Noam, K. W. Fischer et al. (Eds.), *Development and vulnerability in close relationships. The Jean Piaget symposium series.* Mahwah, NJ: Erlbaum.

Shavit, Y. (1990). Stress-induced immune modulation in animals: Opiates and endogenous opioid peptides. In R. Ader, N. Cohen, & D. L. Felten (Eds.), *Psychoneuroimmunology II.* New York: Academic Press.

Shaw, W. S., & Dimsdale, J. E. (2000). Type A personality, Type B personality. In G. Fink (Ed.), *Encyclopedia of stress.* San Diego: Academic Press.

Shek, D. T. L. (1998). A longitudinal study of the relations between parent-adolescent conflict and adolescent psychological well-being. *Journal of Genetic Psychology, 159,* 53–67.

Sheldon, K. M., & Kasser, T. (2001). Getting older, getting better? Personal strivings and psychological maturity across the life span. *Developmental Psychology, 37,* 491–501.

Shepherd, G. (1997). *The synaptic organizer of the brain.* New York: Oxford University Press.

Sherif, M. (1935). A study of some social factors in perception. *Archives of Psychology* (No. 187).

Sherif, M., Harvey, O., White, B., Hood, W., & Sherif, C. (1961). *Intergroup conflict and cooperation: The Robbers Cave experiment.* Norman, OK: University of Oklahoma Press.

Sherman, P. W. (1977). Nepotism and the evolution of alarm calls. *Science, 197,* 1246–1253.

Sherry, J. L. (2001). The effects of violent video games on aggression: A meta-analysis. *Human Communication Research, 27,* 409–431.

Sherwin, B. B. & Gelfand, M. M. (1988). The role of androgen in the maintenance of sexual functioning in oophorectomized women. *Psychosomatic Medicine,* 49: 397–409.

Sherwood, L. (1991). *Fundamentals of physiology: A human perspective.* St. Paul, MN: West.

Shevrin, H., Bond, J. A., Brakel, L. A. W., Hertel, R. K., & Williams, W. J. (1996). *Conscious and unconscious processes: Psychodynamic, cognitive, and neurophysiological convergences.* New York: Guilford Press.

Shevrin, H., Bond, J. A., Brakel, L. A. W., Hertel, R. K., & Williams, W. J. (1998). The Freud-Rapaport theory of consciousness. In R. F. Bronstein, J. M. Masling et al. (Eds.), *Empirical perspectives on the psychoanalytic unconscious. Empirical studies of psychoanalytic theories.* Washington, DC: American Psychological Association.

Shiner, R. L. (1998). How shall we speak of children's personalities in middle childhood? A preliminary taxonomy. *Psychological Bulletin, 124,* 308–332.

Shneidman, E. S. (1998). *The suicidal mind.* New York: Oxford University Press.

Shoda, Y. (1999). Behavioral expressions of a personality system: Generation and perception of behavioral signatures. In D. Cervone & Y. Shoda (Eds.), *The coherence of personality: Social-cognitive bases of consistency, variability, and organization.* New York: Guilford Press.

Shoda, Y., & Mischel, W. (2000). Reconciling contextualism with the core assumptions of personality psychology. *European Journal of Personality, 14,* 462–484.

Shoda, Y., Mischel, W., & Wright, J. C. (1994). Intra-individual stability and patterning of behavior: Incorporating psychological situations into the idiographic analysis of personality. *Journal of Personality and Social Psychology, 65,* 1023–1035.

Shorter, E. (1998). *A history of psychiatry: From the era of the asylum to the age of Prozac.* New York: Wiley.

Shorter, E. (2003). *A history of psychiatry: From the era of the asylum to the age of Prozac.* New York: Wiley.

Shostak, M. (1981). *Nisa: The life and words of a !Kung woman.* Cambridge, MA: Harvard University Press.

Shultz, K. S., Morton, K. R., & Weckerle, J. R. (1998). The influence of push and pull factors on voluntary and involuntary early retirees' retirement decision and adjustment. *Journal of Vocational Behavior, 53,* 45–57.

Shumaker, S. A., & Hill, D. R. (1991). Gender differences in social support and physical health. *Health Psychology, 10,* 102–111.

Sia, C. L., Tan, B. C. Y., & Wei, K. K. (2002). Group polarization and computer mediated communication: Effects of communication cues, social presence, and anonymity. *Information Systems Research, 13,* 70–90.

Siegal, M. P., & Cadida, C. (1998). Preschoolers' understanding of lies and innocent and negligent mistakes. *Developmental Psychology, 34,* 332–341.

Siegel, A., Roeling, T. A. P., Gregg, T. R., & Kruk, M. R. (1999). Neuropharmacology of brain-stimulation-evoked aggression. *Neuroscience and Biobehavioral Reviews, 23,* 359–389.

Siegel, R. K. (1986). MDMA: Medical use and intoxication. *Journal of Psychoactive Drugs, 18,* 349–353.

Siegel, S. (1984). Pavlovian conditioning and heroin overdose: Reports from overdose victims. *Bulletin of the Psychonomic Society, 22,* 428–430.

Siegel, S., & Allan, L. G. (1996). The widespread influence of the Rescorla-Wagner model. *Psychonomic Bulletin and Review, 3,* 314–321.

Siegler, R. S. (1981). Developmental sequences within and between concepts. *Monographs of the Society for Research in Child Development, 46,* 84.

Siegle, G. J., Carter, C. S. and Thase, M. E. (2006). Use of fMRI to predict recovery from unipolar depression with cognitive behavior therapy. *American Journal of Psychiatry, 163,* 735–738.

Siegler, R. S. (1986). *Children's thinking.* Englewood Cliffs, NJ: Prentice Hall.

Siegler, R. S. (1996). *Emerging minds: The process of change in children's thinking.* New York: Oxford University Press.

Siever, L. J., Buchsbaum, M. S., New, A. S., Spiegel, C. J., Wei, T., & Hazlett, E. A., (1999). d,l-Fenfluramine response in impulsive personality disorder assessed with [-sup-1-sup-8F]flurodeoxyglucose positron emission tomography. *Neuropsychopharmacology, 20,* 413–423.

Sigala, N., & Logothetis, N. K. (2002). Visual categorization shapes feature selectivity in the primate temporal cortex. *Nature, 415,* 318–320.

Sigall, H., & Page, R. (1971). Current stereotypes: A little fading, a little faking. *Journal of Personality and Social Psychology, 18,* 247–255.

Sigelman, C. K., & Shaffer, D. R. (1991). *Life-span human development.* Pacific Grove, CA: Brooks/Cole.

Sigman, M. (1995). Nutrition and child development: More food for thought. *Current Directions in Psychological Science, 4,* 52–55.

Silbersweig, D. A., Stern, E., Strain, E. C., Frith, C., Cahill, C., et al. (1995). A functional neuroanatomy of hallucinations in schizophrenia. *Nature, 378*(6553), 176–179.

Silke, A. (1998). Cheshire-Cat logic: The recurring theme of terrorist abnormality in psychological research. *Psychology Crime and Law,* 4(1): 51–69.

Silveri, M. M., Rohan, M. L., Pimentel, P. J., Gruber, S. A., Rosso, I. M., et al. (2006). Sex differences in the relationship between white matter microstructure and impulsivity in adolescents. *Magnetic Resonance Imaging, 24,* 833–841.

Simion, F., Valenza, E., Umilta, C., & Barba, B. D. (1998). Preferential orienting to faces in newborns: A temporal-nasal asymmetry. *Journal of Experimental Psychology: Human Perception and Performance, 24,* 1399–1405.

Simkin, L. R., & Gross, A. M. (1994). Assessment of coping with high risk situations for exercise relapse among healthy women. *Health Psychology, 13,* 274–277.

Simmons, J. V. (1981). *Project sea hunt: A report on prototype development and tests.* Naval Ocean Systems Center, San Diego: Technical Report 746.

Simon, H. A. (1990). Invariants of human behavior. *Annual Review of Psychology, 41,* 1–20.

Simon, L., Greenberg, J., & Brehm, J. (1995). Trivialization: The forgotten mode of dissonance reduction. *Journal of Personality and Social Psychology, 68,* 247–260.

Simons, R. L., & Chao, W. (1996). Conduct problems. In R. L. Simon (Ed.), *Understanding differences between divorced and intact families: Stress, interaction, and child outcome.* Thousand Oaks, CA: Sage Publications.

Simonton, D. K. (1999). Creativity and genius. In L. A. Pervin & O. P. John (Eds.), *Handbook of personality: Theory and research* (2nd ed.). New York: Guilford Press.

Simpaio, E., Maris, S., & Bach-y-Rita, P. (2001). Brain plasticity: "Visual" acuity of blind persons via the tongue. *Brain Research, 908,* 204–207.

Sinclair, S. V., & Mistlberger, R. E. (1997). Scheduled activity reorganizes circadian phase of Syrian hamsters under full and skeleton photoperiods. *Behavioural Brain Research, 87,* 127–137.

Singer, J. A., Singer, J. L., & Zittel, C. (2000). Personality variations in autobiographical memories, self-representations, and daydreaming. In R. G. Kunzendorf & B. Wallace (Eds.), *Individual differences in conscious experience. Advances in consciousness research* (Vol. 20). Amsterdam: John Benjamins.

Singer, J. L. (1988). Sampling ongoing consciousness and emotional experience: Implications for health. In M. J. Horowitz (Ed.), *Psychodynamics and cognition.* Chicago: University of Chicago Press.

Singer, J. L. (1990). *Repression and dissociation.* Chicago: University of Chicago Press.

Singer, J. L. (1999). Repression, dissociation and our human stream of consciousness: Memory as a constructive, creative process. In S. Taub (Ed.), *Recovered memories of child sexual abuse: Psychological, social, and legal perspectives on a contemporary mental health controversy.* Springfield, IL: Charles C Thomas.

Singh, D. (1993). Adaptive significance of waist-to-hip ratio and female physical attractiveness. *Journal of Personality and Social Psychology, 65,* 293–307.

Singh, R., Gupta, M., & Dalal, A. K. (1979). Cultural difference in attribution of performance: An integration-theoretical analysis. *Journal of Personality and Social Psychology, 37,* 1342–1351.

Singh-Manous, A., Hillsdon, M., Brunner, E., & Marmot, M. (2005). Effects of physical activity on cognitive functioning in middle age: evidence from the Whitehall II Prospective Cohort study. *American Journal of Public Health, 95,* 2252–2258.

Single, E., Robson, L., Zie, X., and Rehm, J. (1996). *The costs of substance abuse in Canada.* Published by the Canadian Centre on Substance Abuse.

Sistler, A. B., & Moore, G. M. (1996). Cultural diversity in coping with marital stress. *Journal of Clinical Geropsychology, 2,* 77–82.

Skinner, B. F. (1938). *The behavior of organisms; an experimental analysis.* New York: Appleton-Century.

Skinner, B. F. (1948). *Walden two.* New York: Macmillan.

Skinner, B. F. (1953). *Science and human behavior.* New York: Macmillan.

Skinner, B. F. (1957). *Verbal behavior.* New York: Prentice Hall.

Skinner, B. F. (1968). *The technology of teaching.* New York: Appleton-Century-Crofts.

Skinner, B. F. (1971). *Beyond freedom and dignity.* New York: Knopf.

Skinner, B. F. (1977). *Upon further reflection.* Englewood Cliffs, NJ: Prentice Hall.

Skinner, B. F. (1983). *A matter of consequences.* New York: Knopf.

Skinner, B. F. (1986). The evolution of verbal behavior. *Journal of the Experimental Analysis of Behavior, 45,* 115–122.

Skinner, B. F. (1989a). Teaching machines. *Science, 243,* 1535.

Skinner, B. F. (1989b). The origins of cognitive thought. *American Psychologist, 44,* 13–18.

Skinner, B. F. (1990). Can psychology be a science of mind? *American Psychologist, 45,* 1206–1210.

Sklar, L. S., & Anisman, H. (1981). Stress and cancer. *Psychological Bulletin, 89,* 369–406.

Skorikov, V., & Vondracek, F. W. (1998). Vocational identity development: Its relationship to other identity domains and to overall identity development. *Journal of Career Assessment, 6,* 13–35.

Slater, A. (2000). Visual perception in the young infant: Early organisation and rapid learning. In Muir, D. & Slater, A. (Eds), *Infant Development: The Essential Readings.* Oxford and Massachusetts: Blackwell Publishers.

Slavin, R. E. (1900). *Cooperative learning: Theory, research and practice.* Englewood Cliffs, NJ: Prentice Hall.

Slavney, P. R. (1990). *Perspectives on hysteria.* Baltimore: The Johns Hopkins University Press.

Slobin, D. I. (1996). From "thought and language" to "thinking for speaking." In J. J. Gumperz, et al. (Eds.), *Rethinking linguistic relativity. Studies in the social and cultural foundations of language.* Cambridge, England: Cambridge University Press.

Sloman, S. A., Hayman, C. G., Ohta, N., & Law, J. (1988). Forgetting in primed fragment completion. *Journal of Experimental Psychology: Learning, Memory, and Cognition, 14,* 223–239.

Slone, M. (2000). Responses to media coverage of terrorism. *Journal of Conflict Resolution,* Vol 44(4): 508–522.

Slotnick, S. & Schacter, D. (2004). A sensory signature that distinguishes true from false memories. *Nature Neuroscience, 7,* 664–672.

Smalley, S. L., McGough, J. J., Del'Homme, M., et al. (2000). Familial clustering of symptoms and disruptive behaviors in multiplex families with attention-deficit/hyperactivity disorder. *Journal of the American Academy of Child and Adolescent Psychiatry, 39,* 1135–1143.

Smeets, M. A. M. (1999).Body size categorization in anorexia nervosa using a morphing instrument. *International Journal of Eating Disorders, 25,* 451–455.

Smetana, J. (1988). Adolescents' and parents' conceptions of parental authority. *Child Development, 59,* 321–335.

Smetana, J., & Gaines, C. (1999). Adolescent-parent conflict in middle-class African American families. *Child Development, 70,* 1447–1463.

Smiley, A. (1986). Marijuana: On-road and driving simulator studies. *Alcohol, Drugs and Driving, 2,* 121–134.

Smith, A. T., Snowden, R. J., Milne, A. B. (1995). Is global motion really based on spatial integration of local motion signals? *Ophthalmic Literature, 48,* 228.

Smith, C. (1996). Sleep states, memory processes, and synaptic plasticity. *Behavioural Brain Research, 78,* 49–56.

Smith, C. A., & Ellsworth, P. C. (1985). Patterns of cognitive approach in emotion. *Journal of Personality and Social Psychology, 48,* 813–838.

Smith, C. A., & Lazarus, R. S. (1990). Emotion and adaptation. In L. A. Pervin (Ed.), *Handbook of personality: Theory and research.* New York: Guilford Press.

Smith, C., & Lapp, L. (1991). Increases in number of REMS and REM density in humans following an intensive learning period. *Sleep, 14,* 325–330.

Smith, C., & Rose, G. M. (1997). Posttraining paradoxical sleep in rats is increased after spatial learning in the Morris water maze. *Behavioral Neuroscience, 111,* 1197–1204.

Smith, C. T., Nixon, M. R., & Nader, R. S. (2004). Posttraining increases in REM sleep intensity implicate REM sleep in memory processing and provide a biological marker of learning potential. *Learning and Memory, 11,* 714–719.

Smith, E. R., & Zarate, M. A. (1992). Exemplar-based model of social judgment. *Psychological Review, 99,* 3–21.

Smith, J. W., & Frawley, P. J. (1993). Treatment outcome of 600 chemically dependent patients treated in a multimodal inpatient program including aversion therapy and pentothal interviews. *Journal of Substance Abuse Treatment, 10,* 359–369.

Smith, L. D., & Woodward, W. R. (Eds.) (1996). *B. F. Skinner and behaviorism in American culture.* Bethlehem, PA: Lehigh University Press.

Smith, M. E. (1926). An investigation of the development of the sentence and the extent of vocabulary in young children. *University of Iowa Studies in Child Welfare, 3* (No. 5).

Smith, M. L., & Glass, G. V. (1977). Meta-analyses of psychotherapy outcome studies. *American Psychologist, 32,* 752–760.

Smith, R. E. (1989). Effects of coping skills training on generalized self-efficacy and locus of control. *Journal of Personality and Social Psychology, 56,* 228–233.

Smith, R. E. (1993). *Enhancing human performance: A psychological skills approach.* Minneapolis: West.

Smith, R. E. (1996). Performance anxiety, cognitive interference, and concentration enhancement strategies in sports. In I. G. Sarason, G. R. Pierce, & B. R. Sarason (Eds.), *Cognitive interference: Theories, methods, and findings.* Mahwah, NJ: Erlbaum.

Smith, R. E., & Nye, S. L. (1989). A comparison of induced affect and covert rehearsal in the acquisition of stress management coping skills. *Journal of Counseling Psychology, 36,* 17–23.

Smith, R. E., & Rohsenow, D. J. (1987). Cognitive-affective stress management training: A treatment and resource manual. *Social and Behavioral Science Documents, 17*(2), Document No. 2829.

Smith, R. E., & Smoll, F. L. (1990). Sport performance anxiety. In H. Leitenberg (Ed.), *Handbook of social and evaluation anxiety.* New York: Plenum.

Smith, R. E., & Smoll, F. L. (1997). Coaching the coaches: Youth sports as a scientific and applied behavioral setting. *Current Directions in Psychological Science, 6,* 16–21.

Smith, R. E., Leffingwell, T. R., & Ptacek, J. T. (1999). Can people remember how they coped? Factors associated with discordance between same-day and retrospective reports. *Journal of Personality and Social Psychology, 76,* 1050–1061.

Smith, R. E., Smoll, F. L., & Ptacek, J. T. (1989). Conjunctive moderator variables in vulnerability and resiliency research: Life stress, social support and coping skills, and adolescent sport injuries. *Journal of Personality and Social Psychology, 58,* 360–370.

Smith, R. E., Smoll, F. L., & Schutz, R. W. (1990). Measurement and correlates of sport-specific cognitive and somatic trait anxiety: The Sport Anxiety Scale. *Anxiety Research, 2,* 263–280.

Smith, S. L., & Donnerstein, E. (1998). Harmful effects of exposure to media violence: Learning of aggression, emotional desensitization, and fear. In R. G. Geen, G. Russell, & E. Donnerstein (Eds.), *Human aggression: Theories, research, and implications for social policy.* San Diego: Academic Press.

Smith, S. M., & Rothkopf, E. Z. (1984). Contextual enrichment and distribution of practice in the classroom. *Cognition and Instruction, 1,* 341–358.

Smith, S. M., McIntosh, W. D., & Bazzini, D. G. (1999). Are the beautiful good in Hollywood? An investigation of the beauty-and-goodness stereotype on film. *Basic and Applied Social Psychology, 21,* 69–80.

Snow, M. E., Jacklin, C. N., & Maccoby, E. E. (1983). Sex-of-child-differences in father-child interaction at one year of age. *Child Development, 54,* 227–232.

Snyder, C. R. (Ed.). (2001). *Coping with stress: Effective people and processes.* New York: Oxford University Press.

Snyder, F. (1970). The phenomenology of dreaming. In L. Madow & L. Snow (Eds.), *The psychodynamic implications of the physiological studies on dreams.* Springfield, IL: Charles C Thomas.

Snyder, H. N., & Sickmund, M. (1995). *Juvenile offenders and victims: A national report.* Washington, DC: Office of Juvenile Justice and Delinquency Prevention.

Snyder, M. (1987). *Public appearances/private realities: The psychology of self-monitoring.* New York: W. H. Freeman.

Snyder, M. (2001). Self-fulfilling stereotypes. In A. Branaman (Ed.). *Self and society: Blackwell readers in sociology.* Malden, MA: Blackwell.

Snyder, M., & Gangestad, S. (1986). On the nature of self-monitoring: Matters of assessment, matters of validity. *Journal of Personality and Social Psychology, 51,* 125–139.

Snyder, M., & Swann, W. B., Jr. (1976). When actions reflect attitudes: The politics of impression management. *Journal of Personality and Social Psychology, 34,* 1034–1042.

Snyder, M., Berscheid, E., & Glick, P. (1985). Focusing on the exterior and the interior: Two investigations of the initiation of personal relationships. *Journal of Personality and Social Psychology, 48,* 1427–1439.

Snyder, S. H. (1977). Opiate receptors and internal opiates. *Scientific American, 236,* 44–56.

Sober, E., & Wilson, D. S. (1998). *Unto others: The evolution and psychology of unselfish behavior.* Cambridge, MA: Harvard University Press.

Sohn, C. H. & Lam, R. W. (2005). Update on the biology of seasonal affective disorder. *CNS Spectrums, 10,* 635–646.

Soler, M. J., & Ruiz, J. C. (1996). The spontaneous use of memory aids at different educational levels. *Applied Cognitive Psychology, 10,*41–51.

Solms, M. (2002). Dreaming: Cholinergic and dopaminergic hypotheses. In E. Perry, H. Ashton, & A. Young (Eds.), *Neurochemistry of consciousness: Neurotransmitters in mind. Advances in consciousness research.* Amsterdam: Benjamins.

Solomon, G. F., Segerstrom, S. C., Grohr, P., Kemeny, M., & Fahey, J. (1997). Shaking up immunity: Psychological and immunologic changes after a natural disaster. *Psychosomatic Medicine, 59,* 114–127.

Solomon, R. L., & Wynne, L. C. (1953). Traumatic avoidance learning: Acquisition in normal dogs. *Journal of Abnormal and Social Psychology, 48,* 291–302.

Solomon, Z., & Ginzburg, K. (1998). War trauma and the aged: An Israeli perspective. In J. Lomaranz (Ed.), *Handbook of aging and mental health: An integrative approach.* New York: Plenum.

Solso, R. L. (1999). *Mind and brain sciences in the 21st century.* Cambridge, MA: MIT Press.

Sommer, I. E. C., Aleman, A., Bouma, A., Kahn, R. S. (2004). Do women really have more bilateral language representation than men? A meta-analysis of funtional imaging studies. *Brain, 127*(8), 1845–1852.

Somse, P., Chapko, M. K., Wata, J. B., & et al. (1998). Evaluation of an AIDS training program for traditional healers in the Central African Republic. *AIDS Education and Prevention, 10,* 558–564.

Sorensen, T., & Snow, B. (1991). How children tell: The process of disclosure in child sexual abuse. *Child Welfare, 70,* 3–15.

Sorenson, S. B. (2002). Preventing traumatic stress: Public health approaches. *Journal of Traumatic Stress, 15,* 3–7.

Sotres-Bayon, F., Cain, C. K., and LeDoux, J. E. (2006). Brain mechanisms of fear extinction: Historical perspectives on the contribution of prefrontal cortex. *Biological Psychiatry, 60,* 329–336.

Soussignan, R. (2002). Duchenne smile, emotional experience, and autonomic reactivity: A test of the facial feedback hypothesis. *Emotion, 2,* 52–74.

Soussignan, R., & Schaal, B. (2005) Emotional processes in human newborns: a functionalist perspective. In J. Nadel & D. Muir (Eds.), *Emotional Development: Current and future research directions.* Oxford: Oxford University Press (pp. 127-159).

Soussignan, R., Schaal, B., Marlier, L., & Jiang, T. (1997). Facial and autonomic responses to biological and artificial olfactory stimuli in human neonates: Re-examining early hedonic discrimination of odors. *Physiology and Behavior, 62,* 745–758.

Spanos, N. P. (1986). Hypnotic behavior: A social-psychological interpretation of amnesia, analgesia, and "trance logic." *Behavioral and Brain Sciences, 9,* 449–467.

Spanos, N. P. (1991). A sociocognitive approach to hypnosis. In S. J. Lynn & J. W. Rhue (Eds.), *Theories of hypnosis: Current models and perspectives.* New York: Guilford Press.

Spanos, N. P. (1994). Multiple identity enactments and multiple personality disorder: A sociocognitive perspective. *Psychological Bulletin, 116,* 143–165.

Spanos, N. P. (1996). *Multiple identities and false memories: A sociocognitive perspective.* Washington, DC: American Psychological Association.

Spanos, N. P., & Chaves, J. F. (Eds.) (1988). *Hypnosis: The cognitive-behavioral perspective.* Buffalo, NY: Prometheus Books.

Spanos, N. P., & Katsanis, J. (1989). Effects of institutional set on attributions of nonvolition during hypnotic and nonhypnotic analgesia. *Journal of Personality and Social Psychology, 56,* 182–188.

Spanos, N. P., DuBreuil, S. C., & Gabora, N. J. (1991). Four-month follow-up of skill-training-induced enhancements in hypnotizability. *Contemporary Hypnosis, 8,* 25–32.

Sparkes, S., Grant, V. L., & Lett, B. T. (2003). Role of conditioned taste aversion in the development of activity anorexia. *Appetite, 41,* 161–165.

Spearman, C. (1923). *The nature of "intelligence" and the principles of cognition.* London: Macmillan.

Spector, P. E. (1997). The role of frustration in antisocial behavior at work. In R. A. Giacalone & J. Greenberg (Eds.), *Antisocial behavior in organizations.* Thousand Oaks, CA: Sage Publications.

Speisman, J., Lazarus, R. S., Mordkoff, A., & Davidson, L. (1964). Experimental reduction of stress based on ego-defense theory. *Journal of Abnormal and Social Psychology, 68,* 367–380.

Spencer, H. (1879). *The data of ethics.* New York: Crowell.

Sperling, G. (1960). The information available in brief visual presentations. *Psychological Monographs 74* (Whole No. 11).

Sperling, G. (1984). A unified theory of attention and signal detection. In R. Parasuraman & D. R. Davies (Eds.), *Varieties of attention.* New York: Academic Press.

Sperry, R. W. (1970). Perception in the absence of neocortical commissures. In Association for Research in Nervous and Mental Disease, *Perception and its disorders.* New York: Williams & Wilkins.

Spiegel, D. (2000). Cancer. In G. Fink (Ed.), *Encyclopedia of stress.* San Diego: Academic Press.

Spiegler, M. D., & Guevremont, D. C. (2003). *Contemporary behavior therapy.* Belmont, CA: Wadsworth.

Spielberger, C. D., & DeNike, L. D. (1966). Descriptive behaviorism versus cognitive theory in verbal operant conditioning. *Psychological Review, 73,* 306–326.

Spitzer, R. L. (1975). On pseudoscience in science, logic in remission, and psychiatric diagnosis: a critique of Rosenhan's "On being sane in insane places." *Journal of Abnormal Psychology, 84*(5), 442–452.

Sprafkin, J. N., Liebert, R. M., & Poulos, R. W. (1975). Effects of a prosocial televised example on children's helping. *Journal of Experimental Child Psychology, 20,* 119–126.

Sprecher, S., & Regan, P. C. (1998). Passionate and companionate love in courting and young married couples. *Sociological Inquiry, 68,* 163–185.

Sprecher, S., Barbee, A., & Schwartz, P. (1995). "Was it good for you, too?" Gender differences in first sexual intercourse experiences. *Journal of Sex Research, 32,* 13–15.

Springer, S. (1997). *Left brain, right brain.* San Francisco: W. H. Freeman.

Squier, L. H., & Domhoff, G. W. (1998). The presentation of dreaming and dreams in introductory psychology textbooks: A critical examination with suggestions for textbook authors and course instructors. *Dreaming: Journal of the Association for the Study of Dreams, 8,* 149–168.

Squire, L. R. (1987). *Memory and brain.* Oxford: Oxford University Press.

Squire, L. R. (1992). Memory and the hippocampus: A synthesis from findings with rats, monkeys, and humans. *Psychological Review, 99,* 195–231.

Squire, L. R., & Zola-Morgan, S. (1991). The medial temporal lobe memory system. *Science, 253,* 1380–1386.

Sroufe, L. (2002). From infant attachment to promotion of adolescent autonomy: Prospective, longitudinal data on the role of parents in development. In J. G. Borkowski, S. L. Ramey, & M. Bristol-Power (Eds.), *Parenting and the child's world: Influences on academic, intellectual, and social-emotional development. Monographs in parenting.* Mahwah, NJ: Erlbaum.

Staats, H., van Leeuwen, E., & Wit, A. (2000). A longitudinal study of informational interventions to save energy in an office building. *Journal of Applied Behavior Analysis, 33,* 101–104.

Stahl, S. M. (2000). *Essential psychopharmacology: Neuroscientific basis and clinical applications, 2nd edition.* New York: Cambridge University Press.

Stalder, D. R., & Baron, R. S. (1998). Attributional complexity as a moderator of dissonance-produced attitude change. *Journal of Personality and Social Psychology, 75,* 449–455.

Stanford Center for Narcolepsy (2000). *Basic mechanisms involved in the disease.* [Online]. Available: http://www.med.stanford.edu/school/Psychiatry/narcolepsy/research1.html

Stanley, B. G., Kyrkouli, S. E., Lampert, S., & Leibowitz, S. F. (1986). Neuropeptide Y chronically injected into the hypothalamus: A powerful neurochemical inducer of hyperphagia and obesity. *Peptides, 7,* 1189–1192.

Stanley, S. M., Rhoades, G. K., & Markman, H. (2006). Sliding versus deciding: inertia and the premarital cohabitation effect. Family Relations. Interdisciplinary Journal of Applied Family Studies, 55, 499–509.

Stark, E. (1989, May). Teen sex: Not for love. *Psychology Today,* 10–11.

Statistics Canada (1996). *Health Reports, 40.*

Statistics Canada (1999). *Youth Violent Crime.* The Daily, December 21, 1999.

Staub, E. (1996). Cultural-society roots of violence: The examples of genocidal violence and of contemporary youth violence in the United States. *American Psychologist, 51,* 117–132.

Steele, C. M. & Baumeister, R. F. (1999). The psychology of self-affirmation: Sustaining the integrity of the self. *Key Readings in Social Psychology.* New York: Psychology Press.

Steele, C. M., & Josephs, R. A. (1990). Alcohol myopia: Its prized and dangerous effects. *American Psychologist, 45,* 921–933.

Steele, J., James, J. B., & Barnett, R. C. (2002). Learning in a man's world: Examining the perceptions of undergraduate women in male-dominated academic areas. *Psychology of Women Quarterly, 26,* 46–50.

Steers, R. M., & Porter, L. W. (1991) (Eds.). *Motivation and work behavior* (5th ed.). New York: McGraw-Hill.

Steeves, J. K. E., Culham, J. C., Duchaine, B. C., Pratesi, C. C., Valyear, K.F., Schindler, I., Humphrey, G. K., Milner, D. A., & Goodale, M. A. (2006). The fusiform face area is not sufficient for face recognition: Evidence from a patient with dense prosopagnosia and no occipital face area. *Neuropsychologia, 44,* 594–609.

Stein, D. J. (1997) (Ed.). *Cognitive science and the unconscious.* Washington, DC: American Psychiatric Press.

Stein, D. J., & Hollander, E. (2002). *Textbook of anxiety disorders.* Washington, DC: American Psychiatric Press.

Stein, M., Miller, A. H., & Trestman, R. L. (1990). Depression and the immune system. In R. Ader, N. Cohen, & D. L. Felten (Eds), *Psychoneuroimmunology II.* New York: Academic Press.

Steinberg, L., Lamborn, S. D., Darling, N., & Mount, N. S. (1994). Over-time changes in adjustment and competence among adolescents from authoritative, authoritarian, indulgent, and neglectful families. *Child Development, 65,* 754–770.

Steinberg, R. J. (1986). Intelligence Applied: Understanding and increasing your intellecutal skills. San Diego: Harcourt Brace, Jancovich.

Steinberg, R. J. (1988). *The triarchic mind: A new theory of human intelligence.* New York: Viking Press.

Stella, N., Schweitzer, P., & Piomelli, D. (1997). A second endogenous cannabinoid that modulates long-term potentiation. *Nature, 388* (6644), 773–778.

Stellar, E. (1954). The physiology of motivation. *Psychological Review, 61,* 5–22.

Stephan, W. G. (1990). School desegregation: Short-term and long-term effects. In H. Knopke (Ed.), *Opening Doors: An appraisal of race relations in America.* Tuscaloosa: University of Alabama Press.

Stephan, W. G. (1991). Intergroup relations and prejudice. In R. M. Baron, W. G. Graziano, & C. Stangor (Eds.), *Social psychology.* Ft. Worth, TX: Holt, Rinehart & Winston.

Stephenson, J. (1998). Ethics group drafts guidelines for control of genetic material and information [news]. *Journal of the American Medical Association, 279(3),* 184.

Steptoe, A. (2000). Control and stress. In G. Fink (Ed.), *Encyclopedia of stress.* San Diego: Academic Press.

Steptoe, A. & Wardle, J. (2001). Locus of control and health behaviour revisited: A multivariate analysis of young adults from 18 countries. *British Journal of Psychology, 92,* 659–672.

Sternberg, K. J., Lamb, M. E., Esplin, P. W., Opbach, Y., & Hershkowitz, I. (2002). Using a structure interview protocol to improve the quality of investigative interviews. In M. L. Eisen, (Ed.), *Memory and suggestibility in the forensic interview: Personality and Clinical Psychology Series.* Mahwah, NJ: Erlbaum.

Sternberg, R. J. (1988). Triangulating love. In R. J. Sternberg & M. L. Barnes (Eds.), *The psychology of love.* New Haven, CT: Yale University Press.

Sternberg, R. J. (1997). Construct validation of a triangular love scale. *European Journal of Social Psychology, 27,* 313–335.

Sternberg, R. J. (1998a). Principles of teaching for successful intelligence. *Educational Psychologist, 33,* 65–72.

Sternberg, R. J. (1998b). Applying the triarchic theory of human intelligence in the classroom. In R. J. Sternberg & W. M. Williams (Eds.), *Intelligence, instruction, and assessment: Theory into practice.* Mahwah, NJ: Erlbaum.

Sternberg, R. J., Nokes, C., Geissler, P., Prince, R., Okatcha, F., Bundy, D. A., & Grigorenko, E. L. (2001). The relationship between academic and practical intelligence: A case study in Kenya. *Intelligence, 29,* 401–418.

Sternberg, R. J., Torff, B., & Grigorenko, E. L. (1998). Teaching triarchically improves school achievement. *Journal of Educational Psychology, 90,* 374–384.

Stetson, B. A., Rahn, J. M., Dubbert, P. M., Wilner, B. I., & Mercury, M. G. (1997). Prospective evaluation of the effects of stress on exercise adherence in community-residing women. *Health Psychology, 16,* 515–520.

Stevenson, H. W., Stigler, J. W., Lee, S. Y., Lucker, G. W., Kitamura, S., & Hsu, C. C. (1985). Cognitive performance and academic achievement of Japanese, Chinese, and American children. *Child Development, 56,* 718–734.

Stewart, J. & Wise, R. A. (1992). Reinstatement of heroin self-administration habits: Morphine prompts and naltrexone discourages renewed responding after extinction. *Psychopharmacology,* 108: 79–84.

Stewart, J. (2000). Pathways to relapse: The neurobiology of drug- and stress-induced relapse to drug taking. *Journal of Psychiatry and Neuroscience,* 25:125–136.

Stewart, J. (2002). Modulation of the subjective and physiological effects of drugs by contexts and expectations—The search for mechanisms: Comment on Alessi, Roll, Reilly, and Johanson (2002). *Experimental and Clinical Psychopharmacology, 10,* 96–98.

Stickgold, R., Pace, S. E., & Hobson, J. A. (1994). A new paradigm for dream research: Mentation reports following spontaneous arousal from REM and NREM sleep recorded in a home setting. *Consciousness and Cognition: An International Journal, 3,* 16–29.

Stockhorst, U., Klosterhalfen, S., & Steingrueber, H. J. (1998). Conditioned nausea and further side-effects in cancer chemotherapy: A review. *Journal of Psychophysiology, 12,* 14–33.

Stockhorst, U., Steingrueber H-J., Enck, P., & Klosterhalfen, S. (2006). Pavlovian conditioning of nausea and vomiting. *Autonomic Neuroscience: Basic & Clinical, 129,* 50–57.

Stokols, D. (1995). The paradox of environmental psychology. *American Psychologist, 50,* 821–837.

Stone, A. A., Shiffman, S. S., & DeVries, M. (2000). Rethinking our self-report assessment methodologies: An argument for collecting ecologically valid, momentary measurements. In D. Kahneman, E. Diener, & N. Schwarz (Eds.), *Understanding quality of life: Scientific perspectives on enjoyment and suffering.* New York: Russel Sage Foundation.

Stone, J., & Cooper, J. (2001). A self standards model of cognitive dissonance. *Journal of Experimental Social Psychology, 37,* 228–243.

Storm, L., & Ertel, S. (2001). Does psi exist? Comments on Milton and Wiseman's (1999) meta-analysis of Ganzfield research. *Psychological Bulletin, 12,* 424–433.

Storms, M. D. (1973). Videotape and the attribution process: Reversing actors' and observers' points of view. *Journal of Personality and Social Psychology, 27,* 165–175.

Stormshak, E. A., Bierman, K. L., McMahon, R. J., Lengua, L. J. Conduct Problems Prevention Research Group. (2000). Parenting practices and child disruptive behavior problems in early elementary school. *Journal of Clinical Child Psychology, 29,* 17–29.

Strack, F., Martin, L. L., & Stepper, S. (1988). Inhibiting and facilitating conditions of facial expressions: A non-obtrusive test of the facial feedback hypothesis. *Journal of Personality and Social Psychology, 54,* 768–777.

Stratton, G. (1896). Some preliminary experiments on vision without inversion of the retinal image. *Psychological Review, 3,* 611–617.

Strawbridge, W. J., Shema, S. J., Cohen, R. D., Roberts, R. E., & Kaplan, G. A. (1998). Religion buffers effects of some stressors on depression but exacerbates others. *Journal of Gerontology, 53,* 118–126.

Streissguth, A. P., Bookstein, F. L., Barr, H. M., Press, S., & Sampson, P. D. (1998). A Fetal Alcohol Behavior Scale. *Alcoholism: Clinical and Experimental Research, 22,* 325–333.

Streissguth, A. P., Clarren, S. K., & Jones, K. L. (1985). Natural history of the fetal alcohol syndrome: A 10-year follow-up of eleven patients. *The Lancet, 2* (8446), 85–91.

Streissguth, A. P., Landesman, D. S., Martin, J. C., & Smith, D. W. (1982). Clinical effects of fetal alcohol syndrome. *Digest of Alcoholism Theory and Application, 1,* 5–10.

Strentz, H. (1984, December 25). The road to imbecility. *Cleveland Plain Dealer,* p. B23.

Strentz, T., & Auerbach, S. M. (1988). Adjustment to the stress of simulated captivity: Effects of emotion-focused versus problem-focused preparation on hostages differing in locus of control. *Journal of Personality and Social Psychology, 55,* 652–660.

Stricker, E. M., & Verbalis, J. G. (1987). Biological bases of hunger and satiety. *Annals of Behavioral Medicine, 9,* 3–8.

Strober, M., & Humphrey, L. L. (1987). Familial contributions to the etiology and course of anorexia nervosa and bulimia. *Journal of Consulting and Clinical Psychology, 55,* 654–659.

Strough, J., Berg, C. A., & Sandone, C. (1996). Goals for solving everyday problems across the life span: Age and gender differences in the salience of interpersonal concerns. *Developmental Psychology, 32,* 1106–1115.

Strupp, H. H. (1989). Psychotherapy: Can the practitioner learn from the researcher? *American Psychologist, 44,* 717–724.

Stryer, L. (1987). The molecules of visual excitation. *Scientific American, 257*(1), 42–50.

Stukas, A. A., Snyder, M., & Clary, E. G. (1999). The effects of "mandatory volunteerism" on intentions to volunteer. *Psychological Science, 10,* 59–64.

Stunkard, A. J., Harris, J. R., Pedersen, N. L., & McClearn, G. E. (1990). The body-mass index of twins who have been reared apart. *New England Journal of Medicine, 322,* 1483–1487.

Sue, D. W., & Sue, D. (1999). *Counseling the culturally different: Theory and practice (*2nd ed.). New York: Wiley.

Sue, S. (1977). Community mental health services to minority groups: Some optimism, some pessimism. *American Psychologist, 32,* 616–624.

Sue, S. (1998). In search of cultural competence in psychotherapy and counseling. *American Psychologist, 53,* 440–448.

Sue, S., & Zane, N. (1987). The role of culture and cultural techniques in psychotherapy. *American Psychologist, 42,* 37–45.

Sue, S., Fujino, D., Hu, L. N., Takeuchi, D., & Zane, N. (1991). Community mental health services for ethnic minority groups: A test of the cultural responsiveness hypothesis. *Journal of Consulting and Clinical Psychology, 59,* 533–540.

Suggs, R. (1962). *The hidden worlds of Polynesia.* New York: Harcourt.

Suh, E., Diener, E., & Fujita, F. (1996). Events and subjective well-being: Only recent events matter. *Journal of Personality and Social Psychology, 70,* 1091–1102.

Suh, E., Diener, E., Oishi, S., & Triandis, H. (1998). The shifting basis of life satisfaction judgments across cultures: Emotions versus norms. *Journal of Personality and Social Psychology, 74,* 482–493.

Suinn, R. M., Osborne, D., & Winfree, P. (1962). The self-concept and accuracy of recall of inconsistent self-related information. *Journal of Clinical Psychology, 18,* 473–474.

Sullivan, M. A., & O'Leary, S. G. (1990). Maintenance following reward and cost token programs. *Behavior Therapy, 21,* 139–149.

Suls, J., Green, P., & Hillis, S. (1998). Emotional reactivity to everyday problems, affective inertia, and neuroticism. *Personality and Social Psychology Bulletin, 24,* 127–136.

Suls, J. M., & Wallston, K. A. (2003). *Social psychological foundations of health and illness.* New York: Blackwell.

Suomi, S. J., & Harlow, H. F. (1972). Social rehabilitation of isolate-reared monkeys. *Developmental Psychology, 6,* 487–496.

Super, C. M. (1976). Environmental effects on motor development: A case of African infant precocity. *Developmental Medicine and Child Neurology, 18,* 561–567.

Super, C. M., Harkness, S. (1997). The cultural structuring of child development. In J. W. Berry, P. R. Dasen, & T. S. Saraswathi (Eds.), *Handbook of cross-cultural psychology* (2nd ed., Vol. 2). Boston: Allyn & Bacon.

Super, D. E. (1957). *The psychology of careers.* New York: Harper & Row.

Super, D. E. (1981). A developmental theory: Implementing a self-concept. In D. H. Montross & C. J. Shinkman (Eds.), *Career development in the 1980s: Theory and practice.* Springfield, IL: Charles C Thomas.

Sussman, N. M., & Rosenfeld, H. M. (1982). Influence of culture, language, and sex on conversational distance. *Journal of Personality and Social Psychology, 42,* 66–74.

Sutton, S. K. (2002). Incentive and threat reactivity: Relations with anterior cortical activity. In D. Cervone & W. Mischel (Eds.), *Advances in personality science.* New York: Guilford Press.

Sutton, S. K., & Davidson, R. J. (1997). Prefrontal brain asymmetry: A biological substrate of the behavioral approach and inhibition systems. *Psychological Science, 8,* 204–210.

Swain, I., Zelazo, P.R., & Clifton, R. (1993). Newborn infants' memory for speech sounds retained over 24 hours. *Developmental Psychology, 29,* 312–323.

Swan, G. E., Dame, A., & Carmelli, D. (1991). Involuntary retirement, Type A behavior, and current functioning in elderly men: 27-year followup of the Western Collaborative Group Study. *Psychology and Aging, 6,* 384–391.

Swann, W. B. (1966). *Self-traps: The elusive quest for higher self-esteem.* New York: W. H. Freeman.

Swann, W. B. J. R. (2004). The trouble with change: Self-verification and allegiance to the self. In R. Lowalski and M. R. Leary (Eds.), The interface of social and clinical psychology: key readings. *Key Readings in Social Psychology,* 349–356. New York: Psychology Press.

Swann, W. B., Jr., Stein-Seroussi, A., & Giesler, R. B. (1992). Why people self-verify. *Journal of Personality and Social Psychology, 62,* 392–401.

Swets, J. A. (1992). The science of choosing the right decision threshold in high-stakes diagnostics. *American Psychologist, 47,* 522–532.

Swets, J. A. (1998). Enhancing diagnostic decisions. In R. R. Hoffman & M. F. Sherrick (Eds.), *Viewing psychology as a whole: The integrative science of William N. Dember.* Washington, DC: American Psychological Association.

Symons, D. (1995). Beauty is in the adaptations of the beholder: The evolutionary psychology of human female sexual attractiveness. In P. R. Abramson & S. D. Pinkerton (Eds.), *Sexual nature, sexual culture.* Chicago: University of Chicago Press.

Szasz, T. (1974). *The myth of mental illness* (revised edition). New York: Harper & Row.

Szasz, T. (1987). *Insanity: The idea and its consequences.* New York: Wiley.

Szeszeko, P.R., MacMillan, S., McMeniman, M., Chen, S., Baribault, K., Lim, K.O., et al. (2004). Brain structural abnormalities in psychotropic drug-naïve pediatric patients with obsessive-compulsive disorder. *American Journal of Psychiatry, 161,* 1049–1056.

Szkrybalo, J., & Ruble, D. N. (1999). "God made me a girl": Sex-category constancy judgments and explanations revisited. *Developmental Psychology, 35,* 392–402.

Szymusiak, R., & McGinty, D. (1986). Sleep-related neuronal discharge in the basal forebrain of cats. *Brain Research, 370,* 82–92.

Tait, R. W., & Saladin, M. E. (1986). Concurrent development of excitatory and inhibitory associations during backward conditioning. *Animal Learning and Behavior.* 14: 133–137.

Tajfel, H. (1970). Experiments in intergroup discrimination. *Scientific American,* 223(2), 96–102.

Tajfel, H., & Turner, J. C. (1986). The social identity theory of intergroup behavior. In S. Worchel & W. G. Austin (Eds.), *The psychology of intergroup relations* (2nd ed.). Chicago, IL: Nelson-Hall.

Tajfel, H., Turner, J. C., Jost, J. T., Sidanius, J. (2004). The social identity theory of intergroup behavior. Political psychology: Key readings. *Key readings in social psychology* (276–293). New York: Psychology Press.

Takahashi, Y. (1990). Is multiple personality disorder really rare in Japan? *Dissociation: Progress in the Dissociative Disorders, 3,* 57–59.

Talbot, D. (2003). Advanced brain imaging. *Technological Review,* (Cambridge, Mass), 105, 64.

Talwar, V., & Lee, K. (2002). Development of lying to conceal a transgression: children's control of expressive behavior during verbal deception. *International Journal of Behavioral Development.*

Tamres, L. K., Janicki, D. & Helgeson, V. S. (2002). Sex differences in coping behavior: A meta-analytic review and an examination of relative coping. *Personality and Social Psychology, 6,* 2–30.

Tan, E. S. (1980). Transcultural aspects of anxiety. In G. Burrows and G. Davies (Eds.), *Handbook of studies on anxiety.* Amsterdam, The Netherlands: Elsevier.

Tanaka-Matsumi, J. (1979). Taijin Kyofushu: Diagnostic and cultural issues in Japanese psychiatry. *Culture, Medicine, and Psychiatry, 3,* 231–245.

Tanaka-Matsumi, J., & Draguns, J. (1997). Culture and psychopathology. In J. W. Berry, M. H. Segall, & C. Kagitáibasi (Eds.), *Handbook of cross-cultural psychology* (Vol. 3). Boston: Allyn & Bacon.

Tanda, G., Pontieri, F. E., & Di-Chiara, G. (1997). Cannabinoid and heroin activation of mesolimbic dopamine transmission by a common mu1 opioid receptor mechanism. *Science, 276,* 2048–2050.

Tanner, J. M. (1978). *Fetus into man: Physical growth from conception to maturity.* Cambridge, MA: Harvard University Press.

Tarr, M. J., & Vuong, Q. C. (2002). Visual object recognition. In H. Pashler & S. Yantis (Eds.). *Steven's handbook of experimental psychology: Vol. 1. Sensation and perception* (3rd ed.). New York: Wiley.

Tarumi, S., Ichinaya, A., Yamada, S., Umesue, M., Juroki, T. (2004) Taijin kyofusho in university students: Patterns of fear and predispositions to the offensive variant. *Transcultural Psychiatry, 41*(4), 533–546.

Taylor, F. W. (1911). *The principles of scientific management.* New York: Harper.

Taylor, H. G. (1998). Analysis of the medical use of marijuana and its societal implications. *Journal of the American Pharmaceutical Association, 38,* 126.

Taylor, R. D., & Wang, M. C. (Eds.) (2000). *Resilience across contexts: Family, work, culture, and community.* Mahwah, NJ: Erlbaum.

Taylor, S. E. (1999). *Health Psychology* (2nd ed.). Boston: McGraw-Hill.

Taylor, S. E. (2003). *Health Psychology* (3rd ed.). Boston: McGraw-Hill.

Taylor, S. E., & Brown, J. D. (1988). Illusion and well-being: A social psychological perspective on mental health. *Psychological Bulletin, 103,* 193–210.

Taylor, S. E., & Brown, J. D. (1994). "Illusion" of mental health does not explain positive illusions. *American-Psychologist, 49,* 972–973.

Taylor, S. E., Kemeny, M. E., Reed, G. M., Bower, J. E., & Gruenwald, T. L. (2000). Psychological resources, positive illusions, and health. *American Psychologist, 55,* 99–109.

Teachman, J. D. (2002). Childhood living arrangements and the intergenerational transmission of divorce. *Journal of Marriage and Family, 64,* 717–729.

Teasdale, J. D., & Fogarty, F. J. (1979). Differential affects of induced mood on retrieval of pleasant and unpleasant events from episodic memory. *Journal of Abnormal Psychology, 88,* 248–257.

Teghtsoonian, R. (1971). On the exponents in Stevens' law and the constant in Ekman's law. *Psychological Review, 78,* 71–80.

Teicher, M. H., Glod, C. A., Magnus, E., & Harper, D. (1997). Circadian rest-activity disturbances in seasonal affective disorder. *Archives of General Psychiatry, 54,* 124–130.

Teitelbaum, S., & Geiselman, R. E. (1997). Observer mood and cross-racial cognition of faces. *Journal of Cross-Cultural Psychology, 28,* 93–106.

Tellegen, A., Lykken, D. T., Bouchard, T. J., Wilcox, K. J., Segal, N. L., & Rich, S. (1988). Personality similarity in twins reared apart and together. *Journal of Personality and Social Psychology, 54,* 1031–1039.

Templeton, J. J. (1998). Learning from others' mistakes: A paradox revisited. *Animal Behaviour, 55,* 79–85.

Templeton, L. M., & Wilcox, S. A. (2000). A tale of two representations: The misinformation effect and children's developing theory of mind. *Child Development, 71,* 402–416.

Tenenbaum, H. R. & Leaper, C. (2002). Are parents' gender schemas related to their children's gender-related cognitions? A meta-analysis. *Developmental Psychology, 38,* 615–630.

Tenenbaum, H. R., & Leaper, C. (2003). Parent-child conversations about science: The socialization of gender inequities? *Developmental Psychology, 39,* 34–47.

Terner, J. M., Lomas, L. M., Smith, E. S., Barrett, A. C., & Picker, M. J. (2003). Pharmacogenetic analysis of sex differences in opioid antinociception in rats. *Pain, 106,* 381–391.

Terracciano, A., Abdel-Khalek, A. M. et al. (2005). National character does not reflect mean personality trait levels in 49 cultures. *Science, 310,* 96–100.

Terrace, H. M., Petitto, L. A., Sanders, R. J. & Bever, T. G. (1979). Can an ape create a sentence? *Science, 206,* 891–902.

Terrace, H. S. (1979). *Nim.* New York: Knopf.

Tesser, A. (1988). Toward a self-evaluation maintenance model of social behavior. In L. Berkowitz (Ed.), *Advances in experimental social psychology* (Vol. 21). Orlando, FL: Academic Press.

Tesser, A., & Shaffer, D. (1990). Attitudes and attitude change. *Annual Review of Psychology, 41,* 479–523.

Testa, M. (2002). The impact of men's alcohol consumption on perpetration of sexual aggression. *Clinical Psychology Review, 22,* 1239–1263.

Testa, M., Fillmore, M. T. et al. (2006). Understanding alcohol expectancy effects: revisiting the placebo condition. *Alcoholism: Clinical and Experimental Research, 30,* 339–348.

Teyber, E. (1992). *Interpersonal process in psychotherapy: A guide for clinical training.* Pacific Grove, CA: Brooks/Cole.

Teyber, E., & McClure, F. (2000). Therapist variables. In C. R. Snyder & R. E. Ingram (Eds.), *Handbook of psychological change: Psychotherapy processes and practices for the 21st century.* New York: Wiley.

Thase, M. E., Greenhouse, J. B., Frank, E. et al. (1997). Treatment of major depression with psychotherapy or psychotherapy-pharmacotherapy combinations. *Archives of General Psychiatry, 54,* 1009–1015.

Thatch, W. T., Goodkin, H. P., & Keating, J. G. (1992). The cerebellum and the adaptive coordination of movement. *Annual Review of Neuroscience, 15,* 161–182.

Thatcher, R. W., Hallett, M., Zeffiro, T., John, E. R., & Huerta, M. (Eds.) (1994). *Functional neuroimaging: Technical foundations.* New York: Academic Press.

Thelen, E., Fisher, D. M., Ridley-Johnson, R. (1984). The relationship between physical growth and a newborn reflex. *Infant Behavior and Development, 7,* 479–493.

Thibaut, J. W., & Kelley, H. H. (1959). *The social psychology of groups.* New York: Wiley.

Thoits, P. (1983). Dimensions of life events that influence psychological distress: An evaluation and synthesis of the literature. In H. B. Kaplan (Ed.), *Psychological stress: Trends in theory and research.* New York: Academic Press.

Thomas, A., & Chess, S. (1977). *Temperament and development.* New York: Brunner/Mazel.

Thomas, A., & Chess, S. (1986). The New York Longitudinal Study: From infancy to early adult life. In R. Plomin & J. Dunn (Eds.), *The study of temperament: Changes, continuities, and challenges.* New York: Brunner/Mazel.

Thomas, L. (1974). *The lives of a cell.* New York: Viking Press.

Thomas, R. M. (2000). *Human development theories: Windows on culture.* Thousand Oaks, CA: Sage Publications.

Thomas, S. A., & Palmiter, R. D. (1997). Disruption of the dopamine beta-hydroxylase gene in mice suggests roles for norepinephrine in motor function, learning, and memory. *Behavioral Neuroscience, 111,* 579–589.

Thomas, S. L., Skitka, L. J., Christen, S., & Jurgena, M. (2002). Social facilitation and impression formation. *Basic and Applied Social Psychology, 24,* 67–70.

Thomas, W. P., & Collier, V. P. (1997). *School effectiveness for language minority students.* Washington, DC: National Clearinghouse for Bilingual Education.

Thompson, J. G. (1988). *The psychobiology of emotions.* New York: Plenum.

Thompson, P. M., Giedd, J. N., Woods, R. P., Macdonald, D., Evans, A. C., & Toga, A. W. (2000). Growth patterns in the developing brain detected by using continuum mechanical tensor maps. *Nature, 404,* 190–193.

Thompson, R. F. (1985). *The brain: An introduction to neuroscience.* New York: W. H. Freeman.

Thompson, R. F. (1997). *The brain: Introduction to neuroscience* (3rd ed.). San Francisco: W. H. Freeman.

Thompson, R. F., & Robinson, D. N. (1979). Physiological psychology. In E. Hearsh (Ed.), *The first century of experimental psychology.* Hillsdale, NJ: Erlbaum.

Thompson, R. F., & Steinmetz, J. E. (1992). The essential memory trace circuit for a basic form of associative learning. In I. Gormezano & E. A. Wasserman (Eds.), *Learning and memory: The behavioral and biological substrates.* Hillsdale, NJ: Erlbaum.

Thompson, W.F., Schellengerg, E.G., & Husain, G. (2001). Arousal, mood, and the Mozart effect. *Psychological Science, 12,* 248–251.

Thooft, G. (2000). Physics and the paranormal: A theoretical physicist's view. *Skeptical Inquirer, 24* (2), 27–33.

Thorndike, E. L. (1898). *Animal intelligence, an experimental study of the associative processes in animals.* New York: Macmillan.

Thorndike, E. L. (1911). *Animal intelligence: experimental studies.* New York: Macmillan.

Thorndike, R. L., Hagen, E. P., & Sattler, J. M. (1986). *What is intelligence?: Contemporary viewpoints on its nature and definition.* Chicago: Riverside Press.

Thornhill, R. & Gangestad, S. W. (2006). Facial sexual dimorphism, developmental stability, and susceptibility to disease in men and women. *Evolution and Human Behavior, 27,* 131–144.

Tienari, P., Wynne, L. C., Moring, J., & Lahti, I. et al. (Eds.) (1994). The Finnish adoptive family study of schizophrenia: Implications for family research. *British Journal of Psychiatry, 164,* 20–26.

Tilker, H. A. (1970). Socially responsible behavior as a function of observer responsibility and victim feedback. *Journal of Personality and Social Psychology, 14,* 95–100.

Timiras, P. S. (1972). *Developmental psychology and aging.* New York: Macmillan.

Tinbergen, N. (1951). *The study of instinct.* Oxford: Clarendon Press.

Tincas, I., Benga, O., & Fox, N. A. (2006). Temperamental predictors of anxiety disorders. *Cognition, Brain, Behavior, 10,* 489–515.

Tizard, B., & Hodges, J. (1978). The effect of early institutional rearing on the development of eight-year-old children. *Journal of Child Psychology and Psychiatry, 19,* 99–118.

Tjepkema, M. (2004). Use of cannabis and other illicit drugs. *Health Reports, 15(4),* 43–47.

Tobin, J. J., & Friedman, J. (1983). Spirits, shamans, and nightmare death: Survivor stress in a Hmong refugee. *American Journal of Orthopsychiatry, 53,* 439–448.

Toch, H. (1992). *Violent men: An inquiry into the psychology of violence* (rev. ed.). Washington, DC: American Psychological Association.

Todd, K. J., Serrano, A., Lacaille, J. C., and Robitaille, R. (2006). Glial cells in synaptic plasticity. *Journal of Physiology—Paris, 99,* 75–83.

Todorov, A., & Bargh, J. A. (2002). Automatic sources of aggression. *Aggression and Violent Behavior, 7,* 53–68.

Tollefson, G. D. (1993). Major depression. In D. L. Dunner (Ed.), *Current psychiatric therapy.* Philadelphia: Saunders.

Tollison, C. D., Satterswaithe, J. R., & Tollison, J. W. (2002). *Practical pain management.* New York: Williams & Wilkens.

Tolman, E. C. (1948). Cognitive maps in rats and men. *Psychological Review, 55,* 189–208.

Tolman, E. C., & Honzik, C. H. (1930). Introduction and removal of reward and maze performance in rats. *University of California Publications in Psychology, 4,* 257–275.

Tolson, J. M., & Urberg, K. A. (1993). Similarity between adolescent best friends. *Journal of Adolescent Research, 8,* 274–288.

Tomaka, J., Blascovich, J., Kibler, J., & Ernst, J. M. (1997). Cognitive and physiological antecedents of threat and challenge appraisal. *Journal of Personality and Social Psychology, 73,* 63–72.

Tomarken, A. J., & Keener, A. D. (1998). Frontal brain asymmetry and depression: A self-regulatory perspective. Special Issue: Neuropsychological perspectives on affective and anxiety disorders. *Cognition and Emotion, 12*(3), 387–420.

Tomarken, A. J., Davidson, R. J., Wheeler, R. E., & Doss, R. C. (1992). Individual differences in anterior brain symmetry and fundamental dimensions of emotion. *Journal of Personality and Social Psychology, 62,* 676–687.

Tomarken, A. J., Davidson, R. J., Wheeler, R.W., & Kinney, L. (1992). Psychometric properties of resting anterior EEG asymmetry: Temporal stability and internal consistency. *Psychophysiology, 29,* 576–592.

Tomkins, S. S. (1991). *Affect, imagery, consciousness. Vol. 3: Anger and fear.* New York: Springer.

Tonigan, J. S., Toscova, R., & Miller, W. R. (1996). Meta-analysis of the literature on Alcoholics Anonymous: Sample and study characteristics moderate findings. *Journal of Studies on Alcohol, 57,* 65–72.

Tooby, J., & Cosmides, L. (1992). The psychological foundations of culture. In J. H. Barkow, L. Cosmides, & J. Tooby (Eds.), *The adapted mind.* New York: Oxford University Press.

Toro-Morn, M. & Sprecher, S. (2003). A Cross-Cultural Comparison of Mate Preferences among University Students; The United States vs. The People's Republic of China (PRC). *Journal of Comparative Family Studies, 34,* 151–170.

Torrey, E. F. (1997). *Out of the shadows: Confronting America's mental illness crisis.* New York: Wiley.

Toufexis, A. (1989, June 5). The times of your life. *Time,* 66–67.

Trainor, L. J. & Heinmiller, B. M. (1998). The development of evaluative responses to music: infants prefer to listen to consonance over dissonance. *Infant Behavior and Development, 21,* 77–88.

Trainor, L. J., Tsang, C. D., & Chung, V. H. W. (2002). Preference for sensory consonance in 2- and 4-month-old infants. *Music Perception, 20,* 187–194.

Travis, F., Tecce, J., Arenander, A., & Wallace, R. K. (2002). Patterns of EEG coherence, power, and contingent negative variation characterize the integration of transcendental and waking states. *Biological Psychology, 61,* 293–319.

Traue, H. C., & Deighton, R. M. (2000). Emotional inhibition. In G. Fink (Ed.), *Encyclopedia of stress.* San Diego: Academic Press.

Treffner, P. J. & Barrett, R. (2004). Hands-free mobile phone speech while driving degrades coordination and control. Transportation Research Part F: Traffic *Psychology and Behaviour, 7,* 229–246.

Tremblay, L. K., Naranjo, C. A., Cardenas, L., Hermann, N., & Busto, U. E. (2002). Probing brain reward system function in major depressive disorder: Altered response to dextroamphetamine. *Archives of General Psychiatry, 59,* 409–417.

Tremblay, R. E., Schaal, B., Boulerice, B., Arseneault, L., Soussignan, R., & Perusse, D. (1997). Male physical aggression, social dominance, and testosterone levels at puberty: A developmental perspective. In A. Raine, P. A. Brennan, D. P. Farrington, & S. A. Mednick (Eds.), *Biosocial bases of violence.* New York: Plenum.

Tremblay, R.E., Pagani-Kurtz, L., Mâsse, L.C., Vitaro, F., & Pihl, R.O. (1995). A bimodal preventive intervention for disruptive kindergarten boys: Its impact through mid-adolescence. *Journal of Consulting and Clinical Psychology, 63,* 560–568.

Triandis, H. C. (1989). Cross-cultural studies of individualism and collectivism. In J. J. Berman (Ed.), *Nebraska Symposium on Motivation* (Vol. 37). Lincoln: University of Nebraska Press.

Triandis, H. C. (1994). *Culture and social behavior.* Boston: McGraw-Hill.

Triandis, H. C. (2001). Individualism-collectivism and personality. *Journal of Personality, 69,* 907–924.

Trimble, M. (2003). *Somatoform disorders.* New York: Cambridge University Press.

Triplett, N. (1898). The dynamogenic factors in pacemaking and competition. *American Journal of Psychology, 9,* 507–533.

Trivers, R. (1971). The evolution of reciprocal altruism. *Quarterly Review of Biology, 46,* 35–57.

Trivers, R. (1985). *Social evolution.* Menlo Park, CA: Benjamin/Cummings.

Trivers, R. L. (1972). Parental investment and sexual selection. In B. Campbell (Ed.), *Sexual selection and the descent of man.* Chicago: Aldine-Atherton.

Troiano, R. P., & Flegal, K. M. (1999). Overweight prevalence among youth in the United States: Why so many different numbers? *International Journal of Obesity and Related Metabolic Disorders, 23,* S22–27.

Troll, L. E. (1985). *Early and middle adulthood* (2nd ed.). Monterey, CA: Brooks/Cole.

Trull, T. J., & Geary, D. C. (1997). Comparison of the Big Five Factor structure across samples of Chinese and American adults. *Journal of Personality Assessment, 69,* 324–341.

Trull, T. J., & McCrae, R. R. (2002). A five-factor perspective on personality disorder research. In P. T. Costa, Jr., & T. A. Widiger (Eds.), *Personality disorders and the five-factor model of personality, 2nd edition.* Washington, DC: American Psychological Association.

Trulson, M. E., & Jacobs, B. L. (1979). Dissociations between the effects of LSD on behavior and raphe unit activity in freely moving cats. *Science, 204* (4405), 515–518.

Tryon, W. W. (2002). Network models contribute to cognitive and social neuroscience. *American Psychologist, 57,* 728.

Tsai, J. L., & Levenson, R. W. (1997). Cultural influences of emotional responding: Chinese-American and European-American dating couples during interpersonal conflict. *Journal of Cross-Cultural Psychology, 28,* 600–625.

Tsai, J. L., Levenson, R. W., & McCoy, K. (2006). Cultural temperamental variations in emotional response. *Emotion, 6,* 484–497.

Tsai, J. L., Louie, J. Y., Chen, E. E., & Uchida, Y. (2007). Learning what feelings to desire: Socialization of ideal affect through children's storybooks. *Personality and Social Psychology Bulletin, 33,* 17–30.

Tseng, W. S., Asai, M., Liu, J., Pismai, W. et al. (1990). Multi-cultural study of minor psychiatric disorders in Asia: Symptom manifestations. *International Journal of Social Psychiatry, 36,* 252–264.

Tsujimoto, S., Yahamoto, T., Kawaguchi, H., Koizumi, H,. Sawaguchi, T. (2004). Prefrontal cortical activation associated with working memory in adults and preschool children: An event-related optical topography study. *Cerebral Cortex, 14*(7), 703–712.

Tucker, P., & Aron, A. (1993). Passionate love and marital satisfaction at key transition points in the family life cycle. *Journal of Social and Clinical Psychology, 12,* 135–147.

Tucker, V. A. (2000). The deep fovea, sideways vision and spiral flight paths in raptors. *Journal of Experimental Biology, 203,* 3745–3754.

Tuckfelt, S., Fink, J., & Warren, M. P. (1997). *The psychotherapists' guide to managed care in the 21st century: Surviving big brother.* Northvale, NJ: Jason Aronson.

Tulving, E. (2000) (Ed.). *Memory, consciousness, and the brain: The Tallinn Conference.* Philadelphia: Psychology Press/Taylor & Francis.

Tulving, E. (2002). Episodic memory: From mind to brain. *Annual Review of Psychology, 53,* 1–25.

Tulving, E., & Psotka, J. (1971). Retroactive inhibition in free recall: Inaccessibility of information available in the memory store. *Journal of Experimental Psychology, 87,* 1–8.

Tulving, E., & Schacter, D. L. (1990). Timing and human memory systems. *Science, 247,* 301–306.

Tulving, E., & Thomson, D. M. (1973). Encoding specificity and retrieval processes in episodic memory. *Psychological Review, 80,* 359–380.

Tulving, E., Markowitsch, H. J., Kapur, S., Habib, R., et al. (1994). Novelty encoding networks in the human brain: Positron emission tomography data. *Neuroreport: An International Journal for the Rapid Communication of Research in Neuroscience, 5,* 2525–2528.

Turk, D. C. (2001). Physiological and psychological bases of pain. In A. Baum & T. A. Revenson (Eds.), *Handbook of health psychology.* Mahwah, NJ: Erlbaum.

Turk, D. C., & Melzack, R. (2001). *Handbook of pain assessment* (2nd ed.). New York: Guilford Press.

Turnbull, C. M. (1961). Some observations regarding the experiences and behavior of the Ba Mbuti pygmies. *American Journal of Psychology, 74,* 304–308.

Turner, J. A., & Aaron, L. A. (2001). Pain-related catastrophizing: What is it? *Clinical Journal of Pain, 17,* 65–71.

Turner, J. A., Deyo, R. A., et al. (1994). The importance of placebo effects in pain treatment and research. *Journal of the American Medical Association, 271,* 1609–1614.

Tusing, K. J., & Dillard, J. P. (2000). The psychological reality of the door-in-the-face: It's helping, not bargaining. *Journal of Language and Social Psychology, 19,* 5–25.

Tversky, A., & Kahneman, D. (1980). Causal schemas in judgments under uncertainty. In M. Fishbein (Ed.), *Progress in social psychology.* Hillsdale, NJ: Erlbaum.

Tversky, A., & Kahneman, D. (1981). The framing of decisions and the psychology of choice. *Science, 211,* 453–458.

Tversky, A. & Kahneman, D. (1982). Judgements of and by representativeness. In D. Kahneman, P. Slovic, & A. Tversky (Eds.), *Judgement under uncertainty: Heuristics and biases.* Cambridge, MA: Cambridge University Press.

Tversky, B., & Tuchin, M. (1989). A reconciliation of the evidence on eyewitness testimony: Comments on McCloskey and Zaragoza. *Journal of Experimental Psychology: General, 118,* 86–91.

Tyc, V. L., Mulhern, R. K., & Bieberich, A. A. (1997). Anticipatory nausea and vomiting in pediatric cancer patients: An analysis of conditioning and coping variables. *Journal of Developmental and Behavioral Pediatrics, 18,* 27–33.

Tye, M. (1991). *The imagery debate.* Cambridge, MA: MIT Press.

Tyson, G. A., Hubert, C. J. (2002). Cultural differences in adolescents' explanations of juvenile delinquency. *Journal of Cross-Cultural Psychology, 3*(5), 459–463.

Tzeng, J. M., & Mare, R. D. (1995). Labor market and socioeconomic effects on marital stability. *Social Science Research, 24,* 329–351.

Tzeng, O. J., Hung, W., Cohen, F. J., & Wang, P. (1979). Visual lateralization effect in reading Chinese characters. *Nature, 282,* 499–501.

Tzenova, J., Kaplan, B. J., Petryshen, T. L., & Field, L. L. (2004). Confirmation of a dyslexia susceptibility locus on chromosome 1p34-p36 in a set of 100 Canadian families. *American Journal of Medical Genetics (Neuropsychiatric Genetics), 127,* 117–124.

U.S. Bureau of the Census (1996). *Statistical abstracts of the United States, 1995* (115th ed.). Washington, DC: U.S. Government Printing Office.

U.S. Department of Justice (1999). *National crime victimization survey.* Washington, DC: Author.

U.S. Department of Labor (1998). Supplement to the May 1997 Current Population Survey (CPS). *Bureau of Labor Statistics* [Online]. Available: ftp://146.142.4.23/pub/news.release/flex.txt

U.S. Office of Behavior Technology. (1990). *Provision of professional services to the physically handicapped.* Washington, DC: Author.

U.S. Public Health Service (1979). *Healthy people: The Surgeon General's report on health promotion and disease prevention.* Washington, DC: U.S. Government Printing Office.

Underwood, B. J. (1970). A breakdown of the total-time law in free-recall learning. *Journal of Verbal Learning and Verbal Behavior, 9,* 573–580.

Unger, R. (2001). Them and Us: Hidden Ideologies—Differences in Degree or Kind? in Unger, R. (Ed), *Terrorism and Its Consequences. Analysis of Social Issues and Public Policy, Society for the Psychological Study of Social Issues,* Blackwell Publishers. [Online]. Available: http://www.asap-spssi.org/default.htm.

Urry, H. L., Nitschke, J. B., Dolski, I., Jackson, D. C., Dalton, K. M., Mueller, C. J., Rosenkranz, M. A., Ryff, C. D., Singer, B. H., & Davidson, R. J. (2004). Making a life worth living: Neural correlates of well-being. *Psychological Science, 15,* 367–372.

Urry, H.L., van Reekum, C.M., Johnstone, T., Kalin, N.H., Thurow, M.E., Schaefer, H.S., Jackson, C.A., Frye, C.J., Greischar, L.L., Alexander, A.L., Davidson, R.J. 2006. Amygdala and ventromedial prefrontal cortex are inversely coupled during regulation of negative affect and predict the diurnal pattern of cortisol secretion among older adults. *Journal of Neuroscience, 26,* 4415–4425.

Usher, J. A., & Neisser, U. (1993). Childhood amnesia and the beginnings of memory for four early life events. *Journal of Experimental Psychology: General, 122,* 155–165.

Uttl, B., & Graf, P. (1993). Episodic spatial memory in adulthood. *Psychology and Aging, 8,* 257–273.

Vaillant, G. E. (1977). *Adaptation to life.* Boston: Little, Brown.

Vaillant, C. O. & Vaillant, G. E. (1993). Is the U-curve of marital satisfaction an illusion? A 40-year study of marriage. *Journal of Marriage & the Family, 55,* 230–239.

Valent, P. (2000a). Stress effects of the Holocaust. In G. Fink (Ed.), *Encyclopedia of stress.* San Diego: Academic Press.

Valent, P. (2000b). Survivor guilt. In G. Fink (Ed.), *Encyclopedia of stress.* San Diego: Academic Press.

Valsiner, J., & Lawrence, J. A. (1997). Human development in culture across the life span. In J. W. Berry, P. R. Dasen, & T. S. Saraswathi (Eds.), *Handbook of cross-cultural psychology* (Vol. 2). Boston: Allyn & Bacon.

Valyear, K. F., Culham, J. C., Sharif, N., Westwood, D., & Goodale, M. A. (2006). A double dissociation between sensitivity to changes in object identity and object orientation in the ventral and dorsal visual streams: a human fMRI study. *Neuropsychologia, 44,* 218–28.

vanAsselen, M., Kessels, R. P. C., Neggers, S. F. W., Kappelle, L. J., Frijns, C. J. M., Postma, A. (2006). Brain areas involved in spatial working memory. *Neuropsychologia, 44*(7), 1185–1194.

Van Cauter, E. (2000). Sleep loss, jet lag, and shift work. In G. Fink (Ed.), *Encyclopedia of stress.* San Diego: Academic Press.

Van De Castle, R. L., & Kinder, P. (1968). Dream content during pregnancy. *Psychophysiology, 4,* 375.

van der Heijden, A. H. C. (1991). *Selective attention in vision.* New York: Routledge.

van der Vegt, G., Emans, B., & Van de Vliert, E. (1998). Motivating effects of task and outcome interdependence in work teams. *Group and Organization Management, 23,* 124–143.

Van Houten, R., & Retting, R. A. (2001). Increasing motorist compliance and caution at stop signs. *Journal of Applied Behavior Analysis, 34,* 185–193.

van Ijzendoorn, M. (1995). Adult attachment representations, parental responsiveness, and infant attachment: A meta-analysis of the Adult Attachment Interview. *Psychological Bulletin, 117,* 387–403.

Van Laningham J., Johnson, D. R., & Amato, P. (2001). Marital happiness, marital duration, and the U-shaped curve: evidence from a five-wave panel study. *Social Forces, 79,* 1313–1341.

Van Overschelde, J. P., Rawson, K. A., Dunlosky, J., Hunt, R. R. (2005). Distinctive processing underlies skilled memory. *Psychological Science, 16*(5), 358–361.

van Praag, H. M. (2004). *Stress, vulnerability and depression.* New York: Cambridge University Press.

Van Wel, F. (1994). A culture gap between the generations? Social influences on youth cultural style. *International Journal of Adolescence and Youth, 4,* 211–228.

Van Zomeren, A. H., & Brouwer, W. H. (1994). *Clinical neuropsychology of attention.* New York: Oxford University Press.

Vandell, D. L., & Ramanan, J. (1991). Children of the National Longitudinal Survey of Youth: Choices in after-school care and child development. *Developmental Psychology, 27,* 637–643.

Vander Zanden, J. W. (1997). *Human development* (6th ed.). Boston: McGraw-Hill.

VanItallie, T. B. & Kissileff, H. R. (1990). Human obesity: A problem in body economics. In E. M. Stricker (Ed.), *Handbook of behavioral neurobiology, Volume 10: Neurobiology of food and fluid intake.* New York: Plenum.

Vargha-Khadem, F., Gadian, D. G., Watkins, K. E., Connelly, A., Van Paesschen, W., & Mishkin, M. (1997). Differential effects of early hippocampal pathology on episodic and semantic memory. *Science, 277,* 376–380.

Varney, N. R., & Roberts, R. J. (1999). *The evaluation and treatment of mild traumatic brain injury.* Mahwah, NJ: Erlbaum.

Vartanian, L. R. (1997). Separation-individuation, social support, and adolescent egocentrism: An exploratory study. *Journal of Early Adolescence, 17,* 245–270.

Vartanian, L. R. (2000). Revisiting the imaginary audience and personal fable constructs of adolescent egocentrism: A conceptual review. *Adolescence, 35,* 639–661.

Vaughn, C., & Leff, J. (1976). The measurement of expressed emotion in the families of psychiatric patients. *British Journal of Social and Clinical Psychology, 15,* 157–165.

Venter, J. C., et al. (2001). The sequence of the human genome. *Science, 291,* 1304–51.

Ventura, R. & Harris, K. M. (1999). Three-dimensional relationships between hippocampal synapses and astrocytes. *Journal of Neuroscience, 19,* 6897–6906.

Verbrugge, L. M. (1979). Marital status and health. *Journal of Marriage and the Family, 41,* 267–285.

Vernon, D. T., & Blake, R. L. (1993). *Does problem-based learning work? A meta-analysis of evaluative research. Academic Medicine, 68(7),* 550–563.

Vernon, P.A., Jang, Kerry, L., Aitken-Harris, J., & McCarthy, J.M. (1997). Environmental predictors of personality differences: A twin and sibling study. *Journal of Personality and Social Psychology, 72(1),* 177–183.

Vgonitzas, A. N., Bixler, E. O., & Kales, A. K. (2000). Sleep, sleep disorders, and stress. In G. Fink (Ed.), *Encyclopedia of stress.* San Diego: Academic Press.

Vickery, A. R., & Kirsch, I. (1991). The effects of brief expectancy manipulations on hypnotic responsiveness. *Contemporary Hypnosis, 8,* 167–171.

Viemerö, V. (1996). Factors in childhood that predict later criminal behavior. *Aggressive Behavior, 22,* 87–97.

Villarreal, D. M., Do, V., Haddad, E., & Derrick, B. E. (2002). NMDA receptor antagonists sustain LTP and spatial memory: Active processes mediate LTP decay. *Nature Neuroscience, 5,* 48–52.

Violanti, J. M., & Marshall, J. R. (1996). Cellular phones and traffic accidents: An epidemiological approach. *Accident Analysis and Prevention, 28,* 265–270.

Vogels, W. W. A., Dekker, M. R., Brouwer, W. H., & deJong, R. (2002). Age-related changes in event-related prospective memory performance: A comparison of four prospective memory tasks. *Brain and Cognition, 49,* 341–362.

von Frisch, K. (1974). Decoding the language of the bee. *Science, 185,* 663–668.

Von Melchner, L., Pallas, S. L., & Sur, M. (2000). Visual behaviour mediated by retinal projections directed to the auditory pathway. *Nature, 404,* 871–876.

von Senden, M. (1960). *Space and sight: the perception of space and shape in the congenitally blind before and after operation.* Oxford: Free Press of Glencoe.

Vormfelde, S. V., Hoell, I., Tzvetkov, M., Jamrozinski, K., Sehrt, D., Brockmöller, J., & Leibing, E. (2006). Anxiety- and novelty seeking-related personality traits and serotonin transporter gene polymorphisms. *Journal of Psychiatric Research, 40,* 568–576.

Vrij, A., van der Steen, J., & Koppelaar, L. (1994). Aggression of police officers as a function of temperature: An experiment with the Fire Arms Training System. *Journal of Community and Applied Social Psychology. 1994, 4,* 365–370.

Vurpillot, E. (1968). The development of scanning strategies and their relation to visual differentiations. *Journal of Experimental Child Psychology, 6,* 632–650.

Vygotsky, L. S. (1935/1978). *Mind in society: The development of higher psychological processes.* In Cambridge, MA: Harvard University Press.

Vygotsky, L. S. (1962). *Thought and language.* Cambridge, MA: The MIT Press.

Wacha, V. H. & Obrzut, J. E. (2007). Effects of fetal alcohol syndrome on neuropsychological function. *Journal of Developmental and Physical Disabilities, 19,* 217–226.

Wachtel, P. L. (1997). *Psychoanalysis, behavior therapy, and the relational world.* Washington, DC: American Psychological Association.

Wadden, T. A., Brownell, K. D., & Foster, G. D. (2002). Obesity: Responding to the global epidemic. *Journal of Consulting and Clinical Psychology, 70,* 510–525.

Wadden, T. A., Vogt, R. A., Andersen, R. E., et al. (1997). Exercise in the treatment of obesity: Effects of four interventions on body composition, resting energy expenditure, appetite, and mood. *Journal of Consulting and Clinical Psychology, 654,* 269–277.

Wade, C., & Cirese, S. (1992). *Human sexuality* (2nd ed.). Chicago: Harcourt Brace Jovanovich.

Wade, N. J., & Swanston, M. (2001). *Visual perception: An introduction.* New York: Psychology Press.

Wade, P., & Bernstein, B. (1991). Culture sensitivity training and counselor's race: Effects on Black female client's perceptions and attrition. *Journal of Counseling Psychology, 38,* 9–15.

Wagman, M. (1997). *Cognitive science and the symbolic operations of human and artificial intelligence: Theory and research into the intellective processes.* Westport, CT: Greenwood.

Wagman, M. (1998). *Cognitive science and the mind-body problem: From philosophy to psychology to artificial intelligence to imaging of the brain.* Westport, CT: Greenwood.

Wagner, A.D., Schacter, D., Rotte, M., Koutstaal, W., Meril, A., Dale, A., Rosen, B., & Buckner, R. (1998). Building memories: Remembering and forgetting of verbal experiences as predicted by brain activity. *Science, 281,* 1188–1191.

Wagner, E. H., La Croix, A. Z., Buckner, D. M., & Larson, E. B. (1992). Effects of physical activity on health status in older adults: I: Observational studies. *Annual Review of Public Health, 13,* 368–392.

Wahlberg, K. E., Wynne, L. C., Oja, H., Keskitalo, P., et al. (1997). Gene-environment interaction in vulnerability to schizophrenia: Findings from the Finnish Family Study of Schizophrenia. *American Journal of Psychiatry, 154,* 355–362.

Wainwright, P. E., Simpson, J. R., Cameron, R., Hoffman-Goetz, L., Winfield, D., McCutcheon, D., & MacDonald, M. (1990). Effects of treadmill exercise on weight cycling in female mice. *Physiology and Behavior, 49,* 639–642.

Wakefield, M., Reid, Y., Roberts, L., Mullins, R., & Gillies, P. (1998). Smoking and smoking cessation among men whose partners are pregnant: A qualitative study. *Social Science and Medicine, 47,* 657–664.

Walen, S. (1980). Cognitive factors in sexual behavior. *Journal of Sex and Marital Therapy, 6,* 87–101.

Walen, S. R., & Roth, D. (1987). A cognitive approach. In J. H. Geer & W. T. O'Donohue (Eds.), *Theories of human sexuality.* New York: Plenum.

Walk, R. D. (1981). *Perceptual development.* Monterey, CA: Brooks/Cole.

Walker, L. E. (1999). Psychology and domestic violence around the world. *American Psychologist, 54,* 21–29.

Walker, L. J. (1987, April). *Moral orientations: A comparison of two models.* Paper presented at biennial meetings of Society for Research in Child Development, Baltimore.

Walker, M. P. (2005). A refined model of sleep and the time course of memory formation. *Behavioral and Brain Sciences, 28,* 51–104.

Walker, M. P. & Stickgold, R. (2006). Sleep, memory, and plasticity. *Annual Review of Psychology, 57,* 139–166.

Walker, T. G., & Main, E. C. (1973). Choice-shifts in political decision making: Federal judges and civil liberties cases. *Journal of Applied Social Psychology, 2,* 39–48.

Wallace, B. A. (1999). The Buddhist tradition of Samatha: Methods for refining and examining consciousness. *Journal of Consciousness Studies, 6,* 175–187.

Wallbott, H., & Scherer, K. (1988). How universal and specific is emotional experience? Evidence from 27 countries and five continents. In K. Scherer (Ed.), *Facets of emotion: Recent research.* Hillsdale, NJ: Erlbaum.

Waller, G., & Hartley, P. (1994). Perceived parental style and eating psychopathology. *European Eating Disorders Review, 2,* 76–92.

Wallerstein, J. S. (1984). Children of divorce: Preliminary report of a ten-year follow-up of young children. *American Journal of Orthopsychiatry, 54,* 444–458.

Wallerstein, J. S. (1989). *Second chances.* New York: Tickner & Fields.

Wallerstein, J. S., & Kelly, J. B. (1980). *Surviving the break-up: How children actually cope with divorce.* New York: Basic Books.

Walling, D. P., Baker, J. M., & Dott, S. G. (1998). Scope of hypnosis education in academia: Results of a national survey. *International Journal of Clinical and Experimental Hypnosis, 46,* 150–156.

Wallston, K. A. (1993). Hocus-pocus, the focus isn't strictly on locus: Rotter's social learning theory modified for health. *Cognitive Therapy and Research, 16,* 183–199.

Walsh, B. T., & Devlin, M. J. (1998). Eating disorders: Progress and problems. *Science, 280,* 1387–1390.

Walster, E., Aronson, V., Abrahams, D., & Rottman, L. (1966). The importance of physical attractiveness in dating behavior. *Journal of Personality and Social Psychology, 4,* 508–516.

Walther, E. (2002). Guilty by mere association: Evaluative conditioning and the spreading attitude effect. *Journal of Personality and Social Psychology, 82,* 919–934.

Wand, T., Hudson, S., & Marshall, W. (1996). Attachment style in sex offenders: A preliminary study. *Journal of Sex Research, 33,* 17–26.

Wang, J., Rao, H.,Wetmore, G.S., Furlan, P.M., Korczykowski, M., Dinges, D.F., Detre, J.A. (2005). Perfusion functional MRI reveals cerebral blood flow pattern under psychological stress. *Proceedings of the National Academy of Science, 102,* 17804–17809.

Wang, P. S., Demler, O., & Kessler, R. C. (2002). Adequacy of treatment for serious mental illness in the United States. *American Journal of Public Health, 92,* 92–98.

Wang, T., Brownstein, R., & Katzev, R. (1989). Promoting charitable behaviour with compliance techniques. *Applied Psychology: An International Review, 38,* 165–183.

Ward, R. A. & Spitze, G. D. (2004). Marital implications of parent-adult child coresidence: a longitudinal view. *Journals of Gerontology Series B—Psychological Sciences and Social Sciences, 59,* S2–S8.

Ward, S. L., & Overton, W. F. (1990). Semantic familiarity, relevance, and the development of deductive reasoning. *Developmental Psychology, 26,* 488–493.

Warga, C. (1987). Pain's gatekeeper. *Psychology Today, 21,* 50–59.

Warren, M. P. (1992). Eating, body weight, and menstrual function. In K. D. Brownell, J. Rodin, & J. H. Wilmore (Eds.), *Eating, body weight, and performance in athletes: Disorders of modern society.* Philadelphia: Lea & Febiger.

Washington Post (1994, October 30). Gunman trains rifle fire on White House. *Washington Post,* p. A1.

Wason, P. C., & Johnson-Laird, P. N. (1972). *Psychology of reasoning.* London: Batsford.

Wasserman, E. A, & Berglan, L. R. (1998). Backward blocking and recovery from overshadowing in human causal judgement: The role of within-compound associations. *Quarterly Journal of Experimental Psychology: Comparative and Physiological Psychology, 51B,* 121–138.

Waters, A., Hill, A., & Waller, G. (2001). Bulimics' response to food cravings: Is binge eating a product of hunger or emotional state. *Behaviour Research and Therapy, 39,* 877–886.

Watkins, D., Cheng, C., Mpofu, E., Olowu, S., Singh-Sengupta, S., & Regmi, M. (2003). Gender differences in self-construal: How generalizable are Western findings? *Journal of Social Psychology, 143,* 501–519.

Watkins, L. R., & Maier, S. F. (2000). The pain of being sick: Implications of immune-to-brain communication for understanding pain. *Annual Review of Psychology, 51,* 29–58.

Watkins, L. R., Wiertelak, E. P., McGorry, M., Martinez, J., Schwartz, B., Sisk, D., & Maier, S. F. (1998). Neurocircuitry of conditioned inhibition of analgesia: Effects of amygdala, dorsal raphe, ventral medullary, and spinal cord lesions on antianalgesia in the rat. *Behavioral Neuroscience, 112.*

Watson, C. G., Barnett, M., Nikunen, L., Schultz, C., Randolph, E. T., & Mendez, C. M. (1997). Lifetime prevalences of nine common psychiatric/personality disorders in female domestic abuse survivors. *Journal of Nervous and Mental Disease, 185,* 645–647.

Watson, D., Clark, L. A., & Tellegen, A. (1988). Developmental and validation of brief measures of positive and negative affect: The PANAS scales. *Journal of Personality and Social Psychology, 54,* 1063–1070.

Watson, D. L. & Tharp., R. G. (1989). *Self-directed behavior: Self modification for personal adjustment* (4th ed.). Pacific Grove, CA: Brooks/Cole.

Watson, D. L., & Tharp, R. G. (1997). *Self-directed behavior: Self-modification for personal adjustment* (6th ed.) Belmont, CA: Brooks/Cole.

Watson, J. B. (1924). *Behaviorism.* New York: People's Institute.

Watson, J. B., & Rayner, R. (1920). Conditioned emotional reactions. *Journal of Experimental Psychology, 3,* 1–14.

Watson, J. C., & Greenberg, L. S. (1998). Humanistic and experiential theories of personality. In D. F. Barone, M. Hersen, & V. B. Van Hasselt (Eds.), *Advanced personality.* New York: Plenum.

Watten, R. G., Vassend, D., Myhrer, T., & Syversen, J. L. (1997). Personality factors and somatic symptoms. *European Journal of Personality, 11,* 57–68.

Weaver, C. A. (1993). Do you need a "flash" to form a flashbulb memory? *Journal of Experimental Psychology: General, 122,* 39–46.

Webb, E. J., Campbell, D. T., Schwartz, R. D., & Sechrest, L. (1966). *Unobtrusive measures: Nonreactive research in the social sciences.* Chicago: Rand McNally.

Webb, W. B. (1974). Sleep as an adaptive response. *Perceptual and Motor Skills, 38,* 1023–1027.

Webb, W. B. (1992). *Sleep: The gentle tyrant* (2nd ed.). Bolton, MA: Anker.

Webb, W. B. (1994). Prediction of sleep onset. In R. D. Ogilvie & J. R. Harsh. (Eds.), *Sleep onset: Normal and abnormal processes.* Washington, DC: American Psychological Association.

Webb, W. B., & Campbell, S. S. (1983). Relationships in sleep characteristics of identical and fraternal twins. *Archives of General Psychiatry, 40,* 1093–1095.

Webster, D. M., Richter, L., & Kruglanski, A. W. (1996). On leaping to conclusions when feeling tired: Mental fatigue effects on impressional primacy. *Journal of Experimental Social Psychology, 32,* 181–195.

Webster, J.D. (1997). Attachment style and well-being in elderly adults: A preliminary investigation. *Canadian Journal on Aging, 16,* 101–111.

Wechsler, D. (1991). WISC III: Wechsler Intelligence Scale for Children, third edition (1991). San Antonio, TX: The Psychological Corporation.

Wechsler, D. (1997). Wechsler Adult Intelligence Scale, third edition. San Antonio, TX: The Psycholocial Corporation.

Weg, R. B. (1983). Changing physiology of aging: Normal and pathological. In D. S. Woodruff & J. E. Birren (Eds.), *Aging: Scientific perspectives and social issues* (2nd ed.). Monterey, CA: Brooks/Cole.

Weinberg, R. S., & Genuchi, M. (1980). Relationship between competitive trait anxiety, state anxiety, and golf performance: A field study. *Journal of Sport Psychology, 2,* 148–154.

Weinberger, D. A. (1990). The construct validity of the repressive coping style. In J. L. Singer (Ed.), *Repression and dissociation.* Chicago: University of Chicago Press.

Weinberger, D. R., & McClure, R. K. (2002). Neurotoxicity, neuroplasticity, and magnetic resonance imaging morphometry: What is happening in the schizophrenic brain? *Archives of General Psychiatry, 59,* 553–559.

Weiner, B. (1985). An attributional theory of achievement motivation and emotion. *Psychological Review, 92,* 548–573.

Weiner, B. (1992). *Human motivation: Metaphors, theories, and research.* Newbury Park, CA: Sage Publications.

Weiner, B. (1996). Searching for order in social motivation. *Psychological Inquiry, 7,* 199–216.

Weiner, R. D., & Coffey, C. E. (1988). Indications for the use of electroconvulsive therapy. In A. J. Francis & R. E. Hales (Eds.), *Review of Psychiatry* (Vol. 7), Washington, DC: American Psychiatric Press.

Weinert, F. E., & Hany, E. A. (2003). The stability of individual differences in intellectual development. In R. J. Sternberg, J. Lautrey, & T. I. Lubart (Eds.), *Models of intelligence: International perspectives.* Washington, DC: American Psychological Association.

Weingardt, K. R., & Marlatt, G. A. (1998). Harm reduction and public policy. In G. A. Marlatt (Ed.), *Harm reduction: Pragmatic strategies for managing high-risk behaviors.* New York: Guilford Press.

Weingarten, H. P. (1983). Conditioned cues elicit feeding in sated rats: A role for learning in meal initiation. *Science, 220,* 431–433.

Weinstein, C. S. (1991). The classroom as a social context for learning. *Annual Review of Psychology, 42,* 493–525.

Weinstock, M. (1997). Does prenatal stress impair coping and regulation of hypothalamic-pituitary-adrenal axis? *Neuroscience and Biobehavioral Reviews, 21,* 1–10.

Weisenberg, M. (1998). Cognitive aspects of pain and pain control. *International Journal of Clinical and Experimental Hypnosis, 46,* 44–61.

Weiskrantz, L. (1986). *Blindsight: A case study and implications.* Oxford, England: Oxford University Press.

Weiskrantz, L. (1998). Consciousness and commentaries, *International Journal of Psychology, 33,* 227–223.

Weiss, J. M., Glazer, H. I., & Pohoresky, L. A. (1976). Coping behavior and neurochemical change in rats: An alternative explanation for the original "learned helplessness" experiments. In G. Serban & A. King (Eds.), *Animal models in human psychobiology.* New York: Plenum.

Weissman, M. M., & Markowitz, J. C. (1994). Interpersonal psychotherapy: Current status. *Archives of General Psychiatry, 51,* 599–606.

Weissman, M. M., & Markowitz, J. C. (2002). Interpersonal psychotherapy for depression. In I. H. Gotlib and C. L. Hammen (Eds.), *Handbook of Depression.* (404–421). New York: Guilford Press.

Weissman, M. M., Bland, R. C., Canino, G. J., et al. (1994). The cross-national epidemiology of obsessive-compulsive disorder: The Cross National Collaborative Group. *Journal of Clinical Psychiatry, 55,* 5–10.

Weissman, M. M., Geshon, E. S., Kidd, K. K., Prusoff, B. A., Leckman, J. F., Dibble, E., Hamovit, J., Thompson, W. D., Pauls, D. L., & Guroff, J. J. (1984). Psychiatric disorders in the relatives of probands with affective disorders. *Archives of General Psychiatry, 41,* 13–21.

Weller, A., & Weller, L. (1997). Menstrual synchrony under optimal conditions: Bedouin families. *Journal of Comparative Psychology, 111,* 143–151.

Weller, A., & Weller, L. (1998). Prolonged and very intensive contact may not be conducive to menstrual synchrony. *Psychoneuroendocrinology, 23,* 19–32.

Weller, L., Weller, A., Koresh, H. K., & Shoshan, B. R. (1999). Menstrual synchrony in a sample of working women. *Psychoneuroendocrinology, 24,* 449–459.

Wells, J. A. K., Malenfant, J. E. L., Williams, A. F., & Van Houten, R. (2000). Use of a community program to increase seat belt use among shopping center patrons in Charlotte, North Carolina. *Journal of Safety Research, 31,* 93–99.

Wender, P. H., Kety, S. S., Rosenthal, D., Schulsinger, F., Ortmann, J., & Lunde, I. (1986). Psychiatric disorders in the biological and adoptive families of adopted individuals with affective disorders. *Archives of General Psychiatry, 43,* 923–929.

Wenning, G. K., Odin, P., Morrish, P., et al. (1997). Short- and long-term survival and function of intrastriatal dopaminergic grafts in Parkinson's disease. *Annals of Neurology, 42,* 95–107.

Wenzlaff, R. M., & Wegner, D. M. (2000). Thought suppression. *Annual Review of Psychology, 51,* 59–91.

Wenzlaff, R. M., Wegner, D. M., & Roper, D. W. (1988). Depression and mental control: The resurgence of unwanted negative thoughts. *Journal of Personality and Social Psychology, 55,* 882–892.

Werker, J. (1989). Becoming a native listener. *American Scientist, 77,*

Werker, J. F. & Tees, R. C. (1984). Cross-language speech perception: Evidence for perceptual reorganization during the first year of life. *Infant Behavior and Development, 7,* 49–63.

Werker, J. F., & Tees, R. C. (1992). The organization and reorganization of human speech perception. *Annual Review of Neuroscience, 15,* 86–101.

Werker, J. F. & Tees, R. C. (2002). Cross-language speech perception: evidence for perceptual reorganization during the first year of life. *Infant Behaviour & Development, 25*(1), 121–133.

Werner, E. E., & Smith, R. S. (1982). *Vulnerable but invincible: A longitudinal study of resilient children.* New York: McGraw-Hill.

Westen, D., & Gabbard, G. (1999). Psychoanalytic approaches to personality. In L. A. Pervin & O. P. John (Eds.), *Handbook of personality: Theory and research.* New York: Guilford Press.

Westen, D., & Morrison, K. (2001). A multidimensional meta-analysis of treatments for depression, panic, and generalized anxiety disorder: An empirical examination of the status of empirically supported therapies. *Journal of Consulting and Clinical Psychology, 69,* 875–889.

Westen, D., Nakash, O, Thomas, C. and Bradley, R. (2006). Clinical assessment of attachment patterns and personality disorder in adolescents and adults. *Journal of Consulting and Clinical Psychology, 74,* 1065–1085.

Wethington, E. (2000). Life events scale. In G. Fink (Ed.), *Encyclopedia of stress.* San Diego: Academic Press.

Wetter, D. W., Fiore, M. C., et al. (1998). The Agency for Health Care Policy and Research Smoking cessation clinical practice guideline: Findings and implications for psychologists. *American Psychologist, 53,* 657–669.

Wever, R. A. (1979). *The circadian system of man: Results of experiments under temporal isolation.* New York: Springer-Verlag.

Wever, R. A. (1989). Light effects on human circadian rhythms: A review of recent Andechs experiments. *Journal of Biological Rhythms, 4,* 161–185.

Wexley, K. N., & Yukl, G. A. (1977). *Organizational behavior and personnel psychology.* Homewood, IL: Irwin.

Wheeler, L., & Miyake, K. (1992). Social comparison in everyday life. *Journal of Personality and Social Psychology, 62,* 760–773.

Wheeler, R. E., Davidson, R. J., & Tomarken, A. J. (1993). Frontal brain asymmetry and emotional reactivity: A biological substrate of affective style. *Psychophysiology, 30,* 82–89.

Whitam, F. L., & Mathy, R. M. (1991). Childhood cross-gender behavior of homosexual females in Brazil, Peru, the Philippines, and the United States. *Archives of Sexual Behavior, 20,* 151–170.

Whitbourne, S. K. (1985). *The aging body: Physiological changes and psychological consequences.* New York: Springer-Verlag.

White, D. J., & Galef, B. G Jr. (1999). Social effects on mate choices of male Japanese quail, Coturnix japonica. *Animal Behaviour, 57,* 1005–1012.

White, D. J., & Galef, B. G. Jr. (2000). 'Culture' in quail: Social influences on mate choices of female Coturnix japonica. *Animal Behaviour, 59,* 975–979.

White, G. L. (1980). Physical attractiveness and courtship progress. *Journal of Personality and Social Psychology, 39,* 660–668.

White, K. M., Hogg, M. A., & Terry, D. J. (2002). Improving attitude behavior correspondence through exposure to normative support from a salient ingroup. *Basic and Applied Social Psychology, 24,* 91–103.

White, M. (1987). *The Japanese educational challenge: A commitment to children.* New York: Free Press.

White, N. M., & Milner, P. M. (1992). The psychobiology of reinforcers. *Annual Review of Psychology, 43,* 443–472.

White, R. K. (1968). *Nobody wanted war.* Garden City, NY: Doubleday.

White, T. & Nelson, C. A. (2004). Neurobiological development during childhood and adolescence. In R.L. Findling & S.C. Schulz (Eds.), *Schizophrenia in Adolescents and Children: Assessment, Neurobiology, and Treatment.* Baltimore, MD: Johns Hopkins University Press.

Whiten, A., Goodall, J., McGrew, W. C., Nishida, T., Reynolds, V., Sugiyama, Y., & Tutin, C. E. G. (1999). Cultures in chimpanzees. *Nature, 399,* 682–685.

Whitney, G., McClearn, G. E., & DeFries, J. C. (1970). Heritability of alcohol preference in laboratory mice and rats. *The Journal of Heredity, 61,* 165–169.

Whorf, B. L. (1956). *Language, Thought, and Reality: Selected Writings of Benjamin Lee Whorf.* Ed. John B. Carroll. Cambridge, MA: MIT Press.

Whorf, B. L. (1956). Science and linguistics. In J. B. Carroll (Ed.), *Language, thought and reality: Selected writings of Benjamin Lee Whorf.* Cambridge, MA: MIT Press.

Wicker, A. W. (1969). Attitudes versus actions: The relationship between verbal and overt behavioral responses to attitude objects. *Journal of Social Issues, 25,* 41–78.

Widiger, T. A. (1995). Detection of self-defeating and sadistic personality disorders. In W. J. Livesley (Ed.), *The DSM-IV personality disorders.* New York: Guilford Press.

Widiger, T. A., & Sankis, L. M. (2000). Adult psychopathology: Issues and controversies. *Annual Review of Psychology, 51,* 377–405.

Widom, C. S. (1983). A methodology for studying noninstitutionalized psychopaths. In R. D. Hare & D. A. Schaling (Eds.), *Psychopathic behavior: Approaches to research.* Chichester, England: Wiley.

Wiedenfeld, S. A., O'Leary, A., Bandura, A., Brown, S., Levine, S., & Raska, K. (1990). Impact of perceived self-efficacy in coping with stressors on components of the immune system. *Journal of Personality and Social Psychology, 59,* 1082–1094.

Wiederman, M. W., & Dubois, S. L. (1998). Evolution and sex differences in preferences for short-term mates: Results from a policy capturing study. *Evolution and Human Behavior, 19,* 153–170.

Wiens, A. N., & Menustik, C. E. (1983). Treatment outcome and patient characteristics in an aversion therapy program for alcoholism. *American Psychologist, 38,* 1089–1096.

Wilcox, S., & Storandt, M. (1996). Relations among age, exercise, and psychological variables in a community sample of women. *Health Psychology, 15,* 110–113.

Wilder, D. A. (1986). Social categorization: Implications for creation and reduction of intergroup bias. In L. Berkowitz (Ed.), *Advances in experimental social psychology* (Vol. 19). New York: Academic Press.

Wilk, L. A., & Redmon, W. K. (1998). The effects of feedback and goal setting on the productivity and satisfaction of university admissions staff. *Journal of Organizational Behavior Management, 18,* 45–68.

Wilkins, A. J., & Baddeley, A. D. (1978). Remembering to recall in everyday life: An approach to absentmindedness. In M. M. Grueneberg, P. E. Morris, & R. N. Sykes (Eds.), *Practical aspects of memory.* London: Academic Press.

Willenberg, H. S., Bornstein, S. R., & Crousos, G. P. (2000). Stress-induced disease: Overview. In G. Fink (Ed.), *Encyclopedia of stress.* San Diego: Academic Press.

Williams, C. (2001). *You snooze, you lose?—Sleep patterns in Canada.* Canadian Social Trends, Statistics Canada — Catalogue No. 11-008, 10–14.

Williams, L. M. (1994). Recall of childhood trauma: A prospective study of women's memories of child sexual abuse. *Journal of Consulting and Clinical Psychology, 62,* 1167–1176.

Williams, S. L., Kinney, P. J., & Falbo, J. (1989). Generalization of therapeutic changes in agoraphobia: The role of perceived self-efficacy. *Journal of Consulting and Clinical Psychology, 57,* 436–442.

Williams, T. J., Pepitone, M. E., Christensen, S. E., Cooke, B. M., Huberman, A. D., & Breedlove, N. J. (2000). Finger length patterns and human sexual orientation. *Nature, 404,* 455–456.

Williams, W. M. (1998). Are we raising smarter children today? School- and home-related influences on IQ. In U. Neisser, et al. (Eds.), *The rising curve: Long-term gains in IQ and related measures.* Washington, DC: American Psychological Association.

Willingham, W. W., Rock, D. A., & Pollack, J. (1990). Predictability of college grades: Three tests and three national samples. In W. W. Willingham & C. Lewis (Eds.), *Predicting college grades: An analysis of institutional trends over two decades.* Princeton, NJ: Educational Testing Service.

Wilson, E. O. (1980). *Sociobiology.* Cambridge, MA: Harvard University Press.

Wilson, G. T., & Lawson, D. M. (1976). Expectancies, alcohol, and sexual arousal in male social drinkers. *Journal of Abnormal Psychology, 85,* 587–594.

Wilson, M., & Daly, M. (1985). Competitiveness, risk-taking and violence: The young male syndrome. *Ethology and Sociobiology, 6,* 59–73.

Wilson, M., & Daly, M. (1992). The man who mistook his wife for a chattel. In J. Barkow, L. Cosmides, & J. Tooby (Eds.), *The Adapted Mind: Evolutionary psychology and the generation of culture.* London: Oxford University Press.

Wilson, S. C., & Barber, T. X. (1982). The fantasy-prone personality: Implications for understanding imagery, hypnosis, and parapsycho-logical phenomena. *PSI-Research, 1,* 94–116.

Wilson, S. C., & Barber, T. X. (1983). The fantasy-prone personality: Implications for understanding imagery, hypnosis, and parapsychological phenomena. In A. A. Sheikh (Ed.), *Imagery: Current theory, research and applications.* New York: Wiley.

Windholz, G. (1997). Ivan P. Pavlov: An overview of his life and psychological work. *American Psychologist, 52,* 941–946.

Winkler, I., Korzyukov, O., Gumenyuk, V., Cowan, N., Linkenkaer, H. K., Ilmoniemi, R. J., Alho, K., & Naeaetaenen, R. (2002). Temporary and longer term retention of acoustic information. *Psychophysiology, 39,* 530–534.

Winner, E. (1996). *Gifted children: Myths and realities.* New York: Basic Books.

Winograd, E., Goldstein, F. C., Monarch, E. S., Peluso, J. P., & Goldman, W. P. (1999). The mere exposure effect in patients with Alzheimer's disease. *Neuropsychology, 13,* 41–46.

Wise, R. A. (1996). Addictive drugs and brain stimulation reward. *Annual Review of Neuroscience, 19,* 319–340.

Wise, R. A. (2004). Dopamine, learning and motivation. *Nature Reviews Neuroscience, 5,* 483–494.

Wise, R. A., & Rompre, P. P. (1989). Brain dopamine and reward. *Annual Review of Psychology, 40,* 191–226.

Wiseman, R., Smith, M., & Kornbrot, D. (1996). Exploring possible sender to experimenter acoustic leakage in the PRL autoganzfeld experiments. *Journal of Parapsychology, 60,* 97–128.

Witelson, S. F., Beresh, H., Kigar, D. L. (2006). Intelligence and brain size in 100 postmortem brains: sex, lateralization, and age factors. *Brain, 128*(2), 386–398.

Witelson, S. F., Kigar, D. L., & Harvey, T. (1999). The exceptional brain of Albert Einstein. *Lancet, 353,* 2149–2153.

Witkin, H. A., Dyk, R. B., Faterson, H. F., Goodenough, D. R., & Karp, S. A. (1962). *Psychological differentiation.* New York: Wiley.

Wittchen, H. U., Zhao, S., Kessler, R. C., & Eaton, W. W. (1994). DSM-III-R generalized anxiety disorder in the National Comorbidity Survey. *Archives of General Psychiatry, 51,* 355–364.

Witte, K., & Allen, M. (2000). A meta-analysis of fear appeals: Implications for effective public health campaigns. *Health Education and Behavior, 27,* 591–615.

Witter, R. A., Okun, M. A., Stock, W. A., & Haring, M. J. (1984). Education and subjective well-being: A meta-analysis. *Educational Evaluation and Policy Analysis, 6,* 165–173.

Wixted, J. T. (1991). Conditions and consequences of maintenance rehearsal. *Journal of Experimental Psychology: Learning, Memory, and Cognition, 17,* 963–973.

Wolberg, L. R. (1967). *The technique of psychotherapy* (2nd ed.). New York: Grune & Stratton.

Wolken, J. J. (1995). *Light detectors, photoreceptors, and imaging systems in nature.* New York: Oxford University Press.

Wolpe, J. (1958). *Psychotherapy by reciprocal inhibition.* Stanford, CA: Stanford University Press.

Wolpe, J., & Plau, J. J. (1997). Pavlov's contributions to behavior therapy: The obvious and the not so obvious. *American Psychologist, 52,* 966–972.

Wonderly, D. M. (1996). *The selfish gene pool: An evolutionarily stable system.* Lanham, MD: University Press of America.

Wong, D. F., et al. (1986). Positron emission tomography reveals elevated D2 dopamine receptors in drug-naive schizophrenics. *Science, 234,* 1558–1563.

Wong, M. M., & Csikszentmahalyi, M. (1991). Affiliation motivation and daily experience: Some issues on gender differences. *Journal of Personality and Social Psychology, 60,* 154–164.

Wood, J. M., Bootzin, R. R., Rosenhan, D., Nolen-Hoeksema, S. (1992). Effects of the 1989 San Francisco earthquake on frequency and content of nightmares. *Journal of Abnormal Psychology, 101,* 219–224.

Wood, J. M., Nezworski, M. T., Lilienfeld, S. O., & Garb, H. N. (2003). *What's Wrong With The Rorschach? Science Confronts The Controversial Inkblot Test.* San Francisco, CA: Jossey-Bass.

Wood, J. V., Heimpel, S. A., & Michela, J. L. (2003). Savoring versus dampening: Self-esteem differences in regulating positive affect. *Journal of Personality and Social Psychology, 85,* 566–580.

Wood, J. V., Heimpel, S. A., Newby-Clark. I. R., and Ross, M. (2005). Snatching defeat from the jaws of victory: Self-esteem differences in the experience and anticipation of success. *Journal of Personality and Social Psychology, 89,* 764–780.

Wood, S. L., & Swait, J. (2002). Psychological indicators of innovation adoption: Cross classification based need for cognition and need for change. *Journal of Consumer Psychology, 12,* 1–13.

Wood, W. (2000). Attitude change: Persuasion and social influence. *Annual Review of Psychology, 51,* 539–570.

Wood, W., & Eagly, A. H. (2000). A call to recognize the breadth of evolutionary perspectives: Sociocultural theories and evolutionary psychology. *Psychological Inquiry, 11,* 52–55.

Wood, W., Lundgren, S., Ouellete, J. A., Busceme, S., & Blackstone, T. (1994). Minority influence: A meta-analytic review of social influence processes. *Psychological Bulletin, 115,* 323–345.

Wood, W., Pool, G. J., Leck, K., & Purvis, D. (1996). Self-definition, defensive processing, and influence: The normative impact of majority and minority groups. *Journal of Personality and Social Psychology, 71,* 1181–1193.

Wood, W., Rhodes, N., & Whelan, M. (1989). Sex differences in positive well-being: A consideration of emotional style and marital status. *Psychological Bulletin, 106,* 249–264.

Woodruff-Pak, D. S. (1993). Eyeblink classical conditioning in H. M.: Delay and trace paradigms. *Behavioral Neuroscience, 107,* 911–925.

Woods, S. C., & Seeley, R. J. (2002). Hunger and energy homeostasis. In H. Pashler & R. Gallistel (Eds.), *Steven's handbook of experimental psychology: Vol. 3. Learning, motivation, and emotion* (3rd ed.). New York: Wiley.

Woody, E., & Sadler, P. (1998). On reintegrating dissociated theories: Comment on Kirsch and Lynn. *Psychological Bulletin, 123,* 192–197.

Word, C. O., Zanna, M. P., & Cooper, J. (1974). The nonverbal mediation of self-fulfilling prophecies in interracial interaction. *Journal of Experimental Social Psychology, 10,* 109–120.

Worell, J., & Remer, P. P. (2003). *Feminist perspectives in therapy: Empowering diverse women.* New York: Wiley.

Wrangham, R. W. (1993). The evolution of sexuality in chimpanzees and bonobos. *Human Nature, 4,* 47–79.

Wrangham, R. W., & Peterson, D. (1996). *Demonic males.* Boston: Houghton Mifflin.

Wright, B. A. (1991). Labeling: The need for greater person-environment individuation. In C. R. Snyder & D. R. Forsyth (Eds.), *Handbook of social and clinical psychology: The health perspective.* New York: Pergamon.

Wright, C. I., Martis, B., McMullin, K., Shin, L. M., & Rauch, S. L. (2003). Amygdala and insular responses to emotionally valenced human faces in small animal specific phobia. *Biological Psychiatry, 54,* 1067–1076.

Wright, J. H., & Thase, M. E. (1997) (Eds.). *Cognitive therapy.* Washington, DC: American Psychiatric Press.

Wright, M. J. & Myers, C. R. (1982). *History of Academic Psychology in Canada.* Toronto: C.J. Hogrefe, Inc.

Wu, J. L., Yang, H. M. (2003). Speech perception of Mandarin Chinese speaking young children after cochlear implant use: effect of age at implantation. *International Journal of Pediatric Otorhinolaryngology 67,* 247–253.

Wyer, R. S., Bodenhausen, G. V., & Gorman, T. F. (1985). Cognitive mediators of reactions to rape. *Journal of Personality and Social Psychology, 48,* 324–338.

Wylie, R. C. (1979). *The self-concept* (Vol. 2). Lincoln: University of Nebraska Press.

Wylie, R. C. (1989). *Measures of self-concept.* Lincoln: University of Nebraska Press.

Yablonsky, L. (1962). *The violent gang.* New York: Macmillan.

Yalom, I. D. (1980). *Existential psychotherapy.* New York: Basic Books.

Yamagata, S., Suzuki, A., Ando, J., Ono, Y., Kijima, N., Yoshimura, K., Ostendorf, F., Angleitner, A., Riemann, R., Spinath, F. M., Livesley, W. J., & Jang, K. L. (2006). Is the genetic structure of human personality universal? A cross-cultural twin study from North America, Europe, and Asia. *Journal of Personality and Social Psychology, 90,* 987–998.

Yardley, L., Donovan-Hall, M. (2007). Predicting adherence to exercise-based therapy in rehabilitation. *Rehabilitation Psychology, 52*(1), 56–64.

Yarmey, D. & Yarmey, M. (1997). Eyewitness recall and duration estimates in field settings. *Journal of Applied Social Psychology, 27(4):* 330–344.

Yarmey, D. (1993). Stereotypes and recognition memory for faces and voices of good guys and bad guys. *Applied Cognitive Psychology 7(5):* 419–431.

Yarmey, D. (2001). Expert testimony: Does eyewitness memory research have probative value for the courts? *Canadian Psychology, 42(2):* 92–100.

Yerkes, R. M., & Dodson, J. D. (1908). The relation of strength of stimulus to rapidity of habit-formation. *Journal of Comparative and Physiological Psychology, 18,* 459–482.

Yin, T. C. T., & Kuwada, S. (1984). Neuronal mechanisms of binaural interaction. In G. M. Edelman, W. M. Cowan, & W. E. Gall (Eds.), *Dynamic aspects of neocortical function.* New York: Wiley.

Young, L. R., & Joffe, R. T. (1997). *Bipolar disorder: Biological models and their clinical application.* New York: Marcel Dekker.

Youngstedt, S. D., O'Connor, P. J., & Dishman, R. K. (1997). The effects of acute exercise on sleep: A quantitative synthesis. *Sleep, 20,* 203–214.

Yuille, J.C., & Tollestrup, P. (1990). Some effects of alcohol on eyewitness memory. *Journal of Applied Psychology, 75(3),* 268–273.

Yuille, J.C., Tollestrup. P., Marxsen, D., Porter, S. & Herve, H. (1998). An exploration on the effects of marijuana on eyewitness memory. *International Journal of Law and Psychiatry, 21(1),* 117–128.

Yurgelun-Todd, D. A. & Killgore W. D. S. (2006). Fear-related activity in the prefrontal cortex increases with age during adolescence: A preliminary fMRI study. *Neuroscience Letters, 406,* 194–199.

Zabriskie, J. (1999, February). APA teams with MTV to prevent violence. *APA Monitor,* 24.

Zahn-Waxler, C., Radke-Yarrow, M., & King, R. A. (1979). Child rearing and children's prosocial initiations towards victims of distress. *Child Development, 50,* 319–330.

Zahn-Waxler, C., Radke-Yarrow, M., Wagner, E., & Chapman, M. (1992). Development of concern for others. *Developmental Psychology, 28,* 126–136.

Zajonc, R. B. (1965). Social facilitation. *Science, 149,* 269–274.

Zajonc, R. B. (1968). Attitudinal effects of mere exposure. *Journal of Personality and Social Psychology, 9* (2, Part 2), 1–27.

Zajonc, R. B. (1980). Compresence. In P. Paulus (Ed.), *The psychology of group influence.* Hillsdale, NJ: Erlbaum.

Zajonc, R. B. (1984). On the primacy of affect. *American Psychologist, 39,* 117–123.

Zajonc, R. B. (1985). Emotion and facial efference: A theory reclaimed. *Science,* 228, 15–21.

Zajonc, R. B., Murphy, S. T., & Inglehart, M. (1989). Feeling and facial efference: Implications of a vascular theory of emotion. *Psychological Review, 96,* 395–416.

Zakzanis, K. K. (1998). Neuropsychological correlates of positive vs. negative schizophrenic symptomatology. *Schizophrenia Research, 29,* 227–233.

Zambelis, T., Paparrigopoulos, T., & Soldatos, C.R. (2002). REM sleep behaviour disorder associated with a neurinoma of the left pontocerebellar angle. *Journal of Neurology, Neurosurgery, and Psychiatry, 72,* 821–822.

Zangari, W., & Machado, F. R. (1996). Survey: Incidence and social relevance of Brazilian university students' psychic experiences. *European Journal of Parapsychology, 12,* 75–87.

Zanna, M. P., & Cooper, J. (1974). Dissonance and the pill: An attribution approach to studying the arousal properties of dissonance. *Journal of Personality and Social Psychology, 29,* 703–709.

Zaragoza, M. S., & Mitchell, K. J. (1996). Repeated exposure to suggestion and the creation of false memories. *Psychological Science, 7,* 294–300.

Zatzick, D. F., & Dimsdale, J. E. (1990). Cultural variations in response to painful stimuli. *Psychosomatic Medicine, 52,* 544–557.

Zautra, A. J. (2003). *Emotions, stress, and health.* New York: Oxford University Press.

Zebrowitz, L. A., Voinescu, L., & Collins, M. A. (1996). "Wide-eyed" and "crooked-faced": Determinants of perceived and real honesty across the life span. *Personality and Social Psychology Bulletin, 22,* 1258–1269.

Zelazo, N.A., Zelazo, P.R., Cohen, K.M., & Zelazo, P.D. (1993). Specificity of practice effects on elementary neuromotor patterns. *Developmental Psychology, 29,* 686–691.

Zelazo, P. D., Mueller, U., Frye, D., & Marcovitch, S. (2003). The development of executive funtion in early childhood. *Mongraphs of the Society for Research in Child Development, 68,*(274), 138–151.

Zelazo, P.R., Weiss, M.J., Papageorgiou, A.N. & Laplante, D.P. Recovery and dishabituation of sound localization among normal-, moderate- and high-risk newborns: discriminant validity. *Infant Behavior & Development, 12,* 321–340.

Zelazo, P.R., Zelazo, N.A., & Kolb, S. (1972). "Walking" in the newborn. *Science, 177,* 1058–1059.

Zhang, Q. & Haydon, P. G. (2005). Role for gliotransmission in the nervous system. *Journal of Neural Transmission, 112,* 121–125.

Zhang, A. Y., & Snowden, L. R. (1999). Ethnic characteristics of mental disorders in five U.S. communities. *Cultural Diversity and Ethnic Minority Psychology, 5,* 134–146.

Zhang, Y., Proenca, R., Maffei, M., & Barone, M. et al. (1994). Positional cloning of the mouse obese gene and its human homologue. *Nature, 372,* 425–432.

Zhdanova, I. V., & Wurtman, R. J. (1997). Efficacy of melatonin as a sleep-promoting agent. *Journal of Biological Rhythms, 12,* 644–650.

Zhuikov, A. Y., Couvillon, P. A., & Bitterman, M. E. (1994). Quantitative two-process analysis of avoidance conditioning in goldfish. *Journal of Experimental Psychology: Animal Behavior Processes, 20,* 32–43.

Zillmann, D. (1979). *Hostility and aggression.* New York: Halsted Press.

Zillmann, D. (1984). *Connections between sex and aggression.* Hillsdale, NJ: Erlbaum.

Zillmann, D. (1994). Erotica and family values. In D. Zillmann, J. Bryant, & A. C. Huston (Eds.), *Media, children, and the family: Social scientific, psychodynamic, and clinical perspectives.* Hillsdale, NJ: Erlbaum.

Zimbardo, P. G., Haney, C., Banks, W. C., & Jaffe, D. (1973, April 8). The mind is a formidable jailer: A Pirandellian prison. *New York Times Magazine,* 38–60.

Zimmerman, M. (1995). Diagnosing personality disorders: A review of issues and research methods. *Archives of General Psychiatry, 51,* 225–245.

Zinbarg, R. E., Barlow, D. H., Brown, T. A., & Hertz, R. M. (1992). Cognitive-behavioral approaches to the nature and treatment of anxiety disorders. *Annual Review of Psychology, 43,* 235–268.

Zubieta, J.-K., Smith, Y. R., Bueller, J. A., et al. (2001). Regional mu opioid receptor regulation of sensory and affective dimensions of pain. *Science, 293,* 311–315.

Zubieta, J.-K., & Stohler, C. S. (2002). Response: Measuring our natural painkiller. *Trends in Neuroscience, 69,* 42–51.

Zucker, T. P., Flesche, C. W., Germing, U., Schroeter, S., Willers, R., Wolf, H. H., & Heyll, A. (1998). Patient-controlled versus staff-controlled analgesia with pethidine after allogeneic bone marrow transplantation. *Pain, 75,* 305–312.

Zuckerman, M. (2005). *Psychobiology of Personality* (2nd ed.) New York: Cambridge University Press.

Zuckerman, M., & Link, K. (1968). Construct validity for the Sensation-Seeking Scale. *Journal of Consulting and Clinical Psychology, 32,* 420–426.

Zuckerman, M., Hall, J. A., DeFrank, R. S., & Rosenthal, R. (1976). Encoding and decoding of spontaneous and posed facial expressions. *Journal of Personality and Social Psychology, 34,* 966–977.

Name Index

E

F

G

H

M

N

O

P

T

Z

Subject Index

All page numbers appearing in bold type refer to locations in the text where key terms are defined.

A

B

C

D

E

F

G

N

O

P